Anthology of Romanticism

The late ERNEST BERNBAUM was for many years Professor of English at the University of Illinois. He received his A.B., A.M., and Ph.D. from Harvard University. Dr. Bernbaum is also the author of *Guide Through the Romantic Movement*, Second Edition, published by The Ronald Press Company.

ANTHOLOGY OF
ROMANTICISM

Selected and Edited by

ERNEST BERNBAUM

UNIVERSITY OF ILLINOIS

THIRD EDITION
REVISED AND ENLARGED

A COMPANION VOLUME TO THE
GUIDE THROUGH THE ROMANTIC MOVEMENT

THE RONALD PRESS COMPANY , NEW YORK

LIBRARY OF CONGRESS CATALOG CARD NUMBER: 48-6845

Printed in the United States of America

GRATEFULLY DEDICATED

TO MY FELLOW-STUDENTS

IN MY CLASSES IN THE ROMANTIC MOVEMENT

AT THE UNIVERSITY OF ILLINOIS

AND AT THE UNIVERSITY OF CHICAGO

1927–1945

WHOSE INDIVIDUAL RESEARCHES

CONTRIBUTED MUCH TO THIS VOLUME

PREFACE

George Bernard Shaw has awakened us to the truth that it may be a bright idea to read prefaces. This particular preface is out of the ordinary because, although it opens a textbook, it is really intended to be read by *students* as well as by their teachers. When we say, "Books are for those who can read them," we mean for those who know what the book is trying to do. Whoever skips this preface may never find out what purposes and standards governed the making of this volume, and in what ways it may be best used for profit and delight.

THE PRINCIPLES ON WHICH THESE SELECTIONS WERE CHOSEN

These selections from the voluminous literature of the English Romantic Period (c. 1783-1832) were not chosen merely for historical reasons, or because they were popular in their own time (some were so, others were then almost unknown). This is not an herbarium, nor a museum of fossils; it is not a collection of flora or fauna, once alive, but now dead. It is an anthology in the true sense of the word,—namely a gathering together of the choicest living flowers, the still unfaded efflorescence of the vast and fecund literature of English Romanticism. I have tried to reject any passage that is trash, though it may have been often included in previous books of selections, or though it may still have some curious antiquarian interest. Even in the brief section drawn from the Pre-Romantic Movement, the main purpose of which is historical, I have admitted very few specimens (fewer than in previous editions) that are of historical interest only.

These selections, therefore, whether in prose or in verse, are from what De Quincey calls the Literature of Power, not from the Literature of *mere* Knowledge,—power to arouse and assuage our emotions (of pleasure, pain, sympathy, etc.), power to elevate the understanding and enlighten the reason, power to kindle the imagination, power to reveal the truth, or power to humanize the will. My aim has been to let only what is thus still vital from the Past speak to the living Present. If this book is read in that spirit, it should help its readers to achieve a genuinely liberal education.

I have included not only all the passages that have long been deservedly famous, but also some of those which critics and scholars of our own time have found to be especially significant.

THE CONCURRENT USE OF THE "GUIDE THROUGH THE ROMANTIC MOVEMENT"

Both teachers and students will get the most out of this book if they use it in close connection with its companion-volume, my *Guide Through the Romantic*

Movement. The Introductions in the *Anthology* can give only brief elementary information about the authors and their times. For a deeper appreciation of the purposes, meanings, and values of the selections, it is essential to use concurrently the *Guide,* which has space enough to give reasonably adequate accounts of the lives of the authors, their characters, purposes, merits and limitations; critical estimates of their works; and discussions about that complex era of intellectual and aesthetic revolution, the Romantic Age.

VARIOUS WAYS OF STUDYING THE SELECTIONS

I recommend that the selections from the Pre-Romantic Movement be studied *after* the selections from the Romantic Movement, because the pre-romantic ones will be of greater interest and significance to those readers who are familiar with the characteristics of the main movement itself.

The selections from the Romantic Movement are presented, author by author, in historical sequence, because most readers desire and expect to have them arranged in that order. In my opinion, it is the best order—only, however, in the sense that its advantages outweigh its disadvantages. There are in it some disadvantages. It means beginning with Blake, one of the most difficult of the fourteen Romantics. It also means taking up, near the beginning, the philosophy and criticism of Coleridge, who is more difficult to understand than some of the later critics. If the chief object is to find the easiest approach to the subject, the student should commence with Lamb, Leigh Hunt, Southey, Scott, or with the simpler poems of Wordsworth; and postpone such authors as Blake, Coleridge, and De Quincey. An even better method to follow, if there is sufficient time, is to read the Romantics first in the order of comprehensibility, and thereafter to re-read them in the historical one.

Other methods of reading are frequently suggested in the Notes and Comments, viz., by types, and by topics. Abundant specimens will be found of such forms as blank verse, the ode, the sonnet, the ballad, prose fiction, argumentation, literary criticism, and the familiar essay. Among the recurrent topics are Religion; Nature; the Past, Present, and Future of Mankind; Ethics and Politics; Man and Woman; Childhood, Love, and Marriage; Death and Immortality; Science and Art. To make it an habitual practice to compare selections with one another, in point of style or of substance, offers rich possibilities of genuine education in literary appreciation and critical judgment. When, for example, Wordsworth's *Ode on Intimations of Immortality From Recollections of Early Childhood* is considered in connection with De Quincey's *The Palimpsest of the Human Brain* (both concerned with the importance of childhood impressions), the interest and value of each selection is greatly enhanced. Works of literature, like men, are at their best when they do not live wholly unto themselves. One of the teacher's greatest opportunities is to point out fruitful possibilities of such juxtapositions and comparisons.

NOTES, COMMENTS, BIBLIOGRAPHIES, AND SUGGESTIONS FOR ORAL AND WRITTEN CLASS
DISCUSSIONS

The Notes, Comments, Bibliographies, and Suggestions contain much more than the usual explanations of difficult words or passages. They supplement the general surveys provided in the *Guide*. They bring together from innumerable sources the information—biographical, bibliographical, textual, and interpretive—needed for a better understanding and enjoyment of the selections. Even more important, they offer suggestions which should stimulate teachers and students to discuss, in the classroom or in written essays, live controversial questions—of interpretation, or of taste, or of values. They provide up-to-date references, the use of which should lift the discussions above a merely emotional and impressionistic level into the sphere of adult, informed, realistic argument and criticism. Throughout, the comments try to keep the attention of the reader from wandering into unimportant trivialities, and help to concentrate it upon those problems of literature and life which are meaningful and crucial to all of us as individuals and as members of society. My aim has been, not to provide the student with conclusions, but to stimulate him to form sound opinions of his own.

———

Like the two earlier editions, this Anthology is intended for college courses in the Romantic Movement, or in English Literature from c. 1780 to 1840. The amount of space given to the Selections from the Romantics is half again as long as in the previous edition, thus affording space for all works, both of poetry and prose, which are of the highest importance. It is hoped that new editions of this work will be published from time to time, in order to keep it abreast of the progress of research and criticism. I shall be grateful to readers who send me corrections and suggestions.

E. B.

Freedom's Haven
Jaffrey, New Hampshire
January, 1948

CONTENTS

CONTENTS

SELECTIONS FROM
THE ROMANTIC MOVEMENT

CONTENTS

CONTENTS

INTRODUCTION: THE ROMANTIC MOVEMENT

ITS CHRONOLOGICAL DIVISIONS

WITH few exceptions the chief authors of the late eighteenth century and the early nineteenth were Romantics. Among their precursors were Thomson, Young, Collins, Gray, Macpherson, Chatterton, Cowper, and Burns. The Romantic Movement rose to its heights during the period from about 1783 to 1832. Most of the leading authors were active through nearly the entire period; but it may be subdivided into two parts. The first extends from 1783 to 1812, during which the most important works to appear were the poems of Blake, Coleridge, Wordsworth, and Scott. The second continues from 1812 to 1832, during which the outstanding works were Byron's poems, Scott's Waverley novels, the critical writings and the essays of Coleridge, Hazlitt, Lamb, and De Quincey, the Imaginary Conversations of Landor, and the works of Keats and Shelley. In the latter period the young Carlyle began his work, a link between the Romantic Age and the Victorian.

ITS IMPORTANCE

Today the Romantics may be admired or detested, but no one who is mentally or aesthetically awake can ignore them. For better or worse, the modern outlook is chiefly of their creation—most of the literature of the last one hundred years being either an application of the romantic principles to new themes or a hostile reaction against them. To understand our cultural heritage and our contemporary problems, we must know the Romantics.

ITS GENERAL CHARACTER

A reader will gain more from any one of the selections in this volume if he perceives its relation to some of the other selections. That they are related in one way or another, he will notice again and again; and he may wonder just what it is that seems to bind them together. If he is told that the bond is the spirit of Romanticism, he will ask: what *is* Romanticism? He will demand a definition—a statement of its essential nature in a clear brief sentence which shall enable him to distinguish Romanticism from other kinds of literature. All definitions hitherto proposed have proved unsatisfactory, nor is it likely that any proposed in the future will satisfy.

Romanticism is not the kind of term which can be reduced to a definition. One may define things that are physical, mechanical, practical, or mathematical—water, a rifle, a butcher, a triangle; but the higher one rises into levels of being which involve complex vital, emotional, intellectual, or spiritual elements, the more nearly impossible becomes the making of short clear-cut definitions. Look up the dictionary definitions of "life," "woman," and "democracy"; and observe how far they fall short of expressing the essential or the deeper significances of those words. Romanticism is not even approximately defined by the Romantics themselves. Such treatises as Coleridge's *Biographia Literaria* and Shelley's *Essay on Poetry,* extensive and authoritative as they are, were limited to restricted portions of the entire field. Romanticism was an all-embracing faith, and it was never formulated in a creed or a comprehensive set of dogmas subscribed to by all the Romantics. Nevertheless in romantic literature there are found, as *underlying assumptions,* certain frequently repeated intuitions about the meanings of life and the purposes which lie behind life. In my opinion, those assumptions or intuitions form a fairly coherent though shadowy pattern. It is not the kind of pattern, I repeat, that can be neatly defined in miniature. For that, Romanticism is too vibrant with life; but the most striking features upon its impassioned countenance may perhaps be sketched.

Romanticism is not a systematic philosophy, but an intuitive faith expressed through the emotional and symbolical art of literature. Therefore, during the past fifty years, a principal obstacle to the appreciation of its nature has been the secularization of our thinking and of our criticism (of which secularization, "humanism" is merely an academic form). To recognize the values of Romanticism it is perhaps not necessary to be religious; but it is imperative to have some degree of imaginative sympathy with those who are so: in other words, to appreciate the fact that it is quite possible, and not absurd, for really intelligent human beings confidently to believe in "the evidence of things not seen." Romanticism, like any faith, dwells midway between false fancy and demonstrated certainty. The Romantic is not an escapist dreamer who does not care whether his dreams are fantastic, provided they are pleasing. Nor is he a dogmatist who maintains that his beliefs can be demonstrated scientifically or rationalistically. Yet he is convinced that his faith, though not thus demonstrable, is absolutely true, and that it is in accord with eternal realities.

In trying to set forth the romantic beliefs, it seems to me best to stress a point which was not often raised in romantic literature, which usually was a tacit assumption, but which was fundamental. Believing that the universe was not a meaningless chaos hostile to man, but that it was an harmonious and purposeful whole, created by omnipotence and omniscience, and sustained by justice and by love, the Romantic assumed that *the Universe willed to reveal its essential nature and its eternal purposes to Man.* As Coleridge would put this basic point, the One willed to make itself known to the Many. It spoke to individual men through Nature, and through other men endowed with the gift of conveying truth and beauty. Its utterances might reach all sorts and conditions of men; for a rudimentary capacity for the appreciation of nature and art and literature was implanted in every human soul. All were called, though few responded, and still fewer could express what they had sensed.

The primary means by which truth and virtue and beauty were made known was not the same as that by which men communicate in ordinary practical life: it was not prosy ratiocination; it was inspiration. In other words, the supreme realities were not disclosed by man's unaided thinking ("flesh and blood hath not revealed it unto thee"); they dawned upon his mind briefly, fragmentarily, in fortunate moments, which Wordsworth calls "spots of time" (intersections of the temporal with the eternal), when his percipience was raised above its ordinary level. Hence, as Carlyle said, "no Poet is equal to his Poem." What gave a poem its immortal beauty and power came from a transcendental source, although, of course, its individual and historical traits were derived from the poet's personal life and circumstances.

To receive by inspiration such true glimpses of the real nature of things, the human mind must, at least temporarily, withdraw its attention from practical mundane affairs and concentrate it upon the inner life. It must cultivate that state of mind which is called Imagination, one trait of which is receptivity towards Inspiration. The imaginative state was often accompanied by intense stimulation of the emotions; for the exercise of the imagination did not suppress or supersede the human feelings, but supplemented and exalted them. It was not an escape from normal human nature, but its fulfillment.

What was discovered through inspired imagination was not factual knowledge about nature and man, but intellectual, moral, aesthetic, and spiritual insight into their significance—values in the realm of truth, or of goodness, or of beauty. The chief bearers of these gifts from the realm of Reality were prophets, sages, liberators, artists, and men of letters. Most of what was truest, or noblest, or most beautiful in life, had been apprehended by the Imagination, and communicated by Art and Literature. The good life was an inspired and inspiring life, not a coldly intellectual existence bereft of love. Until mankind accepted these truths of the romantic faith, and lived by them, it could not free itself from its follies and evils; but whenever it did, peace and love and happiness would abide on earth. The faith of Romanticism was humanitarian, democratic, and melioristic.

What the Romantics beheld when they looked at life was a radical difference between the world of *appearances* and the world of *reality*. What seemed important in the world of appearances (the world as it looks to the ordinary man, the man of "common" sense) was revealed as unimportant or false when it was observed by the man of true imagination. The ordinary man judged the values of Nature and of Man by their usefulness for his selfish purposes; he sought to employ them as tools or pawns, forcing or inveigling them to become slaves of his will. His common sense, despite its shrewdness, failed to perceive what lay beneath the superficial appearances, what men really were and could become, what their inmost thoughts and passions were, and what the relationships, political, economic, social, and personal, between them ought to be. Only he who had become capable of imagining himself outside of his own ego, no longer self-centered, could begin to see the world of Reality, his environment and his fellowmen, as they truly were, in themselves and in their relation to one another. Thus freed from unimaginative blindness, the Romantic saw Nature and Man in their true light, their essential character, and their genuine worth. Everything looked wonderfully different, yet authentically real—landscapes, animals, children, men and women, love and death, vices and virtues, follies and wisdom, education and art and literature. Romanticism was a revolutionary transvaluation of all conventional values. It moved men's hearts and minds passionately, and could therefore be communicated fully only through the emotional, symbolical, and beautiful creations of art and of literature. And to communicate those new visions of what life really meant, new forms and styles were needed by the artists and the men of letters, new ones indeed for each markedly individual personality among them.

Because of their faith that the world as it ought to be could be made an actuality, the Romantics scorned the world as it was—full of untruth, evil, ugliness, and wretchedness. Man's inhumanity to man moved them to indignation, sorrow, and at times almost to utter dejection. This mood may be regarded as the *first* state of the romantic mind, a state of rebellion against things as they are. It was powerfully and brilliantly expressed by Lord Byron, and nearly all the other Romantics shared it, at least occasionally. Hence arose, as a part of the Romantic Movement, those realistic works which portrayed bitterly the evils of the times. That realism should, however, be distinguished from the realism of the twentieth century which focuses attention on the most brutish aspects of life, and ends in the depths of despair because it has no hope whatever of happiness for mankind.

Most of the Romantics, after expressing realistically their rebellion against contemporary evils, passed beyond the phase of despondency, and looked expectantly forward towards social betterment. They held that the evils of the world, including poverty and warfare, existed because the kind of men whose motives were greed and pride, and whose Bible was "the Gospel of Getting On," had been allowed to misguide and to misrule it. They had brutalized man; they had standardized, commercialized, mechanized, vulgarized, and metropolitanized his life. Their worldliness had been the deadliest enemy of romantic idealism (as it still is). What was needed, and what could be begun, was a revolt against such worldliness by an awakening of man's imagination to what life really was meant to be—free, natural, peaceful, beautiful, and humane. Under idealistic leadership in the past men had made some progress, though too slowly, towards civilization and towards the improvement of human character; and they could make more and speedier progress in the future.

Much of the literature produced after World War I was rooted in worldliness, and bore the bitter fruits of cynicism and pessimism. Now that World War II has ended, and a new generation is trying to rebuild civilization, there are signs of a revival of the spirit of resolute idealism. If we wish to "move forward with an active faith," to quote the last words of a great modern idealist, we can gain encouragement from the Romantics. In them there is neither fear nor defeatism. Their inspiration and imagination, guiding our own good will, can help to save our world from the abyss of falsehood, evil, and ugliness.

SELECTIONS FROM
THE PRE-ROMANTIC MOVEMENT

SELECTIONS FROM
THE PRE-ROMANTIC MOVEMENT

THE PRE-ROMANTIC MOVEMENT

It has been said by historians of literature that the romantic spirit had two notable manifestations before the Romantic Movement of the early nineteenth century,—one in Palestine in the days of Christ, the other in England in the days of Shakespeare; and it is undeniable that, not only in those periods but in others, many anticipations of modern Romanticism may be found in nearly all periods of literary history. But the most directly influential of these was the so-called Pre-Romantic Movement of the eighteenth century, which prepared the way for the great age itself. It used to be assumed that the differences between the age of Pope and the age of Wordsworth were clear and distinct, and that the passage from the earlier period to the later was abrupt and revolutionary. Students felt that they were mastering the subject when they learned to recognize certain allegedly sharp contrasts between the "neo-classic" and the "romantic." In point of fact, most of the Pre-Romantics were not dissenters from *all* classical tastes and views, even though they departed therefrom in one respect or another. The true history of the change is complicated; it illustrates the general principle that mankind usually advances by steps which are hesitant and meandering. Few of the Pre-Romantics understood fully in what new directions they were wandering. They rarely used the word Romanticism; and they promoted the rise of Romanticism only partially, or superficially, or with respect to merely one or two restricted subjects or phases. The great Romantics were to go further and deeper than these predecessors; they were to see more clearly their objective, and its universal relationships. Each of the authors of the selections which follow contributed something to the beginnings of the movement. But in some cases the fact that they were Pre-Romantics is not the most important or admirable characteristic of their work,—e.g., in the cases of Gray and Burns; while in other instances,—e.g., those of Macpherson, or "Ossian," and Chatterton,—that fact is probably the chief reason why they are still read. All of them are here considered only with respect to the part they played in the new movement.

In the first half of the eighteenth century there began to dawn, both in the popular drama of sensibility and in academic philosophy, a greater faith in man's instinctive and emotional nature, in what Lord Shaftesbury called his "moral sense." James Thomson, writing not in the heroic couplet but in blank verse, combined sentimental sketches of virtue in humble life with fond descriptions of nature in all seasons. The novelist Richardson founded an immensely popular school of sensibility, in fiction. Edward Young began the so-called Graveyard School, which reveled in melancholy. Mark Akenside versified the theory that the response to beauty and truth was a natural impulse; and, in accordance therewith, Joseph and Thomas Warton interpreted Spenser and Shakespeare as great poets because they were poets born, not made. With lyric grace, William Collins stressed rhapsody and wonder as essential elements of poetry, and sought such inspiration in the folk-superstitions of the Scottish Highlands. With even more nearly perfect art, Thomas Gray dwelt on similar themes,—expressing democratic sentiments in his famous *Elegy*, a love of the impassioned in his *Progress of Poesy*, and an interest in ruder and simpler ages of mankind in *The Bard* and *The Descent of Odin*.

In the second half of the century, such tendencies were broadened and accelerated. Goldsmith's *Deserted Village* deplored the decline of country villages with their lovable inhabitants, a decline attributed to the growth of luxurious cities. David Hartley expounded a psychology which derived all the intellectual activities from sensory experiences. "Ossian's" poems, the bold forgeries of Macpherson, seemed to justify the theory that the earlier periods were nobler than civilized modern times, and more conducive to genuine poetry. Chatterton's fabrications set the Middle Ages in a similar favorable light. The genuine *Reliques of Ancient Poetry*, edited by Percy, intensified the growing interest in the life and literature of the past. Pseudo-historical fiction, developing into the melodramatic Gothic Novel, under the hands of Horace Walpole, Mrs. Radcliffe, and "Monk" Lewis, found the past a conveniently pliable setting for sentimental, supernatural, and terrifying actions and for extremely noble or extremely villainous characters. The gentler domestic aspects of Pre-Romanticism were fostered with tenderness and sincerity by William Cowper; while Robert Burns, the ploughman-poet, arose to prove that there was more than sentimental dreaming in the theory that the best poetry ought to spring from life close to nature and to the heart of the common people. Finally, the explosive possibilities in some of the Pre-Romantic ideas and yearnings broke forth in the American Revolution, and even more violently in the French. Those events dramatically indicated to an astonished world that apparently unimportant changes in the feelings and ideals of mere men of letters could ultimately destroy a long-established social order and endeavor to establish one nearer to the heart's desires.

ANTHONY ASHLEY COOPER,
Third Earl of Shaftesbury (1671-1713)

FROM **AN INQUIRY CONCERN-
ING VIRTUE OR MERIT**

[THE MORAL SENSE]

The mind, which is spectator or auditor of other minds, cannot be without its eye and ear, so as to discern proportion, distinguish sound, and scan each sentiment or thought which comes before it. It can let nothing escape its censure. It feels the soft and harsh, the agreeable and disagreeable, in the affections; and finds a foul and fair, a harmonious and a dissonant, as really and truly here, as in any musical numbers or in the outward forms or representations of sensible things. Nor can it withhold its admiration and ecstasy, its aversion and scorn, any more in what relates to one than to the other of these subjects. So that to deny the common and natural sense of a sublime and beautiful in things will appear affectation merely, to anyone who considers duly of this affair.

Now as in the sensible kind of objects the species or images of bodies, colors, and sounds are perpetually moving before our eyes, and acting on our senses, even when we sleep; so in the moral and intellectual kind, the forms and images of things are no less active and incumbent on the mind, at all seasons, and even when the real objects themselves are absent.

In these vagrant characters or pictures of manners which the mind of necessity figures to itself, and carries still about it, the heart cannot possibly remain neutral, but constantly takes part one way or other. However false or corrupt it be within itself, it finds the difference, as to beauty and comeliness, between one heart and another, one turn of affection, one behavior, one senti-ment, and another; and accordingly, in all disinterested cases, must approve in some measure of what is natural and honest, and disapprove what is dishonest and corrupt. . . .

The corruption of moral sense, . . . the wrong sense or false imagination of right and wrong, . . . can proceed only from the force of custom and education in opposition to Nature, as may be noted in those countries where, according to custom or politic institution, certain actions naturally foul and odious are repeatedly viewed with applause and honor ascribed to them. For thus 'tis possible that a man, forcing himself, may eat the flesh of his enemies, not only against his stomach but against his nature, and think it nevertheless both right and honorable, as supposing it to be of considerable service to his community and capable of advancing the name and spreading the terror of his nation. . . .

That it is possible for a creature capable of using reflection to have a liking or dislike of moral actions, and consequently a sense of right and wrong, before such time as he may have any settled notion of a God, is what will hardly be questioned, it being a thing not expected, or any way possible, that a creature such as man, arising from his childhood slowly and gradually to several degrees of reason and reflection, should at the very first be taken up with those speculations, or more refined sort of reflections, about the subject of God's existence.

Let us suppose that a creature who, wanting reason and being unable to reflect, has notwithstanding many good qualities and affections,—as love to his kind, courage, gratitude, or pity. 'Tis certain that if you give to this creature a reflecting faculty it will at the same instant approve of gratitude, kindness, and pity, be taken with any show or representation of the social passion, and think nothing more amiable than this or more odious than the contrary. And this is to be capable of virtue, and to have a sense of right and wrong.

1699(?)   1709

FROM THE MORALISTS: A RHAPSODY

[THE HARMONY OF THE MORAL WORLD AND THE NATURAL]

The balance of Europe, of trade, of power, is strictly sought after; while few have heard of the balance of their passions, or thought of holding these scales even. Few are acquainted with this province, or knowing in these affairs. But were we more so, as this inquiry would make us, we should then see beauty and decorum here as well as elsewhere in Nature, and the order of the moral world would then equal that of the natural. By this the beauty of virtue would appear, and hence, as has been shown, the supreme and sovereign beauty, the original of all which is good or amiable. . . .

Ye fields and woods, my refuge from the toilsome world of business, receive me in your quiet sanctuaries, and favor my retreat and thoughtful solitude.—Ye verdant plains, how gladly I salute ye!—Hail all ye blissful mansions! known seats! delightful prospects! majestic beauties of this earth, and all ye rural powers and graces!— Blessed be ye chaste abodes of happiest mortals, who here in peaceful innocence enjoy a life unenvied, though divine; whilst with its blessed tranquillity it affords a happy leisure and retreat for man, who, made for contemplation, and to search his own and other natures, may here best meditate the cause of things and, placed amidst the various scenes of nature, may nearer view her works.

O glorious Nature! supremely fair, and sovereignly good! All-loving and all-lovely, all-divine! Whose looks are so becoming, and of such infinite grace; whose study brings such wisdom, and whose contemplation such delight; whose every single work affords an ampler scene, and is a nobler spectacle, than all which ever Art presented!—O mighty Nature! wise substitute of Providence! impowered creatress! or thou impowering deity, supreme creator! Thee I invoke, and thee alone adore. To thee this solitude, this place, these rural meditations are sacred; whilst thus inspired with harmony of thought, though unconfined by words, and in loose numbers, I sing of Nature's order in created beings, and celebrate the beauties which resolve in thee, the source and principle of all beauty and perfection. . . .

"The appearances of ill, you say, are not necessarily that ill they represent to you?"

"I own it."

"Therefore what they represent may possibly be good?"

"It may."

"And therefore there may possibly be no real ill in things, but all may be perfectly concurrent to one interest—the interest of that universal One?"

"It may be so."

"Why, then, if it *may* be so (be not surprised), it follows that it *must* be so, on the account of that great unit and simple self-principle which you have granted in the 'Whole.' For whatever is possible in the whole, the nature or mind of the whole will put in execution for the whole's good; and if it be possible to exclude ill, it will exclude it. Therefore, since, notwithstanding the appearances, 'tis possible that ill may actually be excluded, count upon it that actually it is excluded. . . ."

Our element of earth . . . yonder we see cultivated with such care by the early swains now working in the plain below. Unhappy restless men, who first disdained these peaceful labors, gentle rural tasks, performed with such delight! What pride or what ambition bred this scorn? Hence all those fatal evils of your race! Enormous luxury, despising homely fare, ranges through seas and lands, rifles the globe; and men ingenious to their misery work out for themselves the means of heavier labor, anxious cares, and sorrow. Not satisfied to turn and manure for their use the wholesome and beneficial mould of this their earth, they dig yet deeper, and seeking out imaginary wealth, they search its very entrails. . . .

The wildness pleases. We seem to live alone with Nature. We view her in her inmost recesses, and contemplate her with more delight in these original wilds than in the artificial labyrinths and feigned wildernesses of the palace. The objects of the place, the scaly serpents, the savage beasts, and poisonous insects, how terrible soever, or how contrary to human nature, are beauteous in themselves, and fit to raise our thoughts in admiration of that divine wisdom, so far superior to our short views.

Unable to declare the use or service of all things in this universe, we are yet assured of the perfection of all, and of the justice of that economy to which all things are subservient, and in respect of which things seemingly deformed are amiable: disorder becomes regular, corruption wholesome, and poisons . . . prove healing and beneficial.

But behold! through a vast tract of sky before us the mighty Atlas rears his lofty head, covered with snow above the clouds. Beneath the mountain's foot the rocky country rises into hills, a proper basis of the ponderous mass above, where huge embodied rocks lie piled on one another and seem to prop the high arch of heaven.— See with what trembling steps poor mankind tread the narrow brink of the deep precipices! From whence with giddy horror they look down, mistrusting even the ground which bears them, whilst they hear the hollow sound of torrents underneath and see the ruin of the impending rock, with falling trees which hang with their roots upwards and seem to draw more ruin after them. Here thoughtless men, seized with the newness of such objects, become thoughtful and willingly contemplate the incessant changes of this earth's surface. They see, as in one instant, the revolutions of past ages, the fleeting forms of things, and the decay even of this our globe, whose youth and first formation they consider, whilst the apparent spoil and irreparable breaches of the wasted mountain show them the world itself only as a noble ruin, and make them think of its approaching period.—

But here, midway the mountain, a spacious border of thick wood harbors our wearied travelers, who now are come among the ever-green and lofty pines, the firs, and noble cedars, whose towering heads seem endless in the sky, the rest of trees appearing only as shrubs beside them. And here a different horror seizes our sheltered travelers, when they see the day diminished by the deep shapes of the vast wood which, closing thick above, spreads darkness and eternal night below. The faint and gloomy light looks horrid as the shade itself; and the profound stillness of these places imposes silence upon men, struck with the hoarse echoings of every sound within the spacious caverns of the wood. Here space

astonishes. Silence itself seems pregnant, whilst an unknown force works on the mind and dubious objects move the wakeful sense. Mysterious voices are either heard or fancied; and various forms of deity seem to present themselves and appear more manifest in these sacred sylvan scenes, such as of old gave rise to temples and favored the religion of the ancient world. Even we ourselves, who in plain characters may read divinity from so many bright parts of earth, choose rather these obscurer places to spell out that mysterious Being, which to our weak eyes appears at best under a veil of cloud. . . .

"Your Genius, the Genius of the place, and the Great Genius, have at last prevailed. I shall no longer resist the passion growing in me for things of a natural kind; where neither art, nor the conceit or caprice of man, has spoiled their genuine order by breaking in upon that primitive state. Even the rude rocks, the mossy caverns, the irregular unwrought grottoes and broken falls of waters, with all the horrid graces of the wilderness itself, as representing Nature more, will be the more engaging and appear with a magnificence beyond the formal mockery of princely gardens.—But tell me, I entreat you, how comes it that, excepting a few philosophers of your sort, the only people who are enamored in this way, and seek the woods, the rivers, or seashores, are your poor vulgar lovers?"

"Say not this," replied he, "of lovers only. For is it not the same with poets, and all those other students in Nature, and the arts which copy after her? In short, is not this the real case of all who are lovers either of the Muses or the Graces?"

"However," said I, "all those who are deep in this romantic way are looked upon, you know, as a people either plainly out of their wits or overrun with melancholy and enthusiasm. We always endeavor to recall them from these solitary places. And I must own that often when I have found my fancy run this way I have checked myself, not knowing what it was possessed me when I was passionately struck with objects of this kind."

"No wonder," replied he, "if we are at a loss when we pursue the shadow for the substance. . . ."

JAMES THOMSON (1700-1748)

FROM THE SEASONS

PREFACE

Nothing can have a better influence towards the revival of poetry than the choosing of great and serious subjects, such as at once amuse the fancy, enlighten the head, and warm the heart. These give a weight and dignity to the poem; nor is the pleasure—I should say rapture—both the writer and the reader feels unwarranted by reason or followed by repentant disgust. To be able to write on a dry, barren theme is looked upon by some as the sign of a happy, fruitful genius:—fruitful indeed! like one of the pendant gardens in Cheapside, watered every morning by the hand of the Alderman himself. And what are we commonly entertained with on these occasions save forced unaffecting fancies, little glittering prettinesses, mixed turns of wit and expression, which are as widely different from native poetry as buffoonery is from the perfection of human thinking? A genius fired with the charms of truth and nature is tuned to a sublimer pitch, and scorns to associate with such subjects.

I know no subject more elevating, more amusing; more ready to awake the poetical enthusiasm, the philosophical reflection, and the moral sentiment, than the works of nature. Where can we meet with such variety, such beauty, such magnificence? All that enlarges and transports the soul! What more inspiring than a calm, wide survey of them? In every dress nature is greatly charming—whether she puts on the crimson robes of the morning, the strong effulgence of noon, the sober suit of the evening, or the deep sables of blackness and tempest! How gay looks the spring! how glorious the summer! how pleasing the autumn! and how venerable the winter!— But there is no thinking of these things without breaking out into poetry; which is, by-the-by, a plain and undeniable argument of their superior excellence.

For this reason the best, both ancient, and modern, poets have been passionately fond of retirement, and solitude. The wild romantic country was their delight. And they seem never to have been more happy, than when, lost in unfrequented fields, far from the little busy world, they were at leisure, to meditate, and sing the works of nature.

FROM WINTER

[HARDSHIPS AND BENEVOLENCE]

The keener tempests come; and, fuming dun
From all the livid east or piercing north,
Thick clouds ascend, in whose capacious womb
A vapory deluge lies, to snow congealed.
Heavy they roll their fleecy world along,   5
And the sky saddens with the gathered storm.
Through the hushed air the whitening shower descends,
At first thin wavering, till at last the flakes
Fall broad and wide and fast, dimming the day
With a continual flow. The cherished fields   10
Put on their winter robe of purest white;
'Tis brightness all, save where the new snow melts
Along the mazy current; low the woods
Bow their hoar head; and ere the languid sun
Faint from the west emits his evening ray,   15
Earth's universal face, deep-hid and chill,
Is one wild dazzling waste, that buries wide
The works of man. Drooping, the laborer-ox
Stands covered o'er with snow, and then demands
The fruit of all his toil. The fowls of heaven,   20

Tamed by the cruel season, crowd around
The winnowing store, and claim the little boon
Which Providence assigns them.   One alone,
The redbreast, sacred to the household gods,
Wisely regardful of th' embroiling sky,   25
In joyless fields and thorny thickets leaves
His shivering mates, and pays to trusted man
His annual visit: half-afraid, he first
Against the window beats; then brisk alights
On the warm hearth; then, hopping o'er the floor,   30
Eyes all the smiling family askance,
And pecks, and starts, and wonders where he is,
Till, more familiar grown, the table-crumbs
Attract his slender feet.   The foodless wilds
Pour forth their brown inhabitants.   The hare,   35
Though timorous of heart and hard beset
By death in various forms—dark snares, and dogs,
And more unpitying men,—the garden seeks,
Urged on by fearless want.   The bleating kind
Eye the black heaven, and next the glistening earth,   40
With looks of dumb despair; then, sad dispersed,
Dig for the withered herb through heaps of snow.
    Now, shepherds, to your helpless charge be kind:
Baffle the raging year, and fill their pens
With food at will; lodge them below the storm,   45
And watch them strict, for from the bellowing east,
In this dire season, oft the whirlwind's wing
Sweeps up the burthen of whole wintry plains
At one wide waft, and o'er the hapless flocks,
Hid in the hollow of two neighboring hills,   50
The billowy tempest whelms, till, upward urged,
The valley to a shining mountain swells,
Tipped with a wreath high-curling in the sky.
    As thus the snows arise, and foul and fierce
All Winter drives along the darkened air,   55
In his own loose-revolving fields the swain
Disastered stands; sees other hills ascend,
Of unknown, joyless brow, and other scenes,
Of horrid prospect, shag the trackless plain;
Nor finds the river nor the forest, hid   60
Beneath the formless wild, but wanders on
From hill to dale, still more and more astray,
Impatient flouncing through the drifted heaps,
Stung with the thoughts of home.   The thoughts of home
Rush on his nerves, and call their vigor forth   65
In many a vain attempt.   How sinks his soul,
What black despair, what horror fills his heart,
When, for the dusky spot which fancy feigned
His tufted cottage rising through the snow,
He meets the roughness of the middle waste,   70
Far from the track and blest abode of man,
While round him night resistless closes fast,
And every tempest, howling o'er his head,
Renders the savage wilderness more wild!
Then throng the busy shapes into his mind   75
Of covered pits unfathomably deep
(A dire descent!), beyond the power of frost;
Of faithless bogs; of precipices huge,
Smoothed up with snow; and—what is land unknown,

What water—of the still unfrozen spring, 80
In the loose marsh or solitary lake,
Where the fresh fountain from the bottom boils.
These check his fearful steps; and down he sinks
Beneath the shelter of the shapeless drift,
Thinking o'er all the bitterness of death, 85
Mixed with the tender anguish nature shoots
Through the wrung bosom of the dying man—
His wife, his children, and his friends unseen.
In vain for him th' officious wife prepares
The fire fair-blazing and the vestment warm; 90
In vain his little children, peeping out
Into the mingling storm, demand their sire,
With tears of artless innocence.   Alas!
Nor wife nor children more shall he behold,
Nor friends nor sacred home: on every nerve 95
The deadly Winter seizes, shuts up sense,
And, o'er his inmost vitals creeping cold,
Lays him along the snows a stiffened corse,
Stretched out and bleaching in the northern blast.
    Ah, little think the gay licentious proud 100
Whom pleasure, power, and affluence surround;
They who their thoughtless hours in giddy mirth,
And wanton, often cruel, riot waste;
Ah, little think they, while they dance along,
How many feel, this very moment, death 105
And all the sad variety of pain:
How many sink in the devouring flood,
Or more devouring flame; how many bleed,
By shameful variance betwixt man and man;
How many pine in want, and dungeon glooms, 110
Shut from the common air, and common use
Of their own limbs; how many drink the cup
Of baleful grief, or eat the bitter bread
Of misery; sore pierced by wintry winds,
How many shrink into the sordid hut 115
Of cheerless poverty; how many shake
With all the fiercer tortures of the mind,
Unbounded passion, madness, guilt, remorse;
Whence tumbled headlong from the height of life,
They furnish matter for the tragic Muse, 120
Even in the vale, where wisdom loves to dwell,
With friendship, peace, and contemplation joined,
How many, racked with honest passions, droop
In deep retired distress; how many stand
Around the deathbed of their dearest friends, 125
And point the parting anguish. Thought fond man
Of these, and all the thousand nameless ills,
That one incessant struggle render life,
One scene of toil, of suffering, and of fate,
Vice in his high career would stand appalled, 130
And heedless rambling impulse learn to think;
The conscious heart of charity would warm,
And her wide wish benevolence dilate;
The social tear would rise, the social sigh;
And into clear perfection, gradual bliss, 135
Refining still, the social passions work.

1726

FROM SUMMER

[LIFE'S MEANING TO THE GENEROUS MIND]

Forever running an enchanted round,
Passes the day, deceitful vain and void,
As fleets the vision o'er the formful brain,
This moment hurrying wild th' impassioned soul,
The next in nothing lost. 'Tis so to him,   5
The dreamer of this earth, an idle blank;
A sight of horror to the cruel wretch,
Who all day long in sordid pleasure rolled,
Himself an useless load, has squandered vile,
Upon his scoundrel train, what might have cheered   10
A drooping family of modest worth.
But to the generous still-improving mind,
That gives the hopeless heart to sing for joy,
Diffusing kind beneficence around,
Boastless,—as now descends the silent dew,—   15
To him the long review of ordered life
Is inward rapture, only to be felt.

                                                    1727

FROM SPRING

[THE DIVINE FORCE IN SPRING]

Come, gentle Spring, ethereal mildness, come!
And from the bosom of yon dropping cloud,
While music wakes around, veiled in a shower
Of shadowing roses, on our plains descend!
O Hertford, fitted or to shine in courts   5
With unaffected grace, or walk the plain
With Innocence and Meditation joined
In soft assemblage, listen to my song,
Which thy own season paints, when nature all
Is blooming and benevolent, like thee.   10
And see where surly Winter passes off,
Far to the north, and calls his ruffian blasts:
His blasts obey, and quit the howling hill,
The shattered forest, and the ravaged vale;
While softer gales succeed, at whose kind touch—   15
Dissolving snows in livid torrents lost—
The mountains lift their green heads to the sky.
As yet the trembling year is unconfirmed,
And Winter oft at eve resumes the breeze,
Chills the pale morn, and bids his driving sleets   20
Deform the day delightless; so that scarce
The bittern knows his time, with bill engulfed,
To shake the sounding marsh, or from the shore
The plovers when to scatter o'er the heath
And sing their wild notes to the listening waste.   25
At last from Aries rolls the bounteous sun,
And the bright Bull receives him. Then no more
Th' expansive atmosphere is cramped with cold,
But, full of life and vivifying soul,
Lifts the light clouds sublime and spreads them thin,   30

Fleecy and white, o'er all-surrounding heaven;
Forth fly the tepid airs, and, unconfined,
Unbinding earth, the moving softness strays.
Joyous, th' impatient husbandman perceives
Relenting nature, and his lusty steers   35
Drives from their stalls, to where the well-used plough
Lies in the furrow, loosened from the frost;
There, unrefusing, to the harnessed yoke
They lend their shoulder, and begin their toil,
Cheered by the simple song and soaring lark;   40
Meanwhile incumbent o'er the shining share
The master leans, removes th' obstructing clay,
Winds the whole work, and sidelong lays the glebe.
White through the neighboring fields the sower stalks,
With measured step, and liberal throws the grain   45
Into the faithful bosom of the ground;
The harrow follows harsh, and shuts the scene.
   Be gracious, Heaven! for now laborious man
Has done his part. Ye fostering breezes, blow!
Ye softening dews, ye tender showers, descend!   50
And temper all, thou world-reviving sun,
Into the perfect year! Nor ye who live
In luxury and ease, in pomp and pride,
Think these lost themes unworthy of your ear.
Such themes as these the rural Maro sung   55
To wide-imperial Rome, in the full height
Of elegance and taste, by Greece refined.
In ancient times, the sacred plough employed
The kings and awful fathers of mankind;
And some, with whom compared your insect tribes   60
Are but the beings of a summer's day,
Have held the scale of empire, ruled the storm
Of mighty war, then with victorious hand,
Disdaining little delicacies, seized
The plough, and, greatly independent, scorned   65
All the vile stores corruption can bestow.
Ye generous Britons, venerate the plough;
And o'er your hills and long-withdrawing vales
Let Autumn spread his treasures to the sun,
Luxuriant and unbounded! As the sea,   70
Far through his azure, turbulent domain,
Your empire owns, and from a thousand shores
Wafts all the pomp of life into your ports,
So with superior boon may your rich soil,
Exuberant, Nature's better blessings pour   75
O'er every land, the naked nations clothe,
And be th' exhaustless granary of a world.
   Nor only through the lenient air this change,
Delicious, breathes: the penetrative sun,
His force deep-darting to the dark retreat   80
Of vegetation, sets the steaming power
At large, to wander o'er the verdant earth,
In various hues—but chiefly thee, gay green!
Thou smiling Nature's universal robe,
United light and shade, where the sight dwells   85
With growing strength and ever new delight.
From the moist meadow to the withered hill,
Led by the breeze, the vivid verdure runs,
And swells and deepens to the cherished eye.

The hawthorn whitens; and the juicy groves   90
Put forth their buds, unfolding by degrees,
Till the whole leafy forest stands displayed
In full luxuriance to the sighing gales,
Where the deer rustle through the twining brake,
And the birds sing concealed. At once, arrayed   95
In all the colors of the flushing year
By Nature's swift and secret-working hand,
The garden glows, and fills the liberal air
With lavished fragrance, while the promised fruit
Lies yet a little embryo, unperceived,   100
Within its crimson folds. Now from the town,
Buried in smoke and sleep and noisome damps,
Oft let me wander o'er the dewy fields,
Where freshness breathes, and dash the trembling drops
From the bent bush, as through the verdant maze   105
Of sweet-briar hedges I pursue my walk;
Or taste the smell of dairy; or ascend
Some eminence, Augusta, in thy plains,
And see the country, far diffused around,
One boundless blush, one white-empurpled shower   110
Of mingled blossoms, where the raptured eye
Hurries from joy to joy, and, hid beneath
The fair profusion, yellow Autumn spies.

                  . . . .

What is this mighty breath, ye sages, say,
That in a powerful language, felt not heard,   115
Instructs the fowl of heaven, and through their breast
These arts of love diffuses?   What but God?
Inspiring God! who boundless spirit all,
And unremitting energy, pervades,
Adjusts, sustains, and agitates the whole.   120
He ceaseless works alone, and yet alone
Seems not to work; with such perfection framed
Is this complex, stupendous scheme of things.
But, though concealed, to every purer eye
Th' informing author in his works appears: 125
Chief, lovely Spring, in thee, and thy soft scenes,
The smiling God is seen; while water, earth,
And air attest his bounty; which exalts
The brute creation to this finer thought,
And annual melts their undesigning hearts   130
Profusely thus in tenderness and joy.
   Still let my song a nobler note assume,
And sing th' infusive force of Spring on man,
When heaven and earth, as if contending, vie
To raise his being, and serene his soul.   135
Can he forbear to join the general smile
Of nature?   Can fierce passions vex his breast,
While every gale is peace, and every grove
Is melody?   Hence from the bounteous walks
Of flowing Spring, ye sordid sons of earth,   140
Hard, and unfeeling of another's woe;
Or only lavish to yourselves; away!
But come, ye generous minds, in whose wide thought,
Of all his works, creative bounty burns
With warmest beam!   145

                      1728

from AUTUMN

[THE PLEASING SADNESS OF THE DECLINING YEAR]

But see! the fading many-colored woods,
Shade deepening over shade, the country round
Imbrown, a crowded umbrage, dusk and dun,
Of every hue from wan declining green
To sooty dark. These now the lonesome Muse,   5
Low-whispering, lead into their leaf-strown walks,
And give the season in its latest view.
Meantime, light-shadowing all, a sober calm
Fleeces unbounded ether, whose least wave
Stands tremulous, uncertain where to turn   10
The gentle current, while, illumined wide,
The dewy-skirted clouds imbibe the sun,
And through their lucid veil his softened force
Shed o'er the peaceful world. Then is the time,
For those whom wisdom and whom nature charm,   15
To steal themselves from the degenerate crowd,
And soar above this little scene of things,
To tread low-thoughted Vice beneath their feet,
To soothe the throbbing passions into peace,
And woo lone Quiet in her silent walks.   20
Thus solitary, and in pensive guise,
Oft let me wander o'er the russet mead
And through the saddened grove, where scarce is heard
One dying strain to cheer the woodman's toil.
Haply some widowed songster pours his plaint,   25
Far, in faint warblings, through the tawny copse;
While congregated thrushes, linnets, larks,
And each wild throat whose artless strains so late
Swelled all the music of the swarming shades,
Robbed of their tuneful souls, now shivering sit   30
On the dead tree, a dull despondent flock;
With not a brightness waving o'er their plumes,
And naught save chattering discord in their note.
Oh, let not, aimed from some inhuman eye,
The gun the music of the coming year   35
Destroy, and harmless, unsuspecting harm,
Lay the weak tribes a miserable prey,
In mingled murder fluttering on the ground!
The pale descending year, yet pleasing still,
A gentler mood inspires: for now the leaf   40
Incessant rustles from the mournful grove,
Oft startling such as, studious, walk below,
And slowly circles through the waving air;
But should a quicker breeze amid the boughs
Sob, o'er the sky the leafy deluge streams,   45
Till, choked and matted with the dreary shower,
The forest walks, at every rising gale,
Roll wide the withered waste and whistle bleak.
Fled is the blasted verdure of the fields,
And, shrunk into their beds, the flowery race   50
Their sunny robes resign; even what remained
Of stronger fruits fall from the naked tree;
And woods, fields, gardens, orchards, all around,
The desolated prospect thrills the soul.

1730

A HYMN

[CONCLUDING THE SEASONS]

These, as they change, Almighty Father, these,
Are but the varied God.   The rolling year
Is full of Thee.   Forth in the pleasing Spring
Thy beauty walks, thy tenderness and love.
Wide-flush the fields; the softening air is balm; 5
Echo the mountains round; the forest smiles;
And every sense, and every heart is joy.
Then comes thy glory in the summer-months,
With light and heat refulgent.   Then thy sun
Shoots full perfection through the swelling year: 10
And oft thy voice in dreadful thunder speaks;
And oft at dawn, deep noon, or falling eve,
By brooks and groves, in hollow-whispering gales.
Thy bounty shines in autumn unconfined,
And spreads a common feast for all that lives. 15
In winter awful thou! with clouds and storms
Around thee thrown, tempest o'er tempest rolled
Majestic darkness! on the whirlwind's wing,
Riding sublime, thou bidst the world adore,
And humblest nature with thy northern blast. 20
 Mysterious round! what skill, what force Divine,
Deepfelt, in these appear! a simple train,
Yet so delightful mixed, with such kind art,
Such beauty and beneficence combined:
Shade, unperceived, so softening into shade; 25
And all so forming an harmonious whole;
That, as they still succeed, they ravish still.
But wandering oft, with brute unconscious gaze,
Man marks not Thee, marks not the mighty hand;
That, ever-busy, wheels the silent spheres; 30
Works in the secret deep; shoots, steaming, thence
The fair profusion that o'erspreads the spring:
Flings from the sun direct the flaming day;
Feeds every creature; hurls the tempest forth;
And, as on earth this grateful change revolves, 35
With transport touches all the springs of life.
 Nature, attend! join every living soul,
Beneath the spacious temple of the sky,
In adoration join; and ardent raise
One general song!   To Him, ye vocal gales, 40
Breathe soft, whose spirit in your freshness breathes.
Oh, talk of Him in solitary glooms
Where o'er the rock the scarcely waving pine
Fills the brown shade with a religious awe;
And ye, whose bolder note is heard afar, 45
Who shake the astonished world, lift high to heaven
Th' impetuous song, and say from whom you rage.
His praise, ye brooks, attune, ye trembling rills;
And let me catch it as I muse along.
Ye headlong torrents, rapid and profound; 50
Ye softer floods, that lead the humid maze
Along the vale; and thou, majestic main,
A secret world of wonders in thyself,
Sound His stupendous praise, whose greater voice

Or bids you roar, or bids your roarings fall.   55
So roll your incense, herbs, and fruits, and flowers,
In mingled clouds to Him, whose sun exalts,
Whose breath perfumes you, and whose pencil paints.
Ye forests, bend, ye harvests, wave to Him;
Breathe your still song into the reaper's heart,   60
As home he goes beneath the joyous moon.
Ye that keep watch in Heaven, as earth asleep
Unconscious lies, effuse your mildest beams;
Ye constellations, while your angels strike,
Amid the spangled sky, the silver lyre.   65
Great source of day! blest image here below
Of thy Creator, ever pouring wide,
From world to world, the vital ocean round,
On nature write with every beam His praise.
The thunder rolls: be hushed the prostrate world,   70
While cloud to cloud returns the solemn hymn.
Bleat out afresh, ye hills; ye mossy rocks,
Retain the sound; the broad responsive low,
Ye valleys, raise; for the Great Shepherd reigns,
And his unsuffering kingdom yet will come.   75
Ye woodlands, all awake; a boundless song
Burst from the groves; and when the restless day,
Expiring, lays the warbling world asleep,
Sweetest of birds! sweet Philomela, charm
The listening shades, and teach the night His praise.   80
Ye chief, for whom the whole creation smiles;
At once the head, the heart, the tongue of all,
Crown the great hymn! in swarming cities vast,
Assembled men to the deep organ join
The long resounding voice, oft breaking clear,   85
At solemn pauses, through the swelling base;
And, as each mingling flame increases each,
In one united ardor rise to Heaven.
Or if you rather choose the rural shade,
And find a fane in every sacred grove,   90
There let the shepherd's lute, the virgin's lay,
The prompting seraph, and the poet's lyre,
Still sing the God of Seasons as they roll.
For me, when I forget the darling theme,
Whether the blossom blows, the Summer ray   95
Russets the plain, inspiring Autumn gleams,
Or Winter rises in the blackening east—
Be my tongue mute, my fancy paint no more,
And, dead to joy, forget my heart to beat.
    Should Fate command me to the furthest verge   100
Of the green earth, to distant barbarous climes,
Rivers unknown to song; where first the sun
Gilds Indian mountains, or his setting beam
Flames on the Atlantic isles, 'tis nought to me;
Since God is ever present, ever felt,   105
In the void waste as in the city full;
And where He vital breathes, there must be joy.
When even at last the solemn hour shall come,
And wing my mystic flight to future worlds,
I cheerfully will obey; there with new powers,   110
Will rising wonders sing. I cannot go
Where Universal Love not smiles around,
Sustaining all yon orbs, and all their suns;
From seeming evil still educing good,

And better thence again, and better still,   115
In infinite progression. But I lose
Myself in Him, in light ineffable!
Come, then, expressive silence, muse His praise.

                                1730

FROM THE CASTLE OF INDOLENCE

O mortal man, who livest here by toil,
Do not complain of this thy hard estate:
That like an emmet thou must ever moil
Is a sad sentence of an ancient date;
And, certes, there is for it reason great,   5
For though sometimes it makes thee weep and wail,
And curse thy star, and early drudge and late,
Withouten that would come an heavier bale—
Loose life, unruly passions, and diseases pale.

In lowly dale, fast by a river's side,   10
With woody hill o'er hill encompassed round,
A most enchanting wizard did abide,
Than whom a fiend more fell is nowhere found.
It was, I ween, a lovely spot of ground;
And there a season atween June and May,   15
Half prankt with spring, with summer half imbrowned,
A listless climate made, where, sooth to say,
No living wight could work, ne carèd even for play.

Was naught around but images of rest:
Sleep-soothing groves, and quiet lawns between;   20
And flowery beds that slumbrous influence kest,
From poppies breathed; and beds of pleasant green,
Where never yet was creeping creature seen.
Meantime unnumbered glittering streamlets played,
And hurlèd everywhere their waters sheen,   25
That, as they bickered through the sunny glade,
Though restless still themselves, a lulling murmur made.

Joined to the prattle of the purling rills,
Were heard the lowing herds along the vale,
And flocks loud-bleating from the distant hills,   30
And vacant shepherds piping in the dale;
And now and then sweet Philomel would wail,
Or stock doves 'plain amid the forest deep,
That drowsy rustled to the sighing gale;
And still a coil the grasshopper did keep: 35
Yet all these sounds, yblent, inclinèd all to sleep.

Full in the passage of the vale, above,
A sable, silent, solemn forest stood,
Where naught but shadowy forms was seen to move,
As Idless fancied in her dreaming mood;   40
And up the hills, on either side, a wood
Of blackening pines, aye waving to and fro,
Sent forth a sleepy horror through the blood;
And where this valley winded out, below,
The murmuring main was heard, and scarcely heard, to flow.   45

A pleasing land of drowsyhed it was:
Of dreams that wave before the half-shut eye;
And of gay castles in the clouds that pass,
Forever flushing round a summer sky.
There eke the soft delights, that witchingly   50
Instil a wanton sweetness through the breast,
And the calm pleasures, always hovered nigh;
But whate'er smacked of 'noyance or unrest
Was far, far off expelled from this delicious nest.

The landskip such, inspiring perfect ease,   55
Where Indolence (for so the wizard hight)
Close-hid his castle mid embowering trees,
That half shut out the beams of Phœbus bright,
And made a kind of checkered day and night.
Meanwhile, unceasing at the massy gate,   60
Beneath a spacious palm, the wicked wight
Was placed; and, to his lute, of cruel fate
And labor harsh complained, lamenting man's estate.

Thither continual pilgrims crowded still,
From all the roads of earth that pass there by;   65
For, as they chaunced to breathe on neighboring hill,
The freshness of this valley smote their eye,
And drew them ever and anon more nigh,
Till clustering round th' enchanter false they hung,
Ymolten with his syren melody,   70
While o'er th' enfeebling lute his hand he flung,
And to the trembling chords these tempting verses sung:

"Behold, ye pilgrims of this earth, behold!
See all but man with unearned pleasure gay!
See her bright robes the butterfly unfold,   75
Broke from her wintry tomb in prime of May.
What youthful bride can equal her array?
Who can with her for easy pleasure vie?
From mead to mead with gentle wing to stray,
From flower to flower on balmy gales to fly,   80
Is all she has to do beneath the radiant sky.

"Behold the merry minstrels of the morn,
The swarming songsters of the careless grove,
Ten thousand throats that, from the flowering thorn,
Hymn their good God and carol sweet of love,   85
Such grateful kindly raptures then emove!
They neither plough nor sow; ne, fit for flail,
E'er to the barn the nodding sheaves they drove;
Yet theirs each harvest dancing in the gale,
Whatever crowns the hill or smiles along the vale.   90

"Outcast of Nature, man! the wretched thrall
Of bitter-dropping sweat, of sweltry pain,
Of cares that eat away thy heart with gall,
And of the vices, an inhuman train,
That all proceed from savage thirst of gain: 95
For when hard-hearted Interest first began
To poison earth, Astræa left the plain;
Guile, violence, and murder seized on man,
And, for soft milky streams, with blood the rivers ran."

          .   .   .   .

He ceased. But still their trembling ears retained
The deep vibrations of his 'witching song,
That, by a kind of magic power, constrained
To enter in, pell-mell, the listening throng: 175
Heaps poured on heaps, and yet they slipped along
In silent ease; as when beneath the beam
Of summer moons, the distant woods among,
Or by some flood all silvered with the gleam,
The soft-embodied fays through airy portal stream.   180

. . . .

Of all the gentle tenants of the place,   505
There was a man of special grave remark;
A certain tender gloom o'erspread his face,
Pensive, not sad; in thought involved, not dark;
As soote this man could sing as morning lark,
And teach the noblest morals of the heart;   510
But these his talents were yburied stark:
Of the fine stores he nothing would impart,
Which or boon Nature gave, or nature-painting Art.

To noontide shades incontinent he ran,
Where purls the brook with sleep-inviting sound,   515
Or when Dan Sol to slope his wheels began,
Amid the broom he basked him on the ground,
Where the wild thyme and camomil are found;
There would he linger, till the latest ray
Of light sate trembling on the welkin's bound,   520
Then homeward through the twilight shadows stray,
Sauntering and slow: so had he passed many a day.

Yet not in thoughtless slumber were they passed;
For oft the heavenly fire, that lay concealed
Beneath the sleeping embers, mounted fast,   525
And all its native light anew revealed;
Oft as he traversed the cerulean field,
And marked the clouds that drove before the wind,
Ten thousand glorious systems would he build,
Ten thousand great ideas filled his mind: 530
But with the clouds they fled, and left no trace behind.

1748

EDWARD YOUNG (1683-1765)

FROM THE COMPLAINT, OR NIGHT THOUGHTS

[IN THE DARKNESS OF NIGHT]

Tired nature's sweet restorer, balmy Sleep!
He, like the world, his ready visit pays
Where Fortune smiles; the wretched he forsakes,
Swift on his downy pinion flies from woe,
And lights on lids unsullied with a tear.   5
From short (as usual) and disturbed repose,
I wake: how happy they who wake no more!

Yet that were vain, if dreams infest the grave.
I wake, emerging from a sea of dreams
Tumultuous, where my wrecked, desponding thought   10
From wave to wave of fancied misery
At random drove, her helm of reason lost;
Though now restored, 'tis only change of pain,
A bitter change! severer for severe.
The day too short for my distress; and Night,   15
E'en in the zenith of her dark domain,
Is sunshine to the color of my fate.
    Night, sable goddess! from her ebon throne,
In rayless majesty, now stretches forth
Her leaden scepter o'er a slumbering world.   20
Silence how dead! and darkness how profound!
Nor eye nor listening ear an object finds:
Creation sleeps. 'Tis as the general pulse
Of life stood still, and Nature made a pause,
An awful pause, prophetic of her end.   25
And let her prophecy be soon fulfilled!
Fate, drop the curtain! I can lose no more.
    Silence and Darkness, solemn sisters, twins
From ancient Night, who nurse the tender thought
To reason, and on reason build resolve   30
(That column of true majesty in man),
Assist me! I will thank you in the grave,
The grave your kingdom; there this frame shall fall
A victim sacred to your dreary shrine.

                  1742

LIVE EVER HERE?

Live ever here, Lorenzo? Shocking thought!
So shocking, they who wish disown it, too;
Disown from shame what they from folly crave.
Live ever in the womb nor see the light?
For what live ever here? With laboring step   5
To tread our former footsteps? pace the round
Eternal? to climb life's worn, heavy wheel,
Which draws up nothing new? to beat, and beat
The beaten track? to bid each wretched day
The former mock? to surfeit on the same,   10
And yawn our joys? or thank a misery
For change, though sad? to see what we have seen;
Hear, till unheard, the same old slabbered tale?
To taste the tasted, and at each return
Less tasteful? o'er our palates to decant   15
Another vintage? strain a flatter year,
Through loaded vessels and a laxer tone?
Crazy machines, to grind earth's wasted fruits!

                  1743

WELCOME, DEATH!

Then welcome, death! thy dreaded harbingers,
Age and disease; disease, though long my guest;
That plucks my nerves, those tender strings of life;
Which, plucked a little more, will toll the bell,
That calls my few friends to my funeral;   5
Where feeble nature drops, perhaps, a tear,

While reason and religion, better taught.
Congratulate the dead, and crown his tomb
With wreath triumphant. Death is victory;
It binds in chains the raging ills of life: 10
Lust and ambition, wrath and avarice,
Dragged at his chariot-wheel, applaud his power.
That ills corrosive, cares importunate,
Are not immortal too, O death! is thine.
Our day of dissolution!—name it right;   15
'Tis our great pay-day; 'tis our harvest, rich
And ripe: What though the sickle, sometimes keen,
Just scars us as we reap the golden grain?
More than thy balm, O Gilead! heals the wound.
Birth's feeble cry, and death's deep dismal groan,   20
Are slender tributes low-taxed nature pays
For mighty gain: the gain of each, a life!
But O! the last the former so transcends,
Life dies, compared: life lives beyond the grave.
    And feel I, death! no joy from thought of thee,   25
Death, the great counsellor, who man inspires
With every nobler thought and fairer deed!
Death, the deliverer, who rescues man!
Death, the rewarder, who the rescued crowns!
Death, that absolves my birth; a curse without it!   30
Rich death, that realizes all my cares,
Toils, virtues, hopes; without it a chimera!
Death, of all pain the period, not of joy;
Joy's source, and subject, still subsist unhurt;
One, in my soul; and one, in her great sire;   35
Though the four winds were warring for my dust.
Yes, and from winds, and waves, and central night,
Though prisoned there, my dust too I reclaim,
(To dust when drop proud nature's proudest spheres,)
And live entire. Death is the crown of life: 40
Were death denied, poor man would live in vain;
Were death denied, to live would not be life;
Were death denied, e'en fools would wish to die.
Death wounds to cure: we fall; we rise; we reign!
Spring from our fetters; fasten in the skies;   45
Where blooming Eden withers in our sight:
Death gives us more than was in Eden lost.
This king of terrors is the prince of peace.
When shall I die to vanity, pain, death?
When shall I die?—When shall I live for ever?   50

1743

FROM CONJECTURES ON ORIGINAL COMPOSITION

But there are who write with vigor and success, to the world's delight and their own renown. These are the glorious fruits where genius prevails. The mind of a man of genius is a fertile and pleasant field, pleasant as Elysium, and fertile as Tempe; it enjoys a perpetual spring. Of that spring, originals are the fairest flowers; imitations are of quicker growth, but fainter bloom. Imitations are of two kinds; one of nature, one of authors: the first we call Originals, and confine the term Imitation to the second. I shall not enter into the curious inquiry of what is, or is not, strictly speaking, original, content with what all must allow, that some compositions are more so than others; and the more they are so, I say, the better. Originals are and ought to be great favorites, for they are great benefactors; they extend the republic of letters, and add a new province to its dominion. Imitators only give us a sort of duplicates of what we had, possibly much better, before, increasing the mere drug of books, while all that makes them valuable, knowledge and genius, are at a stand. The pen of an original writer, like Armida's wand, out of a barren waste calls a blooming spring. Out of that blooming spring, an imitator is a transplanter of laurels, which sometimes die on removal, [and] always languish in a foreign soil. . . .

We read imitation with somewhat of his languor who listens to a twice-told tale. Our spirits rouse at an original that is a perfect stranger, and all throng to learn what news from a foreign land. And though it comes like an Indian prince, adorned with feathers only, having little of weight, yet of our attention it will rob the more solid, if not equally new. Thus every telescope is lifted at a new-discovered star; it makes a hundred astronomers in a moment, and denies equal notice to the sun. But if an original, by being as excellent as new, adds admiration to surprise, then are we at the writer's mercy; on the strong wind of his imagination, we are snatched from Britain to Italy, from climate to climate, from pleasure to pleasure; we have no home, no thought, of our own till the magician drops his pen. And then falling down into ourselves, we awake to flat realities, lamenting the change, like the beggar who dreamt himself a prince. . . .

But why are originals so few? Not because the writer's harvest is over, the great reapers of antiquity having left nothing to be gleaned after them; nor because the human mind's teeming time is past, or because it is incapable of putting forth unprecedented births; but because illustrious examples engross, prejudice, and intimidate. They engross our attention, and so prevent a due inspection of ourselves; they prejudice our judgment in favor of their abilities, and so lessen the sense of our own; and they intimidate us with the splendor of their renown, and thus under diffidence bury our strength. Nature's impossibilities and those of diffidence lie wide asunder. . . .

Had Milton never wrote, Pope had been less to blame. But when in Milton's genius, Homer, as it were, personally rose to

forbid Britons doing him that ignoble wrong, it is less pardonable, by that effeminate decoration, to put Achilles in petticoats a second time. How much nobler had it been, if his numbers had rolled on in full flow, through the various modulations of masculine melody, into those grandeurs of solemn sound which are indispensably demanded by the native dignity of heroic song! How much nobler, if he had resisted the temptation of that Gothic demon, which modern poesy tasting, became mortal! O how unlike the deathless, divine harmony of three great names (how justly joined!) of Milton, Greece, and Rome! His verse, but for this little speck of mortality in its extreme parts, as his hero had in his heel, like him, had been invulnerable and immortal. But unfortunately, that was undipped in Helicon, as this in Styx. Harmony as well as eloquence is essential to poesy; and a murder of his music is putting half Homer to death. Blank is a term of diminution; what we mean by blank verse is verse unfallen, uncursed; verse reclaimed, reënthroned in the true language of the gods, who never thundered, nor suffered their Homer to thunder, in rhyme. . . .

When such an ample area for renowned adventure in original attempts lies before us, shall we be as mere leaden pipes, conveying to the present age small streams of excellence from its grand reservoir in antiquity, and those too, perhaps, mudded in the pass? Originals shine like comets; have no peer in their path; are rivaled by none, and the gaze of all. All other compositions (if they shine at all) shine in clusters, like the stars in the galaxy, where, like bad neighbors, all suffer from all, each particular being diminished and almost lost in the throng.

If thoughts of this nature prevailed, if ancients and moderns were no longer considered as masters and pupils, but as hardmatched rivals for renown, then moderns, by the longevity of their labors, might one day become ancients themselves. And old time, that best weigher of merits, to keep his balance even, might have the golden weight of an Augustan age in both his scales; or rather our scale might descend, and that of antiquity (as a modern match for it strongly speaks) might kick the beam.
1759　　　　　　　　　　1759

MARK AKENSIDE (1721-1770)

FROM THE PLEASURES OF IMAGINATION

[THE ÆSTHETIC AND MORAL INFLUENCE OF NATURE]

           Fruitless is the attempt,
By dull obedience and by creeping toil
Obscure, to conquer the severe ascent
Of high Parnassus. Nature's kindling breath
Must fire the chosen genius; Nature's hand   5
Must string his nerves, and imp his eagle-wings,
Impatient of the painful steep, to soar
High as the summit, there to breathe at large
Ethereal air, with bards and sages old,
Immortal sons of praise.   10

             Even so did Nature's hand
To certain species of external things
Attune the finer organs of the mind:
So the glad impulse of congenial powers,
Or of sweet sounds, or fair-proportioned form,   15
The grace of motion, or the bloom of light,
Thrills through imagination's tender frame,
From nerve to nerve; all naked and alive
They catch the spreading rays, till now the soul
At length discloses every tuneful spring,   20
To that harmonious movement from without
Responsive.

          What then is taste, but these internal powers
Active, and strong, and feelingly alive
To each fine impulse? a discerning sense   25
Of decent and sublime, with quick disgust
From things deformed, or disarranged, or gross
In species? This, nor gems, nor stores of gold,
Nor purple state, nor culture can bestow;
But God alone, when first his active hand   30
Imprints the secret bias of the soul.
He, mighty parent wise and just in all,
Free as the vital breeze or light of heaven,
Reveals the charms of nature. Ask the swain
Who journeys homeward from a summer day's   35
Long labor, why, forgetful of his toils
And due repose, he loiters to behold
The sunshine gleaming as through amber clouds
O'er all the western sky; full soon, I ween,
His rude expression and untutored airs,   40
Beyond the power of language, will unfold
The form of beauty smiling at his heart—
How lovely! how commanding!

          Oh! blest of Heaven, whom not the languid songs
Of Luxury, the siren! nor the bribes   45
Of sordid Wealth, nor all the gaudy spoils

Of pageant Honor, can seduce to leave
Those ever-blooming sweets which, from the store
Of Nature, fair Imagination culls
To charm th' enlivened soul! What though not all   50
Of mortal offspring can attain the heights
Of envied life, though only few possess
Patrician treasures or imperial state;
Yet Nature's care, to all her children just,
With richer treasure and an ampler state,   55
Endows at large whatever happy man
Will deign to use them. His the city's pomp;
The rural honors his. Whate'er adorns
The princely dome, the column and the arch,
The breathing marbles and the sculptured gold,   60
Beyond the proud possessor's narrow claim,
His tuneful breast enjoys. For him the Spring
Distils her dews, and from the silken gem
Its lucid leaves unfolds; for him the hand
Of Autumn tinges every fertile branch   65
With blooming gold, and blushes like the morn.
Each passing hour sheds tribute from her wings;
And still new beauties meet his lonely walk,
And loves unfelt attract him. Not a breeze
Flies o'er the meadow, not a cloud imbibes   70
The setting sun's effulgence, not a strain
From all the tenants of the warbling shade
Ascends, but whence his bosom can partake
Fresh pleasure unreproved. Nor thence partakes
Fresh pleasure only; for th' attentive mind,   75
By this harmonious action on her powers,
Becomes herself harmonious: wont so oft
In outward things to meditate the charm
Of sacred order, soon she seeks at home
To find a kindred order, to exert   80
Within herself this elegance of love,
This fair-inspired delight; her tempered powers
Refine at length, and every passion wears
A chaster, milder, more attractive mien.
    But if to ampler prospects, if to gaze   85
On Nature's form where, negligent of all
These lesser graces, she assumes the part
Of that Eternal Majesty that weighed
The world's foundations, if to these the mind
Exalts her daring eye; then mightier far   90
Will be the change, and nobler. Would the forms
Of servile custom cramp her generous powers?
Would sordid policies, the barbarous growth
Of ignorance and rapine, bow her down
To tame pursuits, to indolence and fear?   95
Lo! she appeals to Nature, to the winds
And rolling waves, the sun's unwearied course,
The elements and seasons: all declare
For what th' Eternal Maker has ordained
The powers of man: we feel within ourselves   100
His energy divine: he tells the heart
He meant, he made us, to behold and love
What he beholds and loves, the general orb
Of life and being; to be great like him,
Beneficent and active. Thus the men   105
Whom Nature's works can charm, with God himself

Hold converse; grow familiar, day by day,
With his conceptions; act upon his plan;
And form to his, the relish of their souls.

1744

JOSEPH WARTON (1722-1800)

FROM THE ENTHUSIAST; OR, THE LOVER OF NATURE

Ye green-robed Dryads, oft at dusky eve
By wondering shepherds seen, to forests brown
To unfrequented meads, and pathless wilds,
Lead me from gardens decked with art's vain pomps.
Can gilt alcoves, can marble-mimic gods,   5
Parterres embroidered, obelisks, and urns
Of high relief; can the long, spreading lake,
Or vista lessening to the sight; can Stow,
With all her Attic fanes, such raptures raise,
As the thrush-haunted copse, where lightly leaps   10
The fearful fawn the rustling leaves along,
And the brisk squirrel sports from bough to bough,
While from an hollow oak, whose naked roots
O'erhang a pensive rill, the busy bees
Hum drowsy lullabies? The bards of old,   15
Fair Nature's friends, sought such retreats, to charm
Sweet Echo with their songs; oft too they met
In summer evenings, near sequestered bowers,
Or mountain nymph, or Muse, and eager learnt
The moral strains she taught to mend mankind.   20

   . . . .

Rich in her weeping country's spoils, Versailles
May boast a thousand fountains, that can cast
The tortured waters to the distant heavens:
Yet let me choose some pine-topped precipice
Abrupt and shaggy, whence a foamy stream,   25
Like Anio, tumbling roars; or some bleak heath,
Where straggling stands the mournful juniper,
Or yew-tree scathed; while in clear prospect round
From the grove's bosom spires emerge, and smoke
In bluish wreaths ascends, ripe harvests wave,   30
Low, lonely cottages, and ruined tops
Of Gothic battlements appear, and streams
Beneath the sunbeams twinkle.

   . . . .

Happy the first of men, ere yet confined
To smoky cities; who in sheltering groves,   35
Warm caves, and deep-sunk valleys lived and loved,
By cares unwounded; what the sun and showers,
And genial earth untillaged, could produce,
They gathered grateful, or the acorn brown
Or blushing berry; by the liquid lapse   40
Of murmuring waters called to slake their thirst,
Or with fair nymphs their sun-brown limbs to bathe;
With nymphs who fondly clasped their favorite youths,

Unawed by shame, beneath the beechen shade,
Nor wiles nor artificial coyness knew.   45
Then doors and walls were not; the melting maid
Nor frown of parents feared, nor husband's threats;
Nor had cursed gold their tender hearts allured:
Then beauty was not venal. Injured Love,   50
Oh! whither, god of raptures, art thou fled?
      .   .   .   .
What are the lays of artful Addison,
Coldly correct, to Shakespeare's warblings wild?
Whom on the winding Avon's willowed banks
Fair Fancy found, and bore the smiling babe
To a close cavern (still the shepherds show   55
The sacred place, whence with religious awe
They hear, returning from the field at eve,
Strange whisperings of sweet music through the air).
Here, as with honey gathered from the rock,
She fed the little prattler, and with songs   60
Oft soothed his wondering ears; with deep delight
On her soft lap he sat, and caught the sounds.
   Oft near some crowded city would I walk,
Listening the far-off noises, rattling cars,
Loud shouts of joy, sad shrieks of sorrow, knells   65
Full slowly tolling, instruments of trade,
Striking mine ears with one deep-swelling hum.
Or wandering near the sea, attend the sounds
Of hollow winds and ever-beating waves.
Even when wild tempests swallow up the plains,   70
And Boreas' blasts, big hail, and rains combine
To shake the groves and mountains, would I sit,
Pensively musing on the outrageous crimes
That wake Heaven's vengeance: at such solemn hours,
Demons and goblins through the dark air shriek,   75
While Hecat, with her black-browed sisters nine,
Rides o'er the Earth, and scatters woes and death.
Then, too, they say, in drear Egyptian wilds
The lion and the tiger prowl for prey
With roarings loud! The listening traveller   80
Starts fear-struck, while the hollow echoing vaults
Of pyramids increase the deathful sounds.
   But let me never fail in cloudless nights,
When silent Cynthia in her silver car
Through the blue concave slides, when shine the hills,   85
Twinkle the streams, and woods look tipped with gold,
To seek some level mead, and there invoke
Old Midnight's sister, Contemplation sage,
(Queen of the rugged brow and stern-fixed eye,)
To lift my soul above this little earth,   90
This folly-fettered world: to purge my ears,
That I may hear the rolling planet's song,
And tuneful turning spheres: if this be barred
The little fays, that dance in neighboring dales,
Sipping the night-dew, while they laugh and love,   95
Shall charm me with aërial notes.—As thus
I wander musing, lo, what awful forms
Yonder appear! sharp-eyed Philosophy
Clad in dun robes, an eagle on his wrist,
First meets my eye; next, virgin Solitude   100
Serene, who blushes at each gazer's sight;
Then Wisdom's hoary head, with crutch in hand,

Trembling, and bent with age; last Virtue's self,
Smiling, in white arrayed, who with her leads
Sweet Innocence, that prattles by her side,
A naked boy!—Harassed with fear I stop, 105
I gaze, when Virtue thus—"Whoe'er thou art,
Mortal, by whom I deign to be beheld
In these my midnight walks; depart, and say,
That henceforth I and my immortal train 110
Forsake Britannia's isle; who fondly stoops
To vice, her favorite paramour." She spoke,
And as she turned, her round and rosy neck,
Her flowing train, and long ambrosial hair,
Breathing rich odors, I enamored view. 115
　O who will bear me then to western climes,
Since virtue leaves our wretched land, to fields
Yet unpolluted with Iberian swords,
The isles of innocence, from mortal view
Deeply retired, beneath a plantain's shade, 120
Where happiness and quiet sit enthroned,
With simple Indian swains, that I may hunt
The boar and tiger through savannahs wild,
Through fragrant deserts and through citron groves?
There fed on dates and herbs, would I despise 125
The far-fetched cates of luxury, and hoards
Of narrow-hearted avarice; nor heed
The distant din of the tumultuous world.

1744

FROM AN ESSAY ON THE GENIUS
AND WRITINGS OF POPE

To the Rev. Dr. Young:

. . . I revere the memory of Pope, I respect and honor his abilities but I do not think him at the head of his profession. In other words, in that species of poetry wherein Pope excelled, he is superior to all mankind, and I only say that this species of poetry is not the most excellent one of the art.

We do not, it should seem, sufficiently attend to the difference there is betwixt a *man of wit, a man of sense,* and a *true poet.* Donne and Swift were undoubtedly men of wit and men of sense, but what traces have they left of *pure poetry?* It is remarkable that Dryden says of Donne, "He was the greatest wit though not the greatest poet of this nation." Fontenelle and La Motte are entitled to the former character but what can they urge to gain the latter? Which of these characters is the most valuable and useful is entirely out of the question; all I plead for is to have their several provinces kept distinct from each other and to impress on the reader that a clear head and acute understanding are not sufficient alone to make a *poet,* that the most solid observations on human life expressed with the utmost elegance and brevity are *morality,* and not *poetry,* that the *Epistles* of Boileau in *rhyme* are no more poetical than the *Characters* of La Bruyère in *prose,* and that it is a creative and glowing *Imagination,* "acer spiritus ac vis," and that alone that can stamp a writer with this exalted and very uncommon character which so few possess and of which so few can properly judge.

For one person who can adequately relish and enjoy a work of imagination, twenty are to be found who can taste and judge of observations on familiar life and the manners of the age. *The Satires* of Ariosto are more read than the *Orlando Furioso* or even Dante. Are there so many cordial admirers of Spenser and Milton, as of Hudibras if we strike out of the number of these supposed admirers those who appear such out of fashion and not of feeling? Swift's *Rhapsody on Poetry* is far more popular than Akenside's noble *Ode to Lord Huntingdon.* The *Epistles* on the Characters of Men and Women and your sprightly Satires, my good friend, are more frequently perused and quoted than *L'Allegro* and *Il Penseroso* of Milton. Had you written only these Satires, you would, indeed, have gained the title of a man of wit, and a man of sense, but, I am confident would not insist on being denominated a *poet merely* on their account. 5

"Non satis est puris versum prescribere verbis."

It is amazing this matter should ever have been mistaken when Horace has taken particular and repeated pains to settle and 10 adjust the opinion in question. He has more than once disclaimed all right and title to the name of *poet* on the score of his ethic and satiric pieces.

"—Neque enim concludere versum 15
Dixeris esse satis——"

are lines often repeated but whose meaning is not extended and weighed as it ought to be. Nothing can be more judicious than 20 the method he prescribes, of trying whether any composition be essentially poetical or not; which is to drop entirely the measures and numbers and transpose and invert the order of the words; and in this unadorned 25 manner to peruse the passage. If there be really in it a true poetical spirit all your inversions and transpositions will not disguise and extinguish it, but it will retain its luster like a diamond unset and thrown 30 back into the rubbish of the mine. Let us make a little experiment on the following well-known lines, "Yes, you despise the man that is confined to books, who rails at humankind from his study, though what he 35 learns, he speaks, and may perhaps advance some general maxims or may be right by chance. The coxcomb bird, so grave and so talkative that cries, "whore, knave, and cuckold," from his cage, though he rightly 40 call many a passenger, you hold him no philosopher. And yet, such is the fate of all extremes, men may be read too much, as well as books. We grow more partial for the sake of the observer to observations 45 which we ourselves make, less so to written wisdom because another's. Maxims are drawn from notions, and those from guess." What shall we say of this passage? Why, that it is most excellent sense, but just as 50 poetical as the "qui fit Maecenas" of the author who recommends this method of trial. Take ten lines of the *Iliad, Paradise Lost* or even of the *Georgics* of Virgil and see whether by any process of critical chem- 55 istry you can lower and reduce them to the tameness of prose. You will find that they will appear like Ulysses in his disguise of rags, still a hero, though lodged in the cottage of the herdsman Eumaeus.

The sublime and the pathetic are the two chief nerves of all genuine poesy. What is there transcendently sublime or pathetic in Pope? In his works there is, indeed, "nihil inane, nihil arcessitum; puro tamen fonti quam magno flumini proprior," as the excellent Quintilian remarks of Lysias. And because I am, perhaps, unwilling to speak out in plain English, I will adopt the following passage of Voltaire, which, in my opinion, as exactly characterizes Pope as it does his model Boileau, for whom it was originally designed, "Incapable peut-être du sublime qui élève l'ame, et du Sentiment qui l'attendrit, mais fait pour éclairer ceux à qui la nature accorda l'un et l'autre, laborieux, sévère, précis, pur, harmonieux, il devint, enfin, le poète de la Raison."

Our English poets may, I think, be disposed in four different classes and degrees. In the first class I would place our only three sublime and pathetic poets, Spenser, Shakespeare, Milton. In the second class should be ranked such as possessed the true poetical genius in a more moderate degree, but who had noble talents for moral, ethical and panegyrical poesy. At the head of these are Dryden, Prior, Addison, Cowley, Waller, Garth, Fenton, Gay, Denham, Parnell. In the third class may be placed men of wit, of elegant taste and lively fancy in describing familiar life, though not the higher scenes of poetry. Here may be numbered Butler, Swift, Rochester, Donne, Dorset, Oldham. In the fourth class the mere versifiers, however smooth and mellifluous some of them may be thought, should be disposed. Such as Pitt, Sandys, Fairfax, Broome, Buckingham, Landsdown. This enumeration is not intended as a complete catalogue of writers and in their proper order but only to mark out briefly the different species of our celebrated authors. In which of these classes Pope deserves to be placed the following work is intended to determine. . . .

Thus have I endeavored to give a critical account, with freedom, but it is hoped with impartiality, of each of Pope's works; by which review it will appear, that the largest portion of them is of the didactic, moral, and satyric kind; and consequently, not of the most poetic species of poetry; whence it is manifest, that good sense and judgment were his characteristical excellencies, rather than fancy and invention: not that the author of *The Rape of the Lock,* and *Eloisa,* can be thought to want 60 imagination; but because his imagination was not his predominent talent, because he indulged it not, and because he gave not so many proofs of this talent as of the other. This turn of mind led him to admire French models; he studied Boileau attentively; formed himself upon him, as Milton formed himself upon the Grecian and Italian sons of Fancy. He stuck to describing modern manners; but those manners, because they are familiar, uniform, artificial, and polished, are, in their very nature, unfit for any lofty effort of the Muse. He gradually became one of the most correct, even, and exact poets that ever wrote; polishing his pieces with a care and assiduity, that no business or avocation ever interrupted; so that if he does not frequently ravish and transport his reader, yet he does not disgust him with unexpected inequalities, and absurd improprieties. Whatever poetical enthusiasm he actually possessed, he withheld and stifled. The perusal of him affects not our minds with such strong emotions as we feel from Homer and Milton; so that no man of a true poetical spirit, is master of himself while he reads them. Hence, he is a writer fit for universal perusal; adapted to all ages and stations; for the old and for the young; the man of business and the scholar. He who would think *The Fairy Queen, Palamon and Arcite, The Tempest,* or *Comus,* childish and romantic, might relish Pope. Surely, it is no narrow and niggardly encomium, to say he is the great Poet of Reason, the first of ethical authors in verse. And this species of writing is, after all, the surest road to an extensive reputation. It lies more level to the general capacities of men, than the higher flights of more genuine poetry. We all remember when even a Churchill was more in vogue than a Gray.

He that treats of fashionable follies and the topics of the day, that describes present persons and recent events, finds many readers, whose understandings and whose passions he gratifies. The name of Chesterfield on one hand, and of Walpole on the other, failed not to make a poem bought up and talked of. And it cannot be doubted that the *Odes* of Horace which celebrated, and the *Satires* which ridiculed, well-known and real characters at Rome, were more eagerly read and more frequently cited, than the *Æneid* and the *Georgics* of Virgil.

Where then, according to the question proposed at the beginning of this Essay, shall we with justice be authorized to place our admired Pope? Not, assuredly, in the same rank with Spenser, Shakespeare, and Milton; however justly we may applaud the *Eloisa* and *Rape of the Lock;* but, considering the correctness, elegance, and utility of his works, the weight of sentiment, and the knowledge of man they contain, we may venture to assign him a place, next to Milton, and just above Dryden. Yet, to bring our minds steadily to make this decision, we must forget, for a moment, the divine *Music Ode* of Dryden; and may, perhaps, then be compelled to confess, that though Dryden be the greater genius, yet Pope is the better artist.

The preference here given to Pope above other modern English poets, it must be remembered, is founded on the excellencies of his works in general, and taken all together; for there are parts and passages in other modern authors, in Young and in Thomson, for instance, equal to any of Pope; and he has written nothing in a strain so truly sublime, as *The Bard* of Gray.

1756

WILLIAM COLLINS (1721-1759)

A SONG FROM SHAKESPEARE'S CYMBELINE

SUNG BY GUIDERUS AND ARVIRAGUS OVER FIDELE, SUPPOSED TO BE DEAD

To fair Fidele's grassy tomb
Soft maids and village hinds shall bring
Each opening sweet, of earliest bloom,
And rifle all the breathing spring.

No wailing ghost shall dare appear,
To vex with shrieks this quiet grove:
But shepherd lads assemble here,
And melting virgins own their love.

5

No withered witch shall here be seen,
   No goblins lead their nightly crew: 10
The female fays shall haunt the green,
   And dress thy grave with pearly dew.

The redbreast oft at evening hours
   Shall kindly lend his little aid,
With hoary moss, and gathered flowers,   15
   To deck the ground where thou art laid.

When howling winds, and beating rain,
   In tempests shake the sylvan cell,
Or midst the chace on every plain,
   The tender thought on thee shall dwell.   20

Each lonely scene shall thee restore,
   For thee the tear be duly shed:
Beloved, till life could charm no more;
   And mourned, till Pity's self be dead.

                1744

ODE WRITTEN IN THE BEGINNING OF THE YEAR 1746

How sleep the brave who sink to rest
By all their country's wishes blest!
When Spring, with dewy fingers cold,
Returns to deck their hallowed mold,
She there shall dress a sweeter sod   5
Than Fancy's feet have ever trod.

By fairy hands their knell is rung,
By forms unseen their dirge is sung;
There Honor comes, a pilgrim grey,
To bless the turf that wraps their clay;   10
And Freedom shall awhile repair,
To dwell a weeping hermit there!

                1746

ODE TO EVENING

If aught of oaten stop or pastoral song,
May hope, chaste Eve, to soothe thy modest ear,
   Like thy own solemn springs,
   Thy springs and dying gales,

O nymph reserved, while now the bright-haired sun   5
Sits in yon western tent, whose cloudy skirts,
   With brede ethereal wove,
   O'erhang his wavy bed:

Now air is hushed, save where the weak-eyed bat,
With short, shrill shriek, flits by on leathern wing;   10
   Or where the beetle winds
   His small but sullen horn,

As oft he rises 'midst the twilight path,
Against the pilgrim borne in heedless hum:
    Now teach me, maid composed,
    To breathe some softened strain,

Whose numbers, stealing through thy darkening vale,
May not unseemly with its stillness suit,
    As, musing slow, I hail
    Thy genial loved return!

For when thy folding-star, arising, shows
His paly circlet, at his warning lamp
    The fragrant Hours, and elves
    Who slept in flowers the day,

And many a nymph who wreathes her brows with sedge,
And sheds the freshening dew, and, lovelier still,
    The pensive Pleasures sweet,
    Prepare thy shadowy car.

Then lead, calm votaress, where some sheety lake
Cheers the lone heath, or some time-hallowed pile
    Or upland fallows grey
    Reflect its last cool gleam.

But when chill blustering winds or driving rain
Forbid my willing feet, be mine the hut
    That from the mountain's side
    Views wilds, and swelling floods,

And hamlets brown, and dim-discovered spires,
And hears their simple bell, and marks o'er all
    Thy dewy fingers draw
    The gradual dusky veil.

While Spring shall pour his showers, as oft he wont,
And bathe thy breathing tresses, meekest Eve;
    While Summer loves to sport
    Beneath thy lingering light;

While sallow Autumn fills thy lap with leaves;
Or winter, yelling through the troublous air,
    Affrights thy shrinking train,
    And rudely rends thy robes;

So long, sure-found beneath the sylvan shed,
Shall Fancy, Friendship, Science, rose-lipped Health,
    Thy gentlest influence own,
    And hymn thy favorite name!

1747

ODE ON THE POETICAL CHARACTER

STROPHE

As once—if not with light regard
I read aright that gifted bard
(Him whose school above the rest
His loveliest Elfin Queen hast blest)—

One, only one, unrivalled fair
Might hope the magic girdle wear,
At solemn tourney hung on high,
The wish of each love-darting eye;
Lo! to each other nymph in turn applied,
As if, in air unseen, some hovering hand,
Some chaste and angel friend to virgin fame,
With whispered spell had burst the starting band,
It left unblest her loathed, dishonored side;
Happier, hopeless fair, if never
Her baffled hand, with vain endeavor,
Had touched that fatal zone to her denied!
Young Fancy thus, to me divinest name,
To whom, prepared and bathed in heaven,
The cest of amplest power is given,
To few the godlike gift assigns
To gird their blest, prophetic loins,
And gaze her visions wild, and feel unmixed her flame!

EPODE

The band, as fairy legends say,
Was wove on that creating day
When He who called with thought to birth
Yon tented sky, this laughing earth,
And dressed with springs and forests tall,
And poured the main engirting all,
Long by the loved enthusiast wooed,
Himself in some diviner mood,
Retiring, sate with her alone,
And placed her on his sapphire throne,
The whiles, the vaulted shrine around,
Seraphic wires were heard to sound,
Now sublimest triumph swelling,
Now on love and mercy dwelling;
And she, from out the veiling cloud,
Breathed her magic notes aloud,
And thou, thou rich-haired Youth of Morn,
And all thy subject-life, was born!
The dangerous passions kept aloof,
Far from the sainted growing woof:
But near it sate ecstatic Wonder,
Listening the deep applauding thunder;
And Truth, in sunny vest arrayed,
By whose the tarsel's eyes were made;
All the shadowy tribes of mind,
In braided dance, their murmurs joined,
And all the bright uncounted powers
Who feed on heaven's ambrosial flowers.
Where is the bard whose soul can now
Its high presuming hopes avow?
Where he who thinks, with rapture blind,
This hallowed work for him designed?

ANTISTROPHE

High on some cliff, to heaven up-piled,
Of rude access, of prospect wild,
Where, tangled round the jealous steep,
Strange shades o'erbrow the valleys deep,
And holy genii guard the rock,

10
15
20
25
30
35
40
45
50
55

Its glooms embrown, its springs unlock,
While on its rich ambitious head   60
An Eden, like his own, lies spread,
I view that oak, the fancied glades among,
  By which as Milton lay, his evening ear,
From many a cloud that dropped ethereal dew,
  Nigh sphered in heaven, its native strains could hear,   65
On which that ancient trump he reached was hung:
  Thither oft, his glory greeting,
  From Waller's myrtle shades retreating,
With many a vow from Hope's aspiring tongue,
My trembling feet his guiding steps pursue;   70
  In vain—such bliss to one alone
  Of all the sons of soul was known,
  And Heaven and Fancy, kindred powers,
  Have now o'erturned th' inspiring bowers,
Or curtained close such scene from every future view.   75

1746

THE PASSIONS: AN ODE FOR MUSIC

When Music, heavenly maid, was young,
While yet in early Greece she sung,
The Passions oft, to hear her shell,
Thronged around her magic cell,
Exulting, trembling, raging, fainting,   5
Possessed beyond the Muse's painting;
By turns they felt the glowing mind
Disturbed, delighted, raised, refined:

Till once, 'tis said, when all were fired,
Filled with fury, rapt, inspired,   10
From the supporting myrtles round
They snatched her instruments of sound;
And, as they oft had heard apart
Sweet lessons of her forceful art,
Each (for madness ruled the hour)   15
Would prove his own expressive power.

First Fear in hand, its skill to try,
  Amid the chords bewildered laid,
And back recoiled, he knew not why,
  Even at the sound himself had made.   20

Next Anger rushed: his eyes, on fire,
  In lightnings owned his secret stings;
In one rude clash he struck the lyre,
  And swept with hurried hand the strings.

With woeful measures wan Despair
  Low, sullen sounds his grief beguiled;   25
A solemn, strange, and mingled air—
  'Twas sad by fits, by starts 'twas wild.

But thou, O Hope, with eyes so fair,
  What was thy delightful measure?
  Still it whispered promised pleasure,   3C
And bade the lovely scenes at distance hail!

Still would her touch the strain prolong;
    And from the rocks, the woods, the vale,
She called on Echo still, through all the song;   35
    And where her sweetest theme she chose,
A soft responsive voice was heard at every close,
And Hope, enchanted, smiled, and waved her golden hair.

And longer had she sung—but with a frown
    Revenge impatient rose;   40
He threw his blood-stained sword in thunder down.
    And with a withering look
    The war-denouncing trumpet took,
    And blew a blast so loud and dread,
Were ne'er prophetic sounds so full of woe.   45

    And ever and anon he beat
    The doubling drum with furious heat;
And though sometimes, each dreary pause between,
    Dejected Pity, at his side,
    Her soul-subduing voice applied,   50
Yet still he kept his wild unaltered mien,
While each strained ball of sight seemed bursting from his head.
Thy numbers, Jealousy, to naught were fixed,
    Sad proof of thy distressful state;
Of differing themes the veering song was mixed,   55
And now it courted Love, now raving called on Hate.

    With eyes upraised, as one inspired,
    Pale Melancholy sate retired,
    And from her wild sequestered seat,
    In notes by distance made more sweet,   60
Poured through the mellow horn her pensive soul:
    And, dashing soft from rocks around,
    Bubbling runnels joined the sound;
Through glades and glooms the mingled measure stole,
O'er some haunted stream, with fond delay,   65
    Round an holy calm diffusing,
    Love of peace and lonely musing,
    In hollow murmurs died away.

But O how altered was its sprightlier tone,
When Cheerfulness, a nymph of healthiest hue,   70
    Her bow across her shoulder flung,
    Her buskins gemmed with morning dew;
Blew an inspiring air, that dale and thicket rung,
The hunter's call, to faun and dryad known!
The oak-crowned sisters, and their chaste-eyed queen,   75
    Satyrs, and sylvan boys, were seen,
    Peeping from forth their alleys green;
    Brown Exercise rejoiced to hear;
And Sport leaped up, and seized his beechen spear.
    Last came Joy's ecstatic trial: 80
    He, with viny crown advancing,
    First to the lively pipe his hand addressed;
But soon he saw the brisk awakening viol,
    Whose sweet entrancing voice he loved the best.

They would have thought, who heard the strain,   85
They saw in Tempe's vale her native maids,
    Amidst the festal-sounding shades,
    To some unwearied minstrel dancing,

While, as his flying fingers kissed the strings,
  Love framed with Mirth a gay fantastic round;   90
  Loose with her tresses seen, her zone unbound,
    And he, amidst his frolic play,
    As if he would the charming air repay,
  Shook thousand odors from his dewy wings.

O Music! sphere-descended maid!   95
Friend of Pleasure, Wisdom's aid!
Why, goddess, why, to us denied,
Lay'st thou thy ancient lyre aside?
As in that loved Athenian bower
You learned an all-commanding power,   100
Thy mimic soul, O nymph endeared,
Can well recall what then it heard.
Where is thy native simple heart,
Devote to Virtue, Fancy, Art?
Arise as in that elder time,   105
Warm, energic, chaste, sublime!
Thy wonders, in that godlike age,
Fill thy recording sister's page:
'Tis said, and I believe the tale,
Thy humblest reed could more prevail,   110
Had more of strength, diviner rage,
Than all which charms this laggard age,
E'en all at once together found,
Cecilia's mingled world of sound.
O bid our vain endeavors cease: 115
Revive the just designs of Greece;
Return in all thy simple state;
Confirm the tales her sons relate!

                        1746

ODE ON THE POPULAR SUPERSTITIONS
OF THE HIGHLANDS OF SCOTLAND

CONSIDERED AS THE SUBJECT OF POETRY

I

H——, thou return'st from Thames, whose naiads long
  Have seen thee lingering, with a fond delay,
  'Mid those soft friends, whose hearts, some future day,
Shall melt, perhaps, to hear thy tragic song.
Go, not unmindful of that cordial youth   5
  Whom, long-endeared, thou leav'st by Levant's side;
Together let us wish him lasting truth,
  And joy untainted, with his destined bride.
Go! nor regardless, while these numbers boast
  My short-lived bliss, forget my social name;   10
But think, far off, how on the Southern coast
  I met thy friendship with an equal flame!
Fresh to that soil thou turn'st, whose every vale
  Shall prompt the poet, and his song demand:
To thee thy copious subjects ne'er shall fail;   15
  Thou need'st but take the pencil to thy hand,
And paint what all believe who own thy genial land.

II

There must thou wake perforce thy Doric quill;
  'Tis Fancy's land to which thou sett'st thy feet,
  Where still, 'tis said, the fairy people meet
Beneath each birken shade on mead or hill.
There each trim lass that skims the milky store
  To the swart tribes their creamy bowl allots;
By night they sip it round the cottage door,
  While airy minstrels warble jocund notes.
There every herd, by sad experience, knows
  How, winged with fate, their elf-shot arrows fly;
When the sick ewe her summer food foregoes,
  Or, stretched on earth, the heart-smit heifers lie.
Such airy beings awe th' untutored swain:
  Nor thou, though learned, his homelier thoughts neglect;
Let thy sweet Muse the rural faith sustain:
  These are the themes of simple, sure effect,
That add new conquests to her boundless reign,
And fill, with double force, her heart-commanding strain.

20

25

30

35

III

Even yet preserved, how often may'st thou hear,
  Where to the pole the boreal mountains run,
  Taught by the father to his listening son,
Strange lays, whose power had charmed a Spenser's ear.
At every pause, before thy mind possessed,
  Old Runic bards shall seem to rise around,
With uncouth lyres, in many-colored vest,
  Their matted hair with boughs fantastic crowned:
Whether thou bid'st the well-taught hind repeat
  The choral dirge that mourns some chieftain brave,
When every shrieking maid her bosom beat,
  And strewed with choicest herbs his scented grave;
Or whether, sitting in the shepherd's shiel,
  Thou hear'st some sounding tale of war's alarms,
When, at the bugle's call, with fire and steel,
  The sturdy clans poured forth their bony swarms,
And hostile brothers met to prove each other's arms.

40

45

50

IV

'Tis thine to sing, how, framing hideous spells,
  In Skye's lone isle the gifted wizard seer,
  Lodged in the wintry cave with [Fate's fell spear;]
Or in the depth of Uist's dark forests dwells:
How they whose sight such dreary dreams engross,
  With their own visions oft astonished droop,
When o'er the watery strath or quaggy moss
  They see the gliding ghosts unbodied troop;
Or if in sports, or on the festive green,
  Their [destined] glance some fated youth descry,
Who, now perhaps in lusty vigor seen
  And rosy health, shall soon lamented die:
For them the viewless forms of air obey,
  Their bidding heed, and at their beck repair.
They know what spirit brews the stormful day,
  And, heartless, oft like moody madness stare
To see the phantom train their secret work prepare.

55

60

65

V

[To monarchs dear, some hundred miles astray,   70
  Oft have they seen Fate give the fatal blow!
  The seer, in Skye, shrieked as the blood did flow,
When headless Charles warm on the scaffold lay!
As Boreas threw his young Aurora forth,
  In the first year of the first George's reign,   75
And battles raged in welkin of the North,
  They mourned in air, fell, fell Rebellion slain!
And as, of late, they joyed in Preston's fight,
  Saw at sad Falkirk all their hopes near crowned,
They raved, divining, through their second sight,   80
  Pale, red Culloden, where these hopes were drowned!
Illustrious William! Britain's guardian name!
  One William saved us from a tyrant's stroke;
He, for a sceptre, gained heroic fame;
  But thou, more glorious, Slavery's chain hast broke,   85
To reign a private man, and bow to Freedom's yoke!

VI

These, too, thou'lt sing! for well thy magic Muse
  Can to the topmost heaven of grandeur soar!
  Or stoop to wail the swain that is no more!
Ah, homely swains! your homeward steps ne'er lose;   90
Let not dank Will mislead you to the heath:
  Dancing in mirky night, o'er fen and lake,
He glows, to draw you downward to your death,
  In his bewitched, low, marshy willow brake!]
What though far off, from some dark dell espied.   95
His glimmering mazes cheer th' excursive sight,
Yet turn, ye wanderers, turn your steps aside,
  Nor trust the guidance of that faithless light;
For, watchful, lurking 'mid th' unrustling reed,
  At those mirk hours the wily monster lies,   100
And listens oft to hear the passing steed,
  And frequent round him rolls his sullen eyes,
If chance his savage wrath may some weak wretch surprise.

VII

Ah, luckless swain, o'er all unblest indeed!
  Whom, late bewildered in the dank, dark fen,   105
  Far from his flocks and smoking hamlet then,
To that sad spot [where hums the sedgy weed:]
  On him, enraged, the fiend, in angry mood,
  Shall never look with Pity's kind concern,
But instant, furious, raise the whelming flood   110
  O'er its drowned bank, forbidding all return.
Or, if he meditate his wished escape
  To some dim hill that seems uprising near,
To his faint eye the grim and grisly shape,
  In all its terrors clad, shall wild appear.   115
Meantime, the watery surge shall round him rise,
  Poured sudden forth from every swelling source.
What now remains but tears and hopeless sighs?
  His fear-shook limbs have lost their youthly force,
And down the waves he floats, a pale and breathless corse.   120

VIII

For him, in vain, his anxious wife shall wait,
  Or wander forth to meet him on his way;
  For him, in vain, at to-fall of the day,
His babes shall linger at th' unclosing gate.
Ah, ne'er shall he return! Alone, if night   125
  Her travelled limbs in broken slumbers steep,
With dropping willows dressed, his mournful sprite
  Shall visit sad, perchance, her silent sleep:
Then he, perhaps, with moist and watery hand,
  Shall fondly seem to press her shuddering cheek,   130
And with his blue-swoln face before her stand,
  And, shivering cold, these piteous accents speak:
"Pursue, dear wife, thy daily toils pursue
  At dawn or dusk, industrious as before;
Nor e'er of me one hapless thought renew,   135
  While I lie weltering on the oziered shore,
Drowned by the kelpie's wrath, nor e'er shall aid thee more!"

IX

Unbounded is thy range; with varied style
  Thy Muse may, like those feathery tribes which spring
  From their rude rocks, extend her skirting wing   140
Round the moist marge of each cold Hebrid isle
To that hoar pile which still its ruin shows:
  In whose small vaults a pigmy-folk is found,
Whose bones the delver with his spade upthrows,
  And culls them, wondering, from the hallowed ground!   145
Or thither, where, beneath the showery West,
  The mighty kings of three fair realms are laid:
Once foes, perhaps, together now they rest;
  No slaves revere them, and no wars invade:
Yet frequent now, at midnight's solemn hour,   150
  The rifted mounds their yawning cells unfold,
And forth the monarchs stalk with sovereign power,
  In pageant robes, and wreathed with sheeny gold,
And on their twilight tombs aërial council hold.

X

But oh, o'er all, forget not Kilda's race,   155
  On whose bleak rocks, which brave the wasting tides,
  Fair Nature's daughter, Virtue, yet abides.
Go, just as they, their blameless manners trace!
Then to my ear transmit some gentle song
  Of those whose lives are yet sincere and plain,   160
Their bounded walks the rugged cliffs along,
  And all their prospect but the wintry main.
With sparing temperance, at the needful time,
  They drain the sainted spring, or, hunger-pressed,
Along th' Atlantic rock undreading climb,   165
  And of its eggs despoil the solan's nest.
Thus blest in primal innocence they live,
  Sufficed and happy with that frugal fare
Which tasteful toil and hourly danger give.
  Hard is their shallow soil, and bleak and bare;   170
Nor ever vernal bee was heard to murmur there!

XI

Nor need'st thou blush, that such false themes engage
   Thy gentle mind, of fairer stores possessed;
For not alone they touch the village breast,
But filled in elder time th' historic page.   175
There Shakespeare's self, with every garland crowned,—
   [Flew to those fairy climes his fancy sheen!]—
In musing hour, his wayward Sisters found,
   And with their terrors dressed the magic scene.
From them he sung, when, 'mid his bold design,   180
   Before the Scot afflicted and aghast,
The shadowy kings of Banquo's fated line
   Through the dark cave in gleamy pageant passed.
Proceed, nor quit the tales which, simply told,
   Could once so well my answering bosom pierce;   185
Proceed! in forceful sounds and colors bold,
   The native legends of thy land rehearse;
To such adapt thy lyre and suit thy powerful verse.

XII

In scenes like these, which, daring to depart
   From sober truth, are still to nature true,   190
   And call forth fresh delight to Fancy's view,
Th' heroic muse employed her Tasso's art!
How have I trembled, when, at Tancred's stroke,
   Its gushing blood the gaping cypress poured;
When each live plant with mortal accents spoke,   195
   And the wild blast upheaved the vanished sword!
How have I sat, when piped the pensive wind,
   To hear his harp, by British Fairfax strung,—
Prevailing poet, whose undoubting mind
   Believed the magic wonders which he sung!   200
Hence at each sound imagination glows;
   [The MS. lacks a line here.]
Hence his warm lay with softest sweetness flows;
   Melting it flows, pure, numerous, strong, and clear,
And fills th' impassioned heart, and wins th' harmonious ear.   205

XIII

All hail, ye scenes that o'er my soul prevail,
   Ye [splendid] friths and lakes which, far away,
   Are by smooth Annan filled, or pastoral Tay,
Or Don's romantic springs; at distance, hail!
The time shall come when I, perhaps, may tread   210
   Your lowly glens, o'erhung with spreading broom,
Or o'er your stretching heaths by fancy led
[Or o'er your mountains creep, in awful gloom:]
Then will I dress once more the faded bower,
   Where Jonson sat in Drummond's [classic] shade,   215
Or crop from Teviot's dale each [lyric flower]
   And mourn on Yarrow's banks [where Willy's laid!]
Meantime, ye Powers that on the plains which bore
   The cordial youth, on Lothian's plains, attend,
Where'er he dwell, on hill or lowly muir,   220
   To him I lose your kind protection lend,
And, touched with love like mine, preserve my absent friend!
1749   1788

THOMAS WARTON (1728-1790)

FROM THE PLEASURES OF MELANCHOLY

Beneath yon ruined abbey's moss-grown piles
Oft let me sit, at twilight hour of eve,
Where through some western window the pale moon
Pours her long-levelled rule of streaming light,
While sullen, sacred silence reigns around,   5
Save the lone screech-owl's note, who builds his bower
Amid the moldering caverns dark and damp,
Or the calm breeze that rustles in the leaves
Of flaunting ivy, that with mantle green
Invests some wasted tower. Or let me tread   10
Its neighboring walk of pines, where mused of old
The cloistered brothers: through the gloomy void
That far extends beneath their ample arch
As on I pace, religious horror wraps
My soul in dread repose. But when the world   15
Is clad in midnight's raven-colored robe,
'Mid hollow charnel let me watch the flame
Of taper dim, shedding a livid glare
O'er the wan heaps, while airy voices talk
Along the glimmering walls, or ghostly shape,   20
At distance seen, invites with beckoning hand
My lonesome steps through the far-winding vaults.
Nor undelightful is the solemn noon
Of night, when, haply wakeful, from my couch
I start: lo, all is motionless around!   25
Roars not the rushing wind; the sons of men
And every beast in mute oblivion lie;
All nature's hushed in silence and in sleep:
O then how fearful is it to reflect
That through the still globe's awful solitude   30
No being wakes but me! till stealing sleep
My drooping temples bathes in opiate dews.
Nor then let dreams, of wanton folly born,
My senses lead through flowery paths of joy:
But let the sacred genius of the night   35
Such mystic visions send as Spenser saw
When through bewildering Fancy's magic maze,
To the fell house of Busyrane, he led
Th' unshaken Britomart; or Milton knew,
When in abstracted thought he first conceived   40
All Heaven in tumult, and the seraphim
Come towering, armed in adamant and gold.
              .   .   .   .
Through Pope's soft song though all the Graces breathe,
And happiest art adorn his Attic page,
Yet does my mind with sweeter transport glow,   45
As, at the root of mossy trunk reclined,
In magic Spenser's wildly-warbled song
I see deserted Una wander wide
Through wasteful solitudes and lurid heaths,
Weary, forlorn, than when the fated fair   50
Upon the bosom bright of silver Thames
Launches in all the lustre of brocade,
Amid the splendors of the laughing sun:

The gay description palls upon the sense,
And coldly strikes the mind with feeble bliss.   55

. . . .

The tapered choir, at the late hour of prayer,
Oft let me tread, while to th' according voice
The many-sounding organ peals on high
The clear slow-dittied chant or varied hymn,
Till all my soul is bathed in ecstasies   60
And lapped in Paradise. Or let me sit
Far in sequestered aisles of the deep dome;
There lonesome listen to the sacred sounds,
Which, as they lengthen through the Gothic vaults,
In hollow murmurs reach my ravished ear.   65
Nor when the lamps, expiring, yield to night,
And solitude returns, would I forsake
The solemn mansion, but attentive mark
The due clock swinging slow with sweepy sway,
Measuring Time's flight with momentary sound.   70

1747

FROM OBSERVATIONS ON THE FAIRY QUEEN OF SPENSER

It is absurd to think of judging either Ariosto or Spenser by precepts which they did not attend to. We who live in the days of writing by rule are apt to try every composition by those laws which we have been taught to think the sole criterion of excellence. Critical taste is universally diffused, and we require the same order and design which every modern performance is expected to have, in poems where they never were regarded or intended. Spenser, and the same may be said of Ariosto, did not live in an age of planning. His poetry is the careless exuberance of a warm imagination and a strong sensibility. It was his business to engage the fancy, and to interest the attention by bold and striking images, in the formation and the disposition of which, little labor or art was applied. The various and the marvellous were the chief sources of delight. Hence we find our author ransacking alike the regions of reality and romance, of truth and fiction, to find the proper decoration and furniture for his fairy structure. Born in such an age, Spenser wrote rapidly from his own feelings, which at the same time were naturally noble. Exactness in his poem would have been like the cornice which a painter introduced in the grotto of Calypso. Spenser's beauties are like the flowers in Paradise,

Which not nice Art
In beds and curious knots, but Nature boon
Poured forth profuse, on hill, and dale, and
    plain;
Both where the morning sun first warmly
    smote
The open field, or where the unpierced shade
Imbrowned the noon-tide bowers.
                              —*Paradise Lost*, iv, 241.

If *The Fairy Queen* be destitute of that arrangement and economy which epic severity requires, yet we scarcely regret the loss of these while their place is so amply supplied by something which more powerfully attracts us; something which engages the affections, the feelings of the heart, rather than the cold approbation of the head. If there be any poem whose graces please because they are situated beyond the reach of art, and where the force and faculties of creative imagination delight because they are unassisted and unrestrained by those of deliberate judgment, it is this. In reading Spenser, if the critic is not satisfied, yet the reader is transported. . . .

I cannot dismiss this section without a wish that this neglected author [Chaucer], whom Spenser proposed as the pattern of his style, and to whom he is indebted for many noble inventions, should be more universally studied. This is at least what one might expect in an age of research and curiosity. Chaucer is regarded rather as an old, than as a good, poet. We look upon his poems as venerable relics, not as beautiful compositions; as pieces better calculated to gratify the antiquarian than the critic. He abounds not only in strokes of humor, which is commonly supposed to be his sole talent, but of pathos and sublimity not unworthy a more refined age. His old manners, his romantic arguments, his wildness of painting, his simplicity and antiquity of expression, transport us into some fairy region, and are all highly pleasing to the imagination. It is true that his uncouth and unfamiliar language disgusts and deters many readers; but the principal reason of his being so little known and so seldom taken into hand, is the convenient opportunity of reading him with pleasure and facility in modern imitations. For when translation, as such imitations from Chaucer may be justly called, at length becomes substituted as the means of attaining a knowledge of any difficult and ancient author, the original not only begins to be neglected and excluded as less easy, but also despised as less ornamental and elegant. Thus the public taste becomes imperceptibly vitiated, while the genuine model is superseded, and gradually gives way to the establishment of a more specious but false resemblance. Thus, too many readers, happy to find the readiest accommodation for their indolence and their illiteracy, think themselves sufficient masters of Homer from Pope's translation; and thus, by an indiscreet comparison, Pope's translation is commonly preferred to the Grecian text, in proportion as the former is furnished with more frequent and shining metaphors, more lively descriptions, and in general appears to be more full and florid, more elaborate and various. . . .

In reading the works of a poet who lived in a remote age, it is necessary that we should look back upon the customs and manners which prevailed in that age. We should endeavor to place ourselves in the writer's situation and circumstances. Hence we shall become better enabled to discover how his turn of thinking, and manner of composing, were influenced by familiar appearances and established objects which are utterly different from those with which we are at present surrounded. For want of this caution, too many readers view the knights and damsels, the tournaments and enchantments, of Spenser with modern eyes; never considering that the encounters of chivalry subsisted in our author's age, that romances were then most eagerly and universally studied, and that

consequently Spenser from the fashion of the times was induced to undertake a recital of chivalrous achievements, and to become, in short, a *romantic* poet.

Spenser, in this respect, copied real manners no less than Homer. A sensible historian observes that "Homer copied true natural manners, which, however rough and uncultivated, will always form an agreeable and interesting picture; but the pencil of the English poet (Spenser) was employed in drawing the affectations and conceits and fopperies of chivalry." This, however, was nothing more than an imitation of real life; as much, at least, as the plain descriptions in Homer, which corresponded to the simplicity of manners then subsisting in Greece.

Mechanical critics will perhaps be disgusted at the liberties I have taken in introducing so many anecdotes of ancient chivalry. But my subject required frequent proofs of this sort. Nor could I be persuaded that such enquiries were, in other respects, either useless or ridiculous; as they tended, at least, to illustrate an institution of no frivolous or indifferent nature. Chivalry is commonly looked upon as a barbarous sport or extravagant amusement of the dark ages. It had, however, no small influence on the manners, policies, and constitutions of ancient times, and served many public and important purposes. It was the school of fortitude, honor, and affability. Its exercises, like the Grecian games, habituated the youth to fatigue and enterprise, and inspired the noblest sentiments of heroism. It taught gallantry and civility to a savage and ignorant people, and humanized the native ferocity of the Northern nations. It conduced to refine the manners of the combatants by exciting an emulation in the devices and accoutrements, the splendor and parade, of their tilts and tournaments; while its magnificent festivals, thronged with noble dames and courteous knights, produced the first efforts of wit and fancy.

I am still further to hope that, together with other specimens of obsolete literature in general hinted at before, the many references I have made in particular to romances, the necessary appendage of ancient chivalry, will also plead their pardon. For however monstrous and unnatural these compositions may appear to this age of reason and refinement, they merit more attention than the world is willing to bestow. They preserve many curious historical facts, and throw considerable light on the nature of the feudal system. They are the pictures of ancient usages and customs; and represent the manners, genius, and character of our ancestors. Above all, such are their terrible graces of magic and enchantment, so magnificently marvellous are their fictions and fablings, that they contribute, in a wonderful degree, to rouse and invigorate all the powers of imagination; to store the fancy with those sublime and alarming images which poetry best delights to display.   1754

THOMAS GRAY (1716-1771)

HYMN TO ADVERSITY

Daughter of Jove, relentless power,
  Thou tamer of the human breast,
Whose iron scourge and torturing hour
  The bad affright, afflict the best!
Bound in thy adamantine chain,   5
The proud are taught to taste of pain,
And purple tyrants vainly groan
With pangs unfelt before, unpitied and
    alone.

When first thy sire to send on earth
  Virtue, his darling child, designed,   10
To thee he gave the heavenly birth,
  And bade to form her infant mind.
Stern, rugged nurse! thy rigid lore
  With patience many a year she bore;
What sorrow was thou bad'st her
    know,   15
And from her own she learned to melt at
    other's woe.

Scared at thy frown terrific, fly
  Self-pleasing Folly's idle brood,
Wild Laughter, Noise, and thoughtless
    Joy,
  And leave us leisure to be good: 20
Light they disperse, and with them go
The summer friend, the flattering foe;
  By vain Prosperity received,
To her they vow their truth and are again
    believed.

Wisdom in sable garb arrayed,   25
  Immersed in rapturous thought profound,
And Melancholy, silent maid
  With leaden eye, that loves the
    ground,
Still on thy solemn steps attend;
Warm Charity, the genial friend,   30
  With Justice, to herself severe,
And Pity, dropping soft the sadly-pleasing
    tear.

Oh, gently on thy suppliant's head,
  Dread goddess, lay thy chastening
    hand!
Not in thy Gorgon terrors clad,   35
  Nor circled with the vengeful band
(As by the impious thou art seen),
  With thundering voice and threatening
    mien,
With screaming Horror's funeral cry,
Despair, and fell Disease, and ghastly Poverty: 40

Thy form benign, O goddess, wear,
  Thy milder influence impart;
Thy philosophic train be there
  To soften, not to wound, my heart;
The generous spark extinct revive,   45
  Teach me to love and to forgive,
Exact my own defects to scan,
What others are to feel, and know myself
    a man.
                       1748

ELEGY WRITTEN IN A COUNTRY CHURCHYARD

The curfew tolls the knell of parting day,
  The lowing herd winds slowly o'er the lea,
The ploughman homeward plods his weary way,
  And leaves the world to darkness and to me.

Now fades the glimmering landscape on the sight,   5
  And all the air a solemn stillness holds,
Save where the beetle wheels his droning flight,
  And drowsy tinklings lull the distant folds;

Save that from yonder ivy-mantled tower
   The moping owl does to the moon complain   10
Of such, as wandering near her secret bower,
   Molest her ancient solitary reign.

Beneath those rugged elms, that yew-tree's shade,
   Where heaves the turf in many a moldering heap,
Each in his narrow cell forever laid,   15
   The rude forefathers of the hamlet sleep.

The breezy call of incense-breathing morn,
   The swallow twittering from the straw-built shed,
The cock's shrill clarion, or the echoing horn,
   No more shall rouse them from their lowly bed.   20

For them no more the blazing hearth shall burn,
   Or busy housewife ply her evening care:
No children run to lisp their sire's return,
   Or climb his knees the envied kiss to share.

Oft did the harvest to their sickle yield,   25
   Their furrow oft the stubborn glebe has broke;
How jocund did they drive their team afield!
   How bowed the woods beneath their sturdy stroke!

Let not Ambition mock their useful toil,
   Their homely joys, and destiny obscure;   30
Nor Grandeur hear with a disdainful smile,
   The short and simple annals of the poor.

The boast of heraldry, the pomp of power,
   And all that beauty, all that wealth e'er gave,
Awaits alike th' inevitable hour.   35
   The paths of glory lead but to the grave.

Nor you, ye proud, impute to these the fault,
   If Memory o'er their tomb no trophies raise,
Where through the long-drawn aisle and fretted vault
   The pealing anthem swells the note of praise.   40

Can storied urn or animated bust
   Back to its mansion call the fleeting breath?
Can Honor's voice provoke the silent dust,
   Or Flattery soothe the dull cold ear of Death?

Perhaps in this neglected spot is laid   45
   Some heart once pregnant with celestial fire;
Hands that the rod of empire might have swayed,
   Or waked to ecstasy the living lyre.

But Knowledge to their eyes her ample page
   Rich with the spoils of time did ne'er unroll;   50
Chill Penury repressed their noble rage,
   And froze the genial current of the soul.

Full many a gem of purest ray serene,
   The dark unfathomed caves of ocean bear:
Full many a flower is born to blush unseen,   55
   And waste its sweetness on the desert air.

Some village Hampden, that, with dauntless breast
The little tyrant of his fields withstood;
Some mute inglorious Milton here may rest,
Some Cromwell guiltless of his country's blood.   60

Th' applause of listening senates to command,
The threats of pain and ruin to despise,
To scatter plenty o'er a smiling land,
And read their history in a nation's eyes,

Their lot forbade: nor circumscribed alone   65
Their growing virtues, but their crimes confined;
Forbade to wade through slaughter to a throne,
And shut the gates of mercy on mankind,

The struggling pangs of conscious truth to hide,
To quench the blushes of ingenuous shame,   70
Or heap the shrine of Luxury and Pride
With incense kindled at the Muse's flame.

Far from the madding crowd's ignoble strife,
Their sober wishes never learned to stray;
Along the cool sequestered vale of life   75
They kept the noiseless tenor of their way.

Yet even these bones from insult to protect,
Some frail memorial still erected nigh,
With uncouth rhymes and shapeless sculpture decked,
Implores the passing tribute of a sigh.   80

Their names, their years, spelt by th' unlettered Muse,
The place of fame and elegy supply:
And many a holy text around she strews,
That teach the rustic moralist to die.

For who, to dumb forgetfulness a prey,   85
This pleasing anxious being e'er resigned,
Left the warm precincts of the cheerful day,
Nor cast one longing lingering look behind?

On some fond breast the parting soul relies,
Some pious drops the closing eye requires;   90
Even from the tomb the voice of Nature cries,
Even in our ashes live their wonted fires.

For thee, who mindful of th' unhonored dead
Dost in these lines their artless tale relate,
If chance, by lonely contemplation led,   95
Some kindred spirit shall inquire thy fate.

Haply some hoary-headed swain may say,
"Oft have we seen him at the peep of dawn
Brushing with hasty steps the dews away
To meet the sun upon the upland lawn.   100

"There at the foot of yonder nodding beech
That wreathes its old fantastic roots so high,
His listless length at noontide would he stretch,
And pore upon the brook that babbles by.

"Hard by yon wood, now smiling as in scorn,   105
    Muttering his wayward fancies he would rove;
Now drooping, woeful-wan, like one forlorn,
    Or crazed with care, or crossed in hopeless love.

"One morn I missed him on the customed hill,
    Along the heath, and near his favorite tree;   110
Another came; nor yet beside the rill,
    Nor up the lawn, nor at the wood was he;

"The next with dirges due in sad array
    Slow through the church-way path we saw him borne,—
Approach and read (for thou canst read) the lay   115
    Graved on the stone beneath yon agèd thorn."

THE EPITAPH

Here rests his head upon the lap of earth
    A youth to fortune and to fame unknown;
Fair Science frowned not on his humble birth,
    And Melancholy marked him for her own.   120

Large was his bounty, and his soul sincere;
    Heaven did a recompense as largely send:
He gave to Misery (all he had) a tear,
    He gained from Heaven ('twas all he wished) a friend.

No farther seek his merits to disclose,   125
    Or draw his frailties from their dread abode
(There they alike in trembling hope repose,)—
    The bosom of his Father and his God.

                          1751

THE PROGRESS OF POESY

I. 1

Awake, Æolian lyre, awake,
And give to rapture all thy trembling
    strings!
From Helicon's harmonious springs
A thousand rills their mazy progress take;
The laughing flowers that round them
    blow   5
Drink life and fragrance as they flow.
Now the rich stream of music winds along
Deep, majestic, smooth, and strong,
Through verdant vales and Ceres' golden
    reign:
Now rolling down the steep amain,   10
Headlong, impetuous, see it pour;
The rocks and nodding groves rebellow to
    the roar.

I. 2

Oh sovereign of the willing soul,
Parent of sweet and solemn-breathing airs,
Enchanting shell! the sullen Cares   15
And frantic Passions hear thy soft control.
On Thracia's hills the Lord of War

Has curbed the fury of his car
And dropped his thirsty lance at thy com-
    mand.
Perching on the sceptred hand   20
Of Jove, thy magic lulls the feathered king
With ruffled plumes and flagging wing;
Quenched in dark clouds of slumber lie
The terror of his beak and lightnings of
    his eye.

I. 3

Thee the voice, the dance, obey,   25
Tempered to thy warbled lay.
O'er Idalia's velvet-green
The rosy-crownèd Loves are seen,
On Cytherea's day,
With antic Sports and blue-eyed Pleas-
    ures   30
Frisking light in frolic measures:
Now pursuing, now retreating,
Now in circling troops they meet;
To brisk notes in cadence beating
Glance their many-twinkling feet.   35
Slow melting strains their Queen's ap-
    proach declare:
Where'er she turns the Graces homage pay;

With arms sublime, that float upon the air,
In gliding state she wins her easy way;
O'er her warm cheek and rising bosom
    move   40
The bloom of young Desire and purple
    light of Love.

II. 1

Man's feeble race what ills await:
Labor, and Penury, the racks of Pain,
Disease, and Sorrow's weeping train,
And Death, sad refuge from the storms of
    Fate!   45
The fond complaint, my song, disprove,
And justify the laws of Jove.
Say, has he given in vain the heavenly
    Muse?
Night, and all her sickly dews,
Her spectres wan, and birds of boding
    cry,   50
He gives to range the dreary sky;
Till down the eastern cliffs afar
Hyperion's march they spy, and glittering
    shafts of war.

II. 2

In climes beyond the solar road,
Where shaggy forms o'er ice-built moun-
    tains roam,   55
The Muse has broke the twilight-gloom
To cheer the shivering native's dull abode.
And oft, beneath the odorous shade
Of Chili's boundless forests laid,
She deigns to hear the savage youth re-
    peat,   60
In loose numbers wildly sweet,
Their feather-cinctured chiefs and dusky
    loves.
Her track, where'er the goddess roves,
Glory pursue, and generous Shame,
Th' unconquerable Mind, and Freedom's
    holy flame.   65

II. 3

Woods that wave o'er Delphi's steep,
Isles that crown th' Ægean deep,
Fields that cool Ilissus laves,
Or where Mæander's amber waves
In lingering labyrinths creep,   70
How do your tuneful echoes languish,
Mute but to the voice of Anguish?
Where each old poetic mountain
Inspiration breathed around,
Every shade and hallowed fountain   75
Murmured deep a solemn sound;
Till the sad Nine in Greece's evii hour,
Left their Parnassus for the Latian plains:
Alike they scorn the pomp of tyrant Power,
And coward Vice that revels in her chains.   80

When Latium had her lofty spirit lost,
They sought, O Albion! next, thy sea-
    encircled coast.

III. 1

Far from the sun and summer-gale,
In thy green lap was Nature's darling laid,
What time, where lucid Avon strayed,   85
To him the mighty mother did unveil
Her awful face: the dauntless child
Stretched forth his little arms, and smiled.
"This pencil take," she said, "whose colors
    clear
Richly paint the vernal year.   90
Thine too these golden keys, immortal boy!
This can unlock the gates of Joy;
Of Horror that, and thrilling Fears,
Or ope the sacred source of sympathetic
    tears."

III. 2

Nor second he that rode sublime   95
Upon the seraph-wings of Ecstasy,
The secrets of th' abyss to spy.
He passed the flaming bounds of Place and
    Time:
The living throne, the sapphire blaze,
Where angels tremble while they gaze,   100
He saw; but, blasted with excess of light,
Closed his eyes in endless night.
Behold where Dryden's less presumptuous
    car
Wide o'er the fields of glory bear
Two coursers of ethereal race,   105
With necks in thunder clothed, and long-
    resounding pace!

III. 3

Hark! his hands the lyre explore:
Bright-eyed Fancy, hovering o'er,
Scatters from her pictured urn
Thoughts that breathe and words that
    burn.   110
But, ah, 'tis heard no more!
O lyre divine, what daring spirit
Wakes thee now? Though he inherit
Nor the pride nor ample pinion
That the Theban Eagle bear,   115
Sailing with supreme dominion
Through the azure deep of air,
Yet oft before his infant eyes would run
Such forms as glitter in the Muse's ray,
With orient hues unborrowed of the
    sun: 120
Yet shall he mount, and keep his distant
    way
Beyond the limits of a vulgar fate,
Beneath the good how far—but far above
    the great.

1754   **1757**

THE BARD

I. 1

"Ruin seize thee, ruthless king!
Confusion on thy banners wait;
Though fanned by conquest's crimson wing,
They mock the air with idle state.
Helm, nor hauberk's twisted mail, 5
Nor even thy virtues, tyrant, shall avail
To save thy secret soul from nightly fears,
From Cambria's curse, from Cambria's tears!"
Such were the sounds that o'er the crested pride
Of the first Edward scattered wild dismay, 10
As down the steep of Snowdon's shaggy side
He wound with toilsome march his long array.
Stout Gloucester stood aghast in speechless trance;
"To arms!" cried Mortimer, and couched his quivering lance.

I. 2

On a rock, whose haughty brow 15
Frowns o'er old Conway's foaming flood,
Robed in the sable garb of woe,
With haggard eyes the poet stood
(Loose his beard and hoary hair
Streamed, like a meteor, to the troubled air), 20
And with a master's hand and prophet's fire
Struck the deep sorrows of his lyre:
"Hark how each giant oak and desert cave
Sighs to the torrent's awful voice beneath!
O'er thee, oh king! their hundred arms they wave, 25
Revenge on thee in hoarser murmurs breathe,
Vocal no more, since Cambria's fatal day,
To high-born Hoel's harp or soft Llewellyn's lay.

I. 3

"Cold is Cadwallo's tongue,
That hushed the stormy main; 30
Brave Urien sleeps upon his craggy bed;
Mountains, ye mourn in vain
Modred, whose magic song
Made huge Plinlimmon bow his cloud-topped head:
On dreary Arvon's shore they lie, 35
Smeared with gore and ghastly pale;
Far, far aloof th' affrighted ravens sail;

The famished eagle screams, and passes by.
Dear lost companions of my tuneful art,
Dear as the light that visits these sad eyes, 40
Dear as the ruddy drops that warm my heart,
Ye died amidst your dying country's cries—
No more I weep: they do not sleep!
On yonder cliffs, a grisly band,
I see them sit; they linger yet 45
Avengers of their native land:
With me in dreadful harmony they join,
And weave with bloody hands the tissue of thy line.

II. 1

"Weave the warp and weave the woof,
The winding-sheet of Edward's race; 50
Give ample room and verge enough
The characters of hell to trace:
Mark the year, and mark the night,
When Severn shall re-echo with affright
The shrieks of death through Berkley's roofs that ring, 55
Shrieks of an agonizing king!
She-wolf of France, with unrelenting fangs,
That tear'st the bowels of thy mangled mate,
From thee be born who o'er thy country hangs
The scourge of Heaven: what terrors round him wait! 60
Amazement in his van, with Flight combined,
And Sorrow's faded form, and Solitude behind.

II. 2

"Mighty victor, mighty lord!
Low on his funeral couch he lies:
No pitying heart, no eye, afford 65
A tear to grace his obsequies.
Is the Sable Warrior fled?
Thy son is gone; he rests among the dead.
The swarm that in thy noontide beam were born?
Gone to salute the rising morn. 70
Fair laughs the morn and soft the zephyr blows,
While, proudly riding o'er the azure realm,
In gallant trim the gilded vessel goes,
Youth on the prow, and Pleasure at the helm,
Regardless of the sweeping Whirlwind's sway, 75
That, hushed in grim repose, expects his evening prey.

II. 3

"Fill high the sparkling bowl,
The rich repast prepare;
Reft of a crown, he yet may share the
  feast:
Close by the regal chair   80
Fell Thirst and Famine scowl
A baleful smile upon their baffled guest.
Heard ye the din of battle bray,
Lance to lance, and horse to horse?
Long years of havoc urge their destined
  course,   85
And through the kindred squadrons mow
  their way.
Ye towers of Julius, London's lasting
  shame,
With many a foul and midnight murther
  fed,
Revere his consort's faith, his father's fame,
And spare the meek usurper's holy head! 90
Above, below, the rose of snow,
Twined with her blushing foe, we spread:
The bristled Boar in infant gore
Wallows beneath thy thorny shade.
Now, brothers, bending o'er th' accursed
  loom,   95
Stamp we our vengeance deep, and ratify
  his doom!

III. 1

"Edward, lo! to sudden fate
(Weave we the woof: the thread is spun)
Half of thy heart we consecrate.
(The web is wove. The work is done.) 100
Stay, oh stay! nor thus forlorn
Leave me unblessed, unpitied, here to
  mourn!
In yon bright track, that fires the western
  skies,
They melt, they vanish from my eyes.
But oh! what solemn scenes on Snowdon's
  height,   105
Descending slow, their glittering skirts un-
  roll?
Visions of glory, spare my aching sight!
Ye unborn ages, crowd not on my soul!
No more our long-lost Arthur we bewail:
All hail, ye genuine kings, Britannia's issue,
  hail!   110

III. 2

"Girt with many a baron bold,
Sublime their starry fronts they rear;
And gorgeous dames, and statesmen old
In bearded majesty, appear.
In the midst a form divine!   115
Her eye proclaims her of the Briton line;
Her lion-port, her awe-commanding face,
Attempered sweet to virgin-grace.
What strings symphonious tremble in the
  air,
What strains of vocal transport round her
  play   120
Hear from the grave, great Taliessin, hear:
They breathe a soul to animate thy clay.
Bright Rapture calls, and, soaring as she
  sings,
Waves in the eye of Heaven her many-
  colored wings.

III. 3

"The verse adorn again   125
Fierce War and faithful Love
And Truth severe, by fairy Fiction dressed.
In buskined measures move
Pale Grief and pleasing Pain,
With Horror, tyrant of the throbbing
  breast.   130
A voice, as of the cherub-choir,
Gales from blooming Eden bear;
And distant warblings lessen on my ear,
That, lost in long futurity, expire.
Fond impious man, think'st thou yon san-
  guine cloud,   135
Raised by thy breath, has quenched the
  orb of day?
To-morrow he repairs the golden flood,
And warms the nations with redoubled
  ray.
Enough for me; with joy I see
The different doom our Fates assign: 140
Be thine Despair and sceptred Care;
To triumph and to die are mine."
He spoke, and headlong from the moun-
  tain's height
Deep in the roaring tide he plunged to
  endless night.

1757

LETTERS ON MACPHERSON'S OSSIAN

To Horace Walpole

I am so charmed with the two specimens of Erse poetry, that I cannot help giving you the trouble to enquire a little farther about them, and should wish to see a few lines of the original, that I may form some slight idea of the language, the measures, and the rhythm.

Is there anything known of the author or authors, and of what antiquity are they supposed to be? Is there any more to be had of equal beauty, or at all approaching to it? I have been often told that the poem called *Hardycanute* (which I always admired and still admire) was the work of somebody that lived a few years ago. This I do not at all believe, though it has evidently been retouched in places by some modern hand; but however, I am authorized by this report to ask whether the two poems in question are certainly antique and genuine. I make this enquiry in quality of an antiquary, and am not otherwise concerned about it: for, if I were sure that any one now living in Scotland had written them to divert himself, and laugh at the credulity of the world, I would undertake a journey into the Highlands only for the pleasure of seeing him.

1760

To Richard Stonhewer

I have received another Scotch packet with a third specimen, inferior in kind (because it is merely description), but yet full of nature and noble wild imagination. Five bards pass the night at the castle of a chief (himself a principal bard); each goes out in his turn to observe the face of things, and returns with an extempore picture of the changes he has seen; it is an October night (the harvest-month of the Highlands). This is the whole plan; yet there is a contrivance, and a preparation of ideas, that you would not expect. The oddest thing is, that every one of them sees ghosts (more or less). The idea that struck and surprised me most, is the following. One of them (describing a storm of wind and rain) says:

Ghosts ride on the tempest tonight:
Sweet is their voice between the gusts of wind;
Their songs are of other worlds!

Did you never observe (while rocking winds are piping loud) that pause, as the gust is recollecting itself, and rising upon the ear in a shrill and plaintive note, like the swell of an Æolian harp? I do assure you there is nothing in the world so like the voice of a spirit. Thomson had an ear sometimes: he was not deaf to this; and has described it gloriously, but given it another different turn, and of more horror. I cannot repeat the lines: it is in his "Winter." There is another very fine picture in one of them. It describes the breaking of the clouds after the storm before it is settled into a calm, and when the moon is seen by short intervals.

The waves are tumbling on the lake,
And lash the rocky sides.
The boat is brim-full in the cove,
The oars on the rocking tide.
Sad sits a maid beneath a cliff,
And eyes the rolling stream;
Her lover promised to come,
She saw his boat (when it was evening) on the lake;
Are these his groans in the gale?
Is this his broken boat on the shore?

June 29, 1760

To Thomas Warton

If you have seen Stonhewer, he has probably told you of my old Scotch (or rather Irish) poetry. I am gone mad about them. They are said to be translations (literal and in prose) from the Erse-tongue, done by one Macpherson, a young clergyman in the Highlands. He means to publish a collection he has of these specimens of antiquity; but what plagues me is, I cannot come at any certainty on that head. I was so struck, so *extasié* with their infinite beauty, that I writ into Scotland to make a thousand enquiries. The letters I have in return are ill wrote, ill reasoned, unsatisfactory, calculated (one would imagine) to deceive one, and yet not cunning enough to do it cleverly. In short, the whole external evidence would make one believe these fragments (for so he calls them, though nothing can be more entire) counterfeit; but the internal is so strong on the other side, that I am resolved to believe them genuine, spite of the devil and the kirk. It is impossible to convince me that they were invented by the same man that writes me these letters. On the other hand, it is almost as hard to suppose, if they are original, that he should be able to translate them so admirably. What can one do? Since Stonhewer went, I have received another of a very different and inferior kind (being merely descriptive), much more

modern than the former (he says), yet very old too. This too in its way is extremely fine. In short, this man is the very Demon of poetry, or he has lighted on a treasure hid for ages. The Welch poets are also coming to light. I have seen a discourse in MS. about them (by one Mr. Evans, a clergyman) with specimens of their writings. This is in Latin, and though it don't approach the other, there are fine scraps among it. . . .
June, 1760

To The Reverend William Mason

The Erse fragments have been published five weeks ago in Scotland, though I had them not (by a mistake) till last week. As you tell me new things do not reach you soon at Aston, I inclose what I can; the rest shall follow, when you tell me whether you have not got the pamphlet already. I send the two which I had before, for Mr. Wood, because he has not the affectation of not admiring. I continue to think them genuine, though any reasons for believing the contrary are rather stronger than ever: but I will have them antique, for I never knew a Scotchman of my own time that could read, much less write, poetry; and such poetry too! I have one (from Mr. Macpherson) which he has not printed: it is mere description, but excellent, too, in its kind. If you are good, and will learn to admire, I will transcribe it. . . .

As to their authenticity, having made many enquiries about the authenticity of these fragments, I have got a letter from Mr. David Hume (the historian), which is more satisfactory than anything I have yet met with on that subject He says—

"Certain it is that these poems are in everybody's mouth in the Highlands, have been handed down from father to son, and are of an age beyond all memory and tradition. Adam Smith, the celebrated professor in Glasgow, told me that the piper of the Argyleshire Militia repeated to him all of those which Mr. Macpherson had translated, and many more of equal beauty. Major Mackay (Lord Rae's brother) told me that he remembers them perfectly well; as likewise did the Laird of Macfarlane (the greatest antiquarian we have in this country), and who insists strongly on the historical truth as well as the poetical beauty of these productions. I could add the Laird and Lady Macleod, with many more that live in different parts of the Highlands, very remote from each other, and could only be acquainted with what had become (in a manner) national works. There is a country surgeon in Lochaber who has by heart the entire epic poem mentioned by Mr. Macpherson in his preface; and, as he is old, is perhaps the only person living that knows it all. We are in the more haste to recover a monument which will certainly be regarded as a curiosity in the republic of letters. We have, therefore, set about a subscription of a guinea or two guineas apiece, in order to enable Mr. Macpherson to undertake a mission into the Highlands to recover this poem, and other fragments of antiquity."
I forgot to mention to you that the names of Fingal, Ossian, Oscar, etc., are still given in the Highlands to large mastiffs, as we give to ours the names of Cæsar, Pompey, Hector, etc.
Aug. 7, 1760

THE DESCENT OF ODIN

Uprose the King of Men with speed,
And saddled straight his coal-black steed;
Down the yawning steep he rode,
That leads to Hela's drear abode.
Him the Dog of Darkness spied;   5
His shaggy throat he opened wide,
While from his jaws, with carnage filled,
Foam and human gore distilled,
Hoarse he bays with hideous din,
Eyes that glow, and fangs that grin;   10
And long pursues with fruitless yell,
The Father of the powerful spell.
Onward still his way he takes

(The groaning earth beneath him shakes),
Till full before his fearless eyes   15
The portals nine of hell arise.

Right against the eastern gate,
By the moss-grown pile he sate,
Where long of yore to sleep was laid
The dust of the prophetic maid.   20
Facing to the northern clime,
Thrice he traced the Runic rhyme;
Thrice pronounced, in accents dread,
The thrilling verse that wakes the dead;
Till from out the hollow ground   25
Slowly breathed a sullen sound.

Prophetess.   What call unknown, what
    charms, presume
To break the quiet of the tomb?
Who thus afflicts my troubled sprite,
And drags me from the realms of night? 30
Long on these mold'ring bones have beat
The winter's snow, the summer's heat,
The drenching dews, and driving rain!
Let me, let me sleep again!
Who is he, with voice unblest, 35
That calls me from the bed of rest?

Odin.   A traveller, to thee unknown,
Is he that calls, a warrior's son.
Thou the deeds of light shalt know;
Tell me what is done below; 40
For whom yon glitt'ring board is spread,
Dressed for whom yon golden bed?

Prophetess.   Mantling in the goblet see
The pure bev'rage of the bee;
O'er it hangs the shield of gold; 45
'Tis the drink of Balder bold:
Balder's head to death is giv'n;
Pain can reach the sons of Heav'n!
Unwilling I my lips unclose:
Leave me, leave me to repose!

Odin.   Once again my call obey:
Prophetess, arise, and say
What dangers Odin's child await;
Who the author of his fate?

Prophetess.   In Hoder's hand the hero's
    doom; 55
His brother sends him to the tomb.
Now my weary lips I close:
Leave me, leave me to repose!

Odin.   Prophetess, my spell obey:
Once again arise, and say 60
Who th' avenger of his guilt;
By whom shall Hoder's blood be spilt?

Prophetess.   In the caverns of the west,
By Odin's fierce embrace comprest,
A wond'rous boy shall Rinda bear, 65
Who ne'er shall comb his raven-hair,
Nor wash his visage in the stream,
Nor see the sun's departing beam,
Till he on Hoder's corse shall smile
Flaming on the funeral pile. 70
Now my weary lips I close:
Leave me, leave me to repose!

Odin.   Yet a while my call obey:
Prophetess, awake, and say
What virgins these, in speechless woe, 75
That bend to earth their solemn brow,
That their flaxen tresses tear,

And snowy veils that float in air.
Tell me whence their sorrows rose;
Then I leave thee to repose. 80

Prophetess.   Ha! no traveller art thou!
King of Men, I know thee now;
Mightiest of a mighty line—

Odin.   No boding maid of skill divine
Art thou, nor prophetess of good; 85
But mother of the giant-brood!

Prophetess.   Hie thee hence, and boast at
    home,
That never shall enquirer come
To break my iron-sleep again,
Till Lok has burst his tenfold chain; 90
Never, till substantial Night
Has reassumed her ancient right;
Till wrapt in flames, in ruin hurled,
Sinks the fabric of the world.
1761   1768

THE FATAL SISTERS

AN ODE FROM THE NORSE TONGUE

Now the storm begins to lower,
(Haste, the loom of hell prepare!)
Iron-sleet of arrowy shower
Hurtles in the darkened air.

Glittering lances are the loom, 5
Where the dusky warp we strain,
Weaving many a soldier's doom,
Orkney's woe, and Randver's bane.

See the grisly texture grow,
('Tis of human entrails made!) 10
And the weights, that play below,
Each a gasping warrior's head.

Shafts for shuttles, dipped in gore,
Shoot the trembling cords along.
Sword, that once a monarch bore, 15
Keep the tissue close and strong.

Mista black, terrific maid,
Sangrida, and Hilda see,
Join the wayward work to aid:
'Tis the woof of victory. 20

Ere the ruddy sun be set,
Pikes must shiver, javelins sing,
Blade with clattering buckler meet
Hauberk crash, and helmet ring.

(Weave the crimson web of war!)   25
Let us go, and let us fly,
Where our friends the conflict share,
Where they triumph, where they die

As the paths of fate we tread,
Wading through th' ensanguined field: 30
Gondula, and Geira, spread
O'er the youthful king your shield.

We the reins to slaughter give,
Ours to kill, and ours to spare:
Spite of danger he shall live.   35
(Weave the crimson web of war!)

They, whom once the desert-beach
Pent within its bleak domain,
Soon their ample sway shall stretch
O'er the plenty of the plain.   40

Low the dauntless earl is laid,
Gored with many a gaping wound:
Fate demands a nobler head;
Soon a king shall bite the ground.

Long his loss shall Erin weep,   45
Ne'er again his likeness see;
Long her strains in sorrow steep,
Strains of immortality!

Horror covers all the heath,
Clouds of carnage blot the sun.   50
Sisters, weave the web of death;
Sisters, cease, the work is done.

Hail the task, and hail the hands!
Songs of joy and triumph sing!
Joy to the victorious bands;   55
Triumph to the younger king.

Mortal, thou that hear'st the tale,
Learn the tenor of our song.
Scotland, through each winding vale
Far and wide the notes prolong.   60

Sisters, hence with spurs of speed:
Each her thundering falchion wield;
Each bestride her sable steed.
Hurry, hurry to the field!

                     1768

DAVID HARTLEY (1705-1757)

FROM OBSERVATIONS ON MAN

[THE LAWS OF ASSOCIATION]

Sensations are those internal feelings of
the mind, which arise from the impressions
made by external objects upon the several
parts of our bodies.

All of our other internal feelings may be
called ideas. Some of these appear to
spring up in the mind of themselves, some
are suggested by words, others arise in
other ways. Many writers comprehend
sensations under ideas; but I everywhere
use these words in the senses here ascribed
to them.

The ideas which resemble sensations are
called ideas of sensation: all the rest may
therefore be called intellectual ideas.

It will appear in the course of these
observations, that the ideas of sensation
are the elements of which all the rest are
compounded. Hence ideas of sensation
may be termed simple, intellectual ones
complex.

The pleasures and pains are comprehended under the sensations and ideas, as
these are explained above. For all our
pleasures and pains are internal feelings,
and, conversely, all our internal feelings
seem to be attended with some degree
either of pleasure or pain. However, I
shall, for the most part, give the names of
pleasure and pain only to such degrees as
are considerable; referring all low, evanescent ones to the head of mere sensations
and ideas.

The pleasures and pains may be ranged
under seven general classes, viz:

1. Sensation;
2. Imagination;
3. Ambition;
4. Self-interest;
5. Sympathy;
6. Theopathy; and
7. The Moral Sense; according as they
   rise from:
   1. The impressions made on the ex-
      ternal senses;
   2. Natural or artificial beauty or
      deformity;
   3. The opinions of others concern-
      ing us;
   4. Our possession or want of the

means of happiness, and security from, or subjection to, the hazards of misery;

5. The pleasures and pains of our fellow-creatures;

6. The affections excited in us by the contemplation of the Deity; or

7. Moral beauty and deformity. . . .

All the intellectual pleasures and pains are deducible ultimately from the sensible ones, if one can show of each intellectual pleasure and pain in particular, that it takes its rise from other pleasures and pains, either sensible or intellectual. For thus none of the intellectual pleasures and pains can be original. But the sensible pleasures and pains are evidently originals. They are therefore the only ones, i.e., they are the common sources from whence all the intellectual pleasures and pains are ultimately derived. . . .

The sensible pleasures are the first pleasures of which we are capable, and are the foundation of the intellectual ones, which are formed from them in succession, according to the law of association, as before explained. Now which way soever we may turn our view, that which is prior in the order of nature is always less perfect and principal, than that which is posterior, the last of two contiguous states being the end, the first the means subservient to that end, though itself be an end in respect of some foregoing state, the sensible pleasures therefore cannot be supposed of equal value and dignity with the intellectual, to the generation of which they are made subservient. . . .

It is evident, that the pleasures of imagi-

nation were not intended for our primary pursuit, because they are, in general, the first of our intellectual pleasures, which are generated from the sensible ones by association, come to their height early in life, and decline in old age. . . . The pleasures of imagination are the next remove above the sensible ones, and have, in their proper place and degree, a great efficacy in improving and perfecting our natures. They are to men in the early part of their adult age, what playthings are to children; they teach them a love for regularity, exactness, truth, simplicity; they lead them to the knowledge of many important truths relating to themselves, the external world, and its author; they habituate to invent, and reason by analogy and induction; and when the social, moral and religious affections begin to be generated in us, we may make a much quicker progress towards the perfection of our natures by having a due stock of knowledge, in natural and artificial things, of a relish for natural and artificial beauty. It deserves particular notice here, that the language used in respect of the ideas, pleasures, and pains of imagination, is applicable to those of the moral sense, with a peculiar fitness and significancy; as vice versa, the proper language of the moral sense does, in many cases, add great beauty to poetry, oratory, etc., when used catachrestically. And we may observe in general, that as the pleasures of imagination are manifestly intended to generate and augment the higher orders, particularly those of sympathy, theopathy, and the moral sense; so these last may be made to improve and perfect those.

1749

JAMES MACPHERSON (1736-1796)

FROM OSSIAN

[FINGAL'S ROMANTIC GENEROSITY TOWARD HIS CAPTIVE ENEMY]

"King of Lochlin," said Fingal, "thy blood flows in the veins of thy foe. Our fathers met in battle, because they loved the strife of spears. But often did they feast in the hall, and send round the joy of the shell. Let thy face brighten with gladness, and thine ear delight in the harp.

Dreadful as the storm of thine ocean, thou hast poured thy valor forth; thy voice has been like the voice of thousands when they engage in war. Raise, to-morrow, raise thy white sails to the wind, thou brother of Agandecca! Bright as the beam of noon, she comes on my mournful soul. I have seen thy tears for the fair one. I spared thee in the halls of Starno, when my sword was red with slaughter, when my eye was full of tears for the maid. Or dost thou choose the fight? The combat which thy fathers gave to Trenmor is thine! that thou mayest depart renowned, like the sun setting in the west!"

"King of the race of Morven!" said the chief of resounding Lochlin, "never will Swaran fight with thee, first of a thousand heroes! I have seen thee in the halls of Starno: few were thy years beyond my own. When shall I, I said to my soul, lift the spear like the noble Fingal? We have fought heretofore, O warrior, on the side of the shaggy Malmor; after my waves had carried me to thy halls, and the feast of a thousand shells was spread. Let the bards send his name who overcame to future years, for noble was the strife of Malmor! But many of the ships of Lochlin have lost their youths on Lena. Take these, thou king of Morven, and be the friend of Swaran! When thy sons shall come to Gormal, the feast of shells shall be spread, and the combat offered on the vale."

"Nor ship," replied the king, "shall Fingal take, nor land of many hills. The desert is enough to me, with all its deer and woods. Rise on thy waves again, thou noble friend of Agandecca! Spread thy white sails to the beam of the morning; return to the echoing hills of Gormal."

"Blest be thy soul, thou king of shells," said Swaran of the dark-brown shield. "In peace thou art the gale of spring. In war, the mountain-storm. Take now my hand in friendship, king of echoing Selma! Let thy bards mourn those who fell. Let Erin give the sons of Lochlin to earth. Raise high the mossy stones of their fame: that the children of the north hereafter may behold the place where their fathers fought. The hunter may say, when he leans on a mossy tomb, here Fingal and Swaran fought, the heroes of other years. Thus hereafter shall he say, and our fame shall last for ever!"

"Swaran," said the king of hills, "to-day our fame is greatest. We shall pass away like a dream. No sound will remain in our fields of war. Our tombs will be lost in the heath. The hunter shall not know the place of our rest. Our names may be heard in song. What avails it when our strength hath ceased? O Ossian, Carril, and Ullin! you know of heroes that are no more. Give us the song of other years. Let the night pass away on the sound, and morning return with joy."

We gave the song to the kings. A hundred harps mixed their sound with our voice. The face of Swaran brightened, like the full moon of heaven: when the clouds vanish away, and leave her calm and broad in the midst of the sky.

1762

[THE SUN]

O thou that rollest above, round as the shield of my fathers! Whence are thy beams, O sun! thy everlasting light? Thou comest forth, in thy awful beauty; the stars hide themselves in the sky; the moon, cold and pale, sinks in the western wave. But thou thyself movest alone: who can be a companion of thy course? The oaks of the mountains fall: the mountains themselves decay with years; the ocean shrinks and grows again: the moon herself is lost in heaven; but thou art for ever the same; rejoicing in the brightness of thy course. When the world is dark with tempests; when thunder rolls, and lightning flies; thou lookest in thy beauty from the clouds, and laughest at the storm. But to Ossian, thou lookest in vain; for he beholds thy beams no more; whether thy yellow hair flows on the eastern clouds, or thou tremblest at the gates of the west. But thou art perhaps, like me, for a season; thy years will have an end. Thou shalt sleep in the clouds, careless of the voice of the morning. Exult then, O sun! in the strength of thy youth: Age is dark and unlovely; it is like the glimmering light of the moon, when it shines through broken clouds, and the mist is on the hills; the blast of the north is on the plain, the traveller shrinks in the midst of his journey.

[COLMA'S LAMENT]

It is night; I am alone, forlorn on the hill of storms. The wind is heard in the mountain. The torrent pours down the rock. No hut receives me from the rain, forlorn on the hill of winds.

Rise, moon! from behind thy clouds. Stars of the night, arise! Lead me, some light, to the place where my love rests from the chase alone! his bow near him, unstrung; his dogs panting around him. But here I must sit alone, by the rock of the mossy stream. The stream and the wind roar aloud. I hear not the voice of my love! Why delays my Salgar, why the chief of the hill, his promise? Here is the rock, and here the tree! here is the roaring stream! Thou didst promise with night to be here. Ah! whither is my Salgar gone! With thee I would fly, from my father;

with thee, from my brother of pride. Our race have long been foes; we are not foes, O Salgar!

Cease a little while, O wind! stream, be thou silent a while! let my voice be heard around. Let my wanderer hear me! Salgar! it is Colma who calls. Here is the tree and the rock. Salgar, my love! I am here. Why delayest thou thy coming? Lo! the calm moon comes forth. The flood is bright in the vale. The rocks are grey on the steep. I see him not on the brow. His dogs come not before him, with tidings of his near approach. Here I must sit alone!

Who lie on the heath beside me? Are they my love and my brother? Speak to me, O my friends! To Colma they give no reply. Speak to me: I am alone! My soul is tormented with fears! Ah, they are dead! Their swords are red from the fight. O my brother! my brother! why hast thou slain my Salgar? Why, O Salgar! hast thou slain my brother? Dear were ye both to me! what shall I say in your praise? Thou wert fair on the hill among thousands! he was terrible in fight. Speak to me; hear my voice; hear me, sons of my love! They are silent; silent for ever! Cold, cold are their breasts of clay. Oh! from the rock on the hill; from the top of the windy steep, speak, ye ghosts of the dead! speak, I will not be afraid! Whither are ye gone to rest? In what cave of the hill shall I find the departed? No feeble voice is on the gale; no answer half-drowned in the storm!

I sit in my grief! I wait for morning in my tears! Rear the tomb, ye friends of the dead. Close it not till Colma come. My life flies away like a dream! why should I stay behind? Here shall I rest with my friends, by the stream of the sounding rock. When night comes on the hill; when the loud winds arise; my ghost shall stand in the blast, and mourn the death of my friends. The hunter shall hear from his booth. He shall fear, but love my voice! For sweet shall my voice be for my friends: pleasant were her friends to Colma!

1762

[THE LAST WORDS OF OSSIAN]

Such were the words of the bards in the days of song; when the king heard the music of harps, the tales of other times! The chiefs gathered from all their hills and heard the lovely sound. They praised the voice of Cona [Ossian], the first among a thousand bards! But age is now on my tongue; my soul has failed! I hear at times the ghosts of bards, and learn their pleasant song. But memory fails on my mind. I hear the call of years! They say as they pass along, why does Ossian sing? Soon shall he lie in the narrow house, and no bard shall raise his fame! Roll on, ye dark-brown years; ye bring no joy on your course! Let the tomb open to Ossian, for his strength has failed. The sons of song are gone to rest. My voice remains, like a blast that roars lonely on a sea-surrounded rock, after the winds are laid. The dark moss whistles there; the distant mariner sees the waving trees!

1762

CHRISTOPHER SMART (1722-1771)

FROM A SONG TO DAVID

Strong is the lion—like a coal
His eyeball, like a bastion's mole
  His chest against the foes;
Strong the gier-eagle on his sail;
Strong against tide th' enormous whale
  Emerges as he goes:

But stronger still, in earth and air
And in the sea, the man of prayer,
  And far beneath the tide,
And in the seat to faith assigned,

Where ask is have, where seek is find,
  Where knock is open wide.

Beauteous the fleet before the gale;
Beauteous the multitudes in mail,
  Ranked arms and crested heads;
Beauteous the garden's umbrage mild,
Walk, water, meditated wild,
  And all the bloomy beds;

Beauteous the moon full on the lawn;
And beauteous when the veil's withdrawn

The virgin to her spouse;
Beauteous the temple, decked and filled,
When to the heaven of heavens they build
  Their heart-directed vows:

Beauteous, yea beauteous more than
  these,   25
The shepherd King upon his knees,
  For his momentous trust;
With wish of infinite conceit
For man, beast, mute, the small and great,
  And prostrate dust to dust.   30

Precious the bounteous widow's mite;
And precious, for extreme delight,
  The largess from the churl;
Precious the ruby's blushing blaze,
And Alba's blest imperial rays,   35
  And pure cerulean pearl;

Precious the penitential tear;
And precious is the sigh sincere,
  Acceptable to God;
And precious are the winning flowers,   40
In gladsome Israel's feast of bowers,
  Bound on the hallowed sod:

More precious that diviner part
Of David, even the Lord's own heart,
  Great, beautiful, and new;   45
In all things where it was intent,
In all extremes, in each event,
  Proof—answering true to true.

Glorious the sun in mid career;
Glorious th' assembled fires appear;   50
  Glorious the comet's train;
Glorious the trumpet and alarm;
Glorious th' Almighty's stretched-out arm;
  Glorious th' enraptured main;

Glorious the northern lights a-stream;   55
Glorious the song, when God's the theme;
  Glorious the thunder's roar;
Glorious, Hosannah from the den;
Glorious the catholic amen;
  Glorious the martyr's gore: 60

Glorious, more glorious, is the crown
Of Him that brought salvation down,
  By meekness called Thy son;
Thou that stupendous truth believed,
And now the matchless deed's achieved,   65
  Determined, dared, and done.

1763

HORACE WALPOLE (1717-1797)

FROM THE CASTLE OF OTRANTO

Manfred, Prince of Otranto, had one son
and one daughter. The latter, a most
beautiful virgin aged eighteen, was called
Matilda. Conrad, the son, was three years
younger, a homely youth, sickly, and of no
promising disposition; yet he was the darling of his father, who never showed any
symptoms of affection to Matilda. Manfred
had contracted a marriage for his son with
the Marquis of Vicenza's daughter, Isabella; and she had already been delivered
by her guardians into the hands of Manfred that he might celebrate the wedding
as soon as Conrad's infirm state of health
would permit. Manfred's impatience for
this ceremonial was remarked by his family
and neighbors. The former indeed, appre-
hending the severity of their Prince's disposition, did not dare to utter their surmises on this precipitation. Hippolita, his
wife, an amiable lady, did sometimes venture to represent the danger of marrying
their only son so early, considering his
great youth and greater infirmities; but she
never received any other answer than reflections on her own sterility, who had
given him but one heir. His tenants and
subjects were less cautious in their discourses. They attributed this hasty wedding to the Prince's dread of seeing accomplished an ancient prophecy, which was
said to have pronounced that the castle
and lordship of Otranto should pass from
the present family whenever the real owner
should be grown too large to inhabit it.
It was difficult to make any sense of this
prophecy; and still less easy to conceive
what it had to do with the marriage in
question. Yet these mysteries or contradictions did not make the populace adhere
the less to their opinion.

Young Conrad's birthday was fixed for
his espousals. The company was assembled

in the chapel of the castle, and everything ready for beginning the divine office, when Conrad himself was missing. Manfred, impatient of the least delay, and who had not observed his son retire, dispatched one of his attendants to summon the young prince. The servant, who had not stayed long enough to have crossed the court to Conrad's apartment, came running back breathless, in a frantic manner, his eyes staring, and foaming at the mouth. He said nothing, but pointed to the court. The company were struck with terror and amazement. The Princess Hippolita, without knowing what was the matter, but anxious for her son, swooned away. Manfred, less apprehensive than enraged at the procrastination of the nuptials, and at the folly of his domestic, asked imperiously what was the matter. The fellow made no answer, but continued pointing towards the court-yard; and at last, after repeated questions put to him, cried out, "Oh! the helmet! the helmet!" In the meantime, some of the company had run into the court, from whence was heard a confused noise of shrieks, horror, and surprise. Manfred, who began to be alarmed at not seeing his son, went himself to get information of what occasioned this strange confusion. Matilda remained endeavoring to assist her mother, and Isabella staid for the same purpose and to avoid showing any impatience for the bridegroom, for whom, in truth, she had conceived little affection.

The first thing that struck Manfred's eyes was a group of his servants endeavoring to raise something that appeared to him a mountain of sable plumes. He gazed without believing his sight. "What are ye doing?" cried Manfred, wrathfully. "Where is my son?" A volley of voices replied, "Oh! my lord! the prince! the prince! the helmet! the helmet!" Shocked with these lamentable sounds, and dreading he knew not what, he advanced hastily, but what a sight for a father's eyes! He beheld his child dashed to pieces and almost buried under an enormous helmet, an hundred times more large than any casque ever made for human being, and shaded with a proportionable quantity of black feathers.

The horror of the spectacle, the ignorance of all around how this misfortune had happened, and above all, the tremendous phenomenon before him, took away the Prince's speech. Yet his silence lasted longer than even grief could occa-

sion. He fixed his eyes on what he wished in vain to believe a vision; and seemed less attentive to his loss than buried in meditation on the stupendous object that had occasioned it. He touched, he examined the fatal casque; nor could even the bleeding mangled remains of the young Prince divert the eyes of Manfred from the portent before him. All who had known his partial fondness for young Conrad were as much surprised at their Prince's insensibility, as thunder-struck themselves at the miracle of the helmet. They conveyed the disfigured corpse into the hall, without receiving the least direction from Manfred. As little was he attentive to the ladies who remained in the chapel. On the contrary, without mentioning the unhappy princesses, his wife and daughter, the first sounds that dropped from Manfred's lips were, "Take care of the Lady Isabella." . . .

As it was now evening, the servant who conducted Isabella bore a torch before her. When they came to Manfred, who was walking impatiently about the gallery, he started and said hastily: "Take away that light, and begone!" Then shutting the door impetuously, he flung himself upon a bench against the wall, and bade Isabella sit by him. She obeyed trembling. "I sent for you, lady," said he and then stopped under great appearance of confusion. "My lord!" "Yes, I sent for you on a matter of great moment," resumed he. "Dry your tears, young lady. You have lost your bridegroom. Yes, cruel fate! and I have lost the hopes of my race! But Conrad was not worthy of your beauty." "How! my lord," said Isabella. "Sure you do not suspect me of not feeling the concern I ought! My duty and affection would have always"—"Think no more of him," interrupted Manfred; "he was a sickly puny child; and heaven has perhaps taken him away that I might not trust the honors of my house on so frail a foundation. The line of Manfred calls for numerous supports. My foolish fondness for that boy blinded the eyes of my prudence; but it is better as it is. I hope in a few years to have reason to rejoice at the death of Conrad."

Words cannot paint the astonishment of Isabella. At first, she apprehended that grief had disordered Manfred's understanding. Her next thought suggested that this strange discourse was designed to ensnare her. She feared that Manfred had perceived her indifference for his son; and in consequence of that idea she replied:

"Good my lord, do not doubt my tenderness. My heart would have accompanied my hand. Conrad would have engrossed all my care; and wherever fate shall dispose of me, I shall always cherish his memory, and regard your highness and the virtuous Hippolita as my parents." "Curse on Hippolita!" cried Manfred. "Forget her from this moment, as I do. In short, lady, you have missed a husband undeserving of your charms. They shall now be better disposed of. Instead of a sickly boy, you shall have a husband in the prime of his age, who will know how to value your beauties, and who may expect a numerous offspring." "Alas! my lord," said Isabella; "my mind is too sadly engrossed by the recent catastrophe in your family to think of another marriage. If ever my father returns, and it shall be his pleasure, I shall obey, as I did when I consented to give my hand to your son. But until his return, permit me to remain under your hospitable roof, and employ the melancholy hours in assuaging yours, Hippolita's and the fair Matilda's affliction."

"I desired you once before," said Manfred, angrily, "not to name that woman. From this hour she must be a stranger to you as she must be to me. In short, Isabella, since I cannot give you my son, I offer you myself." "Heavens!" cried Isabella, waking from her delusion; "what do I hear? You! my lord! you! my father-in-law! the father of Conrad! the husband of the virtuous Hippolita!" "I tell you," said Manfred, imperiously, "Hippolita is no longer my wife; I divorce her from this hour. Too long has she cursed me by her unfruitfulness. My fate depends on having sons; and this night I trust will give a new date to my hopes." At those words he seized the cold hand of Isabella, who was half dead with fright and horror. She shrieked and started from him. Manfred rose to pursue her, when the moon, which was now up and gleamed in at the opposite casement, presented to his sight the plumes of the fatal helmet, which rose to the height of the windows, waving backwards and forwards, in a tempestuous manner,

and accompanied with a hollow and rustling sound. Isabella, who gathered courage from her situation, and who dreaded nothing so much as Manfred's pursuit of his declaration, cried: "Look! my lord. See! heaven itself declares against your impious intentions." "Heaven nor hell shall impede my designs," said Manfred, advancing again to seize the Princess. At that instant the portrait of his grandfather, which hung over the bench where they had been sitting, uttered a deep sigh and heaved its breast. Isabella, whose back was turned to the picture, saw not the motion, nor knew whence the sound came, but started, and said: "Hark! my lord! What sound was that?" and at the same time made towards the door. Manfred, distracted between the flight of Isabella, who had now reached the stairs, and yet unable to keep his eyes from the picture, which began to move, had, however, advanced some steps after her, still looking backwards on the portrait, when he saw it quit its panel and descend on the floor with a grave and melancholy air. "Do I dream?" cried Manfred, returning; "or are the devils themselves in league against me? Speak, infernal spectre! Or, if thou art my grandsire, why dost thou too conspire against thy wretched descendant, who too dearly pays for—" Ere he could finish the sentence, the vision sighed again, and made a sign to Manfred to follow him. "Lead on!" cried Manfred; "I will follow thee to the gulf of perdition." The spectre marched sedately, but dejected, to the end of the gallery and turned into a chamber on the right-hand. Manfred accompanied him at a little distance, full of anxiety and horror, but resolved. As he would have entered the chamber, the door was clapped to with violence by an invisible hand. The Prince, collecting courage from this delay, would have forcibly burst open the door with his foot, but found that it resisted his utmost efforts. "Since hell will not satisfy my curiosity," said Manfred, "I will use the human means in my power for preserving my race; Isabella shall not escape me."

THOMAS PERCY (1729-1811)

THE ANCIENT BALLAD OF CHEVY-CHASE

THE FIRST FIT

The Persè owt of Northombarlande,
  And a vowe to God mayd he,
That he wolde hunte in the mountayns
  Off Chyviat within dayes thre,
In the mauger of doughtè Dogles,   5
  And all that ever with him be.

The fattiste hartes in all Cheviat
  He sayd he wold kill, and cary them
    away:
"Be my feth," sayd the dougheti Doglas
  agayn,
  "I wyll let that hontyng yf that I
  may."   10

Then the Persè owt of Banborowe cam,
  With him a myghtye meany,
With fifteen hondrith archares bold;
  The wear chosen out of shyars thre.

This begane on a monday at morn   15
  In Cheviat the hillys so he;
The chyld may rue that ys un-born,
  It was the mor pittè.

The dryvars thorowe the woodes went
  For to reas the dear;   20
Bomen bickarte uppone the bent
  With ther browd aras cleare.

Then the wyld thorowe the woodes went
  On every syde shear;
Grea-hondes thorowe the greves glent   25
  For to kyll thear dear.

The begane in Chyviat the hyls abone
  Yerly on a monnyn day;
Be that it drewe to the oware off none
  A hondrith fat hartes ded ther lay.   30

The blewe a mort uppone the bent,
  The semblyd on sydis shear;
To the quyrry then the Persè went
  To se the bryttlyng off the deare.

He sayd, "It was the Duglas promys   35
  This day to meet me hear;

But I wyste he wold faylle verament:"
  A great oth the Persè swear.

At the laste a squyar of Northombelonde
  Lokyde at his hand full ny,   40
He was war ath the doughetie Doglas
  comynge:
  With him a mightè meany,

Both with spear, byll, and brande:
  Yt was a myghti sight to se,
Hardyar men both off hart nar hande   45
  Wear not in Christiantè.

The wear twenty hondrith spear-men good
  Withouten any fayle;
The wear borne a-long be the watter a
  Twyde
Yth bowndes of Tividale.   50

"Leave off the brytlyng of the dear," he
  sayde,
  "And to your bowys look ye tayk good
  heed,
For never sithe ye wear on your mothars
  borne
  Had ye never so mickle need."

The dougheti Dogglas on a stede   55
  He rode all his men beforne;
His armor glytteryde as dyd a glede;
  A bolder barne was never born.

"Tell me what men ye ar," he says,
  "Or whos men that ye be: 60
Who gave youe leave to hunte in this
  Chyviat chays in the spyt of me?"

The first mane that ever him an answear
  mayd,
  Yt was the good lord Persè:
"We wyll not tell the what men we ar," he
  says,   65
  "Nor whos men that we be;
But we wyll hount hear in this chays
  In the spyte of thyne, and of the.

"The fattiste hartes in all Chyviat
  We have kyld, and cast to carry them
  a-way."
  70
"Be my troth," sayd the doughtè Dogglas
  agayn,
  "Ther-for the ton of us shall de this
  day."

Then sayd the doughtè Doglas
  Unto the lord Persè:
"To kyll all thes giltless men,   75
  A-las! it wear great pittè.

"But, Persè, thowe art a lord of lande,
  I am a yerle callyd within my contre;
Let all our men uppone a parti stande;
  And do the battell off the and of me." 80

"Nowe Cristes cors on his crowne," sayd
    the lord Persè,
  "Who-soever ther-to says nay.
Be my troth, doughtè Doglas," he says,
  "Thow shalt never se that day;

"Nethar in Ynglonde, Skottlonde, nar
    France,   85
  Nor for no man of a woman born,
But and fortune be my chance,
  I dar met him on man for on."

Then bespayke a squyar off Northombar-
    londe,
  Ric. Wytharynton was his nam;   90
"It shall never be told in Sothe-Ynglonde,"
    he says,
  "To kyng Herry the fourth for sham.

"I wat youe byn great lordes twaw,
  I am a poor squyar of lande;
I wyll never se my captayne fight on a
    fylde,   95
And stande my-selffe, and looke on,
  But whyll I may my weppone welde,
I wyll not fayl both harte and hande."

That day, that day, that dredfull day:
  The first Fit here I fynde,   100
And you wyll here any mor a the hountyng
    athe Chyviat,
  Yet ys ther mor behynde.

THE SECOND FIT

The Yngglishe men hade ther bowys
    yebent,
  Ther hartes were good yenoughe;
The first of arros that the shote off,   105
  Seven skore spear-men the sloughe.

Yet bydys the yerle Doglas uppon the bent,
  A captayne good yenoughe,
And that was sene verament,
  For he wrought hom both woo and
    wouche.   110

The Dogglas pertyd his ost in thre,
  Lyk a cheffe cheften off pryde,
With suar speares off myghttè tre
  The cum in on every syde.

Thrughe our Yngglishe archery   115
  Gave many a wounde full wyde;
Many a doughetè the garde to dy,
  Which ganyde them no pryde.

The Yngglyshe men let thear bowys be,
  And pulde owt brandes that wer
    bright;   120
It was a hevy syght to se
  Bryght swordes on basnites lyght.

Thorowe ryche male, and myne-ye-ple,
  Many sterne the stroke downe streght:
Many a freyke, that was full free,   125
  Ther undar foot dyd lyght.

At last the Duglas and the Persè met,
  Lyk to captayns of myght and mayne;
The swapte togethar tyll the both swat
  With swordes, that wear of fyn myllàn. 130

Thes worthè freckys for to fyght
  Ther-to the wear full fayne,
Tyll the bloode owte off thear basnetes
    sprente,
  As ever dyd heal or rayne.

"Holde the, Persè," sayd the Doglas,   135
  "And i' feth I shall the brynge
Wher thowe shalte have a yerls wagis
  Of Jamy our Scottish kynge."

"Thoue shalte have thy ransom fre,
  I hight the hear this thinge,   140
For the manfullyste man yet are thowe,
  That ever I conqueryd in filde fightyng."

"Nay, then," sayd the lord Persè,
  "I tolde it the beforne,
That I wolde never yeldyde be   145
  To no man of a woman born."

With that ther cam an arrowe hastely
  Forthe off a mightie wane,
Hit hathe strekene the yerle Duglas
  In at the brest bane.   150

Thoroue lyvar and longs bathe
  The sharp arrowe ys gane,
That never after in all his lyffe days,
  He spake mo wordes but ane,

That was, "Fyghte ye, my merry men,
    whyllys ye may,   155
  For my lyff days ben gan."

The Persè leanyde on his brande,
  And sawe the Duglas de;
He tooke the dede man be the hande,
  And sayd,"Wo ys me for the! 160

"To have savyde thy lyffe, I wold have
    pertyd with
  My landes for years thre,
For a better man of hart, nare of hande
  Was not in all the north countrè."

Off all that se a Skottishe knyght, 165
  Was callyd Sir Hewe the Mongon-byrry,
He sawe the Duglas to the deth was dyght;
  He spendyd a spear a trusti tre:

He rod uppon a corsiare
  Throughe a hondrith archery; 170
He never styntyde, nar never blane
  Tyll he cam to the good lord Persè.

He set uppone the lord Persè
  A dynte, that was full soare;
With a suar spear of a myghtè tre 175
  Clean thorow the body he the Persè
    bore,

Athe tothar syde, that a man myght se,
  A large cloth yard and mare:
Towe bettar captayns wear nat in Chris-
    tiantè,
  Then that day slain wear thare. 180

An archer off Northomberlonde
  Say slean was the lord Persè
He bar a bende-bow in his hande,
  Was made off trusti tre:

An arow, that a cloth yarde was lang, 185
  To th' hard stele halyde he;
A dynt, that was both sad and soar,
  He sat on Sir Hewe the Mongon-byrry.

The dynt yt was both sad and sar,
  That he of Mongon-byrry sete; 190
The swane-fethars, that his arrowe bar,
  With his hart blood the wear wete.

Ther was never a freake wone foot wold
    fle,
  But still in stour dyd stand,
Heawyng on yche othar, whyll the myght
    dre, 195
  With many a bal-ful brande.

This battell begane in Chyviat
  An owar before the none,
And when even-song bell was rang
  The battell was nat half done. 200

The tooke "on" on ethar hand
  Be the lyght off the mone;
Many hade no strength for to stande,
  In Chyviat the hyllys aboun.

Of fifteen hondrith archars of Ynglonde 205
  Went away but fifti and thre;
Of twenty hondrith spear-men of Skot-
    londe,
  But even five and fifti:

But all wear slayne Cheviat within:
  The hade no strengthe to sand on
    hie; 210
The chylde may rue that ys un-borne,
  It was the mor pittè.

Thear were slayne with the lord Persè
  Sir John of Agerstone,
Sir Roge the hinde Hartly, 215
  Sir Wyllyam the bolde Hearone.

Sir Jorg the worthè Lovele
  A knyght of great renowen,
Sir Raff the ryche Rugbè
  With dyntes wear beaten dowene. 220

For Wetharryngton my harte was wo,
  That ever he slayne shulde be;
For when both his leggis wear hewyne
    in to,
  He knyled and fought on hys kne.

Ther was slayne with the dougheti
    Douglas 225
Sir Hewe the Mongon-byrry,
Sir Davye Lwdale, that worthè was,
  His sistars son was he:

Sir Charles a Murrè, in that place,
  That never a foot wolde fle; 230
Sir Hewe Maxwell, a lorde he was,
  With the Duglas dyd he dey.

So on the morrowe the mayde them byears
  Off byrch, and hasell so gray;
Many wedous with wepyng tears 235
  Cam to fach ther makys a-way.

Tivydale may carpe off care,
  Northombarlond may mayk grat mone,
For towe such captayns, as slayne wear
    thear,
  On the March-perti shall never be
    none. 240

Word ys commen to Edden-burrowe,
  To Jamy the Skottishe kyng,
That dougheti Duglas, lyff-tenant of the
    Merches,
  He lay slean Chyviot with-in.

His handdes dyd he weal and wryng,   245
    He sayd, "Alas, and woe ys me!
Such another captayn Skotland within,"
    He sayd, "y-feth shuld never be."

Worde ys commyn to lovly Londone
    Till the fourth Harry our kyng,   250
That lord Persè, leyff-tennante of the
        Merchis,
    He lay slayne Chyviat within.

"God have merci on his soll," sayd kyng
        Harry,
    "Good lord, yf thy will it be!
I have a hondrith captayns in Ynglonde,"
        he sayd,   255
    "As good as ever was hee:
But Persè, and I brook my lyffe,
    Thy deth well quyte shall be."

As our noble kyng made his a-vowe,
    Lyke a noble prince of renowen,   260
For the deth of the lord Persè,
    He dyd the battel of Hombyll-down:

Wher syx and thritte Skottish knyghtes
    On a day wear beaten down:

Glendale glytteryde on ther armor
        bryght,   265
    Over castill, towar, and town.

This was the hontynge off the Cheviat;
    That tear begane this spurn:
Old men that knowen the grownde well
        yenoughe,
    Call it the Battell of Otterburn.   270

At Otterburn began this spurne
    Uppon a monnyn day:
Ther was the dougghtè Doglas slean,
    The Persè never went away.

Ther was never a tym on the march-
        partes   275
    Sen the Doglas and the Persè met,
But yt was marvele, and the redde blude
        ronne not,
    As the reane doys in the stret.

Jhesue Christ our balys bete,
    And to the blys us brynge!   280
Thus was the hountynge of the Chevyat:
    God send us all good ending!
                                    1765

FROM NORTHERN ANTIQUI-
TIES

ODIN, THE ALL-FATHER

The Icelandic chronicles point out Odin
as the most persuasive of men. They tell
us that nothing could resist the force of
his words, that he sometimes enlivened his
harangue with verses, which he composed 10
extempore, and that he was not only a
great poet, but that it was he who first
taught the art of poesy to the Scandanav-
ians. He was also the inventer of the
Runic characters, which so long prevailed 15
among the people. But what most contributed to make him pass for a God was
his skill in magic. He persuaded his followers that he could run over the world in
the twinkling of an eye, that he had the 20
direction of the air and tempests, that he
could transform himself into all sorts of
shapes, could raise the dead, could foretell
things to come, could by enchantments deprive his enemies of health and vigor, and 25
discover all the treasures concealed in the
earth. The same authors add that he also
knew how to sing airs so tender and melodious that the very plains and mountains
would open and expand with delight; and
that the ghosts, attracted by the sweetness
of his songs, would leave their infernal caverns, and stand motionless about him.

But if his eloquence, together with his
august and venerable deportment, procured him love and respect in a calm and
peaceable assembly, he was no less dreadful
and furious in battle. He inspired his
enemies with such terror that they thought
they could not describe it better than by
saying he rendered them blind and deaf;
that he changed himself into the shape of
a bear, a wild-bull, or a lion; that he would
appear like a wolf all desperate; and biting
his very shield for rage, would throw himself amidst the opposing ranks, making
round him the most horrible carnage, without receiving any wounds himself.

NATURE, THE ORGAN OF DIVINITY

Perhaps no religion ever attributed so
much to a Divine Providence as that of the
northern nations. This doctrine served
them for a key, as commodious as it was
universal, to unlock all the phenomena of
nature without exception. The intelligences united to different bodies pene-

trated and moved them, and men needed not to look any farther than to them, to find the cause of everything they observed in them. Thus entire nature, animated and always moved immediately by one or more intelligent causes, was in their system nothing more than the organ or instrument of the divinity, and became a kind of book in which they thought they could read his will, inclinations, and designs. Hence that weakness formerly common to so many nations, and of which the traces still subsist in many places, that makes them regard a thousand indifferent phenomena, such as the quivering of leaves, the crackling and color of flames, the fall of thunderbolts, the flight or singing of a bird, men's involuntary motions, their dreams and visions, the movements of the pulse, etc., as intimations which God gives to wise men, of his will. Hence came oracles, divinations, auspices, presages, and lots; in a word, all that rubbish of dark superstitions called at one time religion, at another magic, a science absurd to the eyes of reason, but suitable to the impatience and restlessness of our desires, and which only betrays the weakness of human nature, in promising to relieve it.

1770

OLIVER GOLDSMITH (1728-1774)

THE DESERTED VILLAGE

Sweet Auburn! loveliest village of the plain;
Where health and plenty cheered the laboring swain,
Where smiling Spring its earliest visit paid,
And parting summer's lingering blooms delayed;
Dear lovely bowers of innocence and ease, 5
Seats of my youth, when every sport could please,
How often have I loitered o'er thy green,
Where humble happiness endeared each scene!
How often have I paused on every charm,
The sheltered cot, the cultivated farm, 10
The never-failing brook, the busy mill,
The decent church that topped the neighboring hill,
The hawthorn bush, with seats beneath the shade
For talking age and whispering lovers made!
How often have I blest the coming day, 15
When toil remitting lent its turn to play,
And all the village train, from labor free,
Led up their sports beneath the spreading tree,
While many a pastime circled in the shade,
The young contending as the old surveyed; 20
And many a gambol frolicked o'er the ground,
And sleights of art and feats of strength went round.
And still, as each repeated pleasure tired,
Succeeding sports the mirthful band inspired;
The dancing pair that simply sought renown 25
By holding out to tire each other down;
The swain mistrustless of his smutted face,
While secret laughter tittered round the place;
The bashful virgin's side-long looks of love,
The matron's glance that would those looks reprove: 30
These were thy charms, sweet village! sports like these,
With sweet succession, taught even toil to please:
These round thy bowers their cheerful influence shed:
These were thy charms—but all these charms are fled.
  Sweet smiling village, loveliest of the lawn, 35

Thy sports are fled, and all thy charms withdrawn;
Amidst thy bowers the tyrant's hand is seen,
And desolation saddens all thy green:
One only master grasps the whole domain,
And half a tillage stints thy smiling plain.   40
No more thy glassy brook reflects the day,
But, choked with sedges, works its weedy way;
Along the glades, a solitary guest,
The hollow sounding bittern guards its nest;
Amidst thy desert walks the lapwing flies.   45
And tires their echoes with unvaried cries;
Sunk are thy bowers in shapeless ruin all,
And the long grass o'ertops the moldering wall;
And trembling, shrinking from the spoiler's hand,
Far, far away thy children leave the land.   50
   Ill fares the land, to hastening ills a prey,
Where wealth accumulates, and men decay:
Princes and lords may flourish, or may fade;
A breath can make them, as a breath has made:
But a bold peasantry, their country's pride,   55
When once destroyed, can never be supplied.
   A time there was, ere England's griefs began,
When every rood of ground maintained its man;
For him light labor spread her wholesome store,
Just gave what life required, but gave no more: 60
His best companions, innocence and health;
And his best riches, ignorance of wealth.
   But times are altered; trade's unfeeling train
Usurp the land and disposses the swain;
Along the lawn, where scattered hamlets rose,   65
Unwieldy wealth and cumbrous pomp repose,
And every want to opulence allied,
And every pang that folly pays to pride.
These gentle hours that plenty bade to bloom,
Those calm desires that asked but little room,   70
Those healthful sports that graced the peaceful scene,
Lived in each look, and brightened all the green;
These, far departing, seek a kinder shore,
And rural mirth and manners are no more.
   Sweet Auburn! parent of the blissful hour,   75
Thy glades forlorn confess the tyrant's power.
Here, as I take my solitary rounds
Amidst thy tangling walks and ruined grounds,
And, many a year elapsed, return to view
Where once the cottage stood, the hawthorn grew,   80
Remembrance wakes with all her busy train,
Swells at my breast, and turns the past to pain.
   In all my wanderings round this world of care,
In all my griefs—and God has given my share—
I still had hopes, my latest hours to crown,   85
Amidst these humble bowers to lay me down;
To husband out life's taper at the close,
And keep the flame from wasting by repose:
I still had hopes, for pride attends us still,
Amidst the swains to show my book-learned skill,   90
Around my fire an evening group to draw,
And tell of all I felt, and all I saw;
And, as an hare whom hounds and horns pursue
Pants to the place from whence at first she flew,
I still had hopes, my long vexations past,   95

Here to return—and die at home at last.
　O blest retirement, friend to life's decline,
Retreats from care, that never must be mine,
How happy he who crowns in shades like these
A youth of labor with an age of ease;   100
Who quits a world where strong temptations try,
And, since 'tis hard to combat, learns to fly!
For him no wretches, born to work and weep,
Explore the mine, or tempt the dangerous deep;
No surly porter stands in guilty state,   105
To spurn imploring famine from the gate;
But on he moves to meet his latter end,
Angels around befriending Virtue's friend;
Bends to the grave with unperceived decay,
While resignation gently slopes the way;   110
And, all his prospects brightening to the last,
His Heaven commences ere the world be past!
　Sweet was the sound, when oft at evening's close
Up yonder hill the village murmur rose.
There, as I passed with careless steps and slow,   115
The mingling notes came softened from below;
The swain responsive as the milk-maid sung,
The sober herd that lowed to meet their young,
The noisy geese that gabbled o'er the pool,
The playful children just let loose from school,   120
The watch-dog's voice that bayed the whispering wind,
And the loud laugh that spoke the vacant mind;—
These all in sweet confusion sought the shade,
And filled each pause the nightingale had made.
But now the sounds of population fail,   125
No cheerful murmurs fluctuate in the gale,
No busy steps the grass-grown foot-way tread,
For all the bloomy flush of life is fled.
All but yon widowed, solitary thing,
That feebly bends beside the plashy spring: 13ᴄ
She, wretched matron, forced in age, for bread,
To strip the brook with mantling cresses spread,
To pick her wintry faggot from the thorn,
To seek her nightly shed, and weep till morn;
She only left of all the harmless train,   135
The sad historian of the pensive plain.
　Near yonder copse, where once the garden smiled,
And still where many a garden flower grows wild;
There, where a few torn shrubs the place disclose.
The village preacher's modest mansion rose.   140
A man he was to all the country dear,
And passing rich with forty pounds a year;
Remote from towns he ran his godly race,
Nor e'er had changed, nor wished to change his place;
Unpractised he to fawn, or seek for power,   145
By doctrines fashioned to the varying hour;
Far other aims his heart had learned to prize,
More skilled to raise the wretched than to rise.
His house was known to all the vagrant train;
He chid their wanderings, but relieved their pain: 150
The long-remembered beggar was his guest.
Whose beard descending swept his aged breast;
The ruined spendthrift, now no longer proud,
Claimed kindred there, and had his claims allowed;
The broken soldier, kindly bade to stay,   155

Sate by his fire, and talked the night away,
Wept o'er his wounds, or, tales of sorrow done,
Shouldered his crutch and showed how fields were won.
Pleased with his guests, the good man learned to glow,
And quite forgot their vices in their woe; 160
Careless their merits or their faults to scan,
His pity gave ere charity began.
     Thus to relieve the wretched was his pride,
And e'en his failings leaned to Virtue's side;
But in his duty prompt at every call, 165
He watched and wept, he prayed and felt, for all;
And, as a bird each fond endearment tries
To tempt its new-fledged offspring to the skies,
He tried each art, reproved each dull delay,
Allured to brighter worlds, and led the way. 170
     Beside the bed where parting life was laid,
And sorrow, guilt, and pain by turns dismayed,
The reverend champion stood. At his control
Despair and anguish fled the struggling soul;
Comfort came down the trembling wretch to raise, 175
And his last faltering accents whispered praise.
     At church, with meek and unaffected grace,
His looks adorned the venerable place;
Truth from his lips prevailed with double sway,
And fools, who came to scoff, remained to pray. 180
The service past, around the pious man,
With steady zeal, each honest rustic ran;
Even children followed with endearing wile,
And plucked his gown to share the good man's smile.
His ready smile a parent's warmth expressed; 185
Their welfare pleased him, and their cares distressed:
To them his heart, his love, his griefs were given,
But all his serious thoughts had rest in Heaven.
As some tall cliff that lifts its awful form,
Swells from the vale, and midway leaves the storm, 190
Though round its breast the rolling clouds are spread,
Eternal sunshine settles on its head.
     Beside yon straggling fence that skirts the way,
With blossomed furze unprofitably gay,
There, in his noisy mansion, skilled to rule, 195
The village master taught his little school.
A man severe he was, and stern to view;
I knew him well, and every truant knew;
Well had the boding tremblers learned to trace
The days' disasters in his morning face; 200
Full well they laughed with counterfeited glee
At all his jokes, for many a joke had he;
Full well the busy whisper circling round
Conveyed the dismal tidings when he frowned.
Yet he was kind, or, if severe in aught, 205
The love he bore to learning was in fault:
The village all declared how much he knew;
'Twas certain he could write, and cipher too;
Lands he could measure, terms and tides presage,
And even the story ran that he could gauge; 210
In arguing, too, the parson owned his skill,
For, even though vanquished, he could argue still;
While words of learned length and thundering sound
Amazed the gazing rustics ranged around;
And still they gazed, and still the wonder grew, 215

That one small head could carry all he knew.
But past is all his fame. The very spot
Where many a time he triumphed is forgot.
Near yonder thorn, that lifts its head on high,
Where once the sign-post caught the passing eye, 220
Low lies that house where nut-brown draughts inspired
Where graybeard mirth and smiling toil retired,
Where village statesmen talked with looks profound,
And news much older than their ale went round.
Imagination fondly stoops to trace 225
The parlor splendors of that festive place:
The whitewashed well, the nicely sanded floor,
The varnished clock that clicked behind the door:
The chest contrived a double debt to pay,
A bed by night, a chest of drawers by day; 230
The pictures placed for ornament and use,
The twelve good rules, the royal game of goose;
The hearth, except when winter chilled the day,
With aspen boughs and flowers and fennel gay;
While broken tea-cups, wisely kept for show, 235
Ranged o'er the chimney, glistened in a row.
Vain transitory splendors could not all
Reprieve the tottering mansion from its fall?
Obscure it sinks, nor shall it more impart
An hour's importance to the poor man's heart. 240
Thither no more the peasant shall repair
To sweet oblivion of his daily care;
No more the farmer's news, the barber's tale,
No more the woodman's ballad shall prevail;
No more the smith his dusky brow shall clear, 245
Relax his ponderous strength, and lean to hear;
The host himself no longer shall be found
Careful to see the mantling bliss go round;
Nor the coy maid, half willing to be pressed,
Shall kiss the cup to pass it to the rest. 250
Yes! let the rich deride, the proud disdain,
These simple blessings of the lowly train;
To me more dear, congenial to my heart,
One native charm, than all the gloss of art.
Spontaneous joys, where Nature has its play, 255
The soul adopts, and owns their first-born sway;
Lightly they frolic o'er the vacant mind,
Unenvied, unmolested, unconfined.
But the long pomp, the midnight masquerade,
With all the freaks of wanton wealth arrayed—— 260
In these, ere triflers half their wish obtain,
The toiling pleasure sickens into pain;
And, e'en while fashion's brightest arts decoy,
The heart distrusting asks if this be joy.
Ye friends to truth, ye statesmen who survey 265
The rich man's joys increase, the poor's decay,
'Tis yours to judge, how wide the limits stand
Between a splendid, and an happy land.
Proud swells the tide with loads of freighted ore,
And shouting Folly hails them from her shore; 270
Hoards e'en beyond the miser's wish abound,
And rich men flock from all the world around.
Yet count our gains! This wealth is but a name
That leaves our useful products still the same.
Not so the loss. The man of wealth and pride 275

Takes up a space that many poor supplied;
Space for his lake, his park's extended bounds,
Space for his horses, equipage, and hounds:
The robe that wraps his limbs in silken sloth
Has robbed the neighboring fields of half their growth;   280
His seat, where solitary sports are seen,
Indignant spurs the cottage from the green:
Around the world each needful product flies,
For all the luxuries the world supplies;
While thus the land adorned for pleasure all   285
In barren splendor feebly waits the fall.
  As some fair female unadorned and plain,
Secure to please while youth confirms her reign,
Slights every borrowed charm that dress supplies,
Nor shares with art the triumph of her eyes;   290
But when those charms are passed, for charms are frail,
When time advances, and when lovers fail,
She then shines forth, solicitous to bless,
In all the glaring impotence of dress.
Thus fares the land by luxury betrayed: 295
In nature's simplest charms at first arrayed,
But verging to decline, its splendors rise,
Its vistas strike, its palaces surprise;
While, scourged by famine from the smiling land
The mournful peasant leads his humble band,   300
And while he sinks, without one arm to save,
The country blooms—a garden and a grave.
  Where then, ah! where, shall poverty reside,
To 'scape the pressure of contiguous pride?
If to some common's fenceless limits strayed,   305
He drives his flock to pick the scanty blade,
Those fenceless fields the sons of wealth divide,
And even the bare-worn common is denied.
  If to the city sped—what waits him there?
To see profusion that he must not share;   310
To see ten thousand baneful arts combined
To pamper luxury, and thin mankind;
To see those joys the sons of pleasure know
Extorted from his fellow-creature's woe.
Here while the courtier glitters in brocade,   315
There the pale artist plies the sickly trade;
Here while the proud their long-drawn pomps display,
There the black gibbet glooms beside the way.
The dome where pleasure holds her midnight reign
Here, richly decked, admits the gorgeous train: 320
Tumultuous grandeur crowds the blazing square,
The rattling chariots clash, the torches glare.
Sure scenes like these no troubles e'er annoy!
Sure these denote one universal joy!
Are these thy serious thoughts?—Ah, turn thine eyes   325
Where the poor houseless shivering female lies.
She once, perhaps, in village plenty blessed,
Has wept at tales of innocence distressed;
Her modest looks the cottage might adorn,
Sweet as the primrose peeps beneath the thorn: 330
Now lost to all; her friends, her virtue fled,
Near her betrayer's door she lays her head,
And, pinched with cold, and shrinking from the shower,
With heavy heart deplores that luckless hour,
When idly first, ambitious of the town,   335

She left her wheel and robes of country brown.
  Do thine, sweet Auburn,—thine, the loveliest train,—
Do thy fair tribes participate her pain?
Even now, perhaps, by cold and hunger led,
At proud men's doors they ask a little bread!   340
  Ah, no! To distant climes, a dreary scene,
Where half the convex world intrudes between,
Through torrid tracts with fainting steps they go,
Where wild Altama murmurs to their woe.
Far different there from all that charmed before   345
The various terrors of that horrid shore;
Those blazing suns that dart a downward ray,
And fiercely shed intolerable day;
Those matted woods, where birds forget to sing,
But silent bats in drowsy clusters cling;   350
Those poisonous fields with rank luxuriance crowned,
Where the dark scorpion gathers death around;
Where at each step the stranger fears to wake
The rattling terrors of the vengeful snake;
Where crouching tigers wait their hapless prey,   355
And savage men more murderous still than they;
While oft in whirls the mad tornado flies,
Mingling the ravaged landscape with the skies.
Far different these from every former scene,
The cooling brook, the grassy vested green,   360
The breezy covert of the warbling grove,
That only sheltered thefts of harmless love.
  Good Heaven! what sorrows gloomed that parting day,
That called them from their native walks away;
When the poor exiles, every pleasure passed,   365
Hung round the bowers, and fondly looked their last,
And took a long farewell, and wished in vain
For seats like those beyond the western main,
And shuddering still to face the distant deep,
Returned and wept, and still returned to weep.   370
The good old sire the first prepared to go
To new-found worlds, and wept for others' woe;
But for himself, in conscious virtue brave,
He only wished for worlds beyond the grave.
His lovely daughter, lovelier in her tears,   375
The fond companion of his helpless years,
Silent went next, neglectful of her charms,
And left a lover's for a father's arms,
With louder plaints the mother spoke her woes,
And blest the cot where every pleasure rose,   380
And kissed her thoughtless babes with many a tear,
And clasped them close, in sorrow doubly dear,
Whilst her fond husband strove to lend relief
In all the silent manliness of grief.
  O luxury! thou cursed by Heaven's decree,   385
How ill exchanged are things like these for thee!
How do thy potions, with insidious joy,
Diffuse their pleasure only to destroy!
Kingdoms by thee, to sickly greatness grown,
Boast of a florid vigor not their own.   390
At every draught more large and large they grow,
A bloated mass of rank unwieldy woe;
Till sapped their strength, and every part unsound,
Down, down, they sink, and spread a ruin round.
  Even now the devastation is begun,   395

And half the business of destruction done;
Even now, methinks, as pondering here I stand,
I see the rural Virtues leave the land.
Down where yon anchoring vessel spreads the sail,
That idly waiting flaps with every gale,   400
Downward they move, a melancholy band,
Pass from the shore, and darken all the strand.
Contented Toil, and hospitable Care,
And kind connubial Tenderness, are there;
And Piety with wishes placed above,   405
And steady Loyalty, and faithful Love.
And thou, sweet Poetry, thou loveliest maid,
Still first to fly where sensual joys invade;
Unfit in these degenerate times of shame
To catch the heart, or strike for honest fame;   410
Dear charming nymph, neglected and decried,
My shame in crowds, my solitary pride;
Thou source of all my bliss, and all my woe,
That found'st me poor at first, and keep'st me so;
Thou guide by which the nobler arts excel,   415
Thou nurse of every virtue, fare thee well!
Farewell, and oh! where'er thy voice be tried,
On Torno's cliffs, or Pambamarca's side,
Whether where equinoctial fervors glow,
Or winter wraps the polar world in snow,   420
Still let thy voice, prevailing over time,
Redress the rigors of th' inclement clime;
Aid slighted truth with thy persuasive strain;
Teach erring man to spurn the rage of gain;
Teach him, that states of native strength possessed,   425
Though very poor, may still be very blessed;
That trade's proud empire hastes to swift decay,
As ocean sweeps the labored mole away;
While self-dependent power can time defy,
As rocks resist the billows and the sky.   430

1770

THOMAS CHATTERTON (1752-1770)

SONGS FROM "ÆLLE, A TRAGYCAL ENTERLUDE WROTENN BIE THOMAS ROWLEIE"

[THE BODDYNGE FLOURETTES BLOSHES ATTE THE LYGHTE]

FYRSTE MYNSTRELLE

The boddynge flourettes bloshes atte the lyghte;
The mees be sprenged wyth the yellowe hue;
Ynn daiseyd mantels ys the mountayne dyghte;
The nesh yonge coweslepe blendethe wyth the dewe;
The trees enlefèd, yntoe Heavenne straughte,   5
Whenn gentle wyndes doe blowe to whestlyng dynne ys brought.

The evenynge commes, and brynges the dewe alonge;
The roddie welkynne sheeneth to the eyne;
Arounde the alestake Mynstrells synge the songe;

Yonge ivie rounde the doore poste do entwyne;   10
I laie mee onn the grasse; yette, to mie wylle,
Albeytte alle ys fayre, there lackethe somethynge stylle.

SECONDE MYNSTRELLE

So Adam thoughtenne, whann, ynn Paradyse,
All Heavenn and Erthe dyd hommage to hys mynde;
Ynn Womman alleyne mannès pleasaunce lyes;   15
As Instrumentes of joie were made the kynde.
Go, take a wyfe untoe thie armes, and see
Wynter and brownie hylles wyll have a charm for thee.

THYRDE MYNSTRELLE

Whanne Autumpne blake and sonne-brente doe appere,
With hys goulde honde guylteynge the falleynge lefe,   20
Bryngeynge oppe Wynterr to folfylle the yere,
Beerynge uponne hys backe the ripèd shefe;
Whan al the hyls wythe woddie sede ys whyte;
Whanne levynne-fyres and lemes do mete from far the syghte;

Whann the fayre apple, rudde as even skie,   25
Do bende the tree unto the fructyle grounde;
When joicie peres, and berries of blacke die,
Doe daunce yn ayre, and call the eyne arounde;
Thann, bee the even foule or even fayre,
Meethynckes mie hartys joie ys steyncèd wyth somme care. 30

SECONDE MYNSTRELLE

Angelles bee wrogte to bee of neidher kynde;
Angelles alleyne fromme chafe desyre bee free:
Dheere ys a somwhatte evere yn the mynde;
Yatte, wythout wommanne, cannot styllèd bee;
Ne seyncte yn celles, botte, havynge blodde and tere, 35
Do fynde the spryte to joie on syghte of wommanne fayre;

Wommen bee made, notte for hemselves, botte manne,
Bone of hys bone, and chyld of hys desire;
Fromme an ynutyle membere fyrste beganne,
Ywroghte with moche of water, lyttele fyre;   40
Therefore theie seke the fyre of love, to hete
The milkyness of kynde, and make hemselfes complete.

Albeytte wythout wommen menne were pheeres
To salvage kynde, and wulde botte lyve to slea,
Botte wommenne efte the spryghte of peace so cheres,   45
Tochelod yn Angel joie heie Angeles bee:
Go, take thee swythyn to thie bedde a wyfe;
Bee bante or blessed hie yn proovynge marryage lyfe.

                    ¹777

AN EXCELENTE BALADE OF CHARITIE

AS WROTEN BIE THE GODE PRIESTE THOMAS ROWLEY, 1464

In Virgynè the sweltrie sun gan sheene,
And hotte upon the mees did caste his raie;
The apple rodded from its palie greene,

And the mole peare did bende the leafy spraie;
The peede chelandri sunge the livelong daie; 5
'Twas nowe the pride, the manhode, of the yeare,
And eke the grounde was dighte in its most defte aumere.

The sun was glemeing in the middle of daie,
Deadde still the aire, and eke the welken blue;
When from the sea arist in drear arraie 10
A hepe of cloudes of sable sullen hue,
The which full fast unto the woodlande drewe,
Hiltring attenes the sunnis fetive face,
And the blacke tempeste swolne and gathered up apace.

Beneathe an holme, faste by a pathwaie side 15
Which dide unto Seyncte Godwine's covent lede,
A hapless pilgrim moneynge dyd abide,
Pore in his viewe, ungentle in his weede,
Longe bretful of the miseries of neede;
Where from the hailstone coulde the almer flie? 20
He had no housen theere, ne anie covent nie.

Look in his glommèd face, his spright there scanne;
Howe woe-be-gone, how withered, forwynd, deade!
Haste to thie church-glebe-house, ashrewed manne;
Haste to thie kiste, thie onlie dorture bedde: 25
Cale as the claie whiche will gre on thie hedde
Is Charitie and Love aminge highe elves;
Knightis and Barons live for pleasure and themselves.

The gathered storm is rype; the bigge drops falle;
The forswat meadowes smethe, and drenche the raine; 30
The comyng ghastness do the cattle pall,
And the full flockes are drivynge ore the plaine;
Dashde from the cloudes, the waters flott againe;
The welkin opes, the yellow levynne flies,
And the hot fierie smothe in the wide lowings dies. 35

Liste! now the thunder's rattling clymmynge sound
Cheves slowie on, and then embollen clangs,
Shakes the hie spyre, and, losst, dispended, drowned,
Still on the gallard eare of terroure hanges;
The windes are up, the lofty elmen swanges; 40
Again the levynne and the thunder poures,
And the full cloudes are braste attenes in stonen showers.

Spurreynge his palfrie oere the watrie plaine,
The Abbote of Seyncte Godwyne's convente came:
His chapournette was drented with the reine, 45
And his pencte gyrdle met with mickle shame;
He aynewards tolde his bederoll at the same.
The storme encreasen, and he drew aside
With the mist almes-craver neere to the holme to bide.

His cope was all of Lyncolne clothe so fyne, 50
With a gold button fastened neere his chynne;
His autremete was edged with golden twynne,
And his shoone pyke a loverds mighte have binne—
Full well it shewn he thoughten coste no sinne;
The trammels of the palfrye pleasde his sighte, 55
For the horse-millanare his head with roses dighte.

"An almes, sir prieste!" the droppynge pilgrim saide;
"Oh let me waite within your covente dore,
Till the sunne sheneth hie above our heade,
And the loude tempeste of the aire is oer.   60
Helpless and ould am I, alas! and poor;
No house, ne friend, ne moneie in my pouche;
All yatte I calle my owne is this my silver crouche."

"Varlet," replyd the Abbatte, "cease your dinne!
This is no season almes and prayers to give.   65
Mie porter never lets a faitour in;
None touch mie rynge who not in honor live."
And now the sonne with the blacke cloudes did stryve
And shettynge on the ground his glairie raie:
The Abbatte spurrde his steede, and eftsoones roadde awaie.   70

Once moe the skie was blacke, the thounder rolde:
Faste reyneynge oer the plaine a prieste was seen,
Ne dighte full proude, ne buttoned up in golde;
His cope and jape were graie, and eke were clene;
A Limitoure he was of order seene.   75
And from the pathwaie side then turnèd hee,
Where the pore almer laie binethe the holmen tree.

"An almes, sir priest!" the droppynge pilgrim sayde,
"For sweete Seyncte Marie and your order sake!"
The Limitoure then loosened his pouche threade,   80
And did thereoute a groate of silver take:
The mister pilgrim dyd for halline shake.
"Here, take this silver; it maie eathe thie care:
We are Goddes stewards all, nete of our owne we bare.

"But ah, unhailie pilgrim, lerne of me   85
Scathe anie give a rentrolle to their Lorde.
Here, take my semecope—thou arte bare, I see;
'Tis thyne; the Seynctes will give me mie rewarde."
He left the pilgrim, and his waie aborde.
Virgynne and hallie Seyncte, who sitte yn gloure,   90
Or give the mittee will, or give the gode man power!

1777

WILLIAM COWPER (1731-1800)

TO A YOUNG LADY

Sweet stream, that winds through yonder
          glade,
Apt emblem of a virtuous maid—
Silent and chaste she steals along,
Far from the world's gay busy throng:
With gentle yet prevailing force,   5
Intent upon her destined course;
Graceful and useful all she does.
Blessing and blest where'er she goes;

Pure-bosomed as that watery glass
And Heaven reflected in her face.   10

1782

FROM THE TASK

[THE INHUMANITY OF MAN]

Oh for a lodge in some vast wilderness,
Some boundless contiguity of shade.
Where rumor of oppression and deceit,

Of unsuccessful or successful war,
Might never reach me more! My ear is
    pained,   5
My soul is sick, with every day's report
Of wrong and outrage with which earth is
    filled.
There is no flesh in man's obdurate heart,
It does not feel for man; the natural bond
Of brotherhood is severed as the flax   10
That falls asunder at the touch of fire.
He finds his fellow guilty of a skin
Not colored like his own, and, having
    power
T'enforce the wrong, for such a worthy
    cause
Dooms and devotes him as his lawful
    prey.   15
Lands intersected by a narrow frith
Abhor each other.   Mountains interposed
Make enemies of nations who had else
Like kindred drops been mingled into one.
Thus man devotes his brother, and de-
    stroys;   20
And worse than all, and most to be de-
    plored,
As human nature's broadest, foulest blot,
Chains him, and tasks him, and exacts his
    sweat
With stripes that Mercy, with a bleeding
    heart,
Weeps when she sees inflicted on a beast. 25
Then what is man? And what man seeing
    this,
And having human feelings, does not blush
And hang his head, to think himself a
    man?
I would not have a slave to till my ground,
To carry me, to fan me while I sleep,   30
And tremble when I wake, for all the
    wealth
That sinews bought and sold have ever
    earned.
No: dear as freedom is, and in my heart's
Just estimation prized above all price,
I had much rather be myself the slave   35
And wear the bonds than fasten them on
    him.
We have no slaves at home: then why
    abroad?
And they themselves, once ferried o'er the
    wave
That parts us, are emancipate and loosed.
Slaves cannot breathe in England; if their
    lungs   40
Receive our air, that moment they are free;
They touch our country, and their shackles
    fall.
That's noble, and bespeaks a nation proud
And jealous of the blessing. Spread it,
    then,

And let it circulate through every vein   45
Of all your empire; that where Britain's
    power
Is felt, mankind may feel her mercy, too.

[LOVE OF ENGLAND]

England, with all thy faults, I love thee
    still,
My country! and, while yet a nook is left
Where English minds and manners may be
    found,
Shall be constrained to love thee. Though
    thy clime
Be fickle, and thy year, most part, de-
    formed   5
With dripping rains, or withered by a frost,
I would not yet exchange thy sullen skies
And fields without a flower, for warmer
    France
With all her vines; nor for Ausonia's groves
Of golden fruitage, and her myrtle
    bowers.   10
To shake thy senate, and from heights
    sublime
Of patriot eloquence to flash down fire
Upon thy foes, was never meant my task;
But I can feel thy fortunes, and partake
Thy joys and sorrows with as true a
    heart   15
As any thunderer there. And I can feel
Thy follies too, and with a just disdain
Frown at effeminates, whose very looks
Reflect dishonor on the land I love.
How, in the name of soldiership and
    sense,   20
Should England prosper, when such things,
    as smooth
And tender as a girl, all-essenced o'er
With odors, and as profligate as sweet,
Who sell their laurel for a myrtle wreath,
And love when they should fight,—when
    such as these   25
Presume to lay their hand upon the ark
Of her magnificent and awful cause?
Time was when it was praise and boast
    enough
In every clime, and travel where we might,
That we were born her children; praise
    enough   30
To fill the ambition of a private man,
That Chatham's language was his mother
    tongue,
And Wolfe's great name compatriot with
    his own.
Farewell those honors, and farewell with
    them
The hope of such hereafter! They have
    fallen   35

Each in his field of glory: one in arms,
And one in council—Wolfe upon the lap
Of smiling Victory that moment won,
And Chatham, heart-sick of his country's
shame!
They made us many soldiers. Chatham
still   40
Consulting England's happiness at home,
Secured it by an unforgiving frown
If any wronged her. Wolfe, where'er he
fought,
Put so much of his heart into his act,
That his example had a magnet's force, 45
And all were swift to follow whom all
loved.
Those suns are set. Oh, rise some other
such!
Or all that we have left is empty talk
Of old achievements, and despair of new.

[COWPER, THE RELIGIOUS RECLUSE]

I was a stricken deer that left the herd
Long since; with many an arrow deep
infixed
My panting side was charged, when I with-
drew
To seek a tranquil death in distant shades.
There was I found by One who had Him-
self   5
Been hurt by th' archers. In His side He
bore,
And in His hands and feet, the cruel scars.
With gentle force soliciting the darts,
He drew them forth, and healed, and bade
me live.
Since then, with few associates, in remote 10
And silent woods I wander, far from those
My former partners of the peopled scene,
With few associates, and not wishing more.
Here much I ruminate, as much I may,
With other views of men and manners
now   15
Than once, and others of a life to come.
I see that all are wanderers, gone astray
Each in his own delusions; they are lost
In chase of fancied happiness, still wooed
And never won; dream after dream en-
sues,   20
And still they dream that they shall still
succeed,
And still are disappointed: rings the world
With the vain stir. I sum up half man-
kind,
And add two-thirds of the remaining half,
And find the total of their hopes and
fears   25
Dreams, empty dreams.

[THE BASTILLE]

Then shame to manhood, and opprobrious
more
To France than all her losses and defeats
Old or of later date, by sea or land,
Her house of bondage worse than that of
old
Which God avenged on Pharaoh—the Bas-
tille!   5
Ye horrid towers, th' abode of broken
hearts,
Ye dungeons and ye cages of despair,
That monarchs have supplied from age to
age
With music such as suits their sovereign
ears—
The sighs and groans of miserable men, 10
There's not an English heart that would
not leap
To hear that ye were fallen at last, to
know
That even our enemies, so oft employed
In forging chains for us, themselves were
free:
For he that values liberty, confines   15
His zeal for her predominance within
No narrow bounds; her cause engages him
Wherever pleaded; 'tis the cause of man.
There dwell the most forlorn of human
kind,
Immured though unaccused, condemned
untried,   20
Cruelly spared, and hopeless of escape.
There, like the visionary emblem seen
By him of Babylon, life stands a stump,
And filleted about with hoops of brass,
Still lives, though all its pleasant boughs
are gone.   25
To count the hour-bell and expect no
change;
And ever as the sullen sound is heard,
Still to reflect that though a joyless note
To him whose moments all have one dull
pace,
Ten thousand rovers in the world at
large   30
Account it music—that it summons some
To theatre, or jocund feast, or ball;
The wearied hireling finds it a release
From labor; and the lover, who has chid
Its long delay, feels every welcome stroke 35
Upon his heart-strings trembling with de-
light:
To fly for refuge from distracting thought
To such amusements as ingenious woe
Contrives, hard-shifting and without her
tools—
To read engraven on the muddy walls,   40
In staggering types, his predecessor's tale.

A sad memorial, and subjoin his own;
To turn purveyor to an overgorged
And bloated spider, till the pampered pest
Is made familiar, watches his approach, 45
Comes at his call, and serves him for a
friend;
To wear out time in numbering to and fro
The studs that thick emboss his iron door,
Then downward and then upward, then
aslant
And then alternate, with a sickly hope 50
By dint of change to give his tasteless task
Some relish, till, the sum exactly found
In all directions, he begins again:—
Oh comfortless existence! hemmed around
With woes, which who that suffers would
not kneel 55
And beg for exile or the pangs of death?
That man should thus encroach on fellow-
man,
Abridge him of his just and native rights,
Eradicate him, tear him from his hold
Upon th' endearments of domestic life 60
And social, nip his fruitfulness and use,
And doom him for perhaps an heedless
word
To barrenness and solitude and tears,
Moves indignation; makes the name of
king
(Of king whom such prerogative can
please) 65
As dreadful as the Manichean god,
Adored through fear, strong only to de-
stroy.

[MEDITATION IN WINTER]

The night was winter in his roughest
mood,
The morning sharp and clear. But now at
noon,
Upon the southern side of the slant hills,
And where the woods fence off the north-
ern blast,
The season smiles, resigning all its rage, 5
And has the warmth of May. The vault is
blue
Without a cloud, and white without a
speck
The dazzling splendor of the scene below.
Again the harmony comes o'er the vale,
And through the trees I view the embattled
tower 10
Whence all the music. I again perceive
The soothing influence of the wafted
strains,
And settle in soft musings as I tread
The walk, still verdant, under oaks and
elms,

Whose outspread branches overarch the
glade. 15
The roof, though moveable through all
its length
As the wind sways it, has yet well sufficed,
And intercepting in their silent fall
The frequent flakes, has kept a path for
me.
No noise is here, or none that hinders
thought. 20
The redbreast warbles still, but is content
With slender notes, and more than half
suppressed:
Pleased with his solitude, and flitting light
From spray to spray, where'er he rests he
shakes
From many a twig the pendent drops of
ice, 25
That tinkle in the withered leaves below.
Stillness, accompanied with sounds so soft,
Charms more than silence. Meditation
here
May think down hours to moments. Here
the heart
May give a useful lesson to the head, 30
And learning wiser grow without his books.
Knowledge and wisdom, far from being
one,
Have ofttimes no connection. Knowledge
dwells
In heads replete with thoughts of other
men,
Wisdom in minds attentive to their own. 35
Knowledge, a rude unprofitable mass,
The mere materials with which wisdom
builds,
Till smoothed and squared and fitted to its
place,
Does but encumber whom it seems to
enrich.
Knowledge is proud that he has learned so
much; 40
Wisdom is humble that he knows no more.
Books are not seldom talismans and spells,
By which the magic art of shrewder wits
Holds an unthinking multitude enthralled.
Some to the fascination of a name 45
Surrender judgment hoodwinked. Some
the style
Infatuates, and through labyrinths and
wilds
Of error leads them, by a tune entranced.
While sloth seduces more, too weak to
bear
The insupportable fatigue of thought, 50
And swallowing therefore, without pause
or choice,
The total grist unsifted, husks and all.
But trees, and rivulets whose rapid course
Defies the check of winter, haunts of deer.

And sheepwalks populous with bleating
lamps,   55
And lanes in which the primrose ere her
time
Peeps through the moss that clothes the
hawthorn root,
Deceive no student.   Wisdom there, and
Truth,
Not shy as in the world, and to be won
By slow solicitation, seize at once   60
The roving thought, and fix it on them-
selves.

[KINDNESS TO ANIMALS]

I would not enter on my list of friends,
Though graced with polished manners and
fine sense,
Yet wanting sensibility, the man
Who needlessly sets foot upon a worm.
An inadvertent step may crush the snail   5
That crawls at evening in the public path;
But he that has humanity, forewarned,
Will tread aside and let the reptile live.
The creeping vermin, loathsome to the
sight,
And charged perhaps with venom, that
intrudes,   10
A visitor unwelcome, into scenes
Sacred to neatness and repose—th' alcove,
The chamber, or refectory,—may die:
A necessary act incurs no blame.
Not so when, held within their proper
bounds   15
And guiltless of offence, they range the air,
Or take their pastime in the spacious field:
There they are privileged; and he that
hunts
Or harms them there is guilty of a wrong,
Disturbs th' economy of Nature's realm, 20
Who, when she formed, designed them an
abode.

1785

ON THE RECEIPT OF MY MOTHER'S PICTURE

O that those lips had language! Life has
passed
With me but roughly since I heard thee
last.
Those lips are thine—thy own sweet smile
I see,
The same that oft in childhood solaced me;
Voice only fails, else how distinct they say, 5
"Grieve not, my child, chase all thy fears
away!"

The meek intelligence of those dear eyes
(Blest be the art that can immortalize,
The art that baffles Time's tyrannic claim
To quench it) here shines on me still the
same.   10
Faithful remembrancer of one so dear,
O welcome guest, though unexpected here!
Who bidd'st me honor with an artless song,
Affectionate, a mother lost so long,
I will obey, not willingly alone,   15
But gladly, as the precept were her own:
And, while that face renews my filial grief,
Fancy shall weave a charm for my relief,
Shall steep me in Elysian revery,
A momentary dream that thou art she.   20
My mother! when I learned that thou
wast dead,
Say, wast thou conscious of the tears I
shed?
Hovered thy spirit o'er thy sorrowing son,
Wretch even then, life's journey just
begun?
Perhaps thou gav'st me, though unfelt, a
kiss;   25
Perhaps a tear, if souls can weep in
bliss—
Ah, that maternal smile! it answers "Yes."
I heard the bell tolled on thy burial day,
I saw the hearse that bore thee slow away,
And, turning from my nursery window,
drew   30
A long, long sigh, and wept a last adieu!
But was it such? It was: where thou art
gone
Adieus and farewells are a sound un-
known.
May I but meet thee on that peaceful
shore,
The parting word shall pass my lips no
more!   35
Thy maidens, grieved themselves at my
concern,
Oft gave me promise of thy quick return.
What ardently I wished I long believed,
And, disappointed still, was still deceived,
By expectation every day beguiled,   40
Dupe of to-morrow even from a child.
Thus many a sad to-morrow came and
went,
Till, all my stock of infant sorrow spent,
I learnt at last submission to my lot,
But, though I less deplored thee, ne'er
forgot.   45
Where once we dwelt our name is heard
no more:
Children not thine have trod my nursery
floor;
And where the gardener Robin, day by
day,
Drew me to school along the public way,

Delighted with my bauble coach, and
 wrapped   50
In scarlet mantle warm, and velvet-capped,
'Tis now become a history little known
That once we called the pastoral house our
 own.
Short-lived possession! But the record fair
That memory keeps, of all thy kindness
 there,   55
Still outlives many a storm that has effaced
A thousand other themes less deeply traced.
Thy nightly visits to my chamber made,
That thou mightst know me safe and
 warmly laid;
Thy morning bounties ere I left my
 home,   60
The biscuit or confectionary plum;
The fragrant waters on my cheeks be-
 stowed
By thy own hand, till fresh they shone and
 glowed;
All this, and, more endearing still than all,
Thy constant flow of love, that knew no
 fall,   65
Ne'er roughened by those cataracts and
 breaks
That humor interposed too often makes;
All this, still legible on memory's page,
And still to be so to my latest age,
Adds joy to duty, makes me glad to pay 70
Such honors to thee as my numbers may,
Perhaps a frail memorial, but sincere,
Not scorned in heaven though little no-
 ticed here.
 Could Time, his flight reversed, restore
 the hours
When, playing with thy vesture's tissued
 flowers,   75
The violet, the pink, the jessamine,
I pricked them into paper with a pin
(And thou wast happier than myself the
 while,
Wouldst softly speak, and stroke my head
 and smile),
Could those few pleasant days again
 appear,   80
Might one wish bring them, would I wish
 them here?
I would not trust my heart—the dear
 delight
Seems so to be desired, perhaps I might.
But no—what here we call our life is
 such,
So little to be loved, and thou so much, 85
That I should ill requite thee to constrain
Thy unbound spirit into bonds again.
 Thou, as a gallant bark from Albion's
 coast,

The storms all weathered and the ocean
 crossed,
Shoots into port at some well-havened
 isle,   90
Where spices breathe and brighter seasons
 smile,
There sits quiescent on the floods, that
 show
Her beauteous form reflected clear below,
While airs impregnated with incense play
Around her, fanning light her streamers
 gay,   95
So thou, with sails how swift, hast reached
 the shore
"Where tempests never beat nor billows
 roar,"
And thy loved consort on the dangerous
 tide
Of life long since has anchored by thy side.
But me, scarce hoping to attain that
 rest,   100
Always from port withheld, always dis-
 tressed,
Me howling blasts drive devious, tempest-
 tossed,
Sails ripped, seams opening wide, and com-
 pass lost,
And day by day some current's thwarting
 force
Sets me more distant from a prosperous
 course.   105
Yet, oh, the thought that thou art safe,
 and he,
That thought is joy, arrive what may to me.
My boast is not that I deduce my birth
From loins enthroned and rulers of the
 earth;
But higher far my proud pretensions
 rise—   110
The son of parents passed into the skies!
 And now, farewell. Time unrevoked
 has run
His wonted course, yet what I wished is
 done:
By contemplation's help, not sought in
 vain,
I seem t' have lived my childhood o'er
 again,   115
To have renewed the joys that once were
 mine,
Without the sin of violating thine;
And while the wings of Fancy still are free,
And I can view this mimic show of thee,
Time has but half succeeded in his
 theft—   120
Thyself removed, thy power to soothe me
 left.
         1798

TO MARY

The twentieth year is well-nigh past,
Since first our sky was overcast;
Ah, would that this might be the last!
    My Mary!

Thy spirits have a fainter flow, 5
I see thee daily weaker grow;
'Twas my distress that brought thee low,
    My Mary!

Thy needles, once a shining store,
For my sake restless heretofore, 10
Now rust disused, and shine no more,
    My Mary!

For though thou gladly wouldst fulfil
The same kind office for me still,
Thy sight now seconds not thy will, 15
    My Mary!

But well thou playedst the housewife's part,
And all thy threads with magic art
Have wound themselves about this heart,
    My Mary! 20

Thy indistinct expressions seem
Like language uttered in a dream;
Yet me they charm, what'er the theme,
    My Mary!

Thy silver locks, once auburn bright, 25
Are still more lovely in my sight
Than golden beams of orient light,
    My Mary!

For, could I view nor them nor thee,
What sight worth seeing could I see? 30
The sun would rise in vain for me,
    My Mary!

Partakers of thy sad decline,
Thy hands their little force resign,
Yet, gently pressed, press gently mine, 35
    My Mary!

Such feebleness of limbs thou provest,
That now at every step thou movest
Upheld by two, yet still thou lovest,
    My Mary! 40

And still to love, though pressed with ill,
In wintry age to feel no chill,
With me is to be lovely still,
    My Mary!

But ah! by constant heed I know, 45
How oft the sadness that I show
Transforms thy smiles to looks of woe,
    My Mary!

And should my future lot be cast
With much resemblance of the past, 50
Thy worn-out heart will break at last,
    My Mary!

c. 1795   1803

THE CASTAWAY

Obscurest night involved the sky,
    The Atlantic billows roared,
When such a destined wretch as I,
    Washed headlong from on board,
Of friends, of hope, of all bereft, 5
His floating home forever left.

No braver chief could Albion boast
    Than he with whom he went,
Nor ever ship left Albion's coast
    With warmer wishes sent. 10
He loved them both, but both in vain,
    Nor him beheld, nor her again.
Not long beneath the whelming brine,
    Expert to swim, he lay;
Nor soon he felt his strength decline, 15
    Or courage die away;
But waged with death a lasting strife,
Supported by despair of life.

He shouted: nor his friends had failed
    To check the vessel's course, 20
But so the furious blast prevailed,
    That, pitiless perforce,
They left their outcast mate behind,
And scudded still before the wind.

Some succor yet they could afford; 25
    And such as storms allow,
The cask, the coop, the floated cord,
    Delayed not to bestow.
But he (they knew) nor ship nor shore,
Whate'er they gave, should visit more. 30

Nor, cruel as it seemed, could he
    Their haste himself condemn,
Aware that flight, in such a sea,
    Alone could rescue them;
Yet bitter felt it still to die 35
Deserted, and his friends so nigh.

He long survives, who lives an hour
    In ocean, self-upheld;
And so long he, with unspent power,
    His destiny repelled; 40
And ever, as the minutes flew,

Entreated help, or cried "Adieu!"
At length, his transient respite past,
  His comrades, who before
Had heard his voice in every blast,   45
  Could catch the sound no more:
For them, by toil subdued, he drank
The stifling wave, and then he sank.

No poet wept him; but the page
  Of narrative sincere,   50
That tells his name, his worth, his age,
  Is wet with Anson's tear:
And tears by bards or heroes shed
Alike immortalize the dead.

I therefore purpose not, or dream,   55
  Descanting on his fate,
To give the melancholy theme
  A more enduring date:
But misery still delights to trace
  Its semblance in another's case.   60

No voice divine the storm allayed,
  No light propitious shone,
When, snatched from all effectual aid,
  We perished, each alone:
But I beneath a rougher sea,   65
And whelmed in deeper gulfs than he.

c. 1790   1803

ROBERT BURNS (1759-1796)

MARY MORISON

O Mary, at thy window be;
  It is the wished, the trysted hour!
Those smiles and glances let me see
  That make the miser's treasure poor!
How blythely wad I bide the stoure,   5
  A weary slave frae sun to sun,
Could I the rich reward secure,
  The lovely Mary Morison.

Yestreen, when to the trembling string
  The dance gaed thro' the lighted ha', 10
To thee my fancy took its wing;
  I sat, but neither heard nor saw:
Tho' this was fair, and that was braw,
  And yon the toast of a' the town,
I sighed, and said amang them a',   15
  "Ye are na Mary Morison."

O Mary, canst thou wreck his peace
  Wha for thy sake wad gladly die?
Or canst thou break that heart of his
  Whase only faut is loving thee?   20
If love for love thou wilt na gie,
  At least be pity to me shown!
A thought ungentle canna be
  The thought o' Mary Morison.

1784?   1800

THE HOLY FAIR

Upon a simmer Sunday morn,
  When Nature's face is fair,
I walkèd forth to view the corn,
  An' snuff the caller air.

The rising sun, owre Galston muirs,   5
  Wi' glorious light was glintin;
The hares were hirplin down the furs,
  The lav'rocks they were chantin
            Fu' sweet that day.

As lightsomely I glowered abroad,   10
  To see a scene sae gay,
Three hizzies, early at the road,
  Cam skelpin up the way.
Twa had manteeles o' dolefu' black,
  But ane wi' lyart lining;   15
The third, that gaed a wee a-back,
  Was in the fashion shining
            Fu' gay that day.

The twa appeared like sisters twin,
  In feature, form, an' claes;   20
Their visage withered, lang an' thin,
  An' sour as onie slaes:
The third cam up, hap-step-an'-lowp,
  As light as onie lambie,
An' wi' a curchie low did stoop,   25
  As soon as e'er she saw me,
            Fu' kind that day.

Wi' bonnet aff, quoth I, "Sweet lass,
  I think ye seem to ken me;
I'm sure I've seen that bonie face,   30
  But yet I canna name ye."
Quo' she, an' laughin as she spak,
  An' taks me by the han's,
"Ye, for my sake, hae gi'en the feck
  Of a' the Ten Comman's   35
            A screed some day.

"My name is Fun—your cronie dear,
  The nearest friend ye hae;
An' this is Superstition here,
  An' that's Hypocrisy.   40
I'm gaun to Mauchline Holy Fair,
  To spend an hour in daffin:
Gin ye'd go there, yon runkled pair,
  We will get famous laughin
        At them this day.   45

. . . .

Here sits a raw of tittlin' jads,
  Wi' heavin breasts an' bare neck;
An' there a batch o' wabster lads,
  Blackguarding frae Kilmarnock,   80
        For fun this day.

Here some are thinkin on their sins,
  An' some upo' their claes;
Ane curses feet that fyled his shins,
  Anither sighs and prays;   85
On this hand sits a chosen swatch,
  Wi' screwed-up grace-proud faces;
On that a set o' chaps, at watch,
  Thrang winkin on the lasses
        To chairs that day.   90

O happy is that man an' blest
  (Nae wonder that it pride him!)
Whase ain dear lass, that he likes best,
  Comes clinkin down beside him!
Wi' arm reposed on the chair-back,   95
  He sweetly does compose him;
Which, by degrees, slips round her neck,
  An's loof upon her bosom,
        Unkend that day.

Now a' the congregation o'er   100
  Is silent expectation;
For Moodie speels the holy door
  Wi' tidings o' damnation.
Should Hornie, as in ancient days,
  'Mang sons o' God present him,   105
The vera sight o' Moodie's face
  To 's ain het hame had sent him
        Wi' fright that day.

Hear how he clears the points o' faith
  Wi' rattlin an wi' thumpin!   110
Now meekly calm, now wild in wrath,
  He's stampin an' he's jumpin!
His lengthened chin, his turned-up snout,
  His eldritch squeel an' gestures,
O how they fire the heart devout—   115
  Like cantharidian plaisters,
        On sic a day!

But hark! the tent has changed its voice;
  There's peace an' rest nae langer;
For a' the real judges rise,   120
  They canna sit for anger:
Smith opens out his cauld harangues
  On practice and on morals;
An' aff the godly pour in thrangs,
  To gie the jars an' barrels   125
        A lift that day.

What signifies his barren shine
  Of moral pow'rs an' reason?
His English style an' gesture fine
  Are a' clean out o' season.   130
Like Socrates or Antonine,
  Or some auld pagan heathen,
The moral man he does define,
  But ne'er a word o' faith in
        That's right that day.   135

In guid time comes an antidote
  Against sic poisoned nostrum;
For Peebles, frae the water-fit,
  Ascends the holy rostrum:
See, up he's got the word o' God,   140
  An' meek an' mim has viewed it,
While Common Sense has taen the road,
  An' aff, an' up the Cowgate
        Fast, fast that day.

Wee Miller niest the guard relieves,   145
  An' orthodoxy raibles,
Tho' in his heart he weel believes
  An' thinks it auld wives' fables;
But faith! the birkie wants a manse,
  So cannilie he hums them,   150
Altho's his carnal wit an' sense
  Like hafflins-wise o'ercomes him
        At times that day.

Now butt an' ben the change-house fills
  Wi' yill-caup commentators;   155
Here's crying out for bakes an' gills,
  An' there the pint-stowp clatters;
While thick an' thrang, an' loud an' lang,
  Wi' logic an' wi' Scripture,
They raise a din that in the end   160
  Is like to breed a rupture
        O' wrath that day.

Leeze me on drink! it gies us mair
  Than either school or college;
It kindles wit, it waukens lear,   165
  It pangs us fou o' knowledge.
Be 't whisky-gill or penny-wheep,
  Or onie stronger potion,
It never fails, on drinkin deep,
  To kittle up our notion,   170
        By night or day.

The lads an' lasses, blythely bent
  To mind baith saul an' body,
Sit round the table weel content,
  An' steer about the toddy. 175
On this ane's dress an' that ane's leuk
  They're makin observations;
While some are cozie i' the neuk,
  An' formin assignations
      To meet some day. 180

But now the Lord's ain trumpet touts,
  Till a' the hills are rairin.
And echoes back return the shouts;
  Black Russell is na spairin:
His piercin words, like Highlan' swords, 185
  Divide the joints an' marrow;
His talk o' hell, whare devils dwell,
  Our verra "sauls does harrow"
      Wi' fright that day!

A vast, unbottomed, boundless pit, 190
  Filled fou o' lowin brunstane,
Whase ragin flame an' scorchin heat
  Wad melt the hardest whun-stane!
The half-asleep start up wi' fear,
  An' think they hear it roarin, 195
When presently it does appear
  'Twas but some neebor snorin,
      Asleep that day.

'Twad be owre lang a tale to tell
  How monie stories passed, 200
An' how they crouded to the yill,
  When they were a' dismissed;
How drink gaed round, in cogs an' caups,
  Amang the furms an' benches,
An' cheese an' bread, frae women's laps, 205
  Was dealt about in lunches
      An' dawds that day.

In comes a gawsie, gash guidwife,
  An' sits down by the fire,
Syne draws her kebbuck an' her knife; 210
  The lasses they are shyer;
The auld guidmen about the grace
  Frae side to side they bother,
Till some ane by his bonnet lays,
  And gi'es them 't, like a tether, 215
      Fu' lang that day.

Waesucks for him that gets nae lass,
  Or lasses that hae naething!
Sma' need has he to say a grace,
  Or melvie his braw claithing! 220
O wives, be mindfu', ance yoursel
  How bonie lads ye wanted,
An' dinna for a kebbuck-heel
  Let lasses be affronted
      On sic a day! 225

Now Clinkumbell, wi' rattlin tow,
  Begins to jow an' croon;
Some swagger hame the best they dow,
  Some wait the afternoon.
At slaps the billies halt a blink, 230
  Till lasses strip their shoon;
Wi' faith an' hope, an' love an' drink,
  They're a' in famous tune
      For crack that day.

How monie hearts this day converts 235
  O' sinners and o' lasses!
Their hearts o' stane, gin night, are gaen
  As saft as onie flesh is.
There's some are fou o' love divine,
  There's some are fou o' brandy; 240
An' monie jobs that day begin,
  May end in houghmagandie
      Some ither day.

1785   1786

FROM EPISTLE TO J. LAPRAIK

I am nae poet, in a sense,
But just a rhymer like by chance, 50
An' hae to learning nae pretence;
  Yet what the matter?
Whene'er my Muse does on me glance,
  I jingle at her.

Your critic-folk may cock their nose, 55
And say, "How can you e'er propose,
You wha ken hardly verse frae prose,
  To mak a sang?"
But, by your leaves, my learnèd foes,
  Ye're maybe wrang. 60

What's a' your jargon o' your schools,
Your Latin names for horns an' stools?
If honest Nature made you fools,
  What sairs your grammers?
Ye'd better taen up spades and shools 65
  Or knappin-hammers.

A set o' dull, conceited hashes
Confuse their brains in college classes;
They gang in stirks, and come out asses,
  Plain truth to speak; 70
An' syne they think to climb Parnassus
  By dint o' Greek!

Gie me ae spark o' Nature's fire,
That's a' the learning I desire;
Then, tho' I drudge thro' dub an' mire 75
  At pleugh or cart,
My Muse, tho' hamely in attire,
  May touch the heart.

1785   1786

THE COTTER'S SATURDAY NIGHT

My loved, my honored, much respected friend!
  No mercenary bard his homage pays;
With honest pride, I scorn each selfish end,
  My dearest meed a friend's esteem and praise:
To you I sing, in simple Scottish lays,   5
The lowly train in life's sequestered scene;
  The native feelings strong, the guileless ways,
What Aiken in a cottage would have been;
Ah, though his worth unknown, far happier there, I ween!

November chill blaws loud wi' angry sugh;   10
  The shortening winter-day is near a close;
The miry beasts retreating frae the pleugh;
  The blackening trains o' craws to their repose:
The toil-worn cotter frae his labor goes—
This night his weekly moil is at an end,—   15
  Collects his spades, his mattocks, and his hoes,
Hoping the morn in ease and rest to spend,
And weary, o'er the moor, his course does hameward bend.

At length his lonely cot appears in view,
  Beneath the shelter of an aged tree;   20
Th' expectant wee-things, toddlin, stacher through
  To meet their dad, wi' flichterin' noise and glee.
His wee bit ingle, blinkin bonilie,
His clean hearth-stane, his thrifty wifie's smile,
  The lisping infant, prattling on his knee,   25
Does a' his weary kiaugh and care beguile,
And makes him quite forget his labor and his toil.

Belyve the elder bairns come drappin in,
  At service out amang the farmers roun';
Some ca' the pleugh, some herd, some tentie rin   30
  A cannie errand to a neebor town.
Their eldest hope, their Jenny, woman-grown,
  In youthfu' bloom, love sparkling in her e'e,
Comes hame, perhaps to shew a braw new gown,
Or deposite her sair-won penny-fee,   35
To help her parents dear if they in hardship be.

With joy unfeigned, brothers and sisters meet,
  And each for other's weelfare kindly spiers;
The social hours, swift-winged, unnoticed fleet;
  Each tells the uncos that he sees or hears.   40
The parents, partial, eye their hopeful years;
Anticipation forward points the view.
  The mother, wi' her needle and her sheers,
Gars auld claes look amaist as weel's the new;
The father mixes a' wi' admonition due: 45

Their master's and their mistress's command
  The younkers a' are warnèd to obey,
And mind their labors wi' an eydent hand,
  And ne'er, tho' out o' sight, to jauk or play:
"And O be sure to fear the Lord alway,   50

And mind your duty duly, morn and night;
　Lest in temptation's path ye gang astray,
Implore His counsel and assisting might:
They never sought in vain that sought the Lord aright!"

But hark! a rap comes gently to the door.　　　　　　　　55
　Jenny, wha kens the meaning o' the same,
Tells how a neebor lad came o'er the moor,
　To do some errands and convoy her hame.
　The wily mother sees the conscious flame
Sparkle in Jenny's e'e, and flush her cheek;　　　　　　60
　With heart-struck anxious care enquires his name,
While Jenny hafflins is afraid to speak;
Weel-pleased the mother hears it's nae wild, worthless rake.

With kindly welcome Jenny brings him ben:
　A strappin' youth, he takes the mother's eye;　　　　　65
Blythe Jenny sees the visit's no ill-taen;
　The father cracks of horses, pleughs, and kye.
　The youngster's artless heart o'erflows wi' joy,
But blate and laithfu', scarce can weel behave;
　The mother, wi' a woman's wiles, can spy　　　　　　70
What makes the youth sae bashfu' and sae grave,
Weel-pleased to think her bairn's respected like the lave.

Oh happy love, where love like this is found!
　Oh heart-felt raptures! bliss beyond compare!
I've pacèd much this weary, mortal round,　　　　　　75
　And sage experience bids me this declare:
　"If Heaven a draught of heavenly pleasure spare,
One cordial in this melancholy vale,
　'Tis when a youthful, loving, modest pair
In other's arms breathe out the tender tale,　　　　　　80
Beneath the milk-white thorn that scents the evening gale."

Is there, in human form, that bears a heart,
　A wretch! a villain! lost to love and truth!
That can, with studied, sly, ensnaring art,
　Betray sweet Jenny's unsuspecting youth?　　　　　　85
　Curse on his perjured arts! dissembling smooth!
Are honor, virtue, conscience, all exiled?
　Is there no pity, no relenting ruth,
Points to the parents fondling o'er their child?
Then paints the ruined maid, and their distraction wild?　　90

But now the supper crowns their simple board:
　The healsome parritch, chief o' Scotia's food:
The soupe their only hawkie does afford,
　That 'yont the hallan snugly chows her cood,
　The dame brings forth, in complimental mood,　　　　95
To grace the lad, her weel-hained kebbuck, fell;
　And aft he's prest, and aft he ca's it guid;
The frugal wifie, garrulous, will tell
How 't was a towmond auld sin' lint was i' the bell.

The cheerfu' supper done, wi' serious face　　　　　　100
　They round the ingle form a circle wide;
The sire turns o'er, wi' patriarchal grace,
　The big ha'-Bible, ance his father's pride;
　His bonnet reverently is laid aside,

His lyart haffets wearing thin and bare;   105
    Those strains that once did sweet in Zion glide,
He wales a portion with judicious care,
And "Let us worship God!" he says, with solemn air.

They chant their artless notes in simple guise;
    They tune their hearts, by far the noblest aim: 110
Perhaps "Dundee's" wild-warbling measures rise,
    Or plaintive "Martyrs," worthy of the name;
    Or noble, "Elgin" beets the heavenward flame,
The sweetest far of Scotia's holy lays.
    Compared with these, Italian trills are tame;   115
The tickled ears no heart-felt raptures raise;
Nae unison hae they with our Creator's praise.

The priest-like father reads the sacred page;
    How Abram was the friend of God on high,
Or Moses bade eternal warfare wage   120
    With Amalek's ungracious progeny;
    Or how the royal bard did groaning lie
Beneath the stroke of Heaven's avenging ire;
    Or Job's pathetic plaint and wailing cry,
    Or rapt Isaiah's wild, seraphic fire;   125
Or other holy seers that tune the sacred lyre.

Perhaps the Christian volume is the theme:
    How guiltless blood for guilty man was shed;
How He Who bore in Heaven the second name
    Had not on earth whereon to lay His head;   130
    How His first followers and servants sped;
The precepts sage they wrote to many a land;
    How he who lone in Patmos banished,
    Saw in the sun a mighty angel stand,
And heard great Bab'lon's doom pronounced by Heaven's command.   135

Then kneeling down to Heaven's Eternal King,
    The saint, the father, and the husband prays;
Hope "springs exulting on triumphant wing,"
    That thus they all shall meet in future days,
    There ever bask in uncreated rays,   140
No more to sigh or shed the bitter tear,
    Together hymning their Creator's praise,
In such society, yet still more dear,
While circling Time moves round in an eternal sphere.

Compared with this, how poor Religion's pride,   145
    In all the pomp of method and of art,
When men display to congregations wide
    Devotion's ev'ry grace except the heart!
    The Power, incensed, the pageant will desert,
The pompous strain, the sacerdotal stole;   150
    But haply, in some cottage far apart,
May hear, well pleased, the language of the soul,
And in His Book of Life the inmates poor enroll.

Then homeward all take off their several way;
    The youngling cottagers retire to rest;   155
The parent-pair their secret homage pay,
    And proffer up to Heaven the warm request
    And He who stills the raven's clamorous nest,

And decks the lily fair in flowery pride,
    Would, in the way His wisdom sees the best,   160
For them and for their little ones provide,
But chiefly in their hearts with grace divine preside.

From scenes like these old Scotia's grandeur springs,
    That makes her loved at home, revered abroad:
Princes and lords are but the breath of kings,   165
    "An honest man's the noblest work of God."
And certes in fair virtue's heavenly road,
    The cottage leaves the palace far behind:
What is a lordling's pomp? a cumbrous load,
    Disguising oft the wretch of human kind,   170
Studied in arts of hell, in wickedness refined!

O Scotia! my dear, my native soil!
    For whom my warmest wish to Heaven is sent!
Long may thy hardy sons of rustic toil
    Be blest with health and peace and sweet content!   175
And O may Heaven their simple lives prevent
    From luxury's contagion, weak and vile!
Then, howe'er crowns and coronets be rent,
    A virtuous populace may rise the while,
And stand a wall of fire around their much-loved isle. 180

O Thou, Who poured the patriotic tide
    That streamed thro' Wallace's undaunted heart,
Who dared to nobly stem tyrannic pride,
    Or nobly die, the second glorious part!
(The patriot's God peculiarly Thou art,   185
    His friend, inspirer, guardian, and reward!)
Oh never, never Scotia's realm desert,
    But still the patriot and the patriot-bard
In bright succession raise, her ornament and guard!
1785-86   1786

FROM THE VISION: DUAN
        SECOND

*The local poetic Muse, Coila, addresses
            Burns*

"With future hope I oft would gaze
Fond, on thy little early ways,
Thy rudely carolled, chiming phrase,
    In uncouth rhymes,
Fired at the simple, artless lays   5
    Of other times.

"I saw thee seek the sounding shore,
Delighted with the dashing roar;
Or when the North his fleecy store
    Drove through the sky,   10
I saw grim Nature's visage hoar
    Struck thy young eye.

"Or when the deep green-mantled earth
Warm cherished every floweret's birth,

And joy and music pouring forth   15
    In every grove,
I saw thee eye the general mirth
    With boundless love.

"When ripened fields, and azure skies,
Called forth the reaper's rustling noise, 20
I saw thee leave their evening joys,
    And lonely stalk,
To vent thy bosom's swelling rise
    In pensive walk.

"When youthful love, warm-blushing,
    strong,   25
Keen-shivering shot thy nerves along,
Those accents, grateful to thy tongue,
    Th' adorèd Name,
I taught thee how to pour in song,
    To soothe thy flame.   30

"I saw thy pulse's maddening play,
Wild send thee Pleasure's devious way,

Misled by Fancy's meteor ray,
　　By Passion driven;
But yet the light that led astray   35
　　Was light from Heaven.

"I taught thy manners-painting strains,
The loves, the ways, of simple swains,
Till now, o'er all my wide domains
　　Thy fame extends;   40
And some, the pride of Coila's plains,
　　Become thy friends.

"Thou canst not learn, nor can I show,
To paint with Thomson's landscape glow;
Or wake the bosom-melting throe   45
　　With Shenstone's art;
Or pour, with Gray, the moving flow
　　Warm on the heart.

"Yet all beneath th' unrivalled rose,
The lowly daisy sweetly blows: 50
Though large the forest's monarch throws
　　His army shade,
Yet green the juicy hawthorn grows
　　Adown the glade.

"Then never murmur or repine;   55
Strive in thy humble sphere to shine;
And trust me, not Potosi's mine,
　　Nor kings' regard,
Can give a bliss o'ermatching thine,
　　A rustic Bard.   60

"To give my counsels all in one—
Thy tuneful flame still careful fan;
Preserve the Dignity of Man,
　　With soul erect;
And trust, the Universal Plan   65
　　Will all protect.

"And wear thou this"—she solemn said,
And bound the holly round my head:
The polished leaves, and berries red,
　　Did rustling play;   70
And, like a passing thought, she fled
　　In light away.
1785-86   1786

TO A MOUSE

ON TURNING HER UP IN HER NEST
WITH THE PLOUGH, NOVEMBER, 1785

Wee, sleekit, cowrin, tim'rous beastie,
O what a panic's in thy breastie!
Thou need na start awa sae hasty,
　　Wi' bickering brattle!
I wad be laith to rin an' chase thee,   5
　　Wi' murdering pattle!

I'm truly sorry man's dominion
Has broken Nature's social union,
An' justifies that ill opinion
　　Which makes thee startle   10
At me, thy poor, earth-born companion,
　　An' fellow-mortal!

I doubt na, whyles, but thou may thieve;
What then? poor beastie, thou maun live!
A daimen icker in a thrave   15
　　'S a sma' request;
I'll get a blessin' wi' the lave,
　　An' never miss 't!

Thy wee-bit housie, too, in ruin!
Its silly wa's the win's are strewin!   20
An' naething now to big a new ane,
　　O' foggage green!
An' bleak December's win's ensuin,
　　Baith snell an' keen!

Thou saw the fields laid bare an' waste, 25
An' weary winter comin fast,
An' cozie here, beneath the blast,
　　Thou thought to dwell—
Till, crash! the cruel coulter passed
　　Out thro' thy cell.   30

That wee bit heap o' leaves an' stibble
Has cost thee monie a weary nibble!
Now thou's turned out, for a' thy trouble,
　　But house or hald,
To thole the winter's sleety dribble,   35
　　An' cranreuch cauld!

But mousie, thou art no thy lane
In proving foresight may be vain:
The best-laid schemes o' mice an' men
　　Gang aft agley,   40
An' lea'e us naught but grief an' pain
　　For promised joy!

Still, thou art blest compared wi' me!
The present only toucheth thee:
But och! I backward cast my e'e,   45
　　On prospects drear!
An' forward, tho' I canna see,
　　I guess an' fear!
1785   1786

TO A MOUNTAIN DAISY

ON TURNING ONE DOWN WITH THE
PLOUGH IN APRIL, 1786

Wee, modest, crimson-tippèd flow'r,
Thou's met me in an evil hour,
For I maun crush among the stoure
　　Thy slender stem;
To spare thee now is past my pow'r,   5
　　Thou bonie gem.

Alas! it's no thy neebor sweet,
The bonie lark, companion meet,
Bending thee 'mang the dewy weet,
   Wi' spreckled breast,   10
When upward springing, blythe, to greet
   The purpling east.

Cauld blew the bitter-biting north
Upon thy early, humble birth;
Yet cheerfully thou glinted forth   15
   Amid the storm,
Scarce reared above the parent-earth
   Thy tender form.

The flaunting flow'rs our gardens yield,
High shelt'ring woods and wa's maun
   shield;   20
But thou, beneath the random bield
   O' clod or stane,
Adorns the histie stibble-field,
   Unseen, alane.

There, in thy scanty mantle clad,   25
Thy snawie bosom sunward spread,
Thou lifts thy unassuming head
   In humble guise;
But now the share uptears thy bed,
   And low thou lies!   30

Such is the fate of artless maid,
Sweet flow'ret of the rural shade!
By love's simplicity betrayed,
   And guileless trust,
Till she, like thee, all soiled is laid,   35
   Low i' the dust.

Such is the fate of simple bard,
On life's rough ocean luckless starred!
Unskilful he to note the card
   Of prudent lore,   40
Till billows rage, and gales blow hard,
   And whelm him o'er!

Such fate to suffering worth is giv'n,
Who long with wants and woes has striv'n,
By human pride or cunning driv'n   45
   To mis'ry's brink;
Till, wrench'd of ev'ry stay but Heav'n,
   He, ruined, sink!

Ev'n thou who mourn'st the daisy's fate,
That fate is thine—no distant date;   50
Stern Ruin's plough-share drives, elate,
   Full on thy bloom,
Till crush'd beneath the furrow's weight
   Shall be thy doom!
              1786

EPISTLE TO A YOUNG FRIEND

I lang hae thought, my youthfu' friend
   A something to have sent you,
Tho' it should serve nae ither end
   Than just a kind memento.
But how the subject-theme may gang,   5
   Let time and chance determine;
Perhaps it may turn out a sang,
   Perhaps turn out a sermon.

Ye'll try the world soon, my lad;
   And, Andrew dear, believe me,   10
Ye'll find mankind an unco squad,
   And muckle they may grieve ye:
For care and trouble set your thought,
   Ev'n when your end's attainèd;
And a' your views may come to nought,   15
   Where ev'ry nerve is strainèd.

I'll no say men are villains a';
   The real, harden'd wicked,
Wha hae nae check but human law,
   Are to a few restricket;   20
But, och! mankind are unco weak,
   An' little to be trusted;
If self the wavering balance shake,
   It's rarely right adjusted!

Yet they wha fa' in fortune's strife,   25
   Their fate we shouldna censure,
For still th' important end of life
   They equally may answer;
A man may hae an honest heart,
   Tho' poortith hourly stare him;   30
A man may tak a neebor's part,
   Yet hae nae cash to spare him.

Aye free, aff-han', your story tell,
   When wi' a bosom crony;
But still keep something to yoursel   35
   Ye scarcely tell to ony.
Conceal yoursel as weel's ye can
   Frae critical dissection;
But keek thro' ev'ry other man,
   Wi' sharpen'd, sly inspection.   40

The sacred lowe o' weel-placed love,
   Luxuriantly indulge it;
But never tempt th' illicit rove,
   Tho' naething should divulge it;
I wave the quantum o' the sin,   45
   The hazard of concealing;
But, och! it hardens a' within,
   And petrifies the feeling!

To catch dame Fortune's golden smile,
   Assiduous wait upon her;   50
And gather gear by ev'ry wile
   That's justified by honor;

Not for to hide it in a hedge,
  Nor for a train attendant;
But for the glorious privilege   55
  Of being independent.

The fear o' hell's a hangman's whip,
  To haud the wretch in order;
But where ye feel your honor grip,
  Let that aye be your border;   60
Its slightest touches, instant pause—
  Debar a' side-pretences;
And resolutely keep its laws,
  Uncaring consequences.

The great Creator to revere,   65
  Must sure become the creature;
But still the preaching cant forbear,
  And ev'n the rigid feature;
Yet ne'er with wits profane to range,
  Be complaisance extended;   70
An atheist-laugh's a poor exchange
  For Deity offended!

When ranting round in pleasure's ring,
  Religion may be blinded;
Or, if she gie a random sting,   75
  It may be little minded;
But when on life we're tempest-driv'n—
  A conscience but a canker,
A correspondence fixed wi' Heav'n
  Is sure a noble anchor!   80

Adieu, dear amiable Youth!
  Your heart can ne'er be wanting!
May prudence, fortitude, and truth,
  Erect your brow undaunting!
In ploughman phrase, "God send you
    speed,"   85
  Still daily to grow wiser;
And may you better reck the rede,
  Than ever did th' adviser!

            1786

A BARD'S EPITAPH

Is there a whim-inspirèd fool,
Owre fast for thought, owre hot for rule,
Owre blate to seek, owre proud to snool?
    Let him draw near;
And owre this grassy heap sing dool,   5
    And drap a tear.

Is there a bard of rustic song
Who, noteless, steals the crowds among,
That weekly this area throng?—
    Oh, pass not by!   10
But with a frater-feeling strong
    Here heave a sigh.

Is there a man whose judgment clear
Can others teach the course to steer,
Yet runs himself life's mad career   15
    Wild as the wave?—
Here pause—and thro' the starting tear
    Survey this grave.

The poor inhabitant below
Was quick to learn and wise to know,   20
And keenly felt the friendly glow
    And softer flame;
But thoughtless follies laid him low,
    And stained his name!

Reader, attend! whether thy soul   25
Soars fancy's flights beyond the pole,
Or darkling grubs this earthly hole
    In low pursuit;
Know, prudent, cautious self-control
    Is wisdom's root.   30

            1786

ADDRESS TO THE UNCO GUID
OR THE RIGIDLY RIGHTEOUS

O ye wha are sae guid yoursel,
  Sae pious and sae holy,
Ye've nought to do but mark and tell
  Your neebor's fauts and folly!
Whase life is like a weel-gaun mill,   5
  Supplied wi' store o' water,
The heapet happer's ebbing still,
  And still the clap plays clatter,—

Hear me, ye venerable core,
  As counsel for poor mortals   10
That frequent pass douce Wisdom's door
  For glaikit Folly's portals;
I for their thoughtless, careless sakes
  Would here propone defences—
Their donsie tricks, their black mistakes,   15
  Their failings and mischances.

Ye see your state wi' theirs compared,
  And shudder at the niffer;
But cast a moment's fair regard,
  What maks the mighty differ?   20
Discount what scant occasion gave,
  That purity ye pride in,
And (what's aft mair than a' the lave)
  Your better art o' hidin.

Think, when your castigated pulse   25
  Gies now and then a wallop,
What ragings must his veins convulse
  That still eternal gallop:

Wi' wind and tide fair i' your tail,
  Right on ye scud your sea-way; 30
But in the teeth o' baith to sail,
  It maks an unco leeway.

See Social Life and Glee sit down,
  All joyous and unthinking,
Till, quite transmugrify'd, they're grown 35
  Debauchery and Drinking:
O would they stay to calculate
  Th' eternal consequences,
Or—your more dreaded hell to state—
  Damnation of expenses! 40

Ye high, exalted, virtuous dames,
  Tied up in godly laces,
Before ye gie poor Frailty names,
  Suppose a change o' cases:
A dear-lov'd lad, convenience snug, 45
  A treach'rous inclination—
But, let me whisper i' your lug,
  Ye're aiblins nae temptation.

Then gently scan your brother man,
  Still gentler sister woman; 50
Tho' they may gang a kennin wrang,
  To step aside is human:
One point must still be greatly dark,
  The moving *why* they do it;
And just as lamely can ye mark 55
  How far perhaps they rue it.

Who made the heart, 'tis He alone
  Decidedly can try us;
He knows each chord, its various tone,
  Each spring, its various bias: 60
Then at the balance, let's be mute,
  We never can adjust it;
What's done we partly may compute,
  But know not what's resisted.

                                  1787

JOHN ANDERSON, MY JO

John Anderson, my jo, John,
  When we were first acquent,
Your locks were like the raven,
  Your bonie brow was brent:
But now your brow is beld, John, 5
  Your locks are like the snaw;
But blessings on your frosty pow,
  John Anderson, my jo!

John Anderson, my jo, John,
  We clamb the hill thegither; 10
And monie a cantie day, John,
  We've had wi' ane anither:

Now we maun totter down, John,
  And hand in hand we'll go,
And sleep thegither at the foot, 15
  John Anderson, my jo!
c. 1788   1796

THE LOVELY LASS OF INVERNESS

The lovely lass of Inverness,
Nae joy nor pleasure can she see;
For e'en to morn she cries, "Alas!"
And aye the saut tear blin's her e'e:

"Drumossie moor—Drumossie day— 5
A waefu' day it was to me!
For there I lost my father dear,
My father dear, and brethren three.

"Their winding-sheet the bluidy clay,
Their graves are growing green to see: 10
And by them lies the dearest lad
That ever blest a woman's e'e!

"Now wae to thee, thou cruel lord,
A bluidy man I trow thou be;
For mony a heart thou hast made sair 15
That ne'er did wrang to thine or thee!"
c. 1788   1796

A RED, RED ROSE

O, my luv is like a red, red rose,
  That's newly sprung in June:
O, my luv is like the melodie
  That's sweetly played in tune.

As fair art thou, my bonie lass, 5
  So deep in luve am I;
And I will luve thee still, my dear,
  Till a' the seas gang dry:

Till a' the seas gang dry, my dear,
  And the rocks melt wi' the sun; 10
And I will luve thee still, my dear,
  While the sands o' life shall run.

And fare thee weel, my only luve!
  And fare thee weel awhile!
And I will come again, my luve, 15
  Tho' it were ten thousand mile!
c. 1788   1796

AULD LANG SYNE

Should auld acquaintance be forgot,
  And never brought to mind?
Should auld acquaintance be forgot,
  And auld lang syne?

Chorus:

  For auld lang syne, my dear,   5
    For auld lang syne,
  We'll tak a cup o' kindness yet,
    For auld lang syne!

And surely ye'll be your pint-stowp,
  And surely I'll be mine;   10
And we'll take a cup o' kindness yet
  For auld lang syne!

We twa hae run about the braes,
  And pou'd the gowans fine;
But we've wandered monie a weary fit   15
  Sin' auld lang syne.

We twa hae paidled in the burn,
  Frae morning sun till dine;
But seas between us braid hae roared
  Sin' auld lang syne.   20

And there's a hand, my trusty fiere,
  And gie's a hand o' thine;
And we'll tak a right guid-willie waught,
  For auld lang syne!

c. 1788   796

SWEET AFTON

Flow gently, sweet Afton, among thy green braes!
Flow gently, I'll sing thee a song in thy praise!
My Mary's asleep by thy murmuring stream,
Flow gently, sweet Afton, disturb not her dream!

Thou stock-dove, whose echo resounds through the glen   5
Ye wild whistling blackbirds in yon thorny den,
Thou green-crested lapwing, thy screaming forbear,
I charge you disturb not my slumbering fair!

How lofty, sweet Afton, thy neighboring hills,
Far marked with the courses of clear winding rills   10
There daily I wander as noon rises high,
My flocks and my Mary's sweet cot in my eye.

How pleasant thy banks and green valleys below,
Where wild in the woodlands the primroses blow!
There oft, as mild evening weeps over the lea,   15
The sweet-scented birk shades my Mary and me.

Thy crystal stream, Afton, how lovely it glides,
And winds by the cot where my Mary resides!
How wanton thy waters her snowy feet lave,
As gathering sweet flowerets she stems thy clear wave!   20

Flow gently, sweet Afton, among thy green braes!
Flow gently, sweet river, the theme of my lays!
My Mary's asleep by thy murmuring stream,
Flow gently, sweet Afton, disturb not her dream!

c. 1789   1796

TO MARY IN HEAVEN

Thou lingering star, with lessening ray,
  That lov'st to greet the early morn,
Again thou usher'st in the day
  My Mary from my soul was torn.
O Mary! dear departed shade!   5
  Where is thy place of blissful rest?

See'st thou thy lover lowly laid?
  Hear'st thou the groans that rend his
    breast?

That sacred hour can I forget,
  Can I forget the hallowed grove,   10
Where by the winding Ayr we met
  To live one day of parting love?

Eternity cannot efface
  Those records dear of transports past,
Thy image at our last embrace— 15
  Ah! little thought we 'twas our last!

Ayr, gurgling, kissed his pebbled shore,
  O'erhung with wild woods, thickening
    green;
The fragrant birch and hawthorn hoar
  Twined amorous round the raptured
    scene: 20
The flowers sprang wanton to be pressed,
  The birds sang love on every spray,

Till too, too soon the glowing west
  Proclaimed the speed of wingèd day.

Still o'er these scenes my memory wakes, 25
  And fondly broods with miser care!
Time but th' impression stronger makes,
  As streams their channels deeper wear.
My Mary, dear departed shade!
  Where is thy place of blissful rest? 30
See'st thou thy lover lowly laid?
  Hear'st thou the groans that rend his
    breast?

1789   1796

WILLIAM BECKFORD (1760-1844)

FROM THE HISTORY OF THE CALIPH VATHEK

Vathek, ninth Caliph of the race of the Abassides, was the son of Motassem, and the grandson of Haroun Al Raschid. From an early accession to the throne, and the talents he possessed to adorn it, his subjects were induced to expect that his reign would be long and happy. His figure was pleasing and majestic; but when he was angry one of his eyes became so terrible, that no person could bear to behold it, and the wretch upon whom it was fixed instantly fell backward, and sometimes expired. For fear, however, of depopulating his dominions and making his palace desolate, he but rarely gave way to his anger.

Being much addicted to women and the pleasures of the table, he sought by his affability to procure agreeable companions; and he succeeded the better as his generosity was unbounded, and his indulgences unrestrained, for he was by no means scrupulous, nor did he think with the Caliph Omar Ben Abdalaziz, that it was necessary to make a hell of this world to enjoy Paradise in the next.

He surpassed in magnificence all his predecessors. The palace of Alkoremmi, which his father Motassem had erected on the hill of Pied Horses, and which commanded the whole city of Samarah, was in his idea far too scanty; he added, therefore, five wings, or rather other palaces, which he destined for the particular gratification of each of his senses.

In the first of these were tables contin-ually covered with the most exquisite dainties, which were supplied both by night and by day according to their constant consumption, whilst the most delicious wines and the choicest cordials flowed forth from a hundred fountains that were never exhausted. This palace was called "The Eternal or Unsatiating Banquet."

The second was styled "The Temple of Melody, or the Nectar of the Soul." It was inhabited by the most skilful musicians and admired poets of the time, who not only displayed their talents within, but, dispersing in bands without, caused every surrounding scene to reverberate their songs, which were continually varied in the most delightful succession.

The palace named "The Delight of the Eyes, or the Support of Memory," was one entire enchantment. Rarities collected from every corner of the earth were there found in such profusion as to dazzle and confound, but for the order in which they were arranged. One gallery exhibited the pictures of the celebrated Mani, and statues that seemed to be alive. Here a well-managed perspective attracted the sight, there the magic of optics agreeably deceived it; whilst the naturalist on his part exhibited, in their several classes, the various gifts that Heaven had bestowed on our globe. In a word, Vathek omitted nothing in this palace that might gratify the curiosity of those who resorted to it, although he was not able to satisfy his own, for he was of all men the most curious.

"The Palace of Perfumes," which was

termed likewise "The Incentive to Pleasure," consisted of various halls where the different perfumes which the earth produces were kept perpetually burning in censers of gold. Flambeaus and aromatic lamps were here lighted in open day. But the too powerful effects of this agreeable delirium might be avoided by descending into an immense garden, where an assemblage of every fragrant flower diffused through the air the purest odors.

The fifth palace, denominated "The Retreat of Joy, or the Dangerous," was frequented by troops of young females beautiful as the houris and not less seducing, who never failed to receive with caresses all whom the Caliph allowed to approach them; for he was by no means disposed to be jealous, as his own women were secluded within the palace he inhabited himself.

Notwithstanding the sensuality in which Vathek indulged, he experienced no abatement in the love of his people, who thought that a sovereign immersed in pleasure was not less tolerable to his subjects than one that employed himself in creating them foes. But the unquiet and impetuous disposition of the Caliph would not allow him to rest there; he had studied so much for his amusement in the lifetime of his father, as to acquire a great deal of knowledge, though not a sufficiency to satisfy himself; for he wished to know everything, even sciences that did not exist. He was fond of engaging in disputes with the learned, but liked them not to push their opposition with warmth; he stopped the mouths of those with presents whose mouths could be stopped, whilst others, whom his liberality was unable to subdue, he sent to prison to cool their blood, a remedy that often succeeded.

[THE HALL OF EBLIS]

After some time Vathek and Nouronihar perceived a gleam brightening through the drapery, and entered a vast tabernacle carpeted with the skins of leopards; an infinity of elders with streaming beards, and Afrits in complete armor, had prostrated themselves before the ascent of a lofty eminence, on the top of which, upon a globe of fire, sat the formidable Eblis. His person was that of a young man, whose noble and regular features seemed to have been tarnished by malignant vapors; in his large eyes appeared both pride and despair; his flowing hair retained some resemblance to that of an angel of light; in his hand, which thunder had blasted, he swayed the iron sceptre that causes the monster Ouranabad, the Afrits, and all the powers of the abyss to tremble; at his presence the heart of the Caliph sank within him, and for the first time, he fell prostrate on his face. Nouronihar, however, though greatly dismayed, could not help admiring the person of Eblis; for she expected to have seen some stupendous Giant. Eblis, with a voice more mild than might be imagined, but such as transfused through the soul the deepest melancholy, said:

"Creatures of clay, I receive you into mine empire; ye are numbered amongst my adorers; enjoy whatever this palace affords; the treasures of the pre-adamite Sultans, their bickering sabres, and those talismans that compel the Dives to open the subterranean expanses of the mountain of Kaf, which communicate with these; there, insatiable as your curiosity may be, shall you find sufficient to gratify it; you shall possess the exclusive privilege of entering the fortress of Aherman, and the halls of Argenk, where are portrayed all creatures endowed with intelligence, and the various animals that inhabited that earth prior to the creation of that contemptible being, whom ye denominate the Father of Mankind."

Vathek and Nouronihar, feeling themselves revived and encouraged by this harangue, eagerly said to the Giaour:

"Bring us instantly to the place which contains these precious talismans."

"Come!" answered this wicked Dive, with his malignant grin, "come! and possess all that my Sovereign hath promised, and more."

He then conducted them into a long aisle adjoining the tabernacle, preceding them with hasty steps, and followed by his disciples with the utmost alacrity. They reached, at length, a hall of great extent, and covered with a lofty dome, around which appeared fifty portals of bronze, secured with as many fastenings of iron; a funereal gloom prevailed over the whole scene; here, upon two beds of incorruptible cedar, lay recumbent the fleshless forms of the Pre-adamite Kings, who had been monarchs of the whole earth; they still possessed enough of life to be conscious of their deplorable condition; their eyes retained a melancholy motion; they regarded each other with looks of the deepest dejection, each holding his right hand motionless on his heart; at their feet were inscribed the events of their several reigns, their power, their pride, and their crimes; Soliman Raad, Soliman Daki, and Soliman Di Gian Ben Gian, who, after having chained up the Dives in the dark caverns of Kaf, became so presumptuous as to doubt of the Supreme Power; all these maintained great state, though not to be compared with the eminence of Soliman Ben Daoud.

This king, so renowned for his wisdom, was on the loftiest elevation, and placed immediately under the dome; he appeared to possess more animation than the rest; though from time to time he labored with profound sighs, and, like his companions, kept his right hand on his heart; yet his countenance was more composed, and he seemed to be listening to the sullen roar of a vast cataract, visible in part through the grated portals; this was the only sound that intruded on the silence of these doleful mansions. A range of brazen vases surrounded the elevation.

"Remove the covers from these cabalistic depositaries," said the Giaour to Vathek, "and avail thyself of the talismans, which will break asunder all these gates of bronze; and not only render thee master of the treasures contained within them, but also of the spirits by which they are guarded."

The Caliph, whom this ominous preliminary had entirely disconcerted, approached the vases with faltering footsteps, and was ready to sink with terror when he heard the groans of Soliman. As he proceeded, a voice from the livid lips of the Prophet articulated these words:

"In my life-time I filled a magnificent throne, having on my right hand twelve thousand seats of gold, where the patriarchs and the prophets heard my doctrines; on my left the sages and doctors, upon as many thrones of silver, were present at all my decisions. Whilst I thus administered justice to innumerable multitude, the birds of the air librating over me served as a canopy from the rays of the sun; my people flourished, and my palace rose to the clouds; I erected a temple to the Most High, which was the wonder of the universe; but I basely suffered myself to be seduced by the love of women, and a curiosity that could not be restrained by sublunary things; I listened to the counsels of Aherman and the daughter of Pharaoh, and adored fire and the hosts of heaven; I forsook the holy city, and commanded the Genii to rear the stupendous palace of Istakhar, and the terrace of the watch-towers, each of which was consecrated to a star; there for a while I enjoyed myself in the zenith of glory and pleasure; not only men, but supernatural existences were subject also to my will. I began to think, as these unhappy monarchs around had already thought, that the vengeance of Heaven was asleep; when at once the thunder burst my structures asunder and precipitated me hither; where, however, I do not remain, like the other inhabitants, totally destitute of hope, for an angel of light hath revealed that, in consideration of the piety of my early youth, my woes shall come to an end when this cataract shall forever cease to flow; till then I am in torments, ineffable torments! an unrelenting fire preys on my heart."

Having uttered this exclamation Soliman raised his hands towards Heaven, in token of supplication, and the Caliph discerned through his bosom, which was transparent as crystal, his heart enveloped in flames. At a sight so full of horror Nouronihar fell back, like one petrified, into the arms of Vathek, who cried out with a convulsive sob:

"O Giaour! whither hast thou brought us? Allow us to depart, and I will relinquish all thou hast promised. O Mahomet! remains there no more mercy?"

"None! none!" replied the malicious Dive. "Know, miserable prince! thou art now in the abode of vengeance and despair; thy heart also will be kindled, like those of the other votaries of Eblis. A few days are allotted thee previous to this fatal period; employ them as thou wilt; recline on these heaps of gold; command the Infernal Potentates; range at thy pleasure through these immense subterranean domains; no barrier shall be shut against thee; as for me, I have fulfilled my mission; I now leave thee to thyself." At these words he vanished.

The Caliph and Nouronihar remained in the most abject affliction. Their tears were unable to flow, and scarcely could they support themselves. At length, taking each other despondingly by the hand, they went faltering from this fatal hall, indifferent which way they turned their steps. Every portal opened at their approach. The dives fell prostrate before them. Every reservoir of riches was disclosed to their view; but they no longer felt the incentives of curiosity, of pride, or avarice. With like apathy they heard the chorus of genii, and saw the stately banquets prepared to regale them. They went wandering on from chamber to chamber, hall to hall, and gallery to gallery; all without bounds or limit; all distinguishable by the same lowering gloom; all adorned with the same awful grandeur; all traversed by persons in search of repose and consolation, but who sought them in vain, for everyone carried within him a heart tormented in flames.

1783   1786

WILLIAM LISLE BOWLES (1762-1850)

EVENING

Evening! as slow thy placid shades descend,
 Veiling with gentlest hush the landscape still,
 The lonely battlement, the farthest hill
And wood, I think of those who have no friend;
Who now, perhaps, by melancholy led,   5
 From the broad blaze of day, where pleasure flaunts,
 Retiring, wander to the ringdove's haunts
Unseen; and watch the tints that o'er thy bed
Hang lovely; oft to musing Fancy's eye
 Presenting fairy vales, where the tired mind   10
 Might rest beyond the murmurs of mankind,
Nor hear the hourly moans of misery!
Alas for man! that Hope's fair views the while
Should smile like you, and perish as they smile!

1789

DOVER CLIFFS

On these white cliffs, that calm above the flood
 Uprear their shadowing heads, and at their feet
 Hear not the surge that has for ages beat,
How many a lonely wanderer has stood!
And, whilst the lifted murmur met his ear,   5
 And o'er the distant billows the still eve
 Sailed slow, has thought of all his heart must leave
To-morrow; of the friends he loved most dear;
Of social scenes, from which he wept to part!
 Oh! if, like me, he knew how fruitless all   10
 The thoughts that would full fain the past recall,
Soon would he quell the risings of his heart,
And brave the wild winds and unhearing tide—
The world his country, and his God his guide.

1789

GILBERT WHITE (1720-1793)

FROM THE NATURAL HISTORY AND ANTIQUITIES OF SELBORNE

[THE TORTOISE]

While I was in Sussex last autumn, my residence was at the village near Lewes, from whence I had formerly the pleasure of writing to you. On the 1st of November I remarked that the old tortoise, formerly mentioned, began first to dig the ground, in order to the forming its hibernaculum, which it had fixed on just beside a great tuft of hepaticas. It scrapes out the ground with its fore-feet, and throws it up over its back with its hind; but the motion of its legs is ridiculously slow, little exceeding the hour-hand of a clock, and suitable to the composure of an animal said to be a whole month in performing one feat of copulation. Nothing can

be more assiduous than this creature, night
and day, in scooping the earth and forcing
its great body into the cavity; but, as the
noons of that season proved unusually
warm and sunny, it was continually inter- 5
rupted and called forth by the heat in the
middle of the day; and though I continued
there till the 13th of November, yet the
w o r k remained unfinished.   Harsher
weather and frosty mornings would have 10
quickened its operations.

No part of its behavior ever struck me
more than the extreme timidity it always expresses with regard to rain; for
though it has a shell that would secure it 15
against the wheel of a loaded cart, yet
does it discover as much solicitude about
rain as a lady dressed in all her best attire, shuffling away on the first sprinklings,
and running its head up in a corner. If 20
attended to, it becomes an excellent
weather-glass; for as sure as it walks elate,
and, as it were, on tiptoe, feeding with
great earnestness in a morning, so sure will
it rain before night. It is totally a diurnal 25
animal, and never pretends to stir after it
becomes dark.

The tortoise, like other reptiles, has an
arbitrary stomach, as well as lungs; and
can refrain from eating as well as breath- 30
ing for a great part of the year. When
first awakened, it eats nothing; nor again
in the autumn, before it retires: through
the height of the summer it feeds vora-
ciously, devouring all the food that comes 35
in its way. I was much taken with its sa-
gacity in discerning those that do it kind
offices; for as soon as the good old lady
comes in sight who has waited on it for
more than thirty years, it hobbles towards 40
its benefactress with awkward alacrity, but
remains inattentive to strangers. Thus
not only "the ox knoweth his owner, and
the ass his master's crib," but the most abject reptile and torpid of beings distin- 45
guishes the hand that feeds it, and is
touched with the feelings of gratitude!

In about three days after I left Sussex
the tortoise retired into the ground under
the hepatica. . . . 50

When one reflects on the state of this
strange being, it is a matter of wonder to
find that Providence should bestow such
a profusion of days, such a seeming waste
of longevity, on a reptile that appears to 55
relish it so little as to squander more than
two-thirds of its existence in a joyless stu-
por, and be lost to all sensation for months
together in the profoundest of slumbers.

Apr. 12, 1772   1789

[THE BEE-LAD]

December 12, 1775. We had in this village, more than twenty years ago, an idiot
boy, whom I well remember, who, from a
child, showed a strong propensity to bees;
they were his food, his amusement, his sole
object; and as people of this cast have seldom more than one point in view, so this
lad exerted all his few faculties on this
one pursuit. In the winter he dozed away
his time, within his father's house by the
fireside, in a kind of torpid state, seldom
departing from the chimney-corner; but in
the summer he was all alert, and in quest
of his game in the fields, and on sunny
banks. Honey bees, humble bees, and
wasps, were his prey wherever he found
them: he had no apprehensions from their
stings, but would seize them *nudis manibus,* and at once disarm them of their
weapons, and suck their bodies for the
sake of their honey bags. Sometimes he
would fill his bosom between his shirt and
his skin with a number of these captives:
and sometimes would confine them in bottles. He was a very *Merops apiaster,* or
bee-bird; and very injurious to men who
kept bees; for he would slide into their
bee-gardens, and, sitting down before the
stools, would rap with his finger on the
hives, and so take the bees as they came
out. He has been known to overturn hives
for the sake of the honey, of which he was
passionately fond. Where metheglin was
making he would linger round the tubs
and vessels, begging a draught of what he
called bee-wine. As he ran about he used
to make a humming noise with his lips,
resembling the buzzing of bees. This lad
was lean and sallow, and of a cadaverous
complexion; and, except in his favorite
pursuit, in which he was wonderfully
adroit, discovered no manner of understanding. Had his capacity been better,
and directed to the same object, he had
perhaps abated much of our wonder at the
feats of a more modern exhibitor of bees;
and we may justly say of him now,

> Thou,
> Had thy presiding star propitious shone,
> Shouldst Wildman be.

When a tall youth, he was removed
from hence to a distant village, where he
died, as I understand, before he arrived at
manhood.

1789

ERASMUS DARWIN (1731-1802)

FROM THE BOTANIC GARDEN

[PROCUL ESTE, PROFANI]

Stay your rude steps! whose throbbing
  breasts infold
The legion-fiends of glory or of gold!
Stay! whose false lips seductive simpers
  part,
While cunning nestles in the harlot-
  heart!—
For you no Dryads dress the roseate bower, 5
For you no Nymphs their sparkling vases
  pour;
Unmarked by you, light Graces swim the
  green,
And hovering Cupids aim their shafts, un-
  seen.
But thou! whose mind the well-attempered
  ray
Of taste and virtue lights with purer day; 10
Whose finer sense each soft vibration owns
With sweet responsive sympathy of tones;
(So the fair flower expands its lucid form
To meet the sun, and shuts it to the storm);
For thee my borders nurse the fragrant
  wreath,   15
My fountains murmur, and my zephyrs
  breathe;
Slow slides the painted snail, the gilded fly.
Smooths his fine down, to charm thy curi-
  ous eye;
On twinkling fins my pearly nations play,
Or win with sinuous train their trackless
  way;   20
My plumy pairs, in gay embroidery dressed,
Form with ingenious bill the pensile nest,
To love's sweet notes attune the listening
  dell,
And Echo sounds her soft symphonious
  shell.
And if with thee some hapless maid should
  stray,   25
Disastrous love companion of her way,
Oh, lead her timid steps to yonder glade,

Whose arching cliffs depending alders
  shade;
There, as meek evening wakes her tem-
  perate breeze,
And moonbeams glimmer through the
  trembling trees,   30
The rills that gurgle round shall soothe her
  ear,
The weeping rocks shall number tear for
  tear;
There as sad Philomel, alike forlorn,
Sings to the night from her accustomed
  thorn;
While at sweet intervals each falling note 35
Sighs in the gale, and whispers round the
  grot;
The sister-woe shall calm her aching breast,
And softer slumbers steal her cares to rest.

[THE SENSITIVE PLANT]

Weak with nice sense, the chaste Mimosa
  stands,
From each rude touch withdraws her timid
  hands;   40
Oft as light clouds o'erpass the summer-
  glade,
Alarmed she trembles at the moving shade;
And feels, alive through all her tender
  form,
The whispered murmurs of the gathering
  storm;
Shuts her sweet eyelids to approaching
  night,   45
And hails with freshened charms the rising
  light.
Veiled, with gay decency and modest pride,
Slow to the mosque she moves, an eastern
  bride,
There her soft vows unceasing love record,
Queen of the bright seraglio of her lord.   50

1789-1792

WILLIAM GILPIN (1724-1804)

[PICTURESQUE BEAUTY]

All forms that are unnatural, displease. A tree lopped into a maypole, as you generally see in the hedge-rows of Surry and some other countries, is disgusting. Clipped yews, lime hedges, and pollards are, for the same reason disagreeable, and yet I have sometimes seen a pollard produce a good effect, when nature has been suffered for some years, to bring it again into form: but I never saw a good effect produced by a pollard on which some single item was left to grow into a tree. The item is of a different growth; it is disproportioned; and always unites awkwardly with the trunk.

Not only all forms that are unnatural, displease; but even natural forms when they bear a resemblance to art, unless indeed these forms are characteristic of the species. A cypress pleases in a conic form; but an oak or an elm trimmed into that appearance would disgust. In the cypress, nature adapts the spray and branches to the form of the tree. In the oak and elm, the spray and branches form a different character.

Lightness also is a characteristic of beauty in a tree; for though there are beautiful trees of a heavy as well as of a light form, yet their extremities must in some parts be separated, and hang with a degree of looseness from the fulness of the foliage, which occupies the middle of the tree, or the whole will only be a large bush. From position, indeed, and contrast, heaviness, though in itself a deformity, may be of singular use in the composition both of natural and of artificial landscape.

A tree also must be *well-balanced* to be beautiful. It may have form and it may have lightness; and yet lose all its effect, by wanting a proper poise. The bole must appear to support the branches. We do not desire to see it supporting its burden with the perpendicular firmness of a column. An easy sweep is always agreeable; but at the same time it should not be such a sweep as discovers one side plainly overbalanced.

On bleak sea-coasts, trees generally take an unbalanced form; and indeed in general, some foreign cause must operate to occasion it; for nature working freely, is as much inclined to balance a tree upon its trunk, as an animal upon its legs.

And yet in some circumstances, I have seen beauty arise even from an unbalanced tree; but it must arise from some peculiar situation, which gives it a local propriety. A tree, for instance, hanging from a rock, though totally unpoised, may be beautiful; or it may have a good effect, when we see it bending over a road; because it corresponds with its peculiar situation. We do not, in these cases, admire it as a tree, but as the adjunct of an effect; the beauty of which does not give the eye leisure to attend to the deformity of the instrument, through which the effect is produced.

Without these requisites, therefore, *form*, *lightness*, and *a proper balance*, no tree can have that *species of beauty*, which we call *picturesque*.

1791

WILLIAM BARTRAM (1739-1823)

[INCIDENTS AND SCENES IN FLORIDA]

The evening was temperately cool and calm. The crocodiles began to roar and appear in uncommon numbers along the shores and in the river. I fixed my camp in an open plain, near the utmost projection of the promontory, under the shelter of a large live oak which stood on the highest part of the ground, and but a few yards from my boat. From this open high situation I had a free prospect of the river, which was a matter of no trivial consideration to me, having good reason to dread the subtle attacks of the alligators who were crowding about my harbor. Having collected a good quantity of wood for the purpose of keeping up a light and smoke during the night, I began to think of preparing my supper, when, upon examining my stores, I found but a scanty provision. I thereupon determined, as the most expeditious way of supplying my necessities, to take my bob and try for some trout. About one hundred yards above my harbor began a cove or bay of the river, out of which opened a large lagoon. The mouth or entrance from the river to it was narrow, but the waters soon after spread and formed a little lake extending into the marshes: its entrance and shores within I observed to be verged with floating lawns of the pistia and nymphea and other aquatic plants; these I knew were excellent haunts for trout.

The verges and islets of the lagoon were elegantly embellished with flowering plants and shrubs; the laughing coots with wings half spread were tripping over the little coves and hiding themselves in the tufts of grass; young broods of the painted summer teal, skimming the still surface of the waters and following the watchful parent unconscious of danger, were frequently surprised by the voracious trout; and he, in turn, as often by the subtle greedy alligator. Behold him rushing forth from the flags and reeds. His enormous body swells. His plaited tail, brandished high, floats upon the lake. The waters like a cataract descend from his opening jaws. Clouds of smoke issue from his dilated nostrils. The earth trembles with his thunder. When immediately from the opposite coast of the lagoon, emerges from the deep his rival champion. They suddenly dart upon each other. The boiling surface of the lake marks their rapid course, and a terrific combat commences. They now sink to the bottom folded together in horrid wreaths. The water becomes thick and discolored. Again they rise, their jaws clap together, re-echoing through the deep surrounding forests. Again they sink, when the contest ends at the muddy bottom of the lake, and the vanquished makes a hazardous escape, hiding himself in the muddy turbulent waters and sedge on a distant shore. The proud victor exulting returns to the place of action. The shores and forests resound his dreadful roar, together with the triumphing shouts of the plaited tribes around, witnesses of the horrid combat. . . .

About noon the weather became extremely sultry, not a breath of wind stirring, hazy or cloudy, with very heavy distant thunder which was answered by the crocodiles, sure presage of a storm!

Soon after ascending this branch of the river, on the right hand presents itself to view a delightful little bluff, consisting chiefly of shells, and covered with a dark grove of red cedar, zanthoxylon, and myrtle. I could not resist the temptation to stop here, although the tremendous thunder all around the hemisphere alarmed me greatly, having a large lake to cross. From this grove appears to view an expansive and pleasing prospect. The beauteous long lake in front, about northeast from me, its most distant east shores adorned with dark high forests of stately trees; north and south almost endless green plains and meadows, embellished with islets and projecting promontories of high dark forests where the pyramidal magnolia grandiflora, palma elata, and shady oak conspicuously tower.

Being heretofore so closely invested by high forests and deep swamps of the great river, I was prevented from seeing the progress and increase of the approaching tempest, the terrific appearance of which now at once confounded me. How purple and fiery appeared the tumultuous clouds swiftly ascending or darting from the horizon upwards! they seemed to oppose and dash against each other; the skies appeared streaked with blood or purple flame overhead, the flaming lightning streaming and darting about in every direction around seemed to fill the world with fire; whilst the heavy thunder kept the earth in a constant tremor. . . .

What a beautiful display of vegetation is here before me! seemingly unlimited in extent and variety: how the dew-drops twinkle and play upon the sight, trembling on the tips of the lucid, green savanna, sparkling as the gem that flames on the turban of the eastern prince. . . .

I was, however, induced to deviate a little from my intended course, and touch at the enchanting little Isle of Palms. This delightful spot, planted by nature, is almost an entire grove of palms with a few pyramidal magnolias, live oaks, golden orange, and the animating zanthoxylon. What a beautiful retreat is here! blessed unviolated spot of earth, rising from the limpid waters of the lake; its fragrant groves and blooming lawns invested and protected by encircling ranks of the yucca gloriosa. A fascinating atmosphere surrounds this blissful garden; the balmy lantana, ambrosial citra, perfumed crinum, perspiring their mingled odors, wafted through zanthoxylon groves. I at last broke away from the enchanting spot and stepped on board my boat, hoisted sail, and soon approached the coast of the main at the cool eve of day: then traversing a capacious semicircular cove of the lake, verged by low extensive grassy meadows, I at length by dusk made a safe harbor in a little lagoon on the sea shore or strand of a bold sandy point which descended from the surf of the lake. . . .

I seated myself upon a swelling green knoll at the head of the crystal basin. Near me on the left was a point or projection of an entire grove of the aromatic *illicium floridanum;* on my right and all around behind me was a fruitful orange grove, with palms and magnolias interspersed; in front, just under my feet, was the enchanting and amazing crystal fountain which incessantly threw up from dark rocky caverns below, tons of water every minute, forming a basin, capacious enough for large shallops to ride in, and a creek of four or five feet depth of water and near twenty yards over, which meanders six miles through green meadows, pouring its limpid waters into the great Lake George where they seem to remain pure and unmixed. About twenty yards from the upper edge of the basin and directly opposite to the mouth or outlet of the creek, is a continual and amazing ebullition where the waters are thrown up in such abundance and amazing force, as to jet and swell up two or three feet above the common surface: white sand and small particles of shells are thrown up with the waters near to the top, when they diverge from the center, subside with the expanding flood, and gently sink again, forming a large rim or funnel round about the aperture or mouth of the fountain which is a vast perforation through a bed of rocks, the ragged points of which are projected out on every side. . . .

The ebullition is astonishing and continual, though its greatest force of fury intermits, regularly, for the space of thirty seconds of time: the waters appear of a lucid sea green color, in some measure owing to the reflection of the leaves above: the ebullition is perpendicular upwards, from a vast ragged orifice through a bed of rocks, a great depth below the common surface of the basin, throwing up small particles or pieces of white shells, which subside with the waters at the moment of intermission, gently settling down round about the orifice, forming a vast funnel. At those moments when the waters rush upwards, the surface of the basin immediately over the orifice is greatly swollen or raised a considerable height; and then it is impossible to keep the boat or any other floating vessel over the fountain; but the ebullition quickly subsides; yet, before the surface becomes quite even, the fountain vomits up the waters again, and so on perpetually. The basin is generally circular, about fifty yards over; and the perpetual stream from it into the river is twelve or fifteen yards wide, and ten or twelve feet in depth; the basin and stream continually peopled with prodigious numbers and variety of fish and other animals; as the alligator, and the manate or sea cow, in the winter season. . . .

This trader being near the place (before it had any visible existence in its present appearance), about three years ago, as he was looking for some horses which he expected to find in these parts, on a sudden was astonished by an inexpressible rushing noise like a mighty hurricane or thunder storm; and looking around, he saw the earth overflowed by torrents of water which came, wave after wave, rushing down a vale or plain very near him, which it filled with water, and soon began to overwhelm the higher grounds, attended with a terrific noise and tremor of the earth. Recovering from his first surprise, he immediately resolved to proceed for the place from whence the noise seemed to come; and soon came in sight of the incomparable fountain, and saw, with amazement, the floods rushing upwards many feet high, and the expanding waters, which prevailed every way, spreading themselves far and near. He at length concluded (he said) that the fountains of the deep were again broken up and that an universal deluge had commenced; and instantly turned about and fled to alarm the town about nine miles distance; but before he could reach it, he met several of the inhabitants, who, already alarmed by the unusual noise, were hurrying on towards the place; upon which he returned with the Indians, taking their stand on an eminence to watch its progress and the event. It continued to jet and flow in this manner for several days forming a large rapid creek or river, descending and following the various courses and windings of the valley for the distance of seven or eight miles, emptying into a vast savanna where was a lake and sink which received and gave vent to its waters.

The fountain, however, gradually ceased

to overflow and finally withdrew itself beneath the common surface of the earth, leaving this capacious basin of waters, which, though continually near full, hath never since overflowed. There yet remains, and will I suppose remain for ages, the dry bed of the river or canal, generally four, five, and six feet below the natural surface of the land; the perpendicular ragged banks of which, on each side, show the different strata of the earth; and at places where ridges or a swelling bank crossed and opposed its course and fury, are vast heaps of fragments of rocks, white chalk, stones, and pebbles, which were collected and thrown into the lateral valleys.

1792

MARY WOLLSTONECRAFT (1759-1797)

FROM THE RIGHTS OF WOMAN

It is vain to expect virtue from women till they are, in some degree, independent of men; nay, it is vain to expect that strength of natural affection which would make them good wives and mothers. Whilst they are absolutely dependent on their husbands they will be cunning, mean, and selfish; and the men who can be gratified by the fawning fondness of spaniel-like affection have not much delicacy, for love is not to be bought, in any sense of the words, its silken wings are instantly shrivelled up when any thing beside a return in kind is sought. Yet whilst wealth enervates men, and women live, as it were, by their personal charms, how can we expect them to discharge those ennobling duties which equally require exertion and self-denial. . . .

The private or public virtue of woman is very problematical; for Rousseau and a numerous list of male writers insist that she should all her life be subjected to a severe restraint, that of propriety. Why subject her to propriety—blind propriety—if she be capable of acting from a nobler spring, if she be an heir of immortality? Is sugar always to be produced by vital blood? Is one half of the human species, like the poor African slaves, to be subject to prejudices that brutalize them, when principles would be a surer guard, only to sweeten the cup of man? Is not this indirectly to deny woman reason? for a gift is a mockery if it be unfit for use. . . .

To render her really virtuous and useful, she must not, if she discharge her civil duties, want, individually, the protection of civil laws; she must not be dependent on her husband's bounty for her subsistence during his life or support after his death—for how can a being be generous who has nothing of its own? or virtuous who is not free? The wife, in the present state of things, who is faithful to her husband and neither suckles nor educates her children, scarcely deserves the name of a wife and has no right to that of a citizen. But take away natural rights and duties become null.

Women, then, must be considered as only the wanton solace of men when they become so weak in mind and body that they cannot exert themselves unless to pursue some frothy pleasure or to invent some frivolous fashion. What can be a more melancholy sight to a thinking mind than to look into the numerous carriages that drive helter-skelter about this metropolis in a morning, full of pale-faced creatures who are flying from themselves! I have often wished, with Dr. Johnson, to place some of them in a little shop with half a dozen children looking up to their languid countenances for support. I am much mistaken, if some latent vigor would not soon give health and spirit to their eyes, and some lines drawn by the exercise of reason on the blank cheeks, which before were only undulated by dimples, might restore lost dignity to the character, or rather enable it to attain the true dignity of its nature. Virtue is not to be acquired even by speculation, much less by the negative supineness that wealth naturally generates.

Besides, when poverty is more disgraceful than even vice, is not morality cut to the quick? Still to avoid misconstruction, though I consider that women in the common walks of life are called to fulfill the duties of wives and mothers by religion and reason, I cannot help lamenting that women of a superior cast have not a road open by which they can pursue more extensive plans of usefulness and independence. I may excite laughter by dropping a hint which I mean to pursue some future time, for I really think that women ought to have representatives, instead of being arbitrarily governed without having any direct share allowed them in the deliberations of government. . . .

It is a melancholy truth; yet such is the blessed effect of civilization! The most respectable women are the most oppressed; and, unless they have understandings far superior to the common run of understandings, taking in both sexes, they must, from being treated like contemptible beings, become contemptible. How many women thus waste life away, the prey of discontent, who might have practised as physicians, regulated a farm, managed a shop, and stood erect supported by their own industry, instead of hanging their heads sur-

charged with the dew of sensibility that consumes the beauty to which it at first gave lustre; nay, I doubt whether pity and love are so near akin as poets feign, for I have seldom seen much compassion excited by the helplessness of females unless they were fair; then, perhaps, pity was the soft handmaid of love, or the harbinger of lust.

How much more respectable is the woman who earns her own bread, by fulfilling any duty, than the most accomplished beauty!—beauty did I say?—so sensible am I of the beauty of moral loveliness or the harmonious propriety that attunes the passions of a well-regulated mind, that I blush at making the comparison; yet I sigh to think how few women aim at attaining this respectability by withdrawing from the giddy whirl of pleasure or the indolent calm that stupefies the good sort of women it sucks in.

1792

WILLIAM GODWIN (1756-1836)

FROM POLITICAL JUSTICE

[THE SUPERIORITY OF REASONING OVER PUNISHMENT]

Punishment is not the appropriate mode of correcting the errors of mankind. It will probably be admitted that the only true end of punishment is correction. That question will be discussed in another part of the present inquiry. "I have done something which, wrong in itself, I believe to be right; or I have done something which I usually admit to be wrong, but my conviction upon the subject is not so clear and forcible as to prevent my yielding to a powerful temptation." There can be no doubt, that the proper way of conveying to my understanding a truth of which I am ignorant, or of impressing upon me a firmer persuasion of a truth with which I am acquainted, is by an appeal to my reason. Even an angry expostulation with me upon my conduct will but excite similar passions in me and cloud instead of illuminate my understanding. There is certainly a way of expressing truth with such benevolence as to command attention and such evidence as to enforce conviction in all cases whatever.

Punishment inevitably excites in the sufferer, and ought to excite, a sense of injustice. Let its purpose be to convince me of the truth of a proposition which I at present believe to be false. It is not abstractedly considered of the nature of an argument, and therefore it cannot begin with producing conviction. Punishment is a specious name, but it is in reality nothing more than force put upon one being by another who happens to be stronger. Now strength apparently does not constitute justice, nor ought "might," according to a trite proverb, to "overcome right." The case of punishment, which we are now considering, is the case of you and I differing in opinion, and your telling me that you must be right, since you have a more brawny arm, or have applied your mind more to the acquiring skill in your weapons than I have.

But let us suppose "that I am convinced of my error, but that my conviction is superficial and fluctuating, and the object you propose is to render it durable and profound." Ought it to be thus durable and profound? There are no doubt arguments and reasons calculated to render it so. Is it in reality problematical, and do you wish by the weight of your blows to make up for the deficiency of your logic? This can never be defended. An appeal to force must appear to both parties, in proportion to the soundness of their understanding, to be a confession of imbecility. He that has recourse to it, would have no occasion for this expedient, if he were sufficiently acquainted with the powers of that truth it is his office to communicate. If there be any man, who, in suffering punishment, is not conscious of injustice, he must have had his mind previously debased to slavery and his sense of moral right and wrong blunted by a series of oppression.

[REASON THE ONLY SANCTION OF LAW AND GOVERNMENT]

Legislation, as it has been usually understood, is not an affair of human competence. Reason is the only legislator and her decrees are irrevocable and uniform. The functions of society extend, not to the making, but the interpreting of law; it cannot decree, it can only declare that which the nature of things has already decreed, and the propriety of which irresistibly flows from the circumstances of the case. Montesquieu says that "in a free state every man will be his own legislator." This is not true, setting apart the functions of the community, unless in the limited sense already explained. It is the office of conscience to determine, "not like an Asiatic cadi, according to the ebbs and flows of his own passions, but like a British judge, who makes no new law but faithfully declares that law which he finds already written."

The same distinction is to be made upon the subject of authority. All political power is strictly speaking executive. It has appeared to be necessary, with respect to men as we at present find them, that force should sometimes be employed in repressing injustice; and for the same reasons it appears that this force should as far as possible be vested in the community. To the public support of justice, therefore, the authority of the community extends. But no sooner does it wander in the smallest degree from the great line of justice than its authority is at an end, it stands upon a level with the obscurest individual, and every man is bound to resist its decisions. . . .

No truth can be more simple, at the same time that no truth has been more darkened by the glosses of interested individuals, than that one man can in no case be bound to yield obedience to any other man or set of men upon earth.

There is one rule to which we are universally bound to conform ourselves: justice, the treating every man precisely as his usefulness and worth demand, the acting under every circumstance in the manner that shall procure the greatest quantity of general good. When we have done thus, what province is there left to the disposal of obedience?

[THE INDIVIDUAL REASON TO BE SUPREME]

Depravity would have gained little ground in the world if every man had been in the exercise of his independent judgment. The instrument by which extensive mischiefs have in all ages been perpetrated has been the principle of many men being reduced to mere machines in the hands of the few. Man while he consults his own understanding is the ornament of the universe. Man when he surrenders his reason and becomes the partisan of implicit faith and passing obedience, is the most mischievous of all animals. Ceasing to examine every proposition that comes before him for the direction of his conduct, he is no longer the capable subject of moral instruction. He is, in the instant of submission, the blind instrument of every nefarious purpose of his principal; and, when left to himself, is open to the seduction of injustice, cruelty, and profligacy.

These reasonings lead to a proper explanation of the word subject. If by the subject of any government we mean a person whose duty it is to obey, the true inference from the preceding principles is, that no government has any subjects. If, on the contrary, we mean a person whom the government is bound to protect or may justly restrain, the word is sufficiently admissible.

[VIRTUE TO FLOURISH IN FREEDOM]

All moral science may be reduced to this one head, calculation of the future. We cannot reasonably expect virtue from the multitude of mankind if they be induced by the perverseness of the conductors of human affairs to believe that it is not their interest to be virtuous. But this is not the point upon which the question turns. Virtue is nothing else but the pursuit of general good. Justice is the standard which discriminates the advantage of the many and of the few, of the whole and a part. If this first and most important of all subjects be involved in obscurity, how shall the well being of mankind be substantially promoted? The most benevolent of our species will be engaged in crusades of error; while the cooler and more phlegmatic spectators, discerning no evident clue that should guide them amidst the labyrinth, sit down in selfish neutrality and leave the complicated scene to produce its own dénouement. . . .

Of all the principles of justice there is none so material to the moral rectitude of mankind as this—that no man can be distinguished but by his personal merit. Why not endeavor to reduce to practice so simple and sublime a lesson? When a man has proved himself a benefactor to the public, when he has already by laudable perseverance cultivated in himself talents which need only encouragement and public favor to bring them to maturity, let that man be honored. In a state of society where fictitious distinctions are unknown, it is impossible he should not be honored. But that a man should be looked up to with servility and awe because the king has bestowed on him a spurious name or decorated him with a ribband; that another should wallow in luxury because his ancestor three centuries ago bled in the quarrel of Lancaster or York; do we imagine that these iniquities can be practised without injury? . . .

Let us for a moment give the reins to reflection and endeavor accurately to conceive the state of mankind where justice should form the public and general principle. In that case our moral feelings would assume a firm and wholesome tone, for they would not be perpetually counteracted by examples that weakened their energy and confounded their clearness. Men would be fearless, because they would know that there were no legal snares lying in wait for their lives. They would be courageous, because no man would be pressed to the earth that another might enjoy immoderate luxury, because every one would be secure of the just reward of his industry and prize of his exertions. Jealousy and hatred would cease, for they are the offspring of injustice. Every man would speak truth with his neighbor, for there would be no temptation to falsehood and deceit. Mind would find its level, for there would be every thing to encourage and to animate. Science would be unspeakably improved, for understanding would convert into a real power, no longer an *ignis fatuus,* shining and expiring by turns, and leading us into sloughs of sophistry, false science, and specious mistake. All men would be disposed to avow their dispositions and actions: none would endeavor to suppress the just eulogium of his neighbor, for, so long as there were tongues to record, the suppression would be possible; none would fear to detect the misconduct of his neighbor, for there would be no laws converting the sincere expression of our convictions into a libel.

[THE EVIL OF MARRIAGE]

All attachments to individuals, except in proportion to their merits, are plainly unjust. It is, therefore, desirable that we should be the friends of man rather than of particular men and that we should pursue the chain of our own reflections with no other interruption than information or philanthropy requires.

This subject of cohabitation is particularly interesting as it includes in it the subject of marriage. It will, therefore, be proper to extend our inquiries somewhat further upon this head. Cohabitation is not only an evil as it checks the independent progress of mind—it is also inconsistent with the imperfections and propensities of man. It is absurd to expect that the inclinations and wishes of two human beings should coincide through any long period of time. To oblige them to act and to live together is to subject them to some inevitable portion of thwarting, bickering, and unhappiness. This cannot be otherwise so long as man has failed to reach the standard of absolute perfection. The supposition that I must have a companion for life is the result of a complication of vices. It is the dictate of cowardice and not of fortitude. It flows from the desire of being loved and esteemed for something that is not desert.

But the evil of marriage as it is practised in European countries lies deeper than this. The habit is, for a thoughtless and romantic youth of each sex to come together, to see each other for a few times and under circumstances full of delusion, and then to vow to each other eternal attachment. What is the consequence of this? In almost every instance they find themselves deceived. They are reduced to make the best of an irretrievable mistake. They are presented with the strongest imaginable temptation to become the dupes of falsehood. They are led to conceive it their wisest policy to shut their eyes upon realities, happy if by any perversion of intellect they can persuade themselves that they were right in their first crude opinion of their companion. The institution of marriage is a system of fraud; and men who carefully mislead their judgments in the daily affair of their life, must always have a crippled judgment in every other concern. We ought to dismiss our mistake as soon as it is detected; but we are taught to cherish it. We ought to be incessant in our search after virtue and worth; but we are taught to check our inquiry, and shut our eyes upon the most attractive and admirable objects. Marriage is law, and the worst of all laws. Whatever our understandings may tell us of the person from whose connection we should derive the greatest improvement, of the worth of one woman and the demerits of another, we are obliged to consider what is law, and not what is justice.

Add to this that marriage is an affair of property, and the worst of all properties. So long as two human beings are forbidden by positive institution to follow the dictates of their own mind, prejudice is alive and vigorous. So long as I seek to engross one woman to myself and to prohibit my neighbor from proving his superior desert and reaping the fruits of it, I am guilty of the most odious of all monopolies. Over this imaginary prize men watch with perpetual jealousy, and one man will find his desires and his capacity to circumvent as much excited as the other is excited to traverse his projects and frustrate his hopes. As long as this state of society continues, philanthropy will be crossed and checked in a thousand ways, and the still augmenting stream of abuse will continue to flow.

The abolition of marriage will be attended with no evils. We are apt to represent it to ourselves as the harbinger of brutal lust and depravity. But it really happens in this, as in other cases, that the positive laws which are made to restrain our vices irritate and multiply them. Not to say, that the same sentiments of justice and happiness which in a state of equal property would destroy the relish for luxury, would decrease our inordinate appetites of every kind, and lead us universally to prefer the pleasures of intellect to the pleasures of sense.

1793

ANN RADCLIFFE (1764-1823)

FROM THE MYSTERIES OF UDOLPHO

[THE CASTLE OF UDOLPHO]

From this sublime scene the travellers continued to ascend among the pines, till they entered a narrow pass of the mountains which shut out every feature of the distant country and in its stead exhibited only tremendous crags impending over the road, where no vestige of humanity or even of vegetation appeared, except here and there the trunk and scathed branches of an oak that hung nearly headlong from the rock into which its strong roots had fastened. This pass, which led into the heart of the Apennines, at length opened to day and a scene of mountains stretched in long perspective as wild as any the travellers had yet passed. Still vast pine forests hung upon their base and crowned the ridgy precipice that rose perpendicularly from the vale, while, above, the rolling mists caught the sunbeams and touched their cliffs with all the magical coloring of light and shade. The scene seemed perpetually changing, and its features to assume new forms as the winding road brought them to the eye in different attitudes; while the shifting vapors, now partially concealing their minuter beauties and now illuminating them with splendid tints, assisted the illusions of the sight.

Though the deep valleys between these mountains were for the most part clothed with pines, sometimes an abrupt opening presented a perspective of only barren rocks with a cataract flashing from their summit among broken cliffs till its waters, reaching the bottom, foamed along with louder fury; and sometimes pastoral scenes exhibited their "green delights" in the narrow vales, smiling amid surrounding horror. There herds and flocks of goats and sheep browsing under the shade of hanging woods and the shepherd's little cabin reared on the margin of a clear stream, presented a sweet picture of repose. 5

Wild and romantic as were these scenes, their character had far less of the sublime than had those of the Alps which guard the entrance of Italy. Emily was often elevated, but seldom felt those emotions of 10 indescribable awe which she had so continually experienced in her passage over the Alps.

Towards the close of day the road wound into a deep valley. Mountains, whose 15 shaggy steeps appeared to be inaccessible, almost surrounded it. To the east a vista opened and exhibited the Apennines in their darkest horrors; and the long perspective of retiring summits rising over each 20 other, their ridges clothed with pines, exhibited a stronger image of grandeur than any that Emily had yet seen. The sun had just sunk below the top of the mountains she was descending, whose long shadows 25 stretched athwart the valley; but his sloping rays, shooting through an opening of the cliffs, touched with a yellow gleam the summits of the forest that hung upon the opposite steeps and streamed in full splen- 30 dor upon the towers and battlements of a castle that spread its extensive ramparts along the brow of a precipice above. The splendor of these illuminated objects was heightened by the contrasted shade which 35 involved the valley below.

"There," said Montoni, speaking for the first time in several hours, "is Udolpho."

Emily gazed with melancholy awe upon the castle, which she understood to be 40 Montoni's, for, though it was now lighted up by the setting sun, the gothic greatness of its features and its moldering walls of dark gray stone rendered it a gloomy and sublime object. As she gazed, the light 45 died away on its walls leaving a melancholy purple tint which spread deeper and deeper as the thin vapor crept up the mountain, while the battlements above were still tipped with splendor. From 50 those, too, the rays soon faded and the whole edifice was invested with the solemn duskiness of evening. Silent, lonely, and sublime, it seemed to stand the sovereign of the scene and to frown defiance on all 55 who dared to invade its solitary reign. As the twilight deepened, its features became more awful in obscurity; and Emily continued to gaze till its clustering towers were alone seen rising over the tops of the 60 woods beneath whose thick shade the carriages soon after began to ascend.

[THE PICTURE BEHIND THE VEIL]

To withdraw her thoughts, however, from the subject of her misfortunes, she attempted to read; but her attention wandered from the page and, at length, she threw aside the book and determined to explore the adjoining chambers of the castle. Her imagination was pleased with the view of ancient grandeur, and an emotion of melancholy awe awakened all its powers as she walked through rooms, obscure and desolate, where no footsteps had passed probably for many years, and remembered the strange history of the former possessor of the edifice. This brought to her recollection the veiled picture which had attracted her curiosity on the preceding night, and she resolved to examine it. As she passed through the chambers that led to this, she found herself somewhat agitated; its connection with the late lady of the castle and the conversation of Annette, together with the circumstances of the veil, throwing a mystery over the object that excited a faint degree of terror. But a terror of this nature, as it occupies and expands the mind and elevates it to high expectation, is purely sublime and leads us, by a kind of fascination, to seek even the object from which we appear to shrink.

Emily passed on with faltering steps; and, having paused a moment at the door before she attempted to open it, she then hastily entered the chamber and went towards the picture, which appeared to be inclosed in a frame of uncommon size, that hung in a dark part of the room. She paused again and then with a timid hand lifted the veil; but instantly let it fall, perceiving that what it had concealed was no picture, and before she could leave the chamber she dropped senseless on the floor.

When she recovered her recollection, the remembrance of what she had seen had nearly deprived her of it a second time. She had scarcely strength to remove from the room and regain her own, and, when arrived there, wanted courage to remain alone. Horror occupied her mind and excluded for a time all sense of past and dread of future misfortune; she seated herself near the casement because from thence she heard voices, though distant, on the terrace and might see people pass; and these, trifling as they were, were reviving circumstances. When her spirits had recovered their tone, she considered whether she should mention what she had seen to Madame Montoni, and various and important motives urged her to do so, among which the least was the hope of the relief which an overburdened mind finds in speaking of the subject of its interest. But she was aware of the terrible consequences which such a communication might lead to; and, dreading the indiscretion of her aunt, at length endeavored to arm herself with resolution to observe a profound silence on the subject.

[THE EXPLANATION OF THE VEILED PORTRAIT]

It may be remembered that in a chamber of Udolpho hung a black veil whose singular situation had excited Emily's curiosity and which afterwards disclosed an object that had overwhelmed her with horror; for on lifting it, there appeared, instead of the picture she had expected, within a recess of the wall a human figure, of ghastly paleness, stretched at its length, and dressed in the habiliments of the grave. What added to the horror of the spectacle was that the face appeared partly decayed and disfigured by worms which were visible on the features and hands. On such an object it will be readily believed that no person could endure to look twice. Emily, it may be recollected had after the first glance let the veil drop, and her terror had prevented her from ever after provoking a renewal of such suffering as she had then experienced. Had she dared to look again her delusion and her fears would have vanished together, and she would have perceived that the figure before her was not human but formed of wax.

The history of it is somewhat extraordinary, though not without example in the records of that fierce severity which monkist superstition has sometimes inflicted on mankind. A member of the house of Udolpho, having committed some offence against the prerogative of the church, had been condemned to the penance of contemplating, during certain hours of the day, a waxen image made to resemble a human body in the state to which it is reduced after death. This penance, serving as a memento of the condition at which he must himself arrive, had been designed to reprove the pride of the Marquis of Udolpho.

1794

MATTHEW GREGORY LEWIS (1775-1818)

FROM THE MONK

[THE CONJURATION OF THE WANDERING JEW]

He was a man of majestic presence; his countenance was strongly marked and his eyes were large, black, and sparkling, yet there was a something in his look which, the moment that I saw him, inspired me with a secret awe, not to say horror. He was dressed plainly, his hair hung wildly upon his brow, and a band of black velvet which encircled his forehead spread over his features an additional gloom. His countenance wore the marks of profound melancholy, his step was slow, and his manner grave, stately, and solemn.

He saluted me with politeness; and having replied to the usual compliments of introduction, he motioned to Theodore to quit the chamber. The page instantly withdrew.

"I know your business," said he without giving me time to speak. "I have the power of releasing you from your nightly visitor, but this cannot be done before Sunday. On the hour when the Sabbath morning breaks, spirits of darkness have least influence over mortals. After Saturday the nun shall visit you no more."

"May I not inquire," said I, "by what means you are in possession of a secret which I have carefully concealed from the knowledge of every one?"

"How can I be so ignorant of your distresses when their cause at this moment stands beside you?"

I started. The stranger continued——

"Though to you only visible for one hour in the twenty-four, neither day or night does she ever quit you; nor will she ever quit you till you have granted her request."

"And what is that request?"

"That she must herself explain; it lies

not in my knowledge. Wait with patience for the night of Saturday; all shall be then cleared up." . . .

The wished-for night arrived. To avoid creating suspicion I retired to bed at my usual hour, but as soon as my attendants had left me I dressed myself again and prepared for the stranger's reception. He entered my room upon the turn of midnight. A small chest was in his hand, which he placed near the stove. He saluted me without speaking; I returned the compliment, observing an equal silence.

The first thing which he produced was a small wooden crucifix. He sunk upon his knees, gazed upon it mournfully, and cast his eyes towards heaven. He seemed to be praying devoutly. At length he bowed his head respectfully, kissed the crucifix thrice, and quitted his kneeling posture. He next drew from the chest a covered goblet. With the liquor which it contained and which appeared to be blood, he sprinkled the floor, and then dipping in it one end of the crucifix, he described a circle in the middle of the room. Round about this he placed various relics, skulls, thigh bones, and so forth. I observed that he disposed them all in the forms of crosses. Lastly, he took out a large Bible and beckoned me to follow him into the circle. I obeyed.

"Be cautious not to utter a syllable," whispered the stranger, "Step not out of the circle, and, as you love yourself, dare not to look upon my face!"

Holding the crucifix in one hand, the Bible in the other, he seemed to read with profound attention. The clock struck one! As usual, I heard the spectre's steps upon the staircase, but I was not seized with the accustomed shivering. I waited her approach with confidence. She entered the room, drew near the circle, and stopped. The stranger muttered some words, to me unintelligible. Then raising his head from the book and extending the crucifix towards the ghost, he pronounced, in a voice distinct and solemn——

"Beatrice! Beatrice! Beatrice!"

"What wouldst thou?" replied the apparition in a hollow faltering tone.

"What disturbs thy sleep? Why dost thou afflict and torture this youth? How can rest be restored to thy unquiet spirit?"

"I dare not tell! I must not tell! Fain would I repose in my grave, but stern commands force me to prolong my punishment."

"Knowest thou this blood? Knowest thou in whose veins it flowed? Beatrice! in his name I charge thee to answer me!"

"I dare not disobey my taskers."

"Darest thou disobey me?"

He spoke in a commanding tone and drew the sable band from his forehead. In spite of his injunctions to the contrary, curiosity would not suffer me to keep my eyes off his face: I raised them and beheld a burning cross impressed upon his brow. For the horror with which this object inspired me I cannot account, but I never felt its equal. My senses left me for some moments, a mysterious dread overcame my courage, and had not the exorciser caught my hand I should have fallen out of the circle.

When I recovered myself, I perceived that the burning cross had produced an effect no less violent upon the spectre. Her countenance expressed reverence and horror, and her visionary limbs were shaken by fear.

"Yes," she said at length, "I tremble at that mark! I respect it! I obey you! Know then, that my bones lie still unburied: they rot in the obscurity of Lindenberg Hole. None but this youth has the right of consigning them to the grave. His own lips have made over to me his body and his soul: never will I give back his promise; never shall he know a night devoid of terror, unless he engages to collect my moldering bones and deposit them in the family vault of his Andalusian castle. Then let thirty masses be said for the repose of my spirit, and I trouble this world no more. Now let me depart. Those flames are scorching!"

He let the hand drop slowly which held the crucifix, and which till then he had pointed towards her. The apparition bowed her head, and her form melted into air. The exorciser led me out of the circle. He replaced the Bible, and so forth, in the chest and then addressed himself to me, who stood near him speechless from astonishment.

"Don Raymond, you have heard the conditions on which repose is promised you. Let it be your business to fulfil them to the letter. For me, nothing more remains than to clear up the darkness still spread over the spectre's history and inform you that when living, Beatrice bore the name of las Cisternas. She was the great aunt of your grandfather. In quality of your relation, her ashes demand respect from you, though the enormity of her crimes must excite your abhorrence."   1795

SELECTIONS FROM
THE ROMANTIC MOVEMENT

WILLIAM BLAKE (1757-1827)

There is something in the madness of this man which interests me more than the sanity of Lord Byron and Walter Scott.

—HENRY CRABB ROBINSON

Before our own century, little attention was given to Blake. Today his reputation resembles that of the founder of a religious cult, and it is clear that he offers something which to many moderns is of fascinating interest. His devotees maintain that it is his *Prophetic Books,* such as *Milton* and *Jerusalem,* that are of the profoundest value; but to the uninitiated beginner they seem too obscure. It is the lyrics of Blake's earlier period that are accepted by everyone as true classics.

Blake was trained to be an engraver and artist. He printed and published his books in an original manner: the illustrations as well as the poems were of his own making. He had less formal schooling than any of the other great Romantics,—which partly accounts for the originality of his genius as well as for its eccentricity. If he had received a conventional education, he might have rejected as heretical or whimsical many of those theological and speculative books which he delighted to read. He was influenced by the mystical teachings of his father's religion,—Swedenborgianism; and he always firmly believed that he held intercourse with angels, prophets, and other "messengers from Heaven." His opinions on politics, morality, love, art, and literature were so contrary to those current that he was mistakenly thought insane. An "affectionate, enthusiastic, hope-fostered visionary," as he called himself, he cheerfully accepted poverty, never did anything inconsistent with his ideals, was diligently devoted to his artistic calling, and thus managed (more successfully than many tiresomely sane people) to find happiness. In reading his works one should not be disconcerted by the queer spellings, the abrupt transitions, or the extreme paradoxes; there is method in his seeming madness.

To Blake the guide to truth was not the critical and sceptical reason, but the free imagination. The Religion of Imagination had two commandments: Be free, and Love all things. Between human nature freely and fully developed and the divine, there was no distinction. If mankind were completely free, it would be completely good. Toward this goal of virtuous anarchy the American Revolution and the French Revolution were gigantic steps. Politicians, moralists, and theologians who feared liberty, supported restrictive laws and commandments, and imposed punishments in this world or the next, were enemies of true virtue. Since classical literature and art fostered ideas contrary to this faith in absolute liberty and individualism, it should not be imitated; a nobler model than Homer or Virgil was the New Testament. Greater even than Liberty was Love,—that bond of universal sympathy, charity, and pity which should unite rich and poor, old and young, mankind and all other creatures. Hence Blake dwelt with peculiar fondness upon the innocence of children, the pitifulness of their suffering, the wickedness of cruelty to animals, and the glory of forgiveness. On such subjects he sang with an exquisite and appealing melody, of a quality that had scarcely been heard in England since the seventeenth century.

The best work of Blake is confined to a few themes. He does not command as wide a range as some of the great Romantics. Yet, when one considers both the sentiments and the style of his *Poetical Sketches* (1783), *Songs of Innocence* (1789), and *Songs of Experience* (1794), one inclines to think that the beginnings of the Romantic Movement may be seen in these poems quite as clearly as in Wordsworth and Coleridge's *Lyrical Ballads* (1798).

———

WILLIAM BLAKE

FROM POETICAL SKETCHES

TO THE EVENING STAR

Thou fair-haired angel of the evening,
Now, whilst the sun rests on the mountains, light
Thy bright torch of love; thy radiant crown
Put on, and smile upon our evening bed!
Smile on our loves, and while thou drawest the
Blue curtains of the sky, scatter thy silver dew
On every flower that shuts its sweet eyes
In timely sleep. Let thy west wind sleep on
The lake; speak silence with thy glimmering eyes,
And wash the dusk with silver. Soon, full soon,   10
Dost thou withdraw; then the wolf rages wide,
And the lion glares through the dun forest:
The fleeces of our flocks are covered with
Thy sacred dew: protect them with thine influence.

1783

SONG

How sweet I roam'd from field to field
  And tasted all the summer's pride,
Till I the prince of love beheld
  Who in the sunny beams did glide!

He show'd me lilies for my hair,   5
  And blushing roses for my brow;
He led me through his gardens fair
  Where all his golden pleasures grow.

With sweet May dews my wings were wet,
  And Phoebus fir'd my vocal rage;   10
He caught me in his silken net,
  And shut me in his golden cage.

He loves to sit and hear me sing,
  Then, laughing, sports and plays with
    me;
Then stretches out my golden wing,   15
  And mocks my loss of liberty.

1783

SONG

My silks and fine array,
  My smiles and languish'd air,
By love are driv'n away;
  And mournful lean Despair
Brings me yew to deck my grave: 5
Such end true lovers have.

His face is fair as heav'n
  When springing buds unfold;
O why to him was't giv'n
  Whose heart is wintry cold?   10

His breast is love's all-worshipp'd tomb,
  Where all love's pilgrims come.

Bring me an axe and spade,
  Bring me a winding sheet;
When I my grave have made   15
  Let winds and tempests beat:
Then down I'll lie as cold as clay.
True love doth pass away!

1783

SONG

I love the jocund dance,
  The softly breathing song,
Where innocent eyes do glance,
  And where lisps the maiden's tongue.

I love the laughing vale,   5
  I love the echoing hill,
Where mirth does never fail,
  And the jolly swain laughs his fill.

I love the pleasant cot,
  I love the innocent bow'r,   10
Where white and brown is our lot,
  Or fruit in the mid-day hour.

I love the oaken seat,
  Beneath the oaken tree,
Where all the old villagers meet,   15
  And laugh our sports to see.

I love our neighbors all,
  But, Kitty, I better love thee;
And love them I ever shall;
  But thou art all to me.   20

1782

SONG

Memory, hither come,
And tune your merry notes:
And, while upon the wind
Your music floats,
I'll pore upon the stream   5
Where sighing lovers dream,
And fish for fancies as they pass
Within the watery glass.

I'll drink of the clear stream,
And hear the linnet's song;   10
And there I'll lie and dream
The day along:
And when night comes, I'll go
To places fit for woe,
Walking along the darken'd valley   15
With silent Melancholy.

                              1783

MAD SONG

The wild winds weep,
And the night is a-cold;
Come hither, Sleep,
And my griefs unfold:
But lo! the morning peeps   5
Over the eastern steeps,
And the rustling beds of dawn
The earth do scorn.

Lo! to the vault
Of paved heaven,   10
With sorrow fraught
My notes are driven:
They strike the ear of night,
Make weep the eyes of day;
They make mad the roaring winds,   15
And with the tempests play.

Like a fiend in a cloud,
With howling woe
After night I do crowd,
And with night will go;   20
I turn my back to the east
From whence comforts have increased;
For light doth seize my brain
With frantic pain.

                              1783

SONG

Fresh from the dewy hill, the merry year
Smiles on my head and mounts his flaming
      car;
Round my young brows the laurel wreathes
      a shade,
And rising glories beam around my head.

My feet are wing'd, while o'er the dewy
      lawn,   5
I meet my maiden risen like the morn:
O bless those holy feet, like angels' feet;
O bless those limbs, beaming with heav'nly
      light!

Like as an angel glitt'ring in the sky
In times of innocence and holy joy;   10
The joyful shepherd stops his grateful song
To hear the music of an angel's tongue.

So when she speaks, the voice of Heaven
      I hear;
So when we walk, nothing impure comes
      near;
Each field seems Eden, and each calm
      retreat;   15
Each village seems the haunt of holy feet.

But that sweet village where my black-eyed
      maid
Closes her eyes in sleep beneath night's
      shade,
Whene'er I enter, more than mortal fire
Burns in my soul, and does my song in-
      spire.   20

                              1783

TO THE MUSES

Whether on Ida's shady brow,
   Or in the chambers of the East,
The chambers of the sun, that now
   From ancient melody have ceased;

Whether in Heaven ye wander fair,   5
   Or the green corners of the earth,
Or the blue regions of the air,
   Where the melodious winds have birth;

Whether on crystal rocks ye rove,
   Beneath the bosom of the sea   10
Wandering in many a coral grove,
   Fair Nine, forsaking Poetry!

How have you left the ancient love
   That bards of old enjoyed in you!
The languid strings do scarcely move, 15
   The sound is forced, the notes are few!

                              1783

FROM SONGS OF INNOCENCE

INTRODUCTION

Piping down the valleys wild,
   Piping songs of pleasant glee,
On a cloud I saw a child,
   And he laughing said to me:

"Pipe a song about a Lamb!"   5
So I piped with merry cheer.
"Piper, pipe that song again;"
So I piped: he wept to hear.

"Drop thy pipe, thy happy pipe;
Sing thy songs of happy cheer:"   10
So I sung the same again,
While he wept with joy to hear.

"Piper, sit thee down and write
In a book, that all may read."
So he vanished from my sight,   15
And I plucked a hollow reed,

And I made a rural pen,
And I stained the water clear,
And I wrote my happy songs
Every child may joy to hear.   20

1789

THE ECHOING GREEN

The Sun does arise,
And make happy the skies;
The merry bells ring
To welcome the Spring;
The skylark and thrush,   5
The birds of the bush,
Sing louder around
To the bells' cheerful sound,
While our sports shall be seen
On the Echoing Green.   10

Old John, with white hair,
Does laugh away care,
Sitting under the oak,
Among the old folk.
They laugh at our play,   15
And soon they all say:
"Such, such were the joys
When we all, girls and boys,
In our youth time were seen
On the Echoing Green."   20

Till the little ones, weary,
No more can be merry;
The sun does descend,
And our sports have an end.
Round the laps of their mothers   25
Many sisters and brothers,
Like birds in their nest,
Are ready for rest,
And sport no more seen
On the darkening Green.   30

1789

THE LAMB

Little Lamb, who made thee?
Dost thou know who made thee?
Gave thee life, and bid thee feed
By the stream and o'er the mead;
Gave thee clothing of delight,   5
Softest clothing, woolly, bright;
Gave thee such a tender voice,
Making all the vales rejoice?
Little Lamb, who made thee?
Dost thou know who made thee?   10

Little Lamb, I'll tell thee,
Little Lamb, I'll tell thee:
He is callèd by thy name,
For he calls himself a Lamb,
He is meek, and he is mild;   15
He became a little child.
I a child, and thou a lamb,
We are callèd by his name.
Little Lamb, God bless thee!
Little Lamb, God bless thee!   20

1789

THE LITTLE BLACK BOY

My mother bore me in the southern wild,
And I am black, but O, my soul is white!
White as an angel is the English child,
But I am black, as if bereaved of light.

My mother taught me underneath a tree,   5
And sitting down before the heat of day,
She took me on her lap and kissèd me,
And, pointing to the East, began to say:

"Look on the rising sun: there God does
live,
And gives his light, and gives his heat
away;   10
And flowers and trees and beasts and men
receive
Comfort in morning, joy in the noonday.

"And we are put on earth a little space,
That we may learn to bear the beams of
love;
And these black bodies and this sun-burnt
face   15
Is but a cloud, and like a shady grove.

"For when our souls have learned the heat
to bear,
The cloud will vanish; we shall hear his
voice,
Saying: 'Come out from the grove, my love
and care,
And round my golden tent like lambs
rejoice'."   20

Thus did my mother say, and kissèd me;
And thus I say to little English boy:
When I from black, and he from white
    cloud free,
And round the tent of God like lambs
    we joy,

I'll shade him from the heat, till he can
    bear   25
To lean in joy upon our Father's knee;
And then I'll stand and stroke his silver
    hair,
And be like him, and he will then love
    me.

1789

THE CHIMNEY SWEEPER

When my mother died I was very young,
And my father sold me while yet my tongue
Could scarcely cry " 'weep! 'weep! 'weep! 'weep!"
So your chimneys I sweep, and in soot I sleep.

There's little Tom Dacre, who cried when his head,   5
That curl'd like a lamb's back, was shav'd: so I said
"Hush, Tom! never mind it, for when your head's bare
You know that the soot cannot spoil your white hair."

And so he was quiet, and that very night,
As Tom was a-sleeping, he had such a sight!—   10
That thousands of sweepers, Dick, Joe, Ned, and Jack,
Were all of them lock'd up in coffins of black.

And by came an Angel who had a bright key,
And he open'd the coffins and set them all free;
Then down a green plain leaping, laughing, they run,   15
And wash in a river, and shine in the sun.

Then naked and white, all their bags left behind,
They rise upon clouds and sport in the wind;
And the Angel told Tom, if he'd be a good boy,
He'd have God for his father, and never want joy.   20

And so Tom awoke; and we rose in the dark,
And got with our bags and our brushes to work.
Tho' the morning was cold, Tom was happy and warm;
So if all do their duty they need not fear harm.

1789

LAUGHING SONG

When the green woods laugh with the voice of joy,
And the dimpling stream runs laughing by;
When the air does laugh with our merry wit,
And the green hill laughs with the noise of it;

When the meadows laugh with lively green,   5
And the grasshopper laughs in the merry scene,
When Mary and Susan and Emily
With their sweet round mouths sing "Ha, Ha, He!"

When the painted birds laugh in the shade,
Where our table with cherries and nuts is spread,   10
Come live, and be merry, and join with me,
To sing the sweet chorus of "Ha, Ha, He!"

1789

A CRADLE SONG

Sweet dreams, form a shade
O'er my lovely infant's head;
Sweet dreams of pleasant streams
By happy, silent, moony beams.

Sweet sleep, with soft down   5
Weave thy brows an infant crown.
Sweet sleep, Angel mild,
Hover o'er my happy child.

Sweet smiles, in the night
Hover over my delight;   10
Sweet smiles, mother's smiles,
All the livelong night beguiles.

Sweet moans, dovelike sighs,
Chase not slumber from thy eyes.
Sweet moans, sweeter smiles,   15
All the dovelike moans beguiles.

Sleep, sleep, happy child,
All creation slept and smiled;
Sleep, sleep, happy sleep,
While o'er thee thy mother weep.   20

Sweet babe, in thy face
Holy image I can trace.
Sweet babe, once like thee
Thy maker lay and wept for me,

Wept for me, for thee, for all,   25
When he was an infant small.
Thou his image ever see,
Heavenly face that smiles on thee,

Smiles on thee, on me, on all;
Who became an infant small.   30
Infant smiles are his own smiles;
Heaven and earth to peace beguiles.
                              1789

THE DIVINE IMAGE

To Mercy, Pity, Peace, and Love
    All pray in their distress;
And to these virtues of delight
    Return their thankfulness.

For Mercy, Pity, Peace, and Love   5
    Is God, our father dear;
And Mercy, Pity, Peace, and Love
    Is Man, his child and care.

For Mercy has a human heart,
    Pity a human face;   10
And Love, the human form divine,
    And Peace, the human dress.

Then every man, of every clime,
    That prays in his distress,
Prays to the human form divine,   15
    Love, Mercy, Pity, Peace.

And all must love the human form,
    In heathen, Turk, or Jew;
Where Mercy, Love, and Pity dwell
    There God is dwelling too.   20
                              1789

HOLY THURSDAY

'Twas on a Holy Thursday, their innocent faces clean,
The children walking two and two, in red and blue and green,
Grey-headed beadles walked before, with wands as white as snow,
Till into the high dome of Paul's they like Thames' waters flow.

O what a multitude they seemed, these flowers of London town!   5
Seated in companies they sit with radiance all their own.
The hum of multitudes was there, but multitudes of lambs,
Thousands of little boys and girls raising their innocent hands.

Now like a mighty wind they raise to heaven the voice of song,
Or like harmonious thunderings the seats of Heaven among.   10
Beneath them sit the agèd men, wise guardians of the poor;
Then cherish pity, lest you drive an angel from your door.
                              1789

NURSE'S SONG

When the voices of children are heard on
    the green,
And laughing is heard on the hill,
My heart is at rest within my breast,
And everything else is still.

"Then come home, my children, the sun is
        gone down,   5
And the dews of night arise;
Come, come, leave off play, and let us
        away
Till the morning appears in the skies."

"No, no, let us play, for it is yet day,
  And we cannot go to sleep; 10
Besides, in the sky the little birds fly,
  And the hills are all cover'd with sheep."

"Well, well, go and play till the light fades
    away,
  And then go home to bed."
The little ones leapèd and shouted and
    laugh'd 15
  And all the hills echoèd.

                    1789

INFANT JOY

"I have no name:
I am but two days old."
What shall I call thee?
"I happy am,
Joy is my name." 5
Sweet joy befall thee!

Pretty Joy!
Sweet Joy, but two days old.
Sweet Joy I call thee:
Thou dost smile, 10
I sing the while,
Sweet joy befall thee!

                    1789

ON ANOTHER'S SORROW

Can I see another's woe,
And not be in sorrow too?
Can I see another's grief,
And not seek for kind relief?

Can I see a falling tear, 5
And not feel my sorrow's share?
Can a father see his child
Weep, nor be with sorrow filled?

Can a mother sit and hear
An infant groan, an infant fear? 10
No, no! never can it be!
Never, never can it be!

And can he who smiles on all
Hear the wren with sorrows small,
Hear the small bird's grief and care, 15
Hear the woes that infants bear,

And not sit beside the nest,
Pouring pity in their breast;
And not sit the cradle near,
Weeping tear on infant's tear; 20

And not sit both night and day,
Wiping all our tears away?
O, no! never can it be!
Never, never can it be!

He doth give his joy to all; 25
He becomes an infant small;
He becomes a man of woe;
He doth feel the sorrow too.

Think not thou canst sigh a sigh
And thy maker is not by; 30
Think not thou canst weep a tear
And thy maker is not near.

O! he gives to us his joy
That our grief he may destroy;
Till our grief is fled and gone 35
He doth sit by us and moan.
                              1789

THE BOOK OF THEL

Thel's Motto

Does the Eagle know what is in the pit?
Or wilt thou go ask the Mole?
Can Wisdom be put in a silver rod?
Or Love in a golden bowl?

I

The daughters of the Seraphim led round their sunny flocks, 5
All but the youngest: she in paleness sought the secret air,
To fade away like morning beauty from her mortal day:
Down by the river of Adona her soft voice is heard,
And thus her gentle lamentation falls like morning dew:

"O life of this our spring! why fades the lotus of the water,   10
Why fade these children of the spring, born but to smile and fall?
Ah! Thel is like a watery bow, and like a parting cloud;
Like a reflection in a glass; like shadows in the water;
Like dreams of infants, like a smile upon an infant's face;
Like the dove's voice; like transient day; like music in the air.   15
Ah! gentle may I lay me down, and gentle rest my head,
And gentle sleep the sleep of death, and gentle hear the voice
Of him that walketh in the garden in the evening time."

The Lily of the valley, breathing in the humble grass,
Answered the lovely maid and said: "I am a wat'ry weed,
And I am very small and love to dwell in lowly vales;   20
So weak, the gilded butterfly scarce perches on my head.
Yet I am visited from heaven, and he that smiles on all
Walks in the valley, and each morn over me spreads his hand,
Saying, 'Rejoice, thou humble grass, thou new-born lily flower,
Thou gentle maid of silent valleys and of modest brooks;   25
For thou shalt be clothèd in light, and fed with morning manna,
Till summer's heat melts thee beside the fountains and the springs,
To flourish in eternal vales.' Then why should Thel complain?
Why should the mistress of the vales of Har utter a sigh?"   30

She ceased, and smiled in tears, then sat down in her silver shrine.
Thel answered: "O thou little virgin of the peaceful valley,
Giving to those that cannot crave, the voiceless, the o'ertired;
Thy breath doth nourish the innocent lamb, he smells thy milky
     garments,
He crops thy flowers while thou sittest smiling in his face,   35
Wiping his mild and meekin mouth from all contagious taints.
Thy wine doth purify the golden honey; thy perfume,
Which thou dost scatter on every little blade of grass that springs,
Revives the milkèd cow, and tames the fire-breathing steed.
But Thel is like a faint cloud kindled at the rising sun: 40
I vanish from my pearly throne, and who shall find my place?"

"Queen of the vales," the Lily answered, "ask the tender cloud,
And it shall tell thee why it glitters in the morning sky,
And why it scatters its bright beauty through the humid air.
Descend, O little Cloud, and hover before the eyes of Thel."   45

The cloud descended, and the Lily bowed her modest head,
And went to mind her numerous charge among the verdant grass.

II

"O little Cloud," the virgin said, "I charge thee tell to me
Why thou complainest not when in one hour thou fade away:
Then we shall seek thee, but not find. Ah! Thel is like to thee: 50
I pass away: yet I complain, and no one hears my voice."

The cloud then showed his golden head and his bright form
     emerged,
Hovering and glittering on the air before the face of Thel.

"O Virgin, know'st thou not our steeds drink of the golden springs
Where Luvah doth renew his horses? Look'st thou on my youth,   55
And fearest thou, because I vanish and am seen no more,
Nothing remains? O maid, I tell thee, when I pass away
It is to tenfold life, to love, to peace, and raptures holy:
Unseen descending, weigh my light wings upon balmy flowers,
And court the fair-eyed dew, to take me to her shining tent: 60
The weeping virgin, trembling, kneels before the risen sun,
Till we arise linked in a golden band and never part,
But walk united, bearing food to all our tender flowers."

"Dost thou, O little Cloud? I fear that I am not like thee,
For I walk through the vales of Har, and smell the sweetest flowers,   65
But I feed not the little flowers; I hear the warbling birds,
But I feed not the warbling birds; they fly and seek their food:
But Thel delights in these no more, because I fade away;
And all shall say, 'Without a use this shining woman lived,
Or did she only live to be at death the food of worms?'"   70

The Cloud reclined upon his airy throne and answered thus:
"Then if thou art the food of worms, O virgin of the skies,
How great thy use, how great thy blessing! Every thing that lives
Lives not alone nor for itself. Fear not, and I will call
The weak worm from its lowly bed, and thou shalt hear its voice.   75
Come forth, worm of the silent valley, to thy pensive queen."

The helpless worm arose, and sat upon the Lily's leaf,
And the bright Cloud sailed on, to find his partner in the vale.

III

Then Thel astonished viewed the worm upon its dewy bed.

"Art thou a worm? Image of weakness, art thou but a worm?   80
I see thee like an infant wrapped in the lily's leaf.
Ah! weep not, little voice, thou canst not speak, but thou canst weep.
Is this a worm? I see thee lay helpless and naked, weeping,
And none to answer, none to cherish thee with mother's smiles."
The clod of clay heard the worm's voice, and raised her pitying head: 85
She bowed over the weeping infant, and her life exhaled
In milky fondness: then on Thel she fixed her humble eyes.

"O Beauty of the vales of Har! we live not for ourselves.
Thou seest me, the meanest thing, and so I am indeed.
My bosom of itself is cold, and of itself is dark;   90
But he that loves the lowly pours his oil upon my head,
And kisses me, and binds his nuptial bands around my breast,
And says: 'Thou mother of my children, I have lovèd thee,
And I have given thee a crown that none can take away.'
But how this is, sweet maid, I know not, and I cannot know;   95
I ponder, and I cannot ponder; yet I live and love."

The daughter of beauty wiped her pitying tears with her white veil,
And said: "Alas! I knew not this, and therefore did I weep.
That God would love a worm I knew, and punish the evil foot
That wilful bruised its helpless form; but that he cherished it   100
With milk and oil I never knew, and therefore did I weep,
And I complained in the mild air, because I fade away,
And lay me down in thy cold bed, and leave my shining lot."

"Queen of the vales." the matron Clay answered, "I heard thy sighs,
And all thy moans flew o'er my roof, but I have called them down.   105
Wilt thou, O Queen, enter my house? 'Tis given thee to enter,
And to return: fear nothing, enter with thy virgin feet."

IV

The eternal gates' terrific porter lifted the northern bar;
Thel entered in and saw the secrets of the land unknown.
She saw the couches of the dead, and where the fibrous roots   110
Of every heart on earth infixes deep its restless twists:
A land of sorrows and of tears where never smile was seen.

She wandered in the land of clouds through valleys dark, listening
Dolours and lamentations; waiting oft beside a dewy grave
She stood in silence, listening to the voices of the ground,   115
Till to her own grave-plot she came, and there she sat down,
And heard this voice of sorrow breathed from the hollow pit.

"Why cannot the ear be closed to its own destruction?
Or the glistening eye to the poison of a smile?
Why are eyelids stored with arrows ready drawn,   120
Where a thousand fighting men in ambush lie?
Or an eye of gifts and graces showering fruits and coined gold?

Why a tongue impressed with honey from every wind?
Why an ear, a whirlpool fierce to draw creations in?
Why a nostril wide inhaling terror, trembling, and affright?   125
Why a tender curb upon the youthful burning boy?
Why a little curtain of flesh on the bed of our desire?"

The virgin started from her seat, and with a shriek
Fled back unhindered till she came into the vales of Har.

1789

FROM THE FRENCH REVOLUTION

[THE BASTILLE—DEMOCRACY—PEACE]

The Commons convene in the Hall of the Nation. France shakes! And the heavens
    of France
Perplexed vibrate round each careful countenance! Darkness of old times around them
Utters loud despair, shadowing Paris; her grey towers groan, and the Bastille trembles.
In its terrible towers the Governor stood, in dark fogs listening the horror;
A thousand his soldiers, old veterans of France, breathing red clouds of power and
    dominion.   20
Sudden seized with howlings, despair, and black night, he stalked like a lion from tower
To tower; his howlings were heard in the Louvre; from court to court restless he
    dragged
His strong limbs; from court to court cursed the fierce torment unquelled,
Howling and giving the dark command; in his soul stood the purple plague,
Tugging his iron manacles, and piercing thro' the seven towers dark and sickly,   25
Panting over the prisoners like a wolf gorged. And the den named Horror held a man
Chained hand and foot; round his neck an iron band, bound to the impregnable wall;
In his soul was the serpent coiled round in his heart, hid from the light, as in a cleft
    rock:
And the man was confined for a writing prophetic. In the tower named Darkness was
    a man

Pinioned down to the stone floor, his strong bones scarce covered with sinews; the iron
    rings   30
Were forged smaller as the flesh decayed: a mask of iron on his face hid the lineaments
Of ancient Kings, and the frown of the eternal lion was hid from the oppressèd earth.
In the tower namèd Bloody, a skeleton yellow remainèd in its chains on its couch
Of stone, once a man who refused to sign papers of abhorrence; the eternal worm
Crept in the skeleton. In the den named Religion, a loathsome sick woman bound
    down   35
To a bed of straw; the seven diseases of earth, like birds of prey, stood on the couch
And fed on the body: she refused to be whore to the Minister, and with a knife smote
    him.
In the tower named Order, an old man, whose white beard covered the stone floor like
    weeds
On margin of the sea, shrivelled up by heat of day and cold of night; his den was short
And narrow as a grave dug for a child, with spiders' webs wove, and with slime   40
Of ancient horrors covered, for snakes and scorpions are his companions; harmless they
    breathe
His sorrowful breath: he, by conscience urged, in the city of Paris raised a pulpit,
And taught wonders to darkened souls. In the den named Destiny a strong man sat,
His feet and hands cut off, and his eyes blinded; round his middle a chain and a band
Fastened into the wall; fancy gave him to see an image of despair in his den,   45
Eternally rushing round, like a man on his hands and knees, day and night without rest:
He was friend to the favorite. In the seventh tower, named the tower of God, was a man
Mad, with chains loose, which he dragged up and down; fed with hopes year by year,
    he pined
For liberty; vain hopes! his reason decayed, and the world of attraction in his bosom
Centered, and the rushing of chaos overwhelmed his dark soul. He was confined   50
For a letter of advice to a King, and his ravings in winds are heard over Versailles.

       .   .   .   .

Aumont went out and stood in the hollow porch, his ivory wand in his hand;
A cold orb of disdain revolved round him, and covered his soul with snows eternal.
Great Henry's soul shuddered, a whirlwind and fire tore furious from his angry
    bosom;   200
He indignant departed on horses of heaven. Then the Abbé de Sieyes raised his feet
On the steps of the Louvre; like a voice of God following a storm, the Abbé followed
The pale fires of Aumont into the chamber; as a father that bows to his son,
Whose rich fields inheriting spread their old glory, so the voice of the people bowed
Before the ancient seat of the kingdom and mountains to be renewed.   205

"Hear, O Heavens of France! the voice of the people, arising from valley and hill,
O'erclouded with power. Hear the voice of valleys, the voice of meek cities,
Mourning oppressed on village and field, till the village and field is a waste.
For the husbandman weeps at blights of the fife, and blasting of trumpets consume
The souls of mild France; the pale mother nourishes her child to the deadly slaughter. 210

When the heavens were sealed with a stone, and the terrible sun closed in an orb, and
    the moon
Rent from the nations, and each star appointed for watchers of night,
The millions of spirits immortal were bound in the ruins of sulphur, heaven
To wander enslaved; black, depressed in dark ignorance, kept in awe with the whip
To worship terrors, bred from the blood of revenge and breath of desire   215
In bestial forms, or more terrible men; till the dawn of our peaceful morning,
Till dawn, till morning, till the breaking of clouds, and swelling of winds, and the uni-
    versal voice;
Till man raise his darkened limbs out of the caves of night: his eyes and his heart
Expand: Where is Space? where, O Sun, is thy dwelling? where thy tent, O faint
    slumb'rous Moon?
Then the valleys of France shall cry to the soldier: 'Throw down thy sword and
    musket,   220

And run and embrace the meek peasant.' Her nobles shall hear and shall weep, and
    put off
The red robe of terror, the crown of oppression, the shoes of contempt, and unbuckle
The girdle of war from the desolate earth; then the Priest in his thunderous cloud
Shall weep, bending to earth, embracing the valleys, and putting his hand to the plough,
Shall say, 'No more I curse thee; but now I will bless thee; no more in deadly black 225
Devour thy labor; nor lift up a cloud in thy heavens, O laborious plough,
That the wild raging millions, that wander in forests, and howl in law-blasted wastes,
Strength maddened with slavery, honesty bound in the dens of superstition,
May sing in the village, and shout in the harvest, and woo in pleasant gardens
Their once savage loves, now beaming with knowledge, with gentle awe adorned;   230
And the saw, and the hammer, the chisel, the pencil, the pen, and the instruments
Of heavenly song sound in the wilds once forbidden, to teach the laborious ploughman
And shepherd, delivered from clouds of war, from pestilence, from night-fear, from
    murder,
From falling, from stifling, from hunger, from cold, from slander, discontent, and sloth,
That walk in beasts and birds of night, driven back by the sandy desert,   235
Like pestilent fogs round cities of men; and the happy earth sings in its course,
The mild peaceable nations are opened to heaven, and men walk with their fathers in
    bliss.'
Then hear the first voice of the morning: 'Depart, O clouds of night, and no more
Return; be withdrawn cloudy war, troops of warriors depart, nor around our peaceable
    city
Breathe fires; but ten miles from Paris let all be peace, nor a soldier be seen!' "   240
1791   1791

FROM THE MARRIAGE OF HEAVEN AND HELL

THE VOICE OF THE DEVIL

All Bibles or sacred codes have been the causes of the following Errors:—

1. That Man has two real existing principles, viz. a Body and a Soul.

2. That Energy, called Evil, is alone 10 from the Body; and that Reason, called Good, is alone from the Soul.

3. That God will torment Man in Eternity for following his Energies.

But the following Contraries to these are 15 True:—

1. Man has no Body distinct from his Soul; for that called Body is a portion of Soul discerned by the five Senses, the chief inlets of the Soul in this age.   20

2. Energy is the only life, and is from the Body; and the Reason is the bound or outward circumference of Energy.

3. Energy is Eternal Delight.

. . . .   25

Note: The reason Milton wrote in fetters when he wrote of Angels and God, and at liberty when of Devils and Hell, is because 30 he was a true Poet and of the Devil's party without knowing it.

A MEMORABLE FANCY

As I was walking among the fires of Hell, delighted with the enjoyments of Genius,
5 which to Angels look like torment and insanity, I collected some of their Proverbs; thinking that as the sayings used in a nation mark its character, so the Proverbs of Hell show the nature of Infernal wisdom better than any description of buildings or garments.

When I came home: on the abyss of the five senses, where a flat sided steep frowns over the present world, I saw a mighty devil folded in black clouds, hovering on the sides of the rock: with corroding fires he wrote the following sentence now perceived by the minds of men, and read by them on earth:—

How do you know but every Bird that cuts the airy way,
Is an immense world of delights, closed by your senses five?

PROVERBS OF HELL

The road of excess leads to the palace of wisdom.

Prudence is a rich, ugly old maid courted by Incapacity . . .

A fool sees not the same tree that a wise man sees . . .

Eternity is in love with the productions of time . . .

The hours of folly are measured by the clock; but of wisdom no clock can measure . . .

If the fool would persist in his folly he would become wise . . .

Prisons are built with stones of Law, Brothels with bricks of Religion.

The pride of the peacock is the glory of God.

The lust of the goat is the bounty of God.

The wrath of the lion is the wisdom of God.

The nakedness of woman is the work of God . . .

The roaring of lions, the howling of wolves, the raging of the stormy sea, and the destructive sword, are portions of eternity, too great for the eye of man . . .

What is now proved was once only imagined . . .

The tigers of wrath are wiser than the horses of instruction . . .

When thou seest an Eagle, thou seest a portion of Genius; lift up thy head!

As the caterpillar chooses the fairest leaves to lay her eggs on, so the priest lays his curse on the fairest joys . . .

Improvement makes straight roads; but the crooked roads without improvement are roads of Genius.

Sooner murder an infant in its cradle than nurse unacted desires . . .

A MEMORABLE FANCY

The prophets Isaiah and Ezekiel dined with me, and I asked them how they dared so roundly to assert that God spoke to them; and whether they did not think at the time that they would be misunderstood, and so be the cause of imposition.

Isaiah answered: "I saw no God, nor heard any, in a finite organical perception; but my senses discovered the infinite in everything, and as I was then persuaded, and remain confirmed, that the voice of honest indignation is the voice of God, I cared not for consequences, but wrote."

Then I asked: "Does a firm persuasion that a thing is so, make it so?"

He replied: "All poets believe that it does, and in ages of imagination this firm persuasion removed mountains; but many are not capable of a firm persuasion of anything."

A MEMORABLE FANCY

Once I saw a Devil in a flame of fire, who arose before an Angel that sat on a cloud, and the Devil uttered these words:—

"The worship of God is: Honoring his gifts in other men, each according to his genius, and loving the greatest men best: those who envy or calumniate great men hate God; for there is no other God."

The Angel hearing this became almost blue; but mastering himself he grew yellow, and at last white, pink, and smiling, and then replied:

"Thou Idolater! is not God One? and is not he visible in Jesus Christ? and has not Jesus Christ given his sanction to the law of ten commandments? and are not all other men fools, sinners, and nothings?"

The Devil answered: "Bray a fool in a mortar with wheat, yet shall not his folly be beaten out of him. If Jesus Christ is the greatest man, you ought to love him in the greatest degree. Now hear how he has given his sanction to the law of ten commandments. Did he not mock at the sabbath, and so mock the sabbath's God? murder those who were murdered because of him? turn away the law from the woman taken in adultery; steal the labor of others to support him? bear false witness when he omitted making a defense before Pilate? covet when he prayed for his disciples, and when he bid them shake off the dust of their feet against such as refused to lodge them? I tell you, no virtue can exist without breaking these ten commandments. Jesus was all virtue, and acted from impulse, not from rules."

When he had so spoken, I beheld the Angel, who stretched out his arms, embracing the flame of fire, and he was consumed and arose as Elijah.

Note: This Angel, who is now become a Devil, is my particular friend. We often read the Bible together in its infernal or diabolical sense, which the world shall have if they behave well.

I have also The Bible of Hell, which the world shall have whether they will or no.

One Law for the Lion and Ox is Oppression.

c. 1793

A SONG OF LIBERTY

The Eternal Female groaned! it was heard over all the Earth.

Albion's coast is sick, silent; the Ameri- 5 can meadows faint!

Shadows of Prophecy shiver along by the lakes and the rivers, and mutter across the ocean: France, rend down thy dun- 10 geon!

Golden Spain, burst the barriers of old Rome!

Cast thy keys, O Rome, into the deep down falling, even to eternity down fall- 15 ing,

And weep.

In her trembling hands she took the new born terror, howling.

On those infinite mountains of light, now barred out by the Atlantic sea, the 20 new born fire stood before the starry king!

Flagged with grey browed snows and thunderous visages, the jealous wings waved over the deep.

The speary hand burned aloft, un- 25 buckled was the shield; forth went the hand of jealousy among the flaming hair, and hurled the new born wonder through the starry night.

The fire, the fire is falling! 30

Look up! look up! O citizen of London, enlarge thy countenance! O Jew, leave counting gold! return to thy oil and wine. O African! black African! (go, winged 35 thought, widen his forehead.)

The fiery limbs, the flaming hair, shot like the sinking sun into the western sea.

Waked from his eternal sleep, the hoary element roaring fled away.

Down rushed, beating his wings in vain, the jealous king; his grey browed coun- 5 sellors, thunderous warriors, curled vet- erans, among helms, and shields, and chariots, horses, elephants, banners, castles, slings, and rocks.

Falling, rushing, ruining! buried in the 10 ruins; on Urthona's dens;

All night beneath the ruins; then, their sullen flames faded, emerge round the gloomy king.

With thunder and fire, leading his 15 starry hosts through the waste wilderness, he promulgates his ten commands, glanc- ing his beamy eyelids over the deep in dark dismay,

Where the son of fire in his eastern 20 cloud, while the morning plumes her golden breast,

Spurning the clouds written with curses, stamps the stony law to dust, loosing the eternal horses from the dens of night, 25 crying: *Empire is no more! and now the lion and wolf shall cease.*

CHORUS

Let the Priests of the Raven of dawn no 30 longer, in deadly black, with hoarse note curse the sons of joy. Nor his accepted brethren—whom, tyrant, he calls free—lay the bound or build the roof. Nor pale 35 Religious lechery call that virginity that wishes but acts not!

For every thing that lives is Holy.

c. 1793

FROM VISIONS OF THE DAUGHTERS OF ALBION

"I cry: Love! Love! Love! happy happy Love! free as the mountain wind!
Can that be Love, that drinks another as a sponge drinks water,
That clouds with jealousy his nights, with weepings all the day,
To spin a web of age around him, grey and hoary, dark;
Till his eyes sicken at the fruit that hangs before his sight? 195
Such is self-love that envies all, a creeping skeleton,
With lamplike eyes watching around the frozen marriage bed!

"But silken nets and traps of adamant will Oothoon spread,
And catch for thee girls of mild silver, or of furious gold.
I'll lie beside thee on a bank, and view their wanton play 200
In lovely copulation, bliss on bliss, with Theotormon:
Red as the rosy morning, lustful as the first-born beam,
Oothoon shall view his dear delight; nor e'er with jealous cloud
Come in the heaven of generous love, nor selfish blightings bring.

"Does the sun walk, in glorious raiment, on the secret floor 205
Where the cold miser spreads his gold; or does the bright cloud drop

On his stone threshold? Does his eye behold the beam that brings
Expansion to the eye of pity; or will he bind himself
Beside the ox to thy hard furrow? Does not that mild beam blot
The bat, the owl, the glowing tiger, and the king of night?   210
The sea-fowl takes the wintry blast for a cov'ring to her limbs,
And the wild snake the pestilence to adorn him with gems and gold;
And trees, and birds, and beasts, and men behold their eternal joy.
Arise, you little glancing wings, and sing your infant joy!
Arise, and drink your bliss, for everything that lives is holy!"   215

Thus every morning wails Oothoon; but Theotormon sits
Upon the margined ocean conversing with shadows dire.

The Daughters of Albion hear her woes, and echo back her sighs.

1793

FROM AMERICA: A PROPHECY

A voice came forth, and shook the temple:—

"The morning comes, the night decays, the watchmen leave their stations;
The grave is burst, the spices shed, the linen wrappèd up;
The bones of death, the cov'ring clay, the sinews shrunk and dried
Reviving shake, inspiring move, breathing, awakening,   40
Spring like redeemèd captives, when their bonds and bars are burst,
Let the slave grinding at the mill run out into the field,
Let him look up into the heavens and laugh in the bright air;
Let the enchainèd soul, shut up in darkness and in sighing,
Whose face has never seen a smile in thirty weary years,   45
Rise and look out; his chains are loose, his dungeon doors are open;
And let his wife and children return from the oppressor's scourge.
They look behind at every step, and believe it is a dream,
Singing: 'The Sun has left his blackness, and has found a fresher morning,
And the fair Moon rejoices in the clear and cloudless night;   50
For Empire is no more, and now the Lion and Wolf shall cease.' "

1793

FROM SONGS OF EXPERIENCE

INTRODUCTION

Hear the voice of the bard!
Who present, past, and future, sees;
   Whose ears have heard
   The Holy Word
That walked among the ancient trees,   5

Calling the lapsèd soul,
And weeping in the evening dew;
   That might control
   The starry pole,
And fallen fallen light renew!   10

"O Earth, O Earth, return!
Arise from out the dewy grass;
   Night is worn,
   And the morn
Rises from the slumberous mass.   15

"Turn away no more;
Why wilt thou turn away?
   The starry floor,
   The wat'ry shore,
Is giv'n thee till the break of day."   20

1794

EARTH'S ANSWER

Earth raised up her head
From the darkness dread and drear.
   Her light fled,
   Stony dread!
And her locks covered with grey despair.   5

"Prisoned on wat'ry shore,
Starry Jealousy does keep my den:
   Cold and hoar,
   Weeping o'er,
I hear the Father of the Ancient Men.   10

"Selfish Father of Men!
Cruel, jealous, selfish Fear!
Can delight,
Chained in night,
The virgins of youth and morning bear? 15

"Does spring hide its joy
When buds and blossoms grow?
Does the sower
Sow by night,
Or the ploughman in darkness plough? 20

"Break this heavy chain
That does freeze my bones around.
Selfish! vain!
Eternal bane!
That free Love with bondage bound." 25

1794

THE CLOD AND THE PEBBLE

"Love seeketh not itself to please,
    Nor for itself hath any care,
But for another gives its ease,
    And builds a Heaven in Hell's despair."

So sung a little clod of clay, 5
    Trodden with the cattle's feet,
But a pebble of the brook
    Warbled out these metres meet:

"Love seeketh only self to please,
    To bind another to its delight, 10
Joys in another's loss of ease,
    And builds a Hell in Heaven's despite."

1794

HOLY THURSDAY

Is this a holy thing to see
    In a rich and fruitful land,—
Babes reduced to misery,
    Fed with cold and usurous hand?

Is that trembling cry a song? 5
    Can it be a song of joy?
And so many children poor?
    It is a land of poverty!

And their sun does never shine,
    And their fields are bleak and bare, 10
And their ways are filled with thorns—
    It is eternal winter there.

For where'er the sun does shine,
    And where'er the rain does fall,
Babe can never hunger there, 15
    Nor poverty the mind appal.

1794

THE CHIMNEY-SWEEPER

A little black thing among the snow,
Crying "'weep! 'weep!" in notes of woe!
"Where are thy father and mother, say?"—
"They are both gone up to the Church to
    pray.

"Because I was happy upon the heath, 5
And smiled among the winter's snow,
They clothèd me in the clothes of death,
And taught me to sing the notes of woe.

"And because I am happy and dance and
    sing,
They think they have done me no in-
    jury, 10
And are gone to praise God and His Priest
    and King,
Who make up a Heaven of our misery."

1794

NURSE'S SONG

When the voices of children are heard on
    the green
And whisp'rings are in the dale,
The days of my youth rise fresh in my
    mind,
My face turns green and pale.

Then come home, my children, the sun is
    gone down, 5
And the dews of night arise;
Your spring and your day are wasted in
    play,
And your winter and night in disguise.

1794

THE SICK ROSE

O rose, thou art sick!
    The invisible worm,
That flies in the night,
    In the howling storm,

Has found out thy bed 5
    Of crimson joy;
And his dark secret love
    Does thy life destroy.

1794

THE FLY

Little Fly,
Thy summer's play
My thoughtless hand
Has brushed away.

Am not I 5
A fly like thee?
Or art not thou
A man like me?

For I dance,
And drink, and sing, 10
Till some blind hand
Shall brush my wing.

1794

THE ANGEL

I dreamt a dream! what can it mean?
And that I was a maiden Queen,
Guarded by an Angel mild:
Witless woe was ne'er beguiled!

And I wept both night and day, 5
And he wiped my tears away,
And I wept both day and night,
And hid from him my heart's delight.

So he took his wings and fled;
Then the morn blushed rosy red; 10
I dried my tears, and armed my fears
With ten thousand shields and spears.

Soon my Angel came again:
I was armed, he came in vain;
For the time of youth was fled, 15
And grey hairs were on my head.

1794

THE TIGER

Tiger! tiger! burning bright
In the forests of the night,
What immortal hand or eye
Could frame thy fearful symmetry?

In what distant deeps or skies 5
Burnt the fire of thine eyes?
On what wings dare he aspire?
What the hand dare seize the fire?

And what shoulder and what art
Could twist the sinews of thy heart? 10
And, when thy heart began to beat,
What dread hand? and what dread feet?

What the hammer? what the chain?
In what furnace was thy brain?
What the anvil? what dread grasp 15
Dare its deadly terrors clasp!

When the stars threw down their spears,
And watered heaven with their tears,
Did he smile his work to see?
Did he who made the lamb make thee? 20

Tiger! tiger! burning bright
In the forests of the night,
What immortal hand or eye
Dare frame thy fearful symmetry?

1794

AH, SUNFLOWER

Ah, Sunflower! weary of time,
Who countest the steps of the sun,
Seeking after that sweet golden clime
Where the traveller's journey is done:

Where the youth pined away with desire, 5
And the pale virgin shrouded in snow,
Arise from their graves, and aspire
Where my Sunflower wishes to go.

1794

THE GARDEN OF LOVE

I went to the Garden of Love
And saw what I never had seen;
A chapel was built in the midst,
Where I used to play on the green.

And the gates of this chapel were shut, 5
And "Thou shalt not" writ over the
door;
So I turned to the Garden of Love
That so many sweet flowers bore;

And I saw it was filled with graves,
And tombstones where flowers should
be; 10
And priests in black gowns were walking
their rounds,
And binding with briars my joys and
desires.

1794

LONDON

I wander through each chartered street,
Near where the chartered Thames does
flow,
And mark in every face I meet
Marks of weakness, marks of woe.

In every cry of every man, 5
In every infant's cry of fear,
In every voice, in every ban,
The mind-forged manacles I hear.

How the chimney-sweeper's cry
Every blackening church appals; 10
And the hapless soldier's sigh
Runs in blood down palace walls.

But most through midnight streets I hear
How the youthful harlot's curse
Blasts the new-born infant's tear, 15
And blights with plagues the marriage
    hearse.

1794

THE HUMAN ABSTRACT

Pity would be no more
If we did not make somebody poor;
And Mercy no more could be
If all were as happy as we.

And mutual fear brings peace, 5
Till the selfish loves increase;
Then Cruelty knits a snare,
And spreads his baits with care.

He sits down with holy fears,
And waters the ground with tears; 10
Then Humility takes its root
Underneath his foot.

Soon spreads the dismal shade
Of Mystery over his head;

And the caterpillar and fly 15
Feed on the Mystery.

And it bears the fruit of Deceit,
Ruddy and sweet to eat;
And the raven his nest has made
In its thickest shade. 20

The Gods of the earth and sea
Sought thro' Nature to find this tree;
But their search was all in vain:
There grows one in the Human brain.

1794

INFANT SORROW

My mother groaned, my father wept,
Into the dangerous world I leapt;
Helpless, naked, piping loud,
Like a fiend hid in a cloud.

Struggling in my father's hands, 5
Striving against my swaddling-bands,
Bound and weary, I thought best
To sulk upon my mother's breast.

1794

FROM THE FOUR ZOAS: NIGHT TWO

THE PRICE OF EXPERIENCE

I am made to sow the thistle for wheat, the nettle for a nourishing dainty: 595
I have planted a false oath in the earth; it has brought forth a Poison Tree:
I have chosen the serpent for a counsellor, and the dog
For a schoolmaster to my children:
I have blotted out from light and living the dove and nightingale,
And I have causèd the earthworm to beg from door to door: 600
I have taught the thief a secret path into the house of the just:
I have taught pale Artifice to spread his nets upon the morning.
My heavens are brass, my earth is iron, my moon a clod of clay,
My sun a pestilence burning at noon, and a vapor of death in night.

What is the price of Experience? Do men buy it for a song, 605
Or Wisdom for a dance in the street? No! it is bought with the price
Of all that a man hath—his house, his wife, his children.
Wisdom is sold in the desolate market where none come to buy,
And in the withered field where the farmer ploughs for bread in vain.

It is an easy thing to triumph in the summer's sun, 610
And in the vintage, and to sing on the waggon loaded with corn:
It is an easy thing to talk of patience to the afflicted,
To speak the laws of prudence to the houseless wanderer,
To listen to the hungry raven's cry in wintry season,
When the red blood is filled with wine and with the marrow of lambs: 615

It is an easy thing to laugh at wrathful elements;
To hear the dog howl at the wintry door, the ox in the slaughterhouse moan;
To see a God on every wind and a blessing on every blast;

To hear sounds of Love in the thunderstorm that destroys our enemy's house;
To rejoice in the blight that covers his field, and the sickness that cuts off his chil-
    dren,   620
While our olive and vine sing and laugh round our door, and our children bring fruits
    and flowers.

Then the groan and the dolor are quite forgotten, and the slave grinding at the mill,
And the captive in chains, and the poor in the prison, and the soldier in the field
When the shattered bone hath laid him groaning among the happier dead:
It is an easy thing to rejoice in the tents of prosperity—   625
Thus would I sing and thus rejoice; but it is not so with me.

1795-1804   1797

[A WORLD OF IMAGINATION AND VISION]

To the Rev. Dr. Trusler

Rev. Sir:

... I perceive that your eye is perverted by caricature prints, which ought not to abound as much as they do. Fun I love, but too much fun is of all things the most loathsome. Mirth is better than fun, and happiness is better than mirth. I feel that a man may be happy in this world. And I know that this world is a world of imagination and vision. I see everything I paint in this world, but everybody does not see alike. To the eyes of a miser a guinea is far more beautiful than the sun, and a bag worn with the use of money has more beautiful proportions than a vine filled with grapes. The tree which moves some to tears of joy is in the eyes of others only a green thing which stands in the way. Some see nature all ridicule and deformity, and by these I shall not regulate my proportions; and some scarce see nature at all. But to the eyes of the man of imagination, nature is imagination itself. As a man is, so he sees. As the eye is formed, such are its powers. You certainly mistake, when you say that the visions of fancy are not to be found in this world. To me this world is all one continued vision of fancy or imagination, and I feel flattered when I am told so. What is it sets Homer, Virgil and Milton in so high a rank of art? Why is the Bible more entertaining and instructive than any other book? Is it not because they are addressed to the imagination, which is spiritual sensation, and but mediately to the understanding or reason? Such is true painting, and such was alone valued by the Greeks and the best modern artists. Consider what Lord Bacon says: "Sense sends over to Imagination before Reason have judged, and Reason sends over to Imagination before the decree can be acted." ...

But I am happy to find a great majority of fellow mortals who can elucidate my visions, and particularly they been elucidated by children, who have taken a greater delight in contemplating my pictures than I even hoped. Neither youth nor childhood is folly or incapacity. Some children are fools and so are some old men. But there is a vast majority on the side of imagination or spiritual sensation. ...

I am, Rev. Sir, your very obedient servant,

Lambeth;
August 23, 1799.

WILLIAM BLAKE

TO TIRZAH

Whate'er is born of mortal birth
Must be consumèd with the earth,
To rise from generation free:
Then what have I to do with thee?

The sexes sprung from shame and pride, 5
Blowed in the morn; in evening died;
But Mercy changed death into sleep;
The sexes rose to work and weep.

Thou, Mother of my mortal part,
With cruelty didst mold my heart,   10
And with false self-deceiving tears
Didst bind my nostrils, eyes, and ears;

Didst close my tongue in senseless clay,
And me to mortal life betray:
The death of Jesus set me free: 15
Then what have I to do with thee?

c. 1801

THE MENTAL TRAVELLER

I travelled through a land of men,
  A land of men and women too,
And heard and saw such dreadful things
  As cold earth-wanderers never knew.

For there the babe is born in joy   5
  That was begotten in dire woe;
Just as we reap in joy the fruit
  Which we in bitter tears did sow.

And, if the babe is born a boy,
  He's given to a woman old,   10
Who nails him down upon a rock,
  Catches his shrieks in cups of gold.

She binds iron thorns around his head,
  She pierces both his hands and feet,
She cuts his heart out at his side   15
  To make it feel both cold and heat.

Her fingers number every nerve,
  Just as a miser counts his gold;
She lives upon his shrieks and cries,
  And she grows young as he grows old.   20

Till he becomes a bleeding youth,
  And she becomes a virgin bright;
Then he rends up his manacles
  And binds her down for his delight.

He plants himself in all her nerves,   25
  Just as a husbandman his mould;
And she becomes his dwelling-place
  And garden fruitful seventy fold.

An aged shadow, soon he fades,
  Wandering round an earthly cot   30
Full filled all with gems and gold
  Which he by industry had got.

And these are the gems of the human soul,
  The rubies and pearls of a lovesick eye,
The countless gold of the aching heart,   35
  The martyr's groan and the lover's sigh.

They are his meat, they are his drink;
  He feeds the beggar and the poor
And the wayfaring traveller:
  Forever open is his door.   40

His grief is their eternal joy;
  They make the roofs and walls to ring;
Till from the fire on the hearth
  A little female babe does spring.

And she is all of solid fire   45
  And gems and gold, that none his hand
Dares stretch to touch her baby form,
  Or wrap her in his swaddling-band.

But she comes to the man she loves,
  If young or old, or rich or poor;   50
They soon drive out the aged host,
  A beggar at another's door.

He wanders weeping far away,
  Until some other take him in;
Oft blind and age-bent, sore distressed,   55
  Until he can a maiden win.

And, to allay his freezing age,
  The poor man takes her in his arms;
The cottage fades before his sight,
  The garden and its lovely charms.   60

The guests are scattered through the land,
  For the eye altering alters all;
The senses roll themselves in fear,
  And the flat earth becomes a ball;

The stars, sun, moon, all shrink away,   65
  A desert vast without a bound,
And nothing left to eat or drink,
  And a dark desert all around.

The honey of her infant lips,
  The bread and wine of her sweet
    smile,   70
The wild game of her roving eye,
  Does him to infancy beguile;

For as he eats and drinks, he grows
  Younger and younger every day;
And on the desert wild they both   75
  Wander in terror and dismay.

Like the wild stag she flees away;
  Her fear plants many a thicket wild;
While he pursues her night and day
  By various arts of love beguiled,   80

By various arts of love and hate,
  Till the wild desert planted o'er
With labyrinths of wayward love,
  Where roam the lion, wolf, and boar,

Till he becomes a wayward babe,   85
  And she a weeping woman old.
Then many a lover wanders here;
  The sun and stars are nearer rolled.

The trees bring forth sweet ecstasy
  To all who in the desert roam;   90
Till many a city there is built
  And many a pleasant shepherd's home.

But, when they find the frowning babe,
  Terror strikes through the region wide:
They cry, "The babe! the babe is born!"   95
  And flee away on every side.

For who dare touch the frowning form,
His arm is withered to its root;
Lions, boars, wolves, all howling flee.
And every tree does shed its fruit.   100

And none can touch that frowning form,
Except it be a woman old;
She nails him down upon the rock,
And all is done as I have told.

c. 1803   1863

FROM AUGURIES OF INNOCENCE

To see a World in a grain of sand,
And a Heaven in a wild flower,
Hold Infinity in the palm of your hand,
And Eternity in an hour.

A robin redbreast in a cage   5
Puts all Heaven in a rage.
A dove-house filled with doves and pigeons
Shudders hell through all its regions.
A dog starved at his master's gate
Predicts the ruin of the state.   10
A horse misused upon the road
Calls to Heaven for human blood.
Each outcry of the hunted hare
A fibre from the brain does tear.
A skylark wounded in the wing,   15
A cherubim does cease to sing.
The game-cock clipped and armed for fight
Does the rising sun affright.
Every wolf's and lion's howl
Raises from hell a human soul.   20
The wild deer, wandering here and there,
Keeps the human soul from care.
The lamb misused breeds public strife,
And yet forgives the butcher's knife.

The bat that flits at close of eve   25
Has left the brain that won't believe.
The owl that calls upon the night
Speaks the unbeliever's fright.
He who shall hurt the little wren
Shall never be beloved by men.   30
He who the ox to wrath has moved
Shall never be by woman loved.
The wanton boy that kills the fly
Shall feel the spider's enmity.
He who torments the chafer's sprite   35
Weaves a bower in endless night.
The caterpillar on the leaf
Repeats to thee thy mother's grief.
Kill not the moth nor butterfly,
For the Last Judgment draweth nigh.   40
He who shall train the horse to war
Shall never pass the polar bar.
The beggar's dog and widow's cat,
Feed them, and thou wilt grow fat.

. . . .

The babe that weeps the rod beneath
Writes revenge in realms of death.
The beggar's rags, fluttering in air,   75
Does to rags the heavens tear.
The soldier, armed with sword and gun,
Palsied strikes the summer's sun.
The poor man's farthing is worth more
Than all the gold on Afric's shore.   80
One mite wrung from the laborer's hands
Shall buy and sell the miser's lands:
Or, if protected from on high,
Does that whole nation sell and buy.
He who mocks the infant's faith   85
Shall be mocked in age and death.
He who shall teach the child to doubt
The rotting grave shall ne'er get out.
He who respects the infant's faith
Triumphs over hell and death.   90

c. 1803

FROM MILTON

PREFACE

And did those feet in ancient time
  Walk upon England's mountains green?
And was the holy Lamb of God
  On England's pleasant pastures seen?

And did the countenance divine   5
  Shine forth upon our clouded hills?
And was Jerusalem builded here
  Among these dark Satanic mills?

Bring me my bow of burning gold:
  Bring me my arrows of desire: 10
Bring me my spear: O clouds, unfold!
  Bring me my chariot of fire.

I will not cease from mental fight,
Nor shall my sword sleep in my hand
Till we have built Jerusalem   15
In England's green and pleasant land.

THE FLOWERS

Thou perceivest the Flowers put forth their precious Odors;
And none can tell how from so small a center comes such sweet,   20
Forgetting that within that center Eternity expands
Its ever-during doors, that Og and Anak fiercely guard.
First, ere the morning breaks, joy opens in the flowery bosoms,
Joy even to tears, which the Sun rising dries: first the Wild Thyme
And Meadow-sweet, downy and soft, waving among the reeds,   25
Light springing on the air, lead the sweet dance; they wake
The Honeysuckle sleeping on the oak; the flaunting beauty
Revels along upon the wind; the White-thorn, lovely May,
Opens her many lovely eyes; listening the Rose still sleeps—
None dare to wake her; soon she bursts her crimson-curtained bed 30
And comes forth in the majesty of beauty. Every Flower,
The Pink, the Jessamine, the Wallflower, the Carnation,
The Jonquil, the mild Lily opes her heavens; every Tree
And Flower and Herb soon fill the air with an innumerable dance,
Yet all in order sweet and lovely. Men are sick with love!   35
Such is a Vision of the lamentation of Beulah over Ololon.

[REASON AND IMAGINATION]

The negation is the Spectre, the reasoning power in man:
This is a false body, an incrustation over my immortal
Spirit, a selfhood which must be put off and annihilated alway.
To cleanse the face of my spirit by self-examination,
To bathe in the waters of life, to wash off the not human,   5
I come in self-annihilation and the grandeur of inspiration,
To cast off rational demonstration by faith in the Savior,
To cast off the rotten rags of memory by inspiration,
To cast off Bacon, Locke, and Newton from Albion's covering,
To take off his filthy garments and clothe him with imagination; 10
To cast aside from poetry all that is not inspiration,
That it no longer shall dare to mock with the aspersion of madness
Cast on the inspired by the tame high finisher of paltry blots
Indefinite, or paltry rhymes, or paltry harmonies,
Who creeps into state government like a caterpillar to destroy;   15
To cast off the idiot questioner, who is always questioning,
But never capable of answering, who sits with a sly grin
Silent plotting when to question, like a thief in a cave,
Who publishes doubt and calls it knowledge, whose science is despair,
Whose pretence to knowledge is envy, whose whole science is   20
To destroy the wisdom of ages to gratify ravenous envy
That rages round him like a wolf day and night without rest:
He smiles with condescension, he talks of benevolence and virtue,
And those who act with benevolence and virtue they murder time on time.
These are the destroyers of Jerusalem, these are the murderers   25
Of Jesus, who deny the faith and mock at eternal life,
Who pretend to poetry that they may destroy imagination
By imitation of nature's images drawn from remembrance.
These are the sexual garments, the abomination of desolation,
Hiding the human lineaments as with an ark and curtains   30
Which Jesus rent and now shall wholly purge away with fire
Till generation is swallowed up in regeneration.

                              1804-08

FROM JERUSALEM

TO THE DEISTS

I saw a Monk of Charlemaine
  Arise before my sight:
I talked with the Grey Monk as we
    stood
  In beams of infernal light.

Gibbon arose with a lash of steel,   5
  And Voltaire with a racking wheel:
The schools, in clouds of learning rolled,
  Arose with war in iron and gold.

"Thou lazy Monk," they sound afar,
  "In vain condemning glorious war;   10
And in your cell you shall ever dwell:
  Rise, War, and bind him in his cell!"

The blood red ran from the Grey Monk's
    side,
  His hands and feet were wounded wide,
His body bent, his arms and knees   15
  Like to the roots of ancient trees.

When Satan first the black bow bent
  And the moral law from the Gospel rent,
He forged the law into a sword,
  And spilled the blood of mercy's Lord. 20

Titus! Constantine! Charlemaine!
  O Voltaire! Rousseau! Gibbon! Vain
Your Grecian mocks and Roman sword
  Against this image of his Lord!

For a tear is an intellectual thing;   25
  And a sigh is the sword of an angel king,
And the bitter groan of a martyr's woe
  Is an arrow from the Almighty's bow.

                    1804-20

TO THE CHRISTIANS

I give you the end of a golden string,
  Only wind it into a ball,
It will lead you in at Heaven's gate
  Built in Jerusalem's wall . . .   5

I know of no other Christianity and of no other Gospel than the liberty both of body and mind to exercise the Divine Arts of Imagination—Imagination, the real and Eternal World of which this Vegetable Universe is but a faint shadow, and in which we shall live in our Eternal or Imaginative Bodies, when these Vegetable Mortal Bodies are no more. The Apostles knew of no other Gospel. What were all their spiritual gifts? What is the Divine Spirit? Is the Holy Ghost any other than an Intellectual Fountain? What is the harvest of the Gospel and its labors? What is that talent which it is a curse to hide? What are the treasures of Heaven which we are to lay up for ourselves? Are they any other than mental studies and performances? What are all the gifts of the Gospel? Are they not all mental gifts? Is God a Spirit who must be worshipped in spirit and in truth? And are not the gifts of the Spirit everything to Man? O ye Religious, discountenance every one among you who shall pretend to despise Art and Science! I call upon you in the name of Jesus! What is the life of Man but Art and Science? Is it meat and drink? Is not the Body more than raiment? What is Mortality but the things relating to the Body, which dies? What is Immortality but the things relating to the Spirit, which lives eternally? What is the Joy of Heaven but improvement in the things of the Spirit? What are the Pains of Hell but Ignorance, Bodily Lust, Idleness, and devastation of the things of the Spirit? Answer this to yourselves, and expel from among you those who pretend to despise the labors of Art and Science, which alone are the labors of the Gospel. Is not this plain and manifest to the thought? Can you think at all, and not pronounce heartily: that to labor in knowledge is to build up Jerusalem; and to despise knowledge is to despise Jerusalem and her Builders. And remember: He who despises and mocks a mental gift in another, calling it pride and selfishness and sin, mocks Jesus, the giver of every mental gift, which always appear to the ignorance-loving hypocrite as sins; but that which is a sin in the sight of cruel Man, is not so in the sight of our kind God. Let every Christian, as much as in him lies, engage himself openly and publicly, before all the World, in some mental pursuit for the Building up of Jerusalem.

                    1804-1820

FROM ANNOTATIONS TO SIR JOSHUA REYNOLDS' DISCOURSES

I consider Reynolds' *Discourses to the Royal Academy* as the simulations of the hypocrite who smiles particularly where he means to betray. His praise of Raphael is like the hysteric smile of revenge. His softness and candor, the hidden trap and poisoned feast. He praises Michael Angelo for qualities which Michael Angelo abhorred, and he blames Raphael for the only qualities which Raphael valued. Whether Reynolds knew what he was doing is nothing to me: the mischief is just the same whether a man does it ignorantly or knowingly. I always considered true art and true artists to be particularly insulted and degraded by the reputation of these *Discourses*, as much as they were degraded by the reputation of Reynolds' paintings, and that such artists as Reynolds are at all times hired by the Satans for the depression of art,—a pretence of art, to destroy art . . .

The rich men of England form themselves into a society to sell and not to buy pictures. The artist who does not throw his contempt on such trading exhibitions,

does not know either his own interest or his duty.

When nations grow old, the arts grow cold
And Commerce settles on every tree,
And the poor and the old can live upon gold,
For all are born poor, aged sixty-three.

Reynolds' opinion was that genius may be taught and that all pretence to inspiration is a lie and a deceit, to say the least of it. For if it is a deceit, the whole Bible is madness. This opinion originates in the Greeks' calling the Muses, Daughters of Memory.

The enquiry in England is not whether a man has talents and genius, but whether he is passive and polite and a virtuous ass and obedient to noblemen's opinions in art and science. If he is, he is a good man. If not, he must be starved . . .

I do not believe that Raphael taught Michael Angelo, or that Michael Angelo taught Raphael, any more than I believe that the rose teaches the lily how to grow, or the apple tree teaches the pear tree how to bear fruit. I do not believe the tales of anecdote writers when they militate against individual character.

c. 1808

DEDICATION OF THE ILLUSTRATIONS TO BLAIR'S GRAVE

TO THE QUEEN

The Door of Death is made of gold,
That mortal eyes cannot behold;
But when the mortal eyes are closed,
And cold and pale the limbs reposed,
The soul awakes; and, wond'ring, sees 5
In her mild hand the golden Keys:
The Grave is Heaven's Golden Gate,
And rich and poor around it wait;
O Shepherdess of England's fold,
Behold this Gate of Pearl and Gold! 10

1808

FROM THE EVERLASTING GOSPEL

Was Jesus chaste? or did he
Give any lessons of chastity?
The Morning blushed fiery red:
Mary was found in adulterous bed;
Earth groaned beneath, and Heaven above 5
Trembled at discovery of Love.
Jesus was sitting in Moses' chair,
They brought the trembling woman there.
Moses commands she be stoned to death,
What was the sound of Jesus' breath? 10
He laid His hand on Moses' law;
The ancient heavens, in silent awe,
Writ with curses from pole to pole,
All away began to roll.

c. 1818

SAMUEL TAYLOR COLERIDGE (1772-1834)

*One of the touchstones of supreme imaginative vision lies in its unerring
recognition of what is universal in the remote and strange.*

JOHN LIVINGSTON LOWES

The contrast is amazing between Coleridge's character, which was shockingly feeble, and his powers as a poet and critic, which were extraordinarily great. He was the son of a clergyman, and from his childhood devoted to reading, day-dreaming, and solitude. Yet he was not unsociable, and his classmates in school and college marveled at his eloquent conversation, or rather monologues, full of mysticism and radical politics. He had received a sound classical education at Christ's Hospital in London, and studied for about two years at Cambridge University; but up to the age of twenty-five he had lived in a visionary and vacillating manner, had drifted into an ill-advised marriage, and could point to no worthy achievement or fixed purpose. He and Southey had married sisters, and planned to emigrate to the United States, where on the banks of the Susquehanna they were to establish a socialistic "Pantisocracy" devoted to simple living and high thinking. Then, fortunately for both, Coleridge met Wordsworth; and in the next four years (1798-1802), aided by the friendship of the Wordsworth family, Coleridge found himself as a poet, becoming co-author of *The Lyrical Ballads*, and producing *The Ancient Mariner, France, Love, Christabel,* and *Kubla Khan.* It was in those years that he and Mrs. Wordsworth's sister, Sarah Hutchinson, fell in love with each other. This was the deepest passion of Coleridge's life (it inspired *Love*); but its hopelessness helped to render him, after his brief golden period as a poet, again wretched, unsettled, and ineffective. His health was poor, and the medical profession of his day did not know how to cure his ailments. To gain relief from his pain, he took opium, only to find the consequences worse than the disease. For a while he abstained entirely from opium, alcoholic beverages, and protein foods; but thus he raised another demon,—insomnia. He relapsed; and from the age of thirty to forty-three he was a slave to opium and alcohol, neglected his family, estranged his friends, and fell into humiliating dependence upon charitable benefactors.

At forty-three he took the step which saved him: he placed himself under the direction of a kind and wise physician, James Gillman, whose residence at Highgate, London, became his home for the remaining nineteen years of his life. There he produced his most notable prose works, including the *Biographia Literaria* (1816), and vainly attempted to compose a comprehensive treatise setting forth his entire philosophic system. His marvelous talk, ingenious and lofty, attracted disciples, even the dour young Carlyle bearing witness to the sublimity of "one who, alone in these dark days, had saved his crown of spiritual manhood; escaping from the black materialism and revolutionary deluges, with 'God, Freedom, Immortality' still his: a king of men." When Coleridge died, his schoolfellow Charles Lamb lamented that he was gone who "was the proof and touchstone of all my cogitations." And Wordsworth mourned him as "the most *wonderful* man" he had ever known.

We read the poetry of Coleridge with a sense of awe, because it expresses the marvelous and eternal mystery of the interpenetration of good and evil, of spirit and matter. It seems at once strange and true, for in showing the effects of the supernatural upon beings like the Ancient Mariner and Christabel, Coleridge remains unerringly faithful to our common human nature. He had the power to evoke an atmosphere of mystery, wonder, and pathos; and his command over the appropriate diction, rhythm, and harmony was complete. Those rationalistic critics who disbelieve in anything that points to the intermingling of the human and the spiritual, try to find faults in Coleridge; but to the unsophisticated spirit of mankind his best poems remain "a warm poetic joy."

In this book, the Selections from Coleridge's Prose (and the introductory remarks thereon) are placed after those from Wordsworth, because some of Coleridge's most important criticism deals with the poetry and the theories of Wordsworth.

PANTISOCRACY

No more my visionary soul shall dwell
On joys that were; no more endure to weigh
The shame and anguish of the evil day,
Wisely forgetful! O'er the ocean swell
Sublime of hope, I seek the cottaged dell　　　　　　5
Where virtue calm with careless step may stray,
And dancing to the moonlight roundelay,
The wizard passions weave an holy spell.
Eyes that have ached with sorrow! Ye shall weep
Tears of doubt-mingled joy, like theirs who start　　10
From precipices of distempered sleep,
On which the fierce-eyed fiends their revels keep,
And see the rising sun, and feel it dart
New rays of pleasance trembling to the heart.

1794　　　　　　　　　　　　　　　　　1849

LA FAYETTE

As when far off the warbled strains are heard
　　That soar on morning's wing the vales among;
　　Within his cage the imprisoned matin bird
Swells the full chorus with a generous song:

He bathes no pinion in the dewy light,　　　　　　5
　　No father's joy, no lover's bliss he shares,
　　Yet still the rising radiance cheers his sight—
His fellows' freedom soothes the captive's cares!

Thou, Fayette! who didst wake with startling voice
　　Life's better sun from that long wintry night,　　10
　　Thus in thy country's triumphs shalt rejoice
And mock with raptures high the dungeon's might:

For lo! the morning struggles into day,
And slavery's spectres shriek and vanish from the ray!

1794　　　　　　　　　　　　　　　　　1794

KOSKIUSKO

O what a loud and fearful shriek was there,
　　As though a thousand souls one death-groan poured!
　　Ah me! they saw beneath a hireling's sword
Their Koskiusko fall! Through the swart air

(As pauses the tired Cossack's barbarous yell　　　5
　　Of triumph) on the chill and midnight gale
　　Rises with frantic burst or sadder swell
The dirge of murdered hope! while freedom pale

Bends in such anguish o'er her destined bier,
　　As if from eldest time some spirit meek　　　　10
　　Had gathered in a mystic urn each tear
That ever on a patriot's furrowed cheek

Fit channel found; and she had drained the bowl
In the mere wilfulness, and sick despair of soul!

1794　　　　　　　　　　　　　　　　　1794

TO THE REVEREND W. L. BOWLES

My heart has thanked thee, Bowles! for those soft strains
   Whose sadness soothes me, like the murmuring
   Of wild-bees in the sunny showers of spring!
For hence not callous to the mourner's pains

Through youth's gay prime and thornless paths I went: 5
   And when the mightier throes of mind began,
   And drove me forth, a thought-bewildered man,
Their mild and manliest melancholy lent

A mingled charm, such as the pang consigned
   To slumber, though the big tear it renewed;   10
   Bidding a strange mysterious pleasure brood
Over the wavy and tumultuous mind,

As the great Spirit erst with plastic sweep
Moved on the darkness of the unformed deep.
1794   1794

TO THE AUTHOR OF "THE ROBBERS"

Schiller! that hour I would have wished to
   die.
If through the shuddering midnight I had
   sent
From the dark dungeon of the tower time-
   rent
That fearful voice, a famish'd father's cry—
Lest in some after moment aught more
   mean   5
Might stamp me mortal! A triumphant
   shout
Black Horror screamed, and all her *goblin*
   rout
Diminished shrunk from the more wither-
   ing scene!
Ah! Bard tremendous in sublimity!
Could I behold thee in thy loftier mood 10
Wandering at eve with finely-frenzied eye
Beneath some vast old tempest-swinging
   wood!
Awhile with mute awe gazing I would
   brood:
Then weep aloud in a wild ecstasy!
                    1794(?)

TO A YOUNG ASS

ITS MOTHER BEING TETHERED NEAR IT

Poor little Foal of an oppressèd race!
I love the languid patience of thy face:
And oft with gentle hand I give thee bread,
And clap thy ragged coat, and pat thy
   head.

But what thy dullèd spirits hath dismayed, 5
That never thou dost sport along the
   glade?
And (most unlike the nature of things
   young)
That earthward still thy moveless head is
   hung?
Do thy prophetic fears anticipate,
Meek child of misery! thy future fate? 10
The starving meal, and all the thousand
   aches
"Which patient merit of the unworthy
   takes"?
Or is thy sad heart thrilled with filial pain
To see thy wretched mother's shortened
   chain?
And truly, very piteous is *her* lot— 15
Chained to a log within a narrow spot,
Where the close-eaten grass is scarcely seen,
While sweet around her waves the tempt-
   ing green!

Poor Ass! thy master should have learnt to
   show
Pity—best taught by fellowship of woe! 20
For much I fear me that *He* lives like thee,
Half famished in a land of luxury!
How *askingly* its footsteps hither bend?
It seems to say, "And have I then **one**
   friend?"
Innocent foal! thou poor despised for-
   lorn! 25
I hail thee *Brother*—spite of the fool's
   scorn!
And fain would take thee with me, in the
   dell

Of peace and mild equality to dwell,
Where toil shall call the charmer health his
    bride,
And laughter tickle plenty's ribless side! 30

How thou wouldst toss thy heels in game-
    some play,
And frisk about, as lamb or kitten gay!
Yea! and more musically sweet to me
Thy dissonant harsh bray of joy would be,
Than warbled melodies that soothe to
    rest   35
The aching of pale fashion's vacant breast!

                                    1794

LEWTI

OR THE CIRCASSIAN LOVE-CHAUNT

At midnight by the stream I roved,
To forget the form I loved.
Image of Lewti! from my mind
Depart; for Lewti is not kind.

The Moon was high, the moonlight gleam 5
    And the shadow of a star
Heaved upon Tamaha's stream;
    But the rock shone brighter far,
The rock half sheltered from my view
By pendant boughs of tressy yew.—   10
So shines my Lewti's forehead fair,
Gleaming through her sable hair,
Image of Lewti! from my mind
Depart; for Lewti is not kind.

J saw a cloud of palest hue,   15
    Onward to the moon it passed:
Still brighter and more bright it grew,
With floating colors not a few,
    Till it reached the moon at last:
Then the cloud was wholly bright,   20
With a rich and amber light!
And so with many a hope I seek,
    And with such joy I find my Lewti;
And even so my pale wan cheek
    Drinks in as deep a flush of beauty! 25
Nay, treacherous image! leave my mind,
If Lewti never will be kind.

The little cloud—it floats away,
    Away it goes; away so soon!
Alas! it has no power to stay: 30
Its hues are dim, its hues are grey—
    Away it passes from the moon!
How mournfully it seems to fly,
    Ever fading more and more,
To joyless regions of the sky—   35
    And now 'tis whiter than before!
As white as my poor cheek will be,

When, Lewti! on my couch I lie,
A dying man for love of thee.
Nay, treacherous image! leave my mind—   40
And yet, thou didst not look unkind.

I saw a vapor in the sky,
Thin, and white, and very high;
I ne'er beheld so thin a cloud:
    Perhaps the breezes that can fly   45
    Now below and now above,
Have snatched aloft the lawny shroud
    Of Lady fair—that died for love.
For maids, as well as youths, have perished
From fruitless love too fondly cherished. 50
Nay, treacherous image! leave my mind—
For Lewti never will be kind.

Hush! my heedless feet from under
    Slip the crumbling banks for ever:
Like echoes to a distant thunder,   55
    They plunge into the gentle river.
The river-swans have heard my tread,
And startle from their reedy bed.
O beauteous birds! methinks ye measure
    Your movements to some heavenly
        tune!   60
O beauteous birds! 'tis such a pleasure
    To see you move beneath the moon,
I would it were your true delight
To sleep by day and wake all night.

I know the place where Lewti lies,   65
When silent night has closed her eyes:
    It is a breezy jasmine-bower,
The nightingale sings o'er her head:
    Voice of the Night! had I the power
That leafy labyrinth to thread,   70
And creep, like thee, with soundless tread,
I then might view her bosom white
Heaving lovely to my sight,
As these two swans together heave
On the gently-swelling wave.   75

Oh! that she saw me in a dream,
    And dreamt that I had died for care;
All pale and wasted I would seem,
    Yet fair withal, as spirits are!
I'd die indeed, if I might see   80
Her bosom heave, and heave for me!
Soothe, gentle image! soothe my mind!
To-morrow Lewti may be kind.

                                    1794

FROM RELIGIOUS MUSINGS

            . . . Lovely was the death
Of Him whose life was Love! Holy with
    power
He on the thought-benighted Sceptic
    beamed   30

Manifest Godhead, melting into day
What floating mists of dark idolatry
Broke and misshaped the omnipresent Sire:
And first by fear uncharmed the drowsèd
  soul.
Till of its nobler nature it 'gan feel   35
Dim recollections; and thence soared to
  hope.
Strong to believe whate'er of mystic good
The Eternal dooms for His immortal sons.
From hope and firmer faith to perfect love
Attracted and absorbed: and centered
  there   40
God only to behold, and know, and feel,
Till by exclusive consciousness of God
All self-annihilated it shall make
God its identity: God all in all!
We and our Father one!   45

. . . .

Believe thou, O my soul, 395
Life is a vision shadowy of truth;
And vice, and anguish, and the wormy
  grave,
Shapes of a dream!   The veiling clouds
  retire,

And lo! the throne of the redeeming God
Forth flashing unimaginable day   400
Wraps in one blaze earth, heaven, and
  deepest hell.

Contemplant Spirits! ye that hover o'er
With untired gaze the immeasurable fount
Ebullient with creative Deity!
And ye of plastic power, that interfused 405
Roll through the grosser and material mass
In organizing surge!   Holies of God!
(And what if Monads of the infinite mind?)
I haply journeying my immortal course
Shall sometime join your mystic choir! Till
  then   410
I discipline my young and novice thought
In ministeries of heart-stirring song,
And aye on meditation's heaven-ward wing
Soaring aloft I breathe the empyreal air
Of Love, omnific, omnipresent Love,   415
Whose day-spring rises glorious in my soul
As the great sun, when he his influence
Sheds on the frost-bound waters—The glad
  stream
Flows to the ray and warbles as it flows.
Dec. 24, 1794   1796

THE EOLIAN HARP

COMPOSED AT CLEVEDON, SOMERSETSHIRE

My pensive Sara! thy soft cheek reclined
Thus on mine arm, most soothing sweet it is
To sit beside our cot, our cot o'ergrown
With white-flowered jasmin, and the broad-leaved myrtle,
(Meet emblems they of innocence and love!)   5
And watch the clouds, that late were rich with light,
Slow saddening round, and mark the star of eve
Serenely brilliant (such should wisdom be)
Shine opposite!   How exquisite the scents
Snatched from yon bean-field! and the world so hushed!   10
The stilly murmur of the distant sea
Tells us of silence.

            And that simplest lute,
Placed length-ways in the clasping casement, hark!
How by the desultory breeze caressed,
Like some coy maid half yielding to her lover,   15
It pours such sweet upbraiding, as must needs
Tempt to repeat the wrong!   And now, its strings
Boldlier swept, the long sequacious notes
Over delicious surges sink and rise,
Such a soft floating witchery of sound   20
As twilight elfins make, when they at eve
Voyage on gentle gales from fairy-land,
Where melodies round honey-dropping flowers,
Footless and wild, like birds of paradise,
Nor pause, nor perch, hovering on untamed wing!   25
O! the one life within us and abroad,

Which meets all motion and becomes its soul,
A light in sound, a sound-like power in light,
Rhythm in all thought, and joyance every where—
Methinks, it should have been impossible 30
Not to love all things in a world so filled;
Where the breeze warbles, and the mute still air
Is music slumbering on her instrument.

And thus, my love! as on the midway slope
Of yonder hill I stretch my limbs at noon, 35
Whilst through my half-closed eye-lids I behold
The sunbeams dance, like diamonds, on the main,
And tranquil muse upon tranquillity;
Full many a thought uncalled and undetained,
And many idle flitting phantasies, 40
Traverse my indolent and passive brain,
As wild and various as the random gales
That swell and flutter on this subject lute!

And what if all of animated nature
Be but organic harps diversely framed, 45
That tremble into thought, as o'er them sweeps
Plastic and vast, one intellectual breeze,
At once the soul of each, and God of all?
But thy more serious eye a mild reproof
Darts, O belovèd woman! nor such thoughts 50
Dim and unhallowed dost thou not reject,
And biddest me walk humbly with my God.
Meek daughter in the family of Christ!
Well hast thou said and holily dispraised
These shapings of the unregenerate mind; 55
Bubbles that glitter as they rise and break
On vain philosophy's aye-babbling spring.
For never guiltless may I speak of him,
The Incomprehensible! save when with awe
I praise him, and with faith that inly feels; 60
Who with his saving mercies healèd me,
A sinful and most miserable man,
Wildered and dark, and gave me to possess
Peace, and this cot, and thee, heart-honored maid!
1795   1796

REFLECTIONS ON HAVING LEFT A PLACE OF RETIREMENT

Low was our pretty cot: our tallest rose
Peeped at the chamber-window. We could hear
At silent noon, and eve, and early morn,
The sea's faint murmur. In the open air
Our myrtles blossomed; and across the porch 5
Thick jasmins twined: the little landscape round
Was green and woody, and refreshed the eye.
It was a spot which you might aptly call
The Valley of Seclusion! Once I saw
(Hallowing his Sabbath-day by quietness) 10
A wealthy son of commerce saunter by,
Bristowa's citizen: methought, it calmed
His thirst of idle gold, and made him muse
With wiser feelings: for he paused, and looked

With a pleased sadness, and gazed all around,   15
Then eyed our cottage, and gazed round again,
And sighed, and said, it was a blessèd place.
And we were blessed. Oft with patient ear
Long-listening to the viewless sky-lark's note
(Viewless, or haply for a moment seen   20
Gleaming on sunny wings) in whispered tones
I've said to my belovèd, "Such, sweet girl!
The inobtrusive song of happiness,
Unearthly minstrelsy! then only heard
When the soul seeks to hear; when all is hushed,   25
And the heart listens!"
                        But the time, when first
From that low dell, steep up the stony mount
I climbed with perilous toil and reached the top,
Oh! what a goodly scene! Here the bleak mount,
The bare bleak mountain speckled thin with sheep;   30
Gray clouds, that shadowing spot the sunny fields;
And river, now with bushy rocks o'er-browed,
Now winding bright and full, with naked banks;
And seats, and lawns, the abbey and the wood,
And cots, and hamlets, and faint city-spire;   35
The Channel there, the Islands and white sails,
Dim coasts, and cloud-like hills, and shoreless ocean—
It seemed like Omnipresence! God, methought,
Had built Him there a temple: the whole world
Seemed imaged in its vast circumference: 40
No wish profaned my overwhelmèd heart.
Blest hour! It was a luxury,—to be!
    Ah! quiet dell! dear cot, and mount sublime!
I was constrained to quit you. Was it right,
While my unnumbered brethren toiled and bled,   45
That I should dream away the entrusted hours
On rose-leaf beds, pampering the coward heart
With feelings all too delicate for use?
Sweet is the tear that from some Howard's eye
Drops on the cheek of one he lifts from earth: 50
And he that works me good with unmoved face,
Does it but half: he chills me while he aids,
My benefactor, not my brother man!
Yet even this, this cold beneficence
Praise, praise it, O my soul! oft as thou scannest   55
The sluggard pity's vision-weaving tribe!
Who sigh for wretchedness, yet shun the wretched,
Nursing in some delicious solitude
Their slothful loves and dainty sympathies!
I therefore go, and join head, heart, and hand,   60
Active and firm, to fight the bloodless fight
Of science, freedom, and the truth in Christ.

Yet oft when after honorable toil
Rests the tired mind, and waking loves to dream,
My spirit shall revisit thee, dear cot!   65
Thy jasmin and thy window-peeping rose,
And myrtles fearless of the mild sea-air.
And I shall sigh fond wishes—sweet abode!
Ah!—had none greater. And that all had such!
It might be so—but the time is not yet.   70
Speed it, O Father! Let thy kingdom come!
1795   1796

ODE ON THE DEPARTING YEAR

I

Spirit who sweepest the wild harp of time!
  It is most hard, with an untroubled ear
  Thy dark inwoven harmonies to hear!
Yet, mine eye fixed on heaven's unchanging clime
Long had I listened, free from mortal fear,   5
  With inward stillness, and a bowèd mind;
  When lo! its folds far waving on the wind,
I saw the train of the departing year!
  Starting from my silent sadness
  Then with no unholy madness,   10
Ere yet the entered cloud foreclosed my sight,
I raised the impetuous song, and solemnized his flight.

II

  Hither, from the recent tomb,
  From the prison's direr gloom,
  From distemper's midnight anguish;   15
And thence, where poverty doth waste and languish;
  Or where, his two bright torches blending,
    Love illumines manhood's maze;
  Or where o'er cradled infants bending,
    Hope has fixed her wishful gaze;   20
  Hither, in perplexèd dance,
  Ye Woes! ye young-eyed Joys! advance!
By Time's wild harp, and by the hand
  Whose indefatigable sweep
  Raises its fateful strings from sleep,   25
I bid you haste, a mixed tumultuous band!
  From every private bower,
    And each domestic hearth,
  Haste for one solemn hour;
  And with a loud and yet a louder voice,   30
O'er nature struggling in portentous birth,
  Weep and rejoice!
Still echoes the dread name that o'er the earth
Let slip the storm, and woke the brood of hell:
  And now advance in saintly jubilee   35
Justice and Truth! They too have heard thy spell,
  They too obey thy name, divinest Liberty!

III

I marked Ambition in his war-array!
  I heard the mailèd monarch's troublous cry—
"Ah! wherefore does the Northern Conqueress stay!   40
Groans not her chariot on its onward way?"
  Fly, mailèd monarch, fly!
  Stunned by death's twice mortal mace,
  No more on murder's lurid face
The insatiate hag shall gloat with drunken eye!   45
  Manes of the unnumbered slain!
  Ye that gasped on Warsaw's plain!
  Ye that erst at Ismail's tower,
When human ruin choked the streams,
  Fell in conquest's glutted hour,   50

Mid women's shrieks and infants' screams!
  Spirits of the uncoffined slain,
  Sudden blasts of triumph swelling,
Oft, at night, in misty train,
  Rush around her narrow dwelling!   55
The exterminating fiend is fled—
  (Foul her life, and dark her doom)
Mighty armies of the dead
  Dance, like death-fires, round her tomb!
Then with prophetic song relate,   60
Each some tyrant-murderer's fate!

IV

Departing Year! 'twas on no earthly shore
  My soul beheld thy vision! Where alone,
  Voiceless and stern, before the cloudy throne,
Aye Memory sits: thy robe inscribed with gore,   65
With many an unimaginable groan
  Thou storied'st thy sad hours!   Silence ensued,
  Deep silence o'er the ethereal multitude,
Whose locks with wreaths, whose wreaths with glories shone.
    Then, his eye wild ardors glancing,   70
    From the choirèd gods advancing,
The spirit of the earth made reverence meet,
And stood up, beautiful, before the cloudy seat.

V

    Throughout the blissful throng,
    Hushed were harp and song: 75
Till wheeling round the throne the Lampads seven,
  (The mystic Words of Heaven)
  Permissive signal make:
The fervent spirit bowed, then spread his wings and spake!
  "Thou in stormy blackness throning   80
  Love and uncreated light,
  By the earth's unsolaced groaning,
  Seize thy terrors, arm of might!
By peace with proffered insult scared,
  Masked hate and envying scorn!   85
  By years of havoc yet unborn!
And hunger's bosom to the frost-winds bared!
  But chief by Afric's wrongs,
  Strange, horrible, and foul!
  By what deep guilt belongs   90
To the deaf Synod, 'full of gifts and lies!'
By wealth's insensate laugh! by torture's howl!
  Avenger, rise!
Forever shall the thankless island scowl,
  Her quiver full, and with unbroken bow?   95
Speak! from thy storm-black heaven, O speak aloud!
    And on the darkling foe
Open thine eye of fire from some uncertain cloud!
  O dart the flash!   O rise and deal the blow!
The past to thee, to thee the future cries!   100
  Hark! how wide nature joins her groans below!
    Rise, God of Nature, rise!"

VI

The voice had ceased, the Vision fled;
Yet still I gasped and reeled with dread.
And ever, when the dream of night   105
Renews the phantom to my sight,
Cold sweat-drops gather on my limbs;
  My ears throb hot; my eye-balls start;
My brain with horrid tumult swims;
  Wild is the tempest of my heart;   110
And my thick and struggling breath
Imitates the toil of death!
No stranger agony confounds
  The soldier on the war-field spread,
When all foredone with toil and wounds,   115
    Death-like he dozes among heaps of dead!
(The strife is o'er, the day-light fled,
  And the night-wind clamors hoarse!
See! the starting wretch's head
Lies pillowed on a brother's corse!)   120

VII

Not yet enslaved, not wholly vile,
O Albion! O my mother isle!
Thy valleys, fair as Eden's bowers
Glitter green with sunny showers;
Thy grassy uplands' gentle swells   125
  Echo to the bleat of flocks;
(Those grassy hills, those glittering dells
  Proudly ramparted with rocks)
And ocean mid his uproar wild
Speaks safety to his island-child!   130
Hence for many a fearless age
Has social quiet loved thy shore;
Nor ever proud invader's rage
Or sacked thy towers, or stained thy fields with gore.

VIII

Abandoned of heaven; mad avarice thy guide,   135
At cowardly distance, yet kindling with pride—
Mid thy herds and thy corn-fields secure thou hast stood,
And joined the wild yelling of famine and blood!
The nations curse thee! They with eager wondering
  Shall hear Destruction, like a vulture, scream!   140
  Strange-eyed Destruction! who with many a dream
Of central fires through nether seas up-thundering
  Soothes her fierce solitude; yet as she lies
  By livid fount, or red volcanic stream,
If ever to her lidless dragon-eyes,   145
  O Albion! thy predestined ruins rise,
The fiend-hag on her perilous couch doth leap,
Muttering distempered triumph in her charmèd sleep.

IX

  Away, my soul, away!
  In vain, in vain the birds of warning sing—   150
And hark! I hear the famished brood of prey

Flap their lank pennons on the groaning wind!
    Away, my soul, away!
    I unpartaking of the evil thing,
      With daily prayer and daily toil   ·   155
      Soliciting for food my scanty soil,
Have wailed my country with a loud lament.
Now I recenter my immortal mind
    In the deep Sabbath of meek self-content;
Cleansed from the vaporous passions that bedim   160
God's image, sister of the Seraphim.
1796   1796

THIS LIME-TREE BOWER MY PRISON

ADDRESSED TO CHARLES LAMB, OF THE INDIA HOUSE, LONDON

In the June of 1797 some long-expected friends paid a visit to the author's cottage; and on the morning of their arrival, he met with an accident, which disabled him from walking during the whole time of their stay. One evening, when they had left him for a few hours, he composed the following lines in the garden-bower.

Well, they are gone, and here must I remain,
This lime-tree bower my prison! I have lost
Beauties and feelings, such as would have been
Most sweet to my remembrance even when age
Had dimmed mine eyes to blindness! They, meanwhile,   5
Friends, whom I never more may meet again,
On springy heath, along the hill-top edge,
Wander in gladness, and wind down, perchance,
To that still roaring dell, of which I told;
The roaring dell, o'erwooded, narrow, deep,   10
And only speckled by the mid-day sun;
Where its slim trunk the ash from rock to rock
Flings arching like a bridge;—that branchless ash,
Unsunned and damp, whose few poor yellow leaves
Ne'er tremble in the gale, yet tremble still,   15
Fanned by the water-fall! and there my friends
Behold the dark green file of long lank weeds,
That all at once (a most fantastic sight!)
Still nod and drip beneath the dripping edge
Of the blue clay-stone.
                Now, my friends emerge   20
Beneath the wide wide Heaven—and view again
The many-steepled tract magnificent
Of hilly fields and meadows, and the sea,
With some fair bark, perhaps, whose sails light up
The slip of smooth clear blue betwixt two Isles   25
Of purple shadow! Yes! they wander on
In gladness all; but thou, methinks, most glad,
My gentle-hearted Charles! for thou hast pined
And hungered after Nature, many a year,
In the great City pent, winning thy way   30
With sad yet patient soul, through evil and pain
And strange calamity! Ah! slowly sink
Behind the western ridge, thou glorious Sun!
Shine in the slant beams of the sinking orb,
Ye purple heath-flowers! richlier burn, ye clouds!   35
Live in the yellow light, ye distant groves!
And kindle, thou blue Ocean! So my friend

Struck with deep joy, may stand, as I have stood,
Silent with swimming sense; yea, gazing round
On the wide landscape, gaze till all doth seem   40
Less gross than bodily, and of such hues
As veil the Almighty Spirit, when yet he makes
Spirits perceive his presence.

             A delight
Comes sudden on my heart, and I am glad
As I myself were there! Nor in this bower,   45
This little lime-tree bower, have I not marked
Much that has soothed me. Pale beneath the blaze
Hung the transparent foliage; and I watched
Some broad and sunny leaf, and loved to see
The shadow of the leaf and stem above   50
Dappling its sunshine! And that walnut-tree
Was richly tinged, and a deep radiance lay
Full on the ancient ivy, which usurps
Those fronting elms, and now, with blackest mass
Makes their dark branches gleam a lighter hue   55
Through the late twilight: and though now the bat
Wheels silent by, and not a swallow twitters,
Yet still the solitary humble-bee
Sings in the bean-flower! Henceforth I shall know
That Nature ne'er deserts the wise and pure;   60
No plot so narrow, be but Nature there,
No waste so vacant, but may well employ
Each faculty of sense, and keep the heart
Awake to Love and Beauty! and sometimes
'Tis well to be bereft of promised good,   65
That we may lift the soul, and contemplate
With lively joy the joys we cannot share.
My gentle-hearted Charles! when the last rook
Beat its straight path along the dusky air
Homewards, I blest it! deeming its black wing   70
(Now a dim speck, now vanishing in light)
Had crossed the mighty Orb's dilated glory,
While thou stood'st gazing; or, when all was still,
Flew creeking o'er thy head, and had a charm
For thee, my gentle-hearted Charles, to whom   75
No sound is dissonant which tells of Life.

June, 1797   1797

THE RIME OF THE ANCIENT MARINER

IN SEVEN PARTS

PART THE FIRST

An ancient Mariner meet-
eth three Gallants bidden to
a wedding-feast, and detain-
eth one.

It is an ancient Mariner
And he stoppeth one of three.
"By thy long grey beard and glittering eye,
Now wherefore stopp'st thou me?

The Bridegroom's doors are opened wide,   5
And I am next of kin;
The guests are met, the feast is set:
May'st hear the merry din."

He holds him with his skinny hand,
"There was a ship," quoth he.   10
"Hold off! unhand me, grey-beard loon!"
Eftsoons his hand dropt he.

The Wedding-Guest is spell-
bound by the eye of the old
seafaring man, and con-
strained to hear his tale.

He holds him with his glittering eye—
The Wedding-Guest stood still,
And listens like a three years' child: 15
The Mariner hath his will.

The Wedding-Guest sat on a stone:
He cannot choose but hear;
And thus spake on that ancient man,
The bright-eyed Mariner.   20

"The ship was cheered, the harbor cleared,
Merrily did we drop
Below the kirk, below the hill,
Below the lighthouse top.

The Mariner tells how the
ship sailed southward with
a good wind and fair weather,
till it reached the Line.

The Sun came up upon the left,   25
Out of the sea came he!
And he shone bright, and on the right
Went down into the sea.

Higher and higher every day,
Till over the mast at noon—"   30
The Wedding-Guest here beat his breast,
For he heard the loud bassoon.

The Wedding-Guest heareth
the bridal music; but the
Mariner continueth his tale.

The bride hath paced into the hall,
Red as a rose is she;
Nodding their heads before her goes   35
The merry minstrelsy.

The Wedding-Guest he beat his breast,
Yet he cannot choose but hear;
And thus spake on that ancient man,
The bright-eyed Mariner.   40

The ship driven by a storm
toward the south pole.

"And now the storm-blast came, and he
Was tyrannous and strong:
He struck with his o'ertaking wings,
And chased us south along.

With sloping masts and dipping prow,   45
As who pursued with yell and blow
Still treads the shadow of his foe
And forward bends his head,
The ship drove fast, loud roared the blast,
And southward aye we fled.   50

And now there came both mist and snow,
And it grew wondrous cold:
And ice, mast-high, came floating by,
As green as emerald.

The land of ice, and of fear-
ful sounds, where no living
thing was to be seen.

And through the drifts the snowy clifts   55
Did send a dismal sheen:
Nor shapes of men nor beasts we ken—
The ice was all between.

The ice was here, the ice was there,
The ice was all around:
It cracked and growled, and roared and howled,
Like noises in a swound!

60

Till a great sea-bird, called the Albatross, came through the snow-fog, and was received with great joy and hospitality.

At length did cross an Albatross:
Thorough the fog it came;
As if it had been a Christian soul,
We hailed it in God's name.

65

It ate the food it ne'er had eat,
And round and round it flew.
The ice did split with a thunder-fit;
The helmsman steered us through!

70

And lo! the Albatross proveth a bird of good omen, and followeth the ship as it returned northward through fog and floating ice.

And a good south wind sprung up behind;
The Albatross did follow,
And every day, for food or play,
Came to the mariners' hollo!

In mist or cloud, on mast or shroud,
It perched for vespers nine;
Whiles all the night, through fog-smoke white,
Glimmered the white Moon-shine."

75

The ancient Mariner inhospitably killeth the pious bird of good omen.

"God save thee, ancient Mariner!
From the fiends, that plague thee thus!—
Why look'st thou so?"—"With my cross-bow
I shot the Albatross.

80

PART THE SECOND

The Sun now rose upon the right:
Out of the sea came he,
Still hid in mist, and on the left
Went down into the sea.

85

And the good south wind still blew behind,
But no sweet bird did follow,
Nor any day for food or play
Came to the mariners' hollo!

90

His shipmates cry out against the ancient Mariner, for killing the bird of good luck.

And I had done a hellish thing,
And it would work 'em woe:
For all averred, I had killed the bird
That made the breeze to blow.
'Ah, wretch!' said they, 'the bird to slay,
That made the breeze to blow!'

95

But when the fog cleared off, they justify the same, and thus make themselves accomplices in the crime.

Nor dim nor red, like God's own head,
The glorious Sun uprist:
Then all averred, I had killed the bird
That brought the fog and mist.
' 'Twas right,' said they, 'such birds to slay,
That bring the fog and mist.'

100

The fair breeze continues; the ship enters the Pacific Ocean, and sails northward, even till it reaches the Line.

The fair breeze blew, the white foam flew,
The furrow followed free;
We were the first that ever burst
Into that silent sea.

105

Down dropt the breeze, the sails dropt down,
'Twas sad as sad could be;

The ship hath been suddenly becalmed.

And we did speak only to break
The silence of the sea! 110

All in a hot and copper sky,
The bloody Sun, at noon,
Right up above the mast did stand,
No bigger than the Moon.

Day after day, day after day, 115
We stuck, nor breath nor motion;
As idle as a painted ship
Upon a painted ocean.

And the Albatross begins to
be avenged.

Water, water, every where,
And all the boards did shrink; 120
Water, water, every where,
Nor any drop to drink.

The very deep did rot: O Christ!
That ever this should be!
Yea, slimy things did crawl with legs 125
Upon the slimy sea.

About, about, in reel and rout
The death-fires danced at night;
The water, like a witch's oils,
Burnt green, and blue, and white. 130

A Spirit had followed them;
one of the invisible inhabitants of this planet, neither
departed souls nor angels;
concerning whom the learned
Jew, Josephus, and the Platonic Constantinopolitan,
Michael Psellus, may be consulted. They are very nu-
merous, and there is no climate or element without one
or more.

And some in dreams assurèd were
Of the Spirit that plagued us so;
Nine fathom deep he had followed us
From the land of mist and snow.

And every tongue, through utter drought, 135
Was withered at the root;
We could not speak, no more than if
We had been choked with soot.

The shipmates, in their sore
distress, would fain throw
the whole guilt on the ancient Mariner: in sign whereof they hang the dead sea-
bird round his neck.

Ah! well-a-day! what evil looks
Had I from old and young! 140
Instead of the cross, the Albatross
About my neck was hung.

PART THE THIRD

There passed a weary time. Each throat
Was parched, and glazed each eye.
A weary time! a weary time! 145
How glazed each weary eye,
When looking westward, I beheld
A something in the sky.

The ancient Mariner be-
holdeth a sign in the element afar off.

At first it seemed a little speck,
And then it seemed a mist; 150
It moved and moved, and took at last
A certain shape, I wist.

A speck, a mist, a shape, I wist!
And still it neared and neared:
As if it dodged a water-sprite,
It plunged and tacked and veered.

At its nearer approach, it
seemeth him to be a ship;
and at a dear ransom he
freeth his speech from the
bonds of thirst.

With throats unslaked, with black lips baked,
We could nor laugh nor wail;
Through utter drought all dumb we stood!
I bit my arm, I sucked the blood,   160
And cried, A sail! a sail!

A flash of joy,

With throats unslaked, with black lips baked,
Agape they heard me call:
Gramercy! they for joy did grin,
And all at once their breath drew in,   165
As they were drinking all.

And horror follows. For can
it be a ship that comes on-
ward without wind or tide?

See! see! (I cried) she tacks no more!
Hither to work us weal;
Without a breeze, without a tide,
She steadies with upright keel!   170

The western wave was all a-flame.
The day was well-nigh done!
Almost upon the western wave
Rested the broad bright Sun;
When that strange shape drove suddenly   175
Betwixt us and the Sun.

It seemeth him but the
skeleton of a ship.

And straight the Sun was flecked with bars,
(Heaven's Mother send us grace!)
As if through a dungeon-grate he peered
With broad and burning face.   180

Alas! (thought I, and my heart beat loud)
How fast she nears and nears!
Are those her sails that glance in the Sun,
Like restless gossameres?

And its ribs are seen as bars
on the face of the setting
Sun. The Spectre-Woman
and her Death-mate, and no
other on board the skeleton-
ship. Like vessel, like crew!

Are those her ribs through which the Sun   185
Did peer, as through a grate?
And is that Woman all her crew?
Is that a Death? and are there two?
Is Death that woman's mate?

Her lips were red, her looks were free,   190
Her locks were yellow as gold:
Her skin was as white as leprosy,
The Night-mare Life-in-Death was she,
Who thicks man's blood with cold.

Death and Life-in-Death
have diced for the ship's
crew, and she (the latter)
winneth the ancient Mariner.

The naked hulk alongside came,   195
And the twain were casting dice;
'The game is done! I've won! I've won!'
Quoth she, and whistles thrice.

No twilight within the courts
of the Sun.

The Sun's rim dips; the stars rush out:
At one stride comes the dark;
With far-heard whisper, o'er the sea,   200
Off shot the spectre-bark.

At the rising of the Moon,	We listened and looked sideways up!
	Fear at my heart, as at a cup,
	My life-blood seemed to sip! 205
	The stars were dim, and thick the night,
	The steersman's face by his lamp gleamed white;
	From the sails the dew did drip—
	Till clomb above the eastern bar
	The hornèd Moon, with one bright star 210
	Within the nether tip.
One after another,	One after one, by the star-dogged Moon,
	Too quick for groan or sigh,
	Each turned his face with a ghastly pang,
	And cursed me with his eye. 215
His shipmates drop down dead.	Four times fifty living men,
	(And I heard nor sigh nor groan)
	With heavy thump, a lifeless lump,
	They dropped down one by one.
But Life-in-Death begins her work on the ancient Mariner.	The souls did from their bodies fly,— 220
	They fled to bliss or woe!
	And every soul, it passed me by,
	Like the whizz of my cross-bow!"

PART THE FOURTH

The Wedding-Guest feareth that a Spirit is talking to him;	"I fear thee, ancient Mariner!
	I fear thy skinny hand! 225
	And thou art long, and lank, and brown,
	As is the ribbed sea-sand.*
But the ancient Mariner assureth him of his bodily life, and proceedeth to relate his horrible penance.	I fear thee and thy glittering eye,
	And thy skinny hand, so brown."—
	"Fear not, fear not, thou Wedding-Guest! 230
	This body dropt not down.
	Alone, alone, all, all alone,
	Alone on a wide wide sea!
	And never a saint took pity on
	My soul in agony. 235
He despiseth the creatures of the calm.	The many men, so beautiful!
	And they all dead did lie:
	And a thousand thousand slimy things
	Lived on; and so did I.
And envieth that they should live, and so many lie dead.	I looked upon the rotting sea, 240
	And drew my eyes away;
	I looked upon the rotting deck,
	And there the dead men lay.
	I looked to Heaven, and tried to pray;
	But or ever a prayer had gusht, 245
	A wicked whisper came, and made
	My heart as dry as dust.

* For the last two lines of this stanza, I am indebted to Mr. Wordsworth. It was on a delightful walk from Nether Stowey to Dulverton, with him and his sister, in the Autumn of 1797, that this Poem was planned, and in part composed.

I closed my lids, and kept them close,
And the balls like pulses beat;
For the sky and the sea, and the sea and the sky   250
Lay like a load on my weary eye,
And the dead were at my feet.

But the curse liveth for him in the eye of the dead men.

The cold sweat melted from their limbs,
Nor rot nor reek did they:
The look with which they looked on me   255
Had never passed away.

An orphan's curse would drag to hell
A spirit from on high;
But oh! more horrible than that
Is the curse in a dead man's eye!   260
Seven days, seven nights, I saw that curse,
And yet I could not die.

In his loneliness and fixedness he yearneth towards the journeying Moon, and the stars that still sojourn, yet still move onward; and everywhere the blue sky belongs to them, and is their appointed rest, and their native country and their own natural homes, which they enter unannounced, as lords that are certainly expected and yet there is a silent joy at their arrival.

The moving Moon went up the sky
And no where did abide:
Softly she was going up,   265
And a star or two beside—

Her beams bemocked the sultry main,
Like April hoar-frost spread;
But where the ship's huge shadow lay,
The charmèd water burnt alway   270
A still and awful red.

By the light of the Moon he beholdeth God's creatures of the great calm.

Beyond the shadow of the ship,
I watched the water-snakes:
They moved in tracks of shining white,
And when they reared, the elfish light
Fell off in hoary flakes.   275

Within the shadow of the ship
I watched their rich attire:
Blue, glossy green, and velvet black,
They coiled and swam; and every track   280
Was a flash of golden fire.

Their beauty and their happiness.

O happy living things! no tongue
Their beauty might declare:
A spring of love gushed from my heart,

He blesseth them in his heart.

And I blessed them unaware: 285
Sure my kind saint took pity on me,
And I blessed them unaware.

The spell begins to break.

The self-same moment I could pray;
And from my neck so free
The Albatross fell off, and sank   290
Like lead into the sea.

PART THE FIFTH

Oh sleep! it is a gentle thing,
Beloved from pole to pole!
To Mary Queen the praise be given!
She sent the gentle sleep from Heaven,   295
That slid into my soul.

By grace of the holy Mother, the ancient Mariner is refreshed with rain.

The silly buckets on the deck,
That had so long remained,
I dreamt that they were filled with dew;
And when I awoke, it rained.   300

My lips were wet, my throat was cold,
My garments all were dank;
Sure I had drunken in my dreams,
And still my body drank.

I moved, and could not feel my limbs: 305
I was so light—almost
I thought that I had died in sleep,
And was a blessèd ghost.

He heareth sounds and seeth strange sights and commotions in the sky and the element.

And soon I heard a roaring wind:
It did not come anear;   310
But with its sound it shook the sails,
That were so thin and sere.

The upper air burst into life!
And a hundred fire-flags sheen,
To and fro they were hurried about!   315
And to and fro, and in and out,
The wan stars danced between.

And the coming wind did roar more loud,
And the sails did sigh like sedge;
And the rain poured down from one black cloud; 320
The Moon was at its edge.

The thick black cloud was cleft, and still
The Moon was at its side:
Like waters shot from some high crag,
The lightning fell with never a jag,   325
A river steep and wide.

The bodies of the ship's crew are inspired and the ship moves on;

The loud wind never reached the ship,
Yet now the ship moved on!
Beneath the lightning and the Moon
The dead men gave a groan.   330

They groaned, they stirred, they all uprose,
Nor spake, nor moved their eyes;
It had been strange, even in a dream,
To have seen those dead men rise.

The helmsman steered, the ship moved on;   335
Yet never a breeze up-blew;
The mariners all 'gan work the ropes,
Where they were wont to do;
They raised their limbs like lifeless tools—
We were a ghastly crew.   340

The body of my brother's son
Stood by me, knee to knee:
The body and I pulled at one rope,
But he said nought to me."

"I fear thee, ancient Mariner!"

"I fear thee, ancient Mariner!"
"Be calm, thou Wedding-Guest!   345
'Twas not those souls that fled in pain,
Which to their corses came again,
But a troop of spirits blest:

But not by the souls of the men, nor by dæmons of earth or middle air, but by a blessed troop of angelic spirits, sent down by the invocation of the guardian saint.

For when it dawned—they dropped their arms,   350
And clustered round the mast;
Sweet sounds rose slowly through their mouths,
And from their bodies passed.

Around, around, flew each sweet sound,
Then darted to the Sun;   355
Slowly the sounds came back again,
Now mixed, now one by one.

Sometimes a-dropping from the sky
I heard the sky-lark sing;
Sometimes all little birds that are,
How they seemed to fill the sea and air   360
With their sweet jargoning!

And now 'twas like all instruments,
Now like a lonely flute;
And now it is an angel's song,
That makes the Heavens be mute.   365

It ceased; yet still the sails made on
A pleasant noise till noon,
A noise like of a hidden brook
In the leafy month of June,
That to the sleeping woods all night   370
Singeth a quiet tune.

Till noon we quietly sailed on,
Yet never a breeze did breathe:
Slowly and smoothly went the ship,   375
Moved onward from beneath.

The lonesome Spirit from the south pole carries on the ship as far as the Line, in obedience to the angelic troop, but still requireth vengeance.

Under the keel nine fathom deep,
From the land of mist and snow,
The spirit slid: and it was he
That made the ship to go.
The sails at noon left off their tune,   380
And the ship stood still also.

The Sun, right up above the mast,
Had fixed her to the ocean:
But in a minute she 'gan stir,
With a short uneasy motion—   385
Backwards and forwards half her length
With a short uneasy motion.

Then like a pawing horse let go,
She made a sudden bound: 390
It flung the blood into my head,
And I fell down in a swound.

The Polar Spirit's fellow-dæmons, the invisible inhabitants of the element, take part in his wrong; and two of them relate, one to the other, that penance long and heavy for the ancient Mariner hath been accorded to the Polar Spirit, who returneth southward.

How long in that same fit I lay,
I have not to declare;
But ere my living life returned,   395
I heard and in my soul discerned
Two voices in the air.

'Is it he?' quoth one, 'Is this the man?
By him who died on cross,
With his cruel bow he laid full low   400
The harmless Albatross.

The spirit who bideth by himself
In the land of mist and snow,
He loved the bird that loved the man
Who shot him with his bow.'   405

The other was a softer voice,
As soft as honey-dew:
Quoth he, 'The man hath penance done,
And penance more will do.'

PART THE SIXTH

FIRST VOICE

'But tell me, tell me! speak again,   410
Thy soft response renewing—
What makes that ship drive on so fast?
What is the ocean doing?'

SECOND VOICE

'Still as a slave before his lord,
The ocean hath no blast;   415
His great bright eye most silently
Up to the Moon is cast—

If he may know which way to go;
For she guides him smooth or grim.
See, brother, see! how graciously   420
She looketh down on him.'

FIRST VOICE

'But why drives on that ship so fast,
Without or wave or wind?'

The Mariner hath been cast into a trance; for the angelic power causeth the vessel to drive northward faster than human life could endure.

SECOND VOICE

'The air is cut away before,
And closes from behind.   425

Fly, brother, fly! more high, more high!
Or we shall be belated:
For slow and slow that ship will go,
When the Mariner's trance is abated.'

The supernatural motion is retarded; the Mariner awakes, and his penance begins anew.

I woke, and we were sailing on   430
As in a gentle weather:
'Twas night, calm night, the Moon was high;
The dead men stood together.

All stood together on the deck,
For a charnel-dungeon fitter:
All fixed on me their stony eyes,
That in the Moon did glitter.   435

The pang, the curse, with which they died,
Had never passed away:
I could not draw my eyes from theirs,
Nor turn them up to pray.   440

The curse is finally expiated.

And now this spell was snapt: once more
I viewed the ocean green,
And looked far forth, yet little saw
Of what had else been seen—   445

Like one, that on a lonesome road
Doth walk in fear and dread,
And having once turned round walks on
And turns no more his head;
Because he knows, a frightful fiend
Doth close behind him tread.   450

But soon there breathed a wind on me,
Nor sound nor motion made:
Its path was not upon the sea,
In ripple or in shade.   455

It raised my hair, it fanned my cheek
Like a meadow-gale of spring—
It mingled strangely with my fears,
Yet it felt like a welcoming.

Swiftly, swiftly flew the ship,   460
Yet she sailed softly too:
Sweetly, sweetly blew the breeze—
On me alone it blew.

And the ancient Mariner beholdeth his native country.

Oh! dream of joy! is this indeed
The light-house top I see?
Is this the hill? is this the kirk?   465
Is this mine own countree?

We drifted o'er the harbor-bar,
And I with sobs did pray—
O let me be awake, my God!
Or let me sleep alway.   470

The harbor-bay was clear as glass,
So smoothly it was strewn!
And on the bay the moonlight lay,
And the shadow of the Moon.   475

The rock shone bright, the kirk no less,
That stands above the rock:
The moonlight steeped in silentness
The steady weathercock.

The angelic spirits leave the
dead bodies,

And the bay was white with silent light, 480
Till rising from the same,
Full many shapes, that shadows were,
In crimson colors came.

And appear in their own
forms of light.

A little distance from the prow
Those crimson shadows were: 485
I turned my eyes upon the deck—
Oh, Christ! what saw I there!

Each corse lay flat, lifeless and flat,
And, by the holy rood!
A man all light, a seraph-man, 490
On every corse there stood.

This seraph-band, each waved his hand:
It was a heavenly sight!
They stood as signals to the land,
Each one a lovely light; 495

This seraph-band, each waved his hand,
No voice did they impart—
No voice; but oh! the silence sank
Like music on my heart.

But soon I heard the dash of oars, 500
I heard the Pilot's cheer;
My head was turned perforce away,
And I saw a boat appear.

The Pilot, and the Pilot's boy,
I heard them coming fast: 507
Dear Lord in Heaven! it was a joy
The dead men could not blast.

I saw a third—I heard his voice:
It is the Hermit good!
He singeth loud his godly hymns 510
That he makes in the wood.
He'll shrieve my soul, he'll wash away
The Albatross's blood.

PART THE SEVENTH

The Hermit of the Wood.

This Hermit good lives in that wood
Which slopes down to the sea. 515
How loudly his sweet voice he rears!
He loves to talk with marineres
That come from a far countree.

He kneels at morn, and noon, and eve—
He hath a cushion plump: 520
It is the moss that wholly hides
The rotted old oak-stump.

The skiff-boat neared: I heard them talk,
'Why this is strange, I trow!
Where are those lights so many and fair, 525
That signal made but now?'

Approacheth the ship with wonder.

'Strange, by my faith!' the Hermit said—
'And they answered not our cheer!
The planks looked warped! and see those sails
How thin they are and sere!
I never saw aught like to them,
Unless perchance it were   530

Brown skeletons of leaves that lag
My forest-brook along;
When the ivy-tod is heavy with snow,
And the owlet whoops to the wolf below,   535
That eats the she-wolf's young.'

'Dear Lord! it hath a fiendish look—
(The Pilot made reply)
I am a-feared'—'Push on, push on!'   540
Said the Hermit cheerily.

The boat came closer to the ship,
But I nor spake nor stirred;
The boat came close beneath the ship,
And straight a sound was heard.   545

The ship suddenly sinketh.

Under the water it rumbled on,
Still louder and more dread:
It reached the ship, it split the bay;
The ship went down like lead.

The ancient Mariner is saved in the Pilot's boat.

Stunned by that loud and dreadful sound,   550
Which sky and ocean smote,
Like one that hath been seven days drowned
My body lay afloat;
But swift as dreams, myself I found
Within the Pilot's boat.   555

Upon the whirl, where sank the ship,
The boat spun round and round;
And all was still, save that the hill
Was telling of the sound.

I moved my lips—the Pilot shrieked   560
And fell down in a fit;
The holy Hermit raised his eyes,
And prayed where he did sit.

I took the oars: the Pilot's boy,
Who now doth crazy go,   565
Laughed loud and long, and all the while
His eyes went to and fro.
'Ha! ha!' quoth he, 'full plain I see,
The Devil knows how to row.'

And now, all in my own countree,   570
I stood on the firm land!
The Hermit stepped forth from the boat,
And scarcely he could stand.

The ancient Mariner earnestly entreateth the Hermit to shrieve him; and the penance of life falls on him.

'O shrieve me, shrieve me, holy man!'
The Hermit crossed his brow.   575
'Say quick,' quoth he, 'I bid thee say—
What manner of man art thou?'

Forthwith this frame of mine was wrenched
With a woeful agony,
Which forced me to begin my tale;   580
And then it left me free.

And ever and anon throughout his future life an agony
constraineth him to travel
from land to land;

Since then, at an uncertain hour,
That agony returns:
And till my ghastly tale is told,
This heart within me burns.   585

I pass, like night, from land to land;
I have strange power of speech;
That moment that his face I see,
I know the man that must hear me:
To him my tale I teach.   590

What loud uproar bursts from that door!
The wedding-guests are there:
But in the garden-bower the bride
And bride-maids singing are:
And hark the little vesper bell,   595
Which biddeth me to prayer!

O Wedding-Guest! this soul hath been
Alone on a wide wide sea:
So lonely 'twas, that God himself
Scarce seemèd there to be.   600

O sweeter than the marriage-feast,
'Tis sweeter far to me,
To walk together to the kirk
With a goodly company!—

To walk together to the kirk,   605
And all together pray,
While each to his great Father bends,
Old men, and babes, and loving friends,
And youths and maidens gay!

Farewell, farewell! but this I tell   610
To thee, thou Wedding-Guest!
He prayeth well, who loveth well
Both man and bird and beast.

And to teach, by his own
example, love and reverence
to all things that God made
and loveth.

He prayeth best, who loveth best
All things both great and small;   615
For the dear God who loveth us,
He made and loveth all."

The Mariner, whose eye is bright,
Whose beard with age is hoar,
Is gone: and now the Wedding-Guest   620
Turned from the bridegroom's door.

He went like one that hath been stunned,
And is of sense forlorn:
A sadder and a wiser man,
He rose the morrow morn.   625

FRANCE: AN ODE

I

Ye Clouds! that far above me float and
  pause,
  Whose pathless march no mortal may
  control!
Ye Ocean-Waves! that, wheresoe'er ye
  roll,
Yield homage only to eternal laws!
Ye Woods! that listen to the night-birds
  singing,   5
  Midway the smooth and perilous slope
  reclined,
Save when your own imperious branches
  swinging,
  Have made a solemn music of the wind!
Where, like a man beloved of God,
Through glooms, which never woodman
  trod,   10
  How oft, pursuing fancies holy,
My moonlight way o'er flowering weeds I
  wound,
Inspired, beyond the guess of folly,
By each rude shape and wild unconquer-
  able sound!
O ye loud Waves! and O ye Forests high! 15
  And O ye Clouds that far above me
  soared!
Thou rising Sun! thou blue rejoicing Sky!
  Yea, every thing that is and will be free!
Bear witness for me, wheresoe'er ye be,
  With what deep worship I have still
  adored   20
  The spirit of divinest Liberty.

II

When France in wrath her giant-limbs up-
  reared,
  And with that oath, which smote air,
  earth, and sea,
Stamped her strong foot and said she
  would be free,
Bear witness for me, how I hoped and
  feared!   25
With what a joy my lofty gratulation
  Unawed I sang, amid a slavish band:
And when to whelm the disenchanted na-
  tion,
  Like fiends embattled by a wizard's
  wand,
  The Monarchs marched in evil day, 30
And Britain joined the dire array;
  Though dear her shores and circling
  ocean,
Though many friendships, many youthful
  loves,
  Had swol'n the patriot emotion,
And flung a magic light o'er all her hills
  and groves;   35

Yet still my voice, unaltered, sang defeat
  To all that braved the tyrant-quelling
  lance,
And shame too long delayed and vain re-
  treat!
For ne'er, O Liberty! with partial aim
I dimmed thy light or damped thy holy
  flame;   40
  But blessed the pæans of delivered
  France,
And hung my head and wept at Britain's
  name.

III

"And what," I said, "though Blasphemy's
  loud scream
  With that sweet music of deliverance
  strove!
Though all the fierce and drunken pas-
  sions wove   45
A dance more wild than e'er was maniac's
  dream!
Ye storms, that round the dawning east
  assembled,
The Sun was rising, though ye hid his
  light!"
And when, to soothe my soul, that hoped
  and trembled,
The dissonance ceased, and all seemed
  calm and bright;   50
When France her front deep-scarred and
  gory
Concealed with clustering wreaths of
  glory;
  When, insupportably advancing,
Her arm made mockery of the warrior's
  ramp;
  While timid looks of fury glancing, 55
Domestic treason, crushed beneath her
  fatal stamp,
Writhed like a wounded dragon in his
  gore;
  Then I reproached my fears that would
  not flee;
"And soon," I said, "shall Wisdom teach
  her lore
In the low huts of them that toil and
  groan!   60
And, conquering by her happiness alone,
  Shall France compel the nations to be
  free,
Till Love and Joy look round, and call the
  Earth their own."

IV

Forgive me, Freedom! O forgive those
  dreams!
I hear thy voice, I hear thy loud lament,   65
  From Bleak Helvetia's icy cavern sent—

I hear thy groans upon her blood-stained
　　streams!
　Heroes, that for your peaceful country
　　perished,
And ye that, fleeing, spot your mountain-
　snows
　With bleeding wounds; forgive me, that
　　I cherished   70
One thought that ever blessed your cruel
　foes!
　　To scatter rage, and traitorous guilt,
　　Where Peace her jealous home had
　　　built;
　　A patriot-race to disinherit
Of all that made their stormy wilds so
　dear;   75
　And with inexpiable spirit
To taint the bloodless freedom of the
　mountaineer—
O France, that mockest Heaven, adulter-
　ous, blind,
　And patriot only in pernicious toils!
Are these thy boasts, Champion of human-
　kind?   80
　To mix with Kings in the low lust of
　　sway,
Yell in the hunt, and share the murderous
　prey;
To insult the shrine of Liberty with
　spoils
　From freemen torn; to tempt and to be-
　　tray?

v

　The Sensual and the Dark rebel in
　　vain,   85
Slaves by their own compulsion! In mad
　game
They burst their manacles and wear the
　name
　Of Freedom, graven on a heavier
　　chain!
O Liberty! with profitless endeavor
Have I pursued thee, many a weary
　hour;   90
But thou nor swell'st the victor's strain,
　nor ever
Didst breathe thy soul in forms of human
　power.
　Alike from all, howe'er they praise thee
　(Nor prayer, nor boastful name delays
　　thee),
　　Alike from Priestcraft's harpy min-
　　ions,   95
And factious Blasphemy's obscener
　slaves.
　　Thou speedest on thy subtle pinions,
The guide of homeless winds, and play-
　mate of the waves!

And there I felt thee!—on that sea-cliff's
　verge,
　Whose pines, scarce travelled by the
　　breeze above,   100
Had made one murmur with the distant
　surge!
Yes, while I stood and gazed, my temples
　bare,
And shot my being through earth, sea, and
　air,
　Possessing all things with intensest love,
　O Liberty! my spirit felt thee there. 105

Feb. 1797   1798

FROST AT MIDNIGHT

The frost performs its secret ministry,
Unhelped by any wind. The owlet's cry
Came loud—and hark, again! loud as be-
　fore.
The inmates of my cottage, all at rest,
Have left me to that solitude, which suits 5
Abstruser musings: save that at my side
My cradled infant slumbers peacefully.
'Tis calm indeed! so calm, that it dis-
　turbs
And vexes meditation with its strange
And extreme silentness. Sea, hill, and
　wood,   10
This populous village! Sea, and hill, and
　wood,
With all the numberless goings-on of life,
Inaudible as dreams! the thin blue flame
Lies on my low-burnt fire, and quivers not;
Only that film, which fluttered on the
　grate,   15
Still flutters there, the sole unquiet thing.
Methinks, its motion in this hush of na-
　ture
Gives it dim sympathies with me who
　live,
Making it a companionable form,
Whose puny flaps and freaks the idling
　spirit   20
By its own moods interprets, everywhere
Echo or mirror seeking of itself,
And makes a toy of thought.

　　　　　　　　　　　But O! how oft,
How oft, at school, with most believing
　mind,
Presageful, have I gazed upon the bars, 25
To watch that fluttering stranger! and as
　oft
With unclosed lids, already had I dreamt
Of my sweet birth-place, and the old
　church-tower,
Whose bells, the poor man's only music,
　rang

From morn to evening, all the hot Fair-
    day,   30
So sweetly, that they stirred and haunted me
With a wild pleasure, falling on mine ear
Most like articulate sounds of things to
    come!
So gazed I, till the soothing things, I
    dreamt,
Lulled me to sleep, and sleep prolonged
    my dreams!   35
And so I brooded all the following morn,
Awed by the stern preceptor's face, mine
    eye
Fixed with mock study on my swimming
    book:
Save if the door half opened, and I
    snatched
A hasty glance, and still my heart leaped
    up,   40
For still I hoped to see the stranger's face,
Townsman, or aunt, or sister more be-
    loved,
My playmate when we both were clothed
    alike!

    Dear babe, that sleepest cradled by my
        side,
Whose gentle breathings, heard in this
    deep calm,   45
Fill up the interspersèd vacancies
And momentary pauses of the thought!
My babe so beautiful! it thrills my heart
With tender gladness, thus to look at thee,
And think that thou shalt learn far other
    lore,   50
And in far other scenes! For I was reared
In the great city, pent 'mid cloisters dim,
And saw nought lovely but the sky and
    stars.
But thou, my babe! shalt wander like a
    breeze
By lakes and sandy shores, beneath the
    crags   55
Of ancient mountain, and beneath the
    clouds,
Which image in their bulk both lakes and
    shores
And mountain crags: so shalt thou see and
    hear
The lovely shapes and sounds intelligible
Of that eternal language, which thy God 60
Utters, who from eternity doth teach
Himself in all, and all things in himself.
Great universal Teacher! he shall mold
Thy spirit, and by giving make it ask.

    Therefore all seasons shall be sweet to
        thee,   65
Whether the summer clothe the general
    earth

With greenness, or the redbreast sit and
    sing
Betwixt the tufts of snow on the bare
    branch
Of mossy apple-tree, while the nigh thatch
Smokes in the sun-thaw; whether the eave·
    drops fall   70
Heard only in the trances of the blast,
Or if the secret ministry of frost
Shall hang them up in silent icicles,
Quietly shining to the quiet moon.
1798   1798

FEARS IN SOLITUDE

WRITTEN IN APRIL, 1798, DURING THE
ALARM OF AN INVASION

A green and silent spot, amid the hills,
A small and silent dell! O'er stiller place
No singing skylark ever poised himself.
The hills are heathy, save that swelling
    slope,
Which hath a gay and gorgeous covering
    on,   5
All golden with the never bloomless furze,
Which now blooms most profusely: but the
    dell,
Bathed by the mist, is fresh and delicate
As vernal corn-field, or the unripe flax,
When, through its half-transparent stalks,
    at eve,   10
The level sunshine glimmers with green
    light.
Oh! 'tis a quiet spirit-healing nook!
Which all, methinks, would love; but
    chiefly he,
The humble man, who, in his youthful
    years,
Knew just so much of folly, as had made 15
His early manhood more securely wise!
Here he might lie on fern or withered
    heath,
While from the singing lark (that sings
    unseen
The minstrelsy that solitude loves best),
And from the sun, and from the breezy
    air,   20
Sweet influences trembled o'er his frame;
And he, with many feelings, many
    thoughts,
Made up a meditative joy, and found
Religious meanings in the forms of nature!
And so, his senses gradually wrapt   25
In a half sleep, he dreams of better worlds,
And dreaming hears thee still, O singing
    lark,
That singest like an angel in the clouds!

My God! it is a melancholy thing
For such a man, who would full fain pre-
  serve 30
His soul in calmness, yet perforce must
  feel
For all his human brethren—O my God!
It weighs upon the heart, that he must
  think
What uproar and what strife may now be
  stirring
This way or that way o'er these silent
  hills— 35
Invasion,—and the thunder and the shout,
And all the crash of onset; fear and rage,
And undetermined conflict—even now,
Even now, perchance, and in his native
  isle:
Carnage and groans beneath this blessed
  sun! 40
We have offended, Oh! my countrymen!
We have offended very grievously,
And been most tyrannous. From east to
  west
A groan of accusation pierces heaven!
The wretched plead against us; multi-
  tudes 45
Countless and vehement, the sons of God,
Our brethren! Like a cloud that travels
  on,
Steamed up from Cairo's swamps of pes-
  tilence,
Even so, my countrymen! have we gone
  forth
And borne to distant tribes slavery and
  pangs, 50
And, deadlier far, our vices, whose deep
  taint
With slow perdition murders the whole
  man,
His body and his soul! Meanwhile, at
  home,
All individual dignity and power
Engulfed in courts, committees, institu-
  tions, 55
Associations and societies,
A vain, speech-mouthing, speech-reporting
  guild,
One benefit-club for mutual flattery,
We have drunk up, demure as at a grace,
Pollutions from the brimming cup of
  wealth; 60
Contemptuous of all honorable rule,
Yet bartering freedom and the poor man's
  life
For gold, as at a market! The sweet words
Of Christian promise, words that even yet
Might stem destruction, were they wisely
  preached, 65
Are muttered o'er by men, whose tones
  proclaim

How flat and wearisome they feel their
  trade:
Rank scoffers some, but most too indolent
To deem them falsehoods or to know their
  truth.
Oh! blasphemous! the Book of Life is
  made 70
A superstitious instrument, on which
We gabble o'er the oaths we mean to
  break;
For all must swear—all and in every place,
College and wharf, council and justice-
  court;
All, all must swear, the briber and the
  bribed, 75
Merchant and lawyer, senator and priest,
The rich, the poor, the old man and the
  young;
All, all make up one scheme of perjury,
That faith doth reel; the very name of
  God
Sounds like a juggler's charm; and, bold
  with joy, 80
Forth from his dark and lonely hiding-
  place,
(Portentous sight!) the owlet Atheism,
Sailing on obscene wings athwart the noon,
Drops his blue-fringèd lids, and holds them
  close,
And hooting at the glorious sun in
  heaven, 85
Cries out, "Where is it?"

    Thankless too for peace,
(Peace long preserved by fleets and peril-
  ous seas)
Secure from actual warfare, we have loved
To swell the war-whoop, passionate for
  war!
Alas! for ages ignorant of all 90
Its ghastlier workings (famine or blue
  plague,
Battle, or siege, or flight through wintry
  snows,)
We, this whole people, have been clamor-
  ous
For war and bloodshed; animating sports,
The which we pay for as a thing we talk
  of, 95
Spectators and not combatants! No guess
Anticipative of a wrong unfelt,
No speculation on contingency,
However dim and vague, too vague and
  dim
To yield a justifying cause; and forth, 100
(Stuffed out with big preamble, holy names,
And adjurations of the God in heaven,)
We send our mandates for the certain
  death

Of thousands and ten thousands! Boys
   and girls,
And women, that would groan to see a
   child   105
Pull off an insect's leg, all read of war,
The best amusement for our morning
   meal!
The poor wretch, who has learnt his only
   prayers
From curses, who knows scarcely words
   enough
To ask a blessing from his Heavenly
   Father,   110
Becomes a fluent phraseman, absolute
And technical in victories and defeats,
And all our dainty terms for fratricide;
Terms which we trundle smoothly o'er our
   tongues
Like mere abstractions, empty sounds to
   which   115
We join no feeling and attach no form!
As if the soldier died without a wound;
As if the fibers of this godlike frame
Were gored without a pang; as if the
   wretch,
Who fell in battle, doing bloody deeds, 120
Passed off to heaven, translated and not
   killed;
As though he had no wife to pine for him,
No God to judge him! Therefore, evil
   days
Are coming on us, O my countrymen!
And what if all-avenging Providence, 125
Strong and retributive, should make us
   know
The meaning of our words, force us to
   feel
The desolation and the agony
Of our fierce doings?

                Spare us yet awhile,
Father and God! Oh! spare us yet
   awhile!   130
Oh! let not English women drag their
   flight
Fainting beneath the burthen of their
   babes,
Of the sweet infants, that but yesterday
Laughed at the breast! Sons, brothers, hus-
   bands, all
Who ever gazed with fondness on the
   forms   135
Which grew up with you round the same
   fire-side,
And all who ever heard the sabbath-bells
Without the infidel's scorn, make your-
   selves pure!
Stand forth! be men! repel an impious foe,
Impious and false, a light yet cruel race, 140
Who laugh away all virtue, mingling mirth

With deeds of murder; and still promising
Freedom, themselves too sensual to be free,
Poison life's amities, and cheat the heart
Of faith and quiet hope, and all that
   soothes,   145
And all that lifts the spirit! Stand we
   forth;
Render them back upon the insulted
   ocean,
And let them toss as idly on its waves
As the vile sea-weed, which some mountain-
   blast
Swept from our shores! And oh! may we
   return   150
Not with a drunken triumph, but with
   fear,
Repenting of the wrongs with which we
   stung
So fierce a foe to frenzy!

                      I have told,
O Britons, O my brethren! I have told
Most bitter truth, but without bitter-
   ness.   155
Nor deem my zeal or factious or mistimed;
For never can true courage dwell with
   them,
Who, playing tricks with conscience, dare
   not look
At their own vices. We have been too
   long
Dupes of a deep delusion! Some, be-
   like,   160
Groaning with restless enmity, expect
All change from change of constituted
   power;
As if a government had been a robe,
On which our vice and wretchedness were
   tagged
Like fancy-points and fringes, with the
   robe   165
Pulled off at pleasure. Fondly these attach
A radical causation to a few
Poor drudges of chastising Providence,
Who borrow all their hues and qualities
From our own folly and rank wicked-
   ness,   170
Which gave them birth and nursed them.
   Others, meanwhile,
Dote with a mad idolatry; and all
Who will not fall before their images,
And yield them worship, they are enemies
Even of their country!

               Such have I been deemed.— 175
But, O dear Britain! O my mother isle!
Needs must thou prove a name most dear
   and holy
To me, a son, a brother, and a friend,
A husband, and a father! who revere

All bonds of natural love, and find them
   all 180
Within the limits of thy rocky shores.
O native Britain! O my mother isle!
How shouldst thou prove aught else but
   dear and holy
To me, who from thy lakes and mountain-
   hills,
Thy clouds, thy quiet dales, thy rocks and
   seas, 185
Have drunk in all my intellectual life,
All   sweet   sensations,   all   ennobling
   thoughts,
All adoration of the God in nature,
All lovely and all honorable things,
Whatever makes this mortal spirit feel 190
The joy and greatness of its future being?
There lives nor form nor feeling in my
   soul
Unborrowed from my country! O divine
And beauteous Island! thou hast been my
   sole
And most magnificent temple, in the
   which 195
I walk with awe, and sing my stately songs,
Loving the God that made me!—

                    May my fears,
My filial fears, be vain! and may the vaunts
And menace of the vengeful enemy
Pass like the gust, that roared and died
   away 200
In the distant tree: which heard, and only
   heard
In this low dell, bowed not the delicate
   grass.

   But now the gentle dew-fall sends abroad
The fruit-like perfume of the golden furze:
The light has left the summit of the
   hill, 205
Though still a sunny gleam lies beautiful,
Aslant the ivied beacon. Now farewell,
Farewell, awhile, O soft and silent spot!
On the green sheep-track, up the heathy
   hill,
Homeward I wind my way; and lo! re-
   called 210
From bodings that have well-nigh wearied
   me,
I find myself upon the brow, and pause
Startled! And after lonely sojourning
In such a quiet and surrounded nook,
This burst of prospect, here the shadowy
   main, 215
Dim-tinted, there the mighty majesty
Of that huge amphitheater of rich
And elmy fields, seems like society—
Conversing with the mind, and giving it

A livelier impulse and a dance of
   thought! 220
And now, belovèd Stowey! I behold
Thy church-tower, and, methinks, the four
   huge elms
Clustering, which mark the mansion of my
   friend;
And close behind them, hidden from my
   view,
Is my own lowly cottage, where my babe 225
And my babe's mother dwell in peace!
   With light
And quickened footsteps thitherward I
   tend,
Remembering thee, O green and silent
   dell!
And grateful, that by nature's quietness
And solitary musings, all my heart 230
Is softened, and made worthy to indulge
Love, and the thoughts that yearn for
   human kind.

1798   1798

FROM THE NIGHTINGALE: A CONVERSATION POEM

                 'Tis the merry Nightingale
That crowds, and hurries, and precipitates
With   fast   thick   warble   his   delicious
   notes, 45
As he were fearful that an April night
Would be too short, for him to utter forth
His love-chant, and disburthen his full soul
Of all its music!
                And I know a grove
Of large extent, hard by a castle huge, 50
Which the great lord inhabits not; and so
This grove is wild with tangling under-
   wood,
And the trim walks are broken up, and
   grass,
Thin grass and king-cups grow within the
   paths.
But never elsewhere in one place I knew 55
So many nightingales; and far and near,
In wood and thicket, over the wide grove,
They answer and provoke each other's
   song,
With skirmish and capricious passagings
And murmurs musical and swift jug jug, 60
And one low piping sound more sweet
   than all—
Stirring the air with such a harmony,
That should you close your eyes, you might
   almost
Forget it was not day! On moonlight
   bushes,
Whose dewy leaflets are but half-dis-
   closed. 65

You may perchance behold them on the
    twigs,
Their bright, bright eyes, their eyes both
    bright and full,
Glistening, while many a glow-worm in the
    shade
Lights up her love-torch.
Apr. 1798   1798

THE BALLAD OF THE DARK
LADIÉ

A FRAGMENT

Beneath yon birch with silver bark,
And boughs so pendulous and fair,
The brook falls scattered down the rock:
    And all is mossy there!

And there upon the moss she sits,   5
The Dark Ladié in silent pain;
The heavy tear is in her eye,
    And drops and swells again.

Three times she sends her little page
Up the castled mountain's breast,   10
If he might find the Knight that wears
    The Griffin for his crest.

The sun was sloping down the sky,
And she had lingered there all day,
Counting moments, dreaming fears—   15
    Oh wherefore can he stay?

She hears a rustling o'er the brook,
She sees far off a swinging bough!
" 'Tis He! 'Tis my betrothéd Knight!
    Lord Falkland, it is Thou!"   20

She springs, she clasps him round the neck,
She sobs a thousand hopes and fears,
Her kisses glowing on his cheeks
    She quenches with her tears.

    *   *   *

"My friends with rude ungentle words   25
They scoff and bid me fly to thee!
O give me shelter in thy breast!
    O shield and shelter me!

"My Henry, I have given thee much,
I gave what I can ne'er recall,   30
I gave my heart, I gave my peace,
    O Heaven! I gave thee all."

The Knight made answer to the Maid,
While to his heart he held her hand,
"Nine castles hath my noble-sire,   35
    None statelier in the land.

"The fairest one shall be my love's,
The fairest castle of the nine!
Wait only till the stars peep out,
    The fairest shall be thine: 40

"Wait only till the hand of eve
Hath wholly closed yon western bars,
And through the dark we two will steal
    Beneath the twinkling stars!"—

"The dark? the dark? No! not the dark? 45
The twinkling stars? How, Henry? How?"
O God! 'twas in the eye of noon
    He pledged his sacred vow!

And in the eye of noon my love
Shall lead me from my mother's door,   50
Sweet boys and girls all clothed in white
    Strewing flowers before:

But first the nodding minstrels go
With music meet for lordly bowers,
The children next in snow-white vests,   55
    Strewing buds and flowers!

And then my love and I shall pace,
My jet black hair in pearly braids,
Between our comely bachelors
    And blushing bridal maids.   60

                1798

ON A CATARACT

FROM A CAVERN NEAR THE SUMMIT
OF A MOUNTAIN PRECIPICE

STROPHE

Unperishing youth!
Thou leapest from forth
The cell of thy hidden nativity;
Never mortal saw
The cradle of the strong one;   5
Never mortal heard
The gathering of his voices;
The deep-murmured charm of the son of
    the rock,
That is lisped evermore at his slumberless
    fountain.
There's a cloud at the portal, a spray-
    woven veil   10
At the shrine of his ceaseless renewing;
It embosoms the roses of dawn,
It entangles the shafts of the noon,
And into the bed of its stillness
The moonshine sinks down as in slumber, 15
That the son of the rock, that the nursling
    of heaven
May be born in a holy twilight!

ANTISTROPHE

The wild goat in awe
Looks up and beholds
Above thee the cliff inaccessible;— 20
Thou art once full-born
Madd'nest in thy joyance,
Whirlest, shatter'st, splitt'st,
Life invulnerable.

1799(?)

THE DEVIL'S THOUGHTS

I

From his brimstone bed at break of day
A walking the Devil is gone,
To visit his snug little farm the earth,
And see how his stock goes on.

II

Over the hill and over the dale, 5
And he went over the plain,
And backward and forward he switched
his long tail
As a gentleman switches his cane.

III

And how then was the Devil drest?
Oh! he was in his Sunday's best: 10
His jacket was red and his breeches were
blue,
And there was a hole where the tail came
through.

IV

He saw a Lawyer killing a Viper
On a dunghill hard by his own stable;
And the Devil smiled, for it put him in
mind 15
Of Cain and his brother, Abel.

V

He saw an Apothecary on a white horse
Ride by on his vocations,
And the Devil thought of his old Friend
Death in the Revelations. 20

VI

He saw a cottage with a double coach-
house,
A cottage of gentility;
And the Devil did grin, for his darling sin
Is pride that apes humility.

VII

He peeped into a rich bookseller's shop, 25
Quoth he! we are both of one college!
For I sate myself, like a cormorant, once
Hard by the tree of knowledge.

VIII

Down the river did glide, with wind and
tide,
A pig with vast celerity; 30
And the Devil looked wise as he saw how
the while,
It cut its own throat. "There!" quoth he
with a smile,
"Goes 'England's commercial prosperity.'"

IX

As he went through Cold-Bath Fields he
saw
A solitary cell; 35
And the Devil was pleased, for it gave him
a hint
For improving his prisons in Hell.

X

He saw a Turnkey in a trice
Fetter a troublesome blade;
"Nimbly," quoth he, "do the fingers move 40
If a man be but used to his trade."

XI

He saw the same Turnkey unfetter a man,
With but little expedition,
Which put him in mind of the long debate
On the Slave-trade abolition. 45

XII

He saw an old acquaintance
As he passed by a Methodist meeting;—
She holds a consecrated key,
And the devil nods her a greeting.

XIII

She turned up her nose, and said, 50
"Avaunt! my name's Religion,"
And she looked to Mr. ——
And leered like a love-sick pigeon.

XIV

He saw a certain minister
(A minister to his mind) 55
Go up into a certain House,
With a majority, behind.

XV

The Devil quoted Genesis
Like a very learnéd clerk,
How "Noah and his creeping things 60
Went up into the Ark."

XVI

He took from the poor,
And he gave to the rich,
And he shook hands with a Scotchman,
For he was not afraid of the —— 65

XVII

General ——'s burning face
  He saw with consternation,
And back to hell his way did he take,
  For the Devil thought by a slight mistake
It was general conflagration.   70

6 Sept. 1799

LINES

WRITTEN IN THE ALBUM AT ELBINGE-RODE, IN THE HARTZ FOREST

I stood on Brocken's sovran height, and
  saw
Woods crowding upon woods, hills over
  hills,
A surging scene, and only limited
By the blue distance. Heavily my way
Downward I dragged through fir groves
  evermore,   5
Where bright green moss heaves in sepul-
  chral forms
Speckled with sunshine; and, but seldom
  heard,
The sweet bird's song became a hollow
  sound;
And the breeze, murmuring indivisibly,
Preserved its solemn murmur most dis-
  tinct   10
From many a note of many a waterfall,
And the brook's chatter; 'mid whose islet-
  stones
The dingy kidling with its tinkling bell
Leaped frolicsome, or old romantic goat
Sat, his white beard slow waving. I moved
  on   15
In low and languid mood: for I had found
That outward forms, the loftiest, still re-
  ceive
Their finer influence from the life with-
  in;—
Fair cyphers else: fair, but of import vague
Or unconcerning, where the heart not
  finds   20
History or prophecy of friend, or child,
Or gentle maid, our first and early love,
Or father, or the venerable name
Of our adorèd country! O thou queen,
Thou delegated deity of earth,   25
O dear, dear England! how my longing eye
Turned westward, shaping in the steady
  clouds
Thy sands and high white cliffs!

                  My native land!
Filled with the thought of thee this heart
  was proud,

Yea, mine eye swam with tears: that all
  the view   30
From sovran Brocken, woods and woody
  hills,
Floated away, like a departing dream,
Feeble and dim! Stranger, these impulses
Blame thou not lightly; nor will I profane,
With hasty judgment or injurious doubt, 35
That man's sublimer spirit, who can feel
That God is everywhere! the God who
  framed
Mankind to be one mighty family,
Himself our Father, and the world our
  home.

1799   1799

LOVE

All thoughts, all passions, all delights,
Whatever stirs this mortal frame,
All are but ministers of Love,
  And feed his sacred flame.

Oft in my waking dreams do I   5
Live o'er again that happy hour,
When midway on the mount I lay,
  Beside the ruined tower.

The moonshine, stealing o'er the scene
Had blended with the lights of eve;   10
And she was there, my hope, my joy,
  My own dear Genevieve!

She leaned against the armed man,
The statue of the armed knight;
She stood and listened to my lay,   15
  Amid the lingering light.

Few sorrows hath she of her own,
My hope! my joy! my Genevieve!
She loves me best, whene'er I sing
  The songs that make her grieve.   20

I played a soft and doleful air,
I sang an old and moving story—
An old rude song, that suited well
  That ruin wild and hoary.

She listened with a flitting blush,   25
With downcast eyes and modest grace;
For well she knew, I could not choose
  But gaze upon her face.

I told her of the Knight that wore
Upon his shield a burning brand;   30
And that for ten long years he wooed
  The Lady of the Land.

I told her how he pined: and ah!
The deep, the low, the pleading tone
With which I sang another's love,   35
      Interpreted my own.

She listened with a flitting blush,
With downcast eyes, and modest grace;
And she forgave me, that I gazed
      Too fondly on her face!   40

But when I told the cruel scorn
That crazed that bold and lovely Knight,
And that he crossed the mountain-woods,
      Nor rested day nor night;

That sometimes from the savage den,   45
And sometimes from the darksome shade,
And sometimes starting up at once
      In green and sunny glade,—

There came and looked him in the face
An angel beautiful and bright;   50
And that he knew it was a fiend,
      This miserable Knight!

And that, unknowing what he did,
He leaped amid a murderous band,
And saved from outrage worse than death   55
      The Lady of the Land!

And how she wept, and clasped his knees;
And how she tended him in vain—
And ever strove to expiate
      The scorn that crazed his brain;—   60

And that she nursed him in a cave;
And how his madness went away,
When on the yellow forest-leaves
      A dying man he lay;—

His dying words—but when I reached   65
That tenderest strain of all the ditty,
My faltering voice and pausing harp
      Disturbed her soul with pity!

All impulses of soul and sense
Had thrilled my guileless Genevieve;   70
The music and the doleful tale,
      The rich and balmy eve;

And hopes, and fears that kindle hope,
An undistinguishable throng,
And gentle wishes long subdued,   75
      Subdued and cherished long!

She wept with pity and delight,
She blushed with love, and virgin-shame;
And like the murmur of a dream,
      I heard her breathe my name.   80

Her bosom heaved—she stepped aside,
As conscious of my look she stept—
Then suddenly, with timorous eye,
      She fled to me and wept.

She half inclosed me with her arms,   85
She pressed me with a meek embrace;
And bending back her head, looked up,
      And gazed upon my face.

'Twas partly love, and partly fear,
And partly 'twas a bashful art,   90
That I might rather feel, than see,
      The swelling of her heart.

I calmed her fears, and she was calm,
And told her love with virgin pride;
And so I won my Genevieve,   95
      My bright and beauteous Bride.

1799   1799

CHRISTABEL

PREFACE

The first part of the following poem was written in the year 1797, at Stowey, in the county of Somerset. The second part, after my return from Germany, in the year 1800, at Keswick, Cumberland. Since the latter date, my poetic powers have been, till very lately, in a state of suspended animation. But as, in my very first conception of the tale, I had the whole present to my mind, with the wholeness, no less than the liveliness of a vision; I trust that I shall be able to embody in verse the three parts yet to come . . .

It is probable that if the poem had been finished at either of the former periods, or if even the first and second part had been published in the year 1800, the impression of its originality would have been much greater than I dare at present expect. But for this, I have only my own indolence to blame. The dates are mentioned for the exclusive purpose of precluding charges of plagiarism or servile imitation from myself. For there is among us a set of critics who seem to hold that every possible thought and image is traditional; who have no notion that there are such things as fountains in the world, small as well as great; and who would therefore charitably derive every rill they behold flowing, from a perforation made in some other man's tank. I am confident, however, that as far as the present poem is concerned, the celebrated poets whose writings I might be suspected of having imitated, either in particular passages, or in the tone and the spirit of the whole, would be among the first to vindicate me from the charge, and who, on any striking coincidence, would permit me to address them in this doggerel version of two monkish Latin hexameters:

'Tis mine and it is likewise yours;
But an if this will not do;
Let it be mine, good friend! for I
Am the poorer of the two.

I have only to add that the metre of the Christabel is not, properly speaking, irregular, though it may seem so from its being founded on a new principle: namely, that of counting in each line the accents, not the syllables. Though the latter may vary from seven to twelve, yet in each line the accents will be found to be only four. Nevertheless, this occasional variation in number of syllables is not introduced wantonly, or for the mere ends of convenience, but in correspondence with some transition in the nature of the imagery or passion.

PART THE FIRST

'Tis the middle of night by the castle
   clock,
And the owls have awakened the crowing
   cock;
Tu—whit!——Tu—whoo!
And hark, again! the crowing cock,
How drowsily it crew.   5

Sir Leoline, the Baron rich,
Hath a toothless mastiff bitch;
From her kennel beneath the rock
She maketh answer to the clock,
Four for the quarters, and twelve for the
   hour;   10
Ever and aye, by shine and shower,
Sixteen short howls, not over loud;
Some say, she sees my lady's shroud.

Is the night chilly and dark?
The night is chilly, but not dark.   15
The thin gray cloud is spread on high,
It covers but not hides the sky.
The moon is behind, and at the full;
And yet she looks both small and dull.
The night is chill, the cloud is gray: 20
'Tis a month before the month of May,
And the Spring comes slowly up this way.

The lovely lady, Christabel,
Whom her father loves so well,
What makes her in the wood so late,   25
A furlong from the castle gate?
She had dreams all yesternight
Of her own betrothed knight;
And she in the midnight wood will pray
For the weal of her lover that's far away. 30

She stole along, she nothing spoke,
The sighs she heaved were soft and low,
And naught was green upon the oak
But moss and rarest mistletoe:
She kneels beneath the huge oak tree,   35
And in silence prayeth she.

The lady sprang up suddenly,
The lovely lady, Christabel!
It moaned as near, as near can be,
But what it is she cannot tell.—   40
On the other side it seems to be,
Of the huge, broad-breasted, old oak tree.

The night is chill; the forest bare;
Is it the wind that moaneth bleak?
There is not wind enough in the air   45
To move away the ringlet curl
From the lovely lady's cheek—
There is not wind enough to twirl
The one red leaf, the last of its clan,
That dances as often as dance it can,   50
Hanging so light, and hanging so high,
On the topmost twig that looks up at the
   sky.

Hush, beating heart of Christabel!
Jesu, Maria, shield her well!
She folded her arms beneath her cloak,   55
And stole to the other side of the oak.
   What sees she there?

There she sees a damsel bright,
Drest in a silken robe of white,
That shadowy in the moonlight shone: 60
The neck that made that white robe wan,
Her stately neck, and arms were bare:
Her blue-veined feet unsandaled were;
And wildly glittered here and there
The gems entangled in her hair.   65
I guess, 'twas frightful there to see
A lady so richly clad as she—
Beautiful exceedingly!

"Mary mother, save me now!"
Said Christabel, "And who art thou?"   70

The lady strange made answer meet,
And her voice was faint and sweet:—
"Have pity on my sore distress,
I scarce can speak for weariness:

Stretch forth thy hand, and have no
   fear!"   75
Said Christabel, "How camest thou here?"
And the lady, whose voice was faint and
   sweet,
Did thus pursue her answer meet:—

"My sire is of a noble line,
And my name is Geraldine: 80
Five warriors seized me yestermorn,
Me, even me, a maid forlorn:
They choked my cries with force and
   fright,
And tied me on a palfrey white.
The palfrey was as fleet as wind,   85
And they rode furiously behind.

They spurred amain, their steeds were
    white:
And once we crossed the shade of night.
As sure as Heaven shall rescue me,
I have no thought what men they be;   90
Nor do I know how long it is
(For I have lain entranced I wis)
Since one, the tallest of the five,
Took me from the palfrey's back,
A weary woman, scarce alive.   95
Some muttered words his comrades spoke:
He placed me underneath this oak;
He swore they would return with haste;
Whither they went I cannot tell—
I thought I heard, some minutes past,   100
Sounds as of a castle bell.
Stretch forth thy hand" (thus ended she),
"And help a wretched maid to flee."

Then Christabel stretched forth her
    hand,
And comforted fair Geraldine: 105
"O well, bright dame! may you command
The service of Sir Leoline;
And gladly our stout chivalry
Will he send forth and friends withal
To guide and guard you safe and free   110
Home to your noble father's hall."

She rose: and forth with steps they
    passed
That strove to be, and were not, fast.
Her gracious stars the lady blest,
And thus spake on the sweet Christabel: 115
"All our household are at rest,
The hall as silent as the cell;
Sir Leoline is weak in health,
And may not well awakened be,
But we will move as if in stealth,   120
And I beseech your courtesy,
This night, to share your couch with me."

They crossed the moat, and Christabel
Took the key that fitted well;
A little door she opened straight,   125
All in the middle of the gate;
The gate that was ironed within and with-
    out,
Where an army in battle-array had
    marched out.
The lady sank, belike through pain,
And Christabel with might and main   130
Lifted her up, a weary weight,
Over the threshold of the gate:
Then the lady rose again,
And moved, as she were not in pain.

So free from danger, free from fear,   135
They crossed the court: right glad they
    were.

And Christabel devoutly cried
To the lady by her side,
"Praise we the Virgin all divine
Who hath rescued thee from thy dis-
    tress!"   140
"Alas, alas!" said Geraldine,
"I cannot speak for weariness."
So free from danger, free from fear,
They crossed the court: right glad they
    were.

Outside her kennel, the mastiff old   145
Lay fast asleep, in moonshine cold.
The mastiff old did not awake,
Yet she an angry moan did make!
And what can ail the mastiff bitch?
Never till now she uttered yell   150
Beneath the eye of Christabel.
Perhaps it is the owlet's scritch:
For what can ail the mastiff bitch?

They passed the hall, that echoes still,
Pass as lightly as you will!   155
The brands were flat, the brands were
    dying,
Amid their own white ashes lying;
But when the lady passed there came
A tongue of light, a fit of flame;
And Christabel saw the lady's eye,   160
And nothing else saw she thereby,
Save the boss of the shield of Sir Leoline
    tall,
Which hung in a murky old niche in the
    wall.
"O softly tread," said Christabel,
"My father seldom sleepeth well."   165

Sweet Christabel her feet doth bare,
And jealous of the listening air
They steal their way from stair to stair,
Now in glimmer, now in gloom,
And now they pass the Baron's room,   170
As still as death, with stifled breath!
And now have reached her chamber door;
And now doth Geraldine press down
The rushes of the chamber floor.

The moon shines dim in the open air,   175
And not a moonbeam enters here.
But they without its light can see
The chamber carved so curiously,
Carved with figures strange and sweet,
All made out of the carver's brain,   180
For a lady's chamber meet:
The lamp with twofold silver chain
Is fastened to an angel's feet.
The silver lamp burns dead and dim;
But Christabel the lamp will trim.   185
She trimmed the lamp, and made it bright,
And left it swinging to and fro,

While Geraldine, in wretched plight,
Sank down upon the floor below.

"O weary lady, Geraldine,   190
I pray you, drink this cordial wine!
It is a wine of virtuous powers;
My mother made it of wild flowers."

"And will your mother pity me,
Who am a maiden most forlorn?"   195
Christabel answered—"Woe is me!
She died the hour that I was born.
I have heard the gray-haired friar tell
How on her death-bed she did say,
That she should hear the castle bell   200
Strike twelve upon my wedding day.
O mother dear; that thou wert here!"
"I would," said Geraldine, "she were!"

But soon with altered voice, said she—
"Off, wandering mother! Peak and pine! 205
I have power to bid thee flee."
Alas! what ails poor Geraldine?
Why stares she with unsettled eye?
Can she the bodiless dead espy?
And why with hollow voice cries she, 210
"Off, woman, off! this hour is mine—
Though thou her guardian spirit be,
Off, woman, off! 'tis given to me."

Then Christabel knelt by the lady's side,
And raised to heaven her eyes so blue— 215
"Alas!" said she, "this ghastly ride—
Dear lady! it hath wildered you!"
The lady wiped her moist cold brow,
And faintly said, " 'tis over now!"

Again the wild-flower wine she drank: 220
Her fair large eyes 'gan glitter bright,
And from the floor whereon she sank,
The lofty lady stood upright:
She was most beautiful to see,
Like a lady of a far countree.   225

And thus the lofty lady spake—
"All they who live in the upper sky,
Do love you, holy Christabel!
And you love them, and for their sake
And for the good which me befell, 230
Even I in my degree will try,
Fair maiden, to requite you well.
But now unrobe yourself; for I
Must pray, ere yet in bed I lie."

Quoth Christabel, "So let it be!" 235
And as the lady bade, did she.
Her gentle limbs did she undress,
And lay down in her loveliness.

But through her brain of weal and woe
So many thoughts moved to and fro, 240
That vain it were her lids to close;
So half-way from the bed she rose,
And on her elbow did recline
To look at the lady Geraldine.

Beneath the lamp the lady bowed, 245
And slowly rolled her eyes around;
Then drawing in her breath aloud,
Like one that shuddered, she unbound
The cincture from beneath her breast:
Her silken robe, and inner vest, 250
Dropt to her feet, and full in view,
Behold! her bosom and half her side—
A sight to dream of, not to tell!
O shield her! shield sweet Christabel!

Yet Geraldine nor speaks nor stirs; 255
Ah! what a stricken look was hers!
Deep from within she seems half-way
To lift some weight with sick assay,
And eyes the maid and seeks delay;
Then suddenly, as one defied, 260
Collects herself in scorn and pride,
And lay down by the Maiden's side!—
And in her arms the maid she took,
   Ah, wel-a-day!
And with low voice and doleful look 265
   These words did say:
"In the touch of this bosom there worketh
   a spell,
Which is lord of thy utterance, Christabel!
Thou knowest to-night, and wilt know to-
   morrow,
This mark of my shame, this seal of my
   sorrow; 270
   But vainly thou warrest
     For this is alone in
   Thy power to declare,
     That in the dim forest
     Thou heard'st a low moaning, 275
And found'st a bright lady, surpassingly
   fair;
And didst bring her home with thee in
   love and in charity,
To shield her and shelter her from the
   damp air."

THE CONCLUSION TO PART THE FIRST

It was a lovely sight to see
The lady Christabel, when she 280
Was praying at the old oak tree.
   Amid the jaggèd shadows
   Of mossy leafless boughs,
   Kneeling in the moonlight,
   To make her gentle vows; 285
Her slender palms together prest,
Heaving sometimes on her breast;

Her face resigned to bliss or bale—
Her face, oh call it fair not pale,
And both blue eyes more bright than
    clear,   290
Each about to have a tear.

With open eyes (ah woe is me!)
Asleep, and dreaming fearfully,
Fearfully dreaming, yet, I wis,
Dreaming that alone, which is—   295
O sorrow and shame! Can this be she,
The lady, who knelt at the old oak tree?
And lo! the worker of these harms,
That holds the maiden in her arms,
Seems to slumber still and mild,   300
As a mother with her child.

A star hath set, a star hath risen,
O Geraldine! since arms of thine
Have been the lovely lady's prison.
O Geraldine! one hour was thine—   305
Thou'st had thy will! By tairn and rill,
The night-birds all that hour were still.
But now they are jubilant anew,
From cliff and tower, tu—whoo! tu—whoo!
Tu—whoo! tu—whoo! from wood and
    fell!   310

And see the lady Christabel
Gathers herself from out her trance;
Her limbs relax, her countenance
Grows sad and soft; the smooth thin lids
Close o'er her eyes; and tears she sheds—   315
Large tears that leave the lashes bright!
And oft the while she seems to smile
As infants at a sudden light!
Yea, she doth smile, and she doth weep,
Like a youthful hermitess,   320
Beauteous in a wilderness,
Who, praying always, prays in sleep.
And, if she move unquietly,
Perchance, 'tis but the blood so free
Comes back and tingles in her feet.   325
No doubt, she hath a vision sweet.
What if her guardian spirit 'twere,
What if she knew her mother near?
But this she knows, in joys and woes,
That saints will aid if men will call: 330
For the blue sky bends over all!

PART THE SECOND

Each matin bell, the Baron saith,
Knells us back to a world of death.
These words Sir Leoline first said,
When he rose and found his lady dead: 335
These words Sir Leoline will say
Many a morn to his dying day!

And hence the custom and law began
That still at dawn the sacristan,
Who duly pulls the heavy bell,   340
Five and forty beads must tell
Between each stroke—a warning knell,
Which not a soul can choose but hear
From Bratha Head to Wyndermere.

Saith Bracy the bard, "So let it knell! 345
And let the drowsy sacristan
Still count as slowly as he can!"
There is no lack of such, I ween,
As well fill up the space between.
In Langdale Pike and Witch's Lair,   350
And Dungeon-ghyll so foully rent,
With ropes of rock and bells of air
Three sinful sextons' ghosts are pent,
Who all give back, one after t'other,
The death-note to their living brother; 355
And oft too, by the knell offended,
Just as their one! two! three! is ended,
The devil mocks the doleful tale
With a merry peal from Borrowdale.

The air is still! through mist and
    cloud   360
That merry peal comes ringing loud;
And Geraldine shakes off her dread,
And rises lightly from the bed;
Puts on her silken vestments white,
And tricks her hair in lovely plight,   365
And nothing doubting of her spell
Awakens the lady Christabel.
"Sleep you, sweet lady Christabel?
I trust that you have rested well."

And Christabel awoke and spied   370
The same who lay down by her side—
O rather say, the same whom she
Raised up beneath the old oak tree!
Nay, fairer yet! and yet more fair!
For she belike hath drunken deep   375
Of all the blessedness of sleep!
And while she spake, her looks, her air
Such gentle thankfulness declare,
That (so it seemed) her girded vests
Grew tight beneath her heaving breasts. 380
"Sure I have sinned!" said Christabel,
"Now Heaven be praised if all be well!"
And in low faltering tones, yet sweet,
Did she the lofty lady greet
With such perplexity of mind   385
As dreams too lively leave behind.

So quickly she rose, and quickly arrayed
Her maiden limbs, and having prayed
That He, who on the cross did groan,
Might wash away her sins unknown,   390
She forthwith led fair Geraldine
To meet her sire, Sir Leoline.

The lovely maid and the lady tall
Are pacing both into the hall,
And pacing on through page and groom 395
Enter the Baron's presence room.

The Baron rose, and while he prest
His gentle daughter to his breast,
With cheerful wonder in his eyes
The lady Geraldine espies, 400
And gave such welcome to the same,
As might beseem so bright a dame!

But when he heard the lady's tale,
And when she told her father's name,
Why waxed Sir Leoline so pale, 405
Murmuring o'er the name again,
Lord Roland de Vaux of Tryermaine?

Alas! they had been friends in youth;
But whispering tongues can poison truth;
And constancy lives in realms above; 410
And life is thorny; and youth is vain;
And to be wroth with one we love
Doth work like madness in the brain.
And thus it chanced, as I divine,
With Roland and Sir Leoline. 415
Each spake words of high disdain
And insult to his heart's best brother:
They parted—ne'er to meet again!
But never either found another
To free the hollow heart from paining— 420
They stood aloof, the scars remaining,
Like cliffs which had been rent asunder;
A dreary sea now flows between,
But neither heat, nor frost, nor thunder,
Shall wholly do away, I ween, 425
The marks of that which once hath been.

Sir Leoline, a moment's space,
Stood gazing on the damsel's face:
And the youthful Lord of Tryermaine
Came back upon his heart again. 430

O then the Baron forgot his age,
His noble heart swelled high with rage:
He swore by the wounds in Jesu's side
He would proclaim it far and wide
With trump and solemn heraldry, 435
That they, who thus had wronged the
        dame,
Were base as spotted infamy!
"And if they dare deny the same,
My herald shall appoint a week,
And let the recreant traitors seek 440
My tourney court—that there and then
I may dislodge their reptile souls
From the bodies and forms of men!"
He spake: his eye in lightning rolls!

For the lady was ruthlessly seized; and he
        kenned 445
In the beautiful lady the child of his
        friend!

And now the tears were on his face,
And fondly in his arms he took
Fair Geraldine, who met the embrace,
Prolonging it with joyous look. 450
Which when she viewed, a vision fell
Upon the soul of Christabel,
The vision of fear, the touch and pain!
She shrunk and shuddered, and saw
        again—
(Ah, woe is me! Was it for thee, 455
Thou gentle maid! such sights to see?)

Again she saw that bosom old,
Again she felt that bosom cold,
And drew in her breath with a hissing
        sound:
Whereat the Knight turned wildly
        round, 460
And nothing saw, but his own sweet maid
With eyes upraised, as one that prayed.

The touch, the sight, had passed away,
And in its stead the vision blest,
Which comforted her after-rest, 465
While in the lady's arms she lay,
Had put a rapture in her breast,
And on her lips and o'er her eyes
Spread smiles like light!
                With new surprise, 470
"What ails then my belovèd child?"
The Baron said—His daughter mild
Made answer, "All will yet be well!"
I ween, she had no power to tell
Aught else: so mighty was the spell. 475

Yet he, who saw this Geraldine,
Had deemed her sure a thing divine,
Such sorrow with such grace she blended,
As if she feared she had offended
Sweet Christabel, that gentle maid! 480
And with such lowly tones she prayed
She might be sent without delay
Home to her father's mansion.
                        "Nay!
Nay, by my soul!" said Leoline, 485
"Ho! Bracy the bard, the charge be thine!
Go thou, with music sweet and loud,
And take two steeds with trappings proud,
And take the youth whom thou lov'st best
To bear thy harp, and learn thy song, 490
And clothe you both in solemn vest,
And over the mountains haste along,
Lest wandering folk, that are abroad,
Detain you on the valley road.

"And when he has crossed the Irthing
    flood,   495
My merry bard! he hastes, he hastes
Up Knorren Moor, through Halegarth
    Wood,
And reaches soon that castle good
Which stands and threatens Scotland's
    wastes.

"Bard Bracy! bard Bracy! your horses are
    fleet,   500
Ye must ride up the hall, your music so
    sweet,
More loud than your horses' echoing feet!
And loud and loud to Lord Roland call,
Thy daughter is safe in Langdale hall!
Thy beautiful daughter is safe and
    free—   505
Sir Leoline greets thee thus through me!
He bids thee come without delay
With all thy numerous array,
And take thy lovely daughter home:
And he will meet thee on the way   510
With all his numerous array
White with their panting palfreys' foam:
And, by mine honor! I will say,
That I repent me of the day
When I spake words of fierce disdain   515
To Roland de Vaux of Tryermaine!—
—For since that evil hour hath flown,
Many a summer's sun hath shone;
Yet ne'er found I a friend again
Like Roland de Vaux of Tryermaine."   520

The lady fell, and clasped his knees,
Her face upraised, her eyes o'erflowing;
And Bracy replied, with faltering voice,
His gracious hail on all bestowing:—
"Thy words, thou sire of Christabel,   525
Are sweeter than my harp can tell;
Yet might I gain a boon of thee,
This day my journey should not be,
So strange a dream hath come to me,
That I had vowed with music loud   530
To clear yon wood from thing unblest,
Warned by a vision in my rest!
For in my sleep I saw that dove,
That gentle bird, whom thou dost love,
And call'st by thy own daughter's
    name—   535
Sir Leoline! I saw the same
Fluttering, and uttering fearful moan,
Among the green herbs in the forest alone.
Which when I saw and when I heard,
I wondered what might ail the bird;   540
For nothing near it could I see,
Save the grass and green herbs underneath
    the old tree.

"And in my dream, methought, I went
To search out what might there be found;
And what the sweet bird's trouble
    meant,   545
That thus lay fluttering on the ground.
I went and peered, and could descry
No cause for her distressful cry;
But yet for her dear lady's sake
I stooped, methought, the dove to take, 550
When lo! I saw a bright green snake
Coiled around its wings and neck,
Green as the herbs on which it couched,
Close by the dove's its head it crouched;
And with the dove it heaves and stirs, 555
Swelling its neck as she swelled hers!
I woke; it was the midnight hour,
The clock was echoing in the tower,
But though my slumber was gone by,
This dream it would not pass away— 560
It seems to live upon my eye!
And thence I vowed this self-same day
With music strong and saintly song
To wander through the forest bare,
Lest aught unholy loiter there."   565

Thus Bracy said: the Baron, the while,
Half-listening heard him with a smile;
Then turned to Lady Geraldine,
His eyes made up of wonder and love;
And said in courtly accents fine,   570
"Sweet maid, Lord Roland's beauteous
    dove,
With arms more strong than harp or song,
Thy sire and I will crush the snake!"
He kissed her forehead as he spake,
And Geraldine in maiden wise   575
Casting down her large bright eyes,
With blushing cheek and courtesy fine
She turned her from Sir Leoline;
Softly gathering up her train,
That o'er her right arm fell again;   580
And folded her arms across her chest,
And couched her head upon her breast,
And looked askance at Christabel—
Jesu, Maria, shield her well!

A snake's small eye blinks dull and
    shy;   585
And the lady's eyes they shrunk in her
    head,
Each shrunk up to a serpent's eye,
And with somewhat of malice, and more
    of dread,
At Christabel she looked askance!—
One moment—and the sight was fled! 590
But Christabel in dizzy trance
Stumbling on the unsteady ground
Shuddered aloud, with a hissing sound;

And Geraldine again turned round,
And like a thing, that sought relief,   595
Full of wonder and full of grief,
She rolled her large bright eyes divine
Wildly on Sir Leoline.

The maid, alas! her thoughts are gone,
She nothing sees—no sight but one!   600
The maid, devoid of guile and sin,
I know not how, in fearful wise,
So deeply had she drunken in
That look, those shrunken serpent eyes,
That all her features were resigned   605
To this sole image in her mind:
And passively did imitate
That look of dull and treacherous hate!
And thus she stood, in dizzy trance,
Still picturing that look askance   610
With forced unconscious sympathy
Full before her father's view—
As far as such a look could be
In eyes so innocent and blue!
And when the trance was o'er, the maid   615
Paused awhile, and inly prayed:
Then falling at the Baron's feet,
"By my mother's soul do I entreat
That thou this woman send away!"
She said; and more she could not say,   620
For what she knew she could not tell,
O'er-mastered by the mighty spell.

Why is thy cheek so wan and wild,
Sir Leoline? Thy only child
Lies at thy feet, thy joy, thy pride,   625
So fair, so innocent, so mild;
The same, for whom thy lady died!
O by the pangs of her dear mother
Think thou no evil of thy child!
For her, and thee, and for no other,   630
She prayed the moment ere she died:
Prayed that the babe for whom she died,
Might prove her dear lord's joy and pride!
That prayer her deadly pangs beguiled,
Sir Leoline!   635
And would'st thou wrong thy only child,
Her child and thine?

Within the Baron's heart and brain
If thoughts, like these, had any share,
They only swelled his rage and pain,   640
And did but work confusion there.
His heart was cleft with pain and rage,
His cheeks they quivered, his eyes were
wild,
Dishonored thus in his old age;
Dishonored by his only child.   645
And all his hospitality
To the wronged daughter of his friend
By more than woman's jealousy
Brought thus to a disgraceful end—

He rolled his eye with stern regard   650
Upon the gentle minstrel bard,
And said in tones abrupt, austere—
"Why, Bracy! dost thou loiter here?
I bade thee hence!" The bard obeyed;
And turning from his own sweet maid,   655
The agèd knight, Sir Leoline,
Led forth the lady Geraldine!

THE CONCLUSION TO PART THE SECOND

A little child, a limber elf,
Singing, dancing to itself,
A fairy thing with red round cheeks   660
That always finds and never seeks,
Makes such a vision to the sight
As fills a father's eyes with light;
And pleasures flow in so thick and fast
Upon his heart, that he at last   665
Must needs express his love's excess
With words of unmeant bitterness.
Perhaps 'tis pretty to force together
Thoughts so all unlike each other;
To mutter and mock a broken charm,   670
To dally with wrong that does no harm.
Perhaps 'tis tender too and pretty
At each wild word to feel within
A sweet recoil of love and pity.
And what, if in a world of sin   675
(O sorrow and shame should this be true!)
Such giddiness of heart and brain
Comes seldom save from rage and pain,
So talks as it's most used to do.
1797-1800   1816

KUBLA KHAN: OR, A VISION IN A DREAM

A FRAGMENT

In the summer of the year 1797, the Author, then in ill-health, had retired to a lonely farm-house between Porlock and Linton, on the Exmoor confines of Somerset and Devonshire. In consequence of a slight indisposition, an anodyne had been prescribed, from the effect of which he fell asleep in his chair at the moment he was reading the following sentence, or words of the same substance, in Purchas's *Pilgrimage:* "Here the Khan Kubla commanded a palace to be built, and a stately garden thereunto: and thus ten miles of fertile ground were inclosed with a wall." The Author continued for about three hours in a profound sleep, at least of the external senses, during which time he has the most vivid confidence, that he could not have composed less than from two to three hundred lines; if that indeed can be called composition in which all the images rose up before him as *things*, with a parallel production of the correspondent expressions, without any sensation or consciousness of effort. On awaking he appeared to himself to have a distinct recollection of the whole, and taking his pen, ink, and paper, instantly and eagerly wrote down the lines that are here preserved. At this moment he was unfortunately called out by a person on business from Porlock, and detained by him above an hour, and on his return to his room, found, to his no small surprise and mortification, that though he still retained some vague and dim recollection of the general purport of the vision, yet, with the exception of some eight or ten scattered lines and images, all the rest had passed away like the images on the surface of a stream into which a stone had been cast, but, alas! without the after restoration of the latter:

          Then all the charm
Is broken—all that phantom-world so fair,
Vanishes, and a thousand circlets spread,
And each mis-shape[s] the other. Stay awhile,
Poor youth! who scarcely dar'st lift up thine
    eyes—
The stream will soon renew its smoothness,
    soon
The visions will return! And lo! he stays,
And soon the fragments dim of lovely forms
Come trembling back, unite, and now once
    more
The pool becomes a mirror.

Yet from the still surviving recollections in his mind, the Author has frequently purposed to finish for himself what had been originally, as it were, given to him Αὔριον ἄδιον ᾄσω: but the to-morrow is yet to come.

In Xanadu did Kubla Khan
A stately pleasure-dome decree:
Where Alph, the sacred river, ran
Through caverns measureless to man
Down to a sunless sea.   5
So twice five miles of fertile ground
With walls and towers were girdled round:
And there were gardens bright with sinuous rills,
Where blossomed many an incense-bearing tree;
And here were forests ancient as the hills,   10
Enfolding sunny spots of greenery.

But oh! that deep romantic chasm which slanted
Down the green hill athwart a cedarn cover!
A savage place! as holy and enchanted
As e'er beneath a waning moon was haunted   15
By woman wailing for her demon-lover!
And from this chasm, with ceaseless turmoil seething,

As if this earth in fast thick pants were breathing,
A mighty fountain momently was forced:
Amid whose swift half-intermitted burst 20
Huge fragments vaulted like rebounding hail,
Or chaffy grain beneath the thresher's flail:
And 'mid these dancing rocks at once and ever
It flung up momently the sacred river.
Five miles meandering with a mazy motion 25
Through wood and dale the sacred river ran,
Then reached the caverns measureless to man,
And sank in tumult to a lifeless ocean:
And 'mid this tumult Kubla heard from far
Ancestral voices prophesying war! 30

    The shadow of the dome of pleasure
    Floated midway on the waves;
    Where was heard the mingled measure
    From the fountain and the caves.
It was a miracle of rare device, 35
A sunny pleasure-dome with caves of ice!
    A damsel with a dulcimer
    In a vision once I saw:
    It was an Abyssinian maid,
    And on her dulcimer she played, 40
    Singing of Mount Abora.
    Could I revive within me
    Her symphony and song,
    To such a deep delight 'twould win me,
That with music loud and long, 45
I would build that dome in air,
That sunny dome! those caves of ice!
And all who heard should see them there,
And all should cry, Beware! Beware!
His flashing eyes, his floating hair! 50
Weave a circle round him thrice,
And close your eyes with holy dread,
For he on honey-dew hath fed,
And drunk the milk of Paradise.
1798   1816

DEJECTION: AN ODE

Late, late yestreen I saw the new Moon,
With the old Moon in her arms:
And I fear, I fear, my Master dear!
We shall have a deadly storm.
          Ballad of Sir Patrick Spence.

Well! If the bard was weather-wise, who made
    The grand old ballad of *Sir Patrick Spence,*
This night, so tranquil now, will not go hence

Unroused by winds, that ply a busier trade
Than those which mold yon cloud in lazy
    flakes,   5
Or the dull sobbing draft, that moans and
    rakes
Upon the strings of this Æolian lute,
    Which better far were mute.
For lo! the new-moon winter-bright!
And overspread with phantom light, 10
(With swimming phantom light o'er-
    spread
But rimmed and circled by a silver
    thread)
I see the old moon in her lap, foretelling
    The coming-on of rain and squally blast.
And oh! that even now the gust were
    swelling,   15
And the slant night-shower driving loud
    and fast!
Those sounds which oft have raised me,
    whilst they awed,
    And sent my soul abroad,
Might now perhaps their wonted impulse
    give,
Might startle this dull pain, and make it
    move and live!

A grief without a pang, void, dark, and
    drear,
    A stifled, drowsy, unimpassioned grief,
Which finds no natural outlet, no relief,
    In word, or sigh, or tear—
O lady! in this wan and heartless mood, 25
To other thoughts by yonder throstle
    wooed,
All this long eve, so balmy and serene,
Have I been gazing on the western sky,
    And its peculiar tint of yellow green:
And still I gaze—and with how blank an
    eye!   30
And those thin clouds above, in flakes and
    bars,
That give away their motion to the stars;
Those stars, that glide behind them or be-
    tween,
Now sparkling, now bedimmed, but al-
    ways seen:
Yon crescent moon, as fixed as if it grew 35
In its own cloudless, starless lake of blue;
I see them all so excellently fair,
I see, not feel, how beautiful they are!

    My genial spirits fail;
    And what can these avail   40
To lift the smothering weight from off my
    breast?
    It were a vain endeavor,
    Though I should gaze forever
On that green light that lingers in the
    west:

I may not hope from outward forms to
    win   45
The passion and the life, whose fountains
    are within.
O lady! we receive but what we give,
And in our life alone does Nature live:
Ours is her wedding garment, ours her
    shroud!
    And would we aught behold, of higher
    worth,   50
Than that inanimate cold world allowed
To the poor loveless ever-anxious crowd,
    Ah! from the soul itself must issue forth
A light, a glory, a fair luminous cloud
    Enveloping the earth—   55
And from the soul itself must there be sent
    A sweet and potent voice, of its own
    birth,
Of all sweet sounds the life and element!

O pure of heart! thou need'st not ask of
    me
What this strong music in the soul may
    be!   60
What, and wherein it doth exist,
This light, this glory, this fair luminous
    mist,
This beautiful and beauty-making power.
    Joy, virtuous lady! Joy that ne'er was
    given,
Save to the pure, and in their purest
    hour,   65
Life, and life's effluence, cloud at once and
    shower,
Joy, lady! is the spirit and the power,
Which wedding nature to us gives in dower
    A new earth and new heaven,
Undreamt of by the sensual and the
    proud—   70
Joy is the sweet voice, joy the luminous
    cloud—
    We in ourselves rejoice!
And thence flows all that charms or ear or
    sight,
    All melodies the echoes of that voice,
All colors a suffusion from that light. 75

There was a time when, though my path
    was rough,
    This joy within me dallied with distress,
And all misfortunes were but as the stuff
    Whence Fancy made me dreams of hap-
    piness:
For hope grew round me, like the twining
    vine,   80
And fruits, and foliage, not my own,
    seemed mine.
But now afflictions bow me down to earth:
Nor care I that they rob me of my mirth;
    But oh! each visitation

Suspends what nature gave me at my
    birth,   85
  My shaping spirit of imagination.
For not to think of what I needs must
    feel,
But to be still and patient, all I can;
And haply by abstruse research to steal
  From my own nature all the natural
    man—   90
  This was my sole resource, my only
    plan:
Till that which suits a part infects the
    whole,
And now is almost grown the habit of my
    soul.

Hence, viper thoughts, that coil around
    my mind,
  Reality's dark dream!   95
I turn from you, and listen to the wind,
  Which long has raved unnoticed. What
    a scream
Of agony by torture lengthened out
That lute sent forth! Thou Wind, that
    rav'st without,
Bare crag, or mountain-tairn, or blasted
    tree,   100
Or pine-grove whither woodman never
    clomb,
Or lonely house, long held the witches'
    home,
  Methinks were fitter instruments for
    thee,
Mad lutanist! who in this month of show-
    ers,
Of dark-brown gardens, and of peeping
    flowers,   105
Mak'st devils' yule, with worse than win-
    try song,
The blossoms, buds, and timorous leaves
    among.
Thou actor, perfect in all tragic sounds!
Thou mighty poet, e'en to frenzy bold!
  What tell'st thou now about?   110
'Tis of the rushing of an host in rout,
With groans, of trampled men, with
    smarting wounds—
At once they groan with pain, and shudder
    with the cold!
But hush! there is a pause of deepest si-
    lence!
And all that noise, as of a rushing
    crowd,   115
With groans, and tremulous shudderings—
    all is over—
  It tells another tale, with sounds less
    deep and loud!
  A tale of less affright,
  And tempered with delight,

As Otway's self had framed the tender
    lay,—   120
  'Tis of a little child
  Upon a lonesome wild,
Not far from home, but she hath lost her
    way:
And now moans low in bitter grief and
    fear,
And now screams loud, and hopes to make
    her mother hear.

'Tis midnight, but small thoughts have I
    of sleep:
Full seldom may my friend such vigils
    keep!
Visit her, gentle sleep! with wings of heal-
    ing,
  And may this storm be but a mountain-
    birth,
May all the stars hang bright above her
    dwelling,   130
  Silent as though they watched the sleep-
    ing earth!
  With light heart may she rise,
  Gay fancy, cheerful eyes,
Joy lift her spirit, joy attune her voice;
To her may all things live, from pole to
    pole,   135
Their life the eddying of her living soul!
  O simple spirit, guided from above,
Dear lady! friend devoutest of my choice,
Thus mayest thou ever, evermore rejoice.
1802   1802

HYMN BEFORE SUNRISE, IN THE VALE OF CHAMOUNI

Hast thou a charm to stay the morning-star
In his steep course? So long he seems to
    pause
On thy bald awful head, O sovran Blanc,
The Arve and Arveiron at thy base
Rave ceaselessly; but thou, most awful
    Form!   5
Risest from forth thy silent sea of pines,
How silently! Around thee and above
Deep is the air and dark, substantial,
    black,
An ebon mass: methinks thou piercest it,
As with a wedge! But when I look
    again,   10
It is thine own calm home, thy crystal
    shrine,
Thy habitation from eternity!
O dread and silent mount! I gazed upon
    thee,
Till thou, still present to the bodily sense,

Didst vanish from my thought: entranced
    in prayer   15
I worshipped the Invisible alone.

Yet, like some sweet beguiling melody,
So sweet, we know not we are listening
    to it,
Thou, the meanwhile, wast blending with
    my thought,
Yea, with my life and life's own secret
    joy: 20
Till the dilating soul, enrapt, transfused,
Into the mighty vision passing—there
As in her natural form, swelled vast to
    heaven!

Awake, my soul! not only passive praise
Thou owest! not alone these swelling
    tears,   25
Mute thanks and secret ecstasy! Awake,
Voice of sweet song! Awake, my heart,
    awake!
Green vales and icy cliffs, all join my
    hymn.

Thou first and chief, sole sovereign of
    the vale!
O struggling with the darkness all the
    night,   30
And visited all night by troops of stars,
Or when they climb the sky or when they
    sink:
Companion of the morning-star at dawn,
Thyself earth's rosy star, and of the dawn
Co-herald: wake, O wake, and utter
    praise!   35
Who sank thy sunless pillars deep in earth?
Who filled thy countenance with rosy light?
Who made thee parent of perpetual
    streams?

And you, ye five wild torrents fiercely
    glad!
Who called you forth from night and utter
    death,   40
From dark and icy caverns called you forth,
Down those precipitous, black, jaggèd
    rocks,
Forever shattered and the same forever?
Who gave you your invulnerable life,
Your strength, your speed, your fury, and
    your joy,   45
Unceasing thunder and eternal foam?
And who commanded (and the silence
    came),
Here let the billows stiffen, and have rest?

Ye ice-falls! ye that from the mountain's
    brow
Adown enormous ravines slope amain— 50
Torrents, methinks, that heard a mighty
    voice,
And stopped at once amid their maddest
    plunge!
Motionless torrents! silent cataracts!
Who made you glorious as the gates of
    heaven
Beneath the keen full moon? Who bade
    the sun   55
Clothe you with rainbows? Who, with
    living flowers
Of loveliest blue, spread garlands at your
    feet?—
God! let the torrents, like a shout of na-
    tions,
Answer! and let the ice-plains echo, God!
God! sing ye meadow-streams with glad-
    some voice!   60
Ye pine-groves, with your soft and soul-
    like sounds!
And they too have a voice, yon piles of
    snow,
And in their perilous fall shall thunder,
    God!

Ye living flowers that skirt the eternal
    frost!
Ye wild goats sporting round the eagle's
    nest!   65
Ye eagles, play-mates of the mountain-
    storm!
Ye lightnings, the dread arrows of the
    clouds!
Ye signs and wonders of the element!
Utter forth God, and fill the hills with
    praise!

Thou too, hoar mount! with thy sky-
    pointing peaks,   70
Oft from whose feet the avalanche, un-
    heard,
Shoots downward, glittering through the
    pure serene
Into the depth of clouds, that veil thy
    breast—
Thou too again, stupendous mountain!
    thou
That as I raise my head, awhile bowed
    low   75
In adoration, upward from thy base
Slow travelling with dim eyes suffused
    with tears,
Solemnly seemest, like a vapory cloud,
To rise before me—Rise, O ever rise,
Rise like a cloud of incense from the
    earth!   80

Thou kingly spirit throned among the hills,
Thou dread ambassador from earth to
    heaven,
Great hierarch! tell thou the silent sky,
And tell the stars, and tell yon rising sun
Earth, with her thousand voices, praises
    God.   85
1802   1802

ANSWER TO A CHILD'S QUESTION

Do you ask what the birds say? The Spar-
    row, the Dove,
The Linnet and Thrush say, "I love and
    I love!"
In the winter they're silent—the wind is
    so strong;
What it says, I don't know, but it sings a
    loud song.
But green leaves, and blossoms, and sunny
    warm weather,   5
And singing, and loving—all come back
    together.
But the Lark is so brimful of gladness and
    love,
The green fields below him, the blue sky
    above,
That he sings, and he sings; and for ever
    sings he—
"I love my Love, and my Love loves
    me!"   10
                                       1802

FROM REMORSE

Hear, sweet spirit, hear the spell,
Lest a blacker charm compel!
So shall the midnight breezes swell
With thy deep long-lingering knell.

And at evening evermore,   5
In a Chapel on the shore,
Shall the Chaunters sad and saintly,
Yellow tapers burning faintly,
Doleful Masses chaunt for thee,
Miserere Domine!   10

Hark! the cadence dies away
    On the quiet moonlight sea:
The boatmen rest their oars and say,
    Miserere Domine!
                                       1812

FROM ZAPOLYA

GLYCINE'S SONG

A sunny shaft did I behold,
    From sky to earth it slanted:
And poised therein a bird so bold—
    Sweet bird, thou wert enchanted!

He sank, he rose, he twinkled, he trolled 5
    Within that shaft of sunny mist;
His eyes of fire, his beak of gold,
    All else of amethyst!

And thus he sang: "Adieu! adieu!
Love's dreams prove seldom true.   10
The blossoms they make no delay:
The sparkling dew-drops will not stay.
    Sweet month of May,
    We must away;
        Far, far away!   15
        Today! today!"

                                       1815

TO WILLIAM WORDSWORTH

COMPOSED ON THE NIGHT AFTER HIS
RECITATION OF A POEM ON THE
GROWTH OF AN INDIVIDUAL
MIND

Friend of the wise! and teacher of the
    good!
Into my heart have I received that lay
More than historic, that prophetic lay
Wherein (high theme by thee first sung
    aright)
Of the foundations and the building up   5
Of a human spirit thou hast dared to tell
What may be told to the understanding
    mind
Revealable; and what within the mind
By vital breathings secret as the soul
Of vernal growth, oft quickens in the
    heart
Thoughts all too deep for words!—   10

        Theme hard as high!
Of smiles spontaneous, and mysterious
    fears
(The first-born they of reason and twin-
    birth),
Of tides obedient to external force,
And currents self-determined, as might
    seem,   15
Or by some inner power; of moments
    awful,

Now in thy inner life, and now abroad,
When power streamed from thee, and thy
    soul received
The light reflected, as a light bestowed—
Of fancies fair, and milder hours of
    youth,   20
Hyblean murmurs of poetic thought
Industrious in its joys, in vales and glens
Native or outland, lakes and famous hills!
Or on the lonely high-road, when the stars
Were rising; or by secret mountain-
    streams,   25
The guides and the companions of thy
    way!

Of more than fancy, of the social sense
Distending wide, and man beloved as man,
Where France in all her towns lay vi-
    brating
Like some becalmèd bark beneath the
    burst   30
Of Heaven's immediate thunder, when no
    cloud
Is visible, or shadow on the main.
For thou wert there, thine own brows gar-
    landed,
Amid the tremor of a realm aglow,
Amid a mighty nation jubilant,   35
When from the general heart of human
    kind
Hope sprang forth like a full-born Deity!
——Of that dear hope afflicted and struck
    down,
So summoned homeward, thenceforth calm
    and sure
From the dread watch-tower of man's ab-
    solute self,   40
With light unwaning on her eyes, to look
Far on—herself a glory to behold,
The angel of the vision! Then (last
    strain)
Of duty, chosen laws controlling choice,
Action and joy!—An Orphic song indeed,
A song divine of high and passionate
    thoughts   45
To their own music chaunted!

                        O great Bard!
Ere yet that last strain dying awed the air,
With stedfast eye I viewed thee in the
    choir
Of ever-enduring men. The truly great   50
Have all one age, and from one visible
    space
Shed influence! They, both in power and
    act,
Are permanent, and Time is not with
    them,
Save as it worketh for them, they in it.
Nor less a sacred roll, than those of old, 55

And to be placed, as they, with gradual
    fame
Among the archives of mankind, thy work
Makes audible a linkèd lay of truth,
Of truth profound a sweet continuous lay,
Not learnt, but native, her own natural
    notes!   60
Ah! as I listened with a heart forlorn,
The pulses of my being beat anew:
And even as life returns upon the
    drowned,
Life's joy rekindling roused a throng of
    pains—
Keen pangs of love, awakening as a babe 65
Turbulent, with an outcry in the heart;
And fears self-willed, that shunned the eye
    of hope;
And hope that scarce would know itself
    from fear;
Sense of past youth, and manhood come in
    vain,
And genius given, and knowledge won in
    vain;   70
And all which I had culled in wood-walks
    wild,
And all which patient toil had reared, and
    all,
Commune with thee had opened out—but
    flowers
Strewed on my corse, and borne upon my
    bier
In the same coffin, for the self-same
    grave!   75

That way no more! and ill beseems it
    me,
Who came a welcomer in herald's guise,
Singing of glory, and futurity,
To wander back on such unhealthful
    road,
Plucking the poisons of self-harm! And
    ill   80
Such intertwine beseems triumphal wreaths
Strew'd before thy advancing!

                        Nor do thou,
Sage Bard! impair the memory of that
    hour
Of thy communion with my nobler mind
By pity or grief, already felt too long! 85
Nor let my words import more blame than
    needs.
The tumult rose and ceased: for peace is
    nigh
Where wisdom's voice has found a listening
    heart.
Amid the howl of more than wintry storms,
The Halcyon hears the voice of vernal
    hours
Already on the wing.   90

Eve following eve,
Dear tranquil time, when the sweet sense
    of home
Is sweetest! moments for their own sake
    hailed
And more desired, more precious, for thy
    song,
In silence listening, like a devout child, 95
My soul lay passive, by thy various strain
Driven as in surges now beneath the stars,
With momentary stars of my own birth,
Fair constellated foam, still darting off
Into the darkness; now a tranquil sea,   100
Outspread and bright, yet swelling to the
    moon.

And when—O Friend! my comforter and
    guide!
Strong in thyself, and powerful to give
    strength!—
Thy long sustainèd song finally closed,
And thy deep voice had ceased—yet thou
    thyself   105
Wert still before my eyes, and round us
    both
That happy vision of belovèd faces—
Scarce conscious, and yet conscious of its
    close
I sate, my being blended in one thought
(Thought was it? or aspiration? or re-
    solve?)   110
Absorbed, yet hanging still upon the
    sound—
And when I rose, I found myself in
    prayer.
January, 1807

FROM A TOMBLESS EPITAPH

'Tis true that, passionate for ancient truths,
And honoring with religious love the Great
Of elder times, he hated to excess,
With an unquiet and intolerant scorn,
The hollow puppets of an hollow age,   10
Ever idolatrous, and changing ever
Its worthless idols! Learning, power, and
    time,
(Too much of all) thus wasting in vain war
Of fervid colloquy. Sickness, 'tis true,
Whole years of weary days, besieged him
    close,   15
Even to the gates and inlets of his life!
But it is true, no less, that strenuous, firm,
And with a natural gladness, he main-
    tained
The citadel unconquered, and in joy
Was strong to follow the delightful
    Muse.   20
For not a hidden path, that to the shades

Of the beloved Parnassian forest leads,
Lurked undiscovered by him; not a rill
There issues from the fount of Hippocrene,
But he had traced it upward to its
    source,   25
Through open glade, dark glen, and secret
    dell,
Knew the gay wild flowers on its banks,
    and culled
Its med'cinable herbs. Yea, oft alone,
Piercing the long-neglected holy cave,
The haunt obscure of old Philosophy,   30
He bade with lifted torch its starry walls
Sparkle, as erst they sparkled to the flame
Of odorous lamps tended by Saint and
    Sage.
O framed for calmer times and nobler
    hearts!
O studious Poet, eloquent for truth!   35
Philosopher! contemning wealth and death,
Yet docile, childlike, full of Life and Love!
                            1809(?)

THE PAINS OF SLEEP

Ere on my bed my limbs I lay,
It hath not been my use to pray
With moving lips or bended knees;
But silently, by slow degrees,
My spirit I to love compose,   5
In humble trust mine eye-lids close,
With reverential resignation,
No wish conceived, no thought exprest,
Only a sense of supplication;
A sense o'er all my soul imprest   10
That I am weak, yet not unblest,
Since in me, round me, everywhere
Eternal strength and wisdom are.

But yester-night I prayed aloud
In anguish and in agony,   15
Up-starting from the fiendish crowd
Of shapes and thoughts that tortured me:
A lurid light, a trampling throng,
Sense of intolerable wrong,
And whom I scorned, those only strong! 20
Thirst of revenge, the powerless will
Still baffled, and yet burning still!
Desire with loathing strangely mixed
On wild or hateful objects fixed.
Fantastic passions! maddening brawl!   25
And shame and terror over all!
Deeds to be hid which were not hid,
Which all confused I could not know
Whether I suffered, or I did:
For all seemed guilt, remorse, or woe, 30
My own or other still the same
Life-stifling fear, soul-stifling shame.

So two nights passed: the night's dismay
Saddened and stunned the coming day.
Sleep, the wide blessing, seemed to me   35
Distemper's worst calamity.
The third night, when my own loud scream
Had waked me from the fiendish dream,
O'ercome with sufferings strange and wild,
I wept as I had been a child;   40
And having thus by tears subdued
My anguish to a milder mood,
Such punishments, I said, were due
To natures deepliest stained with sin,—
For aye entempesting anew   45
The unfathomable hell within,
The horror of their deeds to view,
To know and loathe, yet wish and do!
Such griefs with such men well agree,
But wherefore, wherefore fall on me?   50
To be beloved is all I need,
And whom I love, I love indeed.

1803   1816

FROM LIMBO

'Tis a strange place, this Limbo!—not a
     Place,
Yet name it so;—where Time and weary
     Space
Fettered from flight, with night-mare sense
     of fleeing,
Strive for their last crepuscular half-
     being;—
Lank Space, and scytheless Time with
     branny hands   15
Barren and soundless as the measuring
     sands,
Not marked by flit of Shades,—unmeaning
     they
As moonlight on the dial of the day!
But that is lovely—looks like Human
     Time,—
An Old Man with a steady look sublime, 20
That stops his earthly task to watch the
     skies;
But he is blind—a Statue hath such eyes;—
Yet having moonward turned his face by
     chance,
Gazes the orb with moon-like countenance,
With scant white hairs, with foretop bald
     and high,   25
He gazes still,—his eyeless face all eye;—
As 'twere an organ full of silent sight,
His whole face seemeth to rejoice in light!
Lip touching lip, all moveless, bust and
     limb—
He seems to gaze at that which seems to
     gaze on him!   30
     No such sweet sights doth Limbo den
          immure,

Walled round, and made a spirit-jail se-
     cure,
By the mere horror of blank Naught-at-all,
Whose circumambience doth these ghosts
     enthral.
A lurid thought is growthless, dull Priva-
     tion,   35
Yet that is but a Purgatory curse;
Hell knows a fear far worse,
A fear—a future state;—'tis positive Nega-
     tion!

1817

TIME REAL AND IMAGINARY

AN ALLEGORY

On the wide level of a mountain's head,
(I knew not where, but 'twas some faery
     place)
Their pinions. ostrich-like, for sails out-
     spread,
Two lovely children run an endless race,
     A sister and a brother!   5
     This far outstript the other;
Yet ever runs she with reverted face,
And looks and listens for the boy behind:
     For he, alas! is blind!
O'er rough and smooth with even step he
     passed,   10
And knows not whether he be first or last.

1812   1817

YOUTH AND AGE

Verse, a breeze mid blossoms straying,
Where Hope clung feeding, like a bee—
Both were mine! Life went a-maying
     With Nature, Hope, and Poesy,
          When I was young!   5

When I was young?—Ah, woful When!
Ah! for the change 'twixt Now and Then!
This breathing house not built with hands,
This body that does me grievous wrong,
O'er aery cliffs and glittering sands,   10
How lightly then it flashed along:—
Like those trim skiffs, unknown of yore,
On winding lakes and rivers wide,
That ask no aid of sail or oar,
That fear no spite of wind or tide!   15
Nought cared this body for wind or
     weather
When Youth and I lived in't together.

Flowers are lovely; Love is flower-like;
Friendship is a sheltering tree;
O! the joys, that came down shower-like, 20
Of Friendship, Love, and Liberty,
     Ere I was old!

Ere I was old? Ah woful Ere,
Which tells me, Youth's no longer here!
O Youth! for years so many and sweet,   25
'Tis known, that Thou and I were one,
I'll think it but a fond conceit—
It cannot be that Thou art gone!
Thy vesper-bell hath not yet tolled:—
And thou wert aye a masker bold!   30
What strange disguise hast now put on,
To *make believe,* that thou art gone?
I see these locks in silvery slips,
This drooping gait, this altered size:
But Spring-tide blossoms on thy lips,   35
And tears take sunshine from thine eyes!
Life is but thought: so think I will
That Youth and I are house-mates still.

Dew-drops are the gems of morning,
But the tears of mournful eve!   40
Where no hope is, life's a warning
That only serves to make us grieve,
              When we are old:
That only serves to make us grieve
With oft and tedious taking-leave,   45
Like some poor nigh-related guest,
That may not rudely be dismissed;
Yet hath outstayed his welcome while
And tells the jest without the smile.
1823   1832

WORK WITHOUT HOPE

All nature seems at work. Slugs leave their
    lair—
The bees are stirring—birds are on the
    wing—
And winter slumbering in the open air,

Wears on his smiling face a dream of
    spring!
And I the while, the sole unbusy thing,   5
Nor honey make, nor pair, nor build, nor
    sing.
    Yet well I ken the banks where ama-
        ranths blow,
Have traced the fount whence streams of
    nectar flow.
Bloom, O ye amaranths! bloom for whom
    ye may,
For me ye bloom not! Glide, rich streams,
    away!   10
With lips unbrightened, wreathless brow, I
    stroll:
And would you learn the spells that drowse
    my soul?
Work without hope draws nectar in a sieve,
And hope without an object cannot live.
1825   1828

EPITAPH

Stop, Christian passer-by!—Stop, child of
    God,
And read with gentle breast. Beneath this
    sod
A poet lies, or that which once seemed he.
O, lift one thought in prayer for S. T. C.;
That he who many a year with toil of
    breath   5
Found death in life, may here find life in
    death!
Mercy for praise—to be forgiven for fame
He asked, and hoped, through Christ. Do
    thou the same!
1833   1834

1832

1825

1834

WILLIAM WORDSWORTH (1770-1850)

Time may restore us in his course
Goethe's sage mind and Byron's force;
But where will Europe's latter hour
Again find Wordsworth's healing power?
MATTHEW ARNOLD

There are sound critics of today who maintain that, next to Shakespeare and Milton, Wordsworth is the greatest English poet. He expresses, in a manner closer to the modern than theirs, the ideals and attitudes of the English-speaking peoples. He voices our paradoxical devotion to both the natural and the mystical, to both the commonplace and the sublime. He represents our peculiar conception of liberty, national welfare, morality, duty, the ideal man, the ideal woman, good manners, the relation of nature to self-culture, the true pursuit of happiness, and other matters of profound importance. Not to know and to love Wordsworth is to be out of touch with the soul of our own Anglo-American world. He militates against two of our most dangerous tendencies,—the single-minded pursuit of wealth, and the ostentatious squandering thereof,—by revealing the beauty and happiness of plain living and high thinking.

His wisdom was dearly bought. During his last fifty years, when he was dwelling in the Lake Country, his life was peaceful; but his youth was agitated by visionary plans, vain attempts, and grievous disappointments. By nature he was passionate and rebellious; and in his early twenties, after leaving Cambridge University, believing that nearly everything in the established order was wrong, he eagerly sought truth, liberty, and reform, in radical doctrine and radical action. He was fascinated by the materialistic and anarchial theories of William Godwin. He went to France, fraternized with supporters of the French Revolution, and was disgusted with his own nation's reluctance to accept its principles. He fell in love with Annette Vallon, a Frenchwoman several years older than himself, by whom he had a daughter, Caroline. The political chaos of the time made a marriage ceremony between them impossible; but Wordsworth intended to marry Annette, and returned to France at the risk of his life, but was forced to flee back to England. Before he could join Annette again, war broke out between France and England,—a war which lasted so many years that their plans of marriage were relinquished. Wordsworth never concealed this youthful error from those who had the right to know it; and when, ten years later, he married Mary Hutchinson, she was informed. The Wordsworths remained on friendly terms with Annette and Caroline, and Wordsworth did what he could for them during the rest of his life.

The character of Wordsworth was further chastened by the disappointment of his hopes for the French Revolution, when France embarked upon a career of imperialistic conquest. He now, largely under the influence of Coleridge, ceased to be a revolutionary radical. This did not mean that he reacted to the other false extreme. Indeed one cause of his greatness lies in the fact that, after attaining to maturity and self-mastery, he continued sympathetically to understand the impatience and the questionings of youth. He continued to believe in democracy, liberty, and the free pursuit of happiness. He remained an opponent of the thoughtlessly conventional in life and literature, as his preface to the *Lyrical Ballads* shows. But henceforth he no longer believed that mankind could achieve its goal by political revolutions or materialistic philosophies.

What is fundamental in Wordsworth's views is not only his love of nature, but his idea that human life is a development. Men are not born good, nor can they suddenly achieve goodness: they may grow towards goodness, and consequently towards happiness. There are several stages in life, each of which has its rights and should be freely permitted to develop into the higher. In each stage our relation towards nature is different. In infancy (see *Tintern Abbey*, and elsewhere) we are a thoughtless part of nature; in youth we become passionately aware of its existence, and grow full of fancies concerning it; but not until maturity do we, by exercise of reason and imagination, really understand it. Finally, even higher than the stage of mature culture, we may at times have access to a mystical state, almost inexpressible, of harmony with it. Whatever prevents us from passing from infancy to maturity through these changing relationships towards nature is evil. The memories of each previous stage are a precious heritage to maturity.

In the *Prelude* Wordsworth illustrated his idea of development by recounting those incidents in his life which had contributed towards the formation of his mind and character. His message, though not blindly optimistic, was strong in fortitude; and the *Excursion* was designed as an encouraging revelation to those who had become pessimistic owing to the obvious evils and sorrows of life. Throughout his work, Wordsworth takes a middle ground between naturalism and idyllicism: he neither represents the world as devoid of beauty, truth, and goodness, nor does he invent purely fanciful places or characters to show forth beauty, truth, and goodness; he finds them in scenes and persons such as are known to us all. As Tennyson said of him, he gives us a sense of the permanent amid the transitory. He shows us that to him who rightly lives and rightly feels, life, despite its pains, is full of beauty and delight

When Wordsworth is most himself and at his greatest, he is

> A mind
> That feeds upon infinity, that broods
> Over the dark abyss;

a mind to which

> the least of things
> Seemed infinite;

and which found in them

> Thoughts that do often lie too deep for tears.

FROM AN EVENING WALK

How pleasant, as the sun declines, to view
The spacious landscape change in form and hue!
Here, vanish, as in mist, before a flood
Of bright obscurity, hill, lawn, and wood;   100
There, objects, by the searching beams betrayed,
Come forth, and here retire in purple shade;
Even the white stems of birch, the cottage white,
Soften their glare before the mellow light;
The skiffs, at anchor where with umbrage wide   105
Yon chestnuts half the latticed boat-house hide,
Shed from their sides, that face the sun's slant beam,
Strong flakes of radiance on the tremulous stream:
Raised by yon travelling flock, a dusty cloud   110
Mounts from the road, and spreads its moving shroud;
The shepherd, all involved in wreaths of fire,
Now shows a shadowy speck, and now is lost entire.

1787-89   1793

A NIGHT-PIECE

The sky is overcast
With a continuous cloud of texture close,
Heavy and wan, all whitened by the moon,
Which through that veil is indistinctly seen,
A dull, contracted circle, yielding light   5
So feebly spread that not a shadow falls,
Checkering the ground—from rock, plant,
    tree, or tower.

At length a pleasant instantaneous gleam
Startles the pensive traveler while he treads
His lonesome path, with unobserving
    eye   10
Bent earthwards; he looks up—the clouds
    are split
Asunder—and above his head he sees
The clear moon, and the glory of the
    heavens.
There in a black-blue vault she sails along,

Followed by multitudes of stars, that,
  small 15
And sharp, and bright, along the dark
  abyss
Drive as she drives. How fast they wheel
  away,
Yet vanish not!—the wind is in the tree,
But they are silent; still they roll along
Immeasurably distant; and the vault, 20
Built round by those white clouds, enor-
  mous clouds,
Still deepens its unfathomable depth.
At length the vision closes; and the mind,
Not undisturbed by the delight it feels,
Which slowly settles into peaceful calm, 25
Is left to muse upon the solemn scene.

Jan. 25, 1798   1815

LINES WRITTEN IN EARLY
SPRING

I heard a thousand blended notes,
While in a grove I sate reclined,
In that sweet mood when pleasant thoughts
Bring sad thoughts to the mind.

To her fair works did Nature link 5
The human soul that through me ran;
And much it grieved my heart to think
What man has made of man.

Through primrose tufts, in that green
  bower,
The periwinkle trailed its wreaths; 10
And 'tis my faith that every flower
Enjoys the air it breathes.

The birds around me hopped and played,
Their thoughts I cannot measure:—
But the least motion which they made, 15
It seemed a thrill of pleasure.

The budding twigs spread out their fan,
To catch the breezy air;
And I must think, do all I can,
That there was pleasure there. 20

If this belief from heaven be sent,
If such be Nature's holy plan,
Have I not reason to lament
What man has made of man?

1798   1798

EXPOSTULATION AND REPLY

"Why, William, on that old grey stone,
Thus for the length of half a day,
Why, William, sit you thus alone,
And dream your time away?

"Where are your books?—that light be-
  queathed 5
To Beings else forlorn and blind!
Up! up! and drink the spirit breathed
From dead men to their kind.

"You look round on your Mother Earth,
As if she for no purpose bore you; 10
As if you were her first-born birth,
And none had lived before you!"

One morning thus, by Esthwaite lake,
When life was sweet, I knew not why,
To me my good friend Matthew spake, 15
And thus I made reply:

"The eye—it cannot choose but see;
We cannot bid the ear be still;
Our bodies feel, where'er they be,
Against or with our will. 20

"Nor less I deem that there are Powers
Which of themselves our minds impress;
That we can feed this mind of ours
In a wise passiveness.

"Think you, 'mid all this mighty sum 25
Of things for ever speaking,
That nothing of itself will come,
But we must still be seeking?

"—Then ask not wherefore, here, alone,
Conversing as I may, 30
I sit upon this old grey stone,
And dream my time away."

1798   1798

THE TABLES TURNED

AN EVENING SCENE ON THE SAME
SUBJECT

Up! up! my Friend, and quit your books;
Or surely you'll grow double:
Up! up! my Friend, and clear your looks;
Why all this toil and trouble?

The sun, above the mountain's head, 5
A freshening lustre mellow
Through all the long green fields has
  spread,
His first sweet evening yellow.

Books! 'tis a dull and endless strife:
Come, hear the woodland linnet, 10
How sweet his music! on my life,
There's more of wisdom in it.

And hark! how blithe the throstle sings!
He, too, is no mean preacher:
Come forth into the light of things,   15
Let Nature be your teacher.

She has a world of ready wealth,
Our minds and hearts to bless—
Spontaneous wisdom breathed by health,
Truth breathed by cheerfulness.   20

One impulse from a vernal wood
May teach you more of man,
Of moral evil and of good,
Than all the sages can.

Sweet is the lore which Nature brings;   25
Our meddling intellect
Mis-shapes   the   beauteous   forms   of
            things:—
We murder to dissect.

Enough of Science and of Art;
Close up those barren leaves;   30
Come forth, and bring with you a heart
That watches and receives.

1798   1798

ANECDOTE FOR FATHERS

I have a boy of five years old;
His face is fair and fresh to see;
His limbs are cast in beauty's mold,
And dearly he loves me.

One morn we strolled on our dry walk,   5
Our quiet home all full in view,
And held such intermitted talk
As we are wont to do.

My thoughts on former pleasures ran;
I thought of Kilve's delightful shore,   10
Our pleasant home when spring began,
A long, long year before.

A day it was when I could bear
Some fond regrets to entertain;
With so much happiness to spare,   15
I could not feel a pain.

The green earth echoed to the feet
Of lambs that bounded through the glade,
From shade to sunshine, and as fleet
From sunshine back to shade.   20

Birds warbled round me—and each trace
Of inward sadness had its charm;
Kilve, thought I, was a favored place,
And so is Liswyn farm.

My boy beside me tripped, so slim   25
And graceful in his rustic dress!
And, as we talked, I questioned him,
In very idleness.

"Now tell me, had you rather be,"
I said, and took him by the arm,   30
"On Kilve's smooth shore, by the green sea,
Or here at Liswyn farm?"

In careless mood he looked at me,
While still I held him by the arm,
And said, "At Kilve I'd rather be   35
Than here at Liswyn farm."

"Now, little Edward, say why so:
My little Edward, tell me why."—
"I cannot tell, I do not know."—
"Why, this is strange," said I;   40

"For here are woods, hills smooth and
            warm:
There surely must some reason be
Why you would change sweet Liswyn farm
For Kilve by the green sea."

At this my boy hung down his head,   45
He blushed with shame, nor made reply;
And three times to the child I said,
"Why, Edward, tell me why?"

His head he raised—there was in sight,
It caught his eye, he saw it plain—   50
Upon the house-top, glittering bright,
A broad and gilded vane.

Then did the boy his tongue unlock,
And eased his mind with this reply:
"At Kilve there was no weather-cock;   55
And that's the reason why."

O dearest, dearest boy! my heart
For better lore would seldom yearn,
Could I but teach the hundredth part
Of what from thee I learn.   60
1798   1798

TO MY SISTER

It is the first mild day of March.
Each minute, sweeter than before,
The redbreast sings from the tall larch
That stands beside our door.

There is a blessing in the air,   5
Which seems a sense of joy to yield
To the bare trees, and mountains bare,
And grass in the green field.

My sister! ('tis a wish of mine)
Now that our morning meal is done, 10
Make haste, your morning task resign;
Come forth and feel the sun.

Edward will come with you; and, pray,
Put on with speed your woodland dress;
And bring no book; for this one day 15
We'll give to idleness.

No joyless forms shall regulate
Our living calendar;
We from today, my friend, will date
The opening of the year. 20

Love, now a universal birth,
From heart to heart is stealing,
From earth to man, from man to earth—
It is the hour of feeling.

One moment now may give us more 25
Than years of toiling reason;
Our minds shall drink at every pore
The spirit of the season.

Some silent laws our hearts will make,
Which they shall long obey; 30
We for the year to come may take
Our temper from today.

And from the blessed power that rolls
About, below, above,
We'll frame the measure of our souls; 35
They shall be tuned to love.

Then come, my sister! come, I pray,
With speed put on your woodland dress;
And bring no book; for this one day
We'll give to idleness. 40

1798   1798

LINES

COMPOSED A FEW MILES ABOVE TINTERN ABBEY, ON REVISITING THE BANKS
OF THE WYE DURING A TOUR

Five years have past; five summers, with the length
Of five long winters! and again I hear
These waters, rolling from their mountain-springs
With a soft inland murmur.—Once again
Do I behold these steep and lofty cliffs, 5
That on a wild secluded scene impress
Thoughts of more deep seclusion; and connect
The landscape with the quiet of the sky.
The day is come when I again repose
Here, under this dark sycamore, and view 10
These plots of cottage-ground, these orchard-tufts,
Which at this season, with their unripe fruits,
Are clad in one green hue, and lose themselves
'Mid groves and copses. Once again I see
These hedge-rows, hardly hedge-rows, little lines 15
Of sportive wood run wild: these pastoral farms,
Green to the very door; and wreaths of smoke
Sent up, in silence from among the trees!
With some uncertain notice, as might seem
Of vagrant dwellers in the houseless woods, 20
Or of some Hermit's cave, where by his fire
The Hermit sits alone.
                    These beauteous forms
Through a long absence, have not been to me
As is a landscape to a blind man's eye:
But oft, in lonely rooms, and 'mid the din 25
Of towns and cities, I have owed to them
In hours of weariness, sensations sweet,
Felt in the blood, and felt along the heart;
And passing even into my purer mind,
With tranquil restoration:—feelings too 30
Of unremembered pleasure: such, perhaps,

As have no slight or trivial influence
On that best portion of a good man's life.
His little, nameless, unremembered acts
Of kindness and of love. Nor less, I trust,   35
To them I may have owed another gift,
Of aspect more sublime; that blessed mood,
In which the burthen of the mystery,
In which the heavy and the weary weight
Of all this unintelligible world,   40
Is lightened:—that serene and blessed mood,
In which the affections gently lead us on,—
Until, the breath of this corporeal frame
And even the motion of our human blood
Almost suspended, we are laid asleep   45
In body, and become a living soul:
While with an eye made quiet by the power
Of harmony, and the deep power of joy,
We see into the life of things.
                                If this
Be but a vain belief, yet, oh! how oft   50
In darkness and amid the many shapes
Of joyless daylight; when the fretful stir
Unprofitable, and the fever of the world,
Have hung upon the beatings of my heart—
How oft, in spirit, have I turned to thee,   55
O sylvan Wye! thou wanderer thro' the woods,
How often has my spirit turned to thee!

     And now, with gleams of half-extinguished thought,
With many recognitions dim and faint,
And somewhat of a sad perplexity,   60
The picture of the mind revives again:
While here I stand, not only with the sense
Of present pleasure, but with pleasing thoughts
That in this moment there is life and food
For future years. And so I dare to hope,   65
Though changed, no doubt, from what I was when first
I came among these hills; when like a roe
I bounded o'er the mountains, by the sides
Of the deep rivers, and the lonely streams,
Wherever nature led: more like a man   70
Flying from something that he dreads, than one
Who sought the thing he loved. For nature then
(The coarser pleasures of my boyish days,
And their glad animal movements all gone by)
To me was all in all.—I cannot paint   75
What then I was. The sounding cataract
Haunted me like a passion: the tall rock,
The mountain, and the deep and gloomy wood,
Their colors and their forms, were then to me
An appetite; a feeling and a love,   80
That had no need of a remoter charm,
By thought supplied, nor any interest
Unborrowed from the eye.—That time is past,
And all its aching joys are now no more,
And all its dizzy raptures. Not for this   85
Faint I, nor mourn nor murmur; other gifts
Have followed; for such loss, I would believe,
Abundant recompense. For I have learned
To look on nature, not as in the hour

Of thoughtless youth; but hearing oftentimes 90
The still, sad music of humanity,
Nor harsh nor grating, though of ample power
To chasten and subdue. And I have felt
A presence that disturbs me with the joy
Of elevated thoughts; a sense sublime 95
Of something far more deeply interfused,
Whose dwelling is the light of setting suns,
And the round ocean and the living air,
And the blue sky, and in the mind of man;
A motion and a spirit, that impels 100
All thinking things, all objects of all thought,
And rolls through all things. Therefore am I still
A lover of the meadows and the woods,
And mountains; and of all that we behold
From this green earth; of all the mighty world 105
Of eye, and ear,—both what they half create,
And what perceive; well pleased to recognise
In nature and the language of the sense,
The anchor of my purest thoughts, the nurse,
The guide, the guardian of my heart, and soul 110
Of all my moral being.

            Nor perchance,
If I were not thus taught, should I the more
Suffer my genial spirits to decay:
For thou art with me here upon the banks
Of this fair river; thou my dearest Friend, 115
My dear, dear Friend; and in thy voice I catch
The language of my former heart, and read
My former pleasures in the shooting lights
Of thy wild eyes. Oh! yet a little while
May I behold in thee what I was once, 120
My dear, dear Sister! and this prayer I make,
Knowing that Nature never did betray
The heart that loved her; 'tis her privilege,
Through all the years of this our life, to lead
From joy to joy: for she can so inform 125
The mind that is within us, so impress
With quietness and beauty, and so feed
With lofty thoughts, that neither evil tongues,
Rash judgments, nor the sneers of selfish men,
Nor greetings where no kindness is, nor all 130
The dreary intercourse of daily life,
Shall e'er prevail against us, or disturb
Our cheerful faith, that all which we behold
Is full of blessings. Therefore let the moon
Shine on thee in thy solitary walk; 135
And let the misty mountain-winds be free
To blow against thee: and, in after years,
When these wild ecstasies shall be matured
Into a sober pleasure; when thy mind
Shall be a mansion for all lovely forms, 140
Thy memory be as a dwelling-place
For all sweet sounds and harmonies; oh! then
If solitude, or fear, or pain, or grief,
Should be thy portion, with what healing thoughts
Of tender joy wilt thou remember me, 145
And these my exhortations! Nor, perchance—
If I should be where I no more can hear
Thy voice, nor catch from thy wild eyes these gleams

Of past existence—wilt thou then forget
That on the banks of this delightful stream   150
We stood together, and that I, so long
A worshipper of Nature, hither came
Unwearied in that service: rather say
With warmer love—oh! with far deeper zeal
Of holier love. Nor wilt thou then forget,   155
That after many wanderings, many years
Of absence, these steep woods and lofty cliffs,
And this green pastoral landscape, were to me
More dear, both for themselves and for thy sake!
July 13, 1798   1798

THE REVERIE OF POOR SUSAN

At the corner of Wood Street, when daylight appears,
Hangs a thrush that sings loud, it has sung for three years:
Poor Susan has passed by the spot, and has heard
In the silence of morning the song of the bird.

'Tis a note of enchantment; what ails her? She sees   5
A mountain ascending, a vision of trees;
Bright volumes of vapor through Lothbury glide,
And a river flows on through the vale of Cheapside.

Green pastures she views in the midst of the dale,
Down which she so often has tripped with her pail;   10
And a single small cottage, a nest like a dove's,
The one only dwelling on earth that she loves.

She looks, and her heart is in heaven: but they fade,
The mist and the river, the hill and the shade:
The stream will not flow, and the hill will not rise,   15
And the colors have all passed away from her eyes!
1797   1800

"THERE WAS A BOY"

There was a Boy; ye knew him well, ye cliffs
And islands of Winander!—many a time,
At evening, when the earliest stars began
To move along the edges of the hills,
Rising or setting, would he stand alone,   5
Beneath the trees, or by the glimmering lake;
And there, with fingers interwoven, both hands
Pressed closely palm to palm and to his mouth
Uplifted, he, as through an instrument,
Blew mimic hootings to the silent owls,   10
That they might answer him.—And they would shout
Across the watery vale, and shout again,
Responsive to his call,—with quivering peals,
And long halloos, and screams, and echoes loud
Redoubled and redoubled; concourse wild   15
Of jocund din! And, when there came a pause
Of silence such as baffled his best skill:
Then, sometimes, in that silence, while he hung
Listening, a gentle shock of mild surprise
Has carried far into his heart the voice   20
Of mountain-torrents; or the visible scene

Would enter unawares into his mind
With all its solemn imagery, its rocks,
Its woods, and that uncertain heaven received
Into the bosom of the steady lake.   25
    This boy was taken from his mates, and died
In childhood, ere he was full twelve years old.
Pre-eminent in beauty is the vale
Where he was born and bred: the church-yard hangs
Upon a slope above the village-school;   30
And, through that church-yard when my way has led
On summer-evenings, I believe, that there
A long half-hour together I have stood
Mute—looking at the grave in which he lies!

Nov. or Dec. 1798   1800

WE ARE SEVEN

——A simple Child,
That lightly draws its breath,
And feels its life in every limb,
What should it know of death?

I met a little cottage Girl: 5
She was eight years old, she said:
Her hair was thick with many a curl
That clustered round her head.

She had a rustic, woodland air,
And she was wildly clad: 10
Her eyes were fair, and very fair:
—Her beauty made me glad.

"Sisters and brothers, little Maid,
How many may you be?"
"How many? Seven in all," she said,   15
And wondering looked at me.

"And where are they? I pray you tell."
She answered, "Seven are we;
And two of us at Conway dwell,
And two are gone to sea.   20

"Two of us in the church-yard lie,
My sister and my brother;
And, in the church-yard cottage, I
Dwell near them with my mother."

"You say that two at Conway dwell,   25
And two are gone to sea,
Yet ye are seven!—I pray you tell,
Sweet Maid, how this may be."

Then did the little Maid reply,
"Seven boys and girls are we;   30
Two of us in the church-yard lie,
Beneath the church-yard tree."

"You run about, my little Maid,
Your limbs they are alive;
If two are in the church-yard laid,   35
Then ye are only five."

"Their graves are green, they may be seen,"
The little Maid replied,
"Twelve steps or more from my mother's
                                    door,
And they are side by side.   40

"My stockings there I often knit,
My kerchief there I hem;
And there upon the ground I sit,
And sing a song to them.

"And often after sunset, Sir,   45
When it is light and fair,
I take my little porringer,
And eat my supper there.

"The first that died was sister Jane;
In bed she moaning lay,   50
Till God released her of her pain;
And then she went away.

"So in the church-yard she was laid;
And, when the grass was dry,
Together round her grave we played,   55
My brother John and I.

"And when the ground was white with
                                    snow,
And I could run and slide,
My brother John was forced to go,
And he lies by her side."   60

"How many are you, then," said I,
"If they two are in heaven?"
Quick was the little Maid's reply,
"O Master! we are seven."

"But they are dead; those two are dead! 65
Their spirits are in heaven!"
'Twas throwing words away; for still
The little Maid would have her will,
And said, "Nay, we are seven!"

1798   1800

THE OLD CUMBERLAND BEGGAR

I saw an aged beggar in my walk;
And he was seated, by the highway side,
On a low structure of rude masonry
Built at the foot of a huge hill, that they
Who lead their horses down the steep rough road   5
May thence remount at ease. The aged man
Had placed his staff across the broad smooth stone
That overlays the pile; and, from a bag
All white with flour, the dole of village dames,
He drew his scraps and fragments, one by one;   10
And scanned them with a fixed and serious look
Of idle computation. In the sun,
Upon the second step of that small pile,
Surrounded by those wild unpeopled hills,
He sat, and ate his food in solitude: 15
And ever scattered from his palsied hand,
That, still attempting to prevent the waste,
Was baffled still, the crumbs in little showers
Fell on the ground; and the small mountain birds,
Not venturing yet to peck their destined meal,   20
Approached within the length of half his staff.

Him from my childhood have I known; and then
He was so old, he seems not older now;
He travels on, a solitary man,
So helpless in appearance, that for him   25
The sauntering horseman throws not with a slack
And careless hand his alms upon the ground,
But stops,—that he may safely lodge the coin
Within the old man's hat; nor quits him so,
But still, when he has given his horse the rein,   30
Watches the aged beggar with a look
Sidelong, and half-reverted. She who tends
The toll-gate, when in summer at her door
She turns her wheel, if on the road she sees
The aged beggar coming, quits her work,   35
And lifts the latch for him that he may pass.
The post-boy, when his rattling wheels o'ertake
The aged beggar in the woody lane,
Shouts to him from behind; and, if thus warned
The old man does not change his course, the boy   40
Turns with less noisy wheels to the roadside,
And passes gently by, without a curse
Upon his lips or anger at his heart.

He travels on, a solitary man;
His age has no companion. On the ground   45
His eyes are turned, and, as he moves along,
They move along the ground; and, evermore,
Instead of common and habitual sight
Of fields with rural works, of hill and dale,
And the blue sky, one little span of earth   50
Is all his prospect. Thus, from day to day,
Bow-bent, his eyes forever on the ground,
He plies his weary journey; seeing still,
And seldom knowing that he sees, some straw,
Some scattered leaf, or marks which, in one track,   55

The nails of cart or chariot-wheel have left
Impressed on the white road,—in the same line,
At distance still the same. Poor traveller!
His staff trails with him; scarcely do his feet
Disturb the summer dust; he is so still   60
In look and motion, that the cottage curs,
Ere he has passed the door, will turn away,
Weary of barking at him. Boys and girls,
The vacant and the busy, maids and youths,
And urchins newly breeched—all pass him by: 65
Him even the slow-paced wagon leaves behind.

But deem not this man useless.—Statesmen! ye
Who are so restless in your wisdom, ye
Who have a broom still ready in your hands
To rid the world of nuisances; ye proud,   70
Heart-swoln, while in your pride ye contemplate
Your talents, power, or wisdom, deem him not
A burthen of the earth! 'Tis nature's law
That none, the meanest of created things,
Of forms created the most vile and brute,   75
The dullest or most noxious, should exist
Divorced from good—a spirit and pulse of good,
A life and soul, to every mode of being
Inseparably linked. Then be assured
That least of all can aught—that ever owned   80
The heaven-regarding eye and front sublime
Which man is born to—sink, howe'er depressed,
So low as to be scorned without a sin;
Without offence to God cast out of view;
Like the dry remnant of a garden flower   85
Whose seeds are shed, or as an implement
Worn out and worthless. While from door to door,
This old man creeps, the villagers in him
Behold a record which together binds
Past deeds and offices of charity,   90
Else unremembered, and so keeps alive
The kindly mood in hearts which lapse of years,
And that half-wisdom half-experience gives,
Make slow to feel, and by sure steps resign
To selfishness and cold oblivious cares.   95
Among the farms and solitary huts,
Hamlets and thinly-scattered villages,
Where'er the aged beggar takes his rounds,
The mild necessity of use compels
To acts of love; and habit does the work   100
Of reason; yet prepares that after-joy
Which reason cherishes. And thus the soul,
By that sweet taste of pleasure unpursued,
Doth find herself insensibly disposed
To virtue and true goodness.

                                   Some there are,   105
By their good works exalted, lofty minds,
And meditative, authors of delight
And happiness, which to the end of time
Will live, and spread, and kindle: even such minds
In childhood, from this solitary being,   110
Or from like wanderer haply have received
(A thing more precious far than all that books

Or the solicitudes of love can do!)
That first mild touch of sympathy and thought,
In which they found their kindred with a world   115
Where want and sorrow were. The easy man
Who sits at his own door,—and, like the pear
That overhangs his head from the green wall,
Feeds in the sunshine; the robust and young,
The prosperous and unthinking, they who live   120
Sheltered, and flourish in a little grove
Of their own kindred;—all behold in him
A silent monitor, which on their minds
Must needs impress a transitory thought
Of self-congratulation, to the heart   125
Of each recalling his peculiar boons,
His charters and exemptions; and, perchance,
Though he to no one give the fortitude
And circumspection needful to preserve
His present blessings, and to husband up   130
The respite of the season, he, at least,
And 'tis no vulgar service, makes them felt.

Yet further.—Many, I believe, there are
Who live a life of virtuous decency,
Men who can hear the decalogue and feel   135
No self-reproach; who of the moral law
Established in the land where they abide
Are strict observers; and not negligent
In acts of love to those with whom they dwell,
Their kindred, and the children of their blood.   140
Praise be to such, and to their slumbers peace!
—But of the poor man ask, the abject poor;
Go, and demand of him, if there be here
In this cold abstinence from evil deeds,
And these inevitable charities,   145
Wherewith to satisfy the human soul?
No—man is dear to man; the poorest poor
Long for some moments in a weary life
When they can know and feel that they have been,
Themselves, the fathers and the dealers-out   150
Of some small blessings; have been kind to such
As needed kindness, for this single cause,
That we have all of us one human heart.
—Such pleasure is to one kind being known,
My neighbor, when with punctual care, each week,   155
Duly as Friday comes, though pressed herself
By her own wants, she from her store of meal
Takes one unsparing handful for the scrip
Of this old mendicant, and, from her door
Returning with exhilarated heart,   160
Sits by her fire, and builds her hope in heaven.

Then let him pass, a blessing on his head!
And while in that vast solitude to which
The tide of things has borne him, he appears
To breathe and live but for himself alone,   165
Unblamed, uninjured, let him bear about
The good which the benignant law of heaven
Has hung around him: and, while life is his,
Still let him prompt the unlettered villagers
To tender offices and pensive thoughts.   170

—Then let him pass, a blessing on his head!
And, long as he can wander, let him breathe
The freshness of the valleys; let his blood
Struggle with frosty air and winter snows;
And let the chartered wind that sweeps the heath   175
Beat his gray locks against his withered face.
Reverence the hope whose vital anxiousness
Gives the last human interest to his heart.
May never house, misnamed of industry,
Make him a captive!—for that pent-up din,   180
Those life-consuming sounds that clog the air,
Be his the natural silence of old age!
Let him be free of mountain solitudes;
And have around him, whether heard or not,
The pleasant melody of woodland birds.   185
Few are his pleasures: if his eyes have now
Been doomed so long to settle upon earth
That not without some effort they behold
The countenance of the horizontal sun,
Rising or setting, let the light at least   190
Find a free entrance to their languid orbs,
And let him, where and when he will sit down
Beneath the trees, or on a grassy bank
Of highway side, and with the little birds
Share his chance-gathered meal; and, finally,   195
As in the eye of nature he has lived,
So in the eye of nature let him die!

1798   1800

RUTH

When Ruth was left half desolate,
Her father took another mate;
And Ruth, not seven years old,
A slighted child, at her own will
Went wandering over dale and hill,   5
In thoughtless freedom, bold.

And she had made a pipe of straw,
And music from that pipe could draw
Like sounds of winds and floods;
Had built a bower upon the green,   10
As if she from her birth had been
An infant of the woods.

Beneath her father's roof, alone
She seemed to live; her thoughts her own;
Herself her own delight;   15
Pleased with herself, nor sad, nor gay;
And, passing thus the livelong day,
She grew to woman's height.

There came a youth from Georgia's shore—
A military casque he wore,   20
With splendid feathers dressed;
He brought them from the Cherokees;
The feathers nodded in the breeze,
And made a gallant crest.

From Indian blood you deem him
 sprung—   25
But no! he spake the English tongue,
And bore a soldier's name;
And, when America was free
From battle and from jeopardy,
He 'cross the ocean came.   30

With hues of genius on his cheek
In finest tones the youth could speak.
—While he was yet a boy,
The moon, the glory of the sun,
And streams that murmur as they run, 35
Had been his dearest joy.

He was a lovely youth! I guess
The panther in the wilderness
Was not so fair as he;
And, when he chose to sport and play, 40
No dolphin ever was so gay
Upon the tropic sea.

Among the Indians he had fought,
And with him many tales he brought
Of pleasure and of fear;   45
Such tales as told to any maid
By such a youth, in the green shade,
Were perilous to hear.

He told of girls—a happy rout!
Who quit their fold with dance and
　　shout,　　　　　　　　　　50
Their pleasant Indian town,
To gather strawberries all day long;
Returning with a choral song
When daylight is gone down.

He spake of plants that hourly change　55
Their blossoms, through a boundless range
Of intermingling hues;
With budding, fading, faded flowers
They stand the wonder of the bowers
From morn to evening dews.　　　　60

He told of the magnolia, spread
High as a cloud, high overhead!
The cypress and her spire;
—Of flowers that with one scarlet gleam
Cover a hundred leagues, and seem　　65
To set the hills on fire.

The youth of green savannas spake,
And many an endless, endless lake,
With all its fairy crowds
Of islands, that together lie　　　　70
As quietly as spots of sky
Among the evening clouds.

"How pleasant," then he said, "it were,
A fisher or a hunter there,
In sunshine or in shade　　　　　　75
To wander with an easy mind;
And build a household fire, and find
A home in every glade!

"What days and what bright years! Ah
　　me!
Our life were life indeed, with thee　80
So passed in quiet bliss,
And all the while," said he, "to know
That we were in a world of woe,
On such an earth as this!"

And then he sometimes interwove　85
Fond thoughts about a father's love:
"For there," said he, "are spun
Around the heart such tender ties,
That our own children to our eyes
Are dearer than the sun.　　　　　90

"Sweet Ruth! and could you go with me
My helpmate in the woods to be,
Our shed at night to rear;
Or run, my own adopted bride,
A silvan huntress at my side,　　　95
And drive the flying deer!

"Beloved Ruth!"—No more he said.
The wakeful Ruth at midnight shed
A solitary tear.
She thought again—and did agree　100

With him to sail across the sea,
And drive the flying deer.

"And now, as fitting is and right,
We in the church our faith will plight,
A husband and a wife."　　　　　105
Even so they did; and I may say
That to sweet Ruth that happy day
Was more than human life.

Through dream and vision did she sink,
Delighted all the while to think　　110
That on those lonesome floods
And green savannas, she should share
His board with lawful joy, and bear
His name in the wild woods.

But, as you have before been told,　115
This stripling, sportive, gay, and bold,
And, with his dancing crest,
So beautiful, through savage lands
Had roamed about, with vagrant bands
Of Indians in the west.　　　　　120

The wind, the tempest roaring high,
The tumult of a tropic sky,
Might well be dangerous food
For him, a youth to whom was given
So much of earth—so much of heaven,　125
And such impetuous blood.

Whatever in those climes he found
Irregular in sight or sound
Did to his mind impart
A kindred impulse, seemed allied　　130
To his own powers, and justified
The workings of his heart.

Nor less, to feed voluptuous thought,
The beauteous forms of nature wrought,
Fair trees and gorgeous flowers;　　135
The breezes their own languor lent;
The stars had feelings, which they sent
Into those favored bowers.

Yet, in his worst pursuits I ween
That sometimes there did intervene　140
Pure hopes of high intent;
For passions linked to forms so fair
And stately needs must have their share
Of noble sentiment.

But ill he lived, much evil saw,　　145
With men to whom no better law
Nor better life was known;
Deliberately, and undeceived,
Those wild men's vices he received,
And gave them back his own.　　　150

His genius and his moral frame
Were thus impaired, and he became
The slave of low desires—

A man who without self-control
Would seek what the degraded soul   155
Unworthily admires.

And yet he with no feigned delight
Had wooed the maiden, day and night
Had loved her, night and morn.
What could he less than love a maid   160
Whose heart with so much nature played?
So kind and so forlorn!

Sometimes, most earnestly, he said,
"O Ruth! I have been worse than dead;
False thoughts, thoughts bold and vain, 165
Encompassed me on every side
When I, in confidence and pride,
Had crossed the Atlantic main.

"Before me shone a glorious world—
Fresh as a banner bright, unfurled   170
To music suddenly.
I looked upon those hills and plains,
And seemed as if let loose from chains,
To live at liberty.

"No more of this; for now, by thee   175
Dear Ruth! more happily set free
With nobler zeal I burn;
My soul from darkness is released,
Like the whole sky when to the east
The morning doth return."   180

Full soon that better mind was gone;
No hope, no wish remained, not one—
They stirred him now no more;
New objects did new pleasure give,
And once again he wished to live   185
As lawless as before.

Meanwhile, as thus with him it fared,
They for the voyage were prepared,
And went to the seashore,
But, when they thither came, the youth 190
Deserted his poor bride, and Ruth
Could never find him more.

God help thee, Ruth!—Such pains she had
That she in half a year was mad,
And in a prison housed;   195
And there, with many a doleful song
Made of wild words, her cup of wrong
She fearfully caroused.

Yet sometimes milder hours she knew,
Nor wanted sun, nor rain, nor dew,   200
Nor pastimes of the May;
—They all were with her in her cell;
And a clear brook with cheerful knell
Did o'er the pebbles play.

When Ruth three seasons thus had lain, 205
There came a respite to her pain;
She from her prison fled;
But of the vagrant none took thought;
And where it liked her best she sought
Her shelter and her bread.   210

Among the fields she breathed again;
The master-current of her brain
Ran permanent and free;
And, coming to the Banks of Tone,
There did she rest; and dwell alone   215
Under the greenwood tree.

The engines of her pain, the tools
That shaped her sorrow, rocks and pools,
And airs that gently stir
The vernal leaves—she loved them still; 220
Nor ever taxed them with the ill
Which had been done to her.

A barn her *winter* bed supplies;
But, till the warmth of summer skies
And summer days is gone   225
(And all do in this tale agree),
She sleeps beneath the greenwood tree,
And other home hath none.

An innocent life, yet far astray!
And Ruth will, long before her day,   230
Be broken down and old.
Sore aches she needs must have! but less
Of mind than body's wretchedness,
From damp, and rain, and cold.

If she is pressed by want of food,   235
She from her dwelling in the wood
Repairs to a roadside;
And there she begs at one steep place
Where up and down with easy pace
The horsemen-travelers ride.   240

That oaten pipe of hers is mute,
Or thrown away; but with a flute
Her loneliness she cheers,
This flute, made of a hemlock stalk,
At evening in his homeward walk   245
The Quantock woodman hears.

I, too, have passed her on the hills
Setting her little water-mills
By spouts and fountains wild—
Such small machinery as she turned   250
Ere she had wept, ere she had mourned,
A young and happy child!

Farewell! and when thy days are told,
Ill-fated Ruth, in hallowed mold
Thy corpse shall buried be,   255
For thee a funeral bell shall ring,
And all the congregation sing
A Christian psalm for thee.

1799   1800

NUTTING

—It seems a day
(I speak of one from many singled out),
One of those heavenly days that cannot die;
When, in the eagerness of boyish hope,
I left our cottage threshold, sallying forth   5
With a huge wallet o'er my shoulders slung,
A nutting-crook in hand, and turned my steps
Toward some far-distant wood, a figure quaint,
Tricked out in proud disguise of cast-off weeds
Which for that service had been husbanded,   10
By exhortation of my frugal dame—
Motley accouterment, of power to smile
At thorns, and brakes, and brambles—and in truth
More ragged than need was! O'er pathless rocks,
Through beds of matted fern, and tangled thickets,   15
Forcing my way, I came to one dear nook
Unvisited, where not a broken bough
Drooped with its withered leaves, ungracious sign
Of devastation; but the hazels rose
Tall and erect, with tempting clusters hung,   20
A virgin scene!—A little while I stood,
Breathing with such suppression of the heart
As joy delights in; and with wise restraint
Voluptuous, fearless of a rival, eyed
The banquet; or beneath the trees I sat   25
Amongst the flowers, and with the flowers I played;
A temper known to those who, after long
And weary expectation, have been blessed
With sudden happiness beyond all hope.
Perhaps it was a bower beneath whose leaves   30
The violets of five seasons reappear
And fade, unseen by any human eye;
Where fairy waterbreaks do murmur on
Forever; and I saw the sparkling foam,
And—with my cheek on one of those green stones   35
That, fleeced with moss, under the shady trees,
Lay round me, scattered like a flock of sheep—
I heard the murmur and the murmuring sound,
In that sweet mood when pleasure loves to pay
Tribute to ease; and, of its joy secure,   40
The heart luxuriates with indifferent things,
Wasting its kindliness on stocks and stones,
And on the vacant air. Then up I rose,
And dragged to earth both branch and bough, with crash
And merciless ravage; and the shady nook   45
Of hazels, and the green and mossy bower,
Deformed and sullied, patiently gave up
Their quiet being; and, unless I now
Confound my present feelings with the past,
Ere from the mutilated bower I turned   50
Exulting, rich beyond the wealth of kings,
I felt a sense of pain when I beheld
The silent trees, and saw the intruding sky.
Then, dearest maiden, move along these shades
In gentleness of heart; with gentle hand   55
Touch—for there is a spirit in the woods.

1799   1800

STRANGE FITS OF PASSION
HAVE I KNOWN

Strange fits of passion have I known:
And I will dare to tell,
But in the lover's ear alone,
What once to me befell.

When she I loved looked every day   5
Fresh as a rose in June,
I to her cottage bent my way,
Beneath an evening moon.

Upon the moon I fixed my eye,
All over the wide lea;   10
With quickening pace my horse drew nigh
Those paths so dear to me.

And now we reached the orchard-plot;
And, as we climbed the hill,
The sinking moon to Lucy's cot   15
Came near, and nearer still.

In one of those sweet dreams I slept,
Kind nature's gentlest boon!
And all the while my eyes I kept
On the descending moon.   20

My horse moved on; hoof after hoof
He raised, and never stopped:
When down behind the cottage roof,
At once, the bright moon dropped.

What fond and wayward thoughts will
          slide   25
Into a lover's head!
"O mercy!" to myself I cried,
"If Lucy should be dead!"

1799   1800

LUCY GRAY

OR, SOLITUDE

Oft I had heard of Lucy Gray:
And, when I crossed the wild,
I chanced to see at break of day
The solitary child.

No mate, no comrade Lucy knew;   5
She dwelt on a wide moor,
—The sweetest thing that ever grew
Beside a human door!

You yet may spy the fawn at play,
The hare upon the green;   10
But the sweet face of Lucy Gray
Will never more be seen.

"To-night will be a stormy night—
You to the town must go;
And take a lantern, Child, to light   15
Your mother through the snow."

"That, Father! will I gladly do:
'Tis scarcely afternoon—
The minster-clock has just struck two,
And yonder is the moon!"   20

At this the Father raised his hook,
And snapped a faggot-band;
He plied his work—and Lucy took
The lantern in her hand.

Not blither is the mountain roe: 25
With many a wanton stroke
Her feet disperse the powdery snow,
That rises up like smoke.

The storm came on before its time:
She wandered up and down;   30
And many a hill did Lucy climb:
But never reached the town.

The wretched parents all that night
Went shouting far and wide;
But there was neither sound nor sight   35
To serve them for a guide.

At day-break on a hill they stood
That overlooked the moor;
And thence they saw the bridge of wood,
A furlong from their door.   40

They wept—and, turning homeward, cried,
"In heaven we all shall meet;"
—When in the snow the mother spied
The print of Lucy's feet.

Then downwards from the steep hill's
          edge   45
They tracked the footmarks small;
And through the broken hawthorn hedge,
And by the long stone-wall;

And then an open field they crossed:
The marks were still the same;   50
They tracked them on, nor ever lost;
And to the bridge they came.

They followed from the snowy bank
Those footmarks, one by one,
Into the middle of the plank;   55
And further there were none!

—Yet some maintain that to this day
She is a living child;
That you may see sweet Lucy Gray
Upon the lonesome wild.   60

O'er rough and smooth she trips along,
And never looks behind;
And sings a solitary song
That whistles in the wind.

1799   1800

"SHE DWELT AMONG THE UNTRODDEN WAYS"

She dwelt among the untrodden ways
  Beside the springs of Dove,
A Maid whom there were none to praise
  And very few to love:

A violet by a mossy stone   5
  Half hidden from the eye!
—Fair as a star, when only one
  Is shining in the sky.

She lived unknown, and few could know
  When Lucy ceased to be;   10
But she is in her grave, and, oh,
  The difference to me!

1799   1800

"THREE YEARS SHE GREW IN SUN AND SHOWER"

Three years she grew in sun and shower,
Then Nature said, "A lovelier flower
On earth was never sown;
This Child I to myself will take;
She shall be mine, and I will make   5
A Lady of my own.

"Myself will to my darling be
Both law and impulse: and with me
The Girl, in rock and plain,
In earth and heaven, in glade and bower, 10
Shall feel an overseeing power
To kindle or restrain.

"She shall be sportive as the fawn
That wild with glee across the lawn,
Or up the mountain springs;   15
And hers shall be the breathing balm,
And hers the silence and the calm
Of mute insensate things.

"The floating clouds their state shall lend
To her; for her the willow bend;   20
Nor shall she fail to see
Even in the motions of the Storm
Grace that shall mold the Maiden's form
By silent sympathy.

"The stars of midnight shall be dear   25
To her; and she shall lean her ear
In many a secret place
Where rivulets dance their wayward round,
And beauty born of murmuring sound
Shall pass into her face.   30

"And vital feelings of delight
Shall rear her form to stately height,
Her virgin bosom swell;
Such thoughts to Lucy I will give
While she and I together live   35
Here in this happy dell."

Thus Nature spake—The work was done—
How soon my Lucy's race was run!
She died, and left to me
This heath, this calm, and quiet scene; 40
The memory of what has been,
And never more will be.

1799   1800

"A SLUMBER DID MY SPIRIT SEAL"

A slumber did my spirit seal;
  I had no human fears:
She seemed a thing that could not feel
  The touch of earthly years.

No motion has she now, no force;   5
  She neither hears nor sees;
Rolled round in earth's diurnal course,
  With rocks, and stones, and trees.

1799   1800

A POET'S EPITAPH

Art thou a Statist in the van
Of public conflicts trained and bred?
—First learn to love one living man;
Then may'st thou think upon the dead.

A Lawyer art thou?—draw not nigh!   5
Go, carry to some fitter place
The keenness of that practised eye,
The hardness of that sallow face.

Art thou a Man of purple cheer?
A rosy Man, right plump to see?   10
Approach; yet, Doctor, not too near,
This grave no cushion is for thee.

Or art thou one of gallant pride,
A Soldier and no man of chaff?
Welcome!—but lay the sword aside,   15
And lean upon a peasant's staff.

Physician art thou? one, all eyes,
Philosopher! a fingering slave,
One that would peep and botanise
Upon his mother's grave?   20

Wrapt closely in thy sensual fleece,
O turn aside,—and take, I pray,
That he below may rest in peace,
Thy ever-dwindling soul, away!

A Moralist perchance appears;   25
Led, Heaven knows how! to this poor sod:
And he has neither eyes nor ears;
Himself his world, and his own God;

One to whose smooth-rubbed soul can
     cling
Nor form, nor feeling, great or small;   30
A reasoning, self-sufficing thing,
An intellectual All-in-all!

Shut close the door; press down the latch;
Sleep in thy intellectual crust;
Nor lose ten tickings of thy watch   35
Near this unprofitable dust.

But who is He, with modest looks,
And clad in homely russet brown?
He murmurs near the running brooks
A music sweeter than their own.   40

He is retired as noontide dew,
Or fountain in a noon-day grove;
And you must love him, ere to you
He will seem worthy of your love.

The outward shows of sky and earth,   45
Of hill and valley, he has viewed;
And impulses of deeper birth
Have come to him in solitude.

In common things that round us lie
Some random truths he can impart,—   50
The harvest of a quiet eye
That broods and sleeps on his own heart.

But he is weak; both Man and Boy,
Hath been an idler in the land;
Contented if he might enjoy   55
The things which others understand.

—Come hither in thy hour of strength;
Come, weak as is a breaking wave!
Here stretch thy body at full length;
Or build thy house upon this grave.   60

1799   1800

THE TWO APRIL MORNINGS

We walked along, while bright and red
Uprose the morning sun;
And Matthew stopped, he looked, and
     said,
"The will of God be done!"

A village schoolmaster was he,   5
With hair of glittering gray;
As blithe a man as you could see
On a spring holiday.

And on that morning, through the grass,
And by the steaming rills,   10
We traveled merrily, to pass
A day among the hills.

"Our work," said I, "was well begun,
Then from thy breast what thought,
Beneath so beautiful a sun,   15
So sad a sigh has brought?"

A second time did Matthew stop,
And fixing still his eye
Upon the eastern mountain-top,
To me he made reply: 20

"Yon cloud with that long purple cleft
Brings fresh into my mind
A day like this which I have left
Full thirty years behind.

"And just above yon slope of corn   25
Such colors, and no other,
Were in the sky, that April morn,
Of this the very brother.

"With rod and line I sued the sport
Which that sweet season gave,   30
And, to the churchyard come, stopped
     short
Beside my daughter's grave.

"Nine summers had she scarcely seen,
The pride of all the vale;
And then she sang;—she would have
     been   35
A very nightingale.

"Six feet in earth my Emma lay;
And yet I loved her more,
For so it seemed, than till that day
I e'er had loved before.   40

"And, turning from her grave, I met,
Beside the churchyard yew,
A blooming girl whose hair was wet
With points of morning dew.

"A basket on her head she bare;   45
Her brow was smooth and white.
To see a child so very fair,
It was a pure delight!

"No fountain from its rocky cave
E'er tripped with foot so free;   50
She seemed as happy as a wave
That dances on the sea.

"There came from me a sigh of pain
Which I could ill confine;
I looked at her, and looked again   55
And did not wish her mine!"

Matthew is in his grave, yet now,
Methinks, I see him stand,
As at that moment, with a bough
Of wilding in his hand.   60

1799   1800

THE FOUNTAIN

A CONVERSATION

We talked with open heart, and tongue
Affectionate and true,
A pair of friends, though I was young,
And Matthew seventy-two.

We lay beneath a spreading oak,   5
Beside a mossy seat;
And from the turf a fountain broke,
And gurgled at our feet.

"Now, Matthew!" said I, "let us match
This water's pleasant tune   10
With some old border-song, or catch
That suits a summer's noon;

"Or of the church-clock and the chimes
Sing here beneath the shade,
That half-mad thing of witty rhymes   15
Which you last April made!"

In silence Matthew lay, and eyed
The spring beneath the tree;
And thus the dear old Man replied,
The grey-haired man of glee: 20

"No check, no stay, this Streamlet fears;
How merrily it goes!
'Twill murmur on a thousand years,
And flow as now it flows.

"And here, on this delightful day,   25
I cannot choose but think

How oft, a vigorous man, I lay
Beside this fountain's brink.

"My eyes are dim with childish tears,
My heart is idly stirred,   30
For the same sound is in my ears
Which in those days I heard.

"Thus fares it still in our decay:
And yet the wiser mind
Mourns less for what age takes away   35
Than what it leaves behind.

"The blackbird amid leafy trees,
The lark above the hill,
Let loose their carols when they please,
Are quiet when they will.   40

"With Nature never do *they* wage
A foolish strife; they see
A happy youth, and their old age
Is beautiful and free:

"But we are pressed by heavy laws;   45
And often, glad no more,
We wear a face of joy, because
We have been glad of yore.

"If there be one who need bemoan
His kindred laid in earth,   50
The household hearts that were his own;
It is the man of mirth.

"My days, my Friend, are almost gone,
My life has been approved,
And many love me; but by none   55
Am I enough beloved."

"Now both himself and me he wrongs,
The man who thus complains;
I live and sing my idle songs
Upon these happy plains;   60

"And, Matthew, for thy children dead
I'll be a son to thee!"
At this he grasped my hand, and said,
"Alas! that cannot be."

We rose up from the fountain-side;   65
And down the smooth descent
Of the green sheep-track did we glide;
And through the wood we went;

And, ere we came to Leonard's rock,
He sang those witty rhymes   70
About the crazy old church-clock,
And the bewildered chimes.

1799   1800

MICHAEL

A PASTORAL POEM

If from the public way you turn your steps
Up the tumultuous brook of Greenhead Ghyll,
You will suppose that with an upright path
Your feet must struggle; in such bold ascent
The pastoral mountains front you, face to face.   5
But, courage! for around that boisterous brook
The mountains have all opened out themselves,
And made a hidden valley of their own.
No habitation can be seen; but they
Who journey thither find themselves alone   10
With a few sheep, with rocks and stones, and kites
That overhead are sailing in the sky.
It is in truth an utter solitude;
Nor should I have made mention of this Dell
But for one object which you might pass by,   15
Might see and notice not. Beside the brook
Appears a straggling heap of unhewn stones!
And to that simple object appertains
A story—unenriched with strange events,
Yet not unfit, I deem, for the fireside,   20
Or for the summer shade. It was the first
Of those domestic tales that spake to me
Of shepherds, dwellers in the valleys, men
Whom I already loved; not verily
For their own sakes, but for the fields and hills   25
Where was their occupation and abode.
And hence this Tale, while I was yet a Boy
Careless of books, yet having felt the power
Of Nature, by the gentle agency
Of natural objects, led me on to feel   30
For passions that were not my own, and think
(At random and imperfectly indeed)
On man, the heart of man, and human life.
Therefore, although it be a history
Homely and rude, I will relate the same   35
For the delight of a few natural hearts;
And, with yet fonder feeling, for the sake
Of youthful Poets, who among these hills
Will be my second self when I am gone.

Upon the forest-side in Grasmere Vale   40
There dwelt a Shepherd, Michael was his name;
An old man, stout of heart, and strong of limb.
His bodily frame had been from youth to age
Of an unusual strength: his mind was keen,
Intense, and frugal, apt for all affairs,   45
And in his shepherd's calling he was prompt
And watchful more than ordinary men.
Hence had he learned the meaning of all winds,
Of blasts of every tone; and, oftentimes,
When others heeded not, He heard the South   50
Make subterraneous music, like the noise
Of bagpipers on distant Highland hills.
The Shepherd, at such warning, of his flock
Bethought him, and he to himself would say,

"The winds are now devising work for me!"   55
And, truly, at all times, the storm, that drives
The traveller to a shelter, summoned him
Up to the mountains: he had been alone
Amid the heart of many thousand mists,
That came to him, and left him, on the heights.   60
So lived he till his eightieth year was past.
And grossly that man errs, who should suppose
That the green valleys, and the streams and rocks,
Were things indifferent to the Shepherd's thoughts.
Fields, where with cheerful spirits he had breathed   65
The common air; hills, which with vigorous step
He had so often climbed; which had impressed
So many incidents upon his mind
Of hardship, skill or courage, joy or fear;
Which, like a book, preserved the memory   70
Of the dumb animals, whom he had saved,
Had fed or sheltered, linking to such acts
The certainty of honorable gain;
Those fields, those hills—what could they less?—had laid
Strong hold on his affections, were to him   75
A pleasurable feeling of blind love,
The pleasure which there is in life itself.

   His days had not been passed in singleness.
His Helpmate was a comely matron, old—
Though younger than himself full twenty years.   80
She was a woman of a stirring life,
Whose heart was in her house: two wheels she had
Of antique form; this large, for spinning wool;
That small, for flax; and if one wheel had rest
It was because the other was at work.   85
The Pair had but one inmate in their house,
An only Child, who had been born to them
When Michael, telling o'er his years, began
To deem that he was old,—in shepherd's phrase,
With one foot in the grave. This only Son,   90
With two brave sheep-dogs tried in many a storm,
The one of an inestimable worth,
Made all their household. I may truly say,
That they were as a proverb in the vale
For endless industry. When day was gone,   95
And from their occupations out of doors
The Son and Father were come home, even then,
Their labor did not cease; unless when all
Turned to the cleanly supper-board, and there,
Each with a mess of pottage and skimmed milk,   100
Sat round the basket piled with oaten cakes,
And their plain home-made cheese. Yet when the meal
Was ended, Luke (for so the Son was named)
And his old Father both betook themselves
To such convenient work as might employ   105
Their hands by the fireside; perhaps to card
Wool for the Housewife's spindle, or repair
Some injury done to sickle, flail, or scythe,
Or other implement of house or field.

   Down from the ceiling, by the chimney's edge,   110
That in our ancient uncouth country style
With huge and black projection overbrowed

Large space beneath, as duly as the light
Of day grew dim the Housewife hung a lamp;
An aged utensil, which had performed   115
Service beyond all others of its kind.
Early at evening did it burn—and late,
Surviving comrade of uncounted hours,
Which, going by from year to year, had found,
And left, the couple neither gay perhaps   120
Nor cheerful, yet with objects and with hopes,
Living a life of eager industry.
And now, when Luke had reached his eighteenth year,
There by the light of this old lamp they sate,
Father and Son, while far into the night   125
The Housewife plied her own peculiar work,
Making the cottage through the silent hours
Murmur as with the sound of summer flies.
This light was famous in its neighborhood,
And was a public symbol of the life   130
That thrifty Pair had lived. For, as it chanced,
Their cottage on a plot of rising ground
Stood single, with large prospect, north and south,
High into Easedale, up to Dunmail-Raise,
And westward to the village near the lake;   135
And from this constant light, so regular
And so far seen, the House itself, by all
Who dwelt within the limits of the vale,
Both old and young, was named THE EVENING STAR.

    Thus living on through such a length of years,   140
The Shepherd, if he loved himself, must needs
Have loved his Helpmate; but to Michael's heart
This son of his old age was yet more dear—
Less from instinctive tenderness, the same
Fond spirit that blindly works in the blood of all—   145
Than that a child, more than all other gifts
That earth can offer to declining man,
Brings hope with it, and forward-looking thoughts,
And stirrings of inquietude, when they
By tendency of nature needs must fail.   150
Exceeding was the love he bare to him,
His heart and his heart's joy! For oftentimes
Old Michael, while he was a babe in arms,
Had done him female service, not alone
For pastime and delight, as is the use   155
Of fathers, but with patient mind enforced
To acts of tenderness; and he had rocked
His cradle, as with a woman's gentle hand.

    And, in a later time, ere yet the Boy
Had put on boy's attire, did Michael love,   160
Albeit of a stern unbending mind,
To have the Young-one in his sight, when he
Wrought in the field, or on his shepherd's stool
Sate with a fettered sheep before him stretched
Under the large old oak, that near his door   165
Stood single, and, from matchless depth of shade,
Chosen for the Shearer's covert from the sun,
Thence in our rustic dialect was called
The CLIPPING TREE, a name which yet it bears.
There, while they two were sitting in the shade,   170

With others round them, earnest all and blithe,
Would Michael exercise his heart with looks
Of fond correction and reproof bestowed
Upon the Child, if he disturbed the sheep
By catching at their legs, or with his shouts   175
Scared them, while they lay still beneath the shears.

And when by Heaven's good grace the boy grew up
A healthy Lad, and carried in his cheek
Two steady roses that were five years old;
Then Michael from a winter coppice cut   180
With his own hand a sapling, which he hooped
With iron, making it throughout in all
Due requisites a perfect shepherd's staff,
And gave it to the Boy; wherewith equipped
He as a watchman oftentimes was placed   185
At gate or gap, to stem or turn the flock;
And, to his office prematurely called,
There stood the urchin, as you will divine,
Something between a hindrance and a help;
And for this cause not always, I believe,   190
Receiving from his Father hire of praise;
Though nought was left undone which staff, or voice,
Or looks, or threatening gestures, could perform.

But soon as Luke, full ten years old, could stand
Against the mountain blasts; and to the heights,   195
Not fearing toil, nor length of weary ways,
He with his Father daily went, and they
Were as companions, why should I relate
That objects which the Shepherd loved before
Were dearer now? that from the Boy there came   200
Feelings and emanations—things which were
Light to the sun and music to the wind;
And that the old Man's heart seemed born again?

Thus in his Father's sight the Boy grew up:
And now, when he had reached his eighteenth year,   205
He was his comfort and his daily hope.

While in this sort the simple household lived
From day to day, to Michael's ear there came
Distressful tidings. Long before the time
Of which I speak, the Shepherd had been bound   210
In surety for his brother's son, a man
Of an industrious life, and ample means;
But unforeseen misfortunes suddenly
Had pressed upon him; and old Michael now
Was summoned to discharge the forfeiture,   215
A grievous penalty, but little less
Than half his substance. This unlooked-for claim,
At the first hearing, for a moment took
More hope out of his life than he supposed
That any old man ever could have lost.   220
As soon as he had armed himself with strength
To look his trouble in the face, it seemed
The Shepherd's sole resource to sell at once
A portion of his patrimonial fields.
Such was his first resolve; he thought again,   225

And his heart failed him. "Isabel," said he,
Two evenings after he had heard the news,
"I have been toiling more than seventy years,
And in the open sunshine of God's love
Have we all lived; yet if these fields of ours   230
Should pass into a stranger's hand, I think
That I could not lie quiet in my grave.
Our lot is a hard lot; the sun himself
Has scarcely been more diligent than I;
And I have lived to be a fool at last   235
To my own family. An evil man
That was, and made an evil choice, if he
Were false to us; and, if he were not false,
There are ten thousand to whom loss like this
Had been no sorrow. I forgive him;—but   240
'Twere better to be dumb than to talk thus.

     When I began, my purpose was to speak
Of remedies and of a cheerful hope.
Our Luke shall leave us, Isabel; the land
Shall not go from us, and it shall be free;   245
He shall possess it, free as is the wind
That passes over it. We have, thou know'st,
Another kinsman—he will be our friend
In this distress. He is a prosperous man,
Thriving in trade—and Luke to him shall go,   250
And with his kinsman's help and his own thrift
He quickly will repair this loss, and then
He may return to us. If here he stay,
What can be done? Where every one is poor,
What can be gained?"   255

                    At this the old man paused,
And Isabel sat silent, for her mind
Was busy, looking back into past times.
There's Richard Bateman, thought she to herself,
He was a parish-boy—at the church-door   260
They made a gathering for him, shillings, pence,
And halfpennies, wherewith the neighbors bought
A basket, which they filled with pedlar's wares;
And, with this basket on his arm, the lad
Went up to London, found a master there,   265
Who, out of many, chose the trusty boy
To go and overlook his merchandise
Beyond the seas; where he grew wondrous rich,
And left estates and monies to the poor,
And, at his birth-place, built a chapel, floored   270
With marble, which he sent from foreign lands.
These thoughts, and many others of like sort,
Passed quickly through the mind of Isabel,
And her face brightened. The old Man was glad,
And thus resumed:—"Well, Isabel! this scheme,   275
These two days, has been meat and drink to me
Far more than we have lost is left us yet.
We have enough—I wish indeed that I
Were younger;—but this hope is a good hope.
Make ready Luke's best garments, of the best   280
Buy for him more, and let us send him forth
To-morrow, or the next day, or to-night:
If he *could* go, the Boy should go to-night."

Here Michael ceased, and to the fields went forth
With a light heart. The Housewife for five days   285
Was restless morn and night, and all day long
Wrought on with her best fingers to prepare
Things needful for the journey of her son.
But Isabel was glad when Sunday came
To stop her in her work: for, when she lay   290
By Michael's side, she through the last two nights
Heard him, how he was troubled in his sleep;
And when they rose at morning she could see
That all his hopes were gone. That day at noon
She said to Luke, while they two by themselves   295
Were sitting at the door, "Thou must not go:
We have no other Child but thee to lose,
None to remember—do not go away,
For if thou leave thy Father he will die."
The Youth made answer with a jocund voice;   300
And Isabel, when she had told her fears,
Recovered heart. That evening her best fare
Did she bring forth, and all together sat
Like happy people round a Christmas fire.

With daylight Isabel resumed her work;   305
And all the ensuing week the house appeared
As cheerful as a grove in Spring: at length
The expected letter from their kinsman came,
With kind assurances that he would do
His utmost for the welfare of the Boy;   310
To which, requests were added, that forthwith
He might be sent to him. Ten times or more
The letter was read over; Isabel
Went forth to show it to the neighbors round;
Nor was there at that time on English land   315
A prouder heart than Luke's. When Isabel
Had to her house returned, the old Man said,
"He shall depart to-morrow." To this word
The Housewife answered, talking much of things
Which, if at such short notice he should go,   320
Would surely be forgotten. But at length
She gave consent, and Michael was at ease.

Near the tumultuous brook of Greenhead Ghyll,
In that deep valley, Michael had designed
To build a Sheepfold; and, before he heard   325
The tidings of his melancholy loss,
For this same purpose he had gathered up
A heap of stones, which by the streamlet's edge
Lay thrown together, ready for the work.
With Luke that evening thitherward he walked: 330
And soon as they had reached the place he stopped,
And thus the old Man spake to him:—"My Son,
To-morrow thou wilt leave me: with full heart
I look upon thee, for thou art the same
That wert a promise to me ere thy birth,   335
And all thy life hast been my daily joy.
I will relate to thee some little part
Of our two histories; 'twill do thee good
When thou art from me, even if I should touch
On things thou canst not know of.——After thou   340
First cam'st into the world—as oft befalls

To new-born infants—thou didst sleep away
Two days, and blessings from thy Father's tongue
Then fell upon thee. Day by day passed on,
And still I loved thee with increasing love.   345
Never to living ear came sweeter sounds
Than when I heard thee by our own fireside
First uttering, without words, a natural tune;
While thou, a feeding babe, didst in thy joy
Sing at thy Mother's breast. Month followed month,   350
And in the open fields my life was passed
And on the mountains; else I think that thou
Hadst been brought up upon thy Father's knees.
But we were playmates, Luke: among these hills,
As well thou knowest, in us the old and young   355
Have played together, nor with me didst thou
Lack any pleasure which a boy can know."
Luke had a manly heart; but at these words
He sobbed aloud. The old Man grasped his hand,
And said, "Nay, do not take it so—I see   360
That these are things of which I need not speak
—Even to the utmost I have been to thee
A kind and a good Father: and herein
I but repay a gift which I myself
Received at others' hands; for, though now old   365
Beyond the common life of man, I still
Remember them who loved me in my youth.
Both of them sleep together: here they lived,
As all their Forefathers had done; and when
At length their time was come, they were not loth   370
To give their bodies to the family mould.
I wished that thou should'st live the life they lived:
But 'tis a long time to look back, my Son,
And see so little gain from threescore years.
These fields were burthened when they came to me;   375
Till I was forty years of age, not more
Than half of my inheritance was mine.
I toiled and toiled; God blessed me in my work,
And till these three weeks past the land was free.
—It looks as if it never could endure   380
Another Master. Heaven forgive me, Luke,
If I judge ill for thee, but it seems good
That thou should'st go."
                         At this the old Man paused;
Then, pointing to the stones near which they stood,   385
Thus, after a short silence, he resumed:
"This was a work for us; and now, my Son,
It is a work for me. But, lay one stone—
Here, lay it for me, Luke, with thine own hands.
Nay, Boy, be of good hope;—we both may live   390
To see a better day. At eighty-four
I still am strong and hale;—do thou thy part;
I will do mine.—I will begin again
With many tasks that were resigned to thee:
Up to the heights, and in among the storms,   395
Will I without thee go again, and do
All works which I was wont to do alone,
Before I knew thy face.—Heaven bless thee, Boy!
Thy heart these two weeks has been beating fast
With many hopes; it should be so—yes—yes—   400
I knew that thou could'st never have a wish

To leave me, Luke: thou hast been bound to me
Only by links of love: when thou art gone,
What will be left to us!—But I forget
My purposes. Lay now the corner-stone,   405
As I requested; and hereafter, Luke,
When thou art gone away, should evil men
Be thy companions, think of me, my Son,
And of this moment; hither turn thy thoughts,
And God will strengthen thee: amid all fear   410
And all temptation, Luke, I pray that thou
May'st bear in mind the life thy Fathers lived,
Who, being innocent, did for that cause
Bestir them in good deeds. Now, fare thee well—
When thou return'st, thou in this place wilt see   415
A work which is not here: a covenant
'Twill be between us; but, whatever fate
Befall thee, I shall love thee to the last,
And bear thy memory with me to the grave."

   The Shepherd ended here; and Luke stooped down,   420
And, as his Father had requested, laid
The first stone of the Sheepfold. At the sight
The old Man's grief broke from him; to his heart
He pressed his Son, he kissèd him and wept;
And to the house together they returned.   425
—Hushed was that House in peace, or seeming peace,
Ere the night fell:—with morrow's dawn the Boy
Began his journey, and when he had reached
The public way, he put on a bold face;
And all the neighbors, as he passed their doors,   430
Came forth with wishes and with farewell prayers,
That followed him till he was out of sight.

   A good report did from their Kinsman come,
Of Luke and his well-doing: and the Boy
Wrote loving letters, full of wondrous news,   435
Which, as the Housewife phrased it, were throughout
"The prettiest letters that were ever seen."
Both parents read them with rejoicing hearts.
So, many months passed on: and once again
The Shepherd went about his daily work   440
With confident and cheerful thoughts; and now
Sometimes when he could find a leisure hour
He to that valley took his way, and there
Wrought at the Sheepfold. Meantime Luke began
To slacken in his duty; and, at length,   445
He in the dissolute city gave himself
To evil courses: ignominy and shame
Fell on him, so that he was driven at last
To seek a hiding-place beyond the seas.

   There is a comfort in the strength of love;   450
'Twill make a thing endurable, which else
Would overset the brain, or break the heart:
I have conversed with more than one who well
Remember the old Man, and what he was
Years after he had heard this heavy news.   455
His bodily frame had been from youth to age
Of an unusual strength. Among the rocks
He went, and still looked up to sun and cloud,

And listened to the wind; and, as before,
Performed all kinds of labor for his sheep,   460
And for the land, his small inheritance.
And to that hollow dell from time to time
Did he repair to build the Fold of which
His flock had need. 'Tis not forgotten yet
The pity which was then in every heart   465
For the old Man—and 'tis believed by all
That many and many a day he thither went,
And never lifted up a single stone.

There, by the Sheepfold, sometimes was he seen
Sitting alone, or with his faithful Dog,   470
Then old, beside him, lying at his feet.
The length of full seven years, from time to time,
He at the building of this Sheepfold wrought,
And left the work unfinished when he died.
Three years, or little more, did Isabel   475
Survive her Husband: at her death the estate
Was sold, and went into a stranger's hand.
The Cottage which was named THE EVENING STAR
Is gone—the ploughshare has been through the ground
On which it stood; great changes have been wrought   480
In all the neighborhood:—yet the oak is left
That grew beside their door; and the remains
Of the unfinished Sheepfold may be seen
Beside the boisterous brook of Greenhead Ghyll.

Oct. 11-Dec. 9, 1800   1800

THE DANISH BOY
(A FRAGMENT)

I

Between two sister moorland rills
There is a spot that seems to lie
Sacred to flowerets of the hills,
And sacred to the sky.
And in this smooth and open dell   5
There is a tempest-stricken tree;
A corner-stone by lightning cut,
The last stone of a lonely hut;
And in this dell you see
A thing no storm can e'er destroy,   10
The shadow of a Danish Boy.

II

In clouds above, the lark is heard,
But drops not here to earth for rest;
Within this lonesome nook the bird
Did never build her nest.   15
No beast, no bird, hath here his home;
Bees, wafted on the breezy air,
Pass high above those fragrant bells
To other flowers:—to other dells
Their burdens do they bear;   20
The Danish Boy walks here alone:
The lovely dell is all his own.

III

A Spirit of noon-day is he;
Yet seems a form of flesh and blood;
Nor piping shepherd shall he be,   25
Nor herd-boy of the wood.
A regal vest of fur he wears,
In color like a raven's wing;
It fears not rain, nor wind, nor dew;
But in the storm 'tis fresh and blue   30
As budding pines in spring;
His helmet has a vernal grace,
Fresh as the bloom upon his face.

IV

A harp is from his shoulder slung;
Resting the harp upon his knee,   35
To words of a forgotten tongue
He suits his melody.
Of flocks upon the neighboring hill
He is the darling and the joy;
And often, when no cause appears,   40
The mountain-ponies prick their ears,
—They hear the Danish Boy,
While in the dell he sings alone
Beside the tree and corner-stone.

V

There sits he; in his face you spy   45
No trace of a ferocious air,

Nor ever was a cloudless sky
So steady or so fair.
The lovely Danish Boy is blest
And happy in his flowery cove: 50
From bloody deeds his thoughts are far;
And yet he warbles songs of war,
That seem like songs of love,
For calm and gentle is his mien;
Like a dead Boy he is serene.   55

1799   1800

SONG FOR THE WANDERING JEW

Though the torrents from their fountains
Roar down many a craggy steep,
Yet they find among the mountains
Resting places calm and deep.

Clouds that love through air to hasten,   5
Ere the storm its fury stills,
Helmet-like themselves will fasten
On the heads of towering hills.

What if through the frozen center
Of the Alps the Chamois bound,   10
Yet he has a home to enter
In some nook of chosen ground:

And the Sea-horse, though the ocean
Yield him no domestic cave,
Slumbers without sense of motion,   15
Couched upon the rocking wave.

If on windy days the Raven
Gambol like a dancing skiff,
Not the less she loves her haven
In the bosom of the cliff.   20

The fleet Ostrich, till day closes,
Vagrant over desert sands,
Brooding on her eggs reposes
When chill night that care demands.

Day and night my toils redouble,   25
Never nearer to the goal;
Night and day, I feel the trouble
Of the Wanderer in my soul.

1800   1800

TO A YOUNG LADY

WHO HAD BEEN REPROACHED FOR
TAKING LONG WALKS IN THE COUNTRY

Dear child of Nature, let them rail!
—There is a nest in a green dale,
A harbor and a hold;

Where thou, a wife and friend, shalt see
Thy own heart-stirring days, and be   5
A light to young and old.

There, healthy as a shepherd boy,
And treading among flowers of joy
Which at no season fade,
Thou, while thy babes around thee
    cling,   10
Shalt show us how divine a thing
A woman may be made.

Thy thoughts and feelings shall not die,
Nor leave thee, when gray hairs are nigh,
A melancholy slave;   15
But an old age serene and bright,
And lovely as a Lapland night,
Shall lead thee to thy grave.

1801   1802

I GRIEVED FOR BUONAPARTE

I grieved for Buonaparté with a vain
And an unthinking grief!   The tenderest
    mood
Of that man's mind—what can it be? what
    food
Fed his first hopes? what knowledge could
    he gain?
'Tis not in battles that from youth we
    train   5
The governor who must be wise and good,
And temper with the sternness of the grain
Thoughts motherly, and meek as woman-
    hood.
Wisdom doth live with children round her
    knees:
Books, leisure, perfect freedom, and the
    talk   10
Man holds with week-day man in the
    hourly walk
Of the mind's business: these are the
    degrees
By which true sway doth mount; this is the
    stalk
True power doth grow on; and her rights
    are these.

May 21, 1802   1802

TO TOUSSAINT L'OUVERTURE

Toussaint, the most unhappy man of men!
Whether the whistling Rustic tend his
    plough
Within thy hearing, or thy head be now
Pillowed in some deep dungeon's earless
    den:—

O miserable Chieftain! where and when   5
Wilt thou find patience? Yet die not; do
    thou
Wear rather in thy bonds a cheerful brow:
Though fallen thyself, never to rise again,
Live, and take comfort. Thou hast left
    behind
Powers that will work for thee; air, earth,
    and skies;   10
There's not a breathing of the common
    wind
That will forget thee; thou hast great allies;
Thy friends are exultations, agonies,
And love, and man's unconquerable mind.
c. Aug. 1802   Feb. 2, 1803

"IT IS NOT TO BE THOUGHT OF"

It is not to be thought of that the flood
Of British freedom, which, to the open sea
Of the world's praise, from dark antiquity
Hath flowed, "with pomp of waters, un-
    withstood,"
Roused though it be full often to a mood   5
Which spurns the check of salutary bands,
That this most famous Stream in bogs and
    sands
Should perish; and to evil and to good
Be lost for ever. In our halls is hung
Armoury of the invincible Knights of
    old: 10
We must be free or die, who speak the
    tongue
That Shakespeare spake; the faith and
    morals hold
Which Milton held.—In everything we are
    sprung
Of earth's first blood, have titles manifold.
1802 or 1803   April 16, 1803

"WHEN I HAVE BORNE IN MEMORY"

When I have borne in memory what has
    tamed
Great nations, how ennobling thoughts
    depart
When men change swords for ledgers, and
    desert
The student's bower for gold, some fears
    unnamed
I had, my Country!—am I to be blamed?   5
Now, when I think of thee, and what thou
    art,
Verily, in the bottom of my heart,
Of those unfilial fears I am ashamed.

For dearly must we prize thee; we who find
In thee a bulwark for the cause of men: 10
And I by my affection was beguiled:
What wonder if a poet now and then,
Among the many movements of his mind,
Felt for thee as a lover or a child!
1802 or 1803   Sept. 17, 1803

"I TRAVELLED AMONG UNKNOWN MEN"

I travelled among unknown men,
  In lands beyond the sea;
Nor, England! did I know till then
  What love I bore to thee.

'Tis past, that melancholy dream!   5
  Nor will I quit thy shore
A second time; for still I seem
  To love thee more and more.

Among thy mountains did I feel
  The joy of my desire;   10
And she I cherished turned her wheel
  Beside an English fire.

Thy mornings showed, thy nights con-
    cealed
  The bowers where Lucy played;
And thine too is the last green field   15
  That Lucy's eyes surveyed.
1799   1807

"MY HEART LEAPS UP WHEN I BEHOLD"

My heart leaps up when I behold
  A rainbow in the sky:
So was it when my life began;
So is it now I am a man:
So be it when I shall grow old,   5
  Or let me die!
The Child is father of the Man;
And I could wish my days to be
Bound each to each by natural piety.
March 26, 1802   1807

THE SPARROW'S NEST

Behold, within the leafy shade,
Those bright blue eggs together laid!
On me the chance-discovered sight
Gleamed like a vision of delight.
I started—seeming to espy   5
  The home and sheltered bed,

The sparrow's dwelling, which, hard by
My father's house, in wet or dry
My sister Emmeline and I
    Together visited.   10

She looked at it and seemed to fear it;
Dreading, though wishing, to be near it:
Such heart was in her, being then
A little prattler among men,
The blessing of my later years   15
Was with me when a boy:
She gave me eyes, she gave me ears;
And humble cares, and delicate fears;
A heart, the fountain of sweet tears;
    And love, and thought, and joy.   20
1801   1807

WRITTEN IN MARCH

WHILE RESTING ON THE BRIDGE AT THE
FOOT OF BROTHER'S WATER

The cock is crowing,
The stream is flowing,
The small birds twitter,
The lake doth glitter,
The green field sleeps in the sun;   5
The oldest and youngest
Are at work with the strongest;
The cattle are grazing,
Their heads never raising;
There are forty feeding like one!   10

Like an army defeated
The snow hath retreated,
And now doth fare ill
On the top of the bare hill;
The ploughboy is whooping—anon—
    anon: 15
There's joy in the mountains;
There's life in the fountains;
Small clouds are sailing,
Blue sky prevailing;
The rain is over and gone!
1802   1807

TO THE SMALL CELANDINE

Pansies, lilies, kingcups, daisies,
Let them live upon their praises;
Long as there's a sun that sets,
Primroses will have their glory;
Long as there are violets,   5
They will have a place in story:
There's a flower that shall be mine,
'Tis the little Celandine.

Eyes of some men travel far
For the finding of a star;   10

Up and down the heavens they go,
Men that keep a mighty rout!
I'm as great as they, I trow,
Since the day I found thee out,
Little flower—I'll make a stir,   15
Like a sage astronomer.

Modest, yet withal an elf
Bold, and lavish of thyself;
Since we needs must first have met
I have seen thee, high and low,   20
Thirty years or more, and yet
'Twas a face I did not know;
Thou hast now, go where I may,
Fifty greetings in a day.

Ere a leaf is on a bush,   25
In the time before the thrush
Has a thought about her nest,
Thou wilt come with half a call
Spreading out thy glossy breast
Like a careless prodigal;   30
Telling tales about the sun,
When we've little warmth, or none.

Poets, vain men in their mood!
Travel with the multitude:
Never heed them; I aver   35
That they all are wanton wooers;
But the thrifty cottager,
Who stirs little out of doors,
Joys to spy thee near her home;
Spring is coming, thou art come!   40

Comfort have thou of thy merit,
Kindly, unassuming spirit!
Careless of thy neighborhood,
Thou dost show thy pleasant face
On the moor, and in the wood,   45
In the lane;—there's not a place,
Howsoever mean it be,
But 'tis good enough for thee.

Ill befall the yellow flowers,
Children of the flaring hours!   50
Buttercups, that will be seen,
Whether we will see or no;
Others, too, of lofty mien;
They have done as worldlings do,
Taken praise that should be thine,   55
Little, humble Celandine.

Prophet of delight and mirth,
Ill-requited upon earth;
Herald of a mighty band,
Of a joyous train ensuing,   60
Serving at my heart's command,
Tasks that are not tasks renewing,
I will sing, as doth behove,
Hymns in praise of what I love!
1802   1807

TO THE SAME FLOWER

Pleasures newly found are sweet
When they lie about our feet.
February last, my heart
First at sight of thee was glad.
All unheard of as thou art,   5
Thou must needs, I think, have had,
Celandine! and long ago,
Praise of which I nothing know.

I have not a doubt but he,
Whosoe'er the man might be,   10
Who the first with pointed rays
(Workman worthy to be sainted)
Set the signboard in a blaze,
When the rising sun he painted,
Took the fancy from a glance   15
At thy glittering countenance.

Soon as gentle breezes bring
News of winter's vanishing,
And the children build their bowers—
Sticking 'kerchief-plots of mold   20
All about with full-blown flowers,
Thick as sheep in shepherd's fold—
With the proudest thou art there,
Mantling in the tiny square.

Often have I sighed to measure   25
By myself a lonely pleasure,
Sighed to think I read a book
Only read, perhaps, by me;
Yet I long could overlook
Thy bright coronet and thee,   30
And thy arch and wily ways,
And thy store of other praise.

Blithe of heart, from week to week
Thou dost play at hide-and-seek;
While the patient primrose sits   35
Like a beggar in the cold,
Thou, a flower of wiser wits,
Slip'st into thy sheltering hold;
Liveliest of the vernal train
When ye all are out again.   40

Drawn by what peculiar spell,
By what charm of sight or smell,
Does the dim-eyed curious bee,
Laboring for her waxen cells,
Fondly settle upon thee   45
Prized above all buds and bells
Opening daily at thy side,
By the season multiplied?

Thou art not beyond the moon
But a thing "beneath our shoon."   50
Let the bold discoverer thrid
In his bark the polar sea;
Rear who will a pyramid;

Praise it is enough for me,
If there be but three or four   55
Who will love my little flower.
May 1, 1802   1807

TO H. C.
(HARTLEY COLERIDGE)

SIX YEARS OLD

O thou! whose fancies from afar are
    brought;
Who of thy words dost make a mock
    apparel,
And fittest to unutterable thought
The breeze-like motion and the self-born
    carol;
Thou faery voyager! that dost float   5
In such clear water, that thy boat
May rather seem
To brood on air than on an earthly stream;
Suspended in a stream as clear as sky,
Where earth and heaven do make one
    imagery;   10
O blessed vision! happy child!
Thou art so exquisitely wild,
I think of thee with many fears
For what may be thy lot in future years.
    I thought of times when Pain might be
        thy guest,   15
Lord of thy house and hospitality;
And Grief, uneasy lover! never rest
But when she sate within the touch of thee.
O too industrious folly!
O vain and causeless melancholy!   20
Nature will either end thee quite;
Or, lengthening out thy season of delight,
Preserve for thee, by individual right,
A young lamb's heart among the full-
    grown flocks.
What hast thou to do with sorrow,   25
Or the injuries of to-morrow?
Thou art a dew-drop, which the morn
    brings forth,
Ill fitted to sustain unkindly shocks,
Or to be trailed along the soiling earth;
A gem that glitters while it lives,   30
And no forewarning gives;
But, at the touch of wrong, without a strife
Slips in a moment out of life.
1802   1807

RESOLUTION AND
INDEPENDENCE

There was a roaring in the wind all night;
The rain came heavily and fell in floods;
But now the sun is rising calm and bright;
The birds are singing in the distant woods;

Over his own sweet voice the stock-dove
  broods;   5
The jay makes answer as the magpie
  chatters;
And all the air is filled with pleasant noise
  of waters.

All things that love the sun are out of
  doors;
The sky rejoices in the morning's birth;
The grass is bright with rain-drops;—on
  the moors   10
The hare is running races in her mirth;
And with her feet she from the plashy
  earth
Raises a mist, that, glittering in the sun,
Runs with her all the way, wherever she
  doth run.

I was a traveller then upon the moor;   15
I saw the hare that raced about with joy;
I heard the woods and distant waters roar;
Or heard them not, as happy as a boy:
The pleasant season did my heart employ:
My old remembrances went from me
  wholly;   20
And all the ways of men, so vain and
  melancholy.

But, as it sometimes chanceth, from the
  might
Of joy in minds that can no further go,
As high as we have mounted in delight
In our dejection do we sink as low;   25
To me that morning did it happen so;
And fears and fancies thick upon me came;
Dim sadness—and blind thoughts, I knew
  not, nor could name.

I heard the skylark warbling in the sky;
And I bethought me of the playful hare: 30
Even such a happy child of earth am I;
Even as these blissful creatures do I fare;
Far from the world I walk, and from all
  care;
But there may come another day to me—
Solitude, pain of heart, distress, and pov-
  erty.   35

My whole life I have lived in pleasant
  thought,
As if life's business were a summer mood;
As if all needful things would come un-
  sought
To genial faith, still rich in genial good;
But how can he expect that others
  should   40
Build for him, sow for him, and at his call
Love him, who for himself will take no
  heed at all?

I thought of Chatterton, the marvellous
  boy,
The sleepless soul that perished in his
  pride;
Of him who walked in glory and in joy 45
Following his plough, along the mountain-
  side:
By our own spirits are we deified:
We poets in our youth begin in gladness;
But thereof come in the end despondency
  and madness.

Now, whether it were by peculiar grace, 50
A leading from above, a something given,
Yet it befell that, in this lonely place,
When I with these untoward thoughts had
  striven,
Beside a pool bare to the eye of heaven
I saw a man before me unawares: 55
The oldest man he seemed that ever wore
  gray hairs.

As a huge stone is sometimes seen to lie
Couched on the bald top of an eminence;
Wonder to all who do the same espy,
By what means it could thither come, and
  whence;   60
So that it seems a thing endued with sense:
Like a sea-beast crawled forth, that on a
  shelf
Of rock or sand reposeth, there to sun
  itself;

Such seemed this man, not all alive nor
  dead,
Nor all asleep—in his extreme old age: 65
His body was bent double, feet and head
Coming together in life's pilgrimage;
As if some dire constraint of pain, or rage
Of sickness felt by him in times long past,
A more than human weight upon his frame
  had cast.   70

Himself he propped, limbs, body, and pale
  face,
Upon a long gray staff of shaven wood:
And, still as I drew near with gentle pace,
Upon the margin of that moorish flood
Motionless as a cloud the old man stood, 75
That heareth not the loud winds when
  they call;
And moveth all together, if it move at all.

At length, himself unsettling, he the pond
Stirred with his staff, and fixedly did look
Upon the muddy water, which he
  conned,   80
As if he had been reading in a book:
And now a stranger's privilege I took;
And, drawing to his side, to him did say,
"This morning gives us promise of a
  glorious day."

A gentle answer did the old man make, 85
In courteous speech which forth he slowly
    drew:
And him with further words I thus be-
    spake,
"What occupation do you there pursue?
This is a lonesome place for one like you."
Ere he replied, a flash of mild surprise 90
Broke from the sable orbs of his yet-vivid
    eyes.

His words came feebly, from a feeble chest,
But each in solemn order followed each,
With something of a lofty utterance drest—
Choice word and measured phrase,
    above the reach 95
Of ordinary men; a stately speech;
Such as grave livers do in Scotland use,
Religious men, who give to God and man
    their dues.

He told that to these waters he had come
To gather leeches, being old and poor: 100
Employment hazardous and wearisome!
And he had many hardships to endure:
From pond to pond he roamed, from moor
    to moor;
Housing, with God's good help, by choice
    or chance;
And in this way he gained an honest
    maintenance. 105

The old man still stood talking by my side;
But now his voice to me was like a stream
Scarce heard; nor word from word could I
    divide;
And the whole body of the man did seem
Like one whom I had met with in a
    dream; 110
Or like a man from some far region sent,
To give me human strength, by apt ad-
    monishment.

My former thoughts returned: the fear that
    kills;
And hope that is unwilling to be fed;
Cold, pain, and labor, and all fleshly
    ills; 115
And mighty poets in their misery dead.
—Perplexed, and longing to be comforted,
My question eagerly did I renew,
"How is it that you live, and what is it
    you do?"

He with a smile did then his words re-
    peat; 120
And said that, gathering leeches, far and
    wide
He travelled, stirring thus about his feet
The waters of the pools where they abide.

"Once I could meet with them on every
    side;
But they have dwindled long by slow
    decay; 125
Yet still I persevere, and find them where
    I may."

While he was talking thus, the lonely
    place,
The old man's shape, and speech—all
    troubled me:
In my mind's eye I seemed to see him pace
About the weary moors continually, 130
Wandering about alone and silently.
While I these thoughts within myself pur-
    sued,
He, having made a pause, the same dis-
    course renewed.

And soon with this he other matter
    blended,
Cheerfully uttered, with demeanor kind, 135
But stately in the main; and, when he
    ended,
I could have laughed myself to scorn to
    find
In that decrepit man so firm a mind.
"God," said I, "be my help and stay secure;
I'll think of the leech-gatherer on the
    lonely moor!" 140
1802   1807

"NUNS FRET NOT AT THEIR CONVENT'S NARROW ROOM"

Nuns fret not at their convent's narrow
    room;
And hermits are contented with their cells;
And students with their pensive citadels;
Maids at the wheel, the weaver at his
    loom,
Sit blithe and happy; bees that soar for
    bloom, 5
High as the highest Peak of Furness-fells,
Will murmur by the hour in foxglove
    bells:
In truth the prison, unto which we doom
Ourselves, no prison is: and hence for me,
In sundry moods, 'twas pastime to be
    bound 10
Within the Sonnet's scanty plot of ground;
Pleased if some Souls (for such there needs
    must be)
Who have felt the weight of too much
    liberty,
Should find brief solace there, as I have
    found.
1807

ON THE EXTINCTION OF THE VENETIAN REPUBLIC

Once did She hold the gorgeous east in fee;
And was the safeguard of the west: the worth
Of Venice did not fall below her birth,
Venice, the eldest Child of Liberty.
She was a maiden City, bright and free;   5
No guile seduced, no force could violate;
And, when she took unto herself a Mate,
She must espouse the everlasting Sea.
And what if she had seen those glories fade,
Those titles vanish, and that strength decay;   10
Yet shall some tribute of regret be paid
When her long life hath reached its final day:
Men are we, and must grieve when even the Shade
Of that which once was great is passed away.

c. Aug. 1802   1807

LONDON, 1802

Milton! thou shouldst be living at this hour:
England hath need of thee: she is a fen
Of stagnant waters: altar, sword, and pen,
Fireside, the heroic wealth of hall and bower,
Have forfeited their ancient English dower   5
Of inward happiness. We are selfish men;
Oh! raise us up, return to us again;
And give us manners, virtue, freedom, power.
Thy soul was like a Star, and dwelt apart;
Thou hadst a voice whose sound was like the sea: 10
Pure as the naked heavens, majestic, free,
So didst thou travel on life's common way,
In cheerful godliness; and yet thy heart
The lowliest duties on herself did lay.

1802   1807

COMPOSED BY THE SEASIDE, NEAR CALAIS

AUGUST, 1802

Fair star of evening, splendor of the west,
Star of my country!—on the horizon's brink
Thou hangest, stooping, as might seem, to sink

On England's bosom; yet well pleased to rest,
In courteous speech which forth to rest,
Meanwhile, and be to her a glorious crest   5
Conspicuous to the nations. Thou, I think,
Shouldst be my country's emblem, and shouldst wink,
Bright star! with laughter on her banners, dressed
In thy fresh beauty. There! that dusky spot
Beneath thee, that is England; there she lies.   10
Blessings be on you both! one hope, one lot,
One life, one glory!—I, with many a fear
For my dear country, many heartfelt sighs,
Among men who do not love her, linger here.

Aug. 1802   1807

NEAR DOVER

SEPTEMBER, 1802

Inland, within a hollow vale, I stood;
And saw, while sea was calm and air was clear,
The coast of France—the coast of France how near!
Drawn almost into frightful neighborhood.
I shrunk; for verily the barrier flood   5
Was like a lake, or river bright and fair,
A span of waters; yet what power is there!
What mightiness for evil and for good!
Even so doth God protect us if we be
Virtuous and wise. Winds blow, and waters roll,   10
Strength to the brave, and Power, and Deity;
Yet in themselves are nothing! One decree
Spake laws to them, and said that by the soul
Only, the Nations shall be great and free.

Sept. 1802   1807

WRITTEN IN LONDON

SEPTEMBER, 1802

O friend! I know not which way I must look
For comfort, being, as I am, oppressed,
To think that now our life is only dressed
For show; mean handy-work of craftsman, cook,
Or groom!—We must run glittering like a brook   5
In the open sunshine, or we are unblessed:
The wealthiest man among us is the best:

No grandeur now in nature or in book
Delights us. Rapine, avarice, expense,
This is idolatry; and these we adore: 10
Plain living and high thinking are no
    more:
The homely beauty of the good old cause
Is gone; our peace, our fearful innocence,
And pure religion breathing household
    laws.

1802   1807

COMPOSED UPON WESTMINSTER BRIDGE

SEPTEMBER 3, 1802

Earth has not anything to show more fair:
Dull would he be of soul who could pass
    by
A sight so touching in its majesty:
This City now doth, like a garment, wear
The beauty of the morning; silent, bare,   5
Ships, towers, domes, theatres, and temples
    lie
Open unto the fields, and to the sky;
All bright and glittering in the smokeless
    air.
Never did sun more beautifully steep
In his first splendor, valley, rock, or hill; 10
Ne'er saw I, never felt, a calm so deep!
The river glideth at his own sweet will:
Dear God! the very houses seem asleep;
And all that mighty heart is lying still!

1802   1807

"IT IS A BEAUTEOUS EVENING, CALM AND FREE"

It is a beauteous evening, calm and free,
The holy time is quiet as a Nun
Breathless with adoration; the broad sun
Is sinking down in its tranquillity;
The gentleness of heaven broods o'er the
    Sea: 5
Listen! the mighty Being is awake,
And doth with his eternal motion make
A sound like thunder—everlastingly.
Dear Child! dear Girl! that walkest with
    me here,
If thou appear untouched by solemn
    thought,   10
Thy nature is not therefore less divine:
Thou liest in Abraham's bosom all the
    year,
And worshipp'st at the Temple's inner
    shrine,
God being with thee when we know it not.

1802   1807

"GREAT MEN HAVE BEEN AMONG US"

Great men have been among us; hands
    that penned
And tongues that uttered wisdom—better
    none:
The later Sidney, Marvel, Harrington,
Young Vane, and others who called Milton
    friend.
These moralists could act and compre-
    hend: 5
They knew how genuine glory was put on;
Taught us how rightfully a nation shone
In splendor: what strength was, that would
    not bend
But in magnanimous meekness. France,
    'tis strange,
Hath brought forth no such souls as we
    had then.   10
Perpetual emptiness! unceasing change!
No single volume paramount, no code,
No master spirit, no determined road;
But equally a want of books and men!

1802   1807

TO THE DAISY

Her divine skill taught me this,
That from everything I saw
I could some instruction draw,
And raise pleasure to the height
Through the meanest object's sight.
By the murmur of a spring,
Or the least bough's rustelling;
By a daisy whose leaves spread
Shut when Titan goes to bed;
Or a shady bush or tree;
She could more infuse in me
Than all nature's beauties can
In some other wiser man.
                                    G. WITHER

In youth from rock to rock I went,
From hill to hill in discontent
Of pleasure high and turbulent,
    Most pleased when most uneasy;
But now my own delights I make,—   5
My thirst at every rill can slake,
And gladly nature's love partake,
    Of thee, sweet Daisy!

Thee winter in the garland wears
That thinly decks his few grey hairs;   10
Spring parts the clouds with softest airs,
    That she may sun thee;
Whole summer-fields are thine by right;
And autumn, melancholy wight!
Doth in thy crimson head delight   15
    When rains are on thee.

In shoals and bands, a morrice train,
Thou greet'st the traveller in the lane;
Pleased at his greeting thee again;
　　Yet nothing daunted,   20
Nor grieved if thou be set at nought:
And oft alone in nooks remote
We meet thee, like pleasant thought,
　　When such are wanted.

Be violets in their secret mews   25
The flowers the wanton zephyrs choose;
Proud be the rose, with rains and dews
　　Her head impearling,
Thou liv'st with less ambitious aim,
Yet hast not gone without thy fame;   30
Thou art indeed by many a claim
　　The poet's darling.

If to a rock from rains he fly,
Or, some bright day of April sky,
Imprisoned by hot sunshine lie   35
　　Near the green holly,
And wearily at length should fare;
He needs but look about, and there
Thou art!—a friend at hand, to scare
　　His melancholy.   40

A hundred times, by rock or bower,
Ere thus I have lain couched an hour,
Have I derived from thy sweet power
　　Some apprehension;
Some steady love; some brief delight;   45
Some memory that had taken flight;
Some chime of fancy wrong or right;
　　Or stray invention.

If stately passions in me burn,
And one chance look to thee should
　　turn,   50
I drink out of an humbler urn
　　A lowlier pleasure;
The homely sympathy that heeds
The common life, our nature breeds;
A wisdom fitted to the needs   55
　　Of hearts at leisure.

Fresh-smitten by the morning ray,
When thou art up, alert and gay,
Then, cheerful flower! my spirits play
　　With kindred gladness: 60
And when, at dusk, by dews opprest
Thou sink'st, the image of thy rest
Hath often eased my pensive breast
　　Of careful sadness.

And all day long I number yet,   65
All seasons through, another debt,
Which I, wherever thou art met,
　　To thee am owing;
An instinct call it, a blind sense;

A happy, genial influence,   70
Coming one knows not how, nor whence,
　　Nor whither going.

Child of the year! that round dost run
Thy pleasant course—when day's begun,
As ready to salute the sun   75
　　As lark or leveret,
Thy long-lost praise thou shalt regain;
Nor be less dear to future men
Than in old time—thou not in vain
　　Art nature's favorite.   80
1802   1807

TO THE SAME FLOWER

With little here to do or see
Of things that in the great world be,
Daisy! again I talk to thee,
　　For thou art worthy,
Thou unassuming common-place   5
Of nature, with that homely face,
And yet with something of a grace,
　　Which love makes for thee!

Oft on the dappled turf at ease
I sit, and play with similes,   10
Loose types of things through all degrees,
　　Thoughts of thy raising:
And many a fond and idle name
I give to thee, for praise or blame,
As is the humor of the game,   15
　　While I am gazing.

A nun demure of lowly port;
Or sprightly maiden, of love's court,
In thy simplicity the sport
　　Of all temptations;   20
A queen in crown of rubies dressed;
A starveling in a scanty vest;
Are all, as seems to suit thee best,
　　Thy appellations.

A little cyclops, with one eye   25
Staring to threaten and defy,
That thought comes next—and instantly
　　The freak is over,
The shape will vanish—and behold
A silver shield with boss of gold,   30
That spreads itself, some fairy bold
　　In fight to cover!

I see thee glittering from afar—
And then thou art a pretty star;
Not quite so fair as many are   35
　　In heaven above thee!
Yet like a star, with glittering crest,
Self-poised in air thou seem'st to rest;—
May peace come never to his nest,
　　Who shall reprove thee!   40

Bright *Flower!* for by that name at last,
When all my reveries are past,
I call thee, and to that cleave fast,
  Sweet silent creature!
That breath'st with me in sun and air, 45
Do thou, as thou art wont, repair
My heart with gladness, and a share
  Of thy meek nature!

1802   1807

TO THE DAISY

Bright flower! whose home is everywhere,
Bold in maternal nature's care,
And, all the long year through, the heir
  Of joy and sorrow;
Methinks that there abides in thee 5
Some concord with humanity,
Given to no other flower I see
  The forest thorough!

Is it that man is soon deprest?
A thoughtless thing! who, once unblest, 10
Does little on his memory rest,
  Or on his reason,
And thou wouldst teach him how to find
A shelter under every wind,
A hope for times that are unkind, 15
  And every season?

Thou wander'st the wide world about,
Unchecked by pride or scrupulous doubt,
With friends to greet thee, or without,
  Yet pleased and willing; 20
Meek, yielding to the occasion's call,
And all things suffering from all,
Thy function apostolical
  In peace fulfilling.

1802   1807

TO THE CUCKOO

O blithe newcomer! I have heard,
I hear thee and rejoice,
O Cuckoo! shall I call thee bird,
Or but a wandering voice?

While I am lying on the grass 5
Thy twofold shout I hear,
From hill to hill it seems to pass,
At once far off, and near.

Though babbling only to the vale,
Of sunshine and of flowers, 10
Thou bringest unto me a tale
Of visionary hours.

Thrice welcome, darling of the Spring!
Even yet thou art to me
No bird, but an invisible thing, 15
A voice, a mystery;

The same whom in my school-boy days
I listened to; that cry
Which made me look a thousand ways
In bush, and tree, and sky. 20

To seek thee did I often rove
Through woods and on the green;
And thou wert still a hope, a love;
Still longed for, never seen.

And I can listen to thee yet; 25
Can lie upon the plain
And listen, till I do beget
That golden time again.

O blessèd bird! the earth we pace
Again appears to be 30
An unsubstantial, fairy place;
That is fit home for thee.

1802   1807

THE GREEN LINNET

Beneath these fruit-tree boughs that shed
Their snow-white blossoms on my head,
With brightest sunshine round me spread
  Of spring's unclouded weather,
In this sequestered nook how sweet 5
To sit upon my orchard-seat!
And birds and flowers once more to greet,
  My last year's friends together.

One have I marked, the happiest guest
In all his covert of the blest: 10
Hail to thee, far above the rest
  In joy of voice and pinion!
Thou, Linnet! in thy green array,
Presiding spirit here to-day,
Dost lead the revels of the May; 15
  And this is thy dominion.

While birds, and butterflies, and flowers,
Make all one band of paramours,
Thou, ranging up and down the bowers,
  Art sole in thy employment: 20
A life, a presence like the air,
Scattering thy gladness without care,
Too blest with any one to pair;
  Thyself thy own enjoyment.

Amid yon tuft of hazel trees 25
That twinkle to the gusty breeze,
Behold him perched in ecstasies,
  Yet seeming still to hover;

There! where the flutter of his wings
Upon his back and body flings   30
Shadows and sunny glimmerings,
    That cover him all over.

My dazzled sight he oft deceives,
A brother of the dancing leaves;
Then flits, and from the cottage-eaves   35
    Pours forth his song in gushes;
As if by that exulting strain
He mocked and treated with disdain
The voiceless form he chose to feign,
    While fluttering in the bushes.   40

1803   1807

YARROW UNVISITED

From Stirling castle we had seen
The mazy Fu.. unravelled;
Had trod the banks of Clyde, and Tay,
And with the Tweed had travelled;
And when we came to Clovenford,   5
Then said my *"winsome Marrow,"*
"Whate'er betide, we'll turn aside,
And see the Braes of Yarrow."

"Let Yarrow folk, *frae* Selkirk town,
Who have been buying, selling,   10
Go back to Yarrow, 'tis their own;
Each maiden to her dwelling!
On Yarrow's banks let herons feed,
Hares couch, and rabbits burrow!
But we will downward with the Tweed, 15
Nor turn aside to Yarrow.

"There's Galla Water, Leader Haughs,
Both lying right before us;
And Dryborough, where with chiming
    Tweed
The lintwhites sing in chorus;   20
There's pleasant Tiviot-dale, a land
Made blithe with plough and harrow:
Why throw away a needful day
To go in search of Yarrow?

"What's Yarrow but a river bare,   25
That glides the dark hills under?
There are a thousand such elsewhere
As worthy of your wonder."
—Strange words they seemed of slight and
    scorn:
My True-Love sighed for sorrow;   30
And looked me in the face, to think
I thus could speak of Yarrow!

"Oh! green," said I, "are Yarrow's holms,
And sweet is Yarrow flowing!
Fair hangs the apple frae the rock,   35
But we will leave it growing.

O'er hilly path, and open Strath,
We'll wander Scotland thorough;
But, though so near, we will not turn
Into the dale of Yarrow.   40

"Let beeves and home-bred kine partake
The sweets of Burn-mill meadow;
The swan on still St. Mary's Lake
Float double, swan and shadow!
We will not see them; will not go,   45
To-day, nor yet to-morrow,
Enough if in our hearts we know
There's such a place as Yarrow.

"Be Yarrow stream unseen, unknown!
It must, or we shall rue it: 50
We have a vision of our own;
Ah! why should we undo it?
The treasured dreams of times long past,
We'll keep them, winsome Marrow!
For when we're there, although 'tis fair, 55
'Twill be another Yarrow!

"If Care with freezing years should come,
And wandering seem but folly,—
Should we be loth to stir from home,
And yet be melancholy;   60
Should life be dull, and spirits low,
'Twill soothe us in our sorrow,
That earth has something yet to show,
The bonny holms of Yarrow!"

1803   1807

TO A HIGHLAND GIRL

AT INVERSNEYDE, UPON LOCH LOMOND

Sweet Highland Girl, a very shower
Of beauty is thy earthly dower!
Twice seven consenting years have shed
Their utmost bounty on thy head:
And these grey rocks; that household
    lawn;   5
Those trees, a veil just half withdrawn;
This fall of water that doth make
A murmur near the silent lake;
This little bay; a quiet road
That holds in shelter thy abode—   10
In truth together do ye seem
Like something fashioned in a dream;
Such forms as from their covert peep
When earthly cares are laid asleep!
But, O fair creature! in the light   15
Of common day, so heavenly bright,
I bless thee, vision as thou art,
I bless thee with a human heart;
God shield thee to thy latest years!
Thee, neither know I, nor thy peers;   20

And yet my eyes are filled with tears.
With earnest feeling I shall pray
For thee when I am far away:
For never saw I mien, or face,
In which more plainly I could trace   25
Benignity and home-bred sense
Ripening in perfect innocence.
Here scattered, like a random seed,
Remote from men, Thou dost not need
The embarrassed look of shy distress,   30
And maidenly shamefacedness:
Thou wear'st upon thy forehead clear
The freedom of a mountaineer:
A face with gladness overspread!
Soft smiles, by human kindness bred!   35
And seemliness complete, that sways
Thy courtesies, about thee plays;
With no restraint, but such as springs
From quick and eager visitings
Of thoughts that lie beyond the reach   40
Of thy few words of English speech:
A bondage sweetly brooked, a strife
That gives thy gestures grace and life!
So have I not unmoved in mind,
Seen birds of tempest-loving kind—   45
Thus beating up against the wind.
What hand but would a garland cull
For thee who are so beautiful?
O happy pleasure! here to dwell
Beside thee in some heathy dell;   50
Adopt your homely ways, and dress,
A shepherd, thou a shepherdess!
But I could frame a wish for thee
More like a grave reality:
Thou art to me but as a wave   55
Of the wild sea; and I would have
Some claim upon thee, if I could,
Though but of common neighborhood.
What joy to hear thee, and to see!
Thy elder brother I would be,   60
Thy father—anything to thee!
Now thanks to heaven! that of its grace
Hath led me to this lonely place.
Joy have I had; and going hence
I bear away my recompense.   65
In spots like these it is we prize
Our memory, feel that she hath eyes:
Then, why should I be loth to stir?
I feel this place was made for her;
To give new pleasure like the past,   70
Continued long as life shall last.
Nor am I loth, though pleased at heart,
Sweet Highland Girl! from thee to part:
For I, methinks, till I grow old,
As fair before me shall behold,   75
As I do now, the cabin small,
The lake, the bay, the waterfall;
And thee, the spirit of them all!
1803   1807

THE SOLITARY REAPER

Behold her, single in the field,
Yon solitary Highland Lass!
Reaping and singing by herself;
Stop here, or gently pass!
Alone she cuts and binds the grain,   5
And sings a melancholy strain;
O listen! for the vale profound
Is overflowing with the sound.

No nightingale did ever chaunt
More welcome notes to weary bands   10
Of travellers in some shady haunt,
Among Arabian sands:
A voice so thrilling ne'er was heard
In springtime from the cuckoo bird,
Breaking the silence of the seas   15
Among the farthest Hebrides.

Will no one tell me what she sings?—
Perhaps the plaintive numbers flow
For old, unhappy, far-off things,
And battles long ago: 20
Or is it some more humble lay,
Familiar matter of to-day?
Some natural sorrow, loss, or pain,
That has been, and may be again?

Whate'er the theme, the maiden sang   25
As if her song could have no ending;
I saw her singing at her work,
And o'er the sickle bending;—
I listened, motionless and still;
And, as I mounted up the hill,   30
The music in my heart I bore,
Long after it was heard no more.
1803-05   1807

THE AFFLICTION OF
MARGARET

Where art thou, my beloved son,
Where art thou, worse to me than dead?
Oh find me, prosperous or undone!
Or, if the grave be now thy bed,
Why am I ignorant of the same   5
That I may rest; and neither blame
Nor sorrow may attend thy name?

Seven years, alas! to have received
No tidings of an only child;
To have despaired, have hoped, believed, 10
And been for evermore beguiled;
Sometimes with thoughts of very bliss!
I catch at them, and then I miss;
Was ever darkness like to this?

He was among the prime in worth,   15
An object beauteous to behold;
Well born, well bred; I sent him forth
Ingenuous, innocent, and bold:
If things ensued that wanted grace,
As hath been said, they were not base;   20
And never blush was on my face.

Ah! little doth the young one dream,
When full of play and childish cares,
What power is in his wildest scream,
Heard by his mother unawares!   25
He knows it not, he cannot guess;
Years to a mother bring distress;
But do not make her love the less.

Neglect me! no, I suffered long
From that ill thought; and, being blind,   30
Said, "Pride shall help me in my wrong:
Kind mother have I been, as kind
As ever breathed:" and that is true;
I've wet my path with tears like dew,
Weeping for him when no one knew.   35

My son, if thou be humbled, poor,
Hopeless of honor and of gain,
Oh! do not dread thy mother's door;
Think not of me with grief and pain:
I now can see with better eyes;   40
And worldly grandeur I despise,
And fortune with her gifts and lies.

Alas! the fowls of heaven have wings,
And blasts of heaven will aid their flight;
They mount—how short a voyage brings   45
The wanderers back to their delight!
Chains tie us down by land and sea;
And wishes, vain as mine, may be
All that is left to comfort thee.

Perhaps some dungeon hears thee groan,   50
Maimed, mangled by inhuman men;
Or thou upon a desert thrown
Inheritest the lion's den;
Or hast been summoned to the deep,
Thou, thou and all thy mates, to keep   55
An incommunicable sleep.

I look for ghosts; but none will force
Their way to me: 'tis falsely said
That there was ever intercourse
Between the living and the dead;   60
For, surely, then I should have sight
Of him I wait for day and night,
With love and longing infinite.

My apprehensions come in crowds;
I dread the rustling of the grass;   65
The very shadows of the clouds
Have power to shake me as they pass:

I question things and do not find
One that will answer to my mind;
And all the world appears unkind.   70

Beyond participation lie
My troubles, and beyond relief:
If any chance to heave a sigh,
They pity me, and not my grief.
Then come to me, my son, or send   75
Some tidings that my woes may end;
I have no other earthly friend!

1804   1807

"SHE WAS A PHANTOM OF DELIGHT"

She was a phantom of delight
When first she gleamed upon my sight;
A lovely apparition, sent
To be a moment's ornament;
Her eyes as stars of twilight fair;   5
Like twilight's, too, her dusky hair;
But all things else about her drawn
From Maytime and the cheerful dawn;
A dancing shape, an image gay,
To haunt, to startle, and waylay.   10

I saw her upon nearer view,
A spirit, yet a woman too!
Her household motions light and free,
And steps of virgin liberty;
A countenance in which did meet   15
Sweet records, promises as sweet;
A creature not too bright or good
For human nature's daily food;
For transient sorrows, simple wiles,
Praise, blame, love, kisses, tears, and
        smiles.   20

And now I see with eye serene
The very pulse of the machine;
A being breathing thoughtful breath,
A traveller between life and death;
The reason firm, the temperate will,   25
Endurance, foresight, strength, and skill;
A perfect woman, nobly planned,
To warn, to comfort, and command;
And yet a spirit still, and bright
With something of angelic light.   30

1804   1807

"I WANDERED LONELY AS A CLOUD"

I wandered lonely as a cloud
That floats on high o'er vales and hills,
When all at once I saw a crowd,
A host, of golden daffodils;
Beside the lake, beneath the trees,   5
Fluttering and dancing in the breeze.

Continuous as the stars that shine
And twinkle on the milky way,
They stretched in never-ending line
Along the margin of a bay: 10
Ten thousand saw I at a glance,
Tossing their heads in sprightly dance.

The waves beside them danced; but they
Out-did the sparkling waves in glee:
A poet could not but be gay, 15
In such a jocund company:
I gazed—and gazed—but little thought
What wealth the show to me had brought:

For oft, when on my couch I lie
In vacant or in pensive mood, 20
They flash upon that inward eye
Which is the bliss of solitude;
And then my heart with pleasure fills,
And dances with the daffodils.
1804   1807

STEPPING WESTWARD

While my Fellow-traveller and I were walking
by the side of Loch Ketterine, one fine evening after sunset, in our road to a hut
where, in the course of our tour, we had
been hospitably entertained some weeks before, we met, in one of the loneliest parts
of that solitary region, two well-dressed
women, one of whom said to us, by way of
greeting, "What, you are stepping westward?"

*"What, you are stepping westward?"—
"Yea."*
—'Twould be a *wildish* destiny,
If we, who thus together roam
In a strange land, and far from home,
Were in this place the guests of Chance: 5
Yet who would stop, or fear to advance,
Though home or shelter he had none,
With such a sky to lead him on!

The dewy ground was dark and cold;
Behind, all gloomy to behold; 10
And stepping westward seemed to be
A kind of *heavenly* destiny:
I liked the greeting; 'twas a sound
Of something without place or bound;
And seemed to give me spiritual right 15
To travel through that region bright.

The voice was soft, and she who spake
Was walking by her native lake:
The salutation had to me
The very sound of courtesy: 20
Its power was felt; and while my eye

Was fixed upon the glowing sky,
The echo of the voice enwrought
A human sweetness with the thought
Of travelling through the world that lay 25
Before me in my endless way.
1803-05   1807

TO A SKYLARK

Up with me! up with me into the clouds!
For thy song, lark, is strong;
Up with me, up with me into the clouds!
Singing, singing,
With clouds and sky about thee ringing, 5
Lift me, guide me, till I find
That spot which seems so to thy mind!

I have walked through wildernesses dreary,
And today my heart is weary;
Had I now the wings of a fairy, 10
Up to thee would I fly.
There is madness about thee, and joy
divine
In that song of thine;
Lift me, guide me, high and high
To thy banqueting place in the sky. 15

Joyous as morning,
Thou art laughing and scorning;
Thou hast a nest for thy love and thy rest,
And, though little troubled with sloth,
Drunken lark! thou wouldst be loath 20
To be such a traveler as I.
Happy, happy liver,
With a soul as strong as a mountain river,
Pouring out praise to the Almighty Giver,
Joy and jollity be with us both! 25

Alas! my journey, rugged and uneven,
Through prickly moors or dusty ways must
wind;
But hearing thee, or others of thy kind,
As full of gladness and as free of heaven,
I, with my fate contented, will plod on, 30
And hope for higher raptures, when life's
day is done.
1805   1807

FIDELITY

A barking sound the shepherd hears,
A cry as of a dog or fox;
He halts and searches with his eyes
Among the scattered rocks;
And now at distance can discern
A stirring in a brake of fern;
And instantly a dog is seen,
Glancing through that covert green.

The dog is not of mountain breed;
Its motions, too, are wild and shy;   10
With something, as the shepherd thinks,
Unusual in its cry.
Nor is there anyone in sight
All round, in hollow or on height;
Nor shout, nor whistle strikes his ear;   15
What is the creature doing here?

It was a cove, a huge recess,
That keeps, till June, December's snow;
A lofty precipice in front,
A silent tarn below!   20
Far in the bosom of Helvellyn,
Remote from public road or dwelling,
Pathway, or cultivated land;
From trace of human foot or hand.

There sometimes doth a leaping fish   25
Send through the tarn a lonely cheer;
The crags repeat the raven's croak,
In symphony austere;
Thither the rainbow comes—the cloud—
And mists that spread the flying shroud;   30
And sunbeams; and the sounding blast,
That, if it could, would hurry past;
But that enormous barrier holds it fast.

Not free from boding thoughts, a while
The shepherd stood; then makes his way   35
O'er rocks and stones, following the dog
As quickly as he may;
Nor far had gone before he found
A human skeleton on the ground;
The appalled discoverer with a sigh   40
Looks round, to learn the history.

From those abrupt and perilous rocks
The man had fallen, that place of fear!
At length upon the shepherd's mind
It breaks, and all is clear: 45
He instantly recalled the name,
And who he was, and whence he came;
Remembered, too, the very day
On which the traveller passed this way.

But hear a wonder, for whose sake   50
This lamentable tale I tell!
A lasting monument of words
This wonder merits well.
The dog, which still was hovering nigh,
Repeating the same timid cry,   55
This dog, had been through three months'
     space
A dweller in that savage place.

Yes, proof was plain that, since the day
When this ill-fated traveller died,
The dog had watched about the spot,   60
Or by his master's side:

How nourished here through such long
     time
He knows, who gave that love sublime;
And gave that strength of feeling, great
Above all human estimate!   65
1805   1807

ODE TO DUTY

["Jam non consilio bonus, sed more eo per-
ductus, ut non tantum recte facere possim, sed
nisi recte facere non possim."]

Stern Daughter of the Voice of God!
O Duty! if that name thou love
Who art a light to guide, a rod
To check the erring, and reprove;
Thou, who art victory and law   5
When empty terrors overawe;
From vain temptations dost set free;
And calm'st the weary strife of frail
     humanity!

There are who ask not if thine eye
Be on them; who, in love and truth,   10
Where no misgiving is, rely
Upon the genial sense of youth:
Glad hearts! without reproach or blot
Who do thy work, and know it not:
Oh! if through confidence misplaced   15
They fail, thy saving arms, dread Power!
     around them cast.

Serene will be our days and bright,
And happy will our nature be,
When love is an unerring light,
And joy its own security.   20
And they a blissful course may hold
Even now, who, not unwisely bold,
Live in the spirit of this creed;
Yet seek thy firm support, according to
     their need.

I, loving freedom, and untried;   25
No sport of every random gust,
Yet being to myself a guide,
Too blindly have reposed my trust:
And oft, when in my heart was heard
Thy timely mandate, I deferred   30
The task, in smoother walks to stray;
But thee I now would serve more strictly,
     if I may.

Through no disturbance of my soul,
Or strong compunction in me wrought,
I supplicate for thy control;   35
But in the quietness of thought:
Me this unchartered freedom tires;

I feel the weight of chance-desires:
My hopes no more must change their name,
I long for a repose that ever is the same. 40

Stern Lawgiver! yet thou dost wear
The Godhead's most benignant grace;
Nor know we anything so fair
As is the smile upon thy face:
Flowers laugh before thee on their beds 45
And fragrance in thy footing treads;
Thou dost preserve the stars from wrong;
And the most ancient heavens, through
    Thee, are fresh and strong.

To humbler functions, awful Power!
I call thee: I myself commend 50
Unto thy guidance from this hour;
Oh, let my weakness have an end!
Give unto me, made lowly wise,
The spirit of self-sacrifice;
The confidence of reason give; 55
And in the light of truth thy bondman let
    me live!

1805   1807

ELEGIAC STANZAS

SUGGESTED BY A PICTURE OF PEELE
CASTLE, IN A STORM, PAINTED BY
SIR GEORGE BEAUMONT

I was thy neighbor once, thou rugged pile!
Four summer weeks I dwelt in sight of
    thee:
I saw thee every day; and all the while
Thy form was sleeping on a glassy sea.

So pure the sky, so quiet was the air! 5
So like, so very like, was day to day!
Whene'er I looked, thy image still was
    there;
It trembled, but it never passed away.

How perfect was the calm! it seemed no
    sleep;
No mood, which season takes away, or
    brings: 10
I could have fancied that the mighty deep
Was even the gentlest of all gentle things.

Ah! *then,* if mine had been the painter's
    hand,
To express what then I saw: and add the
    gleam,
The light that never was, on sea or land, 15
The consecration, and the poet's dream;

I would have planted thee, thou hoary pile,

Amid a world how different from this!
Beside a sea that could not cease to smile;
On tranquil land, beneath a sky of bliss. 20

Thou shouldst have seemed a treasure-
    house divine
Of peaceful years; a chronicle of heaven;—
Of all the sunbeams that did ever shine
The very sweetest had to thee been given.

A picture had it been of lasting ease, 25
Elysian quiet, without toil or strife;
No motion but the moving tide, a breeze,
Or merely silent nature's breathing life.

Such, in the fond illusion of my heart,
Such picture would I at that time have
    made: 30
And seen the soul of truth in every part,
A stedfast peace that might not be be-
    trayed.

So once it would have been,—'tis so no
    more;
I have submitted to a new control:
A power is gone, which nothing can re-
    store; 35
A deep distress hath humanized my soul.

Not for a moment could I now behold
A smiling sea, and be what I have been:
The feeling of my loss will ne'er be old;
This, which I know, I speak with mind
    serene. 40

Then, Beaumont, friend! who would have
    been the friend,
If he had lived, of him whom I deplore,
This work of thine I blame not, but com-
    mend;
This sea in anger, and that dismal shore.

O 'tis a passionate work!—yet wise and
    well, 45
Well chosen is the spirit that is here;
That hulk which labors in the deadly swell,
This rueful sky, this pageantry of fear!

And this huge castle, standing here
    sublime,
I love to see the look with which it
    braves, 50
Cased in the unfeeling armor of old time,
The lightning, the fierce wind, and tram-
    pling waves.

Farewell, farewell the heart that lives
    alone,
Housed in a dream, at distance from the
    kind!

Such happiness, wherever it be known, 55
Is to be pitied; for 'tis surely blind.

But welcome fortitude, and patient cheer,
And frequent sights of what is to be borne!
Such sights, or worse, as are before me
    here,—
Not without hope we suffer and we
    mourn. 60

1805   1807

ODE

INTIMATIONS OF IMMORTALITY FROM
RECOLLECTIONS OF EARLY CHILDHOOD

   "The Child is Father of the Man;
   And I could wish my days to be
   Bound each to each by natural piety."

I

There was a time when meadow, grove,
    and stream,
The earth, and every common sight,
    To me did seem
    Apparelled in celestial light,
The glory and the freshness of a dream. 5
It is not now as it hath been of yore;—
    Turn whereso'er I may,
    By night or day,
The things which I have seen I now can
    see no more.

II

    The rainbow comes and goes, 10
    And lovely is the rose,
    The moon doth with delight
Look round her when the heavens are
    bare,
    Waters on a starry night
    Are beautiful and fair; 15
    The sunshine is a glorious birth;
But yet I know, where'er I go,
That there hath passed away a glory from
    the earth.

III

Now, while the birds thus sing a joyous
    song,
    And while the young lambs bound 20
    As to the tabor's sound,
To me alone there came a thought of grief:
A timely utterance gave that thought relief,
    And I again am strong:
The cataracts blow their trumpets from
    the steep; 25
No more shall grief of mine the season
    wrong;
I hear the echoes through the mountains
    throng,

The winds come to me from the fields of
    sleep,
    And all the earth is gay;
    Land and sea 30
    Give themselves up to jollity,
    And with the heart of May
    Doth every beast keep holiday;—
    Thou child of joy,
Shout round me, let me hear thy shouts,
    thou happy shepherd-boy! 35

IV

Ye blessèd creatures, I have heard the call
    Ye to each other make; I see
The heavens laugh with you in your
    jubilee;
    My heart is at your festival,
    My head hath its coronal, 40
The fulness of your bliss, I feel—I feel it
    all.
    Oh evil day! if I were sullen
    While earth herself is adorning,
    This sweet May-morning,
    And the children are culling 45
    On every side
    In a thousand valleys far and wide,
    Fresh flowers; while the sun shines
    warm,
And the babe leaps up on his mother's
    arm:—
    I hear, I hear, with joy I hear! 50
    —But there's a tree, of many, one,
A single field which I have looked upon,
Both of them speak of something that is
    gone:
    The pansy at my feet
    Doth the same tale repeat: 55
Whither is fled the visionary gleam?
Where is it now, the glory and the dream?

V

Our birth is but a sleep and a forgetting:
The soul that rises with us, our life's star,
    Hath had elsewhere its setting, 60
    And cometh from afar:
    Not in entire forgetfulness,
    And not in utter nakedness,
But trailing clouds of glory do we come
    From God, who is our home: 65
Heaven lies about us in our infancy!
Shades of the prison-house begin to close
    Upon the growing boy,
But he beholds the light, and whence it
    flows,
    He sees it in his joy; 70
The youth, who daily farther from the east
    Must travel, still is Nature's priest,
    And by the vision splendid
    Is on his way attended;
At length the man perceives it die away, 75
And fade into the light of common day.

VI

Earth fills her lap with pleasures of her
own;
Yearnings she hath in her own natural
kind,
And, even with something of a mother's
mind,
    And no unworthy aim,   80
The homely nurse doth all she can
To make her foster-child, her inmate man,
    Forget the glories he hath known,
And that imperial palace whence he came.

VII

Behold the child among his new-born
blisses,   85
A six years' darling of a pigmy size!
See, where 'mid work of his own hand he
lies,
Fretted by sallies of his mother's kisses,
With light upon him from his father's
eyes!
See, at his feet, some little plan or chart, 90
Some fragment from his dream of human
life,
Shaped by himself with newly-learned art;
    A wedding or a festival,
    A mourning or a funeral;
    And this hath now his heart,   95
    And unto this he frames his song:
    Then will he fit his tongue
To dialogues of business, love, or strife;
    But it will not be long
    Ere this be thrown aside,   100
    And with new joy and pride
The little actor cons another part;
Filling from time to time his "humorous
stage"
With all the persons, down to palsied age,
That life brings with her in her equip-
age;   105
    As if his whole vocation
    Were endless imitation.

VIII

Thou, whose exterior semblance doth belie
    Thy soul's immensity;
Thou best philosopher, who yet dost
keep   110
Thy heritage, thou eye among the blind,
That, deaf and silent, read'st the eternal
deep,
Haunted for ever by the eternal mind,—
    Mighty prophet! seer blest!
    On whom those truths do rest,   115
Which we are toiling all our lives to find,
In darkness lost, the darkness of the grave;
Thou, over whom thy immortality

Broods like the day, a master o'er a slave,
A presence which is not to be put by;   120
Thou little child, yet glorious in the might
Of heaven-born freedom on thy being's
height,
Why with such earnest pains dost thou
provoke
The years to bring the inevitable yoke,
Thus blindly with thy blessedness at
strife?   125
Full soon thy soul shall have her earthly
freight,
And custom lie upon thee with a weight,
Heavy as frost, and deep almost as life!

IX

    O joy! that in our embers
    Is something that doth live,   130
    That nature yet remembers
    What was so fugitive!
The thought of our past years in me doth
breed
Perpetual benediction: not indeed
For that which is most worthy to be
blest;   135
Delight and liberty, the simple creed
Of childhood, whether busy or at rest,
With new-fledged hope still fluttering in
his breast:—
    Not for these I raise
    The song of thanks and praise;   140
    But for those obstinate questionings
    Of sense and outward things,
    Fallings from us, vanishings;
    Blank misgivings of a creature
Moving about in worlds not realised,   145
High instincts before which our mortal
nature
Did tremble like a guilty thing surprised:
    But for those first affections,
    Those shadowy recollections,
    Which, be they what they may,   150
Are yet the fountain-light of all our day,
Are yet a master-light of all our seeing;
    Uphold us, cherish, and have power to
make
Our noisy years seem moments in the being
Of the eternal silence: truths that wake, 155
    To perish never:
Which neither listlessness, nor mad en-
deavor,
    Nor man nor boy,
Nor all that is at enmity with joy,
Can utterly abolish or destroy!   160
    Hence in a season of calm weather
    Though inland far we be,
Our souls have sight of that immortal sea
    Which brought us hither,
Can in a moment travel thither,   165

And see the children sport upon the shore,
And hear the mighty waters rolling evermore.

X

Then sing, ye birds, sing, sing a joyous
song!
  And let the young lambs bound
  As to the tabor's sound!   170
We in thought will join your throng,
  Ye that pipe and ye that play,
  Ye that through your hearts to-day
  Feel the gladness of the May!
What though the radiance which was once
so bright   175
Be now for ever taken from my sight,
  Though nothing can bring back the
hour
Of splendor in the grass, of glory in the
flower;
  We will grieve not, rather find
  Strength in what remains behind; 180
  In the primal sympathy
  Which having been must ever be;
  In the soothing thoughts that spring
    Out of human suffering;
  In the faith that looks through
death,   185
In years that bring the philosophic mind.

XI

And O, ye fountains, meadows, hills, and
groves,
Forebode not any severing of our loves!
Yet in my heart of hearts I feel your
might;
I only have relinquished one delight 190
To live beneath your more habitual sway.
I love the brooks which down their chan-
nels fret,
Even more than when I tripped lightly as
they;
The innocent brightness of a new-born day
  Is lovely yet;
The clouds that gather round the setting
sun   195
Do take a sober coloring from an eye
That hath kept watch o'er man's mortality;
Another race hath been, and other palms
are won.
Thanks to the human heart by which we
live,
Thanks to its tenderness, its joys, and
fears,   200
To me the meanest flower that blows can
give
Thoughts that do often lie too deep for
tears.

c.1802-06   1807

CHARACTER OF THE HAPPY WARRIOR

Who is the happy Warrior? Who is he
That every man in arms should wish to be?
—It is the generous Spirit, who, when
brought
Among the tasks of real life, hath wrought
Upon the plan that pleased his boyish
thought: 5
Whose high endeavors are an inward light
That makes the path before him always
bright:
Who, with a natural instinct to discern
What knowledge can perform, is diligent
to learn;
Abides by this resolve, and stops not
there,   10
But makes his moral being his prime care;
Who, doomed to go in company with Pain,
And Fear, and Bloodshed, miserable train!
Turns his necessity to glorious gain;
In face of these doth exercise a power 15
Which is our human nature's highest
dower;
Controls them and subdues, transmutes,
bereaves
Of their bad influence, and their good
receives:
By objects, which might force the soul to
abate
Her feeling, rendered more compassion-
ate;   20
Is placable—because occasions rise
So often that demand such sacrifice;
More skilful in self-knowledge, even more
pure,
As tempted more; more able to endure,
As more exposed to suffering and dis-
tress;   25
Thence, also, more alive to tenderness.
—'Tis he whose law is reason; who depends
Upon that law as on the best of friends;
Whence, in a state where men are tempted
still
To evil for a guard against worse ill, 30
And what in quality or act is best
Doth seldom on a right foundation rest,
He labors good on good to fix, and owes
To virtue every triumph that he knows:
—Who, if he rise to station of command, 35
Rises by open means; and there will stand
On honorable terms, or else retire,
And in himself possess his own desire:
Who comprehends his trust, and to the
same
Keeps faithful with a singleness of aim; 40
And therefore does not stoop, nor lie in
wait
For wealth, or honors, or for worldly state;

Whom they must follow; on whose head
  must fall,
Like showers of manna, if they come at all:
Whose powers shed round him in the com-
  mon strife,   45
Or mild concerns of ordinary life,
A constant influence, a peculiar grace;
But who, if he be called upon to face
Some awful moment to which Heaven has
  joined
Great issues, good or bad for human
  kind,   50
Is happy as a Lover; and attired
With sudden brightness, like a Man in-
  spired;
And, through the heat of conflict, keeps
  the law
In calmness made, and sees what he fore-
  saw;
Or if an unexpected call succeed,   55
Come when it will, is equal to the need:
—He who, though thus endued as with a
  sense
And faculty for storm and turbulence,
Is yet a Soul whose master-bias leans
To homefelt pleasures and to gentle
  scenes;   60
Sweet images! which, wheresoe'er he be,
Are at his heart; and such fidelity
It is his darling passion to approve;
More brave for this, that he hath much to
  love:—
'Tis, finally, the Man, who, lifted high,   65
Conspicuous object in a Nation's eye,
Or left unthought-of in obscurity,—
Who, with a toward or untoward lot,
Prosperous or adverse, to his wish or not—
Plays, in the many games of life, that one 70
Where what he most doth value must be
  won:
Whom neither shape of danger can dismay,
Nor thought of tender happiness betray;
Who, not content that former worth stand
  fast,
Looks forward, persevering to the last,   75
From well to better, daily self-surpast:
Who, whether praise of him must walk the
  earth
For ever, and to noble deeds give birth,
Or he must fall, to sleep without his fame,
And leave a dead unprofitable name—   80
Finds comfort in himself and in his cause;
And, while the mortal mist is gathering,
  draws
His breath in confidence of Heaven's
  applause:
This is the happy Warrior; this is He
That every Man in arms should wish to
  be.   85

1805-06   1807

YES, IT WAS THE MOUNTAIN ECHO

Yes, it was the mountain echo,
Solitary, clear, profound,
Answering to the shouting cuckoo,
Giving to her sound for sound!

Unsolicited reply   5
To a babbling wanderer sent;
Like her ordinary cry,
Like—but oh, how different!

Hears not also mortal life?
Hear not we, unthinking creatures!   10
Slaves of folly, love, or strife—
Voices of two different natures?

Have not we too?—yes, we have
Answers, and we know not whence;
Echoes from beyond the grave,   15
Recognized intelligence!

Such rebounds our inward ear
Catches sometimes from afar—
Listen, ponder, hold them dear;
For of God,—of God they are.   20

1806   1807

PERSONAL TALK

I am not one who much or oft delight
To season my fireside with personal talk,—
Of friends, who live within an easy walk,
Or neighbors, daily, weekly, in my sight:
And, for my chance-acquaintance, ladies
  bright,   5
Sons, mothers, maidens withering on the
  stalk,
These all wear out of me, like forms, with
  chalk
Painted on rich men's floors, for one feast-
  night.
Better than such discourse doth silence
  long,
Long, barren silence, square with my de-
  sire;   10
To sit without emotion, hope, or aim,
In the loved presence of my cottage-fire,
And listen to the flapping of the flame,
Or kettle whispering its faint undersong.

"Yet life," you say, "is life; we have seen
  and see,   15
And with a living pleasure we describe;
And fits of sprightly malice do but bribe
The languid mind into activity.
Sound sense, and love itself, and mirth and
  glee

Are fostered by the comment and the
gibe."   20
Even be it so; yet still among your tribe,
Our daily world's true worldlings, rank not
me!
Children are blest, and powerful; their
world lies
More justly balanced; partly at their feet
And part far from them; sweetest melo-
dies   25
Are those that are by distance made more
sweet;
Whose mind is but the mind of his own
eyes,
He is a slave; the meanest we can meet!

Wings have we,—and as far as we can go
We may find pleasure: wilderness and
wood,   30
Blank ocean and mere sky, support that
mood
Which with the lofty sanctifies the low.
Dreams, books, are each a world; and
books, we know,
Are a substantial world, both pure and
good:
Round these, with tendrils strong as flesh
and blood,   35
Our pastime and our happiness will grow.
There find I personal themes, a plenteous
store,
Matter wherein right voluble I am,
To which I listen with a ready ear;
Two shall be named, pre-eminently
dear,—   40
The gentle lady married to the Moor;
And heavenly Una with her milk-white
lamb.

Nor can I not believe but that hereby
Great gains are mine; for thus I live
remote
From evil-speaking; rancor, never sought, 45
Comes to me not; malignant truth, or lie.
Hence have I genial seasons, hence have I
Smooth passions, smooth discourse, and
joyous thought:
And thus from day to day my little boat
Rocks in its harbor, lodging peaceably. 50
Blessings be with them—and eternal praise,
Who gave us nobler loves, and nobler
cares—
The poets, who on earth have made us
heirs
Of truth and pure delight by heavenly lays!
Oh! might my name be numbered among
theirs,   55
Then gladly would I end my mortal days.

    1807

"THE WORLD IS TOO MUCH WITH US; LATE AND SOON"

The world is too much with us; late and
soon,
Getting and spending, we lay waste our
powers:
Little we see in nature that is ours;
We have given our hearts away, a sordid
boon!
The sea that bares her bosom to the
moon;   5
The winds that will be howling at all
hours,
And are up-gathered now like sleeping
flowers;
For this, for everything, we are out of tune;
It moves us not.—Great God! I'd rather
be
A Pagan suckled in a creed outworn;   10
So might I, standing on this pleasant lea,
Have glimpses that would make me less
forlorn;
Have sight of Proteus rising from the
sea;
Or hear old Triton blow his wreathèd
horn.

    1807

THOUGHT OF A BRITON ON THE SUBJUGATION OF SWITZERLAND

Two Voices are there; one is of the sea,
One of the mountains; each a mighty
Voice:
In both from age to age thou didst rejoice
They were thy chosen music, Liberty!
There came a Tyrant, and with holy glee 5
Thou fought'st against him; but hast vainly
striven:
Thou from thy Alpine holds at length art
driven,
Where not a torrent murmurs heard by
thee.
Of one deep bliss thine ear hath been
bereft:
Then cleave, O cleave to that which still
is left;   10
For, high-souled Maid, what sorrow would
it be
That Mountain floods should thunder as
before
And Ocean bellow from his rocky shore,
And neither awful Voice be heard by thee!

    1807   1807

FROM THE ITALIAN OF MICHAEL ANGELO

I

Yes! hope may with my strong desire keep
    pace,
And I be undeluded, unbetrayed;
For if of our affections none finds grace
In sight of Heaven, then, wherefore hath
    God made
The world which we inhabit? Better plea 5
Love cannot have than that in loving thee
Glory to that eternal Peace is paid,
Who such divinity to thee imparts
As hallows and makes pure all gentle
    hearts.
His hope is treacherous only whose love
    dies   10
With beauty, which is varying every hour;
But in chaste hearts, uninfluenced by the
    power
Of outward change, there blooms a death-
    less flower,
That breathes on earth the air of paradise.

II

No mortal object did these eyes behold
When first they met the placid light of
    thine,
And my Soul felt her destiny divine,
And hope of endless peace in me grew
    bold:
Heaven-born, the Soul a heavenward
    course must hold;   5
Beyond the visible world she soars to seek
(For what delights the sense is false and
    weak)
Ideal Form, the universal mold.
The wise man, I affirm, can find no rest
In that which perishes: nor will he lend 10
His heart to aught which doth on time
    depend.
'Tis sense, unbridled will, and not true
    love,
That kills the soul: love betters what is
    best,
Even here below, but more in heaven
    above.

1805   1807

THE ROCK CROWNED WITH SNOWDROPS

Who fancied what a pretty sight
This Rock would be if edged around
With living snowdrops? circlet bright!
How glorious to this orchard-ground!
Who loved the little Rock, and set   5
Upon its head this coronet?

Was it the humor of a child?
Or rather of some gentle maid,
Whose brows, the day that she was styled
The shepherd-queen, were thus arrayed? 10
Of man mature, or matron sage?
Or old man toying with his age?

I asked— 'twas whispered; The device
To each and all might well belong:
It is the Spirit of Paradise   15
That prompts such work, a Spirit strong,
That gives to all the self-same bent
Where life is wise and innocent.
1803   1807

TO SLEEP

A flock of sheep that leisurely pass by,
One after one; the sound of rain, and bees
Murmuring; the fall of rivers, winds and
    seas;
Smooth fields; white sheets of water, and
    pure sky—
I have thought of all by turns, and yet do
    lie   5
Sleepless! and soon the small birds' melo-
    dies
Must hear, first uttered from my orchard
    trees;
And the first cuckoo's melancholy cry.
Even thus last night, and two nights more,
    I lay
And could not win thee, Sleep! by any
    stealth.   10
So do not let me wear tonight away—
Without thee what is all the morning's
    wealth?
Come, blessed barrier between day and day,
Dear mother of fresh thoughts and joyous
    health!

1807

"WHERE LIES THE LAND TO WHICH YON SHIP MUST GO?"

Where lies the land to which yon ship
    must go?
Fresh as a lark mounting at break of day,
Festively she puts forth in trim array;
Is she for tropic suns, or polar snow?
What boots the inquiry?—Neither friend
    nor foe   5
She cares for; let her travel where she may,
She finds familiar names, a beaten way
Ever before her, and a wind to blow.
Yet still I ask, what haven is her mark?
And, almost as it was when ships were
    rare,   10

(From time to time, like pilgrims, here and
    there
Crossing the waters) doubt, and something
    dark,
Of the old sea some reverential fear,
Is with me at thy farewell, joyous bark!

1807

"A GOODLY VESSEL"

With ships the sea was sprinkled far and
    nigh,
Like stars in heaven, and joyously it
    showed;
Some lying fast at anchor in the road,
Some veering up and down, one knew not
    why.
A goodly vessel did I then espy   5
Come like a giant from a haven broad;
And lustily along the bay she strode,
Her tackling rich, and of apparel high.
This ship was nought to me, nor I to her,
Yet I pursued her with a Lover's look;   10
This ship to all the rest did I prefer:
When will she turn, and whither? She will
    brook
No tarrying; where she comes the winds
    must stir:
On went she, and due north her journey
    took.

1807

SONG AT THE FEAST OF BROUGHAM CASTLE

UPON THE RESTORATION OF LORD CLIF-FORD, THE SHEPHERD, TO THE ESTATES AND HONORS OF HIS ANCESTORS.

High in the breathless hall the minstrel
    sate,
And Emont's murmur mingled with the
    song.—
The words of ancient time I thus translate,
A festal strain that hath been silent long:

"From town to town, from tower to
    tower,   5
The red rose is a gladsome flower.
Her thirty years of winter past,
The red rose is revived at last;
She lifts her head for endless spring,
For everlasting blossoming;   10
Both roses flourish, red and white:
In love and sisterly delight
The two that were at strife are blended,
And all old troubles now are ended.—
Joy! joy to both! but most to her   15
Who is the flower of Lancaster!

Behold her how she smiles today
On this great throng, this bright array!
Fair greeting doth she send to all
From every corner of the hall;   20
But chiefly from above the board
Where sits in state our rightful lord,
A Clifford to his own restored!

"They came with banner, spear, and
    shield;
And it was proved in Bosworth Field.   25
Not long the avenger was withstood—
Earth helped him with the cry of blood:
Saint George was for us, and the might
Of blessed angels crowned the right.
Loud voice the land has uttered forth,   30
We loudest in the faithful North.
Our fields rejoice, our mountains ring,
Our streams proclaim a welcoming;
Our strong-abodes and castles see
The glory of their loyalty.   35

"How glad is Skipton at this hour—
Though lonely, a deserted tower;
Knight, squire, and yeoman, page and
    groom:
We have them at the feast of Brough'm.
How glad Pendragon—though the sleep   40
Of years be on her!—She shall reap
A taste of this great pleasure, viewing
As in a dream her own renewing.
Rejoiced is Brough, right glad, I deem,
Beside her little humble stream;   45
And she that keepeth watch and ward
Her statelier Eden's course to guard;
They both are happy at this hour,
Though each is but a lonely tower—
But here is perfect joy and pride   50
For one fair house by Emont's side,
This day, distinguished without peer,
To see her Master and to cheer—
Him, and his Lady-mother dear!

"Oh! it was a time forlorn   55
When the fatherless was born—
Give her wings that she may fly,
Or she sees her infant die!
Swords that are with slaughter wild
Hunt the Mother and the Child.   60
Who will take them from the light?
—Yonder is a man in sight—
Yonder is a house—but where?
No, they must not enter there.
To the caves, and to the brooks,   65
To the clouds of heaven she looks;
She is speechless, but her eyes
Pray in ghostly agonies.
Blissful Mary, Mother mild,
Maid and Mother undefiled,   70
Save a Mother and her Child!

"Now Who is he that bounds with joy
On Carrock's side, a Shepherd-boy?
No thoughts hath he but thoughts that pass
Light as the wind along the grass.   75
Can this be He who hither came
In secret, like a smothered flame?
O'er whom such thankful tears were shed
For shelter, and a poor man's bread!
God loves the Child; and God hath
          willed   80
That those dear words should be fulfilled,
The Lady's words, when forced away,
The last she to her Babe did say:
'My own, my own, thy Fellow-guest
I may not be; but rest thee, rest,   85
For lowly shepherd's life is best!'

"Alas! when evil men are strong
No life is good, no pleasure long.
The Boy must part from Mosedale's groves,
And leave Blencathara's rugged coves,   90
And quit the flowers that summer brings
To Glenderamakin's lofty springs;
Must vanish, and his careless cheer
Be turned to heaviness and fear.
—Give Sir Lancelot Threlkeld praise!   95
Hear it, good man, old in days!
Thou tree of covert and of rest
For this young Bird that is distrest;
Among thy branches safe he lay,
And he was free to sport and play,   100
When falcons were abroad for prey.

"A recreant harp, that sings of fear
And heaviness in Clifford's ear!
I said, when evil men are strong,
No life is good, no pleasure long,   105
A weak and cowardly untruth!
Our Clifford was a happy Youth,
And thankful through a weary time,
That brought him up to manhood's prime.
—Again he wanders forth at will,   110
And tends a flock from hill to hill;
His garb is humble; ne'er was seen
Such garb with such a noble mien;
Among the shepherd grooms no mate
Hath he, a Child of strength and state!   115
Yet lacks not friends for simple glee,
Nor yet for higher sympathy.
To his side the fallow-deer
Came, and rested without fear;
The eagle, lord of land and sea,   120
Stooped down to pay him fealty;
And both the undying fish that swim
Through Bowscale Tarn did wait on him;
The pair were servants of his eye
In their immortality;   125
And glancing, gleaming, dark or bright,
Moved to and fro for his delight.
He knew the rocks which angels haunt

Upon the mountains visitant;
He hath kenned them taking wing.   130
And into caves where fairies sing
He hath entered; and been told
By voices how men lived of old.
Among the heavens his eye can see
The face of thing that is to be;   135
And, if that men report him right,
His tongue could whisper words of might.
—Now another day is come,
Fitter hope, and nobler doom;
He hath thrown aside his crook,   140
And hath buried deep his book;
Armor rusting in his halls
On the blood of Clifford calls—
'Quell the Scot,' exclaims the Lance;
Bear me to the heart of France,   145
Is the longing of the Shield—
Tell thy name, thou trembling Field;
Field of death, where'er thou be,
Groan thou with our victory!
Happy day, and mighty hour,   150
When our shepherd in his power,
Mailed and horsed, with lance and sword,
To his ancestors restored
Like a reappearing star,
Like a glory from afar,   155
First shall head the flock of war!"

Alas! the impassioned minstrel did not
          know
How, by Heaven's grace, this Clifford's
          heart was framed;
How he, long forced in humble walks to
          go,
Was softened into feeling, soothed, and
          tamed.   160

Love had he found in huts where poor
          men lie;
His daily teachers had been woods and
          rills,
The silence that is in the starry sky,
The sleep that is among the lonely hills.

In him the savage virtue of the race,   165
Revenge, and all ferocious thoughts were
          dead;
Nor did he change, but kept in lofty place
The wisdom which adversity had bred.

Glad were the vales and every cottage
          hearth;
The shepherd lord was honored more and
          more;   170
And, ages after he was laid in earth,
"The good Lord Clifford" was the name he
          bore.

1807   1807

YEW TREES

There is a yew tree, pride of Lorton Vale,
Which to this day stands single, in the midst
Of its own darkness, as it stood of yore;
Not loth to furnish weapons for the bands
Of Umfraville or Percy ere they marched 5
To Scotland's heaths; or those that crossed the sea
And drew their sounding bows at Azincour,
Perhaps at earlier Crecy, or Poictiers.
Of vast circumference and gloom profound
This solitary tree! a living thing 10
Produced too slowly ever to decay;
Of form and aspect too magnificent
To be destroyed. But worthier still of note
Are those fraternal four of Borrowdale,
Joined in one solemn and capacious grove; 15
Huge trunks! and each particular trunk a growth
Of intertwisted fibers serpentine
Up-coiling, and inveterately convolved;
Nor uninformed with fantasy, and looks
That threaten the profane; a pillared shade, 20
Upon whose grassless floor of red-brown hue,
By sheddings from the pining umbrage tinged
Perennially—beneath whose sable roof
Of boughs, as if for festal purpose decked
With unrejoicing berries—ghostly shapes 25
May meet at noontide; Fear and trembling Hope,
Silence and Foresight; Death the skeleton
And Time the shadow—there to celebrate,
As in a natural temple scattered o'er
With altars undisturbed of mossy stone, 30
United worship; or in mute repose
To lie, and listen to the mountain flood
Murmuring from Glaramara's inmost caves.

1803   1815

COMPOSED BY THE SIDE OF GRASMERE LAKE

Clouds, lingering yet, extend in solid bars
Through the grey west; and lo! these waters, steeled
By breezeless air to smoothest polish, yield
A vivid repetition of the stars;
Jove, Venus, and the ruddy crest of Mars 5
Amid his fellows beauteously revealed
At happy distance from earth's groaning field,
Where ruthless mortals wage incessant wars.
Is it a mirror?—or the nether sphere
Opening to view the abyss in which she feeds 10
Her own calm fires?—But list! a voice is near;
Great Pan himself low-whispering through the reeds,
"Be thankful, thou; for, if unholy deeds
Ravage the world, tranquillity is here!"

1807   1819

FROM THE CONVENTION OF CINTRA

[NATIONAL INDEPENDENCE ESSENTIAL 5 TO HAPPINESS]

While mechanic arts, manufactures, agriculture, commerce, and all those products of knowledge which are confined to gross— 10 definite—and tangible objects, have, with the aid of experimental philosophy, been every day putting on more brilliant colors; the splendor of the imagination has been fading: sensibility, which was formerly a 15 generous nursling of rude nature, has been chased from its ancient range in the wide domain of patriotism and religion with the weapons of derision by a shadow calling itself good sense: calculations of presump- 20 tuous expediency—groping its way among partial and temporary consequences—have been substituted for the dictates of paramount and infallible conscience, the supreme embracer of consequences: lifeless and circumspect decencies have banished the graceful negligence and unsuspicious dignity of virtue.

The progress of these arts also, by furnishing such attractive stores of outward accommodation, has misled the higher orders of society in their more disinterested exertions for the service of the lower. Animal comforts have been rejoiced over, as if they were the end of being. A neater and more fertile garden; a greener field; implements and utensils more apt; a dwelling more commodious and better furnished;— let these be attained, say the actively benevolent, and we are sure not only of being in the right road, but of having successfully terminated our journey. Now a country may advance, for some time, in this course with apparent profit: these accommodations, by zealous encouragement, may 5 be attained: and still the peasant or artisan, their master, be a slave in mind; a slave rendered even more abject by the very tenure under which these possessions are held: and—if they veil from us this fact, or 10 reconcile us to it—they are worse than worthless. The springs of emotion may be relaxed or destroyed within him; he may have little thought of the past, and less interest in the future.—The great end and 15 difficulty of life for men of all classes, and especially difficult for those who live by manual labor, is a union of peace with innocent and laudable animation. Not by bread alone is the life of man sustained; 20 not by raiment alone is he warmed;—but by the genial and vernal inmate of the breast, which at once pushes forth and cherishes; by self-support and self-sufficing endeavors; by anticipations, apprehensions, 25 and active remembrances; by elasticity under insult, and firm resistance to injury; by joy, and by love; by pride which his imagination gathers in from afar; by patience, because life wants not promises; by admira- 30 tion; by gratitude which—debasing him not when his fellow-being is its object—habitually expands itself, for his elevation, in complacency towards his Creator.

Now, to the existence of these blessings, 35 national independence is indispensable; and many of them it will itself produce and maintain. For it is some consolation to those who look back upon the history of the world to know—that, even without 40 civil liberty, society may possess—diffused through its inner recesses in the minds even of its humblest members—something of dignified enjoyment. But, without national independence, this is impossible. 45 The difference between inbred oppression and that which is from without, is *essential;* inasmuch as the former does not exclude, from the minds of a people, the feeling of being self-governed; does not 50 imply (as the latter does, when patiently submitted to) an abandonment of the first duty imposed by the faculty of reason. In reality, where this feeling has no place, a people are not a society, but a herd; man 55 being indeed distinguished among them from the brute; but only to his disgrace. I am aware that there are too many who think that, to the bulk of the community, this independence is of no value; that it 60

is a refinement with which they feel they have no concern; inasmuch as, under the best frame of government, there is an inevitable dependence of the poor upon the rich—of the many upon the few—so unrelenting and imperious as to reduce this other, by comparison, into a force which has small influence and is entitled to no regard. Super-add civil liberty to national independence; and this position is overthrown at once: for there is no more certain mark of a sound frame of polity than this; that, in all individual instances (and it is upon these generalized that this position is laid down), the dependence is in reality far more strict on the side of the wealthy; and the laboring man leans less upon others than any man in the community—but the case before us is of a country not internally free, yet supposed capable of repelling an external enemy who attempts its subjugation. If a country have put on chains of its own forging, in the name of virtue, let it be conscious that to itself it is accountable: let it not have cause to look beyond its own limits for reproof: and,—in the name of humanity,—if it be self-depressed, let it have its pride and some hope within itself. The poorest peasant, in an unsubdued land, feels this pride. I do not appeal to the example of Britain or of Switzerland, for the one is free, and the other lately was free (and, I trust, will ere long be so again): but talk with the Swede; and you will see the joy he finds in these sensations. With him animal courage (the substitute for many and the friend of all the manly virtues) has space to move in; and is at once elevated by his imagination, and softened by his affections: it is invigorated also; for the whole courage of his country is in his breast.

In fact, the peasant, and he who lives by the fair reward of his manual labor, has ordinarily a larger proportion of his gratifications dependent upon these thoughts—than, for the most part, men in other classes have. For he is in his person attached, by stronger roots, to the soil of which he is the growth: his intellectual notices are generally confined within narrower bounds: in him no partial or antipatriotic interests counteract the force of those nobler sympathies and antipathies which he has in right of his country; and lastly the belt or girdle of his mind has never been stretched to utter relaxation by false philosophy, under a conceit of making it sit more easily and gracefully. These sensations are a social inheritance to him:

more important, as he is precluded from luxurious—and those which are usually called refined—enjoyments.

Love and admiration must push themselves out towards some quarter: otherwise 5 the moral man is killed. Collaterally they advance with great vigor to a certain extent—and they are checked: in that direction, limits hard to pass are perpetually encountered: but upwards and downwards, 10

to ancestry and to posterity, they meet with gladsome help and no obstacles; the tract is interminable.—Perdition to the tyrant who would wantonly cut off an independent nation from its inheritance in past ages; turning the tombs and burial-places of the forefathers into dreaded objects of sorrow, or of shame and reproach, for the children!

1808   1809

THE PRELUDE

OR, GROWTH OF A POET'S MIND
AN AUTOBIOGRAPHICAL POEM

BOOK FIRST

INTRODUCTION—CHILDHOOD AND SCHOOL-TIME

Oh, there is blessing in this gentle breeze,
A visitant that while it fans my cheek
Doth seem half-conscious of the joy it brings
From the green fields, and from yon azure sky.
Whate'er its mission, the soft breeze can come 5
To none more grateful than to me; escaped
From the vast city, where I long had pined,
A discontented sojourner; now free,
Free as a bird to settle where I will.

. . . .

Far better never to have heard the name 255
Of zeal and just ambition than to live
Baffled and plagued by a mind that every hour
Turns recreant to her task; takes heart again,
Then feels immediately some hollow thought
Hang like an interdict upon her hopes. 260
This is my lot; for either still I find
Some imperfection in the chosen theme,
Or see of absolute accomplishment
Much wanting, so much wanting, in myself,
That I recoil and droop, and seek repose 265
In listlessness from vain perplexity,
Unprofitably traveling toward the grave,
Like a false steward who hath much received
And renders nothing back.
                          Was it for this
That one, the fairest of all rivers, loved 270

To blend his murmurs with my nurse's song,
And, from his alder shades and rocky falls,
And from his fords and shallows, sent a voice
That flowed along my dreams? For this, didst thou,
O Derwent! winding among grassy holms 275
Where I was looking on, a babe in arms,
Make ceaseless music that composed my thoughts
To more than infant softness, giving me
Amid the fretful dwellings of mankind
A foretaste, a dim earnest, of the calm 280
That Nature breathes among the hills and groves.

When he had left the mountains and received
On his smooth breast the shadow of those towers
That yet survive, a shattered monument
Of feudal sway, the bright blue river passed 285
Along the margin of our terrace walk—
A tempting playmate whom we dearly loved.
Oh, many a time have I, a five years' child,
In a small mill-race severed from his stream,
Made one long bathing of a summer's day; 290
Basked in the sun, and plunged and basked again
Alternate, all a summer's day, or scoured
The sandy fields, leaping through flowery groves
Of yellow ragwort; or, when rock and hill,
The woods, and distant Skiddaw's lofty height, 295
Were bronzed with deepest radiance, stood alone
Beneath the sky, as if I had been born
On Indian plains, and from my mother's hut

Had run abroad in wantonness, to sport
A naked savage, in the thunder shower. 300

Fair seed-time had my soul, and I grew
    up
Fostered alike by beauty and by fear:
Much favored in my birth-place, and no
    less
In that belovèd Vale to which erelong
We were transplanted;—there were we let
    loose   305
For sports of wider range. Ere I had told
Ten birth-days, when among the mountain
    slopes
Frost, and the breath of frosty wind, had
    snapped
The last autumnal crocus, 'twas my joy
With store of springes o'er my shoulder
    hung   310
To range the open heights where wood-
    cocks run
Along the smooth green turf. Through
    half the night,
Scudding away from snare to snare, I plied
That anxious visitation;—moon and stars
Were shining o'er my head. I was
    alone,   315
And seemed to be a trouble to the peace
That dwelt among them. Sometimes it
    befell
In these night wanderings, that a strong
    desire
O'erpowered my better reason, and the
    bird
Which was the captive of another's toil 320
Became my prey; and when the deed was
    done
I heard among the solitary hills
Low breathings coming after me, and
    sounds
Of undistinguishable motion, steps
Almost as silent as the turf they trod.   325

Nor less when spring had warmed the
    cultured vale,
Moved we as plunderers where the mother
    bird
Had in high places built her lodge; though
    mean
Our object and inglorious, yet the end
Was not ignoble. Oh! when I have
    hung   330
Above the raven's nest, by knots of grass
And half-inch fissures in the slippery rock
But ill sustained, and almost—so it
    seemed—
Suspended by the blast that blew amain.
Shouldering the naked crag, oh, at that
    time   335
While on the perilous ridge I hung alone,

With what strange utterance did the loud,
    dry wind
Blow through my ear! the sky seemed not
    a sky
Of earth—and with what motion moved
    the clouds!

Dust as we are, the immortal spirit
    grows   340
Like harmony in music; there is a dark
Inscrutable workmanship that reconciles
Discordant elements, makes them cling to-
    gether
In one society. How strange that all
The terrors, pains, and early miseries,   345
Regrets, vexations, lassitudes interfused
Within my mind, should e'er have borne a
    part,
And that a needful part, in making up
The calm existence that is mine when I
Am worthy of myself! Praise to the
    end!   350
Thanks to the means which Nature
    deigned to employ;
Whether her fearless visitings, or those
That came with soft alarm, like hurtless
    light
Opening the peaceful clouds; or she may
    use
Severer interventions, ministry   355
More palpable, as best might suit her aim.

One summer evening (led by her) I
    found
A little boat tied to a willow tree
Within a rocky cove, its usual home.
Straight I unloosed her chain, and stepping
    in   360
Pushed from the shore. It was an act of
    stealth
And troubled pleasure, nor without the
    voice
Of mountain echoes did my boat move on;
Leaving behind her still, on either side,
Small circles glittering idly in the moon, 365
Until they melted all into one track
Of sparkling light. But now, like one who
    rows,
Proud of his skill, to reach a chosen point
With an unswerving line, I fixed my view
Upon the summit of a craggy ridge,   370
The horizon's utmost boundary; far above
Was nothing but the stars and the gray sky.
She was an elfin pinnace; lustily
I dipped my oars into the silent lake,
And, as I rose upon the stroke, my boat 375
Went heaving through the water like a
    swan;
When, from behind that craggy steep till
    then

The horizon's bound, a huge peak, black
    and huge,
As if with voluntary power instinct
Upreared its head. I struck and struck
    again,   380
And growing still in stature the grim shape
Towered up between me and the stars, and
    still,
For so it seemed, with purpose of its own
And measured motion like a living thing,
Strode after me. With trembling oars I
    turned,   385
And through the silent water stole my way
Back to the covert of the willow tree;
There in her mooring-place I left my
    bark,—
And through the meadows homeward went,
    in grave
And serious mood; but after I had seen 390
That spectacle, for many days, my brain
Worked with a dim and undetermined
    sense
Of unknown modes of being; o'er my
    thoughts
There hung a darkness, call it solitude
Or blank desertion. No familiar shapes 395
Remained, no pleasant images of trees,
Of sea or sky, no colors of green fields;
But huge and mighty forms, that do not
    live
Like living men, moved slowly through the
    mind
By day, and were a trouble to my
    dreams.   400

    Wisdom and Spirit of the universe!
Thou Soul that art the eternity of thought,
That givest to forms and images a breath
And everlasting motion, not in vain
By day or starlight thus from my first
    dawn   405
Of childhood didst thou intertwine for me
The passions that build up our human
    soul;
Not with the mean and vulgar works of
    man,
But with high objects, with enduring
    things—
With life and nature—purifying thus 410
The elements of feeling and of thought,
And sanctifying, by such discipline,
Both pain and fear, until we recognize
A grandeur in the beatings of the heart.
Nor was this fellowship vouchsafed to
    me   415
With stinted kindness. In November days,
When vapors rolling down the valley made
A lonely scene more lonesome, among
    woods,

At noon and 'mid the calm of summer
    nights,
When, by the margin of the trembling
    lake,   420
Beneath the gloomy hills homeward I went
In solitude, such intercourse was mine;
Mine was it in the fields both day and
    night,
And by the waters, all the summer long.

    And in the frosty season, when the
    sun   425
Was set, and visible for many a mile
The cottage windows blazed through twi-
    light gloom,
I heeded not their summons: happy time
It was indeed for all of us—for me
It was a time of rapture! Clear and
    loud   430
The village clock tolled six,—I wheeled
    about,
Proud and exulting like an untired horse
That cares not for his home. All shod
    with steel,
We hissed along the polished ice in games
Confederate, imitative of the chase   435
And woodland pleasures,—the resounding
    horn,
The pack loud chiming, and the hunted
    hare.
So through the darkness and the cold we
    flew,
And not a voice was idle; with the din
Smitten, the precipices rang aloud;   440
The leafless trees and every icy crag
Tinkled like iron; while far distant hills
Into the tumult sent an alien sound
Of melancholy not unnoticed, while the
    stars
Eastward were sparkling clear, and in the
    west   445
The orange sky of evening died away.
Not seldom from the uproar I retired
Into a silent bay, or sportively
Glanced sideway, leaving the tumultuous
    throng,
To cut across the reflex of a star   450
That fled, and, flying still before me,
    gleamed
Upon the glassy plain; and oftentimes,
When we had given our bodies to the
    wind,
And all the shadowy banks on either side
Came sweeping through the darkness,
    spinning still   455
The rapid line of motion, then at once
Have I, reclining back upon my heels,
Stopped short; yet still the solitary cliffs
Wheeled by me—even as if the earth had
    rolled

With visible motion her diurnal round! 460
Behind me did they stretch in solemn train,
Feebler and feebler, and I stood and
watched
Till all was tranquil as a dreamless sleep.

Ye Presences of Nature in the sky
And on the earth! Ye Visions of the
hills! 465
And Souls of lonely places! can I think
A vulgar hope was yours when ye employed
Such ministry, when ye through many a
year
Haunting me thus among my boyish sports,
On caves and trees, upon the woods and
hills, 470
Impressed upon all forms the characters
Of danger or desire; and thus did make
The surface of the universal earth
With triumph and delight, with hope and
fear,
Work like a sea?
            Not uselessly employed, 475
Might I pursue this theme through every
change
Of exercise and play, to which the year
Did summon us in his delightful round.

We were a noisy crew; the sun in heaven
Beheld not vales more beautiful than
ours; 480
Nor saw a band in happiness and joy
Richer, or worthier of the ground they
trod.
I could record with no reluctant voice
The woods of autumn, and their hazel
bowers
With milk-white clusters hung; the rod and
line, 485
True symbol of hope's foolishness, whose
strong
And unreproved enchantment led us on
By rocks and pools shut out from every
star,
All the green summer, to forlorn cascades
Among the windings hid of mountain
brooks. 490
—Unfading recollections! at this hour
The heart is almost mine with which I felt,
From some hilltop on sunny afternoons,
The paper kite high among fleecy clouds
Pull at her rein like an impetuous
courser; 495
Or, from the meadows sent on gusty days,
Beheld her breast the wind, then suddenly
Dashed headlong, and rejected by the
storm.

   . . . .

Nor, sedulous as I have been to trace
How Nature by extrinsic passion first 545
Peopled the mind with forms sublime or
fair,
And made me love them, may I here omit
How other pleasures have been mine, and
joys
Of subtler origin; how I have felt,
Not seldom even in that tempestuous
time, 550
Those hallowed and pure motions of the
sense
Which seem, in their simplicity, to own
An intellectual charm; that calm delight
Which, if I err not, surely must belong
To those first-born affinities that fit 555
Our new existence to existing things,
And, in our dawn of being, constitute
The bond of union between life and joy.

Yes, I remember when the changeful
earth,
And twice five summers on my mind had
stamped 560
The faces of the moving year, even then
I held unconscious intercourse with beauty
Old as creation, drinking in a pure
Organic pleasure from the silver wreaths
Of curling mist, or from the level plain 565
Of waters colored by impending clouds.

The sands of Westmoreland, the creeks
and bays
Of Cumbria's rocky limits, they can tell
How, when the Sea threw off his evening
shade
And to the shepherd's hut on distant
hills 570
Sent welcome notice of the rising moon,
How I have stood, to fancies such as these
A stranger, linking with the spectacle
No conscious memory of a kindred sight,
And bringing with me no peculiar sense 575
Of quietness or peace; yet have I stood,
Even while mine eye hath moved o'er
many a league
Of shining water, gathering as it seemed,
Through every hair-breadth in that field of
light,
New pleasure like a bee among the
flowers. 580

Thus oft amid those fits of vulgar joy
Which, through all seasons, on a child's
pursuits
Are prompt attendants, 'mid that giddy
bliss
Which, like a tempest, works along the
blood
And is forgotten; even then I felt 585

Gleams like the flashing of a shield;—the
  earth
And common face of Nature spake to me
Rememberable things; sometimes, 'tis true,
By chance collisions and quaint accidents
(Like those ill-sorted unions, work sup-
  posed   590
Of evil-minded fairies), yet not vain
Nor profitless, if haply they impressed
Collateral objects and appearances,
Albeit lifeless then, and doomed to sleep
Until maturer seasons called them forth 595
To impregnate and to elevate the mind.
—And if the vulgar joy by its own weight
Wearied itself out of the memory,
The scenes which were a witness of that joy
Remained in their substantial linea-
  ments   600
Depicted on the brain, and to the eye
Were visible, a daily sight; and thus
By the impressive discipline of fear,
By pleasure and repeated happiness,
So frequently repeated, and by force   605
Of obscure feelings representative
Of things forgotten, these same scenes so
  bright,
So beautiful, so majestic in themselves,
Though yet the day was distant, did be-
  come
Habitually dear, and all their forms   610
And changeful colors by invisible links
Were fastened to the affections.

                            I began
My story early—not misled, I trust,
By an infirmity of love for days
Disowned by memory—ere the breath of
  spring   615
Planting my snowdrops among winter
  snows;
Nor will it seem to thee, O Friend! so
  prompt
In sympathy, that I have lengthened out
With fond and feeble tongue a tedious
  tale.
Meanwhile, my hope has been that I might
  fetch   620
Invigorating thoughts from former years;
Might fix the wavering balance of my
  mind,
And haply meet reproaches, too, whose
  power
May spur me on, in manhood now mature,
To honorable toil. Yet should these
  hopes   625
Prove vain, and thus should neither I be
  taught
To understand myself, nor thou to know
With better knowledge how the heart was
  framed

Of him thou lovest; need I dread from
  thee
Harsh judgments, if the song be loath to
  quit   630
Those recollected hours that have the
  charm
Of visionary things, those lovely forms
And sweet sensations that throw back our
  life,
And almost make remotest infancy
A visible scene, on which the sun is shin-
  ing?   635

  One end at least hath been attained; my
    mind
Hath been revived, and if this genial mood
Desert me not, forthwith shall be brought
  down
Through later years the story of my life.
The road lies plain before me—'tis a
  theme   640
Single and of determined bounds; and
  hence
I choose it rather at this time, than work
Of ampler or more varied argument,
Where I might be discomfited and lost.
And certain hopes are with me, that to
  thee   645
This labor will be welcome, honored
  friend!

BOOK SECOND

SCHOOL-TIME (CONTINUED)

  Midway on long Winander's eastern
    shore,
Within the crescent of a pleasant bay,
A tavern stood; no homely-featured
  house,   140
Primeval like its neighboring cottages,
But 'twas a splendid place, the door beset
With chaises, grooms, and liveries, and
  within
Decanters, glasses, and the blood-red wine.
In ancient times, and ere the Hall was
  built   145
On the large island, had this dwelling been
More worthy of a poet's love, a hut,
Proud of its own bright fire and sycamore
  shade.
But—though the rhymes were gone that
  once inscribed
The threshold, and large golden charac-
  ters,   150
Spread o'er the spangled sign-board, had
  dislodged
The old Lion and usurped his place, in
  slight

And mockery of the rustic painter's hand—
Yet, to this hour, the spot to me is dear
With all its foolish pomp. The garden
   lay   155
Upon a slope surmounted by a plain
Of a small bowling-green; beneath us stood
A grove, with gleams of water through the
   trees
And over the tree-tops; nor did we want
Refreshment, strawberries and mellow
   cream.   160
There, while through half an afternoon we
   played
On the smooth platform, whether skill pre-
   vailed
Or happy blunder triumphed, bursts of
   glee
Made all the mountains ring. But, ere
   night-fall,
When in our pinnace we returned at
   leisure   165
Over the shadowy lake, and to the beach
Of some small island steered our course
   with one,
The minstrel of the troop, and left him
   there,
And rowed off gently, while he blew his
   flute
Alone upon the rock—oh, then, the
   calm   170
And dead still water lay upon my mind
Even with a weight of pleasure, and the
   sky,
Never before so beautiful, sank down
Into my heart, and held me like a dream!
Thus were my sympathies enlarged, and
   thus   175
Daily the common range of visible things
Grew dear to me: already I began
To love the sun; a boy I loved the sun,
Not as I since have loved him, as a pledge
And surety of our earthly life, a light   180
Which we behold and feel we are alive;
Nor for his bounty to so many worlds—
But for this cause, that I had seen him lay
His beauty on the morning hills, had seen
The western mountain touch his setting
   orb,   185
In many a thoughtless hour, when, from
   excess
Of happiness, my blood appeared to flow
For its own pleasure, and I breathed with
   joy.
And, from like feelings, humble though
   intense,
To patriotic and domestic love   190
Analogous, the moon to me was dear;
For I could dream away my purposes,
Standing to gaze upon her while she hung
Midway between the hills, as if she knew

No other region, but belonged to thee, 195
Yea, appertained by a peculiar right
To thee and thy grey huts, thou one dear
   vale!

Those incidental charms which first at
   tached
My heart to rural objects, day by day
Grew weaker, and I hasten on to tell   200
How Nature, intervenient till this time
And secondary, now at length was sought
For her own sake. But who shall parcel out
His intellect by geometric rules,
Split like a province into round and
   square?   205
Who knows the individual hour in which
His habits were first sown, even as a seed?
Who that shall point as with a wand and
   say
"This portion of the river of my mind
Came from yon fountain?" Thou, my
   friend! art one   210
More deeply read in thy own thoughts; to
   thee
Science appears but what in truth she is,
Not as our glory and our absolute boast,
But as a succedaneum, and a prop
To our infirmity. No officious slave   215
Art thou of that false secondary power
By which we multiply distinctions, then
Deem that our puny boundaries are things
That we perceive, and not that we have
   made.
To thee, unblinded by these formal arts, 220
The unity of all hath been revealed,
And thou wilt doubt, with me less aptly
   skilled
Than many are to range the faculties
In scale and order, class the cabinet
Of their sensations, and in voluble
   phrase   225
Run through the history and birth of each
As of a single independent thing.
Hard task, vain hope, to analyse the mind,
If each most obvious and particular
   thought,
Not in a mystical and idle sense,   230
But in the words of reason deeply weighed,
Hath no beginning.   Blest the infant babe,
(For with my best conjecture I would trace
Our being's earthly progress,) blest the
   babe,
Nursed in his mother's arms, who sinks to
   sleep,   235
Rocked on his mother's breast; who with
   his soul
Drinks in the feelings of his mother's eye!
For him, in one dear presence, there exists
A virtue which irradiates and exalts

Objects through widest intercourse of
    sense.   240
No outcast he, bewildered and depressed:
Along his infant veins are interfused
The gravitation and the filial bond
Of nature that connect him with the world.
Is there a flower, to which he points with
    hand   245
Too weak to gather it, already love
Drawn from love's purest earthly fount for
    him
Hath beautified that flower; already shades
Of pity cast from inward tenderness
Do fall around him upon aught that
    bears   250
Unsightly marks of violence or harm.
Emphatically such a being lives,
Frail creature as he is, helpless as frail,
An inmate of this active universe:
For feeling has to him imparted power   255
That through the growing faculties of
    sense
Doth like an agent of the one great mind
Create, creator and receiver both,
Working but in alliance with the works
Which it beholds.—Such, verily, is the
    first   260
Poetic spirit of our human life,
By uniform control of after years,
In most, abated or suppressed; in some,
Through every change of growth and of
    decay,
Pre-eminent till death.
                From early days,   265
Beginning not long after that first time
In which, a babe, by intercourse of touch
I held mute dialogues with my mother's
    heart,
I have endeavored to display the means
Whereby this infant sensibility,   270
Great birthright of our being, was in me
Augmented and sustained. Yet is a path
More difficult before me; and I fear
That in its broken windings we shall need
The chamois' sinews, and the eagle's
    wing: 275
For now a trouble came into my mind
From unknown causes. I was left alone
Seeking the visible world, nor knowing
    why.
The props of my affections were removed,
And yet the building stood, as if sus-
    tained   280
By its own spirit! All that I beheld
Was dear, and hence to finer influxes
The mind lay open, to a more exact
And close communion. Many are our
    joys
In youth, but oh! what happiness to live 285
When every hour brings palpable access

Of knowledge, when all knowledge is
    delight,
And sorrow is not there! The seasons
    came,
And every season wheresoe'er I moved
Unfolded transitory qualities,   290
Which, but for this most watchful power
    of love,
Had been neglected; left a register
Of permanent relations, else unknown.
Hence life, and change, and beauty, soli-
    tude
More active even than "best society"— 295
Society made sweet as solitude
By silent inobtrusive sympathies,
And gentle agitations of the mind
From manifold distinctions, difference
Perceived in things, where, to the unwatch-
    ful eye,   300
No difference is, and hence, from the same
    source,
Sublimer joy! for I would walk alone,
Under the quiet stars, and at that time
Have felt whate'er there is of power in
    sound
To breathe an elevated mood, by form   305
Or image unprofaned; and I would
    stand,
If the night blackened with a coming
    storm,
Beneath some rock, listening to notes that
    are
The ghostly language of the ancient earth,
Or make their dim abode in distant
    winds.   310
Thence did I drink the visionary power;
And deem not profitless those fleeting
    moods
Of shadowy exultation: not for this,
That they are kindred to our purer mind
And intellectual life; but that the soul,   315
Remembering how she felt, but what she
    felt
Remembering not, retains an obscure sense
Of possible sublimity, whereto
With growing faculties she doth aspire,
With faculties still growing, feeling still 320
That whatsoever point they gain, they yet
Have something to pursue.
                And not alone,
'Mid gloom and tumult, but no less 'mid
    fair
And tranquil scenes, that universal power
And fitness in the latent qualities   325
And essences of things, by which the mind
Is moved with feelings of delight, to me
Came strengthened with a superadded soul,
A virtue not its own.

How shall I seek the origin? where find 346
Faith in the marvellous things which then
    I felt?
Oft in these moments such a holy calm
Would overspread my soul, that bodily eyes
Were utterly forgotten, and what I saw 350
Appeared like something in myself, a
    dream,
A prospect in the mind.
                        'Twere long to tell
What spring and autumn, what the winter
    snows,
And what the summer shade, what day and
    night,
Evening and morning, sleep and waking,
    thought   355
From sources inexhaustible, poured forth
To feed the spirit of religious love
In which I walked with Nature. But let
    this
Be not forgotten, that I still retained
My first creative sensibility;   360
That by the regular action of the world
My soul was unsubdued. A plastic power
Abode with me; a forming hand, at times
Rebellious, acting in a devious mood;
A local spirit of his own, at war   365
With general tendency, but, for the most,
Subservient strictly to external things
With which it communed. An auxiliar
    light
Came from my mind, which on the setting
    sun
Bestowed new splendor; the melodious
    birds,   370
The fluttering breezes, fountains that run
    on
Murmuring so sweetly in themselves,
    obeyed
A like dominion, and the midnight storm
Grew darker in the presence of my eye:
Hence my obeisance, my devotion hence, 375
And hence my transport.
                        Nor should this, perchance,
Pass unrecorded, that I still had loved
The exercise and produce of a toil,
Than analytic industry to me
More pleasing, and whose character I
    deem   380
Is more poetic as resembling more
Creative agency. The song would speak
Of that interminable building reared
By observation of affinities
In objects where no brotherhood exists 385
To passive minds. My seventeenth year
    was come;
And, whether from this habit rooted now
So deeply in my mind, or from excess
In the great social principle of life
Coercing all things into sympathy,   390

To unorganic natures were transferred
My own enjoyments; or the power of truth
Coming in revelation, did converse
With things that really are; I, at this time,
Saw blessings spread around me like a
    sea.   395
Thus while the days flew by, and years
    passed on,
From Nature and her overflowing soul
I had received so much, that all my
    thoughts
Were steeped in feeling; I was only then
Contented, when with bliss ineffable   400
I felt the sentiment of Being spread
O'er all that moves and all that seemeth
    still;
O'er all that, lost beyond the reach of
    thought
And human knowledge, to the human eye
Invisible, yet liveth to the heart;   405
O'er all that leaps and runs, and shouts
    and sings,
Or beats the gladsome air; o'er all that
    glides
Beneath the wave, yea, in the wave itself,
And mighty depth of waters. Wonder not
If high the transport, great the joy I felt 410
Communing in this sort through earth and
    heaven
With every form of creature, as it looked
Towards the Uncreated with a counte-
    nance
Of adoration, with an eye of love.
One song they sang, and it was audible, 415
Most audible, then, when the fleshly ear,
O'ercome by humblest prelude of that
    strain,
Forgot her functions, and slept undis-
    turbed.
If this be error, and another faith
Find easier access to the pious mind   420
Yet were I grossly destitute of all
Those human sentiments that make this
    earth
So dear, if I should fail with grateful voice
To speak of you, ye mountains, and ye
    lakes
And sounding cataracts, ye mists and
    winds   425
That dwell among the hills where I was
    born.
If in my youth I have been pure in heart,
If, mingling with the world, I am content
With my own modest pleasures, and have
    lived
With God and Nature communing, re-
    moved   430
From little enmities and low desires,
The gift is yours; if in these times of fear,
This melancholy waste of hopes o'erthrown,

If, 'mid indifference and apathy,
And wicked exultation when good men 435
On every side fall off, we know not how,
To selfishness, disguised in gentle names
Of peace and quiet and domestic love,
Yet mingled not unwillingly with sneers
On visionary minds; if, in this time   440
Of dereliction and dismay, I yet
Despair not of our nature, but retain
A more than Roman confidence, a faith
That fails not, in all sorrow my support,
The blessing of my life; the gift is yours, 445
Ye winds and sounding cataracts! 'tis yours,
Ye mountains! thine, O Nature! Thou
    hast fed
My lofty speculations; and in thee,
For this uneasy heart of ours, I find
A never-failing principle of joy   450
And purest passion.

BOOK THIRD

RESIDENCE AT CAMBRIDGE

The Evangelist St. John my patron was.
Three Gothic courts are his, and in the first
Was my abiding-place, a nook obscure;
Right underneath, the college kitchens
    made
A humming sound, less tunable than
    bees,   50
But hardly less industrious; with shrill
    notes
Of sharp command and scolding inter-
    mixed.
Near me hung Trinity's loquacious clock,
Who never let the quarters, night or day,
Slip by him unproclaimed, and told the
    hours   55
Twice over with a male and female voice.
Her pealing organ was my neignbor, too;
And from my pillow, looking forth by light
Of moon or favoring stars, I could behold
The antechapel where the statue stood 60
Of Newton with his prism and silent face,
The marble index of a mind forever
Voyaging through strange seas of thought,
    alone.

Of college labors, of the lecturer's room
All studaed round, as thick as chairs could
    stand,   65
With loyal students faithful to their books,
Half-and-half idlers, hardy recusants,
And honest dunces—of important days,
Examinations, when the man was weighed
As in a balance! of excessive hopes,   70
Tremblings withal and commendaole fears,
Small jealousies, and triumphs good or
    bad—

Let others that know more speak as they
    know.
Such glory was but little sought by me,
And little won. Yet from the first crude
    days   75
Of settling time in this untried abode,
I was disturbed at times by prudent
    thoughts,
Wishing to hope without a hope, some
    fears
About my future worldly maintenance,
And, more than all, a strangeness in the
    mind,   80
A feeling that I was not for that hour,
Nor for that place. But wherefore be cast
    down?
For (not to speak of reason and her pure
Reflective acts to fix the moral law
Deep in the conscience, nor of Christian
    hope,   85
Bowing her head before her sister faith
As one far mightier), hither I had come,
Bear witness truth, endowed with holy
    powers
And faculties, whether to work or feel.

Oft when the dazzling show no longer
    new   90
Had ceased to dazzle, ofttimes did I quit
My comrades, leave the crowd, buildings
    and groves,
And as I paced alone the level fields
Far from those lovely sights and sounds
    sublime
With which I had been conversant, the
    mind   95
Drooped not; but there into herself re-
    turning,
With prompt rebound seemed fresh as
    heretofore.
At least I more distinctly recognized
Her native instincts: let me dare to speak
A higher language, say that now I felt 100
What independent solaces were mine,
To mitigate the injurious sway of place
Or circumstance, how far soever changed
In youth, or to be changed in after years.

As if awakened, summoned, roused, con-
    strained,   105
I looked for universal things; perused
The common countenance of earth and
    sky:
Earth, nowhere unembellished by some
    trace
Of that first Paradise whence man was
    driven;
And sky, whose beauty and bounty are
    expressed   110

By the proud name she bears—the name of
    Heaven.
I called on both to teach me what they
    might;
Or turning the mind in upon herself,
Pored, watched, expected, listened, spread
    my thoughts
And spread them with a wider creeping;
    felt   115
Incumbencies more awful, visitings
Of the Upholder of the tranquil soul,
That tolerates the indignities of time,
And, from the center of eternity
All finite motions overruling, lives   120
In glory immutable! But peace! enough
Here to record that I was mounting now
To such community with highest truth—
A track pursuing, not untrod before,
From strict analogies by thought sup-
    plied   125
Or consciousnesses not to be subdued.
To every natural form, rock, fruit, or
    flower,
Even the loose stones that cover the high-
    way,
I gave a moral life: I saw them feel,
Or linked them to some feeling: the great
    mass   130
Lay bedded in a quickening soul, and all
That I beheld respired with inward mean-
    ing.
Add that whate'er of terror or of love
Or beauty, Nature's daily face put on
From transitory passion, unto this   135
I was as sensitive as waters are
To the sky's influence in a kindred mood
Of passion; was obedient as a lute
That waits upon the touches of the wind.
Unknown, unthought of, yet I was most
    rich—   140
I had a world about me—'twas my own;
I made it, for it only lived to me,
And to the God who sees into the heart.
Such sympathies, though rarely, were be-
    trayed
By outward gestures and by visible
    looks: 145
Some called it madness—so indeed it was,
If child-like fruitfulness in passing joy,
If steady moods of thoughtfulness matured
To inspiration, sort with such a name;
If prophecy be madness; if things
    viewed   150
By poets in old time, and higher up
By the first men, earth's first inhabitants,
May in these tutored days no more be
    seen
With undisordered sight. But leaving this,

It was no madness, for the bodily eye   155
Amid my strongest workings evermore
Was searching out the lines of difference
As they lie hid in all external forms,
Near or remote, minute or vast; an eye
Which, from a tree, a stone, a withered
    leaf,   160
To the broad ocean and the azure heavens
Spangled with kindred multitudes of stars,
Could find no surface where its power
    might sleep;
Which spake perpetual logic to my soul,
And by an unrelenting agency   165
Did bind my feelings even as in a chain.

And here, O Friend! have I retraced my
    life
Up to an eminence, and told a tale
Of matters which not falsely may be called
The glory of my youth. Of genius,
    power,   170
Creation and divinity itself
I have been speaking, for my theme has
    been
What passed within me. Not of outward
    things
Done visibly for other minds, words, signs,
Symbols or actions, but of my own heart 175
Have I been speaking, and my youthful
    mind.
O Heavens! how awful is the might of
    souls,
And what they do within themselves while
    yet
The yoke of earth is new to them, the
    world
Nothing but a wild field where they were
    sown.   180
This is, in truth, heroic argument,
This genuine prowess, which I wished to
    touch
With hand however weak, but in the
    main
It lies far hidden from the reach of words.
Points have we all of us within our
    souls   185
Where all stand single; this I feel, and
    make
Breathings for incommunicable powers;
But is not each a memory to himself,
And, therefore, now that we must quit this
    theme,
I am not heartless, for there's not a man 190
That lives who hath not known his god-
    like hours,
And feels not what an empire we inherit
As natural beings in the strength of
    Nature.

BOOK FOURTH

SUMMER VACATION

Those walks well worthy to be prized
   and loved—
Regretted!—that word, too, was on my
   tongue,
But they were richly laden with all good,
And cannot be remembered but with
   thanks
And gratitude, and perfect joy of
   heart—   135
Those walks in all their freshness now
   came back
Like a returning spring. When first I
   made
Once more the circuit of our little lake,
If ever happiness hath lodged with man,
That day consummate happiness was
   mine,   140
Wide-spreading, steady, calm, contempla-
   tive.
The sun was set, or setting, when I left
Our cottage door, and evening soon
   brought on
A sober hour, not winning or serene,
For cold and raw the air was, and un-
   tuned;   145
But as a face we love is sweetest then
When sorrow damps it, or, whatever look
It chance to wear, is sweetest if the heart
Have fullness in herself; even so with me
It fared that evening. Gently did my
   soul   150
Put off her veil, and, self-transmuted, stood
Naked, as in the presence of her God.
While on I walked, a comfort seemed to
   touch
A heart that had not been disconsolate:
Strength came where weakness was not
   known to be,   155
At least not felt; and restoration came
Like an intruder knocking at the door
Of unacknowledged weariness. I took
The balance, and with firm hand weighed
   myself.
—Of that external scene which round me
   lay,   160
Little, in this abstraction, did I see;
Remembered less; but I had inward hopes
And swellings of the spirit, was rapt and
   soothed,
Conversed with promises, had glimmering
   views
How life pervades the undecaying
   mind;   165
How the immortal soul with Godlike
   power
Informs, creates, and thaws the deepest
   sleep

That time can lay upon her; how on earth
Man, if he do but live within the light
Of high endeavors, daily spreads abroad   170
His being armed with strength that cannot
   fail.
Nor was there want of milder thoughts, of
   love,
Of innocence, and holiday repose;
And more than pastoral quiet, 'mid the
   stir
Of boldest projects, and a peaceful end   175
At last, or glorious, by endurance won.
Thus musing, in a wood I sat me down
Alone, continuing there to muse. The
   slopes
And heights meanwhile were slowly over-
   spread
With darkness, and before a rippling
   breeze   180
The long lake lengthened out its hoary
   line,
And in the sheltered coppice where I sate,
Around me from among the hazel leaves,
Now here, now there, moved by the strag-
   gling wind,
Came ever and anon a breath-like
   sound,   185
Quick as the pantings of the faithful dog,
The off and on companion of my walk;
And such, at times, believing them to be,
I turned my head to look if he were there;
Then into solemn thought I passed once
   more.   190

. . . .

                       Yet in spite
Of pleasure won, and knowledge not with-
   held,
There was an inner falling off—I loved,
Loved deeply all that had been loved
   before,
More deeply even than ever: but a
   swarm   280
Of heady schemes jostling each other,
   gawds,
And feast and dance, and public revelry,
And sports and games (too grateful in
   themselves,
Yet in themselves less grateful, I believe,
Than as they were a badge glossy and
   fresh   285
Of manliness and freedom) all conspired
To lure my mind from firm habitual quest
Of feeding pleasures, to depress the zeal
And damp those yearnings which had once
   been mine—
A wild, unworldly-minded youth, given
   up   290
To his own eager thoughts. It would de-
   mand

Some skill, and longer time than may be
  spared
To paint these vanities, and how they
  wrought
In haunts where they, till now, had been
  unknown.
It seemed the very garments that I wore 295
Preyed on my strength, and stopped the
  quiet stream
Of self-forgetfulness.
                            Yes, that heartless chase
Of trivial pleasures was a poor exchange
For books and nature at that early age.
'Tis true, some casual knowledge might be
  gained   300
Of character or life; but at that time,
Of manners put to school I took small
  note,
And all my deeper passions lay elsewhere.
Far better had it been to exalt the mind
By solitary study, to uphold   305
Intense desire through meditative peace;
And yet, for chastisement of these regrets,
The memory of one particular hour
Doth here rise up against me. 'Mid a throng
Of maids and youths, old men, and ma-
  trons staid,   310
A medley of all tempers, I had passed
The night in dancing, gaiety, and mirth,
With din of instruments and shuffling feet,
And glancing forms, and tapers glittering,
And unaimed prattle flying up and
  down;   315
Spirits upon the stretch, and here and
  there
Slight shocks of young love-liking inter-
  spersed,
Whose transient pleasure mounted to the
  head,
And tingled through the veins. Ere we
  retired,
The cock had crowed, and now the eastern
  sky   320
Was kindling, not unseen, from humble
  copse
And open field, through which the path-
  way wound,
And homeward led my steps. Magnificent
The morning rose, in memorable pomp,
Glorious as e'er I had beheld—in front, 325
The sea lay laughing at a distance; near,
The solid mountains shone, bright as the
  clouds,
Grain-tinctured, drenched in empyrean
  light;
And in the meadows and the lower
  grounds
Was all the sweetness of a common
  dawn—   330

Dews, vapors, and the melody of birds,
And laborers going forth to till the fields.
Ah! need I say, dear friend! that to the
  brim
My heart was full; I made no vows, but
  vows
Were then made for me; bond unknown
  to me   335
Was given, that I should be, else sinning
  greatly,
A dedicated spirit. On I walked
In thankful blessedness, which yet survives.

BOOK FIFTH

BOOKS

When contemplation, like the night-calm
  felt
Through earth and sky, spreads widely,
  and sends deep
Into the soul its tranquillising power,
Even then I sometimes grieve for thee,
  O man,
Earth's paramount creature! not so much
  for woes   5
That thou endurest; heavy though that
  weight be,
Cloud-like it mounts, or touched with light
  divine
Doth melt away; but for those palms
  achieved
Through length of time, by patient exer-
  cise
Of study and hard thought; there, there,
  it is   10
That sadness finds its fuel. Hitherto,
In progress through this verse, my mind
  hath looked
Upon the speaking face of earth and
  heaven
As her prime teacher, intercourse with man
Established by the sovereign intellect,   15
Who through that bodily image hath dif-
  fused,
As might appear to the eye of fleeting time,
A deathless spirit. Thou also, man! hast
  wrought,
For commerce of thy nature with herself,
Things that aspire to unconquerable life; 20
And yet we feel—we cannot choose but
  feel—
That they must perish. Tremblings of the
  heart
It gives, to think that our immortal being
No more shall need such garments; and yet
  man,
As long as he shall be the child of earth, 25
Might almost "weep to have" what he may
  lose,

Nor be himself extinguished, but survive,
Abject, depressed, forlorn, disconsolate.
A thought is with me sometimes, and I
    say,—
Should the whole frame of earth by inward
    throes   30
Be wrenched, or fire come down from far
    to scorch
Her pleasant habitations, and dry up
Old ocean, in his bed left singed and bare,
Yet would the living present still subsist
Victorious, and composure would ensue, 35
And kindlings like the morning—presage
    sure
Of day returning and of life revived.
But all the meditations of mankind,
Yea, all the adamantine holds of truth
By reason built, or passion, which itself 40
Is highest reason in a soul sublime;
The consecrated works of bard and sage,
Sensuous or intellectual, wrought by men,
Twin laborers and heirs of the same hopes;
Where would they be? Oh! why hath not
    the mind   45
Some element to stamp her image on
In nature somewhat nearer to her own?
Why, gifted with such powers to send
    abroad
Her spirit, must it lodge in shrines so frail?
    . . . .
These mighty workmen of our later age,
Who, with a broad highway, have over-
    bridged
The froward chaos of futurity,
Tamed to their bidding; they who have the
    skill   350
To manage books, and things, and make
    them act
On infant minds as surely as the sun
Deals with a flower; the keepers of our
    time,
The guides and wardens of our faculties,
Sages who in their prescience would con-
    trol   355
All accidents, and to the very road
Which they have fashioned would confine
    us down,
Like engines; when will their presumption
    learn,
That in the unreasoning progress of the
    world
A wiser spirit is at work for us,   360
A better eye than theirs, most prodigal
Of blessings, and most studious of our
    good,
Even in what seem our most unfruitful
    hours?

    There was a boy: ye knew him well, ye
    cliffs

And islands of Winander!—many a time 365
At evening, when the earliest stars began
To move along the edges of the hills,
Rising or setting, would he stand alone
Beneath the trees or by the glimmering
    lake,
And there, with fingers interwoven, both
    hands   370
Pressed closely palm to palm, and to his
    mouth
Uplifted, he, as through an instrument,
Blew mimic hootings to the silent owls,
That they might answer him; and they
    would shout
Across the watery vale, and shout again, 375
Responsive to his call, with quivering peals,
And long halloos and screams, and echoes
    loud,
Redoubled and redoubled, concourse wild
Of jocund din; and, when a lengthened
    pause
Of silence came and baffled his best
    skill,   380
Then sometimes, in that silence while he
    hung
Listening, a gentle shock of mild surprise
Has carried far into his heart the voice
Of mountain torrents; or the visible scene
Would enter unawares into his mind,   385
With all its solemn imagery, its rocks,
Its woods, and that uncertain heaven, re-
    ceived
Into the bosom of the steady lake.

    This boy was taken from his mates, and
    died
In childhood, ere he was full twelve years
    old.   390
Fair is the spot, most beautiful the vale
Where he was born; the grassy churchyard
    hangs
Upon a slope above the village school,
And through that churchyard when my
    way has led
On summer evenings, I believe that
    there   395
A long half hour together I have stood
Mute, looking at the grave in which he
    lies!
Even now appears before the mind's clear
    eye
That selfsame village church; I see her sit
(The thronèd lady whom erewhile we
    hailed)   400
On her green hill, forgetful of this boy
Who slumbers at her feet,—forgetful, too,
Of all her silent neighborhood graves,
And listening only to the gladsome sounds
That, from the rural school ascending,
    play   405

Beneath her and about her. May she long
Behold a race of young ones like to those
With whom I herded! (easily, indeed,
We might have fed upon a fatter soil
Of arts and letters—but be that for-
   given)—   410
A race of real children; not too wise,
Too learned, or too good; but wanton,
   fresh,
And bandied up and down by love and
   hate;
Not unresentful where self-justified;
Fierce, moody, patient, venturous, modest,
   shy;   415
Mad at their sports like withered leaves in
   winds;
Though doing wrong and suffering, and
   full oft
Bending beneath our life's mysterious
   weight
Of pain, and doubt, and fear, yet yielding
   not
In happiness to the happiest upon earth. 420
Simplicity in habit, truth in speech,
Be these the daily strengtheners of their
   minds;
May books and nature be their early joy!
And knowledge, rightly honored with that
   name—
Knowledge not purchased by the loss of
   power!   425

. . . .

And when thereafter to my father's
   house
The holidays returned me, there to find
That golden store of books which I had
   left,
What joy was mine! How often in the
   course   480
Of those glad respites, though a soft west
   wind
Ruffled the waters to the angler's wish,
For a whole day together, have I lain
Down by thy side, O Derwent! murmuring
   stream,
On the hot stones, and in the glaring
   sun,   485
And there have read, devouring as I read,
Defrauding the day's glory, desperate!
Till with a sudden bound of smart re-
   proach,
Such as an idler deals with in his shame,
I to the sport betook myself again.   490

A gracious spirit o'er this earth presides,
And o'er the heart of man; invisibly
It comes, to works of unreproved delight,
And tendency benign, directing those
Who care not, know not, think not, what
   they do.   495

The tales that charm away the wakeful
   night
In Araby, romances; legends penned
For solace by dim light of monkish lamps;
Fictions, for ladies of their love, devised
By youthful squires; adventures endless,
   spun   500
By the dismantled warrior in old age,
Out of the bowels of those very schemes
In which his youth did first extravagate;
These spread like day, and something in
   the shape
Of these will live till man shall be no
   more.   505
Dumb yearnings, hidden appetites, are
   ours,
And *they must* have their food. Our child-
   hood sits,
Our simple childhood, sits upon a throne
That hath more power than all the ele-
   ments.
I guess not what this tells of Being past, 510
Nor what it augurs of the life to come;
But so it is; and, in that dubious hour—
That twilight—when we first begin to see
This dawning earth, to recognise, expect,
And, in the long probation that ensues, 515
The time of trial, ere we learn to live
In reconcilement with our stinted powers;
To endure this state of meagre vassalage,
Unwilling to forego, confess, submit,
Uneasy and unsettled, yoke-fellows   520
To custom, mettlesome, and not yet tamed
And humbled down—oh! then we feel, we
   feel,
We know where we have friends. Ye
   dreamers, then,
Forgers of daring tales! we bless you then.
Impostors, drivellers, dotards, as the ape 525
Philosophy will call you: *then* we feel
With what, and how great might ye are in
   league,
Who make our wish, our power, our
   thought a deed,
An empire, a possession—ye whom time
And seasons serve; all faculties to whom 530
Earth crouches, the elements are potter's
   clay,
Space like a heaven filled up with northern
   lights,
Here, nowhere, there, and everywhere at
   once.

BOOK SIXTH

CAMBRIDGE AND THE ALPS

The poet's soul was with me at that
   time;
Sweet meditations, the still overflow
Of present happiness, while future years

Lacked not anticipations, tender dreams, 45
No few of which have since been realized;
And some remain, hopes for my future life.
Four years and thirty, told this very week,
Have I been now a sojourner on earth,
By sorrow not unsmitten; yet for me   50
Life's morning radiance hath not left the
    hills,
Her dew is on the flowers. Those were the
    days
Which also first emboldened me to trust
With firmness, hitherto but slightly touched
By such a daring thought, that I might
    leave   55
Some monument behind me which pure
    hearts
Should reverence. The instinctive humble-
    ness,
Maintained even by the very name and
    thought
Of printed books and authorship, began
To melt away; and further, the dread awe 60
Of mighty names was softened down and
    seemed
Approachable, admitting fellowship
Of modest sympathy. Such aspect now,
Though not familiarly, my mind put on,
Content to observe, to achieve, and to
    enjoy.   65

All winter long, whenever free to choose,
Did I by night frequent the college groves
And tributary walks; the last, and oft
The only one, who had been lingering
    there
Through hours of silence, till the porter's
    bell,   70
A punctual follower on the stroke of nine,
Rang with its blunt unceremonious voice,
Inexorable summons! Lofty elms,
Inviting shades of opportune recess,
Bestowed composure on a neighborhood 75
Unpeaceful in itself. A single tree
With sinuous trunk, boughs exquisitely
    wreathed,
Grew there; an ash which winter for him-
    self
Decked as in pride, and with outlandish
    grace:
Up from the ground, and almost to the
    top,   80
The trunk and every master branch were
    green
With clustering ivy, and the lightsome
    twigs
And outer spray profusely tipped with
    seeds
That hung in yellow tassels, while the air
Stirred them, not voiceless. Often have I
    stood   85

Foot-bound uplooking at this lovely tree
Beneath a frosty moon. The hemisphere
Of magic fiction, verse of mine perchance
May never tread; but scarcely Spenser's self
Could have more tranquil visions in his
    youth,   90
Or could more bright appearances create
Of human forms with superhuman powers,
Than I beheld loitering on calm clear
    nights
Alone, beneath this fairy work of earth.

.   .   .   .

[*With a guide, they reach the summit of
Simplon Pass*]

Still we had hopes that pointed to the
    clouds,
We questioned him again, and yet again;
But every word that from the peasant's lips
Came in reply, translated by our feel-
    ings,   590
Ended in this,—*that we had crossed the
    Alps.*

    Imagination—here the Power so called
Through sad incompetence of human
    speech,
That awful Power rose from the mind's
    abyss
Like an unfathered vapor that enwraps, 595
At once, some lonely traveller. I was lost;
Halted without an effort to break through;
But to my conscious soul I now can say—
"I recognize thy glory": in such strength
Of usurpation, when the light of sense 600
Goes out, but with a flash that has revealed
The invisible world, doth greatness make
    abode,
There harbors; whether we be young or
    old,
Our destiny, our being's heart and home,
Is with infinitude, and only there;   605
With hope it is, hope that can never die,
Effort, and expectation, and desire,
And something evermore about to be.
Under such banners militant, the soul
Seeks for no trophies, struggles for no
    spoils   610
That may attest her prowess, blest in
    thoughts
That are their own perfection and reward,
Strong in herself and in beatitude
That hides her, like the mighty flood of
    Nile
Poured from his fount of Abyssinian
    clouds   615
To fertilize the whole Egyptian plain.

    The melancholy slackening that ensued
Upon those tidings by the peasant given

Was soon dislodged. Downwards we hur-
    ried fast,
And with the half-shaped road which we
    had missed,   620
Entered a narrow chasm. The brook and
    road
Were fellow-travellers in this gloomy strait,
And with them did we journey several
    hours
At a slow pace. The immeasurable height
Of woods decaying, never to be decayed, 625
The stationary blasts of waterfalls,
And in the narrow rent at every turn
Winds thwarting winds, bewildered and
    forlorn,
The torrent shooting from the clear blue
    sky,
The rocks that muttered close upon our
    ears,   630
Black drizzling crags that spake by the
    way-side
As if a voice were in them, the sick sight
And giddy prospect of the raving stream,
The unfettered clouds and region of the
    heavens,
Tumult and peace, the darkness and the
    light—   635
Were all like workings of one mind, the
    features
Of the same face, blossoms upon one tree;
Characters of the great Apocalypse,
The types and symbols of eternity,
Of first, and last, and midst, and without
    end.   640

BOOK SEVENTH

RESIDENCE IN LONDON

How oft, amid those overflowing streets,
Have I gone forward with the crowd, and
    said
Unto myself, "The face of every one
That passes by me is a mystery!"
Thus have I looked, nor ceased to look,
    oppressed   630
By thoughts of what and whither, when
    and how,
Until the shapes before my eyes became
A second-sight procession, such as glides
Over still mountains, or appears in dreams;
And once, far-travelled in such mood, be-
    yond   635
The reach of common indication, lost
Amid the moving pageant, I was smitten
Abruptly, with the view (a sight not rare)
Of a blind beggar, who, with upright face,
Stood, propped against a wall, upon his
    chest   640
Wearing a written paper, to explain

His story, whence he came, and who he
    was.
Caught by the spectacle my mind turned
    round
As with the might of waters; an apt type
This label seemed of the utmost we can
    know,   645
Both of ourselves and of the universe;
And, on the shape of that unmoving man,
His steadfast face and sightless eyes, I
    gazed,
As if admonished from another world.

. . . .

                        From these sights   675
Take one,—that ancient festival, the Fair,
Holden where martyrs suffered in past
    time,
And named of St. Bartholomew; there, see
A work completed to our hands, that lays,
If any spectacle on earth can do,   680
The whole creative powers of man
    asleep!—
For once, the Muse's help will we implore,
And she shall lodge us, wafted on her
    wings,
Above the press and danger of the crowd,
Upon some showman's platform. What a
    shock   685
For eyes and ears! what anarchy and din,
Barbarian and infernal,—a phantasma,
Monstrous in color, motion, shape, sight,
    sound!
Below, the open space, through every nook
Of the wide area, twinkles, is alive   690
With heads; the midway region, and above,
Is thronged with staring pictures and huge
    scrolls,
Dumb proclamations of the Prodigies;
With chattering monkeys dangling from
    their poles,
And children whirling in their round-
    abouts;   695
With those that stretch the neck and strain
    the eyes,
And crack the voice in rivalship, the crowd
Inviting; with buffoons against buffoons
Grimacing, writhing, screaming,—him who
    grinds
The hurdy-gurdy, at the fiddle weaves,   700
Rattles the salt-box, thumps the kettle-
    drum,
And him who at the trumpet puffs his
    cheeks,
The silver-collared Negro with his timbrel,
Equestrians, tumblers, women, girls, and
    boys,
Blue-breeched, pink-vested, with high-
    towering plumes.—   705
All moveables of wonder, from all parts,

Are here— Albinos, painted Indians,
    Dwarfs,
The Horse of knowledge, and the learned
    Pig,
The Stone-eater, the man that swallows fire,
Giants, Ventriloquists, the Invisible Girl, 710
The Bust that speaks and moves its gog-
    gling eyes,
The Wax-work, Clock-work, all the marvel-
    lous craft
Of modern Merlins, Wild Beasts, Puppet-
    shows,
All out-o'-the-way, far-fetched, perverted
    things,
All freaks of nature, all Promethean
    thoughts   715
Of man, his dulness, madness, and their
    feats
All jumbled up together, to compose
A Parliament of Monsters. Tents and
    booths
Meanwhile, as if the whole were one vast
    mill,
Are vomiting, receiving on all sides,   720
Men, women, three-years' children, babes
    in arms.

Oh, blank confusion! true epitome
Of what the mighty city is herself,
To thousands upon thousands of her sons,
Living amid the same perpetual whirl 725
Of trivial objects, melted and reduced
To one identity, by differences
That have no law, no meaning, and no
    end—
Oppression, under which even highest
    minds
Must labor, whence the strongest are not
    free.   730
But though the picture weary out the eye,
By nature an unmanageable sight,
It is not wholly so to him who looks
In steadiness, who hath among least things
An under-sense of greatest; see the parts 735
As parts, but with a feeling of the whole.
This, of all acquisitions, first awaits
On sundry and most widely different modes
Of education, nor with least delight
On that through which I passed. Atten-
    tion springs,   740
And comprehensiveness and memory flow,
From early converse with the works of God
Among all regions; chiefly where appear
Most obviously simplicity and power.
Think, how the everlasting streams and
    woods,   745
Stretched and still stretching far and wide,
    exalt
The roving Indian, on his desert sands:

What grandeur not unfelt, what pregnant
    show
Of beauty, meets the sun-burnt Arab's eye:
And, as the sea propels, from zone to
    zone,   750
Its currents; magnifies its shoals of life
Beyond all compass; spreads, and sends
    aloft
Armies of clouds,—even so, its powers and
    aspects
Shape for mankind, by principles as fixed,
The views and aspirations of the soul 755
To majesty. Like virtue have the forms
Perennial of the ancient hills; nor less
The changeful language of their counte-
    nances
Quickens the slumbering mind, and aids
    the thoughts,
However multitudinous, to move   760
With order and relation. This, if still,
As hitherto, in freedom I may speak,
Not violating any just restraint,
As may be hoped, of real modesty,—
This did I feel, in London's vast do-
    main.   765
The spirit of Nature was upon me there;
The soul of beauty and enduring life
Vouchsafed her inspiration, and diffused,
Through meagre lines and colors, and the
    press
Of self-destroying, transitory things,   770
Composure, and ennobling harmony.

BOOK EIGHTH

RETROSPECT—LOVE OF NATURE LEADING TO
            LOVE OF MAN

What sounds are those, Helvellvn, that are
    heard
Up to thy summit, through the depth of
    air
Ascending, as if distance had the power
To make the sounds more audible? What
    crowd
Covers, or sprinkles o'er, yon village
    green?   5
Crowd seems it, solitary hill! to thee,
Though but a little family of men,
Shepherds and tillers of the ground—be-
    times
Assembled with their children and their
    wives,
And here and there a stranger inter-
    spersed.   10
They hold a rustic fair—a festival,
Such as, on this side now, and now on that,
Repeated through his tributary vales,
Helvellyn, in the silence of his rest,
Sees annually, if clouds towards either
    ocean   15

Blown from their favorite resting place, or
    mists
Dissolved, have left him an unshrouded
    head.
Delightful day it is for all who dwell
In this secluded glen, and eagerly
They give it welcome. Long ere heat of
    noon,   20
From byre or field the kine were brought;
    the sheep
Are penned in cotes; the chaffering is
    begun.
The heifer lows, uneasy at the voice
Of a new master; bleat the flocks aloud.
Booths are there none; a stall or two is
    here;   25
A lame man or a blind, the one to beg,
The other to make music; hither, too,
From far, with basket, slung upon her arm,
Of hawker's wares—books, pictures, combs,
    and pins—
Some aged woman finds her way again,   30
Year after year, a punctual visitant!
There also stands a speech-maker by rote,
Pulling the strings of his boxed raree-show;
And in the lapse of many years may come
Prouder itinerant, mountebank, or he   35
Whose wonders in a covered wain lie hid.
But one there is, the loveliest of them all,
Some sweet lass of the valley, looking out
For gains, and who that sees her would
    not buy?
Fruits of her father's orchard are her
    wares,   40
And with the ruddy produce she walks
    round
Among the crowd, half pleased with, half
    ashamed
Of her new office, blushing restlessly.
The children now are rich, for the old
    today
Are generous as the young; and, if con-
    tent   45
With looking on, some ancient wedded pair
Sit in the shade together, while they gaze,
"A cheerful smile unbends the wrinkled
    brow,
The days departed start again to life,
And all the scenes of childhood reappear,   50
Faint, but more tranquil, like the changing
    sun
To him who slept at noon and wakes at
    eve."
Thus gaiety and cheerfulness prevail,
Spreading from young to old, from old to
    young,
And no one seems to want his share.—
    Immense   55
Is the recess, the circumambient world
Magnificent, by which they are embraced:

They move about upon the soft green turf:
How little they, they and their doings,
    seem,
And all that they can further or ob-
    struct!   60
Through utter weakness pitiably dear,
As tender infants are: and yet how great!
For all things serve them; them the morn-
    ing light
Loves, as it glistens on the silent rocks;
And them the silent rocks, which now from
    high   65
Look down upon them; the reposing
    clouds;
The wild brooks prattling from invisible
    haunts;
And old Helvellyn, conscious of the stir
Which animates this day their calm abode.

With deep devotion, Nature, did I feel,   70
In that enormous city's turbulent world
Of men and things, what benefit I owed
To thee, and those domains of rural peace,
Where to the sense of beauty first my heart
Was opened; tract more exquisitely fair   75
Than that famed paradise of ten thousand
    trees,
Or Gehol's matchless gardens, for delight
Of the Tartarian dynasty composed
(Beyond that mighty wall, not fabulous,
China's stupendous mound) by patient
    toil   80
Of myriads and boon Nature's lavish help;
There, in a clime from widest empire
    chosen,
Fulfilling (could enchantment have done
    more?)
A sumptuous dream of flowery lawns, with
    domes
Of pleasure sprinkled over, shady dells   85
For eastern monasteries, sunny mounts
With temples crested, bridges, gondolas,
Rocks, dens, and groves of foliage taught
    to melt
Into each other their obsequious hues,
Vanished and vanishing in subtle chase,   90
Too fine to be pursued; or standing forth
In no discordant opposition, strong
And gorgeous as the colors side by side
Bedded among rich plumes of tropic birds;
And mountains over all, embracing all;   95
And all the landscape, endlessly enriched
With waters running, falling, or asleep.

But lovelier far than this, the paradise
Where I was reared; in Nature's primitive
    gifts
Favored no less, and more to every sense   100
Delicious, seeing that the sun and sky,
The elements, and seasons as they change,

Do find a worthy fellow-laborer there—
Man free, man working for himself, with
    choice
Of time, and place, and object; by his
    wants,   105
His comforts, native occupations, cares,
Cheerfully led to individual ends
Or social, and still followed by a train
Unwooed, unthought-of even—simplicity,
And beauty, and inevitable grace.   110

Yea, when a glimpse of those imperial
    bowers
Would to a child be transport over-great,
When but a half-hour's roam through such
    a place
Would leave behind a dance of images,
That shall break in upon his sleep for
    weeks;   115
Even then the common haunts of the green
    earth,
And ordinary interests of man,
Which they embosom, all without regard
As both may seem, are fastening on the
    heart
Insensibly, each with the other's help.   120
For me, when my affections first were led
From kindred, friends, and playmates, to
    partake
Love for the human creature's absolute
    self,
That noticeable kindliness of heart
Sprang out of fountains, there abounding
    most,   125
Where sovereign Nature dictated the tasks
And occupations which her beauty
    adorned,
And shepherds were the men that pleased
    me first;
Not such as Saturn ruled 'mid Latian wilds,
With arts and laws so tempered, that their
    lives   130
Left, even to us toiling in this late day,
A bright tradition of the golden age;
Not such as, 'mid Arcadian fastnesses
Sequestered, handed down among them-
    selves
Felicity, in Grecian song renowned;   135
Nor such as—when an adverse fate had
    driven,
From house and home, the courtly band
    whose fortunes
Entered, with Shakspeare's genius, the wild
    woods
Of Arden—amid sunshine or in shade
Culled the best fruits of Time's uncounted
    hours,   140
Ere Phœbe sighed for the false Ganymede;
Or there where Perdita and Florizel

Together danced, Queen of the feast, and
    King;
Nor such as Spenser fabled. True it is,
That I had heard (what he perhaps had
    seen)   145
Of maids at sunrise bringing in from far
Their May-bush, and along the street in
    flocks
Parading with a song of taunting rhymes,
Aimed at the laggards slumbering within
    doors;
Had also heard, from those who yet remem-
    bered,   150
Tales of the Maypole dance, and wreaths
    that decked
Porch, doorway, or kirk pillar; and of
    youths,
Each with his maid, before the sun was up,
By annual custom, issuing forth in troops,
To drink the waters of some sainted
    well,   155
And hang it round with garlands. Love
    survives;
But, for such purpose, flowers no longer
    grow:
The times, too sage, perhaps too proud,
    have dropped
These lighter graces; and the rural ways
And manners which my childhood looked
    upon   160
Were the unluxuriant produce of a life
Intent on little but substantial needs,
Yet rich in beauty, beauty that was felt.
But images of danger and distress,
Man suffering among awful Powers and
    Forms;   165
Of this I heard, and saw enough to make
Imagination restless; nor was free
Myself from frequent perils; nor were tales
Wanting,—the tragedies of former times,
Hazards and strange escapes, of which the
    rocks   170
Immutable, and everflowing streams,
Where'er I roamed, were speaking monu-
    ments.

Smooth life had flock and shepherd in
    old time,
Long springs and tepid winters, on the
    banks
Of delicate Galesus; and no less   175
Those scattered along Adria's myrtle
    shores:
Smooth life had herdsman, and his snow-
    white herd
To triumphs and to sacrificial rites
Devoted, on the inviolable stream
Of rich Clitumnus; and the goat-herd
    lived   180
As calmly, underneath the pleasant brows

Of cool Lucretilis, where the pipe was
   heard
Of Pan, invisible god, thrilling the rocks
With tutelary music, from all harm
The fold protecting. I myself, mature 185
In manhood then, have seen a pastoral
   tract
Like one of these, where Fancy might run
   wild,
Though under skies less generous, less
   serene:
There, for her own delight had Nature
   framed
A pleasure-ground, diffused a fair ex-
   panse   190
Of level pasture, islanded with groves
And banked with woody risings; but the
   plain
Endless, here opening widely out, and there
Shut up in lesser lakes or beds of lawn
And intricate recesses, creek or bay 195
Sheltered within a shelter, where at large
The shepherd strays, a rolling hut his
   home.
Thither he comes with springtime, there
   abides
All summer, and at sunrise ye may hear
His flageolet to liquid notes of love 200
Attuned, or sprightly fife resounding far.
Nook is there none, nor tract of that vast
   space
Where passage opens, but the same shall
   have
In turn its visitant, telling there his hours
In unlaborious pleasure, with no task 205
More toilsome than to carve a beechen
   bowl
For spring or fountain, which the traveller
   finds,
When through the region he pursues at will
His devious course. A glimpse of such
   sweet life
I saw when, from the melancholy walls 210
Of Goslar, once imperial, I renewed
My daily walk along that wide champaign,
That, reaching to her gates, spreads east
   and west,
And northwards, from beneath the moun-
   tainous verge
Of the Hercynian forest. Yet, hail to
   you   215
Moors, mountains, headlands, and ye hol-
   low vales,
Ye long deep channels for the Atlantic's
   voice,
Powers of my native region! Ye that seize
The heart with firmer grasp! Your snows
   and streams
Ungovernable, and your terrifying
   winds,   220

That howl so dismally for him who treads
Companionless your awful solitudes!
There, 'tis the shepherd's task the winter
   long
To wait upon the storms: of their approach
Sagacious, into sheltering coves he
   drives   225
His flock, and thither from the homestead
   bears
A toilsome burden up the craggy ways,
And deals it out, their regular nourishment
Strewn on the frozen snow. And when the
   spring
Looks out, and all the pastures dance with
   lambs,   230
And when the flock, with warmer weather,
   climbs
Higher and higher, him his office leads
To watch their goings, whatsoever track
The wanderers choose. For this he quits
   his home
At day-spring, and no sooner doth the
   sun   235
Begin to strike him with a fire-like heat,
Than he lies down upon some shining rock,
And breakfasts with his dog. When they
   have stolen,
As is their wont, a pittance from strict
   time,
For rest not needed or exchange of love, 240
Then from his couch he starts; and now
   his feet
Crush out a livelier fragrance from the
   flowers
Of lowly thyme, by Nature's skill en-
   wrought
In the wild turf: the lingering dews of
   morn
Smoke round him, as from hill to hill he
   hies,   245
His staff protending like a hunter's spear,
Or by its aid leaping from crag to crag,
And o'er the brawling beds of unbridged
   streams.
Philosophy, methinks, at Fancy's call,
Might deign to follow him through what
   he does   250
Or sees in his day's march; himself he feels,
In those vast regions where his service lies,
A freeman, wedded to his life of hope
And hazard, and hard labor interchanged
With that majestic indolence so dear 255
To native man. A rambling schoolboy,
   thus,
I felt his presence in his own domain,
As of a lord and master, or a power,
Or genius, under Nature, under God,
Presiding; and severest solitude 260
Had more commanding looks when he was
   there.

When up the lonely brooks on rainy days
Angling I went, or trod the trackless hills
By mists bewildered, suddenly mine eyes
Have glanced upon him distant a few
   steps, 265
In size a giant, stalking through thick fog,
His sheep like Greenland bears; or, as he
   stepped
Beyond the boundary line of some hill-
   shadow,
His form hath flashed upon me, glorified
By the deep radiance of the setting sun: 270
Or him have I descried in distant sky,
A solitary object and sublime,
Above all height! like an aerial cross
Stationed alone upon a spiry rock
Of the Chartreuse, for worship. Thus was
   man 275
Ennobled outwardly before my sight,
And thus my heart was early introduced
To an unconscious love and reverence
Of human nature; hence the human form
To me became an index of delight, 280
Of grace and honor, power and worthiness.
Meanwhile this creature—spiritual almost
As those of books, but more exalted far;
Far more of an imaginative form
Than the gay Corin of the groves, who
   lives 285
For his own fancies, or to dance by the
   hour,
In coronal, with Phyllis in the midst—
Was, for the purposes of kind, a man
With the most common; husband, father;
   learned,
Could teach, admonish; suffered with the
   rest 290
From vice and folly, wretchedness and fear;
Of this I little saw, cared less for it,
But something must have felt.
             Call ye these appearances—
Which I beheld of shepherds in my youth,
This sanctity of Nature given to man— 295
A shadow, a delusion, ye who pore
On the dead letter, miss the spirit of things;
Whose truth is not a motion or a shape
Instinct with vital functions, but a block
Or waxen image which yourselves have
   made 300
And ye adore! But blessèd be the God
Of Nature and of Man that this was so;
That men before my inexperienced eyes
Did first present themselves thus purified,
Removed, and to a distance that was fit: 305
And so we all of us in some degree
Are led to knowledge, wheresoever led,
And howsoever; were it otherwise,
And we found evil fast as we find good
In our first years, or think that it is
   found. 310

How could the innocent heart bear up and
   live!
But doubly fortunate my lot; not here
Alone, that something of a better life
Perhaps was round me than it is the
   privilege
Of most to move in, but that first I
   looked 315
At Man through objects that were great or
   fair;
First communed with him by their help.
   And thus
Was founded a sure safeguard and defence
Against the weight of meanness, selfish
   cares,
Coarse manners, vulgar passions, that beat
   in 320
On all sides from the ordinary world
In which we traffic. Starting from this
   point
I had my face turned toward the truth,
   began
With an advantage furnished by that kind
Of prepossession, without which the
   soul 325
Receives no knowledge that can bring forth
   good,
No genuine insight ever comes to her.
From the restraint of over-watchful eyes
Preserved, I moved about, year after year,
Happy, and now most thankful that my
   walk 330
Was guarded from too early intercourse
With the deformities of crowded life,
And those ensuing laughters and con-
   tempts,
Self-pleasing, which, if we would wish to
   think
With a due reverence on earth's rightful
   lord, 335
Here placed to be the inheritor of heaven,
Will not permit us; but pursue the mind,
That to devotion willingly would rise,
Into the temple and the temple's heart.
   Yet deem not, friend! that human kind
   with me 340
Thus early took a place pre-eminent;
Nature herself was, at this unripe time,
But secondary to my own pursuits
And animal activities, and all
Their trivial pleasures; and when these had
   drooped 345
And gradually expired, and Nature, prized
For her own sake, became my joy, even
   then—
And upwards through late youth, until not
   less
Than two-and-twenty summers had been
   told—
Was Man in my affections and regards 350

Subordinate to her, her visible forms
And viewless agencies: a passion, she,
A rapture often, and immediate love
Ever at hand; he, only a delight
Occasional, an accidental grace,   355
His hour being not yet come. Far less had
  then
The inferior creatures, beast or bird,
  attuned
My spirit to that gentleness of love
(Though they had long been carefully
  observed),
Won from me those minute obeisances 360
Of tenderness, which I may number now
With my first blessings. Nevertheless, on
  these
The light of beauty did not fall in vain,
Or grandeur circumfuse them to no end.
  But when that first poetic faculty   365
Of plain Imagination and severe,
No longer a mute influence of the soul,
Ventured, at some rash muse's earnest call,
To try her strength among harmonious
  words;
And to book-notions and the rules of art 370
Did knowingly conform itself; there came
Among the simple shapes of human life
A wilfulness of fancy and conceit:
And Nature and her objects beautified
These fictions, as in some sort, in their
  turn,   375
They burnished her. From touch of this
  new power
Nothing was safe: the elder tree that grew
Beside the well-known charnel house had
  then
A dismal look; the yew tree had its ghost,
That took his station there for orna-
  ment: 380
The dignities of plain occurrence then
Were tasteless, and truth's golden mean, a
  point
Where no sufficient pleasure could be
  found.
Then, if a widow, staggering with the blow
Of her distress, was known to have turned
  her steps   385
To the cold grave in which her husband
  slept,
One night, or haply more than one,
  through pain
Or half-insensate impotence of mind,
The fact was caught at greedily, and there
She must be visitant the whole year
  through,   390
Wetting the turf with never-ending tears.
  Through quaint obliquities I might pur-
  sue
These cravings; when the foxglove, one by
  one,

Upwards through every stage of the tall
  stem,
Had shed beside the public way its bells, 395
And stood of all dismantled, save the last
Left at the tapering ladder's top, that
  seemed
To bend as doth a slender blade of grass
Tipped with a raindrop, Fancy loved to
  seat,
Beneath the plant despoiled, but crested
  still   400
With this last relic, soon itself to fall,
Some vagrant mother, whose arch little
  ones,
All unconcerned by her dejected plight,
Laughed as with rival eagerness their hands
Gathered the purple cups that round them
  lay,   405
Strewing the turf's green slope.
                      A diamond light
(Whene'er the summer sun, declining,
  smote
A smooth rock wet with constant springs)
  was seen
Sparkling from out a copse-clad bank that
  rose
Fronting our cottage. Oft beside the
  hearth   410
Seated, with open door, often and long
Upon this restless lustre have I gazed,
That made my fancy restless as itself.
'Twas now for me a burnished silver shield
Suspended over a knight's tomb, who
  lay   415
Inglorious, buried in the dusky wood:
An entrance now into some magic cave
Or palace built by fairies of the rock;
Nor could I have been bribed to disenchant
The spectacle by visiting the spot.   420
Thus wilful Fancy, in no hurtful mood,
Engrafted far-fetched shapes on feelings
  bred
By pure Imagination: busy power
She was, and with her ready pupil turned
Instinctively to human passions, then   425
Least understood. Yet, 'mid the fervent
  swarm
Of these vagaries, with an eye so rich
As mine was through the bounty of a
  grand
And lovely region, I had forms distinct
To steady me: each airy thought re-
  volved   430
Round a substantial center, which at once
Incited it to motion, and controlled.
I did not pine like one in cities bred,
As was thy melancholy lot, dear friend!
Great spirit as thou art, in endless
  dreams   435
Of sickliness, disjoining, joining, things

Without the light of knowledge. Where
    the harm,
If, when the woodman languished with dis-
    ease
Induced by sleeping nightly on the ground
Within his sod-built cabin, Indian-wise, 440
I called the pangs of disappointed love,
And all the sad etcetera of the wrong,
To help him to his grave? Meanwhile the
    man,
If not already from the woods retired
To die at home, was haply as I knew, 445
Withering by slow degrees, 'mid gentle airs,
Birds, running streams, and hills so beau-
    tiful
On golden evenings, while the charcoal pile
Breathed up its smoke, an image of his
    ghost
Or spirit that full soon must take her
    flight. 450
Nor shall we not be tending towards that
    point
Of sound humanity to which our tale
Leads, though by sinuous ways, if here I
    show
How Fancy, in a season when she wove
Those slender cords, to guide the uncon-
    scious boy 455
For the man's sake, could feel at Nature's
    call
Some pensive musings which might well
    beseem
Maturer years.
             A grove there is whose boughs
Stretch from the western marge of Thurs-
    ton-mere,
With length of shade so thick, that whoso
    glides 460
Along the line of low-roofed water, moves
As in a cloister. Once—while, in that shade
Loitering, I watched the golden beams of
    light
Flung from the setting sun, as they reposed
In silent beauty on the naked ridge 465
Of a high eastern hill—thus flowed my
    thoughts
In a pure stream of words fresh from the
    heart:
Dear native regions, whereso'er shall close
My mortal course, there will I think on you
Dying, will cast on you a backward
    look; 470
Even as this setting sun (albeit the vale
Is nowhere touched by one memorial
    gleam)
Doth with the fond remains of his last
    power
Still linger, and a farewell lustre sheds
On the dear mountain-tops where first he
    rose. 475

Enough of humble arguments; recall,
My song! those high emotions which thy
    voice
Has heretofore made known; that bursting
    forth
Of sympathy, inspiring and inspired,
When everywhere a vital pulse was felt, 480
And all the several frames of things, like
    stars,
Through every magnitude distinguishable,
Shone mutually indebted, or half lost
Each in the other's blaze, a galaxy
Of life and glory. In the midst stood
    Man, 485
Outwardly, inwardly contemplated,
As, of all visible natures, crown, though
    born
Of dust, and kindred to the worm; a Being,
Both in perception and discernment, first
In every capability of rapture, 490
Through the divine effect of power and
    love;
As, more than anything we know, instinct
With godhead, and, by reason and by will,
Acknowledging dependency sublime.

Ere long, the lonely mountains left, I
    moved, 495
Begirt, from day to day, with temporal
    shapes
Of vice and folly thrust upon my view,
Objects of sport, and ridicule, and scorn,
Manners and characters discriminate,
And little bustling passions that eclipse, 500
As well they might, the impersonated
    thought,
The idea, or abstraction of the kind.

An idler among academic bowers,
Such was my new condition, as at large
Has been set forth; yet here the vulgar
    light 505
Of present, actual, superficial life,
Gleaming, through coloring of other times
Old usages and local privilege,
Was welcome, softened, if not solemnized,
This notwithstanding, being brought more
    near 510
To vice and guilt, forerunning wretched-
    ness,
I trembled,—thought, at times, of human
    life
With an indefinite terror and dismay,
Such as the storms and angry elements
Had bred in me; but gloomier far, a
    dim 515
Analogy to uproar and misrule,
Disquiet, danger, and obscurity.

It might be told (but wherefore speak of
    things
Common to all?) that, seeing I was led
Gravely to ponder—judging between
    good   520
And evil, not as for the mind's delight
But for her guidance—one who was to act,
As sometimes to the best of feeble means
I did, by human sympathy impelled;
And, through dislike and most offensive
    pain,   525
Was to the truth conducted; of this faith
Never forsaken, that, by acting well,
And understanding, I should learn to love
The end of life, and everything we know.

Grave teacher, stern preceptress! for at
    times   530
Thou canst put on an aspect most severe;
London, to thee I willingly return.
Erewhile my verse played idly with the
    flowers
Enwrought upon thy mantle; satisfied
With that amusement, and a simple
    look   535
Of child-like inquisition now and then
Cast upwards on thy countenance, to detect
Some inner meanings which might harbor
    there.
But how could I in mood so light indulge,
Keeping such fresh remembrance of the
    day,   540
When, having thridded the long labyrinth
Of the suburban villages, I first
Entered thy vast dominion? On the roof
Of an itinerant vehicle I sate,
With vulgar men about me, trivial
    forms   545
Of houses, pavement, streets, of men and
    things,—
Mean shapes on every side: but, at the
    instant,
When to myself it fairly might be said,
The threshold now is overpast, (how
    strange
That aught external to the living mind 550
Should have such mighty sway! yet so it
    was),
A weight of ages did at once descend
Upon my heart; no thought embodied, no
Distinct remembrances, but weight and
    power,—
Power growing under weight: alas! I
    feel   555
That I am trifling: 'twas a moment's
    pause,—
All that took place within me came and
    went
As in a moment; yet with Time it dwells,
And grateful memory, as a thing divine.

The curious traveller, who, from open
    day,   560
Hath passed with torches into some huge
    cave,
The grotto of Antiparos, or the den
In old time haunted by that Danish witch,
Yordas; he looks around and sees the vault
Widening on all sides; sees, or thinks he
    sees,   565
Erelong, the massy roof above his head,
That instantly unsettles and recedes,—
Substance and shadow, light and darkness,
    all
Commingled, making up a canopy
Of shapes and forms and tendencies to
    shape   570
That shift and vanish, change and inter-
    change
Like spectres,—ferment silent and sublime!
That after a short space works less and less,
Till, every effort, every motion gone,
The scene before him stands in perfect
    view   575
Exposed, and lifeless as a written book!—
But let him pause awhile, and look again,
And a new quickening shall succeed, at
    first
Beginning timidly, then creeping fast,
Till the whole cave, so late a senseless
    mass,   580
Busies the eye with images and forms
Boldly assembled,—here is shadowed forth
From the projections, wrinkles, cavities,
A variegated landscape,—there the shape
Of some gigantic warrior clad in mail, 585
The ghostly semblance of a hooded monk,
Veiled nun, or pilgrim resting on his staff:
Strange congregation! yet not slow to meet
Eyes that perceive through minds that can
    inspire.

Even in such sort had I at first been
    moved,   590
Nor otherwise continued to be moved,
As I explored the vast metropolis,
Fount of my country's destiny and the
    world's;
That great emporium, chronicle at once
And burial-place of passions, and their
    home   595
Imperial, their chief living residence.

With strong sensations teeming as it did
Of past and present, such a place must
    needs
Have pleased me, seeking knowledge at
    that time
Far less than craving power; yet knowledge
    came,   600
Sought or unsought, and influxes of power

Came, of themselves, or at her call derived
In fits of kindliest apprehensiveness,
From all sides, when whate'er was in itself
Capacious found, or seemed to find, in
   me   605
A correspondent amplitude of mind;
Such is the strength and glory of our youth!
The human nature unto which I felt
That I belonged, and reverenced with love,
Was not a punctual presence, but a
   spirit   610
Diffused through time and space, with aid
   derived
Of evidence from monuments, erect,
Prostrate, or leaning towards their common
   rest
In earth, the widely scattered wreck
   sublime
Of vanished nations, or more clearly
   drawn   615
From books and what they picture and
   record.

'Tis true, the history of our native land,
With those of Greece compared and popu-
   lar Rome,
And in our high-wrought modern narra-
   tives
Stript of their harmonizing soul, the life 620
Of manners and familiar incidents,
Had never much delighted me. And less
Than other intellects had mine been used
To lean upon extrinsic circumstance
Of record or tradition; but a sense   625
Of what in the great city had been done
And suffered, and was doing, suffering, still,
Weighed with me, could support the test
   of thought;
And, in despite of all that had gone by,
Or was departing never to return,   630
There I conversed with majesty and power
Like independent natures. Hence the place
Was thronged with impregnations like the
   wilds
In which my early feelings had been
   nursed—
Bare hills and valleys, full of caverns,
   rocks,   635
And audible seclusions, dashing lakes,
Echoes and waterfalls, and pointed crags
That into music touch the passing wind.
Here then my young imagination found
No uncongenial element; could here   640
Among new objects serve or give command,
Even as the heart's occasions might require,
To forward reason's else too scrupulous
   march.
The effect was, still more elevated views
Of human nature. Neither vice nor
   guilt,   645

Debasement undergone by body or mind,
Nor all the misery forced upon my sight,
Misery not lightly passed, but sometimes
   scanned
Most feelingly, could overthrow my trust
In what we may become; induce belief 650
That I was ignorant, had been falsely
   taught,
A solitary, who with vain conceits
Had been inspired, and walked about in
   dreams.
From those sad scenes when meditation
   turned,
Lo! everything that was indeed divine 655
Retained its purity inviolate,
Nay brighter shone, by this portentous
   gloom
Set off; such opposition as aroused
The mind of Adam, yet in Paradise
Though fallen from bliss, when in the east
   he saw   660
Darkness ere day's mid course, and morn-
   ing light
More orient in the western cloud, that
   drew
O'er the blue firmament a radiant white,
Descending slow with something heavenly
   fraught.

Add also, that among the multitudes 665
Of that huge city, oftentimes was seen
Affectingly set forth, more than elsewhere
Is possible, the unity of man,
One spirit over ignorance and vice
Predominant in good and evil hearts;   670
One sense for moral judgments, as one
   eye
For the sun's light. The soul when smitten
   thus
By a sublime *idea*, whencesoe'er
Vouchsafed for union or communion, feeds
On the pure bliss, and takes her rest with
   God.   675

Thus from a very early age, O friend!
My thoughts by slow gradations had been
   drawn
To human-kind, and to the good and ill
Of human life: Nature had led me on;
And oft amid the "busy hum" I seemed 680
To travel independent of her help,
As if I had forgotten her; but no,
The world of human-kind outweighed not
   hers
In my habitual thoughts; the scale of love,
Though filling daily, still was light, com-
   pared   685
With that in which *her* mighty objects lay.

BOOK NINTH

RESIDENCE IN FRANCE

Hatred of absolute rule, where will of one
Is law for all, and of that barren pride
In them who, by immunities unjust,
Between the sovereign and the people
    stand,   505
His helper and not theirs, laid stronger
    hold
Daily upon me, mixed with pity too
And love; for where hope is, there love
    will be
For the abject multitude. And when we
    chanced
One day to meet a hunger-bitten girl,   510
Who crept along, fitting her languid gait
Unto a heifer's motion, by a cord
Tied to her arm, and picking thus from
    the lane
Its sustenance, while the girl with pallid
    hands
Was busy knitting in a heartless mood 515
Of solitude, and at the sight my friend
In agitation said, " 'Tis against *that*
That we are fighting," I with him believed
That a benignant spirit was abroad
Which might not be withstood, that pov-
    erty   520
Abject as this would in a little time
Be found no more, that we should see the
    earth
Unthwarted in her wish to recompense
The meek, the lowly, patient child of toil,
All institutes forever blotted out   525
That legalized exclusion, empty pomp
Abolished, sensual state and cruel power,
Whether by edict of the one or few;
And finally, as sum and crown of all,
Should see the people having a strong
    hand   530
In framing their own laws; whence better
    days
To all mankind.

BOOK ELEVENTH

RESIDENCE IN FRANCE (CONCLUDED)

              It hath been told 75
That I was led to take an eager part
In arguments of civil polity,
Abruptly, and indeed before my time:
I had approached, like other youths, the
    shield
Of human nature from the golden side, 80
And would have fought, even to the death,
    to attest
The quality of the metal which I saw.
What there is best in individual man,
Of wise in passion, and sublime in power,
Benevolent in small societies,   85
And great in large ones, I had oft revolved,
Felt deeply, but not thoroughly understood
By reason: nay, far from it; they were yet,
As cause was given me afterwards to learn,
Not proof against the injuries of the day; 90
Lodged only at the sanctuary's door,
Not safe within its bosom. Thus prepared,
And with such general insight into evil,
And of the bounds which sever it from
    good,
As books and common intercourse with
    life   95
Must needs have given—to the inexperi-
    enced mind,
When the world travels in a beaten road,
Guide faithful as is needed—I began
To meditate with ardor on the rule
And management of nations; what it is 100
And ought to be; and strove to learn how
    far
Their power or weakness, wealth or
    poverty,
Their happiness or misery, depends
Upon their laws, and fashion of the State.

    O pleasant exercise of hope and joy! 105
For mighty were the auxiliars which then
    stood
Upon our side, us who were strong in love!
Bliss was it in that dawn to be alive,
But to be young was very Heaven! O
    times,
In which the meagre, stale, forbidding
    ways   110
Of custom, law, and statute, took at once
The attraction of a country in romance!
When Reason seemed the most to assert
    her rights
When most intent on making of herself
A prime enchantress—to assist the work, 115
Which then was going forward in her
    name!
Not favored spots alone, but the whole
    Earth,
The beauty wore of promise—that which
    sets
(As at some moments might not be unfelt
Among the bowers of Paradise itself) 120
The budding rose above the rose full
    blown.
What temper at the prospect did not wake
To happiness unthought of? The inert
Were roused, and lively natures rapt away!
They who had fed their childhood upon
    dreams,   125
The play-fellows of fancy, who had made
All powers of swiftness, subtilty, and
    strength

Their ministers,—who in lordly wise had
  stirred
Among the grandest objects of the sense,
And dealt with whatsoever they found
  there   130
As if they had within some lurking right
To wield it;—they, too, who of gentle
  mood
Had watched all gentle motions, and to
  these
Had fitted their own thoughts, schemers
  more mild,
And in the region of their peaceful
  selves;—   135
Now was it that *both* found, the meek and
  lofty
Did both find, helpers to their heart's
  desire,
And stuff at hand, plastic as they could
  wish,—
Were called upon to exercise their skill,
Not in Utopia,—subterranean fields,—   140
Or some secreted island, Heaven knows
  where!
But in the very world, which is the world
Of all of us,—the place where, in the end,
We find our happiness, or not at all!

Why should I not confess that Earth was
  then   145
To me, what an inheritance, new-fallen,
Seems, when the first time visited, to one
Who thither comes to find in it his home?
He walks about and looks upon the spot
With cordial transport, molds it and re-
  molds,   150
And is half-pleased with things that are
  amiss,
'Twill be such joy to see them disappear.

An active partisan, I thus convoked
From every object pleasant circumstance
To suit my ends; I moved among man-
  kind   155
With genial feelings still predominant;
When erring, erring on the better part,
And in the kinder spirit; placable,
Indulgent, as not uninformed that men
See as they have been taught—Antiquity 160
Gives rights to error; and aware, no less,
That throwing off oppression must be work
As well of license as of liberty;
And above all—for this was more than
  all—
Not caring if the wind did now and then 165
Blow keen upon an eminence that gave
Prospect so large into futurity;
In brief, a child of Nature, as at first,
Diffusing only those affections wider

That from the cradle had grown up with
  me,   170
And losing, in no other way than light
Is lost in light, the weak in the more
  strong.

In the main outline, such it might be
  said
Was my condition, till with open war
Britain opposed the liberties of France. 175
This threw me first out of the pale of love;
Soured and corrupted, upwards to the
  source,
My sentiments; was not, as hitherto,
A swallowing up of lesser things in great,
But change of them into their contra-
  ries;   180
And thus a way was opened for mistakes
And false conclusions, in degree as gross,
In kind more dangerous. What had been
  a pride,
Was now a shame; my likings and my loves
Ran in new channels, leaving old ones
  dry;   185
And hence a blow that, in maturer age,
Would but have touched the judgment,
  struck more deep
Into sensations near the heart: meantime,
As from the first, wild theories were afloat,
To whose pretensions, sedulously urged, 190
I had but lent a careless ear, assured
That time was ready to set all things right,
And that the multitude, so long oppressed,
Would be oppressed no more.
                          But when events
Brought less encouragement, and unto
  these   195
The immediate proof of principles no more
Could be entrusted, while the events them-
  selves,
Worn out in greatness, stripped of novelty,
Less occupied the mind, and sentiments
Could through my understanding's natural
  growth   200
No longer keep their ground, by faith
  maintained
Of inward consciousness, and hope that
  laid
Her hand upon her object—evidence
Safer, of universal application, such
As could not be impeached, was sought
  elsewhere.   205

But now, become oppressors in their
  turn,
Frenchmen had changed a war of self-
  defense
For one of conquest, losing sight of all
Which they had struggled for: up mounted
  now,

Openly in the eye of earth and heaven, 210
The scale of liberty. I read her doom,
With anger vexed, with disappointment
    sore,
But not dismayed, nor taking to the shame
Of a false prophet. While resentment
    rose
Striving to hide, what nought could heal,
    the wounds 215
Of mortified presumption, I adhered
More firmly to old tenets, and, to prove
Their temper, strained them more; and
    thus, in heat
Of contest, did opinions every day
Grow into consequence, till round my
    mind 220
They clung, as if they were its life, nay
    more,
The very being of the immortal soul.

. . . .

               A strong shock 270
Was given to old opinions; all men's minds
Had felt its power, and mine was both let
    loose,
Let loose and goaded. After what hath
    been
Already said of patriotic love,
Suffice it here to add, that, somewhat
    stern 275
In temperament, withal a happy man,
And therefore bold to look on painful
    things,
Free likewise of the world, and thence
    more bold,
I summoned my best skill, and toiled,
    intent
To anatomize the frame of social life; 280
Yea, the whole body of society
Searched to its heart. Share with me, friend!
    the wish
That some dramatic tale, endued with
    shapes
Livelier, and flinging out less guarded
    words
Than suit the work we fashion, might set
    forth 285
What then I learned, or think I learned,
    of truth,
And the errors into which I fell, betrayed
By present objects, and by reasonings false
From their beginnings, inasmuch as drawn
Out of a heart that had been turned
    aside 290
From Nature's way by outward accidents,
And which was thus confounded, more and
    more
Misguided, and misguiding. So I fared,
Dragging all precepts, judgments, maxims,
    creeds,

Like culprits to the bar; calling the
    mind, 295
Suspiciously, to establish in plain day
Her titles and her honors; now believing,
Now disbelieving; endlessly perplexed
With impulse, motive, right and wrong, the
    ground
Of obligation, what the rule and whence 300
The sanction; till, demanding formal proof,
And seeking it in everything, I lost
All feeling of conviction, and, in fine,
Sick, wearied out with contrarieties,
Yielded up moral questions in despair. 305

. . . .

Depressed, bewildered thus, I did not
    walk
With scoffers, seeking light and gay revenge
From indiscriminate laughter, nor sate
    down
In reconcilement with an utter waste
Of intellect; such sloth I could not brook 325
(Too well I loved, in that my spring of life,
Painstaking thoughts, and truth, their dear
    reward),
But turned to abstract science, and there
    sought
Work for the reasoning faculty enthroned
Where the disturbances of space and
    time— 330
Whether in matters various, properties
Inherent, or from human will and power
Derived—find no admission. Then it was—
Thanks to the bounteous Giver of all
    good!—
That the belovèd sister in whose sight 335
Those days were passed, now speaking in a
    voice
Of sudden admonition—like a brook
That did but *cross* a lonely road, and now
Is seen, heard, felt, and caught at every
    turn,
Companion never lost through many a
    league— 340
Maintained for me a saving intercourse
With my true self; for, though bedimmed
    and changed
Much, as it seemed, I was no further
    changed
Than as a clouded and a waning moon:
She whispered still that brightness would
    return; 345
She, in the midst of all, preserved me still
A poet, made me seek beneath that name,
And that alone, my office upon earth;
And, lastly, as hereafter will be shown,
If willing audience fail not, Nature's
    self, 350
By all varieties of human love
Assisted, led me back through opening day

To those sweet counsels between head and
    heart
Whence grew that genuine knowledge,
    fraught with peace,
Which, through the later sinkings of this
    cause,   355
Hath still upheld me, and upholds me
    now.

BOOK TWELFTH

IMAGINATION AND TASTE, HOW IMPAIRED AND RESTORED

Long time have human ignorance and guilt
Detained us, on what spectacles of woe
Compelled to look, and inwardly oppressed
With   sorrow,   disappointment,   vexing
    thoughts,
Confusion of the judgment, zeal decayed, 5
And, lastly, utter loss of hope itself
And things to hope for! Not with these
    began
Our song, and not with these our song
    must end.—
Ye motions of delight, that haunt the sides
Of the green hills; ye breezes and soft
    airs,   10
Whose subtle intercourse with breathing
    flowers,
Feelingly   watched,   might   teach   man's
    haughty race
How without injury to take, to give
Without offence; ye who, as if to show
The wondrous influence of power gently
    used,   15
Bend the complying heads of lordly pines,
And, with a touch, shift the stupendous
    clouds
Through the whole compass of the sky; ye
    brooks,
Muttering along the stones, a busy noise
By day, a quiet sound in silent night;   20
Ye waves, that out of the great deep steal
    forth
In a calm hour to kiss the pebbly shore,
Not mute, and then retire, fearing no
    storm;
And you, ye groves, whose ministry it is
To interpose the covert of your shades,   25
Even as a sleep, between the heart of man
And outward troubles, between man him-
    self,
Not seldom, and his own uneasy heart:
Oh! that I had a music and a voice
Harmonious as your own, that I might
    tell   30
What ye have done for me. The morning
    shines,
Nor heedeth Man's perverseness; spring
    returns,—

I saw the spring return, and could rejoice,
In common with the children of her love,
Piping on boughs, or sporting on fresh
    fields,   35
Or boldly seeking pleasure nearer heaven
On wings that navigate cerulean skies.
So neither were complacency, nor peace,
Nor tender yearnings, wanting for my good
Through these distracted times; in Nature
    still   40
Glorying, I found a counterpoise in her,
Which, when the spirit of evil reached its
    height,
Maintained for me a secret happiness.

. . . .

    There are in our existence spots of time,
That with distinct pre-eminence retain
A renovating virtue, whence—depressed 210
By false opinion and contentious thought,
Or aught of heavier or more deadly weight,
In trivial occupations, and the round
Of ordinary intercourse—our minds
Are nourished and invisibly repaired;   215
A virtue, by which pleasure is enhanced,
That penetrates, enables us to mount,
When high, more high, and lifts us up
    when fallen.
This efficacious spirit chiefly lurks
Among those passages of life that give   220
Profoundest knowledge to what point, and
    how,
The mind is lord and master—outward
    sense
The obedient servant of her will. Such
    moments
Are scattered everywhere, taking their date
From our first childhood. I remember
    well,   225
That once, while yet my inexperienced
    hand
Could scarcely hold a bridle, with proud
    hopes
I mounted, and we journeyed towards the
    hills:
An ancient servant of my father's house
Was with me, my encourager and guide: 230
We had not travelled long, ere some mis-
    chance
Disjoined me from my comrade; and,
    through fear
Dismounting, down the rough and stony
    moor
I led my horse, and, stumbling on, at
    length
Came to a bottom, where in former
    times   235
A murderer had been hung in iron chains.
The gibbet-mast had moldered down, the
    bones

And iron case were gone; but on the turf,
Hard by, soon after that fell deed was
    wrought,
Some unknown hand had carved the mur-
    derer's name.
The monumental letters were inscribed 240
In times long past; but still, from year to
    year
By superstition of the neighborhood,
The grass is cleared away, and to this hour
The characters are fresh and visible: 245
A casual glance had shown them, and I
    fled,
Faltering and faint, and ignorant of the
    road:
Then, reascending the bare common, saw
A naked pool that lay beneath the hills,
The beacon on the summit, and, more
    near,   250
A girl, who bore a pitcher on her head,
And seemed with difficult steps to force her
    way
Against the blowing wind. It was, in
    truth,
An ordinary sight; but I should need
Colors and words that are unknown to
    man,   255
To paint the visionary dreariness
Which, while I looked all round for my
    lost guide,
Invested moorland waste and naked pool,
The beacon crowning the lone eminence,
The female and her garments vexed and
    tossed   260
By the strong wind. When, in the blessèd
    hours
Of early love, the loved one at my side,
I roamed, in daily presence of this scene,
Upon the naked pool and dreary crags,
And on the melancholy beacon, fell   265
A spirit of pleasure and youth's golden
    gleam;
And think ye not with radiance more
    sublime
For these remembrances, and for the power
They had left behind? So feeling comes in
    aid
Of feeling, and diversity of strength   270
Attends us, if but once we have been
    strong.
Oh! mystery of man, from what a depth
Proceed thy honors. I am lost, but see
In simple childhood something of the base
On which thy greatness stands; but this I
    feel,   275
That from thyself it comes, that thou must
    give,
Else never canst receive. The days gone by
Return upon me almost from the dawn
Of life: the hiding-places of man's power

Open; I would approach them, but they
    close.   280
I see by glimpses now; when age comes on,
May scarcely see at all; and I would give,
While yet we may, as far as words can give,
Substance and life to what I feel, enshrin-
    ing,
Such is my hope, the spirit of the Past 285
For future restoration.

BOOK THIRTEENTH

IMAGINATION AND TASTE (CONCLUDED)

From Nature doth emotion come, and
    moods
Of calmness equally are Nature's gift:
This is her glory; these two attributes
Are sister horns that constitute her strength.
Hence Genius, born to thrive by inter-
    change   5
Of peace and excitation, finds in her
His best and purest friend; from her re-
    ceives
That energy by which he seeks the truth,
From her that happy stillness of the mind
Which fits him to receive it when un-
    sought.   10

Such benefit the humblest intellects
Partake of, each in their degree; 'tis mine
To speak, what I myself have known and
    felt;
Smooth task! for words find easy way,
    inspired
By gratitude, and confidence in truth.   15
Long time in search of knowledge did I
    range
The field of human life, in heart and mind
Benighted; but, the dawn beginning now
To reappear, 'twas proved that not in vain
I had been taught to reverence a Power 20
That is the visible quality and shape
And image of right reason; that matures
Her processes by stedfast laws; gives birth
To no impatient or fallacious hopes,
No heat of passion or excessive zeal,   25
No vain conceits; provokes to no quick
    turns
Of self-applauding intellect; but trains
To meekness, and exalts by humble faith;
Holds up before the mind intoxicate
With present objects, and the busy dance 30
Of things that pass away, a temperate show
Of objects that endure; and by this course
Disposes her, when over-fondly set
On throwing off incumbrances, to seek
In man, and in the frame of social life, 35
Whate'er there is desirable and good

Of kindred permanence, unchanged in
    form
And function, or, through strict vicissitude
Of life and death, revolving. Above all
Were re-established now those watchful
    thoughts   40
Which, seeing little worthy or sublime
In what the historian's pen so much de-
    lights
To blazon—power and energy detached
From moral purpose—early tutored me
To look with feelings of fraternal love 45
Upon the unassuming things that hold
A silent station in this beauteous world

Thus moderated, thus composed, I found
Once more in Man an object of delight,
Of pure imagination, and of love;   50
And, as the horizon of my mind enlarged,
Again I took the intellectual eye
For my instructor, studious more to see
Great truths, than touch and handle little
    ones.
Knowledge was given accordingly; my
    trust   55
Became more firm in feelings that had
    stood
The test of such a trial; clearer far
My sense of excellence—of right and
    wrong:
The promise of the present time retired
Into its true proportion; sanguine
    schemes,   60
Ambitious projects, pleased me less; I
    sought
For present good in life's familiar face,
And built thereon my hopes of good to
    come.

    . . . .
          When I began to enquire, 160
To watch and question those I met, and
    speak
Without reserve to them, the lonely roads
Were open schools in which I daily read
With most delight the passions of mankind,
Whether by words, looks, sighs, or tears,
    revealed;   165
There saw into the depth of human souls,
Souls that appear to have no depth at all
To careless eyes. And—now convinced at
    heart
How little those formalities, to which
With overweening trust alone we give 170
The name of education, have to do
With real feeling and just sense; how vain
A correspondence with the talking world
Proves to the most; and called to make
    good search
If man's estate, by doom of Nature yoked 175

With toil, be therefore yoked with igno-
    rance;
If virtue be indeed so hard to rear,
And intellectual strength so rare a boon—
I prized such walks still more, for there I
    found
Hope to my hope, and to my pleasure
    peace   180
And steadiness, and healing and repose
To every angry passion. There I heard,
From mouths of men obscure and lowly,
    truths
Replete with honor; sounds in unison
With loftiest promises of good and fair. 185

    . . . .

    Here, calling up to mind what then I
    saw,
A youthful traveller, and see daily now
In the familiar circuit of my home,
Here might I pause, and bend in reverence
To Nature, and the power of human
    minds,   225
To men as they are men within themselves.
How oft high service is performed within,
When all the external man is rude in
    show,—
Not like a temple rich with pomp and gold,
But a mere mountain chapel, that pro-
    tects   230
Its simple worshippers from sun and
    shower.
Of these, said I, shall be my song; of these,
If future years mature me for the task,
Will I record the praises, making verse
Deal boldly with substantial things; in
    truth   235
And sanctity of passion, speak of these,
That justice may be done, obeisance paid
Where it is due: thus haply shall I teach,
Inspire; through unadulterated ears
Pour rapture, tenderness, and hope,—my
    theme   240
No other than the very heart of man,
As found among the best of those who
    live—
Not unexalted by religious faith,
Nor uninformed by books, good books,
    though few—
In Nature's presence: thence may I select 245
Sorrow, that is not sorrow, but delight;
And miserable love, that is not pain
To hear of, for the glory that redounds
Therefrom to human kind, and what we
    are.
Be mine to follow with no timid step 250
Where knowledge leads me: it shall be my
    pride
That I have dared to tread this holy
    ground,

Speaking no dream, but things oracular;
Matter not lightly to be heard by those
Who to the letter of the outward prom-
   ise 255
Do read the invisible soul; by men adroit
In speech, and for communion with the
   world
Accomplished; minds whose faculties are
   then
Most active when they are most eloquent,
And elevated most when most admired. 260
Men may be found of other mould than
   these,
Who are their own upholders, to them-
   selves
Encouragement, and energy, and will,
Expressing liveliest thoughts in lively words
As native passion dictates. Others, too, 265
There are among the walks of homely life
Still higher, men for contemplation framed,
Shy, and unpractised in the strife of phrase;
Meek men, whose very souls perhaps would
   sink
Beneath them, summoned to such inter-
   course: 270
Theirs is the language of the heavens, the
   power,
The thought, the image, and the silent joy:
Words are but under-agents in their souls;
When they are grasping with their greatest
   strength,
They do not breathe among them: this I
   speak 275
In gratitude to God, Who feeds our hearts
For His own service; knoweth us, loveth
   us,
When we are unregarded by the world.

BOOK FOURTEENTH

CONCLUSION

It was a close, warm, breezeless summer
   night,
Wan, dull, and glaring, with a dripping
   fog
Low-hung and thick that covered all the
   sky;
But, undiscouraged, we began to climb
The mountain-side. The mist soon girt us
   round, 15
And, after ordinary travellers' talk
With our conductor, pensively we sank
Each into commerce with his private
   thoughts.
Thus did we breast the ascent, and by
   myself
Was nothing either seen or heard that
   checked 20

Those musings or diverted, save that once
The shepherd's lurcher, who, among the
   crags,
Had to his joy unearthed a hedgehog,
   teased
His coiled-up prey with barkings turbulent.
This small adventure, for even such it
   seemed 25
In that wild place and at the dead of
   night,
Being over and forgotten, on we wound
In silence as before. With forehead bent
Earthward, as if in opposition set
Against an enemy, I panted up 30
With eager pace, and no less eager
   thoughts.
Thus might we wear a midnight hour away,
Ascending at loose distance each from each,
And I, as chanced, the foremost of the
   band;
When at my feet the ground appeared to
   brighten, 35
And with a step or two seemed brighter
   still;
Nor was time given to ask or learn the
   cause,
For instantly a light upon the turf
Fell like a flash, and lo! as I looked up,
The moon hung naked in a firmament 40
Of azure without cloud, and at my feet
Rested a silent sea of hoary mist.
A hundred hills their dusky backs up-
   heaved
All over this still ocean; and beyond,
Far, far beyond the solid vapors
   stretched, 45
In headlands, tongues, and promontory
   shapes,
Into the main Atlantic, that appeared
To dwindle, and give up his majesty,
Usurped upon far as the sight could reach.
Not so the ethereal vault; encroachment
   none 50
Was there, nor loss; only the inferior stars
Had disappeared, or shed a fainter light
In the clear presence of the full-orbed
   moon,
Who, from her sovereign elevation, gazed
Upon the billowy ocean, as it lay 55
All meek and silent, save that through a
   rift—
Not distant from the shore whereon we
   stood,
A fixed, abysmal, gloomy, breathing place—
Mounted the roar of waters, torrents,
   streams
Innumerable, roaring with one voice! 60
Heard over earth and sea, and, in that
   hour,
For so it seemed, felt by the starry heavens.

When into air had partially dissolved
That vision, given to spirits of the night
And three chance human wanderers, in
    calm thought   65
Reflected, it appeared to me the type
Of a majestic intellect, its acts
And its possessions, what it has and craves,
What in itself it is, and would become.
There I beheld the emblem of a mind   70
That feeds upon infinity, that broods
Over the dark abyss, intent to hear
Its voices issuing forth to silent light
In one continuous stream; a mind sus-
    tained
By recognitions of transcendent power, 75
In sense conducting to ideal form,
In soul of more than mortal privilege.
One function, above all, of such a mind
Had Nature shadowed there, by putting
    forth,
Mid circumstances awful and sublime, 80
That mutual domination which she loves
To exert upon the face of outward things,
So molded, joined, abstracted, so endowed
With interchangeable supremacy,
That men, least sensitive, see, hear, per-
    ceive,   85
And cannot choose but feel. The power,
    which all
Acknowledge when thus moved, which
    Nature thus
To bodily sense exhibits, is the express
Resemblance of that glorious faculty
That higher minds bear with them as their
    own.   90
This is the very spirit in which they deal
With the whole compass of the universe:
They from their native selves can send
    abroad
Kindred mutations; for themselves create
A like existence; and, whene'er it dawns 95
Created for them, catch it, or are caught
By its inevitable mastery,
Like angels stopped upon the wing by
    sound
Of harmony from Heaven's remotest
    spheres.
Them the enduring and the transient
    both   100
Serve to exalt; they build up greatest things
From least suggestions; ever on the watch,
Willing to work and to be wrought upon,
They need not extraordinary calls
To rouse them; in a world of life they
    live,   105
By sensible impressions not enthralled,
But by their quickening impulse made
    more prompt
To hold fit converse with the spiritual
    world,

And with the generations of mankind
Spread over time, past, present, and to
    come,   110
Age after age, till time shall be no more.
Such minds are truly from the Deity,
For they are Powers; and hence the highest
    bliss
That flesh can know is theirs—the con-
    sciousness
Of Whom they are, habitually infused 115
Through every image and through every
    thought,
And all affections by communion raised
From earth to heaven, from human to
    divine;
Hence endless occupation for the soul,
Whether discursive or intuitive;   120
Hence cheerfulness for acts of daily life,
Emotions which best foresight need not
    fear,
Most worthy then of trust when most
    intense.
Hence, amid ills that vex and wrongs that
    crush
Our hearts—if here the words of Holy
    Writ   125
May with fit reverence be applied—that
    peace
Which passeth understanding, that repose
In moral judgments which from this pure
    source
Must come, or will by man be sought in
    vain.

Oh! who is he that hath his whole life
    long   130
Preserved, enlarged, this freedom in him-
    self?
For this alone is genuine liberty;
Where is the favored being who hath held
That course unchecked, unerring, and un-
    tired,
In one perpetual progress smooth and
    bright?—   135
A humbler destiny have we retraced,
And told of lapse and hesitating choice,
And backward wanderings along thorny
    ways;
Yet—compassed round by mountain soli-
    tudes,
Within whose solemn temple I received 140
My earliest visitations, careless then
Of what was given me; and which now I
    range,
A meditative, oft a suffering man—
Do I declare—in accents which, from truth
Deriving cheerful confidence, shall blend 145
Their modulation with these vocal
    streams—
That, whatsoever falls my better mind,

Revolving with the accidents of life,
May have sustained, that, howsoe'er misled,
Never did I, in quest of right and wrong, 150
Tamper with conscience from a private
  aim;
Nor was in any public hope the dupe
Of selfish passions; nor did ever yield
Wilfully to mean cares or low pursuits,
But shrunk with apprehensive jealousy 155
From every combination which might aid
The tendency, too potent in itself,
Of use and custom to bow down the soul
Under a growing weight of vulgar sense,
And substitute a universe of death   160
For that which moves with light and life
  informed,
Actual, divine, and true. To fear and love,
To love as prime and chief, for there fear
  ends,
Be this ascribed; to early intercourse,
In presence of sublime or beautiful
  forms,   165
With the adverse principles of pain and
  joy—
Evil as one is rashly named by men
Who know not what they speak. By love
  subsists
All lasting grandeur, by pervading love;
That gone, we are as dust.—Behold the
  fields   170
In balmy springtime full of rising flowers
And joyous creatures; see that pair, the
  lamb
And the lamb's mother, and their tender
  ways
Shall touch thee to the heart; thou callest
  this love,
And not inaptly so, for love it is,   175
Far as it carries thee. In some green bower
Rest, and be not alone, but have thou
  there
The One who is thy choice of all the world:
There linger, listening, gazing, with delight
Impassioned, but delight how pitiable! 180
Unless this love by a still higher love
Be hallowed, love that breathes not with-
  out awe;
Love that adores, but on the knees of
  prayer,
By heaven inspired; that frees from chains
  the soul,
Lifted, in union with the purest, best, 185
Of earth-born passions, on the wings of
  praise
Bearing a tribute to the Almighty's throne.

This spiritual love acts not nor can exist
Without Imagination, which, in truth,
Is but another name for absolute power 190
And clearest insight, amplitude of mind,

And reason in her most exalted mood.
This faculty hath been the feeding source
Of our long labor: we have traced the
  stream
From the blind cavern whence is faintly
  heard   195
Its natal murmur; followed it to light
And open day; accompanied its course
Among the ways of Nature, for a time
Lost sight of it bewildered and engulfed;
Then given it greeting as it rose once
  more   200
In strength, reflecting from its placid breast
The works of man and face of human life;
And lastly, from its progress have we
  drawn
Faith in life endless, the sustaining thought
Of human Being, Eternity, and God. 205

Imagination having been our theme,
So also hath that intellectual Love,
For they are each in each, and cannot
  stand
Dividually.—Here must thou be, O Man!
Power to thyself; no helper hast thou
  here;   210
Here keepest thou in singleness thy state:
No other can divide with thee this work:
No secondary hand can intervene
To fashion this ability; 'tis thine,
The prime and vital principle is thine, 215
In the recesses of thy nature, far
From any reach of outward fellowship,
Else is not thine at all. But joy to him,
Oh, joy to him who here hath sown, hath
  laid
Here, the foundation of his future years! 220
For all that friendship, all that love can do,
All that a darling countenance can look
Or dear voice utter, to complete the man,
Perfect him, made imperfect in himself,
All shall be his: and he whose soul hath
  risen   225
Up to the height of feeling intellect
Shall want no humbler tenderness; his
  heart
Be tender as a nursing mother's heart;
Of female softness shall his life be full,
Of humble cares and delicate desires, 230
Mild interests and gentlest sympathies.

Child of my parents! Sister of my soul!
Thanks in sincerest verse have been else-
  where
Poured out for all the early tenderness
Which I from thee imbibed: and 'tis most
  true   235
That later seasons owed to thee no less;
For, spite of thy sweet influence and the
  touch

Of kindred hands that opened out the
    springs
Of genial thought in childhood, and in
    spite
Of all that unassisted I had marked   240
In life or nature of those charms minute
That win their way into the heart by
    stealth
(Still to the very going-out of youth)
I too exclusively esteemed *that* love,
And sought *that* beauty, which, as Milton
    sings,   245
Hath terror in it. Thou didst soften down
This over-sternness; but for thee, dear
    friend!
My soul, too reckless of mild grace, had
    stood
In her original self too confident,
Retained too long a countenance severe;   250
A rock with torrents roaring, with the
    clouds
Familiar, and a favorite of the stars:
But thou didst plant its crevices with
    flowers,
Hang it with shrubs that twinkle in the
    breeze,
And teach the little birds to build their
    nests   255
And warble in its chambers. At a time
When Nature, destined to remain so long
Foremost in my affections, had fallen back
Into a second place, pleased to become
A handmaid to a nobler than herself,   260
When every day brought with it some new
    sense
Of exquisite regard for common things,
And all the earth was budding with these
    gifts
Of more refined humanity, thy breath,
Dear Sister! was a kind of gentler spring 265
That went before my steps. Thereafter
    came
One whom with thee friendship had early
    paired;
She came, no more a phantom to adorn
A moment, but an inmate of the heart,
And yet a spirit, there for me enshrined 270
To penetrate the lofty and the low;
Even as one essence of pervading light
Shines, in the brightest of ten thousand
    stars
And the meek worm that feeds her lonely
    lamp
Couched in the dewy grass.
               With such a theme, 275
Coleridge! with this my argument, of
    thee
Shall I be silent? O capacious soul!
Placed on this earth to love and under-
    stand,

And from thy presence shed the light of
    love,
Shall I be mute, ere thou be spoken of? 280
Thy kindred influence to my heart of
    hearts
Did also find its way. Thus fear relaxed
Her overweening grasp; thus thoughts and
    things
In the self-haunting spirit learned to take
More rational proportions; mystery, 285
The incumbent mystery of sense and soul,
Of life and death, time and eternity,
Admitted more habitually a mild
Interposition—a serene delight
In closelier gathering cares, such as be-
    come 290
A human creature, howsoe'er endowed,
Poet, or destined for a humbler name.

Whether to me shall be allotted life,
And, with life, power to accomplish aught
    of worth,
That will be deemed no insufficient plea 390
For having given the story of myself,
Is all uncertain: but, beloved friend!
When, looking back, thou seest, in clearer
    view
Than any liveliest sight of yesterday,
That summer, under whose indulgent
    skies, 395
Upon smooth Quantock's airy ridge we
    roved
Unchecked, or loitered 'mid her sylvan
    combs,
Thou in bewitching words, with happy
    heart,
Didst chaunt the vision of that Ancient
    Man,
The bright-eyed Mariner, and rueful
    woes 400
Didst utter of the Lady Christabel;
And I, associate with such labor, steeped
In soft forgetfulness the livelong hours,
Murmuring of him who, joyous hap, was
    found,
After the perils of his moonlight ride, 405
Near the loud waterfall; or her who sate
In misery near the miserable Thorn—
When thou dost to that summer turn thy
    thoughts,
And hast before thee all which then we
    were,
To thee, in memory of that happiness, 410
It will be known, by thee at least, my
    Friend!
Felt, that the history of a Poet's mind
Is labor not unworthy of regard;
To thee the work shall justify itself.

Oh! yet a few short years of useful life, 430
And all will be complete, thy race be run,
Thy monument of glory will be raised;
Then, though (too weak to tread the ways
   of truth)
This age fall back to old idolatry,
Though men return to servitude as fast 435
As the tide ebbs, to ignominy and shame,
By nations sink together, we shall still
Find solace—knowing what we have learnt
   to know,
Rich in true happiness if allowed to be 440
Faithful alike in forwarding a day
Of firmer trust, joint laborers in the work
(Should Providence such grace to us vouch-
   safe)
Of their deliverance, surely yet to come.
Prophets of Nature, we to them will
   speak 445
A lasting inspiration, sanctified
By reason, blest by faith: what we have
   loved,
Others will love, and we will teach them
   how;
Instruct them how the mind of man be-
   comes
A thousand times more beautiful than the
   earth
On which he dwells, above this frame of
   things 450
(Which, 'mid all revolution in the hopes
And fears of men, doth still remain un-
   changed)
In beauty exalted, as it is itself
Of quality and fabric more divine.

1798-1805   1850

THE RECLUSE

[INTRODUCTION TO "THE EXCURSION"]

On Man, on Nature, and on Human
   Life,
Musing in solitude, I oft perceive
Fair trains of imagery before me rise,
Accompanied by feelings of delight
Pure, or with no unpleasing sadness
   mixed; 5
And I am conscious of affecting thoughts
And dear remembrances, whose presence
   soothes
Or elevates the mind, intent to weigh
The good and evil of our mortal state.
—To these emotions, whencesoe'er they
   come, 10
Whether from breath of outward circum-
   stance,
Or from the soul—an impulse to herself—

I would give utterance in numerous verse.
Of Truth, of Grandeur, Beauty, Love, and
   Hope,
And melancholy Fear subdued by Faith; 15
Of blessèd consolations in distress;
Of moral strength, and intellectual Power;
Of joy in widest commonalty spread;
Of the individual Mind that keeps her own
Inviolate retirement, subject there 20
To Conscience only, and the law supreme
Of that Intelligence which governs all—
I sing:—"fit audience let me find though
   few!"
  So prayed, more gaining than he asked,
   the bard—
In holiest mood. Urania, I shall need 25
Thy guidance, or a greater Muse, if such
Descend to earth or dwell in highest
   heaven!
For I must tread on shadowy ground, must
   sink
Deep—and, aloft ascending, breathe in
   worlds
To which the heaven of heavens is but a
   veil. 30
All strength—all terror, single or in bands,
That ever was put forth in personal form—
Jehovah—with his thunder, and the choir
Of shouting angels, and the empyreal
   thrones—
I pass them unalarmed. Not Chaos, not 35
The darkest pit of lowest Erebus,
Nor aught of blinder vacancy, scooped out
By help of dreams—can breed such fear
   and awe
As fall upon us often when we look
Into our minds, into the mind of Man— 40
My haunt, and the main region of my song.
—Beauty—a living presence of the earth,
Surpassing the most fair ideal forms
Which craft of delicate spirits hath com-
   posed
From earth's materials—waits upon my
   steps; 45
Pitches her tents before me as I move,
An hourly neighbor. Paradise, and groves
Elysian, Fortunate Fields—like those of old
Sought in the Atlantic Main—why should
   they be
A history only of departed things, 50
Or a mere fiction of what never was?
For the discerning intellect of Man,
When wedded to this goodly universe
In love and holy passion, shall find these
A simple produce of the common day. 55
—I, long before the blissful hour arrives,
Would chant, in lonely peace, the spousal
   verse
Of this great consummation:—and, by
   words

Which speak of nothing more than what
   we are,
Would I arouse the sensual from their
   sleep   60
Of death, and win the vacant and the vain
To noble raptures; while my voice pro-
   claims
How exquisitely the individual mind
(And the progressive powers perhaps no
   less
Of the whole species) to the external
   world   65
Is fitted:—and how exquisitely, too—
Theme this but little heard of among
   men—
The external world is fitted to the mind;
And the creation (by no lower name
Can it be called) which they with blended
   might   70
Accomplish:—this is our high argument.
—Such grateful haunts foregoing, if I oft
Must turn elsewhere—to travel near the
   tribes
And fellowships of men, and see ill sights
Of madding passions mutually inflamed; 75
Must hear humanity in fields and groves
Pipe solitary anguish; or must hang
Brooding above the fierce confederate
   storm
Of sorrow, barricadoed evermore
Within the walls of cities—may these
   sounds   80
Have their authentic comment; that even
   these
Hearing, I be not downcast or forlorn!—
Descend, prophetic Spirit! that inspir'st
The human soul of universal earth,
Dreaming on things to come; and dost
   possess   85
A metropolitan temple in the hearts
Of mighty poets; upon me bestow
A gift of genuine insight; that my song
With star-like virtue in its place may shine,
Shedding benignant influence, and secure 90
Itself from all malevolent effect
Of those mutations that extend their sway
Throughout the nether sphere!—And if
   with this
I mix more lowly matter; with the thing
Contemplated, describe the mind and
   Man   95
Contemplating; and who, and what he
   was—
The transitory being that beheld
This vision;—when and where, and how he
   lived;
Be not this labor useless. If such theme
May sort with highest objects, then—dread
   Power!   100
Whose gracious favor is the primal source

Of all illumination—may my life
Express the image of a better time,
More wise desires, and simpler manners;—
   nurse
My heart in genuine freedom:—all pure
   thoughts   105
Be with me;—so shall thy unfailing love
Guide, and support, and cheer me to the
   end!

                    1814

THE EXCURSION

BOOK FIRST

THE WANDERER

Such was the Boy—but for the growing
   Youth
What soul was his, when from the naked
   top
Of some bold headland, he beheld the sun
Rise up, and bathe the world in light! He
   looked—   200
Ocean and earth, the solid frame of earth
And ocean's liquid mass, in gladness lay
Beneath him:—Far and wide the clouds
   were touched,
And in their silent faces could he read
Unutterable love. Sound needed none, 205
Nor any voice of joy; his spirit drank
The spectacle: sensation, soul, and form,
All melted into him; they swallowed up
His animal being; in them did he live,
And by them did he live; they were his
   life.   210
In such access of mind, in such high hour
Of visitation from the living God,
Thought was not; in enjoyment it expired.
No thanks he breathed, he proffered no
   request;
Rapt into still communion that tran-
   scends   215
The imperfect offices of prayer and praise,
His mind was a thanksgiving to the power
That made him; it was blessedness and
   love!

A Herdsman on the lonely mountain
   tops,
Such intercourse was his, and in this
   sort   220
Was his existence oftentimes *possessed.*
O then how beautiful, how bright, ap-
   peared
The written promise! Early had he learned
To reverence the volume that displays
The mystery, the life which cannot die; 225
But in the mountains did he *feel* his faith.
All things, responsive to the writing, there

Breathed immortality, revolving life,
And greatness still revolving; infinite:
There littleness was not; the least of
  things   230
Seemed infinite; and there his spirit shaped
Her prospects, nor did he believe,—he *saw*.

. . . .

(*The Wanderer speaks:*)
              "Never did my steps
Approach this door but she who dwelt
  within
A daughter's welcome gave me, and I loved
  her
As my own child. Oh, Sir! the good die
  first,   500
And they whose hearts are dry as summer
  dust
Burn to the socket. Many a passenger
Hath blessed poor Margaret for her gentle
  looks,
When she upheld the cool refreshment
  drawn
From that forsaken spring; and no one
  came   505
But he was welcome; no one went away
But that it seemed she loved him. She is
  dead,
The light extinguished of her lonely hut,
The hut itself abandoned to decay,
And she forgotten in the quiet grave.   510

"I speak," continued he, "of one whose
  stock
Of virtues bloomed beneath this lowly roof.
She was a woman of a steady mind,
Tender and deep in her excess of love;
Not speaking much, pleased rather with
  the joy   515
Of her own thoughts: by some especial care
Her temper had been framed, as if to make
A being, who by adding love to peace
Might live on earth a life of happiness.
Her wedded partner lacked not on his
  side   520
The humble worth that satisfied her heart:
Frugal, affectionate, sober, and withal
Keenly industrious. She with pride would
  tell
That he was often seated at his loom,
In summer, ere the mower was abroad   525
Among the dewy grass,—in early spring,
Ere the last star had vanished.—They who
  passed
At evening, from behind the garden fence
Might hear his busy spade, which he would
  ply,
After his daily work, until the light   530
Had failed, and every leaf and flower were
  lost

In the dark hedges. So their days were
  spent
In peace and comfort; and a pretty boy
Was their best hope, next to the God in
  heaven.

"Not twenty years ago, but you I think   535
Can scarcely bear it now in mind, there
  came
Two blighting seasons, when the fields were
  left
With half a harvest. It pleased Heaven to
  add
A worse affliction in the plague of war;
This happy land was stricken to the
  heart!   540
A wanderer then among the cottages,
I, with my freight of winter raiment, saw
The hardships of the season: many rich
Sank down, as in a dream, among the poor;
And of the poor did many cease to be,   545
And their place knew them not. Mean-
  while, abridged
Of daily comforts, gladly reconciled
To numerous self-denials, Margaret
Went struggling on through those calami-
  tous years
With cheerful hope, until the second
  autumn,   550
When her life's helpmate on a sick-bed lay,
Smitten with perilous fever. In disease
He lingered long; and, when his strength
  returned,
He found the little he had stored, to meet
The hour of accident or crippling age,   555
Was all consumed. A second infant now
Was added to the troubles of a time
Laden, for them and all of their degree,
With care and sorrow: shoals of artisans
From ill-requited labor turned adrift   560
Sought daily bread from public charity,
They, and their wives and children, hap-
  pier far
Could they have lived as do the little birds
That peck along the hedge-rows, or the
  kite
That makes her dwelling on the mountain
  rocks!   565

"A sad reverse it was for him who long
Had filled with plenty, and possessed in
  peace,
This lonely cottage. At the door he stood,
And whistled many a snatch of merry tunes
That had no mirth in them; or with his
  knife   570
Carved uncouth figures on the heads of
  sticks—
Then, not less idly, sought, through every
  nook

In house or gardens, any casual work
Of use or ornament; and with a strange,
Amusing, yet uneasy novelty, 575
He mingled, where he might, the various
tasks
Of summer, autumn, winter, and of spring.
But this endured not; his good humor soon
Became a weight in which no pleasure was:
And poverty brought on a petted mood 580
And a sore temper: day by day he drooped,
And he would leave his work—and to the
town
Would turn without an errand his slack
steps;
Or wander here and there among the fields.
One while he would speak lightly of his
babes, 585
And with a cruel tongue; at other times
He tossed them with a false unnatural joy:
And 'twas a rueful thing to see the looks
Of the poor innocent children. 'Every
smile,'
Said Margaret to me, here beneath these
trees, 590
'Made my heart bleed.'"
        At this the Wanderer paused;
And, looking up to those enormous elms,
He said, " 'Tis now the hour of deepest
noon,
At this still season of repose and peace,
This hour when all things which are not
at rest 595
Are cheerful; while this multitude of flies
With tuneful hum is filling all the air;
Why should a tear be on an old man's
cheek?
Why should we thus, with an untoward
mind,
And in the weakness of humanity, 600
From natural wisdom turn our hearts
away;
To natural comfort shut our eyes and ears;
And, feeding on disquiet, thus disturb
The calm of nature with our restless
thoughts?"

He spake with somewhat of a solemn
tone: 605
But, when he ended, there was in his face
Such easy cheerfulness, a look so mild
That for a little time it stole away
All recollection; and that simple tale
Passed from my mind like a forgotten
sound. 610
A while on trivial things we held discourse,
To me soon tasteless. In my own despite,
I thought of that poor woman as of one
Whom I had known and loved. He had
rehearsed

Her homely tale with such familiar
power, 615
With such an active countenance, an eye
So busy, that the things of which he spake
Seemed present, and, attention now re-
laxed,
A heart-felt chilliness crept along my
veins.
I rose; and, having left the breezy shade, 620
Stood drinking comfort from the warmer
sun,
That had not cheered me long—ere, look-
ing round
Upon that tranquil ruin, I returned,
And begged of the old man that, for my
sake,
He would resume his story.
        He replied, 625
"It were a wantonness, and would demand
Severe reproof, if we were men whose
hearts
Could hold vain dalliance with the misery
Even of the dead; contented thence to
draw
A momentary pleasure, never marked 630
By reason, barren of all future good.
But we have known that there is often
found
In mournful thoughts, and always might
be found
A power to virtue friendly; were't not so,
I am a dreamer among men, indeed 635
An idle dreamer! 'Tis a common tale,
An ordinary sorrow of man's life,
A tale of silent suffering, hardly clothed
In bodily form.—But without further bid-
ding
I will proceed.
        While thus it fared with them, 640
To whom this cottage, till those hapless
years,
Had been a blessèd home, it was my chance
To travel in a country far remote;
And when these lofty elms once more
appeared
What pleasant expectations lured me on 645
O'er the flat common!—With quick step I
reached
The threshold, lifted with light hand the
latch;
But, when I entered, Margaret looked at
me
A little while; then turned her head away
Speechless,—and, sitting down upon a
chair, 650
Wept bitterly. I wist not what to do,
Nor how to speak to her. Poor wretch!
at last
She rose from off her seat, and then,—
O Sir!

I cannot *tell* how she pronounced my
     name:—
With fervent love, and with a face of
     grief   655
Unutterably helpless, and a look
That seemed to cling upon me, she en-
     quired
If I had seen her husband. As she spake
A strange surprise and fear came to my
     heart,
Nor had I power to answer ere she told 660
That he had disappeared—not two months
     gone.
He left his house: two wretched days had
     past,
And on the third, as wistfully she raised
Her head from off her pillow, to look forth,
Like one in trouble, for returning light, 665
Within her chamber-casement she espied
A folded paper, lying as if placed
To meet her waking eyes. This trem-
     blingly
She opened—found no writing, but beheld
Pieces of money carefully enclosed,   670
Silver and gold. 'I shuddered at the sight,'
Said Margaret, 'for I knew it was his hand
That must have placed it there; and ere
     that day
Was ended, that long anxious day, I
     learned,
From one who by my husband had been
     sent   675
With the sad news, that he had joined a
     troop
Of soldiers, going to a distant land.
—He left me thus—he could not gather
     heart
To take a farewell of me; for he feared
That I should follow with my babes, and
     sink   680
Beneath the misery of that wandering life.'

"This tale did Margaret tell with many
     tears:
And when she ended, I had little power
To give her comfort, and was glad to take
Such words of hope from her own mouth
     as served   685
To cheer us both. But long we had not
     talked
Ere we built up a pile of better thoughts,
And with a brighter eye she looked around
As if she had been shedding tears of joy.
We parted.—'Twas the time of early
     spring;   690
I left her busy with her garden tools;
And well remember, o'er that fence she
     looked,
And, while I paced along the foot-way
     path,

Called out, and sent a blessing after me,
With tender cheerfulness, and with a
     voice   695
That seemed the very sound of happy
     thoughts.

"I roved o'er many a hill and many a
     dale,
With my accustomed load; in heat and cold,
Through many a wood and many an open
     ground,
In sunshine and in shade, in wet and
     fair,   700
Drooping or blithe of heart, as might
     befall;
My best companions now the driving
     winds,
And now the 'trotting brooks' and whisper-
     ing trees,
And now the music of my own sad steps,
With many a short-lived thought that
     passed between,   705
And disappeared.

             I journeyed back this way,
When in the warmth of midsummer, the
     wheat
Was yellow; and the soft and bladed grass,
Springing afresh, had o'er the hay-field
     spread
Its tender verdure. At the door arrived, 710
I found that she was absent. In the shade,
Where now we sit, I waited her return.
Her cottage, then a cheerful object, wore
Its customary look,—only, it seemed,
The honeysuckle, crowding round the
     porch,   715
Hung down in heavier tufts; and that
     bright weed,
The yellow stonecrop, suffered to take root
Along the window's edge, profusely grew,
Blinding the lower panes. I turned aside,
And strolled into her garden. It ap-
     peared   720
To lag behind the season, and had lost
Its pride of neatness. Daisy flowers and
     thrift
Had broken their trim borderlines, and
     straggled
O'er paths they used to deck; carnations,
     once
Prized for surpassing beauty, and no less 725
For the peculiar pains they had required,
Declined their languid heads, wanting sup-
     port.
The cumbrous bindweed, with its wreaths
     and bells,
Had twined about her two small rows of
     peas,
And dragged them to the earth.
                         Ere this an hour 730

Was wasted.—Back I turned my restless
    steps;
A stranger passed; and, guessing whom I
    sought,
He said that she was used to ramble far.—
The sun was sinking in the west; and now
I sate with sad impatience. From within 735
Her solitary infant cried aloud;
Then, like a blast that dies away self-stilled,
The voice was silent. From the bench I
    rose;
But neither could divert nor soothe my
    thoughts.
The spot, though fair, was very deso-
    late— 740
The longer I remained, more desolate:
And, looking round me, now I first ob-
    served
The corner stones, on either side the porch,
With dull red stains discolored, and stuck
    o'er
With tufts and hairs of wool, as if the
    sheep, 745
That fed upon the common, thither came
Familiarly, and found a couching place
Even at her threshold. Deeper shadows fell
From these tall elms; the cottage clock
    struck eight;—
I turned, and saw her distant a few steps. 750
Her face was pale and thin—her figure, too,
Was changed. As she unlocked the door,
    she said,
'It grieves me you have waited here so long,
But, in good truth, I've wandered much of
    late;
And, sometimes—to my shame I speak—
    have need 755
Of my best prayers to bring me back again.'
While on the board she spread our evening
    meal,
She told me—interrupting not the work
Which gave employment to her listless
    hands—
That she had parted with her elder
    child; 760
To a kind master on a distant farm
Now happily apprenticed.—'I perceive
You look at me, and you have cause; to-
    day
I have been travelling far, and many days
About the fields I wander, knowing this 765
Only, that what I seek I cannot find;
And so I waste my time: for I am changed;
And to myself,' said she, 'have done much
    wrong
And to this helpless infant. I have slept
Weeping, and weeping have I waked; my
    tears 770
Have flowed as if my body were not such
As others are; and I could never die

But I am now in mind and in my heart
More easy; and I hope,' said she, 'that God
Will give me patience to endure the
    things 775
Which I behold at home.'
               It would have grieved
Your very soul to see her. Sir, I feel
The story linger in my heart; I fear
'Tis long and tedious; but my spirit clings
To that poor woman:—so familiarly 780
Do I perceive her manner, and her look,
And presence; and so deeply do I feel
Her goodness, that, not seldom, in my
    walks
A momentary trance comes over me;
And to myself I seem to muse on one 785
By sorrow laid asleep; or borne away,
A human being destined to awake
To human life, or something very near
To human life, when he shall come again
For whom she suffered. Yes, it would have
    grieved 790
Your very soul to see her: evermore
Her eyelids drooped, her eyes downward
    were cast;
And, when she at her table gave me food,
She did not look at me. Her voice was low,
Her body was subdued. In every act 795
Pertaining to her house affairs, appeared
The careless stillness of a thinking mind
Self-occupied; to which all outward things
Are like an idle matter. Still she sighed,
But yet no motion of the breast was seen, 800
No heaving of the heart. While by the fire
We sate together, sighs came on my ear,
I knew not how, and hardly whence they
    came.

"Ere my departure, to her care I gave,
For her son's use, some tokens of regard, 805
Which with a look of welcome she received;
And I exhorted her to place her trust
In God's good love, and seek his help by
    prayer.
I took my staff, and, when I kissed her
    babe,
The tears stood in her eyes. I left her
    then 810
With the best hope and comfort I could
    give:
She thanked me for my wish;—but for my
    hope
It seemed she did not thank me.
               I returned,
And took my rounds along this road again
When on its sunny bank the primrose
    flower 815
Peeped forth, to give an earnest of the
    spring.

I found her sad and drooping: she had
     learned
No tidings of her husband! if he lived,
She knew not that he lived; if he were
     dead,
She knew not he was dead. She seemed
     the same   820
In person and appearance; but her house
Bespake a sleepy hand of negligence;
The floor was neither dry nor neat, the
     hearth
Was comfortless, and her small lot of books,
Which, in the cottage window, heretofore
Had been piled up against the corner
     panes   825
In seemly order, now, with straggling
     leaves,
Lay scattered here and there, open or shut,
As they had chanced to fall. Her infant
     babe
Had from his mother caught the trick of
     grief,   830
And sighed among its playthings. I with-
     drew,
And once again entering the garden saw,
More plainly still, that poverty and grief
Were now come nearer to her: weeds
     defaced
The hardened soil, and knots of withered
     grass: 835
No ridges there appeared of clear black
     mould,
No winter greenness; of her herbs and
     flowers,
It seemed the better part was gnawed away
Or trampled into earth; a chain of straw,
Which had been twined about the slender
     stem   840
Of a young apple tree, lay at its root;
The bark was nibbled round by truant
     sheep.
—Margaret stood near, her infant in her
     arms,
And, noting that my eye was on the tree,
She said, 'I fear it will be dead and gone 845
Ere Robert come again.' When to the
     house
We had returned together, she enquired
If I had any hope:—but for her babe
And for her little orphan boy, she said,
She had no wish to live, that she must die 850
Of sorrow. Yet I saw the idle loom
Still in its place; his Sunday garments hung
Upon the self-same nail; his very staff
Stood undisturbed behind the door.
                              And when,
In bleak December, I retraced this way, 855
She told me that her little babe was dead,
And she was left alone. She now, released
From her maternal cares, had taken up

The employment common through these
     wilds, and gained,
By spinning hemp, a pittance for her-
     self;   860
And for this end had hired a neighbor's
     boy
To give her needful help. That very time
Most willingly she put her work aside,
And walked with me along the miry road,
Heedless how far; and, in such piteous
     sort   865
That any heart had ached to hear her,
     begged
That, whereso'er I went, I still would ask
For him whom she had lost. We parted
     then—
Our final parting; for from that time forth
Did many seasons pass ere I returned 870
Into this tract again.
                         Nine tedious years;
From their first separation, nine long years,
She lingered in unquiet widowhood;
A wife and widow. Needs must it have
     been
A sore heart-wasting! I have heard, my
     friend,   875
That in yon arbor oftentimes she sate
Alone, through half the vacant Sabbath
     day;
And, if a dog passed by, she still would quit
The shade, and look abroad. On this old
     bench
For hours she sate; and evermore her eye 880
Was busy in the distance, shaping things
That made her heart beat quick. You see
     that path,
Now faint,—the grass has crept o'er its grey
     line;
There, to and fro, she passed through
     many a day
Of the warm summer, from a belt of
     hemp   885
That girt her waist, spinning the long-
     drawn thread
With backward steps. Yet ever as there
     passed
A man whose garments showed the soldier's
     red,
Or crippled mendicant in soldier's garb,
The little child who sate to turn the
     wheel   890
Ceased from his task; and she with falter-
     ing voice
Made many a fond enquiry; and when they
Whose presence gave no comfort, were
     gone by,
Her heart was still more sad. And by yon
     gate,
That bars the traveller's road, she often
     stood,   895

And when a stranger horseman came, the
latch
Would lift, and in his face look wistfully:
Most happy, if, from aught discovered
there
Of tender feeling, she might dare repeat
The same sad question. Meanwhile her
poor hut   900
Sank to decay; for he was gone, whose
hand,
At the first nipping of October frost,
Closed up each chink, and with fresh bands
of straw
Chequered the green-grown thatch. And
so she lived
Through the long winter, reckless and
alone,   905
Until her house, by frost, and thaw, and
rain,
Was sapped; and while she slept, the
nightly damps
Did chill her breast; and in the stormy day
Her tattered clothes were ruffled by the
wind,
Even at the side of her own fire. Yet
still   910
She loved this wretched spot, nor would for
worlds
Have parted hence; and still that length of
road,
And this rude bench, one torturing hope
endeared,
Fast rooted at her heart: and here, my
friend,—
In sickness she remained; and here she
died;   915
Last human tenant of these ruined walls!"

The old man ceased; he saw that I was
moved;
From that low bench, rising instinctively
I turned aside in weakness, nor had power
To thank him for the tale which he had
told.   920
I stood, and leaning o'er the garden wall
Reviewed that woman's sufferings; and it
seemed
To comfort me while with a brother's love
I blessed her in the impotence of grief.
Then towards the cottage I returned; and
traced   925
Fondly, though with an interest more mild,
That secret spirit of humanity
Which, 'mid the calm oblivious tendencies
Of nature, 'mid her plants, and weeds, and
flowers,
And silent overgrowings, still survived.   930
The old man, noting this, resumed, and
said,

"My friend! enough to sorrow you have
given,
The purposes of wisdom ask no more:
Nor more would she have craved as due to
one
Who, in her worst distress, had ofttimes
felt   935
The unbounded might of prayer; and
learned, with soul
Fixed on the cross, that consolation springs,
From sources deeper far than deepest pain,
For the meek sufferer. Why then should
we read
The forms of things with an unworthy
eye?   940
She sleeps in the calm earth, and peace is
here.
I well remember that those very plumes,
Those weeds, and the high spear grass on
that wall,
By mist and silent raindrops silvered o'er,
As once I passed, into my heart con-
veyed   945
So still an image of tranquillity,
So calm and still, and looked so beautiful
Amid the uneasy thoughts which filled my
mind,
That what we feel of sorrow and despair
From ruin and from change, and all the
grief   950
That passing shows of being leave behind,
Appeared an idle dream, that could main-
tain,
Nowhere, dominion o'er the enlightened
spirit
Whose meditative sympathies repose
Upon the breast of Faith. I turned
away,   955
And walked along my road in happiness."

BOOK SECOND

THE SOLITARY

"So was he lifted gently from the ground,
And with their freight homeward the shep-
herds moved
Through the dull mist, I following—when
a step,
A single step, that freed me from the
skirts   830
Of the blind vapor, opened to my view
Glory beyond all glory ever seen
By waking sense or by the dreaming soul!
The appearance, instantaneously disclosed,
Was of a mighty city—boldly say   835
A wilderness of building, sinking far
And self-withdrawn into a boundless depth,
Far sinking into splendor—without end!
Fabric it seemed of diamond and of gold,

With alabaster domes, and silver spires, 840
And blazing terrace upon terrace, high
Uplifted; here, serene pavilions bright,
In avenues disposed; there, towers begirt
With battlements that on their restless
  fronts
Bore stars—illumination of all gems! 845
By earthly nature had the effect been
  wrought
Upon the dark materials of the storm
Now pacified; on them, and on the coves
And mountain steeps and summits, where-
  unto
The vapors had receded, taking there 850
Their station under a cerulean sky.
Oh, 'twas an unimaginable sight!
Clouds, mists, streams, watery rocks and
  emerald turf,
Clouds of all tincture, rocks and sapphire
  sky,
Confused, commingled, mutually in-
  flamed, 855
Molten together, and composing thus,
Each lost in each, that marvellous array
Of temple, palace, citadel, and huge
Fantastic pomp of structure without name,
In fleecy folds voluminous, enwrapped. 860
Right in the midst, where interspace ap-
  peared
Of open court, an object like a throne
Under a shining canopy of state
Stood fixed; and fixed resemblances were
  seen
To implements of ordinary use, 865
But vast in size, in substance glorified;
Such as by Hebrew Prophets were beheld
In vision—forms uncouth of mightiest
  power
For admiration and mysterious awe.
This little vale, a dwelling place of Man, 870
Lay low beneath my feet; 'twas visible—
I saw not, but I felt that it was there.
That which I *saw* was the revealed abode
Of Spirits in beatitude: my heart
Swelled in my breast—'I have been dead,'
  I cried, 875
'And now I live! Oh! wherefore *do* I live?'
And with that pang I prayed to be no
  more!—"

BOOK THIRD

[THE SOLITARY'S LIFE]

"The tenor
Which my life holds, he readily may conceive
Whoe'er hath stood to watch a mountain
  brook
In some still passage of its course, and
  seen, 970

Within the depths of its capacious breast,
Inverted trees, rocks, clouds, and azure sky;
And, on its glassy surface, specks of foam,
And conglobated bubbles undissolved,
Numerous as stars; that, by their onward
  lapse, 975
Betray to sight the motion of the stream,
Else imperceptible. Meanwhile, is heard
A softened roar, or murmur; and the sound
Though soothing, and the little floating
  isles
Though beautiful, are both by Nature
  charged 980
With the same pensive office; and make
  known
Through what perplexing labyrinths,
  abrupt
Precipitations, and untoward straits,
The earth-born wanderer hath passed; and
  quickly
That respite o'er, like traverses and toils 985
Must he again encounter.—Such a stream
Is human life; and so the spirit fares
In the best quiet to her course allowed;
And such is mine,—save only for a hope
That my particular current soon will
  reach 990
The unfathomable gulf, where all is still!"

BOOK FOURTH

DESPONDENCY CORRECTED

"At this day
When a Tartarean darkness overspreads
The groaning nations; when the impious
  rule,
By will or by established ordinance,
Their own dire agents, and constrain the
  good 300
To acts which they abhor; though I bewail
This triumph, yet the pity of my heart
Prevents me not from owning, that the law,
By which mankind now suffers, is most just.
For by superior energies; more strict 305
Affiance in each other; faith more firm
In their unhallowed principles; the bad
Have fairly earned a victory o'er the weak,
The vacillating, inconsistent good.
Therefore, not unconsoled, I wait—in
  hope 310
To see the moment, when the righteous
  cause
Shall gain defenders zealous and devout
As they who have opposed her; in which
  Virtue
Will, to her efforts, tolerate no bounds
That are not lofty as her rights; aspiring 315
By impulse of her own ethereal zeal.
That spirit only can redeem mankind;
And when that sacred spirit shall appear,

Then shall *our* triumph be complete as
   theirs.
Yet should this confidence prove vain, the
   wise   320
Have still the keeping of their proper
   peace;
Are guardians of their own tranquillity.
They act, or they recede, observe, and feel;
'Knowing the heart of man is set to be
The center of this world, about the
   which   325
Those revolutions of disturbances
Still roll; where all the aspects of misery
Predominate; whose strong effects are such
As he must bear, being powerless to redress;
And that unless above himself he can   330
Erect himself, how poor a thing is man!'

"Happy is he who lives to understand,
Not human nature only, but explores
All natures,—to the end that he may find
The law that governs each; and where
   begins   335
The union, the partition where, that makes
Kind and degree, among all visible beings;
The constitutions, powers, and faculties,
Which they inherit,—cannot step be-
   yond,—
And cannot fall beneath; that do assign, 340
To every class its station and its office,
Through all the mighty commonwealth of
   things;
Up from the creeping plant to sovereign
   Man.
Such converse, if directed by a meek,
Sincere, and humble spirit, teaches love: 345
For knowledge is delight; and such delight
Breeds love: yet, suited as it rather is
To thought and to the climbing intellect,
It teaches less to love, than to adore;
If that be not indeed the highest love!" 350

[SOME SCIENTISTS WAGING WARFARE AGAINST
OUR SOULS]

      "Shall men for whom our age
Unbaffled powers of vision hath pre-
   pared,   945
To explore the world without and world
   within,
Be joyless as the blind? Ambitious spirits—
Whom earth, at this late season, hath pro-
   duced
To regulate the moving spheres, and weigh
The planets in the hollow of their hand; 950
And they who rather dive than soar, whose
   pains
Have solved the elements, or analysed
The thinking principle—shall they in fact
Prove a degraded race? and what avails

Renown, if their presumption make them
   such?   955
Oh! there is laughter at their work in
   heaven!
Enquire of ancient Wisdom; go, demand
Of mighty Nature, if 'twas ever meant
That we should pry far off yet be unraised;
That we should pore, and dwindle as we
   pore,   960
Viewing all objects unremittingly
In disconnection dead and spiritless;
And still dividing, and dividing still,
Break down all grandeur, still unsatisfied
With the perverse attempt, while little-
   ness   965
May yet become more little; waging thus
An impious warfare with the very life
Of our own souls!"

[DESPONDENCY CURED BY COMMUNION WITH
NATURE]

      "As men from men
Do, in the constitution of their souls,
Differ, by mystery not to be explained;
And as we fall by various ways, and sink
One deeper than another, self-con-
   demned   1110
Through manifold degrees of guilt and
   shame;
So manifold and various are the ways
Of restoration, fashioned to the steps
Of all infirmity, and tending all
To the same point, attainable by all— 1115
Peace in ourselves, and union with our
   God.
For you, assuredly, a hopeful road
Lies open: we have heard from you a voice
At every moment softened in its course
By tenderness of heart; have seen your
   eye,   1120
Even like an altar lit by fire from heaven.
Kindle before us.—Your discourse this day.
That, like the fabled Lethe, wished to flow
In creeping sadness, through oblivious
   shades
Of death and night, has caught at every
   turn   1125
The colors of the sun. Access for you
Is yet preserved to principles of truth,
Which the imaginative Will upholds
In seats of wisdom, not to be approached
By the inferior faculty that molds,   1130
With her minute and speculative pains,
Opinion, ever changing!
             I have seen
A curious child, who dwelt upon a tract
Of inland ground, applying to his ear
The convolutions of a smooth-lipped
   shell: 1135

To which, in silence hushed, his very soul
Listened intensely; and his countenance
   soon
Brightened with joy; for from within were
   heard
Murmurings, whereby the monitor ex-
   pressed
Mysterious union with its native sea.　1140
Even such a shell the universe itself
Is to the ear of faith; and there are times,
I doubt not, when to you it doth impart
Authentic tidings of invisible things;
Of ebb and flow, and ever-during
   power;　　　　　　　　　　1145
And central peace, subsisting at the heart
Of endless agitation. Here you stand,
Adore, and worship, when you know it not;
Pious beyond the intention of your
   thought;
Devout above the meaning of your will.　1150
—Yes, you have felt, and may not cease to
   feel.
The estate of man would be indeed forlorn
If false conclusions of the reasoning power
Made the eye blind, and closed the passages
Through which the ear converses with the
   heart.　　　　　　　　　　1155
Has not the soul, the being of your life,
Received a shock of awful consciousness,
In some calm season, when these lofty rocks
At night's approach bring down the un-
   clouded sky,
To rest upon their circumambient
   walls;　　　　　　　　　　1160
A temple framing of dimensions vast,
And yet not too enormous for the sound
Of human anthems—choral song, or burst
Sublime of instrumental harmony,
To glorify the Eternal! What if these 1165
Did never break the stillness that prevails
Here—if the solemn nightingale be mute,
And the soft woodlark here did never
   chant
Her vespers—Nature fails not to provide
Impulse and utterance. The whispering
   air　　　　　　　　　　　1170
Sends inspiration from the shadowy heights,
And blind recesses of the caverned rocks;
The little rills, and waters numberless,
Inaudible by daylight, blend their notes
With the loud streams; and often, at the
   hour　　　　　　　　　　1175
When issue forth the first pale stars, is
   heard,
Within the circuit of this fabric huge,
One voice—the solitary raven, flying
Athwart the concave of the dark blue
   dome,
Unseen, perchance above all power of
   sight—　　　　　　　　　1180

An iron knell! with echoes from afar
Faint—and still fainter—as the cry, with
   which
The wanderer accompanies her flight
Through the calm region, fades upon the
   ear,
Diminishing by distance till it seemed　1185
To expire; yet from the abyss is caught
   again,
And yet again recovered!
              But descending
From these imaginative heights, that yield
Far-stretching views into eternity,
Acknowledge that to Nature's humbler
   power　　　　　　　　　　1190
Your cherished sullenness is forced to bend
Even here, where her amenities are sown
With sparing hand. Then trust yourself
   abroad
To range her blooming bowers, and spa-
   cious fields,
Where on the labors of the happy
   throng　　　　　　　　　　1195
She smiles, including in her wide embrace
City, and town, and tower, and sea with
   ships
Sprinkled; be our companion while we
   track
Her rivers populous with gliding life;
While, free as air, o'er printless sands we
   march,　　　　　　　　　　1200
Or pierce the gloom of her majestic woods;
Roaming, or resting under grateful shade
In peace and meditative cheerfulness;
Where living things, and things inanimate,
Do speak, at Heaven's command, to eye
   and ear,　　　　　　　　　1205
And speak to social reason's inner sense,
With inarticulate language.
              For, the man—
Who in this spirit communes with the
   forms
Of nature, who with understanding heart
Both knows and loves such objects as
   excite　　　　　　　　　　1210
No morbid passions, no disquietude,
No vengeance, and no hatred—needs must
   feel
The joy of that pure principle of love
So deeply, that, unsatisfied with aught
Less pure and exquisite, he cannot
   choose　　　　　　　　　　1215
But seek for objects of a kindred love
In fellow-natures and a kindred joy.
Accordingly he by degrees perceives
His feelings of aversion softened down;
A holy tenderness pervade his frame.　1220
His sanity of reason not impaired,
Say rather, all his thoughts now flowing
   clear,

From a clear fountain flowing, he looks
  round
And seeks for good; and finds the good he
  seeks—
Until abhorrence and contempt are
  things   1225
He only knows by name; and, if he hear,
From other mouths, the language which
  they speak,
He is compassionate; and has no thought,
No feeling, which can overcome his love."

FROM BOOK NINTH

[MAN NOT A MERE INSTRUMENT—WISH FOR A
SYSTEM OF NATIONAL EDUCATION]

                          Our life is turned
Out of her course, wherever man is made
An offering, or a sacrifice, a tool   115
Or implement, a passive thing employed
As a brute mean, without acknowledgment
Of common right or interest in the end;
Used or abused, as selfishness may prompt.

. . . .

O for the coming of that glorious time
When, prizing knowledge as her noblest
  wealth
And best protection, this Imperial
  Realm   295
While she exacts allegiance, shall admit
An obligation, on her part, to *teach*
Them who are born to serve her and obey;
Binding herself by statute to secure
For all the children whom her soil main-
  tains   300
The rudiments of letters, and inform
The mind with moral and religious truth,
Both understood and practised,—so that
  none,
However destitute, be left to droop
By timely culture unsustained; or run   305
Into a wild disorder; or be forced
To drudge through a weary life without
  the help
Of intellectual implements and tools.

1795-1814   1814

LAODAMIA

"With sacrifice before the rising morn
Vows have I made by fruitless hope
  inspired;
And from the infernal Gods, 'mid shades
  forlorn
Of night, my slaughtered Lord have I
  required:

Celestial pity I again implore;—   5
Restore him to my sight—great Jove, restore!"

So speaking, and by fervent love endowed
With faith, the suppliant heavenward lifts
  her hands;
While, like the sun emerging from a cloud,
Her countenance brightens—and her eye
  expands;   10
Her bosom heaves and spreads, her stature
  grows;
And she expects the issue in repose.

O terror! what hath she perceived?—O joy!
What doth she look on?—whom doth she
  behold?
Her Hero slain upon the beach of Troy?   15
His vital presence? his corporeal mold?
It is—if sense deceive her not—'tis He!
And a God leads him, wingèd Mercury!

Mild Hermes spake—and touched her with
  his wand
That calms all fear; "Such grace hath
  crowned thy prayer,   20
Laodamía! that at Jove's command
Thy husband walks the paths of upper air:
He comes to tarry with thee three hours'
  space;
Accept the gift, behold him face to face!"

Forth sprang the impassioned Queen her
  Lord to clasp;   25
Again that consummation she essayed;
But unsubstantial form eludes her grasp
As often as that eager grasp was made.
The phantom parts—but parts to reunite,
And reassume his place before her sight.   30

"Protesiláus, lo! thy guide is gone!
Confirm, I pray, the vision with thy voice:
This is our palace,—yonder is thy throne;
Speak, and the floor thou tread'st on will
  rejoice.
Not to appal me have the gods bestowed   35
This precious boon; and blest a sad abode."

"Great Jove, Laodamía! doth not leave
His gifts imperfect:—Spectre though I be,
I am not sent to scare thee or deceive;
But in reward of thy fidelity.   40
And something also did my worth obtain;
For fearless virtue bringeth boundless gain.

"Thou knowest, the Delphic oracle foretold
That the first Greek who touched the
  Trojan strand
Should die; but me the threat could not
  withhold: 45

A generous cause a victim did demand;
And forth I leapt upon the sandy plain;
A self-devoted chief—by Hector slain."

"Supreme of Heroes—bravest, noblest,
      best!
Thy matchless courage I bewail no more, 50
Which then, when tens of thousands were
      depressed
By doubt, propelled thee to the fatal shore;
Thou found'st—and I forgive thee—here
      thou art—
A nobler counsellor than my poor heart.

"But thou, though capable of sternest
      deed,   55
Wert kind as resolute, and good as brave;
And he, whose power restores thee, hath
      decreed
Thou should'st elude the malice of the
      grave:
Redundant are thy locks, thy lips as fair
As when their breath enriched Thessalian
      air.   60

"No spectre greets me,—no vain shadow
      this;
Come, blooming hero, place thee by my
      side!
Give, on this well-known couch, one nup-
      tial kiss
To me, this day, a second time thy bride!"
Jove frowned in heaven: the conscious
      Parcæ threw   65
Upon those roseate lips a Stygian hue.

"This visage tells thee that my doom is
      past:
Nor should the change be mourned, even
      if the joys
Of sense were able to return as fast
And surely as they vanish. Earth destroys 70
Those raptures duly—Erebus disdains:
Calm pleasures there abide—majestic pains.

"Be taught, O faithful consort, to control
Rebellious passion: for the Gods approve
The depth, and not the tumult, of the
      soul;   75
A fervent, not ungovernable, love.
Thy transports moderate; and meekly
      mourn
When I depart, for brief is my sojourn—"

"Ah, wherefore?—Did not Hercules by
      force
Wrest from the guardian monster of the
      tomb   80
Alcestis, a reanimated corse,

Given back to dwell on earth in vernal
      bloom?
Medea's spells dispersed the weight of
      years,
And Æson stood a youth 'mid youthful
      peers.

"The Gods to us are merciful—and they 85
Yet further may relent: for mightier far
Than strength of nerve and sinew, or the
      sway
Of magic potent over sun and star,
Is love, though oft to agony distrest,
And though his favorite seat be feeble
      woman's breast.   90

"But if thou goest, follow—" "Peace!"
      he said,—
She looked upon him and was calmed and
      cheered;
The ghastly color from his lips had fled;
In his deportment, shape, and mien, ap-
      peared
Elysian beauty, melancholy grace,   95
Brought from a pensive though a happy
      place.

He spake of love, such love as spirits feel
In worlds whose course is equable and
      pure;
No fears to beat away—no strife to heal—
The past unsighed for, and the future
      sure;   100
Spake of heroic arts in graver mood
Revived, with finer harmony pursued;

Of all that is most beauteous—imaged
      there
In happier beauty; more pellucid streams,
An ampler ether, a diviner air,   105
And fields invested with purpureal gleams;
Climes which the sun, who sheds the bright-
      est day
Earth knows, is all unworthy to survey.

Yet there the soul shall enter which hath
      earned
That privilege by virtue.—"Ill," said he, 110
"The end of man's existence I discerned,
Who from ignoble games and revelry
Could draw, when we had parted, vain
      delight,
While tears were thy best pastime, day and
      night;

"And while my youthful peers before my
      eyes   115
(Each hero following his peculiar bent)
Prepared themselves for glorious enterprise
By martial sports,—or, seated in the tent,

Chieftains and kings in council were detained;
What time the fleet at Aulis lay enchained.   120

"The wished-for wind was given:—I then
revolved
The oracle, upon the silent sea;
And, if no worthier led the way, resolved
That, of a thousand vessels, mine should be
The foremost prow in pressing to the
strand,—   125
Mine the first blood that tinged the Trojan
sand.

"Yet bitter, oft times bitter, was the pang
When of thy loss I thought, belovèd wife!
On thee too fondly did my memory hang,
And on the joys we shared in mortal
life,—   130
The paths which we had ʌrod—these foun-
tains, flowers,
My new-planned cities, and unfinished
towers.

' But should suspense permit the Foe to
cry,
'Behold they tremble!—haughty their array,
Yet of their number no one dares to
die?'   135
In soul I swept the indignity away:
Old frailties then recurred:—but lofty
thought,
In act embodied, my deliverance wrought.

"And thou, though strong in love, art all
too weak
In reason, in self-government too slow; 140
I counsel thee by fortitude to seek
Our blest reunion in the shades below.
The invisible world with thee hath sympa-
thised;
Be thy affections raised and solemnised.

"Learn, by a mortal yearning, to ascend—145
Seeking a higher object. Love was given,
Encouraged, sanctioned, chiefly for that
end:
For this the passion to excess was driven—
That self might be annulled: her bondage
prove
The fetters of a dream, opposed to
love."—   150

Aloud she shrieked! for Hermes reappears!
Round the dear shade she would have
clung—'tis vain:
The hours are past—too brief had they
been years;

And him no mortal effort can detain:
Swift, toward the realms that know not
earthly day,   155
He through the portal takes his silent way,
And on the palace floor a lifeless corse she
lay.

Thus, all in vain exhorted and reproved,
She perished; and, as for a wilful crime,
By the just Gods whom no weak pity
moved,   160
Was doomed to wear out her appointed
time,
Apart from happy ghosts, that gather
flowers
Of blissful quiet 'mid unfading bowers.

—Yet tears to human suffering are due;
And mortal hopes defeated and o'er-
thrown   165
Are mourned by man, and not by man
alone,
As fondly he believes.—Upon the side
Of Hellespont (such faith was entertained)
A knot of spiry trees for ages grew
From out the tomb of him for whom she
died;   170
And ever, when such stature they had
gained
That Ilium's walls were subject to their
view,
The tree's tall summits withered at the
sight;
A constant interchange of growth and
blight!

1814   1815

" 'WEAK IS THE WILL OF MAN, HIS JUDGMENT BLIND' "

"Weak is the will of Man, his judgment
blind;
Remembrance persecutes, and hope be-
trays;
Heavy is woe;—and joy, for human kind,
A mournful thing, so transient is the
blaze!"
Thus might *he* paint our lot of mortal
days   5
Who wants the glorious faculty assigned
To elevate the more-than-reasoning mind,
And color life's dark cloud with orient
rays.
Imagination is that sacred power,
Imagination lofty and refined: 10
'Tis hers to pluck the amaranthine flower

Of faith, and round the sufferer's temples
  bind
Wreaths that endure affliction's heaviest
  shower,
And do not shrink from sorrow's keenest
  wind.

c. 1815   1815

"SURPRISED BY JOY—IMPA-TIENT AS THE WIND"

Surprised by joy—impatient as the wind
I turned to share the transport—Oh! with
  whom
But thee, deep buried in the silent tomb,
That spot which no vicissitude can find?
Love, faithful love, recalled thee to my
  mind—   5
But how could I forget thee? Through
  what power,
Even for the least division of an hour,
Have I been so beguiled as to be blind
To my most grievous loss!—That
  thought's return
Was the worst pang that sorrow ever
  bore,   10
Save one, one only, when I stood forlorn,
Knowing my heart's best treasure was no
  more;
That neither present time nor years un-
  born
Could to my sight that heavenly face re-
  store.

1812   1815

DION

(SEE PLUTARCH)

I

Serene, and fitted to embrace,
Where'er he turned, a swan-like grace
Of haughtiness without pretence,
And to unfold a still magnificence,
Was princely Dion, in the power   5
And beauty of his happier hour
And what pure homage *then* did wait
On Dion's virtues, while the lunar beam
Of Plato's genius, from its lofty sphere,
Fell round him in the grove of Academe, 10
Softening their inbred dignity austere—
  That he, not too elate
  With self-sufficing solitude,
But with majestic lowliness endued,
  Might in the universal bosom reign,   15
And from affectionate observance gain
Help, under every change of adverse fate.

II

Five thousand warriors—O the rapturous
  day!
Each crowned with flowers, and armed with
  spear and shield,
Or ruder weapon which their course might
  yield,   20
To Syracuse advance in bright array.
Who leads them on?—The anxious people
  see
Long-exiled Dion marching at their head,
He also crowned with flowers of Sicily,
And in a white, far-beaming, corselet
  clad!   25
Pure transport undisturbed by doubt or
  fear
The gazers feel; and, rushing to the plain,
Salute those strangers as a holy train
Or blest procession (to the Immortals dear)
That brought their precious liberty
  again.   30
Lo! when the gates are entered, on each
  hand,
Down the long street, rich goblets filled
  with wine
  In seemly order stand,
On tables set, as if for rites divine;
And, as the great deliverer marches by,   35
He looks on festal ground with fruits be-
  strown;
And flowers are on his person thrown
  In boundless prodigality;
Nor doth the general voice abstain from
  prayer,
Invoking Dion's tutelary care,   40
As if a very deity he were!

III

Mourn, hills and groves of Attica! and
  mourn
Ilissus, bending o'er thy classic urn!
Mourn, and lament for him whose spirit
  dreads
Your once sweet memory, studious walks
  and shades!   45
For him who to divinity aspired,
Not on the breath of popular applause,
But through dependence on the sacred laws
Framed in the schools where Wisdom dwelt
  retired,
Intent to trace the ideal path of right   50
(More fair than heaven's broad causeway
  paved with stars)
Which Dion learned to measure with sub-
  lime delight;
But he hath overleaped the eternal bars;
And, following guides whose craft holds no
  consent

With aught that breathes the ethereal ele-
　　ment,　　　　　　　　　　　　　　55
Hath stained the robes of civil power with
　　blood,
Unjustly shed, though for the public good.
Whence doubts that came too late, and
　　wishes vain,
Hollow excuses, and triumphant pain;
And oft his cogitations sink as low　60
As, through the abysses of a joyless heart,
The heaviest plummet of despair can go—
But whence that sudden check? that fearful
　　start!
He hears an uncouth sound—
　　Anon his lifted eyes　　　　　　65
Saw, at a long-drawn gallery's dusky bound,
A shape of more than mortal size
And hideous aspect, stalking round and
　　round!
A woman's garb the phantom wore,
　　And fiercely swept the marble floor—　70
Like Auster whirling to and fro,
　　His force on Caspian foam to try;
Or Boreas when he scours the snow
That skins the plains of Thessaly,
Or when aloft on Maenalus he stops　75
His flight, 'mid eddying pine-tree tops!

IV

So, but from toil less sign of profit reaping,
The sullen specter to her purpose bowed,
　　Sweeping—vehemently sweeping—
No pause admitted, no design avowed!　80
"Avaunt, inexplicable Guest!—avaunt,"
Exclaimed the chieftain—"let me rather see
The coronal that coiling vipers make;
The torch that flames with many a lurid
　　flake,
And the long train of doleful pageantry　85
Which they behold, whom vengeful Furies
　　haunt;
Who, while they struggle from the scourge
　　to flee,
Move where the blasted soil is not unworn,
And, in their anguish, bear what other
　　minds have borne!"

V

But shapes that come not at an earthly
　　call,　　　　　　　　　　　　　　90
Will not depart when mortal voices bid;
Lords of the visionary eye whose lid,
Once raised, remains aghast, and will not
　　fall!
Ye Gods, thought he, that servile imple-
　　ment
Obeys a mystical intent!　　　　　　95
Your minister would brush away

The spots that to my soul adhere;
But should she labor night and day,
They will not, cannot disappear;
Whence angry perturbations,—and that
　　look　　　　　　　　　　　　　　100
Which no philosophy can brook!

VI

Ill-fated chief! there are whose hopes are
　　built
Upon the ruins of thy glorious name;
Who, through the portal of one moment's
　　guilt,
Pursue thee with their deadly aim!　105
O matchless perfidy! portentous lust
Of monstrous crime!—that horror-striking
　　blade,
Drawn in defiance of the gods, hath laid
The noble Syracusan low in dust!
Shuddered the walls—the marble city
　　wept—　　　　　　　　　　　　110
And silvan places heaved a pensive sigh;
But in calm peace the appointed victim
　　slept,
As he had fallen in magnanimity;
Of spirit too capacious to require
That destiny her course should change;
　　too just　　　　　　　　　　　　115
To his own native greatness to desire
That wretched boon, days lengthened by
　　mistrust.
So were the hopeless troubles, that in-
　　volved
The soul of Dion, instantly dissolved.
Released from life and cares of princely
　　state,　　　　　　　　　　　　　120
He left this moral grafted on his fate:
"Him only pleasure leads, and peace at-
　　tends,
Him, only him, the shield of Jove defends,
Whose means are fair and spotless as his
　　ends."

1816　　　　　　　　　　　　　　1820

COMPOSED UPON AN EVE-
NING OF EXTRAORDINARY
SPLENDOR AND BEAUTY

Had this effulgence disappeared
With flying haste, I might have sent,
Among the speechless clouds, a look
Of blank astonishment;
But 'tis endued with power to stay,　5
And sanctify one closing day,
That frail mortality may see—
What is?—ah no, but what can be!
Time was when field and watery cove

With modulated echoes rang, 10
While choirs of fervent angels sang
Their vespers in the grove;
Or, crowning, star-like, each some sovereign
    height,
Warbled, for heaven above and earth be-
    low,
Strains suitable to both.—Such holy rite, 15
Methinks, if audibly repeated now
From hill or valley, could not move
Sublimer transport, purer love,
Than doth this silent spectacle—the
    gleam—
The shadow—and the peace supreme! 20

No sound is uttered,—but a deep
And solemn harmony pervades
The hollow vale from steep to steep,
And penetrates the glades.
Far-distant images draw nigh, 25
Called forth by wondrous potency
Of beamy radiance, that imbues,
Whate'er it strikes, with gem-like hues!
In vision exquisitely clear,
Herds range along the mountain side; 30
And glistening antlers are descried;
And gilded flocks appear.
Thine is the tranquil hour, purpureal Eve!
But long as god-like wish, or hope divine,
Informs my spirit, ne'er can I believe 35
That this magnificence is wholly thine!
—From worlds not quickened by the sun
A portion of the gift is won;
An intermingling of Heaven's pomp is
    spread
On ground which British shepherds
    tread! 40

And, if there be whom broken ties
Afflict, or injuries assail,
Yon hazy ridges to their eyes
Present a glorious scale,
Climbing suffused with sunny air, 45
To stop—no record hath told where!
And tempting fancy to ascend,
And with immortal spirits blend!
—Wings at my shoulders seem to play;
But, rooted here, I stand and gaze 50
On those bright steps that heavenward
    raise
Their practicable way.
Come forth, ye drooping old men, look
    abroad,
And see to what fair countries ye are
    bound!
And if some traveller, weary of his road, 55
Hath slept since noontide on the grassy
    ground,
Ye Genii! to his covert speed;
And wake him with such gentle heed

As may attune his soul to meet the dower
Bestowed on this transcendent hour! 60

Such hues from their celestial urn
Were wont to stream before mine eye,
Where'er it wandered in the morn
Of blissful infancy.
This glimpse of glory, why renewed? 65
Nay, rather speak with gratitude;
For, if a vestige of those gleams
Survived, 'twas only in my dreams.
Dread power! whom peace and calmness
    serve
No less than Nature's threatening voice, 70
If aught unworthy be my choice,
From THEE if I would swerve;
Oh, let thy grace remind me of the light
Full early lost, and fruitlessly deplored;
Which, at this moment, on my waking
    sight 75
Appears to shine, by miracle restored;
My soul, though yet confined to earth,
Rejoices in a second birth!
—'Tis past, the visionary splendor fades;
And night approaches with her shades. 80
1818   1820

AFTER-THOUGHT

I thought of thee, my partner and my
    guide,
As being past away.—Vain sympathies!
For, backward, Duddon! as I cast my eyes,
I see what was, and is, and will abide;
Still glides the stream, and shall forever
    glide; 5
The form remains, the function never dies;
While we, the brave, the mighty, and the
    wise,
We men, who in our morn of youth defied
The elements, must vanish;—be it so!
Enough, if something from our hands have
    power 10
To live, and act, and serve the future hour;
And if, as toward the silent tomb we go,
Through love, through hope, and faith's
    transcendent dower,
We feel that we are greater than we know.
1819   1820

FROM ECCLESIASTICAL SONNETS

PLACES OF WORSHIP

As star that shines dependent upon star
Is to the sky while we look up in love;
As to the deep fair ships which though
    they move

Seem fixed, to eyes that watch them from
        afar;
As to the sandy desert fountains are,   5
With palm groves shaded at wide intervals,
Whose fruit around the sunburnt Native
        falls
Of roving tired or desultory war
Such to this British Isle her Christian fanes,
Each linked to each for kindred services; 10
Her spires, her steeple towers with glitter-
        ing vanes
Far-kenned, her chapels lurking among
        trees,
Where a few villagers on bended knees
Find solace which a busy world disdains.

c.1821   1822

MUTABILITY

From low to high doth dissolution climb,
And sink from high to low, along a scale
Of awful notes, whose concord shall not
        fail;
A musical but melancholy chime,
Which they can hear who meddle not with
        crime,   5
Nor avarice, nor over-anxious care.
Truth fails not; but her outward forms
        that bear
The longest date do melt like frosty rime,
That in the morning whitened hill and
        plain
And is no more; drop like the tower sub-
        lime   10
Of yesterday, which royally did wear
His crown of weeds, but could not even
        sustain
Some casual shout that broke the silent air,
Or the unimaginable touch of time.

1821   1822

INSIDE OF KING'S COLLEGE CHAPEL, CAMBRIDGE

Tax not the royal saint with vain expense,
With ill-matched aims the architect who
        planned—
Albeit laboring for a scanty band
Of white-robed scholars only—this im-
        mense
And glorious work of fine intelligence!   5
Give all thou canst; high Heaven rejects
        the lore
Of nicely calculated less or more;
So deemed the man who fashioned for the
        sense
These lofty pillars, spread that branching
        roof
Self-poised, and scooped into ten thousand
        cells,   10

Where light and shade repose, where music
        dwells
Lingering—and wandering on as loth to
        die;
Like thoughts whose very sweetness yieldeth
        proof
That they were born for immortality.

THE SAME

What awful pérspective! while from our
        sight
With gradual stealth the lateral windows
        hide
Their portraitures, their stonework glim-
        mers, dyed
In the soft checkerings of a sleepy light.
Martyr, or king, or sainted eremite,   5
Whoe'er ye be, that thus, yourselves unseen,
Imbue your prison bars with solemn sheen,
Shine on, until ye fade with coming
        night!—
But, from the arms of silence—list! O list!
The music bursteth into second life;   10
The notes luxuriate, every stone is kissed
By sound, or ghost of sound, in mazy strife;
Heart-thrilling strains, that cast, before the
        eye
Of the devout, a veil of ecstasy!

CONTINUED

They dreamt not of a perishable home
Who thus could build. Be mine, in hours
        of fear
Or groveling thought, to seek a refuge
        here;
Or through the aisles of Westminster to
        roam;
Where bubbles burst, and folly's dancing
        foam   5
Melts, if it cross the threshold; where the
        wreath
Of awestruck wisdom droops. Or let my
        path
Lead to that younger pile, whose skylight
        dome
Hath typified by reach of daring art
Infinity's embrace; whose guardian crest, 10
The silent cross, among the stars shall
        spread
As now, when she hath also seen her breast
Filled with mementos, satiate with its part
Of grateful England's overflowing dead.

1821   1822

TO THE CUCKOO

Not the whole warbling grove in concert
        heard
When sunshine follows shower, the breast
        can thrill

Like the first summons, Cuckoo! of thy bill.
With its twin notes inseparably paired.
The captive 'mid damp vaults unsunned,
    unaired,   5
Measuring the periods of his lonely doom,
That cry can reach; and to the sick man's
    room
Sends gladness, by no languid smile de-
    clared.
The lordly eagle-race through hostile search
May perish; time may come when never
    more   10
The wilderness shall hear the lion roar;
But, long as cock shall crow from house-
    hold perch
To rouse the dawn, soft gales shall speed
    thy wing,
And thy erratic voice be faithful to the
    spring!

                1827

TO A SKYLARK

Ethereal minstrel! pilgrim of the sky!
Dost thou despise the earth where cares
    abound?
Or, while the wings aspire, are heart and
    eye
Both with thy nest upon the dewy ground?
Thy nest which thou canst drop into at
    will,   5
Those quivering wings composed, that
    music still!
Leave to the nightingale her shady wood;
A privacy of glorious light is thine;
Whence thou dost pour upon the world a
    flood
Of harmony, with instinct more divine; 10
Type of the wise who soar, but never roam;
True to the kindred points of Heaven and
    Home!

1825   1827

"SCORN NOT THE SONNET"

Scorn not the Sonnet; Critic, you have
    frowned,
Mindless of its just honors; with this key
Shakspeare unlocked his heart; the melody
Of this small lute gave ease to Petrarch's
    wound;
A thousand times this pipe did Tasso
    sound;   5
With it Camöens soothed an exile's grief;
The Sonnet glittered a gay myrtle leaf
Amid the cypress with which Dante
    crowned
His visionary brow: a glow-worm lamp

It cheered mild Spenser, called from Faery-
    land   10
To struggle through dark ways; and, when
    a damp
Fell round the path of Milton, in his hand
The thing became a trumpet; whence he
    blew
Soul-animating strains—alas, too few!

                1827

ON THE DEPARTURE OF SIR WALTER SCOTT FROM ABBOTSFORD, FOR NAPLES

A trouble, not of clouds, or weeping rain,
Nor of the setting sun's pathetic light
Engendered, hangs o'er Eildon's triple
    height:
Spirits of power, assembled there, complain
For kindred Power departing from their
    sight;   5
While Tweed, best pleased in chanting a
    blithe strain,
Saddens his voice again, and yet again.
Lift up your hearts, ye mourners! for the
    might
Of the whole world's good wishes with him
    goes;
Blessings and prayers, in nobler retinue 10
Than sceptered king or laurelled con-
    queror knows,
Follow this wondrous potentate. Be true,
Ye winds of ocean, and the midland sea,
Wafting your charge to soft Parthenope!

Sept., 1831   1833

THE TROSSACHS

There's not a nook within this solemn Pass,
But were an apt confessional for one
Taught by his summer spent, his autumn
    gone,
That life is but a tale of morning grass
Withered at eve. From scenes of art which
    chase   5
That thought away, turn, and with watch-
    ful eyes
Feed it 'mid Nature's old felicities,
Rocks, rivers, and smooth lakes more clear
    than glass
Untouched, unbreathed upon. Thrice
    happy quest,
If from a golden perch of aspen spray 10
(October's workmanship to rival May)
The pensive warbler of the ruddy breast
That moral sweeten by a heaven-taught lay,
Lulling the year, with all its cares, to rest!

1831   1835

"MOST SWEET IT IS WITH UNUPLIFTED EYES"

Most sweet it is with unuplifted eyes
To pace the ground, if path be there or
    none,
While a fair region round the traveler lies
Which he forbears again to look upon;
Pleased rather with some soft ideal scene, 5
The work of fancy, or some happy tone
Of meditation, slipping in between
The beauty coming and the beauty gone.
If thought and love desert us, from that
    day
Let us break off all commerce with the
    Muse: 10
With thought and love companions of our
    way,
Whate'er the senses take or may refuse,
The mind's internal heaven shall shed her
    dews
Of inspiration on the humblest lay.
1833   1835

ON THE POWER OF SOUND

I

Thy functions are ethereal,
As if within thee dwelt a glancing mind,
Organ of vision! And a Spirit aërial
Informs the cell of Hearing, dark and
    blind;
Intricate labyrinth, more dread for
    thought   5
To enter than oracular cave;
Strict passage, through which sighs are
    brought,
And whispers for the heart, their slave;
And shrieks, that revel in abuse
Of shivering flesh; and warbled air, 10
Whose piercing sweetness can unloose
The chains of frenzy, or entice a smile
Into the ambush of despair;
Hosannas pealing down the long-drawn
    aisle,
And requiems answered by the pulse that
    beats   15
Devoutly, in life's last retreats!

II

The headlong streams and fountains
Serve Thee, invisible Spirit, with untired
    powers;
Cheering the wakeful tent on Syrian
    mountains,
They lull perchance ten thousand thousand
    flowers.   20

That roar, the prowling lion's *Here I am,*
How fearful to the desert wide!
That bleat, how tender! of the dam
Calling a straggler to her side.
Shout, cuckoo!—let the vernal soul   25
Go with thee to the frozen zone;
Toll from thy loftiest perch, lone bell-bird,
    toll!
At the still hour to Mercy dear,
Mercy from her twilight throne
Listening to nun's faint throb of holy
    fear,   30
To sailor's prayer breathed from a darken-
    ing sea,
Or widow's cottage lullaby.

III

Ye Voices, and ye Shadows
And Images of voice—to hound and horn
From rocky steep and rock-bestudded
    meadows   35
Flung back, and, in the sky's blue caves,
    reborn—
On with your pastime! till the church-
    tower bells
A greeting give of measured glee;
And milder echoes from their cells
Repeat the bridal symphony.   40
Then, or far earlier, let us rove
Where mists are breaking up or gone,
And from aloft look down into a cove
Besprinkled with a careless quire,
Happy milkmaids, one by one   45
Scattering a ditty each to her desire,
A liquid concert matchless by nice Art,
A stream as if from one full heart.

IV

Blest be the song that brightens
The blind man's gloom, exalts the veteran's
    mirth;   50
Unscorned the peasant's whistling breath,
    that lightens
His duteous toil of furrowing the green
    earth.
For the tired slave, Song lifts the languid
    oar,
And bids it aptly fall, with chime
That beautifies the fairest shore,   55
And mitigates the harshest clime.
Yon pilgrims see—in lagging file
They move; but soon the appointed way
A choral *Ave Maria* shall beguile,
And to their hope the distant shrine   60
Glisten with a livelier ray:
Nor friendless he, the prisoner of the mine,
Who from the wellspring of his own clear
    breast
Can draw, and sing his griefs to rest.

V

When civic renovation   65
Dawns on a kingdom, and for needful
    haste
Best eloquence avails not, Inspiration
Mounts with a tune, that travels like a
    blast
Piping through cave and battlemented
    tower;
Then starts the sluggard, pleased to meet 70
That voice of Freedom, in its power
Of promises, shrill, wild, and sweet!
Who, from a martial *pageant*, spreads
Incitements of a battle-day,
Thrilling the unweaponed crowd with
    plumeless heads?—   75
Even She whose Lydian airs inspire
Peaceful striving, gentle play
Of timid hope and innocent desire
Shot from the dancing Graces, as they
    move
Fanned by the plausive wings of Love.   80

VI

How oft along thy mazes,
Regent of sound, have dangerous Passions
    trod!
O Thou, through whom the temple rings
    with praises,
And blackening clouds in thunder speak
    of God,
Betray not by the cozenage of sense   85
Thy votaries, wooingly resigned
To a voluptuous influence
That taints the purer, better, mind;
But lead sick Fancy to a harp
That hath in noble tasks been tried;   90
And, if the virtuous feel a pang too sharp,
Soothe it into patience—stay
The uplifted arm of Suicide;
And let some mood of thine in firm array
Knit every thought the impending issue
    needs   95
Ere martyr burns, or patriot bleeds!

VII

As Conscience, to the center
Of being, smites with irresistible pain,
So shall a solemn cadence, if it enter
The mouldy vaults of the dull idiot's
    brain,   100
Transmute him to a wretch from quiet
    hurled—
Convulsed as by a jarring din;
And then aghast, as at the world
Of reason partially let in
By concords winding with a sway   105
Terrible for sense and soul!
Or awed he weeps, struggling to quell
    dismay.

Point not these mysteries to an Art
Lodged above the starry pole;
Pure modulations flowing from the heart 110
Of divine Love, where Wisdom, Beauty,
    Truth
With Order dwell, in endless youth?

VIII

Oblivion may not cover
All treasures hoarded by the miser, Time.
Orphean Insight! truth's undaunted
    lover   115
To the first leagues of tutored passion
    climb,
When Music deigned within this grosser
    sphere
Her subtle essence to enfold,
And voice and shell drew forth a tear
Softer than Nature's self could mould.   120
Yet *strenuous* was the infant Age:
Art, daring because souls could feel,
Stirred nowhere but an urgent equipage
Of rapt imagination sped her march
Through the realms of woe and weal: 125
Hell to the lyre bowed low; the upper arch
Rejoiced that clamorous spell and magic
    verse
Her wan disasters could disperse.

IX

The gift to King Amphion
That walled a city with its melody   130
Was for belief no dream:—thy skill, Arion!
Could humanize the creatures of the sea,
Where men were monsters. A last grace
    he craves,
Leave for one chant;—the dulcet sound
Steals from the deck o'er willing waves, 135
And listening dolphins gather round.
Self-cast, as with a desperate course,
'Mid that strange audience, he bestrides
A proud one docile as a managed horse;
And singing, while the accordant hand   140
Sweeps his harp, the Master rides;
So shall he touch at length a friendly
    strand,
And he, with his preserver, shine star-
    bright
In memory, through silent night.

X

The pipe of Pan, to shepherds   145
Couched in the shadow of Mænalian pines,
Was passing sweet; the eyeballs of the
    leopards,
That in high triumph drew the Lord of
    vines,
How did they sparkle to the cymbal's clang!
While Fauns and Satyrs beat the ground 150
In cadence,—and Silenus swang

This way and that, with wild flowers
   crowned.
To life, to *life* give back thine ear:
Ye who are longing to be rid
Of fable, though to truth subservient,
   hear   155
The little sprinkling of cold earth that fell
Echoed from the coffin-lid;
The convict's summons in the steeple's
   knell;
"The vain distress-gun," from a leeward
   shore,
Repeated—heard, and heard no more! 160

XI

For terror, joy, or pity,
Vast is the compass and the swell of notes:
From the babe's first cry to voice of regal
   city,
Rolling a solemn sea-like bass, that floats
Far as the woodlands—with the trill to
   blend   165
Of that shy songstress, whose love-tale
Might tempt an angel to descend,
While hovering o'er the moonlight vale.
Ye wandering Utterances, has earth no
   scheme,
No scale of moral music—to unite   170
Powers that survive but in the faintest
   dream
Of memory?—O that ye might stoop to
   bear
Chains, such precious chains of sight
As labored minstrelsies through ages wear!
O for a balance fit the truth to tell   175
Of the Unsubstantial, pondered well!

XII

By one pervading spirit
Of tones and numbers all things are con-
   trolled,
As sages taught, where faith was found to
   merit
Initiation in that mystery old.   180
The heavens, whose aspect makes our
   minds as still
As they themselves appear to be,
Innumerable voices fill
With everlasting harmony;
The towering headlands, crowned with
   mist   185
Their feet among the billows, know
That Ocean is a mighty harmonist;
Thy pinions, universal Air,
Ever waving to and fro,
Are delegates of harmony, and bear   190
Strains that support the Seasons in their
   round;
Stern Winter loves a dirge-like sound.

XIII

Break forth into thanksgiving,
Ye banded instruments of wind and
   chords;
Unite, to magnify the Ever-living,   195
Your inarticulate notes with the voice of
   words!
Nor hushed be service from the lowing
   mead,
Nor mute the forest hum of noon;
Thou too be heard, lone eagle; freed
From snowy peak and cloud, attune   200
Thy hungry barkings to the hymn
Of joy, that from her utmost walls
The six-days' Work by flaming Seraphim
Transmits to Heaven! As Deep to Deep
Shouting through one valley calls,   205
All worlds, all natures, mood and measure
   keep
For praise and ceaseless gratulation, poured
Into the ear of God, their Lord!

XIV

A Voice to Light gave being;
To Time, and Man his earth-born chron-
   icler;   210
A Voice shall finish doubt and dim fore-
   seeing,
And sweep away life's visionary stir;
The trumpet (we, intoxicate with pride,
Arm at its blast for deadly wars)
To archangelic lips applied,   215
The grave shall open, quench the stars.
O Silence! are Man's noisy years
No more than moments of thy life?
Is Harmony, blest queen of smiles and
   tears,
With her smooth tones and discords just, 220
Tempered into rapturous strife,
Thy destined bond-slave? No! though
   earth be dust
And vanish, though the heavens dissolve,
   her stay
Is in the Word, that shall not pass away.
1828   1835

AT THE GRAVE OF BURNS

SEVEN YEARS AFTER HIS DEATH

I shiver, Spirit fierce and bold,
At thought of what I now behold:
As vapors breathed from dungeons cold,
      Strike pleasure dead,
So sadness comes from out the mold   5
      Where Burns is laid.

And have I then thy bones so near,
And thou forbidden to appear?

As if it were thyself that's here
    I shrink with pain; 10
And both my wishes and my fear
    Alike are vain.

Off weight—nor press on weight!—away
Dark thoughts!—they came, but not to
    stay;
With chastened feelings would I pay 15
    The tribute due
To him, and aught that hides his clay
    From mortal view.

Fresh as the flower, whose modest worth
He sang, his genius "glinted" forth, 20
Rose like a star that touching earth,
    For so it seems,
Doth glorify its humble birth
    With matchless beams.

The piercing eye, the thoughtful brow, 25
The struggling heart, where be they now?—
Full soon the aspirant of the plough,
    The prompt, the brave,
Slept, with the obscurest, in the low
    And silent grave. 30

I mourned with thousands, but as one
More deeply grieved, for He was gone
Whose light I hailed when first it shone,
    And showed my youth
How Verse may build a princely throne 35
    On humble truth.

Alas! where'er the current tends,
Regret pursues and with it blends,—
Huge Criffel's hoary top ascends
    By Skiddaw seen,— 40
Neighbors we were, and loving friends
    We might have been;

True friends though diversely inclined;
But heart with heart and mind with mind,
Where the main fibers are entwined, 45
    Through Nature's skill,
May even by contraries be joined
    More closely still.

The tear will start, and let it flow;
Thou "poor inhabitant below," 50
At this dread moment—even so—
    Might we together
Have sate and talked where gowans blow,
    Or on wild heather.

What treasures would have then been
    placed 55
Within my reach; of knowledge graced

By fancy what a rich repast!
    But why go on?—
Oh! spare to sweep, thou mournful blast,
    His grave grass-grown. 60

There, too, a son, his joy and pride,
(Not three weeks past the stripling died,)
Lies gathered to his father's side,
    Soul-moving sight!
Yet one to which is not denied 65
    Some sad delight:

For *he* is safe, a quiet bed
Hath early found among the dead,
Harbored where none can be misled,
    Wronged, or distressed; 70
And surely here it may be said
    That such are blest.

And oh for Thee, by pitying grace
Checked oft-times in a devious race,
May He who halloweth the place 75
    Where Man is laid
Receive thy spirit in the embrace
    For which it prayed!

Sighing I turned away; but ere
Night fell I heard, or seemed to hear, 80
Music that sorrow comes not near,
    A ritual hymn,
Chanted in love that casts out fear
    By Seraphim.

Partly before 1807   1842

A POET!—HE HATH PUT HIS HEART TO SCHOOL

A Poet!—He hath put his heart to school,
Nor dares to move unpropped upon the
    staff
Which art hath lodged within his hand—
    must laugh
By precept only, and shed tears by rule.
Thy art be Nature; the live current quaff, 5
And let the groveller sip his stagnant pool,
In fear that else, when critics grave and
    cool
Have killed him, scorn should write his
    epitaph.
How does the meadow flower its bloom
    unfold?
Because the lovely little flower is free 10
Down to its root, and, in that freedom,
    bold;
And so the grandeur of the forest tree
Comes not by casting in a formal mould,
But from its *own* divine vitality.

1842(?)   1842

PREFACE TO THE SECOND EDITION OF "LYRICAL BALLADS"

The first volume of these poems has already been submitted to general perusal. It was published as an experiment, which, I hoped, might be of some use to ascertain how far, by fitting to metrical arrangement a selection of the real language of men in a state of vivid sensation, that sort of pleasure and that quantity of pleasure may be imparted, which a poet may rationally endeavor to impart.

I had formed no very inaccurate estimate of the probable effect of those poems: I flattered myself that they who should be pleased with them would read them with more than common pleasure; and, on the other hand, I was well aware, that by those who should dislike them, they would be read with more than common dislike. The result has differed from my expectation in this only, that a greater number have been pleased than I ventured to hope I should please.

Several of my friends are anxious for the success of these poems, from a belief that, if the views with which they were composed were indeed realized, a class of poetry would be produced, well adapted to interest mankind permanently, and not unimportant in the quality and in the multiplicity of its moral relations: and on this account they have advised me to prefix a systematic defense of the theory upon which the poems were written. But I was unwilling to undertake the task, knowing that on this occasion the reader would look coldly upon my arguments, since I might be suspected of having been principally influenced by the selfish and foolish hope of *reasoning* him into an approbation of these particular poems: and I was still more unwilling to undertake the task, because adequately to display the opinions, and fully to enforce the arguments, would require a space wholly disproportionate to a preface. For, to treat the subject with the clearness and coherence of which it is susceptible, it would be necessary to give a full account of the present state of the public taste in this country, and to determine how far this taste is healthy or depraved; which, again, could not be determined without pointing out in what manner language and the human mind act and react on each other, and without retracing the revolutions, not of literature alone, but likewise of society itself. I have therefore altogether declined to enter regularly upon this defense; yet I am sensible that there would be something like impropriety in abruptly obtruding upon the public, without a few words of introduction, poems so materially different from those upon which general approbation is at present bestowed.

It is supposed that by the act of writing in verse an author makes a formal engagement that he will gratify certain known habits of association; that he not only thus apprises the reader that certain classes of ideas and expressions will be found in his book, but that others will be carefully excluded. This exponent or symbol held forth by metrical language must in different eras of literature have excited very different expectations: for example, in the age of Catullus, Terence, and Lucretius, and that of Statius or Claudian; and in our own country, in the age of Shakspeare and Beaumont and Fletcher, and that of Donne and Cowley, or Dryden, or Pope. I will not take upon me to determine the exact import of the promise which, by the act of writing in verse, an author in the present day makes to his reader; but it will undoubtedly appear to many persons that I have not fulfilled the terms of an engagement thus voluntarily contracted. They who have been accustomed to the gaudiness and inane phraseology of many modern writers, if they persist in reading this book to its conclusion, will, no doubt, frequently have to struggle with feelings of strangeness and awkwardness; they will look round for poetry, and will be induced to inquire by what species of courtesy these attempts can be permitted to assume that title. I hope, therefore, the reader will not censure me for attempting to state what I have proposed to myself to perform, and also (as far as the limits of a preface will permit) to explain some of the chief reasons which have determined me in the choice of my purpose: that at least he may be spared any unpleasant feeling of disappointment, and that I myself may be protected from one of the most dishonorable accusations which can be brought against an author—namely, that of an indolence which prevents him from endeavoring to ascertain what is his duty, or, when his duty is ascertained, prevents him from performing it.

The principal object, then, proposed in these poems, was to choose incidents and situations from common life, and to relate or describe them throughout, as far as was possible, in a selection of language really used by men, and, at the same time, to throw over them a certain coloring of imagination, whereby ordinary things should be presented to the mind in an unusual aspect, and further, and above all, to make these incidents and situations interesting by tracing in them, truly though not ostentatiously, the primary laws of our nature: chiefly, as far as regards the manner in which we associate ideas in a state of excitement. Humble and rustic life was generally chosen, because in that condition the essential passions of the heart find a better soil in which they can attain their maturity, are less under restraint, and speak a plainer and more emphatic language; because in that condition of life our elementary feelings coexist in a state of greater simplicity, and, consequently, may be more accurately contemplated, and more forcibly communicated; because the manners of rural life germinate from those elementary feelings, and, from the necessary character of rural occupations, are more easily comprehended, and are more durable; and, lastly, because in that condition the passions of men are incorporated with the beautiful and permanent forms of nature. The language, too, of these men has been adopted (purified indeed from what appears to be its real defects, from all lasting and rational causes of dislike or disgust), because such men hourly communicate with the best objects from which the best part of language is originally derived; and, because, from their rank in society and the sameness and narrow circle of their intercourse, being less under the influence of social vanity, they convey their feelings and notions in simple and unelaborated expressions. Accordingly, such a language, arising out of repeated experience and regular feelings, is a more permanent, and a far more philosophical, language than that which is frequently substituted for it by poets, who think that they are conferring honor upon themselves and their art, in proportion as they separate themselves from the sympathies of men, and indulge in arbitrary and capricious habits of expression, in order to furnish food for fickle tastes and fickle appetites of their own creation.*

I cannot, however, be insensible to the present outcry against the triviality and meanness, both of thought and language, which some of my contemporaries have occasionally introduced into their metrical compositions; and I acknowledge that this defect, where it exists, is more dishonorable to the writer's own character than false refinement or arbitrary innovation, though I should contend at the same time that it is far less pernicious in the sum of its consequences. From such verses the poems in these volumes will be found distinguished at least by one mark of difference—that each of them has a worthy *purpose*. Not that I always began to write with a distinct purpose formally conceived; but habits of meditation have, I trust, so prompted and regulated my feelings that my descriptions of such objects as strongly excite those feelings will be found to carry along with them a *purpose*. If this opinion be erroneous, I can have little right to the name of a poet. For all good poetry is the spontaneous overflow of powerful feelings; and though this be true, poems to which any value can be attached were never produced on any variety of subjects but by a man who, being possessed of more than usual organic sensibility, had also thought long and deeply. For our continued influxes of feeling are modified and directed by our thoughts, which are indeed the representatives of all our past feelings; and as, by contemplating the relation of these general representatives to each other, we discover what is really important to men, so, by the repetition and continuance of this act, our feelings will be connected with important subjects, till at length, if we be originally possessed of much sensibility, such habits of mind will be produced that, by obeying blindly and mechanically the impulses of those habits, we shall describe objects, and utter sentiments, of such a nature, and in such connection with each other, that the understanding of the reader must necessarily be in some degree enlightened, and his affections strengthened and purified.

It has been said that each of these poems has a purpose. Another circumstance must be mentioned which distinguishes these poems from the popular poetry of the day; it is this: that the feeling therein developed gives importance to the action and situation, and not the action and situation to the feeling.

A sense of false modesty shall not prevent me from asserting that the reader's attention is pointed to this mark of distinction, far less for the sake of these particular poems than from the general importance of the subject. The subject is indeed im-

* It is worth while here to observe that the affecting parts of Chaucer are almost always expressed in language pure and universally intelligible even to this day.

portant! For the human mind is capable of being excited without the application of gross and violent stimulants; and he must have a very faint perception of its beauty and dignity who does not know this, and who does not further know that one being is elevated above another in proportion as he possesses this capability. It has therefore appeared to me that to endeavor to produce or enlarge this capacity is one of the best services in which, at any period, a writer can be engaged; but this service, excellent at all times, is especially so at the present day. For a multitude of causes, unknown to former times, are now acting with a combined force to blunt the discriminating powers of the mind, and, unfitting it for all voluntary exertion, to reduce it to a state of almost savage torpor. The most effective of these causes are the great national events which are daily taking place, and the increasing accumulation of men in cities, where the uniformity of their occupations produces a craving for extraordinary incident which the rapid communication of intelligence hourly gratifies. To this tendency of life and manners the literature and theatrical exhibitions of the country have conformed themselves. The invaluable works of our elder writers (I had almost said the works of Shakspeare and Milton) are driven into neglect by frantic novels, sickly and stupid German tragedies, and deluges of idle and extravagant stories in verse.—When I think upon this degrading thirst after outrageous stimulation, I am almost ashamed to have spoken of the feeble endeavor made in these volumes to counteract it; and, reflecting upon the magnitude of the general evil, I should be oppressed with no dishonorable melancholy, had I not a deep impression of certain inherent and indestructible qualities of the human mind, and likewise of certain powers in the great and permanent objects that act upon it, which are equally inherent and indestructible, and were there not added to this impression a belief that the time is approaching when the evil will be systematically opposed by men of greater powers, and with far more distinguished success.

Having dwelt thus long on the subjects and aim of these poems, I shall request the reader's permission to apprise him of a few circumstances relating to their *style,* in order, among other reasons, that he may not censure me for not having performed what I never attempted. The reader will find that personifications of abstract ideas rarely occur in these volumes, and are utterly rejected as an ordinary device to elevate the style and raise it above prose. My purpose was to imitate, and, as far as possible, to adopt the very language of men; and assuredly such personifications do not make any natural or regular part of that language. They are, indeed, a figure of speech occasionally prompted by passion, and I have made use of them as such; but have endeavored utterly to reject them as a mechanical device of style, or as a family language which writers in meter seem to lay claim to by prescription. I have wished to keep the reader in the company of flesh and blood, persuaded that by so doing I shall interest him. Others who pursue a different track will interest him likewise; I do not interfere with their claim, but wish to prefer a claim of my own. There will also be found in these volumes little of what is usually called poetic diction; as much pains has been taken to avoid it as is ordinarily taken to produce it; this has been done for the reason already alleged, to bring my language near to the language of men; and, further, because the pleasure which I have proposed to myself to impart is of a kind very different from that which is supposed by many persons to be the proper object of poetry. Without being culpably particular, I do not know how to give my reader a more exact notion of the style in which it was my wish and intention to write than by informing him that I have at all times endeavored to look steadily at my subject; consequently there is, I hope, in these poems, little falsehood of description, and my ideas are expressed in language fitted to their respective importance. Something must have been gained by this practice, as it is friendly to one property of all good poetry—namely, good sense; but it has necessarily cut me off from a large portion of phrases and figures of speech which from father to son have long been regarded as the common inheritance of poets. I have also thought it expedient to restrict myself still further, having abstained from the use of many expressions, in themselves proper and beautiful, but which have been foolishly repeated by bad poets, till such feelings of disgust are connected with them as it is scarcely possible by any art of association to overpower.

If in a poem there should be found a series of lines, or even a single line, in which the language, though naturally arranged, and according to the strict laws of meter, does not differ from that of prose, there is a numerous class of critics who, when they stumble upon these prosaisms, as they call them, imagine that they have made a notable discovery, and exult over the poet as over a man ignorant of his own profession. Now these men would establish a canon of criticism which the reader will conclude he must utterly reject, if he wishes to be pleased with these volumes. And it would be a most easy task to prove to him that not only the language of a large portion of every good poem, even of the most elevated character, must necessarily, except with reference to the meter, in no respect differ from that of good prose, but likewise that some of the most interesting parts of the best poems will be found to be strictly the language of prose when prose is well written. The truth of this assertion might be demonstrated by innumerable passages from almost all the poetical writings, even of Milton himself. To illustrate the subject in a general manner, I will here adduce a short composition of Gray, who was at the head of those who, by their reasonings, have attempted to widen the space of separation betwixt prose and metrical composition, and was more than any other man curiously elaborate in the structure of his own poetic diction:

In vain to me the smiling mornings shine,
And reddening Phoebus lifts his golden fire;
The birds in vain their amorous descant join,
Or cheerful fields resume their green attire.
These ears, alas! for other notes repine;
A different object do these eyes require;
My lonely anguish melts no heart but mine;
And in my breast the imperfect joys expire.
Yet morning smiles the busy race to cheer,
And new-born pleasure brings to happier men;
The fields to all their wonted tribute bear;
To warm their little loves the birds complain.
I fruitless mourn to him that cannot hear,
And weep the more because I weep in vain.

It will easily be perceived that the only part of this sonnet which is of any value is the lines printed in italics; it is equally obvious that, except in the rime, and in the use of the single word "fruitless" for "fruitlessly," which is so far a defect, the language of these lines does in no respect differ from that of prose.

By the foregoing quotation it has been shown that the language of prose may yet be well adapted to poetry; and it was previously asserted that a large portion of the language of every good poem can in no respect differ from that of good prose. We will go further. It may be safely affirmed that there neither is, nor can be, any *essential* difference between the language of prose and metrical composition. We are fond of tracing the resemblance between poetry and painting, and accordingly, we call them sisters; but where shall we find bonds of connection sufficiently strict to typify the affinity betwixt metrical and prose composition? They both speak by and to the same organs; the bodies in which both of them are clothed may be said to be of the same substance, their affections are kindred, and almost identical, not necessarily differing even in degree; poetry * sheds no tears "such as angels weep," but natural and human tears; she can boast of no celestial ichor that distinguishes her vital juices from those of prose; the same human blood circulates through the veins of them both.

If it be affirmed that rime and metrical arrangement of themselves constitute a distinction which overturns what has just been said on the strict affinity of metrical language with that of prose, and paves the way for other artificial distinctions which the mind voluntarily admits, I answer that the language of such poetry as is here recommended is, as far as is possible, a selection of the language really spoken by men; that this selection, wherever it is made with true taste and feeling, will of itself form a distinction far greater than would at first be imagined, and will entirely separate the composition from the vulgarity and meanness of ordinary life, and, if meter be superadded thereto, I believe that a dissimilitude will be produced altogether sufficient for the gratification of a rational mind. What other distinction would we have? Whence is it to come? And where is it to exist? Not, surely, where the poet speaks through the mouths of his characters; it cannot be necessary here, either for elevation of style, or any of its supposed ornaments, for, if the poet's subject be judiciously chosen, it will naturally, and upon fit occasion, lead him to passions, the language of which, if selected truly and judiciously, must necessarily be dignified and variegated, and alive

* I here use the word *poetry* (though against my own judgment) as opposed to the word *prose,* and synonymous with metrical composition. But much confusion has been introduced into criticism by this contradistinction of *poetry* and *prose,* instead of the more philosophical one of *poetry* and *matter of fact,* or *science.* The only strict antithesis to *prose* is *meter;* nor is this, in truth, a *strict* antithesis, because lines and passages of meter so naturally occur in writing prose that it would be scarcely possible to avoid them, even were it desirable.

with metaphors and figures. I forbear to speak of an incongruity which would shock the intelligent reader, should the poet interweave any foreign splendor of his own with that which the passion naturally suggests; it is sufficient to say that such addition is unnecessary. And, surely, it is more probable that those passages, which with propriety abound with metaphors and figures, will have their due effect, if, upon other occasions where the passions are of a milder character, the style also be subdued and temperate.

But, as the pleasure which I hope to give by the poems now presented to the reader must depend entirely on just notions upon this subject, and as it is in itself of high importance to our taste and moral feelings, I cannot content myself with these detached remarks. And if, in what I am about to say, it shall appear to some that my labor is unnecessary, and that I am like a man fighting a battle without enemies, such persons may be reminded that, whatever may be the language outwardly holden by men, a practical faith in the opinions which I am wishing to establish is almost unknown. If my conclusions are admitted, and carried as far as they must be carried if admitted at all, our judgments concerning the works of the greatest poets, both ancient and modern, will be far different from what they are at present, both when we praise and when we censure, and our moral feelings influencing and influenced by these judgments will, I believe, be corrected and purified.

Taking up the subject, then, upon general grounds, let me ask what is meant by the word poet? What is a poet? To whom does he address himself? And what language is to be expected from him?—He is a man speaking to men—a man, it is true, endowed with more lively sensibility, more enthusiasm and tenderness, who has a greater knowledge of human nature, and a more comprehensive soul, than are supposed to be common among mankind; a man pleased with his own passions and volitions, and who rejoices more than other men in the spirit of life that is in him; delighting to contemplate similar volitions and passions as manifested in the goings-on of the universe, and habitually impelled to create them where he does not find them. To these qualities he has added a disposition to be affected more than other men by absent things as if they were present; an ability of conjuring up in himself passions, which are indeed far from being

the same as those produced by real events, yet (especially in those parts of the general sympathy which are pleasing and delightful) do more nearly resemble the passions produced by real events than anything which, from the motions of their own minds merely, other men are accustomed to feel in themselves;—whence, and from practice he has acquired a greater readiness and power in expressing what he thinks and feels, and especially those thoughts and feelings which, by his own choice, or from the structure of his own mind, arise in him without immediate external excitement.

But, whatever portion of this faculty we may suppose even the greatest poet to possess, there cannot be a doubt that the language which it will suggest to him must often, in liveliness and truth, fall short of that which is uttered by men in real life, under the actual pressure of those passions, certain shadows of which the poet thus produces, or feels to be produced, in himself.

However exalted a notion we would wish to cherish of the character of a poet, it is obvious that, while he describes and imitates passions, his employment is in some degree mechanical, compared with the freedom and power of real and substantial action and suffering. So that it will be the wish of the poet to bring his feelings near to those of the persons whose feelings he describes, nay, for short spaces of time, perhaps, to let himself slip into an entire delusion, and even confound and identify his own feelings with theirs; modifying only the language which is thus suggested to him by a consideration that he describes for a particular purpose, that of giving pleasure. Here, then, he will apply the principle of selection which has been already insisted upon. He will depend upon this for removing what would otherwise be painful or disgusting in the passion; he will feel that there is no necessity to trick out or to elevate nature; and, the more industriously he applies this principle the deeper will be his faith that no words, which *his* fancy or imagination can suggest, will be to be compared with those which are the emanations of reality and truth.

But it may be said by those who do not object to the general spirit of these remarks, that, as it is impossible for the poet to produce upon all occasions language as exquisitely fitted for the passion as that which the real passion itself suggests, it is proper that he should consider himself as in the situation of a translator, who does not scruple to substitute excellencies of another kind for those which are unattainable by him, and endeavors occasionally to surpass his original, in order to make some amends for the general inferiority to which he feels that he must submit. But this would be to encourage idleness and unmanly despair. Further, it is the language of men who speak of what they do not understand; who talk of poetry as of a matter of amusement and idle pleasure; who will converse with us as gravely about a *taste* for poetry, as they express it, as if it were a thing as indifferent as a taste for rope-dancing, or Frontiniac or Sherry. Aristotle, I have been told, has said that poetry is the most philosophic of all writing; it is so: its object is truth, not individual and local, but general, and operative; not standing upon external testimony, but carried alive into the heart by passion; truth which is its own testimony, which gives competence and confidence to the tribunal to which it appeals, and receives them from the same tribunal. Poetry is the image of man and nature. The obstacles which stand in the way of the fidelity of the biographer and historian, and of their consequent utility, are incalculably greater than those which are to be encountered by the poet who comprehends the dignity of his art. The poet writes under one restriction only—namely, the necessity of giving immediate pleasure to a human being possessed of that information which may be expected from him, not as a lawyer, a physician, a mariner, an astronomer, or a natural philosopher, but as a man. Except this one restriction, there is no object standing between the poet and the image of things; between this and the biographer and historian, there are a thousand.

Nor let this necessity of producing immediate pleasure be considered as a degradation of the poet's art. It is far otherwise. It is an acknowledgment of the beauty of the universe, an acknowledgment the more sincere because not formal, but indirect; it is a task light and easy to him who looks at the world in the spirit of love; further, it is a homage paid to the native and naked dignity of man, to the grand elementary principle of pleasure, by which he knows, and feels, and lives, and moves. We have no sympathy but what is propagated by pleasure. I would not be misunderstood; but wherever we sympathize with pain, it will be found that the sympathy is produced and carried on by subtle combinations with pleasure. We have no knowledge, that is, no general principles drawn from the contemplation of particular facts, but what has been built up by pleasure, and exists in us by pleasure alone. The man of science, the chemist and mathematician, whatever difficulties and disgusts they may have had to struggle with, know and feel this. However painful may be the objects with which the anatomist's knowledge is connected, he feels that his knowledge is pleasure; and where he has no pleasure has no knowledge. What then does the poet? He considers man and the objects that surround him as acting and reacting upon each other, so as to produce an infinite complexity of pain and pleasure; he considers man in his own nature and in his ordinary life as contemplating this with a certain quantity of immediate knowledge, with certain convictions, intuitions, and deductions, which from habit acquire the quality of intuitions; he considers him as looking upon this complex scene of ideas and sensations, and finding everywhere objects that immediately excite in him sympathies which, from the necessities of his nature, are accompanied by an overbalance of enjoyment.

To this knowledge which all men carry about with them, and to these sympathies in which, without any other discipline than that of our daily life, we are fitted to take delight, the poet principally directs his attention. He considers man and nature as essentially adapted to each other, and the mind of man as naturally the mirror of the fairest and most interesting properties of nature. And thus the poet, prompted by this feeling of pleasure which accompanies him through the whole course of his studies, converses with general nature, with affections akin to those which, through labor and length of time, the man of science has raised up in himself, by conversing with those particular parts of nature which are the objects of his studies. The knowledge both of the poet and the man of science is pleasure; but the knowledge of the one cleaves to us as a necessary part of our existence, our natural and unalienable inheritance; the other is a personal and individual acquisition, slow to come to us, and by no habitual and direct sympathy connecting us with our fellow-beings. The man of science seeks truth as a remote and unknown benefactor; he cherishes and loves it in his solitude; the poet, singing a song in which all human beings join with him, rejoices in the presence of truth as our visible friend and hourly companion. Poetry is the breath and finer spirit of all knowledge; it is the impassioned expression which is in the countenance of all science. Emphatically may it be said of the poet, as Shakspeare hath said of man, that "he looks before and after." He is the rock of defense for human nature; an upholder and preserver, carrying everywhere with him relationship and love. In spite of difference of soil and climate, of language and manners, of laws and customs, in spite of things silently gone out of mind, and things violently destroyed, the poet binds together by passion and knowledge the vast empire of human society, as it is spread over the whole earth, and over all time. The objects of the poet's thoughts are everywhere; though the eyes and senses of man are, it is true, his favorite guides, yet he will follow wheresoever he can find an atmosphere of sensation in which to move his wings. Poetry is the first and last of all knowledge—it is as immortal as the heart of man. If the labors of men of science should ever create any material revolution, direct or indirect, in our condition, and in the impressions which we habitually receive, the poet will sleep then no more than at present; he will be ready to follow the steps of the man of science, not only in those general indirect effects, but he will be at his side, carrying sensation into the midst of the objects of the science itself. The remotest discoveries of the chemist, the botanist, or mineralogist will be as proper objects of the poet's art as any upon which it can be employed, if the time should ever come when these things shall be familiar to us, and the relations under which they are contemplated by the followers of these respective sciences shall be manifestly and palpably material to us as enjoying and suffering beings. If the time should ever come when what is now called science, thus familiarized to men, shall be ready to put on, as it were, a form of flesh and blood, the poet will lend his divine spirit to aid the transfiguration, and will welcome the being thus produced as a dear and genuine inmate of the household of man. It is not, then, to be supposed that anyone who holds that sublime notion of poetry which I have attempted to convey will break in upon the sanctity and truth of his pictures by transitory and accidental ornaments, and endeavor to excite admiration of himself by arts, the necessity of which must manifestly depend upon the assumed meanness of his subject.

What has been thus far said applies to poetry in general, but especially to those parts of composition where the poet speaks through the mouths of his characters; and upon this point it appears to authorize the conclusion that there are few persons of good sense who would not allow that the dramatic parts of composition are defective in proportion as they deviate from the real language of nature, and are colored by a diction of the poet's own, either peculiar to him as an individual poet or belonging simply to poets in general; to a body of men who, from the circumstance of their compositions being in meter, it is expected will employ a particular language. It is not, then, in the dramatic parts of composition that we look for this distinction of language; but still it may be proper and necessary where the poet speaks to us in his own person and character. To this I answer by referring the reader to the description before given of a poet. Among the qualities there enumerated as principally conducing to form a poet, is implied nothing differing in kind from other men, but only in degree. The sum of what was said is that the poet is chiefly distinguished from other men by a greater promptness to think and feel without immediate external excitement, and a greater power in expressing such thoughts and feelings as are produced in him in that manner. But these passions and thoughts and feelings are the general passions and thoughts and feelings of men. And with what are they connected? Undoubtedly with our moral sentiments and animal sensations, and with the causes which excite these; with the operations of the elements, and the appearances of the visible universe, with storm and sunshine, with the revolutions of the seasons, with cold and heat, with loss of friends and kindred, with injuries and resentments, gratitude and hope, with fear and sorrow. These, and the like, are the sensations and objects which the poet describes, as they are the sensations of other men, and the objects which interest them. The poet thinks and feels in the spirit of human passions. How, then, can his language differ in any material degree from that of all other men who feel vividly and see clearly? It might be *proved* that it is impossible. But supposing that this were not the case, the poet might then be allowed to use a peculiar language when expressing his feelings for his own gratification, or that of men like himself. But poets do not write for poets alone, but for men. Unless, therefore, we are advocates for that admiration which subsists upon ignorance, and that pleasure which arises from hearing what we do not understand, the poet must descend from this supposed height, and, in order to excite rational sympathy, he must express himself as other men express themselves. To this it may be added, that while he is only selecting from the real language of men, or, which amounts to the same thing, composing accurately in the spirit of such selection, he is treading upon safe ground, and we know what we are to expect from him. Our feelings are the same with respect to meter; for, as it may be proper to remind the reader, the distinction of meter is regular and uniform, and not, like that which is produced by what is usually called "poetic diction," arbitrary, and subject to infinite caprices upon which no calculation whatever can be made. In the one case, the reader is utterly at the mercy of the poet respecting what imagery or diction he may choose to connect with the passion; whereas, in the other, the meter obeys certain laws, to which the poet and reader both willingly submit because they are certain, and because no interference is made by them with the passion but such as the concurring testimony of ages has shown to heighten and improve the pleasure which coexists with it.

It will now be proper to answer an obvious question, namely, Why, professing these opinions, have I written in verse? To this, in addition to such answer as is included in what has been already said, I reply, in the first place: Because, however I may have restricted myself, there is still left open to me what confessedly constitutes the most valuable object of all writing, whether in prose or verse—the great and universal passions of men, the most general and interesting of their occupations, and the entire world of nature before me—to supply endless combinations of forms and imagery. Now, supposing for a moment that whatever is interesting in these objects may be as vividly described in prose, why should I be condemned for attempting to superadd to such description the charm which, by the consent of all nations, is acknowledged to exist in metrical language? To this, by such as are yet unconvinced, it may be answered that a very small part of the pleasure given by poetry depends upon the meter, and that it is

injudicious to write in meter, unless it be accompanied with the other artificial distinctions of style with which meter is usually accompanied, and that, by such deviation, more will be lost from the shock which will thereby be given to the reader's associations than will be counterbalanced by any pleasure which he can derive from the general power of numbers. In answer to those who still contend for the necessity of accompanying meter with certain appropriate colors of style in order to the accomplishment of its appropriate end, and who also, in my opinion, greatly underrate the power of meter in itself, it might, perhaps, as far as relates to these volumes, have been almost sufficient to observe that poems are extant, written upon more humble subjects, and in a still more naked and simple style, which have continued to give pleasure from generation to generation. Now, if nakedness and simplicity be a defect, the fact here mentioned affords a strong presumption that poems somewhat less naked and simple are capable of affording pleasure at the present day; and, what I wished *chiefly* to attempt, at present, was to justify myself for having written under the impression of this belief.

But various causes might be pointed out why, when the style is manly, and the subject of some importance, words metrically arranged will long continue to impart such a pleasure to mankind as he who proves the extent of that pleasure will be desirous to impart. The end of poetry is to produce excitement in coexistence with an overbalance of pleasure; but, by the supposition, excitement is an unusual and irregular state of the mind; ideas and feelings do not, in that state, succeed each other in accustomed order. If the words, however, by which this excitement is produced be in themselves powerful, or the images and feelings have an undue proportion of pain connected with them, there is some danger that the excitement may be carried beyond its proper bounds. Now the co-presence of something regular, something to which the mind has been accustomed in various moods and in a less excited state, cannot but have great efficacy in tempering and restraining the passion by an intertexture of ordinary feeling, and of feeling not strictly and necessarily connected with the passion. This is unquestionably true; and hence, though the opinion will at first appear paradoxical, from the tendency of meter to divest language, in a certain degree, of its reality, and thus to throw a sort of half-consciousness of unsubstantial existence over the whole composition, there can be little doubt but that more pathetic situations and sentiments (that is, those which have a greater proportion of pain 5 connected with them) may be endured in metrical composition, especially in rime, than in prose. The meter of the old ballads is very artless, yet they contain many passages which would illustrate this opin- 10 ion; and, I hope, if the following poems be attentively perused, similar instances will be found in them. This opinion may be further illustrated by appealing to the reader's own experience of the reluctance 15 with which he comes to the reperusal of the distressful parts of *Clarissa Harlowe,* or *The Gamester;* while Shakspeare's writings, in the most pathetic scenes, never act upon us as pathetic, beyond the bounds of 20 pleasure—an effect which, in a much greater degree than might at first be imagined, is to be ascribed to small, but continual and regular, impulses of pleasurable surprise from the metrical arrangement.— 25 On the other hand (what it must be allowed will much more frequently happen), if the poet's words should be incommensurate with the passion, and inadequate to raise the reader to a height of desirable 30 excitement, then (unless the poet's choice of his meter has been grossly injudicious), in the feelings of pleasure which the reader has been accustomed to connect with meter in general, and in the feeling, 35 whether cheerful or melancholy, which he has been accustomed to connect with that particular movement of meter, there will be found something which will greatly contribute to impart passion to the words, and 40 to effect the complex end which the poet proposes to himself.

If I had undertaken a *systematic* defense of the theory here maintained, it would have been my duty to develop the various 45 causes upon which the pleasure received from metrical language depends. Among the chief of these causes is to be reckoned a principle which must be well known to those who have made any of the arts the 50 object of accurate reflection; namely, the pleasure which the mind derives from the perception of similitude in dissimilitude. This principle is the great spring of the activity of our minds, and their chief 55 feeder. From this principle the direction of the sexual appetite, and all the passions connected with it, take their origin; it is the life of our ordinary conversation; and upon the accuracy with which similitude in 60 dissimilitude, and dissimilitude in similitude, are perceived, depend our taste and our moral feelings. It would not be a useless employment to apply this principle to the consideration of meter, and to show that meter is hence enabled to afford much pleasure, and to point out in what manner that pleasure is produced. But my limits will not permit me to enter upon this subject, and I must content myself with a general summary.

I have said that poetry is the spontaneous overflow of powerful feelings; it takes its origin from emotion recollected in tranquillity; the emotion is contemplated, till, by a species of reaction, the tranquillity gradually disappears, and an emotion, kindred to that which was before the subject of contemplation, is gradually produced, and does itself actually exist in the mind. In this mood successful composition generally begins, and in a mood similar to this it is carried on; but the emotion of whatever kind, and in whatever degree, from various causes, is qualified by various pleasures, so that in describing any passions whatsoever, which are voluntarily described, the mind will, upon the whole, be in a state of enjoyment. If nature be thus cautious to perserve in a state of enjoyment a being so employed, the poet ought to profit by the lesson held forth to him, and ought especially to take care that whatever passions he communicates to his reader, those passions, if his reader's mind be sound and vigorous, should always be accompanied with an overbalance of pleasure. Now the music of harmonious metrical language, the sense of difficulty overcome, and the blind association of pleasure which has been previously received from works of rime or meter of the same or similar construction, an indistinct perception perpetually renewed of language closely resembling that of real life, and yet, in the circumstance of meter, differing from it so widely—all these imperceptibly make up a complex feeling of delight, which is of the most important use in tempering the painful feeling always found intermingled with powerful descriptions of the deeper passions. This effect is always produced in pathetic and impassioned poetry; while, in lighter compositions, the ease and gracefulness with which the poet manages his numbers are themselves confessedly a principal source of the gratification of the reader. All that it is *necessary* to say, however, upon this subject, may be effected by affirming, what few persons will deny, that, of two descriptions either of passions, manners, or characters, each of them equally well executed, the one in prose and the other in verse, the verse will be read a hundred times where the prose 5 is read once.

Having thus explained a few of my reasons for writing in verse, and why I have chosen subjects from common life, and endeavored to bring my language near to the 10 real language of men, if I have been too minute in pleading my own cause, I have at the same time been treating a subject of general interest; and for this reason a few words shall be added with reference 15 solely to these particular poems, and to some defects which will probably be found in them. I am sensible that my associations must have sometimes been particular instead of general, and that, consequently, 20 giving to things a false importance, I may have sometimes written upon unworthy subjects; but I am less apprehensive on this account than that my language may frequently have suffered from those arbi- 25 trary connections of feelings and ideas with particular words and phrases from which no man can altogether protect himself. Hence I have no doubt that, in some instances, feelings, even of the ludicrous, may 30 be given to my readers by expressions which appeared to me tender and pathetic. Such faulty expressions, were I convinced they were faulty at present, and that they must necessarily continue to be so, I would 35 willingly take all reasonable pains to correct. But it is dangerous to make these alterations on the simple authority of a few individuals, or even of certain classes of men; for where the understanding of an 40 author is not convinced, or his feelings altered, this cannot be done without great injury to himself, for his own feelings are his stay and support; and, if he set them aside in one instance, he may be induced 45 to repeat this act till his mind shall lose all confidence in itself, and becomes utterly debilitated. To this it may be added, that the critic ought never to forget that he is himself exposed to the same errors as the 50 poet, and, perhaps, in a much greater degree, for there can be no presumption in saying of most readers that it is not probable they will be so well acquainted with the various stages of meaning through 55 which words have passed, or with the fickleness or stability of the relations of particular ideas to each other; and, above all, since they are so much less interested in the subject, they may decide lightly and carelessly. 60

Long as the reader has been detained, I hope he will permit me to caution him against a mode of false criticism which has been applied to poetry, in which the language closely resembles that of life and nature. Such verses have been triumphed over in parodies of which Dr. Johnson's stanza is a fair specimen:

> I put my hat upon my head
> And walked into the Strand,
> And there I met another man
> Whose hat was in his hand.

Immediately under these lines let us place one of the most justly-admired stanzas of the "Babes in the Wood":

> These pretty babes with hand in hand
> Went wandering up and down;
> But never more they saw the man
> Approaching from the town.

In both these stanzas the words, and the order of the words, in no respect differ from the most unimpassioned conversation. There are words in both, for example, "the Strand," and "the town," connected with none but the most familiar ideas; yet the one stanza we admit as admirable, and the other as a fair example of the superlatively contemptible. Whence arises this difference? Not from the meter, not from the language, not from the order of the words; but the *matter* expressed in Dr. Johnson's stanza is contemptible. The proper method of treating trivial and simple verses, to which Dr. Johnson's stanza would be a fair parallelism, is not to say, this is a bad kind of poetry, or, this is not poetry; but, this wants sense; it is neither interesting in itself, nor can *lead* to anything interesting; the images neither originate in that sane state of feeling which arises out of thought, nor can excite thought or feeling in the reader. This is the only sensible manner of dealing with such verses. Why trouble yourself about the species till you have previously decided upon the genus? Why take pains to prove that an ape is not a Newton, when it is self-evident that he is not a man?

One request I must make of my reader, which is, that in judging these poems he would decide by his own feelings genuinely, and not by reflection upon what will probably be the judgment of others. How common it is to hear a person say, I myself do not object to this style of composition, or this or that expression, but, to such and such classes of people, it will appear mean or ludicrous! This mode of criticism, so destructive of all sound unadulterated judgment, is almost universal; let the reader, then, abide independently by his own feelings, and, if he finds himself affected, let him not suffer such conjectures to inter-5 fere with his pleasure.

If an author, by any single composition, has impressed us with respect for his talents, it is useful to consider this as affording a presumption that on other occasions 10 where we have been displeased he, nevertheless, may not have written ill or absurdly; and further, to give him so much credit for this one composition as may induce us to review what has displeased us 15 with more care than we should otherwise have bestowed upon it. This is not only an act of justice, but, in our decisions upon poetry especially, may conduce, in a high degree, to the improvement of our own 20 taste; for an *accurate* taste in poetry, and in all the other arts, as Sir Joshua Reynolds has observed, is an *acquired* talent, which can only be produced by thought and a long-continued intercourse with the best 25 models of composition. This is mentioned, not with so ridiculous a purpose as to prevent the most inexperienced reader from judging for himself (I have already said that I wish him to judge for himself), 30 but merely to temper the rashness of decision, and to suggest that, if poetry be a subject on which much time has not been bestowed, the judgment may be erroneous, and that, in many cases, it necessarily will 35 be so.

Nothing would, I know, have so effectually contributed to further the end which I have in view, as to have shown of what kind the pleasure is, and how that pleasure 40 is produced, which is confessedly produced by metrical composition essentially different from that which I have here endeavored to recommend, for the reader will say that he has been pleased by such composi-45 tion; and what more can be done for him? The power of any art is limited; and he will suspect that, if it be proposed to furnish him with new friends, that can be only upon condition of his abandoning his old 50 friends. Besides, as I have said, the reader is himself conscious of the pleasure which he has received from such composition, composition to which he has peculiarly attached the endearing name of poetry; and 55 all men feel an habitual gratitude, and something of an honorable bigotry, for the objects which have long continued to please them; we not only wish to be pleased, but to be pleased in that particu-60 lar way in which we have been accustomed to be pleased. There is in these feelings enough to resist a host of arguments; and I should be the less able to combat them successfully, as I am willing to allow that, in order entirely to enjoy the poetry which I am recommending, it would be necessary to give up much of what is ordinarily enjoyed. But would my limits have permitted me to point out how this pleasure is produced, many obstacles might have been removed, and the reader assisted in perceiving that the powers of language are not so limited as he may suppose; and that it is possible for poetry to give other enjoyments, of a purer, more lasting, and more exquisite nature. This part of the subject has not been altogether neglected, but it has not been so much my present aim to prove that the interest excited by some other kinds of poetry is less vivid, and less worthy of the nobler powers of the mind, as to offer reasons for presuming that if my purpose were fulfilled, a species of poetry would be produced which is genuine poetry, in its nature well adapted to interest mankind permanently, and likewise important in the multiplicity and quality of its moral relations.

From what has been said, and from a perusal of the poems, the reader will be able clearly to perceive the object which I had in view; he will determine how far it has been attained, and, what is a much more important question, whether it be worth attaining; and upon the decision of these two questions will rest my claim to the approbation of the public.

1800   1800

APPENDIX

(See page 307, line 21a—"by what is usually called Poetic Diction.")

Perhaps, as I have no right to expect that attentive perusal, without which, confined, as I have been, to the narrow limits of a preface, my meaning cannot be thoroughly understood, I am anxious to give an exact notion of the sense in which the phrase poetic diction has been used; and for this purpose, a few words shall here be added, concerning the origin and characteristics of the phraseology which I have condemned under that name.

The earliest poets of all nations generally wrote from passion excited by real events; they wrote naturally, and as men: feeling powerfully as they did, their lan-

guage was daring, and figurative. In succeeding times, poets, and men ambitious of
the fame of poets, perceiving the influence
of such language, and desirous of producing the same effect without being animated 5
by the same passion, set themselves to a
mechanical adoption of these figures of
speech, and made use of them, sometimes
with propriety, but much more frequently
applied them to feelings and thoughts with 10
which they had no natural connection
whatsoever. A language was thus insensibly
produced, differing materially from the real
language of men in *any situation*. The
reader or hearer of this distorted lan- 15
guage found himself in a perturbed and
unusual state of mind: when affected by
the genuine language of passion he had
been in a perturbed and unusual state of
mind also: in both cases he was willing 20
that his common judgment and understanding should be laid asleep, and he had
no instinctive and infallible perception of
the true to make him reject the false; the
one served as a passport for the other. The 25
emotion was in both cases delightful, and
no wonder if he confounded the one with
the other, and believed them both to be
produced by the same or similar causes.
Besides, the poet spake to him in the char- 30
acter of a man to be looked up to, a man
of genius and authority. Thus, and from a
variety of other causes, this distorted language was received with admiration; and
poets, it is probable, who had before con- 35
tented themselves for the most part with
misapplying only expressions which at first
had been dictated by real passion, carried
the abuse still further, and introduced
phrases composed apparently in the spirit 40
of the original figurative language of passion, yet altogether of their own invention, and characterised by various degrees
of wanton deviation from good sense and
nature.   45
It is indeed true that the language of the
earliest poets was felt to differ materially
from ordinary language, because it was the
language of extraordinary occasions; but
it was really spoken by men, language 50
which the poet himself had uttered when
he had been affected by the events which
he described, or which he had heard
uttered by those around him. To this
language it is probable that metre of some 55
sort or other was early superadded. This
separated the genuine language of poetry
still further from common life, so that
whoever read or heard the poems of these
earliest poets felt himself moved in a way 60

in which he had not been accustomed to
be moved in real life, and by causes manifestly different from those which acted
upon him in real life. This was the great
temptation to all the corruptions which
have followed: under the protection of this
feeling succeeding poets constructed a
phraseology which had one thing, it is true,
in common with the genuine language of
poetry, namely, that it was not heard in
ordinary conversation; that it was unusual.
But the first poets, as I have said, spake a
language which, though unusual, was still
the language of men. This circumstance,
however, was disregarded by their successors; they found that they could please by
easier means: they became proud of modes
of expression which they themselves had
invented, and which were uttered only by
themselves. In process of time meter became a symbol or promise of this unusual
language, and whoever took upon him to
write in meter, according as he possessed
more or less of true poetic genius, introduced less or more of this adulterated
phraseology into his compositions, and the
true and the false were inseparably interwoven until, the taste of men becoming
gradually perverted, this language was received as a natural language, and at length,
by the influence of books upon men, did
to a certain degree really become so.
Abuses of this kind were imported from
one nation to another, and with the progress of refinement this diction became daily
more and more corrupt, thrusting out of
sight the plain humanities of nature by a
motley masquerade of tricks, quaintnesses,
hieroglyphics, and enigmas.
It would not be uninteresting to point
out the causes of the pleasure given by this
extravagant and absurd diction. It depends upon a great variety of causes, but
upon none, perhaps, more than its influence in impressing a notion of the peculiarity and exaltation of the poet's character, and in flattering the reader's self-love
by bringing him nearer to a sympathy with
that character; an effect which is accomplished by unsettling ordinary habits of
thinking, and thus assisting the reader to
approach to that perturbed and dizzy state
of mind in which if he does not find himself, he imagines that he is *balked* of a
peculiar enjoyment which poetry can and
ought to bestow.
The sonnet quoted from Gray in the
preface, except the lines printed in italics,
consists of little else but this diction,
though not of the worst kind; and indeed,

if one may be permitted to say so, it is far too common in the best writers, both ancient and modern. Perhaps in no way, by positive example, could more easily be given a notion of what I mean by the phrase *poetic diction* than by referring to a comparison between the metrical paraphrase which we have of passages in the Old and New Testament, and those passages as they exist in our common translation. See Pope's "Messiah" throughout; Prior's "Did sweeter sounds adorn my flowing tongue," etc. "Though I speak with the tongues of men and of angels," etc. 1st Corinthians, chap. xiii. By way of immediate example, take the following of Dr. Johnson:—

Turn on the prudent ant thy heedless eyes,
Observe her labors, Sluggard, and be wise;
No stern command, no monitory voice,
Prescribes her duties, or directs her choice;
Yet, timely provident, she hastes away
To snatch the blessings of a plenteous day;
When fruitful summer loads the teeming plain,
She crops the harvest, and she stores the grain.
How long shall sloth usurp thy useless hours,
Unnerve thy vigor, and enchain thy powers?
While artful shades thy downy couch enclose,
And soft solicitation courts repose,
Amidst the drowsy charms of dull delight,
Year chases year with unremitted flight,
Till want now following, fraudulent and slow,
Shall spring to seize thee, like an ambushed foe.

From this hubbub of words pass to the original. "Go to the ant, thou sluggard; consider her ways, and be wise: which having no guide, overseer, or ruler, provideth her meat in the summer, and gathereth her food in the harvest. How long wilt thou sleep, O sluggard? when wilt thou arise out of thy sleep? Yet a little sleep, a little slumber, a little folding of the hands to sleep: so shall thy poverty come as one that travelleth, and thy want as an armed man." Proverbs, chap. vi.

One more quotation, and I have done. It is from Cowper's verses supposed to be written by Alexander Selkirk:—

Religion! what treasure untold,
Resides in that heavenly word!
More precious than silver and gold,
Or all that this earth can afford.
But the sound of the church-going bell
These valleys and rocks never heard,
Ne'er sighed at the sound of a knell,
Or smiled when a sabbath appeared.

Ye winds, that have made me your sport,
Convey to this desolate shore
Some cordial endearing report
Of a land I must visit no more.

My Friends, do they now and then send
A wish or a thought after me?
O tell me I yet have a friend,
Though a friend I am never to see.

This passage is quoted as an instance of three different styles of composition. The first four lines are poorly expressed; some critics would call the language prosaic; the fact is, it would be bad prose, so bad, that it is scarcely worse in meter. The epithet "church-going" applied to a bell, and that by so chaste a writer as Cowper, is an instance of the strange abuses which poets have introduced into their language, till they and their readers take them as matters of course, if they do not single them out expressly as objects of admiration. The two lines "Ne'er sighed at the sound," etc., are, in my opinion, an instance of the language of passion wrested from its proper use, and from the mere circumstance of the composition being in meter, applied upon an occasion that does not justify such violent expressions; and I should condemn the passage, though perhaps few readers will agree with me, as vicious poetic diction. The last stanza is throughout admirably expressed: it would be equally good whether in prose or verse, except that the reader has an exquisite pleasure in seeing such natural language so naturally connected with meter. The beauty of this stanza tempts me to conclude with a principle which ought never to be lost sight of, and which has been my chief guide in all I have said,—namely, that in works of *imagination and sentiment,* for of these only have I been treating, in proportion as ideas and feelings are valuable, whether the composition be in prose or in verse, they require and exact one and the same language. Meter is but adventitious to composition, and the phraseology for which that passport is necessary, even where it may be graceful at all, will be little valued by the judicious.

TO LADY BEAUMONT

ON THE RECEPTION OF HIS POEMS

Coleorton, 21 May, 1807

My dear Lady Beaumont,

Though I am to see you so soon, I cannot but write a word or two, to thank you for the interest you take in my poems, as evinced by your solicitude about their immediate reception. I write partly to thank you for this, and to express the pleasure it has given me, and partly to remove any uneasiness from your mind which the disappointments you sometimes meet with in this labor of love, may occasion. I see that you have many battles to fight for me—more than, in the ardor and confidence of your pure and elevated mind, you had even thought of being summoned to; but be assured that this opposition is nothing more than what I distinctly foresaw that you and my other friends would have to encounter. I say this, not to give myself credit for an eye of prophecy, but to allay any vexatious thoughts on my account which this opposition may have produced in you.

It is impossible that any expectations can be lower than mine concerning the immediate effect of this little work upon what is called the public. I do not here take into consideration the envy and malevolence, and all the bad passions which always stand in the way of a work of any merit from a living poet; but merely think of the pure, absolute, honest ignorance in which all worldlings of every rank and situation must be enveloped, with respect to the thoughts, feelings and images on which the life of my poems depends. The things which I have taken, whether from within or without, what have they to do with routs, dinners, morning calls, hurry from door to door, from street to street, on foot or in carriage; with Mr. Pitt, Mr. Fox, Mr. Paul or Sir Francis Burdett, the Westminster election or the borough of Honiton? In a word—for I cannot stop to make my way through the hurry of images that present themselves to me—what have they to do with endless talking about things nobody cares anything for except as far as their own vanity is concerned, and this with persons they care nothing for but as their vanity or *selfishness* is concerned?— what have they to do (to say all at once) with a life without love? In such a life there can be no thought; for we have no thought (save thoughts of pain) but as far as we have love and admiration.

It is an awful truth, that there neither is, nor can be, any genuine enjoyment of poetry among nineteen out of twenty of those persons who live, or wish to live, in the broad light of the world—among those who either are, or are striving to make themselves, people of consideration in society. This is a truth, and an awful one, because to be incapable of a feeling of poetry, in my sense of the word, is to be without love of human nature and reverence for God.

Upon this I shall insist elsewhere; at present let me confine myself to my object, which is to make you, my dear friend, as easy-hearted as myself with respect to these poems. Trouble not yourself upon their present reception; of what moment is that compared with what I trust is their destiny? —to console the afflicted; to add sunshine to daylight, by making the happy happier; to teach the young and the gracious of every age to see, to think, and feel, and, therefore, to become more actively and securely virtuous; this is their office, which I trust they will faithfully perform, long after we (that is, all that is mortal of us) are moldered in our graves. I am well aware how far it would seem to many I overrate my own exertions, when I speak in this way, in direct connection with the volume I have just made public.

I am not, however, afraid of such censure, insignificant as probably the majority of those poems would appear to very respectable persons. I do not mean London wits and witlings, for these have too many foul passions about them to be respectable, even if they had more intellect than the benign laws of Providence will allow to such a heartless existence as theirs is; but grave, kindly natured, worthy persons, who would be pleased if they could. I hope that these volumes are not without some recommendations, even for readers of this class: but their imagination has slept; and the voice which is the voice of my poetry, without imagination, cannot be heard. Leaving these, I was going to say a word to such readers as Mr. ——. Such!—how would he be offended if he knew I considered him only as a representative of a class, and not an unique! "Pity," says Mr. —— "that so many trifling things should be admitted to obstruct the view of those that have merit." Now, let this candid judge take, by way of example, the sonnets, which, probably, with the exception of two or three other poems, for which I will not contend, appear to him the most trifling, as they are the shortest. I would say to him, omitting things of higher consideration, there is one thing which must strike you at once, if you will only read these poems,—that those "to Liberty," at least, have a connection with, or a bearing upon, each other; and, therefore, if individually they want weight, perhaps, as a body, they may not be so deficient. At least, this ought to induce you to suspend your judgment, and qualify it so far as to allow that the writer aims at least at comprehensiveness.

But, dropping this, I would boldly say at once, that these sonnets, while they each fix the attention upon some important sentiment, separately considered, do, at the same time, collectively make a poem on the subject of civil liberty and national independence, which, either for simplicity of style or grandeur of moral sentiment, is, alas! likely to have few parallels in the poetry of the present day. Again, turn to the "Moods of my own Mind." There is scarcely a poem here of above thirty lines, and very trifling these poems will appear to many; but, omitting to speak of them individually, do they not, taken collectively, fix the attention upon a subject eminently poetical, viz., the interest which objects in nature derive from the predominance of certain affections, more or less permanent, more or less capable of salutary renewal in the mind of the being contemplating these objects? This is poetic, and essentially poetic. And why? Because it is creative.

But I am wasting words, for it is nothing more than you know; and if said to those for whom it is intended, it would not be understood.

I see by your last letter, that Mrs. Fermor has entered into the spirit of these "Moods of my own Mind." Your transcript from her letter gave me the greatest pleasure; but I must say that even she has something yet to receive from me. I say this with confidence, from her thinking that I have fallen below myself in the sonnet, beginning,

With ships the sea was sprinkled far and nigh.

As to the other which she objects to, I will only observe, that there is a misprint in the last line but two,

And *though* this wilderness

for

And *through* this wilderness,

that makes it unintelligible. This latter sonnet, for many reasons (though I do not abandon it), I will not now speak of; but upon the other, I could say something important in conversation, and will attempt now to illustrate it by a comment, which, I feel, will be inadequate to convey my meaning. There is scarcely one of my poems which does not aim to direct the attention to some moral sentiment, or to some general principle, or law of thought, or of our intellectual constitution. For instance, in the present case, who is there that has not felt that the mind can have no rest among a multitude of objects, of which it either cannot make one whole, or from which it cannot single out one individual whereupon may be concentrated the attention, divided among or distracted by a multitude? After a certain time, we must either select one image or object, which must put out of view the rest wholly, or must subordinate them to itself while it stands forth as a head:

> Now glowed the firmament
> With living sapphires! Hesperus, that *led*
> The starry host, rode brightest; till the moon,
> Rising in clouded majesty, at length,
> Apparent *Queen*, unveiled *her peerless* light,
> And o'er the dark her silver mantle threw.

Having laid this down as a general principle, take the case before us. I am represented in the sonnet as casting my eyes over the sea, sprinkled with a multitude of ships, like the heavens with stars. My mind may be supposed to float up and down among them, in a kind of dreamy indifference with respect either to this or that one, only in a pleasurable state of feeling with respect to the whole prospect. "Joyously it showed." This continued till that feeling may be supposed to have passed away, and a kind of comparative listlessness or apathy to have succeeded, as at this line,

Some veering up and down, one knew not why.

All at once, while I am in this state, comes forth an object, an individual; and my mind, sleepy and unfixed, is awakened and fastened in a moment.

> Hesperus, that *led*
> The starry host

is a poetical object, because the glory of his own nature gives him the pre-eminence the moment he appears. He calls forth the poetic faculty, receiving its exertions as a tribute. But this ship in the sonnet may, in a manner still more appropriate, be said to come upon a mission of the poetic spirit, because, in its own appearance and attributes, it is barely sufficiently distinguished to rouse the creative faculty of the human mind, to exertions at all times welcome, but doubly so when they come upon us when in a state of remissness. The mind being once fixed and roused, all the rest comes from itself; it is merely a lordly ship, nothing more:

This ship was nought to me, nor I to her,
Yet I pursued her with a lover's look.

My mind wantons with grateful joy in the
exercise of its own powers, and, loving its 5
own creation,

This ship to all the rest I did prefer,

making her a sovereign or a regent, and
thus giving body and life to all the rest; 10
mingling up this idea with fondness and
praise—

where she comes the winds must stir;

and concluding the whole with,

15

On went she, and due north her journey took;

thus taking up again the reader with whom
I began, letting him know how long I must
have watched this favorite vessel, and invit-20
ing him to rest his mind as mine is resting.

Having said so much upon mere fourteen lines, which Mrs. Fermor did not approve, I cannot but add a word or two
upon my satisfaction in finding that my 25
mind has so much in common with hers,
and that we participate so many of each
other's pleasures. I collect this from her
having singled out the two little poems,
"The Daffodils," and "The Rock Crowned 30
With Snowdrops." I am sure that whoever
is much pleased with either of these quiet
and tender delineations must be fitted to
walk through the recesses of my poetry with
delight, and will there recognize, at every 35
turn, something or other in which, and
over which, it has that property and right
which knowledge and life confer. The line,

Come, blessed barrier, etc.,

40

in the "Sonnet upon Sleep," which Mrs. F.
points out, had before been mentioned to
me by Coleridge, and, indeed, by almost
everybody who had heard it, as eminently
beautiful.

My letter (as this second sheet, which I 45
am obliged to take, admonishes me) is
growing to an enormous length; and yet,
saving that I have expressed my calm confidence that these poems will live, I have 50
said nothing which has a particular application to the object of it, which was to
remove all disquiet from your mind on
account of the condemnation they may at
present incur from that portion of my con- 55
temporaries who are called the public. I
am sure, my dear Lady Beaumont, if you
attach any importance to it, it can only
be from an apprehension that it may affect
me, upon which I have already set you at 60

ease; or from a fear that this present blame
is ominous of their future or final destiny.
If this be the case, your tenderness for me
betrays you. Be assured that the decision
of these persons has nothing to do with
the question; they are altogether incompetent judges. These people, in the senseless hurry of their idle lives, do not read
books, they merely snatch a glance at them,
that they may talk about them. And even
if this were not so, never forget what, I
believe, was observed to you by Coleridge,
that every great and original writer, in proportion as he is great or original, must
himself create the taste by which he is to
be relished; he must teach the art by which
he is to be seen; this, in a certain degree,
even to all persons, however wise and pure
may be their lives, and however unvitiated
their taste. But for those who dip into
books in order to give an opinion of them,
or talk about them to take up an opinion
—for this multitude of unhappy and misguided, and misguiding beings, an entire
regeneration must be produced; and if this
be possible, it must be a work of time. To
conclude, my ears are stone-dead to this
idle buzz, and my flesh as insensible as iron
to these petty stings; and after what I have
said, I am sure yours will be the same.
I doubt not that you will share with me an
invincible confidence that my writings (and
among them these little poems) will co-
operate with the benign tendencies in human nature and society, wherever found;
and that they will in their degree be efficacious in making men wiser, better, and
happier. Farewell. I will not apologize
for this letter, though its length demands
an apology. . . .

Most affectionately yours,
W. WORDSWORTH

ESSAY, SUPPLEMENTARY TO THE PREFACE OF "LYRICAL BALLADS"

With the young of both sexes, poetry is,
like love, a passion; but, for much the
greater part of those who have been proud
of its power over their minds, a necessity
soon arises of breaking the pleasing bondage; or it relaxes of itself;—the thoughts
being occupied in domestic cares, or the
time engrossed by business. Poetry then
becomes only an occasional recreation,
while to those whose existence passes away
in a course of fashionable pleasure, it is a

species of luxurious amusement. In middle and declining age, a scattered number of serious persons resort to poetry, as to religion, for a protection against the pressure of trivial employments, and as a consolation for the afflictions of life. And, lastly, there are many who, having been enamored of this art in their youth, have found leisure, after youth was spent, to cultivate general literature; in which poetry has continued to be comprehended *as a study.*

Into the above classes the readers of poetry may be divided; critics abound in them all; but from the last only can opinions be collected of absolute value, and worthy to be depended upon, as prophetic of the destiny of a new work. The young, who in nothing can escape delusion, are especially subject to it in their intercourse with poetry. The cause, not so obvious as the fact is unquestionable, is the same as that from which erroneous judgments in this art, in the minds of men of all ages, chiefly proceed; but upon youth it operates with peculiar force. The appropriate business of poetry (which, nevertheless, if genuine, is as permanent as pure science), her appropriate employment, her privilege and her *duty,* is to treat of things not as they *are,* but as they *appear;* not as they exist in themselves, but as they *seem* to exist to the *senses,* and to the *passions.* What a world of delusion does this acknowledged obligation prepare for the inexperienced! what temptations to go astray are here held forth for them whose thoughts have been little disciplined by the understanding, and whose feelings revolt from the sway of reason!— When a juvenile reader is in the height of his rapture with some vicious passage, should experience throw in doubts, or common sense suggest suspicions, a lurking consciousness that the realities of the muse are but shows, and that her liveliest excitements are raised by transient shocks of conflicting feeling and successive assemblages of contradictory thoughts—is ever at hand to justify extravagance, and to sanction absurdity. But, it may be asked, as these illusions are unavoidable, and, no doubt, eminently useful to the mind as a process, what good can be gained by making observations, the tendency of which is to diminish the confidence of youth in its feelings, and thus to abridge its innocent and even profitable pleasures? The reproach implied in the question could not be warded off, if youth were incapable of being delighted with what is truly excellent; or if these errors always terminated of themselves in due season. But, with the majority, though their force be abated, they continue through life. Moreover, the fire of youth is too vivacious an element to be extinguished or damped by a philosophical remark; and, while there is no danger that what has been said will be injurious or painful to the ardent and the confident, it may prove beneficial to those who, being enthusiastic, are, at the same time, modest and ingenuous. The intimation may unite with their own misgivings to regulate their sensibility, and to bring in, sooner than it would otherwise have arrived, a more discreet and sound judgment.

If it should excite wonder that men of ability, in later life, whose understandings have been rendered acute by practice in affairs, should be so easily and so far imposed upon when they happen to take up a new work in verse, this appears to be the cause;—that, having discontinued their attention to poetry, whatever progress may have been made in other departments of knowledge, they have not, as to this art, advanced in true discernment beyond the age of youth. If, then, a new poem fall in their way, whose attractions are of that kind which would have enraptured them during the heat of youth, the judgment not being improved to a degree that they shall be disgusted, they are dazzled; and prize and cherish the faults for having had power to make the present time vanish before them, and to throw the mind back, as by enchantment, into the happiest season of life. As they read, powers seem to be revived, passions are regenerated, and pleasures restored. The book was probably taken up after an escape from the burden of business, and with a wish to forget the world, and all its vexations and anxieties. Having obtained this wish, and so much more, it is natural that they should make report as they have felt.

If men of mature age, through want of practice, be thus easily beguiled into admiration of absurdities, extravagances, and misplaced ornaments, thinking it proper that their understandings should enjoy a holiday, while they are unbending their minds with verse, it may be expected that such readers will resemble their former selves also in strength of prejudice, and an inaptitude to be moved by the unostentatious beauties of a pure style. In the higher poetry, an enlightened critic chiefly looks for a reflection of the wisdom of the heart and the grandeur of the imagination. Wherever these appear, simplicity accompanies them; magnificence herself, when legitimate, depending upon a simplicity of her own, to regulate her ornaments. But it is a well-known property of human nature, that our estimates are ever governed by comparisons, of which we are conscious with various degrees of distinctness. Is it not, then, inevitable (confining these observations to the effects of style merely) that an eye, accustomed to the glaring hues of diction by which such readers are caught and excited, will for the most part be rather repelled than attracted by an original work, the coloring of which is disposed according to a pure and refined scheme of harmony? It is in the fine arts as in the affairs of life, no man can *serve* (*i.e.* obey with zeal and fidelity) two masters.

As poetry is most just to its own divine origin when it administers the comforts and breathes the spirit of religion, they who have learned to perceive this truth, and who betake themselves to reading verse for sacred purposes, must be preserved from numerous illusions to which the two classes of readers, whom we have been considering, are liable. But as the mind grows serious from the weight of life, the range of its passions is contracted accordingly; and its sympathies become so exclusive that many species of high excellence wholly escape, or but languidly excite, its notice. Besides, men who read from religious or moral inclinations, even when the subject is of that kind which they approve, are beset with misconceptions and mistakes peculiar to themselves. Attaching so much importance to the truths which interest them, they are prone to overrate the authors by whom those truths are expressed and enforced. They come prepared to impart so much passion to the poet's language, that they remain unconscious how little, in fact, they received from it. And, on the other hand, religious faith is to him who holds it so momentous a thing, and error appears to be attended with such tremendous consequences, that, if opinions touching upon religion occur which the reader condemns, he not only cannot sympathise with them, however animated the expression, but there is, for the most part, an end put to all satisfaction and enjoyment. Love, if it before existed, is converted into dislike; and the heart of the reader is set against the author and his book.—To these excesses they, who from their professions ought to be the most guarded against them, are perhaps the most liable; I mean those sects whose religion, being from the calculating understanding, is cold and formal. For when Christianity, the religion of humility, is founded upon the proudest faculty of our nature, what can be expected but contradictions? Accordingly, believers of this cast are at one time contemptuous; at another, being troubled, as they are and must be, with inward misgivings, they are jealous and suspicious;—and at all seasons they are under temptations to supply, by the heat with which they defend their tenets, the animation which is wanting to the constitution of the religion itself.

Faith was given to man that his affections, detached from the treasures of time, might be inclined to settle upon those of eternity:—the elevation of his nature, which this habit produces on earth, being to him a presumptive evidence of a future state of existence, and giving him a title to partake of its holiness. The religious man values what he sees chiefly as an "imperfect shadowing forth" of what he is incapable of seeing. The concerns of religion refer to indefinite objects, and are too weighty for the mind to support them without relieving itself by resting a great part of the burthen upon words and symbols. The commerce between Man and his Maker cannot be carried on but by a process where much is represented in little, and the Infinite Being accommodates himself to a finite capacity. In all this may be perceived the affinity between religion and poetry; between religion—making up the deficiencies of reason by faith; and poetry —passionate for the instruction of reason; between religion—whose element is infinitude, and whose ultimate trust is the supreme of things, submitting herself to circumscription, and reconciled to substitutions; and poetry—ethereal and transcendent, yet incapable to sustain her existence without sensuous incarnation. In this community of nature may be perceived also the lurking incitements of kindred error; —so that we shall find that no poetry has been more subject to distortion than that species, the argument and scope of which is religious; and no lovers of the art have gone farther astray than the pious and devout.

Whither then shall we turn for that union of qualifications which must necessarily exist before the decisions of a critic can be of absolute value? For a mind at once poetical and philosophical; for a critic whose affections are as free and kindly as the spirit of society, and whose understanding is severe as that of dispassionate government? Where are we to look for that [5] initiatory composure of mind which no selfishness can disturb? For a natural sensibility that has been tutored into correctness without losing anything of its quickness; and for active faculties, capable [10] of answering the demands which an author of original imagination shall make upon them, associated with a judgment that cannot be duped into admiration by aught that is unworthy of it?—among those and [15] those only, who, never having suffered their youthful love of poetry to remit much of its force, have applied to the consideration of the laws of this art the best power of their understandings. At the same time it [20] must be observed that, as this class comprehends the only judgments which are trustworthy, so does it include the most erroneous and perverse. For to be mistaught is worse than to be untaught; and [25] no perverseness equals that which is supported by system, no errors are so difficult to root out as those which the understanding has pledged its credit to uphold. In this class are contained censors, who, if [30] they be pleased with what is good, are pleased with it only by imperfect glimpses, and upon false principles; who, should they generalise rightly to a certain point, are sure to suffer for it in the end; who, if [35] they stumble upon a sound rule, are fettered by misapplying it, or by straining it too far; being incapable of perceiving when it ought to yield to one of higher order. In it are found critics too petulant [40] to be passive to a genuine poet, and too feeble to grapple with him; men, who take upon them to report of the course which *he* holds when they are utterly unable to accompany,—confounded if he turn quick [45] upon the wing, dismayed if he soar steadily "into the region;"—men of palsied imaginations and indurated hearts; in whose minds all healthy action is languid, who therefore feed as the many direct them, [50] or, with the many, are greedy after vicious provocatives;—judges, whose censure is auspicious, and whose praise ominous! In this class meet together the two extremes of best and worst. [55]

The observations presented in the foregoing series are of too ungracious a nature to have been made without reluctance; and, were it only on this account, I would invite the reader to try them by the test of [60] comprehensive experience. If the number of judges who can be confidently relied upon be in reality so small, it ought to follow that partial notice only, or neglect, perhaps long continued, or attention wholly inadequate to their merits, must have been the fate of most works in the higher departments of poetry; and that, on the other hand, numerous productions have blazed into popularity, and have passed away, leaving scarcely a trace behind them: it will be further found, that when authors shall have at length raised themselves into general admiration and maintained their ground, errors and prejudices have prevailed concerning their genius and their works, which the few who are conscious of those errors and prejudices would deplore; if they were not recompensed by perceiving that there are select spirits for whom it is ordained that their fame shall be in the world an existence like that of Virtue, which owes its being to the struggles it makes, and its vigor to the enemies whom it provokes;—a vivacious quality, ever doomed to meet with opposition, and still triumphing over it; and, from the nature of its dominion, incapable of being brought to the sad conclusion of Alexander, when he wept that there were no more worlds for him to conquer.

Let us take a hasty retrospect of the poetical literature of this country for the greater part of the last two centuries, and see if the facts support these inferences.

Who is there that now reads the "Creation" of Du Bartas? Yet all Europe once resounded with his praise; he was caressed by kings; and, when his poem was translated into our language, the Faery Queen faded before it. The name of Spenser, whose genius is of a higher order than even that of Ariosto, is at this day scarcely known beyond the limits of the British Isles. And if the value of his works is to be estimated from the attention now paid to them by his countrymen, compared with that which they bestow on those of some other writers, it must be pronounced small indeed.

The laurel, meed of mighty conquerors
And poets *sage*—

are his own words; but his wisdom has, in this particular, been his worst enemy: while its opposite, whether in the shape of folly or madness, has been *their* best friend. But he was a great power, and bears a high name: the laurel has been awarded to [60] him.

A dramatic author, if he write for the stage, must adapt himself to the taste of the audience, or they will not endure him; accordingly the mighty genius of Shakspeare was listened to. The people were delighted; but I am not sufficiently versed in stage antiquities to determine whether they did not flock as eagerly to the representation of many pieces of contemporary authors, wholly undeserving to appear upon the same boards. Had there been a formal contest for superiority among dramatic writers, that Shakspeare, like his predecessors Sophocles and Euripides, would have often been subject to the mortification of seeing the prize adjudged to sorry competitors, becomes too probable, when we reflect that the admirers of Settle and Shadwell were, in a later age, as numerous, and reckoned as respectable in point of talent, as those of Dryden. At all events, that Shakspeare stooped to accommodate himself to the people, is sufficiently apparent; and one of the most striking proofs of his almost omnipotent genius is, that he could turn to such glorious purpose those materials which the prepossessions of the age compelled him to make use of. Yet even this marvellous skill appears not to have been enough to prevent his rivals from having some advantage over him in public estimation; else how can we account for passages and scenes that exist in his works, unless upon a supposition that some of the grossest of them, a fact which in my own mind I have no doubt of, were foisted in by the players, for the gratification of the many?

But that his works, whatever might be their reception upon the stage, made but little impression upon the ruling intellects of the time, may be inferred from the fact that Lord Bacon, in his multifarious writings, nowhere either quotes or alludes to him.—His dramatic excellence enabled him to resume possession of the stage after the Restoration; but Dryden tells us that in his time two of the plays of Beaumont and Fletcher were acted for one of Shakspeare's. And so faint and limited was the perception of the poetic beauties of his dramas in the time of Pope, that, in his edition of the plays, with a view of rendering to the general reader a necessary service, he printed between inverted commas those passages which he thought most worthy of notice.

At this day, the French critics have abated nothing of their aversion to this darling of our nation: "the English, with their bouffon de Shakspeare," is as familiar an expression among them as in the time of Voltaire. Baron Grimm is the only French writer who seems to have perceived his infinite superiority to the first names of the French theater; an advantage which the Parisian critic owed to his German blood and German education. The most enlightened Italians, though well acquainted with our language, are wholly incompetent to measure the proportions of Shakspeare. The Germans only, of foreign nations, are approaching towards a knowledge and feeling of what he is. In some respects they have acquired a superiority over the fellow-countrymen of the poet: for among us it is a current, I might say an established opinion, that Shakspeare is justly praised when he is pronounced to be "a wild irregular genius, in whom great faults are compensated by great beauties." How long may it be before this misconception passes away, and it becomes universally acknowledged that the judgment of Shakspeare in the selection of his materials, and in the manner in which he has made them, heterogeneous as they often are, constitute a unity of their own, and contribute all to one great end, is not less admirable than his imagination, his invention, and his intuitive knowledge of human nature!

There is extant a small volume of miscellaneous poems, in which Shakspeare expresses his own feelings in his own person. It is not difficult to conceive that the editor, George Steevens, should have been insensible to the beauties of one portion of that volume, the Sonnets; though in no part of the writings of this poet is found, in an equal compass, a greater number of exquisite feelings felicitously expressed. But, from regard to the critic's own credit, he would not have ventured to talk of an act of parliament not being strong enough to compel the perusal of those little pieces,* if he had not known that the people of England were ignorant of the treasures contained in them: and if he had not, moreover, shared the too common propensity of human nature to exult over a supposed fall into the mire of a genius whom he had been compelled to regard with admiration,

---

* This flippant insensibility was publicly reprehended by Mr. Coleridge in a course of Lectures upon Poetry given by him at the Royal Institution. For the various merits of thought and language in Shakspeare's Sonnets see Numbers 27, 29, 30, 32, 33, 54, 64, 66, 68, 73, 76, 86, 91, 92, 93, 97, 98, 105, 107, 108, 109, 111, 113, 114, 116, 117, 129, and many others.

as an inmate of the celestial regions—
"there sitting where he durst not soar."

Nine years before the death of Shakspeare, Milton was born; and early in life he published several small poems, which, 5 though on their first appearance they were praised by a few of the judicious, were afterwards neglected to that degree, that Pope in his youth could borrow from them without risk of its being known. Whether 10 these poems are at this day justly appreciated, I will not undertake to decide: nor would it imply a severe reflection upon the mass of readers to suppose the contrary; seeing that a man of the acknowledged 15 genius of Voss, the German poet, could suffer their spirit to evaporate; and could change their character, as is done in the translation made by him of the most popular of those pieces. At all events, it is certain that these poems of Milton are now 20 much read, and loudly praised; yet were they little heard of till more than 150 years after their publication; and of the Sonnets, Dr. Johnson, as appears from Boswell's 25 Life of him, was in the habit of thinking and speaking as contemptuously as Steevens wrote upon those of Shakspeare.

About the time when the Pindaric odes of Cowley and his imitators, and the pro- 30 ductions of that class of curious thinkers whom Dr. Johnson has strangely styled metaphysical poets, were beginning to lose something of that extravagant admiration which they had excited, the Paradise Lost 35 made its appearance. "Fit audience find though few," was the petition addressed by the Poet to his inspiring Muse. I have said elsewhere that he gained more than he asked; this I believe to be true; but Dr. 40 Johnson has fallen into a gross mistake when he attempts to prove, by the sale of the work, that Milton's countrymen were "*just* to it" upon its first appearance. Thirteen hundred copies were sold in two 45 years; an uncommon example, he asserts, of the prevalence of genius in opposition to so much recent enmity as Milton's public conduct had excited. But, be it remembered that, if Milton's political and reli- 50 gious opinions, and the manner in which he announced them, had raised him many enemies, they had procured him numerous friends; who, as all personal danger was passed away at the time of publication, 55 would be eager to procure the master-work of a man whom they revered, and whom they would be proud of praising. Take, from the number of purchasers, persons of this class, and also those who wished to 60

possess the poem as a religious work, and but few, I fear, would be left who sought for it on account of its poetical merits. The demand did not immediately increase; "for," says Dr. Johnson, "many more readers" (he means persons in the habit of reading poetry) "than were supplied at first the nation did not afford." How careless must a writer be who can make this assertion in the face of so many existing title-pages to belie it! Turning to my own shelves, I find the folio of Cowley, seventh edition, 1681. A book near it is Flatman's Poems, fourth edition, 1686; Waller, fifth edition, same date. The Poems of Norris of Bemerton not long after went, I believe, through nine editions. What further demand there might be for these works I do not know; but I well remember that, twenty-five years ago, the booksellers' stalls in London swarmed with the folios of Cowley. This is not mentioned in disparagement of that able writer and amiable man; but merely to show that, if Milton's work were not more read, it was not because readers did not exist at the time. The early editions of the Paradise Lost were printed in a shape which allowed them to be sold at a low price, yet only three thousand copies of the work were sold in eleven years; and the nation, says Dr. Johnson, had been satisfied from 1623 to 1664, that is, forty-one years, with only two editions of the works of Shakspeare, which probably did not together make one thousand copies; facts adduced by the critic to prove the "paucity of readers."—There were readers in multitudes; but their money went for other purposes, as their admiration was fixed elsewhere. We are authorized, then, to affirm that the reception of the Paradise Lost, and the slow progress of its fame, are proofs as striking as can be desired that the positions which I am attempting to establish are not erroneous.* How amusing to shape to one's self such a critique as a Wit of Charles's days, or a Lord of the Miscellanies or trading Journalist of King William's time, would have brought forth, if he had set his faculties industriously to work upon this poem, everywhere impregnated with *original* excellence.

So strange indeed are the obliquities of admiration, that they whose opinions are

* Hughes is express upon this subject: in his dedication of Spenser's Works to Lord Somers, he writes thus: "It was your Lordship's encouraging a beautiful edition of Paradise Lost that first brought that incomparable poem to be generally known and esteemed."

much influenced by authority will often be tempted to think that there are no fixed principles † in human nature for this art to rest upon. I have been honored by being permitted to puruse in MS. a tract composed between the period of the Revolution and the close of that century. It is the work of an English peer of high accomplishments, its object to form the character and direct the studies of his son. Perhaps nowhere does a more beautiful treatise of the kind exist. The good sense and wisdom of the thoughts, the delicacy of the feelings, and the charm of the style, are throughout equally conspicuous. Yet the author, selecting among the poets of his own country those whom he deems most worthy of his son's perusal, particularises only Lord Rochester, Sir John Denham, and Cowley. Writing about the same time, Shaftesbury, an author at present unjustly depreciated, describes the English Muses as only yet lisping in their cradles.

The arts by which Pope, soon afterwards, contrived to procure to himself a more general and a higher reputation than perhaps any English poet ever attained during his lifetime, are known to the judicious. And as well known is it to them, that the undue exertion of those arts is the cause why Pope has for some time held a rank in literature, to which, if he had not been seduced by an over-love of immediate popularity, and had confided more in his native genius, he never could have descended. He bewitched the nation by his melody, and dazzled it by his polished style, and was himself blinded by his own success. Having wandered from humanity in his Eclogues with boyish inexperience, the praise which these compositions obtained tempted him into a belief that Nature was not to be trusted, at least in pastoral poetry. To prove this by example, he put his friend Gay upon writing those Eclogues, which their author intended to be burlesque. The instigator of the work, and his admirers, could perceive in them nothing but what was ridiculous. Nevertheless, though these poems contain some detestable passages, the effect, as Dr. Johnson well observes, "of reality and truth became conspicuous even when the intention was to show them grovelling and degraded." The Pastorals, ludicrous to such as prided themselves upon their refinement, in spite of

† This opinion seems actually to have been entertained by Adam Smith, the worst critic, David Hume not excepted, that Scotland, a soil to which this sort of weed seems natural, has produced.

those disgusting passages, "became popular, and were read with delight, as just representations of rural manners and occupations."

Something less than sixty years after the publication of the Paradise Lost appeared Thomson's Winter; which was speedily followed by his other Seasons. It is a work of inspiration; much of it is written from himself, and nobly from himself. How was it received? "It was no sooner read," says one of his contemporary biographers, "than universally admired: those only excepted who had not been used to feel, or to look for anything in poetry, beyond a *point* of satirical or epigrammatic wit, a smart *antithesis* richly trimmed with rhyme, or the softness of an *elegiac* complaint. To such his manly classical spirit could not readily commend itself; till, after a more attentive perusal, they had got the better of their prejudices, and either acquired or affected a truer taste. A few others stood aloof, merely because they had long before fixed the articles of their poetical creed, and resigned themselves to an absolute despair of ever seeing anything new and original. These were somewhat mortified to find their notions disturbed by the appearance of a poet, who seemed to owe nothing but to nature and his own genius. But, in a short time, the applause became unanimous; every one wondering how so many pictures, and pictures so familiar, should have moved them but faintly to what they felt in his descriptions. His digressions too, the overflowings of a tender benevolent heart, charmed the reader no less; leaving him in doubt, whether he should more admire the poet or love the man."

This case appears to bear strongly against us:—but we must distinguish between wonder and legitimate admiration. The subject of the work is the changes produced in the appearances of nature by the revolution of the year: and, by undertaking to write in verse, Thomson pledged himself to treat his subject as became a poet. Now it is remarkable that, excepting the Nocturnal Reverie of Lady Winchilsea, and a passage or two in the Windsor Forest of Pope, the poetry of the period intervening between the publication of the Paradise Lost and the Seasons does not contain a single new image of external nature, and scarcely presents a familiar one from which it can be inferred that the eye of the poet had been steadily fixed upon his object, much less that his feelings had urged him to work upon it in the spirit of genuine imagination. To what a low state knowledge of the most obvious and important phenomena had sunk, is evident from the style in which Dryden has executed a description of Night in one of his tragedies, and Pope his translation of the celebrated moonlight scene in the Iliad. A blind man, in the habit of attending accurately to descriptions casually dropped from the lips of those around him, might easily depict these appearances with more truth. Dryden's lines are vague, bombastic, and senseless; * those of Pope, though he had Homer to guide him, are throughout false and contradictory. The verses of Dryden, once highly celebrated, are forgotten; those of Pope still retain their hold upon public estimation,—nay, there is not a passage of descriptive poetry, which at this day finds so many and such ardent admirers. Strange to think of an enthusiast, as may have been the case with thousands, reciting those verses under the cope of a moonlight sky, without having his raptures in the least disturbed by a suspicion of their absurdity!— If these two distinguished writers could habitually think that the visible universe was of so little consequence to a poet, that it was scarcely necessary for him to cast his eyes upon it, we may be assured that those passages of the elder poets which faithfully and poetically describe the phenomena of nature, were not at that time holden in much estimation, and that there was little accurate attention paid to those appearances.

Wonder is the natural product of ignorance; and as the soil was *in such good condition* at the time of the publication of the Seasons, the crop was doubtless abundant. Neither individuals nor nations become corrupt all at once, nor are they enlightened in a moment. Thomson was an inspired poet, but he could not work miracles; in cases where the art of seeing had in some degree been learned, the teacher would further the proficiency of his pupils, but he could do little *more;* though so far does vanity assist men in acts of self-deception, that many would often fancy they recognised a likeness when they knew nothing of the original. Having shown that much of what his biographer deemed genu-

ine admiration must in fact have been blind wonderment—how is the rest to be accounted for?— Thomson was fortunate in the very title of his poem, which seemed to bring it home to the prepared sympathies of every one: in the next place, notwithstanding his high powers, he writes a vicious style; and his false ornaments are exactly of that kind which would be most likely to strike the undiscerning. He likewise abounds with sentimental commonplaces that, from the manner in which they were brought forward, bore an imposing air of novelty. In any well-used copy of the Seasons the book generally opens of itself with the rhapsody on love, or with one of the stories (perhaps Damon and Musidora); these also are prominent in our collections of extracts, and are the parts of his work which, after all, were probably most efficient in first recommending the author to general notice. Pope, repaying praises which he had received, and wishing to extol him to the highest, only styles him "an elegant and philosophical Poet"; nor are we able to collect any unquestionable proofs that the true characteristics of Thomson's genius as an imaginative poet † were perceived, till the elder Warton, almost forty years after the publication of the Seasons, pointed them out by a note in his Essay on the Life and Writings of Pope. In the Castle of Indolence (of which Gray speaks so coldly) these characteristics were almost as conspicuously displayed, and in verse more harmonious and diction more pure. Yet that fine poem was neglected on its appearance, and is at this day the delight only of a few!

When Thomson died, Collins breathed forth his regrets in an Elegiac Poem, in which he pronounces a poetical curse upon *him* who should regard with insensibility the place where the poet's remains were deposited. The poems of the mourner himself have now passed through innumerable editions, and are universally known; but if, when Collins died, the same kind of imprecation had been pronounced by a surviving admirer, small is the number whom it would not have comprehended. The notice which his poems attained during his lifetime was so small, and of course the sale so insignificant, that not long be-

---

* CORTES *alone in a night-gown.*

All things are hush'd as Nature's self lay dead;
The mountains seem to nod their drowsy head.
The little birds in dreams their songs repeat,
And sleeping flowers beneath the night-dew sweat:
Even Lust and Envy sleep; yet Love denies
Rest to my soul, and slumber to my eyes.
　　　　DRYDEN's *Indian Emperor.*

† Since these observations upon Thomson were written, I have perused the second edition of his Seasons, and find that even *that* does not contain the most striking passages which Warton points out for admiration; these, with other improvements, throughout the whole work, must have been added at a later period.

fore his death he deemed it right to repay to the bookseller the sum which he had advanced for them, and threw the edition into the fire.

Next in importance to the Seasons of Thomson, though at considerable distance from that work in order of time, come the Reliques of Ancient English Poetry, collected, new-modelled, and in many instances (if such a contradiction in terms may be used) composed by the editor, Dr. Percy. This work did not steal silently into the world, as is evident from the number of legendary tales that appeared not long after its publication; and had been modelled, as the authors persuaded themselves, after the old ballad. The compilation was however ill suited to the then existing taste of city society; and Dr. Johnson, 'mid the little senate to which he gave laws, was not sparing in his exertions to make it an object of contempt. The critic triumphed, the legendary imitators were deservedly disregarded, and, as undeservedly, their ill-imitated models sank, in this country, into temporary neglect; while Bürger, and other able writers of Germany, were translating or imitating these Reliques, and composing, with the aid of inspiration thence derived, poems which are the delight of the German nation. Dr. Percy was so abashed by the ridicule flung upon his labors from the ignorance and insensibility of the persons with whom he lived, that, though while he was writing under a mask he had not wanted resolution to follow his genius into the regions of true simplicity and genuine pathos (as is evinced by the exquisite ballad of Sir Cauline and by many other pieces), yet when he appeared in his own person and character as a poetical writer, he adopted, as in the tale of the Hermit of Warkworth, a diction scarcely in any one of its features distinguishable from the vague, the glossy, and unfeeling language of his day. I mention this remarkable fact * with regret, esteeming the genius of Dr. Percy in this kind of writing superior to that of any other man by whom in modern times it has been cultivated. That even Bürger (to whom Klopstock gave in my

* Shenstone, in his Schoolmistress, gives a still more remarkable instance of this timidity. On its first appearance, (see D'Israeli's 2d Series of the Curiosities of Literature) the poem was accompanied with an absurd prose commentary, showing, as indeed some incongruous expressions in the text imply, that the whole was intended for burlesque. In subsequent editions the commentary was dropped, and the people have since continued to read in seriousness, doing for the author what he had not courage openly to venture upon for himself.

hearing a commendation which he denied to Goethe and Schiller, pronouncing him to be a genuine poet, and one of the few among the Germans whose works would last) had not the fine sensibility of Percy, might be shown from many passages, in which he has deserted his original only to go astray. For example,

"Now daye was gone, and night was come,
And all were fast asleepe,
All save the Lady Emeline,
Who sate in her bowre to weepe:
And soone she heard her true Love's voice
Low whispering at the walle,
Awake, awake, my dear Ladye,
'Tis I thy true-love call."

Which is thus tricked out and dilated:

"Als nun die Nacht Gebirg' und Thal
Vermummt in Rabenschatten,
Und Hochburgs Lampen überall
Schon ausgeflimmert hatten,
Und alles tief entschlafen war;
Doch nur das Fräulein immerdar,
Voll Fieberängst, noch wachte,
Und seinen Ritter dachte:
Da horch! Ein süsser Liebeston
Kam leis' empor geflogen.
"Ho, Trudchen, ho! Da bin ich schon!
Frisch auf! Dich angezogen!"

But from humble ballads we must ascend to heroics.

All hail, Macpherson! hail to thee, Sire of Ossian! The Phantom was begotten by the snug embrace of an impudent Highlander upon a cloud of tradition—it travelled southward, where it was greeted with acclamation, and the thin consistence took its course through Europe, upon the breath of popular applause. The editor of the "Reliques" had indirectly preferred a claim to the praise of invention, by not concealing that his supplementary labors were considerable! how selfish his conduct, contrasted with that of the disinterested Gael, who, like Lear, gives his kingdom away, and is content to become a pensioner upon his own issue for a beggarly pittance!— Open this far-famed book!—I have done so at random, and the beginning of the "Epic Poem Temora," in eight books, presents itself. "The blue waves of Ullin roll in light. The green hills are covered with day. Trees shake their dusky heads in the breeze. Grey torrents pour their noisy streams. Two green hills with aged oaks surround a narrow plain. The blue course of a stream is there. On its banks stood Cairbar of Atha. His spear supports the king; the red eyes of his fear are sad. Cormac rises on his soul with all his ghastly wounds." Precious memorandums from the pocketbook of the blind Ossian!

If it be unbecoming, as I acknowledge that for the most part it is, to speak disrespectfully of works that have enjoyed for a length of time a widely spread reputation, without at the same time producing irrefragable proofs of their unworthiness, let me be forgiven upon this occasion.—Having had the good fortune to be born and reared in a mountainous country, from my very childhood I have felt the falsehood that pervades the volumes imposed upon the world under the name of Ossian. From what I saw with my own eyes, I knew that the imagery was spurious. In nature everything is distinct, yet nothing defined into absolute independent singleness. In Macpherson's work, it is exactly the reverse; everything (that is not stolen) is in this manner defined, insulated, dislocated, deadened,—yet nothing distinct. It will always be so when words are substituted for things. To say that the characters never could exist, that the manners are impossible, and that a dream has more substance than the whole state of society, as there depicted, is doing nothing more than pronouncing a censure which Macpherson defied; when, with the steeps of Morven before his eyes, he could talk so familiarly of his car-borne heroes;—of Morven, which, if one may judge from its appearance at the distance of a few miles, contains scarcely an acre of ground sufficiently accommodating for a sledge to be trailed along its surface. —Mr. Malcolm Laing has ably shown that the diction of this pretended translation is a motley assemblage from all quarters; but he is so fond of making out parallel passages as to call poor Macpherson to account for his *"ands"* and his *"buts!"* and he has weakened his argument by conducting it as if he thought that every striking resemblance was a *conscious* plagiarism. It is enough that the coincidences are too remarkable for its being probable or possible that they could arise in different minds without communication between them. Now as the translators of the Bible, and Shakspeare, Milton, and Pope, could not be indebted to Macpherson, it follows that he must have owed his fine feathers to them; unless we are prepared gravely to assert, with Madame de Staël, that many of the characteristic beauties of our most celebrated English poets are derived from the ancient Fingallian; in which case the mod-ern translator would have been but giving back to Ossian his own.—It is consistent that Lucien Buonaparte, who could censure Milton for having surrounded Satan in the infernal regions with courtly and regal splendor, should pronounce the modern Ossian to be the glory of Scotland; —a country that has produced a Dunbar, a Buchanan, a Thomson, and a Burns! These opinions are of ill omen for the Epic ambition of him who has given them to the world.

Yet, much as those pretended treasures of antiquity have been admired, they have been wholly uninfluential upon the literature of the country. No succeeding writer appears to have caught from them a ray of inspiration; no author, in the least distinguished, has ventured formally to imitate them—except the boy, Chatterton, on their first appearance. He had perceived, from the successful trials which he himself had made in literary forgery, how few critics were able to distinguish between a real ancient medal and a counterfeit of modern manufacture; and he set himself to the work of filling a magazine with *Saxon Poems*,—counterparts of those of Ossian, as like his as one of his misty stars is to another. This incapability to amalgamate with the literature of the Island is, in my estimation, a decisive proof that the book is essentially unnatural; nor should I require any other to demonstrate it to be a forgery, audacious as worthless.—Contrast, in this respect, the effect of Macpherson's publication with the Reliques of Percy, so unassuming, so modest in their pretensions! —I have already stated how much Germany is indebted to this latter work; and for our own country, its poetry has been absolutely redeemed by it. I do not think that there is an able writer in verse of the present day who would not be proud to acknowledge his obligations to the Reliques; I know that it is so with my friends; and, for myself, I am happy in this occasion to make a public avowal of my own.

Dr. Johnson, more fortunate in his contempt of the labors of Macpherson than those of his modest friend, was solicited not long after to furnish Prefaces, biographical and critical, for the works of some of the most eminent English poets. The booksellers took upon themselves to make the collection; they referred probably to the most popular miscellanies, and, unquestionably, to their books of accounts; and decided upon the claim of authors to be admitted into a body of the most eminent from the familiarity of their names with the readers of that day, and by the profits which, from the sale of his works, each had brought and was bringing to the trade. The editor was allowed a limited exercise of discretion, and the authors whom he recommended are scarcely to be mentioned without a smile. We open the volume of Prefatory Lives, and to our astonishment the *first* name we find is that of Cowley!— What is become of the morning star of English poetry? Where is the bright Elizabethan constellation? Or, if names be more acceptable than images, where is the ever-to-be honored Chaucer? where is Spenser? where Sidney? and, lastly, where he, whose rights as a poet, contradistinguished from those which he is universally allowed to possess as a dramatist, we have vindicated, —where Shakspeare?—These, and a multitude of others not unworthy to be placed near them, their contemporaries and successors, we have *not*. But in their stead, we have (could better be expected when precedence was to be settled by an abstract of reputation at any given period made, as in this case before us?) Roscommon, and Stepney, and Phillips, and Walsh, and Smith, and Duke, and King, and Spratt— Halifax, Granville, Sheffield, Congreve, Broome, and other reputed magnates— metrical writers utterly worthless and useless, except for occasions like the present, when their productions are referred to as evidence what a small quantity of brain is necessary to procure a considerable stock of admiration, provided the aspirant will accommodate himself to the likings and fashions of his day.

As I do not mean to bring down this retrospect to our own times, it may with propriety be closed at the era of this distinguished event. From the literature of other ages and countries, proofs equally cogent might have been adduced, that the opinions announced in the former part of this essay are founded upon truth. It was not an agreeable office, nor a prudent undertaking, to declare them; but their importance seemed to render it a duty. It may still be asked, where lies the particular relation of what has been said to these volumes?—The question will be easily answered by the discerning reader who is old enough to remember the taste that prevailed when some of these poems were first published, seventeen years ago; who has also observed to what degree the poetry of this island has since that period been colored by them; and who is further aware of

the unremitting hostility with which, upon some principle or other, they have each and all been opposed. A sketch of my own notion of the constitution of fame has been given; and, as far as concerns myself, I have cause to be satisfied. The love, the admiration, the indifference, the slight, the aversion, and even the contempt, with which these poems have been received, knowing, as I do, the source within my own mind from which they have proceeded, and the labor and pains which, when labor and pains appeared needful, have been bestowed upon them, must all, if I think consistently, be received as pledges and tokens, bearing the same general impression, though widely different in value;— they are all proofs that for the present time I have not labored in vain; and afford assurances, more or less authentic, that the products of my industry will endure.

If there be one conclusion more forcibly pressed upon us than another by the review which has been given of the fortunes and fate of poetical works, it is this,—that every author, as far as he is great and at the same time *original,* has had the task of *creating* the taste by which he is to be enjoyed: so has it been, so will it continue to be. This remark was long since made to me by the philosophical friend for the separation of whose poems from my own I have previously expressed my regret. The predecessors of an original genius of a high order will have smoothed the way for all that he has in common with them;—and much he will have in common; but, for what is peculiarly his own, he will be called upon to clear and often to shape his own road:—he will be in the condition of Hannibal among the Alps.

And where lies the real difficulty of creating that taste by which a truly original poet is to be relished? Is it in breaking the bonds of custom, in overcoming the prejudices of false refinement, and displacing the aversions of inexperience? Or, if he labor for an object which here and elsewhere I have proposed to myself, does it consist in divesting the reader of the pride that induces him to dwell upon those points wherein men differ from each other, to the exclusion of those in which all men are alike, or the same; and in making him ashamed of the vanity that renders him insensible of the appropriate excellence which civil arrangements, less unjust than might appear, and Nature illimitable in her bounty, have conferred on men who may stand below him in the scale of society? Finally, does it lie in establishing that dominion over the spirits of readers by which they are to be humbled and humanised, in order that they may be purified and exalted?

If these ends are to be attained by the mere communication of *knowledge*, it does *not* lie here.—Taste, I would remind the reader, like Imagination, is a word which has been forced to extend its services far beyond the point to which philosophy would have confined them. It is a metaphor, taken from a *passive* sense of the human body, and transferred to things which are in their essence *not* passive,—to intellectual *acts* and *operations*. The word Imagination had been overstrained, from impulses honorable to mankind, to meet the demands of the faculty which is perhaps the noblest of our nature. In the instance of Taste, the process has been reversed; and from the prevalence of dispositions at once injurious and discreditable, being no other than that selfishness which is the child of apathy,—which, as nations decline in productive and creative power, makes them value themselves upon a presumed refinement of judging. Poverty of language is the primary cause of the use which we make of the word Imagination; but the word Taste has been stretched to the sense which it bears in modern Europe by habits of self-conceit, inducing that inversion in the order of things whereby a passive faculty is made paramount among the faculties conversant with the fine arts. Proportion and congruity, the requisite knowledge being supposed, are subjects upon which taste may be trusted; it is competent to this office;—for in its intercourse with these the mind is *passive*, and is affected painfully or pleasurably as by an instinct. But the profound and the exquisite in feeling, the lofty and universal in thought and imagination; or, in ordinary language, the pathetic and the sublime;—are neither of them, accurately speaking, objects of a faculty which could ever without a sinking in the spirit of nations have been designated by the metaphor—*Taste*. And why? Because without the exertion of a co-operating *power* in the mind of the reader, there can be no adequate sympathy with either of these emotions: without this auxiliary impulse, elevated or profound passion cannot exist.

Passion, it must be observed, is derived from a word which signifies *suffering;* but the connection which suffering has with effort, with exertion, and *action,* is immedi-ate and inseparable. How strikingly is this property of human nature exhibited by the fact that, in popular language, to be in a passion is to be angry!—But,

> Anger in hasty *words* or *blows*
> Itself discharges on its foes.

To be moved, then, by a passion, is to be excited, often to external, and always to internal effort; whether for the continuance and strengthening of the passion, or for its suppression, accordingly as the course which it takes may be painful or pleasurable. If the latter, the soul must contribute to its support, or it never becomes vivid,—and soon languishes, and dies. And this brings us to the point. If every great poet with whose writings men are familiar, in the highest exercise of his genius, before he can be thoroughly enjoyed, has to call forth and to communicate *power*, this service, in a still greater degree, falls upon an original writer at his first appearance in the world.—Of genius the only proof is the act of doing well what is worthy to be done, and what was never done before: Of genius, in the fine arts, the only infallible sign is the widening the sphere of human sensibility for the delight, honor, and benefit of human nature. Genius is the introduction of a new element into the intellectual universe: or, if that be not allowed, it is the application of powers to objects on which they had not before been exercised, or the employment of them in such a manner as to produce effects hitherto unknown. What is all this but an advance, or a conquest, made by the soul of the poet? Is it to be supposed that the reader can make progress of this kind, like an Indian prince or general—stretched on his palanquin, and borne by slaves? No; he is invigorated and inspirited by his leader, in order that he may exert himself; for he cannot proceed in quiescence, he cannot be carried like a dead weight. Therefore to create taste is to call forth and bestow power, of which knowledge is the effect; and *there* lies the true difficulty.

As the pathetic participates of an *animal* sensation, it might seem that, if the springs of this emotion were genuine, all men, possessed of competent knowledge of the facts and circumstances, would be instantaneously affected. And, doubtless, in the works of every true poet will be found passages of that species of excellence which is proved by effects immediate and universal. But there are emotions of the pathetic that are simple and direct, and others that are complex and revolutionary; some to which the heart yields with gentleness; others against which it struggles with pride; these varieties are infinite as the combinations of circumstance and the constitutions of character. Remember, also, that the medium through which, in poetry, the heart is to be affected is language; a thing subject to endless fluctuations and arbitrary associations. The genius of the poet melts these down for his purpose; but they retain their shape and quality to him who is not capable of exerting, within his own mind, a corresponding energy. There is also a meditative, as well as a human, pathos; an enthusiastic as well as an ordinary sorrow; a sadness that has its seat in the depths of reason, to which the mind cannot sink gently of itself—but to which it must descend by treading the steps of thought. And for the sublime,—if we consider what are the cares that occupy the passing day, and how remote is the practice and the course of life from the sources of sublimity in the soul of man, can it be wondered that there is little existing preparation for a poet charged with a new mission to extend its kingdom, and to augment and spread its enjoyments?

Away, then, with the senseless iteration of the word *popular* applied to new works in poetry, as if there were no test of excellence in this first of the fine arts but that all men should run after its productions, as if urged by an appetite, or constrained by a spell!—The qualities of writing best fitted for eager reception are either such as startle the world into attention by their audacity and extravagance; or they are chiefly of a superficial kind, lying upon the surfaces of manners; or arising out of a selection and arrangement of incidents, by which the mind is kept upon the stretch of curiosity, and the fancy amused without the trouble of thought. But in everything which is to send the soul into herself, to be admonished of her weakness, or to be made conscious of her power; wherever life and nature are described as operated upon by the creative or abstracting virtue of the imagination; wherever the instinctive wisdom of antiquity and her heroic passions uniting, in the heart of the poet, with the meditative wisdom of later ages, have produced that accord of sublimated humanity, which is at once a history of the remote past and a prophetic enunciation of the remotest future; *there,* the poet must reconcile himself for a season to few and scattered hearers.—Grand thoughts (and Shak-

speare must often have sighed over this truth), as they are most naturally and most fitly conceived in solitude, so can they not be brought forth in the midst of plaudits without some violation of their sanctity. Go to a silent exhibition of the productions of the sister art, and be convinced that the qualities which dazzle at first sight, and kindle the admiration of the multitude, are essentially different from those by which permanent influence is secured. Let us not shrink from following up these principles as far as they will carry us, and conclude with observing that there never has been a period, and perhaps never will be, in which vicious poetry, of some kind or other, has not excited more zealous admiration, and been far more generally read, than good; but this advantage attends the good, that the *individual,* as well as the species, survives from age to age; whereas, of the depraved, though the species be immortal, the individual quickly *perishes;* the object of present admiration vanishes, being supplanted by some other as easily produced; which, though no better, brings with it at least the irritation of novelty,— with adaptation, more or less skilful, to the changing humors of the majority of those who are most at leisure to regard poetical works when they first solicit their attention.

Is it the result of the whole that, in the opinion of the writer, the judgment of the people is not to be respected? The thought is most injurious; and, could the charge be brought against him, he would repel it with indignation. The people have already been justified, and their eulogium pronounced by implication, when it was said above that, of *good* poetry, the *individual,* as well as the species, *survives.* And how does it survive but through the people? What preserves it but their intellect and their wisdom?

"—Past and future, are the wings
On whose support, harmoniously conjoined,
Moves the great Spirit of human knowledge—"
MS.

The voice that issues from this Spirit, is that Vox Populi which the Deity inspires. Foolish must be he who can mistake for this a local acclamation, or a transitory outcry —transitory though it be for years, local though from a nation. Still more lamentable is his error who can believe that there is anything of divine infallibility in the clamor of that small though loud portion of the community, [ever governed by factitious influence,] which, under the name of the PUBLIC, passes itself, upon the unthinking, for the PEOPLE. Towards the public, the writer hopes that he feels as much deference as it is entitled to: but to the people, philosophically characterised, and to the embodied spirit of their knowledge, so far as it exists and moves, at the present, faithfully supported by its two wings, the past and the future, his devout respect, his reverence, is due. He offers it willingly and readily; and, this done, takes leave of his readers, by assuring them that, if he were not persuaded that the contents of these volumes, and the work to which they are subsidiary, evince something of the "Vision and the Faculty divine"; and that, both in words and things, they will operate in their degree to extend the domain of sensibility for the delight, the honor, and the benefit of human nature, notwithstanding the many happy hours which he has employed in their composition, and the manifold comforts and enjoyments they have procured to him, he would not, if a wish could io it, save them from immediate destruction—from becoming at this moment, to the world, as a thing that had never been.

1815

SAMUEL TAYLOR COLERIDGE (1772-1834)

(PROSE SELECTIONS)

For the general introductory remarks on Coleridge, see the Selections from his poetry, preceding the Wordsworth section.

It happened, strangely enough, that it was during the latter period of his life, before he had come under Dr. Gillman's care, and while he was a wretched and conscience-tortured man, at perhaps the lowest point in his moral existence, that Coleridge began to give his now celebrated series of lectures on Shakspeare, Milton, etc., and to produce some of the loftiest, wisest, and most humane criticism of life and literature that has ever been given to the world. One of his American disciples, Ralph Waldo Emerson, said, "He wrote and spoke the only high criticism of his time,"—which may be a slight exaggeration, but points to the truth that Coleridge's criticism was more philosophical than that of Lamb, Hazlitt, and De Quincey, and even than that of Wordsworth. His basic themes were the relationship of the Many to the One, the meaning and value of the imagination, and the way in which poetry revealed the essential nature of the universe. He disclosed the greatness of Shakspeare more profoundly than had any previous critic,—pointing out Shakspeare's exceptional grasp of the complexities of human existence and the amazing vitality of his characters. Better than any contemporary he perceived and praised the unique merits of Wordsworth's poetry; but he opposed Wordsworth's crotchet about the superior value of rustic language, on the ground that culture and education are necessary to discern and fully to express things as they really are. It is doubtful whether one can attain to a sound appreciation of the wisdom that inheres in great poetry, if one has not been guided by Coleridge's insight. His *Biographia Literaria* and Shelley's *Defense of Poetry* are the two high points of Romantic criticism.

If the English Romantics had organized themselves as a school of literature, Coleridge would logically have been their leader; because he was the equal of any of them in his best poems, and because he understood, more philosophically than the others did, the tendencies which united them.

[CHARACTER MORE IMPORTANT THAN POLITICS]

To George Coleridge

April, 1798

I collect from your letter that our opinions and feelings on political subjects are more nearly alike than you imagine them to be. Equally with you (and perhaps with a deeper conviction, for my belief is founded on actual experience), equally with you I deprecate the moral and intellectual habits of those men, both in England and France, who have modestly assumed to themselves the exclusive title of Philosophers and Friends of Freedom. I think them at least as distant from greatness as from goodness. If I know my own opinions, they are utterly untainted with French metaphysics, French politics, French ethics, and French theology. As to *the Rulers* of France, I see in their views, speeches, and actions nothing that distinguishes them to their advantage from other animals of the same species. History has taught me that rulers are much the same in all ages, and under all forms of government; they are as bad as they dare to be. The vanity of ruin and the curse of blindness have clung to them like an hereditary leprosy. Of the French Revolution I can give my thoughts most adequately in the words of Scripture: "A great and strong wind rent the mountains, and brake in pieces the rocks before the Lord; but the Lord was not in the wind; and after the wind an earthquake; and after the earthquake a fire; and the Lord was not in the fire;" and now (believing that no calamities are permitted but as the means of good) I wrap my face in my mantle and wait, with a subdued and patient thought, expecting to hear "the still small voice" which is of God. In America (I have received my information from unquestionable authority) the morals and domestic habits of the people are daily deteriorating; and one good consequence which I expect from revolution is that individuals will see the necessity of individual effort; that they will act as good Christians, rather than as citizens and electors; and so by degrees will purge off . . . the error of attributing to governments a talismanic influence over our virtues and our happiness, as if governments were not rather effects than causes. It is true that all effects react and become causes, and so it must be in some degree with governments; but there are other agents which act more powerfully because by a nigher and more continuous agency, and it remains true that governments are more the *effect* than the cause of that which we are . . . Of guilt I say nothing, but I believe most steadfastly in original sin; that from our mothers' wombs our understandings are darkened; and even where our understandings are in the light, that our organization is depraved and our volitions imperfect; and we sometimes see the good without wishing to attain it, and oftener *wish* it without the energy that wills and performs. And for this inherent depravity I believe that the *spirit* of the Gospel is the sole cure. . . .

You think, my brother, that there can be but two *parties* at present, for the Government and against the Government. It may be so. I am of no party. It is true I think the present Ministry weak and unprincipled men; but I would not with a safe conscience vote for their removal; I could point out no substitutes. . . . I am inclined to consider the aristocrats as the most respectable of our three factions, because they are more decorous. The Opposition and the Democrats are not only vicious, they wear the *filthy garments* of vice.

> He that takes
> Deep in his soft credulity the stamp
> Designed by loud declaimers on the part
> Of liberty, themselves the slaves of lust,
> Incurs derision for his easy faith
> And lack of knowledge, and with cause enough:
> For when was public virtue to be found
> Where private was not? Can he love the whole
> Who loves no part? He be a *nation's* friend,
> Who is, in truth, the friend of *no* man there?
> Can he be strenuous in his country's cause
> Who slights the charities, for whose dear sake
> That country, if at all, must be beloved?
> (Cowper, *The Task*)

. . . I am prepared to suffer without discontent the consequences of my follies and mistakes; and unable to conceive how that which I am of good could have been without that which I have been of evil, it is withheld from me to regret anything. I therefore consent to be deemed a Democrat and a Seditionist. A man's character follows him long after he has ceased to deserve it; but I have snapped my squeaking baby-trumpet of sedition, and the fragments lie scattered in the lumber-room of penitence. I wish to be a good man and a Christian, but I am no Whig, no Reformist, no Republican, and because of the multitude of fiery and undisciplined spirits that lie in wait against the public quiet under these titles, because of them I chiefly accuse the present ministers, to whose folly I attribute, in a great measure, their increased and increasing numbers. You think differently, and if I were called upon by you to prove my assertions, although I imagine I could make them appear plausible, yet I should feel the insufficiency of my data. The Ministers may have had in their possession facts which alter the whole state of the argument, and make my syllogisms fall as flat as a baby's card-house. And feeling this, my brother, I have for some time past withdrawn myself totally from the consideration of *immediate causes,* which are infinitely complex and uncertain, to muse on fundamental and general causes, the *causae causarum.* I devote myself to such works as encroach not on the anti-social passions, —in poetry, to elevate the imagination and set the affections in right tune by the beauty of the inanimate impregnated as with a living soul by the presence of life,— in prose, to the seeking with patience and a slow, very slow mind, *quid sumus, et quidnam victuri gignimus,* what our faculties are and what they are capable of becoming. I love fields and woods and mountains with almost a visionary fondness. And because I have found benevolence and quietness growing within me as that fondness has increased, therefore I should wish to be the means of implanting it in others, and to destroy the bad passions not by combating them but by keeping them in inaction.

> Not useless do I deem
> These shadowy sympathies with things that
>   hold
> An inarticulate Language; for the Man—
> Once taught to love such objects as excite
> No morbid passions, no disquietude.

No vengeance, and no hatred—needs must feel
The joy of that pure principle of love
So deeply, that, unsatisfied with aught
Less pure and exquisite, he cannot choose
But seek for objects of a kindred love
In fellow-nature and a kindred joy.
Accordingly he by degrees perceives
His feelings of aversion softened down;
A holy tenderness pervade his frame!
His sanity of reason not impaired,
Say rather that his thoughts now flowing clear, 10
From a clear fountain flowing, he looks round
And seeks for good; and finds the good he seeks.
(Wordsworth, *The Excursion*)

Your grateful brother

S. T. COLERIDGE

THE STATESMAN'S MANUAL

[SATANIC PRIDE]

In its state of immanence (or indwelling) in reason and religion, the Will appears indifferently, as wisdom or as love: two names of the same power, the former more intelligential, the latter more spiritual, the former more frequent in the Old, the latter in the New Testament. But in its utmost abstraction and consequent state of reprobation, the Will becomes satanic pride and rebellious self-idolatry in the relations of the spirit to itself, and remorseless despotism relatively to others; the more hopeless as the more obdurate by its subjugation of sensual impulses, by its superiority to toil and pain and pleasure; in short, by the fearful resolve to find in itself alone the one absolute motive of action, under which all other motives from within and from without must be either subordinated or crushed.

This is the character which Milton has so philosophically as well as sublimely embodied in the Satan of his Paradise Lost. Alas! too often has it been embodied in real life! Too often has it given a dark and savage grandeur to the historic page! And wherever it has appeared, under whatever circumstances of time and country, the same ingredients have gone to its composition; and it has been identified by the same attributes. Hope in which there is no cheerfulness; steadfastness within and immovable resolve, with outward restlessness and whirling activity; violence with guile; temerity with cunning; and, as the result of all, interminableness of object with perfect indifference of means; these are the qualities that have constituted the commanding genius! these are the marks that have characterised the masters of mischief, the liberticides and mighty hunters of mankind, from Nimrod to Napoleon. And from inattention to the possibility of such a character as well as from ignorance of its elements, even men of honest intentions too frequently become fascinated. Nay, whole nations have been so far duped by this want of insight and reflection as to regard with palliative admiration, instead of wonder and abhorrence, the Molochs of human nature, who are indebted for the far larger portion of their meteoric success to their total want of principle, and who surpass the generality of their fellow-creatures in one act of courage only, that of daring to say with their whole heart, "Evil, be thou my good!" All system so far is power; and a systematic criminal, self-consistent and entire in wickedness, who entrenches villainy within villainy, and barricadoes crime by crime, has removed a world of obstacles by the mere decision, that he will have no obstacles but those of force and brute matter.

1816

FROM BIOGRAPHIA LITERARIA

CHAPTER IV

The Lyrical Ballads with the Preface—Mr.
Wordsworth's earlier poems—On fancy and
imagination—The investigation of the distinction important to the Fine Arts.

I have wandered far from the object in view, but as I fancied to myself readers who would respect the feelings that had tempted me from the main road; so I dare calculate on not a few, who will warmly sympathize with them. At present it will be sufficient for my purpose, if I have proved, that Mr. Southey's writings no more than my own furnished the original occasion to this fiction of a new school of poetry, and to the clamors against its supposed founders and proselytes.

As little do I believe that Mr. Wordsworth's *Lyrical Ballads* were in themselves the cause. I speak exclusively of the two volumes so entitled. A careful and repeated examination of these confirms me in the belief, that the omission of less than a hundred lines would have precluded nine-tenths of the criticism on this work. I hazard this declaration, however, on the supposition, that the reader has taken it up, as he would have done any other collection of poems purporting to derive their subjects or interests from the incidents of domestic or ordinary life, intermingled 5 with higher strains of meditation which the poet utters in his own person and character; with the proviso, that these poems were perused without knowledge of, or reference to, the author's peculiar opin- 10 ions, and that the reader had not had his attention previously directed to those peculiarities. In that case, as actually happened with Mr. Southey's earlier works, the lines and passages which might have of- 15 fended the general taste, would have been considered as mere inequalities, and attributed to inattention, not to perversity of judgment. The men of business who had passed their lives chiefly in cities, and who 20 might therefore be expected to derive the highest pleasure from acute notices of men and manners conveyed in easy, yet correct and pointed language, and all those who, reading but little poetry, are most stimu- 25 lated with that species of it, which seems most distant from prose, would probably have passed by the volumes altogether. Others more catholic in their taste, and yet habituated to be most pleased when most 30 excited, would have contented themselves with deciding, that the author had been successful in proportion to the elevation of his style and subject. Not a few, perhaps, might, by their admiration of the "Lines 35 written near Tintern Abbey," on revisiting the Wye, those "Left upon a Yew Tree Seat," "The Old Cumberland Beggar," and "Ruth," have been gradually led to peruse with kindred feeling "The Brothers," the 40 "Hart-leap Well," and whatever other poems in that collection may be described as holding a middle place between those written in the highest and those in the humblest style; as for instance between the 45 "Tintern Abbey," and "The Thorn," or "Simon Lee." Should their taste submit to no further change, and still remain unreconciled to the colloquial phrases, or the imitations of them, that are, more or less, 50 scattered through the class last mentioned; yet even from the small number of the latter, they would have deemed them but an inconsiderable subtraction from the merit of the whole work; or, what is some- 55 times not unpleasing in the publication of a new writer, as serving to ascertain the natural tendency, and consequently the proper direction of the author's genius.

In the critical remarks, therefore, pre- 60 fixed and annexed to the *Lyrical Ballads,* I believe, we may safely rest, as the true origin of the unexampled opposition which Mr. Wordsworth's writings have been since doomed to encounter. The humbler passages in the poems themselves were dwelt on and cited to justify the rejection of the theory. What in and for themselves would have been either forgotten or forgiven as imperfections, or at least comparative failures, provoked direct hostility when announced as intentional, as the result of choice after full deliberation. Thus the poems, admitted by all as excellent, joined with those which had pleased the far greater number, though they formed twothirds of the whole work, instead of being deemed (as in all right they should have been, even if we take for granted that the reader judged aright) an atonement for the few exceptions, gave wind and fuel to the animosity against both the poems and the poet. In all perplexity there is a portion of fear, which predisposes the mind to anger. Not able to deny that the author possessed both genius and a powerful intellect, they felt *very positive,*—but yet were not *quite certain* that he might not be in the right, and they themselves in the wrong; an unquiet state of mind, which seeks alleviation by quarrelling with the occasion of it, and by wondering at the perverseness of the man, who had written a long and argumentative essay to persuade them, that

Fair is foul, and foul is fair;

in other words, that they had been all their lives admiring without judgment, and were now about to censure without reason.

That this conjecture is not wide from the mark, I am induced to believe from the noticeable fact, which I can state on my own knowledge, that the same general censure has been grounded by almost every different person on some different poem. Among those, whose candor and judgment I estimate highly, I distinctly remember six who expressed their objections to the *Lyrical Ballads* almost in the same words, and altogether to the same purport, at the same time admitting, that several of the poems had given them great pleasure; and, strange as it might seem, the composition which one cited as execrable, another quoted as his favorite. I am indeed convinced in my own mind, that could the same experiment have been tried with these volumes, as was made in the well known story of the picture, the result would have been the same; the parts which had been covered by black spots on the one day, would be found equally *albo lapide notatæ* on the succeeding.

However this may be, it was assuredly hard and unjust to fix the attention on a few separate and insulated poems with as much aversion, as if they had been so many plague-spots on the whole work, instead of passing them over in silence, as so much blank paper, or leaves of a bookseller's catalogue; especially, as no one pretended to have found in them any immorality or indelicacy; and the poems, therefore, at the worst, could only be regarded as so many light or inferior coins in a rouleau of gold, not as so much alloy in a weight of bullion. A friend whose talents I hold in the highest respect, but whose judgment and strong sound sense I have had almost continued occasion to revere, making the usual complaints to me concerning both the style and subjects of Mr. Wordsworth's minor poems; I admitted that there were some few of the tales and incidents, in which I could not myself find a sufficient cause for their having been recorded in metre. I mentioned "Alice Fell" as an instance; "Nay," replied my friend with more than usual quickness of manner, "I cannot agree with you there!—that, I own, does seem to me a remarkably pleasing poem." In the *Lyrical Ballads,* (for my experience does not enable me to extend the remark equally unqualified to the two subsequent volumes,) I have heard at different times, and from different individuals, every single poem extolled and reprobated, with the exception of those of loftier kind, which as was before observed, seem to have won universal praise. This fact of itself would have made me diffident in my censures, had not a still stronger ground been furnished by the strange contrast of the heat and long continuance of the opposition, with the nature of the faults stated as justifying it. The seductive faults, the *dulcia vitia* of Cowley, Marini, or Darwin might reasonably be thought capable of corrupting the public judgment for half a century, and require a twenty years war, campaign after campaign, in order to dethrone the usurper and reestablish the legitimate taste. But that a downright simpleness, under the affectation of simplicity, prosaic words in feeble metre, silly thoughts in childish phrases, and a preference of mean, degrading, or at best trivial associations and characters, should succeed in forming a school of imitators, a company of almost religious admirers, and

this too among young men of ardent minds, liberal education, and not

——with academic laurels unbestowed;

and that this bare and bald counterfeit of poetry, which is characterized as below criticism, should for nearly twenty years have well-nigh engrossed criticism, as the main, if not the only, butt of review, magazine, pamphlet, poem, and paragraph; this is indeed matter of wonder. . . .

During the last year of my residence at Cambridge, 1794, I became acquainted with Mr. Wordsworth's first publication entitled *Descriptive Sketches;* and seldom, if ever, was the emergence of an original poetic genius above the literary horizon more evidently announced. In the form, style, and manner of the whole poem, and in the structure of the particular lines and periods, there is a harshness and acerbity connected and combined with words and images all aglow, which might recall those products of the vegetable world, where gorgeous blossoms rise out of a hard and thorny rind and shell, within which the rich fruit is elaborating. The language is not only peculiar and strong, but at times knotty and contorted, as by its own impatient strength; while the novelty and struggling crowd of images, acting in conjunction with the difficulties of the style, demands always a greater closeness of attention, than poetry,—at all events, than descriptive poetry—has a right to claim. It not seldom therefore justified the complaint of obscurity. In the following extract I have sometimes fancied, that I saw an emblem of the poem itself, and of the author's genius as it was then displayed.——

'Tis storm; and hid in mist from hour to hour,
All day the floods a deepening murmur pour;
The sky is veiled, and every cheerful sight:
Dark is the region as with coming night;
Yet what a sudden burst of overpowering light!
Triumphant on the bosom of the storm,
Glances the fire-clad eagle's wheeling form;
Eastward, in long perspective glittering, shine
The wood-crowned cliffs that o'er the lake recline;
Those Eastern cliffs a hundred streams unfold,
At once to pillars turned that flame with gold;
Behind his sail the peasant strives to shun
The *west,* that burns like one dilated sun,
Where in a mighty crucible expire
The mountains, glowing hot, like coals of fire.

The poetic Psyche, in its process to full development, undergoes as many changes as its Greek namesake, the butterfly. And it is remarkable how soon genius clears and purifies itself from the faults and errors of its earliest products; faults which, in its earliest compositions, are the more obtrusive and confluent, because as heterogeneous elements, which had only a temporary use, they constitute the very ferment, by which themselves are carried off. Or we may compare them to some diseases, which must work on the humors, and be thrown out on the surface, in order to secure the patient from their future recurrence. I was in my twenty-fourth year, when I had the happiness of knowing Mr. Wordsworth personally, and while memory lasts, I shall hardly forget the sudden effect produced on my mind, by his recitation of a manuscript poem, which still remains unpublished, but of which the stanza and tone of style were the same as those of "The Female Vagrant," as originally printed in the first volume of the *Lyrical Ballads.* There was here no mark of strained thought, or forced diction, no crowd or turbulence of imagery; and, as the poet hath himself well described in his Lines on revisiting the Wye, manly reflection and human associations had given both variety, and an additional interest to natural objects, which, in the passion and appetite of the first love, they had seemed to him neither to need nor permit. The occasional obscurities, which had risen from an imperfect control over the resources of his native language, had almost wholly disappeared, together with that worse defect of arbitrary and illogical phrases, at once hackneyed and fantastic, which hold so distinguished a place in the *technique* of ordinary poetry, and will, more or less, alloy the earlier poems of the truest genius, unless the attention has been specially directed to their worthlessness and incongruity. I did not perceive anything particular in the mere style of the poem alluded to during its recitation, except indeed such difference as was not separable from the thought and manner; and the Spenserian stanza, which always, more or less, recalls to the reader's mind Spenser's own style, would doubtless have authorized, in my then opinion, a more frequent descent to the phrases of ordinary life, than could without an ill effect have been hazarded in the heroic couplet.

It was not however the freedom from false taste, whether as to common defects, or to those more properly his own, which made so unusual an impression on my feelings immediately, and subsequently on my judgment. It was the union of deep feeling with profound thought; the fine balance of truth in observing, with the imaginative faculty in modifying, the objects observed; and above all the original gift of spreading the tone, the atmosphere, and with it the depth and height of the ideal world around forms, incidents, and situations, of which, for the common view, custom had bedimmed all the lustre, had dried up the sparkle and the dew drops. . . .

CHAPTER XII

A chapter of requests and premonitions concerning the perusal or omission of the chapter that follows.

. . . I shall now proceed to the nature and *genesis* of the Imagination; but I must first take leave to notice, that after a more accurate perusal of Mr. Wordsworth's remarks on the Imagination, in his preface to the new edition of his poems, I find that my conclusions are not so consentient with his as, I confess, I had taken for granted. In an article contributed by me to Mr. Southey's *Omniana, On the soul and its organs of sense,* are the following sentences. "These (the human faculties) I would arrange under the different senses and powers: as the eye, the ear, the touch, &c.; the imitative power, voluntary and automatic; the imagination, or shaping and modifying power; the fancy, or the aggregative and associative power; the understanding, or the regulative, substantiating and realizing power; the speculative reason, *vis theoretica et scientifica,* or the power by which we produce or aim to produce unity, necessity, and universality in all our knowledge by means of principles *a priori;* the will, or practical reason; the faculty of choice (*Germanice,* Willkühr) and (distinct both from the moral will and the choice) the *sensation* of volition, which I have found reason to include under the head of single and double touch." To this, as far as it relates to the subject in question, namely the words (*the aggregative and associative power*) Mr. Wordsworth's "objection is only that the definition is too general. To aggregate and to associate, to evoke and to combine, belong as well to the Imagination as to the Fancy." I reply, that if, by the power of evoking and combining, Mr. Wordsworth means the same as, and no more than, I meant by the aggregative and associative, I continue to deny, that it belongs at all to the Imagination; and I am disposed to conjecture, that he has mistaken the co-presence of Fancy with Imagination for the operation of the latter singly. A man may work with two very different tools at the same moment; each has its share in the work, but the work effected by each is distinct and different. But it will probably appear in the next chapter, that deeming it necessary to go back much further than Mr. Wordsworth's subject required or permitted, I have attached a meaning to both Fancy and Imagination, which he had not in view, at least while he was writing that preface. He will judge. Would to Heaven, I might meet with many such readers! I will conclude with the words of Bishop Jeremy Taylor: "He to whom all things are one, who draweth all things to one, and seeth all things in one, may enjoy true peace and rest of spirit."

CHAPTER XIV

Occasion of the *Lyrical Ballads*, and the objects originally proposed—Preface to the second edition—The ensuing controversy, its causes and acrimony—Philosophic definitions of a poem and poetry with scholia.

During the first year that Mr. Wordsworth and I were neighbors, our conversations turned frequently on the two cardinal points of poetry, the power of exciting the sympathy of the reader by a faithful adherence to the truth of nature, and the power of giving the interest of novelty by the modifying colors of imagination. The sudden charm, which accidents of light and shade, which moonlight or sunset diffused over a known and familiar landscape, appeared to represent the practicability of combining both. These are the poetry of nature. The thought suggested itself (to which of us I do not recollect) that a series of poems might be composed of two sorts. In the one, the incidents and agents were to be, in part at least, supernatural; and the excellence aimed at was to consist in the interesting of the affections by the dramatic truth of such emotions as would naturally accompany such situations, supposing them real. And real in *this* sense they have been to every human being who, from whatever source of delusion, has at any time believed himself under supernatural agency. For the second class, subjects were to be chosen from ordinary life; the characters and incidents were to be such as will be found in every village and its

vicinity where there is a meditative and feeling mind to seek after them, or to notice them when they present themselves. In this idea originated the plan of the *Lyrical Ballads;* in which it was agreed, that my endeavors should be directed to persons and characters supernatural, or at least romantic; yet so as to transfer from our inward nature a human interest and a semblance of truth sufficient to procure for these shadows of imagination that willing suspension of disbelief for the moment, which constitutes poetic faith. Mr. Wordsworth, on the other hand, was to propose to himself as his object, to give the charm of novelty to things of every day, and to excite a feeling analogous to the supernatural, by awakening the mind's attention to the lethargy of custom, and directing it to the loveliness and the wonders of the world before us; an inexhaustible treasure, but for which, in consequence of the film of familiarity and selfish solicitude we have eyes, yet see not, ears that hear not, and hearts that neither feel nor understand.

With this view I wrote *The Ancient Mariner,* and was preparing, among other poems, *The Dark Ladie,* and the *Christabel,* in which I should have more nearly realized my ideal than I had done in my first attempt. But Mr. Wordsworth's industry had proved so much more successful, and the number of his poems so much greater, that my compositions, instead of forming a balance, appeared rather an interpolation of heterogeneous matter. Mr. Wordsworth added two or three poems written in his own character, in the impassioned, lofty, and sustained diction, which is characteristic of his genius. In this form the *Lyrical Ballads* were published; and were presented by him, as an *experiment,* whether subjects, which from their nature rejected the usual ornaments and extracolloquial style of poems in general, might not be so managed in the langauge of ordinary life as to produce the pleasurable interest, which it is the peculiar business of poetry to impart. To the second edition he added a preface of considerable length, in which, notwithstanding some passages of apparently a contrary import, he was understood to contend for the extension of this style to poetry of all kinds, and to reject as vicious and indefensible all phrases and forms of style that were not included in what he (unfortunately, I think, adopting an equivocal expression) called the language of *real* life. From this preface, prefixed to poems in which it was impossible to deny the presence of original genius, however mistaken its direction might be deemed, arose the whole long-continued controversy. For from the conjunction of perceived power with supposed heresy I explain the inveteracy and in some instances, I grieve to say, the acrimonious passions, with which the controversy has been conducted by the assailants.

Had Mr. Wordsworth's poems been the silly, the childish things, which they were for a long time described as being; had they been really distinguished from the compositions of other poets merely by meanness of language and inanity of thought; had they indeed contained nothing more than what is found in the parodies and pretended imitations of them; they must have sunk at once, a dead weight, into the slough of oblivion, and have dragged the preface along with them. But year after year increased the number of Mr. Wordsworth's admirers. They were found, too, not in the lower classes of the reading public, but chiefly among young men of strong sensibility and meditative minds; and their admiration (inflamed perhaps in some degree by opposition) was distinguished by its intensity, I might almost say, by its *religious* fervor. These facts, and the intellectual energy of the author, which was more or less consciously felt, where it was outwardly and even boisterously denied, meeting with sentiments of aversion to his opinions, and of alarm at their consequences, produced an eddy of criticism, which would of itself have borne up the poems by the violence with which it whirled them round and round. With many parts of this preface, in the sense attributed to them, and which the words undoubtedly seem to authorize, I never concurred; but on the contrary objected to them as erroneous in principle, and as contradictory (in appearance at least) both to other parts of the same preface, and to the author's own practice in the greater number of the poems themselves. Mr. Wordsworth in his recent collection has, I find, degraded this prefatory disquisition to the end of his second volume, to be read or not at the reader's choice. But he has not, as far as I can discover, announced any change in his poetic creed. At all events, considering it as the source of a controversy, in which I have been honored more than I deserve by the frequent conjunction of my name with his, I think it expedient to declare once for all, in what points I coincide with his opinions, and in what points I altogether differ. But in order to render myself intelligible I must previously, in as few words as possible, explain my ideas, first, of a *poem;* and secondly, of *poetry* itself, in *kind,* and in *essence.*

The office of philosophical *disquisition* consists in just *distinction;* while it is the privilege of the philosopher to preserve himself constantly aware, that distinction is not division. In order to obtain adequate notions of any truth, we must intellectually separate its distinguishable parts; and this is the technical *process* of philosophy. But having so done, we must then restore them in our conceptions to the unity, in which they actually coexist; and this is the *result* of philosophy. A poem contains the same elements as a prose composition; the difference therefore must consist in a different combination of them, in consequence of a different object being proposed. According to the difference of the object will be the difference of the combination. It is possible that the object may be merely to facilitate the recollection of any given facts or observations by artificial arrangement; and the composition will be a poem, merely because it is distinguished from prose by metre, or by rhyme, or by both conjointly. In this, the lowest sense, a man might attribute the name of a poem to the well-known enumeration of the days in the several months:

Thirty days hath September,
April, June, and November, &c.

and others of the same class and purpose. And as a particular pleasure is found in anticipating the recurrence of sounds and quantities, all compositions that have this charm superadded, whatever be their contents, *may* be entitled poems.

So much for the superficial *form.* A difference of object and contents supplies an additional ground of distinction. The immediate purpose may be the communication of truths; either of truth absolute and demonstrable, as in works of science; or of facts experienced and recorded, as in history. Pleasure, and that of the highest and most permanent kind, may *result* from the *attainment* of the end; but it is not itself the immediate end. In other works the communication of pleasure may be the immediate purpose; and though truth, either moral or intellectual, ought to be the *ultimate* end, yet this will distinguish the character of the author, not the class to which the work belongs. Blest indeed is that state of society, in which the immediate purpose would be baffled by the perversion of the proper ultimate end; in which no charm of diction or imagery could exempt the *Bathyllus* even of an Anacreon, or the *Alexis* of Virgil, from disgust and aversion!

But the communication of pleasure may be the immediate object of a work not metrically composed; and that object may have been in a high degree attained, as in novels and romances. Would then the mere superaddition of metre, with or without rhyme, entitle *these* to the name of poems? The answer is, that nothing can permanently please, which does not contain in itself the reason why it is so, and not otherwise. If metre be superadded, all other parts must be made consonant with it. They must be such as to justify the perpetual and distinct attention to each part, which an exact correspondent recurrence of accent and sound are calculated to excite. The final definition then, so deduced, may be thus worded. A poem is that species of composition, which is opposed to works of science, by proposing for its *immediate* object pleasure, not truth; and from all other species (having *this* object in common with it) it is discriminated by proposing to itself such delight from the *whole,* as is compatible with a distinct gratification from each component *part*.

Controversy is not seldom excited in consequence of the disputants attaching each a different meaning to the same word; and in few instances has this been more striking, than in disputes concerning the present subject. If a man chooses to call every composition a poem, which is rhyme, or measure, or both, I must leave his opinion uncontroverted. The distinction is at least competent to characterize the writer's intention. If it were subjoined, that the whole is likewise entertaining or affecting, as a tale, or as a series of interesting reflections, I of course admit this as another fit ingredient of a poem, and an additional merit. But if the definition sought for be that of a *legitimate* poem, I answer, it must be one the parts of which mutually support and explain each other; all in their proportion harmonizing with, and supporting the purpose and known influences of metrical arrangement. The philosophic critics of all ages coincide with the ultimate judgment of all countries, in equally denying the praises of a just poem, on the one hand, to a series of striking lines or distiches each of which, absorbing the whole attention of the reader to itself, disjoins it

from its context, and makes it a separate whole, instead of an harmonizing part; and on the other hand, to an unsustained composition, from which the reader collects rapidly the general result, unattracted by the component parts. The reader should be carried forward, not merely or chiefly by the mechanical impulse of curiosity, or by a restless desire to arrive at the final solution; but by the pleasurable activity of mind excited by the attractions of the journey itself. Like the motion of a serpent, which the Egyptians made the emblem of intellectual power; or like the path of sound through the air; at every step he pauses and half recedes, and from the retrogressive movement collects the force which again carries him onward. *Præcipitandus est liber spiritus,* says Petronius Arbiter most happily. The epithet, *liber,* here balances the preceding verb; and it is not easy to conceive more meaning condensed in fewer words.

But if this should be admitted as a satisfactory character of a poem, we have still to seek for a definition of poetry. The writings of Plato, and Bishop Taylor, and the *Theoria Sacra* of Burnet, furnish undeniable proofs that poetry of the highest kind may exist without metre, and even without the contradistinguishing objects of a poem. The first chapter of *Isaiah* (indeed a very large portion of the whole book) is poetry in the most emphatic sense; yet it would not be less irrational than strange to assert, that pleasure, and not truth, was the immediate object of the prophet. In short, whatever *specific* import we attach to the word, poetry, there will be found involved in it, as a necessary consequence, that a poem of any length neither can be, nor ought to be, all poetry. Yet if an harmonious whole is to be produced, the remaining parts must be preserved *in keeping* with the poetry; and this can be no otherwise effected than by such a studied selection and artificial arrangement as will partake of *one,* though not a *peculiar* property of poetry. And this again can be no other than the property of exciting a more continuous and equal attention than the language of prose aims at, whether colloquial or written.

My own conclusions on the nature of poetry, in the strictest use of the word, have been in part anticipated in the preceding disquisition on the fancy and imagination. What is poetry? is so nearly the same question with, what is a poet? that the answer to the one is involved in the solution of the other. For it is a distinction resulting from the poetic genius itself, which sustains and modifies the images, thoughts, and emotions of the poet's own mind.

The poet, described in *ideal* perfection, brings the whole soul of man into activity, with the subordination of its faculties to each other according to their relative worth and dignity. He diffuses a tone and spirit of unity, that blends, and (as it were) *fuses*, each into each, by that synthetic and magical power, to which we have exclusively appropriated the name of imagination. This power, first put in action by the will and understanding, and retained under their irremissive, though gentle and unnoticed, control *(laxis effertur habenis)* reveals itself in the balance or reconciliation of opposite or discordant qualities: of sameness, with difference; of the general, with the concrete; the idea, with the image; the individual, with the representative; the sense of novelty and freshness, with old and familiar objects; a more than usual state of emotion, with more than usual order; judgment ever awake and steady self-possession, with enthusiasm and feeling profound or vehement; and while it blends and harmonizes the natural and the artificial, still subordinates art to nature; the manner to the matter; and our admiration of the poet to our sympathy with the poetry. "Doubtless," as Sir John Davies observes of the soul (and his words may with slight alteration be applied, and even more appropriately, to the poetic imagination),—

Doubtless this could not be, but that she turns
  Bodies to spirit by sublimation strange,
As fire converts to fire the things it burns,
  As we our food into our nature change.

From their gross matter she abstracts their forms,
  And draws a kind of quintessence from things;
Which to her proper nature she transforms,
  To bear them light on her celestial wings.

Thus does she, when from individual states
  She doth abstract the universal kinds;
Which then re-clothed in divers names and fates
  Steal access through the senses to our minds.

Finally, good sense is the body of poetic genius, fancy its drapery, motion its life, and imagination the soul that is everywhere, and in each; and forms all into one graceful and intelligent whole.

CHAPTER XVII

Examination of the tenets peculiar to Mr. Wordsworth—Rustic life (above all, *low* and rustic life) especially unfavorable to the formation of a human diction—The best parts of language the product of philosophers, not of clowns or shepherds—Poetry essentially ideal and generic—The language of Milton as much the language of *real* life, yea, incomparably more so than that of the cottager.

As far, then, as Mr. Wordsworth in his preface contended, and most ably contended, for a reformation in our poetic diction, as far as he has evinced the truth of passion, and the *dramatic* propriety of those figures and metaphors in the original poets, which, stripped of their justifying reasons, and converted into mere artifices of connection or ornament, constitute the characteristic falsity in the poetic style of the moderns; and as far as he has, with equal acuteness and clearness, pointed out the process by which this change was effected, and the resemblances between that state into which the reader's mind is thrown by the pleasurable confusion of thought from an unaccustomed train of words and images, and that state which is induced by the natural language of impassioned feeling; he undertook a useful task, and deserves all praise, both for the attempt and for the execution. The provocations to this remonstrance in behalf of truth and nature were still of perpetual recurrence before and after the publication of this preface. I cannot likewise but add, that the comparison of such poems of merit, as have been given to the public within the last ten or twelve years, with the majority of those produced previously to the appearance of that preface, leave no doubt on my mind, that Mr. Wordsworth is fully justified in believing his efforts to have been by no means ineffectual. Not only in the verses of those who have professed their admiration of his genius, but even of those who have distinguished themselves by hostility to his theory, and depreciation of his writings, are the impressions of his principles plainly visible. It is possible that with these principles others may have been blended, which are not equally evident; and some which are unsteady and subvertible from the narrowness or imperfection of their basis. But it is more than possible that these errors of defect or exaggeration, by kindling and feeding the controversy, may have conduced not only to the wider propagation of the accompanying truths, but that, by their frequent presentation to the mind in an excited state, they may have won for them a more permanent and practical result. A man will borrow a part from his opponent the more easily, if he feels himself justified in continuing to reject a part. While there remain important points in which he can still feel himself in the right, in which he still finds firm footing for continued resistance, he will gradually adopt those opinions, which were the least remote from his own convictions, as not less congruous with his own theory than with that which he reprobates. In like manner with a kind of instinctive prudence, he will abandon by little and little his weakest posts, till at length he seems to forget that they have ever belonged to him, or affects to consider them at most as accidental and "petty annexments," the removal of which leaves the citadel unhurt and unendangered.

My own differences from certain supposed parts of Mr. Wordsworth's theory ground themselves on the assumption that his words had been rightly interpreted, as purporting that the proper diction for poetry in general consists altogether in a language taken, with due exceptions, from the mouths of men in real life, a language which actually constitutes the natural conversation of men under the influence of natural feelings. My objection is, first, that in *any* sense this rule is applicable only to *certain* classes of poetry; secondly, that even to these classes it is not applicable, except in such a sense, as hath never by any one (as far as I know or have read) been denied or doubted; and lastly, that as far as, and in that degree in which it is *practicable,* yet, as a *rule,* it is useless, if not injurious, and therefore either need not or ought not to be practised. The poet informs his reader that he had generally chosen *low and rustic* life; but not *as* low and rustic, or in order to repeat that pleasure of doubtful moral effect, which persons of elevated rank and of superior refinement oftentimes derive from a happy *imitation* of the rude unpolished manners and discourse of their inferiors. For the pleasure so derived may be traced to three exciting causes. The first is the naturalness, in *fact,* of the things represented. The second is the apparent naturalness of the *representation,* as raised and qualified by an imperceptible infusion of the author's own knowledge and talent, which infusion does, indeed, constitute it an *imitation* as distinguished from a mere *copy.* The third cause may be found in the reader's conscious feeling of his superiority, awakened by the contrast presented to him; even as for the same purpose the kings and great barons of yore retained sometimes *actual* clowns and fools, but more frequently shrewd and witty fellows in that *character.* These, however, were not Mr. Wordsworth's objects. *He* chose low and rustic life, "because in that condition the essential passions of the heart find a better soil, in which they can attain their maturity, are less under restraint, and speak a plainer and more emphatic language; because in that condition of life our elementary feelings coexist in a state of greater simplicity, and consequently may be more accurately contemplated, and more forcibly communicated; because the manners of rural life germinate from those elementary feelings; and from the necessary character of rural occupations are more easily comprehended, and are more durable; and lastly, because in that condition the passions of men are incorporated with the beautiful and permanent forms of nature."

Now it is clear to me that in the most interesting of the poems, in which the author is more or less dramatic, as *The Brothers, Michael, Ruth, The Mad Mother,* etc., the persons introduced are by no means taken *from low or rustic life* in the common acceptation of those words; and it is not less clear that the sentiments and language, as far as they can be conceived to have been really transferred from the minds and conversation of such persons, are attributable to causes and circumstances not necessarily connected with "their occupations and abode." The thoughts, feelings, language, and manners of the shepherd-farmers in the vales of Cumberland and Westmoreland, as far as they are actually adopted in those poems, may be accounted for from causes, which will and do produce the same results in *every* state of life, whether in town or country. As the two principal I rank that independence which raises a man above servitude, or daily toil for the profit of others, yet not above the necessity of industry and a frugal simplicity of domestic life; and the accompanying unambitious, but solid and religious, education which has rendered few books familiar but the Bible and the liturgy or hymn book. To this latter cause, indeed, which is so far *accidental* that it is the blessing of particular countries and a particular age, not the product of particular places or employ-ments, the poet owes the show of proba-bility, that his personages might really feel, think, and talk with any tolerable resem-blance to his representation. It is an excel- 5 lent remark of Dr. Henry More's (*Enthusi-asmus Triumpatus,* Sec. xxxv.) that "a man of confined education, but of good parts, by constant reading of the Bible will natu-rally form a more winning and command- 10 ing rhetoric than those that are learned, the intermixture of tongues and of artificial phrases debasing *their* style."

It is, moreover, to be considered that to the formation of healthy feelings and a 15 reflecting mind, *negations* involve impedi-ments not less formidable than sophistica-tion and vicious intermixture. I am con-vinced that for the human soul to prosper in rustic life a certain vantage-ground is 20 prerequisite. It is not every man that is likely to be improved by a country life or by country labors. Education, or original sensibility, or both, must pre-exist, if the changes, forms, and incidents of nature are 25 to prove a sufficient stimulant. And where these are not sufficient, the mind contracts and hardens by want of stimulants; and the man becomes selfish, sensual, gross, and hard-hearted. Let the management of the 30 Poor Laws in Liverpool, Manchester, or Bristol be compared with the ordinary dis-pensation of the poor rates in agricultural villages, where the *farmers* are the overseers and guardians of the poor. If my own ex- 35 perience have not been particularly unfor-tunate, as well as that of the many respect-able country clergymen with whom I have conversed on the subject, the result would engender more than skepticism concerning 40 the desirable influences of low and rustic life in and for itself. Whatever may be concluded on the other side, from the stronger local attachments and enterprising spirit of the Swiss, and other mountaineers, 45 applies to a particular mode of pastoral life, under forms of property that permit and beget manners truly republican, not to rustic life in general, or to the absence of artificial cultivation. On the contrary, 50 the mountaineers, whose manners have been so often eulogized, are in general bet-ter educated and greater readers than men of equal rank elsewhere. But where this is not the case, as among the peasantry of 55 North Wales, the ancient mountains, with all their terrors and all their glories, are pictures to the blind, and music to the deaf.

I should not have entered so much into 60 detail upon this passage, but here seems to be the point to which all the lines of dif-ference converge as to their source and center. (I mean, as far as, and in whatever respect, my poetic creed *does* differ from the doctrines promulgated in this preface.) I adopt with full faith the principle of Aristotle, that poetry as poetry is essentially *ideal,* that it avoids and excludes all *acci-dent;* that its apparent individualities of rank, character, or occupation must be *rep-resentative* of a class; and that the *persons* of poetry must be clothed with *generic* at-tributes, with the *common* attributes of the class; not with such as one gifted individual might *possibly* possess, but such as from his situation it is most probable before-hand that he *would* possess. If my prem-ises are right and my deductions legitimate, it follows that there can be no *poetic* me-dium between the swains of Theocritus and those of an imaginary golden age.

The characters of the vicar and the shepherd-mariner in the poem of *The Brothers,* and that of the shepherd of Greenhead Ghyll in the *Michael,* have all the verisimilitude and representative qual-ity that the purposes of poetry can require. They are persons of a known and abiding class, and their manners and sentiments the natural product of circumstances common to the class. Take *Michael* for instance:

An old man, stout of heart and strong of limb:
His bodily frame had been from youth to age
Of an unusual strength: his mind was keen,
Intense, and frugal, apt for all affairs,
And in his shepherd's calling he was prompt
And watchful more than ordinary men.
Hence he had learned the meaning of all winds,
Of blasts of every tone; and oftentimes
When others heeded not, he heard the South
Make subterraneous music, like the noise
Of bagpipers on distant Highland hills.
The shepherd, at such warning, of his flock
Bethought him, and he to himself would say,
"The winds are now devising work for me!"
And truly, at all times, the storm, that drives
The traveller to a shelter, summoned him
Up to the mountains: he had been alone
Amid the heart of many thousand mists,
That came to him and left him on the heights.
So lived he, until his eightieth year was past.
And grossly that man errs, who should suppose
That the green valleys, and the streams and
    rocks,
Were things indifferent to the shepherd's
    thoughts.
Fields, where with cheerful spirits he had
    breathed
The common air; the hills, which he so oft
Had climbed with vigorous steps; which had
    impressed

So many incidents upon his mind
Of hardship, skill or courage, joy or fear;
Which, like a book, preserved the memory
Of the dumb animals, whom he had saved,
Had fed or sheltered, linking to such acts,
So grateful in themselves, the certainty
Of honorable gain; these fields, these hills
Which were his living being, even more
Than his own blood—who could they less? had
    laid
Strong hold on his affections, were to him
A pleasurable feeling of blind love,
The pleasure which there is in life itself.

On the other hand, in the poems which are pitched at a lower note, as the *Harry Gill*, *The Idiot Boy*, the *feelings* are those of human nature in general; though the poet has judiciously laid the *scene* in the country, in order to place *himself* in the vicinity of interesting images, without the necessity of ascribing a sentimental perception of their beauty to the persons of his drama. In *The Idiot Boy*, indeed, the mother's character is not so much a real and native product of a "situation where the essential passions of the heart find a better soil, in which they can attain their maturity and speak a plainer and more emphatic language," as it is an impersonation of an instinct abandoned by judgment. Hence the two following charges seem to me not wholly groundless; at least, they are the only plausible objections which I have heard to that fine poem. The one is, that the author has not, in the poem itself, taken sufficient care to preclude from the reader's fancy the disgusting images of *ordinary morbid idiocy*, which yet it was by no means his intention to represent. He was even by the "burr, burr, burr," uncounteracted by any preceding description of the boy's beauty, assisted in recalling them. The other is, that the idiocy of the *boy* is so evenly balanced by the folly of the *mother*, as to present to the general reader rather a laughable burlesque on the blindness of anile dotage, than an analytic display of maternal affection in its ordinary workings.

In *The Thorn*, the poet himself acknowledges in a note the necessity of an introductory poem, in which he should have portrayed the character of the person from whom the words of the poem are supposed to proceed: a superstitious man moderately imaginative, of slow faculties and deep feelings, "a captain of a small trading vessel, for example, who, being past the middle age of life, had retired upon an annuity, or small independent income, to some village or country town of which he was not a native, or in which he had not been accustomed to live. Such men having nothing to do become credulous and talkative from indolence." But in a poem, still more in a lyric poem (and the Nurse in Shakspeare's *Romeo and Juliet* alone prevents me from extending the remark even to dramatic *poetry*, if indeed the Nurse itself can be deemed altogether a case in point) it is not possible to imitate truly a dull and garrulous discourser, without repeating the effects of dullness and garrulity. However this may be, I dare assert that the parts (and these form the far larger portion of the whole) which might as well or still better have proceeded from the poet's own imagination, and have been spoken in his own character, are those which have given, and which will continue to give, universal delight; and that the passages exclusively appropriate to the supposed narrator, such as the last couplet of the third stanza, the seven last lines of the tenth, and the five following stanzas, with the exception of the four admirable lines at the commencement of the fourteenth, are felt by many unprejudiced and unsophisticated hearts, as sudden and unpleasant sinkings from the height to which the poet had previously lifted them, and to which he again re-elevates both himself and his reader.

If then I am compelled to doubt the theory, by which the choice of *characters* was to be directed, not only *a priori*, from grounds of reason, but both from the few instances in which the poet himself *need* be supposed to have been governed by it, and from the comparative inferiority of those instances; still more must I hesitate in my assent to the sentence which immediately follows the former citation, and which I can neither admit as particular fact, or as general rule. "The language too of these men is adopted (purified indeed from what appear to be its real defects, from all lasting and rational causes of dislike or disgust) because such men hourly communicate with the best objects from which the best part of language is originally derived; and because, from their rank in society and the sameness and narrow circles of their intercourse, being less under the action of social vanity, they convey their feelings and notions in simple and unelaborated expressions." To this I reply that a rustic's language, purified from all provincialism and grossness, and so far reconstructed as to be made consistent with the rules of grammar (which are in essence no other than the laws of universal logic, applied to psychological materials) will not differ from the language of any other man of common sense, however learned or refined he may be, except as far as the notions, which the rustic has to convey, are fewer and more indiscriminate. This will become still clearer, if we add the consideration (equally important though less obvious) that the rustic, from the more imperfect development of his faculties, and from the lower state of their cultivation, aims almost solely to convey *insulated facts*, either those of his scanty experience or his traditional belief; while the educated man chiefly seeks to discover and express those *connections* of things, or those relative *bearings* of fact to fact, from which some more or less general law is deducible. For *facts* are valuable to a wise man, chiefly as they lead to the discovery of the indwelling *law*, which is the true *being* of things, the sole solution of their modes of existence, and in the knowledge of which consists our dignity and our power.

As little can I agree with the assertion that from the objects with which the rustic hourly communicates, the best part of language is formed. For first, if to communicate with an object implies such an acquaintance with it as renders it capable of being discriminately reflected on, the distinct knowledge of an uneducated rustic would furnish a very scanty vocabulary. The few things and modes of action requisite for his bodily conveniences would alone be individualized; while all the rest of nature would be expressed by a small number of confused general terms. Secondly, I deny that the words and combinations of words derived from the objects with which the rustic is familiar, whether with distinct or confused knowledge, can be justly said to form the *best* part of language. It is more than probable that many classes of the brute creation possess discriminating sounds, by which they can convey to each other notices of such objects as concern their food, shelter, or safety. Yet we hesitate to call the aggregate of such sounds a language, otherwise than metaphorically. The best part of human language, properly so called, is derived from reflection on the acts of the mind itself. It is formed by a voluntary appropriation of fixed symbols to internal acts, to processes and results of imagination, the greater part of which have no place in the consciousness of uneducated man; though in civilized society, by imitation and passive remembrance of what they hear from their religious instructors and other superiors, the most uneducated share in the harvest which they neither sowed [n]or reaped. If the history of the phrases in hourly currency among our peasants were traced, a person not previously aware of the fact would be surprised at finding so large a number which three or four centuries ago were the exclusive property of the universities and the schools, and at the commencement of the Reformation had been transferred from the school to the pulpit, and thus gradually passed into common life. The extreme difficulty, and often the impossibility, of finding words for the simplest moral and intellectual processes of the languages of uncivilized tribes has proved perhaps the weightiest obstacle to the progress of our most zealous and adroit missionaries. Yet these tribes are surrounded by the same nature as our peasants are, but in still more impressive forms; and they are, moreover, obliged to *particularize* many more of them. When, therefore, Mr. Wordsworth adds, "accordingly, such a language" (meaning, as before, the language of rustic life purified from provincialism) "arising out of repeated experience and regular feelings, is a more permanent, and a far more philosophical language, than that which is frequently substituted for it by poets, who think they are conferring honor upon themselves and their art in proportion as they indulge in arbitrary and capricious habits of expression," it may be answered that the language which he has in view can be attributed to rustics with no greater right than the style of Hooker or Bacon to Tom Brown or Sir Roger L'Estrange. Doubtless, if what is peculiar to each were omitted in each, the result must needs be the same. Further, that the poet who uses an illogical diction, or a style fitted to excite only the low and changeable pleasure of wonder by means of groundless novelty, substitutes a language of *folly* and *vanity*, not for that of the *rustic*, but for that of *good sense* and *natural feeling*.

Here let me be permitted to remind the reader that the positions which I controvert are contained in the sentences—"a *selection of the real language of men*";—"*the language of these men*" (i.e. men in low and rustic life) "*I propose to myself to imitate, and, as far as is possible, to adopt the very language of men.*" "*Between the language of prose and that of metrical composition, there neither is, nor can be, any essential difference.*" It is against these exclusively that my opposition is directed.

I object, in the very first instance, to an equivocation in the use of the word "real." Every man's language varies according to the extent of his knowledge, the activity of his faculties, and the depth or quickness of his feelings. Every man's language has, first, its *individuality;* secondly, the common properties of the *class* to which he belongs; and thirdly, words and phrases of *universal* use. The language of Hooker, Bacon, Bishop Taylor, and Burke differs from the common language of the learned class only by the superior number and novelty of the thoughts and relations which they had to convey. The language of Algernon Sidney differs not at all from that which every well-educated gentleman would wish to write, and (with due allowances for the undeliberateness, and less connected train, of thinking natural and proper to conversation) such as he would wish to talk. Neither one nor the other differ half so much from the general language of cultivated society, as the language of Mr. Wordsworth's homeliest composition differs from that of a common peasant. For "real," therefore, we must substitute *ordinary,* or *lingua communis.* And this, we have proved, is no more to be found in the phraseology of low and rustic life than in that of any other class. Omit the peculiarities of each, and the result of course must be common to all. And assuredly the omissions and changes to be made in the language of rustics, before it could be transferred to any species of poem, except the drama or other professed imitation, are at least as numerous and weighty as would be required in adapting to the same purpose the ordinary language of tradesmen and manufacturers. Not to mention that the language so highly extolled by Mr. Wordsworth varies in every county, nay, in every village, according to the accidental character of the clergyman, the existence or nonexistence of schools; or even, perhaps, as the exciseman, publican, or barber happen to be, or not to be, zealous politicians and readers of the weekly newspaper *pro bono publico.* Anterior to cultivation, the *lingua communis* of every country, as Dante has well observed, exists everywhere in parts, and nowhere as a whole.

Neither is the case rendered at all more tenable by the addition of the words, *in a state of excitement.* For the nature of a man's words, where he is strongly affected by joy, grief, or anger, must necessarily depend on the number and quality of the general truths, conceptions, and images, and of the words expressing them, with which his mind had been previously stored. For the property of passion is not to *create,* but to set in increased activity. At least, whatever new connections of thoughts or images, or (which is equally, if not more than equally, the appropriate effect of strong excitement) whatever generalizations of truth or experience the heat of passion may produce, yet the terms of their conveyance must have pre-existed in his former conversations, and are only collected and crowded together by the unusual stimulation. It is indeed very possible to adopt in a poem the unmeaning repetitions, habitual phrases, and other blank counters, which an unfurnished or confused understanding interposes at short intervals, in order to keep hold of his subject, which is still slipping from him, and to give him time for recollection; or, in mere aid of vacancy, as in the scanty companies of a country stage the same player pops backwards and forwards, in order to prevent the appearance of empty spaces, in the procession of *Macbeth,* or *Henry VIII.* But what assistance to the poet, or ornament to the poem, these can supply, I am at a loss to conjecture. Nothing assuredly can differ either in origin or in mode more widely from the *apparent* tautologies of intense and turbulent feeling, in which the passion is greater and of longer endurance than to be exhausted or satisfied by a single representation of the image or incident exciting it. Such repetitions I admit to be a beauty of the highest kind, as illustrated by Mr. Wordsworth himself from the song of Deborah. *"At her feet he bowed, he fell, he lay down; at her feet he bowed, he fell; where he bowed, there he fell down dead."*

CHAPTER XVIII

Language of metrical composition, why and wherein essentially different from that of prose—Origin and elements of metre—Its necessary consequences, and the conditions thereby imposed on the metrical writer in the choice of his diction.

I conclude, therefore, that the attempt is impracticable; and that, were it not impracticable, it would still be useless. For the very power of making the selection implies the previous possession of the language selected. Or where can the poet have lived? And by what rules could he direct his choice, which would not have enabled him to select and arrange his words by the light of his own judgment? We do not adopt the language of a class by the mere adoption of such words exclusively as that class would use, or at least understand; but likewise by following the *order* in which the words of such men are wont to succeed each other. Now this order, in the intercourse of uneducated men, is distinguished from the diction of their superiors in knowledge and power, by the greater *disjunction* and *separation* in the component parts of that, whatever it be, which they wish to communicate. There is a want of that prospectiveness of mind, that *surview*, which enables a man to foresee the whole of what he is to convey, appertaining to any one point; and by this means so to subordinate and arrange the different parts according to their relative importance, as to convey it at once, and as an organized whole.

Now I will take the first stanza, on which I have chanced to open, in the *Lyrical Ballads*. It is one of the most simple, and the least peculiar in its language:

In distant countries have I been,
And yet I have not often seen
A healthy man, a man full grown,
Weep in the public roads, alone.

But such a one, on English ground,
And in the broad highway, I met;
Along the broad highway he came,
His cheeks with tears were wet:
Sturdy he seemed, though he was sad;
And in his arms a lamb he had.

The words here are doubtless such as are current in all ranks of life; and of course not less so in the hamlet and cottage than in the shop, manufactory, college, or palace. But is this the *order*, in which the rustic would have placed the words? I am greviously deceived, if the following less *compact* mode of commencing the same tale be not a far more faithful copy. "I have been in a many parts, far and near, and I don't know that I ever saw before a man crying by himself in the public road; a grown man I mean, that was neither sick nor hurt," etc., etc. But when I turn to the following stanza in *The Thorn*:

At all times of the day and night
This wretched woman thither goes;
And she is known to every star,
And every wind that blows:
And there, beside the thorn, she sits,
When the blue day-light's in the skies;

And when the whirlwind's on the hill,
Or frosty air is keen and still;
And to herself she cries,
"Oh misery! Oh misery!
"Oh woe is me! Oh misery!"

and compare this with the language of ordinary men, or with that which I can conceive at all likely to proceed, in *real* life, from *such* a narrator as is supposed in the note to the poem—compare it either in the succession of the images or of the sentences —I am reminded of the sublime prayer and hymn of praise which Milton, in opposition to an established liturgy, presents as a fair *specimen* of common extemporary devotion, and such as we might expect to hear from every self-inspired minister of conventicle! And I reflect with delight, how little a mere theory, though of his own workmanship, interferes with the processes of genuine imagination in a man of true poetic genius, who possesses, as Mr. Wordsworth, if ever man did, most assuredly does possess,

The Vision and the Faculty divine.

One point then alone remains, but that the most important; its examination having been, indeed, my chief inducement for the preceding inquisition. *"There neither is or can be any essential difference between the language of prose and metrical composition."* Such is Mr. Wordsworth's assertion. Now prose itself, at least in all argumentative and consecutive works, differs, and ought to differ, from the language of conversation; even as reading ought to differ from talking. Unless, therefore, the difference denied be that of the mere *words,* as materials common to all styles of writing, and not of the *style* itself in the universally admitted sense of the term, it might be naturally presumed that there must exist a still greater between the ordonnance of poetic composition and that of prose, than is expected to distinguish prose from ordinary conversation.

There are not, indeed, examples wanting in the history of literature, of apparent paradoxes that have summoned the public wonder as new and startling truths, but which, on examination, have shrunk into tame and harmless truisms; as the eyes of a cat, seen in the dark, have been mistaken for flames of fire. But Mr. Wordsworth is among the last men, to whom a delusion of this kind would be attributed by anyone, who had enjoyed the slightest opportunity of understanding his mind and character. Where an objection has been anticipated by such an author as natural, his answer to it must needs be interpreted in some sense which either is, or has been, or is capable of being controverted. My object then must be to discover some other meaning for the term "essential difference" in this place, exclusive of the indistinction and community of the words themselves. For whether there ought to exist a class of words in the English, in any degree resembling the poetic dialect of the Greek and Italian, is a question of very subordinate importance. The number of such words would be small indeed, in our language; and even in the Italian and Greek, they consist not so much of different words, as of slight differences in the forms of declining and conjugating the same words; forms, doubtless, which having been, at some period more or less remote, the common grammatic flexions of some tribe or province, had been accidentally appropriated to poetry by the general admiration of certain master intellects, the first established lights of inspiration, to whom that dialect happened to be native.

Essence, in its primary signification, means the principle of individuation, the inmost principle of the possibility of any thing, as that particular thing. It is equivalent to the idea of a thing, whenever we use the word, idea, with philosophic precision. Existence, on the other hand, is distinguished from essence, by the superinduction of reality. Thus we speak of the essence, and essential properties of a circle; but we do not therefore assert, that any thing, which really exists, is mathematically circular. Thus too, without any tautology we contend for the existence of the Supreme Being; that is, for a reality correspondent to the idea. There is, next, a secondary use of the word essence, in which it signifies the point or ground of contra-distinction between two modifications of the same substance or subject. Thus we should be allowed to say, that the style of architecture of Westminster Abbey is essentially different from that of St. Paul, even though both had been built with blocks cut into the same form, and from the same quarry. Only in this latter sense of the term must it have been denied by Mr. Wordsworth (for in this sense alone is it affirmed by the general opinion) that the language of poetry (that is the formal construction, or architecture, of the words and phrases) is essentially different from that of prose. Now the burden of the proof lies with the oppugner, not with the supporters of the common belief. Mr. Wordsworth, in consequence, assigns as the proof of his position, "that not only the language of a large portion of every good poem, even of the most elevated character, must necessarily, except with reference to the metre, in no respect differ from that of good prose, but likewise that some of the most interesting parts of the best poems will be found to be strictly the language of prose, when prose is well written. The truth of this assertion might be demonstrated by innumerable passages from almost all the poetical writings, even of Milton himself." He then quotes Gray's sonnet—

"In vain to me the smiling mornings shine,
   And reddening Phœbus lifts his golden fire;
The birds in vain their amorous descant join,
   Or cheerful fields resume their green attire.
These ears, alas! for other notes repine;
   A different object do these eyes require;
My lonely anguish melts no heart but mine;
   And in my breast the imperfect joys expire.
Yet morning smiles the busy race to cheer,
   And new-born pleasure brings to happier
      men;
The fields to all their wonted tribute bear;
   To warm their little loves the birds complain:
I fruitless mourn to him that cannot hear,
And weep the more, because I weep in vain."

and adds the following remark:—"It will easily be perceived, that the only part of this Sonnet which is of any value, is the lines printed in *i*talics; it is equally obvious, that, except in the rhyme, and in the use of the single word 'fruitless' for fruitlessly, which is so far a defect, the language of these lines does in no respect differ from that of prose."

An idealist defending his system by the fact, that when asleep we often believe ourselves awake, was well answered by his plain neighbor, "Ah, but when awake do we ever believe ourselves asleep?" Things identical must be convertible. The preceding passage seems to rest on a similar sophism. For the question is not, whether there may not occur in prose an order of words, which would be equally proper in a poem; nor whether there are not beautiful lines and sentences of frequent occurrence in good poems, which would be equally becoming as well as beautiful in good prose; for neither the one nor the other has ever been either denied or doubted by any one. The true question must be, whether there are not modes of expression, a construction, and an order of sentences, which are in their fit and natural place in a serious prose composition, but would be disproportionate and heterogeneous in metrical poetry; and, *vice versa*, whether in the language of a serious poem there may not be an arrangement both of words and sentences, and a use and selection of (what are called) figures of speech, both as to their kind, their frequency, and their occasions, which on a subject of equal weight would be vicious and alien in correct and manly prose. I contend, that in both cases this unfitness of each for the place of the other frequently will and ought to exist.

And first from the origin of metre. This I would trace to the balance in the mind effected by that spontaneous effort which strives to hold in check the workings of passion. It might be easily explained likewise in what manner this salutary antagonism is assisted by the very state, which it counteracts; and how this balance of antagonists became organized into metre (in the usual acceptation of that term), by a supervening act of the will and judgment, consciously and for the foreseen purpose of pleasure. Assuming these principles, as the *data* of our argument, we deduce from them two legitimate conditions, which the critic is entitled to expect in every metrical work. First, that as the elements of metre owe their existence to a state of increased excitement, so the metre itself should be accompanied by the natural language of excitement. Secondly, that as these elements are formed into metre artificially, by a voluntary act, with the design and for the purpose of blending delight with emotion, so the traces of present volition should throughout the metrical language be proportionately discernible. Now these two conditions must be reconciled and co-present. There must be not only a partnership, but a union; an interpenetration of passion and of will, of spontaneous impulse and of voluntary purpose. Again, this union can be manifested only in a frequency of forms and figures of speech, (originally the offspring of passion, but now the adopted children of power), greater than would be desired or endured, where the emotion is not voluntarily encouraged and kept up for the sake of that pleasure, which such emotion, so tempered and mastered by the will, is found capable of communicating. It not only dictates, but of itself tends to produce a more frequent employment of picturesque and vivifying language, than would be natural in any other case, in which there did not exist, as there does in the present, a previous and well understood, though tacit,

compact between the poet and his reader, that the latter is entitled to expect, and the former bound to supply this species and degree of pleasurable excitement. We may in some measure apply to this union the answer of Polixenes, in the Winter's Tale, to Perdita's neglect of the streaked gilliflowers, because she had heard it said,

"There is an art, which, in their piedness, shares
With great creating nature.
Pol.   Say there be;
Yet nature is made better by no mean,
But nature makes that mean; so, o'er that art,
Which, you say, adds to nature, is an art,
That nature makes. You see, sweet maid, we marry
A gentler scion to the wildest stock;
And make conceive a bark of baser kind
By bud of nobler race. This is an art,
Which does mend nature,—change it rather, but
The art itself is nature."

Secondly, I argue from the effects of metre. As far as metre acts in and for itself, it tends to increase the vivacity and susceptibility both of the general feelings and of the attention. This effect it produces by the continued excitement of surprise, and by the quick reciprocations of curiosity still gratified and still re-excited, which are too slight indeed to be at any one moment objects of distinct consciousness, yet become considerable in their aggregate influence. As a medicated atmosphere, or as wine during animated conversation, they act powerfully, though themselves unnoticed. Where, therefore, correspondent food and appropriate matter are not provided for the attention and feelings thus roused there must needs be a disappointment felt; like that of leaping in the dark from the last step of a stair-case, when we had prepared our muscles for a leap of three or four.

The discussion on the powers of metre in the preface is highly ingenious and touches at all points on truth. But I cannot find any statement of its powers considered abstractly and separately. On the contrary Mr. Wordsworth seems always to estimate metre by the powers, which it exerts during (and, as I think, in consequence of) its combination with other elements of poetry. Thus the previous difficulty is left unanswered, what the elements are, with which it must be combined, in order to produce its own effects to any pleasurable purpose. Double and tri-syllable rhymes, indeed, form a lower species of wit, and, attended to exclusively for their own sake, may become a source of momentary amusement; as in poor Smart's distich to the Welch Squire who had promised him a hare:

Tell me, thou son of great Cadwallader!
Hast sent the hare? or hast thou swallowed
    her?

But for any poetic purposes, metre resembles (if the aptness of the simile may excuse its meanness) yeast, worthless or disagreeable by itself, but giving vivacity and spirit to the liquor with which it is proportionately combined.

The reference to *The Children In The Wood* by no means satisfies my judgment. We all willingly throw ourselves back for a while into the feelings of our childhood. This ballad, therefore, we read under such recollections of our own childish feelings, as would equally endear to us poems, which Mr. Wordsworth himself would regard as faulty in the opposite extreme of gaudy and technical ornament. Before the invention of printing, and in a still greater degree, before the introduction of writing, metre, especially alliterative metre (whether alliterative at the beginning of the words, as in *Pierce Plouman*, or at the end, as in rhymes) possessed an independent value as assisting the recollection, and consequently the preservation, of any series of truths or incidents. But I am not convinced by the collation of facts, that *The Children In The Wood* owes either its preservation, or its popularity, to its metrical form. Mr. Marshal's repository affords a number of tales in prose inferior in pathos and general merit, some of as old a date, and many as widely popular. *Tom Hickathrift, Jack The Giant-Killer, Goody Two-Shoes,* and *Little Red Riding-Hood* are formidable rivals. And that they have continued in prose, cannot be fairly explained by the assumption, that the comparative meanness of their thoughts and images precluded even the humblest forms of metre. The scene of "Goody Two-Shoes" in the church is perfectly susceptible of metrical narration; and, among the Θαυματα θαυμαστότατα even of the present age, I do not recollect a more astonishing image than that of the "whole rookery, that flew out of the giant's beard," scared by the tremendous voice with which this monster answered the challenge of the heroic "Tom Hickathrift"! If from these we turn to compositions universally, and independently of all early associations, beloved and admired; would

the *Maria, The Monk,* or *The Poor Man's Ass* of Sterne, be read with more delight, or have a better chance of immortality, had they without any change in the diction been composed in rhyme, than in their present state? If I am not grossly mistaken, the general reply would be in the negative. Nay, I will confess, that, in Mr. Wordsworth's own volumes, the "Anecdote for Fathers," "Simon Lee," "Alice Fell," "Beggars," and "The Sailor's Mother," notwithstanding the beauties which are to be found in each of them where the poet interposes the music of his own thoughts, would have been more delightful to me in prose, told and managed, as by Mr. Wordsworth they would have been, in a moral essay or pedestrian tour.

Metre in itself is simply a stimulant of the attention, and therefore excites the question: Why is the attention to be thus stimulated? Now the question cannot be answered by the pleasure of the metre itself: for this we have shown to be conditional, and dependent on the appropriateness of the thoughts and expressions, to which the metrical form is superadded. Neither can I conceive any other answer that can be rationally given, short of this: I write in metre, because I am about to use a language different from that of prose. Besides, where the language is not such, how interesting soever the reflections are, that are capable of being drawn by a philosophic mind from the thoughts or incidents of the poem, the metre itself must often become feeble. Take the last three stanzas of "The Sailor's Mother," for instance. If I could for a moment abstract from the effect produced on the author's feelings, as a man, by the incident at the time of its real occurrence, I would dare appeal to his own judgment, whether in the metre itself he found a sufficient reason for *their* being written *metrically?*

And, thus continuing, she said,
"I had a Son, who many a day
Sailed on the seas; but he is dead;
In Denmark he was cast away;
And I have travelled far as Hull to see
What clothes he might have left, or other
    property.

The Bird and Cage they both were his:
'Twas my Son's Bird; and neat and trim
He kept it: many voyages
This Singing-bird hath gone with him;
When last he sailed he left the Bird behind;
As it might be, perhaps, from bodings of his
    mind.

He to a Fellow-lodger's care
Had left it, to be watched and fed,
Till he came back again; and there
I found it when my Son was dead;
And now, God help me for my little wit!
I trail it with me, Sir! he took so much delight 5
in it."

If disproportioning the emphasis we read
these stanzas so as to make the rhymes perceptible, even tri-syllable rhymes could 10
scarcely produce an equal sense of oddity
and strangeness, as we feel here in finding
rhymes at all in sentences so exclusively
colloquial. I would further ask whether,
but for that visionary state, into which the 15
figure of the woman and the susceptibility
of his own genius had placed the poet's
imagination (a state, which spreads its influence and coloring over all, that co-exists
with the exciting cause, and in which 20

The simplest, and the most familiar things
Gain a strange power of spreading awe around
them)

I would ask the poet whether he would not 25
have felt an abrupt downfall in these verses
from the preceding stanza?

The ancient spirit is not dead;
Old times, thought I, are breathing there;
Proud was I that my country bred 30
Such strength, a dignity so fair:
She begged an alms, like one in poor estate;
I looked at her again, nor did my pride abate.

It must not be omitted, and is besides 35
worthy of notice, that those stanzas furnish
the only fair instance that I have been able
to discover in all Mr. Wordsworth's writings, of an actual adoption, or true imitation, of *the real and very language of low* 40
and rustic life, freed from provincialisms.
Thirdly, I deduce the position from all
the causes elsewhere assigned, which render
metre the proper form of poetry, and
poetry imperfect and defective without 45
metre. Metre, therefore, having been connected with poetry most often and by a
peculiar fitness, whatever else is combined
with metre must, though it be not itself
essentially poetic, have nevertheless some 50
property in common with poetry, as an
intermedium of affinity, a sort (if I may
dare to borrow a well-known phrase from
technical chemistry) of *mordaunt* between
it and the super-added metre. Now poetry, 55
Mr. Wordsworth truly affirms, does always
imply passion: which word must be here
understood in its most general sense, as an
excited state of the feelings and faculties.
And as every passion has its proper pulse, 60

so will it likewise have its characteristic
modes of expression. But where there
exists that degree of genius and talent
which entitles a writer to aim at the honors
of a poet, the very act of poetic composition itself is, and is allowed to imply and
to produce, an unusual state of excitement,
which of course justifies and demands a
correspondent difference of language, as
truly, though not perhaps in as marked a
degree, as the excitement of love, fear, rage,
or jealousy. The vividness of the descriptions or declamations in Donne or Dryden,
is as much and as often derived from the
force and fervor of the describer, as from
the reflections, forms or incidents, which
constitute their subject and materials. The
wheels take fire from the mere rapidity of
their motion. To what extent, and under
what modifications, this may be admitted
to act, I shall attempt to define in an after
remark on Mr. Wordsworth's reply to this
objection, or rather on his objection to this
reply, as already anticipated in his preface.
Fourthly, and as intimately connected
with this, if not the same argument in a
more general form, I adduce the high spiritual instinct of the human being impelling
us to seek unity by harmonious adjustment,
and thus establishing the principle that *all*
the parts of an organized whole must be
assimilated to the more *important* and
essential parts. This and the preceding
arguments may be strengthened by the
reflection, that the composition of a poem
is among the imitative arts; and that imitation, as opposed to copying, consists
either in the interfusion of the same
throughout the radically different, or of the
different throughout a base radically the
same.
Lastly, I appeal to the practice of the
best poets, of all countries and in all ages,
as authorizing the opinion (deduced from
all the foregoing) that in every import of
the word essential, which would not here
involve a mere truism, there may be, is,
and ought to be an *essential* difference between the language of prose and of metrical composition.
In Mr. Wordsworth's criticism of Gray's
Sonnet, the reader's sympathy with his
praise or blame of the different parts is
taken for granted rather perhaps too easily.
He has not, at least, attempted to win or
compel it by argumentative analysis. In
my conception at least, the lines rejected
as of no value do, with the exception of
the two first, differ as much and as little
from the language of common life, as those

which he has printed in italics as possessing genuine excellence. Of the five lines thus honorably distinguished, two of them differ from prose even more widely, than the lines which either precede or follow, in the position of the words.

"A different object do these eyes require;
My lonely anguish melts no heart but mine;
And in my breast the imperfect joys expire."

But were it otherwise, what would this prove, but a truth, of which no man ever doubted?—*videlicet,* that there are sentences, which would be equally in their place both in verse and prose. Assuredly it does not prove the point, which alone requires proof; namely, that there are not passages, which would suit the one and not suit the other. The first line of this sonnet is distinguished from the ordinary language of men by the epithet to morning. For we will set aside, at present, the consideration, that the particular word "smiling" is hackneyed, and, as it involves a sort of personification, not quite congruous with the common and material attribute of *"shining."* And, doubtless, this adjunction o. epithets for the purpose of additional description, where no particular attention is demanded for the quality of the thing, would be noticed as giving a poetic cast to a man's conversation. Should the sportsman exclaim, "Come boys! the rosy morning calls you up:"—he will be supposed to have some song in his head. But no one suspects this, when he says, "A wet morning shall not confine us to our beds." This then is either a defect in poetry, or it is not. Whoever should decide in the affirmative, I would request him to re-peruse any one poem, of any confessedly great poet from Homer to Milton, or from Æschylus to Shakspeare; and to strike out (in thought I mean) every instance of this kind. If the number of these fancied erasures did not startle him; or if he continued to deem the work improved by their total omission; he must advance reasons of no ordinary strength and evidence, reasons grounded in the essence of human nature. Otherwise, I should not hesitate to consider him as a man not so much proof against all authority, as dead to it.

The second line,

And reddening Phœbus lifts his golden fire;—

has indeed almost as many faults as words. But then it is a bad line, not because the language is distinct from that of prose; but because it conveys incongruous images; be-

cause it confounds the cause and the effect, the real thing with the personified representative of the thing; in short, because it differs from the language of good sense! That the "Phœbus" is hackneyed, and a school-boy image, is an accidental fault, dependent on the age in which the author wrote, and not deduced from the nature of the thing. That it is part of an exploded mythology, is an objection more deeply grounded. Yet when the torch of ancient learning was re-kindled, so cheering were its beams, that our eldest poets, cut off by Christianity from all accredited machinery, and deprived of all acknowledged guardians and symbols of the great objects of nature, were naturally induced to adopt, as a poetic language, those fabulous personages, those forms of the supernatural in nature, which had given them such dear delight in the poems of their great masters. Nay, even at this day what scholar of genial taste will not so far sympathize with them, as to read with pleasure in Petrarch, Chaucer, or Spenser, what he would perhaps condemn as puerile in a modern poet?

I remember no poet, whose writings would safelier stand the test of Mr. Wordsworth's theory, than Spenser. Yet will Mr. Wordsworth say, that the style of the following stanza is either undistinguished from prose, and the language of ordinary life? Or that it is vicious, and that the stanzas are *blots* in *The Faery Queen?*

By this the northern wagoner had set
His sevenfold teme behind the stedfast starre,
That was in ocean waves yet never wet,
But firme is fixt and sendeth light from farre:
To all that in the wild deep wandering arre:
And chearfull chaunticlere with his note shrill
Had warned once that Phœbus' fiery carre
In hast was climbing up the easterne hill,
Full envious that night so long his roome did fill.

At last the golden orientall gate
Of greatest heaven gan to open fayre,
And Phœbus fresh, as brydegrome to his mate,
Came dauncing forth, shaking his deawie hayre,
And hurled his glist'ring beams through gloomy ayre:
Which when the wakeful elfe perceived, streight way
He started up, and did him selfe prepayre
In sun-bright armes and battailous array;
For with that pagan proud he combat will that day.

On the contrary to how many passages, both in hymn books and in blank verse poems, could I (were it not invidious) direct the reader's attention, the style of which is most unpoetic, because, and only because, it is the style of prose? He will not suppose me capable of having in my mind such verses, as

> I put my hat upon my head
> And walked into the Strand;
> And there I met another man,
> Whose hat was in his hand.

To such specimens it would indeed be a fair and full reply, that these lines are not bad, because they are unpoetic; but because they are empty of all sense and feeling; and that it were an idle attempt to prove that "an ape is not a Newton, when it is self-evident that he is not a man." But the sense shall be good and weighty, the language correct and dignified, the subject interesting and treated with feeling; and yet the style shall, notwithstanding all these merits, be justly blamable as prosaic, and solely because the words and the order of the words would find their appropriate place in prose, but are not suitable to metrical composition. The *Civil Wars* of Daniel is an instructive, and even interesting work; but take the following stanzas (and from the hundred instances which abound I might probably have selected others far more striking):

And to the end we may with better ease
Discern the true discourse, vouchsafe to shew
What were the times foregoing near to these,
That these we may with better profit know.
Tell how the world fell into this disease;
And how so great distemperature did grow;
So shall we see with what degrees it came;
How things at full do soon wax out of frame.

Ten kings had from the Norman Conqu'ror reigned
With intermixed and variable fate,
When England to her greatest height attained
Of power, dominion, glory, wealth, and state;
After it had with much ado sustained
The violence of princes, with debate
For titles and the often mutinies
Of nobles for their ancient liberties.

For first, the Norman, conqu'ring all by might,
By might was forced to keep what he had got;
Mixing our customs and the form of right
With foreign constitutions, he had brought;
Mast'ring the mighty, humbling the poorer wight,
By all severest means that could be wrought;
And, making the succession doubtful, rent
His new-got state, and left it turbulent.

Will it be contended on the one side, that these lines are mean and senseless? Or on the other, that they are not prosaic, and for *that* reason unpoetic? This poet's well-merited epithet is that of the "well-languaged Daniel;" but likewise, and by the consent of his contemporaries no less than of all succeeding critics, "the prosaic Daniel." Yet those, who thus designate this wise and amiable writer from the frequent incorrespondency of his diction to his metre in the majority of his compositions, not only deem them valuable and interesting on other accounts; but willingly admit, that there are to be found throughout his poems, and especially in his *Epistles* and in his *Hymen's Triumph,* many and exquisite specimens of that style which, as the *neutral ground* of prose and verse, is common to both. A fine and almost faultless extract, eminent as for other beauties, so for its perfection in this species of diction, may be seen in Lamb's *Dramatic Specimens,* a work of various interest from the nature of the selections themselves (all from the plays of Shakspeare's contemporaries) and deriving a high additional value from the notes, which are full of just and original criticism, expressed with all the freshness of originality.

Among the possible effects of practical adherence to a theory, that aims to identify the style of prose and verse (if it does not indeed claim for the latter a yet nearer resemblance to the average style of men in the *vivâ voce* intercourse of real life) we might anticipate the following as not the least likely to occur. It will happen, as I have indeed before observed, that the metre itself, the sole acknowledged difference, will occasionally become metre to the eye only. The existence of *prosaisms,* and that they detract from the merit of a poem, *must* at length be conceded, when a number of successive lines can be rendered, even to the most delicate ear, unrecognizable as verse, or as having even been intended for verse, by simply transcribing them as prose; when if the poem be in blank verse, this can be effected without any alteration, or at most by merely restoring one or two words to their proper places, from which they have been transplanted for no assignable cause or reason but that of the author's convenience; but if it be in rhyme, by the mere exchange of the final word of each line for some other of the same meaning, equally appropriate, dignified and euphonic.

The answer or objection in the preface to the anticipated remark "that metre paves the way to other distinctions," is contained in the following words. "The distinction of rhyme and metre is regular and uniform, and not, like that produced by (what is usually called) poetic diction, arbitrary, and subject to infinite caprices, upon which no calculation whatever can be made. In the one case the reader is utterly at the mercy of the poet respecting what imagery or diction he may choose to connect with the passion." But is this a *poet*, of whom a poet is speaking? No surely! rather of a fool or madman: or at best of a vain or ignorant phantast! And might not brains so wild and so deficient make just the same havoc with rhymes and metres, as they are supposed to effect with modes and figures of speech? How is the reader at the mercy of such men? If he continue to read their nonsense, is it not his own fault? The ultimate end of criticism is much more to establish the principles of writing, than to furnish rules how to pass judgment on what has been written by others; if indeed it were possible that the two could be separated. But if it be asked, by what principles the poet is to regulate his own style, if he do not adhere closely to the sort and order of words which he hears in the market, wake, high-road, or plough-field? I reply; by principles, the ignorance or neglect of which would convict him of being no poet, but a silly or presumptuous usurper of the name. By the principles of grammar, logic, psychology. In one word by such a knowledge of the facts, material and spiritual, that most appertain to his art, as, if it have been governed and applied by good sense, and rendered instinctive by habit, becomes the representative and reward of our past conscious reasonings, insights, and conclusions, and acquires the name of Taste. By what *rule* that does not leave the reader at the poet's mercy, and the poet at his own, is the latter to distinguish between the language suitable to suppressed, and the language, which is characteristic of indulged, anger? Or between that of rage and that of jealousy? Is it obtained by wandering about in search of angry or jealous people in uncultivated society, in order to copy their words? Or not far rather by the power of imagination proceeding upon the *all in each* of human nature? By meditation, rather than by observation? And by the latter in consequence only of the former? As eyes, for which the former has predetermined their field of vision, and to which, as to *its* organ, it communicates a microscopic power? There is not, I firmly

believe, a man now living, who has, from his own inward experience, a clearer intuition, than Mr. Wordsworth himself, that the last mentioned are the true sources of *genial* discrimination. Through the same process and by the same creative agency will the poet distinguish the degree and kind of the excitement produced by the very act of poetic composition. As intuitively will he know, what differences of style it at once inspires and justifies; what intermixture of conscious volition is natural to that state; and in what instances such figures and colors of speech degenerate into mere creatures of an arbitrary purpose, cold technical artifices of ornament or connection. For, even as truth is its own light and evidence, discovering at once itself and falsehood, so is it the prerogative of poetic genius to distinguish by parental instinct its proper offspring from the changelings, which the gnomes of vanity or the fairies of fashion may have laid in its cradle or called by its names. Could a rule be given from without, poetry would cease to be poetry, and sink into a mechanical art. It would be μόρφωσις, not ποίησις. The rules of the Imagination are themselves the very powers of growth and production. The words to which they are reducible, present only the outlines and external appearance of the fruit. A deceptive counterfeit of the superficial form and colors may be elaborated; but the marble peach feels cold and heavy, and children only put it to their mouths. We find no difficulty in admitting as excellent, and the legitimate language of poetic fervor self-impassioned, Donne's apostrophe to the Sun in the second stanza of his PROGRESS OF THE SOUL.

"Thee, eye of heaven! this great Soul envies not;
By thy male force is all, we have, begot.
In the first East thou now beginn'st to shine,
Suck'st early balm and island spices there,
And wilt anon in thy loose-reigned career
At Tagus, Po, Seine, Thames, and Danow dine,
And see at night this western world of mine:
Yet hast thou not more nations seen than she
Who before thee one day began to be,
And, thy frail light being quenched, shall long, long outlive thee."

Great Destiny, the commissary of God,
That hast marked out a path and period
For every thing! Who, where we offspring took,
Our ways and ends see'st at one instant: thou
Knot of all causes! Thou, whose changeless brow

Ne'er smiles nor frowns! O! vouchsafe thou
    to look,
And shew my story in thy eternal book, etc.

As little difficulty do we find in exclud-
ing from the honors of unaffected warmth
and elevation the madness prepense of
pseudopoesy, or the startling hysteric of
weakness over-exerting itself, which bursts
on the unprepared reader in sundry odes
and apostrophes to abstract terms. Such
are the Odes to Jealousy, to Hope, to
Oblivion, and the like, in Dodsley's collection and the magazines of that day, which
seldom fail to remind me of an Oxford
copy of verses on the two "Suttons," commencing with

    Inoculation, heavenly maid! descend!

It is not to be denied that men of undoubted talents, and even poets of true,
though not of first-rate, genius, have from
a mistaken theory deluded both themselves
and others in the opposite extreme. I once
read to a company of sensible and well-
educated women the introductory period of
Cowley's preface to his "Pindaric Odes,"
written in imitation of the style and manner of the odes of Pindar. "If," (says
Cowley), "a man should undertake to translate Pindar, word for word, it would be
thought that one madman had translated
another: as may appear, when he, that
understands not the original, reads the
verbal traduction of him into Latin prose,
than which nothing seems more raving."
I then proceeded with his own free version
of the second Olympic, composed for the
charitable purpose of *rationalizing* the
Theban Eagle.

Queen of all harmonious things,
Dancing words and speaking strings,
What god, what hero, wilt thou sing?
What happy man to equal glories bring?
Begin, begin thy noble choice,
And let the hills around reflect the image of
    thy voice.
Pisa does to Jove belong,
Jove and Pisa claim thy song.
The fair first-fruits of war, th' Olympic games,
Alcides, offered up to Jove;
Alcides, too, thy strings may move,
But, oh! what man to join with these can
    worthy prove?
Join Theron boldly to their sacred names;
Theron the next honor claims;
Theron to no man gives place,
Is first in Pisa's and in Virtue's race;
Theron there, and he alone,
Ev'n his own swift forefathers has outgone.

One of the company exclaimed, with the
full assent of the rest, that if the original
were madder than this, it must be incur-
ably mad. I then translated the ode from
the Greek, and as nearly as possible, word
for word; and the impression was, that in
the general movement of the periods, in
the form of the connections and transitions, and in the sober majesty of lofty
sense, it appeared to them to approach
more nearly, than any other poetry they
had heard, to the style of our Bible, in the
prophetic books. The first strophe will
suffice as a specimen:

Ye harp-controlling hymns! (or) ye hymns
    the sovereigns of harps!
What God? what Hero?
What Man shall we celebrate?
Truly Pisa indeed is of Jove,
But the Olympiad (or the Olympic games)
    did Hercules establish,
The first-fruits of the spoils of war.
But Theron for the four-horsed car,
That bore victory to him,
It behoves us now to voice aloud:
The Just, the Hospitable,
The Bulwark of Agrigentum,
Of renowned fathers
The Flower, even him
Who preserves his native city erect and safe.

But are such rhetorical caprices con-
demnable only for their deviation from
the language of real life? and are they by
no other means to be precluded, but by the
rejection of all distinctions between prose
and verse, save that of metre? Surely good
sense, and a moderate insight into the
constitution of the human mind, would be
amply sufficient to prove, that such language and such combinations are the native
product neither of the fancy nor of the
imagination; that their operation consists
in the excitement of surprise by the juxta-
position and *apparent* reconciliation of
widely different or incompatible things. As
when, for instance, the hills are made to
reflect the image of a *voice*. Surely, no
unusual taste is requisite to see clearly, that
this compulsory juxta-position is not produced by the presentation of impressive or
delightful forms to the inward vision, nor
by any sympathy with the modifying powers with which the genius of the poet had
united and inspirited all the objects of his
thought; that it is therefore a species of
wit, a pure work of the *will*, and implies a
leisure and self-possession both of thought
and of feeling, incompatible with the steady
fervor of a mind possessed and filled with
the grandeur of its subject. To sum up

the whole in one sentence. When a poem, or a part of a poem, shall be adduced, which is evidently vicious in the figures and contexture of its style, yet for the condemnation of which no reason can be assigned, except that it differs from the style in which men actually converse, then, and not till then, can I hold this theory to be either plausible, or practicable, or capable of furnishing either rule, guidance, or precaution, that might not, more easily and more safely, as well as more naturally, have been deduced in the author's own mind from considerations of grammar, logic, and the truth and nature of things, confirmed by the authority of works, whose fame is not of one country nor of one age.

CHAPTER XIX

Continuation—Concerning the real object which, it is probable, Mr. Wordsworth had before him in his critical preface—Elucidation and application of this.

It might appear from some passages in the former part of Mr. Wordsworth's preface, that he meant to confine his theory of style, and the necessity of a close accordance with the actual language of men, to those particular subjects from low and rustic life, which by way of experiment he had purposed to naturalize as a new species in our English poetry. But from the train of argument that follows; from the reference to Milton; and from the spirit of his critique on Gray's sonnet; those sentences appear to have been rather courtesies of modesty, than actual limitations of his system. Yet so groundless does this system appear on a close examination; and so strange and overwhelming in its consequences, that I cannot, and I do not, believe that the poet did ever himself adopt it in the unqualified sense, in which his expressions have been understood by others, and which, indeed, according to all the common laws of interpretation they seem to bear. What then did he mean? I apprehend, that in the clear perception, not unaccompanied with disgust or contempt, of the gaudy affectations of a style which passed current with too many for poetic diction (though in truth it had as little pretensions to poetry, as to logic or common sense) he narrowed his view for the time; and feeling a justifiable preference for the language of nature and of good sense, even in its humblest and least ornamented forms, he suffered himself to

express, in terms at once too large and too exclusive, his predilection for a style the most remote possible from the false and showy splendor which he wished to explode. It is possible, that this predilection, at first merely comparative, deviated for a time into direct partiality. But the real object which he had in view, was, I doubt not, a species of excellence which had been long before most happily characterized by the judicious and amiable Garve, whose works are so justly beloved and esteemed by the Germans, in his remarks on Gellert, from which the following is literally translated. "The talent, that is required in order to make excellent verses, is perhaps greater than the philosopher is ready to admit, or would find it in his power to acquire: the talent to seek only the apt expression of the thought, and yet to find at the same time with it the rhyme and the metre. Gellert possessed this happy gift, if ever any one of our poets possessed it; and nothing perhaps contributed more to the great and universal impression which his fables made on their first publication, or conduces more to their continued popularity. It was a strange and curious phænomenon, and such as in Germany had been previously unheard of, to read verses in which everything was expressed just as one would wish to talk, and yet all dignified, attractive, and interesting; and all at the same time perfectly correct as to the measure of the syllables and the rhyme. It is certain, that poetry when it has attained this excellence makes a far greater impression than prose. So much so indeed, that even the gratification which the very rhymes afford, becomes then no longer a contemptible or trifling gratification."

However novel this phænomenon may have been in Germany at the time of Gellert, it is by no means new, nor yet of recent existence in our language. Spite of the licentiousness with which Spenser occasionally compels the orthography of his words into a subservience to his rhymes, the whole *Fairy Queen* is an almost continued instance of this beauty. Waller's song "Go, lovely Rose," is doubtless familiar to most of my readers; but if I had happened to have had by me the Poems of Cotton, more but far less deservedly celebrated as the author of the *Virgil Travestied*, I should have indulged myself, and I think have gratified many, who are not acquainted with his serious works, by selecting some admirable specimens of this style.

There are not a few poems in that volume, replete with every excellence of thought, image, and passion, which we expect or desire in the poetry of the milder muse; and yet so worded, that the reader sees no one reason either in the selection or the order of the words, why he might not have said the very same in an appropriate conversation, and cannot conceive how indeed he could have expressed such thoughts otherwise without loss or injury to his meaning.

But in truth our language is, and from the first dawn of poetry ever has been, particularly rich in compositions distinguished by this excellence. The final *e,* which is now mute, in Chaucer's age was either sounded or dropt indifferently. We ourselves still use either "beloved" or "belov'd" according as the rhyme, or measure, or the purpose of more or less solemnity may require. Let the reader then only adopt the pronunciation of the poet and of the court, at which he lived, both with respect to the final *e* and to the accentuation of the last syllable. . . .

In *The Excursion* the poet has introduced on old man, born in humble but not abject circumstances, who had enjoyed more than usual advantages of education, both from books and from the more awful discipline of nature. This person he represents, as having been driven by the restlessness of fervid feelings, and from a craving intellect to an itinerant life; and as having in consequence passed the larger portion of his time, from earliest manhood, in villages and hamlets from door to door,

A vagrant Merchant bent beneath his load.

Now whether this be a character appropriate to a lofty didactick poem, is perhaps questionable. It presents a fair subject for controversy; and the question is to be determined by the congruity or incongruity of such a character with what shall be proved to be the essential constituents of poetry. But surely the critic who, passing by all the opportunities which such a mode of life would present to such a man; all the advantages of the liberty of nature, of solitude, and of solitary thought; all the varieties of places and seasons, through which his track had lain, with all the varying imagery they bring with them; and lastly, all the observations of men,

Their manners, their enjoyments, and pursuits,
Their passions and their feelings——

which the memory of these yearly journeys must have given and recalled to such a mind—the critic, I say, who from the multitude of possible associations should pass by all these in order to fix his attention exclusively on the *pin-papers,* and *stay-tapes,* which *might* have been among the wares of his pack; this critic, in my opinion, cannot be thought to possess a much higher or much healthier state of moral feeling, than the Frenchmen above recorded.

CHAPTER XXII

The characteristic defects of Wordsworth's poetry, with the principles from which the judgment, that they are defects, is deduced—Their proportion to the beauties—For the greatest part characteristic of his theory only.

If Mr. Wordsworth have set forth principles of poetry which his arguments are insufficient to support, let him and those who have adopted his sentiments be set right by the confutation of those arguments, and by the substitution of more philosophical principles. And still let the due credit be given to the portion and importance of the truths which are blended with this theory; truths, the too exclusive attention to which had occasioned its errors by tempting him to carry those truths beyond their proper limits. If his mistaken theory have at all influenced his poetic compositions, let the effects be pointed out, and the instances given. But let it likewise be shown, how far the influence has acted; whether diffusively, or only by starts; whether the number and importance of the poems and passages thus infected be great or trifling compared with the sound portion; and lastly, whether they are inwoven into the texture of his works, or are loose and separable. The result of such a trial would evince beyond a doubt, what it is high time to announce decisively and aloud, that the *supposed* characteristics of Mr. Wordsworth's poetry, whether admired or reprobated; whether they are simplicity or simpleness; faithful adherence to essential nature, or wilful selections from human nature of its meanest forms and under the least attractive associations; are as little the *real* characteristics of his poetry at large, as of his genius and the constitution of his mind.

In a comparatively small number of poems, he chose to try an experiment; and this experiment we will suppose to have failed. Yet even in these poems it is impossible not to perceive that the natural tendency of the poet's mind is to great objects and elevated conceptions. The poem entitled *Fidelity* is for the greater 5 part written in language as unraised and naked as any perhaps in the two volumes. Yet take the following stanza and compare it with the preceding stanzas of the same poem. 10

There sometimes doth a leaping fish
Send through the tarn a lonely cheer;
The crags repeat the raven's croak,
In symphony austere;
Thither the rainbow comes—the cloud— 15
And mists that spread the flying shroud;
And sun-beams; and the sounding blast,
That, if it could, would hurry past;
But that enormous barrier holds it fast.

Or compare the four last lines of the 20 concluding stanza with the former half.

Yes, proof was plain that, since the day
On which the traveller thus had died,
The dog had watched about the spot,
Or by his master's side: 25
*How nourished there through such long
time
He knows, who gave that love sublime,
And gave that strength of feeling, great
Above all human estimate!* 30

Can any candid and intelligent mind hesitate in determining which of these best represents the tendency and native character of the poet's genius? Will he not decide that the one was written because the 35 poet *would* so write, and the other because he could not so entirely repress the force and grandeur of his mind, but that he must in some part or other of every composition write otherwise? In short, that his only 40 disease is the being out of his element; like the swan, that, having amused himself, for a while, with crushing the weeds on the river's bank, soon returns to his own majestic movements on its reflecting and sus- 45 taining surface. Let it be observed that I am here supposing the imagined judge, to whom I appeal, to have already decided against the poet's theory, as far as it is different from the principles of the art, 50 generally acknowledged.

I cannot here enter into a detailed examination of Mr. Wordsworth's works; but I will attempt to give the main results of my own judgment, after an acquaint- 55 ance of many years, and repeated perusals. And though to appreciate the defects of a great mind it is necessary to understand previously its characteristic excellences, yet I have already expressed myself with suffi- 60

cient fulness to preclude most of the ill effects that might arise from my pursuing a contrary arrangement. I will therefore commence with what I deem the prominent *defects* of his poems hitherto published.

The first characteristic, though only occasional defect, which I appear to myself to find in these poems is the *inconstancy* of the style. Under this name I refer to the sudden and unprepared transitions from lines or sentences of peculiar felicity (at all events striking and original) to a style, not only unimpassioned but undistinguished. He sinks too often and too abruptly to that style which I should place in the second division of language, dividing it into the three species; first, that which is peculiar to poetry; second, that which is only proper in prose; and third, the neutral or common to both. There have been works, such as Cowley's *Essay on Cromwell*, in which prose and verse are intermixed (not as in the *Consolation* of Boetius, or the *Argenis* of Barclay, by the insertion of poems supposed to have been spoken or composed on occasions previously related in prose, but) the poet passing from one to the other, as the nature of the thoughts or his own feelings dictated. Yet this mode of composition does not satisfy a cultivated taste. There is something unpleasant in the being thus obliged to alternate states of feeling so dissimilar, and this too in a species of writing, the pleasure from which is in part derived from the preparation and previous expectation of the reader. A portion of that awkwardness is felt which hangs upon the introduction of songs in our modern comic operas; and to prevent which the judicious Metastasio (as to whose exquisite taste there can be no hesitation, whatever doubts may be entertained as to his poetic genius) uniformly placed the *aria* at the end of the scene, at the same time that he almost always raises and impassions the style of the recitative immediately preceding. Even in real life, the difference is great and evident between words used as the arbitrary marks of thought, our smooth market-coin of intercourse, with the image and superscription worn out by currency; and those which convey pictures either borrowed from one outward object to enliven and particularize some other; or used allegorically to body forth the inward state of the person speaking; or such as are at least the exponents of his peculiar turn and unusual extent of faculty. So much so indeed, that in the social circles of private life we often find a striking use of the latter put a stop to the general flow of conversation, and by the excitement arising from concentered attention produce a sort of damp and interruption for some minutes after. But in the perusal of works of literary art, we prepare ourselves for such language; and the business of the writer, like that of a painter whose subject requires unusual splendor and prominence, is so to raise the lower and neutral tints, that what in a different style would be the commanding colors, are here used as the means of that gentle *degradation* requisite in order to produce the effect of a whole. Where this is not achieved in a poem, the metre merely reminds the reader of his claims in order to disappoint them; and where this defect occurs frequently, his feelings are alternately startled by anticlimax and hyperclimax.

I refer the reader to the exquisite stanzas cited for another purpose from *The Blind Highland Boy*; and then annex, as being in my opinion instances of this *disharmony* in style, the two following:

And one, the rarest, was a shell,
Which he, poor child, had studied well:
The shell of a green turtle, thin
And hollow;—you might sit therein,
    It was so wide, and deep.

Our Highland Boy oft visited
The house which held this prize; and, led
By choice or chance, did thither come
One day, when no one was at home,
    And found the door unbarred.

Or page 172, vol. I.

'Tis gone—forgotten—*let me do
My best.* There was a smile or two—
I can remember them, I see
The smiles worth all the world to me.
Dear baby, I must lay thee down:
Thou troublest me with strange alarms;
Smiles hast thou, sweet ones of thine own;
I cannot keep thee in my arms;
For they confound me: *as it is,*
I have forgot those smiles of his!

Or page 269, vol. I.

Thou hast a nest, for thy love and thy rest,
And though little troubled with sloth,
Drunken lark! thou would'st be loth
To be such a traveller as I.
    Happy, happy liver!
*With a soul as strong as a mountain river
Pouring out praise to the Almighty Giver;*
Joy and jollity be with us both!

Hearing thee or else some other,
    As merry a brother
I on the earth will go plodding on
By myself cheerfully till the day is done.

The incongruity which I appear to find in this passage, is that of the two noble lines in italics with the preceding and following. So vol. II, page 30.

Close by a pond, upon the further side,
He stood alone; a minute's space, I guess,
I watched him, he continuing motionless:
To the pool's further margin then I drew;
He being all the while before me full in view.

Compare this with the repetition of the same image, in the next stanza but two.

And still as I drew near with gentle pace,
Beside the little pond or moorish flood
Motionless as a cloud the old man stood,
That heareth not the loud winds as they call;
And moveth altogether, if it move at all.

Or lastly, the second of the three following stanzas, compared both with the first and the third.

My former thoughts returned; the fear that kills;
And hope that is unwilling to be fed;
Cold, pain, and labor, and all fleshly ills;
And mighty poets in their misery dead.
But now, perplexed by what the old man had said,
My question eagerly did I renew,
"How is it that you live, and what is it you do?"

He with a smile did then his words repeat;
And said, that gathering leeches far and wide
He travelled; stirring thus about his feet
The waters of the ponds where they abide.
"Once I could meet with them on every side,
But they have dwindled long by slow decay;
Yet still I persevere, and find them where I may."

While he was talking thus, the lonely place,
The old man's shape, and speech, all troubled me;
In my mind's eye I seemed to see him pace
About the wary moors continually,
Wandering about alone and silently.

Indeed this fine poem is *especially* characteristic of the author. There is scarce a defect or excellence in his writings of which it would not present a specimen. But it would be unjust not to repeat that this defect is only occasional. From a careful reperusal of the two volumes of poems, I doubt whether the objectionable passages would amount in the whole to one hundred lines; not the eighth part of the number of pages. In *The Excursion* the feeling of incongruity is seldom excited by the diction of any passage considered in itself, but by the sudden superiority of some other passage forming the context.

The second defect I can generalize with tolerable accuracy, if the reader will pardon an uncouth and new-coined word. There is, I should say, not seldom a *matter-of-factness* in certain poems. This may be divided into, first, a laborious minuteness and fidelity in the representation of objects, and their positions, as they appeared to the poet himself; secondly, the insertion of accidental circumstances, in order to the full explanation of his living characters, their dispositions and actions, which circumstances might be necessary to establish the probability of a statement in real life, where nothing is taken for granted by the hearer, but appear superfluous in poetry, where the reader is willing to believe for his own sake. To this *accidentality* I object, as contravening the essence of poetry, which Aristotle pronounces to be σπουδαιότατον καὶ φιλοσοφώτατον γένος, the most intense, weighty and philosophical product of human art; adding, as the reason, that it is the most catholic and abstract. The following passage from Davenant's prefatory letter to Hobbes well expresses this truth. "When I considered the actions which I meant to describe (those inferring the persons), I was again persuaded rather to choose those of a former age, than the present; and in a century so far removed, as might preserve me from their improper examinations, who know not the requisites of a poem, nor how much pleasure they lose (and even the pleasures of heroic poesy are not unprofitable) who take away the liberty of a poet, and fetter his feet in the shackles of an historian. For why should a poet doubt in story to mend the intrigues of fortune by more delightful conveyances of probable fictions, because austere historians have entered into bond to truth? An obligation, which were in poets as foolish and unnecessary, as is the bondage of false martyrs, who lie in chains for a mistaken opinion. *But by this I would imply that truth, narrative and past, is the idol of historians (who worship a dead thing), and truth operative, and by effects continually alive, is the mistress of poets, who hath not her existence in matter, but in reason.*"

For this minute accuracy in the painting of local imagery, the lines in *The Excur-*

sion, pp. 96, 97, and 98, may be taken, if not as a striking instance, yet as an illustration of my meaning. It must be some strong motive (as, for instance, that the description was necessary to the intelligibility of the tale) which could induce me to describe in a number of verses what a draughtsman could present to the eye with incomparably greater satisfaction by half a dozen strokes of his pencil, or the painter with as many touches of his brush. Such descriptions too often occasion in the mind of a reader, who is determined to understand his author, a feeling of labor not very dissimilar to that with which he would construct a diagram, line by line, for a long geometrical proposition. It seems to be like taking the pieces of a dissected map out of its box. We first look at one part, and then at another, then join and dovetail them; and when the successive acts of attention have been completed, there is a retrogressive effort of mind to behold it as a whole. The poet should paint to the imagination, not to the fancy; and I know no happier case to exemplify the distinction between these two faculties. Masterpieces of the former mode of poetic painting abound in the writings of Milton, for example:

The fig-tree; not that kind for fruit renowned,
But such as at this day, to Indians known,
In Malabar or Decan spreads her arms
Branching so broad and long, that in the ground
The bended twigs take root, *and daughters grow*
About the mother tree, a pillared shade
High over-arched and ECHOING WALKS BETWEEN:
There oft the Indian herdsman, shunning heat,
Shelters in cool, and tends his pasturing herds
At loopholes cut through thickest shade.

This is creation rather than painting, or if painting, yet such, and with such copresence of the whole picture flashed at once upon the eye, as the sun paints in a camera obscura. But the poet must likewise understand and command what Bacon calls the *vestigia communia* of the senses, the latency of all in each, and more especially as by a magical *penna duplex,* the excitement of vision by sound and the exponents of sound. Thus, "The echoing walks between," may be almost said to reverse the fable in tradition of the head of Memnon, in the Egyptian statue. Such may be deservedly entitled the *creative words* in the world of imagination.

The second division respects an apparent minute adherence to *matter-of-fact* in character and incidents; *a biographical* attention to probability, and an *anxiety* of explanation and retrospect. Under this head I shall deliver, with no feigned diffidence, the results of my best reflection on the great point of controversy between Mr. Wordsworth and his objectors; namely, on *the choice of his characters.* I have already declared and, I trust, justified, my utter dissent from the mode of argument which his critics have hitherto employed. To *their* question, Why did you choose such a character, or a character from such a rank of life? the poet might, in my opinion, fairly retort: Why with the conception of my character did you make wilful choice of mean or ludicrous associations not furnished by me, but supplied from your own sickly and fastidious feelings? How was it, indeed, probable that such arguments could have any weight with an author whose plan, whose guiding principle, and main object it was to attack and subdue that state of association which leads us to place the chief value on those things on which man differs from man, and to forget or disregard the high dignities, which belong to human nature, the sense and the feeling, which may be, and ought to be, found in all ranks? The feelings with which, as Christians, we contemplate a mixed congregation rising or kneeling before their common Maker, Mr. Wordsworth would have us entertain at all times, as men, and as readers; and by the excitement of this lofty, yet prideless impartiality in poetry, he might hope to have encouraged its continuance in real life. The praise of good men be his! In real life, and, I trust, even in my imagination, I honor a virtuous and wise man, without reference to the presence or absence of artificial advantages. Whether in the person of an armed baron, a laurelled bard, or of an old pedlar, or still older leech-gatherer, the same qualities of head and heart must claim the same reverence. And even in poetry I am not conscious that I have ever suffered my feelings to be disturbed or offended by any thoughts or images which the poet himself has not presented.

But yet I object, nevertheless, and for the following reasons. First, because the object in view, as an *immediate* object, belongs to the moral philosopher, and would be pursued, not only more appropriately, but in my opinion with far greater probability of success, in sermons or moral essays, than in an elevated poem. It seems indeed, to destroy the main fundamental distinction, not only between a poem and prose, but even between philosophy and works of fiction, inasmuch as it proposes *truth* for its immediate object, instead of *pleasure.* Now till the blessed time shall come, when truth itself shall be pleasure, and both shall be so united, as to be distinguishable in words only, not in feeling, it will remain the poet's office to proceed upon that state of association, which actually exists as general; instead of attempting first to make it what it ought to be, and then to let the pleasure follow. But here is unfortunately a small *hysteron-proteron.* For the communication of pleasure is the introductory means by which alone the poet must expect to moralize his readers. Secondly: though I were to admit, for a moment, *this* argument to be groundless: yet how is the moral effect to be produced, by merely attaching the name of some low profession to powers which are *least* likely, and to qualities which are assuredly not *more* likely, to be found in it? The poet, speaking in his own person, may at once delight and improve us by sentiments which teach us the independence of goodness, of wisdom, and even of genius, on the favors of fortune. And having made a due reverence before the throne of Antonine, he may bow with equal awe before Epictetus among his fellow-slaves—

　　　　　　　　　　and rejoice
In the plain presence of his dignity

Who is not at once delighted and improved, when the poet Wordsworth himself exclaims,

O, many are the poets that are sown
By Nature; men endowed with highest gifts,
The vision and the faculty divine,
Yet wanting the accomplishment of verse,
Nor having e'er, as life advanced, been led
By circumstance to take unto the height
The measure of themselves, these favored beings,
All but a scattered few, live out their time,
Husbanding that which they possess within,
And so to the grave, unthought of. Strongest minds
Are often those of whom the noisy world
Hears least.

To use a colloquial phrase, such sentiments, in such language, do one's heart good; though I, for my part, have not the fullest faith in the *truth* of the observation. On the contrary, I believe the instances to be exceedingly rare; and should feel almost as strong an objection to introduce such a character in a poetic fiction, as a pair of black swans on a lake, in a fancy landscape. When I think how many, and how much better books than Homer, or even than Herodotus, Pindar, or Æschylus, could have read, are in the power of almost every man, in a country where almost every man is instructed to read and write; and how restless, how difficultly hidden, the powers of genius are; and yet find even in situations the most favorable, according to Mr. Wordsworth, for the formation of a pure and poetic language—in situations which ensure familiarity with the grandest objects of the imagination—but one Burns, among the shepherds of Scotland, and not a single poet of humble life among those of English lakes and mountains, I conclude, that poetic genius is not only a very delicate, but a very rare plant.

But be this as it may; the feelings with which

I think of Chatterton, the marvellous boy,
The sleepless soul, that perished in his pride;
Of Burns, that walked in glory and in joy
Behind his plough, upon the mountain-side,—

are widely different from those with which I should read a *poem*, where the author, having occasion for the character of a poet and a philosopher in the fable of his narration, had chosen to make him a chimney-sweeper; and then, in order to remove all doubts on the subject, had *invented* an account of his birth, parentage, and education, with all the strange and fortunate accidents which had concurred in making him at once poet, philosopher, and sweep! Nothing but biography can justify this. If it be admissible even in a novel, it must be one in the manner of De Foe's, that were meant to pass for histories, not in the manner of Fielding's: in *The Life of Moll Flanders,* or *Colonel Jack,* not in a *Tom Jones,* or even a *Joseph Andrews.* Much less, then, can it be legitimately introduced in a poem, the characters of which, amid the strongest individualization, must still remain representative. The precepts of Horace, on this point, are grounded on the nature both of poetry and of the human mind. They are not more peremptory, than wise and prudent. For, in the first place, a deviation from them perplexes the reader's feelings, and all the circumstances which are feigned in order to make such accidents less improbable, divide and disquiet his faith, rather than aid and support it. Spite of all attempts, the fiction will

appear, and unfortunately not as fictitious but as false. The reader not only knows that the sentiments and language are the poet's own, and his own, too, in his artificial character, as poet; but by the fruitless endeavors to make him think the contrary, he is not even suffered to forget it. The effect is similar to that produced by an epic poet, when the fable and the characters are *derived* from scripture-history, as in *The Messiah* of Klopstock, or in Cumberland's *Calvary;* and not merely *suggested* by it as in the *Paradise Lost* of Milton. That illusion, contradistinguished from delusion, that negative faith, which simply permits the images presented to work by their own force, without either denial or affirmation of their real existence by the judgment, is rendered impossible by their immediate neighborhood to words and facts of known and absolute truth. A faith which transcends even historic belief must absolutely *put out* this mere poetic *analogon* of faith, as the summer sun is said to extinguish our household fires, when it shines full upon them. What would otherwise have been yielded to as pleasing fiction, is repelled as revolting falsehood. The effect produced in this latter case by the solemn belief of the reader, is in a less degree brought about in the instances to which I have been objecting, by the baffled attempts of the author to *make* him believe.

Add to all the foregoing the seeming uselessness both of the project and of the anecdotes from which it is to derive support. Is there one word, for instance, attributed to the pedlar in *The Excursion,* characteristic of a pedlar? one sentiment that might not more plausibly, even without the aid of any previous explanation, have proceeded from any wise and beneficent old man, of a rank or profession in which the language of learning and refinement are natural and to be expected? Need the rank have been at all particularized, where nothing follows which the knowledge of that rank is to explain or illustrate? when on the contrary this information renders the man's language, feelings, sentiments, and information a riddle, which must itself be solved by episodes of anecdote? Finally, when this, and this alone, could have induced a genuine poet to inweave in a poem of the loftiest style, and on subjects the loftiest and of most universal interest, such minute matters of fact (not unlike those furnished for the obituary of a magazine by the friends of some obscure "ornament of society lately deceased" in some obscure town) as

Among the hills of Athol he was born;
There, on a small hereditary farm,
An unproductive slip of rugged ground,
His father dwelt; and died in poverty;
While he, whose lowly fortune I retrace,
The youngest of three sons, was yet a babe,
A little one—unconscious of their loss.
But ere he had outgrown his infant days
His widowed mother, for a second mate,
Espoused the teacher of the village-school;
Who on her offspring zealously bestowed
Needful instruction.

From his sixth year, the boy of whom I speak,
In summer tended cattle on the hills;
But, through the inclement and the perilous
    days
Of long-continuing winter, he repaired
To his step-father's school, etc.   20

For all the admirable passages interposed in this narration, might, with trifling alterations, have been far more appropriately, and with far greater verisimilitude, told of a poet in the character of a poet; and without incurring another defect which I shall now mention, and a sufficient illustration of which will have been here anticipated.

Third; an undue predilection for the *dramatic* form in certain poems, from which one or other of two evils result. Either the thoughts and diction are different from that of the poet, and then there arises an incongruity of style; or they are the same and indistinguishable, and then it presents a species of ventriloquism, where two are represented as talking, while in truth one man only speaks.

The fourth class of defects is closely connected with the former; but yet are such as arise likewise from an intensity of feeling disproportionate to such knowledge and value of the objects described, as can be fairly anticipated of men in general, even of the most cultivated classes; and with which therefore few only, and those few particularly circumstanced, can be supposed to sympathize. In this class, I comprise occasional prolixity, repetition, and an eddying, instead of progression, of thought. As instances, see pages 27, 28, and 62 of the Poems, Vol. I., and the first eighty lines of the Sixth Book of *The Excursion.*

Fifth and last; thoughts and images too great for the subject. This is an approximation to what might be called mental bombast, as distinguished from verbal: for,

as in the latter there is a disproportion of the expressions to the thoughts, so in this there is a disproportion of thought to the circumstance and occasion. This, by the bye, is a fault of which none but a man of genius is capable. It is the awkwardness and strength of Hercules with the distaff of Omphale.

It is a well-known fact that bright colors in motion both make and leave the strongest impressions on the eye. Nothing is more likely too, than that a vivid image or visual spectrum, thus originated, may become the link of association in recalling the feelings and images that had accompanied the original impression. But if we describe this in such lines as

They flash upon that inward eye,
Which is the bliss of solitude!

in what words shall we describe the joy of retrospection, when the images and virtuous actions of a whole well-spent life pass before that conscience which is indeed the *inward* eye: which is indeed *"the bliss of solitude?"* Assuredly we seem to sink most abruptly, not to say burlesquely, and almost as in a medley, from this couplet to—

And then my heart with pleasure fills,
And dances with the daffodils.

Vol. I., p. 320.

The second instance is from Vol. II., page 12, where the poet, having gone out for a day's tour of pleasure, meets early in the morning with a knot of gipsies, who had pitched their blanket-tents and straw-beds, together with their children and asses, in some field by the roadside. At the close of the day on his return our tourist found them in the same place. "Twelve hours," says he,

Twelve hours, twelve bounteous hours are
    gone, while I
Have been a traveller under open sky,
Much witnessing of change and cheer,
Yet as I left I find them here!

Whereat the poet, without seeming to reflect that the poor tawny wanderers might probably have been tramping for weeks together through road and lane, over moor and mountain, and consequently must have been right glad to rest themselves, their children and cattle, for one whole day; and overlooking the obvious truth, that such repose might be quite as necessary for them, as a walk of the same continuance was pleasing or healthful for the more fortunate poet; expresses his in...

dignation in a series of lines, the diction and imagery of which would have been rather above, than below the mark, had they been applied to the immense empire of China improgressive for thirty centuries:

The weary sun betook himself to rest:—
—Then issued vesper from the fulgent west,
Outshining, like a visible God,
The glorious path in which he trod!
And now, ascending, after one dark hour,
And one night's diminution of her power,
Behold the mighty moon! this way
She looks, as if at them—but they
Regard not her:—oh, better wrong and strife,
Better vain deeds or evil than such life!
The silent heavens have goings on:
The stars have tasks!—But *these* have none!

The last instance of this defect (for I know no other than these already cited) is from the *Ode,* page 351, Vol. II, where, speaking of a child, "a six years' darling of a pigmy size," he thus addresses him:

Thou best philosopher, who yet dost keep
Thy heritage! Thou eye among the blind,
That, deaf and silent, read'st the eternal deep,
Haunted forever by the Eternal Mind,—
Mighty prophet! Seer blest!
On whom those truths do rest,
Which we are toiling all our lives to find!
Thou, over whom thy immortality
Broods like the day, a master o'er a slave,
A presence which is not to be put by!

Now here, not to stop at the daring spirit of metaphor which connects the epithets "deaf and silent," with the apostrophized *eye:* or (if we are to refer it to the preceding word, "philosopher") the faulty and equivocal syntax of the passage; and without examining the propriety of making a "master *brood* o'er a slave," or "the *day*" brood *at all;* we will merely ask, What does all this mean? In what sense is a child of that age a *philosopher?* In what sense does he *read* "the eternal deep"? In what sense is he declared to be *"forever haunted"* by the Supreme Being? or so inspired as to deserve the splendid titles of *a mighty prophet,* a *blessed seer?* By reflection? by knowledge? by conscious intuition? or by *any* form or modification of consciousness? These would be tidings indeed; but such as would presuppose an immediate revelation to the inspired communicator, and require miracles to authenticate his inspiration. Children at this age give us no such information of themselves; and at what time were we dipped in the Lethe, which has produced such utter oblivion of a state so godlike? There are many of us that still possess some remembrances, more or less distinct, respecting themselves at six years old; pity that the worthless straws only should float, while treasures, compared with which all the mines of Golconda and Mexico were but straws, should be absorbed by some unknown gulf into some unknown abyss.

But if this be too wild and exorbitant to be suspected as having been the poet's meaning; if these mysterious gifts, faculties, and operations, are not accompanied with consciousness; who else is conscious of them? or how can it be called the child, if it be no part of the child's conscious being? For aught I know, the thinking spirit within me may be *substantially* one with the principle of life, and of vital operation. For aught I know, it might be employed as a secondary agent in the marvellous organization and organic movements of my body. But, surely, it would be strange language to say that *I* construct my *heart!* or that *I* propel the finer influences through my *nerves!* or that *I* compress my brain, and draw the curtains of sleep round my own eyes! Spinoza and Behmen were, on different systems, both pantheists; and among the ancients there were philosophers, teachers of the ΕΝ ΚΑΙ ΠΑΝ, who not only taught that God was All, but that this All constituted God. Yet not even these would confound the *part, as* a part, with the whole, *as* the whole. Nay, in no system is the distinction between the individual and God, between the modification, and the one only substance, more sharply drawn, than in that of Spinoza. Jacobi indeed relates of Lessing, that, after a conversation with him at the house of the poet Gleim (the Tyrtæus and Anacreon of the German Parnassus) in which conversation Lessing had avowed privately to Jacobi his reluctance to admit any *personal* existence of the Supreme Being, or the *possibility* of personality except in a finite intellect, and while they were sitting at table, a shower of rain came on unexpectedly. Gleim expressed his regret at the circumstance, because they had meant to drink their wine in the garden: upon which Lessing, in one of his half-earnest, half-joking moods, nodded to Jacobi, and said, "It is *I,* perhaps, that am doing *that,*" *i.e., raining!*— and Jacobi answered, "or perhaps *I*"; Gleim contented himself with staring at them both, without asking for any explanation.

So with regard to this passage. In what sense can the magnificent attributes, above quoted, be appropriate to a *child,* which would not make them equally suitable to a *bee,* or a *dog,* or a *field of corn;* or even to a ship, or to the wind and waves that propel it? The omnipresent spirit works equally in them, as in the child; and the child is equally unconscious of it as they. It cannot surely be that the four lines immediately following are to contain the explanation?

> To whom the grave
> Is but a lonely bed without the sense or sight
> Of day or the warm light,
> A place of thought where we in waiting lie.

Surely, it cannot be that this wonder-rousing apostrophe is but a comment on the little poem *We Are Seven?* that the whole meaning of the passage is reducible to the assertion that a child, who, by the bye, at six years old would have been better instructed in most Christian families, has no other notion of death than that of lying in a dark, cold place? And still, I hope, not as in a *place of thought!* not the frightful notion of lying *awake* in his grave! The analogy between death and sleep is too simple, too natural, to render so horrid a belief possible for children; even had they not been in the habit, as all Christian children are, of hearing the latter term used to express the former. But if the child's belief be only that "he is not dead, but sleepeth," wherein does it differ from that of his father and mother, or any other adult and instructed person? To form an idea of a thing's becoming nothing; or of nothing becoming a thing; is impossible to all finite beings alike, of whatever age, and however educated or uneducated. Thus it is with splendid paradoxes in general. If the words are taken in the common sense they convey an absurdity; and if, in contempt of dictionaries and custom, they are so interpreted as to avoid the absurdity, the meaning dwindles into some bald truism. Thus you must at once understand the words *contrary* to their common import, in order to arrive at any *sense;* and *according* to their common import, if you are to receive from them any feeling of *sublimity* or *admiration.*

Though the instances of this defect in Mr. Wordsworth's poems are so few that for themselves it would have been scarcely just to attract the reader's attention toward them, yet I have dwelt on it, and perhaps the more for this very reason. For being so very few, they cannot sensibly detract from the reputation of an author who is even characterized by the number of profound truths in his writings, which will stand the severest analysis; and yet few as they are, they are exactly those passages which his *blind* admirers would be most likely, and best able, to imitate. But Wordsworth, where he is indeed Wordsworth, may be mimicked by copyists, he may be plundered by plagiarists; but he cannot be imitated, except by those who are not born to be imitators. For without his depth of feeling and his imaginative power his *sense* would want its vital warmth and peculiarity; and without his strong sense, his *mysticism* would become *sickly*—mere fog and dimness!

To these defects which, as appears by the extracts, are only occasional, I may oppose, with far less fear of encountering the dissent of any candid and intelligent reader, the following (for the most part correspondent) excellences. First, an austere purity of language both grammatically and logically; in short a perfect appropriateness of the words to the meaning. Of how high value I deem this, and how particularly estimable I hold the example at the present day, has been already stated: and in part, too, the reasons on which I ground both the moral and intellectual importance of habituating ourselves to a strict accuracy of expression. It is noticeable how limited an acquaintance with the masterpieces of art will suffice to form a correct and even a sensitive taste, where none but masterpieces have been seen and admired: while, on the other hand, the most correct notions, and the widest acquaintance with the works of excellence of all ages and countries, will not perfectly secure us against the contagious familiarity with the far more numerous offspring of tastelessness or of a perverted taste. If this be the case, as it notoriously is, with the arts of music and painting, much more difficult will it be to avoid the infection of multiplied and daily examples in the practice of an art which uses words, and words only, as its instruments. In poetry, in which every line, every phrase, may pass the ordeal of deliberation and deliberate choice, it is possible, and barely possible, to attain that ultimatum which I have ventured to propose as the infallible test of a blameless style,—its *untranslatableness* in words of the same language without injury to the meaning. Be it observed, however, that I include in the *meaning* of a word not only its correspondent object, but likewise all the associations which it recalls. For language is framed to convey not the object alone, but likewise the character, mood, and intentions of the person who is representing it. In poetry it *is* practicable to preserve the diction uncorrupted by the affectations and misappropriations which promiscuous authorship, and reading not promiscuous only because it is disproportionately most conversant with the compositions of the day, have rendered general. Yet even to the poet, composing in his own province, it is an arduous work: and as the result and pledge of a watchful good sense, of fine and luminous distinction, and of complete self-possession, may justly claim all the honor which belongs to an attainment equally difficult and valuable, and the more valuable for being rare. It is at *all* times the proper food of the understanding; but in an age of corrupt eloquence it is both food and antidote.

In prose I doubt whether it be even possible to preserve our style wholly unalloyed by the vicious phraseology which meets us everywhere, from the sermon to the newspaper, from the harangue of the legislator to the speech from the convivial chair, announcing a *toast* or sentiment. Our chains rattle, even while we are complaining of them. The poems of Boetius rise high in our estimation when we compare them with those of his contemporaries, as Sidonius Apollinarius, &c. They might even be referred to a purer age, but that the prose in which they are set, as jewels in a crown of lead or iron, betrays the true age of the writer. Much, however, may be effected by education. I believe not only from grounds of reason, but from having in great measure assured myself of the fact by actual though limited experience, that, to a youth led from his first boyhood to investigate the meaning of every word and the reason of its choice and position, logic presents itself as an old acquaintance under new names.

On such future occasion, more especially demanding such disquisition, I shall attempt to prove the close connection between veracity and habits of mental accuracy; the beneficial after-effects of verbal precision in the preclusion of fanaticism, which masters the feelings more especially by indistinct watchwords; and to display the advantages which language alone, at least which language with incomparably greater ease and certainty than any other means, presents to the instructor of impressing modes of intellectual energy so constantly, so imperceptibly, and, as it were, by such elements and atoms, as to secure in due time the formation of a second nature. When we reflect that the cultivation of the judgment is a positive command of the moral law, since the reason can give the *principle* alone, and the conscience bears witness only to the *motive*, while the application and effects must depend on the judgment: when we consider that the greater part of our success and comfort in life depends on distinguishing the similar from the same, that which is peculiar in each thing from that which it has in common with others, so as still to select the most probable, instead of the merely possible or positively unfit, we shall learn to value earnestly and with a practical seriousness a mean, already prepared for us by nature and society, of teaching the young mind to think well and wisely by the same unremembered process and with the same never-forgotten results, as those by which it is taught to speak and converse. Now how much warmer the interest is, how much more genial the feelings of reality and practicability, and thence how much stronger the impulses to imitation are, which a *contemporary* writer, and especially a contemporary *poet*, excites in youth and commencing manhood, has been treated of in the earlier pages of these sketches. I have only to add that all the praise which is due to the exertion of such influence for a purpose so important, joined with that which must be claimed for the infrequency of the same excellence in the same perfection, belongs in full right to Mr. Wordsworth. I am far, however, from denying that we have poets whose *general* style possesses the same excellence, as Mr. Moore, Lord Byron, Mr. Bowles, and, in all his later and more important works, our laurel-honoring Laureate. But there are none in whose works I do not appear to myself to find *more* exceptions than in those of Wordsworth. Quotations or specimens would here be wholly out of place, and must be left for the critic who doubts and would invalidate the justice of this eulogy so applied.

The second characteristic excellence of Mr. W[ordsworth]'s work is: a correspondent weight and sanity of the thoughts and sentiments, won, not from books, but from the poet's own meditative observation. They are *fresh* and have the dew upon them. His muse, at least when in her strength of wing, and when she hovers aloft in her proper element,

Makes audible a linkèd lay of truth,
Of truth profound a sweet continuous lay,
Not learnt, but native, her own natural notes!
                         S. T. C.

Even throughout his smaller poems there
is scarcely one which is not rendered valuable by some just and original reflection.
See page 25, vol. II: or the two following
passages in one of his humblest compositions.

O reader! had you in your mind
Such stores as silent thought can bring,
O gentle reader! you would find
A tale in every thing;

and

I've heard of hearts unkind, kind deeds
With coldness still returning;
Alas! the gratitude of men
Has oftener left me mourning;

or in a still higher strain the six beautiful
quatrains, page 134.

Thus fares it still in our decay:
And yet the wiser mind
Mourns less for what age takes away
Than what it leaves behind.

The blackbird in the summer trees,
The lark upon the hill,
Let loose their carols when they please,
Are quiet when they will.

With Nature never do *they* wage
A foolish strife; they see
A happy youth, and their old age
Is beautiful and free!

But we are pressed by heavy laws;
And often glad no more,
We wear a face of joy, because
We have been glad of yore.

If there is one who need bemoan
His kindred laid in earth,
The household hearts that were his own,
It is the man of mirth.

My days, my friend, are almost gone,
My life has been approved,
And many love me; but by none
Am I enough beloved;

or the sonnet on Buonaparte, page 202,
vol. II; or finally (for a volume would
scarce suffice to exhaust the instances), the
last stanza of the poem on the withered
Celandine, vol. II, p. 212.

To be a prodigal's favorite—then, worse truth,
A miser's pensioner—behold our lot!
O man! that from thy fair and shining youth
Age might but take the things youth needed
    not.

Both in respect of this and of the former
excellence, Mr. Wordsworth strikingly resembles Samuel Daniel, one of the golden
writers of our golden Elizabethan age, now
most causelessly neglected: Samuel Daniel,
whose diction bears no mark of time, no
distinction of age, which has been, and as
long as our language shall last, will be so
far the language of the today and forever,
as that it is more intelligible to us than the
transitory fashions of our own particular
age. A similar praise is due to his sentiments. No frequency of perusal can deprive them of their freshness. For though
they are brought into the full daylight of
every reader's comprehension, yet are they
drawn up from depths which few in any
age are privileged to visit, into which few
in any age have courage or inclination to
descend. If Mr. Wordsworth is not equally
with Daniel alike intelligible to all readers
of average understanding in all passages of
his works, the comparative difficulty does
not arise from the greater impurity of the
ore, but from the nature and uses of the
metal. A poem is not necessarily obscure
because it does not aim to be popular. It
is enough if a work be perspicuous to those
for whom it is written, and

Fit audience find, though few.

To the *Ode on the Intimation[s] of Immortality from Recollections of Early Childhood* the poet might have prefixed the
lines which Dante addresses to one of his
own Canzoni—

Canzon, io credo, che saranno radi
Che tua ragione intendan bene,
Tanto lor sei faticoso ed alto.

O lyric song, there will be few, think I,
Who may thy import understand aright:
Thou art for *them* so arduous and so high!

But the ode was intended for such readers only as had been accustomed to watch
the flux and reflux of their inmost nature,
to venture at times into the twilight realms
of consciousness, and to feel a deep interest
in modes of inmost being, to which they
know that the attributes of time and space
are inapplicable and alien, but which yet
can not be conveyed, save in symbols of
time and space. For such readers the sense
is sufficiently plain, and they will be as
little disposed to charge Mr. Wordsworth
with believing the Platonic pre-existence,
in the ordinary interpretation of the words,
as I am to believe that Plato himself ever
meant or taught it. . .

Third (and wherein he soars far above Daniel), the sinewy strength and originality of single lines and paragraphs: the frequent *curiosa felicitas* of his diction, of which I need not here give specimens, having anticipated them in a preceding page. This beauty, and as eminently characteristic of Wordsworth's poetry, his rudest assailants have felt themselves compelled to acknowledge and admire.

Fourth, the perfect truth of nature in his images and descriptions, as taken immediately from nature, and proving a long and genial intimacy with the very spirit which gives the physiognomic expression to all the works of nature. Like a green field reflected in a calm and perfectly transparent lake, the image is distinguished from the reality only by its greater softness and lustre. Like the moisture or the polish on a pebble, genius neither distorts nor false-colors its objects; but on the contrary brings out many a vein and many a tint, which escapes the eye of common observation, thus raising to the rank of gems what had been often kicked away by the hurrying foot of the traveller on the dusty high road of custom.

Let me refer to the whole description of skating, vol. I, page 42 to 47, especially to the lines

So through the darkness and the cold we flew,
And not a voice was idle: with the din
Meanwhile the precipices rang aloud;
The leafless trees and every icy crag
Tinkled like iron; while the distant hills
Into the tumult sent an alien sound
Of melancholy, not unnoticed, while the stars
Eastward were sparkling clear, and in the west
The orange sky of evening died away.

Or to the poem on *The Green Linnet,* vol. I, page 244. What can be more accurate yet more lovely than the two concluding stanzas?

Upon yon tuft of hazel trees,
That twinkle to the gusty breeze,
Behold him perched in ecstasies,
    Yet seeming still to hover;
There! where the flutter of his wings
Upon his back and body flings
Shadows and sunny glimmerings,
    That cover him all over.

While thus before my eyes he gleams,
A brother of the leaves he seems;
When in a moment forth he teems
    His little song in gushes:
As if it pleased him to disdain
And mock the form which he did feign
While he was dancing with the train
    Of leaves among the bushes.

Or the description of the blue-cap, and of the noontide silence, page 284, or the poem to the cuckoo, page 299; or, lastly, though I might multiply the references to ten times the number, to the poem, so completely Wordsworth's, commencing

Three years she grew in sun and shower, etc.

Fifth, a meditative pathos, a union of deep and subtle thought with sensibility; a sympathy with man as man; the sympathy indeed of a contemplater, rather than a fellow-sufferer or co-mate *(spectator, haud particeps)*, but of a contemplator, from whose view no difference of rank conceals the sameness of the nature; no injuries of wind or weather, or toil, or even of ignorance, wholly disguise the human face divine. The superscription and the image of the Creator still remain legible to *him* under the dark lines with which guilt or calamity had cancelled or cross-barred it. Here the man and the poet lose and find themselves in each other, the one as glorified, the latter as substantiated. In this mild and philosophic pathos, Wordsworth appears to be without a compeer. Such as *he is:* so he *writes.* See vol. I, pages 134 to 136, or that most affecting composition, *The Affliction of Margaret —— of ——,* pages 165 to 168, which no mother, and, if I may judge by my own experience, no parent can read without a tear. Or turn to that genuine lyric, in the former edition, entitled *The Mad Mother,* pages 174 to 178, of which I cannot refrain from quoting two of the stanzas, both of them for their pathos, and the former for the fine transition in the two concluding lines of the stanza, so expressive of that deranged state in which, from the increased sensibility, the sufferer's attention is abruptly drawn off by every trifle, and in the same instant plucked back again by the one despotic thought, bringing home with it, by the blending, *fusing* power of Imagination and Passion, the alien object to which it had been so abruptly diverted, no longer an alien but an ally and an inmate.

Suck, little babe, oh suck again!
It cools my blood; it cools my brain;
Thy lips, I feel them, baby! they
Draw from my heart the pain away.
Oh! press me with thy little hand;
It loosens something at my chest;
About that tight and deadly band
I feel thy little fingers pressed.
The breeze I see is in the tree!
It comes to cool my babe and me.

Thy father cares not for my breast,
'Tis thine, sweet baby, there to rest;
'Tis all thine own—and if its hue
Be changed, that was so fair to view,
'Tis fair enough for thee, my dove! 5
My beauty, little child, is flown,
But thou wilt live with me in love;
And what if my poor cheek be brown?
'Tis well for me, thou canst not see
How pale and wan it else would be. 10

Last, and pre-eminently, I challenge for this poet the gift of Imagination in the highest and strictest sense of the word. In the play of *fancy*, Wordsworth, to my feelings, is not always graceful, and sometimes *recondite*. The *likeness* is occasionally too strange, or demands too peculiar a point of view, or is such as appears the creature of predetermined research, rather than spontaneous presentation. Indeed, his fancy seldom displays itself as mere and unmodified fancy. But in imaginative power he stands nearest of all modern writers to Shakspeare and Milton; and yet in a kind perfectly unborrowed and his own. To employ his own words, which are at once an instance and an illustration, he does indeed to all thoughts and to all objects—

add the gleam,
The light that never was, on sea or land,
The consecration, and the poet's dream.

I shall select a few examples as most obviously manifesting this faculty; but if I should ever be fortunate enough to render my analysis of imagination, its origin and characters, thoroughly intelligible to the reader, he will scarcely open on a page of this poet's works without recognizing, more or less, the presence and the influences of this faculty.

From the poem on the *Yew Trees*, vol. I, page 303, 304.

But worthier still of note
Are those fraternal four of Borrowdale, 45
Joined in one solemn and capacious grove;
Huge trunks!—and each particular trunk a growth
Of intertwisted fibres serpentine
Up-coiling, and inveterately convolved,—
Not uninformed with phantasy, and looks 50
That threaten the profane;—a pillared shade,
Upon whose grassless floor of red-brown hue,
By sheddings from the pinal umbrage tinged
Perennially—beneath whose sable roof
Of boughs, as if for festal purpose, decked 55
With unrejoicing berries, ghostly shapes
May meet at noontide: Fear and trembling Hope,
Silence and Foresight; Death, the skeleton,
And Time, the shadow; there to celebrate, 60

As in a natural temple scattered o'er
With altars undisturbed of mossy stone,
United worship; or in mute repose
To lie, and listen to the mountain flood
Murmuring from Glaramara's inmost caves.

The effect of the old man's figure in the poem of *Re[solution] and Independence,* vol II, page 33.

While he was talking thus, the lonely place,
The old man's shape, and speech, all troubled me:
In my mind's eye I seemed to see him pace
About the weary moors continually,
Wandering about alone and silently.

Or the 8th, 9th, 19th, 26th, 31st, and 33rd, in the collection of miscellaneous sonnets—the sonnet on the subjugation of Switzerland, page 210, or the last ode, from which I especially select the two following stanzas or paragraphs, page 349 to 350.

Our birth is but a sleep and a forgetting;
The soul that rises with us, our life's star,
Hath had elsewhere its setting,
And cometh from afar.
Not in entire forgetfulness,
And not in utter nakedness,
But trailing clouds of glory do we come
From God, who is our home:
Heaven lies about us in our infancy!
Shades of the prison-house begin to close
Upon the growing boy;
But he beholds the light, and whence it flows,
He sees it in his joy!
The youth who daily further from the East
Must travel, still is Nature's priest,
And by the vision splendid
Is on his way attended;
At length the man perceives it die away,
And fade into the light of common day.

And page 352 to 354 of the same ode.

O joy! that in our embers
Is something that doth live,
That nature yet remembers
What was so fugitive!
The thought of our past years in me doth breed
Perpetual benedictions: not indeed
For that which is most worthy to be blest;
Delight and liberty, the simple creed
Of childhood, whether busy or at rest,
With new-fledged hope still fluttering in his breast:—
Not for these I raise
The song of thanks and praise;
But for those obstinate questionings
Of sense and outward things,
Fallings from us, vanishings;
Blank misgivings of a creature
Moving about in worlds not realized,
High instincts, before which our mortal nature

Did tremble like a guilty thing surprised!
But for those first affections,
Those shadowy recollections,
Which, be they what they may,
Are yet the fountain light of all our day,
Are yet a master light of all our seeing;   5
Uphold us—cherish—and have power to
    make
Our noisy years seem moments in the being
Of the eternal silence; truths that wake
    To perish never;   10
Which neither listlessness, nor mad endeavor,
Nor man nor boy,
Nor all that is at enmity with joy,
Can utterly abolish or destroy!
Hence, in a season of calm weather,   15
Though inland far we be,
Our souls have sight of that immortal sea
Which brought us hither,
Can in a moment travel thither,—
And see the children sport upon the shore,
And hear the mighty waters rolling evermore.   20

A solitary doe!
White she is as lily of June,
And beauteous as the silver moon
When out of sight the clouds are driven
And she is left alone in heaven!
Or like a ship some gentle day   5
In sunshine sailing far away—
A glittering ship that hath the plain
Of ocean for her own domain.

* * * * * *

What harmonious pensive changes
Wait upon her as she ranges
Round and through this pile of state
Overthrown and desolate!
Now a step or two her way
Is through space of open day,   15
Where the enamored sunny light
Brightens her that was so bright;
Now doth a delicate shadow fall,
Falls upon her like a breath,
From some lofty arch or wall,
As she passes underneath.   20

And since it would be unfair to conclude with an extract which, though highly characteristic, must yet, from the nature of the thoughts and the subject, be interesting or perhaps intelligible, to but a limited number of readers, I will add, from the poet's last published work, a passage equally Wordsworthian, of the beauty of which, and of the imaginative power displayed therein, there can be but one opinion, and one feeling. See *White Doe*, page 5.

Fast the church-yard fills;—anon
Look again and they [all] are gone;
The cluster round the porch, and the folk
Who sate in the shade of the Prior's Oak!
And scarcely have they disappeared
Ere the prelusive hymn is heard;—
With one consent the people rejoice,
Filling the church with a lofty voice!
They sing a service which they feel,
For 'tis the sun-rise of their zeal;
And faith and hope are in their prime
In great Eliza's golden time.

A moment ends the fervent din.
And all is hushed, without and within;
For though the priest, more tranquilly,
Recites the holy liturgy,
The only voice which you can hear
Is the river murmuring near.
When soft!—the dusky trees between,
And down the path through the open green,
Where is no living thing to be seen;
And through yon gateway, where is found,
Beneath the arch with ivy bound,
Free entrance to the church-yard ground;
And right across the verdant sod,
Towards the very house of God;
Comes gliding in with lovely gleam,
Comes gliding in serene and slow,
Soft and silent as a dream,

The following analogy will, I am apprehensive, appear dim and fantastic, but in reading Bartram's *Travels* I could not help transcribing the following lines as a sort of allegory, or connected simile and metaphor of Wordsworth's intellect and genius.— "The soil is a deep, rich, dark mould, on a deep stratum of tenacious clay; and that on a foundation of rocks, which often break through both strata, lifting their back above the surface. The trees which chiefly grow here are the gigantic black oak, magnolia magniflora, fraximus excelsior, platane, and a few stately tulip trees." What Mr. Wordsworth *will* produce, it is not for me to prophesy: but I could pronounce with the liveliest convictions what he is capable of producing. It is the FIRST GENUINE PHILOSOPHIC POEM.

The preceding criticism will not, I am aware, avail to overcome the prejudices of those, who have made it a business to attack and ridicule Mr. Wordsworth's compositions.

Truth and prudence might be imaged as concentric circles. The poet may perhaps have passed beyond the latter, but he has confined himself far within the bounds of the former, in designating these critics, as "too petulant to be passive to a genuine poet, and too feeble to grapple with him; . . . men of palsied imaginations, in whose minds all healthy action is languid; . . . who, therefore, feed as the many direct them, or with the many are greedy after vicious provocatives."

So much for the detractors from Wordsworth's merits. On the other hand, much as I might wish for their fuller sympathy,

I dare not flatter myself, that the freedom with which I have declared my opinions concerning both his theory and his defects, most of which are more or less connected with his theory, either as cause or effect, will be satisfactory or pleasing to *all* the poet's admirers and advocates. More indiscriminate than mine their admiration may be: deeper and more sincere it cannot be. But I have advanced no opinion either for praise or censure, other than as texts introductory to the reasons which compel me to form it. Above all, I was fully convinced that such a criticism was not only wanted; but that, if executed with adequate ability, it must conduce, in no mean degree, to Mr. Wordsworth's *reputation.* His *fame* belongs to another age, and can neither be accelerated nor retarded. How small the proportion of the defects are to the beauties, I have repeatedly declared; and that no one of them originates in deficiency of poetic genius. Had they been more and greater, I should still, as a friend to his literary character in the present age, consider an analytic display of them as *pure gain;* if only it removed, as surely to all reflecting minds even the foregoing analysis must have removed, the strange mistake, so slightly grounded, yet so widely and industriously propagated, of Mr. Wordsworth's turn for *simplicity!* I am not half as much irritated by hearing his enemies abuse him for vulgarity of style, subject, and conception, as I am disgusted with the gilded side of the same meaning, as displayed by some affected admirers, with whom he is, forsooth, a "sweet, simple poet!" and *so* natural, that little master Charles and his younger sister are *so* charmed with them, that they play at "Goody Blake," or at "Johnny and Betty Foy!"

1815-16   1817

THE CHARACTERISTICS OF SHAKSPEARE'S DRAMAS

In lectures, of which amusement forms a large part of the object, there are some peculiar difficulties. The architect places his foundation out of sight, and the musician tunes his instrument before he makes his appearance; but the lecturer has to try his chords in the presence of the assembly; an operation not likely, indeed, to produce much pleasure, but yet indispensably necessary to a right understanding of the subject to be developed.

Poetry in essence is as familiar to barbarous as to civilized nations. The Laplander and the savage Indian are cheered by it as well as the inhabitants of London and Paris;—its spirit takes up and incorporates surrounding materials, as a plant clothes itself with soil and climate, whilst it exhibits the working of a vital principle within independent of all accidental circumstances. And to judge with fairness of an author's works, we ought to distinguish what is inward and essential from what is outward and circumstantial. It is essential to poetry that it be simple, and appeal to the elements and primary laws of our nature; that it be sensuous, and by its imagery elicit truth at a flash; that it be impassioned, and be able to move our feelings and awaken our affections. In comparing different poets with each other, we should inquire which have brought into the fullest play our imagination and our reason, or have created the greatest excitement and produced the completest harmony. If we consider great exquisiteness of language and sweetness of metre alone, it is impossible to deny to Pope the character of a delightful writer; but whether he be a poet, must depend upon our definition of the word; and, doubtless, if everything that pleases be poetry, Pope's satires and epistles must be poetry. This, I must say, that poetry, as distinguished from other modes of composition, does not rest in metre, and that it is not poetry, if it make no appeal to our passions or our imagination. One character belongs to all true poets, that they write from a principle within, not originating in any thing without; and that the true poet's work in its form, its shapings, and its modifications, is distinguished from all other works that assume to belong to the class of poetry, as a natural from an artificial flower, or as the mimic garden of a child from an enamelled meadow. In the former the flowers are broken from their stems and stuck into the ground; they are beautiful to the eye and fragrant to the sense, but their colors soon fade, and their odor is transient as the smile of the planter;—while the meadow may be visited again and again with renewed delight; its beauty is innate in the soil, and its bloom is of the freshness of nature.

The next ground of critical judgment, and point of comparison, will be as to how far a given poet has been influenced by accidental circumstances. As a living poet must surely write, not for the ages past, but for that in which he lives, and those which are to follow, it is on the one hand natural that he should not violate, and on the other necessary that he should not depend on, the mere manners and modes of his day. See how little does Shakspeare leave us to regret that he was born in his particular age! The great era in modern times was what is called the Restoration of Letters;—the ages preceding it are called the dark ages; but it would be more wise, perhaps, to call them the ages in which we were in the dark. It is usually overlooked that the supposed dark period was not universal, but partial and successive, or alternate; that the dark age of England was not the dark age of Italy, but that one country was in its light and vigor, whilst another was in its gloom and bondage. But no sooner had the Reformation sounded through Europe like the blast of an archangel's trumpet, than from king to peasant there arose an enthusiasm for knowledge; the discovery of a manuscript became the subject of an embassy; Erasmus read by moonlight, because he could not afford a torch, and begged a penny, not for the love of charity, but for the love of learning. The three great points of attention were religion, morals, and taste; men of genius, as well as men of learning, who in this age need to be so widely distinguished, then alike became copyists of the ancients; and this, indeed, was the only way by which the taste of mankind could be improved, or their understandings informed. Whilst Dante imagined himself a humble follower of Virgil, and Ariosto of Homer, they were both unconscious of that greater power working within them, which in many points carried them beyond their supposed originals. All great discoveries bear the stamp of the age in which they are made;— hence we perceive the effects of the purer religion of the moderns, visible for the most part in their lives; and in reading their works we should not content ourselves with the mere narratives of events long since passed, but should learn to apply their maxims and conduct to themselves.

Having intimated that times and manners lend their form and pressure to genius, let me once more draw a slight parallel between the ancient and modern stage,— the stages of Greece and of England. The Greeks were polytheists; their religion was local; almost the only object of all their knowledge, art, and taste, was their god; and, accordingly, their productions were, if the expression may be allowed, statuesque, whilst those of the moderns are picturesque. The Greeks reared a structure, which, in its parts, and as a whole, filled the mind with the calm and elevated impression of perfect beauty, and symmetrical proportion. The moderns also produced a whole—a more striking whole; but it was by blending materials, and fusing the parts together. And as the Pantheon is to York Minster or Westminster Abbey, so is Sophocles compared with Shakspeare; in the one a completeness, a satisfaction, an excellence, on which the mind rests with complacency; in the other a multitude of interlaced materials, great and little, magnificent and mean, accompanied, indeed, with the sense of a falling short of perfection, and yet, at the same time, so promising of our social and individual progression, that we would not, if we could, exchange it for that repose of the mind which dwells on the forms of symmetry in the acquiescent admiration of grace. This general characteristic of the ancient and modern drama might be illustrated by a parallel of the ancient and modern music;—the one consisting of melody arising from a succession only of pleasing sounds,—the modern embracing harmony also, the result of combination, and the effect of a whole.

I have said, and I say it again, that great as was the genius of Shakspeare, his judgment was at least equal to it. Of this any one will be convinced, who attentively considers those points in which the dramas of Greece and England differ, from the dissimilitude of circumstances by which each was modified and influenced. The Greek stage had its origin in the ceremonies of a sacrifice, such as of the goat to Bacchus, whom we most erroneously regard as merely the jolly god of wine;—for among the ancients he was venerable, as the symbol of that power which acts without our consciousness in the vital energies of nature —the *vinum mundi*—as Apollo was that of the conscious agency of our intellectual being. The heroes of old, under the influences of this Bacchic enthusiasm, performed more than human actions; hence tales of the favorite champions soon passed into dialogue. On the Greek stage the chorus was always before the audience; the curtain was never dropped, as we should say; and change of place being therefore, in general, impossible, the absurd notion of condemning it merely as improbable in itself was never entertained by any one. If we can believe ourselves at Thebes in one act, we may believe ourselves at Athens in the next. If a story lasts twenty-four hours or twenty-four years, it is equally improbable. There seems to be no just boundary but what the feelings prescribe. But on the Greek stage, where the same persons were perpetually before the audience, great judgment was necesssary in venturing on any such change. The poets never, therefore, attempted to impose on the senses by bringing places to men, but they did bring men to places, as in the well-known instance in the *Eumenides,* where, during an evident retirement of the chorus from the orchestra, the scene is changed to Athens, and Orestes is first introduced in the temple of Minerva, and the chorus of Furies come in afterwards in pursuit of him.

In the Greek drama there were no formal divisions into scenes and acts; there were no means, therefore, of allowing for the necessary lapse of time between one part of the dialogue and another, and unity of time in a strict sense was, of course, impossible. To overcome that difficulty of accounting for time, which is effected on the modern stage by dropping a curtain, the judgment and great genius of the ancients supplied music and measured motion, and with the lyric ode filled up the vacuity. In the story of the Agamemnon of Æschylus, the capture of Troy is supposed to be announced by a fire lighted on the Asiatic shore, and the transmission of the signal by successive beacons to Mycenæ. The signal is first seen at the 21st line, and the herald from Troy itself enters at the 486th, and Agamemnon himself at the 783rd line. But the practical absurdity of this was not felt by the audience, who, in imagination stretched minutes into hours, while they listened to the lofty narrative odes of the chorus which almost entirely filled up the interspace. Another fact deserves attention here, namely, that regularly on the Greek stage a drama, or acted story, consisted in reality of three dramas, called together a trilogy, and performed consecutively in the course of one day. Now you may conceive a tragedy of Shakspeare's as a trilogy connected in one single representation. Divide *Lear* into three parts, and each would be a play with the ancients; or take the three Æschylean dramas of *Agamemnon,* and divide them into, or call them, as many acts, and they together would be one play. The first act would comprise the usurpation of Ægisthus, and the murder of Agamemnon; the second, the revenge of Orestes, and the murder of his mother; and the third, the penance and absolution of Orestes;—occupying a period of twenty-two years.

The stage in Shakspeare's time was a naked room with a blanket for a curtain; but he made it a field for monarchs. That law of unity, which has its foundations, not in the factitious necessity of custom, but in nature itself, the unity of feeling, is everywhere and at all times observed by Shakspeare in his plays. Read *Romeo and Juliet;*—all is youth and spring;—youth with its follies, its virtues, its precipitancies;—spring with its odors, its flowers, and its transiency; it is one and the same feeling that commences, goes through, and ends the play. The old men, the Capulets and Montagues, are not common old men; they have an eagerness, a heartiness, a vehemence, the effect of spring; with Romeo, his change of passion, his sudden marriage, and his rash death, are all the effects of youth;—whilst in Juliet love has all that is tender and melancholy in the nightingale, all that is voluptuous in the rose, with whatever is sweet in the freshness of spring; but it ends with a long deep sigh like the last breeze of the Italian evening. This unity of feeling and character pervades every drama of Shakspeare.

It seems to me that his plays are distinguished from those of all other dramatic poets by the following characteristics:—

1. Expectation in preference to surprise. It is like the true reading of the passage—"God said, Let there be light, and there was *light;*"—not "there *was* light." As the feeling with which we startle at a shooting star compared with that of watching the sunrise at the pre-established moment, such and so low is surprise compared with expectation.

2. Signal adherence to the great law of nature, that all opposites tend to attract and temper each other. Passion in Shakspeare generally displays libertinism, but involves morality; and if there are exceptions to this, they are, independently of their intrinsic value, all of them indicative of individual character, and, like the farewell admonitions of a parent, have an end beyond the parental relation. Thus the Countess's beautiful precepts to Bertram, by elevating her character, raise that of Helena her favorite, and soften down the point in her which Shakspeare does not mean us not to see, but to see and to forgive, and at length to justify. And so it is in Polonius, who is the personified memory of wisdom no longer actually possessed. This admirable character is always misrep-

resented on the stage. Shakspeare never intended to exhibit him as a buffoon; for although it was natural that Hamlet—a young man of fire and genius, detesting formality, and disliking Polonius on polit- ical grounds, as imagining that he had assisted his uncle in his usurpation—should express himself satirically, yet this must not be taken as exactly the poet's conception of him. In Polonius a certain induration of character had arisen from long habits of business; but take his advice to Laertes, and Ophelia's reverence for his memory, and we shall see that he was meant to be represented as a statesman somewhat past his faculties,—his recollections of life all full of wisdom, and showing a knowledge of human nature, whilst what immediately takes place before him and escapes from him, is indicative of weakness.

But as in Homer all the deities are in armor, even Venus, so in Shakspeare all the characters are strong. Hence real folly and dulness are made by him the vehicles of wisdom. There is no difficulty for one being a fool to imitate a fool; but to be, remain, and speak like a wise man and a great wit, and yet so as to give a vivid representation of a veritable fool,—*hic labor, hoc opus est.* A drunken constable is not uncommon, nor hard to draw; but see and examine what goes to make up a Dogberry.

3. Keeping at all times in the high road of life, Shakspeare has no innocent adulteries, no interesting incests, no virtuous vice; he never renders that amiable which religion and reason alike teach us to detest, or clothes impurity in the garb of virtue, like Beaumont and Fletcher, the Kotzebues of the day. Shakspeare's fathers are roused by ingratitude, his husbands stung by unfaithfulness; in him, in short, the affections are wounded in those points in which all may, nay, must feel. Let the morality of Shakspeare be contrasted with that of the writers of his own, or the succeeding age, or of those of the present day, who boast their superiority in this respect. No one can dispute that the result of such a comparison is altogether in favor of Shakspeare;—even the letters of women of high rank in his age were often coarser than his writings. If he occasionally disgusts a keen sense of delicacy, he never injures the mind; he neither excites, nor flatters, passion, in order to degrade the subject of it; he does not use the faulty thing for a faulty purpose, nor carries on warfare against virtue, by causing wickedness to appear as no wickedness, through the medium of a

morbid sympathy with the unfortunate. In Shakspeare vice never walks as in twilight; nothing is purposely out of place;—he inverts not the order of nature and propriety, —does not make every magistrate a drunkard or glutton, nor every poor man meek, humane, and temperate; he has no benevolent butchers, or sentimental rat-catchers.

4. Independence of the dramatic interest on the plot. The interest in the plot is always in fact on account of the characters, not *vice versa,* as in almost all other writers; the plot is a mere canvas and no more. Hence arises the true justification of the same strategem being used in regard to Benedick and Beatrice,—the vanity in each being alike. Take away from the *Much Ado about Nothing* all that which is not indispensable to the plot, either as having little to do with it, or, at best, like Dogberry and his comrades, forced into the service, when any other less ingeniously absurd watchmen and night-constables would have answered the mere necessities of the action;—take away Benedick, Beatrice, Dogberry, and the reaction of the former on the character of Hero,—and what will remain? In other writers the main agent of the plot is always the prominent character; in Shakspeare it is so, or is not so, as the character is in itself calculated, or not calculated, to form the plot. Don John is the mainspring of the plot of this play; but he is merely shown and then withdrawn.

5. Independence of the interest on the story as the ground-work of the plot. Hence Shakspeare never took the trouble of inventing stories. It was enough for him to select from those that had been already invented or recorded such as had one or other, or both, of two recommendations, namely, suitableness to his particular purpose, and their being parts of popular tradition,—names of which we had often heard, and of their fortunes, and as to which all we wanted was, to see the man himself. So it is just the man himself—the Lear, the Shylock, the Richard—that Shakspeare makes us for the first time acquainted with. Omit the first scene in *Lear,* and yet everything will remain; so the first and second scenes in *The Merchant of Venice.* Indeed it is universally true.

6. Interfusion of the lyrical—that which in its very essence is poetical—not only with the dramatic, as in the plays of Metastasio, where at the end of the scene comes the *aria* as the *exit* speech of the character, —but also in and through the dramatic.

Songs in Shakspeare are introduced as songs only, just as songs are in real life, beautifully as some of them are characteristic of the person who had sung or called for them, as Desdemona's "Willow," and Ophelia's wild snatches, and the sweet carolings in *As You Like It*. But the whole of the *Midsummer Night's Dream* is one continued specimen of the dramatized lyrical. And observe how exquisitely the dramatic of Hotspur;—

Marry, and I'm glad on't with all my heart;
I'd rather be a kitten and cry mew, etc.

melts away into the lyric of Mortimer;—

I understand thy looks; that pretty Welsh
Which thou pour'st down from these swelling
      heavens,
I am too perfect in, etc.
                    Henry IV, part i, act iii, sc. i.

7. The characters of the *dramatis personæ*, like those in real life, are to be inferred by the reader;—they are not told to him. And it is well worth remarking that Shakspeare's characters, like those in real life, are very commonly misunderstood, and almost always understood by different persons in different ways. The causes are the same in either case. If you take only what the friends of the character say, you may be deceived, and still more so, if that which his enemies say; nay, even the character himself sees himself through the medium of his character, and not exactly as he is. Take all together, not omitting a shrewd hint from the clown or the fool, and perhaps your impression will be right; and you may know whether you have in fact discovered the poet's own idea, by all the speeches receiving light from it, and attesting its reality by reflecting it.

Lastly, in Shakspeare the heterogeneous is united, as it is in nature. You must not suppose a pressure or passion always acting on or in the character;—passion in Shakspeare is that by which the individual is distinguished from others, not that which makes a different kind of him. Shakspeare followed the main march of the human affections. He entered into no analysis of the passions or faiths of men, but assured himself that such and such passions and faiths were grounded in our common nature, and not in the mere accidents of ignorance or disease. This is an important consideration, and constitutes our Shakspeare the morning star, the guide and the pioneer, of true philosophy.

FROM AIDS TO REFLECTION

[TWO KINDS OF MYSTICS]

I shall endeavor to describe two ranks of mystics in a sort of allegory or parable. Let us imagine a poor pilgrim benighted in a wilderness or desert, and pursuing his way in the starless dark with a lantern in his hand. Chance or his happy genius leads him to an *oasis* or natural garden, such as in the creations of my youthful fancy I supposed Enos, the child of Cain to have found. And here, hungry and thirsty, the way-wearied man rests at a fountain; and the taper of his lantern throws its light on an over-shadowing tree, a boss of snow-white blossoms, through which the green and growing fruits peeped, and the ripe golden fruitage glowed. Deep, vivid, and faithful are the impressions, which the lovely imagery comprised within the scanty circle of light, makes and leaves on his memory. But scarcely has he eaten of the fruits and drunk of the fountain, ere scared by the roar and howl from the desert he hurries forward; and as he passes with hasty steps through grove and glade, shadows and imperfect beholdings and vivid fragments of things distinctly seen blend with the past and present shapings of his brain. Fancy modifies sight. His dreams transfer their forms to real objects; and these lend a substance and an outness to his dreams. Apparitions greet him; and when at a distance from this enchanted land, and on a different track, the dawn of day discloses to him a caravan, a troop of his fellow-men, his memory, which is itself half fancy, is interpolated afresh by every attempt to recall, connect, and piece out his recollections. His narration is received as a madman's tale. He shrinks from the rude laugh and contemptuous sneer, and retires into himself. Yet the craving for sympathy, strong in proportion to the intensity of his convictions, impels him to unbosom himself to abstract auditors; and the poor quietist becomes a penman, and, all too poorly stocked for the writer's trade, he borrows his phrases and figures from the only writings to which he has had access, the sacred books of his religion. And thus I shadow out the enthusiast Mystic of the first sort; at the head of which stands the illuminated, Teutonic theosopher and shoemaker, honest Jacob Behmen . . . .

To delineate a Mystic of the second or higher order, we need only endow our pilgrim with equal gifts of nature, but these developed and displayed by all the aids and arts of education and favorable fortune. He is on his way to the Mecca of his ancestral and national faith, with a well-guarded and numerous procession of 5 merchants and fellow-pilgrims, on the established track. At the close of day the caravan has halted: the full moon rises on the desert: and he strays forth alone, out of sight but to no unsafe distance; and 10 chance leads him, too, to the same oasis or islet of verdure on the sea of sand. He wanders at leisure in its maze of beauty and sweetness, and thrids his way through the odorous and flowering thickets into 15 open spots of greenery, and discovers statues and memorial characters, grottoes, and refreshing caves. But the moonshine, the imaginative poesy of Nature, spreads its soft shadowy charm over all, conceals 20 distances, and magnifies height, and modifies relations; and fills up vacuities with its own whiteness, counterfeiting substance; and where the dense shadows lie, makes solidity imitate hollowness; and gives to all 25 objects a tender visionary hue and softening. Interpret the moonlight and the shadows as the peculiar genius and sensibility of the individual's own spirit: and here you have the other sort: a Mystic, an 30 enthusiast of a nobler breed—a Fenelon. But the residentiary, or the frequent visitor of the favored spot, who has scanned its beauties by steady daylight, and mastered its true proportions and lineaments, he will 35 discover that both pilgrims have indeed been there. He will know, that the delightful dream, which the latter tells, is a dream of truth; and that even in the bewildered tale of the former there is truth mingled with the dream.   1825

FROM ANIMA POETAE

THE LOVE OF NATURE

The love of Nature is ever returned double to us, not only the delighter in our delight, but by linking our sweetest, but of themselves perishable feelings to distinct and vivid images, which we ourselves, at times, and which a thousand casual recollections, recall to our memory. She is the preserver, the treasurer of our joys. Even in sickness and nervous diseases, she has peopled our imagination with lovely forms which have sometimes overpowered the inward pain and brought with them their old sensations. And even when all men have seemed to desert us and the friend of our heart has passed on, with one glance from his "cold disliking eye"—yet even then the blue heaven spreads it out and bends over us, and the little tree still shelters us its plumage as a second cope, a domestic firmament, and a low creeping gale will sigh in the heath-plant and soothe us by sound of sympathy till the lulled grief lose itself in fixed gaze on the purple heath-bloom, till the present beauty becomes a vision of memory.

1895

CHARLES LAMB (1775-1834)

Working ever close to the concrete, to the details, great or small, of actual things, books, persons, and with no part of them blurred to his vision by the intervention of mere abstract theories, he has reached an enduring moral effect also, in a sort of boundless sympathy. Unoccupied, as he might seem, with great matters, he is in immediate contact with what is real, especially in its caressing littleness.

WALTER PATER

It was Coleridge that Wordsworth praised as "the most *wonderful* man he had ever known", but it was to Lamb that he paid the tribute:

> O, he was *good,* if e'er a good man lived!

Few of those who read the apparently light-hearted essays which began to appear in the *London Magazine* of 1820 could have guessed the thwarting and tragic circumstances of Lamb's life. Born in London, the son of a law-clerk, Lamb's schooling (at Christ's Hospital) had ended at fourteen, his means not permitting him to gratify his studious cravings by going to college. The dark cloud of hereditary insanity hung over his family. Lamb himself at twenty was temporarily afflicted; and his beloved sister Mary, one frightful day in 1796, in a violent fit of madness, slew their mother. Although Mary recovered from that attack, she was subject to occasional recurrences of insanity. Charles, unaided by those who should have helped him, met this situation with quiet heroism, refusing to let Mary be confined permanently, shouldering all responsibility for her, and watching over her until his death. Until he was fifty, he drudged faithfully at the distasteful work of a clerk in the offices of the East India Company. Yet despite the scantiness of his leisure and the burden of his anxieties, he achieved a rare degree of culture and became one of the master-essayists of our literature. Personally he is the most beloved of the great Romantics.

Wordsworth disclosed the satisfactions of the simple life lived in the country; Lamb disclosed how happily that life may be lived, even with modest means, in the city. He showed what delight there was in books, reading, playgoing, evenings by one's fireside or at one's library-table. By his affectionate yet humorous interest in all kinds of human beings, including the shy or apparently unattractive, he notably illustrated and furthered the democratic tendency of Romanticism. A gourmet (not a glutton), he could make even cookery romantic,—a joyous and wonderworking craft. He left high seriousness to others,—to Coleridge, Wordsworth, Keats, Shelley, and Carlyle; but he supplies us what they lack, and our lives would be gloomier without the illumination which, in a whimsical and humorous manner, he casts upon the lesser arts of life and upon the graces of character.

CHILDHOOD FLED

We were two pretty babes, the youngest she,
The youngest, and the loveliest far, I ween,
And Innocence her name. The time has been,
We two did love each other's company;
Time was, we two had wept to have been apart.   5
But when, by show of seeming good beguiled,
I left the garb and manners of a child,
And my first love for man's society,
Defiling with the world my virgin heart—
My loved companion dropped a tear, and fled,   10
And hid in deepest shades her awful head.
Beloved, who shall tell me where thou art—
In what delicious Eden to be found—
That I may seek thee, the wide world around?

1795   1796

THE OLD FAMILIAR FACES

Where are they gone, the old familiar faces?
I had a mother, but she died, and left me,
Died prematurely in a day of horrors—
All, all are gone, the old familiar faces.

I have had playmates, I have had com-
          panions,   5
In my days of childhood, in my joyful
          school-days—
All, all are gone, the old familiar faces.

I have been laughing, I have been carous-
          ing,
Drinking late, sitting late, with my bosom
          cronies—
All, all are gone, the old familiar faces. 10

I loved a love once, fairest among women;
Closed are her doors on me, I must not see
          her—
All, all are gone, the old familiar faces.

I have a friend, a kinder friend has no
          man;
Like an ingrate, I left my friend
          abruptly   15
Left him, to muse on the old familiar faces.

Ghost-like, I paced round the haunts of my
          childhood.
Earth seemed a desert I was bound to
          traverse,
Seeking to find the old familiar faces.

Friend of my bosom, thou more than a
          brother,   20
Why wert not thou born in my father's
          dwelling?
So might we talk of the old familiar faces—

How some they have died, and some they
          have left me,
And some are taken from me; all are
          departed;
All, all are gone, the old familiar faces. 25
Jan., 1798   1798

HESTER

When maidens such as Hester die,
Their place ye may not well supply,
Though ye among a thousand try,
          With vain endeavor.

A month or more hath she been dead,   5
Yet cannot I by force be led
To think upon the wormy bed,
          And her together.

A springy motion in her gait,
A rising step, did indicate   10
Of pride and joy no common rate,
          That flushed her spirit.

I know not by what name beside
I shall it call:—if 'twas not pride,
It was a joy to that allied,   15
          She did inherit.

Her parents held the Quaker rule,
Which doth the human feeling cool,
But she was trained in Nature's school,
          Nature had blest her.   20

A waking eye, a prying mind,
A heart that stirs, is hard to bind,
A hawk's keen sight ye cannot blind,
          Ye could not Hester.

My sprightly neighbor, gone before   25
To that unknown and silent shore,
Shall we not meet, as heretofore,
          Some summer morning,

When from thy cheerful eyes a ray
Hath struck a bliss upon the day,   30
A bliss that would not go away,
          A sweet fore-warning?

1803   1818

PARENTAL RECOLLECTIONS

A child's a plaything for an hour;
          Its pretty tricks we try
For that or for a longer space;
          Then tire, and lay it by.

But I know one, that to itself   5
          All seasons could control;
That would have mocked the sense of pain
          Out of a grieved soul.

Thou straggler into loving arms,
          Young climber up of knees,   10
When I forget thy thousand ways,
          Then life and all shall cease.

1809

WRITTEN AT CAMBRIDGE

I was not trained in Academic bowers,
And to those learned streams I nothing owe
Which copious from those twin fair founts
          do flow;
Mine have been anything but studious
          hours,
Yet I can fancy, wandering 'mid thy
          towers,   5

Myself a nursling, Granta, of thy lap;
My brow seems tightening with the Doc-
    tor's cap,
And I walk *gowned;* feel unusual powers.
Strange forms of logic clothe my admiring
    speech,

Old Ramus' ghost is busy at my brain; 10
And my skull teems with notions infinite.
Be still, ye reeds of Camus, while I teach
Truths, which transcend the searching
    Schoolmen's vein,
And half had staggered that stout Stagirite!

Aug. 15, 1819   Aug. 29-30, 1819

LETTER TO WORDSWORTH

Thanks for your letter and present. I had already borrowed your second volume. What most please me are the "Song of 5 Lucy"—*Simon's sickly daughter* in "The Sexton" made me *cry*. Next to these are the description of the continuous echoes in the story of Joanna's laugh, where the mountains and all the scenery absolutely 10 seem alive—and that fine Shakspearian character of the happy man, in *The Brothers,*

    —that creeps about the fields, 15

Following his fancies by the hour, to bring
Tears down his cheek, or solitary smiles
Into his face, *until the setting sun
Write fool upon his forehead.*

I will mention one more: the delicate 20 and curious feeling in the wish for the Cumberland Beggar, that he may have about him the melody of birds, altho' he hear them not. Here the mind knowingly 25 passes a fiction upon herself, first substitut-ing her own feelings for the Beggar's, and, in the same breath detecting the fallacy, will not part with the wish.—"The Poet's Epitaph" is disfigured, to my taste, by the 30 vulgar satire upon parsons and lawyers in the beginning, and the coarse epithet of pin point in the sixth stanza. All the rest is eminently good, and your own. I will just add that it appears to me a fault in 35 the Beggar that the instructions conveyed in it are too direct and like a lecture: they don't slide into the mind of the reader while he is imagining no such matter. An intelligent reader finds a sort of insult in 40 being told: I will teach you how to think upon this subject. This fault, if I am right, is in a ten-thousandth worse degree to be found in Sterne and many many novelists and modern poets, who continu- 45 ally put a sign post up to show where you are to feel. They set out with assuming their readers to be stupid. Very different from *Robinson Crusoe, The Vicar of Wake-*

field, Roderick Random, and other beauti-ful bare narratives. There is implied an unwritten compact between author and reader: I will tell you a story, and I sup- 5 pose you will understand it. Modern novels, *St. Leons* and the like, are full of such flowers as these: "Let not my reader suppose"—"Imagine, *if you can*"—modest! —etc.—I will here have done with praise and blame. I have written so much, only that you may not think I have passed over your book without observation.—I am sorry that Coleridge has christened his "Ancient Mariner" "a Poet's Reverie"—it is as bad 15 as Bottom the Weaver's declaration that he is not a lion but only the scenical repre-sentation of a lion. What new idea is gained by this title, but one subversive of all credit, which the tale should force upon 20 us, of its truth? For me, I was never so affected with any human tale. After first reading it, I was totally possessed with it for many days—I dislike all the miraculous part of it, but the feelings of the man 25 under the operation of such scenery dragged me along like Tom Piper's magic whistle. I totally differ from your idea that the Mariner should have had a character and profession. This is a beauty in *Gul- 30 liver's Travels,* where the mind is kept in a placid state of little wonderments; but the Ancient Mariner undergoes such trails as overwhelm and bury all individuality or memory of what he was, like the state of 35 a man in a bad dream, one terrible pe-culiarity of which is that all consciousness of personality is gone. Your other obser-vation is, I think, as well a little un-founded: the Mariner from being con- 40 versant in supernatural events *has* acquired a supernatural and strange cast of *phrase,* eye, appearance, etc., which frighten the wedding guest. You will excuse my re-marks, because I am hurt and vexed that 45 you should think it necessary with a prose apology to open the eyes of dead men that cannot see. To sum up a general opinion of the second vol.—I do not feel any one poem in it so forcibly as *The Ancient*

Mariner, The Mad Mother, and the *Lines at Tintern Abbey,* in the first.—I could, too, have wished the critical preface had appeared in a separate treatise. All its dogmas are true and just, and most of them new, *as* criticism. But they associate a *diminishing* idea with the poems which follow, as having been written for *experiment* on the public taste, more than having sprung (as they must have done) from living and daily circumstances.—I am prolix, because I am gratified in the opportunity of writing to you, and I don't well know when to leave off. I ought before this to have replied to your very kind invitation into Cumberland. With you and your sister I could gang anywhere; but I am afraid whether I shall ever be able to afford so desperate a journey. Separate from the pleasure of your company, I don't much care if I never see a mountain in my life. I have passed all my days in London, until I have formed as many and intense local attachments as any of you mountaineers can have done with dead Nature. The lighted shops of the Strand and Fleet Street; the innumerable trades, tradesmen and customers, coaches, wagons, playhouses; all the bustle and wickedness round about Covent Garden; the very women of the town; the watchmen, drunken scenes, rattles; life awake, if you awake, at all hours of the night; the impossibility of being dull in Fleet Street; the crowds, the very dirt and mud, the sun shining upon houses and pavements, the print shops, the old book stalls, parsons cheapening books, coffee houses, steams of soups from kitchens, the pantomimes—London itself a pantomime and a masquerade—all these things work themselves into my mind, and feed me, without a power of satiating me. The wonder of these sights impels me into night-walks about her crowded streets, and I often shed tears in the motley Strand from fulness of joy at so much life. All these emotions must be strange to you. So are your rural emotions to me. But consider, what must I have been doing all my life, not to have lent great portions of my heart with usury to such scenes?

My attachments are all local, purely local. I have no passion (or have had none since I was in love, and then it was the spurious engendering of poetry and books) to groves and valleys. The rooms where I was born, the furniture which has been before my eyes all my life, a book-case which has followed me about (like a faithful dog, only exceeding him in knowledge), wherever I have moved, old chairs, old tables, streets, squares, where I have sunned myself, my old school,—these are my mistresses. Have I not enough, without your mountains? I do not envy you. I should pity you, did I not know that the mind will make friends of anything. Your sun and moon and skies and hills and lakes affect me no more, or scarcely come to me in more venerable characters, than as a gilded room with tapestry and tapers, where I might live with handsome visible objects. I consider the clouds above me but as a roof, beautifully painted, but unable to satisfy my mind; and at last, like the pictures of the apartment of a connoisseur, unable to afford him any longer a pleasure. So fading upon me, from disuse, have been the beauties of Nature, as they have been confinedly called; so ever fresh, and green, and warm are all the inventions of men, and assemblies of men in this great city. I should certainly have laughed with dear Joanna.

Give my kindest love *and my sister's* to D. and yourself, and a kiss from me to little Barbara Lewthwaite. Thank you for liking my play.

1801   C. LAMB

FROM ON THE TRAGEDIES OF SHAKSPEARE, CONSIDERED WITH REFERENCE TO THEIR FITNESS FOR STAGE REPRESENTATION

It may seem a paradox, but I cannot help being of opinion that the plays of Shakspeare are less calculated for performance on a stage, than those of almost any other dramatist whatever. Their distinguished excellence is a reason that they should be so. There is so much in them which comes not under the province of acting, with which eye, and tone, and gesture, have nothing to do.

The glory of the scenic art is to personate passion, and the turns of passion; and the more coarse and palpable the passion is, the more hold upon the eyes and ears of the spectators the performer obviously possesses. For this reason, scolding scenes, scenes where two persons talk themselves into a fit of fury, and then in a surprising manner talk themselves out of it again, have always been the most popular upon our stage. And the reason is plain, because the spectators are here most palpably appealed to; they are the proper judges in this war of words; they are the legitimate ring that should be formed round such "intellectual prize-fighters." Talking is the direct object of the imitation here. But in all the best dramas, and in Shakspeare above all, how obvious it is that the form of *speaking,* whether it be in soliloquy or dialogue, is only a medium, and often a highly artificial one, for putting the reader or spectator into possession of that knowledge of the inner structure and workings of mind in a character, which he could otherwise never have arrived at *in that form of composition* by any gift short of intuition. We do here as we do with novels written in the *epistolary form.* How many improprieties, perfect solecisms in letter-writing, do we put up with in *Clarissa* and other books, for the sake of the delight which that form upon the whole gives us.

But the practice of stage representation reduces everything to a controversy of elocution. Every character, from the boisterous blasphemings of Bajazet to the shrinking timidity of womanhood, must play the orator. The love-dialogues of Romeo and Juliet, their silver-sweet sounds of lovers' tongues by night; the more intimate and sacred sweetness of nuptial colloquy between an Othello or a Posthumus with their married wives, all those delicacies which are so delightful in the reading, as when we read of those youthful dalliances in Paradise—

As beseemed
Fair couple linked in happy nuptial league
Alone:

by the inherent fault of stage representation, how are these things sullied and turned from their very nature by being exposed to a large assembly; when such speeches as Imogen addresses to her lord, come drawling out of the mouth of a hired actress, whose courtship, though nominally addressed to the personated Posthumus, is manifestly aimed at the spectators, who are to judge of her endearments and her returns of love.

The character of Hamlet is perhaps that by which, since the days of Betterton, a succession of popular performers have had the greatest ambition to distinguish themselves. The length of the part may be one of their reasons. But for the character itself, we find it in a play, and therefore we judge it a fit subject of dramatic representation. The play itself abounds in

maxims and reflections beyond any other, and therefore we consider it as a proper vehicle for conveying moral instruction. But Hamlet himself—what does he suffer meanwhile by being dragged forth as a public schoolmaster, to give lectures to the crowd! Why, nine parts in ten of what Hamlet does are transactions between himself and his moral sense; they are the effusions of his solitary musings, which he retires to holes and corners and the most sequestered parts of the palace to pour forth; or rather, they are the silent meditations with which his bosom is bursting, reduced to *words* for the sake of the reader, who must else remain ignorant of what is passing there. These profound sorrows, these light-and-noise-abhorring ruminations, which the tongue scarce dares utter to deaf walls and chambers, how can they be represented by a gesticulating actor, who comes and mouths them out before an audience, making four hundred people his confidants at once? I say not that it is the fault of the actor so to do; he must pronounce them *ore rotundo,* he must accompany them with his eye, he must insinuate them into his auditory by some trick of eye, tone, or gesture, or he fails. *He must be thinking all the while of his appearance, because he knows that all the while the spectators are judging of it.* And this is the way to represent the shy, negligent, retiring Hamlet. . . .

Among the distinguishing features of that wonderful character, one of the most interesting (yet painful) is that soreness of mind which makes him treat the intrusions of Polonius with harshness, and that asperity which he puts on in his interviews with Ophelia. These tokens of an unhinged mind (if they be not mixed in the latter case with a profound artifice of love, to alienate Ophelia by affected discourtesies, so to prepare her mind for the breaking off of that loving intercourse, which can no longer find a place amidst business so serious as that which he has to do) are parts of his character, which to reconcile with our admiration of Hamlet, the most patient consideration of his situation is no more than necessary; they are what we *forgive afterwards,* and explain by the whole of his character, but *at the time* they are harsh and unpleasant. Yet such is the actor's necessity of giving strong blows to the audience, that I have never seen a player in this character who did not exaggerate and strain to the utmost these ambiguous features,—these temporary deformities in the character. They make him express a vulgar scorn at Polonius, which utterly degrades his gentility, and which no explanation can render palatable; they make him show contempt, and curl up the nose at Ophelia's father,—contempt in its very grossest and most hateful form; but they get applause by it: it is natural, people say; that is, the words are scornful, and the actor expresses scorn, and that they can judge of: but why so much scorn, and of that sort, they never think of asking.

So to Ophelia.—All the Hamlets that I have ever seen, rant and rave at her as if she had committed some great crime, and the audience are highly pleased, because the words of the part are satirical, and they are enforced by the strongest expression of satirical indignation of which the face and voice are capable. But then, whether Hamlet is likely to have put on such brutal appearances to a lady whom he loved so dearly, is never thought on. The truth is that in all such deep affections as had subsisted between Hamlet and Ophelia, there is a stock of *supererogatory love* (if I may venture to use the expression), which in any great grief of heart, especially where that which preys upon the mind cannot be communicated, confers a kind of indulgence upon the grieved party to express itself, even to its heart's dearest object, in the language of a temporary alienation; but it is not alienation, it is a distraction purely, and so it always makes itself to be felt by that object: it is not anger, but grief assuming the appearance of anger,—love awkwardly counterfeiting hate, as sweet countenances when they try to frown: but such sternness and fierce disgust as Hamlet is made to show is no counterfeit, but the real face of absolute aversion,—of irreconcilable alienation. It may be said he puts on the madman; but then he should only so far put on this counterfeit lunacy as his own real distraction will give him leave; that is, incompletely, imperfectly; not in that confirmed practiced way, like a master of his art, or, as Dame Quickly would say, "like one of those harlotry players." . . .

The truth is, the characters of Shakspeare are so much the objects of meditation rather than of interest or curiosity as to their actions, that while we are reading any of his great criminal characters,—Macbeth, Richard, even Iago,—we think not so much of the crimes which they commit, as of the ambition, the aspiring spirit, the intellectual activity, which prompts them to overleap those moral fences. . . .

But when we see these things represented, the acts which they do are comparatively everything, their impulses nothing. The state of sublime emotion into which we are elevated by those images of night and horror which Macbeth is made to utter, that solemn prelude with which he entertains the time till the bell shall strike which is to call him to murder Duncan,—when we no longer read it in a book, when we have given up that vantageground of abstraction which reading possesses over seeing, and come to see a man in his bodily shape before our eyes actually preparing to commit a murder, if the acting be true and impressive, as I have witnessed it in Mr. K.'s performance of that part, the painful anxiety about the act, the natural longing to prevent it while it yet seems unperpetrated, the too close pressing semblance of reality, give a pain and an uneasiness which totally destroy all the delight which the words in the book convey, where the deed doing never presses upon us with the painful sense of presence: it rather seems to belong to history,—to something past and inevitable, if it has anything to do with time at all. The sublime images, the poetry alone, is that which is present to our minds in the reading.

So to see Lear acted,—to see an old man tottering about the stage with a walkingstick, turned out of doors by his daughters in a rainy night, has nothing in it but what is painful and disgusting. We want to take him into shelter and relieve him. That is all the feeling which the acting of Lear ever produced in me. But the Lear of Shakspeare cannot be acted. The contemptible machinery by which they mimic the storm which he goes out in, is not more inadequate to represent the horrors of the real elements, than any actor can be to represent Lear: they might more easily propose to personate the Satan of Milton upon a stage, or one of Michael Angelo's terrible figures. The greatness of Lear is not in corporal dimension, but in intellectual: the explosions of his passion are terrible as a volcano: they are storms turning up and disclosing to the bottom that sea, his mind, with all its vast riches. It is his mind which is laid bare. This case of flesh and blood seems too insignificant to be thought on; even as he himself neglects it. On the stage we see nothing but corporal infirmities and weakness, the impotence of rage; while we read it, we see not Lear, but we are Lear,—we are in his mind, we are sustained by a grandeur which baffles the malice of daughters and storms; in the aberrations of his reason, we discover a mighty irregular power of reasoning, immethodized from the ordinary purposes of life, but exerting its powers, as the wind blows where it listeth, at will upon the corruptions and abuses of mankind. What have looks, or tones, to do with that sublime identification of his age with that of the *heavens themselves,* when in his reproaches to them for conniving at the injustice of his children, he reminds them that "they themselves are old"? What gesture shall be appropriate to this? What has the voice or the eye to do with such things? But the play is beyond all art, as the tamperings with it show: it is too hard and stony; it must have love-scenes, and a happy ending. It is not enough that Cordelia is a daughter; she must shine as a lover too. Tate has put his hook in the nostrils of this Leviathan, for Garrick and his followers, the showmen of the scene, to draw the mighty beast about more easily. A happy ending!—as if the living martyrdom that Lear had gone through,—the flaying of his feelings alive, did not make a fair dismissal from the stage of life the only decorous thing for him. If he is to live and be happy after, if he could sustain this world's burden after, why all this pudder and preparation,—why torment us with all this unnecessary sympathy? As if the childish pleasure of getting his gilt robes and sceptre again could tempt him to act over again his misused station,—as if at his years, and with his experience, anything was left but to die! . . .

1811   1811

MODERN GALLANTRY

In comparing modern with ancient manners, we are pleased to compliment ourselves upon the point of gallantry; a certain obsequiousness, or deferential respect, which we are supposed to pay to females, as females.

I shall believe that this principle actuates our conduct, when I can forget, that in the nineteenth century of the era from which we date our civility, we are but just beginning to leave off the very frequent practice of whipping females in public, in common with the coarsest male offenders.

I shall believe it to be influential, when I can shut my eyes to the fact, that in England women are still occasionally—hanged.

I shall believe in it, when actresses are no longer subject to be hissed off a stage by gentlemen.

I shall believe in it, when Dorimant hands a fish-wife across the kennel; or assists the apple-woman to pick up her wandering fruit, which some unlucky dray has just dissipated.

I shall believe in it, when the Dorimants in humbler life, who would be thought in their way notable adepts in this refinement, shall act upon it in places where they are not known, or think themselves not observed—when I shall see the traveler for some rich tradesman part with his admired box-coat, to spread it over the defenseless shoulders of the poor woman, who is passing to her parish on the roof of the same stage-coach with him, drenched in the rain —when I shall no longer see a woman standing up in the pit of a London theater, till she is sick and faint with the exertion, with men about her, seated at their ease, and jeering at her distress; till one, that seems to have more manners or conscience than the rest, significantly declares "she should be welcome to his seat, if she were a little younger and handsomer." Place this dapper warehouseman, or that rider, in a circle of their own female acquaintance, and you shall confess you have not seen a politer-bred man in Lothbury.

Lastly, I shall begin to believe that there is some such principle influencing our conduct, when more than one-half of the drudgery and coarse servitude of the world shall cease to be performed by women.

Until that day comes, I shall never believe this boasted point to be anything more than a conventional fiction; a pageant got up between the sexes, in a certain rank, and at a certain time of life, in which both find their account equally.

I shall be even disposed to rank it among the salutary fictions of life, when in polite circles I shall see the same attentions paid to age as to youth, to homely features as to handsome, to coarse complexions as to clear—to the woman, as she is a woman, not as she is a beauty, a fortune, or a title.

I shall believe it to be something more than a name, when a well-dressed gentleman in a well-dressed company can advert to the topic of *female old age* without exciting, and intending to excite, a sneer:— when the phrases "antiquated virginity," and such a one has "overstood her market," pronounced in good company, shall raise immediate offence in man, or woman, that shall hear them spoken.

Joseph Paice, of Bread-street-hill, merchant, and one of the Directors of the South-Sea company—the same to whom Edwards, the Shakspeare commentator, has addressed a fine sonnet—was the only pattern of consistent gallantry I have met with. He took me under his shelter at an early age, and bestowed some pains upon me. I owe to his precepts and example whatever there is of the man of business (and that is not much) in my composition. It was not his fault that I did not profit more. Though bred a Presbyterian, and brought up a merchant, he was the finest gentleman of his time. He had not *one* system of attention to females in the drawing-room, and *another* in the shop, or at the stall. I do not mean that he made no distinction. But he never lost sight of sex, or overlooked it in the casualties of a disadvantageous situation. I have seen him stand bare-headed—smile if you please— to a poor servant girl, while she has been inquiring of him the way to some street— in such a posture of unforced civility, as neither to embarrass her in the acceptance, nor himself in the offer, of it. He was no dangler, in the common acceptation of the word, after women; but he reverenced and upheld, in every form in which it came before him, *womanhood.* I have seen him —nay, smile not—tenderly escorting a market-woman, whom he had encountered in a shower, exalting his umbrella over her poor basket of fruit, that it might receive no damage, with as much carefulness as if she had been a Countess. To the reverend form of Female Eld he would yield the wall (though it were to an ancient beggar-woman) with more ceremony than we can afford to show our grandams. He was the Preux Chevalier of Age; the Sir Calidore, or Sir Tristan, to those who have no Calidores or Tristans to defend them. The roses, that had long faded thence, still bloomed for him in those withered and yellow cheeks.

He was never married, but in his youth he paid his addresses to the beautiful Susan Winstanley—old Winstanley's daughter of Clapton—who dying in the early days of their courtship, confirmed in him the resolution of perpetual bachelorship. It was during their short courtship, he told me, that he had been one day treating his mistress with a profusion of civil speeches— the common gallantries—to which kind of thing she had hitherto manifested no repugnance—but in this instance with no effect. He could not obtain from her a

decent acknowledgment in return. She rather seemed to resent his compliments. He could not set it down to caprice, for the lady had always shown herself above that littleness. When he ventured on the following day, finding her a little better humored, to expostulate with her on her coldness of yesterday, she confessed, with her usual frankness, that she had no sort of dislike to his attentions; that she could even endure some high-flown compliments; that a young woman placed in her situation had a right to expect all sort of civil things said to her; that she hoped she could digest a dose of adulation, short of insincerity, with as little injury to her humility as most young women: but that—a little before he had commenced his compliments —she had overheard him by accident, in rather rough language, rating a young woman, who had not brought home his cravats quite to the appointed time, and she thought to herself, "As I am Miss Susan Winstanley, and a young lady—a reputed beauty, and known to be a fortune,—I can have my choice of the finest speeches from the mouth of this very fine gentleman who is courting me—but if I had been poor Mary Such-a-one (*naming the milliner*)— and had failed of bringing home the cravats to the appointed hour—though perhaps I had sat up half the night to forward them —what sort of compliments should I have received then?—And my woman's pride came to my assistance; and I thought, that if it were only to do *me* honor, a female, like myself, might have received handsomer usage: and I was determined not to accept any fine speeches, to the compromise of that sex, the belonging to which was after all my strongest claim and title to them."

I think the lady discovered both generosity, and a just way of thinking, in this rebuke which she gave her lover; and I have sometimes imagined, that the uncommon strain of courtesy, which through life regulated the actions and behavior of my friend towards all of woman kind indiscriminately, owed its happy origin to this seasonable lesson from the lips of his lamented mistress.

I wish the whole female world would entertain the same notion of these things that Miss Winstanley showed. Then we should see something of the spirit of consistent gallantry; and no longer witness the anomaly of the same man—a pattern of true politeness to a wife—of cold contempt, or rudeness, to a sister—the idolater of his female mistress—the disparager and despiser of his no less female aunt, or unfortunate—still female—maiden cousin. Just so much respect as a woman derogates from her own sex, in whatever condition placed—her handmaid, or dependent—she deserves to have diminished from herself on that score; and probably will feel the diminution, when youth, and beauty, and advantages, not inseparable from sex, shall lose of their attraction. What a woman should demand of a man in courtship, or after it, is first—respect for her as she is a woman;—and next to that—to be respected by him above all other women. But let her stand upon her female character as upon a foundation; and let the attentions, incident to individual preference, be so many pretty additaments and ornaments—as many, and as fanciful, as you please—to that main structure. Let her first lesson be—with sweet Susan Winstanley—to *reverence her sex.*

1822

DREAM-CHILDREN:
A REVERIE

Children love to listen to stories about their elders, when *they* were children; to stretch their imagination to the conception of a traditionary great-uncle or grandame, whom they never saw. It was in this spirit that my little ones crept about me the other evening to hear about their great-grandmother Field, who lived in a great house in Norfolk (a hundred times bigger than that in which they and papa lived) which had been the scene—so at least it was generally believed in that part of the country—of the tragic incidents which they had lately become familiar with from the ballad of the Children in the Wood. Certain it is that the whole story of the children and their cruel uncle was to be seen fairly carved out in wood upon the chimney-piece of the great hall, the whole story down to the Robin Redbreasts, till a foolish rich person pulled it down to set up a marble one of modern invention in its stead, with no story upon it. Here Alice put out one of her dear mother's looks, too tender to be called upbraiding. Then I went on to say, how religious and how good their great-grandmother Field was, how beloved and respected by everybody, though she was not indeed the mistress of this great house, but had only the charge of it (and yet in some respects she might be said to be the mistress of it too) committed to her by the owner, who preferred living in a newer and more fashionable mansion which he had purchased somewhere in the adjoining county; but still she lived in it in a manner as if it had been her own, and kept up the dignity of the great house in a sort while she lived, which afterwards came to decay, and was nearly pulled down, and all its old ornaments stripped and carried away to the owner's other house, where they were set up, and looked as awkward as if some one were to carry away the old tombs they had seen lately at the Abbey, and stick them up in Lady C.'s tawdry gilt drawing-room. Here John smiled, as much as to say, "that would be foolish indeed." And then I told how, when she came to die, her funeral was attended by a concourse of all the poor, and some of the gentry too, of the neighborhood for many miles round, to show their respect for her memory, because she had been such a good and religious woman; so good indeed that she knew all the Psaltery by heart, ay, and a great part of the Testament besides. Here little Alice spread her hands. Then I told what a tall, upright, graceful person their great-grandmother Field once was; and how in her youth she was esteemed the best dancer—here Alice's little right foot played an involuntary movement, till, upon my looking grave, it desisted—the best dancer, I was saying, in the county, till a cruel disease, called a cancer, came, and bowed her down with pain; but it could never bend her good spirits, or make them stoop, but they were still upright, because she was so good and religious. Then I told how she was used to sleep by herself in a lone chamber of the great lone house; and how she believed that an apparition of two infants was to be seen at midnight gliding up and down the great stair-case near where she slept, but she said "those innocents would do her no harm"; and how frightened I used to be, though in those days I had my maid to sleep with me, because I was never half so good or religious as she—and yet I never saw the infants. Here John expanded all his eyebrows and tried to look courageous. Then I told how good she was to all her grand-children, having us to the great house in the holydays, where I in particular used to spend many hours by myself, in gazing upon the old busts of the Twelve Cæsars, that had been Emperors of Rome, till the old marble heads would seem to live again, or I to be turned into marble with them; how I never could be tired with roaming about that huge mansion, with its vast empty rooms, with their worn-out hangings, fluttering tapestry, and carved oaken panels, with the gilding almost rubbed out —sometimes in the spacious old-fashioned gardens, which I had almost to myself, unless when now and then a solitary gardening man would cross me—and how the nectarines and peaches hung upon the walls, without my ever offering to pluck them, because they were forbidden fruit, unless now and then,—and because I had more pleasure in strolling about among the old melancholy-looking yew trees, or the firs, and picking up the red berries, and the fir apples, which were good for nothing but to look at—or in lying about upon the fresh grass, with all the fine garden smells around me—or basking in the orangery, till I could almost fancy myself ripening too along with the oranges and the limes in that grateful warmth—or in watching the dace that darted to and fro in the fish-pond, at the bottom of the garden, with here and there a great sulky pike hanging midway down the water in silent state, as if it mocked at their impertinent friskings,—I had more pleasure in these busy-idle diversions than in all the sweet flavors of peaches, nectarines, oranges, and such like common baits of children. Here John slyly deposited back upon the plate a bunch of grapes, which, not unobserved by Alice, he had meditated dividing with her, and both seemed willing to relinquish them for the present as irrelevant. Then in somewhat a more heightened tone, I told how, though their great-grandmother Field loved all her grand-children, yet in an especial manner she might be said to love their uncle, John L——, because he was so handsome and spirited a youth, and a king to the rest of us; and, instead of moping about in solitary corners, like some of us, he would mount the most mettlesome horse he could get, when but an imp no bigger than themselves, and make it carry him half over the county in a morning, and join the hunters when there were any out—and yet he loved the old great house and gardens, too, but had too much spirit to be always pent up within their boundaries—and how their uncle grew up to man's estate as brave as he was handsome, to the admiration of everybody, but of their great-grandmother Field most especially; and how he used to carry me upon his back when I was a lame-footed boy—for he was a good bit older than me—many a mile when I could not

walk for pain;—and how in after life he became lame-footed, too, and I did not always (I fear) make allowances enough for him when he was impatient, and in pain, nor remember sufficiently how considerate he had been to me when I was lame-footed; and how when he died, though he had not been dead an hour, it seemed as if he had died a great while ago, such a distance there is betwixt life and death; and how I bore his death as I thought pretty well at first, but afterwards it haunted and haunted me; and though I did not cry or take it to heart as some do, and as I think he would have done if I had died, yet I missed him all day long, and knew not till then how much I had loved him. I missed his kindness, and I missed his crossness, and wished him to be alive again, to be quarreling with him (for we quarreled sometimes), rather than not have him again, and was as uneasy without him, as he their poor uncle must have been when the doctor took off his limb. Here the children fell a-crying, and asked if their little mourning which they had on was not for uncle John, and they looked up, and prayed me not to go on about their uncle, but to tell them some stories about their pretty dead mother. Then I told how for seven long years, in hope sometimes, sometimes in despair, yet persisting ever, I courted the fair Alice W——n; and, as much as children could understand, I explained to them what coyness, and difficulty, and denial meant in maidens—when suddenly, turning to Alice, the soul of the first Alice looked out at her eyes with such a reality of re-presentment, that I became in doubt which of them stood there before me, or whose that bright hair was; and while I stood gazing, both the children gradually grew fainter to my view, receding, and still receding till nothing at last but two mournful features were seen in the uttermost distance, which, without speech, strangely impressed upon me the effects of speech; "We are not of Alice, nor of thee, nor are we children at all. The children of Alice call Bartrum father. We are nothing; less than nothing, and dreams. We are only what might have been, and must wait upon the tedious shores of Lethe millions of ages before we have existence, and a name"—and immediately awakening, I found myself quietly seated in my bachelor armchair, where I had fallen asleep, with the faithful Bridget unchanged by my side—but John L. (or James Elia) was gone for ever.

1822

A DISSERTATION UPON ROAST PIG

Mankind, says a Chinese manuscript, which my friend M. was obliging enough to read and explain to me, for the first seventy thousand ages ate their meat raw, clawing or biting it from the living animal, just as they do in Abyssinia to this day. This period is not obscurely hinted at by their great Confucius in the second chapter of his *Mundane Mutations,* where he designates a kind of golden age by the term Cho-fang, literally the Cooks' Holiday. The manuscript goes on to say, that the art of roasting, or rather broiling (which I take to be the elder brother) was accidentally discovered in the manner following. The swineherd, Ho-ti, having gone out into the woods one morning, as his manner was, to collect mast for his hogs, left his cottage in the care of his eldest son Bo-bo, a great lubberly boy, who being fond of playing with fire, as younkers of his age commonly are, let some sparks escape into a bundle of straw, which kindling quickly, spread the conflagration over every part of their poor mansion, till it was reduced to ashes. Together with the cottage (a sorry antediluvian make-shift of a building, you may think it), what was of much more importance, a fine litter of new-farrowed pigs, no less than nine in number, perished. China pigs have been esteemed a luxury all over the East from the remotest periods that we read of. Bo-bo was in the utmost consternation, as you may think, not so much for the sake of the tenement, which his father and he could easily build up again with a few dry branches, and the labor of an hour or two, at any time, as for the loss of the pigs. While he was thinking what he should say to his father, and wringing his hands over the smoking remnants of one of those untimely sufferers, an odor assailed his nostrils, unlike any scent which he had before experienced. What could it proceed from?—not from the burnt cottage—he had smelt that smell before—indeed, this was by no means the first accident of the kind which had occurred through the negligence of this unlucky young fire brand. Much less did it resemble that of any known herb, weed, or flower. A premonitory moistening at the same time overflowed his nether lip. He knew not what to think. He next stooped down to feel the pig, if there were any signs of life in it. He burnt his fingers, and to cool them he applied them in his booby fashion to his mouth. Some of the crumbs of the scorched skin had come away with his fingers, and for the first time in his life (in the world's life indeed, for before him no man had known it) he tasted—*crackling!* Again he felt and fumbled at the pig. It did not burn him so much now, still he licked his fingers from a sort of habit. The truth at length broke into his slow understanding, that it was the pig that smelt so, and the pig that tasted so delicious; and, surrendering himself up to the new-born pleasure, he fell to tearing up whole handfuls of the scorched skin with the flesh next it, and was cramming it down his throat in his beastly fashion, when his sire entered amid the smoking rafters, armed with retributory cudgel, and finding how affairs stood, began to rain blows upon the young rogue's shoulders, as thick as hail stones, which Bo-bo heeded not any more than if they had been flies. The tickling pleasure, which he experienced in his lower regions, had rendered him quite callous to any inconveniences he might feel in those remote quarters. His father might lay on, but he could not beat him from his pig, till he had fairly made an end of it, when, becoming a little more sensible of his situation, something like the following dialogue ensued.

"You graceless whelp, what have you got there devouring? Is it not enough that you have burnt me down three houses with your dog's tricks, and be hanged to you! but you must be eating fire, and I know not what—what have you got there, I say?"

"O father, the pig, the pig, do come and taste how nice the burnt pig eats."

The ears of Ho-ti tingled with terror. He cursed his son, and he cursed himself that ever he should beget a son that should eat burnt pig.

Bo-bo, whose scent was wonderfully sharpened since morning, soon raked out another pig, and fairly rending it asunder, thrust the lesser half by main force into the fists of Ho-ti, still shouting out "Eat, eat, eat the burnt pig, father, only taste—O Lord!"—with such-like barbarous ejaculations, cramming all the while as if he would choke.

Ho-ti trembled in every joint while he grasped the abominable thing, wavering whether he should not put his son to death for an unnatural young monster, when the crackling scorching his fingers, as it had done his son's, and applying the same remedy to them, he in his turn tasted some of its flavor, which, make what sour mouths he would for a pretence, proved not altogether displeasing to him. In conclusion (for the manuscript here is a little tedious) both father and son fairly sat down to the mess, and never left off till they had despatched all that remained of the litter.

Bo-bo was strictly enjoined not to let the secret escape, for the neighbors would certainly have stoned them for a couple of abominable wretches, who could think of improving upon the good meat which God had sent them. Nevertheless, strange stories got about. It was observed that Ho-ti's cottage was burnt down now more frequently than ever. Nothing but fires from this time forward. Some would break out in broad day, others in the nighttime. As often as the sow farrowed, so sure was the house of Ho-ti to be in a blaze; and Ho-ti himself, which was the more remarkable, instead of chastising his son, seemed to grow more indulgent to him than ever. At length they were watched, the terrible mystery discovered, and father and son summoned to take their trial at Pekin, then an inconsiderable assize town. Evidence was given, the obnoxious food itself produced in court, and verdict about to be pronounced, when the foreman of the jury begged that some of the burnt pig, of which the culprits stood accused, might be handed into the box. He handled it, and they all handled it, and burning their fingers, as Bo-bo and his father had done before them, and nature prompting to each of them the same remedy, against the face of all the facts, and the clearest charge which judge had ever given—to the surprise of the whole court, townsfolk, strangers, reporters, and all present—without leaving the box, or any manner of consultation whatever, they brought in a simultaneous verdict of Not Guilty.

The judge, who was a shrewd fellow, winked at the manifest iniquity of the decision; and, when the court was dismissed, went privily, and bought up all the pigs that could be had for love or money. In a few days his Lordship's town house was observed to be on fire. The thing took wing, and now there was nothing to be seen but fires in every direction. Fuel and pigs grew enormously dear all over the district. The insurance-offices one and all shut up shop. People built slighter and slighter every day, until it was feared that the very science of architecture would in no long time be lost to the world. Thus this custom of firing houses continued, till in process of time, says my manuscript, a

sage arose, like our Locke, who made a discovery, that the flesh of swine, or indeed of any other animal, might be cooked (*burnt,* as they called it) without the necessity of consuming a whole house to dress it. Then first began the rude form of a gridiron. Roasting by the string, or spit, came in a century or two later; I forget in whose dynasty. By such slow degrees, concludes the manuscript, do the most useful, and seemingly the most obvious arts, make their way among mankind.

Without placing too implicit faith in the account above given, it must be agreed, that if a worthy pretext for so dangerous an experiment as setting houses on fire (especially in these days) could be assigned in favor of any culinary object, that pretext and excuse might be found in ROAST PIG.

Of all the delicacies in the whole *mundus edibilis,* I will maintain it to be the most delicate—*princeps obsoniorum.*

I speak not of your grown porkers—things between pig and pork—those hobbledehoys—but a young and tender suckling—under a moon old—guiltless as yet of the sty—with no original speck of the *amor immunditiæ,* the hereditary failing of the first parent, yet manifest—his voice as yet not broken, but something between a childish treble, and a grumble—the mild forerunner, or *præludium,* of a grunt.

He must be roasted. I am not ignorant that our ancestors ate them seethed, or boiled—but what a sacrifice of the exterior tegument!

There is no flavor comparable, I will contend, to that of the crisp, tawny, well-watched, not overroasted, *crackling,* as it is well called—the very teeth are invited to their share of the pleasure at this banquet in overcoming the coy, brittle resistance—with the adhesive oleaginous—O call it not fat!—but an indefinable sweetness growing up to it—the tender blossoming of fat—fat cropped in the bud—taken in the shoot —in the first innocence—the cream and quintessence of the child-pig's yet pure food—the lean, no lean, but a kind of animal manna—or, rather, fat and lean (if it must be so) blended and running into each other, that both together make but one ambrosian result or common substance.

Behold him while he is doing—it seemeth rather a refreshing warmth, than a scorching heat, that he is so passive to. How equably he twirleth round the string! —Now he is just done. To see the extreme sensibility of that tender age! he hath wept out his pretty eyes—radiant jellies—shooting stars.—

See him in the dish, his second cradle, how meek he lieth!—wouldst thou have had this innocent grow up to the grossness and indocility which too often accompany maturer swinehood? Ten to one he would have proved a glutton, a sloven, an obstinate, disagreeable animal—wallowing in all manner of filthy conversation—from these sins he is happily snatched away—

> Ere sin could blight, or sorrow fade,
> Death came with timely care——

his memory is odoriferous—no clown curseth, while his stomach half rejecteth, the rank bacon—no coal-heaver bolteth him in reeking sausages—he hath a fair sepulchre in the grateful stomach of the judicious epicure—and for such a tomb might be content to die.

He is the best of sapors. Pine-apple is great. She is indeed almost too transcendent—a delight, if not sinful, yet so like to sinning, that really a tender-conscienced person would do well to pause—too ravishing for mortal taste, she woundeth and excoriateth the lips that approach her—like lovers' kisses, she biteth—she is a pleasure bordering on pain from the fierceness and insanity of her relish—but she stoppeth at the palate—she meddleth not with the appetite—and the coarsest hunger might barter her consistently for a mutton chop.

Pig—let me speak his praise—is no less provocative of the appetite, than he is satisfactory to the criticalness of the censorious palate. The strong man may batten on him, and the weakling refuseth not his mild juices.

Unlike to mankind's mixed characters, a bundle of virtues and vices, inexplicably intertwisted, and not to be unravelled without hazard, he is—good throughout. No part of him is better or worse than another. He helpeth, as far as his little means extend, all around. He is the least envious of banquets. He is all neighbors' fare.

I am one of those who freely and ungrudgingly impart a share of the good things of this life which fall to their lot (few as mine are in this kind), to a friend. I protest I take as great an interest in my friend's pleasures, his relishes, and proper satisfactions, as in mine own. "Presents," I often say, "endear Absents." Hares, pheasants, partridges, snipes, barn-door chickens (those "tame Villatic fowl"), capons, plovers, brawn, barrels of oysters, I dispense as freely as I receive them. I love to taste them, as it were, upon the tongue of my friend. But a stop must be put somewhere. One would not, like Lear, "give everything." I make my stand upon pig. Methinks it is an ingratitude to the Giver of all good flavors, to extra-domiciliate, or send out of the house, slightingly (under pretext of friendship, or I know not what), a blessing so particularly adapted, predestined, I may say, to my individual palate.—It argues an insensibility.

I remember a touch of conscience in this kind at school. My good old aunt, who never parted from me at the end of a holiday without stuffing a sweetmeat, or some nice thing, into my pocket, had dismissed me one evening with a smoking plum-cake, fresh from the oven. In my way to school (it was over London bridge) a gray-headed old beggar saluted me (I have no doubt at this time of day that he was a counterfeit). I had no pence to console him with, and in the vanity of self-denial, and the very coxcombry of charity, school-boy-like, I made him a present of—the whole cake! I walked on a little, buoyed up, as one is on such occasions, with a sweet soothing of self-satisfaction; but before I had got to the end of the bridge, my better feelings returned, and I burst into tears, thinking how ungrateful I had been to my good aunt, to go and give her good gift away to a stranger, that I had never seen before, and who might be a bad man for aught I knew; and then I thought of the pleasure my aunt would be taking in thinking that I—I myself, and not another—would eat her nice cake—and what should I say to her the next time I saw her—how naughty I was to part with her pretty present!—and the odor of that spicy cake came back upon my recollection, and the pleasure and the curiosity I had taken in seeing her make it, and her joy when she sent it to the oven, and how disappointed she would feel that I had never had a bit of it in my mouth at last—and I blamed my impertinent spirit of alms-giving, and out-of-place hypocrisy of goodness; and above all I wished never to see the face again of that insidious, good-for-nothing, old gray impostor.

Our ancestors were nice in their method of sacrificing these tender victims. We read of pigs whipt to death with something of a shock, as we hear of any other obsolete custom. The age of discipline is gone by, or it would be curious to inquire (in a philosophical light merely) what effect this process might have towards intenerating and dulcifying a substance, naturally so mild and dulcet as the flesh of young pigs. It looks like refining a violet. Yet we should be cautious, while we condemn the inhumanity, how we censure the wisdom of the practice. It might impart a gusto.—

I remember an hypothesis, argued upon by the young students, when I was at St. Omer's and maintained with much learning and pleasantry on both sides, "Whether, supposing that the flavor of a pig who obtained his death by whipping (*per flagellationem extremam*) super-added a pleasure upon the palate of a man more intense than any possible suffering we can conceive in the animal, is man justified in using that method of putting the animal to death?" I forget the decision.

His sauce should be considered. Decidedly, a few bread crumbs, done up with his liver and brains, and a dash of wild sage. But, banish, dear Mrs. Cook, I beseech you, the whole onion tribe. Barbecue your whole hogs to your palate, steep them in shallots, stuff them out with plantations of the rank and guilty garlic; you cannot poison them, or make them stronger than they are—but consider, he is a weakling—a flower.

1822

OLD CHINA

I have an almost feminine partiality for old china. When I go to see any great house, I inquire for the china-closet, and next for the picture-gallery. I cannot defend the order of preference, but by saying that we have all some taste or other, of too ancient a date to admit of our remembering distinctly that it was an acquired one. I can call to mind the first play, and the first exhibition, that I was taken to; but I am not conscious of a time when china jars and saucers were introduced into my imagination.

I had no repugnance then—why should I now have?—to those little, lawless, azure-tinctured grotesques, that, under the notion of men and women, float about, uncircumscribed by any element, in that world before perspective—a china tea-cup.

I like to see my old friends—whom distance cannot diminish—figuring up in the air (so they appear to our optics), yet on terra firma still—for so we must in courtesy interpret that speck of deeper blue, which the decorous artist, to prevent absurdity, had made to spring up beneath their sandals.

I love the men with women's faces, and the women, if possible, with still more womanish expressions.

Here is a young and courtly Mandarin, handing tea to a lady from a salver—two miles off. See how distance seems to set off respect! And here the same lady, or another—for likeness is identity on tea-cups—is stepping into a little fairy boat, moored on the hither side of this calm garden river, with a dainty mincing foot, which in a right angle of incidence (as angles go in our world) must infallibly land her in the midst of a flowery mead—a furlong off on the other side of the same strange stream! Farther on—if far or near can be predicated of their world—see horses, trees, pagodas, dancing the hays.

Here—a cow and rabbit couchant, and co-extensive—so objects show, seen through the lucid atmosphere of fine Cathay.

I was pointing out to my cousin last evening, over our Hyson, (which we are old-fashioned enough to drink unmixed still of an afternoon), some of these *speciosa miracula* upon a set of extraordinary old blue china (a recent purchase) which we were now for the first time using; and could not help remarking, how favorable circumstances had been to us of late years, that we could afford to please the eye sometimes with trifles of this sort—when a passing sentiment seemed to overshade the brows of my companion. I am quick at detecting these summer clouds in Bridget.

"I wish the good old times would come again," she said, "when we were not quite so rich. I do not mean that I want to be poor; but there was a middle state"—so she was pleased to ramble on,—"in which I am sure we were a great deal happier. A purchase is but a purchase, now that you have money enough and to spare. Formerly it used to be a triumph. When we coveted a cheap luxury (and, O! how much ado I had to get you to consent in those times!) —we were used to have a debate two or three days before, and to weigh the for and against, and think what we might spare it out of, and what saving we could hit upon, that should be an equivalent. A thing was worth buying then, when we felt the money that we paid for it.

"Do you remember the brown suit, which you made to hang upon you, till all your friends cried shame upon you, it grew so threadbare—and all because of that folio Beaumont and Fletcher, which you dragged home late at night from Barker's in Covent Garden? Do you remember how we eyed it for weeks before we could make up our minds to the purchase, and had not come to a determination till it was near ten o'clock of the Saturday night, when you set off from Islington, fearing you should be too late—and when the old bookseller with some grumbling opened his shop, and by the twinkling taper (for he was setting bedwards) lighted out the relic from his dusty treasures—and when you lugged it home, wishing it were twice as cumbersome —and when you presented it to me—and when we were exploring the perfectness of it (collating, you called it)—and while I was repairing some of the loose leaves with paste, which your impatience would not suffer to be left till day-break—was there no pleasure in being a poor man? or can those neat black clothes which you wear now, and are so careful to keep brushed, since we have become rich and finical— give you half the honest vanity, with which you flaunted it about in that overworn suit —your old corbeau—for four or five weeks longer than you should have done, to pacify your conscience for the mighty sum of fifteen—or sixteen shillings was it?—a great affair we thought it then—which you had lavished on the old folio. Now you can afford to buy any book that pleases you, but I do not see that you ever bring me home any nice old purchases now.

"When you came home with twenty apologies for laying out a less number of shillings upon that print after Leonardo, which we christened the 'Lady Blanch'; when you looked at the purchase, and thought of the money—and thought of the money, and looked again at the picture— was there no pleasure in being a poor man? Now, you have nothing to do but walk into Colnaghi's, and buy a wilderness of Leonardos. Yet do you?

"Then, do you remember our pleasant walks to Enfield, and Potter's Bar, and Waltham, when we had a holiday—holiday and all other fun are gone now we are rich—and the little hand-basket in which I used to deposit our day's fare of savory cold lamb and salad—and how you would pry about at noon-tide for some decent house, where we might go in, and produce our store—only paying for the ale that you must call for—and speculate upon the looks of the landlady, and whether she was likely to allow us a table-cloth—and wish for such another honest hostess as Izaak Walton has described many a one on the pleasant banks of the Lea, when he went a-fishing—and sometimes they would prove obliging enough, and sometimes they

would look grudgingly upon us—but we had cheerful looks still for one another, and would eat our plain food savorily, scarcely grudging Piscator his Trout Hall? Now, when we go out a day's pleasuring, which is seldom, moreover, we *ride* part of the way—and go into a fine inn, and order the best of dinners, never debating the expense—which, after all, never has half the relish of those chance country snaps, when we were at the mercy of uncertain usage, and a precarious welcome.

"You are too proud to see a play anywhere now but in the pit. Do you remember where it was we used to sit, when we saw the Battle of Hexham, and the Surrender of Calais, and Bannister and Mrs. Bland in the Children in the Wood—when we squeezed out our shillings apiece to sit three or four times in a season in the one-shilling gallery—where you felt all the time that you ought not to have brought me— and more strongly I felt obligation to you for having brought me—and the pleasure was the better for a little shame—and when the curtain drew up, what cared we for our place in the house, or what mattered it where we were sitting, when our thoughts were with Rosalind in Arden, or with Viola at the Court of Illyria? You used to say that the Gallery was the best place of all for enjoying a play socially—that the relish of such exhibitions must be in proportion to the infrequency of going—that the company we met there, not being in general readers of plays, were obliged to attend the more, and did attend, to what was going on, on the stage—because a word lost would have been a chasm, which it was impossible for them to fill up. With such reflections we consoled our pride then— and I appeal to you whether, as a woman, I met generally with less attention and accommodation than I have done since in more expensive situations in the house? The getting in, indeed, and the crowding up those inconvenient staircases, was bad enough—but there was still a law of civility to women recognized to quite as great an extent as we ever found in the other passages—and how a little difficulty overcome heightened the snug seat, and the play, afterwards! Now we can only pay our money and walk in. You cannot see, you say, in the galleries now. I am sure we saw, and heard too, well enough then—but sight and all I think is gone with our poverty.

"There was pleasure in eating strawberries before they became quite common—in the first dish of peas, while they were yet dear—to have them for a nice supper, a treat. What treat can we have now? If we were to treat ourselves now—that is, to have dainties a little above our means, it would be selfish and wicked. It is the very little more that we allow ourselves beyond what the actual poor can get at, that makes what I call a treat—when two people living together, as we have done, now and then indulge themselves in a cheap luxury, which both like; while each apologises, and is willing to take both halves of the blame to his single share. I see no harm in people making much of themselves, in that sense of the word. It may give them a hint how to make much of others. But now— what I mean by the word—we never *do* make much of ourselves. None but the poor can do it. I do not mean the veriest poor of all, but persons as we were, just above poverty.

"I know what you were going to say, that it is mighty pleasant at the end of the year to make all meet,—and much ado we used to have every Thirty-first Night of December to account for our exceedings—many a long face did you make over your puzzled accounts, and in contriving to make it out how we had spent so much—or that we had not spent so much—or that it was impossible we should spend so much next year—and still we found our slender capital decreasing—but then,—betwixt ways, and projects, and compromises of one sort or another, and talk of curtailing this charge, and doing without that for the future—and the hope that youth brings, and laughing spirits (in which you were never poor till now), we pocketed up our loss, and in conclusion, with 'lusty brimmers' (as you used to quote it out of *hearty cheerful Mr. Cotton,* as you called him), we used to welcome in the 'coming guest.' Now we have no reckoning at all at the end of the old year—no flattering promises about the new year doing better for us."

Bridget is so sparing of her speech on most occasions, that when she gets into a rhetorical vein, I am careful how I interrupt it. I could not help however, smiling at the phantom of wealth which her dear imagination had conjured up out of a clear income of a poor —— hundred pounds a year. "It is true we were happier when we were poorer, but we were also younger, my cousin. I am afraid we must put up with the excess, for if we were to shake the superflux into the sea, we should not much mend ourselves. That we had much to

struggle with, as we grew up together, we have reason to be most thankful. It strengthened and knit our compact closer. We could never have been what we have been to each other, if we had always had the sufficiency which you now complain of. The resisting power—those natural dilations of the youthful spirit, which circumstances cannot straiten—with us are long since passed away. Competence to age is supplementary youth; a sorry supplement indeed, but I fear the best that is to be had. We must ride where we formerly walked: live better and lie softer—and shall be wise to do so—than we had means to do in those good old days you speak of. Yet could those days return—could you and I once more walk our thirty miles a day—could Bannister and Mrs. Bland again be young, and you and I be young to see them—could the good old one-shilling gallery days return—they are dreams, my cousin, now—but could you and I at this moment, instead of this quiet argument, by our well-carpeted fireside, sitting on this luxurious sofa—be once more struggling up those inconvenient staircases, pushed about and squeezed, and elbowed by the poorest rabble of poor gallery scramblers—could I once more hear those anxious shrieks of yours—and the delicious *Thank God, we are safe,* which always followed when the topmost stair, conquered, let in the first light of the whole cheerful theatre down beneath us—I know not the fathom line that ever touched a descent so deep as I would be willing to bury more wealth in than Crœsus had, or the great Jew R—— is supposed to have, to purchase it. And now do just look at that merry little Chinese waiter holding an umbrella, big enough for a bed-tester, over the head of that pretty insipid half Madonna-ish chit of a lady in that very blue summer-house."

1823

SANITY OF TRUE GENIUS

So far from the position holding true, that great wit (or genius, in our modern way of speaking) has a necessary alliance with insanity, the greatest wits, on the contrary, will ever be found to be the sanest writers. It is impossible for the mind to conceive of a mad Shakspeare. The greatness of wit, by which the poetic talent is here chiefly to be understood, manifests itself in the admirable balance of all the faculties. Madness is the disproportionate straining or excess of any one of them. "So strong a wit," says Cowley, speaking of a poetical friend,

"——did Nature to him frame,
As all things but his judgment overcame, 5
His judgment like the heavenly moon did show,
Tempering that mighty sea below."

The ground of the mistake is that men, 10 finding in the raptures of the higher poetry a condition of exaltation, to which they have no parallel in their own experience, besides the spurious resemblance of it in dreams and fevers, impute a state of dream- 15 iness and fever to the poet. But the true poet dreams being awake. He is not possessed by his subject, but has dominion over it. In the groves of Eden he walks familiar as in his native paths. He ascends 20 the empyrean heaven, and is not intoxicated. He treads the burning marl without dismay; he wins his flight without self-loss through realms of chaos "and old night." Or if, abandoning himself to that 25 severer chaos of a "human mind untuned," he is content awhile to be mad with Lear, or to hate mankind (a sort of madness) with Timon, neither is that madness, nor this misanthropy, so unchecked, but that,— 30 never letting the reins of reason wholly go, while most he seems to do so,—he has his better genius still whispering at his ear, with the good servant Kent suggesting saner counsels, or with the honest steward 35 Flavius recommending kindlier resolutions. Where he seems most to recede from humanity, he will be found the truest to it. From beyond the scope of Nature if he summon possible existences, he subjugates 40 them to the law of her consistency. He is beautifully loyal to that sovereign directress, even when he appears most to betray and desert her. His ideal tribes submit to policy; his very monsters are tamed to his 45 hand, even as that wild sea-brood, shepherded by Proteus. He tames, and he clothes them with attributes of flesh and blood, till they wonder at themselves, like Indian Islanders forced to submit to Euro- 50 pean vesture. Caliban, the Witches, are as true to the laws of their own nature (ours with a difference), as Othello, Hamlet, and Macbeth. Herein the great and little wits are differenced; that if the latter wan- 55 der ever so little from nature or actual existence, they lose themselves and their readers. Their phantoms are lawless; their visions nightmares. They do not create, which implies shaping and consistency. 60

Their imaginations are not active—for to be active is to call something into act and form—but passive, as men in sick dreams. For the super-natural, or something super-added to what we know of nature, they 5 give you the plainly non-natural. And if this were all, and that these mental hallucinations were discoverable only in the treatment of subjects out of nature, or transcending it, the judgment might with some plea be pardoned if it ran riot, and a little wantonized: but even in the describing of real and everyday life, that which is before their eyes, one of these lesser wits shall more deviate from nature—show more of that inconsequence, which has a natural alliance with frenzy,—than a great genius in his "maddest fits," as Wither somewhere calls them. We appeal to any one that is acquainted with the common run of Lane's novels—as they existed some twenty or thirty years back—those scanty intellectual viands of the whole female reading public, till a happier genius arose, and expelled forever the innutritious phantoms—whether he has not found his brain more "betossed," his memory more puzzled, his sense of when and where more confounded, among the improbable events, the incoherent incidents, the inconsistent characters, or no-characters, of some third-rate love intrigue—where the persons shall be a Lord Glendamour and a Miss Rivers, and the scene only alternate between Bath and Bondstreet—a more bewildering dreaminess induced upon him than he has felt wandering over all the fairy grounds of Spenser. In the productions we refer to, nothing but names and places is familiar; the persons are neither of this world nor of any other conceivable one; an endless string of activities without purpose, of purposes destitute of motive:—we meet phantoms in our known walks; *fantasques* only christened. In the poet we have names which announce fiction; and we have absolutely no place at all, for the things and persons of *The Fairy Queen* prate not of their "whereabout." But in their inner nature, and the law of their speech and actions, we are at home and upon acquainted ground. The one turns life into a dream; the other to the wildest dreams gives the sobrieties of everyday occurrences. By what subtile art of tracing the mental processes it is effected, we are not philosophers enough to explain, but in that wonderful episode of the cave of Mammon, in which the Money God appears first in the lowest form of a miser, is then a worker of metals, and becomes the god of all the treasures of the world; and has a daughter, Ambition, before whom all the world kneels for favors—with the Hesperian fruit, the waters of Tantalus, with Pilate washing his hands vainly, but not impertinently, in the same stream—that we should be at one moment in the cave of an old hoarder of treasures, at the next at the forge of the Cyclops, in a palace and yet in hell, all at once, with the shifting mutations of the most rambling dream, and our judgment yet all the time awake, and neither able nor willing to detect the fallacy,—is a proof of that hidden sanity which still guides the poet in his widest seeming-aberrations.

It is not enough to say that the whole episode is a copy of the mind's conception in sleep; it is, in some sort—but what a copy! Let the most romantic of us, that has been entertained all night with the spectacle of some wild and magnificent vision, recombine it in the morning, and try it by his waking judgment. That which appeared so shifting, and yet so coherent, while that faculty was passive, when it comes under cool examination, shall appear so reasonless and so unlinked, that we are ashamed to have been so deluded; and to have taken, though but in sleep, a monster for a god. But the transitions in this episode are every whit as violent as in the most extravagant dream, and yet the waking judgment ratifies them.

1826

PREFACE TO THE LAST ESSAYS

BY A FRIEND OF THE LATE ELIA

This poor gentleman, who for some months past has been in a declining way, hath at length paid his final tribute to nature.

To say truth, it is time he were gone. The humor of the thing, if ever there was much in it, was pretty well exhausted; and a two years' and a half existence has been a tolerable duration for a phantom.

I am now at liberty to confess, that much which I have heard objected to my late friend's writings was well-founded. Crude they are, I grant you—a sort of unlicked, incondite things—villainously pranked in an affected array of antique modes and phrases. They had not been *his,* if they had been other than such; and better it is,

that a writer should be natural in a self-pleasing quaintness, than to affect a naturalness (so called) that should be strange to him. Egotistical they have been pronounced by some who did not know, that what he tells us, as of himself, was often true only (historically) of another; as in a former Essay (to save many instances)—where under the *first person* (his favorite figure) he shadows forth the forlorn estate of a country-boy placed at a London school, far from his friends and connections —in direct opposition to his own early history. If it be egotism to imply and twine with his own identity the griefs and affections of another—making himself many, or reducing many unto himself—then is the skilful novelist, who all along brings in his hero or heroine, speaking of themselves, the greatest egotist of all; who yet has never, therefore, been accused of that narrowness. And how shall the intenser dramatist escape being faulty, who, doubtless, under cover of passion uttered by another, oftentimes gives blameless vent to his most inward feelings, and expresses his own story modestly?

My late friend was in many respects a singular character. Those who did not like him, hated him; and some, who once liked him, afterwards became his bitterest haters. The truth is, he gave himself too little concern what he uttered, and in whose presence. He observed neither time nor place, and would e'en out with what came uppermost. With the severe religionist he would pass for a free-thinker; while the other faction set him down for a bigot, or persuaded themselves that he belied his sentiments. Few understood him; and I am not certain that at all times he quite understood himself. He too much affected that dangerous figure—irony. He sowed doubtful speeches, and reaped plain, unequivocal hatred. He would interrupt the gravest discussion with some light jest; and yet, perhaps, not quite irrelevant in ears that could understand it. Your long and much talkers hated him. The informal habit of his mind, joined to an inveterate impediment of speech, forbade him to be an orator; and he seemed determined that no one else should play that part when he was present. He was *petit* and ordinary in his person and appearance. I have seen him sometimes in what is called good company, but where he has been a stranger, sit silent, and be suspected for an odd fellow; till some unlucky occasion provoking it, he would stutter out some senseless pun (not altogether senseless, perhaps, if rightly taken), which has stamped his character for the evening. It was hit or miss with him; but nine times out of ten, he contrived by this device to send away a whole company of his enemies. His conceptions rose kindlier than his utterance, and his happiest *impromptus* had the appearance of effort. He has been accused of trying to be witty, when in truth he was but struggling to give his poor thoughts articulation. He chose his companions for some individuality of character which they manifested.—Hence, not many persons of science, and few professed *literati*, were of his councils. They were, for the most part, persons of an uncertain fortune; and, as to such people commonly nothing is more obnoxious than a gentleman of settled (though moderate) income, he passed with most of them for a great miser. To my knowledge this was a mistake. His *intimados,* to confess a truth, were in the world's eye a ragged regiment. He found them floating on the surface of society; and the color, or something else in the weed pleased him. The burrs stuck to him—but they were good and loving burrs for all that. He never greatly cared for the society of what are called good people. If any of these were scandalised (and offenses were sure to arise), he could not help it. When he has been remonstrated with for not making more concessions to the feelings of good people, he would retort by asking, what one point did these good people ever concede to him? He was temperate in his meals and diversions, but always kept a little on this side of abstemiousness. Only in the use of the Indian weed he might be thought a little excessive. He took it, he would say, as a solvent of speech. Marry—

as the friendly vapor ascended, how his prattle would curl up sometimes with it! the ligaments which tongue-tied him, were loosened, and the stammerer proceeded a statist!

I do not know whether I ought to bemoan or rejoice that my old friend is departed. His jests were beginning to grow obsolete, and his stories to be found out. He felt the approaches of age; and while he pretended to cling to life, you saw how slender were the ties left to bind him. Discoursing with him latterly on this subject, he expressed himself with a pettishness, which I thought unworthy of him. In our walks about his suburban retreat (as he called it) at Shacklewell, some children belonging to a school of industry had met us, and bowed and curtseyed, as he thought, in an especial manner to *him.* "They take me for a visiting governor," he muttered eärnestly. He had a horror, which he carried to a foible, of looking like anything important and parochial. He thought that he approached nearer to that stamp daily. He had a general aversion from being treated like a grave or respectable character, and kept a wary eye upon the advances of age that should so entitle him. He herded always, while it was possible, with people younger than himself. He did not conform to the march of time, but was dragged along in the procession. His manners lagged behind his years. He was too much of the boy-man. The *toga virilis* never sate gracefully on his shoulders. The impressions of infancy had burnt into him, and he resented the impertinence of manhood. These were weaknesses; but such as they were, they are a key to explicate some of his writings.

1833

WILLIAM HAZLITT (1778-1830)

To anyone who has made a little progress in criticism himself, to anyone who has either read for himself or is capable of reading for himself, of being guided by what is helpful and of neglecting what is not, there is no greater critic than Hazlitt in any language.

GEORGE SAINTSBURY

Among the romantic critics, Coleridge was the profoundest theorist, but Hazlitt the greatest practitioner. In essays which fill many volumes, he applied the principles of Romanticism to innumerable authors and books, covering more ground than Coleridge, Lamb, or even De Quincey. He lectured and wrote upon almost every important poet, dramatist, and novelist, from Elizabethan times to his own age; and no survey of English literature gives us a more valuable series of critical judgments than Hazlitt provides.

He combined sensitive feelings with a vigorous mind. His life was stormy and full of disappointments. He spent ten years (1798-1808) in vainly trying to become a good painter, but reached only mediocrity in that art. He made an unsuitable marriage, fell in love with a servant-girl, who proved unfaithful to him, was divorced from his first wife, and was deserted by his second. He was intermittently an admirer and friend of Coleridge, Wordsworth, Southey, and especially Lamb; but his emotional outbursts of suspicion or anger tried them sorely, and only Lamb had sufficient charitableness to remain faithful to him unto death. Disillusionment was also the final result of his ardent sympathy with liberal politics. Educated in a sectarian school which exalted freedom in politics and theology, he hoped for the overthrow of the old régimes, through Napoleon particularly; and he was embittered by the conservative reaction which followed Napoleon's defeat at Waterloo (1815). Hence his occasional cynicism,—a prose counterpart to Byron's; hence too that understanding of melancholy which adds so much to his characterization of Hamlet. Most of his mistakes in judgment occurred when he was blinded by political partisanship.

Life taught Hazlitt something of the complexity of human nature and of the intermixture of good and bad motives; and he raised the standards of literary judgment by insisting that to be great (like Shakspeare), an author must portray those complexities, and a critic must discern them. Eighteenth century criticism, he complained, saw merely those features of a work which lay on the surface or were measurable by formal analysis: Dr. Johnson, he boldly asserted, "could not show how the nature of man was modified by the workings of passion, or the infinite fluctuations of thought and accident." "A genuine criticism," said Hazlitt, "should reflect the colors, the light and shade, the soul and body of a work,"—not the body only.

Few critics can describe a work *in its entirety*, and in its *total* effect upon us, as well as Hazlitt can. With sensitiveness, gusto, and subtlety, he combined lucidity. He practised that "unaffected, familiar" style which he recommended: it is idiomatic and natural, but never commonplace or journalistic. "We are fine fellows," Robert Louis Stevenson well said, "but we can't write like William Hazlitt."

FROM MY FIRST ACQUAINTANCE WITH POETS

My father was a Dissenting Minister, at W—m, in Shropshire; and in the year 1798 (the figures that compose that date are to me like the "dreaded name of Demogorgon") Mr. Coleridge came to Shrewsbury, to succeed Mr. Rowe in the spiritual charge of a Unitarian congregation there. He did not come till late on the Saturday afternoon before he was to preach; and Mr. Rowe, who himself went down to the coach, in a state of anxiety and expectation, to look for the arrival of his successor, could find no one at all answering the description but a round-faced man, in a short black coat (like a shooting jacket) which hardly seemed to have been made for him, but who seemed to be talking at a

395

great rate to his fellow-passengers. Mr. Rowe had scarce returned to give an account of his disappointment, when the round-faced man in black entered, and dissipated all doubts on the subject, by beginning to talk. He did not cease while he stayed; nor has he since, that I know of. He held the good town of Shrewsbury in delightful suspense for three weeks that he remained there, "fluttering the proud Salopians, like an eagle in a dovecote"; and the Welsh mountains that skirt the horizon with their tempestuous confusion, agree to have heard no such mystic sounds since the days of

High-born Hoel's harp or soft Llewellyn's lay!

As we passed along between W—m and Shrewsbury, and I eyed their blue tops seen through the wintry branches, or the red rustling leaves of the sturdy oak trees by the roadside, a sound was in my ears as of a Siren's song; I was stunned, startled with it, as from deep sleep; but I had no notion then that I should ever be able to express my admiration to others in motley imagery or quaint allusion, till the light of his genius shone into my soul, like the sun's rays glittering in the puddles of the road. I was at that time dumb, inarticulate, helpless, like a worm by the wayside, crushed, bleeding, lifeless; but now, bursting from the deadly bands that bound them,

With Styx nine times round them,

my ideas float on winged words, and as they expand their plumes, catch the golden light of other years. My soul has indeed remained in its original bondage, dark, obscure, with longings infinite and unsatisfied; my heart, shut up in the prison house of this rude clay, has never found, nor will it ever find, a heart to speak to; but that my understanding also did not remain dumb and brutish, or at length found a language to express itself, I owe to Coleridge. But this is not to my purpose.

My father lived ten miles from Shrewsbury, and was in the habit of exchanging visits with Mr. Rowe, and with Mr. Jenkins of Whitechurch (nine miles farther on) according to the custom of Dissenting Ministers in each other's neighborhood. A line of communication is thus established, by which the flame of civil and religious liberty is kept alive, and nourishes its smouldering fire unquenchable, like the fires in the Agamemnon of Æschylus, placed at different stations, that waited for ten long years to announce with their blazing pyra-

mids the destruction of Troy. Coleridge had agreed to come over to see my father, according to the courtesy of the country, as Mr. Rowe's probable successor; but in the meantime, I had gone to hear him preach the Sunday after his arrival. A poet and a philosopher getting up into a Unitarian pulpit to preach the Gospel, was a romance in these degenerate days, a sort of revival of the primitive spirit of Christianity, which was not to be resisted.

It was in January of 1798, that I rose one morning before daylight, to walk ten miles in the mud, and went to hear this celebrated person preach. Never, the longest day I have to live, shall I have such another walk as this cold, raw, comfortless one, in the winter of the year 1798. Il y a des impressions que ni le tems ni les circonstances peuvent effacer. Dusse-je vivre des siècles entiers, le doux tems de ma jeunesse ne peut renaître pour moi, ni s'effacer jamais dans ma mémoire.* When I got there, the organ was playing the 100th psalm, and when it was done, Mr. Coleridge rose and gave out his text, "And he went up into the mountain to pray, himself, alone." As he gave out this text, his voice "rose like a steam of rich distilled perfume," and when he came to the two last words, which he pronounced loud, deep, and distinct, it seemed to me, who was then young, as if the sounds had echoed from the bottom of the human heart, and as if that prayer might have floated in solemn silence through the universe. The idea of St. John came into my mind, "of one crying in the wilderness, who had his loins girt about, and whose food was locusts and wild honey." The preacher then launched into his subject, like an eagle dallying with the wind. The sermon was upon peace and war; upon church and state—not their alliance but their separation—on the spirit of the world and the spirit of Christianity, not as the same, but as opposed to one another. He talked of those who had "inscribed the cross of Christ on banners dripping with human gore." He made a poetical and pastoral excursion—and to show the fatal effects of war, drew a striking contrast between the simple shepherd boy, driving his team afield, or sitting under the hawthorn, piping to his flock, "as though he should

* Il y a, etc. "There are impressions which neither time nor circumstances can efface. If I should live whole ages, the sweet days of my youth could never return to me, nor ever be effaced from my memory."—Rousseau's Confessions.

never be old," and the same poor country-lad, crimped, kidnapped, brought into town, made drunk, at an alehouse, turned into a wretched drummer-boy, with his hair sticking on end with powder and poma- 5 tum, a long cue at his back, and tricked out in the loathsome finery of the profession of blood.

Such were the notes our once-lov'd poet sung. 10

And for myself, I could not have been more delighted if I had heard the music of the spheres. Poetry and Philosophy had met together. Truth and Genius had em- 15 braced, under the eye and with the sanction of Religion. This was even beyond my hopes. I returned home well satisfied. The sun that was still laboring pale and wan through the sky, obscured by thick 20 mists, seemed an emblem of the *good cause;* and the cold dank drops of dew, that hung half melted on the beard of the thistle, had something genial and refreshing in them; for there was a spirit of hope and youth in 25 all nature, that turned everything into good. The face of nature had not then the brand of *Jus Divinum* on it:

Like to that sanguine flower inscrib'd with 30 woe.

On the Tuesday following, the half-inspired speaker came. I was called down into the room where he was, and went 35 half-hoping, half-afraid. He received me very graciously, and I listened for a long time without uttering a word. I did not suffer in his opinion by my silence. "For those two hours," he afterwards was pleased 40 to say, "he was conversing with W. H.'s forehead!" His appearance was different from what I had anticipated from seeing him before. At a distance, and in the dim light of the chapel, there was to me a 45 strange wildness in his aspect, a dusky obscurity, and I thought him pitted with the smallpox. His complexion was at that time clear, and even bright—

As are the children of yon azure sheen. 50

His forehead was broad and high, light as if built of ivory, with large projecting eyebrows, and his eyes rolling beneath them, 55 like a sea with darkened lustre. "A certain tender bloom his face o'erspread," a purple tinge as we see it in the pale thoughtful complexions of the Spanish portrait-painters, Murillo and Velasquez. His 60

mouth was gross, voluptuous, open, eloquent; his chin good-humored and round; but his nose, the rudder of the face, the index of the will, was small, feeble, nothing —like what he has done. It might seem that the genius of his face as from a height surveyed and projected him (with sufficient capacity and huge aspiration) into the world unknown of thought and imagination, with nothing to support or guide his veering purpose, as if Columbus had launched his adventurous course for the New World in a scallop, without oars or compass. So at least I comment on it after the event. Coleridge in his person was rather above the common size, inclining to the corpulent, or like Lord Hamlet, "somewhat fat and pursy." His hair (now, alas! gray) was then black and glossy as the raven's, and fell in smooth masses over his forehead. This long pendulous hair is peculiar to enthusiasts, to those whose minds tend heavenward; and is traditionally inseparable (though of a different color) from the pictures of Christ. It ought to belong, as a character, to all who preach *Christ crucified,* and Coleridge was at that time one of those! . . .

No two individuals were ever more unlike than were the host and his guest. A poet was to my father a sort of nondescript: yet whatever added grace to the Unitarian cause was to him welcome. He could hardly have been more surprised or pleased, if our visitor had worn wings. Indeed, his thoughts had wings; and as the silken sounds rustled round our little wainscoted parlor, my father threw back his spectacles over his forehead, his white hairs mixing with its sanguine hue; and a smile of delight beamed across his rugged cordial face, to think that Truth had found a new ally in Fancy. Besides, Coleridge seemed to take considerable notice of me, and that of itself was enough. He talked very familiarly, but agreeably, and glanced over a variety of subjects. At dinner-time he grew more animated, and dilated in a very edifying manner on Mary Wolstonecraft and Mackintosh. The last, he said, he considered (on my father's speaking of his *Vindiciæ Gallicæ* as a capital performance) as a clever scholastic man—a master of the topics,—or as the ready warehouseman of letters, who knew exactly where to lay his hand on what he wanted, though the goods were not his own. He thought him no match for Burke, either in style or matter. Burke was a metaphysician, Mackintosh a mere logician. Burke was an orator (almost a poet) who reasoned in figures, because he had an eye for nature: Mackintosh, on the other hand, was a rhetorician, who had only an eye to commonplaces. On this I ventured to say that I had always entertained a great opinion of Burke, and that (as far as I could find) the speaking of him with contempt might be made the test of a vulgar democratical mind. This was the first observation I ever made to Coleridge, and he said it was a very just and striking one. I remember the leg of Welsh mutton and the turnips on the table that day had the finest flavor imaginable. . . .

I forget a great number of things, many more than I remember; but the day passed off pleasantly, and the next morning Mr. Coleridge was to return to Shrewsbury. When I came down to breakfast, I found that he had just received a letter from his friend, T. Wedgwood, making him an offer of 150 *l.* a-year if he chose to waive his present pursuit, and devote himself entirely to the study of poetry and philosophy. Coleridge seemed to make up his mind to close with this proposal in the act of tying on one of his shoes. It threw an additional damp on his departure. It took the wayward enthusiast quite from us to cast him into Deva's winding vales, or by the shores of old romance. Instead of living at ten miles' distance, of being the pastor of a Dissenting congregation at Shrewsbury, he was henceforth to inhabit the Hill of Parnassus, to be a Shepherd on the Delectable Mountains. Alas! I knew not the way thither, and felt very little gratitude for Mr. Wedgwood's bounty. I was presently relieved from this dilemma; for Mr. Coleridge, asking for a pen and ink, and going to a table to write something on a bit of card, advanced towards me with undulating step, and giving me the precious document, said that that was his address, *Mr. Coleridge, Nether Stowey, Somersetshire;* and that he should be glad to see me there in a few weeks' time, and, if I chose, would come half-way to meet me. I was not less surprised than the shepherd-boy (this simile is to be found in *Cassandra*) when he sees a thunderbolt fall close at his feet. I stammered out my acknowledgments and acceptance of this offer (I thought Mr. Wedgwood's annuity a trifle to it) as well as I could; and this mighty business being settled, the poet-preacher took leave, and I accompanied him six miles on the road. It was a fine morning in the middle of winter, and he talked the whole way. The scholar in Chaucer is described as going

——sounding on his way.

So Coleridge went on his. In digressing, in dilating, in passing from subject to subject, he appeared to me to float in air, to slide on ice. He told me in confidence (going along) that he should have preached two sermons before he accepted the situation at Shrewsbury, one on Infant Baptism, the other on the Lord's Supper, showing that he could not administer either, which would have effectually disqualified him for the object in view. I observed that he continually crossed me on the way by shifting from one side of the foot-path to the other. This struck me as an odd movement; but I did not at that time connect it with any instability of purpose or involuntary change of principle, as I have done since. He seemed unable to keep on in a straight line. He spoke slightingly of Hume (whose *Essay on Miracles* he said was stolen from an objection started in one of South's sermons—*Credat Judæus Appella!*) I was not very much pleased at this account of Hume, for I had just been reading, with infinite relish, that completest of all metaphysical *choke-pears,* his *Treatise on Human Nature,* to which the *Essays,* in point of scholastic subtlety and close reasoning, are mere elegant trifling, light summer-reading. Coleridge even denied the excellence of Hume's general style, which I think betrayed a want of taste or candor. He however made me amends by the manner in which he spoke of Berkeley. He dwelt particularly on his *Essay on Vision* as a masterpiece of analytical reasoning. So it undoubtedly is. He was exceedingly angry with Dr. Johnson for striking the stone with his foot, in allusion to this author's theory of matter and spirit, and saying, "Thus I confute him, Sir." Coleridge drew a parallel (I don't know how he brought about the connection) between Bishop Berkeley and Tom Paine. He said the one was an instance of a subtle, the other of an acute mind, than which no two things could be more distinct. The one was a shop-boy's quality, the other the characteristic of a philosopher. . . .

If I had the quaint Muse of Sir Philip Sidney to assist me, I would write a *Sonnet to the Road between W—m and Shrewsbury,* and immortalise every step of it by some fond enigmatical conceit. I would swear that the very milestones had ears, and that Harmer-hill stooped with all its pines, to listen to a poet, as he passed! I remember but one other topic of discourse in this walk. He mentioned Paley, praised the naturalness and clearness of his style, but condemned his sentiments, thought him a mere time-serving casuist, and said that "the fact of his work on Moral and Political Philosophy being made a text-book in our universities was a disgrace to the national character." We parted at the six-mile stone; and I returned homeward pensive but much pleased. I had met with unexpected notice from a person whom I believed to have been prejudiced against me. "Kind and affable to me had been his condescension, and should be honored ever with suitable regard." He was the first poet I had known, and he certainly answered to that inspired name. I had heard a great deal of his powers of conversation, and was not disappointed. In fact, I never met with anything at all like them, either before or since. I could easily credit the accounts which were circulated of his holding forth to a large party of ladies and gentlemen, an evening or two before, on the Berkeleian Theory, when he made the whole material universe look like a transparency of fine words; and another story (which I believe he has somewhere told himself) of his being asked to a party at Birmingham, of his smoking tobacco and going to sleep after dinner on a sofa, where the company found him, to their no small surprise, which was increased to wonder when he started up of a sudden, and rubbing his eyes, looked about him, and launched into a three hours' description of the third heaven, of which he had had a dream, very different from Mr. Southey's *Vision of Judgment,* and also from that other Vision of Judgment, which Mr. Murray, the Secretary of the Bridge-street Junto, has taken into his especial keeping!

On my way back, I had a sound in my ears, it was the voice of Fancy: I had a light before me, it was the face of Poetry. The one still lingers there, the other has not quitted my side. Coleridge in truth met me half-way on the ground of philosophy, or I should not have been won over to his imaginative creed. I had an uneasy, pleasurable sensation all the time, till I was to visit him. During those months the chill breath of winter gave me a welcoming; the vernal air was balm and inspiration to me. The golden sunsets, the silver star of evening, lighted me on my way to new hopes and prospects. *I was to visit Coleridge in the spring.* This circum-stance was never absent from my thoughts, and mingled with all my feelings. I wrote to him at the time proposed, and received an answer postponing my intended visit for a week or two, but very cordially urging me to complete my promise then. This delay did not damp, but rather increased my ardor. In the meantime, I went to Llangollen Vale, by way of initiating myself in the mysteries of natural scenery; and I must say I was enchanted with it. I had been reading Coleridge's description of England in his fine *Ode on the Departing Year,* and I applied it, *con amore,* to the objects before me. That valley was to me (in a manner) the cradle of a new existence: in the river that winds through it, my spirit was baptized in the waters of Helicon!

I returned home, and soon after set out on my journey with unworn heart and untired feet. My way lay through Worcester and Gloucester, and by Upton, where I thought of Tom Jones and the adventure of the muff. I remember getting completely wet through one day, and stopping at an inn (I think it was at Tewkesbury) where I sat up all night to read *Paul and Virginia.* Sweet were the showers in early youth that drenched my body, and sweet the drops of pity that fell upon the books I read! I recollect a remark of Coleridge's upon this very book that nothing could show the gross indelicacy of French manners and the entire corruption of their imagination more strongly than the behavior of the heroine in the last fatal scene, who turns away from a person on board the sinking vessel, that offers to save her life, because he has thrown off his clothes to assist him in swimming. Was this a time to think of such a circumstance? I once hinted to Wordsworth, as we were sailing in his boat on Grasmere lake, that I thought he had borrowed the idea of his *Poems on the Naming of Places* from the local inscriptions of the same kind in *Paul and Virginia.* He did not own the obligation, and stated some distinction without a difference in defense to his claim to originality. Any the slightest variation would be sufficient for this purpose in his mind; for whatever *he* added or omitted would inevitably be worth all that any one else had done, and contain the marrow of the sentiment. I was still two days before the time fixed for my arrival, for I had taken care to set out early enough. I stopped these two days at Bridgewater, and when I was tired of sauntering on the banks of its muddy river, returned to the inn and read *Camilla*. So have I loitered my life away, reading books, looking at pictures, going to plays, hearing, thinking, writing on what pleased me best. I have wanted only one thing to make me happy; but wanting that, have wanted everything!

I arrived, and was well received. The country about Nether Stowey is beautiful, green and hilly, and near the sea-shore. I saw it but the other day, after an interval of twenty years, from a hill near Taunton. How was the map of my life spread out before me, as the map of the country lay at my feet! In the afternoon, Coleridge took me over to All-Foxden, a romantic old family-mansion of the St. Aubins, where Wordsworth lived. It was then in the possession of a friend of the poet's, who gave him the free use of it. Somehow, that period (the time just after the French Revolution) was not a time when *nothing was given for nothing*. The mind opened and a softness might be perceived coming over the heart of individuals, beneath "the scales that fence" our self-interest. Wordsworth himself was from home, but his sister kept house, and set before us a frugal repast; and we had free access to her brother's poems, the *Lyrical Ballads*, which were still in manuscript, or in the form of *Sybilline Leaves*. I dipped into a few of these with great satisfaction, and with the faith of a novice. I slept that night in an old room with blue hangings, and covered with the round-faced family portraits of the age of George I. and II. and from the wooded declivity of the adjoining park that overlooked my window, at the dawn of day, could

——hear the loud stag speak.

In the outset of life (and particularly at this time I felt it so) our imagination has a body to it. We are in a state between sleeping and waking, and have indistinct but glorious glimpses of strange shapes, and there is always something to come better than what we see. As in our dreams the fullness of the blood gives warmth and reality to the coinage of the brain, so in youth our ideas are clothed, and fed, and pampered with our good spirits; we breathe thick with thoughtless happiness, the weight of future years presses on the strong pulses of the heart, and we repose with undisturbed faith in truth and good. As we advance, we exhaust our fund of enjoyment and of hope. We are no longer wrapped in *lamb's-wool*, lulled in Elysium.

As we taste the pleasures of life, their spirit evaporates, the sense palls; and nothing is left but the phantoms, the lifeless shadows of what *has been*!

That morning, as soon as breakfast was over, we strolled out into the park, and seating ourselves on the trunk of an old ash tree that stretched along the ground, Coleridge read aloud with a sonorous and musical voice, the ballad of *Betty Foy*. I was not critically or sceptically inclined. I saw touches of truth and nature, and took the rest for granted. But in the *Thorn*, the *Mad Mother*, and the *Complaint of a Poor Indian Woman*, I felt that deeper power and pathos which have been since acknowledged,

In spite of pride, in erring reason's spite,

as the characteristics of this author; and the sense of a new style and a new spirit in poetry came over me. It had to me something of the effect that arises from the turning up of the fresh soil, or of the first welcome breath of spring,

While yet the trembling year is unconfirmed.

Coleridge and myself walked back to Stowey that evening, and his voice sounded high

Of Providence, foreknowledge, will, and fate, Fixed fate, free-will, foreknowledge absolute.

as we passed through echoing grove, by fairy stream or waterfall, gleaming in the summer moonlight! He lamented that Wordsworth was not prone enough to believe in the traditional superstitions of the place, and that there was a something corporeal, a *matter-of-fact-ness*, a clinging to the palpable, or often to the petty, in his poetry, in consequence. His genius was not a spirit that descended to him through the air; it sprung out of the ground like a flower, or unfolded itself from a green spray, on which the goldfinch sang. He said, however (if I remember right) that this objection must be confined to his descriptive pieces, that his philosophic poetry had a grand and comprehensive spirit in it, so that his soul seemed to inhabit the universe like a palace, and to discover truth by intuition, rather than by deduction. The next day Wordsworth arrived from Bristol at Coleridge's cottage. I think I see him now. He answered in some degree to his friend's description of him, but was more gaunt and Don Quixote-like. He was quaintly dressed (according to the *costume* of that unconstrained period) in a brown fustian jacket and striped pantaloons. There was something of a roll, a lounge in his gait, not unlike his own *Peter Bell*. There was a severe, worn pressure of thought about his temples, a fire in his eye (as if he saw something in objects more than the outward appearance), an intense high narrow forehead, a Roman nose, cheeks furrowed by strong purpose and feeling, and a convulsive inclination to laughter about the mouth, a good deal at variance with the solemn, stately expression of the rest of his face. Chantry's bust wants the marking traits; but he was teased into making it regular and heavy; Haydon's head of him, introduced into the *Entrance of Christ into Jerusalem*, is the most like his drooping weight of thought and expression. He sat down and talked very naturally and freely, with a mixture of clear gushing accents in his voice, a deep guttural intonation, and a strong tincture of the northern *burr*, like the crust on wine. He instantly began to make havoc of the half of a Cheshire cheese on the table, and said triumphantly that "his marriage with experience had not been so unproductive as Mr. Southey's in teaching him a knowledge of the good things of this life." He had been to see the *Castle Specter* by Monk Lewis, while at Bristol, and described it very well. He said "it fitted the taste of the audience like a glove." This *ad captandum* merit was, however, by no means a recommendation of it, according to the severe principles of the new school, which reject rather than court popular effect. Wordsworth, looking out of the low, latticed window, said, "How beautifully the sun sets on that yellow bank!" I thought within myself. "With what eyes these poets see nature!" and ever after, when I saw the sunset stream upon the objects facing it, conceived I had made a discovery, or thanked Mr. Wordsworth for having made one for me! We went over to All-Foxden again the day following, and Wordsworth read us the story of *Peter Bell* in the open air; and the comment made upon it by his face and voice was very different from that of some later critics! Whatever might be thought of the poem, "his face was as a book where men might read strange matters," and he announced the fate of his hero in prophetic tones. There is a *chaunt* in the recitation both of Coleridge and Wordsworth, which acts as a spell upon the hearer, and disarms the judgment. Perhaps they have deceived themselves by making habitual use of this ambiguous accompaniment. Coleridge's manner is more full, animated, and varied; Wordsworth's more equable, sustained, and internal. The one might be termed more *dramatic*, the other more *lyrical*. Coleridge has told me that he himself liked to compose in walking over uneven ground, or breaking through the straggling branches of a copse-wood; whereas Wordsworth always wrote (if he could) walking up and down a straight gravel walk, or in some spot where the continuity of his verse met with no collateral interruption. Returning that same evening, I got into a metaphysical argument with Wordsworth, while Coleridge was explaining the different notes of the nightingale to his sister, in which we neither of us succeeded in making ourselves perfectly clear and intelligible. Thus I passed three weeks at Nether Stowey and in the neighborhood, generally devoting the afternoons to a delightful chat in an arbor made of bark by the poet's friend Tom Poole, sitting under two fine elm trees, and listening to the bees humming round us while we quaffed our flip. . . .

In the morning of the second day, we breakfasted luxuriously in an old-fashioned parlor on tea, toast, eggs, and honey, in the very sight of the beehives from which it had been taken, and a garden full of thyme and wild flowers that had produced it. On this occasion Coleridge spoke of Virgil's *Georgics*, but not well. I do not think he had much feeling for the classical or elegant. It was in this room that we found a little worn-out copy of the *Seasons*, lying in a window-seat, on which Coleridge exclaimed, "*That* is true fame!" He said Thomson was a great poet, rather than a good one; his style was as meretricious as his thoughts were natural. He spoke of Cowper as the best modern poet. He said the *Lyrical Ballads* were an experiment about to be tried by him and Wordsworth to see how far the public taste would endure poetry written in a more natural and simple style than had hitherto been attempted; totally discarding the artifices of poetical diction, and making use only of such words as had probably been common in the most ordinary language since the days of Henry II. Some comparison was introduced between Shakspeare and Milton. He said "he hardly knew which to prefer." Shakspeare appeared to him a mere stripling in the art; he was as tall and as strong, with infinitely more activity than Milton, but he never appeared to have come to man's estate; or if he had, he would not have been a man, but a monster. He spoke with contempt of Gray, and with intolerance of Pope. He did not like the versification of the latter. He observed that "the ears of these couplet-writers might be charged with having short memories, that could not retain the harmony of whole passages." He thought little of Junius as a writer; he had a dislike of Dr. Johnson; and a much higher opinion of Burke as an orator and politician, than of Fox or Pitt. He, however, thought him very inferior in richness of style and imagery to some of our elder prose writers, particularly Jeremy Taylor. He liked Richardson, but not Fielding; nor could I get him to enter into the merits of *Caleb Williams*. In short, he was profound and discriminating with respect to those authors whom he liked, and where he gave his judgment fair play; capricious, perverse, and prejudiced in his antipathies and distastes. We loitered on the "ribbed sea-sands," in such talk as this, a whole morning, and I recollect met with a curious sea-weed, of which John Chester told us the country name! A fisherman gave Coleridge an account of a boy that had been drowned the day before, and that they had tried to save him at the risk of their own lives. He said "he did not know how it was that they ventured, but, Sir, we have a *nature* towards one another." This expression, Coleridge remarked to me, was a fine illustration of that theory of disinterestedness which I (in common with Butler) had adopted.

1823

FROM CHARACTERS OF SHAKSPEARE'S PLAYS

HAMLET

This is that Hamlet the Dane, whom we read of in our youth, and whom we may be said almost to remember in our after-years; he who made that famous soliloquy on life, who gave the advice to the players, who thought "this goodly frame, the earth, a steril promontory, and this brave o'erhanging firmament, the air, this majestical roof fretted with golden fire, a foul and pestilent congregation of vapors"; whom "man delighted not, nor woman neither"; he who talked with the grave-diggers, and moralized on Yorick's skull; the schoolfellow of Rosencrans and Guildenstern at Wittenberg; the friend of Horatio; the lover of Ophelia; he that was mad and sent to England; the slow avenger of his father's death; who lived at the court of Horwendillus five hundred years before we were born, but all whose thoughts we seem to know as well as we do our own, because we have read them in Shakspeare.

Hamlet is a name; his speeches and sayings but the idle coinage of the poet's brain. What then, are they not real? They are as real as our own thoughts. Their reality is in the reader's mind. It is *we* who are Hamlet. This play has a prophetic truth, which is above that of history. Whoever has become thoughtful and melancholy through his own mishaps or those of others; whoever has borne about with him the clouded brow of reflection, and thought himself "too much i' th' sun"; whoever has seen the golden lamp of day dimmed by envious mists rising in his own breast, and could find in the world before him only a dull blank with nothing left remarkable in it; whoever has known "the pangs of despised love, the insolence of office, or the spurns which patient merit of the unworthy takes"; he who has felt his mind sink within him, and sadness cling to his heart like a malady, who has had his hopes blighted and his youth staggered by the apparitions of strange things; who cannot be well at ease, while he sees evil hovering near him like a spectre; whose powers of action have been eaten up by thought, he to whom the universe seems infinite, and himself nothing; whose bitterness of soul makes him careless of consequences, and who goes to a play as his best resource to shove off, to a second remove, the evils of life by a mock representation of them—this is the true Hamlet.

We have been so used to this tragedy that we hardly know how to criticize it any more than we should know how to describe our own faces. But we must make such observations as we can. It is the one of Shakspeare's plays that we think of the oftenest, because it abounds most in striking reflections on human life, and because the distresses of Hamlet are transferred, by the turn of his mind, to the general account of humanity. Whatever happens to him we apply to ourselves, because he applies it to himself as a means of general reasoning. He is a great moralizer; and what makes him worth attending to is that he moralizes on his own feelings and experience. He is not a commonplace pedant. If *Lear* is distinguished by the greatest depth of passion, *Hamlet* is the

most remarkable for the ingenuity, originality, and unstudied development of character. Shakspeare had more magnanimity
than any other poet, and he has shown
more of it in this play than in any other.
There is no attempt to force an interest:
everything is left for time and circumstances to unfold. The attention is excited
without effort, the incidents succeed each
other as matters of course, the characters
think and speak and act just as they might
do, if left entirely to themselves. There
is no set purpose, no straining at a point.
The observations are suggested by the passing scene—the gusts of passion come and
go like sounds of music borne on the wind.
The whole play is an exact transcript of
what might be supposed to have taken
place at the court of Denmark, at the remote period of time fixed upon, before the
modern refinements in morals and manners
were heard of. It would have been interesting enough to have been admitted as a
bystander in such a scene, at such a time,
to have heard and witnessed something of
what was going on. But here we are more
than spectators. We have not only "the
outward pageants and the signs of grief";
but "we have that within which passes
show." We read the thoughts of the heart,
we catch the passions living as they rise.
Other dramatic writers give us very fine
versions and paraphrases of nature: but
Shakspeare, together with his own comments, gives us the original text, that we
may judge for ourselves. This is a very
great advantage.

The character of Hamlet stands quite
by itself. It is not a character marked by
strength of will or even of passion, but by
refinement of thought and sentiment.
Hamlet is as little of the hero as a man can
well be: but he is a young and princely
novice, full of high enthusiasm and quick
sensibility—the sport of circumstances,
questioning with fortune and refining on
his own feelings, and forced from the natural bias of his disposition by the strangeness
of his situation. He seems incapable of
deliberate action, and is only hurried into
extremities on the spur of the occasion,
when he has no time to reflect, as in the
scene where he kills Polonius, and again,
where he alters the letters which Rosencrans and Guildenstern are taking with
them to England, purporting his death. At
other times, when he is most bound to act,
he remains puzzled, undecided, and skeptical, dallies with his purposes, till the occasion is lost, and always finds some pretence

to relapse into indolence and thoughtfulness again. For this reason he refuses to
kill the King when he is at his prayers, and
by a refinement in malice, which is in truth
only an excuse for his own want of resolution, defers his revenge to a more fatal
opportunity, when he shall be engaged in
some act "that has no relish of salvation
in it."

He kneels and prays,
And now I'll do 't, and so he goes to heaven,
And so am I revenged; *that would be scanned;*
He killed my father, and for that,
I, his sole son, send him to heaven.
Why this is reward, not revenge.
Up sword and know thou a more horrid time,
When he is drunk, asleep, or in a rage.

He is the prince of philosophical speculators; and because he cannot have his revenge perfect, according to the most refined
idea his wish can form, he declines it altogether. So he scruples to trust the suggestions of the Ghost, contrives the scene of
the play to have surer proof of his uncle's
guilt, and then rests satisfied with this con-
firmation of his suspicions, and the success
of his experiment, instead of acting upon
it. Yet he is sensible of his own weakness,
taxes himself with it, and tries to reason
himself out of it.

How all occasions do inform against me,
And spur my dull revenge! What is a man,
If his chief good and market of his time
Be but to sleep and feed? A beast; no more.
Sure he that made us with such large dis-
         course,
Looking before and after, gave us not
That capability and god-like reason
To rust in us unused: now whether it be
Bestial oblivion, or some craven scruple
Of thinking too precisely on th' event,—
A thought which quartered, hath but one
         part wisdom,
And ever three parts coward;—I do not know
Why yet I live to say, this thing's to do;
Sith I have cause, and will, and strength, and
         means
To do it. Examples gross as earth exhort me:
Witness this army of such mass and charge,
Led by a delicate and tender prince,
Whose spirit with divine ambition puffed,
Makes mouths at the invisible event,
Exposing what is mortal and unsure
To all that fortune, death and danger dare,
Even for an eggshell. 'Tis not to be great
Never to stir without great argument;
But greatly to find quarrel in a straw,
When honor's at the stake. How stand I then,
That have a father killed, a mother stained,
Excitements of my reason and my blood,
And let all sleep, while to my shame I see
The imminent death of twenty thousand men,

That for a fantasy and trick of fame,
Go to their graves like beds, fight for a plot
Whereon the numbers cannot try the cause,
Which is not tomb enough and continent
To hide the slain?—O, from this time forth,
My thoughts be bloody or be nothing worth.

Still he does nothing; and this very speculation on his own infirmity only affords
him another occasion for indulging it. It
is not for any want of attachment to his
father or abhorrence of his murder that
Hamlet is thus dilatory, but it is more to
his taste to indulge his imagination in reflecting upon the enormity of the crime
and refining on his schemes of vengeance,
than to put them into immediate practice.
His ruling passion is to think, not to act:
and any vague pretext that flatters this
propensity instantly diverts him from his
previous purposes.

The moral perfection of this character
has been called in question, we think, by
those who did not understand it. It is
more interesting than according to rules;
amiable, though not faultless. The ethical
delineations of "that noble and liberal
casuist" (as Shakspeare has been well
called) do not exhibit the drab-colored
quakerism of morality. His plays are not
copied either from *The Whole Duty of
Man* or from *The Academy of Compliments!* We confess we are a little shocked
at the want of refinement in those who are
shocked at the want of refinement in
Hamlet. The neglect of punctilious exactness in his behavior either partakes of the
"license of the time," or else belongs to
the very excess of intellectual refinement
in the character, which makes the common
rules of life, as well as his own purposes,
sit loose upon him. He may be said to be
amenable only to the tribunal of his own
thoughts, and is too much taken up with
the airy world of contemplation to lay as
much stress as he ought on the practical
consequences of things. His habitual principles of action are unhinged and out of
joint with the time. His conduct to
Ophelia is quite natural in his circumstances. It is that of assumed severity only.
It is the effect of disappointed hope, of
bitter regrets, of affection suspended, not
obliterated, by the distractions of the scene
around him! Amidst the natural and pre-
ternatural horrors of his situation, he
might be excused in delicacy from carrying
on a regular courtship. When "his father's
spirit was in arms," it was not a time for
the son to make love in. He could neither
marry Ophelia, nor wound her mind by

explaining the cause of his alienation,
which he durst hardly trust himself to
think of. It would have taken him years
to have come to a direct explanation on
the point. In the harassed state of his
mind, he could not have done much otherwise than he did. His conduct does not
contradict what he says when he sees her
funeral,

I loved Ophelia: forty thousand brothers
Could not with all their quantity of love
Make up my sum.

Nothing can be more affecting or beautiful than the Queen's apostrophe to Ophelia
on throwing the flowers into the grave.

—Sweets to the sweet, farewell.
I hoped thou should'st have been my Hamlet's
wife:
I thought thy bride-bed to have decked, sweet
maid,
And not have strewed thy grave.

Shakspeare was thoroughly a master of
the mixed motives of human character, and
he here shows us the Queen, who was so
criminal in some respects, not without
sensibility and affection in other relations
of life.—Ophelia is a character almost too
exquisitely touching to be dwelt upon. Oh,
rose of May, oh, flower too soon faded!
Her love, her madness, her death, are described with the truest touches of tenderness and pathos. It is a character which nobody but Shakspeare could have drawn in
the way that he has done, and to the conception of which there is not even the
smallest approach, except in some of the
old romantic ballads. Her brother, Laertes,
is a character we do not like so well: he is
too hot and choleric, and somewhat rhodo-
montade. Polonius is a perfect character
in its kind; nor is there any foundation for
the objections which have been made to
the consistency of this part. It is said that
he acts very foolishly and talks very sensibly. There is no inconsistency in that.
Again, that he talks wisely at one time and
foolishly at another; that his advice to
Laertes is very sensible, and his advice to
the King and Queen on the subject of
Hamlet's madness very ridiculous. But he
gives the one as a father, and is sincere in
it; he gives the other as a mere courtier, a
busybody, and is accordingly officious, garrulous, and impertinent. In short, Shakspeare has been accused of inconsistency
in this and other characters, only because
he has kept up the distinction which there
is in nature, between the understandings

and the moral habits of men, between the absurdity of their ideas and the absurdity of their motives. Polonius is not a fool, but he makes himself so. His folly, whether in his actions or speeches, comes under the head of impropriety of intention.

We do not like to see our author's plays acted, and least of all, *Hamlet.* There is no play that suffers so much in being transferred to the stage. Hamlet himself seems hardly capable of being acted. Mr. Kemble unavoidably fails in this character from a want of ease and variety. The character of Hamlet is made up of undulating lines; it has the yielding flexibility of "a wave o' th' sea." Mr. Kemble plays it like a man in armor, with a determined inveteracy of purpose, in one undeviating straight line, which is as remote from the natural grace and refined susceptibility of the character, as the sharp angles and abrupt starts which Mr. Kean introduces into the part. Mr. Kean's Hamlet is as much too splenetic and rash as Mr. Kemble's is too deliberate and formal. His manner is too strong and pointed. He throws a severity, approaching to virulence, into the common observations and answers. There is nothing of this in Hamlet. He is, as it were, wrapped up in his reflections, and only *thinks aloud.* There should therefore be no attempt to impress what he says upon others by a studied exaggeration of emphasis or manner; no *talking at* his hearers. There should be as much of the gentleman and scholar as possible infused into the part, and as little of the actor. A pensive air of sadness should sit reluctantly upon his brow, but no appearances of fixed and sullen gloom. He is full of weakness and melancholy, but there is no harshness in his nature. He is the most amiable of misanthropes.

1817

FROM ON FAMILIAR STYLE

It is not easy to write a familiar style. Many people mistake a familiar for a vulgar style, and suppose that to write without affectation is to write at random. On the contrary, there is nothing that requires more precision, and, if I may so say, purity of expression, than the style I am speaking of. It utterly rejects not only all unmeaning pomp, but all low, cant phrases, and loose, unconnected, *slipshod* allusions. It is not to take the first word that offers, but the best word in common use; it is not to throw words together in any combination

we please, but to follow and avail ourselves of the true idiom of the language. To write a genuine familiar or truly English style, is to write as any one would speak in common conversation, who had a thorough command and choice of words, or who could discourse with ease, force, and perspicuity, setting aside all pedantic and oratorical flourishes. Or to give another illustration, to write naturally is the same thing in regard to common conversation, as to read naturally is in regard to common speech. It does not follow that it is an easy thing to give the true accent and inflection to the words you utter, because you do not attempt to rise above the level of ordinary life and colloquial speaking. You do not assume indeed the solemnity of the pulpit, or the tone of stage-declamation: neither are you at liberty to gabble on at a venture, without emphasis or discretion, or to resort to vulgar dialect or clownish pronunciation. You must steer a middle course. You are tied down to a given and appropriate articulation, which is determined by the habitual associations between sense and sound, and which you can only hit by entering into the author's meaning, as you must find the proper words and style to express yourself by fixing your thoughts on the subject you have to write about. Any one may mouth out a passage with a theatrical cadence, or get upon stilts to tell his thoughts: but to write or speak with propriety and simplicity is a more difficult task. Thus it is easy to affect a pompous style, to use a word twice as big as the thing you want to express: it is not so easy to pitch upon the very word that exactly fits it. Out of eight or ten words equally common, equally intelligible, with nearly equal pretensions, it is a matter of some nicety and discrimination to pick out the very one, the preferableness of which is scarcely perceptible, but decisive. The reason why I object to Dr. Johnson's style is, that there is no discrimination, no selection, no variety in it. He uses none but "tall, opaque words," taken from the "first row of the rubric":—words with the greatest number of syllables, or Latin phrases with merely English terminations. If a fine style depended on this sort of arbitrary pretension, it would be fair to judge of an author's elegance by the measurement of his words, and the substitution of foreign circumlocutions (with no precise associations) for the mother-tongue. How simple it is to be dignified without ease, to be pompous without meaning! Surely, it is but a mechanical rule for avoiding what is low to be always pedantic and affected. It is clear you cannot use a vulgar English word, if you never use a common English word at all. A fine tact is shown in adhering to those which are perfectly common, and yet never falling into any expressions which are debased by disgusting circumstances, or which owe their signification and point to technical or professional allusions. A truly natural or familiar style can never be quaint or vulgar, for this reason, that it is of universal force and applicability, and that quaintness and vulgarity arise out of the immediate connection of certain words with coarse and disagreeable, or with confined ideas. The last form what we understand by *cant* or *slang* phrases.—To give an example of what is not very clear in the general statement. I should say that the phrase *To cut with a knife,* or *To cut a piece of wood,* is perfectly free from vulgarity, because it is perfectly common: but to *cut an acquaintance* is not quite unexceptionable, because it is not perfectly common or intelligible, and has hardly yet escaped out of the limits of slang phraseology. I should hardly therefore use the word in this sense without putting it in italics as a license of expression, to be received *cum grano salis.* All provincial or bye-phrases come under the same mark of reprobation—all such as the writer transfers to the page from his fireside or a particular *coterie,* or that he invents for his own sole use and convenience. I conceive that words are like money, not the worse for being common, but that it is the stamp of custom alone that gives them circulation or value. I am fastidious in this respect, and would almost as soon coin the currency of the realm as counterfeit the King's English. I never invented or gave a new and unauthorized meaning to any word but one single one (the term *impersonal* applied to feelings) and that was in an abstruse metaphysical discussion to express a very difficult distinction. I have been (I know) loudly accused of revelling in vulgarisms and broken English. I cannot speak to that point: but so far I plead guilty to the determined use of acknowledged idioms and common elliptical expressions. I am not sure that the critics in question know the one from the other, that is, can distinguish any medium between formal pedantry and the most barbarous solecism. As an author, I endeavor to employ plain words and popular modes of construction, as were I a chapman and dealer, I should common weights and measures.

The proper force of words lies not in the words themselves, but in their application. A word may be a fine-sounding word, of an unusual length, and very imposing from its learning and novelty, and yet in the connection in which it is introduced, may be quite pointless and irrelevant. It is not pomp or pretension, but the adaptation of the expression to the idea that clenches a writer's meaning:—as it is not the size or glossiness of the materials, but their being fitted each to its place, that gives strength to the arch; or as the pegs and nails are as necessary to the support of the building as the larger timbers, and more so than the mere showy, unsubstantial ornaments. I hate anything that occupies more space than it is worth. I hate to see a load of band-boxes go along the street, and I hate to see a parcel of big words without any thing in them. A person who does not deliberately dispose of all his thoughts alike in cumbrous draperies and flimsy disguises, may strike out twenty varieties of familiar everyday language, each coming somewhat nearer to the feeling he wants to convey, and at last not hit upon that particular and only one, which may be said to be identical with the exact impression in his mind. This would seem to show that Mr. Cobbett is hardly right in saying that the first word that occurs is always the best. It may be a very good one; and yet a better may present itself on reflection or from time to time. It should be suggested naturally, however, and spontaneously, from a fresh and lively conception of the subject. We seldom succeed by trying at improvement, or by merely substituting one word for another that we are not satisfied with, as we cannot recollect the name of a place or person by merely plaguing ourselves about it. We wander farther from the point by persisting in a wrong scent; but it starts up accidentally in the memory when we least expect it, by touching some link in the chain of previous association. There are those who hoard up and make a cautious display of nothing but rich and rare phraseology;—ancient medals, obscure coins, and Spanish pieces of eight. They are very curious to inspect; but I myself would neither offer nor take them in the course of exchange. A sprinkling of archaisms is not amiss; but a tissue of obsolete expressions is more fit *for keep than wear.* I do not say I would not use any phrase that had been brought into fashion before the middle or the end of the last century; but I should be shy of using any that had not been employed by any approved author during the whole of that time. Words, like clothes, get old-fashioned, or mean and ridiculous, when they have been for some time laid aside. Mr. Lamb is the only imitator of old English style I can read with pleasure; and he is so thoroughly imbued with the spirit of his authors that the idea of imitation is almost done away. There is an inward unction, a marrowy vein both in the thought and feeling, an intuition, deep and lively, of his subject, that carries off any quaintness or awkwardness arising from an antiquated style and dress. The matter is completely his own, though the manner is assumed. Perhaps his ideas are altogether so marked and individual, as to require their point and pungency to be neutralized by the affectation of a singular but traditional form of conveyance. Tricked out in the prevailing costume, they would probably seem more startling and out of the way. The old English authors, Burton, Fuller, Coryate, Sir Thomas Browne, are a kind of mediators between us and the more eccentric and whimsical modern, reconciling us to his peculiarities. I do not, however, know how far this is the case or not, till he condescends to write like one of us. I must confess that what I like best of his papers under the signature of Elia (still I do not presume, amidst such excellence, to decide on what is most excellent) is the account of *Mrs. Battle's Opinion on Whist,* which is also the most free from obsolete allusions and turns of expression—

A well of native English undefiled.

To those acquainted with his admired prototypes, these Essays of the ingenious and highly gifted author have the same sort of charm and relish, that Erasmus's *Colloquies* or a fine piece of modern Latin have to the classical scholar. Certainly, I do not know any borrowed pencil that has more power or felicity of execution than the one of which I have here been speaking.

It is as easy to write a gaudy style without ideas, as it is to spread a pallet of showy colors, or to smear in a flaunting transparency. "What do you read?"—"Words, words, words."—"What is the matter?"—*"Nothing,"* it might be answered. The florid style is the reverse of the familiar. The last is employed as an unvarnished medium to convey ideas; the first is re-

sorted to as a spangled veil to conceal the want of them.

1821

LORD BYRON

Lord Byron and Sir Walter Scott are among writers now living the two, who would carry away a majority of suffrages as the greatest geniuses of the age. The former would, perhaps, obtain the preference with the fine gentlemen and ladies (squeamishness apart)—the latter with the critics and the vulgar. We shall treat of them in the same connection, partly on account of their distinguished pre-eminence, and partly because they afford a complete contrast to each other. In their poetry, in their prose, in their politics, and in their tempers, no two men can be more unlike.

If Sir Walter Scott may be thought by some to have been

Born universal heir to all humanity,

it is plain Lord Byron can set up no such pretension. He is, in a striking degree, the creature of his own will. He holds no communion with his kind; but stands alone, without mate or fellow—

As if a man were author of himself,
And owned no other kin.

He is like a solitary peak, all access to which is cut off not more by elevation than distance. He is seated on a lofty eminence, "cloud-capt," or reflecting the last rays of setting suns; and in his poetical moods, reminds us of the fabled Titans, retired to a ridgy steep, playing on their Pan's-pipes, and taking up ordinary men and things in their hands with haughty indifference. He raises his subject to himself, or tramples on it; he neither stoops to, nor loses himself in it. He exists not by sympathy, but by antipathy. He scorns all things, even himself. Nature must come to him to sit for her picture—he does not go to her. She must consult his time, his convenience, and his humor; and wear a *sombre* or a fantastic garb, or his lordship turns his back upon her. There is no ease, no unaffected simplicity of manner, no "golden mean." All is strained, or petulant in the extreme. His thoughts are sphered and crystalline; his style "prouder than when blue Iris bends"; his spirit fiery, impatient, wayward, indefatigable. Instead of taking his impressions from without, in entire and almost unimpaired masses, he molds them according to his own temperament, and heats the materials of his imagination in the furnace of his passions.—Lord Byron's verse glows like a flame, consuming every thing in its way; Sir Walter Scott's glides like a river, clear, gentle, harmless. The poetry of the first scorches, that of the last scarcely warms. The light of the one proceeds from an internal source, ensanguined, sullen, fixed; the other's reflects the hues of heaven, or the face of nature, glancing vivid and various. The productions of the northern bard have the rust and the freshness of antiquity about them; those of the noble poet cease to startle from their extreme ambition of novelty, both in style and matter. Sir Walter's rhymes are "silly sooth"—

And dally with the innocence of thought,
  Like the old age—

his lordship's Muse spurns *the olden time,* and affects all the supercilious airs of a modern fine lady and an upstart. The object of the one writer is to restore us to truth and nature: the other chiefly thinks how he shall display his own power, or vent his spleen, or astonish the reader either by starting new subjects and trains of speculation, or by expressing old ones in a more striking and emphatic manner than they have been expressed before. He cares little what it is he says, so that he can say it differently from others. This may account for the charges of plagiarism which have been repeatedly brought against the noble poet—if he can borrow an image or sentiment from another, and heighten it by an epithet or an allusion of greater force and beauty than is to be found in the original passage, he thinks he shows his superiority of execution in this in a more marked manner than if the first suggestion had been his own. It is not the value of the observation itself he is solicitous about; but he wishes to shine by contrast—even nature only serves as a foil to set off his style. He therefore takes the thoughts of others (whether contemporaries or not) out of their mouths, and is content to make them his own, to set his stamp upon them, by imparting to them a more meretricious gloss, a higher relief, a greater loftiness of tone, and a characteristic inveteracy of purpose. Even in those collateral ornaments of modern style, slovenliness, abruptness, and eccentricity (as well as in terseness and significance), Lord Byron, when he pleases, defies competition and surpasses all his contemporaries. Whatever he does,

he must do in a more decided and daring manner than any one else—he lounges with extravagance, and yawns so as to alarm the reader! Self-will, passion, the love of singularity, a disdain of himself and of others (with a conscious sense that this is among the ways and means of procuring admiration) are the proper categories of his mind: he is a lordly writer, is above his own reputation, and condescends to the Muses with a scornful grace!

Lord Byron, who in his politics is a *liberal,* in his genius is haughty and aristocratic: Walter Scott, who is an aristocrat in principle, is popular in his writings, and is (as it were) equally *servile* to nature and to opinion. The genius of Sir Walter is essentially imitative, or "denotes a foregone conclusion": that of Lord Byron is self-dependent; or at least requires no aid, is governed by no law, but the impulses of its own will. We confess, however much we may admire independence of feeling and erectness of spirit in general or practical questions, yet in works of genius we prefer him who bows to the authority of nature, who appeals to actual objects, to moldering superstitions, to history, observation, and tradition, before him who only consults the pragmatical and restless workings of his own breast, and gives them out as oracles to the world. We like a writer (whether poet or prose-writer) who takes in (or is willing to take in) the range of half the universe in feeling, character, description, much better than we do one who obstinately and invariably shuts himself up in the Bastile of his own ruling passions. In short, we had rather be Sir Walter Scott (meaning thereby the author of Waverley) than Lord Byron, a hundred times over. And for the reason just given, namely, that he casts his descriptions in the mold of nature, ever-varying, never tiresome, always interesting and always instructive, instead of casting them constantly in the mold of his own individual impressions. He gives us man as he is, or as he was, in almost every variety of situation, action, and feeling. Lord Byron makes man after his own image, woman after his own heart; the one is a capricious tyrant, the other a yielding slave; he gives us the misanthrope and the voluptuary by turns; and with these two characters, burning or melting in their own fires, he makes out everlasting cantos of himself. He hangs the cloud, the film of his existence over all outward things —sits in the centre of his thoughts, and enjoys dark night, bright day, the glitter and the gloom "in cell monastic"—we see the mournful pall, the crucifix, the death's heads, the faded chaplet of flowers, the gleaming tapers, the agonized brow of genius, the wasted form of beauty—but we are still imprisoned in a dungeon, a certain intercepts our view, we do not breathe freely the air of nature or of our own thoughts—the other admired author draws aside the curtain, and the veil of egotism is rent, and he shows us the crowd of living men and women, the endless groups, the landscape background, the cloud and the rainbow, and enriches our imaginations and relieves one passion by another, and expands and lightens reflection, and takes away that tightness at the breast which arises from thinking or wishing to think that there is nothing in the world out of a man's self!—In this point of view, the author of Waverley is one of the greatest teachers of morality that ever lived, by emancipating the mind from petty, narrow, and bigoted prejudices: Lord Byron is the greatest pamperer of those prejudices, by seeming to think there is nothing else worth encouraging but the seeds or the full luxuriant growth of dogmatism and self-conceit. In reading the *Scotch Novels*, we never think about the author, except from a feeling of curiosity respecting our unknown benefactor: in reading Lord Byron's works, he himself is never absent from our minds. The coloring of Lord Byron's style, however rich and dipped in Tyrian dyes, is nevertheless opaque, is in itself an object of delight and wonder: Sir Walter Scott's is perfectly transparent. In studying the one, you seem to gaze at the figures cut in stained glass, which exclude the view beyond, and where the pure light of Heaven is only a means of setting off the gorgeousness of art: in reading the other, you look through a noble window at the clear and varied landscape without. Or to sum up the distinction in one word, Sir Walter Scott is the most *dramatic* writer now living; and Lord Byron is the least so. It would be difficult to imagine that the author of Waverley is in the smallest degree a pedant; as it would be hard to persuade ourselves that the author of Childe Harold and Don Juan is not a coxcomb, though a provoking and sublime one. In this decided preference given to Sir Walter Scott over Lord Byron, we distinctly include the prose-works of the former; for we do not think his poetry alone by any means entitles him to that precedence. Sir Walter in his poetry, though pleasing and natural, is a comparative trifler: it is in his anonymous productions that he has shown himself for what he is!—

Intensity is the great and prominent distinction of Lord Byron's writings. He seldom gets beyond force of style, nor has he produced any regular work or masterly whole. He does not prepare any plan beforehand, nor revise and retouch what he has written with polished accuracy. His only object seems to be to stimulate himself and his readers for the moment—to keep both alive, to drive away *ennui*, to substitute a feverish and irritable state of excitement for listless indolence or even calm enjoyment. For this purpose he pitches on any subject at random without much thought or delicacy—he is only impatient to begin—and takes care to adorn and enrich it as he proceeds with "thoughts that breathe and words that burn." He composes (as he himself has said) whether he is in the bath, in his study, or on horseback—he writes as habitually as others talk or think—and whether we have the inspiration of the Muse or not, we always find the spirit of the man of genius breathing from his verse. He grapples with his subject, and moves, penetrates, and animates it by the electric force of his own feelings. He is often monotonous, extravagant, offensive; but he is never dull, or tedious, but when he writes prose. Lord Byron does not exhibit a new view of nature, or raise insignificant objects into importance by the romantic associations with which he surrounds them; but generally (at least) takes commonplace thoughts and events and endeavors to express them in stronger and statelier language than others. His poetry stands like a Martello tower by the side of his subject. He does not, like Mr. Wordsworth, lift poetry from the ground, or create a sentiment out of nothing. He does not describe a daisy or a periwinkle, but the cedar or the cypress: not "poor men's cottages, but princes' palaces." His *Childe Harold* contains a lofty and impassioned review of the great events of history, of the mighty objects left as wrecks of time, but he dwells chiefly on what is familiar to the mind of every schoolboy; has brought out few new traits of feeling or thought; and has done no more than justice to the reader's preconceptions by the sustained force and brilliancy of his style and imagery.

Lord Byron's earlier productions, *Lara,* the *Corsair,* etc. were wild and gloomy romances, put into rapid and shining verse.

They discover the madness of poetry, together with the inspiration: sullen, moody, capricious, fierce, inexorable, gloating on beauty, thirsting for revenge, hurrying from the extremes of pleasure to pain, but with nothing permanent, nothing healthy or natural. The gaudy decorations and the morbid sentiments remind one of flowers strewed over the face of death! In his *Childe Harold* (as has been just observed) he assumes a lofty and philosophic tone, and "reasons high of providence, foreknowledge, will, and fate." He takes the highest points in the history of the world, and comments on them from a more commanding eminence: he shows us the crumbling monuments of time, he invokes the great names, the mighty spirit of antiquity. The universe is changed into a stately mausoleum:—in solemn measures he chaunts a hymn to fame. Lord Byron has strength and elevation enough to fill up the molds of our classical and time-hallowed recollections, and to rekindle the earliest aspirations of the mind after greatness and true glory with a pen of fire. The names of Tasso, of Ariosto, of Dante, of Cincinnatus, of Cæsar, of Scipio, lose nothing of their pomp or their lustre in his hands, and when he begins and continues a strain of panegyric on such subjects, we indeed sit down with him to a banquet of rich praise, brooding over imperishable glories,

Till Contemplation has her fill.

Lord Byron seems to cast himself indignantly from "this bank and shoal of time," or the frail tottering bark that bears up modern reputation, into the huge sea of ancient renown, and to revel there with untired, outspread plume. Even this in him is spleen—his contempt of his contemporaries makes him turn back to the lustrous past, or project himself forward to the dim future!—Lord Byron's tragedies, Faliero,* Sardanapalus, etc. are not equal to his other works. They want the essence of the drama. They abound in speeches and descriptions, such as he himself might make either to himself or others, lolling on his couch of a morning, but do not carry the reader out of the poet's mind to the scenes and events recorded. They have neither action, character, nor interest, but are a sort of *gossamer* tragedies, spun out, and glittering, and spreading a flimsy veil over the face of nature. Yet he spins them on.

* "Don Juan was my Moscow, and Faliero
　My Leipsic, and my Mont St. Jean seems Cain."
　　　　　Don Juan, Canto XI.

Of all that he has done in this way the *Heaven and Earth* (the same subject as Mr. Moore's *Loves of the Angels*) is the best. We prefer it even to *Manfred*. *Manfred* is merely himself, with a fancy-drapery on: but in the dramatic fragment published in the *Liberal*, the space between Heaven and Earth, the stage on which his characters have to pass to and fro, seems to fill his lordship's imagination; and the deluge, which he has so finely described, may be said to have drowned all his own idle humors.

We must say we think little of our author's turn for satire. His "English Bards and Scotch Reviewers" is dogmatical and insolent, but without refinement or point. He calls people names, and tries to transfix a character with an epithet, which does not stick, because it has no other foundation than his own petulance and spite; or he endeavors to degrade by alluding to some circumstance of external situation. He says of Mr. Wordsworth's poetry, that "it is his aversion." That may be: but whose fault is it? This is the satire of a lord, who is accustomed to have all his whims or dislikes taken for gospel, and who cannot be at the pains to do more than signify his contempt or displeasure. If a great man meets with a rebuff which he does not like, he turns on his heel, and this passes for a repartee. The noble author says of a celebrated barrister and critic, that he was "born in a garret sixteen stories high." The insinuation is not true; or if it were, it is low. The allusion degrades the person who makes, not him to whom it is applied. This is also the satire of a person of birth and quality, who measures all merit by external rank, that is, by his own standard. So his lordship, in a "Letter to the Editor of My Grandmother's Review," addresses him fifty times as *"my dear Robarts";* nor is there any other wit in the article. This is surely a mere assumption of superiority from his lordship's rank, and is the sort of *quizzing* he might use to a person who came to hire himself as a valet to him at *Long's*—the waiters might laugh, the public will not. In like manner, in the controversy about Pope, he claps Mr. Bowles on the back with a coarse facetious familiarity, as if he were his chaplain whom he had invited to dine with him, or was about to present to a benefice. The reverend divine might submit to the obligation, but he has no occasion to subscribe to the jest. If it is a jest that Mr. Bowles should be a parson, and Lord Byron a peer, the world knew this before; there was no need to write a pamphlet to prove it.

The *Don Juan* indeed has great power; but its power is owing to the force of the serious writing, and to the oddity of the contrast between that and the flashy passages with which it is interlarded. From the sublime to the ridiculous there is but one step. You laugh and are surprised that any one should turn round and *travestie* himself: the drollery is in the utter discontinuity of ideas and feelings. He makes virtue serve as a foil to vice; *dandyism* is (for want of any other) a variety of genius. A classical intoxication is followed by the splashing of soda-water, by frothy effusions of ordinary bile. After the lightning and the hurricane, we are introduced to the interior of the cabin and the contents of wash-hand basins. The solemn hero of tragedy plays *Scrub* in the farce. This is "very tolerable and not to be endured." The noble lord is almost the only writer who has prostituted his talents in this way. He hallows in order to desecrate; takes a pleasure in defacing the images of beauty his hands have wrought; and raises our hopes and our belief in goodness to heaven only to dash them to the earth again, and break them in pieces the more effectually from the very height they have fallen. Our enthusiasm for genius or virtue is thus turned into a jest by the very person who has kindled it, and who thus fatally quenches the sparks of both. It is not that Lord Byron is sometimes serious and sometimes trifling, sometimes profligate, and sometimes moral—but when he is most serious and most moral, he is only preparing to mortify the unsuspecting reader by putting a pitiful *hoax* upon him. This is a most unaccountable anomaly. It is as if the eagle were to build its eyry in a common sewer, or the owl were seen soaring to the mid-day sun. Such a sight might make one laugh, but one would not wish or expect it to occur more than once.*

In fact, Lord Byron is the spoiled child of fame as well as fortune. He has taken a surfeit of popularity, and is not contented to delight, unless he can shock the public. He would force them to admire in spite of decency and common sense—he would have them read what they would read in no one but himself, or he would not give a rush for their applause. He is to be "a

* This censure applies to the first Cantos of *Don Juan* much more than to the last. It has been called a *Tristram Shandy* in rhyme: it is rather a poem written about itself.

chartered libertine," from whom insults are favors, whose contempt is to be a new incentive to admiration. His lordship is hard to please: he is equally averse to notice or neglect, enraged at censure and scorning praise. He tries the patience of the town to the very utmost, and when they show signs of weariness or disgust, threatens to *discard* them. He says he will write on, whether he is read or not. He would never write another page, if it were not to court popular applause, or to affect a superiority over it. In this respect also, Lord Byron presents a striking contrast to Sir Walter Scott. The latter takes what part of the public favor falls to his share, without grumbling (to be sure he has no reason to complain); the former is always quarreling with the world about his *modicum* of applause, the *spolia opima* of vanity, and ungraciously throwing the offerings of incense heaped on his shrine back in the faces of his admirers. Again, there is no taint in the writings of the author of Waverley, all is fair and natural and *aboveboard:* he never outrages the public mind. He introduces no anomalous character: broaches no staggering opinion. If he goes back to old prejudices and superstitions as a relief to the modern reader, while Lord Byron floats on swelling paradoxes—

Like proud seas under him;

if the one defers too much to the spirit of antiquity, the other panders to the spirit of the age, goes to the very edge of extreme and licentious speculation, and breaks his neck over it. Grossness and levity are the playthings of his pen. It is a ludicrous circumstance that he should have dedicated his *Cain* to the worthy baronet! Did the latter ever acknowledge the obligation? We are not nice, not very nice; but we do not particularly approve those subjects that shine chiefly from their rottenness: nor do we wish to see the Muses dressed out in the flounces of a false or questionable philosophy, like Portia and Nerissa in the garb of Doctors of Law. We like metaphysics as well as Lord Byron; but not to see them making flowery speeches, nor dancing a measure in the fetters of verse. We have as good as hinted, that his lordship's poetry consists mostly of a tissue of superb commonplaces; even his paradoxes are *commonplace.* They are familiar in the schools: they are only new and striking in his dramas and stanzas, by being out of place. In a word, we think that poetry moves best within the circle of nature and received opinion: speculative theory and subtle casuistry are forbidden ground to it. But Lord Byron often wanders into this ground wantonly, wilfully, and unwarrantably. The only apology we can conceive for the spirit of some of Lord Byron's writings, is the spirit of some of those opposed to him. They would provoke a man to write anything. "Farthest from them is best." The extravagance and license of the one seems a proper antidote to the bigotry and narrowness of the other. The first *Vision of Judgment* was a set-off to the second, though

None but itself could be its parallel.

Perhaps the chief cause of most of Lord Byron's errors is, that he is that anomaly in letters and in society, a noble poet. It is a double privilege, almost too much for humanity. He has all the pride of birth and genius. The strength of his imagination leads him to indulge in fantastic opinions; the elevation of his rank sets censure at defiance. He becomes a pampered egotist. He has a seat in the House of Lords, a niche in the Temple of Fame. Everyday mortals, opinions, things are not good enough for him to touch or think of. A mere nobleman is, in his estimation, but "the tenth transmitter of a foolish face": a mere man of genius is no better than a worm. His Muse is also a lady of quality. The people are not polite enough for him: the Court not sufficiently intellectual. He hates the one and despises the other. By hating and despising others, he does not learn to be satisfied with himself. A fastidious man soon grows querulous and splenetic. If there is nobody but ourselves to come up to our idea of fancied perfection, we easily get tired of our idol. When a man is tired of what he is, by a natural perversity he sets up for what he is not. If he is a poet, he pretends to be a metaphysician: if he is a patrician in rank and feeling, he would fain be one of the people. His ruling motive is not the love of the people, but of distinction; not of truth, but of singularity. He patronizes men of letters out of vanity, and deserts them from caprice, or from the advice of friends. He embarks in an obnoxious publication to provoke censure, and leaves it to shift for itself for fear of scandal. We do not like Sir Walter's gratuitous servility: we like Lord Byron's preposterous *liberalism* little better. He may affect the principles of equality, but he resumes his privilege of peerage, upon occasion. His lordship has made great offers of service to the Greeks—money and horses. He is at present in Cephalonia, waiting the event!

We had written thus far when news came of the death of Lord Byron, and put an end at once to a strain of somewhat peevish invective, which was intended to meet his eye, not to insult his memory. Had we known that we were writing his epitaph, we must have done it with a different feeling. As it is, we think it better and more like himself, to let what we had written stand, than to take up our leaden shafts, and try to melt them into "tears of sensibility," or mold them into dull praise, and an affected show of candor. We were not silent during the author's lifetime, either for his reproof or encouragement (such as we could give, and *he* did not disdain to accept) nor can we now turn undertakers' men to fix the glittering plate upon his coffin, or fall into the procession of popular woe.—Death cancels every thing but truth; and strips a man of every thing but genius and virtue. It is a sort of natural canonization. It makes the meanest of us sacred—it installs the poet in his immortality, and lifts him to the skies. Death is the great assayer of the sterling ore of talent. At his touch the drossy particles fall off, the irritable, the personal, the gross, and mingle with the dust—the finer and more ethereal part mounts with the winged spirit to watch over our latest memory, and protect our bones from insult. We consign the least worthy qualities to oblivion, and cherish the nobler and imperishable nature with double pride and fondness. Nothing could show the real superiority of genius in a more striking point of view than the idle contests and the public indifference about the place of Lord Byron's interment, whether in Westminster Abbey or his own family vault. A king must have a coronation—a nobleman a funeral procession.—The man is nothing without the pageant. The poet's cemetery is the human mind, in which he sows the seeds of never-ending thought—his monument is to be found in his works:

Nothing can cover his high fame but Heaven;
No pyramids set off his memory,
But the eternal substance of his greatness.

Lord Byron is dead: he also died a martyr to his zeal in the cause of freedom, for the last, best hopes of man. Let that be his excuse and his epitaph!

1824

SIR WALTER SCOTT (1771-1832)

Sound, sound the clarion, fill the fife!
To all the sensual world proclaim:
One crowded hour of glorious life
Is worth a world without a name!

THOMAS OSBORNE MORDAUNT

It is characteristic of Scott that when he satisfied his heart's desire by acquiring the owner-ship of extensive lands, he busied himself not in making cosy little gardens, but in reforestra-tion,—in planting upon his bare hills great tracts of beautiful woods. In his literary creations he likewise wrought upon a magnificent scale. The scope of his work is wider than that of any other Romantic. He achieved extreme popularity in *both* verse and prose. Even Byron, not given to praising others, acknowledged the sovereign sway of Scott, saying "Of whom could you be jealous?—of none of the living certainly—and of which of the dead?"

Scott's father was a hard-working and conscientious Edinburgh lawyer; his mother, a cheerful woman of ardent feelings and romantic imagination. In their son, the two temperaments inter-mingled, usually in harmony, sometimes in discord. He was sickly as a child, but overcame his weaknesses by strong will-power and through much living out-of-doors. He was from boyhood a great reader, and he became one of the most widely-cultured men of his time; he remembered everything interesting that he read, and he was a born story-teller. His early acquaintance with Percy's *Reliques* and similar fictions fired him with enthusiasm for the traditions of ancient days of stirring action; and this interest was intensified by the oral ballads and tales which he and his companions gathered on long pedestrian excursions in the Scottish Highlands. Insatiable as was his thirst for all kinds of historical lore, it was no greater than his observant interest in the many different kinds of men and women, some of them exceed-ingly odd, with whom he came in contact both in his work and in the pursuit of his hobbies; and he never forgot anything, whether met with in books or in life, that strikingly illustrated the varieties of human experience.

His professional career was that of an attorney, and holder of official legal posts. He also, secretly and unfortunately, ventured into the hazardous business of publishing. For his profes-sional and literary achievements he was knighted. He gradually acquired and developed the great estate which he named Abbotsford, and which became the center of that happy family life and bounteous social hospitality which he loved even more than fame.

His literary life passed through three phases, only the last of which gave him enough scope for the expression of his extensive knowledge of humanity and its history. First he was an antiquary,—an editor of such works as the *Minstrelsy of the Scottish Border* (1802-03). Next he was an indefatigable story-teller in verse, producing his poetical romances, *The Lay of the Last Minstrel* (1805), *Marmion* (1808), *The Lady of the Lake* (1810), etc., which won him celeb-rity. In this field his immediate successor was Lord Byron. Finally Scott unrolled the past of six centuries,—European, Scottish, and English,—in his thirty-two *Waverley Novels* (1814-1832), the popularity of which was immeasurably great not only at home but abroad.

Most of the Romantics were wholly devoted to literature, which was only one of Scott's pursuits. All his experiences are reflected in his poems and novels,—his lives, so to speak, as a lawyer, scholar, sportsman, and country gentleman. In his works he glorified the heroic and the honorable. That this attitude was not merely sentimental was shown by his conduct when the publishing firm with which he was connected failed. Although sick and aging, and not in strict legality obliged to shoulder so great an obligation, he toiled away manfully until his death, and made over his earnings to the creditors. The unheroic type of man would have gone into bankruptcy, and would thereafter have retained what he earned.

Among Americans it is Theodore Roosevelt who best resembles Scott,—in abounding rich-ness and strenuousness of life, and in combining delight in action with delight in books. Partly because of his keen enjoyment of active pursuits, Scott is often belittled by the narrowly literary, the timidly academic, and the neurotic Intelligentsia, who hold it against him (as against Homer) that he is not preoccupied with the introspective, temperamental, morbid, bizarre, subtle, or decadent. In the esteem of men of action, however, the poems and novels of Scott maintain an honored place. Like every great author, he gives us certain values that cannot be obtained elsewhere.

While Wordsworth was disclosing the beauty and significance that lay in contemporaneous life and surroundings, Scott revealed the splendors of the past and the varieties of human experience. His standards and ideals were the same as those of his fellow-Romantics; but he felt that the glory of those ideals could be best manifested by evoking the life of the past and of the frontier. Scotland occupied in British life much the same place as our frontier has held in the American: there both Nature and Man seemed less cultured and conventional; and there lay greater opportunities for the study of the strange, rugged, and picturesque. To this was added Scott's conception of nationality and patriotism. He felt, like Edmund Burke, that a people was not merely an aggregation of individuals, but an organic, complex whole, united by the molding influences of its earlier history. In his Waverley novels he disclosed the ways in which the past has molded the present.

Scott did not attempt to reproduce the past pedantically; but he translated, in terms intelligible to the present, those features of the past which had enduring significance. He evoked the life of those ages in which there was more freedom for the manifestation of character in dramatic deeds, more opportunity for strong passions, natural feelings, and sincere manners to exhibit themselves, more chance for love to show itself as an instinct and a passion rather than a rational preference (this in his poems rather than in his novels), more scope for the development of a multitude of peculiarities in characters from kings and queens to peasants and gypsies. Since Shakspeare, with his chronicle-histories, no British man of letters had thus made the life of the past a vital force in the life of the present.

Scott furthered the revival and vogue of the ballad and the verse-romance (the latter cultivated after him by Byron). He founded the modern historical novel, having not only scores of followers in England and America (Bulwer-Lytton, Cooper, Dickens, Hawthorne, Eliot, Stevenson, etc.) but also hundreds in Europe (Hugo, Mérimée, De Vigny, Freytag, Manzoni, etc.).

WILLIAM AND HELEN

From heavy dreams fair Helen rose,
  And eyed the dawning red:
"Alas, my love, thou tarriest long!
  O art thou false or dead?"

With gallant Frederick's princely power 5
  He sought the bold Crusade,
But not a word from Judah's wars
  Told Helen how he sped.

With Paynim and with Saracen
  At length a truce was made, 10
And every knight returned to dry
  The tears his love had shed.

Our gallant host was homeward bound
  With many a song of joy;
Green waved the laurel in each plume, 15
  The badge of victory.

And old and young, and sire and son,
  To meet them crowd the way,
With shouts and mirth and melody,
  The debt of love to pay. 20

Full many a maid her true-love met,
  And sobbed in his embrace,
And fluttering joy in tears and smiles
  Arrayed full many a face.

Nor joy nor smile for Helen sad, 25
  She sought the host in vain;
For none could tell her William's fate,
  If faithless or if slain.

The martial band is past and gone;
  She rends her raven hair, 30
And in distraction's bitter mood
  She weeps with wild despair.

"O, rise, my child," her mother said,
  "Nor sorrow thus in vain;
A perjured lover's fleeting heart 35
  No tears recall again."

"O mother, what is gone is gone,
  What's lost forever lorn:
Death, death alone can comfort me;
  O had I ne'er been born! 40

"O, break, my heart, O, break at once!
  Drink my life-blood, Despair!
No joy remains on earth for me,
  For me in heaven no share."

"O, enter not in judgment, Lord!"   45
  The pious mother prays;
"Impute not guilt to thy frail child!
  She knows not what she says.

"O, say thy pater-noster, child!
  O, turn to God and grace!   50
His will, that turned thy bliss to bale,
  Can change thy bale to bliss."

"O mother, mother, what is bliss?
  O mother, what is bale?
My William's love was heaven on earth,   55
  Without it earth is hell.

"Why should I pray to ruthless Heaven,
  Since my loved William's slain?
I only prayed for William's sake,
  And all my prayers were vain."   60

"O, take the sacrament, my child,
  And check these tears that flow;
By resignation's humble prayer,
  O, hallowed be thy woe!"

"No sacrament can quench this fire,   65
  Or slake this scorching pain;
No sacrament can bid the dead
  Arise and live again.

"O, break, my heart, O, break at once!
  Be thou my god, Despair!   70
Heaven's heaviest blow has fallen on me,
  And vain each fruitless prayer."

"O, enter not in judgment, Lord,
  With thy frail child of clay!
She knows not what her tongue has
    spoke;   75
  Impute it not, I pray!

"Forbear, my child, this desperate woe,
  And turn to God and grace;
Well can devotion's heavenly glow
  Convert thy bale to bliss."   80

"O, mother, mother, what is bliss?
  O mother, what is bale?
Without my William what were heaven,
  Or with him what were hell?"

Wild she arraigns the eternal doom,   85
  Upbraids each sacred power,
Till, spent, she sought her silent room,
  All in the lonely tower.

She beat her breast, she wrung her hands,
  Till sun and day were o'er,   90
And through the glimmering lattice shone
  The twinkling of the star.

Then, crash! the heavy drawbridge fell
  That o'er the moat was hung;
And, clatter! clatter! on its boards   95
  The hoof of courser rung.

The clank of echoing steel was heard
  As off the rider bounded;
And slowly on the winding stair
  A heavy footstep sounded.   100

And hark! and hark! a knock—tap! tap!
  A rustling stifled noise;—
Door-latch and tinkling staples ring;—
  At length a whispering voice.

"Awake, awake, arise, my love!   105
  How, Helen, dost thou fare?
Wak'st thou, or sleep'st? laugh'st thou, or
    weep'st?
  Hast thought on me, my fair?"

"My love! my love!—so late by night!—
  I waked, I wept for thee: 110
Much have I borne since dawn of morn;
  Where, William, couldst thou be?"

"We saddle late—from Hungary
  I rode since darkness fell;
And to its bourne we both return   115
  Before the matin-bell."

"O, rest this night within my arms,
  And warm thee in their fold!
Chill howls through hawthorn bush the
    wind:—
  My love is deadly cold."   120

"Let the wind howl through hawthorn
    bush!
  This night we must away;
The steed is wight, the spur is bright;
  I cannot stay till day.

"Busk, busk, and boune! Thou mount'st
    behind   125
  Upon my black barb steed:
O'er stock and stile, a hundred miles,
  We haste to bridal bed."

"To-night—to-night a hundred miles!—
  O dearest William, stay!   130
The bell strikes twelve—dark, dismal hour!
  O, wait, my love, till day!"

"Look here, look here—the moon shines
    clear—
  Full fast I ween we ride;
Mount and away! for ere the day   135
  We reach our bridal bed.

"The black barb snorts, the bridle rings;
  Haste, busk, and boune, and seat thee!
The feast is made, the chamber spread,
  The bridal guests await thee." 140

Strong love prevailed: she busks, she
    bounes,
  She mounts the barb behind,
And round her darling William's waist
  Her lily arms she twined.

And, hurry! hurry! off they rode,   145
  As fast as fast might be;
Spurned from the courser's thundering
    heels
  The flashing pebbles flee.

And on the right and on the left,
  Ere they could snatch a view,   150
Fast, fast each mountain, mead, and plain,
  And cot and castle flew.

"Sit fast—dost fear?—The moon shines
    clear—
  Fleet goes my barb—keep hold!
Fear'st thou?"—"O no!" she faintly said; 155
  "But why so stern and cold?"

"What yonder rings? what yonder sings?
  Why shrieks the owlet gray?"
" 'T is death-bells' clang, 't is funeral song,
  The body to the clay.   160

"With song and clang at morrow's dawn
  Ye may inter the dead:
To-night I ride with my young bride
  To deck our bridal bed.

"Come with thy choir, thou coffined
    guest,   165
  To swell our nuptial song!
Come, priest, to bless our marriage feast!
  Come all, come all along!"

Ceased clang and song; down sunk the
    bier;
  The shrouded corpse arose: 170
And hurry! hurry! all the train
  The thundering steed pursues.

And forward! forward! on they go;
  High snorts the straining steed;
Thick pants the rider's laboring breath, 175
  As headlong on they speed.

"O William, why this savage haste?
  And where thy bridal bed?"
" 'T is distant far, low, damp, and chill,
  And narrow, trustless maid."   180

"No room for me?"—"Enough for both;—
  Speed, speed, my barb, thy course!"
O'er thundering bridge, through boiling
    surge,
  He drove the furious horse.

Tramp! tramp! along the land they
    rode,   185
  Splash! splash! along the sea;
The scourge is wight, the spur is bright,
  The flashing pebbles flee.

Fled past on right and left how fast
  Each forest, grove, and bower!   190
On right and left fled past how fast
  Each city, town, and tower!

"Dost fear? dost fear? The moon shines
    clear,
  Dost fear to ride with me?—
Hurrah! hurrah! the dead can ride!"— 195
  "O William, let them be!—

"See there, see there! What yonder swings,
  And creaks mid whistling rain?"—
"Gibbet and steel, the accursed wheel;
  A murderer in his chain.—   200

"Hollo! thou felon, follow here!
  To bridal bed we ride;
And thou shalt prance a fetter dance
  Before me and my bride."

And, hurry! hurry! clash, clash, clash! 205
  The wasted form descends;
And fleet as wind through hazel bush
  The wild career attends.

Tramp! tramp! along the land they rode,
  Splash! splash! along the sea;   210
The scourge is red, the spur drops blood,
  The flashing pebbles flee.

How fled what moonshine faintly showed!
  How fled what darkness hid!
How fled the earth beneath their feet, 215
  The heaven above their head!

"Dost fear? dost fear? The moon shines
    clear,
  And well the dead can ride;
Dost faithful Helen fear for them?"—
  "O leave in peace the dead!"—   220

"Barb! Barb! methinks I hear the cock:
  The sand will soon be run:
Barb! Barb! I smell the morning air;
  The race is well-nigh done."

Tramp! tramp! along the land they
  rode. 225
  Splash! splash! along the sea;
The scourge is red, the spur drops blood,
  The flashing pebbles flee.

"Hurrah! hurrah! well ride the dead;
  The bride, the bride is come; 230
And soon we reach the bridal bed,
  For, Helen, here's my home."

Reluctant on its rusty hinge
  Revolved an iron door,
And by the pale moon's setting beam 235
  Were seen a church and tower.

With many a shriek and cry whiz round
  The birds of midnight scared;
And rustling like autumnal leaves
  Unhallowed ghosts were heard. 240

O'er many a tomb and tombstone pale
  He spurred the fiery horse,
Till sudden at an open grave
  He checked the wondrous course.

The falling gauntlet quits the rein, 245
  Down drops the casque of steel,
The cuirass leaves his shrinking side,
  The spur his gory heel.

The eyes desert the naked skull,
  The mouldering flesh the bone, 250
Till Helen's lily arms entwine
  A ghastly skeleton.

The furious barb snorts fire and foam,
  And with a fearful bound
Dissolves at once in empty air, 255
  And leaves her on the ground.

Half seen by fits, by fits half heard,
  Pale spectres flit along,
Wheel round the maid in dismal dance,
  And howl the funeral song; 260

"E'en when the heart's with anguish cleft
  Revere the doom of Heaven,
Her soul is from her body reft;
  Her spirit be forgiven!"

1796

THE VIOLET

The violet in her greenwood bower,
  Where birchen boughs with hazels mingle,
May boast itself the fairest flower
  In glen or copse or forest dingle.

Though fair her gems of azure hue, 5
  Beneath the dewdrop's weight reclining;
I've seen an eye of lovelier blue,
  More sweet through watery lustre shining.

The summer sun that dew shall dry
  Ere yet the day be past its morrow, 10
Nor longer in my false love's eye
  Remained the tear of parting sorrow.

1797   1813

THE EVE OF SAINT JOHN

The Baron of Smaylho'me rose with day,
  He spurred his courser on,
Without stop or stay, down the rocky way,
  That leads to Brotherstone.

He went not with the bold Buccleuch 5
  His banner broad to rear;
He went not 'gainst the English yew
  To lift the Scottish spear.

Yet his plate-jack was braced and his hel-
    met was laced,
  And his vaunt-brace of proof he wore; 10
At his saddle-gerthe was a good steel
    sperthe,
  Full ten pound weight and more.

The baron returned in three days' space,
  And his looks were sad and sour;
And weary was his courser's pace 15
  As he reached his rocky tower.

He came not from where Ancram Moor
  Ran red with English blood;
Where the Douglas true and the bold
    Buccleuch
  'Gainst keen Lord Evers stood. 20

Yet was his helmet hacked and hewed,
  His acton pierced and tore,
His axe and his dagger with blood im-
    brued,—
  But it was not English gore.

He lighted at the Chapellage, 25
  He held him close and still;
And he whistled thrice for his little foot-
    page,
  His name was English Will.

"Come thou hither, my little foot-page,
  Come hither to my knee; 30
Though thou art young and tender of age,
  I think thou art true to me.

"Come, tell me all that thou hast seen,
  And look thou tell me true!
Since I from Smaylho'me tower have
    been,   35
  What did thy lady do?"

"My lady, each night, sought the lonely
    light
  That burns on the wild Watchfold;
For from height to height the beacons
    bright
  Of the English foemen told.   40

"The bittern clamored from the moss,
  The wind blew loud and shrill;
Yet the craggy pathway she did cross
  To the eiry Beacon Hill.

"I watched her steps, and silent came   45
  Where she sat her on a stone;—
No watchman stood by the dreary flame,
  It burnèd all alone.

"The second night I kept her in sight
  Till to the fire she came,   50
And, my Mary's might! an armèd knight
  Stood by the lonely flame.

"And many a word that warlike lord
  Did speak to my lady there;
But the rain fell fast and loud blew the
    blast,   55
  And I heard not what they were.

"The third night there the sky was fair,
  And the mountain-blast was still,
As again I watched the secret pair
  On the lonesome Beacon Hill.   60

"And I heard her name the midnight hour,
  And name this holy eve;
And say, 'Come this night to thy lady's
    bower;
  Ask no bold baron's leave.

"'He lifts his spear with the bold Buc-
    cleuch;   65
  His lady is all alone;
The door she'll undo to her knight so true
  On the eve of good Saint John.'

"'I cannot come; I must not come;
  I dare not come to thee;   70
On the eve of Saint John I must wander
    alone:
  In thy bower I may not be.'

"'Now, out on thee, faint-hearted knight!
  Thou shouldst not say me nay;

For the eve is sweet, and when lovers
    meet   75
  Is worth the whole summer's day.

"'And I'll chain the blood-hound, and the
    warder shall not sound,
  And rushes shall be strewed on the stair;
So, by the black rood-stone and by holy
    St. John,
  I conjure thee, my love, to be there!' 80

"'Though the blood-hound be mute and
    the rush beneath my foot,
  And the warder his bugle should not
    blow,
Yet there sleepeth a priest in the chamber
    to the east,
  And my footstep he would know.'

"'O, fear not the priest who sleepeth to
    the east,   85
  For to Dryburgh the way he has ta'en;
And there to say mass, till three days do
    pass,
  For the soul of a knight that is slayne.'

"He turned him around and grimly he
    frowned;
  Then he laughed right scornfully— 90
'He who says the mass-rite for the soul of
    that knight
  May as well say mass for me:

"'At the lone midnight hour when bad
    spirits have power
  In thy chamber will I be.'—
With that he was gone and my lady left
    alone,   95
  And no more did I see."

Then changed, I trow, was that bold
    baron's brow
  From the dark to the blood-red high;
"Now, tell me the mien of the knight thou
    hast seen,
  For, by Mary, he shall die!"   100

"His arms shone full bright in the beacon's
    red light;
  His plume it was scarlet and blue;
On his shield was a hound in a silver leash
    bound,
  And his crest was a branch of the yew."

"Thou liest, thou liest, thou little foot-
    page,   105
  Loud dost thou lie to me!
For that knight is cold and low laid in the
    mould,
  All under the Eildon-tree."

"Yet hear but my word, my noble lord!
For I heard her name his name;   110
And that lady bright, she called the knight
Sir Richard of Coldinghame."

The bold baron's brow then changed, I
trow,
From high blood-red to pale—
"The grave is deep and dark—and the
corpse is stiff and stark—   115
So I may not trust thy tale.

"Where fair Tweed flows round holy Mel-
rose,
And Eildon slopes to the plain,
Full three nights ago by some secret foe
That gay gallant was slain.   120

"The varying light deceived thy sight,
And the wild winds drowned the name;
For the Dryburgh bells ring and the white
monks do sing
For Sir Richard of Coldinghame!"

He passed the court-gate and he oped the
tower-gate,   125
And he mounted the narrow stair,
To the bartizan-seat where, with maids that
on her wait,
He found his lady fair.

That lady sat in mournful mood;
Looked over hill and vale;   130
Over Tweed's fair flood and Mertoun's
wood,
And all down Teviotdale.

"Now hail, now hail, thou lady bright!"
"Now hail, thou baron true!
What news, what news, from Ancram
fight?   135
What news from the bold Buccleuch?"

"The Ancram moor is red with gore,
For many a Southern fell;
And Buccleuch has charged us evermore
To watch our beacons well."   140

The lady blushed red, but nothing she
said:
Nor added the baron a word:
Then she stepped down the stair to her
chamber fair,
And so did her moody lord.

In sleep the lady mourned, and the baron
tossed and turned,   145
And oft to himself he said,—

"The worms around him creep, and his
bloody grave is deep—
It cannot give up the dead!"

It was near the ringing of matin-bell,
The night was well-nigh done,   150
When a heavy sleep on that baron fell,
On the eve of good Saint John.

The lady looked through the chamber fair,
By the light of a dying flame;
And she was aware of a knight stood
there—   155
Sir Richard of Coldinghame!

"Alas! away, away!" she cried,
"For the holy Virgin's sake!"
"Lady, I know who sleeps by thy side;
But, lady, he will not awake.   160

"By Eildon-tree for long nights three
In bloody grave have I lain;
The mass and the death-prayer are said for
me,
But, lady, they are said in vain.

"By the baron's brand, near Tweed's fair
strand,   165
Most foully slain I fell;
And my restless spirit on the beacon's
height
For a space is doomed to dwell.

"At our trysting-place, for a certain space,
I must wander to and fro;   170
But I had not had power to come to thy
bower
Hadst thou not conjured me so."

Love mastered fear—her brow she crossed;
"How, Richard, hast thou sped?
And art thou saved or art thou lost?"   175
The vision shook his head!

"Who spilleth life shall forfeit life;
So bid thy lord believe:
That lawless love is guilt above,
This awful sign receive."   180

He laid his left palm on an oaken beam,
His right upon her hand;
The lady shrunk and fainting sunk,
For it scorched like a fiery brand.

The sable score of fingers four   185
Remains on that board impressed;
And forevermore that lady wore
A covering on her wrist.

There is a nun in Dryburgh bower
  Ne'er looks upon the sun;   190
There is a monk in Melrose tower
  He speaketh word to none.

That nun who ne'er beholds the day,
  That monk who speaks to none—
That nun was Smaylho'me's lady gay,   195
  That monk the bold baron.

1801

FROM THE LAY OF THE LAST
MINSTREL

INTRODUCTION

The way was long, the wind was cold,
The Minstrel was infirm and old;
His withered cheek and tresses gray
Seemed to have known a better day;
The harp, his sole remaining joy,   5
Was carried by an orphan boy.
The last of all the bards was he,
Who sung of Border chivalry;
For, well-a-day! their date was fled,
His tuneful brethren all were dead;   10
And he, neglected and oppressed,
Wished to be with them and at rest.
No more on prancing palfrey borne,
He carolled, light as lark at morn;
No longer courted and caressed,   15
High placed in hall, a welcome guest,
He poured, to lord and lady gay,
The unpremeditated lay:
Old times were changed, old manners gone;
A stranger filled the Stuarts' throne;   20
The bigots of the iron time
Had called his harmless art a crime.
A wandering harper, scorned and poor,
He begged his bread from door to door,
And tuned, to please a peasant's ear,   25
The harp a king had loved to hear.
He passed where Newark's stately tower
Looks out from Yarrow's birchen bower:
The Minstrel gazed with wishful eye—
No humbler resting-place was nigh.   30
With hesitating step at last
The embattled portal arch he passed,
Whose ponderous grate and massy bar
Had oft rolled back the tide of war,
But never closed the iron door   35
Against the desolate and poor.
The Duchess marked his weary pace,
His timid mien, and reverend face,
And bade her page the menials tell
That they should tend the old man well: 40
For she had known adversity,
Though born in such a high degree;
In pride of power, in beauty's bloom,
Had wept o'er Monmouth's bloody tomb!

When kindness had his wants supplied, 45
And the old man was gratified,
Began to rise his minstrel pride;
And he began to talk anon
Of good Earl Francis, dead and gone,
And of Earl Walter, rest him God!   50
A braver ne'er to battle rode;
And how full many a tale he knew
Of the old warriors of Buccleuch:
And, would the noble Duchess deign
To listen to an old man's strain,   55
Though stiff his hand, his voice though
    weak,
He thought even yet, the sooth to speak,
That, if she loved the harp to hear,
He could make music to her ear.

The humble boon was soon obtained;   60
The aged Minstrel audience gained.
But when he reached the room of state
Where she with all her ladies sate,
Perchance he wished his boon denied:
For, when to tune his harp he tried,   65
His trembling hand had lost the ease
Which marks security to please;
And scenes, long past, of joy and pain
Came wildering o'er his aged brain—
He tried to tune his harp in vain.   70

The pitying Duchess praised its chime,
And gave him heart, and gave him time,
Till every string's according glee
Was blended into harmony.
And then, he said, he would full fain   75
He could recall an ancient strain
He never thought to sing again.
It was not framed for village churls,
But for high dames and mighty earls;
He had played it to King Charles the
    Good   80
When he kept court in Holyrood;
And much he wished, yet feared, to try
The long-forgotten melody.
Amid the strings his fingers strayed,
And an uncertain warbling made,   85
And oft he shook his hoary head.
But when he caught the measure wild,
The old man raised his face and smiled;
And lightened up his faded eye
With all a poet's ecstasy!   90
In varying cadence, soft or strong,
He swept the sounding chords along:
The present scene, the future lot,
His toils, his wants, were all forgot;
Cold diffidence and age's frost   95
In the full tide of song were lost;
Each blank, in faithless memory void,
The poet's glowing thoughts supplied;
And, while his harp responsive rung,
'T was thus the LATEST MINSTREL sung. 100

SWEET TEVIOT

Sweet Teviot! on thy silver tide
  The glaring bale-fires blaze no more;
No longer steel-clad warriors ride
  Along thy wild and willowed shore;
Where'er thou wind'st, by dale or hill,   5
All, all is peaceful, all is still,
As if thy waves, since Time was born,
Since first they rolled upon the Tweed,
Had only heard the shepherd's reed,
  Nor started at the bugle-horn.   10
Unlike the tide of human time,
  Which, though it change in ceaseless
    flow,
Retains each grief, retains each crime,
  Its earliest course was doomed to know;
And, darker as it downward bears,   15
Is stained with past and present tears.
  Low as that tide has ebbed with me,
It still reflects to Memory's eye
The hour my brave, my only boy,
  Fell by the side of great Dundee.   20
Why, when the volleying musket played
Against the bloody Highland blade,
Why was not I beside him laid!—
Enough—he died the death of fame;
Enough—he died with conquering
    Græme.   25

MY NATIVE LAND

Breathes there the man, with soul so dead,
Who never to himself hath said,
  This is my own, my native land?
Whose heart hath ne'er within him burned,
As home his footsteps he hath turned   5
  From wandering on a foreign strand?
If such there breathe, go, mark him well;
For him no minstrel raptures swell;
High though his titles, proud his name,
Boundless his wealth as wish can claim,— 10
Despite those titles, power, and pelf,
The wretch, concentred all in self,
Living, shall forfeit fair renown,
And, doubly dying, shall go down
To the vile dust from whence he sprung, 15
Unwept, unhonored, and unsung.

O Caledonia, stern and wild,
Meet nurse for a poetic child!
Land of brown heath and shaggy wood,
Land of the mountain and the flood,   20
Land of my sires! what mortal hand
Can e're untie the filial band
That knits me to thy rugged strand!
Still, as I view each well-known scene,
Think what is now and what hath been, 25
Seems as to me, of all bereft,

Sole friends thy woods and streams were
    left;
And thus I love them better still,
Even in extremity of ill.
By Yarrow's stream still let me stray,   30
Though none should guide my feeble way;
Still feel the breeze down Ettrick break,
Although it chill my withered cheek;
Still lay my head by Teviot-stone,
Though there, forgotten and alone,   35
The bard may draw his parting groan.

SONG OF ALBERT GRÆME

It was an English ladye bright,
  (The sun shines fair on Carlisle wall,)
And she would marry a Scottish knight,
  For Love will still be lord of all.

Blithely they saw the rising sun,   195
  When he shone fair on Carlisle wall;
But they were sad ere day was done,
  Though Love was still the lord of all.

Her sire gave brooch and jewel fine,
  Where the sun shines fair on Carlisle
    wall;   200
Her brother gave but a flask of wine,
  For ire that Love was lord of all.

For she had lands, both meadow and lea,
  Where the sun shines fair on Carlisle
    wall,
And he swore her death, ere he would
    see   205
  A Scottish knight the lord of all!

That wine she had not tasted well,
  (The sun shines fair on Carlisle wall,)
When dead, in her true love's arms, she
    fell,
  For Love was still the lord of all!   210

He pierced her brother to the heart,
  Where the sun shines fair on Carlisle
    wall:—
So perish all would true love part,
  That Love may still be lord of all!

And then he took the cross divine,   215
  (Where the sun shines fair on Carlisle
    wall,)
And died for her sake in Palestine,
  So Love was still the lord of all.

Now all ye lovers, that faithful prove,
  (The sun shines fair on Carlisle wall,) 220
Pray for their souls who died for love,
  For Love shall still be lord of all!

HAROLD'S SONG

O, listen, listen ladies gay!
  No haughty feat of arms I tell;
Soft is the note, and sad the lay,
  That mourns the lovely Rosabelle. 355

"Moor, moor the barge, ye gallant crew!
  And, gentle ladye, deign to stay!
Rest thee in Castle Ravensheuch,
  Nor tempt the stormy firth to-day.

"The blackening wave is edged with
    white; 360
  To inch and rock the sea-mews fly;
The fishers have heard the Water Sprite,
  Whose screams forebode that wreck is
    nigh.

"Last night the gifted Seer did view
  A wet shroud swathed round ladye
    gay; 365
Then stay thee, fair, in Ravensheuch:
  Why cross the gloomy firth to-day?"

" 'T is not because Lord Lindesay's heir
  To-night at Roslin leads the ball,
But that my ladye-mother there 370
  Sits lonely in her castle-hall.

" 'T is not because the ring they ride,
  And Lindesay at the ring rides well,
But that my sire the wine will chide,
  If 't is not filled by Rosabelle." 375

O'er Roslin all that dreary night
  A wondrous blaze was seen to gleam;
'T was broader than the watch-fire light,
  And redder than the bright moonbeam.

It glared on Roslin's castled rock, 380
  It ruddied all the copsewood glen;
'T was seen from Dreyden's groves of oak,
  And seen from caverned Hawthornden.

Seemed all on fire that chapel proud
  Where Roslin's chiefs uncoffined lie, 385
Each baron, for a sable shroud,
  Sheathed in his iron panoply.

Seemed all on fire within, around,
  Deep sacristy and altar's pale;
Shone every pillar foliage-bound, 390
  And glimmered all the dead men's mail.

Blazed battlement and pinnet high,
  Blazed every rose-carved buttress fair—
So still they blaze when fate is nigh
  The lordly line of high Saint Clair. 395

There are twenty of Roslin's barons bold
  Lie buried within that proud chapelle;
Each one the holy vault doth hold—
  But the sea holds lovely Rosabelle!

And each Saint Clair was buried there, 400
  With candle, with book, and with knell;
But the sea-caves rung and the wild winds
    sung
  The dirge of lovely Rosabelle.

THE MAID OF NEIDPATH

O, lovers' eyes are sharp to see,
  And lovers' ears in hearing;
And love in life's extremity
  Can lend an hour of cheering.
Disease had been in Mary's bower, 5
  And slow decay from mourning,
Though now she sits on Neidpath's tower
  To watch her love's returning.

All sunk and dim her eyes so bright,
  Her form decayed by pining, 10
Till through her wasted hand at night
  You saw the taper shining;
By fits, a sultry hectic hue
  Across her cheek were flying;
By fits, so ashy pale she grew, 15
  Her maidens thought her dying.

Yet keenest powers to see and hear
  Seemed in her frame residing;
Before the watch-dog pricked his ear,
  She heard her lover's riding; 20
Ere scarce a distant form was kenned,
  She knew, and waved to greet him;
And o'er the battlement did bend,
  As on the wing to meet him.

He came—he passed—an heedless gaze, 25
  As o'er some stranger glancing;
Her welcome, spoke in faltering phrase,
  Lost in his courser's prancing—
The castle arch, whose hollow tone
  Returns each whisper spoken, 30
Could scarcely catch the feeble moan
  Which told her heart was broken.

HUNTING SONG

Waken, lords and ladies gay,
On the mountain dawns the day,
All the jolly chase is here,
With hawk and horse and hunting-spear!
Hounds are in their couples yelling, 5
Hawks are whistling, horns are knelling,
Merrily, merrily, mingle they,
"Waken, lords and ladies gay."

Waken, lords and ladies gay,
The mist has left the mountain gray,   10
Springlets in the dawn are steaming,
Diamonds on the brake are gleaming:
And foresters have busy been
To track the buck in thicket green;
Now we come to chant our lay,   15
"Waken, lords and ladies gay."

Waken, lords and ladies gay,
To the green-wood haste away;
We can show you where he lies,
Fleet of foot and tall of size;   20
We can show the marks he made,
When 'gainst the oak his antlers frayed;
You shall see him brought to bay,
"Waken, lords and ladies gay."

Louder, louder chant the lay,   25
Waken, lords and ladies gay!
Tell them youth and mirth and glee
Run a course as well as we;
Time, stern huntsman, who can balk,
Stanch as hound and fleet as hawk?   30
Think of this and rise with day,
Gentle lords and ladies gay.

                                    1805

FROM MARMION

NELSON, PITT, AND FOX

To mute and to material things
New life revolving summer brings;
The genial call dead Nature hears,   55
And in her glory reappears.
But oh! my country's wintry state
What second spring shall renovate?
What powerful call shall bid arise
The buried warlike and the wise,   60
The mind that thought for Britain's weal,
The hand that grasped the victor steel?
The vernal sun new life bestows
Even on the meanest flower that blows;
But vainly, vainly may he shine   65
Where Glory weeps o'er NELSON's shrine,
And vainly pierce the solemn gloom
That shrouds, O PITT, thy hallowed tomb!

Deep graved in every British heart,
Oh, never let those names depart!   70
Say to your sons,—Lo, here his grave
Who victor died on Gadite wave!
To him, as to the burning levin,
Short, bright, resistless course was given;
Where'er his country's foes were found, 75
Was heard the fated thunder's sound,
Till burst the bolt on yonder shore,
Rolled, blazed, destroyed,—and was no
    more.

Nor mourn ye less his perished worth
Who bade the conqueror go forth,   80
And launched that thunderbolt of war
On Egypt, Hafnia, Trafalgar;
Who, born to guide such high emprise,
For Britain's weal was early wise;
Alas! to whom the Almighty gave,   85
For Britain's sins, an early grave!
His worth who, in his mightiest hour,
A bauble held the pride of power,
Spurned at the sordid lust of pelf,
And served his Albion for herself;   90
Who, when the frantic crowd amain
Strained at subjection's bursting rein,
O'er their wild mood full conquest gained,
The pride, he would not crush, restrained,
Showed their fierce zeal a worthier cause, 95
And brought the freeman's arm to aid the
    freeman's laws.

Hadst thou but lived, though stripped of
    power,
A watchman on the lonely tower,
Thy thrilling trump had roused the land,
When fraud or danger were at hand;   100
By thee, as by the beacon-light,
Our pilots had kept course aright;
As some proud column, though alone,
Thy strength had propped the tottering
    throne.
Now is the stately column broke,   105
The beacon-light is quenched in smoke.
The trumpet's silver sound is still,
The warder silent on the hill!

Oh, think, how to his latest day,
When Death, just hovering, claimed his
    prey,   110
With Palinure's unaltered mood,
Firm at his dangerous post he stood;
Each call for needful rest repelled,
With dying hand the rudder held,
Till, in his fall, with fateful sway, 115
The steerage of the realm gave way!
Then, while on Britain's thousand plains
One unpolluted church remains,
Whose peaceful bells ne'er sent around
The bloody tocsin's maddening sound,   120
But still, upon the hallowed day,
Convoke the swains to praise and pray;
While faith and civil peace are dear,
Grace this cold marble with a tear,
He who preserved them, PITT, lies here. 125

Nor yet suppress the generous sigh
Because his rival slumbers nigh,
Nor be thy requiescat dumb
Lest it be said o'er Fox's tomb;
For talents mourn, untimely lost,   130
When best employed and wanted most;

Mourn genius high, and lore profound,
And wit that loved to play, not wound;
And all the reasoning powers divine,
To penetrate, resolve, combine;   135
And feelings keen, and fancy's glow,
They sleep with him who sleeps below:
And, if thou mourn'st they could not save
From error him who owns this grave,
Be every harsher thought suppressed,   140
And sacred be the last long rest.
Here, where the end of earthly things
Lays heroes, patriots, bards, and kings;
Where stiff the hand, and still the tongue,
Of those who fought, and spoke, and
    sung;   145
Here, where the fretted aisles prolong
The distant notes of holy song,
As if some angel spoke again,
"All peace on earth, good-will to men";
If ever from an English heart,   150
Oh, *here* let prejudice depart,
And, partial feeling cast aside,
Record that Fox a Briton died!

When Europe crouched to France's yoke,
And Austria bent, and Prussia broke,   155
And the firm Russia's purpose brave
Was bartered by a timorous slave,
Even then dishonor's peace he spurned,
The sullied olive-branch returned,
Stood for his country's glory fast,   160
And nailed her colors to the mast!
Heaven, to reward his firmness, gave
A portion in this honored grave,
And ne'er held marble in its trust
Of two such wondrous men the dust.   165

With more than mortal powers endowed,
How high they soared above the crowd!
Theirs was no common party race,
Jostling by dark intrigue for place;
Like fabled Gods, their mighty war   170
Shook realms and nations in its jar;
Beneath each banner proud to stand,
Looked up the noblest of the land,
Till through the British world were known
The names of PITT and Fox alone.   175
Spells of such force no wizard grave
E'er framed in dark Thessalian cave,
Though his could drain the ocean dry,
And force the planets from the sky.
These spells are spent, and, spent with
    these,   180
The wine of life is on the lees,
Genius and taste and talent gone,
Forever tombed beneath the stone,
Where—taming thought to human pride!—
The mighty chiefs sleep side by side.   185
Drop upon Fox's grave the tear,
'T will trickle to his rival's bier;

O'er PITT's the mournful requiem sound,
And Fox's shall the notes rebound.
The solemn echo seems to cry,—   190
"Here let their discord with them die.
Speak not for those a separate doom
Whom Fate made brothers in the tomb;
But search the land, of living men,
Where wilt thou find their like again?"   195

Rest, ardent spirits, till the cries
Of dying nature bid you rise!
Not even your Britain's groans can pierce
The leaden silence of your hearse;
Then, oh, how impotent and vain   200
This grateful tributary strain!
Though not unmarked from northern
    clime,
Ye heard the Border Minstrel's rhyme:
His Gothic harp has o'er you rung;
The Bard you deigned to praise, your
    deathless names has sung.   205

SONG: WHERE SHALL THE LOVER REST?

Where shall the lover rest,
  Whom the fates sever
From his true maiden's breast,   150
  Parted forever?
Where, through groves deep and high,
  Sounds the far billow,
Where early violets die,
  Under the willow.   155

CHORUS

Eleu loro, etc. Soft shall be his pillow.

There, through the summer day,
  Cool streams are laving;
There, while the tempests sway,
  Scarce are boughs waving;   160
There thy rest shalt thou take,
  Parted forever,
Never again to wake,
  Never, O never!

CHORUS

Eleu loro, etc. Never, O never!   165

Where shall the traitor rest,
  He the deceiver,
Who could win maiden's breast,
  Ruin and leave her?
In the lost battle,   170
  Borne down by the flying,
Where mingles war's rattle
  With groans of the dying.

CHORUS   Shame and dishonor sit

By his grave ever;   180

Eleu loro, etc. There shall he be lying.   Blessing shall hallow it,—

Never, O never!

Her wing shall the eagle flap 175
  O'er the false-hearted;   CHORUS

His warm blood the wolf shall lap,
  Ere life be parted.   *Eleu loro, etc.* Never, O never!

LADY HERON'S SONG: LOCHINVAR

Oh! Young Lochinvar is come out of the west,
Through all the wide Border his steed was the best;
And save his good broadsword he weapons had none,   315
He rode all unarmed and he rode all alone.
So faithful in love and so dauntless in war,
There never was knight like the young Lochinvar.

He stayed not for brake and he stopped not for stone,
He swam the Eske river where ford there was none;   320
But ere he alighted at Netherby gate
The bride had consented, the gallant came late:
For a laggard in love and a dastard in war
Was to wed the fair Ellen of brave Lochinvar.

So boldly he entered the Netherby Hall,   325
Among bridesmen, and kinsmen, and brothers, and all:
Then spoke the bride's father, his hand on his sword,—
For the poor craven bridegroom said never a word,—
"Oh! come ye in peace here, or come ye in war,
Or to dance at our bridal, young Lord Lochinvar?"—   330

"I long wooed your daughter, my suit you denied;
Love swells like the Solway, but ebbs like its tide—
And now am I come, with this lost love of mine,
To lead but one measure, drink one cup of wine.
There are maidens in Scotland more lovely by far,   335
That would gladly be bride to the young Lochinvar."

The bride kissed the goblet; the knight took it up,
He quaffed off the wine, and he threw down the cup.
She looked down to blush, and she looked up to sigh,
With a smile on her lips and a tear in her eye.   340
He took her soft hand ere her mother could bar,—
"Now tread we a measure!" said young Lochinvar.

So stately his form, and so lovely her face,
That never a hall such a galliard did grace;
While her mother did fret, and her father did fume,   345
And the bridegroom stood dangling his bonnet and plume;
And the bride-maidens whispered, " 'T were better by far
To have matched our fair cousin with young Lochinvar."

One touch to her hand and one word in her ear,
When they reached the hall-door, and the charger stood near;   350
So light to the croupe the fair lady he swung,
So light to the saddle before her he sprung!

"She is won! we are gone, over bank, bush, and scaur;
They'll have fleet steeds that follow," quoth young Lochinvar.

There was mounting 'mong Græmes of the Netherby clan;   355
Forsters, Fenwicks, and Musgraves, they rode and they ran:
There was racing and chasing on Cannobie Lee,
But the lost bride of Netherby ne'er did they see.
So daring in love and so dauntless in war,
Have ye e'er heard of gallant like young Lochinvar?   360

INTRODUCTION TO CANTO SIXTH:
CHRISTMAS

And well our Christian sires of old
Loved when the year its course had
        rolled,   25
And brought blithe Christmas back again,
With all his hospitable train.
Domestic and religious rite
Gave honor to the holy night;
On Christmas eve the bells were rung;   30
On Christmas eve the mass was sung:
That only night in all the year
Saw the stoled priest the chalice rear.
The damsel donned her kirtle sheen;
The hall was dressed with holly green;   35
Forth to the wood did merrymen go,
To gather in the mistletoe.
Then opened wide the baron's hall
To vassal, tenant, serf, and all;
Power laid his rod of rule aside,   40
And Ceremony doffed his pride.
The heir, with roses in his shoes,
That night might village partner choose;
The lord, underogating, share
The vulgar game of 'post and pair,'   45
All hailed, with uncontrolled delight
And general voice, the happy night
That to the cottage, as the crown,
Brought tidings of salvation down.

The fire, with well-dried logs supplied,   50
Went roaring up the chimney wide;
The huge hall-table's oaken face,
Scrubbed till it shone, the day to grace,
Bore then upon its massive board
No mark to part the squire and lord.   55
Then was brought in the lusty brawn
By old blue-coated serving-man;
Then the grim boar's-head frowned on
        high,
Crested with bays and rosemary.
Well can the green-garbed ranger tell   60
How, when, and where, the monster fell,
What dogs before his death he tore,
And all the baiting of the boar.
The wassail round, in good brown bowls
Garnished with ribbons, blithely trowls.   65
There the huge sirloin reeked; hard by

Plum-porridge stood and Christmas pie;
Nor failed old Scotland to produce
At such high tide her savory goose.
Then came the merry maskers in,   70
And carols roared with blithesome din;
If unmelodious was the song,
It was a hearty note and strong.
Who lists may in their mumming see
Traces of ancient mystery;   75
White shirts supplied the masquerade,
And smutted cheeks the visors made;
But oh! what maskers, richly dight,
Can boast of bosoms half so light!
England was merry England when   80
Old Christmas brought his sports again.
'Twas Christmas broached the mightiest ale,
'Twas Christmas told the merriest tale;
A Christmas gambol oft could cheer
The poor man's heart through half the
        year.   85

Still linger in our northern clime
Some remnants of the good old time,
And still within our valleys here
We hold the kindred title dear,
Even when, perchance, its far-fetched
        claim   90
To Southron ear sounds empty name;
For course of blood, our proverbs deem,
Is warmer than the mountain-stream.
And thus my Christmas still I hold
Where my great-grandsire came of old,   95
With amber beard and flaxen hair
And reverent apostolic air,
The feast and holy-tide to share,
And mix sobriety with wine,
And honest mirth with thoughts divine.   100

MARMION AND DOUGLAS

Then at the altar Wilton kneels,
And Clare the spurs bound on his heels;
And think what next he must have felt
At buckling of the falchion belt!
And judge how Clara changed her hue   355
While fastening to her lover's side
A friend, which, though in danger tried,
He once had found untrue!

Then Douglas struck him with his blade:
"Saint Michael and Saint Andrew aid,　360
　I dub thee knight.
Arise, Sir Ralph, De Wilton's heir!
For king, for church, for lady fair,
　See that thou fight."
And Bishop Gawain, as he rose,　365
Said: "Wilton! grieve not for thy woes,
　Disgrace, and trouble;
For He who honor best bestows
　May give thee double."
De Wilton sobbed, for sob he must:　370
"Where'er I meet a Douglas, trust
　That Douglas is my brother!"
"Nay, nay," old Angus said, "not so;
To Surrey's camp thou now must go,
　Thy wrongs no longer smother.　375
I have two sons in yonder field;
And, if thou meet'st them under shield,
Upon them bravely—do thy worst,
And foul fall him that blenches first!"

Not far advanced was morning day　380
When Marmion did his troop array
　To Surrey's camp to ride;
He had safe-conduct for his band
Beneath the royal seal and hand,
　And Douglas gave a guide.　385
The ancient earl with stately grace
Would Clara on her palfrey place,
And whispered in an undertone,
"Let the hawk stoop, his prey is flown."
The train from out the castle drew,　390
But Marmion stopped to bid adieu:
　"Though something I might plain," he
　　said,
"Of cold respect to stranger guest,
Sent hither by your king's behest,
　While in Tantallion's towers I stayed,　395
Part we in friendship from your land,
And, noble earl, receive my hand."—
But Douglas round him drew his cloak,
Folded his arms, and thus he spoke:—
"My manors, halls, and bowers shall still　400
Be open at my sovereign's will
To each one whom he lists, howe'er
Unmeet to be the owner's peer.
My castles are my king's alone,
From turret to foundation-stone—　405
The hand of Douglas is his own,
And never shall in friendly grasp
The hand of such as Marmion clasp."
Burned Marmion's swarthy cheek like fire
And shook his very frame for ire,　410
　And—"This to me!" he said,
"An 't were not for thy hoary beard,
Such hand as Marmion's had not spared
　To cleave the Douglas' head!
And first I tell thee, haughty peer,　415
He who does England's message here,

Although the meanest in her state,
May well, proud Angus, be thy mate;
And, Douglas, more I tell thee here,
　Even in thy pitch of pride,　420
Here in thy hold, thy vassals near,—
Nay, never look upon your lord,
And lay your hands upon your sword,—
　I tell thee, thou 'rt defied!
And if thou saidst I am not peer　425
To any lord in Scotland here,
Lowland or Highland, far or near,
　Lord Angus, thou hast lied!"
On the earl's cheek the flush of rage
O'ercame the ashen hue of age:　430
Fierce he broke forth,—"And darest thou
　then
To beard the lion in his den,
　The Douglas in his hall?
And hopest thou hence unscathed to go?—
No, by Saint Bride of Bothwell, no!　435
Up drawbridge, grooms—what, warder, ho!
　Let the portcullis fall."—
Lord Marmion turned,—well was his
　need,—
And dashed the rowels in his steed,
Like arrow through the archway sprung,　440
The ponderous grate behind him rung;
To pass there was such scanty room,
The bars descending razed his plume.

The steed along the drawbridge flies
Just as it trembled on the rise;　445
Not lighter does the swallow skim
Along the smooth lake's level brim:
And when Lord Marmion reached his
　band,
He halts, and turns with clenched hand,
And shout of loud defiance pours,　450
And shook his gauntlet at the towers.
"Horse! horse!" the Douglas cried, "and
　chase!"
But soon he reined his fury's pace:
"A royal messenger he came,
Though most unworthy of the name.—　455
A letter forged! Saint Jude to speed!
Did ever knight so foul a deed?
At first in heart it liked me ill
When the king praised his clerkly skill.
Thanks to Saint Bothan, son of mine,　460
Save Gawain, ne'er could pen a line;
So swore I, and I swear it still,
Let my boy-bishop fret his fill.—
Saint Mary mend my fiery mood!
Old age ne'er cools the Douglas blood,　465
I thought to slay him where he stood.
'T is pity of him too," he cried:
"Bold can he speak and fairly ride,
I warrant him a warrior tried."
With this his mandate he recalls,　470
And slowly seeks his castle halls.

THE BATTLE, AND MARMION'S DEATH

Ere yet the bands met Marmion's eye,
Fitz-Eustace shouted loud and high,
"Hark! hark! my lord, an English drum!
And see ascending squadrons come
    Between Tweed's river and the hill, 625
Foot, horse, and cannon! Hap what hap,
My basnet to a prentice cap,
    Lord Surrey's o'er the Till!—
Yet more! yet more!—how fair arrayed
They file from out the hawthorn shade, 630
    And sweep so gallant by!
With all their banners bravely spread,
    And all their armor flashing high,
Saint George might waken from the dead,
    To see fair England's standards
      fly."— 635
"Stint in thy prate," quoth Blount,
    "thou'dst best,
And listen to our lord's behest."—
With kindling brow Lord Marmion said,
"This instant be our band arrayed;
The river must be quickly crossed, 640
That we may join Lord Surrey's host.
If fight King James,—as well I trust
That fight he will, and fight he must,—
The Lady Clare behind our lines
Shall tarry while the battle joins." 645

Himself he swift on horseback threw,
Scarce to the abbot bade adieu,
Far less would listen to his prayer
To leave behind the helpless Clare.
Down to the Tweed his band he drew, 650
And muttered as the flood they view,
"The pheasant in the falcon's claw,
He scarce will yield to please a daw;
Lord Angus may the abbot awe,
    So Clare shall bide with me." 655
Then on that dangerous ford and deep
Where to the Tweed Leat's eddies creep,
    He ventured desperately:
And not a moment will he bide
Till squire or groom before him ride; 660
Headmost of all he stems the tide,
    And stems it gallantly.
Eustace held Clare upon her horse,
    Old Hubert led her rein,
Stoutly they braved the current's course, 665
And, though far downward driven perforce,
    The southern bank they gain.
Behind them straggling came to shore,
    As best they might, the train:
Each o'er his head his yew-bow bore, 670
    A caution not in vain;
Deep need that day that every string,
By wet unharmed, should sharply ring.
A moment then Lord Marmion stayed,

And breathed his steed, his men
    arrayed, 675
    Then forward moved his band,
Until, Lord Surrey's rear-guard won,
He halted by a cross of stone,
That on a hillock standing lone
    Did all the field command. 680

Hence might they see the full array
Of either host for deadly fray;
Their marshalled lines stretched east and
    west,
    And fronted north and south,
And distant salutation passed 685
    From the loud cannon mouth;
Not in the close successive rattle
That breathes the voice of modern battle,
    But slow and far between.
The hillock gained, Lord Marmion
    stayed: 690
"Here, by this cross," he gently said,
    "You well may view the scene.
Here shalt thou tarry, lovely Clare:
O! think of Marmion in thy prayer!—
Thou wilt not?—well,—no less my care 695
Shall, watchful, for thy weal prepare.—
You, Blount and Eustace, are her guard,
    With ten picked archers of my train;
With England if the day go hard,
    To Berwick speed amain.— 700
But, if we conquer, cruel maid,
My spoils shall at your feet be laid,
    When here we meet again."
He waited not for answer there,
And would not mark the maid's despair, 705
    Nor heed the discontented look
From either squire; but spurred amain,
And, dashing through the battle plain,
    His way to Surrey took.

"The good Lord Marmion, by my life! 710
    Welcome to danger's hour!—
Short greeting serves in time of strife:—
    Thus have I ranged my power:
Myself will rule this central host,
Stout Stanley fronts their right, 715
My sons command the vaward post,
    With Brian Tunstall, stainless knight;
Lord Dacre, with his horsemen light,
Shall be in rearward of the fight,
And succor those that need it most. 720
    Now, gallant Marmion, well I know,
Would gladly to the vanguard go;
Edmund, the admiral, Tunstall there,
    With thee their charge will blithely
      share;
There fight thine own retainers too, 725
Beneath De Burgh, thy steward true."—
"Thanks, noble Surrey!" Marmion said,

Nor farther greeting there he paid;
But, parting like a thunderbolt,
First in the vanguard made a halt,   730
  Where such a shout there rose
Of "Marmion! Marmion!" that the cry,
Up Flodden mountain shrilling high,
  Startled the Scottish foes.

Blount and Fitz-Eustace rested still   735
With Lady Clare upon the hill;
On which (for far the day was spent)
The western sunbeams now were bent;
The cry they heard, its meaning knew,
Could plain their distant comrades
    view;   740
Sadly to Blount did Eustace say,
"Unworthy office here to stay!
No hope of gilded spurs to-day.—
But see! look up—on Flodden bent,
The Scottish foe has fired his tent."   745
  And sudden, as he spoke,
From the sharp ridges of the hill,
All downward to the banks of Till,
  Was wreathed in sable smoke.
Volumed and fast, and rolling far,   750
The cloud enveloped Scotland's war,
  As down the hill they broke;
Nor martial shout, nor minstrel tone,
Announced their march; their tread alone,
At times one warning trumpet blown,   755
  At times a stifled hum
Told England, from his mountain throne,
  King James did rushing come.—
Scarce could they hear, or see their foes,
Until at weapon-point they close.—   760
They close, in clouds of smoke and dust,
With sword-sway, and with lance's thrust;
  And such a yell was there,
Of sudden and portentous birth,
As if men fought upon the earth,   765
  And fiends in upper air;
O life and death were in the shout,
Recoil and rally, charge and rout,
  And triumph and despair.
Long looked the anxious squires; their
    eye   770
Could in the darkness naught descry.

At length the freshening western blast
Aside the shroud of battle cast;
And, first, the ridge of mingled spears
Above the brightening cloud appears;   775
And in the smoke the pennons flew,
As in the storm the white sea-mew.
Then marked they, dashing broad and far
The broken billows of the war,
And plumed crest of chieftains brave,   780
Floating like foam upon the wave;
  But naught distinct they see:
Wide raged the battle on the plain;

Spears shook, and falchions flashed amain;
Fell England's arrow-flight like rain;   785
Crests rose, and stooped, and rose again,
  Wild and disorderly.
Amid the scene of tumult, high
They saw Lord Marmion's falcon fly:
And stainless Tunstall's banner white,   790
And Edmund Howard's lion bright,
Still bear them bravely in the fight;
  Although against them come,
Of gallant Gordons many a one,
And many a stubborn Badenoch-man,   795
And many a rugged border clan,
  With Huntley, and with Home.

Far on the left, unseen the while,
Stanley broke Lennox and Argyle;
Though there the western mountaineer   800
Rushed with bare bosom on the spear,
And flung the feeble targe aside,
And with both hands the broadsword plied.
'Twas vain:—But fortune, on the right,
With fickle smile, cheered Scotland's
    fight.   805
Then fell that spotless banner white,
  The Howard's lion fell;
Yet still Lord Marmion's falcon flew
With wavering flight, while fiercer grew
  Around the battle yell.   810
The border slogan rent the sky!
A Home! a Gordon! was the cry;
  Loud were the clanging blows;
Advanced,—forced back,—now low, now
    high
  The pennon sunk and rose;   815
As bends the bark's mast in the gale,
When rent are rigging, shrouds, and sail,
  It wavered 'mid the foes.
No longer Blount the view could bear:
"By heaven, and all its saints! I swear,   820
  I will not see it lost!
Fitz-Eustace, you with Lady Clare
May bid your beads, and patter prayer,—
  I gallop to the host."
And to the fray he rode amain,   825
Followed by all the archer train.
The fiery youth, with desperate charge,
Made, for a space an opening large,—
  The rescued banner rose,—
But darkly closed the war around,   830
Like pine-tree, rooted from the ground,
  It sunk among the foes.
Then Eustace mounted too:—yet staid,
As loath to leave the helpless maid,
  When, fast as shaft can fly,   835
Blood-shot his eyes, his nostrils spread,
The loose rein dangling from his head,
Housing and saddle bloody red,
  Lord Marmion's steed rushed by;
And Eustace, maddening at the sight,   840

A look and sign to Clara cast,
  To mark he would return in haste,
Then plunged into the fight.

Ask me not what the maiden feels,
  Left in that dreadful hour alone: 845
Perchance her reason stoops, or reels;
  Perchance a courage, not her own,
  Braces her mind to desperate tone.—
The scattered van of England wheels;—
  She only said, as loud in air   850
The tumult roared, "Is Wilton there?"—
  They fly, or, maddened by despair,
Fight but to die,—"Is Wilton there?"
With that, straight up the hill there rode,
  Two horsemen drenched with gore,   855
And in their arms, a helpless load,
  A wounded knight they bore.
His hand still strained the broken brand;
His arms were smeared with blood and
      sand.
Dragged from among the horses' feet,   860
With dinted shield and helmet beat,
The falcon-crest and plumage gone,
Can that be haughty Marmion! . . .
Young Blount his armor did unlace,
And, gazing on his ghastly face,   865
  Said, "By Saint George, he 's gone!
That spear-wound has our master sped,
And see the deep cut on his head!
  Good-night to Marmion."—
"Unnurtured Blount! thy brawling
      cease: 870
He opes his eyes," said Eustace; "peace!"

When, doffed his casque, he felt free air,
Around gan Marmion wildly stare:
"Where's Harry Blount? Fitz-Eustace
      where?
Linger ye here, ye hearts of hare!   875
Redeem my pennon,—charge again!
Cry, 'Marmion to the rescue!'—Vain!
Last of my race, on battle-plain
That shout shall ne'er be heard again!—
Yet my last thought is England's—fly,   880
  To Dacre bear my signet-ring;
Tell him his squadrons up to bring.—
Fitz-Eustace, to Lord Surrey hie:
  Tunstall lies dead upon the field,
  His lifeblood stains the spotless
      shield;   885
  Edmund is down; my life is reft;
  The Admiral alone is left.
Let Stanley charge with spur of fire,—
With Chester charge, and Lancashire,
Full upon Scotland's central host,   890
Or victory and England's lost.—
Must I bid twice?—hence, varlets! fly!—
  Leave Marmion here alone—to die."

They parted, and alone he lay;
  Clare drew her from the sight away,   895
Till pain wrung forth a lowly moan,
And half he murmured, "Is there none
  Of all my halls have nurst,
Page, squire, or groom, one cup to bring
Of blessed water from the spring,   900
  To slake my dying thirst!"

O Woman! in our hours of ease
Uncertain, coy, and hard to please,
And variable as the shade
By the light quivering aspen made;   905
When pain and anguish wring the brow,
A ministering angel thou!—
Scarce were the piteous accents said,
When with the baron's casque the maid
  To the nigh streamlet ran: 910
Forgot were hatred, wrongs, and fears;
The plaintive voice alone she hears,
  Sees but the dying man.
She stooped her by the runnel's side,
  But in abhorrence backward drew;   915
For, oozing from the mountain's side
Where raged the war, a dark-red tide
  Was curdling in the streamlet blue.
Where shall she turn?—behold her mark
  A little fountain cell,   920
Where water, clear as diamond spark,
  In a stone basin fell.
Above, some half-worn letters say,
𝔇𝔯𝔦𝔫𝔨 𝔴𝔢𝔞𝔯𝔶 𝔭𝔦𝔩𝔤𝔯𝔦𝔪 𝔡𝔯𝔦𝔫𝔨 𝔞𝔫𝔡 𝔭𝔯𝔞𝔶
𝔉𝔬𝔯 𝔱𝔥𝔢 𝔨𝔦𝔫𝔡 𝔰𝔬𝔲𝔩 𝔬𝔣 𝔖𝔦𝔟𝔶𝔩 𝔊𝔯𝔢𝔶   925
𝔚𝔥𝔬 𝔟𝔲𝔦𝔩𝔱 𝔱𝔥𝔦𝔰 𝔠𝔯𝔬𝔰𝔰 𝔞𝔫𝔡 𝔴𝔢𝔩𝔩
She filled the helm and back she hied,
And with surprise and joy espied
  A monk supporting Marmion's head;
A pious man, whom duty brought   930
To dubious verge of battle fought,
  To shrive the dying, bless the dead.

Deep drank Lord Marmion of the wave,
And, as she stooped his brow to lave—
"Is it the hand of Clare," he said,   935
"Or injured Constance, bathes my head?"
  Then, as remembrance rose,—
"Speak not to me of shrift or prayer!
  I must redress her woes.
Short space, few words, are mine to
      spare;   940
Forgive and listen, gentle Clare!"—
  "Alas!" she said, "the while,—
Oh! think of your immortal weal!
In vain for Constance is your zeal;
  She—died at Holy Isle."—   945
Lord Marmion started from the ground
As light as if he felt no wound,
Though in the action burst the tide
In torrents from his wounded side.
"Then it was truth," he said—"I knew   950

That the dark presage must be true.—
I would the Fiend, to whom belongs
The vengeance due to all her wrongs,
    Would spare me but a day!
For wasting fire, and dying groan,   955
And priests slain on the altar stone,
    Might bribe him for delay.
It may not be!—this dizzy trance—
Curse on yon base marauder's lance,
And doubly cursed my failing brand!   960
A sinful heart makes feeble hand."
Then fainting down on earth he sunk,
Supported by the trembling monk.

With fruitless labor Clara bound
And strove to stanch the gushing
    wound;   965
The monk with unavailing cares
Exhausted all the Church's prayers.
Ever, he said, that, close and near,
A lady's voice was in his ear,
And that the priest he could not hear;   970
    For that she ever sung,
*"In the lost battle, borne down by the
    flying,*
Where mingles war's rattle with groans of
    the dying!"
So the notes rung.—
"Avoid thee, Fiend!—with cruel hand   975
Shake not the dying sinner's sand!—
Oh! look, my son, upon yon sign
Of the Redeemer's grace divine;
    Oh! think on faith and bliss!—
By many a death-bed I have been,   980
And many a sinner's parting seen,
    But never aught like this."—
The war, that for a space did fail,
Now trebly thundering swelled the gale,
    And "Stanley!" was the cry.—   985
A light on Marmion's visage spread,
    And fired his glazing eye;
With dying hand above his head
He shook the fragment of his blade,
    And shouted "Victory!—   990
Charge, Chester, charge! On, Stanley, on!"
Were the last words of Marmion.

By this, though deep the evening fell,
Still rose the battle's deadly swell,
For still the Scots around their king,   995
Unbroken, fought in desperate ring.
Where's now their victor vaward wing,
    Where Huntly, and where Home?—
O, for a blast of that dread horn,
On Fontarabian echoes borne,   1000
    That to king Charles did come,
When Rowland brave, and Olivier,
And every paladin and peer,
    On Roncesvalles died!

Such blast might warn them, not in
    vain,   1005
To quit the plunder of the slain,
And turn the doubtful day again,
    While yet on Flodden side,
Afar, the royal standard flies,
And round it toils, and bleeds, and dies,   1010
    Our Caledonian pride!
In vain the wish—for, far away,
While spoil and havoc mark their way,
Near Sybil's cross the plunderers stray.—
"O, Lady," cried the Monk, "away!"   1015
    And placed her on her steed,
And led her to the chapel fair,
    Of Tilmouth upon Tweed.
There all the night they spent in prayer,
And at the dawn of morning, there   1020
She met her kinsman, Lord Fitz-Clare.

. . . .

Less easy task it were, to show
Lord Marmion's nameless grave, and
    low.   1120
    They dug his grave e'en where he lay,
    But every mark is gone;
    Time's wasting hand has done away
    The simple cross of Sybil Grey,
        And broke her font of stone: 1125
But yet from out the little hill
Oozes the slender springlet still.
    Oft halts the stranger there,
For thence may best his curious eye
    The memorable field descry;   1130
    And shepherd boys repair
To seek the water-flag and rush,
And rest them by the hazel bush,
    And plait their garlands fair;
Nor dream they sit upon the grave,   1135
That holds the bones of Marmion brave.—
When thou shalt find the little hill,
With thy heart commune, and be still.
If ever, in temptation strong,
Thou left'st the right path for the
    wrong;   1140
If every devious step thus trod,
Still led thee farther from the road;
Dread thou to speak presumptuous doom
On noble Marmion's lowly tomb;
But say, "He died a gallant knight,   1145
With sword in hand, for England's right."

1808

FROM THE LADY OF THE LAKE

CANTO FIRST: THE CHASE

Harp of the north! that moldering long
    hast hung
    On the witch-elm that shades Saint
    Fillan's spring,

And down the fitful breeze thy numbers
    flung,
  Till envious ivy did around thee cling,
Muffling with verdant ringlet every
    string,—   5
O minstrel harp, still must thine accents
    sleep?
'Mid rustling leaves and fountains mur-
    muring,
  Still must thy sweeter sounds their
    silence keep,
Nor bid a warrior smile, nor teach a maid
    to weep?

Not thus, in ancient days of Caledon,   10
  Was thy voice mute amid the festal
    crowd,
When lay of hopeless love, or glory won,
  Aroused the fearful, or subdued the
    proud.
At each according pause was heard aloud
Thine ardent symphony sublime and
    high!   15
Fair dames and crested chiefs attention
    bowed;
  For still the burden of thy minstrelsy
Was knighthood's dauntless deed, and
    beauty's matchless eye.

O wake once more! how rude soe'er the
    hand
  That ventures o'er thy magic maze to
    stray;   20
O wake once more! though scarce my skill
    command
  Some feeble echoing of thine earlier lay:
Though harsh and faint, and soon to die
    away,
  And all unworthy of thy nobler strain,
Yet if one heart throb higher at its sway, 25
  The wizard note has not been touched
    in vain.
Then silent be no more! Enchantress,
    wake again!

I

The stag at eve had drunk his fill,
Where danced the moon on Monan's rill,
And deep his midnight lair had made   30
In lone Glenartney's hazel shade;
But, when the sun his beacon red
Had kindled on Benvoirlich's head,
The deep-mouthed bloodhound's heavy
    bay
Resounded up the rocky way,   35
And faint, from farther distance borne,
Were heard the clanging hoof and horn.

II

As chief, who hears his warder call,
"To arms! the foemen storm the wall,"

The antlered monarch of the waste   40
Sprung from his heathery couch in haste,
But, ere his fleet career he took,
The dew-drops from his flanks he shook;
Like crested leader proud and high,
Tossed his beamed frontlet to the sky;   45
A moment gazed adown the dale,
A moment snuffed the tainted gale,
A moment listened to the cry,
That thickened as the chase drew nigh;
Then, as the headmost foes appeared,   50
With one brave bound the copse he
    cleared,
And, stretching forward free and far,
Sought the wild heaths of Uam-Var.

III

Yelled on the view the opening pack;
Rock, glen, and cavern, paid them back;   55
To many a mingled sound at once
The awakened mountain gave response.
A hundred dogs bayed deep and strong,
Clattered a hundred steeds along,
Their peal the merry horns rung out,   60
A hundred voices joined the shout;
With hark and whoop and wild halloo,
No rest Benvoirlich's echoes knew.
Far from the tumult fled the roe,
Close in her covert cowered the doe;   65
The falcon, from her cairn on high,
Cast on the rout a wondering eye,
Till far beyond her piercing ken
The hurricane had swept the glen.
Faint and more faint, its failing din   70
Returned from cavern, cliff, and linn,
And silence settled, wide and still,
On the lone wood and mighty hill.

IV

Less loud the sounds of silvan war
Disturbed the heights of Uam-Var,   75
And roused the cavern, where, 'tis told,
A giant made his den of old;
For ere that steep ascent was won,
High in his pathway hung the sun,
And many a gallant, stayed perforce,   80
Was fain to breathe his faltering horse,
And of the trackers of the deer,
Scarce half the lessening pack was near;
So shrewdly on the mountain side
Had the bold burst their mettle tried.   85

V

The noble stag was pausing now
Upon the mountain's southern brow,
Where broad extended, far beneath,
The varied realms of fair Menteith.
With anxious eye he wandered o'er   90
Mountain and meadow, moss and moor,
And pondered refuge from his toil

By far Lochard or Aberfoyle.
But nearer was the copsewood gray,
That waved and wept on Loch-Achray,　95
And mingled with the pine-trees blue
On the bold cliffs of Benvenue.
Fresh vigor with the hope returned,
With flying foot the heath he spurned,
Held westward with unwearied race,　100
And left behind the panting chase.

VI

'Twere long to tell what steeds gave o'er,
As swept the hunt through Cambusmore:
What reins were tightened in despair,
When rose Benledi's ridge in air;　105
Who flagged upon Bochastle's heath,
Who shunned to stem the flooded Teith,—
For twice that day, from shore to shore,
The gallant stag swam stoutly o'er.
Few were the stragglers, following far,　110
That reached the lake of Vennachar;
And when the Brigg of Turk was won,
The headmost horseman rode alone.

VII

Alone, but with unbated zeal,
That horseman plied the scourge and
　steel;　115
For jaded now, and spent with toil,
Embossed with foam, and dark with soil,
While every gasp with sobs he drew,
The laboring stag strained full in view.
Two dogs of black Saint Hubert's breed, 120
Unmatched for courage, breath, and speed,
Fast on his flying traces came,
And all but won that desperate game;
For, scarce a spear's length from his
　haunch,
Vindictive toiled the bloodhounds
　stanch;　125
Nor nearer might the dogs attain,
Nor farther might the quarry strain.
Thus up the margin of the lake,
Between the precipice and the brake,
O'er stock and rock their race they take. 130

VIII

The hunter marked that mountain high,
The lone lake's western boundary,
And deemed the stag must turn to bay,
Where that huge rampart barred the way;
Already glorying in the prize,　135
Measured his antlers with his eyes;
For the death-wound and death-halloo,
Mustered his breath, his whinyard drew;—
But thundering as he came prepared,
With ready arm and weapon bared,　140
The wily quarry shunned the shock,
And turned him from the opposing rock;
Then, dashing down a darksome glen,

Soon lost to hound and hunter's ken,
In the deep Trosachs' wildest nook　145
His solitary refuge took.
There, while close couched, the thicket
　shed
Cold dews and wild-flowers on his head,
He heard the baffled dogs in vain
Rave through the hollow pass amain,　150
Chiding the rocks that yelled again.

IX

Close on the hounds the hunter came,
To cheer them on the vanished game;
But, stumbling in the rugged dell,
The gallant horse exhausted fell.　155
The impatient rider strove in vain
To rouse him with the spur and rein,
For the good steed, his labors o'er,
Stretched his stiff limbs, to rise no more;
Then, touched with pity and remorse, 160
He sorrowed o'er the expiring horse:
"I little thought, when first thy rein
I slacked upon the banks of Seine,
That Highland eagle e'er should feed
On thy fleet limbs, my matchless steed! 165
Woe worth the chase, woe worth the day,
That costs thy life, my gallant gray!"

X

Then through the dell his horn resounds,
From vain pursuit to call the hounds.
Back limped, with slow and crippled
　pace,　170
The sulky leaders of the chase;
Close to their master's side they pressed,
With drooping tail and humbled crest;
But still the dingle's hollow throat
Prolonged the swelling bugle-note.　175
The owlets started from their dream,
The eagles answered with their scream,
Round and around the sounds were cast,
Till echo seemed an answering blast;
And on the hunter hied his way,　180
To join some comrades of the day;
Yet often paused, so strange the road,
So wondrous were the scenes it showed.

XI

The western waves of ebbing day
Rolled o'er the glen their level way;　185
Each purple peak, each flinty spire,
Was bathed in floods of living fire.
But not a setting beam could glow
Within the dark ravines below,
Where twined the path in shadow hid,　190
Round many a rocky pyramid,
Shooting abruptly from the dell
Its thunder-splintered pinnacle;
Round many an insulated mass,
The native bulwarks of the pass,　195

Huge as the tower which builders vain
Presumptuous piled on Shinar's plain.
The rocky summits, split and rent,
Formed turret, dome, or battlement,
Or seemed fantastically set   200
With cupola or minaret,
Wild crests as pagod ever decked,
Or mosque of Eastern architect.
Nor were these earth-born castles bare,
Nor lacked they many a banner fair;   205
For, from their shivered brows displayed,
Far o'er the unfathomable glade,
All twinkling with the dewdrop sheen,
The brier-rose fell in streamers green,
And creeping shrubs, of thousand dyes,   210
Waved in the west-wind's summer sighs.

XII

Boon nature scattered, free and wild,
Each plant or flower, the mountain's child.
Here eglantine embalmed the air,
Hawthorn and hazel mingled there;   215
The primrose pale, and violet flower,
Found in each cliff a narrow bower;
Fox-glove and night-shade, side by side,
Emblems of punishment and pride,
Grouped their dark hues with every
          stain   220
The weather-beaten crags retain.
With boughs that quaked at every breath,
Gray birch and aspen wept beneath;
Aloft, the ash and warrior oak
Cast anchor in the rifted rock;   225
And, higher yet, the pine-tree hung
His shattered trunk, and frequent flung,
Where seemed the cliffs to meet on high,
His boughs athwart the narrowed sky.
Highest of all, where white peaks
          glanced,   230
Where glist'ning streamers waved and
          danced,
The wanderer's eye could barely view
The summer heaven's delicious blue;
So wondrous wild, the whole might seem
The scenery of a fairy dream.   235

XIII

Onward, amid the copse 'gan peep
A narrow inlet, still and deep,
Affording scarce such breadth of brim
As served the wild duck's brood to swim.
Lost for a space, through thickets veer-
          ing,   240
But broader when again appearing,
Tall rocks and tufted knolls their face
Could on the dark-blue mirror trace;
And farther as the hunter strayed,
Still broader sweep its channels made.   245
The shaggy mounds no longer stood,
Emerging from entangled wood,

But, wave-encircled, seemed to float,
Like castle girdled with its moat;
Yet broader floods extending still   250
Divide them from their parent hill,
Till each, retiring, claims to be
An islet in an inland sea.

XIV

And now, to issue from the glen,
No pathway meets the wanderer's ken.   255
Unless he climb, with footing nice,
A far projecting precipice.
The broom's tough roots his ladder made,
The hazel saplings lent their aid;
And thus an airy point he won,   260
Where, gleaming with the setting sun,
One burnished sheet of living gold,
Loch Katrine lay beneath him rolled;
In all her length far winding lay,
With promontory, creek, and bay,   265
And islands that, empurpled bright,
Floated amid the livelier light,
And mountains, that like giants stand,
To sentinel enchanted land.
High on the south, huge Benvenue   270
Down to the lake in masses threw
Crags, knolls, and mountains, confusedly
          hurled,
The fragments of an earlier world;
A wildering forest feathered o'er
His ruined sides and summit hoar,   275
While on the north, through middle air,
Ben-an heaved high his forehead bare.

XV

From the steep promontory gazed
The stranger, raptured and amazed.
And, "What a scene were here," he
          cried,   280
"For princely pomp, or churchman's pride!
On this bold brow, a lordly tower;
In that soft vale, a lady's bower;
On yonder meadow, far away,
The turrets of a cloister gray;   285
How blithely might the bugle-horn
Chide, on the lake, the lingering morn!
How sweet, at eve, the lover's lute
Chime, when the groves were still and
          mute!
And, when the midnight moon should
          lave   290
Her forehead in the silver wave,
How solemn on the ear would come
The holy matins' distant hum,
While the deep peal's commanding tone
Should wake, in yonder islet lone,   295
A sainted hermit from his cell,
To drop a bead with every knell—
And bugle, lute, and bell, and all,
Should each bewildered stranger call
To friendly feast, and lighted hall.   300

XVI

"Blithe were it then to wander here!
But now,—beshrew yon nimble deer,—
Like that same hermit's, thin and spare,
The copse must give my evening fare;
Some mossy bank my couch must be,   305
Some rustling oak my canopy.
Yet pass we that; the war and chase
Give little choice of resting-place;—
A summer night, in greenwood spent,
Were but tomorrow's merriment: 310
But hosts may in these wilds abound,
Such as are better missed than found;
To meet with Highland plunderers here
Were worse than loss of steed or deer.
I am alone;—my bugle-strain   315
May call some straggler of the train;
Or, fall the worst that may betide,
Ere now this falchion has been tried."

XVII

But scarce again his horn he wound,
When lo! forth starting at the sound,   320
From underneath an aged oak,
That slanted from the islet rock,
A damsel guider of its way,
A little skiff shot to the bay,
That round the promontory steep   325
Led its deep line in graceful sweep,
Eddying, in almost viewless wave,
The weeping willow-twig to lave,
And kiss, with whispering sound and slow,
The beach of pebbles bright as snow.   330
The boat had touched this silver strand,
Just as the hunter left his stand,
And stood concealed amid the brake,
To view this Lady of the Lake.
The maiden paused, as if again   335
She thought to catch the distant strain.
With head up-raised, and look intent,
And eye and ear attentive bent,
And locks flung back, and lips apart,
Like monument of Grecian art,   340
In listening mood, she seemed to stand,
The guardian Naiad of the strand.

XVIII

And ne'er did Grecian chisel trace
A Nymph, a Naiad, or a Grace
Of finer form, or lovelier face!   345
What though the sun, with ardent frown,
Had slightly tinged her cheek with brown;
The sportive toil, which, short and light,
Had dyed her glowing hue so bright,
Served too in hastier swell to show   350
Short glimpses of a breast of snow:
What though no rule of courtly grace
To measured mood had trained her pace;
A foot more light, a step more true,
Ne'er from the heath-flower dashed the
  dew;   355
E'en the slight harebell raised its head,
Elastic from her airy tread:
What though upon her speech there hung
The accents of the mountain tongue;
Those silver sounds, so soft, so dear,   360
The listener held his breath to hear!

XIX

A chieftain's daughter seemed the maid;
Her satin snood, her silken plaid,
Her golden brooch, such birth betrayed.
And seldom was a snood amid   365
Such wild luxuriant ringlets hid,
Whose glossy black to shame might bring
The plumage of the raven's wing;
And seldom o'er a breast so fair,
Mantled a plaid with modest care,   370
And never brooch the folds combined
Above a heart more true and kind.
Her kindness and her worth to spy,
You need but gaze on Ellen's eye;
Not Katrine, in her mirror blue,   375
Gives back the shaggy banks more true,
Than every free-born glance confessed
The guileless movements of her breast;
Whether joy danced in her dark eye,
Or woe or pity claimed a sigh,   380
Or filial love was glowing there,
Or meek devotion poured a prayer,
Or tale of injury called forth
The indignant spirit of the North.
One only passion unrevealed,   385
With maiden pride the maid concealed,
Yet not less purely felt the flame;—
O need I tell that passion's name?

XX

Impatient of the silent horn,
Now on the gale her voice was borne:— 390
"Father!" she cried; the rocks around
Loved to prolong the gentle sound.
Awhile she paused, no answer came;
"Malcolm, was thine the blast?" the name
Less resolutely uttered fell;   395
The echoes could not catch the swell.
"A stranger I," the huntsman said,
Advancing from the hazel shade.
The maid, alarmed, with hasty oar,
Pushed her light shallop from the shore, 400
And when a space was gained between,
Closer she drew her bosom's screen;
(So forth the startled swan would swing,
So turn to prune his ruffled wing.)
Then safe, though fluttered and amazed, 405
She paused, and on the stranger gazed.
Not his the form, nor his the eye,
That youthful maidens wont to fly.

XXI

On his bold visage middle age
Had slightly pressed its signet sage,   410
Yet had not quenched the open truth
And fiery vehemence of youth;
Forward and frolic glee was there,
The will to do, the soul to dare,
The sparkling glance, soon blown to fire,   415
Of hasty love, or headlong ire.
His limbs were cast in manly mold,
For hardy sports or contest bold;
And though in peaceful garb arrayed,
And weaponless, except his blade,   420
His stately mien as well implied
A high-born heart, a martial pride,
As if a baron's crest he wore,
And sheathed in armor trode the shore.
Slighting the petty need he showed,   425
He told of his benighted road;
His ready speech flowed fair and free,
In phrase of gentlest courtesy;
Yet seemed that tone, and gesture bland,
Less used to sue than to command.   430

XXII

Awhile the maid the stranger eyed,
And, reassured, at length replied,
That Highland halls were open still
To wildered wanderers of the hill.
"Nor think you unexpected come   435
To yon lone isle, our desert home;
Before the heath had lost the dew,
This morn, a couch was pulled for you;
On yonder mountain's purple head
Have ptarmigan and heath-cock bled,   440
And our broad nets have swept the mere,
To furnish forth your evening cheer."
"Now, by the rood, my lovely maid,
Your courtesy has erred," he said;
"No right have I to claim, misplaced,   445
The welcome of expected guest.
A wanderer, here by fortune tost,
My way, my friends, my courser lost,
I ne'er before, believe me, fair,
Have ever drawn your mountain air,   450
Till on this lake's romantic strand
I found a fay in fairy land!"

XXIII

"I well believe," the maid replied,
As her light skiff approached the side,
"I well believe that ne'er before   455
Your foot has trod Loch Katrine's shore;
But yet, as far as yesternight,
Old Allan-Bane foretold your plight,—
A gray-haired sire, whose eye intent
Was on the visioned future bent.   460
He saw your steed, a dappled gray,
Lie dead beneath the birchen way;

Painted exact your form and mien,
Your hunting suit of Lincoln green,
That tasselled horn so gaily gilt,   465
That falchion's crooked blade and hilt,
That cap with heron plumage trim,
And yon two hounds so dark and grim.
He bade that all should ready be
To grace a guest of fair degree;   470
But light I held his prophecy,
And deemed it was my father's horn
Whose echoes o'er the lake were borne."

XXIV

The stranger smiled: "Since to your home
A destined errant-knight I come,   475
Announced by prophet sooth and old,
Doomed, doubtless, for achievement bold,
I'll lightly front each high emprise
For one kind glance of those bright eyes.
Permit me, first, the task to guide   480
Your fairy frigate o'er the tide."
The maid, with smile suppressed and sly,
The toil unwonted saw him try;
For seldom sure, if e'er before,
His noble hand had grasped an oar: 485
Yet with main strength his strokes he drew
And o'er the lake the shallop flew;
With heads erect, and whimpering cry,
The hounds behind their passage ply.
Nor frequent does the bright oar break   490
The dark'ning mirror of the lake,
Until the rocky isle they reach,
And moor their shallop on the beach.

XXV

The stranger viewed the shore around;
'Twas all so close with copseweed bound,   495
Nor track nor pathway might declare
That human foot frequented there,
Until the mountain-maiden showed
A clambering unsuspected road,
That winded through the tangled screen   500
And opened on a narrow green,
Where weeping birch and willow round
With their long fibres swept the ground.
Here, for retreat in dangerous hour,
Some chief had framed a rustic bower.   505

XXVI

It was a lodge of ample size,
But strange of structure and device;
Of such materials, as around
The workman's hand had readiest found;
Lopped off their boughs, their hoar trunks
            bared,   510
And by the hatchet rudely squared.
To give the walls their destined height
The sturdy oak and ash unite;
While moss and clay and leaves combined
To fence each crevice from the wind,   515

The lighter pine-trees, over-head,
Their slender length for rafters spread,
And withered heath and rushes dry
Supplied a russet canopy.
Due westward, fronting to the green, 520
A rural portico was seen,
Aloft on native pillars borne,
Of mountain fir, with bark unshorn,
Where Ellen's hand had taught to twine
The ivy and Idaean vine, 525
The clematis, the favored flower
Which boasts the name of virgin-bower,
And every hardy plant could bear
Loch Katrine's keen and searching air.
An instant in this porch she staid, 530
And gaily to the stranger said,
"On heaven and on thy lady call,
And enter the enchanted hall!"

XXVII

"My hope, my heaven, my trust must be,
My gentle guide, in following thee." 535
He crossed the threshold—and a clang
Of angry steel that instant rang.
To his bold brow his spirit rushed,
But soon for vain alarm he blushed
When on the floor he saw displayed, 540
Cause of the din, a naked blade
Dropped from the sheath, that careless
    flung,
Upon a stag's huge antlers swung;
For all around, the walls to grace,
Hung trophies of the fight or chase: 545
A target there, a bugle here,
A battle-axe, a hunting-spear,
And broadswords, bows, and arrows store,
With the tusked trophies of the boar.
Here grins the wolf as when he died, 550
And there the wild-cat's brindled hide
The frontlet of the elk adorns,
Or mantles o'er the bison's horns;
Pennons and flags defaced and stained,
That blackening streaks of blood re-
    tained, 555
And deer-skins, dappled, dun, and white,
With otter's fur and seal's unite,
In rude and uncouth tapestry all,
To garnish forth the silvan hall.

XXVIII

The wondering stranger round him
    gazed, 560
And next the fallen weapon raised:
Few were the arms whose sinewy strength
Sufficed to stretch it forth at length;
And as the brand he poised and swayed,
"I never knew but one," he said, 565
"Whose stalwart arms might brook to wield
A blade like this in battle-field."
She sighed, then smiled and took the word;

"You see the guardian champion's sword;
As light it trembles in his hand, 570
As in my grasp a hazel wand;
My sire's tall form might grace the part
Of Ferragus or Ascabart;
But in the absent giant's hold
Are women now, and menials old." 575

XXIX

The mistress of the mansion came,
Mature of age, a graceful dame;
Whose easy step and stately port
Had well become a princely court;
To whom, though more than kindred
    knew, 580
Young Ellen gave a mother's due.
Meet welcome to her guest she made,
And every courteous rite was paid
That hospitality could claim,
Though all unmasked his birth and
    name. 585
Such then the reverence to a guest,
That fellest foe might join the feast,
And from his deadliest foeman's door
Unquestioned turn, the banquet o'er.
At length his rank the stranger names, 590
"The Knight of Snowdoun, James Fitz-
    James;
Lord of a barren heritage
Which his brave sires, from age to age,
By their good swords have held with toil;
His sire had fallen in such turmoil, 595
And he, God wot, was forced to stand
Oft for his right with blade in hand.
This morning, with Lord Moray's train,
He chased a stalwart stag in vain,
Outstripped his comrades, missed the
    deer, 600
Lost his good steed, and wandered here."

XXX

Fain would the Knight in turn require
The name and state of Ellen's sire.
Well showed the elder lady's mien,
That courts and cities she had seen; 605
Ellen, though more her looks displayed
The simple grace of silvan maid,
In speech and gesture, form and face,
Showed she was come of gentle race.
'Twere strange, in ruder rank to find 610
Such looks, such manners, and such mind.
Each hint the Knight of Snowdoun gave,
Dame Margaret heard with silence grave;
Or Ellen, innocently gay,
Turned all inquiry light away— 615
"Weird women we! by dale and down
We dwell, afar from tower and town.
We stem the flood, we ride the blast,
On wandering knights our spells we cast;

While viewless minstrels touch the
    string,   620
'Tis thus our charmed rhymes we sing."
She sung, and still a harp unseen
Filled up the symphony between.

XXXI

SONG

"Soldier, rest! thy warfare o'er,
    Sleep the sleep that knows not break-
        ing;   625
Dream of battled fields no more,
    Days of danger, nights of waking.
In our isle's enchanted hall,
    Hands unseen thy couch are strewing,
Fairy strains of music fall,   630
    Every sense in slumber dewing.
Soldier, rest! thy warfare o'er,
Dream of fighting fields no more;
Sleep the sleep that knows not breaking,
Morn of toil, nor night of waking.   635

"No rude sound shall reach thine ear,
    Armor's clang of war-steed champing,
Trump nor pibroch summon here
    Mustering clan or squadron tramping.
Yet the lark's shrill fife may come   640
    At the daybreak from the fallow,
And the bittern sound his drum,
    Booming from the sedgy shallow.
Ruder sounds shall none be near,
Guards nor warders challenge here,   645
Here's no war-steed's neigh and champing,
Shouting clans or squadrons stamping."

XXXII

She paused—then, blushing, led the lay
To grace the stranger of the day.
Her mellow notes awhile prolong   650
The cadence of the flowing song,
Till to her lips in measured frame
The minstrel verse spontaneous came:—

"Huntsman, rest! thy chase is done;
    While our slumbrous spells assail ye,   655
Dream not, with the rising sun,
    Bugles here shall sound reveillé.
Sleep! the deer is in his den;
Sleep! thy hounds are by thee lying:
Sleep! nor dream in yonder glen   660
How thy gallant steed lay dying.
Huntsman, rest! thy chase is done;
Think not of the rising sun,
For at dawning to assail ye
Here no bugles sound reveillé."   665

XXXIII

The hall was cleared—the stranger's bed
Was there of mountain heathers spread,
Where oft a hundred guests had lain,
And dreamed their forest sports again.
But vainly did the heath-flower shed   670
Its moorland fragrance round his head;
Not Ellen's spell had lulled to rest
The fever of his troubled breast.
In broken dreams the image rose
Of varied perils, pains, and woes: 675
His steed now flounders in the brake,
Now sinks his barge upon the lake;
Now leader of a broken host,
His standard falls, his honor's lost.
Then,—from my couch may heavenly
    might   680
Chase that worst phantom of the night!—
Again returned the scenes of youth,
On confident undoubting truth;
Again his soul he interchanged
With friends whose hearts were long
    estranged.   685
They come, in dim procession led,
The cold, the faithless, and the dead;
As warm each hand, each brow as gay,
As if they parted yesterday.
And doubt distracts him at the view—   690
O were his senses false or true?
Dreamed he of death, or broken vow,
Or is it all a vision now?

XXXIV

At length, with Ellen in a grove
He seemed to walk, and speak of love;   695
She listened with a blush and sigh,
His suit was warm, his hopes were high.
He sought her yielded hand to clasp,
And a cold gauntlet met his grasp:
The phantom's sex had changed and
    gone,   700
Upon its head a helmet shone;
Slowly enlarged to giant size,
With darkened cheek and threatening eyes,
The grisly visage, stern and hoar,
To Ellen still a likeness bore.   705
He woke, and, panting with affright,
Recalled the vision of the night.
The hearth's decaying brands were red,
And deep and dusky lustre shed,
Half showing, half concealing, all   710
The uncouth trophies of the hall.
'Mid those the stranger fixed his eye,
Where that huge falchion hung on high,
And thoughts on thoughts, a countless
    throng,
Rushed, chasing countless thoughts
    along   715
Until, the giddy whirl to cure,
He rose, and sought the moonshine pure.

XXXV

The wild-rose, eglantine, and broom,
Wasted around their rich perfume;

The birch-trees wept in fragrant balm, 720
The aspens slept beneath the calm;
The silver light, with quivering glance,
Played on the water's still expanse:
Wild were the heart whose passion's sway
Could rage beneath the sober ray! 725
He felt its calm, that warrior guest,
While thus he communed with his breast:
"Why is it, at each turn I trace
Some memory of that exiled race?
Can I not mountain-maiden spy, 730
But she must bear the Douglas eye?
Can I not view a Highland brand,
But it must match the Douglas hand?
Can I not frame a fevered dream,
But still the Douglas is the theme? 735
I'll dream no more; by manly mind
Not even in sleep is will resigned.
My midnight orisons said o'er,
I'll turn to rest, and dream no more."
His midnight orisons he told, 740
A prayer with every bead of gold,
Consigned to heaven his cares and woes,
And sunk in undisturbed repose;
Until the heath-cock shrilly crew,
And morning dawned on Benvenue. 745

FROM CANTO SECOND: HAIL TO THE CHIEF

Hail to the Chief who in triumph advances!
Honored and blessed be the ever-green
Pine! 400
Long may the tree, in his banner that
glances,
Flourish, the shelter and grace of our
line!
Heaven send it happy dew,
Earth lend it sap anew,
Gayly to bourgeon and broadly to
grow, 405
While every Highland glen
Sends our shout back again,
"Roderigh Vich Alpine dhu, ho! ieroe!"

Ours is no sapling, chance-sown by the
fountain,
Blooming at Beltane, in winter to
fade; 410
When the whirlwind has stripped every
leaf on the mountain,
The more shall Clan-Alpine exult in her
shade.
Moored in the rifted rock,
Proof to the tempest's shock,
Firmer he roots him the ruder it blow; 415
Menteith and Breadalbane, then,
Echo his praise again,
"Roderigh Vich Alpine dhu, ho! ieroe!"

Proudly our pibroch has thrilled in Glen
Fruin,
And Bannochar's groans to our slogan
replied; 420
Glen-Luss and Ross-dhu, they are smoking
in ruin,
And the rest of Loch Lomond lie dead
on her side.
Widow and Saxon maid
Long shall lament our raid,
Think of Clan-Alpine with fear and with
woe; 425
Lennox and Leven-glen
Shake when they hear again,
"Roderigh Vich Alpine dhu, ho! ieroe!"

Row, vassals, row, for the pride of the
Highlands!
Stretch to your oars for the ever-green
Pine! 430
O that the rosebud that graces yon islands
Were wreathed in a garland around him
to twine!
O that some seedling gem,
Worthy such noble stem
Honored and blessed in their shadow
might grow! 435
Loud should Clan-Alpine then
Ring from her deepmost glen,
"Roderigh Vich Alpine dhu, ho! ieroe!"

FROM CANTO THIRD: THE FIERY CROSS

'T was all prepared;—and from the rock
A goat, the patriarch of the flock, 180
Before the kindling pile was laid,
And pierced by Roderick's ready blade.
Patient the sickening victim eyed
The life-blood ebb in crimson tide
Down his clogged beard and shaggy
limb, 185
Till darkness glazed his eyeballs dim.
The grisly priest, with murmuring prayer,
A slender crosslet framed with care,
A cubit's length in measure due;
The shaft and limbs were rods of yew, 190
Whose parents in Inch-Cailliach wave
Their shadows o'er Clan-Alpine's grave,
And, answering Lomond's breezes deep,
Soothe many a chieftain's endless sleep.
The Cross, thus formed, he held on
high, 195
With wasted hand, and haggard eye,
And strange and mingled feelings woke,
While his anathema he spoke:

"Woe to the clansman, who shall view
This symbol of sepulchral yew, 200
Forgetful that its branches grew

Where weep the heavens their holiest dew
  On Alpine's dwelling low!
Deserter of his Chieftain's trust,
He ne'er shall mingle with their dust,   205
But, from his sires and kindred thrust,
Each clansman's execration just
  Shall doom him wrath and woe."
He paused;—the word the vassals took,
With forward step and fiery look,   210
On high their naked brands they shook,
  Their clattering targets wildly strook;
  And first in murmur low,
Then, like the billow in his course,
That far to seaward finds his source,   215
And flings to shore his mustered force,
Burst, with loud roar, their answer hoarse,
  "Woe to the traitor, woe!"
Ben-an's gray scalp the accents knew,
The joyous wolf from covert drew,   220
The exulting eagle screamed afar,—
  They knew the voice of Alpine's war.

The shout was hushed on lake and fell,
The monk resumed his muttered spell:
Dismal and low its accents came,   225
The while he scathed the cross with flame;
And the few words that reached the air,
Although the holiest name was there,
Had more of blasphemy than prayer.
But when he shook above the crowd   230
Its kindled points, he spoke aloud:—
"Woe to the wretch, who fails to rear
At this dread sign the ready spear!
For, as the flames this symbol sear,
His home, the refuge of his fear,   235
  A kindred fate shall know;
Far o'er its roof the volumed flame
Clan-Alpine's vengeance shall proclaim,
While maids and matrons on his name
Shall call down wretchedness and shame,   240
  And infamy and woe."
Then rose the cry of females shrill,
As goss-hawk's whistle on the hill,
Denouncing misery and ill,
Mingled with childhood's babbling trill   245
  Of curses stammered slow;
Answering with imprecation dread,
"Sunk be his home in embers red!
And cursed be the meanest shed
That e'er shall hide the houseless head,   250
  We doom to want and woe!"
A sharp and shrieking echo gave,
Coir-Uriskin, thy goblin cave!
And the gray pass where birches wave,
  On Beala-nam-bo.   255

Then deeper paused the priest anew,
And hard his laboring breath he drew,
While, with set teeth and clenched hand,
And eyes that glowed like fiery brand.

He meditated curse more dread,   260
And deadlier, on the clansman's head,
Who, summoned to his Chieftain's aid,
The signal saw and disobeyed.
The crosslet's points of sparkling wood,
He quenched among the bubbling
  blood,   265
And, as again the sign he reared,
Hollow and hoarse his voice was heard:
"When flits this Cross from man to man,
Vich-Alpine's summons to his clan,
Burst be the ear that fails to heed!   270
Palsied the foot that shuns to speed!
May ravens tear the careless eyes,
Wolves make the coward heart their prize!
As sinks that blood-stream in the earth,
So may his heart's-blood drench his
  hearth!   275
As dies in hissing gore the spark,
Quench thou his light, Destruction dark!
And be the grace to him denied,
Bought by this sign to all beside!"
He ceased; no echo gave again   280
The murmur of the deep Amen.

Then Roderick, with impatient look,
From Brian's hand the symbol took:
"Speed, Malise, speed!" he said, and gave
The crosslet to his henchman brave.   285
"The muster-place be Lanrick mead—
Instant the time—speed, Malise, speed!"
Like heath-bird, when the hawks pursue,
A barge across Loch Katrine flew;
High stood the henchman on the prow,   290
So rapidly the barge-men row,
The bubbles, where they launched the
  boat,
Were all unbroken and afloat,
Dancing in foam and ripple still,
When it had neared the mainland hill;   295
And from the silver beach's side
Still was the prow three fathoms wide,
When lightly bounded to the land
The messenger of blood and brand.

Speed Malise, speed! the dun deer's
  hide   300
On fleeter foot was never tied.
Speed, Malise, speed! such cause of haste
Thine active sinews never braced.
Bend 'gainst the steepy hill thy breast,
Burst down like torrent from its crest;   305
With short and springing footstep pass
The trembling bog and false morass;
Across the brook like roebuck bound,
And thread the brake like questing hound,
The crag is high, the scaur is deep   310
Yet shrink not from the desperate leap:
Parched are thy burning lips and brow,
Yet by the fountain pause not now;

Herald of battle, fate, and fear,
Stretch onward in thy fleet career!   315
The wounded hind thou track'st not now,
Pursuest not maid through greenwood
    bough,
Nor pliest thou now thy flying pace,
With rivals in the mountain race;
But danger, death, and warrior deed,   320
Are in thy course—speed, Malise, speed!

Fast as the fatal symbol flies,
In arms the huts and hamlets rise:
From winding glen, from upland brown,
They poured each hardy tenant down.   325
Nor slacked the messenger his pace;
He showed the sign, he named the place,
And, pressing forward like the wind,
Left clamor and surprise behind.
The fisherman forsook the strand,   330
The swarthy smith took dirk and brand;
With changed cheer, the mower blithe
Left in the half-cut swathe the scythe;
The herds without a keeper strayed,
The plough was in mid-furrow staid,   335
The falc'ner tossed his hawk away,
The hunter left the stag at bay;
Prompt at the signal of alarms,
Each son of Alpine rushed to arms;
So swept the tumult and affray   340
Along the margin of Achray.
Alas, thou lovely lake! that e'er
Thy banks should echo sounds of fear!
The rocks, the bosky thickets, sleep
So stilly on thy bosom deep,   345
The lark's blithe carol, from the cloud,
Seems for the scene too gayly loud.

Speed, Malise, speed! the lake is past,
Duncraggan's huts appear at last,
And peep, like moss-grown rocks, half
    seen,   350
Half hidden in the copse so green;
There mayst thou rest, thy labor done,
Their lord shall speed the signal on.—
As stoops the hawk upon his prey,
The henchman shot him down the way. 355
What woeful accents load the gale?
The funeral yell, the female wail!
A gallant hunter's sport is o'er,
A valiant warrior fights no more.
Who, in the battle or the chase,   360
At Roderick's side shall fill his place!—
Within the hall, where torch's ray
Supplies the excluded beams of day,
Lies Duncan on his lowly bier,
And o'er him streams his widow's tear.   365
His stripling son stands mournful by,
His youngest weeps, but knows not why;
The village maids and matrons round
The dismal coronach resound.

CORONACH

He is gone on the mountain,   370
    He is lost to the forest,
Like a summer-dried fountain,
    When our need was the sorest.
The font, reappearing,
    From the rain-drops shall borrow,   375
But to us comes no cheering,
    To Duncan no morrow!

The hand of the reaper
    Takes the ears that are hoary,
But the voice of the weeper   380
    Wails manhood in glory.
The autumn winds rushing
    Waft the leaves that are searest,
But our flower was in flushing,
    When blighting was nearest.   385

Fleet foot on the correi,
    Sage counsel in cumber,
Red hand in the foray,
    How sound is thy slumber!
Like the dew on the mountain,   390
    Like the foam on the river,
Like the bubble on the fountain,
    Thou art gone, and forever.

HYMN TO THE VIRGIN

Ave Maria! maiden mild!
    Listen to a maiden's prayer!
Thou canst hear though from the wild, 715
    Thou canst save amid despair.
Safe may we sleep beneath thy care,
    Though banished, outcast, and reviled—
Maiden! hear a maiden's prayer;
    Mother, hear a suppliant child!   720
                                    Ave Maria!

Ave Maria! undefiled!
    The flinty couch we now must share
Shall seem with down of eider piled,
    If thy protection hover there.
The murky cavern's heavy air   725
    Shall breathe of balm if thou hast
        smiled;
Then, Maiden! hear a maiden's prayer,
    Mother, list a suppliant child!
                                    Ave Maria!

Ave Maria! stainless styled!
    Foul demons of the earth and air,   730
From this their wonted haunt exiled,
    Shall flee before thy presence fair.
We bow us to our lot of care,
    Beneath thy guidance reconciled:
Hear for a maid a maiden's prayer,   735
    And for a father hear a child!
                                    Ave Maria!
                                    1810

FROM ROKEBY: CANTO THIRD

BRIGNALL BANKS

O, Brignall banks are wild and fair,
And Greta woods are green, 395
And you may gather garlands there
Would grace a summer queen.
And as I rode by Dalton-hall,
Beneath the turrets high,
A maiden on the castle wall 400
Was singing merrily,—

CHORUS

"O, Brignall banks are fresh and fair,
And Greta woods are green;
I'd rather rove with Edmund there
Than reign our English queen." 405
"If, maiden, thou wouldst wend with me,
To leave both tower and town,
Thou first must guess what life lead we
That dwell by dale and down?
And if thou canst that riddle read, 410
As read full well you may,
Then to the greenwood shalt thou speed,
As blithe as Queen of May."

CHORUS

Yet sung she, "Brignall banks are fair,
And Greta woods are green; 415
I'd rather rove with Edmund there
Than reign our English queen.

"I read you, by your bugle horn,
And by your palfrey good,
I read you for a ranger sworn 420
To keep the king's greenwood."
"A ranger, lady, winds his horn,
And 't is at peep of light;
His blast is heard at merry morn,
And mine at dead of night." 425

CHORUS

Yet sung she, "Brignall banks are fair,
And Greta woods are gay;
I would I were with Edmund there,
To reign his Queen of May!

"With burnished brand and musketoon 430
So gallantly you come,
I read you for a bold dragoon,
That lists the tuck of drum."
"I list no more the tuck of drum,
No more the trumpet hear; 435
But when the beetle sounds his hum,
My comrades take the spear.

CHORUS

"And O, though Brignall banks be fair,
And Greta woods be gay,
Yet mickle must the maiden dare 440
Would reign my Queen of May!

"Maiden! a nameless life I lead,
A nameless death I'll die;
The fiend whose lantern lights the mead
Were better mate than I! 445
And when I'm with my comrades met
Beneath the greenwood bough,
What once we were we all forget,
Nor think what we are now.

CHORUS

"Yet Brignall banks are fresh and fair, 450
And Greta woods are green,
And you may gather garlands there
Would grace a summer queen."

THE ROVER'S FAREWELL

"A weary lot is thine, fair maid,
A weary lot is thine!
To pull the thorn thy brow to braid,
And press the rue for wine!
A lightsome eye, a soldier's mien, 5
A feather of the blue,
A doublet of the Lincoln green,—
No more of me you knew,
          My love!
No more of me you knew. 10

"This morn is merry June, I trow,
The rose is budding fain;
But she shall bloom in winter snow
Ere we two meet again."
He turned his charger as he spake 15
Upon the river shore,
He gave his bridle-reins a shake,
Said, "Adieu for evermore,
          My love!
And adieu for evermore."

ALLEN-A-DALE

Allen-a-Dale has no fagot for burning,
Allen-a-Dale has no furrow for turning,
Allen-a Dale has no fleece for the spinning, 720
Yet Allen-a-Dale has red gold for the winning.
Come, read me my riddle! come, hearken my tale!
And tell me the craft of bold Allen-a Dale.

The Baron of Ravensworth prances in
    pride,
And he views his domains upon Arkindale
    side.   725
The mere for his net and the land for his
    game,
The chase for the wild and the park for
    the tame;
Yet the fish of the lake and the deer of the
    vale
Are less free to Lord Dacre than Allen-a-
    Dale!

Allen-a-Dale was ne'er belted a knight, 730
Though his spur be as sharp and his blade
    be as bright;
Allen-a-Dale is no baron or lord,
Yet twenty tall yeomen will draw at his
    word;
And the best of our nobles his bonnet will
    vail,
Who at Rere-cross on Stanmore meets
    Allen-a-Dale!   735

Allen-a-Dale to his wooing is come;
The mother, she asked of his household
    and home:
"Though the castle of Richmond stand fair
    on the hill,
My hall," quoth bold Allen, "shows gal-
    lanter still;
'T is the blue vault of heaven, with its
    crescent so pale   740
And with all its bright spangles!" said
    Allen-a-Dale.

The father was steel and the mother was
    stone;
They lifted the latch and they bade him be
    gone;
But loud on the morrow their wail and
    their cry:
He had laughed on the lass with his bonny
    black eye,   745
And she fled to the forest to hear a love-
    tale,
And the youth it was told by was Allen-a-
    Dale!

FROM CANTO FIFTH: THE CYPRESS WREATH

O, Lady, twine no wreath for me,
Or twine it of the cypress tree!
Too lively glow the lilies light,   335
The varnished holly's all too bright,
The mayflower and the eglantine
May shade a brow less sad than mine,
But, Lady, weave no wreath for me,
Or weave it of the cypress tree!   340

Let dimpled Mirth his temples twine
With tendrils of the laughing vine;
The manly oak, the pensive yew,
To patriot and to sage be due;
The myrtle bow bids lovers live,   345
But that Matilda will not give;
Then, Lady, twine no wreath for me,
Or twine it of the cypress tree!

Let merry England proudly rear
Her blended roses, bought so dear;   350
Let Albin bind her bonnet blue
With heath and harebell dipped in dew;
On favored Erin's crest be seen
The flower she loves of emerald green—
But, Lady, twine no wreath for me,   355
Or twine it of the cypress tree.

Strike the wild harp, while maids prepare
The ivy meet for minstrel's hair:
And, while his crown of laurel leaves,
With bloody hand the victor weaves,   360
Let the loud trump his triumph tell;
But when you hear the passing bell,
Then, Lady, twine a wreath for me,
And twine it of the cypress tree.

Yes! twine for me the cypress bough: 365
But, O Matilda, twine not now!
Stay till a few brief months are past,
And I have looked and loved my last!
When villagers my shroud bestrew
With pansies, rosemary, and rue,—   370
Then, Lady, weave a wreath for me,
And weave it of the cypress tree.
                         1813

FLORA MACIVOR'S SONG

There is mist on the mountain, and night on the vale,
But more dark is the sleep of the sons of the Gael.
A stranger commanded—it sunk on the land,
It has frozen each heart and benumbed every hand!

The dirk and the target lie sordid with dust,
The bloodless claymore is but reddened with rust;
On the hill or the glen if a gun should appear,
It is only to war with the heathcock or deer.

The deeds of our sires if our bards should rehearse,
Let a blush or a blow be the meed of their verse!
Be mute every string and be hushed every tone
That shall bid us remember the fame that is flown!

But the dark hours of night and of slumber are past,
The morn on our mountains is dawning at last;
Glenaladale's peaks are illumed with the rays,
And the streams of Glenfinnan leap bright in the blaze.

O high-minded Moray!—the exiled—the dear!—
In the blush of the dawning the *Standard* uprear!
Wide, wide to the winds of the north let it fly,
Like the sun's latest flash when the tempest is nigh!

Ye sons of the strong, when that dawning shall break,
Need the harp of the aged remind you to wake?
That dawn never beamed on your forefather's eye,
But it roused each high chieftain to vanquish or die.

O, sprung from the Kings who in Islay kept state,
Proud chiefs of Clan-Ranald, Glengary, and Sleat!
Combine like three streams from one mountain of snow,
And resistless in union rush down on the foe!

True son of Sir Evan, undaunted Lochiel,
Place thy targe on thy shoulder and burnish thy steel!
Rough Keppoch, give breath to thy bugle's bold swell,
Till far Coryarrick resound to the knell!

Stern son of Lord Kenneth, high chief of Kintail,
Let the stag in thy standard bound wild in the gale!
May the race of Clan-Gillian, the fearless and free,
Remember Glenlivet, Harlaw, and Dundee!

Let the clan of gray Fingon, whose offspring has given
Such heroes to earth and such martyrs to heaven,
Unite with the race of renowned Rorri More,
To launch the long galley and stretch to the oar!

How Mac-Shimei will joy when their chief shall display
The yew-crested bonnet o'er tresses of gray!
How the race of wronged Alpine and murdered Glencoe
Shall shout for revenge when they pour on the foe!

Ye sons of brown Dermid, who slew the wild boar,
Resume the pure faith of the great Callum-More!
Mac-Neil of the Islands, and Moy of the Lake,
For honor, for freedom, for vengeance awake!

Awake on your hills, on your islands awake,
Brave sons of the mountain, the frith, and the lake!
'T is the bugle—but not for the chase is the call;
'T is the pibroch's shrill summons—but not to the hall.

10

15

20

25

30

35

40

45

50

'T is the summons of heroes for conquest or death,
When the banners are blazing on mountain and heath;
They call to the dirk, the claymore, and the targe,   55
To the march and the muster, the line and the charge.

Be the brand of each chieftain like Fin's in his ire!
May the blood through his veins flow like currents of fire!
Burst the base foreign yoke as your sires did of yore!
Or die like your sires, and endure it no more!   60

                                        1813

JOCK OF HAZELDEAN

"Why weep ye by the tide, ladie?
  Why weep ye by the tide?
I'll wed ye to my youngest son,
  And ye sall be his bride:
And ye sall be his bride, ladie,   5
  Sae comely to be seen"—
But aye she loot the tears down fa'
  For Jock of Hazeldean.

"Now let this wilfu' grief be done,
  And dry that cheek so pale;   10
Young Frank is chief of Errington
  And lord of Langley-dale;
His step is first in peaceful ha',
  His sword in battle keen"—
But aye she loot the tears down fa'   15
  For Jock of Hazeldean.

"A chain of gold ye sall not lack,
  Nor braid to bind your hair;
Nor mettled hound, nor managed hawk,
  Nor palfrey fresh and fair;   20
And you, the foremost o' them a',
  Shall ride our forest queen."—
But aye she loot the tears down fa'
  For Jock of Hazeldean.

The kirk was decked at morning-tide,   25
  The tapers glimmered fair;
The priest and bridegroom wait the bride,
  And dame and knight are there.
They sought her baith by bower and ha';
  The ladie was not seen!   30
She's o'er the Border and awa'
  Wi' Jock of Hazeldean.

                                        1816

PIBROCH OF DONUIL DHU

Pibroch of Donuil Dhu,
  Pibroch of Donuil,
Wake thy wild voice anew,
  Summon Clan Conuil.

Come away, come away,   5
  Hark to the summons!
Come in your war array,
  Gentles and commons.

Come from deep glen and
  From mountains so rocky,   10
The war-pipe and pennon
  Are at Inverlochy.
Come every hill-plaid and
  True heart that wears one,
Come every steel blade and   15
  Strong hand that bears one.

Leave untended the herd,
  The flock without shelter;
Leave the corpse uninterred,
  The bride at the altar;   20
Leave the deer, leave the steer,
  Leave nets and barges:
Come with your fighting gear,
  Broadswords and targes.

Come as the winds come when   25
  Forests are rended;
Come as the waves come when
  Navies are stranded:
Faster come, faster come,
  Faster and faster,   30
Chief, vassal, page and groom,
  Tenant and master.

Fast they come, fast they come;
  See how they gather!
Wide waves the eagle plume,   35
  Blended with heather.
Cast your plaids, draw your blades,
  Forward each man set!
Pibroch of Donuil Dhu,
  Knell for the onset!   40

                                        1816

WHY SIT'ST THOU BY THAT RUINED HALL

"Why sit'st thou by that ruined hall,
  Thou aged carle so stern and gray?
Dost thou its former pride recall,
  Or ponder how it passed away?"

"Know'st thou not me?" the Deep Voice
   cried: 5
"So long enjoyed, so oft misused—
Alternate, in thy fickle pride,
   Desired, neglected, and accused!

"Before my breath, like blazing flax,
   Man and his marvels pass away!   10
And changing empires wane and wax,
   Are founded, flourish, and decay.

"Redeem mine hours—the space is brief,
   While in my glass the sand-grains shiver,
And measureless thy joy or grief,   15
   When Time and thou shalt part for-
      ever!"

                  1816

AND WHAT THOUGH WINTER WILL PINCH SEVERE

And what though winter will pinch severe
   Through locks of gray and a cloak that's
      old,
Yet keep up thy heart, bold cavalier,
   For a cup of sack shall fence the cold.

For time will rust the brightest blade,   5
   And years will break the strongest bow;
Was never wight so starkly made,
   But time and years would overthrow.

                  1816

THE SUN UPON THE WEIRDLAW HILL

The sun upon the Weirdlaw Hill
   In Ettrick's vale is sinking sweet;
The westland wind is hush and still,
   The lake lies sleeping at my feet.
Yet not the landscape to mine eye   5
   Bears those bright hues that once it bore,
Though evening with her richest dye
   Flames o'er the hills of Ettrick's shore.

With listless look along the plain
   I see Tweed's silver current glide,   10
And coldly mark the holy fane
   Of Melrose rise in ruined pride.
The quiet lake, the balmy air,
   The hill, the stream, the tower, the
      tree—
Are they still such as once they were,   15
   Or is the dreary change in me?

Alas! the warped and broken board,
   How can it bear the painter's dye?
The harp of strained and tuneless chord,
   How to the minstrel's skill reply?   20
To aching eyes each landscape lowers,
   To feverish pulse each gale blows chill;
And Araby's or Eden's bowers
   Were barren as this moorland hill.

                  1817

PROUD MAISIE

Proud Maisie is in the wood
   Walking so early;
Sweet Robin sits on the bush,
   Singing so rarely.

"Tell me, thou bonny bird,   5
   When shall I marry me?"—
"When six braw gentlemen
   Kirkward shall carry ye."

"Who makes the bridal bed,
   Birdie, say truly?"—   10
"The gray-headed sexton
   That delves the grave duly.

"The glow-worm o'er grave and stone
   Shall light thee steady,
The owl from the steeple sing,   15
   'Welcome, proud lady.'"

                  1818

THE BAREFOOTED FRIAR

I'll give thee, good fellow, a twelvemonth or twain
To search Europe through from Byzantium to Spain;
But ne'er shall you find, should you search till you tire,
So happy a man as the Barefooted Friar.

Your knight for his lady pricks forth in career,   5
And is brought home at even-song pricked through with a spear;
I confess him in haste—for his lady desires
No comfort on earth save the Barefooted Friar's.

Your monarch!—Pshaw! many a prince has been known
To barter his robes for our cowl and our gown,   10
But which of us e'er felt the idle desire
To exchange for a crown the gray hood of a friar?

The Friar has walked out, and where'er he has gone
The land and its fatness is marked for his own;
He can roam where he lists, he can stop where he tires,   15
For every man's house is the Barefooted Friar's.

He's expected at noon, and no wight till he comes
May profane the great chair or the porridge of plums:
For the best of the cheer, and the seat by the fire,
Is the undenied right of the Barefooted Friar.   20

He's expected at night, and the pasty's made hot,
They broach the brown ale and they fill the black pot;
And the good-wife would wish the good-man in the mire,
Ere he lacked a soft pillow, the Barefooted Friar.

Long flourish the sandal, the cord, and the cope,   25
The dread of the devil and trust of the Pope!
For to gather life's roses, unscathed by the briar,
Is granted alone to the Barefooted Friar.

                                                                    1819

REBECCA'S HYMN

When Israel of the Lord beloved
　Out from the land of bondage came,
Her fathers' God before her moved,
　An awful guide in smoke and flame.
By day, along the astonished lands   5
　The cloudy pillar glided slow;
By night, Arabia's crimsoned sands
　Returned the fiery column's glow.

There rose the choral hymn of praise,
　And trump and timbrel answered
　　keen,   10
And Zion's daughters poured their lays,
　With priest's and warrior's voice be-
　　tween.
No portents now our foes amaze,
　Forsaken Israel wanders lone:
Our fathers would not know Thy ways,   15
　And Thou hast left them to their own.

But present still, though now unseen,
　When brightly shines the prosperous day,
Be thoughts of Thee a cloudy screen
　To temper the deceitful ray!   20
And O, when stoops on Judah's path
　In shade and storm the frequent night,
Be Thou, long-suffering, slow to wrath,
　A burning and a shining light!

Our harps we left by Babel's streams,   25
　The tyrant's jest, the Gentile's scorn;
No censer round our altar beams,
　And mute are timbrel, harp, and horn.
But Thou hast said, The blood of goat,
　The flesh of rams I will not prize;   30
A contrite heart, a humble thought,
　Are mine accepted sacrifice.

                                                                    1820

COUNTY GUY

Ah! County Guy, the hour is nigh,
　The sun has left the lea,
The orange flower perfumes the bower,
　The breeze is on the sea.
The lark his lay who thrilled all day   5
　Sits hushed his partner nigh;
Breeze, bird, and flower confess the hour,
　But where is County Guy?

The village maid steals through the shade,
　Her shepherd's suit to hear;   10
To beauty shy by lattice high,
　Sings high-born Cavalier.
The star of Love, all stars above,
　Now reigns o'er earth and sky;
And high and low the influence know—   15
　But where is County Guy?

                                                                    1823

GLEE FOR KING CHARLES

Bring the bowl which you boast,
　Fill it up to the brim;
'T is to him we love most,
　And to all who love him.
Brave gallants, stand up,　　　　　　5
　And avaunt ye, base carles!
Were there death in the cup,
　Here's a health to King Charles!

Though he wanders through dangers,
　Unaided, unknown,　　　　　　　10
Dependent on strangers,
　Estranged from his own;

Though 't is under our breath
　Amidst forfeits and perils,
Here's to honor and faith,　　　　　15
　And a health to King Charles!

Let such honors abound
　As the time can afford,
The knee on the ground,
　And the hand on the sword;　　　20
But the time shall come round
　When, 'mid Lords, Dukes, and Earls,
The loud trumpet shall sound,
　Here's a health to King Charles!

　　　　　　　　　　　　　　1826

BONNY DUNDEE

To the Lords of Convention 't was Claver'se who spoke,
　'Ere the King's crown shall fall there are crowns to be broke;
So let each Cavalier who loves honor and me,
Come follow the bonnet of Bonny Dundee.
　　Come fill up my cup, come fill up my can,
　　Come saddle your horses and call up your men;　　5
　　Come open the West Port and let me gang free,
And it's room for the bonnets of Bonny Dundee!

Dundee he is mounted, he rides up the street,
　The bells are rung backward, the drums they are beat;　10
But the Provost, douce man, said, "Just e'en let him be,
The Gude Town is weel quit of that Deil of Dundee."
　　Come fill up my cup, etc.

As he rode down the sanctified bends of the Bow,
　Ilk carline was flyting and shaking her pow;　　　15
But the young plants of grace they looked couthie and slee,
Thinking, luck to thy bonnet, thou Bonny Dundee!
　　Come fill up my cup, etc.

With sour-featured Whigs the Grassmarket was crammed
　As if half the West had set tryst to be hanged;　　20
There was spite in each look, there was fear in each e'e,
As they watched for the bonnets of Bonny Dundee.
　　Come fill up my cup, etc.

These cowls of Kilmarnock had spits and had spears,
　And lang-hafted gullies to kill Cavaliers;　　　　25
But they shrunk to close-heads and the causeway was free,
At the toss of the bonnet of Bonny Dundee.
　　Come fill up my cup, etc.

He spurred to the foot of the proud Castle rock,
　And with the gay Gordon he gallantly spoke;　　　30
"Let Mons Meg and her marrows speak twa words or three,
For the love of the bonnet of Bonny Dundee."
　　Come fill up my cup, etc.

The Gordon demands of him which way he goes—
"Where'er shall direct me the shade of Montrose!   35
Your Grace in short space shall hear tidings of me,
Or that low lies the bonnet of Bonny Dundee.
    Come fill up my cup, etc.

"There are hills beyond Pentland and lands beyond Forth,
If there's lords in the Lowlands, there's chiefs in the North;   40
There are wild Duniewassals three thousand times three,
Who cry *hoigh!* for the bonnet of Bonny Dundee.
    Come fill up my cup, etc.

"There's brass on the target of barkened bull-hide;
There's steel in the scabbard that dangles beside;   45
The brass shall be burnished, the steel shall flash free,
At a toss of the bonnet of Bonny Dundee.
    Come fill up my cup, etc.

"Away to the hills, to the caves, to the rocks—
Ere I own an usurper, I'll couch with the fox;   50
And tremble, false Whigs, in the midst of your glee,
You have not seen the last of my bonnet and me!"
    Come fill up my cup, etc.

He waved his proud hand and the trumpets were blown,
The kettle-drums clashed, and the horsemen rode on,   55
Till on Ravelston's cliffs and on Clermiston's lee
Died away the wild war-notes of Bonny Dundee.

    Come fill up my cup, come fill up my can,
    Come saddle the horses and call up the men;
    Come open your gates and let me gae free,   60
    For it's up with the bonnets of Bonny Dundee!

1830

FROM GUY MANNERING

THE GYPSY'S CURSE

Little Harry Bertram, one of the hardiest 5
and most lively children that ever made a
sword and grenadier's cap of rushes, now
approached his fifth revolving birthday. A
hardihood of disposition, which early developed itself, made him already a little 10
wanderer; he was well acquainted with
every patch of lea ground and dingle
around Ellangowan, and could tell in his
broken language upon what "baulks" grew
the bonniest flowers, and what copse had 15
the ripest nuts. He repeatedly terrified
his attendants by clambering about the
ruins of the old castle, and had more than
once made a stolen excursion as far as the
gypsy hamlet.   20
On these occasions he was generally
brought back by Meg Merrilies, who,
though she could not be prevailed upon to
enter the Place of Ellangowan after her

nephew had been given up to the pressgang, did not apparently extend her resentment to the child. On the contrary,
she often contrived to waylay him in his
walks, sing him a gypsy song, give him a
ride upon her jackass, and thrust into his
pocket a piece of gingerbread or red-
cheeked apple. This woman's ancient attachment to the family, repelled and
checked in every other direction, seemed
to rejoice in having some object on which
it could yet repose and expand itself. She
prophesied a hundred times, "that young
Mr. Harry would be the pride o' the family, and there hadna been sic a sprout frae
the auld aik since the death of Arthur
Mac-Dingawaie, that was killed in the
battle o' the Bloody Bay; as for the present
stick, it was good for naething but firewood." On one occasion, when the child
was ill, she lay all night below the window,
chanting a rhyme which she believed sovereign as a febrifuge, and could neither be
prevailed upon to enter the house, nor to

leave the station she had chosen, till she was informed that the crisis was over.

The affection of this woman became matter of suspicion, not indeed to the laird, who was never hasty in suspecting evil, but to his wife, who had indifferent health and poor spirits. She was now far advanced in a second pregnancy, and, as she could not walk abroad herself, and the woman who attended upon Harry was young and thoughtless, she prayed Dominie Sampson to undertake the task of watching the boy in his rambles, when he should not be otherwise accompanied. The Dominie loved his young charge, and was enraptured with his own success, in having already brought him so far in his learning as to spell words of three syllables. The idea of this early prodigy of erudition being carried off by the gypsies, like a second Adam Smith, was not to be tolerated; and accordingly, though the charge was contrary to all his habits of life, he readily undertook it, and might be seen stalking about with a mathematical problem in his head, and his eye upon a child of five years old, whose rambles led him into a hundred awkward situations. Twice was the Dominie chased by a cross-grained cow, once he fell into the brook crossing at the stepping-stones, and another time was bogged up to the middle in the slough of Lochend, in attempting to gather a water-lily for the young laird. It was the opinion of the village matrons who relieved Sampson on the latter occasion, "that the laird might as weel trust the care o' his bairn to a potato bogle"; but the good Dominie bore all his disasters with gravity and serenity equally imperturbable. "Pro-di-gi-ous!" was the only ejaculation they ever extorted from the much-enduring man.

The laird had by this time determined to make root-and-branch work with the Maroons of Derncleugh. The old servants shook their heads at his proposal, and even Dominie Sampson ventured upon an indirect remonstrance. As, however, it was couched, in the oracular phrase: "Ne moveas Camerinam," neither the allusion, nor the language in which it was expressed was calculated for Mr. Bertram's edification, and matters proceeded against the gypsies in form of law. Every door in the hamlet was chalked by the ground-officer, in token of a formal warning to remove at next term. Still, however, they showed no symptoms either of submission or of compliance. At length the term-day, the fatal Martinmas, arrived, and violent measures of ejection were resorted to. A strong posse of peace-officers, sufficient to render all resistance vain, charged the inhabitants to depart by noon; and, as they did not obey, the officers, in terms of their warrant, proceeded to unroof the cottages, and pull down the wretched doors and windows,—a summary and effectual mode of ejection, still practiced in some remote parts of Scotland, when a tenant proves refractory. The gypsies, for a time, beheld the work of destruction in sullen silence and inactivity; then set about saddling and loading their asses, and making preparations for their departure. These were soon accomplished, where all had the habits of wandering Tartars; and they set forth on their journey to seek new settlements, where their patrons should neither be of the quorum, nor custos rotulorum.

Certain qualms of feeling had deterred Ellangowan from attending in person to see his tenants expelled. He left the executive part of the business to the officers of the law, under the immediate direction of Frank Kennedy, a supervisor, or riding-officer, belonging to the excise, who had of late become intimate at the Place, and of whom we shall have more to say in the next chapter. Mr. Bertram himself chose that day to make a visit to a friend at some distance. But it so happened, notwithstanding his precautions, that he could not avoid meeting his late tenants during their retreat from his property.

It was in a hollow way, near the top of a steep ascent, upon the verge of the Ellangowan estate, that Mr. Bertram met the gypsy procession. Four or five men formed the advanced guard, wrapped in long loose greatcoats, that hid their tall, slender figures, as the large slouched hats, drawn over their brows, concealed their wild features, dark eyes, and swarthy faces. Two of them carried long fowling pieces, one wore a broadsword without a sheath, and all had the Highland dirk, though they did not wear that weapon openly or ostentatiously. Behind them followed the train of laden asses, and small carts, or "tumblers," as they were called in that country, on which were laid the decrepit and the helpless, the aged and infant part of the exiled community. The women in their red cloaks and straw hats, the elder children with bare heads and bare feet, and almost naked bodies, had the immediate care of the little caravan. The road was narrow, running between two broken banks of sand, and Mr. Bertram's servant rode forward, smacking his whip with an air of authority, and motioning to the drivers to allow free passage to their betters. His signal was unattended to. He then called to the men who lounged idly on before, "Stand to your beasts' heads, and make room for the laird to pass."

"He shall have his share of the road," answered a male gypsy from under his slouched and large-brimmed hat, and without raising his face, "and he shall have nae mair; the highway is as free to our cuddies as to his gelding."

The tone of the man being sulky, and even menacing, Mr. Bertram thought it best to put his dignity in his pocket, and pass by the procession quietly, on such space as they chose to leave for his accommodation, which was narrow enough. To cover with an appearance of indifference his feeling of the want of respect with which he was treated, he addressed one of the men, as he passed him without any show of greeting, salute, or recognition,— "Giles Baillie," he said, "have you heard that your son Gabriel is well?" (The question respected the young man who had been pressed.)

"If I had heard otherwise," said the old man, looking up with a stern and menacing countenance, "you should have heard of it too." And he plodded on his way, tarrying no further question. When the laird had pressed on with difficulty among a crowd of familiar faces, which had on all former occasions marked his approach with the reverence due to that of a superior being, but in which he now only read hatred and contempt, and had got clear of the throng, he could not help turning his horse, and looking back to mark the progress of their march. The group would have been an excellent subject for the pencil of Calotte. The van had already reached a small and stunted thicket, which was at the bottom of the hill, and which gradually hid the line of march until the last stragglers disappeared.

His sensations were bitter enough. The race, it is true, which he had thus summarily dismissed from their ancient place of refuge, was idle and vicious; but had he endeavored to render them otherwise? They were not more irregular characters now, than they had been while they were admitted to consider themselves as a sort of subordinate dependants of his family; and ought the mere circumstance of his becoming a magistrate to have made at once such a change in his conduct towards them? Some means of reformation ought at least to have been tried, before sending seven families at once upon the wide world, and depriving them of a degree of countenance, which withheld them at least from atrocious guilt. There was also a natural yearning of heart on parting with so many known and familiar faces; and to this feeling Godfrey Bertram was peculiarly accessible, from the limited qualities of his mind, which sought its principal amusements among the petty objects around him. As he was about to turn his horse's head to pursue his journey, Meg Merrilies, who had lagged behind the troop, unexpectedly presented herself.

She was standing upon one of those high, precipitous banks, which, as we before noticed, overhung the road; so that she was placed considerably higher than Ellangowan, even though he was on horseback; and her tall figure, relieved against the clear blue sky, seemed almost of supernatural stature. We have noticed, that there was in her general attire, or rather in her mode of adjusting it, somewhat of a foreign costume, artfully adopted perhaps for the purpose of adding to the effect of her spells and predictions, or perhaps from some traditional notions respecting the dress of her ancestors. On this occasion, she had a large piece of red cotton cloth rolled about her head in the form of a turban, from beneath which her dark eyes flashed with uncommon lustre. Her long and tangled black hair fell in elf-locks from the folds of this singular headgear. Her attitude was that of a sibyl in frenzy, and she stretched out, in her right hand, a sapling bough which seemed just pulled.

"I'll be d——d," said the groom, "if she has not been cutting the young ashes in the Dukit park!"—The laird made no answer, but continued to look at the figure which was thus perched above his path.

"Ride your ways," said the gypsy, "ride your ways, laird of Ellangowan—ride your ways, Godfrey Bertram!—This day have ye quenched seven smoking hearths—see if the fire in your ain parlor burn the blyther for that. Ye have riven the thack off seven cottar houses—look if your ain rooftree stand the faster.—Ye may stable your stirks in the shealings at Derncleugh—see that the hare does not couch on the hearthstane at Ellangowan.—Ride your ways, Godfrey Bertram—what do ye glower after our folk for?—There's thirty hearts there that wad hae wanted bread ere ye had wanted sunkets, and spent their life-blood ere ye had scratched your finger. Yes—there's thirty yonder, from the auld wife of an hundred to the babe that was born last week, that ye have turned out o' their bits o' bields, to sleep with the tod and the blackcock in the muirs!—Ride your ways, Ellangowan. —Our bairns are hinging at our weary backs—look that your braw cradle at hame be the fairer spread up: not that I am wishing ill to little Harry, or to the babe that's yet to be born—God forbid—and make them kind to the poor, and better folk than their father!—And now, ride e'en your ways; for these are the last words ye'll ever hear Meg Merrilies speak, and this is the last reise that I'll ever cut in the bonny woods of Ellangowan."

So saying, she broke the sapling she held in her hand, and flung it into the road. Margaret of Anjou, bestowing on her triumphant foes her keen-edged malediction, could not have turned from them with a gesture more proudly contemptuous. The laird was clearing his voice to speak, and thrusting his hand in his pocket to find a half-crown; the gypsy waited neither for his reply nor his donation, but strode down the hill to overtake the caravan.

Ellangowan rode pensively home; and it was remarkable that he did not mention this interview to any of his family. The groom was not so reserved; he told the story at great length to a full audience in the kitchen, and concluded by swearing, that "if ever the Devil spoke by the mouth of a woman, he had spoken by that of Meg Merrilies that blessed day."

1815

FROM THE HEART OF MIDLOTHIAN

JEANIE DEANS AND QUEEN CAROLINE

The Duke made a signal for Jeanie to advance from the spot where she had hitherto remained watching countenances, which were too long accustomed to suppress all apparent signs of emotion, to convey to her any interesting intelligence. Her Majesty could not help smiling at the awe-struck manner in which the quiet demure figure of the little Scotchwoman advanced toward her, and yet more at the first sound of her broad northern accent. But Jeanie had a voice low and sweetly toned, an admirable thing in woman, and eke besought "her Leddyship to have pity on a poor misguided young creature," in tones so affecting, that, like the notes of some of her native songs, provincial vulgarity was lost in pathos.

"Stand up, young woman," said the Queen, but in a kind tone, "and tell me what sort of a barbarous people your countryfolk are, where child-murder is become so common as to require the restraint of laws like yours?"

"If your Leddyship pleases," answered Jeanie, "there are mony places besides Scotland where mothers are unkind to their ain flesh and blood."

It must be observed, that the disputes between George the Second, and Frederick, Prince of Wales, were then at the highest, and that the good-natured part of the public laid the blame on the Queen. She colored highly, and darted a glance of a most penetrating character first at Jeanie, and then at the Duke. Both sustained it unmoved; Jeanie from total unconsciousness of the offence she had given, and the Duke from his habitual composure. But in his heart he thought, My unlucky protégée has, with this luckless answer, shot dead, by a kind of chance-medley, her only hope of success.

Lady Suffolk, good-humoredly and skilfully, interposed in this awkward crisis. "You should tell this lady," she said to Jeanie, "the particular causes which render this crime common in your country."

"Some thinks it's the Kirk-Session—that is—it's the—it's the cutty-stool, if your Leddyship pleases," said Jeanie, looking down, and curtsying.

"The what?" said Lady Suffolk, to whom the phrase was new, and who besides was rather deaf.

"That's the stool of repentance, madam, if it please your Leddyship," answered Jeanie, "for light life and conversation, and for breaking the seventh command." Here she raised her eyes to the Duke, saw his hand at his chin, and, totally unconscious of what she had said out of joint, gave double effect to the innuendo, by stopping short and looking embarrassed.

As for Lady Suffolk, she retired like a covering party, which, having interposed betwixt their retreating friends and the enemy, have suddenly drawn on themselves a fire unexpectedly severe.

The deuce take the lass, thought the Duke of Argyle to himself: there goes another shot—and she has hit with both barrels right and left!

Indeed the Duke had himself his share

of the confusion, for, having acted as master of ceremonies to this innocent offender, he felt much in the circumstances of a country squire, who, having introduced his spaniel into a well-appointed drawing-room, is doomed to witness the disorder and damage which arises to china and to dress-gowns, in consequence of its untimely frolics. Jeanie's last chance-hit, however, obliterated the ill impression which had arisen from the first; for her Majesty had not so lost the feelings of a wife in those of a Queen, but that she could enjoy a jest at the expense of "her good Suffolk." She turned towards the Duke of Argyle with a smile, which marked that she enjoyed the triumph, and observed, "the Scotch are a rigidly moral people." Then again applying herself to Jeanie, she asked, how she travelled up from Scotland.

"Upon my foot mostly, madam," was the reply.

"What, all that immense way upon foot? —How far can you walk in a day?"

"Five and twenty miles and a bittock."

"And a what?" said the Queen, looking towards the Duke of Argyle.

"And about five miles more," replied the Duke.

"I thought I was a good walker," replied the Queen, "but this shames me sadly."

"May your Leddyship never hae sae weary a heart, that ye canna be sensible of the weariness of the limbs!" said Jeanie.

That came better off, thought the Duke; it's the first thing she has said to the purpose.

"And I didna just a'thegither walk the haill way neither, for I had whiles the cast of a cart; and I had the cast of a horse from Ferrybridge—and divers other easements," said Jeanie, cutting short her story, for she observed the Duke made the sign he had fixed upon.

"With all these accommodations," answered the Queen, "you must have had a very fatiguing journey, and, I fear, to little purpose, since, if the King were to pardon your sister, in all probability it would do her little good, for I suppose your people of Edinburgh would hang her out of spite."

She will sink herself now outright, thought the Duke.

But he was wrong. The shoals on which Jeanie had touched in this delicate conversation lay under ground, and were unknown to her; this rock was above water, and she avoided it.

"She was confident," she said, "that baith town and country wad rejoice to see his Majesty taking compassion on a poor unfriended creature."

"His Majesty has not found it so in a late instance," said the Queen; "but, I suppose, my Lord Duke would advise him to be guided by the votes of the rabble themselves, who should be hanged and who spared?"

"No, madam," said the Duke; "but I would advise his Majesty to be guided by his own feelings, and those of his royal consort; and then, I am sure, punishment will only attach itself to guilt, and even then with cautious reluctance."

"Well, my Lord," said her Majesty, "all these fine speeches do not convince me of the propriety of so soon showing any mark of favor to your—I suppose I must not say rebellious?—but, at least, your very disaffected and intractable metropolis. Why, the whole nation is in a league to screen the savage and abominable murderers of that unhappy man; otherwise, how is it possible but that, of so many perpetrators, and engaged in so public an action for such a length of time, one at least must have been recognized? Even this wench, for aught I can tell, may be a depository of the secret.—Hark you, young woman, had you any friends engaged in the Porteous mob?"

"No, madam," answered Jeanie, happy that the question was so framed that she could, with a good conscience, answer it in the negative.

"But I suppose," continued the Queen, "if you were possessed of such a secret, you would hold it matter of conscience to keep it to yourself?"

"I would pray to be directed and guided what was the line of duty, madam," answered Jeanie.

"Yes, and take that which suited your own inclination," replied her Majesty.

"If it like you, madam," said Jeanie, "I would hae gaen to the end of the earth to save the life of John Porteous, or any other unhappy man in his condition; but I might lawfully doubt how far I am called upon to be the avenger of his blood, though it may become the civil magistrate to do so. He is dead and gane to his place, and they that have slain him must answer for their ain act. But my sister, my puir sister Effie, still lives, though her days and hours are numbered!—She still lives, and a word of the King's mouth might restore her to a broken-hearted auld man, that never, in his daily and nightly exercise, forgot to pray that his Majesty might be blessed with a long and a prosperous reign, and that his throne, and the throne of his posterity, might be established in righteousness. O, madam, if ever ye kend what it was to sorrow for and with a sinning and a suffering creature, whose mind is sae tossed that she can be neither ca'd fit to live or die, have some compassion on our misery!—Save an honest house from dishonor, and an unhappy girl, not eighteen years of age, from an early and dreadful death! Alas! it is not when we sleep soft and wake merry ourselves, that we think on other people's sufferings. Our hearts are waxed light within us then, and we are for righting our ain wrangs and fighting our ain battles. But when the hour of trouble comes to the mind or to the body—and seldom may it visit your Leddyship—and when the hour of death comes, that comes to high and low—lang and late may it be yours—Oh, my Leddy, then it isna what we hae dune for oursells, but what we hae dune for others, that we think on maist pleasantly. And the thoughts that ye hae intervened to spare the puir thing's life will be sweeter in that hour, come when it may, than if a word of your mouth could hang the haill Porteous mob at the tail of ae tow."

Tear followed tear down Jeanie's cheeks, as, her features glowing and quivering with emotion, she pleaded her sister's cause with a pathos which was at once simple and solemn.

"This is eloquence," said her Majesty to the Duke of Argyle. "Young woman," she continued, addressing herself to Jeanie, "I cannot grant a pardon to your sister—but you shall not want my warm intercession with his Majesty. Take this housewife case," she continued, putting a small embroidered needle-case into Jeanie's hands; "do not open it now, but at your leisure you will find something in it which will remind you that you have had an interview with Queen Caroline."

Jeanie, having her suspicions thus confirmed, dropped on her knees, and would have expanded herself in gratitude; but the Duke, who was upon thorns lest she should say more or less than just enough, touched his chin once more.

"Our business is, I think, ended for the present, my Lord Duke," said the Queen, "and, I trust, to your satisfaction. Hereafter I hope to see your Grace more frequently, both at Richmond and St. James's. —Come, Lady Suffolk, we must wish his Grace good morning."

They exchanged their parting reverences, and the Duke, so soon as the ladies had turned their backs, assisted Jeanie to rise from the ground, and conducted her back through the avenue, which she trode with the feeling of one who walks in her sleep.

1818

FROM IVANHOE

THE SIEGE OF TORQUILSTONE

A moment of peril is often also a moment of open-hearted kindness and affection. We are thrown off our guard by the general agitation of our feelings, and betray the intensity of those which, at more tranquil periods, our prudence at least conceals, if it cannot altogether suppress them. In finding herself once more by the side of Ivanhoe, Rebecca was astonished at the keen sensation of pleasure which she experienced, even at a time when all around them both was danger, if not despair. As she felt his pulse, and inquired after his health, there was a softness in her touch and in her accents, implying a kinder interest than she would herself have been pleased to have voluntarily expressed. Her voice faltered and her hand trembled, and it was only the cold question of Ivanhoe, "Is it you, gentle maiden?" which recalled her to herself, and reminded her the sensations which she felt were not and could not be mutual. A sigh escaped, but it was scarce audible; and the questions which she asked the knight concerning his state of health were put in the tone of calm friendship. Ivanhoe answered her hastily that he was, in point of health, as well and better than he could have expected— "Thanks," he said, "dear Rebecca, to thy helpful skill."

"He calls me *dear* Rebecca," said the maiden to herself; "but it is in the cold and careless tone which ill suits the word. His war horse, his hunting hound, are dearer to him than the despised Jewess!"

"My mind, gentle maiden," continued Ivanhoe, "is more disturbed by anxiety than my body with pain. From the speeches of these men who were my warders just now, I learn that I am a prisoner and, if I judge aright of the loud hoarse voice which even now dispatched them hence on some military duty, I am in the castle of Front-de-Bœuf. If so, how will this end, or how can I protect Rowena and my father?"

"He names not the Jew or Jewess," said Rebecca internally; "yet what is our portion in him, and how justly am I punished by Heaven for letting my thoughts dwell upon him!" She hastened after this brief self-accusation to give Ivanhoe what information she could; but it amounted only to this, that the Templar Bois-Guilbert and the Baron Front-de-Bœuf were commanders within the castle; that it was beleaguered from without, but by whom she knew not. She added, that there was a Christian priest within the castle, who might be possessed of more information.

"A Christian priest!" said the knight joyfully; "fetch him hither, Rebecca, if thou canst—say a sick man desires his ghostly counsel—say what thou wilt, but bring him —something I must do or attempt, but how can I determine until I know how matters stand without?"

Rebecca, in compliance with the wishes of Ivanhoe, made that attempt to bring Cedric into the wounded knight's chamber, which was defeated as we have already seen by the interference of Urfried, who had been also on the watch to intercept the supposed monk. Rebecca retired to communicate to Ivanhoe the result of her errand.

They had not much leisure to regret the failure of this source of intelligence, or to contrive by what means it might be supplied; for the noise within the castle, occasioned by the defensive preparations, which had been considerable for some time, now increased into tenfold bustle and clamor. The heavy yet hasty step of the men-at-arms traversed the battlements, or resounded on the narrow and winding passages and stairs which led to the various bartizans and points of defence. The voices of the knights were heard, animating their followers, or directing means of defence, while their commands were often drowned in the clashing of armor, or the clamorous shouts of those whom they addressed. Tremendous as these sounds were, and yet more terrible from the awful event which they presaged, there was a sublimity mixed with them, which Rebecca's high-toned mind could feel even in that moment of terror. Her eye kindled, although the blood fled from her cheeks; and there was a strong mixture of fear, and of a thrilling sense of the sublime, as she repeated, half whispering to herself, half speaking to her companion, the sacred text, "The quiver rattleth—the glittering spear and the shield—the noise of the captains and the shouting!"

But Ivanhoe was like the war horse of

that sublime passage, glowing with impatience at his inactivity, and with his ardent desire to mingle in the affray of which these sounds were the introduction. "If I could but drag myself," he said, "to yonder window, that I might see how this brave game is like to go—if I had but bow to shoot a shaft, or battle-axe to strike were it but a single blow for our deliverance! It is in vain—it is in vain; I am alike nerveless and weaponless!"

"Fret not thyself, noble Knight," answered Rebecca, "the sounds have ceased of a sudden; it may be they join not battle."

"Thou knowest nought of it," said Wilfred impatiently. "This dead pause only shows that the men are at their posts on the walls, and expecting an instant attack; what we have heard was but the distant muttering of the storm—it will burst anon in all its fury.—Could I but reach yonder window!"

"Thou wilt but injure thyself by the attempt, noble Knight," replied his attendant. Observing his extreme solicitude, she firmly added, "I myself will stand at the lattice and describe to you as I can what passes without."

"You must not—you shall not!" exclaimed Ivanhoe; "each lattice, each aperture, will be soon a mark for the archers. Some random shaft——"

"It shall be welcome!" murmured Rebecca, as with firm pace she ascended two or three steps which led to the window of which they spoke.

"Rebecca, dear Rebecca!" exclaimed Ivanhoe, "this is no maiden's pastime. Do not expose thyself to wounds and death, and render me for ever miserable for having given the occasion; at least, cover thyself with yonder ancient buckler, and show as little of your person at the lattice as may be."

Following with wonderful promptitude the directions of Ivanhoe, and availing herself of the protection of the large ancient shield, which she placed against the lower part of the window, Rebecca, with tolerable security to herself, could witness part of what was passing without the castle, and report to Ivanhoe the preparations which the assailants were making for the storm. Indeed, the situation which she thus obtained was peculiarly favorable for this purpose, because, being placed on an angle of the main building, Rebecca could not only see what passed beyond the precincts of the castle, but also commanded a view of the outwork likely to be the first object of the meditated assault. It was an exterior fortification of no great height or strength, intended to protect the postern-gate through which Cedric had been recently dismissed by Front-de-Bœuf. The castle moat divided this species of barbican from the rest of the fortress, so that, in case of its being taken, it was easy to cut off the communication with the main building, by withdrawing the temporary bridge. In the outwork was a sally port corresponding to the postern of the castle, and the whole was surrounded by a strong palisade. Rebecca could observe, from the number of men placed for the defence of this post, that the besieged entertained apprehensions for its safety; and, from the mustering of the assailants in a direction nearly opposite to the outwork, it seemed no less plain that it had been selected as a vulnerable point of attack.

These appearances she hastily communicated to Ivanhoe, and added, "The skirts of the wood seem lined with archers, although only a few are advanced from its dark shadow."

"Under what banner?" asked Ivanhoe.

"Under no ensign of war which I can observe," answered Rebecca.

"A singular novelty," muttered the knight, "to advance to storm such a castle without pennon or banner displayed!— Seest thou who they be that act as leaders?"

"A knight, clad in sable armor, is the most conspicuous," said the Jewess; "he alone is armed from head to heel, and seems to assume the direction of all around him."

"What device does he bear on his shield?" replied Ivanhoe.

"Something resembling a bar of iron, and a padlock painted blue on the black shield." *

"A fetterlock and shacklebolt azure," said Ivanhoe. "I know not who may bear the device, but well I ween it might now be mine own.—Canst thou not see the motto?"

"Scarce the device itself at this distance," replied Rebecca; "but when the sun glances fair upon his shield, it shows as I tell you."

"Seem there no other leaders?" exclaimed the anxious enquirer.

"None of mark and distinction that I can behold from this station," said Rebecca; "but, doubtless, the other side of the castle is also assailed. They appear even now preparing to advance.—God of Zion, protect us!—what a dreadful sight! Those who advance first bear huge shields and defences made of plank; the others follow, bending their bows as they come on. They raise their bows!—God of Moses, forgive the creatures Thou hast made!"

Her description was here suddenly interrupted by the signal for assault, which was given by the blast of a shrill bugle, and at once answered by a flourish of the Norman trumpets from the battlements, which, mingled with the deep and hollow clang of the nakers (a species of kettledrum), retorted in notes of defiance the challenge of the enemy. The shouts of both parties augmented the fearful din, the assailants crying, "Saint George for merry England!" and the Normans answering them with loud cries of "En avant De Bracy!—Beauseant! Beauseant!—Front-de-Bœuf à la rescousse!" according to the war cries of their different commanders.

It was not, however, by clamor that the contest was to be decided, and the desperate effort of the assailants were met by an equally vigorous defence on the part of the besieged. The archers, trained by their woodland pastimes to the most effective use of the longbow, shot, to use the appropriate phrase of the time, so "wholly to-

---

* The author has been here upbraided with false heraldry, as having charged metal upon metal. It should be remembered, however, that heraldry had only its first rude origin during the crusades, and that all the minutiæ of its fantastic science were the work of time, and introduced at a much later period. Those who think otherwise must suppose that the Goddess of *Armoirers*, like the Goddess of Arms, sprung into the world completely equipped in all the gaudy trappings of the department she presides over.

In corroboration of what is above stated, it may be observed, that the arms, which were assumed by Godfrey of Boulogne himself, after the conquest of Jerusalem, was a cross counter patent cantoned with four little crosses or, upon a field azure, displaying thus metal upon metal. The heralds have tried to explain this undeniable fact in different modes; but Ferne gallantly contends that a prince of Godfrey's qualities should not be bound by the ordinary rules. The Scottish Nisbet, and the same Ferne, insist that the chiefs of the crusade must have assigned to Godfrey this extraordinary and unwonted coat-of-arms, in order to induce those who should behold them to make inquiries; and hence give them the name of *arma inquirenda*. But with reverence to these grave authorities, it seems unlikely that the assembled princes of Europe should have adjudged to Godfrey a coat armorial so much contrary to the general rule, if such rule had then existed; at any rate, it proves that metal upon metal, now accounted a solecism in heraldry, was admitted in other cases similar to that in the text. See Ferne's *Blazon of Gentrie*, p. 238. Edition 1586. Nisbet's *Heraldry*, vol. i, p. 113. Second Edition.

gether," that no point at which a defender could show the least part of his person escaped their clothyard shafts. By this heavy discharge, which continued as thick and sharp as hail, while, notwithstanding, every arrow had its individual aim, and flew by scores together against each embrasure and opening in the parapets, as well as at every window where a defender either occasionally had post, or might be suspected to be stationed,—by this sustained discharge, two or three of the garrison were slain, and several others wounded. But, confident in their armor of proof, and in the cover which their situation afforded, the followers of Front-de-Bœuf, and his allies, showed an obstinacy in defence proportioned to the fury of the attack, and replied with the discharge of their large crossbows, as well as their longbows, slings, and other missile weapons, to the close and continued shower of arrows, and, as the assailants were necessarily but indifferently protected, did considerably more damage than they received at their hand. The whizzing of shafts and of missiles, on both sides, was only interrupted by the shouts which arose when either side inflicted or sustained some notable loss.

"And I must lie here like a bedridden monk," exclaimed Ivanhoe, "while the game that gives me freedom or death is played out by the hand of others!—Look from the window once again, kind maiden —but beware that you are not marked by the archers beneath—Look out once more, and tell me if they yet advance to the storm."

With patient courage, strengthened by the interval which she had employed in mental devotion, Rebecca again took post at the lattice, sheltering herself, however, so as not to be visible from beneath.

"What dost thou see, Rebecca?" again demanded the wounded knight.

"Nothing but the cloud of arrows flying so thick as to dazzle mine eyes, and to hide the bowmen who shoot them."

"That cannot endure," said Ivanhoe. "If they press not right on to carry the castle by pure force of arms, the archery may avail but little against stone walls and bulwarks. Look for the Knight of the Fetterlock, fair Rebecca, and see how he bears himself; for as the leader is, so will his followers be."

"I see him not," said Rebecca.

"Foul craven!" exclaimed Ivanhoe; "does he blench from the helm when the wind blows highest?"

"He blenches not! he blenches not!" said Rebecca, "I see him now; he leads a body of men close under the outer barrier of the barbican.*—They pull down the piles and palisades; they hew down the barriers with axes.—His high black plume floats abroad over the throng, like a raven over the field of the slain.—They have made a breach in the barriers—they rush in—they are thrust back!—Front-de-Bœuf heads the defenders; I see his gigantic form above the press.— They throng again to the breach, and the pass is disputed hand to hand, and man to man.—God of Jacob! it is the meeting of two fierce tides—the conflict of two oceans moved by adverse winds!"

She turned her head from the lattice, as if unable longer to endure a sight so terrible.

"Look forth again, Rebecca," said Ivanhoe, mistaking the cause of her retiring; "the archery must in some degree have ceased, since they are now fighting hand to hand. Look again, there is now less danger."

Rebecca again looked forth, and almost immediately exclaimed, "Holy prophets of the law! Front-de-Bœuf and the Black Knight fight hand to hand on the breach, amid the roar of their followers, who watch the progress of the strife. Heaven strike with the cause of the oppressed and of the captive!" She then uttered a loud shriek, and exclaimed, "He is down!—he is down!"

"Who is down?" cried Ivanhoe; "for our dear Lady's sake, tell me which has fallen!"

"The Black Knight," answered Rebecca, faintly; then instantly again shouted with joyful eagerness, "But no—but no!—the name of the Lord of Hosts be blessed!—he is on foot again, and fights as if there were twenty men's strength in his single arm— his sword is broken—he snatches an axe from a yeoman—he presses Front-de-Bœuf with blow on blow—the giant stoops and totters like an oak under the steel of the woodman—he falls—he falls!"

"Front-de-Bœuf?" exclaimed Ivanhoe.

"Front-de-Bœuf!" answered the Jewess. "His men rush to the rescue, headed by the haughty Templar—their united force compels the champion to pause—they drag Front-de-Bœuf within the walls."

* Every Gothic castle and city had, beyond the outer walls, a fortification composed of palisades, called the barriers, which were often the scene of severe skirmishes, as these must necessarily be carried before the walls themselves could be approached. Many of those valiant feats of arms which adorn the chivalrous pages of Froissart took place at the barriers of besieged places.

"The assailants have won the barriers, have they not?" said Ivanhoe.

"They have—they have!" exclaimed Rebecca—"and they press the besieged hard upon the outer wall. Some plant ladders, some swarm like bees, and endeavor to ascend upon the shoulders of each other—down go stones, beams, and trunks of trees upon their heads; and as fast as they bear the wounded to the rear, fresh men supply their places in the assault.—Great God! hast Thou given men thine own image, that it should be thus cruelly defaced by the hands of their brethren!"

"Think not of that," said Ivanhoe; "this is no time for such thoughts.—Who yield—who push their way?"

"The ladders are thrown down," replied Rebecca, shuddering; "the soldiers lie grovelling under them like crushed reptiles—the besieged have the better."

"Saint George strike for us!" exclaimed the knight; "do the false yeomen give way?"

"No!" exclaimed Rebecca, "they bear themselves right yeomanly. The Black Knight approaches the postern with his huge axe—the thundering blows which he deals, you may hear them above all the din and shouts of the battle—stones and beams are hailed down on the bold champion—he regards them no more than if they were thistledown or feathers!"

"By Saint Joan of Acre," said Ivanhoe, raising himself joyfully on his couch, "methought there was but one man in England that might do such a deed!"

"The postern gate shakes," continued Rebecca—"it crashes—it is splintered by his blows—they rush in—the outwork is won.—Oh, God!—they hurl the defenders from the battlements—they throw them into the moat.—O men, if ye be indeed men, spare them that can resist no longer!"

"The bridge—the bridge which communicates with the castle—have they won that pass?" exclaimed Ivanhoe.

"No," replied Rebecca; "the Templar has destroyed the plank on which they crossed. Few of the defenders escaped with him into the castle; the shrieks and cries which you hear tell the fate of the others.—Alas! I see it is still more difficult to look upon victory than upon battle."

"What do they now, maiden?" said Ivanhoe. "Look forth yet again—this is no time to faint at bloodshed."

"It is over for the time," answered Rebecca. "Our friends strengthen themselves within the outwork which they have mas-

tered; and it affords them so good a shelter from the foemen's shot, that the garrison only bestow a few bolts on it from interval to interval, as if rather to disquiet than effectually to injure them."

"Our friends," said Wilfred, "will surely not abandon an enterprise so gloriously begun and so happily attained.—Oh, no! I will put my faith in the good knight whose axe hath rent heart of oak and bars of iron.—Singular," he again muttered to himself, "if there be two who can do a deed of such *derring-do!* * A fetterlock and a shacklebolt on a field sable—what may that mean?—Seest thou nought else, Rebecca, by which the Black Knight may be distinguished?"

"Nothing," said the Jewess; "all about him is black as the wing of the night raven. Nothing can I spy that can mark him further; but having once seen him put forth his strength in battle, methinks I could know him again among a thousand warriors. He rushes to the fray as if he were summoned to a banquet. There is more than mere strength, there seems as if the whole soul and spirit of the champion were given to every blow which he deals upon his enemies. God assoilzie him of the sin of bloodshed!—it is fearful, yet magnificent, to behold how the arm and heart of one man can triumph over hundreds."

"Rebecca," said Ivanhoe, "thou hast painted a hero. Surely they rest but to refresh their force, or to provide the means of crossing the moat. Under such a leader as thou hast spoken this knight to be there are no craven fears, no cold-blooded delays, no yielding up a gallant emprize, since the difficulties which render it arduous render it also glorious. I swear by the honor of my house—I vow by the name of my bright lady-love, I would endure ten years' captivity to fight one day by that good knight's side in such a quarrel as this!"

"Alas," said Rebecca, leaving her station at the window, and approaching the couch of the wounded knight, "this impatient yearning after action—this struggling with and repining at your present weakness, will not fail to injure your returning health. How couldst thou hope to inflict wounds on others, ere that be healed which thou thyself hast received?"

"Rebecca," he replied, "thou knowest not how impossible it is for one trained to actions of chivalry to remain passive as a priest, or a woman, when they are acting

* *Derring-do*—desperate courage.

deeds of honor around him. The love of battle is the food upon which we live—the dust of the *mêlée* is the breath of our nostrils! We live not—we wish not to live—longer than while we are victorious and renowned. Such, maiden, are the laws of chivalry to which we are sworn, and to which we offer all that we hold dear."

"Alas!" said the fair Jewess, "and what is it, valiant Knight, save an offering of sacrifice to a demon of vainglory, and a passing through the fire to Moloch? What remains to you as the prize of all the blood you have spilled—of all the travail and pain you have endured—of all the tears which your deeds have caused, when death hath broken the strong man's spear, and overtaken the speed of his war-horse?"

"What remains?" cried Ivanhoe. "Glory, maiden, glory! which gilds our sepulchre and embalms our name."

"Glory?" continued Rebecca. "Alas! is the rusted mail which hangs as a hatchment over the champion's dim and mouldering tomb—is the defaced sculpture of the inscription which the ignorant monk can hardly read to the inquiring pilgrim—are these sufficient rewards for the sacrifice of every kindly affection, for a life spent miserably that ye may make others miserable? Or is there such virtue in the rude rhymes of a wandering bard, that domestic love, kindly affection, peace and happiness are so wildly bartered, to become the hero of those ballads which vagabond minstrels sing to drunken churls over their evening ale?"

"By the soul of Hereward," replied the knight impatiently, "thou speakest, maiden, of thou knowest not what. Thou wouldst quench the pure light of chivalry, which alone distinguishes the noble from the base, the gentle knight from the churl and the savage; which rates our life far, far beneath the pitch of our honor; raises us victorious over pain, toil, and suffering, and teaches us to fear no evil but disgrace. Thou art no Christian, Rebecca; and to thee are unknown those high feelings which swell the bosom of a noble maiden when her lover hath done some deed of emprize which sanctions his flame. Chivalry!—why, maiden, she is the nurse of pure and high affection; the stay of the oppressed, the redresser of grievances, the curb of the power of the tyrant. Nobility were but an empty name without her, and liberty finds the best protection in her lance and her sword."

"I am, indeed," said Rebecca, "sprung from a race whose courage was distinguished in the defence of their own land, but who warred not, even while yet a nation, save at the command of the Deity, or in defending their country from oppression. The sound of the trumpet wakes Judah no longer, and her despised children are now but the unresisting victims of hostile and military oppression. Well hast thou spoken, Sir Knight,—until the God of Jacob shall raise up for His chosen people a second Gideon, or a new Maccabeus, it ill beseemeth the Jewish damsel to speak of battle or of war."

The high-minded maiden concluded the argument in a tone of sorrow, which deeply expressed her sense of the degradation of her people, embittered perhaps by the idea that Ivanhoe considered her as one not entitled to interfere in a case of honor, and incapable of entertaining or expressing sentiments of honor and generosity.

"How little he knows this bosom," she said, "to imagine that cowardice or meanness of soul must needs be its guests, because I have censured the fantastic chivalry of the Nazarenes! Would to Heaven that the shedding of mine own blood, drop by drop, could redeem the captivity of Judah! Nay, would to God it could avail to set free my father, and this his benefactor, from the chains of the oppressor! The proud Christian should then see whether the daughter of God's chosen people dared not to die as bravely as the vainest Nazarene maiden, that boasts her descent from some petty chieftain of the rude and frozen north!"

She then looked towards the couch of the wounded knight.

"He sleeps," she said; "nature exhausted by sufferance and the waste of spirits, his wearied frame embraces the first moment of temporary relaxation to sink into slumber. Alas! is it a crime that I should look upon him, when it may be for the last time?—when yet but a short space, and those fair features will be no longer animated by the bold and buoyant spirit which forsakes them not even in sleep!—when the nostril shall be distended, the mouth agape, the eyes fixed and bloodshot; and when the proud and noble knight may be trodden on by the lowest caitiff of this accursed castle, yet stir not when the heel is lifted up against him! And my father!—oh, my father! evil is it with his daughter, when his grey hairs are not remembered because of the golden locks of youth! What know I but that these evils are the

messengers of Jehovah's wrath to the unnatural child, who thinks of a stranger's
captivity before a parent's? who forgets the
desolation of Judah, and looks upon the
comeliness of a Gentile and a stranger?
But I will tear this folly from my heart,
though every fibre bleed as I rend it
away!"

She wrapped herself closely in her veil,
and sat down at a distance from the couch
of the wounded knight, with her back
turned towards it, fortifying or endeavoring to fortify her mind, not only against
the impending evils from without, but also
against those treacherous feelings which
assailed her from within.

                                    1820

FROM REDGAUNTLET

WANDERING WILLIE'S TALE

Ye maun have heard of Sir Robert Redgauntlet of that Ilk, who lived in these
parts before the dear years. The country
will lang mind him, and our fathers used
to draw breath thick if ever they heard him
named. He was out wi' the Hielandmen
in Montrose's time; and again he was in
the hills wi' Glencairn in the saxteen hundred and fifty-twa; and sae when King
Charles the Second came in, wha was in
sic favor as the Laird of Redgauntlet? He
was knighted at Lonon court, wi' the
King's ain sword; and being a redhot
prelatist, he came down here (rampaging
like a lion, with commissions of lieuten-
ancy (and of lunacy, for what I ken), to
put down a' the Whigs and Covenanters in
the country. Wild wark they made of it;
for the Whigs were as dour as the Cavaliers
were fierce, and it was which should first
tire the other. Redgauntlet was aye for the
strong hand, and his name is kend as wide
in the country as Claverhouse's or Tam
Dalyell's. Glen, nor dargle, nor mountain,
nor cave could hide the puir hill-folk when
Redgauntlet was out with bugle and blood-
hound after them, as if they had been sae
mony deer. And troth, when they fand
them, they didna mak muckle mair ceremony than a Hielandman wi' a roebuck.
It was just, "Will ye tak the test?"—if not,
"Make ready—present—fire!"—and there
lay the recusant.

Far and wide was Sir Robert hated and
feared. Men thought he had a direct compact with Satan; that he was proof against
steel, and that bullets happed aff his buff-
coat like hailstanes from a hearth; that he
had a mear that would turn a hare on the
side of Carrifra Gawns; * and muckle to
the same purpose, of whilk mair anon.
The best blessing they wared on him was,
"Deil scowp wi' Redgauntlet!" He wasna
a bad master to his ain folk though, and
was weel aneugh liked by his tenants; and
as for the lackeys and troopers that raid
out wi' him to the persecutions, as the
Whigs ca'd those killing times, they wad
hae drunken themsells blind to his health
at ony time.

Now you are to ken that my gudesire
lived on Redgauntlet's grund—they ca' the
place Primrose-Knowe. We had lived on
the grund, and under the Redgauntlets,
since the riding days, and lang before. It
was a pleasant bit; and I think the air is
callerer and fresher there than ony where
else in the country. It's a' deserted now;
and I sat on the broken door-cheek three
days since, and was glad I couldna see the
plight the place was in—but that's a' wide
o' the mark. There dwelt my gudesire,
Steenie Steenson, a rambling, rattling chiel
he had been in his young days, and could
play weel on the pipes; he was famous at
"Hoopers and Girders;" a' Cumberland
couldna touch him at "Jockie Lattin;" and
he had the finest finger for the back lilt
between Berwick and Carlisle. The like o'
Steenie wasna the sort that they made
Whigs o'. And so he became a Tory, as
they ca' it, which we now ca' Jacobites, just
out of a kind of needcessity, that he might
belang to some side or other. He had nae
ill-will to the Whig bodies, and liked little
to see the blude rin, though, being obliged
to follow Sir Robert in hunting and host-
ing, watching and warding, he saw muckle
mischief, and maybe did some that he
couldna avoid.

Now Steenie was a kind of favorite with
his master, and kend a' the folks about the
castle, and was often sent for to play the
pipes when they were at their merriment.
Auld Dougal MacCallum, the butler, that
had followed Sir Robert through gude and
ill, thick and thin, pool and stream, was
specially fond of the pipes, and aye gae my
gudesire his gude word wi' the Laird; for
Dougal could turn his master round his
finger.

Weel, round came the Revolution, and
it had like to have broken the hearts baith
of Dougal and his master. But the change
was not a'thegether sae great as they feared
and other folk thought for. The Whigs

* A precipitous side of a mountain in Moffatdale.

made an unco crawing what they wad do with their auld enemies, and in special wi' Sir Robert Redgauntlet. But there were ower mony great folks dipped in the same doings to make a spick and span new warld. So Parliament passed it a' ower easy; and Sir Robert, bating that he was held to hunting foxes instead of Covenanters, remained just the man he was. His revel was as loud, and his hall as weel lighted, as ever it had been, though maybe he lacked the fines of the non-conformists, that used to come to stock his larder and cellar; for it is certain he began to be keener about the rents than his tenants used to find him before, and they behoved to be prompt to the rent-day, or else the Laird wasna pleased. And he was sic an awsome body that naebody cared to anger him; for the oaths he swore, and the rage that he used to get into, and the looks that he put on, made men sometimes think him a devil incarnate.*

Weel, my gudesire was nae manager—no that he was a very great misguider, but he hadna the saving gift—and he got twa terms' rent in arrear. He got the first brash at Whitsunday put ower wi' fair word and piping; but when Martinmas came, there was a summons from the grund-officer to come wi' the rent on a day preceese, or else Steenie behoved to flit. Sair wark he had to get the siller; but he was weel-freended, and at last he got the haill scraped thegither—a thousand merks —the maist of it was from a neighbor they ca'd Laurie Lapraik—a sly tod. Laurie had walth o' gear—could hunt wi' the hound and rin wi' the hare, and be Whig or Tory, saunt or sinner, as the wind stood. He was a professor in this Revolution warld; but he liked an orra sough of this warld, and a tune on the pipes weel aneugh at a bytime; and abune a', he thought he had gude security for the siller he lent my gudesire ower the stocking at Primrose-Knowe.

Away trots my gudesire to Redgauntlet Castle wi' a heavy purse and a light heart, glad to be out of the Laird's danger. Weel, the first thing he learned at the Castle was that Sir Robert had fretted himsel' into a fit of the gout, because he did not appear before twelve o'clock. It wasna a'thegether for sake of the money, Dougal thought, but because he didna like to part wi' my gudesire aff the grund. Dougal was glad to see Steenie, and brought him into the great oak parlor, and there sat the Laird his leesome lane, excepting that he had beside him a great, ill-favored jackanape, that was a special pet of his; a cankered beast it was, and mony an ill-natured trick it played—ill to please it was, and easily angered—ran about the haill castle, chattering and yowling, and pinching and biting folk, specially before ill weather or disturbances in the state. Sir Robert ca'd it Major Weir, after the warlock that was burnt; † and few folk liked either the name or the conditions of the creature—they thought there was something in it by ordinar—and my gudesire was not just easy in his mind when the door shut on him, and he saw himself in the room wi' naebody but the Laird, Dougal MacCallum, and the Major, a thing that hadna chanced to him before.

Sir Robert sat, or, I should say, lay, in a great armed chair, wi' his grand velvet gown, and his feet on a cradle; for he had baith gout and gravel, and his face looked as gash and ghastly as Satan's. Major Weir sat opposite to him, in a red laced coat, and the Laird's wig on his head; and aye as Sir Robert girned wi' pain, the jackanape girned too, like a sheep's-head between a pair of tangs—and ill-faur'd, fearsome couple they were. The Laird's buffcoat was hung on a pin behind him, and his broadsword and his pistols within reach; for he keepit up the auld fashion of having the weapons ready, and a horse saddled day and night, just as he used to do when he was able to loup on horseback and away after ony of the hill-folk he could get speerings of. Some said it was for fear of the Whigs taking vengeance; but I judge it was just his auld custom—he wasna gien to fear onything. The rental-book, wi' its black cover and brass clasps, was lying beside him; and a book of sculduddery sangs was put betwixt the leaves, to keep it open at the place where it bore evidence against the Goodman of Primrose-Knowe, as behind the hand with his mails and duties. Sir Robert gave my gudesire a look, as if he would have withered his heart in his bosom. Ye maun ken he had a way of

* The caution and moderation of King William III., and his principles of unlimited toleration, deprived the Cameronians of the opportunity which they ardently desired, to retaliate the injuries which they had received during the reign of Prelacy, and purify the land, as they called it, from the pollution of blood. They esteemed the Revolution, therefore, only a half measure, which neither comprehended the rebuilding the Kirk in its full splendor, nor the revenge of the death of the saints on their persecutors.

† A celebrated wizard, executed at Edinburgh for sorcery and other crimes.

bending his brows that men saw the visible mark of a horseshoe in his forehead, deep-dinted, as if it had been stamped there.

"Are ye come light-handed, ye son of a toom whistle?" said Sir Robert. "Zounds! if you are——"

My gudesire, with as gude a countenance as he could put on, made a leg, and placed the bag of money on the table wi' a dash, like a man that does something clever. The Laird drew it to him hastily—"Is it all here, Steenie, man?"

"Your honor will find it right," said my gudesire.

"Here, Dougal," said the Laird, "gie Steenie a tass of brandy downstairs, till I count the siller and write the receipt."

But they werena weel out of the room, when Sir Robert gied a yelloch that garred the castle rock. Back ran Dougal—in flew the livery-men—yell on yell gied the Laird, ilk ane mair awfu' than the ither. My gudesire knew not whether to stand or flee, but he ventured back into the parlor, where a' was gaun hirdy-girdy—naebody to say "come in" or "gae out." Terribly the Laird roared for cauld water to his feet and wine to cool his throat; and hell, hell, hell, and its flames, was aye the word in his mouth. They brought him water, and when they plunged his swollen feet into the tub, he cried out it was burning; and folk said that it *did* bubble and sparkle like a seething cauldron. He flung the cup at Dougal's head, and said he had given him blood instead of burgundy; and, sure aneugh, the lass washed clotted blood aff the carpet the neist day. The jackanape they ca'd Major Weir, it jibbered and cried as if it was mocking its master. My gude-sire's head was like to turn; he forgot baith siller and receipt, and downstairs he banged. But as he ran, the shrieks came faint and fainter; there was a deep-drawn shivering groan; and word gaed through the castle that the Laird was dead.

Weel, away came my gudesire, wi' his finger in his mouth, and his best hope was that Dougal had seen the money-bag, and heard the Laird speak of writing the receipt. The young Laird, now Sir John, came from Edinburgh to see things put to rights. Sir John and his father never gree'd weel. Sir John has been bred an advocate, and afterwards sat in the last Scots Parliament and voted for the Union, having gotten, it was thought, a rug of the compensations. If his father could have come out of his grave, he would have brained him for it on his awn hearthstane.

Some thought it was easier counting with the auld rough Knight than the fair-spoken young ane—but mair of that anon.

Dougal MacCallum, poor body, neither grat nor graned, but gaed about the house looking like a corpse, but directing, as was his duty, a' the order of the grand funeral. Now, Dougal looked aye waur and waur when night was coming, and was aye the last to gang to his bed, whilk was in a little round just opposite the chamber of dais, whilk his master occupied while he was living, and where he now lay in state, as they ca'd it, weel-a-day! The night before the funeral, Dougal could keep his awn counsel nae longer; he came doun with his proud spirit, and fairly asked auld Hutch-eon to sit in his room with him for an hour. When they were in the round, Dou-gal took ae tass of brandy to himsel', and gave another to Hutcheon, and wished him all health and lang life, and said that, for himsel', he wasna lang for this world; for that, every night since Sir Robert's death, his silver call had sounded from the state chamber, just as it used to do at nights in his lifetime, to call Dougal to help to turn him in his bed. Dougal said that, being alone with the dead on that floor of the tower (for naebody cared to wake Sir Rob-ert Redgauntlet, like another corpse), he had never daured to answer the call, but that now his conscience checked him for neglecting his duty; for, "though death breaks service," said MacCallum, "it shall never break my service to Sir Robert; and I will answer his next whistle, so be you will stand by me, Hutcheon."

Hutcheon had nae will to the wark, but he had stood by Dougal in battle and broil, and he wad not fail him at this pinch. So down the carles sat ower a stoup of brandy, and Hutcheon, who was something of a clerk, would have read a chapter of the Bible; but Dougal would hear naething but a blaud of Davie Lindsay, whilk was the waur preparation.

When midnight came, and the house was quiet as the grave, sure enough the silver whistle sounded as sharp and shrill as if Sir Robert was blowing it, and up got the twa auld serving-men, and tottered into the room where the dead man lay. Hutch-eon saw aneugh at the first glance; for there were torches in the room, which showed him the foul fiend, in his ain shape, sitting on the Laird's coffin! Ower he cowped as if he had been dead. He could not tell how lang he lay in a trance at the door, but when he gathered himself, he cried on his neighbor, and getting nae answer, raised the house, when Dougal was found lying dead within twa steps of the bed where his master's coffin was placed. As for the whistle, it was gane anes and aye; but mony a time was it heard at the top of the house on the bartizan, and amang the auld chimneys and turrets, where the howlets have their nests. Sir John hushed the matter up, and the funeral passed over without mair bogle-wark.

But when a' was ower, and the Laird was beginning to settle his affairs, every tenant was called up for his arrears, and my gude-sire for the full sum that stood against him in the rental-book. Weel, away he trots to the Castle to tell his story, and there he is introduced to Sir John, sitting in his father's chair, in deep mourning, with weepers and hanging cravat, and a small walking rapier by his side, instead of the auld broadsword that had a hundred-weight of steel about it, what with blade, chape, and basket-hilt. I have heard their communing so often tauld ower that I almost think I was there mysell, though I couldna be born at the time. (In fact, Alan, my companion mimicked, with a good deal of humor, the flattering, conciliating tone of the tenant's address, and the hypocritical melancholy of the Laird's reply. His grandfather, he said, had, while he spoke, his eye fixed on the rental-book, as if it were a mastiff-dog that he was afraid would spring up and bite him.)

"I wuss ye joy, sir, of the head seat, and the white loaf, and the braid lairdship. Your father was a kind man to friends and followers; muckle grace to you, Sir John, to fill his shoon—his boots, I suld say, for he seldom wore shoon, unless it were muils when he had the gout."

"Ay, Steenie," quoth the Laird, sighing deeply, and putting his napkin to his een, "his was a sudden call, and he will be missed in the country; no time to set his house in order—weel prepared Godward, no doubt, which is the root of the matter, but left us behind a tangled hesp to wind, Steenie.—Hem! hem! We maun go to business, Steenie; much to do, and little time to do it in."

Here he opened the fatal volume. I have heard of a thing they call Doomsday-book—I am clear it has been a rental of back-ganging tenants.

"Stephen," said Sir John, still in the same soft, sleekit tone of voice—"Stephen Stevenson, or Steenson, ye are down here for a year's rent behind the hand—due at last term."

Stephen. "Please your honor, Sir John, I paid it to your father."

Sir John. "Ye took a receipt then, doubtless, Stephen, and can produce it?"

Stephen. "Indeed I hadna time, an it like your honor; for nae sooner had I set doun the siller, and just as his honor Sir Robert that's gane drew it till him to count it, and write out the receipt, he was ta'en wi' the pains that removed him."

"That was unlucky," said Sir John, after a pause. "But ye maybe paid it in the presence of somebody. I want but a *talis qualis* evidence, Stephen. I would go ower strictly to work with no poor man."

Stephen. "Troth, Sir John, there was naebody in the room but Dougal Mac-Callum, the butler. But, as your honor kens, he has e'en followed his auld master."

"Very unlucky again, Stephen," said Sir John, without altering his voice a single note. "The man to whom ye paid the money is dead; and the man who witnessed the payment is dead too; and the siller, which should have been to the fore, is neither seen nor heard tell of in repositories. How am I to believe a' this?"

Stephen. "I dinna ken, your honor; but there is a bit of memorandum note of the very coins—for, God help me! I had to borrow out of twenty purses—and I am sure that ilka man there set down will take his grit oath for what purpose I borrowed the money."

Sir John. "I have little doubt ye *borrowed* the money, Steenie. It is the *payment* to my father that I want to have some proof of."

Stephen. "The siller maun be about the house, Sir John. And since your honor never got it, and his honor that was canna have ta'en it wi' him, maybe some of the family may have seen it."

Sir John. "We will examine the servants, Stephen; that is but reasonable."

But lackey and lass, and page and groom, all denied stoutly that they had ever seen such a bag of money as my gudesire described. What was waur, he had unluckily not mentioned to any living soul of them his purpose of paying his rent. Ae quean had noticed something under his arm, but she took it for the pipes.

Sir John Redgauntlet ordered the servants out of the room, and then said to my gudesire, "Now, Steenie, ye see ye have fair play; and, as I have little doubt ye ken better where to find the siller than ony other body, I beg, in fair terms, and for your own sake, that you will end this fasherie; for, Stephen, ye maun pay or flit."

"The Lord forgie your opinion," said Stephen, driven almost to his wit's end; "I am an honest man."

"So am I, Stephen," said his honor; "and so are all the folks in the house, I hope. But if there be a knave amongst us, it must be he that tells the story he cannot prove." He paused, and then added, mair sternly, "If I understand your trick, sir, you want to take advantage of some malicious reports concerning things in this family, and particularly respecting my father's sudden death, thereby to cheat me out of the money, and perhaps take away my character, by insinuating that I have received the rent I am demanding. Where do you suppose this money to be?—I insist upon knowing."

My gudesire saw everything look so muckle against him that he grew nearly desperate. However, he shifted from one foot to another, looked to every corner of the room, and made no answer.

"Speak out, sirrah," said the Laird, assuming a look of his father's, a very particular ane, which he had when he was angry—it seemed as if the wrinkles of his frown made that selfsame fearful shape of a horse's shoe in the middle of his brow. "Speak out, sir! I *will* know your thoughts. Do you supose that I have this money?"

"Far be it frae me to say so," said Stephen.

"Do you charge any of my people with having taken it?"

"I wad be laith to charge them that may be innocent," said my gudesire; "and if there be any one that is guilty, I have nae proof."

"Somewhere the money must be, if there is a word of truth in your story," said Sir John. "I ask where you think it is, and demand a correct answer."

"In hell, if you *will* have my thoughts of it," said my gudesire, driven to extremity— "in hell! with your father, his jackanape, and his silver whistle."

Down the stairs he ran (for the parlor was nae place for him after such a word), and he heard the Laird swearing blood and wounds behind him, as fast as ever did Sir Robert, and roaring for the bailie and the baron-officer.

Away rode my gudesire to his chief creditor (him they caa'd Laurie Lapraik), to try if he could make onything out of him; but when he tauld his story, he got but the warst word in his wame—thief, beggar, and dyvour were the saftest terms; and to the boot of these hard terms Laurie brought up the auld story of his dipping his hand in the blood of God's saunts, just as if a tenant could have helped riding with the Laird, and that a Laird like Sir Robert Redgauntlet. My gudesire was by this time far beyond the bounds of patience, and, while he and Laurie were at deil speed the liars, he was wanchancie aneugh to abuse Lapraik's doctrine as weel as the man, and said things that garr'd folks' flesh grue that heard them—he wasna just himsel', and he had lived wi' a wild set in his day.

At last they parted, and my gudesire was to ride hame through the wood of Pitmurkie, that is a' fou of black firs, as they say. I ken the wood, but the firs may be black or white for what I can tell. At the entry of the wood there is a wild common, and on the edge of the common a little lonely change-house, that was keepit then by an ostler-wife, they suld hae ca'd her Tibbie Faw, and there puir Steenie cried for a mutchkin of brandy, for he had had no refreshment the haill day. Tibbie was earnest wi' him to take a bite of meat, but he couldna think o't, nor would he take his foot out of the stirrup, and took off the brandy wholly at twa draughts, and named a toast at each. The first was, the memory of Sir Robert Redgauntlet, and might he never lie quiet in his grave till he had righted his poor bond-tenant; and the second was, a health to Man's Enemy, if he would but get him back the pock of siller, or tell him what came o't, for he saw the haill world was like to regard him as a thief and a cheat, and he took that waur than even the ruin of his house and hauld.

On he rode, little caring where. It was a dark night turned, and the trees made it yet darker, and he let the beast take its ain road through the wood; when, all of a sudden, from tired and wearied that it was before, the nag began to spring, and flee, and stend, that my gudesire could hardly keep the saddle. Upon the whilk, a horseman, suddenly riding up beside him, said, "That's a mettle beast of yours, freend; will you sell him?" So saying, he touched the horse's neck with his riding-wand, and it fell into its auld heigh-ho of a stumbling trot. "But his spunk's soon out of him, I think," continued the stranger; "and that is like mony a man's courage, that thinks he wad do great things till he come to the proof."

My gudesire scarce listened to this, but spurred his horse, with "Gude e'en to you, freend."

But it's like the stranger was ane that doesna lightly yield his point; for, ride as Steenie liked, he was aye beside him at the self-same pace. At last my gudesire, Steenie Steenson, grew half angry, and, to say the truth, half feared.

"What is it that ye want with me, freend?" he said. "If ye be a robber, I have nae money; if ye be a leal man, wanting company, I have nae heart to mirth or speaking; and if ye want to ken the road, I scarce ken it mysel'."

"If you will tell me your grief," said the stranger, "I am one that, though I have been sair misca'ad in the world, am the only hand for helping my freends."

So my gudesire, to ease his ain heart mair than from any hope of help, told him the story from beginning to end.

"It's a hard pinch," said the stranger; "but I think I can help you."

"If you could lend the money, sir, and take a lang day—I ken nae other help on earth," said my gudesire.

"But there may be some under the earth," the stranger. "Come, I'll be frank wi' you. I could lend you the money on bond, but you would maybe scruple my terms. Now, I can tell you that your auld Laird is disturbed in his grave by your curses, and the wailing of your family, and if ye daur venture to go to see him, he will give you the receipt."

My gudesire's hair stood on end at this proposal, but he thought his companion might be some humorsome chield that was trying to frighten him, and might end with lending him the money. Besides, he was bauld wi' brandy and desperate wi' distress, and he said he had courage to go to the gate of hell, and a step farther, for that receipt. The stranger laughed.

Weel, they rode on through the thickest of the wood, when, all of a sudden, the horse stopped at the door of a great house, and, but that he knew the place was ten miles off, my father would have thought he was at Redgauntlet Castle. They rode into the outer courtyard, through the muckle faulding yetts, and aneath the auld portcullis; and the whole front of the house was lighted, and there were pipes and fiddles, and as much dancing and deray within as used to be in Sir Robert's house at Pace and Yule, and such high seasons. They lap off, and my gudesire, as seemed to him, fastened his horse to the very ring he had tied him to that morning when he gaed to wait on the young Sir John.

"God!" said my gudesire, "if Sir Robert's death be but a dream!"

He knocked at the ha' door just as he was wont, and his auld acquaintance, Dougal MacCallum, just after his wont, too, came to open the door, and said, "Piper Steenie, are ye there, lad? Sir Robert has been crying for you."

My gudesire was like a man in a dream. He looked for the stranger, but he was gane for the time. At last he just tried to say, "Ha! Dougal Driveower, are ye living? I thought ye had been dead."

"Never fash yoursel' wi' me," said Dougal, "but look to yoursel'; and see ye tak naething frae onybody here, neither meat, drink, or siller, except just the receipt that is your ain."

So saying, he led the way out through halls and trances that were weel kend to my gudesire, and into the auld oak parlor; and there was as much singing of profane sangs, and birling of red wine, and speaking blasphemy and sculduddery, as had ever been in Redgauntlet Castle when it was at the blithest.

But, Lord take us in keeping! what a set of ghastly revellers they were that sat round that table! My gudesire kend mony that had long before gane to their place, for often had he piped to the most part in the hall of Redgauntlet. There was the fierce Middleton, and the dissolute Rothes, and the crafty Lauderdale; and Dalyell, with his bald head and a beard to his girdle; and Earlshall, with Cameron's blude on his hand; and wild Bonshaw, that tied blessed Mr. Cargill's limbs till the blude sprung; and Dunbarton Douglas, the twice-turned traitor baith to country and king. There was the Bluidy Advocate MacKenyie, who, for his worldly wit and wisdom, had been to the rest as a god. And there was Claverhouse, as beautiful as when he lived, with his long, dark, curled locks streaming down over his laced buff-coat, and his left hand always on his right spule-blade, to hide the wound that the silver bullet had made. He sat apart from them all, and looked at them with a melancholy, haughty countenance; while the rest halooed, and sung, and laughed, that the room rang. But their smiles were fearfully contorted from time to time; and their laughter passed into such wild sounds as made my gudesire's very nails grow blue, and chilled the marrow in his banes.

They that waited at the table were just

the wicked serving-men and troopers that had done their work and cruel bidding on earth. There was the Lang Lad of the Nethertown, that helped to take Argyle; and the Bishop's summoner, that they called the Deil's Rattle-bag; and the wicked guardsmen, in their laced coats; and the savage Highland Amorites, that shed blood like water; and many a proud serving-man, haughty of heart and bloody of hand, cringing to the rich, and making them wickeder than they would be—grinding the poor to powder when the rich had broken them to fragments. And mony, mony mair were coming and ganging, a' as busy in their vocation as if they had been alive.

Sir Robert Redgauntlet, in the midst of a' this fearful riot, cried, wi' a voice like thunder, on Steenie Piper, to come to the board-head where he was sitting—his legs stretched out before him, and swathed up with flannel, with his holster pistols aside him, while the great broadsword rested against his chair, just as my gudesire had seen him the last time upon earth. The very cushion for the jackanape was close to him, but the creature itself was not there— it wasna its hour, it's likely, for he heard them say as he came forward, "Is not the Major come yet?" And another answered, "The jackanape will be here betimes the morn." And when my gudesire came forward, Sir Robert, or his ghaist, or the deevil in his likeness, said, "Weel, piper, hae ye settled wi' my son for the year's rent?"

With much ado my father gat breath to say that Sir John would not settle without his honor's receipt.

"Ye shall hae that for a tune of the pipes, Steenie," said the appearance of Sir Robert. "Play us up 'Weel hoddler, Luckie.'"

Now this was a tune my gudesire learned frae a warlock, that heard it when they were worshipping Satan at their meetings; and my gudesire had sometimes played it at the ranting suppers in Redgauntlet Castle, but never very willingly; and now he grew cauld at the very name of it, and said, for excuse, he hadna his pipes wi' him.

"MacCallum, ye limb of Beelzebub," said the fearfu' Sir Robert, "bring Steenie the pipes that I am keeping for him!"

MacCallum brought a pair of pipes might have served the piper of Donald of the Isles. But he gave my gudesire a nudge as he offered them; and looking secretly and closely, Steenie saw that the chanter was of steel, and heated to a white heat, so he had fair warning not to trust his fingers with it. So he excused himself again, and said he was faint and frightened, and had not wind aneugh to fill the bag.

"Then ye maun eat and drink, Steenie," said the figure; "for we do little else here, and it's ill speaking between a fou man and a fasting."

Now these were the very words that the bloody Earl of Douglas said to keep the king's messenger in hand, while he cut the head off MacLellan of Bombie, at the Threave Castle; * and that put Steenie mair and mair on his guard. So he spoke up like a man, and said he came neither to eat, or drink, or make minstrelsy, but simply for his ain—to ken what was come o' the money he had paid, and to get a discharge for it. And he was so stout-hearted by this time that he charged Sir Robert for conscience-sake (he had no power to say the holy Name), and as he hoped for peace and rest, to spread no snares for him, but just to give him his ain.

The appearance gnashed its teeth and laughed, but it took from a large pocket-book the receipt, and handed it to Steenie. "There is your receipt, ye pitiful cur; and for the money, my dog-whelp of a son may go look for it in the Cat's Cradle."

My gudesire uttered mony thanks, and was about to retire, when Sir Robert roared aloud, "Stop though, thou sack-doudling son of a whore! I am not done with thee. HERE we do nothing for nothing; and you must return on this very day twelve-month, to pay your master the homage that you owe me for my protection."

My father's tongue was loosed of a suddenty, and he said aloud, "I refer myself to God's pleasure, and not to yours."

He had no sooner uttered the word than all was dark around him, and he sunk on the earth with such a sudden shock that he lost both breath and sense.

How long Steenie lay there he could not tell, but when he came to himsel', he was lying in the auld kirkyard of Redgauntlet parochine just at the door of the family aisle, and the scutcheon of the auld knight, Sir Robert, hanging over his head. There was a deep morning fog on grass and grave-stane around him, and his horse was feeding quietly beside the minister's twa cows. Steenie would have thought the whole was a dream, but he had the receipt in his hand, fairly written and signed by the auld

* The reader is referred for particulars to Pitscottie's History of Scotland.

Laird; only the last letters of his name were a little disorderly, written like one seized with sudden pain.

Sorely troubled in his mind, he left that dreary place, rode through the mist to Redgauntlet Castle, and with much ado he got speech of the Laird.

"Well, you dyvour bankrupt," was the first word, "have you brought me my rent?"

"No," answered my gudesire, "I have not; but I have brought your honor Sir Robert's receipt for it."

"How, sirrah? Sir Robert's receipt! You told me he had not given you one."

"Will your honor please to see if that bit line is right?"

Sir John looked at every line, and at every letter, with much attention; and at last at the date, which my gudesire had not observed. "From my appointed place," he read, "this twenty-fifth of November." "What—That is yesterday! Villain, thou must have gone to hell for this!"

"I got it from your honor's father—whether he be in heaven or hell, I know not," said Steenie.

"I will delate you for a warlock to the Privy Council!" said Sir John. "I will send you to your master, the devil, with the help of a tar-barrel and a torch!"

"I intend to delate mysel' to the Presbytery," said Steenie, "and tell them all I have seen last night, whilk are things fitter for them to judge of than a borrel man like me."

Sir John paused, composed himsel', and desired to hear the full history; and my gudesire told it him from point to point, as I have told it you—word for word, neither more nor less.

Sir John was silent again for a long time, and at last he said, very composedly, "Steenie, this story of yours concerns the honor of many a noble family besides mine; and if it be a leasing-making, to keep yourself out of danger, the least you can expect is to have a red-hot iron driven through your tongue, and that will be as bad as scauding your fingers wi' a red-hot chanter. But yet it may be true, Steenie; and if the money cast up, I shall not know what to think of it. But where shall we find the Cat's Cradle? There are cats enough about the old house, but I think they kitten without the ceremony of bed or cradle."

"We were best ask Hutcheon," said my gudesire; "he kens a' the odd corners about as weel as—another serving-man that is now gane, and that I wad not like to name."

Aweel, Hutcheon, when he was asked, told them that a ruinous turret, lang disused, next to the clock-house, only accessible by a ladder, for the opening was on the outside, and far above the battlements, was called of old the Cat's Cradle.

"There will I go immediately," said Sir John; and he took (with what purpose Heaven kens) one of his father's pistols from the hall-table, where they had lain since the night he died, and hastened to the battlements.

It was a dangerous place to climb, for the ladder was auld and frail, and wanted ane or twa rounds. However, up got Sir John, and entered at the turret door, where his body stopped the only little light that was in the bit turret. Something flees at him wi' a vengeance, maist dang him back ower; bang gaed the knight's pistol, and Hutcheon, that held the ladder, and my gudesire that stood beside him, hears a loud skelloch. A minute after, Sir John flings the body of the jackanape down to them, and cries that the siller is fund, and that they should come up and help him. And there was the bag of siller sure aneugh, and mony orra things besides, that had been missing for mony a day. And Sir John, when he had riped the turret weel, led my gudesire into the dining-parlor, and took him by the hand, and spoke kindly to him, and said he was sorry he should have doubted his word, and that he would hereafter be a good master to him, to make amends.

"And now, Steenie," said Sir John, "although this vision of yours tends, on the whole, to my father's credit, as an honest man, that he should, even after his death, desire to see justice done to a poor man like you, yet you are sensible that ill-disposed men might make bad constructions upon it concerning his soul's health. So, I think, we had better lay the haill dirdum on that ill-deedie creature, Major Weir, and say naething about your dream in the wood of Pitmurkie. You had taken ower muckle brandy to be very certain about onything; and, Steenie, this receipt" (his hand shook while he held it out) "it's but a queer kind of document, and we will do best, I think, to put it quietly in the fire."

"Od, but for as queer as it is, it's a' the voucher I have for my rent," said my gudesire, who was afraid, it may be, of losing the benefit of Sir Robert's discharge.

"I will bear the contents to your credit in the rental-book, and give you a discharge under my own hand," said Sir John, "and that on the spot. And, Steenie, if you can hold your tongue about this matter, you shall sit, from this term downward, at an easier rent."

"Mony thanks to your honor," said Steenie, who saw easily in what corner the wind was; "doubtless I will be conformable to all your honor's commands—only I would willingly speak wi' some powerful minister on the subject, for I do not like the sort of soumons of appointment whilk your honor's father——"

"Do not call the phantom my father!" said Sir John, interrupting him.

"Well, then, the thing that was so like him," said my gudesire. "He spoke of my coming back to see him this time twelve-month, and it's a weight on my conscience."

"Aweel, then," said Sir John, "if you be so much distressed in mind, you may speak to our minister of the parish. He is a douce man, regards the honor of our family, and the mair that he may look for some patronage from me."

"Wi' that, my gudesire readily agreed that the receipt should be burnt, and the Laird threw it into the chimney with his ain hand. Burn it would not for them, though; but away it flew up the lum, wi' a lang train of sparks at its tail, and a hissing noise like a squib.

My gudesire gaed down to the Manse, and the minister, when he had heard the story, said it was his real opinion that, though my gudesire had gaen very far in tampering with dangerous matters, yet, as he had refused the devil's arles (for such was the offer of meat and drink), and refused to do homage by piping at his bidding, he hoped that, if he held a circumspect walk hereafter, Satan could take little advantage by what was come and gane. And, indeed, my gudesire, of his ain accord, lang forswore baith the pipes and the brandy—it was not even till the year was out, and the fatal day passed, that he would so much as take the fiddle, or drink usquebaugh or tippenny.

Sir John made up his story about the jackanape as he liked himsel'; and some believe till this day there was no more in the matter than the filching nature of the brute. Indeed, ye'll no hinder some to threap that it was nane o' the Auld Enemy that Dougal and my gudesire saw in the Laird's room, but only that wanchancy creature, the Major, capering on the coffin; and that, as to the blawing on the Laird's whistle that was heard after he was dead, the filthy brute could do that as well as the Laird himsel', if no better. But Heaven kens the truth, whilk first came out by the minister's wife, after Sir John and her ain gudeman were baith in the moulds. And then my gudesire, wha was failed in his limbs, but not in his judgment or memory —at least nothing to speak of—was obliged to tell the real narrative to his freends, for the credit of his good name. He might else have been charged for a warlock.

1824

FROM REDGAUNTLET

THE FAREWELL OF THE LAST PRETENDER

In the same breath, they were both at the half-opened door of the room, Fairford entreating to speak with the Father Buonaventure, and Lilias, equally vehemently, requesting a moment's interview with her uncle. While the sentinel hesitated what to do, his attention was called to a loud noise at the door, where a crowd had been assembled in consequence of the appalling cry that the enemy were upon them, occasioned, as it afterward proved, by some stragglers having at length discovered the dead bodies of Nanty Ewart and of Nixon. Amid the confusion occasioned by this alarming incident, the sentinel ceased to attend to his duty; and, accepting Alan Fairford's arm, Lilias found no opposition in penetrating even to the inner apartment, where the principal persons in the enterprise, whose conclave had been disturbed by this alarming incident, were now assembled in great confusion, and had been joined by the Chevalier himself.

"Only a mutiny among these smuggling scoundrels," said Redgauntlet.

"*Only* a mutiny, do you say?" said Richard Glendale; "and the lugger, the last hope of escape for"—he looked towards Charles—"stands out to sea under a press of sail!"

"Do not concern yourself about me," said the unfortunate Prince. "This is not the worst emergency in which it has been my lot to stand; and if it were, I fear it not. Shift for yourselves, my lords and gentlemen."

"No, never!" said the young Lord ——. "Our only hope now is an honorable resistance."

"Most true," said Redgauntlet; "let despair renew the union amongst us which accident disturbed. I give my voice for displaying the royal banner instantly, and —— How now!" he concluded sternly, as Lilias, first soliciting his attention by pulling his cloak, put into his hand the scroll, and added it was designed for that of Nixon.

Redgauntlet read, and dropping it on the ground, continued to stare upon the spot where it fell, with raised hands and fixed eyes. Sir Richard Glendale lifted the fatal paper, read it, and saying, "Now all is indeed over," handed it to Maxwell, who said aloud, "Black Colin Campbell, by G—d! I heard he had come post from London last night."

As if in echo to his thoughts, the violin of the blind man was heard playing with spirit, "The Campbells are coming," a celebrated clan march.

"The Campbells are coming in earnest," said MacKellar; "they are upon us with the whole battalion from Carlisle."

There was a silence of dismay, and two or three of the company began to drop out of the room.

Lord —— spoke with the generous spirit of a young English nobleman. "If we have been fools, do not let us be cowards. We have one here more precious than us all, and come hither on our warranty—let us save him at least."

"True, most true," answered Sir Richard Glendale. "Let the King be first cared for."

"That shall be my business," said Redgauntlet; "if we have but time to bring back the brig, all will be well. I will instantly dispatch a party in a fishing skiff to bring her to." He gave his commands to two or three of the most active among his followers. "Let him be once on board," he said, "and there are enough of us to stand to arms and cover his retreat."

"Right, right," said Sir Richard, "and I will look to points which can be made defensible; and the old powder-plot boys could not have made a more desperate resistance than we shall.—Redgauntlet," continued he, "I see some of our friends are looking pale, but methinks your nephew has more mettle in his eye now than when we were in cold deliberation, with danger at a distance."

"It is the way of our house," said Redgauntlet: "our courage ever kindles highest on the losing side. I, too, feel that the catastrophe I have brought on must not be survived by its author. Let me first," he said, addressing Charles, "see your Majesty's sacred person in such safety as can now be provided for it, and then——"

"You may spare all considerations concerning me, gentlemen," again repeated Charles; "yon mountain of Criffell shall fly as soon as I will."

Most threw themselves at his feet with weeping and entreaty; some one or two slunk in confusion from the apartment, and were heard riding off. Unnoticed in such a scene, Darsie, his sister, and Fairford drew together, and held each other by the hands as those who, when a vessel is about to founder in the storm, determine to take their chance of life and death together.

Amid this scene of confusion, a gentleman, plainly dressed in a riding-habit, with a black cockade in his hat, but without any arms except a *couteau-de-chasse,* walked into the apartment without ceremony. He was a tall, thin, gentlemanly man, with a look and bearing decidedly military. He had passed through their guards, if in the confusion they now maintained any, without stop or question, and now stood almost unarmed among armed men, who, nevertheless, gazed on him as on the angel of destruction.

"You look coldly on me, gentlemen," he said. "Sir Richard Glendale—my Lord ——, we were not always such strangers. Ha, Pate-in-Peril, how is it with you? And you, too, Ingoldsby—I must not call you by any other name—why do you receive an old friend so coldly? But you guess my errand."

"And are prepared for it, General," said Redgauntlet: "we are not men to be penned up like sheep for the slaughter."

"Pshaw! you take it too seriously; let me speak but one word with you."

"No words can shake our purpose," said Redgauntlet, "were your whole command, as I suppose is the case, drawn round the house."

"I am certainly not unsupported," said the General; "but if you would hear me——"

"Hear *me*, sir," said the Wanderer, stepping forward. "I suppose I am the mark you aim at. I surrender myself willingly, to save these gentlemen's danger; let this at least avail in their favor."

An exclamation of "Never—never!" broke from the little body of partisans, who threw themselves round the unfortunate prince, and would have seized or struck down Campbell, had it not been that he remained with his arms folded, and a look rather indicating impatience because they would not hear him than the least apprehension of violence at their hand.

At length he obtained a moment's silence. "I do not," he said, "know this gentleman (making a profound bow to the unfortunate prince)—I do not wish to know him; it is a knowledge which would suit neither of us."

"Our ancestors, nevertheless, have been well acquainted," said Charles, unable to suppress, even in that hour of dread and danger, the painful recollections of fallen royalty.

"In one word, General Campbell," said Redgauntlet, "is it to be peace or war? You are a man of honor, and we can trust you."

"I thank you, sir," said the General; "and I reply that the answer to your question rests with yourself. Come, do not be fools, gentlemen; there was perhaps no great harm meant or intended by your gathering together in this obscure corner, for a bear-bait or a cock-fight, or whatever other amusement you may have intended; but it was a little imprudent, considering how you stand with government, and it has occasioned some anxiety. Exaggerated accounts of your purpose have been laid before government by the information of a traitor in your own counsels; and I was sent down post to take the command of a sufficient number of troops, in case these calumnies should be found to have any real foundation. I have come here, of course, sufficiently supported both with cavalry and infantry to do whatever might be necessary; but my commands are—and I am sure they agree with my inclination—to make no arrests, nay, to make no further inquiries of any kind, if this good assembly will consider their own interests so far as to give up their immediate purpose and return quietly home to their own houses."

"What!—all?" exclaimed Sir Richard Glendale—"all, without exception?"

"ALL, without one single exception," said the General; "such are my orders. If you accept my terms, say so, and make haste; for things may happen to interfere with his Majesty's kind purposes towards you all."

"His Majesty's kind purposes!" said the Wanderer. "Do I hear you aright, sir?"

"I speak the King's very words, from his very lips," replied the General. " 'I will,' said his Majesty, 'deserve the confidence of my subjects by reposing my security in the fidelity of the millions who acknowledge my title—in the good sense and prudence of the few who continue, from the errors of education, to disown it.' His Majesty will not even believe that the most zealous Jacobites who yet remain can nourish a thought of exciting a civil war, which must be fatal to their families and themselves, besides spreading bloodshed and ruin through a peaceful land. He cannot even believe of his kinsman, that he would engage brave and generous, though mistaken men, in an attempt which must ruin all who have escaped former calamities; and he is convinced that, did curiosity or any other motive lead that person to visit this country, he would soon see it was his wisest course to return to the Continent, and his Majesty compassionates his situation too much to offer any obstacle to his doing so."

"Is this real?" said Redgauntlet. "Can you mean this? Am I—are all—are any of these gentlemen at liberty, without interruption, to embark in yonder brig, which, I see, is now again approaching the shore?"

"You, sir—all—any of the gentlemen present," said the General—"all whom the vessel can contain, are at liberty to embark, uninterrupted by me; but I advise none to go off who have not powerful reasons unconnected with the present meeting, for this will be remembered against no one."

"Then, gentlemen," said Redgauntlet, clasping his hands together as the words burst from him, "the cause is lost for ever!"

1824

FROM WOODSTOCK

PRESBYTERIAN OUSTED FROM THE PULPIT BY CROMWELLIAN INDEPENDENT

On a morning in the end of September, or beginning of October, in the year 1652, being a day appointed for a solemn thanksgiving for the decisive victory at Worcester, a respectable audience was assembled in the old chantry, or chapel of King John, at Woodstock. The condition of the church and character of the audience both bore witness to the rage of civil war and the peculiar spirit of the times. The sacred edifice showed many marks of dilapidation. The windows, once filled with stained glass, had been dashed to pieces with pikes and muskets, as matters of, and pertaining to, idolatry. The carving on the reading desk was damaged, and two fair screens of beautiful sculptured oak had been destroyed for the same pithy and conclusive reason. The high altar had been removed, and the gilded railing, which was once around it, was broken down and carried off. The effigies of several tombs were mutilated, and now lay scattered about the church,

Torn from their destined niche,—unworthy meed
Of knightly counsel or heroic deed!

The autumn wind piped through empty aisles, in which the remains of stakes and trevisses of rough-hewn timber, as well as a quantity of scattered hay and trampled straw, seemed to intimate that the hallowed precincts had been, upon some late emergency, made the quarters of a troop of horse.

The audience, like the building, was abated in splendor. None of the ancient and habitual worshippers during the peaceful times, were now to be seen in their carved galleries, with hands shadowing their brows, while composing their minds to pray where their fathers had prayed, and after the same mode of worship. The eye of the yeoman and peasant sought in vain the tall form of old Sir Henry Lee of Ditchley, as, wrapped in his laced cloak, and with beard and whiskers duly composed, he moved slowly through the aisles, followed by the faithful mastiff, or blood-hound, which in old time had saved his master by his fidelity, and which regularly followed him to church. Bevis, indeed, fell under the proverb which avers, "He is a good dog which goes to church;" for, bating an occasional temptation to warble along with the accord, he behaved himself as decorously as any of the congregation, and returned as much edified, perhaps, as most of them. The damsels of Woodstock looked as vainly for the laced cloaks, jingling spurs, slashed boots, and tall plumes, of the young cavaliers of this and other high-born houses, moving through the streets and the churchyard with the careless ease, which indicates perhaps rather an overweening degree of self-confidence, yet shows graceful when mingled with good humor and courtesy. The good old dames, too, in their white hoods and black velvet gowns—their daughters, "the cynosure of neighboring eyes,"—where were they all now, who, when they entered the church, used to divide men's thoughts between them and heaven? "But, ah! Alice Lee—

so sweet, so gentle, so condescending in thy loveliness—(thus proceeds a contemporary annalist, whose manuscript we have deciphered)—why is my story to turn upon thy fallen fortunes? and why not rather to the period when, in the very dismounting from your palfrey, you attracted as many eyes as if an angel had descended,—as many blessings as if the benignant being had come fraught with good tidings! No creature wert thou of an idle romancer's imagination—no being fantastically bedizened with inconsistent perfections;—thy merits made me love thee well—and for thy faults—so well did they show amid thy good qualities, that I think they made me love thee better."

With the house of Lee had disappeared from the chantry of King John others of gentle blood and honored lineage—Freemantles, Winklecombs, Drycotts, etc.; for the air that blew over the towers of Oxford was unfavorable to the growth of Puritanism, which was more general in the neighboring counties. There were among the congregation, however, one or two that, by their habits and demeanor, seemed country gentlemen of consideration, and there were also present some of the notables of the town of Woodstock, cutlers or glovers chiefly, whose skill in steel or leather had raised them to a comfortable livelihood. These dignitaries wore long black cloaks, plaited close at the neck, and, like peaceful citizens, carried their Bibles and memorandum-books at their girdles, instead of knife or sword. This respectable, but least numerous part of the audience, were such decent persons as had adopted the Presbyterian form of faith, renouncing the liturgy and hierarchy of the Church of England, and living under the tuition of the Rev. Nehemiah Holdenough, much famed for the length and strength of his powers of predication. With these grave seniors sat their goodly dames in ruff and gorget, like the portraits which in catalogues of paintings are designed "wife of a burgomaster;" and their pretty daughters, whose study, like that of Chaucer's physician, was not always in the Bible, but who were, on the contrary, when a glance could escape the vigilance of their honored mothers, inattentive themselves, and the cause of inattention in others.

But, besides these dignified persons, there were in the church a numerous collection of the lower orders, some brought thither by curiosity, but many of them unwashed artificers, bewildered in the theological discussions of the time, and of as many various sects as there are colors in the rainbow. The presumption of these learned Thebans being in exact proportion to their ignorance, the last was total, and the first boundless. Their behavior in the church was anything but reverential or edifying. Most of them affected a cynical contempt for all that was only held sacred by human sanction. The church was to these men but a steeple house; the clergyman, an ordinary person; her ordinances, dry bran and sapless pottage, unfitted for the spiritualized palates of the saints; and the prayer, an address to Heaven, to which each acceded or not, as in his too critical judgment he conceived fit.

The elder amongst them sat or lay on the benches, with their high steeple-crowned hats pulled over their severe and knitted brows, waiting for the Presbyterian parson as mastiffs sit in dumb expectation of the bull that is to be brought to the stake. The younger mixed, some of them, a bolder license of manners with their heresies; they gazed round on the women, yawned, coughed, and whispered, ate apples, and cracked nuts, as if in the gallery of a theater ere the piece commences.

Besides all these, the congregation contained a few soldiers, some in corselets and steel caps, some in buff, and others in red coats. These men of war had their bandoliers, with ammunition, slung round them, and rested on their pikes and muskets. They, too, had their peculiar doctrines on the most difficult points of religion, and united the extravagances of enthusiasm with the most determined courage and resolution in the field. The burghers of Woodstock looked on these military saints with no small degree of awe; for though not often sullied with deeds of plunder or cruelty, they had the power of both absolutely in their hands, and the peaceful citizens had no alternative, save submission to whatever the ill-regulated and enthusiastic imaginations of their martial guides might suggest.

After some time spent in waiting for him, Mr. Holdenough began to walk up the aisles of the chapel, not with the slow and dignified carriage with which the old rector was of yore wont to maintain the dignity of the surplice, but with a hasty step, like one who arrives too late at an appointment, and bustles forward to make the best use of his time. He was a tall thin man, with an adust complexion, and the vivacity of his eye indicated some irascibility of temperament. His dress was brown, not black, and over his other vestments he wore, in honor of Calvin, a Geneva cloak of a blue color, which fell backwards from his shoulders as he posted on to the pulpit. His grizzled hair was cut as short as shears could perform the feat, and covered with a black silk skull-cap, which stuck so close to his head, that the two ears expanded from under it as if they had been intended as handles by which to lift the whole person. Moreover, the worthy divine wore spectacles, and a long grizzled peaked beard, and he carried in his hand a small pocket-bible with silver clasps. Upon arriving at the pulpit, he paused a moment to take breath, then began to ascend the steps by two at a time.

But his course was arrested by a strong hand, which seized his cloak. It was that of one who had detached himself from the group of soldiery. He was a stout man of middle stature, with a quick eye, and a countenance, which, though plain, had yet an expression that fixed the attention. His dress, though not strictly military, partook of that character. He wore large hose made of calves-leather, and a tuck, as it was then called, or rapier, of tremendous length, balanced on the other side by a dagger. The belt was morocco, garnished with pistols.

The minister, thus intercepted in his duty, faced round upon the party who had seized him, and demanded, in no gentle tone, the meaning of the interruption.

"Friend," quoth the intruder, "is it thy purpose to hold forth to these good people?"

"Ay, marry is it," said the clergyman, "and such is my bounden duty. Woe to me if I preach not the gospel—Prithee, friend, let me not in my labor——"

"Nay," said the man of warlike mien, "I am myself minded to hold forth; therefore, do thou desist, or if thou wilt do by mine advice, remain and fructify with those poor goslings, to whom I am presently about to shake forth the crumbs of comfortable doctrine."

"Give place, thou man of Satan," said the priest, waxing wroth; "respect mine order—my cloth."

"I see no more to respect in the cut of thy cloak, or in the cloth of which it is fashioned," said the other, "than thou didst in the Bishop's rochets—they were black and white, thou art blue and brown. Sleeping dogs every one of you, lying down, loving to slumber; shepherds that starve the flock, but will not watch it, each looking to his own gain—hum!"

Scenes of this indecent kind were so common at the time that no one thought of interfering. The congregation looked on in silence, the better class scandalized, and the lower orders, some laughing, and others backing the soldier or minister as their fancy dictated. Meantime, the struggle waxed fiercer; Mr. Holdenough clamored for assistance.

"Master Mayor of Woodstock," he exclaimed, "wilt thou be among those wicked magistrates who bear the sword in vain?—Citizens, will you not help your pastor?—Worthy Aldermen, will you see me strangled on the pulpit stairs by this man of buff and Belial?—But lo, I will overcome him, and cast his cords from me."

As Holdenough spoke, he struggled to ascend the pulpit stairs, holding hard on the banisters. His tormentor held fast by the skirts of the cloak, which went nigh to the choking of the wearer, until, as he spoke the words last mentioned, in a half-strangled voice, Mr. Holdenough dexterously slipped the string which tied it round his neck, so that the garment suddenly gave way, the soldier fell backwards down the steps, and the liberated divine skipped into the pulpit, and began to give forth a psalm of triumph over his prostrate adversary. But a great hubbub in the church marred his exultation, and although he and his faithful clerk continued to sing the hymn of victory, their notes were only heard by fits, like the whistle of a curlew during a gale of wind.

The cause of the tumult was as follows. The Mayor was a zealous Presbyterian, and witnessed the intrusion of the soldier with great indignation from the very beginning, though he hesitated to interfere with an armed man while on his legs and capable of resistance. But no sooner did he behold the champion of Independency sprawling on his back, with the divine's Geneva cloak fluttering in his hands, than the magistrate rushed forward, exclaiming that such insolence was not to be endured, and ordered his constables to seize the prostrate champion, proclaiming, in the magnanimity of wrath, "I will commit every redcoat of them all—I will commit him were he Noll Cromwell himself!"

The worthy Mayor's indignation had overmastered his reason when he made this mistimed vaunt; for three soldiers, who had hitherto stood motionless like statues, made each a stride in advance, which placed them betwixt the municipal officers and the soldier, who was in the act of rising; then making at once the movement of resting arms according to the manual as then practiced, their musket butts rang on the church pavement, within an inch of the gouty toes of Master Mayor. The energetic magistrate, whose efforts in favor of order were thus checked, cast one glance on his supporters, but that was enough to show him that force was not on his side. All had shrunk back on hearing that ominous clatter of stone and iron. He was obliged to descend to expostulation.

"What do you mean, my masters?" said he; "is it like a decent and God-fearing soldiery, who have wrought such things for the land as have never before been heard of, to brawl and riot in the church, or to aid, abet, and comfort a profane fellow, who hath, upon a solemn thanksgiving, excluded the minister from his own pulpit?"

"We have naught to do with thy church, as thou call'st it," said he who, by a small feather in front of his morion, appeared to be the corporal of the party; "we see not why men of gifts should not be heard within these citadels of superstition, as well as the voice of the men of crape of old, and the men of cloak now. Wherefore, we will pluck yon Jack Presbyter out of his wooden sentinel box, and our own watchman shall relieve the guard, and mount thereon, and cry aloud and spare not."

"Nay, gentlemen," said the Mayor, "if such be your purpose, we have not the means to withstand you, being, as you see, peaceful and quiet men. But let me first speak with this worthy minister, Nehemiah Holdenough, to persuade him to yield up his place for the time without further scandal."

The peace-making Mayor then interrupted the quavering of Holdenough and the clerk, and prayed both to retire, else there would, he said, be certainly strife.

"Strife!" replied the Presbyterian divine with scorn; "no fear of strife among men that dare not testify against this open profanation of the church, and daring display of heresy. Would your neighbors of Banbury have brooked such an insult?"

"Come, come, Master Holdenough," said the Mayor, "put us not to mutiny and cry Clubs. I tell you once more, we are not men of war or blood."

"Not more than may be drawn by the point of a needle," said the preacher scornfully.—"Ye tailors of Woodstock!—for what is a glover but a tailor working on kid skin?—I forsake you, in scorn of your faint hearts and feeble hands, and will seek me elsewhere a flock which will not fly from the shepherd at the braying of the first wild ass which cometh from out the great desert."

So saying, the aggrieved divine departed from his pulpit, and shaking the dust from his shoes, left the church as hastily as he had entered it, though with a different reason for his speed. The citizens saw his retreat with sorrow, and not without a compunctious feeling, as if conscious that they were not playing the most courageous part in the world. The Mayor himself and several others left the church, to follow and appease him.

The independent orator, late prostrate, was now triumphant, and inducting himself into the pulpit without further ceremony, he pulled a Bible from his pocket, and selected his text from the forty-fifth psalm,—"Gird thy sword upon thy thigh, O most mighty, with thy glory and thy majesty: and in thy majesty ride prosperously."—Upon this theme, he commenced one of those wild declamations common at the period, in which men were accustomed to wrest and pervert the language of Scripture, by adapting it to modern events. The language which, in its literal sense, was applied to King David, and typically referred to the coming of the Messiah, was, in the opinion of the military orator, most properly to be interpreted of Oliver Cromwell, the victorious general of the infant Commonwealth, which was never destined to come of age. "Gird on thy sword!" exclaimed the preacher, emphatically; "and was not that a pretty bit of steel as ever dangled from a corselet or rung against a steel saddle? Ay, ye prick up your ears now, ye cutlers of Woodstock, as if ye should know something of a good fox broadsword—Did you forge it, I trow?—was the steel quenched with water from Rosamond's well, or the blade blest by the old cuckoldy priest of Godstow? You would have us think, I warrant me, that you wrought it and welded it, grinded and polished it, and all the while it never came on a Woodstock stithy! You were all too busy making whittles for the lazy crape-men of Oxford, bouncing priests, whose eyes were so closed up with fat, that they could not see Destruction till she had them by the throat. But I can tell you where the sword was forged, and tempered, and welded, and grinded, and polished. When you were, as I said before, making whittles for false

priests, and daggers for dissolute G—d d—n-me cavaliers, to cut the people of England's throat with—it was forged at Long Marston Moor, where blows went faster than ever rung hammer on anvil—and it was tempered at Naseby, in the best blood of the cavaliers—and it was welded in Ireland against the walls of Drogheda—and it was grinded on Scottish lives at Dunbar—and now of late it was polished in Worcester, till it shines as bright as the sun in the middle heaven, and there is no light in England that shall come nigh unto it."

Here the military part of the congregation raised a hum of approbation, which, being a sound like the "Hear, hear!" of the British House of Commons, was calculated to heighten the enthusiasm of the orator, by intimating the sympathy of the audience. "And then," resumed the preacher, rising in energy as he found that his audience partook in these feelings, "what sayeth the text?—Ride on prosperously—do not stop—do not call a halt—do not quit the saddle—pursue the scattered fliers—sound the trumpet—not a levant or a flourish, but a point of war—sound, boot and saddle—to horse and away—a charge!—follow after the young Man!—what part have we in him?—Slay, take, destroy, divide the spoil! Blessed art thou, Oliver, on account of thine honor—thy cause is clear, thy call is undoubted—never has defeat come near thy leading staff, nor disaster attended thy banner. Ride on, flower of England's soldiers! ride on, chosen leader of God's champions! gird up the loins of thy resolution, and be steadfast to the mark of thy high calling!"

Another deep and stern hum, echoed by the ancient embowed arches of the old chantry, gave him an opportunity of an instant's repose; when the people of Woodstock heard him, and not without anxiety, turn the stream of his oratory into another channel.

"But wherefore, ye people of Woodstock, do I say these things to you who claim no portion in our David, no interest in England's son of Jesse?—You, who were fighting as well as your might could (and it was not very formidable) for the late Man, under that old bloodthirsty papist Sir Jacob Aston,—are you not now plotting, or ready to plot, for the restoring, as ye call it, of the young Man, the unclean son of the slaughtered tyrant—the fugitive after whom the true hearts of England are now following, that they may take and slay him?—Come, men of Woodstock, I will ask, and do you answer me. Hunger ye still after the fleshpots of the monks of Godstow? and ye will say, 'Nay';—but wherefore, except that the pots are cracked and broken, and the fire is extinguished wherewith thy oven used to boil? And again, I ask, drink ye still of the well of the fair Rosamond?—ye will say, 'Nay';—but wherefore?"—

Here the orator, ere he could answer the question in his own way, was surprised by the following reply, very pithily pronounced by one of the congregation:—"Because you, and the like of you, have left us no brandy to mix with it."

All eyes turned to the audacious speaker, who stood beside one of the thick sturdy Saxon pillars, which he himself somewhat resembled, being short of stature, but very strongly made, a squat broad Little John sort of figure, leaning on a quarter-staff, and wearing a jerkin, which, though now sorely stained and discolored, had once been of the Lincoln green, and showed remnants of having been laced. There was an air of careless, good-humored audacity about the fellow; and, though under military restraint, there were some of the citizens who could not help crying out,—"Well said, Joceline Joliffe!"

"Jolly Joceline, call ye him?" proceeded the preacher, without showing either confusion or displeasure at the interruption,—"I will make him Joceline of the jail, if he interrupts me again. One of your parkkeepers, I warrant, that can never forget they have borne C. R. upon their badges and bugle-horns, even as a dog bears his owner's name on his collar—a pretty emblem for Christian men! But the brute beast hath the better of him,—the brute weareth his own coat, and the caitliff thrall wears his master's. I have seen such a wag make a rope's end wag ere now. Where was I?—Oh, rebuking you for your backslidings, men of Woodstock.—Yes, then, ye will say ye have renounced Popery, and ye have renounced Prelacy, and then ye wipe your mouth like Pharisees, as ye are; and who but you for purity of religion! But, I tell you, ye are but like Jehu the son of Nimshi, who broke down the house of Baal, yet departed not from the sin of Jeroboam. Even so ye eat not fish on Friday with the blinded Papists, nor minced-pies on the 25th day of December, like the slothful Prelatists; but ye will gorge on sack-posset each night in the year with your blind Presbyterian guide, and ye will speak evil of dignities, and revile the Common-

wealth; and ye will glorify yourselves in your park of Woodstock, and say, 'Was it not walled in first of any other in England, and that by Henry son of William called the Conqueror?' And ye have a princely lodge therein, and call the same a Royal Lodge; and ye have an oak which ye call the King's Oak; and ye steal and eat the venison of the park, and yet say: 'This is the king's venison, we will wash it down with a cup to the king's health—better we eat it than those round-headed Commonwealth knaves.' But listen unto me and take warning. For these things come we to controversy with you. And our name shall be a cannon-shot, before which your Lodge, in the pleasantness whereof ye take pastime, shall be blown into ruins; and we will be as a wedge to split asunder the King's Oak into billets to heat a brown baker's oven; and we will dispark your park, and slay your deer, and eat them ourselves, neither shall you have any portion thereof, whether in neck or haunch. Ye shall not haft a tenpenny knife with the horns thereof, neither shall ye cut a pair of breeches out of the hide, for all ye be cutlers and glovers; and ye shall have no comfort or support neither from the sequestered traitor Henry Lee, who called himself Ranger of Woodstock, nor from any on his behalf; for they are coming hither who shall be called Mahar-shalal-hash-baz, because he maketh haste to the spoil."

Here ended this wild effusion, the latter part of which fell heavy on the souls of the poor citizens of Woodstock, as tending to confirm a report of an unpleasing nature which had been lately circulated. The communication with London was indeed slow, and the news which it transmitted was uncertain, no less uncertain were the times themselves, and the rumors which were circulated, exaggerated by the hopes and fears of so many various factions. But the general stream of report, so far as Woodstock was concerned, had of late run uniformly in one direction. Day after day they had been informed, that the fatal fiat of Parliament had gone out, for selling the park of Woodstock, destroying its lodge, disparking its forest, and erasing, as far as they could be erased, all traces of its ancient fame. Many of the citizens were likely to be sufferers on this occasion, as several of them enjoyed, either by sufferance or right, various convenient privileges of pasturage, cutting firewood, and the like, in the royal chase; and all the inhabitants of the little borough were hurt to think, that the scenery of the place was to be destroyed, its edifices ruined, and its honors rent away. This is a patriotic sensation often found in such places, which ancient distinctions and long-cherished recollections of former days render so different from towns of recent date. The natives of Woodstock felt it in the fullest force. They had trembled at the anticipated calamity; but now, when it was announced by the appearance of those dark,

stern, and at the same time omnipotent soldiers—now that they heard it proclaimed by the mouth of one of their military preachers—they considered their fate as inevitable. The causes of disagreement among themselves were for the time forgotten, as the congregation, dismissed without psalmody or benediction, went slowly and mournfully homeward, each to his own place of abode.

1826

ROBERT SOUTHEY (1774-1843)

His prose is perfect. In his poetry he has passages equal to anything. The "Life of Nelson" is beautiful.
BYRON

Southey was a friend of Wordsworth and of Coleridge, a brother-in-law of the latter, and in his youth a member of the socialistic Pantisocracy. In politics and religion, he began as a radical, as he showed in his epical poems *Joan of Arc* and *Wat Tyler*. After he had become middle-aged and conservative, his enemies taunted him with those early indiscretions, and jeered at his apparent inconsistencies. But he justified himself by pointing out that the principles of the French Revolution which he admired when it began, had been abandoned when France, under Napoleon, became an aggressive autocracy. His contempt for war is well shown in *The Battle of Blenheim;* and liberal and humane sentiments recur throughout his writings.

His first ambition was to become an epic poet. He wrote much verse, and during the last thirty years of his life was the Poet Laureate. But his epics are rarely read today, and his place in English literature is more and more seen to depend upon the excellence of his prose. Even those who, like Byron, ridiculed such poems as his *Vision of Judgment*—an elegy on the death of George III, written in his official capacity—recognized the merits of his prose works. Of these the most notable were the highly popular *Life of Nelson*, one of the best short biographies; the *Life of John Wesley;* the *Life of Bunyan;* and the *History of the Peninsular War*. In them he admirably manifested the sincerity and gravity of his character, his scholarship, his fairness of mind, and his lucidity. The interest in childhood which he shares with Lamb, Wordsworth, De Quincey, and other Romantics, is pleasantly shown in the nursery-favorite, *The Story of the Three Bears*.

THE BATTLE OF BLENHEIM

It was a summer evening,
  Old Kaspar's work was done,
And he before his cottage door
  Was sitting in the sun,
And by him sported on the green   5
His little grandchild Wilhelmine.

She saw her brother Peterkin
  Roll something large and round,
Which he beside the rivulet
  In playing there had found;   10
He came to ask what he had found,
That was so large, and smooth, and round.

Old Kaspar took it from the boy,
  Who stood expectant by;
And then the old man shook his head,   15
  And, with a natural sigh,
" 'Tis some poor fellow's skull," said he,
"Who fell in the great victory.

"I find them in the garden,
  For there's many here about;   20

And often when I go to plough,
  The ploughshare turns them out!
For many a thousand men," said he,
  "Were slain in that great victory."

"Now tell us what 'twas all about,"   25
  Young Peterkin, he cries;
And little Wilhelmine looks up
  With wonder-waiting eyes;
"Now tell us all about the war,
And what they fought each other for."   30

"It was the English," Kaspar cried,
  "Who put the French to rout;
But what they fought each other for,
  I could not well make out;
But everybody said," quoth he,   35
  "That 'twas a famous victory.

"My father lived at Blenheim then,
  Yon little stream hard by;
They burnt his dwelling to the ground,
  And he was forced to fly;   40
So with his wife and child he fled,
Nor had he where to rest his head.

477

"With fire and sword the country round
  Was wasted far and wide,
And many a childing mother then,   45
  And new-born baby died;
But things like that, you know, must be
At every famous victory.

"They say it was a shocking sight
  After the field was won;   50
For many thousand bodies here
  Lay rotting in the sun;
But things like that, you know, must be
After a famous victory.

"Great praise the Duke of Marlbro' won, 55
  And our good Prince Eugene."
"Why 'twas a very wicked thing!"
  Said little Wilhelmine.
"Nay, nay, my little girl," quoth he,
"It was a famous victory.   60

"And everybody praised the Duke
  Who this great fight did win."
"But what good came of it at last?"
  Quoth little Peterkin.
"Why that I cannot tell," said he,   65
"But 'twas a famous victory."

1798   Aug. 9, 1798

THE HOLLY TREE

O reader! hast thou ever stood to see
  The Holly Tree?
The eye that contemplates it well perceives
  Its glossy leaves
Ordered by an intelligence so wise,   5
As might confound the Atheist's sophistries.

Below, a circling fence, its leaves are seen
  Wrinkled and keen;
No grazing cattle through their prickly
  round
  Can reach to wound;   10
But as they grow where nothing is to fear,
Smooth and unarmed the pointless leaves
  appear.

I love to view these things with curious
  eyes,
  And moralize:
And in the wisdom of the Holly Tree   15
  Can emblems see
Wherewith perchance to make a pleasant
  rhyme,
One which may profit in the after time.

Thus, though abroad perchance I might
  appear
  Harsh and austere,   20
To those who on my leisure would intrude
  Reserved and rude,
Gentle at home amid my friends I'd be
Like the high leaves upon the Holly Tree.

And should my youth, as youth is apt I
  know,   25
  Some harshness show,
All vain asperities I day by day
  Would wear away,
Till the smooth temper of my age should
  be
Like the high leaves upon the Holly
  Tree.   30

And as when all the summer trees are seen
  So bright and green,
The Holly leaves a sober hue display
  Less bright than they,
But when the bare and wintry woods we
  see,   35
What then so cheerful as the Holly Tree?

So serious should my youth appear among
  The thoughtless throng,
So would I seem amid the young and gay
  More grave than they,   40
That in my age as cheerful I might be
As the green winter of the Holly Tree.

1798   Dec. 17, 1798

WRITTEN IMMEDIATELY AFTER READING THE SPEECH OF ROBERT EMMET

ON HIS TRIAL AND CONVICTION FOR.
HIGH TREASON, SEPT., 1803

"Let no man write my epitaph; let my
  grave
Be uninscribed, and let my memory rest
Till other times are come, and other men,
Who then may do me justice."
                          Emmet, no!
No withering curse hath dried my spirit
  up,   5
That I should now be silent,—that my soul
Should from the stirring inspiration shrink,
Now when it shakes her, and withhold her
  voice,

Of that divinest impulse never more
Worthy, if impious I withheld it now,   10
Hardening my heart. Here, here in this
  free Isle,
To which in thy young virtue's erring zeal
Thou wert so perilous an enemy,
Here in free England shall an English
  hand
Build thy imperishable monument;   15
Oh,—to thine own misfortune and to ours,
By thine own deadly error so beguiled,
Here in free England shall an English
  voice
Raise up thy mourning-song. For thou hast
  paid
The bitter penalty of that misdeed;   20
Justice hath done her unrelenting part,
If she in truth be Justice who drives on,
Bloody and blind, the chariot wheels of
  death.

So young, so glowing for the general good,
Oh, what a lovely manhood had been
  thine,   25
When all the violent workings of thy youth
Had passed away, hadst thou been wisely
  spared,
Left to the slow and certain influences
Of silent feeling and maturing thought!
How had that heart,—that noble heart of
  thine,   30
Which even now had snapped one spell,
  which beat
With such brave indignation at the shame
And guilt of France, and of her miscreant
  Lord,—
How had it clung to England! With what
  love,
What pure and perfect love, returned to
  her,   35
Now worthy of thy love, the champion now
For freedom,—yea, the only champion now,
And soon to be the Avenger. But the blow
Hath fallen, the indiscriminating blow,
That for its portion to the Grave con-
  signed   40
Youth, Genius, generous Virtue. Oh, grief,
  grief!
Oh, sorrow and reproach! Have ye to
  learn,
Deaf to the past, and to the future blind,
Ye who thus irremissibly exact
The forfeit life, how lightly life is staked,   45
When in distempered times the feverish
  mind
To strong delusion yields? Have ye to
  learn
With what a deep and spirit-stirring voice
Pity doth call Revenge? Have ye no hearts

To feel and understand how Mercy
  tames   50
The rebel nature, maddened by old
  wrongs,
And binds it in the gentle bands of love,
When steel and adamant were weak to
  hold
That Samson-strength subdued!
                    Let no man write
Thy epitaph! Emmet, nay; thou shalt not
  go   55
Without thy funeral strain! Oh, young, and
  good,
And wise, though erring here, thou shalt
  not go
Unhonored nor unsung. And better thus
Beneath that indiscriminating stroke,
Better to fall, than to have lived to
  mourn,   60
As sure thou wouldst, in misery and re-
  morse,
Thine own disastrous triumph; to have
  seen,
If the Almighty at that awful hour
Had turned away his face, wild Ignorance
Let loose, and frantic Vengeance, and dark
  Zeal,   65
And all bad passions tyrannous, and the
  fires
Of Persecution once again ablaze.
How had it sunk into thy soul to see,
Last curse of all, the ruffian slaves of
  France
In thy dear native country lording it!   70
How happier thus, in that heroic mood
That takes away the sting of death, to die,
By all the good and all the wise forgiven,
Yea, in all ages by the wise and good
To be remembered, mourned, and honored
  still.   75

MY DAYS AMONG THE DEAD
ARE PASSED

My days among the dead are passed;
  Around me I behold,
Where'er these casual eyes are cast,
  The mighty minds of old;
My never-failing friends are they,   5
With whom I converse day by day.

With them I take delight in weal,
  And seek relief in woe;
And while I understand and feel
  How much to them I owe,   10
My cheeks have often been bedewed
With tears of thoughtful gratitude.

My thoughts are with the dead, with them
  I live in long-past years,
Their virtues love, their faults condemn, 15
  Partake their hopes and fears,
And from their lessons seek and find
Instruction with an humble mind.

My hopes are with the dead, anon
  My place with them will be, 20
And I with them shall travel on
  Through all futurity;
Yet leaving here a name, I trust,
That will not perish in the dust.

1818   1823

THE DEATH OF JOHN WESLEY

Upon his eighty-sixth birthday, he says, "I now find I grow old. My sight is de- 5 cayed, so that I cannot read a small print, unless in a strong light. My strength is decayed; so that I walk much slower than I did some years since. My memory of names, whether of persons or places, is de- 10 cayed, till I stop a little to recollect them. What I should be afraid of is, if I took thought for the morrow, that my body should weigh down my mind, and create either stubbornness, by the decrease of my 15 understanding, or peevishness, by the increase of bodily infirmities. But thou shalt answer for me, O Lord, my God!" His strength now diminished so much that he found it difficult to preach more than twice 20 a day; and for many weeks he abstained from his five o'clock morning sermons, because a slow and settled fever parched his mouth. Finding himself a little better, he resumed the practice, and hoped to hold 25 on a little longer; but, at the beginning of the year 1790, he writes, "I am now an old man, decayed from head to foot. My eyes are dim; my right hand shakes much; my mouth is hot and dry every morning; I 30 have a lingering fever almost every day; my motion is weak and slow. However, blessed be God! I do not slack my labors; I can preach and write still." In the middle of the same year he closed his cash account- 35 book with the following words, written with a tremulous hand, so as to be scarcely legible: "For upwards of eighty-six years I have kept my accounts exactly: I will not attempt it any longer, being satisfied with 40 the continued conviction, that I save all I can, and give all I can; that is, all I have." His strength was now quite gone, and no glasses would help his sight. "But I feel no pain," he says, "from head to foot; only, 45 it seems, nature is exhausted, and, humanly speaking, will sink more and more, till

The weary springs of life stand still at last."

On the 1st of February, 1791, he wrote his last letter to America. It shows how anxious he was that his followers should consider themselves as one united body. "See," said he, "that you never give place to one thought of separating from your brethren in Europe. Lose no opportunity of declaring to all men, that the Methodists are one people in all the world, and that it is their full determination so to continue." He expressed also a sense that his hour was almost come. "Those that desire to write," said he, "or say anything to me, have no time to lose; for time has shaken me by the hand, and death is not far behind":—words which his father had used in one of the last letters that he addressed to his sons at Oxford. On the 17th of that month he took cold after preaching at Lambeth. For some days he struggled against an increasing fever, and continued to preach till the Wednesday following when he delivered his last sermon. From that time he became daily weaker and more lethargic, and on the 2nd of March he died in peace, being in the eighty-eighth year of his age, and the sixty-fifth of his ministry.

During his illness he said, "Let me be buried in nothing but what is woolen; and let my corpse be carried in my coffin into the chapel." Some years before, he had prepared a vault for himself, and for those itinerant preachers who might die in London. In his will he directed that six poor men should have twenty shillings each for carrying his body to the grave; "for I particularly desire," said he, "that there may be no hearse, no coach, no escutcheon, no pomp except the tears of them that loved me, and are following me to Abraham's bosom. I solemnly adjure my executors, in the name of God, punctually to observe this." At the desire of many of his friends, his body was carried into the chapel the day preceding the interment, and there lay in a kind of state becoming the person, dressed in his clerical habit, with gown, cassock, and band; the old clerical cap on his head; a Bible in one hand, and a white handkerchief in the other. The face was placid, and the expression which death had fixed upon his venerable features was that of a serene and heavenly smile. The 5 crowds who flocked to see him were so great, that it was thought prudent, for fear of accidents, to accelerate the funeral, and perform it between five and six in the morning. The intelligence, however, could 10 not be kept entirely secret, and several hundred persons attended at that unusual hour. Mr. Richardson, who performed the service, had been one of his preachers almost thirty years. When he came to that 15 part of the service, "Forasmuch as it hath pleased Almighty God to take unto himself the soul of our dear *brother,*" his voice changed, and he substituted the word *father;* and the feeling with which he did 20 this was such, that the congregation, who were shedding silent tears, burst at once into loud weeping.

1820

FROM THE HISTORY OF THE PENINSULAR WAR

THE SIEGE OF ZARAGOZA

This most obstinate and murderous contest was continued for eleven successive days and nights, more indeed by night than by day; for it was almost certain death 35 to appear by daylight within reach of those houses which were occupied by the other party. But under cover of darkness, the combatants frequently dashed across the street to attack each other's batteries; and 40 the battles which began there, were often carried on into the houses beyond, where they fought from room to room, and floor to floor. The hostile batteries were so near each other that a Spaniard in one place 45 made way under cover of the dead bodies, which completely filled the space between them, and fastened a rope to one of the French cannons; in the struggle which ensued, the rope broke, and the Zaragozans 50 lost their prize at the very moment when they thought themselves sure of it.

A new horror was added to the dreadful circumstances of war in this ever memorable siege. In general engagements the 55 dead are left upon the field of battle, and the survivors remove to clear ground and an untainted atmosphere; but here—in Spain, and in the month of August, there where the dead lay the struggle was still 60

carried on, and pestilence was dreaded from the enormous accumulation of putrefying bodies. Nothing in the whole course of the siege so embarrassed Palafox as this evil. The only remedy was to tie ropes to the French prisoners, and push them forward amid the dead and dying, to remove the bodies, and bring them away for interment. Even for this necessary office there was no truce, and it would have been certain death to the Aragonese who should have attempted to perform it; but the prisoners were in general secured by the pity of their own soldiers, and in this manner the evil was, in some degree, diminished.

A council of war was held by the Spaniards on the 8th, not for the purpose which is too usual in such councils, but that their heroic resolution might be communicated with authority to the people. It was, that in those quarters of the city where the Aragonese still maintained their ground, they should continue to defend themselves with the same firmness: should the enemy at last prevail, they were then to retire over the Ebro into the suburbs, break down the bridge, and defend the suburbs till they perished. When this resolution was made public, it was received with the loudest acclamations. But in every conflict the citizens now gained ground upon the soldiers, winning it inch by inch, till the space occupied by the enemy, which on the day of their entrance was nearly half the city, was gradually reduced to about an eighth part. Meantime, intelligence of the events in other parts of Spain was received by the French,—all tending to dishearten them; the surrender of Dupont, the failure of Moncey before Valencia, and the news that the Junta of that province had dispatched six thousand men to join the levies in Aragon, which were destined to relieve Zaragoza. During the night of the 13th, their fire was particularly fierce and destructive; after their batteries had ceased, flames burst out in many parts of the buildings which they had won; their last act was to blow up the church of St. Engracia; the powder was placed in the subterranean church,—and this remarkable place,—this monument of fraud and credulity,—this splendid theatre wherein so many feelings of deep devotion had been excited,—which so many thousands had visited in faith, and from which unquestionably many had departed with their imaginations elevated, their principles ennobled, and their hearts strengthened, was laid in ruins. In the morning the French columns, to the great surprise of the Spaniards, were seen at a distance, retreating over the plain, on the road to Pamplona.

The history of a battle, however skillfully narrated, is necessarily uninteresting to all except military men; but in the details of a siege, when time has destroyed those considerations which prejudice or pervert our natural sense of right and wrong, every reader sympathizes with the besieged, and nothing, even in fictitious narratives, excites so deep and animating an interest. There is not, either in the annals of ancient or of modern times, a single event recorded more worthy to be held in admiration, now and for evermore, than the siege of Zaragoza. Will it be said that this devoted people obtained for themselves, by all this heroism and all these sacrifices, nothing more than a short respite from their fate? Woe be to the slavish heart that conceives the thought, and shame to the base tongue that gives it utterance! They purchased for themselves an everlasting remembrance upon earth,— a place in the memory and love of all good men in all ages that are yet to come. They performed their duty; they redeemed their souls from the yoke; they left an example to their country, never to be forgotten, never to be out of mind, and sure to contribute to and hasten its deliverance.

1823

FROM THE LIFE OF HORATIO, LORD NELSON

THE BATTLE OF TRAFALGAR

Unremitting exertions were made to equip the ships which Nelson had chosen, and especially to refit the *Victory*, which was once more to bear his flag. Before he left London he called at his upholsterer's, where the coffin which Captain Hallowell had given him was deposited, and desired that its history might be engraven upon the lid, saying it was highly probable he might want it on his return. He seemed, indeed, to have been impressed with an expectation that he should fall in the battle. In a letter to his brother, written immediately after his return, he had said: "We must not talk of Sir Robert Calder's battle. I might not have done so much with my small force. If I had fallen in with them, you might probably have been a lord before I wished, for I know they meant to make a dead set at the *Victory*." Nelson had once regarded the prospect of death with gloomy satisfaction; it was when he anticipated the upbraidings of his wife and the displeasure of his venerable father. The state of his feelings now was expressed in his private journal in these words: "Friday night (Sept. 13th), at half-past ten, I drove from dear, dear Merton, where I left all which I hold dear in this world, to go to serve my king and country. May the great God whom I adore enable me to fulfill the expectations of my country! And, if it is His good pleasure that I should return, my thanks will never cease being offered up to the throne of His mercy. If it is His good providence to cut short my days upon earth, I bow with the greatest submission; relying that He will protect those so dear to me, whom I may leave behind! His will be done. Amen! Amen! Amen!"

Early on the following morning he reached Portsmouth; and, having despatched his business on shore, endeavored to elude the populace by taking a byway to the beach; but a crowd collected in his train, pressing forward to obtain a sight of his face;—many were in tears, and many knelt down before him, and blessed him as he passed. England has had many heroes, but never one who so entirely possessed the love of his fellow-countrymen as Nelson. All men knew that his heart was as humane as it was fearless; that there was not in his nature the slightest alloy of selfishness or cupidity; but that, with perfect and entire devotion, he served his country with all his heart, and with all his soul, and with all his strength; and, therefore, they loved him as truly and as fervently as he loved England. They pressed upon the parapet to gaze after him when his barge pushed off, and he was returning their cheers by waving his hat. The sentinels, who endeavored to prevent them from trespassing upon this ground, were wedged among the crowd; and an officer, who, not very prudently upon such an occasion, ordered them to drive the people down with their bayonets, was compelled speedily to retreat; for the people would not be debarred from gazing, till the last moment, upon the hero—the darling hero of England. . . .

At daybreak the combined fleets were distinctly seen from the *Victory's* deck, formed in a close line of battle ahead, on the starboard tack, about twelve miles to leeward, and standing to the south. Our fleet consisted of twenty-seven sail of the line and four frigates; theirs of thirty-three and seven large frigates. Their superiority was greater in size and weight of metal than in numbers. They had four thousand troops on board; and the best riflemen who could be procured, many of them Tyrolese, were dispersed through the ships. Little did the Tyrolese, and little did the Spaniards at that day, imagine what horrors the wicked tyrant whom they served was preparing for their country.

Soon after daylight Nelson came upon deck. The 21st of October was a festival in his family, because on that day his uncle, Captain Suckling, in the *Dreadnought,* with two other line-of-battle ships, had beaten off a French squadron of four sail of the line and three frigates. Nelson, with that sort of superstition from which few persons are entirely exempt, had more than once expressed his persuasion that this was to be the day of his battle also; and he was well pleased at seeing his prediction about to be verified. The wind was now from the west,—light breezes, with a long heavy swell. Signal was made to bear down upon the enemy in two lines; and the fleet set all sail. Collingwood, in the *Royal Sovereign,* led the lee-line of thirteen ships; the *Victory* led the weather-line of fourteen. Having seen that all was as it should be, Nelson retired to his cabin, and wrote the following prayer:—

"May the Great God, whom I worship, grant to my country, and for the benefit of Europe in general, a great and glorious victory; and may no misconduct in any one tarnish it! and may humanity after victory be the predominant feature in the British fleet! For myself individually, I commit my life to Him who made me, and may His blessing alight on my endeavors for serving my country faithfully! To Him I resign myself, and the just cause which is intrusted to me to defend. Amen, Amen, Amen." . . .

Having thus discharged his devotional duties, he annexed, in the same diary, the following remarkable writing:—

October 21st, 1805,—then in sight of the combined fleets of France and Spain, distant about ten miles.

Whereas the eminent services of Emma Hamilton, widow of the Right Honorable Sir William Hamilton, have been of the very greatest service to my king and country, to my knowledge, without ever receiving any reward from either our king or country:

First, That she obtained the King of Spain's letter, in 1796, to his brother, the King of Naples, acquainting him of his intention to declare war against England: from which letter the ministry sent out orders to the then Sir John Jervis to strike a stroke, if opportunity offered, against either the arsenals of Spain or her fleets. That neither of these was done is not the fault of Lady Hamilton; the opportunity might have been offered.

Secondly: The British fleet under my command could never have returned the second time to Egypt, had not Lady Hamilton's influence with the Queen of Naples caused letters to be wrote to the governor of Syracuse, that he was to encourage the fleet's being supplied with everything, should they put into any port in Sicily. We put into Syracuse, and received every supply; went to Egypt, and destroyed the French fleet.

Could I have rewarded these services, I would not now call upon my country; but as that has not been in my power, I leave Emma Lady Hamilton, therefore, a legacy to my king and country, that they will give her an ample provision to maintain her rank in life.

I also leave to the beneficence of my country my adopted daughter, Horatia Nelson Thompson; and I desire she will use in future the name of Nelson only.

These are the only favors I ask of my king and country, at this moment when I am going to fight their battle. May God bless my king and country, and all those I hold dear! My relations it is needless to mention: they will, of course, be amply provided for.

Nelson and Bronté

Witness:

Henry Blackwood
T. M. Hardy

The child of whom this writing speaks, was believed to be his daughter, and so, indeed, he called her the last time that he pronounced her name. She was then about five years old, living at Merton, under Lady Hamilton's care. The last minutes which Nelson passed at Merton were employed in praying over this child as she lay sleeping. A portrait of Lady Hamilton hung in his cabin; and no Catholic ever beheld the picture of his patron-saint with devouter reverence. The undisguised and romantic passion with which he regarded it amounted almost to superstition; and when the portrait was now taken down, in clearing for action, he desired the men who removed it to "take care of his guardian angel." In this manner he frequently spoke of it, as if he believed there were a virtue in the image. He wore a miniature of her also next his heart.

Blackwood went on board the *Victory* about six. He found him in good spirits, but very calm; not in that exhilaration which he had felt upon entering into battle at Aboukir and Copenhagen; he knew that his own life would be particularly aimed at, and seems to have looked for death with almost as sure an expectation as for victory. His whole attention was fixed upon the enemy. They tacked to the northward, and formed their line on the larboard tack; thus bringing the shoals of Trafalgar and St. Pedro under the lee of the British, and keeping the port of Cadiz open for themselves. This was judiciously done: and Nelson, aware of all the advantages which it gave them, made signal to prepare to anchor.

Villeneuve was a skilful seaman, worthy of serving a better master and a better cause. His plan of defence was as well conceived, and as original, as the plan of attack. He formed the fleet in a double line, every alternate ship being about a cable's length to windward of her second ahead and astern. Nelson, certain of a triumphant issue to the day, asked Blackwood what he should consider as a victory. That officer answered that, considering the handsome way in which battle was offered by the enemy, their apparent determination for a fair trial of strength, and the situation of the land, he thought it would be a glorious result if fourteen were captured. He replied: "I shall not be satisfied with less than twenty." Soon afterwards he asked him if he did not think there was a signal wanting. Captain Blackwood made answer that he thought the whole fleet seemed very clearly to understand what they were about. These words were scarcely spoken before that signal was made which will be remembered as long as the language or even the memory of England shall endure—Nelson's last signal: "ENG-LAND EXPECTS EVERY MAN WILL DO HIS DUTY!" It was received throughout the fleet with a shout of answering acclamation, made sublime by the spirit which it breathed and the feeling which it expressed. "Now," said Lord Nelson, "I can do no more. We must trust to the great Disposer of all events and the justice of our cause. I thank God for this great opportunity of doing my duty."

He wore that day, as usual, his Admiral's frockcoat, bearing on the left breast four stars of the different orders with which he was invested. Ornaments which rendered him so conspicuous a mark for the enemy were beheld with ominous apprehensions by his officers. It was known that there were riflemen on board the French ships, and it could not be doubted but that his life would be particularly aimed at. They communicated their fears to each other, and the surgeon, Mr. Beatty, spoke to the chaplain, Dr. Scott, and to Mr. Scott, the public secretary, desiring that some person would entreat him to change his dress or cover the stars; but they knew that such a request would highly displease him. "In honor I gained them," he had said when such a thing had been hinted to him formerly, "and in honor I will die with them." Mr. Beatty, however, would not have been deterred by any fear of exciting displeasure from speaking to him himself upon a subject in which the weal of England, as well as the life of Nelson, was concerned; but he was ordered from the deck before he could find an opportunity. This was a point upon which Nelson's officers knew that it was hopeless to remonstrate or reason with him; but both Blackwood and his own captain, Hardy, represented to him how advantageous to the fleet it would be for him to keep out of action as long as possible; and he consented at last to let the *Leviathan* and the *Téméraire*, which were sailing abreast of the *Victory*, be ordered to pass ahead. Yet even here the last infirmity of this noble mind was indulged; for these ships could not pass ahead if the *Victory* continued to carry all her sail; and so far was Nelson from shortening sail, that it was evident he took pleasure in pressing on, and rendering it impossible for them to obey his own orders. A long swell was setting into the Bay of Cadiz: our ships, crowding all sail, moved majestically before it, with light winds from the southwest. The sun shone on the sails of the enemy; and their well-formed line, with their numerous three-deckers, made an appearance which any other assailants would have thought formidable; but the British sailors only admired the beauty and the splendor of the spectacle; and, in full confidence of winning what they saw, remarked to each other, what a fine sight yonder ships would make at Spithead!

The French admiral, from the *Bucentaure*, beheld the new manner in which his enemy was advancing—Nelson and Collingwood each leading his line; and, pointing them out to his officers, he is said to have exclaimed that such conduct could not fail to be successful. Yet Villeneuve had made his own dispositions with the utmost skill, and the fleets under his command waited for the attack with perfect coolness. Ten minutes before twelve they opened their fire. Eight or nine of the ships immediately ahead of the *Victory*, and across her bows, fired single guns at her, to ascertain whether she was yet with- 5 in their range. As soon as Nelson perceived that their shot passed over him, he desired Blackwood and Captain Prowse, of the *Sirius*, to repair to their respective frigates, and on their way to tell all the 10 captains of the line-of-battle ships that he depended on their exertions, and that, if by the prescribed mode of attack they found it impracticable to get into action immediately, they might adopt whatever 15 they thought best, provided it led them quickly and closely alongside an enemy. As they were standing on the front poop, Blackwood took him by the hand, saying he hoped soon to return and find him in 20 possession of twenty prizes. He replied, "God bless you, Blackwood; I shall never see you again."

Nelson's column was steered about two points more to the north than Colling- 25 wood's in order to cut off the enemy's escape into Cadiz. The lee line, therefore, was first engaged. "See," cried Nelson, pointing to the *Royal Sovereign*, as she steered right for the centre of the enemy's 30 line, cut through it astern of the *Santa Anna*, three-decker, and engaged her at the muzzle of her guns on the starboard side; "see how that noble fellow Collingwood carries his ship into action!" Collingwood, 35 delighted at being first in the heat of the fire, and knowing the feelings of his Commander and old friend, turned to his captain and exclaimed, "Rotherham, what would Nelson give to be here!" Both 40 these brave officers perhaps at this moment thought of Nelson with gratitude for a circumstance which had occurred on the preceding day. Admiral Collingwood, with some of the captains, having gone on board 45 the *Victory* to receive instructions, Nelson inquired of him where his captain was, and was told in reply that they were not upon good terms with each other. "Terms!" said Nelson, "good terms with each other!" 50 Immediately he sent a boat for Captain Rotherham, led him, as soon as he arrived, to Collingwood, and saying, "Look, yonder are the enemy!" bade them shake hands like Englishmen. 55

The enemy continued to fire a gun at a time at the *Victory* till they saw that a shot had passed through her main-top-gallant sail; then they opened their broadsides, aiming chiefly at her rigging, in the hope 60 of disabling her before she could close with them. Nelson, as usual, had hoisted several flags, lest one should be shot away. The enemy showed no colors till late in the action, when they began to feel the necessity of having them to strike. For this reason the *Santissima Trinidad*—Nelson's old acquaintance, as he used to call her— was distinguishable only by her four decks; and to the bow of this opponent he ordered the *Victory* to be steered. Meantime an incessant raking fire was kept up upon the *Victory*. The admiral's secretary was one of the first who fell: he was killed by a cannon-shot, while conversing with Hardy. Captain Adair, of the marines, with the help of a sailor, endeavored to remove the body from Nelson's sight, who had a great regard for Mr. Scott; but he anxiously asked, "Is that poor Scott that's gone?" and being informed that it was indeed so, exclaimed, "Poor fellow!" Presently a double-headed shot struck a party of marines, who were drawn up on the poop, and killed eight of them: upon which Nelson immediately desired Captain Adair to disperse his men round the ship, that they might not suffer so much from being together. A few minutes afterwards a shot struck the forebrace bits on the quarter-deck, and passed between Nelson and Hardy, a splinter from the bit tearing off Hardy's buckle and bruising his foot. Both stopped, and looked anxiously at each other: each supposed the other to be wounded. Nelson then smiled, and said, "This is too warm work, Hardy, to last long."

The *Victory* had not yet returned a single gun: fifty of her men had been by this time killed or wounded, and her main-topmast, with all her studding-sails and their booms, shot away. Nelson declared that, in all his battles, he had seen nothing which surpassed the cool courage of his crew on this occasion. At four minutes after twelve she opened her fire from both sides of her deck. It was not possible to break the enemy's line without running on board one of their ships; Hardy informed him of this, and asked him which he would prefer. Nelson replied: "Take your choice, Hardy, it does not signify much." The master was ordered to put the helm to port, and the *Victory* ran on board the *Redoubtable*, just as her tiller ropes were shot away. The French ship received her with a broadside, then instantly let down her lower-deck ports for fear of being boarded through them, and never afterwards fired a great gun during the action. Her tops, like those of all the enemy's ships, were filled with rifle-men. Nelson never placed musketry in his tops; he had a strong dislike to the practice, not merely because it endangers setting fire to the sails, but also because it is a murderous sort of warfare, by which individuals may suffer, and a commander now and then be picked off, but which never can decide the fate of a general engagement.

Captain Harvey, in the *Téméraire,* fell on board the *Redoubtable* on the other side; another enemy was in like manner on board the *Témérairie*; so that these four ships formed as compact a tier as if they had been moored together, their heads all lying the same way. The lieutenants of the *Victory,* seeing this, depressed their guns of the middle and lower decks, and fired with a diminished charge, lest the shot should pass through and injure the *Téméraire*; and because there was danger that the *Redoubtable* might take fire from the lower-deck guns, the muzzles of which touched her side when they were run out, the fireman of each gun stood ready with a bucket of water, which, as soon as the gun was discharged, he dashed into the hole made by the shot. An incessant fire was kept up from the *Victory* from both sides; her larboard guns playing upon the *Bucentaure* and the huge *Santissima Trinidad.*

It had been part of Nelson's prayer that the British fleet might be distinguished by humanity in the victory he expected. Setting an example himself, he twice gave orders to cease firing upon the *Redoubtable,* supposing that she had struck, because her great guns were silent; for, as she carried no flag, there was no means of instantly ascertaining the fact. From this ship, which he had thus twice spared, he received his death. A ball fired from her mizzen-top, which, in the then situation of the two vessels, was not more than fifteen yards from that part of the deck where he was standing, struck the epaulette on his left shoulder,—about a quarter after one, just in the heat of action. He fell upon his face, on the spot which was covered with his poor secretary's blood. Hardy, who was a few steps from him, turning round, saw three men raising him up. "They have done for me at last, Hardy!" said he. "I hope not!" cried Hardy. "Yes," he replied; "my back bone is shot through." Yet even now, not for a moment losing his presence of mind, he observed, as they

were carrying him down the ladder, that the tiller ropes, which had been shot away, were not yet replaced, and ordered that new ones should be rove immediately. Then, that he might not be seen by the crew, he took out his handkerchief, and covered his face and his stars. Had he but concealed these badges of honor from the enemy, England, perhaps, would not have had cause to receive with sorrow the news of the battle of Trafalgar.

The cockpit was crowded with wounded and dying men, over whose bodies he was with some difficulty conveyed, and laid upon a pallet in the midshipmen's berth. It was soon perceived, upon examination, that the wound was mortal. This, however, was concealed from all, except Captain Hardy, the chaplain, and the medical attendants. He himself being certain, from the sensation in his back, and the gush of blood he felt momently within his breast, that no human care could avail him, insisted that the surgeon should leave him, and attend to those to whom he might be useful. "For," said he, "you can do nothing for me." All that could be done was to fan him with paper, and frequently to give him lemonade to alleviate his intense thirst. He was in great pain, and expressed much anxiety for the event of the action, which now began to declare itself. As often as a ship struck, the crew of the *Victory* hurrahed, and at every hurrah a visible expression of joy gleamed in the eyes and marked the countenance of the dying hero. But he became impatient to see Captain Hardy; and as that officer, though often sent for, could not leave the deck, Nelson feared that some fatal cause prevented him, and repeatedly cried: "Will no one bring Hardy to me? He must be killed! He is surely dead!" An hour and ten minutes elapsed from the time when Nelson received his wound before Hardy could come to him. They shook hands in silence; Hardy in vain struggling to suppress the feelings of that most painful and yet sublimest moment. "Well, Hardy," said Nelson, "how goes the day with us?"—"Very well," replied Hardy, "ten ships have struck, but five of the van have tacked, and show an intention to bear down upon the *Victory.* I have called two or three of our fresh ships round, and have no doubt of giving them a drubbing." —"I hope," said Nelson, "none of our ships have struck?" Hardy answered, "There was no fear of that." Then, and not till then, Nelson spoke of himself. "I am a dead man, Hardy," said he; "I am going fast; it will be all over with me soon. Come nearer to me. Let my dear Lady Hamilton have my hair; and all other things belonging to me." Hardy observed that he hoped Mr. Beatty could yet hold out some prospect of life. "Oh no!" he replied, "it is impossible; my back is shot through. Beatty will tell you so." Captain Hardy then once more shook hands with him, and with a heart almost bursting, hastened upon deck.

By this time all feeling below the breast was gone; and Nelson, having bade the surgeon ascertain this, said to him: "You know I am gone. I know it. I feel something rising in my breast"—putting his hand on his left side—"which tells me so." And upon Beatty's inquiring whether his pain was very great, he replied, "So great that he wished he was dead. Yet," said he in a lower voice, "one would like to live a little longer too!" And after a few minutes, in the same under-tone, he added: "What would become of poor Lady Hamilton if she knew my situation!" Next to his country she occupied his thoughts.

Captain Hardy, some fifty minutes after he had left the cockpit, returned, and again taking the hand of his dying friend and Commander, congratulated him on having gained a complete victory. How many of the enemy were taken he did not know, as it was impossible to perceive them distinctly, but fourteen or fifteen at least. "That's well!" cried Nelson, "but I bargained for twenty." And then in a stronger voice he said: "Anchor, Hardy, anchor." Hardy upon this hinted that Admiral Collingwood would take upon himself the direction of affairs. "Not while I live, Hardy," said the dying Nelson, ineffectually endeavoring to raise himself from the bed. "Do you anchor." His previous order for preparing to anchor had shown how clearly he foresaw the necessity of this. Presently, calling Hardy back, he said to him, in a low voice, "Don't throw me overboard"; and he desired that he might be buried by his parents, unless it should please the king to order otherwise. Then, reverting to private feelings: "Take care of my dear Lady Hamilton, Hardy; take care of poor Lady Hamilton.—Kiss me, Hardy," said he. Hardy knelt down, and kissed his cheek; and Nelson said, "Now I am satisfied. Thank God, I have done my duty." Hardy stood over him in silence for a moment or two, then knelt again, and kissed his forehead. "Who is that?" said Nelson; and being informed, he replied, "God bless you, Hardy." And Hardy then left him—for ever.

Nelson now desired to be turned upon his right side, and said: "I wish I had not left the deck; for I shall soon be gone." Death was, indeed, rapidly approaching. He said to the chaplain: "Doctor, I have *not* been a *great* sinner"; and, after a short pause, "Remember that I leave Lady Hamilton, and my daughter Horatia, as a legacy to my country." His articulation now became difficult; but he was distinctly heard to say, "Thank God, I have done my duty!" These words he repeatedly pronounced; and they were the last words he uttered. He expired at thirty minutes after four,—three hours and a quarter after he had received his wound. . . .

Once, amidst his sufferings, Nelson had expressed a wish that he were dead; but immediately the spirit subdued the pains of death, and he wished to live a little longer; doubtless that he might hear the completion of the victory which he had seen so gloriously begun. That consolation—that joy—that triumph, was afforded him. He lived to know that the victory was decisive; and the last guns which were fired at the flying enemy were heard a minute or two before he expired. . . .

It is almost superfluous to add that all the honors which a grateful country could bestow were heaped upon the memory of Nelson. His brother was made an earl, with a grant of £6,000 a-year; £10,000 were voted to each of his sisters; and £100,000 for the purchase of an estate. A public funeral was decreed, and a public monument. Statues and monuments also were voted by most of our principal cities. The leaden coffin in which he was brought home, was cut in pieces, which were distributed as relics of Saint Nelson,—so the gunner of the *Victory* called them,—and when, at his interment, his flag was about to be lowered into the grave, the sailors who assisted at the ceremony, with one accord rent it in pieces, that each might preserve a fragment while he lived.

The death of Nelson was felt in England as something more than a public calamity: men started at the intelligence, and turned pale, as if they had heard of the loss of a dear friend. An object of our admiration and affection, of our pride and of our hopes, was suddenly taken from us; and it seemed as if we had never, till then, known how deeply we loved and reverenced him. What the country had lost in its great naval hero—the greatest of our own, and of all former times—was scarcely taken into the account of grief. So perfectly, indeed, had he performed his part, that the maritime war, after the battle of Trafalgar, was considered at an end; the fleets of the enemy were not merely defeated, but destroyed; new navies must be built, and a new race of seamen reared for them, before the possibility of their invading our shores could again be contemplated. It was not, therefore, from any selfish reflection upon the magnitude of our loss that we mourned for him: the general sorrow was of a higher character. The people of England grieved that funeral ceremonies, and public monuments, and posthumous rewards, were all which they could now bestow upon him, whom the king, the legislature, and the nation, would have alike delighted to honor; whom every tongue would have blessed; whose presence in every village through which he might have passed would have wakened the church bells, have given school-boys a holiday, have drawn children from their sports to gaze upon him, and "old men from the chimney corner," to look upon Nelson ere they died. The victory of Trafalgar was celebrated, indeed, with the usual forms of rejoicing, but they were without joy; for such already was the glory of the British navy through Nelson's surpassing genius, that it scarcely seemed to receive any addition from the most signal victory that ever was achieved upon the seas; and the destruction of this mighty fleet, by which all the maritime schemes of France were totally frustrated, hardly appeared to add to our security or strength; for while Nelson was living, to watch the combined squadrons of the enemy, we felt ourselves as secure as now, when they were no longer in existence.

There was reason to suppose, from the appearances upon opening the body, that in the course of nature he might have attained, like his father, to a good old age. Yet he cannot be said to have fallen prematurely whose work was done, nor ought he to be lamented who died so full of honors and at the height of human fame. The most triumphant death is that of the martyr; the most awful that of the martyred patriot; the most splendid that of the hero in the hour of victory; and if the chariot and the horses of fire had been vouchsafed for Nelson's translation, he could scarcely have departed in a brighter blaze of glory. He has left us, not indeed his mantle of inspiration, but a name and an example which are at this hour inspiring thousands of the youth of England—a name which is our pride, and an example which will continue to be our shield and our strength. Thus it is that the spirits of the great and the wise continue to live and to act after them, verifying in this sense the language of the old mythologist:

Τοὶ μὲν δαίμονές εἰσι, Διὸς μεγάλου διὰ
  βουλας.
Ἐσθλοί, ἐπιχθόνιοι, φύλακες θνητῶν
  ἀνθρώπων.

1813

FROM THE DOCTOR

THE STORY OF THE THREE BEARS

A tale which may content the minds
Of learned men and grave philosophers.

Once upon a time there were Three Bears, who lived together in a house of their own, in a wood. One of them was a Little, Small, Wee Bear; and one was a Middle-sized Bear, and the other was a Great, Huge Bear. They had each a pot for their porridge, a little pot for the Little, Small, Wee Bear; and a middle-sized pot for the Middle Bear; and a great pot for the Great, Huge Bear. And they had each a chair to sit in; a little chair for the Little, Small, Wee Bear; and a middle-sized chair for the Middle Bear; and a great chair for the Great, Huge Bear. And they had each a bed to sleep in; a little bed for the Little, Small, Wee Bear; and a middle-sized bed for the Middle Bear; and a great bed for the Great, Huge Bear.

One day, after they had made the porridge for their breakfast, and poured it into their porridge-pots, they walked out into the wood while the porridge was cooling, that they might not burn their mouths, by beginning too soon to eat it. And while they were walking, a little old Woman came to the house. She could not have been a good, honest old Woman; for first she looked in at the window, and then she peeped in at the keyhole; and seeing nobody in the house, she lifted the latch. The door was not fastened, because the Bears were good Bears, who did nobody any harm, and never suspected that anybody would harm them. So the little old Woman opened the door, and went in; and well pleased she was when she saw the porridge on the table. If she had been a good little old Woman, she would have waited till the Bears came home, and then, perhaps, they would have asked her to breakfast; for they were good Bears,—a little rough or so, as the manner of Bears is, but for all that very good-natured and hospitable. But she was an impudent, bad old Woman, and set about helping herself.

So first she tasted the porridge of the Great, Huge Bear, and that was too hot for her; and she said a bad word about that. And then she tasted the porridge of the Middle Bear, and that was too cold for her; and she said a bad word about that too. And then she went to the porridge of the Little, Small, Wee Bear, and tasted that; and that was neither too hot, nor too cold, but just right; and she liked it so well, that she ate it all up: but the naughty old Woman said a bad word about the little porridge-pot, because it did not hold enough for her.

Then the little old Woman sate down in the chair of the Great, Huge Bear, and that was too hard for her. And then she sate down in the chair of the Middle Bear, and that was too soft for her. And then she sate down in the chair of the Little, Small, Wee Bear, and that was neither too hard, nor too soft, but just right. So she seated herself in it, and there she sate till the bottom of the chair came out, and down came hers, plump upon the ground. And the naughty old Woman said a wicked word about that too.

Then the little old Woman went up stairs into the bed-chamber in which the three Bears slept. And first she lay down upon the bed of the Great, Huge Bear; but that was too high at the head for her. And next she lay down upon the bed of the Middle Bear; and that was too high at the foot for her. And then she lay down upon the bed of the Little, Small, Wee Bear; and that was neither too high at the head, nor at the foot, but just right. So she covered herself up comfortably, and lay there till she fell fast asleep.

By this time the Three Bears thought their porridge would be cool enough; so they came home to breakfast. Now the little old Woman had left the spoon of the Great, Huge Bear, standing in his porridge.

"SOMEBODY HAS BEEN AT MY PORRIDGE!"

said the Great, Huge Bear, in his great, rough, gruff voice. And when the Middle Bear looked at his, he saw that the spoon was standing in it too. They were wooden spoons; if they had been silver ones, the naughty old Woman would have put them in her pocket.

"SOMEBODY HAS BEEN AT MY PORRIDGE!"

said the Middle Bear, in his middle voice.

Then the Little, Small, Wee Bear looked at his, and there was the spoon in the porridge-pot, but the porridge was all gone.

"SOMEBODY HAS BEEN AT MY PORRIDGE, AND HAS EATEN IT ALL UP!"

said the Little, Small, Wee Bear, in his little, small, wee voice.

Upon this the Three Bears, seeing that some one had entered their house, and eaten up the Little, Small, Wee Bear's breakfast, began to look about them. Now the little old Woman had not put the hard cushion straight when she rose from the chair of the Great, Huge Bear.

"SOMEBODY HAS BEEN SITTING IN MY CHAIR!"

said the Great, Huge Bear, in his great, rough, gruff voice.

And the little old Woman had squatted down the soft cushion of the Middle Bear.

"SOMEBODY HAS BEEN SITTING IN MY CHAIR!"

said the Middle Bear, in his middle voice.

And you know what the little old Woman had done to the third chair.

"SOMEBODY HAS BEEN SITTING IN MY CHAIR, AND HAS SATE THE BOTTOM OF IT OUT!"

said the Little, Small, Wee Bear in his little, small, wee voice.

Then the Three Bears thought it necessary that they should make farther search; so they went up stairs into their bed-chamber. Now the little old Woman had pulled the pillow of the Great, Huge Bear, out of its place.

"SOMEBODY HAS BEEN LYING IN MY BED!"

said the Great, Huge Bear, in his great, rough, gruff voice.

And the little old Woman had pulled the bolster of the Middle Bear out of its place.

"SOMEBODY HAS BEEN LYING IN MY BED!"

said the Middle Bear, in his middle voice.

And when the Little, Small, Wee Bear came to look at his bed, there was the bolster in its place; and the pillow in its place upon the bolster; and upon the pillow was the little old Woman's ugly, dirty head,—which was not in its place, for she had no business there.

"SOMEBODY HAS BEEN LYING IN MY BED,— AND HERE SHE IS!"

said the Little, Small, Wee Bear, in his little, small, wee voice.

The little old Woman had heard in her sleep the great, rough, gruff voice of the Great, Huge Bear; but she was so fast asleep that it was no more to her than the roaring of wind, or the rumbling of thunder. And she had heard the middle voice of the Middle Bear, but it was only as if she had heard some one speaking in a dream. But when she heard the little, small, wee voice of the Little, Small, Wee Bear, it was so sharp, and so shrill, that it awakened her at once. Up she started; and when she saw the Three Bears on one side of the bed, she tumbled herself out at the other, and ran to the window. Now the window was open, because the Bears, like good, tidy Bears, as they were, always opened their bed-chamber window when they got up in the morning. Out the little old Woman jumped; and whether she broke her neck in the fall; or ran into the wood and was lost there; or found her way out of the wood, and was taken up by the constable and sent to the House of Correction for a vagrant as she was, I cannot tell. But the Three Bears never saw anything more of her.

1834

THOMAS CAMPBELL (1777-1844)

Campbell, for Hope and fine war-songs renowned.

LEIGH HUNT

Campbell was born in Glasgow, of a mercantile family which became impoverished. While working his way through the law-school in Edinburgh, he wrote *The Pleasures of Hope,* some passages of which raised expectations of future poetic excellence that he was never to attain. During a tour of the continent, however, he gained some lively impressions of battles and warfare, and of the importance of the Navy to the British Isles; and his best poems, *Ye Mariners of England, Hohenlinden,* and *The Battle of the Baltic,* were the widely applauded results. Thereafter he became celebrated and prosperous, received a royal pension, and was elected Lord Rector of Glasgow University. He continued to write verses,—but ceased to be a poet. He had taken a stand in favor of Polish, as well as of Greek, independence; and when he was buried in Westminster Abbey, a grateful Pole cast earth from Kosciusko's grave upon Campbell's coffin. The nationalistic and patriotic strain, which in the greater Romantics is only one of many themes, is in Campbell almost the only note that is struck resonantly.

FROM THE PLEASURES OF HOPE

HOPE ABIDETH

At summer eve, when Heaven's ethereal bow
Spans with bright arch the glittering hills below,
Why to yon mountain turns the musing eye,
Whose sunbright summit mingles with the sky?
Why do those cliffs of shadowy tint appear 5
More sweet than all the landscape smiling near?
'Tis distance lends enchantment to the view,
And robes the mountains in its azure hue.

Thus, with delight, we linger to survey
The promised joys of life's unmeasured way; 10
Thus, from afar, each dim-discovered scene
More pleasing seems than all the past hath been;
And every form, that Fancy can repair
From dark oblivion, glows divinely there.

What potent spirit guides the raptured eye 15
To pierce the shades of dim futurity?
Can Wisdom lend, with all her heavenly power,
The pledge of Joy's anticipated hour?
Ah, no! she darkly sees the fate of man—
Her dim horizon bounded to a span; 20
Or, if she hold an image to the view,
'Tis Nature pictured too severely true.

With thee, sweet Hope! resides the heavenly light
That pours remotest rapture on the sight:
Thine is the charm of life's bewildered way, 25
That calls each slumbering passion into play.
Waked by thy touch, I see the sister band,
On tiptoe watching, start at thy command,
And fly where'er thy mandate bids them steer,
To Pleasure's path or Glory's bright career. 30

Primeval Hope, the Aönian Muses say,
When Man and Nature mourned their first decay;
When every form of death, and every woe,
Shot from malignant stars to earth below;
When Murder bared his arm, and rampant War   35
Yoked the red dragons of her iron car;
When Peace and Mercy, banished from the plain,
Sprung on the viewless winds to heaven again;
All, all forsook the friendless, guilty mind,
But Hope, the charmer, lingered still behind.   40
1796-99   1799

POLAND AND FREEDOM'S CAUSE

Where barbarous hordes of Scythian mountains roam,
Truth, Mercy, Freedom, yet shall find a home;
Where'er degraded Nature bleeds and pines,
From Guinea's coast to Sibir's dreary mines,
Truth shall pervade the unfathomed darkness there,   5
And light the dreadful features of despair.—
Hark! the stern captive spurns his heavy load,
And asks the image back that Heaven bestowed!
Fierce in his eye the fire of valor burns,
And, as the slave departs, the man returns.   10

Oh! sacred Truth! thy triumph ceased awhile,
And Hope, thy sister, ceased with thee to smile,
When leagued Oppression poured to Northern wars
Her whiskered pandoors and her fierce hussars,
Waved her dread standard to the breeze of morn,   15
Pealed her loud drum, and twanged her trumpet horn;
Tumultuous horror brooded o'er her van,
Presaging wrath to Poland—and to man!

Warsaw's last champion from her height surveyed,
Wide o'er the fields, a waste of ruin laid;   20
"Oh! Heaven!" he cried, "my bleeding country save!
Is there no hand on high to shield the brave?
Yet, though destruction sweep those lovely plains,
Rise, fellow-men! our country yet remains!
By that dread name, we wave the sword on high!   25
And swear for her to live!—with her to die!"

He said, and on the rampart-heights arrayed
His trusty warriors, few, but undismayed;
Firm-paced and slow, a horrid front they form,
Still as the breeze, but dreadful as the storm;   30
Low murmuring sounds along their banners fly,
Revenge, or death,—the watchword and reply;
Then pealed the notes, omnipotent to charm,
And the loud tocsin tolled their last alarm!

In vain, alas! in vain, yet gallant few!   35
From rank to rank your volleyed thunder flew:
Oh, bloodiest picture in the book of Time,
Sarmatia fell, unwept, without a crime,
Found not a generous friend, a pitying foe,
Strength in her arms, nor mercy in her woe!   40

Dropped from her nerveless grasp the shattered **spear**,
Closed her bright eye, and curbed her high career;—
Hope, for a season, bade the world farewell,
And Freedom shrieked as Kosciusko fell!

The sun went down, nor ceased the carnage there,   45
Tumultuous murder shook the midnight air;
On Prague's proud arch the fires of ruin glow,
His blood-dyed waters murmuring far below;
The storm prevails, the rampart yields a way;
Bursts the wild cry of horror and dismay!   50
Hark, as the smoldering piles with thunder fall,
A thousand shrieks for hopeless mercy call!
Earth shook; red meteors flashed along the sky,
And conscious Nature shuddered at the cry!

Oh! righteous Heaven; ere Freedom found a grave,   55
Why slept the sword omnipotent to save?
Where was thine arm, O Vengeance! where thy rod,
That smote the foes of Zion and of God;
That crushed proud Ammon, when his iron car
Was yoked in wrath, and thundered from afar?   60
Where was the storm that slumbered till the host
Of blood-stained Pharaoh left their trembling coast;
Then bade the deep in wild commotion flow,
And heaved an ocean on their march below?

Departed spirits of the mighty dead!   65
Ye that at Marathon and Leuctra bled!
Friends of the world! restore your swords to **man**,
Fight in his sacred cause, and lead the van!
Yet for Sarmatia's tears of blood atone,
And make her arm puissant as your own!   70
Oh! once again to Freedom's cause return
The patriot Tell—the Bruce of Bannockburn!

Yes! thy proud lords, unpitied land, shall see
That man hath yet a soul—and dare be free!
A little while, along thy saddening plains,   75
The starless night of Desolation reigns;
Truth shall restore the light by Nature given.
And, like Prometheus, bring the fire of Heaven!
Prone to the dust Oppression shall be hurled,
Her name, her nature, withered from the world!   80

1796-99   1799

YE MARINERS OF ENGLAND

A NAVAL ODE

I

Ye Mariners of England,
That guard our native seas,
Whose flag has braved, a thousand years,
The battle and the breeze—
Your glorious standard launch again   5
To match another foe!
And sweep through the deep,
While the stormy winds do blow,—

While the battle rages loud and long,
And the stormy winds do blow.   10

II

The spirit of your fathers
Shall start from every wave!
For the deck it was their field of fame,
And Ocean was their grave.
Where Blake and mighty Nelson fell,   15
Your manly hearts shall glow,
As ye sweep through the deep,
While the stormy winds do blow,—
While the battle rages loud and long,
And the stormy winds do blow.   20

III

Britannia needs no bulwarks,
No towers along the steep;
Her march is o'er the mountain-waves,
Her home is on the deep.
With thunders from her native oak,   25
She quells the floods below,
As they roar on the shore,
When the stormy winds do blow,—
When the battle rages loud and long,
And the stormy winds do blow.   30

IV

The meteor flag of England
Shall yet terrific burn,
Till danger's troubled night depart,
And the star of peace return.
Then, then, ye ocean-warriors!   35
Our song and feast shall flow
To the fame of your name,
When the storm has ceased to blow,—
When the fiery fight is heard no more,
And the storm has ceased to blow.   40

1799-1800   1801

HOHENLINDEN

On Linden, when the sun was low,
All bloodless lay the untrodden snow,
And dark as winter was the flow
Of Iser, rolling rapidly.

But Linden saw another sight   5
When the drum beat at dead of night,
Commanding fires of death to light
The darkness of her scenery.

By torch and trumpet fast arrayed,
Each horseman drew his battle-blade,   10
And furious every charger neighed
To join the dreadful revelry.

Then shook the hills with thunder riven,
Then rushed the steeds to battle driven,
And louder than the bolts of heaven   15
Far flashed the red artillery.

But redder yet that light shall glow
On Linden's hills of stainèd snow,
And bloodier yet the torrent flow
Of Iser, rolling rapidly.   20

'Tis morn; but scarce yon level sun
Can pierce the war-clouds, rolling dun,
Where furious Frank and fiery Hun
Shout in their sulphurous canopy.

The combat deepens. On, ye brave,   25
Who rush to glory, or the grave!
Wave, Munich! all thy banners wave,
And charge with all thy chivalry!

Few, few, shall part where many meet!
The snow shall be their winding-sheet,   30
And every turf beneath their feet
Shall be a soldier's sepulchre.

1802   1802

THE BATTLE OF THE BALTIC

I

Of Nelson and the North
Sing the glorious day's renown,
When to battle fierce came forth
All the might of Denmark's crown,
And her arms along the deep proudly
          shone,—   5
By each gun and lighted brand,
In a bold determined hand,
And the Prince of all the land
Led them on.

II

Like leviathans afloat   10
Lay their bulwarks on the brine,
While the sign of battle flew
On the lofty British line:
It was ten of April morn by the chime;
As they drifted on their path,   15
There was silence deep as death,
And the boldest held his breath
For a time.

III

But the might of England flushed
To anticipate the scene;   20
And her van the fleeter rushed
O'er the deadly space between.
"Hearts of oak!" our captain cried; when
          each gun
From its adamantine lips
Spread a death-shade round the ships,   25
Like the hurricane eclipse
Of the sun.

IV

Again! again! again!
And the havoc did not slack,
Till a feeble cheer the Dane   30
To our cheering sent us back:
Their shots along the deep slowly boom;
Then ceased—and all is wail
As they strike the shattered sail,
Or in conflagration pale   35
Light the gloom.

V

Out spoke the victor then
As he hailed them o'er the wave:
"Ye are brothers! ye are men!
And we conquer but to save: 40

So peace instead of death let us bring:
But yield, proud foe, thy fleet
With the crews at England's feet,
And make submission meet
To our King."   45

VI

Then Denmark blessed our chief
That he gave her wounds repose;
And the sounds of joy and grief
From her people wildly rose,
As death withdrew his shades from the
          day;   50
While the sun looked smiling bright
O'er a wide and woeful sight,
Where the fires of funeral light
Died away.

VII

Now joy, Old England, raise   55
For the tidings of thy might,
By the festal cities' blaze,
While the wine-cup shines in light;
And yet, amidst that joy and uproar,
Let us think of them that sleep,   60
Full many a fathom deep,
By thy wild and stormy steep,
Elsinore!

VIII

Brave hearts! to Britain's pride
Once so faithful and so true,   65
On the deck of fame that died
With the gallant good Riou:
Soft sigh the winds of Heaven o'er their
          grave!
While the billow mournful rolls
And the mermaid's song condoles,   70
Singing Glory to the souls
Of the brave!
1804-05   1809

THE LAST MAN

All worldly shapes shall melt in gloom,
    The Sun himself must die,
Before this mortal shall assume
    Its Immortality!
I saw a vision in my sleep   5
That gave my spirit strength to sweep
    Adown the gulf of Time!
I saw the last of human mold
That shall Creation's death behold,
    As Adam saw her prime!   10

The Sun's eye had a sickly glare,
    The Earth with age was wan,
The skeletons of nations were
    Around that lonely man!
Some had expired in fight,—the brands   15
Still rusted in their bony hands;
    In plague and famine some!
Earth's cities had no sound nor tread;
And ships were drifting with the dead
    To shores where all was dumb!   29

Yet, prophet-like, that lone one stood
    With dauntless words and high,
That shook the sere leaves from the wood
    As if a storm passed by,
Saying, "We are twins in death, proud
          Sun!   25
Thy face is cold, thy race is run,
    'Tis Mercy bids thee go;
For thou ten thousand thousand years
Hast seen the tide of human tears,
    That shall no longer flow.   30

"What though beneath thee man put forth
    His pomp, his pride, his skill,
And arts that made fire, flood, and earth,
    The vassals of his will?
Yet mourn I not thy parted sway,   35
Thou dim discrownèd king of day,
    For all those trophied arts
And triumphs that beneath thee sprang
Healed not a passion or a pang
    Entailed on human hearts.   40

"Go, let oblivion's curtain fall
    Upon the stage of men,
Nor with thy rising beams recall
    Life's tragedy again.
Its piteous pageants bring not back,   45
Nor waken flesh upon the rack
    Of pain anew to writhe—
Stretched in disease's shapes abhorred,
Or mown in battle by the sword
    Like grass beneath the scythe.   50

"E'en I am weary in yon skies
    To watch thy fading fire;
Test of all sumless agonies,
    Behold not me expire!
My lips that speak thy dirge of death—   55
Their rounded gasp and gurgling breath
    To see thou shalt not boast;
The eclipse of Nature spreads my pall,—
The majesty of Darkness shall
    Receive my parting ghost!   60

"This spirit shall return to Him
  Who gave its heavenly spark;
Yet think not, Sun, it shall be dim
  When thou thyself art dark!
No! it shall live again, and shine   65
In bliss unknown to beams of thine.
  By him recalled to breath
Who captive led captivity,
Who robbed the grave of Victory,
  And took the sting from Death!   70

"Go, Sun, while Mercy holds me up
  On Nature's awful waste
To drink this last and bitter cup
  Of grief that man shall taste—
Go, tell the night that hides thy face   75
Thou saw'st the last of Adam's race
  On Earth's sepulchral clod
The darkening universe defy
To quench his immortality
  Or shake his trust in God!"   80

1823

WALTER SAVAGE LANDOR (1775-1864)

All sweet, all sacred, all heroic things,
All generous names and loyal, and all wise,
With all his heart in all its wayfarings
He sought, and worshipped, seeing them with his eyes
In very present glory, clothed with wings
Of words and deeds and dreams immortal, rise
Visible more than living slaves and kings,
Audible more than actual vows and lies.

ALGERNON CHARLES SWINBURNE

Landor has a more important place in the Romantic revival of the past than is usually accorded him. His chief purpose in his principal works.—*Imaginary Conversations* (1824-53), *Pericles and Aspasia* (1836), and the *Pentameron* (1837),—was to make the past live again in such characters and sentiments as expressed the highest possibilities of human experience. Thus, although he is rarely thought of in connection with Sir Walter Scott, his function was similar to that of the great historical novelist. Landor, however, was less interested than Scott in dramatic action; he concentrated upon moral and intellectual character. He was less preoccupied than Scott with British history. He lived by preference much in Italy. The lives of the ancient Greeks and Romans, and of the Italians of the Renaissance, fascinated him as incarnations of the development of Western culture.

He was one of those men who, though personally prone to outbreaks of violent temper, know that moderation and self-control are two of the noblest human virtues; and, although his life was vexed by quarrels, his works exalt calmness and self-restraint. The other virtues that he chiefly admired were fortitude and compassion. His political principles were democratic: he hated Napoleon, and he admired Washington. He believed that the Periclean Age in Greece was one of the high points in the history of civilization, because its laws were made by the popular will and because it had local self-government. In Pericles and Aspasia he also admired a noble type of love,—one which was pure and unselfish, and set the claims of duty and patriotism even higher than its own passionate desires.

In Landor's longer poems there are dull passages; but his shorter poems are exquisite. They beautifully express his courtesy to women, and his fondness for children and for flowers. Unquestionably one of the finest artists among the Romantics, he is perhaps the least popular among them because his style is so terse and restrained and because his themes, really of the highest importance, can hardly be appreciated without a more than common knowledge of the history of civilization.

ON MAN

In his own image the Creator made,
  His own pure sunbeam quickened thee,
    O man!
Thou breathing dial! Since thy day began
  The present hour was ever marked with
    shade!

1802

ROSE AYLMER

Ah, what avails the sceptred race,
  Ah, what the form divine!
What every virtue, every grace!
  Rose Aylmer, all were thine.

Rose Aylmer, whom these wakeful eyes   5
  May weep, but never see,
A night of memories and of sighs
  I consecrate to thee.

1806

MOTHER, I CANNOT MIND MY WHEEL

Mother, I cannot mind my wheel;
  My fingers ache, my lips are dry:
Oh! if you felt the pain I feel!
  But oh, who ever felt as I!

No longer could I doubt him true,   5
  All other men may use deceit;
He always said my eyes were blue,
  And often swore my lips were sweet.

            1806

REGENERATION

We are what suns and winds and waters
  make us;
The mountains are our sponsors, and the
  rills
Fashion and win their nursling with their
  smiles.
But where the land is dim from tyranny,
There tiny pleasures occupy the place   5
Of glories and of duties; as the feet
Of fabled fairies when the sun goes down
Trip o'er the grass where wrestlers strove
  by day.
Then Justice, called the Eternal One above,
Is more inconstant than the buoyant form 10
That burst into existence from the froth
Of ever-varying ocean: what is best
Then becomes worst; what loveliest, most
  deformed.
The heart is hardest in the softest climes,
The passions flourish, the affections die. 15
O thou vast tablet of these awful truths,
That fillest all the space between the seas,
Spreading from Venice's deserted courts
To the Tarentine and Hydruntine mole,
What lifts thee up? what shakes thee? 'tis
  the breath 20
Of God. Awake, ye nations! spring to life!
Let the last work of his right hand ap-
  pear
Fresh with his image, Man. Thou recreant
  slave
That sittest afar off and helpest not,
O thou degenerate Albion! with what
  shame 25
Do I survey thee, pushing forth the sponge
At thy spear's length, in mockery at the
  thirst
Of holy Freedom in his agony,
And prompt and keen to pierce the
  wounded side!
Must Italy then wholly rot away 30
Amid her slime, before she germinate
Into fresh vigor, into form again?
What thunder bursts upon mine ear! some
  isle
Hath surely risen from the gulfs profound,
Eager to suck the sunshine from the
  breast 35
Of beauteous Nature, and to catch the
  gale
From golden Hermus and Melena's brow.

A greater thing than isle, than continent,
Than earth itself, than ocean circling earth,
Hath risen there; regenerate Man hath
  risen. 40
Generous old bard of Chios! not that Jove
Deprived thee in thy latter days of sight
Would I complain, but that no higher
  theme
Than a disdainful youth, a lawless king,
A pestilence, a pyre, awoke thy song, 45
When on the Chian coast, one javelin's
  throw
From where thy tombstone, where thy
  cradle, stood,
Twice twenty self-devoted Greeks assailed
The naval host of Asia, at one blow
Scattered it into air . . . and Greece was
  free . . . 50
And ere these glories beamed, thy day had
  closed.
Let all that Elis ever saw, give way,
All that Olympian Jove e'er smiled upon:
The Marathonian columns never told
A tale more glorious, never Salamis, 55
Nor, faithful in the centre of the false,
Platea, nor Anthela, from whose mount
Benignant Ceres wards the blessed Laws,
And sees the Amphictyon dip his weary
  foot
In the warm streamlet of the strait below. 60
Goddess! altho' thy brow was never reared
Among the powers that guarded or assailed
Perfidious Ilion, parricidal Thebes,
Or other walls whose war-belt e'er inclosed
Man's congregated crimes and vengeful
  pain, 65
Yet hast thou touched the extremes of grief
  and joy;
Grief upon Enna's mead and Hell's ascent,
A solitary mother; joy beyond,
Far beyond, that thy woe, in this thy fane:
The tears were human, but the bliss
  divine. 70
I, in the land of strangers, and depressed
With sad and certain presage for my own,
Exult at hope's fresh dayspring, tho' afar,
There where my youth was not unexercised
By chiefs in willing war and faithful song: 75
Shades as they were, they were not empty
  shades,
Whose bodies haunt our world and blear
  our sun,
Obstruction worse than swamp and shape-
  less sands.
Peace, praise, eternal gladness, to the souls
That, rising from the seas into the
  heavens, 80
Have ransomed first their country with
  their blood!
O thou immortal Spartan! at whose name

The marble table sounds beneath my palms,
Leonidas! even thou wilt not disdain
To mingle names august as these with thine; 85
Nor thou, twin-star of glory, thou whose rays
Streamed over Corinth on the double sea,
Achaian and Saronic; whom the sons
Of Syracuse, when Death removed thy light,
Wept more than slavery ever made them weep, 90
But shed (if gratitude is sweet) sweet tears.
The hand that then poured ashes o'er their heads
Was loosened from its desperate chain by thee.
What now can press mankind into one mass,
For Tyranny to tread the more secure? 95
From gold alone is drawn the guilty wire
That Adulation trills: she mocks the tone
Of Duty, Courage, Virtue, Piety,
And under her sits Hope. O how unlike
That graceful form in azure vest arrayed, 100
With brow serene, and eyes on heaven alone
In patience fixed, in fondness unobscured!
What monsters coil beneath the spreading tree
Of Despotism! what wastes extend around!
What poison floats upon the distant breeze! 105
But who are those that cull and deal its fruit?
Creatures that shun the light and fear the shade,
Bloated and fierce, Sleep's mien and Famine's cry.
Rise up again, rise in thy dignity,
Dejected Man! and scare this brood away. 110

1824

A FIESOLAN IDYL

Here, where precipitate Spring with one light bound
Into hot Summer's lusty arms expires,
And where go forth at morn, at eve, at night,
Soft airs that want the lute to play with 'em,
And softer sighs that know not what they want, 5
Aside a wall, beneath an orange-tree,
Whose tallest flowers could tell the lowlier ones

Of sights in Fiesolè right up above,
While I was gazing a few paces off
At what they seemed to show me with their nods, 10
Their frequent whispers and their pointing shoots,
A gentle maid came down the garden-steps
And gathered the pure treasure in her lap.
I heard the branches rustle, and stepped forth
To drive the ox away, or mule, or goat, 15
Such I believed it must be. How could I
Let beast o'erpower them? When hath wind or rain
Borne hard upon weak plant that wanted me,
And I (however they might bluster round)
Walked off? 'Twere most ungrateful: for sweet scents 20
Are the swift vehicles of still sweeter thoughts,
And nurse and pillow the dull memory
That would let drop without them her best stores.
They bring me tales of youth and tones of love,
And 'tis and ever was my wish and way 25
To let all flowers live freely, and all die
(Whene'er their Genius bids their souls depart)
Among their kindred in their native place.
I never pluck the rose; the violet's head
Hath shaken with my breath upon its bank 30
And not reproached me; the ever-sacred cup
Of the pure lily hath between my hands
Felt safe, unsoiled, nor lost one grain of gold.
I saw the light that made the glossy leaves 35
More glossy; the fair arm, the fairer cheek
Warmed by the eye intent on its pursuit;
I saw the foot that, although half-erect
From its gray slipper, could not lift her up
To what she wanted: I held down a branch
And gathered her some blossoms; since their hour 40
Was come, and bees had wounded them, and flies
Of harder wing were working their way through
And scattering them in fragments under foot.
So crisp were some, they rattled unevolved,
Others, ere broken off, fell into shells, 45
For such appear the petals when detached,
Unbending, brittle, lucid, white like snow,
And like snow not seen through, by eye or sun:
Yet every one her gown received from me

Was fairer than the first. I thought not
so, 50
But so she praised them to reward my care.
I said, "You find the largest."
"This indeed,"
Cried she, "is large and sweet." She held
one forth,
Whether for me to look at or to take 55
She knew not, nor did I; but taking it
Would best have solved (and this she felt)
her doubt.
I dared not touch it; for it seemed a part
Of her own self; fresh, full, the most
mature
Of blossoms, yet a blossom; with a touch 60
To fall, and yet unfallen. She drew
back
The boon she tendered, and then, finding
not
The ribbon at her waist to fix it in,
Dropped it, as loth to drop it, on the rest.
1831

ABSENCE

Ianthe! you resolve to cross the sea!
A path forbidden me!
Remember, while the sun his blessing sheds
Upon the mountain-heads,
How often we have watched him laying
down 5
His brow, and dropped our own
Against each other's, and how faint and
short
And sliding the support!
What will succeed it now? Mine is unblest,
Ianthe! nor will rest 10
But on the very thought that swells with
pain.
O bid me hope again!
O give me back what Earth, what (without
you)
Not Heaven itself can do,
One of the golden days that we have
passed; 15
And let it be my last!
Or else the gift would be, however sweet,
Fragile and incomplete.
1831

SO LATE REMOVED

So late removed from him she swore,
With clasping arms and vows and tears,
In life and death she would adore,
While memory, fondness, bliss, endears—

Can she forswear! can she forget? 5
Strike, mighty Love! strike Vengeance!—
soft!
Conscience must come, and bring Regret—
These let her feel!—nor these too oft!
1831

PAST RUINED ILION HELEN LIVES

Past ruined Ilion Helen lives,
Alcestis rises from the shades;
Verse calls them forth; 'tis verse that gives
Immortal youth to mortal maids.

Soon shall oblivion's deepening veil 5
Hide all the peopled hills you see,
The gay, the proud, while lovers hail
In distant ages you and me.

The tear for fading beauty check,
For passing glory cease to sigh; 10
One form shall rise above the wreck,
One name, Ianthe, shall not die.
1831

MILD IS THE PARTING YEAR

Mild is the parting year, and sweet
The odor of the falling spray;
Life passes on more rudely fleet,
And balmless is its closing day.

I wait its close, I court its gloom,
But mourn that never must there fall
Or on my breast or on my tomb
The tear that would have soothed it all.
1831

EPITAPH AT FIESOLÈ

Lo! where the four mimosas blend their
shade,
In calm repose at last is Landor laid;
For ere he slept he saw them planted here
By her his soul had ever held most dear,
And he had lived enough when he had
dried her tear.
1831

THE MAID'S LAMENT

I loved him not; and yet now he is gone
I feel I am alone.
I checked him while he spoke; yet could
he speak,
Alas! I would not check.

For reasons not to love him once I sought, 5
  And wearied all my thought
To vex myself and him: I now would give
  My love, could he but live
Who lately lived for me, and when he
  found
    'Twas vain, in holy ground   10
He hid his face amid the shades of death.
I waste for him my breath
Who wasted his for me: but mine returns,
  And this lorn bosom burns
With stifling heat, heaving it up in sleep, 15
  And waking me to weep

Tears that had melted his soft heart: for
  years
  Wept he as bitter tears.
Merciful God! such was his latest prayer,
  These may she never share.   20
Quieter is his breath, his breast more cold,
  Than daisies in the mold,
Where children spell, athwart the church-
  yard gate,
  His name, and life's brief date.
Pray for him, gentle souls, whoe'er you
  be,   25
  And, O! pray too for me.

1834

FROM IMAGINARY CONVERSATIONS

BISHOP BURNET AND HUMPHRY HARDCASTLE

"MR. GEORGE" (LORD BYRON)

Mr. George began with satirising his father's friends, and confounding the bet- 10 ter part of them with all the hirelings and nuisances of the age, with all the scavengers of lust and all the link-boys of literature; with Newgate solicitors, the patrons of adulterers and forgers, who, in the long 15 vacation, turn a penny by puffing a ballad, and are promised a shilling in silver, for their own benefit, on crying down a religious tract. He soon became reconciled to the latter, and they raised him upon their 20 shoulders above the heads of the wittiest and the wisest. This served a whole winter. Afterwards, whenever he wrote a bad poem, he supported his sinking fame by some signal act of profligacy, an elegy by a 25 seduction, an heroic by an adultery, a tragedy by a divorce. On the remark of a learned man, that irregularity is no indication of genius, he began to lose ground rapidly, when on a sudden he cried out at 30 the Haymarket, "There is no God!" It was then surmised more generally and more gravely that there was something in him, and he stood upon his legs almost to the last. "Say what you will," once whis- 35 pered a friend of mine, "there are things in him as strong as poison, and as original as sin." . . .

At last he is removed from among the living: let us hope the best; to wit, that 40 the mercies which have begun with man's forgetfulness will be crowned with God's forgiveness.

1822   1824

NOTE TO THE ABOVE, 1824

Little did I imagine that the extraordinary man, the worst parts of whose character are represented here, should indeed have been carried to the tomb so immaturely. If, before the dialogue was printed, he had performed those services to Greece which will render his name illustrious to eternity, those by which he merited such funereal honors as, in the parsimony of praise, knowing its value in republics, she hardly would have decreed to the most deserving of her heroes, if, I repeat it, he had performed those services, the performance of which I envy him from my soul, and as much as any other does the gifts of heaven he threw away so carelessly, never would I, from whatever provocation, have written a syllable against him. I had avoided him; I had slighted him; he knew it: he did not love me; he could not. While he spoke or wrote against me, I said nothing in print or conversation: the taciturnity of pride gave way to other feelings, when my friends, men so much better, and (let the sincerity of the expression be questioned by those who are unacquainted with us) so much dearer, so much oftener in my thoughts, were assailed by him too intemperately.

Let any man who has been unfair or injurious to me, show that he has been so to me only, and I offer him my hand at once, with more than mere forgiveness.

Alas! my writings are not upon slate: no finger, not of Time himself, who dips it in the clouds of years and in the storm and tempest, can efface the written. Let me be called what I may—I confess it, I am more inconsistent than he was. I do not talk of weeping or bewailing or lamenting, for I hate false words, and seek with care, difficulty, and moroseness, those that fit the thing—why then should I dissemble that, if I have shed no tears, they are at this moment in my eyes! O that I could have clasped his hand before he died! only to make him more enamored of his own virtues, and to keep him with them always!

A word to those who talk of inconsistency. There is as much of it in him who stands while another moves, as in him who moves while another stands. To condemn what is evil, and to commend what is good, is consistent: to retract an error, to soften an asperity, to speak all the good we can, after worse ill than we would, is that and more. If I must understand the word inconsistency as many do, I wish I may be inconsistent with all my enemies. I will take especial care that my inconsistency never makes me a worse man or a richer.

1826

SOUTHEY AND PORSON

WHY WORDSWORTH IS OBJECTED TO

Southey: Mr. Porson, it does not appear to me that anything more is necessary, in the first instance, than to interrogate our hearts in what manner they have been affected. If the ear is satisfied; if at one moment a tumult is aroused in the breast, and tranquillized at another, with a perfect consciousness of equal power exerted in both cases; if we rise up from a perusal of the work with a strong excitement to thought, to imagination, to sensibility; above all, if we sat down with some propensities toward evil, and walk away with much stronger toward good, in the midst of a world which we never had entered and of which we had never dreamed before —shall we perversely put on again the *old man* of criticism, and dissemble that we have been conducted by a most beneficent and most potent genius? Nothing proves to me so manifestly in what a pestiferous condition are its lazarettos, as when I observe how little hath been objected against those who have substituted words for things, and how much against those who have reinstated things for words.

Let Wordsworth prove to the world that there may be animation without blood and broken bones, and tenderness remote from the stews. Some will doubt it; for even things the most evident are often but little perceived and strangely estimated. Swift ridiculed the music of Handel and the generalship of Marlborough; Pope the perspicacity and the scholarship of Bentley; Gray the abilities of Shaftesbury and the eloquence of Rousseau. Shakspeare hardly found those who would collect his tragedies; Milton was read from Godliness; Virgil was antiquated and rustic; Cicero, Asiatic. What a rabble has persecuted my friend! An elephant is born to be consumed by ants in the midst of his unapproachable solitudes: Wordsworth is the prey of Jeffrey. Why repine? Let us rather amuse ourselves with allegories, and recollect that God in the creation left His noblest creature at the mercy of a serpent.

1823

FLORENTINE, ENGLISH VISITOR, AND LANDOR

ROME, KEATS, AND SHELLEY

Landor: I do not assert that my grief remains for days, or even hours together, violent or unremitted, although it has done so once or twice: but seldom have I thought of a friend or companion, be it at the distance of thirty or forty years, that the thought is not as intense and painful, and of as long a visitation, as it was at first. Even those with whom I have not lived, and whom indeed I have never seen, affect me by sympathy, as though I had known them intimately, and I hold with them in my walks many imaginary conversations. If anything could engage me to visit Rome, to endure the sight of her scarred and awful ruins, telling their grave stories upon the ground in the midst of eunuchs and fiddlers; if I could let charnel-houses and opera-houses, consuls and popes, tribunes and cardinals, orators and preachers, clash in my mind, it would be that I might afterwards spend an hour in solitude where the pyramid of Cestius points to the bones of Keats and Shelley. Nothing so attracts my heart as ruins in deserts, or so repels it as ruins in the circle of fashion. What is so shocking as the hard verity of Death swept by the rustling masquerade of Life! and does not Mortality of herself teach us how little we are, without placing us amidst the trivialities of patchwork pomp, where Virgil led the gods to found an empire, where Cicero saved and Caesar shook the world! . . .

Let me return to Shelley. Innocent and careless as a boy, he possessed all the delicate feelings of a gentleman, all the discrimination of a scholar, and united, in just degrees, the ardor of the poet with the patience and forbearance of the philosopher. His generosity and charity went far beyond those of any man (I believe) at present in existence. He was never known to speak evil of an enemy, unless that enemy had done some grievous injustice to another: and he divided his income of only one thousand pounds, with the fallen and afflicted.

This is the man against whom such clamors have been raised by the religious *à la mode*, and by those who live and lap under their tables: this is the man whom, from one false story about his former wife, I had refused to visit at Pisa. I blush in anguish at my prejudice and injustice, and ought hardly to feel it as a blessing or a consolation, that I regret him less than I should have done if I had known him personally. As to what remains of him now life is over, he occupies the third place among our poets of the present age—no humble station—for no other age since that of Sophocles has produced on the whole earth so many of such merits—and is incomparably the most elegant, graceful, and harmonious of the prose writers.

1829

MARCELLUS AND HANNIBAL

Hannibal. Could a Numidian horseman ride no faster? Marcellus! ho! Marcellus! He moves not—he is dead. Did he not stir his fingers? Stand wide, soldiers—wide, forty paces—give him air—bring water—halt! Gather those broad leaves, and all the rest, growing under the brushwood—unbrace his armor. Loose the helmet first—his breast rises. I fancied his eyes were fixed on me—they have rolled back again. Who presumed to touch my shoulder? This horse? It was surely the horse of Marcellus! Let no man mount him. Ha! ha! the Romans, too, sink into luxury: here is gold about the charger.

Gaulish Chieftain. Execrable thief! The golden chain of our king under a beast's grinders! The vengeance of the gods hath overtaken the impure——

Hannibal. We will talk about vengeance when we have entered Rome, and about purity among the priests, if they will hear us. Sound for the surgeon. That arrow may be extracted from the side, deep as it is.—The conqueror of Syracuse lies before me.—Send a vessel off to Carthage. Say Hannibal is at the gates of Rome.—Marcellus, who stood alone between us, fallen. Brave man! I would rejoice and cannot. How awfully serene a countenance! Such as we hear are in the Islands of the Blessed. And how glorious a form and stature! Such too was theirs! They also once lay thus upon the earth wet with their blood—few other enter there. And what plain armor!

Gaulish Chieftain. My party slew him—indeed I think I slew him myself. I claim the chain: it belongs to my king; the glory of Gaul requires it. Never will she endure to see another take it.

Hannibal. My friend, the glory of Marcellus did not require him to wear it. When he suspended the arms of your brave king in the temple, he thought such a trinket unworthy of himself and of Jupiter. The shield he battered down, the breastplate he pierced with his sword—these he showed to the people and to the gods; hardly his wife and little children saw this, ere his horse wore it.

Gaulish Chieftain. Hear me, O Hannibal!

Hannibal. What! when Marcellus lies before me? when his life may perhaps be recalled? when I may lead him in triumph to Carthage? when Italy, Sicily, Greece, Asia, wait to obey me? Content thee! I will give thee mine own bridle, worth ten such.

Gaulish Chieftain. For myself?

Hannibal. For thyself.

Gaulish Chieftain. And these rubies and emeralds, and that scarlet——

Hannibal. Yes, yes.

Gaulish Chieftain. O glorious Hannibal! unconquerable hero! O my happy country! to have such an ally and defender. I swear eternal gratitude—yes, gratitude, love, devotion, beyond eternity.

Hannibal. In all treaties we fix the time: I could hardly ask a longer. Go back to thy station.— I would see what the surgeon is about, and hear what he thinks. The life of Marcellus! the triumph of Hannibal! what else has the world in it? Only Rome and Carthage: these follow.

Marcellus. I must die then? The gods be praised! The commander of a Roman army is no captive.

Hannibal (to the Surgeon). Could not he bear a sea-voyage. Extract the arrow.

Surgeon. He expires that moment.

Marcellus. It pains me: extract it.

Hannibal. Marcellus, I see no expression of pain on your countenance, and never will I consent to hasten the death of an enemy in my power. Since your recovery is hopeless, you say truly you are no captive.

(To the Surgeon.) Is there nothing, man, that can assuage the mortal pain? for, suppress the signs of it as he may, he must feel it. Is there nothing to alleviate and allay it?

Marcellus. Hannibal, give me thy hand —thou hast found it and brought it me, compassion.

(To the Surgeon.) Go, friend; others want thy aid; several fell around me.

Hannibal. Recommend to your country, O Marcellus, while time permits it, reconciliation and peace with me, informing the Senate of my superiority in force, and the impossibility of resistance. The tablet is ready: let me take off this ring—try to write, to sign it, at least. Oh, what satisfaction I feel at seeing you able to rest upon the elbow, and even to smile!

Marcellus. Within an hour or less, with how severe a brow would Minos say to me, "Marcellus, is this thy writing?"

Rome loses one man: she hath lost many such, and she still hath many left.

Hannibal. Afraid as you are of falsehood, say you this? I confess in shame the ferocity of my countrymen. Unfortunately, too, the nearer posts are occupied by Gauls, infinitely more cruel. The Numidians are so in revenge: the Gauls both in revenge and in sport. My presence is required at a distance, and I apprehend the barbarity of one or other, learning, as they must do, your refusal to execute my wishes for the common good, and feeling that by this refusal you deprive them of their country, after so long an absence.

Marcellus. Hannibal, thou art not dying.

Hannibal. What then? What mean you?

Marcellus. That thou mayest, and very justly, have many things yet to apprehend: I can have none. The barbarity of thy soldiers is nothing to me: mine would not dare be cruel. Hannibal is forced to be absent; and his authority goes away with his horse. On the turf lies defaced the semblance of a general; but Marcellus is yet the regulator of his army. Dost thou abdicate a power conferred on thee by thy nation? Or wouldst thou acknowlelge it to have become, by thy own sole fault, less plenary than thy adversary's?

I have spoken too much; let me rest; this mantle oppresses me.

Hannibal. I placed my mantle on your head when the helmet was first removed, and while you were lying in the sun. Let me fold it under, and then replace the ring.

Marcellus. Take it, Hannibal. It was given me by a poor woman who flew to me at Syracuse, and who covered it with her hair, torn off in desperation that she had no other gift to offer. Little thought I that her gift and her words should be mine. How suddenly may the most powerful be in the situation of the most helpless! Let that ring and the mantle under my head be the exchange of guests at parting. The time may come, Hannibal, when thou (and the gods alone know whether as conqueror or conquered) mayest sit under the roof of my children, and in either case it shall serve thee. In thy adverse fortune, they will remember on whose pillow their father breathed his last; in thy prosperous (Heaven grant it may shine upon thee in some other country!), it will rejoice thee to protect them. We feel ourselves the most exempt from affliction when we relieve it, although we are then the most conscious that it may befall us.

There is one thing here which is not at the disposal of either.

Hannibal. What?

Marcellus. This body.

Hannibal. Whither would you be lifted? Men are ready.

Marcellus. I meant not so. My strength is failing. I seem to hear rather what is within than what is without. My sight and other senses are in confusion. I would have said—This body, when a few bubbles of air shall have left it, is no more worthy of thy notice than of mine; but thy glory will not let thee refuse it to the piety of my family.

Hannibal. You would ask something else. I perceive an inquietude not visible till now.

Marcellus. Duty and Death make us think of home sometimes.

Hannibal. Thitherward the thoughts of the conqueror and of the conquered fly together.

Marcellus. Hast thou any prisoners from my escort?

Hannibal. A few dying lie about—and let them lie—they are Tuscans. The remainder I saw at a distance, flying, and but one brave man among them—he appeared a Roman—a youth who turned back, though wounded. They surrounded and dragged him away, spurring his horse with their swords. These Etrurians measure their courage carefully, and tack it well together before they put it on, but throw it off again with lordly ease.

Marcellus, why think about them? or does aught else disquiet your thoughts?

Marcellus. I have suppressed it long enough. My son—my beloved son.

Hannibal. Where is he? Can it be? Was he with you?

Marcellus. He would have shared my fate—and has not. Gods of my country! beneficent throughout life to me, in death surpassingly beneficent: I render you, for the last time, thanks.

1828

METELLUS AND MARIUS

Metellus. Well met, Caius Marius! My orders are to find instantly a centurion who shall mount the walls; one capable of observation, acute in remark, prompt, calm, active, intrepid. The Numantians are sacrificing to the gods in secrecy; they have sounded the horn once only,—and hoarsely and low and mournfully.

Marius. Was that ladder I see yonder among the caper-bushes and purple lilies, under where the fig-tree grows out of the rampart, left for me?

Metellus. Even so, wert thou willing. Wouldst thou mount it?

Marius. Rejoicingly. If none are below or near, may I explore the state of things by entering the city?

Metellus. Use thy discretion in that. What seest thou? Wouldst thou leap down? Lift the ladder.

Marius. Are there spikes in it where it sticks in the turf? I should slip else.

Metellus. How! bravest of the centurions, art even thou afraid? Seest thou any one by?

Marius. Ay; some hundreds close beneath me.

Metellus. Retire, then. Hasten back; I will protect thy descent.

Marius. May I speak, O Metellus, without an offence to discipline?

Metellus. Say.

Marius. Listen! Dost thou not hear?

Metellus. Shame on thee! alight, alight! my shield shall cover thee.

Marius. There is a murmur like the hum of bees in the bean-field of Cereate;

for the sun is hot, and the ground is thirsty. When will it have drunk up for me the blood that has run, and is yet oozing on it, from those fresh bodies!

Metellus. How! We have not fought for many days; what bodies, then, are fresh ones?

Marius. Close beneath the wall are those of infants and of girls; in the middle of the road are youths, emaciated; some either unwounded or wounded months ago; some on their spears, others on their swords: no few have received in mutual death the last interchange of friendship; their daggers unite them, hilt to hilt, bosom to bosom.

Metellus. Mark rather the living,—what are they about?

Marius. About the sacrifice, which portends them, I conjecture, but little good,—it burns sullenly and slowly. The victim will lie upon the pyre till morning, and still be unconsumed, unless they bring more fuel.

I will leap down and walk on cautiously, and return with tidings, if death should spare me.

Never was any race of mortals so unmilitary as these Numantians; no watch, no stations, no palisades across the streets.

Metellus. Did they want, then, all the wood for the altar?

Marius. It appears so—I will return anon.

Metellus. The gods speed thee, my brave, honest Marius!

Marius (returned). The ladder should have been better spiked for that slippery ground. I am down again safe, however. Here a man may walk securely, and without picking his steps.

Metellus. Tell me, Caius, what thou sawest.

Marius. The streets of Numantia.

Metellus. Doubtless; but what else?

Marius. The temples and markets and places of exercise and fountains.

Metellus. Art thou crazed, centurion? what more? Speak plainly, at once, and briefly.

Marius. I beheld, then, all Numantia.

Metellus. Has terror maddened thee? hast thou descried nothing of the inhabitants but those carcasses under the ramparts?

Marius. Those, O Metellus, lie scattered, although not indeed far asunder. The greater part of the soldiers and citizens—of the fathers, husbands, widows, wives, espoused—were assembled together.

Metellus. About the altar?

Marius. Upon it.

Metellus. So busy and earnest in devotion! but how all upon it?

Marius. It blazed under them, and over them, and round about them.

Metellus. Immortal gods! Art thou sane, Caius Marius? Thy visage is scorched: thy speech may wander after such an enterprise; thy shield burns my hand.

Marius. I thought it had cooled again. Why, truly, it seems hot: I now feel it.

Metellus. Wipe off those embers.

Marius. 'Twere better: there will be none opposite to shake them upon for some time.

The funereal horn, that sounded with such feebleness, sounded not so from the faint heart of him who blew it. Him I saw; him only of the living. Should I say it? there was another: there was one child whom its parent could not kill, could not part from. She had hidden it in her robe, I suspect; and, when the fire reached it, either it shrieked or she did. For suddenly a cry pierced through the cıackling pinewood, and something of round in figure fell from brand to brand, until it reached the pavement, at the feet of him who had blown the horn. I rushed toward him, for I wanted to hear the whole story, and felt the pressure of time. Condemn not my weakness, O Cæcilius! I wished an enemy to live an hour longer; for my orders were to explore and bring intelligence. When I gazed on him, in height almost gigantic, I wondered not that the blast of his trumpet was so weak; rather did I wonder that Famine, whose hand had indented every limb and feature, had left him any voice articulate. I rushed toward him, however, ere my eyes had measured either his form or strength. He held the child against me, and staggered under it.

"Behold," he exclaimed, "the glorious ornament of a Roman triumph!"

I stood horror-stricken; when suddenly drops, as of rain, pattered down from the pyre. I looked; and many were the precious stones, many were the amulets and rings and bracelets, and other barbaric ornaments, unknown to me in form or purpose, that tinkled on the hardened and black branches, from mothers and wives and betrothed maids; and some, too, I can imagine, from robuster arms—things of joyance, won in battle. The crowd of incumbent bodies was so dense and heavy, that neither the fire nor the smoke could penetrate upward from among them; and they

sank, whole and at once, into the smoldering cavern eaten out below. He at whose neck hung the trumpet felt this, and started.

"There is yet room," he cried, "and there is strength enough yet, both in the element and in me."

He extended his withered arms, he thrust forward the gaunt links of his throat, and upon gnarled knees, that smote each other audibly, tottered into the civic fire. It—like some hungry and strangest beast on the innermost wild of Africa, pierced, broken, prostrate, motionless, gazed at by its hunter in the impatience of glory, in the delight of awe—panted once more, and seized him.

I have seen within this hour, O Metellus, what Rome in the cycle of her triumphs will never see, what the Sun in his eternal course can never show her, what the Earth has borne but now, and must never rear again for her, what Victory herself has envied her,—a Numantian.

Metellus. We shall feast tomorrow. Hope, Caius Marius, to become a tribune; trust in fortune.

Marius. Auguries are surer: surest of all is perseverance.

Metellus. I hope the wine has not grown vapid in my tent: I have kept it waiting, and must now report to Scipio the intelligence of our discovery. Come after me, Caius.

Marius (alone). The tribune is the discoverer! the centurion is the scout! Caius Marius must enter more Numantias. Lighthearted Cæcilius, thou mayest perhaps hereafter, and not with humbled but with exulting pride, take orders from this hand. If Scipio's words are fate, and to me they sound so, the portals of the Capitol may shake before my chariot, as my horses plunge back at the applauses of the people, and Jove in his high domicile may welcome the citizen of Arpinum.

1829

LEOFRIC AND GODIVA

Godiva. There is a dearth in the land, my sweet Leofric! Remember how many weeks of drought we have had, even in the deep pastures of Leicestershire; and how many Sundays we have heard the same prayers for rain, and supplications that it would please the Lord in his mercy to turn aside his anger from the poor, pining cattle. You, my dear husband, have imprisoned more than one malefactor for leaving his dead ox in the public way; and other hinds have fled before you out of the traces, in which they, and their sons and their daughters, and haply their old fathers and mothers, were dragging the abandoned wain homeward. Although we were accompanied by many brave spearmen and skilful archers, it was perilous to pass the creatures which the farmyard dogs, driven from the hearth by the poverty of their masters, were tearing and devouring; while others, bitten and lamed, filled the air either with long and deep howls or sharp and quick barkings, as they struggled with hunger and feebleness, or were exasperated by heat and pain. Nor could the thyme from the heath, nor the bruised branches of the fir-tree, extinguish or abate the foul odor.

Leofric. And now, Godiva, my darling, thou art afraid we should be eaten up before we enter the gates of Coventry; or perchance that in the gardens there are no roses to greet thee, no sweet herbs for thy mat and pillow.

Godiva. Leofric, I have no such fears. This is the month of roses: I find them everywhere since my blessed marriage. They, and all other sweet herbs, I know not why, seem to greet me wherever I look at them, as though they knew and expected me. Surely they cannot feel that I am fond of them.

Leofric. O light, laughing simpleton! But what wouldst thou? I came not hither to pray; and yet if praying would satisfy thee, or remove the drought, I would ride up straightway to Saint Michael's and pray until morning.

Godiva. I would do the same, O Leofric! but God hath turned away his ear from holier lips than mine. Would my own dear husband hear me, if I implored him for what is easier to accomplish,—what he can do like God?

Leofric. How! what is it?

Godiva. I would not, in the first hurry of your wrath, appeal to you, my loving lord, in behalf of these unhappy men who have offended you.

Leofric. Unhappy! is that all?

Godiva. Unhappy they must surely be, to have offended you so grievously. What a soft air breathes over us! how quiet and serene and still an evening! how calm are the heavens and the earth!—Shall none enjoy them; not even we, my Leofric? The sun is ready to set: let it never set, O Leofric, on your anger. These are not my words: they are better than mine. Should

they lose their virtue from my unworthiness in uttering them?

Leofric. Godiva, wouldst thou plead to me for rebels?

Godiva. They have, then, drawn the sword against you? Indeed, I knew it not.

Leofric. They have omitted to send me my dues, established by my ancestors, well knowing of our nuptials, and of the charges and festivities they require, and that in a season of such scarcity my own lands are insufficient.

Godiva. If they were starving, as they said they were——

Leofric. Must I starve too? Is it not enough to lose my vassals?

Godiva. Enough! O God! too much! too much! May you never lose them! Give them life, peace, comfort, contentment. There are those among them who kissed me in my infancy, and who blessed me at the baptismal font. Leofric, Leofric! the first old man I meet I shall think is one of those; and I shall think on the blessing he gave me, and (ah me!) on the blessing I bring back to him. My heart will bleed, will burst; and he will weep at it! he will weep, poor soul, for the wife of a cruel lord who denounces vengeance on him, who carries death into his family!

Leofric. We must hold solemn festivals.

Godiva. We must, indeed.

Leofric. Well, then?

Godiva. Is the clamorousness that succeeds the death of God's dumb creatures, are crowded halls, are slaughtered cattle, festivals?—are maddening songs, and giddy dances, and hireling praises from parti-colored coats? Can the voice of a minstrel tell us better things of ourselves than our own internal one might tell us; or can his breath make our breath softer in sleep? O my beloved! let everything be a joyance to us: it will, if we will. Sad is the day, and worse must follow, when we hear the blackbird in the garden, and do not throb with joy. But, Leofric, the high festival is strown by the servant of God upon the heart of man. It is gladness, it is thanksgiving; it is the orphan, the starveling, pressed to the bosom, and bidden as its first commandment to remember its benefactor. We will hold this festival; the guests are ready; we may keep it up for weeks, and months, and years together, and always be the happier and richer for it. The beverage of this feast, O Leofric, is sweeter than bee or flower or vine can give us: it flows from heaven; and in heaven will it abundantly be poured out again to him who pours it out here unsparingly.

Leofric. Thou art wild.

Godiva. I have, indeed, lost myself. Some Power, some good kind Power, melts me (body and soul and voice) into tenderness and love. O my husband, we must obey it. Look upon me! look upon me! lift your sweet eyes from the ground! I will not cease to supplicate; I dare not.

Leofric. We may think upon it.

Godiva. Never say that! What! think upon goodness when you can be good? Let not the infants cry for sustenance! The mother of our blessed Lord will hear them; us never, never afterward.

Leofric. Here comes the Bishop: we are but one mile from the walls. Why dismountest thou? no bishop can expect it. Godiva! my honor and rank among men are humbled by this. Earl Godwin will hear of it. Up! up! the Bishop hath seen it: he urgeth his horse onward. Dost thou not hear him now upon the solid turf behind thee?

Godiva. Never, no, never will I rise, O Leofric, until you remit this most impious tax—this tax on hard labor, on hard life.

Leofric. Turn round: look how the fat nag canters, as to the tune of a sinner's psalm, slow and hard-breathing. What reason or right can the people have to complain, while their bishop's steed is so sleek and well caparisoned? Inclination to change, desire to abolish old usages.—Up! up! for shame! They shall smart for it, idlers! Sir Bishop, I must blush for my young bride.

Godiva. My husband, my husband! will you pardon the city?

Leofric. Sir Bishop! I could not think you would have seen her in this plight. Will I pardon? Yea, Godiva, by the holy rood, will I pardon the city when thou ridest naked at noontide through the streets!

Godiva. O my dear, cruel Leofric, where is the heart you gave me? It was not so: can mine have hardened it?

Bishop. Earl, thou abashest thy spouse; she turneth pale, and weepeth. Lady Godiva, peace be with thee.

Godiva. Thanks, holy man! peace will be with me when peace is with your city. Did you hear my lord's cruel word?

Bishop. I did, lady.

Godiva. Will you remember it, and pray against it?

Bishop. Wilt *thou* forget it, daughter?

Godiva. I am not offended.

Bishop. Angel of peace and purity!

Godiva. But treasure it up in your heart: deem it an incense, good only when it is consumed and spent, ascending with prayer and sacrifice. And, now, what was it?

Bishop. Christ save us! that he will pardon the city when thou ridest naked through the streets at noon.

Godiva. Did he not swear an oath?

Bishop. He sware by the holy rood.

Godiva. My Redeemer, thou hast heard it! save the city!

Leofric. We are now upon the beginning of the pavement: these are the suburbs. Let us think of feasting: we may pray afterward; tomorrow we shall rest.

Godiva. No judgments, then, tomorrow, Leofric?

Leofric. None: we will carouse.

Godiva. The saints of heaven have given me strength and confidence; my prayers are heard; the heart of my beloved is now softened.

Leofric (aside). Ay, ay—they shall smart, though.

Godiva. Say, dearest Leofric, is there indeed no other hope, no other mediation?

Leofric. I have sworn. Besides, thou hast made me redden and turn my face away from thee, and all the knaves have seen it: this adds to the city's crime.

Godiva. I have blushed, too, Leofric, and was not rash nor obdurate.

Leofric. But thou, my sweetest, art given to blushing: there is no conquering it in thee. I wish thou hadst not alighted so hastily and roughly: it hath shaken down a sheaf of thy hair. Take heed thou sit not upon it, lest it anguish thee. Well done! it mingleth now sweetly with the cloth of gold upon the saddle, running here and there, as if it had life and faculties and business, and were working thereupon some newer and cunninger device. O my beauteous Eve! there is a Paradise about thee! the world is refreshed as thou movest and breathest on it. I cannot see or think of evil where thou art. I could throw my arms even here about thee. No signs for me! no shaking of sunbeams! no reproof or frown or wonderment—I *will* say it—now, then, for worse—I could close with my kisses thy half-open lips, ay, and those lovely and loving eyes, before the people.

Godiva. Tomorrow you shall kiss me, and they shall bless you for it. I shall be very pale, for tonight I must fast and pray.

Leofric. I do not hear thee; the voice

of the folk are so loud under this archway.

Godiva (to herself). God help them!
good kind souls! I hope they will not
crowd about me so tomorrow. O Leofric!
could my name be forgotten, and yours 5
alone remembered! But perhaps my innocence may save me from reproach; and how
many as innocent are in fear and famine!
No eye will open on me but fresh from
tears. What a young mother for so large 10
a family! Shall my youth harm me? Under
God's hand it gives me courage. Ah! when
will the morning come? Ah! when will
the noon be over?

1829 15

from PERICLES AND ASPASIA

Pericles to Aspasia 20

Do you love me? do you love me? Stay,
reason upon it, sweet Aspasia! doubt, hesitate, question, drop it, take it up again,
provide, raise obstacles, reply directly. 25
Oracles are sacred, and there is a pride in
being a diviner.

Aspasia to Pericles

I will do none of those things you tell
me to do; but I will say something you for- 30
got to say, about the insufficiency of
Phidias.

He may represent a hero with unbent 35
brows, a sage with the lyre of Poetry in his
hand, Ambition with her face half-averted
from the City, but he cannot represent, in
the same sculpture, at the same distance,
Aphrodite higher than Pallas. He would 40
be derided if he did; and a great man can
never do that for which a little man may
deride him.

I shall love you even more than I do, if
you will love yourself more than me. Did 45
ever lover talk so? Pray tell me, for I have
forgotten all they ever talked about. But,
Pericles! Pericles! be careful to lose nothing of your glory, or you lose all that can
be lost of me; my pride, my happiness, my 50
content; everything but my poor weak love;
keep glory then for my sake!

Aspasia to Pericles

When the war is over, as surely it must
be in another year, let us sail among the 55
islands of the Ægean, and be young as
ever. O that it were permitted us to pass
together the remainder of our lives in 60

privacy and retirement! This is never to
be hoped for in Athens.

I inherit from my mother a small yet
beautiful house in Tenos: I remember it
well. Water, clear and cold, ran before
the vestibule: a sycamore shaded the whole
building. I think Tenos must be nearer
to Athens than to Miletus. Could we not
go now for a few days? How temperate
was the air, how serene the sky, how beautiful the country! the people how quiet,
how gentle, how kind-hearted!

Is there any station so happy as an un-
contested place in a small community,
where manners are simple, where wants are
few, where respect is the tribute of probity,
and love is the guerdon of beneficence. O
Pericles! let us go; we can return at any
time.

Aspasia to Pericles

Now the fever is raging, and we are
separated, my comfort and delight is in
our little Pericles. The letters you send
me come less frequently, but I know you
write whenever your duties will allow you,
and whenever men are found courageous
enough to take charge of them. Although
you preserved with little care the speeches
you delivered formerly, yet you promised
me a copy of the latter, and as many of the
earlier as you could collect among your
friends. Let me have them as soon as
possible. Whatever bears the traces of
your hand is precious to me: how greatly
more precious what is imprest with your
genius, what you have meditated and
spoken! I shall see your calm thoughtful
face while I am reading, and will be cautious not to read aloud lest I lose the
illusion of your voice.

Aspasia to Pericles

Gratitude to the immortal Gods overpowers every other impulse of my breast.
You are safe.

Pericles! O my Pericles! come into this
purer air! live life over again in the smiles
of your child, in the devotion of your
Aspasia! Why did you fear for me the
plague within the city, the Spartans round
it? why did you exact the vow at parting,
that nothing but your command should
recall me again to Athens? Why did I
ever make it? Cruel! to refuse me the full
enjoyment of your recovered health!
crueller to keep me in ignorance of its
decline! The happiest of pillows is not

that which Love first presses; it is that which Death has frowned on and passed over.

Aspasia to Pericles

Where on earth is there so much society as in a beloved child? He accompanies me in my walks, gazes into my eyes for what I am gathering from books, tells me more and better things than they do, and asks me often what neither I nor they can answer. When he is absent I am filled with reflections, when he is present I have room for none beside what I receive from him. The charms of his childhood bring me back to the delights of mine, and I fancy I hear my own words in a sweeter voice. Will he (O how I tremble at the mute Oracle of futurity!) will he ever be as happy as I have been? Alas! and must he ever be as subject to fears and apprehensions? No; thanks to the gods! never, never. He carries his father's heart within his breast. I see him already an orator and a leader. I try to teach him daily some of his father's looks and gestures, and I never smile but at his docility and gravity. How his father will love him! the little thunderer! the winner of cities! the vanquisher of Cleones!

Pericles to Aspasia

The pestilence has taken from me both my sons. You, who were ever so kind and affectionate to them, will receive a tardy recompense, in hearing that the least gentle and the least grateful did acknowledge it. I mourn for Paralus, because he loved me; for Xanthippos because he loved me not.

Preserve with all your maternal care our little Pericles. I cannot be fonder of him than I have always been; I can only fear more for him.

Is he not with my Aspasia? What fears then are so irrational as mine? But oh! I am living in a widowed house, a house of desolation! I am living in a city of tombs and torches! and the last I saw before me were for my children.

Pericles to Aspasia

It is right and orderly, that he who has partaken so largely in the prosperity of the Athenians, should close the procession of their calamities. The fever that has depopulated our city, returned upon me last night, and Hippocrates and Acron tell me that my end is near.

When we agreed, O Aspasia, in the beginning of our loves, to communicate our thoughts by writing, even while we were both in Athens, and when we had many reasons for it, we little foresaw the more powerful one that has rendered it necessary of late. We never can meet again. The laws forbid it, and love itself enforces them. Let wisdom be heard by you as imperturbably, and affection as authoritatively, as ever; and remember that the sorrow of Pericles can arise but from the bosom of Aspasia. There is only one word of tenderness we could say, which we have not said oftentimes before; and there is no consolation in it. The happy never say, and never hear said, farewell.

Reviewing the course of my life, it appears to me, at one moment, as if we met but yesterday; at another, as if centuries had past within it; for within it have existed the greater part of those who, since the origin of the world, have been the luminaries of the human race. Damon called me from my music to look at Aristides on his way to exile; and my father pressed the wrist by which he was leading me along, and whispered in my ear,

"Walk quickly by; glance cautiously; it is there Miltiades is in prison."

In my boyhood Pindar took me up in his arms, when he brought to our house the dirge he had composed for the funeral of my grandfather: in my adolescence I offered the rites of hospitality to Empedocles; not long afterward I embraced the neck of Æschylus, about to abandon his country. With Sophocles I have argued on eloquence; with Euripides on polity and ethics; I have discoursed, as became an inquirer, with Protagoras and Democritus, with Anaxagoras and Meton. From Herodotus I have listened to the most instructive history, conveyed in a language the most copious and the most harmonious; a man worthy to carry away the collected suffrages of universal Greece; a man worthy to throw open the temples of Egypt, and to celebrate the exploits of Cyrus. And from Thucydides, who alone can succeed to him, how recently did my Aspasia hear with me the energetic praises of his just supremacy!

As if the festival of life were incomplete, and wanted one great ornament to crown it, Phidias placed before us, in ivory and gold, the tutelary Deity of this land, and the Zeus of Homer and Olympus.

To have lived with such men, to have

enjoyed their familiarity and esteem, over-pays all labors and anxieties. I were un-worthy of the friendships I have commemo-rated, were I forgetful of the latest. Sacred it ought to be, formed as it was under the portico of Death, my friendship with the most sagacious, the most scientific, the most beneficent of philosophers, Acron and Hippocrates. If mortal could war against Pestilence and Destiny, they have been vic-torious. I leave them in the field: unfortu-nate he who finds them among the fallen!

And now, at the close of my day, when every light is dim, and every guest de-parted, let me own that these wane before me, remembering, as I do, in the pride and fulness of my heart, that Athens con-fided her glory and Aspasia her happiness to me.

Have I been a faithful guardian? do I resign them to the custody of the Gods undiminished and unimpaired? Welcome, then, welcome, my last hour! After en-joying for so great a number of years, in my public and my private life, what I be-lieve has never been the lot of any other, I now extend my hand to the urn, and take without reluctance or hesitation what is the lot of all.

1836

FROM THE PENTAMERON: FIFTH DAY

BOCCACCIO'S VISION OF HIS BELOVED

Boccaccio. In vain had I determined not only to mend in future, but to correct the past; in vain had I prayed most fer-vently for grace to accomplish it, with a final aspiration to Fiammetta that she would unite with your beloved Laura, and that, gentle and beatified spirits as they are, they would breathe together their purer prayers on mine. See what follows.

Petrarca. Sigh not at it. Before we can see all that follows from their intercession, we must join them again. But let me hear anything in which they are concerned.

Boccaccio. I prayed; and my breast, after some few tears, grew calmer. Yet sleep did not ensue until the break of morning, when the dropping of soft rain on the leaves of the fig-tree at the window, and the chirping of a little bird, to tell another there was shelter under them, brought me repose and slumber. Scarcely had I closed my eyes, if indeed time can be reckoned any more in sleep than in heaven, when my Fiammetta seemed to have led me into the meadow. You will see it below you: turn away that branch: gently! gently! do not break it; for the little bird sat there.

Petrarca. I think, Giovanni, I can divine the place. Although this fig-tree, growing out of the wall between the cellar and us, is fantastic enough in its branches, yet that other which I see yonder, bent down and forced to crawl along the grass by the pre-potency of the young shapely walnut tree, is much more so. It forms a seat, about a cubit above the ground, level and long enough for several.

Boccaccio. Ha! you fancy it must be a favorite spot with me, because of the two strong forked stakes wherewith it is propped and supported!

Petrarca. Poets know the haunts of poets at first sight; and he who loved Laura—O Laura! did I say he who *loved* thee?—hath whisperings where those feet would wander which have been restless after Fiammetta.

Boccaccio. It is true, my imagination has often conducted her thither; but here in this chamber she appeared to me more visibly in a dream.

"Thy prayers have been heard, O Gio-vanni," said she.

I sprang to embrace her.

"Do not spill the water! Ah! you have spilt a part of it."

I then observed in her hand a crystal vase. A few drops were sparkling on the sides and running down the rim; a few were trickling from the base and from the hand that held it.

"I must go down to the brook," said she, "and fill it again as it was filled before."

What a moment of agony was this to me! Could I be certain how long might be her absence? She went: I was follow-ing: she made a sign for me to turn back: I disobeyed her only an instant: yet my sense of disobedience, increasing my feeble-ness and confusion, made me lose sight of her. In the next moment she was again at my side, with the cup quite full. I stood motionless: I feared my breath might shake the water over. I looked her in the face for her commands—and to see it—to see it so calm, so beneficent, so beautiful. I was forgetting what I had prayed for, when she lowered her head, tasted of the cup, and gave it me. I drank; and suddenly sprang forth before me, many groves and palaces and gardens, and their statues and their avenues, and their labyrinths of alaternus

and bay, and alcoves of citron, and watchful loopholes in the retirements of impenetrable pomegranate. Farther off, just below where the fountain slipt away from its
marble hall and guardian gods, arose, from 5
their beds of moss and drosera and darkest
grass, the sisterhood of oleanders, fond of
tantalizing with their bosomed flowers and
their moist and pouting blossoms the little
shy rivulet, and of covering its face with 10
all the colors of the dawn. My dream expanded and moved forward. I trod again
the dust of Posilippo, soft as the feathers
in the wings of Sleep. I emerged on Baia;
I crossed her innumerable arches; I loitered 15
in the breezy sunshine of her mole; I
trusted the faithful seclusion of her caverns,
the keepers of so many secrets; and I reposed on the buoyancy of her tepid sea.
Then Naples, and her theatres and her 20
churches, and grottoes and dells and forts
and promontories, rushed forward in confusion, now among soft whispers, now
among sweetest sounds, and subsided, and
sank, and disappeared. Yet a memory 25
seemed to come fresh from every one: each
had time enough for its tale, for its pleasure, for its reflection, for its pang. As I
mounted with silent steps the narrow stair-
case of the old palace, how distinctly did 30
I feel against the palm of my hand the
coldness of that smooth stonework, and the
greater of the cramps of iron in it!

"Ah me! is this forgetting?" cried I
anxiously to Fiammetta.   35

"We must recall these scenes before us,"
she replied; "such is the punishment of
them. Let us hope and believe that the
apparition, and the compunction which
must follow it, will be accepted as the full 40
penalty, and that both will pass away almost together."

I feared to lose anything attendant on
her presence: I feared to approach her
forehead with my lips: I feared to touch 45
the lily on its long wavy leaf in her hair,
which filled my whole heart with fragrance.
Venerating, adoring, I bowed my head at
last to kiss her snow-white robe, and trembled at my presumption. And yet the 50
effulgence of her countenance vivified while
it chastened me. I loved her—I must not
say *more* than ever—*better* than ever; it
was Fiammetta who had inhabited the skies.
As my hand opened toward her,   55

"Beware!" said she, faintly smiling; "beware, Giovanni! Take only the crystal;
take it, and drink again."

"Must all be then forgotten?" said I
sorrowfully.

"Remember your prayer and mine, Giovanni. Shall both have been granted—O
how much worse than in vain!"

I drank instantly; I drank largely. How
cool my bosom grew; how could it grow so 5
cool before her! But it was not to remain
in its quiescency; its trials were not yet
over. I will not, Francesco! no, I may not
commemorate the incidents she related to
me, nor which of us said, "I blush for hav- 10
ing loved *first;*" nor which of us replied,
"Say *least,* say *least,* and blush again."

The charm of the words (for I felt not
the encumbrance of the body nor the acuteness of the spirit) seemed to possess me 15
wholly. Although the water gave me
strength and comfort, and somewhat of
celestial pleasure, many tears fell around
the border of the vase as she held it up 20
before me, exhorting me to take courage,
and inviting me with more than exhortation to accomplish my deliverance. She
came nearer, more tenderly, more earnestly;
she held the dewy globe with both hands,
leaning forward, and sighed and shook her 25
head, drooping at my pusillanimity. It was
only when a ringlet had touched the rim,
and perhaps the water (for a sunbeam on
the surface could never have given it such
a golden hue), that I took courage, clasped 30
it, and exhausted it. Sweet as was the
water, sweet as was the serenity it gave me
—alas! that also which it moved away from
me was sweet!

"This time you can trust me alone," said 35
she, and parted my hair, and kissed my
brow. Again she went toward the brook:
again my agitation, my weakness, my doubt,
came over me: nor could I see her while 40
she raised the water, nor knew I whence
she drew it. When she returned, she was
close to me at once: she smiled: her smile
pierced me to the bones: it seemed an
angel's. She sprinkled the pure water on 45
me; she looked most fondly; she took my
hand; she suffered me to press hers to my
bosom; but, whether by design I cannot
tell, she let fall a few drops of the chilly
element between.

"And now, O my beloved!" said she, "we 50
have consigned to the bosom of God our
earthly joys and sorrows. The joys cannot
return, let not the sorrows. These alone
would trouble my repose among the 55
blessed."

"Trouble thy repose! Fiammetta! Give
me the chalice!" cried I—"not a drop will
I leave in it, not a drop."

"Take it!" said that soft voice. "O now 60
most dear Giovanni! I know thou hast

strength enough; and there is but little—
at the bottom lies our first kiss."

"Mine! didst thou say, beloved one? and
is that left thee still?"

"*Mine,*" said she, pensively; and as she
abased her head, the broad leaf of the lily
hid her brow and her eyes; the light of
heaven shone through the flower.

"O Fiammetta! Fiammetta!" cried I in
agony, "God is the God of mercy, God is
the God of love—can I, can I ever?" I
struck the chalice against my head, unmindful that I held it; the water covered
my face and my feet. I started up, not
yet awake, and I heard the name of Fiammetta in the curtains.

Petrarca. Love, O Giovanni, and life
itself, are but dreams at best.

PETRARCH RELATES HIS DREAM OF SLEEP, LOVE, AND DEATH

Wearied with the length of my walk over
the mountains, and finding a soft old mole-
hill, covered with grey grass, by the wayside, I laid my head upon it and slept.
I can not tell how long it was before a
species of dream or vision came over me.
Two beautiful youths appeared beside me;
each was winged; but the wings were hanging down, and seemed ill adapted to flight.
One of them, whose voice was the softest
I ever heard, looking at me frequently, said
to the other, "He is under my guardian-
ship for the present: do not awaken him
with that feather." Methought, on hearing
the whisper, I saw something like the
feather on an arrow; and then the arrow
itself; the whole of it, even to the point;
although he carried it in such a manner
that it was difficult at first to discover more
than a palm's length of it; the rest of the
shaft (and the whole of the barb) was behind his ankles.

"This feather never awakens any one,"
replied he, rather petulantly; "but it brings
more of confident security, and more of
cherished dreams, than you, without me,
are capable of imparting."

"Be it so!" answered the gentler; "none
is less inclined to quarrel or dispute than
I am. Many whom you have wounded
grievously call upon me for succor; but so
little am I disposed to thwart you, it is
seldom I venture to do more for them
than to whisper a few words of comfort in
passing. How many reproaches on these
occasions have been cast upon me for indifference and infidelity! Nearly as many,

and nearly in the same terms, as upon
you!"

"Odd enough that we, O Sleep! should be
thought so alike!" said Love, contemptuously. "Yonder is he who bears a nearer
resemblance to you: the dullest have observed it." I fancied I turned my eyes to
where he was pointing, and saw at a distance the figure he designated. Meanwhile
the contention went on uninterruptedly.
Sleep was slow in asserting his power or
his benefits. Love recapitulated them; but
only that he might assert his own above
them. Suddenly he called on me to decide,
and to choose my patron. Under the influence, first of the one, then of the other,
I sprang from repose to rapture, I alighted
from rapture on repose, and knew not
which was sweetest. Love was very angry
with me, and declared he would cross me
throughout the whole of my existence.
Whatever I might on other occasions have
thought of his veracity, I now felt too
surely the conviction that he would keep
his word. At last, before the close of the
altercation, the third Genius had advanced,
and stood near us. I cannot tell how I
knew him, but I knew him to be the
Genius of Death. Breathless as I was at
beholding him, I soon became familiar
with his features. First they seemed only
calm; presently they grew contemplative;
and lastly beautiful: those of the Graces
themselves are less regular, less harmonious,
less composed. Love glanced at him un-
steadily, with a countenance in which there
was somewhat of anxiety, somewhat of disdain; and cried, "Go away! go away! nothing that thou touchest, lives!"

"Say rather, child!" replied the advancing form, and advancing grew loftier and
statelier, "say rather that nothing of beautiful or of glorious lives its own true life
until my wing hath passed over it."

Love pouted, and rumpled and bent
down with his forefinger the stiff short
feathers on his arrowhead; but replied not.
Although he frowned worse than ever, and
at me, I dreaded him less and less and
scarcely looked toward him. The milder
and calmer Genius, the third, in proportion
as I took courage to contemplate him, regarded me with more and more complacency. He held neither flower nor
arrow as the others did; but throwing back
the clusters of dark curls that overshadowed
his countenance. he presented to me his
hand, openly and benignly. I shrank on
looking at him so near, and yet I sighed to
love him. He smiled, not without an ex-

pression of pity, at perceiving my diffidence, my timidity: for I remembered how soft was the hand of Sleep, how warm and entrancing was Love's. By degrees I became ashamed of my ingratitude; and turning my face away, I held out my arms, and I felt my neck within his. Composure strewed and allayed all the throbbings of my bosom; the coolness of freshest morning breathed around, the heavens seemed to open above me; while the beautiful cheek of my deliverer rested on my head. I would now have looked for those others; but knowing my intention by my gesture, he said consolatorily,

"Sleep is on his way to the earth, where many are calling him; but it is not to these he hastens; for every call only makes him fly farther off. Sedately and gravely as he looks, he is nearly as capricious and volatile as the more arrogant and ferocious one."

"And Love!" said I, "whither is he departed? If not too late, I would propitiate and appease him."

"He who can not follow me, he who can not overtake and pass me," said the Genius, "is unworthy of the name, the most glorious in earth or heaven. Look up! Love is yonder, and ready to receive thee."

I looked: the earth was under me: I saw only the clear blue sky, and something brighter above it.

1837

THE DEATH OF ARTEMIDORA

"Artemidora! Gods invisible,
While thou art lying faint along the couch,
Have tied the sandal to thy veined feet
And stand beside thee, ready to convey
Thy weary steps where other rivers flow. 5
Refreshing shades will waft thy weariness
Away, and voices like thy own come nigh
Soliciting nor vainly thy embrace."
  Artemidora sighed, and would have
    pressed
The hand now pressing hers, but was too
    weak. 10
Fate's shears were over her dark hair un-
    seen
While thus Elpenor spake. He looked into
Eyes that had given light and life erewhile
To those above them, those now dim with
    tears
And watchfulness. Again he spake of
    joy 15
Eternal. At that word, that sad word, joy,
Faithful and fond her bosom heaved once
    more:
Her head fell back; one sob, one loud deep
    sob
Swelled through the darkened chamber;
    'twas not hers.
With her that old boat incorruptible, 20
Unwearied, undiverted in its course,
Had plashed the water up the farther
    strand.

1836

THE HAMADRYAD

Rhaicos was born amid the hills wherefrom
Gnidos, the light of Caria, is discerned,
And small are the white-crested that play
    near,

And smaller onward are the purple waves.
Thence festal choirs were visible, all
    crowned 5
With rose and myrtle if they were inborn;
If from Pandion sprang they, on the coast
Where stern Athene raised her citadel,
Then olive was entwined with violets
Clustered in bosses, regular and large. 10
For various men wore various coronals,
But one was their devotion; 'twas to her
Whose laws all follow, her whose smile
    withdraws
The sword from Ares, thunderbolt from
    Zeus,
And whom in his chill caves the mutable 15
Of mind, Poseidon, the sea-king, reveres,
And whom his brother, stubborn Dis, hath
    prayed
To turn in pity the averted cheek
Of her he bore away, with promises,
Nay, with loud oath before dread Styx
    itself, 20
To give her daily more and sweeter flowers
Than he made drop from her on Enna's
    dell.
  Rhaicos was looking from his father's
    door
At the long trains that hastened to the
    town
From all the valleys, like bright rivulets 25
Gurgling with gladness, wave outrunning
    wave,
And thought it hard he might not also go
And offer up one prayer, and press one
    hand,
He knew not whose. The father called
    him in
And said, "Son Rhaicos! those are idle
    games; 30
Long enough I have lived to find them so."
And ere he ended, sighed; as old men do

Always, to think how idle such games are.
"I have not yet," thought Rhaicos in his
    heart,
And wanted proof. "Suppose thou go and
    help   35
Echeion at the hill, to bark yon oak
And lop its branches off, before we delve
About the trunk and ply the root with axe;
This we may do in winter."
                                    Rhaicos went;
For thence he could see farther, and see
    more   40
Of those who hurried to the city gate.
Echeion he found there, with naked arm
Swart-haired, strong-sinewed, and his eyes
    intent
Upon the place where first the axe should
    fall:
He held it upright. "There are bees
    about,   45
Or wasps, or hornets," said the cautious
    eld,
"Look sharp, O son of Thallinos!" The
    youth
Inclined his ear, afar, and warily,
And caverned in his hand. He heard a
    buzz
At first, and then the sound grew soft and
    clear,   50
And then divided into what seemed tune,
And there were words upon it, plaintive
    words.
He turned, and said, "Echeion! do not
    strike
That tree; it must be hollow, for some god
Speaks from within. Come thyself near."
    Again   55
Both turned toward it; and behold! there
    sat
Upon the moss below, with her two palms
Pressing it, on each side, a maid in form.
Downcast were her long eyelashes, and pale
Her cheek, but never mountain ash dis-
    played   60
Berries of color like her lips so pure,
Nor were the anemones about her hair
Soft, smooth, and wavering like the face
    beneath.
    "What dost thou here?" Echeion, half-
    afraid,
Half-angry, cried. She lifted up her eyes, 65
But nothing spake she. Rhaicos drew one
    step
Backward, for fear came likewise over him,
But not such fear: he panted, gasped,
    drew in
His breath, and would have turned it into
    words,
But could not into one.
                    "O send away   70

That sad old man!" said she. The old
    man went
Without a warning from his master's son,
Glad to escape, for sorely he now feared;
And the axe shone behind him in their
    eyes.
    Hamad.   And wouldst thou too shed the
        most innocent   75
Of blood?   No vow demands it; no god
    wills
The oak to bleed.
    Rhaicos.   Who art thou? whence? why
        here?
And whither wouldst thou go?   Among the
    robed
In white or saffron, or the hue that most
Resembles dawn or the clear sky, is none 80
Arrayed as thou art.   What so beautiful
As that gray robe which clings about thee
    close,
Like moss to stones adhering, leaves to
    trees,
Yet lets thy bosom rise and fall in turn,
As, touched by zephyrs, fall and rise the
    boughs   85
Of graceful platane by the riverside?
    Hamad.   Lovest thou well thy father's
        house?
    Rhaicos.   Indeed
I love it, well I love it, yet would leave
For thine, where'er it be, my father's house,
With all the marks upon the door, that
    show   90
My growth at every birthday since the
    third,
And all the charms, o'erpowering evil eyes,
My mother nailed for me against my bed,
And the Cydonian bow (which thou shalt
    see)
Won in my race last spring from Euty-
    chos.   95
    Hamad.   Bethink thee what it is to leave
        a home
Thou never yet hast left, one night, one
    day.
    Rhaicos.   No, 'tis not hard to leave it;
        'tis not hard
To leave, O maiden, that paternal home,
If there be one on earth whom we may
    love   100
First, last, forever, one who says that she
Will love forever too.   To say which word,
Only to say it, surely is enough—
It shows such kindness—if 'twere possible
We at the moment think she would
    indeed.   105
    Hamad.   Who taught thee all this folly
        at thy age?
    Rhaicos.   I have seen lovers and have
        learned to love.

Hamad. But wilt thou spare the tree?
Rhaicos.   My father wants
The bark; the tree may hold its place
   awhile.
Hamad. Awhile! thy father numbers
   then my days?   110
Rhaicos. Are there no others where the
   moss beneath
Is quite as tufty? Who would send thee
   forth,
Or ask thee why thou tarriest? Is thy flock
Anywhere near?
Hamad.   I have no flock: I kill
Nothing that breathes, that stirs, that feels
   the air,   115
The sun, the dew. Why should the beau-
   tiful
(And thou art beautiful) disturb the source
Whence springs all beauty? Hast thou
   never heard
Of hamadryads?
Rhaicos.   Heard of them I have;
Tell me some tale about them. May I
   sit   120
Beside thy feet? Art thou not tired? The
   herbs
Are very soft; I will not come too nigh;
Do but sit there, nor tremble so, nor doubt.
Stay, stay an instant: let me first explore
If any acorn of last year be left   125
Within it; thy thin robe too ill protects
Thy dainty limbs against the harm one
   small
Acorn may do. Here's none. Another day
Trust me; till then let me sit opposite.
Hamad. I seat me; be thou seated, and
   content.   130
Rhaicos. O sight for gods! ye men below,
   adore
The Aphrodite! *Is* she there below?
Or sits she here before me? as she sate
Before the shepherd on those heights that
   shade
The Hellespont, and brought his kindred
   woe.   135
Hamad. Reverence the higher Powers;
   nor deem amiss
Of her who pleads to thee, and would
   repay—
Ask not how much—but very much. Rise
   not—
No, Rhaicos, no! Without the nuptial
   vow
Love is unholy. Swear to me that none 140
Of mortal maids shall ever taste thy kiss,
Then take thou mine; then take it, not
   before.
Rhaicos. Hearken, all gods above! O
   Aphrodite,
O Herè! Let my vow be ratified!

But wilt thou come into my father's
   house?   145
Hamad. Nay; and of mine I cannot give
   thee part.
Rhaicos. Where is it?
Hamad.   In this oak.
Rhaicos.   Ay, now begins
The tale of Hamadryad; tell it through.
Hamad. Pray of thy father never to cut
   down
My tree; and promise him, as well thou
   mayst,   150
That every year he shall receive from me
More honey than will buy him nine fat
   sheep,
More wax than he will burn to all the
   gods.
Why fallest thou upon thy face? Some
   thorn
May scratch it, rash young man! Rise up;
   for shame!   155
Rhaicos. For shame I cannot rise. O
   pity me!
I dare not sue for love—but do not hate!
Let me once more behold thee—not once
   more,
But many days; let me love on—unloved!
I aimed too high: on my own head the
   bolt   160
Falls back, and pierces to the very brain.
Hamad. Go—rather go than make me
   say I love.
Rhaicos. If happiness is immortality
(And whence enjoy it else the gods above?)
I am immortal too: my vow is heard— 165
Hark! on the left.—Nay, turn not from me
   now,
I claim my kiss.
Hamad. Do men take first, then claim?
Do thus the seasons run their course with
   them?

Her lips were sealed; her head sank on
   his breast.
'Tis said that laughs were heard within the
   wood;   170
But who should hear them? and whose
   laughs? and why?

Savory was the smell, and long past
   noon,
Thallinos, in thy house; for marjoram,
Basil and mint, and thyme and rosemary,
Were sprinkled on the kid's well-roasted
   length,   175
Awaiting Rhaicos. Home he came at last,
Not hungry, but pretending hunger keen,
With head and eyes just o'er the maple
   plate.

"Thou seest but badly, coming from the
    sun,
Boy Rhaicos!" said the father. "That oak's
    bark   180
Must have been tough, with little sap be-
    tween;
It ought to run; but it and I are old."
Rhaicos, although each morsel of the bread
Increased by chewing, and the meat grew
    cold
And tasteless to his palate, took a
    draught   185
Of gold-bright wine, which, thirsty as he
    was,
He thought not of, until his father filled
The cup, averring water was amiss,
But wine had been at all times poured on
    kid—
It was religion.   He, thus fortified,   190
Said, not quite boldly and not quite
    abashed,
"Father, that oak is Zeus's own; that oak
Year after year will bring thee wealth from
    wax
And honey. There is one who fears the
    gods
And the gods love;—that one" (he blushed,
    nor said   195
What one) "hast promised this, and may do
    more.
Thou hast not many moons to wait until
The bees have done their best; if then
    there come
Nor wax nor honey, let the tree be hewn."
    "Zeus hath bestowed on thee a prudent
    mind,"   200
Said the glad sire; "but look thou often
    there,
And gather all the honey thou canst find
In every crevice, over and above
What has been promised; would they
    reckon that?"
    Rhaicos went daily; but the nymph as
    oft,   205
Invisible. To play at love, she knew,
Stopping its breathings when it breathes
    most soft,
Is sweeter than to play on any pipe.
She played on his: she fed upon his sighs;
They pleased her when they gently waved
    her hair,   210
Cooling the pulses of her purple veins;
And when her absence brought them out,
    they pleased.
Even among the fondest of them all,
What mortal or immortal maid is more
Content with giving happiness than
    pain?   215
One day he was returning from the wood

Despondently. She pitied him, and said,
"Come back!" and twined her fingers in
    the hem
Above his shoulder. Then she led his steps
To a cool rill that ran o'er level sand   220
Through lentisk and through oleander;
    there
Bathed she his feet, lifting them on her lap
When bathed, and drying them in both
    her hands.
He dared complain; for those who most
    are loved
Most dare it; but not harsh was his com-
    plaint.   225
"O thou inconstant!" said he, "if stern law
Bind thee, or will, stronger than sternest
    law,
O, let me know henceforward when to
    hope
The fruit of love that grows for me but
    here."
He spake; and plucked it from its pliant
    stem.   230
"Impatient Rhaicos! Why thus intercept
The answer I would give? There is a bee
Whom I have fed, a bee who knows my
    thoughts
And executes my wishes: I will send
That messenger. If ever thou art false, 235
Drawn by another, own it not, but drive
My bee away; then shall I know my fate,
And—for thou must be wretched—weep at
    thine.
But often as my heart persuades to lay
Its cares on thine and throb itself to
    rest,   240
Expect her with thee, whether it be morn
Or eve, at any time when woods are safe."
    Day after day the Hours beheld them
    blest,
And season after season: years had past,
Blest were they still. He who asserts that
    Love   245
Ever is sated of sweet things, the same
Sweet things he fretted for in earlier days,
Never, by Zeus! loved he a hamadryad.
    The nights had now grown longer, and
    perhaps
The hamadryads find them lone and
    dull   250
Among their woods; one did, alas! She
    called
Her faithful bee; 'twas when all bees
    should sleep,
And all did sleep but hers. She was sent
    forth
To bring that light which never wintry
    blast
Blows out, nor rain nor snow extin-
    guishes,   255

The light that shines from loving eyes
    upon
Eyes that love back, till they can see no
    more.
    Rhaicos was sitting at his father's hearth:
Between them stood the table, not o'er-
    spread
With fruits which autumn now profusely
    bore,   260
Nor anise cakes, nor odorous wine, but
    there
The draft-board was expanded; at which
    game
Triumphant sat old Thallinos; the son
Was puzzled, vexed, discomforted, dis-
    traught.
A buzz was at his ear; up went his hand, 265
And it was heard no longer. The poor bee
Returned (but not until the morn shone
    bright),
And found the hamadryad with her head
Upon her aching wrist, and showed one
    wing
Half broken off, the other's meshes
    marred,   270
And there were bruises which no eye could
    see
Saving a hamadryad's. At this sight
Down fell the languid brow, both hands
    fell down;
A shriek was carried to the ancient hall
Of Thallinos: he heard it not; his son 275
Heard it, and ran forthwith into the wood.
No bark was on the tree, no leaf was
    green,
The trunk was riven through. From that
    day forth
Nor word nor whisper soothed his ear, nor
    sound
Even of insect wing; but loud laments 280
The woodmen and the shepherds one long
    year
Heard day and night, for Rhaicos would
    not quit
The solitary place, but moaned and died.
Hence milk and honey wonder not, O
    guest,
To find set duly on the hollow stone. 285
             1846

TWENTY YEARS HENCE MY EYES MAY GROW

Twenty years hence my eyes may grow
If not quite dim, yet rather so,
Still yours from others they shall know
    Twenty years hence.

Twenty years hence though it may hap 5
That I be called to take a nap
In a cool cell where thunderclap
    Was never heard,

There breathe but o'er my arch of grass
A not too sadly sighed *Alas,*   10
And I shall catch, ere you can pass,
    That wingèd word.
             1846

DEATH STANDS ABOVE ME

Death stands above me, whispering low
    I know not what into my ear:
Of his strange language all I know
    Is, there is not a word of fear.
             1853

ON HIS SEVENTY-FIFTH BIRTHDAY

I strove with none; for none was worth my
    strife,
    Nature I loved, and next to Nature, Art;
I warmed both hands before the fire of life,
    It sinks, and I am ready to depart.
             1853

WELL I REMEMBER HOW YOU SMILED

Well I remember how you smiled
    To see me write your name upon
The soft sea-sand. *"O! what a child!*
    You think you're writing upon stone!"
I have since written what no tide 5
    Shall ever wash away, what men
Unborn shall read o'er ocean wide
    And find Ianthe's name again.
             1863

THOMAS MOORE (1779-1852)

From her wilds Ierne sent
The sweetest lyrist of her saddest wrong,
And love taught grief to fall like music from his tongue.

PERCY BYSSHE SHELLEY

Moore was born in Dublin, above the grocery store and wine shop kept by his father. He was of a happy and convivial disposition. By his songs, and by his personal charm, he became popular not only in literary but also in "high" society. He was a special favorite of Byron's, and wrote a biography of him.

Moore's most ambitious poetical effort, the Oriental romance, *Lalla Rookh*, has some fine passages; but it has not proved as enduringly important as are the songs which he wrote to accompany well-known Irish airs. In them he applied to his native country those sentiments of nationalism and patriotism which were characteristic of the Romantic Movement. He will always have an honored place in the history of his people's struggle for independence. It is not the substance of these patriotic songs that constitutes their chief merit: the emotions have the merit of simplicity and sincerity, but they have not the sublimity found in Wordsworth's lyrics of liberty, nor the fiery force of Shelley's. Their distinction is in the perfect adaptation of the words to the music. If publishers and schoolmen were not so timid about departures from uniformity, the following selections from the *Irish Melodies* and *National Airs* would be printed with their musical scores, and would be sung in class rather than read in silence.

[A LETTER FROM NIAGARA FALLS]

My dearest Mother,—

I have seen the Falls, and am all rapture and amazement, I cannot give you a better idea of what I felt than by transcribing what I wrote off hastily in my journal on returning. "Arrived at Chippewa, within three miles of the Falls, on Saturday, July 21, to dinner. That evening walked towards the Falls, but got no farther than the rapids, which gave us a prelibation of the grandeur we had to expect. Next day, July 22, went to visit the Falls. Never shall I forget the impression I felt at the first glimpse of them which we got as the carriage passed over the hill that overlooks them. We were not near enough to be agitated by the terrific effects of the scene; but saw through the trees this mighty flow of waters descending with calm magnificence, and received enough of its grandeur to set imagination on the wing; imagination which, even at Niagara, can outrun reality. I felt as if approaching the very residence of the Deity; the tears started into my eyes; and I remained, for moments after we had lost sight of the scene, in that delicious absorption which pious enthusiasm alone can produce. We arrived at the New Ladder and descended to the bottom. Here all its awful sublimities rushed full upon me. But the former exquisite sensation was gone. I now saw all. The string that had been touched by the first impulse, and which *fancy* would have kept for ever in vibration, now rested at *reality*. Yet, though there was no more to imagine, there was much to feel. My whole heart and soul ascended towards the Divinity in a swell of devout admiration, which I never before experienced. Oh! bring the atheist here, and he cannot return an atheist! I pity the man who can coldly sit down to write a description of these ineffable wonders: much more do I pity him who can submit them to the admeasurement of gallons and yards. It is impossible by pen or pencil to convey even a faint idea of their magnificence. Painting is lifeless, and the most burning words of poetry have all been lavished upon inferior and ordinary subjects. We must have new combinations of language to describe the Fall of Niagara."

24 July, 1804

FROM IRISH MELODIES

OH, BREATHE NOT HIS NAME!

Oh, breathe not his name! let it sleep in
    the shade,
Where cold and unhonored his relics are
    laid;
Sad, silent, and dark be the tears that we
    shed,
As the night-dew that falls on the grass o'er
    his head.

But the night-dew that falls, though in
    silence it weeps,   5
Shall brighten with verdure the grave
    where he sleeps;
And the tear that we shed, though in secret
    it rolls,
Shall long keep his memory green in our
    souls.

1807-28   1807-34

THE HARP THAT ONCE THROUGH TARA'S HALLS

The harp that once through Tara's halls
    The soul of music shed,
Now hangs as mute on Tara's walls
    As if that soul were fled.—
So sleeps the pride of former days,   5
    So glory's thrill is o'er,
And hearts that once beat high for praise
    Now feel that pulse no more!

No more to chiefs and ladies bright
    The harp of Tara swells;   10
The chord alone that breaks at night
    Its tale of ruin tells.
Thus Freedom now so seldom wakes,
    The only throb she gives
Is when some heart indignant breaks,   15
    To show that still she lives.

1834

LET ERIN REMEMBER THE DAYS OF OLD

Let Erin remember the days of old,
    Ere her faithless sons betrayed her;
When Malachi wore the collar of gold,
    Which he won from her proud invader,
When her kings, with standard of green
    unfurled   5
    Led the Red-Branch Knights to dan-
        ger;—
Ere the emerald gem of the western world
    Was set in the crown of a stranger.

On Lough Neagh's bank as the fisherman
    strays,
When the clear cold eve's declining,   10
He sees the round towers of other days
    In the wave beneath him shining;
Thus shall memory often, in dreams sub-
    lime,
    Catch a glimpse of the days that are
        over;
Thus, sighing, look thro' the waves of
    time   15
    For the long-faded glories they cover.

1834

THE SONG OF FIONNUALA

Silent, O Moyle, be the roar of thy water,
    Break not, ye breezes, your chain of
        repose,
While, murmuring mournfully, Lir's lonely
    daughter
Tells to the night star her tale of woes.
When shall the swan, her death note sing-
    ing,   5
    Sleep, with wings in darkness furled?
When will heaven, its sweet bell ringing,
    Call my spirit from this stormy world?

Sadly, O Moyle, to thy winter wave weep-
    ing,
    Fate bids me languish long ages away;   10
Yet still in her darkness doth Erin lie sleep-
    ing,
    Still doth the pure light its dawning
        delay.
When will that daystar, mildly springing.
    Warm our isle with peace and love?
When will heaven, its sweet bell ringing,   15
    Call my spirit to the fields above?

1834

BELIEVE ME, IF ALL THOSE EN-DEARING YOUNG CHARMS

Believe me, if all those endearing young
    charms,
    Which I gaze on so fondly today,
Were to change by tomorrow, and fleet in
    my arms,
    Like fairy gifts fading away,
Thou wouldst still be adored, as this mo-
    ment thou art,   5
    Let thy loveliness fade as it will,
And around the dear ruin each wish of my
    heart
    Would intwine itself verdantly still.

It is not while beauty and youth are thine
    own,
    And thy cheeks unprofaned by a tear,   10

That the fervor and faith of a soul can be
  known,
    To which time will but make thee more
      dear;
No, the heart that has truly loved never
  forgets,
    But as truly loves on to the close,
As the sunflower turns on her god, when
  he sets, 15
The same look which she turned when he
  rose.

1834

SHE IS FAR FROM THE LAND

She is far from the land where her young
  hero sleeps,
  And lovers are round her, sighing:
But coldly she turns from their gaze, and
  weeps,
  For her heart in his grave is lying.

She sings the wild song of her dear native
  plains, 5
  Every note which he loved awaking;—
Ah! little they think who delight in her
  strains
    How the heart of the Minstrel is break-
    ing.

He had lived for his love, for his country
  he died,
  They were all that to life had intwined
  him; 10
Nor soon shall the tears of his country be
  dried,
  Nor long will his love stay behind him.

O, make her a grave where the sunbeams
  rest,
  When they promise a glorious morrow;
They'll shine o'er her sleep, like a smile
  from the West, 15
  From her own loved island of sorrow.

1834

AT THE MID HOUR OF NIGHT

At the mid hour of night, when stars are
  weeping, I fly
To the lone vale we loved, when life shone
  warm in thine eye;
And I think oft, if spirits can steal from
  the regions of air,
To revisit past scenes of delight, thou wilt
  come to me there,
And tell me our love is remembered, even
  in the sky. 5

Then I sing the wild song 'twas once such
  a pleasure to hear!
When our voices commingling breathed,
  like one, on the ear;
And, as Echo far off thro' the vale my sad
  orison rolls,
I think, oh my love! 'tis thy voice from the
  Kingdom of Souls,
Faintly answering still the notes that once
  were so dear. 10

1834

THE YOUNG MAY MOON

The young May moon is beaming, love,
The glow-worm's lamp is gleaming, love,
    How sweet to rove
    Through Morna's grove,
When the drowsy world is dreaming, love! 5
Then awake!—the heavens look bright, my
  dear,
'Tis never too late for delight, my dear,
    And the best of all ways
    To lengthen our days,
Is to steal a few hours from the night, my
  dear! 10

Now all the world is sleeping, love,
But the Sage, his star-watch keeping, love,
    And I, whose star,
    More glorious far,
Is the eye from that casement peeping,
  love. 15
Then awake!—till rise of sun, my dear,
The Sage's glass we'll shun, my dear,
    Or, in watching the flight
    Of bodies of light,
He might happen to take thee for one, my
  dear. 20

1834

THE TIME I'VE LOST IN WOOING

    The time I've lost in wooing,
    In watching and pursuing
      The light that lies
      In woman's eyes,
    Has been my heart's undoing. 5
    Though Wisdom oft has sought me,
    I scorned the lore she brought me,
      My only books
      Were woman's looks,
    And folly's all they've taught me. 10

    Her smile when Beauty granted,
    I hung with gaze enchanted,
      Like him, the Sprite,
      Whom maids by night
Oft meet in glen that's haunted. 15

Like him, too, Beauty won me,
But while her eyes were on me;
   If once their ray
   Was turned away,
Oh! winds could not outrun me.   20

And are those follies going?
And is my proud heart growing
   Too cold or too wise
   For brilliant eyes
Again to set it glowing?   25
No, vain, alas! th' endeavor
From bonds so sweet to sever;
   Poor Wisdom's chance
   Against a glance
Is now as weak as ever.   30

          1834

DEAR HARP OF MY COUNTRY

Dear Harp of my Country! in darkness I
   found thee,
The cold chain of silence had hung o'er
   thee long,
When proudly, my own Island Harp, I unbound thee,
And gave all thy chords to light, freedom, and song!
The warm lay of love and the light note
   of gladness   5
Have wakened thy fondest, thy liveliest
   thrill;
But, so oft hast thou echoed the deep sigh
   of sadness,
That even in thy mirth it will steal from
   thee still.

Dear Harp of my Country! farewell to thy
   numbers,
This sweet wreath of song is the last we
   shall twine!   10
Go, sleep with the sunshine of Fame on thy
   slumbers,
Till touched by some hand less unworthy
   than mine;
If the pulse of the patriot, soldier, or lover,
Have throbbed at our lay, 'tis thy glory
   alone;
I was but as the wind, passing heedlessly
   over,   15
And all the wild sweetness I waked was
   thy own.

          1834

FROM NATIONAL AIRS

OFT, IN THE STILLY NIGHT

SCOTCH AIR

Oft, in the stilly night,
   Ere Slumber's chain has bound me,
Fond Memory brings the light
   Of other days around me;
      The smiles, the tears,   5
      Of boyhood's years,
The words of love then spoken;
      The eyes that shone,
      Now dimmed and gone,
The cheerful hearts now broken!   10
Thus, in the stilly night,
   Ere Slumber's chain has bound me,
Sad Memory brings the light
   Of other days around me.

When I remember all   15
   The friends, so linked together,
I've seen around me fall,
   Like leaves in wintry weather;
      I feel like one
      Who treads alone   20
Some banquet hall deserted,
      Whose lights are fled,
      Whose garlands dead,
And all but he departed!
Thus, in the stilly night,   25
   Ere Slumber's chain has bound me,
Sad Memory brings the light
   Of other days around me.

          1815

HARK! THE VESPER HYMN IS STEALING

RUSSIAN AIR

Hark! the vesper hymn is stealing
   O'er the waters soft and clear;
Nearer yet and nearer pealing,
   And now bursts upon the ear:
      Jubilate, Amen.   5
Farther now, now farther stealing,
   Soft it fades upon the ear:
      Jubilate, Amen.

Now, like moonlight waves retreating
   To the shore, it dies along;   10
Now, like angry surges meeting,
   Breaks the mingled tide of song:
      Jubilate, Amen.
Hush! again, like waves retreating
   To the shore, it dies along: 15
      Jubilate, Amen.

          1815

FROM LALLA ROOKH

THE FIRE-WORSHIPPERS

"How sweetly," said the trembling maid,
Of her own gentle voice afraid,
So long had they in silence stood,
Looking upon than tranquil flood—
"How sweetly does the moonbeam smile 5
To-night upon yon leafy isle!
Oft, in my fancy's wanderings,
I've wished that little isle had wings,
And we, within its fairy bowers,
　　Were wafted off to seas unknown, 10
Where not a pulse would beat but ours,
　　And we might live, love, die alone!
Far from the cruel and the cold,—
　　Where the bright eyes of angels only
Should come around us, to behold 15
　　A paradise so pure and lonely.
Would this be world enough for thee?"
Playful she turned, that he might see
　　The passing smile her cheek put
　　　on;
But when she marked how mournfully 20
　　His eyes met hers, that smile was
　　　gone;
And, bursting into heartfelt tears,
"Yes, yes," she cried, "my hourly fears,
My dreams, have boded all too right—
We part—forever part—tonight! 25
I knew, I knew it could not last—
'Twas bright, 'twas heavenly, but 'tis
　　past!
Oh! ever thus, from childhood's hour,
　　I've seen my fondest hopes decay;
I never loved a tree or flower, 30
　　But 'twas the first to fade away.
I never nursed a dear gazelle,
　　To glad me with its soft black eye,
But when it came to know me well,
　　And love me, it was sure to die! 35
Now too—the joy most like divine
　　Of all I ever dreamt or knew,
To see thee, hear thee, call thee mine,—
　　Oh, misery! must I lose that too?
Yet go—on peril's brink we meet;— 40
　　Those frightful rocks—that treacher-
　　　ous sea—
No, never come again—though sweet,
　　Though heaven, it may be death to
　　　thee.
Farewell—and blessings on thy way,
　　Where'er thou go'st, beloved
　　　stranger! 45
Better to sit and watch that ray,
And think thee safe, though far away,
　　Than have thee near me, and in
　　　danger!"

THE LIGHT OF THE HARAM

Who has not heard of the Vale of Cash-
　　mere,
　　With its roses the brightest that earth
　　　ever gave,
Its temples, and grottos, and fountains as
　　clear
　　As the love-lighted eyes that hang over
　　　their wave?

Oh! to see it at sunset, when warm o'er the
　　lake 5
　　Its splendor at parting a summer eve
　　　throws,
Like a bride, full of blushes, when linger-
　　ing to take
　　A last look of her mirror at night ere she
　　　goes!
When the shrines through the foliage are
　　gleaming half shown,
And each hallows the hour by some rites of
　　its own. 10
Here the music of prayer from a minaret
　　swells,
　　Here the Magian his urn, full of per-
　　　fume, is swinging,
And here, at the altar, a zone of sweet bells
　　Round the waist of some fair Indian
　　　dancer is ringing.
Or to see it by moonlight, when mellowly
　　shines 15
The light o'er its palaces, gardens, and
　　shrines;
When the water-falls gleam, like a quick
　　fall of stars,
And the nightingale's hymn from the Isle
　　of Chenars
Is broken by laughs and light echoes of feet
From the cool, shining walks where the
　　young people meet: 20
Or at morn, when the magic of daylight
　　awakes
A new wonder each minute, as slowly it
　　breaks,—
Hills, cupolas, fountains, called forth every
　　one
Out of darkness, as if but just born of the
　　Sun.
When the Spirit of Fragrance is up with
　　the day, 25
From his Haram of night-flowers stealing
　　away;
And the wind, full of wantonness, wooes
　　like a lover
The young aspen-trees, till they tremble all
　　over.
When the East is as warm as the light of
　　first hopes.

And Day, with his banner of radiance
   unfurled,   30
Shines in through the mountainous portal
   that opes,
   Sublime, from that valley of bliss to the
    world!

But never yet, by night or day,
In dew of spring or summer's ray,
Did the sweet valley shine so gay   35
As now it shines—all love and light,
Visions by day and feasts by night!
A happier smile illumes each brow,
   With quicker spread each heart
    uncloses,   40
And all its ecstasy, for now
   The valley holds its Feast of Roses;
The joyous time, when pleasures pour
Profusely round and, in their shower,
Hearts open, like the season's rose,—
   The floweret of a hundred leaves,   45
Expanding while the dew-fall flows,
   And every leaf its balm receives.

'Twas when the hour of evening came
   Upon the lake, serene and cool,
When Day had hid his sultry flame   50
   Behind the palms of Baramoule,
When maids began to lift their heads,
Refreshed from their embroidered beds,
Where they had slept the sun away,
And waked to moonlight and to play.   55
All were abroad—the busiest hive
On Bela's hills is less alive,
When saffron beds are full in flower,
Than looked the valley in that hour.
A thousand restless torches played   60
Through every grove and island shade;
A thousand sparkling lamps were set
On every dome and minaret;
And fields and pathways, far and near,
Were lighted by a blaze so clear,   65
That you could see, in wandering round,
The smallest rose-leaf on the ground.
Yet did the maids and matrons leave
Their veils at home, that brilliant eve;
And there were glancing eyes about,   70
And cheeks, that would not dare shine out
   In open day, but thought they might
Look lovely then, because 'twas night.
And all were free, and wandering,
And all exclaimed to all they met,   75
That never did the summer bring
   So gay a Feast of Roses yet;
The moon had never shed a light
   So clear as that which blessed them
    there;

The roses ne'er shone half so bright,   80
   Nor they themselves looked half so
    fair.

And what a wilderness of flowers!
It seemed as though from all the bowers
And fairest fields of all the year,
The mingled spoil were scattered here.   85
The lake, too, like a garden breathes,
   With the rich buds that o'er it lie,—
As if a shower of fairy wreaths
   Had fallen upon it from the sky!
And then the sound of joy:—the beat   90
Of tabors and of dancing feet;
The minaret-crier's chant of glee
Sung from his lighted gallery,
And answered by a ziraleet
From neighboring Haram, wild and
   sweet;   95
The merry laughter, echoing
From gardens, where the silken swing
Wafts some delighted girl above
The top leaves of the orange-grove;
Or, from those infant groups at play   100
Among the tents that line the way,
Flinging, unawed by slave or mother,
Handfuls of roses at each other.
Then the sounds from the lake:—the low
   whispering in boats,
   As they shoot through the moonlight;
    the dipping of oars;   105
And the wild, airy warbling that every-
   where floats,
Through the groves, round the islands, as
   if all the shores,
Like those of Kathay, uttered music, and
   gave
An answer in song to the kiss of each wave.
But the gentlest of all are those sounds,
   full of feeling,   110
That soft from the lute of some lover are
   stealing,
Some lover, who knows all the heart-touch-
   ing power
Of a lute and a sigh in this magical hour.
Oh! best of delights as it everywhere is
To be near the loved *One*,—what a rap-
   ture is his   115
Who in moonlight and music thus sweetly
   may glide
O'er the Lake of Cashmere, with that *One*
   by his side!
If woman can make the worst wilderness
   dear,
Think, think what a heaven she must make
   of Cashmere!

1814-17   1817

LORD BYRON (1788-1824)

It is in the contrast between his august conceptions of man, and his contemptuous opinions of men, that much of the almost incomprehensible charm, and power, and enchantment, of his poetry consists.

JOHN WILSON

The play-boy father of Byron was twice married, and treated both of his wives badly. There was a strain of insanity in his mother's family, and her violent temper was one of the bad influences upon him. It was almost inevitable that his own life and character should be turbulent and dissolute. He was strikingly handsome; but the fact that he was lame from birth, increased his self-consciousness and self-pity. Throughout his life, and often unselfishly, he reacted fiercely against injustice or tyranny. In Harrow School and Cambridge University, he was not very proficient in his studies, but he attracted attention by his oratory. His maiden-speech in the House of Lords, in defiance of majority opinion, was on behalf of the working classes. His tour of Europe was not the conventional one, but an adventurous and unsafe journey in the Near East, which included contacts with barbaric chiefs, a visit to the site of ancient Troy, and the swimming of the dangerous Hellespont. He versified some of those experiences in Cantos I and II of *Childe Harold's Pilgrimage;* and upon their publication he could say without exaggeration, "I awoke one morning, and found myself famous." He enjoyed being lionized, and was not backward about letting beautiful and aristocratic ladies make fools of themselves on his account. He wrote *Lines To A Lady Weeping,* in which he pitied the Prince Regent's daughter for having such a disgraceful father; and he visited Leigh Hunt in the prison to which that champion of liberty had been consigned for similar audacities.

Byron married, inappropriately, a very proper young lady, Anne Isabella Milbanke; but, instead of reforming, continued as before, his licentiousness now apparently including the abhorrent crime of incest. His wife left him; and society, whose idol he had been, ostracized him. He felt that he was driven into exile, and he resented what seemed to him excessive punishment for his wrongdoings. From his twenty-eighth year he lived abroad, mostly in Switzerland and Italy, like his friends the Shelleys and Claire Clairmont. For some time he was sunk in debauchery; but after he had met and won the Countess Guiccioli, he abandoned the most evil of his courses and devoted himself assiduously to his poetry. He ended his career with a gesture which was sincere and noble: when the Greeks revolted against the Turks, he volunteered in the Greek service. Before he had an opportunity to take part in battle, he died, in camp, of fever, at the age of thirty-six. His life's close redeemed him in the opinion of some who had previously condemned his conduct. Whatever the moral judgment upon him may be, one cannot deny that his life and death were as romantic and dramatic as his poetry.

The key to an understanding of Byron's peculiar place in the Romantic Movement lies, I believe, in the words quoted above,—"his august conceptions of man, and his contemptuous opinions of men." Man is an idea or an ideal; men are—what they are. Although Byron seems to sneer at everything, he admired, as much as any Romantic, whatever was really true, good, and beautiful. He was enthusiastic about the majestic features of Nature; he admired youth, womanhood, liberty, fame, and the glories of ancient Greece and Rome. He hated oppression and hypocrisy. In his world, so full of pain and evils, the doors are not shut against the *possibility* of all kinds of perfection. England *"might"* have been the noblest nation." But what distinguishes him from romantic idealists like Wordsworth, Keats, and Shelley, is that, perhaps owing to the bitter nature of his experiences, he found it almost impossible to discern any manifestations of ideals in the actual life of mankind. The only happy love that he depicts, Haidée's, is found not among the actualities of life, but in a temporarily idyllic situation. Actual life, as this frustrated idealist saw it, was devoid of present bliss or future promise. The glory that was Greece and the grandeur that was Rome, had no modern successors. Love and happiness might visit us in youth, but the rest of life was disillusionment. The attempts by the clergy to console men in their misery with the orthodox explanations about God, Man, and the Universe, misrepresented man's past history and present status, and were affronts to common sense. In the extremity of his grief and indignation, he is sometimes led to utterances so despairing as to seem quite irreconcilable with the normal fortitude and hopefulness of his contemporaries. The Byronic mood may, however, be regarded as a first phase of Romanticism, which Byron himself rarely passed beyond, in which the emphasis is upon denunciation and ridicule of things as they are and as they seem, with little or no regard as yet to what they may become, or may be made.

The clear and impassioned expression of Byron's feelings did not attain perfect power and brilliance until after Byron had left England forever. The fulness of his strength is first seen in the third canto of *Childe Harold*, after which nearly everything that he wrote, including his superb *Letters*, and his masterpiece *Don Juan*, burns with the unquenchable fire of immortal genius.

LACHIN Y GAIR

Away, ye gay landscapes, ye gardens of roses!
　　In you let the minions of luxury rove;
Restore me the rocks, where the snowflake reposes,
　　Though still they are sacred to freedom and love:
Yet, Caledonia, beloved are thy mountains,   5
　　Round their white summits though elements war;
Though cataracts foam 'stead of smooth-flowing fountains,
　　I sigh for the valley of dark Loch na Garr.

Ah! there my young footsteps in infancy wandered;
　　My cap was the bonnet, my cloak was the plaid;   10
On chieftains long perished my memory pondered,
　　As daily I strode through the pine-covered glade;
I sought not my home till the day's dying glory
　　Gave place to the rays of the bright polar star;
For fancy was cheered by traditional story,   15
　　Disclosed by the natives of dark Loch na Garr.

"Shades of the dead! have I not heard your voices
　　Rise on the night-rolling breath of the gale?"
Surely the soul of the hero rejoices,
　　And rides on the wind, o'er his own Highland vale.   20
Round Loch na Garr while the stormy mist gathers,
　　Winter presides in his cold icy car:
Clouds there encircle the forms of my fathers;
　　They dwell in the tempests of dark Loch na Garr.

"Ill-starred, though brave, did no visions foreboding   25
　　Tell you that fate had forsaken your cause?"
Ah! were you destined to die at Culloden,
　　Victory crowned not your fall with applause:
Still were you happy in death's earthly slumber,
　　You rest with your clan in the caves of Braemar;   30
The pibroch resounds, to the piper's loud number,
　　Your deeds on the echoes of dark Loch na Garr.

Years have rolled on, Loch na Garr, since I left you,
　　Years must elapse ere I tread you again:
Nature of verdure and flowers has bereft you,   35
　　Yet still are you dearer than Albion's plain.
England! thy beauties are tame and domestic
　　To one who has roved o'er the mountains afar:
Oh for the crags that are wild and majestic!
　　The steep frowning glories of dark Loch na Garr.   40

1807

LINES INSCRIBED UPON A CUP FORMED FROM A SKULL

Start not—nor deem my spirit fled;
  In me behold the only skull
From which, unlike a living head,
  Whatever flows is never dull.

I lived, I loved, I quaffed, like thee: 5
  I died: let earth my bones resign;
Fill up—thou canst not injure me;
  The worm hath fouler lips than thine.

Better to hold the sparkling grape,
  Than nurse the earth-worm's slimy
    brood;   10
And circle in the goblet's shape
  The drink of gods, than reptile's food.

Where once my wit, perchance, hath shone,
  In aid of others' let me shine;
And when, alas! our brains are gone, 15
  What nobler substitute than wine?

Quaff while thou canst: another race,
  When thou and thine, like me, are sped,
May rescue thee from earth's embrace,
  And rhyme and revel with the dead. 20

Why not? since through life's little day
  Our heads such sad effects produce;
Redeemed from worms and wasting clay,
  This chance is theirs, to be of use.
1808

WHEN WE TWO PARTED

When we two parted
  In silence and tears,
Half broken-hearted
  To sever for years,
Pale grew thy cheek and cold, 5
  Colder thy kiss;
Truly that hour foretold
  Sorrow to this.

The dew of the morning
  Sunk chill on my brow—   10
It felt like the warning
  Of what I feel now.
Thy vows are all broken,
  And light is thy fame:
I hear thy name spoken,   15
  And share in its shame.

They name thee before me,
  A knell to mine ear;
A shudder comes o'er me—
  Why wert thou so dear?   20

They know not I knew thee,
  Who knew thee too well:—
Long, long shall I rue thee,
  Too deeply to tell.

In secret we met—   25
  In silence I grieve,
That thy heart could forget,
  Thy spirit deceive.
If I should meet thee
  After long years,   30
How should I greet thee?—
  With silence and tears.
1808

INSCRIPTION ON THE MONUMENT OF A NEWFOUNDLAND DOG

When some proud son of man returns to
    earth,
Unknown to glory, but upheld by birth,
The sculptor's art exhausts the pomp of
    woe,
And storied urns record who rest below:
When all is done, upon the tomb is seen, 5
Not what he was, but what he should have
    been:
But the poor dog, in life the firmest friend,
The first to welcome, foremost to defend,
Whose honest heart is still his master's
    own,
Who labors, fights, lives, breathes for him
    alone,   10
Unhonored falls, unnoticed all his worth,
Denied in heaven the soul he held on
    earth:
While man, vain insect! hopes to be for-
    given,
And claims himself a sole exclusive heaven.
Oh man! thou feeble tenant of an hour, 15
Debased by slavery, or corrupt by power,
Who knows thee well must quit thee with
    disgust,
Degraded mass of animated dust!
Thy love is lust, thy friendship all a cheat,
Thy smiles hypocrisy, thy words deceit! 20
By nature vile, ennobled but by name,
Each kindred brute might bid thee blush
    for shame.
Ye! who perchance behold this simple urn,
Pass on—it honors none you wish to
    mourn:
To mark a friend's remains these stones
    arise;   25
I never knew but one,—and here he lies.
Nov. 30, 1808

FROM ENGLISH BARDS AND SCOTCH REVIEWERS

Next comes the dull disciple of thy
    school   235
That mild apostate from poetic rule,
The simple Wordsworth, framer of a lay
As soft as evening in his favorite May,
Who warns his friend "to shake off toil and
    trouble,
And quit his books, for fear of growing
    double";   240
Who, both by precept and example, shows
That prose is verse, and verse is merely
    prose;
Convincing all, by demonstration plain,
Poetic souls delight in prose insane;
And Christmas stories tortured into
    rhyme   245
Contain the essence of the true sublime.
Thus, when he tells the tale of Betty Foy,
The idiot mother of "an idiot boy";
A moon-struck, silly lad, who lost his way,
And, like his bard, confounded night with
    day;   250
So close on each pathetic part he dwells,
And each adventure so sublimely tells,
That all who view the "idiot in his glory"
Conceive the bard the hero of the story.

Shall gentle Coleridge pass unnoticed
    here,   255
To turgid ode and tumid stanza dear?
Though themes of innocence amuse him
    best,
Yet still obscurity's a welcome guest.
If Inspiration should her aid refuse
To him who takes a pixy for a muse,   260
Yet none in lofty numbers can surpass
The bard who soars to elegise an ass.
So well the subject suits his noble mind,
He brays the laureate of the long-eared
    kind.

Oh! wonder-working Lewis! monk, or
    bard,   265
Who fain wouldst make Parnassus a
    church-yard;
Lo! wreaths of yew, not laurel, bind thy
    brow,
Thy muse a sprite, Apollo's sexton thou!
Whether on ancient tombs thou tak'st thy
    stand,
By gibbering specters hailed, thy kindred
    band;   270
Or tracest chaste descriptions on thy page,
To please the females of our modest age;
All hail, M. P.! from whose infernal brain
Thin-sheeted phantoms glide, a grisly train;
At whose command "grim women" throng
    in crowds,   275
And kings of fire, of water, and of clouds,
With "small gray men," "wild yagers," and
    what not,
To crown with honor thee and Walter
    Scott;
Again all hail! if tales like thine may please
St. Luke alone can vanquish the disease; 280
Even Satan's self with thee might dread to
    dwell,
And in thy skull discern a deeper hell.
                    1809

WRITTEN AFTER SWIMMING FROM SESTOS TO ABYDOS

If, in the month of dark December,
    Leander, who was nightly wont
(What maid will not the tale remember?)
    To cross thy stream, broad Hellespont!

If, when the wintry tempest roared,   5
    He sped to Hero, nothing loth,
And thus of old thy current poured,
    Fair Venus! how I pity both!

For *me,* degenerate modern wretch,
    Though in the genial month of May, 10
My dripping limbs I faintly stretch,
    And think I've done a feat to-day.

But since he crossed the rapid tide,
    According to the doubtful story,
To woo,—and—Lord knows what beside, 15
    And swam for Love, as I for Glory;

'T were hard to say who fared the best:
    Sad mortals! thus the gods still plague
        you!
He lost his labor, I my jest;
    For he was drowned, and I've the ague. 20
1810   1812

MAID OF ATHENS, ERE WE PART

Ζώη μου, σᾶς ἀγαπῶ.

Maid of Athens, ere we part,
Give, oh give me back my heart!
Or, since that has left my breast,
Keep it now, and take the rest!
Hear my vow before I go,   5
Ζώη μου, σᾶς ἀγαπῶ.

By those tresses unconfined,
Wooed by each Ægean wind;
By those lids whose jetty fringe

Kiss thy soft cheeks' blooming tinge; 10
By those wild eyes like the roe,
Ζώη μοῦ, σᾶς ἀγαπῶ.

By that lip I long to taste;
By that zone-encircled waist;
By all the token-flowers that tell 15
What words can never speak so well;
By love's alternate joy and woe,
Ζώη μοῦ, σᾶς ἀγαπῶ,

Maid of Athens, I am gone:
Think of me, sweet! when alone. 20
Though I fly to Istambol,
Athens holds my heart and soul:
Can I cease to love thee? No!
Ζώη μοῦ, σᾶς ἀγαπῶ.
1810   1812

FAREWELL! IF EVER FONDEST PRAYER

Farewell! if ever fondest prayer
 For other's weal availed on high,
Mine will not all be lost in air,
 But waft thy name beyond the sky.
'Twere vain to speak, to weep, to sigh: 5
 Oh! more than tears of blood can tell,
When wrung from guilt's expiring eye,
 Are in that word—Farewell!—Farewell!

These lips are mute, these eyes are dry;
 But in my breast and in my brain, 10
Awake the pangs that pass not by,
 The thought that ne'er shall sleep again.
My soul nor deigns nor dares complain,
 Though grief and passion there rebel;
I only know we loved in vain— 15
 I only feel—Farewell!—Farewell!
1808   1814

ODE TO NAPOLEON BUONAPARTE

'Tis done—but yesterday a king!
 And armed with kings to strive—
And now thou art a nameless thing:
 So abject—yet alive!
Is this the man of thousand thrones, 5
Who strewed our earth with hostile bones,
 And can he thus survive?
Since he, miscalled the Morning Star,
Nor man nor fiend hath fallen so far.

Ill-minded man! why scourge thy kind 10
 Who bowed so low the knee?
By gazing on thyself grown blind,
 Thou taught'st the rest to see.

With might unquestioned,—power to
 save,—
Thine only gift hath been the grave, 15
 To those that worshipped thee;
Nor till thy fall could mortals guess
Ambition's less than littleness!

Thanks for that lesson—it will teach
 To after-warriors more, 20
Than high philosophy can preach,
 And vainly preached before.
That spell upon the minds of men
Breaks never to unite again,
 That led them to adore 25
Those Pagod things of sabre sway
With fronts of brass, and feet of clay.

The triumph and the vanity,
 The rapture of the strife—
The earthquake voice of victory, 30
 To thee the breath of life;
The sword, the sceptre, and that sway
Which man seemed made but to obey,
 Wherewith renown was rife—
All quelled!—Dark Spirit! what must be 35
The madness of thy memory!

The desolator desolate!
 The victor overthrown!
The arbiter of others' fate
 A suppliant for his own! 40
Is it some yet imperial hope
That with such change can calmly cope?
 Or dread of death alone?
To die a prince—or live a slave—
Thy choice is most ignobly brave! 45

He who of old would rend the oak
 Dreamed not of the rebound:
Chained by the trunk he vainly broke—
 Alone—how looked he round?
Thou, in the sternness of thy strength, 50
An equal deed hast done at length,
 And darker fate hast found:
He fell, the forest prowlers' prey;
But thou must eat thy heart away!

The Roman, when his burning heart 55
 Was slaked with blood of Rome,
Threw down the dagger—dared depart,
 In savage grandeur, home—
He dared depart in utter scorn
Of men that such a yoke had borne, 60
 Yet left him such a doom!
His only glory was that hour
Of self-upheld abandoned power.

The Spaniard, when the lust of sway
 Had lost its quickening spell, 65
Cast crowns for rosaries away,
 An empire for a cell;

A strict accountant of his beads,
A subtle disputant on creeds,
  His dotage trifled well: 70
Yet better had he neither known
A bigot's shrine—nor despot's throne.

But thou—from thy reluctant hand
  The thunderbolt is wrung—
Too late thou leav'st the high command 75
  To which thy weakness clung;
All Evil Spirit as thou art,
It is enough to grieve the heart
  To see thine own unstrung;
To think that God's fair world hath been 80
The footstool of a thing so mean;

And earth hath spilt her blood for him,
  Who thus can hoard his own!
And monarchs bowed the trembling limb,
  And thanked him for a throne!   85
Fair freedom! we may hold thee dear,
  When thus thy mightiest foes their fear
  In humblest guise have shown.
Oh! ne'er may tyrant leave behind
A brighter name to lure mankind!   90

Thine evil deeds are writ in gore,
  Nor written thus in vain—
Thy triumphs tell of fame no more,
  Or deepen every stain:
If thou hadst died as honor dies,   95
Some new Napoleon might arise,
  To shame the world again—
But who would soar the solar height,
To set in such a starless night?

Weighed in the balance, hero dust   100
  Is vile as vulgar clay;
Thy scales, Mortality! are just
  To all that pass away:
But yet methought the living great
Some higher sparks should animate,   105
  To dazzle and dismay:
Nor deemed contempt could thus make
    mirth
Of these, the conquerors of the earth.

And she, proud Austria's mournful flower,
  Thy still imperial bride;   110
How bears her breast the torturing hour?
  Still clings she to thy side?
Must she too bend, must she too share
Thy late repentance, long despair,
  Thou throneless homicide?   115
If still she loves thee, hoard that gem,—
'Tis worthy thy vanished diadem!

Then haste thee to thy sullen isle,
  And gaze upon the sea;
That element may meet thy smile—   120
  It ne'er was ruled by thee!
Or trace with thine all idle hand
In loitering mood upon the sand
  That earth is now as free!
That Corinth's pedagogue hath now   125
Transferred his by-word to thy brow.

Thou Timour! in his captive's cage
  What thoughts will there be thine,
While brooding in thy prisoned rage?
  But one—"The world *was* mine!"   130
Unless, like he of Babylon,
All sense is with thy sceptre gone,
  Life will not long confine
That spirit poured so widely forth—
So long obeyed—so little worth!   135

Or, like the thief of fire from heaven,
  Wilt thou withstand the shock?
And share with him, the unforgiven,
  His vulture and his rock!
Foredoomed by God—by man accurst,   140
And that last act, though not thy worst,
  The very fiend's arch mock;
He in his fall preserved his pride,
And, if a mortal, had as proudly died!

There was a day—there was an hour,   145
  While earth was Gaul's—Gaul thine—
When that immeasurable power
  Unsated to resign
Had been an act of purer fame
Than gathers round Marengo's name,   150
  And gilded thy decline,
Through the long twilight of all time,
Despite some passing clouds of crime.

But thou forsooth must be a king,
  And don the purple vest,   155
As if that foolish robe could wring
  Remembrance from thy breast.
Where is that faded garment? where
The gewgaws thou wert fond to wear,
  The star, the string, the crest?   160
Vain froward child of empire! say,
Are all thy playthings snatched away?

Where may the wearied eye repose
  When gazing on the Great;
Where neither guilty glory glows,   165
  Nor despicable state?
Yes—one—the first—the last—the best—
The Cincinnatus of the West,
  Whom envy dared not hate,
Bequeathed the name of Washington, 170
To make man blush there was but one!
1814   1814

FROM HEBREW MELODIES

SHE WALKS IN BEAUTY

I

She walks in beauty, like the night
Of cloudless climes and starry skies;
And all that's best of dark and bright
Meet in her aspect and her eyes:
Thus mellowed to that tender light   5
Which heaven to gaudy day denies.

II

One shade the more, one ray the less,
Had half impaired the nameless grace
Which waves in every raven tress,
Or softly lightens o'er her face;   10
Where thoughts serenely sweet express
How pure, how dear their dwelling-place.

III

And on that cheek, and o'er that brow,
So soft, so calm, yet eloquent,
The smiles that win, the tints that glow,   15
But tell of days in goodness spent,
A mind at peace with all below,
A heart whose love is innocent!

June 12, 1814   1815

OH! SNATCHED AWAY IN BEAUTY'S BLOOM

Oh! snatched away in beauty's bloom,
On thee shall press no ponderous tomb;
But on thy turf shall roses rear
Their leaves, the earliest of the year;
And the wild cypress wave in tender
gloom: 5

And oft by yon blue gushing stream
Shall sorrow lean her drooping head,
And feed deep thought with many a dream,
And lingering pause and lightly tread;
Fond wretch! as if her step disturbed the
dead!   10

Away! we know that tears are vain,
That death nor heeds nor hears distress:
Will this unteach us to complain?
Or make one mourner weep the less?
And thou—who tell'st me to forget,   15
Thy looks are wan, thine eyes are wet.
1814   1815

MY SOUL IS DARK

My soul is dark—Oh! quickly string
The harp I yet can brook to hear;
And let thy gentle fingers fling
Its melting murmurs o'er mine ear.

If in this heart a hope be dear,   5
That sound shall charm it forth again:
If in these eyes there lurk a tear,
'Twill flow, and cease to burn my brain.

But bid the strain be wild and deep,
Nor let thy notes of joy be first: 10
I tell thee, minstrel, I must weep,
Or else this heavy heart will burst;
For it hath been by sorrow nursed,
And ached in sleepless silence long;
And now 'tis doomed to know the worst, 15
And break at once—or yield to song.
1814   1815

SONG OF SAUL BEFORE HIS LAST BATTLE

Warriors and chiefs! should the shaft or
the sword
Pierce me in leading the host of the Lord,
Heed not the corse, though a king's, in
your path:
Bury your steel in the bosoms of Gath!

Thou who art bearing my buckler and
bow,   5
Should the soldiers of Saul look away from
the foe,
Stretch me that moment in blood at thy
feet!
Mine be the doom which they dared not to
meet.

Farewell to others, but never we part,
Heir to my royalty, son of my heart!   10
Bright is the diadem, boundless the sway,
Or kingly the death, which awaits us today!
1815   1815

WHEN COLDNESS WRAPS THIS SUFFERING CLAY

1

When coldness wraps this suffering clay,
Ah! whither strays the immortal mind?
It cannot die, it cannot stay,
But leaves its darkened dust behind.
Then, unembodied, doth it trace   5
By steps each planet's heavenly way?
Or fill at once the realms of space,
A thing of eyes, that all survey?

2

Eternal, boundless, undecayed,
A thought unseen, but seeing all,   10
All, all in earth or skies displayed,
Shall it survey, shall it recall:

Each fainter trace that memory holds
  So darkly of departed years,
In one broad glance the soul beholds,   15
  And all, that was, at once appears.

3

Before Creation peopled earth,
  Its eye shall roll through chaos back;
And where the furthest heaven had birth,
  The spirit trace its rising track.   20
And where the future mars or makes,
  Its glance dilate o'er all to be,
While sun is quenched or system breaks,
  Fixed in its own eternity.

4

Above or Love, Hope, Hate, or Fear,   25
  It lives all passionless and pure:
An age shall flee like earthly year;
  Its years as moments shall endure.
Away, away, without a wing,
  O'er all, through all, its thought shall
     fly,   30
A nameless and eternal thing,
  Forgetting what it was to die.

1815

BY THE RIVERS OF BABYLON WE SAT DOWN AND WEPT

1

We sat down and wept by the waters
  Of Babel, and thought of the day
When our foe, in the hue of his slaughters,
  Made Salem's high places his prey;
And ye, oh her desolate daughters!   5
  Were scattered all weeping away.

2

While sadly we gazed on the river
  Which rolled on in freedom below,
They demanded the song; but, oh never
  That triumph the stranger shall know!   10
May this right hand be withered for ever,
  Ere it string our high harp for the foe!

3

On the willow that harp is suspended,
  Oh Salem! its sound should be free;
And the hour when thy glories were
    ended   15
  But left me that token of thee:
And ne'er shall its soft tones be blended
  With the voice of the spoiler by me!

1815

THE DESTRUCTION OF SENNACHERIB

I

The Assyrian came down like the wolf on the fold,
And his cohorts were gleaming in purple and gold;
And the sheen of their spears was like stars on the sea,
When the blue wave rolls nightly on deep Galilee.

II

Like the leaves of the forest when Summer is green,   5
That host with their banners at sunset were seen:
Like the leaves of the forest when Autumn hath blown,
That host on the morrow lay withered and strown.

III

For the Angel of Death spread his wings on the blast,
And breathed in the face of the foe as he passed;   10
And the eyes of the sleepers waxed deadly and chill,
And their hearts but once heaved, and for ever grew still!

IV

And there lay the steed with his nostril all wide,
But through it there rolled not the breath of his pride;
And the foam of his gasping lay white on the turf,   15
And cold as the spray of the rock-beating surf.

V

And there lay the rider distorted and pale,
With the dew on his brow, and the rust on his mail:
And the tents were all silent, the banners alone,
The lances uplifted, the trumpet unblown.   20

VI

And the widows of Ashur are loud in their wail,
And the idols are broke in the temple of Baal;
And the might of the Gentile, unsmote by the sword,
Hath melted like snow in the glance of the Lord!
February 17, 1815   1815

STANZAS FOR MUSIC

There's not a joy the world can give like that it takes away,
When the glow of early thought declines in feeling's dull decay;
'Tis not on youth's smooth cheek the blush alone, which fades so fast,
But the tender bloom of heart is gone, ere youth itself be past.

Then the few whose spirits float above the wreck of happiness   5
Are driven o'er the shoals of guilt or ocean of excess:
The magnet of their course is gone, or only points in vain
The shore to which their shivered sail shall never stretch again.

Then the mortal coldness of the soul like death itself comes down;
It cannot feel for others' woes, it dare not dream its own;   10
That heavy chill has frozen o'er the fountain of our tears,
And though the eye may sparkle still, 'tis where the ice appears.

Though wit may flash from fluent lips, and mirth distract the breast,
Through midnight hours that yield no more their former hope of rest;
'Tis but as ivy-leaves around the ruined turret wreath,   15
All green and wildly fresh without, but worn and gray beneath.

Oh could I feel as I have felt,—or be what I have been,
Or weep as I could once have wept o'er many a vanished scene;
As springs in deserts found seem sweet, all brackish though they be,
So, midst the withered waste of life, those tears would flow to me. 20
1815   1816

THE DREAM

1

Our life is two-fold: Sleep hath its own
      world,
A boundary between the things misnamed
Death and existence: Sleep hath its own
      world,
And a wide realm of wild reality.
And dreams in their development have
      breath,   5
And tears, and tortures, and the touch of
      joy;
They leave a weight upon our waking
      thoughts,
They take a weight from off our waking
      toils,
They do divide our being; they become
A portion of ourselves as of our time,   10
And look like heralds of eternity;
They pass like spirits of the past,—they
      speak

Like Sibyls of the future: they have
      power—
The tyranny of pleasure and of pain;
They make us what we were not—what
      they will,   15
And shake us with the vision that's gone
      by,
The dread of vanished shadows—Are they
      so?
Is not the past all shadow?—What are
      they?
Creations of the mind?—The mind can
      make
Substance, and people planets of its own 20
With beings brighter than have been, and
      give
A breath to forms which can outlive all
      flesh.
I would recall a vision which I dreamed
Perchance in sleep—for in itself a thought,
A slumbering thought, is capable of years, 25
And curdles a long life into one hour.

I saw two beings in the hues of youth
Standing upon a hill, a gentle hill,
Green and of mild declivity, the last
As 't were the cape of a long ridge of
    such,   30
Save that there was no sea to lave its base,
But a most living landscape, and the wave
Of woods and corn-fields, and the abodes
    of men
Scattered at intervals, and wreathing smoke
Arising from such rustic roofs;—the hill 35
Was crowned with a peculiar diadem
Of trees, in circular array, so fixed
Not by the sport of nature, but of man:
These two, a maiden and a youth, were
    there
Gazing—the one on all that was beneath 40
Fair as herself—but the boy gazed on her;
And both were young, and one was beau-
    tiful:
And both were young—yet not alike in
    youth.
As the sweet moon on the horizon's verge,
The maid was on the eve of womanhood; 45
The boy had fewer summers, but his heart
Had far outgrown his years, and to his
    eye
There was but one beloved face on earth,
And that was shining on him: he had
    looked
Upon it till it could not pass away; 50
He had no breath, no being, but in hers;
She was his voice; he did not speak to her,
But trembled on her words; she was his
    sight,
For his eye followed hers, and saw with
    hers,
Which colored all his objects:—he had
    ceased   55
To live within himself; she was his life,
The ocean to the river of his thoughts,
Which terminated all: upon a tone,
A touch of hers, his blood would ebb and
    flow,
And his cheek change tempestuously—his
    heart   60
Unknowing of its cause of agony.
But she in these fond feelings had no share:
Her sighs were not for him; to her he was
Even as a brother—but no more; 't was
    much,
For brotherless she was, save in the name 65
Her infant friendship had bestowed on
    him;
Herself the solitary scion left
Of a time-honored race.—It was a name
Which pleased him, and yet pleased him
    not—and why?

Time taught him a deep answer—when she
    loved   70
Another; even *now* she loved another,
And on the summit of that hill she stood
Looking afar if yet her lover's steed
Kept pace with her expectancy, and flew.

3

A change came o'er the spirit of my
    dream.   75
There was an ancient mansion, and before
Its walls there was a steed caparisoned:
Within an antique Oratory stood
The Boy of whom I spake;—he was alone,
And pale, and pacing to and fro: anon 80
He sate him down, and seized a pen, and
    traced
Words which I could not guess of; then he
    leaned
His bowed head on his hands, and shook as
    't were
With a convulsion—then arose again,
And with his teeth and quivering hands
    did tear   85
What he had written, but he shed no tears,
And he did calm himself, and fix his brow
Into a kind of quiet: as he paused,
The Lady of his love re-entered there;
She was serene and smiling then, and yet 90
She knew she was by him beloved,—she
    knew,
For quickly comes such knowledge, that his
    heart
Was darkened with her shadow, and she
    saw
That he was wretched, but she saw not all.
He rose, and with a cold and gentle
    grasp   95
He took her hand; a moment o'er his face
A tablet of unutterable thoughts
Was traced, and then it faded, as it came;
He dropped the hand he held, and with
    slow steps
Retired, but not as bidding her adieu, 100
For they did part with mutual smiles; he
    passed
From out the massy gate of that old Hall,
And mounting on his steed he went his
    way;
And ne'er repassed that hoary threshold
    more.

4

A change came o'er the spirit of my
    dream.   105
The Boy was sprung to manhood: in the
    wilds
Of fiery climes he made himself a home,
And his soul drank their sunbeams: he was
    girt

With strange and dusky aspects; he was not
Himself like what he had been; on the
    sea 110
And on the shore he was a wanderer;
There was a mass of many images
Crowded like waves upon me, but he was
A part of all; and in the last he lay
Reposing from the noontide sultriness, 115
Couched among fallen columns, in the
    shade
Of ruined walls that had survived the
    names
Of those who reared them; by his sleeping
    side
Stood camels grazing, and some goodly
    steeds
Were fastened near a fountain; and a
    man 120
Clad in a flowing garb did watch the while,
While many of his tribe slumbered around:
And they were canopied by the blue sky,
So cloudless, clear, and purely beautiful,
That God alone was to be seen in
    heaven. 125

5

A change came o'er the spirit of my dream.
The Lady of his love was wed with One
Who did not love her better:—in her
    home,
A thousand leagues from his,—her native
    home,
She dwelt, begirt with growing Infancy, 130
Daughters and sons of Beauty,—but be-
    hold!
Upon her face there was the tint of grief,
The settled shadow of an inward strife,
And an unquiet drooping of the eye,
As if its lid were charged with unshed
    tears. 135
What could her grief be?—she had all she
    loved,
And he who had so loved her was not
    there
To trouble with bad hopes, or evil wish,
Or ill-repressed affliction, her pure
    thoughts.
What could her grief be?—she had loved
    him not, 140
Nor given him cause to deem himself be-
    loved,
Nor could he be a part of that which
    preyed
Upon her mind—a specter of the past.

6

A change came o'er the spirit of my dream.
The Wanderer was returned.—I saw him
    stand 145
Before an Altar—with a gentle bride;

Her face was fair, but was not that which
    made
The Starlight of his Boyhood;—as he stood
Even at the altar, o'er his brow there came
The self-same aspect, and the quivering
    shock 150
That in the antique Oratory shook
His bosom in its solitude; and then—
As in that hour—a moment o'er his face
The tablet of unutterable thoughts
Was traced,—and then it faded as it
    came, 155
And he stood calm and quiet, and he spoke
The fitting vows, but heard not his own
    words,
And all things reeled around him; he could
    see
Not that which was, nor that which should
    have been—
But the old mansion, and the accustomed
    hall, 160
And the remembered chambers, and the
    place,
The day, the hour, the sunshine, and the
    shade,
All things pertaining to that place and
    hour,
And her who was his destiny, came back
And thrust themselves between him and the
    light: 165
What business had they there at such a
    time?

7

A change came o'er the spirit of my dream.
The Lady of his love:—Oh! she was
    changed
As by the sickness of the soul; her mind
Had wandered from its dwelling, and her
    eyes 170
They had not their own luster, but the
    look
Which is not of the earth; she was become
The queen of a fantastic realm; her
    thoughts
Were combinations of disjointed things;
And forms impalpable and unperceived 175
Of others' sight familiar were to hers.
And this the world calls frenzy; but the
    wise
Have a far deeper madness, and the glance
Of melancholy is a fearful gift;
What is it but the telescope of truth? 180
Which strips the distance of its fantasies,
And brings life near in utter nakedness,
Making the cold reality too real!

8

A change came o'er the spirit of my dream.
The Wanderer was alone as heretofore, 185

The beings which surrounded him were
    gone,
Or were at war with him; he was a mark
For blight and desolation, compassed round
With Hatred and Contention; Pain was
    mixed
In all which was served up to him, until, 190
Like to the Pontic monarch of old days,
He fed on poisons, and they had no power,
But were a kind of nutriment; he lived
Through that which had been death to
    many men,
And made him friends of mountains: with
    the stars   195
And the quick Spirit of the Universe
He held his dialogues; and they did teach
To him the magic of their mysteries;
To him the book of Night was opened
    wide,
And voices from the deep abyss re-
    vealed,   200
A marvel and a secret—Be it so.

9

My dream was past; it had no further
    change.
It was of a strange order, that the doom
Of these two creatures should be thus
    traced out
Almost like a reality—the one   205
To end in madness—both in misery.
July, 1816   1816

SONNET ON CHILLON

Eternal Spirit of the chainless Mind!
Brightest in dungeons, Liberty! thou art,
For there thy habitation is the heart—
The heart which love of thee alone can
    bind;
And when thy sons to fetters are con-
    signed—   5
To fetters, and the damp vault's dayless
    gloom,
Their country conquers with their martyr-
    dom,
And Freedom's fame finds wings on every
    wind.
Chillon! thy prison is a holy place,
And thy sad floor an altar—for 'twas
    trod,   10
Until his very steps have left a trace
Worn, as if thy cold pavement were a sod,
By Bonnivard!   May none those marks
    efface!
For they appeal from tyranny to God.
1816   1816

THE PRISONER OF CHILLON

My hair is gray, but not with years,
    Nor grew it white
    In a single night,
As men's have grown from sudden fears:
My limbs are bowed, though not with toil, 5
    But rusted with a vile repose,
For they have been a dungeon's spoil,
    And mine has been the fate of those
To whom the goodly earth and air
Are banned, and barred—forbidden fare: 10
But this was for my father's faith
I suffered chains and courted death;
That father perished at the stake
For tenets he would not forsake;
And for the same his lineal race   15
In darkness found a dwelling-place;
We were seven—who now are one,
    Six in youth, and one in age,
Finished as they had begun,
    Proud of Persecution's rage;   20
One in fire, and two in field,
Their belief with blood have sealed,
Dying as their father died,
For the God their foes denied;
Three were in a dungeon cast,   25
Of whom this wreck is left the last.

There are seven pillars of Gothic mold,
In Chillon's dungeons deep and old,
There are seven columns, massy and gray,
Dim with a dull imprisoned ray,   30
A sunbeam which hath lost its way,
And through the crevice and the cleft
Of the thick wall is fallen and left;
Creeping o'er the floor so damp,
Like a marsh's meteor lamp: 35
And in each pillar there is a ring,
    And in each ring there is a chain;
That iron is a cankering thing,
    For in these limbs its teeth remain,
With marks that will not wear away,   40
Till I have done with this new day,
Which now is painful to these eyes,
Which have not seen the sun so rise
For years—I cannot count them o'er,
I lost their long and heavy score,   45
When my last brother drooped and died,
And I lay living by his side.

They chained us each to a column stone,
And we were three—yet, each alone;
We could not move a single pace,   50
We could not see each other's face,
But with that pale and livid light
That made us strangers in our sight:
And thus together—yet apart,
Fettered in hand, but joined in heart,   55
'Twas still some solace, in the dearth

Of the pure elements of earth,
To hearken to each other's speech,
And each turn comforter to each
With some new hope, or legend old,   60
Or song heroically bold;
But even these at length grew cold.
Our voices took a dreary tone,
An echo of the dungeon stone,
    A grating sound, not full and free   65
    As they of yore were wont to be:
    It might be fancy, but to me
They never sounded like our own.

I was the eldest of the three,
    And to uphold and cheer the rest   70
    I ought to do—and did my best;
And each did well in his degree.
    The youngest, whom my father loved,
Because our mother's brow was given
To him, with eyes as blue as heaven—   75
    For him my soul was sorely moved;
And truly might it be distressed
To see such bird in such a nest;
For he was beautiful as day
    (When day was beautiful to me   80
    As to young eagles, being free)—
    A polar day, which will not see
A sunset till its summer's gone,
    Its sleepless summer of long light,
The snow-clad offspring of the sun: 85
    And thus he was as pure and bright,
And in his natural spirit gay,
With tears for nought but others' ills,
And then they flowed like mountain rills,
Unless he could assuage the woe   90
Which he abhorred to view below.

The other was as pure of mind,
But formed to combat with his kind;
Strong in his frame, and of a mood
Which 'gainst the world in war had
    stood,   95
And perished in the foremost rank
    With joy:—but not in chains to pine:
His spirit withered with their clank,
    I saw it silently decline—
    And so perchance in sooth did mine: 100
But yet I forced it on to cheer
Those relics of a home so dear.
He was a hunter of the hills,
    Had followed there the deer and wolf;
    To him his dungeon was a gulf,   105
And fettered feet the worst of ills.

    Lake Leman lies by Chillon's walls:
A thousand feet in depth below,
Its massy waters meet and flow;
Thus much the fathom-line was sent   110
From Chillon's snowy-white battlement,
    Which round about the wave inthrals:

A double dungeon wall and wave
Have made—and like a living grave.
Below the surface of the lake   115
The dark vault lies wherein we lay;
We heard it ripple night and day;
    Sounding o'er our heads it knocked;
And I have felt the winter's spray
Wash through the bars when winds were
    high   120
And wanton in the happy sky;
    And then the very rock hath rocked,
    And I have felt it shake, unshocked,
Because I could have smiled to see
The death that would have set me free.   125

I said my nearer brother pined,
I said his mighty heart declined,
He loathed and put away his food;
It was not that 'twas coarse and rude,
For we were used to hunters' fare,   130
And for the like had little care:
The milk drawn from the mountain goat
Was changed for water from the moat,
Our bread was such as captives' tears
Have moistened many a thousand years, 135
Since man first pent his fellow men
Like brutes within an iron den;
But what were these to us or him?
These wasted not his heart or limb;
My brother's soul was of that mold   140
Which in a palace had grown cold,
Had his free breathing been denied
The range of the steep mountain's side;
But why delay the truth?—he died.
I saw, and could not hold his head,   145
Nor reach his dying hand—nor dead,—
Though hard I strove, but strove in vain,
To rend and gnash my bonds in twain.
He died—and they unlocked his chain,
And scooped for him a shallow grave   150
Even from the cold earth of our cave.
I begged them, as a boon, to lay
His corse in dust whereon the day
Might shine—it was a foolish thought,
But then within my brain it wrought,   155
That even in death his freeborn breast
In such a dungeon could not rest.
I might have spared my idle prayer—
They coldly laughed, and laid him there:
The flat and turfless earth above   160
The being we so much did love;
His empty chain above it leant,
Such murder's fitting monument!

But he, the favorite and the flower,
Most cherished since his natal hour,   165
His mother's image in fair face,
The infant love of all his race,
His martyred father's dearest thought,
My latest care, for whom I sought

To hoard my life, that his might be   170
Less wretched now, and one day free;
He, too, who yet had held untired
A spirit natural or inspired—
He, too, was struck, and day by day
Was withered on the stalk away.   175
Oh, God! it is a fearful thing
To see the human soul take wing
In any shape, in any mood:
I've seen it rushing forth in blood,
I've seen it on the breaking ocean   180
Strive with a swoln convulsive motion,
I've seen the sick and ghastly bed
Of Sin delirious with its dread;
But these were horrors—this was woe
Unmixed with such—but sure and slow: 185
He faded, and so calm and meek,
So softly worn, so sweetly weak,
So tearless, yet so tender—kind,
And grieved for those he left behind;
With all the while a cheek whose bloom 190
Was as a mockery of the tomb,
Whose tints as gently sunk away
As a departing rainbow's ray;
An eye of most transparent light,
That almost made the dungeon bright, 195
And not a word of murmur, not
A groan o'er his untimely lot,—
A little talk of better days,
A little hope my own to raise,
For I was sunk in silence—lost   200
In this last loss, of all the most;
And then the sighs he would suppress
Of fainting nature's feebleness,
More slowly drawn, grew less and less:
I listened, but I could not hear;   205
I called, for I was wild with fear;
I knew 'twas hopeless, but my dread
Would not be thus admonished;
I called, and thought I heard a sound—
I burst my chain with one strong bound, 210
And rushed to him:—I found him not,
I only stirred in this black spot,
I only lived, *I* only drew
The accursed breath of dungeon-dew;
The last, the sole, the dearest link 215
Between me and the eternal brink,
Which bound me to my failing race,
Was broken in this fatal place.
One on the earth, and one beneath—
My brothers—both had ceased to
    breathe: 220
I took that hand which lay so still,
Alas! my own was full as chill;
I had not strength to stir, or strive,
But felt that I was still alive—
A frantic feeling, when we know   225
That what we love shall ne'er be so.
    I know not why
    I could not die,

I had no earthly hope—but faith,
And that forbade a selfish death.   230

What next befell me then and there
    I know not well—I never knew;
First came the loss of light, and air,
    And then of darkness too:
I had no thought, no feeling—none; 235
Among the stones I stood a stone,
And was, scarce conscious what I wist,
As shrubless crags within the mist;
For all was blank, and bleak, and gray;
It was not night, it was not day;   240
It was not even the dungeon-light,
So hateful to my heavy sight,
But vagrancy absorbing space,
And fixedness—without a place;
There were no stars, no earth, no time, 245
No check, no change, no good, no crime—
But silence, and a stirless breath
Which neither was of life nor death;
A sea of stagnant idleness,
Blind, boundless, mute, and motionless! 250

A light broke in upon my brain,—
    It was the carol of a bird;
It ceased, and then it came again,
    The sweetest song ear ever heard,
And mine was thankful till my eyes 255
Ran over with the glad surprise,
And they that moment could not see
I was the mate of misery;
But then by dull degrees came back
My senses to their wonted track;   260
I saw the dungeon walls and floor
Close slowly round me as before;
I saw the glimmer of the sun
Creeping as it before had done,
But through the crevice where it came 265
That bird was perched, as fond and tame,
    And tamer than upon the tree;
A lovely bird, with azure wings,
And song that said a thousand things,
    And seemed to say them all for me! 270
I never saw its like before,
I ne'er shall see its likeness more:
It seemed like me to want a mate,
But was not half so desolate,
And it was come to love me when   275
None lived to love me so again,
And cheering from my dungeon's brink,
Had brought me back to feel and think.
I know not if it late were free,
    Or broke its cage to perch on mine, 280
But knowing well captivity,
    Sweet bird! I could not wish for thine!
Or if it were, in winged guise,
    A visitant from Paradise;
For—Heaven forgive that thought! the
    while   285

Which made me both to weep and smile—
I sometimes deemed that it might be
My brother's soul come down to me;
But then at last away it flew,
And then 'twas mortal—well I knew,   290
For he would never thus have flown,
And left me twice so doubly lone,—
Lone—as the corse within its shroud,
Lone—as a solitary cloud,
  A single cloud on a sunny day,   295
While all the rest of heaven is clear,
A frown upon the atmosphere,
That hath no business to appear
  When skies are blue, and earth is gay.
A kind of change came in my fate,   300
My keepers grew compassionate;
I know not what had made them so,
They were inured to sights of woe,
But so it was:—my broken chain
With links unfastened did remain,   305
And it was liberty to stride
Along my cell from side to side,
And up and down, and then athwart,
And tread it over every part;
And round the pillars one by one,   310
Returning where my walk begun,
Avoiding only, as I trod,
My brothers' graves without a sod;
For if I thought with heedless tread
My step profaned their lowly bed,   315
My breath came gaspingly and thick,
And my crushed heart fell blind and sick.

I made a footing in the wall,
  It was not therefrom to escape,
For I had buried one and all   320
  Who loved me in a human shape;
And the whole earth would henceforth be
A wider prison unto me:
No child, no sire, no kin had I,
No partner in my misery;   325
I thought of this, and I was glad,
For thought of them had made me mad;
But I was curious to ascend
To my barred windows, and to bend
Once more, upon the mountains high,   330
The quiet of a loving eye.

I saw them—and they were the same,
They were not changed like me in frame;
I saw their thousand years of snow
On high—their wide long lake below,   335
And the blue Rhone in fullest flow;
I heard the torrents leap and gush
O'er channeled rock and broken bush;
I saw the white-walled distant town,
And whiter sails go skimming down,   340
And then there was a little isle,
Which in my very face did smile,
  The only one in view;

A small green isle, it seemed no more,
Scarce broader than my dungeon floor,   345
But in it there were three tall trees,
And o'er it blew the mountain breeze,
And by it there were waters flowing,
And on it there were young flowers grow-
  ing,
  Of gentle breath and hue.   350
The fish swam by the castle wall,
And they seemed joyous each and all;
The eagle rode the rising blast,
Methought he never flew so fast
As then to me he seemed to fly;   355
And then new tears came in my eye,
And I felt troubled—and would fain
I had not left my recent chain;
And when I did descend again,
The darkness of my dim abode   360
Fell on me as a heavy load;
It was as in a new-dug grave,
Closing o'er one we sought to save,—
And yet my glance, too much oppressed
Had almost need of such a rest.   365

It might be months, or years, or days—
  I kept no count, I took no note,
I had no hope my eyes to raise,
  And clear them of their dreary mote.
At last men came to set me free;   370
  I asked not why, and recked not where;
It was at length the same to me,
Fettered or fetterless to be,
  I learned to love despair.
And thus when they appeared at last,   375
And all my bonds aside were cast,
These heavy walls to me had grown
A hermitage—and all my own!
And half I felt as they were come
To tear me from a second home.   380
With spiders I had friendship made,
And watched them in their sullen trade,
Had seen the mice by moonlight play,
And why should I feel less than they?
We were all inmates of one place,   385
And I, the monarch of each race,
Had power to kill—yet, strange to tell!
In quiet we had learned to dwell;
My very chains and I grew friends,
So much a long communion tends   390
To make us what we are:—even I
Regained my freedom with a sigh.

1816

POEMS OF THE SEPARATION

FARE THEE WELL

"Alas! they had been friends in youth:
But whispering tongues can poison truth;
And constancy lives in realms above;

And life is thorny; and youth is vain;
And to be wroth with one we love,
Doth work like madness in the brain;

———

But never either found another
To free the hollow heart from paining—
They stood aloof, the scars remaining,
Like cliffs which had been rent asunder;
A dreary sea now flows between,
But neither heat, nor frost, nor thunder,
Shall wholly do away, I ween,
The marks of that which once hath been."
　　　　　—COLERIDGE's *Christabel*.

Fare thee well! and if for ever,
　Still for ever, fare thee well:
Even though unforgiving, never
　'Gainst thee shall my heart rebel.

Would that breast were bared before thee 5
　Where thy head so oft hath lain,
While that placid sleep came o'er thee
　Which thou ne'er canst know again:

Would that breast, by thee glanced over,
　Every inmost thought could show! 10
Then thou wouldst at last discover
　'Twas not well to spurn it so.

Though the world for this commend thee—
　Though it smile upon the blow,
Even its praises must offend thee, 15
　Founded on another's woe:

Though my many faults defaced me,
　Could no other arm be found,
Than the one which once embraced me,
　To inflict a cureless wound? 20

Yet, oh yet, thyself deceive not;
　Love may sink by slow decay,
But by sudden wrench, believe not
　Hearts can thus be torn away:

Still thine own its life retaineth, 25
　Still must mine, though bleeding, beat;
And the undying thought which paineth
　Is—that we no more may meet.

These are words of deeper sorrow
　Than the wail above the dead; 30
Both shall live, but every morrow
　Wake us from a widowed bed.

And when thou wouldst solace gather,
　When our child's first accents flow,
Wilt thou teach her to say "Father!" 35
　Though his care she must forego?

When her little hands shall press thee,
　When her lip to thine is pressed,
Think of him whose prayer shall bless thee,
　Think of him thy love had blessed! 40

Should her lineaments resemble
　Those thou never more may'st see,
Then thy heart will softly tremble
　With a pulse yet true to me.

All my faults perchance thou knowest, 45
　All my madness none can know;
All my hopes, where'er thou goest,
　Wither, yet with *thee* they go.

Every feeling hath been shaken;
　Pride, which not a world could bow, 50
Bows to thee—by thee forsaken,
　Even my soul forsakes me now:

But 'tis done—all words are idle—
　Words from me are vainer still;
But the thoughts we cannot bridle 55
　Force their way without the will.

Fare thee well! thus disunited,
　Torn from every nearer tie,
Seared in heart, and lone, and blighted,
　More than this I scarce can die. 60

March 18, 1816　　　　　　1816

A SKETCH

Born in the garret, in the kitchen bred,
Promoted thence to deck her mistress'
　　head;
Next—for some gracious service unex-
　　pressed,
And from its wages only to be guessed—
Raised from the toilette to the table,—
　　where 5
Her wondering betters wait behind her
　　chair.
With eye unmoved, and forehead un-
　　abashed,
She dines from off the plate she lately
　　washed.
Quick with the tale, and ready with the lie,
The genial confidante, and general spy, 10
Who could, ye gods! her next employment
　　guess—
An only infant's earliest governess!
She taught the child to read, and taught
　　so well,
That she herself, by teaching, learned to
　　spell.
An adept next in penmanship she grows, 15
As many a nameless slander deftly shows:
What she had made the pupil of her art

None know—but that high Soul secured
    the heart,
And panted for the truth it could not
    hear,
With longing breast and undeluded ear. 20
Foiled was perversion by that youthful
    mind,
Which Flattery fooled not, Baseness could
    not blind,
Deceit infect not, near Contagion soil,
Indulgence weaken, nor Example spoil,
Nor mastered Science tempt her to look
    down   25
On humbler talents with a pitying frown,
Nor Genius swell, nor Beauty render vain,
Nor Envy ruffle to retaliate pain,
Nor Fortune change, Pride raise, nor Pas-
    sion bow,
Nor Virtue teach austerity—till now.   30
Serenely purest of her sex that live,
But wanting one sweet weakness—to for-
    give,
Too shocked at faults her soul can never
    know,
She deems that all could be like her be-
    low:
Foe to all vice, yet hardly Virtue's friend 35
For Virtue pardons those she would amend.

But to the theme, now laid aside too
    long,
The baleful burthen of this honest song,
Though all her former functions are no
    more,
She rules the circle which she served be-
    fore.   40
If mothers—none know why—before her
    quake;
If daughters dread her for the mothers'
    sake;
If early habits—those false links, which
    bind
At times the loftiest to the meanest mind—
Have given her power too deeply to instil 45
The angry essence of her deadly will;
If like a snake she steal within your walls,
Till the black slime betray her as she
    crawls;
If like a viper to the heart she wind,
And leave the venom there she did not
    find;   50
What marvel that this hag of hatred works
Eternal evil latent as she lurks,
To make a Pandemonium where she
    dwells,
And reign the Hecate of domestic hells?
Skilled by a touch to deepen scandal's
    tints   55
With all the kind mendacity of hints,

While mingling truth with falsehood,
    sneers with smiles,
A thread of candor with a web of wiles:
A plain blunt show of briefly-spoken seem-
    ing,
To hide her bloodless heart's soul-hardened
    scheming;   60
A lip of lies; a face formed to conceal,
And, without feeling, mock at all who feel:
With a vile mask the Gorgon would dis-
    own,—
A cheek of parchment, and an eye of stone.
Mark, how the channels of her yellow
    blood   65
Ooze to her skin, and stagnate there to
    mud,
Cased like the centipede in saffron mail,
Or darker greenness of the scorpion's
    scale—
(For drawn from reptiles only may we
    trace
Congenial colors in that soul or face)—   70
Look on her features! and behold her mind
As in a mirror of itself defined:
Look on the picture! deem it not o'er-
    charged—
There is no trait which might not be
    enlarged:
Yet true to "Nature's journeymen," who
    made   75
This monster when their mistress left off
    trade—
This female dog-star of her little sky,
Where all beneath her influence droop or
    die.

Oh! wretch without a tear—without a
    thought,
Save joy above the ruin thou hast
    wrought—   80
The time shall come, nor long remote,
    when thou
Shalt feel far more than thou inflictest
    now;
Feel for thy vile self-loving self in vain,
And turn thee howling in unpitied pain.
May the strong curse of crushed affections
    light   85
Back on thy bosom with reflected blight!
And make thee in thy leprosy of mind
As loathsome to thyself as to mankind!
Till all thy self-thoughts curdle into hate,
Black—as thy will for others would
    create;   90
Till thy hard heart be calcined into dust,
And thy soul welter in its hideous crust.
Oh, may thy grave be sleepless as the bed,
The widowed couch of fire, that thou hast
    spread!

Then, when thou fain wouldst weary
   Heaven with a prayer,   95
Look on thine earthly victims—and de-
   spair!
Down to the dust!—and, as thou rott'st
   away,
Even worms shall perish on thy poisonous
   clay.
But for the love I bore, and still must
   bear,
To her thy malice from all ties would
   tear—   100
Thy name—thy human name—to every eye
The climax of all scorn should hang on
   high
Exalted o'er thy less abhorred compeers—
And festering in the infamy of years.
March 29, 1816   1819

STANZAS TO AUGUSTA

I

Though the day of my destiny's over,
   And the star of my fate hath declined,
Thy soft heart refused to discover
   The faults which so many could find;
Though thy soul with my grief was ac-
   quainted,   5
   It shrunk not to share it with me,
And the love which my spirit hath painted
   It never hath found but in *thee*.

II

Then when nature around me is smiling,
   The last smile which answers to mine,   10
I do not believe it beguiling,
   Because it reminds me of thine;
And when winds are at war with the ocean,
   As the breasts I believed in with me,
If their billows excite an emotion,   15
   It is that they bear me from *thee*.

III

Though the rock of my last hope is
   shivered,
   And its fragments are sunk in the wave,
Though I feel that my soul is delivered
   To pain—it shall not be its slave.   20
There is many a pang to pursue me:
   They may crush, but they shall not con-
   temn;
They may torture, but shall not subdue
   me;
   'Tis of *thee* that I think—not of them.

IV

Though human, thou didst not deceive
   me,   25
   Though woman, thou didst not forsake,

Though loved, thou forborest to grieve me,
   Though slandered, thou never couldst
   shake:
Though trusted, thou didst not disclaim
   me,
   Though parted, it was not to fly,   30
Though watchful, 'twas not to defame me,
   Nor, mute, that the world might belie.

V

Yet I blame not the world, nor despise it,
   Nor the war of the many with one;
If my soul was not fitted to prize it,   35
   'Twas folly not sooner to shun:
And if dearly that error hath cost me,
   And more than I once could foresee,
I have found that, whatever it lost me,
   It could not deprive me of *thee*.   40

VI

From the wreck of the past, which hath
   perished,
   Thus much I at least may recall,
It hath taught me that what I most cher-
   ished
   Deserved to be dearest of all:
In the desert a fountain is springing,   45
   In the wide waste there still is a tree,
And a bird in the solitude singing,
   Which speaks to my spirit of *thee*.
1816   1816

STANZAS FOR MUSIC

There be none of Beauty's daughters
   With a magic like thee;
And like music on the waters
   Is thy sweet voice to me:
When, as if its sound were causing   5
The charmed ocean's pausing,
The waves lie still and gleaming,
And the lulled winds seem dreaming:

And the midnight moon is weaving
   Her bright chain o'er the deep;   10
Whose breast is gently heaving,
   As an infant's asleep:
So the spirit bows before thee,
To listen and adore thee;
With a full but soft emotion,   15
Like the swell of Summer's ocean.
March 28, 1816   1816

EPISTLE TO AUGUSTA

My sister! my sweet sister! if a name
Dearer and purer were, it should be
   thine;
Mountains and seas divide us, but I
   claim

No tears, but tenderness to answer mine:
Go where I will, to me thou art the
    same—   5
A loved regret which I would not resign.
There are yet two things in my destiny,—
A world to roam through, and a home with
    thee.

The first were nothing—had I still the
    last,
It were the haven of my happiness;   10
But other claims and other ties thou hast,
And mine is not the wish to make them
    less.
A strange doom is thy father's son's, and
    past
Recalling, as it lies beyond redress;
Reversed for him our grandsire's fate of
    yore,—   15
He had no rest at sea, nor I on shore.

If my inheritance of storms hath been
In other elements, and on the rocks
Of perils, overlooked or unforeseen,
I have sustained my share of worldly
    shocks,   20
The fault was mine; nor do I seek to
    screen
My errors with defensive paradox;
I have been cunning in mine overthrow,
The careful pilot of my proper woe.

Mine were my faults, and mine be their
    reward.   25
My whole life was a contest, since the
    day
That gave me being, gave me that which
    marred
The gift,—a fate, or will, that walked
    astray;
And I at times have found the struggle
    hard,
And thought of shaking off my bonds of
    clay: 30
But now I fain would for a time survive,
If but to see what next can well arrive.

Kingdoms and empires in my little day
I have outlived, and yet I am not old;
And when I look on this, the petty
    spray   35
Of my own years of trouble, which have
    rolled
Like a wild bay of breakers, melts away:
Something—I know not what—does still
    uphold
A spirit of slight patience;—not in vain,
Even for its own sake, do we purchase
    pain.   40

Perhaps the workings of defiance stir
Within me,—or perhaps a cold despair,
Brought on when ills habitually recur,—
Perhaps a kinder clime, or purer air
(For even to this may change of soul
    refer,   45
And with light armor we may learn to
    bear),
Have taught me a strange quiet, which
    was not
The chief companion of a calmer lot.

I feel almost at times as I have felt
In happy childhood; trees, and flowers,
    and brooks,   50
Which do remember me of where I dwelt
Ere my young mind was sacrificed to
    books,
Come as of yore upon me, and can melt
My heart with recognition of their looks;
And even at moments I could think I
    see   55
Some living thing to love—but none like
    thee.

Here are the Alpine landscapes which
    create
A fund for contemplation;—to admire
Is a brief feeling of a trivial date;
But something worthier do such scenes
    inspire: 60
Here to be lonely is not desolate,
For much I view which I could most
    desire,
And, above all, a lake I can behold
Lovelier, not dearer, than our own of old.

Oh that thou wert but with me!—but I
    grow   65
The fool of my own wishes, and forget
The solitude, which I have vaunted so,
Has lost its praise in this but one regret;
There may be others which I less may
    show;—
I am not of the plaintive mood, and
    yet   70
I feel an ebb in my philosophy,
And the tide rising in my altered eye.

I did remind thee of our own dear lake,
By the old hall which may be mine no
    more.
Leman's is fair; but think not I forsake   75
The sweet remembrance of a dearer
    shore:
Sad havoc time must with my memory
    make,
Ere *that* or *thou* can fade these eyes
    before;

Though, like all things which I have
  loved, they are
Resigned forever, or divided far.   80

The world is all before me; I but ask
Of nature that with which she will
  comply—
It is but in her summer's sun to bask,
To mingle with the quiet of her sky,
To see her gentle face without a mask, 85
And never gaze on it with apathy.
She was my early friend, and now shall
  be
My sister—till I look again on thee.

I can reduce all feelings but this one;
And that I would not;—for at length I
  see   90
Such scenes as those wherein my life
  begun,
The earliest—even the only paths for
  me;
Had I but sooner learnt the crowd to
  shun,
I had been better than I now can be;
The passions which have torn me would
  have slept;   95
I had not suffered, and *thou* hadst not
  wept.

With false ambition what had I to do?
Little with love, and least of all with
  fame;
And yet they came unsought, and with
  me grew,
And made me all which they can make—
  a name.   100
Yet this was not the end I did pursue;
Surely I once beheld a nobler aim.
But all is over—I am one the more
To baffled millions which have gone before.

And for the future, this world's future
  may   105
From me demand but little of my care;
I have outlived myself by many a day,
Having survived so many things that
  were;
My years have been no slumber, but the
  prey
Of ceaseless vigils; for I had the share 110
Of life which might have filled a century,
Before its fourth in time had passed me by.

And for the remnant which may be to
  come
I am content; and for the past I feel
Not thankless,—for within the crowded
  sum   115

Of struggles, happiness at times would
  steal;
And for the present, I would not be-
  numb
My feelings further.—Nor shall I conceal
That with all this I still can look around,
And worship nature with a thought pro-
  found.   120

For thee, my own sweet sister, in thy
  heart
I know myself secure, as thou in mine;
We were and are—I am, even as thou
  art—
Beings who ne'er each other can resign;
It is the same, together or apart,   125
From life's commencement to its slow
  decline
We are entwined—let death come slow
  or fast,
The tie which bound the first endures the
  last!

1816   1830

DARKNESS

I had a dream, which was not all a dream.
The bright sun was extinguished, and the
  stars
Did wander darkling in the eternal space,
Rayless, and pathless, and the icy earth
Swung blind and blackening in the moon-
  less air;   5
Morn came and went—and came, and
  brought no day,
And men forgot their passions in the dread
Of this their desolation; and all hearts
Were chilled into a selfish prayer for light:
And they did live by watchfires—and the
  thrones,   10
The palaces of crowned kings—the huts,
The habitations of all things which dwell,
Were burnt for beacons; cities were con-
  sumed,
And men were gathered round their blaz-
  ing homes
To look once more into each other's
  face;   15
Happy were those who dwelt within the
  eye
Of the volcanos, and their mountain-torch:
A fearful hope was all the world contained;
Forests were set on fire—but hour by hour
They fell and faded—and the crackling
  trunks   20
Extinguished with a crash—and all was
  black.
The brows of men by the despairing light
Wore an unearthly aspect, as by fits

The flashes fell upon them; some lay down
And hid their eyes and wept; and some did
    rest   25
Their chins upon their clenched hands,
    and smiled;
And others hurried to and fro, and fed
Their funeral piles with fuel, and looked
    up
With mad disquietude on the dull sky,
The pall of a past world; and then again 30
With curses cast them down upon the
    dust,
And gnashed their teeth and howled: the
    wild birds shrieked
And, terrified, did flutter on the ground,
And flap their useless wings; the wildest
    brutes
Came tame and tremulous; and vipers
    crawled   35
And twined themselves among the multi-
    tude,
Hissing, but stingless—they were slain for
    food!
And war, which for a moment was no
    more,
Did glut himself again:—a meal was
    bought
With blood, and each sate sullenly apart 40
Gorging himself in gloom: no love was left;
All earth was but one thought—and that
    was death
Immediate and inglorious; and the pang
Of famine fed upon all entrails—men
Died, and their bones were tombless as
    their flesh;   45
The meagre by the meagre were devoured,
Even dogs assailed their masters, all save
    one,
And he was faithful to a corse, and kept
The birds and beasts and famished men at
    bay,
Till hunger clung them, or the dropping
    dead   50
Lured their lank jaws; himself sought out
    no food,
But with a piteous and perpetual moan,
And a quick desolate cry, licking the hand
Which answered not with a caress—he
    died.
The crowd was famished by degrees; but
    two   55
Of an enormous city did survive,
And they were enemies: they met beside
The dying embers of an altar-place,
Where had been heaped a mass of holy
    things
For an unholy usage; they raked up,   60
And shivering scraped with their cold skele-
    ton hands
The feeble ashes. and their feeble breath

Blew for a little life, and made a flame
Which was a mockery; then they lifted up
Their eyes as it grew lighter, and beheld 65
Each other's aspects—saw, and shrieked,
    and died—
Even of their mutual hideousness they
    died,
Unknowing who he was upon whose brow
Famine had written Fiend. The world was
    void,
The populous and the powerful was a
    lump   70
Seasonless, herbless, treeless, manless, life-
    less—
A lump of death—a chaos of hard clay.
The rivers, lakes, and ocean all stood still,
And nothing stirred within their silent
    depths;
Ships sailorless lay rotting on the sea,   75
And their masts fell down piecemeal: as
    they dropped
They slept on the abyss without a surge—
The waves were dead; the tides were in
    their grave,
The Moon, their mistress, had expired
    before;
The winds were withered in the stagnant
    air,   80
And the clouds perished; Darkness had
    no need
Of aid from them—She was the Universe.
1816   1816

PROMETHEUS

Titan! to whose immortal eyes
    The sufferings of mortality,
    Seen in their sad reality,
Were not as things that gods despise;
What was thy pity's recompense?   5
A silent suffering, and intense;
The rock, the vulture, and the chain,
All that the proud can feel of pain,
The agony they do not show,
The suffocating sense of woe,   10
    Which speaks but in its loneliness,
And then is jealous lest the sky
Should have a listener, nor will sigh
    Until its voice is echoless.

Titan! to thee the strife was given   15
    Between the suffering and the will,
    Which torture where they cannot kill;
And the inexorable Heaven,
And the deaf tyranny of Fate,
The ruling principle of Hate,   20
Which for its pleasure doth create
The things it may annihilate,

Refused thee even the boon to die:
The wretched gift eternity
Was thine—and thou hast borne it well. 25
All that the thunderer wrung from thee
Was but the menace which flung back
On him the torments of thy rack;
The fate thou didst so well foresee,
But would not to appease him tell; 30
And in thy silence was his sentence,
And in his soul a vain repentance,
And evil dread so ill dissembled,
That in his hand the lightnings trembled.

Thy Godlike crime was to be kind, 35
  To render with thy precepts less
  The sum of human wretchedness,
And strengthen man with his own mind;
But baffled as thou wert from high,
Still in thy patient energy, 40
In the endurance, and repulse
  Of thine impenetrable spirit,
Which Earth and Heaven could not con-
  vulse,
  A mighty lesson we inherit:
Thou art a symbol and a sign 45
  To mortals of their fate and force;
Like thee, man is in part divine,
  A troubled stream from a pure source;
And man in portions can foresee
His own funereal destiny; 50
His wretchedness, and his resistance,
And his sad unallied existence:
To which his spirit may oppose

Itself—and equal to all woes,
  And a firm will, and a deep sense, 55
Which even in torture can descry
  Its own concentered recompense,
Triumphant where it dares defy,
And making death a victory.
1816   1816

SONNET TO LAKE LEMAN

Rousseau, Voltaire, our Gibbon, and De
    Staël—
Leman! these names are worthy of thy
    shore,
Thy shore of names like these!—Wert thou
    no more
Their memory thy remembrance would
    recall:
To them thy banks were lovely as to all, 5
But they have made them lovelier, for the
    lore
Of mighty minds doth hallow in the core
Of human hearts the ruin of a wall
Where dwelt the wise and wondrous; but
    by *thee*
How much more, Lake of Beauty! do we
    feel, 10
In sweetly gliding o'er thy crystal sea,
The wild glow of that not ungentle zeal,
Which of the heirs of immortality
Is proud, and makes the breath of glory
    real!
1816   1816

FROM CHILDE HAROLD'S PILGRIMAGE

CANTO III

I

Is thy face like thy mother's, my fair child!
Ada! sole daughter of my house and heart?
When last I saw thy young blue eyes they smiled,
And then we parted,—not as now we part,
But with a hope.—
                    Awaking with a start, 5
The waters heave around me; and on high
The winds lift up their voices: I depart,
Whither I know not; but the hour's gone by,
When Albion's lessening shores could grieve or glad mine eye.

II

Once more upon the waters! yet once more! 10
And the waves bound beneath me as a steed
That knows his rider. Welcome to their roar!
Swift be their guidance, wheresoe'er it lead!
Though the strained mast should quiver as a reed,
And the rent canvas fluttering strew the gale, 15

Still must I on; for I am as a weed,
Flung from the rock, on Ocean's foam to sail
Where'er the surge may sweep, the tempest's breath prevail.

III

In my youth's summer I did sing of one,
The wandering outlaw of his own dark mind; 20
Again I seize the theme, then but begun,
And bear it with me, as the rushing wind
Bears the cloud onwards: in that tale I find
The furrows of long thought, and dried-up tears,
Which, ebbing, leave a sterile track behind, 25
O'er which all heavily the journeying years
Plod the last sands of life,—where not a flower appears.

IV

Since my young days of passion—joy, or pain,
Perchance my heart and harp have lost a string,
And both may jar: it may be, that in vain 30
I would essay as I have sung to sing.
Yet, though a dreary strain, to this I cling;
So that it wean me from the weary dream
Of selfish grief or gladness—so it fling
Forgetfulness around me—it shall seem 35
To me, though to none else, a not ungrateful theme.

V

He, who grown aged in this world of woe,
In deeds, not years, piercing the depths of life,
So that no wonder waits him; nor below
Can love or sorrow, fame, ambition, strife, 40
Cut to his heart again with the keen knife
Of silent, sharp endurance: he can tell
Why thought seeks refuge in lone caves, yet rife
With airy images, and shapes which dwell
Still unimpaired, though old, in the soul's haunted cell. 45

VI

'Tis to create, and in creating live
A being more intense that we endow
With form our fancy, gaining as we give
The life we image, even as I do now.
What am I? Nothing: but not so art thou, 50
Soul of my thought! with whom I traverse earth,
Invisible, but gazing, as I glow
Mixed with thy spirit, blended with thy birth,
And feeling still with thee in my crushed feelings' dearth.

VII

Yet must I think less wildly:—I *have* thought 55
Too long and darkly, till my brain became,
In its own eddy boiling and o'erwrought,
A whirling gulf of phantasy and flame:
And thus, untaught in youth my heart to tame,
My springs of life were poisoned. 'Tis too late! 60
Yet am I changed; though still enough the same
In strength to bear what time cannot abate,
And feed on bitter fruits without accusing Fate.

VIII

Something too much of this:—but now 'tis past,
And the spell closes with its silent seal. 65

Long absent Harold reappears at last;
He of the breast which fain no more would feel,
Wrung with the wounds which kill not, but ne'er heal;
Yet Time, who changes all, had altered him
In soul and aspect as in age: years steal 70
Fire from the mind as vigor from the limb;
And life's enchanted cup but sparkles near the brim.

IX

His had been quaffed too quickly, and he found
The dregs were wormwood; but he filled again,
And from a purer fount, on holier ground, 75
And deemed its spring perpetual; but in vain!
Still round him clung invisible a chain
Which galled forever, fettering though unseen,
And heavy though it clanked not; worn with pain,
Which pined although it spoke not, and grew keen, 80
Entering with every step he took through many a scene.

X

Secure in guarded coldness, he had mixed
Again in fancied safety with his kind,
And deemed his spirit now so firmly fixed
And sheathed with an invulnerable mind, 85
That, if no joy, no sorrow lurked behind;
And he, as one, might 'midst the many stand
Unheeded, searching through the crowd to find
Fit speculation; such as in strange land
He found in wonder-works of God and Nature's hand. 90

XI

But who can view the ripened rose, nor seek
To wear it? who can curiously behold
The smoothness and the sheen of beauty's cheek,
Nor feel the heart can never all grow old?
Who can contemplate Fame through clouds unfold 95
The star which rises o'er her steep, nor climb?
Harold, once more within the vortex, rolled
On with the giddy circle, chasing Time,
Yet with a nobler aim than in his youth's fond prime.

XII

But soon he knew himself the most unfit 100
Of men to herd with man; with whom he held
Little in common; untaught to submit
His thoughts to others, though his soul was quelled
In youth by his own thoughts; still uncompelled,
He would not yield dominion of his mind 105
To spirits against whom his own rebelled;
Proud though in desolation; which could find
A life within itself, to breathe without mankind.

XIII

Where rose the mountains, there to him were friends;
Where rolled the ocean, thereon was his home; 110
Where a blue sky, and glowing clime, extends,
He had the passion and the power to roam;
The desert, forest, cavern, breaker's foam,
Were unto him companionship; they spake
A mutual language, clearer than the tome 115
Of his land's tongue, which he would oft forsake
For Nature's pages glassed by sunbeams on the lake.

XIV

Like the Chaldean, he could watch the stars,
Till he had peopled them with beings bright
As their own beams; and earth, and earth-born jars, 120
And human frailties, were forgotten quite:
Could he have kept his spirit to that flight
He had been happy; but this clay will sink
Its spark immortal, envying it the light
To which it mounts, as if to break the link 125
That keeps us from yon heaven which woos us to its brink.

XV

But in man's dwellings he became a thing
Restless and worn, and stern and wearisome,
Drooped as a wild-born falcon with clipt wing,
To whom the boundless air alone were home: 130
Then came his fit again, which to o'ercome,
As eagerly the barred-up bird will beat
His breast and beak against his wiry dome
Till the blood tinge his plumage, so the heat
Of his impeded soul would through his bosom eat. 135

XVI

Self-exiled Harold wanders forth again,
With nought of hope left, but with less of gloom;
The very knowledge that he lived in vain,
That all was over on this side the tomb,
Had made Despair a smilingness assume, 140
Which, though 'twere wild,—as on the plundered wreck
When mariners would madly meet their doom
With draughts intemperate on the sinking deck,—
Did yet inspire a cheer, which he forbore to check.

XVII

Stop!—for thy tread is on an empire's dust! 145
An earthquake's spoil is sepulchred below!
Is the spot marked with no colossal bust?
Nor column trophied for triumphal show?
None; but *the moral's truth* tells simpler so,
As the ground was before, thus let it be;— 150
How that red rain hath made the harvest grow!
And is this all the world has gained by thee,
Thou first and last of fields! king-making Victory?

XVIII

And Harold stands upon this place of skulls,
The grave of France, the deadly Waterloo! 155
How in an hour the power which gave annuls
Its gifts, transferring fame as fleeting too!
In "pride of place" here last the eagle flew,
Then tore with bloody talon the rent plain,
Pierced by the shaft of banded nations through; 160
Ambition's life and labors all were vain;
He wears the shattered links of the world's broken chain.

XIX

Fit retribution! Gaul may champ the bit
And foam in fetters;—but is Earth more free?
Did nations combat to make *one* submit; 165
Or league to teach all kings true sovereignty?

What! shall reviving Thraldom again be
The patched-up idol of enlightened days?
Shall we, who struck the Lion down, shall we
Pay the Wolf homage? proffering lowly gaze   170
And servile knees to thrones? No; *prove* before ye praise!

XX

If not, o'er one fallen despot boast no more!
In vain fair cheeks were furrowed with hot tears
For Europe's flowers long rooted up before
The trampler of her vineyards; in vain, years   175
Of death, depopulation, bondage, fears,
Have all been borne, and broken by the accord
Of roused-up millions; all that most endears
Glory, is when the myrtle wreathes a sword
Such as Harmodius drew on Athens' tyrant lord.   180

XXI

There was a sound of revelry by night,
And Belgium's capital had gathered then
Her Beauty and her Chivalry, and bright
The lamps shone o'er fair women and brave men;
A thousand hearts beat happily; and when   185
Music arose with its voluptuous swell,
Soft eyes looked love to eyes which spake again,
And all went merry as a marriage bell;
But hush! hark! a deep sound strikes like a rising knell!

XXII

Did ye not hear it?—No; 'twas but the wind,   190
Or the car rattling o'er the stony street;
On with the dance! let joy be unconfined;
No sleep till morn, when Youth and Pleasure meet
To chase the glowing Hours with flying feet—
But hark!—that heavy sound breaks in once more,   195
As if the clouds its echo would repeat;
And nearer, clearer, deadlier than before!
Arm! Arm! it is—it is—the cannon's opening roar!

XXIII

Within a windowed niche of that high hall
Sate Brunswick's fated chieftain; he did hear   200
That sound the first amidst the festival,
And caught its tone with Death's prophetic ear;
And when they smiled because he deemed it near,
His heart more truly knew that peal too well
Which stretched his father on a bloody bier,   205
And roused the vengeance blood alone could quell;
He rushed into the field, and, foremost fighting, fell.

XXIV

Ah! then and there was hurrying to and fro,
And gathering tears, and tremblings of distress,
And cheeks all pale, which but an hour ago   210
Blushed at the praise of their own loveliness;
And there were sudden partings, such as press
The life from out young hearts, and choking sighs
Which ne'er might be repeated; who could guess
If ever more should meet those mutual eyes,   215
Since upon night so sweet such awful morn could rise!

XXV

And there was mounting in hot haste: the steed,
The mustering squadron, and the clattering car,
Went pouring forward with impetuous speed,
And swiftly forming in the ranks of war; 220
And the deep thunder peal on peal afar;
And near, the beat of the alarming drum
Roused up the soldier ere the morning star;
While thronged the citizens with terror dumb,
Or whispering, with white lips—"The foe! They come! they come!" 225

XXVI

And wild and high the *Cameron's Gathering* rose!
The war-note of Lochiel, which Albyn's hills
Have heard, and heard, too, have her Saxon foes:—
How in the noon of night that pibroch thrills,
Savage and shrill! But with the breath which fills 230
Their mountain-pipe, so fill the mountaineers
With the fierce native daring which instils
The stirring memory of a thousand years,
And Evan's, Donald's fame rings in each clansman's ears!

XXVII

And Ardennes waves above them her green leaves, 235
Dewy with Nature's tear-drops, as they pass,
Grieving, if aught inanimate e'er grieves,
Over the unreturning brave,—alas!
Ere evening to be trodden like the grass
Which now beneath them, but above shall grow 240
In its next verdure, when this fiery mass
Of living valor, rolling on the foe
And burning with high hope shall moulder cold and low.

XXVIII

Last noon beheld them full of lusty life,
Last eve in Beauty's circle proudly gay, 245
The midnight brought the signal-sound of strife,
The morn the marshalling in arms,—the day
Battle's magnificently stern array!
The thunder-clouds close o'er it, which when rent
The earth is covered thick with other clay, 250
Which her own clay shall cover, heaped and pent,
Rider and horse,—friend, foe,—in one red burial blent!

XXIX

Their praise is hymned by loftier harps than mine:
Yet one I would select from that proud throng,
Partly because they blend me with his line, 255
And partly that I did his sire some wrong,
And partly that bright names will hallow song;
And his was of the bravest, and when showered
The death-bolts deadliest the thinned files along,
Even where the thickest of war's tempest lowered, 260
They reached no nobler breast than thine, young gallant Howard!

XXX

There have been tears and breaking hearts for thee,
And mine were nothing had I such to give;
But when I stood beneath the fresh green tree,
Which living waves where thou didst cease to live, 265

And saw around me the wide field revive
With fruits and fertile promise, and the spring
Came forth her work of gladness to contrive,
With all her reckless birds upon the wing,
I turned from all she brought to those she could not bring.   270

XXXI

I turned to thee, to thousands, of whom each
And one as all a ghastly gap did make
In his own kind and kindred, whom to teach
Forgetfulness were mercy for their sake;
The Archangel's trump, not Glory's, must awake   275
Those whom they thirst for; though the sound of fame
May for a moment soothe, it cannot slake
The fever of vain longing, and the name
So honored but assumes a stronger, bitterer claim.

XXXII

They mourn, but smile at length; and, smiling, mourn   280
The tree will wither long before it fall;
The hull drives on, though mast and sail be torn;
The roof-tree sinks, but molders on the hall
In massy hoariness; the ruined wall
Stands when its wind-worn battlements are gone;   285
The bars survive the captive they enthral;
The day drags through, though storms keep out the sun;
And thus the heart will break, yet brokenly live on:

XXXIII

Even as a broken mirror, which the glass
In every fragment multiplies; and makes   290
A thousand images of one that was,
The same, and still the more, the more it breaks;
And thus the heart will do which not forsakes,
Living in shattered guise; and still, and cold,
And bloodless, with its sleepless sorrow aches,   295
Yet withers on till all without is old,
Showing no visible sign, for such things are untold.

XXXIV

There is a very life in our despair,
Vitality of poison,—a quick root
Which feeds these deadly branches; for it were   300
As nothing did we die; but life will suit
Itself to sorrow's most detested fruit,
Like to the apples on the Dead Sea's shore,
All ashes to the taste. Did man compute
Existence by enjoyment, and count o'er   305
Such hours 'gainst years of life,—say, would he name threescore?

XXXV

The Psalmist numbered out the years of man:
They are enough; and if thy tale be *true*,
Thou, who didst grudge him even that fleeting span,
More than enough, thou fatal Waterloo!   310
Millions of tongues record thee, and anew
Their children's lips shall echo them, and say—
"Here, where the sword united nations drew,
Our countrymen were warring on that day!"
And this is much, and all which will not pass away.   315

XXXVI

There sunk the greatest, nor the worst of men,
Whose spirit, antithetically mixt,
One moment of the mightiest, and again
On little objects with like firmness fixt;
Extreme in all things! hadst thou been betwixt,   320
Thy throne had still been thine, or never been;
For daring made thy rise as fall: thou seek'st
Even now to re-assume the imperial mien,
And shake again the world, the thunderer of the scene!

XXXVII

Conqueror and captive of the earth art thou!   325
She trembles at thee still, and thy wild name
Was ne'er more bruited in men's minds than now
That thou art nothing, save the jest of fame,
Who wooed thee once, thy vassal, and became
The flatterer of thy fierceness, till thou wert   330
A god unto thyself! nor less the same
To the astounded kingdoms all inert,
Who deemed thee for a time whate'er thou didst assert.

XXXVIII

Oh, more or less than man—in high or low,
Battling with nations, flying from the field;   335
Now making monarchs' necks thy footstool, now
More than thy meanest soldier taught to yield;
An empire thou couldst crush, command, rebuild,
But govern not thy pettiest passion, nor,
However deeply in men's spirits skilled,   340
Look through thine own, nor curb the lust of war,
Nor learn that tempted fate will leave the loftiest star.

XXXIX

Yet well thy soul hath brooked the turning tide
With that untaught innate philosophy,
Which, be it wisdom, coldness, or deep pride,   345
Is gall and wormwood to an enemy.
When the whole host of hatred stood hard by,
To watch and mock thee shrinking, thou hast smiled
With a sedate and all-enduring eye;—
When fortune fled her spoiled and favorite child,   350
He stood unbowed beneath the ills upon him piled.

XL

Sager than in thy fortunes; for in them
Ambition steeled thee on too far to show
That just habitual scorn, which could contemn
Men and their thoughts; 'twas wise to feel, not so   355
To wear it ever on thy lip and brow,
And spurn the instruments thou wert to use
Till they were turned unto thine overthrow:
'Tis but a worthless world to win or lose;
So hath it proved to thee, and all such lot who choose.   360

XLI

If, like a tower upon a headland rock,
Thou hadst been made to stand or fall alone,
Such scorn of man had helped to brave the shock;
But men's thoughts were the steps which paved thy throne,

Their admiration thy best weapon shone; 365
The part of Philip's son was thine, not then
(Unless aside thy purple had been thrown)
Like stern Diogenes to mock at men;
For sceptred cynics earth were far too wide a den.

XLII

But quiet to quick bosoms is a hell, 370
And *there* hath been thy bane; there is a fire
And motion of the soul which will not dwell
In its own narrow being, but aspire
Beyond the fitting medium of desire;
And, but once kindled, quenchless evermore, 375
Preys upon high adventure, nor can tire
Of aught but rest; a fever at the core,
Fatal to him who bears, to all who ever bore.

XLIII

This makes the madmen who have made men mad
By their contagion; conquerors and kings, 380
Founders of sects and systems, to whom add
Sophists, bards, statesmen, all unquiet things
Which stir too strongly the soul's secret springs,
And are themselves the fools to those they fool;
Envied, yet how unenviable! what stings 385
Are theirs! One breast laid open were a school
Which would unteach mankind the lust to shine or rule:

XLIV

Their breath is agitation, and their life
A storm whereon they ride, to sink at last,
And yet so nursed and bigoted to strife, 390
That should their days, surviving perils past,
Melt to calm twilight, they feel overcast
With sorrow and supineness, and so die;
Even as a flame unfed, which runs to waste
With its own flickering, or a sword laid by, 395
Which eats into itself, and rusts ingloriously.

XLV

He who ascends to mountain-tops, shall find
The loftiest peaks most wrapt in clouds and snow;
He who surpasses or subdues mankind,
Must look down on the hate of those below. 400
Though high *above* the sun of glory glow,
And far *beneath* the earth and ocean spread,
Round him are icy rocks, and loudly blow
Contending tempests on his naked head,
And thus reward the toils which to those summits led. 405

XLVI

Away with these! true wisdom's world will be
Within its own creation, or in thine,
Maternal nature! for who teems like thee,
Thus on the banks of thy majestic Rhine?
There Harold gazes on a work divine, 410
A blending of all beauties; streams and dells,
Fruit, foliage, crag, wood, cornfield, mountain. vine,
And chiefless castles breathing stern farewells
From gray but leafy walls, where ruin greenly dwells.

XLVII

And there they stand, as stands a lofty mind,   415
Worn, but unstooping to the baser crowd,
All tenantless, save to the crannying wind,
Or holding dark communion with the cloud.
There was a day when they were young and proud;
Banners on high, and battles passed below;   420
But they who fought are in a bloody shroud,
And those which waved are shredless dust ere now,
And the bleak battlements shall bear no future blow.

XLVIII

Beneath these battlements, within those walls,
Power dwelt amidst her passions; in proud state   425
Each robber chief upheld his armed halls,
Doing his evil will, nor less elate
Than mightier heroes of a longer date.
What want these outlaws conquerors should have
But history's purchased page to call them great?   430
A wider space, an ornamental grave?
Their hopes were not less warm, their souls were full as brave.

XLIX

In their baronial feuds and single fields,
What deeds of prowess unrecorded died!
And love, which lent a blazon to their shields,   435
With emblems well devised by amorous pride,
Through all the mail of iron hearts would glide;
But still their flame was fierceness, and drew on
Keen contest and destruction near allied,
And many a tower for some fair mischief won,   440
Saw the discolored Rhine beneath its ruin run.

L

But thou, exulting and abounding river!
Making thy waves a blessing as they flow
Through banks whose beauty would endure forever
Could man but leave thy bright creation so,   445
Nor its fair promise from the surface mow
With the sharp scythe of conflict,—then to see
Thy valley of sweet waters, were to know
Earth paved like heaven; and to seem such to me,
Even now what wants thy stream?—that it should Lethe be.   450

LI

A thousand battles have assailed thy banks,
But these and half their fame have passed away,
And slaughter heaped on high his weltering ranks;
Their very graves are gone, and what are they?
Thy tide washed down the blood of yesterday,   455
And all was stainless, and on thy clear stream
Glassed, with its dancing light, the sunny ray;
But o'er the blackened memory's blighting dream
Thy waves would vainly roll, all sweeping as they seem.

LII

Thus Harold inly said, and passed along,   460
Yet not insensible to all which here
Awoke the jocund birds to early song
In glens which might have made even exile dear:

Though on his brow were graven lines austere,
And tranquil sternness, which had ta'en the place 465
Of feelings fierier far but less severe,
Joy was not always absent from his face,
But o'er it in such scenes would steal with transient trace.

LIII

Nor was all love shut from him, though his days
Of passion had consumed themselves to dust. 470
It is in vain that we would coldly gaze
On such as smile upon us; the heart must
Leap kindly back to kindness, though disgust
Hath weaned it from all worldlings: thus he felt,
For there was soft remembrance, and sweet trust 475
In one fond breast, to which his own would melt,
And in its tenderer hour on that his bosom dwelt.

LIV

And he had learned to love,—I know not why,
For this in such as him seems strange of mood,—
The helpless looks of blooming infancy, 480
Even in its earliest nurture; what subdued,
To change like this, a mind so far imbued
With scorn of man, it little boots to know;
But thus it was; and though in solitude
Small power the nipped affections have to grow, 485
In him this glowed when all beside had ceased to glow.

LV

And there was one soft breast, as hath been said,
Which unto his was bound by stronger ties
Than the church links withal; and, though unwed,
That love was pure, and, far above disguise, 490
Had stood the test of mortal enmities
Still undivided, and cemented more
By peril, dreaded most in female eyes;
But this was firm, and from a foreign shore
Well to that heart might his these absent greetings pour! 495

THE CASTLED CRAG OF DRACHENFELS

1

The castled crag of Drachenfels
Frowns o'er the wide and winding Rhine,
Whose breast of waters broadly swells
Between the banks which bear the vine,
And hills all rich with blossomed trees, 500
And fields which promise corn and wine,
And scattered cities crowning these,
Whose far white walls along them shine,
Have strewed a scene, which I should see
With double joy wert *thou* with me. 505

2

And peasant girls, with deep blue eyes,
And hands which offer early flowers,
Walk smiling o'er this paradise;
Above, the frequent feudal towers
Through green leaves lift their walls of gray; 510
And many a rock which steeply lowers,

And noble arch in proud decay,
Look o'er this vale of vintage-bowers;
But one thing want these banks of Rhine,—
Thy gentle hand to clasp in mine!   515

3

I send the lilies given to me;
Though long before thy hand they touch,
I know that they must withered be,
But yet reject them not as such;
For I have cherished them as dear,   520
Because they yet may meet thine eye,
And guide thy soul to mine even here,
When thou behold'st them drooping nigh,
And know'st them gathered by the Rhine,
And offered from my heart to thine!   525

4

The river nobly foams and flows,
The charm of this enchanted ground,
And all its thousand turns disclose
Some fresher beauty varying round:
The haughtiest breast its wish might bound   530
Through life to dwell delighted here;
Nor could on earth a spot be found
To nature and to me so dear,
Could thy dear eyes in following mine
Still sweeten more these banks of Rhine!   535

LVI

By Coblentz, on a rise of gentle ground,
There is a small and simple pyramid,
Crowning the summit of the verdant mound;
Beneath its base are heroes' ashes hid,
Our enemy's—but let not that forbid   540
Honor to Marceau! o'er whose early tomb
Tears, big tears, gushed from the rough soldier's lid,
Lamenting and yet envying such a doom,
Falling for France, whose rights he battled to resume.

LVII

Brief, brave, and glorious was his young career,—   545
His mourners were two hosts, his friends and foes;
And fitly may the stranger lingering here
Pray for his gallant spirit's bright repose;
For he was freedom's champion, one of those,
The few in number, who had not o'erstept   550
The charter to chastise which she bestows
On such as wield her weapons; he had kept
The whiteness of his soul, and thus men o'er him wept.

LVIII

Here Ehrenbreitstein, with her shattered wall
Black with the miner's blast, upon her height   555
Yet shows of what she was, when shell and ball
Rebounding idly on her strength did light:
A tower of victory! from whence the flight
Of baffled foes was watched along the plain:
But Peace destroyed what war could never blight,   560
And laid those proud roofs bare to summer's rain—
On which the iron shower for years had poured in vain.

LIX

Adieu to thee, fair Rhine!   How long delighted
The stranger fain would linger on his way!
Thine is a scene alike where souls united   565
Or lonely contemplation thus might stray;
And could the ceaseless vultures cease to prey
On self-condemning bosoms, it were here,
Where nature, nor too sombre nor too gay,
Wild but not rude, awful yet not austere,   570
Is to the mellow earth as autumn to the year.

LX

Adieu to thee again! a vain adieu!
There can be no farewell to scene like thine;
The mind is colored by thy every hue;
And if reluctantly the eyes resign   575
Their cherished gaze upon thee, lovely Rhine!
'Tis with the thankful heart of parting praise;
More mighty spots may rise, more glaring shine,
But none unite in one attaching maze
The brilliant, fair, and soft,—the glories of old days.   580

LXI

The negligently grand, the fruitful bloom
Of coming ripeness, the white city's sheen,
The rolling stream, the precipice's gloom,
The forest's growth, and Gothic walls between,
The wild rocks shaped as they had turrets been,   585
In mockery of man's art; and these withal
A race of faces happy as the scene,
Whose fertile bounties here extend to all,
Still springing o'er thy banks, though empires near them fall.

LXII

But these recede.   Above me are the Alps,   590
The palaces of nature, whose vast walls
Have pinnacled in clouds their snowy scalps,
And throned eternity in icy halls
Of cold sublimity, where forms and falls
The avalanche—the thunderbolt of snow!   595
All that expands the spirit, yet appals,
Gather around these summits, as to show
How earth may pierce to heaven, yet leave vain man below.

LXIII

But ere these matchless heights I dare to scan,
There is a spot should not be passed in vain,—   600
Morat! the proud, the patriot field! where man
May gaze on ghastly trophies of the slain,
Nor blush for those who conquered on that plain;
Here Burgundy bequeathed his tombless host,
A bony heap, through ages to remain,   605
Themselves their monument;—the Stygian coast
Unsepulchred they roamed, and shrieked each wandering ghost.

LXIV

While Waterloo with Cannæ's carnage vies,
Morat and Marathon twin names shall stand;
They were true Glory's stainless victories,   610
Won by the unambitious heart and hand

Of a proud, brotherly, and civic band,
All unbought champions in no princely cause
Of vice-entailed corruption; they no land
Doomed to bewail the blasphemy of laws   615
Making kings' rights divine, by some Draconic clause.

LXV

By a lone wall a lonelier column rears
A gray and grief-worn aspect of old days;
'Tis the last remnant of the wreck of years,
And looks as with the wild-bewildered gaze   620
Of one to stone converted by amaze,
Yet still with consciousness; and there it stands
Making a marvel that it not decays,
When the coeval pride of human hands,
Levelled Adventicum, hath strewed her subject lands.   625

LXVI

And there—oh! sweet and sacred be the name!—
Julia—the daughter, the devoted—gave
Her youth to heaven; her heart, beneath a claim
Nearest to heaven's broke o'er a father's grave.
Justice is sworn 'gainst tears, and hers would crave   630
The life she lived in; but the judge was just,
And then she died on him she could not save.
Their tomb was simple, and without a bust,
And held within their urn one mind, one heart, one dust.

LXVII

But these are deeds which should not pass away,   635
And names that must not wither, though the earth
Forgets her empires with a just decay,
The enslavers and the enslaved, their death and birth;
The high, the mountain-majesty of worth
Should be, and shall, survivor of its woe,   640
And from its immortality look forth
In the sun's face, like yonder Alpine snow,
Imperishably pure beyond all things below.

LXVIII

Lake Leman woos me with its crystal face,
The mirror where the stars and mountains view   645
The stillness of their aspect in each trace
Its clear depth yields of their far height and hue:
There is too much of man here, to look through
With a fit mind the might which I behold;
But soon in me shall Loneliness renew   650
Thoughts hid, but not less cherished than of old,
Ere mingling with the herd had penned me in their fold.

LXIX

To fly from, need not be to hate, mankind:
All are not fit with them to stir and toil,
Nor is it discontent to keep the mind   655
Deep in its fountain, lest it overboil
In the hot throng, where we become the spoil
Of our infection, till too late and long
We may deplore and struggle with the coil,
In wretched interchange of wrong for wrong   660
Midst a contentious world, striving where none are strong.

LXX

There, in a moment we may plunge our years
In fatal penitence, and in the blight
Of our own soul turn all our blood to tears,
And color things to come with hues of Night;　　　665
The race of life becomes a hopeless flight
To those that walk in darkness: on the sea
The boldest steer but where their ports invite;
But there are wanderers o'er Eternity
Whose bark drives on and on, and anchored ne'er shall be.　　　670

LXXI

Is it not better, then, to be alone,
And love Earth only for its earthly sake?
By the blue rushing of the arrowy Rhone,
Or the pure bosom of its nursing lake,
Which feeds it as a mother who doth make　　　675
A fair but froward infant her own care,
Kissing its cries away as these awake;—
Is it not better thus our lives to wear,
Than join the crushing crowd, doomed to inflict or bear?

LXXII

I live not in myself, but I become　　　680
Portion of that around me; and to me
High mountains are a feeling, but the hum
Of human cities torture: I can see
Nothing to loathe in nature, save to be
A link reluctant in a fleshly chain,　　　685
Classed among creatures, when the soul can flee,
And with the sky, the peak, the heaving plain
Of ocean, or the stars, mingle, and not in vain.

LXXIII

And thus I am absorbed, and this is life:
I look upon the peopled desert past,　　　690
As on a place of agony and strife,
Where, for some sin, to sorrow I was cast,
To act and suffer, but remount at last
With a fresh pinion; which I feel to spring,
Though young, yet waxing vigorous as the blast　　　695
Which it would cope with, on delighted wing,
Spurning the clay-cold bonds which round our being cling.

LXXIV

And when, at length, the mind shall be all free
From what it hates in this degraded form,
Reft of its carnal life, save what shall be　　　700
Existent happier in the fly and worm,—
When elements to elements conform,
And dust is as it should be, shall I not
Feel all I see, less dazzling, but more warm?
The bodiless thought? the spirit of each spot?　　　705
Of which, even now, I share at times the immortal lot?

LXXV

Are not the mountains, waves, and skies, a part
Of me and of my soul, as I of them?
Is not the love of these deep in my heart
With a pure passion? should I not contemn　　　710

All objects, if compared with these? and stem
A tide of suffering, rather than forego
Such feelings for the hard and worldly phlegm
Of those whose eyes are only turned below,
Gazing upon the ground, with thoughts which dare not glow? 715

LXXVI

But this is not my theme; and I return
To that which is immediate, and require
Those who find contemplation in the urn,
To look on one, whose dust was once all fire,
A native of the land where I respire 720
The clear air for a while—a passing guest,
Where he became a being,—whose desire
Was to be glorious; 'twas a foolish quest,
The which to gain and keep, he sacrificed all rest.

LXXVII

Here the self-torturing sophist, wild Rousseau, 725
The apostle of affliction, he who threw
Enchantment over passion, and from woe
Wrung overwhelming eloquence, first drew
The breath which made him wretched; yet he knew
How to make madness beautiful, and cast 730
O'er erring deeds and thoughts a heavenly hue
Of words, like sunbeams, dazzling as they past
The eyes, which o'er them shed tears feelingly and fast.

LXXVIII

His love was passion's essence:—as a tree
On fire by lightning, with ethereal flame 735
Kindled he was, and blasted; for to be
Thus, and enamored, were to him the same.
But his was not the love of living dame,
Nor of the dead who rise upon our dreams,
But of ideal beauty, which became 740
In him existence, and o'erflowing teems
Along his burning page, distempered though it seems.

LXXIX

This breathed itself to life in Julie, *this*
Invested her with all that's wild and sweet;
This hallowed, too, the memorable kiss 745
Which every morn his fevered lip would greet,
From hers, who but with friendship his would meet;
But to that gentle touch through brain and breast
Flashed the thrilled spirit's love-devouring heat;
In that absorbing sigh perchance more blest 750
Than vulgar minds may be with all they seek possest.

LXXX

His life was one long war with self-sought foes,
Or friends by him self-banished; for his mind
Had grown suspicion's sanctuary, and chose,
For its own cruel sacrifice, the kind, 755
'Gainst whom he raged with fury strange and blind.
But he was phrensied,—wherefore, who may know?
Since cause might be which skill could never find;
But he was phrensied by disease or woe,
To that worst pitch of all. which wears a reasoning show. 766

LXXXI

For then he was inspired, and from him came,
As from the Pythian's mystic cave of yore,
Those oracles which set the world in flame,
Nor ceased to burn till kingdoms were no more:
Did he not this for France? which lay before   765
Bowed to the inborn tyranny of years?
Broken and trembling to the yoke she bore,
Till by the voice of him and his compeers
Roused up to too much wrath which follows o'ergrown fears?

LXXXII

They made themselves a fearful monument!   770
The wreck of old opinions—things which grew,
Breathed from the birth of time: the veil they rent,
And what behind it lay, all earth shall view.
But good with ill they also overthrew,
Leaving but ruins, wherewith to rebuild   775
Upon the same foundations, and renew
Dungeons and thrones, which the same hour refilled,
As heretofore, because ambition was self-willed.

LXXXIII

But this will not endure, nor be endured!
Mankind have felt their strength, and made it felt.   780
They might have used it better, but allured
By their new vigor, sternly have they dealt
On one another; pity ceased to melt
With her once natural charities. But they,
Who in oppression's darkness caved had dwelt,   785
They were not eagles, nourished with the day;
What marvel then, at times, if they mistook their prey?

LXXXIV

What deep wounds ever closed without a scar?
The heart's bleed longest, and but heal to wear
That which disfigures it; and they who war   790
With their own hopes, and have been vanquished, bear
Silence, but not submission: in his lair
Fixed Passion holds his breath, until the hour
Which shall atone for years; none need despair:
It came, it cometh, and will come,—the power   795
To punish or forgive—in *one* we shall be slower.

LXXXV

Clear, placid Leman! thy contrasted lake,
With the wild world I dwelt in, is a thing
Which warns me, with its stillness, to forsake
Earth's troubled waters for a purer spring.   800
This quiet sail is as a noiseless wing
To waft me from distraction; once I loved
Torn Ocean's roar, but thy soft murmuring
Sounds sweet as if a sister's voice reproved,
That I with stern delights should e'er have been so moved.   805

LXXXVI

It is the hush of night, and all between
Thy margin and the mountains, dusk, yet clear,
Mellowed and mingling, yet distinctly seen,
Save darkened Jura, whose capt heights appear

Precipitously steep; and drawing near,   810
There breathes a living fragrance from the shore,
Of flowers yet fresh with childhood; on the ear
Drops the light drip of the suspended oar,
Or chirps the grasshopper one good-night carol more.

LXXXVII

He is an evening reveller, who makes   815
His life an infancy, and sings his fill;
At intervals, some bird from out the brakes
Starts into voice a moment, then is still.
There seems a floating whisper on the hill,
But that is fancy, for the starlight dews   820
All silently their tears of love instil,
Weeping themselves away, till they infuse
Deep into Nature's breast the spirit of her hues.

LXXXVIII

Ye stars which are the poetry of heaven!
If in your bright leaves we would read the fate   825
Of men and empires,—'tis to be forgiven,
That in our aspirations to be great,
Our destinies o'erleap their mortal state,
And claim a kindred with you; for ye are
A beauty and a mystery, and create   830
In us such love and reverence from afar,
That fortune, fame, power, life, have named themselves a star.

LXXXIX

All heaven and earth are still—though not in sleep,
But breathless, as we grow when feeling most;
And silent, as we stand in thoughts too deep:—   835
All heaven and earth are still. From the high host
Of stars, to the lulled lake and mountain-coast,
All is concentered in a life intense,
Where not a beam, nor air, nor leaf is lost,
But hath a part of being, and a sense   840
Of that which is of all Creator and defence.

XC

Then stirs the feeling infinite, so felt
In solitude, where we are *least* alone;
A truth, which through our being then doth melt,
And purifies from self: it is a tone,   845
The soul and source of music, which makes known
Eternal harmony, and sheds a charm
Like to the fabled Cytherea's zone,
Binding all things with beauty;—'twould disarm
The spectre Death, had he substantial power to harm.   850

XCI

Not vainly did the early Persian make
His altar the high places, and the peak
Of earth-o'ergazing mountains, and thus take
A fit and unwalled temple, there to seek
The Spirit, in whose honor shrines are weak,   855
Upreared of human hands. Come, and compare
Columns and idol-dwellings, Goth or Greek,
With Nature's realms of worship, earth and air,
Nor fix on fond abodes to circumscribe thy prayer!

XCII

Thy sky is changed!—and such a change! Oh night,   860
And storm, and darkness, ye are wondrous strong,
Yet lovely in your strength, as is the light
Of a dark eye in woman! Far along,
From peak to peak, the rattling crags among
Leaps the live thunder! Not from one lone cloud,   865
But every mountain now hath found a tongue,
And Jura answers, through her misty shroud,
Back to the joyous Alps, who call to her aloud!

XCIII

And this is in the night:—Most glorious night!
Thou wert not sent for slumber! let me be
A sharer in thy fierce and far delight,—   870
A portion of the tempest and of thee!
How the lit lake shines, a phosphoric sea,
And the big rain comes dancing to the earth!
And now again 'tis black,—and now, the glee   875
Of the loud hills shakes with its mountain-mirth,
As if they did rejoice o'er a young earthquake's birth.

XCIV

Now, where the swift Rhone cleaves his way between
Heights which appear as lovers who have parted
In hate, whose mining depths so intervene,   880
That they can meet no more, though broken-hearted;
Though in their souls, which thus each other thwarted,
Love was the very root of the fond rage
Which blighted their life's bloom, and then departed:
Itself expired, but leaving them an age   885
Of years all winters,—war within themselves to wage.

XCV

Now, where the quick Rhone thus hath cleft his way,
The mightiest of the storms hath ta'en his stand:
For here, not one, but many, make their play,
And fling their thunder-bolts from hand to hand,   890
Flashing and cast around; of all the band,
The brightest through these parted hills hath forked
His lightnings,—as if he did understand
That in such gaps as desolation worked,
There the hot shaft should blast whatever therein lurked.   895

XCVI

Sky, mountains, rivers, winds, lake, lightnings, ye!
With night, and clouds, and thunder, and a soul
To make these felt and feeling, well may be
Things that have made me watchful; the far roll
Of your departing voices, is the knoll   900
Of what in me is sleepless,—if I rest.
But where of ye, O tempests! is the goal?
Are ye like those within the human breast?
Or do ye find, at length, like eagles, some high nest?

XCVII

Could I embody and unbosom now   905
That which is most within me,—could I wreak
My thoughts upon expression, and thus throw
Soul, heart, mind, passions, feelings, strong or weak,

All that I would have sought, and all I seek,
Bear, know, feel, and yet breathe—into *one* word, 910
And that one word were Lightning, I would speak;
But as it is, I live and die unheard,
With a most voiceless thought, sheathing it as a sword.

XCVIII

The morn is up again, the dewy morn,
With breath all incense, and with cheek all bloom, 915
Laughing the clouds away with playful scorn,
And living as if earth contained no tomb,—
And glowing into day: we may resume
The march of our existence: and thus I,
Still on thy shores, fair Leman! may find room 920
And food for meditation, nor pass by
Much that may give us pause, if pondered fittingly.

XCIX

Clarens! sweet Clarens, birthplace of deep Love!
Thine air is the young breath of passionate thought;
Thy trees take root in love; the snows above 925
The very glaciers have his colors caught,
And sun-set into rose-hues sees them wrought
By rays which sleep there lovingly: the rocks,
The permanent crags, tell here of love, who sought
In them a refuge from the worldly shocks, 930
Which stir and sting the soul with hope that woos, then mocks.

C

Clarens! by heavenly feet thy paths are trod,—
Undying love's, who here ascends a throne
To which the steps are mountains; where the god
Is a pervading life and light,—so shown 935
Not on those summits solely nor alone
In the still cave and forest; o'er the flower
His eye is sparkling, and his breath hath blown,
His soft and summer breath, whose tender power
Passes the strength of storms in their most desolate hour. 940

CI

All things are here of *him;* from the black pines,
Which are his shade on high, and the loud roar
Of torrents, where he listeneth, to the vines
Which slope his green path downward to the shore,
Where the bowed waters meet him, and adore, 945
Kissing his feet with murmurs; and the wood,
The covert of old trees, with trunks all hoar,
But light leaves, young as joy, stands where it stood,
Offering to him, and his, a populous solitude.

CII

A populous solitude of bees and birds, 950
And fairy-formed and many-colored things,
Who worship him with notes more sweet than words,
And innocently open their glad wings,
Fearless and full of life: the gush of springs,
And fall of lofty fountains, and the bend 955
Of stirring branches, and the bud which brings
The swiftest thought of beauty, here extend,
Mingling, and made by love, unto one mighty end.

CIII

He who hath loved not, here would learn that lore,
And make his heart a spirit; he who knows
That tender mystery, will love the more;   960
For this is love's recess, where vain men's woes,
And the world's waste, have driven him far from those,
For 'tis his nature to advance or die;
He stands not still, but or decays, or grows   965
Into a boundless blessing, which may vie
With the immortal lights, in its eternity!

CIV

'Twas not for fiction chose Rousseau this spot,
Peopling it with affections; but he found
It was the scene which passion must allot   970
To the mind's purified beings; 'twas the ground
Where early love his Psyche's zone unbound,
And hallowed it with loveliness; 'tis lone,
And wonderful, and deep, and hath a sound,
And sense, and sight of sweetness; here the Rhone   975
Hath spread himself a couch, the Alps have reared a throne.

CV

Lausanne! and Ferney! ye have been the abodes
Of names which unto you bequeathed a name;
Mortals, who sought and found, by dangerous roads,
A path to perpetuity of fame: 980
They were gigantic minds, and their steep aim
Was, Titan-like, on daring doubts to pile
Thoughts which should call down thunder, and the flame
Of heaven again assailed, if heaven the while
On man and man's research could deign do more than smile   985

CVI

The one was fire and fickleness, a child,
Most mutable in wishes, but in mind
A wit as various,—gay, grave, sage, or wild,—
Historian, bard, philosopher, combined;
He multiplied himself among mankind,   990
The Proteus of their talents; but his own
Breathed most in ridicule,—which, as the wind,
Blew where it listed, laying all things prone,—
Now to o'erthrow a fool, and now to shake a throne.

CVII

The other, deep and slow, exhausting thought,   995
And hiving wisdom with each studious year,
In meditation dwelt, with learning wrought,
And shaped his weapon with an edge severe,
Sapping a solemn creed with solemn sneer;
The lord of irony,—that master-spell,   1000
Which stung his foes to wrath, which grew from fear,
And doomed him to the zealot's ready hell,
Which answers to all doubts so eloquently well.

CVIII

Yet, peace be with their ashes,—for by them,
If merited, the penalty is paid;   1005
It is not ours to judge,—far less condemn;
The hour must come when such things shall be made

Known unto all, or hope and dread allayed
By slumber, on one pillow, in the dust,
Which, thus much we are sure, must lie decayed; 1010
And when it shall revive, as is our trust,
'Twill be to be forgiven, or suffer what is just.

CIX

But let me quit man's works, again to read
His Maker's, spread around me, and suspend
This page, which from my reveries I feed, 1015
Until it seems prolonging without end.
The clouds above me to the white Alps tend,
And I must pierce them, and survey whate'er
May be permitted, as my steps I bend
To their most great and growing region, where 1020
The earth to her embrace compels the powers of air.

CX

Italia too, Italia! looking on thee,
Full flashes on the soul the light of ages,
Since the fierce Carthaginian almost won thee,
To the last halo of the chiefs and sages 1025
Who glorify thy consecrated pages;
Thou wert the throne and grave of empires; still
The fount at which the panting mind assuages
Her thirst of knowledge, quaffing there her fill,
Flows from the eternal source of Rome's imperial hill. 1030

CXI

Thus far have I proceeded in a theme
Renewed with no kind auspices:—to feel
We are not what we have been, and to deem
We are not what we should be, and to steel
The heart against itself; and to conceal, 1035
With a proud caution, love, or hate, or aught,—
Passion or feeling, purpose, grief or zeal,—
Which is the tyrant spirit of our thought,
Is a stern task of soul:—no matter,—it is taught.

CXII

And for these words, thus woven into song, 1040
It may be that they are a harmless wile,—
The coloring of the scenes which fleet along,
Which I would seize, in passing, to beguile
My breast, or that of others, for a while.
Fame is the thirst of youth, but I am not 1045
So young as to regard men's frown or smile,
As loss or guerdon of a glorious lot;
I stood and stand alone,—remembered or forgot.

CXIII

I have not loved the world, nor the world me;
I have not flattered its rank breath, nor bowed 1050
To its idolatries a patient knee,
Nor coined my cheek to smiles, nor cried aloud
In worship of an echo; in the crowd
They could not deem me one of such; I stood
Amongst them, but not of them; in a shroud 1055
Of thoughts which were not their thoughts, and still could,
Had I not filed my mind. which thus itself subdued.

CXIV

I have not loved the world, nor the world me,—
But let us part fair foes; I do believe,
Though I have found them not, that there may be   1060
Words which are things, hopes which will not deceive,
And virtues which are merciful, nor weave
Snares for the failing; I would also deem
O'er others' griefs that some sincerely grieve;
That two, or one, are almost what they seem,   1065
That goodness is no name, and happiness no dream.

CXV

My daughter! with thy name this song begun;
My daughter! with thy name thus much shall end;
I see thee not, I hear thee not, but none
Can be so wrapt in thee; thou art the friend   1070
To whom the shadows of far years extend:
Albeit my brow thou never shouldst behold,
My voice shall with thy future visions blend,
And reach into thy heart, when mine is cold,
A token and a tone, even from thy father's mould.   1075

CXVI

To aid thy mind's development, to watch
Thy dawn of little joys, to sit and see
Almost thy very growth, to view thee catch
Knowledge of objects,—wonders yet to thee!
To hold thee lightly on a gentle knee,   1080
And print on thy soft cheek a parent's kiss,—
This, it should seem, was not reserved for me;
Yet this was in my nature: as it is,
I know not what is there, yet something like to this.

CXVII

Yet, though dull hate as duty should be taught,   1085
I know that thou wilt love me; though my name
Should be shut from thee, as a spell still fraught
With desolation, and a broken claim:
Though the grave closed between us,—'twere the same,
I know that thou wilt love me; though to drain   1090
My blood from out thy being were an aim,
And an attainment,—all would be in vain,—
Still thou wouldst love me, still that more than life retain.

CXVIII

The child of love, though born in bitterness,
And nurtured in convulsion,—of thy sire   1095
These were the elements, and thine no less.
As yet such are around thee, but thy fire
Shall be more tempered, and thy hope far higher.
Sweet be thy cradled slumbers! O'er the sea
And from the mountains where I now respire,   1100
Fain would I waft such blessing upon thee,
As, with a sigh, I deem thou might'st have been to me.

1816   1816

CANTO IV

I

I stood in Venice, on the "Bridge of Sighs";
A palace and a prison on each hand:
I saw from out the wave her structures rise
As from the stroke of the enchanter's wand:
A thousand years their cloudy wings expand   5
Around me, and a dying Glory smiles
O'er the far times, when many a subject land
Looked to the winged Lion's marble piles,
Where Venice sate in state, throned on her hundred isles!

II

She looks a sea Cybele, fresh from ocean,   10
Rising with her tiara of proud towers
At airy distance, with majestic motion,
A ruler of the waters and their powers:
And such she was;—her daughters had their dowers
From spoils of nations, and the exhaustless East   15
Poured in her lap all gems in sparkling showers.
In purple was she robed, and of her feast
Monarchs partook, and deemed their dignity increased.

III

In Venice Tasso's echoes are no more,
And silent rows the songless gondolier;   20
Her palaces are crumbling to the shore,
And music meets not always now the ear:
Those days are gone—but Beauty still is here.
States fall, arts fade—but Nature doth not die,
Nor yet forget how Venice once was dear,   25
The pleasant place of all festivity,
The revel of the earth, the masque of Italy!

IV

But unto us she hath a spell beyond
Her name in story, and her long array
Of mighty shadows, whose dim forms despond   30
Above the dogeless city's vanished sway;
Ours is a trophy which will not decay
With the Rialto; Shylock and the Moor,
And Pierre, cannot be swept or worn away—
The keystones of the arch! though all were o'er,   35
For us repeopled were the solitary shore.

V

The beings of the mind are not of clay;
Essentially immortal, they create
And multiply in us a brighter ray
And more beloved existence: that which Fate   40
Prohibits to dull life, in this our state
Of mortal bondage, by these spirits supplied,
First exiles, then replaces what we hate;
Watering the heart whose early flowers have died,
And with a fresher growth replenishing the void.   45

VIII

I've taught me other tongues, and in strange eyes
Have made me not a stranger; to the mind   55
Which is itself, no changes bring surprise,

Nor is it harsh to make, nor hard to find
A country with—ay, or without mankind;
Yet was I born where men are proud to be,—
Not without cause; and should I leave behind
The inviolate island of the sage and free,   70
And seek me out a home by a remoter sea,

IX

Perhaps I loved it well: and should I lay
My ashes in a soil which is not mine,
My spirit shall resume it—if we may
Unbodied choose a sanctuary. I twine   75
My hopes of being remembered in my line
With my land's language: if too fond and far
These aspirations in their scope incline,—
If my fame should be, as my fortunes are,   80
Of hasty growth and blight, and dull Oblivion bar

X

My name from out the temple where the dead
Are honored by the nations—let it be—
And light the laurels on a loftier head!
And be the Spartan's epitaph on me—   85
"Sparta hath many a worthier son than he."
Meantime I seek no sympathies, nor need;
The thorns which I have reaped are of the tree
I planted: they have torn me, and I bleed:
I should have known what fruit would spring from such a seed.   90

. . . .

XIII

Before St. Mark still glow his steeds of brass,
Their gilded collars glittering in the sun;
But is not Doria's menace come to pass?   110
Are they not *bridled?*—Venice, lost and won,
Her thirteen hundred years of freedom done,
Sinks, like a seaweed, into whence she rose!
Better be whelmed beneath the waves, and shun,
Even in destruction's depth, her foreign foes,   115
From whom submission wrings an infamous repose.

XIV

In youth she was all glory,—a new Tyre;
Her very by-word sprung from victory,
The "Planter of the Lion," which through fire
And blood she bore o'er subject earth and sea;   120
Though making many slaves, herself still free,
And Europe's bulwark 'gainst the Ottomite;
Witness Troy's rival, Candia! Vouch it, ye
Immortal waves that saw Lepanto's fight!   125
For ye are names no time nor tyranny can blight.

XV

Statues of glass—all shivered—the long file
Of her dead Doges are declined to dust;
But where they dwelt, the vast and sumptuous pile
Bespeaks the pageant of their splendid trust;
Their sceptre broken, and their sword in rust,   130
Have yielded to the stranger: empty halls,
Thin streets, and foreign aspects, such as must
Too oft remind her who and what enthrals,
Have flung a desolate cloud o'er Venice' lovely walls.   135

XVI

When Athens' armies fell at Syracuse,
And fettered thousands bore the yoke of war,
Redemption rose up in the Attic muse,
Her voice their only ransom from afar:
See! as they chant the tragic hymn, the car   140
Of the o'ermastered victor stops, the reins
Fall from his hands, his idle scimitar
Starts from its belt—he rends his captive's chains,
And bids him thank the bard for freedom and his strains.

XVII

Thus, Venice, if no stronger claim were thine,   145
Were all thy proud historic deeds forgot,
Thy choral memory of the bard divine,
Thy love of Tasso, should have cut the knot
Which ties thee to thy tyrants; and thy lot
Is shameful to the nations,—most of all,   150
Albion! to thee: the ocean queen should not
Abandon ocean's children; in the fall
Of Venice, think of thine, despite thy watery wall.

XVIII

I loved her from my boyhood; she to me
Was as a fairy city of the heart,   155
Rising like water-columns from the sea,
Of joy the sojourn, and of wealth the mart;
And Otway, Radcliffe, Schiller, Shakspeare's art,
Had stamped her image in me, and even so,
Although I found her thus, we did not part;   160
Perchance even dearer in her day of woe,
Than when she was a boast, a marvel, and a show.

XIX

I can repeople with the past—and of
The present there is still for eye and thought,
And meditation chastened down, enough;   16!
And more, it may be, than I hoped or sought;
And of the happiest moments which were wrought
Within the web of my existence, some
From thee, fair Venice! have their colors caught:
There are some feelings time cannot benumb   170
Nor torture shake, or mine would now be cold and dumb.

XX

But from their nature will the tannen grow
Loftiest on loftiest and least sheltered rocks,
Rooted in barrenness, where nought below
Of soil supports them 'gainst the Alpine shocks   175
Of eddying storms; yet springs the trunk and mocks
The howling tempest, till its height and frame
Are worthy of the mountains from whose blocks
Of bleak, gray granite into life it came,
And grew a giant tree;—the mind may grow the same.   180

XXI

Existence may be borne, and the deep root
Of life and sufferance make its firm abode
The bare and desolated bosoms: mute
The camel labors with the heaviest load,

And the wolf dies in silence,—not bestowed
In vain should such example be; if they, 185
Things of ignoble or of savage mood,
Endure and shrink not, we of nobler clay
May temper it to bear,—it is but for a day.

XXII

All suffering doth destroy, or is destroyed,
Even by the sufferer; and, in each event, 190
Ends: Some, with hope replenished and rebuoyed,
Return to whence they came—with like intent,
And weave their web again; some, bowed and bent,
Wax gray and ghastly, withering ere their time,
And perish with the reed on which they leant; 195
Some seek devotion, toil, war, good or crime,
According as their souls were formed to sink or climb.

. . . .

XXV

But my soul wanders; I demand it back
To meditate amongst decay, and stand
A ruin amidst ruins; there to track
Fall'n states and buried greatness, o'er a land 220
Which *was* the mightiest in its old command,
And *is* the loveliest, and must ever be
The master-mold of nature's heavenly hand;
Wherein were cast the heroic and the free,
The beautiful, the brave, the lords of earth and sea, 225

XXVI

The commonwealth of kings, the men of Rome!
And even since, and now, fair Italy!
Thou art the garden of the world, the home
Of all art yields, and nature can decree;
Even in thy desert, what is like to thee? 230
Thy very weeds are beautiful, thy waste
More rich than other climes' fertility;
Thy wreck a glory, and thy ruin graced
With an immaculate charm which cannot be defaced.

XXVII

The moon is up, and yet it is not night;
Sunset divides the sky with her; a sea 235
Of glory streams along the Alpine height
Of blue Friuli's mountains; heaven is free
From clouds, but of all colors seems to be,—
Melted to one vast Iris of the west,— 240
Where the day joins the past eternity,
While, on the other hand, meek Dian's crest
Floats through the azure air—an island of the blest!

XXVIII

A single star is at her side, and reigns
With her o'er half the lovely heaven; but still 245
Yon sunny sea heaves brightly, and remains
Rolled o'er the peak of the far Rhætian hill,
As day and night contending were, until
Nature reclaimed her order:—gently flows
The deep-dyed Brenta, where their hues instil 250
The odorous purple of a new-born rose,
Which streams upon her stream, and glassed within it glows,

XXIX

Filled with the face of heaven, which, from afar,
Comes down upon the waters; all its hues,
From the rich sunset to the rising star, 255
Their magical variety diffuse:
And now they change; a paler shadow strews
Its mantle o'er the mountains; parting day
Dies like the dolphin, whom each pang imbues
With a new color as it gasps away, 260
The last still loveliest,—till—'tis gone—and all is gray.

XXXV

Ferrara! in thy wide and grass-grown streets,
Whose symmetry was not for solitude,
There seems as 't were a curse upon the seats
Of former sovereigns, and the antique brood 310
Of Este, which for many an age made good
Its strength within thy walls, and was of yore
Patron or tyrant, as the changing mood
Of petty power impelled, of those who wore
The wreath which Dante's brow alone had worn before. 315

XXXVI

And Tasso is their glory and their shame.
Hark to his strain! and then survey his cell!
And see how dearly earned Torquato's fame,
And where Alfonso bade his poet dwell:
The miserable despot could not quell 320
The insulted mind he sought to quench, and blend
With the surrounding maniacs, in the hell
Where he had plunged it. Glory without end
Scattered the clouds away; and on that name attend

XXXVII

The tears and praises of all time; while thine 325
Would rot in its oblivion—in the sink
Of worthless dust, which from thy boasted line
Is shaken into nothing—but the link
Thou formest in his fortunes bids us think
Of thy poor malice, naming thee with scorn: 330
Alfonso! how thy ducal pageants shrink
From thee! if in another station born,
Scarce fit to be the slave of him thou madest to mourn:

XLII

Italia! oh Italia! thou who hast 370
The fatal gift of beauty, which became
A funeral dower of present woes and past,
On thy sweet brow is sorrow ploughed by shame,
And annals graved in characters of flame.
Oh, God! that thou wert in thy nakedness 375
Less lovely or more powerful, and couldst claim
Thy right, and awe the robbers back, who press
To shed thy blood, and drink the tears of thy distress;

XLIII

Then might'st thou more appal; or, less desired,
Be homely and be peaceful, undeplored 380
For thy destructive charms; then, still untired,
Would not be seen the armed torrents poured

Down the deep Alps; nor would the hostile horde
Of many-nation'd spoilers from the Po
Quaff blood and water; nor the stranger's sword   385
Be thy sad weapon of defence, and so,
Victor or vanquished, thou the slave of friend or foe.

· · · · · · ·

XLVII

Yet, Italy! through every other land   415
Thy wrongs should ring, and shall, from side to side;
Mother of Arts! as once of arms; thy hand
Was then our guardian, and is still our guide;
Parent of our religion! whom the wide
Nations have knelt to for the keys of heaven!   420
Europe, repentant of her parricide,
Shall yet redeem thee, and, all backward driven,
Roll the barbarian tide, and sue to be forgiven.

· · · · · · ·

LIV

In Santa Croce's holy precincts lie
Ashes which make it holier, dust which is
Even in itself an immortality,   480
Though there were nothing save the past, and this,
The particle of those sublimities
Which have relapsed to chaos: here repose
Angelo's, Alfieri's bones, and his,
The starry Galileo, with his woes;   485
Here Machiavelli's earth returned to whence it rose.

LV

These are four minds, which, like the elements,
Might furnish forth creation:—Italy!
Time, which hath wronged thee with ten thousand rents
Of thine imperial garment, shall deny,
And hath denied, to every other sky,
Spirits which soar from ruin: thy decay
Is still impregnate with divinity,
Which gilds it with revivifying ray;
Such as the great of yore, Canova is to-day.   495

LVI

But where repose the all Etruscan three—
Dante, and Petrarch, and, scarce less than they,
The Bard of Prose, creative spirit! he
Of the Hundred Tales of love—where did they lay
Their bones, distinguished from our common clay   500
In death as life? Are they resolved to dust,
And have their country's marbles nought to say?
Could not her quarries furnish forth one bust?
Did they not to her breast their filial earth intrust?

LVII

Ungrateful Florence! Dante sleeps afar,   505
Like Scipio, buried by the upbraiding shore:
Thy factions, in their worse than civil war,
Proscribed the bard whose name for evermore
Their children's children would in vain adore
With the remorse of ages, and the crown   510
Which Petrarch's laureate brow supremely wore,
Upon a far and foreign soil had grown,
His life, his fame, his grave, though rifled—not thine own.

LVIII

Boccaccio to his parent earth bequeathed
His dust,—and lies it not her great among, 515
With many a sweet and solemn requiem breathed
O'er him who formed the Tuscan's siren tongue?
That music in itself, whose sounds are song,
The poetry of speech? No;—even his tomb
Uptorn, must bear the hyæna bigot's wrong, 520
No more amidst the meaner dead find room,
Nor claim a passing sigh, because it told for *whom!*

. . . .

LXXVIII

Oh Rome! my country! city of the soul!
The orphans of the heart must turn to thee, 695
Lone mother of dead empires! and control
In their shut breasts their petty misery.
What are our woes and sufferance? Come and see
The cypress, hear the owl, and plod your way
O'er steps of broken thrones and temples, Ye! 700
Whose agonies are evils of a day—
A world is at our feet as fragile as our clay.

LXXIX

The Niobe of nations! there she stands,
Childless and crownless, in her voiceless woe;
An empty urn within her withered hands, 705
Whose holy dust was scattered long ago;
The Scipios' tomb contains no ashes now;
The very sepulchres lie tenantless
Of thy heroic dwellers: dost thou flow,
Old Tiber! through a marble wilderness? 710
Rise, with thy yellow waves, and mantle her distress.

LXXX

The Goth, the Christian, Time, War, Flood, and Fire,
Have dealt upon the seven-hilled city's pride;
She saw her glories star by star expire,
And up the steep barbarian monarchs ride, 715
Where the car climbed the Capitol; far and wide
Temple and tower went down, nor left a site:
Chaos of ruins! who shall trace the void,
O'er the dim fragments cast a lunar light,
And say, "here was, or is," where all is doubly night? 720

LXXXI

The double night of ages, and of her,
Night's daughter, Ignorance, hath wrapped and wrap
All round us: we but feel our way to err:
The ocean hath its chart, the stars their map,
And Knowledge spreads them on her ample lap; 725
But Rome is as the desert, where we steer
Stumbling o'er recollections; now we clap
Our hands, and cry "Eureka!" it is clear—
When but some false mirage of ruin rises near.

LXXXII

Alas! the lofty city! and alas! 730
The trebly hundred triumphs! and the day
When Brutus made the dagger's edge surpass
The conqueror's sword in bearing fame away!

Alas, for Tully's voice, and Virgil's lay,
And Livy's pictured page!—but these shall be
Her resurrection; all beside—decay.
Alas, for Earth, for never shall we see
That brightness in her eye she bore when Rome was free!   735

.·.·.·.·.·.·.

XCIII

What from this barren being do we reap?
Our senses narrow, and our reason frail,   830
Life short, and truth a gem which loves the deep,
And all things weighed in custom's falsest scale;
Opinion an omnipotence,—whose veil
Mantles the earth with darkness, until right
And wrong are accidents, and men grow pale   835
Lest their own judgments should become too bright,
And their free thoughts be crimes, and earth have too much light.

XCIV

And thus they plod in sluggish misery,
Rotting from sire to son, and age to age,
Proud of their trampled nature, and so die,   840
Bequeathing their hereditary rage
To the new race of inborn slaves, who wage
War for their chains, and rather than be free,
Bleed gladiator-like, and still engage
Within the same arena where they see   845
Their fellows fall before, like leaves of the same tree.

XCV

I speak not of men's creeds—they rest between
Man and his Maker—but of things allowed,
Averred, and known, and daily, hourly seen:—
The yoke that is upon us doubly bowed,   850
And the intent of tyranny avowed,
The edict of Earth's rulers, who are grown
The apes of him who humbled once the proud,
And shook them from their slumbers on the throne—
Too glorious, were this all his mighty arm had done.   855

XCVI

Can tyrants but by tyrants conquered be,
And Freedom find no champion and no child
Such as Columbia saw arise when she
Sprung forth a Pallas, armed and undefiled?
Or must such minds be nourished in the wild,   860
Deep in the unpruned forest, 'midst the roar
Of cataracts, where nursing Nature smiled
On infant Washington? Has Earth no more
Such seeds within her breast, or Europe no such shore?

XCVII

But France got drunk with blood to vomit crime,   865
And fatal have her Saturnalia been
To Freedom's cause, in every age and clime;
Because the deadly days which we have seen,
And vile Ambition, that built up between
Man and his hopes an adamantine wall,   870
And the base pageant last upon the scene,
Are grown the pretext for the eternal thrall
Which nips life's tree, and dooms man's worst—his second fall.

XCVIII

Yet, Freedom! yet thy banner, torn but flying,
Streams like the thunder-storm *against* the wind;
Thy trumpet voice, though broken now and dying,   875
The loudest still the tempest leaves behind;
Thy tree hath lost its blossoms, and the rind,
Chopped by the axe, looks rough and little worth,
But the sap lasts, and still the seed we find   880
Sown deep, even in the bosom of the North:
So shall a better Spring less bitter fruit bring forth.

. . . .

CVIII

There is the moral of all human tales;
'T is but the same rehearsal of the past,
First Freedom, and then Glory—when that fails,   965
Wealth, vice, corruption,—barbarism at last.
And History, with all her volumes vast,
Hath but *one* page,—'t is better written here
Where gorgeous Tyranny hath thus amassed   970
All treasures, all delights, that eye or ear,
Heart, soul could seek, tongue ask—Away with words! draw near.

CIX

Admire, exult, despise, laugh, weep,—for here
There is such matter for all feeling:—Man!
Thou pendulum betwixt a smile and tear,   975
Ages and realms are crowded in this span,
This mountain, whose obliterated plan
This pyramid of empires pinnacled,
Of Glory's gewgaws shining in the van
Till the sun's rays with added flame were filled!   980
Where are its golden roofs? where those who dared to build?

. . . .

CXX

Alas! our young affections run to waste,
Or water but the desert; whence arise
But weeds of dark luxuriance, tares of haste,
Rank at the core, though tempting to the eyes,   1075
Flowers whose wild odors breathe but agonies,
And trees whose gums are poisons; such the plants
Which spring beneath her steps as Passion flies
O'er the world's wilderness, and vainly pants
For some celestial fruit forbidden to our wants.   1080

CXXI

Oh, Love! no habitant of earth thou art—
An unseen seraph, we believe in thee,—
A faith whose martyrs are the broken heart,—
But never yet hath seen, nor e'er shall see
The naked eye, thy form, as it should be;   1085
The mind hath made thee, as it peopled heaven,
Even with its own desiring phantasy,
And to a thought such shape and image given,
As haunts the unquenched soul—parched, wearied, wrung, and riven.

CXXII

Of its own beauty is the mind diseased,   1090
And fevers into false creation:—where,
Where are the forms the sculptor's soul hath seized?
In him alone. Can Nature show so fair?

Where are the charms and virtues which we dare
Conceive in boyhood and pursue as men,   1095
The unreached Paradise of our despair,
Which o'er-informs the pencil and the pen,
And overpowers the page where it would bloom again?

CXXIII

Who loves, raves—'t is youth's frenzy—but the cure
Is bitterer still, as charm by charm unwinds   1100
Which robed our idols, and we see too sure
Nor worth nor beauty dwells from out the mind's
Ideal shape of such; yet still it binds
The fatal spell, and still it draws us on,
Reaping the whirlwind from the oft-sown winds;   1105
The stubborn heart, its alchemy begun,
Seems ever near the prize—wealthiest when most undone.

CXXIV

We wither from our youth, we gasp away—
Sick—sick; unfound the boon, unslaked the thirst,
Though to the last, in verge of our decay,   1110
Some phantom lures, such as we sought at first—
But all too late,—so are we doubly cursed.
Love, fame, ambition, avarice—'t is the same,
Each idle, and all ill, and none the worst—
For all are meteors with a different name,   1115
And Death the sable smoke where vanishes the flame.

CXXV

Few—none—find what they love or could have loved,
Though accident, blind contact, and the strong
Necessity of loving, have removed
Antipathies—but to recur, ere long,   1120
Envenomed with irrevocable wrong;
And Circumstance, that unspiritual god
And miscreator, makes and helps along
Our coming evils with a crutch-like rod,
Whose touch turns Hope to dust,—the dust we all have trod.   1125

CXXVI

Our life is a false nature: 't is not in
The harmony of things,—this hard decree,
This uneradicable taint of sin,
This boundless upas, this all-blasting tree,
Whose root is earth, whose leaves and branches be   1130
The skies which rain their plagues on men like dew—
Disease, death, bondage—all the woes we see,
And worse, the woes we see not—which throb through
The immedicable soul, with heart-aches ever new.

CXXVII

Yet let us ponder boldly—'t is a base   1135
Abandonment of reason to resign
Our right of thought—our last and only place
Of refuge; this, at least, shall still be mine:
Though from our birth the faculty divine
Is chained and tortured—cabined, cribbed, confined,   1140
And bred in darkness, lest the truth should shine
Too brightly on the unprepared mind,
The beam pours in, for time and skill will couch the blind.

CXXVIII

Arches on arches! as it were that Rome,
Collecting the chief trophies of her line,   1145
Would build up all her triumphs in one dome,
Her Coliseum stands; the moonbeams shine
As 'twere its natural torches, for divine
Should be the light which streams here to illume
This long-explored but still exhaustless mine   1150
Of contemplation; and the azure gloom
Of an Italian night, where the deep skies assume

CXXIX

Hues which have words, and speak to ye of heaven,
Floats o'er this vast and wondrous monument,
And shadows forth its glory. There is given   1155
Unto the things of earth, which Time hath bent,
A spirit's feeling, and where he hath leant
His hand, but broke his scythe, there is a power
And magic in the ruined battlement,
For which the palace of the present hour   1160
Must yield its pomp, and wait till ages are its dower.

CXXX

Oh Time! the beautifier of the dead,
Adorner of the ruin, comforter
And only healer when the heart hath bled;
Time! the corrector when our judgments err,   1165
The test of truth, love—sole philosopher,
For all beside are sophists—from thy thrift,
Which never loses though it doth defer—
Time, the avenger! unto thee I lift
My hands, and eyes, and heart, and crave of thee a gift: 1170

CXXXI

Amidst this wreck, where thou hast made a shrine
And temple more divinely desolate,
Among thy mightier offerings here are mine,
Ruins of years, though few, yet full of fate:
If thou hast ever seen me too elate,   1175
Hear me not; but if calmly I have borne
Good, and reserved my pride against the hate
Which shall not whelm me, let me not have worn
This iron in my soul in vain—shall *they* not mourn?

CXXXII

And thou, who never yet of human wrong   1180
Left the unbalanced scale, great Nemesis!
Here, where the ancient paid thee homage long—
Thou who didst call the furies from the abyss,
And round Orestes bade them howl and hiss
For that unnatural retribution—just,   1185
Had it but been from hands less near—in this
Thy former realm, I call thee from the dust!
Dost thou not hear my heart?—Awake! thou shalt, and must.

CXXXIII

It is not that I may not have incurred
For my ancestral faults or mine the wound   1190
I bleed withal, and, had it been conferred
With a just weapon, it had flowed unbound;

But now my blood shall not sink in the ground;
To thee I do devote it—*thou* shalt take
The vengeance, which shall yet be sought and found,   1195
Which if *I* have not taken for the sake——
But let that pass—I sleep, but thou shalt yet awake.

CXXXIV

And if my voice break forth, 'tis not that now
I shrink from what is suffered: let him speak
Who hath beheld decline upon my brow,   1200
Or seen my mind's convulsion leave it weak;
But in this page a record will I seek.
Not in the air shall these my words disperse,
Though I be ashes; a far hour shall wreak
The deep prophetic fulness of this verse,   1205
And pile on human heads the mountain of my curse!

CXXXV

That curse shall be forgiveness.—Have I not—
Hear me, my mother earth! behold it, heaven!
Have I not had to wrestle with my lot?
Have I not suffered things to be forgiven?   1210
Have I not had my brain seared, my heart riven,
Hopes sapped, name blighted, life's life lied away?
And only not to desperation driven,
Because not altogether of such clay
As rots into the souls of those whom I survey.   1215

CXXXVI

From mighty wrongs to petty perfidy
Have I not seen what human things could do?
From the loud roar of foaming calumny
To the small whisper of the as paltry few,
And subtler venom of the reptile crew,   1220
The Janus glance of whose significant eye,
Learning to lie with silence, would *seem* true,
And without utterance, save the shrug or sigh,
Deal round to happy fools its speechless obloquy.

CXXXVII

But I have lived, and have not lived in vain: 1225
My mind may lose its force, my blood its fire,
And my frame perish even in conquering pain;
But there is that within me which shall tire
Torture and time, and breathe when I expire;
Something unearthly, which they deem not of,   1230
Like the remembered tone of a mute lyre,
Shall on their softened spirits sink, and move
In hearts all rocky now the late remorse of love.

CXXXVIII

The seal is set.—Now welcome, thou dread power!
Nameless, yet thus omnipotent, which here   1235
Walk'st in the shadow of the midnight hour
With a deep awe, yet all distinct from fear;
Thy haunts are ever where the dead walls rear
Their ivy mantles, and the solemn scene
Derives from thee a sense so deep and clear   1240
That we become a part of what has been,
And grow unto the spot, all-seeing but unseen.

CXXXIX

And here the buzz of eager nations ran,
In murmured pity, or loud-roared applause,
As man was slaughtered by his fellow-man.   1245
And wherefore slaughtered? wherefore, but because
Such were the bloody Circus' genial laws,
And the imperial pleasure.—Wherefore not?
What matters where we fall to fill the maws
Of worms—on battle-plains or listed spot?   1250
Both are but theatres where the chief actors rot.

CXL

I see before me the Gladiator lie:
He leans upon his hand—his manly brow
Consents to death, but conquers agony,
And his drooped head sinks gradually low—   1255
And through his side the last drops, ebbing slow
From the red gash, fall heavy, one by one,
Like the first of a thunder-shower; and now
The arena swims around him—he is gone,
Ere ceased the inhuman shout which hailed the wretch who won.   1260

CXLI

He heard it, but he heeded not—his eyes
Were with his heart, and that was far away;
He recked not of the life he lost nor prize,
But where his rude hut by the Danube lay,
There were his young barbarians all at play,   1265
There was their Dacian mother—he, their sire,
Butchered to make a Roman holiday—
All this rushed with his blood—Shall he expire
And unavenged? Arise, ye Goths, and glut your ire!

CXLII

But here, where Murder breathed her bloody stream;   1270
And here, where buzzing nations choked the ways,
And roared or murmured like a mountain stream
Dashing or winding as its torrent strays;
Here, where the Roman million's blame or praise,
Was death or life, the playthings of a crowd,   1275
My voice sounds much—and fall the stars' faint rays
On the arena void—seats crushed—walls bowed—
And galleries, where my steps seem echoes strangely loud.

CXLIII

A ruin—yet what ruin! from its mass
Walls, palaces, half-cities, have been reared;   1280
Yet oft the enormous skeleton ye pass,
And marvel where the spoil could have appeared.
Hath it indeed been plundered, or but cleared?
Alas! developed, opens the decay,
When the colossal fabric's form is neared: 1285
It will not bear the brightness of the day,
Which streams too much on all, years, man, have reft away.

CXLIV

But when the rising moon begins to climb
Its topmost arch, and gently pauses there;
When the stars twinkle through the loops of time,   1290
And the low night-breeze waves along the air

The garland-forest, which the gray walls wear,
Like laurels on the bald first Cæsar's head;
When the light shines serene but doth not glare,
Then in this magic circle raise the dead: 1295
Heroes have trod this spot—'tis on their dust ye tread.

CXLV

"While stands the Coliseum, Rome shall stand;
When falls the Coliseum, Rome shall fall;
And when Rome falls—the World." From our own land
Thus spake the pilgrims o'er this mighty wall   1300
In Saxon times, which we are wont to call
Ancient; and these three mortal things are still
On their foundations, and unaltered all;
Rome and her Ruin past Redemption's skill,
The World, the same wide den—of thieves, or what ye will.   1305

. . . .

CLIII

But lo! the dome—the vast and wondrous dome,
To which Diana's marvel was a cell—
Christ's mighty shrine above his martyr's tomb!   1370
I have beheld the Ephesian's miracle:—
Its columns strew the wilderness, and dwell
The hyæna and the jackal in their shade;
I have beheld Sophia's bright roofs swell   1375
Their glittering mass i' the sun, and have surveyed
Its sanctuary the while the usurping Moslem prayed;

CLIV

But thou, of temples old, or altars new,
Standest alone, with nothing like to thee—
Worthiest of God, the holy and the true.   1380
Since Zion's desolation, when that He
Forsook his former city, what could be,
Of earthly structures, in his honor piled,
Of a sublimer aspect? Majesty,
Power, Glory, Strength, and Beauty all are aisled   1385
In this eternal ark of worship undefiled.

CLV

Enter: its grandeur overwhelms thee not;
And why? It is not lessened; but thy mind,
Expanded by the genius of the spot,
Has grown colossal, and can only find   1390
A fit abode wherein appear enshrined
Thy hopes of immortality; and thou
Shalt one day, if found worthy, so defined,
See thy God face to face, as thou dost now
His Holy of Holies, nor be blasted by his brow.   1395

CLVI

Thou movest, but increasing with the advance,
Like climbing some great Alp, which still doth rise,
Deceived by its gigantic elegance;
Vastness which grows, but grows to harmonise—
All musical in its immensities;   1400
Rich marbles, richer painting—shrines where flame

The lamps of gold—and haughty dome which vies
In air with Earth's chief structures, though their frame
Sits on the firm-set ground, and this the clouds must claim.

. . . .

CLXXVII

Oh! that the desert were my dwelling-place,　　　　1585
With one fair Spirit for my minister,
That I might all forget the human race,
And, hating no one, love but only her!
Ye elements!—in whose ennobling stir
I feel myself exalted—Can ye not　　　　　　　　1590
Accord me such a being? Do I err
In deeming such inhabit many a spot?
Though with them to converse can rarely be our lot.

CLXXVIII

There is a pleasure in the pathless woods,
There is a rapture on the lonely shore,
There is society, where none intrudes,　　　　　　1595
By the deep sea, and music in its roar:
I love not man the less, but Nature more,
From these our interviews, in which I steal
From all I may be, or have been before,　　　　　1600
To mingle with the Universe, and feel
What I can ne'er express, yet cannot all conceal.

CLXXIX

Roll on, thou deep and dark blue Ocean—roll!
Ten thousand fleets sweep over thee in vain;
Man marks the earth with ruin—his control　　　1605
Stops with the shore; upon the watery plain
The wrecks are all thy deed, nor doth remain
A shadow of man's ravage, save his own,
When, for a moment, like a drop of rain,
He sinks into thy depths with bubbling groan,　　1610
Without a grave, unknelled, uncoffined, and unknown.

CLXXX

His steps are not upon thy paths,—thy fields
Are not a spoil for him,—thou dost arise
And shake him from thee; the vile strength he wields
For earth's destruction thou dost all despise,　　1615
Spurning him from thy bosom to the skies,
And send'st him, shivering in thy playful spray
And howling, to his gods, where haply lies
His petty hope in some near port or bay,
And dashest him again to earth:—there let him lay.　1620

CLXXXI

The armaments which thunderstrike the walls
Of rock-built cities, bidding nations quake,
And monarchs tremble in their capitals,
The oak leviathans, whose huge ribs make
Their clay creator the vain title take　　　　　　1625
Of lord of thee, and arbiter of war—
These are thy toys, and, as the snowy flake,
They melt into thy yeast of waves, which mar
Alike the Armada's pride or spoils of Trafalgar.

CLXXXII

Thy shores are empires, changed in all save thee—
Assyria, Greece, Rome, Carthage, what are they?
Thy waters washed them power while they were free,
And many a tyrant since; their shores obey
The stranger, slave, or savage; their decay
Has dried up realms to deserts:—not so thou;—
Unchangeable, save to thy wild waves' play,
Time writes no wrinkle on thine azure brow:
Such as creation's dawn beheld, thou rollest now.

      1630

      1635

CLXXXIII

Thou glorious mirror, where the Almighty's form
Glasses itself in tempests; in all time,—
Calm or convulsed, in breeze, or gale, or storm,
Icing the pole, or in the torrid clime
Dark-heaving—boundless, endless, and sublime,
The image of Eternity, the throne
Of the Invisible; even from out thy slime
The monsters of the deep are made; each zone
Obeys thee; thou goest forth, dread, fathomless, alone.

      1640

      1645

CLXXXIV

And I have loved thee, Ocean! and my joy
Of youthful sports was on thy breast to be
Borne, like thy bubbles, onward: from a boy
I wantoned with thy breakers—they to me
Were a delight; and if the freshening sea
Made them a terror—'twas a pleasing fear,
For I was as it were a child of thee,
And trusted to thy billows far and near,
And laid my hand upon thy mane—as I do here.

      1650

      1655

CLXXXV

My task is done, my song hath ceased, my theme
Has died into an echo; it is fit
The spell should break of this protracted dream.
The torch shall be extinguished which hath lit
My midnight lamp—and what is writ, is writ;
Would it were worthier! but I am not now
That which I have been—and my visions flit
Less palpably before me—and the glow
Which in my spirit dwelt is fluttering, faint, and low.

      1660

      1665

CLXXXVI

Farewell! a word that must be, and hath been—
A sound which makes us linger;—yet—farewell!
Ye! who have traced the Pilgrim to the scene
Which is his last, if in your memories dwell
A thought which once was his, if on ye swell
A single recollection, not in vain
He wore his sandal-shoon and scallop-shell;
Farewell! with *him* alone may rest the pain,
If such there were—with *you*, the moral of his strain.

      1670

     1817   1818

MANFRED

A DRAMATIC POEM

There are more things in heaven and earth, Horatio,
Than are dreamt of in your philosophy.

DRAMATIS PERSONÆ

MANFRED	WITCH OF THE ALPS
CHAMOIS HUNTER	ARIMANES
ABBOT OF ST. MAURICE	NEMESIS
MANUEL	THE DESTINIES
HERMAN	SPIRITS, &c

The SCENE of the Drama is amongst the Higher Alps—partly in the Castle of Manfred, and partly in the Mountains.

ACT I

SCENE I

MANFRED *alone.—Scene, a Gothic Gallery. Time, Midnight*

Man. The lamp must be replenished, but even then
It will not burn so long as I must watch:
My slumbers—if I slumber—are not sleep,
But a continuance of enduring thought,
Which then I can resist not: in my heart   5
There is a vigil, and these eyes but close
To look within; and yet I live, and bear
The aspect and the form of breathing men.
But grief should be the instructor of the wise;
Sorrow is knowledge: they who know the most   10
Must mourn the deepest o'er the fatal truth,
The tree of knowledge is not that of life.
Philosophy and science, and the springs
Of wonder, and the wisdom of the world,
I have essayed, and in my mind there is   15
A power to make these subject to itself—
But they avail not: I have done men good,
And I have met with good even among men—
But this availed not: I have had my foes,
And none have baffled, many fallen before me—   20
But this availed not:—Good, or evil, life,
Powers, passions, all I see in other beings,
Have been to me as rain unto the sands,
Since that all-nameless hour. I have no dread,
And feel the curse to have no natural fear,   25
Nor fluttering throb, that beats with hopes or wishes,
Or lurking love of something on the earth.
Now to my task.—
                    Mysterious agency!
Ye spirits of the unbounded universe!
Whom I have sought in darkness and in light—   30
Ye, who do compass earth about, and dwell
In subtler essence—ye, to whom the tops
Of mountains inaccessible are haunts,
And earth's and ocean's cave familiar things—
I call upon ye by the written charm   35
Which gives me power upon you—Rise! Appear!

                                        [*A pause.*

They come not yet.—Now by the voice of him
Who is the first among you—by this sign,
Which makes you tremble—by the claims of him
Who is undying,—Rise! Appear——Appear!   40

                                       [A pause.

If it be so—Spirits of earth and air,
Ye shall not thus elude me: by a power,
Deeper than all yet urged, a tyrant-spell,
Which had its birthplace in a star condemned,
The burning wreck of a demolished world,   45
A wandering hell in the eternal space
By the strong curse which is upon my soul,
The thought which is within me and around me,
I do compel ye to my will—Appear!

        [A star is seen at the darker end of the gallery:
          it is stationary; and a voice is heard singing.

First Spirit

Mortal! to thy bidding bowed,   50
From my mansion in the cloud,
Which the breath of twilight builds
And the summer's sunset gilds
With the azure and vermilion,
Which is mixed for my pavilion;   55
Though thy quest may be forbidden,
On a star-beam I have ridden:
To thine adjuration bowed,
Mortal—be thy wish avowed!

Voice of the Second Spirit

Mont Blanc is the monarch of mountains;   60
  They crowned him long ago
On a throne of rocks, in a robe of clouds,
  With a diadem of snow.
Around his waist are forests braced,
  The avalanche in his hand;   65
But ere it fall, that thundering ball
  Must pause for my command.
The glacier's cold and restless mass
  Moves onward day by day;
But I am he who bids it pass,   70
  Or with its ice delay.
I am the spirit of the place,
  Could make the mountain bow
And quiver to his caverned base—
  And what with me would *thou?*   75

Voice of the Third Spirit

In the blue depth of the waters,
  Where the wave hath no strife,
Where the wind is a stranger,
  And the sea-snake hath life,
Where the mermaid is decking   80
  Her green hair with shells,
Like the storm on the surface
  Came the sound of thy spells;

O'er my calm Hall of Coral
  The deep echo rolled—
To the Spirit of Ocean
  Thy wishes unfold!   85

Fourth Spirit

Where the slumbering earthquake
  Lies pillowed on fire,
And the lakes of bitumen   90
  Rise boilingly higher;
Where the roots of the Andes
  Strike deep in the earth,
As their summits to heaven
  Shoot soaringly forth;   95
I have quitted my birthplace
  Thy bidding to bide—
Thy spell hath subdued me,
  Thy will be my guide!

Fifth Spirit

I am the rider of the wind,   100
  The stirrer of the storm;
The hurricane I left behind
  Is yet with lightning warm;
To speed to thee, o'er shore and sea
  I swept upon the blast: 105
The fleet I met sailed well, and yet
  'Twill sink ere night be past.

Sixth Spirit

My dwelling is the shadow of the night,
Why doth thy magic torture me with light?

Seventh Spirit

The star which rules thy destiny   110
Was ruled, ere earth began, by me:
It was a world as fresh and fair
As e'er revolved round sun in air;
Its course was free and regular,
Space bosomed not a lovelier star.   115
The hour arrived—and it became
A wandering mass of shapeless flame,
A pathless comet, and a curse,
The menace of the universe;
Still rolling on with innate force,   120
Without a sphere, without a course,
A bright deformity on high,
The monster of the upper sky!
And thou! beneath its influence born—
Thou worm! whom I obey and scorn—   125
Forced by a power (which is not thine,
And lent thee but to make thee mine)
For this brief moment to descend,
Where these weak spirits round thee bend
And parley with a thing like thee——   130
What wouldst thou, child of clay! with me?

The Seven Spirits

Earth, ocean, air, night, mountains, winds, thy star,
  Are at thy beck and bidding, child of clay!
Before thee at thy quest their spirits are—
  What wouldst thou with us, son of mortals—say?   135
  Man. Forgetfulness—
  First Spirit. Of what—of whom—and why?
  Man. Of that which is within me; read it there—
Ye know it, and I cannot utter it.
  Spirit. We can but give thee that which we possess: 140
Ask of us subjects, sovereignty, the power
O'er earth—the whole, or portion—or a sign
Which shall control the elements, whereof
We are the dominators,—each and all,
These shall be thine.   145
  Man.   Oblivion, self-oblivion.
Can ye not wring from out the hidden realms
Ye offer so profusely what I ask?
  Spirit. It is not in our essence, in our skill;
But—thou may'st die.
  Man.   Will death bestow it on me?
  Spirit. We are immortal, and do not forget;   150
We are eternal; and to us the past
Is, as the future, present. Art thou answered?
  Man. Ye mock me—but the power which brought ye here
Hath made you mine. Slaves, scoff not at my will!
The mind, the spirit, the Promethean spark,   155
The lightning of my being, is as bright,
Pervading, and far darting as your own,
And shall not yield to yours, though cooped in clay!
Answer, or I will teach you what I am.
  Spirit. We answer as we answered; our reply   160
Is even in thine own words.
  Man.   Why say ye so?
  Spirit. If, as thou say'st, thine essence be as ours,
We have replied in telling thee, the thing
Mortals call death hath naught to do with us.
  Man. I then have called ye from your realms in vain; 165
Ye cannot, or ye will not, aid me.
  Spirit.   Say,
What we possess we offer; it is thine:
Bethink ere thou dismiss us; ask again—
Kingdom, and sway, and strength, and length of days—
  Man. Accursed! what have I to do with days?   170
They are too long already.—Hence—begone!
  Spirit. Yet pause: being here, our will would do thee service;
Bethink thee, is there then no other gift
Which we can make not worthless in thine eyes?
  Man. No, none: yet stay—one moment, ere we part, 175
I would behold ye face to face. I hear
Your voices, sweet and melancholy sounds,
As music on the waters; and I see
The steady aspect of a clear large star;
But nothing more. Approach me as ye are,   180
Or one, or all, in your accustomed forms.
  Spirit. We have no forms, beyond the elements
Of which we are the mind and principle:
But choose a form—in that we will appear.
  Man. I have no choice; there is no form on earth 185

Hideous or beautiful to me. Let him,
  Who is most powerful of ye, take such aspect
As unto him may seem most fitting—Come!
  Seventh Spirit (appearing in the shape of a beautiful female
    figure). Behold!
    Man. Oh God! if it be thus, and *thou*   190
Art not a madness and a mockery,
I yet might be most happy, I will clasp thee,
And we again will be—
                              [The figure vanishes.
            My heart is crushed!
                          *[*MANFRED *falls senseless.*

    (A voice is heard in the Incantation which follows.)

      When the moon is on the wave,
        And the glow-worm in the grass,
      And the meteor on the grave,   195
        And the wisp on the morass;
      When the falling stars are shooting,
      And the answered owls are hooting,
      And the silent leaves are still
      In the shadow of the hill,   200
      Shall my soul be upon thine,
      With a power and with a sign.

      Though thy slumber may be deep,
      Yet thy spirit shall not sleep;
      There are shades that will not vanish,   205
      There are thoughts thou canst not banish;
      By a power to thee unknown,
      Thou canst never be alone;
      Thou art wrapt as with a shroud,
      Thou art gathered in a cloud;   210
      And forever shalt thou dwell
      In the spirit of this spell.

      Though thou seest me not pass by,
      Thou shalt feel me with thine eye
      As a thing that, though unseen,   215
      Must be near thee, and hath been;
      And when in that secret dread
      Thou hast turned around thy head,
      Thou shalt marvel I am not
      As thy shadow on the spot,   220
      And the power which thou dost feel
      Shall be what thou must conceal.

      And a magic voice and verse
      Hath baptized thee with a curse;
      And a spirit of the air   225
      Hath begirt thee with a snare;
      In the wind there is a voice
      Shall forbid thee to rejoice;
      And to thee shall night deny
      All the quiet of her sky;   230
      And the day shall have a sun,
      Which shall make thee wish it done.

From thy false tears I did distil
An essence which hath strength to kill;
From thy own heart I then did wring 235
The black blood in its blackest spring;
From thy own smile I snatched the snake,
For there it coiled as in a brake;
From thy own lip I drew the charm
Which gave all these their chiefest harm; 240
In proving every poison known,
I found the strongest was thine own.

By thy cold breast and serpent smile,
By thy unfathomed gulfs of guile,
By that most seeming virtuous eye, 245
By thy shut soul's hypocrisy;
By the perfection of thine art
Which passed for human thine own heart;
By thy delight in others' pain,
And by thy brotherhood of Cain, 250
I call upon thee! and compel
Thyself to be thy proper hell!

And on thy head I pour the vial
Which doth devote thee to this trial;
Nor to slumber, nor to die, 255
Shall be in thy destiny;
Though thy death shall still seem near
To thy wish, but as a fear;
Lo! the spell now works around thee,
And the clankless chain hath bound thee; 260
O'er thy heart and brain together
Hath the word been passed—now wither!

Scene II

The Mountain of the Jungfrau.—Time, Morning.—

Manfred *alone upon the Cliffs.*

Man. The spirits I have raised abandon me,
The spells which I have studied baffle me,
The remedy I recked of tortured me;
I lean no more on superhuman aid;
It hath no power upon the past, and for 5
The future, till the past be gulfed in darkness,
It is not of my search.—My mother earth!
And thou fresh breaking day, and you, ye mountains,
Why are ye beautiful? I cannot love ye.
And thou, the bright eye of the universe, 10
That openest over all, and unto all
Art a delight—thou shin'st not on my heart.
And you, ye crags, upon whose extreme edge
I stand, and on the torrent's brink beneath
Behold the tall pines dwindled as to shrubs 15
In dizziness of distance; when a leap,
A stir, a motion, even a breath, would bring
My breast upon its rocky bosom's bed
To rest forever—wherefore do I pause?
I feel the impulse—yet I do not plunge; 20
I see the peril—yet do not recede;

And my brain reels—and yet my foot is firm:
There is a power upon me which withholds,
And makes it my fatality to live;
If it be life to wear within myself   25
This barrenness of spirit, and to be
My own soul's sepulchre, for I have ceased
To justify my deeds unto myself—
The last infirmity of evil. Ay,
Thou winged and cloud-cleaving minister,   30
                            [*An eagle passes.*

Whose happy flight is highest into heaven,
Well may'st thou swoop so near me—I should be
Thy prey, and gorge thine eaglets; thou art gone
Where the eye cannot follow thee; but thine
Yet pierces downward, onward, or above,   35
With a pervading vision.—Beautiful!
How beautiful is all this visible world!
How glorious in its action and itself!
But we, who name ourselves its sovereigns, we,
Half dust, half deity, alike unfit   40
To sink or soar, with our mixed essence make
A conflict of its elements, and breathe
The breath of degradation and of pride,
Contending with low wants and lofty will,
Till our mortality predominates,   45
And men are—what they name not to themselves,
And trust not to each other. Hark! the note,
                    [*The Shepherd's pipe in the distance
                                            is heard.*

The natural music of the mountain reed—
For here the patriarchal days are not
A pastoral fable—pipes in the liberal air,   50
Mixed with the sweet bells of the sauntering herd;
My soul would drink those echoes. Oh, that I were
The viewless spirit of a lovely sound,
A living voice, a breathing harmony,
A bodiless enjoyment—born and dying   55
With the blest tone which made me!

Enter from below a CHAMOIS HUNTER.

  Chamois Hunter.   Even so
This way the chamois leapt: her nimble feet
Have baffled me; my gains today will scarce
Repay my break-neck travail.—What is here?
Who seems not of my trade, and yet hath reached   60
A height which none even of our mountaineers,
Save our best hunters, may attain: his garb
Is goodly, his mien manly, and his air
Proud as a free-born peasant's, at this distance:
I will approach him nearer.   65
  Man. (*not perceiving the other*). To be thus—
Gray-haired with anguish, like these blasted pines,
Wrecks of a single winter, barkless, branchless,
A blighted trunk upon a cursed root,
Which but supplies a feeling to decay—
And to be thus, eternally but thus,   70
Having been otherwise! Now furrowed o'er
With wrinkles, ploughed by moments,—not by years,—
And hours, all tortured into ages—hours
Which I outlive!—Ye toppling crags of ice!

Ye avalanches, whom a breath draws down   75
In mountainous o'erwhelming, come and crush me!
I hear ye momently above, beneath,
Crash with a frequent conflict; but ye pass,
And only fall on things that still would live;
On the young flourishing forest, or the hut   80
And hamlet of the harmless villager.
    C. Hun. The mists begin to rise from up the valley;
I'll warn him to descend, or he may chance
To lose at once his way and life together.
    Man. The mists boil up around the glaciers; clouds   85
Rise curling fast beneath me, white and sulphury,
Like foam from the roused ocean of deep hell,
Whose every wave breaks on a living shore,
Heaped with the damned like pebbles.—I am giddy.
    C. Hun. I must approach him cautiously; if near,   90
A sudden step will startle him, and he
Seems tottering already.
    Man.   Mountains have fallen,
Leaving a gap in the clouds, and with the shock
Rocking their Alpine brethren; filling up
The ripe green valleys with destruction's splinters;   95
Damming the rivers with a sudden dash,
Which crushed the waters into mist and made
Their fountains find another channel—thus,
Thus, in its old age, did Mount Rosenberg—
Why stood I not beneath it?   100
    C. Hun.   Friend! have a care,
Your next step may be fatal!—for the love
Of him who made you, stand not on that brink!
    Man. (not hearing him). Such would have been for me a
               fitting tomb;
My bones had then been quiet in their depth;
They had not then been strewn upon the rocks   105
For the wind's pastime—as thus—thus they shall be—
In this one plunge.—Farewell, ye opening heavens!
Look not upon me thus reproachfully—
Ye were not meant for me—Earth! take these atoms!
                [*As* MANFRED *is in act to spring from the*
                      cliff, the CHAMOIS HUNTER *seizes and*
                      retains him with a sudden grasp.
    C. Hun. Hold, madman!—though aweary of thy life,   110
Stain not our pure vales with thy guilty blood:
Away with me—I will not quit my hold.
    Man. I am most sick at heart—nay, grasp me not—
I am all feebleness—the mountains whirl
Spinning around me—I grow blind—   115
          What art thou?
    C. Hun. I'll answer that anon. Away with me!
The clouds grow thicker—there—now lean on me—
Place your foot here—here, take this staff, and cling
A moment to that shrub—now give me your hand,
And hold fast by my girdle—softly—well—   120
The Chalet will be gained within an hour:
Come on, we'll quickly find a surer footing,
And something like a pathway, which the torrent
Hath washed since winter.—Come, 'tis bravely done—
You should have been a hunter.—Follow me.   125
                [*As they descend the rocks with difficulty,*
                the scene closes.

ACT II

Scene I

A Cottage amongst the Bernese Alps.

Manfred *and the* Chamois Hunter

C. Hun. No, no—yet pause—thou must not yet go forth:
Thy mind and body are alike unfit
To trust each other, for some hours, at least;
When thou art better, I will be thy guide—
But whither?   5
  Man.   It imports not: I do know
My route full well, and need no further guidance.
  C. Hun. Thy garb and gait bespeak thee of high lineage—
One of the many chiefs, whose castled crags
Look o'er the lower valleys—which of these
May call thee lord? I only know their portals;   10
My way of life leads me but rarely down
To bask by the huge hearths of those old halls,
Carousing with the vassals; but the paths,
Which step from out our mountains to their doors,
I know from childhood—which of these is thine?   15
  Man. No matter.
  C. Hun.   Well, sir, pardon me the question,
And be of better cheer. Come, taste my wine;
'Tis of an ancient vintage; many a day
'T has thawed my veins among our glaciers, now
Let it do thus for thine. Come, pledge me fairly.   20
  Man. Away, away! there's blood upon the brim!
Will it then never—never sink in the earth?
  C. Hun. What dost thou mean? thy senses wander from thee.
  Man. I say 'tis blood—my blood! the pure warm stream
Which ran in the veins of my fathers, and in ours   25
When we were in our youth, and had one heart,
And loved each other as we should not love,
And this was shed: but still it rises up,
Coloring the clouds, that shut me out from heaven,
Where thou art not—and I shall never be.   30
  C. Hun. Man of strange words, and some half-maddening sin,
Which makes thee people vacancy, whate'er
Thy dread and sufferance be, there's comfort yet—
The aid of holy men, and heavenly patience—
  Man. Patience and patience! Hence—that word was made   35
For brutes of burthen, not for birds of prey;
Preach it to mortals of a dust like thine,—
I am not of thine order.
  C. Hun.   Thanks to heaven!
I would not be of thine for the free fame
Of William Tell; but whatsoe'er thine ill,   40
It must be borne, and these wild starts are useless.
  Man. Do I not bear it?—Look on me—I live.
  C. Hun. This is convulsion, and no healthful life.
  Man. I tell thee, man! I have lived many years,
Many long years, but they are nothing now   45
To those which I must number: ages—ages—
Space and eternity—and consciousness,
With the fierce thirst of death—and still unslaked!
  C. Hun. Why, on thy brow the seal of middle age

Hath scarce been set; I am thine elder far.   50
    Man.   Think'st thou existence doth depend on time?
It doth; but actions are our epochs: mine
Have made my days and nights imperishable,
Endless, and all alike, as sands on the shore,
Innumerable atoms; and one desert,   55
Barren and cold, on which the wild waves break,
But nothing rests, save carcasses and wrecks,
Rocks, and the salt-surf weeds of bitterness.
    C. Hun.   Alas! he's mad—but yet I must not leave him.
    Man.   I would I were—for then the things I see   60
Would be but a distempered dream.
    C. Hun.   What is it
That thou dost see, or think thou look'st upon?
    Man.   Myself, and thee—a peasant of the Alps—
Thy humble virtues, hospitable home,
And spirit patient, pious, proud, and free;   65
Thy self-respect, grafted on innocent thoughts;
Thy days of health, and nights of sleep; thy toils,
By danger dignified, yet guiltless; hopes
Of cheerful old age and a quiet grave,
With cross and garland over its green turf,   70
And thy grandchildren's love for epitaph;
This do I see—and then I look within—
It matters not—my soul was scorched already!
    C. Hun.   And wouldst thou then exchange thy lot for mine?
    Man.   No, friend! I would not wrong thee, nor exchange   75
My lot with living being: I can bear—
However wretchedly, 'tis still to bear—
In life what others could not brook to dream,
But perish in their slumber.
    C. Hun.   And with this—
This cautious feeling for another's pain,   80
Canst thou be black with evil?—say not so.
Can one of gentle thoughts have wreaked revenge
Upon his enemies?
    Man.   Oh! no, no, no!
My injuries came down on those who loved me—
On those whom I best loved: I never quelled   85
An enemy, save in my just defence—
But my embrace was fatal.
    C. Hun.   Heaven give thee rest!
And penitence restore thee to thyself;
My prayers shall be for thee.
    Man.   I need them not—
But can endure thy pity. I depart—   90
'Tis time—farewell!—Here's gold, and thanks for thee;
No words—it is thy due. Follow me not—
I know my path—the mountain peril's past:
And once again I charge thee, follow not!
                             [*Exit* MANFRED.

SCENE II

A lower Valley in the Alps.—A Cataract.

Enter MANFRED.

It is not noon—the sunbow's rays still arch
The torrent with the many hues of heaven,
And roll the sheeted silver's waving column

O'er the crag's headlong perpendicular,
And fling its lines of foaming light along
And to and fro, like the pale courser's tail,
The giant steed, to be bestrode by death,
As told in the Apocalypse. No eyes
But mine now drink this sight of loveliness;
I should be sole in this sweet solitude,
And with the Spirit of the place divide
The homage of these waters.—I will call her.

        [MANFRED *takes some of the water into the*
        palm of his hand, and flings it into the air
        muttering the adjuration. After a pause,
        the WITCH OF THE ALPS *rises beneath*
        the arch of the sunbow of the torrent.

Beautiful spirit! with thy hair of light,
And dazzling eyes of glory, in whose form
The charms of earth's least mortal daughters grow
To an unearthly stature, in an essence
Of purer elements; while the hue of youth,—
Carnationed like a sleeping infant's cheek,
Rocked by the beating of her mother's heart,
Or the rose tints, which summer's twilight leaves
Upon the lofty glacier's virgin snow,
The blush of earth embracing with her heaven,—
Tinge thy celestial aspect, and make tame
The beauties of the sunbow which bends o'er thee.
Beautiful Spirit! in thy calm clear brow,
Wherein is glassed serenity of soul,
Which of itself shows immortality,
I read that thou wilt pardon to a son
Of Earth, whom the abstruser powers permit
At times to commune with them—if that he
Avail him of his spells—to call thee thus,
And gaze on thee a moment.
    Witch.   Son of Earth!
I know thee, and the powers which give thee power;
I know thee for a man of many thoughts,
And deeds of good and ill, extreme in both,
Fatal and fated in thy sufferings.
I have expected this—what wouldst thou with me?
    Man. To look upon thy beauty—nothing further.
The face of the earth hath maddened me, and I
Take refuge in her mysteries, and pierce
To the abodes of those who govern her—
But they can nothing aid me. I have sought
From them what they could not bestow, and now
I search no further.
    Witch.   What could be the quest
Which is not in the power of the most powerful,
The rulers of the invisible?
    Man.   A boon;
But why should I repeat it? 'twere in vain.
    Witch. I know not that; let thy lips utter it.
    Man. Well, though it torture me, 'tis but the same;
My pangs shall find a voice. From my youth upwards
My spirit walked not with the souls of men,
Nor looked upon the earth with human eyes;
The thirst of their ambition was not mine,
The aim of their existence was not mine;
My joys, my griefs, my passions, and my powers,

Made me a stranger; though I wore the form
I had no sympathy with breathing flesh,
Nor midst the creatures of clay that girded me
Was there but one who—but of her anon.
I said with men, and with the thoughts of men,   60
I held but slight communion; but instead,
My joy was in the wilderness,—to breathe
The difficult air of the iced mountain's top,
Where the birds dare not build, nor insect's wing
Flit o'er the herbless granite; or to plunge   65
Into the torrent, and to roll along
On the swift whirl of the new breaking wave
Of river-stream, or ocean, in their flow.
In these my early strength exulted; or
To follow through the night the moving moon,   70
The stars and their development; or catch
The dazzling lightnings till my eyes grew dim;
Or to look, list'ning, on the scattered leaves,
While autumn winds were at their evening song.
These were my pastimes, and to be alone;   75
For if the beings, of whom I was one,—
Hating to be so,—crossed me in my path,
I felt myself degraded back to them,
And was all clay again. And then I dived,
In my lone wanderings, to the caves of death,   80
Searching its cause in its effect; and drew
From withered bones, and skulls, and heaped up dust,
Conclusions most forbidden. Then I passed
The nights of years in sciences untaught,
Save in the old time; and with time and toil,   85
And terrible ordeal, and such penance
As in itself hath power upon the air,
And spirits that do compass air and earth,
Space, and the peopled infinite, I made
Mine eyes familiar with Eternity,   90
Such as, before me, did the Magi, and
He who from out their fountain dwellings raised
Eros and Anteros, at Gadara,
As I do thee;—and with my knowledge grew
The thirst of knowledge, and the power and joy   95
Of this most bright intelligence, until—
    Witch. Proceed.
    Man. Oh! I but thus prolonged my words,
Boasting these idle attributes, because
As I approach the core of my heart's grief—   100
But to my task. I have not named to thee
Father, or mother, mistress, friend, or being,
With whom I wore the chain of human ties;
If I had such, they seemed not such to me;
Yet there was one—   105
    Witch.   Spare not thyself—proceed.
    Man. She was like me in lineaments; her eyes,
Her hair, her features, all, to the very tone
Even of her voice, they said were like to mine;
But softened all, and tempered into beauty:
She had the same lone thoughts and wanderings,   110
The quest of hidden knowledge, and a mind
To comprehend the universe: nor these
Alone, but with them gentler powers than mine,
Pity, and smiles, and tears—which I had not;

And tenderness—but that I had for her; 115
Humility—and that I never had.
Her faults were mine—her virtues were her own—
I loved her, and destroyed her!
    Witch.   With thy hand?
    Man. Not with my hand, but heart—which broke her heart;
It gazed on mine, and withered. I have shed 120
Blood, but not hers—and yet her blood was shed;
I saw—and could not stanch it.
    Witch.   And for this—
A being of the race thou dost despise,
The order, which thine own would rise above,
Mingling with us and ours,—thou dost forego 125
The gifts of our great knowledge, and shrink'st back
To recreant mortality—Away!
    Man. Daughter of air! I tell thee, since that hour—
But words are breath—look on me in my sleep,
Or watch my watchings—Come and sit by me! 130
My solitude is solitude no more,
But peopled with the furies;—I have gnashed
My teeth in darkness till returning morn,
Then cursed myself till sunset;—I have prayed
For madness as a blessing—'tis denied me. 135
I have affronted death—but in the war
Of elements the waters shrunk from me,
And fatal things passed harmless; the cold hand
Of an all-pitiless demon held me back,
Back by a single hair, which would not break. 140
In fantasy, imagination, all
The affluence of my soul—which one day was
A Crœsus in creation—I plunged deep,
But, like an ebbing wave, it dashed me back
Into the gulf of my unfathomed thought. 145
I plunged amidst mankind—Forgetfulness
I sought in all, save where 'tis to be found,
And that I have to learn; my sciences,
My long-pursued and superhuman art,
Is mortal here: I dwell in my despair— 150
And live—and live forever.
    Witch.   It may be
That I can aid thee.
    Man.   To do this thy power
Must wake the dead, or lay me low with them.
Do so—in any shape—in any hour—
With any torture—so it be the last. 155
    Witch. That is not in my province; but if thou
Wilt swear obedience to my will, and do
My bidding, it may help thee to thy wishes.
    Man. I will not swear—Obey! and whom? the spirits
Whose presence I command, and be the slave 160
Of those who served me—Never!
    Witch.   Is this all?
Hast thou no gentler answer?—Yet bethink thee,
And pause ere thou rejectest.
    Man.   I have said it.
    Witch. Enough! I may retire then—say!
    Man.   Retire!   [*The* WITCH *disappears.*
    Man. (alone). We are the fools of time and terror. Days 165
Steal on us, and steal from us; yet we live,
Loathing our life, and dreading still to die.

In all the days of this detested yoke—
This vital weight upon the struggling heart,
Which sinks with sorrow, or beats quick with **pain,**   170
Or joy that ends in agony or faintness—
In all the days of past and future, for
In life there is no present, we can number
How few—how less than few—wherein the soul
Forbears to pant for death, and yet draws back   175
As from a stream in winter, though the chill
Be but a moment's. I have one resource
Still in my science—I can call the dead,
And ask them what it is we dread to be:
The sternest answer can but be the grave,   180
And that is nothing. If they answer not—
The buried prophet answered to the Hag
Of Endor; and the Spartan Monarch drew
From the Byzantine maid's unsleeping spirit
An answer and his destiny—he slew   185
That which he loved, unknowing what he slew,
And died unpardoned—though he called in aid
The Phyxian Jove, and in Phigalia roused
The Arcadian Evocators to compel
The indignant shadow to depose her wrath,   190
Or fix her term of vengeance—she replied
In words of dubious import, but fulfilled.
If I had never lived, that which I love
Had still been living; had I never loved,
That which I love would still be beautiful,   195
Happy and giving happiness. What is she?
What is she now?—a sufferer for my sins—
A thing I dare not think upon—or nothing.
Within few hours I shall not call in vain—
Yet in this hour I dread the thing I dare: 200
Until this hour I never shrunk to gaze
On spirit, good or evil—now I tremble,
And feel a strange cold thaw upon my heart.
But I can act even what I most abhor,
And champion human fears.—The night approaches.   205
                                                         [*Exit.*

SCENE III

The Summit of the Jungfrau Mountain.

Enter FIRST DESTINY.

The moon is rising broad, and round, and bright;
And here on snows, where never human foot
Of common mortal trod, we nightly tread,
And leave no traces: o'er the savage sea,
The glassy ocean of the mountain ice,   5
We skim its rugged breakers, which put on
The aspect of a tumbling tempest's foam,
Frozen in a moment—a dead whirlpool's image:
And this most steep fantastic pinnacle,
The fretwork of some earthquake—where the clouds   10
Pause to repose themselves in passing by—
Is sacred to our revels, or our vigils;
Here do I wait my sisters, on our way
To the Hall of Arimanes, for tonight
Is our great festival—'tis strange they come not.   15

A Voice without, singing

The captive usurper,
  Hurled down from the throne,
Lay buried in torpor,
  Forgotten and lone;
I broke through his slumbers,   20
  I shivered his chain,
I leagued him with numbers—
  He's tyrant again!
With the blood of a million he'll answer my care,
With a nation's destruction—his flight and despair.   25

Second Voice, without

The ship sailed on, the ship sailed fast,
But I left not a sail, and I left not a mast;
There is not a plank of the hull or the deck,
And there is not a wretch to lament o'er his wreck;
Save one, whom I held, as he swam, by the hair,   30
And he was a subject, well worthy my care;
A traitor on land, and a pirate at sea—
But I saved him to wreak further havoc for me!

First Destiny, answering

The city lies sleeping;
  The morn, to deplore it,   35
May dawn on it weeping:
  Sullenly, slowly,
The black plague flew o'er it—
  Thousands lie lowly;
Tens of thousands shall perish;   40
  The living shall fly from
The sick they should cherish;
  But nothing can vanquish
The touch that they die from.
  Sorrow and anguish,   45
And evil and dread,
  Envelop a nation;
The blest are the dead,
  Who see not the sight
Of their own desolation;   50
  This work of a night—
This wreck of a realm—this deed of my doing—
For ages I've done, and shall still be renewing!

Enter the SECOND and THIRD DESTINIES.

The Three

Our hands contain the hearts of men,
  Our footsteps are their graves;   55
We only give to take again
  The spirits of our slaves!

First Des. Welcome!—Where's Nemesis?
Second Des.   At some great work;
But what I know not, for my hands were full.
  Third Des. Behold she cometh.   60

Enter NEMESIS.

First Des. Say, where hast thou been?
My sisters and thyself are slow tonight.
  Nem. I was detained repairing shattered thrones,
Marrying fools, restoring dynasties,
Avenging men upon their enemies,
And making them repent their own revenge;   65
Goading the wise to madness; from the dull
Shaping out oracles to rule the world
Afresh, for they were waxing out of date,
And mortals dared to ponder for themselves,
To weigh kings in the balance, and to speak   70
Of freedom, the forbidden fruit.—Away!
We have outstayed the hour—mount we our clouds.

                                  [*Exeunt.*

SCENE IV

*The Hall of Arimanes. Arimanes on his Throne, a Globe of
Fire, surrounded by the Spirits.*

Hymn of the Spirits

Hail to our Master!—Prince of earth and air!
  Who walks the clouds and waters—in his hand
The sceptre of the elements, which tear
  Themselves to chaos at his high command!
He breatheth—and a tempest shakes the sea;   5
  He speaketh—and the clouds reply in thunder;
He gazeth—from his glance the sunbeams flee;
  He moveth—earthquakes rend the world asunder.
Beneath his footsteps the volcanoes rise;
  His shadow is the pestilence; his path   10
The comets herald through the crackling skies;
  And planets turn to ashes at his wrath.
To him war offers daily sacrifice;
  To him death pays his tribute; life is his,
With all its infinite of agonies—   15
  And his the spirit of whatever is!

Enter the DESTINIES *and* NEMESIS.

First Des. Glory to Arimanes! on the earth
His power increaseth—both my sisters did
His bidding, nor did I neglect my duty!
  Second Des. Glory to Arimanes! we who bow   20
The necks of men, bow down before his throne!
  Third Des. Glory to Arimanes! we await His nod!
  Nem. Sovereign of sovereigns! we are thine,
And all that liveth, more or less, is ours,
And most things wholly so; still to increase   25
Our power, increasing thine, demands our care,
And we are vigilant. Thy late commands
Have been fulfilled to the utmost.

Enter MANFRED

  A Spirit.   What is here?
A mortal!—Thou most rash and fatal wretch,
Bow down and worship!   30
  Second Spirit.   I do know the man—

A magian of great power, and fearful skill!
  Third Spirit. Bow down and worship, slave!—
    What, know'st thou not
Thine and our sovereign?—Tremble, and obey!
  All the Spirits. Prostrate thyself, and thy condemned clay, 35
Child of the earth! or dread the worst.
  Man.   I know it;
And yet ye see I kneel not.
  Fourth Spirit.   'Twill be taught thee.
  Man. 'Tis taught already;—many a night on the earth,
On the bare ground, have I bowed down my face,
And strewed my head with ashes; I have known 40
The fullness of humiliation, for
I sunk before my vain despair, and knelt
To my own desolation.
  Fifth Spirit.   Dost thou dare
Refuse to Arimanes on his throne
What the whole earth accords, beholding not 45
The terror of his glory?—Crouch, I say.
  Man. Bid *him* bow down to that which is above him,
The overruling Infinite—the Maker
Who made him not for worship—let him kneel,
And we will kneel together. 50
  The Spirits.   Crush the worm!
Tear him in pieces!—
  First Des.   Hence! avaunt!—he's mine.
Prince of the powers invisible! This man
Is of no common order, as his port
And presence here denote; his sufferings
Have been of an immortal nature, like 55
Our own; his knowledge, and his powers and will,
As far as is compatible with clay,
Which clogs the ethereal essence, have been such
As clay hath seldom borne; his aspirations
Have been beyond the dwellers of the earth, 60
And they have only taught him what we know—
That knowledge is not happiness, and science
But an exchange of ignorance for that
Which is another kind of ignorance.
This is not all—the passions, attributes 65
Of earth and heaven, from which no power, nor being,
Nor breath from the worm upwards is exempt,
Have pierced his heart, and in their consequence
Made him a thing which I, who pity not,
Yet pardon those who pity. He is mine, 70
And thine, it may be; be it so, or not,
No other spirit in this region hath
A soul like his—or power upon his soul.
  Nem. What doth he here then?
  First Des.   Let him answer that.
  Man. Ye know what I have known; and without power 75
I could not be amongst ye: but there are
Powers deeper still beyond—I come in quest
Of such, to answer unto what I seek.
  Nem. What wouldst thou?
  Man.   Thou canst not reply to me.
Call up the dead—my question is for them. 80
  Nem. Great Arimanes, doth thy will avouch
The wishes of this mortal?
  Ari.   Yea.

Nem.   Whom wouldst thou
Uncharnel?
Man.   One without a tomb—call up
Astarte.

Nemesis

Shadow! or spirit!   85
    Whatever thou art,
Which still doth inherit
    The whole or a part
Of the form of thy birth,
    Of the mould of thy clay,   90
Which returned to the earth,—
    Reappear to the day!
Bear what thou borest,
    The heart and the form,
And the aspect thou worest   95
    Redeem from the worm.
Appear!—Appear!—Appear!
Who sent thee there requires thee here!

[*The Phantom of* ASTARTE *rises and stands
                                    in the midst.*

Man. Can this be death? there's bloom upon her cheek;
But now I see it is no living hue,   100
But a strange hectic—like the unnatural red
Which autumn plants upon the perished leaf.
It is the same! Oh, God! that I should dread
To look upon the same—Astarte!—No,
I cannot speak to her—but bid her speak—   105
Forgive me or condemn me.

Nemesis

By the power which hath broken
    The grave which enthralled thee,
Speak to him who hath spoken,
    Or those who have called thee!   110
Man.   She is silent,
And in that silence I am more than answered.
Nem. My power extends no further. Prince of Air!
It rests with thee alone—command her voice.
Ari. Spirit—obey this sceptre!
Nem.   Silent still!
She is not of our order, but belongs   115
To the other powers. Mortal! thy quest is vain,
And we are baffled also.
Man.   Hear me, hear me—
Astarte! my beloved! speak to me:
I have so much endured—so much endure—
Look on me! the grave hath not changed thee more   120
Than I am changed for thee. Thou lovedst me
Too much, as I loved thee: we were not made
To torture thus each other, though it were
The deadliest sin to love as we have loved.
Say that thou loath'st me not—that I do bear   125
This punishment for both—that thou wilt be
One of the blessed—and that I shall die;
For hitherto all hateful things conspire
To bind me in existence—in a life

Which makes me shrink from immortality— 130
A future like the past. I cannot rest.
I know not what I ask, nor what I seek:
I feel but what thou art, and what I am;
And I would hear yet once before I perish
The voice which was my music—Speak to me! 135
For I have called on thee in the still night,
Startled the slumbering birds from the hushed boughs,
And woke the mountain wolves, and made the caves
Acquainted with thy vainly echoed name,
Which answered me—many things answered me— 140
Spirits and men—but thou wert silent all.
Yet speak to me! I have outwatched the stars,
And gazed o'er heaven in vain in search of thee.
Speak to me! I have wandered o'er the earth,
And never found thy likeness—Speak to me! 145
Look on the fiends around—they feel for me:
I fear them not, and feel for thee alone—
Speak to me! though it be in wrath;—but say—
I reck not what—but let me hear thee once—
This once—once more!

    Phantom of Astarte. Manfred!
    Man.   Say on, say on— 150
I live but in the sound—it is thy voice!
    Phan. Manfred! Tomorrow ends thine earthly ills.
Farewell!
    Man.   Yet one word more—am I forgiven?
    Phan. Farewell!
    Man.   Say, shall we meet again?
    Phan. Farewell!
    Man.   One word for mercy! 155
      Say, thou lovest me.
    Phan. Manfred!
                     [*The Spirit of* ASTARTE *disappears.*
    Nem. She's gone, and will not be recalled;
Her words will be fulfilled. Return to the earth.
    A Spirit. He is convulsed.—This is to be a mortal
And seek the things beyond mortality. 160
    Another Spirit. Yet, see, he mastereth himself, and makes
His torture tributary to his will.
Had he been one of us, he would have made
An awful spirit.
    Nem.   Hast thou further question
Of our great sovereign, or his worshippers? 165
    Man. None.
    Nem.   Then for a time farewell.
    Man. We meet then! Where? On the earth?—
Even as thou wilt: and for the grace accorded
I now depart a debtor. Fare ye well!
                          [*Exit* MANFRED.

    (*Scene closes.*)

ACT III

SCENE I

A Hall in the Castle of Manfred.

MANFRED *and* HERMAN.

Man. What is the hour?
Her.   It wants but one till sunset,
And promises a lovely twilight.
Man.   Say,
Are all things so disposed of in the tower
As I directed?
Her.   All, my lord, are ready:
Here is the key and casket.
Man.   It is well: 5
Thou may'st retire.   [*Exit* HERMAN.
Man. (alone). There is a calm upon me—
Inexplicable stillness! which till now,
Did not belong to what I knew of life.
If that I did not know philosophy
To be of all our vanities the motliest,   10
The merest word that ever fooled the ear
From out the schoolman's jargon, I should deem
The golden secret, the sought "Kalon," found,
And seated in my soul. It will not last,
But it is well to have known it, though but once: 15
It hath enlarged my thoughts with a new sense,
And I within my tablets would note down
That there is such a feeling. Who is there?

Re-enter HERMAN.

Her. My lord, the abbot of St. Maurice craves
To greet your presence.   20

Enter the ABBOT OF ST. MAURICE.

Abbot.   Peace be with Count Manfred!
Man. Thanks, holy father! welcome to these walls;
Thy presence honors them, and blesseth those
Who dwell within them.
Abbot.   Would it were so, Count!—
But I would fain confer with thee alone.
Man. Herman, retire.—What would my reverend guest?   25
Abbot. Thus, without prelude:—Age and zeal, my office,
And good intent, must plead my privilege;
Our near, though not acquainted neighborhood,
May also be my herald. Rumors strange,
And of unholy nature, are abroad,   30
And busy with thy name; a noble name
For centuries: may he who bears it now
Transmit it unimpaired!
Man.   Proceed,—I listen.
Abbot. 'Tis said thou holdest converse with the things
Which are forbidden to the search of man;   35
That with the dwellers of the dark abodes,
The many evil and unheavenly spirits
Which walk the valley of the shade of death,
Thou communest. I know that with mankind,
Thy fellows in creation, thou dost rarely   40

Exchange thy thoughts, and that thy solitude
Is as an anchorite's, were it but holy.
   Man. And what are they who do avouch these things?
   Abbot. My pious brethren—the scared peasantry—
Even thy own vassals—who do look on thee   45
With most unquiet eyes. Thy life's in peril.
   Man. Take it.
   Abbot. I come to save, and not destroy:
I would not pry into thy secret soul;
But if these things be sooth, there still is time
For penitence and pity: reconcile thee   50
With the true church, and through the church to heaven.
   Man. I hear thee. This is my reply: whate'er
I may have been, or am, doth rest between
Heaven and myself. I shall not choose a mortal
To be my mediator. Have I sinned   55
Against your ordinances? prove and punish!
   Abbot. My son! I did not speak of punishment,
But penitence and pardon;—with thyself
The choice of such remains—and for the last,
Our institutions and our strong belief   60
Have given me power to smooth the path from sin
To higher hope and better thoughts; the first
I leave to heaven,—"Vengeance is mine alone!"
So saith the Lord, and with all humbleness
His servant echoes back the awful word.   65
   Man. Old man! there is no power in holy men,
Nor charm in prayer, nor purifying form
Of penitence, nor outward look, nor fast,
Nor agony—nor, greater than all these,
The innate tortures of that deep despair,   70
Which is remorse without the fear of hell,
But all in all sufficient to itself
Would make a hell of heaven—can exorcise
From out the unbounded spirit the quick sense
Of its own sins, wrongs, sufferance, and revenge   75
Upon itself; there is no future pang
Can deal that justice on the self-condemned
He deals on his own soul.
   Abbot.   All this is well;
For this will pass away, and be succeeded
By an auspicious hope, which shall look up   80
With calm assurance to that blessed place,
Which all who seek may win, whatever be
Their earthly errors, so they be atoned:
And the commencement of atonement is
The sense of its necessity. Say on—   85
And all our church can teach thee shall be taught;
And all we can absolve thee shall be pardoned.
   Man. When Rome's sixth emperor was near his last,
The victim of a self-inflicted wound,
To shun the torments of a public death   90
From senates once his slaves, a certain soldier,
With show of loyal pity, would have stanched
The gushing throat with his officious robe;
The dying Roman thrust him back, and said—
Some empire still in his expiring glance—   95
"It is too late—is this fidelity?"
   Abbot. And what of this?
   Man.   I answer with the Roman—

"It is too late!"

Abbot.   It never can be so,
To reconcile thyself with thy own soul,
And thy own soul with heaven. Hast thou no hope?   100
'Tis strange—even those who do despair above,
Yet shape themselves some fantasy on earth,
To which frail twig they cling, like drowning men.

Man. Ay—father! I have had those earthly visions,
And noble aspirations in my youth,   105
To make my own the mind of other men,
The enlightener of nations; and to rise
I knew not whither—it might be to fall;
But fall, even as the mountain-cataract,
Which, having leapt from its more dazzling height,   110
Even in the foaming strength of its abyss
(Which casts up misty columns that become
Clouds raining from the re-ascended skies),
Lies low but mighty still.—But this is past,
My thoughts mistook themselves.   115

Abbot.   And wherefore so?

Man. I could not tame my nature down; for he
Must serve who fain would sway; and soothe, and sue,
And watch all time, and pry into all place,
And be a living lie, who would become
A mighty thing amongst the mean, and such   120
The mass are; I disdained to mingle with
A herd, though to be leader—and of wolves.
The lion is alone, and so am I.

Abbot. And why not live and act with other men?

Man. Because my nature was averse from life;   125
And yet not cruel; for I would not make,
But find a desolation. Like the wind,
The red-hot breath of the most lone simoom,
Which dwells but in the desert, and sweeps o'er
The barren sands which bear no shrubs to blast,   130
And revels o'er their wild and arid waves,
And seeketh not, so that it is not sought,
But being met is deadly,—such hath been
The course of my existence; but there came
Things in my path which are no more.   135

Abbot.   Alas!
I 'gin to fear that thou art past all aid
From me and from my calling; yet so young,
I still would—

Man.   Look on me! there is an order
Of mortals on the earth, who do become
Old in their youth, and die ere middle age,   140
Without the violence of warlike death;
Some perishing of pleasure, some of study,
Some worn with toil, some of mere weariness,
Some of disease, and some insanity,
And some of withered or of broken hearts;   145
For this last is a malady which slays
More than are numbered in the lists of fate,
Taking all shapes, and bearing many names.
Look upon me! for even of all these things
Have I partaken; and of all these things,   150
One were enough; then wonder not that I
Am what I am, but that I ever was,
Or having been, that I am still on earth.

Abbot. Yet, hear me still—
Man.   Old man! I do respect
Thine order, and revere thine years; I deem   155
Thy purpose pious, but it is in vain:
Think me not churlish; I would spare thyself,
Far more than me, in shunning at this time
All further colloquy; and so—farewell.
                                        [*Exit* MANFRED.

Abbot. This should have been a noble creature: he   160
Hath all the energy which would have made
A goodly frame of glorious elements,
Had they been wisely mingled; as it is,
It is an awful chaos—light and darkness,
And mind and dust, and passions and pure thoughts   165
Mixed, and contending without end or order,—
All dormant or destructive; he will perish,
And yet he must not; I will try once more.
For such are worth redemption; and my duty
Is to dare all things for a righteous end.   170
I'll follow him—but cautiously, though surely.
                                        [*Exit* ABBOT.

SCENE II

Another Chamber.

MANFRED *and* HERMAN.

Her. My lord, you bade me wait on you at sunset:
He sinks behind the mountain.
Man.   Doth he so?
I will look on him.
            [MANFRED *advances to the Window of the Hall.*
                    Glorious orb! the idol
Of early nature, and the vigorous race
Of undiseased mankind, the giant sons   5
Of the embrace of angels, with a sex
More beautiful than they, which did draw down
The erring spirits who can ne'er return.—
Most glorious orb! that wert a worship, ere
The mystery of thy making was revealed!   10
Thou earliest minister of the Almighty,
Which gladdened, on their mountain tops, the hearts
Of the Chaldean shepherds, till they poured
Themselves in orisons! Thou material God!
And representative of the unknown—   15
Who chose thee for his shadow! Thou chief star!
Center of many stars! which mak'st our earth
Endurable, and temperest the hues
And hearts of all who walk within thy rays!
Sire of the seasons! Monarch of the climes,   20
And those who dwell in them! for near or far,
Our inborn spirits have a tint of thee
Even as our outward aspects;—thou dost rise,
And shine, and set in glory. Fare thee well!
I ne'er shall see thee more. As my first glance   25
Of love and wonder was for thee, then take
My latest look; thou wilt not beam on one
To whom the gifts of life and warmth have been
Of a more fatal nature. He is gone:
I follow.   [*Exit* MANFRED.   30

SCENE III

The Mountains—The Castle of Manfred at some distance—A Terrace before a Tower.—Time, Twilight.

HERMAN, MANUEL, *and other Dependants of* MANFRED.

Her. 'Tis strange enough; night after night, for years,
He hath pursued long vigils in this tower,
Without a witness. I have been within it,—
So have we all been ofttimes; but from it,
Or its contents, it were impossible
To draw conclusions absolute, of aught   5
His studies tend to. To be sure, there is
One chamber where none enter: I would give
The fee of what I have to come these three years,
To pore upon its mysteries.
    Manuel.   'Twere dangerous: 10
Content thyself with what thou know'st already.
    Her. Ah! Manuel! thou art elderly and wise,
And couldst say much; thou hast dwelt within the castle—
How many years is 't?
    Manuel.   Ere Count Manfred's birth,
I served his father, whom he nought resembles.   15
    Her. There be more sons in like predicament.
But wherein do they differ?
    Manuel.   I speak not
Of features or of form, but mind and habits;
Count Sigismund was proud, but gay and free,—
A warrior and a reveller; he dwelt not   20
With books and solitude, nor made the night
A gloomy vigil, but a festal time,
Merrier than day; he did not walk the rocks
And forests like a wolf, nor turn aside
From men and their delights.
    Her.   Beshrew the hour,   25
But those were jocund times! I would that such
Would visit the old walls again; they look
As if they had forgotten them.
    Manuel.   These walls
Must change their chieftain first. Oh! I have seen
Some strange things in them, Herman.
    Her.   Come, be friendly,   30
Relate me some to while away our watch:
I've heard thee darkly speak of an event
Which happened hereabouts, by this same tower.
    Manuel.   That was a night indeed! I do remember
'Twas twilight, as it may be now, and such
Another evening;—yon red cloud, which rests   35
On Eigher's pinnacle, so rested then,—
So like that it might be the same; the wind
Was faint and gusty, and the mountain snows
Began to glitter with the climbing moon;
Count Manfred was, as now, within his tower,—   40
How occupied, we knew not, but with him
The sole companion of his wanderings
And watchings—her, whom of all earthly things
That lived, the only thing he seemed to love,
As he, indeed, by blood was bound to do,   45
The lady Astarte, his—
            Hush! who comes here?

Enter the ABBOT.

Abbot. Where is your master?
Her.   Yonder in the **tower.**
Abbot. I must speak with him.
Manuel.   'T is impossible;
He is most private, and must not be thus   50
Intruded on.
Abbot.   Upon myself I take
The forfeit of my fault, if fault there be—
But I must see him.
Her.   Thou hast seen him once
This eve already.
Abbot.   Herman! I command thee,
Knock, and apprize the Count of my approach.   55
Her. We dare not.
Abbot.   Then it seems I must be herald
Of my own purpose.
Manuel.   Reverend father stop—
I pray you pause.
Abbot.   Why so?
Manuel.   But step this way,
And I will tell you further.   [*Exeunt.*

SCENE IV

Interior of the Tower

MANFRED *alone*

The stars are forth, the moon above the tops
Of the snow-shining mountains.—Beautiful!
I linger yet with nature, for the night
Hath been to me a more familiar face
Than that of man; and in her starry shade   5
Of dim and solitary loveliness,
I learned the language of another world.
I do remember me, that in my youth,
When I was wandering,—upon such a night
I stood within the Coliseum's wall,   10
'Midst the chief relics of almighty Rome;
The trees which grew along the broken arches
Waved dark in the blue midnight, and the stars
Shone through the rents of ruin; from afar
The watch-dog bayed beyond the Tiber; and   15
More near from out the Cæsar's palace came
The owl's long cry, and, interruptedly,
Of distant sentinels the fitful song
Begun and died upon the gentle wind.
Some cypresses beyond the time-worn breach   20
Appeared to skirt the horizon, yet they stood
Within a bowshot. Where the Cæsars dwelt,
And dwell the tuneless birds of night, amidst
A grove which springs through levelled battlements,
And twines its roots with the imperial hearths,   25
Ivy usurps the laurel's place of growth;
But the gladiator's bloody Circus stands,
A noble wreck in ruinous perfection,
While Cæsar's chambers, and the Augustan halls,
Grovel on earth in indistinct decay.   30
And thou didst shine, thou rolling moon, upon
All this, and cast a wide and tender light,

Which softened down the hoar austerity
Of rugged desolation, and filled up,
As 't were anew, the gaps of centuries;   35
Leaving that beautiful which still was so,
And making that which was not, till the place
Became religion, and the heart ran o'er
With silent worship of the great of old,—
The dead but sceptred sovereigns, who still rule   40
Our spirits from their urns.
              'Twas such a night!
'Tis strange that I recall it at this time;
But I have found our thoughts take wildest flight
Even at the moment when they should array
Themselves in pensive order.   45

Enter the ABBOT

   Abbot.   My good lord!
I crave a second grace for this approach;
But yet let not my humble zeal offend
By its abruptness—all it hath of ill
Recoils on me; its good in the effect
May light upon your head—could I say *heart*—   50
Could I touch *that,* with words or prayers, I should
Recall a noble spirit which hath wandered;
But is not yet all lost.
   Man.   Thou know'st me not;
My days are numbered, and my deeds recorded;
Retire, or 't will be dangerous—Away!   55
   Abbot.   Thou dost not mean to menace me?
   Man.   Not I;
I simply tell thee peril is at hand,
And would preserve thee.
   Abbot.   What dost thou mean?
   Man.   Look there!
What dost thou see?
   Abbot.   Nothing.
   Man.   Look there, I say,
And steadfastly;—now tell me what thou seest.   60
   Abbot.   That which should shake me, but I fear it not:
I see a dusk and awful figure rise,
Like an infernal god, from out the earth;
His face wrapt in a mantle, and his form
Robed as with angry clouds: he stands between   65
Thyself and me—but I do fear him not.
   Man.   Thou hast no cause; he shall not harm thee, but
His sight may shock thine old limbs into palsy.
I say to thee—Retire!
   Abbot.   And I reply—
Never—till I have battled with this fiend:—   70
What doth he here?
   Man.   Why—ay—what doth he here?
I did not send for him,—he is unbidden.
   Abbot.   Alas! lost mortal! what with guests like these
Hast thou to do? I tremble for thy sake:
Why doth he gaze on thee, and thou on him?   75
Ah! he unveils his aspect: on his brow
The thunder-scars are graven: from his eye
Glares forth the immortality of hell—
Avaunt!—
   Man.   Pronounce—what is thy mission?

Spirit.   Come!
Abbot. What art thou, unknown being? answer!—speak!   80
Spirit. The genius of this mortal.—Come! 'tis time.
Man. I am prepared for all things, but deny
The power which summons me. Who sent thee here?
Spirit. Thou 'lt know anon—Come! come!
Man.   I have commanded
Things of an essence greater far than thine,   85
And striven with thy masters. Get thee hence!
Spirit. Mortal! thine hour is come—Away! I say.
Man. I knew, and know my hour is come, but not
To render up my soul to such as thee:
Away! I'll die as I have lived—alone.   90
Spirit. Then I must summon up my brethren.—Rise!

                      [Other Spirits rise up.
Abbot. Avaunt! ye evil ones!—Avaunt! I say;
Ye have no power where piety hath power,
And I do charge ye in the name—
Spirit.   Old man!
We know ourselves, our mission, and thine order;   95
Waste not thy holy words on idle uses,
It were in vain: this man is forfeited.
Once more I summon him—Away! Away!
Man. I do defy ye,—though I feel my soul
Is ebbing from me, yet I do defy ye;   100
Nor will I hence, while I have earthly breath
To breathe my scorn upon ye—earthly strength
To wrestle, though with spirits; what ye take
Shall be ta'en limb by limb.
Spirit.   Reluctant mortal!
Is this the Magian who would so pervade   105
The world invisible, and make himself
Almost our equal? Can it be that thou
Art thus in love with life? the very life
Which made thee wretched!
Man.   Thou false fiend, thou liest!
My life is in its last hour,—*that* I know,   110
Nor would redeem a moment of that hour;
I do not combat against death, but thee
And thy surrounding angels; my past power,
Was purchased by no compact with thy crew,
But by superior science—penance, daring,   115
And length of watching, strength of mind, and skill
In knowledge of our fathers—when the earth
Saw men and spirits walking side by side,
And gave ye no supremacy: I stand
Upon my strength—I do defy—deny—   120
Spurn back, and scorn ye!—
Spirit.   But thy many crimes
Have made thee—
Man.   What are they to such as thee?
Must crimes be punished but by other crimes,
And greater criminals?—Back to thy hell!
Thou hast no power upon me, *that* I feel;   125
Thou never shalt possess me, *that* I know:
What I have done is done; I bear within
A torture which could nothing gain from thine:
The mind which is immortal makes itself
Requital for its good or evil thoughts,—   130
Is its own origin of ill and end

And its own place and time; its innate sense,
When stripped of this mortality, derives
No color from the fleeting things without,
But is absorbed in sufferance or in joy,   135
Born from the knowledge of its own desert.
Thou didst not tempt me, and thou couldst not tempt me;
I have not been thy dupe, nor am thy prey—
But was my own destroyer, and will be
My own hereafter.—Back, ye baffled fiends!—   140
The hand of death is on me—but not yours.
                              [*The Demons disappear.*
    Abbot. Alas! how pale thou art—thy lips are white—
And thy breast heaves—and in thy gasping throat
The accents rattle: Give thy prayers to heaven—
Pray—albeit but in thought,—but die not thus.   145
    Man. 'Tis over—my dull eyes can fix thee not;
But all things swim around me, and the earth
Heaves as it were beneath me. Fare thee well!
Give me thy hand.
    Abbot.   Cold—cold—even to the heart—
But yet one prayer—Alas! how fares it with thee?   150
    Man. Old man! 'tis not so difficult to die.
                              [MANFRED *expires.*
    Abbot. He's gone—his soul hath ta'en its earthless flight;
Whither? I dread to think—but he is gone.
1816-17   1817

FROM BEPPO

ITALY AND ENGLAND

XLI

With all its sinful doings, I must say,
    That Italy's a pleasant place to me,
Who love to see the sun shine every day,
    And vines (not nailed to walls) from tree to tree
Festooned, much like the back scene of a play,   325
    Or melodrame, which people flock to see,
When the first act is ended by a dance
In vineyards copied from the south of France.

XLII

I like on autumn evenings to ride out,
    Without being forced to bid my groom be sure   330
My cloak is round his middle strapped about,
    Because the skies are not the most secure;
I know too that, if stopped upon my route,
    Where the green alleys windingly allure,
Reeling with *grapes* red wagons choke the way,—   335
In England 'twould be dung, dust, or a dray.

XLIII

I also like to dine on becaficas,
    To see the sun set, sure he'll rise tomorrow,
Not through a misty morning twinkling weak as
    A drunken man's dead eye in maudlin sorrow,   340
But with all Heaven t'himself; the day will break as
    Beauteous as cloudless, nor be forced to borrow
That sort of farthing candlelight which glimmers
Where reeking London's smoky cauldron simmers.

XLIV

I love the language, that soft bastard Latin,   345
  Which melts like kisses from a female mouth,
And sounds as if it should be writ on satin,
  With syllables which breathe of the sweet South,
And gentle liquids gliding all so pat in,
  That not a single accent seems uncouth,   350
Like our harsh northern whistling, grunting guttural,
Which we're obliged to hiss, and spit, and sputter all.

XLV

I like the women too (forgive my folly!)
  From the rich peasant cheek of ruddy bronze,
And large black eyes that flash on you a volley   355
  Of rays that say a thousand things at once,
To the high dama's brow, more melancholy,
  But clear, and with a wild and liquid glance,
Heart on her lips, and soul within her eyes,
Soft as her clime, and sunny as her skies.   360

XLVI

Eve of the land which still is Paradise!
  Italian Beauty! Did'st thou not inspire
Raphael, who died in thy embrace, and vies
  With all we know of Heaven, or can desire,
In what he hath bequeathed us?—in what guise,   365
  Though flashing from the fervor of the lyre,
Would *words* describe thy past and present glow,
While yet Canova can create below?

XLVII

"England! with all thy faults I love thee still,"
  I said at Calais, and have not forgot it;   370
I like to speak and lucubrate my fill;
  I like the government (but that is not it);
I like the freedom of the press and quill;
  I like the Habeas Corpus (when we've got it);
I like a parliamentary debate,   375
Particularly when 'tis not too late;

XLVIII

I like the taxes, when they're not too many;
  I like a sea-coal fire, when not too dear;
I like a beef-steak, too, as well as any;
  Have no objection to a pot of beer;   380
I like the weather, when it is not rainy,
  That is, I like two months of every year,
And so God save the Regent, Church, and King!
Which means that I like all and everything.

XLIX

Our standing army, and disbanded seamen,   385
  Poor's rate, Reform, my own, the nation's debt,
Our little riots just to show we're free men,
  Our trifling bankruptcies in the Gazette,
Our cloudy climate, and our chilly women,
  All these I can forgive, and those forget,   390
And greatly venerate our recent glories,
And wish they were not owing to the Tories.

1818

MAZEPPA

I

'Twas after dread Pultowa's day,
  When fortune left the royal Swede,
Around a slaughtered army lay,
  No more to combat and to bleed.
The power and glory of the war,   5
  Faithless as their vain votaries, men,
Had passed to the triumphant Czar,
  And Moscow's walls were safe again,
Until a day more dark and drear,
And a more memorable year,   10
Should give to slaughter and to shame
A mightier host and haughtier name;
A greater wreck, a deeper fall,
A shock to one—a thunderbolt to all.

II

Such was the hazard of the die;   15
The wounded Charles was taught to fly
By day and night through field and flood,
Stained with his own and subjects' blood;
For thousands fell that flight to aid:
And not a voice was heard t' upbraid   20
Ambition in his humbled hour,
When truth had nought to dread from
    power.
His horse was slain, and Gieta gave
His own—and died the Russians' slave.
This too sinks after many a league   25
Of well sustained but vain fatigue;
And in the depth of forests darkling,
The watch-fires in the distance sparkling—
  The beacons of surrounding foes—
A king must lay his limbs at length.   30
  Are these the laurels and repose
For which the nations strain their strength?
They laid him by a savage tree,
In outworn nature's agony;
His wounds were stiff, his limbs were
    stark;   35
The heavy hour was chill and dark;
The fever in his blood forbade
A transient slumber's fitful aid:
And thus it was; but yet through all,
Kinglike the monarch bore his fall,   40
And made, in this extreme of ill,
His pangs the vassals of his will:
All silent and subdued were they,
As once the nations round him lay.

III

A band of chiefs!—alas! how few,   45
  Since but the fleeting of a day
Had thinned it; but this wreck was true
  And chivalrous: upon the clay
Each sate him down, all sad and mute,
  Beside his monarch and his steed;   50

For danger levels man and brute,
  And all are fellows in their need.
Among the rest, Mazeppa made
His pillow in an old oak's shade—
Himself as rough, and scarce less old,   55
The Ukraine's Hetman, calm and bold;
But first, outspent with this long course,
The Cossack prince rubbed down his horse,
And made for him a leafy bed,
  And smoothed his fetlocks and his
    mane,   60
  And slacked his girth, and stripped his
    rein,
And joyed to see how well he fed;
For until now he had the dread
His wearied courser might refuse
To browse beneath the midnight dews: 65
But he was hardy as his lord,
And little cared for bed and board;
But spirited and docile, too,
Whate'er was to be done, would do.
Shaggy and swift, and strong of limb,   70
All Tartar-like he carried him;
Obeyed his voice, and came to call,
And knew him in the midst of all:
Though thousands were around,—and
    night,
Without a star, pursued her flight,—   75
That steed from sunset until dawn
His chief would follow like a fawn.

IV

This done, Mazeppa spread his cloak
And laid his lance beneath his oak,
Felt if his arms in order good   80
The long day's march had well withstood—
If still the powder filled the pan,
  And flints unloosened kept their lock—
His sabre's hilt and scabbard felt,
And whether they had chafed his belt;   85
And next the venerable man,
From out his haversack and can
  Prepared and spread his slender stock;
And to the monarch and his men
The whole or portion offered then   90
With far less of inquietude
Than courtiers at a banquet would.
And Charles of this his slender share
With smiles partook a moment there,
To force of cheer a greater show,   95
And seem above both wounds and woe;
And then he said—"Of all our band,
Though firm of heart and strong of hand,
In skirmish, march, or forage, none
Can less have said or more have done   100
Than thee, Mazeppa! on the earth
So fit a pair had never birth,
Since Alexander's days till now,
As thy Bucephalus and thou:
All Scythia's fame to thine should yield 105

For pricking on o'er flood and field."
Mazeppa answered—"Ill betide
The school wherein I learned to ride!"
Quoth Charles—"Old Hetman, wherefore so,
Since thou hast learned the art so well?" 110
Mazeppa said—" 'T were long to tell;
And we have many a league to go,
With every now and then a blow,
And ten to one at least the foe,
Before our steeds may graze at ease 115
Beyond the swift Borysthenes:
And, Sire, your limbs have need of rest,
   And I will be the sentinel
Of this your troop."—"But I request,"
   Said Sweden's monarch, "thou wilt
      tell 120
This tale of thine, and I may reap,
Perchance, from this the boon of sleep;
For at this moment from my eyes
The hope of present slumber flies."

"Well, Sire, with such a hope, I'll track 125
My seventy years of memory back:
I think 't was in my twentieth spring,—
Ay, 't was,—when Casimir was king—
John Casimir,—I was his page
Six summers, in my earlier age: 130
A learned monarch, faith! was he,
And most unlike your majesty;
He made no wars, and did not gain
New realms to lose them back again;
And (save debates in Warsaw's diet) 135
He reigned in most unseemly quiet;
Not that he had no cares to vex;
He loved the muses and the sex;
And sometimes these so froward are,
They made him wish himself at war; 140
But soon his wrath being o'er, he took
Another mistress—or new book:
And then he gave prodigious fêtes—
All Warsaw gathered round his gates
To gaze upon his splendid court, 145
And dames, and chiefs, of princely port:
He was the Polish Solomon,
So sung his poets, all but one,
Who, being unpensioned, made a satire,
And boasted that he could not flatter. 150
It was a court of jousts and mimes,
Where every courtier tried at rhymes;
Even I for once produced some verses,
And signed my odes 'Despairing Thyrsis.'
There was a certain Palatine, 155
   A count of far and high descent,
Rich as a salt or silver mine;
And he was proud, ye may divine,
   As if from heaven he had been sent:
He had such wealth in blood and ore 160
   As few could match beneath the throne;
And he would gaze upon his store,

And o'er his pedigree would pore,
Until by some confusion led,
Which almost looked like want of head, 165
   He thought their merits were his own.
His wife was not of his opinion;
   His junior she by thirty years,
Grew daily tired of his dominion;
   And, after wishes, hopes, and fears, 170
   To virtue a few farewell tears,
A restless dream or two, some glances
At Warsaw's youth, some songs, and dances,
Awaited but the usual chances,
Those happy accidents which render 175
The coldest dames so very tender,
To deck her Count with titles given,
'T is said, as passports into heaven;
But, strange to say, they rarely boast
Of these, who have deserved them most. 180

V

"I was a goodly stripling then;
   At seventy years I so may say,
That there were few, or boys or men,
   Who, in my dawning time of day,
Of vassal or of knight's degree, 185
Could vie in vanities with me;
For I had strength, youth, gaiety,
A port, not like to this ye see,
But smooth, as all is rugged now;
For time, and care, and war, have
      ploughed 190
My very soul from out my brow;
   And thus I should be disavowed
By all my kind and kin, could they
Compare my day and yesterday;
This change was wrought, too, long ere
      age 195
Had ta'en my features for his page;
With years, ye know, have not declined
My strength, my courage, or my mind,
Or at this hour I should not be
Telling old tales beneath a tree, 200
With starless skies my canopy
   But let me on: Theresa's form—
Methinks it glides before me now,
Between me and yon chestnut's bough,
   The memory is so quick and warm; 205
And yet I find no words to tell
The shape of her I loved so well:
She had the Asiatic eye,
   Such as our Turkish neighborhood
Hath mingled with our Polish blood, 210
Dark as above us is the sky;
But through it stole a tender light,
Like the first moonrise of midnight;
Large, dark, and swimming in the stream,
Which seemed to melt to its own beam; 215
All love, half languor, and half fire,
Like saints that at the stake expire,
And lift their raptured looks on high,

As though it were a joy to die.
A brow like a midsummer lake,　　　220
Transparent with the sun therein,
When waves no murmur dare to make,
　And heaven beholds her face within.
A cheek and lip—but why proceed?
　I loved her then, I love her still;　　225
And such as I am, love indeed
　In fierce extremes—in good and ill.
But still we love even in our rage,
And haunted to our very age
With the vain shadow of the past,　　230
As is Mazeppa to the last.

VI

"We met—we gazed—I saw, and sighed;
She did not speak, and yet replied;
There are ten thousand tones and signs
We hear and see, but none defines—　　235
Involuntary sparks of thought,
Which strike from out the heart o'er-
　　wrought,
And form a strange intelligence,
Alike mysterious and intense,
Which link the burning chain that
　　binds,　　　240
Without their will, young hearts and
　　minds;
Conveying, as the electric wire,
We know not how, the absorbing fire.
I saw, and sighed—in silence wept,
And still reluctant distance kept,　　245
Until I was made known to her,
And we might then and there confer
Without suspicion—then, even then,
　I longed, and was resolved to speak;
But on my lips they died again,　　250
　The accents tremulous and weak,
Until one hour.—There is a game,
　A frivolous and foolish play,
　Wherewith we while away the day;
It is—I have forgot the name—　　255
And we to this, it seems, were set,
By some strange chance, which I forget:
I recked not if I won or lost,
　It was enough for me to be
　So near to hear, and oh! to see　　260
The being whom I loved the most.
I watched her as a sentinel,
(May ours this dark night watch as well!)
　Until I saw, and thus it was,
That she was pensive, nor perceived　　265
Her occupation, nor was grieved
Nor glad to lose or gain; but still
Played on for hours, as if her will
Yet bound her to the place, though not
That hers might be the winning lot.　　270
　Then through my brain the thought did
　　pass
Even as a flash of lightning there,

That there was something in her air
Which would not doom me to despair;
And on the thought my words broke
　　forth,　　　275
　All incoherent as they were;
Their eloquence was little worth,
But yet she listened—'t is enough—
　Who listens once will listen twice;
　Her heart, be sure, is not of ice,　　280
And one refusal no rebuff.

VII

"I loved, and was beloved again—
　They tell me, Sire, you never knew
　Those gentle frailties; if 't is true,
I shorten all my joy or pain;　　285
To you 't would seem absurd as vain;
But all men are not born to reign,
Or o'er their passions, or as you
Thus o'er themselves and nations too.
I am—or rather *was*—a prince,　　290
　A chief of thousands, and could lead
　Them on where each would foremost
　　bleed;
But could not o'er myself evince
The like control—But to resume:
　I loved, and was beloved again;　　295
In sooth, it is a happy doom,
　But yet where happiest ends in pain.
We met in secret, and the hour
Which led me to that lady's bower
Was fiery Expectation's dower.　　300
My days and nights were nothing—all
Except that hour, which doth recall,
In the long lapse from youth to age,
　No other like itself: I'd give
　The Ukraine back again to live　　305
It o'er once more, and be a page,
The happy page, who was the lord
Of one soft heart, and his own sword,
And had no other gem nor wealth
Save nature's gift of youth and health.　310
We met in secret—doubly sweet,
Some say, they find it so to meet;
I know not that—I would have given
　My life but to have called her mine
In the full view of earth and heaven;　315
　For I did oft and long repine
That we could only meet by stealth.

VIII

"For lovers there are many eyes,
　And such there were on us; the devil
　On such occasions should be civil—　320
The devil!—I'm loth to do him wrong,
　It might be some untoward saint,
Who would not be at rest too long,
　But to his pious bile gave vent—
But one fair night, some lurking spies　325
Surprised and seized us both.

The Count was something more than
    wroth—
I was unarmed; but if in steel,
All cap-à-pie from head to heel,
What 'gainst their numbers could I do? 330
'T was near his castle, far away
    From city or from succor near,
And almost on the break of day;
I did not think to see another,
    My moments seemed reduced to few; 335
And with one prayer to Mary Mother,
    And, it may be, a saint or two,
As I resigned me to my fate,
They led me to the castle gate:
    Theresa's doom I never knew,   340
Our lot was henceforth separate.
An angry man, ye may opine,
Was he, the proud Count Palatine;
And he had reason good to be,
    But he was most enraged lest such   345
    An accident should chance to touch
Upon his future pedigree;
Nor less amazed, that such a blot
His noble 'scutcheon should have got,
While he was highest of his line;   350
    Because unto himself he seemed
    The first of men, nor less he deemed
In others' eyes, and most in mine.
'Sdeath! with a *page*—perchance a king
Had reconciled him to the thing;   355
But with a stripling of a page—
I felt, but cannot paint his rage.

IX

" 'Bring forth the horse!'—the horse was
    brought;
    In truth, he was a noble steed,
    A Tartar of the Ukraine breed,   360
Who looked as though the speed of
    thought
Were in his limbs; but he was wild,
    Wild as the wild deer, and untaught,
With spur and bridle undefiled—
    'T was but a day he had been caught; 365
And snorting, with erected mane,
And struggling fiercely, but in vain,
In the full foam of wrath and dread
To me the desert-born was led:
They bound me on, that menial throng; 370
Upon his back with many a thong;
Then loosed him with a sudden lash—
Away!—away!—and on we dash!
Torrents less rapid and less rash.

X

"Away!—away! My breath was gone,   375
I saw not where he hurried on:
'T was scarcely yet the break of day,
And on he foamed—away!—away!
The last of human sounds which rose,

As I was darted from my foes,   380
Was the wild shout of savage laughter,
Which on the wind came roaring after
A moment from that rabble rout:
With sudden wrath I wrenched my head,
    And snapped the cord, which to the
    mane   385
Had bound my neck in lieu of rein,
And, writhing half my form about,
Howled back my curse; but 'midst the
    tread,
The thunder of my courser's speed,
Perchance they did not hear nor heed: 390
It vexes me—for I would fain
Have paid their insult back again.
I paid it well in after days:
There is not of that castle gate,
Its drawbridge and portcullis' weight, 395
Stone, bar, moat, bridge, or barrier left;
Nor of its fields a blade of grass,
    Save what grows on a ridge of wall,
    Where stood the hearth-stone of the hall;
And many a time ye there might pass, 400
Nor dream that e'er that fortress was.
I saw its turrets in a blaze,
Their crackling battlements all cleft,
    And the hot lead pour down like rain
From off the scorched and blackening
    roof,   405
Whose thickness was not vengeance-proof.
They little thought that day of pain,
When launched, as on the lightning's flash,
They bade me to destruction dash,
    That one day I should come again,   410
With twice five thousand horse, to thank
    The Count for his uncourteous ride.
They played me then a bitter prank,
    When, with the wild horse for my guide,
They bound me to his foaming flank: 415
At length I played them one as frank—
For time at last sets all things even—
    And if we do but watch the hour,
    There never yet was human power
Which could evade, if unforgiven,   420
The patient search and vigil long
Of him who treasures up a wrong.

XI

"Away, away, my steed and I,
    Upon the pinions of the wind,
    All human dwellings left behind;   425
We sped like meteors through the sky,
When with its crackling sound the night
Is chequered with the northern light.
Town—village—none were on our track,
    But a wild plain of far extent,   430
And bounded by a forest black;
    And, save the scarce seen battlement
On distant heights of some strong hold,
Against the Tartars built of old,

No trace of man. The year before   435
A Turkish army had marched o'er;
And where the Spahi's hoof hath trod,
The verdure flies the bloody sod:
The sky was dull, and dim, and gray,
  And a low breeze crept moaning by— 440
  I could have answered with a sigh—
But fast we fled, away, away—
And I could neither sigh nor pray;
And my cold sweat-drops fell like rain
Upon the courser's bristling mane;   445
But, snorting still with rage and fear,
He flew upon his far career:
At times I almost thought, indeed,
He must have slackened in his speed;
But no—my bound and slender frame 450
  Was nothing to his angry might,
And merely like a spur became:
Each motion which I made to free
My swoln limbs from their agony
  Increased his fury and affright: 455
I tried my voice,—'t was faint and low—
But yet he swerved as from a blow;
And, starting to each accent, sprang
As from a sudden trumpet's clang:
Meantime my cords were wet with gore, 460
Which, oozing through my limbs, ran o'er;
And in my tongue the thirst became
A something fierier far than flame.

XII

"We neared the wild wood—'t was so wide,
I saw no bounds on either side   465
'T was studded with old sturdy trees,
That bent not to the roughest breeze
Which howls down from Siberia's waste,
And strips the forest in its haste,—
But these were few and far between, 470
Set thick with shrubs more young and
    green,
Luxuriant with their annual leaves,
Ere strown by those autumnal eves
That nip the forest's foliage dead,
Discolored with a lifeless red,   475
Which stands thereon like stiffened gore
Upon the slain when battle's o'er,
And some long winter's night hath shed
Its frost o'er every tombless head,
So cold and stark the raven's beak 480
May peck unpierced each frozen cheek:
'T was a wild waste of underwood,
And here and there a chestnut stood,
The strong oak, and the hardy pine;
  But far apart—and well it were,   485
Or else a different lot were mine—
  The boughs gave way, and did not tear
My limbs; and I found strength to bear
My wounds, already scarred with cold;
My bonds forbade to loose my hold. 490
We rustled through the leaves like wind,

Left shrubs, and trees, and wolves behind;
By night I heard them on the track,
Their troop came hard upon our back,
With their long gallop, which can tire 495
The hound's deep hate, and hunter's fire:
Where'er we flew they followed on,
Nor left us with the morning sun;
Behind I saw them, scarce a rood,
At day-break winding through the wood, 500
And through the night had heard their feet
Their stealing, rustling step repeat.
Oh! how I wished for spear or sword,
  At least to die amidst the horde,
And perish—if it must be so—   505
At bay, destroying many a foe!
  When first my courser's race begun,
I wished the goal already won
But now I doubted strength and speed:
Vain doubt! his swift and savage breed 510
Had nerved him like the mountain-roe;
Nor faster falls the blinding snow
Which whelms the peasant near the door
Whose threshold he shall cross no more,
Bewildered with the dazzling blast, 515
Than through the forest-paths he passed—
Untired, untamed, and worse than wild;
All furious as a favored child
Balked of its wish; or fiercer still—
A woman piqued—who has her will! 520

XIII

"The wood was past; 't was more than
    noon,
But chill the air, although in June!
Or it might be my veins ran cold—
Prolonged endurance tames the bold;
And I was then not what I seem,   525
But headlong as a wintry stream,
And wore my feelings out before
I well could count their causes o'er:
And what with fury, fear, and wrath,
The tortures which beset my path,   530
Cold, hunger, sorrow, shame, distress,
Thus bound in nature's nakedness
(Sprung from a race whose rising blood,
When stirred beyond its calmer mood,
And trodden hard upon, is like   535
The rattle-snake's, in act to strike),
What marvel if this worn-out trunk
Beneath its woes a moment sunk?
The earth gave way, the skies rolled round,
I seemed to sink upon the ground;   540
But erred, for I was fastly bound.
My heart turned sick, my brain grew sore,
And throbbed awhile, then beat no more:
The skies spun like a mighty wheel;
I saw the trees like drunkards reel,   545
And a slight flash sprang o'er my eyes,
Which saw no farther: he who dies
Can die no more than then I died,

O'ertortured by that ghastly ride.
I felt the blackness come and go, 550
  And strove to wake; but could not make
My senses climb up from below:
I felt as on a plank at sea,
When all the waves that dash o'er thee,
At the same time upheave and whelm, 555
And hurl thee towards a desert realm.
My undulating life was as
The fancied lights that flitting pass
Our shut eyes in deep midnight, when
Fever begins upon the brain; 560
But soon it passed, with little pain,
  But a confusion worse than such:
I own that I should deem it much,
Dying, to feel the same again;
And yet I do suppose we must 565
Feel far more ere we turn to dust:
No matter; I have bared my brow
Full in death's face—before—and now.

XIV

"My thoughts came back; where was I?
  Cold,
  And numb, and giddy: pulse by pulse 570
Life reassumed its lingering hold,
And throb by throb,—till grown a pang
  Which for a moment would convulse,
  My blood reflowed, though thick and
    chill;
My ear with uncouth noises rang, 575
  My heart began once more to thrill;
My sight returned, though dim; alas!
And thickened, as it were, with glass.
Methought the dash of waves was nigh;
There was a gleam too of the sky, 580
Studded with stars;—it is no dream;
The wild horse swims the wilder stream!
The bright broad river's gushing tide
Sweeps, winding onward, far and wide,
And we are half-way, struggling o'er 585
To yon unknown and silent shore.
The waters broke my hollow trance,
And with a temporary strength
  My stiffened limbs were rebaptized.
My courser's broad breast proudly
    braves, 590
And dashes off the ascending waves,
And onward we advance!
We reach the slippery shore at length,
  A haven I but little prized,
For all behind was dark and drear, 595
And all before was night and fear.
How many hours of night or day
In those suspended pangs I lay,
I could not tell; I scarcely knew
If this were human breath I drew. 600

XV

"With glossy skin, and dripping mane,
  And reeling limbs, and reeking flank,

The wild steed's sinewy nerves still strain
  Up the repelling bank.
We gain the top: a boundless plain 605
Spreads through the shadow of the night,
  And onward, onward, onward, seems,
  Like precipices in our dreams,
To stretch beyond the sight;
And here and there a speck of white, 610
  Or scattered spot of dusky green,
In masses broke into the light,
As rose the moon upon my right:
  But nought distinctly seen
In the dim waste would indicate 615
The omen of a cottage gate;
No twinkling taper from afar
Stood like a hospitable star;
Not even an ignis-fatuus rose
To make him merry with my woes: 620
  That very cheat had cheered me then!
Although detected, welcome still,
Reminding me, through every ill,
  Of the abodes of men.

XVI

"Onward we went—but slack and slow; 625
  His savage force at length o'erspent,
The drooping courser, faint and low,
  All feebly foaming went:
A sickly infant had had power
To guide him forward in that hour; 630
  But, useless all to me,
His new-born tameness nought availed—
My limbs were bound; my force had failed,
  Perchance, had they been free.
With feeble effort still I tried 635
To rend the bonds so starkly tied,
  But still it was in vain;
My limbs were only wrung the more,
And soon the idle strife gave o'er,
  Which but prolonged their pain. 640
The dizzy race seemed almost done,
Although no goal was nearly won:
Some streaks announced the coming sun—
  How slow, alas! he came!
Methought that mist of dawning gray 645
Would never dapple into day;
How heavily it rolled away—
  Before the eastern flame
Rose crimson, and deposed the stars,
And called the radiance from their cars, 650
And filled the earth, from his deep throne,
With lonely lustre, all his own.

XVII

"Up rose the sun; the mists were curled
Back from the solitary world
Which lay around, behind, before. 655
What booted it to traverse o'er
Plain, forest, river? Man nor brute,
Nor dint of hoof, nor print of foot,

Lay in the wild luxuriant soil;
No sign of travel, none of toil; 660
The very air was mute;
And not an insect's shrill small horn,
Nor matin bird's new voice was borne
From herb nor thicket. Many a werst,
Panting as if his heart would burst, 665
The weary brute still staggered on;
And still we were—or seemed—alone.
At length, while reeling on our way,
Methought I heard a courser neigh,
From out yon tuft of blackening firs. 670
Is it the wind those branches stirs?
No, no! from out the forest prance
  A trampling troop; I see them come!
In one vast squadron they advance!
  I strove to cry—my lips were dumb! 675
The steeds rush on in plunging pride;
But where are they the reins to guide?
A thousand horse—and none to ride!
With flowing tail, and flying mane,
Wide nostrils never stretched by pain, 680
Mouths bloodless to the bit or rein,
And feet that iron never shod,
And flanks unscarred by spur or rod,
A thousand horse, the wild, the free,
Like waves that follow o'er the sea, 685
  Came thickly thundering on,
As if our faint approach to meet.
The sight re-nerved my courser's feet,
A moment staggering, feebly fleet,
A moment, with a faint low neigh, 690
  He answered, and then fell;
With gasps and blazing eyes he lay,
  And reeking limbs immovable—
  His first and last career is done!
On came the troop—they saw him stoop, 695
  They saw me strangely bound along
His back with many a bloody thong.
They stop—they start—they snuff the air,
Gallop a moment here and there,
Approach, retire, wheel round and
    round, 700
Then plunging back with sudden bound,
Headed by one black mighty steed,
Who seemed the patriarch of his breed,
  Without a single speck or hair
Of white upon his shaggy hide; 705
They snort—they foam—neigh—swerve
    aside,
And backward to the forest fly,
By instinct, from a human eye.
  They left me there to my despair,
  Linked to the dead and stiffening
    wretch, 710
Whose lifeless limbs beneath me stretch,
Relieved, from that unwonted weight,
From whence I could not extricate
Nor him nor me—and there we lay,
  The dying on the dead! 715

I little deemed another day
  Would see my houseless, helpless head.

"And there from morn to twilight bound,
I felt the heavy hours toil round,
With just enough of life to see 720
My last of suns go down on me,
In hopeless certainty of mind,
That makes us feel at length resigned
To that which our foreboding years
Present the worst and last of fears: 725
Inevitable—even a boon,
Nor more unkind for coming soon,
Yet shunned and dreaded with such care,
As if it only were a snare
  That Prudence might escape: 730
At times both wished for and implored,
At times sought with self-pointed sword,
Yet still a dark and hideous close
To even intolerable woes,
  And welcome in no shape. 735
And, strange to say, the sons of pleasure,
They who have revelled beyond measure
In beauty, wassail, wine, and treasure,
Die calm, or calmer, oft than he
Whose heritage was misery. 740
For he who hath in turn run through
All that was beautiful and new,
  Hath nought to hope, and nought to
    leave;
And, save the future (which is viewed
Not quite as men are base or good, 745
But as their nerves may be endued),
  With nought perhaps to grieve:
The wretch still hopes his woes must end,
And death, whom he should deem his
    friend,
Appears, to his distempered eyes, 750
Arrived to rob him of his prize,
The tree of his new paradise.
Tomorrow would have given him all,
Repaid his pangs, repaired his fall;
Tomorrow would have been the first 755
Of days no more deplored or cursed,
But bright, and long, and beckoning years,
Seen dazzling through the mist of tears,
Guerdon of many a painful hour;
Tomorrow would have given him power 760
To rule, to shine, to smite, to save—
And must it dawn upon his grave?

XVIII

"The sun was sinking—still I lay
  Chained to the chill and stiffening steed;
I thought to mingle there our clay, 765
  And my dim eyes of death had need;
  No hope arose of being freed.
I cast my last looks up the sky,
  And there between me and the sun
I saw the expecting raven fly, 770

Who scarce would wait till both should die,
  Ere his repast begun;
He flew, and perched, then flew once more,
And each time nearer than before;
I saw his wing through twilight flit, 775
And once so near me he alit
  I could have smote, but lacked the
      strength;
But the slight motion of my hand,
And feeble scratching of the sand,
The exerted throat's faint struggling
      noise, 780
Which scarcely could be called a voice,
Together scared him off at length.—
I know no more—my latest dream
  Is something of a lovely star
  Which fixed my dull eyes from afar, 785
  And went and came with wandering
      beam,
And of the cold, dull, swimming, dense
Sensation of recurring sense,
And then subsiding back to death,
And then again a little breath, 790
A little thrill, a short suspense,
  An icy sickness curdling o'er
My heart, and sparks that crossed my
      brain—
A gasp, a throb, a start of pain,
A sigh, and nothing more. 795

XIX

"I woke—where was I?—Do I see
A human face look down on me?
And doth a roof above me close?
Do these limbs on a couch repose?
Is this a chamber where I lie? 800
And is it mortal yon bright eye,
That watches me with gentle glance?
  I closed my own again once more,
As doubtful that my former trance
  Could not as yet be o'er. 805
A slender girl, long-haired, and tall,
Sate watching by the cottage wall;
The sparkle of her eye I caught,
Even with my first return of thought;
For ever and anon she threw 810
  A prying, pitying glance on me
  With her black eyes so wild and free:
I gazed, and gazed, until I knew
  No vision it could be,—
But that I lived, and was released 815
From adding to the vulture's feast:
And when the Cossack maid beheld
My heavy eyes at length unsealed,
She smiled—and I essayed to speak,

But failed—and she approached, and
      made 820
With lip and finger signs that said,
I must not strive as yet to break
The silence, till my strength should be
Enough to leave my accents free;
And then her hand on mine she laid; 825
And smoothed the pillow for my head,
And stole along on tiptoe tread,
  And gently oped the door, and spake
In whispers—ne'er was voice so sweet!
Even music followed her light feet: 830
But those she called were not awake,
And she went forth; but, ere she passed,
  Another look on me she cast,
  Another sign she made, to say,
That I had nought to fear, that all 835
Were near, at my command or call,
  And she would not delay
Her due return:—while she was gone,
Methought I felt too much alone.

XX

"She came with mother and with sire— 840
What need of more?—I will not tire
With long recital of the rest,
Since I became the Cossack's guest.
They found me senseless on the plain,
  They bore me to the nearest hut, 845
They brought me into life again—
Me—one day o'er their realm to reign!
  Thus the vain fool who strove to glut
His rage, refining on my pain,
Sent me forth to the wilderness, 850
Bound, naked, bleeding, and alone,
To pass the desert to a throne,—
  What mortal his own doom may guess?
Let none despond, let none despair!
Tomorrow the Borysthenes 855
May see our coursers graze at ease
Upon his Turkish bank, and never
Had I such welcome for a river
  As I shall yield when safely there.
Comrades, good night!"—The Hetman
      threw 860
  His length beneath the oak-tree shade,
  With leafy couch already made,
A bed nor comfortless nor new
To him, who took his rest whene'er
The hour arrived, no matter where: 865
  His eyes the hastening slumbers steep.
And if ye marvel Charles forgot
To thank his tale, *he* wondered not,—
  The king had been an hour asleep.

1818   1819

DON JUAN

Difficile est proprie communia dicere.—HORACE.

Dost thou think, because thou art virtuous, there shall be no more cakes and
ale? Yes, by St. Anne, and ginger shall be hot i' the mouth, too!
Shakespeare, *Twelfth Night, or What You Will.*

CANTO THE FIRST

DEDICATION

I

Bob Southey! You 're a poet—Poet-laureate,
  And representative of all the race;
Although 't is true that you turned out a Tory at
  Last,—yours has lately been a common case;
And now, my Epic Renegade! what are ye at?   5
  With all the Lakers, in and out of place?
A nest of tuneful persons, to my eye
Like "four and twenty Blackbirds in a pye;

II

"Which pye being opened they began to sing"
  (This old song and new simile holds good),   10
"A dainty dish to set before the King,"
  Or Regent, who admires such kind of food;—
And Coleridge, too, has lately taken wing,
  But like a hawk encumbered with his hood,—
Explaining metaphysics to the nation—   15
  I wish he would explain his Explanation.

III

You, Bob! are rather insolent, you know,
  At being disappointed in your wish
To supersede all warblers here below,
  And be the only Blackbird in the dish;   20
And then you overstrain yourself, or so,
  And tumble downward like the flying fish
Gasping on deck, because you soar too high, Bob,
And fall, for lack of moisture quite a-dry, Bob!

IV

And Wordsworth, in a rather long "Excursion"   25
  (I think the quarto holds five hundred pages),
Has given a sample from the vasty version
  Of his new system to perplex the sages;
'T is poetry—at least by his assertion,
  And may appear so when the dog-star rages—   30
And he who understands it would be able
To add a story to the Tower of Babel.

V

You—Gentlemen! by dint of long seclusion
  From better company, have kept your own
At Keswick, and, through still continued fusion   35
  Of one another's minds, at last have grown
To deem as a most logical conclusion,
  That Poesy has wreaths for you alone:
There is a narrowness in such a notion,
Which makes me wish you'd change your lakes for ocean.   40

VI

I would not imitate the petty thought,
  Nor coin my self-love to so base a vice,
For all the glory your conversion brought,
  Since gold alone should not have been its price.
You have your salary: was 't for that you wrought?   45
  And Wordsworth has his place in the Excise.
You're shabby fellows—true—but poets still,
And duly seated on the immortal hill.

VII

Your bays may hide the baldness of your brows—
  Perhaps some virtuous blushes;—let them go—   50
To you I envy neither fruit nor boughs—
  And for the fame you would engross below,
The field is universal, and allows
  Scope to all such as feel the inherent glow;
Scott, Rogers, Campbell, Moore, and Crabbe, will try   55
'Gainst you the question with posterity.

VIII

For me, who, wandering with pedestrian Muses,
  Contend not with you on the winged steed,
I wish your fate may yield ye, when she chooses,
  The fame you envy, and the skill you need;   60
And recollect a poet nothing loses
  In giving to his brethren their full meed
Of merit, and complaint of present days
Is not the certain path to future praise.

IX

He that reserves his laurels for posterity   65
  (Who does not often claim the bright reversion)
Has generally no great crop to spare it, he
  Being only injured by his own assertion;
And although here and there some glorious rarity
  Arise like Titan from the sea's immersion,   70
The major part of such appellants go
To—God knows where—for no one else can know.

X

If, fallen in evil days on evil tongues,
  Milton appealed to the Avenger, Time,
If Time, the Avenger, execrates his wrongs,   75
  And makes the word "Miltonic" mean "sublime,"
He deigned not to belie his soul in songs,
  Nor turn his very talent to a crime;
He did not loathe the Sire to laud the Son,
But closed the tyrant-hater he begun.   80

XI

Think'st thou, could he—the blind Old Man—arise,
  Like Samuel from the grave, to freeze once more
The blood of monarchs with his prophecies,
  Or be alive again—again all hoar
With time and trials, and those helpless eyes,   85
  And heartless daughters—worn—and pale—and poor;
Would he adore a sultan? he obey
The intellectual eunuch Castlereagh?

XII

Cold-blooded, smooth-faced, placid miscreant!
  Dabbling its sleek young hands in Erin's gore,   90
And thus for wider carnage taught to pant,
  Transferred to gorge upon a sister shore,
The vulgarest tool that Tyranny could want,
  With just enough of talent, and no more,
To lengthen fetters by another fixed,   95
And offer poison long already mixed.

XIII

An orator of such set trash of phrase
  Ineffably—legitimately vile,
That even its grossest flatterers dare not praise,
  Nor foes—all nations—condescend to smile;   100
Not even a sprightly blunder's spark can blaze
  From that Ixion grindstone's ceaseless toil,
That turns and turns to give the world a notion
Of endless torments and perpetual motion.

XIV

A bungler even in its disgusting trade,   105
  And botching, patching, leaving still behind
Something of which its masters are afraid,
  States to be curbed, and thoughts to be confined,
Conspiracy or Congress to be made—
  Cobbling at manacles for all mankind—   110
A tinkering slave-maker, who mends old chains,
With God and man's abhorrence for its gains.

XV

If we may judge of matter by the mind,
  Emasculated to the marrow *It*
Hath but two objects, how to serve, and bind,   115
  Deeming the chain it wears even men may fit,
Eutropius of its many masters,—blind
  To worth as freedom, wisdom as to wit,
Fearless—because *no* feeling dwells in ice,
Its very courage stagnates to a vice.   120

XVI

Where shall I turn me not to *view* its bonds,
  For I will never *feel* them;—Italy!
Thy late reviving Roman soul desponds
  Beneath the lie this State-thing breathed o'er thee—
Thy clanking chain, and Erin's yet green wounds,   125
  Have voices—tongues to cry aloud for me.
Europe has slaves, allies, kings, armies still,
And Southey lives to sing them very ill.

XVII

Meantime, Sir Laureate, I proceed to dedicate,
  In honest simple verse, this song to you.   130
And, if in flattering strains I do not predicate,
  'T is that I still retain my "buff and blue";
My politics as yet are all to educate:
  Apostasy 's so fashionable, too,
To keep *one* creed's a task grown quite Herculean:
Is it not so, my Tory, Ultra-Julian?

                 VENICE, September 16, 1818

[DON JUAN'S FIRST INTRIGUE]

I

I want a hero: an uncommon want,
    When every year and month sends forth a new one,
Till, after cloying the gazettes with cant,
    The age discovers he is not the true one:
Of such as these I should not care to vaunt,   5
    I'll therefore take our ancient friend Don Juan—
We all have seen him, in the pantomime,
Sent to the devil somewhat ere his time.

II

Vernon, the butcher Cumberland, Wolfe, Hawke,
    Prince Ferdinand, Granby, Burgoyne, Keppel, Howe,   10
Evil and good, have had their tithe of talk,
    And filled their sign-posts then, like Wellesley now;
Each in their turn like Banquo's monarchs stalk,
    Followers of fame, "nine farrow" of that sow:
France, too, had Buonaparté and Dumourier   15
Recorded in the Moniteur and Courier.

III

Barnave, Brissot, Condorcet, Mirabeau,
    Pétion, Clootz, Danton, Marat, La Fayette,
Were French, and famous people, as we know;
    And there were others, scarce forgotten yet,   20
Joubert, Hoche, Marceau, Lannes, Desaix, Moreau,
    With many of the military set,
Exceedingly remarkable at times,
But not at all adapted to my rhymes.

IV

Nelson was once Britannia's god of war,   25
    And still should be so, but the tide is turned;
There's no more to be said of Trafalgar,
    'T is with our hero quietly inurned;
Because the army 's grown more popular,
    At which the naval people are concerned,   30
Besides, the prince is all for the land-service,
Forgetting Duncan, Nelson, Howe, and Jervis.

V

Brave men were living before Agamemnon
    And since, exceeding valorous and sage,
A good deal like him too, though quite the same none;   35
    But then they shone not on the poet's page,
And so have been forgotten:—I condemn none,
    But can't find any in the present age
Fit for my poem (that is, for my new one);
So, as I said, I'll take my friend Don Juan.   40

VI

Most epic poets plunge "in medias res"
    (Horace makes this the heroic turnpike road),
And then your hero tells, whene'er you please,
    What went before—by way of episode,

While seated after dinner at his ease,   45
  Beside his mistress in some soft abode,
Palace, or garden, paradise, or cavern,
Which serves the happy couple for a tavern.

VII

That is the usual method, but not mine—
  My way is to begin with the beginning;   50
The regularity of my design
  Forbids all wandering as the worst of sinning,
And therefore I shall open with a line
  (Although it cost me half an hour in spinning)
Narrating somewhat of Don Juan's father,   55
And also of his mother, if you'd rather.

VIII

In Seville was he born, a pleasant city,
  Famous for oranges and women—he
Who has not seen it will be much to pity,
  So says the proverb—and I quite agree;   60
Of all the Spanish towns is none more pretty,
  Cadiz, perhaps—but that you soon may see:—
Don Juan's parents lived beside the river,
A noble stream, and called the Guadalquivir.

IX

His father's name was Jóse—*Don*, of course,   65
  A true Hidalgo, free from every stain
Of Moor or Hebrew blood, he traced his source
  Through the most Gothic gentlemen of Spain;
A better cavalier ne'er mounted horse,
  Or, being mounted, e'er got down again,   70
Than Jóse, who begot our hero, who
Begot—but that's to come—Well, to renew:

X

His mother was a learned lady, famed
  For every branch of every science known—
In every Christian language ever named,   75
  With virtues equalled by her wit alone:
She made the cleverest people quite ashamed,
  And even the good with inward envy groan,
Finding themselves so very much exceeded
In their own way by all the things that she did.   80

XI

Her memory was a mine: she knew by heart
  All Calderon and greater part of Lopé,
So that if any actor missed his part
  She could have served him for the prompter's copy;
For her Feinagle's were an useless art,   85
  And he himself obliged to shut up shop—he
Could never make a memory so fine as
That which adorned the brain of Donna Inez.

XII

Her favorite science was the mathematical,
  Her noblest virtue was her magnanimity;   90
Her wit (she sometimes tried at wit) was Attic all,
  Her serious sayings darkened to sublimity;

In short, in all things she was fairly what I call
  A prodigy—her morning dress was dimity,
Her evening silk, or, in the summer, muslin,   95
  And other stuffs, with which I won't stay puzzling.

XIII

She knew the Latin—that is, "the Lord's prayer,"
  And Greek—the alphabet—I'm nearly sure;
She read some French romances here and there,
  Although her mode of speaking was not pure;   100
For native Spanish she had no great care,
  At least her conversation was obscure;
Her thoughts were theorems, her words a problem,
As if she deemed that mystery would ennoble 'em.

XIV

She liked the English and the Hebrew tongue,   105
  And said there was analogy between 'em;
She proved it somehow out of sacred song,
  But I must leave the proofs to those who've seen 'em,
But this I heard her say, and can't be wrong,
  And all may think which way their judgments lean 'em,   110
" 'T is strange—the Hebrew noun which means 'I am,'
The English always use to govern d—n."

XV

Some women use their tongues—she *looked* a lecture,
  Each eye a sermon, and her brow a homily,
An all-in-all sufficient self-director,   115
  Like the lamented late Sir Samuel Romilly,
The Law's expounder, and the State's corrector,
  Whose suicide was almost an anomaly—
One sad example more, that "All is vanity,"—
(The jury brought their verdict in "Insanity.")   120

XVI

In short, she was a walking calculation,
  Miss Edgeworth's novels stepping from their covers,
Or Mrs. Trimmer's books on education,
  Or "Cœlebs' Wife" set out in quest of lovers,
Morality's prim personification,   125
  In which not Envy's self a flaw discovers;
To others' share let "female errors fall,"
For she had not even one—the worst of all.

XVII

Oh! she was perfect past all parallel—
  Of any modern female saint's comparison;   130
So far above the cunning powers of hell,
  Her guardian angel had given up his garrison;
Even her minutest motions went as well
  As those of the best time-piece made by Harrison:
In virtues nothing earthly could surpass her,
Save thine "incomparable oil," Macassar!   135

XVIII

Perfect she was, but as perfection is
  Insipid in this naughty world of ours,
Where our first parents never learned to kiss
  Till they were exiled from their earlier bowers,   140

Where all was peace, and innocence, and bliss
   (I wonder how they got through the twelve hours),
Don Jóse, like a lineal son of Eve,
Went plucking various fruit without her leave.

XIX

He was a mortal of the careless kind,   145
   With no great love for learning, or the learned,
Who chose to go where'er he had a mind,
   And never dreamed his lady was concerned;
The world, as usual, wickedly inclined
   To see a kingdom or a house o'erturned,   150
Whispered he had a mistress, some said *two,*
But for domestic quarrels *one* will do.

XX

Now Donna Inez had, with all her merit,
   A great opinion of her own good qualities;
Neglect, indeed, requires a saint to bear it,   155
   And such, indeed, she was in her moralities;
But then she had a devil of a spirit,
   And sometimes mixed up fancies with realities,
And let few opportunities escape
Of getting her liege lord into a scrape.   160

XXI

This was an easy matter with a man
   Oft in the wrong, and never on his guard;
And even the wisest, do the best they can,
   Have moments, hours, and days, so unprepared,
That you might "brain them with their lady's fan";   165
   And sometimes ladies hit exceeding hard,
And fans turn into falchions in fair hands,
And why and wherefore no one understands.

XXII

'T is pity learned virgins ever wed
   With persons of no sort of education,
Or gentlemen, who, though well born and bred,   170
   Grow tired of scientific conversation;
I don't choose to say much upon this head,
   I'm a plain man, and in a single station,
But—Oh! ye lords of ladies intellectual,   175
Inform us truly, have they not hen-pecked you all?

XXIII

Don Jóse and his lady quarrelled—*why,*
   Not any of the many could divine,
Though several thousand people chose to try,
   'T was surely no concern of theirs nor mine;   180
I loathe that low vice—curiosity;
   But if there 's anything in which I shine,
'T is in arranging all my friends' affairs,
Not having, of my own, domestic cares.

XXIV

And so I interfered, and with the best   185
   Intentions, but their treatment was not kind;
I think the foolish people were possessed,
   For neither of them could I ever find,

Although their porter afterwards confessed—
  But that 's no matter, and the worst 's behind,   190
For little Juan o'er me threw, down stairs,
A pail of housemaid's water unawares.

XXV

A little curly-headed, good-for-nothing,
  And mischief-making monkey from his birth;
His parents ne'er agreed except in doting   195
  Upon the most unquiet imp on earth;
Instead of quarrelling, had they been but both in
  Their senses, they'd have sent young master forth
To school, or had him soundly whipped at home,
To teach him manners for the time to come.   200

XXVI

Don Jóse and tne Donna Inez led
  For some time an unhappy sort of life,
Wishing each other, not divorced, but dead;
  They lived respectably as man and wife,
Their conduct was exceedingly well-bred,   205
  And gave no outward signs of inward strife,
Until at length the smothered fire broke out,
And put the business past all kind of doubt.

XXVII

For Inez called some druggists and physicians,
  And tried to prove her loving lord was *mad,*   210
But as he had some lucid intermissions,
  She next decided he was only *bad;*
Yet when they asked her for her depositions,
  No sort of explanation could be had,
Save that her duty both to man and God   215
Required this conduct—which seemed very odd.

XXVIII

She kept a journal, where his faults were noted,
  And opened certain trunks of books and letters,
All which might, if occasion served, be quoted;
  And then she had all Seville for abettors,   220
Besides her good old grandmother (who doted);
  The hearers of her case became repeaters,
Then advocates, inquisitors, and judges,
Some for amusement, others for old grudges.

XXIX

And then this best and meekest woman bore   225
  With such serenity her husbands' woes,
Just as the Spartan ladies did of yore,
  Who saw their spouses killed, and nobly chose
Never to say a word about them more—
  Calmly she heard each calumny that rose,   230
And saw *his* agonies with such sublimity,
That all the world exclaimed, "What magnanimity!"

XXX

No doubt this patience, when the world is damning us,
  Is philosophic in our former friends:
'T is also pleasant to be deemed magnanimous,   235
  The more so in obtaining our own ends;

And what the lawyers call a *"malus animus"*
  Conduct like this by no means comprehends:
Revenge in person 's certainly no virtue,
But then 't is not *my* fault, if *others* hurt you.   240

XXXI

And if our quarrels should rip up old stories,
  And help them with a lie or two additional,
I'm not to blame, as you well know—no more is
  Any one else—they were become traditional;
Besides, their resurrection aids our glories   245
  By contrast, which is what we just were wishing all:
And science profits by this resurrection—
Dead scandals form good subjects for dissection.

XXXII

Their friends had tried at reconciliation,
  Then their relations, who made matters worse,   250
('T were hard to tell upon a like occasion
  To whom it may be best to have recourse—
I can't say much for friend or yet relation):
  The lawyers did their utmost for divorce;
But scarce a fee was paid on either side   255
Before, unluckily, Don Jóse died.

XXXIII

He died: and most unluckily, because,
  According to all hints I could collect
From counsel learned in those kinds of laws
  (Although their talk 's obscure and circumspect),   260
His death contrived to spoil a charming cause;
  A thousand pities also with respect
To public feeling, which on this occasion
Was manifested in a great sensation.

XXXIV

But ah! he died; and buried with him lay   265
  The public feeling and the lawyers' fees:
His house was sold, his servants sent away,
  A Jew took one of his two mistresses,
A priest the other—at least so they say:
  I asked the doctors after his disease—   270
He died of the slow fever called the tertian,
And left his widow to her own aversion.

XXXV

Yet Jóse was an honorable man,
  That I must say, who knew him very well;
Therefore his frailties I 'll no further scan,   275
  Indeed there were not many more to tell:
And if his passions now and then outran
  Discretion, and were not so peaceable
As Numa's (who was also named Pompilius),
He had been ill brought up, and was born bilious.   280

XXXVI

Whate'er might be his worthlessness or worth,
  Poor fellow! he had many things to wound him,
Let's own—since it can do no good on earth—
  It was a trying moment that which found him

Standing alone beside his desolate hearth,   285
  Where all his household gods lay shivered round him:
No choice was left his feelings or his pride,
  Save death or Doctors' Commons—so he died.

XXXVII

Dying intestate, Juan was sole heir
  To a chancery suit, and messuages and lands,   290
Which, with a long minority and care,
  Promised to turn out well in proper hands:
Inez became sole guardian, which was fair,
  And answered but to nature's just demands;
An only son left with an only mother   295
Is brought up much more wisely than another.

XXXVIII

Sagest of women, even of widows, she
  Resolved that Juan should be quite a paragon,
And worthy of the noblest pedigree:
  (His sire was of Castile, his dam from Aragon).   300
Then for accomplishments of chivalry,
  In case our lord the king should go to war again,
He learned the arts of riding, fencing, gunnery,
And how to scale a fortress—or a nunnery.

XXXIX

But that which Donna Inez most desired,   305
  And saw into herself each day before all
The learned tutors whom for him she hired,
  Was, that his breeding should be strictly moral:
Much into all his studies she inquired,
  And so they were submitted first to her, all,   310
Arts, sciences, no branch was made a mystery
To Juan's eyes, excepting natural history.

XL

The languages, especially the dead,
  The sciences, and most of all the abstruse,
The arts, at least all such as could be said   315
  To be the most remote from common use,
In all these he was much and deeply read:
  But not a page of anything that 's loose,
Or hints continuation of the species,
Was ever suffered, lest he should grow vicious.   320

XLI

His classic studies made a little puzzle,
  Because of filthy loves of gods and goddesses,
Who in the earlier ages raised a bustle,
  But never put on pantaloons or bodices;
His reverend tutors had at times a tussle,   325
  And for their Æneids, Iliads, and Odysseys,
Were forced to make an odd sort of apology,
For Donna Inez dreaded the Mythology.

XLII

Ovid's a rake, as half his verses show him,
  Anacreon's morals are a still worse sample,   330
Catullus scarcely has a decent poem,
  I don't think Sappho's Ode a good example,

Although Longinus tells us there is no hymn
  Where the sublime soars forth on wings more ample;
But Virgil's songs are pure, except that horrid one   335
Beginning with "Formosum Pastor Corydon."

XLIII

Lucretius' irreligion is too strong
  For early stomachs, to prove wholesome food;
I can't help thinking Juvenal was wrong,
  Although no doubt his real intent was good,   340
For speaking out so plainly in his song,
  So much indeed as to be downright rude;
And then what proper person can be partial
To all those nauseous epigrams of Martial?

XLIV

Juan was taught from out the best edition,   345
  Expurgated by learned men, who place,
Judiciously, from out the schoolboy's vision,
  The grosser parts; but, fearful to deface
Too much their modest bard by this omission,
  And pitying sore this mutilated case,   350
They only add them all in an appendix,
Which saves, in fact, the trouble of an index;

XLV

For there we have them all "at one fell swoop,"
  Instead of being scattered through the pages;
They stand forth marshalled in a handsome troop,   355
  To meet the ingenuous youth of future ages,
Till some less rigid editor shall stoop
  To call them back into their separate cages,
Instead of standing staring all together,
Like garden gods—and not so decent either.   360

XLVI

The Missal too (it was the family Missal)
  Was ornamented in a sort of way
Which ancient mass-books often are, and this all
  Kinds of grotesques illumined; and how they,
Who saw those figures on the margin kiss all,   365
  Could turn their optics to the text and pray,
Is more than I know—But Don Juan's mother
Kept this herself, and gave her son another.

XLVII

Sermons he read, and lectures he endured,
  And homilies, and lives of all the saints;
To Jerome and to Chrysostom inured,   370
  He did not take such studies for restraints;
But how faith is acquired, and then insured,
  So well not one of the aforesaid paints
As Saint Augustine in his fine Confessions,   375
Which make the reader envy his transgressions.

XLVIII

This, too, was a sealed book to little Juan—
  I can't but say that his mamma was right,
If such an education was the true one.
  She scarcely trusted him from out her sight;   380

Her maids were old, and if she took a new one,
  You might be sure she was a perfect fright,
She did this during even her husband's life—
I recommend as much to every wife.

XLIX

Young Juan waxed in godliness and grace;
  At six a charming child, and at eleven
With all the promise of as fine a face
  As e'er to man's maturer growth was given.
He studied steadily and grew apace,
  And seemed, at least, in the right road to heaven,
For half his days were passed at church, the other
Between his tutors, confessor, and mother.

L

At six, I said, he was a charming child,
  At twelve he was a fine, but quiet boy;
Although in infancy a little wild,
  They tamed him down amongst them: to destroy
His natural spirit not in vain they toiled,
  At least it seemed so; and his mother's joy
Was to declare how sage, and still, and steady,
Her young philosopher was grown already.

LI

I had my doubts, perhaps I have them still,
  But what I say is neither here nor there:
I knew his father well, and have some skill
  In character—but it would not be fair
From sire to son to augur good or ill:
  He and his wife were an ill sorted pair—
But scandal 's my aversion—I protest
Against all evil speaking, even in jest.

LII

For my part I say nothing—nothing—but
  This I will say—my reasons are my own—
That if I had an only son to put
  To school (as God be praised that I have none),
'T is not with Donna Inez I would shut
  Him up to learn his catechism alone,
No—no—I'd send him out betimes to college,
For there it was I picked up my own knowledge.

LIII

For there one learns—'t is not for me to boast,
  Though I acquired—but I pass over *that,*
As well as all the Greek I since have lost:
  I say that there 's the place—but *"Verbum sat,"*
I think I picked up too, as well as most,
  Knowledge of matters—but no matter *what*—
I never married—but, I think, I know
That sons should not be educated so.

LIV

Young Juan now was sixteen years of age,
  Tall, handsome, slender, but well knit: he seemed
Active, though not so sprightly, as a page;
  And everybody but his mother deemed

385

390

395

400

405

410

415

420

425

Him almost man; but she flew in a rage
   And bit her lips (for else she might have screamed) 430
If any said so, for to be precocious
Was in her eyes a thing the most atrocious.

LV

Amongst her numerous acquaintance, all
   Selected for discretion and devotion,
There was the Donna Julia, whom to call 435
   Pretty were but to give a feeble notion
Of many charms in her as natural
   As sweetness to the flower, or salt to ocean,
Her zone to Venus, or his bow to Cupid,
(But this last simile is trite and stupid). 440

LVI

The darkness of her Oriental eye
   Accorded with her Moorish origin;
(Her blood was not all Spanish, by the by;
   In Spain, you know, this is a sort of sin).
When proud Granada fell, and, forced to fly, 445
   Boabdil wept, of Donna Julia's kin
Some went to Africa, some stayed in Spain,
Her great great grandmamma chose to remain.

LVII

She married (I forget the pedigree)
   With an Hidalgo, who transmitted down 450
His blood less noble than such blood should be;
   At such alliances his sires would frown,
In that point so precise in each degree
   That they bred *in and in,* as might be shown,
Marrying their cousins—nay, their aunts, and nieces, 455
Which always spoils the breed, if it increases.

LVIII

This heathenish cross restored the breed again,
   Ruined its blood, but much improved its flesh;
For from a root the ugliest in old Spain
   Sprung up a branch as beautiful as fresh; 460
The sons no more were short, the daughters plain:
   But there 's a rumor which I fain would hush,
'T is said that Donna Julia's grandmamma
Produced her Don more heirs at love than law.

LIX

However this might be, the race went on 465
   Improving still through every generation,
Until it centered in an only son,
   Who left an only daughter: my narration
May have suggested that this single one
   Could be but Julia (whom on this occasion 470
I shall have much to speak about), and she
Was married, charming, chaste, and twenty-three.

LX

Her eye (I 'm very fond of handsome eyes)
   Was large and dark, suppressing half its fire
Until she spoke, then through its soft disguise 475
   Flashed an expression more of pride than ire,

And love than either; and there would arise
  A something in them which was not desire,
But would have been, perhaps, but for the soul
Which struggled through and chastened down the whole.   480

LXI

Her glossy hair was clustered o'er a brow
  Bright with intelligence, and fair, and smooth;
Her eyebrow's shape was like the aërial bow,
  Her cheek all purple with the beam of youth,
Mounting, at times, to a transparent glow,   485
  As if her veins ran lightning; she, in sooth,
Possessed an air and grace by no means common:
Her stature tall—I hate a dumpy woman.

LXII

Wedded she was some years, and to a man
  Of fifty, and such husbands are in plenty;   490
And yet, I think, instead of such a ONE
  'T were better to have TWO of five-and-twenty,
Especially in countries near the sun:
  And now I think on 't, "mi vien in mente,"
Ladies even of the most uneasy virtue   495
Prefer a spouse whose age is short of thirty.

LXIII

'T is a sad thing, I cannot choose but say,
  And all the fault of that indecent sun,
Who cannot leave alone our helpless clay,
  But will keep baking, broiling, burning on,   500
That howsoever people fast and pray,
  The flesh is frail, and so the soul undone:
What men call gallantry, and gods adultery,
Is much more common where the climate's sultry.

LXIV

Happy the nations of the moral North!   505
  Where all is virtue, and the winter season
Sends sin, without a rag on, shivering forth
  ('T was snow that brought St. Anthony to reason);
Where juries cast up what a wife is worth,
  By laying whate'er sum, in mulct, they please on   510
The lover, who must pay a handsome price,
Because it is a marketable vice.

LXV

Alfonso was the name of Julia's lord,
  A man well looking for his years, and who
Was neither much beloved nor yet abhorred: 515
  They lived together as most people do,
Suffering each others' foibles by accord,
  And not exactly either one or two;
Yet he was jealous, though he did not show it,
For jealousy dislikes the world to know it.   520

LXVI

Julia was—yet I never could see why—
  With Donna Inez quite a favorite friend;
Between their tastes there was small sympathy,
  For not a line had Julia ever penned:

Some people whisper (but, no doubt, they lie,   525
   For malice still imputes some private end)
That Inez had, ere Don Alfonso's marriage,
Forgot with him her very prudent carriage;

LXVII

And that still keeping up the old connexion,
   Which time had lately rendered much more chaste,   530
She took his lady also in affection,
   And certainly this course was much the best:
She flattered Julia with her sage protection,
   And complimented Don Alfonso's taste;
And if she could not (who can?) silence scandal,   535
At least she left it a more slender handle.

LXVIII

I can't tell whether Julia saw the affair
   With other people's eyes, or if her own
Discoveries made, but none could be aware
   Of this, at least no symptom e'er was shown;   540
Perhaps she did not know, or did not care,
   Indifferent from the first, or callous grown:
I'm really puzzled what to think or say,
She kept her counsel in so close a way.

LXIX

Juan she saw, and, as a pretty child,   545
   Caressed him often—such a thing might be
Quite innocently done, and harmless styled,
   When she had twenty years, and thirteen he;
But I am not so sure I should have smiled
   When he was sixteen, Julia twenty-three;   550
These few short years make wondrous alterations,
Particularly amongst sun-burnt nations.

LXX

Whate'er the cause might be, they had become
   Changed; for the dame grew distant, the youth shy,
Their looks cast down, their greetings almost dumb,   555
   And much embarrassment in either eye;
There surely will be little doubt with some
   That Donna Julia knew the reason why,
But as for Juan, he had no more notion
Than he who never saw the sea of ocean.   560

LXXI

Yet Julia's very coldness still was kind,
   And tremulously gentle her small hand
Withdrew itself from his, but left behind
   A little pressure, thrilling, and so bland
And slight, so very slight, that to the mind   565
   'T was but a doubt; but ne'er magician's wand
Wrought change with all Armida's fairy art
Like what this light touch left on Juan's heart.

LXXII

And if she met him, though she smiled no more,
   She looked a sadness sweeter than her smile,
As if her heart had deeper thoughts in store   570
   She must not own, but cherished more the while

For that compression in its burning core;
　　Even innocence itself has many a wile,
And will not dare to trust itself with truth,   575
　　And love is taught hypocrisy from youth.

LXXIII

But passion most dissembles, yet betrays
　　Even by its darkness; as the blackest sky
Foretells the heaviest tempest, it displays
　　Its workings through the vainly guarded eye,   58з
And in whatever aspect it arrays
　　Itself, 't is still the same hypocrisy:
Coldness or anger, even disdain or hate,
Are masks it often wears, and still too late.

LXXIV

Then there were sighs, the deeper for suppression,   585
　　And stolen glances, sweeter for the theft,
And burning blushes, though for no transgression,
　　Tremblings when met, and restlessness when left;
All these are little preludes to possession,
　　Of which young passion cannot be bereft,   59ı
And merely tend to show how greatly love is
Embarrassed at first starting with a novice.

LXXV

Poor Julia's heart was in an awkward state;
　　She felt it going, and resolved to make
The noblest efforts for herself and mate,   595
　　For honor's, pride's, religion's, virtue's sake.
Her resolutions were most truly great,
　　And almost might have made a Tarquin quake:
She prayed the Virgin Mary for her grace,
As being the best judge of a lady's case.   600

LXXVI

She vowed she never would see Juan more,
　　And next day paid a visit to his mother,
And looked extremely at the opening door,
　　Which, by the Virgin's grace, let in another;
Grateful she was, and yet a little sore—   605
　　Again it opens, it can be no other,
'T is surely Juan now—No! I'm afraid
That night the Virgin was no further prayed.

LXXVII

She now determined that a virtuous woman
　　Should rather face and overcome temptation,   610
That flight was base and dastardly, and no man
　　Should ever give her heart the least sensation;
That is to say, a thought beyond the common
　　Preference, that we must feel upon occasion,
For people who are pleasanter than others,   61ь
But then they only seem so many brothers.

LXXVIII

And even if by chance—and who can tell?
　　The devil's so very sly—she should discover
That all within was not so very well,
　　And, if still free, that such or such a lover   620

Might please perhaps, a virtuous wife can quell
  Such thoughts, and be the better when they're over;
And if the man should ask, 't is but denial:
I recommend young ladies to make trial.

LXXIX

And then there are such things as love divine,   625
  Bright and immaculate, unmixed and pure,
Such as the angels think so very fine,
  And matrons, who would be no less secure,
Platonic, perfect, "just such love as mine":
  Thus Julia said—and thought so, to be sure;   630
And so I'd have her think, were I the man
On whom her reveries celestial ran.

LXXX

Such love is innocent, and may exist
  Between young persons without any danger:
A hand may first, and then a lip be kist;   635
  For my part, to such doings I'm a stranger,
But *hear* these freedoms form the utmost list
  Of all o'er which such love may be a ranger:
If people go beyond, 't is quite a crime,
But not my fault—I tell them all in time.   640

LXXXI

Love, then, but love within its proper limits
  Was Julia's innocent determination
In young Don Juan's favor, and to him its
  Exertion might be useful on occasion;
And, lighted at too pure a shrine to dim its   645
  Ethereal lustre, with what sweet persuasion
He might be taught, by love and her together—
I really don't know what, nor Julia either.

LXXXII

Fraught with this fine intention, and well fenced
  In mail of proof—her purity of soul,   650
She, for the future of her strength convinced,
  And that her honor was a rock, or mole,
Exceeding sagely from that hour dispensed
  With any kind of troublesome control;
But whether Julia to the task was equal   655
Is that which must be mentioned in the sequel.

LXXXIII

Her plan she deemed both innocent and feasible,
  And, surely, with a stripling of sixteen
Not scandal's fangs could fix on much that's seizable,
  Or if they did so, satisfied to mean   660
Nothing but what was good, her breast was peaceable:
  A quiet conscience makes one so serene!
Christians have burnt each other, quite persuaded
That all the Apostles would have done as they did.

LXXXIV

And if in the mean time her husband died,   665
  But Heaven forbid that such a thought should cross
Her brain, though in a dream! (and then she sighed)
  Never could she survive that common loss;

But just suppose that moment should betide,
   I only say suppose it—*inter nos*.   670
(This should be *entre nous*, for Julia thought
In French, but then the rhyme would go for nought.)

LXXXV

I only say, suppose this supposition:
   Juan being then grown up to man's estate
Would fully suit a widow of condition,   675
   Even seven years hence it would not be too late;
And in the interim (to pursue this vision)
   The mischief, after all, could not be great,
For he would learn the rudiments of love,
I mean the seraph way of those above.   680

LXXXVI

So much for Julia. Now we'll turn to Juan.
   Poor little fellow! he had no idea
Of his own case, and never hit the true one;
   In feelings quick as Ovid's Miss Medea,
He puzzled over what he found a new one,   685
   But not as yet imagined it could be a
Thing quite in course, and not at all alarming,
Which, with a little patience, might grow charming.

LXXXVII

Silent and pensive, idle, restless, slow,
   His home deserted for the lonely wood,   690
Tormented with a wound he could not know,
   His, like all deep grief, plunged in solitude:
I'm fond myself of solitude or so,
   But then, I beg it may be understood,
By solitude I mean a Sultan's, not   695
A hermit's, with a haram for a grot.

LXXXVIII

"Oh Love! in such a wilderness as this,
   Where transport and security entwine,
Here is the empire of thy perfect bliss,
   And here thou art a god indeed divine."   700
The bard I quote from does not sing amiss,
   With the exception of the second line,
For that same twining "transport and security"
Are twisted to a phrase of some obscurity.

LXXXIX

The poet meant, no doubt, and thus appeals   705
   To the good sense and senses of mankind,
The very thing which everybody feels,
   As all have found on trial, or may find,
That no one likes to be disturbed at meals
   Or love.—I won't say more about "entwined"   710
Or "transport," as we knew all that before,
But beg "Security" will bolt the door.

XC

Young Juan wandered by the glassy brooks,
   Thinking unutterable things; he threw
Himself at length within the leafy nooks   715
   Where the wild branch of the cork forest grew;

There poets find materials for their books,
  And every now and then we read them through,
So that their plan and prosody are eligible,
Unless, like Wordsworth, they prove unintelligible.   720

XCI

He, Juan (and not Wordsworth), so pursued
  His self-communion with his own high soul,
Until his mighty heart, in its great mood,
  Had mitigated part, though not the whole
Of its disease; he did the best he could   725
  With things not very subject to control,
And turned, without perceiving his condition,
Like Coleridge, into a metaphysician.

XCII

He thought about himself, and the whole earth,
  Of man the wonderful, and of the stars,   730
And how the deuce they ever could have birth;
  And then he thought of earthquakes, and of wars,
How many miles the moon might have in girth,
  Of air-balloons, and of the many bars
To perfect knowledge of the boundless skies;—   735
And then he thought of Donna Julia's eyes.

XCIII

In thoughts like these true wisdom may discern
  Longings sublime, and aspirations high,
Which some are born with, but the most part learn
  To plague themselves withal, they know not why:
'T was strange that one so young should thus concern   740
  His brain about the action of the sky;
If *you* think 't was philosophy that this did,
I can't help thinking puberty assisted.

XCIV

He pored upon the leaves, and on the flowers,   745
  And heard a voice in all the winds; and then
He thought of wood-nymphs and immortal bowers,
  And how the goddesses came down to men:
He missed the pathway, he forgot the hours,
  And when he looked upon his watch again,   750
He found how much old Time had been a winner—
He also found that he had lost his dinner.

XCV

Sometimes he turned to gaze upon his book,
  Boscan, or Garcilasso;—by the wind
Even as the page is rustled while we look,   755
  So by the poesy of his own mind
Over the mystic leaf his soul was shook,
  As if 't were one whereon magicians bind
Their spells, and give them to the passing gale
According to some good old woman's tale.   760

XCVI

Thus would he while his lonely hours away
  Dissatisfied, nor knowing what he wanted;
Nor glowing reverie, nor poet's lay,
  Could yield his spirit that for which it panted,

A bosom whereon he his head might lay, 765
  And hear the heart beat with the love it granted,
With—several other things which I forget,
Or which, at least, I need not mention yet.

XCVII

Those lonely walks, and lengthening reveries,
  Could not escape the gentle Julia's eyes; 770
She saw that Juan was not at his ease;
  But that which chiefly may, and must surprise,
Is, that the Donna Inez did not tease
  Her only son with question or surmise;
Whether it was she did not see, or would not, 775
Or, like all very clever people, could not.

XCVIII

This may seem strange, but yet 't is very common;
  For instance—gentlemen, whose ladies take
Leave to o'erstep the written rights of woman,
  And break the——Which commandment is 't they break? 780
(I have forgot the number, and think no man
  Should rashly quote, for fear of a mistake.)
I say, when these same gentlemen are jealous,
They make some blunder, which their ladies tell us.

XCIX

A real husband always is suspicious, 785
  But still no less suspects in the wrong place,
Jealous of some one who had no such wishes,
  Or pandering blindly to his own disgrace,
By harboring some dear friend extremely vicious;
  The last indeed's infallibly the case: 790
And when the spouse and friend are gone off wholly,
He wonders at their vice, and not his folly.

C

Thus parents also are at times short-sighted;
  Though watchful as the lynx, they ne'er discover,
The while the wicked world beholds delighted, 795
  Young Hopeful's mistress, or Miss Fanny's lover,
Till some confounded escapade has blighted
  The plan of twenty years, and all is over;
And then the mother cries, the father swears,
And wonders why the devil he got heirs. 800

CI

But Inez was so anxious, and so clear
  Of sight, that I must think, on this occasion,
She had some other motive much more near
  For leaving Juan to this new temptation,
But what that motive was, I shan't say here; 805
  Perhaps to finish Juan's education,
Perhaps to open Don Alfonso's eyes,
In case he thought his wife too great a prize.

CII

It was upon a day, a summer's day;—
  Summer 's indeed a very dangerous season, 810
And so is spring about the end of May;
  The sun, no doubt, is the prevailing reason;

But whatsoe'er the cause is, one may say,
　And stand convicted of more truth than treason,
That there are months which nature grows more merry in,— 815
March has its hares, and May must have its heroine.

CIII

'T was on a summer's day—the sixth of June:—
　I like to be particular in dates,
Not only of the age, and year, but moon;
　They are a sort of post-house, where the Fates 820
Change horses, making history change its tune,
　Then spur away o'er empires and o'er states,
Leaving at last not much besides chronology,
Excepting the post-obits of theology.

CIV

'T was on the sixth of June, about the hour 825
　Of half-past six—perhaps still nearer seven—
When Julia sate within as pretty a bower
　As e'er held houri in that heathenish heaven
Described by Mahomet, and Anacreon Moore,
　To whom the lyre and laurels have been given, 830
With all the trophies of triumphant song—
He won them well, and may he wear them long!

CV

She sate, but not alone; I know not well
　How this same interview had taken place,
And even if I knew, I should not tell— 835
　People should hold their tongues in any case;
No matter how or why the thing befell,
　But there were she and Juan, face to face—
When two such faces are so, 't would be wise,
But very difficult, to shut their eyes. 840

CVI

How beautiful she looked! her conscious heart
　Glowed in her cheek, and yet she felt no wrong.
Oh Love! how perfect is thy mystic art,
　Strengthening the weak, and trampling on the strong!
How self-deceitful is the sagest part 845
　Of mortals whom thy lure hath led along!—
The precipice she stood on was immense,
So was her creed in her own innocence.

CVII

She thought of her own strength, and Juan's youth,
　And of the folly of all prudish fears, 850
Victorious virtue, and domestic truth,
　And then of Don Alfonso's fifty years:
I wish these last had not occurred, in sooth,
　Because that number rarely much endears,
And through all climes, the snowy and the sunny, 855
Sounds ill in love, whate'er it may in money.

CVIII

When people say, "I 've told you fifty times,"
　They mean to scold, and very often do;
When poets say, "I 've written fifty rhymes,"
　They make you dread that they 'll recite them too; 860

In gangs of *fifty*, thieves commit their crimes;
　At *fifty* love for love is rare, 't is true,
But then, no doubt, it equally as true is,
　A good deal may be bought for *fifty* Louis.

CIX

Julia had honor, virtue, truth, and love　　　　　865
　For Don Alfonso; and she inly swore,
By all the vows below to powers above,
　She never would disgrace the ring she wore,
Nor leave a wish which wisdom might reprove;
　And while she pondered this, besides much more,　870
One hand on Juan's carelessly was thrown,
Quite by mistake—she thought it was her own;

CX

Unconsciously she leaned upon the other,
　Which played within the tangles of her hair;
And to contend with thoughts she could not smother　875
　She seemed, by the distraction of her air,
'T was surely very wrong in Juan's mother
　To leave together this imprudent pair,
She who for many years had watched her son so—
I'm very certain *mine* would not have done so.　880

CXI

The hand which still held Juan's, by degrees
　Gently, but palpably confirmed its grasp,
As if it said, "Detain me, if you please";
　Yet there 's no doubt she only meant to clasp
His fingers with a pure Platonic squeeze;　　　885
　She would have shrunk as from a toad or asp,
Had she imagined such a thing could rouse
A feeling dangerous to a prudent spouse.

CXII

I cannot know what Juan thought of this,
　But what he did, is much what you would do;　890
His young lip thanked it with a grateful kiss,
　And then, abashed at its own joy, withdrew
In deep despair, lest he had done amiss,—
　Love is so very timid when 't is new:
She blushed, and frowned not, but she strove to speak,　895
And held her tongue, her voice was grown so weak.

CXIII

The sun set, and up rose the yellow moon;
　The devil 's in the moon for mischief; they
Who called her CHASTE, methinks, began too soon
　Their nomenclature; there is not a day,　　900
The longest, not the twenty-first of June,
　Sees half the business in a wicked way,
On which three single hours of moonshine smile—
And then she looks so modest all the while.

CXIV

There is a dangerous silence in that hour,　　905
　A stillness, which leaves room for the full soul
To open all itself, without the power
　Of calling wholly back its self-control;

The silver light which, hallowing tree and tower,
  Sheds beauty and deep softness o'er the whole.
Breathes also to the heart, and o'er it throws   910
A loving languor, which is not repose.

CXV

And Julia sate with Juan, half embraced
  And half retiring from the glowing arm,
Which trembled like the bosom where 't was placed;   915
  Yet still she must have thought there was no harm,
Or else 't were easy to withdraw her waist;
  But then the situation had its charm,
And then—— God knows what next—I can't go on;
I 'm almost sorry that I e'er begun.   920

CXVI

Oh Plato! Plato! you have paved the way,
  With your confounded phantasies, to more
Immoral conduct by the fancied sway
  Your system feigns o'er the controlless core
Of human hearts, than all the long array   925
  Of poets and romancers:—You're a bore,
A charlatan, a coxcomb—and have been,
At best, no better than a go-between.

CXVII

And Julia's voice was lost, except in sighs,
  Until too late for useful conversation;   930
The tears were gushing from her gentle eyes,
  I wish, indeed, they had not had occasion;
But who, alas! can love, and then be wise?
  Not that remorse did not oppose temptation;
A little still she strove, and much repented,   935
And whispering "I will ne'er consent"—consented.

CXVIII

'T is said that Xerxes offered a reward
  To those who could invent him a new pleasure
Methinks the requisition 's rather hard,
  And must have cost his majesty a treasure;   940
For my part, I 'm a moderate-minded bard,
  Fond of a little love (which I call leisure);
I care not for new pleasures, as the old
Are quite enough for me, so they but hold.

CXIX

Oh Pleasure! you 're indeed a pleasant thing,   945
  Although one must be damned for you, no doubt:
I make a resolution every spring
  Of reformation, ere the year run out,
But somehow, this my vestal vow takes wing,
  Yet still, I trust, it may be kept throughout;   950
I 'm very sorry, very much ashamed,
And mean, next winter, to be quite reclaimed.

CXX

Here my chaste Muse a liberty must take—
  Start not; still chaster reader—she 'll be nice hence-
Forward, and there is no great cause to quake;   955
  This liberty is a poetic licence,

Which some irregularity may make
  In the design, and as I have a high sense
Of Aristotle and the Rules, 't is fit
To beg his pardon when I err a bit.   960

This licence is to hope the reader will
  Suppose from June the sixth (the fatal day
Without whose epoch my poetic skill
  For want of facts would all be thrown away),
But keeping Julia and Don Juan still   965
  In sight, that several months have passed; we'll say
'T was in November, but I 'm not so sure
About the day—the era 's more obscure.

We 'll talk of that anon.—'T is sweet to hear
  At midnight on the blue and moonlit deep   970
The song and oar of Oria's gondolier,
  By distance mellowed, o'er the waters sweet;
'T is sweet to see the evening star appear;
  'T is sweet to listen as the night-winds creep
From leaf to leaf; 't is sweet to view on high   975
The rainbow, based on ocean, span the sky.

'T is sweet to hear the watch-dog's honest bark
  Bay deep-mouthed welcome as we draw near home;
'T is sweet to know there is an eye will mark
  Our coming, and look brighter when we come;   980
'T is sweet to be awakened by the lark,
  Or lulled by falling waters; sweet the hum
Of bees, the voice of girls, the song of birds,
The lisp of children, and their earliest words.

Sweet is the vintage, when the showering grapes   985
  In Bacchanal profusion reel to earth,
Purple and gushing; sweet are our escapes
  From civic revelry to rural mirth;
Sweet to the miser are his glittering heaps,
  Sweet to the father is his first-born's birth,   990
Sweet is revenge—especially to women,
Pillage to soldiers, prize-money to seamen.

Sweet is a legacy, and passing sweet
  The unexpected death of some old lady
Or gentleman of seventy years complete,   995
  Who 've made "us youth" wait too—too long already
For an estate, or cash, or country seat,
  Still breaking, but with stamina so steady
That all the Israelites are fit to mob its
Next owner for their double-damned post-obits.   1000

'T is sweet to win, no matter how, one's laurels,
  By blood or ink; 't is sweet to put an end
To strife; 't is sometimes sweet to have our quarrels,
  Particularly with a tiresome friend:

Sweet is old wine in bottles, ale in barrels;
   Dear is the helpless creature we defend
Against the world; and dear the schoolboy spot
We ne'er forget, though there we are forgot.   1005

CXXVII

But sweeter still than this, than these, than all,
   Is first and passionate love—it stands alone,   1010
Like Adam's recollection of his fall;
   The tree of knowledge has been plucked—all 's known—
And life yields nothing further to recall
   Worthy of this ambrosial sin, so shown,
No doubt in fable, as the unforgiven   1015
Fire which Prometheus filched for us from heaven.

CXXVIII

Man 's a strange animal, and makes strange use
   Of his own nature, and the various arts,
And likes particularly to produce
   Some new experiment to show his parts;   1020
This is the age of oddities let loose,
   Where different talents find their different marts;
You 'd best begin with truth, and when you've lost your
Labor, there 's a sure market for imposture.

CXXIX

What opposite discoveries we have seen!   1025
   (Signs of true genius, and of empty pockets.)
One makes new noses, one a guillotine,
   One breaks your bones, one sets them in their sockets;
But vaccination certainly has been
   A kind antithesis to Congreve's rockets,   1030
With which the Doctor paid off an old pox,
By borrowing a new one from an ox.

CXXX

Bread has been made (indifferent) from potatoes;
   And galvanism has set some corpses grinning,
But has not answered like the apparatus   1035
   Of the Humane Society's beginning,
By which men are unsuffocated gratis:
   What wondrous new machines have late been spinning!
I said the small pox has gone out of late;
Perhaps it may be followed by the great.   1040

CXXXI

'T is said the great came from America;
   Perhaps it may set out on its return,—
The population there so spreads, they say
   'T is grown high time to thin it in its turn,
With war, or plague, or famine, any way,   1045
   So that civilisation they may learn;
And which in ravage the more loathsome evil is—
Their real lues, or our pseudo-syphilis?

CXXXII

This is the patent age of new inventions
   For killing bodies, and for saving souls,   1050
All propagated with the best intentions;
   Sir Humphrey Davy's lantern, by which coals

Are safely mined for in the mode he mentions,
  Tombuctoo travels, voyages to the Poles,
Are ways to benefit mankind, as true
  Perhaps, as shooting them at Waterloo.

1055

CXXXIII

Man 's a phenomenon, one knows not what,
  And wonderful beyond all wondrous measure;
'T is pity though, in this sublime world, that
  Pleasure 's a sin, and sometimes sin 's a pleasure;
Few mortals know what end they would be at,
  But whether glory, power, or love, or treasure,
The path is through perplexing ways, and when
The goal is gained, we know, you know—and then——

1060

CXXXIV

What then?—I do not know, no more do you——
  And so good night.—Return we to our story:
'T was in November, when fine days are few,
  And the far mountains wax a little hoary,
And clap a white cape on their mantles blue;
  And the sea dashes round the promontory,
And the loud breaker boils against the rock,
And sober suns must set at five o'clock.

1065

1070

CXXXV

'T was, as the watchmen say, a cloudy night;
  No moon, no stars, the wind was low or loud
By gusts, and many a sparkling hearth was bright
  With the piled wood, round which the family crowd;
There 's something cheerful in that sort of light,
  Even as a summer sky 's without a cloud;
I 'm fond of fire, and crickets, and all that,
A lobster salad, and champagne, and chat.

1075

1080

CXXXVI

'T was midnight—Donna Julia was in bed,
  Sleeping, most probably,—when at her door
Arose a clatter might awake the dead,
  If they had never been awoke before,
And that they have been so we all have read,
  And are to be so, at the least, once more;—
The door was fastened, but with voice and fist
First knocks were heard, then "Madam—Madam—hist!

1085

CXXXVII

"For God's sake, Madam—Madam—here's my master,
  With more than half the city at his back—
Was ever heard of such a curst disaster!
  'T is not my fault—I kept good watch—Alack!
Do pray undo the bolt a little faster—
  They 're on the stair just now, and in a crack
Will all be here; perhaps he yet may fly—
Surely the window 's not so very high!"

1090

1095

CXXXVIII

By this time Don Alfonso was arrived,
  With torches, friends, and servants in great number;
The major part of them had long been wived,
  And therefore paused not to disturb the slumber

1100

Of any wicked woman, who contrived
  By stealth her husband's temples to encumber:
Examples of this kind are so contagious,
Were *one* not punished, *all* would be outrageous.

CXXXIX

I can't tell how, or why, or what suspicion   1105
  Could enter into Don Alfonso's head;
But for a cavalier of his condition
  It surely was exceedingly ill-bred,
Without a word of previous admonition,
  To hold a levee round his lady's bed,   1110
And summon lackeys, armed with fire and sword,
To prove himself the thing he most abhorred.

CXL

Poor Donna Julia! starting as from sleep
  (Mind—that I do not say—she had not slept),
Began at once to scream, and yawn, and weep;   1115
  Her maid, Antonia, who was an adept,
Contrived to fling the bed-clothes in a heap,
  As if she had just now from out them crept:
I can't tell why she should take all this trouble
To prove her mistress had been sleeping double.   1120

CXLI

But Julia mistress, and Antonia maid,
  Appeared like two poor harmless women, who
Of goblins, but still more of men afraid,
  Had thought one man might be deterred by two,
And therefore side by side were gently laid,   1125
  Until the hours of absence should run through,
And truant husband should return, and say,
"My dear, I was the first who came away."

CXLII

Now Julia found at length a voice, and cried,
  "In heaven's name, Don Alfonso, what d' ye mean?   1130
Has madness seized you? would that I had died
  Ere such a monster's victim I had been!
What may this midnight violence betide,
  A sudden fit of drunkenness or spleen?
Dare you suspect me, whom the thought would kill?   1135
Search, then, the room!"—Alfonso said, "I will."

CXLIII

He searched, *they* searched, and rummaged everywhere,
  Closet and clothes-press, chest and window-seat.
And found much linen, lace, and several pair
  Of stockings, slippers, brushes, combs, complete,   1140
With other articles of ladies fair,
  To keep them beautiful, or leave them neat:
Arras they pricked and curtains with their swords,
And wounded several shutters, and some boards.

CXLIV

Under the bed they searched, and there they found—   1145
  No matter what—it was not that they sought;
They opened windows, gazing if the ground
  Had signs of footmarks, but the earth said nought;

And then they stared each other's faces round:
    'T is odd, not one of all these seekers thought,
And seems to me almost a sort of blunder,
Of looking *in* the bed as well as under.   1150

CXLV

During this inquisition Julia's tongue
    Was not asleep—"Yes, search and search," she cried,
"Insult on insult heap, and wrong on wrong!
    It was for this that I became a bride!   1155
For this in silence I have suffered long
    A husband like Alfonso at my side;
But now I 'll bear no more, nor here remain,
If there be law or lawyers in all Spain.   1160

CXLVI

"Yes, Don Alfonso! husband now no more.
    If ever you indeed deserved the name,
Is 't worthy of your years?—you have three-score—
    Fifty, or sixty, it is all the same—
Is 't wise or fitting, causeless to explore   1165
    For facts against a virtuous woman's fame?
Ungrateful, perjured, barbarous Don Alfonso,
How dare you think your lady would go on so?

CXLVII

"Is it for this I have disdained to hold
    The common privileges of my sex?   1170
That I have chosen a confessor so old
    And deaf, that any other it would vex,
And never once he has had cause to scold,
    But found my very innocence perplex
So much, he always doubted I was married—   1175
How sorry you will be when I 've miscarried!

CXLVIII

"Was it for this that no Cortejo e'er
    I yet have chosen from out the youth of Seville?
Is it for this I scarce went anywhere,
    Except to bull-fights, mass, play, rout, and revel?   1180
Is it for this, whate'er my suitors were,
    I favored none—nay, was almost uncivil?
Is it for this that General Count O'Reilly,
Who took Algiers, declares I used him vilely?

CXLIX

"Did not the Italian Musico Cazzani   1185
    Sing at my heart six months at least in vain?
Did not his countryman, Count Corniani,
    Call me the only virtuous wife in Spain?
Were there not also Russians, English, many?
    The Count Strongstroganoff I put in pain,   1190
And Lord Mount Coffeehouse, the Irish peer,
Who killed himself for love (with wine) last year.

CL

"Have I not had two bishops at my feet?
    The Duke of Ichar, and Don Fernan Nunez?
And is it thus a faithful wife you treat?   1195
    I wonder in what quarter now the moon is:

I praise your vast forbearance not to beat
  Me also, since the time so opportune is—
Oh, valiant man! with sword drawn and cocked trigger,
Now, tell me, don't you cut a pretty figure?   1200

CLI

"Was it for this you took your sudden journey,
  Under pretence of business indispensable,
With that sublime of rascals your attorney,
  Whom I see standing there, and looking sensible
Of having played the fool? though both I spurn, he   1205
  Deserves the worst, his conduct 's less defensible,
Because, no doubt, 't was for his dirty fee,
And not from any love to you nor me.

CLII

"If he comes here to take a deposition,
  By all means let the gentleman proceed;   1210
You 've made the apartment in a fit condition:—
  There 's pen and ink for you, sir, when you need—
Let everything be noted with precision,
  I would not you for nothing should be fee'd—
But as my maid 's undrest, pray turn your spies out."   1215
"Oh!" sobbed Antonia, "I could tear their eyes out."

CLIII

"There is the closet, there is the toilet, there
  The antechamber—search them under, over;
There is the sofa, there the great arm-chair,
  The chimney—which would really hold a lover.   1220
I wish to sleep, and beg you will take care
  And make no further noise, till you discover
The secret cavern of this lurking treasure—
And when 't is found, let me, too, have that pleasure.

CLIV

"And now, Hidalgo! now that you have thrown   1225
  Doubt upon me, confusion over all,
Pray have the courtesy to make it known
  Who is the man you search for? how d' ye call
Him? what 's his lineage? let him but be shown—
  I hope he 's young and handsome—is he tall?   1230
Tell me—and be assured, that since you stain
Mine honor thus, it shall not be in vain.

CLV

"At least, perhaps, he has not sixty years,
  At that age he would be too old for slaughter
Or for so young a husband's jealous fears—   1235
  (Antonia! let me have a glass of water.)
I am ashamed of having shed these tears,
  They are unworthy of my father's daughter;
My mother dreamed not in my natal hour,
That I should fall into a monster's power.   1240

CLVI

"Perhaps 't is of Antonia you are jealous.
  You saw that she was sleeping by my side,
When you broke in upon us with your fellows;
  Look where you please—we 've nothing, sir, to hide;

Only another time, I trust, you 'll tell us,   1245
  Or for the sake of decency abide
A moment at the door, that we may be
Dressed to receive so much good company.

CLVII

"And now, sir, I have done, and say no more;
  The little I have said may serve to show   1250
The guileless heart in silence may grieve o'er
  The wrongs to whose exposure it is slow:—
I leave you to your conscience as before,
  'T will one day ask you, *why* you used me so?
God grant you feel not then the bitterest grief!   1255
Antonia! where 's my pocket-handkerchief?"

CLVIII

She ceased, and turned upon her pillow; pale
  She lay, her dark eyes flashing through their tears,
Like skies that rain and lighten; as a veil,
  Waved and o'ershading her wan cheek, appears   1260
Her streaming hair; the black curls strive, but fail,
  To hide the glossy shoulder, which uprears
Its snow through all;—her soft lips lie apart,
And louder than her breathing beats her heart.

CLIX

The Senhor Don Alfonso stood confused;   1265
  Antonia bustled round the ransacked room,
And, turning up her nose, with looks abused
  Her master, and his myrmidons, of whom
Not one, except the attorney, was amused;
  He, like Achates, faithful to the tomb,   1270
So there were quarrels, cared not for the cause,
Knowing they must be settled by the laws.

CLX

With prying snub-nose, and small eyes, he stood,
  Following Antonia's motions here and there,
With much suspicion in his attitude;   1275
  For reputations he had little care;
So that a suit or action were made good,
  Small pity had he for the young and fair,
And ne'er believed in negatives, till these
Were proved by competent false witnesses.   1280

CLXI

But Don Alfonso stood with downcast looks,
  And, truth to say, he made a foolish figure;
When, after searching in five hundred nooks,
  And treating a young wife with so much rigor,
He gained no point, except some self-rebukes,   1285
  Added to those his lady with such vigor
Had poured upon him for the last half hour,
Quick, thick, and heavy—as a thunder-shower.

CLXII

At first he tried to hammer an excuse,
  To which the sole reply was tears and sobs,   1290
And indications of hysterics, whose
  Prologue is always certain throes, and throbs,

Gasps, and whatever else the owners choose:
　　Alfonso saw his wife, and thought of Job's;
He saw too, in perspective, her relations,
　　And then he tried to muster all his patience. 　　　　　　　1295

CLXIII

He stood in act to speak, or rather stammer,
　　But sage Antonia cut him short before
The anvil of his speech received the hammer,
　　With "Pray, sir, leave the room and say no more, 　　　　1300
Or madam dies."—Alfonso muttered, "D—n her."
　　But nothing else, the time of words was o'er;
He cast a rueful look or two, and did,
He knew not wherefore, that which he was bid.

CLXIV

With him retired his *"posse comitatus,"* 　　　　　　　　　1305
　　The attorney last, who lingered near the door
Reluctantly, still tarrying there as late as
　　Antonia let him—not a little sore
At this most strange and unexplained *"hiatus"*
　　In Don Alfonso's facts, which just now wore 　　　　　　1310
An awkward look; as he revolved the case,
The door was fastened in his legal face.

CLXV

No sooner was it bolted, than—Oh shame!
　　Oh sin! Oh sorrow! and Oh womankind!
How can you do such things and keep your fame, 　　　　　1315
　　Unless this world, and t' other too, be blind?
Nothing so dear as an unfilched good name!
　　But to proceed—for there is more behind:
With much heartfelt reluctance be it said,
Young Juan slipped, half-smothered, from the bed. 　　　　　1320

CLXVI

He had been hid—I don't pretend to say
　　How, nor can I indeed describe the where—
Young, slender, and packed easily, he lay,
　　No doubt, in little compass, round or square;
But pity him I neither must nor may 　　　　　　　　　　1325
　　His suffocation by that pretty pair;
'T were better, sure, to die so, than be shut
With maudlin Clarence in his Malmsey butt.

CLXVII

And, secondly, I pity not, because
　　He had no business to commit a sin, 　　　　　　　　1330
Forbid by heavenly, fined by human laws,
　　At least 't was rather early to begin;
But at sixteen the conscience rarely gnaws
　　So much as when we call our old debts in
At sixty years, and draw the accompts of evil, 　　　　　　1335
And find a deuced balance with the devil.

CLXVIII

Of his position I can give no notion:
　　'T is written in the Hebrew Chronicle,
How the physicians, leaving pill and potion,
　　Prescribed, by way of blister, a young belle, 　　　　　1340

When old King David's blood grew dull in motion,
  And that the medicine answered very well;
Perhaps 't was in a different way applied,
For David lived, but Juan nearly died.

CLXIX

What 's to be done? Alfonso will be back   1345
  The moment he has sent his fools away.
Antonia's skill was put upon the rack,
  But no device could be brought into play—
And how to parry the renewed attack?
  Besides, it wanted but few hours of day: 1350
Antonia puzzled; Julia did not speak,
But pressed her bloodless lip to Juan's cheek.

CLXX

He turned his lip to hers, and with his hand
  Called back the tangles of her wandering hair;
Even then their love they could not all command,   1355
  And half forgot their danger and despair:
Antonia's patience now was at a stand—
  "Come, come, 't is no time now for fooling there,"
She whispered in great wrath—"I must deposit
This pretty gentleman within the closet: 1360

CLXXI

"Pray, keep your nonsense for some luckier night—
  Who can have put my master in this mood?
What will become on 't—I 'm in such a fright.
  The devil's in the urchin, and no good—
Is this a time for giggling? this a plight?   1365
  Why, don't you know that it may end in blood?
You 'll lose your life, and I shall lose my place,
My mistress all, for that half-girlish face.

CLXXII

"Had it but been for a stout cavalier
  Of twenty-five or thirty—(come, make haste)   1370
But for a child, what piece of work is here!
  I really, madam, wonder at your taste—
(Come, sir, get in)—my master must be near:
  There, for the present, at the least, he's fast,
And if we can but till the morning keep   1375
Our counsel—(Juan, mind, you must not sleep)."

CLXXIII

Now, Don Alfonso entering, but alone,
  Closed the oration of the trusty maid:
She loitered, and he told her to be gone,
  An order somewhat sullenly obeyed;   1380
However, present remedy was none,
  And no great good seemed answered if she staid;
Regarding both with slow and sidelong view,
She snuffed the candle, curtsied, and withdrew.

CLXXIV

Alfonso paused a minute—then begun   1385
  Some strange excuses for his late proceeding:
He would not justify what he had done,
  To say the best, it was extreme ill-breeding;

But there were ample reasons for it, none
  Of which he specified in this his pleading: 1390
His speech was a fine sample, on the whole,
  Of rhetoric, which the learned call *"rigmarole."*

CLXXV

Julia said nought; though all the while there rose
  A ready answer, which at once enables
A matron, who her husband's foible knows,   1395
  By a few timely words to turn the tables,
Which, if it does not silence, still must pose,—
  Even if it should comprise a pack of fables;
'T is to retort with firmness, and when he
Suspects with *one*, do you reproach with *three*.   1400

CLXXVI

Julia, in fact, had tolerable grounds,—
  Alfonso's loves with Inez were well known;
But whether 't was that one's own guilt confounds—
  But that can't be, as has been often shown,
A lady with apologies abounds;—   1405
  It might be that her silence sprang alone
From delicacy to Don Juan's ear,
To whom she knew his mother's fame was dear.

CLXXVII

There might be one more motive, which makes two,
  Alfonso ne'er to Juan had alluded,—   1410
Mentioned his jealousy, but never who
  Had been the happy lover, he concluded,
Concealed amongst his premises; 't is true,
  His mind the more o'er this its mystery brooded
To speak of Inez now were, one may say,   1415
Like throwing Juan in Alfonso's way.

CLXXVIII

A hint, in tender cases, is enough;
  Silence is best: besides there is a *tact*—
(That modern phrase appears to me sad stuff,
  But it will serve to keep my verse compact)—   1420
Which keeps, when pushed by questions rather rough,
  A lady always distant from the fact:
The charming creatures lie with such a grace,
There's nothing so becoming to the face.

CLXXIX

They blush, and we believe them, at least I   1425
  Have always done so; 't is of no great use,
In any case, attempting a reply,
  For then their eloquence grows quite profuse;
And when at length they're out of breath, they sigh,
  And cast their languid eyes down, and let loose   1430
A tear or two, and then we make it up;
And then—and then—and then—sit down and sup.

CLXXX

Alfonso closed his speech, and begged her pardon,
  Which Julia half withheld, and then half granted,
And laid conditions, he thought very hard, on,   1435
  Denying several little things he wanted:

He stood like Adam lingering near his garden,
  With useless penitence perplexed and haunted,
Beseeching she no further would refuse,
When, lo! he stumbled o'er a pair of shoes.   1440

CLXXXI

A pair of shoes!—what then? not much, if they
  Are such as fit with ladies' feet, but these
(No one can tell how much I grieve to say)
  Were masculine; to see them, and to seize,
Was but a moment's act.—Ah! well-a-day!   1445
  My teeth begin to chatter, my veins freeze—
Alfonso first examined well their fashion,
And then flew out into another passion.

CLXXXII

He left the room for his relinquished sword,
  And Julia instant to the closet flew.   1450
"Fly, Juan, fly; for heaven's sake—not a word—
  The door is open—you may yet slip through
The passage you so often have explored—
  Here is the garden-key—Fly—fly—Adieu!
Haste—haste! I hear Alfonso's hurrying feet—   1455
Day has not broke—there's no one in the street."

CLXXXIII

None can say that this was not good advice.
  The only mischief was, it came too late;
Of all experience 't is the usual price,
  A sort of income-tax laid on by fate: 1460
Juan had reached the room-door in a trice,
  And might have done so by the garden-gate,
But met Alfonso in his dressing-gown,
Who threatened death—so Juan knocked him down.

CLXXXIV

Dire was the scuffle, and out went the light;   1465
  Antonia cried out "Rape!" and Julia "Fire!"
But not a servant stirred to aid the fight.
  Alfonso, pommelled to his heart's desire,
Swore lustily he 'd be revenged this night;
  And Juan, too, blasphemed an octave higher;   1470
His blood was up: though young, he was a Tartar,
And not at all disposed to prove a martyr.

CLXXXV

Alfonso's sword had dropped ere he could draw it,
  And they continued battling hand to hand,
For Juan very luckily ne'er saw it;   1475
  His temper not being under great command,
If at that moment he had chanced to claw it,
  Alfonso's days had not been in the land
Much longer.—Think of husbands', lovers' lives!
And how ye may be doubly widows—wives!   1480

CLXXXVI

Alfonso grappled to detain the foe,
  And Juan throttled him to get away,
And blood ('t was from the nose) began to flow;
  At last, as they more faintly wrestling lay,

Juan contrived to give an awkward blow,   1485
  And then his only garment quite gave way;
He fled, like Joseph, leaving it; but there,
I doubt, all likeness ends between the pair.

CLXXXVII

Lights came at length, and men, and maids, who found
  An awkward spectacle their eyes before;   1490
Antonia in hysterics, Julia swooned,
  Alfonso leaning, breathless, by the door;
Some half-torn drapery scattered on the ground,
  Some blood, and several footsteps, but no more:
Juan the gate gained, turned the key about,   1495
And liking not the inside, locked the out.

CLXXXVIII

Here ends this canto.—Need I sing, or say,
  How Juan, naked, favored by the night,
Who favors what she should not, found his way,
  And reached his home in an unseemly plight?   1500
The pleasant scandal which arose next day,
  The nine days' wonder which was brought to light,
And how Alfonso sued for a divorce,
Were in the English newspapers, of course.

CLXXXIX

If you would like to see the whole proceedings,   1505
  The depositions and the cause at full,
The names of all the witnesses, the pleadings
  Of counsel to nonsuit, or to annul,
There 's more than one edition, and the readings
  Are various, but they none of them are dull;   1510
The best is that in short-hand ta'en by Gurney,
Who to Madrid on purpose made a journey.

CXC

But Donna Inez, to divert the train
  Of one of the most circulating scandals
That had for centuries been known in Spain,
  At least since the retirement of the Vandals,   1515
First vowed (and never had she vowed in vain)
  To Virgin Mary several pounds of candles;
And then, by the advice of some old ladies,
She sent her son to be shipped off from Cadiz.   1520

CXCI

She had resolved that he should travel through
  All European climes, by land or sea,
To mend his former morals, and get new,
  Especially in France and Italy
(At least this is the thing most people do).   1525
  Julia was sent into a convent: she
Grieved, but, perhaps, her feelings may be better
Shown in the following copy of her Letter:—

CXCII

"They tell me 't is decided you depart:
  'T is wise—'t is well, but not the less a pain;   1530
I have no further claim on your young heart,
  Mine is the victim, and would be again:

To love too much has been the only art
  I used;—I write in haste, and if a stain
Be on this sheet, 't is not what it appears;
My eyeballs burn and throb, but have no tears.

CXCIII

"I loved, I love you, for this love have lost
  State, station, heaven, mankind's, my own esteem,
And yet cannot regret what it hath cost,
  So dear is still the memory of that dream;
Yet, if I name my guilt, 't is not to boast,
  None can deem harshlier of me than I deem:
I trace this scrawl because I cannot rest—
I 've nothing to reproach or to request.

CXCIV

"Man's love is of man's life a thing apart,
  'T is woman's whole existence; man may range
The court, camp, church, the vessel, and the mart;
  Sword, gown, gain, glory, offer in exchange
Pride, fame, ambition, to fill up his heart,
  And few there are whom these cannot estrange;
Men have all these resources, we but one,
To love again, and be again undone.

CXCV

"You will proceed in pleasure, and in pride,
  Beloved and loving many; all is o'er
For me on earth, except some years to hide
  My shame and sorrow deep in my heart's core:
These I could bear, but cannot cast aside
  The passion which still rages as before,—
And so farewell—forgive me, love me—No,
That word is idle now—but let it go.

CXCVI

"My breast has been all weakness, is so yet;
  But still I think I can collect my mind;
My blood still rushes where my spirit 's set,
  As roll the waves before the settled wind;
My heart is feminine, nor can forget—
  To all, except one image, madly blind;
So shakes the needle, and so stands the pole,
As vibrates my fond heart to my fixed soul.

CXCVII

"I have no more to say, but linger still,
  And dare not set my seal upon this sheet,
And yet I may as well the task fulfil,
  My misery can scarce be more complete:
I had not lived till now, could sorrow kill;
  Death shuns the wretch who fain the blow would meet,
And I must even survive this last adieu,
And' bear with life to love and pray for you!"

CXCVIII

This note was written upon gilt-edged paper
  With a neat little crow-quill, slight and new;
Her small white hand could hardly reach the taper,
  It trembled as magnetic needles do,

1535

1540

1545

1550

1555

1560

1̠565

1570

1575

⁊580

And yet she did not let one tear escape her:
  The seal a sun-flower; *"Elle vous suit partout,"*
The motto, cut upon a white cornelian;
  The wax was superfine, its hue vermilion.

CXCIX

This was Don Juan's earliest scrape; but whether   1585
  I shall proceed with his adventures is
Dependent on the public altogether;
  We 'll see, however, what they say to this,
Their favor in an author's cap 's a feather,
  And no great mischief 's done by their caprice;   1590
And if their approbation we experience,
Perhaps they 'll have some more about a year hence.

CC

My poem 's epic, and is meant to be
  Divided in twelve books; each book containing,
With love, and war, a heavy gale at sea,   1595
  A list of ships, and captains, and kings reigning,
New characters; the episodes are three:
  A panoramic view of hell 's in training
After the style of Virgil and of Homer,
So that my name of Epic 's no misnomer.   1600

CCI

All these things will be specified in time,
  With strict regard to Aristotle's rules,
The *Vade Mecum* of the true sublime,
  Which makes so many poets, and some fools:
Prose poets like blank-verse, I 'm fond of rhyme,   1605
  Good workmen never quarrel with their tools;
I 've got new mythological machinery,
And very handsome supernatural scenery.

CCII

There 's only one slight difference between
  Me and my epic brethren gone before,   1610
And here the advantage is my own, I ween
  (Not that I have not several merits more,
But this will more peculiarly be seen);
  They so embellish, that 't is quite a bore
Their labyrinth of fables to thread through,   1615
Whereas this story 's actually true.

CCIII

If any person doubt it, I appeal
  To history, tradition, and to facts,
To newspapers, whose truth all know and feel,
  To plays in five, and operas in three acts: 1620
All these confirm my statement a good deal,
  But that which more completely faith exacts
Is, that myself, and several now in Seville,
Saw Juan's last elopement with the devil.

CCIV

If ever I should condescend to prose,   1625
  I 'll write poetical commandments, which
Shall supersede beyond all doubt all those
  That went before; in these I shall enrich
My text with many things that no one knows,
  And carry precept to the highest pitch: 1630

I 'll call the work "Longinus o'er a Bottle,
Or, Every Poet his *own* Aristotle."

CCV

Thou shalt believe in Milton, Dryden, Pope;
  Thou shalt not set up Wordsworth, Coleridge, Southey;
Because the first is crazed beyond all hope,   1635
  The second drunk, the third so quaint and mouthy:
With Crabbe it may be difficult to cope,
  And Campbell's Hippocrene is somewhat drouthy:
Thou shalt not steal from Samuel Rogers, nor
Commit—flirtation with the muse of Moore.   1640

CCVI

Thou shalt not covet Mr. Sotheby's Muse,
  His Pegasus, nor anything that 's his;
Thou shalt not bear false witness like "the Blues"—
  (There 's one, at least, is very fond of this);
Thou shalt not write, in short, but what I choose;   1645
  This is true criticism, and you may kiss—
Exactly as you please, or not,—the rod;
And if you don't, I'll lay it on, by G—d!

CCVII

If any person should presume to assert
  This story is not moral, first, I pray,   1650
That they will not cry out before they 're hurt,
  Then that they 'll read it o'er again, and say
(But, doubtless, nobody will be so pert),
  That this is not a moral tale, though gay;
Besides, in Canto Twelfth, I mean to show,   1655
The very place where wicked people go.

CCVIII

If, after all, there should be some so blind
  To their own good this warning to despise,
Led by some tortuosity of mind,
  Not to believe my verse and their own eyes,   1660
And cry that they "the moral cannot find,"
  I tell him, if a clergyman, he lies;
Should captains the remark, or critics, make,
They also lie too—under a mistake.

CCIX

The public approbation I expect,   1665
  And beg they 'll take my word about the moral,
Which I with their amusement will connect
  (So children cutting teeth receive a coral);
Meantime they 'll doubtless please to recollect
  My epical pretensions to the laurel: 1670
For fear some prudish readers should grow skittish,
I 've bribed my grandmother's review—the British.

CCX

I sent it in a letter to the Editor,
  Who thanked me duly by return of post—
I'm for a handsome article his creditor;   1675
  Yet, if my gentle Muse he please to roast,
And break a promise after having made it her,
  Denying the receipt of what it cost,
And smear his page with gall instead of honey,
All I can say is—that he had the money.   1680

CCXI

I think that with this holy new alliance
    I may ensure the public, and defy
All other magazines of art or science,
    Daily, or monthly, or three monthly; I
Have not essayed to multiply their clients,   1685
    Because they tell me 't were in vain to try,
And that the Edinburgh Review and Quarterly
Treat a dissenting author very martyrly.

CCXII

"*Non ego hoc ferrem calida juventâ*
    Consule Planco," Horace said, and so   1690
Say I; by which quotation there is meant a
    Hint that some six or seven good years ago
(Long ere I dreamt of dating from the Brenta)
    I was most ready to return a blow,
And would not brook at all this sort of thing   1695
In my hot youth—when George the Third was King.

CCXIII

But now at thirty years my hair is gray—
    (I wonder what it will be like at forty?
I thought of a peruke the other day—)
    My heart is not much greener; and, in short, I   1700
Have squandered my whole summer while 't was May,
    And feel no more the spirit to retort; I
Have spent my life, both interest and principal,
And deem not, what I deemed, my soul invincible.

CCXIV

No more—no more—Oh! never more on me   1705
    The freshness of the heart can fall like dew,
Which out of all the lovely things we see
    Extracts emotions beautiful and new;
Hived in our bosoms like the bag o' the bee.
    Think'st thou the honey with those objects grew?   1710
Alas! 't was not in them, but in thy power
To double even the sweetness of a flower.

CCXV

No more—no more—Oh! never more, my heart,
    Canst thou be my sole world, my universe!
Once all in all, but now a thing apart,   1715
    Thou canst not be my blessing or my curse:
The illusion 's gone for ever, and thou art
    Insensible, I trust, but none the worse,
And in thy stead I 've got a deal of judgment
Though heaven knows how it ever found a lodgment.   1720

CCXVI

My days of love are over; me no more
    The charms of maid, wife, and still less of widow,
Can make the fool of which they made before,—
    In short, I must not lead the life I did do;
The credulous hope of mutual minds is o'er,   1725
    The copious use of claret is forbid too,
So for a good old-gentlemanly vice,
I think I must take up with avarice.

CCXVII

Ambition was my idol, which was broken
  Before the shrines of Sorrow, and of Pleasure;
And the two last have left me many a token
  O'er which reflection may be made at leisure;
Now, like Friar Bacon's brazen head, I 've spoken
  "Time is, Time was, Time 's past":—a chymic treasure
Is glittering youth, which I have spent betimes—
My heart in passion, and my head on rhymes.

CCXVIII

What is the end of fame? 't is but to fill
  A certain portion of uncertain paper:
Some liken it to climbing up a hill,
  Whose summit, like all hills, is lost in vapor;
For this men write, speak, preach, and heroes kill,
  And bards burn what they call their "midnight taper,"
To have, when the original is dust,
A name, a wretched picture, and worse bust.

CCXIX

What are the hopes of man? Old Egypt's King
  Cheops erected the first pyramid
And largest, thinking it was just the thing
  To keep his memory whole, and mummy hid:
But somebody or other rummaging,
  Burglariously broke his coffin's lid
Let not a monument give you or me hopes,
Since not a pinch of dust remains of Cheops.

CCXX

But I, being fond of true philosophy,
  Say very often to myself, "Alas!
All things that have been born were born to die,
  And flesh (which Death mows down to hay) is grass;
You 've passed your youth not so unpleasantly,
  And if you had it o'er again—'t would pass—
So thank your stars that matters are no worse,
And read your Bible, sir, and mind your purse."

CCXXI

But for the present, gentle reader! and
  Still gentler purchaser! the bard—that 's I—
Must, with permission, shake you by the hand,
  And so your humble servant, and good-bye!
We meet again, if we should understand
  Each other; and if not, I shall not try
Your patience further than by this short sample—
'T were well if others followed my example.

CCXXII

"Go, little book, from this my solitude!
  I cast thee on the waters—go thy ways!
And if, as I believe, thy vein be good,
  The world will find thee after many days."
When Southey's read, and Wordsworth understood,
  I can't help putting in my claim to praise—
The four first rhymes are Southey's, every line:
For God's sake, reader! take them not for mine!

1819

1730

1735

1740

1745

1750

1755

1760

1765

1770

1775

CANTO THE SECOND

[HIS SHIPWRECK AND HAIDÉE]

XLIV

The ship was evidently settling now　　　　　　　　　345
　　Fast by the head; and, all distinction gone,
Some went to prayers again, and made a vow
　　Of candles to their saints—but there were none
To pay them with! and some looked o'er the bow;
　　Some hoisted out the boats; and there was one　　350
That begged Pedrillo for an absolution,
Who told him to be damned—in his confusion.

XLV

Some lashed them in their hammocks; some put on
　　Their best clothes, as if going to a fair;
Some cursed the day on which they saw the sun,　　355
　　And gnashed their teeth, and howling, tore their hair;
And others went on as they had begun,
　　Getting the boats out, being well aware
That a tight boat will live in a rough sea,
Unless with breakers close beneath her lee.　　　360

XLVI

The worst of all was, that in their condition,
　　Having been several days in great distress,
'Twas difficult to get out such provision
　　As now might render their long suffering less:
Men, even when dying, dislike inanition;　　　365
　　Their stock was damaged by the weather's stress:
Two casks of biscuits, and a keg of butter,
Were all that could be thrown into the cutter.

XLVII

But in the long-boat they contrived to stow
　　Some pounds of bread, though injured by the wet:
Water, a twenty-gallon cask or so;　　　　370
　　Six flasks of wine; and they contrived to get
A portion of their beef up from below,
　　And with a piece of pork, moreover, met,
But scarce enough to serve them for a luncheon—　　375
Then there was rum, eight gallons in a puncheon.

XLVIII

The other boats, the yawl and pinnace, had
　　Been stove in the beginning of the gale;
And the long-boat's condition was but bad,
　　As there were but two blankets for a sail,　　　380
And one oar for a mast, which a young lad
　　Threw in by good luck over the ship's rail;
And two boats could not hold, far less be stored,
To save one half the people then on board.

XLIX

'Twas twilight, and the sunless day went down　　385
　　Over the waste of waters; like a veil,
Which, if withdrawn, would but disclose the frown
　　Of one whose hate is masked but to assail.

Thus to their hopeless eyes the night was shown,
   And grimly darkled o'er the faces pale,
And the dim desolate deep: twelve days had Fear   390
Been their familiar, and now Death was here.

L

Some trial had been making at a raft,
   With little hope in such a rolling sea,
A sort of thing at which one would have laughed,   395
   If any laughter at such times could be,
Unless with people who too much have quaffed,
   And have a kind of wild and horrid glee,
Half epileptical, and half hysterical:—
Their preservation would have been a miracle.   400

LI

At half-past eight o'clock, booms, hencoops, spars
   And all things, for a chance, had been cast loose
That still could keep afloat the struggling tars,
   For yet they strove, although of no great use:
There was no light in heaven but a few stars,   405
   The boats put off o'ercrowded with their crews;
She gave a heel, and then a lurch to port,
And, going down head foremost—sunk, in short.

LII

Then rose from sea to sky the wild farewell—
   Then shrieked the timid, and stood still the brave—   410
Then some leaped overboard with dreadful yell,
   As eager to anticipate their grave;
And the sea yawned around her like a hell,
   And down she sucked with her the whirling wave,
Like one who grapples with his enemy,   415
And strives to strangle him before he die.

LIII

And first one universal shriek there rushed,
   Louder than the loud ocean, like a crash
Of echoing thunder; and then all was hushed,
   Save the wild wind and the remorseless dash   420
Of billows; but at intervals there gushed,
   Accompanied by a convulsive splash,
A solitary shriek, the bubbling cry
Of some strong swimmer in his agony.

LIV

The boats, as stated, had got off before,   425
   And in them crowded several of the crew;
And yet their present hope was hardly more
   Than what it had been, for so strong it blew
There was slight chance of reaching any shore;
   And then they were too many, though so few—   430
Nine in the cutter, thirty in the boat,
Were counted in them when they got afloat.

    . . . .

LXII

The sun rose red and fiery, a sure sign
   Of the continuance of the gale: to run   490
Before the sea until it should grow fine,
   Was all that for the present could be done:

A few tea-spoonfuls of their rum and wine
   Were served out to the people, who begun
To faint, and damaged bread wet through the bags,   495
   And most of them had little clothes but rags.

LXIII

They counted thirty, crowded in a space
   Which left scarce room for motion or exertion;
They did their best to modify their case,
   One half sate up, though numbed with the immersion,   500
While t' other half were laid down in their place,
   At watch and watch; thus, shivering like the tertian
Ague in its cold fit, they filled their boat,
With nothing but the sky for a great coat.

LXIV

'T is very certain the desire of life   505
   Prolongs it: this is obvious to physicians,
When patients, neither plagued with friends nor wife,
   Survive through very desperate conditions,
Because they still can hope, nor shines the knife
   Nor shears of Atropos before their visions: 510
Despair of all recovery spoils longevity,
And makes men's miseries of alarming brevity.

LXV

'T is said that persons living on annuities
   Are longer lived than others,—God knows why,
Unless to plague the grantors,—yet so true it is,   515
   That some, I really think, *do* never die;
Of any creditors the worst a Jew it is,
   And *that* 's their mode of furnishing supply:
In my young days they lent me cash that way,
Which I found very troublesome to pay.   520

LXVI

'T is thus with people in an open boat,
   They live upon the love of life, and bear
More than can be believed, or even thought,
   And stand like rocks the tempest's wear and tear;
And hardship still has been the sailor's lot,   525
   Since Noah's ark went cruising here and there;
She had a curious crew as well as cargo,
Like the first old Greek privateer, the Argo.

LXVII

But man is a carnivorous production,
   And must have meals, at least one meal a day;   530
He cannot live, like woodcocks, upon suction,
   But, like the shark and tiger, must have prey;
Although his anatomical construction
   Bears vegetables, in a grumbling way,
Your laboring people think beyond all question   535
Beef, veal, and mutton, better for digestion.

LXVIII

And thus it was with this our hapless crew;
   For on the third day there came on a calm,
And though at first their strength it might renew,
   And lying on their weariness like balm,   540

Lulled them like turtles sleeping on the blue
  Of ocean, when they woke they felt a qualm,
And fell all ravenously on their provision,
Instead of hoarding it with due precision.

LXIX

The consequence was easily foreseen—   545
  They ate up all they had, and drank their wine,
In spite of all remonstrances, and then
  On what, in fact, next day were they to dine?
They hoped the wind would rise, these foolish men!
  And carry them to shore; these hopes were fine,   550
But as they had but one oar, and that brittle,
It would have been more wise to save their victual.

LXX

The fourth day came, but not a breath of air,
  And Ocean slumbered like an unweaned child:
The fifth day, and their boat lay floating there,   555
  The sea and sky were blue, and clear, and mild—
With their one oar (I wish they had had a pair)
  What could they do? and hunger's rage grew wild:
So Juan's spaniel, spite of his entreating,
Was killed, and portioned out for present eating.   560

LXXI

On the sixth day they fed upon his hide,
  And Juan, who had still refused, because
The creature was his father's dog that died,
  Now feeling all the vulture in his jaws,
With some remorse received (though first denied)   565
  As a great favor one of the fore-paws,
Which he divided with Pedrillo, who
Devoured it, longing for the other too.

LXXII

The seventh day, and no wind—the burning sun
  Blistered and scorched, and, stagnant on the sea,   570
They lay like carcasses; and hope was none,
  Save in the breeze that came not: savagely
They glared upon each other—all was done,
  Water, and wine, and food,—and you might see
The longings of the cannibal arise   575
(Although they spoke not) in their wolfish eyes.

LXXIII

At length one whispered his companion, who
  Whispered another, and thus it went round,
And then into a hoarser murmur grew,
  An ominous, and wild, and desperate sound;   580
And when his comrade's thought each sufferer knew,
  'T was but his own, suppressed till now, he found:
And out they spoke of lots for flesh and blood,
And who should die to be his fellow's food.

LXXIV

But ere they came to this, they that day shared   585
  Some leathern caps, and what remained of shoes;
And then they looked around them, and despaired,
  And none to be the sacrifice would choose;

At length the lots were torn up, and prepared,
  But of materials that must shock the Muse—
Having no paper, for the want of better,
They took by force from Juan Julia's letter.   590

LXXV

Then lots were made, and marked, and mixed, and handed
  In silent horror, and their distribution
Lulled even the savage hunger which demanded,   595
  Like the Promethean vulture, this pollution;
None in particular had sought or planned it,
  'T was nature gnawed them to this resolution,
By which none were permitted to be neuter—
And the lot fell on Juan's luckless tutor.   600

LXXVI

He but requested to be bled to death:
  The surgeon had his instruments, and bled
Pedrillo, and so gently ebbed his breath,
  You hardly could perceive when he was dead.
He died as born, a Catholic in faith,   605
  Like most in the belief in which they 're bred,
And first a little crucifix he kissed,
And then held out his jugular and wrist.

LXXVII

The surgeon, as there was no other fee,
  Had his first choice of morsels for his pains;   610
But being thirstiest at the moment, he
  Preferred a draught from the fast-flowing veins:
Part was divided, part thrown in the sea,
  And such things as the entrails and the brains
Regaled two sharks, who followed o'er the billow—   615
The sailors ate the rest of poor Pedrillo.

LXXVIII

The sailors ate him, all save three or four,
  Who were not quite so fond of animal food;
To these was added Juan, who, before
  Refusing his own spaniel, hardly could   620
Feel now his appetite increased much more;
  'T was not to be expected that he should,
Even in extremity of their disaster,
Dine with them on his pastor and his master.

LXXIX

'T was better that he did not; for, in fact,   625
  The consequence was awful in the extreme;
For they, who were most ravenous in the act,
  Went raging mad—Lord! how they did blaspheme!
And foam, and roll, with strange convulsions racked,
  Drinking salt-water like a mountain-stream;   630
Tearing, and grinning, howling, screeching, swearing,
And, with hyæna-laughter, died despairing.

LXXX

Their numbers were much thinned by this infliction,
  And all the rest were thin enough, Heaven knows;
And some of them had lost their recollection,   635
  Happier than they who still perceived their woes;

But others pondered on a new dissection,
  As if not warned sufficiently by those
Who had already perished, suffering madly,
For having used their appetites so sadly.   640

LXXXI

And next they thought upon the master's mate,
  As fattest; but he saved himself, because,
Besides being much averse from such a fate,
  There were some other reasons: the first was,
He had been rather indisposed of late;   645
  And that which chiefly proved his saving clause,
Was a small present made to him at Cadiz,
By general subscription of the ladies.

LXXXII

Of poor Pedrillo something still remained,
  But was used sparingly,—some were afraid,   650
And others still their appetites constrained,
  Or but at times a little supper made;
All except Juan, who throughout abstained,
  Chewing a piece of bamboo, and some lead:
At length they caught two boobies, and a noddy,   655
And then they left off eating the dead body.

LXXXIII

And if Pedrillo's fate should shocking be,
  Remember Ugolino condescends
To eat the head of his arch-enemy
  The moment after he politely ends   660
His tale: if foes be food in hell, at sea
  'T is surely fair to dine upon our friends,
When shipwreck's short allowance grows too scanty,
Without being much more horrible than Dante.

LXXXIV

And the same night there fell a shower of rain,   665
  For which their mouths gaped, like the cracks of earth
When dried to summer dust; till taught by pain,
  Men really know not what good water's worth;
If you had been in Turkey or in Spain,
  Or with a famished boat's-crew had your berth,   670
Or in the desert heard the camel's bell,
You 'd wish yourself where Truth is—in a well.

LXXXV

It poured down torrents, but they were no richer,
  Until they found a ragged piece of sheet,
Which served them as a sort of spongy pitcher,   675
  And when they deemed its moisture was complete,
They wrung it out, and though a thirsty ditcher
  Might not have thought the scanty draught so sweet
As a full pot of porter, to their thinking
They ne'er till now had known the joys of drinking.   680

LXXXVI

And their baked lips, with many a bloody crack,
  Sucked in the moisture, which like nectar streamed;
Their throats were ovens, their swoln tongues were black
  As the rich man's in hell, who vainly screamed

To beg the beggar, who could not rain back
   A drop of dew, when every drop had seemed   685
To taste of heaven—If this be true, indeed,
Some Christians have a comfortable creed.

LXXXVII

There were two fathers in this ghastly crew,
   And with them their two sons, of whom the one   690
Was more robust and hardy to the view,
   But he died early; and when he was gone,
His nearest messmate told his sire, who threw
One glance at him, and said, "Heaven's will be done!
I can do nothing," and he saw him thrown   695
Into the deep without a tear or groan.

LXXXVIII

The other father had a weaklier child,
   Of a soft cheek, and aspect delicate;
But the boy bore up long, and with a mild
   And patient spirit held aloof his fate;
Little he said, and now and then he smiled,   700
   As if to win a part from off the weight
He saw increasing on his father's heart,
With the deep deadly thought, that they must part.

LXXXIX

And o'er him bent his sire, and never raised   705
   His eyes from off his face, but wiped the foam
From his pale lips, and ever on him gazed,
   And when the wished-for shower at length was come,
And the boy's eyes, which the dull film half glazed,
   Brightened, and for a moment seemed to roam,   710
He squeezed from out a rag some drops of rain
Into his dying child's mouth—but in vain.

XC

The boy expired—the father held the clay,
   And looked upon it long, and when at last
Death left no doubt, and the dead burthen lay   715
   Stiff on his heart, and pulse and hope were past,
He watched it wistfully, until away
   'T was borne by the rude wave wherein 't was cast;
Then he himself sunk down all dumb and shivering,
And gave no sign of life, save his limbs quivering.   720

XCI

Now overhead a rainbow, bursting through
   The scattering clouds, shone, spanning the dark sea,
Resting its bright base on the quivering blue;
   And all within its arch appeared to be
Clearer than that without, and its wide hue   725
   Waxed broad and waving, like a banner free,
Then changed like to a bow that 's bent, and then
Forsook the dim eyes of these shipwrecked men.

XCII

It changed, of course; a heavenly chameleon,
   The airy child of vapor and the sun,
Brought forth in purple, cradled in vermilion,   730
   Baptized in molten gold, and swathed in dun,

Glittering like crescents o'er a Turk's pavilion,
   And blending every color into one,
Just like a black eye in a recent scuffle 735
(For sometimes we must box without the muffle).

XCIII

Our shipwrecked seamen thought it a good omen—
   It is as well to think so, now and then;
'T was an old custom of the Greek and Roman,
   And may become of great advantage when 740
Folks are discouraged; and most surely no men
   Had greater need to nerve themselves again
Than these, and so this rainbow looked like hope—
Quite a celestial kaleidoscope.

XCIV

About this time a beautiful white bird, 745
   Web-footed, not unlike a dove in size
And plumage (probably it might have erred
   Upon its course), passed oft before their eyes,
And tried to perch, although it saw and heard
   The men within the boat, and in this guise 750
It came and went, and fluttered round them till
Night fell:—this seemed a better omen still.

XCV

But in this case I also must remark,
   'T was well this bird of promise did not perch,
Because the tackle of our shattered bark 755
   Was not so safe for roosting as a church;
And had it been the dove from Noah's ark,
   Returning there from her successful search,
Which in their way that moment chanced to fall,
They would have eat her, olive-branch and all. 760

XCVI

With twilight it again came on to blow,
   But not with violence; the stars shone out,
The boat made way; yet now they were so low,
   They knew not where nor what they were about;
Some fancied they saw land, and some said "No!" 765
   The frequent fog-banks gave them cause to doubt—
Some swore that they heard breakers, others guns,
And all mistook about the latter once.

XCVII

As morning broke, the light wind died away,
   When he who had the watch sung out and swore, 770
If 't was not land that rose with the sun's ray,
   He wished that land he never might see more:
And the rest rubbed their eyes, and saw a bay,
   Or thought they saw, and shaped their course for shore;
For shore it was, and gradually grew 775
Distinct, and high, and palpable to view.

XCVIII

And then of these some part burst into tears,
   And others, looking with a stupid stare,
Could not yet separate their hopes from fears,
   And seemed as if they had no further care; 780

While a few prayed—(the first time for some years)—
   And at the bottom of the boat three were
Asleep: they shook them by the hand and head,
And tried to awaken them, but found them dead.

XCIX

The day before, fast sleeping on the water,   785
   They found a turtle of the hawk's-bill kind,
And by good fortune, gliding softly, caught her,
   Which yielded a day's life, and to their mind
Proved even still a more nutritious matter,
   Because it left encouragement behind: 790
They thought that in such perils, more than chance
Had sent them this for their deliverance.

C

The land appeared a high and rocky coast,
   And higher grew the mountains as they drew,
Set by a current, toward it: they were lost   795
   In various conjectures, for none knew
To what part of the earth they had been tost,
   So changeable had been the winds that blew;
Some thought it was Mount Ætna, some the highlands
Of Candia, Cyprus, Rhodes, or other islands.   800

CI

Meantime the current, with a rising gale,
   Still set them onwards to the welcome shore,
Like Charon's bark of spectres, dull and pale:
   Their living freight was now reduced to four,
And three dead, whom their strength could not avail   805
   To heave into the deep with those before,
Though the two sharks still followed them, and dashed
The spray into their faces as they splashed.

CII

Famine, despair, cold, thirst, and heat, had done
   Their work on them by turns, and thinned them to   810
Such things a mother had not known her son
   Amidst the skeletons of that gaunt crew;
By night chilled, by day scorched, thus one by one
   They perished, until withered to these few,
But chiefly by a species of self-slaughter,   815
In washing down Pedrillo with salt water.

CIII

As they drew nigh the land, which now was seen
   Unequal in its aspect here and there,
They felt the freshness of its growing green,
   That waved in forest-tops, and smoothed the air,   820
And fell upon their glazed eyes like a screen
   From glistening waves, and skies so hot and bare—
Lovely seemed any object that should sweep
Away the vast, salt, dread, eternal deep.

CIV

The shore looked wild, without a trace of man,   825
   And girt by formidable waves; but they
Were mad for land, and thus their course they ran,
   Though right ahead the roaring breakers lay:

A reef between them also now began
  To show its boiling surf and bounding spray,   830
But finding no place for their landing better,
They ran the boat for shore,—and overset her.

CV

But in his native stream, the Guadalquivir,
  Juan to lave his youthful limbs was wont;
And having learnt to swim in that sweet river,   835
  Had often turned the art to some account:
A better swimmer you could scarce see ever,
  He could, perhaps, have passed the Hellespont,
As once (a feat on which ourselves we prided)
Leander, Mr. Ekenhead, and I did.   840

CVI

So here, though faint, emaciated, and stark,
  He buoyed his boyish limbs, and strove to ply
With the quick wave, and gain, ere it was dark,
  The beach which lay before him, high and dry:
The greatest danger here was from a shark,   845
  That carried off his neighbor by the thigh;
As for the other two, they could not swim,
So nobody arrived on shore but him.

CVII

Nor yet had he arrived but for the oar,
  Which, providentially for him, was washed   850
Just as his feeble arms could strike no more,
  And the hard wave o'erwhelmed him as 'twas dashed
Within his grasp; he clung to it, and sore
  The waters beat while he thereto was lashed;
At last, with swimming, wading, scrambling, he   855
Rolled on the beach, half senseless, from the sea:

CVIII

There, breathless, with his digging nails he clung
  Fast to the sand, lest the returning wave,
From whose reluctant roar his life he wrung,
  Should suck him back to her insatiate grave: 860
And there he lay, full length, where he was flung,
  Before the entrance of a cliff-worn cave,
With just enough of life to feel its pain,
And deem that it was saved, perhaps in vain.

CIX

With slow and staggering effort he arose,   865
  But sunk again upon his bleeding knee
And quivering hand; and then he looked for those
  Who long had been his mates upon the sea;
But none of them appeared to share his woes,
  Save one, a corpse, from out the famished three,   870
Who died two days before, and now had found
An unknown barren beach for burial-ground.

CX

And as he gazed, his dizzy brain spun fast,
  And down he sunk; and as he sunk, the sand
Swam round and round, and all his senses passed: 875
  He fell upon his side, and his stretched hand

Drooped dripping on the oar (their jury-mast),
  And, like a withered lily, on the land
His slender frame and pallid aspect lay,
As fair a thing as e'er was formed of clay.   880

CXI

How long in his damp trance young Juan lay
  He knew not, for the earth was gone for him,
And time had nothing more of night nor day
  For his congealing blood, and senses dim;
And how this heavy faintness passed away   885
  He knew not, till each painful pulse and limb,
And tingling vein, seemed throbbing back to life,
For Death, though vanquished, still retired with strife.

CXII

His eyes he opened, shut, again unclosed,
  For all was doubt and dizziness; he thought   890
He still was in the boat, and had but dozed,
  And felt again with his despair o'erwrought,
And wished it death in which he had reposed,
  And then once more his feelings back were brought,
And slowly by his swimming eyes was seen   895
A lovely female face of seventeen.

CXIII

'Twas bending close o'er his, and the small mouth
  Seemed almost prying into his for breath;
And chafing him, the soft warm hand of youth
  Recalled his answering spirits back from death;   900
And, bathing his chill temples, tried to soothe
  Each pulse to animation, till beneath
Its gentle touch and trembling care, a sigh
To these kind efforts made a low reply.

CXIV

Then was the cordial poured, and mantle flung   905
  Around his scarce-clad limbs; and the fair arm
Raised higher the faint head which o'er it hung;
  And her transparent cheek, all pure and warm,
Pillowed his death-like forehead; then she wrung
  His dewy curls, long drenched by every storm;   910
And watched with eagerness each throb that drew
A sigh from his heaved bosom—and hers, too.

CXV

And lifting him with care into the cave,
  The gentle girl, and her attendant,—one
Young, yet her elder, and of brow less grave,   915
  And more robust of figure—then begun
To kindle fire, and as the new flames gave
  Light to the rocks that roofed them, which the sun
Had never seen, the maid, or whatsoe'er
She was, appeared distinct, and tall, and fair.   920

CXVI

Her brow was overhung with coins of gold,
  That sparkled o'er the auburn of her hair,
Her clustering hair, whose longer locks were rolled
  In braids behind; and though her stature were

Even of the highest for a female mold.   925
   They nearly reached her heel; and in her air
There was a something which bespoke command,
   As one who was a lady in the land.

CXVII

Her hair, I said, was auburn; but her eyes
   Were black as death, their lashes the same hue,   930
Of downcast length, in whose silk shadow lies
   Deepest attraction; for when to the view
Forth from its raven fringe the full glance flies,
   Ne'er with such force the swiftest arrow flew;
'Tis as the snake late coiled, who pours his length,   935
And hurls at once his venom and his strength.

CXVIII

Her brow was white and low, her cheek's pure dye
   Like twilight rosy still with the set sun;
Short upper lip—sweet lips! that make us sigh
   Ever to have seen such; for she was one   940
Fit for the model of a statuary
   (A race of mere impostors, when all's done—
I've seen much finer women, ripe and real,
Than all the nonsense of their stone ideal).

CXIX

I'll tell you why I say so, for 'tis just   945
   One should not rail without a decent cause:
There was an Irish lady, to whose bust
   I ne'er saw justice done, and yet she was
A frequent model; and if e'er she must
   Yield to stern time and nature's wrinkling laws,   950
They will destroy a face which mortal thought
Ne'er compassed, nor less mortal chisel wrought.

CXX

And such was she, the lady of the cave:
   Her dress was very different from the Spanish,
Simpler, and yet of colors not so grave;   955
   For, as you know, the Spanish women banish
Bright hues when out of doors, and yet, while wave
   Around them (what I hope will never vanish)
The basquina and the mantilla, they
Seem at the same time mystical and gay.   960

CXXI

But with our damsel this was not the case:
   Her dress was many-colored, finely spun;
Her locks curled negligently round her face.
   But through them gold and gems profusely shone:
Her girdle sparkled, and the richest lace   965
   Flowed in her veil, and many a precious stone
Flashed on her little hand; but, what was shocking,
Her small snow feet had slippers, but no stocking.

CXXII

The other female's dress was not unlike,
   But of inferior materials: she   970
Had not so many ornaments to strike.
   Her hair had silver only, bound to be

Her dowry; and her veil, in form alike,
  Was coarser; and her air, though firm, less free;
Her hair was thicker, but less long; her eyes   975
As black, but quicker, and of smaller size.

CXXIII

And these two tended him, and cheered him both
  With food and raiment, and those soft attentions,
Which are—(as I must own)—of female growth,
  And have ten thousand delicate inventions: 980
They made a most superior mess of broth,
  A thing which poesy but seldom mentions,
But the best dish that e'er was cooked since Homer's
Achilles ordered dinner for new comers.

CXXIV

I'll tell you who they were, this female pair,   985
  Lest they should seem princesses in disguise;
Besides, I hate all mystery, and that air
  Of clap-trap, which your recent poets prize;
And so, in short, the girls they really were
  They shall appear before your curious eyes,   990
Mistress and maid; the first was only daughter
Of an old man, who lived upon the water.

CXXV

A fisherman he had been in his youth,
  And still a sort of fisherman was he;
But other speculations were, in sooth,   995
  Added to his connection with the sea,
Perhaps not so respectable, in truth:
  A little smuggling, and some piracy,
Left him, at last, the sole of many masters
Of an ill-gotten million of piastres.   1000

CXXVI

A fisher, therefore, was he,—though of men,
  Like Peter the Apostle,—and he fished
For wandering merchant vessels, now and then,
  And sometimes caught as many as he wished;
The cargoes he confiscated, and gain   1005
  He sought in the slave-market too, and dished
Full many a morsel for that Turkish trade,
By which, no doubt, a good deal may be made.

CXXVII

He was a Greek, and on his isle had built
  (One of the wild and smaller Cyclades)
A very handsome house from out his guilt,   1010
  And there he lived exceedingly at ease;
Heaven knows what cash he got, or blood he spilt,
  A sad old fellow was he, if you please;
But this I know, it was a spacious building,
Full of barbaric carving, paint, and gilding.   1015

CXXVIII

He had an only daughter, called Haidée,
  The greatest heiress of the Eastern Isles;
Besides, so very beautiful was she,
  Her dowry was as nothing to her smiles:

Still in her teens, and like a lovely tree   1020
  She grew to womanhood, and between whiles
Rejected several suitors, just to learn
How to accept a better in his turn.

CXXIX

And walking out upon the beach, below
  The cliff, towards sunset, on that day she found,   1025
Insensible,—not dead, but nearly so,—
  Don Juan, almost famished, and half drowned;
But being naked, she was shocked, you know,
  Yet deemed herself in common pity bound,
As far as in her lay, "to take him in,   1030
A stranger," dying, with so white a skin.

CXXX

But taking him into her father's house
  Was not exactly the best way to save,
But like conveying to the cat the mouse,
  Or people in a trance into their grave;   1035
Because the good old man had so much "νοῦς,"
  Unlike the honest Arab thieves so brave,
He would have hospitably cured the stranger
And sold him instantly when out of danger.

CXXXI

And therefore, with her maid, she thought it best   1040
  (A virgin always on her maid relies)
To place him in the cave for present rest:
  And when, at last, he opened his black eyes,
Their charity increased about their guest;
  And their compassion grew to such a size,   1045
It opened half the turnpike gates to heaven—
(St. Paul says, 'tis the toll which must be given).

CXXXII

They made a fire,—but such a fire as they
  Upon the moment could contrive with such
Materials as were cast up round the bay,—   1050
  Some broken planks, and oars, that to the touch
Were nearly tinder, since so long they lay
  A mast was almost crumbled to a crutch;
But, by God's grace, here wrecks were in such plenty,
That there was fuel to have furnished twenty.   1055

CXXXIII

He had a bed of furs, and a pelisse,
  For Haidée stripped her sables off to make
His couch; and, that he might be more at ease,
  And warm, in case by chance he should awake,
They also gave a petticoat apiece,   1060
  She and her maid,—and promised by daybreak
To pay him a fresh visit, with a dish
For breakfast, of eggs, coffee, bread, and fish.

CXXXIV

And thus they left him to his lone repose:
  Juan slept like a top, or like the dead,   1065
Who sleep at last, perhaps (God only knows),
  Just for the present; and in his lulled head

Not even a vision of his former woes
    Throbbed in accursed dreams, which sometimes spread
Unwelcome visions of our former years,   1070
    Till the eye, cheated, opens thick with tears.

CXXXV

Young Juan slept all dreamless:—but the maid,
    Who smoothed his pillow, as she left the den
Looked back upon him, and a moment staid,
    And turned, believing that he called again.   1075
He slumbered; yet she thought, at least she said
    (The heart will slip, even as the tongue and pen),
He had pronounced her name—but she forgot
That at this moment Juan knew it not.

CXXXVI

And pensive to her father's house she went,   1080
    Enjoining silence strict to Zoe, who
Better than her knew what, in fact, she meant,
    She being wiser by a year or two:
A year or two's an age when rightly spent,
    And Zoe spent hers, as most women do,   1085
In gaining all that useful sort of knowledge
Which is acquired in nature's good old college.

CXXXVII

The morn broke, and found Juan slumbering still
    Fast in his cave, and nothing clashed upon
His rest: the rushing of the neighboring rill,   1090
    And the young beams of the excluded sun,
Troubled him not, and he might sleep his fill;
    And need he had of slumber yet, for none
Had suffered more—his hardships were comparative
To those related in my grand-dad's "Narrative."   1095

CXXXVIII

Not so Haidée: she sadly tossed and tumbled,
    And started from her sleep, and, turning o'er,
Dreamed of a thousand wrecks, o'er which she stumbled,
    And handsome corpses strewed upon the shore;
And woke her maid so early that she grumbled,   1100
    And called her father's old slaves up, who swore
In several oaths—Armenian, Turk, and Greek—
They knew not what to think of such a freak.

CXXXIX

But up she got, and up she made them get,
    With some pretence about the sun, that makes   1105
Sweet skies just when he rises, or is set;
    And 't is, no doubt, a sight to see when breaks
Bright Phœbus, while the mountains still are wet
    With mist, and every bird with him awakes,
And night is flung off like a mourning suit   1110
Worn for a husband,—or some other brute.

CXL

I say, the sun is a most glorious sight:
    I 've seen him rise full oft, indeed of late
I have sat up on purpose all the night,
    Which hastens, as physicians say, one's fate;   1115

And so all ye, who would be in the right
  In health and purse, begin your day to date
From daybreak, and when confined at four-score
Engrave upon the plate, you rose at four.

CXLI

And Haidée met the morning face to face;
  Her own was freshest, though a feverish flush
Had dyed it with the headlong blood, whose race
  From heart to cheek is curbed into a blush,
Like to a torrent which a mountain's base,
  That overpowers some Alpine river's rush,
Checks to a lake, whose waves in circles spread;
Or the Red Sea—but the sea is not red.

CXLII

And down the cliff the island virgin came,
  And near the cave her quick light footsteps drew,
While the sun smiled on her with his first flame,
  And young Aurora kissed her lips with dew,
Taking her for a sister; just the same
  Mistake you would have made on seeing the two,
Although the mortal, quite as fresh and fair,
Had all the advantage, too, of not being air.

CXLIII

And when into the cavern Haidée stepped
  All timidly, yet rapidly, she saw
That like an infant Juan sweetly slept;
  And then she stopped, and stood as if in awe
(For sleep is awful), and on tiptoe crept
  And wrapped him closer, lest the air, too raw,
Should reach his blood, then o'er him still as death
Bent, with hushed lips, that drank his scarce-drawn breath.

CXLIV

And thus like to an angel o'er the dying
  Who die in righteousness, she leaned; and there
All tranquilly the shipwrecked boy was lying,
  As o'er him lay the calm and stirless air:
But Zoe the meantime some eggs was frying,
  Since, after all, no doubt the youthful pair
Must breakfast, and betimes—lest they should ask it,
She drew out her provision from the basket.

CXLV

She knew that the best feelings must have victual,
  And that a shipwrecked youth would hungry be;
Besides, being less in love, she yawned a little,
  And felt her veins chilled by the neighboring sea;
And so, she cooked their breakfast to a tittle;
  I can't say that she gave them any tea,
But there were eggs, fruit, coffee, bread, fish, honey,
With Scio wine,—and all for love, not money.

CXLVI

And Zoe, when the eggs were ready, and
  The coffee made, would fain have wakened Juan;
But Haidée stopped her with her quick small hand,
  And without word, a sign her finger drew on

1120

1125

1130

1135

1140

1145

1150

1155

1160

Her lip, which Zoe needs must understand;
　　And, the first breakfast spoilt, prepared a new one, 1165
Because her mistress would not let her break
That sleep which seemed as it would ne'er awake.

CXLVII

For still he lay, and on his thin worn cheek
　　A purple hectic played like dying day
On the snow-tops of distant hills; the streak 1170
　　Of sufferance yet upon his forehead lay,
Where the blue veins looked shadowy, shrunk, and weak;
　　And his black curls were dewy with the spray,
Which weighed upon them yet, all damp and salt,
Mixed with the stony vapors of the vault. 1175

CXLVIII

And she bent o'er him, and he lay beneath,
　　Hushed as the babe upon its mother's breast,
Drooped as the willow when no winds can breathe,
　　Lulled like the depth of ocean when at rest,
Fair as the crowning rose of the whole wreath, 1180
　　Soft as the callow cygnet in its nest;
In short, he was a very pretty fellow,
Although his woes had turned him rather yellow.

CXLIX

He woke and gazed, and would have slept again,
　　But the fair face which met his eyes forbade 1185
Those eyes to close, though weariness and pain
　　Had further sleep a further pleasure made;
For woman's face was never formed in vain
　　For Juan, so that even when he prayed
He turned from grisly saints, and martyrs hairy, 1190
To the sweet portraits of the Virgin Mary.

CL

And thus upon his elbow he arose,
　　And looked upon the lady, in whose cheek
The pale contended with the purple rose,
　　As with an effort she began to speak; 1195
Her eyes were eloquent, her words would pose,
　　Although she told him, in good modern Greek,
With an Ionian accent, low and sweet,
That he was faint, and must not talk, but eat.

CLI

Now Juan could not understand a word, 1200
　　Being no Grecian; but he had an ear,
And her voice was the warble of a bird,
　　So soft, so sweet, so delicately clear,
That finer, simpler music ne'er was heard;
　　The sort of sound we echo with a tear, 1205
Without knowing why—an overpowering tone,
Whence melody descends as from a throne.

CLII

And Juan gazed as one who is awoke
　　By a distant organ, doubting if he be
Not yet a dreamer, till the spell is broke 1210
　　By the watchman, or some such reality,

Or by one's early valet's cursed knock;
   At least it is a heavenly sound to me,
Who like a morning slumber—for the night
Shows stars and women in a better light.   1215

CLIII

And Juan, too, was helped out from his dream,
   Or sleep, or whatsoe'er it was, by feeling
A most prodigious appetite; the steam
   Of Zoe's cookery no doubt was stealing
Upon his senses, and the kindling beam   1220
   Of the new fire, which Zoe kept up, kneeling,
To stir her viands, made him quite awake
And long for food, but chiefly a beef-steak.

CLIV

But beef is rare within these oxless isles;
   Goat's flesh there is, no doubt, and kid, and mutton,   1225
And, when a holiday upon them smiles,
   A joint upon their barbarous spits they put on:
But this occurs but seldom, between whiles,
   For some of these are rocks with scarce a hut on;
Others are fair and fertile, among which   1230
This, though not large, was one of the most rich.

CLV

I say that beef is rare, and can't help thinking
   That the old fable of the Minotaur—
From which our modern morals, rightly shrinking,
   Condemn the royal lady's taste who wore   1235
A cow's shape for a mask—was only (sinking
   The allegory) a mere type, no more,
That Pasiphae promoted breeding cattle,
To make the Cretans bloodier in battle.

CLVI

For we all know that English people are   1240
   Fed upon beef—I won't say much of beer,
Because 't is liquor only, and being far
   From this my subject, has no business here;
We know, too, they are very fond of war,
   A pleasure—like all pleasures—rather dear;   1245
So were the Cretans—from which I infer
That beef and battles both were owing to her.

CLVII

But to resume. The languid Juan raised
   His head upon his elbow, and he saw
A sight on which he had not lately gazed,   1250
   As all his latter meals had been quite raw,
Three or four things, for which the Lord he praised,
   And, feeling still the famished vulture gnaw,
He fell upon whate'er was offered, like
A priest, a shark, an alderman, or pike.   1255

CLVIII

He ate, and he was well supplied; and she,
   Who watched him like a mother, would have fed
Him past all bounds, because she smiled to see
   Such appetite in one she had deemed dead;

But Zoe, being older than Haidée,
   Knew (by tradition, for she ne'er had read)
That famished people must be slowly nurst,
   And fed by spoonfuls, else they always burst.

1260

CLIX

And so she took the liberty to state,
   Rather by deeds than words, because the case
Was urgent, that the gentleman, whose fate
   Had made her mistress quit her bed to trace
The sea-shore at this hour, must leave his plate,
   Unless he wished to die upon the place—
She snatched it, and refused another morsel,
Saying, he had gorged enough to make a horse ill.

1265
1270

CLX

Next they—he being naked, save a tattered
   Pair of scarce decent trousers—went to work,
And in the fire his recent rags they scattered,
   And dressed him, for the present, like a Turk,
Or Greek—that is, although it not much mattered,
   Omitting turban, slippers, pistols, dirk,—
They furnished him, entire, except some stitches,
With a clean shirt, and very spacious breeches.

1275

CLXI

And then fair Haidée tried her tongue at speaking,
   But not a word could Juan comprehend,
Although he listened so that the young Greek in
   Her earnestness would ne'er have made an end;
And, as he interrupted not, went eking
   Her speech out to her protégé and friend,
Till pausing at the last her breath to take,
She saw he did not understand Romaic.

1280
1285

CLXII

And then she had recourse to nods, and signs,
   And smiles, and sparkles of the speaking eye,
And read (the only book she could) the lines
   Of his fair face, and found, by sympathy,
The answer eloquent, where the soul shines
   And darts in one quick glance a long reply;
And thus in every look she saw expressed
A world of words, and things at which she guessed.

1290
1295

CLXIII

And now, by dint of fingers and of eyes,
   And words repeated after her, he took
A lesson in her tongue; but by surmise,
   No doubt, less of her language than her look:
As he who studies fervently the skies
   Turns oftener to the stars than to his book,
Thus Juan learned his alpha beta better
From Haidée's glance than any graven letter.

1300

CLXIV

'T is pleasing to be schooled in a strange tongue
   By female lips and eyes—that is, I mean,
When both the teacher and the taught are young,
   As was the case, at least, where I have been;

1305

They smile so when one 's right, and when one 's wrong
　　They smile still more, and then there intervene
Pressure of hands, perhaps even a chaste kiss;—
I learned the little that I know by this:　　　　　　　　　　1310

CLXV

That is, some words of Spanish, Turk, and Greek,
　　Italian not at all, having no teachers;
Much English I cannot pretend to speak,
　　Learning that language chiefly from its preachers,　　　1315
Barrow, South, Tillotson, whom every week
　　I study, also Blair, the highest reachers
Of eloquence in piety and prose—
I hate your poets, so read none of those.

CLXVI

As for the ladies, I have naught to say,　　　　　　　　　1320
　　A wanderer from the British world of fashion.
Where I, like other "dogs, have had my day,"
　　Like other men, too, may have had my passion—
But that, like other things, has passed away,
　　And all her fools whom I *could* lay the lash on:　　　　1325
Foes, friends, men, women, now are nought to me
But dreams of what has been, no more to be.

CLXVII

Return we to Don Juan. He begun
　　To hear new words, and to repeat them; but
Some feelings, universal as the sun,　　　　　　　　　　　1330
　　Were such as could not in his breast be shut
More than within the bosom of a nun:
　　He was in love,—as you would be, no doubt,
With a young benefactress,—so was she,
Just in the way we very often see.　　　　　　　　　　　　1335

CLXVIII

And every day by daybreak—rather early
　　For Juan, who was somewhat fond of rest—
She came into the cave, but it was merely
　　To see her bird reposing in his nest;
And she would softly stir his locks so curly,　　　　　　　1340
　　Without disturbing her yet slumbering guest,
Breathing all gently o'er his cheek and mouth,
As o'er a bed of roses the sweet south.

CLXIX

And every morn his color freshlier came,
　　And every day helped on his convalescence;　　　　　　　1345
'T was well, because health in the human frame
　　Is pleasant, besides being true love's essence,
For health and idleness to passion's flame
　　Are oil and gunpowder; and some good lessons
Are also learnt from Ceres and from Bacchus,　　　　　　　1350
Without whom Venus will not long attack us.

CLXX

While Venus fills the heart (without heart really
　　Love, though good always, is not quite so good),
Ceres presents a plate of vermicelli,—
　　For love must be sustained like flesh and blood,　　　　1355

While Bacchus pours out wine, or hands a jelly:
  Eggs, oysters, too, are amatory food;
But who is their purveyor from above
Heaven knows,—it may be Neptune, Pan, or Jove.

CLXXI

When Juan woke he found some good things ready,   1360
  A bath, a breakfast, and the finest eyes
That ever made a youthful heart less steady,
  Besides her maid's, as pretty for their size;
But I have spoken of all this already—
  And repetition's tiresome and unwise,—   1365
Well—Juan, after bathing in the sea,
Came always back to coffee and Haidée.

CLXXII

Both were so young, and one so innocent,
  That bathing passed for nothing; Juan seemed
To her, as 't were, the kind of being sent,   1370
  Of whom these two years she had nightly dreamed,
A something to be loved, a creature meant
  To be her happiness, and whom she deemed
To render happy: all who joy would win
Must share it,—Happiness was born a twin.   1375

CLXXIII

It was such pleasure to behold him, such
  Enlargement of existence to partake
Nature with him, to thrill beneath his touch,
  To watch him slumbering, and to see him wake;
To live with him for ever were too much;   1380
  But then the thought of parting made her quake:
He was her own, her ocean-treasure, cast
Like a rich wreck—her first love, and her last.

CLXXIV

And thus a moon rolled on, and fair Haidée
  Paid daily visits to her boy, and took   1385
Such plentiful precautions, that still he
  Remained unknown within his craggy nook;
At last her father's prows put out to sea,
  For certain merchantmen upon the look,
Not as of yore to carry off an Io,   1390
But three Ragusan vessels bound for Scio.

CLXXV

Then came her freedom, for she had no mother,
  So that, her father being at sea, she was
Free as a married woman, or such other
  Female, as where she likes may freely pass,   1395
Without even the encumbrance of a brother,
  The freest she that ever gazed on glass:
I speak of Christian lands in this comparison,
Where wives, at least, are seldom kept in garrison.

CLXXVI

Now she prolonged her visits and her talk   1400
  (For they must talk), and he had learnt to say
So much as to propose to take a walk,—
  For little had he wandered since the day

On which, like a young flower snapped from the stalk,
  Drooping and dewy on the beach he lay,— 1405
And thus they walked out in the afternoon,
And saw the sun set opposite the moon.

CLXXVII

It was a wild and breaker-beaten coast,
  With cliffs above, and a broad sandy shore,
Guarded by shoals and rocks as by an host, 1410
  With here and there a creek, whose aspect wore
A better welcome to the tempest-tost;
  And rarely ceased the haughty billow's roar,
Save on the dead long summer days, which make
The outstretched ocean glitter like a lake. 1415

CLXXVIII

And the small ripple spilt upon the beach
  Scarcely o er passed the cream of your champagne,
When o'er the brim the sparkling bumpers reach,
  That spring-dew of the spirit! the heart's rain!
Few things surpass old wine; and they may preach 1420
  Who please,—the more because they preach in vain,—
Let us have wine and women, mirth and laughter,
Sermons and soda-water the day after.

CLXXIX

Man, being reasonable, must get drunk;
  The best of life is but intoxication: 1425
Glory, the grape, love, gold, in these are sunk
  The hopes of all men, and of every nation;
Without their sap, how branchless were the trunk
  Of life's strange tree, so fruitful on occasion!
But to return,—Get very drunk, and when 1430
You wake with headache, you shall see what then.

CLXXX

Ring for your valet—bid him quickly bring
  Some hock and soda-water, then you'll know
A pleasure worthy Xerxes the great king;
  For not the blest sherbet, sublimed with snow, 1435
Nor the first sparkle of the desert spring,
  Nor Burgundy in all its sunset glow,
After long travel, ennui, love, or slaughter,
Vie with that draught of hock and soda-water.

CLXXXI

The coast—I think it was the coast that I 1440
  Was just describing—Yes, it *was* the coast—
Lay at this period quiet as the sky,
  The sands untumbled, the blue waves untossed
And all was stillness, save the sea-bird's cry,
  And dolphin's leap, and little billow crossed 1445
By some low rock or shelve, that made it fret
Against the boundary it scarcely wet.

CLXXXII

And forth they wandered, her sire being gone,
  As I have said, upon an expedition;
And mother, brother, guardian, she had none, 1450
  Save Zoe, who, although with due precision

She waited on her lady with the sun,
   Thought daily service was her only mission,
Bringing warm water, wreathing her long tresses,
And asking now and then for cast-off dresses.   1455

CLXXXIII

It was the cooling hour, just when the rounded
   Red sun sinks down behind the azure hill,
Which then seems as if the whole earth it bounded,
   Circling all nature, hushed, and dim, and still,
With the far mountain-crescent half surrounded   1460
   On one side, and the deep sea calm and chill,
Upon the other, and the rosy sky,
With one star sparkling through it like an eye.

CLXXXIV

And thus they wandered forth, and hand in hand,
   Over the shining pebbles and the shells,   1465
Glided along the smooth and hardened sand,
   And in the worn and wild receptacles
Worked by the storms, yet worked as it were planned,
   In hollow halls, with sparry roofs and cells,
They turned to rest; and, each clasped by an arm,   1470
Yielded to the deep twilight's purple charm.

CLXXXV

They looked up to the sky, whose floating glow
   Spread like a rosy ocean, vast and bright;
They gazed upon the glittering sea below,
   Whence the broad moon rose circling into sight;   1475
They heard the waves' splash, and the wind so low,
   And saw each other's dark eyes darting light
Into each other—and, beholding this,
Their lips drew near, and clung into a kiss;

CLXXXVI

A long, long kiss, a kiss of youth, and love,   1480
   And beauty, all concentrating like rays
Into one focus, kindled from above;
   Such kisses as belong to early days,
Where heart, and soul, and sense, in concert move,
   And the blood's lava, and the pulse a blaze,   1485
Each kiss a heart-quake,—for a kiss's strength,
I think it must be reckoned by its length.

CLXXXVII

By length I mean duration; theirs endured
   Heaven knows how long—no doubt they never reckoned;
And if they had, they could not have secured   1490
   The sum of their sensations to a second:
They had not spoken; but they felt allured,
   As if their souls and lips each other beckoned,
Which, being joined, like swarming bees they clung—
Their hearts the flowers from whence the honey sprung.   1495

CLXXXVIII

They were alone, but not alone as they
   Who shut in chambers think it loneliness;
The silent ocean, and the starlight bay,
   The twilight glow, which momently grew less,

The voiceless sands, and drooping caves, that lay 1500
  Around them, made them to each other press,
As if there were no life beneath the sky
Save theirs, and that their life could never die.

CLXXXIX

They feared no eyes nor ears on that lone beach,
  They felt no terrors from the night; they were 1505
All in all to each other; though their speech
  Was broken words, they *thought* a language there,—
And all the burning tongues the passions teach
  Found in one sigh the best interpreter
Of nature's oracle—first love,—that all 1510
Which Eve has left her daughters since her fall.

CXC

Haidée spoke not of scruples, asked no vows,
  Nor offered any; she had never heard
Of plight and promises to be a spouse,
  Or perils by a loving maid incurred; 1515
She was all which pure ignorance allows,
  And flew to her young mate like a young bird,
And never having dreamt of falsehood, she
Had not one word to say of constancy.

CXCI

She loved, and was beloved—she adored, 1520
  And she was worshipped; after nature's fashion,
Their intense souls, into each other poured,
  If souls could die, had perished in that passion,—
But by degrees their senses were restored,
  Again to be o'ercome, again to dash on; 1525
And, beating 'gainst *his* bosom, Haidée's heart
Felt as if never more to beat apart.

CXCII

Alas! they were so young, so beautiful,
  So lonely, loving, helpless, and the hour
Was that in which the heart is always full, 1530
  And, having o'er itself no further power,
Prompts deeds eternity cannot annul,
  But pays off moments in an endless shower
Of hell-fire—all prepared for people giving
Pleasure or pain to one another living. 1535

CXCIII

Alas! for Juan and Haidée! they were
  So loving and so lovely—till then never,
Excepting our first parents, such a pair
  Had run the risk of being damned for ever;
And Haidée, being devout as well as fair, 1540
  Had, doubtless, heard about the Stygian river,
And hell and purgatory—but forgot
Just in the very crisis she should not.

CXCIV

They look upon each other, and their eyes
  Gleam in the moonlight; and her white arm clasps 1545
Round Juan's head, and his around her lies
  Half buried in the tresses which it grasps;

She sits upon his knee, and drinks his sighs,
  He hers, until they end in broken gasps;
And thus they form a group that 's quite antique,   1550
Half naked, loving, natural, and Greek.

CXCV

And when those deep and burning moments passed,
  And Juan sunk to sleep within her arms,
She slept not, but all tenderly, though fast,
  Sustained his head upon her bosom's charms;   1555
And now and then her eye to heaven is cast,
  And then on the pale cheek her breast now warms,
Pillowed on her o'erflowing heart, which pants
With all it granted, and with all it grants.

CXCVI

An infant when it gazes on a light,   1560
  A child the moment when it drains the breast,
A devotee when soars the Host in sight,
  An Arab with a stranger for a guest,
A sailor when the prize has struck in fight,
  A miser filling his most hoarded chest,   1565
Feel rapture; but not such true joy are reaping
As they who watch o'er what they love while sleeping.

CXCVII

For there it lies so tranquil, so beloved,
  All that it hath of life with us is living;
So gentle, stirless, helpless, and unmoved,   1570
  And all unconscious of the joy 't is giving;
All it hath felt, inflicted, passed, and proved,
  Hushed into depths beyond the watcher's diving;
There lies the thing we love with all its errors
And all its charms, like death without its terrors.   1575

CXCVIII

The lady watched her lover—and that hour
  Of Love's, and Night's, and Ocean's solitude,
O'erflowed her soul with their united power;
  Amidst the barren sand and rocks so rude
She and her wave-worn love had made their bower,   1580
  Where nought upon their passion could intrude,
And all the stars that crowded the blue space
Saw nothing happier than her glowing face.

CXCIX

Alas! the love of women! it is known
  To be a lovely and a fearful thing;   1585
For all of theirs upon that die is thrown,
  And if 'tis lost, life hath no more to bring
To them but mockeries of the past alone,
  And their revenge is as the tiger's spring,
Deadly, and quick, and crushing; yet, as real   1590
Torture is theirs, what they inflict they feel.

CC

They are right; for man, to man so oft unjust,
  Is always so to women; one sole bond
Awaits them, treachery is all their trust;
  Taught to conceal, their bursting hearts despond   1595

Over their idol, till some wealthier lust
  Buys them in marriage—and what rests beyond?
A thankless husband, next a faithless lover,
  Then dressing, nursing, praying, and all's over.

CCI

Some take a lover, some take drams or prayers,   1600
  Some mind their household, others dissipation,
Some run away, and but exchange their cares,
  Losing the advantage of a virtuous station;
Few changes e'er can better their affairs,
  Theirs being an unnatural situation,   1605
From the dull palace to the dirty hovel:
Some play the devil, and then write a novel.

CCII

Haidée was Nature's bride, and knew not this:
  Haidée was Passion's child, born where the sun
Showers triple light, and scorches even the kiss   1610
  Of his gazelle-eyed daughters; she was one
Made but to love, to feel that she was his
  Who was her chosen: what was said or done
Elsewhere was nothing. She had nought to fear,
Hope, care, nor love beyond,—her heart beat *here*.   1615

CCIII

And oh! that quickening of the heart, that beat!
  How much it costs us! yet each rising throb
Is in its cause as its effect so sweet,
  That Wisdom, ever on the watch to rob
Joy of its alchemy, and to repeat   1620
  Fine truths; even Conscience, too, has a tough job
To make us understand each good old maxim,
So good—I wonder Castlereagh don't tax 'em.

CCIV

And now 'twas done—on the lone shore were plighted
  Their hearts; the stars, their nuptial torches, shed   1625
Beauty upon the beautiful they lighted:
  Ocean their witness, and the cave their bed,
By their own feelings hallowed and united,
  Their priest was Solitude, and they were wed:
And they were happy, for to their young eyes   1630
Each was an angel, and earth paradise.

1819

CANTO THE THIRD

[ECSTASY AND DANGER]

I

Hail, Muse! *et cetera*.—We left Juan sleeping,
  Pillowed upon a fair and happy breast,
And watched by eyes that never yet knew weeping,
  And loved by a young heart, too deeply blest
To feel the poison through her spirit creeping,   5
  Or know who rested there, a foe to rest,
Had soiled the current of her sinless years,
And turned her pure heart's purest blood to tears!

II

Oh, Love, what is it in this world of ours
    Which makes it fatal to be loved? Ah why   10
With cypress branches hast thou wreathed thy bowers,
    And made thy best interpreter a sigh?
As those who dote on odors pluck the flowers,
    And place them on their breast—but place to die—
Thus the frail beings we would fondly cherish   15
Are laid within our bosoms but to perish.

III

In her first passion woman loves her lover,
    In all the others all she loves is love,
Which grows a habit she can ne'er get over
    And fits her loosely—like an easy glove,   20
As you may find, whene'er you like to prove her:
    One man alone at first her heart can move;
She then prefers him in the plural number,
Not finding that the additions much encumber.

IV

I know not if the fault be men's or theirs;   25
    But one thing's pretty sure; a woman planted
(Unless at once she plunge for life in prayers)—
    After a decent time must be gallanted;
Although, no doubt, her first of love affairs
    Is that to which her heart is wholly granted;   30
Yet there are some, they say, who have had *none,*
But those who have ne'er end with only *one.*

V

'T is melancholy, and a fearful sign
    Of human frailty, folly, also crime,
That love and marriage rarely can combine,   35
    Although they both are born in the same clime;
Marriage from love, like vinegar from wine—
    A sad, sour, sober beverage—by time
Is sharpened from its high celestial flavor,
Down to a very homely household savor.   40

VI

There 's something of antipathy, as 't were,
    Between their present and their future state;
A kind of flattery that 's hardly fair
    Is used until the truth arrives too late—
Yet what can people do, except despair?   45
    The same things change their names at such a rate;
For instance—passion in a lover 's glorious,
But in a husband is pronounced uxorious.

VII

Men grow ashamed of being so very fond;
    They sometimes also get a little tired   50
(But that, of course, is rare), and then despond:
    The same things cannot always be admired.
Yet 't is "so nominated in the bond,"
    That both are tied till one shall have expired.
Sad thought! to lose the spouse that was adorns   55
Our days, and put one's servants into mourning.

VIII

There 's doubtless something in domestic doings
  Which forms, in fact, true love's antithesis;
Romances paint at full length people's wooings,
  But only give a bust of marriages; 60
For no one cares for matrimonial cooings,
  There's nothing wrong in a connubial kiss:
Think you, if Laura had been Petrarch's wife,
He would have written sonnets all his life?

IX

All tragedies are finished by a death, 65
  All comedies are ended by a marriage;
The future states of both are left to faith,
  For authors fear description might disparage
The worlds to come of both, or fall beneath,
  And then both worlds would punish their miscarriage; 70
So leaving each their priest and prayer-book ready,
They say no more of Death or of the Lady.

X

The only two that in my recollection
  Have sung of heaven and hell, or marriage, are
Dante and Milton, and of both the affection 75
  Was hapless in their nuptials, for some bar
Of fault or temper ruined the connexion
  (Such things, in fact, it don't ask much to mar);
But Dante's Beatrice and Milton's Eve
Were not drawn from their spouses, you conceive. 80

XI

Some persons say that Dante meant theology
  By Beatrice, and not a mistress—I,
Although my opinion may require apology,
  Deem this a commentator's phantasy,
Unless indeed it was from his own knowledge he 85
  Decided thus, and showed good reason why;
I think that Dante's more abstruse ecstatics
Meant to personify the mathematics.

XII

Haidée and Juan were not married, but
  The fault was theirs, not mine; it is not fair, 90
Chaste reader, then, in any way to put
  The blame on me, unless you wish they were;
Then if you 'd have them wedded, please to shut
  The book which treats of this erroneous pair,
Before the consequences grow too awful; 95
'T is dangerous to read of loves unlawful.

XIII

Yet they were happy,—happy in the illicit
  Indulgence of their innocent desires;
But more imprudent grown with every visit,
  Haidée forgot the island was her sire's; 100
When we have what we like, 't is hard to miss it,
  At least in the beginning, ere one tires;
Thus she came often, not a moment losing,
Whilst her piratical papa was cruising.

XIV

Let not his mode of raising cash seem strange,   105
   Although he fleeced the flags of every nation,
For into a prime minister but change
   His title, and 't is nothing but taxation;
But he, more modest, took an humbler range
   Of life, and in an honester vocation   110
Pursued o'er the high seas his watery journey,
And merely practised as a sea-attorney.

XV

The good old gentleman had been detained
   By winds and waves, and some important captures;
And, in the hope of more, at sea remained,   115
   Although a squall or two had damped his raptures,
By swamping one of the prizes; he had chained
   His prisoners, dividing them like chapters
In numbered lots; they all had cuffs and collars,
And averaged each from ten to a hundred dollars.   120

XVI

Some he disposed of off Cape Matapan,
   Among his friends the Mainots; some he sold
To his Tunis correspondents, save one man
   Tossed overboard unsaleable (being old):
The rest—save here and there some richer one,   125
   Reserved for future ransom—in the hold,
Were linked alike, as for the common people he
Had a large order from the Dey of Tripoli.

XVII

The merchandise was served in the same way,
   Pieced out for different marts in the Levant,   130
Except some certain portions of the prey,
   Light classic articles of female want,
French stuffs, lace, tweezers, toothpicks, teapot, tray,
   Guitars and castanets from Alicant,
All which selected from the spoil he gathers,   135
Robbed for his daughter by the best of fathers.

XVIII

A monkey, a Dutch mastiff, a mackaw,
   Two parrots, with a Persian cat and kittens,
He chose from several animals he saw—
   A terrier, too, which once had been a Briton's,   140
Who dying on the coast of Ithaca,
   The peasants gave the poor dumb thing a pittance.
These to secure in this strong blowing weather,
He caged in one huge hamper all together.

XIX

Then having settled his marine affairs,   145
   Despatching single cruisers here and there,
His vessel having need of some repairs,
   He shaped his course to where his daughter fair
Continued still her hospitable cares;
   But that part of the coast being shoal and bare,   150
And rough with reefs which ran out many a mile,
His port lay on the other side o' the isle.

XX

And there he went ashore without delay,
  Having no custom-house nor quarantine
To ask him awkward questions on the way,   155
  About the time and place where he had been:
He left his ship to be hove down next day,
  With orders to the people to careen;
So that all hands were busy beyond measure,
In getting out goods, ballast, guns, and treasure.   160

XXI

Arriving at the summit of a hill
  Which overlooked the white walls of his home,
He stopped.—What singular emotions fill
  Their bosoms who have been induced to roam!
With fluttering doubts if all be well or ill—   165
  With love for many, and with fears for some;
All feelings which o'erleap the years long lost,
And bring our hearts back to their starting-post.

XXII

The approach of home to husbands and to sires,
  After long travelling by land or water,   170
Most naturally some small doubt inspires—
  A female family 's a serious matter;
(None trusts the sex more, or so much admires—
  But they hate flattery, so I never flatter;)
Wives in their husbands' absences grow subtler,   175
And daughters sometimes run off with the butler.

XXIII

An honest gentleman at his return
  May not have the good fortune of Ulysses;
Not all lone matrons for their husbands mourn,
  Or show the same dislike to suitors' kisses;   180
The odds are that he finds a handsome urn
  To his memory—and two or three young misses
Born to some friend, who holds his wife and riches;—
And that his Argus bites him by—the breeches.

XXIV

If single, probably his plighted fair   185
  Has in his absence wedded some rich miser;
But all the better, for the happy pair
  May quarrel, and the lady growing wiser,
He may resume his amatory care
  As cavalier servente, or despise her;   190
And that his sorrow may not be a dumb one,
Writes odes on the Inconstancy of Woman.

XXV

And oh! ye gentlemen who have already
  Some chaste *liaison* of the kind—I mean
An honest friendship with a married lady—   195
  The only thing of this sort ever seen
To last—of all connections the most steady,
  And the true Hymen, (the first 's but a screen)—
Yet for all that keep not too long away;
I 've known the absent wronged four times a day.   200

XXVI

Lambro, our sea-solicitor, who had
　　Much less experience of dry land than ocean,
On seeing his own chimney-smoke, felt glad;
　　But not knowing metaphysics, had no notion
Of the true reason of his not being sad,
　　Or that of any other strong emotion;　　　　　　　　205
He loved his child, and would have wept the loss of her,
But knew the cause no more than a philosopher.

XXVII

He saw his white walls shining in the sun,
　　His garden trees all shadowy and green;　　　　　　210
He heard his rivulet's light bubbling run,
　　The distant dog-bark; and perceived between
The umbrage of the wood so cool and dun,
　　The moving figures, and the sparkling sheen
Of arms (in the East all arm)—and various dyes　　　215
Of colored garbs, as bright as butterflies.

XXVIII

And as the spot where they appear he nears,
　　Surprised at these unwonted signs of idling,
He hears—alas! no music of the spheres,
　　But an unhallowed, earthly sound of fiddling!　　220
A melody which made him doubt his ears,
　　The cause being past his guessing or unriddling;
A pipe, too, and a drum, and shortly after,
A most unoriental roar of laughter.

XXIX

And still more nearly to the place advancing,　　　　225
　　Descending rather quickly the declivity,
Through the waved branches, o'er the greensward glancing,
　　'Midst other indications of festivity,
Seeing a troop of his domestics dancing
　　Like dervishes, who turn as on a pivot, he　　　　230
Perceived it was the Pyrrhic dance so martial,
To which the Levantines are very partial.

XXX

And further on a group of Grecian girls,
　　The first and tallest her white kerchief waving,
Were strung together like a row of pearls,　　　　　235
　　Linked hand in hand, and dancing: each too having
Down her white neck long floating auburn curls—
　　(The least of which would set ten poets raving);
Their leader sang—and bounded to her song,
With choral step and voice, the virgin throng.　　　240

XXXI

And here, assembled cross-legged round their trays,
　　Small social parties just begun to dine;
Pilaus and meats of all sorts met the gaze,
　　And flasks of Samian and of Chian wine,
And sherbet cooling in the porous vase;　　　　　　245
　　About them their dessert grew on its vine,
The orange and pomegranate nodding o'er
Dropped in their laps, scarce plucked, their mellow store.

XXXII

A band of children, round a snow-white ram,
  There wreathe his venerable horns with flowers;   250
While peaceful as if still an unweaned lamb,
  The patriarch of the flock all gently cowers
His sober head, majestically tame,
  Or eats from out the palm, or playfully lowers
His brow, as if in act to butt, and then   255
Yielding to their small hands, draws back again.

XXXIII

Their classical profiles, and glittering dresses,
  Their large black eyes, and soft seraphic cheeks,
Crimson as cleft pomegranates, their long tresses,
  The gesture which enchants, the eye that speaks,   260
The innocence which happy childhood blesses,
  Made quite a picture of these little Greeks;
So that the philosophical beholder
Sighed for their sakes—that they should e'er grow older.

XXXIV

Afar, a dwarf buffoon stood telling tales   265
  To a sedate grey circle of old smokers,
Of secret treasures found in hidden vales,
  Of wonderful replies from Arab jokers,
Of charms to make good gold and cure bad ails,
  Of rocks bewitched that open to the knockers,   270
Of magic ladies who, by one sole act,
Transformed their lords to beasts (but that 's a fact).

XXXV

Here was no lack of innocent diversion
  For the imagination or the senses,
Song, dance, wine, music, stories from the Persian,   275
  All pretty pastimes in which no offence is;
But Lambro saw all these things with aversion,
  Perceiving in his absence such expenses,
Dreading that climax of all human ills
The inflammation of his weekly bills.   280

XXXVI

Ah! what is man? what perils still environ
  The happiest mortals even after dinner!
A day of gold from out an age of iron
  Is all that life allows the luckiest sinner;
Pleasure (whene'er she sings, at least) 's a siren,   285
  That lures, to flay alive, the young beginner;
Lambro's reception at his people's banquet
Was such as fire accords to a wet blanket.

XXXVII

He—being a man who seldom used a word
  Too much, and wishing gladly to surprise   290
(In general he surprised men with the sword)
  His daughter—had not sent before to advise
Of his arrival, so that no one stirred;
  And long he paused to re-assure his eyes,
In fact much more astonished than delighted,   295
To find so much good company invited.

XXXVIII

He did not know (alas! how men will lie!)
  That a report (especially the Greeks)
Avouched his death (such people never die),
  And put his house in mourning several weeks,—   300
But now their eyes and also lips were dry;
  The bloom, too, had returned to Haidée's cheeks.
Her tears, too, being returned into their fount,
She now kept house upon her own account.

XXXIX

Hence all this rice, meat, dancing, wine and fiddling,   305
  Which turned the isle into a place of pleasure;
The servants all were getting drunk or idling,
  A life which made them happy beyond measure.
Her father's hospitality seemed middling,
  Compared with what Haidée did with his treasure;   310
'T was wonderful how things went on improving,
While she had not one hour to spare from loving.

XL

Perhaps you think, in stumbling on this feast,
  He flew into a passion, and in fact
There was no mighty reason to be pleased;   315
  Perhaps you prophesy some sudden act,
The whip, the rack, or dungeon at least,
  To teach his people to be more exact,
And that, proceeding at a very high rate,
He showed the royal *penchants* of a pirate.   320

XLI

You're wrong.—He was the mildest mannered man
  That ever scuttled ship or cut a throat,
With such true breeding of a gentleman,
  You never could divine his real thought,
No courtier could, and scarcely woman can   325
  Gird more deceit within a petticoat;
Pity he loved adventurous life's variety,
He was so great a loss to good society.

XLII

Advancing to the nearest dinner tray,
  Tapping the shoulder of the nighest guest,   330
With a peculiar smile, which, by the way,
  Boded no good, whatever it expressed,
He asked the meaning of this holiday;
  The vinous Greek to whom he had addressed
His question, much too merry to divine   335
The questioner, filled up a glass of wine,

XLIII

And without turning his facetious head,
  Over his shoulder, with a Bacchant air,
Presented the o'erflowing cup, and said,
  "Talking 's dry work, I have no time to spare."   340
A second hiccuped, "Our old master 's dead,
  You 'd better ask our mistress who 's his heir."
"Our mistress!" quoth a third: "Our mistress!—pooh—
You mean our master—not the old, but new."

XLIV

These rascals, being new comers, knew not whom   345
　　They thus addressed—and Lambro's visage fell—
And o'er his eye a momentary gloom
　　Passed, but he strove quite courteously to quell
The expression, and endeavoring to resume
　　His smile, requested one of them to tell   350
The name and quality of his new patron,
Who seemed to have turned Haidée into a matron.

XLV

"I know not," quoth the fellow, "who or what
　　He is, nor whence he came—and little care;
But this I know, that this roast capon 's fat,   355
　　And that good wine ne'er washed down better fare;
And if you are not satisfied with that,
　　Direct your questions to my neighbor there;
He 'll answer all for better or for worse,
For none likes more to hear himself converse."   360

XLVI

I said that Lambro was a man of patience,
　　And certainly he showed the best of breeding,
Which scarce even France, the paragon of nations,
　　E'er saw her most polite of sons exceeding;
He bore these sneers against his near relations,   365
　　His own anxiety, his heart, too, bleeding,
The insults, too, of every servile glutton,
Who all the time was eating up his mutton.

XLVII

Now in a person used to much command—
　　To bid men come, and go, and come again—   370
To see his orders done, too, out of hand—
　　Whether the word was death, or but the chain—
It may seem strange to find his manners bland;
　　Yet such things are, which I cannot explain,
Though doubtless he who can command himself   375
Is good to govern—almost as a Guelf.

XLVIII

Not that he was not sometimes rash or so,
　　But never in his real and serious mood;
Then calm, concentrated, and still, and slow,
　　He lay coiled like the boa in the wood;   380
With him it never was a word and blow,
　　His angry word once o'er, he shed no blood,
But in his silence there was much to rue,
And his *one* blow left little work for *two.*

XLIX

He asked no further questions, and proceeded   385
　　On to the house, but by a private way,
So that the few who met him hardly heeded,
　　So little they expected him that day;
If love paternal in his bosom pleaded
　　For Haidée's sake, is more than I can say,   390
But certainly to one deemed dead returning,
This revel seemed a curious mode of mourning.

▼

LXVII

Haidée and Juan carpeted their feet
  On crimson satin, bordered with pale blue;   530
Their sofa occupied three parts complete
  Of the apartment—and appeared quite new;
The velvet cushions (for a throne more meet)
  Were scarlet, from whose glowing center grew
A sun embossed in gold, whose rays of tissue,   535
Meridian-like, were seen all light to issue.

LXVIII

Crystal and marble, plate and porcelain,
  Had done their work of splendor; Indian mats
And Persian carpets, which the heart bled to stain,
  Over the floors were spread; gazelles and cats,   540
And dwarfs and blacks, and such like things that gain
  Their bread as ministers and favorites—(that 's
To say, by degradation)—mingled there
As plentiful as in a court or fair.

LXIX

There was no want of lofty mirrors, and   545
  The tables most of ebony inlaid
With mother of pearl or ivory, stood at hand,
  Or were of tortoise-shell or rare woods made,
Fretted with gold or silver:—by command,
  The greater part of these were ready spread   550
With viands and sherbets in ice—and wine—
Kept for all comers at all hours to dine.

LXX

Of all the dresses I select Haidée's:
  She wore two jelicks—one was of pale yellow;
Of azure, pink, and white was her chemise—   555
  'Neath which her breast heaved like a little billow,
With buttons formed of pearls as large as peas,
  All gold and crimson shone her jelick's fellow,
And the striped white gauze baracan that bound her,
Like fleecy clouds about the moon, flowed round her.   560

LXXI

One large gold bracelet clasped each lovely arm,
  Lockless—so pliable from the pure gold
That the hand stretched and shut it without harm,
  The limb which it adorned its only mold;
So beautiful—its very shape would charm,   565
  And clinging as if loath to lose its hold,
The purest ore enclosed the whitest skin
That e'er by precious metal was held in.

LXXII

Around, as princess of her father's land,
  A like gold bar above her instep rolled   570
Announced her rank; twelve rings were on her hand;
  Her hair was starred with gems; her veil's fine fold
Below her breast was fastened with a band
  Of lavish pearls, whose worth could scarce be told;
Her orange silk full Turkish trousers furled   575
About the prettiest ankle in the world.

LXXIII

Her hair's long auburn waves down to her heel
  Flowed like an Alpine torrent which the sun
Dyes with his morning light,—and would conceal
  Her person if allowed at large to run,   580
And still they seemed resentfully to feel
  The silken fillet's curb, and sought to shun
Their bonds, whene'er some Zephyr caught began
To offer his young pinion as her fan.

LXXIV

Round her she made an atmosphere of life,   585
  The very air seemed lighter from her eyes,
They were so soft and beautiful, and rife
  With all we can imagine of the skies,
And pure as Psyche ere she grew a wife—
  Too pure even for the purest human ties;   590
Her overpowering presence made you feel
It would not be idolatry to kneel.

LXXV

Her eyelashes, though dark as night, were tinged
  (It is the country's custom), but in vain;
For those large black eyes were so blackly fringed,   595
  The glossy rebels mocked the jetty stain,
And in their native beauty stood avenged:
  Her nails were touched with henna; but again
The power of art was turned to nothing, for
They could not look more rosy than before.   600

LXXVI

The henna should be deeply dyed to make
  The skin relieved appear more fairly fair;
She had no need of this, day ne'er will break
  On mountain-tops more heavenly white than her:
The eye might doubt if it were well awake,   605
  She was so like a vision; I might err,
But Shakspeare also says, 't is very silly
"To gild refined gold, or paint the lily."

LXXVII

Juan had on a shawl of black and gold
  But a white baracan, and so transparent   610
The sparkling gems beneath you might behold,
  Like small stars through the milky way apparent;
His turban furled in many a graceful fold,
  An emerald aigrette with Haidée's hair in 't
Surmounted, as its clasp, a glowing crescent,   615
Whose rays shone ever trembling, but incessant.

LXXVIII

And now they were diverted by their suite,
  Dwarfs, dancing-girls, black eunuchs, and a poet,
Which made their new establishment complete;
  The last was of great fame, and liked to show it;   620
His verses rarely wanted their due feet—
  And for his theme—he seldom sung below it,
He being paid to satirise or flatter,
As the psalm says, "inditing a good matter."

. . . . . .

1

The isles of Greece, the isles of Greece!
  Where burning Sappho loved and sung,   690
Where grew the arts of war and peace,
  Where Delos rose, and Phœbus sprung!
Eternal summer gilds them yet,
But all, except their sun, is set.

2

The Scian and the Teian muse,   695
  The hero's harp, the lover's lute,
Have found the fame your shores refuse:
  Their place of birth alone is mute
To sounds which echo further west
Than your sires' "Islands of the Blest."   700

3

The mountains look on Marathon—
  And Marathon looks on the sea;
And musing there an hour alone,
  I dreamed that Greece might still be free,
For standing on the Persians' grave,   705
I could not deem myself a slave.

4

A king sate on the rocky brow
  Which looks o'er sea-born Salamis;
And ships, by thousands, lay below,
  And men in nations;—all were his!   710
He counted them at break of day—
And when the sun set where were they?

5

And where are they? and where art thou
  My country? On thy voiceless shore
The heroic lay is tuneless now—   715
  The heroic bosom beats no more!
And must thy lyre, so long divine,
Degenerate into hands like mine?

6

'Tis something, in the dearth of fame,
  Though linked among a fettered race,   720
To feel at least a patriot's shame,
  Even as I sing, suffuse my face;
For what is left the poet here?
For Greeks a blush—for Greeks a tear.

7

Must *we* but weep o'er days more blest?   725
  Must *we* but blush?—Our fathers bled.
Earth! render back from out thy breast
  A remnant of our Spartan dead!
Of the three hundred grant but three,
To make a new Thermopylæ!   730

8

What, silent still? and silent all?
  Ah! no;—the voices of the dead
Sound like a distant torrent's fall,
  And answer, "Let one living head,
But one arise,—we come, we come!"   735
'Tis but the living who are dumb.

9

In vain—in vain: strike other chords;
　Fill high the cup with Samian wine!
Leave battles to the Turkish hordes,
　And shed the blood of Scio's vine!
Hark! rising to the ignoble call—
How answers each bold Bacchanal! 740

10

You have the Pyrrhic dance as yet;
　Where is the Pyrrhic phalanx gone?
Of two such lessons, why forget 745
　The nobler and the manlier one?
You have the letters Cadmus gave—
Think ye he meant them for a slave?

11

Fill high the bowl with Samian wine!
　We will not think of themes like these! 750
It made Anacreon's song divine:
　He served—but served Polycrates—
A tyrant; but our masters then
Were still, at least, our countrymen.

12

The tyrant of the Chersonese 755
　Was freedom's best and bravest friend;
That tyrant was Miltiades!
　Oh! that the present hour would lend
Another despot of the kind!
Such chains as his were sure to bind. 760

13

Fill high the bowl with Samian wine!
　On Suli's rock, and Parga's shore,
Exists the remnant of a line
　Such as the Doric mothers bore;
And there, perhaps, some seed is sown, 765
The Heracleidan blood might own.

14

Trust not for freedom to the Franks—
　They have a king who buys and sells;
In native swords, and native ranks,
　The only hope of courage dwells: 770
But Turkish force, and Latin fraud,
Would break your shield, however broad.

15

Fill high the bowl with Samian wine!
　Our virgins danced beneath the shade—
I see their glorious black eyes shine; 775
　But gazing on each glowing maid,
My own the burning tear-drop laves,
To think such breasts must suckle slaves.

16

Place me on Sunium's marbled steep,
　Where nothing, save the waves and I, 780
May hear our mutual murmurs sweep;
　There, swan-like, let me sing and die:
A land of slaves shall ne'er be mine—
Dash down yon cup of Samian wine!

LXXXVII

Thus sung, or would, or could, or should have sung,   785
  The modern Greek, in tolerable verse;
If not like Orpheus quite, when Greece was young,
  Yet in these times he might have done much worse:
His strain displayed some feeling—right or wrong:
  And feeling, in a poet, is the source   790
Of others' feelings; but they are such liars,
And take all colors—like the hands of dyers.

LXXXVIII

But words are things, and a small drop of ink,
  Falling like dew, upon a thought, produces
That which makes thousands, perhaps millions, think;   795
  'Tis strange, the shortest letter which man uses
Instead of speech, may form a lasting link
  Of ages; to what straits old Time reduces
Frail man, when paper—even a rag like this,
Survives himself, his tomb, and all that's his!   800

LXXXIX

And when his bones are dust, his grave a blank,
  His station, generation, even his nation,
Become a thing, or nothing, save to rank
  In chronological commemoration,
Some dull MS. oblivion long has sank,   805
  Or graven stone found in a barrack's station
In digging the foundation of a closet,
May turn his name up, as a rare deposit.

XC

And glory long has made the sages smile;
  'Tis something, nothing, words, illusion, wind—   810
Depending more upon the historian's style
  Than on the name a person leaves behind:
Troy owes to Homer what whist owes to Hoyle:
  The present century was growing blind
To the great Marlborough's skill in giving knocks,   815
Until his late life by Archdeacon Coxe.

XCI

Milton's the prince of poets—so we say;
  A little heavy, but no less divine:
An independent being in his day—
  Learned, pious, temperate in love and wine;   820
But his life falling into Johnson's way
  We're told this great high priest of all the nine
Was whipt at college—a harsh sire—odd spouse,
For the first Mrs. Milton left his house.

XCII

All these are, *certes*, entertaining facts,   825
  Like Shakspeare's stealing deer, Lord Bacon's bribes;
Like Titus' youth, and Cæsar's earliest acts;
  Like Burns (whom Doctor Currie well describes);
Like Cromwell's pranks;—but although truth exacts
  These amiable descriptions from the scribes,   830
As most essential to their hero's story,
They do not much contribute to his glory.

XCIII

All are not moralists, like Southey, when
  He prated to the world of "Pantisocrasy;"
Or Wordsworth unexcised, unhired, who then   835
  Seasoned his pedlar poems with democracy;
Or Coleridge, long before his flighty pen
  Let to *The Morning Post* its aristocracy;
When he and Southey, following the same path,
Espoused two partners (milliners of Bath.)   840

XCIV

Such names at present cut a convict figure,
  The very Botany Bay in moral geography;
Their loyal treason, renegado rigor,
  Are good manure for their more bare biography,
Wordsworth's last quarto, by the way, is bigger   845
  Than any since the birthday of typography;
A drowsy frowzy poem, called *The Excursion,*
Writ in a manner which is my aversion.

XCV

He there builds up a formidable dyke
  Between his own and others' intellect:
But Wordsworth's poem, and his followers, like   850
  Joanna Southcote's Shiloh, and her sect,
Are things which in this century don't strike
  The public mind,—so few are the elect;
And the new births of both their stale virginities   855
Have proved but dropsies, taken for divinities.

XCVI

But let me to my story: I must own,
  If I have any fault, it is digression—
Leaving my people to proceed alone,
  While I soliloquize beyond expression: 860
But these are my addresses from the throne,
  Which put off business to the ensuing session:
Forgetting each omission is a loss to
The world, not quite so great as Ariosto.

XCVII

I know that what our neighbors call *"longueurs"*   865
  (We've not so good a *word,* but have the *thing,*
In that complete perfection which insures
  An epic from Bob Southey every spring),
Form not the true temptation which allures
  The reader; but 'twould not be hard to bring   870
Some fine examples of the *epopée,*
To prove its grand ingredient is *ennui.*

XCVIII

We learn from Horace, "Homer sometimes sleeps;"
  We feel without him, Wordsworth sometimes wakes,—
To show with what complacency he creeps,   875
  With his dear *"Waggoners,"* around his lakes.
He wishes for "a boat" to sail the deeps—
  Of ocean?—No, of air; and then he makes
Another outcry for "a little boat,"
And drivels seas to set it well afloat.   880

XCIX

If he must fain sweep o'er the ethereal plain,
  And Pegasus runs restive in his "Waggon,"
Could he not beg the loan of Charles's Wain?
  Or pray Medea for a single dragon?
Or if, too classic for his vulgar brain,   885
  He feared his neck to venture such a nag on,
And he must needs mount nearer to the moon,
Could not the blockhead ask for a balloon?

C

"Pedlars," and "Boats," and "Waggons!" Oh! ye shades
  Of Pope and Dryden, are we come to this?   890
That trash of such sort not alone evades
  Contempt, but from the bathos' vast abyss
Floats scumlike uppermost, and these Jack Cades
  Of sense and song above your graves may hiss—
The "little boatman" and his "Peter Bell"   895
Can sneer at him who drew "Achitophell!"

                   1821

CANTO THE FOURTH

[THE DEATH OF HAIDÉE]

I

Nothing so difficult as a beginning
  In poesy, unless, perhaps the end;
For oftentimes when Pegasus seems winning
  The race, he sprains a wing, and down we tend,
Like Lucifer when hurled from heaven for sinning;   5
  Our sin the same, and hard as his to mend,
Being pride, which leads the mind to soar too far,
Till our own weakness shows us what we are.

II

But Time, which brings all beings to their level,
  And sharp Adversity, will teach at last   10
Man,—and, as we would hope,—perhaps the devil,
  That neither of their intellects are vast;
While youth's hot wishes in our red veins revel,
  We know not this—the blood flows on too fast:
But as the torrent widens towards the ocean,   15
We ponder deeply on each past emotion.

III

As boy, I thought myself a clever fellow,
  And wished that others held the same opinion;
They took it up when my days grew more mellow,
  And other minds acknowledged my dominion: 20
Now my sere fancy "falls into the yellow
  Leaf," and Imagination droops her pinion,
And the sad truth which hovers o'er my desk
Turns what was once romantic to burlesque.

IV

And if I laugh at any mortal thing,   25
  'Tis that I may not weep; and if I weep,
'Tis that our nature cannot always bring
  Itself to apathy, for we must steep

Our hearts first in the depths of Lethe's spring,
 Ere what we least wish to behold will sleep:
Thetis baptized her mortal son in Styx;
A mortal mother would on Lethe fix.   30

V

Some have accused me of a strange design
 Against the creed and morals of the land;
And trace it in this poem every line;   35
 I don't pretend that I quite understand
My own meaning when I would be *very* fine;
 But the fact is that I have nothing planned,
Unless it were to be a moment merry,
A novel word in my vocabulary.   40

VI

To the kind reader of our sober clime
 This way of writing will appear exotic;
Pulci was sire of the half-serious rhyme,
 Who sang when chivalry was more Quixotic,
And revelled in the fancies of the time,   45
 True knights, chaste dames, huge giants, kings despotic:
But all these, save the last, being obsolete,
I chose a modern subject as more meet.

VII

How I have treated it, I do not know;
 Perhaps no better than *they* have treated me,   50
Who have imputed such designs as show
 Not what they saw, but what they wished to see;
But if it gives them pleasure, be it so,
 This is a liberal age, and thoughts are free:
Meantime Apollo plucks me by the ear,   55
And tells me to resume my story here.

VIII

Young Juan and his lady-love were left
 To their own hearts' most sweet society;
Even Time the pitiless in sorrow cleft
 With his rude scythe such gentle bosoms; he   60
Sighed to behold them of their hours bereft,
 Though foe to love; and yet they could not be
Meant to grow old, but die in happy spring,
Before one charm or hope had taken wing.

IX

Their faces were not made for wrinkles, their   65
 Pure blood to stagnate, their great hearts to fail!
The blank gray was not made to blast their hair,
 But like the climes that know nor snow nor hail,
They were all summer; lightning might assail
 And shiver them to ashes, but to trail   70
A long and snake-like life of dull decay
Was not for them—they had too little clay.

X

They were alone once more; for them to be
 Thus was another Eden; they were never
Weary, unless when separate: the tree   7!
 Cut from its forest root of years—the river

Dammed from its fountain—the child from the knee
  And breast maternal weaned at once forever,—
Would wither less than these two torn apart;
  Alas! there is no instinct like the human heart—   80

XI

The heart—which may be broken: happy they!
  Thrice fortunate! who of that fragile mold,
The precious porcelain of human clay,
  Break with the first fall: they can ne'er behold
The long year linked with heavy day on day,   85
  And all which must be borne, and never told;
While life's strange principle will often lie
Deepest in those who long the most to die.

XII

"Whom the gods love die young" was said of yore,
  And many deaths do they escape by this   90
The death of friends, and that which slays even more—
  The death of friendship, love, youth, all that is,
Except mere breath; and since the silent shore
  Awaits at last even those who longest miss
The old archer's shafts, perhaps the early grave   95
Which men weep over may be meant to save!

XIII

Haidée and Juan thought not of the dead—
  The heavens, and earth, and air seemed made for them:
They found no fault with Time, save that he fled;
  They saw not in themselves aught to condemn;   100
Each was the other's mirror, and but read
  Joy sparkling in their dark eyes like a gem,
And knew such brightness was but the reflection
Of their exchanging glances of affection.

XIV

The gentle pressure, and the thrilling touch,   105
  The least glance better understood than words,
Which still said all, and ne'er could say too much;
  A language, too, but like to that of birds,
Known but to them, at least appearing such
  As but to lovers a true sense affords;   110
Sweet playful phrases, which would seem absurd
To those who have ceased to hear such, or ne'er heard—

XV

All these were theirs, for they were children still,
  And children still they should have ever been;
They were not made in the real world to fill   115
  A busy character in the dull scene,
But like two beings born from out a rill,
  A nymph and her beloved, all unseen
To pass their lives in fountains and on flowers,
And never know the weight of human hours.   120

XVI

Moons changing had rolled on, and changeless found
  Those their bright rise had lighted to such joys
As rarely they beheld throughout their round;
  And these were not of the vain kind which cloys,

For theirs were buoyant spirits, never bound
 By the mere senses; and that which destroys
Most love, possession, unto them appeared
A thing which each endearment more endeared.   125

XVII

Oh beautiful! and rare as beautiful!
 But theirs was love in which the mind delights
To lose itself, when the old world grows dull,   130
 And we are sick of its hack sounds and sights,
Intrigues, adventures of the common school,
 Its petty passions, marriages, and flights,
Where Hymen's torch but brands one strumpet more,   135
Whose husband only knows her not a whore.

XVIII

Hard words; harsh truth; a truth which many know.
 Enough.—The faithful and the fairy pair,
Who never found a single hour too slow,
 What was it made them thus exempt from care?   140
Young innate feelings all have felt below,
 Which perish in the rest, but in them were
Inherent—what we mortals call romantic,
And always envy, though we deem it frantic.

XIX

This is in others a factitious state,   145
 An opium dream of too much youth and reading,
But was in them their nature or their fate:
 No novels e'er had set their young hearts bleeding,
For Haidée's knowledge was by no means great,
 And Juan was a boy of saintly breeding;   150
So that there was no reason for their loves
More than for those of nightingales or doves.

XX

They gazed upon the sunset; 'tis an hour
 Dear unto all, but dearest to *their* eyes,
For it had made them what they were: the power   155
 Of love had first o'erwhelmed them from such skies,
When happiness had been their only dower,
 And twilight saw them linked in passion's ties;
Charmed with each other, all things charmed that brought
The past still welcome as the present thought.   160

XXI

I know not why, but in that hour tonight,
 Even as they gazed, a sudden tremor came,
And swept, as 'twere, across their hearts' delight,
 Like the wind o'er a harp-string, or a flame,
When one is shook in sound, and one in sight: 165
 And thus some boding flashed through either frame,
And called from Juan's breast a faint low sigh,
While one new tear arose in Haidée's eye.

XXII

That large black prophet eye seemed to dilate
 And follow far the disappearing sun,   170
As if their last day of a happy date
 With his broad, bright, and dropping orb were gone;

Juan gazed on her as to ask his fate—
   He felt a grief, but knowing cause for none,
His glance inquired of hers for some excuse,   175
For feelings causeless, or at least abstruse.

XXIII

She turned to him, and smiled, but in that sort
   Which makes not others smile; then turned aside:
Whatever feeling shook her, it seemed short,
   And mastered by her wisdom or her pride;   180
When Juan spoke, too—it might be in sport—
   Of this their mutual feeling, she replied—
"If it should be so,—but—it cannot be—
Or I at least shall not survive to see."

XXIV

Juan would question further, but she pressed   185
   His lips to hers, and silenced him with this,
And then dismissed the omen from her breast,
   Defying augury with that fond kiss;
And no doubt of all methods 'tis the best:
   Some people prefer wine—'tis not amiss;   190
I have tried both; so those who would a part take
May choose between the headache and the heartache.

XXV

One of the two according to your choice,
   Woman or wine, you'll have to undergo;
Both maladies are taxes on our joys: 195
   But which to choose, I really hardly know;
And if I had to give a casting voice,
   For both sides I could many reasons show,
And then decide, without great wrong to either,
It were much better to have both than neither.   200

XXVI

Juan and Haidée gazed upon each other
   With swimming looks of speechless tenderness,
Which mixed all feelings—friend, child, lover, brother—
   All that the best can mingle and express
When two pure hearts are poured in one another,   205
   And love too much, and yet cannot love less;
But almost sanctify the sweet excess
By the immortal wish and power to bless.

XXVII

Mixed in each other's arms, and heart in heart,
   Why did they not then die?—they had lived too long   210
Should an hour come to bid them breathe apart;
   Years could but bring them cruel things or wrong;
The world was not for them, nor the world's art
   For beings passionate as Sappho's song;
Love was born *with* them, *in* them, so intense,   215
It was their very spirit—not a sense.

XXVIII

They should have lived together deep in woods,
   Unseen as sings the nightingale; they were
Unfit to mix in these thick solitudes
   Called social, haunts of Hate, and Vice, and Care;   220

How lonely every freeborn creature broods!
  The sweetest song-birds nestle in a pair;
The eagle soars alone; the gull and crow
Flock o'er their carrion, just like men below.

XXIX

Now pillowed cheek to cheek, in loving sleep,   225
  Haidée and Juan their siesta took,
A gentle slumber, but it was not deep,
  For ever and anon a something shook
Juan, and shuddering o'er his frame would creep;
  And Haidée's sweet lips murmured like a brook   230
A wordless music, and her face so fair
Stirred with her dream, as rose-leaves with the air;—

XXX

Or as the stirring of a deep clear stream
  Within an Alpine hollow, when the wind
Walks o'er it, was she shaken by the dream,   235
  The mystical usurper of the mind—
O'erpowering us to be whate'er may seem
  Good to the soul which we no more can bind:
Strange state of being! (for 'tis still to be),
Senseless to feel, and with sealed eyes to see.   240

XXXI

She dreamed of being alone on the seashore,
  Chained to a rock; she knew not how, but stir
She could not from the spot, and the loud roar
  Grew, and each wave rose roughly, threatening her;
And o'er her upper lip they seemed to pour,   245
  Until she sobbed for breath, and soon they were
Foaming o'er her lone head, so fierce and high—
Each broke to drown her, yet she could not die.

XXXII

Anon—she was released, and then she strayed
  O'er the sharp shingles with her bleeding feet,   250
And stumbled almost every step she made;
  And something rolled before her in a sheet,
Which she must still pursue howe'er afraid:
  'Twas white and indistinct, nor stopped to meet
Her glance nor grasp, for still she gazed and grasped, 255
And ran, but it escaped her as she clasped.

XXXIII

The dream changed:—in a cave she stood, its walls
  Were hung with marble icicles; the work
Of ages on its water-fretted halls,
  Where waves might wash, and seals might breed and lurk; 260
Her hair was dripping, and the very balls
  Of her black eyes seemed turned to tears, and mirk
The sharp rocks looked below each drop they caught,
Which froze to marble as it fell,—she thought.

XXXIV

And wet, and cold, and lifeless at her feet,   265
  Pale as the foam that frothed on his dead brow,
Which she essayed in vain to clear, (how sweet
  Were once her cares, how idle seemed they now!),

Lay Juan, nor could aught renew the beat
  Of his quenched heart; and the sea dirges low   270
Rang in her sad ears like a mermaid's song,
And that brief dream appeared a life too long.

XXXV

And gazing on the dead, she thought his face
  Faded, or altered into something new—
Like to her father's features, till each trace   275
  More like and like to Lambro's aspect grew—
With all his keen worn look and Grecian grace;
  And starting, she awoke, and what to view?
Oh! Powers of Heaven! what dark eye meets she there
'Tis—'tis her father's—fixed upon the pair!   280

XXXVI

Then shrieking, she arose, and shrieking fell,
  With joy and sorrow, hope and fear, to see
Him whom she deemed a habitant where dwell
  The ocean-buried, risen from death, to be
Perchance the death of one she loved too well;   285
  Dear as her father had been to Haidée,
It was a moment of that awful kind—
I have seen such—but must not call to mind.

XXXVII

Up Juan sprang to Haidée's bitter shriek,
  And caught her falling, and from off the wall   290
Snatched down his sabre, in hot haste to wreak
  Vengeance on him who was the cause of all:
Then Lambro who till now forebore to speak,
  Smiled scornfully, and said, "Within my call,
A thousand scimitars await the word;   295
Put up, young man, put up your silly sword."

XXXVIII

And Haidée clung around him; "Juan, 'tis—
  'Tis Lambro—'tis my father! Kneel with me—
He will forgive us—yes—it must be—yes.
  Oh! dearest father, in this agony   300
Of pleasure and of pain—even while I kiss
  Thy garment's hem with transport, can it be
That doubt should mingle with my filial joy?
Deal with me as thou wilt, but spare this boy."

XXXIX

High and inscrutable the old man stood,   305
  Calm in his voice, and calm within his eye—
Not always signs with him of calmest mood:
  He looked upon her, but gave no reply;
Then turned to Juan, in whose cheek the blood
  Oft came and went, as there resolved to die;   310
In arms, at least, he stood, in act to spring
On the first foe whom Lambro's call might bring.

XL

"Young man, your sword;" so Lambro once more said:
  Juan replied, "Not while this arm is free."
The old man's cheek grew pale, but not with dread,   315
  And drawing from his belt a pistol, he

Replied, "Your blood be then on your own head."
Then looked close at the flint, as if to see
'Twas fresh—for he had lately used the lock—
And next proceeded quietly to cock. 320

XLI

It has a strange quick jar upon the ear,
  That cocking of a pistol, when you know
A moment more will bring the sight to bear
  Upon your person, twelve yards off, or so; 325
A gentlemanly distance, not too near,
  If you have got a former friend for foe;
But after being fired at once or twice,
The ear becomes more Irish, and less nice.

XLII

Lambro presented, and one instant more
  Had stopped this Canto, and Don Juan's breath, 330
When Haidée threw herself her boy before;
  Stern as her sire: "On me," she cried, "let death
Descend—the fault is mine; this fatal shore
  He found—but sought not. I have pledged my faith;
I love him—I will die with him: I knew 335
Your nature's firmness—know your daughter's too."

XLIII

A minute past, and she had been all tears,
  And tenderness, and infancy; but now
She stood as one who championed human fears—
  Pale, statue-like, and stern, she wooed the blow; 340
And tall beyond her sex, and their compeers,
  She drew up to her height, as if to show
A fairer mark; and with a fixed eye scanned
Her father's face—but never stopped his hand.

XLIV

He gazed on her, and she on him; 'twas strange 345
  How like they looked! the expression was the same;
Serenely savage, with a little change
  In the large dark eye's mutual-darted flame;
For she, too, was as one who could avenge,
  If cause should be—a lioness, though tame; 350
Her father's blood before her father's face
Boiled up, and proved her truly of his race.

XLV

I said they were alike, their features and
  Their stature, differing but in sex and years:
Even to the delicacy of their hand 355
  There was resemblance, such as true blood wears;
And now to see them, thus divided, stand
  In fixed ferocity, when joyous tears,
And sweet sensations, should have welcomed both,
Shows what the passions are in their full growth. 360

XLVI

The father paused a moment, then withdrew
  His weapon, and replaced it; but stood still,
And looking on her, as to look her through,
  "Not I," he said, "have sought this stranger's ill;

Not *I* have made this desolation: few   365
  Would bear such outrage, and forbear to kill;
But I must do my duty—how thou hast
Done thine, the present vouches for the past.

XLVII

"Let him disarm; or, by my father's head,
  His own shall roll before you like a ball!"   370
He raised his whistle as the word he said,
  And blew; another answered to the call,
And rushing in disorderly, though led,
  And armed from boot to turban, one and all,
Some twenty of his train came, rank on rank;   375
He gave the word, "Arrest or slay the Frank."

XLVIII

Then, with a sudden movement, he withdrew
  His daughter; while compressed within his clasp,
'Twixt her and Juan interposed the crew;
  In vain she struggled in her father's grasp—   380
His arms were like a serpent's coil: then flew
  Upon their prey, as darts an angry asp,
The file of pirates: save the foremost, who
Had fallen, with his right shoulder half cut through.

XLIX

The second had his cheek laid open; but   385
  The third, a wary, cool old sworder, took
The blows upon his cutlass, and then put
  His own well in; so well, ere you could look,
His man was floored, and helpless at his foot,
  With the blood running like a little brook   390
From two smart sabre gashes, deep and red—
One on the arm, the other on the head.

L

And then they bound him where he fell, and bore
  Juan from the apartment: with a sign
Old Lambro bade them take him to the shore,   395
  Where lay some ships which were to sail at nine.
They laid him in a boat, and plied the oar
  Until they reached some galliots, placed in line;
On board of one of these, and under hatches,
They stowed him, with strict orders to the watches.   400

LI

The world is full of strange vicissitudes,
  And here was one exceedingly unpleasant:
A gentleman so rich in the world's goods,
  Handsome and young, enjoying all the present,
Just at the very time when he least broods   405
  On such a thing, is suddenly to sea sent,
Wounded and chained, so that he cannot move,
And all because a lady fell in love.

LII

Here I must leave him, for I grow pathetic,
  Moved by the Chinese nymph of tears, green tea!   410
Than whom Cassandra was not more prophetic;
  For if my pure libations exceed three,

I feel my heart become so sympathetic,
   That I must have recourse to black Bohea.
'Tis pity wine should be so deleterious,   415
For tea and coffee leave us much more serious,

LIII

Unless when qualified with thee, Cogniac!
   Sweet Naïad of the Phlegethontic rill!
Ah! why the liver wilt thou thus attack,
   And make, like other nymphs, thy lovers ill?   420
I would take refuge in weak punch, but *rack*
   (In each sense of the word), whene'er I fill
My mild and midnight beakers to the brim,
Wakes me next morning with its synonym.

LIV

I leave Don Juan for the present, safe—   425
   Not sound, poor fellow, but severely wounded;
Yet could his corporal pangs amount to half
   Of those with which his Haidée's bosom bounded!
She was not one to weep, and rave, and chafe,
   And then give way, subdued because surrounded;   430
Her mother was a Moorish maid from Fez,
Where all is Eden, or a wilderness.

LV

There the large olive rains its amber store
   In marble fonts; there grain, and flour, and fruit,
Gush from the earth until the land runs o'er;   435
   But there, too, many a poison-tree has root,
And midnight listens to the lion's roar,
   And long, long deserts scorch the camel's foot,
Or heaving whelm the helpless caravan;
And as the soil is, so the heart of man.   440

LVI

Afric is all the sun's, and as her earth
   Her human clay is kindled; full of power
For good or evil, burning from its birth,
   The Moorish blood partakes the planet's hour,
And like the soil beneath it will bring forth: 445
   Beauty and love were Haidée's mother's dower;
But her large dark eye showed deep Passion's force,
Though sleeping like a lion near a source.

LVII

Her daughter, tempered with a milder ray,
   Like summer clouds all silvery, smooth, and fair,   450
Till slowly charged with thunder they display
   Terror to earth, and tempest to the air,
Had held till now her soft and milky way,
   But overwrought with passion and despair,
The fire burst forth from her Numidian veins,   455
Even as the Simoom sweeps the blasted plains.

LVIII

The last sight which she saw was Juan's gore,
   And he himself o'ermastered and cut down;
His blood was running on the very floor
   Where late he trod, her beautiful, her own;   460

Thus much she viewed an instant and no more,—
　Her struggles ceased with one convulsive groan;
On her sire's arm, which until now scarce held
Her writhing, fell she like a cedar felled.

LIX

A vein had burst, and her sweet lips' pure dyes   465
　Were dabbled with the deep blood which ran o'er;
And her head drooped, as when the lily lies
　O'ercharged with rain: her summoned handmaids bore
Their lady to her couch with gushing eyes;
　Of herbs and cordials they produced their store,   470
But she defied all means they could employ,
Like one life could not hold, nor death destroy.

LX

Days lay she in that state unchanged, though chill—
　With nothing livid, still her lips were red;
She had no pulse, but death seemed absent still;   475
　No hideous sign proclaimed her surely dead;
Corruption came not in each mind to kill
　All hope; to look upon her sweet face bred
New thoughts of life, for it seemed full of soul—
She had so much, earth could not claim the whole.   480

LXI

The ruling passion, such as marble shows
　When exquisitely chiselled, still lay there,
But fixed as marble's unchanged aspect throws
　O'er the fair Venus, but forever fair;
O'er the Laocoön's all eternal throes,   485
　And ever-dying Gladiator's air,
Their energy like life forms all their fame,
Yet looks not life, for they are still the same.

LXII

She woke at length, but not as sleepers wake,
　Rather the dead, for life seemed something new,   490
A strange sensation which she must partake
　Perforce, since whatsoever met her view
Struck not on memory, though a heavy ache
　Lay at her heart, whose earliest beat still true
Brought back the sense of pain without the cause,   495
For, for a while, the furies made a pause.

LXIII

She looked on many a face with vacant eye,
　On many a token without knowing what;
She saw them watch her without asking why,
　And recked not who around her pillow sat;   500
Not speechless, though she spoke not; not a sigh
　Relieved her thoughts; dull silence and quick chat
Were tried in vain by those who served; she gave
No sign, save breath, of having left the grave.

LXIV

Her handmaids tended, but she heeded not;   505
　Her father watched, she turned her eyes away;
She recognized no being, and no spot,
　However dear or cherished in their day;

They changed from room to room—but all forgot—
　Gentle, but without memory she lay;
At length those eyes, which they would fain be weaning
Back to old thoughts, waxed full of fearful meaning.

510

LXV

And then a slave bethought her of a harp;
　The harper came, and tuned his instrument;
At the first notes, irregular and sharp,
　On him her flashing eyes a moment bent,
Then to the wall she turned as if to warp
　Her thoughts from sorrow through her heart resent;
And he began a long low island song
Of ancient days, ere tyranny grew strong.

515

520

LXVI

Anon her thin wan fingers beat the wall
　In time to his old tune; he changed the theme,
And sung of love; the fierce name struck through all
　Her recollection; on her flashed the dream
Of what she was, and is, if ye could call
　To be so being; in a gushing stream
The tears rushed forth from her o'erclouded brain,
Like mountain mists at length dissolved in rain.

525

LXVII

Short solace, vain relief!—thought came too quick,
　And whirled her brain to madness; she arose
As one who ne'er had dwelt among the sick,
　And flew at all she met, as on her foes;
But no one ever heard her speak or shriek,
　Although her paroxysm drew towards its close;—
Hers was a frenzy which disdained to rave,
Even when they smote her, in the hope to save.

530

535

LXVIII

Yet she betrayed at times a gleam of sense;
　Nothing could make her meet her father's face,
Though on all other things with looks intense
　She gazed, but none she ever could retrace;
Food she refused, and raiment; no pretence
　Availed for either; neither change of place,
Nor time, nor skill, nor remedy, could give her
Senses to sleep—the power seemed gone forever.

540

LXIX

Twelve days and nights she withered thus; at last,
　Without a groan, or sigh, or glance, to show
A parting pang, the spirit from her passed:
　And they who watched her nearest could not know
The very instant, till the change that cast
　Her sweet face into shadow, dull and slow,
Glazed o'er her eyes—the beautiful, the black—
Oh! to possess such luster—and then lack!

545

550

LXX

She died, but not alone; she held within
　A second principle of life, which might
Have dawned a fair and sinless child of sin;
　But closed its little being without light,

555

And went down to the grave unborn, wherein
  Blossom and bough lie withered with one blight;
In vain the dews of Heaven descend above
The bleeding flower and blasted fruit of love.   560

LXXI

Thus lived—thus died she; never more on her
  Shall sorrow light, or shame. She was not made
Through years or moons the inner weight to bear,
  Which colder hearts endure till they are laid
By age in earth: her days and pleasures were   565
  Brief, but delightful—such as had not staid
Long with her destiny; but she sleeps well
By the sea-shore, whereon she loved to dwell.

LXXII

That isle is now all desolate and bare,
  Its dwellings down, its tenants passed away;   570
None but her own and father's grave is there,
  And nothing outward tells of human clay;
Ye could not know where lies a thing so fair,
  No stone is there to show, no tongue to say,
What was; no dirge, except the hollow sea's,   575
Mourns o'er the beauty of the Cyclades.

LXXIII

But many a Greek maid in a loving song
  Sighs o'er her name; and many an islander
With her sire's story makes the night less long;
  Valor was his, and beauty dwelt with her: 580
If she loved rashly, her life paid for wrong—
  A heavy price must all pay who thus err,
In some shape; let none think to fly the danger,
For soon or late Love is his own avenger.

            1821

CANTO THE TENTH

[WHAT MIGHT HAVE BEEN THE NOBLEST NATION]

LXVI

I've no great cause to love that spot of earth
  Which holds what *might have been* the noblest nation;
But though I owe it little but my birth,
  I feel a mixed regret and veneration
For its decaying fame and former worth.   525
  Seven years (the usual term of transportation)
Of absence lay one's old resentments level,
When a man's country's going to the devil.

LXVII

Alas! could she but fully, truly, know
  How her great name is now throughout abhorred;   530
How eager all the earth is for the blow
  Which shall lay bare her bosom to the sword;
How all the nations deem her their worst foe,
  That worse than *worst of foes*, the once adored
False friend, who held out freedom to mankind,   535
And now would chain them, to the very mind;—

LXVIII

Would she be proud, or boast herself the free,
  Who is but first of slaves? The nations are
In prison,—but the gaoler, what is he?
  No less a victim to the bolt and bar.
Is the poor privilege to turn the key
  Upon the captive, freedom? He's as far
From the enjoyment of the earth and air
Who watches o'er the chain, as they who wear.   540

1823

CANTO THE ELEVENTH

[HIGH SOCIETY IN ENGLAND]

LIII

Juan knew several languages—as well
  He might—and brought them up with skill, in time
To save his fame with each accomplished belle,
  Who still regretted that he did not rhyme.   420
There wanted but this requisite to swell
  His qualities (with them) into sublime:
Lady Fitz-Frisky, and Miss Mævia Mannish,
Both longed extremely to be sung in Spanish.

LIV

However, he did pretty well, and was   425
  Admitted as an aspirant to all
The coteries, and, as in Banquo's glass,
  At great assemblies or in parties small,
He saw ten thousand living authors pass,
  That being about their average numeral;   430
Also the eighty "greatest living poets,"
As every paltry magazine can show *its*.

LV

In twice five years the "greatest living poet,"
  Like to the champion in the fisty ring,
Is called on to support his claim, or show it,   435
  Although 'tis an imaginary thing,
Even I—albeit I'm sure I did not know it,
  Nor sought of foolscap subjects to be king—
Was reckoned, a considerable time,
The grand Napoleon of the realms of rhyme.   440

LVI

But Juan was my Moscow, and Faliero
  My Leipsic, and my Mont Saint Jean seems Cain:
La Belle Alliance of dunces down at zero,
  Now that the Lion's fallen, may rise again:
But I will fall at least as fell my hero;   445
  Nor reign at all, or as a *monarch* reign;
Or to some lonely isle of gaolers go,
With turncoat Southey for my turnkey Lowe.

LVII

Sir Walter reigned before me; Moore and Campbell
 Before and after: but now grown more holy, 450
The Muses upon Sion's hill must ramble
 With poets almost clergymen, or wholly:
And Pegasus has a psalmodic amble
 Beneath the very Reverend Rowley Powley,
Who shoes the glorious animal with stilts, 455
A modern Ancient Pistol—"by these hilts"!

. . . .

LIX

Then there's my gentle Euphues, who, they say, 465
 Sets up for being a sort of *moral me;*
He'll find it rather difficult some day
 To turn out both, or either, it may be.
Some persons think that Coleridge hath the sway;
 And Wordsworth has supporters, two or three; 470
And that deep-mouth'd Bœotian "Savage Landor"
Has taken for a swan rogue Southey's gander.

LX

John Keats, who was killed off by one critique,
 Just as he really promised something great,
If not intelligible, without Greek 475
 Contrived to talk about the gods of late,
Much as they might have been supposed to speak.
 Poor fellow! His was an untoward fate;
'Tis strange the mind, that fiery particle,
Should let itself be snuffed out by an article. 480

LXI

The list grows long of live and dead pretenders
 To that which none will gain—or none will know
The conqueror at least; who, ere Time renders
 His last award, will have the long grass grow
Above his burnt-out brain, and sapless cinders. 485
 If I might augur, I should rate but low
Their chances;—they're too numerous, like the thirty
Mock tyrants, when Rome's annals waxed but dirty.

LXII

This is the literary *lower* empire,
 Where the prætorian bands take up the matter;— 490
A "dreadful trade," like his who "gathers samphire,"
 The insolent soldiery to soothe and flatter,
With the same feelings as you'd coax a vampire.
 Now, were I once at home, and in good satire,
I'd try conclusions with those Janizaries, 495
And show them *what* an intellectual war is.

LXIII

I think I know a trick or two, would turn
 Their flanks;—but it is hardly worth my while
With such small gear to give myself concern:
 Indeed I've not the necessary bile; 500
My natural temper's really aught but stern,
 And even my Muse's worst reproof's a smile;
And then she drops a brief and modern curtsy,
And glides away, assured she never hurts ye.

LXIV

My Juan, whom I left in deadly peril　　　505
　Amongst live poets and *blue* ladies, passed
With some small profit through that field so sterile,
　Being tired in time, and neither least nor last,
Left it before he had been treated very ill;
　And henceforth found himself more gaily classed　510
Among the higher spirits of the day,
The sun's true son, no vapor, but a ray.

LXV

His morns he passed in business—which dissected,
　Was like all business, a laborious nothing
That leads to lassitude, the most infected　　　515
　And Centaur Nessus garb of mortal clothing,
And on our sofas makes us lie dejected,
　And talk in tender horrors of our loathing
All kinds of toil, save for our country's good—
Which grows no better, though 'tis time it should.　520

LXVI

His afternoons he passed in visits, luncheons,
　Lounging, and boxing; and the twilight hour
In riding round those vegetable puncheons
　Called "Parks," where there is neither fruit nor flower
Enough to gratify a bee's slight munchings;　　525
　But after all it is the only "bower"
(In Moore's phrase) where the fashionable fair
Can form a slight acquaintance with fresh air.

LXVII

Then dress, then dinner, then awakes the world!
　Then glare the lamps, then whirl the wheels, then roar　530
Through street and square fast flashing chariots hurled
　Like harnessed meteors; then along the floor
Chalk mimics painting; then festoons are twirled;
　Then roll the brazen thunders of the door,
Which opens to the thousand happy few　　　535
An earthly Paradise of *Or Molu.*

LXVIII

There stands the noble hostess, nor shall sink
　With the three-thousandth curtsy; there the waltz,
The only dance which teaches girls to think,
　Makes one in love even with its very faults.　540
Saloon, room, hall, o'erflow beyond their brink,
　And long the latest of arrivals halts,
'Midst royal dukes and dames condemned to climb,
And gain an inch of staircase at a time.

LXIX

Thrice happy he who, after a survey　　　545
　Of the good company, can win a corner,
A door that's *in* or boudoir *out* of the way,
　Where he may fix himself like small "Jack Horner,"
And let the Babel round run as it may,
　And look on as a mourner, or a scorner,　　550
Or an approver, or a mere spectator,
Yawning a little as the night grows later.

LXX

But this won't do, save by and by; and he
  Who, like Don Juan, takes an active share,
Must steer with care through all that glittering sea   555
  Of gems and plumes and pearls and silks, to where
He deems it is his proper place to be;
  Dissolving in the waltz to some soft air,
Or proudlier prancing with mercurial skill,
Where Science marshals forth her own quadrille.   560

LXXI

Or, if he dance not, but hath higher views
  Upon an heiress or his neighbor's bride,
Let him take care that that which he pursues
  Is not at once too palpably descried.
Full many an eager gentleman oft rues   565
  His haste; impatience is a blundering guide,
Amongst a people famous for reflection,
Who like to play the fool with circumspection.

LXXII

But, if you can contrive, get next at supper;
  Or if forestalled, get opposite and ogle:—   570
Oh, ye ambrosial moments! always upper
  In mind, a sort of sentimental bogle,
Which sits for ever upon memory's crupper,
  The ghost of vanished pleasures once in vogue! Ill
Can tender souls relate the rise and fall   575
Of hopes and fears which shake a single ball.

LXXIII

But these precautionary hints can touch
  Only the common run, who must pursue,
And watch, and ward; whose plans a word too much
  Or little overturns; and not the few   580
Or many (for the number's sometimes such)
  Whom a good mien, especially if new,
Or fame, or name, for wit, war, sense, or nonsense,
Permits whate'er they please, or *did* not long since.

LXXIV

Our hero, as a hero, young and handsome,   585
  Noble, rich, celebrated, and a stranger,
Like other slaves of course must pay his ransom,
  Before he can escape from so much danger
As will environ a conspicuous man. Some
  Talk about poetry, and "rack and manger,"   590
And ugliness, disease, as toil and trouble;—
I wish they knew the life of a young noble.

LXXV

They are young, but know not youth—it is anticipated;
  Handsome but wasted, rich without a sou;
Their vigor in a thousand arms is dissipated;   595
  Their cash comes *from*, their wealth goes *to* a Jew;
Both senates see their nightly votes participated
  Between the tyrant's and the tribunes' crew;
And having voted, dined, drunk, gamed, and whored,
The family vault receives another lord.   600

LXXVI

"Where is the world?" cries Young, at eighty—"Where
  The world in which a man was born?" Alas!
Where is the world of eight years past? 'Twas there—
  I look for it—'tis gone, a globe of glass!
Cracked, shivered, vanished, scarcely gazed on, ere   604
  A silent change dissolves the glittering mass.
Statesmen, chiefs, orators, queens, patriots, kings,
And dandies, all are gone on the wind's wings.

    . . . .

LXXXV

I have seen small poets, and great prosers, and
  Interminable—not eternal—speakers—
I have seen the funds at war with house and land—   675
  I have seen the country gentlemen turn squeakers—
I have seen the people ridden o'er like sand
  By slaves on horseback—I have seen malt liquors
Exchanged for "thin potations" by John Bull—
I have seen John half detect himself a fool.—   680

LXXXVI

But *"Carpe diem,"* Juan, *"carpe, carpe!"*
  Tomorrow sees another race as gay
And transient, and devoured by the same harpy.
  "Life's a poor player,"—then "play out the play,
Ye villains!" and above all keep a sharp eye   685
  Much less on what you do than what you say:
Be hypocritical, be cautious, be
Not what you *seem,* but always what you *see.*

LXXXVII

But how shall I relate in other cantos
  Of what befell our hero in the land,   690
Which 'tis the common cry and lie to vaunt as
  A moral country? But I hold my hand—
For I disdain to write an Atalantis;
  But 'tis well at once to understand,
You are *not* a moral people, and you know it   695
Without the aid of too sincere a poet.

LXXXVIII

What Juan saw and underwent shall be
  My topic, with of course the due restriction
Which is required by proper courtesy;
  And recollect the work is only fiction,   700
And that I sing of neither mine nor me,
  Though every scribe, in some slight turn of diction,
Will hint allusions never *meant.* Ne'er doubt
This—when I speak, I *don't hint,* but *speak out.*

LXXXIX

Whether he married with the third or fourth   705
  Offspring of some sage husband-hunting countess,
Or whether with some virgin of more worth
  (I mean in Fortune's matrimonial bounties),
He took to regularly peopling Earth,
  Of which your lawful, awful wedlock fount is—   710
Or whether he was taken in for damages,
For being too excursive in his homages,—

XC

Is yet within the unread events of time.
  Thus far, go forth, thou lay, which I will back
Against the same given quantity of rhyme,   715
  For being as much the subject of attack
As ever yet was any work sublime,
  By those who love to say that white is black.
So much the better!—I may stand alone,   720
But would not change my free thoughts for a throne.
                                                        1823

WHEN A MAN HATH NO FREEDOM
TO FIGHT FOR AT HOME

When a man hath no freedom to fight for at home,
  Let him combat for that of his neighbors;
Let him think of the glories of Greece and of Rome,
  And get knocked on his head for his labors.

To do good to mankind is the chivalrous plan,   5
  And is always as nobly requited;
Then battle for freedom wherever you can,
  And, if not shot or hanged, you'll get knighted.
1820   1824

THE WORLD IS A BUNDLE OF HAY

        The world is a bundle of hay,
          Mankind are the asses who pull;
        Each tugs it a different way,
          And the greatest of all is John Bull.
        1821   1830

WHO KILLED JOHN KEATS

          "Who killed John Keats?"
          "I," says *The Quarterly*,
          So savage and Tartarly;
          " 'Twas one of my feats."

          "Who shot the arrow?"   5
          "The poet-priest **Milman**
          (So ready to kill man),
          Or Southey, or Barrow."
          1821   1830

FROM CAIN: A MYSTERY

Cain *and* Abel *have dressed their altars, and kindled
a flame upon them.*

  Abel. My brother, as the elder, offer first   220
Thy prayer and thanksgiving with sacrifice.
  Cain. No—I am new to this; lead thou the way,
And I will follow—as I may.
  Abel (kneeling).   Oh. God!

Who made us, and who breathed the breath of life
Within our nostrils, who hath blessed us, 225
And spared, despite our father's sin, to make
His children all lost, as they might have been,
Had not thy justice been so tempered with
The mercy which is thy delight, as to
Accord a pardon like a Paradise, 230
Compared with our great crimes:—Sole Lord of Light,
Of good, and glory, and eternity!
Without whom all were evil, and with whom
Nothing can err, except to some good end
Of thine omnipotent benevolence— 235
Inscrutable, but still to be fulfilled—
Accept from out thy humble first of shepherd's
First of the first-born flocks—an offering,
In itself nothing—as what offering can be
Aught unto thee?—but yet accept it for 240
The thanksgiving of him who spreads it in
The face of thy high heaven, bowing his own
Even to the dust, of which he is, in honor
Of thee, and of thy name, for evermore!
    Cain (standing erect during this speech). Spirit!
        whate'er or whosoe'er thou art, 245
Omnipotent, it may be—and, if good,
Shown in the exemption of thy deeds from evil;
Jehovah upon earth! and God in heaven!
And it may be with other names, because
Thine attributes seem many, as thy works:— 250
If thou must be propitiated with prayers,
Take them! If thou must be induced with altars,
And softened with a sacrifice, receive them!
Two beings here erect them unto thee.
If thou lov'st blood, the shepherd's shrine, which
    smokes 255
On my right hand, hath shed it for thy service
In the first of his flock, whose limbs now reek
In sanguinary incense to thy skies;
Or if the sweet and blooming fruits of earth,
And milder seasons, which the unstained turf 260
I spread them on now offers in the face
Of the broad sun which ripened them, may seem
Good to thee, inasmuch as they have not
Suffered in limb or life, and rather form
A sample of thy works, than supplication 265
To look on ours! If a shrine without victim,
And altar without gore, may win thy favor,
Look on it! and for him who dresseth it,
He is—such as thou mad'st him; and seeks nothing
Which must be won by kneeling: if he's evil, 270
Strike him! thou art omnipotent, and may'st—
For what can he oppose? If he be good,
Strike him, or spare him, as thou wilt! since all
Rests upon thee; and good and evil seem
To have no power themselves, save in thy will; 275
And whether that be good or ill I know not,
Not being omnipotent, nor fit to judge
Omnipotence, but merely to endure
Its mandate; which thus far I have endured.
    (*The fire upon the altar of* ABEL *kindles into a*
      column of the brightest flame, and ascends to

*heaven; while a whirlwind throws down the
altar of* CAIN, *and scatters the fruits abroad
upon the earth.*)

Abel (kneeling). Oh, brother, pray! Jehovah's
    wroth with thee.

Cain. Why so?   280

Abel.   Thy fruits are scattered on the
    earth.

Cain. From earth they came, to earth let them
    return;
Their seed will bear fresh fruit there ere the summer:
Thy burnt flesh-off'ring prospers better; see
How heaven licks up the flames, when thick with
    blood!   285

Abel. Think not upon my offering's acceptance,
But make another of thine own before
It is too late.

Cain.   I will build no more altars,
Nor suffer any——

Abel (rising).   Cain! what meanest thou?

Cain. To cast down yon vile flatt'rer of the clouds,   290
The smoky harbinger of thy dull prayers—
Thine altar, with its blood of lambs and kids,
Which fed on milk, to be destroyed in blood.

Abel (opposing him). Thou shalt not:—add not
    impious works to impious
Words! let that altar stand—'t is hallowed now   295
By the immortal pleasure of Jehovah,
In his acceptance of the victims.

Cain.   His!
His pleasure! what was his high pleasure in
The fumes of scorching flesh and smoking blood,
To the pain of the bleating mothers, which   300
Still yearn for their dead offspring? or the pangs
Of the sad ignorant victims underneath
Thy pious knife? Give way! this bloody record
Shall not stand in the sun, to shame creation!

Abel. Brother, give back, thou shalt not touch my
    altar   305
With violence: if that thou wilt adopt it,
To try another sacrifice, 't is thine.

Cain. Another sacrifice! Give way, or else
That sacrifice may be——

Abel.   What mean'st thou?

Cain.   Give—
Give way!—thy God loves blood!—then look to it:—   310
Give way, ere he hath *more!*

Abel.   In his great name,
I stand between thee and the shrine which hath
Had his acceptance.

Cain.   If thou lov'st thyself,
Stand back till I have strew'd this turf along
Its native soil:—else——   315

Abel (opposing him). I love God far more
Than life.

*Cain (striking him with a brand, on the temples,
which he snatches from the altar.)*
      Then take thy life unto thy God,
Since he loves lives.

Abel (falls). What hast thou done, my brother?

Cain. Brother!
Abel. Oh, God! receive thy servant, and
Forgive his slayer, for he knew not what
He did—Cain, give me—give me thy hand, and tell   320
Poor Zillah——
Cain (after a moment's stupefaction). My hand!
'T is all red, and with——
What?
  (A long pause.—Looking slowly round.) Where
   am I? alone? Where's Abel? where
Cain? Can it be that I am he? My brother,
Awake!—why liest thou so on the green earth?   325
'T is not the hour of slumber;—why so pale?
What, hast thou!—thou wert full of life this morn!
Abel! I pray thee, mock me not! I smote
Too fiercely, but not fatally. Ah, why
Wouldst thou oppose me? This is mockery;   330
And only done to daunt me:—'t was a blow—
And but a blow. Stir—stir—nay, only stir!
Why, so—that 's well!—thou breath'st! breathe upon
 me!
Oh, God! Oh, God!
  Abel (very faintly). What's he who speaks of God?
Cain. Thy murderer.
  Abel.   Then may God forgive him!
   Cain,
Comfort poor Zillah:—she has but one brother   335
Now.   (ABEL *dies.*)
 Cain. And I none!—Who makes me brotherless?
His eyes are open! then he is not dead!
Death is like sleep; and sleep shuts down our lids.
His lips, too, are apart; why then he breathes;
And yet I feel it not.—His heart!—his heart!   340
Let me see, doth it beat? methinks—No!—no!
This is a vision, else I am become
The native of another and worse world.
The earth swims round me:—what is this?— 't is wet;
     (Puts his hand to his brow,
      and then looks at it.)
And yet there are no dews! 'T is blood—my blood—   345
My brother's and my own! and shed by me!
Then what have I further to do with life,
Since I have taken life from my own flesh?
But he cannot be dead!—Is silence death?
No, he will wake; then let me watch by him.   350
Life cannot be so slight, as to be quenched
Thus quickly!—he hath spoken to me since—
What shall I say to him?—My brother!—No:
He will not answer to that name; for brethren
Smite not each other. Yet—yet—speak to me.   355
Oh! for a word more of that gentle voice,
That I may bear to hear my own again!

1821

THE VISION OF JUDGMENT

I

Saint Peter sat by the celestial gate:
　　His keys were rusty, and the lock was
　　　　dull,
So little trouble had been given of late;
　　Not that the place by any means was full,
But since the Gallic era "eighty-eight"　　5
　　The devils had ta'en a longer, stronger
　　　　pull,
And "a pull altogether," as they say
At sea—which drew most souls another
　　way.

II

The angels all were singing out of tune,
　　And hoarse with having little else to
　　　　do,　　10
Excepting to wind up the sun and moon,
　　Or curb a runaway young star or two,
Or wild colt of a comet, which too soon
　　Broke out of bounds o'er the ethereal
　　　　blue,
Splitting some planet with its playful tail, 15
As boats are sometimes by a wanton whale.

III

The guardian seraphs had retired on high,
　　Finding their charges past all care below;
Terrestrial business filled nought in the sky
　　Save the recording angel's black bu-
　　　　reau;　　20
Who found, indeed, the facts to multiply
　　With such rapidity of vice and woe,
That he had stripped off both his wings in
　　quills,
And yet was in arrear of human ills.

IV

His business so augmented of late years, 25
　　That he was forced, against his will no
　　　　doubt,
(Just like those cherubs, earthly ministers,)
　　For some resource to turn himself about,
And claim the help of his celestial peers,
　　To aid him ere he should be quite worn
　　　　out　　30
By the increased demand for his remarks:
Six angels and twelve saints were named
　　his clerks.

V

This was a handsome board—at least for
　　heaven;
　　And yet they had even then enough to
　　　　do,
So many conquerors' cars were daily
　　driven,　　35
　　So many kingdoms fitted up anew;

Each day, too, slew its thousands six or
　　seven,
　　Till at the crowning carnage, Waterloo,
They threw their pens down in divine
　　disgust—
The page was so besmeared with blood
　　and dust.　　40

VI

This by the way; 'tis not mine to record
　　What angels shrink from: even the very
　　　　devil
On this occasion his own work abhorred,
　　So surfeited with the infernal revel:
Though he himself had sharpened every
　　sword,　　45
　　It almost quenched his innate thirst of
　　　　evil,
(Here Satan's sole good work deserves in-
　　sertion—
'Tis, that he has both generals in rever-
　　sion.)

VII

Let's skip a few short years of hollow peace,
　　Which peopled earth no better, hell as
　　　　wont,　　50
And heaven none—they form the tyrant's
　　lease,
　　With nothing but new names subscribed
　　　　upon 't;
'Twill one day finish: meantime they in-
　　crease,
　　"With seven heads and ten horns," and
　　　　all in front,
Like Saint John's foretold beast; but ours
　　are born　　55
Less formidable in the head than horn.

VIII

In the first year of freedom's second dawn
　　Died George the Third; although no
　　　　tyrant, one
Who shielded tyrants, till each sense with-
　　drawn
Left him nor mental nor external sun:　　60
A better farmer ne'er brushed dew from
　　lawn,
　　A worse king never left a realm undone!
He died—but left his subjects still behind,
One half as mad—and t'other no less blind.

IX

He died! his death made no great stir on
　　earth:　　65
　　His burial made some pomp; there was
　　　　profusion
Of velvet, gilding, brass, and no great
　　dearth
　　Of aught but tears—save those shed by
　　　　collusion.

For these things may be bought at their
true worth;
Of elegy there was the due infusion— 70
Bought also; and the torches, cloaks, and
banners,
Heralds, and relics of old Gothic manners,

X

Formed a sepulchral melodrame. Of all
The fools who flocked to swell or see the
show,
Who cared about the corpse? The
funeral 75
Made the attraction, and the black the
woe.
There throbbed not there a thought which
pierced the pall;
And when the gorgeous coffin was laid
low,
It seemed the mockery of hell to fold
The rottenness of eighty years in gold. 80

XI

So mix his body with the dust! It might
Return to what it *must* far sooner, were
The natural compound left alone to fight
Its way back into earth, and fire, and air;
But the unnatural balsams merely blight 85
What nature made him at his birth, as
bare
As the mere million's base unmummied
clay—
Yet all his spices but prolong decay.

XII

He's dead—and upper earth with him has
done;
He's buried; save the undertaker's bill, 90
Or lapidary scrawl, the world is gone
For him, unless he left a German will:
But where's the proctor who will ask his
son?
In whom his qualities are reigning still,
Except that household virtue, most un-
common, 95
Of constancy to a bad, ugly woman.

XIII

"God save the king!" It is a large economy
In God to save the like; but if he will
Be saving, all the better; for not one am I
Of those who think damnation better
still: 100
I hardly know too if not quite alone am I
In this small hope of bettering future ill
By circumscribing, with some slight re-
striction,
The eternity of hell's hot jurisdiction.

XIV

I know this is unpopular; I know 105
'Tis blasphemous; I know one may be
damned
For hoping no one else may e'er be so;
I know my catechism; I know we're
crammed
With the best doctrines till we quite o'er-
flow;
I know that all save England's church
have shammed, 110
And that the other twice two hundred
churches
And synagogues have made a *damned* bad
purchase.

XV

God help us all! God help me too! I am,
God knows, as helpless as the devil can
wish,
And not a whit more difficult to damn, 115
Than is to bring to land a late-hooked
fish,
Or to the butcher to purvey the lamb;
Not that I'm fit for such a noble dish,
As one day will be that immortal fry
Of almost everybody born to die. 120

XVI

Saint Peter sat by the celestial gate,
And nodded o'er his keys; when, lo!
there came
A wondrous noise he had not heard of
late—
A rushing sound of wind, and stream,
and flame;
In short, a roar of things extremely
great, 125
Which would have made aught save a
saint exclaim;
But he, with first a start and then a wink,
Said, "There's another star gone out, I
think!"

XVII

But ere he could return to his repose,
A cherub flapped his right wing o'er his
eyes— 130
At which St. Peter yawned, and rubbed his
nose:
"Saint porter," said the angel, "prithee
rise!"
Waving a goodly wing, which glowed, as
glows
An earthly peacock's tail, with heavenly
dyes:
To which the saint replied, "Well, what's
the matter? 135
Is Lucifer come back with all this clatter?"

XVIII

"No," quoth the cherub; "George the
  Third is dead."
  "And who *is* George the Third?" replied
  the apostle:
"What George? what Third?" "The king
  of England," said
The angel. "Well! he won't find kings
  to jostle   140
Him on his way; but does he wear his
  head?
  Because the last we saw here had a tustle,
And ne'er would have got into heaven's
  good graces,
Had he not flung his head in all our faces.

XIX

"He was, if I remember, king of France; 145
  That head of his, which could not keep a
  crown
On earth, yet ventured in my face to
  advance
  A claim to those of martyrs—like my
  own:
If I had had my sword, as I had once
  When I cut ears off, I had cut him
  down;   150
But having but my *keys*, and not my brand,
I only knocked his head from out his hand.

XX

"And then he set up such a headless howl,
  That all the saints came out and took
  him in;
And there he sits by St. Paul, cheek by
  jowl;   155
  That fellow Paul—the parvenù! The
  skin
Of St. Bartholomew, which makes his
  cowl
  In heaven, and upon earth redeemed his
  sin,
So as to make a martyr, never sped
Better than did this weak and wooden
  head.   160

XXI

"But had it come up here upon his shoul-
  ders,
  There would have been a different tale
  to tell:
The fellow-feeling in the saint's beholders
  Seems to have acted on them like a spell;
And so this very foolish head heaven
  solders   165
  Back on its trunk; it may be very well,
And seems the custom here to overthrow
Whatever has been wisely done below."

XXII

The angel answered, "Peter! do not pout:
  The king who comes has head and all
  entire,   170
And never knew much what it was about—
  He did as doth the puppet—by its wire,
And will be judged like all the rest, no
  doubt:
  My business and your own is not to
  inquire
Into such matters, but to mind our cue— 175
Which is to act as we are bid to do."

XXIII

While thus they spake, the angelic caravan,
  Arriving like a rush of mighty wind,
Cleaving the fields of space, as doth the
  swan
  Some silver stream (say Ganges, Nile, or
  Inde,   180
Or Thames, or Tweed), and midst them an
  old man
  With an old soul, and both extremely
  blind,
Halted before the gate, and in his shroud
Seated their fellow-traveller on a cloud.

XXIV

But bringing up the rear of this bright
  host   185
  A Spirit of a different aspect waved
His wings, like thunder-clouds above some
  coast
  Whose barren beach with frequent
  wrecks is paved;
His brow was like the deep when tempest-
  tossed;
  Fierce and unfathomable thoughts en-
  graved   190
Eternal wrath on his immortal face,
And *where* he gazed a gloom pervaded
  space.

XXV

As he drew near, he gazed upon the gate
  Ne'er to be entered more by him or Sin,
With such a glance of supernatural hate, 195
  As made Saint Peter wish himself within;
He pottered with his keys at a great rate,
  And sweated through his apostolic skin:
Of course his perspiration was but ichor,
Or some such other spiritual liquor.   200

XXVI

The very cherubs huddled all together,
  Like birds when soars the falcon, and
  they felt
A tingling to the tip of every feather,
  And formed a circle like Orion's belt

Around their poor old charge; who scarce
  knew whither   205
His guards had led him, though they
  gently dealt
With royal manes (for by many stories,
And true, we learn the angels are all
  Tories).

XXVII

As things were in this posture, the gate flew
  Asunder, and the flashing of its hinges 210
Flung over space an universal hue
  Of many-colored flame, until its tinges
Reached even our speck of earth, and made
  a new
  Aurora borealis spread its fringes
O'er the North Pole; the same seen, when
  icebound,   215
By Captain Parry's crew, in "Melville's
  Sound."

XXVIII

And from the gate thrown open issued
  beaming
  A beautiful and mighty Thing of Light,
Radiant with glory, like a banner stream-
  ing
  Victorious from some world-o'erthrowing
  fight: 220
My poor comparisons must need be teem-
  ing
  With earthly likenesses, for here the
  night
Of clay obscures our best conceptions, sav-
  ing
Johanna Southcote, or Bob Southey raving.

XXIX

'Twas the archangel Michael: all men
  know   225
  The make of angels and archangels, since
There's scarce a scribbler has not one to
  show,
  From the fiends' leaders to the angels'
  prince.
There also are some altar-pieces, though
  I really can't say that they much
  evince   230
One's inner notions of immortal spirits;
But let the connoisseurs explain *their*
  merits.

XXX

Michael flew forth in glory and in good;
  A goodly work of him from whom all
  glory
And good arise; the portal past—he
  stood;   235
  Before him the young cherubs and saints
  hoary—

(I say *young,* begging to be understood
  By looks, not years; and should be very
  sorry
To state, they were not older than St.
  Peter,
But merely that they seemed a little
  sweeter.)   240

XXXI

The cherubs and the saints bowed down
  before
  That arch-angelic hierarch, the first
Of essences angelical, who wore
  The aspect of a god; but this ne'er
  nursed
Pride in his heavenly bosom, in whose
  core   245
  No thought, save for his Master's service,
  durst
Intrude, however glorified and high;
He knew him but the viceroy of the sky.

XXXII

He and the sombre, silent Spirit met—
  They knew each other both for good and
  ill;   250
Such was their power, that neither could
  forget
  His former friend and future foe; but
  still
There was a high, immortal, proud regret
  In either's eye, as if 'twere less their will
Than destiny to make the eternal years 255
  Their date of war, and their "champ clos"
  the spheres.

XXXIII

But here they were in neutral space: we
  know
  From Job, that Satan hath the power to
  pay
A heavenly visit thrice a year or so;
  And that the "sons of God," like those of
  clay,   260
Must keep him company; and we might
  show
  From the same book, in how polite a way
The dialogue is held between the Powers
Of Good and Evil—but 'twould take up
  hours.

XXXIV

And this is not a theologic tract,   265
  To prove with Hebrew and with Arabic,
If Job be allegory or a fact,
  But a true narrative; and thus I pick
From out the whole but such an act
  As sets aside the slightest thought of
  trick.   270
'Tis every tittle true, beyond suspicion,
And accurate as any other vision.

XXXV

The spirits were in neutral space, before
  The gate of heaven; like eastern thresh-
    olds is
The place where Death's grand cause is
  argued o'er,   275
  And souls despatched to that world or to
    this;
And therefore Michael and the other wore
  A civil aspect: though they did not kiss,
Yet still between his Darkness and his
  Brightness
There passed a mutual glance of great
  politeness.   280

XXXVI

The Archangel bowed, not like a modern
  beau,
  But with a graceful oriental bend,
Pressing one radiant arm just where below
  The heart in good men is supposed to
    tend:
He turned as to an equal, not too low, 285
  But kindly; Satan met his ancient friend
With more hauteur, as might an old
  Castilian
Poor noble meet a mushroom rich civilian.

XXXVII

He merely bent his diabolic brow
  An instant; and then raising it, he
    stood   290
In act to assert his right or wrong, and
  show
  Cause why King George by no means
    could or should
Make out a case to be exempt from woe
  Eternal, more than other kings, endued
With better sense and hearts, whom history
  mentions,   295
Who long have "paved hell with their good
  intentions."

XXXVIII

Michael began: "What wouldst thou with
  this man,
  Now dead, and brought before the Lord?
    What ill
Hath he wrought since his mortal race
  began,
  That thou canst claim him? Speak! and
    do thy will,   300
If it be just: if in this earthly span
  He hath been greatly failing to fulfil
His duties as a king and mortal, say,
And he is thine; if not, let him have way."

XXXIX

"Michael!" replied the Prince of Air, "even
  here   305
  Before the gate of Him thou servest,
    must
I claim my subject: and will make appear
  That as he was my worshipper in dust,
So shall he be in spirit, although dear
  To thee and thine, because nor wine nor
    lust   310
Were of his weaknesses; yet on the throne
He reigned o'er millions to serve me alone.

XL

"Look to our earth, or rather mine; it was,
  Once, more thy master's; but I triumph
    not
In this poor planet's conquest; nor,
  alas!   315
  Need he thou servest envy me my lot:
With all the myriads of bright worlds
  which pass
  In worship round him, he may have
    forgot
Yon weak creation of such paltry things:
I think few worth damnation save their
  kings,—   320

XLI

"And these but as a kind of quit-rent, to
  Assert my right as lord: and even had
I such an inclination, 'twere (as you
  Well know) superfluous; they are grown
    so bad,
That hell has nothing better left to do 325
  Than leave them to themselves: so much
    more mad
And evil by their own internal curse,
Heaven cannot make them better, nor I
  worse.

XLII

"Look to the earth, I said, and say again:
  When this old, blind, mad, helpless,
    weak, poor worm   330
Began in youth's first bloom and flush to
  reign,
  The world and he both wore a different
    form,
And much of earth, and all the watery
  plain
  Of ocean called him king; through many
    a storm
His isles had floated on the abyss of
  time;   335
For the rough virtues chose them for their
  clime.

XLIII

"He came to his sceptre young; he leaves it
 old:
 Look to the state in which he found his
  realm,
And left it; and his annals too behold,
 How to a minion first he gave the
  helm; 340
How grew upon his heart a thirst for gold,
 The beggar's vice, which can but over-
  whelm
The meanest hearts; and for the rest, but
 glance
Thine eye along America and France.

XLIV

" 'Tis true, he was a tool from first to
 last 345
 (I have the workmen safe); but as a tool
So let him be consumed. From out the
 past
 Of ages, since mankind have known the
  rule
Of monarchs—from the bloody rolls
 amassed
 Of sin and slaughter—from the Cæsar's
  school, 350
Take the worst pupil; and produce a reign
More drenched with gore, more cumbered
 with the slain.

XLV

"He ever warred with freedom and the
 free:
 Nations as men, home subjects, foreign
  foes,
So that they uttered the word 'Liberty!' 355
 Found George the Third their first op-
  ponent. Whose
History was ever stained as his will be
 With national and individual woes?
I grant his household abstinence; I grant
His neutral virtues, which most monarchs
 want; 360

XLVI

"I know he was a constant consort; own
 He was a decent sire, and middling lord.
All this is much, and most upon a throne;
 As temperance, if at Apicius' board,
Is more than at an anchorite's supper
 shown. 365
I grant him all the kindest can accord;
And this was well for him, but not for
 those
Millions who found him what oppression
 chose.

XLVII

"The New World shook him off; the Old
 yet groans
 Beneath what he and his prepared, if
  not 370
Completed: he leaves heirs on many
 thrones
 To all his vices, without what begot
Compassion for him—his tame virtues;
 drones
 Who sleep, or despots who have now
  forgot
A lesson which shall be re-taught them,
 wake 375
Upon the thrones of earth; but let them
 quake!

XLVIII

"Five millions of the primitive, who hold
 The faith which makes ye great on earth,
  implored
A *part* of that vast *all* they held of old,—
 Freedom to worship—not alone your
  Lord, 380
Michael, but you, and you, Saint Peter!
 Cold
 Must be your souls, if you have not
  abhorred
The foe to Catholic participation
In all the license of a Christian nation.

XLIX

"True! he allowed them to pray God; but
 as 385
 A consequence of prayer, refused the law
Which would have placed them upon the
 same base
 With those who did not hold the saints
  in awe."
But here Saint Peter started from his place,
 And cried, "You may the prisoner with-
  draw: 390
Ere heaven shall ope her portals to this
 Guelph,
While I am guard, may I be damned my-
 self!

L

"Sooner will I with Cerberus exchange
 My office (and *his* is no sinecure)
Than see this royal Bedlam bigot range 395
 The azure fields of heaven, of that be
  sure!"
"Saint!" replied Satan, "you do well to
 avenge
 The wrongs he made your satellites en-
  dure;

And if to this exchange you should be
　given,
I'll try to coax *our* Cerberus up to
　heaven!"　　　　　　　　　　　400

LI

Here Michael interposed: "Good saint! and
　devil!
　Pray, not so fast; you both outrun dis-
　cretion.
Saint Peter! you were wont to be more
　civil:
　Satan! excuse this warmth of his expres-
　sion,
And condescension to the vulgar's level;　405
　Even saints sometimes forget themselves
　in session.
Have you got more to say?"—"No."—"If
　you please,
I'll trouble you to call your witnesses."

LII

Then Satan turned and waved his swarthy
　hand,
　Which stirred with its electric qualities　410
Clouds farther off than we can understand,
　Although we find him sometimes in our
　skies;
Infernal thunder shook both sea and land
　In all the planets, and hell's batteries
Let off the artillery, which Milton men-
　tions　　　　　　　　　　　　415
As one of Satan's most sublime inventions.

LIII

This was a signal unto such damned souls
　As have the privilege of their damnation
Extended far beyond the mere control
　Of worlds past, present, or to come; no
　station　　　　　　　　　　　420
Is theirs particularly in the rolls
　Of Hell assigned; but where their in-
　clination
Or business carries them in search of game,
They may range freely—being damned the
　same.

LIV

They are proud of this—as very well they
　may,　　　　　　　　　　　　425
　It being a sort of knighthood, or gilt key
Stuck in their loins; or like to an "entrée"
　Up the back stairs, or such free-masonry.
I borrow my comparisons from clay,
　Being clay myself. Let not those spirits
　be　　　　　　　　　　　　430
Offended with such base low likenesses;
We know their posts are nobler far than
　these.

LV

When the great signal ran from heaven to
　hell—
　About ten million times the distance
　reckoned
From our sun to its earth, as we can tell　435
　How much time it takes up, even to a
　second,
For every ray that travels to dispel
　The fogs of London, through which,
　dimly beaconed,
The weathercocks are gilt some thrice a
　year,
If that the *summer* is not too severe:　　440

LVI

I say that I can tell—'twas half a minute;
　I know the solar beams take up more
　time
Ere, packed up for their journey, they
　begin it;
　But then their telegraph is less sublime,
And if they ran a race, they would not
　win it　　　　　　　　　　　445
　'Gainst Satan's couriers bound for their
　own clime.
The sun takes up some years for every ray
To reach its goal—the devil not half a day.

LVII

Upon the verge of space, about the size
　Of half-a-crown, a little speck
　appeared　　　　　　　　　　450
(I've seen a something like it in the skies
　In the Ægean, ere a squall); it neared,
And, growing bigger, took another guise;
　Like an aërial ship it tacked, and steered,
Or *was* steered (I am doubtful of the gram-
　mar　　　　　　　　　　　455
Of the last phrase, which makes the stanza
　stammer;—

LVIII

But take your choice): and then it grew a
　cloud:
　And so it was—a cloud of witnesses.
But such a cloud! No land e'er saw a
　crowd
　Of locusts numerous as the heavens saw
　these;
They shadowed with their myriads space;
　their loud
　And varied cries were like those of wild
　geese
(If nations may be likened to a goose),
And realized the phrase of "hell broke
　loose."

LIX

Here crashed a sturdy oath of stout John
 Bull, 465
Who damned away his eyes as hereto-
 fore:
There Paddy brogued "By Jasus!"—
 "What's your wull?"
The temperate Scot exclaimed: the
 French ghost swore
In certain terms I shan't translate in full,
 As the first coachman will; and 'midst
 the war, 470
The voice of Jonathan was heard to ex-
 press,
"*Our* President is going to war, I guess."

LX

Besides there were the Spaniard, Dutch,
 and Dane;
 In short, an universal shoal of shades,
From Otaheite's isle to Salisbury Plain, 475
 Of all climes and professions, years and
 trades,
Ready to swear against the good king's
 reign,
 Bitter as clubs in cards are against
 spades,
All summoned by this grand "subpœna," to
Try if kings mayn't be damned like me or
 you. 480

LXI

When Michael saw this host, he first grew
 pale,
 As angels can; next, like Italian twilight,
He turned all colors—as a peacock's tail,
 Or sunset streaming through a Gothic
 skylight
In some old abbey, or a trout not stale, 485
 Or distant lightning on the horizon *by*
 night,
Or a fresh rainbow, or a grand review
Of thirty regiments in red, green, and blue.

LXII

Then he addressed himself to Satan:
 "Why—
 My good old friend, for such I deem you,
 though 490
Our different parties make us fight so shy,
 I ne'er mistake you for a *personal* foe;
Our difference is *political,* and I
 Trust that, whatever may occur below,
You know my great respect for you: and
 this 495
Makes me regret whate'er you do amiss—

LXIII

"Why, my dear Lucifer, would you abuse
 My call for witnesses? I did not mean

That you should half of earth and hell
 produce;
'Tis even superfluous, since two honest,
 clean, 500
True testimonies are enough: we lose
 Our time, nay, our eternity, between
The accusation and defence: if we
Hear both, 'twill stretch our immortality."

LXIV

Satan replied, "To me the matter is 505
 Indifferent, in a personal point of view:
I can have fifty better souls than this
 With far less trouble than we have gone
 through
Already; and I merely argued his
 Late Majesty of Britain's case with
 you 510
Upon a point of form: you may dispose
Of him; I've kings enough below, God
 knows!"

LXV

Thus spoke the Demon (late called "multi-
 faced"
 By multo-scribbling Southey). "Then
 we'll call
One or two persons of the myriads
 placed 515
 Around our congress, and dispense with
 all
The rest," quoth Michael: "Who may be so
 graced
 As to speak first? there's choice enough—
 who shall
It be?" Then Satan answered, "There are
 many;
But you may choose Jack Wilkes as well
 as any." 520

LXVI

A merry, cock-eyed, curious-looking sprite
 Upon the instant started from the
 throng,
Dressed in a fashion now forgotten quite;
 For all the fashions of the flesh stick long
By people in the next world; where
 unite 525
 All the costumes since Adam's, right or
 wrong,
From Eve's fig-leaf down to the petticoat,
Almost as scanty, of days less remote.

LXVII

The spirit looked around upon the crowds
 Assembled, and exclaimed, "My friends
 of all 530
The spheres, we shall catch cold amongst
 these clouds;
 So let's to business: why this general call?

If those are freeholders I see in shrouds,
    And 'tis for an election that they bawl,
Behold a candidate with unturned coat! 535
Saint Peter, may I count upon your vote?"

LXVIII

"Sir," replied Michael, "you mistake; these
        things
    Are of a former life, and what we do
Above is more august; to judge of kings
    Is the tribunal met; so now you
        know."   540
"Then I presume those gentlemen with
        wings,"
    Said Wilkes, "are cherubs; and that soul
        below
Looks much like George the Third, but to
        my mind
A good deal older—Bless me! is he blind?"

LXIX

"He is what you behold him, and his
        doom   545
    Depends upon his deeds," the Angel
        said;
"If you have aught to arraign in him, the
        tomb
    Gives license to the humblest beggar's
        head
To lift itself against the loftiest."—"Some,"
    Said Wilkes, "don't wait to see them
        laid in lead,   550
For such a liberty—and I, for one,
Have told them what I thought beneath
        the sun."

LXX

"*Above* the sun repeat, then, what thou
        hast
    To urge against him," said the Arch-
        angel. "Why,"
Replied the spirit, "since old scores are
        past,   555
    Must I turn evidence? In faith, not I.
Besides, I beat him hollow at the last,
    With all his Lords and Commons: in the
        sky
I don't like ripping up old stories, since
His conduct was but natural in a prince. 560

LXXI

"Foolish, no doubt, and wicked, to oppress
    A poor unlucky devil without a shilling;
But then I blame the man himself much
        less
    Than Bute and Grafton, and shall be
        unwilling

To see him punished here for their
        excess,   565
    Since they were both damned long ago,
        and still in
Their place below: for me, I have forgiven,
And vote his *habeas corpus* into heaven."

LXXII

"Wilkes," said the Devil, "I understand all
        this;
    You turned to half a courtier ere you
        died,   570
And seem to think it would not be amiss
    To grow a whole one on the other side
Of Charon's ferry; you forget that *his*
    Reign is concluded; whatsoe'er betide,
He won't be sovereign more; you've lost
        your labor,   575
For at the best he will but be your neigh-
        bor.

LXXIII

"However, I knew what to think of it,
    When I beheld you in your jesting way,
Flitting and whispering round about the
        spit
    Where Belial, upon duty for the day, 580
With Fox's lard was basting William Pitt,
    His pupil; I knew what to think, I say:
That fellow even in hell breeds farther ills;
I'll have him *gagged*—'twas one of his own
        bills.

LXXIV

"Call Junius!" From the crowd a shadow
        stalked,   585
    And at the name there was a general
        squeeze,
So that the very ghosts no longer walked
    In comfort, at their own aërial ease,
But were all rammed, and jammed (but to
        be balked,
    As we shall see), and jostled hands and
        knees,   590
Like wind compressed and pent within a
        bladder,
Or like a human colic, which is sadder.

LXXV

The shadow came—a tall, thin, grey-haired
        figure,
    That looked as it had been a shade on
        earth;
Quick in its motions, with an air of
        vigor,   595
    But nought to mark its breeding or its
        birth;

Now it waxed little, then again grew
  bigger,
  With now an air of gloom, or savage
    mirth;
But as you gazed upon its features, they
Changed every instant—to *what,* none
    could say.   600

LXXVI

The more intently the ghosts gazed, the less
  Could they distinguish whose the fea-
    tures were;
The Devil himself seemed puzzled even to
    guess;
  They varied like a dream—now here,
    now there;
And several people swore from out the
    press,   605
  They knew him perfectly; and one could
    swear
He was his father: upon which another
Was sure he was his mother's cousin's
    brother:

LXXVII

Another, that he was a duke, or knight,
  An orator, a lawyer, or a priest,   610
A nabob, a man-midwife; but the wight
  Mysterious changed his countenance at
    least
As oft as they their minds: though in full
    sight
  He stood, the puzzle only was increased;
The man was a phantasmagoria in   615
  Himself—he was so volatile and thin.

LXXVIII

The moment that you had pronounced him
    one,
  Presto! his face changed, and he was an-
    other;
And when that change was hardly well put
    on,
  It varied, till I don't think his own
    mother   620
(If that he had a mother) would her son
  Have known, he shifted so from one to
    t'other;
Till guessing from a pleasure grew a task,
At this epistolary "Iron Mask."

LXXIX

For sometimes he like Cerberus would
    seem—   625
  "Three gentlemen at once" (as sagely
    says
Good Mrs. Malaprop); then you might
    deem
  That he was not even *one;* now many
    rays

Were flashing round him; and now a thick
    steam
  Hid him from sight—like fogs on Lon-
    don days: 630
Now Burke, now Tooke, he grew to peo-
    ple's fancies,
And certes often like Sir Philip Francis.

LXXX

I've an hypothesis—'tis quite my own;
  I never let it out till now, for fear
Of doing people harm about the throne, 635
  And injuring some minister or peer,
On whom the stigma might perhaps be
    blown;
  It is—my gentle public, lend thine ear!
'Tis, that what Junius we are wont to call
Was *really, truly,* nobody at all.   640

LXXXI

I don't see wherefore letters should not be
  Written without hands, since we daily
    view
Them written without heads; and books,
    we see,
  Are filled as well without the latter too:
And really till we fix on somebody   645
  For certain sure to claim them as his due,
Their author, like the Niger's mouth, will
    bother
The world to say if *there* be mouth or
    author.

LXXXII

"And who and what art thou?" the Arch-
    angel said.
  "For *that* you may consult my title-
    page,"   650
Replied this mighty shadow of a shade:
  "If I have kept my secret half an age,
I scarce shall tell it now."—"Canst thou
    upbraid,"
  Continued Michael, "George Rex, or
    allege
Aught further?" Junius answered, "You
    had better   655
First ask him for *his* answer to my letter:

LXXXIII

"My charges upon record will outlast
  The brass of both his epitaph and tomb."
"Repent'st thou not," said Michael, "of
    some past
  Exaggeration? something which may
    doom   660
Thyself if false, as him if true? Thou wast
  Too bitter—is it not so—in thy gloom
Of passion?"—"Passion!" cried the phan-
    tom dim,
  "I loved my country, and I hated him.

LXXXIV

"What I have written, I have written: let 665
  The rest be on his head or mine!" So spoke
Old "Nominis Umbra"; and while speaking yet,
  Away he melted in celestial smoke.
Then Satan said to Michael, "Don't forget
  To call George Washington, and John Horne Tooke, 670
And Franklin;"—but at this time there was heard
  A cry for room, though not a phantom stirred.

LXXXV

At length with jostling, elbowing, and the aid
  Of cherubim appointed to that post,
The devil Asmodeus to the circle made 675
  His way, and looked as if his journey cost
Some trouble. When his burden down he laid,
  "What's this?" cried Michael; "why, 'tis not a ghost?"
"I know it," quoth the incubus; "but he
Shall be one, if you leave the affair to me. 680

LXXXVI

"Confound the renegado! I have sprained
  My left wing, he's so heavy; one would think
Some of his works about his neck were chained.
  But to the point; while hovering o'er the brink
Of Skiddaw (where as usual it still rained), 685
  I saw a taper, far below me, wink,
And stooping, caught this fellow at a libel—
No less on history than the Holy Bible.

LXXXVII

"The former is the devil's scripture, and
  The latter yours, good Michael: so the affair 690
Belongs to all of us, you understand.
  I snatched him up just as you see him there,
And brought him off for sentence out of hand:
  I've scarcely been ten minutes in the air—
At least a quarter it can hardly be: 695
I dare say that his wife is still at tea."

LXXXVIII

Here Satan said, "I know this man of old,
  And have expected him for some time here;
A sillier fellow you will scarce behold,
  Or more conceited, in his petty sphere: 700
But surely it was not worth while to fold
  Such trash below your wing, Asmodeus dear:
We had the poor wretch safe (without being bored
With carriage) coming of his own accord.

LXXXIX

"But since he's here, let's see what he has done." 705
  "Done!" cried Asmodeus, "he anticipates
The very business you are now upon,
  And scribbles as if head clerk to the Fates.
Who knows to what his ribaldry may run,
  When such an ass as this, like Balaam's, prates?" 710
"Let's hear," quoth Michael, "what he has to say:
You know we're bound to that in every way."

XC

Now the bard, glad to get an audience, which
  By no means often was his case below,
Began to cough, and hawk, and hem, and pitch 715
  His voice into that awful note of woe
To all unhappy hearers within reach
  Of poets when the tide of rhyme's in flow;
But stuck fast with his first hexameter,
Not one of all whose gouty feet would stir. 720

XCI

But ere the spavined dactyls could be spurred
  Into recitative, in great dismay
Both cherubim and seraphim were heard
  To murmur loudly through their long array;
And Michael rose ere he could get a word 725
  Of all his foundered verses under way,
And cried, "For God's sake stop, my friend! 'twere best—
Non Di, non homines—you know the rest."

XCII

A general bustle spread throughout the throng,
　Which seemed to hold all verse in detestation;　730
The angels had of course enough of song
　When upon service; and the generation
Of ghosts had heard too much in life, not long
　Before, to profit by a new occasion:
The monarch, mute till then, exclaimed, "What! what!　735
Pye come again? No more—no more of that!"

XCIII

The tumult grew; an universal cough
　Convulsed the skies, as during a debate,
When Castlereagh has been up long enough
　(Before he was first minister of state　740
I mean—the slaves hear now); some cried "Off, off!"
　As at a farce; till, grown quite desperate,
The bard Saint Peter prayed to interpose
(Himself an author) only for his prose.

XCIV

The varlet was not an ill-favored knave;　745
　A good deal like a vulture in the face,
With a hook nose and a hawk's eye, which gave
　A smart and sharper-looking sort of grace
To his whole aspect, which, though rather grave,
　Was by no means so ugly as his case;　750
But that, indeed, was hopeless as can be,
Quite a poetic felony "de se."

XCV

Then Michael blew his trump, and stilled the noise
　With one still greater, as is yet the mode
On earth besides; except some grumbling voice,　755
　Which now and then will make a slight inroad
Upon decorous silence, few will twice
　Lift up their lungs when fairly overcrowed;
And now the bard could plead his own bad cause,
With all the attitudes of self-applause.　760

XCVI

He said—(I only give the heads)—he said,
　He meant no harm in scribbling; 'twas his way

Upon all topics; 'twas, besides, his bread,
　Of which he buttered both sides; 'twould delay
Too long the assembly (he was pleased to dread),　765
　And take up rather more time than a day,
To name his works—he would but cite a few—
"Wat Tyler"—"Rhymes on Blenheim"—"Waterloo."

XCVII

He had written praises of a regicide;
　He had written praises of all kings whatever;　770
He had written for republics far and wide,
　And then against them bitterer than ever;
For pantisocracy he once had cried
　Aloud, a scheme less moral than 'twas clever,
Then grew a hearty anti-jacobin—　775
Had turned his coat—and would have turned his skin.

XCVIII

He had sung against all battles, and again
　In their high praise and glory; he had called
Reviewing "the ungentle craft," and then
　Become as base a critic as e'er crawled—　780
Fed, paid, and pampered by the very men
　By whom his muse and morals had been mauled:
He had written much blank verse, and blanker prose,
And more of both than anybody knows.

XCIX

He had written Wesley's life:—here turning round　785
　To Satan, "Sir, I'm ready to write yours,
In two octavo volumes, nicely bound,
　With notes and preface, all that most allures
The pious purchaser; and there's no ground
　For fear, for I can choose my own reviewers:　790
So let me have the proper documents,
That I may add you to my other saints."

C

Satan bowed, and was silent. "Well, if you,
　With amiable modesty, decline

My offer, what says Michael? There are
few   795
Whose memoirs could be rendered more
divine.
Mine is a pen of all work; not so new
As it was once, but I would make you
shine
Like your own trumpet. By the way, my
own
Has more of brass in it, and is as well
blown.   800

CI

"But talking about trumpets, here's my
Vision!
Now you shall judge, all people; yes, you
shall
Judge with my judgment, and by my de-
cision
Be guided who shall enter heaven or fall.
I settle all these things by intuition, 805
Times present, past, to come, heaven,
hell, and all,
Like King Alfonso. When I thus see
double,
I save the Deity some worlds of trouble."

CII

He ceased, and drew forth an MS.; and no
Persuasion on the part of devils,
saints,   810
Or angels, now could stop the torrent; so
He read the first three lines of the con-
tents;
But at the fourth, the whole spiritual show
Had vanished, with variety of scents,
Ambrosial and sulphureous, as they
sprang,   815
Like lightning, off from his "melodious
twang."

CIII

Those grand heroics acted as a spell;
The angels stopped their ears and plied
their pinions;
The devils ran howling, deafened, down to
hell;
The ghosts fled, gibbering, for their own
dominions—   820
(For 'tis not yet decided where they dwell,
And I leave every man to his opinions);
Michael took refuge in his trump—but, lo!
His teeth were set on edge, he could not
blow!

CIV

Saint Peter, who has hitherto been
known   825
For an impetuous saint, upraised his
keys,

And at the fifth line knocked the poet
down;
Who fell like Phæton, but more at ease,
Into his lake, for there he did not drown;
A different web being by the Destinies 830
Woven for the Laureate's final wreath,
whene'er
Reform shall happen either here or there.

CV

He first sank to the bottom—like his works,
But soon rose to the surface—like him-
self;
For all corrupted things are buoyed like
corks,   835
By their own rottenness, light as an elf,
Or wisp that flits o'er a morass: he lurks,
It may be, still, like dull books on a shelf,
In his own den, to scrawl some "Life" or
"Vision,"
As Welborn says—"the devil turned pre-
cisian."   840

CVI

As for the rest, to come to the conclusion
Of this true dream, the telescope is gone
Which kept my optics free from all delu-
sion,
And showed me what I in my turn have
shown.
All I saw further, in the last confusion, 845
Was, that King George slipped into
heaven for one;
And when the tumult dwindled to a calm,
I left him practising the hundredth psalm.

1822

ON THIS DAY I COMPLETE MY THIRTY-SIXTH YEAR

'Tis time this heart should be unmoved,
Since others it hath ceased to move:
Yet, though I cannot be beloved,
Still let me love!

My days are in the yellow leaf;   5
The flowers and fruits of love are gone;
The worm, the canker, and the grief
Are mine alone!

The fire that on my bosom preys
Is lone as some volcanic isle;   10
No torch is kindled at its blaze—
A funeral pile.

The hope, the fear, the jealous care,
  The exalted portion of the pain
And power of love, I cannot share,   15
  But wear the chain.

But 'tis not *thus*—and 'tis not *here*—
  Such thoughts should shake my soul, nor
    now,
Where glory decks the hero's bier,
  Or binds his brow.   20

The sword, the banner, and the field,
  Glory and Greece, around me see!
The Spartan, borne upon his shield,
  Was not more free.

Awake! (not Greece—she *is* awake!)   25
  Awake, my spirit! Think through *whom*
Thy life-blood tracks its parent lake,
  And then strike home!

Tread those reviving passions down,
  Unworthy manhood!—unto thee   30
Indifferent should the smile or frown
  Of beauty be.

If thou regrett'st thy youth, *why live?*
  The land of honorable death
Is here:—up to the field, and give   35
  Away thy breath!

Seek out—less often sought than found—
  A soldier's grave, for thee the best;
Then look around, and choose thy ground,
  And take thy rest.   40
1824   1824

STANZAS WRITTEN ON THE ROAD BETWEEN FLORENCE AND PISA

Oh, talk not to me of a name great in story;
The days of our youth are the days of our
    glory;
And the myrtle and ivy of sweet two-and-
    twenty
Are worth all your laurels, though ever so
    plenty.

What are garlands and crowns to the brow
    that is wrinkled?   5
'Tis but as a dead-flower with May-dew be-
    sprinkled.
Then away with all such from the head
    that is hoary!
What care I for the wreaths that can *only*
    give glory!

O FAME!—if I e'er took delight in thy
    praises,
'Twas less for the sake of thy high-sound-
    ing phrases,   10
Than to see the bright eyes of the dear one
    discover,
She thought that I was not unworthy to
    love her.

There chiefly I sought thee, *there* only I
    found thee;
Her glance was the best of the rays that
    surround thee;
When it sparkled o'er aught that was bright
    in my story,   15
I knew it was love, and I felt it was glory.
Nov. 6, 1821   1830

LORD BYRON: LETTERS

ANNOUNCING HIS ENGAGEMENT

To Thomas Moore

Newstead Abbey, Sept. 20, 1814

  Here's to her who long
    Hath waked the poet's sigh!
  The girl who gave to song
    What gold could never buy.

My dear Moore,—

  I am going to be married—that is, I am
accepted, and one usually hopes the rest
will follow. My mother of the Gracchi
(that *are* to be), *you* think too strait-laced
for me, although the paragon of only children, and invested with "golden opinions
of all sorts of men," and full of "most blest
conditions" as Desdemona herself. Miss
Milbanke is the lady, and I have her
father's invitation to proceed there in my
elect capacity,—which, however, I cannot
do till I have settled some business in
London, and got a blue coat.
  She is said to be an heiress, but of that
I really know nothing certainly, and shall
not enquire. But I do know, that she has
talents and excellent qualities; and you

will not deny her judgment, after having refused six suitors and taken me.

Now, if you have anything to say against this, pray do; my mind's made up, positively fixed, determined, and therefore I will listen to reason, because now it can do no harm. Things may occur to break it off, but I will hope not. In the meantime, I tell you (a *secret*, by the by,—at least, till I know she wishes it to be public) that I have proposed and am accepted. You need not be in a hurry to wish me joy, for one mayn't be married for months. I am going to town tomorrow: but expect to be here, on my way there, within a fortnight.

If this had not happened, I should have gone to Italy. In my way down, perhaps, you will meet me at Nottingham, and come over with me here. I need not say that nothing will give me greater pleasure. I must, of course, reform thoroughly; and, seriously, if I can contribute to her happiness, I shall secure my own. She is so good a person, that—that—in short, I wish I was a better.

Ever, etc.

BYRON

HIS MANNER OF LIFE IN VENICE

To John Murray

Venice, December 27, 1816

Dear Sir,—

As the news of Venice must be very interesting to you, I will regale you with it.

Yesterday being the feast of St. Stephen, every mouth was put in motion. There was nothing but fiddling and playing on the virginals, and all kinds of conceits and divertisements, on every canal of this aquatic city. I dined with the Countess Albrizzi and a Paduan and Venetian party, and afterwards went to the opera, at the Fenice theatre (which opens for the Carnival on that day),—the finest, by the way, I have ever seen; it beats *our* theatres hollow in beauty and scenery, and those of Milan and Brescia bow before it. The opera and its sirens were much like all other operas and women, but the subject of the said opera was something edifying; it turned—the plot and conduct thereof—upon a fact narrated by Livy of a hundred and fifty married ladies having poisoned a hundred and fifty husbands in the good old times. The bachelors of Rome believed this extraordinary mortality to be merely the common effect of matrimony or a pestilence; but the surviving Benedicts, being all seized with the colic, examined into the matter, and found that "their possets had been drugged"; the consequence of which was much scandal and several suits at law. This is really and truly the subject of the musical piece at the Fenice; and you can't conceive what pretty things are sung and recitativoed about the *horrenda strage*. The conclusion was a lady's head about to be chopped off by a lictor, but (I am sorry to say) he left it on, and she got up and sung a trio with the two consuls, the Senate in the background being chorus.

The ballet was distinguished by nothing remarkable, except that the principal she-dancer went into convulsions because she was not applauded on her first appearance; and the manager came forward to ask if there was "ever a physician in the theatre." There was a Greek one in my box, whom I wished very much to volunteer his services, being sure that in this case these would have been the last convulsions which would have troubled the *ballerina;* but he would not.

The crowd was enormous; and in coming out, having a lady under my arm, I was obliged, in making way, almost to "beat a Venetian and traduce the state," being compelled to regale a person with an English punch in the guts, which sent him as far back as the squeeze and the passage would admit. He did not ask for another; but, with great signs of disapprobation and dismay, appealed to his compatriots, who laughed at him.

I am going on with my Armenian studies in a morning, and assisting and stimulating in the English portion of an English and Armenian grammar, now publishing at the convent of St. Lazarus. The Superior of the Friars is a bishop, and a fine old fellow, with the beard of a meteor. My spiritual preceptor, pastor, and master, Father Paschal, is also a learned and pious soul: he was two years in England.

I am still dreadfully in love with the Adriatic lady whom I spoke of in a former letter (and *not* in *this*—I add, for fear of mistakes; for the only one mentioned in the first part of this epistle is elderly and bookish, two things which I have ceased to admire); and love in this part of the world is no sinecure. This is also the season when everybody make [*sic*] up their intrigues for the ensuing year, and cut for partners for the next deal.

And now, if you don't write, I don't know what I won't say or do, nor what I will: send me some news—good news.

Yours very truly, etc., etc., etc.

B

P.S. Remember me to Mr. G[ifford], with all duty.

I hear that the E[dinburgh] R[eview] has cut up Coleridge's Christabel, and me for praising it, which omen, I think, bodes no great good to your forthcome or coming Canto and Castle (of Chillon): my run of luck within the last year seems to have taken a turn every way; but never mind, I will bring myself through in the end— if not, I can but be where I began: in the meantime, I am not displeased to be where I am—I mean, at Venice. My Adriatic nymph is this moment here, and I must therefore repose from this letter, "rocked by the beating of her heart."

SIR SAMUEL ROMILLY'S SUICIDE

To Lady Byron

Venice, Nov. 18, 1818

Sir Samuel Romilly has cut this throat for the loss of his wife. It is now nearly three years since he became, in the face of his compact (by a retainer—previous, and, I believe, general), the advocate of the measures and the approver of the proceedings, which deprived me and mine. I would not exactly, like Mr. Thwackum, when Philosopher Square bit his own tongue— "saddle him with a judgement;" but

"This even-handed justice
Commends the ingredients of our poisoned chalice
To our own lips."

This man little thought, when he was lacerating my heart according to law, while he was poisoning my life at its sources, aiding and abetting in the blighting, branding, and exile that was to be the result of his counsels in their indirect effects, that in less than thirty-six moons—in the pride of his triumph as the highest candidate for the representation of the Sister-City of the mightiest of Capitals—in the fullness of his professional career—in the greenness of a healthy old age—in the radi-

ance of fame, and the complacency of self-earned riches—that a domestic affliction would lay him in the earth, with the meanest of malefactors, in a cross-road with the stake in his body, if the verdict of insanity did not redeem his ashes from the sentence of the laws he had lived upon by interpreting or misinterpreting, and died in violating.

This man had eight children, lately deprived of their mother: could he not live? Perhaps, previous to his annihilation, he felt a portion of what he contributed his legal mite to make me feel; but I have lived—lived to see him a sexagenary suicide.

It was not in vain that I invoked Nemesis in the midnight of Rome from the awfullest of her ruins.

Fare you well.

BYRON

"I HAVE NOT WRITTEN FOR THEIR PLEASURE"

To John Murray

Venice, April 6, 1819

So you and Mr. Foscolo, etc. want me to undertake what you call a "great work?" an Epic Poem, I suppose, or some such pyramid. I'll try no such thing; I hate tasks. And then "seven or eight years!" God send us all well this day three months, let alone years. If one's years can't be better employed than in sweating poesy, a man had better be a ditcher. And works, too!—is Childe Harold nothing? You have so many "divine" poems, is it nothing to have written a human one? without any of your worn-out machinery. Why, man, I could have spun the thoughts of the four cantos of that poem into twenty, had I wanted to book-make, and its passion into as many modern tragedies. Since you want length, you shall have enough of Juan, for I'll make fifty cantos.

And Foscolo, too! Why does he not do something more than the Letters to Ortis, and a tragedy, and pamphlets? He has good fifteen years more at his command than I have: what has he done all that time?—proved his genius, doubtless, but not fixed its fame, nor done his utmost.

Besides, I mean to write my best work in Italian, and it will take me nine years more thoroughly to master the language; and then if my fancy exists, and I exist too.

I will try what I *can* do *really*. As to the estimation of the English which you talk of, let them calculate what it is worth, before they insult me with their insolent condescension.

I have not written for their pleasure. If they are pleased, it is that they chose to be so; I have never flattered their opinions, nor their pride; nor will I. Neither will I make "Ladies' books" *al dilettar le femine e la plebe.* I have written from the fulness of my mind, from passion, from impulse, from many motives, but not for their "sweet voices."

I know the precise worth of popular applause, for few scribblers have had more of it; and if I chose to swerve into their paths, I could retain it, or resume it. But I neither love ye, nor fear ye; and though I buy with ye and sell with ye, I will neither eat with ye, drink with ye, nor pray with ye. They made me, without my search, a species of popular idol; they, without reason or judgment, beyond the caprice of their good pleasure, threw down the image from its pedestal: it was not broken with the fall, and they would, it seems, again replace it,—but they shall not.

You ask about my health: about the beginning of the year I was in a state of great exhaustion, attended by such debility of stomach that nothing remained upon it; and I was obliged to reform my "way of life," which was conducting me from the "yellow leaf" to the ground, with all deliberate speed. I am better in health and morals, and very much yours, etc.

BYRON

GRAVES, AND DAYS OF RECKONING

To John Murray

Bologna, June 7, 1819

I have been picture-gazing this morning at the famous Domenichino and Guido, both of which are superlative. I afterwards went to the beautiful cemetery of Bologna, beyond the walls, and found, besides the superb burial-ground, an original of a Custode, who reminded one of the grave-digger in Hamlet. He has a collection of Capuchins' skulls, labelled on the forehead, and taking down one of them said, "This was Brother Desiderio Berro, who died at forty —one of my best friends. I begged his head of his brethren after decease, and they gave it me. I put it in lime, and then boiled it. Here it is, teeth and all, in excellent preservation. He was the merriest, cleverest fellow I ever knew. Wherever he went, he brought joy; and whenever any one was melancholy, the sight of him was enough to make him cheerful again. He walked so actively, you might have taken him for a dancer—he joked—he laughed— oh! he was such a Frate as I never saw before, nor ever shall again!"

He told me that he had himself planted all the cypresses in the cemetery; that he had the greatest attachment to them and to his dead people; that since 1801 they had buried fifty-three thousand persons. In showing some older monuments, there was that of a Roman girl of twenty with a bust by Bernini. She was a princess Bartorini, dead two centuries ago; he said that, on opening her grave, they had found her hair complete, and "as yellow as gold." Some of the epitaphs at Ferrara pleased me more than the more splendid monuments at Bologna; for instance—

> "Martini Luigi
>   Implora pace."

> "Lucrezia Picini
>   Implora eterna quiete."

Can any thing be more full of pathos? Those few words say all that can be said or sought: the dead had had enough of life; all they wanted was rest, and this they *implored!* There is all the helplessness, and humble hope, and deathlike prayer, that can arise from the grave—"implora pace." I hope whoever may survive me, and shall see me put in the foreigners' burying-ground at the Lido, within the fortress by the Adriatic, will see those two words, and no more, put over me; I trust they won't think of "pickling, and bringing me home to Clod or Blunderbuss Hall." I am sure my bones would not rest in an English grave, or my clay mix with the earth of that country. I believe the thought would drive me mad on my deathbed, could I suppose that any of my friends would be base enough to convey my carcass back to your soil.—I would not even feed your worms, if I could help it.

So, as Shakspeare says of Mowbray, the banished Duke of Norfolk, who died at Venice (see Richard II), that he, after fighting

"Against black Pagans, Turks, and Saracens, And toiled with works of war, retired himself

To Italy, and there, at *Venice,* gave
His body to that *pleasant* country's earth,
And his pure soul unto his captain, Christ,
Under whose colors he had fought so long."

. . . There will come a day of reckoning, even if I should not live to see it. I have at last seen Romilly shivered, who was one of my assassins. When that man was doing his worst to uproot my whole family tree, branch, and blossoms—when, after taking my retainer, he went over to them—when he was bringing desolation on my hearth, and destruction on my household gods— did he think that, in less than three years, a natural event—a severe domestic, but an expected and common calamity—would lay his carcass in a cross-road, or stamp his name in a verdict of lunacy! Did he . . . reflect or consider what my feelings must have been, when wife, and child, and sister, and name, and fame, and country, were to be my sacrifice on his legal altar—and this at a moment when my health was declining, my fortune embarrassed, and my mind had been shaken by many kinds of disappointment—while I was yet young, and might have reformed what might be wrong in my conduct, and retrieved what was perplexing in my affairs! But he is in his grave, and—what a long letter I have scribbled!

Yours, etc.

BYRON

P.S. Here, as in Greece, they strew flowers on the tombs. I saw a quantity of rose-leaves, and entire roses, scattered over the graves at Ferrara. It has the most pleasing effect you can imagine.

AMOR MIO

To the Countess Guiccioli

Bologna, August 25, 1819

My dearest Teresa,—

I have read this book in your garden;— my love, you were absent, or else I could not have read it. It is a favorite book of yours, and the writer was a friend of mine. You will not understand these English words, and *others* will not understand them,—which is the reason I have not scrawled them in Italian. But you will recognize the handwriting of him who passionately loved you, and you will divine that, over a book which was yours, he could only think of love. In that word, beautiful in all languages, but most so in yours—*Amor mio*—is comprised my existence here and hereafter. I feel I exist here, and I fear that I shall exist hereafter,—as to *what* purpose you will decide; my destiny rests with you, and you are a woman, seventeen years of age, and two out of a convent. I wish that you had staid there, with all my heart,—or, at least, that I had never met you in your married state.

But all this is too late. I love you, and you love me,—at least, you *say so,* and *act* as if you *did* so, which last is a great consolation in all events. But I more than love you, and cannot cease to love you.

Think of me, sometimes, when the Alps and the ocean divide us,—but they never will, unless you *wish* it.

B.

ON KEATS

To Percy Bysshe Shelley

Ravenna, April 26, 1821

The child continues doing well, and the accounts are regular and favorable. It is gratifying to me that you and Mrs. Shelley do not disapprove of the step which I have taken, which is merely temporary.

I am very sorry to hear what you say of Keats—is it *actually* true? I did not think criticism had been so killing. Though I differ from you essentially in your estimate of his performances, I so much abhor all unnecessary pain, that I would rather he had been seated on the highest peak of Parnassus than have perished in such a manner. Poor fellow! though with such inordinate self-love he would probably have not been very happy. I read the review of "Endymion" in the Quarterly. It was severe,—but surely not so severe as many reviews in that and other journals upon others.

I recollect the effect on me of the Edinburgh on my first poem; it was rage, and resistance, and redress—but not despondency nor despair. I grant that those are not amiable feelings; but, in this world of bustle and broil, and especially in the career of writing, a man should calculate upon his powers of *resistance* before he goes into the arena.

"Expect not life from pain nor danger free,
Nor deem the doom of man reversed for thee."

You know my opinion of *that second-hand* school of poetry. You also know my high opinion of your own poetry,—because it is of *no* school. I read Cenci—but, besides that I think the *subject* essentially undramatic, I am not an admirer of our old dramatists, *as models.* I deny that the English have hitherto had a drama at all. Your Cenci, however, was a work of power, and poetry. As to *my* drama, pray revenge yourself upon it, by being as free as I have been with yours.

I have not yet got your Prometheus, which I long to see. I have heard nothing of mine, and do not know that it is yet published. I have published a pamphlet on the Pope controversy, which you will not like. Had I known that Keats was dead—or that he was alive and so sensitive —I should have omitted some remarks upon his poetry, to which I was provoked by his *attack* upon *Pope,* and my disapprobation of *his own* style of writing.

You want me to undertake a great Poem —I have not the inclination nor the power. As I grow older, the indifference—*not* to life, for we love it by instinct—but to the stimuli of life, increases. Besides, this late failure of the Italians has latterly disappointed me for many reasons,—some public, some personal. My respects to Mrs. S.

Yours ever.
BYRON

P.S. Could not you and I contrive to meet this summer? Could not you take a run here *alone?*

NO ENEMY TO RELIGION

To Thomas Moore

Pisa, March 4, 1822

Since I wrote the enclosed, I have waited another post, and now have your answer acknowledging the arrival of the packet—a troublesome one, I fear, to you in more ways than one, both from weight external and internal. . . .

I am sorry you think Werner even *approaching* to any fitness for the stage, which, with my notions upon it, is very far from my present object. With regard to the publication, I have already explained that I have no exorbitant expectations of either fame or profit in the present instances; but wish them published because they are written, which is the common feeling of all scribblers.

With respect to "Religion," can I never convince you that *I* have no such opinions as the characters in that drama, which seems to have frightened everybody? Yet *they* are nothing to the expressions in Goethe's Faust (which are ten times hardier), and not a whit more bold than those of Milton's Satan. My ideas of a character may run away with me: like all imaginative men, I, of course, embody myself with the character while I *draw* it, but not a moment after the pen is from off the paper.

I am no enemy to religion, but the contrary. As a proof, I am educating my natural daughter a strict Catholic in a convent of Romagna, for I think people can never have *enough* of religion, if they are to have any. I incline, myself, very much to the Catholic doctrines; but if I am to write a drama, I must make my characters speak as I conceive them likely to argue.

As to poor Shelley, who is another bugbear to you and the world, he is, to my knowledge, the *least* selfish and the mildest of men—a man who has made more sacrifices of his fortune and feelings for others than any I ever heard of. With his speculative opinions I have nothing in common, nor desire to have.

The truth is, my dear Moore, you live near the *stove* of society, where you are unavoidably influenced by its heat and its vapors. I did so once—and too much— and enough to give a color to my whole future existence. As my success in society was *not* inconsiderable, I am surely not a prejudiced judge upon the subject, unless in its favor; but I think it, as now constituted, *fatal* to all great original undertakings of every kind. I never courted it *then,* when I was young and high in blood and one of its "curled darlings"; and do you think I would do so *now,* when I am living in a clearer atmosphere? One thing *only* might lead me back to it, and that is, to try once more if I could do any good in *politics;* but *not* in the petty politics I see now preying upon our miserable country.

Do not let me be misunderstood, however. If you speak your *own* opinions, they ever had, and will have, the greatest weight with *me.* But if you merely *echo* the "monde" (and it is difficult not to do so, being in its favor and its ferment), I can only regret that you should ever repeat anything to which I cannot pay attention. But I am prosing. The gods go with you, and as much immortality of all kinds as may suit your present and all other existence.

Yours, etc.

BYRON 5

REMEMBER ME IN YOUR SMILES AND WINE

To Thomas Moore

Cephalonia, December 27, 1823

I received a letter from you some time ago. I have been too much employed latterly to write as I could wish, and even now must write in haste.

I embark for Missolonghi to join Mavrocordato in four-and-twenty hours. The state of parties (but it were a long story) has kept me here till *now;* but now that Mavrocordato (their Washington, or their Kosciusko) is employed again, I can act with a *safe conscience.* I carry money to pay the squadron, etc., and I have influence with the Suliotes, *supposed* sufficient to keep them in harmony with some of the dissentients;—for there are plenty of differences, but trifling.

It is imagined that we shall attempt either Patras, or the castles on the Straits; and it seems, by most accounts, that the Greeks,—at any rate, the Suliotes, who are in affinity with me of "bread and salt,"— expect that I should march with them, and —be it even so! If any thing in the way of fever, fatigue, famine, or otherwise, should cut short the middle age of a brother warbler,—like Garcilasso de la Vega, Kleist, Korner, Joukoffsky (a Russian nightingale —see Bowring's Anthology), or Thersander, or,—or somebody else—but never mind—I pray you to remember me in your "smiles and wine."

I have hopes that the cause will triumph; but, whether it does or no, still "Honor must be minded as strictly as a milk diet." I trust to observe both.

Ever, etc.

BYRON

JOHN KEATS (1795-1821)

In what other English poet (however superior to him in other respects) are you so certain of never opening a page without lighting upon the loveliest imagery and the most eloquent expressions? Name one.

LEIGH HUNT

The life and the poetry of Keats constitute a most amazing exception to the rule that formal training and long practice are necessary for the highest achievement. Keats, the son of a servant at an inn in London, was taken out of school at fifteen, was a student of surgery and medicine until twenty-one, and died of consumption at twenty-five. Even when due allowance is made for the fact that his poetical development was encouraged by his school teacher, Charles Cowden Clarke, by Leigh Hunt, by the artist Benjamin Haydon, and by Wordsworth, Keats must be regarded as almost entirely a "self-made" poet. He enthusiastically appreciated great poetry, and, to a degree unusual even among poets, reverenced the poet's calling. One of the best traits of his amiable character was his modesty. He was ever dissatisfied with his own works, always strove to surpass himself, and stood ready to profit even by the savagely hostile criticism which greeted his first efforts.

In Keats's life there was a poignant conflict of fortunes during the four years from 1816 to 1820,—the upward surge of his astounding literary power on the one hand; on the other, the decline of his health and happiness. In 1816 he was a joyful youth, enthusiastically devoted to poetry and nature, encouraged by Leigh Hunt, Hazlitt, Wordsworth, boundlessly hopeful; then followed blow after blow,—the emigration of one of his brothers to the United States; the slow dying of his other brother by tuberculosis; the journalistic sneers, politically motivated, against his *Endymion* (1818); dreadful warnings of his own fatal illness; and, most unbearable of all, his realization, after he and Fanny Brawne had fallen in love with each other, that the state of his health prevented their marriage. He had died to all personal hope months before he left for Italy "as a soldier marches up to a battery." He died in Rome in 1821. His only consolation during that tragic series of outward events (and he was too passionately human a being for it to be a sufficient recompense) was his consciousness that he had really become a true poet, and that there was a steady advance both in the depth and in the art of his poetry. By the Spring of 1819 (see the dates of composition in the selections) he had already reached a glorious height; in 1820 he ascended even higher, and he did not cease to rise until the approach of death stayed his flight.

The distinctive qualities of Keats's poems were their sensuous appeal, their exquisite rhythm and melody, and the richness of their colors and forms. The loveliness of his style is well set forth in Leigh Hunt's essay, given below; and his favorite images are evoked to deck his bier in Shelley's *Adonais*.

Some of Keats's critics have been so preoccupied with the beauties of his style that they have ignored his thoughts,—a tendency which Keats himself would have deplored, for he adhered strongly to the faith that poetry is not only an epicurean enjoyment but also a revelation of truth. His view of life had points of contact with those of the other Romantics, but had distinctly individual peculiarities. Like Byron, he was made melancholy by the vanity and dreariness of ordinary life, and by the transitoriness of much that is lovely and joyous. But he conceived a strong antipathy to the Byronic, because Byron would not transcend a merely gloomy or mocking state of mind. To Keats it was possible, though difficult, to find happiness in human life. It could be found in art and in aesthetic appreciation of the universe, in the pursuit of knowledge, and, best of all, in a sincere love of humanity. This vision of the completely human life he expressed in what may be called his last testament, *The Fall of Hyperion*.

O SOLITUDE!

O Solitude! if I must with thee dwell,
  Let it not be among the jumbled heap
  Of murky buildings; climb with me the steep,—
Nature's observatory—whence the dell,
In flowery slopes, its river's crystal swell,   5
  May seem a span; let me thy vigils keep
  'Mongst boughs pavilioned, where the deer's swift leap
Startles the wild bee from the foxglove bell.
But though I'll gladly trace these scenes with thee,
  Yet the sweet converse of an innocent mind,   10
  Whose words are images of thoughts refined,
Is my soul's pleasure; and it sure must be
  Almost the highest bliss of human-kind,
When to thy haunts two kindred spirits flee.

Nov., 1815   1816

IMITATION OF SPENSER

Now Morning from her orient chamber came,
  And her first footsteps touched a verdant hill;
Crowning its lawny crest with amber flame,
  Silvering the untainted gushes of its rill;
Which, pure from mossy beds, did down distill,   5
  And after parting beds of simple flowers,
By many streams a little lake did fill,
  Which round its marge reflected woven bowers,
And, in its middle space, a sky that never lowers.

There the kingfisher saw his plumage bright   10
  Vying with fish of brilliant dye below;
Whose silken fins, and golden scales' light
  Cast upward, through the waves, a ruby glow:
There saw the swan his neck of archèd snow,
  And oared himself along with majesty;   15
Sparkled his jetty eyes; his feet did show
  Beneath the waves like Afric's ebony,
And on his back a fay reclined voluptuously.

Ah! could I tell the wonders of an isle
  That in that fairest lake had placèd been,   20
I could e'en Dido of her grief beguile;
  Or rob from agèd Lear his bitter teen:
For sure so fair a place was never seen,
  Of all that ever charmed romantic eye:
It seemed an emerald in the silver sheen   25
  Of the bright waters; or, as when on high,
Through clouds of fleecy white, laughs the cœrulean sky.

And all around it dipped luxuriously
  Slopings of verdure through the glossy tide,
Which, as it were in gentle amity,   30
  Rippled delighted up the flowery side;
As if to glean the ruddy tears, it tried,
  Which fell profusely from the rose-tree stem!
Haply it was the workings of its pride,
  In strife to throw upon the shore a gem   35
Outvying all the buds in Flora's diadem.

1812 or 1813   1817

WOMAN! WHEN I BEHOLD THEE FLIPPANT, VAIN

Woman! when I behold thee flippant, vain,
  Inconstant, childish, proud, and full of fancies;
  Without that modest softening that enhances
The downcast eye, repentant of the pain
That its mild light creates to heal again: 5
  E'en then, elate, my spirit leaps, and prances,
  E'en then my soul with exultation dances
For that to love, so long, I've dormant lain:
But when I see thee meek, and kind, and tender,
  Heavens! how desperately do I adore   10
Thy winning graces;—to be thy defender
  I hotly burn—to be a Calidore—
A very Red Cross Knight—a stout Leander—
  Might I be loved by thee like these of yore.

Light feet, dark violet eyes, and parted hair;   15
  Soft dimpled hands, white neck, and creamy breast,
  Are things on which the dazzled senses rest
Till the fond, fixed eyes, forget they stare.
From such fine pictures, heavens! I cannot dare
  To turn my admiration, though unpossessed   20
  They be of what is worthy,—though not drest
In lovely modesty, and virtues rare.
Yet these I leave as thoughtless as a lark;
  These lures I straight forget,—e'en ere I dine,
Or thrice my palate moisten: but when I mark   25
  Such charms with mild intelligences shine,
My ear is open like a greedy shark,
  To catch the tunings of a voice divine.

Ah! who can e'er forget so fair a being?
  Who can forget her half-retiring sweets?   30
  God! she is like a milk-white lamb that bleats
For man's protection. Surely the All-seeing,
Who joys to see us with his gifts agreeing,
  Will never give him pinions, who intreats
  Such innocence to ruin,—who vilely cheats   35
A dove-like bosom. In truth there is no freeing
One's thoughts from such a beauty; when I hear
  A lay that once I saw her hand awake,
Her form seems floating palpable, and near;
  Had I e'er seen her from an arbor take   40
A dewy flower, oft would that hand appear,
  And o'er my eyes the trembling moisture shake.
    1815   1817

HOW MANY BARDS

How many bards gild the lapses of time!
  A few of them have ever been the food
  Of my delighted fancy,—I could brood
Over their beauties, earthly, or sublime:
And often, when I sit me down to rhyme,   5
  These will in throngs before my mind intrude:
  But no confusion, no disturbance rude
Do they occasion; 'tis a pleasing chime.

So the unnumbered sounds that evening store;
  The songs of birds—the whispering of the leaves—   10
  The voice of waters—the great bell that heaves
With solemn sound,—and thousand others more,
  That distance of recognizance bereaves,
Make pleasing music, and not wild uproar.

March, 1816   1817

ON AN ENGRAVED GEM OF LEANDER

Come hither all sweet maidens soberly,
  Down-looking aye, and with a chastened light,
  Hid in the fringes of your eyelids white,
And meekly let your fair hands joinèd be,
As if so gentle that ye could not see,   5
  Untouched, a victim of your beauty bright,
  Sinking away to his young spirit's night,—
Sinking bewildered 'mid the dreary sea:
'Tis young Leander toiling to his death;
  Nigh swooning, he doth purse his weary lips   10
  For Hero's cheek, and smiles against her smile.
O horrid dream! see how his body dips
  Dead-heavy; arms and shoulders gleam awhile:
He's gone: up bubbles all his amorous breath!

c. March, 1817   1829

TO ONE WHO HAS BEEN LONG IN CITY PENT

To one who has been long in city pent,
'Tis very sweet to look into the fair
And open face of heaven,—to breathe a
    prayer
Full in the smile of the blue firmament.
Who is more happy, when, with heart's
    content,   5
Fatigued he sinks into some pleasant lair
Of wavy grass, and reads a debonair
And gentle tale of love and languishment?
Returning home at evening, with an ear
Catching the notes of Philomel,—an eye   10
Watching the sailing cloudlet's bright
    career,
He mourns that day so soon has glided by:
E'en like the passage of an angel's tear
That falls through the clear ether silently.

June, 1816   1817

I STOOD TIPTOE

"Places of nestling green for Poets made."
                              Story of Rimini.

I stood tiptoe upon a little hill,
The air was cooling, and so very still,
That the sweet buds which with a modest
    pride
Pull droopingly, in slanting curve aside,

Their scantly leaved, and finely tapering
    stems,   5
Had not yet lost their starry diadems
Caught from the early sobbing of the morn.
The clouds were pure and white as flocks
    new shorn,
And fresh from the clear brook; sweetly
    they slept
On the blue fields of heaven, and then
    there crept   10
A little noiseless noise among the leaves,
Born of the very sigh that silence heaves:
For not the faintest motion could be seen
Of all the shades that slanted o'er the
    green.
There was wide wandering for the greed-
    iest eye,   15
To peer about upon variety;
Far round the horizon's crystal air to skim,
And trace the dwindled edgings of its brim;
To picture out the quaint, and curious
    bending
Of a fresh woodland alley, never ending;   20
Or by the bowery clefts, and leafy shelves,
Guess where the jaunty streams refresh
    themselves.
I gazed awhile, and felt as light, and free
As though the fanning wings of Mercury
Had played upon my heels: I was light-
    hearted,   25
And many pleasures to my vision started;
So I straightway began to pluck a posey
Of luxuries bright, milky, soft and rosy.

A bush of May flowers with the bees about
   them:
Ah, sure no tasteful nook could be without
   them;   30
And let a lush laburnum oversweep them,
And let long grass grow round the roots to
   keep them
Moist, cool and green; and shade the
   violets,
That they may bind the moss in leafy nets.

A filbert hedge with wild briar over-
   twined,   35
And clumps of woodbine taking the soft
   wind
Upon their summer thrones; there too
   should be
The frequent chequer of a youngling tree,
That with a score of light green brethren
   shoots
From the quaint mossiness of agèd roots: 40
Round which is heard a spring-head of
   clear waters
Babbling so wildly of its lovely daughters
The spreading blue bells: it may haply
   mourn
That such fair clusters should be rudely
   torn
From their fresh beds, and scattered
   thoughtlessly   45
By infant hands, left on the path to die.

Open afresh your round of starry folds,
Ye ardent marigolds!
Dry up the moisture from your golden lids,
For great Apollo bids   50
That in these days your praises should be
   sung
On many harps, which he has lately strung;
And when again your dewiness he kisses,
Tell him, I have you in my world of
   blisses:
So haply when I rove in some far vale,   55
His mighty voice may come upon the gale.

Here are sweet peas, on tiptoe for a flight:
With wings of gentle flush o'er delicate
   white,
And taper fingers catching at all things,
To bind them all about with tiny rings.   60

Linger awhile upon some bending planks
That lean against a streamlet's rushy banks,
And watch intently Nature's gentle doings:
They will be found softer than ring-dove's
   cooings.
How silent comes the water round that
   bend;   65
Not the minutest whisper does it send
To the o'erhanging sallows: blades of grass
Slowly across the chequered shadows pass.

Why, you might read two sonnets, ere they
   reach
To where the hurrying freshnesses aye
   preach   70
A natural sermon o'er their pebbly beds;
Where swarms of minnows show their little
   heads,
Staying their wavy bodies 'gainst the
   streams,
To taste the luxury of sunny beams
Tempered with coolness. How they ever
   wrestle   75
With their own sweet delight, and ever
   nestle
Their silver bellies on the pebbly sand.
If you but scantily hold out the hand,
That very instant not one will remain;
But turn your eye, and there they are
   again.   80
The ripples seem right glad to reach those
   cresses,
And cool themselves among the emerald
   tresses;
The while they cool themselves, they fresh-
   ness give,
And moisture, that the bowery green may
   live:
So keeping up an interchange of favors, 85
Like good men in the truth of their be-
   haviors.
Sometimes goldfinches one by one will
   drop
From low hung branches; little space they
   stop;
But sip, and twitter, and their feathers
   sleek;
Then off at once, as in a wanton freak; 90
Or perhaps, to show their black and golden
   wings,
Pausing upon their yellow flutterings.
Were I in such a place, I sure should
   pray
That naught less sweet, might call my
   thoughts away,
Than the soft rustle of a maiden's gown 95
Fanning away the dandelion's down;
Than the light music of her nimble toes
Patting against the sorrel as she goes.
How she would start, and blush, thus to be
   caught
Playing in all her innocence of thought. 100
O let me lead her gently o'er the brook,
Watch her half-smiling lips, and downward
   look;
O let me for one moment touch her wrist;
Let me one moment to her breathing list;
And as she leaves me may she often turn 105
Her fair eyes looking through her locks
   auburne.
What next? A tuft of evening primroses,

O'er which the mind may hover till it
    dozes;
O'er which it well might take a pleasant
    sleep,
But that 'tis ever startled by the leap   110
Of buds into ripe flowers; or by the flitting
Of diverse moths, that aye their rest are
    quitting:
Or by the moon lifting her silver rim
Above a cloud, and with a gradual swim
Coming into the blue with all her light. 115
O Maker of sweet poets, dear delight
Of this fair world, and all its gentle livers;
Spangler of clouds, halo of crystal rivers,
Mingler with leaves, and dew and tumbling
    streams,
Closer of lovely eyes to lovely dreams,   120
Lover of loneliness, and wandering,
Of upcast eye, and tender pondering!
Thee must I praise above all other glories
That smile us on to tell delightful stories.
For what has made the sage or poet write 125
But the fair paradise of Nature's light?
In the calm grandeur of a sober line,
We see the waving of the mountain pine;
And when a tale is beautifully staid,
We feel the safety of a hawthorn glade: 130
When it is moving on luxurious wings,
The soul is lost in pleasant smotherings:
Fair dewy roses brush against our faces,
And flowering laurels spring from diamond
    vases;
O'erhead we see the jasmine and sweet
    briar,   135
And bloomy grapes laughing from green
    attire;
While at our feet, the voice of crystal
    bubbles
Charms us at once away from all our
    troubles:
So that we feel uplifted from the world,
Walking upon the white clouds wreathed
    and curled.   140
So felt he, who first told, how Psyche went
On the smooth wind to realms of wonder-
    ment;
What Psyche felt, and Love, when their
    full lips
First touched; what amorous, and fondling
    nips
They gave each other's cheeks; with all
    their sighs,   145
And how they kissed each other's tremulous
    eyes:
The silver lamp,—the ravishment,—the
    wonder—
The darkness,—loveliness,—the fearful
    thunder;
Their woes gone by, and both to heaven
    upflown,

To bow for gratitude before Jove's
    throne.   150
So did he feel, who pulled the boughs
    aside,
That we might look into a forest wide,
To catch a glimpse of Fawns, and Dryades
Coming with softest rustle through the
    trees;
And garlands woven of flowers wild, and
    sweet,   155
Upheld on ivory wrists, or sporting feet:
Telling us how fair, trembling Syrinx fled
Arcadian Pan, with such a fearful dread.
Poor nymph,—poor Pan,—how did he
    weep to find
Naught but a lovely sighing of the wind 160
Along the reedy stream; a half heard strain,
Full of sweet desolation—balmy pain.

What first inspired a bard of old to sing
Narcissus pining o'er the untainted spring?
In some delicious ramble, he had found 165
A little space, with boughs all woven round;
And in the midst of all, a clearer pool
Than e'er reflected in its pleasant cool,
The blue sky here, and there, serenely
    peeping
Through tendril wreaths fantastically
    creeping.   170
And on the bank a lonely flower he spied,
A meek and forlorn flower, with naught of
    pride,
Drooping its beauty o'er the watery clear-
    ness,
To woo its own sad image into nearness:
Deaf to light Zephyrus it would not
    move;   175
But still would seem to droop, to pine, to
    love.
So while the Poet stood in this sweet spot,
Some fainter gleamings o'er his fancy shot;
Nor was it long ere he had told the tale
Of young Narcissus, and sad Echo's bale. 180

Where had he been, from whose warm
    head outflew
That sweetest of all songs, that ever new,
That aye refreshing, pure deliciousness,
Coming ever to bless
The wanderer by moonlight? to him bring-
    ing   185
Shapes from the invisible world, unearthly
    singing
From out the middle air, from flowery
    nests,
And from the pillowy silkiness that rests
Full in the speculation of the stars.
Ah! surely he had burst our mortal bars; 190
Into some wond'rous region he had gone,
To search for thee, divine Endymion!

He was a poet, sure a lover too,
Who stood on Latmus' top, what time
    there blew
Soft breezes from the myrtle vale below; 195
And brought in faintness solemn, sweet,
    and slow
A hymn from Dian's temple; while up-
    swelling,
The incense went to her own starry dwell-
    ing.
But though her face was clear as infant's
    eyes,
Though she stood smiling o'er the sacri-
    fice,   200
The Poet wept at her so piteous fate,
Wept that such beauty should be desolate:
So in fine wrath some golden sounds he
    won,
And gave meek Cynthia her Endymion.

Queen of the wide air; thou most lovely
    queen   205
Of all the brightness that mine eyes have
    seen!
As thou exceedest all things in thy shine,
So every tale, does this sweet tale of thine.
O for three words of honey, that I might
Tell but one wonder of thy bridal night! 210

Where distant ships do seem to show their
    keels,
Phœbus awhile delayed his mighty wheels,
And turned to smile upon thy bashful eyes,
Ere he his unseen pomp would solemnize.
The evening weather was so bright and
    clear,   215
That men of health were of unusual cheer;
Stepping like Homer at the trumpet's call,
Or young Apollo on the pedestal:
And lovely women were as fair and warm,
As Venus looking sideways in alarm.   220
The breezes were ethereal, and pure,
And crept through half closed lattices to
    cure
The languid sick; it cooled their fevered
    sleep,
And soothed them into slumbers full and
    deep.
Soon they awoke clear eyed: nor burnt with
    thirsting,   225
Nor with hot fingers, nor with temples
    bursting:
And springing up, they met the wond'ring
    sight
Of their dear friends, nigh foolish with
    delight;
Who feel their arms, and breasts, and kiss
    and stare,
And on their placid foreheads part the
    hair.   230

Young men, and maidens at each other
    gazed
With hands held back, and motionless,
    amazed
To see the brightness in each other's eyes;
And so they stood, filled with a sweet sur-
    prise,
Until their tongues were loosed in poesy. 235
Therefore no lover did of anguish die:
But the soft numbers, in that moment
    spoken,
Made silken ties, that never may be broken.
Cynthia! I cannot tell the greater blisses,
That followed thine, and thy dear shep-
    herd's kisses: 240
Was there a Poet born?—but now no more,
My wand'ring spirit must no further
    soar.—

June-Dec., 1816   1817

OH! HOW I LOVE

Oh! how I love, on a fair summer's eve,
    When streams of light pour down the
        golden west,
    And on the balmy zephyrs tranquil rest
The silver clouds, far—far away to leave
All meaner thoughts, and take a sweet re-
        prieve   5
    From little cares; to find, with easy quest,
    A fragrant wild, with Nature's beauty
        dressed,
And there into delight my soul deceive.
There warm my breast with patriotic lore,
    Musing on Milton's fate—on Sydney's
        bier—   10
      Till their stern forms before my mind
        arise:
Perhaps on wings of Poesy upsoar,
    Full often dropping a delicious tear,
      When some melodious sorrow spells
        mine eyes.

Summer, 1816   1848

ON FIRST LOOKING INTO CHAPMAN'S HOMER

Much have I travelled in the realms of
    gold,
    And many goodly states and kingdoms
        seen;
    Round many western islands have I been
Which bards in fealty to Apollo hold.
Oft of one wide expanse had I been told   5
    That deep-browed Homer ruled as his
        demesne;
    Yet did I never breathe its pure serene

Till I heard Chapman speak out loud and
    bold:
Then felt I like some watcher of the skies
    When a new planet swims into his
      ken;   10
Or like stout Cortez when with eagle eyes
    He stared at the Pacific—and all his men
Looked at each other with a wild surmise—
    Silent, upon a peak in Darien.

Oct., 1816   Dec. 1, 1816

SLEEP AND POETRY

What is more gentle than a wind in
    summer?
What is more soothing than the pretty
    hummer
That stays one moment in an open flower,
And buzzes cheerily from bower to bower?
What is more tranquil than a musk-rose
    blowing   5
In a green island, far from all men's know-
    ing?
More healthful than the leafiness of dales?
More secret than a nest of nightingales?
More serene than Cordelia's countenance?
More full of visions than a high ro-
    mance?   10
What, but thee, Sleep? Soft closer of our
    eyes!
Low murmurer of tender lullabies!
Light hoverer around our happy pillows!
Wreather of poppy buds, and weeping wil-
    lows!
Silent entangler of a beauty's tresses!   15
Most happy listener! when the morning
    blesses
Thee for enlivening all the cheerful eyes
That glance so brightly at the new sun-rise.

But what is higher beyond thought than
    thee?
Fresher than berries of a mountain tree? 20
More strange, more beautiful, more smooth,
    more regal,
Than wings of swans, than doves, than
    dim-seen eagle?
What is it? And to what shall I compare
    it?
It has a glory, and nought else can share it:
The thought thereof is awful, sweet, and
    holy,   25
Chasing away all worldliness and folly;
Coming sometimes like fearful claps of
    thunder,
Or the low rumblings earth's regions under;
And sometimes like a gentle whispering
Of all the secrets of some wondrous thing 30
That breathes about us in the vacant air;

So that we look around with prying stare,
Perhaps to see shapes of light, aerial lim-
    ning,
And catch soft floatings from a faint-heard
    hymning;
To see the laurel wreath, on high sus-
    pended,   35
That is to crown our name when life is
    ended.
Sometimes it gives a glory to the voice,
And from the heart up-springs, rejoice!
    rejoice!
Sounds which will reach the Framer of all
    things,
And die away in ardent mutterings.   40

No one who once the glorious sun has seen,
And all the clouds, and felt his bosom clean
For his great Maker's presence, but must
    know
What 'tis I mean, and feel his being glow:
Therefore no insult will I give his spirit, 45
By telling what he sees from native merit.

    O Poesy! for thee I hold my pen
That am not yet a glorious denizen
Of thy wide heaven—should I rather kneel
Upon some mountain-top until I feel 50
A glowing splendor round about me hung,
And echo back the voice of thine own
    tongue?
O Poesy! for thee I grasp my pen
That am not yet a glorious denizen
Of thy wide heaven; yet, to my ardent
    prayer,   55
Yield from thy sanctuary some clear air,
Smoothed for intoxication by the breath
Of flowering bays, that I may die a death
Of luxury, and my young spirit follow
The morning sunbeams to the great
    Apollo   60
Like a fresh sacrifice; or, if I can bear
The o'erwhelming sweets, 'twill bring to
    me the fair
Visions of all places: a bowery nook
Will be elysium—an eternal book
Whence I may copy many a lovely saying 65
About the leaves, and flowers—about the
    playing
Of nymphs in woods, and fountains; and
    the shade
Keeping a silence round a sleeping maid;
And many a verse from so strange influence
That we must ever wonder how, and
    whence   70
It came. Also imaginings will hover
Round my fireside, and haply there dis-
    cover
Vistas of solemn beauty, where I'd wander
In happy silence, like the clear Meander

Through its lone vales; and where I found
   a spot   75
Of awfuller shade, or an enchanted grot,
Or a green hill o'erspread with chequered
   dress
Of flowers, and fearful from its loveliness,
Write on my tablets all that was permitted,
All that was for our human senses fitted. 80
Then the events of this wide world I'd seize
Like a strong giant, and my spirit teaze
Till at its shoulders it should proudly see
Wings to find out an immortality.

Stop and consider! life is but a day;   85
A fragile dewdrop on its perilous way
From a tree's summit; a poor Indian's sleep
While his boat hastens to the monstrous
   steep
Of Montmorenci. Why so sad a moan?
Life is the rose's hope while yet un-
   blown;   90
The reading of an ever-changing tale;
The light uplifting of a maiden's veil;
A pigeon tumbling in clear summer air;
A laughing school-boy, without grief or
   care,
Riding the springy branches of an elm. 95

O for ten years, that I may overwhelm
Myself in poesy; so I may do the deed
That my own soul has to itself decreed.
Then will I pass the countries that I see
In long perspective, and continually   100
Taste their pure fountains. First the realm
   I'll pass
Of Flora, and old Pan: sleep in the grass,
Feed upon apples red, and strawberries,
And choose each pleasure that my fancy
   sees;
Catch the white-handed nymphs in shady
   places,   105
To woo sweet kisses from averted faces,—
Play with their fingers, touch their shoul-
   ders white
Into a pretty shrinking with a bite
As hard as lips can make it; till agreed,
A lovely tale of human life we'll read. 110
And one will teach a tame dove how it best
May fan the cool air gently o'er my rest;
Another, bending o'er her nimble tread,
Will set a green robe floating round her
   head,
And still will dance with ever varied
   ease,   115
Smiling upon the flowers and the trees:
Another will entice me on, and on
Through almond blossoms and rich cinna-
   mon;
Till in the bosom of a leafy world

We rest in silence, like two gems up
   curled   120
In the recesses of a pearly shell.

And can I ever bid these joys farewell?
Yes, I must pass them for a nobler life,
Where I may find the agonies, the strife
Of human hearts: for lo! I see afar,   125
O'ersailing the blue cragginess, a car
And steeds with streamy manes—the chario-
   teer
Looks out upon the winds with glorious
   fear:
And now the numerous tramplings quiver
   lightly
Along a huge cloud's ridge; and now with
   sprightly   130
Wheel downward come they into fresher
   skies,
Tipt round with silver from the sun's
   bright eyes.
Still downward with capacious whirl they
   glide;
And now I see them on a green-hill's side
In breezy rest among the nodding stalks. 135
The charioteer with wondrous gesture talks
To the trees and mountains; and there
   soon appear
Shapes of delight, of mystery, and fear,
Passing along before a dusky space
Made by some mighty oaks: as they would
   chase   140
Some ever-fleeting music on they sweep.
Lo! how they murmur, laugh, and smile,
   and weep:
Some with upholden hand and mouth
   severe;
Some with their faces muffled to the ear
Between their arms; some, clear in youthful
   bloom,   145
Go glad and smilingly athwart the gloom;
Some looking back, and some with upward
   gaze;
Yes, thousands in a thousand different ways
Flit onward—now a lovely wreath of girls
Dancing their sleek hair into tangled
   curls;   150
And now broad wings. Most awfully in-
   tent
The driver of those steeds is forward bent,
And seems to listen: O that I might know
All that he writes with such a hurrying
   glow!

The visions all are fled—the car is fled 155
Into the light of heaven, and in their stead
A sense of real things comes doubly strong,
And, like a muddy stream, would bear
   along
My soul to nothingness: but I will strive

Against all doubtings, and will keep
   alive   160
The thought of that same chariot, and the
   strange
Journey it went.

                    Is there so small a range
In the present strength of manhood, that
   the high
Imagination cannot freely fly
As she was wont of old? prepare her
   steeds,   165
Paw up against the light, and do strange
   deeds
Upon the clouds? Has she not shown us
   all?
From the clear space of ether, to the small
Breath of new buds unfolding? From the
   meaning
Of Jove's large eyebrow, to the tender
   greening   170
Of April meadows? Here her altar shone,
E'en in this isle; and who could paragon
The fervid choir that lifted up a noise
Of harmony, to where it aye will poise
Its mighty self of convoluting sound,   175
Huge as a planet, and like that roll round,
Eternally around a dizzy void?
Aye, in those days the Muses were nigh
   cloyed
With honors; nor had any other care
Than to sing out and sooth their wavy
   hair.   180

Could all this be forgotten? Yes, a schism
Nurtured by foppery and barbarism,
Made great Apollo blush for this his land.
Men were thought wise who could not
   understand
His glories: with a puling infant's force 185
They swayed about upon a rocking horse,
And thought it Pegasus. Ah, dismal
   souled!
The winds of heaven blew, the ocean rolled
Its gathering waves—ye felt it not. The
   blue
Bared its eternal bosom, and the dew   190
Of summer night collected still to make
The morning precious; beauty was awake!
Why were ye not awake? But ye were
   dead
To things ye knew not of.—were closely
   wed
To musty laws lined out with wretched
   rule   195
And compass vile: so that ye taught a
   school
Of dolts to smooth, inlay, and clip, and fit,
Till, like the certain wands of Jacob's wit,
Their verses tallied. Easy was the task:

A thousand handicraftsmen wore the
   mask   200
Of Poesy. Ill-fated, impious race!
That blasphemed the bright Lyrist to his
   face,
And did not know it,—no, they went about,
Holding a poor, decrepid standard out
Marked with most flimsy mottoes, and in
   large   205
The name of one Boileau!

                    O ye whose charge
It is to hover round our pleasant hills!
Whose congregated majesty so fills
My boundly reverence, that I cannot trace
Your hallowed names, in this unholy
   place,   210
So near those common folk; did not their
   shames
Affright you? Did our old lamenting
   Thames
Delight you? Did ye never cluster round
Delicious Avon, with a mournful sound,
And weep? Or did ye wholly bid adieu 215
To regions where no more the laurel grew?
Or did ye stay to give a welcoming
To some lone spirits who could proudly
   sing
Their youth away, and die? 'Twas even so:
But let me think away those times of
   woe: 220
Now 'tis a fairer season; ye have breathed
Rich benedictions o'er us; ye have wreathed
Fresh garlands: for sweet music has been
   heard
In many places;—some has been upstirred
From out its crystal dwelling in a lake, 225
By a swan's ebon bill; from a thick brake,
Nested and quiet in a valley mild,
Bubbles a pipe; fine sounds are floating
   wild
About the earth: happy are ye and glad.

These things are doubtless: yet in truth
   we've had   230
Strange thunders from the potency of song;
Mingled indeed with what is sweet and
   strong,
From majesty: but in clear truth the themes
Are ugly clubs, the Poets Polyphemes
Disturbing the grand sea. A drainless
   shower   235
Of light is poesy; 'tis the supreme of
   power;
'Tis might half slumb'ring on its own right
   arm.
The very archings of her eyelids charm
A thousand willing agents to obey,
And still she governs with the mildest
   sway: 240

But strength alone though of the Muses
    born
Is like a fallen angel: trees uptorn,
Darkness, and worms, and shrouds, and
    sepulchres
Delight it; for it feeds upon the burrs
And thorns of life; forgetting the great
    end   245
Of Poesy, that it should be a friend
To soothe the cares, and lift the thoughts
    of man.

Yet I rejoice: a myrtle fairer than
E'er grew in Paphos, from the bitter weeds
Lifts its sweet head into the air, and
    feeds   250
A silent space with ever sprouting green.
All tenderest birds there find a pleasant
    screen,
Creep through the shade with jaunty flut-
    tering,
Nibble the little cuppèd flowers and sing.
Then let us clear away the choking
    thorns   255
From round its gentle stem; let the young
    fawns,
Yeanèd in after times, when we are flown,
Find a fresh sward beneath it, overgrown
With simple flowers; let there nothing be
More boisterous than a lover's bended
    knee;   260
Nought more ungentle than the placid
    look
Of one who leans upon a closèd book;
Nought more untranquil than the grassy
    slopes
Between two hills. All hail delightful
    hopes!
As she was wont, th' imagination   265
Into most lovely labyrinths will be gone,
And they shall be accounted poet kings
Who simply tell the most heart-easing
    things.
O may these joys be ripe before I die!

Will not some say that I presumptuously 270
Have spoken? that from hastening disgrace
'Twere better far to hide my foolish face?
That whining boyhood should with rever-
    ence bow
Ere the dread thunderbolt could reach?
    How!
If I do hide myself, it sure shall be   275
In the very fane, the light of Poesy:
If I do fall, at least I will be laid
Beneath the silence of a poplar shade;
And over me the grass shall be smooth
    shaven;
And there shall be a kind memorial
    graven.   280

But off Despondence! miserable bane!
They should not know thee, who athirst to
    gain
A noble end, are thirsty every hour.
What though I am not wealthy in the
    dower
Of spanning wisdom; though I do not
    know   285
The shiftings of the mighty winds that
    blow
Hither and thither all the changing
    thoughts
Of man: though no great minist'ring reason
    sorts
Out the dark mysteries of human souls
To clear conceiving: yet there ever rolls 290
A vast idea before me, and I glean
Therefrom my liberty; thence too I've seen
The end and aim of Poesy. 'Tis clear
As anything most true; as that the year
Is made of the four seasons—manifest 295
As a large cross, some old cathedral's crest,
Lifted to the white clouds. Therefore
    should I
Be but the essence of deformity,
A coward, did my very eyelids wink
At speaking out what I have dared to
    think.   300
Ah! rather let me like a madman run
Over some precipice; let the hot sun
Melt my Dedalian wings, and drive me
    down
Convulsed and headlong! Stay! an inward
    frown
Of conscience bids me be more calm
    awhile.   305
An ocean dim, sprinkled with many an isle,
Spreads awfully before me. How much toil!
How many days! what desperate turmoil!
Ere I can have explored its widenesses.
Ah, what a task! upon my bended knees, 310
I could unsay those—no, impossible!
Impossible!

        For sweet relief I'll dwell
On humbler thoughts, and let this strange
    assay
Begun in gentleness die so away.
E'en now all tumult from my bosom
    fades: 315
I turn full hearted to the friendly aids
That smooth the path of honor; brother-
    hood,
And friendliness the nurse of mutual good.
The hearty grasp that sends a pleasant
    sonnet
Into the brain ere one can think upon
    it;   320
The silence when some rhymes are coming
    out;

And when they're come, the very pleasant
rout:
The message certain to be done tomorrow.
'Tis perhaps as well that it should be to
borrow
Some precious book from out its snug re-
treat,   325
To cluster round it when we next shall
meet.
Scarce can I scribble on; for lovely airs
Are fluttering round the room like doves in
pairs;
Many delights of that glad day recalling,
When first my senses caught their tender
falling.   330
And with these airs come forms of elegance
Stooping their shoulders o'er a horse's
prance,
Careless, and grand—fingers soft and round
Parting luxuriant curls;—and the swift
bound
Of Bacchus from his chariot, when his
eye   335
Made Ariadne's cheek look blushingly.
Thus I remember all the pleasant flow
Of words at opening a portfolio.

Things such as these are ever harbingers
To trains of peaceful images: the stirs 340
Of a swan's neck unseen among the rushes:
A linnet starting all about the bushes:
A butterfly, with golden wings broad
parted,
Nestling a rose, convulsed as though it
smarted
With over pleasure—many, many more, 345
Might I indulge at large in all my store
Of luxuries: yet I must not forget
Sleep, quiet with his poppy coronet:
For what there may be worthy in these
rhymes
I partly owe to him: and thus, the chimes 350
Of friendly voices had just given place
To as sweet a silence, when I 'gan retrace
The pleasant day, upon a couch at ease.
It was a poet's house who keeps the keys
Of pleasure's temple. Round about were
hung   355
The glorious features of the bards who
sung
In other ages—cold and sacred busts
Smiled at each other. Happy he who trusts
To clear Futurity his darling fame!
Then there were fauns and satyrs taking
aim   360
At swelling apples with a frisky leap
And reaching fingers, 'mid a luscious heap
Of vine-leaves. Then there rose to view a
fane
Of liny marble, and thereto a train

Of nymphs approaching fairly o'er the
sward: 365
One, loveliest, holding her white hand to-
ward
The dazzling sunrise: two sisters sweet
Bending their graceful fingers till they
meet
Over the trippings of a little child:
And some are hearing, eagerly, the wild 370
Thrilling liquidity of dewy piping.
See, in another picture, nymphs are wiping
Cherishingly Diana's timorous limbs;—
A fold of lawny mantle dabbling swims
At the bath's edge, and keeps a gentle
motion   375
With the subsiding crystal: as when ocean
Heaves calmly its broad swelling smooth-
ness o'er
Its rocky marge, and balances once more
The patient weeds; that now unshent by
foam
Feel all about their undulating home.   380

Sappho's meek head was there half smiling
down
At nothing; just as though the earnest
frown
Of over thinking had that moment gone
From off her brow, and left her all alone.

Great Alfred's too, with anxious, pitying
eyes,   385
As if he always listened to the sighs
Of the goaded world; and Kosciusko's,
worn
By horrid suffrance—mightily forlorn.
Petrarch, outstepping from the shady green,
Starts at the sight of Laura; nor can
wean   390
His eyes from her sweet face. Most happy
they!
For over them was seen a free display
Of outspread wings, and from between
them shone
The face of Poesy: from off her throne
She overlooked things that I scarce could
tell.   395
The very sense of where I was might well
Keep Sleep aloof: but more than that there
came
Thought after thought to nourish up the
flame
Within my breast; so that the morning
light
Surprised me even from a sleepless night; 400
And up I rose refreshed, and glad, and gay,
Resolving to begin that very day
These lines; and howsoever they be done,
I leave them as a father does his son.
Autumn-Winter, 1816   1817

KEEN, FITFUL GUSTS

Keen, fitful gusts are whisp'ring here and
    there
  Among the bushes half leafless and dry;
  The stars look very cold about the sky,
And I have many miles on foot to fare.
Yet feel I little of the cool bleak air,   5
  Or of the dead leaves rustling drearily,
  Or of those silver lamps that burn on
    high,
Or of the distance from home's pleasant
    lair:
For I am brimful of the friendliness
  That in a little cottage I have found; 10
Of fair-haired Milton's eloquent distress,
  And all his love for gentle Lycid
    drowned;
Of lovely Laura in her light green dress,
  And faithful Petrarch gloriously crowned.
Winter, 1816   1817

ADDRESSED TO HAYDON

Great spirits now on earth are sojourning;
  He of the cloud, the cataract, the lake,
  Who on Helvellyn's summit, wide awake,
Catches his freshness from Archangel's
    wing:
He of the rose, the violet, the spring,   5
  The social smile, the chain for Freedom's
    sake:
  And lo!—whose steadfastness would
    never take
A meaner sound than Raphael's whisper-
    ing.
And other spirits there are standing apart
  Upon the forehead of the age to come; 10
These, these will give the world another
    heart,
  And other pulses. Hear ye not the hum
Of mighty workings?——
    Listen awhile, ye nations, and be dumb.
Nov., 1816   1817

TO G. A. W.

Nymph of the downward smile and side-
    long glance,
  In what diviner moments of the day
  Art thou most lovely? When gone far
    astray
Into the labyrinths of sweet utterance?
Or when serenely wand'ring in a trance 5
  Of sober thought? Or when starting
    away,

With careless robe, to meet the morning
    ray,
Thou spar'st the flowers in thy mazy dance?
Haply 'tis when thy ruby lips part sweetly,
  And so remain, because thou listenest: 10
But thou to please wert nurtured so com-
    pletely
  That I can never tell what mood is best.
I shall as soon pronounce which Grace
    more neatly
  Trips it before Apollo than the rest.
Dec., 1816   1817

ON THE GRASSHOPPER AND
CRICKET

The poetry of earth is never dead:
  When all the birds are faint with the
    hot sun,
  And hide in cooling trees, a voice will
    run
From hedge to hedge about the new-mown
    mead;
That is the Grasshopper's—he takes the
    lead   5
  In summer luxury,—he has never done
  With his delights; for when tired out
    with fun
He rests at ease beneath some pleasant
    weed.
The poetry of earth is ceasing never:
  On a lone winter evening, when the
    frost   10
    Has wrought a silence, from the stove
    there shrills
The Cricket's song, in warmth increasing
    ever,
  And seems to one in drowsiness half lost,
    The Grasshopper's among some grassy
    hills.
Dec. 30, 1816   1817

AFTER DARK VAPORS

After dark vapors have oppressed our
    plains
  For a long dreary season, comes a day
  Born of the gentle South, and clears
    away
From the sick heavens all unseemly stains.
The anxious month, relievèd of its pains, 5
  Takes as a long-lost right the feel of
    May;
    The eyelids with the passing coolness
    play

Like rose leaves with the drip of Summer
    rains.
The calmest thoughts come round us; as
    of leaves
    Budding—fruit ripening in stillness—
    Autumn suns   10
Smiling at eve upon the quiet sheaves—
Sweet Sappho's cheek—a smiling infant's
    breath—
    The gradual sand that through an hour-
        glass runs—
A woodland rivulet—a Poet's death.

Jan. 31, 1817   1817

TO LEIGH HUNT, Esq.

Glory and loveliness have passed away;
    For if we wander out in early morn,
    No wreathèd incense do we see upborne
Into the east, to meet the smiling day:
No crowds of nymphs soft voiced and
    young, and gay,   5
    In woven baskets bringing ears of corn,
    Roses, and pinks, and violets, to adorn
The shrine of Flora in her early May.
But there are left delights as high as these,
    And I shall ever bless my destiny,   10
That in a time, when under pleasant trees
    Pan is no longer sought, I feel a free,
A leafy luxury, seeing I could please
    With these poor offerings, a man like
        thee.

                    1817

WRITTEN ON THE BLANK SPACE AT THE END OF CHAUCER'S TALE OF "THE FLOWRE AND THE LEFE"

This pleasant tale is like a little copse:
The honied lines do freshly interlace
To keep the reader in so sweet a place,
So that he here and there full-hearted
    stops;
And oftentimes he feels the dewy drops 5
Come cool and suddenly against his face,
And by the wandering melody may trace
Which way the tender-legged linnet hops.
Oh! what a power has white simplicity!
What mighty power has this gentle story! 10
I that forever feel athirst for glory
Could at this moment be content to lie
Meekly upon the grass, as those whose sob-
    bings
Were heard of none beside the mournful
    robins.

Feb., 1817   1817

ON SEEING THE ELGIN MARBLES

My spirit is too weak—mortality
    Weighs heavily on me like unwilling
        sleep,
    And each imagined pinnacle and steep
Of godlike hardship, tells me I must die
Like a sick eagle looking at the sky.   5
    Yet 'tis a gentle luxury to weep
    That I have not the cloudy winds to
        keep,
Fresh for the opening of the morning's eye.
Such dim conceivèd glories of the brain
    Bring round the heart an indescribable
        feud;   10
So do these wonders a most dizzy pain,
    That mingles Grecian grandeur with the
        rude
Wasting of old Time—with a billowy
    main—
A sun—a shadow of a magnitude.

March, 1817   1817

ON THE SEA

It keeps eternal whisperings around
    Desolate shores, and with its mighty swell
    Gluts twice ten thousand Caverns, till the
        spell
Of Hecate leaves them their old shadowy
    sound.
Often 'tis in such gentle temper found,   5
    That scarcely will the very smallest shell
    Be moved for days from where it some-
        time fell,
When last the winds of Heaven were un-
    bound.
Oh ye! who have your eye-balls vexed and
    tired,
    Feast them upon the wideness of the
        Sea;   10
    Oh ye! whose ears are dinned with
        uproar rude,
    Or fed too much with cloying melody—
        Sit ye near some old Cavern's Mouth,
        and brood
Until ye start, as if the sea-nymphs quired!

April, 1817   1817

FROM ENDYMION

A POETIC ROMANCE

BOOK I

A thing of beauty is a joy for ever:
Its loveliness increases; it will never
Pass into nothingness; but still will keep
A bower quiet for us, and a sleep

Full of sweet dreams, and health, and quiet
  breathing. 5
Therefore, on every morrow, are we
  wreathing
A flowery band to bind us to the earth,
Spite of despondence, of the inhuman
  dearth
Of noble natures, of the gloomy days,
Of all the unhealthy and o'er-darkened
  ways 10
Made for our searching: yes, in spite of all,
Some shape of beauty moves away the pall
From our dark spirits. Such the sun, the
  moon,
Trees old and young, sprouting a shady
  boon
For simple sheep; and such are daffodils 15
With the green world they live in; and
  clear rills
That for themselves a cooling covert make
'Gainst the hot season; the mid forest
  brake,
Rich with a sprinkling of fair musk-rose
  blooms:
And such too is the grandeur of the
  dooms 20
We have imagined for the mighty dead;
All lovely tales that we have heard or read:
An endless fountain of immortal drink,
Pouring unto us from the heaven's brink.

Nor do we merely feel these essences 25
For one short hour; no, even as the trees
That whisper round a temple become soon
Dear as the temple's self, so does the moon,
The passion poesy, glories infinite,
Haunt us till they become a cheering
  light 30
Unto our souls, and bound to us so fast,
That, whether there be shine, or gloom
  o'ercast,
They alway must be with us, or we die.

Therefore, 'tis with full happiness that I
Will trace the story of Endymion. 35
The very music of the name has gone
Into my being, and each pleasant scene
Is growing fresh before me as the green
Of our own valleys: so I will begin
Now while I cannot hear the city's din; 40
Now while the early budders are just new,
And run in mazes of the youngest hue
About old forests; while the willow trails
Its delicate amber; and the dairy pails
Bring home increase of milk. And, as the
  year 45
Grows lush in juicy stalks, I'll smoothly
  steer
My little boat, for many quiet hours,

With streams that deepen freshly into
  bowers.
Many and many a verse I hope to write,
Before the daisies, vermeil rimmed and
  white, 50
Hide in deep herbage; and ere yet the bees
Hum about globes of clover and sweet peas,
I must be near the middle of my story.
O may no wintry season, bare and hoary,
See it half finished: but let Autumn bold, 55
With universal tinge of sober gold,
Be all about me when I make an end.
And now at once, adventuresome, I send
My herald thought into a wilderness:
There let its trumpet blow, and quickly
  dress 60
My uncertain path with green, that I may
  speed
Easily onward, through flowers and weed.

Upon the sides of Latmos was outspread
A mighty forest; for the moist earth fed
So plenteously all weed-hidden roots 65
Into o'er-hanging boughs, and precious
  fruits.
And it had gloomy shades, sequestered
  deep,
Where no man went; and if from shep-
  herd's keep
A lamb strayed far a-down those inmost
  glens,
Never again saw he the happy pens 70
Whither his brethren, bleating with con-
  tent,
Over the hills at every nightfall went.
Among the shepherds, 'twas believed ever,
That not one fleecy lamb which thus did
  sever
From the white flock, but passed unwor-
  ried 75
By angry wolf, or pard with prying head,
Until it came to some unfooted plains
Where fed the herds of Pan: aye great his
  gains
Who thus one lamb did lose. Paths there
  were many,
Winding through palmy fern, and rushes
  fenny, 80
And ivy banks; all leading pleasantly
To a wide lawn, whence one could only see
Stems thronging all around between the
  swell
Of turf and slanting branches: who could
  tell
The freshness of the space of heaven
  above, 85
Edged round with dark tree tops? through
  which a dove
Would often beat its wings, and often too
A little cloud would move across the blue.

Full in the middle of this pleasantness
There stood a marble altar, with a tress   90
Of flowers budded newly; and the dew
Had taken fairy phantasies to strew
Daisies upon the sacred sward last eve,
And so the dawned light in pomp receive.
For 'twas the morn: Apollo's upward fire 95
Made every eastern cloud a silvery pyre
Of brightness so unsullied, that therein
A melancholy spirit well might win
Oblivion, and melt out his essence fine
Into the winds: rain-scented eglantine   100
Gave temperate sweets to that well-wooing
      sun;
The lark was lost in him; cold springs had
      run
To warm their chilliest bubbles in the
      grass;
Man's voice was on the mountains; and the
      mass
Of nature's lives and wonders pulsed ten-
      fold,   105
To feel this sunrise and its glories old.

Now while the silent workings of the
      dawn
Were busiest, into that self-same lawn
All suddenly, with joyful cries, there sped
A troop of little children garlanded;   110
Who gathering round the altar, seemed to
      pry
Earnestly round as wishing to espy
Some folk of holiday: nor had they waited
For many moments, ere their ears were
      sated
With a faint breath of music, which ev'n
      then   115
Filled out its voice, and died away again.
Within a little space again it gave
Its airy swellings, with a gentle wave,
To light-hung leaves, in smoothest echoes
      breaking
Through copse-clad valleys,—ere their
      death, o'ertaking   120
The surgy murmurs of the lonely sea.

And now, as deep into the wood as we
Might mark a lynx's eye, there glimmered
      light
Fair faces and a rush of garments white,
Plainer and plainer showing, till at last 125
Into the widest alley they all past,
Making directly for the woodland altar.
O kindly muse! let not my weak tongue
      falter
In telling of this goodly company,
Of their old piety, and of their glee: 130
But let a portion of ethereal dew
Fall on my head, and presently unmew

My soul; that I may dare, in wayfaring,
To stammer where old Chaucer used to
      sing.

Leading the way, young damsels danced
      along,   135
Bearing the burden of a shepherd song;
Each having a white wicker over brimmed
With April's tender younglings: next, well
      trimmed,
A crowd of shepherds with as sunburnt
      looks
As may be read of in Arcadian books;   140
Such as sat listening round Apollo's pipe,
When the great deity, for earth too ripe,
Let his divinity o'erflowing die
In music, through the vales of Thessaly:
Some idly trailed their sheep-hooks on the
      ground,   145
And some kept up a shrilly mellow sound
With ebon-tipped flutes: close after these,
Now coming from beneath the forest trees,
A venerable priest full soberly,
Begirt with minist'ring looks: always his
      eye   150
Steadfast upon the matted turf he kept,
And after him his sacred vestments swept.
From his right hand there swung a vase,
      milk-white,
Of mingled wine, out-sparkling generous
      light;
And in his left he held a basket full   155
Of all sweet herbs that searching eye could
      cull:
Wild thyme, and valley-lilies whiter still
Than Leda's love, and cresses from the rill.
His aged head, crowned with beechen
      wreath,
Seemed like a poll of ivy in the teeth   160
Of winter hoar. Then came another crowd
Of shepherds, lifting in due time aloud
Their share of the ditty. After them ap-
      peared,
Up-followed by a multitude that reared
Their voices to the clouds, a fair wrought
      car,   165
Easily rolling so as scarce to mar
The freedom of three steeds of dapple
      brown:
Who stood therein did seem of great re-
      nown
Among the throng. His youth was fully
      blown,
Showing like Ganymede to manhood
      grown;   170
And, for those simple times, his garments
      were
A chieftain king's: beneath his breast, half
      bare,
Was hung a silver bugle, and between

His nervy knees there lay a boar-spear
  keen.
A smile was on his countenance; he
  seemed,   175
To common lookers-on, like one who
  dreamed
Of idleness in groves Elysian:
But there were some who feelingly could
  scan
A lurking trouble in his nether lip,
And see that oftentimes the reins would
  slip   180
Through his forgotten hands: then would
  they sigh,
And think of yellow leaves, of owlet's cry,
Of logs piled solemnly.—Ah, well-a-day,
Why should our young Endymion pine
  away?

  Soon the assembly, in a circle ranged, 185
Stood silent round the shrine: each look
  was changed
To sudden veneration: women meek
Beckoned their sons to silence; while each
  cheek
Of virgin bloom paled gently for slight
  fear.
Endymion too, without a forest peer,   190
Stood, wan and pale, and with an awed
  face,
Among his brothers of the mountain chace.
In midst of all, the venerable priest
Eyed them with joy from greatest to the
  least,
And, after lifting up his aged hands,   195
Thus spake he: "Men of Latmos! shepherd
  bands!
Whose care it is to guard a thousand flocks:
Whether descended from beneath the rocks
That overtop your mountains; whether
  come
From valleys where the pipe is never
  dumb;   200
Or from your swelling downs, where sweet
  air stirs
Blue harebells lightly, and where prickly
  furze
Buds lavish gold; or ye, whose precious
  charge
Nibble their fill at ocean's very marge,
Whose mellow reeds are touched with
  sounds forlorn   205
By the dim echoes of old Triton's horn:
Mothers and wives! who day by day pre-
  pare
The scrip, with needments, for the moun-
  tain air;
And all ye gentle girls who foster up
Udderless lambs, and in a little cup   210

Will put choice honey for a favored youth:
Yea, every one attend! for in good truth
Our vows are wanting to our great god
  Pan.
Are not our lowing heifers sleeker than
Night-swollen mushrooms? Are not our
  wide plains   215
Speckled with countless fleeces? Have not
  rains
Greened over April's lap? No howling sad
Sickens our fearful ewes; and we have had
Great bounty from Endymion our lord.
The earth is glad: the merry lark has
  poured   220
His early song against yon breezy sky
That spreads so clear o'er our solemnity."

  Thus ending, on the shrine he heaped a
  spire
Of teeming sweets, enkindling sacred fire;
Anon he stained the thick and spongy
  sod   225
With wine, in honor of the shepherd god.
Now while the earth was drinking it, and
  while
Bay leaves were crackling in the fragrant
  pile,
And gummy frankincense was sparkling
  bright
'Neath smothering parsley, and a hazy
  light   230
Spread grayly eastward, thus a chorus sang:

"O thou, whose mighty palace roof doth
  hang
From jagged trunks, and overshadoweth
Eternal whispers, glooms, the birth, life,
  death
Of unseen flowers in heavy peacefulness; 235
Who lov'st to see the hamadryads dress
Their ruffled locks where meeting hazels
  darken;
And through whole solemn hours dost sit,
  and hearken
The dreary melody of bedded reeds—
In desolate places, where dank moisture
  breeds   240
The pipy hemlock to strange overgrowth;
Bethinking thee, how melancholy loth
Thou wast to lose fair Syrinx—do thou
  now,
By thy love's milky brow!
By all the trembling mazes that she ran, 245
Hear us, great Pan!

"O thou, for whose soul-soothing quiet,
  turtles
Passion their voices cooingly 'mong
  myrtles
What time thou wanderest at eventide

Through sunny meadows, that outskirt the
   side   250
Of thine enmossed realms; O thou, to
   whom
Broad leaved fig trees even now foredoom
Their ripened fruitage; yellow girted bees
Their golden honeycombs; our village leas
Their fairest blossomed beans and poppied
   corn;   255
The chuckling linnet its five young unborn,
To sing for thee; low creeping strawberries
Their summer coolness; pent up butterflies
Their freckled wings; yea, the fresh bud-
   ding year
All its completions—be quickly near,   260
By every wind that nods the mountain
   pine,
O forester divine!

"Thou, to whom every faun and satyr
   flies
For willing service; whether to surprise
The squatted hare while in half sleeping
   fit;   265
Or upward ragged precipices flit,
To save poor lambkins from the eagle's
   maw;
Or by mysterious enticement draw
Bewildered shepherds to their path again;
Or to tread breathless round the frothy
   main,   270
And gather up all fancifullest shells
For thee to tumble into Naiad's cells,
And, being hidden, laugh at their out-
   peeping;
Or to delight thee with fantastic leaping,
The while they pelt each other on the
   crown   275
With silvery oak apples, and fir cones
   brown—
By all the echoes that about thee ring,
Hear us, O satyr king!

"O Hearkener to the loud clapping
   shears,
While ever and anon to his shorn peers 280
A ram goes bleating: Winder of the horn,
When snouted wild-boars routing tender
   corn
Anger our huntsmen: Breather round our
   farms,
To keep off mildews, and all weather
   harms:
Strange ministrant of undescribed
   sounds,   285
That come a-swooning over hollow
   grounds,
And wither drearily on barren moors:
Dread opener of the mysterious doors
Leading to universal knowledge—see,

Great son of Dryope,   290
The many that are come to pay their vows
With leaves about their brows!

"Be still the unimaginable lodge
For solitary thinkings; such as dodge
Conception to the very bourne of
   heaven,   295
Then leave the naked brain: be still the
   leaven,
That spreading in this dull and clodded
   earth
Gives it a touch ethereal—a new birth:
Be still a symbol of immensity;
A firmament reflected in a sea;   300
An element filling the space between,
An unknown—but no more; we humbly
   screen
With uplift hands our foreheads, lowly
   bending,
And giving out a shout most heaven rend-
   ing,
Conjure thee to receive our humble
   Pæan,   305
Upon thy Mount Lycean!"

Even while they brought the burden to a
   close,
A shout from the whole multitude arose,
That lingered in the air like dying rolls
Of abrupt thunder, when Ionian shoals 310
Of dolphins bob their noses through the
   brine.
Meantime, on shady levels, mossy fine,
Young companies nimbly began dancing
To the swift treble pipe, and humming
   string.
Aye, those fair living forms swam heav-
   enly   315
To tunes forgotten—out of memory:
Fair creatures! whose young children's chil-
   dren bred
Thermopylæ its heroes—not yet dead,
But in old marbles ever beautiful.
High genitors, unconscious did they cull 320
Time's sweet first-fruits—they danced to
   weariness,
And then in quiet circles did they press
The hillock turf, and caught the latter end
Of some strange history, potent to send
A young mind from its bodily tenement. 325
Or they might watch the quoit-pitchers,
   intent
On either side; pitying the sad death
Of Hyacinthus, when the cruel breath
Of Zephyr slew him,—Zephyr penitent,
Who now, ere Phœbus mounts the firma-
   ment,   330
Fondles the flower amid the sobbing rain.
The archers too, upon a wider plain,

Beside the feathery whizzing of the shaft,
And the dull twanging bowstring, and the
    raft
Branch down sweeping from a tall ash
    top,   335
Called up a thousand thoughts to envelope
Those who would watch. Perhaps, the
    trembling knee
And frantic gape of lonely Niobe,
Poor, lonely Niobe! when her lovely young
Were dead and gone, and her caressing
    tongue   340
Lay a lost thing upon her paly lip,
And very, very deadliness did nip
Her motherly cheeks. Aroused from this
    sad mood
By one, who at a distance loud hallooed,
Uplifting his strong bow into the air,   345
Many might after brighter visions stare:
After the Argonauts, in blind amaze
Tossing about on Neptune's restless ways,
Until, from the horizon's vaulted side,
There shot a golden splendor far and
    wide,   350
Spangling those million poutings of the
    brine
With quivering ore: 'twas even an awful
    shine
From the exaltation of Apollo's bow;
A heavenly beacon in their dreary woe.
Who thus were ripe for high contemplat-
    ing,   355
Might turn their steps towards the sober
    ring
Where sat Endymion and the aged priest
'Mong shepherds gone in eld, whose looks
    increased
The silvery setting of their mortal star.
There they discoursed upon the fragile
    bar   360
That keeps us from our homes ethereal;
And what our duties there: to nightly call
Vesper, the beauty-crest of summer
    weather;
To summon all the downiest clouds to-
    gether
For the sun's purple couch; to emulate   365
In minist'ring the potent rule of fate
With speed of fire-tailed exhalations;
To tint her pallid cheek with bloom, who
    cons
Sweet poesy by moonlight: besides these,
A world of other unguessed offices.   370
Anon they wandered, by divine converse,
Into Elysium; vying to rehearse
Each one his own anticipated bliss.
One felt heart-certain that he could not
    miss
His quick-gone love, among fair blossomed
    boughs,   375

Where every zephyr-sigh pouts, and endows
Her lips with music for the welcoming.
Another wished, 'mid that eternal spring,
To meet his rosy child, with feathery sails,
Sweeping, eye-earnestly, through almond
    vales: 380
Who, suddenly, should stoop through the
    smooth wind,
And with the balmiest leaves his temples
    bind;
And, ever after, through those regions be
His messenger, his little Mercury.
Some were athirst in soul to see again   385
Their fellow huntsmen o'er the wide cham-
    paign
In times long past; to sit with them, and
    talk
Of all the chances in their earthly walk;
Comparing, joyfully, their plenteous stores
Of happiness, to when upon the moors,   390
Benighted, close they huddled from the
    cold,
And shared their famished scrips. Thus all
    out-told
Their fond imaginations,—saving him
Whose eyelids curtained up their jewels
    dim,
Endymion: yet hourly had he striven   395
To hide the cankering venom, that had
    riven
His fainting recollections. Now indeed
His senses had swooned off: he did not
    heed
The sudden silence, or the whispers low,
Or the old eyes dissolving at his woe,   400
Or anxious calls, or close of trembling
    palms,
Or maiden's sigh, that grief itself embalms:
But in the self-same fixed trance he kept,
Like one who on the earth had never stept.
Aye, even as dead-still as a marble man,   405
Frozen in that old tale Arabian.

Who whispers him so pantingly and
    close?
Peona, his sweet sister: of all those,
His friends, the dearest. Hushing signs she
    made,
And breathed a sister's sorrow to per-
    suade   410
A yielding up, a cradling on her care.
Her eloquence did breathe away the curse:
She led him, like some midnight spirit
    nurse
Of happy changes in emphatic dreams,
Along a path between two little
    streams,—   415
Guarding his forehead, with her round
    elbow,

From low-grown branches, and his footsteps
  slow
From stumbling over stumps and hillocks
  small;
Until they came to where these streamlets
  fall,
With mingled bubblings and a gentle
  rush,   420
Into a river, clear, brimful, and flush
With crystal mocking of the trees and sky.
A little shallop, floating there hard by,
Pointed its beak over the fringed bank;
And soon it lightly dipt, and rose, and
  sank,   425
And dipt again, with the young couple's
  weight,—
Peona guiding, through the water straight,
Towards a bowery island opposite;
Which gaining presently, she steered light
Into a shady, fresh, and ripply cove,   430
Where nested was an arbor, overwove
By many a summer's silent fingering;
To whose cool bosom she was used to bring
Her playmates, with their needle broidery,
And minstrel memories of times gone by. 435

  So she was gently glad to see him laid
Under her favorite bower's quiet shade,
On her own couch, new made of flower
  leaves,
Dried carefully on the cooler side of
  sheaves
When last the sun his autumn tresses
  shook,   440
And the tanned harvesters rich armfuls
  took.
Soon was he quieted to slumbrous rest:
But, ere it crept upon him, he had prest
Peona's busy hand against his lips,
And still, a-sleeping, held her fingertips 445
In tender pressure. And as a willow keeps
A patient watch over the stream that creeps
Windingly by it, so the quiet maid
Held her in peace: so that a whispering
  blade
Of grass, a wailful gnat, a bee bustling 450
Down in the blue-bells, or a wren light-
  rustling
Among sere leaves and twigs, might all be
  heard.

  O magic sleep! O comfortable bird,
That broodest o'er the troubled sea of the
  mind
Till it is hushed and smooth! O uncon-
  fined   455
Restraint! imprisoned liberty! great key
To golden palaces, strange minstrelsy,
Fountains grotesque, new trees, bespangled
  caves,

Echoing grottoes, full of tumbling waves
And moonlight; aye, to all the mazy
  world   460
Of silvery enchantment!—who, upfurled
Beneath thy drowsy wing a triple hour,
But renovates and lives?—Thus, in the
  bower,
Endymion was calmed to life again.
Opening his eyelids with a healthier
  brain,   465
He said: "I feel this thine endearing love
All through my bosom: thou art as a dove
Trembling its closed eyes and sleeked wings
About me; and the pearliest dew not brings
Such morning incense from the fields of
  May,   470
As do those brighter drops that twinkling
  stray
From those kind eyes,—the very home and
  haunt
Of sisterly affection. Can I want
Aught else, aught nearer heaven, than such
  tears?
Yet dry them up, in bidding hence all
  fears   475
That, any longer, I will pass my days
Alone and sad. No, I will once more raise
My voice upon the mountain heights; once
  more
Make my horn parley from their foreheads
  hoar:
Again my trooping hounds their tongues
  shall loll   480
Around the breathed boar: again I'll poll
The fair-grown yew tree, for a chosen bow:
And, when the pleasant sun is getting low,
Again I'll linger in a sloping mead
To hear the speckled thrushes, and see
  feed   485
Our idle sheep. So be thou cheered, sweet,
And, if thy lute is here, softly intreat
My soul to keep in its resolved course."

  Hereat Peona, in their silver source,
Shut her pure sorrow-drops with glad ex-
  claim,   490
And took a lute, from which there pulsing
  came
A lively prelude, fashioning the way
In which her voice should wander. 'Twas
  a lay
More subtle cadenced, more forest wild
Than Dryope's lone lulling of her child; 495
And nothing since has floated in the air
So mournful strange. Surely some influ-
  ence rare
Went, spiritual, through the damsel's hand;
For still, with Delphic emphasis, she
  spanned

The quick invisible strings, even though
she saw 500
Endymion's spirit melt away and thaw
Before the deep intoxication.
But soon she came, with sudden burst,
upon
Her self-possession—swung the lute aside,
And earnestly said: "Brother, 'tis vain to
hide 505
That thou dost know of things mysterious,
Immortal, starry; such alone could thus
Weigh down thy nature. Hast thou sinned
in aught
Offensive to the heavenly powers? Caught
A Paphian dove upon a message sent? 510
Thy deathful bow against some deer-herd
bent
Sacred to Dian? Haply, thou hast seen
Her naked limbs among the alders green;
And that, alas! is death. No, I can trace
Something more high perplexing in thy
face!" 515

Endymion looked at her, and pressed her
hand,
And said, "Art thou so pale, who wast so
bland
And merry in our meadows? How is this?
Tell me thine ailment: tell me all amiss!—
Ah! thou hast been unhappy at the
change 520
Wrought suddenly in me? What indeed
more strange?
Or more complete to overwhelm surmise?
Ambition is no sluggard: 'tis no prize,
That toiling years would put within my
grasp,
That I have sighed for: with so deadly
gasp 525
No man e'er panted for a mortal love.
So all have set my heavier grief above
These things which happen. Rightly have
they done:
I, who still saw the horizontal sun
Heave his broad shoulder o'er the edge of
the world, 530
Out-facing Lucifer, and then had hurled
My spear aloft, as signal for the chase—
I, who for very sport of heart, would
race
With my own steed from Araby; pluck
down
A vulture from his towery perching;
frown 535
A lion into growling, loth retire—
To lose, at once, all my toil-breeding fire,
And sink thus low! but I will ease my
breast
Of secret grief, here in this bowery nest.

"This river does not see the naked sky, 540
Till it begins to progress silverly
Around the western border of the wood,
Whence, from a certain spot, its winding
flood
Seems at the distance like a crescent moon:
And in that nook, the very pride of
June, 545
Had I been used to pass my weary eves;
The rather for the sun unwilling leaves
So dear a picture of his sovereign power,
And I could witness his most kingly hour,
When he doth tighten up the golden
reins, 550
And paces leisurely down amber plains
His snorting four. Now when his chariot
last
Its beams against the zodiac-lion cast,
There blossomed suddenly a magic bed
Of sacred ditamy, and poppies red: 555
At which I wondered greatly, knowing well
That but one night had wrought this
flowery spell;
And, sitting down close by, began to muse
What it might mean. Perhaps, thought I,
Morpheus,
In passing here, his owlet pinions shook; 560
Or, it may be, ere matron Night uptook
Her ebon urn, young Mercury, by stealth,
Had dipped his rod in it: such garland
wealth
Came not by common growth. Thus on I
thought,
Until my head was dizzy and distraught. 565
Moreover, through the dancing poppies
stole
A breeze, most softly lulling to my soul:
And shaping visions all about my sight
Of colors, wings, and bursts of spangly
light;
The which became more strange, and
strange, and dim, 570
And then were gulfed in a tumultuous
swim:
And then I fell asleep. Ah, can I tell
The enchantment that afterwards befell?
Yet it was but a dream: yet such a dream
That never tongue, although it overteem 575
With mellow utterance, like a cavern
spring,
Could figure out and to conception bring
All I beheld and felt. Methought I lay
Watching the zenith, where the milky way
Among the stars in virgin splendor
pours; 580
And travelling my eye, until the doors
Of heaven appeared to open for my flight,
I became loth and fearful to alight
From such high soaring by a downward
glance:

So kept me steadfast in that airy trance, 585
Spreading imaginary pinions wide.
When presently, the stars began to glide,
And faint away, before my eager view:
At which I sighed that I could not pursue,
And dropped my vision to the horizon's
    verge; 590
And lo! from opening clouds, I saw emerge
The loveliest moon, that ever silvered o'er
A shell for Neptune's goblet: she did soar
So passionately bright, my dazzled soul
Commingling with her argent spheres did
    roll 595
Through clear and cloudy, even when she
    went
At last into a dark and vapory tent—
Whereat, methought, the lidless-eyed train
Of planets all were in the blue again.
To commune with those orbs, once more I
    raised 600
My sight right upward: but it was quite
    dazed
By a bright something, sailing down apace,
Making me quickly veil my eyes and face:
Again I looked, and, O ye deities,
Who from Olympus watch our destinies! 605
Whence that completed form of all com-
    pleteness?
Whence came that high perfection of all
    sweetness?
Speak, stubborn earth, and tell me where,
    O where
Hast thou a symbol of her golden hair?
Not oat-sheaves drooping in the western
    sun; 610
Not—thy soft hand, fair sister! let me shun
Such follying before thee—yet she had,
Indeed, locks bright enough to make me
    mad;
And they were simply gordianed up and
    braided,
Leaving, in naked comeliness, unshaded, 615
Her pearl round ears, white neck, and
    orbèd brow;
The which were blended in, I know not
    how,
With such a paradise of lips and eyes,
Blush-tinted cheeks, half smiles, and faint-
    est sighs,
That, when I think thereon, my spirit
    clings 620
And plays about its fancy, till the stings
Of human neighborhood envenom all.
Unto what awful power shall I call?
To what high fane?—Ah! see her hovering
    feet,
More bluely veined, more soft, more
    whitely sweet 625
Than those of sea-born Venus, when she
    rose

From out her cradle shell. The wind out-
    blows
Her scarf into a fluttering pavilion;
'Tis blue, and over-spangled with a million
Of little eyes, as though thou wert to
    shed, 630
Over the darkest, lushest blue-bell bed,
Handfuls of daisies."—"Endymion, how
    strange!
Dream within dream!"—"She took an airy
    range,
And then, towards me, like a very maid,
Came blushing, waning, willing, and
    afraid, 635
And pressed me by the hand: Ah! 'twas
    too much;
Methought I fainted at the charmèd touch,
Yet held my recollection, even as one
Who dives three fathoms where the waters
    run
Gurgling in beds of coral: for anon, 640
I felt upmounted in that region
Where falling stars dart their artillery
    forth,
And eagles struggle with the buffeting
    north
That balances the heavy meteor-stone;—
Felt too, I was not fearful, nor alone, 645
But lapped and lulled along the dangerous
    sky.
Soon, as it seemed, we left our journeying
    high,
And straightway into frightful eddies
    swooped;
Such as aye muster where grey time has
    scooped
Huge dens and caverns in a mountain's
    side: 650
There hollow sounds aroused me, and I
    sighed
To faint once more by looking on my
    bliss—
I was distracted; madly did I kiss
The wooing arms which held me, and did
    give
My eyes at once to death: but 'twas to
    live, 655
To take in draughts of life from the gold
    fount
Of kind and passionate looks; to count,
    and count
The moments, by some greedy help that
    seemed
A second self, that each might be redeemed
And plundered of its load of blessed-
    ness. 660
Ah, desperate mortal! I e'en dared to press
Her very cheek against my crownèd lip,
And, at that moment, felt my body dip
Into a warmer air: a moment more,

Our feet were soft in flowers. There was
 store 665
Of newest joys upon that alp. Sometimes
A scent of violets, and blossoming limes,
Loitered around us; then of honey cells,
Made delicate from all white-flower bells;
And once, above the edge of our nest, 670
An arch face peeped,—an Oread as I
 guessed.

"Why did I dream that sleep o'erpow-
 ered me
In midst of all this heaven? Why not see,
Far off, the shadows of his pinions dark,
And stare them from me? But no, like a
 spark 675
That needs must die, although its little
 beam
Reflects upon a diamond, my sweet dream
Fell into nothing—into stupid sleep.
And so it was, until a gentle creep,
A careful moving caught my waking ears, 680
And up I started: Ah! my sighs, my tears,
My clenchèd hands;—for lo! the poppies
 hung
Dew-dabbled on their stalks, the ouzel sung
A heavy ditty, and the sullen day
Had chidden herald Hesperus away, 685
With leaden looks: the solitary breeze
Blustered, and slept, and its wild self did
 teaze
With wayward melancholy; and I thought
Mark me, Peona! that sometimes it brought
Faint fare-thee-wells, and sigh-shrilled
 adieus!— 690
Away I wandered—all the pleasant hues
Of heaven and earth had faded: deepest
 shades
Were deepest dungeons; heaths and sunny
 glades
Were full of pestilent light; our taintless
 rills
Seemed sooty, and o'erspread with up-
 turned gills 695
Of dying fish; the vermeil rose had blown
In frightful scarlet, and its thorns out-
 grown
Like spikèd aloe. If an innocent bird
Before my heedless footsteps stirred, and
 stirred
In little journeys, I beheld in it 700
A disguised demon, missioned to knit
My soul with under darkness; to entice
My stumblings down some monstrous preci-
 pice:
Therefore I eager followed, and did curse
The disappointment. Time, that agèd
 nurse, 705
Rocked me to patience. Now, thank gen-
 tle heaven

These things, with all their comfortings,
 are given
To my down-surken hours, and with thee,
Sweet sister, help to stem the ebbing sea
Of weary life."

 Thus ended he, and both 710
Sat silent: for the maid was very loth
To answer; feeling well that breathèd
 words
Would all be lost, unheard, and vain as
 swords
Against the enchased crocodile, or leaps
Of grasshoppers against the sun. She
 weeps 715
And wonders; struggles to devise some
 blame;
To put on such a look as would say, Shame
On this poor weakness! but, for all her
 strife,
She could as soon have crushed away the
 life
From a sick dove. At length, to break the
 pause, 720
She said with trembling chance: "Is this
 the cause?
This all? Yet it is strange, and sad, alas!
That one who through this middle earth
 should pass
Most like a sojourning demi-god, and leave
His name upon the harp-string, should
 achieve 725
No higher bard than simple maidenhood,
Singing alone, and fearfully,—how the
 blood
Left his young cheek; and how he used to
 stray
He knew not where; and how he would
 say, nay,
If any said 'twas love: and yet 'twas
 love; 730
What could it be but love? How a ring-
 dove
Let fall a sprig of yew tree in his path;
And how he died: and then, that love doth
 scathe
The gentle heart, as northern blasts do
 roses;
And then the ballad of his sad life closes 735
With sighs, and an alas!—Endymion!
Be rather in the trumpet's mouth,—anon
Among the winds at large—that all may
 hearken!
Although, before the crystal heavens
 darken,
I watch and dote upon the silver lakes 740
Pictured in western cloudiness, that takes
The semblance of gold rocks and bright
 gold sands,

Islands, and creeks, and amber-fretted
    strands
With horses prancing o'er them, palaces
And towers of amethyst—would I so
    teaze   745
My pleasant days, because I could not
    mount
Into those regions? The Morphean fount
Of that fine element that visions, dreams,
And fitful whims of sleep are made of,
    streams
Into its airy channels with so subtle,   750
So thin a breathing, not the spider's
    shuttle,
Circled a million times within the space
Of a swallow's nest-door, could delay a
    trace,
A tinting of its quality: how light
Must dreams themselves be; seeing they're
    more slight   755
Than the mere nothing that engenders
    them!
Then wherefore sully the entrusted gem
Of high and noble life with thoughts so
    sick?
Why pierce high-fronted honor to the quick
For nothing but a dream?" Hereat the
    youth   760
Looked up: a conflicting of shame and ruth
Was in his plaited brow: yet, his eyelids
Widened a little, as when Zephyr bids
A little breeze to creep between the fans
Of careless butterflies: amid his pains 765
He seemed to taste a drop of manna-dew,
Full palatable; and a color grew
Upon his cheek, while thus he lifeful spake.

"Peona! ever have I longed to slake
My thirst for the world's praises: nothing
    base,   770
No merely slumberous phantasm, could
    unlace
The stubborn canvas for my voyage pre-
    pared—
Though now 'tis tattered; leaving my bark
    bared
And sullenly drifting: yet my higher hope
Is of too wide, too rainbow-large a scope, 775
To fret at myriads of earthly wrecks.
Wherein lies happiness? In that which
    becks
Our ready minds to fellowship divine,
A fellowship with essence; till we shine,
Full alchemized, and free of space. Be-
    hold   780
The clear religion of heaven! Fold
A rose leaf round thy finger's taperness,
And soothe thy lips: hist, when the airy
    stress

Of music's kiss impregnates the free winds,
And with a sympathetic touch unbinds 785
Æolian magic from their lucid wombs:
Then old songs waken from enclouded
    tombs;
Old ditties sigh above their father's grave;
Ghosts of melodious prophesyings rave
Round every spot where trod Apollo's
    foot;   790
Bronze clarions awake, and faintly bruit,
Where long ago a giant battle was;
And, from the turf, a lullaby doth pass
In every place where infant Orpheus slept.
Feel we these things?—that moment have
    we stepped   795
Into a sort of oneness, and our state
Is like a floating spirit's. But there are
Richer entanglements, enthralments far
More self-destroying, leading, by degrees,
To the chief intensity: the crown of
    these   800
Is made of love and friendship, and sits
    high
Upon the forehead of humanity.
All its more ponderous and bulky worth
Is friendship, whence there ever issues forth
A steady splendor; but at the tip-top,   805
There hangs by unseen film, an orbèd drop
Of light, and that is love: its influence,
Thrown in our eyes, genders a novel sense,
At which we start and fret; till in the end,
Melting into its radiance, we blend,   810
Mingle, and so become a part of it,—
Nor with aught else can our souls interknit
So wingedly: when we combine therewith,
Life's self is nourished by its proper pith,
And we are nurtured like a pelican
    brood.   815
Aye, so delicious is the unsating food,
That men, who might have towered in the
    van
Of all the congregated world, to fan
And winnow from the coming step of time
All chaff of custom, wipe away all slime 820
Left by men-slugs and human serpentry,
Have been content to let occasion die,
Whilst they did sleep in love's elysium.
And, truly, I would rather be struck dumb,
Than speak against this ardent listless-
    ness: 825
For I have ever thought that it might bless
The world with benefits unknowingly;
As does the nightingale, up-perchèd high,
And cloistered among cool and bunchèd
    leaves—
She sings but to her love, nor e'er con-
    ceives   830
How tiptoe Night holds back her dark-grey
    hood.
Just so may love, although 'tis understood

The mere commingling of passionate
breath,
Produce more than our searching wit-
nesseth:
What I know not: but who, of men, can
tell   835
That flowers would bloom, or that green
fruit would swell
To melting pulp, that fish would have
bright mail,
The earth its dower of river, wood, and
vale,
The meadows runnels, runnels pebble-
stones,
The seed its harvest, or the lute its
tones,   840
Tones ravishment, or ravishment its sweet,
If human souls did never kiss and greet?

"Now, if this earthly love has power to
make
Men's being mortal, immortal; to shake
Ambition from their memories, and brim 845
Their measure of content; what merest
whim,
Seems all this poor endeavor after fame,
To one, who keeps within his steadfast
aim
A iove immortal, an immortal too.
Look not so wildered; for these things are
true,   850
And never can be born of atomies
That buzz about our slumbers, like brain-
flies,
Leaving us fancy-sick. No, no, I'm sure,
My restless spirit never could endure
To brood so long upon one luxury,   855
Unless it did, though fearfully espy
A hope beyond the shadow of a dream.

My sayings will the less obscured seem,
When I have told thee how my waking
sight
Has made me scruple whether that same
night   860
Was passed in dreaming. Hearken, sweet
Peona!
Beyond the matron-temple of Latona,
Which we should see but for these dark-
ening boughs,
Lies a deep hollow, from whose ragged
brows
Bushes and trees do lean all round
athwart   865
And meet so nearly, that with wings out-
raught,
And spreaded tail, a vulture could not glide
Past them, but he must brush on every side.
Some moldered steps lead into this cool
cell,

Far as the slabbed margin of a well,   870
Whose patient level peeps its crystal eye
Right upward, through the bushes, to the
sky.
Oft have I brought thee flowers, on their
stalks set
Like vestal primroses, but dark velvet
Edges them round, and they have golden
pits: 875
'Twas there I got them, from the gaps and
slits
In a mossy stone, that sometimes was my
seat,
When all above was faint with mid-day
heat.
And there in strife no burning thoughts to
heed,
I'd bubble up the water through a reed; 880
So reaching back to boyhood: make me
ships
Of molted feathers, touchwood, alder chips,
With leaves stuck in them; and the Nep-
tune be
Of their pretty ocean. Oftener, heavily,
When lovelorn hours had left me less a
child,   885
I sat contemplating the figures wild
Of o'er-head clouds melting the mirror
through.
Upon a day, while thus I watched, by flew
A cloudy Cupid, with his bow and quiver;
So plainly charactered, no breeze would
shiver   890
The happy chance; so happy, I was fain
To follow it upon the open plain,
And, therefore, was just going, when, be-
hold!
A wonder, fair as any I have told—
The same bright face I tasted in my
sleep,   895
Smiling in the clear well. My heart did
leap
Through the cool depth.—It moved as if to
flee—
I started up, when lo! refreshfully,
There came upon my face, in plenteous
showers,
Dew-drops, and dewy buds, and leaves,
and flowers,   900
Wrapping all objects from my smothered
sight,
Bathing my spirit in a new delight.
Aye, such a breathless honey-feel of bliss
Alone preserved me from the drear abyss
Of death, for the fair form had gone
again.   905
Pleasure is oft a visitant; but pain
Clings cruelly to us, like the gnawing sloth
On the deer's tender haunches: late, and
loth,

'Tis scared away by slow returning pleas-
ure.
How sickening, how dark the dreadful
leisure 910
Of weary days, made deeper exquisite,
By a foreknowledge of unslumbrous night!
Like sorrow came upon me, heavier still,
Than when I wandered from the poppy
hill:
And a whole age of lingering moments
crept 915
Sluggishly by, ere more contentment swept
Away at once the deadly yellow spleen.
Yes, thrice have I this fair enchantment
seen;
Once more been tortured with renewed
life.
When last the wintry gusts gave over
strife 920
With the conquering sun of spring, and
left the skies
Warm and serene, but yet with moistened
eyes
In pity of the shattered infant buds,—
That time thou didst adorn, with amber
studs,
My hunting cap, because I laughed and
smiled, 925
Chatted with thee, and many days exiled
All torment from my breast;—'twas even
then,
Straying about, yet cooped up in the den
Of helpless discontent,—hurling my lance
From place to place, and following at
chance, 930
At last, by hap, through some young trees
it struck,
And, plashing among bedded pebbles, stuck
In the middle of a brook,—whose silver
ramble
Down twenty little falls, through reeds and
bramble,
Tracing along, it brought me to a cave, 935
Whence it ran brightly forth, and white
did lave
The nether sides of mossy stones and
rock,—
'Mong which it gurgled blythe adieus, to
mock
Its own sweet grief at parting. Overhead,
Hung a lush screen of drooping weeds, and
spread 940
Thick, as to curtain up some wood-nymph's
home.
"Ah! impious mortal, whither do I roam?"
Said I, low-voiced: "Ah, whither! 'Tis the
grot
Of Proserpine, when Hell, obscure and hot,
Doth her resign; and where her tender
hands 945

She dabbles, on the cool and sluicy sands:
Or 'tis the cell of Echo, where she sits,
And babbles thorough silence, and anon,
Are gone in tender madness, and anon,
Faints into sleep, with many a dying
tone 950
Of sadness. O that she would take my
vows,
And breathe them sighingly among the
boughs,
To sue her gentle ears for whose fair head,
Daily, I pluck sweet flowerets from their
bed,
And weave them dyingly—send honey-
whispers 955
Round every leaf, that all those gentle
lispers
May sigh my love unto her pitying!
O charitable Echo! hear, and sing
This ditty to her!—tell her"—So I stayed
My foolish tongue, and listening, half-
afraid, 960
Stood stupefied with my own empty folly.
And blushing for the freaks of melancholy.
Salt tears were coming, when I heard my
name
Most fondly lipped, and then these accents
came:
"Endymion! the cave is secreter 965
Than the isle of Delos. Echo hence shall
stir
No sighs but sigh-warm kisses, or light noise
Of thy combing hand, the while it travel-
ling cloys
And trembles through my labyrinthine
hair."
At that oppressed I hurried in.—Ah!
where 970
Are those swift moments? Whither are
they fled?
I'll smile no more, Peona; nor will wed
Sorrow the way to death; but patiently
Bear up against it: so farewell, sad sigh;
And come instead demurest meditation, 975
To occupy me wholly, and to fashion
My pilgrimage for the world's dusky brink.
No more will I count over, link by link,
My chain of grief: no longer strive to
find
A half-forgetfulness in mountain wind 980
Blustering about my ears: aye, thou shalt
see,
Dearest of sisters, what my life shall be;
What a calm round of hours shall make
my days.
There is a paly flame of hope that plays
Where'er I look: but yet, I'll say 'tis
naught— 985
And here I bid it die. Have not I caught,
Already, a more healthy countenance?

By this the sun is setting; we may chance
Meet some of our near-dwellers with my
  car."

This said, he rose, faint-smiling like a
  star   990
Through autumn mists, and took Peona's
  hand:
They stept into the boat, and launched
  from land.

BOOK II

O sovereign power of love! O grief! O
  balm!
All records, saving thine, come cool, and
  calm,
And shadowy, through the mist of passed
  years:
For others, good or bad, hatred and tears
Have become indolent; but touching
  thine,   5
One sigh doth echo, one poor sob doth
  pine,
One kiss brings honey-dew from buried
  days.
The woes of Troy, towers smothering o'er
  their blaze,
Stiff-holden shields, far-piercing spears, keen
  blades,
Struggling, and blood, and shrieks—all
  dimly fades   10
Into some backward corner of the brain;
Yet, in our very souls, we feel amain
The close of Troilus and Cressid sweet.
Hence, pageant history! hence, gilded
  cheat!
Swart planet in the universe of deeds!   15
Wide sea, that one continuous murmur
  breeds
Along the pebbled shore of memory!
Many old rotten-timbered boats there be
Upon thy vaporous bosom, magnified
To goodly vessels; many a sail of pride, 20
And golden keeled, is left unlaunched and
  dry.
But wherefore this? What care, though owl
  did fly
About the great Athenian admiral's mast?
What care, though striding Alexander past
The Indus with his Macedonian num-
  bers?   25
Though old Ulysses tortured from his
  slumbers
The glutted Cyclops, what care?—Juliet
  leaning
Amid her window-flowers,—sighing,—
  weaning
Tenderly her fancy from its maiden snow,

Doth more avail than these: the silver
  flow   30
Of Hero's tears, the swoon of Imogen,
Fair Pastorella in the bandit's den,
Are things to brood on with more ardency
Than the death-day of empires. Fearfully
Must such conviction come upon his
  head,   35
Who, thus far, discontent, has dared to
  tread,
Without one muse's smile, or kind behest,
The path of love and poesy. But rest,
In chaffing restlessness, is yet more drear
Than to be crushed, in striving to uprear 40
Love's standard on the battlements of song.
So once more days and nights aid me along,
Like legioned soldiers.

    After a thousand mazes overgone,
At last, with sudden step, he came upon
A chamber, myrtle-walled, embowered high,
Full of light, incense, tender minstrelsy, 390
And more of beautiful and strange beside:
For on a silken couch of rosy pride,
In midst of all, there lay a sleeping youth
Of fondest beauty; fonder, in fair sooth,
Than sighs could fathom, or contentment
  reach: 395
And coverlids gold-tinted like the peach,
Or ripe October's faded marigolds,
Fell sleek about him in a thousand folds—
Not hiding up an Apollonian curve
Of neck and shoulder, nor the tenting
  swerve   400
Of knee from knee, nor ankles pointing
  light;
But rather, giving them to the filled sight
Officiously. Sideway his face reposed
On one white arm, and tenderly unclosed,
By tenderest pressure, a faint damask
  mouth   405
To slumbery pout; just as the morning
  south
Disparts a dew-lipped rose. Above his
  head,
Four lily stalks did their white honors wed
To make a coronal; and round him grew
All tendrils green, of every bloom and
  hue,   410
Together intertwined and trammelled
  fresh:
The vine of glossy sprout; the ivy mesh,
Shading its Ethiop berries; and woodbine,
Of velvet-leaves and bugle-blooms divine;
Convolvulus in streaked vases flush;   415
The creeper, mellowing for an autumn
  blush;
And virgin's bower, trailing airily;
With others of the sisterhood. Hard by,

Stood serene Cupids watching silently.
One, kneeling to a lyre, touched the
    strings,   420
Muffling to death the pathos with his
    wings;
And, ever and anon, uprose to look
At the youth's slumber; while another took
A willow bough, distilling odorous dew,
And shook it on his hair; another flew   425
In through the woven roof, and fluttering-
    wise
Rained violets upon his sleeping eyes.

BOOK III

Are then regalities all gilded masks?
No, there are thronèd seats unscalable
But by a patient wing, a constant spell,
Or by ethereal things that, unconfined,   25
Can make a ladder of the eternal wind,
And poise about in cloudy thunder-tents
To watch the abysm-birth of elements.
Aye, 'bove the withering of old-lipped Fate
A thousand Powers keep religious state,   30
In water, fiery realm, and airy bourne;
And, silent as a consecrated urn,
Hold sphery sessions for a season due.
Yet few of these far majesties, ah, few!
Have bared their operations to this
    globe—   35
Few, who with gorgeous pageantry enrobe
Our piece of heaven—whose benevolence
Shakes hand with our own Ceres; every
    sense
Filling with spiritual sweets to plenitude,
As bees gorge full their cells. And, by the
    feud   40
'Twixt Nothing and Creation, I here swear,
Eterne Apollo! that thy Sister fair
Is of all these the gentlier-mightiest.
When thy gold breath is misting in the
    west,
She unobservèd steals unto her throne,   45
And there she sits most meek and most
    alone;
As if she had not pomp subservient;
As if thine eye, high Poet! was not bent
Towards her with the Muses in thine heart;
As if the ministering stars kept not apart,   50
Waiting for silver-footed messages.
O Moon! the oldest shades 'mong oldest
    trees
Feel palpitations when thou lookest in:
O Moon! old boughs lisp forth a holier din
The while they feel thine airy fellowship.   55
Thou dost bless every where, with silver lip
Kissing dead things to life. The sleeping
    kine,
Couched in thy brightness, dream of fields
    divine:

Innumerable mountains rise and rise,
Ambitious for the hallowing of thine
    eyes;   60
And yet thy benediction passeth not
One obscure hiding-place, one little spot
Where pleasure may be sent: the nested
    wren
Has thy fair face within its tranquil ken,
And from beneath a sheltering ivy leaf   65
Takes glimpses of thee; thou art a relief
To the poor patient oyster, where it sleeps
Within its pearly house.—The mighty
    deeps,
The monstrous sea is thine—the myriad
    sea!
O Moon! far-spooming Ocean bows to
    thee,   70
And Tellus feels his forehead's cumbrous
    load.

. . . .

"What is there in thee, Moon! that thou
    shouldst move   142
My heart so potently? When yet a child
I oft have dried my tears when thou hast
    smiled.
Thou seem'dst my sister: hand in hand we
    went   145
From eve to morn across the firmament.
No apples would I gather from the tree,
Till thou hadst cooled their cheeks de-
    liciously:
No tumbling water ever spake romance,
But when my eyes with thine thereon could
    dance: 150
No woods were green enough, no bower
    divine,
Until thou liftedst up thine eyelids fine:
In sowing-time ne'er would I dibble take,
Or drop a seed, till thou wast wide awake;
And, in the summer tide of blossoming,   155
No one but thee hath heard me blithely
    sing
And mesh my dewy flowers all the night.
No melody was like a passing spright
If it went not to solemnize thy reign.
Yes, in my boyhood, every joy and pain 160
By thee were fashioned to the self-same
    end;
And as I grew in years, still didst thou
    blend
With all my ardors; thou wast the deep
    glen;
Thou wast the mountain-top—the sage's
    pen—
The poet's harp—the voice of friends—the
    sun;   165
Thou wast the river—thou wast glory won;
Thou wast my clarion's blast—thou wast
    my steed—

My goblet full of wine—my topmost
deed:—
Thou wast the charm of women, lovely
Moon!
O what a wild and harmonized tune   170
My spirit struck from all the beautiful!
On some bright essence could I lean, and
lull
Myself to immortality: I prest
Nature's soft pillow in a wakeful rest.
But gentle Orb! there came a nearer
bliss—   175
My strange love came—Felicity's abyss!
She came, and thou didst fade, and fade
away—
Yet not entirely; no, thy starry sway
Has been an under-passion to this hour.
Now I begin to feel thine orby power   180
Is coming fresh upon me: O be kind,
Keep back thine influence, and do not
blind
My sovereign vision.—Dearest love, forgive
That I can think away from thee and
live!—
Pardon me, airy planet, that I prize   185
One thought beyond thine argent luxuries!
How far beyond!"

BOOK IV

Muse of my native land! loftiest Muse!
O first-born on the mountains! by the hues
Of heaven on the spiritual air begot:
Long didst thou sit alone in northern grot,
While yet our England was a wolfish den; 5
Before our forests heard the talk of men;
Before the first of Druids was a child;—
Long didst thou sit amid our regions wild
Rapt in a deep prophetic solitude.
There came an eastern voice of solemn
mood:—   10
Yet wast thou patient. Then sang forth
the Nine,
Apollo's garland:—yet didst thou divine
Such home-bred glory, that they cried in
vain,
"Come hither, Sister of the Island!" Plain
Spake fair Ausonia; and once more she
spake   15
A higher summons:—still didst thou betake
Thee to thy native hopes. O thou hast
won
A full accomplishment! The thing is done,
Which undone, these our latter days had
risen
On barren souls. Great Muse, thou know'st
what prison   20
Of flesh and bone curbs, and confines, and
frets

Our spirit's wings: despondency besets
Our pillows; and the fresh tomorrow morn
Seems to give forth its light in very scorn
Of our dull, uninspired, snail-paced lives. 25
Long have I said, how happy he who
shrives
To thee! But then I thought on poets
gone,
And could not pray:—nor can I now—
so on
I move to the end in lowliness of heart.—

"Ah, woe is me! that I should fondly
part   30
From my dear native land! Ah, foolish
maid!
Glad was the hour, when, with thee,
myriads bade
Adieu to Ganges and their pleasant fields!
To one so friendless the clear freshet yields
A bitter coolness; the ripe grape is sour: 35
Yet I would have, great gods! but one short
hour
Of native air—let me but die at home."

Endymion to heaven's airy dome
Was offering up a hecatomb of vows,
When these words reached him. Where-
upon he bows   40
His head through thorny-green entangle-
ment
Of underwood, and to the sound is bent,
Anxious as hind towards her hidden fawn.

"Is no one near to help me? No fair
dawn
Of life from charitable voice? No sweet
saying   45
To set my dull and saddened spirit play-
ing?
No hand to toy with mine? No lips so
sweet
That I may worship them? No eyelids
meet
To twinkle on my bosom? No one dies
Before me, till from these enslaving eyes 50
Redemption sparkles!—I am sad and lost."

Thou, Carian lord, hadst better have
been tost
Into a whirlpool. Vanish into air,
Warm mountaineer! for canst thou only
bear
A woman's sigh alone and in distress? 55
See not her charms! Is Phœbe passionless?
Phœbe is fairer far—O gaze no more:—
Yet if thou wilt behold all beauty's store,
Behold her panting in the forest grass!
Do not those curls of glossy jet surpass 60
For tenderness the arms so idly lain

Amongst them?   Feelest not a kindred
   pain,
To see such lovely eyes in swimming search
After some warm delight, that seems to
   perch
Dovelike in the dim cell lying beyond   65
Their upper lids?—Hist!

               "O for Hermes' wand,
To touch this flower into human shape!
That woodland Hyacinthus could escape
From his green prison, and here kneeling
   down
Call me his queen, his second life's fair
   crown!   70
Ah me, how could I love!—My soul doth
   melt
For the unhappy youth—Love! I have felt
So faint a kindness, such a meek surrender
To what my own full thoughts had made
   too tender,
That but for tears my life had fled
   away!—   75
Ye deaf and senseless minutes of the day,
And thou, old forest, hold ye this for true,
There is no lightning, no authentic dew
But in the eye of love: there's not a sound,
Melodious howsoever, can confound   80
The heavens and earth in one to such a
   death
As doth the voice of love: there's not a
   breath
Will mingle kindly with the meadow air,
Till it has panted round, and stolen a share
Of passion from the heart!—

                Upon a bough   85
He leant, wretched.   He surely cannot now
Thirst for another love: O impious,
That he can ever dream upon it thus!—
Thought he, "Why am I not as are the
   dead,
Since to a woe like this I have been led   90
Through the dark earth, and through the
   wondrous sea?
Goddess! I love thee not the less: from
   thee
By Juno's smile I turn not—no, no, no—
While the great waters are at ebb and
   flow.—
I have a triple soul! O fond pretence—   95
For both, for both my love is so immense,
I feel my heart is cut for them in twain."

    And so he groaned, as one by beauty
   slain.
The lady's heart beat quick, and he could
   see
Her gentle bosom heave tumultuously.   100

He sprang from his green covert: there she
   lay,
Sweet as a muskrose upon new-made hay;
With all her limbs on tremble, and her eyes
Shut softly up alive.   To speak he tries.
"Fair damsel, pity me! forgive that I   105
Thus violate thy bower's sanctity!
O pardon me, for I am full of grief—
Grief born of thee, young angel! fairest
   thief!
Who stolen hast away the wings wherewith
I was to top the heavens.   Dear maid,
   sith   110
Thou art my executioner, and I feel
Loving and hatred, misery and weal,
Will in a few short hours be nothing to
   me,
And all my story that much passion slew
   me;
Do smile upon the evening of my days: 115
And, for my tortured brain begins to craze,
Be thou my nurse; and let me understand
How dying I shall kiss that lily hand.—
Dost weep for me?   Then should I be con-
   tent.
Scowl on, ye fates! until the firmament   120
Outblackens Erebus, and the full-caverned
   earth
Crumbles into itself.   By the cloud-girth
Of Jove, those tears have given me a thirst
To meet oblivion."—As her heart would
   burst
The maiden sobbed awhile, and then re-
   plied: 125
"Why must such desolation betide
As that thou speakest of?   Are not these
   green nooks
Empty of all misfortune?   Do the brooks
Utter a gorgon voice?   Does yonder thrush,
Schooling its half-fledged little ones to
   brush   130
About the dewy forest, whisper tales?—
Speak not of grief, young stranger, or cold
   snails
Will slime the rose tonight.   Though if
   thou wilt,
Methinks 'twould be a guilt—a very guilt—
Not to companion thee, and sigh away   135
The light—the dusk—the dark—till break
   of day!"
"Dear lady," said Endymion, "'tis past:
I love thee! and my days can never last.
That I may pass in patience still speak:
Let men have music dying, and I seek   140
No more delight—I bid adieu to all.
Didst thou not after other climates call,
And murmur about Indian streams?"—
         Then she,
Sitting beneath the midmost forest tree,
For pity sang this roundelay—   145

"O Sorrow,
Why dost borrow
The natural hue of health, from vermeil
lips?—
To give maiden blushes
To the white rose bushes?   150
Or is't thy dewy hand the daisy tips?

"O Sorrow,
Why dost borrow
The lustrous passion from a falcon-eye?—
To give the glow-worm light?   155
Or, on a moonless night,
To tinge, on syren shores, the salt sea-
spray?

"O Sorrow,
Why dost borrow
The mellow ditties from a mourning
tongue?—   160
To give at evening pale
Unto the nightingale,
That thou mayest listen the cold dews
among?

"O Sorrow,
Why dost borrow   165
Heart's lightness from the merriment of
May?—
A lover would not tread
A cowslip on the head,
Though he should dance from eve till peep
of day—
Nor any drooping flower   170
Held sacred for thy bower,
Wherever he may sport himself and play.

"To Sorrow,
I bade good-morrow,
And thought to leave her far away be-
hind;   175
But cheerly, cheerly,
She loves me dearly;
She is so constant to me, and so kind:
I would deceive her
And so leave her,   180
But ah; she is so constant and so kind.

"Beneath my palm trees, by the river side,
I sat a weeping: in the whole world wide
There was no one to ask me why I wept,—
And so I kept   185
Brimming the water-lily cups with tears
Cold as my fears.

"Beneath my palm trees, by the river side,
I sat a weeping: what enamoured bride,
Cheated by shadowy wooer from the
clouds,   190
But hides and shrouds
Beneath dark palm trees by a river side?

"And as I sat, over the light blue hills
There came a noise of revellers: the rills
Into the wide stream came of purple
hue—   195
'Twas Bacchus and his crew!
The earnest trumpet spake, and silver
thrills
From kissing cymbals made a merry din—
'Twas Bacchus and his kin!
Like to a moving vintage down they
came,   200
Crowned with green leaves, and faces all
on flame;
All madly dancing through the pleasant
valley,
To scare thee, Melancholy!
O then, O then, thou wast a simple name!
And I forgot thee, as the berried holly   205
By shepherds is forgotten, when, in June,
Tall chestnuts keep away the sun and
moon:—
I rushed into the folly!

"Within his car, aloft, young Bacchus
stood,
Trifling his ivy-dart, in dancing mood,   210
With sidelong laughing;
And little rills of crimson wine imbrued
His plump white arms, and shoulders,
enough white
For Venus' pearly bite:
And near him rode Silenus on his ass,   215
Pelted with flowers as he on did pass
Tipsily quaffing.

"Whence came ye, merry Damsels! whence
came ye!
So many, and so many, and such glee?
Why have ye left your bowers desolate,   220
Your lutes, and gentler fate?—
'We follow Bacchus! Bacchus on the wing,
A conquering!
Bacchus, young Bacchus! good or ill betide,
We dance before him thorough kingdoms
wide:—   225
Come hither, lady fair, and joinèd be
To our wild minstrelsy!'

"Whence came ye, jolly Satyrs! whence
came ye!
So many, and so many, and such glee?
Why have ye left your forest haunts, why
left   230
Your nuts in oak-tree cleft?—
'For wine, for wine we left our kernel tree;
For wine we left our heath, and yellow
brooms,
And cold mushrooms;
For wine we follow Bacchus through the
earth;   235

Great god of breathless cups and chirping
　　　　mirth!—
Come hither, lady fair, and joinèd be
　　To our mad minstrelsy!'

"Over wide streams and mountains great
　　　　we went,
And, save when Bacchus kept his ivy
　　　　tent,　　　　　　　　　　240
Onward the tiger and the leopard pants,
　　With Asian elephants:
Onward these myriads—with song and
　　dance,
With zebras striped, and sleek Arabians'
　　prance,
Web-footed alligators, crocodiles,　　245
Bearing upon their scaly backs, in files,
Plump infant laughers mimicking the coil
Of seamen, and stout galley-rowers' toil:
With toying oars and silken sails they glide,
　　Nor care for wind and tide.　　250

"Mounted on panthers' furs and lions'
　　manes,
From rear to van they scour about the
　　plains;
A three days' journey in a moment done:
And always, at the rising of the sun,
About the wilds they hunt with spear and
　　horn,　　　　　　　　　　255
　　On spleenful unicorn.

"I saw Osirian Egypt kneel adown
　　Before the vine-wreath crown!
I saw parched Abyssinia rouse and sing
　　To the silver cymbals' ring!　　260
I saw the whelming vintage hotly pierce
　　Old Tartary the fierce!
The kings of Ind their jewel-sceptres vail,
And from their treasures scatter pearled
　　hail;
Great Brahma from his mystic heaven
　　groans,　　　　　　　　　　265
　　And all his priesthood moans;
Before young Bacchus' eye-wink turning
　　pale.—
Into these regions came I following him,
Sick-hearted, weary—so I took a whim
To stray away into these forests drear　　270
　　Alone, without a peer:
And I have told thee all thou mayest hear.

"Young stranger!
　　I've been a ranger
In search of pleasure throughout every
　　clime:　　　　　　　　　　275
　　Alas, 'tis not for me!
　　Bewitched I sure must be,
To lose in grieving all my maiden prime.

"Come then, Sorrow!
　　Sweetest Sorrow!　　　　　　280
Like an own babe I nurse thee on my
　　breast:
　　I thought to leave thee
　　And deceive thee,
But now of all the world I love thee best.

"There is not one,　　　　　　285
　　No, no, not one
But thee to comfort a poor lonely maid;
　　Thou art her mother,
　　And her brother,
Her playmate, and her wooer in the
　　shade."　　　　　　　　　　290

O what a sigh she gave in finishing,
And look, quite dead to every worldly
　　thing!
Endymion could not speak, but gazed on
　　her;
And listened to the wind that now did stir
About the crisped oaks full drearily,　　295
Yet with as sweet a softness as might be
Remembered from its velvet summer song.
At last he said: "Poor lady, how thus long
Have I been able to endure that voice?
Fair Melody! kind Siren! I've no choice; 300
I must be thy sad servant evermore:
I cannot choose but kneel here and adore.
Alas, I must not think—by Phœbe, no!
Let me not think, soft Angel! shall it be so?
Say, beautifullest, shall I never think?　　305
O thou could'st foster me beyond the brink
Of recollection! make my watchful care
Close up its bloodshot eyes, nor see despair!
Do gently murder half my soul, and I
Shall feel the other half so utterly!—　　310
I'm giddy at that cheek so fair and smooth;
O let it blush so ever! let it soothe
My madness! let it mantle rosy-warm
With the tinge of love, panting in safe
　　alarm.—
This cannot be thy hand, and yet it is;　　315
And this is sure thine other softling—this
Thine own fair bosom, and I am so near!
Wilt fall asleep? O let me sip that tear!
And whisper one sweet word that I may
　　know
This is this world—sweet dewy blossom!"—
　　Woe!　　　　　　　　　　320
*Woe! Woe to that Endymion! Where is
he?—*
Even these words went echoing dismally
Through the wide forest—a most fearful
　　tone,
Like one repenting in his latest moan;
And while it died away a shade passed
　　by,　　　　　　　　　　325
As of a thundercloud. When arrows fly

Through the thick branches, poor ring-
doves sleek forth
Their timid necks and tremble; so these
both
Leant to each other trembling, and sat so
Waiting for some destruction—when lo! 330
Foot-feathered Mercury appeared sublime
Beyond the tall tree tops; and in less time
Than shoots the slanted hail-storm, down
he dropt
Towards the ground; but rested not, nor
stopt
One moment from his home: only the
sward 335
He with his wand light touched, and
heavenward
Swifter than sight was gone—even before
The teeming earth a sudden witness bore
Of his swift magic. Diving swans appear
Above the crystal circlings white and
clear; 340
And catch the cheated eye in wide surprise,
How they can dive in sight and unseen
rise—
So from the turf outsprang two steeds jet-
black,
Each with large dark-blue wings upon his
back.
The youth of Caria placed the lovely
dame 345
On one, and felt himself in spleen to tame
The other's fierceness. Through the air
they flew,
High as the eagles. Like two drops of dew
Exhaled to Phœbus' lips, away they are
gone,
Far from the earth away—unseen, alone, 350
Among cool clouds and winds, but that the
free,
The buoyant life of song can floating be
Above their heads, and follow them un-
tired.—
Muse of my native land, am I inspired?
This is the giddy air, and I must spread 355
Wide pinions to keep here; nor do I dread
Or height, or depth, or width, or any
chance
Precipitous: I have beneath my glance
Those towering horses and their mournful
freight.
Could I thus sail, and see, and thus await 360
Fearless for power of thought, without
thine aid?—

There is a sleepy dusk, an odorous shade
From some approaching wonder, and behold
Those winged steeds, with snorting nostrils
bold

Snuff at its faint extreme, and seem to
tire, 365
Dying to embers from their native fire!

There curled a purple mist around them;
soon,
It seemed as when around the pale new
moon
Sad Zephyr droops the clouds like weeping
willow:
'Twas Sleep slow journeying with head on
pillow. 370
For the first time, since he came nigh dead-
born
From the old womb of night, his cave for-
lorn
Had he left more forlorn; for the first time,
He felt aloof the day and morning's
prime—
Because into his depth Cimmerian 375
There came a dream, showing how a young
man,
Ere a lean bat could plump its wintery
skin,
Would at high Jove's empyreal footstool
win
An immortality, and how espouse
Jove's daughter, and be reckoned of his
house. 380
Now was he slumbering towards heaven's
gate,
That he might at the threshold one hour
wait
To hear the marriage melodies, and then
Sink downward to his dusky cave again.
His litter of smooth semilucent mist, 385
Diversely tinged with rose and amethyst,
Puzzled those eyes that for the center
sought;
And scarcely for one moment could be
caught
His sluggish form reposing motionless.
Those two on winged steeds, with all the
stress 390
Of vision searched for him, as one would
look
Athwart the sallows of a river nook
To catch a glance at silver-throated eels,—
Or from old Skiddaw's top, when fog con-
ceals
His rugged forehead in a mantle pale, 395
With an eye-guess towards some pleasant
vale
Descry a favorite hamlet faint and far.

These raven horses, though they fostered
are
Of earth's splenetic fire, dully drop
Their full-veined ears, nostrils blood wide,
and stop; 400

Upon the spiritless mist have they out-
spread
Their ample feathers, are in slumber
dead,—
And on those pinions, level in mid air,
Endymion sleepeth and the lady fair.
Slowly they sail, slowly as icy isle   405
Upon a calm sea drifting: and meanwhile
The mournful wanderer dreams. Behold!
he walks
On heaven's pavement; brotherly he talks
To divine powers: from his hand full fain
Juno's proud birds are pecking pearly
grain: 410
He tries the nerve of Phœbus' golden bow,
And asketh where the golden apples grow:
Upon his arm he braces Pallas' shield,
And strives in vain to unsettle and wield
A Jovian thunderbolt: arch Hebe brings 415
A full-brimmed goblet, dances lightly, sings
And tantalizes long; at last he drinks
And lost in pleasure at her feet he sinks,
Touching with dazzled lips her starlight
hand.
He blows a bugle,—an ethereal band 420
Are visible above: the seasons four,—
Green-kirtled spring, flush summer, golden
store
In autumn's sickle, winter frosty hoar,
Join dance with shadowy hours; while still
the blast,
In swells unmitigated, still doth last 425
To sway their floating morris. "Whose is
this?
Whose bugle?" he inquires; they smile—
"O Dis!
Why is this mortal here? Dost thou not
know
Its mistress' lips? Not thou?—'Tis Dian's:
lo!
She rises crescented!" He looks, 'tis she, 430
His very goddess: good-bye earth, and sea,
And air, and pains, and care, and suffering;
Good-bye to all but love! Then doth he
spring
Towards her, and awakes—and, strange,
o'erhead,
Of those same fragrant exhalations bred, 435
Beheld awake his very dream: the gods
Stood smiling; merry Hebe laughs and
nods;
And Phœbe bends towards him crescented.
O state perplexing! On the pinion bed,
Too well awake, he feels the panting
side 440
Of his delicious lady. He who died
For soaring too audacious in the sun,
When that same treacherous wax began to
run,
Felt not more tongue-tied than Endymion.

His heart leapt up as to its rightful
throne, 445
To that fair-shadowed passion pulsed its
way—
Ah, what perplexity! Ah, well a day!
So fond, so beauteous, was his bedfellow,
He could not help but kiss her: then he
grew
Awhile forgetful of all beauty save 450
Young Phœbe's, golden haired; and so 'gan
crave
Forgiveness: yet he turned once more to
look
At the sweet sleeper,—all his soul was
shook,—
She pressed his hand in slumber; so once
more
He could not help but kiss her and
adore. 455
At this the shadow wept, melting away.
The Latmian started up: "Bright goddess,
stay!
Search my most hidden breast! By truth's
own tongue,
I have no dædale heart: why is it wrung
To desperation? Is there nought for me, 460
Upon the bourne of bliss, but misery?"

These words awoke the stranger of dark
tresses:
Her dawning love-look rapt Endymion
blesses
With 'havior soft. Sleep yawned from un-
derneath.
"Thou swan of Ganges, let us no more
breathe 465
This murky phantasm! thou contented,
seem'st
Pillowed in lovely idleness, nor dream'st
What horrors may discomfort thee and me.
Ah, shouldst thou die from my heart-
treachery!—
Yet did she merely weep—her gentle
soul 470
Hath no revenge in it: as it is whole
In tenderness, would I were whole in love!
Can I prize thee, fair maid, all price above,
Even when I feel as true as innocence?
I do, I do.—What is this soul then?
Whence 475
Came it? It does not seem my own, and I
Have no self-passion or identity.
Some fearful end must be: where, where
is it?
By Nemesis, I see my spirit flit
Alone about the dark—Forgive me,
sweet: 480
Shall we away?" He roused the steeds:
they beat

Their wings chivalrous into the clear air,
Leaving old sleep within his vapory lair.

The good-night blush of eve was waning
    slow,
And Vesper, risen star, began to throe 485
In the dusk heavens silverly, when they
Thus sprang direct towards the Galaxy.
Nor did speed hinder converse soft and
    strange—
Eternal oaths and vows they interchange,
In such wise, in such temper, so aloof 490
Up in the winds, beneath a starry roof,
So witless of their doom, that verily
'Tis well-nigh past man's search their
    hearts to see;
Whether they wept, or laughed, or grieved,
    or toyed—
Most like with joy gone mad, with sorrow
    cloyed. 495

Full facing their swift flight, from ebon
    streak,
The moon put forth a little diamond peak,
No bigger than an unobserved star,
Or tiny point of fairy scimitar;
Bright signal that she only stooped to tie 500
Her silver sandals, ere deliciously
She bowed into the heavens her timid
    head.
Slowly she rose, as though she would have
    fled,
While to his lady meek the Carian turned,
To mark if her dark eyes had yet dis-
    cerned 505
This beauty in its birth—Despair! despair!
He saw her body fading gaunt and spare
In the cold moonshine. Straight he seized
    her wrist;
It melted from his grasp: her hand he
    kissed,
And, horror! kissed his own—he was
    alone. 510
Her steed a little higher soared, and then
Dropt hawkwise to the earth.

                  There lies a den,
Beyond the seeming confines of the space
Made for the soul to wander in and trace
Its own existence, of remotest glooms. 515
Dark regions are around it, where the
    tombs
Of buried griefs the spirit sees, but scarce
One hour doth linger weeping, for the
    pierce
Of new-born woe it feels more inly smart:
And in these regions many a venomed
    dart 520
At random flies; they are the proper home
Of every ill: the man is yet to come

Who hath not journeyed in this native
    hell.
But few have ever felt how calm and well
Sleep may be had in that deep den of all. 525
There anguish does not sting; nor pleasure
    pall:
Woe-hurricanes beat ever at the gate,
Yet all is still within and desolate.
Beset with plainful gusts, within ye hear
No sound so loud as when on curtained
    bier 530
The death-watch tick is stifled. Enter none
Who strive therefore: on the sudden it is
    won.
Just when the sufferer begins to burn,
Then it is free to him; and from an urn,
Still fed by melting ice, he takes a
    draught— 535
Young Semele such richness never quaffed
In her maternal longing! Happy gloom!
Dark paradise! where pale becomes the
    bloom
Of health by due; where silence dreariest
Is most articulate; where hopes infest; 540
Where those eyes are the brightest far that
    keep
Their lids shut longest in a dreamless sleep.
O happy spirit-home! O wondrous soul!
Pregnant with such a den to save the whole
In thine own depth. Hail, gentle Carian! 545
For, never since thy griefs and woes began
Hast thou felt so content: a grievous feud
Hath led thee to this cave of quietude
Aye, his lulled soul was there, although
    upborne
With dangerous speed: and so he did not
    mourn 550
Because he knew not whither he was going.
So happy was he, not the aerial blowing
Of trumpets at clear parley from the east
Could rouse from that fine relish, that high
    feast.
They stung the feathered horse: with fierce
    alarm 555
He flapped towards the sound. Alas, no
    charm
Could lift Endymion's head, or he had
    viewed
A skyey mask, a pinioned multitude,—
And silvery was its passing: voices sweet 560
Warbling the while as if to lull and greet
The wanderer in his path. Thus warbled
    they,
While past the vision went in bright array.

"Who, who from Dian's feast would be
    away?
For all the golden bowers of the day
Are empty left? Who, who away would
    be 565

From Cynthia's wedding and festivity?
Not Hesperus: lo! upon his silver wings
He leans away for highest heaven and
  sings,
Snapping his lucid fingers merrily!—
Ah, Zephyrus! art here, and Flora too! 570
Ye tender bibbers of the rain and dew,
Young playmates of the rose and daffodil,
Be careful, ere ye enter in, to fill
  Your baskets high
With fennel green, and balm, and golden
  pines, 575
Savory, latter-mint, and columbines,
Cool parsley, basil sweet, and sunny thyme;
Yea, every flower and leaf of every clime,
All gathered in the dewy morning: hie
  Away! fly! fly!— 580
Crystalline brother of the belt of heaven,
Aquarius! to whom king Jove has given
Two liquid pulse streams 'stead of feath-
  ered wings,
Two fan-like fountains,—thine illuminings
  For Dian play: 585
Dissolve the frozen purity of air;
Let thy white shoulders silvery and bare
Show cold through watery pinions; make
  more bright
The Star-Queen's crescent on her marriage
  night:
  Haste, haste away!— 590
Castor has tamed the planet Lion, see!
And of the Bear has Pollux mastery:
A third is in the race! who is the third
Speeding away swift as the eagle bird?
  The ramping Centaur! 595
The Lion's mane's on end: the Bear how
  fierce!
The Centaur's arrow ready seems to pierce
Some enemy: far forth his bow is bent
Into the blue of heaven. He'll be shent,
  Pale unrelentor, 600
When he shall hear the wedding lutes
  a-playing.—
Andromeda! sweet woman! why delaying
So timidly among the stars: come hither!
Join this bright throng, and nimbly follow
  whither
  They all are going. 605
Danaë's son, before Jove newly bowed,
Has wept for thee, calling to Jove aloud.
Thee, gentle lady, did he disenthral:
Ye shall forever live and love, for all
  Thy tears are flowing.— 610
By Daphne's fright, behold Apollo!—"

        More
Endymion heard not: down his steed him
  bore,
Prone to the green head of a misty hill.

His first touch of the earth went nigh to
  kill.
"Alas!" said he, "were I but always
  borne 615
Through dangerous winds, had but my
  footsteps worn
A path in hell, for ever would I bless
Horrors which nourish an uneasiness
For my own sullen conquering: to him
Who lives beyond earth's boundary, grief
  is dim, 620
Sorrow is but a shadow: now I see
The grass; I feel the solid ground—Ah, me!
It is thy voice—divinest! Where?—who?
  who
Left thee so quiet on this bed of dew?
Behold upon this happy earth we are; 625
Let us aye love each other; let us fare
On forest fruits, and never, never go
Among the abodes of mortals here below,
Or be by phantoms duped. O destiny!
Into a labyrinth now my soul would fly, 630
But with thy beauty will I deaden it.
Where didst thou melt to? By thee will
  I sit
For ever: let our fate stop here—a kid
I on this spot will offer: Pan will bid
Us live in peace, in love and peace
  among 635
His forest wildernesses. I have clung
To nothing, loved a nothing, nothing seen
Or felt but a great dream! O I have been
Presumptuous against love, against the sky,
Against all elements, against the tie 640
Of mortals each to each, against the
  blooms
Of flowers, rush of rivers, and the tombs
Of heroes gone! Against his proper glory
Has my own soul conspired: so my story
Will I to children utter, and repent. 645
There never lived a mortal man, who bent
His appetite beyond his natural sphere,
But starved and died. My sweetest Indian,
  here,
Here will I kneel, for thou redeemèd hast
My life from too thin breathing: gone and
  past 650
Are cloudy phantasms. Caverns lone, fare-
  well!
And air of visions, and the monstrous swell
Of visionary seas! No, never more
Shall airy voices cheat me to the shore
Of tangled wonder, breathless and
  aghast. 655
Adieu, my daintiest Dream! although so
  vast
My love is still for thee. The hour may
  come
When we shall meet in pure elysium.

On earth I may not love thee; and there-
fore
Doves will I offer up, and sweetest store 660
All through the teeming year: so thou wilt
shine
On me, and on this damsel fair of mine,
And bless our simple lives. My Indian
bliss!
My river-lily bud! one human kiss!
One sigh of real breath—one gentle
squeeze, 665
Warm as a dove's nest among summer
trees,
And warm with dew at ooze from living
blood!
Whither didst melt? Ah, what of that!—
all good
We'll talk about—no more of dreaming.—
Now,
Where shall our dwelling be? Under the
brow 670
Of some steep mossy hill, where ivy dun
Would hide us up, although spring leaves
were none;
And where dark yew trees, as we rustle
through,
Will drop their scarlet berry cups of dew?
O thou wouldst joy to live in such a
place; 675
Dusk for our loves, yet light enough to
grace
Those gentle limbs on mossy bed reclined:
For by one step the blue sky shouldst thou
find,
And by another, in deep dell below,
See, through the trees, a little river go 680
All in its mid-day gold and glimmering.
Honey from out the gnarled hive I'll bring,
And apples, wan with sweetness, gather
thee,—
Cresses that grow where no man may them
see,
And sorrel untorn by the dew-clawed
stag; 685
Pipes will I fashion of the syrinx flag,
That thou mayst always know whither I
roam,
When it shall please thee in our quiet
home
To listen and think of love. Still let me
speak;
Still let me dive into the joy I seek,— 690
For yet the past doth prison me. The rill,
Thou haply mayst delight in, will I fill
With fairy fishes from the mountain tarn,
And thou shalt feed them from the squir-
rel's barn.
Its bottom will I strew with amber shells, 695
And pebbles blue from deep enchanted
wells.

Its sides I'll plant with dew-sweet eglantine,
And honeysuckles full of clear bee-wine.
I will entice this crystal rill to trace
Love's silver name upon the meadow's
face. 700
I'll kneel to Vesta, for a flame of fire;
And to god Phœbus, for a golden lyre;
To Empress Dian, for a hunting spear;
To Vesper, for a taper silver-clear,
That I may see thy beauty through the
night; 705
To Flora, and a nightingale shall light
Tame on thy finger; to the River gods,
And they shall bring thee taper fishing
rods
Of gold, and lines of Naiads' long bright
tress.
Heaven shield thee for thine utter loveli-
ness! 710
Thy mossy footstool shall the altar be
'Fore which I'll bend, bending, dear love,
to thee:
Those lips shall be my Delphos, and shall
speak
Laws to my footsteps, color to my cheek,
Trembling or steadfastness to this same
voice, 715
And of three sweetest pleasurings the
choice:
And that affectionate light, those diamond
things,
Those eyes, those passions, those supreme
pearl springs,
Shall be my grief, or twinkle me to
pleasure.
Say, is not bliss within our perfect
seizure? 720
O that I could not doubt!"

The mountaineer
Thus strove by fancies vain and crude to
clear
His briared path to some tranquillity.
It gave bright gladness to his lady's eye,
And yet the tears she wept were tears of
sorrow; 725
Answering thus, just as the golden morrow
Beamed upward from the valleys of the
east:
"O that the flutter of this heart had ceased,
Or the sweet name of love had passed
away.
Young feathered tyrant! by a swift decay 730
Wilt thou devote this body to the earth:
And I do think that at my very birth
I lisped thy blooming titles inwardly;
For at the first, first dawn and thought of
thee,
With uplift hands I blest the stars of
heaven. 735

Art thou not cruel? Ever have I striven
To think thee kind, but ah, it will not do!
When yet a child, I heard that kisses drew
Favor from thee, and so I kisses gave
To the void air, bidding them find out
    love: 740
But when I came to feel how far above
All fancy, pride, and fickle maidenhood,
All earthly pleasure, all imagined good,
Was the warm tremble of a devout kiss,—
Even then, that moment, at the thought of
    this,   745
Fainting I fell into a bed of flowers,
And languished there three days. Ye
    milder powers,
Am I not cruelly wronged? Believe, believe
Me, dear Endymion, were I to weave
With my own fancies garlands of sweet
    life,   750
Thou shouldst be one of all. Ah, bitter
    strife!
I may not be thy love: I am forbidden—
Indeed I am—thwarted, affrighted, chidden,
By things I trembled at, and gorgon wrath.
Twice hast thou asked whither I went:
    henceforth   755
Ask me no more! I may not utter it,
Nor may I be thy love. We might commit
Ourselves at once to vengeance; we might
    die;
We might embrace and die: voluptuous
    thought!
Enlarge not to my hunger, or I'm
    caught   760
In trammels of perverse deliciousness.
No, no, that shall not be: thee will I bless,
And bid a long adieu."

The Carian

No word returned: both lovelorn, silent,
    wan,
Into the valleys green together went.   765
Far wandering, they were perforce content
To sit beneath a fair lone beechen tree;
Nor at each other gazed, but heavily
Pored on its hazel cirque of shedded leaves.

  Endymion! unhappy! it nigh grieves   770
Me to behold thee thus in last extreme:
Enskied ere this, but truly that I deem
Truth the best music in a first-born song,
Thy lute-voiced brother will I sing ere
    long,
And thou shalt aid—hast thou not aided
    me?   775
Yes, moonlight emperor! felicity
Has been thy meed for many thousand
    years;
Yet often have I, on the brink of tears,

Mourned as if yet thou wert a forester;—
Forgetting the old tale.

                      He did not stir   780
His eyes from the dead leaves, or one small
    pulse
Of joy he might have felt. The spirit culls
Unfaded amaranth, when wild it strays
Through the old garden-ground of boyish
    days.
A little onward ran the very stream   785
By which he took his first soft poppy
    dream;
And on the very bark 'gainst which he
    leant
A crescent he had carved, and round it
    spent
His skill in little stars. The teeming tree
Had swollen and greened the pious charac-
    tery,   790
But not ta'en out. Why, there was not a
    slope
Up which he had not feared the antelope;
And not a tree, beneath whose rooty shade
He had not with his tamed leopards
    played:
Nor could an arrow light, or javelin,   795
Fly in the air where his had never been—
And yet he knew it not.

                        O treachery!
Why does his lady smile, pleasing her eye
With all his sorrowing? He sees her not.
But who so stares on him? His sister
    sure!   800
Peona of the woods!—Can she endure—
Impossible—how dearly they embrace!
His lady smiles; delight is in her face;
It is no treachery.

                      "Dear brother mine!
Endymion, weep not so! Why shouldst
    thou pine   805
When all great Latmos so exalt will be?
Thank the great gods, and look not bit-
    terly;
And speak not one pale word, and sigh no
    more.
Sure I will not believe thou hast such store
Of grief, to last thee to my kiss again.   810
Thou surely canst not bear a mind in pain,
Come hand in hand with one so beautiful.
Be happy both of you! for I will pull
The flowers of autumn for your coronals.
Pan's holy priest for young Endymion
    calls;   815
And when he is restored, thou, fairest
    dame,
Shalt be our queen. Now, is it not a shame
To see ye thus,—not very, very sad?

Perhaps ye are too happy to be glad:
O feel as if it were a common day; 820
Free-voiced as one who never was away.
No tongue shall ask, whence come ye? but
ye shall
Be gods of your own rest imperial.
Not even I, for one whole month, will pry
Into the hours that have passed us by, 825
Since in my arbor I did sing to thee.
O Hermes! on this very night will be
A hymning up to Cynthia, queen of light;
For the soothsayers old saw yesternight
Good visions in the air, whence will be-
fall, 830
As say these sages, health perpetual
To shepherds and their flocks; and further-
more,
In Dian's face they read the gentle lore:
Therefore for her these vesper-carols are.
Our friends will all be there from nigh and
far. 835
Many upon thy death have ditties made;
And many, even now, their foreheads shade
With cypress, on a day of sacrifice.
New singing for our maids shalt thou
devise,
And pluck the sorrow from our huntsmen's
brows. 840
Tell me, my lady-queen, how to espouse
This wayward brother to his rightful joys!
His eyes are on thee bent, as thou didst
poise
His fate most goddess-like. Help me, I
pray,
To lure—Endymion, dear brother, say 845
What ails thee?" He could bear no more,
and so
Bent his soul fiercely like a spiritual bow,
And twanged it inwardly, and calmly said:
"I would have thee my only friend, sweet
maid!
My only visitor! not ignorant though, 850
That those deceptions which for pleasure
go
'Mong men, are pleasures real as real may
be:
But there are higher ones I may not see,
If impiously an earthly realm I take.
Since I saw thee, I have been wide
awake 855
Night after night, and day by day, until
Of the empyrean I have drunk my fill.
Let it content thee, sister, seeing me
More happy than betides mortality.
A hermit young, I'll live in mossy cave, 860
Where thou alone shalt come to me, and
lave
Thy spirit in the wonders I shall tell.
Through me the shepherd realm shall pros-
per well;

For to thy tongue will I all health confide.
And, for my sake, let this young maid
abide 865
With thee as a dear sister. Thou alone,
Peona, mayst return to me. I own
This may sound strangely: but when, dear-
est girl,
Thou seest it for my happiness, no pearl
Will trespass down those cheeks. Compan-
ion fair! 870
Wilt be content to dwell with her, to share
This sister's love with me?" Like one
resigned
And bent by circumstance, and thereby
blind
In self-commitment, thus that meek un-
known:
"Aye, but a buzzing by my ears has
flown, 875
Of jubilee to Dian:—truth I heard?
Well then, I see there is no little bird,
Tender soever, but is Jove's own care.
Long have I sought for rest, and, unaware,
Behold I find it! so exalted too! 880
So after my own heart! I knew, I knew
There was a place untenanted in it:
In that same void white Chastity shall sit,
And monitor me nightly to lone slumber.
With sanest lips I vow me to the num-
ber 885
Of Dian's sisterhood; and, kind lady,
With thy good help, this very night shall
see
My future days to her fane consecrate."

As feels a dreamer what doth most create
His own particular fright, so these three
felt: 890
Or like one who, in after ages, knelt
To Lucifer or Baal, when he'd pine
After a little sleep: or when in mine
Far under-ground, a sleeper meets his
friends
Who know him not. Each diligently
bends 895
Towards common thoughts and things for
very fear;
Striving their ghastly malady to cheer,
By thinking it a thing of yes and no,
That housewives talk of. But the spirit-
blow
Was struck, and all were dreamers. At the
last 900
Endymion said: "Are not our fates all cast?
Why stand we here? Adieu, ye tender pair!
Adieu!" Whereat those maidens, with wild
stare,
Walked dizzily away. Pained and hot
His eyes went after them, until they got 905
Near to a cypress grove, whose deadly maw,

In one swift moment, would what then he
    saw
Engulf forever. "Stay!" he cried, "ah stay!
Turn damsels! hist! one word I have to
    say.
Sweet Indian, I would see thee once
    again.   910
It is a thing I dote on: so I'd fain,
Peona, ye should hand in hand repair
Into those holy groves, that silent are
Behind great Dian's temple. I'll be yon,
At Vesper's earliest twinkle—they are
    gone—   915
But once, once, once again—" At this he
    pressed
His hands against his face, and then did
    rest
His head upon a mossy hillock green,
And so remained as he a corpse had been
All the long day; save when he scantly
    lifted   920
His eyes abroad, to see how shadows shifted
With the slow move of time,—sluggish and
    weary
Until the poplar tops, in journey dreary,
Had reached the river's brim. Then up he
    rose,
And, slowly as that very river flows,   925
Walked towards the temple grove with this
    lament:
"Why such a golden eve? The breeze is
    sent
Careful and soft, that not a leaf may fall
Before the serene father of them all
Bows down his summer head below the
    west.   930
Now am I of breath, speech, and speed
    possessed,
But at the setting I must bid adieu
To her for the last time. Night will strew
On the damp grass myriads of lingering
    leaves,
And with them shall I die; nor much it
    grieves   935
To die, when summer dies on the cold
    sward.
Why, I have been a butterfly, a lord
Of flowers, garlands, love-knots, silly posies,
Groves, meadows, melodies, and arbor
    roses;
My kingdom's at its death, and just it is 940
That I should die with it: so in all this
We miscall grief, bale, sorrow, heartbreak,
    woe,
What is there to plain of? By Titan's foe
I am but rightly served." So saying, he
Tripped lightly on, in sort of deathful
    glee;   945
Laughing at the clear stream and setting
    sun.

As though they jests had been: nor had he
    done
His laugh at nature's holy countenance,
Until that grove appeared, as if perchance,
And then his tongue with sober seem-
    lihed   950
Gave utterance as he entered: "Ha! I said,
King of the butterflies; but by this gloom,
And by old Rhadamanthus' tongue of
    doom,
This dusk religion, pomp of solitude,
And the Promethean clay by thief en-
    dued,   955
By old Saturnus' forelock, by his head
Shook with eternal palsy, I did wed
Myself to things of light from infancy;
And thus to be cast out, thus lorn to die,
Is sure enough to make a mortal man   960
Grow impious." So he inwardly began
On things for which no wording can be
    found;
Deeper and deeper sinking, until drowned
Beyond the reach of music: for the choir
Of Cynthia he heard not, though rough
    briar   965
Nor muffling thicket interposed to dull
The vesper hymn, far swollen, soft and full,
Through the dark pillars of those sylvan
    aisles.
He saw not the two maidens, nor their
    smiles,
Wan as primroses gathered at midnight 970
By chilly-fingered spring. "Unhappy wight!
Endymion!" said Peona, "we are here!
What wouldst thou ere we all are laid on
    bier?"
Then he embraced her, and his lady's hand
Pressed, saying: "Sister, I would have com-
    mand,   975
If it were heaven's will, on our sad fate."
At which that dark-eyed stranger stood
    elate
And said, in a new voice, but sweet as love,
To Endymion's amaze: "By Cupid's dove,
And so thou shalt! and by the lily truth 980
Of my own breast thou shalt, beloved
    youth!"
And as she spake, into her face there came
Light, as reflected from a silver flame:
Her long black hair swelled ampler, in
    display
Full golden; in her eyes a brighter day 985
Dawned blue and full of love. Aye, he
    beheld
Phœbe, his passion! joyous she upheld
Her lucid bow, continuing thus: "Drear,
    drear
Has our delaying been; but foolish fear
Withheld me first; and then decrees of
    fate;   990

And then 'twas fit that from this mortal
  state
Thou shouldst, my love, by some unlooked-
  for change
Be spiritualized. Peona, we shall range
These forests, and to thee they safe shall be
As was thy cradle; hither shalt thou flee 995
To meet us many a time."   Next Cynthia
  bright
Peona kissed, and blessed with fair good
  night:
Her brother kissed her too, and knelt
  adown
Before his goddess, in a blissful swoon.
She gave her fair hands to him, and be-
  hold,   1000
Before three swiftest kisses he had told,
They vanished far away!—Peona went
Home through the gloomy wood in won-
  derment.

Apr.-Nov., 1817   1818

Dressed as though bold Robin Hood   10
Would, with his maid Marian,
Sup and bowse from horn and can.

  I have heard that on a day
Mine host's signboard flew away,
Nobody knew whither, till   15
An astrologer's old quill
To a sheepskin gave the story,
Said he saw you in your glory,
Underneath a new old-sign
Sipping beverage divine,   20
And pledging with contented smack
The Mermaid in the Zodiac.

  Souls of Poets dead and gone,
What Elysium have ye known,
Happy field or mossy cavern,   25
Choicer than the Mermaid Tavern?
Feb. 3, 1818   1820

WHEN I HAVE FEARS

When I have fears that I may cease to be
  Before my pen has gleaned my teeming
    brain,
Before high-pilèd books, in charactery,
  Hold like rich garners the full ripened
    grain;
When I behold, upon the night's starred
    face,   5
  Huge cloudy symbols of a high romance,
And think that I may never live to trace
  Their shadows, with the magic hand of
    chance;
And when I feel, fair creature of an hour,
  That I shall never look upon thee
    more,   10
Never have relish in the fairy power
  Of unreflecting love;—then on the shore
Of the wide world I stand alone, and think
Till love and fame to nothingness do sink.
Jan., 1818   1848

LINES ON THE MERMAID
TAVERN

Souls of Poets dead and gone,
What Elysium have ye known,
Happy field or mossy cavern,
Choicer than the Mermaid Tavern?
Have ye tippled drink more fine   5
Than mine host's Canary wine?
Or are fruits of Paradise
Sweeter than those dainty pies
Of venison? O generous food!

ISABELLA

OR

THE POT OF BASIL

A STORY FROM BOCCACCIO

Fair Isabel, poor simple Isabel!
  Lorenzo, a young palmer in Love's eye!
They could not in the self-same mansion
    dwell
  Without some stir of heart, some malady;
They could not sit at meals but feel how
    well   5
  It soothèd each to be the other by;
They could not, sure, beneath the same
    roof sleep,
But to each other dream, and nightly weep.

With every morn their love grew tenderer,
  With every eve deeper and tenderer
    still;   10
He might not in house, field, or garden stir,
  But her full shape would all his seeing
    fill;
And his continual voice was pleasanter
  To her, than noise of trees or hidden rill;
Her lute-string gave an echo of his name, 15
She spoilt her half-done broidery with the
    same.

He knew whose gentle hand was at the
    latch,
  Before the door had given her to his
    eyes;

And from her chamber window he would
     catch
   Her beauty farther than the falcon
     spies;   20
And constant as her vespers would he
     watch,
   Because her face was turned to the same
     skies;
And with sick longing all the night out-
     wear,
   To hear her morning-step upon the stair.

A whole long month of May in this sad
     plight   25
   Made their cheeks paler by the break of
     June:
"Tomorrow will I bow to my delight,
   Tomorrow will I ask my lady's boon."—
"O may I never see another night,
   Lorenzo, if thy lips breathe not love's
     tune."—   30
So spake they to their pillows; but, alas,
Honeyless days and days did he let pass;

Until sweet Isabella's untouched cheek
   Fell sick within the rose's just domain,
Fell thin as a young mother's, who doth
     seek   35
   By every lull to cool her infant's pain:
"How ill she is," said he, "I may not speak,
   And yet I will, and tell my love all plain:
If looks speak love-laws, I will drink her
     tears,
And at the least 'twill startle off her
     cares."   40

So said he one fair morning, and all day
   His heart beat awfully against his side;
And to his heart he inwardly did pray
   For power to speak; but still the ruddy
     tide
Stifled his voice, and pulsed resolve
     away—   45
   Fevered his high conceit of such a bride,
Yet brought him to the meekness of a child:
Alas! when passion is both meek and wild!

So once more he had waked and anguishèd
   A dreary night of love and misery,   50
If Isabel's quick eye had not been wed
   To every symbol on his forehead high;
She saw it waxing very pale and dead,
   And straight all flushed; so lispèd ten-
     derly,
"Lorenzo!"—here she ceased her timid
     quest,   55
But in her tone and look he read the rest.

"O Isabella, I can half perceive
   That I may speak my grief into thine
     ear;

If thou didst ever any thing believe,
   Believe how I love thee, believe how
     near   60
My soul is to its doom: I would not grieve
   Thy hand by unwelcome pressing, would
     not fear
Thine eyes by gazing; but I cannot live
   Another night, and not my passion shrive.

"Love! thou art leading me from wintry
     cold,   65
   Lady! thou leadest me to summer clime,
And I must taste the blossoms that unfold
   In its ripe warmth this gracious morning
     time."
So said, his erewhile timid lips grew bold,
   And poesied with hers in dewy rhyme: 70
Great bliss was with them, and great happi-
     ness
   Grew, like a lusty flower in June's caress.

Parting they seemed to tread upon the air,
   Twin roses by the zephyr blown apart
Only to meet again more close, and share 75
   The inward fragrance of each other's
     heart.
She, to her chamber gone, a ditty fair
   Sang, of delicious love and honeyed dart;
He with light steps went up a western hill,
   And bade the sun farewell, and joyed his
     fill.   80

All close they met again, before the dusk
   Had taken from the stars its pleasant
     veil,
All close they met, all eves, before the dusk
   Had taken from the stars its pleasant
     veil,
Close in a bower of hyacinth and musk, 85
   Unknown of any, free from whispering
     tale.
Ah! better had it been for ever so,
   Than idle ears should pleasure in their
     woe.

Were they unhappy then?—It cannot be—
   Too many tears for lovers have been
     shed,   90
Too many sighs give we to them in fee,
   Too much of pity after they are dead,
Too many doleful stories do we see
   Whose matter in bright gold were best
     be read;
Except in such a page where Theseus'
     spouse   95
Over the pathless waves towards him bows.

But, for the general award of love,
   The little sweet doth kill much bitter-
     ness;

Though Dido silent is in under-grove,
　And Isabella's was a great distress,　100
Though young Lorenzo in warm Indian
　　clove
　Was not embalmed, this truth is not the
　　less—
Even bees, the little almsmen of spring
　　bowers,
Know there is richest juice in poison
　　flowers.

With her two brothers this fair lady
　　dwelt,　105
　Enrichèd from ancestral merchandise,
And for them many a weary hand did swelt
　In torchèd mines and noisy factories,
And many once proud-quivered loins did
　　melt
　In blood from stinging whip;—with hol-
　　low eyes　110
Many all day in dazzling river stood,
To take the rich-ored driftings of the flood.

For them the Ceylon diver held his breath,
　And went all naked to the hungry shark;
For them his ears gushed blood; for them
　　in death　115
　The seal on the cold ice with piteous
　　bark
Lay full of darts; for them alone did seethe
　A thousand men in troubles wide and
　　dark:
Half-ignorant, they turned an easy wheel,
That set sharp racks at work, to pinch and
　　peel.　120

Why were they proud? Because their mar-
　　ble founts
　Gushed with more pride than do a
　　wretch's tears?—
Why were they proud? Because fair orange-
　　mounts
　Were of more soft ascent than lazar
　　stairs?—
Why were they proud? Because red-lined
　　accounts　125
　Were richer than the songs of Grecian
　　years?—
Why were they proud? again we ask aloud,
Why in the name of Glory were they
　　proud?

Yet were these Florentines as self-retired
　In hungry pride and gainful cowar-
　　dice,　130
As two close Hebrews in that land inspired,
　Paled in and vineyarded from beggar-
　　spies;
The hawks of shipmast forests—the untired
　And panniered mules for ducats and old
　　lies—

Quick catspaws on the generous stray-
　　away,—　135
Great wits in Spanish, Tuscan, and Malay.

How was it these same ledger-men could
　　spy
　Fair Isabella in her downy nest?
How could they find out in Lorenzo's eye
　A straying from his toil? Hot Egypt's
　　pest　140
Into their vision covetous and sly!
　How could these money bags see east and
　　west?—
Yet so they did—and every dealer fair
Must see behind, as doth the hunted hare.

O eloquent and famed Boccaccio!　145
　Of thee we now should ask forgiving
　　boon,
And of thy spicy myrtles as they blow,
　And of thy roses amorous of the moon,
And of thy lilies, that do paler grow
　Now they can no more hear thy ghittern's
　　tune,　150
For venturing syllables that ill beseem
The quiet glooms of such a piteous theme.

Grant thou a pardon here, and then the
　　tale
　Shall move on soberly, as it is meet;
There is no other crime, no mad assail　155
　To make old prose in modern rhyme
　　more sweet:
But it is done—succeed the verse or fail—
　To honor thee, and thy gone spirit greet;
To stead thee as a verse in English tongue,
An echo of thee in the north wind sung.　160

These brethren having found by many signs
　What love Lorenzo for their sister had,
And how she loved him too, each uncon-
　　fines
　His bitter thoughts to other, well nigh
　　mad
That he, the servant of their trade de-
　　signs,　165
　Should in their sister's love be blithe and
　　glad,
When 'twas their plan to coax her by de-
　　grees
To some high noble and his olive trees.

And many a jealous conference had they,
　And many times they bit their lips
　　alone,　170
Before they fixed upon a surest way
　To make the youngster for his crime
　　atone;

And at the last, these men of cruel clay
  Cut Mercy with a sharp knife to the
    bone;
For they resolvèd in some forest dim   175
To kill Lorenzo, and there bury him.

So on a pleasant morning, as he leant
  Into the sunrise, o'er the balustrade
Of the garden terrace, towards him they
    bent
  Their footing through the dews; and to
    him said,   180
"You seem there in the quiet of content,
  Lorenzo, and we are most loth to invade
Calm speculation; but if you are wise,
  Bestride your steed while cold is in the
    skies.

"Today we purpose, aye, this hour we
    mount   185
  To spur three leagues towards the Apen-
    nine;
Come down, we pray thee, ere the hot sun
    count
  His dewy rosary on the eglantine."
Lorenzo, courteously as he was wont,
  Bowed a fair greeting to these serpents'
    whine;   190
And went in haste to get in readiness,
  With belt, and spur, and bracing hunts-
    man's dress.

And as he to the courtyard passed along,
  Each third step did he pause, and listened
    oft
If he could hear his lady's matin song,   195
  Or the light whisper of her footstep soft;
And as he thus over his passion hung,
  He heard a laugh full musical aloft;
When, looking up, he saw her features
    bright
Smile through an in-door lattice, all de-
    light.   200

"Love, Isabel!" said he, "I was in pain
  Lest I should miss to bid thee a good
    morrow:
Ah! what if I should lose thee, when so
    fain
I am to stifle all the heavy sorrow
Of a poor three hours' absence? but we'll
    gain   205
  Out of the amorous dark what day doth
    borrow.
Good bye! I'll soon be back."—"Good
    bye!" said she:—
And as he went she chanted merrily.

So the two brothers and their murdered
    man
  Rode past fair Florence, to where Arno's
    stream   210
Gurgles through straitened banks, and still
    doth fan
  Itself with dancing bulrush, and the
    bream
Keeps head against the freshets. Sick and
    wan
  The brothers' faces in the ford did seem,
Lorenzo's flush with love.—They passed the
    water   215
Into a forest quiet for the slaughter.

There was Lorenzo slain and buried in,
  There in that forest did his great love
    cease;
Ah! when a soul doth thus its freedom win,
  It aches in loneliness—is ill at peace 220
As the break-covert bloodhounds of such
    sin:
  They dipped their swords in the water,
    and did tease
Their horses homeward, with convulsèd
    spur,
Each richer by his being a murderer.

They told their sister how, with sudden
    speed,   225
  Lorenzo had ta'en ship for foreign lands,
Because of some great urgency and need
  In their affairs, requiring trusty hands.
Poor girl! put on thy stifling widow's weed,
  And 'scape at once from Hope's accursèd
    bands;   230
Today thou wilt not see him, nor tomor-
    row,
And the next day will be a day of sorrow.

She weeps alone for pleasures not to be;
  Sorely she wept until the night came on,
And then, instead of love, O misery!   235
  She brooded o'er the luxury alone:
His image in the dusk she seemed to see,
  And to the silence made a gentle moan,
Spreading her perfect arms upon the air,
And on her couch low murmuring "Where?
    O where?"   240

But Selfishness, Love's cousin, held not long
  Its fiery vigil in her single breast;
She fretted for the golden hour, and hung
  Upon the time with feverish unrest—
Not long—for soon into her heart a
    throng   245
  Of higher occupants, a richer zest,
Came tragic; passion not to be subdued,
And sorrow for her love in travels rude.

In the mid days of autumn, on their eves
  The breath of Winter comes from far
    away,   250
And the sick west continually bereaves
  Of some gold tinge, and plays a rounde-
    lay
Of death among the bushes and the leaves,
  To make all bare before he dares to stray
From his north cavern. So sweet Isabel 255
By gradual decay from beauty fell,

Because Lorenzo came not. Oftentimes
  She asked her brothers, with an eye all
    pale,
Striving to be itself, what dungeon climes
  Could keep him off so long? They spake
    a tale   260
Time after time, to quiet her. Their crimes
  Came on them, like a smoke from Hin-
    nom's vale;
And every night in dreams they groaned
    aloud,
To see their sister in her snowy shroud.

And she had died in drowsy ignorance, 265
  But for a thing more deadly dark than
    all;
It came like a fierce potion, drunk by
    chance,
  Which saves a sick man from the feath-
    ered pall
For some few gasping moments; like a
    lance,
  Waking an Indian from his cloudy
    hall   270
With cruel pierce, and bringing him again
Sense of the gnawing fire at heart and
    brain.

It was a vision.—In the drowsy gloom,
  The dull of midnight, at her couch's foot
Lorenzo stood, and wept: the forest
    tomb   275
  Had marred his glossy hair which once
    could shoot
Lustre into the sun, and put cold doom
  Upon his lips, and taken the soft lute
From his lorn voice, and past his loamèd
    ears
Had made a miry channel for his tears. 280

Strange sound it was, when the pale shadow
    spake;
  For there was striving, in its piteous
    tongue,
To speak as when on earth it was awake,
  And Isabella on its music hung:
Langour there was in it, and tremulous
    shake,   285
  As in a palsied Druid's harp unstrung;

And through it moaned a ghostly under-
    song,
Like hoarse night-gusts sepulchral briars
    among.

Its eyes, though wild, were still all dewy
    bright
  With love, and kept all phantom fear
    aloof   290
From the poor girl by magic of their light,
  The while it did unthread the horrid
    woof
Of the late darkened time,—the murderous
    spite
  Of pride and avarice,—the dark pine
    roof
In the forest,—and the sodden turfed
    dell,   295
Where, without any word, from stabs he
    fell.

Saying moreover, "Isabel, my sweet!
  Red whortle-berries droop above my
    head
And a large flintstone weighs upon my feet;
  Around me beeches and high chestnuts
    shed   300
Their leaves and prickly nuts; a sheepfold
    bleat
  Comes from beyond the river to my bed:
Go, shed one tear upon my heather bloom,
And it shall comfort me within the tomb.

"I am a shadow now, alas! alas!   305
  Upon the skirts of human nature dwell-
    ing
Alone: I chant alone the holy mass,
  While little sounds of life are round me
    knelling,
And glossy bees at noon do fieldward pass,
  And many a chapel bell the hour is tell-
    ing,   310
Paining me through: those sounds grow
    strange to me,
And thou art distant in Humanity.

"I know what was, I feel full well what is,
  And I should rage, if spirits could go
    mad;
Though I forget the taste of earthly bliss, 315
  That paleness warms my grave, as though
    I had
A Seraph chosen from the bright abyss
  To be my spouse: thy paleness makes me
    glad;
Thy beauty grows upon me, and I feel
A greater love through all my essence
    steal."   320

The Spirit mourned "Adieu!"—dissolved,
    and left
The atom darkness in a slow turmoil;
As when of healthful midnight sleep bereft,
    Thinking on rugged hours and fruitless
        toil,
We put our eyes into a pillowy cleft,   325
    And see the spangly gloom froth up and
        boil:
It made sad Isabella's eyelids ache,
And in the dawn she started up awake;

"Ha! ha!" said she, "I knew not this hard
    life,
    I thought the worst was simple misery; 330
I thought some Fate with pleasure or with
    strife
    Portioned us—happy days, or else to die;
But there is crime—a brother's bloody
    knife!
    Sweet Spirit, thou hast schooled my in-
        fancy:
I'll visit thee for this, and kiss thine
    eyes,   335
And greet thee morn and even in the skies."

When the full morning came, she had de-
    vised
    How she might secret to the forest hie;
How she might find the clay, so dearly
    prized,
    And sing to it one latest lullaby;   340
How her short absence might be unsur-
    mised,
    While she the inmost of the dream
        would try.
Resolved, she took with her an aged nurse,
And went into that dismal forest-hearse.

See, as they creep along the river side,   345
    How she doth whisper to that aged dame,
And, after looking round the champaign
    wide,
    Shows her a knife.—"What feverish hec-
        tic flame
Burns in thee, child?—What good can thee
    betide,
    That thou shouldst smile again?"—The
        evening came,   350
And they had found Lorenzo's earthy bed;
The flint was there, the berries at his head.

Who hath not' loitered in a green church-
    yard,
    And let his spirit, like a demon mole,
Work through the clayey soil and gravel
    hard,   355
    To see skull, coffined bones, and funeral
        stole;

Pitying each form that hungry Death hath
    marred,
    And filling it once more with human
        soul?
Ah! this is holiday to what was felt
When Isabella by Lorenzo knelt.   360

She gazed into the fresh-thrown mould, as
    though
    One glance did fully all its secrets tell;
Clearly she saw, as other eyes would know
    Pale limbs at bottom of a crystal well;
Upon the murderous spot she seemed to
    grow,   365
    Like to a native lily of the dell:
Then with her knife, all sudden, she began
To dig more fervently than misers can.

Soon she turned up a soilèd glove, whereon
    Her silk had played in purple fan-
        tasies,   370
She kissed it with a lip more chill than
    stone,
    And put it in her bosom, where it dries
And freezes utterly unto the bone
    Those dainties made to still an infant's
        cries:
Then 'gan she work again; nor stayed her
    care,   375
But to throw back at times her veiling hair.

That old nurse stood beside her wondering,
    Until her heart felt pity to the core
At sight of such a dismal laboring,
    And so she kneelèd, with her locks al!
        hoar,   380
And put her lean hands to the horrid
    thing:
    Three hours they labored at this travail
        sore;
At last they felt the kernel of the grave,
And Isabella did not stamp and rave.

Ah! wherefore all this wormy circum-
    stance?   385
    Why linger at the yawning tomb so long?
O for the gentleness of old Romance,
    The simple plaining of a minstrel's song!
Fair reader, at the old tale take a glance,
    For here, in truth, it doth not well be-
        long   390
To speak:—O turn thee to the very tale,
And taste the music of that vision pale.

With duller steel than the Perséan sword
    They cut away no formless monster's
        head,
But one, whose gentleness did well ac-
    cord   395
    With death, as life. The ancient harps
        have said,

Love never dies, but lives, immortal Lord:
  If Love impersonate was ever dead,
Pale Isabella kissed it, and low moaned.
'Twas love; cold,—dead indeed, but not de-
    throned.   400

In anxious secrecy they took it home.
  And then the prize was all for Isabel:
She calmed its wild hair with a golden
    comb,
  And all around each eye's sepulchral cell
Pointed each fringèd lash; the smearèd
    loam   405
With tears, as chilly as a dripping well,
  She drenched away:—and still she combed,
    and kept
Sighing all day—and still she kissed, and
    wept.

Then in a silken scarf,—sweet with the dews
  Of precious flowers plucked in Araby,   410
And divine liquids come with odorous ooze
  Through the cold serpent-pipe refresh-
    fully,—
She wrapped it up, and for its tomb did
    choose
  A garden pot wherein she laid it by,
And covered it with mould, and o'er it
    set   415
Sweet Basil, which her tears kept ever wet.

And she forgot the stars, the moon, and
    sun,
  And she forgot the blue above the trees,
And she forgot the dells where waters run,
  And she forgot the chilly autumn
    breeze;   420
She had no knowledge when the day was
    done,
  And the new morn she saw not: but in
    peace
Hung over her sweet Basil evermore,
And moistened it with tears unto the core.

And so she ever fed it with thin tears,   425
  Whence thick, and green, and beautiful
    it grew,
So that it smelt more balmy than its peers
  Of Basil-tufts in Florence; for it drew
Nurture besides, and life, from human
    fears,
  From the fast mouldering head there
    shut from view   430
So that the jewel, safely casketed,
Came forth, and in perfumèd leafits spread.

O Melancholy, linger here awhile!
  O Music, Music, breathe despondingly!

O Echo, Echo, from some sombre isle,   435
  Unknown, Lethean, sigh to us—O sigh!
Spirits in grief, lift up your heads, and
    smile;
  Lift up your heads, sweet Spirits, heavily,
And make a pale light in your cypress
    glooms,
  Tinting with silver wan your marble
    tombs.   440

Moan hither, all ye syllables of woe,
  From the deep throat of sad Melpomene!
Through bronzèd lyre in tragic order go,
  And touch the strings into a mystery;
Sound mournfully upon the winds and
    low;   445
  For simple Isabel is soon to be
Among the dead: She withers, like a palm
Cut by an Indian for its juicy balm.

O leave the palm to wither by itself;
  Let not quick Winter chill its dying
    hour!—   450
It may not be—those Baälites of pelf,
  Her brethren, noted the continual
    shower
From her dead eyes; and many a curious
    elf,
  Among her kindred, wondered that such
    dower
Of youth and beauty should be thrown
    aside   455
By one marked out to be a Noble's bride.

And, furthermore, her brethren wondered
    much
  Why she sat drooping by the Basil green,
And why it flourished, as by magic touch;
  Greatly they wondered what the thing
    might mean: 460
They could not surely give belief, that such
  A very nothing would have power to
    wean
Her from her own fair youth, and pleasures
    gay,
And even remembrance of her love's delay.

Therefore they watched a time when they
    might sift   465
  This hidden whim; and long they
    watched in vain;
For seldom did she go to chapel-shrift,
  And seldom felt she any hunger-pain;
And when she left, she hurried back, as
    swift
  As bird on wing to breast its eggs
    again;   470
And, patient as a hen-bird, sat her there
Beside her Basil, weeping through her hair,

Yet they contrived to steal the Basil-pot,
    And to examine it in secret place:
The thing was vile with green and livid
        spot,   475
    And yet they knew it was Lorenzo's face:
The guerdon of their murder they had got,
    And so left Florence in a moment's space,
Never to turn again.—Away they went,
With blood upon their heads, to banish-
        ment.   480

O Melancholy, turn thine eyes away!
    O Music, Music, breathe despondingly!
O Echo, Echo, on some other day,
    From isles Lethean, sigh to us—O sigh!
Spirits of grief, sing not your "Well-a-
        way!"   485
    For Isabel, sweet Isabel, will die;
Will die a death too lone and incomplete,
Now they have ta'en away her Basil sweet.

Piteous she looked on dead and senseless
        things,
    Asking for her lost Basil amorously;   490
And with melodious chuckle in the strings
    Of her lorn voice, she oftentimes would
        cry
After the Pilgrim in his wanderings,
    To ask him where her Basil was; and
        why
'Twas hid from her: "For cruel 'tis," said
        she,   495
"To steal my Basil-pot away from me."

And so she pined, and so she died forlorn,
    Imploring for her Basil to the last.
No heart was there in Florence but did
        mourn
    In pity of her love, so overcast.   500
And a sad ditty of this story born
    From mouth to mouth through all the
        country passed:
Still is the burthen sung—"O cruelty,
To steal my Basil-pot away from me!"

Feb.-Apr., 1818   1820

THE HUMAN SEASONS

Four Seasons fill the measure of the year;
    There are four seasons in the mind of
        man:
He has his lusty Spring, when fancy clear
    Takes in all beauty with an easy span:
He has his Summer, when luxuriously   5
    Spring's honeyed cud of youthful thought
        he loves
To ruminate, and by such dreaming nigh
    His nearest unto heaven: quiet coves

His soul has in its Autumn, when his wings
    He furleth close: contented so to look 10
On mists in idleness—to let fair things
    Pass by unheeded as a threshold brook.
He has his Winter too of pale misfeature,
Or else he would forego his mortal nature.

March, 1818   1819

MEG MERRILIES

I

Old Meg she was a Gipsy,
    And lived upon the Moors:
Her bed it was the brown heath turf,
    And her house was out of doors.

II

Her apples were swart blackberries,   5
    Her currants pods o' broom;
Her wine was dew of the wild white rose,
    Her book a churchyard tomb.

III

Her Brothers were the craggy hills,
    Her Sisters larchen trees—   10
Alone with her great family
    She lived as she did please.

IV

No breakfast had she many a morn,
    No dinner many a noon,
And 'stead of supper she would stare   15
    Full hard against the Moon.

V

But every morn of woodbine fresh
    She made her garlanding,
And every night the dark glen Yew
    She wove, and she would sing.   20

VI

And with her fingers old and brown
    She plaited Mats o' Rushes,
And gave them to the Cottagers
    She met among the Bushes.

VII

Old Meg was brave as Margaret Queen 25
    And tall as Amazon:
An old red blanket cloak she wore;
    A chip hat had she on.
God rest her aged bones somewhere—
    She died full long agone!   30

c. July 2, 1818   1844

WRITTEN UPON THE TOP OF BEN NEVIS

Read me a lesson, Muse, and speak it loud
  Upon the top of Nevis, blind in mist!
I look into the chasms, and a shroud
  Vaporous doth hide them,—just so much
      I wist
Mankind do know of hell; I look o'er-
      head,   5
  And there is sullen mist,—even so much
Mankind can tell of heaven; mist is spread
  Before the earth, beneath me,—even
      such,
Even so vague is man's sight of himself!
  Here are the craggy stones beneath my
      feet,—   10
Thus much I know that, a poor witless elf,
  I tread on them,—that all my eye doth
      meet
Is mist and crag, not only on this height,
But in the world of thought and mental
      might!

Aug. 2, 1818   1838

TO AILSA ROCK

Hearken, thou craggy ocean pyramid!
  Give answer by thy voice, the sea-fowls'
      screams!
  When were thy shoulders mantled in
      huge streams?
When from the sun was thy broad fore-
      head hid?
How long is 't since the mighty Power
      bid   5
  Thee heave to airy sleep from fathom
      dreams?
Sleep in the lap of thunder or sunbeams,
Or when grey clouds are thy cold coverlid.
Thou answer'st not; for thou art dead
      asleep;
  Thy life is but two dead eternities—   10
The last in air, the former in the deep;
  First with the whales, last with the eagle-
      skies—
Drowned wast thou till an earthquake
      made thee steep,
  Another cannot wake thy giant size!

c. July 10, 1818   1819

HYPERION

BOOK I

Deep in the shady sadness of a vale
Far sunken from the healthy breath of
      morn,
Far from the fiery noon, and eve's one star,
Sat grey-haired Saturn, quiet as a stone,
Still as the silence round about his lair;   5
Forest on forest hung about his head
Like cloud on cloud. No stir of air was
      there
Not so much life as on a summer's day
Robs not one light seed from the feathered
      grass,
But where the dead leaf fell, there did it
      rest.   10
A stream went voiceless by, still deadened
      more
By reason of his fallen divinity
Spreading a shade: the Naiad 'mid her
      reeds
Pressed her cold finger closer to her lips.

Along the margin-sand large foot-marks
      went,   15
No further than to where his feet had
      strayed,
And slept there since. Upon the sodden
      ground
His old right hand lay nerveless, listless,
      dead,
Unsceptred; and his realmless eyes were
      closed;
While his bowed head seemed list'ning to
      the Earth,   20
His ancient mother, for some comfort yet.

It seemed no force could wake him from
      his place;
But there came one, who with a kindred
      hand
Touched his wide shoulders, after bending
      low
With reverence, though to one who knew
      it not,   25
She was a Goddess of the infant world;
By her in stature the tall Amazon
Had stood a pigmy's height; she would
      have ta'en
Achilles by the hair and bent his neck;
Or with a finger stayed Ixion's wheel.   30
Her face was large as that of Memphian
      sphinx,
Pedestaled haply in a palace court,
When sages looked to Egypt for their lore.
But oh! how unlike marble was that face:
How beautiful, if sorrow had not made   35
Sorrow more beautiful than Beauty's self.
There was a listening fear in her regard,
As if calamity had but begun;
As if the vanward clouds of evil days
Had spent their malice, and the sullen
      rear   40
Was with its stored thunder laboring up.
One hand she pressed upon that aching
      spot

Where beats the human heart, as if just
there,
Though an immortal, she felt cruel pain:
The other upon Saturn's bended neck 45
She laid, and to the level of his ear
Leaning with parted lips, some words she
spake
In solemn tenor and deep organ tone;
Some mourning words, which in our feeble
tongue
Would come in these like accents; O how
frail 50
To that large utterance of the early Gods!
"Saturn, look up!—though wherefore, poor
old King?
"I have no comfort for thee, no not one:
"I cannot say 'O wherefore sleepest thou?'
"For heaven is parted from thee, and the
earth 55
"Knows thee not, thus afflicted, for a God;
"And ocean too, with all its solemn noise,
"Has from thy sceptre passed; and all the
air
"Is emptied of thine hoary majesty.
"Thy thunder, conscious of the new com-
mand, 60
"Rumbles reluctant o'er our fallen house;
"And thy sharp lightning in unpractised
hands
"Scorches and burns our once serene do-
main.
"O aching time! O moments big as years!
"All as ye pass swell out the monstrous
truth, 65
"And press it so upon our weary griefs
"That unbelief has not a space to breathe.
"Saturn, sleep on:—O thoughtless, why did
I
"Thus violate thy slumbrous solitude?
"Why should I ope thy melancholy eyes? 70
"Saturn, sleep on! while at thy feet I weep."

As when, upon a tranced summer night,
Those green-robed senators of mighty
woods,
Tall oaks, branch-charmed by the earnest
stars,
Dream, and so dream all night without a
stir, 75
Save from one gradual solitary gust
Which comes upon the silence, and dies off,
As if the ebbing air had but one wave;
So came these words and went; the while
in tears,
She touched her fair large forehead to the
ground, 80
Just where her falling hair might be out-
spread
A soft and silken mat for Saturn's feet.
One moon, with alteration slow, had shed

Her silver seasons four upon the night,
And still these two were postured motion-
less, 85
Like natural sculpture in cathedral cavern;
The frozen God still couchant on the earth,
And the sad Goddess weeping at his feet:
Until at length old Saturn lifted up
His faded eyes, and saw his kingdom
gone, 90
And all the gloom and sorrow of the place,
And that fair kneeling Goddess; and then
spake,
As with a palsied tongue, and while his
beard
Shook horrid with such aspen-malady:
"O tender spouse of gold Hyperion, 95
"Thea, I feel thee ere I see thy face;
"Look up, and let me see our doom in it;
"Look up, and tell me if this feeble shape
"Is Saturn's; tell me, if thou hear'st the
voice
"Of Saturn; tell me, if this wrinkling
brow 100
"Naked and bare of its great diadem,
"Peers like the front of Saturn. Who had
power
"To make me desolate? whence came the
strength?
"How was it nurtured to such bursting
forth,
"While Fate seemed strangled in my nerv-
ous grasp? 105
"But it is so; and I am smothered up,
"And buried from all godlike exercise
"Of influence benign on planets pale,
"Of admonitions to the winds and seas,
"Of peaceful sway above man's harvest-
ing, 110
"And all those acts which Deity supreme
"Doth ease its heart of love in.—I am gone
"Away from my own bosom: I have left
"My strong identity, my real self,
"Somewhere between the throne, and where
I sit 115
"Here on this spot of earth. Search, Thea,
search!
"Open thine eyes eterne, and sphere them
round
"Upon all space: space starred, and lorn of
light;
"Space regioned with life-air; and barren
void;
"Spaces of fire, and all the yawn of
hell.— 120
"Search, Thea, search! and tell me, if thou
seest
"A certain shape or shadow, making way
"With wings or chariot fierce to repossess
"A heaven he lost erewhile: it must—it
must

"Be of ripe progress—Saturn must be
      king.   125
"Yes, there must be a golden victory;
"There must be Gods thrown down, and
      trumpets
"Of triumph calm, and hymns of festival
"Upon the gold clouds metropolitan,
"Voices of soft proclaim, and silver stir   130
"Of strings in hollow shells; and there shall
      be
"Beautiful things made new, for the sur-
      prise
"Of the sky-children; I will give command:
"Thea! Thea! Thea! where is Saturn?"

This passion lifted him upon his feet,   135
And made his hands to struggle in the air,
His Druid locks to shake and ooze with
      sweat,
His eyes to fever out, his voice to cease.
He stood, and heard not Thea's sobbing
      deep;
A little time, and then again he
      snatched,   140
Utterance thus.—"But cannot I create?
"Cannot I form? Cannot I fashion forth
"Another world, another universe,
"To overbear and crumble this to nought?
"Where is another chaos? Where?"—That
      word   145
Found way unto Olympus, and made quake
The rebel three.—Thea was startled up,
And in her bearing was a sort of hope,
As thus she quick-voiced spake, yet full of
      awe.

"This cheers our fallen house: come to
      our friends,   150
"O Saturn! come away, and give them
      heart;
"I know the covert, for thence come I
      hither."
Thus brief; then with beseeching eyes she
      went
With backward footing through the shade
      a space:
He followed, and she turned to lead the
      way   155
Through aged boughs, that yielded like the
      mist
Which eagles cleave upmounting from
      their nest.

Meanwhile in other realms big tears were
      shed,
More sorrow like to this, and such like woe,
Too huge for mortal tongue or pen of
      scribe: 160
The Titans fierce, self-hid, or prison-bound,

Groaned for the old allegiance once more,
And listened in sharp pain for Saturn's
      voice.
But one of the whole mammoth-brood still
      kept
His sov'reignty, and rule, and majesty;— 165
Blazing Hyperion on his orbed fire
Still sat, still snuffed the incense, teeming
      up
From man to the sun's God; yet unsecure:
For as among us mortals omens drear
Fright and perplex, so also shuddered
      he—   170
Not at dog's howl, or gloom-bird's hated
      screech,
Or the familiar visiting of one
Upon the first toll of his passing-bell,
Or prophesyings of the midnight lamp;
But horrors, portioned to a giant nerve, 175
Oft made Hyperion ache. His palace
      bright
Bastioned with pyramids of glowing gold,
And touched with shade of bronzed obe-
      lisks,
Glared a blood-red through all its thousand
      courts,
Arches, and domes, and fiery galleries;   180
And all its curtains of Aurorian clouds
Flushed angerly: while sometimes eagles'
      wings,
Unseen before by Gods or wondering men,
Darkened the place; and neighing steeds
      were heard,
Not heard before by Gods or wondering
      men.   185
Also, when he would taste the spicy wreaths
Of incense, breathed aloft from sacred hills,
Instead of sweets, his ample palate took
Savor of poisonous brass and metal sick:
And so, when harbored in the sleepy
      west,   190
After the full completion of fair day,—
For rest divine upon exalted couch
And slumber in the arms of melody
He paced away the pleasant hours of ease
With stride colossal, on from hall to
      hall;   195
While far within each aisle and deep recess,
His winged minions in close clusters stood,
Amazed and full of fear; like anxious men
Who on wide plains gather in panting
      troops,
When earthquakes jar their battlements
      and towers.   200
Even now, while Saturn, roused from icy
      trance,
Went step for step with Thea through the
      woods,
Hyperion, leaving twilight in the rear,
Came slope upon the threshold of the west;

Then, as was wont, his palace door flew
　　ope　　　　　　　　　　　　　　205
In smoothest silence, save what solemn
　　tubes,
Blown by the serious Zephyrs, gave of sweet
And wandering sounds, slow-breathed
　　melodies;
And like a rose in vermeil tint and shape,
In fragrance soft, and coolness to the
　　eye,　　　　　　　　　　　　　210
That inlet to severe magnificence
Stood full blown, for the God to enter in.

　　He entered, but he entered full of wrath;
His flaming robes streamed out beyond his
　　heels,
And gave a roar, as if of earthly fire,　215
That scared away the meek ethereal Hours
And made their dove-wings tremble. On
　　he flared,
From stately nave to nave, from vault to
　　vault,
Through bowers of fragrant and en-
　　wreathed light,
And diamond-paved lustrous long ar-
　　cades,　　　　　　　　　　　　220
Until he reached the great main cupola;
There standing fierce beneath, he stamped
　　his foot,
And from the basements deep to the high
　　towers
Jarred his own golden region; and before
The quavering thunder thereupon had
　　ceased,　　　　　　　　　　　225
His voice leaped out, despite of godlike
　　curb,
To this result: "O dreams of day and night!
"O monstrous forms! O effigies of pain!
"O spectres busy in a cold, cold gloom!
"G lank-eared Phantoms of black-weeded
　　pools!　　　　　　　　　　　230
"Why do I know ye? why have I seen ye?
　　why
"Is my eternal essence thus distraught
"To see and to behold these horrors new?
"Saturn is fallen, am I too to fall?
"Am I to leave this haven of my rest,　235
"This cradle of my glory, this soft clime,
"This calm luxuriance of blissful light,
"These crystalline pavilions, and pure
　　fanes,
"Of all my lucent empire? It is left
"Deserted, void, nor any haunt of mine. 240
"The blaze, the splendor, and the sym-
　　metry,
"I cannot see—but darkness, death and
　　darkness.
"Even here, into my center of repose,
"The shady visions come to domineer,

"Insult, and blind, and stifle up my
　　pomp.—　　　　　　　　　　245
"Fall!—No, by Tellus and her briny robes!
"Over the fiery frontier of my realms
"I will advance a terrible right arm
"Shall scare the infant thunderer, rebel
　　Jove,
"And bid old Saturn take his throne
　　again."—　　　　　　　　　　250
He spake, and ceased, the while a heavier
　　threat
Held struggle with his throat but came not
　　forth;
For as in theatres of crowded men
Hubbub increases more they call out
　　"Hush!"
So at Hyperion's words the Phantoms
　　pale　　　　　　　　　　　　255
Bestirred themselves, thrice horrible and
　　cold;
And from the mirrored level where he
　　stood
A mist arose, as from a scummy marsh.
At this, through all his bulk an agony
Crept gradual, from the feet unto the
　　crown,　　　　　　　　　　　260
Like a lithe serpent vast and muscular
Making slow way, with head and neck con-
　　vulsed
From over-strained might. Released, he
　　fled
To the eastern gates, and full six dewy
　　hours
Before the dawn in season due should
　　blush,　　　　　　　　　　　265
He breathed fierce breath against the
　　sleepy portals,
Cleared them of heavy vapors, burst them
　　wide
Suddenly on the ocean's chilly streams.
The planet orb of fire, whereon he rode
Each day from east to west the heavens
　　through,　　　　　　　　　　270
Spun round in sable curtaining of clouds;
Not therefore veiled quite, blindfold, and
　　hid,
But ever and anon the glancing spheres,
Circles, and arcs, and broad-belting colure,
Glowed through, and wrought upon the
　　muffling dark　　　　　　　　275
Sweet-shaped lightnings from the nadir
　　deep
Up to the zenith,—hieroglyphics old,
Which sages and keen-eyed astrologers
Then living on the earth, with laboring
　　thought
Won from the gaze of many centuries: 280
Now lost, save what we find on remnants
　　huge

Of stone, or marble swart; their import
    gone,
Their wisdom long since fled.—Two wings
    this orb
Possessed for glory, two fair argent wings,
Ever exalted at the God's approach: 285
And now, from forth the gloom their
    plumes immense
Rose, one by one, till all outspreaded were;
While still the dazzling globe maintained
    eclipse,
Awaiting for Hyperion's command.
Fain would he have commanded, fain took
    throne   290
And bid the day begin, if but for change.
He might not:—No, though a primeval
    God:
The sacred seasons might not be disturbed.
Therefore the operations of the dawn
Stayed in their birth, even as here 'tis
    told.   295
Those silver wings expanded sisterly,
Eager to sail their orb; the porches wide
Opened upon the dusk demesnes of night;
And the bright Titan, phrenzied with new
    woes,
Unused to bend, by hard compulsion
    bent   300
His spirit to the sorrow of the time;
And all along a dismal rack of clouds,
Upon the boundaries of day and night,
He stretched himself in grief and radiance
    faint.
There as he lay, the Heaven with its
    stars   305
Looked down on him with pity, and the
    voice
Of Cœlus, from the universal space,
Thus whispered low and solemn in his ear.
"O brightest of my children dear, earth-
    born
"And sky-engendered, Son of Mysteries 310
"All unrevealed even to the powers
"Which met at thy creating; at whose joys
"And palpitations sweet, and pleasures soft,
"I, Cœlus, wonder, how they came and
    whence;
"And at the fruits thereof what shapes they
    be,   315
"Distinct, and visible; symbols divine,
"Manifestations of that beauteous life
"Diffused unseen throughout eternal space:
"Of these new-formed art thou, oh bright-
    est child!
"Of these, thy brethren and the God-
    desses!   320
"There is sad feud among ye, and rebellion
"Of son against his sire. I saw him fall,
"I saw my first-born tumbled from his
    throne!

"To me his arms were spread, to me his
    voice
"Found way from forth the thunders round
    his head!   325
"Pale wox I, and in vapors hid my face.
"Art thou, too, near such doom? vague fear
    there is:
"For I have seen my sons most unlike Gods.
"Divine ye were created, and divine
"In sad demeanor, solemn, undisturbed, 330
"Unruffled, like high Gods, ye lived and
    ruled:
"Now I behold in you fear, hope, and
    wrath;
"Actions of rage and passion; even as
"I see them, on the mortal world beneath,
"In men who die.—This is the grief, O
    Son!   335
"Sad sign of ruin, sudden dismay, and fall!
"Yet do thou strive; as thou art capable,
"As thou canst move about, an evident
    God;
"And canst oppose to each malignant hour
"Ethereal presence:—I am but a voice; 340
"My life is but the life of winds and tides,
"No more than winds and tides can I
    avail:—
"But thou canst.—Be thou therefore in the
    van
"Of circumstance; yea, seize the arrow's
    barb
"Before the tense string murmur.—To the
    earth!   345
"For there thou wilt find Saturn, and his
    woes.
"Meantime I will keep watch on thy bright
    sun,
"And on thy seasons be a careful nurse."—
Ere half this region-whisper had come
    down,
Hyperion arose, and on the stars   350
Lifted his curved lids, and kept them wide
Until it ceased; and still he kept them
    wide:
And still they were the same bright, pa-
    tient stars.
Then with a slow incline of his broad
    breast,
Like to a diver in the pearly seas,   355
Forward he stooped over the airy shore,
And plunged all noiseless into the deep
    night.

BOOK II

Just at the self-same beat of Time's wide
    wings
Hyperion slid into the rustled air,
And Saturn gained with Thea that sad
    place

Where Cybele and the bruised Titans
    mourned.
It was a den where no insulting light   5
Could glimmer on their tears; where their
    own groans
They felt, but heard not, for the solid roar
Of thunderous waterfalls and torrents
    hoarse,
Pouring a constant bulk, uncertain where.
Crag jutting forth to crag, and rocks that
    seemed   10
Ever as if just rising from a sleep,
Forehead to forehead held their monstrous
    horns;
And thus in thousand hugest phantasies
Made a fit roofing to this nest of woe.
Instead of thrones, hard flint they sat
    upon,   15
Couches of rugged stone, and slaty ridge
Stubborned with iron. All were not assem-
    bled:
Some chained in torture, and some wander-
    ing.
Cœus, and Gyges, and Briareüs,
Typhon, and Dolor, and Porphyrion,   20
With many more, the brawniest in assault,
Were pent in regions of laborious breath;
Dungeoned in opaque elements, to keep
Their clenched teeth still clenched, and all
    their limbs
Locked up like veins of metal, crampt and
    screwed;   25
Without a motion, save of their big hearts
Heaving in pain, and horribly convulsed
With sanguine feverous boiling gurge of
    pulse,
Mnemosyne was straying in the world;
Far from her moon had Phœbe wan-
    dered;   30
And many else were free to roam abroad,
But for the main, here found they covert
    drear.
Scarce images of life, one here, one there,
Lay vast and edgeways; like a dismal cirque
Of Druid stones, upon a forlorn moor,   35
When the chill rain begins at shut of eve,
In dull November, and their chancel vault,
The Heaven itself, is blinded throughout
    night.
Each one kept shroud, nor to his neigh-
    bor gave
Or word, or look, or action of despair.   40
Creüs was one; his ponderous iron mace
Lay by him, and a shattered rib of rock
Told of his rage, ere he thus sank and
    pined.
Iäpetus another; in his grasp,
A serpent's plashy neck, its barbed tongue   45
Squeezed from the gorge, and all its un-
    curled length

Dead; and because the creature could not
    spit
Its poison in the eyes of conquering Jove.
Next Cottus: prone he lay, chin uppermost,
As though in pain; for still upon the flint   50
He ground severe his skull, with open
    mouth
And eyes at horrid working, Nearest him
Asia, born of most enormous Caf,
Who cost her mother Tellus keener pangs,
Though feminine, than any of her sons: 55
More thought than woe was in her dusky
    face,
For she was prophesying of her glory;
And in her wide imagination stood
Palm-shaded temples, and high rival fanes,
By Oxus or in Ganges' sacred isles.   60
Even as Hope upon her anchor leans,
So leant she, not so fair, upon a tusk
Shed from the broadest of her elephants.
Above her, on a crag's uneasy shelve,
Upon his elbow raised, all prostrate else, 65
Shadowed Enceladus; once tame and mild
As grazing ox unworried in the meads;
Now tiger-passioned, lion-thoughted, wroth,
He meditated, plotted, and even now
Was hurling mountains in that second
    war,   70
Not long delayed, that scared the younger
    Gods
To hide themselves in forms of beast and
    bird.
Not far hence Atlas; and beside him prone
Phorcus, the sire of Gorgons. Neighbored
    close
Oceanus, and Tethys, in whose lap   75
Sobbed Clymene among her tangled hair.
In midst of all lay Themis, at the feet
Of Ops the queen all clouded round from
    sight;
No shape distinguishable, more than when
Thick night confounds the pine-tops with
    the clouds: 80
And many else whose names may not be
    told.
For when the Muse's wings are air-ward
    spread,
Who shall delay her flight? And she must
    chaunt
Of Saturn, and his guide, who now had
    climbed
With damp and slippery footing from a
    depth   85
More horrid still. Above a sombre cliff
Their heads appeared, and up their stature
    grew
Till on the level height their steps found
    ease:
Then Thea spread abroad her trembling
    arms

Upon the precincts of this nest of pain, 90
And sidelong fixed her eye on Saturn's
   face:
There saw she the direst strife; the supreme
   God
At war with all the frailty of grief,
Of rage, of fear, anxiety, revenge,
Remorse, spleen, hope, but most of all
   despair. 95
Against these plagues he strove in vain; for
   Fate
Had poured a mortal oil upon his head,
A disanointing poison: so that Thea,
Affrighted, kept her still, and let him pass
First onwards in, among the fallen tribe. 100

As with us mortal men, the laden heart
Is persecuted more, and fevered more,
When it is nighing to the mournful house
Where other hearts are sick of the same
   bruise;
So Saturn, as he walked into the midst, 105
Felt faint, and would have sunk among the
   rest,
But that he met Enceladus's eye,
Whose mightiness, and awe of him, at once
Came like an inspiration; and he shouted,
"Titans, behold your God!" at which some
   groaned: 110
Some started on their feet; some also
   shouted;
Some wept, some wailed, all bowed with
   reverence;
And Ops, uplifting her black folded veil,
Showed her pale cheeks, and all her fore-
   head wan,
Her eyebrows thin and jet, and hollow
   eyes. 115
There is a roaring in the bleak-grown pines
When Winter lifts his voice; there is a noise
Among immortals when a God gives sign,
With hushing finger, how he means to load
His tongue with the full weight of utterless
   thought, 120
With thunder, and with music, and with
   pomp:
Such noise is like the roar of bleak-grown
   pines;
Which, when it ceases in this mountained
   world,
No other sound succeeds; but ceasing here,
Among these fallen, Saturn's voice there-
   from 125
Grew up like organ, that begins anew
Its strain, when other harmonies, stopt
   short,
Leave the dinned air vibrating silverly.
Thus grew it up—"Not in my own sad
   breast,

"Which is its own great judge and searcher
   out, 130
"Can I find reason why ye should be thus:
"Not in the legends of the first of days,
"Studied from that old spirit-leaved book
"Which starry Uranus with finger bright
"Saved from the shores of darkness, when
   the waves 135
"Low-ebbed still hid it up in shallow
   gloom;—
"And the which book ye know I ever kept
"For my firm-based footstool:—Ah, infirm!
"Not there, nor in sign, symbol, or portent
"Of element, earth, water, air, and fire,— 140
"At war, at peace, or inter-quarreling
"One against one, or two, or three, or all
"Each several one, against the other three,
"As fire with air loud warring when rain-
   floods
"Drown both, and press them both against
   earth's face, 145
"Where, finding sulphur, a quadruple
   wrath
"Unhinges the poor world;—not in that
   strife,
"Wherefrom I take strange lore, and read
   it deep,
"Can I find reason why ye should be thus:
"No, nowhere can unriddle, though I
   search, 150
"And pore on Nature's universal scroll
"Even to swooning, why ye, Divinities,
"The first-born of all shaped and palpable
   Gods,
"Should cower beneath what, in compari-
   son,
"Is untremendous might. Yet ye are
   here, 155
"O'erwhelmed, and spurned, and battered,
   ye are here!
"O Titans, shall I say 'Arise!'—Ye groan:
"Shall I say 'Crouch!'—Ye groan. What
   can I then?
"O Heaven wide! O unseen parent dear!
"What can I? Tell me, all ye brethren
   Gods, 160
"How we can war, how engine our great
   wrath!
"O speak your counsel now, for Saturn's
   ear
"Is all a-hungered. Thou, Oceanus,
"Ponderest high and deep; and in thy face
"I see, astonied, that severe content 165
"Which comes of thought and musing: give
   us help!"

So ended Saturn; and the God of the
   Sea,
Sophist and sage, from no Athenian grove,
But cogitation in his watery shades,

Arose, with locks not oozy, and began, 170
In murmurs, which his first-endeavoring
    tongue
Caught infant-like from the far-foamed
    sands.
"O ye, whom wrath consumes! who, pas-
    sion-strung,
"Writhe at defeat, and nurse your agonies!
"Shut up your senses, stifle up your ears, 175
"My voice is not a bellows unto ire.
"Yet listen, ye who will, whilst I bring
    proof
"How ye, perforce, must be content to
    stoop:
"And in the proof much comfort will I
    give,
"If ye will take that comfort in its truth. 180
"We fall by course of Nature's law, not
    force
"Of thunder, or of Jove. Great Saturn,
    thou
"Hast sifted well the atom-universe;
"But for this reason, that thou art the
    King,
"And only blind from sheer supremacy, 185
"One avenue was shaded from thine eyes,
"Through which I wandered to eternal
    truth.
"And first, as thou wast not the first of
    powers,
"So art thou not the last; it cannot be:
"Thou art not the beginning nor the
    end. 190
"From chaos and parental darkness came
"Light, the first fruits of that intestine
    broil,
"That sullen ferment, which for wondrous
    ends
"Was ripening in itself. The ripe hour
    came,
"And with it light, and light, engender-
    ing 195
"Upon its own producer, forthwith touched
"The whole enormous matter into life.
"Upon that very hour, our parentage,
"The Heavens and the Earth, were mani-
    fest:
"Then thou first born, and we the giant
    race, 200
"Found ourselves ruling new and beaute-
    ous realms.
"Now comes the pain of truth, to whom
    'tis pain;
"O folly; for to bear all naked truths,
"And to envisage circumstance, all calm,
"That is the top of sovereignty. Mark
    well! 205
"As Heaven and Earth are fairer, fairer far
"Than Chaos and blank Darkness, though
    once chiefs;

"And as we show beyond that Heaven and
    Earth
"In form and shape compact and beautiful,
"In will, in action free, companionship, 210
"And thousand other signs of purer life;
"So on our heels a fresh perfection treads,
"A power more strong in beauty, born of us
"And fated to excel us, as we pass
"In glory that old Darkness: nor are we 215
"Thereby more conquered, than by us the
    rule
"Of shapeless Chaos. Say, doth the dull
    soil
"Quarrel with the proud forests it hath fed,
"And feedeth still, more comely than itself?
"Can it deny the chiefdom of green
    groves? 220
"Or shall the tree be envious of the dove
"Because it cooeth, and hath snowy wings
"To wander wherewithal and find its joys?
"We are such forest trees, and our fair
    boughs
"Have bred forth, not pale solitary
    doves, 225
"But eagles golden-feathered, who do tower
"Above us in their beauty, and must reign
"In right thereof; for 'tis the eternal law
"That first in beauty should be first in
    might:
"Yea, by that law, another race may
    drive 230
"Our conquerors to mourn as we do now.
"Have ye beheld the young God of the
    Seas,
"My dispossessor? Have ye seen his face?
"Have ye beheld his chariot, foamed along
"By noble winged creatures he hath
    made? 235
"I saw him on the calmed waters scud,
"With such a glow of beauty in his eyes,
"That it enforced me to bid sad farewell
"To all my empire: farewell sad I took,
"And hither came, to see how dolorous
    fate 240
"Had wrought upon ye; and how I might
    best
"Give consolation in this woe extreme.
"Receive the truth, and let it be your
    balm."

Whether through pozed conviction, or
    disdain,
They guarded silence, when Oceanus 245
Left murmuring, what deepest thought can
    tell?
But so it was, none answered for a space,
Save one whom none regarded, Clymene;
And yet she answered not, only com
    plained.

With hectic lips, and eyes up-looking
mild,   250
Thus wording timidly among the fierce:
"O Father, I am here the simplest voice,
"And all my knowledge is that joy is gone,
"And this thing woe crept in among our
hearts,
"There to remain for ever, as I fear: 255
"I would not bode of evil, if I thought
"So weak a creature could turn off the
help
"Which by just right should come of
mighty Gods;
"Yet let me tell my sorrow, let me tell
"Of what I heard, and how it made me
weep,   260
"And know that we had parted from all
hope.
"I stood upon a shore, a pleasant shore,
"Where a sweet clime was breathed from a
land
"Of fragrance, quietness, and trees, and
flowers.
"Full of calm joy it was, as I of grief;   265
"Too full of joy and soft delicious warmth;
"So that I felt a movement in my heart
"To chide, and to reproach that solitude
"With songs of misery, music of our woes;
"And sat me down, and took a mouthed
shell   270
"And murmured into it, and made mel-
ody—
"O melody no more! for while I sang,
"And with poor skill let pass into the
breeze
"The dull shell's echo, from a bowery
strand
"Just opposite, an island of the sea,   275
"There came enchantment with the shift-
ing wind,
"That did both drown and keep alive my
ears.
"I threw my shell away upon the sand,
"And a wave filled it, as my sense was filled
"With that new blissful golden melody. 280
"A living death was in each gush of sounds,
"Each family of rapturous hurried notes,
"That fell, one after one, yet all at once,
"Like pearl beads dropping sudden from
their string:
"And then another, then another strain, 285
"Each like a dove leaving its olive perch,
"With music winged instead of silent
plumes,
"To hover round my head, and make me
sick
"Of joy and grief at once. Grief overcame,
"And I was stopping up my frantic ears, 290
"When, past all hindrance of my trembling
hands,

"A voice came sweeter, sweeter than all
tune,
"And still it cried, 'Apollo! young Apollo!
"'The morning-bright Apollo! young
Apollo!'
"I fled, it followed me, and cried
'Apollo!'   295
"O Father, and O Brethren, had ye felt
"Those pains of mine; O Saturn, hadst
thou felt,
"Ye would not call this too indulged
tongue
"Presumptuous, in thus venturing to be
heard."

So far her voice flowed on, like timorous
brook   300
That, lingering along a pebbled coast,
Doth fear to meet the sea: but sea it met,
And shuddered; for the overwhelming
voice
Of huge Enceladus swallowed it in wrath:
The ponderous syllables, like sullen
waves   305
In the half-glutted hollows of reef-rocks,
Came booming thus, while still upon his
arm
He leaned; not rising, from supreme con-
tempt,
"Or shall we listen to the over-wise,
"Or to the over-foolish, Giant-Gods?   310
"Not thunderbolt on thunderbolt, till all
"That rebel Jove's whole armory were
spent,
"Not world on world upon these shoul-
ders piled,
"Could agonize me more than baby-words
"In midst of this dethronement horrible. 315
"Speak! roar! shout! yell! ye sleepy Titans
all.
"Do ye forget the blows, the buffets vile?
"Are ye not smitten by a youngling arm?
"Dost thou forget, sham Monarch of the
Waves,
"Thy scalding in the seas? What, have I
roused   320
"Your spleens with so few simple words as
these?
"O joy! for now I see ye are not lost:
"O joy! for now I see a thousand eyes
"Wide glaring for revenge!"—As this he
said,
He lifted up his stature vast, and stood, 325
Still without intermission speaking thus:
"Now ye are flames, I'll tell you how to
burn,
"And purge the ether of our enemies;
"How to feed fierce the crooked stings of
fire,

"And singe away the swollen clouds of
Jove,   330
"Stifling that puny essence in its tent.
"O let him feel the evil he hath done;
"For though I scorn Oceanus's lore,
"Much pain have I for more than loss of
realms:
"The days of peace and slumberous calm
are fled;   335
"Those days, all innocent of scathing war,
"When all the fair Existences of heaven
"Came open-eyed to guess what we would
speak:—
"That was before our brows were taught to
frown,
"Before our lips knew else but solemn
sounds;   340
"That was before we knew the winged
thing,
'Victory, might be lost, or might be won.
'And be ye mindful that Hyperion,
"Our brightest brother, still is undis-
graced—
"Hyperion, lo! his radiance is here!"   345

All eyes were on Enceladus's face,
And they beheld, while still Hyperion's
name
Flew from his lips up to the vaulted rocks,
A pallid gleam across his features stern:
Not savage, for he saw full many a God 350
Wroth as himself. He looked upon them
all,
And in each face he saw a gleam of light,
But splendider in Saturn's, whose hoar
locks
Shone like the bubbling foam about a
keel
When the prow sweeps into a midnight
cove.   355
In pale and silver silence they remained,
Till suddenly a splendor, like the morn,
Pervaded all the beetling gloomy steeps,
All the sad spaces of oblivion,
And every gulf, and every chasm old,   360
And every height, and every sullen depth,
Voiceless, or hoarse with loud tormented
streams:
And all the everlasting cataracts,
And all the headlong torrents far and near,
Mantled before in darkness and huge
shade,   365
Now saw the light and made it terrible.
It was Hyperion:—a granite peak
His bright feet touched, and there he
stayed to view
The misery his brilliance had betrayed
To the most hateful seeing of itself.   370
Golden his hair of short Numidian curl,
Regal his shape majestic, a vast shade

In midst of his own brightness, like the
bulk
Of Memnon's image at the set of sun
To one who travels from the dusking
East: 375
Sighs, too, as mournful as that Memnon's
harp
He uttered, while his hands contemplative
He pressed together, and in silence stood.
Despondence seized again the fallen Gods
At sight of the dejected King of Day,   380
And many hid their faces from the light:
But fierce Enceladus sent forth his eyes
Among the brotherhood; and, at their
glare,
Uprose Iäpetus, and Creüs, too,
And Phorcus, sea-born, and together
strode   385
To where he towered on his eminence.
There those four shouted forth old Saturn's
name;
Hyperion from the peak loud answered,
"Saturn!"
Saturn sat near the Mother of the Gods,
In whose face was no joy, though all the
Gods   390
Gave from their hollow throats the name
of "Saturn!"

BOOK III

Thus in alternate uproar and sad peace,
Amazed were those Titans utterly.
O leave them, Muse! O leave them to their
woes:
For thou art weak to sing such tumults
dire:
A solitary sorrow best befits   5
Thy lips, and antheming a lonely grief.
Leave them, O Muse! for thou anon wilt
find
Many a fallen old Divinity
Wandering in vain about bewildered
shores.
Meantime touch piously the Delphic
harp,   10
And not a wind of heaven but will breathe
In aid soft warble from the Dorian flute;
For lo! 'tis for the Father of all verse.
Flush every thing that hath a vermeil hue,
Let the rose glow intense and warm the
air,   15
And let the clouds of even and of morn
Float in voluptuous fleeces o'er the hills;
Let the red wine within the goblet boil,
Cold as a bubbling well; let faint-lipped
shells,
On sands, or in great deeps, vermilion
turn   20

Through all their labyrinths; and let the
  maid
Blush keenly, as with some warm kiss sur-
  prised.
Chief isle of the embowered Cyclades,
Rejoice, O Delos, with thine olives green,
And poplars, and lawn-shading palms, and
  beech,   25
In which the Zephyr breathes the loudest
  song,
And hazels thick, dark-stemmed beneath
  the shade:
Apollo is once more the golden theme!
Where was he, when the Giant of the Sun
Stood bright, amid the sorrow of his
  peers?   30
Together had he left his mother fair
And his twin-sister sleeping in their bower,
And in the morning twilight wandered
  forth
Beside the osiers of a rivulet,
Full ankle-deep in lilies of the vale.   35
The nightingale had ceased, and a few
  stars
Were lingering in the heavens, while the
  thrush
Began calm-throated. Throughout all the
  isle
There was no covert, no retired cave
Unhaunted by the murmurous noise of
  waves,   40
Though scarcely heard in many a green
  recess.
He listened, and he wept, and his bright
  tears
Went trickling down the golden bow he
  held.
Thus with half-shut suffused eyes he stood,
While from beneath some cumbrous
  boughs hard by   45
With solemn step an awful Goddess came,
And there was purport in her looks for
  him,
Which he with eager guess began to read
Perplexed, the while melodiously he said:
"How cam'st thou over the unfooted sea? 50
"Or hath that antique mien and robed
  form
"Moved in these vales invisible till now?
"Sure I have heard those vestments sweep-
  ing o'er
"The fallen leaves, when I have sat alone
"In cool mid-forest. Surely I have traced 55
"The rustle of those ample skirts about
"The grassy solitudes, and seen the flowers
"Lift up their heads, as still the whisper
  passed.
"Goddess! I have beheld those eyes before,
"And their eternal calm, and all that
  face,   5c

"Or I have dreamed."—"Yes," said the su-
  preme shape,
"Thou hast dreamed of me, and awaking
  up
"Didst find a lyre all golden by thy side,
"Whose strings touched by thy fingers, all
  the vast
"Unwearied ear of the whole universe   65
"Listened in pain and pleasure at the birth
"Of such new tuneful wonder. Is't not
  strange
"That thou shouldst weep, so gifted? Tell
  me, youth,
"What sorrow thou canst feel; for I am sad
"When thou dost shed a tear: explain thy
  griefs   70
"To one who in this lonely isle hath been
"The watcher of thy sleep and hours of life,
"From the young day when first thy infant
  hand
"Plucked witless the weak flowers, till thine
  arm
"Could bend that bow heroic to all
  times.   75
"Show thy heart's secret to an ancient
  Power
"Who hath forsaken old and sacred thrones
"For prophecies of thee, and for the sake
"Of loveliness new born."—Apollo then,
With sudden scrutiny and gloomless eyes, 80
Thus answered, while his white melodious
  throat
Throbbed with the syllables.—"Mne-
  mosyne!
"Thy name is on my tongue, I know not
  how;
"Why should I tell thee what thou so well
  seest?
"Why should I strive to show what from
  thy lips   85
"Would come no mystery? For me, dark,
  dark,
"And painful vile oblivion seals my eyes:
"I strive to search wherefore I am so sad,
"Until a melancholy numbs my limbs;
"And then upon the grass I sit, and
  moan,   90
"Like one who once had wings.—O why
  should I
"Feel cursed and thwarted, when the liege-
  less air
"Yields to my step aspirant? why should I
"Spurn the green turf as hateful to my feet?
"Goddess benign, point forth some un-
  known thing: 95
"Are there not other regions than this isle?
"What are the stars? There is the sun, the
  sun!
"And the most patient brilliance of the
  moon!

"And stars by thousands! Point me out
　　the way
"To any one particular beauteous star, 100
"And I will flit into it with my lyre,
"And make its silvery splendor pant with
　　bliss.
"I have heard the cloudy thunder: Where
　　is power?
"Whose hand, whose essence, what divinity
"Makes this alarum in the elements, 105
"While I here idle listen on the shores
"In fearless yet in aching ignorance?
"O tell me, lonely Goddess, by thy harp,
"That waileth every morn and eventide.
"Tell me why thus I rave, about these
　　groves! 110
"Mute thou remainest—Mute! yet I can
　　read
"A wondrous lesson in thy silent face:
"Knowledge enormous makes a God of me.
"Names, deeds, grey legends, dire events,
　　rebellions,
"Majesties, sovran voices, agonies, 115
"Creations and destroyings, all at once
"Pour into the wide hollows of my brain,
"And deify me, as if some blithe wine
"Or bright elixir peerless I had drunk,
"And so become immortal."—Thus the
　　God, 120
While his enkindled eyes, with level glance
Beneath his white soft temples, steadfast
　　kept
Trembling with light upon Mnemosyne.
Soon wild commotions shook him, and
　　made flush
All the immortal fairness of his limbs: 125
Most like the struggle at the gate of death;
Or liker still to one who should take leave
Of pale immortal death, and with a pang
As hot as death's is chill, with fierce convulse
Die into life: so young Apollo an-
　　guished: 130
His very hair, his golden tresses famed
Kept undulation round his eager neck.
During the pain Mnemosyne upheld
Her arms as one who prophesied.—At
　　length
Apollo shrieked;—and lo! from all his
　　limbs 135
Celestial . . . .

Aug.-Dec., 1819　　　　　　　　1856

IN A DREAR-NIGHTED
DECEMBER

In a drear-nighted December,
　　Too happy, happy tree,
Thy branches ne'er remember
　　Their green felicity:

The north cannot undo them, 5
　　With a sleety whistle through them;
Nor frozen thawings glue them
　　From budding at the prime.

In a drear-nighted December,
　　Too happy, happy brook, 10
Thy bubblings ne'er remember
　　Apollo's summer look;
But with a sweet forgetting,
　　They stay their crystal fretting,
Never, never petting 15
　　About the frozen time.

Ah! would 'twere so with many
　　A gentle girl and boy!
But were there ever any
　　Writhed not at passèd joy? 20
To know the change and feel it,
When there is none to heal it,
Nor numbèd sense to steel it,
　　Was never said in rhyme.

Dec., 1818　　　　　　　　　　1829

FANCY

Ever let the Fancy roam,
Pleasure never is at home:
At a touch sweet Pleasure melteth,
Like to bubbles when rain pelteth;
Then let wingèd Fancy wander 5
Through the thought still spread beyond
　　her:
Open wide the mind's cage-door,
She'll dart forth, and cloudward soar.
O sweet Fancy! let her loose;
Summer's joys are spoilt by use, 10
And the enjoying of the Spring
Fades as does its blossoming;
Autumn's red-lipped fruitage too,
Blushing through the mist and dew,
Cloys with tasting: What do then? 15
Sit thee by the ingle, when
The sear fagot blazes bright,
Spirit of a winter's night;
When the soundless earth is muffled,
And the cakèd snow is shuffled 20
From the ploughboy's heavy shoon;
When the Night doth meet the Noon
In a dark conspiracy
To banish Even from her sky.
Sit thee there, and send abroad, 25
With a mind self-overawed,
Fancy, high-commissioned:—send her!
She has vassals to attend her:
She will bring, in spite of frost,

Beauties that the earth hath lost; 30
She will bring thee, all together,
All delights of summer weather;
All the buds and bells of May,
From dewy sward or thorny spray;
All the heapèd Autumn's wealth, 35
With a still, mysterious stealth:
She will mix these pleasures up
Like three fit wines in a cup,
And thou shalt quaff it:—thou shalt hear
Distant harvest-carols clear; 40
Rustle of the reapèd corn;
Sweet birds antheming the morn:
And, in the same moment—hark!
'Tis the early April lark,
Or the rooks, with busy caw, 45
Foraging for sticks and straw.
Thou shalt, at one glance, behold
The daisy and the marigold;
White-plumed lilies, and the first
Hedge-grown primrose that hath burst; 50
Shaded hyacinth, alway
Sapphire queen of the mid-May;
And every leaf, and every flower
Pearlèd with the self-same shower.
Thou shalt see the field mouse peep 55
Meagre from its cellèd sleep;
And the snake all winter-thin
Cast on sunny bank its skin;
Freckled nest-eggs thou shalt see
Hatching in the hawthorn tree, 60
When the hen-bird's wing doth rest
Quiet on her mossy nest;
Then the hurry and alarm
When the beehive casts its swarm;
Acorns ripe down-pattering, 65
While the autumn breezes sing.

Oh, sweet Fancy! let her loose;
Every thing is spoilt by use:
Where's the cheek that doth not fade,
Too much gazed at? Where's the maid 70
Whose lip mature is ever new?
Where's the eye, however blue
Doth not weary? Where's the face
One would meet in every place?
Where's the voice, however soft, 75
One would hear so very oft?
At a touch sweet Pleasure melteth
Like to bubbles when rain pelteth.
Let, then, wingèd Fancy find
Thee a mistress to thy mind: 80
Dulcet-eyed as Ceres' daughter,
Ere the God of Torment taught her
How to frown and how to chide;
With a waist and with a side
White as Hebe's, when her zone 85
Slipped its golden clasp, and down

Fell her kirtle to her feet,
While she held the goblet sweet,
And Jove grew languid.—Break the mesh
Of the Fancy's silken leash; 90
Quickly break her prison-string
And such joys as these she'll bring—
Let the wingèd Fancy roam,
Pleasure never is at home.

Dec., 1818   1820

ODE: BARDS OF PASSION

Bards of Passion and of Mirth,
Ye have left your souls on earth!
Have ye souls in heaven too,
Double-lived in regions new?
Yes, and those of heaven commune 5
With the spheres of sun and moon;
With the noise of fountains wondrous,
And the parle of voices thund'rous,
With the whisper of heaven's trees
And one another, in soft ease 10
Seated on Elysian lawns
Browsed by none but Dian's fawns;
Underneath large bluebells tented,
Where the daisies are rose-scented,
And the rose herself has got 15
Perfume which on earth is not;
Where the nightingale doth sing
Not a senseless, trancèd thing,
But divine melodious truth;
Philosophic numbers smooth; 20
Tales and golden histories
Of heaven and its mysteries.

Thus ye live on high, and then
On the earth ye live again;
And the souls ye left behind you 25
Teach us, here, the way to find you,
Where your other souls are joying,
Never slumbered, never cloying,
Here, your earth-born souls still speak
To mortals, of their little week; 30
Of their sorrows and delights;
Of their passions and their spites;
Of their glory and their shame;
What doth strengthen and what maim.
Thus ye teach us, every day, 35
Wisdom, though fled far away.

Bards of Passion and of Mirth,
Ye have left your souls on earth!
Ye have souls in heaven too,
Double-lived in regions new! 40

Dec., 1818   1820

SONG

The stranger lighted from his steed,
　And ere he spake a word,
He seized my lady's lily hand,
　And kissed it all unheard.

The stranger walked into the hall,　　5
　And ere he spake a word,
He kissed my lady's cherry lips,
　And kissed 'em all unheard.

The stranger walked into the bower,—
　But my lady first did go,—　　10
Aye hand in hand into the bower,
　Where my lord's roses blow.

My lady's maid had a silken scarf,
　And a golden ring had she,
And a kiss from the stranger, as off he
　　went　　15
Again on his palfrey. . . .
c. 1818　　　　　　　　　　　　1848

THE EVE OF ST. AGNES

St. Agnes' Eve—Ah, bitter chill it was!
The owl, for all his feathers, was a-cold;
The hare limped trembling through the frozen grass,
And silent was the flock in woolly fold:
Numb were the Beadsman's fingers, while he told　　5
His rosary, and while his frosted breath,
Like pious incense from a censer old,
Seemed taking flight for heaven, without a death,
Past the sweet Virgin's picture, while his prayer he saith.

His prayer he saith, this patient, holy man;　　10
Then takes his lamp, and riseth from his knees,
And back returneth, meagre, barefoot, wan,
Along the chapel aisle by slow degrees:
The sculptured dead, on each side, seem to freeze,
Emprisoned in black, purgatorial rails:　　15
Knights, ladies, praying in dumb orat'ries,
He passeth by; and his weak spirit fails
To think how they may ache in icy hoods and mails.

Northward he turneth through a little door,
And scarce three steps, ere Music's golden tongue　　20
Flattered to tears this agèd man and poor;
But no—already had his deathbell rung;
The joys of all his life were said and sung:
His was harsh penance on St. Agnes' Eve:
Another way he went, and soon among　　25
Rough ashes sat he for his soul's reprieve,
And all night kept awake, for sinners' sake to grieve.

That ancient Beadsman heard the prelude soft;
And so it chanced, for many a door was wide,
From hurry to and fro. Soon, up aloft,　　30
The silver, snarling trumpets 'gan to chide:
The level chambers, ready with their pride,
Were glowing to receive a thousand guests:
The carvèd angels, ever eager-eyed,
Stared, where upon their heads the cornice rests,　　35
With hair blown back, and wings put cross-wise on their breasts.

At length burst in the argent revelry,
With plume, tiara, and all rich array,
Numerous as shadows, haunting fairily
The brain, new stuffed, in youth, with triumphs gay   40
Of old romance.   These let us wish away,
And turn, sole-thoughted, to one Lady there,
Whose heart had brooded, all that wintry day,
On love, and winged St. Agnes' saintly care,
As she had heard old dames full many times declare.   45

They told her how, upon St. Agnes' Eve,
Young virgins might have visions of delight,
And soft adorings from their loves receive
Upon the honeyed middle of the night,
If ceremonies due they did aright;   50
As, supperless to bed they must retire,
And couch supine their beauties, lily white;
Nor look behind, nor sideways, but require
Of Heaven with upward eyes for all that they desire.

Full of this whim was thoughtful Madeline: 55
The music, yearning like a God in pain,
She scarcely heard: her maiden eyes divine,
Fixed on the floor, saw many a sweeping train
Pass by—she heeded not at all: in vain
Came many a tiptoe, amorous cavalier,   60
And back retired: not cooled by high disdain,
But she saw not: her heart was otherwhere:
She sighed for Agnes' dreams, the sweetest of the year.

She danced along with vague, regardless eyes,
Anxious her lips, her breathing quick and short: 65
The hallowed hour was near at hand: she sighs
Amid the timbrels, and the thronged resort
Of whisperers in anger, or in sport;
'Mid looks of love, defiance, hate, and scorn,
Hoodwinked with fairy fancy; all amort,   70
Save to St. Agnes and her lambs unshorn,
And all the bliss to be before tomorrow morn.

So, purposing each moment to retire,
She lingered still.   Meantime, across the moors,
Had come young Porphyro, with heart on fire   75
For Madeline.   Beside the portal doors,
Buttressed from moonlight, stands he, and implores
All saints to give him sight of Madeline,
But for one moment in the tedious hours,
That he might gaze and worship all unseen;   80
Perchance speak, kneel, touch, kiss—in sooth such things have been.

He ventures in: let no buzzed whisper tell:
All eyes be muffled, or a hundred swords
Will storm his heart, Love's fev'rous citadel:
For him, those chambers held barbarian hordes,   85
Hyena foemen, and hot-blooded lords,
Whose very dogs would execrations howl
Against his lineage: not one breast affords
Him any mercy, in that mansion foul,
Save one old beldame, weak in body and in soul.   90

Ah, happy chance! the agèd creature came,
Shuffling along with ivory-headed wand,
To where he stood, hid from the torch's flame,
Behind a broad hall-pillar, far beyond
The sound of merriment and chorus bland: 95
He startled her; but soon she knew his face,
And grasped his fingers in her palsied hand,
Saying, "Mercy, Porphyro! hie thee from this place;
"They are all here to-night, the whole blood-thirsty race!

"Get hence! get hence! there's dwarfish Hildebrand;   100
"He had a fever late, and in the fit
"He cursèd thee and thine, both house and land:
"Then there's that old Lord Maurice, not a whit
"More tame for his grey hairs—Alas me! flit!
"Flit like a ghost away."—"Ah, Gossip dear,   105
"We're safe enough; here in this arm-chair sit,
"And tell me how"—"Good Saints! not here, not here;
"Follow me, child, or else these stones will be thy bier."   10

He followed through a lowly archèd way,
Brushing the cobwebs with his lofty plume,   110
And as she muttered "Well-a—well-a-day!"
He found him in a little moonlight room,
Pale, latticed, chill, and silent as a tomb.
"Now tell me where is Madeline," said he,
"O tell me, Angela, by the holy loom   115
"Which none but secret sisterhood may see,
"When they St. Agnes' wool are weaving piously."

"St. Agnes! Ah! it is St. Agnes' Eve—
"Yet men will murder upon holy days:
"Thou must hold water in a witch's sieve,   120
"And be liege lord of all the Elves and Fays,
"To venture so: it fills me with amaze
"To see thee, Porphyro!—St. Agnes' Eve!
"God's help! my lady fair the conjuror plays
"This very night: good angels her deceive!   125
"But let me laugh awhile, I've mickle time to grieve."

Feebly she laugheth in the languid moon,
While Porphyro upon her face doth look,
Like puzzled urchin on an agèd crone
Who keepeth closed a wondrous riddle-book,   130
As spectacled she sits in chimney nook.
But soon his eyes grew brilliant, when she told
His lady's purpose; and he scarce could brook
Tears, at the thought of those enchantments cold,
And Madeline asleep in lap of legends old.   135

Sudden a thought came like a full-blown rose,
Flushing his brow, and in his painèd heart
Made purple riot: then doth he propose
A stratagem, that makes the beldame start:
"A cruel man and impious thou art: 140
"Sweet lady, let her pray, and sleep, and dream
"Alone with her good angels, far apart
"From wicked men like thee. Go, go!—I deem
"Thou canst not surely be the same that thou didst seem."

"I will not harm her, by all saints I swear,"   145
Quoth Porphyro: "O may I ne'er find grace
"When my weak voice shall whisper its last prayer,
"If one of her soft ringlets I displace,
"Or look with ruffian passion in her face:
"Good Angela, believe me by these tears;   150
"Or I will, even in a moment's space,
"Awake, with horrid shout, my foemen's ears,
"And beard them, though they be more fanged than wolves and bears."

"Ah! why wilt thou affright a feeble soul?
"A poor, weak, palsy-stricken, churchyard thing,   155
"Whose passing-bell may ere the midnight toll;
"Whose prayers for thee, each morn and evening,
"Were never missed."—Thus plaining, doth she bring
A gentler speech from burning Porphyro;
So woeful, and of such deep sorrowing,   160
That Angela gives promise she will do
Whatever he shall wish, betide her weal or woe.

Which was, to lead him, in close secrecy,
Even to Madeline's chamber, and there hide
Him in a closet, of such privacy   165
That he might see her beauty unespied,
And win perhaps that night a peerless bride,
While legioned fairies paced the coverlet,
And pale enchantment held her sleepy-eyed.
Never on such a night have lovers met,   170
Since Merlin paid his Demon all the monstrous debt.

"It shall be as thou wishest," said the Dame:
"All cates and dainties shall be storèd there
"Quickly on this feast night: by the tambour frame
"Her own lute thou wilt see: no time to spare,   175
"For I am slow and feeble, and scarce dare
"On such a catering trust my dizzy head.
"Wait here, my child, with patience; kneel in prayer
"The while: Ah! thou must needs the lady wed,
"Or may I never leave my grave among the dead."   180

So saying, she hobbled off with busy fear.
The lover's endless minutes slowly passed;
The Dame returned, and whispered in his ear
To follow her; with agèd eyes aghast
From fright of dim espial. Safe at last,   185
Through many a dusky gallery, they gain
The maiden's chamber, silken, hushed, and chaste;
Where Porphyro took covert, pleased amain.
His poor guide hurried back with agues in her brain.

Her falt'ring hand upon the balustrade,   190
Old Angela was feeling for the stair,
When Madeline, St. Agnes' charmèd maid,
Rose, like a missioned spirit, unaware:
With silver taper's light, and pious care,
She turned, and down the agèd gossip led   195
To a safe level matting. Now prepare,
Young Porphyro, for gazing on that bed;
She comes, she comes again, like ring-dove frayed and fled.

Out went the taper as she hurried in;
Its little smoke, in pallid moonshine, died: 200
She closed the door, she panted, all akin
To spirits of the air, and visions wide:
No uttered syllable, or, woe betide!
But to her heart, her heart was voluble,
Paining with eloquence her balmy side;   205
As though a tongueless nightingale should swell
Her throat in vain, and die, heart-stifled, in her dell.

A casement high and triple-arched there was,
All garlanded with carven imag'ries
Of fruits, and flowers, and bunches of knot-grass,   210
And diamonded with panes of quaint device,
Innumerable of stains and splendid dyes,
As are the tiger-moth's deep-damasked wings;
And in the midst, 'mong thousand heraldries,
And twilight saints, and dim emblazonings,   215
A shielded scutcheon blushed with blood of queens and kings.

Full on this casement shone the wintry moon,
And threw warm gules on Madeline's fair breast,
As down she knelt for heaven's grace and boon;
Rose-bloom fell on her hands, together pressed,   220
And on her silver cross soft amethyst,
And on her hair a glory, like a saint:
She seemed a splendid angel, newly dressed,
Save wings, for heaven:—Porphyro grew faint:
She knelt, so pure a thing, so free from mortal taint.   225

Anon his heart revives: her vespers done,
Of all its wreathèd pearls her hair she frees;
Unclasps her warmèd jewels one by one;
Loosens her fragrant bodice; by degrees
Her rich attire creeps rustling to her knees: 230
Half-hidden, like a mermaid in seaweed,
Pensive awhile she dreams awake, and sees,
In fancy, fair St. Agnes in her bed,
But dares not look behind, or all the charm is fled.

Soon, trembling in her soft and chilly nest,   235
In sort of wakeful swoon, perplexed she lay,
Until the poppied warmth of sleep oppressed
Her soothèd limbs, and soul fatigued away;
Flown, like a thought, until the morrow-day;
Blissfully havened both from joy and pain;   240
Clasped like a missal where swart Paynims pray;
Blinded alike from sunshine and from rain,
As though a rose should shut, and be a bud again.

Stolen to this paradise, and so entranced,
Porphyro gazed upon her empty dress,   245
And listened to her breathing, if it chanced
To wake into a slumberous tenderness:
Which when he heard, that minute did he bless,
And breathed himself: then from the closet crept,
Noiseless as fear in a wide wilderness,   250
And over the hushed carpet, silent, stepped,
And 'tween the curtains peeped, where, lo!—how fast she slept.

Then by the bedside, where the faded moon
Made a dim, silver twilight, soft he set
A table and, half anguished, threw thereon   255
A cloth of woven crimson, gold, and jet:—
O for some drowsy Morphean amulet!
The boisterous, midnight, festive clarion,
The kettledrum, and far-heard clarinet,
Affray his ears, though but in dying tone:—   260
The hall door shuts again, and all the noise is gone.

And still she slept an azure-lidded sleep,
In blanchèd linen, smooth, and lavendered,
While he from forth the closet brought a heap
Of candied apple, quince, and plum, and gourd: 265
With jellies soother than the creamy curd,
And lucent syrops, tinct with cinnamon;
Manna and dates, in argosy transferred
From Fez; and spicèd dainties, every one,
From silken Samarcand to cedared Lebanon.   270

These delicates he heaped with glowing hand
On golden dishes and in baskets bright
Of wreathèd silver: sumptuous they stand
In the retirèd quiet of the night,
Filling the chilly room with perfume light.—   275
"And now, my love, my seraph fair, awake!
"Thou art my heaven, and I thine eremite:
"Open thine eyes, for meek St. Agnes' sake,
"Or I shall drowse beside thee, so my soul doth ache."

Thus whispering, his warm, unnervèd arm   280
Sank in her pillow. Shaded was her dream
By the dusk curtains:—'twas a midnight charm
Impossible to melt as icèd stream:
The lustrous salvers in the moonlight gleam;
Broad golden fringe upon the carpet lies: 285
It seemed he never, never could redeem
From such a steadfast spell his lady's eyes;
So mused awhile, entoiled in woofèd fantasies.

Awakening up, he took her hollow lute,—
Tumultuous,—and, in chords that tenderest be,   290
He played an ancient ditty, long since mute,
In Provence called, "La belle dame sans mercy:"
Close to her ear touching the melody;—
Wherewith disturbed, she uttered a soft moan:
He ceased—she panted quick—and suddenly   295
Her blue affrayèd eyes wide open shone:
Upon his knees he sank, pale as smooth-sculptured stone.

Her eyes were open, but she still beheld,
Now wide awake, the vision of her sleep:
There was a painful change, that nigh expelled   300
The blisses of her dream so pure and deep,
At which fair Madeline began to weep,
And moan forth witless words with many a sigh;
While still her gaze on Porphyro would keep;
Who knelt, with joinèd hands and piteous eye,   305
Fearing to move or speak, she looked so dreamingly.

"Ah, Porphyro!" said she, "but even now
"Thy voice was at sweet tremble in mine ear,
"Made tuneable with every sweetest vow;
"And those sad eyes were spiritual and clear: 310
"How changed thou art! how pallid, chill, and drear!
"Give me that voice again, my Porphyro,
"Those looks immortal, those complainings dear!
"Oh leave me not in this eternal woe,
"For if thou diest, my Love, I know not where to go."   315

Beyond a mortal man impassioned far
At these voluptuous accents, he arose,
Ethereal, flushed, and like a throbbing star
Seen mid the sapphire heaven's deep repose;
Into her dream he melted, as the rose   320
Blendeth its odor with the violet,—
Solution sweet: meantime the frost-wind blows
Like Love's alarum pattering the sharp sleet
Against the windowpanes; St. Agnes' moon hath set.

'Tis dark: quick pattereth the flaw-blown sleet.   325
"This is no dream, my bride, my Madeline!"
'Tis dark: the icèd gusts still rave and beat:
"No dream, alas! alas! and woe is mine!
"Porphyro will leave me here to fade and pine.—
"Cruel! what traitor could thee hither bring?   330
"I curse not, for my heart is lost in thine,
"Though thou forsakest a deceivèd thing;—
"A dove forlorn and lost with sick unprunèd wing."

"My Madeline! sweet dreamer! lovely bride!
"Say, may I be for aye thy vassal blest?   335
"Thy beauty's shield, heart-shaped and vermeil dyed?
"Ah, silver shrine, here will I take my rest
"After so many hours of toil and quest,
"A famished pilgrim,—saved by miracle.
"Though I have found, I will not rob thy nest   340
"Saving of thy sweet self; if thou think'st well
"To trust, fair Madeline, to no rude infidel.

"Hark! 'tis an elfin-storm from fairy land
"Of haggard seeming, but a boon indeed:
"Arise—arise! the morning is at hand;—   345
"The bloated wassailers will never heed:—
"Let us away, my love, with happy speed;
"There are no ears to hear, or eyes to see,—
"Drowned all in Rhenish and the sleepy mead:
"Awake! arise! my love, and fearless be,   350
"For o'er the southern moors I have a home for thee."

She hurried at his words, beset with fears,
For there were sleeping dragons all around,
At glaring watch, perhaps, with ready spears—
Down the wide stairs a darkling way they found.—   355
In all the house was heard no human sound.
A chain-drooped lamp was flickering by each door;
The arras, rich with horseman, hawk, and hound,
Fluttered in the besieging wind's uproar;
And the long carpets rose along the gusty floor.   360

They glide, like phantoms, into the wide hall;
Like phantoms, to the iron porch, they glide;
Where lay the Porter, in uneasy sprawl,
With a huge empty flagon by his side:
The wakeful bloodhound rose, and shook his hide,   365
But his sagacious eye an inmate owns:
By one, and one, the bolts full easy slide:—
The chains lie silent on the footworn stones;—
The key turns, and the door upon its hinges groans.

And they are gone: aye, ages long ago   370
These lovers fled away into the storm.
That night the Baron dreamt of many a woe,
And all his warrior-guests, with shade and form
Of witch, and demon, and large coffin-worm,
Were long be-nightmared. Angela the old   375
Died palsy-twitched, with meagre face deform;
The Beadsman, after thousand aves told,
For aye unsought-for slept among his ashes cold.

1819   1820

THE EVE OF SAINT MARK

A FRAGMENT

Upon a Sabbath day it fell;
Twice holy was the Sabbath bell,
That called the folk to evening prayer;
The city streets were clean and fair
From wholesome drench of April rains;   5
And, on the western window panes
The chilly sunset faintly told
Of unmatured green vallies cold,
Of the green thorny bloomless hedge,
Of rivers new with spring-tide sedge,   10
Of primroses by sheltered rills,
And daisies on the aguish hills.
Twice holy was the Sabbath bell:
The silent streets were crowded well
With staid and pious companies,   15
Warm from their fireside orat'ries;
And moving, with demurest air,
To evensong, and vesper prayer.
Each archèd porch, and entry low,
Was filled with patient folk and slow,   20
With whispers hush, and shuffling feet,
While played the organ loud and sweet.

The bells had ceased, the prayers began,
And Bertha had not yet half done
A curious volume, patched and torn,   25
That all day long, from earliest morn,
Had taken captive her two eyes,
Among its golden broideries;
Perplexed her with a thousand things,—
The stars of Heaven, and angels' wings,   30
Martyrs in a fiery blaze,

Azure saints and silver rays,
Aaron's breastplate, and the seven
Candlesticks John saw in Heaven,
The winged Lion of Saint Mark,   35
And the Covenantal Ark,
With its many mysteries,
Cherubim and golden mice.

Bertha was a maiden fair,
Dwelling in th' old Minster-square;   40
From her fireside she could see,
Sidelong, its rich antiquity,
Far as the Bishop's garden wall;
Where sycamores and elm-trees tall,
Full-leaved, the forest had outstript,   45
By no sharp north wind ever nipt,
So sheltered by the mighty pile,
Bertha arose, and read awhile,
With forehead 'gainst the windowpane.
Again she tried, and then again,   50
Until the dusk eve left her dark
Upon the legend of St. Mark.
From pleated lawn-frill, fine and thin,
She lifted up her soft warm chin,
With aching neck and swimming eyes,   55
And dazed with saintly imageries.

All was gloom, and silent all,
Save now and then the still footfall
Of one returning homewards late,
Past the echoing minster-gate.   60
The clamorous daws, that all the day
Above treetops and towers play,
Pair by pair had gone to rest,
Each in its ancient belfry nest,

Where asleep they fall betimes,   65
To music and the drowsy chimes.

All was silent, all was gloom,
Abroad and in the homely room:
Down she sat, poor cheated soul!
And struck a swart lamp from the coal;   70
Leaned forward, with bright drooping hair
And slant book, full against the glare,
Her shadow, in uneasy guise,
Hovered about, a giant size,
On ceiling-beam and old oak chair,   75
The parrot's cage, and panel square;
And the warm angled winter-screen,
On which were many monsters seen,
Called Doves of Siam, Lima mice,
And legless birds of Paradise,   80
Macaw, and tender Av'davat,
And silken-furred Angora cat.
Untired she read, her shadow still
Glowered about, as it would fill
The room with wildest forms and shades, 85
As though some ghostly queen of spades
Had come to mock behind her back,
And dance, and ruffle her garments black.
Untired she read the legend page,
Of holy Mark, from youth to age,   90
On land, on sea, in pagan chains,
Rejoicing for his many pains.
Sometimes the learnèd eremite,
With golden star, or dagger bright,
Referred to pious poesies   95
Written in smallest crow-quill size
Beneath the text; and thus the rhyme
Was parcelled out from time to time: . . .
——"Als writith he of swevenis,
Men han beforne they waken in bliss, 100
Whanne that hir friendes thinke him
      bounde
In crimpede shroude farre under grounde;
And how a litling child mote be
A saint er its nativitie,
Gif that the modre (God her blesse!) 105
Kepen in solitarinesse,
And kissen devoute the holy croce.
Of Goddes love, and Sathan's force,—
He writith; and thinges many moe—
Of swiche thinges I may not show.   110
Bot I must tellen verilie
Somdele of Saintè Cicilie,
And chieflie what he auctorethe
Of Saintè Markis life and dethe."

At length her constant eyelids come 115
Upon the fervent martydom;
Then lastly to his holy shrine,
Exalt amid the tapers' shine
At Venice,—
Feb. 13-17, 1819   1848

WHY DID I LAUGH TO-NIGHT? NO VOICE WILL TELL

Why did I laugh tonight? No voice will
      tell:
No God, no Demon of severe response,
Deigns to reply from Heaven or from Hell.
Then to my human heart I turn at once.
Heart! Thou and I are here sad and
      alone;   5
I say, why did I laugh! O mortal pain!
O Darkness! Darkness! ever must I moan,
      To question Heaven and Hell and Heart
      in vain.
Why did I laugh? I know this Being's
      lease,
My fancy to its utmost blisses spreads; 10
Yet would I on this very midnight cease,
      And the world's gaudy ensigns see in
      shreds;
Verse, Fame, and Beauty are intense in-
      deed,
But Death intenser—Death is Life's high
      meed.
March, 1819   1848

ON A DREAM

As Hermes once took to his feathers light,
When lullèd Argus, baffled, swooned and
      slept,
So, on a Delphic reed, my idle spright,
So played, so charmed, so conquered, so
      bereft
The dragon world of all its hundred eyes; 5
And, seeing it asleep, so fled away—
Not to pure Ida with its snow-cold skies,
Nor unto Tempe, where Jove grieved a
      day;
But to that second circle of sad Hell,
Where 'mid the gust, the whirlwind, and
      the flaw   10
Of rain and hailstones, lovers need not tell
Their sorrows. Pale were the sweet lips
      I saw,
Pale were the lips I kissed, and fair the
      form
I floated with, about that melancholy
      storm.
April, 1819   1820

TO SLEEP

O soft embalmer of the still midnight,
      Shutting, with careful fingers and benign,
Our gloom-pleased eyes, embowered from
      the light,
      Enshaded in forgetfulness divine:

O soothest Sleep! if so it please thee,
   close,   5
  In midst of this thine hymn, my willing
    eyes,
Or wait the "Amen," ere thy poppy throws
  Around my bed its lulling charities.
Then save me, or the passèd day will
   shine
Upon my pillow, breeding many woes,— 10
  Save me from curious conscience, that
   still lords
Its strength for darkness, burrowing like a
   mole;
Turn the key deftly in the oilèd wards,
And seal the hushèd casket of my soul.

April, 1819   1838

ON FAME

How fevered is the man, who cannot look
  Upon his mortal days with temperate
   blood,
Who vexes all the leaves of his life's book,
  And robs his fair name of its maiden-
   hood;
It is as if the rose should pluck herself, 5
  Or the ripe plum finger its misty bloom,
As if a Naiad, like a meddling elf,
  Should darken her pure grot with muddy
   gloom,
But the rose leaves herself upon the briar,
  For winds to kiss and grateful bees to
   feed,   10
And the ripe plum still wears its dim attire,
  The undisturbèd lake has crystal space.
Why then should man, teasing the world
   for grace,
Spoil his salvation for a fierce miscreed?

April, 1819   1848

ON THE SONNET

If by dull rhymes our English must be
   chained,
And, like Andromeda, the Sonnet sweet
Fettered, in spite of painèd loveliness,
Let us find out, if we must be constrained,
Sandals more interwoven and complete 5
To fit the naked foot of Poesy:
Let us inspect the Lyre, and weigh the
   stress
Of every chord, and see what may be
   gained
By ear industrious, and attention meet;
Misers of sound and syllable, no less   10
Than Midas of his coinage, let us be

Jealous of dead leaves in the bay wreath
   crown;
So, if we may not let the Muse be free,
She will be bound with garlands of her
   own.

c. 3 May, 1819   1848

LA BELLE DAME SANS MERCY

Ah, what can ail thee, wretched wight,
  Alone and palely loitering;
The sedge is withered from the lake,
  And no birds sing.

Ah, what can ail thee, wretched wight, 5
  So haggard and so woe-begone?
The squirrel's granary is full,
  And the harvest's done.

I see a lily on thy brow,
  With anguish moist and fever dew; 10
And on thy cheek a fading rose
  Fast withereth too.

I met a Lady in the meads
  Full beautiful, a fairy's child;
Her hair was long, her foot was light, 15
  And her eyes were wild.

I set her on my pacing steed,
  And nothing else saw all day long;
For sideways would she lean, and sing
  A fairy's song.   20

I made a garland for her head,
  And bracelets too, and fragrant zone;
She looked at me as she did love,
  And made sweet moan.

She found me roots of relish sweet, 25
  And honey wild, and manna dew;
And sure in language strange she said,
  "I love thee true."

She took me to her elfin grot,
  And there she gazed and sighèd deep, 30
And there I shut her wild sad eyes—
  So kissed to sleep.

And there we slumbered on the moss,
  And there I dreamed, ah woe betide,
The latest dream I ever dreamed 35
  On the cold hill side.

I saw pale kings, and princes too,
  Pale warriors, death-pale were they all;
Who cried—"La belle Dame sans mercy
  Hath thee in thrall!"   40

I saw their starved lips in the gloom
  With horrid warning gapèd wide,
And I awoke, and found me here
  On the cold hill side.

And this is why I sojourn here   45
  Alone and palely loitering,
Though the sedge is withered from the
    lake,
  And no birds sing.

April, 1819   1820

ODE TO PSYCHE

O Goddess! hear these tuneless numbers,
    wrung
  By sweet enforcement and remembrance
    dear,
And pardon that thy secrets should be sung
Even into thine own soft-conchèd ear:
Surely I dreamt today, or did I see   5
  The wingèd Psyche with awakened eyes?
I wandered in a forest thoughtlessly,
  And, on the sudden, fainting with sur-
    prise,
Saw two fair creatures, couchèd side by side
  In deepest grass, beneath the whisp'ring
    roof   10
Of leaves and trembled blossoms, where
    there ran
  A brooklet, scarce espied:

'Mid hushed, cool-rooted flowers, fragrant-
    eyed,
  Blue, silver-white, and budded Tyrian,
They lay calm-breathing, on the bedded
    grass;   15
  Their arms embracèd, and their pinions
    too;
  Their lips touched not, but had not bade
    adieu,
As if disjoinèd by soft-handed slumber,
And ready still past kisses to outnumber
  At tender eye-dawn of aurorean love: 20
    The wingèd boy I knew;
  But who wast thou, O happy, happy
    dove?
    His Psyche true!

O latest born and loveliest vision far
  Of all Olympus' faded hierarchy!   25
Fairer than Phœbe's sapphire-regioned star,
  Or Vesper, amorous glow-worm of the
    sky;

Fairer than these, though temple thou hast
    none,
  Nor altar heaped with flowers;
Nor virgin-choir to make delicious moan 30
  Upon the midnight hours;
No voice, no lute, no pipe, no incense
    sweet
  From chain-swung censer teeming;
No shrine, no grove, no oracle, no heat
  Of pale-mouthed prophet dreaming.   35

O brightest! though too late for antique
    vows,
  Too, too late for the fond believing lyre,
When holy were the haunted forest boughs,
  Holy the air, the water, and the fire;
Yet even in these days so far retired   40
  From happy pieties, thy lucent fans,
    Fluttering among the faint Olympians,
I see, and sing, by my own eyes inspired.
So let me be thy choir, and make a moan
  Upon the midnight hours;   45
Thy voice, thy lute, thy pipe, thy incense
    sweet
  From swingèd censer teeming;
Thy shrine, thy grove, thy oracle, thy heat
  Of pale-mouthed prophet dreaming.

Yes, I will be thy priest, and build a fane 50
  In some untrodden region of my mind,
Where branchèd thoughts, new grown with
    pleasant pain
  Instead of pines shall murmur in the
    wind:
Far, far around shall those dark-clustered
    trees
  Fledge the wild-ridgèd mountains steep
    by steep;   55
And there by zephyrs, streams, and birds,
    and bees,
  The moss-lain Dryads shall be lulled to
    sleep;
And in the midst of this wide quietness
A rosy sanctuary will I dress
With the wreathed trellis of a working
    brain,   60
  With buds, and bells, and stars without
    a name,
  With all the gardener Fancy e'er could
    feign,
  Who breeding flowers, will never breed
    the same:
And there shall be for thee all soft delight
  That shadowy thought can win,   65
A bright torch, and a casement ope at
    night,
  To let the warm Love in!

April, 1819   1820

["THE LAST SONNET"]

WRITTEN ON A BLANK PAGE IN SHAKESPEARE'S POEMS, FACING "A LOVER'S COMPLAINT"

Bright star, would I were steadfast as thou
art—
Not in lone splendor hung aloft the
night
And watching, with eternal lids apart,
Like nature's patient, sleepless Eremite,
The moving waters at their priest-like
task   5
Of pure ablution round earth's human
shores,
Or gazing on the new soft-fallen mask
Of snow upon the mountains and the
moors—
No—yet still steadfast, still unchangeable,
Pillowed upon my fair love's ripening
breast,   10
To feel for ever its soft fall and swell,
Awake for ever in a sweet unrest,
Still, still to hear her tender-taken breath,
And so live ever—or else swoon to death.

c. Feb., 1819   1838

ODE ON INDOLENCE

"They toil not, neither do they spin."

I

One morn before me were three figures
seen,
With bowed necks, and joined hands,
side-faced;
And one behind the other stepped serene,
In placid sandals, and in white robes
graced;
They passed, like figures on a marble
urn,   5
When shifted round to see the other
side;
They came again; as when the urn
once more
Is shifted round, the first seen shades return;
And they were strange to me, as may
betide
With vases, to one deep in Phidian
lore.   10

II

How is it, Shadows! that I knew ye not?
How came ye muffled in so hush a mask?
Was it a silent deep-disguised plot
To steal away, and leave without a task

My idle days? Ripe was the drowsy
hour;   15
The blissful cloud of summer indolence
Benumbed my eyes; my pulse grew less
and less;
Pain had no sting, and pleasure's wreath
no flower:
O, why did ye not melt, and leave my
sense
Unhaunted quite of all but—nothing-
ness?   20

III

A third time passed they by, and, passing,
turned
Each one the face a moment whiles to
me;
Then faded, and to follow them I burned
And ached for wings, because I knew
the three;
The first was a fair Maid, and Love her
name;   25
The second was Ambition, pale of cheek,
And ever watchful with fatigued eye;
The last, whom I love more, the more of
blame
Is heaped upon her, maiden most un-
meek,—
I knew to be my demon Poesy.   30

IV

They faded, and, forsooth! I wanted
wings:
O folly! What is Love? and where is it?
And for that poor Ambition! it springs
From a man's little heart's short fever-
fit;
For Poesy!—no,—she has not a joy,—   35
At least for me,—so sweet as drowsy
noons,
And evenings steeped in honied indo-
lence;
O, for an age so sheltered from annoy,
That I may never know how change the
moons,
Or hear the voice of busy common
sense!   40

V

And once more came they by;—alas! where-
fore?
My sleep had been embroidered with dim
dreams;
My soul had been a lawn besprinkled o'er
With flowers, and stirring shades, and
baffled beams:
The morn was clouded, but no shower
fell,   45
Tho' in her lids hung the sweet tears of
May;

The open casement pressed a new-
   leaved vine,
Let in the budding warmth and throstle's
   lay;
O Shadows! 't was a time to bid farewell!
Upon your skirts had fallen no tears
   of mine.   50

VI

So, ye three Ghosts, adieu! Ye cannot raise
My head cool-bedded in the flowery
   grass;

For I would not be dieted with praise,
   A pet lamb in a sentimental farce!
Fade softly from my eyes and be once
     more   55
In masque-like figures on the dreamy
   urn;
   Farewell! I yet have visions for the
     night,
And for the day faint visions there is store;
   Vanish, ye Phantoms! from my idle
     spright,
Into the clouds, and nevermore return! 60
May, 1819   1848

ODE TO A NIGHTINGALE

My heart aches, and a drowsy numbness pains
   My sense, as though of hemlock I had drunk,
Or emptied some dull opiate to the drains
   One minute past, and Lethe-wards had sunk:
'Tis not through envy of thy happy lot,   5
   But being too happy in thy happiness,—
     That thou, light-wingèd Dryad of the trees,
       In some melodious plot
   Of beechen green, and shadows numberless,
     Singest of summer in full-throated ease.   10

O for a draught of vintage! that hath been
   Cooled a long age in the deep-delvèd earth,
Tasting of Flora and the country green,
   Dance, and Provençal song, and sunburnt mirth!
O for a beaker full of the warm South,   15
   Full of the true, the blushful Hippocrene,
     With beaded bubbles winking at the brim,
       And purple-stainèd mouth;
   That I might drink, and leave the world unseen,
     And with thee fade away into the forest dim: 20

Fade far away, dissolve, and quite forget
   What thou among the leaves hast never known,
The weariness, the fever, and the fret
   Here, where men sit and hear each other groan;
Where palsy shakes a few, sad, last grey hairs,   25
   Where youth grows pale, and spectre-thin, and dies;
     Where but to think is to be full of sorrow
       And leaden-eyed despairs,
   Where Beauty cannot keep her lustrous eyes,
     Or new Love pine at them beyond to-morrow.   30

Away! away! for I will fly to thee,
   Not charioted by Bacchus and his pards,
But on the viewless wings of Poesy,
   Though the dull brain perplexes and retards:
Already with thee! tender is the night,   35
   And haply the Queen-Moon is on her throne,
     Clustered around by all her starry Fays;
       But here there is no light,
   Save what from heaven is with the breezes blown
     Through verdurous glooms and winding mossy ways.   40

I cannot see what flowers are at my feet,
  Nor what soft incense hangs upon the boughs,
But, in embalmèd darkness, guess each sweet
  Wherewith the seasonable month endows
The grass, the thicket, and the fruit tree wild;   45
  White hawthorn, and the pastoral eglantine;
     Fast fading violets covered up in leaves;
       And mid-May's eldest child,
The coming musk rose, full of dewy wine,
  The murmurous haunt of flies on summer eves.   50

Darkling I listen; and, for many a time
  I have been half in love with easeful Death,
Called him soft names in many a musèd rhyme,
  To take into the air my quiet breath;
Now more than ever seems it rich to die,   55
  To cease upon the midnight with no pain,
     While thou art pouring forth thy soul abroad
       In such an ecstasy!
  Still wouldst thou sing, and I have ears in vain—
  To thy high requiem become a sod.   60

Thou wast not born for death, immortal Bird!
  No hungry generations tread thee down;
The voice I hear this passing night was heard
  In ancient days by emperor and clown:
Perhaps the self-same song that found a path   65
  Through the sad heart of Ruth, when, sick for home,
     She stood in tears amid the alien corn;
       The same that oft-times hath
Charmed magic casements, opening on the foam
  Of perilous seas, in faery lands forlorn.   70

Forlorn! the very word is like a bell
  To toll me back from thee to my sole self!
Adieu! the fancy cannot cheat so well
  As she is famed to do, deceiving elf.
Adieu! adieu! thy plaintive anthem fades   75
  Past the near meadows, over the still stream,
     Up the hillside; and now 'tis buried deep
       In the next valley glades:
  Was it a vision, or a waking dream?
  Fled is that music:—Do I wake or sleep?   80
May, 1819   1819

ODE ON A GRECIAN URN

Thou still unravished bride of quietness,
  Thou foster-child of silence and slow time,
Sylvan historian, who canst thus express
  A flowery tale more sweetly than our rhyme:
What leaf-fringed legend haunts about thy shape   5
  Of deities or mortals, or of both,
     In Tempe or the dales of Arcady?
  What men or gods are these? What maidens loth?
What mad pursuit? What struggle to escape?
  What pipes and timbrels? What wild ecstasy?   10

Heard melodies are sweet, but those unheard
  Are sweeter; therefore, ye soft pipes, play on;
Not to the sensual ear, but, more endeared,
  Pipe to the spirit ditties of no tone:
Fair youth, beneath the trees, thou canst not leave   15
  Thy song, nor ever can those trees be bare;
    Bold Lover, never, never canst thou kiss,
Though winning near the goal—yet, do not grieve;
  She cannot fade, though thou hast not thy bliss,
    For ever wilt thou love, and she be fair!   20

Ah, happy, happy boughs! that cannot shed
  Your leaves, nor ever bid the Spring adieu;
And, happy melodist, unwearièd,
  For ever piping songs for ever new;
More happy love! more happy, happy love!   25
  For ever warm and still to be enjoyed,
    For ever panting, and for ever young;
All breathing human passion far above,
  That leaves a heart high-sorrowful and cloyed,
    A burning forehead, and a parching tongue.   30

Who are these coming to the sacrifice?
  To what green altar, O mysterious priest,
Lead'st thou that heifer lowing at the skies,
  And all her silken flanks with garlands dressed?
What little town by river or sea-shore,   35
  Or mountain-built with peaceful citadel,
    Is emptied of its folk, this pious morn?
And, little town, thy streets for evermore
  Will silent be; and not a soul to tell
    Why thou art desolate, can e'er return.   40

O Attic shape! Fair attitude! with brede
  Of marble men and maidens overwrought,
With forest branches and the trodden weed;
  Thou, silent form, dost tease us out of thought
As doth eternity: Cold Pastoral!   45
  When old age shall this generation waste,
    Thou shalt remain, in midst of other woe
Than ours, a friend to man, to whom thou say'st,
  "Beauty is truth, truth beauty,"—that is all
    Ye know on earth, and all ye need to know.   50
May, 1819   1820

ODE ON MELANCHOLY

No, no, go not to Lethe, neither twist
  Wolfsbane, tight-rooted, for its poisonous wine;
Nor suffer thy pale forehead to be kissed
  By nightshade, ruby grape of Proserpine;
Make not your rosary of yew-berries,   5
  Nor let the beetle, nor the death-moth be
    Your mournful Psyche, nor the downy owl
A partner in your sorrow's mysteries;
  For shade to shade will come too drowsily,
    And drown the wakeful anguish of the soul.   10

But when the melancholy fit shall fall
  Sudden from heaven like a weeping cloud,
That fosters the droop-headed flowers all,
  And hides the green hill in an April shroud;
Then glut thy sorrow on a morning rose,   15
  Or on the rainbow of the salt sand-wave,
    Or on the wealth of globèd peonies;
Or if thy mistress some rich anger shows,
  Emprison her soft hand, and let her rave,
  And feed deep, deep upon her peerless eyes.   20

She dwells with Beauty—Beauty that must die;
  And Joy, whose hand is ever at his lips
Bidding adieu; and aching Pleasure nigh,
  Turning to poison while the bee-mouth sips:
Aye, in the very temple of Delight   25
  Veiled Melancholy has her sovran shrine,
    Though seen of none save him whose strenuous tongue
Can burst Joy's grape against his palate fine;
  His soul shall taste the sadness of her might,
    And be among her cloudy trophies hung.   30
May, 1819   1820

LAMIA

PART I

Upon a time, before the faery broods
Drove nymph and satyr from the prosper-
    ous woods,
Before King Oberon's bright diadem,
Sceptre, and mantle, clasped with dewy
    gem,
Frighted away the dryads and the fauns 5
From rushes green, and brakes, and cow-
    slipped lawns,
The ever-smitten Hermes empty left
His golden throne, bent warm on amorous
    theft:
From high Olympus had he stolen light,
On this side of Jove's clouds, to escape
    the sight   10
Of his great summoner, and made retreat
Into a forest on the shores of Crete.
For somewhere in that sacred island dwelt
A nymph, to whom all hoofed Satyrs knelt;
At whose white feet the languid Tritons
    poured   15
Pearls, while on land they withered and
    adored.
Fast by the springs where she to bathe was
    wont,
And in those meads where sometime she
    might haunt,
Were strewn rich gifts, unknown to any
    muse,
Though fancy's casket were unlocked to
    choose.   20

Ah, what a world of love was at her feet!
So Hermes thought, and a celestial heat
Burnt from his winged heels to either ear,
That from a whiteness, as the lily clear,
Blushed into roses 'mid his golden hair, 25
Fallen in jealous curls about his shoulders
    bare.

From vale to vale, from wood to wood,
    he flew,
Breathing upon the flowers his passion
    new,
And wound with many a river to its head,
To find where this sweet nymph prepared
    her secret bed: 30
In vain; the sweet nymph might nowhere
    be found,
And so he rested, on the lonely ground,
Pensive, and full of painful jealousies
Of the wood-gods, and even the very trees.
There as he stood, he heard a mournful
    voice,   35
Such as once heard, in gentle heart, de-
    stroys
All pain but pity: thus the lone voice
    spake:
"When from this wreathèd tomb shall I
    awake!
"When move in a sweet body fit for life,
"And love, and pleasure, and the ruddy
    strife   40
"Of hearts and lips! Ah, miserable me!"
The god, dove-footed, glided silently
Round bush and tree, soft-brushing, in his
    speed,

The taller grasses and full-flowering weed,
Until he found a palpitating snake.   45
Bright, and cirque-couchant in a dusky
  brake.

She was a gordian shape of dazzling hue,
Vermilion-spotted, golden, green, and blue;
Striped like a zebra, freckled like a pard,
Eyed like a peacock, and all crimson
  barred;   50
And full of silver moons, that, as she
  breathed,
Dissolved, or brighter shone, or inter-
  wreathed
Their lustres with the gloomier tapestries—
So rainbow-sided, touched with miseries,
She seemed, at once, some penanced lady
  elf,   55
Some demon's mistress, or the demon's self.
Upon her crest she wore a wannish fire
Sprinkled with stars, like Ariadne's tiar.
Her head was serpent, but ah, bitter-sweet!
She had a woman's mouth with all its
  pearls complete: 60
And for her eyes—what could such eyes do
  there
But weep, and weep, that they were born
  so fair?
As Proserpine still weeps for her Sicilian
  air.
Her throat was serpent, but the words she
  spake
Came, as through bubbling honey, for
  love's sake,   65
And thus; while Hermes on his pinions lay,
Like a stooped falcon ere he takes his prey.

  "Fair Hermes, crowned with feathers,
    fluttering light,
"I had a splendid dream of thee last night:
"I saw thee sitting, on a throne of gold, 70
"Among the Gods, upon Olympus old,
"The only sad one, for thou didst not hear
"The soft, lute-fingered Muses chanting
  clear,
"Nor even Apollo when he sang alone,
"Deaf to his throbbing throat's long, long
  melodious moan.   75
"I dreamt I saw thee, robed in purple
  flakes,
"Break amorous through the clouds, as
  morning breaks,
"And, swiftly as a bright Phœbean dart,
"Strike for the Cretan isle; and here thou
  art!
"Too gentle Hermes, hast thou found the
  maid?"   80
Whereat the star of Lethe not delayed
His rosy eloquence, and thus inquired:

"Thou smooth-lipped serpent, surely high
  inspired!
"Thou beauteous wreath, with melancholy
  eyes,
"Possess whatever bliss thou canst devise, 85
"Telling me only where my nymph is
  fled,—
"Where she doth breathe!"—"Bright
  planet, thou hast said,"
Returned the snake, "but seal with oaths,
  fair God!"
"I swear," said Hermes, "by my serpent
  rod,
"And by thine eyes, and by thy starry
  crown!"   90
Light flew his earnest words, among the
  blossoms blown.

Then thus again the brilliance feminine:
"Too frail of heart! for this lost nymph of
  thine,
"Free as the air, invisibly, she strays
"About these thornless wilds; her pleasant
  days   95
"She tastes unseen; unseen her nimble feet
"Leave traces in the grass and flowers
  sweet;
"From weary tendrils, and bowed branches
  green,
"She plucks the fruit unseen, she bathes
  unseen:
"And by my power is her beauty veiled 100
"To keep it unaffronted, unassailed
"By the love-glances of unlovely eyes,
"Of satyrs, fauns, and bleared Silenus' sighs.
"Pale grew her immortality, for woe
"Of all these lovers, and she grieved so 105
"I took compassion on her, bade her steep
"Her hair in weird syrups, that would keep
"Her loveliness invisible, yet free
"To wander as she loves, in liberty.
"Thou shalt behold her, Hermes, thou
  alone,   110
"If thou wilt, as thou swearest, grant my
  boon!"

Then, once again, the charmed god began
An oath, and through the serpent's ears it
  ran
Warm, tremulous, devout, psalterian.
Ravished, she lifted her Circean head, 115
Blushed a live damask, and swift-lisping
  said,
"I was a woman, let me have once more
"A woman's shape, and charming as before.
"I love a youth of Corinth—O the bliss!
"Give me my woman's form, and place me
  where he is.   120
"Stoop, Hermes, let me breathe upon thy
  brow,
"And thou shalt see thy sweet nymph even
  now."

The god on half-shut feathers sank serene,
She breathed upon his eyes, and swift was
      seen
Of both the guarded nymph near-smiling
      on the green.   125
It was no dream; or say a dream it was,
Real are the dreams of gods, and smoothly
      pass
Their pleasures in a long immortal dream.
One warm, flushed moment, hovering, it
      might seem
Dashed by the wood nymph's beauty, so he
      burned;   130
Then, lighting on the printless verdure,
      turned
To the swooned serpent, and with languid
      arm,
Delicate, put to proof the lithe Caducean
      charm.
So done, upon the nymph his eyes he bent
Full of adoring tears and blandishment, 135
And towards her stept: she, like a moon in
      wane,
Faded before him, cowered, nor could re-
      strain
Her fearful sobs, self-folding like a flower
That faints into itself at evening hour:
But the god fostering her chillèd hand, 140
She felt the warmth, her eyelids opened
      bland,
And, like new flowers at morning song of
      bees,
Bloomed, and gave up her honey to the
      lees.
Into the green-recessèd woods they flew;
Nor grew they pale, as mortal lovers do. 145

Left to herself, the serpent now began
To change; her elfin blood in madness ran,
Her mouth foamed, and the grass, there-
      with bespent,
Withered at dew so sweet and virulent;
Her eyes in torture fixed, and anguish
      drear,   150
Hot, glazed, and wide, with lid-lashes all
      sear,
Flashed phosphor and sharp sparks, with-
      out one cooling tear.
The colors all inflamed throughout her
      train,
She writhed about, convulsed with scarlet
      pain:
A deep volcanian yellow took the place 155
Of all her milder-moonèd body's grace;
And, as the lava ravishes the mead,
Spoilt all her silver mail, and golden brede;
Made gloom of all her frecklings, streaks,
      and bars,
Eclipsed her crescents, and licked up her
      stars: 160

So that, in moments few, she was undrest
Of all her sapphires, greens, and amethyst,
And rubious-argent: of all these bereft,
Nothing but pain and ugliness were left.
Still shone her crown; that vanished, also
      she   165
Melted and disappeared as suddenly;
And in the air, her new voice luting soft,
Cried, "Lycius! gentle Lycius!"—Borne
      aloft
With the bright mists about the mountains
      hoar
These words dissolved: Crete's forests heard
      no more.   170

Whither fled Lamia, now a lady bright,
A full-born beauty new and exquisite?
She fled into that valley they pass o'er
Who go to Corinth from Cenchreas' shore;
And rested at the foot of those wild
      hills,   175
The rugged founts of the Peræan rills,
And of that other ridge whose barren back
Stretches, with all its mist and cloudy rack,
South-westward to Cleone. There she stood
About a young bird's flutter from a
      wood,   180
Fair, on a sloping green of mossy tread,
By a clear pool, wherein she passionèd
To see herself escaped from so sore ills,
While her robes flaunted with the daffodils.

Ah, happy Lycius!—for she was a
      maid   185
More beautiful than ever twisted braid,
Or sighed, or blushed, or on spring-flow'red
      lea
Spread a green kirtle to the minstrelsy:
A virgin purest lipped, yet in the lore
Of love deep learned to the red heart's
      core: 190
Not one hour old, yet of sciential brain
To unperplex bliss from its neighbor pain;
Define their pettish limits, and estrange
Their points of contact, and swift counter-
      change;
Intrigue with the specious chaos, and dis-
      part   195
Its most ambiguous atoms with sure art;
As though in Cupid's college she had spent
Sweet days a lovely graduate, still unshent,
And kept his rosy terms in idle languish-
      ment.

Why this fair creature chose so fairily 200
By the wayside to linger, we shall see;
But first 'tis fit to tell how she could muse
And dream, when in the serpent prison-
      house,
Of all she list, strange or magnificent:

How, ever, where she willed, her spirit
 went;   205
Whether to faint Elysium, or where
Down through tress-lifting waves the
 Nereids fair
Wind into Thetis' bower by many a pearly
 stair;
Or where God Bacchus drains his cups
 divine,
Stretched out, at ease, beneath a glutinous
 pine;   210
Or where in Pluto's gardens palatine
Mulciber's columns gleam in far piazzian
 line.
And sometimes into cities she would send
Her dream, with feast and rioting to blend;
And once, while among mortals dreaming
 thus,   215
She saw the young Corinthian Lycius
Charioting foremost in the envious race,
Like a young Jove with calm uneager face,
And fell into a swooning love of him.
Now on the moth-time of that evening
 dim   220
He would return that way, as well she
 knew,
To Corinth from the shore; for freshly blew
The eastern soft wind, and his galley now
Grated the quaystones with her brazen
 prow
In port Cenchreas, from Egina isle 225
Fresh anchored; whither he had been
 awhile
To sacrifice to Jove, whose temple there
Waits with high marble doors for blood
 and incense rare.
Jove heard his vows, and bettered his de-
 sire;
For by some freakful chance he made
 retire   230
From his companions, and set forth to
 walk,
Perhaps grown wearied of their Corinth
 talk:
Over the solitary hills he fared,
Thoughtless at first, but ere eve's star ap-
 peared
His phantasy was lost, where reason
 fades,   235
In the calmed twilight of Platonic shades.
Lamia beheld him coming, near, more
 near—
Close to her passing, in indifference drear,
His silent sandals swept the mossy green;
So neighbored to him, and yet so unseen 240
She stood: he passed, shut up in mysteries,
His mind wrapped like his mantle, while
 her eyes
Followed his steps, and her neck regal
 white

Turned—syllabling thus, "Ah, Lycius
 bright,
"And will you leave me on the hills
 alone?   245
"Lycius, look back! and be some pity
 shown."
He did; not with cold wonder fearingly,
But Orpheus-like at an Eurydice;
For so delicious were the words she sung,
It seemed he had loved them a whole sum-
 mer long: 250
And soon his eyes had drunk her beauty
 up,
Leaving no drop in the bewildering cup,
And still the cup was full,—while he, afraid
Lest she should vanish ere his lip had paid
Due adoration, thus began to adore; 255
Her soft look growing coy, she saw his
 chain so sure:
"Leave thee alone! Look back! Ah, god-
 dess, see
"Whether my eyes can ever turn from thee!
"For pity do not this sad heart belie—
"Even as thou vanishest so shall I die. 260
"Stay! though a naiad of the rivers, stay!
"To thy far wishes will thy streams obey:
"Stay! though the greenest woods be thy
 domain,
"Alone they can drink up the morning
 rain:
"Though a descended Pleiad, will not
 one   265
"Of thine harmonious sisters keep in tune
"Thy spheres, and as thy silver proxy
 shine?
"So sweetly to these ravished ears of mine
"Came thy sweet greeting, that if thou
 shouldst fade
"Thy memory will waste me to a
 shade:—   270
"For pity do not melt!"—"If I should stay,"
Said Lamia, "here, upon this floor of clay,
"And pain my steps upon these flowers too
 rough,
"What canst thou say or do of charm
 enough
"To dull the nice remembrance of my
 home?   275
"Thou canst not ask me with thee here to
 roam
"Over these hills and vales, where no joy
 is,—
"Empty of immortality and bliss!
"Thou art a scholar, Lycius, and must
 know
"That finer spirits cannot breathe below 280
"In human climes, and live. Alas! poor
 youth,
"What taste of purer air hast thou to
 soothe

"My essence? What serener palaces,
"Where I may all my many senses please,
"And by mysterious sleights a hundred
    thirsts appease?   285
"It cannot be—Adieu!" So said, she rose
Tiptoe with white arms spread. He, sick
    to lose
The amorous promise of her lone com-
    plain,
Swooned, murmuring of love, and pale
    with pain.
The cruel lady, without any show   290
Of sorrow for her tender favorite's woe,
But rather, if her eyes could brighter be,
With brighter eyes and slow amenity,
Put her new lips to his, and gave afresh
The life she had so tangled in her mesh:295
And as he from one trance was wakening
Into another, she began to sing,
Happy in beauty, life, and love, and every
    thing,
A song of love, too sweet for earthly lyres,
While, like held breath, the stars drew in
    their panting fires.   300
And then she whispered in such trembling
    tone,
As those who, safe together met alone
For the first time through many anguished
    days,
Use other speech than looks; bidding him
    raise
His drooping head, and clear his soul of
    doubt,   305
For that she was a woman, and without
Any more subtle fluid in her veins
Than throbbing blood, and that the self-
    same pains
Inhabited her frail-strung heart as his.
And next she wondered how his eyes could
    miss   310
Her face so long in Corinth, where, she
    said,
She dwelt but half retired, and there had
    led
Days happy as the gold coin could invent
Without the aid of love; yet in content
Till she saw him, as once she passed him
    by,   315
Where 'gainst a column he leant thought-
    fully
At Venus' temple porch, 'mid baskets
    heaped
Of amorous herbs and flowers, newly
    reaped
Late on that eve, as 'twas the night before
The Adonian feast; whereof she saw no
    more,   320
But wept alone those days, for why should
    she adore?
Lycius from death awoke into amaze.

To see her still, and singing so sweet lays;
Then from amaze into delight he fell
To hear her whisper woman's lore so
    well;   325
And every word she spake enticed him on
To unperplexed delight and pleasure
    known.
Let the mad poets say whate'er they please
Of the sweets of fairies, Peris, goddesses,
There is not such a treat among them
    all,   330
Haunters of cavern, lake, and waterfall,
As a real woman, lineal indeed
From Pyrrha's pebbles or old Adam's seed.
Thus gentle Lamia judged, and judged
    aright,
That Lycius could not love in half a
    fright,   335
So threw the goddess off, and won his heart
More pleasantly by playing woman's part,
With no more awe than what her beauty
    gave,
That, while it smote, still guaranteed to
    save,
Lycius to all made eloquent reply,   340
Marrying to every word a twin-born sigh;
And last, pointing to Corinth, asked her
    sweet,
If 'twas too far that night for her soft feet.
The way was short, for Lamia's eagerness
Made, by a spell, the triple league de-
    crease   345
To a few paces; not at all surmised
By blinded Lycius, so in her comprised.
They passed the city gates, he knew not
    how,
So noiseless, and he never thought to know.

    As men talk in a dream, so Corinth
    all,   350
Throughout her palaces imperial,
And all her populous streets and temples
    lewd,
Muttered, like tempest in the distance
    brewed,
To the wide-spreaded night above her
    towers,
Men, women, rich and poor, in the cool
    hours,   355
Shuffled their sandals o'er the pavement
    white,
Companioned or alone; while many a light
Flared, here and there, from wealthy festi-
    vals,
And threw their moving shadows on the
    walls,
Or found them clustered in the corniced
    shade   360
Of some arched temple door, or dusky
    colonnade.

Muffling his face, of greeting friends in
　　fear,
Her fingers he pressed hard, as one came
　　near
With curled gray beard, sharp eyes, and
　　smooth bald crown,
Slow-stepped, and robed in philosophic
　　gown:　　　　　　　　　　　　　　365
Lycius shrank closer, as they met and past,
Into his mantle, adding wings to haste,
While hurried Lamia trembled: "Ah," said
　　he,
"Why do you shudder, love, so ruefully?
"Why does your tender palm dissolve in
　　dew?"—　　　　　　　　　　　　370
"I'm wearied," said fair Lamia: "tell me
　　who
"Is that old man?　I cannot bring to mind
"His features:—Lycius! wherefore did you
　　blind
"Yourself from his quick eyes?"　Lycius re-
　　plied,
" 'Tis Apollonius sage, my trusty guide 375
"And good instructor; but tonight he seems
"The ghost of folly haunting my sweet
　　dreams."

While yet he spake they had arrived be-
　　fore
A pillared porch, with loftly portal door,
Where hung a silver lamp, whose phosphor
　　glow　　　　　　　　　　　　　　380
Reflected in the slabbed steps below,
Mild as a star in water; for so new,
And so unsullied was the marble's hue,
So through the crystal polish, liquid fine,
Ran the dark veins, that none but feet
　　divine　　　　　　　　　　　　　385
Could e'er have touched there.　Sounds
　　Æolian
Breathed from the hinges. as the ample
　　span
Of the wide doors disclosed a place un-
　　known
Some time to any, but those two alone,
And a few Persian mutes, who that same
　　year　　　　　　　　　　　　　　390
Were seen about the markets: none knew
　　where
They could inhabit; the most curious
Were foiled, who watched to trace them to
　　their house:
And but the flitter-winged verse must tell,
For truth's sake, what woe afterwards be-
　　fell,　　　　　　　　　　　　　395
'Twould humor many a heart to leave them
　　thus,
Shut from the busy world of more incredu-
　　lous.

PART II

Love in a hut, with water and a crust,
Is—Love, forgive us!—cinders, ashes, dust;
Love in a palace is perhaps at last
More grievous torment than a hermit's
　　fast:—
That is a doubtful tale from fairy land, 5
Hard for the non-elect to understand.
Had Lycius lived to hand his story down,
He might have given the moral a fresh
　　frown,
Or clenched it quite: but too short was
　　their bliss
To breed distrust and hate, that make the
　　soft voice hiss.　　　　　　　　　10
Besides, there, nightly, with terrific glare,
Love, jealous grown of so complete a pair,
Hovered and buzzed his wings, with fearful
　　roar,
Above the lintel of their chamber door,
And down the passage cast a glow upon the
　　floor.　　　　　　　　　　　　15

For all this came a ruin: side by side
They were enthronèd, in the even tide,
Upon a couch, near to a curtaining
Whose airy texture, from a golden string,
Floated into the room, and let appear　20
Unveiled the summer heaven, blue and
　　clear,
Betwixt two marble shafts:—there they re-
　　posed,
Where use had made it sweet, with eyelids
　　closed,
Saving a tithe which love still open kept,
That they might see each other while they
　　almost slept;　　　　　　　　　25
When from the slope side of a suburb hill,
Deafening the swallow's twitter, came a
　　thrill
Of trumpets—Lycius started—the sounds
　　fled,
But left a thought, a buzzing in his head.
For the first time, since first he harbored
　　in　　　　　　　　　　　　　　30
That purple-lined palace of sweet sin,
His spirit passed beyond its golden bourn
Into the noisy world almost forsworn.
The lady, ever watchful, penetrant,
Saw this with pain, so arguing a want　35
Of something more, more than her empery
Of joys; and she began to moan and sigh
Because he mused beyond her, knowing
　　well
That but a moment's thought is passion's
　　passing bell.
"Why do you sigh, fair creature?" whis-
　　pered he:　　　　　　　　　　40

"Why do you think?" returned she ten-
    derly:
"You have deserted me;—where am I now?
"Not in your heart while care weighs on
    your brow:
"No, no, you have dismissed me; and I go
"From your breast houseless: aye, it must
    be so."   45
He answered, bending to her open eyes,
Where he was mirrored small in paradise,
"My silver planet, both of eve and morn!
"Why will you plead yourself so sad for-
    lorn,
"While I am striving how to fill my heart 50
"With deeper crimson, and a double smart?
"How to entangle, trammel up, and snare
"Your soul in mine, and labyrinth you
    there
"Like the hid scent in an unbudded rose?
"Aye, a sweet kiss—you see your mighty
    woes.   55
"My thoughts! shall I unveil them? Listen
    then!
"What mortal hath a prize, that other men
"May be confounded and abashed withal,
"But lets it sometimes pace abroad majest-
    ical,
"And triumph, as in thee I should rejoice 60
"Amid the hoarse alarm of Corinth's voice.
"Let my foes choke, and my friends shout
    afar,
"While through the thronged streets your
    bridal car
"Wheels round its dazzling spokes."—The
    lady's cheek
Trembled; she nothing said, but, pale and
    meek,   65
Arose and knelt before him, wept a rain
Of sorrows at his words; at last with
    pain
Beseeching him, the while his hand she
    wrung,
To change his purpose. He thereat was
    stung,
Perverse, with stronger fancy to reclaim 70
Her wild and timid nature to his aim:
Besides, for all his love, in self despite,
Against his better self, he took delight
Luxurious in her sorrows, soft and new.
His passion, cruel grown, took on a hue 75
Fierce and sanguineous as 'twas possible
In one whose brow had no dark veins to
    swell.
Fine was the mitigated fury, like
Apollo's presence when in act to strike
The serpent—Ha, the serpent! certes, she 80
Was none. She burnt, she loved the
    tyranny,
And, all subdued, consented to the hour

When to the bridal he should lead his
    paramour.
Whispering in midnight silence, said the
    youth,
"Sure some sweet name thou hast, though,
    by my truth,   85
"I have not asked it, ever thinking thee
"Not mortal, but of heavenly progeny,
"As still I do. Hast any mortal name,
"Fit appellation for this dazzling frame?
"Or friends or kinsfolk on the citied
    earth,   90
"To share our marriage feast and nuptial
    mirth?"
"I have no friends," said Lamia, "no, not
    one;
"My presence in wide Corinth hardly
    known:
"My parents' bones are in their dusty urns
"Sepulchred, where no kindled incense
    burns,   95
"Seeing all their luckless race are dead,
    save me,
"And I neglect the holy rite for thee.
"Even as you list invite your many guests;
"But if, as now it seems, your vision rests
"With any pleasure on me, do not bid 100
"Old Apollonius—from him keep me hid."
Lycius, perplexed at words so blind and
    blank,
Made close inquiry; from whose touch she
    shrank,
Feigning a sleep; and he to the dull shade
Of deep sleep in a moment was betrayed. 105

    It was the custom then to bring away
The bride from home at blushing shut of
    day,
Veiled, in a chariot, heralded along
By strewn flowers, torches, and a marriage
    song,
With other pageants: but this fair un-
    known   110
Had not a friend. So being left alone,
(Lycius was gone to summon all his kin)
And knowing surely she could never win
His foolish heart from its mad pompous-
    ness,
She set herself, high-thoughted, how to
    dress   115
The misery in fit magnificence.
She did so, but 'tis doubtful how and
    whence
Came, and who were her subtle servitors.
About the halls, and to and from the doors,
There was a noise of wings, till in short
    space   120
The glowing banquet room shone with
    wide-arched grace.

A haunting music, sole perhaps and lone
Supportress of the fairy roof, made moan
Throughout, as fearful the whole charm
    might fade.
Fresh carvèd cedar, mimicking a glade   125
Of palm and plantain, met from either
    side,
High in the midst, in honor of the bride:
Two palms and then two plantains, and so
    on,
From either side their stems branched one
    to one
All down the aisled place; and beneath
    all   130
There ran a stream of lamps straight on
    from wall to wall.
So canopied, lay an untasted feast
Teeming with odors. Lamia, regal dressed,
Silently paced about, and as she went,
In pale contented sort of discontent,   135
Missioned her viewless servants to enrich
The fretted splendor of each nook and
    niche.
Between the tree-stems, marbled plain at
    first,
Came jasper panels; then, anon, there burst
Forth creeping imagery of slighter trees, 140
And with the larger wove in small intrica-
    cies.
Approving all, she faded at self-will,
And shut the chamber up, close, hushed
    and still,
Complete and ready for the revels rude,
When dreadful guests would come to spoil
    her solitude.   145

The day appeared, and all the gossip
    rout.
O senseless Lycius! Madman! wherefore
    flout
The silent-blessing fate, warm cloistered
    hours,
And show to common eyes these secret
    bowers?
The herd approached; each guest, with
    busy brain,   150
Arriving at the portal, gazed amain,
And entered marveling: for they knew the
    street,
Remembered it from childhood all com-
    plete
Without a gap, yet ne'er before had seen
That royal porch, that high-built fair de-
    mesne;   155
So in they hurried all, amazed, curious,
    and keen:
Save one, who looked thereon with eye
    severe.
And with calm-planted steps walked in
    austere;

'Twas Apollonius: something too he
    laughed,
As though some knotty problem, that had
    daft   160
His patient thought, had now begun to
    thaw,
And solve, and melt:—'twas just as he fore-
    saw.

He met within the murmurous vestibule
His young disciple. " 'Tis no common rule,
Lycius," said he, "for uninvited guest   165
"To force himself upon you, and infest
"With an unbidden presence the bright
    throng
"Of younger friends; yet must I do this
    wrong,
"And you forgive me." Lycius blushed, and
    led
The old man through the inner doors
    broad-spread;   170
With reconciling words and courteous mien
Turning into sweet milk the sophist's
    spleen.

Of wealthy lustre was the banquet room,
Filled with pervading brilliance and per-
    fume;
Before each lucid panel fuming stood   175
A censer fed with myrrh and spicèd wood,
Each by a sacred tripod held aloft.
Whose slender feet wide-swerved upon the
    soft
Wool-woofed carpets: fifty wreaths of
    smoke
From fifty censers their light voyage took 180
To the high roof, still mimicked as they
    rose
Along the mirrored walls by twin clouds
    odorous.
Twelve sphered tables, by silk seats in-
    sphered,
High as the level of a man's breast reared
On libbard's paws, upheld the heavy
    gold   185
Of cups and goblets, and the store thrice
    told
Of Ceres' horn, and, in huge vessels, wine
Come from the gloomy tun with merry
    shine.
Thus loaded with a feast the tables stood,
Each shrining in the midst the image of a
    god.   190

When in an antechamber every guest
Had felt the cold full sponge to pleasure
    pressed,
By minist'ring slaves, upon his hands and
    feet,
And fragrant oils with ceremony meet

Poured on his hair, they all moved to the
   feast   195
In white robes, and themselves in order
   placed
Around the silken couches, wondering
Whence all this mighty cost and blaze of
   wealth could spring.

Soft went the music the soft air along,
While fluent Greek a voweled undersong 200
Kept up among the guests, discoursing low
At first, for scarcely was the wine at flow;
But when the happy vintage touched their
   brains,
Louder they talk, and louder come the
   strains
Of powerful instruments:—the gorgeous
   dyes,   205
The space, the splendor of the draperies,
The roof of awful richness, nectarous cheer,
Beautiful slaves, and Lamia's self, appear,
Now, when the wine has done its rosy deed,
And every soul from human trammels
   freed,   210
No more so strange; for merry wine, sweet
   wine,
Will make Elysian shades not too fair, too
   divine.
Soon was God Bacchus at meridian height;
Flushed were their cheeks, and bright eyes
   double bright:
Garlands of every green, and every scent 215
From vales deflowered, or forest trees
   branch-rent,
In baskets of bright osiered gold were
   brought
High as the handles heaped, to suit the
   thought
Of every guest; that each, as he did please,
Might fancy-fit his brows, silk-pillowed at
   his ease.   220

What wreath for Lamia? What for
   Lycius?
What for the sage, old Apollonius?
Upon her aching forehead be there hung
The leaves of willow and of adder's tongue;
And for the youth, quick, let us strip for
   him   225
The thyrsus, that his watching eyes may
   swim
Into forgetfulness; and, for the sage,
Let spear grass and the spiteful thistle wage
War on his temples. Do not all charms fly
At the mere touch of cold philosophy? 230
There was an awful rainbow once in
   heaven:
We know her woof, her texture; she is
   given
In the dull catalogue of common things.

Philosophy will clip an Angel's wings,
Conquer all mysteries by rule and line, 235
Empty the haunted air, and gnomèd mine—
Unweave a rainbow, as its erewhile made
The tender-personed Lamia melt into a
   shade.

By her glad Lycius sitting, in chief place,
Scarce saw in all the room another face, 240
Till, checking his love trance, a cup he took
Full brimmed, and opposite sent forth a
   look
'Cross the broad table, to beseech a glance
From his old teacher's wrinkled counte-
   nance,
And pledge him. The bald-head phi-
   losopher   245
Had fixed his eye, without a twinkle or stir
Full on the alarmed beauty of the bride,
Brow-beating her fair form, and troubling
   her sweet pride.
Lycius then pressed her hand, with devout
   touch,
As pale it lay upon the rosy couch: 250
'Twas icy, and the cold ran through his
   veins;
Then sudden it grew hot, and all the pains
Of an unnatural heat shot to his heart.
"Lamia, what means this? Wherefore dost
   thou start?
"Know'st thou that man?" Poor Lamia
   answered not.   255
He gazed into her eyes, and not a jot
Owned they the lovelorn piteous appeal:
More, more he gazed: his human senses
   reel:
Some hungry spell that loveliness absorbs;
There was no recognition in those orbs. 260
"Lamia!" he cried—and no soft-toned
   reply.
The many heard, and the loud revelry
Grew hush; the stately music no more
   breathes;
The myrtle sickened in a thousand wreaths.
By faint degrees, voice, lute, and pleasure
   ceased;   265
A deadly silence step by step increased
Until it seemed a horrid presence there,
And not a man but felt the terror in his
   hair.
"Lamia!" he shrieked; and nothing but the
   shriek
With its sad echo did the silence break. 270
"Begone, foul dream!" he cried, gazing
   again
In the bride's face, where now no azure
   vein
Wandered on fair-spaced temples; no soft
   bloom
Misted the cheek; no passion to illume

The deep-recessed vision: — all was
    blight;
                                        275
Lamia, no longer fair, there sat a deadly
    white.
"Shut, shut those juggling eyes, thou ruth-
    less man!
"Turn them aside, wretch! or the righteous
    ban
"Of all the gods, whose dreadful images
"Here represent their shadowy pres-
    ences,
                                        280
"May pierce them on the sudden with the
    thorn
"Of painful blindness; leaving thee forlorn,
"In trembling dotage to the feeblest fright
"Of conscience, for their long-offended
    might,
"For all thine impious proud-heart sophis-
    tries,
                                        285
"Unlawful magic, and enticing lies.
"Corinthians! look upon that gray-beard
    wretch!
"Mark how, possessed, his lashless eyelids
    stretch
"Around his demon eyes! Corinthians, see!
"My sweet bride withers at their po-
    tency."
                                        290
"Fool!" said the sophist in an undertone
Gruff with contempt; which a death-nigh-
    ing moan
From Lycius answered, as heart-struck and
    lost,
He sank supine beside the aching ghost.
"Fool! Fool!" repeated he, while his eyes
    still
                                        295
Relented not, nor moved; "from every ill
"Of life have I preserved thee to this day,
"And shall I see thee made a serpent's
    prey?"
Then Lamia breathed death breath; the
    sophist's eye,
Like a sharp spear, went through her ut-
    terly,
                                        300
Keen, cruel, perceant, stinging: she, as well
As her weak hand could any meaning tell,
Motioned him to be silent; vainly so,
He looked and looked again a level—No!
"A serpent!" echoed he; no sooner said, 305
Than with a frightful scream she vanished:
And Lycius' arms were empty of delight,
As were his limbs of life, from that same
    night.
On the high couch he lay!—his friends
    came round—
Supported him—no pulse, or breath they
    found,
                                        310
And, in its marriage robe, the heavy body
    wound.

July-Sept., 1819   1820

TO AUTUMN

Season of mists and mellow fruitfulness,
    Close bosom-friend of the maturing sun;
Conspiring with him how to load and bless
    With fruit the vines that round the
        thatch-eves run;
To bend with apples the mossed cottage
    trees,   5
    And fill all fruit with ripeness to the
        core;
        To swell the gourd, and plump the
            hazel shells
    With a sweet kernel; to set budding
        more,
And still more, later flowers for the bees,
Until they think warm days will never
    cease,   10
    For Summer has o'er-brimmed their
        clammy cells.

Who hath not seen thee oft amid thy store?
    Sometimes whoever seeks abroad may
        find
Thee sitting careless on a granary floor,
    Thy hair soft-lifted by the winnowing
        wind;   15
Or on a half-reaped furrow sound asleep,
    Drowsed with the fume of poppies, while
        thy hook
        Spares the next swath and all its
            twinèd flowers:
And sometimes like a gleaner thou dost
    keep
    Steady thy laden head across a brook; 20
Or by a cider-press, with patient look,
    Thou watchest the last oozings hours
        by hours.

Where are the songs of Spring? Aye, where
    are they?
    Think not of them, thou hast thy music
        too,—
While barrèd clouds bloom the soft-dying
    day,   25
    And touch the stubble plains with rosy
        hue;
Then in a wailful choir the small gnats
    mourn
    Among the river sallows, borne aloft
        Or sinking as the light wind lives or
            dies;
And full-grown lambs loud bleat from hilly
    bourn;   30
    Hedge-crickets sing; and now with treble
        soft
The red-breast whistles from a garden-
    croft;
    And gathering swallows twitter in the
        skies.

Sept. 19, 1819   1820

THE FALL OF HYPERION, A VISION

CANTO I

Fanatics have their dreams, wherewith
   they weave
A paradise for a sect; the savage, too,
From forth the loftiest 'fashion of his sleep
Guesses at heaven; pity these have not
Traced upon vellum or wild Indian leaf 5
The shadows of melodious utterance,
But bare of laurel they live, dream, and
   die;
For Poesy alone can tell her dreams,—
With the fine spell of words alone can save
Imagination from the sable chain   10
And dumb enchantment. Who alive can
   say,
"Thou art no Poet—may'st not tell thy
   dreams?"
Since every man whose soul is not a clod
Hath visions and would speak, if he had
   loved,
And been well nurtured in his mother
   tongue.   15
Whether the dream now purposed to re-
   hearse
Be poet's or fanatic's will be known
When this warm scribe, my hand, is in the
   grave.

   Methought I stood where trees of every
   clime,
Palm, myrtle, oak, and sycamore, and
   beech,   20
With plantane and spice-blossoms, made a
   screen,
In neighborhood of fountains (by the noise
Soft-showering in my ears), and (by the
   touch
Of scent) not far from roses. Turning
   round
I saw an arbor with a drooping roof   25
Of trellis vines, and bells, and larger
   blooms,
Like floral censers, swinging light in air;
Before its wreathèd doorway, on a mound
Of moss, was spread a feast of summer
   fruits,
Which, nearer seen, seemed refuse of a
   meal   30
By angel tasted or our Mother Eve;
For empty shells were scattered on the
   grass,
And grape-stalks but half-bare, and rem-
   nants more
Sweet-smelling, whose pure kinds I could
   not know.

Still was more plenty than the fabled
   horn   35
Thrice emptied could pour forth at ban-
   queting
For Proserpine returned to her own fields,
Where the white heifers low. And appe-
   tite,
More yearning than on earth I ever felt,
Growing within, I ate deliciously,—   40
And, after not long, thirsted; for thereby
Stood a cool vessel of transparent juice
Sipped by the wandered bee, the which I
   took,
And pledging all the mortals of the world,
And all the dead whose names are in our
   lips,   45
Drank. That full draught is parent of my
   theme.
No Asian poppy nor elixir fine
Of the soon-fading, jealous, Caliphat,
No poison gendered in close monkish cell,
To thin the scarlet conclave of old men, 50
Could so have rapt unwilling life away.
Among the fragrant husks and berries
   crushed
Upon the grass, I struggled hard against
The domineering potion, but in vain:
The cloudy swoon came on, and down I
   sank,   55
Like a Silenus on an antique vase.
How long I slumbered 'tis a chance to
   guess.
When sense of life returned, I started up
As if with wings, but the fair trees were
   gone,
The mossy mound and arbor were no
   more: 60
I looked around upon the carvèd sides
Of an old sanctuary, with roof august,
Builded so high, it seemed that filmèd
   clouds
Might spread beneath as o'er the stars of
   heaven.
So old the place was, I remembered none 65
The like upon the earth: what I had seen
Of gray cathedrals, buttressed walls, rent
   towers,
The superannuations of sunk realms,
Or Nature's rocks toiled hard in waves and
   winds,
Seemed but the faulture of decrepit
   things   70
To that eternal domèd monument.
Upon the marble at my feet there lay
Store of strange vessels and large draperies,
Which needs had been of dyed asbestos
   wove,
Or in that place the moth could not cor-
   rupt,   75
So white the linen, so, in some, distinct

Ran imageries from a sombre loom.
All in a mingled heap confused there lay
Robes, golden tongs, censer and chafing-
     dish,
Girdles, and chains, and holy jewelries.   80

     Turning from these with awe, once more
         I raised
My eyes to fathom the space every way:
The embossèd roof, the silent massy range
Of columns north and south, ending in
     mist
Of nothing; then to eastward, where black
     gates   85
Were shut against the sunrise evermore.
Then to the west I looked, and saw far off
An image, huge of feature as a cloud,
At level of whose feet an altar slept,
To be approached on either side by steps 90
And marble balustrade, and patient travail
To count with toil the innumerable de-
     grees.
Towards the altar sober-paced I went,
Repressing haste as too unholy there;
And, coming nearer, saw beside the shrine 95
One ministering; and there arose a flame.
When in mid-day the sickening east wind
Shifts sudden to the south, the small warm
     rain
Melts out the frozen incense from all
     flowers,
And fills the air with so much pleasant
     health 100
That even the dying man forgets his
     shroud;—
Even so that lofty sacrificial fire,
Sending forth Maian incense, spread
     around
Forgetfulness of everything but bliss,
And clouded all the altar with soft
     smoke;   105
From whose white fragrant curtains thus I
     heard
Language pronounced: "If thou canst not
     ascend
These steps, die on that marble where thou
     art.
Thy flesh, near cousin to the common dust,
Will parch for lack of nutriment; thy
     bones   110
Will wither in few years, and vanish so
That not the quickest eye could find a
     grain
Of what thou now art on that pavement
     cold.
The sands of thy short life are spent this
     hour,
And no hand in the universe can turn   115
Thy hour-glass, if these gummèd leaves be
     burnt

Ere thou canst mount up these immortal
     steps."
I heard, I looked: two senses both at once,
So fine, so subtle, felt the tyranny
Of that fierce threat and the hard task
     proposed.   120
Prodigious seemed the toil; the leaves were
     yet
Burning, when suddenly a palsied chill
Struck from the pavèd level up my limbs,
And was ascending quick to put cold grasp
Upon those streams that pulse beside the
     throat.   125
I shrieked, and the sharp anguish of my
     shriek
Stung my own ears; I strove hard to escape
The numbness, strove to gain the lowest
     step.
Slow, heavy, deadly was my pace: the cold
Grew stifling, suffocating at the heart;   130
And when I clasped my hands I felt them
     not.
One minute before death my iced foot
     touched
The lowest stair; and, as if touched, life
     seemed
To pour in at the toes; I mounted up
As once fair angels on a ladder flew   135
From the green turf to heaven. "Holy
     Power,"
Cried I, approaching near the hornèd
     shrine,
"What am I that should so be saved from
     death?
"What am I that another death come not
"To choke my utterance sacrilegious,
     here?"   140
Then said the veilèd shadow: "Thou hast
     felt
"What 'tis to die and live again before
"Thy fated hour; that thou hadst power to
     do so
"Is thine own safety; thou hast dated on
"Thy doom." "High Prophetess," said I,
     "purge off,   145
"Benign, if so it please thee, my mind's
     film."
"None can usurp this height," returned
     that shade,
"But those to whom the miseries of the
     world
"Are misery, and will not let them rest.
"All else who find a haven in the world, 150
"Where they may thoughtless sleep away
     their days,
"If by a chance into this fane they come,
"Rot on the pavement where thou rottedst
     half."
"Are there not thousands in the world,"
     said I,

Encouraged by the sooth voice of the
    shade, 155
"Who love their fellows even to the death,
"Who feel the giant agony of the world,
"And more, like slaves to poor humanity,
"Labor for mortal good? I sure should see
"Other men here, but I am here alone." 160
"Those whom thou spak'st of are no
    vision'ries,"
Rejoined that voice; "they are no dreamers
    weak;
"They seek no wonder but the human face,
"No music but a happy-noted voice:
"They come not here; they have no thought
    to come; 165
"And thou art here, for thou art less than
    they.
"What benefit canst thou, or all thy tribe,
"To the great world? Thou art a dreaming
    thing,
"A fever of thyself: think of the earth;
"What bliss, even in hope, is there for
    thee? 170
"What haven? every creature hath its
    home,
"Every sole man hath days of joy and pain,
"Whether his labors be sublime or low—
"The pain alone, the joy alone, distinct:
"Only the dreamer venoms all his days, 175
"Bearing more woe than all his sins de-
    serve.
"Therefore, that happiness be somewhat
    shared,
"Such things as thou art are admitted oft
"Into like gardens thou didst pass erewhile,
"And suffered in these temples: for that
    cause 180
"Thou standest safe beneath this statue's
    knees."
"That I am favored for unworthiness,
"By such propitious parley medicined
"In sickness not ignoble, I rejoice,
"Aye, and could weep for love of such
    award." 185
So answered I, continuing, "If it please,
"Majestic shadow, tell me: sure not all
"Those melodies sung into the world's ear
"Are useless; sure a poet is a sage;
"A humanist, physician to all men. 190
"That I am none I feel, as vultures feel
"They are no birds when eagles are abroad.
"What am I then: Thou spakest of my
    tribe:
"What tribe?" The tall shade veiled in
    drooping white
Then spake. so much more earnest, that
    the breath 195
Moved the thin linen folds that drooping
    hung
About a golden censer from the hand

Pendent—"Art thou not of the dreamer
    tribe?
"The poet and the dreamer are distinct,
"Diverse, sheer opposite, antipodes. 200
"The one pours out a balm upon the
    world,
"The other vexes it." Then shouted I
Spite of myself, and with a Pythia's spleen.
"Apollo! faded! O far flown Apollo!
"Where is thy misty pestilence to creep 205
"Into the dwellings, through the door cran-
    nies
"Of all mock lyrists, large self worshippers
"And careless Hectorers in proud bad verse.
"Though I breathe death with them it will
    be life
"To see them sprawl before me into
    graves. 210
"Majestic shadow, tell me where I am,
"Whose altar this, for whom this incense
    curls;
"What image this whose face I cannot see
"For the broad marble knees; and who
    thou art,
"Of accent feminine so courteous?" 215

Then the tall shade, in drooping linens
    veiled,
Spoke out, so much more earnest, that her
    breath
Stirred the thin folds of gauze that droop-
    ing hung
About a golden censer from her hand
Pendent; and by her voice I knew she
    shed 220
Long-treasured tears. "This temple, sad
    and lone,
"Is all spared from the thunder of a war
"Foughten long since by giant hierarchy
"Against rebellion: this old image here,
"Whose carvèd features wrinkled as he
    fell, 225
"Is Saturn's; I, Moneta, left supreme,
"Sole priestess of this desolation."
I had no words to answer, for my tongue,
Useless, could find about its roofèd home
No syllable of a fit majesty 230
To make rejoinder to Moneta's mourn:
There was a silence, while the altar's blaze
Was fainting for sweet food. I looked
    thereon,
And on the pavèd floor, where nigh were
    piled
Fagots of cinnamon, and many heaps 235
Of other crispèd spicewood: then again
I looked upon the altar, and its horns
Whitened with ashes, and its lang'rous
    flame,
And then upon the offerings again;
And so, by turns, till sad Moneta cried: 240

"The sacrifice is done, but not the less
"Will I be kind to thee for thy good will.
"My power, which to me is still a curse,
"Shall be to thee a wonder; for the scenes
"Still swooning vivid through my globèd
    brain,   245
"With an electral changing misery,
"Thou shalt with these dull mortal eyes
    behold
"Free from all pain, if wonder pain thee
    not."
As near as an immortal's spherèd words
Could to a mother's soften were these
    last: 250
And yet I had a terror of her robes,
And chiefly of the veils that from her brow
Hung pale, and curtained her in mysteries,
That made my heart too small to hold its
    blood.
This saw that Goddess, and with sacred
    hand   255
Parted the veils. Then saw I a wan face,
Not pined by human sorrows, but bright-
    blanched
By an immortal sickness which kills not;
It works a constant change, which happy
    death
Can put no end to; deathwards progress-
    ing   260
To no death was that visage; it had passed
The lily and the snow; and beyond these
I must not think now, though I saw that
    face.
But for her eyes I should have fled away;
They held me back with a benignant
    light,   265
Soft mitigated by divinest lids
Half-closed, and visionless entire they
    seemed
Of all external things; they saw me not,
But, in blank splendor, beamed, like the
    mild moon,
Who comforts those she sees not, who
    knows not   270
What eyes are upward cast. As I had found
A grain of gold upon a mountain's side,
And, twinged with avarice, strained out my
    eyes
To search its sullen entrails rich with ore,
So, at the view of sad Moneta's brow,   275
I ached to see what things the hollow brow
Behind enwombed: what high tragedy
In the dark secret chambers of her skull
Was acting, that could give so dread a
    stress
To her cold lips, and fill with such a
    light   280
Her planetary eyes, and touch her voice
With such a sorrow.—"Shade of Memory!"
Cried I, with act adorant at her feet,

"By all the gloom hung round thy fallen
    house,
"By this last temple, by the golden age, 285
"By great Apollo, thy dear foster child,
"And by thyself, forlorn divinity,
"The pale Omega of a withered race,
"Let me behold, according as thou saidst,
"What in thy brain so ferments to and
    fro!"   290
No sooner had this conjuration past
My devout lips, than side by side we stood
(Like a stunt bramble by a solemn pine)
Deep in the shady sadness of a vale
Far sunken from the healthy breath of
    morn,   295
Far from the fiery noon and eve's one star.
Onward I looked beneath the gloomy
    boughs,
And saw what first I thought an image
    huge,
Like to the image pedestalled so high
In Saturn's temple; then Moneta's voice 300
Came brief upon mine ear. "So Saturn sat
"When he had lost his realms:" whereon
    there grew
A power within me of enormous ken
To see as a god sees, and take the depth
Of things as nimbly as the outward eye 305
Can size and shape pervade. The lofty
    theme
At those few words hung vast before my
    mind
With half-unravelled web. I set myself
Upon an eagle's watch, that I might see,
And seeing ne'er forget. No stir of life 310
Was in this shrouded vale,—not so much
    air
As in the zoning of a summer's day
Robs not one light seed from the feathered
    grass;
But where the dead leaf fell there did it
    rest.
A stream went voiceless by, still deadened
    more   315
By reason of the fallen divinity
Spreading more shade; the Naiad 'mid her
    reeds
Pressed her cold finger closer to her lips.

Along the margin-sand large footmarks
    went
No farther than to where old Saturn's
    feet   320
Had rested, and there slept how long a
    sleep!
Degraded, cold, upon the sodden ground
His old right hand lay nerveless, listless,
    dead,
Unsceptred, and his realmless eyes were
    closed;

While his bowed head seemed listening to
   the Earth,   325
His ancient mother, for some comfort yet.

It seemed no force could wake him from
   his place;
But there came one who, with a kindred
   hand,
Touched his wide shoulders, after bending
   low
With reverence, though to one who knew
   it not.   330
Then came the grievèd voice of Mne-
   mosyne,
And grieved I hearkened. "That divinity
"Whom thou saw'st step from yon forlorn-
   est wood,
"And with slow pace approach our fallen
   king,
"Is Thea, softest-natured of our brood." 335
I marked the Goddess, in fair statuary
Surpassing wan Moneta by the head,
And in her sorrow nearer woman's tears.
There was a listening fear in her regard,
As if calamity had but begun;   340
As if the vanward clouds of evil days
Had spent their malice, and the sullen rear
Was with its storèd thunder laboring up.
One hand she pressed upon that aching
   spot
Where beats the human heart, as if just
   there,   345
Though an immortal, she felt cruel pain;
The other upon Saturn's bended neck
She laid, and to the level of his hollow ear
Leaning, with parted lips some words she
   spake
In solemn tenor and deep organ-tone;   350
Some mourning words, which in our feeble
   tongue
Would come in this-like accenting; how
   frail
To that large utterance of the early gods!

"Saturn, look up! and for what, poor lost
   king?
"I have no comfort for thee; no, not
   one;   355
"I cannot cry, wherefore thus sleepest thou?
"For Heaven is parted from thee, and the
   Earth
"Knows thee not, so afflicted, for a god;
"And Ocean, too, with all its solemn noise,
"Has from thy sceptre passed; and all the
   air   360
"Is emptied of thine hoary majesty.
"Thy thunder, captious at the new com-
   mand,

"Rumbles reluctant o'er our fallen house;
"And thy sharp lightning, in unpractised
   hands,
"Scorches and burns our once serene do-
   main.   365
"With such remorseless speed still come
   new woes,
"That unbelief has not a space to breathe.
"Saturn! sleep on: me thoughtless, why
   should I
"Thus violate thy slumbrous solitude?
"Why should I ope thy melancholy eyes? 370
"Saturn! sleep on, while at thy feet I
   weep."

As when upon a trancèd summer-night
Forests, branch-charmèd by the earnest
   stars,
Dream, and so dream all night without a
   noise,
Save from one gradual solitary gust   375
Swelling upon the silence, dying off,
As if the ebbing air had but one wave,
So came these words and went; the while
   in tears
She pressed her fair large forehead to the
   earth,
Just where her fallen hair might spread in
   curls,   380
A soft and silken mat for Saturn's feet.
Long, long these two were postured mo-
   tionless,
Like sculpture builded-up upon the grave
Of their own power. A long awful time
I looked upon them: still they were the
   same;   385
The frozen God still bending to the earth,
And the sad Goddess weeping at his feet;
Moneta silent. Without stay or prop
But my own weak mortality, I bore
The load of this eternal quietude,   390
The unchanging gloom and the three fixed
   shapes
Ponderous upon my senses, a whole moon;
For by my burning brain I measured sure
Her silver seasons shedded on the night,
And every day by day methought I grew 395
More gaunt and ghostly. Oftentimes I
   prayed
Intense, that death would take me from
   the vale
And all its burthens; gasping with despair
Of change, hour after hour I cursed my-
   self,
Until old Saturn raised his faded eyes, 400
And looked around and saw his kingdom
   gone,
And all the gloom and sorrow of the place,
And that fair kneeling Goddess at his feet.

As the moist scent of flowers, and grass,
    and leaves,
Fills forest dells with a pervading air,   405
Known to the woodland nostril, so the
    words
Of Saturn filled the mossy glooms around,
Even to the hollows of time-eaten oaks,
And to the windings in the foxes' hole,
With sad low tones, while thus he spake,
    and sent   410
Strange musings to the solitary Pan.
"Moan, brethren, moan, for we are swal-
    lowed up
"And buried from all godlike exercise
"Of influence benign on planets pale,
"And peaceful sway above man's harvest-
    ing,   415
"And all those acts which Deity supreme
"Doth ease its heart of love in. Moan and
    wail;
"Moan, brethren, moan; for lo, the rebel
    spheres
"Spin round; the stars their ancient courses
    keep;
"Clouds still with shadowy moisture haunt
    the earth,   420
"Still suck their fill of light from sun and
    moon;
"Still buds the tree, and still the seashores
    murmur;
"There is no death in all the universe,
"No smell of death.—There shall be death.
    Moan, moan;
"Moan, Cybele, moan; for thy pernicious
    babes   425
"Have changed a god into an aching palsy.
"Moan, brethren, moan, for I have no
    strength left;
"Weak as the reed, weak, feeble as my
    voice,—
"O, O, the pain, the pain of feebleness;
"Moan, moan, for still I thaw; or give me
    help;   430
"Throw down those imps, and give me vic-
    tory.
"Let me hear other groans, and trumpets
    blown
"Of triumph calm, and hymns of festival,
"From the gold peaks of heaven's high-
    pilèd clouds;
"Voices of soft proclaim, and silver stir   435
"Of strings in hollow shells; and let there
    be
"Beautiful things made new, for the sur-
    prise
"Of the sky-children." So he feebly ceased,
With such a poor and sickly-sounding
    pause,
Methought I heard some old man of the
    earth   440

Bewailing earthly loss; nor could my eyes
And ears act with that pleasant unison of
    sense
Which marries sweet sound with the grace
    of form,
And dolorous accent from a tragic harp
With large-limbed visions. More I scruti-
    nized.   445
Still fixed he sat beneath the sable trees,
Whose arms spread straggling in wild ser-
    pent forms,
With leaves all hushed; his awful presence
    there
(Now all was silent) gave a deadly lie
To what I erewhile heard: only his lips 450
Trembled amid the white curls of his
    beard;
They told the truth, though round the
    snowy locks
Hung nobly, as upon the face of heaven
A mid-day fleece of clouds. Thea arose,
And stretched her white arm through the
    hollow dark,   455
Pointing some whither: whereat he too
    rose,
Like a vast giant, seen by men at sea
To grow pale from the waves at dull mid-
    night.
They melted from my sight into the woods;
Ere I could turn, Moneta cried, "These
    twain   460
"Are speeding to the families of grief,
"Where, roofed in by black rocks, they
    waste in pain
"And darkness, for no hope." And she
    spake on,
As ye may read who can unwearied pass
Onward from th' antechamber of this
    dream,   465
Where, even at the open doors, awhile
I must delay, and glean my memory
Of her high phrase—perhaps no further
    dare.

CANTO II

"Mortal, that thou may'st understand
    aright,
"I humanize my sayings to thine ear,
"Making comparisons of earthly things;
"Or thou might'st better listen to the wind,
"Whose language is to thee a barren noise, 5
"Though it blows legend-laden thro' the
    trees.
"In melancholy realms big tears are shed,
"More sorrow like to this, and such like
    woe,
"Too huge for mortal tongue or pen of
    scribe.

"The Titans fierce, self-hid or prison-
          bound,   10
"Groan for the old allegiance once more,
"Listening in their doom for Saturn's voice.
"But one of our whole eagle-brood still
          keeps
"His sovereignty, and rule, and majesty:
"Blazing Hyperion on his orbèd fire   15
"Still sits, still snuffs the incense teeming
          up
"From Man to the Sun's God—yet unse-
          cure.
"For as upon the earth dire prodigies
"Fright and perplex, so also shudders he;
"Not at dog's howl or gloom-bird's Even
          screech,   20
"Or the familiar visitings of one
"Upon the first toll of his passing bell,
"But horrors, portioned to a giant nerve,
"Make great Hyperion ache. His palace
          bright,
"Bastioned with pyramids of glowing
          gold,   25
"And touched with shade of bronzèd
          obelisks,
"Glares a blood-red through all the thou-
          sand courts,
"Arches, and domes, and fiery galleries;
"And all its curtains of Aurorian clouds
"Flush angrily; when he would taste the
          wreaths   30
"Of incense, breathed aloft from sacred
          hills,
"Instead of sweets, his ample palate takes
"Savor of poisonous brass and metals sick;
"Wherefore when harbored in the sleepy
          West,
"After the full completion of fair day, 35
"For rest divine upon exalted couch,
"And slumber in the arms of melody,
"He paces through the pleasant hours of
          ease,
"With strides colossal, on from hall to hall,
"While far within each aisle and deep re-
          cess   40
"His winged minions in close clusters stand
"Amazed, and full of fear; like anxious
          men,
"Who on a wide plain gather in sad troops,
"When earthquakes jar their battlements
          and towers.
"Even now while Saturn, roused from icy
          trance,   45
"Goes step for step with Thea from yon
          woods,
"Hyperion, leaving twilight in the rear,
"Is sloping to the threshold of the West.
"Thither we tend." Now in clear light I
          stood,
Relieved from the dusk vale. Mnemosyne 50

Was sitting on a square-edged polished
          stone,
That in its lucid depth reflected pure
Her priestess' garments. My quick eyes ran
          on
From stately nave to nave, from vault to
          vault,
Through bow'rs of fragrant and enwreathèd
          light,   55
And diamond-pavèd lustrous long arcades.
Anon rushed by the bright Hyperion;
His flaming robes streamed out beyond his
          heels,
And gave a roar as if of earthly fire,
That scared away the meek ethereal
          hours,   60
And made their dove-wings tremble. On
          he flared.

c. Aug.-Dec., 1819   1856

THE DAY IS GONE

The day is gone, and all its sweets are
          gone!
Sweet voice, sweet lips, soft hand, and softer
          breast,
Warm breath, tranced whisper, tender semi-
          tone,
Bright eyes, accomplished shape, and lan-
          gorous waist!
Vanished unseasonably at shut of eve,   5
When the dusk holiday—or holinight
Of fragrant-curtained love begins to weave
The woof of darkness thick, for hid delight;
Faded the flower and all its budded charms,
Faded the sight of beauty from my eyes, 10
Faded the shape of beauty from my arms,
Faded the voice, warmth, whiteness, para-
          dise;—
But, as I've read love's missal through to-
          day,
He'll let me sleep, seeing I fast and pray.

Oct. 10, 1819   1838

LINES SUPPOSED TO HAVE
BEEN ADDRESSED TO
FANNY BRAWNE

This living hand, now warm and capable
Of earnest grasping, would, if it were cold
And in the icy silence of the tomb,
So haunt thy days and chill thy dreaming
          nights
That thou would[st] wish thine own heart
          dry of blood   5

So in my veins red life might stream again,
And thou be conscience-calmed—see here it
   is—
I hold it towards you.

Autumn, 1819   1898

TO FANNY

I cry your mercy—pity—love!—aye, love!
  Merciful love that tantalizes not,
One-thoughted, never-wandering, guileless
   love,
  Unmasked, and being seen—without a
   blot!

O! let me have thee whole,—all—all—be
  mine!   5
That shape, that fairness, that sweet
  minor zest
Of love, your kiss,—those hands, those eyes
  divine,
That warm, white, lucent, million-pleas-
  ured breast,—
Yourself—your soul—in pity give me all,
  Withhold no atom's atom or I die,   10
Or living on perhaps, your wretched thrall,
  Forget, in the mist of idle misery,
Life's purposes,—the palate of my mind
Losing its gust, and my ambition blind!

Nov., 1819   1848

LETTERS OF KEATS

ETERNAL POETRY

To John Hamilton Reynolds

Carisbrooke, April 18, 1817   5

My dear Reynolds,—
  On the 23rd was Shakespeare born. Now
if I should receive a letter from you and
another from my Brothers on that day
'twould be a parlous good thing. When- 10
ever you write say a word or two on some
Passage in Shakespeare that may have come
rather new to you, which must be continually happening, notwithstanding that we
read the same Play forty times—for in- 15
stance, the following from the Tempest
never struck me so forcibly as at present,

             "Urchins
Shall, for the vast of night that they may work,
All exercise on thee—"   20

How can I help bringing to your mind the
line—

In the dark backward and abysm of time—   25

I find I cannot exist without Poetry— without eternal Poetry—half the day will not
do—the whole of it—I began with a little,
but habit has made me a Leviathan. I
had become all in a Tremble from not 30
having written any thing of late—the Sonnet overleaf did me good. I slept the
better last night for it—this Morning, however, I am nearly as bad again. Just now
I opened Spenser, and the first Lines I 35
saw were these—

"The noble heart that harbors virtuous
  thought,
And is with child of glorious great intent.
Can never rest until it forth have brought
Th' eternal brood of glory excellent—"

              Your sincere friend,
               JOHN KEATS

MATERIALS OF IMAGINA-TION

To Benjamin Robert Haydon

Margate, Saturday Eve [May 10, 1817].

My Dear Haydon,

"Let Fame, which all hunt after in their lives,
Live registered upon our brazen tombs,
And so grace us in the disgrace of death:
When spite of cormorant devouring Time
The endeavor of this present breath may buy
That Honor which shall bate his Scythe's keen
  edge
And make us heirs of all eternity."
          [*Love's Labor's Lost*, I. i. 1-7.]

  To think that I have no right to couple
myself with you in this speech would be
death to me, so I have e'en written it, and
I pray God that our "brazen tombs" be
nigh neighbors. It cannot be long first;
the "endeavor of this present breath" will
soon be over, and yet it is as well to breathe
freely during our sojourn—it is as well as
if you have not been teased with that

Money affair, that bill-pestilence. However, I must think that difficulties nerve the Spirit of a Man—they make our Prime Objects a Refuge as well as a Passion. The Trumpet of Fame is as a tower of Strength, the ambitious bloweth it and is safe. I suppose, by your telling me not to give way to forebodings, George has mentioned to you what I have lately said in my Letters to him—truth is I have been in such a state of Mind as to read over my Lines and hate them. I am one that "gathers Samphire, dreadful trade"—the Cliff of Poesy towers above me—yet when Tom who meets with some of Pope's Homer in Plutarch's Lives reads some of those to me they seem like Mice to mine. I read and write about eight hours a day. There is an old saying "well begun is half done"—'tis a bad one. I would use instead, "Not begun at all till half done;" so according to that I have not begun my Poem and consequently (à priori) can say nothing about it. Thank God! I do begin arduously where I leave off, notwithstanding occasional depressions; and I hope for the support of a High Power while I climb this little eminence, and especially in my Years of more momentous Labor. I remember your saying that you had notions of a good Genius presiding over you. I have of late had the same thought, for things which I do half at Random are afterwards confirmed by my judgment in a dozen features of Propriety. Is it too daring to fancy Shakespeare this Presider? When in the Isle of Wight I met with a Shakespeare in the Passage of the House at which I lodged—it comes nearer to my idea of him than any I have seen—I was but there a Week, yet the old woman made me take it with me though I went off in a hurry. Do you not think this is ominous of good? I am glad you say every man of great views is at times tormented as I am. . . . I am extremely glad that a time must come when everything will leave not a wrack behind. You tell me never to despair—I wish it was as easy for me to observe the saying—truth is I have a horrid Morbidity of Temperament which has shown itself at intervals—it is I have no doubt the greatest Enemy and stumbling-block I have to fear—I may even say that it is likely to be the cause of my disappointment. However every ill has its share of good—this very bane would at any time enable me to look with an obstinate eye on the Devil Himself—aye to be as proud of being the lowest of the human race as Alfred could be in being of the highest. I feel confident I should have been a rebel angel had the opportunity been mine. I am very sure that you do love me as your own Brother—I have seen it in your continual anxiety for me—and I assure you that your welfare and fame is and will be a chief pleasure to me all my Life. I know no one but you who can be fully sensible of the turmoil and anxiety, the sacrifice of all what is called comfort, the readiness to measure time by what is done and to die in six hours could plans be brought to conclusions—the looking upon the Sun, the Moon, the Stars, the Earth and its contents, as materials to form greater things—that is to say ethereal things—but here I am talking like a Madman,—greater things than our Creator himself made!!

I wrote to Hunt yesterday—scarcely know what I said in it. I could not talk about Poetry in the way I should have liked for I was not in humor with either his or mine. His self-delusions are very lamentable—they have enticed him into a Situation which I should be less eager after than that of a galley Slave—what you observe thereon is very true must be in time.

Perhaps it is a self-delusion to say so—but I think I could not be deceived in the manner that Hunt is—may I die tomorrow if I am to be. There is no greater Sin after the seven deadly than to flatter oneself into an idea of being a great Poet—or one of those beings who are privileged to wear out their Lives in the pursuit of Honor—how comfortable a feel it is that such a Crime must bring its heavy Penalty? That if one be a Self-deluder accounts will be balanced? I am glad you are hard at work—'twill now soon be done—I long to see Wordsworth's as well as to have mine in: but I would rather not show my face in Town till the end of the Year—if that will be time enough—if not I shall be disappointed if you do not write for me even when you think best. I never quite despair and I read Shakespeare—indeed I shall I think never read any other Book much. Now this might lead me into a long Confab but I desist. I am very near agreeing with Hazlitt that Shakespeare is enough for us.

Your everlasting friend,
JOHN KEATS

A LIFE OF SENSATIONS RATHER THAN OF THOUGHTS

To Benjamin Bailey

November 22, 1817

My dear Bailey:

I wish I was as certain of the end of all your troubles as that of your momentary start about the authenticity of the Imagination. I am certain of nothing but of the holiness of the heart's affections, and the truth of imagination. What the imagination seizes as beauty must be truth—whether it existed before or not,—for I have the same idea of all our passions as of love: they are all, in their sublime, creative of essential beauty. In a word, you may know my favorite speculation by my first book, and the little song I sent in my last, which is a representation from the fancy of the probable mode of operating in these matters. The imagination may be compared to Adam's dream,—he awoke and found it truth. I am more zealous in this affair because I have never yet been able to perceive how anything can be known for truth by consecutive reasoning —and yet it must be. Can it be that even the greatest philosopher ever arrived at his goal without putting aside numerous objections? However it may be, O for a life of sensations rather than of thoughts! It is "a Vision in the form of Youth," a shadow of reality to come. And this consideration has further convinced me,—for it has come as auxiliary to another favorite speculation of mine,—that we shall enjoy ourselves hereafter by having what we called happiness on earth repeated in a finer tone and so repeated. And yet such a fate can only befall those who delight in sensation, rather than hunger as you do after truth. Adam's dream will do here, and seems to be a conviction that imagination and its empyreal reflection is the same as human life and its spiritual repetition. But, as I was saying, the simple imaginative mind may have its rewards in the repetition of its own silent working coming continually on the spirit with a fine suddenness. To compare great things with small, have you never by being surprised with an old melody, in a delicious place by a delicious voice, *felt* over again your very speculations and surmises at the time it first operated on your soul? Do you not remember forming to yourself the singer's face—more beautiful than it was possible, and yet with the elevation of the moment you did not think so? Even then you were mounted on the wings of imagination, so high that the prototype must be hereafter—that delicious face you will see. What a time! I am continually running away from the subject. Sure this cannot be exactly the case with a complex mind—one that is imaginative, and at the same time careful of its fruits,—who would exist partly on sensation, partly on thought —to whom it is necessary that years should bring the philosophic mind? Such a one I consider yours, and therefore it is necessary to your eternal happiness that you not only drink this old wine of heaven, which I shall call the redigestion of our most ethereal musings on earth, but also increase in knowledge and know all things. . . .

You perhaps at one time thought there was such a thing as worldly happiness to be arrived at, at certain periods of time marked out,—you have of necessity from your disposition been thus led away—I scarcely remember counting upon any happiness—I look not for it if it be not in the present hour,—nothing startles me beyond the moment. The setting sun will always set me to rights, or if a sparrow come before my window, I take part in its existence and pick about the gravel. The first thing that strikes me on hearing a misfortune having befallen another is this— "Well, it cannot be helped: he will have the pleasure of trying the resources of his spirit"—and I beg now, my dear Bailey, that hereafter should you observe anything cold in me not to put it to the account of heartlessness, but abstraction—for I assure you I sometimes feel not the influence of a passion or affection during a whole week —and so long this sometimes continues, I begin to suspect myself, and the genuineness of my feelings at other times—thinking them a few barren tragedy tears.

Your affectionate friend,

JOHN KEATS

WHAT THE THRUSH SAID

To John Hamilton Reynolds

[Hampstead, February 19, 1818.]

My dear Reynolds—

I had an idea that a Man might pass a very pleasant life in this manner—Let him

on a certain day read a certain page of full
Poesy or distilled Prose, and let him wander with it, and muse upon it, and reflect
upon it, and bring home to it, and prophesy upon it, and dream upon it: until it 5
becomes stale—But when will it do so?
Never—When Man has arrived at a certain
ripeness in intellect any one grand and
spiritual passage serves him as a starting-
post towards all "the two-and-thirty Pal- 10
aces." How happy is such a voyage of conception, what delicious diligent Indolence!
A doze upon a sofa does not hinder it, and
a nap upon Clover engenders ethereal
finger-pointings—the prattle of a child gives 15
it wings, and the converse of middle age a
strength to beat them—a strain of music
conducts to "an odd angle of the Isle," and
when the leaves whisper it puts a girdle
round the earth.—Nor will this sparing 20
touch of noble Books be any irreverence
to their Writers—for perhaps the honors
paid by Man to Man are trifles in comparison to the Benefit done by great works to
the "spirit and pulse of good" by their 25
mere passive existence. Memory should
not be called Knowledge—Many have original minds who do not think it—they are
led away by Custom. Now it appears to
me that almost any Man may like the 30
spider spin from his own inwards his own
airy Citadel—the points of leaves and twigs
on which the spider begins her work are
few, and she fills the air with a beautiful
circuiting. Man should be content with as 35
few points to tip with the fine Web of his
Soul, and weave a tapestry empyrean—full
of symbols for his spiritual eye, of softness
for his spiritual touch, of space for his
wandering, of distinctness for his luxury. 40
But the Minds of Mortals are so different
and bent on such diverse journeys that it
may at first appear impossible for any common taste and fellowship to exist between
two or three under these suppositions. It 45
is however quite the contrary. Minds
would leave each other in contrary directions, traverse each other in numberless
points, and at last greet each other at the
journey's end. An old Man and a child 50
would talk together and the old Man be
led on his path and the child left thinking.
Man should not dispute or assert but whisper results to his neighbor and thus by
every germ of spirit sucking the sap from 55
mould ethereal every human might become
great, and Humanity instead of being a
wide heath of Furze and Briars with here
and there a remote Oak or Pine, would
become a grand democracy of Forest Trees! 60

It has been an old comparison for our
urging on—the Beehive; however it seems
to me that we should rather be the flower
than the Bee—for it is a false notion that
more is gained by receiving than giving—
no, the receiver and the giver are equal in
their benefits. The flower, I doubt not,
receives a fair guerdon from the Bee—its
leaves blush deeper in the next spring—
and who shall say between Man and
Woman which is the most delighted? Now
it is more noble to sit like Jove than to
fly like Mercury—let us not therefore go
hurrying about and collecting honey, bee-
like buzzing here and there impatiently
from a knowledge of what is to be aimed
at; but let us open our leaves like a flower
and be passive and receptive—budding patiently under the eye of Apollo and taking
hints from every noble insect that favors
us with a visit—sap will be given us for
meat and dew for drink. I was led into
these thoughts, my dear Reynolds, by the
beauty of the morning operating on a
sense of Idleness—I have not read any
books—the Morning said I was right—I
had no idea but of the morning, and the
thrush said I was right—seeming to say,

O thou whose face hath felt the winter's
    wind,
Whose eye has seen the snow-clouds hung in
    mist,
And the black elm tops 'mong the freezing
    stars,
To thee the spring will be a harvest-time.
O thou whose only book has been the light
Of supreme darkness, which thou feddest on
Night after night, when Phoebus was away,
To thee the spring shall be a triple morn.
O fret not after knowledge—I have none,
And yet my song comes native with the
    warmth.
O fret not after knowledge—I have none,
And yet the Evening listens. He who saddens
At thought of idleness cannot be idle,
And he's awake who thinks himself asleep.

Now I am sensible all this is a mere
sophistication (however it may neighbor
to any truths), to excuse my own indolence
—so I will not deceive myself that man
should be equal with Jove—but think himself very well off as a sort of scullion-
Mercury, or even a humble Bee. It is no
matter whether I am right or wrong, either
one way or another, if there is sufficient
to lift a little time from your shoulders.

Your affectionate friend,

JOHN KEATS

AXIOMS IN POETRY

To John Taylor

Hampstead, February 27 [1818]. [5]

My dear Taylor—

Your alteration strikes me as being a great Improvement—And now I will attend to the punctuations you speak of—The [10] comma should be at *soberly,* and in the other passage, the Comma should follow *quiet.* I am extremely indebted to you for this attention, and also for your after admonitions. It is a sorry thing for me that [15] any one should have to overcome prejudices in reading my verses—that affects me more than any hypercriticism on any particular passage—In Endymion, I have most likely but moved into the go-cart from the [20] leading-strings—In poetry I have a few axioms, and you will see how far I am from their centre.

1st. I think poetry should surprise by a fine excess, and not by singularity; It [25] should strike the reader as a wording of his own highest thoughts, and appear almost a remembrance.

2d. Its touches of beauty should never be half-way, thereby making the reader [30] breathless, instead of content. The rise, the progress, the setting of Imagery should, like the sun, come natural to him, shine over him, and set soberly, although in magnificence, leaving him in the luxury of twi- [35] light. But it is easier to think what poetry should be, than to write it—And this leads me to

Another axiom—That if poetry comes not as naturally as the leaves to a tree, it [40] had better not come at all.—However it may be with me, I cannot help looking into new countries with "O for a Muse of Fire to ascend!" If Endymion serves me as a pioneer, perhaps I ought to be content [45] —I have great reason to be content, for thank God I can read, and perhaps understand Shakespeare to his depths; and I have I am sure many friends, who, if I fail, will attribute any change in my life [50] and temper to humbleness rather than pride—to a cowering under the wings of great poets, rather than to a bitterness that I am not appreciated. I am anxious to get Endymion printed that I may forget it and [55] proceed. I have copied the 3rd Book and begun the 4th.

Your sincere and obliged friend,

JOHN KEATS

MILTON, WORDSWORTH, AND THE DARKENING CHAMBER OF MAIDEN-THOUGHT

To John Hamilton Reynolds

Teignmouth, May 3, 1818

My dear Reynolds,—

Were I to study physic, or rather medicine, again, I feel it would not make the least difference in my Poetry; when the mind is in its infancy a bias is in reality a bias; but when we have acquired more strength, a bias becomes no bias. Every department of knowledge we see excellent and calculated towards a great whole—I am so convinced of this that I am glad at not having given away my medical Books, which I shall again look over to keep alive the little I know thitherwards; and moreover intend through you and Rice to become a sort of pip-civilian. An extensive knowledge is needful to thinking people— [25] it takes away the heat and fever; and helps, by widening speculation, to ease the Burden of the Mystery, a thing which I begin to understand a little, and which weighed upon you in the most gloomy and true [30] sentence in your Letter. The difference of high Sensations with and without knowledge appears to me this: in the latter case we are falling continually ten thousand fathoms deep and being blown up again, [35] without wings, and with all horror of a bare-shouldered Creature—in the former case, our shoulders are fledge, and we go through the same air and space without fear. . . .

My branchings out have been numerous; one of them is the consideration of Wordsworth's genius and as a help, in the manner of gold being the meridian line of worldly wealth, how he differs from Milton. [45] And here I have nothing but surmises, from an uncertainty whether Milton's apparently less anxiety for humanity proceeds from his seeing further or no than Wordsworth: and whether Wordsworth has in truth epic [50] passion, and martyrs himself to the human heart, the main region of his song. In regard to his genius alone, we find what he says true as far as we have experienced; and we can judge no further but by larger [55] experience; for axioms in philosophy are not axioms until they are proved upon our pulses. We read fine things, but never feel them to the full until we have gone the same steps as the author.—I know this is [60] not plain; you will know exactly my meaning when I say that now I shall relish Hamlet more than I ever have done. Or, better—you are sensible no man can set down venery as ∴ bestial or joyless thing until he is sick of it, and therefore all philosophising on it would be mere wording. Until we are sick, we understand not; in fine, as Byron says, "Knowledge is sorrow"; and I go on to say that "Sorrow is wisdom"—and further for aught we can know for certainty "Wisdom is folly" . . . I will return to Wordsworth: whether or no he has an extended vision or a circumscribed grandeur, whether he is an eagle in his nest or on the wing. And to be more explicit and to show you how tall I stand by the giant, I will put down a simile of human life as far as I now perceive it; that is, to the point to which I say we both have arrived at. Well, I compare human life to a large mansion of many apartments, two of which I can only describe, the doors of the rest being as yet shut upon me. The first we step into we call the infant or thoughtless chamber, in which we remain as long as we do not think. We remain there a long while, and notwithstanding the doors of the second chamber remain wide open, showing a bright appearance, we care not to hasten to it; but are at length imperceptibly impelled by the awakening of the thinking principle within us. We no sooner get into the second chamber, which I shall call the chamber of maiden-thought, than we become intoxicated with the light and the atmosphere, we see nothing but pleasant wonders, and think of delaying there for ever in delight. However, among the effects this breathing is father of, is that tremendous one of sharpening one's vision into the heart and nature of Man, of convincing one's nerves that the world is full of misery and heartbreak, pain, sickness, and oppression—whereby this chamber of maiden-thought becomes gradually darkened, and at the same time, on all sides of it, many doors are set open—but all dark—all leading to dark passages. We see not the balance of good and evil—we are in a mist—*we* are now in that state. We feel the "burden of the mystery."

To this point was Wordsworth come, as far as I can conceive, when he wrote *Tintern Abbey,* and it seems to me that his genius is explorative of those dark passages. Now if we live, and go on thinking, we too shall explore them. He is a genius and superior to us, in so far as he can, more than we, make discoveries and shed a

light in them. Here I must think Wordsworth is deeper than Milton, though I think it has depended more upon the general and gregarious advance of intellect, than individual greatness of mind. From the *Paradise Lost* and the other works of Milton, I hope it is not too presuming, even between ourselves, to say that his philosophy, human and divine, may be tolerably understood by one not much advanced in years. In his time, Englishmen were just emancipated from a great superstition, and men had got hold of certain points and resting places in reasoning which were too newly born to be doubted, and too much opposed by the mass of Europe not to be thought ethereal and authentically divine. Who could gainsay his ideas on virtue, vice, and chastity in *Comus,* just at the time of the dismissal of cod-pieces and a hundred other disgraces? Who would not rest satisfied with his hintings at good and evil in the *Paradise Lost,* when just free from the inquisition and burning in Smithfield? The Reformation produced such immediate and great benefits, that Protestantism was considered under the immediate eye of heaven, and its own remaining dogmas and superstitions then, as it were, regenerated, constituted those resting places and seeming sure points of Reasoning. From that I have mentioned, Milton, whatever he may have thought in the sequel, appears to have been content with these by his writings. He did not think into the human heart as Wordsworth has done. Yet Milton as a philosopher had sure as great powers as Wordsworth. What is then to be inferred? O many things! It proves there is really a grand march of intellect. It proves that a mighty providence subdues the mightiest minds to the service of the time being, whether it be in human knowledge or religion. . . .

Your affectionate friend,

JOHN KEATS

LIFE MUST BE UNDERGONE

To Benjamin Bailey

London; June 10, 1818

My dear Bailey,—

I was in hopes some little time back to be able to relieve your dullness by my spirits—to point out things in the world worth your enjoyment—and now I am never alone without rejoicing that there is such a thing as death—without placing my ultimate in the glory of dying for a great human purpose. Perhaps if my affairs were in a different state, I should not have written the above—you shall judge: I have two brothers; one is driven, by the "burden of Society," to America; the other with an exquisite love of life, is in a lingering state. —My love for my brothers, from the early loss of our parents, and even for earlier misfortunes, has grown into an affection "passing the love of women." I have been ill-tempered with them—I have vexed them —but the thought of them has always stifled the impression that any woman might otherwise have made upon me. I have a sister too, and may not follow them either to America or to the grave. Life must be undergone, and I certainly derive some consolation from the thought of writing one or two more poems before it ceases.

Your affectionate friend,

JOHN KEATS

I SHALL NEVER MARRY

To George and Georgiana Keats

[Hampstead; c. Oct. 25, 1818]

My dear George,—

. . . I shall in a short time write you as far as I know how I intend to pass my Life—I cannot think of those things now Tom is so unwell and weak. Notwithstanding your Happiness and your recommendation I hope I shall never marry. Though the most beautiful Creature were waiting for me at the end of a Journey or a Walk; though the Carpet were of Silk, the Curtains of the morning Clouds; the chairs and Sofa stuffed with Cygnet's down; the food Manna, the Wine beyond Claret, the Window opening on Winander mere, I should not feel—or rather my Happiness would not be so fine, as my Solitude is sublime. Then instead of what I have described, there is a sublimity to welcome me home—The roaring of the wind is my wife and the Stars through the window pane are my Children. The mighty abstract Idea I have of Beauty in all things stifles the more divided and minute domestic happiness—an amiable wife and sweet Children I contemplate as a part of that Beauty, but I must have a thousand of those beautiful particles to fill up my heart. I feel more and more every day, as my imagination strengthens, that I do not live in this world alone but in a thousand worlds—No sooner am I alone than shapes of epic greatness are stationed around me, and serve my Spirit the office which is equivalent to a King's bodyguard—then "Tragedy with sceptred pall comes sweeping by." According to my state of mind I am with Achilles shouting in the Trenches or with Theocritus in the Vales of Sicily. Or I throw my whole being into Troilus, and repeating those lines, "I wander like a lost Soul upon the stygian Banks staying for waftage," I melt into the air with a voluptuousness so delicate that I am content to be alone. These things, combined with the opinion I have of the generality of women—who appear to me as children to whom I would rather give a sugar Plum than my time, form a barrier against Matrimony which I rejoice in.

I have written this that you might see I have my share of the highest pleasures, and that though I may choose to pass my days alone I shall be no Solitary. You see there is nothing spleenical in all this. The only thing that can ever affect me personally for more than one short passing day, is any doubt about my powers for poetry —I seldom have any, and I look with hope to the nighing time when I shall have none. I am as happy as a Man can be—that is, in myself I should be happy if Tom was well, and I knew you were passing pleasant days. Then I should be most enviable—with the yearning Passion I have for the beautiful, connected and made one with the ambition of my intellect. Think of my Pleasure in Solitude in comparison of my commerce with the world—there I am a child—there they do not know me, not even my most intimate acquaintance— I give in to their feelings as though I were refraining from irritating a little child. Some think me middling, others silly, others foolish—every one thinks he sees my weak side against my will, when in truth it is with my will—I am content to be thought all this because I have in my own breast so great a resource. This is one great reason why they like me so: because they can all show to advantage in a room and eclipse from a certain tact one who is reckoned to be a good Poet. I hope I am not here playing tricks "to make the angels weep": I think not: for I have not the least contempt for my species, and though it may sound paradoxical, my greatest elevations of soul leave me every time more humbled—Enough of this—though in your Love for me you will not think it enough.

Your anxious and affectionate Brother

JOHN

THE POET HAS NO IDENTITY

To Richard Woodhouse

Hampstead; Oct. 27, 1818

My dear Woodhouse,—

Your letter gave me a great satisfaction, more on account of its friendliness than any relish of that matter in it which is accounted so acceptable to the "genus irritabile." The best answer I can give you is in a clerklike manner to make some observations on two principal points which seem to point like indices into the midst of the whole pro and con about genius, and views, and achievements, and ambition, et cætera. 1st. As to the poetical Character itself (I mean that sort, of which, if I am anything, I am a member; that sort distinguished from the Wordsworthian, or egotistical sublime; which is a thing per se, and stands alone,) it is not itself—it has no self—It is everything and nothing—It has no character—it enjoys light and shade; it lives in gusto, be it foul or fair, high or low, rich or poor, mean or elevated—It has as much delight in conceiving an Iago as an Imogen. What shocks the virtuous philosopher delights the chameleon poet. It does no harm from its relish of the dark side of things, any more than from its taste for the bright one, because they both end in speculation. A poet is the most unpoetical of anything in existence, because he has no Identity—he is continually in for and filling some other body. The Sun,—the Moon,—the Sea, and men and women who are creatures of impulse, are poetical, and have about them an unchangeable attribute; the poet has none, no identity—he is certainly the most unpoetical of all God's creatures.—If then he has no self, and if I am a poet, where is the wonder that I should say I would write no more? Might I not at that very instant have been cogitating on the Characters of Saturn and Ops? It is a wretched thing to confess; but it is a very fact, that not one word I ever utter can be taken for granted as an opinion growing out of my identical Nature—how can it, when I have no

Nature? When I am in a room with people, if I ever am free from speculating on creations of my own brain, then, not myself goes home to myself, but the identity of every one in the room begins to press upon me, that I am in a very little time annihilated—not only among men; it would be the same in a nursery of Children. I know not whether I make myself wholly understood: I hope enough so to let you see that no dependence is to be placed on what I said that day.

In the second place, I will speak of my views, and of the life I purpose to myself. I am ambitious of doing the world some good: if I should be spared, that may be the work of maturer years—in the interval I will assay to reach to as high a summit in poetry as the nerve bestowed upon me will suffer. The faint conceptions I have of poems to come brings the blood frequently into my forehead—All I hope is, that I may not lose all interest in human affairs—that the solitary indifference I feel for applause, even from the finest spirits, will not blunt any acuteness of vision I may have. I do not think it will. I feel assured I should write from the mere yearning and fondness I have for the beautiful, even if my night's labors should be burnt every morning, and no eye ever shine upon them. But even now I am perhaps not speaking from myself, but from some character in whose soul I now live.

I am sure however that this next sentence is from myself—I feel your anxiety, good opinion, and friendship, in the highest degree, and am

Yours most sincerely

JOHN KEATS.

HAZLITT AND GIFFORD

To George and Georgiana Keats

March 12-13, 1819

My dear Brother and Sister,—

I have by me at present Hazlitt's Letter to Gifford—perhaps you would like an extract or two from the high-seasoned parts. It begins thus:

Sir, you have an ugly trick of saying what is not true of any one you do not like; and it will be the object of this Letter to cure you of it. You say what you please of others; it is time you were told what you are. In doing this give me leave to borrow the familiarity of your style:—for the fidelity of the picture I shall be answerable. You are a little person but a considerable cat's paw; and so far worthy of notice. Your clandestine connection with persons high in office constantly influences your opinions and alone gives importance to them. You are the government critic, a character nicely differing from that of a government spy—the invisible link which connects literature with the Police.

Again:

Your employers, Mr. Gifford, do not pay their hirelings for nothing—for condescending to notice weak and wicked sophistry; for pointing out to contempt what excites no admiration; for cautiously selecting a few specimens of bad taste and bad grammar where nothing else is to be found. They want your invincible pertness, your mercenary malice, your impenetrable dullness, your bare-faced impudence, your pragmatical self-sufficiency, your hypocritical zeal, your pious frauds to stand in the gap of their Prejudices and pretensions, to flyblow and taint public opinion, to defeat independent efforts, to apply not the touch of the scorpion but the touch of the Torpedo to youthful hopes, to crawl and leave the slimy track of sophistry and lies over every work that does not dedicate its sweet leaves to some Luminary of the treasury bench, or is not fostered in the hotbed of corruption. This is your office; "this is what is looked for at your hands, and this you do not baulk"—to sacrifice what little honesty and prostitute what little intellect you possess to any dirty job you are commissioned to execute. "They keep you as an ape does an apple in the corner of his jaw, first mouthed to be at last swallowed." You are by appointment literary toadeater to greatness and taster to the court. You have a natural aversion to whatever differs from your own pretensions, and an acquired one for what gives offence to your superiors. Your vanity panders to your interest, and your malice truckles only to your love of Power. If your instinctive or premeditated abuse of your enviable trust were found wanting in a single instance; if you were to make a single slip in getting up your select committee of enquiry and green bag report of the state of Letters, your occupation would be gone. You would never after obtain a squeeze of the hand from a great man, or a smile from a Punk of Quality. The great and powerful whom you call wise and good do not like to have the privacy of their self-love startled by the obtrusive and unmanageable claims of Literature and Philosophy, except through the intervention of people like you, whom, if they have common penetration, they soon find out to be without any superiority of intellect; or if they do not, whom they can despise for their meanness of soul. You "have the office opposite to Saint Peter." You "keep a corner in the public mind for foul prejudice and corrupt power to knot and gender in"; you volunteer your services

to people of quality to ease scruples of mind and qualms of conscience; you lay the flattering unction of venal prose and laurell'd verse to their souls. You persuade them that there is neither purity of morals, nor depth of understanding, except in themselves and their hangers-on; and would prevent the unhallow'd names of Liberty and humanity from ever being whispered in ears polite! You, sir, do you not all this? I cry you mercy then: I took you for the Editor of the Quarterly Review.

This is the sort of feu de joie he keeps up. There is another extract or two—one especially which I will copy tomorrow—for the candles are burnt down and I am using the wax taper—which has a long snuff on it—the fire is at its last click—I am sitting with my back to it with one foot rather askew upon the rug and the other with the heel a little elevated from the carpet—I am writing this on the Maid's Tragedy, which I have read since tea with great pleasure—Besides this volume of Beaumont and Fletcher, there are on the table two volumes of Chaucer and a new work of Tom Moore's, called Tom Cribb's Memorial to Congress—nothing in it. These are trifles—but I require nothing so much of you but that you will give one a like description of yourselves, however it may be when you are writing to me. Could I see the same thing done of any great Man long since dead it would be a great delight: as to know in what position Shakespeare sat when he began "To be or not to be"—such things become interesting from distance of time or place. I hope you are both now in that sweet sleep which no two beings deserve more than you do—I must fancy you so—and please myself in the fancy of speaking a prayer and a blessing over you and your lives—God bless you —I whisper good-night in your ears, and you will dream of me. . . .

I know not why Poetry and I have been so distant lately; I must make some advances soon or she will cut me entirely. Hazlitt has this fine Passage in his Letter: Gifford in his Review of Hazlitt's characters of Shakespeare's plays attacks the Coriolanus critique. He says that Hazlitt has slandered Shakespeare in saying that he had a leaning to the arbitrary side of the question. Hazlitt thus defends himself:

My words are, "Coriolanus is a storehouse of political common-places. The Arguments for and against aristocracy and democracy on the Privileges of the few and the claims of the many, on Liberty and slavery, power and the abuse of it, peace and war, are here very ably handled, with the spirit of a Poet and the acuteness of a Philosopher. Shakespeare himself seems to have had a leaning to the arbitrary side of the question, perhaps from some feeling of contempt for his own origin, and to have spared no occasion of bating the rabble. What he says of them is very true; what he says of their betters is also very true, though he dwells less upon it." I then proceed to account for this by showing how it is that "the cause of the people is but little calculated for a subject for poetry; or that the language of Poetry naturally falls in with the language of power." I affirm, Sir, that Poetry, that the imagination generally speaking, delights in power, in strong excitement, as well as in truth, in good, in right, whereas pure reason and the moral sense approve only of the true and good. I proceed to show that this general love or tendency to immediate excitement or theatrical effect, no matter how produced, gives a Bias to the imagination often [in]consistent with the greatest good, that in Poetry it triumphs over principle, and bribes the passions to make a sacrifice of common humanity. You say that it does not, that there is no such original Sin in Poetry, that it makes no such sacrifice or unworthy compromise between poetical effect and the still small voice of reason. And how do you prove that there is no such principle giving a bias to the imagination and a false coloring to poetry? Why, by asking in reply to the instances where this principle operates, and where no other can with much modesty and simplicity—"But are these the only topics that afford delight in Poetry, etc.?" No; but these objects do afford delight in poetry, and they afford it in proportion to their strong and often tragical effect, and not in proportion to the good produced, or their desirableness in a moral point of view. "Do we read with more pleasure of the ravages of a beast of prey than of the Shepherd's pipe upon the Mountain?" No; but we do read with pleasure of the ravages of a beast of prey, and we do so on the principle I have stated, namely, from the sense of power abstracted from the sense of good; and it is the same principle that makes us read with admiration and reconciles us in fact to the triumphant progress of the conquerors and mighty Hunters of mankind, who come to stop the Shepherd's Pipe upon the Mountains and sweep away his listening flock. Do you mean to deny that there is anything imposing to the imagination in power, in grandeur, in outward show, in the accumulation of individual wealth and luxury, at the expense of equal justice and the common weal? Do you deny that there is anything in the "Pride, Pomp, and Circumstances of glorious war, that makes ambition virtue" in the eyes of admiring multitudes? Is this a new theory of the pleasures of the imagination, which says that the pleasures of the imagination do not take rise solely in the calculation of the understanding? Is it a paradox of my creating that "one murder makes a villain, millions a Hero"? or is it not true that here, as in other cases, the enormity of the evil overpowers and makes a convert of the imagination by its very magnitude? You contradict my reasoning because you know nothing of the question, and you think that no one has a right to understand what you do not. My offence against purity in the passage alluded to, "which contains the concentrated venom of my malignity," is that I have admitted that there are tyrants and slaves abroad in the world; and you would hush the matter up and pretend that there is no such thing in order that there may be nothing else. Further, I have explained the cause, the subtle sophistry of the human mind, that tolerates and pampers the evil in order to guard against its approaches; you would conceal the cause in order to prevent the cure, and to leave the proud flesh about the heart to harden and ossify into one impenetrable mass of selfishness and hypocrisy, that we may not "sympathise in the distresses of suffering virtue" in any case in which they come in competition with the fictitious wants and "imputed weaknesses of the great." You ask, "Are we gratified by the cruelties of Domitian or Nero?" No, not we—they were too petty and cowardly to strike the imagination at a distance; but the Roman senate tolerated them, addressed their perpetrators, exalted them into gods, the fathers of the people, they had pimps and scribblers of all sorts in their pay, their Senecas, etc., till a turbulent rabble, thinking there were no injuries to Society greater than the endurance of unlimited and wanton oppression, put an end to the farce and abated the nuisance as well as they could. Had you and I lived in those times we should have been what we are now, I "a sour malcontent," and you "a sweet courtier."

The manner in which this is managed: the force and innate power with which it yeasts and works up itself—the feeling for the costume of society; is in a style of genius. He hath a demon, as he himself says of Lord Byron. . . .

THE CASTLE OF INDOLENCE

March 19, 1819

This morning I have been reading "the False One." Shameful to say, I was in bed at ten—I mean this morning. The Blackwood Reviewers have committed themselves in a scandalous heresy—they have been putting up Hogg, the Ettrick Shepherd, against Burns: the senseless villains! The Scotch cannot manage by themselves at all, they want imagination, and that is why they are so fond of Hogg, who has a little of it. This morning I am in a sort of temper, indolent and supremely careless— I long after a Stanza or two of Thomson's Castle of Indolence—my passions are all asleep, from my having slumbered till nearly eleven, and weakened the animal fibre all over me to a delightful sensation about three degrees on this side of faintness. If I had teeth of pearl and the breath of lilies I should call it languor, but as I am I must call it laziness. In this state of effeminacy the fibres of the brain are relaxed in common with the rest of the body, and to such a happy degree that pleasure has no show of enticement and pain no unbearable frown. Neither Poetry, nor Ambition, nor Love have any alertness of countenance as they pass by me; they seem rather like figures on a Greek vase—a Man and two women whom no one but myself could distinguish in their disguisement. This is the only happiness, and is a rare instance of the advantage of the body overpowering the Mind. I have this moment received a note from Haslam, in which he expects the death of his Father, who has been for some time in a state of insensibility; his mother bears up he says very well—I shall go to town to-morrow to see him. This is the world—thus we can not expect to give way many hours to pleasure. Circumstances are like Clouds continually gathering and bursting—While we are laughing, the seed of some trouble is put into the wide arable land of events—while we are laughing it sprouts it grows and suddenly bears a poison fruit which we must pluck. Even so we have leisure to reason on the misfortunes of our friends; our own touch us too nearly for words. Very few men have ever arrived at a complete distinterestedness of Mind: very few have been influenced by a pure desire of the benefit of others,—in the greater part of the Benefactors to Humanity some meretricious motive has sullied their greatness—some melodramatic scenery has fascinated them. From the manner in which I feel Haslam's misfortune I perceive how far I am from any humble standard of disinterestedness. Yet this feeling ought to be carried to its highest pitch, as there is no fear of its ever injuring society—which it would do, I fear, pushed to an extremity. For in wild nature the Hawk would lose his Breakfast of Robins and the Robin his of Worms—The Lion must starve as well as the swallow. The greater part of Men make their way with the same instinctiveness, the same unwandering eye from their purposes, the same animal eagerness as the Hawk. The Hawk wants a Mate, so does the Man—look at them both, they set about it and procure one in the same manner. They want both a nest and they both set about one in the same manner—they get their food in the same manner. The noble animal Man for his amusement smokes his pipe—the Hawk balances about the Clouds—that is the only difference of their leisures. This it is that makes the Amusement of Life—to a speculative Mind—I go among the Fields and catch a glimpse of a Stoat or a fieldmouse peeping out of the withered grass— the creature hath a purpose, and its eyes are bright with it. I go amongst the buildings of a city and I see a Man hurrying along—to what? The Creature has a purpose and his eyes are bright with it. But then, as Wordsworth says, "we have all one human heart——" There is an electric fire in human nature tending to purify—so that among these human creatures there is continually some birth of new heroism. The pity is that we must wonder at it, as we should at finding a pearl in rubbish. I have no doubt that thousands of people never heard of have had hearts completely disinterested: I can remember but two— Socrates and Jesus—Their histories evince it. What I heard a little time ago, Taylor observe with respect to Socrates, may be said of Jesus—That he was so great a man that though he transmitted no writing of his own to posterity, we have his Mind and his sayings and his greatness handed to us by others. It is to be lamented that the history of the latter was written and revised by Men interested in the pious frauds of Religion. Yet through all this I see his splendor. Even here, though I myself am pursuing the same instinctive course as the veriest human animal you can think of, I am, however young, writing at random, straining at particles of light in the midst of a great darkness, without knowing the bearing of any one assertion, of any one opinion. Yet may I not in this be free from sin? May there not be superior beings amused with any graceful, though instinctive, attitude my mind may fall into as I am entertained with the alertness of a Stoat or the anxiety of a Deer? Though a quarrel in the Streets is a thing to be hated, the energies displayed in it are fine; the commonest Man shows a grace in his quarrel. By a superior Being our reasonings may take the same tone—though erioneous they may be fine. This is the very thing in which consists Poetry, and if so it is not so fine a thing as philosophy— For the same reason that an eagle is not so fine a thing as a truth. Give me this credit —Do you not think I strive—to know myself? Give me this credit, and you will not think that on my own account I repeat Milton's lines—

How charming is divine Philosophy,
Not harsh and crabbed, as dull fools suppose,
But musical as is Apollo's lute.

No—not for myself—feeling grateful as I do to have got into a state of mind to relish them properly. Nothing ever becomes real till it is experienced—Even a Proverb is no proverb to you till your Life has illustrated it. I am ever afraid that your anxiety for me will lead you to fear for the violence of my temperament continually smothered down: for that reason I did not intend to have sent you the following sonnet—but look over the two last pages and ask yourselves whether I have not that in me which will well bear the buffets of the world. It will be the best comment on my sonnet; it will show you that it was written with no Agony but that of ignorance; with no thirst of anything but Knowledge when pushed to the point though the first steps to it were through my human passions—they went away and I wrote with my Mind— and perhaps I must confess a little bit of my heart—

Why did I laugh to-night? No voice will tell;
    No God, no Demon of severe response,
Deigns to reply from Heaven or from Hell:
    Then to my human heart I turn at once.
Heart! Thou and I are here sad and alone;
    I say, why did I laugh? O mortal pain!
O Darkness! Darkness! ever must I moan,
    To question Heaven and Hell and Heart in vain.
Why did I laugh? I know this Being's lease,
    My fancy to its utmost blisses spreads;
Yet could I on this very midnight cease,
    And the world's gaudy ensigns see in shreds;
Verse, Fame, and Beauty are intense indeed,
But Death intenser—Death is Life's high meed.

I went to bed, and enjoyed an uninterrupted sleep. Sane I went to bed, and sane I arose. . . .

                              JOHN KEATS

THE VALE OF SOUL-MAKING

April, 1819

I have been reading lately two very different books, Robertson's *America* and Vol-

taire's *Siècle de Louis XIV*. It is like walking arm and arm between Pizarro and the great-little monarch. In how lamentable a case do we see the great body of the people in both instances; in the first, where men might seem to inherit quiet of mind from unsophisticated senses: from uncontamination of civilisation, and especially from their being, as it were, estranged from the mutual helps of society and its mutual injuries—and thereby more immediately under the protection of providence—even there they had mortal pains to bear as bad, or even worse, than bailiffs, debts, and poverties of civilised life. The whole appears to resolve into this—that man is originally a poor forked creature subject to the same mischances as the beasts of the forest, destined to hardships and disquietude of some kind or other. If he improves by degrees his bodily accommodations and comforts, at each stage, at each ascent there are waiting for him a fresh set of annoyances: he is mortal, and there is still a heaven with its stars above his head. The most interesting question that can come before us is: How far by the persevering endeavors of a seldom appearing Socrates mankind may be made happy. I can imagine such happiness carried to an extreme, but what must it end in?—death—and who could in such a case bear with death? The whole troubles of life, which are now frittered away in a series of years, would then be accumulated for the last days of a being who instead of hailing its approach would leave this world as Eve left Paradise.

But in truth I do not at all believe in this sort of perfectibility—the nature of the world will not admit of it—the inhabitants of the world will correspond to itself. Let the fish philosophise the ice away from the rivers in winter time, and they shall be at continual play in the tepid delight of summer. Look at the poles and at the sands of Africa, whirlpools and volcanoes. Let men exterminate them and I will say that they may arrive at earthly happiness. The point at which man may arrive is as far as the parallel state in inanimate nature, and no further. For instance, suppose a rose to have sensation, it blooms on a beautiful morning, it enjoys itself, but then comes a cold wind, a hot sun—it cannot escape it, it cannot destroy its annoyances—they are as native to the world as itself: no more can man be happy in spite, the worldly elements will prey upon his nature.

The common cognomen of this world

among the misguided and superstitious is "a vale of tears," from which we are to be redeemed by a certain arbitrary interposition of God and taken to Heaven. What a little circumscribed straightened notion! Call the world if you please "The vale of soul-making." Then you will find out the use of the world (I am speaking now in the highest terms for human nature admitting it to be immortal, which I will here take for granted for the purpose of showing a thought which has struck me concerning it). I say *"soul-making"*—soul as distinguished from an intelligence. There may be intelligences or sparks of the divinity in millions, but they are not souls till they acquire identities, till each one is personally itself. Intelligences are atoms of perception; they know and they see and they are pure, in short, they are God. How then are souls to be made? How then are these sparks which are God to have identity given them, so as ever to possess a bliss peculiar to each one's individual existence? How, but by the medium of a world like this? This point I sincerely wish to consider because I think it a grander system of salvation than the Christian religion; or rather it is a system of spirit-creation. This is effected by three grand materials acting the one upon the other for a series of years. These three materials are the *intelligence* —the *human heart* (as distinguished from intelligence or mind), and the *world* or *elemental space* suited for the proper action of *mind and heart* on each other for the purpose of forming the *soul* or *intelligence destined to possess the sense of identity.* I can scarcely express what I but dimly perceive, and yet I think I perceive it. That you may judge the more clearly I will put it in the most homely form possible. I will call the *world* a school instituted for the purpose of teaching little children to read. I will call the *human heart* the *horn book* used in that school. And I will call the *child able to read, the soul* made from that *school* and its *horn book.* Do you not see how necessary a world of pains and troubles is to school an intelligence and make it a soul,—a place where the heart must feel and suffer in a thousand diverse ways? Not merely is the heart a horn book, it is the mind's Bible, it is the mind's experience, it is the teat from which the mind or intelligence sucks its identity. As various as the lives of men are, so various become their souls, and thus does God make individual beings, souls, identical souls of the sparks of his own essence. This appears to

me a faint sketch of a system of salvation which does not offend our reason and humanity . . .

Your ever affectionate brother,

JOHN KEATS

TWO LUXURIES

To Fanny Brawne

July 25, 1819

My Sweet Girl,—

I hope you did not blame me much for not obeying your request of a Letter on Saturday: we have had four in our small room playing at cards night and morning leaving me no undisturbed opportunity to write. Now Rice and Martin are gone I am at liberty. Brown to my sorrow confirms the account you give of your ill health. You cannot conceive how I ache to be with you: how I would die for one hour—for what is in the world? I say you cannot conceive; it is impossible you should look with such eyes upon me as I have upon you: it cannot be. Forgive me if I wander a little this evening, for I have been all day employed in a very abstract Poem and I am in deep love with you—two things which must excuse me. I have, believe me, not been an age in letting you take possession of me; the very first week I knew you I wrote myself your vassal; but burnt the Letter as the very next time I saw you I thought you manifested some dislike to me. If you should ever feel for Man at the first sight what I did for you, I am lost. Yet I should not quarrel with you, but hate myself if such a thing were to happen—only I should burst if the thing were not as fine as a Man as you are as a Woman. Perhaps I am too vehement, then fancy me on my knees, especially when I mention a part of your Letter which hurt me; you say speaking of Mr. Severn "but you must be satisfied in knowing that I admired you much more than your friend." My dear love, I cannot believe there ever was or ever could be any thing to admire in me especially as far as sight goes—I cannot be admired, I am not a thing to be admired. You are, I love you; all I can bring you is a swooning admiration of your Beauty. I hold that place among Men which snub-nosed brunettes with meeting eyebrows do among women—they are trash to me—unless I should find one among them with a fire in her heart like the one that burns in mine. You absorb me in spite of myself—you alone: for I look not forward with any pleasure to what is called being settled in the world; I tremble at domestic cares—yet for you I would meet them, though if it would leave you the happier I would rather die than do so. I have two luxuries to brood over in my walks, your Loveliness and the hour of my death. O that I could have possession of them both in the same minute. I hate the world: it batters too much the wings of my self-will, and would I could take a sweet poison from your lips to send me out of it. From no others would I take it. I am indeed astonished to find myself so careless of all charms but yours—remembering as I do the time when even a bit of ribband was a matter of interest with me. What softer words can I find for you after this—what it is I will not read. Nor will I say more here, but in a postscript answer anything else you may have mentioned in your letter in so many words—for I am distracted with a thousand thoughts. I will imagine you Venus tonight and pray, pray, pray to your star like a heathen.

Yours ever, fair Star,

JOHN KEATS

I HAVE LOVED BEAUTY

To Fanny Brawne

Feb. (?), 1820

My dear Fanny,—

Do not let your mother suppose that you hurt me by writing at night. For some reason or other your last night's note was not so treasurable as former ones. I would fain that you call me *Love* still. To see you happy and in high spirits is a great consolation to me—still let me believe that you are not half so happy as my restoration would make you. I am nervous, I own, and may think myself worse than I really am; if so you must indulge me, and pamper with that sort of tenderness you have manifested towards me in different Letters. My sweet creature when I look back upon the pains and torments I have suffered for you from the day I left you to go to the Isle of Wight; the ecstasies in which I have passed some days and the miseries in their turn, I wonder the more at the Beauty which has kept up the spell so fervently. When I send this round I shall be in the front parlor watching to see you show yourself for a minute in the garden. How illness stands

as a barrier betwixt me and you! Even if I was well—I must make myself as good a Philosopher as possible. Now I have had opportunities of passing nights anxious and awake I have found other thoughts intrude upon me. "If I should die," said I to myself, "I have left no immortal work behind me—nothing to make my friends proud of my memory—but I have loved the principle of beauty in all things, and if I had had time I would have made myself remembered." Thoughts like these came very feebly whilst I was in health and every pulse beat for you—now you divide with this (may *I* say it?) "last infirmity of noble minds" all my reflection.

God bless you, Love

J. KEATS

LOAD EVERY RIFT WITH ORE

To Percy Bysshe Shelley

Hampstead; Aug. 16, 1820

My dear Shelley,—

I am very much gratified that you, in a foreign country, and with a mind almost over-occupied, should write to me in the strain of the letter beside me. If I do not take advantage of your invitation, it will be prevented by a circumstance I have very much at heart to prophesy. There is no doubt that an English winter would put an end to me, and do so in a lingering hateful manner. Therefore, I must either voyage or journey to Italy, as a soldier marches up to a battery. My nerves at present are the worst part of me, yet they feel soothed that, come what extreme may, I shall not be destined to remain in one spot long enough to take a hatred of any four particular bedposts. I am glad you take any pleasure in my poor poem, which I would willingly take the trouble to unwrite, if possible, did I care so much as I have done about reputation. I received a copy of the Cenci, as from yourself, from Hunt. There is only one part of it I am judge of—the poetry and dramatic effect, which by many spirits nowadays is considered the Mammon. A modern work, it is said, must have a purpose, which may be the God. An artist must serve Mammon; he must have "self-concentration"—selfishness, perhaps. You, I am sure, will forgive me for sincerely remarking that you might curb your magnanimity, and be more of an artist, and load every rift of your subject with ore.

The thought of such discipline must fall like cold chains upon you, who perhaps never sat with your wings furled for six months together. And is this not extraordinary talk for the writer of Endymion, whose mind was like a pack of scattered cards? I am picked up and sorted to a pip. My imagination is a monastery, and I am its monk. You must explain my metap[hors] to yourself. I am in expectation of Prometheus every day. Could I have my own wish effected, you would have it still in manuscript, or be but now putting an end to the second act. I remember you advis-

ing me not to publish my first-blights, on Hampstead Heath. I am returning advice upon your hands. Most of the poems in the volume I send you have been written above two years, and would never have been published but from a hope of gain; so you see I am inclined enough to take your advice now. I must express once more my deep sense of your kindness, adding my sincere thanks and respects for Mrs. Shelley.

In the hope of soon seeing you, I remain

most sincerely yours
JOHN KEATS

PERCY BYSSHE SHELLEY (1792-1822)

Alike remote from Byron's scorn
And Keats's magic as of morn,
Bursting forever newly-born
  On forest old,
To wake a hoary world forlorn
  With touch of gold;

Impatient of the world's fixed way,
He ne'er could suffer God's delay,
But all the future in a day
  Would build divine.
    WILLIAM WATSON

So much political and philosophical partisanship embitters the discussions about Shelley that the real truth concerning his character, and concerning the meaning and value of his poems, is hard to discern. His worshipers assert that his lyrical powers are nothing short of marvelous, and even his enemies concede the point; but every other important matter is hotly disputed. The scorners of Shelley make much of his early period (before the age of twenty-three). In those years, he was expelled from Oxford for engaging in atheistical propaganda, he entered into an unwise marriage, he deserted his wife and children, he eloped with Mary Godwin, and he professed those principles of philosophical anarchy (including free love and communism) of which her father, William Godwin, was an advocate. The young Shelley's failure to adjust himself to the world was clear; and his opponents then and now have found plenty of evidence in his youthful acts and words to indict him as rash, impious, and wicked, and to suggest that the poetry of such a man can hardly be of true light and leading.

It seems, however, unnecessary to concentrate attention upon Shelley's conduct during that period (although there are facts which mitigate his offenses); for the reason,—which his enemies ignore,—that those poems of Shelley which are his greatest belong to the later period of his life (1815-22), when there was some change in the manner of his life, and a decidedly important change in his views. In March, 1818, he left England for Italy; and there, during the last four years of his life, encouraged by the companionship of kindred spirits,—his wife, Mary, Byron, Claire Clairmont, Trelawny, Leigh Hunt, etc., he devoted himself to his studies in philosophy, and produced his greatest poetry. While sailing his boat off Leghorn, he was caught in a sudden squall and drowned on July 8, 1822. He died, like Keats, when at the height of his poetic power.

During his last eight years Shelley, who had been a materialist and rationalist, scornful of the spiritual and the imaginative, became, under the influence of Plato, Plotinus, and Spinoza, a transcendental idealist, with a mystical religion and a highly imaginative theory of poetry. From his earlier period he retained his political opposition to autocratic tyranny and privilege, his rebelliousness against senseless conventions, and his impatience with the slowness of human progress. He retained his interest in the bolder speculations of contemporary scientists. He retained, too, his love of nature; but he now felt that the poet's highest opportunity lay in not merely describing phenomena objectively but in evoking that ideal beauty which the visual appearance tended to veil. The Shelley of the great poems believed in a Soul of the Universe, a Spirit of Love, revealed through poetry and art. He believed that the will of mankind could be more successfully exerted against our besetting evils than it had been in the past, and that soon it would be thus exerted; but this liberation of mankind would be achieved, not by cool reason, but rather by ardent love and faith. Those who struggled onwards in that spirit were the truly great and good:

To suffer woes which Hope thinks infinite;
To forgive wrongs darker than death or night;
To defy Power, which seems omnipotent;
To love, and bear; to hope till Hope creates
From its own wreck the thing it contemplates;
Neither to change, nor falter, nor repent;
This, like thy glory, Titan, is to be
Good, great and joyous, beautiful and free;
This is alone Life, Joy, Empire, and Victory.

(Close of *Prometheus Unbound*)

STANZAS.—APRIL, 1814

Away! the moor is dark beneath the moon,
  Rapid clouds have drank the last pale beam of even:
Away! the gathering winds will call the darkness soon,
  And profoundest midnight shroud the serene lights of heaven.

Pause not! the time is past! Every voice cries, Away!   5
  Tempt not with one last tear thy friend's ungentle mood:
Thy lover's eye, so glazed and cold, dares not entreat thy stay:
  Duty and dereliction guide thee back to solitude.

Away, away! to thy sad and silent home;
  Pour bitter tears on its desolated hearth;   10
Watch the dim shades as like ghosts they go and come,
  And complicate strange webs of melancholy mirth.

The leaves of wasted autumn woods shall float around thine head:
  The blooms of dewy spring shall gleam beneath thy feet:
But thy soul or this world must fade in the frost that binds the dead,   15
  Ere midnight's frown and morning's smile, ere thou and peace may meet.

The cloud shadows of midnight possess their own repose,
  For the weary winds are silent, or the moon is in the deep:
Some respite to its turbulence unresting ocean knows;
  Whatever moves, or toils, or grieves, hath its appointed sleep.   20

Thou in the grave shalt rest—yet till the phantoms flee
  Which that house and heath and garden made dear to thee erewhile,
Thy remembrance, and repentance, and deep musings are not free
  From the music of two voices and the light of one sweet smile.

TO WORDSWORTH

Poet of Nature, thou hast wept to know
  That things depart which never may return:
Childhood and youth, friendship and love's first glow,
  Have fled like sweet dreams, leaving thee to mourn.
These common woes I feel. One loss is mine   5
  Which thou too feel'st, yet I alone deplore.
Thou wert as a lone star, whose light did shine
  On some frail bark in winter's midnight roar:
Thou hast like to a rock-built refuge stood
Above the blind and battling multitude: 10
In honored poverty thy voice did weave
  Songs consecrate to truth and liberty,—
Deserting these, thou leavest me to grieve,
  Thus having been, that thou shouldst cease to be.

c. 1815   March, 1816

FROM ALASTOR

PREFACE

The poem entitled "ALASTOR," may be ₅
considered as allegorical of one of the most
interesting situations of the human mind.
It represents a youth of uncorrupted feelings and adventurous genius led forth by
an imagination inflamed and purified 10
through familiarity with all that is excellent and majestic, to the contemplation of
the universe. He drinks deep of the fountains of knowledge, and is still insatiate.
The magnificence and beauty of the ex- 15
ternal world sinks profoundly into the
frame of his conceptions, and affords to
their modifications a variety not to be exhausted. So long as it is possible for his
desires to point towards objects thus in- 20
finite and unmeasured, he is joyous, and
tranquil, and self-possessed. But the period
arrives when these objects cease to suffice.
His mind is at length suddenly awakened
and thirsts for intercourse with an intelli- 25
gence similar to itself. He images to himself the Being whom he loves. Conversant
with speculations of the sublimest and most
perfect natures, the vision in which he embodies his own imaginations unites all of 30
wonderful, or wise, or beautiful, which the
poet, the philosopher, or the lover could
depicture. The intellectual faculties, the
imagination, the functions of sense, have
their respective requisitions on the sym- 35
pathy of corresponding powers in other
human beings. The Poet is represented as
uniting these requisitions, and attaching
them to a single image. He seeks in vain
for a prototype of his conception. Blasted 40
by his disappointment, he descends to an
untimely grave.

The picture is not barren of instruction

to actual men. The Poet's self-centered
seclusion was avenged by the furies of an
irresistible passion pursuing him to speedy
ruin. But that Power which strikes the
luminaries of the world with sudden darkness and extinction, by awakening them to
too exquisite a perception of its influences,
dooms to a slow and poisonous decay those
meaner spirits that dare to abjure its dominion. Their destiny is more abject and
inglorious as their delinquency is more con
temptible and pernicious. They who, deluded by no generous error, instigated by
no sacred thirst of doubtful knowledge,
duped by no illustrious superstition, loving
nothing on this earth, and cherishing no
hopes beyond, yet keep aloof from sympathies with their kind, rejoicing neither in
human joy nor mourning with human
grief; these, and such as they, have their
apportioned curse. They languish, because
none feel with them their common nature.
They are morally dead. They are neither
friends, nor lovers, nor fathers, nor citizens
of the world, nor benefactors of their country. Among those who attempt to exist
without human sympathy, the pure and
tender-hearted perish through the intensity
and passion of their search after its com-
munities, when the vacancy of their spirit
suddenly makes itself felt. All else, selfish,
blind, and torpid, are those unforeseeing
multitudes who constitute, together with
their own, the lasting misery and loneliness of the world. Those who love not
their fellow-beings, live unfruitful lives,
and prepare for their old age a miserable
grave.

                    The good die first,
And those whose hearts are dry as summer
    dust,
Burn to the socket!

Dec. 14, 1815

ALASTOR

OR

THE SPIRIT OF SOLITUDE

Nondum amabam, et amare amabam, quær-
ebam quid amarem, amans amare.
            Confess. St. August.

Earth, ocean, air, belovèd brotherhood!
If our great Mother has imbued my soul
With aught of natural piety to feel
Your love, and recompense the boon with
    mine;

If dewy morn, and odorous noon, and
    even,   5
With sunset and its gorgeous ministers,
And solemn midnight's tingling silentness;
If autumn's hollow sighs in the sere wood,
And winter robing with pure snow and
    crowns
Of starry ice the gray grass and bare
    boughs;   10
If spring's voluptuous pantings when she
    breathes
Her first sweet kisses, have been dear to me;
If no bright bird, insect, or gentle beast
I consciously have injured, but still loved

And cherished these my kindred; then forgive   15
This boast, belovèd brethren, and withdraw
No portion of your wonted favor now!

Mother of this unfathomable world!
Favor my solemn song, for I have loved
Thee ever, and thee only; I have watched 20
Thy shadow, and the darkness of thy steps,
And my heart ever gazes on the depth
Of thy deep mysteries. I have made my bed
In charnels and on coffins, where black
   death
Keeps record of the trophies won from
   thee,   25
Hoping to still these obstinate questionings
Of thee and thine, by forcing some lone
   ghost,
Thy messenger, to render up the tale
Of what we are. In lone and silent hours,
When night makes a weird sound of its
   own stillness,   30
Like an inspired and desperate alchemist
Staking his very life on some dark hope,
Have I mixed awful talk and asking looks
With my most innocent love, until strange
   tears
Uniting with those breathless kisses, made 35
Such magic as compels the charmèd night
To render up thy charge. . . . and, though
   ne'er yet
Thou hast unveiled thy inmost sanctuary,
Enough from incommunicable dream,
And twilight phantasms, and deep noonday
   thought,   40
Has shone within me, that serenely now
And moveless, as a long-forgotten lyre
Suspended in the solitary dome
Of some mysterious and deserted fane,
I wait thy breath, Great Parent, that my
   strain   45
May modulate with murmurs of the air,
And motions of the forests and the sea,
And voice of living beings, and woven
   hymns
Of night and day, and the deep heart of
   man.

   There was a Poet, whose untimely tomb 50
No human hands with pious reverence
   reared,
But the charmed eddies of autumnal winds
Built o'er his moldering bones a pyramid
Of moldering leaves in the waste wilder-
   ness:—
A lovely youth,—no mourning maiden
   decked   55
With weeping flowers, or votive cypress
   wreath,

The lone couch of his everlasting sleep:—
Gentle, and brave, and generous,—no lorn
   bard
Breathed o'er his dark fate one melodious
   sigh:
He lived, he died, he sung, in solitude. 60
Strangers have wept to hear his passionate
   notes,
And virgins, as unknown he passed, have
   pined
And wasted for fond love of his wild eyes.
The fire of those soft orbs has ceased to
   burn,
And Silence, too enamored of that voice, 65
Locks its mute music in her rugged cell.

   By solemn vision, and bright silver
   dream,
His infancy was nurtured. Every sight
And sound from the vast earth and ambi-
   ent air,
Sent to his heart its choicest impulses. 70
The fountains of divine philosophy
Fled not his thirsting lips, and all of great,
Or good, or lovely, which the sacred past
In truth or fable consecrates, he felt
And knew. When early youth had passed,
   he left   75
His cold fireside and alienated home
To seek strange truths in undiscovered
   lands.
Many a wide waste and tangled wilderness
Has lured his fearless steps; and he has
   bought
With his sweet voice and eyes, from savage
   men,   80
His rest and food. Nature's most sacred
   steps
He like her shadow has pursued, where'er
The red volcano overcanopies
Its fields of snow and pinnacles of ice
With burning smoke, or where bitumen
   lakes   85
On black bare pointed islets ever beat
With sluggish surge, or where the secret
   caves
Rugged and dark, winding among the
   springs
Of fire and poison, inaccessible
To avarice or pride, their starry domes 90
Of diamond and of gold expand above
Numberless and immeasurable halls,
Frequent with crystal column, and clear
   shrines
Of pearl, and thrones radiant with chryso-
   lite.
Nor had that scene of ampler majesty 95
Than gems or gold, the varying roof of
   heaven

And the green earth, lost in his heart its
    claims
To love and wonder; he would linger long
In lonesome vales, making the wild his
    home,
Until the doves and squirrels would par-
    take   100
From his innocuous hand his bloodless
    food,
Lured by the gentle meaning of his looks,
And the wild antelope, that starts whene'er
The dry leaf rustles in the brake, suspend
Her timid steps to gaze upon a form   105
More graceful than her own.
                          His wandering step,
Obedient to high thoughts, has visited
The awful ruins of the days of old:
Athens, and Tyre, and Balbec, and the
    waste
Where stood Jerusalem, the fallen tow-
    ers   110
Of Babylon, the eternal pyramids,
Memphis and Thebes, and whatsoe'er of
    strange
Sculptured on alabaster obelisk
Or jasper tomb, or mutilated sphynx,
Dark Æthiopia in her desert hills   115
Conceals. Among the ruined temples there,
Stupendous columns, and wild images
Of more than man, where marble dæmons
    watch
The Zodiac's brazen mystery, and dead men
Hang their mute thoughts on the mute
    walls around,   120
He lingered, poring on memorials
Of the world's youth, through the long
    burning day
Gazed on those speechless shapes, nor, when
    the moon
Filled the mysterious halls with floating
    shades,
Suspended he that task, but ever gazed 125
And gazed, till meaning on his vacant mind
Flashed like strong inspiration, and he saw
The thrilling secrets of the birth of time.

Meanwhile an Arab maiden brought his
    food,
Her daily portion, from her father's
    tent,   130
And spread her matting for his couch, and
    stole
From duties and repose to tend his steps:—
Enamored, yet not daring for deep awe
To speak her love:—and watched his
    nightly sleep,
Sleepless herself, to gaze upon his lips 135
Parted in slumber, whence the regular
    breath

Of innocent dreams arose: then, when red
    morn
Made paler the pale moon, to her cold
    home
Wildered, and wan, and panting, she re-
    turned.

The Poet wandering on, through
    Arabie   140
And Persia, and the wild Carmanian waste,
And o'er the aërial mountains which pour
    down
Indus and Oxus from their icy caves,
In joy and exultation held his way;
Till in the vale of Cashmire, far within 145
Its loneliest dell, where odorous plants en-
    twine
Beneath the hollow rocks a natural bower,
Beside a sparkling rivulet he stretched
His languid limbs. A vision on his sleep
There came, a dream of hopes that never
    yet   150
Had flushed his cheek. He dreamed a
    veilèd maid
Sat near him, talking in low solemn tones.
Her voice was like the voice of his own soul
Heard in the calm of thought; its music
    long,
Like woven sounds of streams and breezes,
    held   155
His inmost sense suspended in its web
Of many-colored woof and shifting hues.
Knowledge and truth and virtue were her
    theme,
And lofty hopes of divine liberty,
Thoughts the most dear to him, and
    poesy,   160
Herself a poet. Soon the solemn mood
Of her pure mind kindled through all her
    frame
A permeating fire: wild numbers then
She raised, with voice stifled in tremendous
    sobs
Subdued by its own pathos: her fair
    hands   165
Were bare alone, sweeping from some
    strange harp
Strange symphony, and in their branching
    veins
The eloquent blood told an ineffable tale.
The beating of her heart was heard to fill
The pauses of her music, and her breath 170
Tumultuously accorded with those fits
Of intermitted song. Sudden she rose,
As if her heart impatiently endured
Its bursting burthen: at the sound he
    turned,
And saw by the warm light of their own
    life   175
Her glowing limbs beneath the sinuous veil

Of woven wind, her outspread arms now
  bare,
Her dark locks floating in the breath of
  night,
Her beamy bending eyes, her parted lips
Outstretched, and pale, and quivering
  eagerly.   180
His strong heart sunk and sickened with
  excess
Of love. He reared his shuddering limbs
  and quelled
His gasping breath, and spread his arms to
  meet
Her panting bosom: . . . she drew back a
  while,
Then, yielding to the irresistible joy,   185
With frantic gesture and short breathless
  cry
Folded his frame in her dissolving arms.
Now blackness veiled his dizzy eyes, and
  night
Involved and swallowed up the vision;
  sleep,
Like a dark flood suspended in its
  course,   190
Rolled back its impulse on his vacant
  brain.

Roused by the shock he started from his
  trance—
The cold white light of morning, the blue
  moon
Low in the west, the clear and garish hills,
The distinct valley and the vacant woods, 195
Spread round him where he stood.
  Whither have fled
The hues of heaven that canopied his
  bower
Of yesternight? The sounds that soothed
  his sleep,
The mystery and the majesty of Earth,
The joy, the exultation? His wan eyes 200
Gaze on the empty scene as vacantly
As ocean's moon looks on the moon in
  heaven.
The spirit of sweet human love has sent
A vision to the sleep of him who spurned
Her choicest gifts. He eagerly pursues 205
Beyond the realms of dream that fleeting
  shade;
He overleaps the bounds. Alas! alas!
Were limbs, and breath, and being inter-
  twined
Thus treacherously? Lost, lost, for ever
  lost,
In the wide pathless desert of dim sleep, 210
That beautiful shape! Does the dark gate
  of death
Conduct to thy mysterious paradise,

O Sleep? Does the bright arch of rainbow
  clouds,
And pendent mountains seen in the calm
  lake,
Lead only to a black and watery depth, 215
While death's blue vault, with loathliest
  vapors hung,
Where every shade which the foul grave
  exhales
Hides its dead eye from the detested day,
Conduct, O Sleep, to thy delightful realms?
This doubt with sudden tide flowed on his
  heart,   220
The insatiate hope which it awakened
  stung
His brain even like despair.
                 While daylight held
The sky, the Poet kept mute conference
With his still soul. At night the passion
  came,
Like the fierce fiend of a distempered
  dream,   225
And shook him from his rest, and led him
  forth
Into the darkness.—As an eagle grasped
In folds of the green serpent, feels her
  breast
Burn with the poison, and precipitates
Through night and day, tempest, and calm,
  and cloud,   230
Frantic with dizzying anguish, her blind
  flight
O'er the wide aëry wilderness: thus driven
By the bright shadow of that lovely dream,
Beneath the cold glare of the desolate
  night,
Through tangled swamps and deep precip-
  itous dells,   235
Startling with careless step the moon-light
  snake,
He fled. Red morning dawned upon his
  flight,
Shedding the mockery of its vital hues
Upon his cheek of death. He wandered on
Till vast Aornos seen from Petra's steep 240
Hung o'er the low horizon like a cloud;
Through Balk, and where the desolated
  tombs
Of Parthian kings scatter to every wind
Their wasting dust, wildly he wandered on,
Day after day, a weary waste of hours, 245
Bearing within his life the brooding care
That ever fed on its decaying flame.
And now his limbs were lean; his scattered
  hair
Sered by the autumn of strange suffering
Sung dirges in the wind; his listless
  hand   250
Hung like dead bone within its withered
  skin;

Life, and the lustre that consumed it, shone
As in a furnace burning secretly
From his dark eyes alone. The cottagers,
Who ministered with human charity   255
His human wants, beheld with wondering
  awe
Their fleeting visitant. The mountaineer,
Encountering on some dizzy precipice
That spectral form, deemed that the Spirit
  of wind
With lightning eyes, and eager breath, and
  feet   260
Disturbing not the drifted snow, had
  paused
In its career: the infant would conceal
His troubled visage in his mother's robe
In terror at the glare of those wild eyes,
To remember their strange light in many a
  dream   265
Of after-times; but youthful maidens,
  taught
By nature, would interpret half the woe
That wasted him, would call him with
  false names
Brother, and friend, would press his pallid
  hand
At parting, and watch, dim through tears,
  the path   270
Of his departure from their father's door.

At length upon the lone Chorasmian
  shore
He paused, a wide and melancholy waste
Of putrid marshes. A strong impulse urged
His steps to the seashore. A swan was
  there,   275
Beside a sluggish stream among the reeds.
It rose as he approached, and with strong
  wings
Scaling the upward sky, bent its bright
  course
High over the immeasurable main.
His eyes pursued its flight.—"Thou hast a
  home,   280
Beautiful bird; thou voyagest to thine
  home,
Where thy sweet mate will twine her
  downy neck
With thine, and welcome thy return with
  eyes
Bright in the lustre of their own fond joy.
And what am I that I should linger
  here,   285
With voice far sweeter than thy dying
  notes,
Spirit more vast than thine, frame more
  attuned
To beauty, wasting these surpassing powers
In the deaf air, to the blind earth, and
  heaven

That echoes not my thoughts?" A gloomy
  smile   290
Of desperate hope wrinkled his quivering
  lips.
For sleep, he knew, kept most relentlessly
Its precious charge, and silent death ex-
  posed,
Faithless perhaps as sleep, a shadowy lure,
With doubtful smile mocking its own
  strange charms.   295

Startled by his own thoughts, he looked
  around.
There was no fair fiend near him, not a
  sight
Or sound of awe but in his own deep mind.
A little shallop floating near the shore
Caught the impatient wandering of his
  gaze.   300
It had been long abandoned, for its sides
Gaped wide with many a rift, and its frail
  joints
Swayed with the undulations of the tide.
A restless impulse urged him to embark
And meet lone Death on the drear ocean's
  waste;   305
For well he knew that mighty Shadow loves
The slimy caverns of the populous deep.

The day was fair and sunny, sea and sky
Drank its inspiring radiance, and the wind
Swept strongly from the shore, blackening
  the waves.   310
Following his eager soul, the wanderer
Leaped in the boat, he spread his cloak
  aloft
On the bare mast, and took his lonely seat,
And felt the boat speed o'er the tranquil
  sea
Like a torn cloud before the hurricane.   315

As one that in a silver vision floats
Obedient to the sweep of odorous winds
Upon resplendent clouds, so rapidly
Along the dark and ruffled waters fled
The straining boat.—A whirlwind swept it
  on,   320
With fierce gusts and precipitating force,
Through the white ridges of the chafèd sea.
The waves arose. Higher and higher still
Their fierce necks writhed beneath the
  tempest's scourge
Like serpents struggling in a vulture's
  grasp.   325
Calm and rejoicing in the fearful war
Of wave ruining on wave and blast on blast
Descending, and black flood on whirlpool
  driven
With dark obliterating course, he sate:
As if their genii were the ministers   330

Appointed to conduct him to the light
Of those belovèd eyes, the Poet sate
Holding the steady helm. Evening came on,
The beams of sunset hung their rainbow
    hues
High 'mid the shifting domes of sheeted
    spray   335
That canopied his path o'er the waste
    deep;
Twilight, ascending slowly from the east,
Entwined in duskier wreaths her braided
    locks
O'er the fair front and radiant eyes of day;
Night followed, clad with stars. On every
    side   340
More horribly the multitudinous streams
Of ocean's mountainous waste to mutual
    war
Rushed in dark tumult thundering, as to
    mock
The calm and spangled sky. The little
    boat
Still fled before the storm; still fled, like
    foam   345
Down the steep cataract of a wintry river;
Now pausing on the edge of the riven
    wave;
Now leaving far behind the bursting mass
That fell, convulsing ocean. Safely fled—
As if that frail and wasted human form, 350
Had been an elemental god.
                    At midnight
The moon arose: and lo! the etherial cliffs
Of Caucasus, whose icy summits shone
Among the stars like sunlight, and around
Whose caverned base the whirlpools and
    the waves   355
Bursting and eddying irresistibly
Rage and resound forever.—Who shall
    save?—
The boat fled on,—the boiling torrent
    drove,—
The crags closed round with black and
    jaggèd arms,
The shattered mountain overhung the
    sea,   360
And faster still, beyond all human speed,
Suspended on the sweep of the smooth
    wave,
The little boat was driven. A cavern there
Yawned, and amid its slant and winding
    depths
Ingulfed the rushing sea. The boat fled
    on   365
With unrelaxing speed.—"Vision and
    Love!"
The Poet cried aloud, "I have beheld
The path of thy departure. Sleep and
    death
Shall not divide us long!"

                    The boat pursued
The windings of the cavern. Daylight
    shone   370
At length upon that gloomy river's flow;
Now, where the fiercest war among the
    waves
Is calm, on the unfathomable stream
The boat moved slowly. Where the moun-
    tain, riven,
Exposed those black depths to the azure
    sky,   375
Ere yet the flood's enormous volume fell
Even to the base of Caucasus, with sound
That shook the everlasting rocks, the
    mass
Filled with one whirlpool all that ample
    chasm;
Stair above stair the eddying waters rose 380
Circling immeasurably fast, and laved
With alternating dash the gnarled roots
Of mighty trees, that stretched their giant
    arms
In darkness over it. I' the midst was left,
Reflecting, yet distorting every cloud,   385
A pool of treacherous and tremendous
    calm.
Seized by the sway of the ascending stream,
With dizzy swiftness, round, and round,
    and round,
Ridge after ridge the straining boat arose,
Till on the verge of the extremest curve, 390
Where through an opening of the rocky
    bank,
The waters overflow, and a smooth spot
Of glassy quiet 'mid those battling tides
Is left, the boat paused shuddering.—Shall
    it sink
Down the abyss? Shall the reverting
    stress   395
Of that resistless gulf embosom it?
Now shall it fall?—A wandering stream of
    wind,
Breathed from the west, has caught the
    expanded sail,
And, lo! with gentle motion, between
    banks
Of mossy slope, and on a placid stream, 400
Beneath a woven grove it sails, and, hark!
The ghastly torrent mingles its far roar,
With the breeze murmuring in the musical
    woods.
Where the embowering trees recede, and
    leave
A little space of green expanse, the cove 405
Is closed by meeting banks, whose yellow
    flowers
For ever gaze on their own drooping eyes,
Reflected in the crystal calm. The wave
Of the boat's motion marred their pensive
    task,

Which nought but vagrant bird, or wanton
    wind,   410
Or falling spear-grass, or their own decay
Had e'er disturbed before. The Poet
    longed
To deck with their bright hues his with-
    ered hair,
But on his heart its solitude returned,
And he forbore. Not the strong impulse
    hid   415
In those flushed cheeks, bent eyes, and
    shadowy frame
Had yet performed its ministry: it hung
Upon his life, as lightning in a cloud
Gleams, hovering ere it vanish, ere the
    floods
Of night close over it.
          The noonday sun 420
Now shone upon the forest, one vast mass
Of mingling shade, whose brown magnifi-
    cence
A narrow vale embosoms. There, huge
    caves,
Scooped in the dark base of their aëry rocks
Mocking its moans, respond and roar for
    ever.   425
The meeting boughs and implicated leaves
Wove twilight o'er the Poet's path, as led
By love, or dream, or god, or mightier
    Death,
He sought in Nature's dearest haunt, some
    bank,
Her cradle, and his sepulchre. More
    dark   430
And dark the shades accumulate. The
    oak,
Expanding its immense and knotty arms,
Embraces the light beech. The pyramids
Of the tall cedar overarching, frame
Most solemn domes within, and far be-
    low,   435
Like clouds suspended in an emerald sky,
The ash and the acacia floating hang
Tremulous and pale. Like restless ser-
    pents, clothed
In rainbow and in fire, the parasites,
Starred with ten thousand blossoms, flow
    around   440
The gray trunks, and, as gamesome infants'
    eyes,
With gentle meanings, and most innocent
    wiles,
Fold their beams round the hearts of those
    that love,
These twine their tendrils with the wedded
    boughs
Uniting their close union; the woven
    leaves   445
Make network of the dark blue light of
    day,

And the night's noontide clearness, muta-
    ble
As shapes in the weird clouds. Soft mossy
    lawns
Beneath these canopies extend their swells,
Fragrant with perfumed herbs, and eyed
    with blooms   450
Minute yet beautiful. One darkest glen
Sends from its woods of musk-rose, twined
    with jasmine,
A soul-dissolving odor, to invite
To some more lovely mystery. Through
    the dell,
Silence and Twilight here, twin sisters,
    keep   455
Their noonday watch, and sail among the
    shades,
Like vaporous shapes half seen; beyond, a
    well,
Dark, gleaming, and of most translucent
    wave,
Images all the woven boughs above,
And each depending leaf, and every
    speck   460
Of azure sky, darting between their chasms;
Nor aught else in the liquid mirror laves
Its portraiture, but some inconstant star
Between one foliaged lattice twinkling fair,
Or, painted bird, sleeping beneath the
    moon,   465
Or gorgeous insect floating motionless,
Unconscious of the day, ere yet his wings,
Have spread their glories to the gaze of
    noon.

    Hither the Poet came. His eyes beheld
Their own wan light through the reflected
    lines   470
Of his thin hair, distinct in the dark depth
Of that still fountain; as the human heart,
Gazing in dreams over the gloomy grave,
Sees its own treacherous likeness there. He
    heard
The motion of the leaves, the grass that
    sprung   475
Startled and glanced and trembled even to
    feel
An unaccustomed presence, and the sound
Of the sweet brook that from the secret
    springs
Of that dark fountain rose. A Spirit
    seemed
To stand beside him—clothed in no bright
    robes   480
Of shadowed silver or enshrining light,
Borrowed from aught the visible world
    affords
Of grace, or majesty, or mystery;—
But, undulating woods, and silent well,
And leaping rivulet, and evening gloom 485

Now deepening the dark shades, for speech
   assuming
Held commune with him, as if he and it
Were all that was,—only . . . when his
   regard
Was raised by intense pensiveness, . . . two
   eyes,
Two starry eyes, hung in the gloom of
   thought,   490
And seemed with their serene and azure
   smiles
To beckon him. . . .

. . . .

When on the threshold of the green
   recess   625
The wanderer's footsteps fell, he knew that
   death
Was on him. Yet a little, ere it fied,
Did he resign his high and holy soul
To images of the majestic past,
That paused within his passive being
   now,   630
Like winds that bear sweet music, when
   they breathe
Through some dim latticed chamber. He
   did place
His pale lean hand upon the rugged trunk
Of the old pine. Upon an ivied stone
Reclined his languid head, his limbs did
   rest,   635
Diffused and motionless, on the smooth
   brink
Of that obscurest chasm;—and thus he lay,
Surrendering to their final impulses
The hovering powers of life. Hope and
   despair,
The tortures, slept; no mortal pain or
   fear   640
Marred his repose, the influxes of sense,
And his own being unalloyed by pain,
Yet feebler and more feeble, calmly fed
The stream of thought, till he lay breath-
   ing there
At peace, and faintly smiling:—his last
   sight   645
Was the great moon, which o'er the western
   line
Of the wide world her mighty horn sus-
   pended.
With whose dun beams inwoven darkness
   seemed
To mingle. Now upon the jaggèd hills
It rests, and still as the divided frame   650
Of the vast meteor sunk, the Poet's blood,
That ever beat in mystic sympathy
With nature's ebb and flow, grew feebler
   still:
And when two lessening points of light
   alone

Gleamed through the darkness, the alter-
   nate gasp   655
Of his faint respiration scarce did stir
The stagnate night:—till the minutest ray
Was quenched, the pulse yet lingered in
   his heart,
It paused—it fluttered. But when heaven
   remained
Utterly black, the murky shades in-
   volved   660
An image, silent, cold, and motionless,
As their own voiceless earth and vacant air.
Even as a vapor fed with golden beams
That ministered on sunlight, ere the west
Eclipses it, was now that wondrous
   frame—   665
No sense, no motion, no divinity—
A fragile lute, on whose harmonious strings
The breath of heaven did wander—a
   bright stream
Once fed with many-voicèd waves—a dream
Of youth, which night and time have
   quenched for ever,   670
Still, dark, and dry, and unremembered
   now.

O, for Medea's wondrous alchemy,
Which wheresoe'er it fell made the earth
   gleam
With bright flowers, and the wintry boughs
   exhale
From vernal blooms fresh fragrance! Oh,
   that God,   675
Profuse of poisons, would concede the
   chalice
Which but one living man has drained,
   who now,
Vessel of deathless wrath, a slave that feels
No proud exemption in the blighting curse
He bears, over the world wanders for
   ever,   680
Lone as incarnate death! O, that the
   dream
Of dark magician in his visioned cave,
Raking the cinders of a crucible
For life and power, even when his feeble
   hand
Shakes in its last decay, were the true
   law   685
Of this so lovely world! But thou art fled
Like some frail exhalation; which the dawn
Robes in its golden beams,—ah! thou hast
   fled!
The brave, the gentle, and the beautiful,
The child of grace and genius. Heartless
   things   690
Are done and said i' the world, and many
   worms
And beasts and men live on, and mighty
   Earth

From sea and mountain, city and wilder-
ness,
In vesper low or joyous orison,
Lifts still its solemn voice:—but thou art
fled—   695
Thou canst no longer know or love the
shapes
Of this phantasmal scene, who have to thee
Been purest ministers, who are, alas!
Now thou art not. Upon those pallid lips
So sweet even in their silence, on those
eyes   700
That image sleep in death, upon that form
Yet safe from the worm's outrage, let no
tear
Be shed—not even in thought. Nor, when
those hues
Are gone, and those divinest lineaments,
Worn by the senseless wind, shall live
alone   705
In the frail pauses of this simple strain,
Let not high verse, mourning the memory
Of that which is no more, or painting's woe
Or sculpture, speak in feeble imagery
Their own cold powers. Art and elo-
quence,   710
And all the shows o' the world are frail
and vain
To weep a loss that turns their light to
shade.
It is a woe too "deep for tears," when all
Is reft at once, when some surpassing
Spirit,
Whose light adorned the world around it,
leaves   715
Those who remain behind, not sobs or
groans,
The passionate tumult of a clinging hope;
But pale despair and cold tranquillity,
Nature's vast frame, the web of human
things,
Birth and the grave, that are not as they
were.   720

1815   March, 1816

HYMN TO INTELLECTUAL
BEAUTY

1

The awful shadow of some unseen Power
Floats though unseen amongst us,—visiting
This various world with as inconstant
wing
As summer winds that creep from flower to
flower,—
Like moonbeams that behind some piny
mountain shower.   5

It visits with inconstant glance
Each human heart and countenance;
Like hues and harmonies of evening,—
Like clouds in starlight widely
spread,—
Like memory of music fled,—   10
Like aught that for its grace may be
Dear, and yet dearer for its mystery.

2

Spirit of BEAUTY, that dost consecrate
With thine own hues all thou dost shine
upon
Of human thought or form,—where art
thou gone?   15
Why dost thou pass away and leave our
state,
This dim vast vale of tears, vacant and
desolate?
Ask why the sunlight not for ever
Weaves rainbows o'er yon mountain
river,
Why aught should fail and fade that once
is shown,   20
Why fear and dream and death and
birth
Cast on the daylight of this earth
Such gloom,—why man has such a
scope
For love and hate, despondency and hope?

3

No voice from some sublimer world hath
ever   25
To sage or poet these responses given—
Therefore the names of Demon, Ghost,
and Heaven,
Remain the records of their vain endeavor,
Frail spells—whose uttered charm might
not avail to sever,
From all we hear and all we see,   30
Doubt, chance, and mutability.
Thy light alone—like mist o'er mountains
driven,
Or music by the night wind sent,
Through strings of some still instru-
ment,
Or moonlight on a midnight stream, 35
Gives grace and truth to life's unquiet
dream.

4

Love, Hope, and Self-esteem, like clouds
depart
And come, for some uncertain moments
lent,
Man were immortal, and omnipotent,
Didst thou, unknown and awful as thou
art,   40

Keep with thy glorious train firm state
within his heart.
  Thou messenger of sympathies,
  That wax and wane in lovers' eyes—
Thou—that to human thought art nour-
  ishment,
    Like darkness to a dying flame!   45
    Depart not as thy shadow came,
    Depart not—lest the grave should be,
Like life and fear, a dark reality.

5

While yet a boy I sought for ghosts, and
  sped
  Through many a listening chamber, cave
    and ruin,   50
  And starlight wood, with fearful steps
    pursuing
Hopes of high talk with the departed dead,
I called on poisonous names with which
    our youth is fed,
    I was not heard—I saw them not—
    When musing deeply on the lot   55
Of life, at the sweet time when winds are
  wooing
    All vital things that wake to bring
    News of birds and blossoming,—
    Sudden, thy shadow fell on me;
I shrieked, and clasped my hands in
  ecstasy!   60

6

I vowed that I would dedicate my powers
  To thee and thine—have I not kept the
    vow?
  With beating heart and streaming eyes,
    even now
I call the phantoms of a thousand hours
Each from his voiceless grave: they have in
    visioned bowers   65
    Of studious zeal or love's delight
    Outwatched with me the envious
    night—
They know that never joy illumed my
  brow
    Unlinked with hope that thou wouldst
    free
    This world from its dark slavery,   70
    That thou—O awful LOVELINESS,
Wouldst give whate'er these words cannot
  express.

7

The day becomes more solemn and serene
  When noon is past—there is a harmony
  In autumn, and a luster in its sky,   75
Which through the summer is not heard or
  seen,

As if it could not be, as if it had not been!
  Thus let thy power, which like the
    truth
  Of nature on my passive youth
Descended, to my onward life supply   80
  Its calm—to one who worships thee,
  And every form containing thee,
  Whom, SPIRIT fair, thy spells did bind
To fear himself, and love all human kind.
June 30, 1816   Jan. 19, 1817

MONT BLANC

LINES WRITTEN IN THE VALE OF
CHAMOUNI

I

The everlasting universe of things
Flows through the mind, and rolls its rapid
  waves,
Now dark—now glittering—now reflecting
  gloom—
Now lending splendor, where from secret
  springs
The source of human thought its tribute
  brings   5
Of waters,—with a sound but half its own,
Such as a feeble brook will oft assume
In the wild woods, among the mountains
  lone,
Where waterfalls around it leap for ever,
Where woods and winds contend, and a
  vast river   10
Over its rocks ceaselessly bursts and raves.

II

Thus thou, Ravine of Arve—dark, deep
  Ravine—
Thou many-colored, many-voicèd vale,
Over whose pines, and crags, and caverns
  sail
Fast cloud-shadows and sunbeams: awful
  scene,   15
Where Power in likeness of the Arve comes
  down
From the ice gulfs that gird his secret
  throne,
Bursting through these dark mountains like
  the flame
Of lightning through the tempest;—thou
  dost lie,
Thy giant brood of pines around thee
  clinging,   20
Children of elder time, in whose devotion
The chainless winds still come and ever
  came
To drink their odors, and their mighty
  swinging

To hear—an old and solemn harmony;
Thine earthly rainbows stretched across the sweep 25
Of the ætherial waterfall, whose veil
Robes some unsculptured image; the strange sleep
Which when the voices of the desert fail
Wraps all in its own deep eternity;—
Thy caverns echoing to the Arve's commotion, 30
A loud, lone sound no other sound can tame;
Thou art pervaded with that ceaseless motion,
Thou art the path of that unresting sound—
Dizzy Ravine! and when I gaze on thee
I seem as in a trance sublime and strange 35
To muse on my own separate phantasy,
My own, my human mind, which passively
Now renders and receives fast influencings,
Holding an unremitting interchange
With the clear universe of things around; 40
One legion of wild thoughts, whose wandering wings
Now float above thy darkness, and now rest
Where that or thou art no unbidden guest,
In the still cave of the witch Poesy,
Seeking among the shadows that pass by 45
Ghosts of all things that are, some shade of thee,
Some phantom, some faint image; till the breast
From which they fled recalls them, thou art there!

III

Some say that gleams of a remoter world
Visit the soul in sleep,—that death is slumber, 50
And that its shapes the busy thoughts outnumber
Of those who wake and live.—I look on high;
Has some unknown omnipotence unfurled
The veil of life and death? or do I lie
In dream, and does the mightier world of sleep 55
Spread far around and inaccessibly
Its circles? For the very spirit fails,
Driven like a homeless cloud from steep to steep
That vanishes among the viewless gales!
Far, far above, piercing the infinite sky, 60
Mont Blanc appears,—still, snowy, and serene—
Its subject mountains their unearthly forms
Pile around it, ice and rock; broad vales between
Of frozen floods, unfathomable deeps,

Blue as the overhanging heaven, that spread 65
And wind among the accumulated steeps;
A desert peopled by the storms alone,
Save when the eagle brings some hunter's bone,
And the wolf tracks her there—how hideously
Its shapes are heaped around! rude, bare, and high, 70
Ghastly, and scarred, and riven.—Is this the scene
Where the old Earthquake-dæmon taught her young
Ruin? Were these their toys? or did a sea
Of fire envelope once this silent snow?
None can reply—all seems eternal now. 75
The wilderness has a mysterious tongue
Which teaches awful doubt, or faith so mild,
So solemn, so serene, that man may be
But for such faith with nature reconciled;
Thou hast a voice, great Mountain, to repeal 80
Large codes of fraud and woe; not understood
By all, but which the wise, and great, and good
Interpret, or make felt, or deeply feel.

IV

The fields, the lakes, the forests, and the streams,
Ocean, and all the living things that dwell 85
Within the dædal earth; lightning, and rain,
Earthquake, and fiery flood, and hurricane,
The torpor of the year when feeble dreams
Visit the hidden buds, or dreamless sleep
Holds every future leaf and flower;—the bound 90
With which from that detested trance they leap;
The works and ways of man, their death and birth,
And that of him and all that his may be;
All things that move and breathe with toil and sound
Are born and die; revolve, subside and swell. 95
Power dwells apart in its tranquillity
Remote, serene, and inaccessible:
And this, the naked countenance of earth,
On which I gaze, even these primeval mountains
Teach the adverting mind. The glaciers creep 100
Like snakes that watch their prey, from their far fountains,

Slow rolling on; there, many a precipice,
Frost and the Sun in scorn of mortal power
Have piled: dome, pyramid, and pinnacle,
A city of death, distinct with many a
    tower   105
And wall impregnable of beaming ice.
Yet not a city, but a flood of ruin
Is there, that from the boundaries of the
    sky
Rolls its perpetual stream; vast pines are
    strewing
Its destined path, or in the mangled soil 110
Branchless and shattered stand; the rocks,
    drawn down
From yon remotest waste, have overthrown
The limits of the dead and living world,
Never to be reclaimed. The dwelling-place
Of insects, beasts, and birds, becomes its
    spoil;   115
Their food and their retreat for ever gone,
So much of life and joy is lost. The race
Of man, flies far in dread; his work and
    dwelling
Vanish, like smoke before the tempest's
    stream,
And their place is not known. Below, vast
    caves   120
Shine in the rushing torrent's restless
    gleam,
Which from those secret chasms in tumult
    welling
Meet in the vale, and one majestic River,
The breath and blood of distant lands, for
    ever
Rolls its loud waters to the ocean waves, 125
Breathes its swift vapors to the circling air.

v

Mont Blanc yet gleams on high:—the
    power is there,
The still and solemn power of many sights,
And many sounds, and much of life and
    death.
In the calm darkness of the moonless
    nights,   130
In the lone glare of day, the snows descend
Upon that Mountain; none beholds them
    there,
Nor when the flakes burn in the sinking
    sun,
Or the star-beams dart through them:—
    Winds contend
Silently there, and heap the snow with
    breath   135
Rapid and strong, but silently! Its home
The voiceless lightning in these solitudes
Keeps innocently, and like vapor broods
Over the snow. The secret strength of
    things

Which governs thought, and to the infinite
    dome   140
Of heaven is as a law, inhabits thee!
And what were thou, and earth, and stars,
    and sea,
If to the human mind's imaginings
Silence and solitude were vacancy?

July 23, 1816   Dec. 10, 1817

TO MARY —— ——

DEDICATION TO THE REVOLT OF ISLAM

So now my summer task is ended, Mary,
And I return to thee, mine own heart's
    home;
As to his Queen some victor Knight of
    Fairy,
Earning bright spoils for her enchanted
    dome;
Nor thou disdain, that ere my fame be-
    come   5
A star among the stars of mortal night,
If it indeed may cleave its natal gloom,
Its doubtful promise thus I would unite
With thy belovèd name, thou child of love
    and light.

The toil which stole from thee so many an
    hour,   10
Is ended,—and the fruit is at thy feet!
No longer where the woods to frame a
    bower
With interlacèd branches mix and meet,
Or where with sound like many voices
    sweet,
Waterfalls leap among wild islands green, 15
Which framed for my lone boat a lone
    retreat
Of moss-grown trees and weeds, shall I be
    seen:
But beside thee, where still my heart has
    ever been.

Thoughts of great deeds were mine, dear
    friend, when first
The clouds which wrap this world from
    youth did pass.   20
I do remember well the hour which burst
My spirit's sleep. A fresh May-dawn it was,
When I walked forth upon the glittering
    grass,
And wept, I knew not why; until there
    rose
From the near schoolroom, voices, that,
    alas!   25
Were but one echo from a world of woes—
The harsh and grating strife of tyrants and
    of foes.

And then I clasped my hands and looked
  around,
But none was near to mock my streaming
  eyes,
Which poured their warm drops on the
  sunny ground—   30
So, without shame, I spake:—"I will be
  wise,
And just, and free, and mild, if in me lies
Such power, for I grow weary to behold
The selfish and the strong still tyrannize
Without reproach or check." I then con-
  trolled   35
My tears, my heart grew calm, and I was
  meek and bold.

And from that hour did I with earnest
  thought
Heap knowledge from forbidden mines of
  lore;
Yet nothing that my tyrants knew or taught
I cared to learn, but from that secret
  store   40
Wrought linkèd armor for my soul, before
It might walk forth to war among man-
  kind;
Thus power and hope were strengthened
  more and more
Within me, till there came upon my mind
A sense of loneliness, a thirst with which
  I pined.   45

Alas, that love should be a blight and
  snare
To those who seek all sympathies in one!
Such once I sought in vain; then black
  despair,
The shadow of a starless night, was thrown
Over the world in which I moved alone: 50
Yet never found I one not false to me,
Hard hearts, and cold, like weights of icy
  stone
Which crushed and withered mine, that
  could not be
Aught but a lifeless clod, until revived by
  thee.

Thou friend, whose presence on my wintry
  heart   55
Fell, like bright spring upon some herbless
  plain;
How beautiful and calm and free thou
  wert
In thy young wisdom, when the mortal
  chain
Of Custom thou didst burst and rend in
  twain,
And walked as free as light the clouds
  among,   60

Which many an envious slave then breathed
  in vain
From his dim dungeon, and my spirit
  sprung
To meet thee from the woes which had
  begirt it long!

No more alone through the world's wilder-
  ness,
Although I trod the paths of high intent, 65
I journeyed now: no more companionless,
Where solitude is like despair, I went.
There is the wisdom of a stern content
When Poverty can blight the just and good,
When Infamy dares mock the innocent, 70
And cherished friends turn with the multi-
  tude
To trample: this was ours, and we un-
  shaken stood!

Now has descended a serener hour,
And with inconstant fortune, friends return;
Though suffering leaves the knowledge and
  the power   75
Which says:—Let scorn be not repaid with
  scorn.
And from thy side two gentle babes are
  born
To fill our homes with smiles, and thus are
  we
Most fortunate beneath life's beaming
  morn;
And these delights, and thou, have been to
  me   80
The parents of the song I consecrate to
  thee.

Is it that now my inexperienced fingers
But strike the prelude of a loftier strain?
Or must the lyre on which my spirit lingers
Soon pause in silence, ne'er to sound
  again,   85
Though it might shake the Anarch Cus-
  tom's reign,
And charm the minds of men to Truth's
  own sway
Holier than was Amphion's? I would fain
Reply in hope—but I am worn away,
And Death and Love are yet contending
  for their prey.   90

And what art thou? I know, but dare not
  speak:
Time may interpret to his silent years.
Yet in the paleness of thy thoughtful cheek,
And in the light thine ample forehead
  wears,
And in thy sweetest smiles, and in thy
  tears,   95

And in thy gentle speech, a prophecy
Is whispered, to subdue my fondest fears:
And through thine eyes, even in thy soul
    I see
A lamp of vestal fire burning internally.

They say that thou wert lovely from thy
    birth,   100
Of glorious parents, thou aspiring child.
I wonder not—for one then left this earth
Whose life was like a setting planet mild,
Which clothed thee in the radiance unde-
    filed
Of its departing glory; still her fame   105
Shines on thee, through the tempests dark
    and wild
Which shake these latter days; and thou
    canst claim
The shelter, from thy sire, of an immortal
    name.

One voice came forth from many a mighty
    spirit,
Which was the echo of three thousand
    years;   110
And the tumultuous world stood mute to
    hear it,
As some lone man who in a desert hears
The music of his home:—unwonted fears
Fell on the pale oppressors of our race,
And Faith, and Custom, and low-thoughted
    cares,   115
Like thunder-stricken dragons, for a space
Left the torn human heart, their food and
    dwelling-place.

Truth's deathless voice pauses among man-
    kind!
If there must be no response to my cry—
If men must rise and stamp with fury
    blind   120
On his pure name who loves them,—thou
    and I,
Sweet friend! can look from our tranquillity
Like lamps into the world's tempestuous
    night,—
Two tranquil stars, while clouds are passing
    by
Which wrap them from the foundering sea-
    man's sight,   125
That burn from year to year with unextin-
    guished light.

1817   1818

TO CONSTANTIA, SINGING

I

Thus to be lost and thus to sink and die,
  Perchance were death indeed!—Con-
    stantia, turn!

In thy dark eyes a power like light doth lie,
  Even though the sounds which were thy
    voice, which burn
Between thy lips, are laid to sleep;   5
  Within thy breath, and on thy hair, like
    odor, it is yet,
And from thy touch like fire doth leap.
  Even while I write, my burning cheeks
    are wet,
  Alas, that the torn heart can bleed, but
    not forget!

II

A breathless awe, like the swift change   10
  Unseen, but felt in youthful slumbers,
Wild, sweet, but uncommunicably strange,
  Thou breathest now in fast ascending
    numbers.
The cope of heaven seems rent and cloven
  By the enchantment of thy strain,   15
And on my shoulders wings are woven,
  To follow its sublime career,
Beyond the mighty moons that wane
  Upon the verge of Nature's utmost
    sphere,
    Till the world's shadowy walls are past
    and disappear.   20

III

Her voice is hovering o'er my soul—it
    lingers
  O'ershadowing it with soft and lulling
    wings,
The blood and life within those snowy
    fingers
  Teach witchcraft to the instrumental
    strings.
My brain is wild, my breath comes
    quick—   25
  The blood is listening in my frame,
And thronging shadows, fast and thick,
  Fall on my overflowing eyes;
My heart is quivering like a flame;
  As morning dew, that in the sunbeam
    dies,   30
  I am dissolved in these consuming ec-
    stasies.

IV

I have no life, Constantia, now, but thee,
  Whilst, like the world-surrounding air,
    thy song
Flows on, and fills all things with melody.—
  Now is thy voice a tempest swift and
    strong,   35
On which, like one in trance upborne,
  Secure o'er rocks and waves I sweep,
Rejoicing like a cloud of morn.
Now 'tis the breath of summer night,

Which when the starry waters sleep,   40
　Round western isles, with incense-blos-
　　soms bright,
Lingering, suspends my soul in its
　voluptuous flight.
1817   1824

OZYMANDIAS

I met a traveller from an antique land
Who said: Two vast and trunkless legs of
　stone
Stand in the desert. Near them, on the
　sand,
Half sunk, a shattered visage lies, whose
　frown,
And wrinkled lip, and sneer of cold com-
　mand,   5
Tell that its sculptor well those passions
　read
Which yet survive, stamped on these life-
　less things,
The hand that mocked them and the heart
　that fed:
And on the pedestal these words appear:
"My name is Ozymandias, king of kings: 10
Look on my works, ye Mighty, and de-
　spair!"
Nothing beside remains. Round the decay
Of that colossal wreck, boundless and bare
The lone and level sands stretch far away.
1817   1818

LINES WRITTEN AMONG THE
EUGANEAN HILLS

Many a green isle needs must be
In the deep wide sea of misery,
Or the mariner, worn and wan,
Never thus could voyage on
Day and night, and night and day,   5
Drifting on his dreary way,
With the solid darkness black
Closing round his vessel's track;
Whilst above the sunless sky,
Big with clouds, hangs heavily,   10
And behind the tempest fleet
Hurries on with lightning feet,
Riving sail, and cord, and plank,
Till the ship has almost drank
Death from the o'er-brimming deep;   15
And sinks down, down, like that sleep
When the dreamer seems to be
Weltering through eternity;
And the dim low line before
Of a dark and distant shore   20
Still recedes, as ever still

Longing with divided will,
But no power to seek or shun,
He is ever drifted on
O'er the unreposing wave   25
To the haven of the grave.
What if there no friends will greet;
What if there no heart will meet
His with love's impatient beat;
Wander wheresoe'er he may,   30
Can he dream before that day
To find refuge from distress
In friendship's smile, in love's caress?
Then 'twill wreak him little woe
Whether such there be or no: 35
Senseless is the breast, and cold,
Which relenting love would fold;
Bloodless are the veins and chill
Which the pulse of pain did fill;
Every little living nerve   40
That from bitter words did swerve
Round the tortured lips and brow,
Are like sapless leaflets now
Frozen upon December's bough.
On the beach of a northern sea   45
Which tempests shake eternally,
As once the wretch there lay to sleep,
Lies a solitary heap,
One white skull and seven dry bones,
On the margin of the stones,   50
Where a few gray rushes stand,
Boundaries of the sea and land:
Nor is heard one voice of wail
But the sea-mews', as they sail
O'er the billows of the gale;   55
Or the whirlwind up and down
Howling, like a slaughtered town,
When a king in glory rides
Through the pomp of fratricides:
Those unburied bones around   60
There is many a mournful sound;
There is no lament for him,
Like a sunless vapor, dim,
Who once clothed with life and thought
What now moves nor murmurs not.   65

Aye, many flowering islands lie
In the waters of wide Agony:
To such a one this morn was led,
My bark by soft winds piloted:
'Mid the mountains Euganean   70
I stood listening to the pæan,
With which the legioned rooks did hail
The sun's uprise majestical;
Gathering round with wings all hoar,
Through the dewy mist they soar   75
Like gray shades, till the eastern heaven
Bursts, and then, as clouds of even,
Flecked with fire and azure, lie
In the unfathomable sky,
So their plumes of purple grain,   80

Starred with drops of golden rain,
Gleam above the sunlight woods,
As in silent multitudes
On the morning's fitful gale
Through the broken mist they sail, 85
And the vapors cloven and gleaming
Follow down the dark steep streaming,
Till all is bright, and clear, and still,
Round the solitary hill.

Beneath is spread like a green sea 90
The waveless plain of Lombardy,
Bounded by the vaporous air,
Islanded by cities fair;
Underneath day's azure eyes,
Ocean's nursling, Venice lies, 95
A peopled labyrinth of walls,
Amphitrite's destined halls,
Which her hoary sire now paves
With his blue and beaming waves.
Lo! the sun upsprings behind, 100
Broad, red, radiant, half reclined
On the level quivering line
Of the waters crystalline;
And before that chasm of light,
As within a furnace bright, 105
Column, tower, and dome, and spire,
Shine like obelisks of fire,
Pointing with inconstant motion
From the altar of dark ocean
To the sapphire-tinted skies; 110
As the flames of sacrifice
From the marble shrines did rise,
As to pierce the dome of gold
Where Apollo spoke of old.

Sun-girt City, thou hast been 115
Ocean's child, and then his queen;
Now is come a darker day,
And thou soon must be his prey,
If the power that raised thee here
Hallow so thy watery bier. 120
A less drear ruin then than now,
With thy conquest-branded brow
Stooping to the slave of slaves
From thy throne, among the waves
Wilt thou be, when the sea mew 125
Flies, as once before it flew,
O'er thine isles depopulate,
And all is in its ancient state,
Save where many a palace gate
With green sea-flowers overgrown 130
Like a rock of ocean's own,
Topples o'er the abandoned sea
As the tides change sullenly.
The fisher on his watery way,
Wandering at the close of day, 135
Will spread his sail and seize his oar
Till he pass the gloomy shore,
Lest thy dead should, from their sleep

Bursting o'er the starlight deep,
Lead a rapid mask of death 140
O'er the waters of his path.

Those who alone thy towers behold
Quivering through aërial gold,
As I now behold them here,
Would imagine not they were 145
Sepulchres, where human forms,
Like pollution-nourished worms
To the corpse of greatness cling,
Murdered, and now moldering:
But if Freedom should awake 150
In her omnipotence, and shake
From the Celtic Anarch's hold
All the keys of dungeons cold,
Where a hundred cities lie
Chained like thee, ingloriously, 155
Thou and all thy sister band
Might adorn this sunny land,
Twining memories of old time
With new virtues more sublime;
If not, perish thou and they, 160
Clouds which stain truth's rising day
By her sun consumed away,
Earth can spare ye: while like flowers,
In the waste of years and hours,
From your dust new nations spring 165
With more kindly blossoming.
Perish—let there only be
Floating o'er thy hearthless sea
As the garment of thy sky
Clothes the world immortally, 170
One remembrance, more sublime
Than the tattered pall of time,
Which scarce hides thy visage wan;—
That a tempest-cleaving Swan
Of the songs of Albion, 175
Driven from his ancestral streams
By the might of evil dreams,
Found a nest in thee; and Ocean
Welcomed him with such emotion
That its joy grew his, and sprung 180
From his lips like music flung
O'er a mighty thunder-fit
Chastening terror:—what though yet
Poesy's unfailing River,
Which through Albion winds for ever 185
Lashing with melodious wave
Many a sacred Poet's grave,
Mourn its latest nursling fled?
What though thou with all thy dead
Scarce can for this fame repay 190
Aught thine own? oh, rather say
Though thy sins and slaveries foul
Overcloud a sunlike soul?
As the ghost of Homer clings
Round Scamander's wasting springs; 195
As divinest Shakespeare's might
Fills Avon and the world with light

Like omniscient power which he
Imaged 'mid mortality;
As the love from Petrarch's urn,　200
Yet amid yon hills doth burn,
A quenchless lamp by which the heart
Sees things unearthly;—so thou art,
Mighty spirit—so shall be
The City that did refuge thee.　205

Lo, the sun floats up the sky
Like thought-wingèd Liberty,
Till the universal light
Seems to level plain and height;
From the sea a mist has spread,　210
And the beams of morn lie dead
On the towers of Venice now,
Like its glory long ago.
By the skirts of that gray cloud
Many-domèd Padua proud　215
Stands, a peopled solitude,
'Mid the harvest-shining plain,
Where the peasant heaps his grain
In the garner of his foe,
And the milk-white oxen slow　220
With the purple vintage strain,
Heaped upon the creaking wain,
That the brutal Celt may swill
Drunken sleep with savage will;
And the sickle to the sword　225
Lies unchanged, though many a lord,
Like a weed whose shade is poison,
Overgrows this region's foison,
Sheaves of whom are ripe to come
To destruction's harvest home:　230
Men must reap the things they sow,
Force from force must ever flow,
Or worse; but 'tis a bitter woe
That love or reason cannot change
The despot's rage, the slave's revenge.　235

Padua, thou within whose walls
Those mute guests at festivals,
Son and Mother, Death and Sin,
Played at dice for Ezzelin,
Till Death cried, "I win, I win!"　240
And Sin cursed to lose the wager,
But Death promised, to assuage her,
That he would petition for
Her to be made Vice-Emperor,
When the destined years were o'er,　245
Over all between the Po
And the eastern Alpine snow,
Under the mighty Austrian.
Sin smiled so as Sin only can,
And since that time, aye, long before,　250
Both have ruled from shore to shore,
That incestuous pair, who follow
Tyrants as the sun the swallow,
As Repentance follows Crime,
And as changes follow Time.　255

In thine halls the lamp of learning,
Padua, now no more is burning;
Like a meteor, whose wild way
Is lost over the grave of day,
It gleams betrayed and to betray:　260
Once remotest nations came
To adore that sacred flame,
When it lit not many a hearth
On this cold and gloomy earth:
Now new fires from antique light　265
Spring beneath the wide world's might;
But their spark lies dead in thee,
Trampled out by tyranny.
As the Norway woodman quells,
In the depth of piny dells,　270
One light flame among the brakes,
While the boundless forest shakes,
And its mighty trunks are torn
By the fires thus lowly born:
The spark beneath his feet is dead,　275
He starts to see the flames it fed
Howling through the darkened sky
With a myriad tongues victoriously,
And sinks down in fear: so thou,
O Tyranny, beholdest now　280
Light around thee, and thou hearest
The loud flames ascend, and fearest:
Grovel on the earth: aye, hide
In the dust thy purple pride!

Noon descends around me now:　285
'Tis the noon of autumn's glow,
When a soft and purple mist
Like a vaporous amethyst,
Or an air-dissolvèd star
Mingling light and fragrance, far　290
From the curved horizon's bound
To the point of heaven's profound,
Fills the overflowing sky;
And the plains that silent lie
Underneath, the leaves unsodden　295
Where the infant frost has trodden
With his morning-wingèd feet,
Whose bright print is gleaming yet;
And the red and golden vines,
Piercing with their trellised lines　300
The rough, dark-skirted wilderness;
The dun and bladed grass no less,
Pointing from this hoary tower
In the windless air; the flower
Glimmering at my feet; the line　305
Of the olive-sandalled Apennine
In the south dimly islanded;
And the Alps, whose snows are spread
High between the clouds and sun;
And of living things each one;　310
And my spirit which so long
Darkened this swift stream of song,
Interpenetrated lie
By the glory of the sky:

Be it love, light, harmony,   315
Odor, or the soul of all
Which from heaven like dew doth fall,
Or the mind which feeds this verse
Peopling the lone universe.

Noon descends, and after noon   320
Autumn's evening meets me soon,
Leading the infantine moon,
And that one star, which to her
Almost seems to minister
Half the crimson light she brings   325
From the sunset's radiant springs:
And the soft dreams of the morn,
(Which like wingèd winds had borne
To that silent isle, which lies
'Mid remembered agonies,   330
The frail bark of this lone being,)
Pass, to other sufferers fleeing,
And its ancient pilot, Pain,
Sits beside the helm again.

Other flowering isles must be   335
In the sea of life and agony:
Other spirits float and flee
O'er that gulf: even now, perhaps,
On some rock the wild wave wraps,
With folded wings they waiting sit   340
For my bark, to pilot it
To some calm and blooming cove,
Where for me, and those I love,
May a windless bower be built,
Far from passion, pain, and guilt,   345
In a dell 'mid lawny hills,
Which the wild sea-murmur fills,
And soft sunshine, and the sound
Of old forests echoing round,
And the light and smell divine   350
Of all flowers that breathe and shine:
We may live so happy there,
That the spirits of the air,
Envying us, may even entice
To our healing paradise   355
The polluting multitude;
But their rage would be subdued
By that clime divine and calm,
And the winds whose wings rain balm
On the uplifted soul, and leaves   360
Under which the bright sea heaves;
While each breathless interval
In their whisperings musical
The inspired soul supplies
With its own deep melodies,   365
And the love which heals all strife
Circling, like the breath of life,
All things in that sweet abode
With its own mild brotherhood:
They, not it, would change; and soon   370

Every sprite beneath the moon
Would repent its envy vain,
And the earth grow young again.

Oct., 1818   1819

STANZAS

WRITTEN IN DEJECTION, NEAR NAPLES

The sun is warm, the sky is clear,
     The waves are dancing fast and bright;
Blue isles and snowy mountains wear
     The purple noon's transparent might;
     The breath of the moist earth is light 5
Around its unexpanded buds;
     Like many a voice of one delight,
The winds, the birds, the ocean floods,
The City's voice itself, is soft like Solitude's.

     I see the Deep's untrampled floor   10
     With green and purple seaweeds
         strown;
I see the waves upon the shore,
     Like light dissolved in star-showers,
         thrown:
     I sit upon the sands alone,—
The lightning of the noontide ocean   15
     Is flashing round me, and a tone
Arises from its measured motion,
How sweet! did any heart now share in my
     emotion.

Alas! I have nor hope nor health,
     Nor peace within nor calm around, 20
Nor that content surpassing wealth
     The sage in meditation found,
     And walked with inward glory
         crowned—
Nor fame, nor power, nor love, nor
     leisure.
     Others I see whom these surround— 25
Smiling they live, and call life pleasure;—
To me that cup has been dealt in another
     measure.

Yet now despair itself is mild,
     Even as the winds and waters are;
I could lie down like a tired child,   30
     And weep away the life of care
     Which I have borne and yet must bear,
Till death like sleep might steal on me,
     And I might feel in the warm air
My cheek grow cold, and hear the sea 35
Breathe o'er my dying brain its last monot-
     ony.

Some might lament that I were cold,
  As I, when this sweet day is gone,
Which my lost heart, too soon grown old,
  Insults with this untimely moan;   40
They might lament—for I am one
Whom men love not,—and yet regret,
Unlike this day, which, when the sun
  Shall on its stainless glory set,
Will linger, though enjoyed, like joy in
    memory yet.   45
1818   1824

SONNET

Lift not the painted veil which those who
    live
Call Life: though unreal shapes be pic-
    tured there,
And it but mimic all we would believe
With colors idly spread,—behind, lurk Fear
And Hope, twin Destinies; who ever
    weave   5
Their shadows, o'er the chasm, sightless
    and drear.
I knew one who had lifted it—he sought,
For his lost heart was tender, things to
    love,
But found them not, alas! nor was there
    aught
The world contains, the which he could
    approve.   10
Through the unheeding many he did move,
A splendor among shadows, a bright blot
Upon this gloomy scene, a Spirit that
    strove
For truth, and like the Preacher found it
    not.
1818

LOVE'S PHILOSOPHY

I

The Fountains mingle with the River
  And the Rivers with the Ocean,
The winds of Heaven mix for ever
  With a sweet emotion;
Nothing in the world is single;   5
  All things by a law divine
In one spirit meet and mingle.
  Why not I with thine?—

II

See the mountains kiss high Heaven
  And the waves clasp one another;   10
No sister-flower would be forgiven
  If it disdained its brother,
And the sunlight clasps the earth
  And the moonbeams kiss the sea:
What is all this sweet work worth   15
  If thou kiss not me?
1819   1819

ODE TO THE WEST WIND

I

O, wild West Wind, thou breath of Au-
    tumn's being,
Thou, from whose unseen presence the
    leaves dead
Are driven, like ghosts from an enchanter
    fleeing,

Yellow, and black, and pale, and hectic red,
Pestilence-stricken multitudes: O, thou,   5
Who chariotest to their dark wintry bed

The wingèd seeds, where they lie cold and
    low,
Each like a corpse within its grave, until
Thine azure sister of the spring shall blow

Her clarion o'er the dreaming earth, and
    fill   10
(Driving sweet buds like flocks to feed in
    air)
With living hues and odors plain and hill:

Wild Spirit, which art moving every where;
Destroyer and preserver; hear, O, hear!

II

Thou on whose stream, 'mid the steep sky's
    commotion,   15
Loose clouds like earth's decaying leaves
    are shed,
Shook from the tangled boughs of Heaven
    and Ocean,

Angels of rain and lightning: there are
    spread
On the blue surface of thine airy surge,
Like the bright hair uplifted from the
    head   20

Of some fierce Mænad, even from the dim
    verge
Of the horizon to the zenith's height
The locks of the approaching storm.
    Thou dirge

Of the dying year, to which this closing
    night
Will be the dome of a vast sepulchre,   25
Vaulted with all thy congregated might

Of vapors, from whose solid atmosphere
Black rain, and fire, and hail will burst: O,
    hear!

III

Thou who didst waken from his summer
    dreams
The blue Mediterranean, where he lay, 30
Lulled by the coil of his crystalline streams,

Beside a pumice isle in Baiæ's bay,
And saw in sleep old palaces and towers
Quivering within the wave's intenser day,

All overgrown with azure moss and
    flowers 35
So sweet, the sense faints picturing them!
    Thou
For whose path the Atlantic's level powers

Cleave themselves into chasms, while far
    below
The sea-blooms and the oozy woods which
    wear
The sapless foliage of the ocean, know 40

Thy voice, and suddenly grow grey with
    fear,
And tremble and despoil themselves: O,
    hear!

IV

If I were a dead leaf thou mightest bear;
If I were a swift cloud to fly with thee;
A wave to pant beneath thy power, and
    share 45

The impulse of thy strength, only less free
Than thou, O, uncontrollable! If even
I were as in my boyhood, and could be

The comrade of thy wanderings over
    heaven,
As then, when to outstrip thy skiey speed 50
Scarce seemed a vision; I would ne'er have
    striven

As thus with thee in prayer in my sore
    need,
Oh! lift me as a wave, a leaf, a cloud!
I fall upon the thorns of life! I bleed!

A heavy weight of hours has chained and
    bowed 55
One too like thee: tameless, and swift, and
    proud.

V

Make me thy lyre, even as the forest is:
What if my leaves are falling like its own!
The tumult of thy mighty harmonies

Will take from both a deep, autumnal
    tone, 60
Sweet though in sadness. Be thou, spirit
    fierce,
My spirit! Be thou me, impetuous one!

Drive my dead thoughts over the universe
Like withered leaves to quicken a new
    birth!
And, by the incantation of this verse, 65

Scatter, as from an unextinguished hearth
Ashes and sparks, my words among man-
    kind!
Be through my lips to unawakened earth

The trumpet of a prophecy! O, wind,
If Winter comes, can Spring be far be-
    hind? 70
1819   1820

THE INDIAN SERENADE

I arise from dreams of thee
    In the first sweet sleep of night,
When the winds are breathing low,
    And the stars are shining bright:
I arise from dreams of thee, 5
    And a spirit in my feet
Hath led me—who knows how?
    To thy chamber window, sweet!

The wandering airs, they faint
    On the dark, the silent stream; 10
The champak odors fail
    Like sweet thoughts in a dream;
The nightingale's complaint,
    It dies upon her heart,
As I must die on thine, 15
    Oh, belovèd as thou art!

Oh, lift me from the grass!
    I die! I faint! I fail!
Let thy love in kisses rain
    On my lips and eyelids pale. 20
My cheek is cold and white, alas!
    My heart beats loud and fast;—
Oh! press it close to thine again,
    Where it will break at last.
1819   1822

FROM THE CENCI: A TRAGEDY

DEDICATION: TO LEIGH HUNT

My dear Friend,—
    I inscribe with your name, from a distant
country, and after an absence whose months

have seemed years, this the latest of my literary efforts.

Those writings which I have hitherto published have been little else than visions which impersonate my own apprehensions of the beautiful and the just. I can also perceive in them the literary defects incidental to youth and impatience; they are dreams of what ought to be, or may be. The drama which I now present to you is a sad reality. I lay aside the presumptuous attitude of an instructor, and am content to paint, with such colors as my own heart furnishes, that which has been.

Rome; May 29, 1819

PREFACE

A manuscript was communicated to me during my travels in Italy, which was copied from the archives of the Cenci Palace at Rome, and contains a detailed account of the horrors which ended in the extinction of one of the noblest and richest families of that city during the Pontificate of Clement VIII., in the year 1599. The story is that an old man, having spent his life in debauchery and wickedness, conceived at length an implacable hatred towards his children; which showed itself towards one daughter under the form of an incestuous passion, aggravated by every circumstance of cruelty and violence. This daughter, after long and vain attempts to escape from what she considered a perpetual contamination both of body and mind, at length plotted with her mother-in-law and brother to murder their common tyrant. The young maiden who was urged to this tremendous deed by an impulse which overpowered its horror was evidently a most gentle and amiable being, a creature formed to adorn and be admired, and thus violently thwarted from her nature by the necessity of circumstance and opinion. The deed was quickly discovered, and, in spite of the most earnest prayers made to the Pope by the highest persons in Rome, the criminals were put to death. The old man had during his life repeatedly bought his pardon from the Pope for capital crimes of the most enormous and unspeakable kind, at the price of a hundred thousand crowns; the death therefore of his victims can scarcely be accounted for by the love of justice. The Pope, among other motives for severity, probably felt that whoever killed the Count Cenci deprived his treasury of a certain and copious source of revenue. Such a story, if told so as to present to the reader all the feelings of those who once acted it, their hopes and fears, their confidences and misgivings, their various interests, passions and opinions, acting upon and with each other, yet all conspiring to one tremendous end, would be as a light to make apparent some of the most dark and secret caverns of the human heart.

ACT IV

SCENE II. *Before the Castle of Petrella*

Enter BEATRICE *and* LUCRETIA *above on the Ramparts*

Beatrice

They come not yet.

Lucretia

'Tis scarce midnight.

Beatrice

How slow
Behind the course of thought, even sick with speed,
Lags leaden-footed time!

Lucretia

The minutes pass . . .
If he should wake before the deed is done?

Beatrice

O, Mother! He must never wake again.   5
What thou hast said persuades me that our act
Will but dislodge a spirit of deep hell
Out of a human form.

Lucretia

'Tis true he spoke
Of death and judgment with strange confidence
For one so wicked; as a man believing   10
In God, yet recking not of good or ill.
And yet to die without confession! . . .

Beatrice

Oh!
Believe that Heaven is merciful and just,
And will not add our dread necessity
To the amount of his offences.

Enter OLIMPIO *and* MARZIO *below*

Lucretia

See,   15
They come.

Beatrice

All mortal things must hasten thus
To their dark end. Let us go down.
[*Exeunt* LUCRETIA *and* BEATRICE *from above.*

Olimpio

How feel you to this work?

Marzio

              As one who thinks
A thousand crowns excellent market price
For an old murderer's life. Your cheeks
    are pale.   20

Olimpio

It is the white reflection of your own,
Which you call pale.

Marzio

              Is that their natural hue?

Olimpio

Or 'tis my hate and the deferred desire
To wreak it, which extinguishes their
    blood.

Marzio

You are inclined then to this business?

Olimpio

                      Aye. 25
If one should bribe me with a thousand
    crowns
To kill a serpent which had stung my child,
I could not be more willing.

Enter BEATRICE *and* LUCRETIA *below*

                  Noble ladies!

Beatrice

Are ye resolved?

Olimpio

              Is he asleep?

Marzio

                    Is all
Quiet?

Lucretia

      I mixed an opiate with his drink: 30
He sleeps so soundly . . .

Beatrice

           That his death will be
But as a change of sin-chastising dreams,
A dark continuance of the Hell within him,
Which God extinguish! But ye are re-
    solved?
Ye know it is a high and holy deed? 35

Olimpio

We are resolved.

Marzio

          As to the how this act
Be warranted, it rests with you.

Beatrice

                Well, follow!

Olimpio

Hush! Hark! What noise is that?

Marzio

                Ha! some one comes!

Beatrice

Ye conscience-stricken cravens, rock to rest
Your baby hearts. It is the iron gate, 40
Which ye left open, swinging to the wind,
That enters whistling as in scorn. Come,
    follow!
And be your steps like mine, light, quick,
    and bold.

                          [*Exeunt.*

SCENE III. *An Apartment in the Castle*

Enter BEATRICE *and* LUCRETIA

Lucretia

They are about it now.

Beatrice

             Nay, it is done.

Lucretia

I have not heard him groan.

Beatrice

             He will not groan.

Lucretia

What sound is that?

Beatrice

           List! 'tis the tread of feet
About his bed.

Lucretia

          My God!
If he be now a cold stiff corpse . . .

Beatrice

                O, fear not 5
What may be done, but what is left undone:
The act seals all.

Enter OLIMPIO *and* MARZIO

          Is it accomplished?

Marzio

                  What?

Olimpio

Did you not call?

Beatrice

When?

Olimpio

Now.

Beatrice

I ask if all is over?

Olimpio

We dare not kill an old and sleeping man;
His thin grey hair, his stern and reverent
  brow,   10
His veinèd hands crossed on his heaving
  breast,
And the calm innocent sleep in which he
  lay,
Quelled me. Indeed, indeed, I cannot do
  it.

Marzio

But I was bolder; for I chid Olimpio,
And bade him bear his wrongs to his own
  grave   15
And leave me the reward. And now my
  knife
Touched the loose wrinkled throat, when
  the old man
Stirred in his sleep, and said, "God! hear,
  O, hear,
A father's curse! What, art thou not our
  father?"
And then he laughed. I knew it was the
  ghost   20
Of my dead father speaking through his
  lips,
And could not kill him.

Beatrice

Miserable slaves!
Where, if ye dare not kill a sleeping man,
Found ye the boldness to return to me
With such a deed undone? Base palter-
  ers!   25
Cowards and traitors! Why, the very con-
  science
Which ye would sell for gold and for
  revenge
Is an equivocation: it sleeps over
A thousand daily acts disgracing men;
And when a deed where mercy insults
  heaven . . .   30
Why do I talk?
[*Snatching a dagger from one of them and
  raising it.*

Hadst thou a tongue to say,
She murdered her own father, I must do it!
But never dream ye shall outlive him long!

Olimpio

Stop, for God's sake!

Marzio

I will go back and kill him.

Olimpio

Give me the weapon, we must do thy
  will.   35

Beatrice

Take it! Depart! Return!
[*Exeunt* OLIMPIO *and* MARZIO.
How pale thou art!
We do but that which 'twere a deadly crime
To leave undone.

Lucretia

Would it were done!

Beatrice

Even whilst
That doubt is passing through your mind,
  the world
Is conscious of a change. Darkness and
  hell   40
Have swallowed up the vapor they sent
  forth
To blacken the sweet light of life. My
  breath
Comes, methinks, lighter, and the jellied
  blood
Runs freely through my veins. Hark!

Enter OLIMPIO *and* MARZIO.
He is . . .

Olimpio

Dead!

Marzio

We strangled him that there might be no
  blood;   45
And then we threw his heavy corpse i' the
  garden
Under the balcony; 'twill seem it fell.

Beatrice [*giving them a bag of coin.*

Here, take this gold, and hasten to your
  homes.
And, Marzio, because thou wast only awed
By that which made me tremble, wear thou
  this!   50
[*Clothes him in a rich mantle.*

It was the mantle which my grandfather
Wore in his high prosperity, and men
Envied his state: so may they envy thine.
Thou wert a weapon in the hand of God
To a just use. Live long and thrive! And,
    mark,   55
If thou hast crimes, repent: this deed is
    none.
                            [*A horn is sounded.*

Lucretia

Hark, 'tis the castle horn; my God! it
    sounds
Like the last trump.

Beatrice

                Some tedious guest is coming.

Lucretia

The drawbridge is let down; there is a
    tramp
Of horses in the court; fly, hide your-
    selves!   60
            [*Exeunt* OLIMPIO *and* MARZIO.

Beatrice

Let us retire to counterfeit deep rest;
I scarcely need to counterfeit it now:
The spirit which doth reign within these
    limbs
Seems strangely undisturbed. I could even
    sleep
Fearless and calm: all ill is surely past. 65
                                    [*Exeunt.*

SCENE IV. *Another Apartment in the Castle*

Enter on one side the Legate SAVELLA, *in-
    troduced by a* Servant, *and on the other*
    LUCRETIA *and* BERNARDO

Savella

Lady, my duty to his Holiness
Be my excuse that thus unseasonably
I break upon your rest. I must speak with
Count Cenci; doth he sleep?

Lucretia [in a hurried and confused
                            manner
                        I think he sleeps;
Yet wake him not, I pray, spare me awhile, 5
He is a wicked and a wrathful man;
Should he be roused out of his sleep to-
    night,
Which is, I know, a hell of angry dreams,
It were not well; indeed it were not well.

Wait till day break . . . *(Aside)* O, I am
    deadly sick!   10

Savella

I grieve thus to distress you, but the Count
Must answer charges of the gravest import,
And suddenly; such my commission is.

Lucretia [with increased agitation
I dare not rouse him: I know none who
    dare. . . .
'Twere perilous; . . . you might as safely
    waken   15
A serpent; or a corpse in which some fiend
Were laid to sleep.

Savella

                Lady, my moments here
Are counted. I must rouse him from his
    sleep,
Since none else dare.

Lucretia (aside)

                    O, terror! O, despair!
(To Bernardo.) Bernardo, conduct you the
    Lord Legate to   20
Your father's chamber.
            [*Exeunt* SAVELLA *and* BERNARDO.

Enter BEATRICE

Beatrice

                'Tis a messenger
Come to arrest the culprit who now stands
Before the throne of unappealable God.
Both Earth and Heaven, consenting arbi-
    ters,
Acquit our deed.

Lucretia

                Oh, agony of fear!   25
Would that he yet might live! Even now I
    heard
The Legate's followers whisper as they
    passed
They had a warrant for his instant death.
All was prepared by unforbidden means
Which we must pay so dearly, having
    done.   30
Even now they search the tower, and find
    the body;
Now they suspect the truth; now they con-
    sult
Before they come to tax us with the fact;
O, horrible, 'tis all discovered!

Beatrice

                    Mother,
What is done wisely, is done well. Be
    bold   35
As thou art just. 'Tis like a truant child
To fear that others know what thou hast
    done,
Even from thine own strong consciousness,
    and thus
Write on unsteady eyes and altered cheeks
All thou wouldst hide. Be faithful to thy-
    self,   40
And fear no other witness but thy fear.
For if, as cannot be, some circumstance
Should rise in accusation, we can blind
Suspicion with such cheap astonishment,
Or overbear it with such guiltless pride,   45
As murderers cannot feign. The deed is
    done,
And what may follow now regards not me.
I am as universal as the light;
Free as the earth-surrounding air; as firm
As the world's center. Consequence, to
    me,   50
Is as the wind which strikes the solid rock
But shakes it not.
                    [*A cry within and tumult.*

Voices

Murder! Murder! Murder!

Enter BERNARDO AND SAVELLA

Savella (to his followers)

Go search the castle round; sound the
    alarm;
Look to the gates that none escape!

Beatrice

                         What now?

Bernardo

I know not what to say . . . my father's
    dead.   55

Beatrice

How; dead! he only sleeps; you mistake,
    brother.
His sleep is very calm, very like death;
'Tis wonderful how well a tyrant sleeps.
He is not dead?

Bernardo

        Dead; murdered.

Lucretia (with extreme agitation)

                         Oh, no, no
He is not murdered though he may be
    dead;   60
I have alone the keys of those apartments.

Savella

Ha! Is it so?

Beatrice

        My Lord, I pray excuse us;
We will retire; my mother is not well:
She seems quite overcome with this strange
    horror.
                [*Exeunt* LUCRETIA *and* BEATRICE.

Savella

Can you suspect who may have murdered
    him?   65

Bernardo

I know not what to think.

Savella

                    Can you name any
Who had an interest in his death?

Bernardo

                         Alas!
I can name none who had not, and those
    most
Who most lament that such a deed is done;
My mother, and my sister, and myself.   70

Savella

'Tis strange! There were clear marks of
    violence.
I found the old man's body in the moon-
    light
Hanging beneath the window of his cham-
    ber,
Among the branches of a pine: he could
    not
Have fallen there, for all his limbs lay
    heaped   75
And effortless; 'tis true there was no
    blood. . . .
Favor me, Sir,—it much imports your house
That all should be made clear,—to tell the
    ladies
That I request their presence.
                         [*Exit* BERNARDO.

Enter Guards *bringing in* MARZIO

Guard

                    We have one.

Officer

My Lord, we found this ruffian and an-
    other   80
Lurking among the rocks; there is no doubt
But that they are the murderers of Count
    Cenci:
Each had a bag of coin; this fellow wore
A gold-inwoven robe, which shining bright

Under the dark rocks to the glimmering
    moon   85
Betrayed them to our notice: the other fell
Desperately fighting.

Savella

          What does he confess?

Officer

He keeps firm silence: but these lines
    found on him
May speak.

Savella

        Their language is at least sincere.
    (Reads.)

TO THE LADY BEATRICE

"That the atonement of what my nature 90
sickens to conjecture may soon arrive, I
send thee, at thy brother's desire, those who
will speak and do more than I dare write.
. . . Thy devoted servant, ORSINO."

Enter LUCRETIA, BEATRICE, *and* BERNARDO

Knowest thou this writing, Lady?

Beatrice

                No.

Savella

                Nor thou?

Lucretia

*(Her conduct throughout the scene is
marked by extreme agitation)*
Where was it found? What is it? It should
    be   95
Orsino's hand! It speaks of that strange
    horror
Which never yet found utterance, but
    which made
Between that hapless child and her dead
    father
A gulf of obscure hatred.

Savella

                Is it so?
Is it true, Lady, that thy father did   100
Such outrages as to awaken in thee
Unfilial hate?

Beatrice

        Not hate—'twas more than hate:
This is most true, yet wherefore question
    me?

Savella

There is a deed demanding question done;
Thou hast a secret which will answer
    not.   105

Beatrice

What sayest? My Lord, your words are
    bold and rash.

Savella

I do arrest all present in the name
Of the Pope's Holiness. You must to
    Rome.

Lucretia

O, not to Rome! Indeed we are not guilty.

Beatrice

Guilty! Who dares talk of guilt? My
    Lord,   110
I am more innocent of parricide
Than is a child born fatherless. . . . Dear
    Mother,
Your gentleness and patience are no shield
For this keen-judging world, this two-edged
    lie,
Which seems, but is not. What! will human
    laws,   115
Rather will ye who are their ministers,
Bar all access to retribution first,
And then, when heaven doth interpose to
    do
What ye neglect, arming familiar things
To the redress of an unwonted crime, 120
Make ye the victims who demanded it
Culprits? 'Tis ye are culprits! That poor
    wretch
Who stands so pale, and trembling, and
    amazed,
If it be true he murdered Cenci, was
A sword in the right hand of justest
    God.   125
Wherefore should I have wielded it? Unless
The crimes which mortal tongue dare
    never name
God therefore scruples to avenge.

Savella

                  You own
That you desired his death?

Beatrice

              It would have been
A crime no less than his, if for one mo-
    ment   130
That fierce desire had faded in my heart.
'Tis true I did believe, and hope, and pray,
Aye, I even knew,—for God is wise and
    just,
That some strange sudden death hung over
    him.
'Tis true that this did happen, and most
    true   135

There was no other rest for me on earth,
No other hope in Heaven . . . now what
of this?

Savella

Strange thoughts beget strange deeds; and
   here are both:
I judge thee not.

Beatrice

         And yet, if you arrest me,
You are the judge and executioner   140
Of that which is the life of life: the breath
Of accusation kills an innocent name,
And leaves for lame acquittal the poor life
Which is a mask without it. 'Tis most false
That I am guilty of foul parricide;   145
Although I must rejoice, for justest cause,
That other hands have sent my father's
   soul
To ask the mercy he denied to me.
Now leave us free: stain not a noble house
With vague surmises of rejected crime; 150
Add to our sufferings and your own neglect
No heavier sum: let them have been
   enough:
Leave us the wreck we have.

Savella

             I dare not, Lady.
I pray you that you prepare yourselves for
   Rome:
There the Pope's further pleasure will be
   known.   155

Lucretia

O, not to Rome! O, take us not to Rome!

Beatrice

Why not to Rome, dear mother? There as
   here
Our innocence is as an armèd heel
To trample accusation. God is there
As here, and with his shadow ever
   clothes   160
The innocent, the injured and the weak;
And such are we. Cheer up, dear Lady,
   lean
On me; collect your wandering thoughts.
   My Lord,
As soon as you have taken some refresh-
   ment,
And had all such examinations made   165
Upon the spot, as may be necessary
To the full understanding of this matter,
We shall be ready. Mother; will you come?

Lucretia

Ha! they will bind us to the rack, and wrest
Self-accusation from our agony!   170
Will Giacomo be there? Orsino? Marzio?
All present; all confronted; all demanding
Each from the other's countenance the
   thing
Which is in every heart! O, misery!

               [*She faints, and is borne out.*

Savella

She faints: an ill appearance this.

Beatrice

              My Lord,   175
She knows not yet the uses of the world.
She fears that power is as a beast which
   grasps
And loosens not: a snake whose look trans-
   mutes
All things to guilt which is its nutriment.
She cannot know how well the supine
   slaves   180
Of blind authority read the truth of things
When written on a brow of guilelessness:
She sees not yet triumphant Innocence
Stand at the judgment-seat of mortal man,
A judge and an accuser of the wrong   185
Which drags it there. Prepare yourself, my
   Lord;
Our suite will join yours in the court
   below.

                         [*Exeunt.*

May-Aug., 1819   1819

ENGLAND IN 1819

An old, mad, blind, despised, and dying
   king;
Princes, the dregs of their dull race, who
   flow
Through public scorn—mud from a muddy
   spring;
Rulers who neither see, nor feel, nor know,
But leech-like to their fainting country
   cling   5
Till they drop, blind in blood, without a
   blow;
A people starved and stabbed in the un-
   tilled field;
An army, which liberticide and prey
Makes as a two-edged sword to all who
   wield;
Golden and sanguine laws which tempt and
   slay;   10
Religion Christless, Godless—a book sealed;

A Senate—Time's worst statute unre-
    pealed,—
Are graves, from which a glorious Phantom
    may
Burst, to illumine our tempestuous day.
1819   1839

SONG TO THE MEN OF ENGLAND

I

Men of England, wherefore plough
For the lords who lay ye low?
Wherefore weave with toil and care
The rich robes your tyrants wear?

II

Wherefore feed, and clothe, and save,   5
From the cradle to the grave,
Those ungrateful drones who would
Drain your sweat—nay, drink your blood?

III

Wherefore, Bees of England, forge
Many a weapon, chain, and scourge,   10
That these stingless drones may spoil
The forced produce of your toil?

IV

Have ye leisure, comfort, calm,
Shelter, food, love's gentle balm?
Or what is it ye buy so dear   15
With your pain and with your fear?

V

The seed ye sow, another reaps;
The wealth ye find, another keeps;
The robes ye weave, another wears;
The arms ye forge, another bears.   20

VI

Sow seed,—but let no tyrant reap;
Find wealth,—let no impostor heap;
Weave robes,—let not the idle wear;
Forge arms,—in your defence to bear.

VII

Shrink to your cellars, holes, and cells;   25
In halls ye deck another dwells.
Why shake the chains ye wrought? Ye see
The steel ye tempered glance on ye.

VIII

With plough and spade, and hoe and loom,
Trace your grave, and build your tomb,   30
And weave your winding sheet, till fair
England be your sepulchre.
1819   1819

FROM THE MASK OF ANARCHY

WRITTEN ON THE OCCASION OF THE MASSACRE AT MANCHESTER

As I lay asleep in Italy
There came a voice from over the Sea,
And with great power it forth led me
To walk in the visions of Poesy.

I met Murder on the way—   5
He had a mask like Castlereagh—
Very smooth he looked, yet grim;
Seven bloodhounds followed him:

All were fat; and well they might
Be in admirable plight,   10
For one by one, and two by two,
He tossed them human hearts to chew
Which from his wide cloak he drew.

Next came Fraud, and he had on,
Like Eldon, an ermined gown;   15
His big tears, for he wept well,
Turned to millstones as they fell.

And the little children, who
Round his feet played to and fro,
Thinking every tear a gem,   20
Had their brains knocked out by them.

Clothed with the Bible, as with light,
And the shadows of the night,
Like Sidmouth, next, Hypocrisy
On a crocodile rode by.   25

And many more Destructions played
In this ghastly masquerade,
All disguised, even to the eyes,
Like Bishops, lawyers, peers or spies.

Last came Anarchy: he rode   30
On a white horse, splashed with blood;
He was pale even to the lips,
Like Death in the Apocalypse.

And he wore a kingly crown;
And in his grasp a sceptre shone;   35
On his brow this mark I saw—
"I AM GOD, AND KING, AND LAW!"

With a pace stately and fast,
Over English land he passed,
Trampling to a mire of blood   40
The adoring multitude. . . .
c. Sept., 1819   1832

PROMETHEUS UNBOUND

A LYRICAL DRAMA IN FOUR ACTS

DRAMATIS PERSONÆ

PROMETHEUS	ASIA ⎫
DEMOGORGON	PANTHEA ⎬ Oceanides.
JUPITER	IONE ⎭
THE EARTH	THE PHANTASM OF JUPITER
OCEAN	THE SPIRIT OF THE EARTH
APOLLO	THE SPIRIT OF THE MOON
MERCURY	SPIRITS OF THE HOURS
HERCULES	SPIRITS ECHOES
	FAUNS FURIES

ACT I

SCENE.—*A ravine of icy rocks in the Indian Caucasus.*
PROMETHEUS *is discovered bound to the Precipice.* PAN-
THEA *and* IONE *are seated at his feet.   Time, night.
During the scene, morning slowly breaks.*

Prometheus. Monarch of gods and dæmons, and all spirits
But one, who throng those bright and rolling worlds
Which thou and I alone of living things
Behold with sleepless eyes! regard this earth
Made multitudinous with thy slaves, whom thou   5
Requitest for knee-worship, prayer, and praise,
And toil, and hecatombs of broken hearts,
With fear and self-contempt and barren hope.
Whilst me, who am thy foe, eyeless in hate,
Hast thou made reign and triumph, to thy scorn,   10
O'er mine own misery and thy vain revenge.
Three thousand years of sleep-unsheltered hours,
And moments aye divided by keen pangs
Till they seemed years, torture and solitude,
Scorn and despair,—these are mine empire:—   15
More glorious far than that which thou surveyest
From thine unenvied throne, O mighty god!
Almighty, had I deigned to share the shame
Of thine ill tyranny, and hung not here
Nailed to this wall of eagle-baffling mountain,   20
Black, wintry, dead, unmeasured; without herb,
Insect, or beast, or shape or sound of life.
Ah me! alas, pain, pain ever, forever!

No change, no pause, no hope! Yet I endure.
I ask the earth, have not the mountains felt?   25
I ask yon heaven, the all-beholding sun,
Has it not seen? The sea, in storm or calm,
Heaven's ever-changing shadow, spread below,
Have its deaf waves not heard my agony?
Ah me! alas, pain, pain ever, forever!   30

The crawling glaciers pierce me with the spears
Of their moon-freezing crystals; the bright chains
Eat with their burning cold into my bones.
Heaven's wingèd hound, polluting from thy lips
His beak in poison not his own, tears up   35

My heart; and shapeless sights come wandering by,
The ghastly people of the realm of dream,
Mocking me: and the earthquake-fiends are charged
To wrench the rivets from my quivering wounds
When the rocks split and close again behind: 40
While from their loud abysses howling throng
The genii of the storm, urging the rage
Of whirlwind, and afflict me with keen hail.
And yet to me welcome is day and night,
Whether one breaks the hoar frost of the morn,   45
Or starry, dim, and slow, the other climbs
The leaden-colored east; for then they lead
The wingless, crawling hours, one among whom—
As some dark priest hales the reluctant victim—
Shall drag thee, cruel king, to kiss the blood   50
From these pale feet, which then might trample thee
If they disdained not such a prostrate slave.
Disdain! Ah, no! I pity thee. What ruin
Will hunt thee undefended through the wide heaven!
How will thy soul, cloven to its depth with terror,   55
Gape like a hell within! I speak in grief,
Not exultation, for I hate no more,
As then ere misery made me wise. The curse
Once breathed on thee I would recall. Ye mountains,
Whose many-voicèd echoes, through the mist   60
Of cataracts, flung the thunder of that spell!
Ye icy springs, stagnant with wrinkling frost,
Which vibrated to hear me, and then crept
Shuddering through India! Thou serenest air,
Through which the sun walks burning without beams!   65
And ye swift whirlwinds, who on poisèd wings
Hung mute and moveless o'er yon hushed abyss,
As thunder, louder than your own, made rock
The orbèd world! If then my words had power,
Though I am changed so that aught evil wish   70
Is dead within; although no memory be
Of what is hate, let them not lose it now!
What was that curse? for ye all heard me speak.

First Voice (from the Mountains)

Thrice three hundred thousand years
   O'er the Earthquake's couch we stood: 75
Oft, as men convulsed with fears,
   We trembled in our multitude.

Second Voice (from the Springs)

Thunderbolts had parched our water,
   We had been stained with bitter blood,
And had run mute, 'mid shrieks of slaughter,   80
   Thro' a city and a solitude.

Third Voice (from the Air)

I had clothed, since Earth uprose,
   Its wastes in colors not their own,
And oft had my serene repose
   Been cloven by many a rending groan.   85

Fourth Voice (from the Whirlwinds)

We had soared beneath these mountains
    Unresting ages; nor had thunder,
Nor yon volcano's flaming fountains,
    Nor any power above or under
    Ever made us mute with wonder.   90

First Voice

But never bowed our snowy crest
As at the voice of thine unrest.

Second Voice

Never such a sound before
To the Indian waves we bore.
A pilot asleep on the howling sea   95
Leaped up from the deck in agony,
And heard, and cried, "Ah, woe is me!"
And died as mad as the wild waves be.

Third Voice

By such dread words from Earth to Heaven
My still realm was never riven: 100
When its wound was closed, there stood
Darkness o'er the day like blood.

Fourth Voice

And we shrank back: for dreams of ruin
To frozen caves our flight pursuing
Made us keep silence—thus—and thus—   105
Though silence is as hell to us.

The Earth. The tongueless Caverns of the craggy hills
Cried, "Misery!" then; the hollow Heaven replied,
"Misery!" And the Ocean's purple waves,
Climbing the land, howled to the lashing winds,   110
And the pale nations heard it, "Misery!"
    Prometheus. I heard a sound of voices: not the voice
Which I gave forth. Mother, thy sons and thou
Scorn him, without whose all-enduring will
Beneath the fierce omnipotence of Jove,   115
Both they and thou had vanished, like thin mist
Unrolled on the morning wind. Know ye not me,
The Titan? He who made his agony
The barrier to your else all-conquering foe?
Oh, rock-embosomed lawns, and snow-fed streams,   120
Now seen athwart frore vapors, deep below,
Through whose o'ershadowing woods I wandered once
With Asia, drinking life from her loved eyes;
Why scorns the spirit which informs ye, now
To commune with me? me alone, who checked,   125
As one who checks a fiend-drawn charioteer,
The falsehood and the force of him who reigns
Supreme, and with the groans of pining slaves
Fills your dim glens and liquid wildernesses:
Why answer ye not, still? Brethren!
    The Earth.   They dare not.   130
    Prometheus. Who dares? for I would hear that curse again.
Ha, what an awful whisper rises up!

'Tis scarce like sound: it tingles through the frame
As lightning tingles, hovering ere it strike.
Speak, Spirit! from thine inorganic voice   135
I only know that thou art moving near
And love. How cursed I him?
    The Earth.   How canst thou hear
Who knowest not the language of the dead?
    Prometheus. Thou art a living spirit; speak as they.
    The Earth. I dare not speak like life, lest Heaven's fell King   140
Should hear, and link me to some wheel of pain
More torturing than the one whereon I roll.
Subtle thou art and good, and though the Gods
Hear not this voice, yet thou art more than God,
Being wise and kind: earnestly hearken now.   145
    Prometheus. Obscurely through my brain, like shadows dim,
Sweep awful thoughts, rapid and thick. I feel
Faint, like one mingled in entwining love;
Yet 'tis not pleasure.
    The Earth.   No, thou canst not hear:
Thou art immortal, and this tongue is known   150
Only to those who die.
    Prometheus.   And what art thou,
O, melancholy Voice?
    The Earth.   I am the earth,
Thy mother; she within whose stony veins,
To the last fiber of the loftiest tree
Whose thin leaves trembled in the frozen air,   155
Joy ran, as blood within a living frame,
When thou didst from her bosom, like a cloud
Of glory, arise, a spirit of keen joy!
And at thy voice her pining sons uplifted
Their prostrate brows from the polluting dust,   160
And our almighty tyrant with fierce dread
Grew pale, until his thunder chained thee here.
Then—see those million worlds which burn and roll
Around us—their inhabitants beheld
My spherèd light wane in wide heaven; the sea   165
Was lifted by strange tempest, and new fire
From earthquake-rifted mountains of bright snow
Shook its portentous hair beneath heaven's frown;
Lightning and inundation vexed the plains;
Blue thistles bloomed in cities; foodless toads   170
Within voluptuous chambers panting crawled:
When plague had fallen on man and beast and worm,
And famine; and black blight on herb and tree;
And in the corn, and vines, and meadow-grass,
Teemed ineradicable poisonous weeds   175
Draining their growth; for my wan breast was dry
With grief; and the thin air, my breath, was stained
With the contagion of a mother's hate
Breathed on her child's destroyer; aye, I heard
Thy curse, the which, if thou rememberest not,   180
Yet my innumerable seas and streams,
Mountains, and caves, and winds, and yon wide air,
And the inarticulate people of the dead,
Preserve, a treasured spell. We meditate
In secret joy and hope those dreadful words,   185
But dare not speak them.
    Prometheus.   Venerable mother!
All else who live and suffer take from thee

Some comfort; flowers, and fruits, and happy sounds,
And love, though fleeting; these may not be mine,
But mine own words, I pray, deny me not.   190
   The Earth. They shall be told. Ere Babylon was dust,
The Magus Zoroaster, my dead child,
Met his own image walking in the garden.
That apparition, sole of men, he saw.
For know there are two worlds of life and death: 195
One that which thou beholdest; but the other
Is underneath the grave, where do inhabit
The shadows of all forms that think and live
Till death unite them and they part no more;
Dreams and the light imaginings of men,   200
And all that faith creates or love desires,
Terrible, strange, sublime and beauteous shapes.
There thou art, and dost hang, a writhing shade,
'Mid whirlwind-peopled mountains; all the gods
Are there, and all the powers of nameless worlds,   205
Vast, sceptred phantoms; heroes, men, and beasts;
And Demogorgon, a tremendous gloom;
And he, the supreme Tyrant, on his throne
Of burning gold. Son, one of these shall utter
The curse which all remember. Call at will   210
Thine own ghost, or the ghost of Jupiter,
Hades or Typhon, or what mightier Gods
From all-prolific Evil, since thy ruin
Have sprung, and trampled on my prostrate sons.
Ask, and they must reply: so the revenge   215
Of the Supreme may sweep through vacant shades,
As rainy wind through the abandoned gate
Of a fallen palace.
   Prometheus.   Mother, let not aught
Of that which may be evil, pass again
My lips, or those of aught resembling me.   220
Phantasm of Jupiter, arise, appear!

Ione

My wings are folded o'er mine ears:
  My wings are crossèd o'er mine eyes:
Yet through their silver shade appears,
  And through their lulling plumes arise,   225
A Shape, a throng of sounds;
  May it be no ill to thee
  O thou of many wounds!
Near whom, for our sweet sister's sake,
Ever thus we watch and wake.   230

Panthea

The sound is of whirlwind underground,
  Earthquake, and fire, and mountains cloven;
The shape is awful like the sound,
  Clothed in dark purple, star-inwoven.
A sceptre of pale gold   235
  To stay steps proud, o'er the slow cloud
  His veinèd hand doth hold.
Cruel he looks, but calm and strong,
Like one who does, not suffers wrong.

Phantasm of Jupiter. Why have the secret powers of this
  strange world   240
Driven me, a frail and empty phantom, hither
On direst storms? What unaccustomed sounds
Are hovering on my lips, unlike the voice
With which our pallid race hold ghastly talk
In darkness? And, proud sufferer, who art thou? 245
 Prometheus. Tremendous Image, as thou art must be
He whom thou shadowest forth. I am his foe,
The Titan. Speak the words which I would hear,
Although no thought inform thine empty voice.
 The Earth. Listen! And though your echoes must be mute, 250
Gray mountains, and old woods, and haunted springs,
Prophetic caves, and isle-surrounding streams,
Rejoice to hear what yet ye cannot speak.
 Phantasm. A spirit seizes me and speaks within:
It tears me as fire tears a thundercloud.   255
 Panthea. See, how he lifts his mighty looks, the Heaven
Darkens above.
 Ione.   He speaks! O shelter me!
 Prometheus. I see the curse on gestures proud and cold,
And looks of firm defiance, and calm hate,
And such despair as mocks itself with smiles, 260
Written as on a scroll: yet speak: Oh, speak!

Phantasm

Fiend, I defy thee! with a calm, fixed mind,
 All that thou canst inflict I bid thee do;
Foul tyrant both of gods and human-kind,
  One only being shalt thou not subdue. 265
  Rain then thy plagues upon me here,
  Ghastly disease, and frenzying fear;
  And let alternate frost and fire
  Eat into me, and be thine ire
Lightning, and cutting hail, and legioned forms 270
Of furies, driving by upon the wounding storms.

Aye, do thy worst. Thou art omnipotent.
 O'er all things but thyself I gave thee power,
And my own will. Be thy swift mischiefs sent
 To blast mankind, from yon ethereal tower. 275
Let thy malignant spirit move
In darkness over those I love:
On me and mine I imprecate
The utmost torture of thy hate;
And thus devote to sleepless agony, 280
This undeclining head while thou must reign on high.

But thou, who art the God and Lord: O thou
 Who fillest with thy soul this world of woe,
To whom all things of earth and heaven do bow
 In fear and worship—all-prevailing foe! 285
I curse thee! let a sufferer's curse
Clasp thee, his torturer, like remorse;
Till thine infinity shall be
A robe of envenomed agony;
And thine omnipotence a crown of pain, 290
To cling like burning gold round thy dissolving brain.

Heap on thy soul, by virtue of this curse,
  Ill deeds, then be thou damned, beholding good;
Both infinite as is the universe,
And thou, and thy self-torturing solitude.   295
An awful image of calm power
Though now thou sittest, let the hour
Come, when thou must appear to be
That which thou art internally;
And after many a false and fruitless crime   300
Scorn track thy lagging fall through boundless space and time.
Prometheus. Were these my words, O Parent?
The Earth.   They were thine.
Prometheus. It doth repent me: words are quick and vain;
Grief for awhile is blind, and so was mine.   305
I wish no living thing to suffer pain.

The Earth

  Misery, Oh misery to me,
  That Jove at length should vanquish thee.
  Wail, howl aloud, Land and Sea,
  The Earth's rent heart shall answer ye.
Howl, Spirits of the living and the dead,   310
Your refuge, your defence lies fallen and vanquishèd.

First Echo

Lies fallen and vanquishèd!

Second Echo

          Fallen and vanquishèd!

Ione

Fear not: 'tis but some passing spasm,
  The Titan is unvanquished still.   315
But see, where through the azure chasm
  Of yon forked and snowy hill
Trampling the slant winds on high
  With golden-sandalled feet, that glow
Under plumes of purple dye,   320
Like rose-ensanguined ivory,
    A Shape comes now,
  Stretching on high from his right hand
  A serpent-cinctured wand.

Panthea. 'Tis Jove's world-wandering herald, Mercury.   325

Ione

And who are those with hydra tresses
  And iron wings that climb the wind,
Whom the frowning God represses
  Like vapors steaming up behind,
Clanging loud, an endless crowd—   330

Panthea

These are Jove's tempest-walking hounds
Whom he gluts with groans and blood,
When charioted on sulphurous cloud
  He bursts Heaven's bounds.

Ione

Are they now led, from the thin dead   335
On new pangs to be fed?

Panthea

The Titan looks as ever, firm, not proud.

First Fury. Ha! I scent life!
Second Fury. Let me but look into his eyes!
Third Fury. The hope of torturing him smells like a heap   340
Of corpses to a death-bird after battle.
  First Fury. Darest thou delay, O Herald! take cheer, Hounds
Of Hell: what if the Son of Maia soon
Should make us food and sport—who can please long
The Omnipotent?
  Mercury. Back to your towers of iron,   345
And gnash, beside the streams of fire and wail,
Your foodless teeth. Geryon, arise! and Gorgon,
Chimæra, and thou Sphinx, subtlest of fiends
Who ministered to Thebes Heaven's poisoned wine,
Unnatural love, and more unnatural hate: 350
These shall perform your task.
  First Fury.   Oh, mercy! mercy!
We die with our desire: drive us not back!
  Mercury. Crouch then in silence.
                                          Awful Sufferer!
To thee unwilling, most unwillingly
I come, by the great Father's will driven down,   355
To execute a doom of new revenge.
Alas! I pity thee, and hate myself
That I can do no more: aye from thy sight
Returning, for a season, Heaven seems Hell,
So thy worn form pursues me night and day,   360
Smiling reproach. Wise art thou, firm and good,
But vainly wouldst stand forth alone in strife
Against the Omnipotent; as yon clear lamps
That measure and divide the weary years
From which there is no refuge, long have taught   365
And long must teach. Even now thy Torturer arms
With the strange might of unimagined pains
The powers who scheme slow agonies in Hell,
And my commission is to lead them here,
Or what more subtle, foul, or savage fiends   370
People the abyss, and leave them to their task.
Be it not so! there is a secret known
To thee, and to none else of living things,
Which may transfer the sceptre of wide Heaven,
The fear of which perplexes the Supreme: 375
Clothe it in words, and bid it clasp his throne
In intercession; bend thy soul in prayer,
And like a suppliant in some gorgeous fane,
Let the will kneel within thy haughty heart:
For benefits and meek submission tame   380
The fiercest and the mightiest.
  Prometheus.   Evil minds
Change good to their own nature. I gave all
He has; and in return he chains me here
Years, ages, night and day: whether the Sun
Split my parched skin, or in the moony night   385

The crystal-wingèd snow cling round my hair:
Whilst my belovèd race is trampled down
By his thought-executing ministers.
Such is the tyrant's recompense: 'tis just:
He who is evil can receive no good;   390
And for a world bestowed, or a friend lost,
He can feel hate, fear, shame; not gratitude:
He but requites me for his own misdeed.
Kindness to such is keen reproach, which breaks
With bitter stings the light sleep of Revenge.   395
Submission, thou dost know I cannot try:
For what submission but that fatal word,
The death-seal of mankind's captivity,
Like the Sicilian's hair-suspended sword,
Which trembles o'er his crown, would he accept,   400
Or could I yield? Which yet I will not yield.
Let others flatter Crime, where it sits throned
In brief Omnipotence: secure are they:
For Justice, when triumphant, will weep down
Pity, not punishment, on her own wrongs,   405
Too much avenged by those who err. I wait,
Enduring thus, the retributive hour
Which since we spake is even nearer now.
But hark, the hell-hounds clamor: fear delay:
Behold! Heaven lowers under thy Father's frown.   410
  Mercury. Oh, that we might be spared: I to inflict
And thou to suffer! Once more answer me:
Thou knowest not the period of Jove's power?
  Prometheus. I know but this, that it must come.
  Mercury.   Alas!
Thou canst not count thy years to come of pain?   415
  Prometheus. They last while Jove must reign: nor more, nor less
Do I desire or fear.
  Mercury.   Yet pause, and plunge
Into Eternity, where recorded time,
Even all that we imagine, age on age,
Seems but a point, and the reluctant mind   420
Flags wearily in its unending flight,
Till it sink, dizzy, blind, lost, shelterless;
Perchance it has not numbered the slow years
Which thou must spend in torture, unreprieved?
  Prometheus. Perchance no thought can count them, yet they pass.   425
  Mercury. If thou might'st dwell among the Gods the while
Lapped in voluptuous joy?
  Prometheus. I would not quit
This bleak ravine, these unrepentant pains.
  Mercury. Alas! I wonder at, yet pity thee.
  Prometheus. Pity the self-despising slaves of Heaven,   430
Not me, within whose mind sits peace serene,
As light in the sun, throned: how vain is talk!
Call up the fiends.
  Ione.   O, sister, look! White fire
Has cloven to the roots yon huge snow-loaded cedar;
How fearfully God's thunder howls behind!   435
  Mercury. I must obey his words and thine: alas!
Most heavily remorse hangs at my heart!
  Panthea. See where the child of Heaven, with wingèd feet,
Runs down the slanted sunlight of the dawn.
  Ione. Dear sister, close thy plumes over thine eyes   440
Lest thou behold and die: they come: they come

Blackening the birth of day with countless wings,
And hollow underneath, like death.
 First Fury.   Prometheus!
 Second Fury. Immortal Titan!
 Third Fury.   Champion of Heaven's slaves!
 Prometheus. He whom some dreadful voice invokes is here, 445
Prometheus, the chained Titan. Horrible forms,
What and who are ye? Never yet there came
Phantasms so foul through monster-teeming Hell
From the all-miscreative brain of Jove;
Whilst I behold such execrable shapes,   450
Methinks I grow like what I contemplate,
And laugh and stare in loathsome sympathy.
 First Fury. We are the ministers of pain, and fear,
And disappointment, and mistrust, and hate,
And clinging crime; and as lean dogs pursue   455
Through wood and lake some struck and sobbing fawn,
We track all things that weep, and bleed, and live,
When the great King betrays them to our will.
 Prometheus. Oh! many fearful natures in one name,
I know ye; and these lakes and echoes know   460
The darkness and the clangor of your wings.
But why more hideous than your lothèd selves
Gather ye up in legions from the deep?
 Second Fury. We knew not that: Sisters, rejoice, rejoice!
 Prometheus. Can aught exult in its deformity?   465
 Second Fury. The beauty of delight makes lovers glad,
Gazing on one another: so are we.
As from the rose which the pale priestess kneels
To gather for her festal crown of flowers
The aërial crimson falls, flushing her cheek,   470
So from our victim's destined agony
The shade which is our form invests us round,
Else we are shapeless as our mother Night.
 Prometheus. I laugh your power, and his who sent you here,
To lowest scorn. Pour forth the cup of pain.   475
 First Fury. Thou thinkest we will rend thee bone from bone,
And nerve from nerve, working like fire within?
 Prometheus. Pain is my element, as hate is thine;
Ye rend me now: I care not.
 Second Fury.   Dost imagine
We will but laugh into thy lidless eyes?   480
 Prometheus. I weigh not what ye do, but what ye suffer,
Being evil. Cruel was the power which called
You, or aught else so wretched, into light.
 Third Fury. Thou think'st we will live through thee, one by one,
Like animal life, and though we can obscure not   485
The soul which burns within, that we will dwell
Beside it, like a vain loud multitude
Vexing the self-content of wisest men:
That we will be dread thought beneath thy brain,
And foul desire round thine astonished heart,   490
And blood within thy labyrinthine veins
Crawling like agony?
 Prometheus.   Why, ye are thus now;
Yet am I king over myself, and rule
The torturing and conflicting throngs within,
As Jove rules you when Hell grows mutinous.   495

Chorus of Furies

From the ends of the earth, from the ends of the earth,
Where the night has its grave and the morning its birth,
          Come, come, come!
Oh, ye who shake hills with the scream of your mirth,
When cities sink howling in ruin; and ye   500
Who with wingless footsteps trample the sea,
And close upon Shipwreck and Famine's track,
Sit chattering with joy on the foodless wreck;
          Come, come, come!
Leave the bed, low, cold, and red,   505
     Strewed beneath a nation dead;
     Leave the hatred, as in ashes
          Fire is left for future burning:
     It will burst in bloodier flashes
          When ye stir it, soon returning: 510
     Leave the self-contempt implanted
     In young spirits, sense-enchanted,
          Misery's yet unkindled fuel:
     Leave Hell's secrets half unchanted,
          To the maniac dreamer; cruel   515
     More than ye can be with hate
          Is he with fear.
          Come, come, come!
We are steaming up from Hell's wide gate
And we burthen the blast of the atmosphere,   520
But vainly we toil till ye come here.

     Ione.   Sister, I hear the thunder of new wings.
     Panthea.   These solid mountains quiver with the sound
Even as the tremulous air: their shadows make
The space within my plumes more black than night.   525

First Fury

Your call was as wingèd car
Driven on whirlwinds fast and far;
It rapped us from red gulfs of war.

Second Fury

From wide cities, famine-wasted;

Third Fury

Groans half heard, and blood untasted;   530

Fourth Fury

Kingly conclaves stern and cold,
Where blood with gold is bought and sold;

Fifth Fury

From the furnace, white and hot,
In which—

A Fury

          Speak not: whisper not:
I know all that ye would tell,   535
But to speak might break the spell
Which must bend the Invincible,
     The stern of thought;
He yet defies the deepest power of Hell.

A Fury

Tear the veil!

Another Fury

It is torn.

Chorus

The pale stars of the morn   540
Shine on a misery, dire to be borne.
Dost thou faint, mighty Titan? We laugh thee to scorn.
Dost thou boast the clear knowledge thou waken'dst for man?
Then was kindled within him a thirst which outran
Those perishing waters; a thirst of fierce fever,   545
Hope, love, doubt, desire, which consume him for ever.
One came forth of gentle worth
Smiling on the sanguine earth;
His words outlived him, like swift poison
Withering up truth, peace, and pity.   550
Look! where round the wide horizon
Many a million-peopled city
Vomits smoke in the bright air.
Hark that outcry of despair!
'Tis his mild and gentle ghost   555
Wailing for the faith he kindled:
Look again, the flames almost
To a glowworm's lamp have dwindled:
The survivors round the embers
Gather in dread.
Joy, joy, joy!   560
Past ages crowd on thee, but each one remembers,
And the future is dark, and the present is spread
Like a pillow of thorns for thy slumberless head.

Semichorus I

Drops of bloody agony flow   565
From his white and quivering brow.
Grant a little respite now:
See a disenchanted nation
Springs like day from desolation;
To Truth its state is dedicate,   570
And Freedom leads it forth, her mate;
A legioned band of linkèd brothers
Whom Love calls children—

Semichorus II

'Tis another's:
See how kindred murder kin:
'Tis the vintage-time for death and sin: 575
Blood, like new wine, bubbles within:
Till Despair smothers
The struggling world, which slaves and tyrants win.
                [*All the* FURIES *vanish, except one.*
Ione. Hark, sister! what a low yet dreadful groan
Quite unsuppressed is tearing up the heart   580
Of the good Titan, as storms tear the deep,
And beasts hear the sea moan in inland caves.
Darest thou observe how the fiends torture him?
Panthea. Alas! I looked forth twice, but will no more

Ione. What didst thou see?
Panthea.   A woeful sight: a youth   585
With patient looks nailed to a crucifix.
Ione. What next?
Panthea.   The heaven around, the earth below
Was peopled with thick shapes of human death,
All horrible, and wrought by human hands,
And some appeared the work of human hearts.   590
For men were slowly killed by frowns and smiles:
And other sights too foul to speak and live
Were wandering by. Let us not tempt worse fear
By looking forth: those groans are grief enough.
    Fury. Behold an emblem: those who do endure   595
Deep wrongs for man, and scorn, and chains, but heap
Thousandfold torment on themselves and him.
    Prometheus. Remit the anguish of that lighted stare;
Close those wan lips; let that thorn-wounded brow
Stream not with blood; it mingles with thy tears!   600
Fix, fix those tortured orbs in peace and death,
So thy sick throes shake not that crucifix,
So those pale fingers play not with thy gore.
O, horrible! Thy name I will not speak,
It hath become a curse. I see, I see   605
The wise, the mild, the lofty, and the just,
Whom thy slaves hate for being like to thee,
Some hunted by foul lies from their heart's home,
An early-chosen, late-lamented home;
As hooded ounces cling to the driven hind;   610
Some linked to corpses in unwholesome cells:
Some—hear I not the multitude laugh loud?—
Impaled in lingering fire: and mighty realms
Float by my feet, like sea-uprooted isles,
Whose sons are kneaded down in common blood   615
By the red light of their own burning homes.
    Fury. Blood thou canst see, and fire; and canst hear groans;
Worse things, unheard, unseen, remain behind.
    Prometheus. Worse?
    Fury.   In each human heart terror survives
The ravin it has gorged: the loftiest fear   620
All that they would disdain to think were true:
Hypocrisy and custom make their minds
The fanes of many a worship, now outworn.
They dare not devise good for man's estate,
And yet they know not that they do not dare.   625
The good want power, but to weep barren tears.
The powerful goodness want: worse need for them.
The wise want love; and those who love want wisdom;
And all best things are thus confused to ill.
Many are strong and rich, and would be just,   630
But live among their suffering fellow-men
As if none felt: they know not what they do.
    Prometheus. Thy words are like a cloud of wingèd snakes;
And yet I pity those they torture not.
    Fury. Thou pitiest them? I speak no more!
                                        [*Vanishes.*
    Prometheus.   Ah woe!   635
Ah woe! Alas! pain, pain ever, for ever!
I close my tearless eyes, but see more clear
Thy works within my woe-illumèd mind,
Thou subtle tyrant! Peace is in the grave.

The grave hides all things beautiful and good: 640
I am a God and cannot find it there,
Nor would I seek it: for, though dread revenge,
This is defeat, fierce king, not victory.
The sights with which thou torturest gird my soul
With new endurance, till the hour arrives
When they shall be no types of things which are.   645
   Panthea. Alas! what sawest thou more?
   Prometheus.   There are two woes:
To speak, and to behold; thou spare me one.
Names are there, Nature's sacred watchwords, they
Were borne aloft in bright emblazonry;   650
The nations thronged around, and cried aloud,
As with one voice, Truth, liberty, and love!
Suddenly fierce confusion fell from heaven
Among them: there was strife, deceit, and fear:
Tyrants rushed in, and did divide the spoil.   655
This was the shadow of the truth I saw.
   The Earth. I felt thy torture, son; with such mixed joy
As pain and virtue give. To cheer thy state
I bid ascend those subtle and fair spirits,
Whose homes are the dim caves of human thought,   660
And who inhabit, as birds wing the wind,
Its world-surrounding æther: they behold
Beyond that twilight realm, as in a glass,
The future: may they speak comfort to thee!
   Panthea. Look, sister, where a troop of spirits gather,   665
Like flocks of clouds in spring's delightful weather,
Thronging in the blue air!
   Ione.   And see! more come,
Like fountain-vapors when the winds are dumb,
That climb up the ravine in scattered lines.
And, hark! is it the music of the pines?   670
Is it the lake? Is it the waterfall?
   Panthea. 'Tis something sadder, sweeter far than all.

Chorus of Spirits

From unremembered ages we
Gentle guides and guardians be
Of heaven-oppressed mortality;   675
And we breathe, and sicken not,
The atmosphere of human thought:
Be it dim, and dank, and gray,
Like a storm-extinguished day,
Travelled o'er by dying gleams;   680
Be it bright as all between
Cloudless skies and windless streams,
  Silent, liquid, and serene;
As the birds within the wind,
  As the fish within the wave,   685
As the thoughts of man's own mind
  Float through all above the grave;
We make there our liquid lair,
Voyaging cloudlike and unpent
  Through the boundless element: 690
Thence we bear the prophecy
Which begins and ends in thee!
   Ione. More yet come, one by one: the air around them
Looks radiant as the air around a star.

First Spirit

On a battle-trumpet's blast
I fled hither, fast, fast, fast,   695
'Mid the darkness upward cast.
From the dust of creeds outworn,
From the tyrant's banner torn,
Gathering 'round me, onward borne,
There was mingled many a cry—   700
Freedom! Hope! Death! Victory!
Till they faded through the sky;
And one sound, above, around,
One sound beneath, around, above,
Was moving; 'twas the soul of Love;   705
'Twas the hope, the prophecy,
Which begins and ends in thee.

Second Spirit

A rainbow's arch stood on the sea,
Which rocked beneath, immovably;
And the triumphant storm did flee,   710
Like a conqueror, swift and proud,
Between, with many a captive cloud,
A shapeless, dark and rapid crowd,
Each by lightning riven in half:
I heard the thunder hoarsely laugh: 715
Mighty fleets were strewn like chaff
And spread beneath a hell of death
O'er the white waters. I alit
On a great ship lightning-split,   720
And speeded hither on the sigh
Of one who gave an enemy,
His plank, then plunged aside to die.

Third Spirit

I sate beside a sage's bed,
And the lamp was burning red   725
Near the book where he had fed,
When a Dream with plumes of flame,
To his pillow hovering came,
And I knew it was the same
Which had kindled long ago   730
Pity, eloquence, and woe;
And the world awhile below
Wore the shade, its lustre made.
It has borne me here as fleet
As Desire's lightning feet: 735
I must ride it back ere morrow,
Or the sage will wake in sorrow.

Fourth Spirit

On a poet's lips I slept
Dreaming like a love-adept
In the sound his breathing kept;   740
Nor seeks nor finds he mortal blisses,
But feeds on the aërial kisses
Of shapes that haunt thought's wildernesses.
He will watch from dawn to gloom
The lake-reflected sun illume   745

The yellow bees in the ivy-bloom,
Nor heed nor see, what things they be;
But from these create he can
Forms more real than living man,
Nursling of immortality!   750
One of these awakened me,
And I sped to succor thee.

Ione

Behold'st thou not two shapes from the east and west
Come, as two doves to one belovèd nest,
Twin nurslings of the all-sustaining air   755
On swift still wings glide down the atmosphere?
And, hark! their sweet, sad voices! 'tis despair
Mingled with love and then dissolved in sound.
    Panthea. Canst thou speak, sister? all my words are drowned.
    Ione. Their beauty gives me voice. See how they float   760
On their sustaining wings of skiey grain,
Orange and azure deepening into gold:
Their soft smiles light the air like a star's fire.

Chorus of Spirits

Hast thou beheld the form of Love?

Fifth Spirit

               As over wide dominions
I sped, like some swift cloud that wings the wide air's
    wildernesses,   765
That planet-crested shape swept by on lightning-braided
    pinions,
Scattering the liquid joy of life from his ambrosial tresses:
His footsteps paved the world with light; but as I passed
    'twas fading,
And hollow Ruin yawned behind: great sages bound in
    madness,
And headless patriots, and pale youths who perished, un-
    upbraiding,   770
Gleamed in the night. I wandered o'er, till thou, O
    King of sadness,
Turned by thy smile the worst I saw to recollected gladness.

Sixth Spirit

Ah, sister! Desolation is a delicate thing:
It walks not on earth, it floats not on the air,
But treads with lulling footsteps, and fans with silent wing   775
The tender hopes which in their hearts the best and
    gentlest bear;
Who, soothed to false repose by the fanning plumes above
And the music-stirring motion of its soft and busy feet,
Dream visions of aërial joy, and call the monster, Love,
And wake, and find the shadow Pain, as he whom now
    we greet.   780

Chorus

Though Ruin now Love's shadow be,
Following him, destroyingly,
    On Death's white and wingèd steed,
Which the fleetest cannot flee,
    Trampling down both flower and weed,   785

Man and beast, and foul and fair,
Like a tempest through the air;
Thou shalt quell this horseman grim,
Woundless though in heart or limb.

 Prometheus. Spirits! how know ye this shall be?   790

Chorus

In the atmosphere we breathe,
As buds grow red when the snow-storms flee,
 From Spring gathering up beneath,
Whose mild winds shake the elder brake,
And the wandering herdsmen know   795
That the white-thorn soon will blow:
  Wisdom, Justice, Love, and Peace,
  When they struggle to increase,
   Are to us as soft winds be
    To shepherd boys, the prophecy 800
   Which begins and ends in thee.

 Ione. Where are the Spirits fled?
 Panthea.   Only a sense
Remains of them, like the omnipotence
Of music, when the inspired voice and lute
Languish, ere yet the responses are mute,   805
Which through the deep and labyrinthine soul,
Like echoes through long caverns, wind and roll.
 Prometheus. How fair these airborn shapes! and yet I feel
Most vain all hope but love; and thou art far,
Asia! who, when my being overflowed,   810
Wert like a golden chalice to bright wine
Which else had sunk into the thirsty dust.
All things are still: alas! how heavily
This quiet morning weighs upon my heart;
Though I should dream I could even sleep with grief 815
If slumber were denied not. I would fain
Be what it is my destiny to be,
The saviour and the strength of suffering man,
Or sink into the original gulf of things:
There is no agony, and no solace left;   820
Earth can console, Heaven can torment no more.
 Panthea. Hast thou forgotten one who watches thee
The cold dark night, and never sleeps but when
The shadow of thy spirit falls on her?
 Prometheus. I said all hope was vain but love: thou lovest. 825
 Panthea. Deeply in truth; but the eastern star looks white,
And Asia waits in that far Indian vale,
The scene of her sad exile; rugged once
And desolate and frozen, like this ravine;
But now invested with fair flowers and herbs, 830
And haunted by sweet airs and sounds, which flow
Among the woods and waters, from the ether
Of her transforming presence, which would fade
If it were mingled not with thine. Farewell!

   END OF THE FIRST ACT

ACT II

Scene I.—*Morning. A lovely vale in the Indian Caucasus.*
Asia *alone.*

Asia. From all the blasts of heaven thou hast descended:
Yes, like a spirit, like a thought, which makes
Unwonted tears throng to the horny eyes,
And beatings haunt the desolated heart,
Which should have learnt repose: thou hast descended   5
Cradled in tempests; thou dost wake, O spring!
O child of many winds! As suddenly
Thou comest as the memory of a dream,
Which now is sad because it hath been sweet;
Like genius, or like joy which riseth up   10
As from the earth, clothing with golden clouds
The desert of our life.
This is the season, this the day, the hour;
At sunrise thou shouldst come, sweet sister mine,
Too long desired, too long delaying, come!   15
How like death-worms the wingless moments crawl!
The point of one white star is quivering still
Deep in the orange light of widening morn
Beyond the purple mountains: through a chasm
Of wind-divided mist the darker lake   20
Reflects it: now it wanes: it gleams again
As the waves fade, and as the burning threads
Of woven cloud unravel in pale air:
'Tis lost! and through yon peaks of cloud-like snow
The roseate sunlight quivers: hear I not   25
The Æolian music of her sea-green plumes
Winnowing the crimson dawn?
                                        [Panthea *enters.*
                        I feel, I see
Those eyes which burn through smiles that fade in tears,
Like stars half-quenched in mists of silver dew.
Belovèd and most beautiful, who wearest   30
The shadow of that soul by which I live,
How late thou art! the spherèd sun had climbed
The sea; my heart was sick with hope, before
The printless air felt thy belated plumes.
    Panthea. Pardon, great sister! but my wings were **faint** 35
With the delight of a remembered dream,
As are the noontide plumes of summer winds
Satiate with sweet flowers. I was wont to sleep
Peacefully, and awake refreshed and calm
Before the sacred Titan's fall and thy   40
Unhappy love had made, through use and pity,
Both love and woe familiar to my heart
As they had grown to thine: erewhile I slept
Under the glaucous caverns of old ocean
Within dim bowers of green and purple moss,   45
Our young Ione's soft and milky arms
Locked then, as now, behind my dark, moist hair,
While my shut eyes and cheek were pressed within
The folded depth of her life-breathing bosom:
But not as now, since I am made the wind   50
Which fails beneath the music that I bear
Of thy most wordless converse; since dissolved
Into the sense with which love talks, my rest
Was troubled and yet sweet; my waking hours

Too full of care and pain.
 Asia.   Lift up thine eyes, 55
And let me read thy dream.
 Panthea.   As I have said
With our sea-sister at his feet I slept.
The mountain mists, condensing at our voice
Under the moon, had spread their snowy flakes,
From the keen ice shielding our linkèd sleep. 60
Then two dreams came. One, I remember not.
But in the other his pale wound-worn limbs
Fell from Prometheus, and the azure night
Grew radiant with the glory of that form
Which lives unchanged within, and his voice fell 65
Like music which makes giddy the dim brain,
Faint with intoxication of keen joy:
"Sister of her whose footsteps pave the world
With loveliness—more fair than aught but her,
Whose shadow thou art—lift thine eyes on me." 70
I lifted them: the overpowering light
Of that immortal shape was shadowed o'er
By love; which, from his soft and flowing limbs,
And passion-parted lips, and keen, faint eyes,
Steamed forth like vaporous fire; an atmosphere 75
Which wrapped me in its all-dissolving power,
As the warm ether of the morning sun
Wraps ere it drinks some cloud of wandering dew.
I saw not, heard not, moved not, only felt
His presence flow and mingle through my blood 80
Till it became his life, and his grew mine,
And I was thus absorbed, until it passed,
And like the vapors when the sun sinks down,
Gathering again in drops upon the pines,
And tremulous as they, in the deep night 85
My being was condensed; and as the rays
Of thought were slowly gathered, I could hear
His voice, whose accents lingered ere they died
Like footsteps of weak melody: thy name
Among the many sounds alone I heard 90
Of what might be articulate; though still
I listened through the night when sound was none.
Ione wakened then, and said to me:
"Canst thou divine what troubles me tonight?
I always knew what I desired before, 95
Nor ever found delight to wish in vain.
But now I cannot tell thee what I seek;
I know not; something sweet, since it is sweet
Even to desire; it is thy sport, false sister;
Thou hast discovered some enchantment old, 100
Whose spells have stolen my spirit as I slept
And mingled it with thine: for when just now
We kissed, I felt within thy parted lips
The sweet air that sustained me, and the warmth
Of the life-blood, for loss of which I faint, 105
Quivered between our intertwining arms."
I answered not, for the eastern star grew pale,
But fled to thee.
 Asia.   Thou speakest, but thy words
Are as the air: I feel them not. Oh, lift
Thine eyes, that I may read his written soul! 110
 Panthea. I lift them though they droop beneath the load

Of that they would express; what canst thou see
But thine own fairest shadow imaged there?
　　Asia.　Thine eyes are like the deep, blue, boundless heaven
Contracted to two circles underneath   115
Their long, fine lashes; dark, far, measureless,
Orb within orb, and line through line inwoven.
　　Panthea.　Why lookest thou as if a spirit passed?
　　Asia.　There is a change; beyond their inmost depth
I see a shade, a shape: 'tis he, arrayed   120
In the soft light of his own smiles, which spread
Like radiance from the cloud-surrounded moon.
Prometheus, it is thine! depart not yet!
Say not those smiles that we shall meet again
Within that bright pavilion which their beams   125
Shall build on the waste world? The dream is told.
What shape is that between us? Its rude hair
Roughens the wind that lifts it, its regard
Is wild and quick, yet 'tis a thing of air,
For through its gray robe gleams the golden dew   130
Whose stars the noon has quenched not
　　Dream.　　　　　　　　　　　Follow! Follow!
　　Panthea.　It is mine other dream.
　　Asia.　　　　　　　　　　　It disappears.
　　Panthea.　It passes now into my mind. Methought
As we sate here, the flower-infolding buds
Burst on yon lightning-blasted almond tree,   135
When swift from the white Scythian wilderness
A wind swept forth wrinkling the earth with frost:
I looked, and all the blossoms were blown down;
But on each leaf was stamped, as the blue bells
Of Hyacinth tell Apollo's written grief,   140
OH, FOLLOW, FOLLOW!
　　Asia.　　　　　　　As you speak, your words
Fill, pause by pause, my own forgotten sleep
With shapes. Methought among these lawns together
We wandered, underneath the young gray dawn,
And multitudes of dense white fleecy clouds   145
Were wandering in thick flocks along the mountains
Shepherded by the slow, unwilling wind;
And the white dew on the new-bladed grass,
Just piercing the dark earth, hung silently;
And there was more which I remember not: 150
But on the shadows of the morning clouds,
Athwart the purple mountain slope, was written
FOLLOW, OH, FOLLOW! as they vanished by;
And on each herb, from which heaven's dew had fallen,
The like was stamped, as with a withering fire;   155
A wind arose among the pines; it shook
The clinging music from their boughs, and then
Low, sweet, faint sounds, like the farewell of ghosts,
Were heard: OH, FOLLOW, FOLLOW, FOLLOW ME!
And then I said: "Panthea, look on me."   160
But in the depth of those belovèd eyes
Still I saw, FOLLOW, FOLLOW!
　　Echo.　　　　　　　　　　Follow, follow!
　　Panthea.　The crags, this clear spring morning, mock our
　　　voices
As they were spirit-tongued.
　　Asia.　　　　　　　　　It is some being
Around the crags. What fine clear sounds! Oh list!   165

Echoes (unseen)

Echoes we: listen!
We cannot stay:
As dew-stars glisten
Then fade away—
Child of Ocean!   170

Asia. Hark! Spirits speak. The liquid responses
Of their aërial tongues yet sound.
Panthea.   I hear.

Echoes

Oh, follow, follow
As our voice recedeth
Through the caverns hollow.
Where the forest spreadeth;   175

(More distant)

Oh, follow, follow!
Through the caverns hollow,
As the song floats thou pursue,
Where the wild bee never flew,
Through the noontide darkness deep,   180
By the odor-breathing sleep
Of faint night-flowers, and the waves
At the fountain-lighted caves,
While our music, wild and sweet,
Mocks thy gently falling feet,   185
Child of Ocean!

Asia. Shall we pursue the sound? It grows more faint
and distant.
Panthea. List! the strain floats nearer now.

Echoes

In the world unknown   190
Sleeps a voice unspoken;
By thy step alone
Can its rest be broken;
Child of Ocean!

Asia. How the notes sink upon the ebbing wind!   195

Echoes

Oh, follow, follow!
Through the caverns hollow,
As the song floats thou pursue,
By the woodland noontide dew;
By the forest, lakes, and fountains,   200
Through the many-folded mountains;
To the rents, and gulfs, and chasms,
Where the Earth reposed from spasms,
On the day when he and thou
Parted, to commingle now;   205
Child of Ocean!

Asia. Come, sweet Panthea, link thy hand in mine,
And follow, ere the voices fade away.

SCENE II.—*A forest, intermingled with rocks and caverns.*
ASIA *and* PANTHEA *pass into it. Two young fauns are sitting on a rock listening.*

Semichorus I of Spirits

The path through which that lovely twain
　Have passed, by cedar, pine, and yew,
　And each dark tree that ever grew,
Is curtained out from heaven's wide blue;
Nor sun, nor moon, nor wind, nor rain,　　　　　　　5
　Can pierce its interwoven bowers,
Nor aught, save where some cloud of dew,
Drifted along the earth-creeping breeze,
Between the trunks of the hoar trees,
　Hangs each a pearl in the pale flowers　　　　　　10
Of the green laurel, blown anew;
And bends, and then fades silently,
One frail and fair anemone:
Or when some star of many a one
That climbs and wanders through steep night,　　　15
Has found the cleft through which alone
Beams fall from high those depths upon
Ere it is borne away, away,
By the swift heavens that cannot stay,
It scatters drops of golden light,　　　　　　　　20
Like lines of rain that ne'er unite:
And the gloom divine is all around,
And underneath is the mossy ground.

Semichorus II

There the voluptuous nightingales,
　Are awake through all the broad noonday.　　　　25
When one with bliss or sadness fails,
　And through the windless ivy-boughs,
　Sick with sweet love, droops dying away
On its mate's music-panting bosom;
Another from the swinging blossom,　　　　　　　30
　Watching to catch the languid close
Of the last strain, then lifts on high
The wings of the weak melody,
Till some new strain of feeling bear
　The song, and all the woods are mute;　　　　　35
When there is heard through the dim air
The rush of wings, and rising there
　Like many a lake-surrounded flute,
Sounds overflow the listener's brain
So sweet, that joy is almost pain.　　　　　　　40

Semichorus I

There those enchanted eddies play
　Of echoes, music-tongued, which draw,
　By Demogorgon's mighty law,
　With melting rapture, or sweet awe,
All spirits on that secret way;　　　　　　　　45
　As inland boats are driven to Ocean
Down streams made strong with mountain-thaw:
　And first there comes a gentle sound
　To those in talk or slumber bound,
And wakes the destined soft emotion,—　　　　　50

Attracts, impels them; those who saw
  Say from the breathing earth behind
  There steams a plume-uplifting wind
Which drives them on their path, while they
  Believe their own swift wings and feet 55
The sweet desires within obey:
And so they float upon their way,
Until, still sweet, but loud and strong,
The storm of sound is driven along,
  Sucked up and hurrying: as they fleet 60
  Behind, its gathering billows meet
And to the fatal mountain bear
Like clouds amid the yielding air.

    First Faun. Canst thou imagine where those spirits live
Which make such delicate music in the woods? 65
We haunt within the least frequented caves
And closest coverts, and we know these wilds,
Yet never meet them, though we hear them oft:
Where may they hide themselves?

    Second Faun.   'Tis hard to tell:
I have heard those more skilled in spirits say, 70
The bubbles, which the enchantment of the sun
Sucks from the pale faint water flowers that pave
The oozy bottom of clear lakes and pools,
Are the pavilions where such dwell and float
Under the green and golden atmosphere 75
Which noontide kindles through the woven leaves;
And when these burst, and the thin fiery air,
The which they breathed within those lucent domes,
Ascends to flow like meteors through the night,
They ride on them, and rein their headlong speed, 80
And bow their burning crests, and glide in fire
Under the waters of the earth again.

    First Faun. If such live thus, have others other lives,
Under pink blossoms or within the bells
Of meadow flowers, or folded violets deep, 85
Or on their dying odors, when they die,
Or in the sunlight of the spherèd dew?

    Second Faun. Ay, many more which we may well divine.
But, should we stay to speak, noontide would come,
And thwart Silenus find his goats undrawn, 90
And grudge to sing those wise and lovely songs
Of Fate, and Chance, and God, and Chaos old,
And Love, and the chained Titan's woful doom,
And how he shall be loosed, and make the earth
One brotherhood: delightful strains which cheer 95
Our solitary twilights, and which charm
To silence the unenvying nightingales.

    Scene III.—*A Pinnacle of Rock among Mountains.*
        Asia *and* Panthea.

    Panthea. Hither the sound has borne us—to the realm
Of Demogorgon, and the mighty portal,
Like a volcano's meteor-breathing chasm,
Whence the oracular vapor is hurled up
Which lonely men drink wandering in their youth,
And call truth, virtue, love, genius, or joy,
That maddening wine of life, whose dregs they drain
To deep intoxication; and uplift,

Like Mænads who cry aloud, Evoe! Evoe!
The voice which is contagion to the world.　　10
　　Asia. Fit throne for such a power! Magnificent!
How glorious art thou, earth! And if thou be
The shadow of some spirit lovelier still,
Though evil stain its work, and it should be
Like its creation, weak yet beautiful,　　15
I could fall down and worship that and thee.
Even now my heart adoreth. Wonderful!
Look, sister, ere the vapor dim thy brain:
Beneath is a wide plain of billowy mist,
As a lake, paving in the morning sky,　　20
With azure waves which burst in silver light,
Some Indian vale. Behold it, rolling on
Under the curdling winds, and islanding
The peak whereon we stand, midway, around,
Encinctured by the dark and blooming forests,　　25
Dim twilight-lawns, and stream-illumined caves,
And wind-enchanted shapes of wandering mist;
And far on high the keen sky-cleaving mountains
From icy spires of sun-like radiance fling
The dawn, as lifted Ocean's dazzling spray,　　30
From some Atlantic islet scattered up,
Spangles the wind with lamp-like water-drops.
The vale is girdled with their walls, a howl
Of cataracts from their thaw-cloven ravines,
Satiates the listening wind, continuous, vast,　　35
Awful as silence. Hark! the rushing snow!
The sun-awakened avalanche! whose mass,
Thrice sifted by the storm, had gathered there
Flake after flake, in heaven-defying minds
As thought by thought is piled, till some great truth　　40
Is loosened, and the nations echo round,
Shaken to their roots, as do the mountains now.
　　Panthea. Look how the gusty sea of mist is breaking
In crimson foam, even at our feet! it rises
As Ocean at the enchantment of the moon　　45
Round foodless men wrecked on some oozy isle.
　　Asia. The fragments of the cloud are scattered up;
The wind that lifts them disentwines my hair;
Its billows now sweep o'er mine eyes; my brain
Grows dizzy; I see shapes within the mist.　　50
　　Panthea. A countenance with beckoning smiles: there burns
An azure fire within its golden locks!
Another and another: hark! they speak!

Song of Spirits

To the deep, to the deep,
　　　　Down, down!　　55
Through the shade of sleep,
Through the cloudy strife
Of death and of life;
Through the veil and the bar
Of things which seem and are　　60
Even to the steps of the remotest throne,
　　　　Down, down!

While the sound whirls around,
　　　　Down, down!
As the fawn draws the hound,　　65

As the lightning the vapor,
As the weak moth the taper;
Death, despair; love, sorrow;
Time, both; today, tomorrow;
As steel obeys the spirit of the stone,   70
　　　Down, down!

Through the gray, void abysm,
　　　Down, down!
Where the air is no prism,
And the moon and stars are not,   75
And the cavern-crags wear not
The radiance of heaven,
Nor the gloom to earth given,
Where there is one pervading, one alone,
　　　Down, down!   80

In the depth of the deep,
　　　Down, down!
Like veiled lightning asleep,
Like the spark nursed in embers,
The last look love remembers,   85
Like a diamond, which shines
On the dark wealth of mines,
A spell is treasured but for thee alone.
　　　Down, down!

We have bound thee, we guide thee;   90
　　　Down, down!
With the bright form beside thee;
Resist not the weakness,
Such strength is in meekness
That the Eternal, the Immortal,   95
Must unloose through life's portal
The snake-like Doom coiled underneath his throne
　　　By that alone.

SCENE IV.—*The Cave of Demogorgon.*
ASIA *and* PANTHEA.

Panthea. What veilèd form sits on that ebon throne?
Asia. The veil has fallen.
Panthea.　　　　　　　I see a mighty darkness
Filling the seat of power, and rays of gloom
Dart round, as light from the meridian sun,
Ungazed upon and shapeless; neither limb,   5
Nor form, nor outline; yet we feel it is
A living spirit.
Demogorgon. Ask what thou wouldst know.
Asia. What canst thou tell?
Demogorgon. All things thou dar'st demand.
Asia. Who made the living world?
Demogorgon.　　　　　God.
Asia.　　　　　　　　　Who made all
That it contains? thought, passion, reason, will,   10
Imagination?
Demogorgon. God: Almighty God.
Asia. Who made that sense which, when the winds of spring
In rarest visitation, or the voice
Of one belovèd heard in youth alone.

Fills the faint eyes with falling tears which dim   15
The radiant looks of unbewailing flowers,
And leaves this peopled earth a solitude
When it returns no more?
   Demogorgon.   Merciful God.
   Asia. And who made terror, madness, crime, remorse,
Which from the links of the great chain of things,   20
To every thought within the mind of man
Sway and drag heavily, and each one reels
Under the load towards the pit of death:
Abandoned hope, and love that turns to hate;
And self-contempt, bitterer to drink than blood;   25
Pain, whose unheeded and familiar speech
Is howling, and keen shrieks, day after day;
And hell, or the sharp fear of hell?
   Demogorgon.   He reigns.
   Asia. Utter his name; a world pining in pain
Asks but his name; curses shall drag him down.   30
   Demogorgon. He reigns.
   Asia.   I feel, I know it: who?
   Demogorgon.   He reigns.
   Asia. Who reigns? There was the heaven and earth at first,
And Light and Love; then Saturn, from whose throne
Time fell, an envious shadow: such the state
Of the earth's primal spirits beneath his sway,   35
As the calm joy of flowers and living leaves
Before the wind or sun has withered them
And semivital worms; but he refused
The birthright of their being, knowledge, power,
The skill which wields the elements, the thought   40
Which pierces this dim universe like light,
Self-empire, and the majesty of love;
For thirst of which they fainted. Then Prometheus
Gave wisdom, which is strength, to Jupiter,
And with this law alone, "Let man be free,"   45
Clothed him with the dominion of wide heaven.
To know nor faith, nor love, nor law; to be
Omnipotent but friendless, is to reign;
And Jove now reigned; for on the race of man
First famine, and then toil, and then disease,   50
Strife, wounds, and ghastly death unseen before,
Fell; and the unseasonable seasons drove
With alternating shafts of frost and fire,
Their shelterless, pale tribes to mountain caves:
And in their desert hearts fierce wants he sent,   55
And mad disquietudes, and shadows idle
Of unreal good, which levied mutual war,
So ruining the lair wherein they raged.
Prometheus saw, and waked the legioned hopes
Which sleep within folded Elysian flowers,   60
Nepenthe, Moly, Amaranth, fadeless blooms,
That they might hide with thin and rainbow wings
The shape of Death; and Love he sent to bind
The disunited tendrils of that vine
Which bears the wine of life, the human heart;   65
And he tamed fire which, like some beast of prey,
Most terrible, but lovely, played beneath
The frown of man; and tortured to his will
Iron and gold; the slaves and signs of power,
And gems and poisons, and all subtlest forms   70

Hidden beneath the mountains and the waves.
He gave man speech, and speech created thought,
Which is the measure of the universe;
And science struck the thrones of earth and heaven,
Which shook, but fell not; and the harmonious mind   75
Poured itself forth in all-prophetic song;
And music lifted up the listening spirit
Until it walked, exempt from mortal care,
Godlike, o'er the clear billows of sweet sound;
And human hands first mimicked and then mocked,   80
With molded limbs more lovely than its own,
The human form, till marble grew divine;
And mothers, gazing, drank the love men see
Reflected in their race, behold, and perish.
He told the hidden power of herbs and springs,   85
And Disease drank and slept. Death grew like sleep.
He taught the implicated orbits woven
Of the wide-wandering stars; and how the sun
Changes his lair, and by what secret spell
The pale moon is transformed, when her broad eye   90
Gazes not on the interlunar sea:
He taught to rule, as life directs the limbs,
The tempest-wingèd chariots of the Ocean,
And the Celt knew the Indian. Cities then
Were built, and through their snow-like columns flowed   95
The warm winds, and the azure ether shone,
And the blue sea and shadowy hills were seen.
Such, the alleviations of his state,
Prometheus gave to man, for which he hangs
Withering in destined pain: but who rains down   100
Evil, the immedicable plague, which, while
Man looks on his creation like a god
And sees that it is glorious, drives him on,
The wreck of his own will, the scorn of earth,
The outcast, the abandoned, the alone?   105
Not Jove: while yet his frown shook heaven, ay, when
His adversary from adamantine chains
Cursed him, he trembled like a slave. Declare
Who is his master? Is he too a slave?
   Demogorgon. All spirits are enslaved which serve things evil: 110
Thou knowest if Jupiter be such or no.
   Asia. Whom calledst thou God?
   Demogorgon. I spoke but as ye speak,
For Jove is the supreme of living things.
   Asia. Who is the master of the slave?
   Demogorgon. If the abysm
Could vomit forth its secrets—but a voice   115
Is wanting, the deep truth is imageless;
For what would it avail to bid thee gaze
On the revolving world? What to bid speak
Fate, Time, Occasion, Chance, and Change? To these
All things are subject but eternal Love.   120
   Asia. So much I asked before, and my heart gave
The response thou hast given; and of such truths
Each to himself must be the oracle.
One more demand; and do thou answer me
As mine own soul would answer, did it know   125
That which I ask. Prometheus shall arise
Henceforth the sun of this rejoicing world:
When shall the destined hour arrive?

Demogorgon.   Behold!
Asia. The rocks are cloven, and through the purple night
I see cars drawn by rainbow-wingèd steeds   130
Which trample the dim winds; in each there stands
A wild-eyed charioteer urging their flight.
Some look behind, as fiends pursued them there,
And yet I see no shapes but the keen stars:
Others, with burning eyes, lean forth, and drink   135
With eager lips the wind of their own speed,
As if the thing they loved fled on before,
And now, even now, they clasped it. Their bright locks
Stream like a comet's flashing hair; they all
Sweep onward.
          Demogorgon. These are the immortal Hours,   140
Of whom thou didst demand. One waits for thee.
     Asia. A spirit with a dreadful countenance
Checks its dark chariot by the craggy gulf.
Unlike thy brethren, ghastly charioteer,
Who art thou? Whither wouldst thou bear me? Speak!   145
     Spirit. I am the shadow of a destiny
More dread than is my aspect; ere yon planet
Has set, the darkness which ascends with me
Shall wrap in lasting night heaven's kingless throne.
     Asia. What meanest thou?
     Panthea.   That terrible Shadow floats   150
Up from its throne, as may the lurid smoke
Of earthquake-ruined cities o'er the sea.
Lo! it ascends the car; the coursers fly
Terrified; watch its path among the stars
Blackening the night!
     Asia.   Thus I am answered: strange!   155
     Panthea. See, near the verge, another chariot stays;
An ivory shell inlaid with crimson fire,
Which comes and goes within its sculptured rim
Of delicate strange tracery; the young Spirit
That guides it has the dove-like eyes of hope;   160
How its soft smiles attract the soul! as light
Lures wingèd insects through the lampless air.

Spirit

My coursers are fed with the lightning,
     They drink of the whirlwind's stream,
And when the red morning is bright'ning   165
     They bathe in the fresh sunbeam;
     They have strength for their swiftness I deem,
Then ascend with me, daughter of Ocean.

I desire—and their speed makes night kindle;
     I fear—they outstrip the typhoon;   170
Ere the cloud piled on Atlas can dwindle,
     We encircle the earth and the moon.
     We shall rest from long labors at noon:
Then ascend with me, daughter of Ocean.

SCENE V.—*The car pauses within a cloud on the top of a
snowy mountain.* ASIA, PANTHEA, *and the* SPIRIT OF THE
HOUR.

Spirit

On the brink of the night and the morning
  My coursers are wont to respire;
But the Earth has just whispered a warning
  That their flight must be swifter than fire:
  They shall drink the hot speed of desire!   5

Asia. Thou breathest on their nostrils, but my breath
Would give them swifter speed.
    Spirit.   Alas! it could not.
    Panthea. O Spirit! pause, and tell whence is the light
Which fills this cloud? the sun is yet unrisen.
    Spirit. The sun will rise not until noon. Apollo   10
Is held in heaven by wonder; and the light
Which fills this vapor, as the aërial hue
Of fountain-gazing roses fills the water,
Flows from thy mighty sister.
    Panthea.   Yes, I feel—
    Asia. What is it with thee, sister? Thou art pale.   15
    Panthea. How thou art changed! I dare not look on thee;
I feel but see thee not. I scarce endure
The radiance of thy beauty. Some good change
Is working in the elements, which suffer
Thy presence thus unveiled. The Nereids tell   20
That on the day when the clear hyaline
Was cloven at thy uprise, and thou didst stand
Within a veinèd shell, which floated on
Over the calm floor of the crystal sea,
Among the Ægean isles, and by the shores   25
Which bear thy name,—love, like the atmosphere
Of the sun's fire filling the living world,
Burst from thee, and illumined earth and heaven
And the deep ocean and the sunless caves
And all that dwells within them; till grief cast   30
Eclipse upon the soul from which it came:
Such art thou now; nor is it I alone,
Thy sister, thy companion, thine own chosen one,
But the whole world which seeks thy sympathy.
Hearest thou not sounds i' the air which speak the love   35
Of all articulate beings? Feelest thou not
The inanimate winds enamoured of thee? List!
                                         [Music.
    Asia. Thy words are sweeter than aught else but his
Whose echoes they are: yet all love is sweet,
Given or returned. Common as light is love,   40
And its familiar voice wearies not ever.
Like the wide heaven, the all-sustaining air,
It makes the reptile equal to the god:
They who inspire it most are fortunate,
As I am now; but those who feel it most   45
Are happier still, after long sufferings,
As I shall soon become.
    Panthea.   List! Spirits speak.

Voice in the Air, singing

Life of Life! thy lips enkindle
  With their love the breath between them;
And thy smiles before they dwindle   50

Make the cold air fire; then screen them
In those looks, where whoso gazes
Faints, entangled in their mazes.

Child of Light! thy limbs are burning
    Through the vest which seems to hide them;   55
As the radiant lines of morning
    Through the clouds ere they divide them;
And this atmosphere divinest
Shrouds thee wheresoe'er thou shinest.

Fair are others; none beholds thee,   60
    But thy voice sounds low and tender
Like the fairest, for it folds thee
    From the sight, that liquid splendor,
And all feel, yet see thee never,
As I feel now, lost forever!   65

Lamp of Earth! where'er thou movest
    Its dim shapes are clad with brightness,
And the souls of whom thou lovest
    Walk upon the winds with lightness,
Till they fail, as I am failing,   70
Dizzy, lost, yet unbewailing!

Asia

My soul is an enchanted boat,
    Which, like a sleeping swan, doth float
Upon the silvery waves of thy sweet singing;
    And thine doth like an angel sit   75
    Beside a helm conducting it.
Whilst all the winds with melody are ringing,
    It seems to float ever, forever,
    Upon that many-winding river,
    Between mountains, woods, abysses,   80
    A paradise of wildernesses!
Till, like one in slumber bound,
Borne to the ocean, I float down, around,
Into a sea profound, of ever-spreading sound:

    Meanwhile thy spirit lifts its pinions   85
    In music's most serene dominions;
Catching the winds that fan that happy heaven.
    And we sail on, away, afar,
    Without a course, without a star,
But, by the instinct of sweet music driven;   90
    Till through Elysian garden islets
    By thee, most beautiful of pilots,
    Where never mortal pinnace glided,
    The boat of my desire is guided:
Realms where the air we breathe is love,   95
Which in the winds and on the waves doth move,
Harmonizing this earth with what we feel above.

    We have passed age's icy caves,
    And manhood's dark and tossing waves,
And youth's smooth ocean, smiling to betray: 100
    Beyond the glassy gulfs we flee
    Of shadow-peopled infancy,
Through death and birth, to a diviner day;

A paradise of vaulted bowers,
Lit by downward-gazing flowers, 105
And watery paths that wind between
Wildernesses calm and green,
Peopled by shapes too bright to see,
And rest, having beheld; somewhat like thee;
Which walk upon the sea, and chant melodiously! 110

ACT III

SCENE I.—*Heaven.* JUPITER *on his throne;* THETIS *and the
other Deities assembled.*

Jupiter. Ye congregated powers of heaven, who share
The glory and the strength of him ye serve,
Rejoice! henceforth I am omnipotent.
All else had been subdued to me; alone
The soul of man, like unextinguished fire, 5
Yet burns towards heaven with fierce reproach and doubt,
And lamentation, and reluctant prayer,
Hurling up insurrection, which might make
Our antique empire insecure, though built
On eldest faith, and hell's coeval, fear; 10
And though my curses through the pendulous air,
Like snow on herbless peaks, fall flake by flake,
And cling to it; though under my wrath's night
It climb the crags of life, step after step,
Which wound it, as ice wounds unsandalled feet, 15
It yet remains supreme o'er misery,
Aspiring, unrepressed, yet soon to fall:
Even now have I begotten a strange wonder,
That fatal child, the terror of the earth,
Who waits but till the destined hour arrive, 20
Bearing from Demogorgon's vacant throne
The dreadful might of ever-living limbs
Which clothed that awful spirit unbeheld,
To redescend, and trample out the spark.
Pour forth heaven's wine, Idæan Ganymede, 25
And let it fill the dædal cups like fire,
And from the flower-inwoven soil divine,
Ye all-triumphant harmonies, arise,
As dew from earth under the twilight stars:
Drink! be the nectar circling through your veins 30
The soul of joy, ye ever-living gods,
Till exultation burst in one wide voice
Like music from Elysian winds.
                                            And thou
Ascend beside me, veilèd in the light
Of the desire which makes thee one with me, 35
Thetis, bright image of eternity!
When thou didst cry, "Insufferable might!
God! Spare me! I sustain not the quick flames,
The penetrating presence; all my being,
Like him whom the Numidian seps did thaw 40
Into a dew with poison, is dissolved,
Sinking through its foundations," even then
Two mighty spirits, mingling, made a third
Mightier than either, which, unbodied now,
Between us floats, felt, although unbeheld, 45

Waiting the incarnation, which ascends.
(Hear ye the thunder of the fiery wheels
Griding the winds?) from Demogorgon's throne.
Victory! victory! Feel'st thou not, O world,
The earthquake of his chariot thundering up   50
Olympus?
      [*The car of the* HOUR *arrives.* DEMOGORGON *descends,*
         and moves towards the throne of JUPITER.
    Awful shape, what art thou? Speak!
    Demogorgon. Eternity. Demand no direr name.
Descend, and follow me down the abyss.
I am thy child, as thou wert Saturn's child;
Mightier than thee: and we must dwell together   55
Henceforth in darkness. Lift thy lightnings not.
The tyranny of heaven none may retain,
Or reassume, or hold, succeeding thee:
Yet if thou wilt, as 'tis the destiny
Of trodden worms to writhe till they are dead,   60
Put forth thy might.
    Jupiter.   Detested prodigy!
Even thus beneath the deep Titanian prisons
I trample thee! Thou lingerest?
                     Mercy! mercy!
No pity, no release, no respite! Oh,
That thou wouldst make mine enemy my judge,   65
Even where he hangs, seared by my long revenge,
On Caucasus! he would not doom me thus.
Gentle, and just, and dreadless, is he not
The monarch of the world? What then art thou?
No refuge! no appeal!
                Sink with me then,   70
We two will sink on the wide waves of ruin,
Even as a vulture and a snake outspent
Drop, twisted in inextricable fight,
Into a shoreless sea. Let hell unlock
Its mounded oceans of tempestuous fire,   75
And whelm on them into the bottomless void
This desolated world, and thee, and me,
The conqueror and the conquered, and the wreck
Of that for which they combated.
                       Ai! Ai!
The elements obey me not. I sink   80
Dizzily down, ever, forever, down.
And, like a cloud, mine enemy above
Darkens my fall with victory! Ai, Ai!

SCENE II.—*The mouth of a great river in the Island Atlantis.*
OCEAN *is discovered reclining near the shore;* APOLLO
stands beside him.

    Ocean. He fell, thou sayest, beneath his conqueror's frown?
    Apollo. Aye, when the strife was ended which made dim
The orb I rule, and shook the solid stars,
The terrors of his eye illumined heaven
With sanguine light, through the thick ragged skirts   5
Of the victorious darkness, as he fell:
Like the last glare of day's red agony,
Which, from a rent among the fiery clouds,
Burns far along the tempest-wrinkled deep.
    Ocean. He sunk to the abyss? To the dark void?   10

Apollo. An eagle so caught in some bursting cloud
On Caucasus, his thunder-baffled wings
Entangled in the whirlwind, and his eyes
Which gazed on the undazzling sun, now blinded
By the white lightning, while the ponderous hail   15
Beats on his struggling form, which sinks at length
Prone, and the aërial ice clings over it.
    Ocean. Henceforth the fields of heaven-reflecting sea
Which are my realm, will heave, unstained with blood,
Beneath the uplifting winds, like plains of corn   20
Swayed by the summer air; my streams will flow
Round many-peopled continents, and round
Fortunate isles; and from their glassy thrones
Blue Proteus and his humid nymphs shall mark
The shadow of fair ships, as mortals see   25
The floating bark of the light-laden moon
With that white star, its sightless pilot's crest,
Borne down the rapid sunset's ebbing sea,
Tracking their path no more by blood and groans,
And desolation, and the mingled voice   30
Of slavery and command; but by the light
Of wave-reflected flowers, and floating odors,
And music soft, and mild, free, gentle voices,
And sweetest music, such as spirits love.
    Apollo. And I shall gaze not on the deeds which made   35
My mind obscure with sorrow, as eclipse
Darkens the sphere I guide; but list, I hear
The small, clear, silver lute of the young Spirit
That sits i' the morning star.
    Ocean.   Thou must away;
Thy steeds will pause at even, till when farewell: 40
The loud deep calls me home even now to feed it.
With azure calm out of the emerald urns
Which stand forever full beside my throne.
Behold the Nereids under the green sea,
Their wavering limbs borne on the wind-like stream,   45
Their white arms lifted o'er their streaming hair
With garlands pied and starry sea-flower crowns,
Hastening to grace their mighty sister's joy.
                    [*A sound of waves is heard.*
It is the unpastured sea hungering for calm.
Peace, monster; I come now. Farewell.
    Apollo.   Farewell.   50

SCENE III.—*Caucasus.* PROMETHEUS, HERCULES, IONE, *the*
    EARTH, SPIRITS, ASIA, *and* PANTHEA, *borne in the car with*
    the SPIRIT OF THE HOUR. HERCULES *unbinds* PROME-
    THEUS, *who descends.*

    Hercules. Most glorious among spirits, thus doth strength
To wisdom, courage, and long-suffering love,
And thee, who art the form they animate,
Minister like a slave.
    Prometheus.   Thy gentle words
Are sweeter even than freedom long desired   5
And long delayed.
                    Asia, thou light of life,
Shadow of beauty unbeheld; and ye,
Fair sister nymphs who made long years of pain
Sweet to remember, through your love and care:

Henceforth we will not part. There is a cave, 10
All overgrown with trailing odorous plants,
Which curtain out the day with leaves and flowers,
And paved with veinèd emerald, and a fountain
Leaps in the midst with an awakening sound.
From its curved roof the mountain's frozen tears 15
Like snow, or silver, or long diamond spires,
Hang downward, raining forth a doubtful light;
And there is heard the ever-moving air,
Whispering without from tree to tree, and birds,
And bees; and all around are mossy seats, 20
And the rough walls are clothed with long soft grass;
A simple dwelling, which shall be our own;
Where we will sit and talk of time and change,
As the world ebbs and flows, ourselves unchanged.
What can hide man from mutability? 25
And if ye sigh, then I will smile; and thou,
Ione, shalt chant fragments of sea-music,
Until I weep, when ye shall smile away
The tears she brought, which yet were sweet to shed.
We will entangle buds and flowers and beams 30
Which twinkle on the fountain's brim, and make
Strange combinations out of common things,
Like human babes in their brief innocence;
And we will search, with looks and words of love,
For hidden thoughts, each lovelier than the last, 35
Our unexhausted spirits; and like lutes
Touched by the skill of the enamored wind,
Weave harmonies divine, yet ever new,
From difference sweet where discord cannot be;
And hither come, sped on the charmèd winds, 40
Which meet from all the points of heaven, as bees
From every flower aërial Enna feeds,
At their known island-homes in Himera,
The echoes of the human world, which tell
Of the low voice of love, almost unheard, 45
And dove-eyed pity's murmured pain, and music,
Itself the echo of the heart, and all
That tempers or improves man's life, now free;
And lovely apparitions—dim at first,
Then radiant, as the mind arising bright 50
From the embrace of beauty (whence the forms
Of which these are the phantoms) casts on them
The gathered rays which are reality—
Shall visit us, the progeny immortal
Of painting, sculpture, and rapt poesy, 55
And arts, though unimagined, yet to be.
The wandering voices and the shadows these
Of all that man becomes, the mediators
Of that best worship love, by him and us
Given and returned; swift shapes and sounds, which grow 60
More fair and soft as man grows wise and kind,
And, veil by veil, evil and error fall.
Such virtue has the cave and place around.
[*Turning to the* SPIRIT OF THE HOUR.
For thee, fair Spirit, one toil remains. Ione
Give her that curvèd shell, which Proteus old 65
Made Asia's nuptial boon, breathing within it
A voice to be accomplished, and which thou
Didst hide in grass under the hollow rock.

Ione. Thou most desired Hour, more loved and lovely
Than all thy sisters, this is the mystic shell;
See the pale azure fading into silver
Lining it with a soft yet glowing light.
Looks it not like lulled music sleeping there?
   Spirit. It seems in truth the fairest shell of ocean:
Its sound must be at once both sweet and strange.
   Prometheus. Go, borne over the cities of mankind
On whirlwind-footed coursers; once again
Outspeed the sun around the orbèd world;
And as thy chariot cleaves the kindling air,
Thou breathe into the many-folded shell,
Loosening its mighty music; it shall be
As thunder mingled with clear echoes: then
Return; and thou shalt dwell beside our cave.
And thou, O Mother Earth!—
   The Earth.   I hear, I feel;
Thy lips are on me, and their touch runs down
Even to the adamantine central gloom
Along these marble nerves; 'tis life, 'tis joy,
And through my withered, old, and icy frame
The warmth of an immortal youth shoots down
Circling. Henceforth the many children fair
Folded in my sustaining arms; all plants,
And creeping forms, and insects rainbow-winged,
And birds, and beasts, and fish, and human shapes,
Which drew disease and pain from my wan bosom,
Draining the poison of despair, shall take
And interchange sweet nutriment; to me
Shall they become like sister-antelopes
By one fair dam, snow-white and swift as wind,
Nursed among lilies near a brimming stream.
The dew-mists of my sunless sleep shall float
Under the stars like balm; night-folded flowers
Shall suck unwithering hues in their repose;
And men and beasts in happy dreams shall gather
Strength for the coming day, and all its joy;
And death shall be the last embrace of her
Who takes the life she gave, even as a mother
Folding her child, says, "Leave me not again."
   Asia. Oh, mother! wherefore speak the name of death?
Cease they to love, and move, and breathe, and speak,
Who die?
   The Earth. It would avail not to reply;
Thou art immortal, and this tongue is known
But to the uncommunicating dead.
Death is the veil which those who live call life;
They sleep, and it is lifted: and meanwhile
In mild variety and the seasons mild
With rainbow-skirted showers, and odorous winds,
And long blue meteors cleansing the dull night,
And the life-kindling shafts of the keen sun's
All-piercing bow, and the dew-mingled rain
Of the calm moonbeans, a soft influence mild,
Shall clothe the forests and the fields, aye, even
The crag-built deserts of the barren deep,
With ever-living leaves, and fruits, and flowers.
And thou! there is a cavern where my spirit
Was panted forth in anguish whilst thy pain
Made my heart mad, and those who did inhale it

70

75

80

85

90

95

100

105

110

115

120

125

Became mad too, and built a temple there,
And spoke, and were oracular, and lured
The erring nations round to mutual war,
And faithless faith, such as Jove kept with thee;   130
Which breath now rises, as amongst tall weeds
A violet's exhalation, and it fills
With a serener light and crimson air
Intense, yet soft, the rocks and woods around;
It feeds the quick growth of the serpent vine,   135
And the dark linkèd ivy tangling wild,
And budding, blown, or odor-faded blooms
Which star the winds with points of colored light,
As they rain through them, and bright golden globes
Of fruit, suspended in their own green heaven,   140
And through their veinèd leaves and amber stems
The flowers whose purple and translucid bowls
Stand ever mantling with aërial dew,
The drink of spirits; and it circles round,
Like the soft waving wings of noonday dreams,   145
Inspiring calm and happy thoughts, like mine,
Now thou art thus restored. This cave is thine.
Arise! Appear!
            [A SPIRIT *rises in the likeness of a winged child.*
            This is my torch-bearer;
Who let his lamp out in old time with gazing
On eyes from which he kindled it anew   150
With love, which is as fire, sweet daughter mine,
For such is that within thine own. Run, wayward,
And guide this company beyond the peak
Of Bacchic Nysa, Mænad-haunted mountain,
And beyond Indus and its tribute rivers,   155
Trampling the torrent streams and glassy lakes
With feet unwet, unwearied, undelaying,
And up the green ravine, across the vale,
Beside the windless and crystalline pool,
Where ever lies, on unerasing waves,   160
The image of a temple, built above,
Distinct with column, arch, and architrave,
And palm-like capital, and overwrought,
And populous most with living imagery,
Praxitelean shapes, whose marble smiles   165
Fill the hushed air with everlasting love.
It is deserted now, but once it bore
Thy name, Prometheus; there the emulous youths
Bore to thy honor through the divine gloom
The lamp which was thine emblem; even as those   170
Who bear the untransmitted torch of hope
Into the grave, across the night of life,
As thou hast borne it most triumphantly
To this far goal of time. Depart, farewell.
Beside that temple is the destined cave.   175

SCENE IV.—*A forest. In the background a cave.* PROME-
THEUS, ASIA, PANTHEA, IONE, *and the* SPIRIT OF THE EARTH.

Ione. Sister, it is not earthly; how it glides
Under the leaves! how on its head there burns
A light, like a green star, whose emerald beams
Are twined with its fair hair! how, as it moves,
The splendor drops in flakes upon the grass!   5
Knowest thou it?

Panthea.   It is the delicate spirit
That guides the earth through heaven. From afar
The populous constellations call that light
The loveliest of the planets; and sometimes
It floats along the spray of the salt sea,   10
Or makes its chariot of a foggy cloud,
Or walks through fields or cities while men sleep,
Or o'er the mountain tops, or down the rivers,
Or through the green waste wilderness, as now,
Wondering at all it sees. Before Jove reigned   15
It loved our sister Asia, and it came
Each leisure hour to drink the liquid light
Out of her eyes, for which it said it thirsted
As one bit by a dipsas, and with her
It made a childish confidence, and told her   20
All it had known or seen, for it saw much,
Yet idly reasoned what it saw; and called her—
For whence it sprung it knew not, nor do I—
Mother, dear mother.
　　The Spirit of the Earth (running to ASIA*).* Mother, dearest
　　　　mother;
May I then talk with thee as I was wont?   25
May I then hide my eyes in thy soft arms,
After thy looks have made them tired of joy?
May I then play beside thee the long noons,
When work is none in the bright silent air?
　　Asia. I love thee, gentlest being, and henceforth   30
Can cherish thee unenvied. Speak, I pray;
Thy simple talk once solaced, now delights.
　　Spirit of the Earth. Mother, I am grown wiser, though
　　　　a child
Cannot be wise like thee, within this day;
And happier too; happier and wiser both.   35
Thou knowest that toads, and snakes, and loathly worms,
And venomous and malicious beasts, and boughs
That bore ill berries in the woods, were ever
An hindrance to my walks o'er the green world;
And that, among the haunts of humankind,   40
Hard-featured men, or with proud, angry looks,
Or cold, staid gait, or false and hollow smiles,
Or the dull sneer of self-loved ignorance,
Or other such foul masks, with which ill thoughts
Hide that fair being whom we spirits call man;   45
And women too, ugliest of all things evil
(Though fair, even in a world where thou art fair,
When good and kind, free and sincere like thee),
When false or frowning made me sick at heart
To pass them, though they slept, and I unseen.   50
Well, my path lately lay through a great city
Into the woody hills surrounding it;
A sentinel was sleeping at the gate;
When there was heard a sound, so loud, it shook
The towers amid the moonlight, yet more sweet   55
Than any voice but thine, sweetest of all;
A long, long sound, as it would never end;
And all the inhabitants leaped suddenly
Out of their rest, and gathered in the streets,
Looking in wonder up to heaven, while yet   60
The music pealed along. I hid myself
Within a fountain in the public square

Where I lay like the reflex of the moon
Seen in a wave under green leaves; and soon
Those ugly human shapes and visages   65
Of which I spoke as having wrought me pain,
Passed floating through the air, and fading still
Into the winds that scattered them; and those
From whom they passed seemed mild and lovely forms
After some foul disguise had fallen, and all   70
Were somewhat changed, and after brief surprise
And greetings of delighted wonder, all
Went to their sleep again: and when the dawn
Came, wouldst thou think that toads, and snakes, and efts,
Could e'er be beautiful? yet so they were,   75
And that with little change of shape or hue:
All things had put their evil nature off:
I cannot tell my joy, when o'er a lake,
Upon a drooping bough with nightshade twined,
I saw two azure halcyons clinging downward   80
And thinning one bright bunch of amber berries,
With quick long beaks, and in the deep there lay
Those lovely forms imaged as in a sky;
So, with my thoughts full of these happy changes,
We meet again, the happiest change of all.   85
    Asia.   And never will we part, till thy chaste sister,
Who guides the frozen and inconstant moon,
Will look on thy more warm and equal light
Till her heart thaw like flakes of April snow
And love thee.
    Spirit of the Earth.   What! as Asia loves Prometheus?   90
    Asia.   Peace, wanton, thou art yet not old enough.
Think ye by gazing on each other's eyes
To multiply your lovely selves, and fill
With sphered fire the interlunar air?
    Spirit of the Earth.   Nay, mother, while my sister trims
      her lamp   95
'Tis hard I should go darkling.
    Asia.   Listen; look!

            [*The* SPIRIT OF THE HOUR *enters.*

    Prometheus.   We feel what thou hast heard and seen: yet
      speak.
    Spirit of the Hour.   Soon as the sound had ceased whose
      thunder filled
The abysses of the sky and the wide earth,
There was a change; the impalpable thin air   100
And the all-circling sunlight were transformed,
As if the sense of love dissolved in them
Had folded itself round the sphered world.
My vision then grew clear, and I could see
Into the mysteries of the universe,   105
Dizzy as with delight I floated down;
Winnowing the lightsome air with languid plumes,
My coursers sought their birthplace in the sun,
Where they henceforth will live exempt from toil,
Pasturing flowers of vegetable fire;   110
And where my moonlike car will stand within
A temple, gazed upon by Phidian forms
Of thee, and Asia, and the Earth, and me,
And you fair nymphs looking the love we feel,—

In memory of the tidings it has borne,—   115
Beneath a dome fretted with graven flowers,
Poised on twelve columns of resplendent stone,
And open to the bright and liquid sky.
Yoked to it by an amphisbenic snake
The likeness of those wingèd steeds will mock   120
The flight from which they find repose. Alas,
Whither has wandered now my partial tongue
When all remains untold which ye would hear?
As I have said, I floated to the earth;
It was, as it is still, the pain of bliss   125
To move, to breathe, to be; I wandering went
Among the haunts and dwellings of mankind,
And first was disappointed not to see
Such mighty change as I had felt within
Expressed in outward things; but soon I looked,   130
And behold, thrones were kingless, and men walked
One with the other even as spirits do—
None fawned, none trampled; hate, disdain, or fear,
Self-love or self-contempt, on human brows
No more inscribed, as o'er the gate of hell,   135
"All hope abandon ye who enter here;"
None frowned, none trembled, none with eager fear
Gazed on another's eye of cold command,
Until the subject of a tyrant's will
Became, worse fate, the abject of his own,   140
Which spurred him, like an outspent horse, to death.
None wrought his lips in truth-entangling lines
Which smiled the lie his tongue disdained to speak;
None, with firm sneer, trod out in his own heart
The sparks of love and hope till there remained   145
Those bitter ashes, a soul self-consumed,
And the wretch crept a vampire among men,
Infecting all with his own hideous ill;
None talked that common, false, cold, hollow talk
Which makes the heart deny the *yes* it breathes,   150
Yet question that unmeant hypocrisy
With such a self-mistrust as has no name.
And women, too, frank, beautiful, and kind
As the free heaven which rains fresh light and dew
On the wide earth, passed; gentle, radiant forms,   155
From custom's evil taint exempt and pure;
Speaking the wisdom once they could not think,
Looking emotions once they feared to feel,
And changed to all which once they dared not be,
Yet being now, made earth like heaven; nor pride,   160
Nor jealousy, nor envy, nor ill shame,
The bitterest of those drops of treasured gall,
Spoiled the sweet taste of the nepenthe, love.

Thrones, altars, judgment-seats, and prisons, wherein,
And beside which, by wretched men were borne   165
Sceptres, tiaras, swords, and chains, and tomes
Of reasoned wrong, glozed on by ignorance,
Were like those monstrous and barbaric shapes,
The ghosts of a no-more-remembered fame,
Which, from their unworn obelisks, look forth   170
In triumph o'er the palaces and tombs
Of those who were their conquerors; moldering round,
These imaged to the pride of kings and priests

A dark yet mighty faith, a power as wide
As is the world it wasted, and are now
But an astonishment; even so the tools   175
And emblems of its last captivity,
Amid the dwellings of the peopled earth,
Stand, not o'erthrown, but unregarded now.
And those foul shapes, abhorred by god and man,—   180
Which, under many a name and many a form
Strange, savage, ghastly, dark, and execrable,
Were Jupiter, the tyrant of the world,
And which the nations, panic-stricken, served
With blood, and hearts broken by long hope, and love   185
Dragged to his altars soiled and garlandless,
And slain amid men's unreclaiming tears,
Flattering the thing they feared, which fear was hate,—
Frown, moldering fast, o'er their abandoned shrines.
The painted veil, by those who were, called life,   190
Which mimicked, as with colors idly spread,
All men believed or hoped, is torn aside;
The loathsome mask has fallen, the man remains
Sceptreless, free, uncircumscribed, but man
Equal, unclassed, tribeless, and nationless,   195
Exempt from awe, worship, degree, the king
Over himself; just, gentle, wise; but man
Passionless—no, yet free from guilt or pain,
Which were, for his will made or suffered them;
Nor yet exempt, though ruling them like slaves,   200
From chance, and death, and mutability,
The clogs of that which else might oversoar
The loftiest star of unascended heaven,
Pinnacled dim in the intense inane.

ACT IV

SCENE I.—*A part of the forest near the cave of* PROMETHEUS.
PANTHEA *and* IONE *are sleeping: they awaken gradually
during the first song.*

Voice of unseen Spirits

The pale stars are gone!
For the sun, their swift shepherd,
To their folds them compelling,
In the depths of the dawn,
Hastes, in meteor-eclipsing array, and they flee   5
Beyond his blue dwelling,
As fawns flee the leopard.
But where are ye?

*A train of dark Forms and Shadows passes by con-
fusedly, singing.*

Here, oh here!
We bear the bier
Of the father of many a cancelled year!   10
Specters we
Of the dead Hours be,
We bear Time to his tomb in eternity.

Strew, oh strew   15
Hair, not yew!
Wet the dusty pall with tears, not dew.
    Be the faded flowers
    Of Death's bare bowers
Spread on the corpse of the King of Hours!   20

    Haste, oh, haste!
    As shades are chased,
Trembling, by day, from heaven's blue waste.
    We melt away,
    Like dissolving spray,   25
From the children of a diviner day,
    With the lullaby
    Of winds that die
On the bosom of their own harmony!

Ione

What dark forms were they?   30

Panthea

The past Hours weak and gray,
With the spoil which their toil
    Raked together
From the conquest but One could foil.

Ione

Have they passed?   35

Panthea

            They have passed;
They outspeeded the blast,
While 'tis said, they are fled:

Ione

Whither, oh, whither?

Panthea

To the dark, to the past, to the dead.

Voice of Unseen Spirits

Bright clouds float in heaven,   40
Dew-stars gleam on earth,
Waves assemble on ocean,
    They are gathered and driven
By the storm of delight, by the panic of glee!
    They shake with emotion,   45
    They dance in their mirth.
        But where are ye?

The pine boughs are singing
Old songs with new gladness,
The billows and fountains   50
Fresh music are flinging,

Like the notes of a spirit from land and from sea;
  The storms mock the mountains
  With the thunder of gladness.
    But where are ye?   55

Ione. What charioteers are these?
Panthea.   Where are their chariots?

Semichorus of Hours

The voice of the Spirits of Air and of Earth
Have drawn back the figured curtain of sleep
Which covered our being and darkened our birth
  In the deep.

A Voice

In the deep?

Semichorus II

                Oh! below the deep.   60

Semichorus I

An hundred ages we had been kept
  Cradled in visions of hate and care,
And each one who waked as his brother slept,
  Found the truth—

Semichorus II

             Worse than his visions were!

Semichorus I

We have heard the lute of Hope in sleep;   65
  We have known the voice of Love in dreams;
We have felt the wand of Power, and leap—

Semichorus II

As the billows leap in the morning beams!

Chorus

Weave the dance on the floor of the breeze,
  Pierce with song heaven's silent light,
Enchant the day that too swiftly flees,   70
  To check its flight ere the cave of night.

Once the hungry Hours were hounds
  Which chased the day like a bleeding deer,
And it limped and stumbled with many wounds   75
  Through the nightly dells of the desert year.

But now, oh, weave the mystic measure
  Of music, and dance, and shapes of light,
Let the Hours, and the Spirits of might and pleasure,
  Like the clouds and sunbeams, unite—

A Voice

Unite!   80

Panthea. See, where the Spirits of the human mind,
Wrapped in sweet sounds, as in bright veils, approach.

Chorus of Spirits

We join the throng
Of the dance and the song,
By the whirlwind of gladness borne along;   85
As the flying fish leap
From the Indian deep,
And mix with the sea birds, half asleep.

Chorus of Hours

Whence come ye, so wild and so fleet,
For sandals of lightning are on your feet,   90
And your wings are soft and swift as thought,
And your eyes are as love which is veilèd not?

Chorus of Spirits

We come from the mind
Of human kind,
Which was late so dusk, and obscene, and blind;   95
Now 'tis an ocean
Of clear emotion,
A heaven of serene and mighty motion.

From that deep abyss
Of wonder and bliss,   100
Whose caverns are crystal palaces;
From those skyey towers
Where thought's crowned powers
Sit watching your dance, ye happy Hours!

From the dim recesses   105
Of woven caresses,
Where lovers catch ye by your loose tresses;
From the azure isles,
Where sweet wisdom smiles,
Delaying your ships with her siren wiles.   110

From the temples high
Of man's ear and eye,
Roofed over sculpture and poesy;
From the murmurings
Of the unsealed springs   115
Where science bedews her dædal wings.

Years after years,
Through blood, and tears,
And a thick hell of hatreds, and hopes, and fears;
We waded and flew,   120
And the islets were few
Where the bud-blighted flowers of happiness grew.

Our feet now, every palm,
  Are sandalled with calm,
And the dew of our wings is a rain of balm;   125
  And, beyond our eyes,
  The human love lies,
Which makes all it gazes on, paradise.

Chorus of Spirits and Hours

Then weave the web of the mystic measure;
From the depths of the sky and the ends of the earth,   130
  Come, swift Spirits of might and of pleasure,
Fill the dance and the music of mirth,
  As the waves of a thousand streams rush by
  To an ocean of splendor and harmony!

Chorus of Spirits

Our spoil is won,
  Our task is done,   135
We are free to dive, or soar, or run;
  Beyond and around,
  Or within the bound
Which clips the world with darkness round.   140

We'll pass the eyes
  Of the starry skies
Into the hoar deep to colonize:
  Death, Chaos, and Night,
  From the sound of our flight,
Shall flee, like mist from a tempest's might.   145

And Earth, Air, and Light,
  And the Spirit of Might,
Which drives round the stars in their fiery flight;
  And Love, Thought, and Breath,   150
  The powers that quell Death,
Wherever we soar shall assemble beneath.

And our singing shall build
  In the void's loose field
A world for the Spirit of Wisdom to wield;   155
  We will take our plan
  From the new world of man,
And our work shall be called the Promethean.

Chorus of Hours

Break the dance, and scatter the song;
  Let some depart, and some remain.   160

Semichorus I

We, beyond heaven, are driven along:

Semichorus II

Us the enchantments of earth retain:

Semichorus I

Ceaseless, and rapid, and fierce, and free,
With the Spirits which build a new earth and sea,
And a heaven where yet heaven could never be;   165

Semichorus II

Solemn, and slow, and serene, and bright,
Leading the day and outspeeding the night,
With the powers of a world of perfect light;

Semichorus I

We whirl, singing loud, round the gathering sphere,
Till the trees, and the beasts, and the clouds appear   170
From its chaos made calm by love, not fear.

Semichorus II

We encircle the ocean and mountains of earth,
And the happy forms of its death and birth
Change to the music of our sweet mirth.

Chorus of Hours and Spirits

Break the dance, and scatter the song;   175
  Let some depart, and some remain;
Wherever we fly we lead along
In leashes, like starbeams, soft yet strong,
  The clouds that are heavy with love's sweet rain.

Panthea. Ha! they are gone!
Ione.   Yet feel you no delight   180
From the past sweetness?
  Panthea.   As the bare green hill
When some soft cloud vanishes into rain,
Laughs with a thousand drops of sunny water
To the unpavilioned sky!
  Ione.   Even whilst we speak
New notes arise. What is that awful sound?   185
  Panthea. 'Tis the deep music of the rolling world
Kindling within the strings of the waved air
Æolian modulations.
  Ione.   Listen too,
How every pause is filled with under-notes,
Clear, silver, icy, keen awakening tones,   190
Which pierce the sense, and live within the soul,
As the sharp stars pierce winter's crystal air
And gaze upon themselves within the sea.
  Panthea. But see where, through two openings in the forest
Which hanging branches overcanopy,   195
And where two runnels of a rivulet,
Between the close moss violet-inwoven,
Have made their path of melody, like sisters
Who part with sighs that they may meet in smiles,
Turning their dear disunion to an isle   200
Of lovely grief, a wood of sweet sad thoughts;
Two visions of strange radiance float upon
The ocean-like enchantment of strong sound.

Which flows intenser, keener, deeper yet,
Under the ground and through the windless air.   205
   Ione. I see a chariot like that thinnest boat,
In which the Mother of the Months is borne
By ebbing light into her western cave,
When she upsprings from interlunar dreams;
O'er which is curved an orblike canopy   210
Of gentle darkness, and the hills and woods,
Distinctly seen through that dusk airy veil,
Regard like shapes in an enchanter's glass;
Its wheels are solid clouds, azure and gold,
Such as the genii of the thunderstorm   215
Pile on the floor of the illumined sea
When the sun rushes under it; they roll
And move and grow as with an inward wind;
Within it sits a wingèd infant, white
Its countenance, like the whiteness of bright snow,   220
Its plumes are as feathers of sunny frost,
Its limbs gleam white, through the wind-flowing folds
Of its white robe, woof of ethereal pearl.
Its hair is white, the brightness of white light
Scattered in strings; yet its two eyes are heavens   225
Of liquid darkness, which the Deity
Within seems pouring, as a storm is poured
From jaggèd clouds, out of their arrowy lashes,
Tempering the cold and radiant air around,
With fire that is not brightness; in its hand   230
It sways a quivering moonbeam, from whose point
A guiding power directs the chariot's prow
Over its wheelèd clouds, which as they roll
Over the grass, and flowers, and waves, wake sounds,
Sweet as a singing rain of silver dew.   235
   Panthea. And from the other opening in the wood
Rushes, with loud and whirlwind harmony,
A sphere, which is as many thousand spheres,
Solid as crystal, yet through all its mass
Flow, as through empty space, music and light;   240
Ten thousand orbs involving and involved,
Purple and azure, white, green, and golden,
Sphere within sphere; and every space between
Peopled with unimaginable shapes,
Such as ghosts dream dwell in the lampless deep,   245
Yet each inter-transpicuous; and they whirl
Over each other with a thousand motions,
Upon a thousand sightless axles spinning,
And with the force of self-destroying swiftness,
Intensely, slowly, solemnly roll on,   250
Kindling with mingled sounds, and many tones,
Intelligible words and music wild.
With mighty whirl the multitudinous orb
Grinds the bright brook into an azure mist
Of elemental subtlety, like light;   255
And the wild odor of the forest flowers,
The music of the living grass and air,
The emerald light of leaf-entangled beams
Round its intense yet self-conflicting speed,
Seem kneaded into one aërial mass   260
Which drowns the sense. Within the orb itself,
Pillowed upon its alabaster arms,
Like to a child o'erwearied with sweet toil,

On its own folded wings, and wavy hair,
The Spirit of the Earth is laid asleep,   265
And you can see its little lips are moving,
Amid the changing light of their own smiles,
Like one who talks of what he loves in dream.
    Ione. 'Tis only mocking the orb's harmony.
    Panthea. And from a star upon its forehead, shoot,   270
Like swords of azure fire, or golden spears
With tyrant-quelling myrtle overtwined,
Embleming heaven and earth united now,
Vast beams like spokes of some invisible wheel
Which whirl as the orb whirls, swifter than thought,   275
Filling the abyss with sun-like lightnings,
And perpendicular now, and now transverse,
Pierce the dark soil, and as they pierce and pass,
Make bare the secrets of the earth's deep heart;
Infinite mines of adamant and gold,   280
Valueless stones, and unimagined gems,
And caverns on crystalline columns poised
With vegetable silver overspread;
Wells of unfathomed fire, and watersprings
Whence the great sea, even as a child, is fed,   285
Whose vapors clothe earth's monarch mountain-tops
With kingly, ermine snow.   The beams flash on
And make appear the melancholy ruins
Of cancelled cycles; anchors, beaks of ships;
Planks turned to marble; quivers, helms, and spears,   290
And gorgon-headed targes, and the wheels
Of scythèd chariots, and the emblazonry
Of trophies, standards, and armorial beasts,
Round which death laughed, sepulchred emblems
Of dead destruction, ruin within ruin!   295
The wrecks beside of many a city vast,
Whose population which the earth grew over
Was mortal, but not human; see, they lie,
Their monstrous works, and uncouth skeletons,
Their statues, homes, and fanes; prodigious shapes   300
Huddled in gray annihilation, split,
Jammed in the hard, black deep; and over these,
The anatomies of unknown wingèd things,
And fishes which were isles of living scale,
And serpents, bony chains, twisted around   305
The iron crags, or within heaps of dust
To which the tortuous strength of their last pangs
Had crushed the iron crags; and over these
The jaggèd alligator, and the might
Of earth-convulsing behemoth, which once   310
Were monarch beasts, and on the slimy shores,
And weed-overgrown continents of earth,
Increased and multiplied like summer worms
On an abandoned corpse, till the blue globe
Wrapped deluge round it like a cloak, and they   315
Yelled, gasped, and were abolished; or some god
Whose throne was in a comet, passed, and cried,
"Be not!"   And like my words they were no more.

The Earth

The joy, the triumph, the delight, the madness!
The boundless, overflowing, bursting gladness,   320

The vaporous exultation not to be confined!
  Ha! ha! the animation of delight
  Which wraps me, like an atmosphere of light,
And bears me as a cloud is borne by its own wind.

The Moon

    Brother mine, calm wanderer,   325
     Happy globe of land and air,
  Some Spirit is darted like a beam from thee,
     Which penetrates my frozen frame,
     And passes with the warmth of flame,
  With love, and odor, and deep melody   330
     Through me, through me!

The Earth

Ha! ha! the caverns of my hollow mountains,
  My cloven fire-crags, sound-exulting fountains,
Laugh with a vast and inextinguishable laughter.
  The oceans, and the deserts, and the abysses,   335
  And the deep air's unmeasured wildernesses,
Answer from all their clouds and billows, echoing after.

  They cry aloud as I do. Sceptered curse,
  Who all our green and azure universe
Threatenedst to muffle round with black destruction, sending   340
  A solid cloud to rain hot thunderstones,
  And splinter and knead down my children's bones,
All I bring forth, to one void mass battering and blending,—

  Until each crag-like tower, and storied column,
  Palace, and obelisk, and temple solemn,   345
My imperial mountains crowned with cloud, and snow, and fire,
  My sea-like forests, every blade and blossom
  Which finds a grave or cradle in my bosom,
Were stamped by thy strong hate into a lifeless mire:

  How art thou sunk, withdrawn, covered, drunk up   350
  By thirsty nothing, as the brackish cup
Drained by a desert troop, a little drop for all;
  And from beneath, around, within, above,
  Filling thy void annihilation, love
Burst in like light on coves cloven by the thunder-ball.   355

The Moon

  The snow upon my lifeless mountains
   Is loosened into living fountains,
My solid oceans flow, and sing, and shine:
   A spirit from my heart bursts forth,
   It clothes with unexpected birth   360
My cold bare bosom. Oh! it must be thine
    On mine, on mine!

  Gazing on thee I feel, I know,
   Green stalks burst forth, and bright flowers grow,
And living shapes upon my bosom move: 365
   Music is in the sea and air,
   Wingèd clouds soar here and there,
Dark with the rain new buds are dreaming of:
    'Tis love, all love!

The Earth

It interpenetrates my granite mass,
Through tangled roots and trodden clay doth pass
Into the utmost leaves and delicatest flowers;
  Upon the winds, among the clouds 'tis spread,
  It wakes a life in the forgotten dead,—
They breathe a spirit up from their obscurest bowers; 375

And like a storm bursting its cloudy prison
With thunder, and with whirlwind, has arisen
Out of the lampless caves of unimagined being:
  With earthquake shock and swiftness making shiver
  Thought's stagnant chaos, unremoved forever, 380
Till hate, and fear, and pain, light-vanquished shadows, fleeing,

Leave man, who was a many-sided mirror,
Which could distort to many a shape of error,
This true fair world of things, a sea reflecting love;
  Which over all his kind, as the sun's heaven
  Gliding o'er ocean, smooth, serene, and even, 385
Darting from starry depths radiance and life, doth move:

Leave man, even as a leprous child is left,
Who follows a sick beast to some warm cleft
Of rocks, through which the might of healing springs is poured;
  Then when it wanders home with rosy smile, 390
  Unconscious, and its mother fears awhile
It is a spirit, then, weeps on her child restored.

Man, oh, not men! a chain of linkèd thought,
Of love and might to be divided not,
Compelling the elements with adamantine stress; 395
  As the sun rules, even with a tyrant's gaze,
  The unquiet republic of the maze
Of planets, struggling fierce towards heaven's free wilderness.

Man, one harmonious soul of many a soul, 400
Whose nature is its own divine control,
Where all things flow to all, as rivers to the sea;
  Familiar acts are beautiful through love;
  Labor, and pain, and grief, in life's green grove
Sport like tame beasts; none knew how gentle they could be! 405

His will, with all mean passions, bad delights,
And selfish cares, its trembling satellites,
A spirit ill to guide, but mighty to obey,
  Is as a tempest-wingèd ship, whose helm
  Love rules, through waves which dare not overwhelm, 410
Forcing life's wildest shores to own its sovereign sway.

All things confess his strength. Through the cold mass
Of marble and of color his dreams pass—
Bright threads whence mothers weave the robes their children wear;
  Language is a perpetual Orphic song, 415
  Which rules with dædal harmony a throng
Of thoughts and forms, which else senseless and shapeless were.

The lightning is his slave; heaven's utmost deep
Gives up her stars, and like a flock of sheep
They pass before his eye, are numbered, and roll on!   420
The tempest is his steed, he strides the air;
And the abyss shouts from her depth laid bare,
"Heaven, hast thou secrets? Man unveils me; I have none."

The Moon

The shadow of white death has passed
From my path in heaven at last,   425
A clinging shroud of solid frost and sleep;
And through my newly-woven bowers,
Wander happy paramours,
Less mighty, but as mild as those who keep
Thy vales more deep.   430

The Earth

As the dissolving warmth of dawn may fold
A half unfrozen dew-globe, green, and gold,
And crystalline, till it becomes a wingèd mist,
And wanders up the vault of the blue day,
Outlives the moon, and on the sun's last ray   435
Hangs o'er the sea, a fleece of fire and amethyst.

The Moon

Thou art folded, thou art lying
In the light which is undying
Of thine own joy, and heaven's smile divine;
All suns and constellations shower   440
On thee a light, a life, a power,
Which doth array thy sphere; thou pourest thine
On mine, on mine!

The Earth

I spin beneath my pyramid of night,
Which points into the heavens dreaming delight,   445
Murmuring victorious joy in my enchanted sleep;
As a youth lulled in love-dreams faintly sighing,
Under the shadow of his beauty lying,
Which round his rest a watch of light and warmth doth keep.

The Moon

As in the soft and sweet eclipse,   450
When soul meets soul on lovers' lips,
High hearts are calm, and brightest eyes are dull;
So when thy shadow falls on me,
Then am I mute and still, by thee
Covered; of thy love, Orb most beautiful,   455
Full, oh, too full!

Thou art speeding round the sun
Brightest world of many a one;
Green and azure sphere which shinest
With a light which is divinest   460
Among all the lamps of heaven

To whom life and light is given;
I, thy crystal paramour
Borne beside thee by a power
Like the polar paradise,   465
Magnet-like of lovers' eyes;
I, a most enamored maiden
Whose weak brain is overladen
With the pleasure of her love,
Maniac-like around thee move   470
Gazing, an insatiate bride,
On thy form from every side
Like a Mænad, round the cup
Which Agave lifted up
In the weird Cadmæan forest.   475
Brother, wheresoe'er thou soarest
I must hurry, whirl, and follow
Through the heavens wide and hollow,
Sheltered by the warm embrace
Of thy soul from hungry space,   480
Drinking from thy sense and sight
Beauty, majesty, and might,
As a lover or a chameleon
Grows like what it looks upon,
As a violet's gentle eye   485
Gazes on the azure sky
Until its hue grows like what it beholds,
As a gray and watery mist
Glows like solid amethyst
Athwart the western mountain it enfolds,   490
When the sunset sleeps
    Upon its snow—

The Earth

And the weak day weeps
    That it should be so.
O gentle Moon, the voice of thy delight   495
Falls on me like thy clear and tender light
Soothing the seaman, borne the summer night,
    Through isles forever calm;
O gentle Moon, thy crystal accents pierce
The caverns of my pride's deep universe,   500
Charming the tiger joy, whose tramplings fierce
    Made wounds which need thy balm.

    Panthea. I rise as from a bath of sparkling water,
A bath of azure light, among dark rocks,
Out of the stream of sound.
    Ione.   Ah me! sweet sister,   505
The stream of sound has ebbed away from us,
And you pretend to rise out of its wave,
Because your words fall like the clear, soft dew
Shaken from a bathing wood-nymph's limbs and hair.
    Panthea. Peace! peace! A mighty power, which is as
        darkness,   510
Is rising out of Earth, and from the sky
Is showered like night, and from within the air
Bursts, like eclipse which had been gathered up
Into the pores of sunlight: the bright visions,
Wherein the singing Spirits rode and shone,   515

Gleam like pale meteors through a watery night.
Ione. There is a sense of words upon mine ear.
Panthea. An universal sound like words: Oh, list!

Demogorgon

Thou, Earth, calm empire of a happy soul,
  Sphere of divinest shapes and harmonies,   520
Beautiful orb! gathering as thou dost roll
  The love which paves thy path along the skies:

The Earth

I hear: I am as a drop of dew that dies.

Demogorgon

Thou, Moon, which gazest on the nightly Earth
  With wonder, as it gazes upon thee;   525
Whilst each to men, and beasts, and the swift birth
  Of birds, is beauty, love, calm, harmony:

The Moon

I hear: I am a leaf shaken by thee!

Demogorgon

Ye kings of suns and stars, Dæmons and Gods,
  Etherial Dominations, who possess   530
Elysian, windless, fortunate abodes
  Beyond Heaven's constellated wilderness:

A Voice from above

Our great republic hears: we are blest, and bless.

Demogorgon

Ye happy dead, whom beams of brightest verse
  Are clouds to ride, not colors to portray,   535
Whether your nature is that universe
  Which once ye saw and suffered—

A Voice from beneath

          Or, as they
Whom we have left, we change and pass away.

Demogorgon

Ye elemental Genii, who have homes
  From man's high mind even to the central stone   540
Of sullen lead; from Heaven's star-fretted domes
  To the dull weed some sea-worm battens on:

A confused Voice

We hear: thy words waken Oblivion.

Demogorgon

Spirits, whose homes are flesh: ye beasts and birds,
  Ye worms, and fish; ye living leaves and buds;   545
Lightning and wind; and ye untameable herds,
  Meteors and mists, which throng air's solitudes:—

A Voice

Thy voice to us is wind among still woods.

Demogorgon

Man, who wert once a despot and a slave,
  A dupe and a deceiver, a decay,   550
A traveller from the cradle to the grave
  Through the dim night of this immortal day:

All

Speak: thy strong words may never pass away.

Demogorgon

This is the day which down the void abysm
At the Earth-born's spell yawns for Heaven's despotism,   555
  And Conquest is dragged captive through the deep:
Love, from its awful throne of patient power
In the wise heart, from the last giddy hour
  Of dread endurance, from the slippery, steep,
And narrow verge of crag-like agony, springs   560
And folds over the world its healing wings.

Gentleness, Virtue, Wisdom, and Endurance,—
These are the seals of that most firm assurance
  Which bars the pit over Destruction's strength;
And if, with infirm hand, Eternity,   565
Mother of many acts and hours, should free
  The serpent that would clasp her with his length,
These are the spells by which to reassume
An empire o'er the disentangled doom.

To suffer woes which Hope thinks infinite;   570
To forgive wrongs darker than death or night;
  To defy Power, which seems omnipotent;
To love, and bear; to hope till Hope creates
From its own wreck the thing it contemplates;
  Neither to change, nor falter, nor repent;—   575
This, like thy glory, Titan, is to be
Good, great and joyous, beautiful and free;
This is alone Life, Joy, Empire, and Victory!

1818-19   Aug., 1820

THE SENSITIVE PLANT

PART FIRST

A Sensitive Plant in a garden grew,
And the young winds fed it with silver dew,
And it opened its fan-like leaves to the light,
And closed them beneath the kisses of
    night.

And the Spring arose on the garden fair, 5
Like the Spirit of Love felt every where;
And each flower and herb on Earth's dark
    breast
Rose from the dreams of its wintry rest.

But none ever trembled and panted with
    bliss
In the garden, the field, or the wilder-
    ness, 10
Like a doe in the noontide with love's
    sweet want,
As the companionless Sensitive Plant.

The snow-drop, and then the violet,
Arose from the ground with warm rain
    wet,
And their breath was mixed with fresh
    odor, sent 15
From the turf, like the voice and the in-
    strument.

Then the pied wind-flowers and the tulip
    tall,
And narcissi, the fairest among them all,
Who gaze on their eyes in the stream's
    recess,
Till they die of their own dear loveli-
    ness; 20

And the Naiad-like lily of the vale,
Whom youth makes so fair and passion so
    pale,
That the light of its tremulous bells is seen
Through their pavilions of tender green;

And the hyacinth purple, and white, and
    blue, 25
Which flung from its bells a sweet peal
    anew
Of music so delicate, soft, and intense,
It was felt like an odor within the sense;

And the rose like a nymph to the bath
    addressed,
Which unveiled the depth of her glowing
    breast, 30
Till, fold after fold, to the fainting air
The soul of her beauty and love lay bare:

And the wand-like lily, which lifted up,
As a Mænad, its moonlight-colored cup,
Till the fiery star, which is its eye, 35
Gazed through clear dew on the tender sky;

And the jessamine faint, and the sweet
    tuberose,
The sweetest flower for scent that blows;
And all rare blossoms from every clime
Grew in that garden in perfect prime. 40

And on the stream whose inconstant bosom
Was prankt under boughs of embowering
    blossom,
With golden and green light, slanting
    through
Their heaven of many a tangled hue,

Broad water lilies lay tremulously, 45
And starry river-buds glimmered by,
And around them the soft stream did glide
    and dance
With a motion of sweet sound and radi-
    ance.

And the sinuous paths of lawn and of moss,
Which led through the garden along and
    across, 50
Some open at once to the sun and the
    breeze,
Some lost among bowers of blossoming
    trees,

Were all paved with daisies and delicate
    bells
As fair as the fabulous asphodels,
And flowrets which drooping as day
    drooped too 55
Fell into pavilions, white, purple, and blue,
To roof the glow-worm from the evening
    dew.

And from this undefiled Paradise
The flowers (as an infant's awakening eyes
Smile on its mother, whose singing sweet 60
Can first lull, and at last must awaken it),

When Heaven's blithe winds had unfolded
    them,
As mine-lamps enkindle a hidden gem,
Shone smiling to Heaven, and every one
Shared joy in the light of the gentle sun; 65

For each one was interpenetrated
With the light and the odor its neighbor
    shed,
Like young lovers whom youth and love
    make dear
Wrapped and filled by their mutual atmos-
    phere.

But the Sensitive Plant, which could give
    small fruit   70
Of the love which it felt from the leaf to
    the root,
Received more than all,—it loved more
    than ever,
(Where none wanted but it) could belong
    to the giver:

For the Sensitive Plant has no bright
    flower;
Radiance and odor are not its dower;   75
It loves, even like Love; its deep heart is
    full;
It desires what it has not, the beautiful!

The light winds which from unsustaining
    wings
Shed the music of many murmurings;
The beams which dart from many a star 80
Of the flowers whose hues they bear afar;

The plumèd insects swift and free,
Like golden boats on a sunny sea,
Laden with light and odor, which pass
Over the gleam of the living grass;   85

The unseen clouds of the dew, which lie
Like fire in the flowers till the sun rides
    high,
Then wander like spirits among the
    spheres,
Each cloud faint with the fragrance it
    bears;

The quivering vapors of dim noontide, 90
Which like a sea o'er the warm earth glide,
In which every sound, and odor, and beam,
Move, as reeds in a single stream;

Each and all like ministering angels were
For the Sensitive Plant sweet joys to
    bear,   95
Whilst the lagging hours of the day went
    by
Like windless clouds o'er a tender sky.

And when evening descended from heaven
    above,
And the Earth was all rest, and the air was
    all love,
And delight, though less bright, was far
    more deep,   100
And the day's veil fell from the world of
    sleep,

And the beasts, and the birds, and the in-
    sects were drowned
In an ocean of dreams without a sound;

Whose waves never mark, though they ever
    impress
The light sand which paves it, conscious-
    ness;   105

(Only over head the sweet nightingale
Ever sang more sweet as the day might fail,
And snatches of its Elysian chant
Were mixed with the dreams of the Sensi-
    tive Plant.)

The Sensitive Plant was the earliest   110
Up-gathered into the bosom of rest;
A sweet child weary of its delight,
The feeblest and yet the favorite,
Cradled within the embrace of night.

PART SECOND

There was a Power in this sweet place, 115
An Eve in this Eden; a ruling grace
Which to the flowers, did they waken or
    dream,
Was as God is to the starry scheme.

A Lady, the wonder of her kind,
Whose form was upborne by a lovely
    mind   120
Which, dilating, had molded her mien and
    motion
Like a sea-flower unfolded beneath the
    ocean,

Tended the garden from morn to even:
And the meteors of that sublunar heaven,
Like the lamps of the air when night walks
    forth,   125
Laughed round her footsteps up from the
    Earth!

She had no companion of mortal race,
But her tremulous breath and her flushing
    face
Told, whilst the morn kissed the sleep
    from her eyes,
That her dreams were less slumber than
    Paradise: 130

As if some bright Spirit for her sweet sake
Had deserted heaven while the stars were
    awake,
As if yet around her he lingering were,
Though the veil of daylight concealed him
    from her.

Her step seemed to pity the grass it
    pressed;   135
You might hear by the heaving of her
    breast,

That the coming and going of the wind
Brought pleasure there and left passion be-
    hind.

And wherever her airy footstep trod,
Her trailing hair from the grassy sod   140
Erased its light vestige, with shadowy
    sweep,
Like a sunny storm o'er the dark green
    deep.

I doubt not the flowers of that garden
    sweet
Rejoiced in the sound of her gentle feet;
I doubt not they felt the spirit that
    came   145
From her glowing fingers through all their
    frame.

She sprinkled bright water from the stream
On those that were faint with the sunny
    beam;
And out of the cups of the heavy flowers
She emptied the rain of the thunder
    showers.   150

She lifted their heads with her tender
    hands,
And sustained them with rods and ozier
    bands;
If the flowers had been her own infants
    she
Could never have nursed them more ten-
    derly.

And all killing insects and gnawing
    worms,   155
And things of obscene and unlovely forms,
She bore in a basket of Indian woof,
Into the rough woods far aloof,

In a basket, of grasses and wild flowers full,
The freshest her gentle hands could pull 160
For the poor banished insects, whose intent,
Although they did ill, was innocent.

But the bee and the beamlike ephemeris
Whose path is the lightning's, and soft
    moths that kiss
The sweet lips of the flowers, and harm
    not, did she   165
Make her attendant angels be.

And many an antenatal tomb,
Where butterflies dream of the life to come,
She left clinging round the smooth and
    dark
Edge of the odorous cedar bark.   170

This fairest creature from earliest spring
Thus moved through the garden minister-
    ing
All the sweet season of summer tide,
And ere the first leaf looked brown—she
    died!

PART THIRD

Three days the flowers of the garden
    fair   175
Like stars when the moon is awakened
    were,
Or the waves of Baiæ, ere luminous
She floats up through the smoke of Vesu-
    vius.

And on the fourth, the Sensitive Plant
Felt the sound of the funeral chant   180
And the steps of the bearers, heavy and
    slow,
And the sobs of the mourners deep and
    low;

The weary sound and the heavy breath,
And the silent motions of passing death,
And the smell, cold, oppressive, and
    dank,   185
Sent through the pores of the coffin plank;

The dark grass, and the flowers among the
    grass,
Were bright with tears as the crowd did
    pass;
From their sighs the wind caught a mourn-
    ful tone,
And sate in the pines, and gave groan for
    groan.   190

The garden, once fair, became cold and
    foul,
Like the corpse of her who had been its
    soul,
Which at first was lovely as if in sleep,
Then slowly changed, till it grew a heap
To make men tremble who never weep.   195

Swift summer into the autumn flowed,
And frost in the mist of morning rode,
Though the noonday sun looked clear and
    bright,
Mocking the spoil of the secret night.

The rose leaves, like flakes of crimson
    snow,   200
Paved the turf and the moss below,
The lilies were drooping, and white, and
    wan,
Like the head and the skin of a dying man.

And Indian plants, of scent and hue
The sweetest that ever were fed on dew, 205
Leaf by leaf, day after day,
Were massed into the common clay.

And the leaves, brown, yellow, and gray,
and red,
And white with the whiteness of what is
dead,
Like troops of ghosts on the dry wind
passed; 210
Their whistling noise made the birds
aghast.

And the gusty winds waked the wingèd
seeds,
Out of their birthplace of ugly weeds,
Till they clung round many a sweet
flower's stem,
Which rotted into the earth with them. 215

The water blooms under the rivulet
Fell from the stalks on which they were set;
And the eddies drove them here and there,
As the winds did those of the upper air.

Then the rain came down, and the broken
stalks, 220
Were bent and tangled across the walks;
And the leafless network of parasite bowers
Massed into ruin; and all sweet flowers.

Between the time of the wind and the snow,
All loathliest weeds began to grow, 225
Whose coarse leaves were splashed with
many a speck,
Like the water snake's belly and the toad's
back.

And thistles, and nettles, and darnels rank,
And the dock, and henbane, and hemlock
dank,
Stretched out its long and hollow shank, 230
And stifled the air till the dead wind stank.

And plants, at whose names the verse feels
loath,
Filled the place with a monstrous under-
growth,
Prickly, and pulpous, and blistering, and
blue,
Livid, and starred with a lurid dew. 235

And agarics, and fungi, with mildew and
mold
Started like mist from the wet ground
cold;
Pale, fleshy, as if the decaying dead
With a spirit of growth had been animated!

Spawn, weeds, and filth, a leprous scum, 240
Made the running rivulet thick and dumb,
And at its outlet flags huge as stakes
Damned it up with roots knotted like water
snakes.

And hour by hour, when the air was still,
The vapors arose which have strength to
kill: 245
At morn they were seen, at noon they were
felt,
At night they were darkness no star could
melt.

And unctuous meteors from spray to spray
Crept and flitted in broad noonday
Unseen; every branch on which they alit 250
By a venomous blight was burned and bit.

The Sensitive Plant like one forbid
Wept, and the tears within each lid
Of its folded leaves which together grew
Were changed to a blight of frozen glue. 255

For the leaves soon fell, and the branches
soon
By the heavy axe of the blast were hewn;
The sap shrank to the root through every
pore
As blood to a heart that will beat no more.

For Winter came: the wind was his
whip: 260
One choppy finger was on his lip:
He had torn the cataracts from the hills
And they clanked at his girdle like man-
acles;

His breath was a chain which without a
sound
The earth, and the air, and the water
bound; 265
He came, fiercely driven, in his chariot-
throne,
By the tenfold blasts of the arctic zone.

Then the weeds which were forms of living
death
Fled from the frost to the earth beneath.
Their decay and sudden flight from
frost 270
Was but like the vanishing of a ghost!

And under the roots of the Sensitive Plant
The moles and the dormice died for want:
The birds dropped stiff from the frozen air
And were caught in the branches naked
and bare. 275

First there came down a thawing rain
And its full drops froze on the boughs
  again;
Then there steamed up a freezing dew
Which to the drops of the thaw-rain grew;

And a northern whirlwind, wandering
  about   280
Like a wolf that had smelt a dead child out,
Shook the boughs thus laden, and heavy
  and stiff,
And snapped them off with his rigid griff.

When winter had gone and spring came
  back
The Sensitive Plant was a leafless wreck; 285
But the mandrakes, and toadstools, and
  docks and darnels,
Rose like the dead from their ruined
  charnels.

CONCLUSION

Whether the Sensitive Plant, or that
Which within its boughs like a spirit sat
Ere its outward form had known decay, 290
Now felt this change, I cannot say.

Whether that Lady's gentle mind,
No longer with the form combined
Which scattered love, as stars do light,
Found sadness, where it left delight,   295

I dare not guess; but in this life
Of error, ignorance, and strife,
Where nothing is, but all things seem,
And we the shadows of the dream,

It is a modest creed, and yet   300
Pleasant if one considers it,
To own that death itself must be,
Like all the rest, a mockery.

That garden sweet, that Lady fair,
And all sweet shapes and odors there, 305
In truth have never passed away;
'Tis we, 'tis ours, are changed; not they.

For love, and beauty, and delight,
There is no death nor change: their might
Exceeds our organs, which endure   310
No light, being themselves obscure.
March, 1820   Aug., 1820

THE CLOUD

I bring fresh showers for the thirsting
  flowers
  From the seas and the streams;
I bear light shade for the leaves when laid
  In their noonday dreams.

From my wings are shaken the dews that
  waken   5
  The sweet buds every one,
When rocked to rest on their mother's
  breast,
  As she dances about the sun.
I wield the flail of the lashing hail,
  And whiten the green plains under, 10
And then again I dissolve it in rain,
  And laugh as I pass in thunder.

I sift the snow on the mountains below,
  And their great pines groan aghast;
And all the night 'tis my pillow white, 15
  While I sleep in the arms of the blast.
Sublime on the towers of my skiey bowers,
  Lightning my pilot sits;
In a cavern under is fettered the thunder,—
  It struggles and howls at fits;   20
Over earth and ocean, with gentle motion,
  This pilot is guiding me,
Lured by the love of the genii that move
  In the depths of the purple sea;
Over the rills, and the crags, and the
  hills,   25
  Over the lakes and the plains,
Wherever he dream, under mountain or
  stream,
  The Spirit he loves remains;
And I all the while bask in heaven's blue
  smile,
  Whilst he is dissolving in rains.   30

The sanguine sunrise, with his meteor eyes,
  And his burning plumes outspread,
Leaps on the back of my sailing rack,
  When the morning star shines dead,
As on the jag of a mountain crag,   35
  Which an earthquake rocks and swings,
An eagle alit one moment may sit
  In the light of its golden wings.
And when sunset may breathe, from the lit
  sea beneath
  Its ardors of rest and of love,   40
And the crimson pall of eve may fall
  From the depth of heaven above,
With wings folded I rest, on mine airy
  nest,
  As still as a brooding dove.

That orbèd maiden with white fire laden, 45
  Whom mortals call the moon,
Glides glimmering o'er my fleece-like floor,
  By the midnight breezes strewn;
And wherever the beat of her unseen feet,
  Which only the angels hear,   50
May have broken the woof of my tent's
  thin roof,
  The stars peep behind her and peer;

And I laugh to see them whirl and flee,
   Like a swarm of golden bees,
When I widen the rent in my wind-built
      tent,   55
   Till the calm rivers, lakes, and seas,
Like strips of the sky fallen through me on
      high,
      Are each paved with the moon and
         these.

I bind the sun's throne with a burning
      zone,
      And the moon's with a girdle of
         pearl;   60
The volcanoes are dim and the stars reel
      and swim,
   When the whirlwinds my banner un-
      furl.
From cape to cape, with a bridge-like
      shape,
      Over a torrent sea,
Sunbeam-proof, I hang like a roof,   65
   The mountains its columns be.
The triumphal arch through which I march
   With hurricane, fire, and snow,
When the powers of the air are chained to
      my chair,
      Is the million-colored bow;   70
The sphere-fire above its soft colors wove,
   While the moist earth was laughing
      below.

I am the daughter of earth and water,
   And the nursling of the sky;
I pass through the pores of the ocean and
      shores;   75
   I change, but I cannot die.
For after the rain when, with never a stain,
   The pavilion of heaven is bare,
And the winds and sunbeams with their
      convex gleams
      Build up the blue dome of air,   80
I silently laugh at my own cenotaph,
   And out of the caverns of rain,
Like a child from the womb, like a ghost
      from the tomb,
   I arise and unbuild it again.

1819   Aug., 1820

TO A SKYLARK

   Hail to thee, blithe spirit!
      Bird thou never wert,
   That from heaven, or near it,
      Pourest thy full heart
In profuse strains of unpremeditated art. 5

Higher still and higher
   From the earth thou springest
Like a cloud of fire;
   The blue deep thou wingest,
And singing still dost soar, and soaring ever
   singest.   10

In the golden lightning
   Of the sunken sun,
O'er which clouds are bright'ning,
   Thou dost float and run;
Like an unbodied joy whose race is just
   begun.   15

The pale purple even
   Melts around thy flight;
Like a star of heaven
   In the broad daylight
Thou art unseen, but yet I hear thy shrill
   delight,   20

Keen as are the arrows
   Of that silver sphere,
Whose intense lamp narrows
   In the white dawn clear,
Until we hardly see, we feel that it is
   there.   25

All the earth and air
   With thy voice is loud,
As, when night is bare,
   From one lonely cloud
The moon rains out her beams, and heaven
   is overflowed.   30

What thou art we know not;
   What is most like thee?
From rainbow clouds there flow not
   Drops so bright to see
As from thy presence showers a rain of
   melody.   35

Like a poet hidden
   In the light of thought,
Singing hymns unbidden,
   Till the world is wrought
To sympathy with hopes and fears it
   heeded not—   40

Like a high-born maiden
   In a palace tower,
Soothing her love-laden
   Soul in secret hour
With music sweet as love, which overflows
   her bower—   45

Like a glowworm golden
In a dell of dew,
Scattering unbeholden
Its aërial hue
Among the flowers and grass which screen
   it from the view—   50

Like a rose embowered
In its own green leaves,
By warm winds deflowered,
Till the scent it gives
Makes faint with too much sweet these
   heavy-wingèd thieves.   55

Sound of vernal showers
On the twinkling grass,
Rain-awakened flowers,
All that ever was
Joyous, and clear, and fresh, thy music
   doth surpass.   60

Teach us, sprite or bird,
What sweet thoughts are thine;
I have never heard
Praise of love or wine
That panted forth a flood of rapture so
   divine: 65

Chorus Hymenæal,
Or triumphal chaunt,
Matched with thine, would be all
But an empty vaunt,
A thing wherein we feel there is some hid-
   den want.   70

What objects are the fountains
Of thy happy strain?
What fields, or waves, or mountains?
What shapes of sky or plain?
What love of thine own kind? what igno-
   rance of pain?   75

With thy clear keen joyance
Languor cannot be—
Shadow of annoyance
Never came near thee:
Thou lovest—but ne'er knew love's sad
   satiety.   80

Waking or asleep,
Thou of death must deem
Things more true and deep
Than we mortals dream,
Or how could thy notes flow in such a
   crystal stream?   85

We look before and after
And pine for what is not:
Our sincerest laughter
With some pain is fraught;
Our sweetest songs are those that tell of
   saddest thought.   90

Yet if we could scorn
Hate, and pride, and fear;
If we were things born
Not to shed a tear,
I know not how thy joy we ever should
   come near.   95

Better than all measures
Of delightful sound—
Better than all treasures
That in books are found—
Thy skill to poet were, thou scorner of the
   ground!   100

Teach me half the gladness
That thy brain must know,
Such harmonious madness
From my lips would flow,
The world should listen then—as I am
   listening now.   105

   1819   Aug., 1820

FROM ODE TO LIBERTY

Yet, Freedom, yet, thy banner, torn but flying,
Streams like a thunderstorm against the wind.
                    BYRON

XV

Oh, that the free would stamp the impious name
   Of KING into the dust! or write it there,
So that this blot upon the page of fame
   Were as a serpent's path, which the light air
Erases, and the flat sands close behind!   215
      Ye the oracle have heard:
      Lift the victory-flashing sword,

And cut the snaky knots of this foul gordian word,
　Which, weak itself as stubble, yet can bind
　　Into a mass, irrefragably firm,
　The axes and the rods which awe mankind; 　　　　220
　　The sound has poison in it, 'tis the sperm
Of what makes life foul, cankerous, and abhorred;
　Disdain not thou, at thine appointed term,
　To set thine armèd heel on this reluctant worm. 　　225

XVI

Oh, that the wise from their bright minds would kindle
　Such lamps within the dome of this dim world,
That the pale name of PRIEST might shrink and dwindle
　Into the hell from which it first was hurled,
A scoff of impious pride from fiends impure: 　　　　230
　　Till human thoughts might kneel alone,
　　Each before the judgment throne
Of its own aweless soul, or of the Power unknown!
　　Oh, that the words which make the thoughts obscure
　　From which they spring, as clouds of glimmering dew 　　233
　From a white lake blot Heaven's blue portraiture,
　　Were stripped of their thin masks and various hue
And frowns and smiles and splendors not their own,
　　Till in the nakedness of false and true
　They stand before their Lord, each to receive its due! 　　240

XVII

He who taught man to vanquish whatsoever
　Can be between the cradle and the grave
Crowned him the King of Life. O vain endeavor!
　If on his own high will, a willing slave,
He has enthroned the oppression and the oppressor. 　　245
　　What if earth can clothe and feed
　　Amplest mill'ons at their need,
And power in thought be as the tree within the seed?
　　O, what if Art, an ardent intercessor,
　　Driving on fiery wings to Nature's throne, 　　　　250
　Checks the great mother stooping to caress her,
　　And cries: Give me, thy child, dominion
Over all height and depth? if Life can breed
　New wants, and wealth from those who toil and groan
　Rend of thy gifts and hers a thousand fold for one. 　　255
1820　　　　　　　　　　　　　　　　　1820

THE QUESTION

I

I dreamed that, as I wandered by the way,
　Bare winter suddenly was changed to spring,
And gentle odors led my steps astray,
　Mixed with a sound of waters murmuring
Along a shelving bank of turf, which lay 　　　　5
　Under a copse, and hardly dared to fling
Its green arms round the bosom of the stream,
But kissed it and then fled, as thou mightest in dream.

II

There grew pied wind-flowers and violets,
  Daisies, those pearled Arcturi of the earth,   10
The constellated flower that never sets;
  Faint oxlips; tender bluebells, at whose birth
The sod scarce heaved; and that tall flower that wets
  (Like a child, half in tenderness and mirth)
Its mother's face with heaven-collected tears,   15
When the low wind, its playmate's voice, it hears.

III

And in the warm hedge grew lush eglantine,
  Green cowbind and the moonlight-colored May,
And cherry blossoms, and white cups, whose wine
  Was the bright dew, yet drained not by the day;   20
And wild roses, and ivy serpentine,
  With its dark buds and leaves, wandering astray;
And flowers azure, black, and streaked with gold,
Fairer than any wakened eyes behold.

IV

And nearer to the river's trembling edge   25
  There grew broad flag-flowers, purple prankt with white,
And starry river-buds among the sedge,
  And floating water lilies broad and bright,
Which lit the oak that overhung the hedge
  With moonlight beams of their own watery light;   30
And bulrushes and reeds of such deep green
As soothed the dazzled eye with sober sheen.

V

Methought that of these visionary flowers
  I made a nosegay, bound in such a way
That the same hues, which in their natural bowers   35
  Were mingled or opposed, the like array
Kept these imprisoned children of the Hours
  Within my hand,—and then, elate and gay,
I hastened to the spot whence I had come,
That I might there present it!—oh! to whom?   40
1820   1822

HYMN OF PAN

I

From the forests and highlands
    We come, we come;
From the river-girt islands,
    Where loud waves are dumb
      Listening to my sweet pipings.   5
The wind in the reeds and the rushes,
    The bees on the bells of thyme,
The birds on the myrtle bushes,
    The cicale above in the lime,
And the lizards below in the grass,   10
Were as silent as ever old Tmolus was,
      Listening to my sweet pipings.

II

Liquid Peneus was flowing,
    And all dark Tempe lay
In Pelion's shadow, outgrowing 15
    The light of the dying day,
    Speeded by my sweet pipings.
The Sileni, and Sylvans, and Fauns,
    And the Nymphs of the woods and waves,
To the edge of the moist river-lawns, 20
    And the brink of the dewy caves,
And all that did then attend and follow
Were silent with love, as you now, Apollo,
    With envy of my sweet pipings.

III

I sang of the dancing stars, 25
    I sang of the dædal Earth,
And of Heaven—and the giant wars,
    And Love, and Death, and Birth,—
    And then I changed my pipings,—
Singing how down the vale of Menalus 30
    I pursued a maiden and clasped a reed:
Gods and men, we are all deluded thus!
    It breaks in our bosom and then we bleed:
All wept, as I think both ye now would,
    If envy or age had not frozen your blood, 35
    At the sorrow of my sweet pipings.

1820   1824

TO ———

I

I fear thy kisses, gentle maiden,
  Thou needest not fear mine;
My spirit is too deeply laden
  Ever to burthen thine.

II

I fear thy mien, thy tones, thy motion, 5
  Thou needest not fear mine;
Innocent is the heart's devotion
  With which I worship thine.

1820   1824

THE TWO SPIRITS: AN ALLEGORY

First Spirit

O thou, who plumed with strong desire
Wouldst float above the earth, beware!
A shadow tracks thy flight of fire—
    Night is coming!
Bright are the regions of the air, 5
And among the winds and beams
  It were delight to wander there—
    Night is coming!

Second Spirit

The deathless stars are bright above;
  If I would cross the shade of night, 10
Within my heart is the lamp of love,
    And that is day!
And the moon will smile with gentle light
On my golden plumes where'er they move;
  The meteors will linger round my flight, 15
    And make night day.

First Spirit

But if the whirlwinds of darkness waken
  Hail, and lightning, and stormy rain;
See, the bounds of the air are shaken—
    Night is coming! 20
The red swift clouds of the hurricane
Yon declining sun have overtaken,
  The clash of the hail sweeps over the plain—
    Night is coming!

Second Spirit

I see the light, and I hear the sound; 25
  I'll sail on the flood of the tempest dark,
With the calm within and the light around
    Which makes night day:

And thou, when the gloom is deep and
    stark,
Look from thy dull earth, slumber-bound, 30
My moon-like flight thou then mayst
    mark
    On high, far away.

* * *

Some say there is a precipice
  Where one vast pine is frozen to ruin
O'er piles of snow and chasms of ice   35
    Mid Alpine mountains;
  And that the languid storm pursuing
That wingèd shape, for ever flies
    Round those hoar branches, aye renew-
      ing
    Its aëry fountains.   40

Some say when nights are dry and clear,
  And the death-dews sleep on the morass,
Sweet whispers are heard by the traveller,
    Which make night day:
  And a silver shape like his early love
    doth pass   45
Upborne by her wild and glittering hair,
  And when he awakes on the fragrant
    grass,
    He finds night day.

1820   1824

TO THE MOON

I

Art thou pale for weariness
Of climbing heaven and gazing on the
    earth,
  Wandering companionless
Among the stars that have a different
    birth,—
And ever changing, like a joyless eye   5
That finds no object worth its constancy?

II

Thou chosen sister of the spirit,
That gazes on thee till in thee it pities . . .

1820   1824

TO NIGHT

I

Swiftly walk o'er the western wave,
    Spirit of Night!
Out of the misty eastern cave,
Where all the long and lone daylight,
Thou wovest dreams of joy and fear,   5
  Which make thee terrible and dear,—
    Swift be thy flight!

II

Wrap thy form in a mantle grey,
    Star-inwrought!
Blind with thine hair the eyes of Day;   10
Kiss her until she be wearied out,
Then wander o'er city, and sea, and land,
Touching all with thine opiate wand—
    Come, long sought!

III

When I arose and saw the dawn,   15
    I sighed for thee;
When light rode high, and the dew was
    gone,
And noon lay heavy on flower and tree,
And the weary Day turned to his rest,
Lingering like an unloved guest,   20
    I sighed for thee.

IV

Thy brother Death came, and cried,
    Wouldst thou me?
Thy sweet child Sleep, the filmy-eyed,
Murmured like a noontide bee,   25
Shall I nestle near thy side?
Wouldst thou me?—And I replied,
    No, not thee!

V

Death will come when thou art dead,
    Soon, too soon—   30
Sleep will come when thou art fled;
Of neither would I ask the boon
I ask of thee, belovèd Night—
Swift be thine approaching flight,
    Come soon, soon!   35

1821   1824

TIME

Unfathomable Sea! whose waves are years,
  Ocean of Time, whose waters of deep
    woe
Are brackish with the salt of human tears!
  Thou shoreless flood, which in thy ebb
    and flow
  Claspest the limits of mortality,   5
  And sick of prey, yet howling on for
    more,
Vomitest thy wrecks on its inhospitable
    shore;
  Treacherous in calm, and terrible in
    storm,
    Who shall put forth on thee,
    Unfathomable Sea?   10

1821   1824

TO ———

Music, when soft voices die,
Vibrates in the memory;
Odors, when sweet violets sicken,
Live within the sense they quicken.
Rose leaves, when the rose is dead,   5
Are heaped for the belovèd's bed;
And so thy thoughts, when thou art gone,
Love itself shall slumber on.

1821   1824

SONG

I

Rarely, rarely, comest thou,
    Spirit of Delight!
Wherefore hast thou left me now
    Many a day and night?
Many a weary night and day   5
'Tis since thou art fled away.

II

How shall ever one like me
    Win thee back again?
With the joyous and the free
    Thou wilt scoff at pain.   10
Spirit false! thou hast forgot
All but those who need thee not.

III

As a lizard with the shade
    Of a trembling leaf,
Thou with sorrow art dismayed;   15
    Even the sighs of grief
Reproach thee, that thou art not near,
And reproach thou wilt not hear.

IV

Let me set my mournful ditty
    To a merry measure,   20
Thou wilt never come for pity,
    Thou wilt come for pleasure,
Pity then will cut away
Those cruel wings, and thou wilt stay.

V

I love all that thou lovest,   25
    Spirit of Delight!
The fresh Earth in new leaves dressed,
    And the starry night;
Autumn evening, and the morn
When the golden mists are born.   30

VI

I love snow, and all the forms
    Of the radiant frost;
I love waves, and winds, and storms,
    Every thing almost
Which is Nature's, and may be   35
Untainted by man's misery.

VII

I love tranquil solitude,
    And such society
As is quiet, wise and good;
    Between thee and me   40
What difference? but thou dost possess
The things I seek, not love them less.

VIII

I love Love—though he has wings,
    And like light can flee,
But above all other things,   45
    Spirit, I love thee—
Thou art love and life! O come,
Make once more my heart thy home.

1820 or 1821   1824

MUTABILITY

I

The flower that smiles to-day
        Tomorrow dies;
All that we wish to stay
        Tempts and then flies.
What is this world's delight?   5
Lightning that mocks the night,
        Brief even as bright.

II

Virtue, how frail it is!
        Friendship how rare!
Love, how it sells poor bliss   10
        For proud despair!
But we, though soon they fall,
Survive their joy, and all
        Which ours we call.

III

Whilst skies are blue and bright,   15
        Whilst flowers are gay,
Whilst eyes that change ere night
        Make glad the day;
Whilst yet the calm hours creep,
Dream thou—and from thy sleep   20
        Then wake to weep.

1821   1824

POLITICAL GREATNESS

Nor happiness, nor majesty, nor fame,
Nor peace, nor strength, nor skill in arms
        or arts,
Shepherd those herds whom tyranny makes
        tame;
Verse echoes not one beating of their
        hearts,
History is but the shadow of their shame. 5

Art veils her glass, or from the pageant
  starts
As to oblivion their blind millions fleet,
Staining that Heaven with obscene imagery
Of their own likeness. What are numbers
  knit
By force of custom? Man who man would
  be,   10
Must rule the empire of himself; in it
Must be supreme, establishing his throne
On vanquished will, quelling the anarchy
Of hopes and fears, being himself alone.
1821   1824

A LAMENT

I

Oh, world! oh, life! oh, time!
On whose last steps I climb
  Trembling at that where I had stood
    before;
When will return the glory of your prime?
  No more—O, never more!   5

II

Out of the day and night
A joy has taken flight;
  Fresh spring, and summer, and winter
    hoar,
Move my faint heart with grief, but with
    delight
  No more—O, never more!   10
1821   1824

TO ――――

I

One word is too often profaned
  For me to profane it,
One feeling too falsely disdained
  For thee to disdain it.
One hope is too like despair   5
  For prudence to smother,
And pity from thee more dear
  Than that from another.

II

I can give not what men call love,
  But wilt thou accept not   10
The worship the heart lifts above
  And the Heavens reject not,—
The desire of the moth for the star,
  Of the night for the morrow,
The devotion to something afar   15
  From the sphere of our sorrow?
1821   1824

TO ――――

I

When passion's trance is overpast,
If tenderness and truth could last,
Or live, whilst all wild feelings keep
Some mortal slumber, dark and deep,
I should not weep, I should not weep!   5

II

It were enough to feel, to see,
Thy soft eyes gazing tenderly,
And dream the rest—and burn and be
The secret food of fires unseen,
Couldst thou but be as thou hast been.   10

III

After the slumber of the year
The woodland violets reappear;
All things revive in field or grove,
And sky and sea, but two, which move
And form all others, life and love.   15
1821   1824

FROM EPIPSYCHIDION

VERSES ADDRESSED TO THE NOBLE AND
UNFORTUNATE LADY, EMILIA V――――,
NOW IMPRISONED IN THE CONVENT
OF――――

Sweet Spirit! Sister of that orphan one,
Whose empire is the name thou weepest
    on,
In my heart's temple I suspend to thee
These votive wreaths of withered memory.

Poor captive bird! who, from thy narrow
    cage,   5
Pourest such music, that it might assuage
The rugged hearts of those who prisoned
    thee,
Were they not deaf to all sweet melody;
This song shall be thy rose: its petals pale
Are dead, indeed, my adored Nightin-
    gale!   10
But soft and fragrant is the faded blossom,
And it has no thorn left to wound thy
    bosom.

High, spirit-wingèd Heart! who dost for
    ever
Beat thine unfeeling bars with vain en-
    deavor,
Till those bright plumes of thought, in
    which arrayed   15

It over-soared this low and worldly shade,
Lie shattered; and thy panting, wounded
   breast
Stains with dear blood its unmaternal nest!
I weep vain tears: blood would less bitter
   be,
Yet poured forth gladlier, could it profit
   thee.   20

   Seraph of Heaven! too gentle to be
   human,
Veiling beneath that radiant form of
   Woman
All that is insupportable in thee
Of light, and love, and immortality!
Sweet Benediction in the eternal Curse! 25
Veiled Glory of this lampless Universe!
Thou Moon beyond the clouds! Thou
   living Form
Among the Dead! Thou Star above the
   Storm!
Thou Wonder, and thou Beauty, and thou
   Terror!
Thou Harmony of Nature's art! Thou
   Mirror   30
In whom, as in the splendor of the Sun,
All shapes look glorious which thou gazest
   on!
Ay, even the dim words which obscure thee
   now
Flash, lightning-like, with unaccustomed
   glow;
I pray thee that thou blot from this sad
   song   35
All of its much mortality and wrong,
With those clear drops, which start like
   sacred dew
From the twin lights thy sweet soul darkens
   through,
Weeping, till sorrow becomes ecstasy:
Then smile on it, so that it may not die. 40

   I never thought before my death to see
Youth's vision thus made perfect. Emily,
I love thee; though the world by no thin
   name
Will hide that love from its unvalued
   shame.
Would we two had been twins of the same
   mother!   45
Or, that the name my heart lent to another
Could be a sister's bond for her and thee,
Blending two beams of one eternity!
Yet were one lawful and the other true,
These names, though dear, could paint not,
   as is due,   50
How beyond refuge I am thine. Ah me!
I am not thine: I am a part of *thee.*

Sweet Lamp! my moth-like Muse has
   burned its wings
Or, like a dying swan who soars and sings,
Young Love should teach Time, in his own
   gray style,   55
All that thou art. Art thou not void of
   guile,
A lovely soul formed to be blessed and
   bless?
A well of sealed and secret happiness,
Whose waters like blithe light and music
   are,
Vanquishing dissonance and gloom?   A
   Star   60
Which moves not in the moving heavens,
   alone?
A Smile amid dark frowns? a gentle tone
Amid rude voices? a belovèd light?
A Solitude, a Refuge, a Delight?
A Lute, which those whom Love has taught
   to play   65
Make music on, to soothe the roughest day
And lull fond Grief asleep? a buried treas-
   ure?
A cradle of young thoughts of wingless
   pleasure?
A violet-shrouded grave of Woe?—I meas-
   ure
The world of fancies, seeking one like
   thee,   70
And find—alas! mine own infirmity.

   She met me, Stranger, upon life's rough
   way,
And lured me towards sweet Death; as
   Night by Day,
Winter by Spring, or Sorrow by swift
   Hope,
Led into light, life, peace. An antelope, 75
In the suspended impulse of its lightness,
Were less ethereally light: the brightness
Of her divinest presence trembles through
Her limbs, as underneath a cloud of dew
Embodied in the windless heaven of
   June   80
Amid the splendor-wingèd stars, the Moon
Burns, inextinguishably beautiful:
And from her lips, as from a hyacinth full
Of honey-dew, a liquid murmur drops,
Killing the sense with passion; sweet as
   stops   85
Of planetary music heard in trance.
In her mild lights the starry spirits dance,
The sunbeams of those wells which ever
   leap
Under the lightnings of the soul—too deep
For the brief fathom-line of thought or
   sense.   90
The glory of her being, issuing thence,

Stains the dead, blank, cold air with a
　　warm shade
Of unentangled intermixture, made
By Love, of light and motion: one intense
Diffusion, one serene Omnipresence,　　95
Whose flowing outlines mingle in their
　　flowing,
Around her cheeks and utmost fingers
　　glowing
With the unintermitted blood, which there
Quivers, (as in a fleece of snow-like air
The crimson pulse of living morning
　　quiver,)　　100
Continuously prolonged, and ending never,
Till they are lost, and in that Beauty furled
Which penetrates and clasps and fills the
　　world;
Scarce visible from extreme loveliness.
Warm fragrance seems to fall from her
　　light dress　　105
And her loose hair; and where some heavy
　　tress
The air of her own speed has disentwined,
The sweetness seems to satiate the faint
　　wind;
And in the soul a wild odor is felt,
Beyond the sense, like fiery dews that
　　melt　　110
Into the bosom of a frozen bud.—
See where she stands! a mortal shape in-
　　dued
With love and life and light and deity,
And motion which may change but cannot
　　die;
An image of some bright Eternity;　　115
A shadow of some golden dream; a Splen-
　　dor
Leaving the third sphere pilotless; a tender
Reflection of the eternal Moon of Love
Under whose motions life's dull billows
　　move;
A Metaphor of Spring and Youth and
　　Morning;　　120
A Vision like incarnate April, warning,
With smiles and tears, Frost the Anatomy
Into his summer grave.
　　　　　　　Ah, woe is me!
What have I dared? where am I lifted? how
Shall I descend, and perish not? I know 125
That Love makes all things equal: I have
　　heard
By mine own heart this joyous truth
　　averred:
The spirit of the worm beneath the sod
In love and worship, blends itself with God.

Spouse! Sister! Angel! Pilot of the
　　Fate　　130
Whose course has been so starless! O too
　　late

Belovèd! O too soon adored, by me!
For in the fields of Immortality
My spirit should at first have worshipped
　　thine,
A divine presence in a place divine;　　135
Or should have moved beside it on this
　　earth,
A shadow of that substance, from its birth;
But not as now:—I love thee; yes, I feel
That on the fountain of my heart a seal
Is set, to keep its waters pure and bright 140
For thee, since in those *tears* thou hast
　　delight.
We—are we not formed, as notes of music
　　are,
For one another, though dissimilar;
Such difference without discord, as can
　　make
Those sweetest sounds, in which all spirits
　　shake　　145
As trembling leaves in a continuous air?

Thy wisdom speaks in me, and bids me
　　dare
Beacon the rocks on which high hearts are
　　wrecked.
I never was attached to that great sect,
Whose doctrine is, that each one should
　　select　　150
Out of the crowd a mistress or a friend,
And all the rest, though fair and wise,
　　commend
To cold oblivion, though it is in the code
Of modern morals, and the beaten road
Which those poor slaves with weary foot-
　　steps tread,　　155
Who travel to their home among the dead
By the broad highway of the world. and so
With one chained friend, perhaps a jealous
　　foe,
The dreariest and the longest journey go.

True Love in this differs from gold and
　　clay,　　160
That to divide is not to take away.
Love is like understanding, that grows
　　bright,
Gazing on many truths; 'tis like thy light,
Imagination! which from earth and sky,
And from the depths of human fantasy, 165
As from a thousand prisms and mirrors,
　　fills
The Universe with glorious beams, and
　　kills
Error, the worm, with many a sun-like
　　arrow
Of its reverberated lightning.　Narrow
The heart that loves, the brain that con-
　　templates,　　170

The life that wears, the spirit that creates
One object, and one form, and builds
thereby
A sepulchre for its eternity.

Mind from its object differs most in this:
Evil from good; misery from happiness; 175
The baser from the nobler; the impure
And frail, from what is clear and must
endure.
If you divide suffering and dross, you may
Diminish till it is consumed away;
If you divide pleasure and love and
thought, 180
Each part exceeds the whole; and we know
not
How much, while any yet remains un-
shared,
Of pleasure may be gained, of sorrow
spared:
This truth is that deep well, whence sages
draw
The unenvied light of hope; the eternal
law 185
By which those live, to whom this world of
life
Is as a garden ravaged, and whose strife
Tills for the promise of a later birth
The wilderness of this Elysian earth.

There was a Being whom my spirit
oft 190
Met on its visioned wanderings, far aloft,
In the clear golden prime of my youth's
dawn,
Upon the fairy isles of sunny lawn,
Amid the enchanted mountains, and the
caves
Of divine sleep, and on the air-like
waves 195
Of wonder-level dream, whose tremulous
floor
Paved her light steps;—on an imagined
shore,
Under the gray beak of some promontory
She met me, robed in such exceeding glory,
That I beheld her not. In solitudes 200
Her voice came to me through the whisper-
ing woods,
And from the fountains, and the odors
deep
Of flowers, which, like lips murmuring in
their sleep
Of the sweet kisses which had lulled them
there,
Breathed but of *her* to the enamored
air; 205
And from the breezes whether low or loud,
And from the rain of every passing cloud,
And from the singing of the summer-birds,

And from all sounds, all silence. In the
words
Of antique verse and high romance,—in
form, 210
Sound, color—in whatever checks that
Storm
Which with the shattered present chokes
the past;
And in that best philosophy, whose taste
Makes this cold common hell, our life, a
doom
As glorious as a fiery martyrdom; 215
Her Spirit was the harmony of truth.—

Then, from the caverns of my dreamy
youth
I sprang, as one sandalled with plumes of
fire,
And towards the lodestar of my one desire,
I flitted, like a dizzy moth, whose flight 220
Is as a dead leaf's in the owlet light,
When it would seek in Hesper's setting
sphere
A radiant death, a fiery sepulchre,
As if it were a lamp of earthly flame.—
But She, whom prayers or tears then could
not tame, 225
Passed, like a God throned on a wingèd
planet,
Whose burning plumes to tenfold swiftness
fan it,
Into the dreary cone of our life's shade;
And as a man with mighty loss dismayed,
I would have followed, though the grave
between 230
Yawned like a gulf whose spectres are un-
seen:
When a voice said:—"O thou of hearts the
weakest,
The phantom is beside thee whom thou
seekest."
Then I—"Where?"—the world's echo an-
swered "where?"
And in that silence, and in my despair, 235
I questioned every tongueless wind that
flew
Over my tower of mourning, if it knew
Whither 'twas fled, this soul out of my
soul;
And murmured names and spells which
have control
Over the sightless tyrants of our fate; 240
But neither prayer nor verse could dissi-
pate
The night which closed on her; nor un-
create
That world within this Chaos, mine and
me,
Of which she was the veiled Divinity,

The world I say of thoughts that wor-
shipped her: 245
And therefore I went forth, with hope and
fear
And every gentle passion sick to death,
Feeding my course with expectation's
breath,
Into the wintry forest of our life;
And struggling through its error with vain
strife, 250
And stumbling in my weakness and my
haste,
And half bewildered by new forms, I
passed,
Seeking among those untaught foresters
If I could find one form resembling hers,
In which she might have masked herself
from me. 255
There,—One, whose voice was venomed
melody
Sate by a well, under blue nightshade
bowers:
The breath of her false mouth was like
faint flowers,
Her touch was as electric poison,—flame
Out of her looks into my vitals came, 260
And from her living cheeks and bosom
flew
A killing air, which pierced like honey-dew
Into the core of my green heart, and lay
Upon its leaves; until, as hair grown gray
O'er a young brow, they hid its unblown
prime 265
With ruins of unseasonable time.

In many mortal forms I rashly sought
The shadow of that idol of my thought.
And some were fair—but beauty dies away:
Others were wise—but honeyed words be-
tray: 270
And One was true—oh! why not true to
me?
Then, as a hunted deer that could not flee,
I turned upon my thoughts, and stood at
bay,
Wounded and weak and panting; the cold
day
Trembled, for pity of my strife and
pain. 275
When, like a noonday dawn, there shone
again
Deliverance. One stood on my path who
seemed
As like the glorious shape which I had
dreamed
As is the Moon, whose changes ever run
Into themselves, to the eternal Sun; 280
The cold chaste Moon, the Queen of
Heaven's bright isles,

Who makes all beautiful on which she
smiles,
That wandering shrine of soft yet icy flame
Which ever is transformed, yet still the
same,
And warms not but illumines. Young and
fair 285
As the descended Spirit of that sphere,
She hid me, as the Moon may hide the
night
From its own darkness, until all was bright
Between the Heaven and Earth of my calm
mind,
And, as a cloud charioted by the wind, 290
She led me to a cave in that wild place,
And sate beside me, with her downward
face
Illumining my slumbers, like the Moon
Waxing and waning o'er Endymion.
And I was laid asleep, spirit and limb, 295
And all my being became bright or dim
As the Moon's image in a summer sea,
According as she smiled or frowned on me;
And there I lay, within a chaste cold bed:
Alas, I then was nor alive nor dead:— 300
For at her silver voice came Death and
Life,
Unmindful each of their accustomed strife,
Masked like twin babes, a sister and a
brother,
The wandering hopes of one abandoned
mother,
And through the cavern without wings they
flew, 305
And cried, "Away, he is not of our crew."
I wept, and though it be a dream, I weep.

What storms then shook the ocean of my
sleep,
Blotting that Moon, whose pale and wan-
ing lips
Then shrank as in the sickness of
eclipse;— 310
And how my soul was as a lampless sea,
And who was then its Tempest; and when
She,
The Planet of that hour, was quenched,
what frost
Crept o'er those waters, till from coast to
coast
The moving billows of my being fell 315
Into a death of ice, immovable;—
And then—what earthquake made it gape
and split,
The white Moon smiling all the while
on it,
These words conceal:—If not, each word
would be
The key of staunchless tears. Weep not
for me! 320

At length into the obscure Forest came
The Vision I had sought through grief and
    shame.
Athwart that wintry wilderness of thorns
Flashed from her motion splendor like the
    Morn's,
And from her presence life was radiated 325
Through the gray earth and branches bare
    and dead;
So that her way was paved, and roofed
    above
With flowers as soft as thoughts of budding
    love;
And music from her respiration spread
Like light,—all other sounds were pene-
    trated   330
By the small, still, sweet spirit of that
    sound,
So that the savage winds hung mute
    around;
And odors warm and fresh fell from her
    hair
Dissolving the dull cold in the frore air:
Soft as an Incarnation of the Sun,   335
When light is changed to love, this glorious
    One
Floated into the cavern where I lay,
And called my Spirit, and the dreaming
    clay
Was lifted by the thing that dreamed below
As smoke by fire, and in her beauty's
    glow   340
I stood, and felt the dawn of my long night
Was penetrating me with living light:
I knew it was the Vision veiled from me
So many years—that it was Emily.

Twin Spheres of light who rule this
    passive Earth,   345
This world of love, this *me;* and into birth
Awaken all its fruits and flowers, and dart
Magnetic might into its central heart;
And lift its billows and its mists, and guide
By everlasting laws, each wind and tide 350
To its fit cloud, and its appointed cave;
And lull its storms, each in the craggy grave
Which was its cradle, luring to faint bowers
The armies of the rainbow-wingèd showers;
And, as those married lights, which from
    the towers   355

Of Heaven look forth and fold the wander-
    ing globe
In liquid sleep and splendor, as a robe;
And all their many-mingled influence
    blend,
If equal, yet unlike, to one sweet end;—
So ye, bright regents, with alternate
    sway   360
Govern my sphere of being, night and day!
Thou, not disdaining even a borrowed
    might;
Thou, not eclipsing a remoter light;
And, through the shadow of the seasons
    three,
From Spring to Autumn's sere maturity, 365
Light it into the Winter of the tomb,
Where it may ripen to a brighter gloom.
Thou too, O Comet beautiful and fierce,
Who drew the heart of this frail Universe
Towards thine own; till, wrecked in that
    convulsion,   370
Alternating attraction and repulsion,
Thine went astray and that was rent in
    twain;
Oh, float into our azure heaven again!
Be there Love's folding-star at thy return;
The living Sun will feed thee from its
    urn   375
Of golden fire; the Moon will veil her
    horn
In thy last smiles; adoring Even and Morn
Will worship thee with incense of calm
    breath
And lights and shadows; as the star of
    Death
And Birth is worshipped by those sisters
    wild   380
Called Hope and Fear—upon the heart are
    piled
Their offerings,—of this sacrifice divine
A World shall be the altar.
                              Lady mine,
Scorn not these flowers of thought, the fad-
    ing birth
Which from its heart of hearts that plant
    puts forth   385
Whose fruit, made perfect by thy sunny
    eyes,
Will be as of the trees of Paradise. . . .

Jan.-Feb., 1821   1821

ADONAIS

AN ELEGY ON THE DEATH OF JOHN KEATS

'Αστὴρ πρὶν μὲν ἔλαμπες ἐνὶ ζώοισιν ἑῷος.
Νῦν δὲ θανὼν λάμπεις ἕσπερος ἐν φθιμένοις.
PLATO

I

I weep for Adonais—he is dead!
O, weep for Adonais! though our tears
Thaw not the frost which binds so dear a head!
And thou, sad Hour, selected from all years
To mourn our loss, rouse thy obscure compeers,
And teach them thine own sorrow, say: with me
Died Adonais; till the Future dares
Forget the Past, his fate and fame shall be
An echo and a light unto eternity.

II

Where wert thou, mighty Mother, when he lay,   10
When thy Son lay, pierced by the shaft which flies
In darkness? where was lorn Urania
When Adonais died? With veilèd eyes,
'Mid listening Echoes, in her Paradise
She sat, while one, with soft enamored breath,   15
Rekindled all the fading melodies,
With which, like flowers that mock the corse beneath,
He had adorned and hid the coming bulk of death.

III

O, weep for Adonais—he is dead!
Wake, melancholy Mother, wake and weep!   20
Yet wherefore? Quench within their burning bed
Thy fiery tears, and let thy loud heart keep,
Like his, a mute and uncomplaining sleep;
For he is gone, where all things wise and fair
Descend;—oh, dream not that the amorous Deep   25
Will yet restore him to the vital air;
Death feeds on his mute voice, and laughs at our despair.

IV

Most musical of mourners, weep again!
Lament anew, Urania!—He died,
Who was the Sire of an immortal strain,   30
Blind, old, and lonely, when his country's pride,
The priest, the slave, and the liberticide,
Trampled and mocked with many a loathèd rite
Of lust and blood; he went, unterrified,
Into the gulf of death; but his clear Sprite   35
Yet reigns o'er earth; the third among the sons of light.

V

Most musical of mourners, weep anew!
Not all to that bright station dared to climb;
And happier they their happiness who knew,
Whose tapers yet burn through that night of time   40

In which suns perished; others more sublime,
Struck by the envious wrath of man or God,
Have sunk, extinct in their refulgent prime;
And some yet live, treading the thorny road,
Which leads, through toil and hate, to Fame's serene abode.   45

VI

But now, thy youngest, dearest one has perished,
The nursling of thy widowhood, who grew,
Like a pale flower by some sad maiden cherished,
And fed with true love tears, instead of dew;
Most musical of mourners, weep anew!   50
Thy extreme hope, the loveliest and the last,
The bloom, whose petals, nipped before they blew,
Died on the promise of the fruit, is waste;
The broken lily lies—the storm is overpast.

VII

To that high Capital, where kingly Death   55
Keeps his pale court in beauty and decay.
He came; and bought, with price of purest breath,
A grave among the eternal.—Come away!
Haste, while the vault of blue Italian day
Is yet his fitting charnel-roof! while still   60
He lies, as if in dewy sleep he lay;
Awake him not! surely he takes his fill
Of deep and liquid rest, forgetful of all ill.

VIII

He will awake no more, oh, never more!—
Within the twilight chamber spreads apace,   65
The shadow of white Death, and at the door
Invisible Corruption waits to trace
His extreme way to her dim dwelling-place;
The eternal Hunger sits, but pity and awe
Soothe her pale rage, nor dares she to deface   70
So fair a prey, till darkness, and the law
Of change, shall o'er his sleep the mortal curtain draw.

IX

O, weep for Adonais!—The quick Dreams,
The passion-wingèd Ministers of thought,
Who were his flocks, whom near the living streams   75
Of his young spirit he fed, and whom he taught
The love which was its music, wander not,—
Wander no more, from kindling brain to brain,
But droop there, whence they sprung; and mourn their lot
Round the cold heart, where, after their sweet pain,   80
They ne'er will gather strength, or find a home again.

X

And one with trembling hands clasps his cold head,
And fans him with her moonlight wings, and cries;
"Our love, our hope, our sorrow, is not dead;
See, on the silken fringe of his faint eyes,   85
Like dew upon a sleeping flower, there lies
A tear some Dream has loosened from his brain."
Lost Angel of a ruined Paradise!
She knew not 'twas her own; as with no stain
She faded, like a cloud which had outwept its rain.   90

XI

One from a lucid urn of starry dew
Washed his light limbs as if embalming them;
Another clipped her profuse locks, and threw
The wreath upon him, like an anadem,
Which frozen tears instead of pearls begem;　　　　95
Another in her wilful grief would break
Her bow and wingèd reeds, as if to stem
A greater loss with one which was more weak;
And dull the barbèd fire against his frozen cheek.

XII

Another Splendor on his mouth alit,　　　　100
That mouth, whence it was wont to draw the breath
Which gave it strength to pierce the guarded wit,
And pass into the panting heart beneath
With lightning and with music: the damp death
Quenched its caress upon his icy lips;　　　　105
And, as a dying meteor stains a wreath
Of moonlight vapor, which the cold night clips,
It flushed through his pale limbs, and passed to its eclipse.

XIII

And others came . . . Desires and Adorations,
Wingèd Persuasions and veiled Destinies,　　　　110
Splendors, and Glooms, and glimmering Incarnations
Of hopes and fears, and twilight Phantasies;
And Sorrow, with her family of Sighs,
And Pleasure, blind with tears, led by the gleam
Of her own dying smile instead of eyes,　　　　115
Came in slow pomp;—the moving pomp might seem
Like pageantry of mist on an autumnal stream.

XIV

All he had loved, and molded into thought,
From shape, and hue, and odor, and sweet sound,
Lamented Adonais. Morning sought　　　　120
Her eastern watch-tower, and her hair unbound,
Wet with the tears which should adorn the ground,
Dimmed the aërial eyes that kindle day;
Afar the melancholy thunder moaned,
Pale Ocean in unquiet slumber lay,　　　　125
And the wild winds flew round, sobbing in their dismay.

XV

Lost Echo sits amid the voiceless mountains,
And feeds her grief with his remembered lay,
And will no more reply to winds or fountains,
Or amorous birds perched on the young green spray,　　　　130
Or herdsman's horn, or bell at closing day;
Since she can mimic not his lips, more dear
Than those for whose disdain she pined away
Into a shadow of all sounds:—a drear
Murmur, between their songs, is all the woodmen hear.　　　　135

XVI

Grief made the young Spring wild, and she threw down
Her kindling buds, as if she Autumn were,
Or they dead leaves; since her delight is flown
For whom should she have waked the sullen year?

To Phœbus was not Hyacinth so dear   140
Nor to himself Narcissus, as to both
Thou, Adonais: wan they stand and sere
Amid the faint companions of their youth,
With dew all turned to tears; odor, to sighing ruth.

XVII

Thy spirit's sister, the lorn nightingale,   145
Mourns not her mate with such melodious pain;
Not so the eagle, who like thee could scale
Heaven, and could nourish in the sun's domain
Her mighty youth with morning, doth complain,
Soaring and screaming round her empty nest,   150
As Albion wails for thee: the curse of Cain
Light on his head who pierced thy innocent breast,
And scared the angel soul that was its earthly guest!

XVIII

Ah woe is me! Winter is come and gone,
But grief returns with the revolving year;   155
The airs and streams renew their joyous tone;
The ants, the bees, the swallows reappear;
Fresh leaves and flowers deck the dead Seasons' bier;
The amorous birds now pair in every brake,
And build their mossy homes in fields and brere;   160
And the green lizard, and the golden snake,
Like unimprisoned flames, out of their trance awake.

XIX

Through wood and stream and field and hill and Ocean
A quickening life from the Earth's heart has burst
As it has ever done, with change and motion   165
From the great morning of the world when first
God dawned on Chaos; in its stream immersed
The lamps of Heaven flash with a softer light;
All baser things pant with life's sacred thirst;
Diffuse themselves; and spend in love's delight   170
The beauty and the joy of their renewèd might.

XX

The leprous corpse touched by this spirit tender
Exhales itself in flowers of gentle breath;
Like incarnations of the stars, when splendor
Is changed to fragrance, they illumine death   175
And mock the merry worm that wakes beneath;
Naught we know, dies. Shall that alone which knows
Be as a sword consumed beneath the sheath
By sightless lightning?—th' intense atom glows
A moment, then is quenched in a most cold repose.   180

XXI

Alas! that all we loved of him should be,
But for our grief, as if it had not been,
And grief itself be mortal! Woe is me!
Whence are we, and why are we? of what scene
The actors or spectators? Great and mean   185
Meet massed in death, who lends what life must borrow.
As long as skies are blue, and fields are green,
Evening must usher night, night urge the morrow,
Month follow month with woe, and year wake year to sorrow.

XXII

He will awake no more, oh, never more!   190
"Wake thou," cried Misery, "childless Mother, rise
Out of thy sleep, and slake, in thy heart's core,
A wound more fierce than his with tears and sighs."
And all the dreams that watched Urania's eyes,
And all the Echoes whom their sister's song   195
Had held in holy silence, cried: "Arise!"
Swift as a Thought by the snake Memory stung,
From her ambrosial rest the fading Splendor sprung.

XXIII

She rose like an autumnal Night, that springs
Out of the East, and follows wild and drear   200
The golden Day, which, on eternal wings,
Even as a ghost abandoning a bier,
Had left the Earth a corpse. Sorrow and fear
So struck, so roused, so rapt Urania;
So saddened round her like an atmosphere   205
Of stormy mist; so swept her on her way
Even to the mournful place where Adonais lay.

XXIV

Out of her secret Paradise she sped,
Through camps and cities rough with stone, and steel,
And human hearts, which to her aëry tread   210
Yielding not, wounded the invisible
Palms of her tender feet where'er they fell:
And barbèd tongues, and thoughts more sharp than they,
Rent the soft Form they never could repel,
Whose sacred blood, like the young tears of May,   215
Paved with eternal flowers that undeserving way.

XXV

In the death chamber for a moment Death,
Shamed by the presence of that living Might,
Blushed to annihilation, and the breath
Revisited those lips, and life's pale light   220
Flashed through those limbs, so late her dear delight.
"Leave me not wild and drear and comfortless,
As silent lightning leaves the starless night!
Leave me not!" cried Urania: her distress
Roused Death: Death rose and smiled, and met her vain caress.   225

XXVI

"Stay yet awhile! speak to me once again;
Kiss me, so long but as a kiss may live;
And in my heartless breast and burning brain
That word, that kiss shall all thoughts else survive,   230
With food of saddest memory kept alive,
Now thou art dead, as if it were a part
Of thee, my Adonais! I would give
All that I am to be as thou now art!
But I am chained to Time, and cannot thence depart!

XXVII

"Oh gentle child, beautiful as thou wert,   235
Why didst thou leave the trodden paths of men
Too soon, and with weak hands though mighty heart
Dare the unpastured dragon in his den?

Defenceless as thou wert, oh where was then
Wisdom the mirrored shield, or scorn the spear?   240
Or hadst thou waited the full cycle, when
Thy spirit should have filled its crescent sphere,
The monsters of life's waste had fled from thee like deer.

XXVIII

"The herded wolves, bold only to pursue;
The obscene ravens, clamorous o'er the dead;   245
The vultures to the conqueror's banner true,
Who feed where Desolation first has fed,
And whose wings rain contagion; how they fled,
When like Apollo, from his golden bow,
The Pythian of the age one arrow sped   250
And smiled!—The spoilers tempt no second blow;
They fawn on the proud feet that spurn them lying low.

XXIX

"The sun comes forth, and many reptiles spawn;
He sets, and each ephemeral insect then
Is gathered into death without a dawn,   255
And the immortal stars awake again;
So is it in the world of living men:
A godlike mind soars forth, in its delight
Making earth bare and veiling heaven, and when
It sinks, the swarms that dimmed or shared its light   260
Leave to its kindred lamps the spirit's awful night."

XXX

Thus ceased she: and the mountain shepherds came,
Their garlands sere, their magic mantles rent;
The Pilgrim of Eternity, whose fame
Over his living head like Heaven is bent,   265
An early but enduring monument,
Came, veiling all the lightnings of his song
In sorrow; from her wilds Ierne sent
The sweetest lyrist of her saddest wrong,
And love taught grief to fall like music from his tongue.   270

XXXI

Midst others of less note, came one frail Form,
A phantom among men, companionless
As the last cloud of an expiring storm
Whose thunder is its knell; he, as I guess,
Had gazed on Nature's naked loveliness,   275
Actæon-like, and now he fled astray
With feeble steps o'er the world's wilderness,
And his own thoughts, along that rugged way,
Pursued, like raging hounds, their father and their prey.

XXXII

A pardlike Spirit beautiful and swift—   280
A Love in desolation masked;—a Power
Girt round with weakness;—it can scarce uplift
The weight of the superincumbent hour;
It is a dying lamp, a falling shower,
A breaking billow;—even whilst we speak   285
Is it not broken? On the withering flower
The killing sun smiles brightly; on a cheek
The life can burn in blood, even while the heart may break.

XXXIII

His head was bound with pansies overblown,
And faded violets, white, and pied, and blue;   290
And a light spear topped with a cypress cone,
Round whose crude shaft dark ivy tresses grew
Yet dripping with the forest's noonday dew,
Vibrated, as the ever-beating heart
Shook the weak hand that grasped it; of that crew   295
He came the last, neglected and apart;
A herd-abandoned deer struck by the hunter's dart.

XXXIV

All stood aloof, and at his partial moan
Smiled through their tears; well knew that gentle band
Who in another's fate now wept his own;   300
As, in the accents of an unknown land,
He sung new sorrow; sad Urania scanned
The Stranger's mien, and murmured: "Who art thou?"
He answered not, but with a sudden hand
Made bare his branded and ensanguined brow,   305
Which was like Cain's or Christ's—Oh! that it should be so!

XXXV

What softer voice is hushed over the dead?
Athwart what brow is that dark mantle thrown?
What form leans sadly o'er the white death-bed,
In mockery of monumental stone,   310
The heavy heart heaving without a moan?
If it be He, who, gentlest of the wise,
Taught, soothed, loved, honored the departed one,
Let me not vex with inharmonious sighs
The silence of that heart's accepted sacrifice.   315

XXXVI

Our Adonais has drunk poison—oh!
What deaf and viperous murderer could crown
Life's early cup with such a draught of woe?
The nameless worm would now itself disown:
It felt; yet could escape the magic tone   320
Whose prelude held all envy, hate, and wrong,
But what was howling in one breast alone,
Silent with expectation of the song,
Whose master's hand is cold, whose silver lyre unstrung.

XXXVII

Live thou, whose infamy is not thy fame!   325
Live! fear no heavier chastisement from me,
Thou noteless blot on a remembered name!
But be thyself, and know thyself to be!
And ever at thy season be thou free
To spill the venom when thy fangs o'erflow: 330
Remorse and Self-contempt shall cling to thee;
Hot Shame shall burn upon thy secret brow,
And like a beaten hound, tremble thou shalt—as now.

XXXVIII

Nor let us weep that our delight is fled
Far from these carrion kites that scream below;
He wakes or sleeps with the enduring dead;   335
Thou canst not soar where he is sitting now.—

Dust to the dust! but the pure spirit shall flow
Back to the burning fountain whence it came,
A portion of the Eternal, which must glow   340
Through time and change, unquenchably the same,
Whilst thy cold embers choke the sordid hearth of shame.

XXXIX

Peace, peace! he is not dead, he doth not sleep—
He hath awakened from the dream of life—
'Tis we who, lost in stormy visions, keep   345
With phantoms an unprofitable strife,
And in mad trance strike with our spirit's knife
Invulnerable nothings.—*We* decay
Like corpses in a charnel; fear and grief
Convulse us and consume us day by day,   350
And cold hopes swarm like worms within our living clay.

XL

He has outsoared the shadow of our night;
Envy and calumny and hate and pain,
And that unrest which men miscall delight,
Can touch him not and torture not again;   355
From the contagion of the world's slow stain
He is secure, and now can never mourn
A heart grown cold, a head grown gray in vain;
Nor, when the spirit's self has ceased to burn,
With sparkless ashes load an unlamented urn.   360

XLI

He lives, he wakes—'tis Death is dead, not he;
Mourn not for Adonais.—Thou young Dawn
Turn all thy dew to splendor, for from thee
The spirit thou lamentest is not gone;
Ye caverns and ye forests, cease to moan!   365
Cease ye faint flowers and fountains, and thou Air
Which like a mourning veil thy scarf hadst thrown
O'er the abandoned Earth, now leave it bare
Even to the joyous stars which smile on its despair!

XLII

He is made one with Nature: there is heard   370
His voice in all her music, from the moan
Of thunder, to the song of night's sweet bird;
He is a presence to be felt and known
In darkness and in light, from herb and stone,
Spreading itself where'er that Power may move   375
Which has withdrawn his being to its own:
Which wields the world with never wearied love,
Sustains it from beneath and kindles it above.

XLIII

He is a portion of the loveliness
Which once he made more lovely: he doth bear   380
His part, while the one Spirit's plastic stress
Sweeps through the dull dense world, compelling there
All new successions to the forms they wear;
Torturing th' unwilling dross that checks its flight
To its own likeness, as each mass may bear;   385
And bursting in its beauty and its might
From trees and beasts and men into the Heaven's light.

XLIV

The splendors of the firmament of time
May be eclipsed, but are extinguished not;
Like stars to their appointed height they climb   390
And death is a low mist which cannot blot
The brightness it may veil. When lofty thought
Lifts a young heart above its mortal lair,
And love and life contend in it, for what
Shall be its earthly doom, the dead live there   395
And move like winds of light on dark and stormy air.

XLV

The inheritors of unfulfilled renown
Rose from their thrones, built beyond mortal thought,
Far in the Unapparent. Chatterton
Rose pale, his solemn agony had not   400
Yet faded from him; Sidney, as he fought
And as he fell and as he lived and loved
Sublimely mild, a Spirit without spot,
Arose; and Lucan, by his death approved:
Oblivion as they rose shrank like a thing reproved.   405

XLVI

And many more, whose names on Earth are dark
But whose transmitted effluence cannot die
So long as fire outlives the parent spark,
Rose, robed in dazzling immortality.
"Thou art become as one of us," they cry,   410
"It was for thee yon kingless sphere has long
Swung blind in unascended majesty,
Silent alone amid an Heaven of Song.
Assume thy wingèd throne, thou Vesper of our throng!"

XLVII

Who mourns for Adonais? oh come forth   415
Fond wretch! and know thyself and him aright.
Clasp with thy panting soul the pendulous Earth;
As from a center, dart thy spirit's light
Beyond all worlds, until its spacious might
Satiate the void circumference: then shrink   420
Even to a point within our day and night;
And keep thy heart light lest it make thee sink
When hope has kindled hope, and lured thee to the brink.

XLVIII

Or go to Rome, which is the sepulchre,
O, not of him, but of our joy: 'tis naught   425
That ages, empires, and religions there
Lie buried in the ravage they have wrought;
For such as he can lend,—they borrow not
Glory from those who made the world their prey;
And he is gathered to the kings of thought   430
Who waged contention with their time's decay,
And of the past are all that cannot pass away.

XLIX

Go thou to Rome,—at once the Paradise,
The grave, the city, and the wilderness;
And where its wrecks like shattered mountains rise,   435
And flowering weeds and fragrant copses dress

The bones of Desolation's nakedness
Pass, till the Spirit of the spot shall lead
Thy footsteps to a slope of green access
Where, like an infant's smile, over the dead,   440
A light of laughing flowers along the grass is spread.

L

And gray walls moulder round, on which dull Time
Feeds, like slow fire upon a hoary brand;
And one keen pyramid with wedge sublime,
Pavilioning the dust of him who planned   445
This refuge for his memory, doth stand
Like flames transformed to marble; and beneath,
A field is spread, on which a newer band
Have pitched in Heaven's smile their camp of death
Welcoming him we lose with scarce extinguished breath.   450

LI

Here pause: these graves are all too young as yet
To have outgrown the sorrow which consigned
Its charge to each; and if the seal is set,
Here, on one fountain of a mourning mind,
Break it not thou! too surely shalt thou find   455
Thine own well full, if thou returnest home,
Of tears and gall. From the world's bitter wind
Seek shelter in the shadow of the tomb.
What Adonais is, why fear we to become?

LII

The One remains, the many change and pass;   460
Heaven's light forever shines, Earth's shadows fly;
Life, like a dome of many-colored glass,
Stains the white radiance of Eternity,
Until Death tramples it to fragments.—Die,
If thou wouldst be with that which thou dost seek!   465
Follow where all is fled!—Rome's azure sky,
Flowers, ruins, statues, music, words, are weak
The glory they transfuse with fitting truth to speak.

LIII

Why linger, why turn back, why shrink, my Heart?
Thy hopes are gone before: from all things here   470
They have departed; thou shouldst now depart!
A light is past from the revolving year,
And man, and woman; and what still is dear
Attracts to crush, repels to make thee wither.
The soft sky smiles,—the low wind whispers near;   475
'Tis Adonais calls! oh, hasten thither,
No more let Life divide what Death can join together.

LIV

That Light whose smile kindles the Universe,
That Beauty in which all things work and move,
That Benediction which the eclipsing Curse
Of birth can quench not, that sustaining Love   480
Which, through the web of being blindly wove
By man and beast and earth and air and sea,
Burns bright or dim, as each are mirrors of
The fire for which all thirst, now beams on me,   485
Consuming the last clouds of cold mortality.

LV

The breath whose might I have invoked in song
Descends on me; my spirit's bark is driven,
Far from the shore, far from the trembling throng
Whose sails were never to the tempest given;
The massy earth and spheréd skies are riven!   490
I am borne darkly, fearfully, afar:
Whilst burning through the inmost veil of Heaven,
The soul of Adonais, like a star,
Beacons from the abode where the Eternal are.

June, 1821   1821

FROM HELLAS

LIFE MAY CHANGE, BUT IT MAY FLY NOT

Life may change, but it may fly not;
Hope may vanish, but can die not;
Truth be veiled, but still it burneth;
Love repulsed,—but it returneth!

Yet were life a charnel where   5
Hope lay coffined with Despair;
Yet were truth a sacred lie,
Love were lust—

                    If Liberty
Lent not life its soul of light,
Hope its iris of delight,   10
Truth its prophet's robe to wear,
Love its power to give and bear.

WORLDS ON WORLDS ARE ROLLING EVER

Worlds on worlds are rolling ever
From creation to decay,
Like the bubbles on a river
Sparkling, bursting, borne away.
But they are still immortal   5
Who, through birth's orient portal
And death's dark chasm hurrying to and
fro,
Clothe their unceasing flight
In the brief dust and light
Gathered around their chariots as they
go;   10
New shapes they still may weave,
New gods, new laws receive,
Bright or dim are they as the robes they
last
On Death's bare ribs had cast.

A power from the unknown God,   15
A Promethean conqueror, came;
Like a triumphal path he trod
The thorns of death and shame.

A mortal shape to him
Was like the vapor dim   20
Which the orient planet animates with
light;
Hell, Sin, and Slavery came,
Like bloodhounds mild and tame,
Nor preyed, until their lord had taken
flight;
The moon of Mahomet   25
Arose, and it shall set:
While blazoned as on Heaven's immortal
noon
The cross leads generations on.

Swift as the radiant shapes of sleep
From one whose dreams are Paradise,   30
Fly, when the fond wretch wakes to
weep,
And Day peers forth with her blank
eyes;
So fleet, so faint, so fair,
The Powers of earth and air
Fled from the folding-star of Bethlehem: 35
Apollo, Pan, and Love,
And even Olympian Jove
Grew weak, for killing Truth had glared
on them;
Our hills and seas and streams,
Dispeopled of their dreams,   40
Their waters turned to blood, their dew to
tears,
Wailed for the golden years.

DARKNESS HAS DAWNED IN THE EAST

Darkness has dawned in the east
On the noon of time:
The death-birds descend to their feast
From the hungry clime.
Let Freedom and Peace flee far   5
To a sunnier strand,
And follow Love's folding-star
To the Evening land!

The young moon has fed
    Her exhausted horn   10
With the sunset's fire:
    The weak day is dead,
    But the night is not born;
And, like loveliness panting with wild desire
While it trembles with fear and delight,   15
Hesperus flies from awakening night,
And pants in its beauty and speed with light
Fast-flashing, soft, and bright.
Thou beacon of love! thou lamp of the free!
    Guide us far, far away,   20
To climes where now veiled by the ardor of day
    Thou art hidden
From waves on which weary Noon
Faints in her summer swoon,
Between kingless continents sinless as Eden,   25
Around mountains and islands inviolably
    Pranked on the sapphire sea.

Through the sunset of hope,
Like the shapes of a dream,
What Paradise islands of glory gleam!   30
    Beneath Heaven's cope,
Their shadows more clear float by—
The sound of their oceans, the light of their sky,
The music and fragrance their solitudes breathe
Burst, like morning on dream, or like Heaven on death,   35
    Through the walls of our prison;
    And Greece, which was dead, is arisen!

THE WORLD'S GREAT AGE BEGINS ANEW

The world's great age begins anew,
    The golden years return,
The earth doth like a snake renew
    Her winter weeds outworn:
Heaven smiles, and faiths and empires gleam,   5
Like wrecks of a dissolving dream.

A brighter Hellas rears its mountains
    From waves serener far;
A new Peneus rolls his fountains
    Against the morning star.   10
Where fairer Tempes bloom, there sleep
Young Cyclads on a sunnier deep.

A loftier Argo cleaves the main,
    Fraught with a later prize;
Another Orpheus sings again,   15
    And loves, and weeps, and dies.
A new Ulysses leaves once more
Calypso for his native shore.

Oh, write no more the tale of Troy,
    If earth Death's scroll must be!   20
Nor mix with Laian rage the joy
    Which dawns upon the free:
Although a subtler Sphinx renew
Riddles of death Thebes never knew.

Another Athens shall arise,   25
    And to remoter time
Bequeath, like sunset to the skies,
    The splendor of its prime;
And leave, if nought so bright may live,
All earth can take or Heaven can give.   30

Saturn and Love their long repose
    Shall burst, more bright and good
Than all who fell, than One who rose,
    Than many unsubdued:
Not gold, not blood, their altar dowers,   35
But votive tears and symbol flowers.

Oh, cease! must hate and death return?
    Cease! must men kill and die?
Cease! drain not to its dregs the urn
    Of bitter prophecy.   40
The world is weary of the past,
Oh, might it die or rest at last!
1821

March, 1822

LINES

I

When the lamp is shattered
The light in the dust lies dead—
When the cloud is scattered
The rainbow's glory is shed.
When the lute is broken,   5
Sweet tones are remembered not;
When the lips have spoken,
Loved accents are soon forgot.

II

As music and splendor
Survive not the lamp and the lute,   10
    The heart's echoes render
No song when the spirit is mute,—
    No song but sad dirges,
Like the wind through a ruined cell,
    Or the mournful surges   15
That ring the dead seaman's knell.

III

When hearts have once mingled
Love first leaves the well-built nest,—
    The weak one is singled
To endure what it once possessed.   20
    O, Love! who bewailest
The frailty of all things here,
    Why choose you the frailest
For your cradle, your home and your bier?

IV

Its passions will rock thee   25
As the storms rock the ravens on high:
    Bright reason will mock thee,
Like the sun from a wintry sky.
    From thy nest every rafter
Will rot, and thine eagle home   30
    Leave thee naked to laughter,
When leaves fall and cold winds come.
1822   1824

WITH A GUITAR: TO JANE

Ariel to Miranda:—Take
This slave of Music, for the sake
Of him who is the slave of thee,
And teach it all the harmony
In which thou canst, and only thou,   5
Make the delighted spirit glow,
Till joy denies itself again,
And, too intense, is turned to pain;
For by permission and command
Of thine own Prince Ferdinand,   10
Poor Ariel sends this silent token
Of more than ever can be spoken;
Your guardian spirit, Ariel, who,
From life to life, must still pursue
Your happiness,—for thus alone   15
Can Ariel ever find his own.
From Prospero's enchanted cell,
As the mighty verses tell,
To the throne of Naples, he
Lit you o'er the trackless sea,   20
Flitting on, your prow before,
Like a living meteor.
When you die, the silent Moon,
In her interlunar swoon,
Is not sadder in her cell   25
Than deserted Ariel.
When you live again on earth,
Like an unseen star of birth,
Ariel guides you o'er the sea
Of life from your nativity.   30
Many changes have been run
Since Ferdinand and you begun
Your course of love. and Ariel still

Has tracked your steps, and served your
    will;
Now, in humbler, happier lot,   35
This is all remembered not;
And now, alas! the poor sprite is
Imprisoned, for some fault of his,
In a body like a grave.
From you he only dares to crave,   40
For his service and his sorrow,
A smile today, a song tomorrow.

The artist who this idol wrought
To echo all harmonious thought,
Felled a tree, while on the steep   45
The woods were in their winter sleep,
Rocked in that repose divine
On the wind-swept Apennine;
And dreaming, some of autumn past,
And some of spring approaching fast,   50
And some of April buds and showers,
And some of songs in July bowers,
And all of love; and so this tree—
Oh, that such our death may be!—
Died in sleep, and felt no pain,   55
To live in happier form again:
From which, beneath Heaven's fairest star,
The artist wrought this loved guitar,
And taught it justly to reply,
To all who question skilfully,   60
In language gentle as thine own;
Whispering in enamored tone
Sweet oracles of woods and dells,
And summer winds in sylvan cells;
For it had learned all harmonies   65
Of the plains and of the skies,
Of the forests and the mountains,
And the many voicèd fountains;
The clearest echoes of the hills,
The softest notes of falling rills,   70
The melodies of birds and bees,
The murmuring of summer seas,
And pattering rain, and breathing dew,
And airs of evening; and it knew
That seldom-heard mysterious sound,   75
Which, driven on its diurnal round,
As it floats through boundless day,
Our world enkindles on its way.—
All this it knows but will not tell
To those who cannot question well   80
The Spirit that inhabits it;
It talks according to the wit
Of its companions; and no more
Is heard than has been felt before,
By those who tempt it to betray   85
These secrets of an elder day:
But, sweetly as its answers will
Flatter hands of perfect skill,
It keeps its highest, holiest tone
For our belovèd Jane alone.   90
1822   Oct. 20, 1832

A DIRGE

Rough wind, that moanest loud
  Grief too sad for song;
Wild wind, when sullen cloud
  Knells all the night long;
Sad storm, whose tears are vain,
Bare woods, whose branches strain,
Deep caves and dreary main,—
  Wail, for the world's wrong!

1822

THE TRIUMPH OF LIFE

Swift as a spirit hastening to his task
Of glory and of good, the Sun sprang forth
Rejoicing in his splendor, and the mask

Of darkness fell from the awakened
  Earth—
The smokeless altars of the mountain
  snows   5
Flamed above crimson clouds, and at the
  birth

Of light, the Ocean's orison arose,
To which the birds tempered their matin
  lay.
All flowers in field or forest which unclose

Their trembling eyelids to the kiss of
  day,   10
Swinging their censers in the element,
With orient incense lit by the new ray

Burned slow and inconsumably, and sent
Their odorous sighs up to the smiling air;
And, in succession due, did continent, 15

Isle, ocean, and all things that in them
  wear
The form and character of mortal mold,
Rise as the Sun their father rose, to bear

Their portion of the toil, which he of old
Took as his own, and then imposed on
  them: 20
But I, whom thoughts which must remain
  untold

Had kept as wakeful as the stars that gem
The cone of night, now they were laid
  asleep
Stretched my faint limbs beneath the hoary
  stem

Which an old chestnut flung athwart the
  steep   25
Of a green Apennine: before me fled
The night; behind me rose the day; the
  deep

Was at my feet, and Heaven above my
  head,—
When a strange trance over my fancy grew
Which was not slumber, for the shade it
  spread   30

Was so transparent, that the scene came
  through
As clear as when a veil of light is drawn
O'er evening hills they glimmer; and I
  knew

That I had felt the freshness of that dawn
Bathe in the same cold dew my brow and
  hair,   35
And sate as thus upon that slope of lawn

Under the self-same bough, and heard as
  there
The birds, the fountains and the ocean
  hold
Sweet talk in music through the enamored
  air,
And then a vision on my brain was rolled. 40

As in that trance of wondrous thought I
  lay,
This was the tenor of my waking dream:—
Methought I sate beside a public way

Thick strewn with summer dust, and a
  great stream
Of people there was hurrying to and fro, 45
Numerous as gnats upon the evening
  gleam,

All hastening onward, yet none seemed to
  know
Whither he went, or whence he came, or
  why
He made one of the multitude, and so

Was borne amid the crowd, as through the
  sky   50
One of the million leaves of summer's bier;
Old age and youth, manhood and infancy,

Mixed in one mighty torrent did appear,
Some flying from the thing they feared,
  and some
Seeking the object of another's fear; 55

And others, as with steps towards the tomb,
Pored on the trodden worms that crawled
  beneath,
And others mournfully within the gloom

Of their own shadow walked, and called it
  death;
And some fled from it as it were a ghost, 60
Half fainting in the affliction of vain
  breath:

But more, with motions which each other
    crossed,
Pursued or shunned the shadows the clouds
    threw,
Or birds within the noonday ether lost,

Upon that path where flowers never
    grew,—   65
And, weary with vain toil and faint for
    thirst,
Heard not the fountains, whose melodious
    dew

Out of their mossy cells forever burst;
Nor felt the breeze which from the forest
    told
Of grassy paths and wood-lawns inter-
    spersed   70

With overarching elms and caverns cold,
And violet banks where sweet dreams
    brood, but they
Pursued their serious folly as of old.

And as I gazed, methought that in the way
The throng grew wilder, as the woods of
    June   75
When the south wind shakes the extin-
    guished day,

And a cold glare, intenser than the noon,
But icy cold, obscured with blinding light
The sun, as he the stars. Like the young
    moon—

When on the sunlit limits of the night   80
Her white shell trembles amid crimson air,
And whilst the sleeping tempest gathers
    might—

Doth, as the herald of its coming, bear
The ghost of its dead mother, whose dim
    form
Bends in dark ether from her infant's
    chair,—   85

So came a chariot on the silent storm
Of its own rushing splendor, and a Shape
So sate within, as one whom years deform,

Beneath a dusky hood and double cape,
Crouching within the shadow of a tomb; 90
And o'er what seemed the head a cloud-like
    crape

Was bent, a dun and faint ethereal gloom
Tempering the light. Upon the chariot-
    beam
A Janus-visaged Shadow did assume

The guidance of that wonder-wingèd
    team;   95
The shapes which drew it in thick light-
    enings
Were lost:—I heard alone on the air's soft
    stream

The music of their ever-moving wings.
All the four faces of that Charioteer
Had their eyes banded; little profit
    brings   100

Speed in the van and blindness in the rear,
Nor then avail the beams that quench the
    sun,—
Or that with banded eyes could pierce the
    sphere

Of all that is, has been or will be done;
So ill was the car guided—but it passed 105
With solemn speed majestically on.

The crowd gave way, and I arose aghast,
Or seemed to rise, so mighty was the trance,
And saw, like clouds upon the thunder-
    blast,

The million with fierce song and maniac
    dance   110
Raging around—such seemed the jubilee
As when to greet some conqueror's advance

Imperial Rome poured forth her living sea
From senate-house, and forum, and theater,
When   upon the free 15
their odorous sighs up to the smiling air;

Had bound a yoke, which soon they
    stooped to bear.
Nor wanted here the just similitude
Of a triumphal pageant, for where'er

The chariot rolled, a captive multitude
Was driven;—all those who had grown old
    in power   120
Or misery,—all who had their age subdued

By action or by suffering, and whose hour
Was drained to its last sand in weal or
    woe,
So that the trunk survived both fruit and
    flower;—

All those whose fame or infamy must
    grow   125
Till the great winter lay the form and
    name
Of this green earth with them for ever
    low;—

All but the sacred few who could not tame
Their spirits to the conquerors—but as
    soon
As they had touched the world with living
    flame,   130

Fled back like eagles to their native noon,
Or those who put aside the diadem
Of earthly thrones or gems . . .

Were there, of Athens or Jerusalem,
Were neither mid the mighty captives
    seen,   135
Nor mid the ribald crowd that followed
    them,

Nor those who went before fierce and
    obscene.
The wild dance maddens in the van, and
    those
Who lead it—fleet as shadows on the green,

Outspeed the chariot, and without re-
    pose   140
Mix with each other in tempestuous meas-
    ure
To savage music, wilder as it grows,

They, tortured by their agonizing pleasure,
Convulsed and on the rapid whirlwinds
    spun
Of that fierce Spirit, which unholy lei-
    sure   145

Was soothed by mischief since the world
    begun,
Throw back their heads and loose their
    streaming hair;
And in their dance round her who dims
    the sun,

Maidens and youths fling their wild arms
    in air
As their feet twinkle; they recede, and
    now   150
Bending within each other's atmosphere,

Kindle invisibly—and as they glow,
Like moths by light attracted and repelled,
Oft to their bright destruction come and
    go,

Till like two clouds into one vale im-
    pelled,   155
That shake the mountains when their light-
    nings mingle
And die in rain—the fiery band which held

Their natures, snaps—while the shock still
    may tingle;
One falls and then another in the path
Senseless—nor is the desolation single,   160

Yet ere I can say *where*—the chariot hath
Passed over them—nor other trace I find
But as of foam after the ocean's wrath

Is spent upon the desert shore;—behind,
Old men and women foully disarrayed,   165
Shake their gray hairs in the insulting
    wind,

And follow in the dance, with limbs de-
    cayed,
Seeking to reach the light which leaves
    them still
Farther behind and deeper in the shade.

But not the less with impotence of will   170
They wheel, though ghastly shadows inter-
    pose
Round them and round each other, and
    fulfill

Their work, and in the dust from whence
    they rose
Sink, and corruption veils them as they lie,
And past in these performs what   in
    those.   175

Struck to the heart by this sad pageantry,
Half to myself I said—"And what is this?"
Whose shape is that within the car? And
    why—"

I would have added—"is all here amiss?—"
But a voice answered—"Life!—I turned,
    and knew   180
(O Heaven, have mercy on such wretched-
    ness!)

That what I thought was an old root which
    grew
To strange distortion out of the hill side,
Was indeed one of those deluded crew,

And that the grass, which methought hung
    so wide   185
And white, was but his thin discolored
    hair,
And that the holes he vainly sought to
    hide,

Were or had been eyes:—"If thou canst,
    forbear
To join the dance, which I had well for-
    borne!"
Said the grim Feature (of my thought
    aware),   190

"I will unfold that which to this deep scorn
Led me and my companions, and relate
The progress of the pageant since the
    morn;

"If thirst of knowledge shall not then
    abate,
Follow it thou even to the night, but I 195
Am weary."—Then like one who with the
    weight

Of his own words is staggered, wearily
He paused; and ere he could resume, I
    cried:
"First, who art thou?"—"Before thy mem-
    ory,

"I feared, loved, hated, suffered, did and
    died, 200
And if the spark with which Heaven lit my
    spirit
Had been with purer nutriment supplied,

"Corruption would not now thus much
    inherit
Of what was once Rousseau,—nor this dis-
    guise
Stain that which ought to have disdained
    to wear it; 205

"If I have been extinguished, yet there rise
A thousand beacons from the spark I
    bore"—
"And who are those chained to the car?"—
    "The wise,

"The great, the unforgotten,—they who
    wore
Mitres and helms and crowns, or wreaths
    of light, 210
Signs of thought's empire over thought—
    their lore

"Taught them not this, to know them-
    selves; their might
Could not repress the mystery within,
And for the morn of truth they feigned,
    deep night

"Caught them ere evening."—"Who is he
    with chin 215
Upon his breast, and hands crossed on his
    chain?"—
"The child of a fierce hour; he sought to
    win

"The world, and lost all that it did contain
Of greatness, in its hope destroyed; and
    more
Of fame and peace than virtue's self can
    gain 220

"Without the opportunity which bore
Him on its eagle pinions to the peak
From which a thousand climbers have be-
    fore

"Fallen, as Napoleon fell."—I felt my
    cheek
Alter, to see the shadow pass away, 225
Whose grasp had left the giant world so
    weak

That every pigmy kicked it as it lay;
And much I grieved to think how power
    and will
In opposition rule our mortal day,

And why God made irreconcilable 230
Good and the means of good; and for
    despair
I half disdained mine eyes' desire to fill

With the spent vision of the times that were
And scarce have ceased to be.—"Dost thou
    behold,"
Said my guide, "those spoilers spoiled,
    Voltaire, 235

"Frederick, and Paul, Catherine, and Leo-
    pold,
And hoary anarchs, demagogues, and sage—
    names which the world thinks always
    old,

"For in the battle Life and they did wage,
She remained conqueror, I was over-
    come 240
By my own heart alone, which neither age,

"Nor tears, nor infamy, nor now the tomb
Could temper to its object."—"Let them
    pass,"
I cried, "the world and its mysterious doom

"Is not so much more glorious than it
    was, 245
That I desire to worship those who drew
New figures on its false and fragile glass

"As the old faded."—"Figures ever new
Rise on the bubble, paint them as you may;
We have but thrown, as those before us
    threw, 250

"Our shadows on it as it passed away.
But mark how chained to the triumphal
    chair
The mighty phantoms of an elder day;

"All that is mortal of great Plato there
Expiates the joy and woe his master knew
    not; 255
The star that ruled his doom was far too
    fair.

"And life, where long that flower of
Heaven grew not,
Conquered that heart by love, which gold,
or pain,
Or age, or sloth, or slavery could subdue
not.

"And near him walk the   twain, 260
The tutor and his pupil, whom Dominion
Followed as tame as vulture in a chain.

"The world was darkened beneath either
pinion
Of him whom from the flock of conquerors
Fame singled out for her thunder-bearing
minion;   265

"The other long outlived both woes and
wars,
Throned in the thoughts of men, and still
had kept
The jealous key of Truth's eternal doors,

"If Bacon's eagle spirit had not lept
Like lightning out of darkness—he com-
pelled   270
The Proteus shape of Nature, as it slept

"To wake, and lead him to the caves that
held
The treasure of the secrets of its reign.
See the great bards of elder time, who
quelled

"The passions which they sung, as by their
strain   275
May well be known: their living melody
Tempers its own contagion to the vein

"Of those who are infected with it—I
Have suffered what I wrote, or viler pain!
And so my words have seeds of misery— 280

"Even as the deeds of others, not as theirs."
And then he pointed to a company,

'Midst whom I quickly recognized the heirs
Of Caesar's crime, from him to Constantine;
The anarch chiefs, whose force and murderous snares   285

Had founded many a sceptre-bearing line,
And spread the plague of gold and blood
abroad:
And Gregory and John, and men divine,

Who rose like shadows between man and
God;
Till that eclipse, still hanging over
heaven,   290
Was worshipped by the world o'er which
they strode,

For the true sun it quenched—"Their
power was given
But to destroy," replied the leader:—"I
Am one of those who have created, even

"If it be but a world of agony."—   295
"Whence camest thou? and whither goest
thou?
How did thy course begin?" I said, "and
why?

"Mine eyes are sick of this perpetual flow
Of people, and my heart sick of one sad
thought—
Speak!"—"Whence I am, I partly seem to
know,   300

"And how and by what paths I have been
brought
To this dread pass, methinks even thou
mayst guess;—
Why this should be my mind can compass
not;

"Whither the conqueror hurries me, still
less;—
But follow thou, and from spectator
turn   305
Actor or victim in this wretchedness,

"And what thou wouldst be taught I then
may learn
From thee. Now listen:—In the April
prime,
When all the forest-tips began to burn

"With kindling green, touched by the azure
clime   310
Of the young season, I was laid asleep
Under a mountain, which from unknown
time

"Had yawned into a cavern, high and deep;
And from it came a gentle rivulet,
Whose water, like clear air, in its calm
sweep   315

"Bent the soft grass, and kept for ever wet
The stems of the sweet flowers, and filled
the grove
With sounds, which whoso hears must
needs forget

"All pleasure and all pain, all hate and
love,
Which they had known before that hour
of rest;   320
A sleeping mother then would dream not of

"Her only child who died upon the breast
At eventide—a king would mourn no more
The crown of which his brows were dis-
possessed

"When the sun lingered o'er his ocean
  floor   325
To gild his rival's new prosperity.
Thou wouldst forget thus vainly to deplore

"Ills, which if ills can find no cure from
  thee,
The thought of which no other sleep will
  quell,
Nor other music blot from memory,   330

"So sweet and deep is the oblivious spell;
And whether life had been before that
  sleep
The Heaven which I imagine, or a Hell

"Like this harsh world in which I wake to
  weep,
I know not. I arose, and for a space   335
The scene of woods and waters seemed to
  keep,

"Though it was now broad day, a gentle
  trace
Of light diviner than the common sun
Sheds on the common earth, and all the
  place

"Was filled with magic sounds woven into
  one   340
Oblivious melody, confusing sense
Amid the gliding waves and shadows dun;

"And, as I looked, the bright omnipresence
Of morning through the orient cavern
  flowed,
And the sun's image radiantly intense.   345

"Burned on the waters of the well that
  glowed
Like gold, and threaded all the forest's
  maze
With winding paths of emerald fire; there
  stood

"Amid the sun, as he amid the blaze
Of his own glory, on the vibrating   350
Floor of the fountain, paved with flashing
  rays,

"A Shape all light, which with one hand
  did fling
Dew on the earth, as if she were the dawn,
And the invisible rain did ever sing

"A silver music on the mossy lawn;   355
And still before me on the dusky grass,
Iris her many-colored scarf had drawn:

"In her right hand she bore a crystal glass,
Mantling with bright Nepenthe; the fierce
  splendor
Fell from her as she moved under the
  mass   360

"Of the deep cavern, and with palms so
  tender,
Their tread broke not the mirror of its
  billow,
Glided along the river, and did bend her

"Head under the dark boughs, till like a
  willow
Her fair hair swept the bosom of the
  stream   365
That whispered with delight to be its pillow.

"As one enamored is upborne in dream
O'er lily-paven lakes, mid silver mist,
To wondrous music, so this shape might
  seem

"Partly to tread the waves with feet which
  kissed   370
The dancing foam; partly to glide along
The air which roughened the moist amethyst,

"Or the faint morning beams that fell
  among
The trees or the soft shadows of the trees;
And her feet, ever to the ceaseless song   375

"Of leaves, and winds, and waves, and
  birds, and bees,
And falling drops, moved in a measure
  new
Yet sweet, as on the summer evening
  breeze,

"Up from the lake a shape of golden dew
Between two rocks, athwart the rising
  moon,   380
Dances i' the wind, where never eagle flew;

"And still her feet, no less than the sweet
  tune
To which they moved, seemed as they
  moved to blot
The thoughts of him who gazed on them;
  and soon

"All that was, seemed as if it had been
  not;   385
And all the gazer's mind was strewn beneath
Her feet like embers; and she, thought by
  thought,

"Trampled its sparks into the dust of
death;
As day upon the threshold of the east
Treads out the lamps of night, until the
breath   390

"Of darkness re-illumine even the least
Of heaven's living eyes—like day she came,
Making the night a dream; and ere she
ceased

"To move, as one between desire and
shame
Suspended, I said—If, as it doth seem, 395
Thou comest from the realm without a
name

"Into this valley of perpetual dream,
Show whence I came, and where I am, and
why—
Pass not away upon the passing stream.

"Arise and quench thy thirst, was her
reply.   400
And as a shut lily stricken by the wand
Of dewy morning's vital alchemy,

"I rose; and, bending at her sweet com-
mand,
Touched with faint lips the cup she raised,
And suddenly my brain became as sand 405

"Where the first wave had more than half
erased
The track of deer on desert Labrador;
Whilst the wolf, from which they fled
amazed,

"Leaves his stamp visibly upon the shore,
Until the second bursts;—so on my
sight   410
Burst a new vision, never seen before,

"And the fair shape waned in the coming
light,
As veil by veil the silent splendor drops
From Lucifer, amid the chrysolite

"Of sunrise, ere it tinge the mountain-
tops;   415
And as the presence of that fairest planet,
Although unseen, is felt by one who hopes

"That his day's path may end as he began
it,
In that star's smile, whose light is like the
scent
Of a jonquil when evening breezes fan
it,   420

"Or the soft note in which his dear lament
The Brescian shepherd breathes, or the
caress
That turned his weary slumber to content;

"So knew I in that light's severe excess
The presence of that Shape which on the
stream   425
Moved, as I moved along the wilderness,

"More dimly than a day-appearing dream,
The ghost of a forgotten form of sleep;
A light of heaven, whose half-extinguished
beam

"Through the sick day in which we wake
to weep   430
Glimmers, for ever sought, for ever lost;
So did that shape its obscure tenor keep

"Beside my path, as silent as a ghost;
But the new Vision, and the cold bright
car,
With solemn speed and stunning music,
crossed   435

"The forest, and as if from some dread war
Triumphantly returning, the loud million
Fiercely extolled the fortune of her star.

"A moving arch of victory, the vermilion
And green and azure plumes of Iris had 440
Built high over her wind-wingèd pavilion,

"And underneath ethereal glory clad
The wilderness, and far before her flew
The tempest of the splendor, which for-
bade

"Shadow to fall from leaf and stone; the
crew   445
Seemed in that light, like atomies to dance
Within a sunbeam;—some upon the
new

"Embroidery of flowers, that did enhance
The grassy vesture of the desert, played,
Forgetful of the chariot's swift advance; 450

"Others stood gazing, till within the shade
Of the great mountain its light left them
dim;
Others outspeeded it; and others made

"Circles around it, like the clouds that
swim
Round the high moon in a bright sea of
air;   455
And more did follow, with exulting hymn,

"The chariot and the captives fettered
there:—
But all like bubbles on an eddying flood
Fell into the same track at last, and were

"Borne onward.—I among the multi-
tude   460
Was swept—me, sweetest flowers delayed
not long;
Me, not the shadow nor the solitude;

"Me, not that falling stream's Lethean
song;
Me, not the phantom of that early Form
Which moved upon its motion—but
among   465

'The thickest billows of that living storm
I plunged, and bared my bosom to the
clime
Of that cold light, whose airs too soon deform.

"Before the chariot had begun to climb
The opposing steep of that mysterious
dell,   470
Behold a wonder worthy of the rhyme

"Of him who from the lowest depths of
hell,
Through every paradise and through all
glory,
Love led serene, and who returned to tell

"The words of hate and awe; the wondrous
story   475
How all things are transfigured except
Love;
For deaf as is a sea, which wrath makes
hoary,

"The world can hear not the sweet notes
that move
The sphere whose light is melody to
lovers—
A wonder worthy of his rhyme.—The
grove   480

"Grew dense with shadows to its inmost
covers,
The earth was gray with phantoms, and
the air
Was peopled with dim forms, as when
there hovers

"A flock of vampire bats before the glare
Of the tropic sun, bringing, ere evening, 485
Strange night upon some Indian isle;—thus
were

"Phantoms diffused around; and some did
fling
Shadows of shadows, yet unlike themselves,
Behind them; some like eaglets on the wing

"Were lost in the white day; others like
elves   490
Danced in a thousand unimagined shapes
Upon the sunny streams and grassy shelves;

"And others sate chattering like restless
apes
On vulgar hands, . . .
Some made a cradle of the ermined capes 495

"Of kingly mantles; some across the tiar
Of pontiffs sate like vultures; others played
Under the crown which girt with empire

"A baby's or an idiot's brow, and made
Their nests in it. The old anatomies   500
Sate hatching their bare broods under the
shade

"Of demon wings, and laughed from their
dead eyes
To reassume the delegated power,
Arrayed in which those worms did mon-
archize,

"Who made this earth their charnel. Others
more   505
Humble, like falcons, sate upon the fist
Of common men, and round their heads
did soar;

"Or like small gnats and flies, as thick as
mist
On evening marshes, thronged about the
brow
Of lawyers, statesmen, priest and the-
orist;—   510

"And others, like discolored flakes of snow
On fairest bosoms and the sunniest hair,
Fell, and were melted by the youthful glow

"Which they extinguished; and, like tears,
they were
A veil to those from whose faint lids they
rained   515
In drops of sorrow. I became aware

"Of whence those forms proceeded which
thus stained
The track in which we moved. After brief
space,
From every form the beauty slowly waned;

"From every firmest limb and fairest face 520
The strength and freshness fell like dust,
    and left
The action and the shape without the grace

"Of life. The marble brow of youth was
    cleft
With care; and in those eyes where once
    hope shone,
Desire, like a lioness bereft   525

"Of her last cub, glared ere it died; each
    one
Of that great crowd sent forth incessantly
These shadows, numerous as the dead
    leaves blown

"In autumn evening from a poplar tree.
Each like himself and like each other
    were   530
At first; but some distorted seemed to be

"Obscure clouds, molded by the casual air;
And of this stuff the car's creative ray
Wrought all the busy phantoms that were
    there,

"As the sun shapes the clouds; thus on the
    way   535
Mask after mask fell from the countenance
And form of all; and long before the day

"Was old, the joy which waked like
    heaven's glance
The sleepers in the oblivious valley died;
And some grew weary of the ghastly
    dance,   540

"And fell, as I have fallen, by the way-
    side;—
Those soonest from whose forms most
    shadows passed,
And least of strength and beauty did
    abide.

"Then, what is life? I cried."—

1822   1824

A DEFENSE OF POETRY

According to one mode of regarding those two classes of mental action, which are called reason and imagination, the former may be considered as mind contemplating the relations borne by one thought to another, however produced, and the latter as mind acting upon those thoughts so as to color them with its own light, and composing from them, as from elements, other thoughts, each containing within itself the principle of its own integrity. The one is the τὸ ποιεῖν, or the principle of synthesis, and has for its object those forms which are common to universal nature and existence itself; the other is the τὸ λογίζειν, or principle of analysis, and its action regards the relations of things simply as relations; considering thoughts not in their integral unity, but as the algebraical representations which conduct to certain general results. Reason is the enumeration of quantities already known; imagination is the perception of the value of those quantities, both separately and as a whole. Reason respects the differences, and imagination the similitudes of things. Reason is to imagination as the instrument to the agent, as the body to the spirit, as the shadow to the substance.

Poetry, in a general sense, may be defined to be "the expression of the imagination"; and poetry is connate with the origin of man. Man is an instrument over which a series of external and internal impressions are driven, like the alternations of an ever-changing wind over an Æolian lyre, which move it by their motion to ever-changing melody. But there is a principle within the human being, and perhaps within all sentient beings, which acts otherwise than in a lyre, and produces not melody alone, but harmony, by an internal adjustment of the sounds or motions thus excited to the impressions which excite them. It is as if the lyre could accommodate its chords to the motions of that which strikes them, in a determined proportion of sound; even as the musician can accommodate his voice to the sound of the lyre. A child at play by itself will express its delight by its voice and motions; and every inflection of tone and every gesture will bear exact relation to a corresponding antitype in the pleasurable impressions which awakened it; it will be the reflected image of that impression; and as the lyre trembles and sounds after the wind has died away, so the child seeks, by prolonging in its voice and motions, the duration of the effect, to prolong also a consciousness of the cause. In relation to the objects which delight a child, these expressions are what poetry is to higher objects. The savage (for the savage is to ages what the child is to years) expresses the emotions produced in him by surrounding objects in a similar manner; and language and gesture, together with plastic or pictorial imitation, become the image of the combined effect of those objects and of his apprehension of them. Man in society, with all his passions and his pleasures, next becomes the object of the passions and pleasures of man; an additional class of emotions produces an augmented treasure of expressions; and language, gesture, and the imitative arts become at once the representation and the medium, the pencil and the picture, the chisel and the statue, the chord and the harmony. The social sympathies, or those laws from which, as from its elements, society results, begin to develop themselves from the moment that two human beings co-exist; the future is contained within the present as the plant within the seed; and equality, diversity, unity, contrast, mutual dependence, become the principles alone capable of affording the motives according to which the will of a social being is determined to action, inasmuch as he is social; and constitute pleasure in sensation, virtue in sentiment, beauty in art, truth in reasoning, and love in the intercourse of kind. Hence men, even in the infancy of society, observe a certain order in their words and actions, distinct from that of the objects and the impressions represented by them, all expression being subject to the laws of that from which it proceeds. But let us dismiss those more general considerations which might involve an inquiry into the principles of society itself, and restrict our view to the manner in which the imagination is expressed upon its forms.

In the youth of the world, men dance and sing and imitate natural objects, observing in these actions, as in all others, a certain rhythm or order. And, although all men observe a similar, they observe not the same order in the motions of the dance, in the melody of the song, in the combinations of language, in the series of their imitations of natural objects. For there is a certain order or rhythm belonging to each of these classes of mimetic representation, from which the hearer and the spectator receive an intenser and purer pleasure than from any other; the sense of an approximation to this order has been called taste by modern writers. Every man, in the in-

fancy of art, observes an order which approximates more or less closely to that from which this highest delight results; but the diversity is not sufficiently marked as that its gradations should be sensible, except in those instances where the predominance of this faculty of approximation to the beautiful (for so we may be permitted to name the relation between this highest pleasure and its cause) is very great. Those in whom it exists in excess are poets, in the most universal sense of the word; and the pleasure resulting from the manner in which they express the influence of society or nature upon their own minds, communicates itself to others, and gathers a sort of reduplication from that community. Their language is vitally metaphorical; that is, it marks the before unapprehended relations of things and perpetuates their apprehension, until the words, which represent them, become, through time, signs for portions or classes of thought instead of pictures of integral thoughts; and then, if no new poets should arise to create afresh the associations which have been thus disorganized, language will be dead to all the nobler purposes of human intercourse. These similitudes or relations are finely said by Lord Bacon to be "the same footsteps of nature impressed upon the various subjects of the world"—and he considers the faculty which perceives them as the storehouse of axioms common to all knowledge. In the infancy of society every author is necessarily a poet, because language itself is poetry; and to be a poet is to apprehend the true and the beautiful, in a word, the good which exists in the relation subsisting, first between existence and perception, and secondly between perception and expression. Every original language near to its source is in itself the chaos of a cyclic poem; the copiousness of lexicography and the distinctions of grammar are the works of a later age, and are merely the catalogue and the form of the creations of poetry.

But poets, or those who imagine and express this indestructible order, are not only the authors of language and of music, of the dance, and architecture, and statuary, and painting: they are the institutors of laws, and the founders of civil society, and the inventors of the arts of life, and the teachers who draw into a certain propinquity with the beautiful and the true that partial apprehension of the agencies of the invisible world which is called religion. Hence all original religions are allegorical, or susceptible of allegory, and, like Janus, have a double face of false and true. Poets, according to the circumstances of the age and nation in which they appeared, were called, in the earlier epochs of the world, 5 legislators or prophets; a poet essentially comprises and unites both these characters. For he not only beholds intensely the present as it is, and discovers those laws according to which present things ought to be 10 ordered, but he beholds the future in the present, and his thoughts are the germs of the flower and the fruit of latest time. Not that I assert poets to be prophets in the gross sense of the word, or that they can 15 foretell the form as surely as they foreknow the spirit of events; such is the pretence of superstition, which would make poetry an attribute of prophecy, rather than prophecy an attribute of poetry. A 20 poet participates in the eternal, the infinite, and the one; as far as relates to his conceptions, time and place and number are not. The grammatical forms which express the moods of time, and the difference 25 of persons, and the distinction of place, are convertible with respect to the highest poetry without injuring it as poetry; and the choruses of Æschylus, and the *Book of Job,* and Dante's *Paradise,* would afford, 30 more than any other writings, examples of this fact, if the limits of this essay did not forbid citation. The creations of sculpture, painting, and music are illustrations still more decisive. 35

Language, color, form, and religious and civil habits of action, are all the instruments and materials of poetry; they may be called poetry by that figure of speech which considers the effect as a synonym of the 40 cause. But poetry in a more restricted sense expresses those arrangements of language, and especially metrical language, which are created by that imperial faculty whose throne is curtained within the in- 45 visible nature of man. And this springs from the nature itself of language, which is a more direct representation of the actions and passions of our internal being, and is susceptible of more various and delicate 50 combinations, than color, form, or motion, and is more plastic and obedient to the control of that faculty of which it is a creation. For language is arbitrarily produced by the imagination, and has relation to 55 thoughts alone; but all other materials, instruments, and conditions of art have relations among each other, which limit and interpose between conception and expression. The former is as a mirror which re- 60

flects, the latter as a cloud which enfeebles, the light of which both are mediums of communication. Hence the fame of sculptors, painters, and musicians, although the intrinsic powers of the great masters of 5 these arts may yield in no degree to that of those who have employed language as the hieroglyphic of their thoughts, has never equalled that of poets in the restricted sense of the term; as two performers of 10 equal skill will produce unequal effects from a guitar and a harp. The fame of legislators and founders of religions, so long as their institutions last, alone seems to exceed that of poets in the restricted sense; 15 but it can scarcely be a question, whether, if we deduct the celebrity which their flattery of the gross opinions of the vulgar usually conciliates, together with that which belonged to them in their higher character 20 of poets, any excess will remain.

We have thus circumscribed the word *poetry* within the limits of that art which is the most familiar and the most perfect expression of the faculty itself. It is neces- 25 sary, however, to make the circle still narrower, and to determine the distinction between measured and unmeasured language; for the popular division into prose and verse is inadmissible in accurate philos- 30 ophy.

Sounds as well as thoughts have relation both between each other and towards that which they represent, and a perception of the order of those relations has always been 35 found connected with the perception of the order of the relations of thoughts. Hence the language of poets has ever affected a certain uniform and harmonious recurrence of sound, without which it were 40 not poetry, and which is scarcely less indispensable to the communication of its influence than the words themselves without reference to that peculiar order. Hence the vanity of translation; it were as wise to 45 cast a violet into a crucible that you might discover the formal principle of its color and odor, as to seek to transfuse from one language into another the creations of a poet. The plant must spring again from 50 its seed, or it will bear no flower—and this is the burthen of the curse of Babel.

An observation of the regular mode of the recurrence of harmony in the language of poetical minds, together with its relation 55 to music, produced metre, or a certain system of traditional forms of harmony and language. Yet it is by no means essential that a poet should accommodate his language to this traditional form, so that the 60 harmony, which is its spirit, be observed. The practice is indeed convenient and popular, and to be preferred especially in such composition as includes much action; but every great poet must inevitably inno- 5 vate upon the example of his predecessors in the exact structure of his peculiar versification. The distinction between poets and prose writers is a vulgar error. The distinction between philosophers and poets has 10 been anticipated. Plato was essentially a poet—-the truth and splendor of his imagery, and the melody of his language, are the most intense that it is possible to conceive. He rejected the measure of the epic, dra- 15 matic, and 'lyrical forms, because he sought to kindle a harmony in thoughts divested of shape and action, and he forebore to invent any regular plan of rhythm which would include, under determinate forms, 20 the varied pauses of his style. Cicero sought to imitate the cadence of his periods, but with little success. Lord Bacon was a poet. His language has a sweet and majestic rhythm which satisfies the sense, 25 no less than the almost superhuman wisdom of his philosophy satisfies the intellect; it is a strain which distends and then bursts the circumference of the reader's mind, and pours itself forth together with it into the 30 universal element with which it has perpetual sympathy. All the authors of revolutions in opinion are not only necessarily poets as they are inventors, nor even as their words unveil the permanent analogy 35 of things by images which participate in the life of truth; but as their periods are harmonious and rhythmical, and contain in themselves the elements of verse, being the echo of the eternal music. Nor are those 40 supreme poets, who have employed traditional forms of rhythm on account of the form and action of their subjects, less capable of perceiving and teaching the truth of things, than those who have omitted that 45 form. Shakespeare, Dante, and Milton (to confine ourselves to modern writers) are philosophers of the very loftiest power.

A poem is the very image of life expressed in its eternal truth. There is this 50 difference between a story and a poem, that a story is a catalogue of detached facts, which have no other connection than time, place, circumstance, cause and effect; the other is the creation of actions according to 55 the unchangeable forms of human nature, as existing in the mind of the creator, which is itself the image of all other minds. The one is partial, and applies only to a definite period of time, and a certain com- 60

bination of events which can never again recur; the other is universal, and contains within itself the germ of a relation to whatever motives or actions have place in all possible varieties of human nature. Time, which destroys the beauty and the use of the story of particular facts, stripped of the poetry which should invest them, augments that of poetry, and for ever develops new and wonderful applications of the eternal truth which it contains. Hence epitomes have been called the moths of just history; they eat out the poetry of it. A story of particular facts is as a mirror which obscures and distorts that which should be beautiful; poetry is a mirror which makes beautiful that which is distorted.

The parts of a composition may be poetical, without the composition as a whole being a poem. A single sentence may be considered as a whole, though it may be found in the midst of a series of unassimilated portions; a single word even may be a spark of inextinguishable thought. And thus all the great historians, Herodotus, Plutarch, Livy, were poets; and although the plan of these writers, especially that of Livy, restrained them from developing this faculty in its highest degree, they made copious and ample amends for their subjection, by filling all the interstices of their subjects with living images.

Having determined what is poetry, and who are poets, let us proceed to estimate its effects upon society.

Poetry is ever accompanied with pleasure: all spirits on which it falls open themselves to receive the wisdom which is mingled with its delight. In the infancy of the world, neither poets themselves nor their auditors are fully aware of the excellence of poetry, for it acts in a divine and unapprehended manner, beyond and above consciousness; and it is reserved for future generations to contemplate and measure the mighty cause and effect in all the strength and splendor of their union. Even in modern times, no living poet ever arrived at the fulness of his fame; the jury which sits in judgment upon a poet, belonging as he does to all time, must be composed of his peers; it must be impanelled by Time from the selectest of the wise of many generations. A poet is a nightingale, who sits in darkness and sings to cheer its own solitude with sweet sounds; his auditors are as men entranced by the melody of an unseen musician, who feel that they are moved and softened, yet know not whence or why. The poems of Homer and his contemporaries were the delight of infant Greece; they were the elements of that social system which is the column upon which all succeeding civilization has reposed. Homer embodied the ideal perfection of his age in human character; nor can we doubt that those who read his verses were awakened to an ambition of becoming like to Achilles, Hector, and Ulysses; the truth and beauty of friendship, patriotism, and persevering devotion to an object, were unveiled to their depths in these immortal creations; the sentiments of the auditors must have been refined and enlarged by a sympathy with such great and lovely impersonations, until from admiring they imitated, and from imitation they identified themselves with the objects of their admiration. Nor let it be objected that these characters are remote from moral perfection, and that they are by no means to be considered as edifying patterns for general imitation. Every epoch, under names more or less specious, has deified its peculiar errors; Revenge is the naked idol of the worship of a semi-barbarous age; and Self-Deceit is the veiled image of unknown evil, before which luxury and satiety lie prostrate. But a poet considers the vices of his contemporaries as a temporary dress in which his creations must be arrayed, and which cover without concealing the eternal proportions of their beauty. An epic or dramatic personage is understood to wear them around his soul, as he may the ancient armor or the modern uniform around his body, whilst it is easy to conceive a dress more graceful than either. The beauty of the internal nature can not be so far concealed by its accidental vesture, but that the spirit of its form shall communicate itself to the very disguise, and indicate the shape it hides from the manner in which it is worn. A majestic form and graceful motions will express themselves through the most barbarous and tasteless costume. Few poets of the highest class have chosen to exhibit the beauty of their conceptions in its naked truth and splendor; and it is doubtful whether the alloy of costume, habit, etc., be not necessary to temper this planetary music for mortal ears.

The whole objection, however, of the immorality of poetry rests upon a misconception of the manner in which poetry acts to produce the moral improvement of man. Ethical science arranges the elements which poetry has created, and propounds schemes and proposes examples of civil and domestic life; nor is it for want of admirable doctrines that men hate, and despise, and censure, and deceive, and subjugate one another. But poetry acts in another and diviner manner. It awakens and enlarges the mind itself by rendering it the receptacle of a thousand unapprehended combinations of thought. Poetry lifts the veil from the hidden beauty of the world, and makes familiar objects be as if they were not familiar; it reproduces all that it represents, and the impersonations clothed in its Elysian light stand thenceforward in the minds of those who have once contemplated them, as memorials of that gentle and exalted content which extends itself over all thoughts and actions with which it co-exists. The great secret of morals is love; or a going out of our own nature, and an identification of ourselves with the beautiful which exists in thought, action, or person, not our own. A man, to be greatly good, must imagine intensely and comprehensively; he must put himself in the place of another and of many others; the pains and pleasures of his species must become his own. The great instrument of moral good is the imagination; and poetry administers to the effect by acting upon the cause. Poetry enlarges the circumference of the imagination by replenishing it with thoughts of ever new delight, which have the power of attracting and assimilating to their own nature all other thoughts, and which form new intervals and interstices whose void forever craves fresh food. Poetry strengthens the faculty which is the organ of the moral nature of man, in the same manner as exercise strengthens a limb. A poet therefore would do ill to embody his own conceptions of right and wrong, which are usually those of his place and time, in his poetical creations, which participate in neither. By this assumption of the inferior office of interpreting the effect, in which perhaps after all he might acquit himself but imperfectly, he would resign a glory in the participation of the cause. There was little danger that Homer, or any of the eternal poets, should have so far misunderstood themselves as to have abdicated this throne of their widest dominion. Those in whom the poetical faculty, though great, is less intense, as Euripides, Lucan, Tasso, Spenser, have frequently affected a moral aim, and the effect of their poetry is diminished in exact proportion to the degree in which they compel us to advert to this purpose.

Homer and the cyclic poets were followed at a certain interval by the dramatic and lyrical poets of Athens, who flourished contemporaneously with all that is most perfect in the kindred expressions of the poetical faculty; architecture, painting, music, the dance, sculpture, philosophy, and, we may add, the forms of civil life. For although the scheme of Athenian society was deformed by many imperfections which the poetry existing in chivalry and Christianity has erased from the habits and institutions of modern Europe; yet never at any other period has so much energy, beauty, and virtue, been developed; never was blind strength and stubborn form so disciplined and rendered subject to the will of man, or that will less repugnant to the dictates of the beautiful and the true, as during the century which preceded the death of Socrates. Of no other epoch in the history of our species have we records and fragments stamped so visibly with the image of the divinity in man. But it is poetry alone, in form, in action, or in language, which has rendered this epoch memorable above all others, and the storehouse of examples to everlasting time. For written poetry existed at that epoch simultaneously with the other arts, and it is an idle inquiry to demand which gave and which received the light, which all, as from a common focus, have scattered over the darkest periods of succeeding time. We know no more of cause and effect than a constant conjunction of events: poetry is ever found to co-exist with whatever other arts contribute to the happiness and perfection of man. I appeal to what has already been established to distinguish between the cause and the effect.

It was at the period here adverted to, that the drama had its birth; and however a succeeding writer may have equalled or surpassed those few great specimens of the Athenian drama which have been preserved to us, it is indisputable that the art itself never was understood or practised according to the true philosophy of it, as at Athens. For the Athenians employed language, action, music, painting, the dance, and religious institutions, to produce a common effect in the representation of the highest idealisms of passion and of power; each division in the art was made perfect in its kind by artists of the most consummate skill, and was disciplined into a beautiful proportion and unity one towards the other. On the modern stage a few only of the elements capable of expressing the image of the poet's conception are employed at once. We have tragedy without music and dancing; and music and dancing without the highest impersonations of which they are the fit accompaniment, and both without religion and solemnity. Religious institution has indeed been usually banished from the stage. Our system of divesting the actor's face of a mask, on which the many expressions appropriated to his dramatic character might be molded into one permanent and unchanging expression, is favorable only to a partial and inharmonious effect; it is fit for nothing but a monologue, where all the attention may be directed to some great master of ideal mimicry. The modern practice of blending comedy with tragedy, though liable to great abuse in point of practice, is undoubtedly an extension of the dramatic circle; but the comedy should be as in *King Lear*, universal, ideal, and sublime. It is perhaps the intervention of this principle which determines the balance in favor of *King Lear* against the *Oedipus Tyrannus* or the *Agamemnon*, or, if you will, the trilogies with which they are connected; unless the intense power of the choral poetry, especially that of the latter, should be considered as restoring the equilibrium. *King Lear*, if it can sustain this comparison, may be judged to be the most perfect specimen of the dramatic art existing in the world; in spite of the narrow conditions to which the poet was subjected by the ignorance of the philosophy of the drama which has prevailed in modern Europe. Calderon, in his religious *Autos*, has attempted to fulfil some of the high conditions of dramatic representation neglected by Shakespeare; such as the establishing a relation between the drama and religion, and the accommodating them to music and dancing; but he omits the observation of conditions still more important, and more is lost than gained by the substitution of the rigidly defined and ever-repeated idealisms of a distorted superstition for the living impersonations of the truth of human passion.

But I digress.—The connection of scenic exhibitions with the improvement or corruption of the manners of men, has been universally recognized: in other words, the presence or absence of poetry in its most perfect and universal form, has been found to be connected with good and evil in conduct or habit. The corruption which has been imputed to the drama as an effect, begins, when the poetry employed in its constitution ends: I appeal to the history or manners whether the periods of the growth of the one and the decline of the other have not corresponded with an exactness equal to any example of moral cause and effect.

The drama at Athens, or wheresoever else it may have approached to its perfection, ever co-existed with the moral and intellectual greatness of the age. The tragedies of the Athenian poets are as mirrors in which the spectator beholds himself, under a thin disguise of circumstance, stripped of all but that ideal perfection and energy which every one feels to be the internal type of all that he loves, admires, and would become. The imagination is enlarged by a sympathy with pains and passions so mighty, that they distend in their conception the capacity of that by which they are conceived; the good affectations are strengthened by pity, indignation, terror, and sorrow; and an exalted calm is prolonged from the satiety of this high exercise of them into the tumult of familiar life: even crime is disarmed of half its horror and all its contagion by being represented as the fatal consequence of the unfathomable agencies of nature; error is thus divested of its wilfulness; men can no longer cherish it as the creation of their choice. In a drama of the highest order there is little food for censure or hatred; it teaches rather self-knowledge and self-respect. Neither the eye nor the mind can see itself, unless reflected upon that which it resembles. The drama, so long as it continues to express poetry, is a prismatic and many-sided mirror, which collects the brightest rays of human nature and divides and reproduces them from the simplicity of these elementary forms, and touches them with majesty and beauty, and multiplies all that it reflects, and endows it with the power of propagating its like wherever it may fall.

But in periods of the decay of social life, the drama sympathizes with that decay. Tragedy becomes a cold imitation of the forms of the great masterpieces of antiquity, divested of all harmonious accompaniment of the kindred arts; and often the very form misunderstood, or a weak attempt to teach certain doctrines, which the writer considers as moral truths; and which are usually no more than specious flatteries of some gross vice or weakness with which the author, in common with his auditors, are infected. Hence what has been called the classical and domestic drama. Addison's *Cato* is a specimen of the one; and would

it were not superfluous to cite examples of the other! To such purposes poetry cannot be made subservient. Poetry is a sword of lightning, ever unsheathed, which consumes the scabbard that would contain it. And thus we observe that all dramatic writings of this nature are unimaginative in a singular degree; they affect sentiment and passion, which, divested of imagination, are other names for caprice and appetite. The period in our own history of the grossest degradation of the drama is the reign of Charles II, when all forms in which poetry had been accustomed to be expressed became hymns to the triumph of kingly power over liberty and virtue. Milton stood alone, illuminating an age unworthy of him. At such periods the calculating principle pervades all the forms of dramatic exhibition, and poetry ceases to be expressed upon them. Comedy loses its ideal universality: wit succeeds to humor; we laugh from self-complacency and triumph, instead of pleasure; malignity, sarcasm, and contempt, succeed to sympathetic merriment; we hardly laugh, but we smile. Obscenity, which is ever blasphemy against the divine beauty in life, becomes, from the very veil which it assumes, more active if less disgusting: it is a monster for which the corruption of society for ever brings forth new food, which it devours in secret.

The drama being that form under which a greater number of modes of expression of poetry are susceptible of being combined than any other, the connection of poetry and social good is more observable in the drama than in whatever other form. And it is indisputable that the highest perfection of human society has ever corresponded with the highest dramatic excellence; and that the corruption or the extinction of the drama in a nation where it has once flourished, is a mark of a corruption of manners, and an extinction of the energies which sustain the soul of social life. But, as Machiavelli says of political institutions, that life may be preserved and renewed, if men should arise capable of bringing back the drama to its principles. And this is true with respect to poetry in its most extended sense: all language, institution and form, require not only to be produced but to be sustained: the office and character of a poet participates in the divine nature as regards providence, no less than as regards creation.

Civil war, the spoils of Asia, and the fatal predominance first of the Macedonian, and then of the Roman arms, were so many symbols of the extinction or suspension of the creative faculty in Greece. The bucolic writers, who found patronage under the lettered tyrants of Sicily and Egypt, were the latest representatives of its most glorious reign. Their poetry is intensely melodious; like the odor of the tuberose, it overcomes and sickens the spirit with excess of sweetness; whilst the poetry of the preceding age was as a meadow-gale of June, which mingles the fragrance of all the flowers of the field, and adds a quickening and harmonizing spirit of its own, which endows the sense with a power of sustaining its extreme delight. The bucolic and erotic delicacy in written poetry is correlative with that softness in statuary, music, and the kindred arts, and even in manners and institutions, which distinguished the epoch to which I now refer. Nor is it the poetical faculty itself, or any misapplication of it, to which this want of harmony is to be imputed. An equal sensibility to the influence of the senses and the affections is to be found in the writings of Homer and Sophocles: the former, especially, has clothed sensual and pathetic images with irresistible attraction. Their superiority over these succeeding writers consists in the presence of those thoughts which belong to the inner faculties of our nature, not in the absence of those which are connected with the external: their incomparable perfection consists in a harmony of the union of all. It is not what the erotic poets have, but what they have not, in which their imperfection consists. It is not inasmuch as they were poets, but inasmuch as they were not poets, that they can be considered with any plausibility as connected with the corruption of their age. Had that corruption availed so as to extinguish in them the sensibility to pleasure, passion, and natural scenery, which is imputed to them as an imperfection, the last triumph of evil would have been achieved. For the end of social corruption is to destroy all sensibility to pleasure; and, therefore, it is corruption. It begins at the imagination and the intellect as at the core, and distributes itself thence as a paralysing venom, through the affections into the very appetites, until all become a torpid mass in which hardly sense survives. At the approach of such a period, poetry ever addresses itself to those faculties which are the last to be destroyed, and its voice is heard, like the footsteps of Astræa, departing from the world. Poetry ever communicates all the pleasure which men are capable of receiving: it is ever still the light of life; the source of whatever of beautiful or generous or true can have place in an evil time. It will readily be confessed that those among the luxurious citizens of Syracuse and Alexandria, who were delighted with the poems of Theocritus, were less cold, cruel, and sensual than the remnant of their tribe. But corruption must utterly have destroyed the fabric of human society before poetry can ever cease. The sacred links of that chain have never been entirely disjoined, which descending through the minds of many men is attached to those great minds, whence as from a magnet the invisible effluence is sent forth, which at once connects, animates, and sustains the life of all. It is the faculty which contains within itself the seeds at once of its own and of social renovation. And let us not circumscribe the effects of the bucolic and erotic poetry within the limits of the sensibility of those to whom it was addressed. They may have perceived the beauty of those immortal compositions, simply as fragments and isolated portions: those who are more finely organized, or born in a happier age, may recognize them as episodes to that great poem, which all poets, like the co-operating thoughts of one great mind, have built up since the beginning of the world.

The same revolution within a narrower sphere had place in ancient Rome; but the actions and forms of its social life never seem to have been perfectly saturated with the poetical element. The Romans appear to have considered the Greeks as the selectest treasuries of the selectest forms of manners and of nature, and to have abstained from creating in measured language, sculpture, music, or architecture, anything which might bear a particular relation to their own condition, whilst it should bear a general one to the universal constitution of the world. But we judge from partial evidence, and we judge perhaps partially. Ennius, Varro, Pacuvius, and Accius, all great poets, have been lost. Lucretius is in the highest, and Virgil in a very high sense, a creator. The chosen delicacy of expressions of the latter, are as a mist of light which conceal from us the intense and exceeding truth of his conceptions of nature. Livy is instinct with poetry. Yet Horace, Catullus, Ovid, and generally the other great writers of the Virgilian age, saw man and nature in the mirror of Greece. The institutions also, and the religion of Rome were less poetical than those of Greece, as the shadow is less vivid than the substance. Hence poetry in Rome, seemed to follow, rather than accompany, the perfection of political and domestic society. The true poetry of Rome lived in its institutions; for whatever of beautiful, true, and majestic, they contained, could have sprung only from the faculty which creates the order in which they consist. The life of Camillus, the death of Regulus; the expectation of the senators, in their godlike state, of the victorious Gauls: the refusal of the republic to make peace with Hannibal, after the battle of Cannæ, were not the consequences of a refined calculation of the probable personal advantage to result from such a rhythm and order in the shows of life, to those who were at once the poets and the actors of these immortal dramas. The imagination beholding the beauty of this order, created it out of itself according to its own idea; the consequence was empire, and the reward everliving fame. These things are not the less poetry *quia carent vate sacro*. They are the episodes of that cyclic poem written by Time upon the memories of men. The Past, like an inspired rhapsodist, fills the theatre of everlasting generations with their harmony.

At length the ancient system of religion and manners had fulfilled the circle of its evolutions. And the world would have fallen into utter anarchy and darkness, but that there were found poets among the authors of the Christian and chivalric systems of manners and religion, who created forms of opinion and action never before conceived; which, copied into the imaginations of men, became as generals to the bewildered armies of their thoughts. It is foreign to the present purpose to touch upon the evil produced by these systems: except that we protest, on the ground of the principles already established, that no portion of it can be attributed to the poetry they contain.

It is probable that the poetry of Moses, Job, David, Solomon, and Isaiah, had produced a great effect upon the mind of Jesus and his disciples. The scattered fragments preserved to us by the biographers of this extraordinary person, are all instinct with the most vivid poetry. But his doctrines seem to have been quickly distorted. At a certain period after the prevalence of a system of opinions founded upon those promulgated by him, the three forms into which Plato had distributed the faculties of mind underwent a sort of apotheosis, and became the object of the worship of the civilized world. Here it is to be confessed that "Light seems to thicken",

And the crow makes wing to the rooky wood, Good things of day begin to droop and drowse, Whiles night's black agents to their preys do rouse.

But mark how beautiful an order has sprung from the dust and blood of this fierce chaos! how the world, as from a resurrection, balancing itself on the golden wings of knowledge and of hope, has reassumed its yet unwearied flight into the heaven of time. Listen to the music, unheard by outward ears, which is as a ceaseless and invisible wind, nourishing its everlasting course with strength and swiftness.

The poetry in the doctrines of Jesus Christ, and the mythology and institutions of the Celtic conquerors of the Roman empire, outlived the darkness and the convulsions connected with their growth and victory, and blended themselves in a new fabric of manners and opinion. It is an error to impute the ignorance of the dark ages to the Christian doctrines or the predominance of the Celtic nations. Whatever of evil their agencies may have contained sprang from the extinction of the poetical principle, connected with the progress of despotism and superstition. Men, from causes too intricate to be here discussed, had become insensible and selfish: their own will had become feeble, and yet they were its slaves, and thence the slaves of the will of others: lust, fear, avarice, cruelty, and fraud, characterized a race amongst whom no one was to be found capable of *creating* in form, language, or institution. The moral anomalies of such a state of society are not justly to be charged upon any class of events immediately connected with them, and those events are most entitled to our approbation which could dissolve it most expeditiously. It is unfortunate for those who cannot distinguish words from thoughts, that many of these anomalies have been incorporated into our popular religion.

It was not until the eleventh century that the effects of the poetry of the Christian and chivalric systems began to manifest themselves. The principle of equality had been discovered and applied by Plato in his *Republic*, as the theoretical rule of the mode in which the materials of pleasure and of power, produced by the common skill and labor of human beings, ought to be distributed among them. The limitations of this rule were asserted by him to be determined only by the sensibility of each, or the utility to result to all. Plato, following the doctrines of Timaeus and Pythagoras, taught also a moral and intellectual system of doctrine, comprehending at once the past, present, and the future condition of man. Jesus Christ divulged the sacred and eternal truths contained in these views to mankind, and Christianity, in its abstract purity, became the exoteric expression of the esoteric doctrines of the poetry and wisdom of antiquity. The incorporation of the Celtic nations with the exhausted population of the south, impressed upon it the figure of the poetry existing in their mythology and institutions. The result was a sum of the action and reaction of all the causes included in it; for it may be assumed as a maxim that no nation or religion can supersede any other without incorporating into itself a portion of that which it supersedes. The abolition of personal and domestic slavery, and the emancipation of women from a great part of the degrading restraints of antiquity, were among the consequences of these events.

The abolition of personal slavery is the basis of the highest political hope that it can enter into the mind of man to conceive. The freedom of women produced the poetry of sexual love. Love became a religion, the idols of whose worship were ever present. It was as if the statues of Apollo and the Muses had been endowed with life and motion, and had walked forth among their worshippers; so that earth became peopled by the inhabitants of a diviner world. The familiar appearance and proceedings of life became wonderful and heavenly, and a paradise was created as out of the wrecks of Eden. And as this creation itself is poetry, so its creators were poets; and language was the instrument of their art: "Galeotto fù il libro, e chi lo scrisse." The Provençal Trouveurs, or inventors, preceded Petrarch, whose verses are as spells which unseal the inmost enchanted fountains of the delight which is in the grief of love. It is impossible to feel them without becoming a portion of that beauty which we contemplate: it were superfluous to explain how the gentleness and the elevation of mind connected with these sacred emotions can render men more amiable, more generous and wise, and lift them out of the dull vapors of the little world of self. Dante understood the secret things of love even

more than Petrarch. His *Vita Nuova* is an inexhaustible fountain of purity of sentiment and language: it is the idealized history of that period, and those intervals of his life which were dedicated to love. His apotheosis of Beatrice in Paradise, and the gradations of his own love and her loveliness, by which as by steps he feigns himself to have ascended to the throne of the Supreme Cause, is the most glorious imagination of modern poetry. The acutest critics have justly reversed the judgment of the vulgar, and the order of the great acts of the *Divina Commedia,* in the measure of the admiration which they accord to the Hell, Purgatory, and Paradise. The latter is a perpetual hymn of everlasting love. Love, which found a worthy poet in Plato alone of all the ancients, has been celebrated by a chorus of the greatest writers of the renovated world; and the music has penetrated the caverns of society, and its echoes still drown the dissonance of arms and superstition. At successive intervals, Ariosto, Tasso, Shakespeare, Spenser, Calderon, Rousseau, and the great writers of our own age, have celebrated the dominion of love, planting as it were trophies in the human mind of that sublimest victory over sensuality and force. The true relation borne to each other by the sexes into which human kind is distributed, has become less misunderstood; and if the error which confounded diversity with inequality of the powers of the two sexes has been partially recognized in the opinions and institutions of modern Europe, we owe this great benefit to the worship of which chivalry was the law, and poets the prophets.

The poetry of Dante may be considered as the bridge thrown over the stream of time, which unites the modern and ancient world. The distorted notions of invisible things which Dante and his rival Milton have idealized, are merely the mask and the mantle in which these great poets walk through eternity enveloped and disguised. It is a difficult question to determine how far they were conscious of the distinction which must have subsisted in their minds between their own creeds and that of the people. Dante at least appears to wish to mark the full extent of it by placing Riphaeus, whom Virgil calls *justissimus unus,* in Paradise, and observing a most heretical caprice in his distribution of rewards and punishments. And Milton's poem contains within itself a philosophical refutation of that system, of which, by a strange and natural antithesis, it has been a chief popular support. Nothing can exceed the energy and magnificence of the character of Satan as expressed in *Paradise Lost*. It is a mistake to suppose that he could ever have been intended for the popular personification of evil. Implacable hate, patient cunning, and a sleepless refinement of device to inflict the extremest anguish on an enemy, these things are evil; and, although venial in a slave, are not to be forgiven in a tyrant; although redeemed by much that ennobles his defeat in one subdued, are marked by all that dishonors his conquest in the victor. Milton's Devil as a moral being is as far superior to his God, as one who perseveres in some purpose which he has conceived to be excellent in spite of adversity and torture, is to one who in the cold security of undoubted triumph inflicts the most horrible revenge upon his enemy, not from any mistaken notion of inducing him to repent of a perseverance in enmity, but with the alleged design of exasperating him to deserve new torments. Milton has so far violated the popular creed (if this shall be judged to be a violation) as to have alleged no superiority of moral virtue to his God over his Devil. And this bold neglect of a direct moral purpose is the most decisive proof of the supremacy of Milton's genius. He mingled as it were the elements of human nature as colors upon a single pallet, and arranged them in the composition of his great picture according to the laws of epic truth; that is, according to the laws of that principle by which a series of actions of the external universe and of intelligent and ethical beings is calculated to excite the sympathy of succeeding generations of mankind. The *Divina Commedia* and *Paradise Lost* have conferred upon modern mythology a systematic form; and when change and time shall have added one more superstition to the mass of those which have arisen and decayed upon the earth, commentators will be learnedly employed in elucidating the religion of ancestral Europe, not only utterly forgotten because it will have been stamped with the eternity of genius.

Homer was the first and Dante the second epic poet: that is, the second poet, the series of whose creations bore a defined and intelligible relation to the knowledge and sentiment and religion of the age in which he lived, and of the ages which followed it: developing itself in correspondence with their development. For Lucretius had limed the wings of his swift spirit in the dregs of the sensible world; and Virgil, with a modesty that ill became his genius, had affected the fame of an imitator, even whilst he created anew all that he copied; and none among the flock of mock-birds, though their notes are sweet, Apollonius Rhodius, Quintus (Calaber) Smyrnæus, Nonnus, Lucan, Statius, or Claudian, have sought even to fulfil a single condition of epic truth. Milton was the third epic poet. For if the title of epic in its highest sense be refused to the *Aeneid,* still less can it be conceded to the *Orlando Furioso,* the *Gerusalemme Liberata,* the *Lusiad,* or the *Fairy Queen.*

Dante and Milton were both deeply penetrated with the ancient religion of the civilized world; and its spirit exists in their poetry probably in the same proportion as its forms survived in the unreformed worship of modern Europe. The one preceded and the other followed the Reformation at almost equal intervals. Dante was the first religious reformer, and Luther surpassed him rather in the rudeness and acrimony, than in the boldness of his censures of papal usurpation. Dante was the first awakener of entranced Europe; he created a language, in itself music and persuasion, out of a chaos of inharmonious barbarisms. He was the congregator of those great spirits who presided over the resurrection of learning; the Lucifer of that starry flock which in the thirteenth century shone forth from republican Italy, as from a heaven, into the darkness of the benighted world. His very words are instinct with spirit; each is as a spark, a burning atom of inextinguishable thought; and many yet lie covered in the ashes of their birth, and pregnant with a lightning which has yet found no conductor. All high poetry is infinite; it is as the first acorn, which contained all oaks potentially. Veil after veil may be undrawn, and the inmost naked beauty of the meaning never exposed. A great poem is a fountain for ever overflowing with the waters of wisdom and delight; and after one person and one age has exhausted all its divine effluence which their peculiar relations enable them to share, another and yet another succeeds, and new relations are ever developed, the source of an unforeseen and an unconceived delight.

The age immediately succeeding to that of Dante, Petrarch, and Boccaccio, was characterized by a revival of painting, sculpture, and architecture. Chaucer caught the sacred inspiration, and the superstructure of English literature is based upon the materials of Italian invention.

But let us not be betrayed from a defense into a critical history of poetry and its influence on society. Be it enough to have pointed out the effects of poets, in the large and true sense of the word, upon their own and all succeeding times.

But poets have been challenged to resign the civic crown to reasoners and mechanists, on another plea. It is admitted that the exercise of the imagination is most delightful, but it is alleged that that of reason is more useful. Let us examine as the grounds of this distinction, what is here meant by utility. Pleasure or good, in a general sense, is that which the consciousness of a sensitive and intelligent being seeks, and in which, when found, it acquiesces. There are two kinds of pleasure, one durable, universal and permanent; the other transitory and particular. Utility may either express the means of producing the former or the latter. In the former sense, whatever strengthens and purifies the affections, enlarges the imagination, and adds spirit to sense, is useful. But a narrower meaning may be assigned to the word utility, confining it to express that which banishes the importunity of the wants of our animal nature, the surrounding men with security of life, the dispersing the grosser delusions of superstition, and the conciliating such a degree of mutual forbearance among men as may consist with the motives of personal advantage.

Undoubtedly the promoters of utility, in this limited sense, have their appointed office in society. They follow the footsteps of poets, and copy the sketches of their creations into the book of common life. They make space, and give time. Their exertions are of the highest value, so long as they confine their administration of the concerns of the inferior powers of our nature within the limits due to the superior ones. But whilst the sceptic destroys gross superstitions, let him spare to deface, as some of the French writers have defaced, the eternal truths charactered upon the imaginations of men. Whilst the mechanist abridges, and the political economist combines labor, let them be aware that their speculations, for want of correspondence with those first principles which belong to the imagination, do not tend, as they have in modern England, to exasperate at once the extremes of luxury and want. They have exemplified the saying, "To him that hath, more shall be given; and from him hath not, the little that he hath shall be taken away." The rich have become richer, and the poor have become poorer; and the vessel of the state is driven between the Scylla and Charybdis of anarchy and despotism. Such are the effects which must ever flow from an unmitigated exercise of the calculating faculty.

It is difficult to define pleasure in its highest sense; the definition involving a number of apparent paradoxes. For, from an inexplicable defect of harmony in the constitution of human nature, the pain of the inferior is frequently connected with the pleasures of the superior portions of our being. Sorrow, terror, anguish, despair itself, are often the chosen expressions of an approximation to the highest good. Our sympathy in tragic fiction depends on this principle; tragedy delights by affording a shadow of the pleasure which exists in pain. This is the source also of the melancholy which is inseparable from the sweetest melody. The pleasure that is in sorrow is sweeter than the pleasure of pleasure itself. And hence the saying, "It is better to go to the house of mourning than to the house of mirth." Not that this highest species of pleasure is necessarily linked with pain. The delight of love and friendship, the ecstasy of the admiration of nature, the joy of the perception and still more of the creation of poetry, is often wholly unalloyed.

The production and assurance of pleasure in this highest sense is true utility. Those who produce and preserve this pleasure are poets or poetical philosophers.

The exertions of Locke, Hume, Gibbon, Voltaire, Rousseau, and their disciples, in favor of oppressed and deluded humanity, are entitled to the gratitude of mankind. Yet it is easy to calculate the degree of moral and intellectual improvement which the world would have exhibited, had they never lived. A little more nonsense would have been talked for a century or two; and perhaps a few more men, women, and children, burnt as heretics. We might not at this moment have been congratulating each other on the abolition of the Inquisition in Spain. But it exceeds all imagination to conceive what would have been the moral condition of the world if neither Dante, Petrarch, Boccaccio, Chaucer, Shakespeare, Calderon, Lord Bacon, nor Milton, had ever existed; if Raphael and Michael Angelo had never been born; if the Hebrew poetry had never been translated; if a revival of the study of Greek literature had never taken place; if no monuments of ancient sculpture had been handed down to us; and if the poetry of the religion of the ancient world had been extinguished together with its belief The human mind could never, except by the intervention of these excitements, have been awakened to the invention of the grosser sciences, and that application of analytical reasoning to the aberrations of society, which it is now attempted to exalt over the direct expression of the inventive and creative faculty itself.

We have more moral, political and historical wisdom than we know how to reduce into practice; we have more scientific and economical knowledge than can be accommodated to the just distribution of the produce which it multiplies. The poetry in these systems of thought, is concealed by the accumulation of facts and calculating processes. There is no want of knowledge respecting what is wisest and best in morals, government, and political economy, or at least, what is wiser and better than what men now practise and endure. But we let "I dare not wait upon I would, like the poor cat in the adage." We want the creative faculty to imagine that which we know; we want the generous impulse to act that which we imagine; we want the poetry ot life: our calculations have outrun conception; we have eaten more than we can digest. The cultivation of those sciences which have enlarged the limits of the empire of man over the external world, has, for want of the poetical faculty, proportionally circumscribed those of the internal world; and man, having enslaved the elements, remains himself a slave. To what but a cultivation of the mechanical arts in a degree disproportioned to the presence of the creative faculty, which is the basis of all knowledge, is to be attributed the abuse of all invention for abridging and combining labor, to the exasperation of the inequality of mankind? From what other cause has it arisen that the discoveries which should have lightened, have added a weight to the curse imposed on Adam? Poetry, and the principle of Self, of which money is the visible incarnation, are the God and Mammon of the world.

The functions of the poetical faculty are twofold: by one it creates new materials of knowledge, and power, and pleasure; by the other it engenders in the mind a desire to reproduce and arrange them according to a certain rhythm and order which may be called the beautiful and the good. The

cultivation of poetry is never more to be desired than at periods when, from an excess of the selfish and calculating principle, the accumulation of the materials of external life exceed the quantity of the power of assimilating them to the internal laws of human nature. The body has then become too unwieldy for that which animates it.

Poetry is indeed something divine. It is at once the center and circumference of knowledge; it is that which comprehends all science, and that to which all science must be referred. It is at the same time the root and blossom of all other systems of thought; it is that from which all spring, and that which adorns all; and that which, if blighted, denies the fruit and the seed, and withholds from the barren world the nourishment and the succession of the scions of the tree of life. It is the perfect and consummate surface and bloom of all things; it is as the odor and the color of the rose to the texture of the elements which compose it, as the form and splendor of unfaded beauty to the secrets of anatomy and corruption. What were virtue, love, patriotism, friendship; what were the scenery of this beautiful universe which we inhabit; what were our consolations on this side of the grave, and what were our aspirations beyond it,—if poetry did not ascend to bring light and fire from those eternal regions where the owl-winged faculty of calculation dare not ever soar? Poetry is not like reasoning, a power to be exerted according to the determination of the will. A man cannot say, "I will compose poetry." The greatest poet even cannot say it; for the mind in creation is as a fading coal, which some invisible influence, like an inconstant wind, awakens to transitory brightness; this power arises from within, like the color of a flower which fades and changes as it is developed, and the conscious portions of our natures are unprophetic either of its approach or its departure. Could this influence be durable in its original purity and force, it is impossible to predict the greatness of the results; but when composition begins, inspiration is already on the decline, and the most glorious poetry that has ever been communicated to the world is probably a feeble shadow of the original conceptions of the poet. I appeal to the greatest poets of the present day whether it is not an error to assert that the finest passages of poetry are produced by labor and study. The toil and the delay recommended by critics can be justly interpreted to mean no more than a careful observation of the inspired moments, and an artificial connection of the spaces between their suggestions by the intertexture of conventional expressions—a necessity only imposed by the limitedness of the poetical faculty itself; for Milton conceived the *Paradise Lost* as a whole before he executed it in portions. We have his own authority also for the muse having "dictated" to him the "unpremeditated song." And let this be an answer to those who would allege the fifty-six various readings of the first line of the *Orlando Furioso*. Compositions so produced are to poetry what mosaic is to painting. The instinct and intuition of the poetical faculty is still more observable in the plastic and pictorial arts: a great statue or picture grows under the power of the artist as a child in the mother's womb; and the very mind which directs the hands in formation, is incapable of accounting to itself for the origin, the gradations, or the media of the process.

Poetry is the record of the best and happiest moments of the happiest and best minds. We are aware of evanescent visitations of thought and feeling, sometimes associated with place or person, sometimes regarding our own mind alone, and always arising unforeseen and departing unbidden, but elevating and delightful beyond all expression; so that even in the desire and the regret they leave, there cannot but be pleasure, participating as it does in the nature of its object. It is, as it were, the interpenetration of a diviner nature through our own; but its footsteps are like those of a wind over the sea, which the morning calm erases, and whose traces remain only, as on the wrinkled sand which paves it. These and corresponding conditions of being are experienced principally by those of the most delicate sensibility and the most enlarged imagination; and the state of mind produced by them is at war with every base desire. The enthusiasm of virtue, love, patriotism, and friendship is essentially linked with such emotions; and whilst they last, self appears as what it is, an atom to a universe. Poets are not only subject to these experiences as spirits of the most refined organization, but they can color all that they combine with the evanescent hues of this ethereal world; a word, a trait in the representation of a scene or a passion will touch the enchanted chord, and reanimate, in those who have ever experienced these emotions, the sleeping, the cold, the buried image of the past. Poetry thus makes immortal all that is best and most beautiful in the world; it arrests the vanishing apparitions which haunt the interlunations of life, and veiling them or in language or in form, sends them forth among mankind, bearing sweet news of kindred joy to those with whom their sisters abide—abide, because there is no portal of expression from the caverns of the spirit which they inhabit into the universe of things. Poetry redeems from decay the visitations of the divinity in man.

Poetry turns all things to loveliness; it exalts the beauty of that which is most beautiful, and it adds beauty to that which is most deformed; it marries exultation and horror, grief and pleasure, eternity and change; it subdues to union under its light yoke all irreconcilable things. It transmutes all that it touches, and every form moving within the radiance of its presence is changed by wondrous sympathy to an incarnation of the spirit which it breathes; its secret alchemy turns to potable gold the poisonous waters which flow from death through life; it strips the veil of familiarity from the world, and lays bare the naked and sleeping beauty which is the spirit of its forms.

All things exist as they are perceived: at least in relation to the percipient.

The mind is its own place, and of itself
Can make a Heaven of Hell, a Hell of Heaven.

But poetry defeats the curse which binds us to be subjected to the accident of surrounding impressions. And whether it spreads its own figured curtain, or withdraws life's dark veil from before the scene of things, it equally creates for us a being within our being. It makes us the inhabitants of a world to which the familiar world is a chaos. It reproduces the common universe of which we are portions and percipients, and it purges from our inward sight the film of familiarity which obscures from us the wonder of our being. It compels us to feel that which we perceive, and to imagine that which we know. It creates anew the universe, after it has been annihilated in our minds by the recurrence of impressions blunted by reiteration. It justifies the bold and true words of Tasso: *Non merita nome di creatore, se non Iddio ed il Poeta.*

A poet, as he is the author to others of the highest wisdom, pleasure, virtue, and glory, so he ought personally to be the happiest, the best, the wisest, and the most illustrious of men. As to his glory, let time be challenged to declare whether the fame of any other institutor of human life be comparable to that of a poet. That he is the wisest, the happiest, and the best, inasmuch as he is a poet, is equally incontrovertible; the greatest poets have been men of the most spotless virtue, of the most consummate prudence, and, if we would look into the interior of their lives, the most fortunate of men; and the exceptions, as they regard those who possessed the poetic faculty in a high yet inferior degree, will be found on consideration to confirm rather than destroy the rule. Let us for a moment stoop to the arbitration of popular breath, and usurping and uniting in our own persons the incompatible characters of accuser, witness, judge, and executioner, let us decide without trial, testimony, or form, that certain motives of those who are "there sitting where we dare not soar," are reprehensible. Let us assume that Homer was a drunkard, that Virgil was a flatterer, that Horace was a coward, that Tasso was a madman, that Lord Bacon was a peculator, that Raphael was a libertine, that Spenser was a poet laureate. It is inconsistent with this division of our subject to cite living poets, but posterity has done ample justice to the great names now referred to. Their errors have been weighed and found to have been dust in the balance; if their sins were as scarlet, they are now white as snow, they have been washed in the blood of the mediator and redeemer, Time. Observe in what a ludicrous chaos the imputations of real or fictitious crime have been confused in the contemporary calumnies against poetry and poets; consider how little is as it appears— or appears as it is; look to your own motives, and judge not, lest ye be judged.

Poetry, as has been said, differs in this respect from logic, that it is not subject to the control of the active powers of the mind, and that its birth and recurrence have no necessary connection with the consciousness or will. It is presumptuous to determine that these are the necessary conditions of all mental causation, when mental effects are experienced unsusceptible of being referred to them. The frequent recurrence of the poetical power, it is obvious to suppose, may produce in the mind a habit of order and harmony correlative with its own nature and with its effects upon other minds. But in the intervals of inspiration—and they may be frequent without being durable—a poet becomes a man, and is abandoned to the sudden reflux of the influences under which others habitually live. But as he is more delicately organized than other men, and sensible to pain and pleasure, both his own and that of others, in a degree unknown to them, he will avoid the one and pursue the other with an ardor proportioned to this difference. And he renders himself obnoxious to calumny when he neglects to observe the circumstances under which these objects of universal pursuit and flight have disguised themselves in one another's garments.

But there is nothing necessarily evil in this error, and thus cruelty, envy, revenge, avarice, and the passions purely evil, have never formed any portion of the popular imputations on the lives of poets.

I have thought it most favorable to the cause of truth to set down these remarks according to the order in which they were suggested to my mind, by a consideration of the subject itself, instead of observing the formality of a polemical reply; but if the view which they contain be just, they will be found to involve a refutation of the arguers against poetry, so far at least as regards the first division of the subject. I can readily conjecture what should have moved the gall of some learned and intelligent writers who quarrel with certain versifiers; I confess myself like them, unwilling to be stunned by the Theseids of the hoarse Codri of the day. Bavius and Mævius undoubtedly are, as they ever were, insufferable persons. But it belongs to a philosophical critic to distinguish rather than confound.

The first part of these remarks has related to poetry in its elements and principles; and it has been shown, as well as the narrow limits assigned them would permit, that what is called poetry in a restricted sense, has a common source with all other forms of order and of beauty according to which the materials of human life are susceptible of being arranged, and which is poetry in a universal sense.

The second part will have for its object an application of these principles to the present state of the cultivation of poetry, and a defense of the attempt to idealize the modern forms of manners and opinions, and compel them into a subordination to the imaginative and creative faculty. For the literature of England, an energetic development of which has ever preceded or accompanied a great and free development of the national will, has arisen as it were from a new birth. In spite of the low-thoughted envy which would undervalue contemporary merit, our own will be a memorable age in intellectual achievements, and we live among such philosophers and poets as surpass beyond comparison any who have appeared since the last national struggle for civil and religious liberty. The most unfailing herald, companion, and follower of the awakening of a great people to work a beneficial change in opinion or institution, is poetry. At such periods there is an accumulation of the power of communicating and receiving intense and impassioned conceptions respecting man and nature. The persons in whom this power resides may often, as far as regards many portions of their nature, have little apparent correspondence with that spirit of good of which they are the ministers. But even whilst they deny and abjure, they are yet compelled to serve the power which is seated on the throne of their own soul. It is impossible to read the compositions of the most celebrated writers of the present day without being startled with the electric life which burns within their words. They measure the circumference and sound the depths of human nature with a comprehensive and all-penetrating spirit, and they are themselves perhaps the most sincerely astonished at its manifestations; for it is less their spirit than the spirit of the age. Poets are the hierophants of an unapprehended inspiration; the mirrors of the gigantic shadows which futurity casts upon the present; the words which express what they understand not; the trumpets which sing to battle and feel not what they inspire; the influence which is moved not, but moves. Poets are the unacknowledged legislators of the world.

Feb.-Mar., 1821   1840

LETTERS OF SHELLEY

THE CATARACT OF TERNI

To Thomas Love Peacock

Rome; November 20, 1818

My dear P.,—

We passed on day after day, until we came to Spoleto, I think the most romantic city I ever saw. There is here an aqueduct of astonishing elevation, which unites two rocky mountains—there is the path of a torrent below, whitening the green dell with its broad and barren track of stones, and above there is a castle, apparently of great strength and tremendous magnitude, which overhangs the city, and whose marble bastions are perpendicular with the precipice. I never saw a more impressive picture; in which the shapes of nature are of the grandest order, but over which the creations of man, sublime from their antiquity and greatness, seem to predominate. The castle was built by Belisarius or Narses, I forget which, but was of that epoch.

From Spoleto we went to Terni, and saw the cataract of the Velino. The glaciers of Montanvert and the source of the Arveiron is the grandest spectacle I ever saw. This is the second. Imagine a river sixty feet in breadth, with a vast volume of waters, the outlet of a great lake among the higher mountains, falling 300 feet into a sightless gulf of snow-white vapor, which bursts up for ever and for ever, from a circle of black crags, and thence leaping downwards, made five or six other cataracts, each fifty or a hundred feet high, which exhibit, on a smaller scale, and with beautiful and sublime variety, the same appearances. But words (and far less could painting) will not express it. Stand upon the brink of the platform of cliff, which is directly opposite. You see the ever-moving water stream down. It comes in thick and tawny folds, flaking off like solid snow gliding down a mountain. It does not seem hollow within, but without it is unequal, like the folding of linen thrown carelessly down; your eye follows it, and it is lost below; not in the black rocks which gird it around, but in its own foam and spray, in the cloud-like vapors boiling up from below, which is not like rain, nor mist, nor spray, nor foam, but water, in a shape wholly unlike anything I ever saw before. It is as white as snow, but thick and impenetrable to the eye. The very imagination is bewildered in it. A thunder comes up from the abyss wonderful to hear; for, though it ever sounds, it is never the same, but, modulated by the changing motion, rises and falls intermittingly; we passed half an hour in one spot looking at it, and thought but a few minutes had gone by. The surrounding scenery is, in its kind, the loveliest and most sublime that can be conceived. In our first walk we passed through some olive groves, of large and ancient trees, whose hoary and twisted trunks leaned in all directions. We then crossed a path of orange trees by the river side, laden with their golden fruit, and came to a forest of ilex of a large size, whose evergreen and acorn-bearing boughs were intertwined over our winding path. Around, hemming in the narrow vale, were pinnacles of lofty mountains of pyramidical rock clothed with all evergreen plants and trees; the vast pine, whose feathery foliage trembled in the blue air, the ilex, that ancestral inhabitant of these mountains, the arbutus with its crimson-colored fruit and glittering leaves. After an hour's walk, we came beneath the cataract of Terni, within the distance of half a mile; nearer you cannot approach, for the Nar, which has here its confluence with the Velino, bars the passage. We then crossed the river formed by this confluence, over a narrow natural bridge of rock, and saw the cataract from the platform I first mentioned. We think of spending some time next year near this waterfall. The inn is very bad, or we should have stayed there longer.

Adieu,—very faithfully yours,

P. B. S.

ROME, NAPLES, AND VESUVIUS

To Thomas Love Peacock

Naples; December 22, 1818

My dear P.,—

Since I last wrote you, I have seen the ruins of Rome, the Vatican, St. Peter's, and all the miracles of ancient and modern art contained in that majestic city. The impression of it exceeds anything I have ever experienced in my travels. We stayed there only a week, intending to return at the end of February, and devote two or three months to its mines of inexhaustible contemplation, to which period I refer you for a minute account of it. We visited the Forum and the ruins of the Coliseum every day. The Coliseum is unlike any work of human hands I ever saw before. It is of enormous height and circuit, and the arches built of massy stones are piled on one another, and jut into the blue air, shattered into the forms of overhanging rocks. It has been changed by time into the image of an amphitheater of rocky hills over-

grown by the wild olive, the myrtle, and the fig tree, and threaded by little paths, which wind among its ruined stairs and immeasurable galleries: the copsewood overshadows you as you wander through its labyrinths, and the wild weeds of this climate of flowers bloom under your feet. The arena is covered with grass, and pierces, like the skirts of a natural plain, the chasms of the broken arches around. But a small part of the exterior circumference remains—it is exquisitely light and beautiful; and the effect of the perfection of its architecture, adorned with ranges of Corinthian pilasters, supporting a bold cornice, is such as to diminish the effect of its greatness. The interior is all ruin. I can scarcely believe that even when encrusted with Dorian marble and ornamented by columns of Egyptian granite, its effect could have been so sublime and so impressive as in its present state. It is open to the sky, and it was the clear and sunny weather of the end of November in this climate when we visited it, day after day.

Near it is the arch of Constantine, or rather the arch of Trajan; for the servile and avaricious senate of degraded Rome ordered that the monument of his prede-cessor should be demolished in order to dedicate one to the Christian reptile, who had crept among the blood of his murdered family to the supreme power. It is exquisitely beautiful and perfect. The Forum is a plain in the midst of Rome, a kind of desert full of heaps of stones and pits; and though so near the habitations of men, is the most desolate place you can conceive. The ruins of temples stand in and around it, shattered columns and ranges of others complete, supporting cornices of exquisite workmanship, and vast vaults of shattered domes distinct with regular compartments, once filled with sculptures of ivory or brass. The temples of Jupiter, and Concord, and Peace, and the Sun, and the Moon, and Vesta, are all within a short distance of this spot. Behold the wrecks of what a great nation once dedicated to the abstractions of the mind! Rome is a city, as it were, of the dead, or rather of those who cannot die, and who survive the puny generations which inhabit and pass over the spot which they have made sacred to eternity. In Rome, at least in the first enthusiasm of your recognition of ancient time, you see nothing of the Italians. The nature of the city assists the delusion, for its vast and antique walls describe a circum-ference of sixteen miles, and thus the population is thinly scattered over this space, nearly as great as London. Wide wild fields are enclosed within it, and there are grassy lanes and copses winding among the ruins, and a great green hill, lonely and bare, which overhangs the Tiber. The gardens of the modern palaces are like wild woods of cedar, and cypress, and pine, and the neglected walks are overgrown with weeds. The English burying-place is a green slope near the walls, under the pyramidal tomb of Cestius, and is, I think, the most beautiful and solemn cemetery I ever beheld. To see the sun shining on its bright grass, fresh, when we first visited it, with the autumnal dews, and hear the whispering of the wind among the leaves of the trees which have overgrown the tomb of Cestius, and the soil which is stirring in the sun-warm earth, and to mark the tombs, mostly of women and young people who were buried there, one might, if one were to die, desire the sleep they seem to sleep. Such is the human mind, and so it peoples with its wishes vacancy and oblivion. . . .

External nature in these delightful regions contrasts with and compensates for the deformity and degradation of humanity. We have a lodging divided from the sea by the royal gardens, and from our windows we see perpetually the blue waters of the bay, forever changing, yet forever the same, and encompassed by the mountainous island of Capri, the lofty peaks which overhang Salerno, and the woody hill of Posilipo, whose promontories hide from us Misenum and the lofty isle Inarime, which, with its divided summit, forms the opposite horn of the bay. From the pleasant walks of the garden we see Vesuvius; a smoke by day and a fire by night is seen upon its summit, and the glassy sea often reflects its light or shadow. The climate is delicious. We sit without a fire, with the windows open, and have almost all the productions of an English summer. The weather is usually like what Wordsworth calls "the first fine day of March"; sometimes very much warmer, though perhaps it wants that "each minute sweeter than before," which gives an intoxicating sweetness to the awakening of the earth from its winter's sleep in England. . . .

Vesuvius is, after the Glaciers, the most impressive exhibition of the energies of nature I ever saw. It has not the immeasurable greatness, the overpowering magnificence, nor, above all, the radiant beauty of the glaciers; but it has all their character of tremendous and irresistible strength.

From Resina to the hermitage you wind up the mountain, and cross a vast stream of hardened lava, which is an actual image of the waves of the sea, changed into hard black stone by enchantment. The lines of the boiling flood seem to hang in the air, and it is difficult to believe that the billows which seem hurrying down upon you are not actually in motion. This plain was once a sea of liquid fire. From the hermitage we crossed another vast stream of lava, and then went on foot up the cone—this is the only part of the ascent in which there is any difficulty, and that difficulty has been much exaggerated. It is composed of rocks of lava, and declivities of ashes; by ascending the former and descending the latter, there is very little fatigue. On the summit is a kind of irregular plain, the most horrible chaos that can be imagined; riven into ghastly chasms, and heaped up with tumuli of great stones and cinders, and enormous rocks blackened and calcined, which had been thrown from the volcano upon one another in terrible confusion. In the midst stands the conical hill from which volumes of smoke, and the fountains of liquid fire, are rolled forth forever. The mountain is at present in a slight state of eruption; and a thick heavy white smoke is perpetually rolled out, interrupted by enormous columns of an impenetrable black bituminous vapor, which is hurled up, fold after fold, into the sky with a deep hollow sound, and fiery stones are rained down from its darkness, and a black shower of ashes fell even where we sat. The lava, like the glacier, creeps on perpetually, with a crackling sound as of suppressed fire. There are several springs of lava; and in one place it rushes precipitously over a high crag, rolling down the half-molten rocks and its own overhanging waves; a cataract of quivering fire. We approached the extremity of one of the rivers of lava; it is about twenty feet in breadth and ten in height; and as the inclined plane was not rapid, its motion was very slow. We saw the masses of its dark exterior surface detach themselves as it moved, and betray the depth of the liquid flame. In the day the fire is but slightly seen; you only observe a tremulous motion in the air, and streams and fountains of white sulphurous smoke.

At length we saw the sun sink, between Capri and Inarime, and, as the darkness increased, the effect of the fire became more beautiful. We were, as it were, surrounded by streams and cataracts of the red and radiant fire; and in the midst, from the column of bituminous smoke shot up into the air, fell the vast masses of rock, white with the light of their intense heat, leaving behind them through the dark vapor trains of splendor. We descended by torchlight, and I should have enjoyed the scenery on my return, but they conducted me, I know not how, to the hermitage in a state of intense bodily suffering, the worst effect of which was spoiling the pleasure of Mary and C—. Our guides on the occasion were complete savages. You have no idea of the horrible cries which they suddenly utter, no one knows why; the clamor, the vociferation, the tumult. C— in her palanquin suffered most from it; and when I had gone on before, they threatened to leave her in the middle of the road, which they would have done had not my Italian servant promised them a beating, after which they became quiet. Nothing, however, can be more picturesque than the gestures and the physiognomies of these savage people. And when, in the darkness of night, they unexpectedly begin to sing in chorus some fragments of their wild but sweet national music, the effect is exceedingly fine.

Since I wrote this, I have seen the museum of this city. Such statues! There is a Venus; an ideal shape of the most winning loveliness. A Bacchus, more sublime than any living being. A Satyr, making love to a youth: in which the expressed life of the sculpture, and the inconceivable beauty of the form of the youth, overcome one's repugnance to the subject. There are multitudes of wonderfully fine statues found in Herculaneum and Pompeii. We are going to see Pompeii the first day that the sea is waveless. Herculaneum is almost filled up; no more excavations are made; the king bought the ground and built a palace upon it . . . .

Adieu, my dear P.— Affectionately your friend,

P. B. S.

LEIGH HUNT (1784-1859)

Wit, poet, prose-man, party-man, translator,
Hunt, your best title yet is INDICATOR.

CHARLES LAMB

Hunt was the son of parents devoted to intellectual and humanitarian reforms, and through-out almost a century of prolific journalistic and literary endeavors he was an ardent opponent of ultra-conservative attitudes in politics, ethics, and criticism. The trend of his labors is shown in some of the titles of his periodicals and books,—*The Examiner, The Indicator, The Liberal,* and *Christianism: the Religion of the Heart.* He fought bravely on all fronts,—constitutional reform, sectarian toleration, prison-reform, emancipation from slavery, abolition of child-labor, prevention of cruelty to animals, etc. When the Tory press adulated the Prince Regent on his accession to power, Hunt dared to tell the truth about him,—that he was "a disgraceful libertine, without one single claim on the gratitude of his country or the respect of posterity,"—and was sentenced to prison for this freedom of speech. When, largely for political reasons, stuffy and complacent sneers were uttered against the personal character of the Romantics, Hunt courageously counterattacked in essays which are of permanent interest and value as exposures of Pharisaism.

Among his friends were Lamb, Hazlitt, Moore, Byron, and Shelley. If it had not been for Leigh Hunt's discernment and enthusiasm, the true greatness of several of the Romantics,—notably Coleridge, Keats, and Shelley,—would have received slower recognition. He himself was a talented writer of verse and prose, but his creative work is of uneven merit, and he wrote far too much. His chief service lay in pointing out the merits of writers of genius, before the public had recognized them. Remarkably few of his judgments concerning the writers of his own age, or of earlier periods, have been rejected by the verdicts of later times. His good taste in judging the work of others than himself was almost impeccable; and his skill in showing the special qualities of a poet by means of apt quotation was extraordinary. His essay, *What Is Poetry?*, though not as profound as Coleridge's or Shelley's discussions on the subject, is one of the clearest and most persuasive statements ever written on the aesthetic beliefs of the Romantic School.

TO HAMPSTEAD

WRITTEN DURING THE AUTHOR'S IMPRISONMENT,
AUGUST, 1813

Sweet upland, to whose walks, with fond repair,
Out of thy western slope I took my rise
Day after day, and on these feverish eyes
Met the moist fingers of the bathing air;—
If health, unearned of thee, I may not share,   5
Keep it, I pray thee, where my memory lies,
In thy green lanes, brown dells, and breezy skies,
Till I return, and find thee doubly fair.

Wait then my coming, on that lightsome land,
Health, and the joy that out of nature springs,   10
And Freedom's air-blown locks;—but stay with me,
Friendship, frank entering with the cordial hand,
And Honor, and the Muse with growing wings,
And Love Domestic, smiling equably.

1813   1813

THE POETS

Were I to name, out of the times gone by,
  The poets dearest to me, I should say,
  Pulci for spirits, and a fine, free way;
Chaucer for manners, and close, silent eye;
Milton for classic taste, and harp strung high; 5
Spenser for luxury, and sweet, sylvan play;
  Horace for chatting with, from day to day;
Shakespeare for all, but most, society.

But which take with me, could I take but one?
  Shakespeare,—as long as I was unoppressed 10
  With the world's weight, making sad thoughts intenser;
But did I wish, out of the common sun,
To lay a wounded heart in leafy rest,
And dream of things far off and healing,—Spenser.

                                    1815

FROM THE STORY OF RIMINI

  A noble range it was, of many a rood,
Walled and tree-girt, and ending in a wood.
A small sweet house o'erlooked it from a nest
Of pines:—all wood and garden was the rest, 385
Lawn, and green lane, and covert:—and it had
A winding stream about it, clear and glad,
With here and there a swan, the creature born
To be the only graceful shape of scorn.
The flower-beds all were liberal of delight; 390
Roses in heaps were there, both red and white,
Lilies angelical, and gorgeous glooms
Of wall-flowers, and blue hyacinths, and blooms
Hanging thick clusters from light boughs; in short,
All the sweet cups to which the bees resort, 395
With plots of grass, and leafier walks between
Of red geraniums, and of jessamine,
And orange, whose warm leaves so finely suit,
And look as if they shade a golden fruit;
And midst the flow'rs, turfed round beneath a shade 400
Of darksome pines, a babbling fountain played,
And 'twixt their shafts you saw the water bright,
Which through the tops glimmered with show'ring light.
So now you stood to think what odors best
Made the air happy in that lovely nest; 405
And now you went beside the flowers, with eyes
Earnest as bees, restless as butterflies;
And then turned off into a shadier walk,
Close and continuous, fit for lover's talk;
And then pursued the stream, and as you trod 410
Onward and onward o'er the velvet sod,
Felt on your face an air, watery and sweet,
And a new sense in your soft-lighting feet.
At last you entered shades indeed, the wood,
Broken with glens and pits, and glades fair-viewed, 415
Through which the distant palace now and then
Looked lordly forth with many-windowed ken;
A land of trees,—which reaching round about

In shady blessing stretched their old arms out;
With spots of sunny openings, and with nooks   420
To lie and read in, sloping into brooks,
Where at her drink you startled the slim deer,
Retreating lightly with a lovely fear.
And all about, the birds kept leafy house,
And sung and darted in and out the boughs;   425
And all about, a lovely sky of blue
Clearly was felt, or down the leaves laughed through.
And here and there, in ev'ry part, were seats,—
Some in the open walks, some in retreats,—
With bow'ring leaves o'erhead, to which the eye   430
Looked up half sweetly and half awfully,—
Places of nestling green, for poets made,
Where, when the sunshine struck a yellow shade,
The rugged trunks, to inward peeping sight,
Thronged in dark pillars up the gold green light.   435

But 'twixt the wood and flowery walks, half-way,
And formed of both, the loveliest portion lay,—
A spot, that struck you like enchanted ground:—
It was a shallow dell, set in a mound
Of sloping orchards,—fig, and almond trees,   440
Cherry and pine, with some few cypresses;
Down by whose roots, descending darkly still,
(You saw it not, but heard) there gushed a rill,
Whose low sweet talking seemed as if it said
Something eternal to that happy shade.   445
The ground within was lawn, with fruits and flowers
Heaped towards the center, half of citron bowers;
And in the middle of those golden trees,
Half seen amidst the globy oranges,
Lurked a rare summer-house, a lovely sight,—   450
Small, marble, well-proportioned, creamy white,
Its top with vine-leaves sprinkled,—but no more,—
And a young bay tree either side the door.
The door was to the wood, forward and square,
The rest was domed at top and circular;   455
And through the dome the only light came in,
Tinged as it entered by the vine-leaves thin.

It was a beauteous piece of ancient skill,
Spared from the rage of war, and perfect still;
By some supposed the work of fairy hands,—   460
Famed for luxurious taste, and choice of lands,
Alcina or Morgana,—who from fights
And errant fame inveigled amorous knights,
And lived with them in a long round of blisses,
Feasts, concerts, baths, and bower-enshaded kisses.   465
But 'twas a temple, as its sculpture told,
Built to the Nymphs that haunted there of old;
For o'er the door was carved a sacrifice
By girls and shepherds brought, with reverent eyes,
Of sylvan drinks and foods, simple and sweet,   470
And goats with struggling horns and planted feet:
And round about ran, on a line with this,
In like relief, a world of pagan bliss,
That showed, in various scenes, the nymphs themselves;
Some by the water-side, on bowery shelves   475
Leaning at will,—some in the stream of play,—

Some pelting the young Fauns with buds of May,—
Or half asleep pretending not to see
The latter in the brakes come creepingly,
While from their careless urns, lying aside   480
In the long grass, the straggling waters glide.
Never, be sure, before or since was seen
A summer-house so fine in such a nest of green.
1812-16   1816

TO THE GRASSHOPPER AND THE CRICKET

Green little vaulter in the sunny grass,
Catching your heart up at the feel of June,
Sole voice that's heard amidst the lazy noon,
When even the bees lag at the summoning brass,
And you, warm little housekeeper, who class   5
With those who think the candles come too soon,
Loving the fire, and with your tricksome tune
Nick the glad silent moments as they pass;

Oh sweet and tiny cousins, that belong,
One to the fields, the other to the hearth,   10
Both have your sunshine; both, though small, are strong
At your clear hearts; and both seem given to earth
To ring in thoughtful ears this natural song—
In doors and out, summer and winter, mirth.
1816   1817

THE NILE

It flows through old hushed Egypt and its sands,
Like some grave mighty thought threading a dream,
And times and things, as in that vision, seem
Keeping along it their eternal stands,—
Caves, pillars, pyramids, the shepherd bands   5
That roamed through the young world, the glory extreme
Of high Sesostris, and that southern beam,
The laughing queen that caught the world's great hands.

Then comes a mightier silence, stern and strong,
As of a world left empty of its throng,   10
And the void weighs on us; and then we wake,
And hear the fruitful stream lapsing along
'Twixt villages, and think how we shall take
Our own calm journey on for human sake.
1818

ON A LOCK OF MILTON'S HAIR

It lies before me there, and my own breath
    Stirs its thin outer threads, as though beside
    The living head I stood in honored pride,
Talking of lovely things that conquer death.
Perhaps he pressed it once, or underneath   5
    Ran his fine fingers, when he leant, blank-eyed,
    And saw, in fancy, Adam and his bride
With their heaped locks, or his own Delphic wreath.

There seems a love in hair, though it be dead.
It is the gentlest, yet the strongest thread
Of our frail plant,—a blossom from the tree   10
Surviving the proud trunk;—as if it said,
Patience and Gentleness is Power. In me
Behold affectionate eternity.

1818

FROM THE NYMPHS

Dique petitorum, dixit, salvete locorum,
    Tuque novos coelo terra datura Deos;
Fluminaque, et Fontes, quibus utitur hospita
    tellus
    Et Nemorum Divae, Naiadumque chori.—
                                                            OVID

Spirit, who waftest me where'er I will,
And seest, with finer eyes what infants see,
Feeling all lovely truth
With the wise health of everlasting youth,
Beyond the motes of Bigotry's sick eye,   5
Or the blind feel of false Philosophy,—
O Spirit, O Muse of mine,
Frank, and quick-dimpled to all social glee,
And yet most sylvan of the earnest Nine,
Who on the fountain-shedding hill,   10
Leaning about among the clumpy bays
Look at the clear Apollo while he plays;—
Take me, now, now, and let me stand
On some such lovely land,
Where I may feel me, as I please,   15
In dells among the trees,
Or on some outward slope, with ruffling
    hair,
Be level with the air;
For a new smiling sense has shot down
    through me,
And from the clouds, like stars, bright eyes
    are beckoning to me.   20

Arrived!   Arrived!   O shady spots of
    ground,
What calmness ye strike round,
Hushing the soul as if with hand on lips!
And are ye seen then but of animal eyes,
Prone, or side-looking with a blank sur-
    mise?   25
And do ye hear no finer-fancied words
Than the sweet whistle of the repeating
    birds?
And are ye haunted of no lovelier trips
Than the poor stag's, who startled, as he
    sips,
Perks up with timid mouth, from which
    the water drips?   30

O ye whom ancient wisdom, in its graces,
Made guardians of these places;
Etherial human shapes, perhaps the souls
Of poets and poetic women, staying
To have their fill of pipes and leafy play-
    ing,   35
Ere they drink heavenly change from nec-
    tar-bowls;
You finer people of the earth,
Nymphs of all names, and woodland
    Geniuses,
I see you, here and there, among the trees,
Shrouded in noonday respite of your
    mirth;   40
This hum in air, which the still ear per-
    ceives,
Is your unquarreling voice among the
    leaves;
And now I find whose are the laughs and
    stirrings
That made the delicate birds dart so in
    whisks and whirrings.

There are the fair-limbed Nymphs o' the
    Woods, (look ye   45
Whom kindred Fancies have brought after
    me!)
These are the tawny Dryads, who love
    nooks
In the dry depth of oaks;
Or feel the air in groves, or pull green
    dresses
For their glad heads in rooty wilder-
    nesses;   50
Or on the golden turf, o'er the dark lines,
Which the sun makes when he declines,
Bend their linked dances in and out the
    pines.
They tend all forests old, and meeting
    trees,
Wood, copse, or queach, or slippery dell
    o'erhung   55
With firs, and with their dusty apples
    strewn;
And let the visiting beams the bows among,
And bless the trunks from clingings of dis-
    ease
And wasted hearts that to the night-wind
    groan.

They screen the cuckoo when he sings; and
　　teach　　　　　　　　　　　　　　　60
The mother blackbird how to lead astray
The unformed spirit of the foolish boy
From thick to thick, from hedge to layery
　　beech,
When he would steal the huddled nest
　　away
Of yellow bills, up-gaping for their food, 65
And spoil the song of the free solitude.
And they, at sound of the brute, insolent
　　horn,
Hurry the deer out of the dewy morn;
And take into their sudden laps with joy
The startled hare that did but peep
　　abroad;　　　　　　　　　　　　70
And from the trodden road
Help the bruised hedgehog. And at rest,
　　they love
The back-turned pheasant, hanging from
　　the tree
His sunny drapery;
And handy squirrel, nibbling hastily;　75
And fragrant-living bee,
So happy, that he will not move, not he,
Without a song; and hidden, amorous
　　dove,
With his deep breath; and bird of wakeful
　　glow,
Whose louder song is like the voice of
　　life,　　　　　　　　　　　　　80
Triumphant o'er death's image; but whose
　　deep,
Low, lovelier note is like a gentle wife,
A poor, a pensive, yet a happy one,

Stealing when daylight's common tasks are
　　done,
An hour for mother's work; and singing
　　low,　　　　　　　　　　　　　85
While her tired husband and her children
　　sleep.

　　　　　　　　　　　　　　　　1818

THE PRAYER IN THE BOWER

Turning down, goatherd, by the oaks,
　　you'll see
A fig-tree statue, put up recently,
Three-footed, with the bark on, without
　　ears;
Yet plain enough Priapus it appears.
A sacred hedge runs round it; and a brook, 5
Flowing from out a little gravelly nook,
Keeps green the laurel and the myrtle
　　trees,
And odorous cypresses:
And there's a vine there, heaping all about
Its tendrilled clusters out;　　　　　10
And vernal blackbirds through the sprays
Shake their shrill notes a thousand ways;
And yellow nightingales reply,
Murmuring a honied song deliciously.
Sit you down there; and the kind god
　　implore,　　　　　　　　　　　15
That I may yearn for Psamathe no more;
Myself with a fine kid will follow you,
And sacrifice; and should the deity nod,
A heifer and a goat shall thank him too,
And a house-lamb. Hear then, kind-
　　hearted god.　　　　　　　　　20

　　　　　　　　　　　　　　　　1818

THE FISH, THE MAN, AND THE SPIRIT

To Fish

You strange, astonished-looking, angle-faced,
Dreary-mouthed, gaping wretches of the sea,
Gulping salt water everlastingly,
Cold-blooded, though with red your blood be graced,
And mute, though dwellers in the roaring waste;　　　5
And you, all shapes beside, that fishy be,—
Some round, some flat, some long, all devilry,
Legless, unloving, infamously chaste:—

O scaly, slippery, wet, swift, staring wights,
What is't ye do? what life lead? eh, dull goggles?　　10
How do ye vary your vile days and nights?
How pass your Sundays? Are ye still but joggles
In ceaseless wash? Still nought but gapes and bites,
And drinks, and stares, diversified with boggles?

A Fish Answers

Amazing monster! that, for aught I know,   15
With the first sight of thee didst make our race
Forever stare! Oh flat and shocking face,
Grimly divided from the breast below!
Thou that on dry land horribly dost go
With a split body and most ridiculous pace,   20
Prong after prong, disgracer of all grace,
Long-useless-finned, haired, upright, unwet, slow!

O breather of unbreathable, sword-sharp air,
How canst exist? How bear thyself, thou dry
And dreary sloth? What particle canst share   25
Of the only blessed life, the watery?
I sometimes see of ye an actual *pair*
Go by! linked fin by fin! most odiously.

The Fish turns into a Man, and then into a Spirit,
and again speaks

Indulge thy smiling scorn, if smiling still,
O man! and loathe, but with a sort of love: 30
For difference must its use by difference prove,
And, in sweet clang, the spheres with music fill.
One of the spirits am I, that at his will
Live in whate'er has life—fish, eagle, dove—
No hate, no pride, beneath nought, nor above,   35
A visitor of the rounds of God's sweet skill.

Man's life is warm, glad, sad, 'twixt loves and graves,
Boundless in hope, honored with pangs austere,
Heaven-gazing; and his angel-wings he craves:
The fish is swift, small-needing, vague yet clear,   40
A cold, sweet, silver life, wrapped in round waves,
Quickened with touches of transporting fear.

                                                    1836

ABOU BEN ADHEM

Abou Ben Adhem, may his tribe increase!
Awoke one night from a deep dream of peace,
And saw, within the moonlight in his room,
Making it rich, and like a lily in bloom,
An angel writing in a book of gold:—   5

Exceeding peace had made Ben Adhem bold,
And to the presence in the room he said,
"What writest thou?"—The vision raised its head,
And with a look made of all sweet accord,
Answered, "The names of those who love the Lord."   10
"And is mine one?" said Abou. "Nay, not so,"
Replied the angel. Abou spoke more low,
But cheerly still; and said, "I pray thee then,
"Write me as one that loves his fellow men."

The angel wrote and vanished. The next night   15
It came again with a great wakening light,
And showed the names whom love of God had blessed,
And lo! Ben Adhem's name led all the rest.

                                                    1838

RONDEAU

Jenny kissed me when we met,
  Jumping from the chair she sat in;
Time, you thief, who love to get
  Sweets into your list, put that in:
Say I'm weary, say I'm sad,
  Say that health and wealth have missed me,
Say I'm growing old, but add,
  Jenny kissed me.

1838

THE OLD LADY

If the old lady is a widow and lives alone, the manners of her condition and time of life are so much the more apparent. She generally dresses in plain silks, that make a gentle rustling as she moves about the silence of her room; and she wears a nice cap with a lace border, that comes under the chin. In a placket at her side is an old enamelled watch, unless it is locked up in a drawer of her toilet, for fear of accidents. Her waist is rather tight and trim than otherwise, and she had a fine one when young; and she is not sorry if you see a pair of her stockings on a table, that you may be aware of the neatness of her leg and foot. Contented with these and other evident indications of a good shape, and letting her young friends understand that she can afford to obscure it a little, she wears pockets, and uses them well too. In the one is her handkerchief, and any heavier matter that is not likely to come out with it, such as the change of a sixpence; in the other is a miscellaneous assortment, consisting of a pocketbook, a bunch of keys, a needle-case, a spectacle-case, crumbs of biscuits, a nutmeg and grater, a smelling-bottle, and, according to the season, an orange or apple, which after many days she draws out, warm and glossy, to give to some little child that has well behaved itself. She generally occupies two rooms, in the neatest condition possible. In the chamber is a bed with a white coverlet, built up high and round, to look well, and with curtains of a pastoral pattern, consisting alternately of large plants, and shepherds and shepherdesses. On the mantelpiece are more shepherds and shepherdesses, with dot-eyed sheep at their feet, all in colored ware: the man, perhaps, in a pink jacket and knots of ribbons at his knees and shoes, holding his crook lightly in one hand, and with the other at his breast, turning his toes out and looking tenderly at the shepherdess; the woman holding a crook, also, and modestly returning his look, with a gipsy-hat jerked up behind a very slender waist, with petticoat and hips to counteract, and with the petticoat pulled up through the pocket-holes, in order to show the trimness of her ankles. But these patterns, of course, are various. The toilet is ancient, carved at the edges, and tied about with a snow-white drapery of muslin. Beside it are various boxes, mostly japan; and the set of drawers are exquisite things for a little girl to rummage, if ever little girl be so bold,—containing ribbons and laces of various kinds; linen smelling of lavender, of the flowers of which there is always dust in the corners; a heap of pocketbooks for a series of years; and pieces of dress long gone by, such as head-fronts, stomachers, and flowered satin shoes, with enormous heels. The stock of letters are under especial lock and key. So much for the bedroom. In the sitting room is rather a spare assortment of shining old mahogany furniture, or carved armchairs equally old, with chintz draperies down to the ground; a folding or other screen, with Chinese figures, their round little-eyed, meek faces perking sideways; a stuffed bird, perhaps in a glass case (a living one is too much for her); a portrait of her husband over the mantelpiece, in a coat with frog-buttons, and a delicate frilled hand lightly inserted in the waistcoat; and opposite him on the wall, is a piece of embroidered literature, framed and glazed, containing some moral distich or maxim, worked in angular capital letters, with two trees or parrots below, in their proper colors; the whole concluding with an ABC and numerals, and the name of the fair industrious, expressing it to be "her work, Jan. 14, 1762." The rest of the furniture consists of a looking-glass with carved edges, perhaps a settee, a hassock for the feet, a mat for the little dog, and a small set of shelves, in which are *The Spectator* and *Guardian*, *The Turkish Spy*, a *Bible* and *Prayer Book*, Young's *Night Thoughts* with a piece of lace in it to flatten, Mrs. Rowe's *Devout Exercises of the Heart*, Mrs. Glasse's *Cookery*, and perhaps *Sir Charles Grandison*, and *Clarissa*. *John Buncle* is in the closet among the pickles and preserves. The clock is on the landing-place between the two room doors, where it ticks audibly but quietly; and the landing-place is carpeted to a nicety. The house is most in character, and properly coeval, if it is in a retired suburb, and strongly built, with wainscot rather than paper inside, and lockers in the windows. Before the windows should be some quivering poplars. Here the Old Lady receives a few quiet visitors to tea, and perhaps an early game at cards: or you may see her going out on the same kind of visit herself, with a light umbrella running up into a stick and crooked ivory handle, and her little dog, equally famous for his love to her and captious antipathy to strangers. Her grandchildren dislike him on holidays, and the boldest sometimes ventures to give him a sly kick under the table. When she returns at night, she appears, if the weather happens to be doubtful, in a calash; and her servant in pattens follows half behind and half at her side, with a lantern.

Her opinions are not many nor new. She thinks the clergyman a nice man. The Duke of Wellington, in her opinion, is a very great man; but she has a secret preference for the Marquis of Granby. She thinks the young women of the present day too forward, and the men not respectful enough; but hopes her grandchildren will be better; though she differs with her daughter in several points respecting their management. She sets little value on the new accomplishments; is a great though delicate connoisseur in butcher's meat and all sorts of housewifery; and if you mention waltzes, expatiates on the grace and fine breeding of the minuet. She longs to have seen one danced by Sir Charles Grandison, whom she almost considers as a real person. She likes a walk of a summer's evening, but avoids the new streets, canals, etc., and sometimes goes through the churchyard, where her children and her husband lie buried, serious, but not melancholy. She has had three great epochs in her life:—her marriage, her having been at court to see the King and Queen and Royal Family, and a compliment on her figure she once received, in passing, from Mr. Wilkes, whom she describes as a sad, loose man, but engaging. His plainness she thinks much exaggerated. If anything takes her at a distance from home, it is still the court; but she seldom stirs, even for that. The last time but one that she went, was to see the Duke of Wirtemberg; and most probably for the last time of all, to see the Princess Charlotte and Prince Leopold. From this beatific vision she returned with the same admiration as ever for the fine comely appearance of the Duke of York and the rest of the family, and great delight at having had a near view of the Princess, whom she speaks of with smiling pomp and lifted mittens, clasping them as passionately as she can together, and calling her, in a transport of mixed loyalty and self-love, a fine royal young creature, and "Daughter of England."

1816

ON BYRON'S "DON JUAN": CANTOS FIRST AND SECOND

Some persons consider this the finest work of Lord Byron,—or at least that in which he displays most power. It is at all events the most extraordinary that he has yet published. His other poems, with the exception of that amusing satire—*Beppo*, are written for the most part with one sustained serious feeling throughout,—either of pathos, or grandeur, or passion, or all united. But *Don Juan* contains specimens of all the author's modes of writing, which are mingled together and push one another about in a strange way. The groundwork (if we may so speak of a stile [*sic*]) is the satirical and humorous; but you are sometimes surprised and moved by a touching piece of human nature, and again startled and pained by the sudden transition from loveliness or grandeur to ridicule or the mock-heroic. The delicious and deep descriptions of love, and youth, and hope, came upon us like the "young beams" of the sun breaking through the morning dew, and the terrific pictures of the misery of man and his most appalling sensations, like awful flashes of lightning;—but when the author reverses this change, he trifles too much with our feelings, and occasionally goes on, turning to ridicule or hopelessness all the fine ideas he has excited, with a recklessness that becomes extremely unpleasant and mortifying.

Don Juan is accused of being an "immoral" work, which we cannot at all discover. We suppose that this charge more particularly alludes to the first canto. Let us see then on what foundation it rests. The son of a Spanish patrician, educated in the most prudish manner by a licentious, yet affectedly virtuous mother, falls in love with the young wife of an old man. She returns his affection, and their passion being favored by opportunity, she gives way to her natural feelings, and is unfaithful to her marriage vows, the example (observe) being set her by this very husband's intrigues with *Juan's* mother. Now Lord Byron speaks lightly of the effect of any scruples of conscience upon her, and of her infidelity; and this, it is said, has tendency to corrupt the minds of "us youth," and to make us *think* lightly of breaking the matrimonial contract. But if to do this be immoral, we can only say that Nature is immoral. Lord Byron does no more than relate the consequences of certain absurdities. If he speaks slightingly of the ties between a girl and a husband old enough for her father, it is because the ties themselves *are* slight. He does not ridicule the bonds of marriage generally, or where they are formed as they should be: he merely shows the folly and wickedness of setting forms and opinions against nature. If stupid and selfish parents will make up matches between persons whom difference of age or disposition disqualifies for mutual affection, they must take the consequences: —but we do not think it fair that a poet should be exclaimed against as a promoter of nuptial infidelity because he tells them what those consequences are. In this particular case, too, the author does not omit some painful consequences to those who have sinned according to "nature's law." *Julia*, the victim of selfishness and "damned custom," is shut up in a convent, where no consolation remains to her but the remembrance of her entire and hapless love; but even that was perhaps pleasanter to her than living in the constant irksomeness of feigning an affection she could not feel.

There are a set of prudish and very suspicious moralists who endeavor to make vice appear to inexperienced eyes much more hateful than it really is. They would correct Nature;—and they always overreach themselves. Nature has made vice to a certain degree pleasurable, though its painful consequences outweigh its present gratification. Now the said prudes, in their lectures and sermons and moral discourses (for they are chiefly priests) are constantly declaiming on the *deformity* of vice, and its almost total want of attraction. The consequence is, that when they are found to have deceived (as they always are) and immoral indulgence is discovered to be not without its charms,—the minds of young persons are apt to confound their true with their false maxims, and to think the threats of future pain and repentance mere fables invented to deter them from their rightful enjoyments. Which then, we would ask, are the immoral writings,—those which, by misrepresenting the laws of nature, lead to false views of morality and consequent licentiousness?—or those, which ridicule and point out the effects of absurd contradictions of human feelings and passions, and help to bring about a reformation of such practises.

Of the story in the second canto it is unnecessary to say much, for these remarks will apply to both. We suppose there has been some sermonizing on the description of the delight arising from the "illicit intercourse" of *Juan* and *Haidee*. People who talk in this way can perceive no distinctions. It certainly is not to be inculcated, that every handsome young man and woman will find their account in giving way to all their impulses, because the very violent breaking through the habits and forms of society would create a great deal of unhappiness, both to the individuals, and to others. But what is there to blame in a beautiful and affectionate girl who gives way to a passion for a young shipwrecked human creature bound to her by gratitude as well as love? She exacts no promises, says the bard, because she fears no inconstancy. Her father had exposed her to the first temptation that comes across her, because he had not provided against it by allowing her to know more of mankind. And does she not receive, as well as bestow, more real pleasure (for that is the question) in the enjoyment of a first and deep passion, than in becoming the wife of some brother in iniquity to whom her pirating father would have trucked her for lucre?

The fact is, at the bottom of all these questions, that many things are made vicious, which are not so by nature; and many things made virtuous, which are only so by calling and agreement: and it is on the horns of this self-created dilemma, that society is continually writhing and getting desperate.

Oct. 31, 1819

GETTING UP ON COLD MORNINGS

An Italian author, Giulio Cordara, a Jesuit, has written a poem upon insects, which he begins by insisting, that those troublesome and abominable little animals were created for our annoyance, and that they were certainly not inhabitants of Paradise. We of the north may dispute this piece of theology; but on the other hand, it is as clear as the snow on the house tops, that Adam was not under the necessity of shaving; and that when Eve walked out of her delicious bower, she did not step upon ice three inches thick.

Some people say it is a very easy thing to get up of a cold morning. You have only, they tell you, to take the resolution; and the thing is done. This may be very true; just as a boy at school has only to take a flogging, and the thing is over. But we have not at all made up our minds upon it; and we find it a very pleasant exercise to discuss the matter, candidly, before we get up. This, at least, is not idling, though it may be lying. It affords an excellent answer to those who ask how lying in bed can be indulged in by a reasoning being,—a rational creature. How! Why, with the argument calmly at work in one's head, and the clothes over one's shoulder. Oh! it is a fine way of spending a sensible, impartial half-hour.

If these people would be more charitable, they would get on with their argument better. But they are apt to reason so ill, and to assert so dogmatically, that one could wish to have them stand round one's bed of a bitter morning, and *lie* before their faces. They ought to hear both sides of the bed, the inside and out. If they cannot entertain themselves with their own thoughts for half-an-hour or so, it is not the fault of those who can.

Candid inquiries into one's decumbency, besides the greater or less privileges to be allowed a man in porportion to his ability of keeping early hours, the work given his faculties, etc., will at least concede their due merits to such representations as the following. In the first place, says the in-

jured but calm appealer, I have been warm all night, and find my system in a state perfectly suitable to a warm-blooded animal. To get out of this state into the cold —besides the inharmonious and uncritical abruptness of the transition, is so unnatural to such a creature, that the poets, refining upon the tortures of the damned, make one of their greatest agonies consist in being suddenly transported from heat to cold, from fire to ice. They are "haled" out of their "beds," says Milton, by "harpy-footed furies,"—fellows who come to call them. On my first movement towards the anticipation of getting up I find that such parts of the sheets and bolster as are exposed to the air of the room are stone-cold. On opening my eyes, the first thing that meets them is my own breath rolling forth, as if in the open air, like smoke out of a chimney. Think of this symptom. Then I turn my eyes sideways and see the window all frozen over. Think of that. Then the servant comes in. "It is very cold this morning, is it not?"—"Very cold, sir."—"Very cold indeed, isn't it?"—"Very cold indeed, sir."—"More than usually so, isn't it, even for this weather?" Here the servant's wit and good nature are put to a considerable test, and the inquirer lies on thorns for the answer. "Why, sir, I think it *is*." (Good creature! There is not a better or more truth-telling servant going.) "I must rise, however—get me some warm water."—Here comes a fine interval between the departure of the servant and the arrival of the hot water, during which, of course, it is of "no use?" to get up. The hot water comes. "Is it quite hot?"—"Yes, sir."—"Perhaps too hot for shaving; I must wait a little?"—"No, sir, it will just do." (There is an over-nice propriety sometimes, an officious zeal of virtue, a little troublesome.) "Oh—the shirt—you must air my clean shirt;—linen gets very damp this weather."—"Yes, sir." Here another delicious five minutes. A knock at the door. "Oh, the shirt—very well. My stockings— I think the stockings had better be aired too."—"Very well, sir."—Here another interval. At length everything is ready, except myself. I now, continues our incumbent (a happy word, by the bye, for a country vicar)—I now cannot help thinking a good deal—who can?—upon the unnecessary and villainous custom of shaving; it is a thing so unmanly (here I nestle closer)— so effeminate (here I recoil from an unlucky step into the colder part of the bed). —No wonder that the Queen of France took part with the rebels against that degenerate King, her husband, who first affronted her smooth visage with a face like her own. The Emperor Julian never showed the luxuriancy of his genius to better advantage than in reviving the flowing beard. Look at Cardinal Bembo's picture—at Michael Angelo's—at Titian's—at Shakespeare's—at Fletcher's—at Spenser's—at Chaucer's—at Alfred's—at Plato's—I could name a great man for every tick of my watch.—Look at the Turks, a grave and otiose people.—Think of Haroun Al Raschid and Bed-ridden Hassan.—Think of Wortley Montague, the worthy son of his mother, above the prejudice of his time.—Look at the Persian gentlemen, whom one is ashamed of meeting about the suburbs, their dress and appearance are so much finer than our own.—Lastly, think of the razor itself—how totally opposed to every sensation of bed—how cold, how edgy, how hard! how utterly different from anything like the warm and circling amplitude, which

> Sweetly recommends itself
> Unto our gentle senses.

Add to this, benumbed fingers, which may help you to cut yourself, a quivering body, a frozen towel, and a ewer full of ice; and he that says there is nothing to oppose in all this, only shows that he has no merit in opposing it.

Thomson, the poet, who exclaims in his *Seasons*—

> Falsely luxurious! Will not man awake?

used to lie in bed till noon, because he said he had no motive in getting up. He could imagine the good of rising; but then he could also imagine the good of lying still; and his exclamation, it must be allowed, was made upon summertime, not winter. We must proportion the argument to the individual character. A money-getter may be drawn out of his bed by three or four pence; but this will not suffice for a student. A proud man may say, "What shall I think of myself, if I don't get up?" but the more humble one will be content to waive this prodigious notion of himself out of respect to his kindly bed. The mechanical man shall get up without any ado at all; and so shall the barometer. An ingenious lier-in-bed will find hard matter of discussion even on the score of health and longevity. He will ask us for our proofs and precedents of the ill effects of lying later in cold weather; and sophisticate much on the advantages of an even temperature of body; of the natural propensity (pretty universal) to have one's way; and of the animals that roll themselves up and sleep all the winter. As to longevity, he will ask whether the longest is of necessity the best; and whether Holborn is the handsomest street in London.

1820

ON THE REALITIES OF IMAGINATION

We may say of the love of nature what Shakespeare says of another love, that it

> Adds a precious seeing to the eye.

And we may say also, upon the like principle, that it adds a precious hearing to the ear. This and imagination, which ever follows upon it, are the two purifiers of our sense, which rescue us from the deafening babble of common cares, and enable us to hear all the affectionate voices of earth and heaven. The starry orbs, lapsing about in their smooth and sparkling dance, sing to us. The brooks talk to us of solitude. The birds are the animal spirits of nature, carolling in the air, like a careless lass.

> The gentle gales,
> Fanning their odoriferous wings, dispense
> Native perfumes; and whisper whence they stole
> Those balmy spoils.—*Paradise Lost*, iv, 156-9.

The poets are called creators, (ποιηταί, makers), because with their magical words they bring forth to our eyesight the abundant images and beauties of creation. They put them there, if the reader pleases; and so are literally creators. But whether put there or discovered, whether created or invented (for invention means nothing but finding out), there they are. If they touch us, they exist to as much purpose as anything else which touches us. If a passage in *King Lear* brings the tears into our eyes, it is real as the touch of a sorrowful hand. If the flow of a song of Anacreon's intoxicates us, it is as true to a pulse within us as the wine he drank. We hear not their sounds with ears, not see their sights with eyes; but we hear and see both so truly, that we are moved with pleasure; and the advantage, nay even the test, of seeing and hearing, at any time, is not in the seeing and hearing, but in the ideas we realize, and the pleasure we derive. Intellectual objects, therefore, inasmuch as they come home to us, are as true a part of the stock of nature as visible ones; and they are infinitely more abundant. Between the tree of a country clown and the tree of a Milton or Spenser, what a difference in point of productiveness! Between the plodding of a sexton through a churchyard and the walk of a Gray, what a difference! What a difference between the Bermudas of a shipbuilder and the Bermoothes of Shakespeare! the isle

> Full of noises,
> Sounds, and sweet airs, that give deiight, and
>   hurt not;

the isle of elves and fairies, that chased the tide to and fro on the sea-shore; of coralbones and the knell of sea-nymphs; of spirits dancing on the sands, and singing amidst the hushes of the wind; of Caliban, whose brute nature enchantment had made poetical; of Ariel, who lay in cowslip bells, and rode upon the bat; of Miranda, who wept when she saw Ferdinand work so hard, and begged him to let her help; telling him,

> I am your wife, if you will marry me;
> If not, I'll die your maid. To be your fellow
> You may deny me; but I'll be your servant,
> Whether you will or no.

Such are the discoveries which the poets make for us; worlds to which that of Columbus was but a handful of brute matter. America began to be richer for us the other day, when Humboldt came back and told us of its luxuriant and gigantic vegetation; of the myriads of shooting lights, which revel at evening in the southern sky; and of that grand constellation, at which Dante seems to have made so remarkable a guess (*Purgatorio*, cant., I, 5, 22). The natural warmth of the Mexican and Peruvian genius, set free from despotism, will soon do all the rest for it; awaken the sleeping riches of its eyesight, and call forth the glad music of its affections.

Imagination enriches everything. A great library contains not only books, but

> The assembled souls of all that men held wise.
>   DAVENANT

The moon is Homer's and Shakespeare's moon, as well as the one we look at. The sun comes out of his chamber in the east, with a sparkling eye, "rejoicing like a bridegroom." The commonest thing becomes like Aaron's rod, that budded. Pope called up the spirits of the Cabala to wait

upon a lock of hair, and justly gave it the honors of a constellation; for he has hung it, sparkling forever in the eyes of posterity. A common meadow is a sorry thing to a ditcher or a coxcomb; but by the help of its dues from imagination and the love of nature, the grass brightens for us, the air soothes us, we feel as we did in the daisied hours of childhood. Its verdures, its sheep, its hedge-row elms,—all these, and all else which sight, and sound, and associations can give it, are made to furnish a treasure of pleasant thoughts. Even brick and mortar are vivified, as of old, at the harp of Orpheus. A metropolis becomes no longer a mere collection of houses or of trades. It puts on all the grandeur of its history, and its literature; its towers, and rivers; its art, and jewelry, and foreign wealth; its multitude of human beings all intent upon excitement, wise or yet to learn; the huge and sullen dignity of its canopy of smoke by day; the wide gleam upwards of its lighted lustre at nighttime; and the noise of its many chariots, heard at the same hour, when the wind sets gently towards some quiet suburb.   1820

ON A QUARTERLY-REVIEWER'S ATTACK ON SHELLEY'S "PROMETHEUS UNBOUND"

As a conclusive proof of Mr. Shelley's nonsense, the Reviewer selects one of his passages which most require attention, separates it from its proper context, and turns it into prose: after which he triumphantly informs the reader that this prose is not prose, but "the conclusion of the third act of *Prometheus verbatim et literatim.*" Now poetry has often a language as well as music of its own, so distinct from prose, and so universally allowed a right to the distinction (which none are better aware of than the versifiers in the *Quarterly Review*), that secretly to decompose a poetical passage into prose, and then call for a criticism of a reader upon it, is like depriving a body of its distinguishing properties, or confounding their rights and necessities, and then asking where they are. Again, to take a passage abruptly from its context, especially when a context is more than usually necessary to its illustration, is like cutting out a piece of shade from a picture, and reproaching it for want of light. And finally, to select an obscure passage or two from an author, or even to show that he is often obscure, and then to pretend from these specimens, that he is nothing but obscurity and nonsense, is mere dishonesty.

For instance, Dante is a great genius who is often obscure; but suppose a critic were to pick out one of his obscurest passages, and assert that Dante was a mere writer of jargon. Suppose he were to select one of the metaphysical odes from his *Amoroso Convivio;* or to take a passage from Mr. Cary's translation of his great poem, and turn it into prose for the better mystification of the reader. Here is a specimen:—

"Every orb, corporeal, doth proportion its extent unto the virtue through its parts diffused. The greater blessedness preserves the more. The greater is the body (if all parts share equally) the more is to preserve. Therefore the circle, whose swift course enwheels the universal frame, answers to that, which is supreme in knowledge and in love. Thus by the virtue, not the seeming breadth of substance, measuring, thou shalt see the heavens, each to the intelligence that ruleth it, greater to more, and smaller unto less, suited in strict and wondrous harmony."—*Paradise,* Canto 28.

The lines in question from Mr. Shelley's poem are as follows. A spirit is describing a mighty change that has just taken place on earth. It is the consummation of a state of things, for which all the preceding part of the poem has been yearning:

The painted veil, by those who were, called life,
Which mimicked, as with colors idly spread,
All men believed and hoped, is torn aside;
The loathsome mask is fallen, the man remains
Sceptreless, free, uncircumscribed, but man
Equal, unclassed, tribeless, and nationless,
Exempt from awe, worship, degree, the king
Over himself; just, gentle, wise; but man.
Passionless? no,—yet free from guilt or pain,
Which were, for his will made or suffered them;
Nor yet exempt, tho' ruling them like slaves,
From chance, and death, and mutability,
The clogs of that which else might oversoar
The loftiest star of unascended heaven,
Pinnacled dim in the intense inane.

That is to say,—The veil, or superficial state of things, which was called life by those who lived before us, and which had nothing but an idle resemblance to that proper state of things, which we would fain have thought it, is no longer existing. The loathsome mask is fallen; and the being who was compelled to wear it, is now what he ought to be, one of a great family who are their own rulers, just, gentle, wise and passionless; no, not passionless, though free from guilt or pain, which were only the consequences of their former wilful mistakes; nor are they exempt, though they turn them to the best and most philosophical account, from chance, and death, and mutability; things, which are the clogs of that lofty spirit of humanity, which else might rise beyond all that we can conceive of the highest and happiest star of heaven, pinnacled, like an almost viewless atom, in the space of the universe.—*The intense inane* implies excess of emptiness, and is a phrase of Miltonian construction, like "the palpable obscure" and "the vast abrupt." Where is the unintelligible nonsense of all this? and where is the want of "grammar," with which the "pride" of the Reviewer, as *Mr. Looney M'Twoulter* says, would "come over" him?

Mr. Shelley has written a great deal of poetry equally unmetaphysical and beautiful. The whole of the tragedy of the *Cenci,* which the Reviewers do not think it to their interest to notice, is written in a style equally plain and noble. But we need not go farther than the volume before us, though, according to the Reviewer, the "whole" of it does not contain "*one* original image of nature, *one* simple expression of human feeling, or *one* new association of the appearances of the moral with those of the material world." We really must apologize to all intelligent readers who know anything of Mr. Shelley's genius, for appearing to give more notice to these absurdities than they are worth; but there are good reasons why they ought to be exposed. The *Prometheus* has already spoken for itself. Now take the *Ode to a Skylark,* of which I will venture to say, that there is not in the whole circle of lyric poetry a piece more *full* of "original images of nature, of simple expressions of human feeling, and of the associations of the appearances of the moral with those of the material world." . . . I know of nothing more beautiful than this,—more choice of tones, more natural in words, more abundant in exquisite, cordial, and most poetical associations. One gets the stanzas by heart unawares, and repeats them like "snatches of old tunes." To say that nobody who writes in the *Quarterly Review* could produce anything half as good (unless Mr. Wordsworth writes in it, which I do not believe he does) would be sorry praise. When Mr. Gifford "sings" as the phrase is, one is reminded of nothing but snarling. Mr. Southey, though the gods have made him more poetical than Mr. Gifford, is always affecting something original, and tiring one to death with commonplace. "Croker," as Goldsmith says, "rhymes to joker;" and as to the chorus of priests and virgins,—of scribes and pharisees,—which make up the poetical undersong of the Review, it is worthy of the discordant mixture of worldliness and religion, of faith and bad practice, of Christianity and malignity, which finds in it something ordinary enough to merit its approbation.

One passage more from this immoral and anti-christian volume, that contains, "not one simple expression of human feeling," and I will close my letter. It is part of *"An Ode, written October 1819, before the Spaniards had recovered their liberty:"*—

Glory, glory, glory,
To those who have greatly suffered and done!
  Never name in story
Was greater than that which ye shall have
  won.
Conquerors have conquered their foes alone,
Whose revenge, pride, and power they have
  overthrown:
Ride ye, more victorious, over your own.

Hear that, ye reverend and pugnacious Christians of the Quarterly!

Bind, bind every brow
With crownals of violet, ivy, and pine:
  Hide the bloodstains now
With hues which sweet nature has made
  divine;
Green strength, azure hope, and eternity;
But let not the pansy among them be;
Ye were injured, and that means memory.

How well the Spaniards have acted up to this infidel injunction is well known to the whole of wondering Christendom, and affords one of the happiest presages to the growth of true freedom and philosophy. Why did not the Reviewer quote such passages as these by way of specimens of the author's powers and moral feeling? Why did his boasted Christianity lead him to conceal these, as well as to omit what was necessary to the one quoted in my last? You pretty well understand why by this time.

June 23, 1822

FROM WHAT IS POETRY?

Poetry, strictly and artistically so called, that is to say, considered not merely as poetic feeling, which is more or less shared by all the world, but as the operation of that feeling, such as we see it in the poet's book, is the utterance of a passion for truth, beauty, and power, embodying and illustrating its conceptions by imagination and fancy, and modulating its language on the principle of variety in uniformity. Its means are whatever the universe contains; and its ends, pleasure and exaltation. Poetry stands between nature and convention, keeping alive among us the enjoyment of the external and the spiritual world; it has constituted the most enduring fame of nations and, next to Love and Beauty which are its parents, is the greatest proof to man of the pleasure to be found in all things, and of the probable riches of infinitude.

Poetry is a passion, because it seeks the deepest impressions; and because it must undergo, in order to convey them.

It is a passion for truth, because without truth the impression would be false or defective.

It is a passion for beauty, because its office is to exalt and refine by means of pleasure, and because beauty is nothing but the loveliest form of pleasure.

It is a passion for power, because power is impression triumphant, whether over the poet as desired by himself, or over the reader as affected by the poet.

It embodies and illustrates its impressions by imagination, or images of the objects of which it treats, and other images brought in to throw light on those objects, in order that it may enjoy and impart the feeling of their truth in its utmost conviction and affluence.

It illustrates them by fancy, which is a lighter play of imagination or the feeling of analogy coming short of seriousness, in order that it may laugh with what it loves, and show how it can decorate it with fairy ornament.

It modulates what it utters because in running the whole round of beauty it must needs include beauty of sound, and because, in the height of its enjoyment, it must show the perfection of its triumph, and make difficulty itself become part of its facility and joy.

And lastly, Poetry shapes this modulation into uniformity for its outline and variety for its parts, because it thus realizes the last idea of beauty itself, which includes the charm of diversity within the flowing round of habit and ease.

Poetry is imaginative passion. The quickest and subtlest test of the possession of its essence is in expression; the variety of things to be expressed shows the amount of its resources; and the continuity of the song completes the evidence of its strength and greatness. He who has thought, feeling, expression, imagination, action, character, and continuity, all in the largest amount and highest degree, is the greatest poet.

Poetry includes whatsoever of painting can be made visible to the mind's eye, and whatsoever of music can be conveyed by sound and proportion without singing or instrumentation. But it far surpasses those divine arts in suggestiveness, range, and intellectual wealth;—the first, in expression of thought, combination of images, and the triumph over space and time; the second, in all that can be done by speech apart from the tones and modulations of pure sound. Painting and music, however, include all those portions of the gift of poetry that can be expressed and heightened by the visible and melodious. Painting, in a certain apparent manner, is things themselves; music, in a certain audible manner, is their very emotion and grace. Music and painting are proud to be related to poetry, and poetry loves and is proud of them.

Poetry begins where matter of fact or of science ceases to be merely such and to exhibit a further truth, that is to say, the connection it has with the world of emotion, and its power to produce imaginative pleasure. Inquiring of a gardener, for instance, what flower it is we see yonder, he answers, "A lily." This is matter of fact. The botanist pronounces it to be of the order of "Hexandria monogynia." This is matter of science. It is the "lady" of the garden, says Spenser; and here we begin to have a poetical sense of its fairness and grace. It is

> The plant and flower of *light,*

says Ben Jonson; and poetry then shows us the beauty of the flower in all its mystery and splendor.

If it be asked how we know perceptions like these to be true, the answer is, by the fact of their existence—by the consent and delight of poetic readers. And as feeling is the earliest teacher, and perception the only final proof of things the most demon-

strable by science, so the remotest imaginations of the poets may often be found to have the closest connection with matter of fact; perhaps might always be so, if the subtlety of our perceptions were a match for the causes of them. Consider this image of Ben Jonson's—of a lily being the flower of light. Light, undecomposed, is white; and as the lily is white, and light is white, and whiteness itself is nothing *but* light, the two things, so far, are not merely similar, but identical. A poet might add, by an analogy drawn from the connection of light and color, that there is a "golden dawn" issuing out of the white lily in the rich yellow of the stamens. I have no desire to push this similarity farther than it may be worth. Enough has been stated to show that, in poetical as well as in other analogies, "the same feet of Nature", as Bacon says, may be seen "treading in different paths"; and that the most scornful, that is to say, dullest disciple of fact, should be cautious how he betrays the shallowness of his philosophy by discerning no poetry in its depths.

But the poet is far from dealing only with these subtle and analogical truths. Truth of every kind belongs to him, provided it can bud into any kind of beauty, or is capable of being illustrated and impressed by the poetic faculty. Nay, the simplest truth is often so beautiful and impressive of itself that one of the greatest proofs of his genius consists in his leaving it to stand alone, illustrated by nothing but the light of its own tears or smiles, its own wonder, might, or playfulness. Hence the complete effect of many a simple passage in our old English ballads and romances, and of the passionate sincerity in general of the greatest early poets, such as Homer and Chaucer, who flourished before the existence of a "literary world", and were not perplexed by a heap of notions and opinions, or by doubts how emotion ought to be expressed. The greatest of their successors never write equally to the purpose, except when they can dismiss everything from their minds but the like simple truth. In the beautiful poem of *Sir Eger, Sir Graham, and Sir Gray-Steel* (see it in Ellis's *Specimens* or Laing's *Early Metrical Tales*), a knight thinks himself disgraced in the eyes of his mistress:—

> Sir Eger said, "If it be so,
> Then wot I well I must forgo
> Love-liking, and manhood, all clean!"
> *The water rushed out of his een!*

Sir Gray-Steel is killed:—

> Gray-Steel into his death thus thraws
> He *walters and the grass up draws;*
> . . . .
> *A little while then lay he still*
> (*Friends that him saw, liked full ill*)
> *And bled into his armor bright.*

The abode of Chaucer's Reve, or Steward, in the *Canterbury Tales,* is painted in two lines which nobody ever wished longer:—

> His wonning was full fair upon an heath,
> With greeny trees yshadowed was his place.

Every one knows the words of Lear, "most *matter-of-fact,* most melancholy":—

> Pray, do not mock me;
> I am a very foolish fond old man,
> Fourscore and upwards:
> Not an hour more, nor less; and, to deal plainly,
> I fear I am not in my perfect mind.

It is thus by exquisite pertinence, melody, and the implied power of writing with exuberance, if need be, that beauty and truth become identical in poetry, and that pleasure, or at the very worst, a balm in our tears, is drawn out of pain.

It is a great and rare thing, and shows a lovely imagination when the poet can write a commentary, as it were, of his own on such sufficing passages of nature, and be thanked for the addition. There is an instance of this kind in Warner, an old Elizabethan poet, than which I know nothing sweeter in the world. He is speaking of Fair Rosamond and of a blow given her by Queen Eleanor:—

> With that she dashed her on the lips,
> *So dyèd double red:*
> *Hard was the heart that gave the blow,*
> *Soft were those lips that bled.*

There are different kinds and degrees of imagination, some of them necessary to the formation of every true poet, and all of them possessed by the greatest. Perhaps they may be enumerated as follows: first, that which presents to the mind any object or circumstance in everyday life, as when we imagine a man holding a sword, or looking out of a window; second, that which presents real, but not everyday circumstances, as King Alfred tending the loaves, or Sir Philip Sidney giving up the water to the dying soldier; third, that which combines character and events

directly imitated from real life, with imitative realities of its own invention, as the probable parts of the histories of Priam and Macbeth, or what may be called natural fiction as distinguished from supernatural; fourth, that which conjures up things and events not to be found in nature, as Homer's gods and Shakespeare's witches, enchanted horses and spears, Ariosto's hippogriff, &c.; fifth, that which, in order to illustrate or aggravate one image, introduces another: sometimes in simile, as when Homer compares Apollo descending in his wrath at noon-day to the coming of night-time; sometimes in metaphor, or simile comprised in a word, as in Milton's "motes that *people* the sunbeams"; sometimes in concentrating into a word the main history of any person or thing, past or even future, as in the "starry Galileo" of Byron, and that ghastly foregone conclusion of the epithet "murdered" applied to the yet living victim in Keats's story from Boccaccio,—

> So the two brothers and their *murdered* man
> Rode towards fair Florence;—

sometimes in the attribution of a certain representative quality which makes one circumstance stand for others, as in Milton's gray-fly winding its *"sultry* horn," which epithet contains the heat of a summer's day; sixth, that which reverses this process, and makes a variety of circumstances take color from one, like nature seen with jaundiced or glad eyes, or under the influence of storm or sunshine; as when in *Lycidas,* or the Greek pastoral poets, the flowers and the flocks are made to sympathize with a man's death; or, in the Italian poet, the river flowing by the sleeping Angelica seems talking of love—

> Parea che l'erba le fiorisse intorno,
> *E d'amor ragionasse quella riva!*
> *Orlando Innamorato,* Canto iii.

or in the voluptuous homage paid to the sleeping Imogen by the very light in the chamber and the reaction of her own beauty upon itself; or in the "witch element" of the tragedy of *Macbeth* and the May-day night of *Faust;* seventh, and last, that which by a single expression, apparently of the vaguest kind, not only meets but surpasses in its effect the extremest force of the most particular description; as in that exquisite passage of Coleridge's *Christabel* where the unsuspecting object of the witch's malignity is bidden to go to bed:—

> Quoth Christabel, So let it be!
> And as the lady bade, did she.
> Her gentle limbs did she undress,
> *And lay down in her loveliness;*—

a perfect verse surely, both for feeling and music. The very smoothness and gentleness of the limbs is in the series of the letter *l*'s.

I am aware of nothing of the kind surpassing that most lovely inclusion of physical beauty in moral, neither can I call to mind any instances of the imagination that turns accompaniments into accessories, superior to those I have alluded to. Of the class of comparison, one of the most touching (many a tear must it have drawn from parents and lovers) is in a stanza which has been copied into the *Friar of Orders Gray* out of Beaumont and Fletcher:—

> Weep no more, lady, weep no more,
>   Thy sorrow is in vain;
> *For violets plucked the sweetest showers*
>   *Will ne'er make grow again.*

And Shakespeare and Milton abound in the very grandest; such as Antony's likening his changing fortunes to the cloud-rack; Lear's appeal to the old age of the heavens; Satan's appearance in the horizon, like a fleet "hanging in the clouds"; and the comparisons of him with the comet and the eclipse. Nor unworthy of this glorious company for its extraordinary combination of delicacy and vastness is that enchanting one of Shelley's in the Adonais:—

> Life, like a dome of many-colored glass,
> Stains the white radiance of eternity.

I multiply these particulars in order to impress upon the reader's mind the great importance of imagination in all its phases as a constituent part of the highest poetic faculty.

The happiest instance I remember of imaginative metaphor is Shakespeare's moonlight "sleeping" on a bank; but half his poetry may be said to be made up of it, metaphor indeed being the common coin of discourse. Of imaginary creatures, none out of the pale of mythology and the East are equal, perhaps, in point of invention to Shakespeare's Ariel and Caliban, though poetry may grudge to prose the discovery of a Winged Woman, especially such as she has been described by her inventor in the story of *Peter Wilkins*, and, in point of treatment, the Mammon and Jealousy of

Spenser, some of the monsters in Dante, particularly his Nimrod, his interchangements of creatures into one another, and (if I am not presumptuous in anticipating what I think will be the verdict of posterity) the Witch in Coleridge's *Christabel* may rank even with the creations of Shakespeare.

1844

COLERIDGE

Coleridge lived in the most extraordinary and agitated period of modern history; and to a certain extent he was so mixed up with its controversies, that he was at one time taken for nothing but an apostate republican, and at another for a dreaming theosophist. The truth is, that both his politics and theosophy were at the mercy of a discursive genius, intellectually bold but educationally timid, which, anxious, or rather willing, to bring conviction and speculation together, mooting all points as it went, and throwing the subtlest glancing lights on many, ended in satisfying nobody, and concluding nothing. Charles Lamb said of him, that he had "the art of making the unintelligible appear intelligible." He was the finest dreamer, the most eloquent talker, and the most original thinker of the day; but for want of complexional energy, did nothing with all the vast *prose* part of his mind but help the Germans to give a subtler tone to criticism, and sow a few valuable seeds of thought in minds worthy to receive them. Nine-tenths of his theology would apply equally well to their own creeds in the mouths of a Brahmin or a Mussulman.

His poetry is another matter. It is so beautiful, and was so quietly content with its beauty, making no call on the critics, and receiving hardly any notice, that people are but now beginning to awake to a full sense of its merits. Of pure poetry, strictly so called, that is to say, consisting of nothing but its essential self, without conventional and perishing helps, he was the greatest master of his time. If you would see it in a phial, like a distillation of roses (taking it, I mean, at its best), it would be found without a speck. The poet is happy with so good a gift, and the reader is "happy in his happiness." Yet so little, sometimes, are a man's contemporaries and personal acquaintances able or disposed to estimate him properly, that while Coleridge, unlike Shakespeare, lavished praises on his poetic friends, he had all the merit of the generosity to himself; and even Hazlitt, owing perhaps to causes of political alienation, could see nothing to admire in the exquisite poem of *Christabel,* but the description of the quarrel between the friends! After speaking, too, of the Ancient Mariner as the only one of his poems that he could point out to any one as giving an adequate idea of his great natural powers, he adds, "It is high German, however, and in it he seems to conceive of poetry but as a drunken dream, reckless, careless, and heedless of past, present, and to come." This is said of a poem, with which fault has been found for the exceeding conscientiousness of its moral! O, ye critics, the best of ye, what havoc does personal difference play with your judgments! It was Mr. Hazlitt's only or most unwarrantable censure, or one which friendship found hardest to forgive. But peace, and honor too, be with his memory! If he was a splenetic and sometimes jealous man, he was a disinterested politician and an admirable critic: and lucky were those whose natures gave them the right and the power to pardon him.

Coleridge, though a born poet, was in his style and general musical feeling the disciple partly of Spenser, and partly of the fine old English ballad-writers in the collection of Bishop Percy. But if he could not improve on them in some things, how he did in others, especially in the art of being thoroughly musical! Of all our writers of the briefer narrative poetry, Coleridge is the finest since Chaucer; and assuredly he is the sweetest of all our poets. Waller's music is but a court-flourish in comparison; and though Beaumont and Fletcher, Collins, Gray, Keats, Shelley, and others, have several as sweet passages, and Spenser is in a certain sense musical throughout, yet no man has written whole poems, of equal length, so perfect in the sentiment of music, so varied with it, and yet leaving on the ear so unbroken and single an effect.

1844

KEATS

Keats was born a poet of the most poetical kind. All his feelings came to him through a poetical medium, or were speedily colored by it. He enjoyed a jest as heartily as any one, and sympathized with the lowliest commonplace; but the next minute his thoughts were in a garden of enchantment, with nymphs, and fauns, and shapes of exalted humanity:

> Elysian beauty, melancholy grace.

It might be said of him that he never beheld an oak tree without seeing the Dryad. His fame may now forgive the critics who disliked his politics, and did not understand his poetry. Repeated editions of him in England, France, and America attest its triumphant survival of all obloquy; and there can be no doubt that he has taken a permanent station among the British poets, of a very high, if not thoroughly mature, description.

Keats's early poetry, indeed, partook plentifully of the exuberance of youth; and even in most of his later, his sensibility, sharpened by mortal illness, tended to a morbid excess. His region is "a wilderness of sweets,"—flowers of all hue, and "weeds of glorious feature,"—where, as he says, the luxuriant soil brings

> The pipy hemlock to strange undergrowth.

But there also is the "rain-scented eglantine," and bushes of May-flowers, with bees, and myrtle, and bay,—and endless paths into forests haunted with the loveliest as well as gentlest beings; and the gods live in the distance, amid notes of majestic thunder. I do not say that no "surfeit" is ever there; but I do, that there is no end of the "nectared sweets." In what other English poet (however superior to him in other respects) are you so *certain* of never opening a page without lighting upon the loveliest imagery and the most eloquent expressions? Name one. Compare any succession of their pages at random, and see if the young poet is not sure to present his stock of beauty; crude it may be, in many instances; too indiscriminate in general; never, perhaps, thoroughly perfect in cultivation; but there it is, exquisite of its kind, and filling envy with despair. He died at five-and-twenty; he had not revised his earlier works, nor given his genius its last pruning. His *Endymion,* in resolving to be free from all critical trammels, had no versification; and his last noble fragment, *Hyperion,* is not faultless,—but it is nearly so. *The Eve of St. Agnes* betrays morbidity only in one instance (noticed in the comment). Even in his earliest productions, which are to be considered as those of youth just emerging from boyhood, are to be found passages of as masculine a beauty as ever were written. Witness the

Sonnet on Reading Chapman's Homer,— epical in the splendor and dignity of its images, and terminating with the noblest Greek simplicity. Among his finished productions, however, of any length, *The Eve of St. Agnes* still appears to me the most delightful and complete specimen of his genius. It stands midway between his most sensitive ones (which, though of rare beauty, occasionally sink into feebleness) and the less generally characteristic majesty of the fragment of *Hyperion.* Doubtless his greatest poetry is to be found in *Hyperion;* and had he lived, there is as little doubt he would have written chiefly in that strain; rising superior to those languishments of love which made the critics so angry, and which they might so easily have pardoned at his time of life. But *The Eve of St. Agnes* had already bid most of them adieu,—exquisitely loving as it is. It is young, but full-grown poetry of the rarest description; graceful as the beardless Apollo; glowing and gorgeous with the colors of romance. I have therefore reprinted the whole of it in the present volume, together with the comment alluded to in the Preface; especially as, in addition to felicity of treatment, its subject is in every respect a happy one, and helps to "paint" this our bower of "poetry with delight." Melancholy, it is true, will "break in" when the reader thinks of the early death of such a writer; but it is one of the benevolent provisions of nature that all good things tend to pleasure in the recollection, when the bitterness of their loss is past, their own sweetness embalms them.

A thing of beauty is a joy forever.

While writing this paragraph, a handorgan out-of-doors has been playing one of the mournfullest and loveliest of the airs of Bellini—another genius who died young. The sound of music always gives a feeling either of triumph or tenderness to the state of mind in which it is heard: in this instance it seemed like one departed spirit come to bear testimony to another, and to say how true indeed may be the union of sorrowful and sweet recollections.

Keats knew the youthful faults of his poetry as well as any man, as the reader may see by the preface to *Endymion,* and its touching though manly acknowledgment of them to critical candor. I have this moment read it again, after a lapse of years, and have been astonished to think how anybody could answer such an appeal to the mercy of strength, with the cruelty of weakness. All the good for which Mr. Gifford pretended to be zealous, he might have effected with pain to no one, and glory to himself; and therefore all the evil he mixed with it was of his own making. But the secret at the bottom of such unprovoked censure is exasperated inferiority. Young poets, upon the whole,—at least very young poets,—had better not publish at all. They are pretty sure to have faults; and jealousy and envy are as sure to find them out, and wreak upon them their own disappointments. The critic is often an unsuccessful author, almost always an inferior one to a man of genius, and possesses his sensibility neither to beauty nor to pain. If he does,—if by any chance he is a man of genius himself (and such things have been), sure and certain will be his regret, some day, for having given pains which he might have turned into noble pleasures; and nothing will console him but that very charity towards himself, the grace of which can only be secured to us by our having denied it to no one.

Let the student of poetry observe that in all the luxury of *The Eve of St. Agnes* there is nothing of the conventional craft of artificial writers; no heaping up of words or similes for their own sakes or the rhyme's sake; no gaudy commonplaces; no borrowed airs of earnestness; no tricks of inversion; no substitution of reading or of ingenious thoughts for feeling or spontaneity; no irrelevancy or unfitness of any sort. All flows out of sincerity and passion. The writer is as much in love with the heroine as his hero is; his description of the painted window, however gorgeous, has not an untrue or superfluous word; and the only speck of a fault in the whole poem arises from an excess of emotion.

1844

THOMAS DE QUINCEY (1785-1859)

De Quincey, a dreamer of beautiful dreams, disdained an obstinate vassalage to mere matters of fact, but sought with intense concentration of effort after a conscientious and profound psychology of letters.

EDMUND GOSSE

De Quincey was the son of a merchant in Manchester, and was educated at Oxford. His disposition and manner of life was that of a scholar; but he earned his living as a contributor to magazines and as an editor. Some years of his life he spent in the Lake Country, and some in London; but the last thirty, in Edinburgh. His addiction to opium was during a few years only; and neither that weakness, nor his inclination to solitude, prevented his being very happy in his relationship with his wife and children. He knew nearly all the leading Romantics personally. He greatly admired Coleridge, revered Wordsworth; and although estrangements arose between him and them, he was always one of their most devoted students and interpreters.

De Quincey accepted the basic doctrines of Romanticism about life and literature, but he applied its principles to so many diverse subjects that he greatly enriched its literature. A scholar, a sympathetic observer of life, and a dreamer, he appreciated the intellectual, the emotional, and the mystical. Much of his work, including his historical narratives and *The English Mail Coach,* is predominantly factual, and cannot fairly be called escapist. And those of his writings which used to be called so, and were scornfully dismissed by some critics as mere opium-dreams, of value only as rhetorical fireworks, are now seen to have important exploratory purposes and values. In the age of Freud and Jung we can understand the real significance and originality of De Quincey, not only in the *Confessions of an Opium-Eater,* but also in *The Affliction of Childhood,* in *Dreaming,* and in *The Palimpsest of the Human Brain.* In such essays he was trying to extend the psychological gropings of Romanticism, trying to fathom the lower depths of the subconscious and to reach upwards to the higher altitudes of the soul; he is wondering about their interrelationship, and about the possible governance of the lower impulses and memories by the higher will.

Only in poetic prose could such experiences and thoughts and questionings be approximately communicated, only in a style like De Quincey's,—rich, sonorous, orchestrated. There are faults in his writings: sometimes he becomes too vague or rhapsodical, sometimes ostentatious. There are irritating prejudices, also lapses from good taste, particularly when he tries to be humorous. But at his best, and especially in his realm, the mysterious depths of human nature, he has few equals.

FROM CONFESSIONS OF AN ENGLISH OPIUM-EATER: BEING AN EXTRACT FROM THE LIFE OF A SCHOLAR

THE PLEASURES OF OPIUM

Markets and theatres are not the appropriate haunts of the opium-eater, when in the divinest state incident to his enjoyment. In that state, crowds become an oppression to him; music even, too sensual and gross. He naturally seeks solitude and silence, as indispensable conditions of those trances and profoundest reveries which are the crown or consummation of what opium can do for human nature. I, whose disease it was to meditate too much, and to observe too little, and who upon my first entrance at college was nearly falling into a deep melancholy from brooding too much on the sufferings which I had witnessed in London, was sufficiently aware of the tendencies of my own thoughts to do all I could to counteract them.—I was, indeed, like a person who, according to the old legend, had entered the cave of Trophonius: and the remedies I sought were to force myself into society, and to keep my understanding in continual activity upon matters of science. But for these remedies, I should certainly have become hypochondriacally melancholy. In after years, however, when my cheerfulness was more fully re-established, I yielded to my natural inclination for a solitary life. And, at that time, I often fell into these reveries upon taking opium; and more than once it has happened to me, on a summer night, when I have been at an open window, in a room from which I could overlook the sea at a mile below me, and could command a view of the great town of L[iverpool], at about the same distance, that I have sat, from sunset to sunrise, motionless, and without wishing to move.

I shall be charged with mysticism, Behmenism, quietism, etc., but *that* shall not alarm me. Sir H. Vane, the younger, was one of our wisest men: and let my readers see if he, in his philosophical works, be half as unmystical as I am.—I say, then, that it has often struck me that the scene itself was somewhat typical of what took place in such a reverie. The town of L[iverpool] represented the earth, with its sorrows and its graves left behind, yet not out of sight, nor wholly forgotten. The ocean, in everlasting but gentle agitation, and brooded over by a dove-like calm, might not unfitly typify the mind and the mood which then swayed it. For it seemed to me as if then first I stood at a distance, and aloof from the uproar of life, as if the tumult, the fever, and the strife, were suspended; a respite granted from the secret burthens of the heart: a sabbath of repose; a resting from human labors. Here were the hopes which blossom in the paths of life, reconciled with the peace which is in the grave; motions of the intellect as unwearied as the heavens, yet for all anxieties a halcyon calm: a tranquillity that seemed no product of inertia, but as if resulting from mighty and equal antagonisms; infinite activities, infinite repose.

Oh! just, subtle, and mighty opium! that to the hearts of poor and rich alike, for the wounds that will never heal, and for "the pangs that tempt the spirit to rebel," bringest an assuaging balm; eloquent opium! that with thy potent rhetoric stealest away the purposes of wrath; and to the guilty man for one night givest back the hopes of his youth, and hands washed pure from blood; and to the proud man a brief oblivion for

Wrongs unredressed and insults unavenged;

that summonest to the chancery of dreams, for the triumphs of suffering innocence, false witnesses; and confoundest perjury; and dost reverse the sentences of unrighteous judges:—thou buildest upon the bosom of darkness, out of the fantastic imagery of the brain, cities and temples beyond the art of Phidias and Praxiteles—beyond the splendor of Babylon and Hekatompylos: and "from the anarchy of dreaming sleep," callest into sunny light the faces of long-buried beauties, and the blessed household countenances, cleansed from the "dishonors of the grave." Thou only givest these gifts to man; and thou hast the keys of Paradise, oh, just, subtle, and mighty opium! . . .

But now farewell—a long farewell to happiness—winter or summer! farewell to smiles and laughter! farewell to peace of mind! farewell to hope and to tranquil dreams, and to the blessed consolation of sleep! for more than three years and a half I am summoned away from these: I am now arrived at an *Iliad* of woes: for I have now to record

THE PAINS OF OPIUM

——as when some great painter dips
His pencil in the gloom of earthquake and
   eclipse.

SHELLEY'S *Revolt of Islam*

Many years ago, when I was looking over Piranesi's *Antiquities of Rome,* Coleridge, then standing by, described to me a set of plates from that artist, called his *Dreams,* and which record the scenery of his own visions during the delirium of a fever. Some of these (I describe only from memory of Coleridge's account) represented vast Gothic halls; on the floor of which stood mighty engines and machinery, wheels, cables, catapults, etc., expressive of enormous power put forth, or resistance overcome. Creeping along the sides of the walls, you perceived a staircase; and upon this, groping his way upwards, was Piranesi himself. Follow the stairs a little farther, and you perceive them reaching an abrupt termination, without any balustrade, and allowing no step onwards to him who should reach the extremity, except into the depths below. Whatever is to become of poor Piranesi, at least you suppose that his labors must now in some way terminate. But raise your eyes, and behold a second flight of stairs still higher, on which again Piranesi is perceived, by this time standing on the very brink of the abyss. Once again elevate your eye, and a still more aërial flight is descried; and there, again, is the delirious Piranesi, busy on his aspiring labors: and so on, until the unfinished stairs and the hopeless Piranesi both are lost in the upper gloom of the hall. With the same power of endless growth and self-reproduction did my architecture proceed in dreams. In the early stage of the malady, the splendors of my dreams were indeed chiefly architectural; and I beheld such pomp of cities and palaces as never yet was beheld by the waking eye, unless in the clouds. . . .

May, 1818.—The Malay has been a fearful enemy for months. Every night, through his means, I have been transported into Asiatic scenery. I know not whether others share in my feelings on this point; but I have often thought that if I were compelled to forego England, and to live in China, among Chinese manners and modes of life and scenery, I should go mad. The causes of my horror lie deep, and some of them must be common to others. Southern Asia, in general, is the seat of awful images and associations. As the cradle of the human race, if on no other ground, it would have a dim, reverential feeling connected with it. But there are other reasons. No man can pretend that the wild, barbarous, and capricious superstitions of Africa, or of savage tribes elsewhere, affect him in the way that he is affected by the ancient, monumental, cruel, and elaborate religions of Hindostan. The mere antiquity of Asiatic things, of their institutions, histories, above all, of their mythologies, &c., is so impressive, that to me the vast age of the race and name overpowers the sense of youth in the individual. A young Chinese seems to me an antediluvian man renewed. Even Englishmen, though not bred in any knowledge of such institutions, cannot but shudder at the mystic sublimity of *castes* that have flowed apart, and refused to mix, through such immemorial tracts of time; nor can any man fail to be awed by the sanctity of the Ganges, or by the very name of the Euphrates. It contributes much to these feelings that Southeastern Asia is, and has been for thousands of years, the part of the earth most swarming with human life, the great *officina gentium.* Man is a weed in those regions. The vast empires, also, into which the enormous population of Asia has always been cast, give a further

sublimity to the feelings associated with all Oriental names or images. In China, over and above what it has in common with the rest of southern Asia, I am terrified by the modes of life, by the manners, by the barrier of utter abhorrence placed between myself and *them,* by counter-sympathies deeper than I can analyze. I could sooner live with lunatics, with vermin, with crocodiles or snakes. All this, and much more than I can say, the reader must enter into before he can comprehend the unimaginable horror which these dreams of Oriental imagery and mythological tortures impressed upon me. Under the connecting feeling of tropical heat and vertical sunlights, I brought together all creatures, birds, beasts, reptiles, all trees and plants, usages and appearances, that are found in all tropical regions, and assembled them together in China or Hindostan. From kindred feelings, I soon brought Egypt and her gods under the same law. I was stared at, hooted at, grinned at, chattered at, by monkeys, by paroquets, by cockatoos. I ran into pagodas, and was fixed for centuries at the summit, or in secret rooms; I was the idol; I was the priest; I was worshipped; I was sacrificed. I fled from the wrath of Brama through all the forests of Asia; Vishnu hated me; Seeva lay in wait for me. I came suddenly upon Isis and Osiris: I had done a deed, they said, which the ibis and the crocodile trembled at. Thousands of years I lived and was buried in stone coffins, with mummies and sphinxes, in narrow chambers at the heart of eternal pyramids. I was kissed, with cancerous kisses by crocodiles, and was laid, confounded with all unutterable abortions, amongst reeds and Nilotic mud.

Some slight abstraction I thus attempt of my oriental dreams, which filled me always with such amazement at the monstrous scenery, that horror seemed absorbed for a while in sheer astonishment. Sooner or later came a reflux of feeling that swallowed up the astonishment, and left me, not so much in terror, as in hatred and abomination of what I saw. Over every form, and threat, and punishment, and dim sightless incarceration, brooded a sense of eternity and infinity that drove me into an oppression as of madness. Into these dreams only, it was, with one or two slight exceptions, that any circumstances of physical horror entered. All before had been moral and spiritual terrors. But here the main agents were ugly birds, or snakes, or crocodiles; especially the last. The cursed crocodile became to me the object of more horror than almost all the rest. I was compelled to live with him; and (as was always the case almost in my dreams) for centuries. I escaped sometimes, and found myself in 5 Chinese houses, with cane tables, etc. All the feet of the tables, sofas, etc., soon became instinct with life: the abominable head of the crocodile, and his leering eyes, looked out at me, multiplied into a thou- 10 sand repetitions: and I stood loathing and fascinated. And so often did this hideous reptile haunt my dreams, that many times the very same dream was broken up in the very same way: I heard gentle voices 15 speaking to me (I hear everything when I am sleeping); and instantly I awoke: it was broad noon; and my children were standing, hand in hand, at my bedside; come to show me their colored shoes, or 20 new frocks, or to let me see them dressed for going out. I protest that so awful was the transition from the damned crocodile, and the other unutterable monsters and abortions of my dreams, to the sight of 25 innocent *human* natures and of infancy, that, in the mighty and sudden revulsion of mind, I wept, and could not forbear it, as I kissed their faces.

Then suddenly would come a dream 30 of far different character,—a tumultuous dream,—commencing with a music such as now I often heard in sleep,—music of preparation and of awakening suspense. The undulations of fast-gathering tumults were 35 like the opening of the Coronation Anthem; and, like *that*, gave the feeling of a multitudinous movement, of infinite cavalcades filing off, and the tread of innumerable armies. The morning was come of a 40 mighty day—a day of crisis and of ultimate hope for human nature, then suffering mysterious eclipse, and laboring in some dread extremity. Somewhere, but I knew not where—somehow, but I knew not how—by 45 some beings, but I knew not by whom—a battle, a strife, an agony, was traveling through all its stages—was evolving itself, like the catastrophe of some mighty drama, with which my sympathy was the more insupportable, from deepening confusion as 50 to its local scene, its cause, its nature, and its undecipherable issue. I (as is usual in dreams where, of necessity, we make ourselves central to every movement) had the 55 power, and yet had not the power, to decide it. I had the power, if I could raise myself to will it; and yet again had not the power, for the weight of twenty Atlantics was upon me, or the oppression of inexpia- 60

ble guilt. "Deeper than ever plummet sounded," I lay inactive. Then, like a chorus, the passion deepened. Some·greater interest was at stake, some mightier cause, than ever yet the sword had pleaded, or 5 trumpet had proclaimed. Then came sudden alarms; hurryings to and fro; trepidations of innumerable fugitives, I knew not whether from the good cause or the bad; darkness and lights; tempest and human 10 faces; and at last, with the sense that all was lost, female forms, and the features that were worth all the world to me; and but a moment allowed—and clasped hands, with heart-breaking partings, and then— 15 everlasting farewells! and, with a sigh such as the caves of hell sighed when the incestuous mother uttered the abhorred name of Death, the sound was reverberated— everlasting farewells! and again, and yet 20 again reverberated—everlasting farewells!

And I awoke in struggles, and cried aloud, "I will sleep no more!"

1821

ON THE KNOCKING AT THE GATE IN MACBETH

From my boyish days I had always felt a great perplexity on one point in *Macbeth*. It was this:—the knocking at the gate which succeeds to the murder of Duncan produced to my feelings an effect for which 35 I never could account. The effect was that it reflected back upon the murderer a peculiar awfulness and a depth of solemnity; yet, however obstinately I endeavored with my understanding to comprehend this, for 40 many years I never could see *why* it should produce such an effect.

Here I pause for one moment to exhort the reader never to pay any attention to his understanding when it stands in opposi- 45 tion to any other faculty of his mind. The mere understanding, however useful and indispensable, is the meanest faculty in the human mind, and the most to be distrusted; and yet the great majority of peo- 50 ple trust to nothing else,—which may do for ordinary life, but not for philosophical purposes. Of this, out of ten thousand instances that I might produce, I will cite one. Ask of any person whatsoever who is 55 not previously prepared for the demand by a knowledge of the perspective, to draw in the rudest way the commonest appearance which depends upon the laws of that 60 science,—as, for instance, to represent the effect of two walls standing at right angles to each other, or the appearance of the houses on each side of a street as seen by a person looking down the street from one extremity. Now, in all cases, unless the person has happened to observe in pictures how it is that artists produce these effects, he will be utterly unable to make the smallest approximation to it. Yet why? For he has actually seen the effect every day of his life. The reason is that he allows his understanding to overrule his eyes. His understanding, which includes no intuitive knowledge of the laws of vision, can furnish him with no reason why a line which is known and can be proved to be a horizontal line should not *appear* a horizontal line; a line that made any angle with the perpendicular less than a right angle would seem to him to indicate that his houses were all tumbling down together. Accordingly, he makes the line of his houses a horizontal line, and fails, of course, to produce the effect demanded. Here, then, is one instance out of many in which not only the understanding is allowed to overrule the eyes, but where the understanding is positively allowed to obliterate the eyes, as it were; for not only does the man believe the evidence of his understanding in opposition to that of his eyes, but (what is monstrous) the idiot is not aware that his eyes ever gave such evidence. He does not know that he has seen (and therefore, *quoad,* his consciousness has *not* seen) that which he *has* seen every day of his life.

But to return from this digression. My understanding could furnish no reason why the knocking at the gate in *Macbeth* should produce any effect, direct or reflected. In fact, my understanding said positively that it could *not* produce any effect. But I knew better; I felt that it did; and I waited and clung to the problem until further knowledge should enable me to solve it. At length, in 1812, Mr. Williams made his *début* on the stage of Ratcliffe Highway, and executed those unparalleled murders which have procured for him such a brilliant and undying reputation. On which murders, by the way, I must observe, that in one respect they have had an ill effect, by making the connoisseur in murder very fastidious in his taste, and dissatisfied by anything that has been since done in that line. All other murders look pale by the deep crimson of his; and, as an amateur once said to me in a querulous tone, "There has been absolutely nothing *doing* since his time, or nothing that's worth

speaking of." But this is wrong; for it is unreasonable to expect all men to be great artists, and born with the genius of Mr. Williams. Now it will be remembered that in the first of these murders (that of the Marrs) the same incident (of a knocking at the door soon after the work of extermination was complete) did actually occur which the genius of Shakespeare has invented; and all good judges, and the most eminent dilettanti, acknowledged the felicity of Shakespeare's suggestion as soon as it was actually realized. Here, then, was a fresh proof that I was right in relying on my own feeling, in opposition to my understanding; and I again set myself to study the problem. At length I solved it to my own satisfaction; and my solution is this:— Murder, in ordinary cases, where the sympathy is wholly directed to the case of the murdered person, is an incident of coarse and vulgar horror; and for this reason,— that it flings the interest exclusively upon the natural but ignoble instinct by which we cleave to life: an instinct which, as being indispensable to the primal law of self-preservation, is the same in kind (though different in degree) amongst all living creatures. This instinct, therefore, because it annihilates all distinctions, and degrades the greatest of men to the level of "the poor beetle that we tread on," exhibits human nature in its most abject and humiliating attitude. Such an attitude would little suit the purposes of the poet. What then must he do? He must throw the interest on the murderer. Our sympathy must be with *him* (of course I mean a sympathy of comprehension, a sympathy by which we enter into his feelings, and are made to understand them,—not a sympathy of pity or approbation). In the murdered person, all strife of thought, all flux and reflux of passion and of purpose, are crushed by one overwhelming panic; the fear of instant death smites him "with its petrific mace." But in the murderer, such a murderer as a poet will condescend to, there must be raging some great storm of passion,—jealousy, ambition, vengeance, hatred,—which will create a hell within him; and into this hell we are to look.

In *Macbeth,* for the sake of gratifying his own enormous and teeming faculty of creation, Shakespeare has introduced two murderers: and, as usual in his hands, they are remarkably discriminated: but,—though in Macbeth the strife of mind is greater than in his wife, the tiger spirit not so awake, and his feelings caught chiefly by contagion from her,—yet, as both were finally involved in the guilt of murder, the murderous mind of necessity is finally to be presumed in both. This was to be expressed; and, on its own account, as well as to make it a more proportionable antagonist to the unoffending nature of their victim, "the gracious Duncan," and adequately to expound "the deep damnation of his taking off," this was to be expressed with peculiar energy. We were to be made to feel that the human nature,—i. e., the divine nature of love and mercy, spread through the hearts of all creatures, and seldom utterly withdrawn from man,—was gone, vanished, extinct, and that the fiendish nature had taken its place. And, as this effect is marvellously accomplished in the *dialogues* and *soliloquies* themselves, so it is finally consummated by the expedient under consideration; and it is to this that I now solicit the reader's attention. If the reader has ever witnessed a wife, daughter, or sister in a fainting fit, he may chance to have observed that the most affecting moment in such a spectacle is *that* in which a sigh and a stirring announce the recommencement of suspended life. Or, if the reader has ever been present in a vast metropolis on the day when some great national idol was carried in funeral pomp to his grave, and, chancing to walk near the course through which it passed, has felt powerfully, in the silence and desertion of the streets, and in the stagnation of ordinary business, the deep interest which at that moment was possessing the heart of man,—if all at once he should hear the death-like stillness broken up by the sound of wheels rattling away from the scene, and making known that the transitory vision was dissolved, he will be aware that at no moment was his sense of the complete suspension and pause in ordinary human concerns so full and affecting as at that moment when the suspension ceases, and the goings-on of human life are suddenly resumed. All action in any direction is best expounded, measured, and made apprehensible, by reaction. Now, apply this to the case in *Macbeth.* Here, as I have said, the retiring of the human heart and the entrance of the fiendish heart was to be expressed and made sensible. Another world has stepped in; and the murderers are taken out of the region of human things, human purposes, human desires. They are transfigured: Lady Macbeth is "unsexed"; Macbeth has forgot that he was born of woman; both are conformed to the image of devils; and the world of devils is suddenly revealed. But how shall this be conveyed and made palpable? In order that a new world may step in, this world must for a time disappear. The murderers and the murder must be insulated—cut off by an immeasurable gulf from the ordinary tide and succession of human affairs—locked up and sequestered in some deep recess; we must be made sensible that the world of ordinary life is suddenly arrested, laid asleep, tranced, racked into a dread armistice; time must be annihilated, relation to things without abolished; and all must pass self-withdrawn into a deep syncope and suspension of earthly passion. Hence it is that, when the deed is done, when the work of darkness is perfect, then the world of darkness passes away like a pageantry in the clouds: the knocking at the gate is heard, and it makes known audibly that the reaction has commenced; the human has made its reflux upon the fiendish; the pulses of life are beginning to beat again; and the re-establishment of the goings-on of the world in which we live first makes us profoundly sensible of the awful parenthesis that had suspended them.

O mighty poet! Thy works are not as those of other men, simply and merely great works of art, but are also like the phenomena of nature, like the sun and the sea, the stars and the flowers, like frost and snow, rain and dew, hailstorm and thunder, which are to be studied with entire submission of our own faculties, and in the perfect faith that in them there can be no too much or too little, nothing useless or inert, but that, the farther we press in our discoveries, the more we shall see proofs of design and self-supporting arrangement where the careless eye had seen nothing but accident!

1823

DREAM-VISION OF THE INFINITE

God called up from dreams a man into the vestibule of heaven, saying "Come thou hither and see the glory of my house." And to the servants that stood around his throne he said "Take him, and undress him from his robes of flesh; cleanse his vision, and put a new breath into his nostrils; arm him with sail-broad wings for flight. Only touch not with any change his human heart—the heart that weeps and trembles." It was done; and, with a mighty angel for his guide, the man stood ready for his infinite voyage; and from the terraces of heaven, without sound or farewell, they wheeled away into endless space. 5

Sometimes with the solemn flight of angel-wing they fled through Zaarahs of darkness, through wildernesses of death that divided the worlds of life: sometimes they swept over frontiers that were quick- 10 ening under prophetic motions towards a life not yet realized. Then, from a distance that is counted only in heaven, light dawned for a time through a sleepy film: by unutterable pace the light swept to 15 *them,* they by unutterable pace to the light: in a moment the rushing of planets was upon them: in a moment the blazing of suns was around them. Then came eternities of twilight, that revealed, but were 20 not revealed. To the right hand and to the left towered mighty constellations, that by self-repetitions and by answers from afar, that by counterpositions, that by mysterious combinations, built up triumphal 25 gates, whose architraves, whose archways—horizontal, upright—rested, rose—at altitudes, by spans, that seemed ghostly from infinitude. Without measure were the architraves, past number were the archways, 30 beyond memory the gates. Within were stairs that scaled the eternities above, that descended to the eternities below: above was below, below was above, to the man stripped of gravitating body: depth was 35 swallowed up in height insurmountable, height was swallowed up in depth unfathomable.

Suddenly as thus they rode from infinite to infinite, suddenly as thus they tilted over 40 abysmal worlds, a mighty cry arose—that systems more mysterious, worlds more billowy, other heights and other depths, were dawning, were nearing, were at hand. Then the man sighed, stopped, shuddered, 45 and wept. His overladen heart uttered itself in tears; and he said "Angel, I will go no further. For the spirit of man aches under this infinity. Insufferable is the glory of God's house. Let me lie down in 50 the grave, that I may find rest from the persecutions of the Infinite; for end, I see, there is none." And from all the listening stars that shone around issued one choral chant: "Even so it is; Angel, thou 55 knowest that it is; end there is none that ever yet we heard of."

"End is there none?" the Angel solemnly demanded. "And is this the sorrow that kills you?" But no voice answered, that he 60 might answer himself. Then the Angel threw up his glorious hands to the heaven of heavens, saying, "End—there is none to the Universe of God? Lo! also THERE IS NO BEGINNING."

1824

FROM AUTOBIOGRAPHIC SKETCHES

THE AFFLICTION OF CHILDHOOD

A CHILD'S GRIEF FOR HIS SISTER'S DEATH, AND HIS SENSE OF SOLITUDE

At this time, and under this impulse of rapacious grief, that grasped at what it could not obtain, the faculty of shaping images in the distance out of slight elements, and grouping them after the yearnings of the heart, grew upon me in morbid excess. And I recall at the present moment one instance of that sort, which may show how merely shadows, or a gleam of brightness, or nothing at all, could furnish a sufficient basis for this creative faculty.

On Sunday mornings I went with the rest of my family to church: it was a church on the ancient model of England, having aisles, galleries, organ, all things ancient and venerable, and the proportions majestic. Here, whilst the congregation knelt through the long litany, as often as we came to that passage, so beautiful amongst many that are so, where God is supplicated on behalf of "all sick persons and young children," and that he would "show his pity upon all prisoners and captives," I wept in secret; and raising my streaming eyes to the upper windows of the galleries, saw, on days when the sun was shining, a spectacle as affecting as ever prophet can have beheld. The *sides* of the windows were rich with storied glass; through the deep purples and crimsons streamed the golden light; emblazonries of heavenly illumination (from the sun) mingling with the earthly emblazonries (from art and its gorgeous coloring) of what is grandest in man. *There* were the apostles that had trampled upon earth, and the glories of earth, out of celestial love to man. *There* were the martyrs that had borne witness to the truth through flames, through torments, and through armies of fierce, insulting faces. *There* were the saints who, under intolerable pangs, had 60 glorified God by meek submission to his will. And all the time, whilst this tumult of sublime memorials held on as the deep chords from some accompaniment in the bass, I saw through the wide central field of the window, where the glass was un-colored, white, fleecy clouds sailing over the azure depths of the sky; were it but a fragment or a hint of such a cloud, imme-diately under the flash of my sorrow-haunted eye, it grew and shaped itself into visions of beds with white lawny curtains; and in the beds lay sick children, dying children, that were tossing in anguish, and weeping clamorously for death. God, for some mysterious reason, could not sud-denly release them from their pain; but he suffered the beds, as it seemed, to rise slowly through the clouds; slowly the beds ascended into the chambers of the air; slowly also his arms descended from the heavens, that he and his young children, whom in Palestine, once and forever, he had blessed, though they *must* pass slowly through the dreadful chasm of separation, might yet meet the sooner. These visions were self-sustained. These visions needed not that any sound should speak to me, or music mold my feelings. The hint from the litany, the fragment from the clouds—those and the storied windows were suffi-cient. But not the less the blare of the tumultuous organ wrought its own separate creations. And oftentimes in anthems, when the mighty instrument threw its vast columns of sound, fierce yet melodious, over the voices of the choir—high in arches, when it seemed to rise, surmounting and overriding the strife of the vocal parts, and gathering by strong coercion the total storm into unity—sometimes I seemed to rise and walk triumphantly upon those clouds which, but a moment before, I had looked up to as mementos of prostrate sorrow; yes, sometimes under the transfigurations of music, felt of grief itself as of a fiery chariot for mounting victoriously above the causes of grief.

God speaks to children, also, in dreams, and by the oracles that lurk in darkness. But in solitude, above all things, when made vocal to the meditative heart by the truths and services of a national church, God holds with children "communion un-disturbed." Solitude, though it may be silent as light, is, like light, the mightiest of agencies; for solitude is essential to man. All men come into this world *alone;* all leave it *alone.* Even a little child has a dread, whispering consciousness, that, if he should be summoned to travel into God's

presence, no gentle nurse will be allowed to lead him by the hand, nor mother to carry him in her arms, nor little sister to share his trepidations. King and priest, warrior and maiden, philosopher and child, all must walk those mighty galleries alone. The solitude, therefore, which in this world appals or fascinates a child's heart, is but the echo of a far deeper solitude, through which already he has passed, and of an-other solitude, deeper still, through which he *has* to pass: reflex of one solitude—prefiguration of another.

Oh, burden of solitude, that cleavest to man through every stage of his being! in his birth, which *has* been—in his life, which *is*—in his death, which *shall* be—mighty and essential solitude! that wast, and art, and art to be; thou broodest, like the Spirit of God moving upon the surface of the deeps, over every heart that sleeps in the nurseries of Christendom. Like the vast laboratory of the air, which, seeming to be nothing, or less than the shadow of a shade, hides within itself the principle of all things, solitude for the meditating child is the Agrippa's mirror of the unseen uni-verse. Deep is the solitude of millions who, with hearts welling forth love, have none to love them. Deep is the solitude of those who under secret griefs, have none to pity them. Deep is the solitude of those who, fighting with doubts or darkness, have none to counsel them. But deeper than the deepest of these solitudes is that which broods over childhood under the passion of sorrow — bringing before it, at intervals, the final solitude which watches for it, and is waiting for it within the gates of death. Oh, mighty and essential solitude, that wast, and art, and art to be! thy kingdom is made perfect in the grave; but even over those that keep watch outside the grave, like myself, an infant of six years old, thou stretchest out a sceptre of fascination.

1845

FROM SUSPIRIA DE PROFUNDIS

DREAMING

In 1821, as a contribution to a periodical work,—in 1822, as a separate volume,—ap-peared the "Confessions of an English Opium-Eater." The object of that work was to reveal something of the grandeur which belongs *potentially* to human dreams. Whatever may be the number of those in whom this faculty of dreaming splendidly can be supposed to lurk, there are not, perhaps, very many in whom it is developed. He whose talk is of oxen will probably dream of oxen; and the condition of human life which yokes so vast a major- 5 ity to a daily experience incompatible with much elevation of thought oftentimes neutralizes the tone of grandeur in the reproductive faculty of dreaming, even for those whose minds are populous with solemn 10 imagery. Habitually to dream magnificently, a man must have a constitutional determination to reverie. This in the first place; and even this, where it exists strongly, is too much liable to disturbance 15 from the gathering agitation of our present English life. Already, what by the procession through fifty years of mighty revolutions amongst the kingdoms of the earth, what by the continual development of vast 20 physical agencies,—steam in all its applications, light getting under harness as a slave for man, powers from heaven descending upon education and accelerations of the press, powers from hell (as it might seem, 25 but these also celestial) coming round upon artillery and the forces of destruction,— the eye of the calmest observer is troubled; the brain is haunted as if by some jealousy of ghostly beings moving amongst us; and 30 it becomes too evident that, unless this colossal pace of advance can be retarded (a thing not to be expected), or, which is happily more probable, can be met by counter-forces of corresponding magnitude, 35 —forces in the direction of religion or profound philosophy that shall radiate centrifugally against this storm of life so perilously centripetal towards the vortex of the merely human,—left to itself, the natural 40 tendency of so chaotic a tumult must be to evil; for some minds to lunacy, for others a reagency of fleshly torpor. How much this fierce condition of eternal hurry upon an arena too exclusively human in its in- 45 terests is likely to defeat the grandeur which is latent in all men, may be seen in the ordinary effect from living too constantly in varied company. The word *dissipation*, in one of its uses, expresses 50 that effect; the action of thought and feeling is consciously dissipated and squandered. To reconcentrate them into meditative habits, a necessity is felt by all observing persons for sometimes retiring from 55 crowds. No man ever will unfold the capacities of his own intellect who does not at least checker his life with solitude. How much solitude, so much power. Or, if not true in that rigor of expression, to 60

this formula undoubtedly it is that the wise rule of life must approximate. 1845

THE PALIMPSEST OF THE HUMAN BRAIN

A palimpsest is a membrane or roll cleansed of its manuscript by reiterated successions . . . Here, for instance, is a parchment which contained some Grecian tragedy,—the Agamemnon of Æschylus, or the Phœnissæ of Euripides. This had possessed a value almost inappreciable in the eyes of accomplished scholars, continually growing rarer through generations. But four centuries are gone by since the destruction of the Western Empire. Christianity, with towering grandeurs of another class, has founded a different empire; and some bigoted, yet perhaps holy monk has washed away (as he persuades himself) the heathen's tragedy, replacing it with a monastic legend; which legend is disfigured with fables in its incidents, and yet in a higher sense is true, because interwoven with Christian morals, and with the sublimest of Christian revelations. Three, four, five, centuries more find man still devout as ever; but the language has become obsolete; and even for Christian devotion a new era has arisen, throwing it into the channel of crusading zeal or of chivalrous enthusiasm. The *membrana* is wanted now for a knightly romance—for "My Cid" or Cœur de Lion, for Sir Tristrem or Lybœus Disconus. In this way, by means of the imperfect chemistry known to the medieval period, the same roll has served as a conservatory for three separate generations of flowers and fruits, all perfectly different, and yet all specially adapted to the wants of the successive possessors. The Greek tragedy, the monkish legend, the knightly romance, each has ruled its own period. One harvest after another has been gathered into the garners of man through ages far apart. And the same hydraulic machinery has distributed, through the same marble fountains, water, milk, or wine, according to the habits and training of the generations that came to quench their thirst. Such were the achievements of rude monastic chemistry. But the more elaborate chemistry of our own days has reversed all these motions of our simple ancestors, with results in every stage that to *them* would have realised the most fantastic amongst the promises of thaumaturgy. Insolent vaunt of Paracelsus, that he would restore the original rose or violet out of the ashes settling from its combustion—*that* is now rivalled in this modern achievement. The traces of each successive handwriting, regularly effaced, as had been imagined, have, in the inverse order, been regularly called back; the footsteps of the game pursued, wolf or stag, in each several chase, have been unlinked, and hunted back through all their doubles; and, as the chorus of the Athenian stage unwove through the antistrophe every step that had been mystically woven through the strophe, so, by our modern conjurations of science, secrets of ages remote from each other have been exorcised from the accumulated shadows of centuries. Chemistry, a witch as potent as the Erictho of Lucan (*Pharsalia,* lib. vi or vii), has extorted by her torments, from the dust and ashes of forgotten centuries, the secrets of a life extinct from the general eye, but still glowing in the embers. Even the fable of the Phœnix, that secular bird who propagated his solitary existence, and his solitary births, along the line of centuries, through eternal relays of funeral mists, is but a type of what we have done with Palimpsests. We have backed upon each phœnix in the long *regressus,* and forced him to expose his ancestral phœnix, sleeping in the ashes below his own ashes. Our good old forefathers would have been aghast at our sorceries; and, if they speculated on the propriety of burning Dr. Faustus, *us* they would have burned by acclamation. Trial there would have been none; and they could not otherwise have satisfied their horror of the brazen profligacy marking our modern magic than by ploughing up the houses of all who had been parties to it, and sowing the ground with salt. . . .

What else than a natural and mighty palimpsest is the human brain? Such a palimpsest is my brain; such a palimpsest, oh reader! is yours. Everlasting layers of ideas, images, feelings, have fallen upon your brain softly as light. Each succession has seemed to bury all that went before. And yet, in reality, not one has been extinguished. And, if in the vellum palimpsest, lying amongst the other *diplomata* of human archives or libraries, there is anything fantastic or which moves to laughter, as oftentimes there is in the grotesque collisions of those successive themes, having no natural connection, which by pure accident have consecutively occupied the roll, yet, in our own heaven-created palimpsest, the deep memorial palimpsest of the brain, there are not and cannot be such incoherencies. The fleeting accidents of a man's life, and its external shows, may indeed be irrelate and incongruous; but the organising principles which fuse into harmony, and gather about fixed predetermined centers, whatever heterogeneous elements life may have accumulated from without, will not permit the grandeur of human unity greatly to be violated, or its ultimate repose to be troubled, in the retrospect from dying moments, or from other great convulsions.

Such a convulsion is the struggle of gradual suffocation, as in drowning; and in the original Opium Confessions I mentioned a case of that nature communicated to me by a lady from her own childish experience. The lady was then still living, though of unusually great age; and I may mention that amongst her faults never was numbered any levity of principle, or carelessness of the most scrupulous veracity, but, on the contrary, such faults as arise from austerity, too harsh, perhaps, and gloomy, indulgent neither to others nor herself. And, at the time of relating this incident, when already very old, she had become religious to asceticism. According to my present belief, she had completed her ninth year when, playing by the side of a solitary brook, she fell into one of its deepest pools. Eventually, but after what lapse of time nobody ever knew, she was saved from death by a farmer, who, riding in some distant lane, had seen her rise to the surface; but not until she had descended within the abyss of death and looked into its secrets, as far, perhaps, as ever human eye *can* have looked that had permission to return. At a certain stage of this descent, a blow seemed to strike her; phosphoric radiance sprang forth from her eyeballs; and immediately a mighty theater expanded within her brain. In a moment, in the twinkling of an eye, every act, every design of her past life, lived again, arraying themselves not as a succession, but as parts of a coexistence. Such a light fell upon the whole path of her life backwards into the shades of infancy as the light, perhaps, which wrapped the destined Apostle on his road to Damascus. Yet that light blinded for a season; but hers poured celestial vision upon the brain, so that her consciousness became omnipresent at one moment to every feature in the infinite review.

This anecdote was treated sceptically at the time by some critics. But, besides that it has since been confirmed by other experience essentially the same, reported by other parties in the same circumstances, who had never heard of each other, the true point for astonishment is not the *simultaneity* of arrangement under which the past events of life, though in fact successive, had formed their dread line of revelation. This was but a secondary phenomenon; the deeper lay in the resurrection itself, and the possibility of resurrection for what had so long slept in the dust. A pall, deep as oblivion, had been thrown by life over every trace of these experiences; and yet suddenly, at a silent command, at the signal of a blazing rocket sent up from the brain, the pall draws up, and the whole depths of the theater are exposed. Here was the greater mystery. Now, this mystery is liable to no doubt; for it is repeated and ten thousand times repeated, by opium, for those who are its martyrs.

Yes, reader, countless are the mysterious handwritings of grief or joy which have inscribed themselves successively upon the palimpsest of your brain; and, like the annual leaves of aboriginal forests, or the undissolving snows on the Himalaya, or light falling upon light, the endless strata have covered up each other in forgetfulness. But by the hour of death, but by fever, but by the searchings of opium, all these can revive in strength. They are not dead, but sleeping. In the illustration imagined by myself from the case of some individual palimpsest, the Grecian tragedy had seemed to be displaced, but was *not* displaced, by the monkish legend; and the monkish legend had seemed to be displaced, but was *not* displaced, by the knightly romance. In some potent convulsion of the system, all wheels back into its earliest elementary stage. The bewildering romance, light tarnished with darkness, the semi-fabulous legend, truth celestial mixed with human falsehoods, these fade even of themselves as life advances. The romance has perished that the young man adored; the legend has gone that deluded the boy; but the deep, deep tragedies of infancy, as when the child's hands were unlinked forever from his mother's neck, or his lips forever from his sister's kisses, these remain lurking below all, and these lurk to the last. Alchemy there is none of passion or disease that can scorch away these immortal impresses; and the dream

which closed the preceding section, together with the succeeding dreams of this (which may be viewed as in the nature of choruses winding up the overture contained in Part I), are but illustrations of this truth, such as every man probably will meet experimentally who passes through similar convulsions of dreaming or delirium from any similar or equal disturbance in his nature.

1845

LEVANA AND OUR LADIES OF SORROW

Oftentimes at Oxford I saw Levana in my dreams. I knew her by her Roman symbols. Who is Levana? Reader, that do not pretend to have leisure for very much scholarship, you will not be angry with me for telling you. Levana was the Roman goddess that performed for the new-born infant the earliest office of ennobling kindness,—typical, by its mode, of that grandeur which belongs to man everywhere, and of that benignity in powers invisible which even in Pagan worlds sometimes descends to sustain it. At the very moment of birth, just as the infant tasted for the first time the atmosphere of our troubled planet, it was laid on the ground. *That* might bear different interpretations. But immediately, lest so grand a creature should grovel there for more than one instant, either the paternal hand, as proxy for the goddess Levana, or some near kinsman, as proxy for the father, raised it upright, bade it look erect as the king of all this world, and presented its forehead to the stars, saying, perhaps, in his heart, "Behold what is greater than yourselves!" This symbolic act represented the function of Levana. And that mysterious lady, who never revealed her face (except to me in dreams), but always acted by delegation, had her name from the Latin verb (as still it is the Italian verb) *levare,* to raise aloft.

This is the explanation of Levana. And hence it has arisen that some people have understood by Levana the tutelary power that controls the education of the nursery. She, that would not suffer at his birth even a prefigurative or mimic degradation for her awful ward, far less could be supposed to suffer the real degradation attaching to the non-development of his powers. She therefore watches over human education. Now, the word *edŭco,* with the penultimate short, was derived (by a process often exemplified in the crystallization of languages) from the word *edúco,* with the penultimate long. Whatsoever *educes,* or develops, *educates.* By the education of Levana, therefore, is meant,—not the poor machinery that moves by spelling books and grammars, but by that mighty system of central forces hidden in the deep bosom of human life, which by passion, by strife, by temptation, by the energies of resistance, works forever upon children,—resting not day or night, any more than the mighty wheel of day and night themselves, whose moments, like restless spokes, are glimmering forever as they revolve.

If, then, *these* are the ministries by which Levana works, how profoundly must she reverence the agencies of grief! But you, reader, think that children generally are not liable to grief such as mine. There are two senses in the word *generally,*—the sense of Euclid, where it means *universally* (or in the whole extent of the *genus*), and a foolish sense of this word, where it means *usually.* Now, I am far from saying that children universally are capable of grief like mine. But there are more than you ever heard of who die of grief in this island of ours. I will tell you a common case. The rules of Eton require that a boy on the *foundation* should be there twelve years: he is superannuated at eighteen; consequently he must come at six. Children torn away from mothers and sisters at that age not unfrequently die. I speak of what I know. The complaint is not entered by the registrar as grief; but *that* it is. Grief of that sort, and at that age, has killed more than ever have been counted amongst its martyrs.

Therefore it is that Levana often communes with the powers that shake man's heart; therefore it is that she dotes upon grief. "These ladies," said I softly to myself, on seeing the ministers with whom Levana was conversing, "these are the Sorrows; and they are three in number: as the *Graces* are three, who dress man's life with beauty; the *Parcœ* are three, who weave the dark arras of man's life in their mysterious loom always with colors sad in part, sometimes angry with tragic crimson and black; the *Furies* are three, who visit with retributions called from the other side of the grave offences that walk upon this; and once even the *Muses* were but three, who fit the harp, the trumpet, or the lute, to the great burdens of man's impassioned creations. These are the Sorrows; all three of whom I know." The last words I say

now; but in Oxford I said, "one of whom I know, and the others too surely I *shall* know." For already, in my fervent youth, I saw (dimly relieved upon the dark background of my dreams) the imperfect lineaments of the awful Sisters.

These Sisters—by what name shall we call them? If I say simply "The Sorrows," there will be a chance of mistaking the term; it might be understood of individual sorrow,—separate cases of sorrow,—whereas I want a term expressing the mighty abstractions that incarnate themselves in all individual sufferings of man's heart, and I wish to have these abstractions presented as impersonations,—that is, as clothed with human attributes of life, and with functions pointing to flesh. Let us call them, therefore, *Our Ladies of Sorrow.*

I know them thoroughly, and have walked in all their kingdoms. Three sisters they are, of one mysterious household; and their paths are wide apart; but of their dominion there is no end. Them I saw often conversing with Levana, and sometimes about myself. Do they talk, then? O no! Mighty phantoms like these disdain the infirmities of language. They may utter voices through the organs of man when they dwell in human hearts, but amongst themselves is no voice nor sound; eternal silence reigns in *their* kingdoms. They spoke not as they talked with Levana; they whispered not; they sang not; though oftentimes methought they *might* have sung: for I upon earth had heard their mysteries oftentimes deciphered by harp and timbrel, by dulcimer and organ. Like God, whose servants they are, they utter their pleasure not by sounds that perish, or by words that go astray, but by signs in heaven, by changes on earth, by pulses in secret rivers, heraldries painted on darkness, and hieroglyphics written on the tablets of the brain. *They* wheeled in mazes; *I* spelled the steps. *They* telegraphed from afar; *I* read the signals. *They* conspired together; and on the mirrors of darkness *my* eye traced the plots. *Theirs* were the symbols; *mine* are the words.

What is it the Sisters are? What is it that they do? Let me describe their form and their presence, if form it were that still fluctuated in its outline, or presence it were that forever advanced to the front or forever receded amongst shades.

The eldest of the three is named *Mater Lachrymarum,* Our Lady of Tears. She it is that night and day raves and moans, calling for vanished faces. She stood in Rama, where a voice was heard of lamentation,—Rachel weeping for her children, and refusing to be comforted. She it was that stood in Bethlehem on the night when Herod's sword swept its nurseries of Innocents, and the little feet were stiffened forever which, heard at times as they trotted along floors overhead, woke pulses of love in household hearts that were not unmarked in heaven. Her eyes are sweet and subtle, wild and sleepy, by turns; oftentimes rising to the clouds, oftentimes challenging the heavens. She wears a diadem round her head. And I knew by childish memories that she could go abroad upon the winds, when she heard the sobbing of litanies, or the thundering of organs, and when she beheld the mustering of summer clouds. This Sister, the elder, it is that carries keys more than papal at her girdle, which open every cottage and every palace. She, to my knowledge, sat all last summer by the bedside of the blind beggar, him that so often and so gladly I talked with, whose pious daughter, eight years old, with the sunny countenance, resisted the temptations of play and village mirth, to travel all day long on dusty roads with her afflicted father. For this did God send her a great reward. In the springtime of the year, and whilst yet her own spring was budding, He recalled her to himself. But her blind father mourns forever over *her:* still he dreams at midnight that the little guiding hand is locked within his own; and still he wakens to a darkness that is *now* within a second and a deeper darkness. This *Mater Lachrymarum* also has been sitting all this winter of 1844-5 within the bedchamber of the Czar, bringing before his eyes a daughter (not less pious) that vanished to God not less suddenly, and left behind her a darkness not less profound. By the power of the keys it is that Our Lady of Tears glides, a ghostly intruder, into the chambers of sleepless men, sleepless women, sleepless children, from Ganges to the Nile, from Nile to Mississippi. And her, because she is the first-born of her house, and has the widest empire, let us honor with the title of "Madonna."

The second Sister is called *Mater Suspiriorum,* Our Lady of Sighs. She never scales the clouds, nor walks abroad upon the winds. She wears no diadem. And her eyes, if they were ever seen, would be neither sweet nor subtle; no man could read their story; they would be found filled with perishing dreams, and with wrecks of forgotten delirium. But she raises not her eyes; her head, on which sits a dilapidated turban, droops forever, forever fastens on the dust. She weeps not. She groans not. But she sighs inaudibly at intervals. Her sister, Madonna, is oftentimes stormy and frantic, raging in the highest against heaven, and demanding back her darlings. But Our Lady of Sighs never clamors, never defies, dreams not of rebellious aspirations. She is humble to abjectness. Hers is the meekness that belongs to the hopeless. Murmur she may, but it is in her sleep. Whisper she may, but it is to herself in the twilight. Mutter she does at times, but it is in solitary places that are desolate as she is desolate, in ruined cities, and when the sun has gone down to his rest. This Sister is the visitor of the Pariah, of the Jew, of the bondsman to the oar in the Mediterranean galleys; of the English criminal in Norfolk Island, blotted out from the books of remembrance in sweet far-off England; of the baffled penitent reverting his eyes forever upon a solitary grave, which to him seems the altar overthrown of some past and bloody sacrifice, on which altar no oblations can now be availing, whether towards pardon that he might implore, or towards reparation that he might attempt. Every slave that at noonday looks up to the tropical sun with timid reproach, as he points with one hand to the earth, our general mother, but for *him* a stepmother, as he points with the other hand to the Bible, our general teacher, but against *him* sealed and sequestered; every woman sitting in darkness, without love to shelter her head, or hope to illumine her solitude, because the heaven-born instincts kindling in her nature germs of holy affections, which God implanted in her womanly bosom, having been stifled by social necessities, now burn sullenly to waste, like sepulchral lamps amongst the ancients; every nun defrauded of her unreturning May-time by wicked kinsman, whom God will judge; every captive in every dungeon; all that are betrayed, and all that are rejected; outcasts by traditionary law, and children of *hereditary* disgrace: all these walk with Our Lady of Sighs. She also carries a key; but she needs it little. For her kingdom is chiefly amongst the tents of Shem, and the houseless vagrant of every clime. Yet in the very highest ranks of man she finds chapels of her own; and even in glorious England there are some that, to the world, carry their heads as proudly as the reindeer, who yet secretly have received her mark upon their foreheads.

But the third Sister, who is also the youngest ——! Hush! whisper whilst we talk of *her.* Her kingdom is not large, or else no flesh should live: but within that kingdom all power is hers. Her head, turreted like that of Cybele, rises almost beyond the reach of sight. She droops not; and her eyes, rising so high, *might* be hidden by distance. But, being what they are, they cannot be hidden: through the treble veil of crape which she wears the fierce light of a blazing misery, that rests not for matins or for vespers, for noon of day or noon of night, for ebbing or for flowing tide, may be read from the very ground. She is the defier of God. She also is the mother of lunacies, and the suggestress of suicides. Deep lie the roots of her power; but narrow is the nation that she rules. For she can approach only those in whom a profound nature has been upheaved by central convulsions; in whom the heart trembles and the brain rocks under conspiracies of tempest from without and tempest from within. Madonna moves with uncertain steps, fast or slow, but still with tragic grace. Our Lady of Sighs creeps timidly and stealthily. But this youngest Sister moves with incalculable motions, bounding, and with tiger's leaps. She carries no key; for, though coming rarely amongst men, she storms all doors at which she is permitted to enter at all. And *her* name is *Mater Tenebrarum,*—Our Lady of Darkness.

1845

FROM JOAN OF ARC

What is to be thought of *her?* What is to be thought of the poor shepherd girl from the hills and forests of Lorraine, that —like the Hebrew shepherd boy from the hills and forests of Judea—rose suddenly out of the quiet, out of the safety, out of the religious inspiration, rooted in deep pastoral solitudes, to a station in the van of armies, and to the more perilous station at the right hand of kings? The Hebrew boy inaugurated his patriotic mission by an *act,* by a victorious *act,* such as no man could deny. But so did the girl of Lorraine, if we read her story as it was read by those who saw her nearest. Adverse armies bore witness to the boy as no pretender; but so they did to the gentle girl.

Judged by the voices of all who saw them *from a station of good-will,* both were found true and loyal to any promises involved in their first acts. Enemies it was that made the difference between their subsequent fortunes. The boy rose to a splendor and a noonday prosperity, both personal and public, that rang through the records of his people, and became a byword among his posterity for a thousand years, until the sceptre was departing from Judah. The poor, forsaken girl, on the contrary, drank not herself from that cup of rest which she had secured for France. She never sang together with the songs that rose in her native Domrémy as echoes to the departing steps of invaders. She mingled not in the festal dances at Vaucouleurs which celebrated in rapture the redemption of France. No! for her voice was then silent; no! for her feet were dust. Pure, innocent, noble-hearted girl! whom, from earliest youth, ever I believed in as full of truth and self-sacrifice, this was amongst the strongest pledges for *thy* truth, that never once—no, not for a moment of weakness—didst thou revel in the vision of coronets and honor from man. Coronets for thee! Oh no! Honors, if they come when all is over, are for those that share thy blood. Daughter of Domrémy, when the gratitude of thy king shall awaken, thou wilt be sleeping the sleep of the dead. Call her, King of France, but she will not hear thee. Cite her by the apparitors to come and receive a robe of honor, but she will be found *en contumace.* When the thunders of universal France, as even yet may happen, shall proclaim the grandeur of the poor shepherd girl that gave up all for her country, thy ear, young shepherd girl, will have been deaf for five centuries. To suffer and to do, that was thy portion in this life; that was thy destiny; and not for a moment was it hidden from thyself. Life, thou saidst, is short; and the sleep which is in the grave is long; let me use that life, so transitory, for the glory of those heavenly dreams destined to comfort the sleep which is so long! This pure creature—pure from every suspicion of even a visionary self-interest, even as she was pure in senses more obvious—never once did this holy child, as regarded herself, relax from her belief in the darkness that was travelling to meet her. She might not prefigure the very manner of her death; she saw not in vision, perhaps, the aerial altitude of the fiery scaffold, the spectators without end on every road pouring into

Rouen as to a coronation, the surging smoke, the volleying flames, the hostile faces all around, the pitying eye that lurked but here and there, until nature and imperishable truth broke loose from artificial restraints;—these might not be apparent through the mists of the hurrying future. But the voice that called her to death, *that* she heard forever . . .

Bishop of Beauvais! thy victim died in fire upon a scaffold—thou upon a down bed. But, for the departing minutes of life, both are oftentimes alike. At the farewell crisis, when the gates of death are opening, and flesh is resting from its struggles, oftentimes the tortured and the torturer have the same truce from carnal torment; both sink together into sleep; together both sometimes kindle into dreams. When the mortal mists were gathering fast upon you two, bishop and shepherd girl— when the pavilions of life were closing up their shadowy curtains about you—let us try, through the gigantic glooms, to decipher the flying features of your separate visions.

The shepherd girl that had delivered France—she, from her dungeon, she, from her baiting at the stake, she, from her duel with fire, as she entered her last dream— saw Domrémy, saw the fountain of Domrémy, saw the pomp of forests in which her childhood had wandered. That Easter festival which man had denied to her languishing heart—that resurrection of springtime, which the darkness of dungeons had intercepted from *her,* hungering after the glorious liberty of forests—were by God given back into her hands, as jewels that had been stolen from her by robbers. With those, perhaps (for the minutes of dreams can stretch into ages), was given back to her by God the bliss of childhood. By special privilege for *her* might be created, in this farewell dream, a second childhood, innocent as the first; but not, like *that,* sad with the gloom of a fearful mission in the rear. This mission had now been fulfilled. The storm was weathered; the skirts even of that mighty storm were drawing off. The blood that she was to reckon for had been exacted; the tears that she was to shed in secret had been paid to the last. The hatred to herself in all eyes had been faced steadily, had been suffered, had been survived. And in her last fight upon the scaffold she had triumphed gloriously; victoriously she had tasted the stings of death. For all, except this comfort from her farewell dream. she

had died—died, amidst the tears of ten thousand enemies—died, amidst the drums and trumpets of armies—died, amidst peals redoubling upon peals, volleys upon volleys, from the saluting clarions of martyrs.

Bishop of Beauvais! because the guilt-burdened man is in dreams haunted and waylaid by the most frightful of his crimes, and because upon that fluctuating mirror —rising (like the mocking mirrors of *mirage* in Arabian deserts) from the fens of death —most of all are reflected the sweet countenances which the man has laid in ruins; therefore I know, bishop, that you also entering your final dream, saw Domrémy. That fountain, of which the witnesses spoke so much, showed itself to your eyes in pure morning dews: but neither dews, nor the holy dawn, could cleanse away the bright spots of innocent blood upon its surface. By the fountain, bishop, you saw a woman seated, that hid her face. But, as *you* draw near, the woman raises her wasted features. Would Domrémy know them again for the features of her child? Ah, but *you* know them, bishop, well! Oh, mercy! what a groan was *that* which the servants, waiting outside the bishop's dream at his bedside, heard from his laboring heart, as at this moment he turned away from the fountain and the woman, seeking rest in the forests afar off. Yet not *so* to escape the woman, whom once again he must behold before he dies. In the forests to which he prays for pity, will he find a respite? What a tumult, what a gathering of feet is there! In glades where only wild deer should run, armies and nations are assembling; towering in the fluctuating crowd are phantoms that belong to departed hours. There is the great English Prince, Regent of France. There is my Lord of Winchester, the princely cardinal, that died and made no sign. There is the Bishop of Beauvais, clinging to the shelter of thickets. What building is that which hands so rapid are raising? Is it a martyr's scaffold? Will they burn the child of Domrémy a second time? No: it is a tribunal that rises to the clouds; and two nations stand around it, waiting for a trial. Shall my Lord of Beauvais sit again upon the judgment seat, and again number the hours for the innocent? Ah no! he is the prisoner at the bar. Already all is waiting: the mighty audience is gathered, the Court is hurrying to their seats, the witnesses are arrayed, the trumpets are sounding, the judge is taking his place. Oh! but this is sudden. My lord, have you no counsel? "Counsel I have none: in heaven above, or on earth beneath, counsellor there is none now that would take a brief from *me:* all are silent." Is it, indeed, come to this? Alas! the time is short, the tumult is wondrous, the crowd stretches away into infinity; but yet I will search in it for somebody to take your brief: I know of somebody that will be your counsel. Who is this that cometh from Domrémy? Who is she in bloody coronation robes from Rheims? Who is she that cometh with blackened flesh from walking the furnaces of Rouen? This is she, the shepherd girl, counsellor that had none for herself, whom I choose, bishop, for yours. She it is, I engage, that shall take my lord's brief. She it is, bishop, that would plead for you: yes, bishop, SHE— when heaven and earth are silent.

1847

THE LITERATURE OF KNOWL-
EDGE AND THE LITERATURE
OF POWER

In that great social organ which, collectively we call literature, there may be distinguished two separate offices, that may blend and often *do* so, but capable, severally, of a severe insulation, and naturally fitted for reciprocal repulsion. There is first, the literature of *knowledge;* and, secondly, the literature of *power.* The function of the first is to *teach;* the function of the second is to—*move:* the first is a rudder; the second, an oar or a sail. The first speaks to the *mere* discursive understanding; the second speaks ultimately, it may happen, to the higher understanding or reason, but always *through* affections of pleasure and sympathy. Remotely, it may travel towards an object seated in what Lord Bacon calls *dry* light; but proximately, it does and must operate,—else it ceases to be a literature of *power,*—on and through that *humid* light which clothes itself in the mists and glittering *iris* of human passions, desires, and genial emotions. Men have so little reflected on the higher functions of literature as to find it a paradox if one should describe it as a mean or subordinate purpose of books to give information. But this is a paradox only in the sense which makes it honorable to be paradoxical. Whenever we talk in ordinary language of seeking information or gaining knowledge, we understand the words as

connected with something of absolute novelty. But it is the grandeur of all truth which *can* occupy a very high place in human interests that it is never absolutely novel to the meanest of minds: it exists eternally, by way of germ or latent principle, in the lowest as in the highest, needing to be developed, but never to be planted. To be capable of transplantation is the immediate criterion of a truth that ranges on a lower scale. Besides which, there is a rarer thing than truth, namely,— *power,* or deep sympathy with truth. What is the effect, for instance, upon society, of children? By the pity, by the tenderness, and by the peculiar modes of admiration, which connect themselves with the helplessness, with the innocence, and with the simplicity of children, not only are the primal affections strengthened and continually renewed, but the qualities which are dearest in the sight of heaven,—the frailty, for instance, which appeals to forbearance, the innocence which symbolizes the heavenly, and the simplicity which is most alien from the worldly,—are kept up in perpetual remembrance, and their ideals are continually refreshed. A purpose of the same nature is answered by the higher literature, *viz.,* the literature of power. What do you learn from *Paradise Lost?* Nothing at all. What do you learn from a cookery book? Something new, something that you did not know before, in every paragraph. But would you therefore put the wretched cookery book on a higher level of estimation than the divine poem? What you owe to Milton is not any knowledge, of which a million separate items are still but a million of advancing steps on the same earthly level; what you owe is *power,*—that is, exercise and expansion to your own latent capacity of sympathy with the infinite, where every pulse and each separate influx is a step upwards, a step ascending as upon a Jacob's ladder from earth to mysterious altitudes above the earth. *All* the steps of knowledge, from first to last, carry you further on the same plane, but could never raise you one foot above your ancient level of earth: whereas the very *first* step in power is a flight—is an ascending movement into another element where earth is forgotten.

Were it not that human sensibilities are ventilated and continually called out into exercise by the great phenomena of infancy, or of real life as it moves through chance and change, or of literature as it recombines these elements in the mimicries of poetry, romance, etc., it is certain that, like any animal power or muscular energy falling into disuse, all such sensibilities would gradually droop and dwindle. It is in relation to these great *moral* capacities of man that the literature of power, as contradistinguished from that of knowledge, lives and has its field of action. It is concerned with what is highest in man; for the Scriptures themselves never condescended to deal by suggestion or cooperation with the mere discursive understanding: when speaking of man in his intellectual capacity, the Scriptures speak not of the understanding, but of *"the understanding heart,"*—making the heart, *i. e.,* the great *intuitive* (or nondiscursive) organ, to be the interchangeable formula for man in his highest state of capacity for the infinite. Tragedy, romance, fairy tale, or epopee, all alike restore to man's mind the ideals of justice, of hope, of truth, of mercy, of retribution, which else (left to the support of daily life in its realities) would languish for want of sufficient illustration. What is meant, for instance, by *poetic justice?*—It does not mean a justice that differs by its object from the ordinary justice of human jurisprudence; for then it must be confessedly a very bad kind of justice; but it means a justice that differs from common forensic justice by the degree in which it *attains* its object, a justice that is more omnipotent over its own ends, as dealing—not with the refractory elements of earthly life, but with the elements of its own creation, and with materials flexible to its own purest preconceptions. It is certain that, were it not for the Literature of Power, these ideals would often remain amongst us as mere arid notional forms; whereas, by the creative forces of man put forth in literature, they gain a vernal life of restoration, and germinate into vital activities. The commonest novel, by moving in alliance with human fears and hopes, with human instincts of wrong and right, sustains and quickens those affections. Calling them into action, it rescues them from torpor. And hence the pre-eminence, over all authors that merely *teach* of the meanest that moves, or that teaches, if at all, indirectly *by* moving. The very highest work that has ever existed in the literature of Knowledge is but a *provisional* work: a book upon trial and sufferance, and *quamdiu bene se gesserit*. Let its teaching be even partially revised, let it be but expanded,— nay, even let its teaching be but placed in a better order,—and instantly it is super-

seded. Whereas the feeblest works in the Literature of Power, surviving at all, survive as finished and unalterable amongst men. For instance, the *Principia* of Sir Isaac Newton was a book *militant* on earth from the first. In all stages of its progress it would have to fight for its existence: 1st, as regards absolute truth; 2dly, when that combat was over, as regards its form or mode of presenting the truth. And as soon as a La Place, or anybody else, builds higher upon the foundations laid by this book, effectually he throws it out of the sunshine into decay and darkness; by weapons won from this book he superannuates and destroys this book, so that soon the name of Newton remains as a mere *nominis umbra,* but his book, as a living power, has transmigrated into other forms. Now, on the contrary, the *Iliad,* the *Prometheus* of Æschylus, the *Othello* or *King Lear,* the *Hamlet* or *Macbeth,* and the *Paradise Lost* are not militant but triumphant forever as long as the languages exist in which they speak or can be taught to speak. They never *can* transmigrate into new incarnations. To reproduce *these* in new forms, or variations, even if in some things they should be improved, would be to plagiarize. A good steam engine is properly superseded by a better. But one lovely pastoral valley is not superseded by another, nor a statue of Praxiteles by a statue of Michael Angelo. These things are separated not by imparity, but by disparity. They are not thought of as unequal under the same standard, but as different in *kind,* and, if otherwise equal, as equal under a different standard. Human works of immortal beauty and works of nature in one respect stand on the same footing: they never absolutely repeat each other, never approach so near as not to differ; and they differ not as better and worse, or simply by more and less: they differ by undecipherable and incommunicable differences, that cannot be caught by mimicries, that cannot be reflected in the mirror of copies, that cannot become ponderable in the scales of vulgar comparison.

1848

GOING DOWN WITH VICTORY

The grandest chapter of our experience within the whole mail coach service was on those occasions when we went down from London with the news of victory. A period of about ten years stretched from Trafalgar to Waterloo; the second and third years of which period (1806 and 1807) were comparatively sterile; but the other nine (from 1805 to 1815 inclusively) furnished a long succession of victories, the least of which, in such a contest of Titans, had an inappreciable value of position: partly for its absolute interference with the plans of our enemy, but still more from its keeping alive through central Europe the sense of a deep-seated vulnerability in France. Even to tease the coasts of our enemy, to mortify them by continual blockades, to insult them by capturing if it were but a baubling schooner under the eyes of their arrogant armies, repeated from time to time a sullen proclamation of power lodged in one quarter to which the hopes of Christendom turned in secret. How much more loudly must this proclamation have spoken in the audacity of having bearded the *élite* of their troops, and having beaten them in pitched battles! Five years of life it was worth paying down for the privilege of an outside place on a mail coach, when carrying down the first tidings of any such event. And it is to be noted that, from our insular situation, and the multitude of our frigates disposable for the rapid transmission of intelligence, rarely did any unauthorized rumor steal away a prelibation from the first aroma of the regular despatches. The government news was generally the earliest news.

From eight P.M. to fifteen or twenty minutes later imagine the mails assembled on parade in Lombard Street; where, at that time, and not in St. Martin's-le-Grand, was seated the General Post-Office. In what exact strength we mustered I do not remember; but, from the length of each separate *attelage,* we filled the street, though a long one, and though we were drawn up in double file. On *any* night the spectacle was beautiful. The absolute perfection of all the appointments about the carriages and the harness, their strength, their brilliant cleanliness, their beautiful simplicity —but, more than all, the royal magnificence of the horses—were what might first have fixed the attention. Every carriage on every morning in the year was taken down to an official inspector for examination: wheels, axles, linchpins, pole, glasses, lamps, were all critically probed and tested. Every part of every carriage had been cleaned, every horse had been groomed, with as much rigor as if they belonged to a private gentleman; and that part of the spectacle offered itself always. But the

night before us is a night of victory; and, behold! to the ordinary display what a heart-shaking addition!—horses, men, carriages, all are dressed in laurels and flowers, oakleaves and ribbons. The guards, as being officially his Majesty's servants, and of the coachmen such as are within the privilege of the post-office, wear the royal liveries of course; and, as it is summer (for all the *land* victories were naturally won in summer), they wear, on this fine evening, these liveries exposed to view, without any covering of upper coats. Such a costume, and the elaborate arrangement of the laurels in their hats, dilate their hearts, by giving to them openly a personal connection with the great news in which already they have the general interest of patriotism. That great national sentiment surmounts and quells all sense of ordinary distinctions. Those passengers who happen to be gentlemen are now hardly to be distinguished as such except by dress; for the usual reserve of their manner in speaking to the attendants has on this night melted away. One heart, one pride, one glory, connects every man by the transcendent bond of his national blood. The spectators, who are numerous beyond precedent, express their sympathy with these fervent feelings by continual hurrahs. Every moment are shouted aloud by the post-office servants, and summoned to draw up, the great ancestral names of cities known to history through a thousand years—Lincoln, Winchester, Portsmouth, Gloucester, Oxford, Bristol, Manchester, York, Newcastle, Edinburgh, Glasgow, Perth, Stirling, Aberdeen —expressing the grandeur of the empire by the antiquity of its towns, and the grandeur of the mail establishment by the diffusive radiation of its separate missions. Every moment you hear the thunder of lids locked down upon the mail bags. That sound to each individual mail is the signal for drawing off, which process is the finest part of the entire spectacle. Then come the horses into play. Horses! can these be horses that bound off with the action and gestures of leopards? What stir!—what sea-like ferment!—what a thundering of wheels!—what tramping of hoofs!—what a sounding of trumpets!—what farewell cheers—what redoubling peals of brotherly congratulation, connecting the name of the particular mail—"Liverpool forever!"— with the name of the particular victory— "Badajoz forever!" or "Salamanca forever!" The half-slumbering consciousness that all night long, and all the next day—perhaps for even a longer period—many of these mails, like fire racing along a train of gunpowder, will be kindling at every instant new successions of burning joy, has an obscure effect of multiplying the victory itself, by multiplying to the imagination into infinity the stages of its progressive diffusion. A fiery arrow seems to be let loose, which from that moment is destined to travel, without intermission, westwards for three hundred miles—northwards for six hundred; and the sympathy of our Lombard Street friends at parting is exalted a hundredfold by a sort of visionary sympathy with the yet slumbering sympathies which in so vast a succession we are going to awake.

Liberated from the embarrassments of the city, and issuing into the broad uncrowded avenues of the northern suburbs, we soon begin to enter upon our natural pace of ten miles an hour. In the broad light of the summer evening, the sun, perhaps, only just at the point of setting, we are seen from every story of every house. Heads of every age crowd to the windows; young and old understand the language of our victorious symbols; and rolling volleys of sympathizing cheers run along us, behind us, and before us. The beggar, rearing himself against the wall, forgets his lameness—real or assumed—thinks not of his whining trade, but stands erect, with bold exulting smiles, as we pass him. The victory has healed him, and says, Be thou whole!

1849

THOMAS CARLYLE (1795-1881)

To "recover the life of things," past or present, as Carlyle does, and with his fidelity and intensity, has been granted to no English writer since he died.

OLIVER ELTON

Carlyle, whose early works belong to the Romantic Movement, was the son of a Scotch stonemason, and was sent to Edinburgh University in the hope that he would become a minister. Instead, he became a schoolmaster, and thereafter a contributor to an encyclopedia and to magazines, often writing on German romantic authors. He married the sensitive and brilliant Jane Welsh. His distaste for metropolitan life, and preference for the country, are shown in the two letters given below. The Carlyles at first lived on Craigenputtock Farm, in Scotland. It seemed a narrow and obscure kind of life, burdened with ill health and narrow means; but it was illumined by love and by the pursuit of learning. Carlyle's best works are those which he produced during the first portion of his career,—his essays on Burns and Goethe, *Sartor Resartus* (1834), *The French Revolution* (1837), and *Heroes and Hero-Worship* (1841).

Much in Carlyle's temper and views was characteristic of that rugged Scotch type from which he descended,—people who were heroic in their self-reliance, self-denial, and strenuous labor, who obeyed their consciences unflinchingly, and who deeply believed in literal Biblical Christianity. The literalness, and some of the theological concepts, the young Carlyle forsook. For a time, indeed, he was tempted by Gibbon and Hume into that state of disbelief which he was to call "the Everlasting No,"—namely, the despairing conviction that whatever may rule the Universe it is not a force making for righteousness and considerate of man's spiritual aspirations. This skepticism Carlyle put behind him in his celebrated crisis, or self-conversion in Leith Walk in June, 1821, when he embraced that "Everlasting Yea" which he witnesses to in the famous passage from *Sartor Resartus*.

The beliefs of Carlyle were influenced by Coleridge, and by German romantic authors and philosophers such as Goethe, Jean Paul Richter, and Fichte. The chief tenets of his faith were the following. (1) The universe is a mystery; but to the imaginative intuition of faith, its secret is revealed by symbols. (2) The soul of the universe is good, and though often balked by evil, ultimately secures the victory of righteousness. (3) The individual is not meant to become carefree and happy through the gratification of his personal desires; indeed, since he is a spark of the Infinite, hemmed within the Finite, the very divinity of his nature makes it inevitable that he should be unhappy in this world. (4) To each individual a special capability (his "idea") has been intrusted, which he is unselfishly "to strive to work out, into Faithfulness and Doing" for the benefit of his fellow-men. (5) The individual who fully does so is the Great Man, the Hero; and it is he, rather than circumstances, who has made history. (6) The function of the poet, accordingly, is to see and disclose the "idea," the "inmost heart and generic secret" of those persons and things that he observes.

Carlyle preferred history and biography to poetry and fiction, because he distrusted any types of literature into which the fanciful and illusory might easily creep, and because he wished to emphasize that the ideal lives in actual persons and events. In his later years he fell into the error of opining that the "strong man" who knows the right should force his will upon the people; but in his early period, which alone concerns us here, he had not yet abandoned his romantic faith in freedom.

Carlyle felt that he was addressing himself to a world which doubted or ignored the truths he preached. Hence his style is vehement, indignant, abrupt, and explosive. But its prophetlike sincerity and force are superb. Few prose writers can equal Carlyle in that kind of delineation of character which reveals the inner moral and spiritual life of a person through his outward appearance.

LONDON A MONSTROUS WEN

To Alexander Carlyle

Pentonville; December 14, 1824

My dear Alick,—

Of this enormous Babel of a place I can give you no account in writing: it is like the heart of all the universe; and the flood of human effort rolls out of it and into it with a violence that almost appals one's very sense. Paris scarcely occupies a quarter of the ground, and does not seem to have the twentieth part of the business. O that our father saw Holborn in a fog! with the black vapor brooding over it, absolutely like fluid ink; and coaches and wains and sheep and oxen and wild people rushing on with bellowings and shrieks and thundering din, as if the earth in general were gone distracted. Today I chanced to pass through Smithfield, when the market was three-fourths over. I mounted the steps of a door, and looked abroad upon the area, an irregular space of perhaps thirty acres in extent, encircled with old dingy brick-built houses, and intersected with wooden pens for the cattle. What a scene! Innumerable herds of fat oxen, tied in long rows, or passing at a trot to their several shambles; and thousands of graziers, drovers, butchers, cattle-brokers with their quilted frocks and long goads pushing on the hapless beasts; hurrying to and fro in confused parties, shouting, jostling, cursing, in the midst of rain and *shairn,* and braying discord such as the imagination cannot figure. Then there are stately streets and squares, and calm green recesses to which nothing of this abomination is permitted to enter. No wonder Cobbett calls the place a Wen. It is a monstrous Wen! The thick smoke of it beclouds a space of thirty square miles; and a million of vehicles, from the dog or cuddy-barrow to the giant wagon, grind along its streets forever. I saw a six-horse wain the other day with, I think, Number 200,000 and odds upon it!

There is an excitement in all this, which is pleasant as a transitory feeling, but much against my taste as a permanent one. I had much rather visit London from time to time, than live in it. There is in fact no *right* life in it that I can find: the people are situated here like plants in a hothouse, to which the quiet influences of sky and earth are never in their unadulterated state admitted. It is the case with all ranks: the car-man with his huge slouch-hat hanging half-way down his back, consumes his breakfast of bread and tallow or hog's lard, sometimes as he swags along the streets, always in a hurried and precarious fashion, and supplies the deficit by continual pipes, and pots of beer. The fashionable lady rises at three in the afternoon, and begins to live towards midnight. Between these two extremes, the same false and tumultuous manner of existence more or less infests all ranks. It seems as if you were for ever in "an inn," the feeling of *home* in our acceptation of the term is not known to one of a thousand. You are packed into paltry shells of brick houses (calculated to endure for forty years, and then fall); every door that slams to in the street is audible in your most secret chamber; the necessaries of life are hawked about through multitudes of hands, and reach you, frequently adulterated, always at rather more than *twice* their cost elsewhere; people's friends must visit them by rule and measure; and when you issue from your door, you are assailed by vast shoals of quacks, and showmen, and street sweepers, and pickpockets, and mendicants of every degree and shape, all plying in noise or silent craft their several vocations, all in their hearts like "lions ravening for their prey." The blackguard population of the place is the most consummately blackguard of anything I ever saw.

Yet the people are in general a frank, jolly, *well-living,* kindly people. You get a certain way in their good graces with great ease: they want little more with you than now and then a piece of recreating conversation, and you are quickly on terms for giving and receiving it. Farther, I suspect, their nature or their habits seldom carry or admit them. I have found one or two strange mortals, whom I sometimes stare to see myself beside. There is Crabbe Robinson, an old Templar (Advocate dwelling in the Temple), who gives me coffee and *Sally-Lunns* (a sort of buttered roll), and German books, and talk by the gallon in a minute. His windows look into Alsatia! With the Montagus I, once a week or so, step in and chat away a friendly hour: they are good clever people, though their goodness and cleverness are strangely mingled with absurdity in word and deed. They like me very well: I saw Badams there last night; I am to see him more at large tomorrow or soon after. Mrs. Strachey has twice been here to see me—in her carriage, a circumstance of strange omen to our worthy friend. . . . Among the poets I see Procter and Allan Cunningham as often as I like: the other night I had a second and much longer talk with Campbell. I went over with one Macbeth, not the "Usurper," but a hapless Preacher from Scotland, whose gifts, coupled with their drawbacks, cannot earn him bread in London, though Campbell and Irving and many more are doing all they can for him. Thomas is a clever man, and we had a much more pleasant conversation than our first: but I do not think my view of him was materially altered. He is vain and dry in heart; the brilliancy of his mind (which will not dazzle you to death after all) is like the glitter of an iceberg in the Greenland seas; parts of it are beautiful, but it is cold, cold, and you would rather look at it than touch it. I partly feel for Campbell: his early life was a tissue of wretchedness (here in London he has lived upon a pennyworth of milk and a penny roll per day); and at length his soul has got encrusted as with a case of iron; and he has betaken himself to sneering and selfishness —a common issue! . . .

Good night! my dear Alick!—I am, ever your affectionate Brother,

T. CARLYLE

PLAIN LIVING AND HIGH THINKING

To Thomas De Quincey

Craigenputtock; December 11, 1828

My dear Sir,—

Having the opportunity of a frank, I cannot resist the temptation to send you a few lines, were it only to signify that two well-wishers of yours are still alive in these remote moors, and often thinking of you with the old friendly feelings. My wife encourages me in this innocent purpose: she has learned lately that you were inquiring for her of some female friend; nay, even promising to visit us here—a fact of the most interesting sort to both of us. I am to say, therefore, that your presence at this fireside will diffuse no ordinary gladness over all members of the household; that our warmest welcome, and such solacements as even the desert does not refuse, are at any time and at all times in store for one we love so well. Neither is this expedition so impracticable. We lie but a short way out of your direct route to Westmore-

land; communicate by gravelled roads with Dumfries and other places in the habitable globe. Were you to warn us of your approach, it might all be made easy enough. And then such a treat it would be to hear the sound of philosophy and literature in the hitherto quite savage wolds, where since the creation of the world no such music, scarcely even articulate speech, had been uttered or dreamed of! Come, therefore, come and see us; for we often long after you. Nay, I can promise, too, that we are almost a unique sight in the British Empire; such a quantity of German periodicals and mystic speculation embosomed in plain Scottish *Peatmoor* being nowhere else that I know of to be met with.

In idle hours we sometimes project founding a sort of colony here, to be called the "Misanthropic Society"; the settlers all to be men of a certain philosophic depth, and intensely sensible of the present state of literature; each to have his own cottage, encircled with roses or thistles as he might prefer; a library and pantry within, and huge stack of turf-fuel without; fenced off from his neighbors by fir woods, and, when he pleased, by cast-metal railing, so that each might feel himself strictly an individual, and free as a son of the wilderness; but the whole settlement to meet weekly over coffee, and there unite in their *Miserere*, or what were better, hurl forth their defiance, pity, expostulation, over the whole universe, civil, literary, and religious. I reckon this place a much fitter site for such an establishment than your Lake Country—a region abounding in natural beauty, but blown on by coach-horns, betrodden by picturesque tourists, and otherwise exceedingly desecrated by too frequent resort; whereas here, though still in communication with the manufacturing world, we have a solitude altogether Druidical— grim hills tenanted chiefly by the wild grouse, tarns and brooks that have soaked and slumbered unmolested since the Deluge of Noah, and nothing to disturb you with speech, except Arcturus and Orion, and the Spirit of Nature, in the heaven and in the earth, as it manifests itself in anger or love, and utters its inexplicable tidings, unheard by the mortal ear. But the misery is the almost total want of colonists! Would *you* come hither and be king over us; *then* indeed we had made a fair beginning, and the "Bog School" might snap its fingers at the "Lake School" itself, and hope to be one day recognised of all men.

But enough of this fooling. Better were it to tell you in plain prose what little can be said of my own welfare, and inquire in the same dialect after yours. It will gratify you to learn that here, in the desert, as in the crowded city, I am moderately active and well; better in health, not worse; and though active only on the small scale, yet in my own opinion honestly, and to as much result as has been usual with me at any time. We have horses to ride on, gardens to cultivate, tight walls and strong fires to defend us against winter; books to read, paper to scribble on; and no man or thing, at least in this visible earth, to make us afraid; for I reckon that so securely sequestered are we, not only would no Catholic rebellion, but even no new Hengist and Horsa invasion, in anywise disturb our tranquillity. True, we have no society; but who has, in the strict sense of that word? I have never had any worth speaking much about since I came into this world: in the next, it may be, they will order matters better. Meanwhile, if we have not the *wheat* in great quantity, we are nearly altogether free from the *chaff*, which often in this matter is highly annoying to weak nerves. My wife and I are busy learning Spanish; far advanced in *Don Quixote* already. I purpose writing mystical *Reviews* for somewhat more than a twelvemonth to come; have Greek to read, and the whole universe to study (for I understand less and less of it); so that here as well as elsewhere I find that a man may *"dree his wierd"* (serve out his earthly apprenticeship) with reasonable composure, and wait what the flight of years may bring him, little disappointed (unless Le is a fool) if it brings him mere *nothing* save what he has already—a body and a soul—more cunning and costly treasures than all Golconda and Potosi could purchase for him. What would the vain worm, man, be at? Has he not a head, to speak of nothing else—a head (be it *with* a hat or without one) full of far richer things than Windsor Palace, or the Brighton Teapot added to it? What are all Dresden picture galleries and magazines *des arts et des métiers* to the strange painting and thrice precious workmanship that goes on under the cranium of a beggar? What *can* be added to him or taken from him by the hatred or love of all men? The grey paper or the white silk paper in which the gold ingot is wrapped; the gold is inalienable; *he* is the gold. But truce also to this moralising. I had a thousand things to ask concerning you: your employments, purposes, sufferings and pleasures. Will you not write to me? will you not come to me and tell? Believe it, you are well loved here, and none feels better than I what a spirit is for the present eclipsed in clouds. For the present it can only be; time and chance are for all men; that troublous season will end; and one day with more joyful, not deeper or truer regard, I shall see you "yourself again." Meanwhile, pardon me this intrusion; and write, if you have a vacant hour which you would fill with a good action . . .

With all friendly sentiments, I am ever, my dear sir, most faithfully yours,

T. CARLYLE

FROM JEAN PAUL FRIEDRICH RICHTER

We defy the most careless or prejudiced reader to peruse these works without an impression of something splendid, wonderful and daring. But they require to be studied as well as read, and this with no ordinary patience, if the reader, especially the foreign reader, wishes to comprehend rightly either their truth or their want of truth. Tried by many an accepted standard, Richter would be speedily enough disposed of; pronounced a mystic, a German dreamer, a rash and presumptuous innovator; and so consigned, with equanimity, perhaps with a certain jubilee, to the Limbo appointed for all such windbags and deceptions. Originality is a thing we constantly clamor for, and constantly quarrel with; as if, observes our author himself, any originality but our own could be expected to content us! In fact, all strange things are apt, without faults of theirs, to estrange us at first view; unhappily scarcely anything is perfectly plain, but what is also perfectly common. The current coin of the realm passes into all hands; and be it gold, silver, or copper, is acceptable and of known value: but with new ingots, with foreign bars, and medals of Corinthian brass, the case is widely different.

There are few writers with whom deliberation and careful distrust of first impressions are more necessary than with Richter. He is a phenomenon from the very surface; he presents himself with a professed and determined singularity: his language itself is a stone of stumbling to the critic; to critics of the grammarian species, an unpardonable, often an insuperable, rock of offence. Not that he is ignorant of grammar, or disdains the sciences of spelling and parsing; but he exercises both in a certain latitudinarian spirit; deals with astonishing liberality in parentheses, dashes, and subsidiary clauses; invents hundreds of new words, alters old ones, or by hyphen chains and pairs and packs them together into most jarring combination; in short, produces sentences of the most heterogeneous, lumbering, interminable kind. Figures without limit; indeed the whole is one tissue of metaphors, and similes, and allusions to all the provinces of the Earth, Sea, and Air; interlaced with epigrammatic breaks, vehement bursts, or sardonic turns, interjections, quips, puns, and even oaths! A perfect Indian jungle it seems; a boundless, unparalleled, imbroglio; nothing on all sides but darkness, dissonance, confusion worse confounded! Then the style of the whole corresponds, in perplexity and extravagance, with that of the parts. Every work, be it fiction or serious treatise, is embaled in some fantastic wrappage, some mad narrative accounting for its appearance, and connecting it with the author, who generally becomes a person in the drama himself, before all is over. He has a whole imaginary geography of Europe in his novels; the cities of Flachsenfingen, Haarhaar, Scheerau, and so forth, with their princes, and privy councillors, and serene highnesses; most of whom, odd enough fellows every way, are Richter's private acquaintances, talk with him of state matters (in the purest Tory dialect), and often incite him to get on with his writing. No story proceeds without the most erratic digressions, and voluminous tagrags rolling after it in many a snaky twine. Ever and anon there occurs some "Extra-leaf," with its satirical petition, program, or other wonderful intercalation, no mortal can foresee on what. It is, indeed, a mighty maze; and often the panting reader toils after him in vain; or, baffled and spent, indignantly stops short, and retires, perhaps forever.

All this, we must admit, is true of Richter; but much more is true also. Let us not turn from him after the first cursory glance, and imagine we have settled his account by the words Rhapsody and Affectation. They are cheap words, and of sovereign potency; we should see, therefore, that they be not rashly applied. Many things in Richter accord ill with such a theory. There are rays of the keenest truth, nay, steady pillars of scientific light rising through this chaos: Is it in fact a chaos; or may it be that our eyes are of finite, not of infinite vision, and have only missed the plan? Few "rhapsodists" are men of science, of solid learning, of rigorous study, and accurate, extensive, nay universal knowledge; as he is. With regard to affectation also, there is much to be said. The essence of affectation is that it be *assumed:* the character is, as it were, forcibly crushed into some foreign mold, in the hope of being thereby reshaped and beautified; the unhappy man persuades himself that he has in truth become a new creature, of the wonderfulest symmetry; and so he moves about with a conscious air, though every movement betrays not symmetry but dislocation. This it is to be affected, to walk in a vain show. But the strangeness alone is no proof of the vanity. Many men that move smoothly in the old-established railways of custom will be found to have their affectation; and perhaps here and there some divergent genius be accused of it unjustly. The *show*, though common, may not cease to be *vain;* nor become so for being uncommon. Before we censure a man for seeming what he is not, we should be sure that we know what he *is.* As to Richter in particular, we cannot but observe, that, strange and tumultuous as he is, there is a certain benign composure visible in his writings; a mercy, a gladness, a reverence, united in such harmony as bespeaks not a false, but a genuine state of mind; not a feverish and morbid, but a healthy and robust state.

The secret of the matter is, that Richter requires more study than most readers care to give him. As we approach more closely, many things grow clearer. In the man's own sphere there is consistency; the farther we advance into it, we see confusion more and more unfold itself into order, till at last, viewed from its proper center, his intellectual universe, no longer a distorted incoherent series of air-landscapes, coalesces into compact expansion; a vast, magnificent and variegated scene; full of wondrous products; rude, it may be, and irregular; but gorgeous, benignant, great; gay with the richest verdure and foliage, glittering in the brightest and kindest sun.

Richter has been called an intellectual Colossus; and in truth it is somewhat in this light that we view him. His faculties are all of gigantic mold; cumbrous, awkward in their movements; large and splendid, rather than harmonious or beautiful; yet joined in living union; and of force and compass altogether extraordinary. He has an intellect vehement, rugged, irresistible; crushing in pieces the hardest problems; piercing into the most hidden combinations of things, and grasping the most distant: an imagination vague, somber, splendid, or appalling; brooding over the abysses of Being; wandering through Infinitude, and summoning before us, in its dim religious light, shapes of brilliancy, solemnity, or terror: a fancy of exuberance literally unexampled; for it pours its treasures with a lavishness which knows no limit, hanging, like the sun, a jewel on every grass-blade, and sowing the earth at large with orient pearl. But deeper than all these lies Humor, the ruling quality with Richter; as it were the central fire that pervades and vivifies his whole being. He is a humorist from his inmost soul; he thinks as a humorist, he feels, imagines, acts as a humorist: Sport is the element in which his nature lives and works. A tumultuous element for such a nature, and wild work he makes in it! A Titan in his sport as in his earnestness, he oversteps all bound, and riots without law or measure. He heaps Pelion upon Ossa, and hurls the universe together and asunder like a case of playthings. The Moon "bombards" the Earth, being a rebellious satellite; Mars "preaches" to the other planets, very singular doctrine; nay, we have Time and Space themselves playing fantastic tricks: it is an infinite masquerade; all Nature is gone forth mumming in the strangest guises.

Yet the anarchy is not without its purpose: these vizards are not mere hollow masks; there are living faces under them, and this mumming has its significance. Richter is a man of mirth, but he seldom or never condescends to be a merry-andrew. Nay, in spite of its extravagance, we should say that his humor is of all his gifts intrinsically the finest and most genuine. It has such witching turns; there is something in it so capricious, so quaint, so heartfelt. From his Cyclopean workshop, and its fuliginous limbecs, and huge unwieldy machinery, the little shrivelled twisted Figure comes forth at last, so perfect and so living, to be forever laughed at and forever loved! Wayward as he seems, he works not without forethought: like Rubens, by a single stroke he can change a laughing face into a sad one. But in his smile itself a touching pathos may lie hidden, a pity too deep for tears.

He is a man of feeling, in the noblest sense of that word; for he loves all living with the heart of a brother; his soul rushes forth, in sympathy with gladness and sorrow, with goodness or grandeur, over all Creation. Every gentle and generous affection, every thrill of mercy, every glow of nobleness, awakens in his bosom a response; nay strikes his spirit into harmony; a wild music as of wind-harps, floating round us in fitful swells, but soft sometimes, and pure and soul-entrancing as the song of angels! Aversion itself with him is not hatred; he despises much, but justly, with tolerance also, with placidity, and even a sort of love. Love, in fact, is the atmosphere he breathes in, the medium through which he looks. His is the spirit which gives life and beauty to whatever it embraces. Inanimate Nature itself is no longer an insensible assemblage of colors and perfumes, but a mysterious Presence, with which he communes in unutterable sympathies. We might call him, as he once called Herder, "a Priest of Nature, a mild Bramin," wandering amid spicy groves, and under benignant skies. The infinite Night with her solemn aspects, Day, and the sweet approach of Even and Morn, are full of meaning for him. He loves the green Earth with her streams and forests, her flowery leas and eternal skies; loves her with a sort of passion, in all her vicissitudes of light and shade; his spirit revels in her grandeur and charms; expands like the breeze over wood and lawn, over glade and dingle, stealing and giving odors.

1828

FROM REVIEW OF LOCKHART'S LIFE OF BURNS

We do not think that the blame of Burns's failure lies chiefly with the world. The world, it seems to us, treated him with more rather than with less kindness than it usually shows to such men. It has ever, we fear, shown but small favor to its Teachers: hunger and nakedness, perils and revilings, the prison, the cross, the poison chalice have, in most times and countries, been the market price it has offered for Wisdom, the welcome with which it has greeted those who have come to enlighten and purify it. Homer and Socrates, and the Christian Apostles, belong to old days; but the world's Martyrology was not completed with these. Roger Bacon and

Galileo languish in priestly dungeons; Tasso pines in the cell of a madhouse; Camoens dies begging on the streets of Lisbon. So neglected, so "persecuted they the Prophets," not in Judea only, but in all places where men have been. We reckon that every poet of Burns's order is, or should be, a prophet and teacher to his age; that he has no right to expect great kindness from it, but rather is bound to do it great kindness; that Burns, in particular, experienced fully the usual proportion of the world's goodness; and that the blame of his failure, as we have said, lies not chiefly with the world.

Where, then, does it lie? We are forced to answer: With himself; it is his inward, not his outward misfortunes that bring him to the dust. Seldom, indeed, is it otherwise; seldom is a life morally wrecked but the grand cause lies in some internal malarrangement, some want less of good fortune than of good guidance. Nature fashions no creature without implanting in it the strength needful for its action and duration; least of all does she so neglect her masterpiece and darling, the poetic soul. Neither can we believe that it is in the power of *any* external circumstances utterly to ruin the mind of a man; nay, if proper wisdom be given him, even so much as to affect its essential health and beauty. The sternest sum-total of all worldly misfortunes is Death; nothing more *can* lie in the cup of human woe: yet many men, in all ages, have triumphed over Death, and led it captive; converting its physical victory into a moral victory for themselves, into a seal and immortal consecration for all that their past life had achieved. What has been done, may be done again; nay, it is but the degree and not the kind of such heroism that differs in different seasons; for without some portion of this spirit, not of boisterous daring, but of silent fearlessness, of Self-denial in all its forms, no good man, in any scene or time, has ever attained to be good.

We have already stated the error of Burns; and mourned over it, rather than blamed it. It was the want of unity in his purposes, of consistency in his aims; the hapless attempt to mingle in friendly union the common spirit of the world with the spirit of poetry, which is of a far different and altogether irreconcilable nature. Burns was nothing wholly, and Burns could be nothing, no man formed as he was can be anything, by halves. The heart, not of a mere hot-blooded, popular Verse-monger, or poetical *Restaurateur,* but of a true Poet and Singer, worthy of the old religious heroic times, had been given him: and he fell in an age, not of heroism and religion, but of skepticism, selfishness and triviality, when true Nobleness was little understood, and its place supplied by a hollow, dissocial, altogether barren and unfruitful principle of Pride. The influences of that age, his open, kind, susceptible nature, to say nothing of his highly untoward situation, made it more than usually difficult for him to cast aside, or rightly subordinate; the better spirit that was within him ever sternly demanded its rights, its supremacy: he spent his life in endeavoring to reconcile these two; and lost it, as he must lose it, without reconciling them.

Burns was born poor; and born also to continue poor, for he would not endeavor to be otherwise: this it had been well could he have once for all admitted, and considered as finally settled. He was poor, truly; but hundreds even of his own class and order of minds have been poorer, yet have suffered nothing deadly from it: nay, his own Father had a far sorer battle with ungrateful destiny than his was; and he did not yield to it, but died courageously warring, and to all moral intents prevailing, against it. True, Burns had little means, had even little time for poetry, his only real pursuit and vocation; but so much the more precious was what little he had. In all these external respects his case was hard; but very far from the hardest. Poverty, incessant drudgery and much worse evils, it has often been the lot of Poets and wise men to strive with, and their glory to conquer. Locke was banished as a traitor; and wrote his *Essay on the Human Understanding* sheltering himself in a Dutch garret. Was Milton rich or at his ease when he composed *Paradise Lost?* Not only low, but fallen from a height; not only poor, but impoverished; in darkness and with dangers compassed round, he sang his immortal song, and found fit audience, though few. Did not Cervantes finish his work, a maimed soldier and in prison? Nay, was not the *Araucana,* which Spain acknowledges as its Epic, written without even the aid of paper; on scraps of leather, as the stout fighter and voyager snatched any moment from that wild warfare?

And what, then, had these men, which Burns wanted? Two things; both which, it seems to us, are indispensable for such men. They had a true, religious principle of morals; and a single, not a double aim in their activity. They were not self-seekers and self-worshippers; but seekers and worshippers of something far better than Self. Not personal enjoyment was their object; but a high, heroic idea of Religion, of Patriotism, of heavenly Wisdom, in one or the other form, ever hovered before them; in which cause they neither shrank from suffering, nor called on the earth to witness it as something wonderful; but patiently endured, counting it blessedness enough so to spend and be spent. Thus the "golden calf of Self-love," however curiously carved, was not their Deity; but the Invisible Goodness, which alone is man's reasonable service. This feeling was as a celestial fountain, whose streams refreshed into gladness and beauty all the provinces of their otherwise too desolate existence. In a word, they willed one thing, to which all other things were subordinated and made subservient; and therefore they accomplished it. The wedge will rend rocks; but its edge must be sharp and single: if it be double, the wedge is bruised in pieces and will rend nothing.

Part of this superiority these men owed to their age; in which heroism and devotedness were still practised, or at least not yet disbelieved in: but much of it likewise they owed to themselves. With Burns, again, it was different. His morality, in most of its practical points, is that of a mere worldly man; enjoyment, in a finer or coarser shape, is the only thing he longs and strives for. A noble instinct sometimes raises him above this; but an instinct only, and acting only for moments. He has no Religion; in the shallow age, where his days were cast, Religion was not discriminated from the New and Old Light *forms* of Religion; and was, with these, becoming obsolete in the minds of men. His heart, indeed, is alive with a trembling adoration, but there is no temple in his understanding. He lives in darkness and in the shadow of doubt. His religion, at best, is an anxious wish; like that of Rabelais, "a great Perhaps."

He loved Poetry warmly, and in his heart; could he but have loved it purely, and with his whole undivided heart, it had been well. For Poetry, as Burns could have followed it, is but another form of Wisdom, of Religion; is itself Wisdom and Religion. But this also was denied him. His poetry is a stray vagrant gleam, which will not be extinguished within him, yet rises not to be the true light of his path,

but is often a wildfire that misleads him. It was not necessary for Burns to be rich, to be, or to seem, "independent;" but it *was* necessary for him to be at one with his own heart; to place what was highest in his nature highest also in his life; "to seek within himself for that consistency and sequence, which external events would forever refuse him." He was born a poet; poetry was the celestial element of his being, and should have been the soul of his whole endeavors. Lifted into that serene ether, whither he had wings given him to mount, he would have needed no other elevation: poverty, neglect and all evil, save the desecration of himself and his Art, were a small matter to him; the pride and the passions of the world lay far beneath his feet; and he looked down alike on noble and slave, on prince and beggar, and all that wore the stamp of man, with clear recognition, with brotherly affection, with sympathy, with pity. Nay, we question whether for his culture as a Poet poverty and much suffering for a season were not absolutely advantageous. Great men, in looking back over their lives, have testified to that effect. "I would not for much," says Jean Paul, "that I had been born richer." And yet Paul's birth was poor enough; for, in another place, he adds: "The prisoner's allowance is bread and water; and I had often only the latter." But the gold that is refined in the hottest furnace comes out the purest; or, as he has himself expressed it, "the canary bird sings sweeter the longer it has been trained in a darkened cage."

A man like Burns might have divided his hours between poetry and virtuous industry; industry which all true feeling sanctions, nay, prescribes, and which has a beauty, for that cause, beyond the pomp of thrones: but to divide his hours between poetry and rich men's banquets was an ill-starred and inauspicious attempt. How could he be at ease at such banquets? What had he to do there, mingling his music with the coarse roar of altogether earthly voices; brightening the thick smoke of intoxication with fire lent him from heaven? Was it his aim to *enjoy* life? Tomorrow he must go drudge as an Exciseman! We wonder not that Burns became moody, indignant, and at times an offender against certain rules of society; but rather that he did not grow utterly frantic, and run *amuck* against them all. How could a man, so falsely placed, by his own or others' fault, ever know contentment or peaceable diligence for an hour? What he did, under such perverse guidance, and what he forbore to do, alike fill us with astonishment at the natural strength and worth of his character.

Doubtless there was a remedy for this perverseness; but not in others; only in himself; least of all in simple increase of wealth and worldly "respectability." We hope we have now heard enough about the efficacy of wealth for poetry, and to make poets happy. Nay, have we not seen another instance of it in these very days? Byron, a man of an endowment considerably less ethereal than that of Burns, is born in the rank not of a Scottish ploughman, but of an English peer: the highest worldly honors, the fairest worldly career, are his by inheritance; the richest harvest of fame he soon reaps, in another province, by his own hand. And what does all this avail him? Is he happy, is he good, is he true? Alas, he has a poet's soul, and strives towards the Infinite and the Eternal; and soon feels that all this is but mounting to the house-top to reach the stars! Like Burns, he is only a proud man; might, like him, have "purchased a pocket-copy of Milton to study the character of Satan;" for Satan also is Byron's grand exemplar, the hero of his poetry, and the model apparently of his conduct. As in Burns's case, too, the celestial element will not mingle with the clay of earth; both poet and man of the world he must not be; vulgar Ambition will not live kindly with poetic Adoration; he *cannot* serve God and Mammon. Byron, like Burns, is not happy; nay, he is the most wretched of all men. His life is falsely arranged: the fire that is in him is not a strong, still, central fire, warming into beauty the products of a world; but it is the mad fire of a volcano; and now—we look sadly into the ashes of a crater, which ere long will fill itself with snow!

Byron and Burns were sent forth as missionaries to their generation, to teach it a higher Doctrine, a purer Truth; they had a message to deliver, which left them no rest till it was accomplished; in dim throes of pain, this divine behest lay smoldering within them; for they knew not what it meant, and felt it only in mysterious anticipation, and they had to die without articulately uttering it. They are in the camp of the Unconverted; yet not as high messengers of rigorous though benignant truth, but as soft flattering singers, and in pleasant fellowship will they live there:

they are first adulated, then persecuted; they accomplish little for others; they find no peace for themselves, but only death and the peace of the grave. We confess, it is not without a certain mournful awe that we view the fate of these noble souls, so richly gifted, yet ruined to so little purpose with all their gifts. It seems to us there is a stern moral taught in this piece of history,—*twice* told us in our own time! Surely to men of like genius, if there be any such, it carries with it a lesson of deep impressive significance. Surely it would become such a man, furnished for the highest of all enterprises, that of being the Poet of his Age, to consider well what it is that he attempts, and in what spirit he attempts it. For the words of Milton are true in all times, and were never truer than in this: "He who would write heroic poems must make his whole life a heroic poem." If he cannot first so make his life, then let him hasten from this arena; for neither its lofty glories, nor its fearful perils, are fit for him. Let him dwindle into a modish balladmonger; let him worship and besing the idols of the time, and the time will not fail to reward him. If, indeed, he can endure to live in that capacity! Byron and Burns could not live as idol-priests, but the fire of their own hearts consumed them; and better it was for them that they could not. For it is not in the favor of the great or of the small, but in a life of truth, and in the inexpugnable citadel of his own soul, that a Byron's or a Burns's strength must lie. Let the great stand aloof from him, or know how to reverence him. Beautiful is the union of wealth with favor and furtherance for literature; like the costliest flower-jar enclosing the loveliest amaranth. Yet let not the relation be mistaken. A true poet is not one whom they can hire by money or flattery to be a minister of their pleasures, their writer of occasional verses, their purveyor of table wit; he cannot be their menial, he cannot even be their partisan. At the peril of both parties, let no such union be attempted! Will a Courser of the Sun work softly in the harness of a Dray-horse? His hoofs are of fire, and his path is through the heavens, bringing light to all lands; will he lumber on mud highways, dragging ale for earthly appetites from door to door?

But we must stop short in these considerations, which would lead us to boundless lengths. We had something to say on the public moral character of Burns; but this also we must forbear. We are far from regarding him as guilty before the world, as guiltier than the average; nay, from doubting that he is less guilty than one of ten thousand. Tried at a tribunal far more rigid than that where the *Plebiscita* of common civic reputations are pronounced, he has seemed to us even there less worthy of blame than of pity and wonder. But the world is habitually unjust in its judgments of such men; unjust on many grounds, of which this one may be stated as the substance: It decides, like a court of law, by dead statutes; and not positively but negatively, less on what is done right, than on what is or is not done wrong. Not the few inches of deflection from the mathematical orbit, which are so easily measured, but the *ratio* of these to the whole diameter, constitutes the real aberration. This orbit may be a planet's, its diameter the breadth of the solar system; or it may be a city hippodrome; nay, the circle of a gin-horse, its diameter a score of feet or paces. But the inches of deflection only are measured: and it is assumed that the diameter of the gin-horse, and that of the planet, will yield the same ratio when compared with them! Here lies the root of many a blind, cruel condemnation of Burnses, Swifts, Rousseaus, which one never listens to with approval. Granted, the ship comes into harbor with shrouds and tackle damaged; the pilot is blameworthy; he has not been all-wise and all-powerful: but to know *how* blameworthy, tell us first whether his voyage has been round the Globe, or only to Ramsgate and the Isle of Dogs.

With our readers in general, with men of right feeling anywhere, we are not required to plead for Burns. In pitying admiration he lies enshrined in all our hearts, in a far nobler mausoleum than that one of marble; neither will his Works, even as they are, pass away from the memory of men. While the Shakespeares and Miltons roll on like mighty rivers through the country of Thought, bearing fleets of traffickers and assiduous pearl-fishers on their waves; this little Valclusa Fountain will also arrest our eye: for this also is of Nature's own and most cunning workmanship, bursts from the depths of the earth, with a full gushing current, into the light of day; and often will the traveller turn aside to drink of its clear waters, and muse among its rocks and pines!

1828

FROM SIGNS OF THE TIMES

These dark features, we are aware, belong more or less to other ages, as well as to ours. This faith in Mechanism, in the all-importance of physical things, is in every age the common refuge of weakness and blind discontent; of all who believe, as many will ever do, that man's true good lies without him, not within. We are aware also, that, as applied to ourselves in all their aggravation, they form but half the picture; that in the whole picture there are bright lights as well as gloomy shadows. If we here dwell chiefly on the latter, let us not be blamed: it is in general more profitable to reckon up our defects than to boast of our attainments.

Neither, with all these evils more or less clearly before us, have we at any time despaired of the fortunes of society. Despair, or even despondency, in that respect, appears to us, in all cases, a groundless feeling. We have a faith in the imperishable dignity of man; in the high vocation to which, throughout this his earthly history, he has been appointed. However it may be with individual nations, whatever melancholic speculators may assert, it seems a well-ascertained fact, that in all times, reckoning even from those of the Heraclides and Pelasgi, the happiness and greatness of mankind at large have been continually progressive. Doubtless this age also is advancing. Its very unrest, its ceaseless activity, its discontent contains matter of promise. Knowledge, education are opening the eyes of the humblest; are increasing the number of thinking minds without limit. This is as it should be; for not in turning back, not in resisting, but only in resolutely struggling forward, does our life consist.

Nay, after all, our spiritual maladies are but of Opinion; we are but fettered by chains of our own forging, and which ourselves also can rend asunder. This deep, paralyzed subjection to physical objects comes not from Nature, but from our own unwise mode of *viewing* Nature. Neither can we understand that man wants, at this hour, any faculty of heart, soul or body, that ever belonged to him. "He, who has been born, has been a First Man;" has had lying before his young eyes, and as yet unhardened into scientific shapes, a world as plastic, infinite, divine, as lay before the eyes of Adam himself. If Mechanism, like some glass bell, encircles and imprisons us; if the soul looks forth on a fair heavenly country which it cannot reach, and pines, and in its scanty atmosphere is ready to perish,—yet the bell is but of glass; "one bold stroke to break the bell in pieces, and thou art delivered!" Not the invisible world is wanting, for it dwells in man's soul, and this last is still here. Are the solemn temples, in which the Divinity was once visibly revealed among us, crumbling away? We can repair them, we can re-build them. The wisdom, the heroic worth of our forefathers, which we have lost, we can recover. That admiration of old noble-ness, which now so often shows itself as a faint *dilettantism,* will one day become a generous emulation, and man may again be all that he has been, and more than he has been. Nor are these the mere day-dreams of fancy; they are clear possibilities; nay, in this time they are even assuming the character of hopes. Indications we do see in other countries and in our own, signs infinitely cheering to us, that Mecha-nism is not always to be our hard task-master, but one day to be our pliant, all-ministering servant; that a new and brighter spiritual era is slowly evolving itself for all men. But on these things our present course forbids us to enter.

Meanwhile, that great outward changes are in progress can be doubtful to no one. The time is sick and out of joint. Many things have reached their height; and it is a wise adage that tells us, "the darkest hour is nearest the dawn." Wherever we can gather indication of the public thought, whether from printed books, as in France or Germany, or from Carbonari rebellions and other political tumults, as in Spain, Portugal, Italy and Greece, the voice it utters is the same. The thinking minds of all nations call for change. There is a deep-lying struggle in the whole fabric of society; a boundless grinding collision of the New with the Old. The French Revolution, as is now visible enough, was not the parent of this mighty movement, but its offspring. Those two hostile in-fluences, which always exist in human things, and on the constant intercom-munion of which depends their health and safety, had lain in separate masses, accumu-lating through generations, and France was the scene of their fiercest explosion; but the final issue was not unfolded in that country: nay it is not yet anywhere un-folded. Political freedom is hitherto the object of these efforts; but they will not and cannot stop there. It is towards a higher freedom than mere freedom from oppression by his fellow-mortal, that man dimly aims. Of this higher, heavenly free-dom, which is "man's reasonable service," all his noble institutions, his faithful en-deavors and loftiest attainments, are but the body, and more and more approxi-mated emblem.

On the whole, as this wondrous planet, Earth, is journeying with its fellows through infinite Space, so are the wondrous destinies embarked on it journeying through infinite Time, under a higher guidance than ours. For the present, as our astronomy informs us, its path lies to-wards *Hercules,* the constellation of *Phys-ical Power:* but that is not our most press-ing concern. Go where it will, the deep HEAVEN will be around it. Therein let us have hope and sure faith. To reform a world, to reform a nation, no wise man will undertake; and all but foolish men know, that the only solid, though a far slower reformation, is what each begins and perfects on *himself.*

1829

FROM BIOGRAPHY

In some *Boswell's Life of Johnson,* how indelible and magically bright does many a little *Reality* dwell in our remembrance! There is no need that the personages on the scene be a King and Clown; that the scene be the Forest of the Royal Oak, "on the borders of Staffordshire"; need only that the scene lie on this old firm Earth of ours, where we also have so surprisingly arrived; that the personages be *men,* and *seen* with the eyes of a man. Foolish enough, how some slight, perhaps mean and even ugly incident, if *real* and well presented, will fix itself in a susceptive memory, and lie ennobled there; silvered over with the pale cast of thought, with the pathos which belongs only to the Dead. For the Past is all holy to us; the Dead are all holy, even they that were base and wicked while alive. Their baseness and wickedness was not *They,* was but the heavy and unmanageable Environment that lay round them, with which they fought unprevailing: *they* (the ethereal god-given Force that dwelt in them, and was their *Self*) have now shuffled off that heavy Environment, and are free and pure: their life-long Battle, go how it might, is all ended, with many wounds or with fewer; they have been recalled from it, and the once harsh-jarring battlefield has become a silent awe-inspiring Golgotha and *Gottesacker* (Field of God)!—Boswell relates this in itself smallest and poorest of occurrences: "As we walked along the Strand tonight, arm in arm, a woman of the town accosted us in the usual enticing manner. 'No, no, my girl,' said Johnson; 'it won't do.' He, however, did not treat her with harshness; and we talked of the wretched life of such women." Strange power of *Reality!* Not even this poorest of occurrences, but now, after seventy years are come and gone, has a meaning for us. Do but consider that it is *true;* that it did in very deed occur! That unhappy Outcast, with all her sins and woes, her lawless desires, too complex mischances, her wailings and her riotings, has departed utterly; alas! her siren finery has got all besmutched, ground, generations since, into dust and smoke; of her degraded body, and whole miserable earthly existence, all is away: *she* is no longer here, but far from us, in the bosom of Eternity,—whence we too came, whither we too are bound! Johnson said, "No, no, my girl; it won't do"; and then "we talked";—and herewith the wretched one, seen but for the twinkling of an eye, passes on into the utter Darkness. No high Calista, that ever issued from Story-teller's brain, will impress us more deeply than this meanest of the mean; and for a good reason: That *she* issued from the Maker of Men.

It is well worth the Artist's while to examine for himself what it is that gives such pitiable incidents their memorableness; his aim likewise is, above all things, to be memorable. Half the effect, we already perceive, depends on the object; on its being *real;* on its being really *seen.* The other half will depend on the observer; and the question now is: How are real objects to be *so* seen; on what quality of observing, or of style in describing, does this so intense pictorial power depend? Often a slight circumstance contributes curiously to the result: some little, and perhaps to appearance accidental, feature is presented; a light-gleam, which instantaneously *excites* the mind, and urges it to complete the picture, and evolve the meaning thereof for itself. By critics, such light-gleams and their almost magical influence have frequently been noted: but the power to produce such, to select such features as will produce them, is generally treated as a knack, or trick of the trade, a secret for being "graphic"; whereas these magical feats are, in truth, rather inspirations; and the gift of performing them, which acts unconsciously, without forethought, and as if by nature alone, is properly a *genius* for description.

One grand, invaluable secret there is, however, which includes all the rest, and, what is comfortable, lies clearly in every man's power: *To have an open loving heart, and what follows from the possession of such.* Truly, it has been said, emphatically in these days ought it to be repeated: A loving Heart is the beginning of all Knowledge. This it is that opens the whole mind, quickens every faculty of the intellect to do its fit work, that of *knowing;* and therefrom, by sure consequence, of *vividly uttering-forth.* Other secret for being "graphic" is there none, worth having: but this is an all-sufficient one. See, for example, what a small Boswell can do! Hereby, indeed, is the whole man made a living mirror, wherein the wonders of this ever-wonderful Universe are, in their true light (which is ever a magical, miraculous one) represented, and reflected back on us. It has been said, "the heart sees farther than the head": but, indeed, without the seeing heart, there is no true seeing for the head so much as possible; all is mere *oversight,* hallucination and vain superficial phantasmagoria, which can permanently profit no one.

Here, too, may we not pause for an instant, and make a practical reflection? Considering the multitude of mortals that handle the Pen in these days, and can mostly spell, and write without glaring violations of grammar, the question naturally arises: How is it, then, that no Work proceeds from them, bearing any stamp of authenticity and permanence; of worth for more than one day? Shiploads of Fashionable Novels, Sentimental Rhymes, Tragedies, Farces, Diaries of Travel, Tales by flood and field, are swallowed monthly into the bottomless Pool: still does the Press toil; innumerable Paper makers, Compositors, Printers' Devils, Bookbinders, and Hawkers grown hoarse with loud proclaiming, rest not from their labor; and still, in torrents, rushes on the great array of Publications, unpausing, to their final home; and still Oblivion, like the Grave, cries, Give! Give! How is it that of all these countless multitudes, no one can attain to the smallest mark of excellence, or produce aught that shall endure longer than "snowflake on the river," or the foam of penny-beer? We answer: Because they *are* foam; because there is no *Reality* in them. These

'Three Thousand men, women and children, that make up the army of British Authors, do not, if we will well consider it, *see* anything whatever; consequently *have* nothing that they can record and utter, only more or fewer things that they can plausibly pretend to record. The Universe, of Man and Nature, is still quite shut-up from them; the "open secret" still utterly a secret; because no sympathy with Man or Nature, no love and free simplicity of heart has yet unfolded the same. Nothing but a pitiful Image of their own pitiful Self, with its vanities, and grudgings, and ravenous hunger of all kinds, hangs forever painted in the retina of these unfortunate persons; so that the starry All, with whatsoever it embraces, does but appear as some expanded, magic-lantern shadow of that same Image, and naturally looks pitiful enough.

It is vain for these persons to allege that they are naturally without gift, naturally stupid and sightless, and so *can* attain to no knowledge of anything; therefore, in writing of anything, must needs write falsehoods of it, there being in it no truth for them. Not so, good Friends. The stupidest of you has a certain faculty; were it but that of articulate speech (say, in the Scottish, the Irish, the Cockney dialect, or even in "Governess-English"), and of physically discerning what lies under your nose. The stupidest of you would perhaps grudge to be compared in faculty with James Boswell; yet see what he has produced! You do not use your faculty honestly; your heart is shut up; full of greediness, malice, discontent; so your intellectual sense cannot be open. It is vain also to urge that James Boswell had opportunities; saw great men and great things, such as you can never hope to look on. What make ye of Parson White in Selborne? He had not only no great men to look on, but not even men; merely sparrows and cockchafers: yet has he left us a *Biography* of these; which, under its title *Natural History of Selborne*, still remains valuable to us; which has copied a little sentence or two *faithfully* from the Inspired Volume of Nature, and so is itself not without inspiration. Go ye and do likewise. Sweep away utterly all frothiness and falsehood from your heart; struggle unweariedly to acquire, what is possible for every god-created Man, a free, open, humble soul: *speak not at all in any wise, till you have somewhat to speak;* care not for the *reward* of your speaking, but simply and with undivided mind for the truth of your speaking: then be placed in what section of Space and of Time soever, do but open your eyes, and they shall actually *see,* and bring you real *knowledge,* wondrous, worthy of *belief;* and instead of one Boswell and one White, the world will rejoice in a thousand,—stationed on their thousand several watchtowers, to instruct us by indubitable documents, of whatsoever in our so stupendous World comes to light and *is!* O, had the Editor of this Magazine but a magic rod to turn all that not inconsiderable Intellect, which now deluges us with artificial fictitious soap-lather, and mere Lying, into the faithful study of Reality,—what knowledge of great, everlasting Nature, and of Man's ways and doings therein, would not every year bring us in! Can we but change one single soap-latherer and mountebank Juggler, into a true Thinker and Doer, who even *tries* honestly to think and do,—great will be our reward.

Feb., 1832

FROM THE DEATH OF GOETHE

There are now, what some years ago there were not, English hearts that know something of what those three words, "Death of Goethe," mean; to such men, among their many thoughts on the event, which are not to be translated into speech, may these few, through that imperfect medium, prove acceptable.

"Death," says the philosopher, "is a commingling of Eternity with Time; in the death of a good man Eternity is seen looking through Time." With such a sublimity here offered to eye and heart, it is not unnatural to look with new earnestness before and behind, and ask, What space in those years and æons of computed Time, this man with his activity may influence; what relation to the world of change and mortality, which the earthly name Life, he who is even now called to the Immortals has borne and may bear. Goethe, it is commonly said, made a New Era in Literature; a Poetic Era began with him, the end or ulterior tendencies of which are yet nowise generally visible. This common saying is a true one; and true with a far deeper meaning than, to the most, it conveys. Were the Poet but a sweet sound and singer, solacing the ear of the idle with pleasant songs; and the new Poet one who could sing his idle pleasant song to a new air,—we should account him a small matter, and his performance small. But this man, it is not unknown to many, was a Poet in such a sense as the late generations have witnessed no other; as it is, in this generation, a kind of distinction to believe in the existence of, in the possibility of. The true Poet is ever, as of old, the Seer; whose eye has been gifted to discern the godlike Mystery of God's Universe, and decipher some new lines of its celestial writing; we can still call him a *Vates* and Seer; for he *sees* into this greatest of secrets, "the open secret"; hidden things become clear; how the Future (both resting on Eternity) is but another phasis of the Present: thereby are his words in very truth prophetic; what he has spoken shall be done.

It begins now to be everywhere surmised that the real Force, which in this world all things must obey, is Insight, Spiritual Vision and Determination. The Thought is parent of the Deed, nay is living soul of it, and last and continual, as well as first mover of it; is the foundation and beginning and essence, therefore, of man's whole existence here below. In this sense, it has been said, the Word of man (the uttered Thought of man) is still a magic formula, whereby he rules the world. Do not the winds and waters, and all tumultuous powers, inanimate and animate, obey him? A poor, quite mechanical Magician speaks; and fire-winged ships cross the Ocean at his bidding. Or mark, above all, that "raging of the nations," wholly in contention, desperation and dark chaotic fury; how the meek voice of a Hebrew Martyr and Redeemer stills it into order, and a savage Earth becomes kind and beautiful, and the habitation of horrid cruelty a temple of peace. The true Sovereign of the world, who molds the world like soft wax, according to his pleasure, is he who lovingly *sees* into the world; the "inspired Thinker," whom in these days we name Poet. The true Sovereign is the Wise Man.

However, as the Moon, which can heave up the Atlantic, sends not in her obedient billows at once, but gradually; and the Tide, which swells today on our shores, and washes every creek, rose in the bosom of the great Ocean (astronomers assure us) eight-and-forty-hours ago; and indeed, all world-movements, by nature deep, are by nature calm, and flow and swell onwards with a certain majestic slowness: so too with the Impulse of a Great Man, and the effect he has to manifest on other men. To such a one we may grant some generation or two, before the celestial Impulse he impressed on the world will universally proclaim itself, and become (like the working of the Moon) if still not intelligible, yet palpable, to all men; some generation or two more, wherein it has to grow, and expand, and envelop all things, before it can reach its acme; and thereafter mingling with other movements and new impulses, at length cease to require a specific observation or designation. Longer or shorter such period may be, according to the nature of the Impulse itself, and of the elements it works in; according, above all, as the Impulse was intrinsically great and deepreaching, or only wide-spread, superficial and transient. Thus, if David Hume is at this hour pontiff of the world, and rules most hearts, and guides most tongues (the hearts and tongues even of those that in vain rebel against him), there are nevertheless symptoms that his task draws towards completion; and now in the distance his successor becomes visible. On the other hand, we have seen a Napoleon, like some gunpowder force (with which sort, indeed, he chiefly worked), explode his whole virtue suddenly, and thunder himself out and silent, in a space of five-and-twenty years. While again, for a man of true greatness, working with spiritual implements, two centuries is no uncommon period; nay, on this Earth of ours, there have been men whose Impulse has not completed its development till after fifteen hundred years and might perhaps be seen still individually subsistent after two thousand.

But, as was once written, "though our clock strikes when there is a change from hour to hour, no hammer in the Horologe of Time peals through the Universe to proclaim that there is a change from era to era." The true Beginning is oftenest unnoticed and unnoticeable. Thus do men go wrong in their reckoning; and grope hither and thither, not knowing where they are, in what course their history runs. Within this last century, for instance, with its wild doings and destroyings, what hope, grounded on miscalculation, ending in disappointment! How many world-famous victories were gained and lost, dynasties founded and subverted, revolutions accomplished, constitutions sworn to; and ever the "new era" was come, was coming, yet still it came not, but the time continued sick! Alas, all these were but spasmodic convulsions of the death-sick time: the crisis of cure and regeneration to the time was not there indicated. The real new era was when a Wise Man came into the world, with clearness of vision and greatness of soul to accomplish this old high enterprise, amid these new difficulties, yet again: A Life of Wisdom. Such a man became, by Heaven's pre-appointment, in very deed the Redeemer of the time. Did he not bear the curse of the time? He was filled full with its skepticism, bitterness, hollowness and thousandfold contradictions, till his heart was like to break; but he subdued all this, rose victorious over this, and manifoldly by word and act showed others that come after, how to do the like. Honor to him who first "through the impassable paves a road!" Such, indeed, is the task of every great man; nay of every good man in one or the other sphere, since goodness is greatness, and the good man, high or humble, is ever a martyr and "spiritual hero that ventures forward into the gulf for our deliverance." The gulf into which this man ventured, which he tamed and rendered habitable, was the greatest and most perilous of all, wherein truly all others lie included: *The whole distracted Existence of man in an age of Unbelief.* Whoso lives, whoso with earnest mind studies to live wisely in that mad element, may yet know, perhaps too well, what an enterprise was here; and for the Chosen Man of our time who could prevail in it, have the higher reverence, and a gratitude such as belongs to no other.

How far he prevailed in it, and by what means, with what endurances and achievements, will in due season be estimated. Those volumes called *Goethe's Works* will now receive no further addition or alteration; and the record of his whole spiritual Endeavor lies written there,—were the man or men but ready that could read it rightly! A glorious record; wherein he who would understand himself and his environment, who struggles for escape out of darkness into light as for the one thing needful, will long thankfully study. For the whole chaotic Time, what it has suffered, attained and striven after, stands imaged there; interpreted, ennobled into poetic clearness. From the passionate longings and wailings of *Werter,* spoken as from the heart of all Europe; onwards through the wild unearthly melody of *Faust,* like the spirit-song of falling worlds; to that serenely smiling wisdom of *Meisters Lehrjahre, and the German Hafiz,*—what an interval; and all enfolded in an ethereal music, as from unknown spheres, harmoniously uniting all! A long interval; and wide as well as long;

for this was a universal man. History, Science, Art, human Activity under every aspect; the laws of Light in his *Farbenlehre;* the laws of wild Italian Life in his *Benvenuto Cellini;*—nothing escaped him; nothing that he did not look into, that he did not see into. Consider, too, the genuineness of whatsoever he did; his hearty, idiomatic way; simplicity with loftiness, and nobleness, and aerial grace! Pure works of Art, completed with an antique Grecian polish, as *Torquato Tasso* as *Iphigenie; Proverbs; Xenien;* Patriarchal Sayings, which, since the Hebrew Scriptures were closed, we know not where to match; in whose homely depths lie often the materials for volumes.

To measure and estimate all this, as we said, the time is not come; a century hence will be the fitter time. He who investigates it best will find its meaning greatest, and be the readiest to acknowledge that it transcends him. Let the reader have *seen,* before he attempts to *oversee.* A poor reader, in the meanwhile, were he who discerned not here the authentic rudiments of that same New Era, whereof we have so often had false warning. Wondrously, the wrecks and pulverized rubbish of ancient things, institutions, religions, forgotten nobleness, made alive again by the breath of Genius, lie here in new coherence and incipient union, the spirit of Art working creative through the mass; that *chaos,* into which the eighteenth century with its wild war of hypocrites and skeptics had reduced the Past, begins here to be once more a *world.*—This, the highest that can be said of written Books, is to be said of these: there is in them a New Time, the prophecy and beginning of a New Time. The cornerstone of a new social edifice for mankind is laid there; firmly, as before, on the natural rock: far-extending traces of a ground-plan we can also see; which future centuries may go on to enlarge, to amend and work into reality. These sayings seem strange to some; nevertheless they are not empty exaggerations, but expressions, in their way, of a belief, which is not now of yesterday; perhaps when Goethe has been read and meditated for another generation, they will not seem so strange.

Precious is the new light of Knowledge which our Teacher conquers for us; yet small to the new light of Love which also we derive from him: the most important element of any man's performance is the Life he has accomplished. Under the intellectual union of man and man, which works by precept, lies a holier union of affection, working by example; the influences of which latter, mystic, deep-reaching, all-embracing, can still less be computed. For Love is ever the beginning of Knowledge, as fire is of light; and works also more in the manner of *fire*. That Goethe was a great Teacher of men means already that he was a good man; that he had himself learned; in the school of experience had striven and proved victorious. To how many hearers, languishing, nigh dead, in the airless dungeon of Unbelief (a true vacuum and nonentity), has the assurance that there was such a man, that such a man was still possible, come like tidings of great joy! He who would learn to reconcile reverence with clearness; to deny and defy what is False, yet believe and worship what is True; amid raging factions, bent on what is either altogether empty or has substance in it only for a day, which stormfully convulse and tear hither and thither a distracted expiring system of society, to adjust himself aright, and, working for the world and in the world, keep himself unspotted from the world,—let him look here. This man, we may say, became morally great, by being in his own age, what in some other ages many might have been, a genuine man. His grand excellency was this, that he was genuine. As his primary faculty, the foundation of all others, was Intellect, depth and force of Vision; so his primary virtue was Justice, was the courage to be just. A giant's strength we admired in him; yet strength ennobled into softest mildness; even like that "silent rock-bound strength of a world," on whose bosom, which rests on the adamant, grow flowers. The greatest of hearts was also the bravest; fearless, unwearied, peacefully invincible. A completed man: the trembling sensibility, the wild enthusiasm of a Mignon can assort with the scornful world-mockery of a Mephistopheles; and each side of many-sided life receives its due from him.

Goethe reckoned Schiller happy that he died young, in the full vigor of his days; that we could "figure him as a youth forever." To himself a different, higher destiny was appointed. Through all the changes of man's life, onwards to its extreme verge he was to go; and through them all nobly. In youth, flatterings of fortune, uninterrupted outward prosperity cannot corrupt him; a wise observer has to remark: "None but a Goethe, at the Sun of earthly happiness, can keep his phœnix-wings unsinged."—Through manhood, in the most complex relation, as poet, courtier, politician, man of business, man of speculation; in the middle of revolutions and counter-revolutions, outward and spiritual; with the world loudly for him, with the world loudly or silently against him; in all seasons and situations, he holds equally on his way. Old age itself, which is called dark and feeble, he was to render lovely: who that looked upon him there, venerable in himself, and in the world's reverence ever the clearer, the purer, but could have prayed that he too were such an old man? And did not the kind Heavens continue kind, and grant to a career so glorious a worthiest end?

Such was Goethe's life; such has his departure been. He sleeps now beside his Schiller and his Carl August of Weimar: so had the Prince willed it, that between these two should be his own final rest. In life they were united, in death they are not divided. The unwearied Workman now rests from his labors; the fruit of these is left growing, and to grow. His earthly years have been numbered and ended: but of his Activity, for it stood rooted in the Eternal, there is no end. All that we mean by the higher Literature of Germany, which is the higher Literature of Europe, already gathers round this man, as its creator; of which grand object, dawning mysterious on a world that hoped not for it, who is there that can measure the significance and far-reaching influences? The Literature of Europe will pass away; Europe itself, the Earth itself will pass away: this little life-boat of an Earth, with its noisy crew of a Mankind, and all their troubled History, will one day have vanished; faded like a cloud-speck from the azure of the All! What, then, is man! What, then, is man! He endures but for an hour, and is crushed before the moth. Yet in the being and in the working of a faithful man is there already (as all faith, from the beginning, gives assurance) a something that pertains not to this wild death-element of Time; that triumphs over Time; and *is*, and will be, when Time shall be no more.

And now we turn back into the world, withdrawing from this new-made grave. The man whom we love lies there: but glorious, worthy; and his spirit yet lives in us with an authentic life. Could each here vow to do his little task, even as the Departed did his great one; in the manner of a true man, not for a Day, but for Eternity! To live, as he counselled and commanded, not commodiously in the Reputable, the Plausible, the Half, but resolutely in the Whole, the Good, the True:

Im Ganzen, Guten, Wahren resolut zu leben.
1832

FROM SARTOR RESARTUS

THE EVERLASTING YEA

"Man's Unhappiness, as I construe, comes of his Greatness; it is because there is an Infinite in him, which with all his cunning he cannot quite bury under the Finite. Will the whole Finance Ministers and Upholsterers and Confectioners of modern Europe undertake, in joint-stock company, to make one Shoeblack HAPPY? They cannot accomplish it, above an hour or two; for the Shoeblack also has a Soul quite other than his Stomach: and would require, if you consider it, for his permanent satisfaction and saturation, simply this allotment, no more, and no less: *God's infinite Universe altogether to himself, therein to enjoy infinitely, and fill every wish as fast as it rose.* Oceans of Hochheimer, a Throat like that of Ophiuchus: speak not of them; to the infinite Shoeblack they are as nothing. No sooner is your ocean filled, than he grumbles that it might have been of better vintage. Try him with half of a Universe, of an Omnipotence, he sets to quarreling with the proprietor of the other half, and declares himself the most maltreated of men.—Always there is a black spot in our sunshine: it is even, as I said, the *Shadow of Ourselves.*

"But the whim we have of Happiness is somewhat thus. By certain valuations, and averages, of our own striking, we come upon some sort of average terrestrial lot; this we fancy belongs to us by nature, and of indefeasible right. It is simply payment of our wages, of our deserts; requires neither thanks nor complaint; only such *overplus* as there may be do we account Happiness; any *deficit* again is Misery. Now consider that we have made the valuation of our own deserts ourselves, and what a fund of Self-conceit there is in each of us,—do you wonder that the balance should so often dip the wrong way, and many a Blockhead cry: See there, what a payment; was ever worthy gentleman so used!—I tell thee, Blockhead, it all comes of thy Vanity; of what thou *fanciest* those same deserts of thine to be. Fancy that

thou deservest to be hanged (as is most likely), thou wilt feel it happiness to be only shot: fancy that thou deservest to be hanged in a hair-halter, it will be a luxury to die in hemp.

"So true it is, what I then said, that *the Fraction of Life can be increased in value not so much by increasing your Numerator as by lessening your Denominator.* Nay, unless my Algebra deceive me, *Unity* itself divided by *Zero* will give *Infinity.* Make thy claim of wages a zero, then; thou hast the world under thy feet. Well did the Wisest of our times write: 'It is only with Renunciation (*Entsagen*) that Life, properly speaking, can be said to begin.'

"I asked myself: What is this that, ever since earliest years, thou hast been fretting and fuming, and lamenting and self-tormenting, on account of? Say it in a word: is it not because thou art not HAPPY? Because the THOU (sweet gentleman) is not sufficiently honored, nourished, soft-bedded, and lovingly cared for? Foolish soul! What Act of Legislature was there that *thou* shouldst be Happy? A little while ago thou hadst no right to *be* at all. What if thou wert born and predestined not to be Happy, but to be Unhappy! Art thou nothing other than a Vulture, then, that fliest through the Universe seeking after somewhat to *eat;* and shrieking dolefully because carrion enough is not given thee? Close thy *Byron;* open thy *Goethe.*"

"*Es leuchtet mir ein,* I see a glimpse of it!" cries he elsewhere "there is in man a HIGHER than Love of Happiness: he can do without Happiness, and instead thereof find Blessedness! Was it not to preach-forth this same HIGHER that sages and martyrs, the Poet and the Priest, in all times, have spoken and suffered; bearing testimony, through life and through death, of the Godlike that is in Man, and how in the Godlike only has he Strength and Freedom? Which God-inspired Doctrine art thou also honored to be taught; O Heavens! and broken with manifold merciful Afflictions, even till thou become contrite, and learn it! O thank thy Destiny for these; thankfully bear what yet remain: thou hadst need of them; the Self in thee needed to be annihilated. By benignant fever-paroxysms is Life rooting out the deep-seated chronic Disease, and triumphs over Death. On the roaring billows of Time, thou art not engulfed, but borne aloft into the azure of Eternity. Love not Pleasure; love God. This is the EVERLASTING YEA, wherein all contradiction is solved; wherein whoso walks and works, it is well with him." . . .

"Conviction, were it never so excellent, is worthless till it convert itself into Conduct. Nay, properly Conviction is not possible till then; inasmuch as all Speculation is by nature endless, formless, a vortex amid vortices: only by a felt indubitable certainty of Experience does it find any center to revolve round, and so fashion itself into a system. Most true is it, as a wise man teaches us, that 'Doubt of any sort cannot be removed except by Action.' On which ground, too, let him who gropes painfully in darkness or uncertain light, and prays vehemently that the dawn may ripen into day, lay this other precept well to heart, which to me was of invaluable service: 'Do the Duty which lies nearest thee,' which thou knowest to be a Duty! Thy second Duty will already have become clearer.

"May we not say, however, that the hour of Spiritual Enfranchisement is even this: When your Ideal World, wherein the whole man has been dimly struggling and inexpressibly languishing to work, becomes revealed and thrown open; and you discover, with amazement enough, like the Lothario in Wilhelm Meister, that your 'America is here or nowhere'? The Situation that has not its Duty, its Ideal, was never yet occupied by man. Yes here, in this poor, miserable, hampered, despicable Actual, wherein thou even now standest, here or nowhere is thy Ideal: work it out therefrom; and working, believe, live, be free. Fool! the Ideal is in thyself, the impediment too is in thyself: thy Condition is but the stuff thou art to shape that same Ideal out of: what matters whether such stuff be of this sort or that, so the Form thou give it be heroic, be poetic? O thou that pinest in the imprisonment of the Actual, and criest bitterly to the gods for a kingdom wherein to rule and create, know this of a truth: the thing thou seekest is already with thee, 'here or nowhere,' couldst thou only see."

"But it is with man's Soul as it was with Nature: the beginning of Creation is— Light. Till the eye have vision, the whole members are in bonds. Divine moment, when over the tempest-tost Soul, as once over the wild-weltering Chaos, it is spoken: Let there be light! Ever to the greatest that has felt such moment, is it not miraculous and God-announcing; even as, under simpler figures, to the simplest and least. The mad primeval Discord is hushed; the

rudely jumbled conflicting elements bind themselves into separate Firmaments: deep silent rock-foundations are built beneath; and the skyey vault with its everlasting Luminaries above: instead of a dark wasteful Chaos, we have a blooming, fertile, Heaven-encompassed World.

"I too could now say to myself: Be no longer a Chaos, but a World, or even Worldkin. Produce! Produce! Were it but the pitifullest infinitesimal fraction of a Product, produce it, in God's name! 'Tis the utmost thou hast in thee: out with it, then. Up, up! Whatsoever thy hand findeth to do, do it with thy whole might. Work while it is called Today; for the Night cometh, wherein no man can work."

1833-1834

FROM THE FRENCH REVOLUTION

THE FAILURE TO BE A KING

[Louis XVI and Marie Antoinette, disguised, are fleeing in a berline (carriage) towards the border. They have nearly reached the place where assistance awaits them. It is the king's last chance to save his life.]

One figure . . . we do note at the last door of the Village: that figure in looseflowing nightgown, of Jean Baptiste Drouet, Master of the Post here. An acrid choleric man, rather dangerous looking; still in the prime of life, though he has served, in his time, as a Conde Dragoon. This day, from an early hour Drouet got his choler stirred, and has been kept fretting. Hussar Goguelat in the morning saw good, by way of thrift, to bargain with his own Innkeeper, not with Drouet regular Maitre de Post, about some gig-horse for the sending back of his gig; which thing Drouet perceiving came over in red ire, menacing the Innkeeper, and would not be appeased. Wholly an unsatisfactory day. For Drouet is an acrid Patriot too, was at the Paris Feast of Pikes: and what do these Bouille soldiers mean? Hussars,—with their gig, and a vengeance to it!—have hardly been thrust out, when Dandoins and his fresh Dragoons arrive from Clermont, and stroll. For what purpose? Choleric Drouet steps out and steps in, with long-flowing nightgown; looking abroad, with that sharpness of faculty which stirred choler gives to man. On the other hand, mark Captain

Dandoins on the street of that same Village; sauntering with a face of indifference, a heart eaten of black care! For no Korff Berline makes its appearance. The great Sun flames broader towards setting: one's heart flutters on the verge of dread unutterabilities.

By Heaven! here is the yellow Bodyguard Courier; spurring fast, in the ruddy evening light! Steady, O Dandoins, stand with inscrutable indifferent face; though the yellow blockhead spurs past the Posthouse; inquires to find it; and stirs the Village, all delighted with his fine livery.— Lumbering along with its mountains of bandboxes, and Chaise behind, the Korff Berline rolls in; huge Acapulco ship with its Cockboat, having got thus far. The eyes of the Villagers look enlightened, as such eyes do when a coach-transit, which is an event, occurs for them. Strolling Dragoons respectfully, so fine are the yellow liveries, bring hand to helmet; and a Lady in gypsy-hat responds with a grace peculiar to her. Dandoins stands with folded arms, and what look of indifference and disdainful garrison-air a man can, while the heart is like leaping out of him. Curled disdainful mustachio; careless glance,—which, however surveys the Village-groups, and does not like them. With his eye he bespeaks the yellow Courier, Be Quick, be quick! Thickheaded Yellow cannot understand the eye; comes up mumbling, to ask in words: seen of the Village!

Nor is Postmaster Drouet unobservant all this while: but steps out and steps in, with his long-flowing nightgown, in the level sunlight; prying into several things. When a man's faculties, at the right time, are sharpened by choler, it may lead to much. That Lady in slouched gypsy-hat, though sitting back in Carriage, does she not resemble some one we have seen, some time;—at the Feast of Pikes, or elsewhere? And this *Grosse-Tete* in round hat and peruke, which, looking rearward, pokes itself out from time to time, methinks there are features in it—? Quick, Sieur Guillaume, Clerk of the *Directoire,* bring me a new Assignat! Drouet scans the new Assignat; compares the Paper-money Picture with the Gross Head in round hat there: by Day and Night! you might say the one was an attempted Engraving of the other. And this march of Troops; this sauntering and whispering,—I see it!

Drouet, Postmaster of this Village, hot Patriot, Old-Dragoon of Conde, consider, therefore, what thou wilt do. And fast, for behold the new Berline, expeditiously yoked, cracks whipcord, and rolls away!— Drouet dare not, on the spur of the instant, clutch the bridles in his own two hands; Dandoins, with broadsword, might hew you off. Our poor Nationals, not one of them here, have three hundred fusils, but then no powder; besides one is not sure, only morally certain. Drouet, as an adroit Old-Dragoon of Conde, does what is advisablest; privily bespeaks Clerk Guillaume, Old-Dragon of Conde he too; privily, while Clerk Guillaume is saddling two of the fleetest horses, slips over to the Townhall to whisper a word; then mounts with Clerk Guillaume; and the two bound eastward in pursuit, to *see* what can be done.

. . . .

The Korff Berline, fairly ahead of all this riding Avalanche, reached the little paltry Village of Varennes about eleven o'clock; hopeful, in spite of that hoarse-whispering Unknown. Do not all Towns now lie behind us; Verdun avoided, on our right? Within wind of Bouille himself, in a manner; and the darkest of midsummer nights favoring us! And so we halt on the hilltop at the South end of the Village; expecting our relay; which young Bouille, Bouille's own son, with his Escort of Hussars, was to have ready; for in this Village is no Post. Distracting to think of: neither horse nor Hussar is here! Ah, and stout horses, a proper relay belonging to Duke Choiseul, do stand at hay, but in the Upper Village over the Bridge; and we know not of them. Hussars likewise do wait, but drinking in the taverns. For indeed it is six hours beyond the time; young Bouille, silly stripling, thinking the matter over for this night, has retired to bed. And so our yellow Couriers, inexperienced, must rove, groping, bungling, through a village mostly asleep: Postillions will not, for any money, go on with the tired horses; not at least without refreshment; not they, let the Valet in round hat argue as he likes.

Miserable! "For five-and-thirty minutes" by the King's watch, the Berline is at a dead stand: Round-hat arguing with Churn-boots; tired horses slobbering their meal-and-water; yellow Couriers groping, bungling; young Bouille asleep, all the while, in the Upper Village, and Choiseul's fine team standing there at hay. No help for it; not with a King's ransom; the horses deliberately slobber, Round-hat argues, Bouille sleeps. And mark now, in the

thick night, do not two Horsemen, with
jaded trot, come clank-clanking; and start
with half-pause, if one noticed them, at
sight of this dim mass of a Berline, and its
dull slobbering and arguing; then prick off 5
faster, into the Village? It is Drouet, he
and Clerk Guillaume! Still ahead, they
two, of the whole riding hurlyburly; un-
shot, though some brag of having chased
them. Perilous is Drouet's errand also; but 10
he is an Old-Dragoon, with his wits shaken
thoroughly awake.

The Village of Varennes lies dark and
slumberous; a most unlevel Village, of inverse saddle-shape, as men write. It sleeps; 15
the rushing of the River Aire singing lullaby to it. Nevertheless from the Golden
Arm, *Bras d'Or* Tavern, across that sloping
Marketplace, there still comes shine of social
light, comes voice of rude drovers, or the 20
like, who have not yet taken the stirrup-
cup; Boniface Le Blanc, in white apron,
serving them: cheerful to behold. To this
Bras d'Or Drouet enters, alacrity looking
through his eyes; he nudges Boniface, in 25
all privacy, *"Camarade, es-tu bon Patriote,*
Art thou a good Patriot?"—*"Si je suis!"*
answers Boniface.—"In that case," eagerly
whispers Drouet—what whisper is needful,
heard of Boniface alone. 30

And now see Boniface Le Blanc bustling,
as he never did for the jolliest toper. See
Drouet and Guillaume, dexterous Old-
Dragoons, instantly down blocking the
Bridge, with a "furniture wagon they find 35
there," with whatever wagons, tumbrils,
barrels, barrows their hands can lay hold
of;—till no carriage can pass. Then swiftly,
the Bridge once blocked, see them take station hard by, under Varennes Archway 40
joined by Le Blanc, Le Blanc's Brother,
and one or two alert Patriots he has roused.
Some half-dozen in all, with National muskets, they stand close, waiting under the
Archway, till that same Korff Berline rum- 45
ble up.

It rumbles up: *Alte la!* lanterns flash out
from under coat-skirts, bridles chuck in
strong fists, two National muskets level
themselves fore and aft through the two 50
Coach-doors: "Mesdames, your Passports?"
—Alas, alas! Sieur Sausse, Procureur of
the Township, Tallow-chandler also and
Grocer, is there, with official grocer-polite-
ness; Drouet with fierce logic and ready 55
wit:—The respected Travelling Party, be
it Baroness de Korff's, or persons of still
higher consequence, will perhaps please to
rest itself in M. Sausse's till the dawn strike
up! 60

O Louis; O hapless Marie Antoinette,
fated to pass thy life with such men!
Phlegmatic Louis, art thou but lazy semi-
animate phlegm, then, to the center of
thee? King, Captain General, Sovereign
Frank! if thy heart ever formed, since it
began beating under the name of heart,
any resolution at all, be it now then, or
never in this world:—"Violent nocturnal
individuals, and if it were persons of high
consequence? And if it were the King himself? Has the King not the power which
all beggars have, of travelling unmolested
on his own Highway? Yes: it is the King;
and tremble ye to know it! The King has
said, in this one small matter; and in
France, or under God's Throne, is no
power that shall gainsay. Not the King
shall ye stop here under this your miserable
Archway; but his dead body only, and answer it to Heaven and Earth. To me,
Bodyguards; Postillions, *en avant!"*—One
fancies in that case the pale paralysis of
these two Le Blanc musketeers; the drooping of Drouet's underjaw; and how Procureur Sausse had melted like tallow in
furnace-heat; Louis faring on; in some few
steps awakening Young Bouille, awakening
relays and Hussars: triumphant entry, with
cavalcading high-brandishing Escort, and
Escorts, into Montmédi; and the whole
course of French History different!

Alas, it was not *in* the poor phlegmatic
man. Had it been in him, French History
had never come under this Varennes Archway to decide itself.—He steps out; all step
out. Procureur Sausse gives his grocer-arms
to the Queen and Sister Elizabeth; Majesty
taking the two children by the hand. And
thus they walk, coolly back, over the
Market-place to Procureur Sausse's; mount
into his small upper story; where straightway his Majesty "demands refreshments."
Demands refreshments, as is written; gets
bread-and-cheese with a bottle of Burgundy; and remarks, that it is the best
Burgundy he ever drank!

1837

FROM HEROES AND HERO-WORSHIP

THE HERO AS POET

You will say, there must be a difference
between true Poetry and true Speech not
poetical: what is the difference? On this
point many things have been written, espe-

cially by late German Critics, some of which are not very intelligible at first. They say, for example, that the Poet has an *infinitude* in him; communicates an *Unendlichkeit*, a certain character of "infinitude," to whatsoever he delineates. This, though not very precise, yet on so vague a matter is worth remembering: if well meditated, some meaning will gradually be found in it. For my own part, I find considerable meaning in the old vulgar distinction of Poetry being metrical, having music in it, being a Song. Truly, if pressed to give a definition, one might say this as soon as anything else: If your delineation be authentically *musical*, musical not in word only, but in heart and substance, in all the thoughts and utterances of it, in the whole conception of it, then it will be poetical; if not, not.—Musical: how much lies in that! A *musical* thought is one spoken by a mind that has penetrated into the inmost heart of the thing; detected the inmost mystery of it, namely the *melody* that lies hidden in it; the inward harmony of coherence which is its soul, whereby it exists, and has a right to be, here in this world. All inmost things, we may say, are melodious; naturally utter themselves in Song. The meaning of Song goes deep. Who is there that, in logical words, can express the effect music has on us? A kind of inarticulate unfathomable speech, which leads us to the edge of the Infinite, and lets us for moments gaze into that!

Nay all speech, even the commonest speech, has something of song in it: not a parish in the world but has its parish-accent;—the rhythm or *tune* to which the people there *sing* what they have to say! Accent is a kind of chanting; all men have accent of their own,—though they only *notice* that of others. Observe too how all passionate language does of itself become musical,—with a finer music than the mere accent; the speech of a man even in zealous anger becomes a chant, a song. All deep things are Song. It seems somehow the very central essence of us, Song; as if all the rest were but wrappages and hulls! The primal element of us; of us, and of all things. The Greeks fabled of Sphere-Harmonies: it was the feeling they had of the inner structure of Nature: that the soul of all her voices and utterances was perfect music. Poetry, therefore, we will call *musical Thought*. The Poet is he who *thinks* in that manner. At bottom, it turns still on power of intellect; it is a man's sincerity and depth of vision that makes him a Poet. See deep enough, and you see musically; the heart of Nature *being* everywhere music, if you can only reach it.

The *Vates* Poet, with his melodious Apocalypse of Nature, seems to hold a poor rank among us, in comparison with the *Vates* Prophet; his function, and our esteem of him for his function, alike slight. The Hero taken as Divinity; the Hero taken as Prophet; then next the Hero taken only as Poet: does it not look as if our estimate of the Great Man, epoch after epoch, were continually diminishing? We take him first for a god, then for one god-inspired; and now in the next stage of it, his most miraculous word gains from us only the recognition that he is a Poet, beautiful verse-maker, man of genius, or suchlike!—It looks so; but I persuade myself that intrinsically it is not so. If we consider well, it will perhaps appear that in man still there is the *same* altogether peculiar admiration for the Heroic Gift, by what name soever called, that there is at any time was.

I should say, if we do not now reckon a Great Man literally divine, it is that our notions of God, of the supreme unattainable Fountain of Splendor, Wisdom, and Heroism, are ever rising *higher;* not altogether that our reverence for these qualities, as manifested in our like, is getting lower. This is worth taking thought of. Skeptical Dilettantism, the curse of these ages, a curse which will not last for ever, does indeed in this the highest province of human things, as in all provinces, make sad work; and our reverence for great men, all crippled, blinded, paralytic as it is, comes out in poor plight, hardly recognisable. Men worship the shows of great men; the most disbelieve that there is any reality of great men to worship. The dreariest, fatalest faith; believing which, one would literally despair of human things. Nevertheless look, for example, at Napoleon! A Corsican lieutenant of artillery; that is the show of *him:* yet is he not obeyed, *worshipped* after his sort, as all the Tiaraed and Diademed of the world put together could not be? High Duchesses, and ostlers of inns, gather round the Scottish rustic, Burns;—a strange feeling dwelling in each that they never heard a man like this; that, on the whole, this is the man! In the secret heart of these people it still dimly reveals itself, though there is no accredited way of uttering it at present, that this rustic, with his black brows and flashing sun-eyes, and strange words moving laughter and tears, is of a dignity far beyond all others, incommensurable with all others. Do not we feel it so? But now, were Dilettantism, Skepticism, Triviality, and all that sorrowful brood, cast-out of us,—as, by God's blessing, they shall one day be; were faith in the shows of things entirely swept-out, replaced by clear faith in the *things*, so that a man acted on the impulse of that only, and counted the other non-extant; what a new livelier feeling towards this Burns were it!

Nay here in these ages, such as they are, have we not two mere Poets, if not deified, yet we may say beatified? Shakespeare and Dante are Saints of Poetry; really, if we will think of it, *canonised*, so that it is impiety to meddle with them. The un-guided instinct of the world, working across all these perverse impediments, has arrived at such result. Dante and Shakespeare are a peculiar Two. They dwell apart, in a kind of royal solitude; none equal, none second to them: in the general feeling of the world, a certain transcendentalism, a glory as of complete perfection, invests these two. They *are* canonised, though no Pope or Cardinals took hand in doing it! Such, in spite of every perverting influence, in the most unheroic times, is still our in-destructible reverence for heroism. . . .

It is in what I called Portrait painting, delineating of men and things, especially of men, that Shakespeare is great. All the greatness of the man comes out decisively here. It is unexampled, I think, that calm creative perspicacity of Shakespeare. The thing he looks at reveals not this or that face of it, but its inmost heart, and generic secret: it dissolves itself as in light before him, so that he discerns the perfect structure of it. Creative, we said: poetic creation, what is this too but *seeing* the thing sufficiently? The *word* that will describe the thing, follows of itself from such clear intense sight of the thing. And is not Shakespeare's *morality*, his valor, candor, tolerance, truthfulness; his whole victorious strength and greatness, which can triumph over such obstructions, visible there too? Great as the world! No *twisted*, poor con-vex-concave mirror, reflecting all objects with its own convexities and concavities; a perfectly *level* mirror;—that is to say withal, if we will understand it, a man justly related to all things and men, a good

man. It is truly a lordly spectacle how this great soul takes in all kinds of men and objects, a Falstaff, an Othello, a Juliet, a Coriolanus; sets them all forth to us in their round completeness; loving, just, the equal brother of all. Novum Organum, and all the intellect you will find in Bacon, is of a quite secondary order; earthly, ma-terial, poor in comparison with this. Among modern men, one finds, in strict-ness, almost nothing of the same rank. Goethe alone, since the days of Shakes-peare, reminds me of it. Of him too you say that he *saw* the object; you may say what he himself says of Shakespeare: "His characters are like watches with dial-plates of transparent crystal; they show you the hours like others, and the inward mecha-nism also is all visible."

The seeing eye! It is this that discloses the inner harmony of things; what Nature meant, what musical idea Nature has wrapped up in these often rough embodi-ments. Something she did mean. To the seeing eye that something were discernible. Are they base, miserable things? You can laugh over them, you can weep over them; you can in some way or other genially re-late yourself to them;—you can, at lowest, hold your peace about them, turn away your own and others' face from them, till the hour come for practically exterminat-ing and extinguishing them! At bottom, it is the Poet's first gift, as it is all men's, that he have intellect enough. He will be a Poet if he have: a Poet in word; or failing that, perhaps still better, a Poet in act. Whether he write at all; and if so, whether in prose or in verse, will depend on acci-dents: who knows on what extremely triv-ial accidents,—perhaps on his having had a singing master, on his being taught to sing in his boyhood! But the faculty which en-ables him to discern the inner heart of things, and the harmony that dwells there (for whatsoever exists has a harmony in the heart of it, or it would not hold together and exist), is not the result of habits or accidents, but the gift of Nature herself; the primary outfit for a Heroic Man in what sort soever. To the Poet, as to every other, we say first of all, See. If you can-not do that, it is of no use to keep string-ing rhymes together, jingling sensibilities against each other, and *name* yourself a Poet; there is no hope for you.

1841

NOTES, COMMENTS, BIBLIOGRAPHIES, AND
SUGGESTIONS FOR ORAL AND WRITTEN
CLASS DISCUSSIONS

THE TEXT OF THE SELECTIONS

The text is based on the last edition of the original known to have been approved by the author. Variants which are unusually significant are given in the Notes.

The spelling, capitalization, and punctuation, have as a rule been brought into conformity with modern American usage, especially whenever the retention of the original peculiarities would merely distract the attention of the reader without any compensating advantage. But in cases where such peculiarities seem to reflect an essential characteristic of the substance or the tone of the passage, they have been retained (e.g., in Chatterton, Blake, and Carlyle), "queer" as they may seem today. The mechanical redaction of all the text, without any exceptions, to one system, would have been easy, since it requires no exercise of judgment; but it would obliterate distinctions which were of real importance to the authors. Sometimes, for example, Wordsworth spells such general terms as "Man" and "man," "Nature" and "nature," differently not out of caprice or carelessness, but because by the capitalized form he signifies a meaning distinct from the one he conveys by the uncapitalized.

ABBREVIATIONS

The abbreviations most frequently used are the following:

Anth.	*Anthology of Romanticism*
DISC.	Topics for Discussion, Oral or Written

ELH	*Journal of English Literary History*
EXP	*The Explicator*
JEGP	*Journal of English and Germanic Philology*
JHI	*Journal of the History of Ideas*
KR	*Kenyon Review*
MLN	*Modern Language Notes*
MLQ	*Modern Language Quarterly*
MP	*Modern Philology*
N&Q	*Notes and Queries*
NYT	*New York Times Book Review*
PMLA	*Publication of the Modern Language Association*
PQ	*Philological Quarterly*
RES	*Review of English Studies*
RLC	*Revue de Littérature Comparée*
SAQ	*South Atlantic Quarterly*
SP	*Studies in Philology*
TLS	*Times Literary Supplement* (London)
UTQ	*University of Toronto Quarterly*

For other abbreviations, see the key prefixed to *The Romantic Movement: A Selective and Critical Bibliography*, ELH (annually).

GENERAL BIBLIOGRAPHY OF THE ROMANTIC MOVEMENT

I.—On the History of the Romantic Movement

*Herford, C. H. *The Age of Wordsworth*, 1897.
Beers, H. A. *A History of English Romanticism in the Nineteenth Century*, 1901.
Elton, Oliver. *A Survey of English Literature: 1780-1830*, 2 vols., 1912.
Pierce, F. E. *Currents and Eddies in the English Romantic Generation*, 1918.
Legouis, Emile, and Cazamian, Louis. *A History of English Literature*, 1924; rev. ed., 1935.
Bernbaum, Ernest. "The Views of the Great Critics on the Historical Novel," PMLA, XLI, 424; 1926.
Stockley, V. *German Literature as Known in England: 1750-1830*, 1929.
Nicoll, Allardyce. *A History of Early Nineteenth Century Drama: 1800-1850*, 2 vols., 1930.
Fairchild, H. N. *The Romantic Quest*, 1931.
Baker, E. A. *The History of the English Novel*, vols. VI, VII, and VIII, 1935-1937.
Sherwood, Margaret. *Undercurrents of Influence in English Romantic Poetry*, 1935.
Lovejoy, A. O. *The Great Chain of Being*, 1936.
*Beach, J. W. *The Concept of Nature in Nineteenth-Century English Poetry*, 1936.
Colum, Mary M. *From These Roots: The Ideas That Have Made Modern Literature*, 1937.
*Bush, Douglas. *Mythology and the Romantic Tradition in English Poetry*, 1937.
Tinker, C. B. *Painter and Poet*, 1939.
Evans, B. I. *Tradition and Romanticism*, 1939.
*Fairchild, Nitchie, et al. "Romanticism: A Symposium," PMLA, LV, 1; 1940.
Hungerford, E. B. *Shores of Darkness*, 1941.
Larrabee, S. A. *English Bards and Grecian Marbles*, 1942.
Barzun, Jacques. *Romanticism and the Modern Ego*, 1943.
Bate, W. J. *From Classic to Romantic*, 1946.

II.—On the Nature and the Value of Romanticism

A.—Attempts to Define

Grierson, H. J. C. "Classical and Romantic," 1923; rptd. in *The Background of English Literature*, 1925.
Smith, Logan Pearsall. *Four Words: Romantic, Originality, Creative, Genius*, 1924; rptd. in *Words and Idioms*, 1925.
Robertson, J. S. "The Reconciliation of Classic and Romantic," *Publ. Mod. Hum. Research Asso.*, 1925.—Cf. R. S. Crane, PQ, Oct., 1926.
Pierce, F. E. "Romanticism and Other Isms," JEGP, Mch., 1926.
*Lucas, F. L. *The Decline and Fall of the Romantic Ideal*, 1936.
Borgerhoff, E. B. O. "*Realisme* and Kindred Words," PMLA, LIII, 837; 1938.
*Ash, David. "Creative Romanticism," *College English*, IV, 100; 1942.

B.—The Attack on Romanticism by Humanism, and the Defense

*More, P. E. "The Drift of Romanticism," *Shelburne Essays*, VIII, 1913.
*Babbitt, Irving. *Rousseau and Romanticism*, 1919.
Herford, C. H. "Romanticism in the Modern World," *Engl. Asso. Essays and Studies*, VIII, 109; 1922.

Foerster, Norman. *Humanism and America*, 1929.
*Fausset, H. I'A. *The Proving of Psyche*, 1929.
Bernbaum, Ernest. "The Practical Result of the Humanistic Theories," *Engl. Journal*, xx, 103; 1931.
*Beach, J. W. *A Romantic View of Poetry*, 1944.

C.—The Attack by the New Criticism, and the Defense

*Eliot, T. S. *The Sacred Wood*, 1920.
*Richards, I. A. *Principles of Literary Criticism*, 1924.
Empson, William. *Seven Types of Ambiguity*, 1930.
Wilson, Edmund. *Axel's Castle*, 1931.
Richards, I. A. *Coleridge on Imagination*, 1934.
Hamilton, G. R. *Poetry and Contemplation*, 1937.
*James, D. J. *Scepticism and Poetry*, 1937.
*Ransom, J. C. *The World's Body*, 1938.
*Brooks, Cleanth. *Modern Poetry and the Tradition*, 1939.
Tate, Allen, ed. *The Language of Poetry*, 1942.
Abel, Darel. "Intellectual Criticism," *Amer. Scholar*, XII, 414; 1943.—Cf. Brooks, Cleanth, "The New Criticism," Do., XIII, 285; 1944.
*Fogle, R. H. "Romantic Bards and Metaphysical Reviewers," ELH, XII, 221; 1945.

D.—Appreciative Enthusiasts

*Murry, J. M. *Keats and Shakespeare*, 1925; and *Heroes of Thought*, 1938.
Williams, Charles. *The English Poetic Mind*, 1932.
*Knight, G. Wilson. *The Burning Oracle: Studies in the Poetry of Action*, 1939; and *The Starlit Dome: Studies in the Poetry of Vision*, 1941.
Du Bos, Charles. *What Is Literature?*, 1940.

E.—Other Important Criticisms

*Pater, Walter. *Appreciations*, 1889.
*Watts-Dunton, Theodore. "The Renaissance of Wonder in Poetry," *Chambers's Cyclopaedia of Engl. Lit.*, III, 1903.
Campbell, Olwen W. *Shelley and the Unromantics*, ch. 9, 1924.
Powell, Annie E. *The Romantic Theory of Poetry*, 1926.
Praz, Mario. *The Romantic Agony*, 1933.
*Leavis, F. R. *Revaluation: Tradition and Development in English Poetry*, 1936.
Bronowski, J. *The Poet's Defence*, 1939.

Bibliographical Aids

For descriptive and critical comments on the books and articles listed in these Notes, and for more extensive references for each author, consult the *Guide Through the Romantic Movement*.

*Starred works in the lists given in the *Anthology* are those which are of the greatest importance for the beginner. They should therefore be available in any library where serious study of the subject is attempted.

To supplement the bibliographies in the *Anthology* and in the *Guide*, consult:

Bateson, F. W., ed. *Cambridge Bibliography of English Literature*, esp. vols. II and III, 1941.
Modern Humanities Research Association. *Annual Bibliography*, 1920 ff.
The Romantic Movement: A Selective and Critical Bibliography, annually in ELH, since 1937.
English Literature: 1660-1800, annually in PQ, since 1926, (esp. for Pre-Romanticism, and for Blake).
The English Association (London). *The Year's Work in English Studies*, annually since 1919.

NOTES, COMMENTS, BIBLIOGRAPHIES, AND SUGGESTIONS FOR ORAL AND WRITTEN CLASS DISCUSSIONS

SELECTIONS FROM THE PRE-ROMANTIC MOVEMENT

In this section the Selections, Notes, etc., elucidate the authors *only in their relationship to Romanticism.* For selections and comments dealing with these authors *in general,* see *Eighteenth Century Poetry and Prose,* edited by L. I. Bredvold, A. D. McKillop, and Lois Whitney (1939), to which I am much indebted.

GENERAL BIBLIOGRAPHY OF THE PRE-ROMANTIC MOVEMENT

*Phelps, W. L. *The Beginnings of the English Romantic Movement,* 1893.
Reynolds, Myra. *The Treatment of Nature in Poetry Between Pope and Wordsworth,* 1896.
Beers, H. A. *A History of English Romanticism in the Eighteenth Century,* 1898.
Farley, F. E. *Scandinavian Influence in the English Romantic Movement,* 1903.
Conant, Martha. *The Oriental Tale in England in the Eighteenth Century,* 1908.
Havens, R. D. "Romantic Aspects of the Age of Pope," PMLA, xxvii, 297; 1912.
Bernbaum, Ernest. *The Drama of Sensibility: English Sentimental Comedy and Domestic Tragedy: 1696-1780,* 1915.
Scarborough, Dorothy. *The Supernatural in Modern English Fiction,* 1917.
Bernbaum, Ernest. Introduction to *English Poets of the Eighteenth Century,* 1918.
Birkhead, Edith. *The Tale of Terror,* 1921.
Tinker, C. B. *Nature's Simple Plan: Radical Thought in the Mid-Eighteenth Century,* 1922.
Snyder, E. D. *The Celtic Revival in English Literature: 1760-1800,* 1923.
Van Tieghem, Paul. *Le Pré-Romantisme,* 1924; Second Series, 1930.
Reed, Amy L. *The Background of Gray's Elegy: Melancholy Poetry, 1700-51,* 1924.
Railo, Eino. *The Haunted Castle: A Study of the Elements of English Romanticism,* 1927.
Smith, D. N. *Shakespeare in the Eighteenth Century,* 1928.—Cf. Babcock, R. W., *The Genesis of Shakespeare Idolatry,* 1931; and Ralli, Augustus, *A History of Shakesperian Criticism,* 1932.
*Fairchild, H. N. *The Noble Savage: A Study in Romantic Naturalism,* 1928.
Clark, Kenneth. *The Gothic Revival,* 1928.—Cf. Manwaring, Elizabeth, *Italian Landscape in Eighteenth Century England,* 1926; and Hussey, Christopher, *The Picturesque,* 1927.
*Elton, Oliver. *A Survey of English Literature: 1730-1780,* 2 vols., 1929.
Draper, J. W. *The Funeral Elegy and the Rise of English Romanticism,* 1929.
Warner, W. J. *The Wesleyan Movement and the Industrial Revolution,* 1930.—Cf. Lee, Umphry, *The Historical Background of Early Methodist Enthusiasm,* 1931; also *Hibbert Journal,* July, 1933.
Sickels, Eleanor M. *The Gloomy Egoist: Moods and Themes of Melancholy from Gray to Keats,* 1932.
Whitney, Lois. *Primitivism and the Idea of Progress in English Popular Literature of the Eighteenth Century,* 1934.
Monk, S. H. *The Sublime: A Study of Critical Theories in Eighteenth-Century England,* 1935.
Allen, B. Sprague. *Tides in English Taste: 1619-1800,* 2 vols., 1937.
Wright, W. F. *Sensibility in English Prose Fiction: 1760-1814,* 1937.
Summers, Montagu. *The Gothic Quest: A History of the Gothic Novel,* 1938; *A Gothic Bibliography,* 1941.

Fairchild, H. N. *Religious Trends in English Poetry.*—Vol. I: *Protestantism and the Cult of Sentiment: 1700-1740;* Vol. II: *Religious Sentimentalism in the Age of Johnson* (1939, 1942).
*Willey, Basil. *The Eighteenth Century Background: Studies on the Idea of Nature in the Thought of the Period,* 1940.
Nicolson, Marjorie H. *Newton Demands the Muse,* 1945.
*Bate, W. J. *From Classic to Romantic: Premises of Taste in Eighteenth-Century England,* 1946.

GENERAL TOPICS FOR ORAL AND WRITTEN CLASS DISCUSSIONS

Notice and discuss in the Selections the appearance of one or more of the following tendencies or features, which are commonly regarded as characteristic of the Pre-Romantic Movement:

1. Faith in the instinctive goodness of human beings
2. Faith in the relatively high moral and religious value of sympathy or benevolence (School of Sensibility)
3. Accurate observation of nature, though without mysticism
4. The same as (3), with the suggestion that nature has a religious significance
5. Elegiac interest, in death, mutability, mourning, melancholy (Graveyard School)
6. Interest in humanitarian movements and reforms
7. Interest in kindness towards animals
8. A democratic attitude,—insistence on the rights and dignity of man, and on the freedom of the individual socially and politically
9. Attacks upon wrongs in the established order or conventional usages,—political, economic, social, or educational
10. Interest in the state-of-nature, the "noble savage," preference for the simple life of earlier ages, primitive religions, folk-poetry
11. Interest in the medieval period,—as an age of faith, chivalry, and poetry
12. Attacks on Pope and other neo-classical authors
13. Revival or imitation of older forms of verse,—ballads, sonnets, blank verse, Spenserian stanzas, etc.
14. Use of local dialects and color
15. Translation or imitation of Oriental tales
16. Translation or imitation of old Scandinavian literature
17. Translation or imitation of old Celtic literature
18. Development of the historical novel, the Gothic School, and the School of Terror
19. Development of literary theories and literary criticism stressing the relatively greater importance (over the rational and formal) of the imaginative, emotional, intuitive, free, individual, and particular (rather than general)
20. Exaltation of Shakespeare, Spenser, and Milton

ANTHONY ASHLEY COOPER, LORD SHAFTESBURY (1671-1713)

See Alexander Lyons, *Shaftesbury's Ethical Principle of Adaptation to Universal Harmony,* 1909; and C. A. Moore, "Shaftesbury and the Ethical Poets in England," PMLA, June, 1916, and "The Return to Nature in the English Poetry of the Eighteenth Century," SP, July, 1917.

4. AN INQUIRY CONCERNING VIRTUE OR MERIT

Shaftesbury asserts that all men naturally and without education feel the difference between good and evil. This instinctive feeling he calls the moral sense, a term not invented by him but brought into vogue through his work.—Acceptance of this doctrine encouraged faith in the instinctive goodness of man.

    4a. 11. *affections:* all kinds of feelings.
    17. *sensible:* perceptible by the senses.
    36. *still:* always.

4b. **3.** *honest:* good, just, honorable.—Observe the tacit assumption that the good is the natural, and evil a corruption thereof.

26. *a sense of right and wrong before,* etc.: Our moral sense is not a consequence of our spiritual nature. It precedes our religious development. Morality is accordingly not dependent upon religion.

5a. **1.** *be taken with any show:* be attracted by any manifestation.

2. *social passion:* sympathy for humanity,—in modern jargon, "social-mindedness."

5.   THE MORALIST: A RHAPSODY

This is mainly a dialogue between Theocles, an enthusiast, and his friend Philocles, who begins as a skeptic but is finally persuaded to accept Theocles' new religion, worship of the Genius of Nature. Nature is absolutely good and harmonious, and evil is only an appearance caused by our imperfect vision.—The style conforms to the subtitle, "A Rhapsody." The Hymn to Nature was translated by the German Romantic, Herder (*Naturhymnus von Shaftesburi*), and became famous in European literatures.

5a. **15.** *balance of Europe:* The political balance, the equilibrium of strength between the rival powers.

23. *order . . . would then equal:* The constitution of the moral world would then manifestly be as harmonious as the constitution of physical nature.

35. *known seats:* famous estates of noblemen.

36. *prospects:* views, landscapes.

5b. **3.** *in loose numbers:* not in regular verse (actually in a kind of prose-poetry).

5. *resolve:* unite.

26. *if it be possible to exclude ill, it will exclude it:* DISC.—Can you see any ambiguity or other weakness in this argument?

47. *imaginary wealth:* gold and precious stones, which Shaftesbury regarded as corrupting mankind.

53. *artificial labyrinths:* the mazes, grottoes, etc., of overelaborate landscape gardening.

58. *beauteous in themselves:* somewhat anticipates William Blake's sentiment in *The Tiger; Anth.* p. 127.

6a. **4.** *Economy:* general system.

11. *Atlas:* the wildly romantic mountain region, here beheld in a vision, in which Shelley a century later laid the scene of his *Witch of Atlas.*

20. *horror:* an agitation of the senses, in the eighteenth century, not always signifying fear and dread only, but sometimes also the astonishment and fascination with which we behold strange and mighty objects, hence the commonplace, "a pleasing horror." The "horrid" might mean not merely the revolting but also anything rugged or gloomy,—e.g., "a horrid wood."

6b. **13.** *that mysterious Being:* the Genius of Nature, the Spirit of the Universe, God.—Observe that the "horrid" scenes just described have ultimately a sublime effect upon the beholder, in whom they awaken the consciousness of the divine.

17. *have at last prevailed:* i.e., the skeptical Philocles is convinced that the Universe is spiritual, and that the natural is the good.

20. *conceit:* vain ingenuity.

29. *formal gardens:* Note the attack upon them.

34. *vulgar:* ordinary (without the modern sense of "coarse," "low").

40. *lovers of the Muses or . . . Graces:* lovers of the beautiful or the civilized.

43. *romantic:* Like "enthusiasm" (l. 46), a word then used contemptuously.

54. *shadow:* the vanities pursued by the worldly in contrast to the really substantial values enjoyed by the devotee of Nature.

JAMES THOMSON   (1700-1748)

See A. D. McKillop, *The Background of Thomson's 'Seasons',* 1942; and the studies of Herbert Drennon on Thomson and Newtonism in Univ. of Chic. *Abstracts,* 1930; PMLA, 1934 and 1938; *Engl. Studien,* 1934 and 1936; and SP, 1934.—See what Coleridge said to Hazlitt; *Anth.,* p. 401, 41b.

7. PREFACE OF "THE SEASONS"

7a. 7. *amuse:* pleasantly entertain and divert (in the eighteenth century the word did not usually suggest "funny").

15. *pendant gardens:* flowering plants in hanging baskets, window-boxes, etc., on the houses.

15. *Cheapside:* a business street in the heart of London. The shopkeepers (some of whom were aldermen) often lived above their shops.

7. WINTER

DISC.—Try to distinguish between passages in the new style,—i.e., comparatively simple and objective (such as, generally speaking, ll. 7-10 and 28-34 in the first selection) and passages in the older manner (such as "the bleating kind," l. 39, and the last seven lines).

7. 1. *fuming dun:* arising dark.

8. 39. *bleating kind:* sheep.

45. *at will:* freely.

45. *below the storm:* e.g., in such a sheltered hollow as is described below, l. 50.

56. *loose-revolving fields:* In the whirling snowstorm the boundaries of the fields seem to move around.

59. *shag:* roughen.

76. *covered pits,* etc.: He fears to walk onward, since the snow may conceal fatal pits and precipices.

9. 89. *officious:* duteous.

89-93. Gray remembered these lines; see below, the *Elegy,* ll. 21-24, "For them no more the blazing hearth shall burn," etc. (*Anth.,* p. 43).

109. *variance:* discord.

110. *dungeon glooms:* Thomson was sympathetically interested in the humanitarian efforts of the prison-reformers of his time.

123. *honest passions:* feelings that are honorable—such as grief and pity.

130. *vice . . . impulse,* etc.: Observe his reverting to personification.

10. SUMMER

10. 3. *formful brain:* mind full of images or fancies.

12. *still:* constantly.

13. *gives:* causes.

10. SPRING

10. 5. Hertford: *"Spring,"* writes Dr. Johnson (*Lives of the Poets,* ed. G. B. Hill, III, 287) "was published next year, with a dedication to the Countess of Hertford, whose practice it was to invite every summer some poet into the country to hear her verses and assist her studies. This honor was one summer conferred on Thomson, who took more delight in carousing with Lord Hertford and his friends than assisting her ladyship's poetical operations, and therefore never received another summons."

22. *bittern:* a wading bird. It makes a noise which Goldsmith calls "booming."

26. *Aries . . . Bull:* The signs of the Zodiac, Aries and Taurus. When the sun enters the first, on March 21, Spring begins.

11. 41. *share:* plough.

43. *winds:* controls, guides.

55. *Maro:* Virgil.

98. *liberal:* free.

12. 108. *Augusta:* London.

118. *God . . . pervades,* etc.: Observe how such a passage prepares the way for a more mystical interpretation of the relation of Nature to God.

13. AUTUMN

13. 5. *These:* the woods, which attract the Muse.
31. *dull, despondent:* DISC.—Are birds thus in autumn, or is this a pathetic fallacy?
53. *woods . . . all around:* the prospect all around the woods, etc., thrills the soul.

14. A HYMN CONCLUDING THE SEASONS

Cf. *Psalm* 148, and the morning hymn of Adam and Eve in Milton's *Paradise Lost*, v, 153-208.

DISC.—Distinguish between (a) the passages in which God and Nature seem to melt into one another, and (b) those in which Nature remains, as in the *Psalms,* only one of the wonderful works of God.

14. 47. *from whom you rage:* who it is (God) that gives you the power to storm.
48. *His praise, ye brooks attune,* etc.: Compare the majestic Canticle in the *Bock of Common Prayer,* "Benedicite, omnia Opera," "O all ye works of the Lord, bless ye the Lord."
15. 72. *Bleat . . . hills,* etc.: They are thought of as the flock of the Great Shepherd.
81. *Ye chief:* You human beings.
114. *seeming evil:* Cf., above p. 5, Shaftesbury's doctrine that evil is only apparent not real.

16. THE CASTLE OF INDOLENCE

"This poem being writ in the manner of Spenser," says Thomson in his preface, "the obsolete words, and a simplicity of diction in some of the lines which borders on the ludicrous, were necessary to make the imitation more perfect."

16. 3. *emmet:* ant.
8. *bale:* sorrow.
10. *fast:* close.
21. *kest:* cast.
33. *plain:* complain.
35. *coil:* noise.
36. *yblent:* blended together.

17. 46. *drowsyhed:* drowsiness.
70. *Ymolten:* Melted.
87. *ne:* nor.
97. *Astræa:* Justice.

18. 113. *soote:* sweetly.

DISC.—Wordsworth's appreciation of Thomson's poetry in the *Essay Supplementary to the Preface, Anth.,* p. 321b, 5 ff.

EDWARD YOUNG (1683-1765)

18. THE COMPLAINT, OR NIGHT THOUGHTS

The full title is *The Complaint, or Night Thoughts on Life, Death, and Immortality.* The theology is orthodox (see Isabel St. J. Bliss, "Young's Night Thoughts in Relation to Contemporary Christian Apologetics," PMLA, 1934). But, as often in the pre-romantics, there are inconsistencies,—gloomy reflections on death and mutability, interspersed with strong hopes for man's future and faith in his "original genius." The poem is in blank verse instead of the heroic couplet, but observe the retention of balance and antithesis.—Some of the passages furnished, in the next century, congenial subjects for illustrations by William Blake.

19.   WELCOME DEATH!

DISC.—Compare the most famous romantic treatment of the theme, as to both thoughts and style,—Shelley's *Adonais*, XXXIX-XL, *Anth.*, p. 961.

20.   CONJECTURES ON ORIGINAL COMPOSITION

20a. 1. *there are who:* there are those who.
    9. *Elysium and Tempe:* Paradise, and a fertile valley in Greece.

21a. 7. *Armida:* an enchantress in Tasso's *Jerusalem Delivered.* Scarcely an apt simile, since her wizardry was exerted chiefly on the side of evil.
    54. *Pope:* an historically important attack upon Pope's celebrated translation of Homer on the grounds that the translation should have been more virile, and the meter, blank verse.
—See D. M. Foerster, *Homer in English Criticism*, 1947.

21b. 17. *extreme parts:* jocose for the endings of the lines.
    18. *his heel:* Achilles' heel was not hardened because it had not been dipped into the river Styx,—and Pope's translation had not been refreshed by the waters of the Muses' spring.
    54. *Augustan age:* any supreme age of literature; in Latin literature, the age of Augustus.

MARK AKENSIDE (1721-1770)

22.   THE PLEASURES OF IMAGINATION

His poetry was influenced by Shaftesbury and glorified a universe, each part of which showed perfection in some degree. Well known to Wordsworth, Keats, etc.—See G. R. Potter, "Akenside, Prophet of Evolution," MP, 1926; C. T. Houpt, *Mark Akenside*, 1944; and A. O. Aldridge, JHI, 1944; SP, 1945; and MLQ, 1947.

22. 6. *imp:* strengthen.
    29. *nor culture:* i.e., good taste is innate, like the moral sense.

JOSEPH WARTON (1722-1800)

24.   THE ENTHUSIAST

24. 8. *Stow:* A typically formal park.
    9. *Attic fanes:* Greek temples.
    21. *Versailles:* Typical of French classical taste.
    26. *Anio:* A romantic stream in Italy, with a high waterfall.

25. 71. *Boreas:* The North Wind.
    76. *Hecat:* Goddess of witchcraft.

26. 118. *Iberean:* Spanish.
    124. *deserts:* any untilled region.
    126. *cates:* delicacies.

26.   AN ESSAY ON THE GENIUS AND WRITINGS OF POPE

26a. 17. *Donne and Swift:* Today all would agree so far as Swift is concerned; but the "New Criticism," which is anti-romantic, considers John Donne's poetry admirable.
    22. *Fontenelle . . . La Motte:* French authors, the latter almost forgotten, the former remembered only for his prose.

26b. 8. *acer spiritus ac vis:* vehement spirit and power.

27a. 6. *Non satis est,* etc.: It does not suffice to set down correct words in the line.
    15. *Neque enim,* etc.: You would not assert that it is enough merely to fill out the line of verse.

33. *Yes, you despise,* etc.: Paraphrased from Pope's verse.

51. *qui fit Mæcenas:* Horace's first satire.

27b. 5. *nihil inane,* etc.: nothing meaningless, nothing dragged in; but he is a pure spring rather than a great river.

8. *Lysias:* A famous Greek orator (c. 400 B.C.)

12. *Boileau:* The greatest critic of the French classical school (c. 1660-1700).

13. *Incapable peut-être:* incapable perhaps of that sublimity which elevates the soul, and of those sentiments which move it, but created to enlighten those whom nature had given those two gifts; laborious, severe, exact, harmonious, he became, in short, the poet of the Reason.

29. *Dryden,* etc.: Few in this list would be placed so high today, except Dryden and perhaps Cowley.

35. *Butler,* etc.: We should probably place Donne in a different class, and omit all the others except Butler and Swift.

39. *Pitt,* etc.: All of these have failed to survive.

28a. 31. *Palamon and Arcite:* Dryden's version of Chaucer's *Knight's Tale.*

39. *lies more level to:* is more nearly on the same level as.

42. *Churchill:* Charles Churchill (1731-1764) a satirical poet who wrote on topics momentarily interesting, and alluded to contemporary celebrities like Lord Chesterfield and Walpole, the Prime Minister.

28b. 28. *Music Ode:* Either the *Song for St. Cecilia's Day* (1687) or *Alexander's Feast* (1697).

WILLIAM COLLINS (1721-1759)

See *W. C. Bronson, ed., *Poetical Works,* 1898; and A. L. Poole, ed., *Poems of Gray and Collins,* 3rd. ed., 1937. Also A. S. P. Woodhouse, in Toronto *Studies in English,* 1931. E. G. Ainsworth, Jr., *Poor Collins,* 1937; and Wilma L. Kennedy, *English Heritage of Coleridge,* 1947.— Coleridge thought Collins had more genius than Gray (*Table Talk;* Apr. 21, 1811).

28.   A SONG FROM SHAKESPEARE'S CYMBELINE

See Act IV, ii,—the obsequies of Imogen (Fidele). Guiderus and Arviragus are huntsmen,— hence *chace,* l. 19.

29.   ODE WRITTEN IN THE BEGINNING OF THE YEAR 1746

In 1745 and 1746 British troops had suffered heavy losses in the battles of Fontenoy, Preston-pans, and Falkirk.

29.   ODE TO EVENING

The absence of rhyme is noteworthy. In the older manner are the personifications; in the newer, the prevalent tone and the exquisitely chosen details which sustain it.

The dependent clause which begins with l. 1 and ends with l. 14, describes phenomena created by Evening herself, which may please her better than the poet's song.

29. 11. *winds . . . his horn:* hums.

30. 21. *folding-star:* evening star. "The star that bids the shepherd fold" (Milton).

32. *its:* perhaps the reading should be "thy."

30.   ODE ON THE POETICAL CHARACTER

In the Epode, Collins boldly associates poetic imagination with God's creation of the universe. Cf. Dorothy L. Sayers, *The Mind of the Maker* (1941). "That part of it," says Coleridge (Letter to Thelwall, December, 1796), "beginning with 'The band, as fairy legends say,

Was wove on that creating day.'

has inspired and whirled *me* along with greater agitations of enthusiasm than any the most *impassioned* scene in Schiller or Shakespeare."

30. 1-22. Even as only one lady was permitted to wear the magic girdle, so Fancy permits few to enjoy the gift of poetry.

2. *bard:* Spenser.

31. 19. *cest:* girdle.

23. *band:* girdle (emblem of poetical genius).

24. *wove on that creating day,* etc.: Poetic genius was created by God at the same time with the Universe.

29. *enthusiast:* Fancy.

46. *tarsel:* falcon.

54. *work:* the girdle.

55. *cliff,* etc.: symbolically, Milton.

32. 69. *Waller:* A seventeenth-century poet, here typifying the neo-classic style.

72. *one alone:* Milton.

32.   THE PASSIONS: AN ODE FOR MUSIC

In the days of Greece, Collins says, the passions successfully expressed themselves; now they fail to. Some decades later (see below, *Anth.,* p. 113) William Blake still complains, in *To The Muses:*

> The languid strings do scarcely move,
> The sound is forced, the notes are few!

32. 3. *shell:* lyre.

33. 65. *haunted stream . . . holy calm:* A passage in Coleridge's mind when he wrote Kubla Khan (J. L. Lowes, *Xanadu,* 399).

34.   ODE ON THE POPULAR SUPERSTITIONS OF THE HIGHLANDS

The long interval between the date of composition (c. 1749) and that of publication (1788) is noteworthy. The bracketed passages, filling out gaps in an imperfect copy are probably not by Collins, but illustrate the ordinary stylistic standards of the time. For the best discussion of the complicated problem of the true text, see *Poems of Collins,* ed. W. C. Bronson, 1898, pp. 121-132.

Collins' knowledge of Scotch superstitions was derived partly from Martin Martin's *Late Voyage to Kilda* (1698) and *Description of the Western Islands of Scotland* (rev. ed., 1716), which helped to arouse in Dr. Johnson's mind (c. 1763) a desire to visit those islands,—a desire which Boswell thought "a very romantick fancy" (ed. G. B. Hill, I, 521). Collins also learned Scotch lore from the lips of John Home, the Scotch dramatist to whom his poem is addressed, and who was returning to the Highlands after a sojourn in London.

34. 4. *shall melt,* etc.: A prediction fulfilled in 1757, when Home's tragedy *Douglas* began its successful career in London.

5. *cordial youth:* John Barrow, a mutual friend of Home and Collins, who lived in Essex near the river Levant (6).

17. *own:* call it theirs.

35. 18. *Doric:* simple, natural.

23. *swart tribes:* Brownies.

27. *elf-shot:* arrows shot by elves were supposed to cause diseases in men and animals.

37. *boreal:* northern.

39. *had:* would have.

41. *Runic:* northern and ancient.

42. *uncouth:* strange (probably not in a contemptuous sense).

45. *dirge,* etc.: Sir Walter Scott may be said to have taken this advice when he imitated the coronach (see below, IV, 49) and the pibroch (IV, 59) of the Highlands.

48. *shiel:* a rude shelter.

57. *dreary dreams,* etc.: Martin (pp. 300, 321) tells of the "second-sight" and of the fatal predictions of witchcraft.

59. *strath:* valley.

65. *them:* those possessed of evil powers.

36. 73. *Charles:* Charles I, beheaded in 1649. The Highlanders were pro-Stuart, sympathized with the rebellion against George I, and consequently rejoiced at the victories of Prestonpans and Falkirk, and lamented the defeat of Colloden (where the victor was William, Duke of Cumberland). Observe that this stanza is a digression from the chief theme, out of tune with it, and not a very happy topic to touch upon in a poem addressed to a Scotch friend.

83. *one William:* William III, King of England, whose accession in 1689 brought the reign of the Stuarts to an end.

91. *dank Will:* the will-o'-the-wisp.

100. *wily monster:* The water-demon, or kelpie,—again mentioned in ll. 108 and 137.

37. 121. *For him in vain:* An echo of Thomson's passage (above p. 9, 89 ff.) directly, or through Gray (below, p. 43, 21 ff.).

123. *to-fall:* close.

142. *hoar pile:* An island on which the bones of pigmies were believed to have been found (Martin, p. 82).

147. *three fair realms:* Scotland, Ireland, and Norway, many of whose kings were supposed to be buried on the island of St. Iona (Martin, pp. 260-261).

155. *Kilda:* Martin (pp. 280-295) ascribed a high moral character to the natives of St. Kilda.

38. 177. *sheen:* bright.

180. *From them he sung,* etc.: In those scenes he laid *Macbeth.*

192. *Tasso,* etc.: Alluding to *Jerusalem Delivered* (translated by Fairfax in 1600), canto XIII, 41-43, 46.

215. *Jonson,* etc.: Ben Jonson visited William Drummond, the poet, at his estate near Edinburgh in 1619. Their conversation was upon topics unlike those which Collins is interested in.

THOMAS WARTON (1728-1790)

The brothers Joseph and Thomas Warton, and their friend William Collins "longed for a revival of imagination and passion on what they conceived to be the ancient Greek model" (Bredvold, McKillop, and Whitney, *Eighteenth Century Poetry and Prose,* p. 559).

39. THE PLEASURES OF MELANCHOLY

DISC.—Before reading this, read Milton's *Il Penseroso;* then discuss the similarities and differences.

39. 17. *charnel:* tomb.

38. *Busyrane,* etc.: Spenser (*Fairie Queene,* III, XI-XII) describes the brave female knight Britomart venturing to the house of the dreaded enchanter Busyrane.

42. *towering, armed,* etc.: From *Paradise Lost,* VI, 110.

50. *fated fair:* Pope's Belinda who was fated to lose her lock (See *The Rape of the Lock,* II).—Observe that this attack on Pope preceded Joseph Warton's prose *Essay on Pope* (above, p. 26).

40. OBSERVATIONS ON THE FAIRY QUEEN OF SPENSER

40a. 15. *Spenser did not live in an age of planning:* but see the plan for the *Fairy Queen* in his prefatory letter,—"to portray in Arthur. . . . the image of a brave knight, perfected in the twelve moral virtues, which is the purpose of these first twelve books."

41a. 13. *disgusts:* displeases.

41b. 6. *sensible:* i.e., as a rule sensible, though mistaken in the following remark so far as Spenser is concerned.

THOMAS GRAY (1716-1771)

42.   HYMN TO ADVERSITY

DISC.—Compare with Wordsworth's *Ode to Duty, Anth.*, p. 230.—The classical background may be seen in Aeschylus, *Agamemnon* (ll. 167-171, "Wisdom comes by suffering,"—Gray's motto); and in Horace, *Ode to Fortune* (I, xxxv).

42.   ELEGY WRITTEN IN A COUNTRY CHURCHYARD

Perhaps begun as early as 1742, after the death of Gray's friend Richard West; but not finished until 1750; for the improvements in style (mostly in the romantic direction) gradually made, see H. W. Starr, "Gray's Craftmanship," JEGP, XLV, 415; 1946.—Note the perfect harmonizing of the three themes (1) reflections on death, (2) the dignity of humble life, and (3) the young poet, unknown to fame, who loved nature and humanity.

42. 2. *lea:* grassy field.

43. 21. *For them no more,* etc.: Perhaps a reminiscence of Thomson's *Seasons* (above, p. 9, l. 89).

35. *awaits,* not "await."

41. *storied urn:* An urn, containing the ashes, with an inscription giving the history of the departed.

41. *animated:* looking alive.

44. 57. *Hampden:* The patriot who resisted Charles I's attempt to impose a tax unconstitutionally. Originally Gray chose classical personages for this passage,—Cato, Cicero, and Caesar.

78. *still:* always.

85. *who, to dumb forgetfulness,* etc.: who, about to become a prey to forgetfulness, ever resigned?

45. 105-112. These stanzas are inscribed on the monument to Gray at Stoke Poges; but this does not prove that Gray intended the unknown young poet to represent himself. He may have had Richard West in mind. See Odell Shepard, MP, xx, 347; 1923.

119. *Science:* knowledge.

45.   THE PROGRESS OF POESY

To this Pindaric ode Gray prefixed a motto from Pindar's *Olympics* (II, 153-154): "This is intelligible to the wise, but for the world at large needs interpretation." He provided an outline in prose, quoted in the following notes.

45. 1. *Awake,* etc.: "The various sources of poetry, which gives life and lustre to all it touches are here described; its quiet majestic progress, enriching every subject (otherwise dry and barren) with a pomp of diction and luxuriant harmony of numbers, and its more rapid and irresistible course, when swoln and hurried away by the conflict of tumultuous passions."—Gray.

9. *Ceres' reign:* grain fields.

13-24. "Power of harmony to calm the turbulent passions of the soul."—Gray.

21. *feathered king:* eagle.

21-41. "Power of harmony to produce all the graces of motion in the body."—Gray.

27. *Idalia:* A town famous for its temple of Venus.

36. *Queen:* Venus.

46. 42-53. "To compensate the real and the imaginary ills of life, the Muse was given to mankind by the same Providence that sends the Day, by its cheerful presence, to dispel the gloom and terrors of the Night."—Gray.

46. *fond:* foolish.

53. *Hyperion:* The Sun.

54-65. "Extensive influence of poetic genius over the remotest and most uncivilized nations, its connection with liberty, and the virtues that naturally attend on it. (See the Erse, Norwegian, and Welsh fragments, the Lapland and American songs)."—Gray.

66-82. "Progress of Poesy from Greece to Italy and from Italy to England."—Gray.

78. *Latian:* Roman.

84. *Nature's Darling:* Shakespeare.

95. *Nor secord he,* etc.: Milton.

112. *what daring spirit:* Gray himself.

115. *Theban eagle:* Pindar.

123. *great:* worldly great.

47.   THE BARD

After Edward I had conquered Wales (1277-1284), he issued the usual edicts against strolling minstrels. By the seventeenth century his act had come to be misrepresented as an order to exterminate all the Welsh bards; and in this form the tradition reached Gray, who had recently been aroused to enthusiasm for Welsh poetical remains by his acquaintance Parry and in other ways. In his preface to *The Bard*, Gray said: "The following ode is founded on a tradition current in Wales, that Edward I, when he completed the conquest of the country, ordered all the bards that fell into his hands to be put to death." Gray's own outline of the poem is as follows:

"The army of Edward I as they march through a deep valley, are suddenly stopped by the appearance of a venerable figure seated on the summit of an inaccessible rock, who, with a voice more than human, reproaches the King with all the misery and desolation which he had brought on his country; foretells the misfortunes of the Norman race, and with prophetic spirit declares, that all his cruelty shall never extinguish the noble ardor of poetic genius in this island; and that men shall never be wanting to celebrate true virtue and valor in immortal strains, to expose vice and infamous pleasure, and boldly censure tyranny and oppression. His song ended, he precipitates himself from the mountain, and is swallowed up by the river that rolls at its foot."

47. 8. *Cambria:* Wales.

28. *Hoel:* a prince and poet.

28. *Llewellyn:* a gentle prince.

29. *Cadwallo:* a poet.

29. *Urien:* a poet.

33. *Modred:* an unknown.

48-100. In these lines, the ghosts of the slain bards join. Gray says: "See the Norwegian Ode,—*The Fatal Sisters;*" below, p. 51.

55. *Berkley's roofs,* etc.: Edward II was murdered at Berkley Castle, his queen, Isabel of France, being in rebellion against him. Their son Edward III won victories in France.

64. "Death of that king, abandoned by his children, and even robbed in his last moments by his courtiers and his mistress."—Gray.

67. "The Black Prince, dead some time before his father."—Gray.

70. "Magnificence of Richard II's reign."—Gray.

48. 77-82. "Richard II was starved to death."—Gray.

83-86. "Ruinous civil wars of York and Lancaster."—Gray.

87. "Henry VI, George Duke of Clarence, Edward V, Richard Duke of York, etc.: believed to be murdered secretly in the Tower of London."—Gray.

89. *his consort:* Margaret of Anjou, Henry VI's queen.

89. *his father:* Henry V.

90. *Usurper:* Henry VI.

91. *rose,* etc.: "The white and red roses, devices of York and Lancaster."—Gray.

93. *boar:*—The villainous Richard III.

99. *Half of thy heart:* Edward I's beloved queen Eleanor, who died soon after the conquest of Wales.

102. *me:* the Bard.

110. *ye genuine kings,* etc.: When Henry VIII of the house of Tudor (Welsh), ascended the throne, the Welsh were appeased.

115. *a form divine:* Queen Elizabeth.

121. *Taliessin:* "Chief of the Bards."—Gray.

128. *buskin'd measure:* dramatic form, the age of Shakespeare.

131. *a voice:* Milton.

133. *distant warblings:*—"The succession of poets after Milton's time."—Gray.

49. LETTERS ON MACPHERSON'S OSSIAN

The first letter refers, not to the printed edition, but to manuscript copies of the samples which Macpherson had submitted to John Howe.

49a. 6. *Erse:* Gaelic, the ancient language of Scotland.

17. *Hardycanute:* Gray was mistaken in believing it ancient; it was a good imitation of an old ballad, composed by Lady Elizabeth Wardlaw, published in 1719, and later admired by Walter Scott.

49b. 1. *recollecting:* gathering itself for a new onslaught.

39. *so extasie:* in such ecstasy.

51. *devil and kirk:* powers of evil and of good.

50a. 7. *Mr. Evans:* Evan Evans, who in 1764 published *Specimens of the Poetry of the Ancient Welsh Bards.*

50b. 5. *Adam Smith; etc.:* This array of reputable believers in Macpherson's fabrications shows the low state of philological learning in that time.

50. THE DESCENT OF ODIN

From the Old Norse *Poetic Edda,* through Bartholin's Latin verse translation (1689). Odin, disguised as a traveller, descends to the lower world to learn the future fate of his favorite son Balder. Balder is destined to be killed by a mistletoe shot by his blind brother Hoder; and Hoder, in turn, will be slain by the child of Odin and Rinda.

50. 4. *Hela:* a goddess of the lower world.

22. *Runic:* magical.

51. 44. *bev'rage of the bee:* Rather "from the bee," it being mead, fermented from honey.

75. *what virgins:* Odin sees the Fates, whom mortal eyes cannot see; therefore the Prophetess recognizes his divinity. He in turn now knows her to be the ruling goddess of the lower world.

90. *Lok:* The evil god, bound in chains until the crack of doom.

51. THE FATAL SISTERS

Based upon a Latin version of an Old Norse poem. It was supposed to have been sung by the Valkyrs, or Choosers of the Slain, before they flew to the battle between the Scandinavians and the Irish in which (1014) the Earl of the Orkneys was slain.—On this and the preceding poem, see G. L. Kittredge, "Gray's Knowledge of Old Norse," in W. L. Phelps's *Selections from Gray* (1894).— When Walter Scott visited the Orkneys, he was greatly interested in the survival of this legend there; see his Diary, Aug. 14, 1814, in Lockhart's *Life of Scott.*

51. 17. *Mista,* etc.: names of the Valkyrs, as likewise Gondula, etc., below.

52. 41. *dauntless earl:* the earl of Orkney.

44. *a king:* of Ireland.

DAVID HARTLEY (1705-1757)

The psychologist and philosopher whose *Observations on Man, His Frame, His Duty, and His Expectations* was to have a great influence on Wordsworth, Coleridge, and other Romantics. For recent discussions of associationism see N. P. Stallknecht, *Strange Seas of Thought,* 1945; and J. R. Caldwell, *John Keats' Fancy,* 1945.

53a. 11. *sensible:* those derived from sensations.

53b. 33. *catachrestically:* figuratively.

JAMES MACPHERSON (1736-1796)

Published as genuine translations, Macpherson's Ossianic epics were fabricated elaborations of very slightly genuine, orally transmitted, remains of ancient Scottish traditions. They portrayed the past as Macpherson wished and supposed it to be, rather than as it was; but they had an enormous influence upon the imagination of literary Europe, which temporarily was pleased with the notion that the North had had a poet as great as Homer. See J. S. Smart, *Macpherson*, 1905; P. Van Tieghem, *Ossian en France;* 1917, and *Le Préromantisme*, 1924; and R. T. Clark, Jr., "Herder, Percy, and the Song of Songs," PMLA, LXI, 1087; 1946.

53. FINGAL'S ROMANTIC GENEROSITY

Swaran, King of Lochlin (Scandinavia), has been captured in battle by Fingal, King of Morven (Scotland); but Fingal gives him life and liberty, recalling that they have the same ancestor Trenmor (whose deeds have just been sung), and being especially moved by love and gratitude to Swaran's sister Agandecca, who was slain by her father Starno because she warned Fingal of a plot against his life.

54a. 25. *desert:* uncultivated wilderness.
    35. *Erin:* North Britain.
    52. *Ossian, Carril, and Ullin:* the bards.

54. COLMA'S LAMENT

Sung before Fingal by the female bard Minona.

55. THE LAST WORDS OF OSSIAN

55b. 25. *ghosts of the bards:* it is curious that five years before Macpherson, Gray had imagined them joining in chorus with his Bard (see above, p. 47).

DISC.—Wordsworth's rejection of Macpherson for falsifying, not history, but nature,--*Essay Supplementary, Anth.*, p. 323b, 34 ff.

CHRISTOPHER SMART (1722-1771)

See W. F. Stead, ed., Smart's *Rejoice In The Lamb* (1939), and E. G. Ainsworth and C. E. Noyes, *Christopher Smart* (1943).—Browning exaggerated when, in *Parleyings with Certain People of Importance in Their Day*, he asserted that no other poet beside Smart between Milton and Keats spoke "language straight from the soul"; nevertheless, in spiritual sincerity, he sometimes anticipates William Blake.—In this selection from his best known poem, the lion, the eagle, etc., in all their mightiness are less potent and sublime than King David when at prayer.

55. A SONG TO DAVID

    55. 2. *bastion's mole·* projecting part of a fortification.
    4. *gier-eagle:* vulture (Biblical word).
    9. *and far beneath the tide:* should follow immediately after "in the sea." The man of prayer is in the seat to faith assigned.

    56. 29. *mute:* the inanimate.
    33. *largess:* alms.
    35. *Alba:* the sun (?).
    59. *catholic:* general, congregational.
    64. *that stupendous truth:* namely, that the Son of God will triumph; see, e.g., *Psalm* **2.**

HORACE WALPOLE (1717-1797)

56. THE CASTLE OF OTRANTO

First notable romance of the "Gothic" School, or School of Terror, other authors of which were Beckford (*Anth.*, p. 92), Mrs. Radcliffe (p. 105), and "Monk" Lewis (p. 107). For the influence of Gothic novels and dramas on Byron and other Romantics, see Bertrand Evans, "Manfred's Remorse and Dramatic Tradition," PMLA, LXII, 752; 1947.—The scene of *The Castle of Otranto* is supposed to be medieval Italy.

THOMAS PERCY (1729-1811)

See Leah A. Dennis, "Thomas Percy: Antiquarian vs. Man of Taste," PMLA, LVII, 140; 1942. —Bishop Percy's *Reliques of Ancient English Poetry*, and his translation of Mallet's *Northern Antiquities*, gave a picture of medieval culture that was nearer the truth than Macpherson's *Ossian;* but, on the continent as well as in England, those three works were indiscriminately admired, and were believed to demonstrate that the perfection of poetry had been reached in a supposedly primitive and nobler state of society (see R. T. Clark, Jr., "Herder, Percy, and the Song of Songs," PMLA, LXI, 1087; 1946).

59.   THE ANCIENT BALLAD OF CHEVY-CHASE

For the best text, see Child's *English and Scottish Popular Ballads*,—"The Hunting of the Cheviot." Percy's text is fairly good.—The battle described in the ballad was probably that fought in 1388 between the Scotch under the Earl of Douglas and the English under Sir Henry Percy ("Hotspur"), which is likewise the subject of the ballad, "The Battle of Otterburn." Ben Jonson is said to have declared that he had rather have been the author of "Chevy-Chase" than of all his works. Addison (see his noble appreciation in *The Spectator*, Nos. 70 and 74) says it was the favorite ballad of the common people.—In "Chevy-Chase," Percy is represented as starting the conflict by hunting in Douglas' territory. As this is an English ballad, and not a Scottish, everything is put into the best light from the English point of view.

The difficulty of reading these ballads will be much lessened if you will read them aloud, for the unfamiliar appearance of the words is often due only to their spelling; thus if you will speak "owar" (l. 29.) you will recognize it as "hour," and so with "Percè" (for Percy), bomen (for bowmen), the (for they). Such words are therefore not glossed here.

59. *Fit:* part.
    5. *in the mauger:* despite.
    10. *let:* hinder.
    12. *meany:* company.
    16. *he:* high.
    20. *reas:* rouse.
    21. *bickarte:* coursed; *bent:* field.
    22. *aras:* arrows.
    25. *greves glent:* groves glanced.
    27. *abone:* above.
    28. *yerly:* early; *monnyn:* Monday.
    31. *mort:* note signifying the death.
    32. *sydis shear:* all sides.
    33. *guyrry:* dead game.
    34. *bryttling:* quartering.
    37. *verament:* truly.
    40. *at his hand:* shading his eyes with his hand.
    57. *glede:* glowing coal.
    58. *barne:* fellow.
    70. *cast:* intend.
    72. *ten:* one.

60. **78.** *yerte:* earl.
    81. *cors:* curse.
    101. *And you:* If you.
    106. *sloughe:* slew.
    107. *bydys:* abides; *bent:* business.
    110. *wouche:* harm.
    117. *garde:* caused.
    122. *basnites:* helmets.
    123. *male:* armor; *myne-ye-ple:* gauntlet.
    124. *sterne:* stern warriors.
    125. *freyke:* man.

130. *myllàn:* Milan steel.

134. *heal:* hail.

61. 165. *se:* saw.

214. *Sir John,* etc.: The heroes named in this list are mostly identifiable, although the names have in some cases been corrupted.

62. 236. *makys:* husbands.

237. *carpe:* talk.

268. *that tear,* etc.: The meaning of this line is unknown.

279. *balys bete:* remedy our evils.

62. NORTHERN ANTIQUITIES

Although Mallet, a man of the rationalistic enlightment, speaks scornfully of the ancient nature-worship, it is easy to understand what an appeal to the romantic spirit was made by the faith that "entire nature" was "an instrument of the divinity."—The romantic young Carlyle chose Odin as a representative divine hero in his *Heroes and Hero-Worship (Anth.,* p. 1054).

DISC.—The reasons why Wordsworth, in his *Essay Supplementary (Anth.,* p. 323a, 5 ff.), placed Percy's *Reliques,* in the Pre-Romantic Movement, next in importance to Thomson's *Seasons.*

OLIVER GOLDSMITH (1728-1774)

The situation described in *The Deserted Village,* and the anxieties arising therefrom, were set forth eight years earlier in "The Revolution in Low Life" (*New Essays by Oliver Goldsmith,* ed., R. S. Crane, p. 104, 1927). In his dedication of the poem to Sir Joshua Reynolds, Goldsmith said: "I know you will object that the depopulation it deplores is nowhere to be seen, and the disorders it laments are only to be found in the poet's own imagination. To this I can scarce make any other answer, than that I sincerely believe what I have written; that I have taken all possible pains in my country excursions, for these four or five years past, to be certain of what I allege; and that all my views and inquiries have led me to believe those miseries real which I here attempt to display. . . In regretting the depopulation of the country, I inveigh against the increase of our luxuries, . . . those luxuries prejudicial to states, by which so many vices are introduced and so many kingdoms have been undone." There was nevertheless in the picture of the village some intensification both of the light and of the shade.

63. THE DESERTED VILLAGE

63. 12. *decent:* seemly, in good taste.

65. 122. *vacant:* untroubled, at ease.

66. 209. *terms and tides presage:* tell beforehand the dates when rents, wages, etc., fell due; and the seasons or holy days of the church calendar.

210. *gauge:* calculate the capacity of a barrel.

67. 232. *twelve good rules:* supposed to be King Charles's rules of life.

232. *game of goose:* in which dice were cast, and counters moved on a board.

249. *pressed:* urged to do so.

69. 343. *Altama:* the river Altamaha in Georgia.

70. 418. *Torno:* the river Tornea in northern Sweden ("the polar world").

418. *Pambamarca:* a mountain in Ecuador.

DISC.—Goldsmith as a precursor of Wordsworth with respect to "plain living," country life, and the dangers of luxury.

THOMAS CHATTERTON (1752-1770)

See M. C. Hare's edition of the *Rowley Poems*, 1911; and E. H. W. Meyerstein's *Life of Thomas Chatterton*, 1930.—To the Romantics the life of Chatterton was even more significant than his works,—because he was precocious, poetically gifted, rejected by worldlings, and a suicide at eighteen. Hence Wordsworth's

> I thought of Chatterton, the marvellous boy,
> The sleepless soul that perished in his pride . . .
> We poets in our youth begin in gladness
> But thereof come in the end despondency and madness.
> (*Resolution and Independence; Anth.*, p. 220.)

In Shelley's *Adonais* (*Anth.*, p. 962) he is one of "the inheritors of unfulfilled renown," worthy to attend the obsequies of Keats.

Chatterton attributed his poems to an imaginary fifteenth-century monk, Thomas Rowley. He borrowed words from Chaucer and from Percy's *Reliques*, but chiefly from Spenser. Sometimes he used the archaic words in a wrong sense; the following glosses give only the meanings he attributed to them. Many of the unfamiliar looking words you will recognize if you read them aloud.

70.   SONGS FROM ÆLLE, BIE THOMAS ROWLEIE

- **70. 1.** *boddynge:* budding.
- **1.** *flourettes:* flowers.
- **2.** *mees:* meadows.
- **4.** *nesh:* tender.
- **5.** *straughte:* stretched.
- **6.** *dynne:* noise.
- **9.** *alestake:* alehouse sign.
- **71. 12.** *albeytte:* albeit.
- **23.** *woddie sede:* willow seed.
- **24.** *levynne:* lightning.
- **24.** *lemes:* gleams.
- **30.** *steyncèd:* stained.
- **31.** *neidher:* neither.
- **32.** *chafe:* warm.
- **43.** *pheeres:* mates.
- **48.** *bante:* accursed.
- **48.** *hie:* highly.

71.   AN EXCELENTE BALADE OF CHARITIE

- **71. 1.** *Virgynè:* The sign of the Virgin (Zodiac).
- **72. 4.** *mole:* soft.
- **5.** *peede chelandri:* pied goldfinch.
- **7.** *aumere:* mantle.
- **13.** *hiltring:* hiding.
- **13.** *fetive:* festive.
- **15.** *holme:* oak.
- **16.** *covent:* convent.
- **19.** *bretful:* brimful.
- **22.** *glommed:* gloomy.
- **22.** *spright:* spirit.
- **23.** *frowynd:* withered.
- **25.** *dorture:* sleeping.

26. *gre:* grow.
30. *forswat:* sunbu.ned.
30. *smethe:* smoke.
30. *drenche:* drink.
35. *lowings:* flashings.
36. *clymmynge:* noisy.
37. *Cheves:* moves.
37. *embollen:* swelled.
39. *gallard:* frightened.
45. *chapournette:* round hat.
49. *mist:* poor.
52. *autremette:* white robe.
56. *horse-millanare:* saddler; one who decks out a horse.
73. 63. *crouche:* cross.
66. *faitour:* vagabond.
75. *Limitoure:* begging friar.
82. *halline:* joy.
85. *unhailie:* unhappy.
87. *semecope:* coat.
91. *mittee:* mighty.

WILLIAM COWPER (1731-1800)

H. S. Milford, ed., *Poems*, 3rd. ed., 1926; David Cecil, ed., *Selections*, 1933. *Life of Cowper*, by Thomas Wright, 2nd ed., 1921; by H. I'A. Fausset, 1928. See also L. C. Hartley, *William Cowper, Humanitarian*, 1938; Adelaide E. Thein, "The Religion of John Newton," PQ, XXI, 146 (1942); and M. J. Quinlan, "Cowper and the Unpardonable Sin," *Journal of Religion*, XXIII, 110 (1943).

Cowper's poetry is largely religious,—in reaction against the rationalism and formalism of the Anglican Church, and in favor of Methodism, which strove to make religious experience sincerely personal, deeply emotional, and actively democratic and humanitarian. He said that his purpose was "to discountenance the modern enthusiasm after a London life, and to recommend rural ease and leisure, as friendly to the cause of piety and virtue."

73.   THE TASK: THE INHUMANITY OF MAN

Since 1772, slaves were free if they entered England; but not until 1834 were they emancipated in the British colonies.

74.   LOVE OF ENGLAND

74b. 9. *Ausonia:* Italy.
32. *Chatham:* William Pitt, first Earl of Chatham, brilliant statesman and orator, who died in 1778.
33. *Wolfe:* General James Wolfe, who fell in the victorious battle of Quebec, Sept. 13, 1759.

75.   COWPER, THE RELIGIOUS RECLUSE

Though Methodism is a hopeful form of Christianity, Cowper was at times personally melancholy, feeling that his own salvation was very doubtful (cf. *The Castaway*, below p. 79).

75.   THE BASTILLE

Four years after these lines were published, this prison in Paris, in which political prisoners were incarcerated, was stormed by the populace (July 14, 1789). The Romantics regarded its fall as a symbolic event of the highest importance. See the Notes on Blake's *The French*

Revolution, Anth., p. 120, where comparison with passages in Wordsworth and Carlyle is suggested.

75b. 22. *visionary emblem:* the tree seen in a dream by Nebuchadnezzar (*Daniel,* 4, 10).

76a. 66. *Manichean god:* Evil, by the ancient Manicheans regarded as coeternal with Good, and as a creator of Man.

76.   MEDITATION IN WINTER

The closing lines ("But trees and rivulets," 53b. ff.) anticipate Wordsworth's attitude in *Expostulation and Reply, Anth.,* p. 189.

77.   KINDNESS TO ANIMALS

The best-known passage of this kind in eighteenth-century literature is that in Laurence Sterne's *Tristram Shandy* (1759), where Uncle Toby lets the fly which had tormented him escape, saying, "Go, poor devil. . . Why should I hurt thee? This world surely is wide enough to hold both thee and me."

77.   ON THE RECEIPT OF MY MOTHER'S PICTURE

Cowper was only five years old when his mother died, and he had no picture of her until fifty-two years later, a cousin sent him one.

79.   TO MARY

Addressed to his "second mother," Mrs. Unwin, then in her second childhood.

79.   THE CASTAWAY

The incident of the sailor whom it was impossible to save, Cowper had read in George Anson's *Voyage Round the World* (1748), and he saw in it a parallel to his own spiritual doom. His belief that he had committed the unpardonable sin is shown in the *Spiritual Diary* which he wrote in 1795 (ed. by Kenneth Povey, *London Mercury,* xv, 493; 1927). In the second stanza, the allusion in "braver chief" is to Christ, and in "ship" to the Church (see Lodwick Hartley, EXP, Dec., 1946).

DISC.—In what ways, (considering both substance and style) does Cowper anticipate Wordsworth? In what ways is Wordsworth different?

Consider for what reasons Coleridge probably (c. 1798) "spoke of Cowper as the best modern poet," as Hazlitt says (*My First Acquaintance With Poets, Anth.,* p. 401b. 43).

Why does Cowper bore our "New Critics"? Edmund Wilson finds him "only a little above mediocrity" (*New Yorker,* May 17, 1947).

ROBERT BURNS (1759-1796)

W. E. Henley and T. F. Henderson, eds., *The Centenary Burns,* 1896-1897; J. C. Dick, ed., *The Songs of Robert Burns* (with their music); and J. DeL. Ferguson, ed., *The Letters of Robert Burns,* 1931. Biography and criticism by F. B. Snyder, 1932; J. DeL. Ferguson, 1939; and R. T. Fitzhugh, 1943. See also Russell Noyes, "Wordsworth and Burns," PMLA, LIX, 813; 1944.

Burns was misinterpreted in two opposite ways. On the one hand, he was represented as a "heaven-taught plowman, of humble and unlettered station," (Henry Mackenzie) although he had more than the rudiments of a sound liberal and religious education. On the other hand, his weaknesses and errors were exaggerated, and he was slandered as grossly immoral and intemperate,—largely because he had satirized narrow sectarianism, hypocritical righteousness, snobbishness, and political conservatism. The Romantics defended Burns as a man and as a poet, Wordsworth taking the lead in his *Letter to a Friend of Robert Burns* (1816), and Hazlitt doing justice to his genius in *On Burns and the Old English Ballads* (1817).

Perhaps the best introduction to Burns is the selection (p. 86) from his *Vision*, in which he modestly touches upon his chief purposes and themes,—his love of nature, simple life, sincere religion, and the "dignity of man." "With the exception of Burns and Cowper," Wordsworth wrote (to R. P. Gillies; Dec. 22, 1814) "there is very little of recent verse, however much it may interest me, that sticks to my memory,—I mean which I get by heart."— In his devotion to the dialect and airs of his native land, he pointed the way to Walter Scott, Thomas Moore, and the romantic movement in general.

80. MARY MORISON

80. 5. *bide the stoure:* endure the tumult of life.

80. THE HOLY FAIR

A church gathering, to which throng both the zealously religious and those who make a picnic of it.

80. 7. *hirplin:* limping.
7. *furs:* furrows.
8. *lav'rocks:* larks.
12. *hizzies:* jades.
13. *skelpin:* proceeding noisily.
16. *lyart:* gray.
25. *curchie:* curtsy.
34. *feck:* most.
36. *screed:* rip.
81. 42. *daffin:* merriment.
43. *gin:* if.
43. *runkl'd:* wrinkled.
77. *tittlin:* whispering.
79. *wabster:* weaver.
84. *fyled:* soiled.
86. *swatch:* sample.
98. *an's loof:* and his hand.
102. *Moodie* etc.: The names are those of actual ministers of the district. They differed in doctrine or in method; *speels the holy door:* climbs the pulpit.
104. *Hornie:* the devil.
114. *eldritch:* unearthly.
116. *cantharidian:* blistering.
138. *water-fit:* river's mouth.
141 *mim:* prim.
142. *Common Sense:* Burn's friend, Dr. Mackenzie, leaves the meeting.
146. *raibles:* rattles off.
149. *manse:* parsonage.
152. *hafflins-wise:* halfways.
154. *butt an' ben:* quickly.
154. *change-house:* tavern.—The preaching tent had a convenient back-entrance into it.
155. *yill-caup:* ale cup.
163. *Leeze me on:* Bless.
165. *lear:* learning.
166. *pangs:* crams.
167. *penny-wheep:* weak beer.
82. 175. *toddy:* whiskey and hot water.
193. *whun-stane:* mill-stone.
203. *cogs:* basins.
207. *dawds:* hunks.
208. *gawsie:* buxom.
208. *gash:* shrewd.
210. *kebbuck:* cheese.
215. *gi'es them 't,* etc.: gives them a free rein.

217. *waesucks:* alas.
220. *melvie:* soil with meal.
230. *slaps:* fence gaps.
230. *billies:* fellows.
234. *crack:* talking.
242. *houghmagandie:* fornication.

82.   EPISTLE TO J. LAPRAIK

Lapraik was a local wit and poet, admired by Burns.

82. 64. *sairs:* serves.
66. *knappin-hammers:* stone-hammers.
69. *stirks:* young steers.

83.   THE COTTER'S SATURDAY NIGHT

83. 1. *friend:* Robert Aiken a lawyer in Ayr, and a friend and patron of Burns.
21. *stacher:* stagger.
22. *flichterin':* fluttering.
23. *ingle:* fireside.
26. *kiaugh:* worry.
30. *tentie:* heedful.
40. *uncos:* news.
48. *eydent:* diligent.
49. *jauk:* trifle.

84. 69. *blate:* shy.
69. *laithfu':* sheepish.
92. *parritch:* porridge.
93. *hawkie:* cow.
94. *hallan:* partition.
96. *weel-hained:* carefully saved.
99. *towmond:* twelve-month.
99. *lint:* flax.
99. *bell:* flower.

85. 105. *lyart haffets:* gray locks.
107. *wales:* selects.
133. *he:* St. John.

86. 166. *An honest man,* etc.: Pope, *Essay on Man,* IV, 248.
182. *Wallace:* The thirteenth-century Scotch patriot who resisted the English conquest unto death.

86.   THE VISION: DUAN SECOND

See the above general comment on Burns. Duan means Canto.

87.   TO A MOUSE

See Dix Harwood, *Love for Animals, and How It Developed in Great Britain,* 1928.—Burns saved the mouse from being killed by the boy who was leading his plough-horses.

87. 1. *sleekit:* sleek.
4. *bickering brattle:* hurrying scamper.
6. *pattle:* paddle to clean the plough with.
15. *daimen icker in a thrave:* an ear or two in a whole shock.
29. *coulter:* the part of the plough which cuts the sward first.
35. *thole:* endure.
36. *canreuch:* hoar-frost.

87. TO A MOUNTAIN DAISY

See the Note on Wordsworth's *To The Daisy, Anth.,* p. 223.

87. 3. *stoure:* dust.
88. 23. *histie:* dry.

88. EPISTLE TO A YOUNG FRIEND

88. 30. *poortith:* poverty.
  30. *stare:* watches.
89. 87. *reck the rede:* take the advice.

89. ADDRESS TO THE UNCO GUID, OR THE RIGIDLY RIGHTEOUS

89. 7. *heapit happer:* full hopper.
  11. *douce:* prudent.
  12. *glaikit:* foolish.
  15. *donsie:* unlucky.
  18. *niffer:* difference.
90. 47. *lug:* ear.
  48. *aiblins:* maybe.
  51. *kennin:* trifle.

90. JOHN ANDERSON, MY JO

90. 4. *brent:* smooth.
  5. *beld:* bald.
  7. *pow:* pate, head.

91. AULD LANG SYNE

91. 9. *be your pint-stowp:* be good for your two-quart flagon.
  21. *fiere:* chum.
  23. *guid-willie waught:* good-will draught.

DISC.—Burns's life and character as seen in his poems, and as interpreted by Wordsworth (*At the Grave of Burns, Anth.,* p. 298) and by Carlyle (*Review of Lockhart's Life of Burns, Anth.,* p. 1040).

The scope of Burns's poetry, and of Wordsworth's.—Consider Wordsworth's self-belittling statement to Crabb Robinson: "I want flesh and blood; even coarse nature and truth, where there is a want of refinement and beauty, is better than the other extreme. At the head of this natural and sensual school is Chaucer, the greatest poet of his class. Next comes Burns."

92. WILLIAM BECKFORD (1760-1844)

Guy Chapman, ed.; *Vathek, with the Episodes of Vathek,* 2 vols., 1929; *The Travel-Diaries,* 2 vols., 1928.—J. W. Oliver, *The Life of William Beckford,* 1932.

The theme, in Beckford's words: "The Caliph Vathek, who for the sake of empty pomp and forbidden power, had sullied himself with a thousand crimes, became a prey to grief without end, and remorse without mitigation."

95. WILLIAM LISLE BOWLES (1762-1850)

See Coleridge's grateful appreciation, *To The Reverend W. L. Bowles, Anth.,* p. 137. In the first book of *Biographia Literaria* (ed. Shawcross, p. 15) he describes the effect produced on him by Bowles's poems.

GILBERT WHITE (1720-1793)

95.   THE NATURAL HISTORY AND ANTIQUITIES OF SELBORNE

If Izaak Walton's *Complete Angler* (1653) is the first classic of nature writing in English, the Rev. Gilbert White's *Natural History* is the second. Notable for accurate, loving, and humorous observation of fauna and flora (and, now and then, of men). For a well annotated reading list of the best nature writers, many of whom were Romantics, see H. F. West, *The Nature Writers*, 1939.

95b. 2. *hibernaculum:* winter-quarters.

96b. 17. *humble bees:* bumble bees.
20. *nudis manibus:* with his bare hands.
35. *metheglin:* mead, an ancient fermented drink, brewed of honey, malt, and water.
52. *Wildman:* Thomas Wildman, author of *A Treatise on the Management of Bees,* 1768.

97.   ERASMUS DARWIN (1731-1802)

A physician, and a scientist who abounded in ingenious speculations about "the loves of plants," etc. An instructive contrast to the unforgotten Gilbert White, Darwin made the mistake of casting his observations and theories into an old fashioned and inappropriate literary form.

97a. 1. *Procul este, profani:* Away, ye profane!

97b. 11. *The Sensitive Plant:* For the opposite extreme in poetical experience, see Shelley's *The Sensitive Plant, Anth.,* p. 936.

98.   WILLIAM GILPIN (1724-1804)

W. D. Templeman, *Gilpin: Master of the Picturesque,* 1939.—Gilpin's *Remarks on Forest Scenery and Other Woodland Views* (1791) displayed that careful observation of the elements of beautiful landscape which the Romantics fostered, and which was to culminate in Ruskin's *Modern Painters* (see, e.g., vol. v. ch. 60, "The Living Tree").

98.   WILLIAM BARTRAM (1739-1823)

Mark Van Doren, ed., *The Travels of William Bartram,* 1947; N. Bryllion Fagin, *William Bartram: Interpreter of the American Landscape,* 1933.—This adventurous scientist, a Quaker of percipient imagination, in the 1770's explored the deep South from Charleston to Baton Rouge. His *Travels,* an important link between Romanticism in England and in America, stimulated the imagination of Wordsworth and Coleridge; see the Notes on *The Ancient Mariner* and *Kubla Khan* (*Anth.,* pp. 146 and 176).

98a. 5. *crocodiles:* probably alligators, the words being then loosely interchangeable.

99a. 14. *pistia and nympea:* water lettuce and water lilies.

99b. 50. *zanthoxylon:* the prickly pear (?).
57. *lantana:* a shrub with bright-colored flowers.
58. *crinum:* amaryllis.

100a. 15. *illicium floridanum:* magnolia grandiflora.

101.   MARY WOLLSTONECRAFT (1759-1797)

Pioneer feminist. Five years after *The Rights of Woman* was published she married William
Godwin; their daughter Mary became the second wife of Shelley.—Observe that what she em-
phasizes is the cultivation of the reason.—See Godwin's *Memoirs of Mary Wollstonecraft*, ed.
W. C. Durant, 1927.

102.   WILLIAM GODWIN (1756-1836)

F. E. L. Priestley, ed., *Enquiry Concerning Political Justice and Its Influence on Morals and
Happiness*, 3 vols., 1947 (first two vols., photographic facsimile of 1798 ed.); and George Wood-
cock, *William Godwin*, 1946.
  Radical critic of established institutions; a believer in the gradual perfectibility of mankind
through rationalistic culture; an opponent of force, and therefore of any kind of political government, i.e., a philosophical anarchist.   Temporarily influential upon Wordsworth and
Coleridge, and even more so upon Shelley.   "He is," Lamb wrote to Manning (Feb. 13, 1800),
"a well-behaved, decent man, nothing very brilliant about him, or imposing, as you may suppose; quite another-guess sort of gentleman from what your anti-Jacobin Christians imagine
him.   I was well pleased to find he has neither horns nor claws; quite a tame creature, I
assure you.   A middle-sized man, both in stature and understanding; whereas, from his noisy
fame, you would expect to find a Briareus Centimanus, or a Tityus tall enough to pull
Jupiter from his heavens."

103a. 29. *Montesquieu:* the philosophic and liberal author of *The Spirit of Laws* (1748).   The
   quotation is from XI, 6.
     35. *not like,* etc.: from Laurence Sterne's admirable sermon, "On A Good Conscience,"
   which Corporal Trim reads aloud in *Tristram Shandy;* see II, 17.

104b. 4. *ignis fatuus:* will-o'-the-wisp.

105.   ANN RADCLIFFE (1764-1823)

Clara F. MacIntyre, *Ann Radcliffe in Relation to Her Time*, 1920; A. A. Wieten, *Mrs. Radcliffe: Her Relation to Romanticism*, 1926.
  This was the Gothic novelist whom Walter Scott and other Romantics most generally admired, especially for her exciting incidents and lavish descriptions (though often it was of
scenery she had never seen); but Coleridge condemned her *The Italian*, as well as Lewis' *The
Monk*, for the falsity of its characterization.   As shown in the last selection, she habitually
explained away in the conclusion those supernatural phenomena which she had utilized for
melodramatic purposes.—For a criticism of her work based on Marxian principles, see Wylie
Sypher, "Social Ambiguity in a Gothic Novel," *Partisan Review*, XII, 50; 1945.

107.   MATTHEW GREGORY LEWIS (1775-1818)

Montague Summers, *The Gothic Quest*, ch. 5.—Correct the date of publication of *The Monk*
to 1796; it was composed, in ten weeks, in 1795.—There is no rationalizing, as in Mrs. Radcliffe;
but more terror and sensationalism—to such an extreme that it caused scandal and forced a
revision of the first edition.—On the Wandering Jew, who had jeered at Christ on his way to
crucifixion, see the Note on Wordsworth's *Song for the Wandering Jew, Anth.*, p. 216.
  DISC.—Compare the Selections from the novelists of the Gothic School, or School of
Terror,—Walpole (p. 56), Beckford (p. 92), Mrs. Radcliffe (p. 105), and "Monk" Lewis.—The
chief authorities on the subject, listed in the Bibliography under the following dates, are:
Scarborough, 1917; Birkhead, 1921; Railo, 1927; Wright, 1937; and Summers, 1938.

  DISC.—For discussion topics on Pre-Romanticism in general, see the list at the beginning
of the Notes, p. 1062.

SELECTIONS FROM THE ROMANTIC MOVEMENT

WILLIAM BLAKE (1757-1827)

I. EDITIONS

*Keynes, Geoffrey, ed. *Poetry and Prose of William Blake* (Nonesuch), 1927.
Sampson, John, ed. *The Poetical Works of William Blake*, 1913.
Sloss, D. J., and Wallis, J. P. R., eds. *The Prophetic Writings of William Blake*, 2 vols., 1926.
Selincourt, Basil De, ed. *Selected Poems* (World's Classics), 1927.
Binyon, Laurence, ed. *Poems of Blake*, 1931.
*Kazin, Alfred., ed. *The Portable Blake*, 1946.

II. BIOGRAPHY AND CRITICISM

Gilchrist, Alexander. *Life of William Blake;* 1st ed., 1863; in Everyman's Libr., 1942.
Swinburne, A. C. *William Blake*, 1868.
*Yeats, W. B. "William Blake and the Imagination" (1897), *Essays*, 1924.—See also *Ideas of Good and Evil*, 1903.
More, Paul Elmer. *Shelburne Essays*, Vol. IV, 1906.
Chesterton, Gilbert K. *William Blake*, 1910.
Berger, Pierre. *William Blake, Poet and Mystic*, 1914.
*Damon, S. Foster. *William Blake: His Philosophy and Symbols*, 1924; rptd., 1947.
Bruce, Harold L. *William Blake in This World*, 1925.
*Wilson, Mona. *The Life of William Blake*, 1927; 2nd ed., 1932.
*Plowman, Max. *Introduction to the Study of Blake*, 1927.
White, Helen C. *The Mysticism of William Blake*, 1927.
*De Selincourt, Basil. Introduction to *Selected Poems*, 1927; also Ernest De Selincourt, "Blake" in *Oxford Lectures on Poetry*, 1934.
Binyon, Laurence. Introductory Essay to *Poems of Blake*, 1931.
Murry, J. Middleton. *William Blake*, 1933.
*Percival, Milton O. *William Blake's Circle of Destiny*, 1938.
Jameson, Grace. "Irish Poets of Today and William Blake," PMLA, LIII, 575 (1938).
Lowery, Margaret R. *Windows of the Morning: A Critical Study of the "Poetical Sketches,"* 1940.
Bronowski, Jacob. *A Man Without a Mask*, 1943.
Cheney, Sheldon. *Men Who Have Walked With God*, 1945.
*Schorer, Mark. *William Blake*, 1946.
Nicolson, Marjorie H. "Epilogue on Blake," *Newton Demands The Muse*, 1946.
Kazin, Alfred. Introduction to *The Portable Blake*, 1946.
Witcutt, W. P. *Blake: A Psychological Study*, 1946.
Frye, Northrup. *Fearful Symmetry*, 1947.
Todd, Ruthven. *Tracks in the Snow*, 1947.

Figgis, Darrell. *The Paintings of William Blake*, 1925.
Binyon, Laurence. *The Engraved Designs of William Blake*, 1926.

NOTES, COMMENTS, AND TOPICS FOR DISCUSSION

POETICAL SKETCHES

112.

See Lowery, Margaret R., *Windows of the Morning*, 1940; also Geoffrey Keynes, TLS, Mch. 10 and 17, 1945.

All the poems in this volume were written before Blake completed his twentieth year, some perhaps when he was only twelve years old.—Observe the date, 1783,—fifteen years earlier than Wordsworth and Coleridge's *Lyrical Ballads*.

DISC.—In some passages the style seems typical of the eighteenth century; in others, of the new age. Try to point out examples of each. What do you think Pope would have said about the rhymes in the first three stanzas of "Fresh from the Dewy Hill"?

112.   **TO THE EVENING STAR**

112. 8-10. Note the rhythm and imagery.

113.   **MAD SONG**

To appreciate the metrical beauty, read this aloud.

113a. 7. Blake changed the original "beds" to "birds" in some later copies. "Birds" is clearer, but is it imaginatively better?

113.   **SONG: FRESH FROM THE DEWY HILL**

It is doubtful whether any English lyric better expresses the purity of the dawn of love.

113.   **TO THE MUSES**

In the manner of the eighteenth century, yet voicing a desire for what that century missed. "In these lines the eighteenth century dies to music" (Arthur Symons).

113.   **SONGS OF INNOCENCE**

See Joseph H. Wicksteed's beautiful facsimile, 1928; and for interpretation, Pierre Berger's *William Blake*, 1914; pp. 284-304.

113.   **INTRODUCTION**

"This poem was carefully planned to show: first, the Divine command; next, the inner revelation of the song's meaning; then the fitting of the words to the wordless melody; and finally its appearance in visible form" (Damon).

114.   **THE LITTLE BLACK BOY**

Of all Blake's poems, Coleridge liked this best.—In EXP, June, 1943, someone asked: "Can this poem be reconciled with the known humanitarian sympathies of Blake?" An affirmative answer in EXP, Apr., 1947, is in general satisfactory, but in details is discussible. Blake conceives of whiteness as a sign of less constant exposure to light (i.e. to God). The abolition of slavery was energetically advocated in England for several decades before the date of this poem.

116.   **THE DIVINE IMAGE**

May be regarded as a protest against the kind of idealism that is abstract or sentimental instead of concrete and practical.

The contrasting poem "A Divine Image" was added to the *Songs of Experience* c. 1794:

> Cruelty has a Human Heart,
> And Jealousy a Human Face;
> Terror the Human Form Divine,
> And Secrecy the Human Dress.
>
> The Human Dress is forged Iron,
> The Human Form a fiery Forge,
> The Human Face a Furnace sealed,
> The Human Heart its hungry Gorge.

Herein Man has fallen under the sway of Urizen the God of this world, and has become perverted and satanic. Ultimately the ideals of "The Divine Image," Blake believes, will overcome the sins described in "A Divine Image." S. A. Larrabee, "An Interpretation of Blake's *A Divine Image,*" MLN, May, 1932).

117. THE BOOK OF THEL

Usually considered the first of Blake's "symbolic" poems.—The *Motto* implies that it is only by personal experience that we learn.

119. 55. *Luvah:* love, passion.

120. 108. *The eternal gates terrific porter:* probably Los, the god of poetry (Damon).—In this section (IV), Thel enters the world of matter and beholds her own grave (her body). She flees from the strangeness and terror of the five senses, through which she would experience passion. She is reluctant to sacrifice herself through passion and thus become a part of the endless chain of being.

120. THE FRENCH REVOLUTION

Proofs of the first book, c. 16 pages, were struck off in 1791, with the announcement, "The remaining books of this poem are finished, and will be published in their order." There were to be seven books; but only the first is extant, and it was not published until 1913 (by John Sampson) in the Oxford *Poetical Works of William Blake.*

120. 16. *The Commons convene:* On June 17, 1789, the representatives of the Third Estate (the others being the Nobles and the Clergy) constituted themselves the National Assembly,—that act marking the first step in the French Revolution. See Carlyle's *French Revolution,* Bk. V, ch. 1: "They, then, are the Nation? Triumvirate of Princes, Queen, refractory Noblesse and Clergy, what, then, are *you?*"

18. *the Bastille:* "Tyranny's stronghold, which they name *Bastille,* or *Building,* as if there were no other building" (*do.,* IV, 3; cf. V, 6-9). "The key of that Robber-Den shall cross the Atlantic; shall lie on Washington's hall-table."

121. 201. *Abbé de Sieyes:* "System-builder, Constitution-builder General,—as many as wanted" (IV, 4).

DISC.—Compare with Blake: Cowper on the Bastille, *Anth.,* p. 75; Wordsworth, "Residence in France," p. 267; and Carlyle, "The Failure to Be a King," p. 1052.

122. THE MARRIAGE OF HEAVEN AND HELL

Probably written in 1793, perhaps begun as early as 1790.—Full-color facsimile, with an essay by Max Plowman (Dent, c. 1930).—Allusions to Swedenborgianism are frequent, e.g. "A Memorable Fancy," Swedenborg having called his visions "Memorable Relations" (Damon).

The bold paradoxes were meant to stab broad awake the Philistines whose morality is conventional, afraid of the natural feelings and desires the Creator has implanted in us, and confined to the do-not commandments. They have mistakenly condemned to Hell some human qualities which really belong in Heaven. Blake insists on freedom from repression, and imaginative appreciation of human beings.

DISC.—"The whole of Freud's teachings may be found in *The Marriage of Heaven and Hell*" (W. H. Auden). On the other hand, N. P. Witcutt sees in Blake, not Freud's psychology, but Jung's (*Blake, A Psychological Study,* 1947).

123b. 42. *Jesus acted from impulse:* "impulse meaning not romantic whim, but the spontaneous action that comes from perfect imaginative sympathy" (Percival, *Blake's Circle of Destiny,* p. 130).

124. A SONG OF LIBERTY

The Marriage of Heaven and Hell culminates in a prophecy of universal brotherhood, achieved by the defeat of mere rationalizing and of jealousy, and by the victory of imagination and of love. Compare Shelley's *Prometheus Unbound, Anth.,* p. 883.

124.   VISIONS OF THE DAUGHTERS OF ALBION

Full-color facsimile, with a note by J. Middleton Murry (1932).

"The Daughters of Albion, in their slavish obedience to Reason (Urizen), weave the world of spiritual depravity . . . They personify hate masquerading as mercy and pity in the cruel and spurious forms of the moral law. . . . They bind down man's immortal senses" (Percival, p. 45).—The "argument" of the *Visions* begins:

> I loved Theotormon,
> And I was not ashamed.

In the given selection, Oothoon pleads for freedom in love; "for everything that lives is holy." "No phase of Blake's mythology has mystified his commentators more. For this the ascetic tradition of the Christian Church is largely responsible. Blake's symbolism disturbs us because it follows the less familiar paths of heterodoxy." (Percival, p. 107. See his entire ch. 6, "Sex Symbolism"). For another kind of defense, see Kazin's Introduction to *The Portable Blake*, pp. 37-38.

125.   AMERICA: A PROPHECY

Expresses the prophetic confidence, of both English and American Romantics that the independence of the United States marked the dawn of world brotherhood and peace. Can you find similar sentiments in Emerson and Whitman?

125.   SONGS OF EXPERIENCE

When Blake printed this in the same volume with the *Songs of Innocence*, he added the significant subtitle: *Shewing the Two Contrary States of the Human Soul.*—In this second state, Man and his World have fallen away from their original innocence and joy. Materialism is a barrier against their return. To childhood, experience often proves dark, cruel, sinister, or tyrannous.

DISC.—Compare *The Chimney Sweep, Nurse's Song*, etc., with corresponding poems in the *Songs of Innocence*.

126.   THE CLOD AND THE PEBBLE

DISC.—Obviously two kinds of love,—unselfish and selfish,—are presented. Is the theme the *superiority* of the first, or is it the *existence* in experience of both? (See EXP., Nov., 1942; Feb., Nov., 1943). Would the *tension* between them especially interest the New Critics?

127.   THE TIGER

DISC.—The greatest of Blake's short poems,—and, as to the meaning, the most disputed. Poses the problem of good and evil,—"Did he who made the Lamb make thee?"—the problem of God and his creation, his wrathful justice and his boundless mercy. Are they even partly reconcilable? Does Blake suggest an answer, or merely raise the question? Elizabeth Nitchie believes it is closely connected in Blake's religion with *Vala, or the Four Zoas*, Night V, where also occurs the line "The stars threw down their spears," and therefore with the Fall of the Universe. "Both lamb and tiger are parts of eternity in material form, results of the act of creation by which Divine Mercy stopped the fall of Urizen and preserved the possibility of regeneration and return to divine unity" (EXP, Feb., 1943; cf. Oct. and Dec., 1942).—For an elaborate new-style interpretation of the symbolism ("it is a hymn to pure being") see Kazin's Introduction, pp. 43-46.

127.   AH, SUNFLOWER

Rooted in the earth, yet ever turning towards the sun, the sunflower symbolizes humanity.

127.   THE GARDEN OF LOVE

See, *Anth.*, the note on the *Visions of the Daughters of Albion.*

127.   LONDON

To those who especially value in Blake the note of revolutionary social protest, this is "one of his greatest poems" (Kazin, Intr., p. 12). See Carlyle's letter, "London a Monstrous Wen," *Anth.*, p. 1036; and contrast Lamb's "Letter to Wordsworth," p. 377.

127. 2. *chartered Thames:* In the first version Blake wrote "dirty Thames." Why did he change it?

128.   THE HUMAN ABSTRACT

The general idea seems clear enough,—that the source of evils like deceitfulness is not in nature but in the human mind. But as to some of the details there may be differences of opinion. Just what do ll. 5 and 6 mean? Is the sequence,—Cruelty, Hypocrisy, Humility, and Mystery,—accidental, or does it signify a regular causal relationship? Does "Mystery" mean "mystification"?

128.   THE FOUR ZOAS

The Zoas, or "living creatures," were powers which precipitated the Fall. They became the four elements,—earth, air, fire, and water,—to which Man is temporally subject, and which hamper his spiritual well-being. Man's experience in this world is bought at the price of his real happiness,—except by those who are unscrupulous and hypocritical, and contrive for themselves a specious kind of success and complacency (Percival, pp. 18-46).

The poem is c. 85 pages long. The title, in its first form, was *Vala, or the Death and Judgment of the Ancient Man.* In its second, it became *The Four Zoas: The Torment of Love and Jealousy in the Death and Judgment of Albion the Ancient Man.* The motto, given in the original Greek of the New Testament (*Ephesians,* 6, 12) indicated Blake's main interest: "For we wrestle not against flesh and blood, but against principalities, against powers, against the rulers of the darkness of this world, against spiritual wickedness in high places."

128. 605. *What is the price of Experience?* See *Job,* 28, 12; "Where shall wisdom be found? . . . Man knoweth not the price thereof."

129.   A WORLD OF IMAGINATION

Trusler had raised some objections to "moral paintings" which were intended to convey "visions of Eternity."—To understand Blake's doctrines about Imagination, consider together the chief statements in this selection; in "Reason and Imagination," p. 132; and in "To the Christians," p. 133.—Jakob Boehme (1575-1624) one of Blake's inspirers, said: "All things are created out of Imagination" (*Signature of All Things,* ed. Everyman, p. 207).

129.   TO TIRZAH

129a. 3. *generation:* creation into this fallen world, a barrier to moral and spiritual freedom.

130.   THE MENTAL TRAVELLER

Any new idea in the intellectual history of the world has had to struggle against worldly conventions. It is persecuted: and, although temporarily it may conquer, it becomes deadened by custom; and it must again be awakened to itself.

130. 10. *a woman old:* Intellectualized, materialized being. She delights in conventionalizing the vital idea.

130. 69-92. *The honey of her infant lips:* In the next six stanzas, the searcher after truth is reanimated, coming to see things with the innocence and clearness of a child, while his original ideal is withered.

131. 97-104. This process is repeated for ever and ever.

131.   AUGURIES OF INNOCENCE

Not revised for publication by Blake, this remains a disconnected series of aphorisms, inveighing against cruelty to animals, physical punishment, militarism, agnosticism, etc.

131. 1-4. *To see the world:* "The secret of art, as Blake saw, is definiteness. No stanza in our poetry has more mystical depth than this; yet here is no unconscious expression of a state of soul, but a beautifully clear statement of recognizable spiritual experience" De Selincourt, *Oxford Lectures,* p. 11).

131.   MILTON

The entire poem, c. 86 pages, is in two books. Blake, whose admiration for Milton was intense, conceives of him as inspiring a new reign of the Imagination in poetry and life. In this poem, the center of Blake's universe becomes "Jesus the Saviour."

The "Preface" ends with the significant quotation from Moses: "Would to God that all the Lord's people were prophets!" (*Numbers,* 11, 29). Blake's moral fervor and style are inspired by the Old Testament prophets; see especially *Isaiah,* 52 and 66; and *Jeremiah,* 4. (EXP., Mch., 1943). See also Saurat's *Blake and Modern Thought,* pp. 51-85.

"The Flowers" and "Reason and Imagination" are from Book II (in Nonesuch ed., pp. 527 and 545).

133.   TO THE DEISTS

The Monk represents meek and nonresistant Christianity; Charlemagne, government by the sword; Voltaire, Rousseau, and Gibbon, skeptical doubt. Blake believed that the Deists, who tried to construct a rationalistic Christianity, had materialized God and debased a spiritual religion into a mechanistic monism.

133.   TO THE CHRISTIANS

From *Jerusalem,* Book IV.—Imagination is Reality, the human existence itself, the true Being (Percival, p. 130).

134.   ANNOTATIONS TO REYNOLDS' DISCOURSES

These pungent strictures on some anti-romantic tendencies which Blake saw, or believed he saw, in the famous *Discourses* should not be taken as a fair judgment on them as a whole. A more judicious verdict is that of Blake's contemporary, the romantic artist Henry Fuseli (1741-1825): "They are written in an easy agreeable manner, and contain many just observations, much excellent criticism, and valuable advice; but being undertaken before he had profoundly considered the subject, they are frequently vague and unintelligible, and sometimes contradictory."—See especially the Sixth Discourse, "The Contemplation of Excellence." There is an ed. in the World's Classics.

134.   DEDICATION OF BLAIR'S GRAVE

Robert Blair's *The Grave* (1743), one of the pre-romantic poems of death, like Young's *Night Thoughts* and William Cullen Bryant's *Thanatopsis.* Blake's illustrations are much finer than the poem. The queen was Charlotte Sophia, wife of George III.

134.   THE EVERLASTING GOSPEL

Not revised for publication by Blake. Observe the metrical freedom of the verse, and compare that of Coleridge's *Christabel* (1816).

SAMUEL TAYLOR COLERIDGE (1772-1834)

I. EDITIONS

Shedd, W. G. T., ed. *Complete Works*, 7 vols., 1853, 1884.
Ashe, Thomas, ed. *Works* (Bohn Libr.), 8 vols., 1885.
*Campbell, J. D., ed. *Poetical Works*, 1893, 1909.
Coleridge, E. H., ed. *Complete Poetical Works*, 2 vols., 1912.

Garrod, H. W., ed. *Coleridge—Poetry and Prose, With Essays by Hazlitt, Jeffrey, De Quincey, Carlyle and Others*; 1925.
*Griggs, E. L., ed. *The Best of Coleridge*, 1932.
*Potter, Stephen, ed. *Coleridge: Select Poetry and Prose* (Nonesuch), 1934.

Shawcross, John, ed. *Biographia Literaria*, 2 vols., 1907.
Raysor, T. M., ed. *Shakespearean Criticism*, 2 vols., 1930.
Raysor, T. M., ed. *Miscellaneous Criticism*, 1936.
Griggs, E. L., ed. *Unpublished Letters*, 2 vols., 1933.

II. BIOGRAPHY AND CRITICISM

Pater, Walter. "Coleridge," in *Appreciations*, 1889.
*Campbell, J. D. *Coleridge*, 1894.
Symons, Arthur. "Coleridge," in *The Romantic Movement in Poetry*, 1909.
Vaughan, C. E. "Coleridge," in *The Cambridge History of English Literature*, XI, 1914.
Stork, C. W. "The Influence of the Popular Ballad on Wordsworth and Coleridge," PMLA, XXIX, 299-326; 1914.
Snyder, Alice D. *The Critical Principle of the Reconciliation of Opposites as Employed by Coleridge*, 1918.
Howard, Claud. *Coleridge's Idealism: Kant and the Cambridge Platonists*, 1924.
Potter, G. R. "Coleridge and the Idea of Evolution," PMLA, XL, 370-397, 1925.
*Fausset, H. I'A. *Coleridge*, 1926.
Shafer, Robert. "Coleridge" in *Christianity and Naturalism*, 1926.
*Lowes, John Livingston. *The Road to Xanadu*, 1927.
Raysor, T. M. "The Study of Shakespeare's Characters in the Eighteenth Century," MLN, XLII, 495-500, 1927.
Raysor, T. M. "Coleridge and Asra," SP, XXVI, 305-324, 1929.
Garrod, H. W. "Coleridge," in *The Profession of Poetry*, 1929.
Charpentier, John. *Coleridge, the Sublime Somnambulist*, 1929.
*Muirhead, J. H. *Coleridge as Philosopher*, 1930.
Fairchild, H. N. *The Romantic Quest*, 1931.
Blunden, Edmund, and Griggs, E. L. *Studies by Several Hands*, 1934.
*Richards, I. A. *Coleridge on Imagination*, 1934.
Potter, Stephen. *Coleridge and S. T. C.*, 1935.
James, D. J. *Scepticism and Poetry: an Essay on the Poetic Imagination*, 1937.
*Hanson, Lawrence. *The Life of Coleridge; The Early Years*, 1938.
*Chambers, E. K. *S. T. Coleridge*, 1938.
Griggs, E. L. ed. *Wordsworth and Coleridge: Studies in Honor of G. McL. Harper*, 1939.
Thorpe, Clarence D. "The Imagination: Coleridge vs. Wordsworth," PQ, XVIII, 1-18, 1939.
McKenzie, Gordon. "Organic Unity in Coleridge," Univ. of Cal. Publ., VII, 1939.
Raysor, T. M. "Coleridge's Criticism of Wordsworth," PMLA, LIV, 456-510, 1939.
Lovejoy, Arthur O. "Coleridge and Kant's Two Worlds," ELH, VII, 341-362, 1940.
Sanders, C. R. *Coleridge and the Broad Church Movement*, 1942.
Thorpe, Clarence D. "Coleridge as Aesthetician and Critic," JHI, V, 387-414, 1944.
Willey, Basil. *Coleridge on Imagination and Fancy* (Warton Lecture), 1946.
Creed, Howard H. "Coleridge on Taste," ELH, XIII, 143-155, 1946.

Shapiro, Karl. "English Prosody and Modern Poetry," ELH, XIV, 77-92, 1947.

Kennedy, Wilma L. *The English Heritage of Coleridge of Bristol, 1798,* 1947.

Warren, Robert Penn. "A Poem of Pure Imagination," *Kenyon Review,* VIII, 391-427, 1946.— To be expanded, and published as a book, 1948 (?).

III. MISCELLANEOUS

Logan, (Sister) Eugenia. *A Concordance to the Poetry of S. T. Coleridge,* 1940.

Kennedy, Virginia W., and Barton, Mary N., comps. *Coleridge: A Selected Bibliography,* 1935.

NOTES, COMMENTS, AND TOPICS FOR DISCUSSION

136. PANTISOCRACY

The Utopian community which Coleridge and Southey planned to establish in the United States.

136. LAFAYETTE

After aiding the American Revolution, he likewise supported the French Revolution, but in 1792 fled from France because the extremists (Jacobins) sought to kill him. But the Prussians and Austrians imprisoned him, and he did not escape until shortly after this sonnet was written.

136. 1. *the warbled strains:* those of the lark.

136. KOSKIUSKO

See Thomas Campbell, *Poland and Freedom's Cause (Anth.,* p. 492).—Tadeusz Kosciuszko (as his name is now spelled), is the national hero of Poland. Born in that oppressed country in 1746, he volunteered his services in the American Revolution, distinguished himself at Yorktown, and was given by Congress the rank of brigadier general and the status of an American citizen. He led an insurrection against Russia in his own country (1794), was defeated, and imprisoned. On his release he lived in the United States until 1798. He refused to support Napoleon. He died, an exile in Switzerland, in 1817. In the literature of Romanticism he ranks among the great liberators,—Washington, Lafayette, Toussaint l'Ouverture, and Simon Bolivar. In Landor's *Southey and Landor,* the author says: "I never saw any man in whose presence I felt inferiority excepting Kosciuszko."

137. TO THE REVEREND W. L. BOWLES

In the first book of *Biographia Literaria* (ed. Shawcross p. 15) Coleridge records the influence of Bowles upon his early work. See *Anth.,* p. 95.

137. TO THE AUTHOR OF "THE ROBBERS"

Friedrich von Schiller (1759-1805) whose storm-and-stress drama, *Die Räuber* (1781), was important in the German Romantic movement; and whose greatest work, *Wallenstein,* Coleridge translated (1799-1800).—"The famished father" is the father of *The Robbers.*

137. TO A YOUNG ASS

The brash choice of this subject gave the Anti-Romantics an obvious opportunity for cheap ridicule (especially if they forgot the entry into Jerusalem; *Matthew,* 21). Even Charles Lamb thought it trivial.

DISC.—Compare Victor Hugo's *La Vache (The Cow), Oxford Bk. Fr. Verse,* p. 130; W. B. Yeats's *The Second Coming* (Collected Poems, 1946; p. 215); and G. K. Chesterton's *The Donkey* (Untermeyer, Mod. Brit. Poetry, p. 281).

137b. 12. *Which patient merit: Hamlet,* III, 1, 74. (not "aches," but "spurns").

26. *dell of peace:* the Pantisocratic colony in the valley of the Susquehanna.

138. LEWTI

The Circassians were a fiercely independent tribe in the region of the Caucasus Mountains, famed for the beauty of their persons, and the patriarchal simplicity of their manners. This is an early specimen of the many attempts by the Romantics to write dramatic lyrics which should characterize the spirit of other peoples, e.g., Thomas Moore's *Irish Melodies*.

DISC.—Find other examples in *Anth.*, and compare them. On the connection with *Bartram's Travels* see J. L. Lowes, *Xanadu*, p. 513.

138. RELIGIOUS MUSINGS

This is the longest of Coleridge's early poems (419 ll.), and for some years he considered it his most important effort, although he felt that the *Eolian Harp* was his most successful one. It suggests the kind of sermons he must have preached, one of which Hazlitt describes (*Anth.*, p. 396). Lamb admired it. In a second edition, however, Coleridge confessed that it suffered from "a profusion of double epithets and a general turgidness."

139. 35-45. This passage was influenced by David Hartley, as Coleridge indicated in a footnote in the 1797 edition (H. N. Fairchild, "Hartley, Pistorius, and Coleridge," PMLA, LXII, 1010-1021; 1947).

395. *Believe thou, O my soul:* On this, relatively clear passage, Coleridge makes this characteristic comment: "This paragraph is intelligible to those who, like the author, believe and feel the sublime system of Berkeley [idealism], and the doctrine of the final happiness of all men."

139. THE EOLIAN HARP

The Eolian (or Aeolian) harp, named after Eolus, the god of the Winds, was invented in the 1740's by James Oswald. It consists of an uncovered box, with strings across the top. Placed in a draught of air, e.g. at an open window, it may give forth musical sounds. It was to become one of the favorite symbols of Romanticism, its relation to Nature, Inspiration, etc., being obvious. Coleridge and Sara Fricker had an Eolian harp, and took it on their wedding journey, about six weeks after he wrote this poem.—See E. von Erhardt-Siebold, "Some Inventions," *Engl. Studien*, 1932.

Many pre-Romantics and Romantics mention this harp,—including Macpherson (in *Ossian!*). A collection of passages on the subject, *Nature's Music* (1808) was made by the "farmer-poet" Robert Bloomfield; republished in his *Remains*. (See the excellent note in Grigson, *The Romantics*, pp. 342-343). The young Carlyle speaks of Jean-Paul Richter's soul as moved by "a wild music as of wind-harps" (*Anth.*, 1040b. 10). John Constable, whose landscapes were likened to Eolian music, said he valued *The Ancient Mariner* highest among contemporary poems because it sounded "the full harmonies of the Eolian lyre" (Letter to John Fisher; Dec. 17, 1824).

In later years Coleridge, perhaps thinking that the Eolian harp symbolism overemphasized the passive aspect of composition and neglected the actively creative mind, wrote this warning: "The mind does not resemble an Aeolian harp, nor even a barrel-organ turned by a stream of water, conceive as many tunes mechanized in it as you like, but rather, as far as objects are concerned, a violin or other instrument of few strings yet vast compass, played on by a musician of Genius" (Alice D. Snyder, RLC, VII, 529; 1927).—Likewise Shelley in *A Defense of Poetry* (*Anth.*, 975b. 4) points out that the human soul, unlike the harp, has "a power of internal adjustment of the sounds or motions" that impinge upon it.

H. J. W. Milley, MP, XXXVI, 359-375 (1939), calls attention to striking similarities between this poem and Wordsworth's *Tintern Abbey* (*Anth.*, p. 191), and also to Coleridge's anticipations of Wordsworth's theories about poetical inspiration.

140. 44-48. Heresy-hunters considered these lines unorthodox.

140. REFLECTIONS

DISC.—G. M. Harper's "Coleridge's Conversation Poems," *Quarterly Review*, CCXLIV, 284-298, 1925, is an admirable appreciation of such poems as *The Eolian Harp*, *Reflections on Having Left a Place of Retirement*, *This Lime-Tree Bower*, *Frost at Midnight*, *Fears in Solitude*, *The Nightingale*, *Dejection*, and *To William Wordsworth*. But it is not necessary to read that essay before considering this question: What do these autobiographical poems reveal concerning Coleridge's personal traits and feelings from c. 1795 to 1807?

140. 12. *Bristowa:* Bristol.

141. 49. *Howard:* John Howard (1726-1790), pioneer in prison reform.—*State of Prisons*, 1777.

142. ODE ON THE DEPARTING YEAR

In an earlier version of this poem, the first stanza was Strophe I; the second, Strophe II; the third, Epode; the fourth Antistrophe I; the fifth, Antistrophe II; the rest, Epode II. Coleridge summarizes the ode as follows: "The ode commences with an address to the Divine Providence that regulates into one vast harmony all the events of time, however calamitous some of them may appear to mortals. The second strophe calls on men to suspend their private joys and sorrows, and devote them for a while to the cause of human nature in general. The first epode speaks of the Empress of Russia, who died of an apoplexy on the 17th of November, 1796; having just concluded a subsidiary treaty with the kings combined against France. The first and second antistrophe describe the Image of the Departing Year, etc., as in a vision. The second epode prophesies, in anguish of spirit, the downfall of this country." The Empress of Russia, Catherine the Great (1729-1796), was as famous for her amours as for her military conquests. She helped to subjugate Poland. Her General Suvaroff massacred 38,000 Turks at Ismail in 1790 (see Byron's *Don Juan*, Canto VIII). To Coleridge she typified bloodthirsty tyranny.

142. 33. *the dread name:* "The name of Liberty, which at the commencement of the French Revolution was both the occasion and the pretext of unnumbered crimes" (Coleridge).

40. *the Northern Conqueress:* Coleridge comments as follows: "A subsidiary treaty had been just concluded; and Russia was to have furnished more effectual aid than that of pious manifestoes to the Powers combined against France. I rejoice—not over the deceased woman (I never dared figure the Russian sovereign to my imagination under the dear and venerable character of Woman—Woman, that complex term for mother, sister, wife!) I rejoice, as at the disenshrining of a demon! I rejoice, as at the extinction of the evil principle impersonated! This very day, six years ago, the massacre of Ismail was perpetrated. *Thirty Thousand Human Beings, Men, Women, and Children*, murdered in cold blood, for no other crime than that their garrison had defended the place with perseverance and bravery. Why should I recall the poisoning of her husband, her iniquities in Poland, or her late unmotived attack on Persia, the desolating ambition of her public life or the libidinous excesses of her private hours! I have no wish to qualify myself for the office of Historiographer to the King of Hell!"

43. *death's twice mortal mace:* Catherine earned the wages of sin twice,—by public crimes and by private "libidinous excesses." (See EXP, June and Dec., 1943.)

76. *the Lampads seven: Revelations*, 4, 5.

135. *Abandoned of heaven:* Coleridge comments as follows: "The poet from having considered the peculiar advantages, which this country has enjoyed, passes in rapid transition to the uses which we have made of these advantages. We have been preserved by our insular situation, from suffering the actual horrors of war ourselves, and we have shown our gratitude to Providence for this immunity by our eagerness to spread those horrors over nations less happily situated. In the midst of plenty and safety we have raised or joined the yell for famine and blood. Of the one hundred and seven last years, fifty have been years of war. Such wickedness cannot pass unpunished. We have been proud and confident in our alliances and our fleets—but God has prepared the cankerworm, and will smite the *gourds* of our pride. 'Art thou better than populous No, that was situate among the rivers, that had the waters round about it, whose rampart was the Sea? Ethiopia and Egypt were her strength and it was infinite: Put and Lubim were her helpers. Yet she was carried away, she went into captivity: and they cast lots for her honorable men, and all her great men were bound in chains. Thou also shalt be drunken: all thy strongholds shall be like fig trees with the first ripe figs; if they be shaken, they shall even fall into the mouth of the eater. Thou hast multiplied thy merchants above the stars of heaven. Thy crowned are as the locusts; and thy captains as the great grasshoppers which camp in the hedges in the cool-day; but when the sun ariseth they flee away, and their place is not known where they are. There is no healing of thy bruise; thy wound is grievous: all, that hear the report of thee, shall

clap hands over thee: for upon whom hath not thy wickedness passed continually?'
Nahum, ch. 3."

When the *Ode* was written England was at war with France. "Let it not be forgotten,"
Coleridge said in justification of his change of attitude subsequently, "that the *Ode* was written many years before the abolition of the slave-trade (1807), likewise before the invasion of
Switzerland by the French Republic (1798)." The effect of the latter event on Coleridge is seen
in *France: An Ode (Anth.,* 160).

145.   **THIS LIME-TREE BOWER**

Correct the date of publication to 1800 (Annual Anthology of that year).—Besides Lamb,
the friends were William and Dorothy Wordsworth.

145. 28. *gentle-hearted Charles:* Lamb wrote to Coleridge: "For God's sake, don't make me
ridiculous any more by terming me gentle-hearted in print. . . . it almost always means
poor-spirited."

146. 74. *creeking:* Coleridge quotes Bartram's statement that when the Savanna crane moves
its wings "their shafts and webs upon one another creek."

146.   THE RIME OF THE ANCIENT MARINER

How the Composition of the Poem Originated

There are three accounts of this much-studied subject. The first is Coleridge's narrative
in the first two paragraphs of the fourteenth chapter of his *Biographia Literaria,* given in this
Anth., p. 335.

The second is Wordsworth's statement (c. 1835) to Alexander Dyce, as follows:

> *The Ancient Mariner* was founded on a strange dream, which a friend of Cole-
> ridge had, who fancied he saw a skeleton ship, with figures in it. We had both
> determined to write some poetry for a monthly magazine, the profits of which were
> to defray the expenses of a little excursion we were to make together. *The Ancient
> Mariner* was intended for this periodical, but was too long. I had very little share
> in the composition of it, for I soon found that the style of Coleridge and myself
> would not assimilate. Besides the lines (in the fourth part):
>
> > And thou art long, and lank, and brown,
> > As is the ribbed sea-sand—
>
> I wrote the stanza (in the first part):
>
> > He holds him with his glittering eye—
> > The Wedding-Guest stood still,
> > And listens like a three-years' child:
> > The Mariner hath his will—
>
> and four or five lines more in different parts of the poem, which I could not now
> point out. The idea of *'shooting an albatross' was mine; for I had been reading*
> *Shelvocke's Voyages, which probably Coleridge never saw.* I also suggested the
> reanimation of the dead bodies, to work the ship.

The third account Wordsworth dictated in 1843 to Miss Fenwick, as part of a comment
on *We Are Seven.* It is as follows:

> In reference to this poem I will here mention one of the most remarkable
> facts in my own poetic history and that of Mr. Coleridge. In the autumn of
> 1797 he, my sister, and myself, started from Alfoxden, pretty late in the afternoon,
> with a view to visit Linton and the Valley of Stones near to it; and as our united
> funds were very small, we agreed to defray the expense of the tour by writing a
> poem, to be sent to *The New Monthly Magazine* set up by Phillips the bookseller,
> and edited by Dr. Aikin. Accordingly we set off and proceeded along the Quan-
> tock Hills towards Watchet, and in the course of this walk was planned the poem
> of *The Ancient Mariner,* founded on a dream, as Mr. Coleridge said, of his friend,

Mr. Cruikshank. Much the greatest part of the story was Mr. Coleridge's invention; but certain parts I suggested:—for example, some crime was to be committed which should bring upon the Old Navigator, as Coleridge afterwards delighted to call him, the spectral persecution, as a consequence of that crime and his own wanderings. I had been reading in Shelvocke's *Voyages* a day or two before that while doubling Cape Horn they frequently saw albatrosses in that latitude, the largest sort of sea-fowl, some extending their wings twelve or fifteen feet. "Suppose," said I, "you represent him as having killed one of these birds on entering the South Sea, and that the tutelary spirits of these regions take upon them to avenge the crime." The incident was thought fit for the purpose and adopted accordingly. I also suggested the navigation of the ship by the dead men, but do not recollect that I had anything more to do with the scheme of the poem. The gloss with which it was subsequently accompanied was not thought of by either of us at the time; at least, not a hint of it was given to me, and I have no doubt it was a gratuitous afterthought. We began the composition together on that to me memorable evening. I furnished two or three lines at the beginning of the poem, in particular:—

> And listened like a three years' child;
> The Mariner had his will.

These trifling contributions, all but one (which Mr. Coleridge has with unnecessary scrupulosity recorded) slipped out of his mind as they well might. As we endeavored to proceed conjointly (I speak of the same evening) our respective manners proved so widely different that it would have been quite presumptuous in me to do anything but separate from an undertaking upon which I could only have been a clog. We returned after a few days from a delightful tour, of which I have many pleasant, and some of them droll enough, recollections. We returned by Dulverton to Alfoxden. *The Ancient Mariner* grew and grew till it became too important for our first object, which was limited to our expectation of five pounds, and we began to think of a volume, which was to consist, as Mr. Coleridge has told the world, of poems chiefly on supernatural subjects taken from common life, but looked at, as much as might be, through an imaginative medium. Accordingly I wrote *The Idiot Boy, Her Eyes Are Wild*, etc., *We Are Seven, The Thorn,* and some others.

The History of the Text

The form of *The Ancient Mariner* which, after several revisions, Coleridge finally brought it to, and in which we now read it, differs in notable ways from his first version. That version was published in the *Lyrical Ballads* in 1798. In it there were many archaic words, after the manner of the ancient ballads; e.g., "Marinere," "withouten," "yspread," "eldritch," "ne" (for "nor"), "ee" (for "eye"). Such archaisms were reduced in number when the next version of the poem appeared, in the second edition of the *Lyrical Ballads* (1800). At some unknown time between 1800 and 1817 (Professor Lowes plausibly suggests c. 1802), Coleridge made the last important changes in the poem; viz. (1) he modified some of the passages, (2) he added that marginal prose gloss which adds incalculably to the artistic effect, and (3) he prefixed the following Latin motto concerning dæmons, which he took from the *Archaeologiae Philosophicae* (p. 68) of the seventeenth-century divine, Thomas Burnet. These three changes did not appear in print until 1817, when what is essentially the final form of *The Ancient Mariner* was published in Coleridge's *Sibylline Leaves*.

In the Nonesuch *Coleridge: Select Poetry and Prose*, the first version and the final version are printed on opposite pages. (A comparison of the changes Coleridge made, the possible reasons for them, and their respective merits makes an excellent subject for discussion.) See B. R. McElderry, Jr., "Coleridge's Revision of the Ancient Mariner," SP, XXIX, 68-94, 1932.

The Latin Motto and Its Translation

Facile credo, plures esse Naturas invisibiles quam visibiles in rerum universitate. Sed horum omnium familiam quis nobis enarrabit, et gradus et cognationes et discrimina et singulorum munera? Quid agunt? quæ loca habitant? Harum rerum notitiam semper ambivit ingenium humanum, nunquam attigit. Juvat, interea, non diffiteor, quandoque in animo, tanquam in tabulâ, majoris et melioris mundi imaginem contemplari: ne mens assuefacta hodiernæ vitæ minutiis se contrahat nimis, et tota subsidat in pusillas cogitationes. Sed veritati interea invigilandum est, modusque servandus, ut certa ab incertis, diem a nocte, distinguamus.

I readily believe that there are more invisible beings in the universe than visible. But who shall explain to us the nature, the rank and kinship, the distinguishing marks and graces of each? What do they do? Where do they dwell? The human mind has circled round this knowledge, but never attained to it. Yet there is profit, I do not doubt, in sometimes contemplating in the mind, as in a picture, the image of a greater and better world: lest the intellect, habituated to the petty details of daily life, should be contracted within too narrow limits and settle down wholly on trifles. But, meanwhile, a watchful eye must be kept on truth, and proportion observed, that we may distinguish the certain from the uncertain, day from night.

The Sources of The Ancient Mariner

As will appear from the following notes, the great commentary on *The Ancient Mariner* and *Kubla Khan* is Professor John Livingston Lowes's *The Road to Xanadu: A Study in the Ways of the Imagination* (1927), which renders obsolete all previous suggestions as to the sources of these poems, and all previous annotation of them. The most significant point in this learned treatise, to anyone who is beginning the serious study of poetry, is this: that, although these wonderfully beautiful poems of Coleridge seem the product of mere visionary fantasy, there is scarcely a notable detail in them which is not drawn from actual human experience. In other words, what seems so fantastic is much more realistic (objectively and subjectively) than one would suppose. When Coleridge quoted Burnet's "a watchful eye must be kept on truth," in the motto of the poem, he quoted to the point.

Supplementing or modifying Lowes's conclusions is R. C. Bald's "Coleridge and *The Ancient Mariner:* Addenda to *The Road to Xanadu,*" in *Nineteenth-Century Studies* (Ithaca, N. Y.), 1940.—See also W. W. Beyer, "Coleridge, Wieland's *Oberon,* and *The Ancient Mariner,*" RES, XV, 401-411, 1939.

The "Moral," or the Inner Meaning

This issue is debated in many of the books and articles listed above. See also: Elizabeth Nitchie, "The Moral of *The Ancient Mariner* Reconsidered," PMLA, XLVIII, 867-876, 1933; Louise S. Boas in EXP, May, 1944; N. P. Stallknecht, "The Moral of The Ancient Mariner," in *Strange Seas of Thought,* ch. 5, 1945; and Robert Penn Warren, "Coleridge's Rime," *Kenyon Review,* VIII, 391-427, 1946, which is expected to be extended into a book in the near future.

Topics for Discussion

Read some of the ballads in the Pre-Romantic Selections, and compare *The Ancient Mariner* with them.

Compare it with some of Blake's poems.

J. W. Beach, in *A Romantic View of Poetry* (1944), p. 15 ff., apropos of the realism in the poem, contrasts it with Keats's verse narratives. Do you agree that it is in that respect superior to, say, *Isabella* or *Lamia?*—Southey called it "a Dutch attempt at sublimity," implying perhaps that some of the details were too realistic and homely to sustain the dignity of the true sublime. Consider some passages in the light of that contention.

The four articles listed above, on the "moral" or inner meaning, raise important controversial points. Is *any* plain moral intended? Is it: "He prayeth best who loveth best," or is that merely the sentiment of the simple-minded mariner? Is G. K. Chesterton's maxim pertinent, "The bad fable has a moral, while the good fable is a moral"? Is the central idea the faith in imaginative love, similar to that of Wordsworth's *Prelude?* (Stallknecht). Is it "the theme of the One Life," with "a strain of terror in all this"? (Warren). Some of these questions involve the appropriateness of the symbolism to convey the deeper significance of the poem.—Debatable also is the ultra-modern attack of E. M. Bewley and F. R. Leavis, "Revaluations," in *Scrutiny,* VIII, 406-420; IX, 57-69; 1940.

Coleridge's Summary

Coleridge's "argument," i.e., summary, reads: "How a ship, having passed the Line [Equator] was driven by storms to the cold Country towards the South Pole; and how from thence she made her course to the tropical latitude of the Great Pacific Ocean; and of the strange things that befell; and in what manner the Ancient Mariner came back to his own country."—See the map in Lowes, opposite page 228, describing Captain Shelvocke's voyage round the world. Many British explorers had sailed the Ancient Mariner's course, and recorded their adventures. "The basic structure of the voyage regarded as a voyage is as austerely true to fact as an Admiralty report." (Lowes, 124.)

147. **12.** *Eftsoons:* Immediately.

14. *The Wedding Guest:* The impressiveness of the tale is enhanced by its enthralling one bent on so urgent an occasion as a wedding. William Taylor's translation of Bürger's *Lenore,* and Schiller's *Ghostseer* (which Coleridge dramatized), may have suggested this feature (See Lowes, 251 and notes).

30. Shows they are crossing the Equator.

32. *Bassoon:* A deep-toned musical wind-instrument. Coleridge's friend, Thomas Poole, had recently been acquiring a bassoon for the Stowey church choir.

55. Coleridge had read much about the polar regions, including *The Memoirs and Travels of Count de Benyowsky,* translated in 1790; and Frederick Martens's *Voyage into Spitzbergen and Greenland,* translated in 1694. The latter work (Hamburg edition, 1675) has a picture of "snowy clifts"; see Lowes, opposite page 144.

148. **61-62.** These noises, according to the arctic travelers whose voyages Coleridge had read, are characteristic features of the region.

63. *Albatross:* Wordsworth, and probably Coleridge after him, read in Capt. George Shelvocke's *Voyage Round the World by Way of the Great South Sea* (1726) pp. 71-72, an impressive description of the desolate, almost uninhabited Antarctic—sunless, dismal, where, says Shelvocke "one would think it impossible any thing living could subsist," and where they "had not had the sight of one fish of any kind . . . nor one sea bird, except a disconsolate black Albatross." Shelvocke's mate, Hatley, regarding the bird as responsible for the foul weather, shot it (See De Quincey's comments on this: *Works,* II, 145). This was not the great albatross, which has a wingspread of about twelve feet, and could not be hung about a mariner's neck; but the "sooty" albatross, a much smaller species (Lowes, 226-227).

67. *The food it ne'er had eat:* The first version had "The Marineres gave it biscuit-worms," a realistic touch taken from such experiences of half-starved sailors as are recorded in Eden's *History of Travayle* (Lowes, 150).

75. *shroud:* rope.

76. *vespers:* evenings, or evening church services.

81. *cross-bow:* Note the artistry of this choice of a weapon,—which, like other touches in the poem, suggests the past.—c. the sixteenth century.

83. *upon the right:* Indicating that the vessel has rounded Cape Horn and turned northwards into the Pacific.

85. Originally, "And broad as a weft, upon the left," a weft being a fine old sea-term for an ensign, which Coleridge had probably picked up in the harbor of Bristol, but which was condemned as obscure by landlubber reviewers (Lowes, 261).

97. See the picture of the glorious sun, in the guise of the trinitarian godhead, in Lowes, opposite p. 138, from a seventeenth-century book of travels.

98. *uprist:* uprose.

103. *The fair breeze:* The trade winds, constantly mentioned by the voyagers.

149. **111.** *hot and copper sky:* Mr. Herbert Wright (*Nineteenth Century and After,* XCIX, 732-744 (May, 1926) would derive this from a personal experience of Coleridge's, previously expressed in his poem *Respiration.* On the other hand, Lowes, 158, quotes Gilbert White, *Selborne,* ch. 65, and Thomas Burnet's *Telluris Theoria Sacra.*

125-130. Coleridge had read Capt. James Cook's *Voyage to the Pacific Ocean,* from which Lowes, 81, quotes such passages as these: "During a calm . . . some parts of the sea seemed covered with a kind of slime; and some small sea animals were swimming about . . . that had a white, or shining appearance . . . . When they began to swim about, which they did, with equal ease, upon their back, sides, or belly, they emitted the brightest colors of the most precious gems. . . . Sometimes they . . . assumed various tints of blue . . . But . . . the color was chiefly a beautiful, pale green, tinged with a burnished gloss; and, in the dark, it had a faint appearance of glowing fire. They . . . proved to be . . . probably an animal which has a share in producing . . . that lucid appearance, often observed near ships at sea, in the night." Coleridge had also read much about "slime-fishes" in Martens's *Voyage into Spitzbergen* (Lowes, 88).

128. *death fires:* Phosphorescent gleams which appear on ships' riggings, actually electrical, but by sailors regarded with superstitious dread.

141. *Instead of the cross:* It was with a cross upon the forehead that, according to some legends, the Wandering Jew, who forbade Christ to rest upon his way to Golgotha, was branded; and this was also reputed to be the brand of Cain (Lowes, 259, 245).

152. *wist:* knew.

150. **168.** *weal:* good.

169. Phantom ships were common in the travelers' tales (see Lowes, 275, 168).

196. "A tale of two spectral figures casting dice on a phantom ship for the soul of an eternal wanderer was current on the seas" (Lowes, 277, referring to the Dutch tale of Falkenberg).

200. This vivid description of a tropical sunset is not extravagant, but based upon travelers' reports.

151. **210.** *The hornèd Moon:* Has been condemned as fantastic, because the new moon does not rise at dawn. But this is the waning moon, which may rise at that time. The bright star within the moon's tip may be said to be an American star, for it was originally observed in New England, and was reported by Cotton Mather to the Royal Society in London, a quotation from whose letter was noted by Coleridge in the *Philosophical Transactions* (Lowes, 180).

The luminosity seen as a star might actually be a reflection from the lunar mountain Aristarchus. As for the "nether tip," W. A. Osborn, an Australian scientist, points out that in the tropics the moon would be seen on her back, and therefore there would be no "nether." In Coleridge's first version, line 221 read: "Almost atween the tips." See "Off The Track," TLS editorial, Nov. 2, 1946; and the comment by O. H. T. Dudley, "The Hornèd Moon," do., Dec. 7, 1946.—Whether such an astronomical phenomenon could occur actually, or is here only described approximately, is from a literary point of view less important than whether the passage is in harmony with its context and with the general atmosphere of the whole poem.

152. **254.** The travelers told of climates in which dead bodies lay "without any stinke or corruption" (Lowes, 292).

273-280. Again, not fantastical, but suggested by voyagers like Father Bourzes, Bartram, Capt. Cook, Sir Richard Hawkins, and Dampier(Lowes, 40-53).

291 ff. Up to this, daemons have controlled the vessel; but, after the mariner's blessing of the creatures of the deep, it is guided (not, as Wordsworth had originally suggested by the dead men, but rather) by angelic spirits. This is partly from a pious legend by the fourth-century Bishop Paulinus (Lowes, 283).

153. **297.** *Silly:* Futile, because dry.

314-317. *Fire-flags . . . wan stars:* Travelers had given accounts of seeing the stars through the Aurora Borealis (Lowes, 190).

154. **359-362.** *Sky-lark:* In the first version, *lavrock* (lark), a pseudo-Chaucerian reminiscence, like *jargoning* below (Lowes, 334).

156. **446.** This stanza resembles a passage in a forgotten poem of 1747 by G. Masters (cited by H. O. White in TLS., Jan. 14, 1926).

464-467. There was not only exquisite art in ending "the whole night-mare story among the clear fresh sounds and lights of the bay where it began," as Walter Pater has observed; but Coleridge was still remaining true to the spirit of the voyagers' tales, which not infrequently strike this note, half-incredulous, of "Home at last!" (Cf. Lowes, 154).

157. **520.** *a cushion:* The Wordsworths and Coleridge had at this time "a mild obsession" with such rustic seats. See Charles S. Bouslog, "The Symbol of the Sod-Seat in Coleridge," PMLA, LX, 802-810, 1945.

158. 535. *Ivy-tod:* ivy-bush.

545. *Sound:* The scientific transactions which Coleridge had been reading dwelt much upon the sound accompanying earthquakes (Lowes, 289).

159. 582. This stanza, and the marginal prose, imply that the Ancient Mariner must undergo a penance similar to that of the Wandering Jew. (Lowes, 249).

160. FRANCE: AN ODE

Provoked by the French attack upon a sister-republic ("Helvetia," line 66) early in 1798. See G. Bounard, "The Invasion of Switzerland and English Public Opinion," *Engl. Studies* (Amsterdam), XXII, 1-26, 1940. A later edition is prefaced by this summary: *"First Stanza.* An invocation to those objects in nature the contemplation of which had inspired the poet with a devotional love of liberty. *Second Stanza.* The exultation of the poet at the commencement of the French Revolution, and his unqualified abhorrence of the Alliance against the Republic. *Third Stanza.* The blasphemies and horrors during the domination of the Terrorists regarded by the poet as a transient storm, and as the natural consequence of the former despotism and of the foul superstition of Popery. Reason, indeed, began to suggest many apprehensions; yet still the poet struggled to retain the hope that France would make conquests by no other means than by presenting to the observation of Europe a people more happy and better instructed than under other forms of government. *Fourth Stanza.* Switzerland, and the poet's recantation. *Fifth Stanza.* An address to liberty, in which the poet expresses his conviction that those feelings and that grand *ideal* of freedom which the mind attains by its contemplation of its individual nature, and of the sublime surrounding objects (see stanza the first) do not belong to men, as a society, nor can possibly be either gratified or realized, under any form of human government; but belong to the individual man, so far as he is pure, and inflamed with the love and adoration of God in nature."

DISC.—The change of political views from those in the *Ode On The Departing Year.* See also the letter to George Coleridge, April, 1798; *Anth.,* p. 329. Compare the change in Wordsworth, *Prelude,* IX and XI; *Anth.,* p. 267; also x, 263-288.

160. 30. *Monarchs:* of Prussia and Austria, against whom France declared war in 1792. Great Britain became their ally in 1793.

43. *Blasphemy:* For example, in the "Feast of Reason," November, 1793, when "Reason," impersonated by an actress, was enthroned on the high altar of the cathedral of Notre Dame.

54. *ramp:* threatening posture.—In some early editions the misprint "tramp" crept in.

161. 85-86. Recalls Milton's insistence, in *Areopagitica* and elsewhere, that without education and self-restraint, liberty becomes license.

161. FROST AT MIDNIGHT

161. 7. *My cradled infant:* his son Hartley. See E. L. Griggs, *Hartley Coleridge* (1929).

15. *that film:* "These films," says Coleridge, "are called strangers and supposed to portend the arrival of some absent friend."

162. 37. *preceptor:* The master of Christ's Hospital, Boyer, who had flogged Coleridge when he said he did not want to become a clergyman but a shoemaker.

43. *playmate:* his sister Ann.

52. *In the great city:* Wordsworth alludes to this, *Prelude,* VIII, 433; *Anth.,* p. 263.

162. FEARS IN SOLITUDE

DISC.—Coleridge's autograph note: "The above is perhaps not Poetry,—but rather a sort of middle thing between Poetry and Oratory—*sermoni propriora.* Some parts are, I am conscious, too tame even for animated prose."

165. THE NIGHTINGALE

"What false notions," writes Wordsworth, "have prevailed from generation to generation of the true character of the nightingale! As far as my friend's poem, in the *Lyrical Ballads,* is read, it will contribute greatly to rectify these."

166. THE BALLAD OF THE DARK LADIÉ

When *Love*, below p. 168, was first published (in the *Morning Post*, Dec. 21, 1799), it was entitled "Introduction to the Tale of the Dark Ladié."

167. THE DEVIL'S THOUGHTS

This satire caused a sensation on its appearance in the *Post*. Southey wrote a longer version; and it was not forgotten by Byron ("The Devil's Drive," 1813) and Shelley ("The Devil's Walk," 1812).

168. LINES WRITTEN IN THE ALBUM

When Coleridge was staying at an inn in Germany, he was asked to write something in the inn album. He sent a copy of these lines to his wife, saying that they recorded his experiences and feelings on this woodland journey.

168. LOVE

The connection between this poem and Coleridge's love for Sarah Hutchinson (Mrs. Wordsworth's sister) is disclosed in Thomas M. Raysor's "Coleridge and 'Asra'," SP, XXVI, 305, 1929.

169. CHRISTABEL

169b. 53. *1797:* perhaps a mistake for 1798.

56. *Since the latter date,* etc.: These two sentences were omitted in later editions.

59. *I had the whole present to my mind:* Although Wordsworth doubted whether Coleridge ever had any definite plan for the conclusion, Dr. Gillman, in his *Life of Coleridge* (1838), says it was to have concluded as follows:

Over the mountains, the Bard, as directed by Sir Leoline, hastes with his disciple; but in consequence of one of those inundations supposed to be common to this country, the spot only where the castle once stood is discovered, the edifice itself being washed away. He determines to return. Geraldine, being acquainted with all that is passing, like the weird sisters in *Macbeth*, vanishes. Reappearing, however, she awaits the return of the Bard, exciting in the meantime, by her wily arts, all the anger she could rouse in the Baron's breast, as well as that jealousy of which he is described to have been susceptible.

The old Bard and the youth at length arrive, and therefore she can no longer personate the character of Geraldine, the daughter of Lord Roland de Vaux, but changes her appearance to that of the accepted, though absent, lover of Christabel. Next ensues a courtship most distressing to Christabel, who feels—she knows not why—great disgust for her once favored knight.

This coldness is very painful to the Baron, who has no more conception than herself of the supernatural transformation. She at last yields to her father's entreaties, and consents to approach the altar with the hated suitor. The real lover, returning, enters at this moment, and produces the ring which she had once given him in sign of her betrothment. Thus defeated, the supernatural being Geraldine disappears. As predicted, the castle bell tolls, the mother's voice is heard, and, to the exceeding great joy of the parties, the rightful marriage takes place, after which follows a reconcilation and explanation between father and daughter.

74. *celebrated poets:* During the many years before *Christabel* was published, manuscript copies were circulated. Scott knew and admired the poem as early as 1801, and imitated the metrical form in some passages of *The Lay of the Last Minstrel* (1805). It influenced *The Siege of Corinth* (XIX, 521-532), Byron having heard it in 1811; and it was Byron who induced Murray to publish it in 1816. Hence Coleridge tries to ward off "charges of plagiarism" by those who were unaware of his priority.

170a. 5. *The metre is not irregular:* This opens a field of almost ferocious debate today. See Karl Shapiro, "English Prosody and Modern Poetry," ELH, XIV, 77-92; 1947,—where it is contended that Gerard Manley Hopkins and Coleridge "were for the same prosody," and that "in *Christabel* the syllabic structure of the line is subordinated to the time structure, supernumerary syllables being accounted for by what Coleridge calls accent, and by which it is now understood that he meant something like musical beat."

On the sources and composition of the poem, divergent views will be found in D. R. Tuttle, "Christabel Sources in Percy's Reliques and the Gothic Romance," PMLA, LIII, 445-474, 1938; A. H. Nethercot, *The Road to Tryermaine*, 1939; and N. C. Starr, "Coleridge's 'Sir Leoline'," PMLA, LXI, 157-163, 1946.

170. 49. *The one red leaf:* Dorothy Wordsworth's *Journal*, March 7, 1798: "William and I drank tea at Coleridge's . . . One only leaf upon the top of a tree—the sole remaining leaf—danced round and round like a rag blown by the wind." Many other passages in the *Journal* show the closeness of the companionship of these kindred spirits. See Lowes, *Xanadu*, ch. 11.

171. 129-132. She pretended to faint because, being an evil spirit, she could not cross the threshold except by being carried.

149. Animals were believed to have an instinctive perception of the supernatural.

172. 253. There is some evidence that in one of the manuscripts, now lost, this passage stood:

> A sight to dream of, not to tell,
> Hideous, deformed, and pale of hue.

173. 350. *Pike:* peak.
351. *ghyll:* valley.
365. *Plight:* Perhaps "state"; but more likely archaic for "plait."

174. 408. "The best and sweetest lines that I ever wrote," remarks Coleridge to Poole in 1813. Contrast it with Byron's treatment of the same theme in *Childe Harold*, III, stanza XCIV; *Anth.*, p. 564.—Coleridge's estrangement from Southey may have intensified the poignancy of these lines.

176. KUBLA KHAN

In the Preface, "1797" is a mistake for May, 1798.—The exact reading of the passage from Samuel Purchas' *Pilgrimage* (ed. 1617, p. 472) is: "In Xamdu did Cubla Can build a stately Palace, encompassing sixteen miles of plaine ground with a wall, wherein are fertile Meddowes, pleasant springs, delightfull Streames, and all sorts of beasts of chace and game, and in the middest thereof a sumptuous house of pleasure, which may be removed from place to place." The historical Kubla Khan was a Mongol emperor of the thirteenth century. Mrs. Alfred Wingate's *A Servant of the Mightiest* (1927) describes one of his imperial palaces as a circular Temple of Heaven, wherein the Emperor mediated between God and Man.

Lowes's *Xanadu* shows that loosely remembered picturesque passages were borrowed by Coleridge from about eight other travelers, ancient and modern, besides Purchas, including James Bruce's *Travels to Discover the Source of the Nile* (1790) and William Bartram's *Travels* (in America, 1792). Geoffrey Grigson, George Whalley, and Keidrych Rhys suggest that some touches may have been derived from contemporary romantic landscapes (TLS, June 21 and Aug. 16, 1947).

The quotation in the Preface, "Then all the charm," is from Coleridge's *The Picture*, ll. 91-100. The Greek passage near the end is from Theocritus, *Idyls*, 1, 132, "to sing a sweeter song tomorrow."

The most important statement in the Preface is that the poem is "a distinct recollection" of an opium dream. This has been generally accepted as the truth. Lowes emphasized the contrast between the consciously planned *Ancient Mariner* and the automatic dream-composition of *Kubla Khan*. Strong reasons for doubting Coleridge's assertions are given in Elisabeth Schneider's "The 'Dream' of Kubla Khan," PMLA, LX, 784-801, 1945.

DISC.—What do you think of G. Wilson Knight's suggestion that *Christabel* corresponds to the *Inferno*, *The Ancient Mariner* to the *Purgatorio*, and *Kubla Khan* to the *Paradiso?*

Discuss Lamb's comment (Letter to Wordsworth, Apr. 26, 1816): "Coleridge repeats his vision so enchantingly that it irradiates and brings heaven and elysian bowers into my parlor when he sings it or says it," but he fears lest it should be discovered by printing to be "no better than nonsense or no sense."

177. 3. *Alph:* Virgil and other ancients told of the Alpheus, which, like the Nile of the legends, sank beneath earth and ocean, and rose again in a fountain (Lowes, 393).

4. *caverns measureless to man:* Explorers recorded such unfathomable caverns in the Nile regions (Lowes, 391).

8-9. Purchas, in his *Pilgrimes* (not the same work as that quoted above), tells of Aloadine, the Old Man of the Mountain, having "a goodly garden, furnished with the best trees and fruits he could find, adorned with divers Palaces and houses of pleasure" (Lowes, 361).— As for the remaining touches in the picture, see the passages from Bartram's *Travels,* in *Anth.,* pp. 98-101 (Lowes, 366).

12. *That deep romantic chasm,* etc.: Recollected from Abyssinian landscapes described in Bruce's *Nile* (Lowes, 377).

14. Lowes (399) cites from William Collins' *The Passions,* 64-66:

> Thro' glades and glooms the mingled measure stole;
> Or o'er some haunted stream, with fond delay
> Round an holy calm diffusing . . .

Professor Lane Cooper (MP, Jan. 1906; PMLA, June, 1928) finds the association of "holy" with demoniac love a repulsive blemish. But does it not merely suggest that such a spot, to the awestruck listener, would seem unapproachable?

17-28. Many recollections of fountainous scenes in Bartram's *Travels* (Lowes, 367). See *Anth.,* p. 100.

30. Both in Purchas and in Bruce, near passages read by Coleridge, there is mention of priests counseling concerning war (Lowes, 397).

33. *Mingled measure:* See note on l. 14.

37-54. Aloadine (see on l. 8 above), according to Purchas, maintained such a "Paradise," where his young warriors were ministered unto by "Damosells skilfull in Songs and Instruments of Musicke," to their undoing (Lowes, 362).

39. Bruce's *Nile* deals largely with Abyssinia.

41. *Mount Abora:* In Coleridge's dream, there apparently coalesced Purchas' hill Amara, Bruce's river Abola, and Milton's

> . . . where Abassin kings their issue guard
> Mount Amara (though this by some supposed
> True Paradise) under the Ethiop line
> By Nilus' head.—*Par. Lost,* IV, 280-283

49. A recollection of the passage about the savage king in Bruce's *Nile.*

177. DEJECTION: AN ODE

Ernest De Selincourt edits the earliest version of this poem, "as it was written on 4 April, 1802, and sent to Sara Hutchinson"; and he sets forth its important place in the lives of Coleridge and the Wordsworths (Engl. Asso., *Essays and Studies,* XXII, 1936; rptd. in *Wordsworthian and Other Studies,* 1947). For the names "William" and "Wordsworth," found in Ms versions, Coleridge on publication substituted "lady" (ll. 25 and 42) and "Otway" (l. 120). The poem first appeared in the *Morning Post,* Oct. 4, 1802, which was Wordsworth's wedding day. Originally the following lines appeared after line 75:

> Calm steadfast Spirit, guided from above,
> O Wordsworth! friend of my devoutest choice,
> Great son of genius! full of light and love
> Thus, thus dost thou rejoice.
> To thee do all things live from pole to pole,
> Their life the eddying of thy living soul.
> Brother and friend of my devoutest choice,
> Thus may'st thou ever, evermore rejoice!

The happiness of Wordsworth by contrast deepens the darkness of Coleridge's melancholy.

The poet declares that because his afflictions have robbed him of joy his "shaping spirit of Imagination" has fled, and therewith the consciousness of communion with Nature ("I see, not *feel,* how beautiful they are"). Since "in our life *alone* does Nature live," the death of the Imagination is paralyzing to poetic creativeness; and nature poetry becomes merely an indulgence in the pathetic fallacy. In other words, Coleridge goes so far as to deny that Imagination can bring him into genuine communion with Reality,—a skeptical and anti-romantic attitude.—This was not the first time that he had "roamed the black Heath of Distress" (*To William Godwin*, 1795), nor was his despair permanent: in *Biographia Literaria* he returned to idealism, i.e., to his usual faith in the harmonious relationship between the mind and its universe (Stallknecht, *Strange Seas of Thought*, pp. 159-171; 1945).

Coleridge's temporary state of mind is not uncommon in the lives of great poets. Charles Williams opines that all the greatest have been assailed by moods of catastrophic disillusionment,—Shakespeare, Milton, Wordsworth, etc. (*The English Poetic Mind*, 1932).

DISC.—The relation of the feelings and thoughts in *Dejection* with those in (1) *The Ancient Mariner* (breach of communion with Nature); (2) Wordsworth's *Ode on Intimations of Immortality*, the first four stanzas of which are by some considered a restatement of Coleridge's feelings; and (3) possibly Wordsworth's *Resolution and Independence*, which also has been regarded as a rejoinder (Fred M. Smith, "The Relation of the Ode on Dejection to the Ode on Intimations," PMLA, L, 224-234; 1935).

178. 45-46: These lines give the motto and title to Charles Morgan's novel, *The Fountain* (1932).

179. 121. *'Tis of a little child:* Wordsworth's Lucy Gray; *Anth.*, p. 203.

179.   HYMN BEFORE SUNRISE

When the poem appeared in the *Morning Post*, Sept 11, 1802, it had this preface: "Chamouni is one of the highest mountain valleys of the Barony of Faucigny in the Savoy Alps; and exhibits a kind of fairy world, in which the wildest appearances (I had almost said horrors) of nature alternate with the softest and most beautiful. The chain of Mont Blanc is its boundary; and besides the Arve it is filled with sounds from the Arveiron, which rushes from the melted glaciers, like a giant, mad with joy, from a dungeon, and forms other torrents of snow-water, having their rise in the glaciers which slope down into the valley. The beautiful *Gentiana Major*, or great gentian, with blossoms of the brightest blue, grows in large companies a few steps from the never-melted ice of the glaciers. I thought it an affecting emblem of the boldness of human hope, venturing near, and, as it were, leaning over the brink of the grave. Indeed, the whole vale, its every light, its every sound, must needs impress every mind not utterly callous with the thought—Who *would* be, who *could* be an atheist in this valley of wonders! If any of the readers of *The Morning Post* have visited this vale in their journeys among the Alps, I am confident that they will not find the sentiments and feeling expressed, or attempted to be expressed, in the following poem, extravagant."

Adrien Bonjour, *Coleridge's "Hymn Before Sunrise"* (Lausanne, 1942), devotes more than 200 pages to this first attempt by Coleridge, after writing *Dejection*, to recapture his poetic powers. The *Hymn* is a fourfold expansion of a twenty-line German poem by Fredericke Brun, published without proper acknowledgment.

DISC.—Compare with Shelley's *Mont Blanc; Anth.*, p. 864.

181.   TO WILLIAM WORDSWORTH

On Coleridge's return from Malta, in an ill and unhappy state, Wordsworth read to him in the course of several evenings those books of *The Prelude* (beginning with Book VI) which he had composed during his friend's absence.

182. 65-75. At the end of ch. 10 of *Biographia Literaria* Coleridge quotes these self-condemning lines, and hints that they are too severe.

84. *my nobler mind:* alluding to his golden period, in 1797.

183.   THE PAINS OF SLEEP

In a letter to Thomas Poole, October 3, 1803, Coleridge wrote: "God forbid that my worst enemy should ever have the nights and the sleeps that I have had night after night—surprised by sleep, while I struggled to remain awake, starting up to bless my own loud scream that had awakened me—yea, dear friend! till my repeated night-yells had made me a nuisance in my own house. As I live and am a man, this is an unexaggerated tale. My dreams became the substances of my life."

184. TIME, REAL AND IMAGINARY

Whether it is the boy or the girl who represents "real" time, is disputed: see EXP, Oct., 1944, and Feb., 1945. In *Anima Poetae* Coleridge writes: "How marked the contrast between troubled manhood and joyously active youth in the sense of time! To the former, time like the sun in an empty sky is never seen to move, but only to have moved. . . . To the latter it is as a full moon in a fine breezy October night, driving on amid clouds of all shapes and hues, . . . and yet seems not to have moved at all. This I feel to be a just image of time real and time as felt, in two different states of being. The title of the poem therefore (for poem it ought to be) should be time real and time felt (in the sense of time) in active youth, or activity with hope and fullness of aim in any period, and in despondent, objectless manhood—time objective and subjective." A simpler explanation is found in the Preface to the *Sibylline Leaves:* "By imaginary Time, I meant the state of a schoolboy's mind when on his return to school he projects his being in his day-dreams, and lives in his next holidays, six months hence; and this I contrasted with real Time."

WILLIAM WORDSWORTH (1770-1850)

I. EDITIONS

Selincourt, E. De, and Darbishire, Helen, eds. *The Poetical Works of William Wordsworth,* 3 vols., 1941-1946.
*Hutchinson, Thomas, ed. *The Poems of William Wordsworth,* 1923.—With Intr. and Notes by G. McL. Harper, 1928.
Selincourt, E. De, ed. *The Prelude, Edited from the Mss.,* 1926.—Abridgment, 1935.
Reynolds, E. E., ed. *The Excursion,* 1935.
Knight, W. A., ed. *Prose Works,* 2 vols., 1896.
Selincourt, E. De, ed. *The Journals of Dorothy Wordsworth,* 2 vols, 1942.
Selincourt, E. De, ed. *The Letters of William and Dorothy Wordsworth,* 7 vols., 1935 ff.

Selected Poems:
    Arnold, Matthew; 1879.
    Grey (Viscount); 1910.
    Hall, Howard J.; 1918.
    Harper, G. McL.; 1923.

II. BIOGRAPHY AND CRITICISM

Wordsworth, Christopher. *Memoir of William Wordsworth,* 2 vols., 1851.
Stephen, Leslie. "Wordsworth's Ethics" (1874), rptd. in *Hours in a Library.*
*Arnold, Matthew. In *Essays in Criticism,* II; 1888.
Pater, Walter. In *Appreciations,* 1889.
*Legouis, Emile. *The Early Life of Wordsworth,* 1896; 2nd ed., 1921.
Raleigh, Walter. *Wordsworth,* 1903.
*Bradley, A. C. In *Oxford Lectures on Poetry,* 1909.
*Harper, George McL. *William Wordsworth: His Life, Works, and Influence,* 2 vols., 1916.--Abridgment, 1929.
*Dicey, A. V. *The Statesmanship of Wordsworth,* 1917.
Harper, G. McL. *Wordsworth's French Daughter,* 1921.
*Beatty, Arthur. *William Wordsworth: His Doctrine and Art,* 1922; 2nd ed., 1927.
*Whitehead, A. N. In *Science and the Modern World,* 1925.
Huxley, Aldous. "Wordsworth in the Tropics," 1929; rptd. in *Do What You Will,* 1930.
Herford, C. H. *Wordsworth,* 1930.
Read, Herbert. *Wordsworth,* 1930.
Rader, Melvin M. *Presiding Ideas in Wordsworth's Poetry,* 1931.
Maclean, Catherine M. *Dorothy Wordsworth,* 1932.
Fausset, Hugh I'A. *Lost Leader,* 1933.

*Selincourt, Ernest De. *Dorothy Wordsworth*, 1933.

*Batho, Edith C. *The Later Wordsworth*, 1933.

Campbell, O. J., and Mueschke, P. *Wordsworth's Aesthetic Development: 1795-1802*, 1933.

Sperry, Willard L. *Wordsworth's Anti-Climax*, 1935.

*Beach, J. W. *The Concept of Nature in Nineteenth-Century Poetry*, 1936.

Martin, A. D. *The Religion of Wordsworth*, 1936.

*Bush, Douglas. *Mythology and the Romantic Tradition in English Poetry*, 1937.

*James, D. G. *Scepticism and Poetry*, 1937.

Grierson, H. J. C. *Milton and Wordsworth*, 1937.

Murry, J. Middleton. *Heroes of Thought*, 1938.

Wilson, J. Dover. *Leslie Stephen and Matthew Arnold as Critics of Wordsworth*, 1939.

Griggs, E. L., ed. *Wordsworth and Coleridge: Studies in Honor of G. M. Harper*, 1939.

Thorpe, C. D. "The Imagination: Coleridge vs. Wordsworth," PQ, XVIII, 1-18; 1939.

Beach, J. W. "Reason and Nature in Wordsworth," JHI, I, 335-351; 1940.

Bernbaum, Ernest. "Is Wordsworth's Nature-Poetry Antiquated?," ELH, VII, 333-340.

*Knight, G. Wilson. *The Starlit Dome*, 1941.

*Havens, R. D. *The Mind of a Poet*, 1941.

Noyes, Russell. *Wordsworth and Jeffrey*, 1941.

Miles, Josephine. *Wordsworth and the Vocabulary of Emotion*, 1942.

Burton, Mary E. *The One Wordsworth*, 1942.

Meyer, George W. *Wordsworth's Formative Years*, 1943.

Geen, Elizabeth. "The Concept of Grace in Wordsworth's Poetry," PMLA, LVIII, 689-716; 1943.

*Peek, Katherine M. *Wordsworth in England*, 1943.

Noyes, Russell. "Wordsworth and Burns," PMLA, LIX, 813-833; 1944.

Smith, J. C. *Wordsworth*, 1944.

*Stallknecht, N. P. *Strange Seas of Thought*, 1945.

Worthington, Jane. *Wordsworth's Reading of Roman Prose*, 1946.

Christensen, Francis. "Creative Sensibility in Wordsworth," JEGP, XLV, 361-368; 1946.

*Selincourt, Ernest De. *Wordsworthian and Other Studies*, 1947.

Cooper, Lane. *A Concordance to the Poems of William Wordsworth*, 1911.

NOTES, COMMENTS, AND TOPICS FOR DISCUSSION

188.   AN EVENING WALK

Here, as throughout Wordsworth's nature poetry, the best references are not to books but to nature itself; hence he should be studied in the country, where his precision and sensitivity can be appreciated. "The present-day connoisseur of either poetry or painting is delighted to find Wordsworth characterizing shadows as *purple* (l. 103) nearly a century before the impressionist painters discovered that they might actually have that color" (Beach, *Romantic View of Poetry*, pp. 10-11).

189.   LINES WRITTEN IN EARLY SPRING

One of the basic themes: the Universe is fair and harmonious, but Man perverts it.

189.   EXPOSTULATION AND REPLY

"William" is Wordsworth in his youth; "Matthew" is his teacher, "a friend," says Wordsworth, "somewhat unreasonably attached to modern books of natural philosophy." The passage, ll. 21-24, about a wise passiveness is said to be a favorite with Quakers. The state of mind was to be more fully described in *Tintern Abbey*, 38-50. Observe that Wordsworth does not represent wise passiveness as the *only* way to find truth, but as one way, too much neglected by the merely intellectual seeker.

189. 26. *things forever speaking*: This belief is an essential part of the faith in Inspiration.
    30. *Conversing*: communing with the universe.

THE TABLES TURNED

189.

Lane Cooper (MLN, Mch., 1907) warns us not to overlook the "half playful" character of this poem. The provocative lines are 21-24 about *one impulse from a vernal wood.* Note that Wordsworth does not say "always will teach you," but "may teach you." To those who damn the lines as unorthodox, T. E. Casson (TLS, Apr. 29, 1939) retorts with Saint Bernard's dictum: "Believe one who has tried: trees and stones will teach you what you cannot learn from any master." The kind of misshaping intellectualism which is attacked is that of Godwin (Beach, *Rom. View,* p. 42).

ANECDOTE FOR FATHERS

190.

Characteristic of the Romantics,—an effort to enter sympathetically into the mind of a child, and to respect its individuality. "What from thee I learn," (l. 60), is chiefly an insight into human nature and its state in infancy, rather than anything comparable to adult theories.

LINES COMPOSED ABOVE TINTERN ABBEY

191.

Tintern Abbey was a ruin in Monmouthshire, long celebrated for its historical interest and its beauty. The scientist Humphrey Davy in his early notebooks tells how deeply he was stirred by seeing it in the moonlight (quoted in Grigson, *The Romantics;* p. 170). "No poem of mine," says Wordsworth, "was composed under circumstances more pleasant for me to remember than this. I began it upon leaving Tintern, after crossing the Wye, and concluded it just as I was entering Bristol, in the evening, after a ramble of four or five days, with my sister. Not a line of it was altered, and not any part of it written down till I reached Bristol." It is the most important of his early poems.

The general meaning is clear: the beauty of Nature enables the poet to feel, despite the apparent evils of life, that the Universe is fundamentally harmonious. Tennyson praised it (esp. ll. 95 ff.) as "giving the sense of the permanent in the transitory." Also noteworthy are the distinctions drawn between childhood, youth, and maturity.—G. W. Meyer (*Wordsworth's Formative Years,* ch. 6) attempts a step-by-step retracing of Wordsworth's changes in attitude toward Nature. He stresses, perhaps overmuch, the importance of "still" in "Therefore am I still a lover" (l. 102).

193. 93-102. These lines are commonly considered pantheistic; but A. E. Garvie, quoting them, says: "We must not call pantheism the sense which poets have had of God's presence in nature" (*Encl. of Religion and Ethics,* art. "Pantheism"). The "tension of uncertainty" which some critics have felt in the poem may reflect the fact that Wordsworth was groping for complex truths rather than feeling cocksure about the precise interrelationships between God, Nature, and Man. It is easy for those who have no better account of the relationship to propose, to call the passage "muddled" and "shuffling," as Empson arbitrarily does (*Seven Types of Ambiguity,* p. 191).

115. *my dearest Friend:* Dorothy Wordsworth.

DISC.—Norman Foerster: "*Tintern Abbey* is great aesthetically, as we have come increasingly to see; it is ethically vital, but unsound; in sum, this poem is a superb expression of unwisdom" (Quoted in McElderry, "Grapes of Wrath," *College English,* Mch., 1944).

See Charles H. Gray, "Wordsworth's First Visit to Tintern Abbey," PMLA, XLIX, 123-133; 1934; J. C. Ransom, *The New Criticism,* pp. 115-119; 1941; and J. B. McNulty, SP, XLII, 81-86; and MLN, LX, 291-295; 1945.

THE REVERIE OF POOR SUSAN

194.

The places named are in the very center of London, where thoughts of the country would be the least likely to arise. "This arose," says Wordsworth, "out of my observation of the affecting music of these birds hanging in this way in the London streets during the freshness and stillness of the spring morning."

194.   THERE WAS A BOY

Later used in *The Prelude*, v, 364-397.—See the remarkable biographical passage, with a striking quotation from Wordsworth, in De Quincey's *Literary Reminiscences*, pp. 312-317; omitted in his *Collected Writings*, but found in Beatty, pp. 160-162, and in Stallknecht, p. 58-61.

194. 2. *Winander:* Lake Windermere, Westmoreland.

     10. *Blew mimic hootings:* From Buckinghamshire, England, Harold Morland writes: "There is an owl hooting outside my room now. If I interlace my fingers, *but not my thumbs,* as Wordsworth suggests, I leave a very slight gap towards the top of my palms. Blowing through this and making a voiced sound, and at the same time making my hands quiver against my lips, I give a very fair imitation indeed of an owl-call. It is a game much indulged in by small boys in the north of England, of whom I was once one" (EXP., Oct., 1946).

     The relation to nature in childhood is represented as close, but neither conscious nor reflective, an attitude perhaps impossible to recapture later, but precious as a memory.

195. 24-25. *uncertain heaven received,* etc.: Of these lines Coleridge said: "I should have recognized them anywhere; and had I met these lines running wild in the deserts of Arabia, I should have instantly screamed out, 'Wordsworth!'."

195.   WE ARE SEVEN

"The little girl who is the heroine I met within the area of Goodrich Castle in the year 1793." Wordsworth.—The little maid's inability to conceive of death as the ordinary understanding conceives of it was not in Wordsworth's view mere ignorance. "Forlorn, and cut off from communication with the best part of his nature must that man be who should derive the sense of immortality, as it exists in the mind of a child, from the same unthinking gaiety or liveliness of animal spirits with which the lamb in the meadow, or any other irrational creature, is endowed" (Wordsworth's *Essays on Epitaphs*). Compare the theme with that of the *Ode: Intimations of Immortality from Recollections of Early Childhood*. In the *Ode*, the lofty theme is treated in the grand manner; here, in the simplest.

In that simplicity of its style, *We Are Seven* was one of the boldest of the experiments attempted in the *Lyrical Ballads*. "When," says Wordsworth, "it was all but finished, I came in and recited it to Mr. Coleridge and my sister, and said, 'A prefatory stanza must be added, and I should sit down to our little tea-meal with greater pleasure if my task were finished.' I mentioned in substance what I wished to be expressed, and Coleridge immediately threw off the stanza thus:—

'A little child, dear brother Jem,'—

I objected to the rhyme, 'dear brother Jem,' as being ludicrous, but we all enjoyed the joke of hitching-in our friend, James T[obin]'s name, who was familiarly called Jem. He was the brother of the dramatist, and this reminds me of an anecdote which it may be worth while here to notice. The said Jem got a sight of the *Lyrical Ballads* as it was going through the press at Bristol, during which time I was residing in that city. One evening he came to me with a grave face, and said, 'Wordsworth, I have seen the volume that Coleridge and you are about to publish. There is one poem in it which I earnestly entreat you to cancel, for, if published, it will make you everlastingly ridiculous.' I answered that I felt much obliged by the interest he took in my good name as a writer, and begged to know what was the unfortunate piece he alluded to. He said, 'It is called *We Are Seven*.'—'Nay,' said I, 'that shall take its chance, however,' and he left me in despair."

Observe that in 1815 Wordsworth omitted the too prosaic "dear brother Jim" from the first line.

Coleridge disagreed with Wordsworth on this subject of a child's alleged perception of immortality; and in 1817, in *Biographia Literaria*, ch. 22, cited *We Are Seven* and Stanza VIII of the *Ode* as instances of Wordsworth's addiction to "thoughts and images too great for the subject."

Marcel Kessel (EXP., Apr., 1944) warns us against reading too much into this child's mind.

DISC.—How much further in this respect does the *Ode on Intimations of Immortality* go?

195. 37 and **39.** Note the internal rhymes, like those often used in *The Ancient Mariner*.

196. ### THE OLD CUMBERLAND BEGGAR

Of this poem Wordsworth writes as follows: "Observed, and with great benefit to my own heart, when I was a child: written at Racedown and Alfoxden in my twenty-third year. The political economists were about that time beginning their war upon mendicity in all its forms, and by implication, if not directly, on alms-giving also. This heartless process has been carried as far as it can go by the amended poor-law bill, though the inhumanity that prevails in this measure is somewhat disguised by the profession that one of its objects is to throw the poor upon the voluntary donations of their neighbors; that is, if rightly interpreted, to force them into a condition between relief in the Union poor-house, and alms robbed of their Christian grace and spirit, as being *forced* rather from the benevolent than given by them; while the avaricious and selfish, and all in fact but the humane and charitable, are at liberty to keep all they possess from their distressed brethren.

"The class of beggars, to which the old man here described belongs, will probably soon be extinct. It consisted of poor, and, mostly, old and infirm persons, who confined themselves to a stated round in their neighborhood, and had certain fixed days, on which, at different houses, they regularly received alms, sometimes in money, but mostly in provisions."

199. 179. *house, misnamed of industry:* workhouse, poorhouse.

184. *Whether heard or not:* On this exquisite touch, see Lamb's comment, *Anth.*, p. 377a, 21. On the concern for social welfare in the poem, see Dyson, "The Old Cumberland Beggar," *Essays of the Eighteenth Century Presented to D. N. Smith*, 1945.

199. ### RUTH

Refutes the notion that Wordsworth believed that the influences of nature were always beneficent. See esp. ll. 121 ff.

202. ### NUTTING

"Written," says Wordsworth, "in Germany . . . Arose out of remembrance of feelings I had often when a boy."

203. ### STRANGE FITS OF PASSION HAVE I KNOWN

First of the "Lucy" poems. The others are: "She Dwelt," "Three Years" (p. 204) and "I Travelled" (p. 217).

203. ### LUCY GRAY: OR, SOLITUDE

"Written at Goslar in Germany. It was founded on a circumstance told me by my sister, of a little girl who, not far from Halifax in Yorkshire, was bewildered in a snowstorm. Her footsteps were traced by her parents to the middle of the lock of a canal, and no other vestige of her, backward or forward, could be traced. The body however was found in the canal. The way in which the incident was treated and the spiritualizing of the character might furnish hints for contrasting the imaginative influences which I have endeavored to throw over common life with Crabbe's matter of fact style of treating subjects of the same kind. This is not spoken to his disparagement, far from it, but to direct the attention of thoughtful readers, into whose hands these notes may fall, to a comparison that may both enlarge the circle of their sensibilities, and tend to produce in them a catholic judgment." Wordsworth.—Observe that in Wordsworth's version the child's body is not found, this change helping the plausibility of the belief in her apparition.

204. ### SHE DWELT AMONG THE UNTRODDEN WAYS

The Lucy poems are Wordsworth's most poignant expressions of love and grief. Who Lucy was has been much debated. She may have been a purely imaginary character; but the apparently deeply personal sentiments of the poem, combined with Wordsworth's customary avoidance in this period of subjects not drawn from his own experience, make this hypothesis unlikely. Professor De Selincourt (ed. *Prelude,* p. 595) suggests that Lucy may have been Mary Hutchinson, later the poet's wife, but there is evidence against that possibility. Professor Harper is "convinced that the Lucy poems record, in the delicate distillation of memory, a real experience of youthful love and bewildering grief. The maiden whom he loved was a child. He loved her with the ennobling passion of a high-minded boy. She died, but her image survived in his heart." He thinks it likely that Lucy died in the summer of 1788 (TLS, Nov. 11, 1926). See the lively debate in TLS, July 15, 22, Dec. 9, 1926; Apr. 3, 17, May 8, 1930. Also: J. D. Rea, "Hartley Coleridge and Wordsworth's Lucy," SP, XXVIII, 118-135; 1931; Herbert Hartman, "Wordsworth's Lucy Poems," PMLA, XLIX, 134-142; 1934; and J. R. Harris, *Wordsworth's Lucy* (After-glow Essays), 1935. In his Life of Dorothy Wordsworth, De Selincourt intimates that the poet's deep affection for his sister contributed to the poignancy of these poems.

204. 2. *Dove:* A stream in the Lake country. Professor Harper inclines to believe that Hartsop Hall, a farmhouse in this region, a region familiar to Wordsworth at the time in question, may have been the home of Lucy or at least near it.

204. ### THREE YEARS SHE GREW

Francis Christensen (EXP., Dec., 1945) gives reasons for believing that Wordsworth distinguished between infancy, during which the mother is everything to the child, and childhood —at approximately three—when Nature begins to take over some of the parent's functions.

Interesting as such speculations are, still more important is the kind of education which Nature gives to Lucy (without Lucy's thinking of it as an education).

204a. 8. *law and impulse:* Does not the next stanza indicate what this means,—the last three lines, the law; the first three, the impulse?

204. ### A SLUMBER DID MY SPIRIT SEAL

The appalling unexpectedness, suddenness, and finality of Death, expressed in one of the sublimest dirges of our tongue.

DISC.—Compare with some of Landor's elegiac poems; and in the light of such poems, ask whether diffuseness and unrestraint are as characteristic of the Romantics as is alleged.

204. ### A POET'S EPITAPH

204b. 1. *Statist:* statesman.
11. *Doctor:* of Divinity.

205. ### THE TWO APRIL MORNINGS

"Some of Wordsworth's pieces prompted by a sort of half-playful mysticism, like the *Daffodils* and *The Two April Mornings* are distinguished by a certain quaint gayety of metre, and rival by their perfect execution, similar pieces among our own Elizabethan or contemporary French poetry." Walter Pater, *Appreciations.*

207. ### MICHAEL: A PASTORAL POEM

Wordsworth once said that there was some foundation in fact, however slight, for every poem he had ever written of a narrative kind; and this was certainly true of *Michael.*

"The sheepfold, on which so much of the poem turns, remains, or rather the ruins of it. The character and circumstances of Luke were taken from a family to whom had belonged, many years before, the house we lived in at Town-end, along with some fields and woodlands on the eastern shore of Grasmere. The name of the Evening Star was not in fact given to this house, but to another on the same side of the valley, more to the north."—Wordsworth.

"In the two poems, *The Brothers* and *Michael,* I have attempted to draw a picture of the domestic affections, as I know they exist amongst a class of men who are now almost confined to the north of England. They are small independent *proprietors* of land, here called statesmen, men of respectable education, who daily labor on their own little properties. The domestic affections will always be strong amongst men who live in a country not crowded with population, if these men are placed above poverty. But if they are proprietors of small estates which have descended to them from their ancestors, the power which these affections acquire amongst such men is inconceivable by those who have only had an opportunity of observing hired laborers, farmers, and the manufacturing poor. Their little tract of land serves as a kind of permanent rallying point for their domestic feelings, as a tablet on which they are written, which makes them objects of memory in a thousand instances, when they would otherwise be forgotten. It is a fountain fitted to the nature of social man, from which supplies of affection, as pure as his heart was intended for, are daily drawn. This class of men is rapidly disappearing. . . . The two poems which I have mentioned were written with a view to show that men who do not wear fine clothes can feel deeply. . . . The poems are faithful copies from Nature." Wordsworth to Charles James Fox, 14 Jan., 1801.

"I have attempted to give a picture of a man, of strong mind and lively sensibility, agitated by two of the most powerful affections of the human heart: the parental affection, and the love of property (landed property), including the feelings of inheritance, home, and personal and family independence. . . . In writing it I had your character often before my eyes; and sometimes thought that I was delineating such a man as you yourself would have been under the same circumstances." Wordsworth to Thomas Poole, 1801.

207. 2. *Greenhead Ghyll:* A narrow valley, with steep sides, near Wordsworth's cottage. All the places named are in the vicinity—Grasmere, Easedale, Dummail—Raise, etc.

211. 259. *Richard Bateman:* "The story alluded to is well known in the country. The chapel is called Ings Chapel, and it is on the right-hand side of the road leading from Kendal to Ambleside" (Wordsworth).

215.

THE DANISH BOY

"These stanzas were designed to introduce a Ballad upon the story of a Danish Prince who had fled from battle and, for the sake of valuables about him, was murdered by the inhabitant of a cottage in which he had taken refuge. The house fell under a curse, and the Spirit of the youth, it was believed, haunted the valley where the crime had been committed" (Wordsworth).

216.

SONG FOR THE WANDERING JEW

This legendary figure was of great interest to the Romantics; he was ever seeking death yet unable to find it, and he could be made to typify various tragic plights of man. See George K. Anderson, "The Wandering Jew Returns to England." JEGP, XLV, 237-251; 1946.—Grigson (*The Romantics*, p. 50) gives an anonymous poem like Wordsworth's, which was quoted by De Quincey, and which Grigson opines Wordsworth rewrote and ruined.

215.

I GRIEVED FOR BUONAPARTÉ

Written when Napoleon's power was growing greater and greater, and it seemed foolish to try to resist "the wave of the future."—This is the first important sonnet inspired by Milton. He preferred the Miltonic form to the Shakespearian and the Spenserian, but "he contributed quite as much as he borrowed" (see J. B. McNulty, "Milton's Influence on Wordsworth's Early Sonnets," PMLA, LXII, 745; 1947).—On the war-sonnets in general, see James V. Logan, *Sewanee Review*, Oct., 1942.

216.

TOUSSAINT L'OUVERTURE

Toussaint, a Negro, was one of the liberator-heroes to the Romantics, and to Abolitionists like Wendell Phillips and Whittier; see the latter's poem on him. He freed Haiti, was called L'Ouverture because of his military skill in breaking through enemy lines, and defied Napoleon when that tyrant tried to reintroduce slavery. He was finally captured, and brought to France, where he died in prison about two months after Wordsworth wrote this sonnet. See Ralph Korngold, *Citizen Toussaint*, 1944; also Kenneth Roberts' novel, *Lydia Bailey*, 1947.— Observe the alliance of "Powers," in Nature and in Man, that sustain the struggle towards Justice and Freedom.

217. IT IS NOT TO BE THOUGHT OF

The patriotic poems of Wordsworth, written during the military ascendancy of Napoleon, stress the moral basis of national fortitude; and they steeled the heart of England during World Wars I and II.

217a. 4. *pomp of waters:* quoted from Samuel Daniels, an Elizabethan poet loved by Wordsworth.

217. WHEN I HAVE BORNE IN MEMORY

Quoted by our war-time British Ambassador, Lord Halifax, in his farewell address to the United States, May 11, 1946.

217. I TRAVELLED AMONG UNKNOWN MEN

On the intertwining of the patriotic and the personal themes, see Walter Gierasch, EXP, June, 1943.

217. MY HEART LEAPS UP WHEN I BEHOLD

217b. 7. *The Child:*   The childhood shows the man
As morning shows the day.
(Milton; *Par. Reg.,* IV, 220)

9. *natural piety:* reverence towards Nature; or, as Santayana puts it, "a devout attach-ment to the sources of one's being." Blake misunderstood the phrase when he wrote in the margin: "There is no such thing as natural piety, because the natural man is at enmity with God." The child unconsciously has this bond with Nature. The last three lines became the motto of the *Ode on Intimations of Immortality (Anth.,* p. 232).

217. THE SPARROW'S NEST

A tribute to Dorothy Wordsworth ("Emmeline").

218. TO THE SMALL CELANDINE

Ranunculus ficaria, the small celandine, flowers in early spring, and, as Wordsworth ob-serves, "shuts itself up and opens out according to the degree of light and temperature." Also called the swallow-wort, it is found in the eastern United States as an escape from gardens.

219. RESOLUTION AND INDEPENDENCE

Based upon actual experience. "I describe myself," says Wordsworth "as having been exalted to the highest pitch of delight by the joyousness and beauty of nature; and then as depressed, even in the midst of those beautiful objects, to the lowest dejection and despair. A young poet in the midst of the happiness of nature is described as overwhelmed by the thoughts of the miserable reverses which have befallen the happiest of all men, *viz.,* poets. I think of this till I am so deeply impressed with it, that I consider the manner in which I was rescued from my dejection and despair almost as an interposition of Providence. A person reading the poem with feelings like mine will have been awed and controlled, expecting something spiritual or supernatural. What is brought forward? A lonely place, 'a pond by which an old man *was,* far from all house or home': not *stood,* nor *sat,* but *was*—the figure presented in the most naked simplicity possible. This feeling of spirituality or supernatural-ness is again referred to as being strong in my mind in this passage. How came he here? thought I, or what can he be doing? I then describe him, whether ill or well is not for me to judge with perfect confidence; but this I *can* confidently affirm, that though I believe God has given me a strong imagination, I cannot conceive a figure more impressive than that of an old man like this, the survivor of a wife and ten children, travelling alone among the mountains and all lonely places, carrying with him his own fortitude, and the necessities which an unjust state of society has laid upon him."

220b. 43. *Chatterton;* see *Anth.,* p. 70.

45. *Of him:* Robert Burns; *Anth.,* p. 80.

222. ON THE EXTINCTION OF THE VENETIAN REPUBLIC

In 1177 the Venetian navy defeated that of the German Emperor, whereupon the Pope gave the Doge a ring and bade him wed the Adriatic Sea in token of his mastery thereof, a ceremony annually performed by a naval procession and the casting of a ring into the sea. In the thirteenth century the Venetian Republic, which had captured Constantinople, was the bulwark against the Turks; and for centuries it remained, although the discovery of America resulted in the moving of the center of commerce to the English Channel, prosperous, powerful, and free. In 1797, however, Napoleon destroyed its independence.

On the espousing of the everlasting sea, and for a characteristically different treatment of the whole subject, see Byron's *Childe Harold,* Canto IV; *Anth.,* p. 569.

222. LONDON, 1802

This sonnet, and the next two, carry a message of the highest importance to any nation threatened, like our own, by the temptations of prosperity. "This was written immediately after my return from France to London, when I could not but be struck, as here described, with the vanity and parade of our own country, especially in great towns and cities, as contrasted with the quiet, and I may say the desolation, that the revolution had produced in France. This must be borne in mind, or else the reader may think that in this and the succeeding sonnets I have exaggerated the mischief engendered and fostered among us by undisturbed wealth" (Wordsworth).

222a. 1. To Milton, Wordsworth was bound by a common love of liberty, and by addiction to the simple life and to the studious. His enthusiasm for his great predecessor was already strong in his college days; see *The Prelude,* III, 283 ff.

14. *the lowliest duties:* For many years, obedient to a sense of citizenship, Milton rendered political and literary services to the cause of the Puritan Commonwealth, as pamphleteer and as secretary of state.

DISC.—Brooks and Warren, *Approach to Literature,* pp. 496-498, in what has been called "a heavy-handed treatment," say this poem is poorly organized. Is it? See EXP., Dec., 1942; Apr., 1944.

222. NEAR DOVER

222b. 12-13. The antecedents of "themselves" and "them" are "winds" and "waters."

222. WRITTEN IN LONDON

222b. 1. *friend:* Coleridge.

223a. 13. *our fearful innocence:* our innocence full of awe and reverence.

14. *pure religion breathing household laws:* "breathing" is an example of Wordsworth's remarkable gift for choosing exactly the right word. He means, as De Quincey says (*On Christianity*) "not *teaching* such laws, not formally *prescribing* a new economy of life, so much as *inspiring* it indirectly through a new atmosphere surrounding all objects with new attributes."

223. COMPOSED UPON WESTMINSTER BRIDGE

To be borne in mind whenever we think of Wordsworth as a poet only of nature and of moral being. The majesty of a great city about to awaken into life has never been more beautifully expressed. "To Wordsworth," says Walter Bagehot, "has been vouchsafed the last grace of the self-denying artist: you think neither of him nor of his style, but you cannot help thinking of—you must recall—the exact phrase, the very sentiment he wished" (*Pure, Ornate, and Grotesque Art*).

Earl Wasserman has discovered a sonnet, "On the Prospect from Westminster Bridge, March, 1750," in Elizabeth Tollet's *Poems on Several Occasions,* 1755, a prosy performance.

223. IT IS A BEAUTEOUS EVENING

223a. 9. *Dear Child!:* Caroline, the natural daughter of Wordsworth and Annette Vallon. See Carl J. Weber, "Thanks to the Censor," *On Wordsworth's Birthday,* Waterville, Maine; 1932.

223. GREAT MEN HAVE BEEN AMONG US

223b. 3. *Sidney,* etc.: Algernon Sidney, Andrew Marvell, James Harrington, and Sir Richard Vane, heroes in the struggle to establish the Puritan Commonwealth, and admired by Wordsworth also for their unselfishness.

223. TO THE DAISY

Not the daisy we know best, *chrysanthemum leucanthemum,* but *bellis perennis,* a little white or pinkish blossom that hugs the English turf, and is called the day's eye because it closes at dusk and opens at dawn,—the daisy of Chaucer, Shakespeare, and Burns (wee, modest, crimson-tippit flower; *Anth.,* p. 87). See the passable illustration in "The World in Your Garden," *Nat. Geog. Mag.,* July, 1947, p. 18.

225a. 23. *apostolical:* Some critics objected that to call a daisy apostolical was "little less than profane." Wordsworth replied: "The word is adopted with reference to its derivation, implying something sent on a mission; and assuredly this little flower, especially when the subject of verse, may be regarded in its humble degree, as administering both to moral and to spiritual purposes."

225. TO THE CUCKOO

Wordsworth's favorite among his shorter poems.—In the course of a discussion of the functions of the imagination, in his preface to the 1815 edition of his poems, Wordsworth comments on ll. 3 and 4 as follows: "This concise interrogation characterises the seeming ubiquity of the voice of the cuckoo, and dispossesses the creature almost of a corporeal existence,— the Imagination being tempted to this exertion of her power by a consciousness in the memory that the cuckoo is almost perpetually heard through the season of spring, but seldom becomes an object of sight."

"This poem has an exultation and a glory, joined with an exquisiteness of expression, which place it in the highest rank among the many masterpieces of its illustrious author." Francis Turner Palgrave.

225. THE GREEN LINNET

"What can be more accurate yet more lovely than the two concluding stanzas?" (Coleridge).

DISC.—Compare Robert Bridges' *I Heard a Linnet Courting,* and Walter De La Mare's *The Linnet.*

226. YARROW UNVISITED

This poem, as well as "To a Highland Girl," "The Solitary Reaper," "She Was a Phantom of Delight," and "The Grave of Burns," were memorials of a tour in Scotland.

226a. 17. *Galla Water, Leader Haughs:* The Galla and the Leader are streams not far from Sir Walter Scott's Abbotsford. Haughs, like holms (l. 33), are riverside meadows, often submerged.

20. *lintwhites:* linnets.

226b. 37. *Strath:* valley.

43. *The swan:* Sir Walter Scott wrote to Wordsworth: "I like your swan upon St. Mary's Lake. How came you to know that it is actually frequented by that superb bird?" Subsequently Sir Walter misquoted the passage as "swans," which distressed Wordsworth, who wished to convey a sense of utter loneliness. "It was for that reason," says Wordsworth, "that I recorded the swan and its shadow. Had there been many swans and many shadows, they would have implied nothing as regards the character of that place." Observe that it is fidelity to the essential character of the object that Wordsworth desires.

TO A HIGHLAND GIRL

Dorothy Wordsworth, in *Recollections of a Tour Made in Scotland* (Aug. 28, 1803) relates the origin of this poem as follows: "When beginning to descend the hill toward Loch Lomond, we overtook two girls, who told us we could not cross the ferry till evening, for the boat was gone with a number of people to church. One of the girls was exceedingly beautiful; and the figures of both of them, in gray plaids falling to their feet, their faces only being uncovered, excited our attention before we spoke to them; but they answered us so sweetly that we were quite delighted, at the same time that they stared at us with an innocent look of wonder. I think I never heard the English language sound more sweetly than from the mouth of the elder of these girls, while she stood at the gate answering our inquiries, her face flushed with the rain; her pronunciation was clear and distinct: without difficulty, yet slow, like that of a foreign speech. They told us we might sit in the ferry-house till the return of the boat, went in with us, and made a good fire as fast as possible to dry our wet clothes. We learnt that the taller was the sister of the ferryman, and had been left in charge with the house for the day, that the other was his wife's sister, and was come with her mother on a visit,—an old woman, who sate in a corner beside the cradle, nursing her little grand-child. We were glad to be housed, with our feet upon a warm hearth-stone; and our attendants were so active and good-humored that it was pleasant to have to desire them to do anything. The younger was a delicate and unhealthy-looking girl; but there was an uncommon meekness in her countenance, with an air of premature intelligence, which is often seen in sickly young persons. The other made me think of Peter Bell's Highland Girl:

'As light and beauteous as a squirrel,
As beautous and as wild.'
(Wordsworth's *Peter Bell*, 889-890)

She moved with unusual activity, which was chastened very delicately by a certain hesitation in her looks when she spoke, being able to understand us but imperfectly. . . .

"The hospitality we had met with . . . gave us very favorable impressions on this our first entrance into the Highlands, and at this day the innocent merriment of the girls, with their kindness to us, and the beautiful figure and face of the elder, come to my mind whenever I think of the ferry-house and waterfall of Loch Lomond, and I never think of the two girls but the whole image of that romantic spot is before me, a living image, as it will be to my dying day."

Observe that what Wordsworth emphasizes in his characterization is the absence of artificiality and embarrassed self-consciousness, and the presence of spontaneity, kindliness, home-bred sense, and independence.

227. ## THE SOLITARY REAPER

Partly from Wordsworth's own experience, and partly from that of Thomas Wilkinson, who had written in his *Tour of Scotland:* "Passed a female who was reaping alone; she sung in Erse, as she bended over her sickle; the sweetest human voice I ever heard: her strains were tenderly melancholy, and felt delicious, long after they were heard no more." Note that the final phrase is almost literally quoted in the last line of the poem.

227. ## THE AFFLICTION OF MARGARET

"This was taken," says Wordsworth, "from the case of a poor widow who lived in the town of Penrith. Her sorrow was well known to Mrs. Wordsworth, to my sister, and, I believe, to the whole town. She kept a shop, and when she saw a stranger passing by, she was in the habit of going out into the street to enquire of him after her son."

228. SHE WAS A PHANTOM OF DELIGHT

At once a tribute to Wordsworth's wife, Mary Hutchinson, and his characterization of ideal womanhood. The word "machine" (l. 22) was not as prosaic in 1804 as it has become.—Well interpreted in EXP, Dec., 1944.

228. I WANDERED LONELY AS A CLOUD

"Written at Town-end, Grasmere. The daffodils grew and still grow on the margin of Ullswater, and probably may be seen to this day as beautiful in the month of March, nodding their golden heads beside the dancing and foaming waves" (Wordsworth).

"When we were in the woods beyond Gowbarrow Park we saw a few daffodils close to the water-side. . . . As we went along there were more, and yet more; and, at last, under the boughs of the trees, we saw there was a long belt of them along the shore. . . . I never saw daffodils so beautiful. They grew among the mossy stones, about and about them; some rested their heads on these stones as on a pillow for weariness; and the rest tossed, and reeled, and danced, and seemed as if they verily laughed with the wind that blew upon them over the lake. They looked so gay, ever glancing, ever changing. . . . There was here and there a little knot, and a few stragglers higher up; but they were so few as not to disturb the simplicity, unity, and life of that one busy highway." Dorothy Wordsworth, *Journal*, April 15, 1802.

"In Scotland it is possible to find some countryman bred to the land, broad and harsh in his use of the Doric, who will softly recite 'I wandered lonely as a cloud' " (TLS, July 20, 1946).

229. 21-22. Mrs. Wordsworth wrote these lines.

229. STEPPING WESTWARD

"I cannot describe how affecting this simple expression was in that remote place, with the western sky in front, yet glowing with the departed sun" (Dorothy Wordsworth, *Tour*, Sept. 11, 1803).

DISC.—The poems of the Highland tour should be considered together, especially the ways in which they illustrate the Wordsworthian association of the simplest life in wild and beautiful regions with the highest hopes of man and with his relation to eternity ("Our destiny is with infinitude," *Prelude*, VI, 605). See the admirable appreciation in Beach, *Rom. View*, pp. 71-75.

On the personal side, discuss Beach's remark: "A circumstance out of which Shelley would have developed an *Epipsychidion*, and Byron a *Maid of Athens* and an *affaire du coeur*, was used by Wordsworth merely to add the human note to a set of associations forever dear to him on other grounds than those supplied by Eros." The poems to be compared are in *Anth.*, pp. 528 and 948.

229. FIDELITY

DISC.—Compare with Byron's *Inscription on the Monument of a Newfoundland Dog; Anth.*, p. 527.

230. ODE TO DUTY

The motto: "What urges me on now is not so much good counsel as habit; so that my condition is not that I am able to do right, but rather that I am unable to do wrong."

"The ode is on the model of Gray's *Ode to Adversity*, which is copied from Horace's *Ode to Fortune*" (Wordsworth).

N. P. Stallknecht (*Strange Seas*) stresses the influence of Kant and Schiller's ideas of duty; Jane Worthington (*Reading of Roman Prose*), the influence of the Stoics.

231. 40. After this line, the 1807 edition contained the following stanza, which Wordsworth did not include in later editions:

> Yet not the less would I throughout
> Still act according to the voice
> Of my own wish; and feel past doubt
> That my submissiveness was choice:
> Not seeking in the school of pride
> For 'precepts over dignified',
> Denial and restraint I prize
> No farther than they breed a second Will more wise.

Whether this was withdrawn because of the substance or the style is not known.

231. 45. *Flowers laugh before thee:* Edith Batho likens "the great declaration" in the rest of this stanza with Dante's faith that Love moves the sun and stars in their courses.

DISC.—Is Wordsworth's attitude toward man's freedom different in the *Ode to Duty* and *The Prelude?* Stallknecht (*Strange Seas*, VII and VIII) believes he had more confidence in man's ability to make his own moral decisions in *The Prelude* than he had in the *Ode*.

231.   ELEGIAC STANZAS

Sir George Beaumont was a landscape painter.—See Martha H. Shackford, *Wordsworth's Interest in Painters and Pictures*, 1945.

231a. 15. *The light that never was:* In this passage Wordsworth renounces art which is merely idyllic .

231b. 39. *my loss:* His brother, Capt. John Wordsworth, had recently been drowned at sea. "His grief turned him towards the Christian faith in the form it was familiar to him" (Batho, *Later Wordsworth*, p. 276).

232.   ODE: INTIMATIONS OF IMMORTALITY

De Selincourt holds that it "seems to have been finished by March, 1804" (TLS, May 9, 1942).

As this celebrated ode expresses a complex train of thoughts and feelings, its entire course should be followed before its details are examined. It passes through three phases: (1) the perception that in youth the universe has a freshness and glory which later fades (stanzas I-IV); (2) a suggestion that this childish intuition of the divine and the immortal may be explained by the pre-existence of the soul (stanzas V-VIII); and (3) the assertion of a reconciling faith that the loss of the childish vision is recompensed for by the love and wisdom attainable in maturity (stanzas IX-XI). The second movement in this succession of ideas has received, partly because of its supposedly heretical nature, more attention than the others. That the conclusion to which Wordsworth comes at the end is the most important part of the poem is insisted upon by Arthur Beatty (*William Wordsworth: His Doctrine and Art*, 2nd ed., 1927).

In the following passage Wordsworth himself asserts his firm belief in the truth of what may be called the child-psychology of the first part of the ode, and protests that he did not intend to be prosaically dogmatic about the theory of pre-existence suggested in the second:

"This was composed during my residence at Town-end, Grasmere. Two years at least passed between the writing of the four first stanzas and the remaining part. To the attentive and competent reader the whole sufficiently explains itself; but there may be no harm in adverting here to particular feelings or *experiences* of my own mind on which the structure of the poem partly rests. Nothing was more difficult for me in childhood than to admit the notion of death as a state applicable to my own being. I have said elsewhere:—

> 'A simple child,
> That lightly draws its breath,
> And feels its life in every limb,
> What should it know of death?'
> (*We Are Seven*, 1-4)

But it was not so much from feelings of animal vivacity that *my* difficulty came as from a sense of the indomitableness of the spirit within me. I used to brood over the stories of Enoch and Elijah, and almost to persuade myself that, whatever might become of others, I should be translated, in something of the same way, to heaven. With a feeling congenial to this, I was often unable to think of external things as having external existence, and I communed with all that I saw as something not apart from, but inherent in. my own immaterial nature. Many times while going to school have I grasped at a wall or tree to recall myself from this abyss of idealism to the reality. At that time I was afraid of such processes. In later periods of life I have deplored, as we have all reason to do, a subjugation of an opposite character, and have rejoiced over the remembrances, as is expressed in the lines—

> 'Obstinate questionings
> Of sense and outward things,
> Fallings from us, vanishings': etc.

To that dream-like vividness and splendor which invest objects of sight in childhood, every one, I believe, if he would look back, could bear testimony, and I need not dwell upon it here: but having in the poem regarded it as presumptive evidence of a prior state of existence, I think it right to protest against a conclusion, which has given pain to some good and pious persons, that I meant to inculcate such a belief. It is far too shadowy a notion to be recommended to faith, as more than an element in our instincts of immortality. But let us bear in mind that, though the idea is not advanced in revelation, there is nothing there to contradict it, and the fall of man presents an analogy in its favor. Accordingly, a pre-existent state has entered into the popular creeds of many nations; and, among all persons acquainted with classic literature, is known as an ingredient in Platonic philosophy. Archimedes said that he could move the world if he had a point whereon to rest his machine. Who has not felt the same aspirations as regards the world of his own mind? Having to wield some of its elements when I was impelled to write this poem on the Immortality of the Soul, I took hold of the notion of pre-existence as having sufficient foundation in humanity for authorizing me to make for my purpose the best use of it I could as a poet."

The notion of pre-existence, i.e., of descent from Heaven and of gradual forgetfulness, is Neo-Platonic and is found in a well-known chapter in the fifth-century philosopher Proclus, a chapter already drawn upon by the poet Vaughan in *The Retreat*, and one which Coleridge may have called to Wordsworth's attention. In any case, conversations with Coleridge were influential upon the *Ode* (see J. D. Rea, "Coleridge's Intimations of Immortality," MP, XXVI, 201; 1928). It should be noted, however, that by 1817 Coleridge is protesting against Wordsworth's terming "a six years' darling" "thou best philosopher" (*Biog. Lit.*, ch. 22; *Anth.*, p. 361).— Emerson regarded the *Ode* as "the high-water mark which the intellect has reached in this age."

Modern criticism of the *Ode* is at least a hundred times as long as the *Ode* itself. In much of it, the above statements by Wordsworth about poetic license are prosaically ignored. The child's intuitions of eternality make him to the imaginative mind a witness, or an immortality-symbol. In trying to understand Wordsworth's religion as a whole, and the relation of his psychology of childhood thereto, *The Prelude*, as critics sometimes forget, is more important than the *Ode*, which cannot carry alone all the weight which some interpreters place upon it.— In studying the modern criticism, it is best to begin with the clear explication by Lionel Trilling in the *English Institute Annual: 1941;* and thereafter read Stallknecht, *Strange Seas*, Appendix to ch. 5; H. I'A, Fausset, *Proving of Psyche* (1929), p. 178; G. Knight Wilson, *Christian Renaissance* (1933), pp. 69 and 265; Herbert Hartman, "The Intimations," RES, VI, 129-148 (1930); D. A. Stauffer, "Cooperative Criticism," *Kenyon Review*, IV, 133-144 (1942); and Cleanth Brooks, "The Intimations," *Kenyon Review*, VIII, 80-102 (1946) and in *The Well Wrought Urn* (1947).

232. 23. *A timely utterance:* It is likely that this utterance was *Resolution and Independence* (Trilling).
28. *the fields of sleep:* probably "the fields where the winds slept," although an allusion to the subconscious was suspected by Dowden.
56. *visionary gleam:* This does not refer to the poetic or creative power, but to the bright recollections with which we come into the world, and to the nonobjective way in which a child regards his world. See *The Prelude*, II, 232 ff. (*Anth.*, p. 247), and *Elegiac Stanzas: Peele Castle*, 15-16 (p. 231).
58. *Our birth is but a sleep and a forgetting:* Compare Plato (*Phaedo*): "Your favorite doctrine, Socrates, that knowledge is simply recollection, if true, also necessarily implies a previous time in which we learned that which now we recollect. But this would be impossible unless our soul was in some place before existing in the human form; here then is another argument of the soul's immortality." See J. G. Fraser, *The Magic Art*, I, 104.

233. **88.** *fretted:* not "irritated by," but "chequered" Elisabeth Schneider, EXP, Feb., 1947).

145. *not realized:* not yet truly made real, not yet poetically perceived and manifested.

151. *the fountain-light:* the positive intuition of Being, of eternity, of our relation to the World-Soul (Stallknecht).

234. **181.** *the primal sympathy:* the sense of a filial bond, of a mind fitted to the Universe, which still remains in maturity, though not as constantly as in childhood, because in maturity we are also bound to our finite earthly existence (Trilling).

186. *the philosophic mind:* this is not opposed to the poetic function, but includes it (Trilling).

DISC.—The relation between the *Ode, Tintern Abbey, Elegiac Stanzas,* and the passage referred to above from *The Prelude.*

The contrast between the *Ode* and Coleridge's *Dejection: An Ode (Anth.,* p. 177).

234. CHARACTER OF THE HAPPY WARRIOR

Admirable traits in Wordsworth's brother, and in his French friend Beaupuy, contributed to this study. He would have alluded to Nelson, if the affair with Lady Hamilton had not shown too great a flaw in that hero.

235. PERSONAL TALK

236a. **51-54.** These lines are inscribed on the pedestal of the statue of Wordsworth in Westminster Abbey.

236. THE WORLD IS TOO MUCH WITH US

236b. **4.** *a sordid boon:* Our hearts are the boon, or gift; but it is what we get in exchange for them that is sordid.

10. *A Pagan,* etc.: Almost any kind of religion is better than materialism; see *The Excursion,* IV, "Superstition better than Apathy." Proteus and Triton were Greek sea gods. "The suggestion is from Proclus, the phrasing in part from Spenser and Milton (Rea, MP, XXVI, 211). On the balance of the images in the octave and sestet, see EXP, Oct., 1942.

236. SUBJUGATION OF SWITZERLAND

Wordsworth thought this his best sonnet. The "two voices" are those of Great Britain and Switzerland. At this time Napoleon was making ready to cross the Channel.

237. FROM THE ITALIAN OF MICHAEL ANGELO

Michael Angelo (1475-1564), the superb sculptor, painter, poet, and "universal man" of the Renaissance, whose power, intensity, and "terribilita" Blake adored, appealed to Wordsworth as one of the most religious men in a dissolute age, a Christian Platonist who regarded true love, virtue, earthly beauty, and artistic genius as inspirations from God. Michael Angelo's sonnets of Platonic love, of which Wordsworth translated five, were addressed to the illustrious poet Vittoria Colonna, and glorified the kind of love which transcends time and mutability.

DISC.—Compare with Landor's *Pentameron; Anth.,* p. 511.

Blake particularly admired the second of these sonnets.

238. SONG AT THE FEAST OF BROUGHAM CASTLE

DISC.—Contrast Lord Clifford with the heroes of Scott's lays.

The Cliffords were a noble family of the Westmoreland region. The action takes place during the War of the Roses (1455-1485), and the main facts about the Shepherd-Lord are historical.

240. YEW TREES

An evergreen (*Taxus baccata*) with rich lustrous foliage, its strong wood used for the bows which won English victories in the battles named in the poem. The only American relative is a shrub, *Taxus canadensis*, miscalled the ground hemlock. The yew was revered in Britain from heathen times; see Vaughan Cornish, *The Churchyard Yew and Immortality* (1946).

240. THE CONVENTION OF CINTRA

Napoleon had conquered the Spanish Peninsula; but aided by a British army under Sir Arthur Wellesley (later the Duke of Wellington), the Spaniards and Portuguese had defeated a French army. By the Convention, or Agreement, of Cintra, August 30, 1808, however, this army was permitted to return to France with its equipment—a concession which seemed to Wordsworth a betrayal of the great cause of national independence. In the passage here selected from his tract, he insists that to the humblest citizen national independence is an even greater boon than peace and prosperity. In his sonnet, "I dropped my pen," he said that he feared his tract would pass as unregarded as the wind; but, with his patriotic sonnets, it became of outstanding importance in the literature of democracy and nationalism.—See A. V. Dicey's edition, 1915, and his *The Statesmanship of Wordsworth*, 1917; also J. E. Wells, "Story of Wordsworth's 'Cintra'," SP, XVIII, 15-76 (1921), and "Wordsworth and De Quincey," PMLA, LV, 1080-1128 (1940).—Note that the justification of patriotism is not racial but psychological and ethical.

242. THE PRELUDE: OR, GROWTH OF A POET'S MIND

The stages through which this poetical autobiography passed are shown in the admirable edition by Professor Ernest De Selincourt (Oxford, Clarendon Press, 1926). It was intended to be the introduction to a long poem, *The Recluse*, of which only the second part, *The Excursion*, was actually completed.

"Several years ago, when the author retired to his native mountains with the hope of being enabled to construct a literary work that might live, it was a reasonable thing that he should take a review of his own mind, and examine how far nature and education had qualified him for such an employment. As subsidiary to this preparation, he undertook to record, in verse, the origin and progress of his own powers, as far as he was acquainted with them. That work, addressed to a dear friend, most distinguished for his knowledge and genius, and to whom the author's intellect is deeply indebted, has been long finished; and the result of the investigation which gave rise to it, was a determination to compose a philosophical poem, containing views of man, nature, and society, and to be entitled *The Recluse*; as having for its principal subject the sensations and opinions of a poet living in retirement.

"The preparatory poem is biographical, and conducts the history of the author's mind to the point when he was emboldened to hope that his faculties were sufficiently matured for entering upon the arduous labor which he had proposed to himself; and the two works have the same kind of relation to each other, if he may so express himself, as the antechapel has to the body of a Gothic church. Continuing this allusion, he may be permitted to add, that his minor pieces, which have been long before the public, when they shall be properly arranged, will be found by the attentive reader to have such connection with the main work as may give them claim to be likened to the little cells, oratories, and sepulchral recesses, ordinarily included in those edifices. . . . The friend to whom the present poem is addressed was the late Samuel Taylor Coleridge" (Wordsworth).

See Coleridge's poem, *To William Wordsworth*, "composed on the night after his recitation" of parts of *The Prelude; Anth.*, pp. 181-183:

> A song divine of high and passionate thoughts
> To their own music chaunted!

By many critics *The Prelude* is regarded as the greatest English poem of the nineteenth century.

Basically important, besides De Selincourt's notes in his edition, is R. D. Havens' learned explication, *The Mind of a Poet* (1941). See also: D. H. Bishop, "The Origin of 'The Prelude'," SP, XXXVIII, 494-520 (1941); Mary E. Burton, "How Wordsworth Changed the Diction," CE, Oct., 1941; and Francis Christensen, "Creative Sensibility in Wordsworth," JEGP, XLV, 361-368 (1946).

243b. 371. *far above:* Probably should read "for above."

244a. 401. *Wisdom and Spirit:* The following 63 lines are a slightly changed version of those composed in 1799, and published in 1809, with the significant title, "Influence of Natural Objects in Calling Forth and Strengthening the Imagination in Boyhood and Early Youth."

246a. 615. *breath of spring:* Probably should read "birth of spring."

247. 232-272. *the infant babe,* etc.: the basic importance of this passage, describing the rise of infant sensibility and its relation to the "poetic spirit of our human life," is stressed by Trilling, "Ode: Intimations," *Engl. Inst. Annual: 1941;* and by Christensen, "Creative Sensibility," JEGP, XLV, 361; 1946.

249b. 432. *these times of fear:* The aftermath of the French Revolution. Coleridge wrote to Wordsworth in 1799: "I wish you would write a poem, in blank verse, addressed to those who, in consequence of the complete failure of the French Revolution, have thrown up all hopes of the amelioration of mankind, and are sinking into an almost epicurean selfishness, disguising the same under the soft titles of domestic attachment and contempt for visionary *philosophers.* It would do a great good, and might form a part of the *Recluse."*

250a. 46. *Evangelist St. John:* Wordsworth's college was St. John's, Cambridge University.
53. *Trinity:* Another of the Cambridge colleges.

250b. 106. *I looked for universal things:* "He sought the one behind the many, the real behind the appearance, the abiding behind the flux, the eternal behind the transitory, the changeless behind the mutable, the perfect behind the incomplete" (Havens, p. 2).

251. 127-132. "In so far as he felt there is no dead matter he is in accord with the scientific thought of today" (Havens, p. 344).

253b. 337. *A dedicated spirit:* Edith Batho (*Later Wordsworth,* p. 308) considers this a *religious* conversion. Compare Carlyle's experience of the Everlasting Yea; *Anth.,* p. 1051.

254b. 373. *mimic hootings:* See the note on *There Was A Boy,* p. 194.

255a. 479. *golden store of books:* His father encouraged his wide reading in poetry, and Wordsworth also read much of the best eighteenth-century fiction.

256b. 593. *incompetence of human speech:* A glance at semantics, the science of meanings, today so anxiously studied.

257a. 621-640. See the excellent appreciation of this passage in Beach, *Rom. View,* pp. 9-10,— "This ethereal flight of the abstracting mind." **DISC.**—Compare Shelley's *Mont Blanc, Anth.,* p. 864.

259b. 77. *Gehol:* Jehol, in Mongolia, summer residence of Chinese emperors.

260a. 139. *Arden:* In *As You Like It.*
142. *Perdita and Florizel:* In *The Winter's Tale,* IV, 4.

260b. 144. *Spenser:* In *The Shepherd's Calendar.*—Throughout this passage the contrast is between the imaginary shepherds of pastoral poetry and the real shepherds Wordsworth knew.

261a. 211. *Goslar:* In Germany, in the Hartz mountain region (hence *Hercynian,* l. 215).

262b. 349. *two-and-twenty:* i.e., in 1791-1792, when Wordsworth became interested in humanitarian movements (ed. De Selincourt, pp. 561-562).

264b. 485. *In the midst stood Man,* etc.: **DISC.**—Compare with two other famous characterizations: *Hamlet,* II, II, 316; and Pope's *Essay on Man,* Epistle II.

265b. 562. *den:* a cave in Yorkshire.

267a. 77. *arguments of civil polity:* e.g., William Godwin's.

267b. 108. *Bliss was it,* etc.: This great passage was quoted in the *London Times Lit. Suppl.,* Mch. 8, 1947, in an editorial "The Call To A New Britain."

275a. 164. *Be this ascribed:* "this" refers to his own habitual effort to avoid worldliness and meanness.

DISC.—Consider the significance of the fact that one of the most important romantic works is an autobiography.

Do you find that *The Prelude* follows these stages of growth: "first the age of sensation, or childhood; then the age of simple ideas, or youth; and finally the age of complex ideas, or maturity"? (Herbert Read).

Vladimir Mayakovsky, Soviet poet, in his autobiography *I Myself*, boldly says: "I am a poet. That is what makes me interesting. That is what I am writing about." Would Wordsworth endorse that sentiment? Is a poet a being essentially different from typical Man? Or is he typical Man fully developed?

Is the omission of the Annette Vallon affair justifiable?

277.   THE RECLUSE

"The best single key to Wordsworth's life-work" (G. Wilson Knight, *Starlit Dome*, p. 1). A summary of his message, reminding us of its broad scope and its profundity.

277b. 23. *fit audience:* From Milton, *Paradise Lost*, VII, 31.

278a. 86. *metropolitan:* of the mother church, i.e., supreme.

278.   THE EXCURSION

The theme is: What causes despondency, and by what means,—nature, religion, etc.,—it may be overcome. In discussing it, truisms are unavoidable; but, as Coleridge says, in *The Excursion* they arise not because the poet thoughtlessly accepted second-hand assertions, but because he had become convinced through "the joint operation of his own experience, feelings, and reason" that certain old truths were important which had been too much taken for granted or ignored.

Two of the chief characters, besides the Author, are the contemplative Wanderer, a pedlar by trade (a fact derided by the anti-Romantics), and the Solitary, who is melancholy because he is disappointed and disgusted by the outcome of the French Revolution. In the last two of the nine books Wordsworth deplores the degradation of the common people by the Industrial Revolution, but holds out the hope of betterment through educational and humanitarian reforms. In the first book the character of the Wanderer is revealed through his attitude toward the pathetic experiences of Margaret. Parts of this Ruined Cottage episode were composed years earlier than the rest of *The Excursion;* and their importance in the poet's development is stressed by G. W. Meyer (*Formative Years*, p. 220 ff.), who thinks they show, in place of the "crude juxtaposing" in *The Borderers* of social sympathy and philosophical love of nature a "really characteristic synthesis" of the two.

285b. 296. *Despondency Corrected:* The lines 296-331 were a favorite quotation of John Stuart Mill when he was troubled by the presence in liberal ranks of too many "half-honest men, and men of feeble purposes." They should be recalled whenever the enemies of freedom and democracy seem more efficient and better organized than their defenders.

286a. 324-331. Quoted from the Elizabethan poet, Samuel Daniel, whose style is astonishingly modern.

287a. 1139. *Murmurings:* If the child supposes that they are stored up sounds of the sea, he is mistaken; but it is a legitimate poetic metaphor to introduce the sublime line "Authentic tidings of invisible things."

288.   LAODAMIA

In interpreting this classical legend, Wordsworth says, "I wrote with the hope of giving it a loftier tone than, so far as I know, has been given to it by any of the ancients who have treated of it. It cost me more trouble than almost anything of equal length I have ever written."

Protesilaus was the first of the Greeks slain at Troy. His wife Laodamia died of excessive grief. Virgil placed her in the dismal fields of mourning, with Phaedra, Dido, etc. (*Aeneid*, VI, 441-448).

To deal with excessive love in a spirit combining justice and mercy is almost impossible; and neither Wordsworth nor his critics found it easy to determine what Laodamia's ultimate fate ought to have been. Wordsworth wrote two different versions of lines 158-163, one gentler, and the other even sterner, before he settled on the present one. In the 1815 and 1820 editions, the lines read:

> Ah, judge her gently who so deeply loved!
> Her, who, in reason's spite, yet without crime,
> Was in a trance of passion thus removed;

> Delivered from the galling yoke of time
> And these frail elements—to gather flowers
> Of blissful quiet 'mid unfading bowers.

In 1827 the severest of the three judgments was passed:

> By no weak pity might the Gods be moved;
> She who thus perished not without the crime
> Of lovers that in Reason's spite have loved,
> Was doomed to wander in a grosser clime
> Apart from happy ghosts—that gather flowers
> Of blissful quiet 'mid unfading bowers.

In explanation of this severity, Wordsworth in 1831 wrote: "As first written, the heroine was dismissed to happiness in Elysium. To what purpose then the mission of Protesilaus? He exhorts her to moderate her passion; the exhortation is fruitless, and no punishment follows. So it stood: at present she is placed among the unhappy ghosts for disregard of that exhortation. Virgil also places her there."

He changed his mind again, and the present version was the result. It is gentler towards Laodamia than the previous version; but it does not retract Wordsworth's main point: "Her error was not merely that she clung passionately to earthly love, which was now forbidden by divine decree, but that she failed to lift up her heart to a higher object."

DISC.—The debatable issue is presented in its clearest form by Stallknecht (*Strange Seas*, pp. 22, 26, 227, 235), who calls the ethics of *Laodamia* "authoritarian and traditional" and maintains that Wordsworth in this poem, the *Ode to Duty*, and others of his later years, had ceased to be "the great prophet of romantic individualism" that he was in *The Prelude* and *The Recluse*. The question is whether these attitudes are reconcilable. Do the crucial lines 74-76 contradict Wordsworth's earlier work?

E. B. Hungerford, *Shores of Darkness* (1941), p. 103, rebukes Wordsworth for not revealing how lustful the classical sources showed Laodamia.—See also, for more important general principles, Douglas Bush, "Wordsworth and the Classics," *Toronto Univ. Quart.* (1933), pp. 359-379.

288b. 19. *Hermes:* the Greek name of Mercury.

289a. 65. *Parcæ threw a Stygian hue:* the Fates cast the hue of death.
71. *Erebus:* the region of darkness through which the soul passed to Hades.
81. *Alcestis:* She had offered to die in place of her king (Euripides' tragedy).

289b. 83. *Medea:* In Ovid's *Metamorphoses,* she rejuvenated by magic the aged Aeson.

290a. 120. *enchained:* becalmed because Agamemnon had offended the goddess Diana.

290b. 73. *summits withered:* This legend is in Livy, *Nat. Hist.*, XVI, 44. "The incident," says Wordsworth, "of the trees growing and withering put the subject into my thoughts."— See C. L. Shaver, "Wordsworth's Adaptation of Pliny," MLN, LXI, 400; 1946.

290. WEAK IS THE WILL OF MAN

May be regarded as Wordsworth's answer to Byronic despair. Note that hope is based on imagination, because he believes that imagination reveals truth.

291. SURPRISED BY JOY

"Suggested by (remembrance of) my daughter Catherine, long after her death" (Wordsworth).

291. DION

From Plutarch's *Life of Dion*, who compares him with Marcus Brutus. But the characterization of Dion is Wordsworth's own, and even more so the ethical judgment. Dion (408-353 B. C.) had noble Platonic ideals, and wished to establish liberty and justice in Syracuse; but he was persuaded to allow foul means, the murder of an unscrupulous opponent, to be used for attaining good ends; hence his tragic failure.

DISC.—The use of bad means for good ends in modern politics.

292. COMPOSED UPON AN EVENING OF EXTRAORDINARY SPLENDOR

DISC.—Do you think that this poem, and those that follow, show a serious falling off in Wordsworth's poetic powers, as some critics do?

293. AFTER-THOUGHT

Beach (*Rom. View*, p. 38) comments on the last line: "Was anything profounder ever uttered by philosopher, any statement more moving ever framed by poet, on the subject of man's fate, 'la condition humaine'? And how utterly romantic! How uncongenial to the taste of those whose stern motto is, 'We know we should be stricter than we feel.' "

294. MUTABILITY

Persons unfamiliar with the Prayer Book have wondered why Wordsworth, in a series of sonnets celebrating rites and ceremonies, should introduce the idea of change; but the Prayer Book itself in at least three places admits the need of revision from age to age of external forms (Edith Batho, *Later Wordsworth*, pp. 242-244).

294. INSIDE OF KING'S COLLEGE CHAPEL

St. Peter's in Rome awed him even more than the Coliseum and the Pantheon.

295. TO A SKYLARK

DISC.—Compare with Shelley's *To A Skylark*, Anth., p. 941.

295. SCORN NOT THE SONNET

295a. 4. *wound:* May refer to the hopelessness of Petrarch's love for Laura, or to his grief at her death.
6. *Camoens:* Portuguese poet (1524-1580), banished from Lisbon because of his beloved, after whose death he wrote elegiac sonnets.

296. ON THE POWER OF SOUND

Before reading this poem try to imagine what a poet might say on the subject.—It is an almost forgotten poem; but G. Wilson Knight (*Starlit Dome*, pp. 78-81) says: "Probably his genius attains its most characteristic expression in this ode."
Wordsworth's summary: "The ear addressed, as occupied by a spiritual functionary, in communion with sounds, individual, or combined in studied harmony. Sources and effects of those sounds (to the close of 6th stanza). The power of music, whence proceeding . . . effect in early ages (to middle of 10th). Sounds acting casually. Wish that these could be united into a system for moral interests (12th). The Pythagorean theory of numbers, and their supposed power over the motions of the universe. Wish (11th) realized by the representation of all sounds under the form of thanksgiving to the Creator. (Last) the destruction of the universe, and the survival of audible harmony in the Divine Nature."

298. AT THE GRAVE OF BURNS

William and Dorothy visited the grave August 18, 1803; and repeated to each other the third stanza of Burns's *A Bard's Epitaph* (Anth., p. 89), the measure of which is here followed. Wordsworth judged the character of Burns more generously than was customary in his time, and protested against Dr. Currie's censorious *Life of Burns*.—See Russell Noyes, "Wordsworth and Burns," PMLA, LIX, 813-832; 1944.

299a. 53. *gowans:* daisies.

300. PREFACE TO THE SECOND EDITION OF "THE LYRICAL BALLADS"

The reviews of the first edition were condemnatory; as Mrs. Coleridge put it, "they are not liked at all by any." This proved fortunate for posterity, for it provoked this famous *Preface*, which, as Herbert Read says, is "probably the most careful definition of the poet's function ever made" (*The Politics of the Unpolitical*, p. 155; 1943), despite flaws due to ambiguity or exaggeration.

300b. 19. *Catullus*, etc.: The contrast, both in ancient literature and in modern, is between poets whom Wordsworth considers natural in style and those whom he considers artificial.

308a. 17. *Clarissa*, etc.: Both Richardson's novel, *Clarissa Harlowe*, and Edward Moore's tragedy, *The Gamester*, are in prose.

DISC.—After the whole *Preface* has been read, the following passages should be carefully pondered and discussed:

300b. 59. *a selection of language really used by men.*

301a. 10. *humble and rustic life chosen.*

54. *triviality and meanness:* He himself was charged with encouraging it.

302a. 32. *frantic novels*, etc.: These were just the kinds of literature that hostile critics accused the Lake School of fostering.

302a. 56 to 302b. 23. *style . . . poetic diction:* The *Appendix*, p. 310, should be considered in connection with this passage.

303b. 2. *essential difference:* None such existent between prose and verse.

304a. 43. *A poet—a man speaking to men.*

304b. 43. *the principle of selection.*

305a. 45. *immediate pleasure:* whence is the pleasure drawn?

305b. 36. *men and nature as essentially adapted to each other:* what has this faith to do with the other principles?

306a. 3. *Poetry is the breath and finer spirit of all knowledge.*

307a. 37. *Why have I written in verse?*

308b. 12. *spontaneous over flow of powerful feelings.*

14. *emotion recollected in tranquillity.*

DISC.—Point out illustrations of the above principles, or deviations from them, in Wordsworth's poems. Blake asserted they were "directly contrary to Wordsworth's own practice"; and Coleridge (see *Biog. Lit.*), in a less extreme way, saw discrepancies.

Discuss whether, as some maintain, T. S. Eliot and other poets of today, in striving to give poetry a direct relation to common speech, are progressing in the path Wordsworth recommended. See T. S. Eliot, *The Use of Poetry and the Use of Criticism*, 1933; and Henry W. Wells, *New Poets from Old*, 1940. Also, on the relation of poetry to country life, W. Kenneth Richmond, *Poetry and the People*, 1947.

312. TO LADY BEAUMONT

This perennial problem is the subject of Henri Peyre's *Writers and Their Critics: A Study of Misunderstanding* (1944); see the review in JEGP, July, 1945.

315. ESSAY, SUPPLEMENTARY

Significant as an interpretation of literary history from the point of view of the romantic school. Not always factually accurate, but especially interesting for its appreciation of the authors whom we now call the Pre-Romantics.

321b. 54. *not a single new image:* This is now known to be too broad a generalization; see the Pre-Romantic section of the *Anthology* for other passages showing appreciation of nature.

DISC.—Contrast the treatment of country-folk in Wordsworth and in Thomas Hardy's poems and novels.

Search Louis Untermeyer's *Modern American Poetry* and *Modern British Poetry* for poems which show marked relationship (either influence or reaction) to Wordsworth.

What is Wordsworthian in Robert Bridges' *Testament of Beauty*, and what is modern?

SAMUEL TAYLOR COLERIDGE—PROSE

329.   CHARACTER MORE IMPORTANT THAN POLITICS

Written in the same month as *Fears In Solitude*, *Anth.*, p. 162.

331.   THE STATESMAN'S MANUAL: SATANIC PRIDE

DISC.—Point out modern instances.

331.   BIOGRAPHIA LITERARIA

See J. M. Murry, "Coleridge's Criticism," *Aspects of Literature* (1920); Shawcross's Introduction and Notes to his edition of *Biographia Literaria* (1907); T. M. Raysor's "Coleridge's Criticism of Wordsworth," PMLA, LIV, 494-511 (1939); and H. H. Creed's "Coleridge on Taste," ELH, XIII, 143-155 (1946).

In the selections which follow, Coleridge discusses some of the literary theories set forth by Wordsworth in the *Preface* to the *Lyrical Ballads*. In that *Preface*, written about eighteen years earlier, Coleridge had been, in a way, a collaborator; for it was intended to justify their styles of poetry, and its general principles originated in their conversations together. Coleridge's attack, it is important to note, is not directed against Wordsworth's whole case, but only against certain parts thereof. If after reading Coleridge's objections, the student will mark in Wordsworth's *Preface* those parts which Coleridge disagrees with, he may be surprised at their fewness. Coleridge himself repeatedly emphasizes that his strictures are not general. He implies, moreover, that Wordsworth's practice in these respects is usually better than his theory; and in chapter 22 he holds that the defects of Wordsworth's poems are far outweighed by the excellences.

A careful comparison of Wordsworth's case with what may be called Coleridge's improvements upon it will give the student a better understanding of the nature of poetry and of the nature of criticism. Both the difficulties and the rewards of criticism,—i.e., of precise and philosophic thinking about literature,—are here illustrated brilliantly.

DISC.—The following passages should be marked, pondered, and discussed:

335b. 57-59.	338b. 32-34.	343a. 1.
336b. 3-5.	339a. 24-34.	343a. 56.
337a. 23-32.	339b. 28-34.	343b. 5.
337a. 48-54.	340a. 23-26.	344a. 44-45.
337b. 24-26.	340b. 7-16	345b. 47.
338a. 6-10.	341b. 56.	346a. 12.
338a. 19-20.	342a. 7.	351a. 25-42.
338a. 56-60.	342a. 51-59.	351a. 52-54.
338b. 13-16.	342b. 50.	353a. 1-19.

332b. 2. *the true origin:* a safer statement would have been "one of the origins."

333a. 3. *albo lapide notatae:* marked with a white stone.

47. *dulcia vitia:* seductive faults (because they were pretentious, whereas Wordsworth's were simple).

334b. 1-11. Perhaps the characteristics of Wordsworth's poetry have never been better delineated than in this sentence.

39. *vis theoretica et scientifica:* theoretical and scientific power.

335b. 58. *the language of real life:* Wordsworth's actual words are "the real language of men," and "the very language of men."

337b. 18. *Praecipitandus est liber spiritus:* Headlong should be the free spirit.

28. *Burnet:* See H. V. S. Ogden, "Thomas Burnet's 'Telluris Theoria Sacra' and Mountain Scenery," ELH, XIV, 139-150 (1947).—From Burnet was taken the Latin motto of *The Ancient Mariner*, given above in the Notes on that poem.

338a. 18. *laxis effertur habenis:* it is driven with reins relaxed.

19-20. *balance or reconciliation of opposite:* One of his basic ideas. See Alice D. Snyder, *The Reconciliation of Opposites as Employed by Coleridge* (1918).

34. *Davies:* Sir John Davies (1569-1626), philosophical poet.

339b. 49-53. To test the soundness of this opinion, apply it to Burns.

340a. 7. *Triumpatus:* Error for "Triumphatus."

340b. 7-17. This acceptance of Aristotle's *Poetics* should be borne in mind whenever it is alleged that the Romantics and the Classicists are diametrically opposed to each other.

341a. 13. Most of the poems of Wordsworth that Coleridge criticized adversely did not achieve permanent fame.

343a. 28. *real:* Perhaps if instead of "real" Wordsworth had written "natural," Coleridge would not have objected; for the latter held "it is a general but mistaken notion that because some forms of writing, and some combinations of thought, are not usual, they are not natural."

344b. 38-40. Coleridge is probably mistaken here. Wordsworth meant to restrict his denial of a difference to words. T. M. Raysor, however, believes Coleridge's interpretation correct.

347a. 3. *Smart:* Christopher Smart, one of the Pre-Romantics.

30. *Pierce Plouman:* William Langland's *Pierce Plowman* (1362).

51. Θαύματα Θαυμαστότατα: wonder of wonders.

348a. 54. *mordaunt:* connective.

349a. 13. *videlicet:* namely (viz.).

350a. 6. Dr. Johnson's parody (misquoted) of the ballad style.

27. *Daniel:* Samuel Daniel (1562-1619).

351a. 25-42. *Taste:* See Creed's article, listed above, and quoted in connection with Shakespeare below.

353b. 12-14. *Garve . . . Gellert:* Christian Garve (1742-1798), a philosopher; and the poet C. F. Gellert (1715-1769).

55. *Cotton:* Charles Cotton (1630-1687). See his *Ode to Winter.*

354a. 27. *(Correction):* The rest of this passage is from Ch. 21.

28. *an old man:* The Wanderer.—The passages from *The Excursion* alluded to are in Book I, ll. 108, 324, and 342.

49. *the critic:* The sneering critic was Jeffrey, in the *Edinburgh Review*, XXIV, 30, who asked: "Did Mr. Wordsworth really imagine that his favorite doctrines were likely to gain anything in point of effect or authority by being put into the mouth of a person accustomed to higgle about tape or brass sleeve-buttons?"

355a. 23. *On which:* Wordsworth changed this line to: "When this ill-fated traveller died."

355b. 25. *Boetius:* Boethius, Roman philosopher of the sixth century; *Barclay:* John Barclay (1582-1621), whose *Argenis* is a political romance.

42. *Metastasio:* An Italian poet (1698-1782).

356a. 31. *The shell of a green turtle:* This is quoted from the edition of 1815. In that of 1807, the boy carried "a household tub." In that of 1820, the lines became:

> A shell of ample size, and light
> As the pearly car of Amphitrite,
> That sportive dolphins drew.

42. *'Tis gone, etc.:* From the *Emigrant Mother*, composed in 1802 and published in 1807. In 1820, Wordsworth changed the passage to:

> 'Tis gone, like dreams that we forget

54. *Thou hast a nest, etc.:* From *To A Skylark*, composed in 1805 and published in 1807. In the edition of 1820 the last lines were changed to:

> Alas! my journey, rugged and uneven,
> Through prickly moors or dusty ways must wind;
> But hearing thee, or others of thy kind,
> As full of gladness and as free as heaven,
> I, with my fate contented, will plod on,
> And hope for higher raptures, when life's day is done.

356b. 10. *Close by a pond*, etc.: From *Resolution and Independence*, which see above p. 219. The first stanza that Coleridge quotes was omitted in the edition of 1820.

357a. 31. *Davenant*: Sir William Davenant (1608-1668) wrote a preface to his epic *Gondibert*, addressed to the philosopher Thomas Hobbes.

    60. *Excursion*: Book III, 50.

357b. 31. *The fig-tree: Paradise Lost*, IX, 1101.

    51. *vestigia communia*: common traces.

    53. *penna duplex*: double wing,—vision in sound, and sound in vision.

    58. *Memnon*: It was fabled that when the sun rose the statue of Memnon gave forth a sound.

358b. 16. *hysteron-proteron*: inversion of the natural order.

    33. *Antonine*: The Emperor Marcus Aurelius (121-180 A.D.).

    35. *and rejoice: The Excursion*, I, 75.

    41. *O, many: The Excursion*, I, 77.

359a. 24. *Chatterton: Resolution and Independence*, l. 42 (loosely quoted).

359b. 11. *Klopstock . . . Cumberland*: Friedrich Klopstock (1724-1803), German poet; and Richard Cumberland (1732-1811), dramatist.

    23. *analogon*: analogue, imitation.

360a. 3. *Among the hills: The Excursion*, I, 108.—In later versions, some of the particulars were stricken out.

    53. The references are to *Anecdote for Fathers*, and probably to *Song at the Feast of Brougham Castle*.

360b. 8. *Omphale*: the mistress of Hercules.

    18. *They flash*: from *I Wandered Lonely as a Cloud*.

    33. *The second instance*: from *Gipsies*.

361b. 5. *Golconda*: Near Hyderabad, India, famous for its diamonds.

    27. *Spinoza*: Jewish philosopher (1632-1677).

    27. *Behmen*: Jakob Böhme (1575-1624), German mystic.

    30. EN KAI IIAN: One and All.

    38. *Jacobi*: Friederich Jacobi (1743-1819), German philosopher.

    39. *Lessing*: Gotthold Ephraim Lessing (1729-1781), celebrated German dramatist and critic.

    48. *Gleim*: Johan Gleim (1718-1803), like the Greek Tyrtœus, a versifier successful only in war songs.

362a. 11. *To whom the grave*, etc.: Wordsworth omitted these lines in later editions.

363b. 44. *Laureate*: Southey.

364a. 1. The quotations in this column are from Wordsworth's *Star Gazers, Simon Lee*, and *Fountain*.

365a. 32. *So through*: From *Influence of Natural Objects*.

366a. 30. *add the gleam*: An unfortunate quotation, because Wordsworth in this poem on *Peele Castle* expressed his opposition to this conception of the Imagination. To him it does not *add* the gleam (though it may discover it already in the object).

367b. 24. *Bartram's Travels*: Used, as is noted above, in *The Ancient Mariner* and *Kubla Khan*. The quotation is not literally accurate, but essentially correct.

368.   THE CHARACTERISTICS OF SHAKSPEARE'S DRAMAS

See T. M. Raysor's learned edition, *Coleridge's Shakespearian Criticism*, 2 vols., 1930.—Also Roberta Morgan, "The Philosophic Basis of Coleridge's Hamlet Criticism," ELH, VI, 256-270

(1939); and H. H. Creed, "Coleridge on Taste," ELH, XIII, 143-155 (1946), from which is quoted: "The prime characteristic of the imagination is the interpretive power that shows in the external world a spiritual principle; and this faculty is at its highest in Shakspeare."

Coleridge gave public lectures on Shakspeare in 1808, 1810-1813, and 1818. His notes were published in *Literary Remains*, 1837-1839. The passage here given is probably what he said in 1818.—Coleridge is the leader in the romantic reinterpretation of Shakspeare. In this selection, the following ideas are especially characteristic:

1. that Shakspeare's wisdom and art are almost perfect (373a. 57-59)
2. that he was influenced by his age, but not dominated by it (369a. 1-5)
3. that his works have a unity, not mechanical, but organic (368b. 36-39; and 370b. 5-10)
4. that his characters are so true to human nature that they may be discussed almost as if they were real (implied in 370b. 57 ff.).

DISC.—Test Coleridge's principles by applying them to Shakspearian dramas which you know.

Compare Coleridge's interpretations with those of Lamb, *On the Tragedies of Shakspeare;* of Hazlitt, *Hamlet;* of De Quincey, *The Knocking at the Gate;* and of Carlyle, *The Hero as Poet;* all in *Anth.*, pp. 378, 402, 1018, 1054.

368b. 13. Milton had casually remarked (*Education*) that poetry was more simple, sensuous, and passionate, than logic.

36-54. This is one of the passages in which Coleridge took the substance from August Wilhelm Schlegel's *Lectures on Shakspeare* (Lecture I). The eloquence, however, is often Coleridge's own.

58. *As a living poet:* An admirable sentence, exhibiting Coleridge's genius in the higher type of criticism. Reconciles two false extremes,—the theory that an author's work is wholly determined by the conditions of his age, and the theory that real genius is entirely independent of them.

369b. 9. The comparison is Schlegel's (Lecture I).
23. This parallel became a commonplace.

370a. 2. *equally improbable.* Dr. Johnson, in his *Preface to Shakspeare,* had previously remarked: "Delusion, if delusion be admitted, has no certain limitation."
51-56. From Schlegel (Lecture IV).

370b. 22-27. From Schlegel (Lecture XII).
52. *Bertram:* In *All's Well That Ends Well*, I, 1, 70-79.
58. *Polonius:* In *Hamlet.*

371a. 32. *Dogberry:* In *Much Ado About Nothing.*
39. *Kotzebue:* A melodramatic German playwright, whose works were translated and played in London. An attack upon dangerous tendencies in Romanticism, like that on "frantic novels."

372a. 49-56. Another passage to be recommended to those who accuse the Romantics of encouraging the abnormal or bizarre.

372.   AIDS TO REFLECTION

Contrasts Jakob Boehme (1575-1624), the enthusiastic German mystic, with the gentle French idealist, Archbishop François de Fénelon (1651-1715), author of the philosophical romance, *The Adventures of Telemachus.* There is much about Boehme and his influence in Stallknecht's *Strange Seas*, 1945.

CHARLES LAMB (1775-1834)

I. EDITIONS

Lucas, E. V., ed. *Works of Charles and Mary Lamb*, rev. ed., 6 vols., 1912.
*Hutchinson, Thomas, ed. *Works in Prose and Verse of Charles and Mary Lamb*, 2 vols. in 1. 1924.

Complete Works and Letters. (Mod. Libr. Giant), 1935.
Letters. (Everyman's Libr.), 2 vols., 1946.

Ward, A. C., ed. *Everybody's Lamb,* 1933.
Reynolds, E. E., ed. *A Shorter Lamb,* 1930 (Essays and Letters arranged as a kind of auto-biography).

II. Biography and Criticism

Pater, Walter. In *Appreciations,* 1889.
*Lucas, E. V. *Life of Charles Lamb,* 2 vols., rev. ed., 1921.
Morley, F. V. *Lamb Before Elia,* 1932.
*Johnson, Edith C. *Lamb Always Elia,* 1935.
*Howe, Will D. *Charles Lamb and His Friends,* 1944.
"The Letters of Charles Lamb," TLS, June 15, 1946.
Johnson, Edith C. "Lamb and Manning," TLS, Aug. 31, 1946.
Bald, R. C. "Lamb and the Elizabethans," *Studies in Honor of A. H. R. Fairchild,* 1946.
"Charles Lamb's Best Friend [Mary]." TLS, May 24, 1947.

NOTES, COMMENTS, AND TOPICS FOR DISCUSSION

376.   THE OLD FAMILIAR FACES

These lines were written under great emotional stress. "They pretend," says Lamb, "to little like metre, but they will portray the disorder I was in" (E. V. Lucas ed. of the *Letters;* I, 121).

376a. 3. *a day of horrors:* the day when his sister Mary went insane and killed their mother.
    11. *fairest among women:* Ann Simons,—the "Alice" of the essay below, *Dream-Children.*
    14. *a friend:* perhaps Charles Lloyd.
    24. *taken from me:* Mary had again been taken to an asylum shortly before this was written.

376.   HESTER

In 1800 Lamb fell in love with a young Quakeress, Hester Savory. She died in 1803.

376.   WRITTEN AT CAMBRIDGE

Wordsworth said that Lamb was a good Latin scholar, and probably would have gone to college but for the impediment in his speech.

377b. 10. *Ramus:* Sixteenth-century French logician.
    12. *Camus:* Personification of the river Cam.

377.   LETTER TO WORDSWORTH

Observe the candor with which Lamb mentions defects as well as merits in Wordsworth's poetry, like Coleridge's candor in *Biog. Lit.*

377a. 3. *present:* The second edition of *Lyrical Ballads,* 2 vols.
    5. *Song of Lucy: Lucy Gray,* above p. 203.
377b. 6. *St. Leon:* A novel by William Godwin.
    15. *Bottom:* Shakspeare's *Midsummer Night's Dream,* III, I, 40.
    27-29. In an unfortunate comment on *The Ancient Mariner,* Wordsworth had remarked: "The poem of my friend has, indeed, great defects: first, that the principal person has no distinct character, either in his profession of mariner or as a human being who, having been long under the control of supernatural impressions, might be supposed himself to partake of something supernatural."
378a. 21. *Don't much care if I never see a mountain,* etc.: A passage which is characteristic of Lamb, and which strikingly shows that not all the Romantics were nature poets, but that

some of them saw the beauty of cities. They complement one another. Moreover, in a letter of Sept. 8, 1802, Lamb writes in a different mood, and says, "mountains haunt me perpetually."

378. ON THE TRAGEDIES OF SHAKSPEARE

One will get profit and pleasure from this essay if one does not take it too literally. The proposition that Shakspeare's plays should *never* be acted is absurd; he wrote them for that purpose. But Lamb's paradox is delightfully true in implying that Shakspeare's plays are so great and profound that they had better not be performed at all than by actors and actresses deficient in genius or culture. The real difficulty is stated on p. 380b, l. 53,—that it is the *mind,* and not merely the bodily appearance, of the characters that has to be presented.—In the passage preceding the given selection, Lamb, referring to Garrick's tomb in Westminster Abbey, protests that no actor, however talented, ought to be considered as great a man as such a dramatist as Shakspeare.

379a. **20.** *Clarissa:* Richardson's novel, *Clarissa Harlowe.*
  36. Milton's *Paradise Lost,* IV, 338-340.
  45. *Imogen:* Shakspeare's *Cymbeline,* I, 1.
  53. *Betterton:* A great actor of the period of the Restoration.

379b. **26.** *ore rotundo:* in a mouth-filling voice.

380a. **49.** *Henry IV,* II, 4, 437.

380b. **17.** *Mr. K.:* The celebrated actor, John Phillip Kemble.

381a. **21.** *Tate:* Nahum Tate, one of several Restoration playwrights who made misguided attempts to "improve" Shakspeare's plays.

381. MODERN GALLANTRY

DISC.—A contribution by a Romantic to the cause of democracy in a broader sense than the merely political. Find other instances.

383. DREAM-CHILDREN: A REVERIE

Note the confluence of two main streams of romantic interest,—the dream and the auto-biography. Strangely enough, this classic is omitted from Walter De La Mare's anthology, *Behold This Dreamer!* (1939).

385. A DISSERTATION UPON ROAST PIG

The title itself is humorous, for by a "dissertation" we mean, speaking literally, an elaborate and learned discourse upon an intellectually important subject. Observe throughout the delightful use of hyperbole.

385a. **2.** *my friend M:* Thomas Manning who had been in China and was interested in Chinese jest-books. In a letter of March 11, 1823, Lamb said: "The idea of the discovery of roasting pigs, I borrowed from my friend Manning."—See references to him in the Bibliography.

On Lamb's archaisms in this and other essays, the best comment is Hazlitt's in "On Familiar Style," *Anth.,* p. 407a, l. 8 ff.
  12. *Mundane Mutations:* Of course Confucius wrote no such work.
  21. *mast:* The nuts of forest-trees, chestnuts, acorns, etc.

385b. **5.** *crackling:* The crisp skin of roast pork.

386a. **26.** *assize town:* county town.

386b. **1.** *Locke:* The English philosopher.
  21. *mundus edibilis:* edible world.
  23. *princeps obsoniorum:* the chief of delicacies.
  29. *amor immunditiae:* love of evil.

387a. 1. *radiant jellies:* Shooting stars were supposed to turn into jelly where they fell.

12. From Coleridge's *Epitaph on an Infant.*

20. *For such a tomb:* Milton wrote in his epitaph to Shakspeare:

> . . . So sepulchered in such pomp dost lie
> That kings for such a tomb would wish to die.

22. *sapors:* savors.

58. *tame Villatic fowl:* In Milton's poetic diction, domestic fowl.

59. *brawn:* boar's flesh, pickled or potted.

388a. 8. *St. Omer's:* In France. A college of the Jesuits, who were famous for their training in logic and disputation. Lamb was not at school there.

12. *per flagellationem extremam:* By flogging to death.

26. *shallot:* An onion-like plant.

388.   OLD CHINA

This famous essay, revealing the possibility of enjoying happiness despite narrow means, was especially beloved by Wordsworth; and it may be termed a city-variation upon his theme, the blessings of the simple life.

388b. 17. *hays:* An old English country dance.

22. *Hyson:* green tea.

24. *speciosa miracula:* shining wonders (Horace, *Ars Poetica*, 144, referring to the *Odyssey*).

34. *Bridget:* Lamb's sister, Mary Lamb.

58. *Barker's:* There actually was an old bookstore in London by that name, and at one time the Lambs had lodgings above it.

389a. 23. *corbeau:* tailor's cant for black (literally, raven) goods.

34. *Leonardo:* Mary Lamb had written a poem on this picture by Leonardo da Vinci.

57. *Walton:* In his *Complete Angler.*

389b. 16. *Battle of Hexham*, etc.: Actual plays and actors of the time, and favorites with Lamb.

390a. 53. *Mr. Cotton:* The seventeenth-century poet, Charles Cotton, wrote:

> Then let us welcome the new guest
> With lusty brimmers of the best.

390b. 38. *the great Jew R.:* Nathan Meyer Rothschild (1777-1836), the famous banker.

42. *tester:* canopy.

390.   SANITY OF TRUE GENIUS

Dryden, in *Absalom and Achitophel*, 1, 163-164, wrote:

> Great wits are sure to madness near allied,
> And thin partitions do their bounds divide.

Dryden did not intend this satirical couplet to be taken as a serious generalization that geniuses are abnormal; but Lamb believed there was a popular notion that such was the truth, and, like Wordsworth and Coleridge, he regarded the notion as a fallacy.

391a. 18. *has dominion over it:* The sentence is a useful one to quote to those who allege that the Romantics encouraged unrestrained improvisation.

19-23. The allusions are to Milton in *Paradise Lost.*

391b. 18. *Wither:* George Wither, seventeenth-century poet, in his *Shepherd's Hunting,* Eclogue IV.

21. *Lane's novels:* Trashy best sellers.

24. *a happier genius:* No doubt Sir Walter Scott.

44. *fantasques:* They have been given names, but they have no real character.

WILLIAM HAZLITT (1778-1830)

I. EDITIONS

Howe, P. P., ed. *The Complete Works of William Hazlitt*, 21 vols., 1930-1934.

Selections by:
 *Will D. Howe, 1913.
 P. P. Howe, 1923.
 P. V. D. Shelley, 1924.
 *Geoffrey Keynes (Nonesuch Press), 1930.
*Zeitlin, Jacob. *Hazlitt on English Literature*, 1913.

II. BIOGRAPHY AND CRITICISM

*Howe, P. P. *Life of William Hazlitt*, new ed. 1928, 1947.
Birrell, Augustine. *Life of Hazlitt*, 1902.
Saintsbury, George. *Essays in English Literature*, 1890.
Schneider, Elisabeth. *The Aesthetics of William Hazlitt*, 1933.
*Maclean, Catherine M. *Born Under Saturn*, 1943.
Bullitt, J. M. "Hazlitt and the Romantic Conception of the Imagination," PQ, XXIV, 343; 1945.

NOTES, COMMENTS, AND TOPICS FOR DISCUSSION

MY FIRST ACQUAINTANCE WITH POETS
395.

In reading this famous account of Coleridge, bear in mind that it was written 25 years after the event. In 1798 Coleridge had been opposed to England's war against France. By 1823 he had become a conservative in many respects, while Hazlitt continued a radical. That explains why Hazlitt's general admiration for Coleridge is here occasionally intermixed with fault-finding, cropping out in such remarks as "our once loved poet," "his nose small, feeble, nothing—like what he has done," "instability of purpose," and "not much feeling for the classical or elegant."

This memoir was first published in Leigh Hunt's anti-conservative journal, *The Liberal*.

395a. 5. *W--m:* Wem.
 7. *like . . . Demogorgon:* Another way of saying, "They strike me with an inexplicable awe."—*Paradise Lost*, II, 294.

396a. 11. *Salopians:* The Latin name of Shropshire is Salopia.
 16. Gray's *The Bard*, l. 28.

396b. 37. *St. John:* John the Baptist.
 49. *banners dripping with gore:* Those of Great Britain and her allies. See *France: An Ode*, stanza II; *Anth.*, p. 160.

397a. 1. *never be old:* Sidney's *Arcadia*, Bk. I.
 10. Pope, *Epistle to the Earl of Oxford*.
 28. *Jus Divinum:* the divine right (of kings), odious to Hazlitt.
 30. Milton, *Lycidas*, l. 106.
 42. *forehead:* his tongue being silent.
 50. Thomson, *Castle of Indolence*, II, st. 33.
 57. Do., I, st. 57.

397b. 49. *Wolstonecraft . . . Mackintosh:* Mary Wollstonecraft, author of *The Vindication of the Rights of Woman;* and Sir James Mackintosh, who wrote a vindication of the French Revolution in reply to Burke's attack upon it.

398a. 21. *a letter:* Actually not from Tom Wedgwood, but from his brother Josiah, the famous manufacturer of fine earthenware. See Mrs. Henry Sandford, *Thomas Poole and His Friends*, I, 236-238.

31. *Deva:* the river Dee.

37. *Delectable Mountains:* those to which Christian, in Bunyan's *Pilgrim's Progress,* escapes after being imprisoned by Giant Despair.

52. *Cassandra:* One of the French heroic romances, popular in the seventeenth century.

398b. 23. *Hume:* David Hume (1711-1776), anti-orthodox philosopher.

26. *Credat,* etc.: Let the Jew Apella (who believes everything) believe it (Horace).

30. *choke-pears:* an astringent pear,—implying the realistically honest and tart flavor of Hume's work.

38. *Berkeley:* George Berkeley (1685-1753) the idealistic philosopher who maintained that the universe is the manifestation of divine ideas, and who was a leading opponent of materialism.—Hazlitt was at this time brooding over the anti-cynical principles which he later published in *The Natural Disinterestedness of the Human Mind* (1807).

48. *Tom Paine:* author of *Common Sense* (1776), in support of the American Revolution, and of *The Rights of Man* (1791).

58. *conceit:* extravagant fancy.

399a. 3. *Paley:* William Paley (1743-1805), theologian.

15. *Par. Lost,* VIII, 648.

41. *Vision:* Southey's *Vision* glorified George III, and Byron's (published by Murray) burlesqued it; *Anth.,* p. 724.—The *Junto* was the Bridge-Street Association, which opposed radical publications.

399b. 24. *Tom Jones:* Fielding's novel; Bk. X, ch. 5.

47. *Paul and Virginia:* an idyllic French story by Bernardin de Saint Pierre.

53-55. Note the bitterness against Wordsworth.

400a. 2. *Camilla:* Fanny Burney's novel.

20. *free use:* a mistake; Wordsworth paid rent.

30. *Lyrical Ballads:* they were published in the autumn of 1798. Coleridge's *Sybilline Leaves* appeared in 1817.

400b. 2. *the sense palls:* It is doleful passages such as this that make Hazlitt seem a prose-Byron.

10. *Betty Foy:* This poem, and those mentioned in ll. 13-15, are in the *Lyrical Ballads.*

17. Pope, *Essay on Man,* I, 293.

26. Thomson, *Seasons, Spring,* 18.

31. *Par. Lost,* II, 559.

40. *matter-of-fact-ness:* Observe that, although his *Biog. Lit.,* was not published until many years later, Coleridge seems already to have held some of the opinions which he therein expressed.

401a. 17. *Entrance of Christ:* The picture is now in a Roman Catholic institution in Cincinnati, Ohio.

23. *burr:* i.e., he "rolled" his r's.

23. *crust on wine:* deposit on the sides of the bottle.

30. *Castle Specter:* The contempt expressed for this melodrama is another illustration that the Romantics had ceased to sympathize with pre-romantic extravagances.

34. *ad captandum:* a merit only in capturing popularity.

53. *His face: Macbeth,* I, v, 63.

401b. 24. *Tom Poole:* a Bristol tanner.

27. *flip:* a mixture of beer with some stronger liquor, whipped up, and heated with a hot iron.

40. *He said,* etc.: It is difficult to judge the reliability of the statements in this paragraph about Coleridge's attitude toward the authors mentioned, especially since his reasons are not fully reported. I doubt whether his "contempt of Gray" was complete; for it is clear from *Biog. Lit.,* ch. 2, that although Wordsworth had persuaded him that there were imperfections in *The Bard* and even in the *Elegy,* he retained his admiration for that poet.

402a. 17. *Richardson:* Either this was inaccurately remembered, or Coleridge changed his mind; for in *Table Talk* (July 5, 1833) he prefers Fielding (as Hazlitt also did).

18. *Caleb Williams:* by William Godwin.

24. *ribbed sea-sands: The Ancient Mariner,* l. 227.

404.   CHARACTERS OF SHAKSPEARE'S PLAYS: HAMLET

In the Preface of this book, Hazlitt wrote: "The only work which seemed to supersede the necessity of an attempt like the present was Schlegel's very admirable *Lectures on the Drama,* which give by far the best account of the plays of Shakspeare that has hitherto appeared. The only circumstances in which it was thought not impossible to improve on the manner in which the German critic has executed this part of his design, were in avoiding an appearance of mysticism in his style, not very attractive to the English reader, and in bringing illustrations from particular passages of the plays themselves, of which Schlegel's work, from the extensiveness of his plan, did not admit. We will at the same time confess that some little jealousy of the character of the national understanding was not without its share in producing the following undertaking, for we were piqued that it should be reserved for a foreign critic to give reasons for the faith which we English have in Shakspeare."—This was followed by a long quotation from Schlegel, and a contrast between his estimate of Shakspeare and that of Dr. Johnson, much to the disadvantage of the latter.—The study of *Hamlet* first appeared in the *Morning Chronicle,* Mch. 14, 1814.

Hazlitt's general soundness as a critic is shown by the fact that, although *Hamlet* has been learnedly investigated and thoughtfully discussed for more than a century since this essay was composed, there is little in Hazlitt's interpretation of Hamlet's character that is contra-dicted by the most competent modern Shakspearian scholars.

DISC.—See the suggested discussion in the Notes on Coleridge's *Characteristics of Shakspeare Anth.,* p. 368. Consider Hazlitt's statement that, although other authors may give fine imita-tions of nature, Shakspeare gives us nature itself (p. 403a. 32).

403a. 6-8. George Saintsbury, *Hist. of Criticism,* III, 258, calls this passage one of the high points in Shakspearian criticism.

    42. Is not this at least a faint anticipation of one of the most widely accepted modern interpretations of Hamlet.—A. C. Bradley's *Shakespearian Tragedy?*

404a. 30. *Whole Duty:* a didactic treatise. The *Academy* was a manual of courtship (known to Sheridan's Lydia Languish).

405a. 7. DISC.—Compare with Lamb's views; *Anth.,* p. 378.

    11. *Kemble:* John Philip Kemble, a great tragic actor, whom Hazlitt on the whole admired, as he likewise admired Edmund Kean, perhaps the greatest of all Shakspearian actors.

405.   ON FAMILIAR STYLE

Another essay to be commended to those who believe the Romantics encourage the merely instinctive, impulsive, crotchety, vulgar, centrifugal, etc. Observe Hazlitt's protests against Cobbett's notion that "the first word that occurs is always the best," and against those who would "write at random." The gist of his advice is to "steer a middle course" between the pompous and the vulgar or technical.

405b. 46. This is truer of Dr. Johnson's imitators than of Johnson himself, whose diction was as simple and direct as anyone's when he thought it appropriate to the subject.

406a. 31. *cum grano salis:* with a grain of salt; i.e., not unreservedly.

406b. 33. *Cobbett:* William Cobbett (1762-1835), liberal reformer, who had written on Gram-mar, but is better known for his *Rural Rides.*

407a. 41. *well of native English:* Spenser's praise of Chaucer's diction (*Fairie Queene,* IV, II, 32).

    46. *Erasmus:* the celebrated humanist (1466-1538), whose *Colloquies* were imaginary con-versations on current topics.

407.   LORD BYRON

DISC.—It may be best to read the Selections from Scott and Byron before reading this essay, and thereafter to discuss it in relation to their works.—Hazlitt wrote this essay shortly before Lord Byron's death; hence the apologetic postscript.

410b. 59. *Bowles:* William Lisle Bowles; see his Sonnets, *Anth.,* p. 95.

411a. 21. *Scrub:* In Farquhar's *The Beaux' Stratagem* (1707).

412a. 13. *Vision:* See Byron's, *Anth.,* p. 724.

DISC.—How would you explain that Hazlitt, the so-called "prose-Byron," much preferred Keats to Byron? See C. D. Thorpe, "Keats and Hazlitt," PMLA, LXII, 487-502; 1947.

SIR WALTER SCOTT (1771-1832)

I. EDITIONS

*Scudder, H. E., ed. *Complete Poetical Works,* 1900.
*Lang, Andrew, ed. *Waverley Novels,* 25 vols., 1902-1904.—Many other satisfactory editions.
Henderson, Thomas, ed. *Minstrelsy of the Scottish Border,* 1931.
Grierson, H. J. C., ed. *Letters of Sir Walter Scott,* 12 vols., 1932-1937.
Tait, J. G., and Parker, W. M. *The Journal of Sir Walter Scott,* 1947.

Holmes, John Haynes, ed. *The Heart of Scott's Poetry,* 1932.
*Walpole, Hugh, ed. *The Waverley Pageant* [Selections from the Novels], 1932.

II. BIOGRAPHY AND CRITICISM

*Lockhart, J. G. *Life of Sir Walter Scott,* 5 vols., 1837-1838; best mod. ed. Houghton Mifflin, 1901.—Abbreviated ed. in Everyman's Libr.
Hazlitt, William. In *On the English Novelists, The Spirit of the Age,* etc.
Carlyle, Thomas. "Sir Walter Scott" (1838), in *Critical and Miscellaneous Essays.*
Bagehot, Walter. "The Waverley Novels" (1858), in *Literary Studies.*
Shairp, John C. "The Homeric Spirit in Walter Scott," in *Aspects of English Poetry,* 1881.
Stevenson, R. L. "A Gossip on Romance," in *Memories and Portraits,* 1887.
Saintsbury, George. "The Historical Novel," *Essays in English Literature,* II, 1895.
*Saintsbury, George. *Sir Walter Scott,* 1897.
Hudson, W. H. *Sir Walter Scott,* 1901.
*Lang, Andrew. Introductions to the Border Edition of the Novels, 1902-1904.
Young, Charles A. *The Waverley Novels,* 1907.
Ball, Margaret. *Sir Walter Scott as a Critic of Literature,* 1907.
Verrall, A. W. "The Prose of Sir Walter Scott," *Collected Literary Essays,* 1913.
*Emerson, O. F. "The Early Literary Life of Sir Walter Scott," JEGP, XXIX, 29, 241, 389; 1924.
Baldensperger, F. "La Grande Communion Romantique de 1827," RLC, VII, 47; 1927.
Buchan, John. *Sir Walter Scott,* 5th ed., 1932.
McKillop, A. D. *Sir Walter Scott in the Twentieth Century* (Rice Inst.), 1933.
Dargan, E. P. "Scott and the French Romantics," PMLA, XLIX, 599-629; 1934.
Boatright, Mody C. "Demonology in the Novels" and "Witchcraft in the Novels," *Univ. of Texas Studies,* 1934 and 1935; "The Use of the Supernatural," PMLA, l, 235-261; 1935.
*Baker, Ernest A. *The History of the English Novel,* VI, ch. 6-9; 1935.
Hillhouse, J. T. *The Waverley Novels and Their Critics,* 1936.
Landis, P. N. "The Waverley Novels," PMLA, LII, 461-473; 1937.
*Grierson, H. J. C. *Sir Walter Scott, Bart.,* 1938.
Fiske, Christabel F. *Epic Suggestion in the Imagery of the Waverley Novels,* 1940.
Orians, G. H. "Walter Scott, Mark Twain, and the Civil War," SAQ, XL, 342-359; 1941.
Wenger, Jared. "Character-Types of Scott, Balzac, Dickens, Zola," PMLA, LXII, 213-232; 1947

Corson, James C. *A Bibliography of Sir Walter Scott,* 1943.
Burr, Alston. *Sir Walter Scott: An Index,* 1936.

NOTES, COMMENTS, AND TOPICS FOR DISCUSSION

414.   WILLIAM AND HELEN

This version of Bürger's *Lenore* closely links the earliest literary work of Scott with previous English imitators of German literature, and especially with William Taylor of Norwich. "A lady of high rank in the literary world [Mrs. Anna Letitia Barbauld]," says Scott, "read this romantic tale, as translated by Mr. Taylor, in the house of the celebrated Professor Dugald Stewart of Edinburgh. The author [Scott] was not present, nor indeed in Edinburgh at the time; but a gentleman who had the pleasure of hearing the ballad, afterwards told him the story, and repeated the remarkable chorus—

> Tramp, tramp, across the land they speede,
> Splash, splash, across the sea;
> Hurrah, the dead can ride apace!
> Dost fear to ride with me?

In attempting a translation, then intended only to circulate among friends, the present author did not hesitate to make use of this impressive stanza; for which freedom he has since obtained the forgiveness of the ingenious gentleman to whom it properly belongs."

414a. 5. *Frederick:* Frederick Barbarossa, King of Germany and Emperor of the Holy Roman Empire,—a leader in the Third Crusade, A. D. 1189.

7. *Judah's wars:* The wars in Palestine.

9. *Paynim:* Heathen.

415b. 116. *matin:* Early morning.

123. *wight:* Ready for action.

125. *Busk, busk, and boune:* Dress thyself and make ready.

126. *barb:* Steed of Barbary—powerful and swift.

417.   THE VIOLET

The "false love" was Williamina Stuart, whose fickleness had caused young Walter Scott, as he put it, "three years of dreaming and two years of wakening." Although written in 1797, the poem was not published until after her death in 1810.

417.   THE EVE OF ST. JOHN

417b. 5. *Buccleuch:* The clan-name of the Scotts.

22. *acton:* a stuffed jacket worn under the armor.

418a. 41. *bittern:* a species of heron, sometimes called stake-drivers.

418b. 79. *black rood-stone:* At Melrose Abbey there was a crucifix of black marble.

419a. 127. *bartizan:* A small structure projecting from a castle, for observation and defense.

420a. 193. *ne'er beholds the day:* Scott knew of an unfortunate young woman who, because her lover never returned, immured herself for the rest of her life from the light of day.

420.   THE LAY OF THE LAST MINSTREL

"The poem now offered to the public," says Scott in the preface to the first edition, "is intended to illustrate the customs and manners which anciently prevailed on the Borders of Scotland and England. The inhabitants living in a state partly pastoral and partly warlike, and combining habits of constant depredation with the influence of a rude spirit of chivalry, were often engaged in scenes highly susceptible of poetical ornament. As the description of scenery and manners was more the object of the author than a combined and regular narrative, the plan of the ancient metrical romance was adopted, which allows greater latitude, in this respect than would be consistent with the dignity of a regular poem. . . . For these reasons, the poem was put into the mouth of an ancient minstrel, the last of the race, who as he is supposed to have survived the Revolution, might have caught somewhat of the refinement of modern poetry, without losing the simplicity of his original model. The date of the tale itself is about the middle of the sixteenth century, when most of the persons actually flourished."

The metre of the poem was taken from Coleridge's *Christabel*, which had not yet been published, but which a friend of Coleridge's recited on a visit to Scott in 1801 (four years before the publication of the *Lay*). In 1831 Scott acknowledged this indebtedness as an "acknowledgment due from the pupil to his master."

420a. 20-21. The allusion is to Cromwell and the Puritans.

44. *Monmouth:* Executed in 1685 for rebellion against King James II.

420b. 80. *Charles:* King Charles I, when he visited Edinburgh.

421a. 17. *Caledonia:* Scotland.

422.   THE MAID OF NEIDPATH

"There is a tradition in Tweeddale that, when Neidpath Castle, near Peebles, was inhabited by the Earls of March, a mutual passion subsisted between a daughter of that noble family and a son of the Laird of Tushielaw, in Ettrick Forest. As the alliance was thought unsuitable by her parents, the young man went abroad. During his absence the lady fell into a consumption; and at length, as the only means of saving her life, her father consented that her lover should be recalled. On the day when he was expected to pass through Peebles, on the road to Tushielaw, the young lady, though much exhausted, caused herself to be carried to the balcony of a house in Peebles belonging to the family, that she might see him as he rode past. Her anxiety and eagerness gave such force to her organs that she is said to have distinguished the horse's footsteps at an incredible distance. But Tushielaw, unprepared for the change in her appearance, and not expecting to see her in that place, rode on without recognizing her, or even slackening his pace. The lady was unable to support the shock; and, after a short struggle, died in the arms of her attendants."—Scott.

DISC.—How has Scott changed the story, and with what effect?

422b. 21. *kenned:* recognized.

422.   HUNTING SONG

422b. 5. *coupled:* the hounds are linked together in couples.

423.   MARMION

Of the differences between the *Lay* and *Marmion*, Buchan says: "The new work, unlike the *Lay*, had not its origin in the Border lore of his youth, for it was a concocted tale of chivalry, with an elaborate plot, culminating in the great national tragedy of Flodden [in Northumberland, where the English defeated the Scots, Sept. 9, 1513]. Its inspiration was the martial fervor which ran in Scott's veins, the ardent patriotism with which the spectacle of great events on the Continent filled his mind . . . The speed of the verse is due to the fact that passages like the description of Flodden were conceived while with his regiment on Portobello sands, or galloping among the hills between Tweed and Yarrow. He made no parade of a high poetic purpose" (Buchan, *Scott*, p. 84).

The Introduction celebrates the memory of three of the greatest British leaders during the war against France, all of whom had died within less than one year: (1) Nelson, in the Battle of Trafalgar, October 21, 1805; (2) William Pitt, twice Prime Minister, January 23, 1806; and (3) Charles James Fox, the famous orator and liberal statesman, September 13, 1806.

423a. 72. *Gadite:* Spanish, referring to Trafalgar.

     73. *levin:* lightning.

423b. 82. *On Egypt, Hafnia,* etc.: Nelson's chief victories,—the first being commonly called the Battle of the Nile; and the second, the Battle of Copenhagen (of which "Hafnia" is the Latin name).

     104. *tottering throne:* Alluding to the insanity of George III.

     111. *Palinure:* The helmsman in Virgil's *Aeneid*, whose vigilance not even the God of Sleep could relax.

     127. *slumbers nigh:* They lie near one another in Westminster.

     128. *requiescat:* May he rest in peace.

424a. 139. *error:* Fox's personal habits were dissolute. Scott's allusion to that fact aroused the anger of Jeffrey (in *Edinburgh Review*) and of other partisans.

     157. *timorous slave:* A Russian ambassador, D'Oubril, in negotiations after Napoleon's victory at Austerlitz, was willing to agree to a supine peace.

     158. Fox's unwillingness to make peace with the triumphant Napoleon was all the more noteworthy since in the early days of the war he had been an advocate of a pacific policy.

     177. *Thessalian:* Thessaly was famed as a land of wizardry.

424b. 204. *you deigned to praise:* Both Pitt and Fox admired *The Lay of the Last Minstrel.*

424.   SONG: WHERE SHALL THE LOVER REST?

Scott regarded this "wild and sad air" as characteristically Scotch, and introduced it as follows:

> Such have I heard in Scottish land
> Rise from the busy harvest band,
> When falls before the mountaineer
> On Lowland plains the ripened ear.
> Now one shrill voice the notes prolong,
> Now a wild chorus swells the song:
> Oft have I listened and stood still
> As it came softened up the hill,
> And deemed it the lament of men
> Who languished for their native glen,
> And thought how sad would be such sound
> On Susquehanna's swampy ground,
> Kentucky's wood-encumbered brake,
> Or wild Ontario's boundless lake,
> Where heart-sick exiles in the strain
> Recalled fair Scotland's hills again!
>   (*Marmion*, III, 132-147)

425.   LADY HERON'S SONG: LOCHINVAR

DISC.—"The ballad of Lochinvar is in a very slight degree founded on a ballad called 'Katharine Janfarie'" (Scott). The usual title for it is *Katharine Jaffray*. Read it in Child's *English and Scottish Popular Ballads*, and consider the purpose and value of Scott's changes. Compare Browning's *How They Brought the Good News from Ghent to Aix*, in which Scott's galloping metre was used.

  425. **321.** *brake:* thicket.
  332. *like the Solway:* i.e., violently, the Firth of Solway being noted for its powerful tides. Scott later described them in *Redgauntlet*, ch. 4.
  344. *galliard:* a lively dance for two persons.

  426. **353.** *scaur:* cliff.

426.   MARMION AND DOUGLAS

This scene of defiance between the English villain-hero Marmion and his turbulent host Douglas, Earl of Angus, is a passage typical of the spirited action of Scott's romances; and it may be sufficiently appreciated without a detailed knowledge of its context. The main point in the situation is that Douglas has received Marmion into his castle because Marmion is on an official mission, but Douglas will not countenance any suggestion of personal friendship between them.

The following annotations by Scott are characteristic illustrations of his scholarship and of his desire to be true to historical facts.

  427b. 429. *the flush of rage:* "This ebullition of violence in the potent Earl of Angus is not without its examples in the real history of the house of Douglas, whose chieftains possessed the ferocity with the heroic virtues of a savage state. The most curious instance occurred in the case of Maclellan, tutor of Bomby, who, having refused to acknowledge the pre-eminence claimed by Douglas over the gentlemen and Barons of Galloway, was seized and imprisoned by the Earl, in his castle of the Thrieve, on the borders of Kirkcudbright-shire. Sir Patrick Gray, commander of King James the Second's guard, was uncle to the tutor of Bomby, and obtained from the King 'a sweet letter of supplication,' praying the Earl to deliver his prisoner into Gray's hand. When Sir Patrick arrived at the castle, he was received with all the honor due to a favorite servant of the King's household; but while he was at dinner, the Earl, who suspected his errand, caused his prisoner to be led forth and beheaded. After dinner, Sir Patrick presented the King's letter to the Earl, who received it with great affectation of reverence; 'and took him by the hand, and led him forth to the green, where the gentleman was lying dead, and showed him the manner, and said, "Sir Patrick, you are come a little too late; yonder is your sister's son lying, but he wants the head: take his body, and do with it what you will." Sir Patrick answered again with a sore heart, and said, "My lord, if ye have taken from him his head, dispone upon the body as ye please": and with that called for his horse, and leaped thereon; and when he was on horseback, he said to the Earl on this manner, "My lord, if I live, you shall be rewarded for your labors, that you have used at this time, according to your demerits." At this saying the Earl was highly offended, and cried for horse. Sir Patrick, seeing the Earl's fury, spurred his horse but he was chased near Edinburgh ere they left him: and had it not been his lead horse was so tried and good, he had been taken' (Pitscottie's *History*)."—Scott.

456. *A letter forged:* "Lest the reader should partake of the Earl's astonishment, and consider the crime as inconsistent with the manners of the period, I have to remind him of the numerous forgeries (partly executed by a female assistant) devised by Robert of Artois, to forward his suit against the Countess Matilda; which, being detected, occasioned his flight into England, and proved the remote cause of Edward the Third's memorable wars in France. John Harding, also, was expressly hired by Edward IV to forge such documents as might appear to establish the claim of fealty asserted over Scotland by the English monarchs."—Scott.

Despite this plea, the introduction of a forgery into this kind of tale has been almost universally deemed a blemish. Byron, in *English Bards and Scotch Reviewers*, 166 ff., scoffed at

> The golden-crested haughty Marmion,
> Now forging scrolls, now foremost in the fight,
> Not quite a felon, yet but half a knight.

428. THE BATTLE, AND MARMION'S DEATH

Marmion is riding with his band to join the English army before the battle of Flodden Field. Clare, whom circumstances have put in his power, loves another man and fears Marmion. The battle scene in Marmion was extravagantly praised by Landor.

431. THE LADY OF THE LAKE

"The scene of the following poem is laid chiefly in the vicinity of Loch Katrine, in the Western Highlands of Perthshire."—Scott.

"The ancient manners, the habits, and customs of the aboriginal race by whom the Highlands of Scotland were inhabited, had always appeared to me peculiarly adapted to poetry. The change in their manners, too, had taken place almost within my own time, or at least I had learned many particulars concerning the ancient state of the Highlands from the old men of the last generation. I had always thought the old Scottish Gael highly adapted for poetical composition. The feuds, and political dissensions, which, half a century earlier, would have rendered the richer and wealthier part of the kingdom indisposed to countenance a poem, the scene of which was laid in the Highlands, were now sunk in the generous compassion which the English, more than any other nation, feel for the misfortunes of an honorable foe. The poems of Ossian had, by their popularity, sufficiently shown, that if writings on Highland subjects were qualified to interest the reader, mere national prejudices were, in the present day, very unlikely to interfere with their success.

"I had also read a great deal, seen much, and heard more, of that romantic country, where I was in the habit of spending some time every autumn; and the scenery of Loch Katrine was connected with the recollection of many a dear friend and merry expedition of former days. This poem, the action of which lay among scenes so beautiful, and so deeply imprinted on my recollection, was a labor of love; and it was no less so to recall the manners and incidents introduced."—Scott.

The interspersed lyrics, perhaps even more than the narrative parts of *The Lady of the Lake*, express the spirit of the Highlands.

431b. 2. *witch-elm:* elm with broad leaves.

432a. 10. *Caledon:* Scotland.

433a. 138. *whinyard:* huntsman's sword or dagger.

433b. 166. *woe worth:* of poor value.

434a. 202. *pagod:* pagoda, oriental tower.

436a. 440. *ptarmigan and heath-cock:* game birds.

441. *mere:* lake.

443. *by the rood:* by the Cross.

437a. 525. *Idaean vine:* Whortleberry, associated with Mt. Ida, in Crete.

437b. 573. *Ferragus or Oscabart:* Gigantic heroes of old.

438a. 638. *pibroch:* music played on the bagpipe, especially before going into battle.

641. *fallow:* pasture, or other uncultivated land.

439.　　　　　　　　　HAIL TO THE CHIEF

Sung by boatmen who are rowing their chieftain. "The song itself is intended as an imita-tion of the *jorrams*, or boat songs of the Highlanders, which were usually composed in honor of a favorite chief. They are so adapted as to keep time with the sweep of the oars, and it is easy to distinguish between those intended to be sung to the oars of a galley, where the stroke is lengthened and doubled, as it were, and those which were timed to the rowers of an ordinary boat."—Scott.

439a. 408. *Roderigh Vich,* etc.: Black Roderick, the descendant of Alpine.

410. *Beltane:* May day.

439b. 426. "The Lennox, as the district is called which encircles the lower extremity of Loch Lomond, was peculiarly exposed to the incursions of the mountaineers, who inhabited the inaccessible fastnesses at the upper end of the lake, and the neighboring district of Loch Katrine. These were often marked by circumstances of great ferocity."—Scott.

441.　　　　　　　　　CORONACH

Sung by the women, lamenting the death of the chieftain. "The *Coronach* of the high-landers, like the *Ululatus* of the Romans, and the *Ululoo* of the Irish, was a wild expression of lamentation, poured forth by the mourners over the body of a departed friend. When the words of it were articulate, they expressed the praises of the deceased, and the loss the clan would sustain by his death."—Scott.

Observe that the imagery is "in character,"—i.e., drawn from such objects and experiences as are familiar to the Highlanders.

441b. 386. *correi:* A hollow in a hillside, where game hides.

387. *cumber:* trouble (Cf. "encumbered").

442.　　　　　　ROKEBY: BRIGNALL BANKS

"The banks of the Greta [a river in Yorkshire], below Rutherford Bridge, abound in seams of grayish slate, which are wrought in some places to a very great depth under ground, thus forming artificial caverns, which, when the seam has been exhausted, are gradually hidden by the underwood which grows in profusion upon the romantic banks of the river. In times of public confusion, they might be well adapted to the purposes of banditti."—Scott. In the dialogue between the maiden and her lover, it is gradually disclosed to her that he is an outlaw.

442.　　　　　　　THE ROVER'S FAREWELL

442b. 4. *the rue:* signifying the wine of bitterness.

442.　　　　　　　　　ALLEN-A-DALE

The minstrel of Robin Hood's outlaw band, contrasted with a noble. Lord Dacre. Baron of Ravensworth.

443a. 734. *vail:* take off.

443.   FLORA MACIVOR'S SONG

A link between Scott the poet and Scott the author of *Waverley*, in ch. 22 of which novel the Highland heroine sings this song. She expresses her enthusiasm for the Jacobite Rebellion of 1745 in favor of the young Stuart Pretender and against the "stranger" (l. 3), the Hanoverian King George II. Many Highland clans supported the Pretender's cause, as they had done in the previous rebellion of 1715.

443. 6. *claymore:* a great sword.
444. 17. *Moray:* The Pretender. The Stuarts were Earls of Moray.
    36. *Remember,* etc.: Scenes of former battles.
    50. *frith:* firth, narrow inlet from the sea.

445.   JOCK OF HAZELDEAN

The first stanza is from an old ballad, which in Child's *Ballads* is entitled *John of Hazelgreen.*—See M. C. Kelly, MLN, XLVI, 304-306; 1931.
445a. 19. *managed:* trained.

445.   PIBROCH OF DONUIL DHU

"This is a very ancient pibroch belonging to Clan MacDonald, and supposed to refer to the expedition of Donald Balloch, who, in 1431, launched from the Isles with a considerable force, invaded Lochaber, and at Inverlochy defeated and put to flight the Earls of Mar and Caithness, though at the head of an army superior to his own. The words of the set, theme, or melody, to which the pipe variations are applied, run thus in Gaelic:—

> Piobaireachd Dhonuil Dhuidh, piobaireachd Dhonuil;
> Piobaireachd Dhonuil Dhuidh, piobaireachd Dhonuil;
> Piobaireachd Dhonuil Dhuidh, piobaireachd Dhonuil;
> Piob agus bratach air faiche Inverlochi.

> The pipe-summons of Donald the Black,
> The pipe-summons of Donald the Black,
> The war-pipe and the pennon are on the gathering-place at Inverlochy."—Scott.

445b. 11. *pennon:* pennant.
    24. *targes:* shields.

445.   WHY SIT'ST THOU BY THAT RUINED HALL

From *The Antiquary,* ch. 10, where a woman sings it. The Deep Voice (l. 5) is that of Time, and the poem is sometimes entitled Time.

446.   AND WHAT THOUGH WINTER WILL PINCH SEVERE

From *Old Mortality,* ch. 19. Expresses the spirit of the seventeenth-century cavaliers,—cheerful in adversity.
446a. 4. *sack:* a dry Spanish wine, like sherry.
    7. *starkly:* strongly.

446.   THE SUN UPON THE WEIRDLAW HILL

Lockhart (*Life of Scott,* ch. 39) comments upon this pathetic poem as follows: "It was while struggling with such languor, on one lovely evening of this autumn [1817], that he composed the following beautiful verses. They mark the very spot of their birth,—namely, the then naked height overhanging the northern side of the Cauldshields Loch, from which Melrose Abbey to the eastward, and the hills of Ettrick and Yarrow to the west, are now visible over a wide range of woodland,—all the work of the poet's hand."

446. PROUD MAISIE

This ballad (from *The Heart of Midlothian*, ch. 45) is sung by the crazed Madge Wildfire upon her deathbed. "Only a fragment or two," says Scott, "could be collected."

446. THE BAREFOOTED FRIAR

Sung by the jolly friar in *Ivanhoe*, ch. 17.

447. REBECCA'S HYMN

From *Ivanhoe*, ch. 39. Sung in a time of great adversity by the lovely Jewess at her evening devotions.

447a. 4. *flame*: see *Exodus*, 13.
10. *timbrel*: a kind of drum.

447. COUNTY GUY

From *Quentin Durward*, ch. 4. Supposed to be sung by a maiden in the days of chivalry. "The words," says Scott, "had neither so much sense, wit, and fancy, as to withdraw the attention from the music, nor the music so much of art as to drown all feeling of the words. The one seemed fitted to the other; and if the song had been recited without the notes, or the air played without the words, neither would have been worth noting. It is, therefore, scarcely fair to put upon record lines intended not to be said or read, but only to be sung."

447. *County*: Count, earl, or lord.

448. GLEE FOR KING CHARLES

From *Woodstock*, ch. 20. Like *What Though Winter Will Pinch Severe*, expresses the Cavaliers' defiance of misfortune and danger. At the time when they are supposed to be singing it, their king was defeated and in deadly peril.

448a. 6. *carles*: churls.

448. BONNY DUNDEE

From Scott's forgotten play, *The Doom of Devorgoil*.

Dundee is John Graham of Claverhouse, Viscount Dundee, gallant soldier and supporter of a lost cause, much admired by Scott, who had depicted his character in *Old Mortality*. During the reigns of the Stuart kings Charles II and James II, Dundee persecuted the rebellious Scotch Dissenters. When the Stuart cause was lost, and James II fled to France, Dundee remained loyal, as described in the poem. Defying the "Lords of Convention," i.e., the Scottish Parliament, he left Edinburgh with a small escort, vainly attempted to persuade the Duke of Gordon to hold Edinburgh Castle for King James, raised an army in the Highlands, and led it to victory at Killiecrankie, in which battle he was mortally wounded. His exit from Edinburgh was not quite so dramatic as Scott imagined, but the poem is in general harmony with the temper and staunchness of Dundee.

448. 10. *backwards*: in sign of alarm.
11. *douce*: prudent (somewhat sarcastically).
14. *sanctified*: So called because the Bow was a street mainly occupied by Dissenters or Covenanters, whom their opponents thought ostentatiously and hypocritically devout.
15. *Ilk carline*, etc.: Every old woman was scolding and wagging her head.
16. *young plants*, etc.: The young Covenanters looked not unsympathetically.
19. *crammed*: Stewart A. Robertson and S. M. Ellis have established the fact that in the first publication of the poem (in *The Christmas Box*, 1828) the reading was *pang'd*, i.e., "stuffed full." See *Times Lit. Suppl.*, Feb. 28, Mch. 7, Mch. 14, and Apr. 4, 1929. An obviously better rhyme, and almost certainly the correct reading.
24. *cowls of Kilmarnock*: wearers of hooded garments, made in Kilmarnock, a town west of Edinburgh.

25. *lang-hafted gullies:* long-handled knives.

26. *close-heads:* The innermost ends of the blind alleys leading out of the causeway or main street.

31. *Mons Meg:* Dundee is asking Gordon, commander of the castle, to turn the huge cannon called Meg, and supposed to have been made in Mons, Belgium, against the Covenanters.

31. *marrows:* mates.

449. **35.** *Where'er shall direct me,* etc.: Wherever loyalty and bravery in the Stuart cause may require, for the Marquis of Montrose had been a valient royalist leader, who was finally captured and executed by the Covenanters.

41. *Duniewassals:* Highland gentlemen in the service of the chiefs.

44. *barkened:* tanned with bark.

449. GUY MANNERING

Mr. Bertram, laird (i.e., squire) of Ellangowan, having recently been appointed a magistrate, feels that he must enforce the law forbidding the harboring of gypsies.

449a. **12.** *lea ground and dingle:* pasture and wooded ravine.

14. *baulks:* sloping uncultivated places.

449b. **1.** *pressgang:* Those who drafted men into the army.

16. *aik:* oak.

22. *sovereign,* etc.: cure for fever.

450a. **21.** *Adam Smith:* The famous economist.

38. *potato bogle:* potato-scarecrow.

45. *Maroons:* The gypsies.

49. *Ne moveas,* etc.: A pedant's way of saying: "Let sleeping dogs lie."

60. *Martinmas:* The feast of St. Martin, November 11.

450b. **20.** *of the quorum,* etc.: Alluding to Mr. Bertram's having been made one of the magistrates and the custodian of their records.

451a. **12.** *nae mair:* no more.

13. *cuddies:* donkeys.

44. *Calotte:* Jacques Callot (1592-1635), artist, master of the grotesque, precursor of Hogarth and Goya.

451b. **36.** *elf-locks:* Entangled locks.

50. *blyther:* more cheerfully.

51. *riven the thack,* etc.: torn the thatch from seven cottages.

53. *stirks in the shealings:* heifers in the gypsy shelters.

59. *sunkets:* delicacies.

452a. **4.** *bields:* shelters.

5. *tod and blackcock,* etc.: fox and grouse upon the moors.

16. *reise:* sapling.

20. *Margaret of Anjou:* The unfortunate queen of Henry VI. Scott probably had in mind her denunciations of her enemies in Shakespeare's *Henry VI,* I, v, 5.

452. THE HEART OF MIDLOTHIAN

From ch. 37. Jeanie Deans, whose sister Effie lies in Edinburgh under sentence of death for child-murder, has tramped on foot to London to pray for a pardon from Queen Caroline, and the Duke of Argyll has brought her before Her Majesty. The difficulty of Jeanie's bold effort is increased by the circumstance that the Queen has lately been angered by the unruliness of the Scotch, manifested in the Porteous riots. Capt. Porteous had ordered his troops to fire upon a crowd which had become excited at a public execution. More than a dozen persons having been killed and wounded, he was found guilty of murder; and when the Government respited him, a mob dragged him out of prison and lynched him.

452b. **36.** *cutty-stool:* A low but conspicuous stool in Scottish churches, upon which offenders against morality were condemned to sit. Lady Suffold's reputation was none too good.

47. *his hand at his chin:* The Duke and Jeanie had previously agreed that whenever she seemed to be saying the wrong things he should raise his hand to his chin.

453a. 32. *hae sae:* have so.
    39. *haill:* whole.
    39. *whiles the cast:* sometimes a lift.
453b. 23. *that unhappy man:* Capt. Porteous (see above).
    54. *puir:* poor.
454a. 3. *kend:* knew.
    6. *ca'd:* called.
    22. *dune for oursells:* done for ourselves.
    24. *maist:* most.
    29. *ae tow:* one rope.

454.
IVANHOE

The previous passages from the Waverley novels have illustrated Scott's power in discerning and depicting the noble and beautiful in characters drawn from humble life (Meg Merrilies and Jeanie Deans). The present selection illustrates his command over the grand style in historical fiction,—his successful mingling of the sublime and the human.

The hero Ivanhoe is a wounded prisoner in the castle of his enemy Front-de-Boeuf, and the beautiful Jewess Rebecca is nursing him, when the mysterious Black Knight attacks the castle.

456b. 34. *En avant*, etc.: Forward, De Bracy! . . . Front-de-Boeuf to the rescue!
458b. 30. *assoilzie:* shrive, forgive.
459a. 12. *Moloch:* A heathen god, craving human sacrifices.
459b. 12. *Gideon . . . Maccabeus:* Jewish patriots and liberators.

460.
WANDERING WILLIE'S TALE

From *Redgauntlet*, ch. 11. An illustration of Scott's sense of humor, and one of the most famous short stories of the world's literature.

Glossary

a'	all	*carles*	fellows
abune	above	*cauld*	cold
ae	a, one	*chanter*	finger-pipe of a bagpipe
aff	off	*chiel, chield*	child, fellow
ain	own	*cowped*	fell
aneath	beneath	*crawing*	crowing
anes	once		
aneugh	enough	*dang*	knocked over
arles	earnest-money	*dargle*	dell
a' thegether	altogether	*daur*	dare
auld	old	*deedie*	mischievous
		deil	devil
baith	both	*delate*	accuse
banes	bones	*deray*	mirthful noise
bauld	bold	*dinna*	don't
birling	drinking	*dirdum*	disturbance
blaud	ballad	*door-cheek*	door-post
blude	blood	*douce*	sensible
bogle	bogy, ghost	*dour*	stubborn
borrel	rough, common	*dyvour*	bankrupt
braid	broad		
brash	outburst of anger	*een*	eyes
by ordinar	out of the ordinary	*e'en*	evening
ca'	call	*fand*	found
ca'd	called	*fash*	trouble
callerer	cooler	*fasherie*	nonsense

faulding	folding	*mony*	many
flit	move	*muckle*	much
fou	full	*muils*	slippers
frae	from		
fund	found	*na*	not
		nae	no
gaed	went	*needcessity*	necessity
ganging	going	*neist*	next
garred	forced, jarred		
gash	shrewd, calm	*ony*	any
gat	got	*orra*	other
gear	property	*o't*	of it
gied	gave	*otten*	often
gien	given	*ower*	over
girned	grimaced		
ghaist	ghost	*Pace*	Easter
graned	groaned	*parochine*	parish
grat	wept	*pock*	bag
gree'd	agreed	*precesse*	precise
grit	great	*puir*	poor
grue	creep, shiver		
grund	ground	*quean*	woman
gude	good		
gudesire	grandfather	*raid*	rode
		rin	run
hae	have	*riped*	searched
haill	whole	*rug*	a good share
happed	hopped		
hauld	hold	*sack-doudling*	bagpiping
hesp	hank of yarn	*sae*	so
Hielandmen	Highlanders	*saftest*	softest
hoddled	waddled	*sair*	very much
hosting	mustering	*saunt*	saint
howlets	small owls	*scaud*	scald
		scowp	take
ilk	same; place of the same name	*sculduddery*	ribald
ilka	each	*shoon*	shoes
ill-faur'd	ill-favored	*sic*	such
		siller	silver, money
keepit	kept	*skelloch*	screech
ken	know	*sleekit*	smooth
		sough	tune
laith	loath	*speerings*	tidings
lang	long	*spule-blade*	shoulder-blade
lap	leaped	*stend*	stride
leal	loyal, honest	*suld*	should
leasing	lying		
leesome lane	all alone	*tass*	glass
Lonon	London	*tauld*	told
loup	leaped	*thick*	hard
lum	chimney	*threap*	hint
		tippenny	twopenny ale
mails	rents	*tod*	fox
mair	more	*toom*	empty
maist	most	*twa*	two
maister	master		
maun	must	*unco*	uncommon
mear	mare	*usquebaugh*	whiskey
merks	marks		
misca'd	miscalled	*wad*	would

wame	belly	*weel*	well
wanchancy	unlucky	*weel-freended*	well-befriended
warding	awarding	*wha*	who
wared	wished	*whilk*	which
wark	work	*wuss*	wish
warld	world		
warlock	magician	*yelloch*	yell
warst	worst	*yetts*	gates
waur	worse		

460a. 26. *the dear years:* the hard times.

29 ff. Sir Robert, in other words, was a cavalier, fighting under Montrose and Glencairn against the Puritans, and therefore rewarded when the Stuarts were restored.

37. *prelatist:* He supported the Church of England (prelates instead of presbyters), and persecuted the dissenting Covenanters, who politically were Whigs.

54. *tak the test:* take the oath of loyalty to king and church.

56. *recusant:* refuser.

460b. 18. *riding days:* wartimes.

29. *Hoopers and Girders:* Like *Jockie Lattin,* the name of a country dance, which Steenie could skillfully play upon the bagpipe.

40. *hunting,* etc.: Referring to the persecuting of Whigs and Covenanters.

461a. 12. *fines,* etc.: i.e., formerly he got fines from Covenanters, with which money he could purchase food and drink more plentifully than now.

41. *a professor,* etc.: He pretended to be religious.

461b. 10. *jackanape:* monkey.—Observe the cautious introduction of the uncanny.

462a. 56. *last Scots Parliament:* It passed the Act of Union, uniting the kingdoms of England and Scotland, in 1706; and the intimation is that Sir John was bribed to cast his vote in favor of it.

462b. 46. *a blaud of Davie Lindsay:* If the Bible had been read, no diabolic whistle could have sounded; but there were unsanctified lines enough in the poems of Sir David Lyndesay (c. 1490-1555),—e.g., in *Kitty's Confession.*

463a. 20. *weepers:* a white band around the sleeve, in token of mourning. Everything about Sir John, including the little rapier, suggests, in contrast to his rough father, the sleek and dapper.

24. *chape:* the loop by which the scabbard is attached.

463b. 15. *talis qualis:* such as it is; passably acceptable.

464a. 32. *horse's shoe:* This horseshoe frown is a curious instance of artistic economy. Scott originally ran across it in the accounts of the villainous wizard Major Weir (after whom the rascally monkey was named), whose sister was said to have such a frown. By transferring it to the Redgauntlets, Scott enhanced the impression of them that he wished to give.

464b. 23. *change-house:* a public house, an inn.

26. *a mutchin:* An imperial pint, i.e., about a pint and a quarter. Taken as Steenie took it, rapidly, and upon an empty stomach, this quantity of brandy might muddle the perceptions of even as hardy a drinker as the Scotch bagpiper. No doubt Scott purposely stressed these circumstances because it permitted the skeptical reader of Steenie's subsequent adventures to regard them as a drunkard's fantasy. Observe here, as throughout, the careful skill in rendering plausible the apparently supernatural.

36. This profane toast placed Steenie in the power of the Devil.

465b. 16. If Steenie had disregarded this warning, he would have had to remain in Hell.

30. *ghastly revellers:* The names that follow are those of notorious persecutors of the Covenanters, including Sir George Mackenzie. Scott's partiality for Claverhouse (Bonny Dundee) is shown.

466a. 42. *Weel hoddler,* etc.: A dance-tune of supposedly diabolic origin.

466b. 42. The mention of the sacred name looses the spell.

468a. **33.** *away it flew,* etc.: Here again Scott puts in a touch which will seem supernatural to some, and realistically explicable to others.

48. *lang forswore:* To Steenie, total abstinence for an entire year would seem long indeed.

DISC.—Compare *Wandering Willie's Tale* (1824) with Washington Irving's *Rip Van Winkle,* which appeared in *The Sketch-Book* (1819).

468.   REDGAUNTLET: THE FAREWELL OF THE LAST PRETENDER

When this incident opens, the cause of the "Chevalier," i.e., the last Stuart to land in England, and attempt an uprising against the Hanoverian king, has been betrayed. He, Charles Edward (Redgauntlet), and his small remaining band of devoted followers, had hoped to escape by sea, but are surrounded, and are about to be arrested by the forces of General Campbell. All of them are legally guilty of treason and subject to the penalty of death.

470.   WOODSTOCK

The scene is Woodstock Parish Church, eight miles north of Oxford; the time, shortly after the battle of Worcester, 1651 (not 1652 as the text has it). During the Puritan Revolution, quarrels like this were common among the different sects, not only in England but in the American colonies.

472a. **4.** *learned Theban:* originally Oedipus, who solved the riddle of the Sphinx, and became king of Thebes.

13. *dry bran and sapless porridge:* the Anglican Prayer Book.

472b. **57.** *rochets:* linen vestments.

474a. **46.** *Rosamond:* mistress of Henry II in the twelfth century; poisoned by his wife.

48. *Godstow:* a monastery.

474b. **4.** *Marston Moor:* Marston Moor, Naseby, Dunbar, and Drogheda, were scenes of victories by Cromwell,—the last being a massacre in Ireland.

26. *levant:* a fanciful strain, in contrast to a signal for attack.

29. *the young Man:* contemptuous for King Charles.

475b. **12.** *round-headed:* with hair cropped short.

29. *sequestered:* his properties confiscated.

33. *Mahar:* signifying make-speed-hasten-spoil; *Isaiah,* 8.

DISC.—In what ways are historical novels, and historical verse-romances, like Sir Walter Scott's *romantic* in the sense described in the Introduction of the *Anthology?*

ROBERT SOUTHEY (1774-1843)

I. Editions

*Fitzgerald, M. H., ed. *Poems of Robert Southey,* 1909.

Roberts, R. E., ed. Southey's and Byron's *Vision of Judgment,* 1932.

Fitzgerald, M. H., ed. *Life of Wesley,* 2 vols., 1925.

*Gollancz, Emma, ed. *Life of Nelson* (Temple Classics), 1896.

Fitzgerald, M. H., ed. *The Doctor* (abridged), 1930.

Selections by:

    *Dowden, Edward (Poems), 1895

    Zeitlin, Jacob (Prose), 1916

    Fitzgerald, M. H. (Letters), World's Classics, 1912

II. Biography and Criticism

*Dowden, Edward. *Southey* (Engl. Men of Letters), 1876.

Saintsbury, George. *Essays in English Literature,* 1895.

*Haller, William. *The Early Life of Southey,* 1917.—Cf. his "Southey's Later Radicalism," PMLA, XXVII, 281; 1922.

Kaufman, Paul. "The Reading of Southey and Coleridge," MP, XXI, 317; 1924.
Knowlton, E. C. "Southey's Eclogues," PQ, VII, 231; 1928.
Feiling, Keith. "Southey and Wordsworth," *Sketches in Nineteenth Century Biography*, 1930.
Wright, H. G. "Three Aspects of Southey," RES, IX, 37; 1933.
Brown, W. C. "Southey and the English Interest in the Near East," ELH, V, 218; 1938.
Cameron, K. N. "Shelley vs. Southey," PMLA, LVII, 489; 1942.
Havens, R. D. "Southey's 'Specimens of the Later English Poets'," PMLA, LX, 1066; 1945.
*Simmons, Jack. *Southey*, 1945.—See TLS, Apr. 21, 1945.

NOTES, COMMENTS, AND TOPICS FOR DISCUSSION

THE BATTLE OF BLENHEIM

477.

Old Kaspar lives at Blenheim, in Bavaria, Germany; where, in 1704, under the leadership of the Duke of Marlborough and the Austrian Prince Eugene, an allied army of English, Germans, Dutch, and Danes, defeated a numerically superior French and Bavarian force. Southey's poem is one of the best-known attacks upon the futility of war. In selecting the battle of Blenheim as an instance, he made a shrewd choice; for although the victory was a brilliant exhibition of military skill, the ultimate outcome of the war was that the defeated French achieved their purpose,—viz. the recognition of Philip of Anjou as King of Spain. A devil's advocate might retort to Southey, however, that although the immediate results of Marlborough's victories seemed disappointing, their ultimate consequences in enhancing the prestige and influence of Great Britain were fully worth the sacrifice. Moreover, the ambition of Louis XIV to dominate Europe was checked.

DISC.—Contrast the glorification of Blenheim in Addison's poem, *The Campaign* (1704). The style is typical of the young Romantics of that time (1798),—the expression of idealistic conceptions in a simple, almost naïve, manner. Compare Southey's poem in that respect with some of Wordsworth's and Coleridge's contributions to the *Lyrical Ballads*.

WRITTEN AFTER READING THE SPEECH OF ROBERT EMMET

478.

Robert Emmet (1778-1803) planned a revolution in Ireland; but when the rising took place, July 23, 1803, he was horrified at what seemed to him the unnecessary violence of his followers. At his trial he said "Let my character and motives repose in obscurity and peace, till other times and other men can do them justice." Southey's poem is another instance of a Romantic courageously taking issue with his own country's political conduct, on moral grounds.

MY DAYS AMONG THE DEAD ARE PAST

479.

Southey was a great lover of books and lived mostly in his library, which finally contained 14,000 volumes. De Quincey said that in conversation Southey's heart was "continually reverting to his wife, viz. his library. . . . The library . . . was in all senses a good one. The books were chiefly English, Spanish, and Portuguese; well selected, being the great cardinal classics of the three literatures; fine copies, and decorated externally with a reasonable elegance, so as to make them in harmony with the other embellishments of the room. This effect was aided by the horizontal arrangement upon brackets of many rare manuscripts, Spanish and Portuguese." (De Quincey, *Literary and Lake Reminiscences*, 1839, ch. 5.). "His dearly prized books," says his son, "indeed were a pleasure to him almost to the end, and he would walk slowly round his library, looking at them and taking them down mechanically" (Cuthbert Southey, *Life and Correspondence of Robert Southey*, 1849, ch. 38).

THE DEATH OF JOHN WESLEY

480.

Sectarian and literary conservatives had despised and derided the Methodists during the eighteenth century, largely because of their emotionally enthusiastic methods of popularizing their faith. Although Southey by 1820, the date of the *Life of Wesley*, was a devout member of the Church of England, he was broadminded enough to write the first sympathetic biography of Wesley composed by one who was not a Methodist. Another staunch Churchman, Coleridge, called it "the favorite of my library, the book I can read for the twentieth time, when I can read nothing else."

480b. 49. *clerical cap:* This seems to be one of the surprisingly few mistakes in the *Life;* for an eyewitness asserts that there was no cap, nor any handkerchief. (Moore's *Life of Wesley;* 1825, II, 394, n.).

481.   THE HISTORY OF THE PENINSULAR WAR

From 1808 to 1814, the Spanish and Portuguese peninsula was the scene of a war against Napoleon to regain the national independence of Spain and Portugal, a war in which the native forces were aided by the British. A victory in the first year of that war had resulted in the disappointing Convention of Cintra, concerning which Wordsworth wrote the pamphlet from which a selection is given, *Anth.,* p. 240 ff. Southey's *History* was soon to be superseded, especially in military matters, by one written by a participant, Sir William Napier's *History of the War in the Peninsula* (1828-1840); but it remains a noteworthy illustration of his sympathy with some of the national achievements of his time as well as one of the best specimens of his admirable prose.

In 1808-1809, the first year of the war, the Spanish city Zaragoza (better known to us as Saragossa) was twice besieged by the French, who captured it on the second attempt. The passage here given relates to the first siege.

481b. 4. *Palafox:* The Spanish commander.

11. *Aragonese:* Saragossa is the capital of the district of Aragon.

42. *Junta:* A legislative assembly.

482b. 19-21. *obtained . . . nothing more:* alluding to the fact that the city was taken in the second siege.—DISC.—Can you reconcile the sentiments concluding this passage with those of *The Battle of Blenheim?*

482.   THE LIFE OF HORATIO, LORD NELSON

The best brief biography written in the romantic period. Nelson fell on October 21, 1805. Southey's *Life* appeared eight years later; but we should bear in mind that the overthrow of Napoleon had not yet been achieved at that time, and that Southey's purpose was to strengthen the courage and perseverance of British sailors and soldiers by recalling the sublime example of Nelson's character and prowess.

An admirable feature of Southey's style is that, unlike the "smart" biographical style fashionable today, it never directs attention to itself at the expense of the subject.

See Geoffrey Callender's edition, 1922; and J. A. R. Jones, "Corrigenda to Southey's *Life*," NQ, CXLVII, 62; 1924.—For modern (controversial) views of Nelson, see Arthur Bryant's *Years of Endurance* (1942) and *Years of Victory* (1944); also Charles Morgan's admirable essay in *Reflections in a Mirror* (Second Series), 1947; and Carola Oman's *Nelson*, 1947.

482a. 56. *Sir Robert Calder:* Several weeks previously Calder had fought against the French fleet in a battle which was disappointingly indecisive. Note Nelson's unwillingness to criticize or to boast.

60. *a lord:* If Nelson had been killed, since he had no son, his brother would have succeeded to his title.

482b. 4. *upbraidings . . . displeasure:* Alluding to the tragic passion of Nelson's life. In 1798, when his fleet lay idle at Naples, he had become infatuated with the beautiful Lady Hamilton, the wife of the British envoy there. She was 35 years younger than her husband, and had led a loose life before her marriage. The liaison between her and Nelson, which lasted until his death, was notorious.

39. *all his heart,* etc.: From *St. Luke,* 10, 27.

56. *at daybreak:* i.e., on the morning of October 21, 1805, the day of the battle.

483a. 9. *Tyrolese . . . Spaniards:* For Napoleon's attack upon the latter, see above, the notes on the Peninsular War. The Tyrolese he ruthlessly subdued in 1809, and had their national hero, Andreas Hofer, shot (see the German Romantic, Julius Mosen's famous poem on Hofer).

30. *lee-line:* The line farthest from the direction whence the wind blows. The weather-line is the opposite.

484a. 10. *Trafalgar:* Correctly accented on the last syllable, as in Byron's.

> Oft did he mark the scenes of vanished war,
> Actium, Lepanto, fatal Trafalgar.

But the modern accent is usually on the second syllable.

10. *under the lee:* A coast on the leeward side, i.e., on the side the wind is blowing toward, is always dangerous.

16. *Villeneuve:* Commander of the French fleet.

42. *England expects:* As first drafted, the signal read: "Nelson expects . . ." Who suggested the more superb "England expects . . ." seems to be unknown; but when Nelson heard it he said, "Certainly, certainly." This immortal sentence is often misquoted as "England expects every man *to do* his duty."

484b. 4. *Mr. Beatty:* Southey had before him Beatty's account of Nelson's death, and in the first edition acknowledged his indebtedness thereto.

30. *last infirmity:* the love of fame,—alluding to Milton's lines in *Lycidas,* 70-72:

> Fame is the spur which the clear spirit doth raise
> (That last infirmity of noble mind)
> To scorn delights, and live laborious days.

49. *Spithead:* A stretch of water affording good anchorage near the British naval base of Portsmouth.

485a. 24. *two points:* i.e., slightly; there being 32 points in the complete circle of a compass.

485b. 6. *to strike:* to lower, in sign of surrender.

8. *old acquaintance:* He had fought her in the Battle of the Nile.

30. *forbrace bits:* Frames to which the ropes of the foresail were fastened.

39. *not yet returned:* Because she was not wasting her ammunition by firing before she was close to the enemy.

486a. 3. *filled with riflemen:* Southey may be mistaken here. The French deny the charge, and Beatty says that Nelson was killed, not by a rifle-ball, but by a musket-ball.

40. *struck:* surrendered.

486b. 4. *rove:* passed through the holes, so that the ship could be steered. These details are significant as showing that Nelson did his duty to the last.

488b. 10. The Greek quotation is from Hesiod's *Works and Days,* and may be translated as follows: "There are some whom we may call pure spirits dwelling on the earth; they are kindly, they deliver from harm, and they are guardians of mortal men."

488.   THE STORY OF THE THREE BEARS

This nursery tale, originally composed for his own children, and later included in his hodgepodge of a novel, *The Doctor,* illustrates the Romantics' sympathetic understanding of the minds of children, and their efforts to create a new and more suitable kind of literature for them (e.g., Charles and Mary Lamb's *Tales from Shakspeare*). On Southey's sources, see Mary I. Shamburger and Vera R. Lachmann, *Jour. Amer. Folklore,* Oct., 1946; cf. E. B. Vest, *Sat. Rev. Lit.,* May 24 and Sept. 6, 1947 (Phoenix Nest).

The motto is humorously quoted from the sixteenth-century author, George Gascoigne.

DISC.—Are contemporary stories for children in accord with the Romantics' ideas about children?

THOMAS CAMPBELL (1777-1844)

I. EDITIONS

*Robertson, J. L., ed. *Complete Poetical Works,* 1907.
Campbell, Lewis, ed. Selected Poems (Golden Treasury Series), 1904.

II. BIOGRAPHY AND CRITICISM

*Hadden, J. C. *Thomas Campbell*, 1899.
Saintsbury, George. *Essays in English Literature, Second Series*, 1895.
Elton, Oliver. *Survey of English Literature: 1780-1830*, 1912.
Turner, A. M. "Wordsworth's Influence on Campbell," PMLA, xxxviii, 253; 1923.
*Dixon, W. Macneile. "Thomas Campbell," *An Apology for the Arts*, 1944.

NOTES, COMMENTS, AND TOPICS FOR DISCUSSION

491.   THE PLEASURES OF HOPE

DISC.—Observe the contrast between the spirit of this poem and its form. In an almost neoclassically strict kind of heroic couplet, it expresses sympathy with the French Revolution, scorn for the oppressors of Poland, and opposition to Negro slavery. What style of heroic couplet, or what other metres, can you suggest as better suited to the emotions and ideas?

492. 4. *Guinea . . . Sibir:* The Guinea, Africa, of the slave trade, and the Siberia of the Russian exiles and prisoners.

13. *leagued Oppression:* alluding to the conquest and partition of Poland by Russia, Prussia, and Austria in the 1790's, a wrong not righted until World War I, and repeated after World War II.

14. *pandoors:* an Austrian regiment well known for its bravery and ferocity.

19. *Warsaw's last champion:* See the note on Coleridge's *Koskiusko*, *Anth.*, p. 136. Kosciuszko "fell" (l. 44) only in the sense that he was wounded and captured. He died in exile.

493. 69. *Sarmatia:* Poland.

493.   YE MARINERS OF ENGLAND

Written in the early years of the conflict against Napoleon, when, as always, the retention of sea power was Great Britain's crucial need.

DISC.—Compare the poem with the following seventeenth-century ballad, by Martyn Parker, which is in part its source:

> Ye gentlemen of England
>   That live at home in ease
> Ah! little do you think upon
>   The dangers of the seas.
> Give ear unto the mariners,
>   And they will plainly show
> All the cares and all the fears
>   When the stormy winds do blow
>   When the stormy winds do blow.
>
> If enemies oppose us
>   When England is at war
> With any foreign nation,
>   We fear not wound nor scar;
> Our roaring guns shall teach 'em
>   Our valor for to know
> Whilst they reel on the keel,
>   And the stormy winds do blow
>   And the stormy winds do blow.
>
> Then courage all brave mariners,
>   And never be dismayed;
> While we have bold adventurers,
>   We ne'er shall want a trade:
> Our merchants will employ us
>   To fetch them wealth we know:

Then be bold—work for gold,
When the stormy winds do blow
When the stormy winds do blow.

By what changes in the contents and in the diction has Campbell elevated the tone of the poem?
Contrast Blake's fiery "War Song to Englishmen," *Poetical Sketches*, Nonesuch ed. of Blake,
p. 40.

494a. 31. *meteor flag:* see, in any large dictionary, a colored picture of the British flag, its design and hue suggesting a meteor.

494 ## HOHENLINDEN

In December, 1800, at Hohenlinden, Bavaria, near the river Iser, the French defeated the Austro-Hungarians. The battle was very bloody, a fourth of the combatants being killed or badly wounded.

DISC.—Contrast with Southey's *Blenheim; Anth.*, p. 477.
"In the genuine success of *Hohenlinden* every line is a separate emphasis, but all the emphasis is required by the subject, is in its place. The thud and brief monotony of the metre give the very sound of cannonading; each line is like a crackle of musketry. What is obvious in it, even, comes well into a poem which depends on elements so simple for its success; indeed, its very existence" (Arthur Symons).

494. ## THE BATTLE OF THE BALTIC

The Danes, who had the only fleet that in alliance with the French would be very dangerous to Great Britain, had entered into an armed league of neutrality, directed against the British. Nelson was sent to destroy or capture the Danish fleet, which was protected by land-batteries in the harbor of Copenhagen. The victory was won on April 2, 1801, the defeated being treated generously. Nelson was wounded, and Captain Edward Riou was killed.
"It is an attempt," says Campbell, "to write an English ballad on the battle of Copenhagen, as much as possible in that plain, strong style peculiar to our old ballads, which tell us the when, where, and how the event happened—without gaud or ornament but what the subject essentially and easily affords" (Letter to Dr. Currie, April 24, 1805).

495. 63. *Elsinore:* A seaport near the scene of the action. Immortal in English literature as the name of Hamlet's castle.

495. ## THE LAST MAN

DISC.—Campbell had mentioned this subject to Lord Byron, who subsequently treated it in the poem called *Darkness (Anth.*, p. 544). Campbell's last man, and Byron's, face extinction in a very different spirit; contrast them.
For modern attitudes, see the Swiss novelist, C. F. Ramuz, *The End of All Men,* and the French essayist, Denis de Rougemont, *The Last Trump.*

WALTER SAVAGE LANDOR (1775-1864)

I. EDITIONS

Welby, T. E., and Wheeler, Stephen, eds. *Complete Works of Landor*, 16 vols., 1927-1936

———

Selections by:
  *Sidney Colvin (Golden Treasury), 1882.
  Havelock Ellis (Everyman's Libr.), 1933.
  J. B. Sidgwick, *Shorter Poems,* 1947.
  *Ernest De Selincourt, *Imaginary Conversations,* 1915.

II. Biography and Criticism

Forster, John. *Walter Savage Landor*, 2 vols., 1869.

*Colvin, Sidney. *Landor* (Engl. Men of Letters), 1878.

Saintsbury, George. *Essays in English Literature, Second Series;* 1895.

Goldmark, Ruth I. *Studies in the Influence of the Classics*, 1918.

Williams, Stanley T. "Landor as a Critic of Literature," PMLA, XXXVIII, 906; 1923.

Bailey, John. "Notes on the Unpopularity of Landor," *Essays by Divers Hands*, 1925.

Minchin, H. C. *Last Days, Letters, and Conversations*, 1934.

Elkin, Felice. *Landor's Studies of Italian Life and Literature*, 1934.

Becker, G. J. "Landor's Political Purpose," SP, XXXV, 446; 1938.

*Elwin, Malcolm. *Savage Landor*, 1940.

Super, R. H. "Extraordinary Action for Libel," PMLA, XLI, 736; 1941.

Selincourt, Ernest De; *Wordsworthian and Other Studies*, 1947.

Morgan, Charles. *Reflections in a Mirror, Second Series*, 1947.

497.   ROSE AYLMER

She was the daughter of Lord Aylmer (hence *sceptred race*), and from 1794 a friend of Landor. She died in Calcutta in 1800, and these lines are carved in marble on her tomb. The elegy, Lamb wrote to Landor in 1833, "has a charm I cannot explain; I lived upon it for weeks." For a defense against a "New Critic," see R. H. Super, EXP, Feb., 1945.

498.   REGENERATION

Provoked by the plight of Landor's beloved Italy and Greece, with allusions to their former freedom and present subjection.

DISC.—To be compared with Wordsworth's *Extinction of the Venetian Republic, Subjection of Switzerland*, and *Convention of Cintra* (*Anth.*, pp. 222, 236, 240); and with the many similar strains in Byron and Shelley.

498. 19. *Tarentine and Hydruntine:* of Tarentum and Otranto.

     37. *Hermus and Melena:* a river and a promontory in ancient Greece.

     41. *bard of Chios:* Homer, born in Scio.

     48. *twenty Greeks:* alluding to a daring exploit, c. 1822, in the preliminary skirmishes of the Greek War of Independence.

     55. *Salamis,* etc.: allusions to victories of ancient Greece.

     67. *Enna's mead:* the vale in Sicily from which the daughter of the goddess Ceres was carried off to the nether world.

499. 84. *Leonidas:* victor in the pass of Thermopylae against the huge armies of Xerxes, and one of the few historic characters whom the skeptical Byron admired.

     86. *twin-star of glory:* Archimedes, Syracusan mathematician, slain in 212 B. C.

499.   A FIESOLAN IDYL

Fiesole, in which the Villa Landor still stands, and where he indulged his passionate love of flowers, is a beautiful old town near Florence. See Lilian Whiting, *The Florence of Landor*, 1905.

501.   IMAGINARY CONVERSATIONS

The first three extracts are given to show Landor's opinions of Byron, Wordsworth, and Shelley; they characterize the writer quite as much as those he writes about.

501a. 30. *cried out at the Haymarket:* made his atheism public.

501b. 30. *my friends:* probably Wordsworth and Southey.

DISC.—Compare Landor's criticism of Byron with Hazlitt's (*Anth.*, p. 407).

502. SOUTHEY AND PORSON

A conversation between two scholarly critics, Richard Porson (1759-1808) being a famous classical scholar.

502a. 50. *the old man of criticism:* the critic with uninspired standards, alluding to St. Paul's evil old man (*Colossians,* 3, 9).

502b. 14. *Asiatic:* over-ornate.

502. FLORENTINE, ENGLISH VISITOR, AND LANDOR

The contrast is between the dignity of ancient Rome and the flashy modern Roman society.

502b. 51. *pyramid:* this ancient monument "points to" the graves only in the sense that it stands near the Protestant cemetery.

503a. 21. *one false story:* gossip which exaggerated Shelley's coldness toward the wife whom he had left.

28. *third place:* the other two were Wordsworth, and probably Byron.

503. MARCELLUS AND HANNIBAL

Hannibal, the famous Carthaginian general who in the third century B.C. almost conquered Rome, regarded Marcellus as his most dangerous opponent. Marcellus had made a brilliant campaign against the Gauls, whose king he slew in single combat; and he had taken Syracuse after a most difficult siege. He was ambushed while attended by only a small force, near Venusia. "Marcellus," says Plutarch (*Life of Marcellus,* 30) "was pierced through the side with a lance. Then even the few survivors of the Fregellans left him lying there, and snatching up his son, who was wounded, made their way back to camp. . . . Hannibal heard of the fate of all the rest with indifference, but when he was told that Marcellus had fallen he himself hastened to the place and stood for a long time beside the corpse, admiring his strength and beauty. He made no boastful speech, and showed no joy in his countenance, as a man who had slain a troublesome and dangerous enemy; but, wondering at the strangeness of his ending, he drew the ring from the dead man's finger, and had the corpse decently attired and burned. The relics he gathered into a silver urn, upon which he placed a golden crown, and sent it to Marcellus's son." Observe that Landor modified the incidents freely, but was faithful in his characterization of the magnanimous Hannibal and the resolute Marcellus.

503a. 39. *a Numidian horseman:* One of Hannibal's cavalry, perhaps with orders to take Marcellus alive.

503b. 9. *Islands of the Blessed:* Where heroes approved by the gods dwell in eternal bliss.

504a. 29. *Minos:* Judge in the next world.

504b. 59. *Tuscans:* The Tuscans or Etrurians in Marcellus' troops had become panic stricken.

505a. 15. The Roman father rejoices that his son tried to die in the battle, yet also that he survived.

505. METELLUS AND MARIUS

In 132 B.C., Scipio Africanus besieged Numantia, a fortified city in Spain. After enduring dreadful privations, the surviving citizens agreed to surrender after three days' delay, during which those who preferred death to captivity might make an end to themselves. "Many," says Appian (*History,* VI, 97), "directly after the surrender, killed themselves in whatever way they chose, some in one way and some in another. The remainder congregated on the third day at the appointed place, a strange and shocking spectacle. Their bodies were foul, their hair and nails long, and they were smeared with dirt. They smelt most horribly, and the clothes they wore were likewise squalid and emitted an equally foul odour. For these reasons they appeared pitiable even to their enemies. At the same time there was something fearful to the beholders in the expression of their eyes—an expression of anger, grief, toil, and the consciousness of having eaten human flesh." Upon this basis Landor invented the consuming sacrificial fire and the ghastly famished sentinel.

He also imagined that Scipio had directed one of his tribunes, Metellus, a haughty aristocrat whom Scipio once termed asinine, to have a centurion spy upon the city; and that he picked for the task Marius, who was later to become famous as a leader of the popular party in the civil wars. Landor's sympathy is of course on the side of Marius.

505a. 57. The slow-witted Metellus rebukes Marius for not withdrawing before the citizens **see** him.

506b. 35. These hopes of Marius came true.

DISC.—Compare this selection with Scott's account of the siege of Torquilstone (*Anth.*, p. 454), discussing both similarities and dissimilarities in the methods and styles.

506. ### LEOFRIC AND GODIVA

The annals of the ancient city of Coventry (which Hitler subjected to a "cultural bombing") contained the legend that about the middle of the eleventh century, the wife of Leofric, Earl of Mercia, had begged him to relieve the city of a burdensome tax. He refused unless she should ride naked through the marketplace. She did so, veiled only by her long hair. To this day Coventry celebrates her festival. Tennyson's *Godiva* appeared thirteen years after Landor's and was highly praised by him.

507a. 3. *hinds:* peasants.

507b. 35 ff. Note the characteristic preference for the festival of benevolence over the festival of gayety and ostentation.

508a. 43. *holy rood:* the cross of Christ.

508b. 32. *adds to the city's crime:* How?

509. ### PERICLES AND ASPASIA

Not one of the *Imaginary Conversations*, but a prose fiction in the form of letters supposed to be written by the celebrated Greek statesman Pericles (fifth century B. C.), to his mistress Aspasia, and their friends. The letters here selected are Nos. 69, 70, 173, 192, 194, 231, 234, and 235. Observe particularly the ideals of conduct animating these noble lovers, and the relative place of love and duty in their scale of values.

509b. 46. The plague has broken out in Athens.

510a. 56 ff. Compare the spirit of fortitude in this letter with that of Wordsworth's *Laodamia*, (*Anth.*, p. 288).

510b. 20. *Reviewing the course of my life.* Pericles proceeds to name those whom he remembers,—viz., the greatest men of the greatest age of Greece: soldiers like Aristides and Miltiades; historians like Herodotus and Thucydides; philosophers like Empedocles, Protagoras, and Hippocrates; a sculptor like Phidias; and poets and dramatists like Pindar, Æschylus, Sophocles, and Euripides.

511. ### THE PENTAMERON

Boccaccio was Landor's favorite Italian author (Felice Elkins, *Landor's Studies*, p. 166). There was a tradition that the Villa Landor had been the abode of that fourteenth-century poet and novelist, who wrote the *Decameron. The Pentameron* consists of five conversations between Boccaccio and his equally famous contemporary, Petrarch. In this selection, Boccaccio, recovering from an illness, relates how his old love Fiammetta, daughter of the King of Naples, appeared to him in a dream. Noteworthy is the sympathetic understanding of a type of love (sometimes called Petrarchan) consisting less of passion than of veneration and adoration.

DISC.—On the basis of the above *Imaginary Conversations*, what do you think of George Bernard Shaw's provocative statement (*Sat. Rev. Lit.*, Oct. 12, 1946): "Consider Walter Savage Landor, whose *Imaginary Conversations* will show you how boring characters are which are not idiosyncratically differentiated like those of Shakspeare, Shaw, Scott, and Dumas"?

514. ### THE DEATH OF ARTEMIDORA

From *Pericles and Aspasia*, letter 85. Artemidora, betrothed to Elpenor, is dying.—In later editions Landor omitted the last three lines, about Charon's ferry conveying Artemidora to the realms of the dead.

514.   THE HAMADRYAD

First published in the *Foreign Quarterly Review*, 1842; then in the *Hellenics*, 1846. The introductory note said, "Our hope is that it will be found of that order of simplicity which is simple in the manner of Theocritus." Hamadryads were spirits of trees, and each lived and died even as the tree did. J. G. Fraser's *Golden Bough* is rich in instances, especially in vol. II (*The Magic Art*). The original Greek story about Rhaicos, who lived in Asia Minor, was of the fifth century. J. R. Lowell retold it in his *Rhaecus*. Landor was attracted to the theme by his intense love of trees, as well as by his admiration for ancient times and manners.

514b. 7. *Pandion:* mythical king of Athens.

515b. 94. *Cydonian:* of a city in Crete, famous for archers.

518.   ON HIS SEVENTY-FIFTH BIRTHDAY

(Correction): Add the date of composition, Jan. 30, 1849; and change the date of publication from "1853" to "1849." Charles Dickens, and Forster (later his biographer), had called upon him on that day. Landor had intended to entitle the epigram: *Dying Speech of an Old Philosopher*.

518.   WELL I REMEMBER HOW YOU SMILED

Ianthe, who inspired several of Landor's loveliest poems, was Jane Sophia Swifte (Mrs. Godwin Swifte), to whom he was long affectionately devoted.

DISC.—Regarding the general tone of Landor's poetry and prose, consider whether he was justified in saying: "I deliver its possessor from the limitations of a fanatical or one-track mind, and from the confused hesitations of a mind divided."

Do you think these lines from Ben Jonson at all like Landor's poetry?

> It is not growing like a tree
> In bulk, doth make man better be;
> Or standing long an oak, three hundred year,
> To fall a log at last, dry, bald, and sere:
> A lily of a day
> Is fairer far in May,
> Although it fall and die that night;
> It was the plant and flower of light.
> In small proportions we just beauties see;
> And in short measures, life may perfect be.

THOMAS MOORE (1779-1852)

I. Editions

*Godley, A. D., ed. *Poetical Works of Thomas Moore,* 1910.
Falkiner, C. L., ed. *Selected Poems* (Golden Treasury), 1903.
Priestley, J. B., ed. *Tom Moore's Diary,* 1925.

II. Biography and Criticism

Brandes, Georg. *Main Currents in Nineteenth Century Literature,* 1871 ff., transl., 1901 ff
*Symington, A. J. *Thomas Moore: His Life and Works,* 1880.
Saintsbury, George. *Essays in English Literature,* 1890.
*Gwynn, S. L. *Thomas Moore* (Engl. Men of Letters), 2nd ed., 1924.
Godley, A. D. Introduction to *Poetical Works,* 1910.
Strahan, J. A.—"Byron's Biographer," *Blackwood's,* ccxv, 574; 1924.
Priestley, J. B. Introduction to *Diary,* 1925.
*Jones, Howard M. *The Harp That Once: A Chronicle of the Life of Thomas Moore,* 1937.

519.   A LETTER FROM NIAGARA FALLS

Since Moore is one of the least mystical of the Romantics, his spontaneous religious feelings in the presence of Nature should be noted.

520.   OH, BREATHE NOT HIS NAME!

DISC.—On Robert Emmet, the Irish patriot. Contrast with Southey's poem on the same subject; *Anth.*, p. 478.

520.   THE HARP THAT ONCE THROUGH TARA'S HALLS

Tara, northwest of Dublin, was a stronghold of the ancient Irish kings.

520.   LET ERIN REMEMBER

520a. 3. *Malachi:* a tenth-century Irish king who bested a Danish invader and took from his neck a collar of gold.
  6. *Red-Branch Knights:* legendary Irish knights.
520b. 9. *Lough Neagh:* originally a fountain, supposed to have flooded a wide region.

521.   AT THE MID HOUR OF NIGHT

"It is impossible not to regret that Moore has written so little in this sweet and genuinely national style" (F. T. Palgrave, *The Golden Treasury*).

521.   THE TIME I'VE LOST IN WOOING

521b. 13. *the Sprite:* this is the Irish fairy which is in your power only as long as you keep your gaze fixed upon him.

522.   DEAR HARP OF MY COUNTRY

DISC.—In connection with this song, and the *Irish Melodies* in general, consider the brilliant Irish literary renaissance at the end of the nineteenth century—Lady Gregory, Synge, Yeats, etc. What do you find in those authors that is lacking in Moore's simpler expression of the Irish spirit and character?

522.   NATIONAL AIRS

Whenever Romanticism is charged with having created too strong a sense of nationalism, it should be remembered that the movement also stimulated a sympathetic interest in the traits of other nations than one's own.

523.   LALLA ROOKH

This romance in verse is more than a hundred pages in length, and is furnished with elaborate historical introductions and notes. The story is that of the Indian princess Lalla Rookh, who is journeying to her betrothed, and to whom these passages are recited for her entertainment on the way. Some of the local color is drawn from reports of famous travelers like Bernier and Ouseley.

Saintsbury calls *Lalla Rookh* a "very respectable poem of the second rank," but his standard for inclusion in that rank are rather high.

523b. 11. *minaret:* a lofty slender tower, with balconies from which to chant prayers.
  12. *Magian:* a priest.
524b. 94. *ziraleet:* a chorus of women.

LORD BYRON (1788-1824)

I. EDITIONS

The Works of Lord Byron, 13 vols., 1898-1903; new ed., 1922:—
    Coleridge, E. H., ed. *Poetical Works,* 7 vols.
    Prothero, R. E., ed. *Letters and Journals,* 6 vols.
*Coleridge, E. H., ed. *Poetical Works,* 1905.

Selections by:
  *R. A. Rice, 1933 (*The Best of Byron*).
  R. G. Howarth, 1933 (*Letters of Lord Byron*).

II. BIOGRAPHY AND CRITICISM

Moore, Thomas. *The Life of Lord Byron, with His Letters and Journals,* 1830.
Brandes, Georg. *Main Currents in Nineteenth Century Literature,* Vol. IV; 1875.
Nichol, John. *Byron* (Engl. Men of Letters), 1887.
*Arnold, Matthew. *Essays in Criticism, Second Series,* 1888.
More, Paul Elmer. Introduction to Byron's *Poetical Works,* 1905.
Lovelace, Ralph, Earl of. *Astarte,* 1905; 2nd ed., 1921.
Elton, Oliver. *Survey of English Literature: 1780-1830,* 1912.
*Mayne, Ethel C. *Byron,* 2 vols., 1912; rev. ed., 1924.
Goode, C. T. *Byron as a Critic,* 1923.
*Fox, Sir John C. *The Byron Mystery,* 1924.
Elliott, G. R. "Byron and the Comic Spirit," PMLA, XXXIX, 897; 1924.
Rice, R. A. *Lord Byron's British Reputation,* 1924.
Chew, S. C. *Byron in England,* 1924.
*Nicolson, H. G. *The Last Journey: 1823-1824,* 1924; 2nd. ed., 1948.
*Grierson, H. J. C. "Byron and English Society," in W. A. Briscoe, ed., *Byron the Poet,* 1924.
*Drinkwater, John. *The Pilgrim of Eternity,* 1925.
Maurois, André. *Byron,* 1930.
Du Bos, Charles. *Byron and the Need of Fatality,* transl. by E. C. Mayne, 1932.
*Quennell, Peter. *Byron,* 1934.
Quennell, Peter. *The Years of Fame,* 1935.
Marjarum, E. W. *Byron as Skeptic and Believer,* 1938.
*Knight, G. Wilson. *The Burning Oracle: Studies in the Poetry of Action,* 1939.
Wiener, H. S. L. *Byron and the East: Literary Sources of the Turkish Tales,* 1940.
Russell, Bertrand. "Byron and the Modern World," JHI, I, 34; 1940.
Hentschel, Cedric. *The Byronic Teuton: Aspects of German Pessimism, 1800-1933,* 1940.
Quennell, Peter. *Byron in Italy,* 1941.
Erdman, D. V. "Byron and the Genteel Reformers," PMLA, LVI, 1065; 1941.
Erdman, D. V. "Byron as Rinaldo," PMLA, LVII, 189; 1942.
"Menander." "The English View of Byron," TLS, Jan. 22, 1944.
Trueblood, P. G. *The Flowering of Byron's Genius,* 1945.
Russell, Bertrand. "Byron," in *History of Western Philosophy,* 1946.

NOTES, COMMENTS, AND TOPICS FOR DISCUSSION

526.   LACHIN Y GAIR

Links Byron with "Ossian" and Scott.—Lochnagar (modern spelling) is a mountain in northern Scotland ("Caledonia"), often snow-capped.

526. 27. *Culloden:* a moor where the Highlanders who supported the young Stuart Pretender were defeated in 1746.

527.   INSCRIPTION ON THE MONUMENT OF A NEWFOUNDLAND DOG

The prose inscription which preceded the verse reads in part:

> One who possessed Beauty without Vanity
> Strength without Insolence
> Courage without Ferocity
> And all the Virtues of Man without his Vices

528.   ENGLISH BARDS AND SCOTCH REVIEWERS

The reviewers were Francis Jeffrey of the *Edinburgh Review*, William Gifford of the *Quarterly Review*, etc. The "Bards," besides those satirized in the selection, were Southey, Bowles, Cottle, etc.

528. 265. *Lewis:* See *Anth.*, p. 107. His *Monk* made Parnassus a churchyard by its superabundance of deaths and ghosts.

280. *St. Luke:* See *Colossians*, 4, 14. It would take a physician who had apostolic or supernatural power.

DISC.—Byron's judgment as a critic is a controversial subject; (see C. T. Goode, 1923). He changed his mind frequently. Four years later than *English Bards*, viz. in 1813, he ranked Scott highest; Samuel Rogers, second; Moore and Campbell, third; and, reluctantly, Wordsworth, Coleridge, and Southey, fourth. If you bear in mind his admiration for Pope, you can perhaps explain this ranking.

528.   WRITTEN AFTER SWIMMING FROM SESTOS TO ABYDOS

528b. 2. *Leander:* In the Greek legend, he nightly swam the Hellespont (Dardanelles) to be with his beloved, Hero, and finally was drowned. The actual breadth of the strait is only about one mile, but when Byron repeated Leander's feat, he had, owing to the fierce current, to swim at least four. See *Don Juan*, II, cv; *Anth.*, p. 671.

528.   MAID OF ATHENS, ERE WE PART

The Greek motto means: "My life, I love you."

DISC.—What do you think of J. Donald Adams' opinion (NYT, Apr. 20, 1947) that poetry such as this—and the *Stanzas for Music*, p. 533—being poetry of the heart rather than of the brain, "has vanished from our world"? Ultra-moderns praise and practice poetry much more intellectual and complex.

529.   ODE TO NAPOLEON BUONAPARTE

Written in April, 1814, on hearing the news that Napoleon had abdicated "the throne of the world."

529a. 8. *miscalled the Morning Star:* Satan was miscalled Lucifer, through a misreading of *Isaiah*, 14, 12 (Isaiah was referring to a king of Babylon).

529b. 36-40. It would have pleased Byron that a member of the American House of Representatives, in 1815, quoted these lines in a speech against conscription, which Napoleon was the first to impose, saying "Napoleon split on this rock of conscription."

46. *He who of old:* the Greek athlete Milo, who, caught in the cleft of the oak, was devoured by wolves.

55. *The Roman:* Sulla, who, after seizing supreme power, resigned.

64. *The Spaniard:* the Emperor Charles V, who abdicated and, though he did not become a monk, retired to a monastery.

530a. 95. *hadst died as honor dies:* Leigh Hunt (*Examiner*, Apr. 24) protested against the idea that Napoleon ought to have committed suicide.

109. *And she:* Maria Louisa, Princess of Austria.

530b. 127. *Timour:* Tamerlane, a Mongolian world-conquerer who carried a vanquished enemy in his train in an iron cage.

131. *he of Babylon:* Nebuchadnezzar, who went insane.

136. *thief of fire:* Prometheus.

150. *Marengo:* a village in Northern Italy near which Napoleon won one of his most brilliant victories.

160. *the string:* a chain of eagles.

251. *Washington:* Cf. *Don Juan,* VIII, 5:

> Leonidas and Washington,
> Whose every battle-field is holy ground,
> Which breathes of nations saved, not worlds undone.
> How sweetly on the ear such echoes sound!
> While the mere victor's may appal or stun
> The servile and the vain, such names will be
> A watchword till the future shall be free.

Byron's praises of Washington were quoted in R. C. Winthrop's oration at the dedication of the Washington Monument, Feb. 21, 1885.—Compare Lincoln's words: "Washington is the mightiest name of earth,—long since mightiest in the cause of civil liberty, still mightiest in *moral reformation.*" Napoleon, on the other hand, said: "I am not a man like other men, and the laws of morality or custom cannot be applied to me."

531. ## SHE WALKS IN BEAUTY

Inspired by his meeting for the first time his cousin, the beautiful Mrs. Wilmot, at an evening party (she wore a black dress with spangles; hence "night" and "starry skies").

531. ## SONG OF SAUL

Saul and his three sons were defeated by the Philistines, and he fell upon his sword (*I Samuel,* 31).

532. ## THE DESTRUCTION OF SENNACHERIB

DISC.—Read II *Kings,* 19, esp. verse 35. What does Byron add that is not in the Old Testament story?

533. 21-22. *Ashur . . . Baal:* Assyria, and its god.

533. ## STANZAS FOR MUSIC

"An event—the death of poor Dorset," says Byron, "and the recollection of what I had once felt, and ought to have felt now, but could not, set me pondering, and finally into the train of thought which you have in your hands." To Moore he wrote: "I pique myself on these lines as being the *truest,* though the most melancholy, I ever wrote." (*Letters;* March 8, 1816.)

533. ## THE DREAM

Tries to recapture, about thirteen years later, his boyhood love for Mary Chaworth, two years older than himself, who also made an unhappy marriage.

536. 191. *Pontic Monarch:* Mithridates of Pontus, who vainly tried to kill himself by poison.

536. ## THE PRISONER OF CHILLON

Shelley and Byron visited the Castle of Chillon c. June 26, 1816. Since 1820 visitors to the dungeon have been shown Byron's name carved on the third column, but its authenticity is questionable. Byron began his poem within a day or two after his visit, while staying at Ouchy on Lake Geneva.

The historic prisoner of Chillon, François Bonivard (1493-1570), was a prelate in Geneva, then under the rule of Duke Charles III of Savoy. An ardent reformer and controversialist, he strove to make Geneva an independent republic. The Duke twice cast him into prison, the second time in violation of a promise of safe conduct. The second imprisonment, the subject of the poem, lasted from 1530 to 1535. To later ages Bonivard became a hero and martyr of liberty; and several traits in his actual character, which was morally far from perfect, were obscured in a legendary sanctification. In the eighteenth century Rousseau contributed much to his fame by laying the catastrophe of his famous novel, *La Nouvelle Héloise,* near the castle of Chillon, and by remarking: "It was there that François Bonivard was kept a prisoner for six years, . . . a man of rare merit, whose righteousness and fortitude sustained every test,—a friend of liberty, although a Savoyard; and tolerant, although a priest" (Pt. VI, Letter 8, note).

Byron, as he himself later admitted, was imperfectly acquainted with the historical facts in the case. No brothers suffered with Bonivard (he had but two). Although his dungeon was foul enough, his assertion that it was "lower than the lake," was unwarranted, it being some six feet higher. Finally, upon his release, he cannot realistically be described as one who "had learned to love despair" and who "regained freedom with a sigh," his subsequent career being turbulent and strenuous.

See A. van Amstel, "The True Story of the Prisoner of Chillon," *Nineteenth Century,* May, 1900, pp. 821-829.

The poem, therefore, is best regarded not as an historical account of the particular sufferer to whose name Byron attached it, but rather as an imaginative interpretation of what the martyrs of liberty have in general endured. And such is the history of human cruelty that, thus regarded, the poem contains no exaggerations.

536b. 10. *banned:* An example of Byron's bold use of language. When he wrote, "banned" was exclusively used in the sense of "laid a curse upon." He here introduced the new sense, "prohibited."

35. *meteor lamp:* will-o'-the-wisp.

537a. 107. *Leman;* Geneva.

538b. 236. *stood a stone:* Probably influenced by Dante's famous line, "I wept not; so all stone I felt within" (*Inferno,* XXXIII). This canto of the *Inferno,* with its horrible picture of the prisoner seeing his beloved sons die before his eyes, should be compared with Byron's poem. Are there not other borrowed features besides the present one?

539a. 294. *solitary cloud:* Cf. Wordsworth's "I wandered lonely as a cloud."

331. *quiet of a loving eye:* Another Wordsworthian reminiscence; cf. Wordsworth's "the harvest of a quiet eye."

539.   POEMS OF THE SEPARATION: FARE THEE WELL

This poem and the next were written in grief and anger when Lady Byron left him. They were not at first published in the ordinary way, but circulated among "the initiated." The propriety of writing them, and letting them be known to others, was furiously debated at the time; particularly as regards the savage *Sketch,* on his mother-in-law. Wordsworth thought the publicity pitiable, the sentiments disgusting, and the style contemptible. The uninhibited Mme. de Staël, a leading French Romantic, on the other hand, is credited with remarking that "if her husband had bade her such a farewell she could not have avoided running into his arms, and being reconciled immediately."

DISC.—The Poems of the Separation raise the question of Byron's emotional audacities and his contempt for conventional opinion, which were to endear him to opponents of Victorianism. Such audacities should be noted in his later work, esp. *Childe Harold* and *Don Juan,* and discussed as an important characteristic of his work.

542.   STANZAS TO AUGUSTA

This and the *Epistle* are addressed to his beloved half-sister, who had remained loyal to him when the world turned against him.

543a. 16. *no rest at sea:* it was said of John Byron ("Foulweather Jack"), eighteenth-century admiral, that whenever he put to sea, he met with a storm.

543b. 63. *a lake:* Lake Leman (or Geneva) contrasted with their own at Newstead Abbey.

544a. 112. *its fourth:* before my twenty-fifth year was finished.

544.   DARKNESS

DISC.—Contrast Byron's characterization of the last man with Campbell's; *Anth.,* p. 495 and note.

545. PROMETHEUS

Prometheus, who knew the secret of why Jupiter would ultimately fall, refused to disclose it; and was therefore condemned to unending torture.—DISC.—In due course, this should be contrasted with Shelley's *Prometheus Unbound, Anth.*, p. 883. Here note that Byron's Prometheus has no possibility of a different future.

546. SONNET TO LAKE LEMAN

The famous authors named in the first line had dwelt near this beautiful Swiss lake. Mme. de Staël's estate was a rendezvous for men of letters and artists of the romantic school—French, German, Scandinavian, Italian, etc.,—including Byron himself.

546. CHILDE HAROLD'S PILGRIMAGE

"Childe" was a kind of title prefixed to the name of the oldest son of a noble family, until he became knighted or inherited his father's title.

Knowing that the public would assume that Childe Harold was Byron himself, the author protested in the preface (1811) of the first and second cantos as follows: "A fictitious character is introduced for the sake of giving some connection to the piece, which, however, makes no pretension to regularity. It has been suggested to me by friends, on whose opinions I set a high value, that in this fictitious character, Childe Harold, I may incur the suspicion of having intended some real personage: this I beg leave, once for all, to disclaim—Harold is the child of imagination, for the purpose I have stated. In some very trivial particulars, and those merely local, there might be grounds for such a notion; but in the main points, I should hope, none whatever."

This declaration has not been taken very seriously, Childe Harold obviously being the mouthpiece of his creator. In the later cantos (from which the selections are taken) the allusions to Byron's own life are obvious; and much of the power of the poem arises from intimately personal feelings and experiences.

Cantos III and IV, written by one who felt that his transgressions had been punished too severely, were inspired, as Goethe said, by the Genius of Pain. "I was half mad," Byron says, "during the time of the composition of Canto III, between metaphysics, mountains, lakes, love unextinguishable, thoughts unutterable, and the nightmare of my own delinquencies" (Jan. 28, 1817). In this canto, the best of the four, the main theme is the flight of a social outcast to the companionship of ocean, lake, and mountain; the method is intensely dramatic and rhetorical. The influence of this work on romantic literature was probably greater than that of any other of Byron's poems.

546. 1. *my fair child:* His daughter Augusta Ada, who was only five weeks old when Byron saw her for the last time.

547. 19. *my youth's summer:* When he began to write *Childe Harold*, he was c. twenty-one years old.

46. *in creating live a being more intense:* A passage of some importance as expressing Byron's conception of the purpose of poetry. The idealistic influence of Shelley has been seen here, and of "Wordsworth, as preached by Shelley." As Ernest Hartley Coleridge interprets this stanza (Byron's *Works*, II, 219) Byron " 'got religion', went over for a while to the Church of the mystics." On careful reading of the stanza, this interpretation will seem mistaken. What Byron characteristically values in poetry is its intensifying and exalting his own ego; and since he says nothing here of its also bringing him into communion with a higher truth (as the other great Romantics believed), we cannot justly term this a "religious" aesthetics. His view is not absolutely contradictory of Shelley's and Wordsworth's, but in comparison with theirs it is incomplete.

547. 64. He will endeavor to cease speaking of himself.

548. 74. *wormwood:* a plant of very bitter taste.
91. *nor:* and not.
100. *the most unfit of men to herd with man:* A typical passage. Cf. *Manfred*, II, II, 50-58.

> From my youth upwards
> My spirit walked not with the souls of men
> Nor looked upon the earth with human eyes;
> The thirst of their ambition was not mine,
> The aim of their existence was not mine;
> My joys, my griefs, my passions, and my powers,
> Made me a stranger; though I wore the form,
> I had no sympathy with breathing flesh.

DISC.—Stanzas XII-XIV are the first of about six outstanding passages in this canto in which a mind sick of society seeks comfort in Nature. Find and discuss the others.

549. 123. *clay will sink:* the body will cause the soul to burn low.

131. *came his fit again:* his mood returned. When Macbeth learns that Fleance has escaped his fears return, and he says: "Then comes my fit again" (III, IV, 21).

145 ff. Stanzas XVII-XIX on Waterloo, Wellington and Bluecher's decisive victory over Napoleon, June 18, 1815. An authentic description of the ball at Brussels on the eve of the battle, which is also the subject of Thackeray's well-known ch. 30 in *Vanity Fair*, may be found in Mrs. J. R. Swinton's *Life of Lady de Ros* (1893), p. 122.—There are celebrated literary treatments of Waterloo in Stendhal, Erckmann-Chatrain, and especially Victor Hugo (*Les Miserables*, II, i; and the poem, "l'Expiation" in *Les Chatiments*).

Byron visited the scene a year after the battle. He raises the question whether it was anything better than a "king-making Victory," since in several nations it settled sovereigns like the Bourbons more firmly on their tyrannous thrones.

DISC.—Contrast Wordsworth's attitude in the following lines from his *Ode for a General Thanksgiving;* Jan. 18, 1816:

> O Britain! dearer far than life is dear,
> 　　If one there be
> 　　Of all thy progeny
> Who can forget thy prowess, never more
> Be that ungrateful Son allowed to hear
> Thy green leaves rustle or thy torrents roar.
> As springs the lion from his den,
> 　　As from a forest-brake
> 　　Upstarts a glistering snake,
> The bold Arch-despot re-appeared;—again
> Wide Europe heaves, impatient to be cast,
> 　　With all her armed Powers,
> 　　On that offensive soil, like waves upon a thousand shores.
> The trumpet blew a universal blast!
> But Thou art foremost in the field:—there stand:
> Receive the triumph destined to thy hand!
> All States have glorified themselves;—their claims
> Are weighed by Providence, in balance even;
> And now, in preference to the mightiest names,
> To thee the exterminating sword is given.
> Dread mark of approbation, justly gained!
> Exalted office, worthily sustained!
> 　．　．　．　．　．　．　．　．　．　．
> Bless Thou the hour, or ere the hour arrive,
> When a whole people shall kneel down in prayer,
> And, at one moment, in one rapture, strive
> With lip and heart to tell their gratitude
> 　　For thy protecting care,
> Their solemn joy—praising the Eternal Lord
> 　　For tyranny subdued,
> And for the sway of equity renewed,
> For liberty confirmed, and peace restored!

158. *In pride of place:* at the top of his flight (falconry).

164. *is Earth more free?:* An immediate, unreflecting "No!" is the reply expected.

DISC.—Consider this passage, and similar ones to come, raising doubts whether anything was really achieved by apparent victories of right and justice. Byron is the voice of modern recurrent post-war disillusionments, felt by the Lost Generation of the 1920's, and perhaps to be felt again in the 1940's. Look up the protests made, justly or unjustly, by Archibald MacLeish, Van Wyck Brooks, etc., c. 1940, against the Lost Generation literature which interpreted the victory of the Allies in World War I as entirely futile; and the violent debate that ensued.

550. 180. *Harmodius:* The assassin of a tyrant.

200. *Brunswick's fated chieftain:* Frederick William, Duke of Brunswick (Braunschweig), Germany. His father (l. 205) had been killed in the battle of Auerstädt in 1806.

551. 226. *Cameron's Gathering:* Battle music; cf. Scott's *Pibroch of Donuil Dhu; Anth.,* p. 445. This stanza celebrates the gallant Camerons, of whom Evan fought against Cromwell in the seventeenth century; and Donald, celebrated by Thomas Campbell in *Lochiel's Warning,* was wounded in the battle of Culloden in 1746.—Remember Byron's Scottish ancestry.

235. *Ardennes:* Byron in his note on this word made the mistake of confusing the forest near Waterloo with Shakspeare's Forest of Arden ("connected," as he remarks, "with nobler associations than those of mere slaughter").

553. 316. *the greatest:* Napoleon.

554. 366. *Philip's son:* Alexander the Great.

555. 429. *What want these outlaws,* etc.: What do conquerors have that these outlaws did not have, except history's purchased page?

435. *love lent a blazon:* the shields bore the emblem of a bleeding heart.

556. 496. *Drachenfels:* German for Dragon's Rock, the dragon being the one slain by Siegfried, the mythical Teutonic hero. The castle is on the right bank of the Rhine, near Bonn. The poem is addressed to Byron's half-sister.

557. 541. *Marceau:* a popular French general, François Marceau (1769-1796).

558. 601. *Morat:* a small Swiss village whose citizens defeated in 1476 the invading Duke of Burgundy.

608. *Cannae:* The site of Hannibal's bloody victory over the Romans, 216 B.C.

559. 625. *Adventicum:* The capital of Switzerland in Roman times, fallen into ruin.

627. *Julia:* An inscription, subsequently shown to be a forgery, suggested to Byron that this heroine, after trying in vain to save her father's life, was buried in this spot.

645. *Lake Leman:* Observe that this and similar passages are not mere description. The poet, having found the life of mankind sordid or senseless, seeks solitude in Nature. The important question is: what can Nature give to such a one?

560. 666. *The race of life:* Instead of running a successful course to a noble goal, human beings, their minds darkened by ignorance of the real purpose of life, are fleeing hopelessly they know not where.

668. *The boldest steer:* Instead of making life an enterprising exploration, even the boldest seek nothing but a harbor with a safe anchorage.

669. *wanderers o'er Eternity:* Five years later, Shelley (*Adonais,* xxx), in an immortal phrase, styled Byron "the Pilgrim of Eternity." Hence the title of John Drinkwater's biography of Byron.

682. *High mountains are a feeling:* As Ernest Hartley Coleridge remarks, the sentiment is Wordsworthian (*Tintern Abbey,* 78-85) so far as it goes; but with Wordsworth the love of nature regardless of humanity was only a youthful phase. (Byron's *Works,* II, 261 n.).

561. 725. *Rousseau:* Jean Jacques Rousseau (1712-1778), famous for his novels, *La Nouvelle Héloïse* and *Émile,* as well as for his *Confessions,* and by some considered the founder of Romanticism.

743. *Julie:* heroine of *La Nouvelle Héloïse.*

745. *the memorable kiss:* See the *Confessions,* ch. 9.

562. 762. *Pythian's:* Apollo's oracle at Delphi.

770. This stanza illustrates the paradox that a political radical may retain a love for old institutions (Marjarum, *Byron,* p. 77).

563. 851 ff. *the early Persian:* Two years earlier, Wordsworth (*The Excursion,* iv) had admired the Persian priests who performed their rites not in temples and at altars but on "loftiest heights."

"The most beautiful and impressive doctrines of the divine Founder of Christianity," says Byron in his lengthy note on this stanza, "were delivered, not in the *Temple*, but on the *Mount.*" After giving many other instances of the superiority of out-of-doors worship and oratory, he quotes a passage from Rousseau's *Confessions*, II, xi, of which the following is a translation: "I cannot find a worthier homage to God than the mute admiration evoked by contemplation of his works and not expressed by definite actions. I understand how it is that dwellers in cities, who see only walls, streets, and crimes, have little faith; but I cannot understand how country-folk, and especially those who live there alone, can fail to have it. Why are their souls not uplifted with ecstasy a hundred times daily to the Creator of the wonders which strike them? . . . Within my chamber I pray more rarely and less fervently; but at the sight of a beautiful landscape I feel myself moved by something I cannot express."

859. *fond:* With a suggestion of "foolish" as well as "cherished."

564. 906. *could I wreak:* could I furiously throw my thoughts completely into expression, and thus rid myself of them.

565. 923. *Clarens:* Scene of *La Nouvelle Héloïse.*

566. 968. This stanza links Byron with the gentler moods of the Romantics, and is exceptional in his work. Contrast Canto IV, stanzas CXXI-CXXII, for the more usual melancholy strain.

977. *Lausanne:* where Gibbon lived from 1753 to 1758 and from 1783 to his death.

977. *Ferney:* Voltaire's residence from 1758-1778. Both Gibbon and Voltaire were skeptics, and hostile to Christianity.

986. *The one:* Voltaire.

995. *The other:* Gibbon.

567. 1024. *Carthaginian:* Hannibal.

1049. Hazlitt quotes the superb stanzas CXIII-CXIV in his essay, *On Living to One's-Self.*

568. 1064. *some grieve:* alluding to the cynic Rochefoucault's saying that in the adversity of our friends we are apt to find something not displeasing.

1085. *dull hate taught:* Lady Byron indignantly denied the truth of this insinuation.

569.
CHILDE HAROLD'S PILGRIMAGE: CANTO IV

In the dedication, Byron announces that he has given up the vain effort to distinguish between the pilgrim and himself. In this canto he gives less attention to Nature, and to what he calls "metaphysics," than to the glories of Italian history and art, especially to sculpture, which interested him more than painting. The descriptions are amazingly successful in combining realistic observation with depth of feeling.

569. 1. *Venice:* For this city, long a defender of Western civilization in the Mediterranean, victor against the Turks in the battle of Lepanto (1571), but now in subjection, the Romantics had an ardent admiration. Cf. Wordsworth's *On the Extinction of the Venetian Republic; Anth.,* p. 222 and note. See the fine illustrations in *Life,* Aug. 4, 1947.

8. *winged Lion:* emblem of the city, it stood on the top of a pillar near the palace.

10. *Cybele:* a goddess who wore a mural crown (tiara).

19. *Tasso's echoes:* In former days the gondoliers used alternately to sing stanzas of the sixteenth-century poet Tasso's epic, *Jerusalem Delivered.* Thirty years before Byron's visit, the custom was dying: Goethe had to bespeak a special performance of such singing (see his *Letters from Italy,* October 6, 1786).

27. *masque:* the favorite place of entertainment.

33. *Rialto:* the chief place of commerce and exchange.

33. *Shylock and the Moor:* Shakspeare's Shylock and Othello.

34. *Pierre:* A tragic character in Otway's *Venice Preserved,* formerly almost as well known as the Shakspearean personages.

37. *The beings of the mind:* See the note on 547. 46, above.

570. 109. *steeds of brass:* The Genoese general Doria, in 1379, boasted that he would bridle these celebrated bronze horses.

120. *Planter of the Lion:* A wingèd lion was the emblem of Venice.

124. *Candia . . . Le Panto:* The Venetians defended Candia (Crete) for twenty-four years against the Turks.—In the Gulf of Lepanto (west of Greece) the Venetians participated in a decisive naval victory over the Turks.

571. **136 ff.** *When Athens' armies,* etc.: The Athenians in the fifth century B. C. besieged Syracuse, Sicily, but were defeated and captured. It was related that those who could recite passages from Euripides were released.

148. *Tasso:* Torquoto Tasso (1544-1595), celebrated poet, some of whose work was published at Venice.

158. *Radcliffe;* Mrs. Radcliffe (1764-1823), the scenes of several of whose novels are laid in Italy.—Schiller's *Ghost-Seer* is the story alluded to.

573. **316.** *Tasso:* The poet, while in the service of Duke Alfonso of Ferrara, was ill-treated and went mad. Legend had it that he had been so bold as to fall in love with the Duke's sister, on which subject Goethe wrote a tragedy of great importance in the Romantic Movement.

370. *Italia:* Stanzas XLII and XLIII are translated from a sonnet by Filicaja.

574. **478.** *Santa Croce:* the church in Florence which Byron calls the Westminster Abbey of Italy. Besides Michelangelo and the others named, Ugo Foscolo, the Italian Romantic of Byron's own time, lies buried there.

495. *Canova:* celebrated contemporary Italian sculptor.

575. **694.** *Oh Rome!:* The theme is that of Gibbon's *Decline and Fall of the Roman Empire,* to which Byron alludes in his notes. The first stanza is characteristic in that he does not forget his own "petty misery" while contemplating the imperial woes of Rome. If that be somewhat egotistic, contrast the even greater self-regard of André Gide's remark in his *Journals:* "I have found the secret of my boredom in Rome: I do not find myself interesting here."

703. *Niobe:* The ultimate in sorrow; in Greek myth, the queen-mother whose twelve children were slain before her eyes.

707. *contains no ashes:* The remains had been removed in 1780. There was much rifling of tombs and sepulchres.

576. **853.** *him who humbled:* Napoleon.

868. *deadly days,* etc.: A swift and bilious review of recent history: first, the Reign of Terror; next, the imperial ambitions of France; and finally, the peace which strengthened despotic power. See the note on *Waterloo, Anth.,* **549.** **145.**

577. **874-875.** *Freedom's banner . . . against the wind:* One of the sublimest metaphors in Byron, true to nature and to history, and prophetic also.

881. *the North:* Great Britain.

579. **1147.** *Coliseum . . . moonlight:* Before Byron, Goethe (*Letters from Italy*, February 2, 1787) had observed: "Of the beauty of a walk through Rome by moonlight it is impossible to form a conception . . . Peculiarly beautiful at such a time is the Coliseum." After Byron, another great Romantic, Mme. de Staël, in *Corinne,* expressed the same enthusiasm.

1184. *Orestes:* He slew his mother and her lover, who had murdered Agamemnon, his father.

580. **1221.** *Janus glance:* A god represented with two faces, seeing the past and the future simultaneously. Here equivalent to double-faced.

1225-1229. "There is in these lines from the apostrophe to the Coliseum a sublimity of accent which was fully justified in Byron's case; for here, perhaps more than in any other instance, force of personality is everything, and, as he rightly divined, his was proof against wear and tear" (Du Bos, *Byron and Fatality,* p. 30).

581. **1252.** *Gladiator:* a famous statue in the Vatican. If you will find and study a good picture of it, you will appreciate these two stanzas, which admirably combine descriptive realism and historical imagination.

1261. *Arise, ye Goths:* The wish was fulfilled when the Goths under Alaric sacked Rome in 410 A. D.

582. **1293.** *bald first Caesar's head:* "Suetonius," notes Byron, "informs us that Julius Caesar was particularly gratified by that decree of the senate which enabled him to wear a wreath of laurel on all occasions. He was anxious, not to show that he was the conqueror of the world, but to hide that he was bald." This backstairs psychology is in the manner of some modern biography. See the note on *Waterloo, Anth.,* **549.** **145;** and bear in mind that Suetonius wrote a hundred years after Caesar's death.

1297. Byron takes this quotation from Gibbon, who quoted it from the Venerable Bede (8th century), who in turn probably obtained it from Anglo-Saxon pilgrims to Rome. **1370.** *Diana's marvel:* the temple of Diana at Ephesus.

583. 1586. *one fair Spirit:* his sister?

1620. *there let him lay:* A notoriously incorrect use of "lay." Attempts to regularize Byron's grammar by alleging that "lay" is the predicate of "The armaments" in the next line collapsed before the plain fact that Byron's manuscript shows a period after "lay."

583. 1629. Byron's note on this passage is characteristic: "The gale of wind which succeeded the battle of Trafalgar destroyed the greater part (if not all) of the prizes—nineteen sail of the line—taken on that memorable day. I should be ashamed to specify particulars which should be known to all, did we not know that in France the people were kept in ignorance of the event of this most glorious victory in modern times, and that in England it is the present fashion to talk of Waterloo as though it were entirely an English triumph, and a thing to be named with Blenheim and Agincourt, Trafalgar and Aboukir. Posterity will decide; but if it be remembered as a skilful or as a wonderful action, it will be like the battle of Zama, where we think of Hannibal more than of Scipio. For assuredly we dwell on this action, not because it was gained by Blücher or Wellington, but because it was lost by Buonaparte—a man who, with all his vices and his faults, never yet found an adversary with a tithe of his talents (as far as the expression can apply to a conqueror) or his good intentions, his clemency or his fortitude. Look at his successors throughout Europe, whose imitation of the worst parts of his policy is only limited by their comparative impotence, and their positive imbecility."

584. 1639. One of the sublimest and truest stanzas in the poem.

DISC.—Swinburne ("Wordsworth and Byron") and others have asserted that the verse of *Childe Harold* is not admirable, and that it would be improved if translated into good prose. Try it, and see.

585.   MANFRED: A DRAMATIC POEM

The reviewers of Manfred discussed resemblances between it and such works as Marlowe's *Dr. Faustus,* Goethe's *Faust,* and Æschylus' *Prometheus.* Writing to Murray, Oct. 12, 1817, Byron remarked: "Many thanks for *The Edinburgh Review,* which is very kind about *Manfred,* and defends its originality, which I did not know that anybody had attacked. I *never read,* and do not know that I ever saw, the *Faustus* of Marlowe, and had, and have, no dramatic works by me in English, except the recent things you sent me; but I heard Mr. Lewis translate verbally some scenes of Goethe's *Faust* (which were some good, and some bad) last summer;— which is all I know of the history of that magical personage; and as to the germs of *Manfred,* they may be found in the Journal which I sent to Mrs. Leigh . . . shortly before I left Switzerland. I have the whole scene of *Manfred* before me, as if it was but yesterday, and could point it out, spot by spot, torrent and all. Of the *Prometheus* of Æschylus I was passionately fond as a boy (it was one of the Greek plays we read thrice a year at Harrow) . . . As to the *Faustus* of Marlowe, I never read, never saw, nor heard of it—at least, thought of it, except that I think Mr. Gifford mentioned in a note of his which you sent me, something about the catastrophe, but not as having anything to do with mine, which may or may not resemble it, for anything I know. The *Prometheus,* if not exactly in my plan, has always been so much in my head that I can easily conceive its influence over all or anything that I have written;—but I deny Marlowe, and his progeny, and beg that you will do the same."

Goethe wrote a review of *Manfred* in June, 1820, saying: "Byron's tragedy, *Manfred,* was to me a wonderful phenomenon, and one that closely touched me. This singular intellectual poet has taken my *Faustus* to himself, and extracted from it the strangest nourishment for his hypochondriac humor. He has made use of the impelling principles in his own way, for his own purposes, so that no one of them remains the same; and it is particularly on this account that I cannot enough admire his genius. The whole is in this way so completely formed anew that it would be an interesting task for the critic to point out, not only the alterations he has made, but their degree of resemblance with, or dissimilarity to, the original; in the course of which I cannot deny that the gloomy heat of an unbounded and exuberant despair becomes at last oppressive to us. Yet is the dissatisfaction we feel always connected with esteem and admiration."

Byron sent this to Murray, June 7, 1820, with the following comment: "Enclosed is something which will interest you, to-wit, the opinion of *the* Greatest man of Germany—perhaps of Europe—upon one of the great men of your advertisements, (all 'famous hands,' as Jacob Tonson used to say of his ragamuffins,)—in short, a critique of *Goethe's* upon Manfred. There is the original, Mr. Hoppner's translation, and an Italian one; keep them all in your archives,— for the opinions of such a man as Goethe, whether favorable or not, are always interesting, and this is, moreover, favorable. His *Faust* I never read, for I don't know German; but Matthew Monk Lewis, in 1816, at Coligny, translated most of it to me *viva voce*, and I was naturally much struck with it; but it was the *Staubach* and the *Jungfrau*, and something else, much more than *Faustus*, that made me write *Manfred*. The first scene, however, and that of *Faustus* are very similar."

In recent times, the discovery of Byron's relations with his half-sister causes one to attach a deep significance to the apparently unimportant words "and something else." Without that passionate experience and the consequent remorse there would have been no *Manfred;* but it also drew from the "Gothic" novels and dramas (Walpole, Beckford, Lewis, etc.). See Bertrand Evans, "Manfred's Remorse and Dramatic Tradition," PMLA, LXII, 752; 1947.

585. 5. *in my heart there is a vigil:* It is significant that Byron chose as the motto (from Tasso) of *The Corsair:* "His inmost thoughts could never slumber." "Though that vigil did not assume all its tragic intensity," says Du Bos (*Byron and Fatality*, p. 34) until after the intercourse with Augusta, I think that there can be no doubt that the terrible scenes with his mother, in his childhood, were what sowed the first seeds of it."

593. 40. *William Tell:* Celebrated Swiss patriot on whom Schiller wrote a play.

596. 92. *He who,* etc.: The Neo-Platonic philosopher Jamblicus who called the two gods of love out of the Springs at Gadara in Syria.

598. 182. *Hag of Endor:* The witch of Endor who raised up Samuel from the dead, see *I Samuel,* 28.

183. *the Spartan monarch:* Pausanias, who by mistake slew his beloved. When the priests (Evocators) summoned up her ghost and asked for a message of pardon, she darkly replied that he would soon be freed from his agony. He died soon thereafter. See Plutarch's *Life of Cimon.*

605. 88. *Rome's sixth emperor:* Nero.

607. 4-29. *Glorious orb!:* G. Wilson Knight (*The Burning Oracle*) emphasizes the importance of this nature-passage, and of the passage 610, 38-41, about those "who still rule our spirits from their urns."

DISC.—Assuming that *Childe Harold* and *Manfred* are in large measure personal confessions, do you think Grierson right in saying (Briscoe, *Byron the Poet*, 1924) that Byron remorsefully admits he has committed wrongs, but does not feel responsible for them since God created him as he is and ought not to punish him for doing what his nature compelled him to do? Is that the attitude of the Childe and of Manfred? Is it also the attitude of Prometheus?

Prometheus, Childe Harold, and *Manfred* present the Byronic "hero," widely imitated in all European literatures. A modern (Symbolist) descendant or variant of the type is Villiers de l'Isle Adam's hero in *Axel*, a "dramatic poem in prose," who lives, however, for art only. Huysmans and other moderns have created similar characters, whose likenesses and differences in relation to Byron's are worth discussing. See Edmund Wilson, *Axel's Castle*, ch. 8.

612. BEPPO: ITALY AND ENGLAND

Noteworthy for its sarcastic praise of Byron's native land.

612. 337. *becaficas:* a small bird, highly prized by Italian gourmets.

614. MAZEPPA

The foundation of this tale is a passage in Voltaire's *History of Charles XII*, which told of a young Polish gentleman Mazeppa who made love to his master's wife, and was cruelly punished by being bound upon the back of a wild horse. After becoming a Cossack chieftain Mazeppa fought against the Russians under the great King of Sweden Charles XII, who was defeated at Poltava in 1709.

614. 56. *Hetman:* Chieftain of Cossacks.—Ukraine is a district in Russia.

104. *Bucephalus:* Alexander's favorite horse.

622.   DON JUAN: CANTO I

Motto: It is difficult to speak about ordinary subjects in an appropriate manner.—See Hazlitt, *On Familiar Style, Anth.,* p. 405.

Don Juan, Byron's masterpiece, has been variously termed "a picaresque novel in verse," "*the* epic of modern life," and Byron's "most serious criticism of life." A brilliant appreciation of both its merits and its faults is found in Taine's *Hist. of Engl. Lit.,* IV, II.—Elizabeth F. Boyd's *Byron's 'Don Juan'* (1945), and T. G. Steffan's "Byron At Work On Canto I," MP, XLIV, 141 (1947), analyze the complex environmental, emotional, and intellectual forces in the poem. P. G. Trueblood's *The Flowering of Byron's Genius* (1945) finds its main theme an attack against "all insincerity which obstructs individual and national freedom." See also S. de Madariaga, *Don Juan as a European Figure* (1946).

On the Countess Guiccioli, the most important personal influence on Byron during his *Don Juan* period, see Austin K. Gray's *Teresa or Her Demon Lover,* (1945); also E. C. Smith in PMLA, XLVI, 1221 (1931).

622. 15. *explaining metaphysics:* in *Biographia Literaria.*

623. 46. *Wordsworth:* Byron's savage note on this passage calls him a "poetical charlatan and political parasite."

86. *heartless daughters:* it was said that Milton was cheated by them; Byron compares him to Lear.

88. *Castlereagh:* the great Tory statesman largely responsible for Napoleon's defeat and the peace-treaty, whose faults were bitterly exaggerated by Byron and Shelley.

624. 102. *Ixion:* fixed in hell to an ever-turning wheel.

117. *Eutropius:* a eunuch, and the despicable minister of a Roman emperor; see Gibbon, ch. 32.

132. buff and blue: the colors of the Whigs (Liberals).

136. *Ultra-Julian:* alluding to Julian the Apostate.

626. 73. *a learned lady:* Lady Byron is lampooned in the character of Juan's mother.

85. *Feinagle:* a charlatan who professed to train the memory.

627. 117. *Romilly:* the judge who condemned Byron; see Byron's exultant letter on his suicide; *Anth.,* p. 739.

135. *Macassar:* hair-oil.

629. 210. *tried to prove her lord mad:* Lady Byron had Byron's sanity inquired into.

631. 288. *Doctor's Commons:* divorce court.

635. 508. *St. Anthony:* Byron refers to Alban Butler's *Lives of the Saints.*

637. 598. *Tarquin:* the ravisher in Shakspeare's *Rape of Lucrece.*

639. 701. *the bard:* Thomas Campbell.

642. 829. *Anacreon Moore:* Thomas Moore translated the Odes of the Greek poet Anacreon.

646. 1030. *Congreve's rockets:* explosives invented by William Congreve, (1772-1828).

1052. *lantern:* miner's lamp, first used in 1816.

649. 1077. *Cortejo:* lover.

1083. *O'Reilly:* in a note, Byron says Donna Julia made a mistake, O'Reilly was defeated.

652. 1328. *Clarence:* see Shakspeare's *Richard III,* Act I, Sc. IV.

660. 1690. *Consule Planco:* in the consulship of Plancus, Horace was young and foolish, and ever ready to fight.

662.   DON JUAN: CANTO II

In dramatic contrast to the light-hearted tone of Canto I comes this grim realism. Byron's idea of what Wordsworth called "the ordinary language of men" must have shocked the "Laker."—The situation is that Juan, on the way from Spain to Italy, is wrecked in a storm. Pedrillo is his tutor. Many of the realistic details are taken from Dalzell's *Shipwrecks and Disasters at Sea* (1812).

662. 376. *puncheon:* barrel.

663. 392. *familiar:* attendant spirit.

667. 659. *Ugolino:* Dante, *Inferno*, XXXIII.

671. 840. *Leander:* See Byron's *Written After Swimming from Sestos to Abydos, Anth.,* p. 528 and note.

675. 1036. The Greek word means intelligence.

676. 1095. *my grand-dad's:* John Byron's *Narrative* of his expedition around the world.

679. 1232. *Minotaur:* the mythical bull with whom Pasiphae, queen of Crete, fell in love. Byron delights to burlesque classic myths—in which, too, he has many modern imitators.

687. 1607. *then write a novel:* alluding to Lady Caroline Lamb, who ardently pursued him and afterwards told her side of the story in the novel *Glenarvon*. See the amusing *Young Melbourne and his Marriage with Caroline Lamb* (1939), by Lord David Cecil.

DISC.—What do you think of the arguments in Leigh Hunt's defense of Cantos First and Second against objections raised on moral grounds? See Hunt's *On Byron's 'Don Juan', Anth.,* p. 1003.

Another live topic for discussion is furnished by the defense of the first five cantos entitled *John Bull's Letter to Lord Byron* (ed. A. L. Strout, 1947), which its editor has found to be the work of J. G. Lockhart, Scott's son-in-law.

687.   **DON JUAN: CANTO III**

698. 690. *Sappho:* The earliest celebrated poetess of Greece.

701. *Marathon:* Scene of a victory which freed Greece from Persian domination.

730. *Thermopylæ:* The pass where the Spartan Leonidas defeated the Persian king Xerxes.

699. 739. *Turkish:* When this was written, Greece was subject to Turkey.

752. *Polycrates:* He ruled in the days of the poet Anacreon, but he was a Greek, not a foreign, tyrant.

767. *the Franks:* Any foreign ruler.

700. 815. *Marlborough:* The eighteenth-century English general, famed for his brilliant victories.

827. *Titus,* etc.: The allusions are to amatory escapades.—Titus was emperor of Rome 79-81.—Currie's *Life of Burns* exaggerates the dissipation.—It was said that Cromwell as a lad was skilful in robbing orchards.

701. 852. *Joanna Southcote:* (1750-1814). She was a religious fanatic who founded a sect, and prophesied that she would bear a second "Shiloh" or Messiah.

865. *longueurs:* Tiresome passages.

871. *epopée:* Epic.

702. 893. *Jack Cade:* He led an insurrection in the fifteenth century, and his name became a byword for ignorant rebelliousness.

896. *him who drew:* Dryden.

702.   **DON JUAN: CANTO IV**

In the pathetic close of the story of Haidée the idyllic nature of the episode is stated in lines 115 and 213; the lovers "were not made in the real world to fill a busy character," "the world was not for them," etc.

Stanzas III and IV, about "turning what was once romantic to burlesque," are noteworthy explanations of so-called romantic irony.

703. 29. *Lethe:* the spring of forgetfulness.

43. *Pulci:* Luigi Pulci (1432-1487), an Italian poet, wrote a half-serious, half-comic epic. *Morgante Maggiore.*

709. 360. *shows what the passions are in their full growth:* one of the objectives of this style of poetry.

711. 414. *Bohea:* an inferior kind of tea.

417. *qualified with Cogniac:* mixed with brandy.

418. *Phlegethontic:* fiery.

421. *rack:* a mixture of liquors, a punch; also a hangover.

456. *Simoom:* a hot wind from the desert.

714.   DON JUAN: CANTOS X-XI

In the intervening cantos, Don Juan escapes from slavery in a harem to service in the Russian army and the court of Catherine the Great, and finally visits England. E. D. H. Johnson, "Don Juan in England," ELH, XI, 135 (1944) maintains that the satire, although just so far as "high Society" was concerned, suffers through Byron's ignorance of the great middle class.

715. 427. *Banquo's glass:* in a mirror Macbeth sees Banquo and his descendants as kings of Scotland (*Macbeth*, IV, 1).

441. *Moscow, Leipsic, Mont Saint Jean:* scenes of Napoleon's defeats.

448. *Lowe:* Sir Hudson Lowe, governor of St. Helena during Napoleon's capitivity.

716. 471. *Boeotian:* implies that Landor was heavy and dull.

473. Stanza LX,—its tone should be contrasted with Shelley's *Adonais; Anth.,* p. 954.

717. 516. *Centaur Nessus garb:* burning garb.

535. *Or Molu:* brass made to look like gold.

718. 571. *bogle:* ghost.

719. 681. *carpe diem:* make the most of the present day.

DISC.—Consider Byron as the precursor of the modern "hard-boiled" school, with its ironic, amoral attitude—his sense that social life is almost wholly a game of make-believe, and that it is bourgeois hypocrisy to pretend otherwise, or self-deception.

What do you think of Andrew Lang's lines on *Don Juan?*

> This kind of writing is my pet aversion,
> I hate the slang, I hate the personalities,
> I loathe the aimless, reckless, loose dispersion,
> Of every rhyme that in the singer's wallet is,
> I hate it as you hated the *Excursion.* . . .

Has George Bernard Shaw learned anything from Byron? See his *Man and Superman* (1904), especially the amusing interlude in which Don Juan debates with the Devil. Shaw makes woman the pursuer; man, the pursued. Is that as new as Shaw seems to have supposed?

720.   WHO KILLED JOHN KEATS?

See Shelley's *Adonais, Anth.,* p. 954 and the notes.

720.   CAIN: A MYSTERY

Goethe admired *Cain,* and regretted that Byron did not live to reinterpret more of the Old Testament; but to most readers in England it was a frightfully shocking performance to make the first murderer a free-thinker and a critic of God or God's worshippers, a critic moreover who seemed to have the best of the argument. For the issues involved, see above, the first topic for discussion at the end of the notes on *Manfred.*

724.   THE VISION OF JUDGMENT

There is a good edition, by Ellis Roberts, of both Southey's *Vision* and Byron's (1932), with an Introduction covering the controversy.

When George III died, in 1820, the Poet Laureate, Robert Southey, in duty bound, praised his virtues in verses entitled *A Vision of Judgment.* In the preface thereof he unfortunately spoke ill of Byron's character. Byron's retort, one of the most incisive satires in our tongue, was published with the following preface:

> It hath been wisely said, that "One fool makes many"; and it hath been poet-
> ically observed—
> "That fools rush in where angels fear to tread."—Pope.
> If Mr. Southey had not rushed in where he had no business, and where he never
> was before, and never will be again, the following poem would not have been
> written. It is not impossible that it may be as good as his own, seeing that it can-
> not, by any species of stupidity, natural or acquired, be *worse.* The gross flattery,

the dull impudence, the renegado intolerance, and impious cant, of the poem by the author of *Wat Tyler*, are something so stupendous as to form the sublime of himself—containing the quintessence of his own attributes.

So much for his poem—a word on his Preface. In this Preface it has pleased the magnanimous Laureate to draw the picture of a supposed "Satanic School," the which he doth recommend to the notice of the legislature; thereby adding to his other laurels the ambition of those of an informer. If there exists anywhere, except in his imagination, such a School, is he not sufficiently armed against it by his own intense vanity? The truth is that there are certain writers whom Mr. S. imagines, like Scrub, to have "talked" of *him;* for they laughed consumedly.

I think I know enough of most of the writers to whom he is supposed to allude, to assert, that they, in their individual capacities have done more good, in the charities of life, to their fellow-creatures, in any one year, than Mr. Southey has done harm to himself by his absurdities in his whole life; and this is saying a great deal. But I have a few questions to ask.

1stly, Is Mr. Southey the author of *Wat Tyler?*

2ndly, Was he not refused a remedy at law by the highest judge of his beloved England, because it was a blasphemous and seditious publication?

3rdly, Was he not entitled by William Smith, in full parliament, "a rancorous renegado"?

4thly, Is he not poet laureate, with his own lines on Martin the regicide staring him in the face?

And, 5thly, Putting the four preceding items together, with what conscience dare *he* call the attention of the laws to the publications of others, be they what they may?

I say nothing of the cowardice of such a proceeding, its meanness speaks for itself; but I wish to touch upon the *motive*, which is neither more nor less than that Mr. S. has been laughed at a little in some recent publications, as he was of yore in the *Anti-Jacobin*, by his present patrons. Hence all this "skimble-scamble stuff" about "Satanic," and so forth. However, it is worthy of him—*"qualis ab incepto."* ["the same as he always was"].

If there is anything obnoxious to the political opinions of a portion of the public in the following poem, they may thank Mr. Southey. He might have written hexameters, as he has written everything else, for aught that the writer cared— had they been upon another subject. But to attempt to canonize a monarch, who, whatever were his household virtues, was neither a successful nor a patriot king,— inasmuch as several years of his reign passed in war with America and Ireland, to say nothing of the aggression upon France,—like all other exaggeration, necessarily begets opposition. In whatever manner he may be spoken of in this new *Vision*, his *public* career will not be more favorably transmitted by history. Of his private virtues (although a little expensive to the nation) there can be no doubt.

With regard to the supernatural personages treated of, I can only say that I know as much about them, and (as an honest man) have a better right to talk of them than Robert Southey. I have also treated them more tolerantly. The way in which that poor insane creature, the Laureate, deals about his judgments in the next world, is like his own judgment in this. If it was not completely ludicrous, it would be something worse. I don't think that there is much more to say at present.

724. 5. *eighty-eight:* The last year of the old régime. The French Revolution broke out in 1789.

726. 142. *the last we saw here:* the guillotined Louis XVI.

729. 364. *Apicius:* A celebrated epicure of the days of Augustus.

383. *Catholic participation:* Alluding to the fact that Catholics still lay under some disabilities.

391. *Guelph:* Anti-Catholic.

731. 520. *Jack Wilkes:* A leader of the extreme opposition to the king.

732. 564. *Bute and Grafton:* The king's ministers.

585. *Junius:* The most brilliant pamphleteer who opposed the government of George III; his identity is still unknown.

733. 632. *Sir Philip Francis:* Believed to be Junius.

734. 667. *Nominis Umbra:* Merely the shadow of a name.
670. *Tooke:* Another Republican.
728. *Non Di, non homines:* neither gods nor men ("the rest" is "will tolerate mediocre poetry."—Horace).

735. 736. *Pye:* Henry James Pye, a wretched poet, who was Southey's predecessor as poet laureate.
745. *the varlet:* Southey.

736. 807. *Alfonso:* a proud King of Spain who said that if he had been consulted at the time of the Creation, he would have spared God some absurdities.
828. *Phaeton:* The son of the sun who, trying to drive the sun's chariot, fell from heaven.
840. *Welborn:* a character in *A New Way To Pay Old Debts,* by the seventeenth-century playwright Massinger.

736.   ON THIS DAY I COMPLETE MY THIRTY-SIXTH YEAR

Written a few weeks before his death. T. O. Mabbott (EXP, Mch., 1946) points out the rich allusions to classical tradition. Byron moves closer to Landor here.

737. 23. *The Spartan was not more free:* free from selfish considerations. Having done his duty to his country, and being dead or wounded, he is borne away upon his shield.
26. *through whom:* alluding to his warlike ancestry.

737.   STANZAS WRITTEN BETWEEN FLORENCE AND PISA

737. 3. *myrtle and ivy:* love and friendship.

737.   LORD BYRON: LETTERS

Those who believe that *Childe Harold* and *Don Juan* would have been even better in the form of prose fiction, point to the admirable style of his letters—informal, frank, intense, and terse.

737b. 1. *mother of the Gracchi:* the Gracchi were two honorable Roman tribunes, whose mother declared that they were her true jewels.

738a. 35. *John Murray:* a great publisher, and devoted friend of many of the Romantics.
44. *virginals:* a musical instrument like a small piano.
44. *conceits:* displays and games thought up for amusement.
58. *Livy:* bk. VIII, ch. 18.

738b. 13. *horrenda strage:* awful downfall.
34. *beat a Venetian:* Othello, V, II.

739a. 26. *Romilly:* the judge whom Byron thought unjust to him. Romilly, upon the death of his wife, killed himself at the age of 61.

740a. 6-14. A sincere and noteworthy statement of his purposes in writing ("not to delight women and the populace").

740b. 26. What they implore is peace and eternal rest.
50. His friends did convey his body home to Newstead.

741a. 50. *this book:* a celebrated romantic novel, Mme. de Staël's *Corinne,* in which Italy and England are contrasted.

741b. 29. *The child:* Allegra, aged four, daughter of Byron and Claire Clairmont. He placed her in a convent near Ravenna, where she died a year later.—See R. G. Grylls, *Claire Clairmont,* 1939.

742a. 53. *Werner:* a tragedy by Byron, based on a German story, and dedicated to Goethe.

742b. 41. *fatal to all great original undertakings:* again, the romantic revolt against worldliness.

743a. 15. Written less than four months before his death. The authors named towards the end of the letter died, or were wounded, on a battlefield.

DISC.—Continental Europeans place Byron higher than any other English author except Shakspeare. What do you think of the suggestion that the reason why Englishmen and Americans do not place him so high is because he is so different from the main current of Anglo American literary tradition—such a contrast to Shakspeare, Milton, Wordsworth, Keats, Emerson, Whitman, etc.?

Discuss Hazlitt's criticism of Byron (*Anth.*, p. 407), and Landor's (*Anth.*, p. 502).

JOHN KEATS (1795-1821)

I. EDITIONS

Forman, H. Buxton, ed. *The Poetical Works and Other Writings of John Keats* (Hampstead Edition), 8 vols., 1938-1939).—If that ed. is not accessible, use Forman's ed., *Complete Works,* 5 vols., 1901.

Selincourt, Ernest De, ed. *Poems*, 5th ed., 1926.

Garrod, H. W., ed. *Poetical Works*, 2nd ed., 1939.

*Thorpe, C. DeW., ed. *Complete Poems and Selected Letters*, 1935.

Forman, H. Buxton, ed. *Letters*, 3rd ed., 1947.

Weller, E. V., ed. *Autobiography* (compiled from his letters), 1934.

II. BIOGRAPHY AND CRITICISM

Brown, Charles Armitage (contemporary). *Life of Keats*, 1939.

Milnes, R. M. (Lord Houghton). *Life, Letters, and Literary Remains* (Everyman's Libr.), 1927.

Arnold, Matthew. *Essays in Criticism, Second Series*, 1888.

*Selincourt, Ernest De. Introduction and Notes to *Poems*, 5th ed., 1926.

Bridges, Robert. Introduction to Muses Libr. ed. of *Poems*, 1896.

Elliott, G. R. "The Real Tragedy of Keats," PMLA, XXXVI, 315; 1921.

Fausset, H. I'A. *Keats: A Study in Development*, 1922.

*Colvin, Sidney. *John Keats: His Life and Poetry*, new ed., 1925.

*Lowell, Amy. *John Keats*, 2 vols., 1925.

Murry, J. M. *Keats and Shakespeare*, 1925.

Thorpe, C. D. *The Mind of John Keats*, 1926.

Garrod, H. W. *Keats*, 1926.

Thorpe, C. D. "Wordsworth and Keats," PMLA, XLII, 1010; 1927.

Spurgeon, Caroline F. E. *Keats' Shakespeare*, 1928.

Roberts, J. H. "Poetry of Sensation or of Thought," PMLA, XLV, 1129; 1930.

Fairchild, H. N. *The Romantic Quest*, 1931.

Thorpe, C. D. "Keats's Interest in Politics," PMLA, XLVI, 1228; 1931.

*Ridley, M. R. *Keats' Craftsmanship*, 1933.

Marsh, G. L., and White, N. I. "Keats and the Periodicals of his Time," MP, XXXII, 37; 1934.

*Evans, B. I. *Keats* (Great Lives), 1934.

Havens, R. D. "Unreconciled Opposites in Keats," PQ, XIV, 289; 1935.

*Finney, C. L. *The Evolution of Keats's Poetry*, 2 vols., 1936.

James, D. G. *Scepticism and Poetry*, 1937.

Bate, W. J. *Negative Capability: The Intuitive Approach in Keats*, 1939.

Haber, T. B. "The Unifying Influence of Love in Keats's Poetry," PQ, XVI, 192; 1937.

Wagenblass, J. H. "Keats's Roaming Fancy," *Harvard Studies in Philol.*, XX, 123; 1938.

*Murry, J. M. *Studies in Keats: New and Old*, 1939.

Du Bos, Charles. *What Is Literature?* 1940.

Wright, W. F. "A Sudden Development in Keats's Poetic Method," *State Coll. of Wash. Studies*, VIII, 113; 1940.

Ford, G. H. *Keats and the Victorians*, 1944.

Spender, Stephen. "The Sensuous World of Keats," *Penguin New Writing*, 1944.

*Bate, W. J. *The Stylistic Development of Keats*, 1945.

Caldwell, J. R. *John Keats' Fancy*, 1945.

Tate, Allen. "A Reading of Keats," *Amer. Scholar*, Winter, 1945-1946.

Rollins, H. E. *Keats' Reputation in America to 1848*, 1946.

Fogle, R. H. "Empathic Imagery in Keats and Shelley," PMLA, LXI, 163; 1946.
Beyer, W. W. *Keats and the Daemon King*, 1947.
Thorpe, C. D. "Keats and Hazlitt," PMLA, LXII, 487; 1947.

III. MISCELLANEOUS

Baldwin, D. L., Broughton, L. N., et al. *A Concordance to the Poems of John Keats*, 1917.
Forman, M. Buxton. *List of Principal Works Concerning Keats* (Hampstead Ed., vol. I), 1938.

NOTES, COMMENTS, AND TOPICS FOR DISCUSSION

In the following annotations I am frequently and gratefully indebted to the scholarly editions and studies of Keats, listed above, by De Selincourt, Finney, and Thorpe.

746.   O SOLITUDE!

Written while he was a medical student, "in city pent." The first of his poems to be published.

746.   IMITATION OF SPENSER

The first of his poems that is extant. He was self-taught in Spenser, borrowing a copy of the *Faerie Queene,* and reading through it with intense delight in such imaginative phrases as "sea-shouldering whales."

> **746. 12.** *scales:* two syllables.
>   **15.** *oared:* Milton speaks of the swan's "oary" feet.
>   **21.** *Dido:* deserted by Virgil's Aeneas.
>   **24.** *romantic:* eighteenth-century diction rather than Elizabethan.

747.   WOMAN! WHEN I BEHOLD THEE

Reflects his permanent attitude towards the grace, beauty, and tenderness of womanhood. But the style is very uneven.—**DISC.**—Point out the better and the feebler lines in these sonnets, in *To One Who Has Been Long in City Pent,* and in the other selections from his early work.

> **747. 12.** *Calidore:* the type of knightly courtesy in the *Fairie Queene.* The Red Cross Knight, St. George, is the hero of the first book of the same poem.
>   **13.** *Leander:* the swimmer whom Byron imitated; *Anth.,* p. 528 and note. See *On an Engraved Gem of Leander,* below.

747.   HOW MANY BARDS

DISC.—Observe the boldly irregular metre of the first line (accent "gild" and "lap"). Does the substance and spirit justify the irregularities?

748.   I STOOD TIPTOE

The motto is from Leigh Hunt's poem, published the previous year. See the passage from which it is taken; *Anth.,* p. 997, l. 432.—The title was originally *Endymion.*

The scene was not far from Hunt's cottage, Hampstead Heath and the countryside immediately adjacent to it. The time was autumn. The style and metre were influenced by Hunt as well as by the seventeenth-century poet William Browne's *Brittania's Pastorals.* Observe the freedom from neoclassic rules shown by the frequency of overrun lines, and the use of short lines (48, 50, 184).

> **749. 51.** *in these days:* referring to the Romantic Movement.
>   **67.** *sallows:* willows.
>   **71.** *A natural sermon:* Alluding to Shakspeare's description of the contemplative man in the Forest of Arden who perceived "tongues in trees, books in the running brooks, sermons in stones."

749. **85.** *interchange of favors:* Is it fantastic to see in this passage a recognition of what science calls the symbiosis in nature, which Maeterlinck and other neo-romantics make so much of?

750. **113 ff.** This description is praised by Amy Lowell (I, 147). Observe the implied theory of poetry: the relationship between Nature, Man, and Poetry felt to be so close that they are regarded as variant manifestations of the same Being, and the moving cause of poetry being delight in nature.

750. **129.** *Staid:* held, its action suspended; in contrast to *moving* in 131. The general idea of the passage is that pleasures of literature are counterparts of the pleasures of nature.

134. *diamond:* sparkling with dew.

141. *first told, how Psyche went:* The lovely tale of Cupid and Psyche was, strangely enough, not in the ancient orthodox Greek mythology but was first told, in Latin, by Apuleius, in his *Metamorphoses, or the Golden Ass* (IV, 28), as late as the second century A. D. Keats probably knew the story chiefly through John Lemprière's *Classical Dictionary* (1788), and through contemporary versions such as Mrs. Tighe's *Psyche, or the Legend of Love* (1811) and Thomas Moore's *Cupid and Psyche*.

The story is as follows (incidents alluded to by Keats being italicised): Cupid fell in love with Psyche, a beautiful princess. He caused *Zephyr to bear her to his marvelous palace,* where he visited her only at night and commanded her to make no attempt to behold him. But her curiosity, intensified by the suggestions of her jealous sisters that her husband must be a monster, caused her to light *a lamp.* She was *transported with joy* to see that he was a handsome young god; but he awoke and, since she had suspected him, sadly left her prostrate with grief and fear. Not until after she had endured many *woes* and trials was she, on *Cupid's appeal to Jove,* made an immortal and *reunited to him in heaven.*

Psyche, exemplifying the soul searching for the highest kind of love, and sometimes blundering and suffering in its quest, had a strong appeal to the Romantics. See Keats's *Ode to Psyche,* below, p. 816.

157. *Syrinx:* A nymph who fled from the wooing of Pan, the god of nature, who overtook her when she was stopped by coming upon a river. The water nymphs saved her by turning her into a tuft of reeds. As he embraced them, sighing, a faint melody was heard.

163 ff. Keats's theory of the origin of myths. This is drawn from Wordsworth, who in *The Excursion* (1814), IV, 717-762, 846-887, had refused to regard the ancient myths as idle and nonsensical fictions and suggested that they constituted one of the necessary phases in man's mental evolution towards an understanding of nature. He suggested

> The face which rural solitude might wear
> To the unenlightened swains of pagan Greece;

for example, how distant music heard by a shepherd might be by him attributed to the god of the sun; how the moon, lighting the track of the nightly hunter, might be by him invoked to share his sport; the myth of Diana, the goddess of the chase, thus arising; etc. What in Wordsworth is psychology and philosophy poetized, here in Keats becomes the poetry of action and description.

164. *Narcissus:* A beautiful young god, who had rejected the nymph Echo (hence "sad," l. 180) and all other nymphs who wooed him, and who was punished for his self-sufficiency by falling in love with his own image in a pool (Ovid, *Metamorphoses*). For such Ovidian materials as the myths of Syrinx, Narcissus, and Endymion, Keats was indebted to the "folio edition with full commentaries" of the seventeenth-century English translation of Ovid by George Sandys (Selincourt, 391), a work which has been somewhat daringly termed the first American poem, because Sandys may have written part of it during his stay in Virginia.

189. *speculation:* sight, vision (Murry).

751. **204.** *Gave Cynthia:* Gave Diana, the goddess of the moon, Endymion, the shepherd of Mount Latmus whom she loved—meaning that he invented the story associating him with her.

211 ff. A wondrously beautiful evening so beautifies and exalts all that they find words (poetry) expressive of love.

217. *Stepping like Homer at the trumpet's call:* Stepping forth as eagerly and proudly as gods and heroes in Homer. The line has puzzled commentators because Keats did not write "Homer's heroes." But surely there is no extreme poetical license in attributing to Homer himself a trait which Homer so loved in others and so frequently describes—e.g., when the furious Neptune rushes to help the Greeks: (a passage we know Keats to have read in Chapman's translation):

> The woods and all the great hills near trembled beneath the weight
> Of his immortal moving feet. Three steps he only took,
> Before he far-off Aegas reached, but, with the fourth, it shook
> With his dread entry.

The objection that there is extant no statue showing Homer in such an attitude seems to me prosaic.

Perhaps Keats recalled that in a vision in *Gulliver's Travels* (III, VIII) Homer "walked very erect for one of his age" (H. E. Briggs, "Swift and Keats," PMLA, LXI, 1102; 1946).

218. *Apollo:* presumably the statue of Apollo Belvidere in the Vatican at Rome.

220. *Venus:* as she looks in the statue, Venus de Medici, in Florence.

751.   ON FIRST LOOKING INTO CHAPMAN'S HOMER

George Chapman's "loud and bold" Homer, as romantic as Pope's is classical, appeared in 1598-1616. To Keats, who knew no Greek, and to whom some of the finest passages in Chapman's translation were read by Charles Cowden Clarke in October, 1816, it was a revelation. In this sonnet he touched, for the first time, the sublime—especially in its close. The conception of the discoverer of the Pacific (actually not Cortez but Balboa) was drawn from Titian's portrait of Cortez and either from William Robertson's *History of America* or (more likely) from a note in Wordsworth's *The Excursion* quoting the obscure William Gilbert's splendid sentence: "When he walks along the river of the Amazons, when he rests his eye on the unrivalled Andes, when he measures the long and watered savannah, or contemplates, from a sudden promontory, the distant vast Pacific, and feels himself a freeman in this vast theatre, . . . his exaltation is not less than imperial."

The controversies raging about the sources, Cortez, etc., may be pursued through the following: Grace W. Landrum, PMLA, XLII, 986 (1927); B. I. Evans, *Essays and Studies*, XVI, 26 (1930); J. L. Lowes, TLS, Oct. 12, 1933; J. W. Beach, PMLA, XLIX, 246 (1934); K. G. Pfeiffer, N&Q, CLXXV, 203 (1938); H. E. Briggs, PMLA, LIX, 184 (1944); and especially Harris, Mabbott, and Walcutt, EXP, Mch. and Dec., 1946; and June, 1947.

752.   SLEEP AND POETRY

One of the many works in which the Romantics tried to fathom the significance in human life of dream, reverie, and sleep. On their place in Keats's work, see Thorpe, Introduction (1935), pp. XXII-XXIII.—This poem was conceived in Leigh Hunt's library, where one night a makeshift resting place had been arranged for Keats. The closing lines describe pictures and other objects in the room. The chief themes are the greatness of poetry, the poet's ambition and how he might achieve it, his anxiety that he may not succeed, and his dislike of the pseudo-poetry of the neoclassical school.

752. 2. *hummer:* hummingbird.

9. *Cordelia:* in *King Lear.*

753. 89. *Montmorenci:* river and cataract in Quebec, Canada.

122 ff. Observe the influence of Wordsworth.

754. 180. *sooth:* arrange.

181. Here begins the attack on the school of Pope and Boileau. It was resented by Byron.—DISC.—Similarity of the views to Wordsworth's *Essay Supplementary, Anth.,* p. 315.

186. *a rocking horse:* Hazlitt (*The Round Table*, Aug. 20, 1815) had said that Pope and Johnson would have converted Milton's Pegasus into a rocking horse (TLS, Mch. 14 and 21, 1935). Hazlitt's influence on Keats was great.

198. *Jacob's wit:* alluding to a trick by which Jacob fooled his silly sheep (*Genesis,* 30, 37).

209. *boundly:* bounden.

218. *lone spirits:* e.g., Chatterton.

224 ff. Again a tribute to Wordsworth and Leigh Hunt.

230. *doubtless:* unquestionable (a loose use of the word).

234. *clubs:* Homer's Polyphemus threw rocks, not clubs, at the fleeing Ulysses.—In this passage, Byron is attacked, whose gigantic power Keats believed to be misdirected. He preferred the serenity of Wordsworth.

237. *might half slumb'ring on its own right arm:* John Middleton Murry (*Keats and Shakespeare*, p. 23) says that in this single line Keats "reveals more of the essential nature of poetry than a critic could do in many paragraphs; it is a definition of poetry by poetry."

755. 303. *Dedalian:* presumptuously youthful. Icarus, son of Dædalus, flew too high with the waxen wings invented by his father, and perished.

756. 322. *very pleasant rout:* This phrase, like the monosyllabic *perhaps* in 324, exemplifies what has been condemned as crude cockneyism in Keats's early work.

376 ff. *ocean:* Seen for the first time by Keats at Margate shortly before. These lines are justly admired for their union of accurate observation with dignity of expression.

757.

KEEN, FITFUL GUSTS

Another tribute to Leigh Hunt, from whose hospitable cottage Keats is walking homeward on a chilly autumn night, after delighting with him in Milton's *Lycidas* and Petrarch's poems in honor of Laura.

757.

ADDRESSED TO HAYDON

A tribute to Wordsworth (1-4) and Hunt (5-6) as well as to Benjamin Robert Haydon (1786-1846), their mutual friend, the idealistic painter of historical subjects on large canvases. Reynolds had spoken of him as a modern Raphael.—See C. Olney, "Keats and Haydon," PMLA, XLIX, 258 (1934); and Thorpe, "Keats and Hazlitt," listed in Bibl., above.

757a. 7. *And lo!:* possibly a misprint for "And thou" (TLS, July 4, 1929).

757.

TO G. A. W.

Georgiana Wylie, who was to marry his brother George Keats

757.

ON THE GRASSHOPPER AND CRICKET

One evening, while a cricket chirped on the hearth, Hunt proposed to Keats that they write sonnets on this subject in friendly competition. See Hunt's, *Anth.*, p. 998.—DISC.—What differences do you find, especially with respect to elevation of tone?

758.

TO LEIGH HUNT, ESQ.

The dedication of the volume of poems of 1817. It was Leigh Hunt who, as editor of *The Examiner*, had published the first of Keats's poems that appeared in print, *O Solitude!*, May 3, 1816; and thenceforth had encouraged him in many ways.

This sonnet is said to have been written extemporaneously, while the printer's messenger was waiting for it. The first line is not to be regarded as a settled conviction; for, despite the fact that it expresses a mood which often came upon him, his general tendency is rather to find glory and loveliness here and now.

758.

WRITTEN ON THE BLANK SPACE

On Chaucer's "The Flower and the Leaf."

758.

ON SEEING THE ELGIN MARBLES

Addressed to Haydon, who had helped Keats to appreciate the beauty of the sculptures from the Parthenon which Lord Elgin had removed to London, and which are still one of the greatest glories of the British Museum.—See Hyder Rollins, "Keats's Elgin Marble Sonnets," *Studies in Honor of A. H. R. Fairchild*, 1946.

758.　　　　　　　　　　　ON THE SEA

An illustration of how Nature and Poetry combined to elevate Keats's imagination. Inspired partly by the line in *King Lear* (IV, VI, 4), "Hark, do you hear the sea?"; and partly by the sight of the sea from Shanklin Cliffs.

758.　　　　　　　　　　ENDYMION: BOOK I

Keats's very modest Preface is perhaps the most disparaging comment any great poet ever prefixed to his work: he apologizes for letting it be published when it is so obviously youthful. "The imagination," he says, "of a boy is healthy, and the mature imagination of a man is healthy; but there is a space of life between, in which the soul is in a ferment, the character undecided, the way of life uncertain, the ambition thick-sighted: thence proceeds mawkishness . . ." He was then twenty-two years old. Two years later he wrote Shelley (*Anth.*, p. 852), still in the same modest vein, that his mind during the composition of *Endymion* had been "like a pack of scattered cards."

Besides the important interpretations of *Endymion* listed in the Bibliography above, under Colvin, Selincourt, Bridges, Murry, Finney, and Thorpe, see the following: Leonard Brown, "The Genesis, Growth, and Meaning of Endymion," SP, xxx, 618 (1933); E. S. Le Comte, *Endymion in England*, (1944); H. E. Briggs, "Keats's Conscious and Unconscious Reactions to Criticism," PMLA, LX, 1106 (1945); and W. W. Beyer, *Keats and the Daemon King* (Wieland's influence) (1947).

Nearly all leading critics are agreed that the main story is an allegory in which Endymion represents Man and the Poet in quest of supersensuous ideal Beauty. In contradiction, Amy Lowell (p. 365) calls the poem an "idealization of sexual love"; and N. F. Ford, (ELH, XIV, 64; 1947) tries to prove that the theme is merely "Endymion's quest of an everlasting erotism," an interpretation which is not accepted in the following Notes and Comments.

The first 33 lines declare the poet's purpose, "spite of despondence," to try to add one more to those "shapes of beauty" which, in nature and in literature, make life worth living.

759. *18. Brake:* thicket.

　　20. grandeur of the dooms, etc.: immortal rewards of the heroic.

　　41-57. He will begin in the Spring, reach the middle of the poem by Summer, and finish by Autumn. This schedule of work—the most poetically expressed in our entire literature—was more faithfully adhered to than would be supposed by those who hold the popular notions about the artistic temperament. Keats began the poem in April, was working on the third book by September, and finished the last by November.

　　76. *pard:* leopard.

760. **140.** *Arcadian books:* Books describing the simple pastoral life legendarily associated with Arcadia, a mountainous region of Greece.

　　158. *Leda's love:* Leda was the mother of Helen and was wooed by Zeus in the form of a swan.

　　170. *Ganymede:* A beautiful Trojan youth made cupbearer to the gods.

761. **232.** In this hymn to Pan, Endymion and the other shepherds render thanks to the god of nature for his bounteousness, a chorus singing the hymn.—Keats recited it to Wordsworth, December 28, 1817, at Haydon's.

　　232. *palace roof:* the forest foliage.

　　236. *hamadryads:* tree nymphs.

　　241. *hemlock:* a poisonous herb.

　　243. *Syrinx:* See above, note on **750, 157.**

　　247. *turtles:* turtle doves.

762. **255.** *poppied corn:* grain, with poppies growing among it.

　　267. *maw:* crop.

　　272. *Naiad:* water-nymph.

　　294. *such as dodge,* etc.: so aspiring that they pursue the power of imagination to the boundary of Heaven.

　　318. *Thermopylæ:* The narrow pass where a small army of Greeks under Leonidas fought to death against the overwhelming host of the Persians.

328. *Hyacinthus:* In the earliest versions of the legend Apollo slew him, but Keats follows later versions in which Zephyr, jealous of Apollo's love for Hyacinth, committed the crime.—The exquisite allusion to those mornings in which wind and rain precede the sunrise (Zephyr preceding Phoebus Apollo) is original and characteristic (Selincourt).

763. 338. *Niobe:* The proud mother who boasted superiority over the wife of Zeus because she (Niobe) had twelve children and Leto only two. In punishment the gods slew all her children.

347. *Argonauts:* The heroes who sailed with Jason in the ship Argo to capture the Golden Fleece.

358. *gone in eld:* advanced in age.

406. *that old tale Arabian:* In *The Arabian Nights,* the story told by the Eldest Lady in "The Porter And the Three Ladies of Bagdad."

764. 495. *Dryope:* A shepherdess who had a child by Apollo.

765. 510. *Paphian dove:* Dove sent by the goddess of love, Aphrodite, who had a temple at Paphos (in Cypress).

516. *Endymion looked at her,* etc.: This passage, in which Endymion relates how he was borne aloft to his beloved goddess of the moon Cynthia, of his rapture and bliss there, and of his dejection when he again found himself on earth, allegorically expresses the poet's yearning for an unworldly ideal, and the tragic difficulty of attaining it.

530. *Lucifer:* The morning star.

553. *zodiac-lion:* The sign of the lion in the zodiac, through which the sun passes in midsummer.

555. *ditamy:* the dittany, an herb, formerly believed of medicinal value.

559. *Morpheus:* God of sleep.

573. *enchantment:* Accented on the first syllable.

766. 595. *argent:* silvery

598. *lidless:* never sleeping.

614. *gordianed:* knotted.

624. *fane:* sacred place.

632. Peona speaks.

644. *balances:* holds back the rushing meteor.

654. *give my eyes to death:* beheld what he supposed would be death for mortal to behold.

767. 671. *Oread:* woodland nymph.

683. *ouzel:* blackbird.

714. *enchased:* armored.

721. *with trembling chance:* trembling, but taking a chance.

721. *the cause:* the cause for dejection.

725. *achieve no higher bard:* make himself into a poet who could rise to no higher themes than those which a simple maiden might sing of.

768. 760. *nothing but a dream.* The rest of the passage expresses his feeing that the dream was something more than mere fantasy: he "espies a hope beyond the shadow of a dream" (l. 857). Allegorically it is suggested that high ideals are greater realities than the apparent actualities of common sense, that they give us "a fellowship with essence" (I. 779).

771. *unlace the canvas:* unloosen the sails.

779. *A fellowship with essence:* N. F. Ford (PMLA, LXII, 1061; 1947) rejects the generally accepted transcendental interpretations of this famous passage, and maintains that it is only "a young poet's description, albeit not very precise, of imaginative 'empathy'." DISC.— This article should be discussed together with Dr. Ford's other one on *Endymion,* referred to above in the introductory Note.

796. *oneness:* harmony within ourselves and with the universe.

801. *love and friendship:* This part of the complex theme shows the influence of both Plato and Wordsworth. "The true order of going," says Plato (*Symposium*), "or being led by another to the things of love, is to begin from the beauties of earth and mount upwards for the sake of that other beauty, using these as steps only, and from one going on to two, and from two to all fair forms, and from fair forms to fair practices, and from fair practices to fair notions, until from fair notions he arrives at the idea of absolute beauty, and at last knows what the essence of beauty is." The Platonic influence may have come through Shelley. From Wordsworth probably comes the insistence that the true ideal is not one which severs us from humanity. In his letter to his publisher, enclosing these lines, Keats said that they clarified in his mind the "gradations of happiness," and seemed to him very true and important. From this point onwards *Endymion* may be said to struggle with the problem of how to reconcile an unworldly ideal with a love for humanity.

815. *like a pelican brood:* The pelican was fabled to nurture its young with its own blood.

771. ENDYMION: BOOKS II AND III

771. 1-43. Critics unsympathetic towards Keats cite this passage, which praises love as of superior human interest to ambition, as an illustration of Keats's alleged effeminacy. It is not the whole of his philosophy; and in its context it is dramatically appropriate since Endymion is about to set forth on his quest for love.

13. *close of Troilus:* embrace of Shakspeare's famous lovers, Troilus and Cressida.

22. *what care, though owl,* etc.: What do we care (in comparison with our interest in great love stories) about History telling us that an owl (of good omen) alighted upon Themistocles' ship at a critical moment?

26. *Ulysses tortured,* etc.: Even adventures in Homer are of inferior interest. The Cyclops was Polyphemus, the giant who, glutted with human flesh and with wine, fell asleep; whereupon Ulysses plunged a burning stake into his eye.

27. *Juliet:* Shakspeare's, in the balcony.

31. *Hero:* The Greek priestess, whose lover nightly swam the Hellespont (Musaeus, and Marlowe).

31. *Imogen:* The faithful and long-suffering heroine of Shakspeare's "Cymbeline."

32. *Pastorella:* An ill-used maiden in Spenser's *Fairie Queene*, vi, 2.

34. *Fearfully,* etc.: The very fact that Love is a sublime theme causes Keats, in his modesty, to fear he may fail.

37. *Without one muse's smile:* I believe this signified his own doubts as to whether he had as yet been truly inspired, rather than the frown of the critics upon his 1817 volume of poems.

39. *chaffing:* chafing.

387-427. Endymion comes upon Adonis in slumber.

772. 21. This passage near the beginning of Book III is preceded by an attack upon the then rulers of Great Britain, whom Keats regarded as "gilded masks," or incompetents.

42. *Sister:* Cynthia.

70. *Ocean,* etc.: Tellus, goddess of the earth, feels the moonlit breakers of the Ocean dashing upon her rocky shore.

142. Endymion addresses the moon, now knowing that it is the goddess of the moon whom he is pursuing.

773. ENDYMION: BOOK IV

DISC.—For the meaning of the allegory as a whole, this book is the most important one. What did Keats intend to signify by the *outcome* of Endymion meeting the Indian maid, falling in love with her, being shocked by his apparent infidelity to Cynthia, etc.?

773. 15. *Ausonia:* Italy, where as in Palestine and in Greece poetry flourished earlier than in England.

774. 145. *roundelay:* A roundelay, or rondeau, is a lyric containing a refrain.—This is sung by an Indian maiden, Phoebe, to Endymion, who first pities and then loves her.

775. 148. *borrow:* i.e., take away.

151. *is't:* Correct to "is it,"—a preferable variant.

157. *tinge:* i.e., with phosphorescence.

196. *Bacchus:* This is the kind of Sorrow which not even Bacchus, god of wine and mirth, can dispel. The brilliant description owes something to Rabelais, and perhaps even more to Titian's picture, *Bacchus and Ariadne,* which hung in the National Gallery and was of much interest to the Romantics. See the reproduction in Craven's *Treasury of Art Masterpieces.* Plate 40. See also the note below **(786. 95)**; Wordsworth's *On The*

Power of Sound, line 147, *Anth.*, p. 297; Charles Lamb's *Barrenness of the Imaginative Faculty in Modern Art;* and M. H. Shackford's *Wordsworth's Interest in Painters*. pp. 58-59.

776. 215. *Silenus:* Foster-father of Bacchus, an old toper.

247. *Coil:* bustle.

263. *vail:* lower respectfully.

777. 375. *Cimmerian:* Gloomy.—The legendary people called Cimmerii dwelt in perpetual night.

394. *Skiddaw:* The mountain in the lake country.

778. 441. *He who died:* Icarus, son of Dædalus, who flew with wings of wax too near the sun.

459. *dædale:* cunning, deceptive.

779. 536. *Semele:* The mother of Dionysus by Zeus.

780. 582. *Aquarius*, etc.: The constellations of the zodiac attend the wedding of the Star Queen.

614. *His first touch of the earth*, etc.: Endymion returns to earth, and temporarily, in his love for the Indian maid, tries to forget all heavenly aspiration. This idyllic description of merely earthly sensuous content, however beautifully expressed, is nevertheless immediately thereafter condemned by Keats as "fancies vain and crude," not permanently satisfying to the human spirit. It is not until he discovers, at the close of the poem, that the Indian maid is the goddess Cynthia in human guise that he happily realizes the possibility of finding the ideal in the actual.

781. 671. *dun:* dark.

686. *syrinx flag:* reed.

713. *Delphos:* oracle.

784. 953. *Rhadamanthus:* A judge in the next world.

955. *Promethean clay*, etc.: Man, whom Prometheus made of clay and to whom he had given the fire which he had stolen from heaven.

LINES ON THE MERMAID TAVERN

785.

Traditionally believed to be the favorite tavern of such authors as Ben Jonson, Sir Walter Raleigh, and perhaps Shakspeare, c. 1600.

785a. 6. *Canary wine:* a dry Spanish wine, made in the Canary Islands.

785b. 12. *bowse:* to booze, to drink greedily.

ISABELLA, OR THE POT OF BASIL

785.

Boccaccio in the *Decameron*, IV, 5, told this story, emphasizing the horror of the incidents. Keats changed the action very little (he has two brothers instead of one, and moves the scene from Messina to Florence), but elaborated the pathos of Isabella's and Lorenzo's emotions. The verse form was a favorite with Italian poets, and had been recently introduced into English by Byron and others—but not for serious verse.

Again Keats was a severe self-critic; "there is," he said, "too much inexperience of life and simplicity of knowledge in it . . ." with an amusing sober-sadness about it."—Ridley's *Keats' Craftsmanship*, pp. 18-56, is a good study of this poem.

785b. 5. *palmer:* pilgrim, devotee.

786. 95. *Theseus' spouse:* Ariadne, ungratefully deserted by Theseus; see note above **(775, 196).**

787. 105 ff. Characteristically George Bernard Shaw calls this stanza an epitome of the "immense indictment of the profiteers and exploiters with which Marx has shaken capitalistic civilization to its foundations." He also praises ll. 137-152 as "some of the sanest stanzas in Keats's work." **DISC.**—Comment on this kind of criticism.

123. *orange-mounts . . . lazar stairs:* Noble staircases of orange wood in their palace, pleasanter than the stairs of a hospital for infectious diseases.

159. *stead thee:* keep thee in memory.

789. 262. *smoke from Hinnom's vale:* Alluding to 2 *Chronicles*, 28, and Ahaz who "burnt his children in the fire, after the abominations of the heathen."

790. 321-328. Admired by Browning for supreme mastery of language.

352 ff. Charles Lamb said of the description of Isabella disinterring the body "there is nothing more awfully simple in diction, more nakedly grand and moving in sentiment, in Dante, in Chaucer, or in Spenser" (Blunden, *Lamb and His Contemporaries*, 1933; p. 113).

393. *Perséan:* of Perseus, who decapitated the monstrous Gorgon Medusa.

791. 416. *Basil:* a fragrant herb, like mint.

442. *Melpomene:* the Muse of tragedy.

451. *Baälites of pelf:* worshippers of money.

792.   THE HUMAN SEASONS

The influence of Wordsworth (e.g., *The Excursion*, v, 394-410) has been suggested (TLS, Feb. 9, 1946), but that of Shakspeare is at least as strong here. See Keats's letter to Bailey, Mch. 13, 1818, where this sonnet first appears.

792.   MEG MERRILIES

See Scott's *Guy Mannering; Anth.*, p. 449.

793.   WRITTEN UPON THE TOP OF BEN NEVIS

The highest mountain in Scotland (4,406 ft.).—The utterance of a humble heart which, like St. Paul's, confesses that "now I know only *in part.*" **DISC.**—Have you found this mood in Wordsworth?

793.   TO AILSA ROCK

An island, conical in form, off the west coast of Scotland; seen by Keats in the summer of 1818.

793.   HYPERION

Keats intended this poem to deal with even nobler beings than *Endymion*—with an Apollo who would "shape his actions as a *fore-seeing* god"—and therefore it must be written in a grander style, Miltonic, in "a more naked and Grecian manner" (Letter to Haydon, Jan. 23, 1818). The sublimity and intensity he achieved forced even those contemporary critics who had sneered at his previous work to express astonishment and reluctant admiration. Today some leading critics think *Hyperion* is the summit of Keats's genius, though others look upon the second version, and some of the *Odes*, as even greater.

On the question, which of the two versions was the earlier, see the Notes on the *Fall of Hyperion*, below. For a close study of the differences, see Bate, *Stylistic Development* (1945).—On the tone and imagery,—ancient, monumental—see Helen Darbishire, "Keats and Egypt," RES, III, 9 (1927); also Ridley, *Craftsmanship* (1933).

In the first age after chaos, the Titans reigned, the children of Uranus (Heaven) and Gaea (Earth),—among them Saturn, who succeeded Uranus, and blazing Hyperion, god of the sun. The Titans, before the action of the poem begins, were overthrown by "the rebel three," Jupiter, Neptune, and Pluto. Jupiter, by Latona, was the father of Apollo and his twin-sister Diana. In the unwritten conclusion, Hyperion was to be overcome by Apollo.

DISC.—What are the causes for these defeats and victories? Saturn (II, 149) confesses he can't understand them. One reason is suggested in II, 181,—"Nature's law"—what does that mean? The whole speech of Oceanus is revelatory. Apollo, (III, 103) is groping after the answer to "Where *is* power?" The questions involved are even more crucial today than they were in Keats's time.

793b. 23. *came one:* Thea, sister and wife of Hyperion.

794. 73. *branch-charmed by the earnest stars:* One of those typically Keatsian lines which glorify his poetry. **DISC.**—Gather others in the rest of his work, compare them, and try to characterize their special beauty.

115-121. Exemplifies Miltonic "inversion" or "repeats." Other examples are ll. 182-185 and 283-285.

798. 19 ff. *Coeus,* etc.: the names of these Titans are used in Miltonic fashion, for their sound.
53. *Asia . . . Caf:* Asia, mother of Prometheus, was to become important in Shelley's *Prometheus Unbound.* Caf is probably from Beckford's frightful Kaf in *Vathek.*

799. 167. *God of the Sea:* Oceanus. See the DISC. recommended above. This introduction of a debate is similar to Milton's procedure in *Paradise Lost,* II, 109 ff., where Belial and Mammon hold forth.

800. 212. *a fresh perfection:* Here Keats inclines in the direction that became so important in Shelley's poetry.

802. 374. *Memnon:* son of Aurora, the dawn; hence his statue near Thebes at sunrise gave forth harplike music.

803. 29. *Giant of the Sun:* Hyperion.
46. *Goddess:* Mnemosyne (memory), mother of the Muses.
63. *a lyre all golden:* Apollo was to become the god of music and poetry.

804. 103. *Where is power?:* Apollo, not yet fully a god, is in a state of wonderment and uncertainty—a stage of growth which Keats was himself undergoing and deeply sympathized with.
136. *Apollo shrieked:* now he was a god.

At this point Keats gave up the attempt to treat the theme in this style; "there were," he wrote, "too many Miltonic inversions in it," too much art, not enough feeling (Letter to Reynolds, Sept. 21, 1819).

804. IN A DREAR-NIGHTED DECEMBER

804b. 15. *petting:* fussing, fretting.
21. *To know,* etc.: For this line Murry would substitute "The feel of *not* to feel it" (*Studies in Keats*). Is it preferable?

806. SONG

Elizabethan in tone. Some surmise the influence of Blake, although there is no evidence that Keats knew his songs.

806. THE EVE OF ST. AGNES

The best study and appreciation is in Ridley, *Craftsmanship,* p. 96 ff.—On the "heady mixture" of romance, superstition, and passion, see EXP., Nov. and Dec., 1942; June, 1943: and Oct., 1944.
For details Keats drew on much reading of very different kinds, Shakspeare, the *Arabian Nights,* Mrs. Radcliffe, folklore, etc.; but his main source was in a sixteenth-century French translation of Boccaccio's *Il Filocolo,* the episode of Biancofiore and her lover Florio. But he elevated the quality of the passion. In the source, the maiden's desire is for the actual presence of her lover, and it is aroused by the amorous chatter of her nurse; in place thereof Keats substituted the belief that on St. Agnes' eve (Jan. 21) a maiden may behold a vision of her future husband.

806. 1. *bitter chill:* Whether this stanza is the "coldest passage in English poetry" was debated in *Sat. Rev. Lit.* during 1947 (Apr. 19, June 21, etc.).

807. 54. At this point the published version omitted the following stanza:

'Twas said her future lord would there appear
Offering as sacrifice—all in the dream—
Delicious food even to her lips brought near:
Viands and wine and fruit and sugar'd cream,
To touch her palate with the fine extreme
Of relish: then soft music heard; and then
More pleasures followed in a dizzy stream
Palpable almost: then to wake again
Warm in the virgin morn, no weeping Magdalen.

70. *amort:* as if dead, unresponsive.

71. *St. Agnes' lambs:* On the saint's day, two lambs were brought to the altar at Mass as an offering. Their wool was afterwards woven by the nuns (see below, l. 117).

808. 120. *a witch's sieve:* a sieve so enchanted that water will not run through it.

809. 171. *Merlin:* A wizard in Arthurian story. He owed his existence to a fiend, and paid his debt by deeds of evil deceit.

   173. *cates:* dainties.

810. 218. *gules:* red colors (from the stained glass).

   241. *clasped like a missal,* etc.: Shut in as safely as a prayer book with its clasps in a heathen land.

811. 292. *La belle dame:* Anticipating the title of his later poem, *Anth.,* p. 815.

812. 349. *Rhenish . . . mead:* Wine from the Rhine country, and mead (fermented honey and malt).

DISC.—Contrast the manner of telling the story with Scott's in *Lochinvar* (*Anth.,* p. 425). and compare the descriptions with those in Coleridge's *Christabel* (*Anth.,* p. 169).

813.

THE EVE OF ST. MARK: A FRAGMENT

The theme is the contrast between the commonplace familiar English cathedral town, and the glorious life and martyrdom of St. Mark which Bertha is perusing with ecstatic longing, the tension being almost tragic (W. E. Houghton, "The Meaning of the Eve of St. Mark," ELH, xiii, 64; 1946).—See Caxton's *Golden Legend* for the kind of saint's life Bertha is supposed to be reading. The exotic creatures on the screen, including the "Av'davat," (an Indian finch), help to bridge the gap imaginatively.—This is one of the poems which links Keats with Chatterton, especially lines 99 ff.

814. 99. *swevenis:* dreams.

   103. *litling:* very little (allusion to the Children's Crusade).

   112. *Sainte Cicile:* Roman maiden who was martyred in the third century.

814.

ON A DREAM

He had dreamed of amorously floating about like Dante's lovers, Paolo and Francesca (*Inferno,* v).

814.

TO SLEEP

Keats sent a copy of this to his brother George in America. It was published in *The Dial* in April, 1843, less than five years after its appearance in an English journal.

815.

ON FAME

Perhaps "On Personal Ambition" would be a clearer title. The "mis-creed" in the last line is the false belief that such ambition is defensible.—Keats prefixed the proverb: "You cannot eat your cake and have it too."

815.

ON THE SONNET

Keats's constant effort was to find a prosody really congenial to Poesy—forms which would be completely appropriate means of expressing the substance. The last two lines of this sonnet, emphasizing *of her own,* are significant.—On his dissatisfaction with the sonnet-form, see Bate, *Stylistic Development,* pp. 125-132.

815.

LA BELLE DAME SANS MERCY

"Mercy" in *The Indicator* ed.; "Merci" elsewhere.

"No one else could have done anything like it. Keats here shows at full his power to isolate materials from the actual world and put them, still holding the essence of human passion and aspiration, into a half-world of spiritual reality" (Thorpe, *Poems and Selected Letters,* p. 340 n.).

For the title, "The Beautiful Lady Without Pity," he was indebted to a translation, mistakenly attributed to Chaucer, from a French medieval poet, Alain Chartier; but the important influences are chiefly Spenser, William Browne, and Coleridge. It has been suggested that he is closely following the conventional five steps in medieval courtly love—"le regard, le parler, l'attouchement, le baiser, le don de mercy"—the last favor being denied the knight; but this theory is dubious (See Locke, Keister, and Mabbott, EXP, Oct., 1946; Feb. and May, 1947). —The Lady is a *supernatural* creature; and traditionally human love for such was tragic, though also exalting. Allegorically the Lady may represent Poetry.—The reticence in the elfin-grot stanza is comparable to that in *The Eve of St. Agnes*, st. XXXVI.

The poem is historically important for its great influence on the Pre-Raphaelites, especially Rossetti and William Morris. The latter preferred the earlier version, saying "Why that was the germ from which all the poetry of my group has sprung!".—See EXP, Dec., 1947.

815. 13. *I met a Lady:* The "wretched wight's" answer begins here.

DISC.—The text gives the final version; the earlier, given below, is by some critics considered the better one. Do you agree with them? Why?

> O what can ail thee, knight at arms,
> Alone and palely loitering?
> The sedge has withered from the lake,
> And no birds sing!
>
> O what can ail thee, knight at arms,
> So haggard and so woe-begone?
> The squirrel's granary is full,
> And the harvest's done.
>
> I see a lily on thy brow,
> With anguish moist and fever dew;
> And on thy cheeks a fading rose
> Fast withereth too.
>
> I met a lady in the meads,
> Full beautiful, a faery's child;
> Her hair was long, her foot was light,
> And her eyes were wild.
>
> I made a garland for her head,
> And bracelets, too, and fragrant zone;
> She looked at me as she did love,
> And made sweet moan.
>
> I set her on my pacing steed,
> And nothing else saw, all day long;
> For sidelong would she bend, and sing
> A faery's song.
>
> She found me roots of relish sweet,
> And honey wild, and manna dew;
> And sure in language strange she said,
> "I love thee true."
>
> She took me to her elfin grot,
> And there she wept and sighed full sore;
> And there I shut her wild, wild eyes
> With kisses four.
>
> And there she lullèd me asleep,
> And there I dreamed, ah woe betide!
> The latest dream I ever dreamt,
> On the cold hill side.
>
> I saw pale kings, and princes too,
> Pale warriors, death pale were they all,
> Who cried, "La belle dame sans merci
> Thee hath in thrall!"

> I saw their starved lips in the gloam
> With horrid warning gapèd wide—
> And I awoke, and found me here,
> On the cold hill's side.
>
> And this is why I sojourn here,
> Alone and palely loitering;
> Though the sedge is withered from the lake,
> And no birds sing.

816.   ODE TO PSYCHE

On the subject, see above, Note on p. 750, 141. —In a letter to his brother (Apr., 1819) Keats wrote:

"The following poem, the last I have written, is the first and only one with which I have taken even moderate pains; I have, for the most part, dashed off my lines in a hurry. This one I have done leisurely; I think it reads the more richly for it, and it will, I hope, encourage me to write other things in even a more peaceable and healthy spirit. You must recollect that Psyche was not embodied as a goddess before the time of Apuleius the Platonist, who lived after the Augustan age, and consequently the goddess was never worshipped or sacrificed to with any of the ancient fervor, and perhaps never thought of in the old religion. I am more orthodox than to let a heathen goddess be so neglected."

816. 20. *aurorean:* dawning.

26. *Phœbe's:* Diana's (the moon).

35. *pale-mouthed prophet:* The passage is reminiscent of Milton's Ode on the Nativity, XIX: "the pale-eyed priest from his prophetic cell."

52. *thoughts:* He will worship Psyche (who is the soul) not with material sacrifices but with the gifts of the mind.

T. S. Eliot (*Use of Poetry*, p. 91) considers this to be Keats's best ode. **DISC.**—Mr. Eliot's reasons.

817.   "THE LAST SONNET"

Used to be so entitled, but now known to have been composed in Feb., 1819.

817. 5. *priest-like task of pure ablution:* On this "right and beautiful metaphor, which adds subtlety to simplicity, and sanctification to the obvious," see Havelock Ellis, *Fountain of Life;* pp. 90 and 410.—The *Eremite* is a solitary, a devotee of Nature.

12. *Awake in a sweet unrest:* These apparent contradictions, but real truths, like "pleasant pain" in *Psyche,* 52, are characteristic of Keats (see Knight, *Christian Renaissance*, pp. 295-296). The need of man is to awaken to them.

817.   ODE ON INDOLENCE

Read Keats's letter (The Castle of Indolence), *Anth.*, p. 847.

817. 54. *A pet lamb in a sentimental farce:* Amy Lowell, *Keats,* makes this the title of her ch. 4, and thinks it refers to Keats's association with Hunt's circle in the winter of 1816-1817.

818.   ODE TO A NIGHTINGALE

Keats's friend, C. A. Brown (*Life of Keats*, p. 53) says that this arose out of "the tranquil and continual joy" he felt in the song of a nightingale near Brown's house.

It is the first of the great poems of Keats's maturity, which are closely interrelated in feeling and thought, feelings and thoughts which are harmonious but so rich and varied that critics often go astray by stressing only one strain in that harmony. The *Odes*, as R. H. Fogle says in the best brief criticism of this poem (MLQ, VIII, 81; 1947), "express an exquisite awareness of the existence of joy and melancholy, pleasure and pain, and art and life. They express a feeling that these are inseparable, although not identical, and they express acceptance of this insep-arability of the elements of human experience." See also Charles Williams, *Reason and Beauty in the Poetic Mind* (1933), pp. 63-81; A. W. Crawford, *The Genius of Keats* (1932); and S. M. Pitcher, EXP, Mch., 1945.

818. 4. *Lethe-wards:* into forgetfulness.

16. *Hippocrene:* a fountain, the waters of which inspired poets.

26. *youth . . . dies:* probably an allusion to the death of Keats's brother, and perhaps to his own precarious health.

32. *not charioted:* Wine, first resorted to (stanza 2) for relief from the oppressiveness of life, is now rejected in favor of poetry. See *Anth.*, p. 775; *Endymion*, IV, 145 ff.

35. *with thee!.* Keats used exclamation points very freely. It has been suggested that his meaning would be clearer if they were omitted in this line, and possibly also in l. 11 (C. S. Kilby, EXP, Feb., 1947).

819. 51. *Darkling:* in the dark.

61 ff. "This stanza would, I suppose, by common consent be taken along with *Kubla Khan* as offering us the distilled sorceries of Romanticism" (Ridley, *Craftsmanship*, p. 227). DISC.—Compare them.

66. *Ruth:* In the Bible; *Ruth*, 2.

DISC.—Compare the *Ode to a Nightingale* with Shelley's *To a Skylark* (*Anth.*, p. 941), the movement, the tone, the adjectives, etc.

Contrast the differences, in substance and style, between Keats's *Ode* and Coleridge's *The Nightingale* (*Anth.*, p. 165), the peasant-poet John Clare's *Early Nightingale,* and Matthew Arnold's *Philomela.*

819. ODE ON A GRECIAN URN

Inspired by the Elgin marbles (procession to the sacrifice) and the urns in the British Museum, and by an exhibit of Raphael's drawings, especially "The Sacrifice at Lystra," about all of which Haydon was enthusiastic (Macgillivray and Roberts, TLS, July 9 and Aug. 20, 1938). On the artistry of Grecian urns, see J. D. Beazley, *Potter and Painter in Ancient Athens.*

R. H. Snow, "Heresy Concerning Keats," PMLA, XLIII, 1142 (1928), overstresses the sensory elements in the poem; refuted by Mary E. Shipman, "Orthodoxy Concerning Keats," PMLA, XLIV, 929 (1929).—See also R. D. Havens on the relation of this Ode to that on *Melancholy* (MP, XXIV, 209; 1926); and "Keats and Ourselves," TLS, Nov. 10, Dec. 22, 1945, Jan. 26, Feb. 2, 1946); Cleanth Brooks, *The Well Wrought Urn* (1947), and EXP., Oct., 1947.

820. 13. *sensual ear:* the ear of sense, contrasted with that of the spirit or imagination.

41. *brede:* embroidery, embellishment, sculptural relief.

44. *tease us out of thought:* draw us away from worried thinking.

49. *Beauty is truth,* etc.: T. S. Eliot says the last two lines "spoil a good poem," and J. M. Murry (*Studies in Keats,* p. 73), strangely enough, agrees.—DISC.—What do you think?

The context shows what kind of truth Keats is feeling here. For the marble men and maidens, Time stands still; there is no change or decay; their characters and relationships are not blurred; hence the artist can seize and hold *the essential inner meaning* of the object, which is its beauty, and likewise is its truth. Such art is "a friend to man," especially in times of woe, because it helps him to become conscious of the meaning in life. This interpretation agrees, I believe, with Keats's views in his letter to Bailey, Nov. 22, 1817 (*Anth.*, p. 840): "What the imagination seizes as beauty must be the truth . . . The imagination may be compared to Adam's dream,—he awoke and found it truth."

For other recent interpretations see Hamm, Basler, and Pettigrew, EXP, May and Oct. 1945, Nov., 1946.

DISC.—Do you find the following comment helpful: "When beauty is truth and truth is beauty, the complete satisfaction of sensation is the complete satisfaction of exalted reason" (Charles Williams, *Reason and Beauty,* 1933; p. 77).

An ultra-modern interpretation is Kenneth Burke's "Symbolic Action in a Poem by Keats," *Accent,* Autumn, 1943, p. 30.—What does it mean? What is its value?

820. ODE ON MELANCHOLY

Keats had been reading Robert Burton's wonderful *Anatomy of Melancholy* (1621). The general theme is that to satisfy the "fit" (mood) of melancholy you need not seek forgetfulness

(Lethe) or death; for melancholy can find something to feed upon among even the loveliest experiences of life. See the quotation from R. H. Fogle in the Notes on the *Ode To a Nightingale*. For a strained interpretation, see Empson, *Seven Types of Ambiguity*, p. 272.

821.   LAMIA

The story is found in Philostratus' biography of Apollonius Tyanæus, a Greek philosopher of the first century. Keats came upon it in the following passage from Robert Burton's *Anatomy of Melancholy* (1621):

> Philostratus, in his fourth book *de Vita Apollonii*, hath a memorable instance in this kind, which I may not omit, of one Menippus Lycius, a young man twenty-five years of age, that going betwixt Cenchreas and Corinth, met such a phantasm in the habit of a fair gentlewoman, which, taking him by the hand, carried him home to her house, in the suburbs of Corinth, and told him she was a Phœnician by birth, and if he would tarry with her, he should hear her sing and play, and drink such wine as never any drank, and no man should molest him; but she, being fair and lovely, would live and die with him, that was fair and lovely to behold. The young man, a philosopher, otherwise staid and discreet, able to moderate his passions, though not this of love, tarried with her a while to his great content, and at last married her, to whose wedding, amongst other guests, came Apollonius; who, by some probable conjectures, found her out to be a serpent, a lamia; and that all her furniture was, like Tantalus' gold, described by Homer, no substance but mere illusions. When she saw herself descried, she wept, and desired Apollonius to be silent, but he would not be moved, and thereupon she, plate, house, and all that was in it, vanished in an instant: many thousands took notice of this fact, for it was done in the midst of Greece.

Critics agree that Keats's poetical recasting of the story is masterful, but there is much controversy about what he intended to emphasize. Unacceptable are J. H. Roberts' belief that it shows a reaffirmation of the sensuous ("The Significance of *Lamia*," PMLA, L, 550; 1935); and Finney's elaborate allegorical interpretation, according to which Lycius represents Keats, and Apollonius his reviewers (*Evolution of Keats's Poetry*, p. 698).—Dubious too is the theory that *Lamia* reflects Keats's alleged uncertainties about Fanny Brawne.

In my opinion Thorpe's interpretation is the soundest (Intr. to *Poems*, p. xliv),—that *Lamia* shows a conflict of two extremes, both falsities, false fantasies in the lovers and false, coldly factual knowledge in Apollonius. By contrast the true ideal of Keats was shown in the Apollo of *Hyperion,* and the Poet of the *Fall*.

Lamia is thus a moral allegory written in a realistic mood, and required a different kind of style, a couplet which, as Bate says, "would express what he had to say with rapidity, with emphasis, and even epigrammatic succinctness" (closely studied in *Stylistic Development of Keats,* pp. 146-171).

821. **7.** *ever-smitten Hermes:* the messenger of the gods, who often fell in love.

822. **46.** *cirque-couchant:* coiled in a circle.

58. *Ariadne's tiar:* Her crown. After her death she became a constellation.

63. *Proserpine:* She was carried off into the lower world by Pluto.

81. *star of Lethe:* Hermes guided souls into oblivion.

823. **133.** *Caducean:* Hermes' wand, the Caduceus, had the power of enchanting.

157. *brede:* embroidery.

198. *unshent:* innocent.

199. *terms:* semesters.

824. **248.** *Orpheus-like:* Like Orpheus who was permitted to lead his wife Eurydice out of the realm of death provided he would not gaze on her while he did so. He violated the restriction.

825. **320.** *Adonian:* Of Adonis who was beloved by Venus.

332. *a real woman:* reflects Keats's personal experience as a lover.

352. *temples lewd:* those of Venus, in which lascivious rites were performed.

826. **36.** *empery:* empire.

828. **185.** *libbard's:* leopard's.

829. 231. *awful rainbow:* awe-inspiring. A significant allusion to Sir Isaac Newton, At a party, Hazlitt and Keats (not too seriously) maintained that the great scientist had "destroyed all the poetry of the rainbow by reducing it to its prismatic colors."

DISC.—Compare *Lamia* with its source, given above.

Contrast *Lamia* with *Endymion* with respect to its realism (including realism of characterization), the speed of its action, and the style of the couplets (esp., I, 350-361, and II, 199-220).

Compare the attitude towards Apollonius with the passage from Wordsworth's *The Excursion* on scientists; *Anth.*, p. 286.

830. **TO AUTUMN**

De Selincourt regards this (except for the *Fall of Hyperion*) as Keats's "last work of full and conscious power," and wishes that he "had been spared the agony of mind which can be read in the fevered attempts at self-expression" in the rest of his works.—*To Autumn* seems to show that he had brought the problems and tensions so evident in the previous Odes to a solution,—a sombre but serene acceptance of life and death (see the appreciation by Anna J. Mill, TLS, Feb. 2, 1946).

831. **THE FALL OF HYPERION: A DREAM**

Often called "A Vision."—Amy Lowell and C. L. Finney (JEGP, 1927) believed that this was the earlier of the two versions of *Hyperion;* but that has been disproved by J. M. Murry (*Keats and Shakespeare*) and Douglas Bush (MLN, XLIX, 281; 1934).—It is not a mere revision, but a new poem, with a different conception of the theme, and an appropriately different style (see Bate, *Stylistic Development*, pp. 171-182).—See also J. L. Lowes, "Moneta's Temple," PMLA, LI, 1098 (1936).

From a garden where he "ate deliciously" (19-40) after the enchanted draught (41-59), the poet passes through the richly stored temple (60-85) to the altar, where the true nature of poetry is disclosed to him (87-215). It is an allegory of the stages in the highest development of human character. (Compare it with Wordsworth's ages of man, for similarities in substance and contrasts in style.) The garden is the youthful period of merely sensuous delight; the temple, that of knowledge, art, and philosophy, serves the period of intellectual curiosity, in which likewise one may wander purposeless; the altar, that of inspired truth and unselfish dedication, marks the hour when true self-knowledge is attained.

Keats felt that up to this time his work had been too largely that of a dreamer, a self-indulgent wanderer in the garden and through the temple, too detached from his fellow beings and of too little service to them. (This self-condemning opinion was either entirely mistaken or a considerable exaggeration, but it was sincerely and strongly held.) He imagines that at the altar he is given a last opportunity to rise to a higher understanding of a true poet's functions, and by a most painful effort he succeeds in mounting the first step (105-133). He is rewarded by new strength, and by the disclosure to him through the prophetess Moneta of the secret of great poetry—its sympathy with human suffering, a sympathy which dreamers and self-worshippers [Byron] lack (134-210).

After this prelude, the poet is privileged, under Moneta's guidance, to behold the Fall of Hyperion, one of Saturn's Titans, who, when the action of the poem begins, is still the ruler of the sun, but who is to be overthrown by Apollo. In Keats's view, Hyperion fell because he was a god of mere power. Apollo won because he was a god of enlightenment, of beauty, and of beneficence to mankind. That portion of the poem had previously been written (from l. 294 onwards), but in a different style, that of a Miltonic epic which Keats came to regard as too imitative, and also as too objective to permit that amplitude of interpretation which he now desired.

831. 48. *soon-fading:* Possibly meaning that the califs "faded," i.e., "murdered" their enemies quickly, or that (by assassins using poison) they themselves died soon one after the other.
76. *some:* Misprint for "zone"?

832. 97. *mid-day:* Probably a misprint for "mid-May" (TLS, May 24, 1924).
147. *None can usurp,* etc.: Shows the influence not only of Wordsworth but also (see A. C. Bradley, *Oxford Lectures on Poetry*, p. 242) of Shelley's *Alastor;* see especially the prose preface, and ll. 42-49 (*Anth.*, 855-856).

833. 167. *canst thou:* canst thou do.

187-210. *Majestic shadow,* etc.: This passage, highly important for an understanding of Keats's philosophy, was unfortunately omitted in the first edition.

208. *careless Hectorers:* This attack on Byron regrettably lowers the noble tone of the poem.

834. 294. *Deep in the shady:* The first version of the poem began at this point.

835. 365. *scorches:* Possibly Keats wrote "scourges."

DISC.—What are the chief differences between the two versions of Hyperion? Do you agree with the opinion that both versions are "the superb imaginative expression of a passionate concern for humanity which rivals Shelley's own"? (TLS editorial; Aug. 9, 1947).

837. THE DAY IS GONE

On Fanny Brawne. She has been criticized as too shallow to deserve the love of Keats; but see F. Edgcumbe's ed. of the *Letters of Fanny Brawne to Fanny Keats: 1820-1824* (1937), which should silence her detractors. They show her "a young woman of remarkable perception and imagination, keen in the observance of character and events, possessing an unusual critical faculty, and intellectually fitted to become the wife of Keats."

838. LETTERS OF KEATS

They were dashed off in haste, with no thought that they would ever be published, and no regard for details of composition, punctuation, etc.—to illustrate which I give the first two and the fourth with most of the irregularities. In the other letters I have brought the spelling and punctuation nearer to normal usages.

The letters are a precious record of the absolutely sincere emotions and thoughts of a noble nature gifted with genius, modestly but eagerly groping its way toward beauty, truth, and goodness.

DISC.—The letters contain some of Keats's most important sentiments about life and literature. They should be discussed in close connection with his poems. They are not absolutely consistent throughout: one of the most interesting topics is, which of the views harmonize with his practice and with one another, and which seem to be temporary notions?

838a. 4. *John Hamilton Reynolds:* a lawyer, writer of verse, and staunch friend.—The letters are strewn with quotations from Shakspeare, often the ones he had underlined in his copy (Spurgeon, *Keats' Shakespeare*).

838b. 14. *Haydon:* see the sonnets on *Haydon* and *Elgin Marbles, Anth.,* pp. 757-758.

840a. 26. *Adam's dream:* in *Paradise Lost,* VIII, 449-489.

34. *sensations,* etc.: The contrast is not between a sensuous life and an intellectual; but between the vivid concreteness of art and literature, and the pale abstractions of formal philosophy.

840b. 14. *the philosophic mind:* quoted from Wordsworth's *Immortality Ode,* which, Bailey says, Keats was never weary of repeating.

841a. 10. *two-and-thirty Palaces:* the palaces of delight of the Buddhists.

25. *spirit and pulse of good:* Wordsworth's *Old Cumberland Beggar,* l. 77.

841b. 28. *the thrush:* the thrush of Keats is a less rapturous bird than Browning's (*Home Thoughts*), John Clare's (*Thrush's Nest*), and Siegfried Sassoon's (*Thrushes*).
DISC.—Compare them.

842a. 4. *John Taylor:* partner in the firm that published Keats's *Endymion* and *Lamia.*

842b. 27. *Burden of the Mystery: Tintern Abbey,* l. 38.

51. *main region of his song: The Recluse,* l. 41.

843a. 9. *Knowledge is sorrow:* What Byron (or Manfred) really said was "Sorrow is knowledge," a very different assertion (*Manfred;* I, 1. 10).

843b. 53. *Benjamin Bailey:* clergyman, and a good friend to Keats.

845a. 11. *Richard Woodhouse:* a young lawyer, adviser to Keats's publishers.

19. *genus irritabile:* the irritable race of poets.—Stallknecht (*Strange Seas,* p. 264), though chiefly interested in Wordsworth, calls this letter of Keats "the most memorable statement

of the operation of esthetic sensibility"; but he also notes that this deals only with the first half of poetic composition; the second, the creative activity, or the unifying imagination, is dealt with best by Coleridge.

44. *in for and filling:* perhaps "informing" would be a clearer reading.

55. *Ops:* goddess of the harvest, wife of Saturn.

845b. 43. *Hazlitt and Gifford:* Shows Keats capable of enjoying righteous indignation, and links him with Byron, Shelley, Hunt, etc., against Tory "Scotch Reviewers." See Thorpe, "Keats and Hazlitt," PMLA, LXII, 487; 1947.

846b. 12. *feu de joie:* a firing of guns in token of joy.

847b. 48. *The Castle of Indolence:* see *Anth.*, p. 817 and Note.

53. *The False One:* by Beaumont and Fletcher.

57. *Hogg against Burns:* in *Blackwood's Magazine*, Feb., 1819.

848b. 22. *one human heart: Old Cumberland Beggar*, l. 153.

45. *I am, however, young:* Perhaps the passage would be clearer if these words were placed in brackets.

849b. 2. *Pizarro:* conqueror of Peru, hence in William Robertson's *History of America;* see Note on p. 751, *On First Looking Into Chapman's Homer*.

850b. 10. *Fanny Brawne:* See the Note on *The Day Is Gone*, p. 837; also *The Last Sonnet*, p. 817.

852b. 4. *the volume I send you:* the 1820 volume, containing *Lamia, Isabella*, etc. When Shelley's drowned body was recovered, Hunt's copy of this edition was found in his pocket; it was placed upon the funeral pyre.

DISC.—Compare the narrative poetry of Wordsworth, Scott, Coleridge, Landor, and Keats with respect to (a) choice of subjects, (b) swiftness of action, (c) proportion of description to narration, (d) simplicity or richness of details, and (e) clarity and profundity of characterization. —Then do likewise with some of the narrative poetry of our time—S. V. Benet, MacLeish, T. S. Eliot, etc.—for contrast with the Romantics.

Which features of nature, and what meanings seen in Nature, do Keats and Wordsworth respectively emphasize?

Contrast the treatment of love in Wordsworth (including the Lucy poems) and in Keats.

One of the most characteristic notes in Keats, yielding rich poetical effects, is his sense of *wonderment* at the strangeness and complexity of human life and growth. Trace this in such passages as *Ben Nevis* (p. 793); *Hyperion*, III (p. 804), *Why Did I Laugh Tonight* (p. 814), the greater *Odes* (p. 816 ff.), and the Letters. Have you found comparable strains in any of the other Romantics?

Gather a dozen examples of *word magic* in Keats (e.g., Embalmed darkness, No hungry generations tread thee down, deep-delved earth); do likewise with, say, Coleridge or Wordsworth; and try to express the differences in style that thus come into view.

PERCY BYSSHE SHELLEY (1792-1822)

I. EDITIONS

Ingpen, Roger, and Peck, Walter E., eds. *Complete Works of Shelley*, 10 vols., 1926-1930.

Forman, H. Buxton, ed. *Complete Works*, 8 vols., 1882.

*Woodberry, G. E., ed. *Complete Poetical Works*, 1901

Hutchinson, Thomas, ed. *Complete Poetical Works*, 1933.

Shawcross, John, ed. *Literary and Philosophical Criticism*, 1909.

Jones, F. L., ed. *The Letters of Mary Wollstonecraft Shelley*, 2 vols., 1944.—*Mary Shelley's Journal*, 1947.

*White, Newman I., ed. *The Best of Shelley*, 1932.

II. BIOGRAPHY AND CRITICISM

Browning, Robert. "An Essay on Shelley," 1852 (In *Complete Poetical Works*, 1895).

Arnold, Matthew. *Essays in Criticism: Second Series*, 1888.

Yeats, W. B. *Ideas of Good and Evil*, 1903.

*Thompson, Francis. "Shelley," *Collected Works*, III; 1913.

More, P. E. *Shelburne Essays: Seventh Series*, 1910.

Strong, A. T. *Three Studies in Shelley*, 1921.

*Campbell, Mrs. O. W. *Shelley and the Unromantics*, 1924.

Maurois, André. *Ariel: A Shelley Romance*, 1924.

Peck, W. E. *Shelley: His Life and Work*, 2 vols., 1927.

Grabo, C. H. *A Newton Among Poets*, 1930.

Hotson, John Leslie. *Shelley's Lost Letters to Harriet*, 1930.

Fairchild, H. N. *The Romantic Quest*, 1931.

Stovall, Floyd. *Desire and Restraint in Shelley*, 1931.

Weaver, Bennett. *Toward the Understanding of Shelley*, 1932.

Kurtz, B. P. *The Pursuit of Death*, 1933.

Read, Herbert. *In Defense of Shelley, and Other Essays*, 1935.

*Grabo, C. H. *The Magic Plant: The Growth of Shelley's Mind*, 1936.

Barnard, Ellsworth. *Shelley's Religion*, 1937.

Firkins, O. W. *Power and Elusiveness in Shelley*, 1937.

Grylls, R. Glynn. *Mary Shelley: A Biography*, 1938.

White, N. I. *The Unextinguished Hearth: Shelley and His Contemporary Critics*, 1938.

Grylls, R. Glynn. *Claire Clairmont*, 1939.—Cf. J. H Smith, "Shelley and Claire Clairmont,"
    PMLA, LIV, 785; 1939; and F. L. Jones, "Mary Shelley," SAQ, XLII, 406; 1943.

Powers, Julia. *Shelley in America*, 1940.

*White, N. I. *Shelley*, 2 vols., 1940 (condensed, 1 vol., 1945).

*Knight, G. Wilson. "The Naked Seraph," in *The Starlit Dome*, 1941.

Clark, D. L. "What Was Shelley's Indebtedness to Keats?" PMLA, LVI, 479; 1941.

Cluck, Julia. "Elinor Wylie's Shelley Obsession," PMLA, LVI, 841; 1941.

Cameron, K. N. "The Social Philosophy of Shelley," *Sewanee Rev.*, l. 457; 1942.

Notopoulos, J. A. "The Dating of Shelley's Prose," PMLA, LVIII, 477; 1943

Smith, R. M. *The Shelley Legend*, 1945.—See N. I. White, SP, XLIII, 522; F L. Jones, PMLA,
    XLI, 848; and K. N. Cameron, JEGP, XLV, 369; 1946.

Cameron, K. N. "Shelley and the Reformers," ELH, XII, 62; 1945.

*Fogle, R. H. "Romantic Bards and Metaphysical Reviewers," ELH, XII, 221; 1945.

Fogle, R. H. "The Abstractness of Shelley," PQ, XXIV, 362; 1945.

Fogle, R. H. "Empathic Imagery in Keats and Shelley," PMLA, LXI, 163; 1946.

Jones, F. L. "The Vision Theme in Shelley's 'Alastor' and Related Works," SP, XLIV, 108
    (1947); and "Shelley's *On Life*," PMLA, LXII, 774 (1947).

Hughes, A. M. D. *The Nascent Mind of Shelley*, 1947.

Barrell, Joseph. *Shelley and the Thought of His Time*, 1947.

III. Miscellaneous

Ellis, F. S. *A Lexical Concordance to the Poetical Works of Shelley*, 1892.

Salt, H. S. A. *A Shelley Primer*, 1887.

NOTES, COMMENTS, AND TOPICS FOR DISCUSSION

854.   STANZAS.—APRIL, 1814

Mrs. Campbell (*Shelley and the Unromantics*, p. 125), after surveying all the previous writings of Shelley, exclaims on coming to this lyric: "Suddenly and wonderfully, the *poet* has arisen." That is more important than the personal allusions to the fact that Shelley had been happy, staying with his friends at Bracknell, and was now returning to his home, from which he felt that love had departed.

854.   TO WORDSWORTH

He had long admired Wordsworth's poetry, but he was angered when Wordsworth accepted a government position. Thirty years later, Browning expressed a similar feeling in *The Lost Leader*.

855.   ALASTOR, OR THE SPIRIT OF SOLITUDE

The Greek "alastor" signifies an avenging spirit, here that of solitude destroying those who isolate themselves. The motto: "I loved not yet,—I loved to love,—I sought something to love, for I loved to love."

Shelley was distraught. His youthful attempts at radical political and social reforms had been baffled. He was in poor health, and believed himself near death. Having deserted Harriet, and eloped with Mary Godwin, he had been driven into exile. "I am," he wrote Leigh Hunt, "an outcast from human society; my name is execrated,—by those very beings whose happiness I ardently desired." Hence the tragedy of the idealist who vainly seeks the embodiment of his ideals in actuality, weighed upon his mind. Chatterton lived in his memory; and there are borrowings from Johnson's *Rasselas*, Volney's *Ruins*, Lady Morgan's *The Missionary*, and Wordsworth's *Elegiac Stanzas* ("the light that never was, on sea or land,"—*Anth.*, p. 231). See K. N. Cameron, SP, XL, 58 (1943); and the references in the next paragraph.

Do not look for consistency within the poem itself, nor between it and its preface; Shelley's emotions and ideas are in ferment . Hence the following learned debate about the inconsistencies, and why they exist: R. D. Havens, PMLA, XLV, 1098 (1930); H. L. Hoffman, *An Odyssey of the Soul* (1933), A. E. Du Bois, JEGP, XXV, 530 (1936); M. Kessel, PMLA, LI, 302 (1936); F. L. Jones, ELH, XIII, 291 (1946) and SP, XLIV, 108 (1947) and E. K. Gibson, PMLA, LXII, 1022 (1947). —Better than the "plot" is the style—the flexible colorful blank verse, much improved over that of his earlier poems.

855a. 14. *still insatiate:* DISC.—Contrast this seeker with Byron's Manfred (*Anth.*, p. 585).

855b. 4. *that Power*, etc.: The ruler of the Universe. The contrast is between two false extremes—the idealist (luminary) who fancies he can live without the world in his devotion to abstract perfection, and the practical man (meaner spirit) who fancies he can live without ideals.

39. *The good die first:* It is significant that the preface should end with a quotation from Wordsworth (*Excursion*, I, 500). Notice in the poem such Wordsworthian phrases as "natural piety" (3) and "obstinate questionings" (26).

856. 93. *frequent with:* with many.

857. 109. *Balbec:* Syrian city famous for its ruins.

119. *Zodiac*, etc.: The statues are gazing upon brazen representations of such mythological creatures as appear in the signs of the Zodiac.

141. *Carmania:* Southern Persia, mod. Kerman.

145. *Cashmire:* see Moore's *Light of the Haram*, *Anth.*, p. 523.

151. *veiled maid:* the Spirit of Solitude.

858. 211. *gate of death:* the thought of suicide enters his mind.

859. 272. *Chorasmian:* he has wandered to Khiva, a desolate region in central Asia.

861. 479. *Spirit:* the Spirit of Nature, perhaps the "Mother" of l. 18.

862. 490. *starry eyes:* those of the Vision.

676. *chalice . . . one living man:* the cup of unending life, forced upon the Wandering Jew. See the Note on Wordsworth's *Wandering Jew; Anth.*, p. 216. Note the resentment against the alleged injustice of God.

863.   HYMN TO INTELLECTUAL BEAUTY

Shelley's world is no longer ruled solely by rigid Necessity. There is in it Intellectual—or Ideal—Beauty, which visits us infrequently and which we never behold abstractly. Its existence is felt by us through those actual phenomena which it creates and which, in "studious zeal and love's delight" (65), we come to know and experience. These phenomena that visit us with "inconstant wing" fade and die sooner or later; they lack the eternal reality of the Ideal Beauty.—The general conception is Plato's (*Symposium*, 211-212). See J. A. Notopoulos on the Platonic sources, PMLA, LVIII, 582; 1943.

864. 49. *I sought for ghosts*, etc.: the contrast is between vainly seeking for supermundane beings which have no existence, and obtaining glimpses of "thy shadow" (58), i.e., of the divine reality of beauty.

DISC.—Compare the *Hymn* with Wordsworth's *Ode: Intimations of Immortality*, which strongly influenced it (see Frederick L. Jones, "Shelley's *On Life*," PMLA, LXII, 774; 1947).

864.   MONT BLANC

Written immediately after Shelley, with a guide, had ascended to the Boisson glacier, feeling the wild desolation and majestic beauty flowing from the secret fastnesses of the mountain, where "Power dwells apart in its tranquillity."—As in *Alastor,* there are obscurities. It has been asserted that Shelley in most of the poem implies that man is ruled by Necessity, but that in the last three lines he contradicts that assumption. The pros and cons are well weighed by I. J. Kapstein, PMLA, LXII, 1046 (1947).

DISC.—Similarities and dissimilarities between this poem and Wordsworth's *Prelude,* VI, 621-640; *Anth.,* p. 257.—Such passages created enthusiasm for mountain climbing, the passion for which is one of the consequences of the Romantic Movement. A classic is Edward Whymper's *Scrambles Among the Alps,* 1873, incidents from which are versified in Kenneth Rexroth's *The Phoenix and the Tortoise,* 1947—another subject for discussion.

866.   TO MARY: DEDICATION TO THE REVOLT OF ISLAM

The *Revolt,* a poem of radical tendencies, was dedicated to his second wife, Mary Godwin Shelley. At this time Claire Clairmont, daughter of the Mrs. Clairmont who became William Godwin's second wife, was living with the Shelleys. The important activity of this household was the study of literature, with a view of fighting against prejudice, injustice, and tyranny.

867. 46. *Alas that love,* etc.: This stanza alludes to his unhappy marriage with Harriet West-brook, and his elopement with Mary.
58. *the mortal chain of Custom:* Alluding to the fact that Mary eloped with a married man.
86. *Anarch Custom:* Blind adherence to convention, destroying, rather than establishing, the right relations among mankind.
88. *Amphion:* In mythology, a musician whose lyre produced magical effects.
868. 101. *glorious parents:* William Godwin and Mary Wollstonecraft. (See *Anth.,* pp. 101-102.)

868.   TO CONSTANTIA, SINGING

Claire Clairmont, see preceding Note.

869.   OZYMANDIAS

Shelley and Horace Smith agreed to enter into a sonnet-writing competition, the subject being a passage they had been reading together in the Greek historian Diodorus Siculus, which related that the largest statue in Egypt bore the following inscription: "I am Ozymandias, king of kings; if anyone wishes to know what I am and where I lie, let him surpass me in some of my exploits." Observe that Shelley has intensified the boast, and has imagined that the sculptor ("the hand that mocked") would dare to mock.

DISC.—Collect some of the boastful sayings of Caesar, Napoleon, the Emperor Wilhelm II, Hitler, and some of our own contemporaneous "thrasonical braggers."—See Morris Bishop's amusing sidelight, *Ozymandias Revisited.*
Soon after Shelley's poem was published, a colossal bust, now called that of "Young Memnon," but then thought to be that of Ozymandias, was transported to the British Museum; see the *Narrative* (1820) of the engineer, G. Belzoni.—See also D. W. Thompson, PQ, XVI, 59; 1937.

869.   LINES WRITTEN AMONG THE EUGANEAN HILLS

These beautiful hills in Lombardy are near Padua and Venice, in a region then under the despotic foreign (hence "Celtic") rule of Austria. The melancholy expressed is partly owing to Shelley's regrets that Italy did not have national independence, and partly owing to the poor state of his health and the recent death of his child Clara. Characteristic is the overcoming of this sad mood at the close, by means of delight in the glories of nature and of hope in a better future.—DISC.—Which parts of this poem seem to you to harmonize with the attitude of Byron, and which do not? Compare also Wordsworth's treatment of the theme of national independence,—*Venetian Republic, Subjugation of Switzerland, Cintra,* etc.

869. 45-65. It is plausibly suggested by Louise S. Boas (EXP, Nov., 1944) that "the wretch" may be the man-made man of Mary Shelley's *Frankenstein,* published in the same year as these *Lines.*

72. *rooks:* small crows.

80. *grain:* color.

870. 97. *Amphitrite:* Goddess of the sea, of which her "hoary sire" Nereus, was also a divinity.

116. *his queen:* Compare Wordsworth's *On the Extinction of the Venetian Republic, Anth.,* p. 222.

123. *slave of slaves:* The Austrian emperor, Francis I.

152. *Celtic Anarch:* Foreign tyrant.

174. *tempest-cleaving swan:* Byron, who had left England two years before.

871. 222. *wain:* wagon.

228. *foison:* fertility.

239. *Ezzelin:* Tyrant of Padua in the thirteenth century.

240. *"I win":* Allusion to Life-in-Death winning the game of dice in *The Ancient Mariner.*

256. *lamp of learning:* The University of Padua was more than half a millennium old. Napoleon and other foreign rulers of Italy suppressed, on slight provocation, the liberty of teaching in her universities.

Shelley's *Lines* preface a book by another lover of Italy, Walter Starkie. In his *Waveless Plain* (1937), he tells of having learned it in boyhood, and of later reciting it before Petrarch's house in Arqua.

872.   STANZAS WRITTEN IN DEJECTION, NEAR NAPLES

A deeply moving passage in Kurtz's *Pursuit of Death,* pp. 151-153, describes the torturing afflictions under which Shelley was struggling.—Lines 35-36 seem prophetic of his death.—The last stanza plumbs the depths, suggesting that even those who might mourn his death would regret that he had lived (EXP., Feb., 1943).—DISC.—Ought this stanza to please the Eliot school of criticism, who on the whole dislike Shelley?

873.   SONNET

His despondency discourages even the pursuit of truth.—The unreal shadows are probably those of Plato's famous cave (*The Republic,* VII), distorted reflections of ideal reality. The Preacher is the Old Testament *Ecclesiastes* (1, 2; 12, 12).

873.   ODE TO THE WEST WIND

The melancholy mood is passing. The influence of Wordsworth has been noted by F. A. Pottle (TLS, June 20, 1936).—In Mediterranean regions strong winds from the West presage winter. Shelley, once "tameless, and swift, and proud," like the West Wind, but of late despondent, prays that its spirit may reanimate his own, and may bear his message (the Spring that shall succeed Winter) throughout the world.—See EXP., May and Oct., 1947.

873. 21. *Maenad:* a priestess or devotee of Bacchus, god of wine and revelry.

874. 32. *pumice isle in Baiae:* island of volcanic lava, near Naples.

38. *cleave themselves,* etc.: Shelley's note points out that the wind actually has this effect upon the bottom of the sea.

60. *autumnal tone:* Is Shelley's spirit really autumnal?

63. *my dead thoughts:* They are vital, but as he is still in a partly depressed state of mind, they seem lifeless to him.

874.   THE INDIAN SERENADE

874. 11. *champak:* a tree somewhat like a magnolia.

874.   THE CENCI: A TRAGEDY

See G. E. Woodberry's edition in the Belles Lettres Series, 1909. Also: Sara R. Watson on *Othello* and *The Cenci;* PMLA, LV, 611 (1940); K. G. Pfeiffer, "Landor's Critique," SP, XXXIX, 670 (1942); and Cameron and Frenz, "Stage History," PMLA, LX, 1080 (1945).

Shelley kept close to the historical facts as he knew them, except that he did not show Beatrice's repentance before her execution. The chief literary influences were Calderon, Shakspeare, and John Webster. By coming much closer to actual life, Shelley hoped to win public favor; but the incest theme rendered that impossible. He regarded *The Cenci* as much less important than *Prometheus Unbound* and *Adonais;* but Mrs. Shelley thought it his masterpiece, and some critics agree with her.

At the beginning of the scene given in the selections, Beatrice and her mother Lucretia are awaiting the arrival of Olimpio and Marzio, whom they have hired to murder Cenci.—In the following scene, Savelli is the legate, or executive officer, of the Pope.

DISC.—Contrast the diction of *The Cenci* with that of *Prometheus Unbound,* and the mastery over the varieties of style which the differences show. (*The Cenci* was written between Acts III and IV of *Prometheus*).

881. ENGLAND IN 1819—THE MASK OF ANARCHY

On August 19, 1819, an enthusiastic rally of Manchester citizens advocating parliamentary reforms led to disorders which resulted in an attack by the military forces and in several deaths. On these deplorable "Manchester massacres" Shelley wrote these three poems. The attack on the "despised king," George III, who had been insane for nine years, precedes that of Byron in *The Vision of Judgment (Anth.,* p. 724 and Notes).—DISC.—Point out similarities and differences in their political views, and in their manner of expressing them.

881. 9. *who wield:* who wield it (to their own danger).

882b. 15. *Eldon:* Lord Chancellor, one of the highest officials.

24. *Sidmouth:* Home Secretary, directly responsible for repressive measures.

883. PROMETHEUS UNBOUND: A LYRICAL DRAMA

All the authorities listed in the Bibliography give much attention to this masterpiece, and should be consulted, especially the most learned and judicious,—N. I. White, *Shelley* (1940). Vida D. Scudder's edition (1897) is still valuable, including its Introduction. On the scientific side, see Grabo's two books (1930 and 1936); on the religious, G. Wilson Knight's *Christian Renaissance* (1933) and *Starlit Dome* (1941). See also Stovall (1931); and among recent contributions K. N. Cameron, "Political Symbolism," PMLA, LVIII, 728 (1943); and J. S. Thomson "The Unbinding of Prometheus," UTQ, XV, 1 (1945).

The title page bore a Latin motto—"Hear ye not these things, hidden under the earth?"

Shelley's Preface

The Greek tragic writers, in selecting as their subject any portion of their national history or mythology, employed in their treatment of it a certain arbitrary discretion. They by no means conceived themselves bound to adhere to the common interpretation or to imitate in story as in title their rivals and predecessors. Such a system would have amounted to a resignation of those claims to a preference over their competitors which incited the composition. The Agamemnonian story was exhibited on the Athenian theatre with as many variations as dramas.

I have presumed to employ a similar license. The *Prometheus Unbound* of Æschylus supposed the reconciliation of Jupiter with his victim as the price of the disclosure of the danger threatened to his empire by the consummation of his marriage with Thetis. Thetis, according to this view of the subject, was given in marriage to Peleus, and Prometheus, by the permission of Jupiter, delivered from his captivity by Hercules. Had I framed my story on this model, I should have done no more than have attempted to restore the lost drama of Æschylus; an ambition which, if my preference to this mode of treating the subject had incited me to cherish, the recollection of the high comparison such an attempt would challenge might well abate. But, in truth, I was averse from a catastrophe so feeble as that of reconciling the champion with the oppressor of mankind. The moral interest of the fable, which is so powerfully sustained by the sufferings and endurance of Prometheus, would be annihilated if we could conceive of him as unsaying his high language and quailing before his successful and perfidious adversary. The only imaginary being resembling in any degree Prometheus, is Satan; and Prometheus is, in my judgment, a more poetical character than Satan, because, in addition to courage, and majesty, and firm and patient opposition to omnipotent force, he is susceptible of being described as exempt from the taints of ambition, envy, revenge, and a desire for personal aggrandizement, which, in the hero of *Paradise Lost*, interfere with the interest. The character of Satan engenders in the mind a pernicious casuistry which leads us to weigh his faults with his wrongs, and to excuse the former because the latter exceed all measure. In the minds of those who consider that magnificent fiction with a religious feeling it engenders something worse. But Prometheus is, as it were, the type of the highest perfection of moral and intellectual nature, impelled by the purest and the truest motives to the best and noblest ends.

This poem was chiefly written upon the mountainous ruins of the Baths of Caracalla, among the flowery glades, and thickets of odoriferous blossoming trees, which are extended in ever winding labyrinths upon its immense platforms and dizzy arches suspended in the air. The bright blue sky of Rome, and the effect of the vigorous awakening spring in that divinest climate, and the new life with which it drenches the spirits even to intoxication, were the inspiration of this drama.

The imagery which I have employed will be found, in many instances, to have been drawn from the operations of the human mind, or from those external actions by which they are expressed. This is unusual in modern poetry, although Dante and Shakespeare are full of instances of the same kind: Dante indeed more than any other poet, and with greater success. But the Greek poets, as writers to whom no resource of awakening the sympathy of their contemporaries was unknown, were in the habitual use of this power; and it is the study of their works (since a higher merit would probably be denied me) to which I am willing that my readers should impute this singularity.

One word is due in candor to the degree in which the study of contemporary writings may have tinged my composition, for such has been a topic of censure with regard to poems far more popular, and indeed more deservedly popular, than mine. It is impossible that any one who inhabits the same age with such writers as those who stand in the foremost ranks of our own, can conscientiously assure himself that his language and tone of thought may not have been modified by the study of the productions of those extraordinary intellects. It is true that, not the spirit of their genius, but the forms in which it has manifested itself, are due less to the peculiarities of their own minds than to the peculiarity of the moral and intellectual condition of the minds among which they have been produced. Thus a number of writers possess the form, whilst they want the spirit of those whom, it is alleged, they imitate; because the former is the endowment of the age in which they live, and the latter must be the uncommunicated lightning of their own mind.

The peculiar style of intense and comprehensive imagery which distinguishes the modern literature of England, has not been, as a general power, the product of the imitation of any particular writer. The mass of capabilities remains at every period materially the same; the circumstances which awaken it to action perpetually change. If England were divided into forty republics, each equal in population and extent to Athens, there is no reason to suppose but that, under institutions not more perfect than those of Athens, each would produce philosophers and poets equal to those who (if we except Shakespeare) have never been surpassed. We owe the great writers of the golden age of our literature to that fervid awakening of the public mind which shook to dust the oldest and most oppressive form of the Christian religion. We owe Milton to the progress and development of the same spirit: the sacred Milton was, let it ever be remembered, a republican, and a bold inquirer into morals and religion. The great writers of our own age are, we have reason to suppose, the companions and forerunners of some unimagined change in our social condition or the opinions which cement it. The cloud of mind is discharging its collected lightning, and the equilibrium between institutions and opinions is now restoring, or is about to be restored.

As to imitation, poetry is a mimetic art. It creates, but it creates by combination and representation. Poetical abstractions are beautiful and new, not because the portions of which they are composed had no previous existence in the mind of man or in nature, but because the whole produced by their combination has some intelligible and beautiful analogy with those sources of emotion and thought, and with the contemporary condition of them: one great poet is a masterpiece of nature which another not only ought to study but must study. He might as wisely and as easily determine that his mind should no longer be the mirror of all that is lovely in the visible universe, as exclude from his contemplation the beautiful which exists in the writings of a great contemporary. The pretence of doing it would be a presumption in any but the greatest; the effect, even in him, would be strained, unnatural, and ineffectual. A poet is the combined product of such internal powers as modify the nature of others; and of such external influences as excite and sustain these powers; he is not one, but both. Every man's mind is, in this respect, modified by all the objects of nature and art; by every word and every suggestion which he ever admitted to act upon his consciousness; it is the mirror upon which all forms are reflected, and in which they compose one form. Poets, not otherwise than philosophers, painters, sculptors, and musicians, are, in the one sense, the creators, and, in another, the creations, of their age. From this subjection the loftiest do not escape. There is a similarity between Homer and Hesiod, between Æschylus and Euripides, between Virgil and Horace, between Dante and Petrarch, between Shakespeare and Fletcher, between Dryden and Pope; each has a generic resemblance under which their specific distinctions are arranged. If this similarity be the result of imitation, I am willing to confess that I have imitated.

Let this opportunity be conceded to me of acknowledging that I have, what a Scotch philosopher characteristically terms, "a passion for reforming the world": what passion incited him to write and publish his book, he omits to explain. For my part I had rather be damned with Plato and Lord Bacon, than go to Heaven with Paley and Malthus. But it is a mistake to suppose that I dedicate my poetical compositions solely to the direct enforcement of reform, or that I consider them in any degree as containing a reasoned system on the theory of human life. Didactic poetry is my abhorrence; nothing can be equally well expressed in prose that is not tedious and supererogatory in verse. My purpose has hitherto been simply to familiarize the highly refined imagination of the more select classes of poetical readers with beautiful idealisms of moral excellence; aware that until the mind can love, and admire, and trust, and hope, and endure, reasoned principles of moral conduct are seeds cast upon the highway of life which the unconscious passenger tramples into dust, although they would bear the harvest of his happiness. Should I live to accomplish what I purpose, that is, produce a systematical history of what appear to me to be the genuine elements of human society, let not the advocates of injustice and superstition flatter themselves that I should take Æschylus rather than Plato as my model.

The having spoken of myself with unaffected freedom will need little apology with the candid, and let the uncandid consider that they injure me less than their own hearts and minds by misrepresentation. Whatever talents a person may possess to amuse and instruct others, be they ever so inconsiderable, he is yet bound to exert them: if his attempt be ineffectual, let the punishment of an unaccomplished purpose have been sufficient; let none trouble themselves to heap the dust of oblivion upon his efforts; the pile they raise will betray his grave which might otherwise have been unknown.

Mrs. Shelley's Note

["An excellent statement of the circumstances under which *Prometheus Unbound* was composed and the general ideas it embodies" (N. I. White).]

He meditated three subjects as the groundwork for lyrical dramas. One was the story of Tasso; of this a slight fragment of a song of Tasso remains. The other was one founded on the *Book of Job*, which he never abandoned in idea, but of which no trace remains among his papers. The third was the *Prometheus*

Unbound. The Greek tragedians were now his most familiar companions in his wanderings, and the sublime majesty of Æschylus filled him with wonder and delight. The father of Greek tragedy does not possess the pathos of Sophocles, nor the variety and tenderness of Euripides; the interest on which he founds his dramas is often elevated above human vicissitudes into the mighty passions and throes of gods and demi-gods: such fascinated the abstract imagination of Shelley.

. . . .

At first he completed the drama in three acts. It was not till several months after, when at Florence, that he conceived that a fourth act, a sort of hymn of rejoicing in the fulfillment of the prophecies with regard to Prometheus, ought to be added to complete the composition.

The prominent feature of Shelley's theory of the destiny of the human species was that evil is not inherent in the system of the creation, but an accident that might be expelled. This also forms a portion of Christianity: God made earth and man perfect, till he, by his fall,

'Brought death into the world and all our woe.'

Shelley believed that mankind had only to will that there should be no evil, and their would be none. It is not my part in these notes to notice the arguments that have been urged against this opinion, but to mention the fact that he entertained it, and was indeed attached to it with fervent enthusiasm. That man could be so perfectionized as to be able to expel evil from his own nature, and from the greater part of the creation, was the cardinal point of his system. And the subject he loved best to dwell on was the image of One warring with the Evil Principle, oppressed not only by it, but by all—even the good, who were deluded into considering evil a necessary portion of humanity; a victim full of fortitude and hope and the spirit of triumph emanating from a reliance in the ultimate omnipotence of Good. Such he had depicted in his last poem [*The Revolt of Islam*] when he made Laon the enemy and the victim of tyrants. He now took a more idealized image of the same subject. He followed certain classical authorities in figuring Saturn as the good principle, Jupiter the usurping evil one, and Prometheus as the regenerator, who, unable to bring mankind back to primitive innocence, used knowledge as a weapon to defeat evil, by leading mankind, beyond the state wherein they are sinless through ignorance, to that in which they are virtuous through wisdom. Jupiter punished the temerity of the Titan by chaining him to a rock of Caucasus, and causing a vulture to devour his still-renewed heart. There was a prophecy afloat in heaven portending the fall of Jove, the secret of averting which was known only to Prometheus; and the god offered freedom from torture on condition of its being communicated to him. According to the mythological story, this referred to the off-spring of Thetis, who was destined to be greater than his father. Prometheus at last bought pardon for his crime of enriching mankind with his gifts, by revealing the prophecy. Hercules killed the vulture, and set him free; and Thetis was married to Peleus, the father of Achilles.

Shelley adapted the catastrophe of this story to his peculiar views. The son greater than his father, born of the nuptials of Jupiter and Thetis, was to dethrone Evil, and bring back a happier reign than that of Saturn. Prometheus defies the power of his enemy, and endures centuries of torture; till the hour arrives when Jove, blind to the real event, but darkly guessing that some great good to himself will flow, espouses Thetis. At the moment, the Primal Power of the world drives him from his usurped throne, and Strength, in the person of Hercules, liberates Humanity, typified in Prometheus, from the tortures generated by evil done or suffered. Asia, one of the Oceanides, is the wife of Prometheus— she was, according to other mythological interpretations, the same as Venus and Nature. When the benefactor of mankind is liberated, Nature resumes the beauty of her prime, and is united to her husband, the emblem of the human race, in perfect and happy union. In the Fourth Act, the poet gives further scope to his imagination, and idealizes the forms of creation—such as we know them, instead of such as they appeared to the Greeks. Maternal Earth, the mighty parent, is superseded by the Spirit of the Earth, the guide of our planet through the realms of sky; while his fair and weaker companion and attendant, the Spirit of the Moon, receives bliss from the annihilation of Evil in the superior sphere.

Shelley develops, more particularly in the lyrics of this drama, his abstruse and imaginative theories with regard to the Creation. It requires a mind as subtle and penetrating as his own to understand the mystic meanings scattered throughout the poem. They elude the ordinary reader by their abstraction and delicacy of distinction, but they are far from vague. It was his design to write prose metaphysical essays on the nature of man, which would have served to explain much of what is obscure in his poetry; a few scattered fragments of observations and remarks alone remain. He considered these philosophical views of mind and nature to be instinct with the intensest spirit of poetry.

More popular poets clothe the ideal with familiar and sensible imagery. Shelley loved to idealize the real—to gift the mechanism of the material universe with a soul and a voice, and to bestow such also on the most delicate and abstract emotions and thoughts of the mind. . . .

Through the whole poem there reigns a sort of calm and holy spirit of love; it soothes the tortured, and is hope to the expectant, till the prophecy is fulfilled, and love, untainted by any evil, becomes the law of the world. . . .

The charm of the Roman climate helped to clothe his thoughts in greater beauty than they had ever worn before. And, as he wandered among the ruins made one with nature in their decay, or gazed on the Praxitelean shapes that throng the Vatican, the Capitol, and the palaces of Rome, his soul imbibed forms of loveliness which became a portion of itself. There are many passages in the *Prometheus* which show the intense delight he received from such studies, and give back the impression with a beauty of poetical description peculiarly his own.

Outline of the Drama

Prometheus, who at the beginning of his torture had pronounced a horrible curse against Jupiter, has suffered ages of pain and thereby gained insight and wisdom. Hatred has now left his soul, he despises revenge, and would recall his curse. Jupiter, mistakenly supposing that this means feebleness, demands that Prometheus disclose the secret of what he must not do if he would avoid downfall; and when Prometheus refuses to bow to unjust power, inflicts further tortures upon him. Far away, in an Indian vale, dwells Asia, the beloved of Prometheus, and the very spirit of Love. She is, however, passive and ineffectual until, roused by messengers from Prometheus, she yearns for enlightenment, whereupon she is borne through the dark forest of human experience into the presence of the most dread of beings, Demogorgon, that mysterious Eternal Fate which is even greater than the gods of Olympus. She implores him to disclose the fate of Prometheus, and their future is shown to her in a vision, culminating in his adoration of her. There follows the downfall of Jupiter, who has incurred the fatal danger by marrying Thetis. Their child, Hercules, overthrows Jupiter and frees Prometheus, whereupon all the spirits of the universe chant a paean of rejoicing over the downfall of tyranny and the victory of forgiveness, love, and unconquerable resistance to force.

General Editorial Comments

The statements in Shelley's Preface and in his wife's Note are even more important than the best modern interpretations, and they should be carefully studied and borne in mind during the reading of the drama.

Prometheus Unbound was condemned by many contemporary critics as blasphemous, as immoral, and (not quite so unfairly) as obscure. Its later admirers included, besides Robert Browning and Francis Thompson, political radicals like Karl Marx, Robert Owen, and George Bernard Shaw. N. I. White calls Shelley "the greatest radical voice in poetry since Lucretius." But the youthful *Queen Mab* is much nearer Marxian philosophy than is *Prometheus Unbound*, in which Shelley moves much closer toward Christian ethics, especially in the key thought (indicated in the Preface and Note) that Evil is not inherent in creation, has existed only by the consent of the human mind and will. In *Prometheus* Love means, not compromise with Evil, but pity for its slaves; and Love is perfected in man only when he rises, usually through suffering, above the desire for personal vengeance. Shelley planned to expound in prose treatises the application of these principles to practical problems, but unfortunately did not live to do so. In the drama itself, his enthusiasm for ideals of moral excellence and his faith in the future of mankind is expressed in a style of extraordinary lyrical splendor and richness. The following passages are of especial importance in the understanding of Shelley's beliefs:—

884. 48-53. Prometheus' moral transformation, the true cause of the ultimate victory of the good. "Do good to them that hate you." See 889, 304: "It doth repent me."

890. 382. "I gave all he has." Man makes gods that are cruel.

894. 542 ff. The evil Furies tempt Prometheus by showing him how Good has been corrupted or has suffered. Shelley calls this "the sophistry of the Furies," and has it repudiated by the Chorus of Spirits, 898, 781 ff.

895. 585 ff. The attitude of love toward Christ on the cross.

909. 119 ff. Fate, Time, Occasion, Chance, and Change—formerly considered omnipotent Necessity—still have power over men and gods, including Jupiter, but not over the redeemed Prometheus; for Love is the all-important exception, the Ultimate Omnipotence.

---

883. 2. But one: except Prometheus himself.
7. hecatombs: huge sacrifices (literally, one hundred oxen).
9. eyeless in hate: in your blind hate.
34. Heaven's winged hound: the vulture, which daily tore his entrails.

887. 192. Zoroaster: founder of the Persian religion. Shelley makes dramatic use of his doctrine that there is a real world and a corresponding one of phantasms—e.g., Jupiter's phantasm below, l. 282, who repeats what Jupiter himself had said thousands of years before.

889. 7. should vanquish thee: Earth naturally mistakes a moral victory as a defeat.

890. 343. son of Maia: Mercury.

891. 399. Sicilian's sword: that of Damocles.

900. 27. Panthea: She is the messenger of love between Prometheus and his divine consort Asia.
44. glaucous: greyish green.

902. 140. Hyacinth: A youth accidentally killed by Apollo. The god caused the flower to spring from his blood, and marked its petals with AI (woe).

904. 1. Scene II. A forest: Allegorically, the forest is human experience through which Love (Asia) and Faith (Panthea) pursue their way.

906. 9. Mœnads: The frenzied nymphs who were the attendants of the god of wine.
54. To the deep, etc.: We leave the phenomenal world to seek the one reality, the "one pervading, one alone" (l. 79).

907. 12. when the winds, etc.: "at the winds" would be clearer.

908. 61. Nepenthe, Moly, Amaranth: The drug which banished sorrow, the herb which protected against witchcraft, and the flower that never faded.

911. 20. Nereids tell: the sea nymphs tell of the goddess arising out of the ocean (hyaline).

913. 40. Numidian seps: a serpent whose bite caused torment and death.

914. 72. vulture . . . snake: in Shelleyan symbolism, the vulture is evil, the snake good.

915. 24. Blue Proteus: a sea deity, hence blue. See Wordsworth's The World Is Too Much With Us, Anth., p. 236.

916. 15. frozen tears: stalactites. One of the many passages showing Shelley's intense interest in natural phenomena—like the hydrogen-chain above, p. 905, 70-82.
42. Enna . . . Himera: in Sicily.

918. 165. Praxitelean shapes: statues as beautiful as those of the celebrated Greek sculptor Praxiteles.

919. 6. the delicate spirit: the crude material earth is now replaced by a new-born spirit of reason and love.
19. dipsas: a snake whose bite caused intense thirst.

921. 119. amphisbenic snake: the mythical serpent with a head at each end, and therefore able to move in either direction. On the appropriateness of the metaphor here, see EXP, Dec., 1943.

922. 193. *man remains:* Man is at last freed from the tyranny of force. He is not without passions, but governs them in self-control.

922. *Act IV:* The main action ends with Act III, but Act IV lyrically expresses the new freedom of all the elements and forces of the universe.

DISC.—*Prometheus Unbound* is the supreme expression of faith in human perfectibility. It is largely on that account that Arnold calls Shelley "a beautiful but ineffectual angel," that P. E. More talks of his "illusive yet rapturous emanation of hope devoid of specific content," and George Santayana (*Winds of Doctrine*) considers him incapable of understanding reality. That is a principal reason why the "New Criticism" is even more contemptuous of Shelley than of Wordsworth and Keats. Do you believe in the possibility of human nature being radically improved, or do you not? For self-knowledge, an honest answer to that question is needed, also for clarifying your preferences among authors.

Discuss the significance of Shelley's entitling *Prometheus* a *lyrical* drama.

How sound is Leigh Hunt's defence (*Anth.*, p. 1007) of *Prometheus Unbound* against charges of obscurity, immorality, and irreligion?

One of the few poetical dramas of our time worthy to be compared, both in thought and in style, with *Prometheus* is Thomas Hardy's *The Dynasts*. Discuss the resemblances and differences.

The spirit of Byron is probably closer to that of today's literature than Shelley's. In what ways?

936. THE SENSITIVE PLANT

Unequalled among the many lovely poems on gardens. The essence, the reality, the soul of a garden, is the love and skill of her who tends it.

The actual garden described was that of Lady Mountcasbel, near Oxford; although Shelley characteristically said that the "exact antetype" of the lady was Jane Williams, whom he did not meet until a year after he had written the poem. Allegorically, the Sensitive Plant may represent Shelley himself.

936. 17. *pied wind-flowers:* anemones, variegated with spots of different colors.
    42. *prankt:* adorned.

938. 162. *was innocent:* Compare Sterne's Uncle Toby letting the fly escape (*Tristram Shandy*).
    163. *ephemeris:* a swift-flying insect.
    177. *Baiæ:* Near Naples.

939. 236. *agarics:* mushrooms.
    273. *dormice:* squirrel-like mice.
    283. *griff:* grasp.

940. THE CLOUD

Here, as in the case of all the best romantic nature poems, your appreciation of the truth-beauty (Keats) will be enhanced by closely observing nature itself—the clouds through the four seasons. This is the most perfect brief example of Shelley's using the best scientific knowledge of his day to symbolize higher truths. See Grabo, *A Newton Among Poets*, pp. 119, 154, for the borrowings from Beccaria's *Artificial Electricity*.

940. 33. *rack:* broken clouds.

941. 81. *cenotaph:* an unoccupied tomb, a monument to one buried elsewhere.

941. TO A SKYLARK

See Thomas Hardy's poem, *Shelley's Skylark*.—On the symbolism, see E. W. Marjarum, PMLA, LII, 911; 1937.

941. 22. *silver sphere:* morning star.

942. 71. *the fountains:* the inspiration.
    83. *more true:* mortals fear death; the singing skylark seems not to.

DISC.—Can you find anything except blind malice in Aldous Huxley's attack on this poem in *Point Counter Point* (p. 119)? "Shelley? Don't talk to me of Shelley . . . Blithe spirit! . . . Just pretending, just lying to himself as usual. The lark couldn't be allowed to be a mere bird. . . ."

For a striking contrast between the Romantics and the moderns compare Shelley's *Skylark* and Wordsworth's two poems on the subject (*Anth.*, pp. 229 and 295) with Gerard Manley Hopkins' *The Caged Skylark* (Untermeyer, *Mod. Brit. Poetry*, p. 102), beginning:

> As a dare-gale skylark scanted in a dull cage
> Man's mounting spirit in his bone-house, mean house, dwells.

How would you arbitrate the disagreement on this poem between two of our "New Critics," T. S. Eliot and William Empson, shown in the latter's *Seven Types of Ambiguity*, p. 197?

941. ODE TO LIBERTY

Contains obscure passages, especially in st. XVII, whose meaning is debated (EXP., June 1944; Dec., 1946); but the main idea seems clear: that the chief obstacles to liberty lie in the distortions of truth and misuse of words by man's *own mind,* not merely in the institutions which those distortions created.—A prose parallel, discussing specific reforms, is Shelley's *Philosophical View of Reform.*—DISC.—Is there here an anticipation of the modern interest in semantics and propaganda slogans?

943. THE QUESTION

944. 10. *Arcturi:* one of the greater stars.
13. *tall flower:* the tulip?
18. *cowbind:* bryony.
18. *May:* hawthorn.

DISC.—Compare the garden passage in Keats, *Nightingale*, ll. 41-50; *Anth.*, p. 819.

944. HYMN OF PAN

"Written at the request of a friend, to be inserted in a drama on the subject of Midas. Apollo and Pan contend before Tmolus, a mountain god, for the prize in music" (Mrs. Shelley).

944. 9. *cicale:* locusts.
945. 13. *Peneus:* a river in Sicily.
14. *Tempe . . . Pelion:* a valley and a mountain in Thessaly.
26. *daedal:* cunningly wrought.
30. *Menalus:* a mountain range in Sicily sacred to Pan.
31. *a maiden:* Syrinx, who fled from Pan and was changed into a reed.

DISC.—Compare with the Hymn to Pan in *Endymion*, I, 246; *Anth.*, p. 761.

945. THE TWO SPIRITS: AN ALLEGORY

DISC.—The Second Spirit apparently is Love; but who is the First? Science? Prudence? Prose?

947. SONG: RARELY, RARELY, COMEST THOU

The biographer who knows Shelley best, N. I. White, points out: "The assurance which Shelley gives in the last four stanzas is one of his most delightful bits of self-portraiture, built as authentic as the self-pity passages in other poems" (*Best of Shelley*, p. 504).

947. POLITICAL GREATNESS

DISC.—Does this remind you in sentiment and tone of passages in Wordsworth's political sonnets and Coleridge's Ode to France?

As will be seen in the *Defense of Poetry*, Shelley maintained that there was a correlation between the rise and decline of social and political liberty and the rise and decline of the arts.

948. A LAMENT

It is possible that this, and similarly sad lyrics of this period, may express Shelley's regret at the marriage of Emilia Viviani.

948 EPIPSYCHIDION

See Stopford Brooke, "Epipsychidion," *Studies in Poetry* (1920); and P. N. Roy's monograph (Calcutta, 1938) which utilizes an Italian *Life of Emilia Viviani* (1936).—Emilia, the beautiful daughter of a Pisan nobleman, was befriended by the Shelleys and, when a *marriage de convenance* was arranged for her, seemed to the poet a victim of parental tyranny—and also (for about a year) an embodiment of ideal beauty, truth, and love.—The poem was privately printed. It was condemned as immoral, incoherent as a whole, and obscure in details.

Though *Epipsychidion* retains some hold upon actual experience by its personal and autobiographical allusions, and by indications of the disturbances caused by the intrusion of passion upon ideals, it is of importance mainly as an expression—the most intense and beautiful in Shelley—of what the highest kind of love means to him. He is inspired chiefly by Plato's exaltation (in the *Symposium*, which he had been translating) of spiritual love above physical; and by Dante's and Petrarch's glorifying of romantic love between man and woman as the highest perfection and guide of human life. The main theme is spiritual affinity. G. Wilson Knight (*Christian Renaissance*, p. 305) maintains that *Epipsychidion* is not immoral "though the corresponding action in 'real life' probably would be so because inexpedient in relation to society as a whole," a verdict which will of course be hotly disputed by some. Mrs. Shelley dismissed the matter by calling the poem his "Italian Platonics."

948. 1-20. Here Emilia is merely a lovely young girl in distress.—J. H. Roberts (EXP, Apr., 1943) suggests that the "sweet Spirit" is Emilia; the "orphan," Mary; and "the name," marriage, the prospect of which grieves Emilia.

949. 21-123. According to N. I. White's excellent analysis, these lines as well as 321-348, describe Emilia as the realization of the poet's vision of Love.
42. *Youth's vision:* that of *Alastor*.
50. *these names:* sister and wife.
68. *wingless:* not fleeting.

950. 117. *third sphere:* that of Venus.
123-180. The poet's conviction that they are "formed for each other" (White).

951. 180-216. The Poet's devotion to ideal beauty.—The "Being" in l. 190 is the Vision in "Alastor," but there the search was less successful.
216-320. The poet's earlier attempts to find ideal beauty in human form.
238. *This soul out of my soul:* These words give the meaning of the title.

952. 256 ff. Identification of some of the persons alluded to is controversial; but there is general agreement that "the Moon" in l. 279 refers to Mary Shelley.

953. 321 ff. Again the poet returns to Emilia as the Vision realized (White).—In the rest of the poem, not given in this selection, the poet envisages their flight together.
368. *Comet:* Claire Clairmont (?).

DISC.—Compare Petrarchan love as interpreted by Landor, *The Pentameron, Anth.,* p. 511 and Note.

954. ADONAIS: AN ELEGY ON THE DEATH OF JOHN KEATS

The motto from Plato is translated by Shelley as follows:

Thou wert the morning star among the living,
Ere thy fair light had fled;—
Now, having died, thou art as Hesperus, giving
New splendor to the dead.

No great English poet has a nobler memorial than this; and few elegies in any language have a worthier subject. Shelley was acquainted with Keats, but not intimately; and he was moved to utter this tribute, not merely by personal friendship, but by just admiration of Keats's poetry and by consciousness of what Poesy had lost by his early death. To these sound motives was, unhappily, added another, one which did not rest upon as true a foundation in fact—

Shelley's indignation against the anonymous hostile reviewer in the *Quarterly* of Apr., 1818, the savagery of whose attack upon Keats's poem Shelley erroneously believed to have caused the young poet's death. Hence we hear, amid the otherwise lovely elegiac tones of *Adonais*, harsh notes in such epithets as "deaf and viperous murderer," "vulture," "nameless worm," "carrion kites," and "obscene ravens." Shelley's introduction of invective into an elegy might be defended by the precedent set in a famous passage in Miltons *Lycidas*—

> such as for their bellies' sake
> Creep, and intrude, and climb into the fold,

but the defence would be stronger if the object of Shelley's indignation had been as actual as that of Milton's. On the other hand, although no reviewer was guilty of murdering Keats, Shelley was fully justified in denouncing the failure of the world to recognize gratefully his genius.

The first edition of *Adonais* was printed at Pisa, Italy. Shelley's feelings at the time find characteristic expression in his preface, as follows:

> It is my intention to subjoin to the London edition of this poem a criticism upon the claims of its lamented object to be classed among the writers of the highest genius who have adorned our age. My known repugnance to the narrow principles of taste on which several of his earlier compositions were modeled prove at least that I am an impartial judge. I consider the fragment of *Hyperion* as second to nothing that was ever produced by a writer of the same years.
>
> John Keats died at Rome of a consumption, in his twenty-fourth year, on the [23rd] of [Feb.], 1821; and was buried in the romantic and lonely cemetery of the Protestants in that city, under the pyramid which is the tomb of Cestius, and the massy walls and towers, now moldering and desolate, which formed the circuit of ancient Rome. The cemetery is an open space among the ruins, covered in winter with violets and daisies. It might make one in love with death, to think that one should be buried in so sweet a place.
>
> The genius of the lamented person to whose memory I have dedicated these unworthy verses was not less delicate and fragile than it was beautiful; and where cankerworms abound, what wonder if its young flower was blighted in the bud? The savage criticism on his *Endymion*, which appeared in *The Quarterly Review*, produced the most violent effect on his susceptible mind; the agitation thus originated ended in the rupture of a blood-vessel in the lungs; a rapid consumption ensued, and the succeeding acknowledgments from more candid critics of the true greatness of his powers were ineffectual to heal the wound thus wantonly inflicted.
>
> It may be well said that these wretched men know not what they do. They scatter their insults and their slanders without heed as to whether the poisoned shaft lights on a heart made callous by many blows or one like Keats's composed of more penetrable stuff. One of their associates[1] is, to my knowledge, a most base and unprincipled calumniator. As to *Endymion*, was it a poem, whatever might be its defects, to be treated contemptuously by those who had celebrated, with various degrees of complacency and panegyric, *Paris*, and *Woman*, and a *Syrian Tale*, and Mrs. Lefanu, and Mr. Barrett, and Mr. Howard Payne, and a long list of the illustrious obscure? Are these the men who in their venal good nature presumed to draw a parallel between the Rev. Mr. Milman and Lord Byron? What gnat did they strain at here, after having swallowed all those camels? Against what woman taken in adultery dares the foremost of these literary prostitutes to cast his opprobrious stone? Miserable man! you, one of the meanest, have wantonly defaced one of the noblest specimens of the workmanship of God. Nor shall it be your excuse, that, murderer as you are, you have spoken daggers, but used none.
>
> The circumstances of the closing scene of poor Keats's life were not made known to me until the *Elegy* was ready for the press. I am given to understand that the wound which his sensitive spirit had received from the criticism of *Endymion* was exasperated by the bitter sense of unrequited benefits; the poor fellow seems to have been hooted from the stage of life, no less by those on whom he had wasted

---

[1] Henry Hart Milman, who had written several romantic dramas and poems. It may be added that Shelley suspected him to be the author of the "murderous" review. The actual author was John Wilson Croker, who may be said to have met his Nemesis when Macaulay reviewed his edition of Boswell's *Johnson* and dealt with him as he had dealt with Keats.

the promise of his genius, than those on whom he had lavished his fortune and his care. He was accompanied to Rome, and attended in his last illness by Mr. Severn, a young artist of the highest promise, who, I have been informed, "almost risked his own life, and sacrificed every prospect to unwearied attendance upon his dying friend." Had I known these circumstances before the completion of my poem, I should have been tempted to add my feeble tribute of applause to the more solid recompense which the virtuous man finds in the recollection of his own motives. Mr. Severn can dispense with a reward from "such stuff as dreams are made of." His conduct is a golden augury of the success of his future career—may the unextinguished Spirit of his illustrious friend animate the creations of his pencil, and plead against Oblivion for his name!

The Greek pastoral poets Moschus and Bion (third century A.D., of whom Shelley was fond, and of whom he translated some fragments, are occasionally mentioned as "the sources" of *Adonais.* They furnished, indeed, some of the pastoral conventions and descriptive touches. The extent of their contributions may be judged by comparing with the poem the following passages:

> "This kiss will I treasure, even as thyself, Adonis, since, ah ill-fated, thou art fleeing me, thou art fleeing far, Adonis, and art faring to Acheron, to that hateful king and cruel, while wretched I yet live, being a goddess, and may not follow thee! . . . For why, ah overbold, didst thou follow the chase, and, being so fair, why wert thou thus overhardy to fight with beasts? . . . He reclines, the delicate Adonis, in his raiment of purple, and around him the Loves are weeping, and groaning aloud, clipping their locks for Adonis. And one upon his shafts, another on his bow is treading, and one hath loosed the sandal of Adonis, and another hath broken his own feathered quiver, and one in a golden vessel bears water, and another laves the wound, and another from behind him with his wings is fanning Adonis."—Bion, *Lament for Adonis.*

> "Ye flowers, now in sad clusters breathe yourselves away. Now redden, ye roses, in your sorrow, and now wax red, ye wind-flowers; now, thou hyacinth, whisper the letters on thee graven, and add a deeper *ai ai* to thy petals; he is dead, the beautiful singer. . . . Ye nightingales that lament among the thick leaves of the trees, tell ye to the Sicilian waters of Arethusa the tidings that Bion the herdsman is dead. . . . And Echo in the rocks laments that thou are silent, and no more she mimics thy voice. And in sorrow for thy fall the trees cast down their fruit, and all the flowers have faded. . . . Poison came, Bion, to thy mouth, thou didst know poison. To such lips as thine did it come, and was not sweetened. What mortal was so cruel that could mix poison for thee, or who could give thee the venom that heard thy voice? Surely he had no music in his soul."—Moschus, *Lament for Bion.*

[The last four sentences of this *Lament,* in the original Greek, were given in the first edition as a second motto.]

The chief "source" is commonly not mentioned, perhaps because it is so obvious—viz., Keats's own poems. To Shelley, Keats survived in what he had created, and what he had created appeared to deck his bier.—

> All he had loved, and molded into thought,
> From shape, and hue, and odor, and sweet sound,   10
> Lamented Adonais.

To those who have just been reading Keats, therefore, *Adonais* will again and again afford the pleasure of recognition.

The sources of the philosophy of the poem are Platonic and, despite the absence of any expression of faith in *personal* immortality, Christian. The most important, and characteristically romantic, themes (more important than the personal allusions) are: 1. that only those *really* live who dwell with eternal truth and beauty; 2. that Keats survives in the recurrent Beauty of the Nature he disclosed in his poetry; and 3. that he lives forever in the "firmament of Time" with the immortal dead.

954. 1. *Adonais:* The name is normally Adonis, that of the youth whom Venus loved and who was slain by a wild boar. (To Shelley, the boar was the critic.) Various explanations for

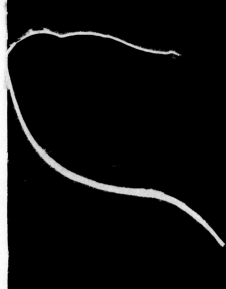

Shelley's form of the name have been suggested, none completely convincing. The best seems that of Professors Dixon and Grierson (*English Parnassus*): "Adonais is just a modification of Adonis intended to suggest that Keats was as dear to Urania, the Goddess of Heavenly Love and Muse of high poetry, poetry that quickens in men's souls the love of liberty (notice the poets with whom Shelley associates Keats,—Milton and Lucan, as well as Sidney and Chatterton), as Adonis was to Aphrodite."

5. *obscure compeers:* hours not as notable as that in which Keats died.

15. *one:* Echo. Keats's sad Echo; see *Anth.*, p. 750. 180.

29. *He died:* Milton, at whose death his cause seemed lost, owing to the Restoration of the Stuart kings and the reaction against Puritanism (alluded to in 32-34).

36. *the third:* probably the other two are Homer and Dante; see *A Defense of Poetry; Anth.*, p. 985a. 52.

40. *tapers . . . suns . . . sublime:* The threefold contrast is between (a) talented poets who did not attempt work beyond their powers, and therefore survived, (b) over-ambitious poets who perished, and (c) geniuses struck down before maturity.

955. 48. *a pale flower:* the basil in Keats's *Isabella.* See *Anth.*, and note, p. 791. 416.

51. *extreme:* last.

55. *Capital:* Rome.

58. *Come away:* Descend from Heaven to the chamber of Keats.

69. *Hunger:* Corruption.

956. 94. *anadem:* garland.

97. *stem:* oppose, put away.

102. *wit:* intellect.

107. *clips:* embraces.

957. 140. *Phoebus:* Apollo, who loved the youth Hyacinth, and who caused the flower to spring up, after Hyacinth's death, from his blood.

141. *Narcissus:* See in Keats's poems; *Anth.*, p. 750. 180.

145. *nightingale:* Alluding to Keats's *Ode* (*Anth.*, p. 818).

149. *Her mighty youth:* In Milton's *Areopagitica*, the classic of free speech, England is called "an eagle mewing her mighty youth."

160. *brere:* briar.

177. *dies:* is wholly annihilated.

177-179. *that alone which knows . . . th' intense atom:* the mind, the soul, greater than material atomic power.

180. *quenched . . . in . . . repose:* falls asleep, and to common sense appears to be dead.

186. *death, who lends,* etc.: To melancholy perception, seeing that billions are dead and comparatively few alive, Death seems the capitalist who lends, and Life the borrower.

958. 198. *the fading Splendor:* Urania.

211. *wounded,* etc.: Alluding to the world's rejection of genius.

229. *heartless breast:* She has given her heart to Keats.

959. 250. *the Pythian:* the Apollo, i.e., Byron, who had attacked reviewers in *English Bards* and *Scotch Reviewers* (1809). It was hardly true that thereafter the reviewers "tempted no second blow."

264. *Pilgrim of Eternity:* Byron, who in *Childe Harold* had spoken of "wanderers o'er Eternity"; see, *Anth.*, p. 560. 669. and note. Shelley had received a letter from him, dated April 26, 1821, in which he wrote: "I am very sorry to hear what you say of Keats, —is it actually true? I did not think that criticism had been so killing. Though I differ from you essentially in your estimate of his performances, I so much abhor all unnecessary pain that I would rather he had been seated on the highest peak of Parnassus than have perished in such a manner."

268. *Ierne sent the sweetest lyrist:* Ireland sent Thomas Moore. He had no special claim to a place here.

271. *of less note:* i.e., than Byron and Moore.

271. *one frail Form:* Shelley himself.

276. *Actæon-like:* Because Actæon could not resist gazing upon Diana bathing, he was changed into a stag and hunted to death. Even so Shelley had had glimpses of Nature's secrets, which left him a prey to unrest.

280. *pardlike:* leopard-like.

960. 300. *in another's fate now wept his own:* Shelley felt that he as well as Keats had been ill-used by the world in general, and the reviewers in particular; hence his "moan" was "partial."

301. *accents of an unknown land:* A passage of which the meaning is disputed. Perhaps "in English, a tongue unknown to the Greek gods"; or "in English, a tongue strange to the land where Keats is buried."

306. *Cain's or Christ's:* This daring phrase signifies that the world has branded with shame not only evildoers but also saviors. The passage aroused such horrified protests as the following (from the *Literary Gazette*, December 8, 1821):

"Memorable and ferocious blasphemy! . . . What can be said to the wretched person capable of this daring profanation? The name of the first murderer—the accursed of God—brought into the same aspect and image with that of the Savior of the World! We are scarcely satisfied that even to quote such passages may not be criminal."

307. *What softer voice,* etc.: Leigh Hunt, whose lifelong devotion to Keats deserved this tribute.

319. *nameless worm:* the anonymous reviewer of *Endymion.*

336. *wakes or sleeps:* White (*Best of Shelley*, p. 519) finds the uncertainty significant; "there is an immortality of fame, but whether it is accompanied by personal survival is a point he carefully leaves open."

961. 343 ff. *Peace, peace! he is not dead:* These two stanzas, the sublimest in the poem, express the Platonic-Christian paradox that a worldly life is death. J. W. Beach (*Romantic View*, p. 40) calls the passage "perhaps the finest recital in English poetry of the sufferings and humiliations to which the spirit lies open in the mortal state."

375. *that Power:* God.

381. *the one Spirit's plastic stress,* etc.: A notable assertion of the romantic faith that the Ideal struggles to mold the reluctant actual into forms as near perfection as possible.

962. 395. *the dead:* the masters of literature illumine the problems of youth.

397. *unfulfilled renown:* They died so young that the fame which their work promised was not fully attained. Chatterton died at seventeen; Sir Philip Sidney, the Elizabethan poet and author of the *Arcadia*, fell in battle at thirty-two; and Lucan, an epic poet in the days of Nero, committed suicide to avoid a shameful death, at twenty-six. Shelley himself was to die at twenty-nine.

404. *Lucan:* There are differences of opinion as to why Shelley thought he was "approved" by his death—probably because he was a lover of liberty (see T. O. Mabbott and Elizabeth Nitchie, EXP, Mch., 1943).

406. *whose names are dark:* the dimly remembered benefactors.

414. *Vesper:* the Evening Star; see the translated motto at the beginning of the Notes on *Adonais.*

416. *Fond wretch,* etc.: The wretch who foolishly is sorry for Keats because Keats is dead, is in this obscure stanza asked to fly in imagination through the universe in order to realize what a minute particle he is. And if he takes a hopeful interest in life, he had better make it a light-hearted sort of hope, lest he be too bitterly disappointed.

963. 439. *slope of green access:* Keats's grave in the Protestant burial ground. See the description in Shelley's preface, above. The "keen pyramid" of Cestius stands nearby.— Shelley's son, William, was buried there in 1819; and Shelley's ashes also, in 1822.

453. *if the seal is set:* probably a dark allusion to the burial of William Shelley.

460. *The One:* See stanza LIV, where the One is manifested as Love, Light, Beauty, and Benediction.

463. *Stains the white radiance:* the pure white eternal Light is on earth distorted into many colors.—Used in the title of G. Wilson Knight's *The Starlit Dome*, containing a notable chapter on Shelley.

DISC.—Compare with *Adonais* two other noble elegies, Milton's *Lycidas* and Tennyson's *In Memoriam.*

What is the poetic or imaginative (and religious) value of the kinds of immortality envisaged in *Adonais?*

964. CHORUSES FROM HELLAS: A LYRICAL DRAMA

Written in sympathy with the Greek War of Independence.—R. D. Havens, " 'Hellas' and 'Charles the First,' " SP, XLIII, 545 (1946), finds in the last poems of Shelley, including *The Tri-*

umph of Life, a deeper sense for the complexity of human emotions and a kindlier attitude toward Christianity; "he was growing up."

964b. 34. *The Powers,* etc.: The flight of the pagan gods at the birth of Christ is one of the themes of Milton's *Ode on the Nativity.*

8. *Evening land:* Havens points out that there are several suggestions in Shelley's last writings that it is in the United States that Liberty and Plato's Great Age will rise again.

965a. 1 ff. Shelley has a highly characteristic note on this Chorus: "It is indistinct and obscure . . . Prophecies of wars, and rumors of wars, etc., may safely be made by a poet or prophet in any age, but to anticipate however darkly a period of regeneration and happiness is a more hazardous exercise of the faculty which bards possess or feign. It will remind the reader, at a great interval, of Isaiah and Virgil."—This chorus was based on the ancient idea that the history of the world proceeded in cycles, and that after the present era a new beginning would be made, with a second Golden Age even lovelier than the first.

965b. 17. *Ulysses:* may allude to the contemporary revolutionist Odysseus (Margaret Armstrong, *Trelawney,* p. 301).

19. *Oh, write no more:* "The obscure fourth stanza means that it is useless to repeat the victories of the Trojan War if they are to be gained by bloodshed, or to achieve freedom if it is to be mingled with rage like that of the fatal quarrel between Laius and his son Oedipus" (White, *Best of Shelley,* p. 508).

33. *One who rose:* Christ.

DISC.—Compare the choruses from *Hellas* with Byron's *The Isles of Greece, Anth.,* p. 698.

965. **LINES: WHEN THE LAMP IS SHATTERED**

Love has in the human heart a frail abode; and, in the weak, it passes too easily from ecstatic possession into mere suffering. On the beautiful form and intricate meanings of this poem, see the excellent discussions in EXP, Mch., Apr., May, Oct., 1943, and Nov. 1944.

966. **WITH A GUITAR: TO JANE**

Mr. and Mrs. Edward Williams were close friends of Shelley. In Shakspeare's *Tempest,* Ariel is the Spirit imprisoned in the cloven pine; Miranda is the princess who releases him, and Ferdinand is her lover. So in this allegory, the Spirit of Music is imprisoned in the guitar (made of Swiss pine); Jane Williams is Miranda; and Mr. Williams, Ferdinand. The guitar is now in the Bodleian Library, Oxford.

967. **THE TRIUMPH OF LIFE**

At Shelley's death this was unfinished and unrevised; hence gaps and obscurities.—There is a splendor and impetus in the vision inspired by Dante (e.g., ll. 282-286); also the strong influence of Petrarch's *Trionfi* ("The Triumph of Love Over Man"). The resemblance to the contemporary Leopardi's *Appressamento alla Morte* (a vision of the omnipotence of Death) is striking. This is the most Italian of Shelley's works.

See F. Melian Stawell, *Engl. Asso. Essays and Studies,* v, 112 (1919), and William Cherubini, "Shelley's Own Symposium," SP, xxxix, 559 (1942).

Probably the main purpose was like that stated in the last sentence of the Preface to *The Cenci,*—"to make apparent some of the most dark and secret caverns of the human heart." It is a powerful, though fragmentary and unfinished, picture of the alluring yet terrible attractions of the world, enchaining, degenerating, or destroying human character. The mass of mankind succumb; they become selfish, deceitful, or cruel. Only a few escape back to Light and Love (Socrates? Christ? l. 128). Even love may contribute in weak souls to the collapse; but on the whole, as in Dante, it is the only force that can pass through Hell without metamorphosis (l. 475, "all things are transfigured except Love"). In short, "Life" is worldliness; and its "Triumph" is a tragedy.—Even if this analysis is accepted as a valid account of the main theme, many of the details will remain debatable.

968. 99. *four faces:* Past, Present, Future, Eternity (?).

969. 180. *a voice:* Rousseau.

970. 217. *the child of a fierce hour:* Napoleon.

971. 258. *by love:* how?

    261. *the tutor and his pupil:* Aristotle and Alexander the Great.

972. 359. *Nepenthe:* a potion giving forgetfulness of pain and sorrow.

974. 468. *that cold light:* life?

    472. *him . . . from . . . hell:* Dante

DISC.—Which passages in the *Triumph of Life* seem to you to conform with the analysis given above, and which do not?

Is the view of mankind in some ways like Byron's; and, if so, how does the manner of conveying it differ?

975.   A DEFENSE OF POETRY

A. S. Cook's well-annotated edition (1891) includes Peacock's *Four Ages of Poetry*. H. F. B. Brett-Smith's (1929) also has Peacock, and adds Browning's *Essay on Shelley*.—See A. C. Bradley, "Shelley's Views of Poetry," *Oxford Lectures on Poetry* (1911); M. T. Solve, *Shelley: His Theory of Poetry* (1927); Lucas Verkoren, *A Study of Shelley's Defense* (1937); K. N. Cameron, "A New Source," SP, XXXVIII, 629 (1941); and B. R. McElderry, Jr., "Common Elements in Wordsworth's Preface and Shelley's Defense," MLQ, v, 175 (1944).

In *Ollier's Literary Miscellany* (1820) Shelley's friend, Thomas Love Peacock, published an essay, *The Four Ages of Poetry*, which maintained that in savage and barbarous ages poetry had been appropriate, but that in modern times it had become an anachronism. Wordsworth, Scott, Byron, Southey, Coleridge, et al., were engaged in a pretentious and antiquated pastime. "A poet in our times," said Peacock, "is a semi-barbarian in a civilized community," "a morbid dreamer," "a driveler and mountebank," not "a useful or rational man" such as a mathematician, politician, or chemist. Peacock's malicious, pungent, and Philistine squib (compare some of Mencken's sallies) "excited me," says Shelley, "to a sacred rage," and the result was one of our noblest vindications of poetry.

Shelley (Letter to Peacock, Mch., 1821) said the *Defense* was "the first part of an essay intended to consist of three parts"; but only the first part is extant.

Influential upon the *Defense* were ideas about imagination and poetry by Plato (esp. *Ion, Philebus, Phaedrus,* and *Symposium*), by Sir Philip Sidney (*Defense of Poesy*), and by Wordsworth.—With Sidney, Shelley agrees on many points; but Sidney is more Aristotelian, Horatian, and realistic than Shelley, who is closer to Plato, and in general to the Greeks rather than to the Romans (see Cook's ed., Intr., Sect. 2).

Observe that Shelley is dealing with three subjects which, though distinguishable, are interrelated: (a) the nature of poetry, (b) its history, and (c) its effects upon mankind. The assertions concerning (b) are probably not as important, or as valid, as those concerning (a) and (c).

976b. 39. *the relation subsisting between existence and perception:* Recalls one of Wordsworth's chief interests.

977a. 1. *Janus:* Roman deity of gates, represented with two faces.

977b. 29. *division into prose and verse:* Cf. Coleridge, *Biog. Lit.*, XIV and elsewhere: "Poetry of the highest kind may exist without metre" (*Anth.*, 67b. 6).

    Cf. Wordsworth, *Anth.*, 303a. 10 (*Pref. to Lyrical Ballads*) "the language of a large portion of every good poem . . . must necessarily . . . in no respect differ from that of good prose." Leigh Hunt, in *What Is Poetry?* goes farther: "Poetry need not be written in verse at all." And Hazlitt, in *Lectures on the English Poets*, says, "I will mention three works which come as near to poetry as possible without absolutely being so; namely, the *Pilgrim's Progress, Robinson Crusoe,* and the *Tales of Boccaccio* [i.e., the *Decameron*] . . . If it is of the essence of poetry to strike and fix the imagination, whether we will or no, to make the eye of childhood glisten with the starting tear, to be never thought of afterwards with indifference, John Bunyan and Daniel Defoe may be permitted to pass for poets in their way."

978a. 51. *difference between a story and a poem:* Aristotle drew this distinction. "Poetry is a more philosophical and a higher thing than history: for poetry tends to express the universal, history the particular" (*Poetics*, Book IX, 1-3).

978b. 52. *untrammeled by Time:* Cf. Wordsworth's Letter to Lady Beaumont (*Anth.*, 312).

979b. 40. *A poet would do ill:* Is this carrying the caution too far? Is it necessary to the main argument?

980b. 8. *divesting the actor's face of a mask:* Coleridge, in his lecture on *Macbeth*, expressed the wish that in such a tragedy "an attempt should be made to introduce the flexible character-mask," perhaps by an artist like Flaxman. In our time Maeterlinck has suggested the same experiment. (R. M. Alden, ed., *Crit. Essays*, 1921: p. 157).

24. Sophocles *Oedipus,* Æschylus' *Agamemnon.*

37. Calderon (1600-1681) *Autos Sacramentales* (1653), allegorical dramas on the mysteries of the Holy Communion.

981a. 59. *domestic drama:* Or, "bourgeois tragedy," like *George Barnwell* (1731).

982a. 35. *the erotic poets . . . what they have not:* Obscenity lacks the sense for "the divine beauty in life" (*Anth.,* 981b. 28).

982b. 11. *The sacred links of that chain:* Plato's Socrates says: "This gift which you have is not an art, but an inspiration; there is a divinity moving you, like that in the stone which Euripides calls a magnet. . . . This is like the Muse, who first gives to men inspiration herself, and from these inspired persons a chain of other persons is suspended, who take the inspiration from them" (*Ion,* 533-536)

983a. 9. *Camillus,* etc.: These great persons and deeds arose in the history of Rome because Imagination was then strong enough to beget enthusiastic devotion to noble personal characteristics and to magnanimous deeds. See Plutarch's *Lives* for Camillus and Hannibal, and for some of the incidents, interpreted in an idealistic mood similar to Shelley's. He would have maintained, in our day, that imaginatively *beholding of the beauty of this order* (l. 20) was essential to the practical realization of such an organization as the United Nations.

983b. 3. *The crow: Macbeth,* III, II, 50.

21. *Celtic:* A better term would be "Germanic" or "Gothic."

54. *The principle of equality:* Plato, *Republic,* Book III. Plato's "guardians" or leaders of the people were to be equal in the sense that none of them was to have any property, but all "live together like soldiers in a camp." Shelley's theory that Plato was a forerunner of Christ in teaching a genuinely democratic idea of equality is hardly tenable.

984a. 46. *Galeotto:* "Galeotto was the book, and he who wrote it." Dante's lovers, Paolo and Francesca, read it together before their first kiss (*Inferno,* V, 137).

47. *Trouveurs:* Troubadours, Provençal poets of c. 1000-1300.—On Petrarch, see Landor's *Pentameron, Anth.,* 511. Elsewhere (in *Discourse on the Manners of the Ancients*) Shelley speaks of "the sublime and chivalric sensibility of Petrarch."

984b. 1. *Vita Nuova:* His "New Life," a prose narrative with lyrics, written (1292-1294) in honor of his beloved Beatrice, who had died in June, 1290.

18. *poet in Plato:* See Agathon's speech in the *Symposium.*

54. *Riphaeus:* a Trojan, therefore technically a "heathen." See Dante's *Paradiso,* XX, 67 and 118; and Virgil's *Aeneid* II, 426.

985a. 14. *Milton's Devil:* See the second paragraph of Shelley's *Preface to Prometheus Unbound, Anth.,* 883, where Shelley gives a somewhat different interpretation of the character of Milton's so-called "hero."

985b. 6. *Apollonius Rhodius,* etc.: Minor Roman poets.

12. *Aeneid,* etc.: The respective authors are Virgil, Ariosto, Tasso, Camoens, and Spenser.

37-55. *His very words . . . unconceived delight:* "That is one of our grandest passages of aesthetic philosophy. I know of none more universally true, none more important. Symbolic language is indeed inexhaustible." (G. Wilson Knight, *The Christian Renaissance,* 1933; p. 33).

986a. 37. *the promoters of utility:* On their aptitude for "defacing eternal truths," see J. B. Selkirk, *Ethics and Aesthetics of Modern Poetry,* 1878, esp., pp. 205-206.

57. *exasperate:* to make rougher and more grievous.

986b. 5. *Scylla and Charybdis:* Scylla, a rock, and Charybdis, a whirlpool, between the Italian mainland and Sicily.

22. *melancholy inseparable from the sweetest melody:* Cf. Shelley's *To a Skylark,* l. 86-90 (*Anth.,* p. 941).

26. *It is better to go,* etc.: *Ecclesiastes,* 7, 2.

51. *Inquisition:* It had been suppressed, for the second time, in 1820.

987a. 14. DISC.—In what particulars are the following two paragraphs applicable to events and problems of today? Cf. Wordsworth, *Excursion,* IV, 967; *Anth.,* 285.

27. *I dare not:* Macbeth, I, VII, 44.

987b. 59. *produced by labor:* To say "solely produced" would be nearer the truth. See Cook's Introduction, pp. xx-xxv, on "The Provinces of Inspiration and Labor." George Saintsbury comments: "There is an obvious fallacy here. The finest passages are not originally inspired by labor and study, but in their finest shape they are the result of labor and study spent on the immediate result of inspiration" (*Specimens of English Prose,* p. 346).

988a. 11. *unpremeditated song: Paradise Lost,* IX, 24. For "song" read "verse."

36. DISC.—Find and compare in Blake, Wordsworth, Coleridge, etc., similar expressions of belief in poetry being inspired by *the interpenetration of a diviner nature through our own.* See Socrates' enthusiastic speech on inspiration in Plato's *Ion.*

988b. 31. *The mind: Paradise Lost,* I, 254.

54. *Non merita:* None merits the name of Creator, save God and the Poet.

989a. 13. *confirm:* Perhaps Shelley wrote "confine."

989b. 33. *Theseids of Codri . . . Bavius and Mævius:* Fictitious names of bad poets, scorned by Horace, Virgil, etc. Codrus was fabled to have composed a wretched tragedy on Theseus. William Gifford wrote satires entitled, *The Baviad* (1794) and *The Mæviad* (1795).

56. DISC.—Is it tenable that *an energetic development of English literature has always preceded or accompanied a great and free development of the national will?* Is it true of the era of King Alfred? of Queen Elizabeth? or Oliver Cromwell? etc.? Is it true of American literature and American history?

990b. 2-12. *the electric life which burns within their words:* These two sentences express what is probably the most exalted praise of the Romantic Movement uttered by one of its leaders. It is curious that Hazlitt's survey, published four years after Shelley's *Defense* was composed, was entitled *The Spirit of the Age.*

12. *hierophants:* high priests, i.e., those who serve a Spirit which they themselves do not completely apprehend. Shelley is thinking of such as Milton, who, in "the last national struggle for civil and religious liberty" (l. 6a) wrote *Areopagitica,* on the freedom of speech and press.

DISC.—At least half a dozen of the sentences, broad generalizations about the nature and functions of poetry, have become famous. Which sentences do you think they are?

N. I. White (*Best of Shelley,* p. 487) maintains that Shelley's idea of the poet in *The Sensitive Plant* and *Adonais* (*Anth.,* pp. 936 and 954) is somewhat morbid, and "curiously at variance with his more virile attitude toward the poet and himself" in the *Defense.* Do you agree? Also consider *Alastor* (*Anth.,* p. 855).

Make an outline of the *Defense,* and compare its main points with those of Wordsworth's *Preface* (*Anth.,* p. 300) and Coleridge's *Biographia Literaria* (p. 331). Which ideas of Shelley are *like* Wordsworth's, which like Coleridge's? Which *supplement* their ideas? Which, if any, *differ* from theirs? Compare your answers with B. R. McElderry's analysis in his article (listed above) on the common elements in Wordsworth and Shelley.

Among ultramoderns, Shelley is not admired. They are interested in aspects and functions of poetry to which Shelley pays little or no attention. What are those aspects and functions? Does Shelley's inattention to them invalidate those principles which he does dwell upon?

990. LETTERS OF SHELLEY

Shelley's letters from Italy admirably combine the aesthetic delights of a percipient lover of nature with the historical enthusiasms of a classical scholar.—On Thomas Love Peacock (1785-1866) see the Notes on *A Defense of Poetry, Anth.,* p. 975. Though they differed on that and other subjects, they had many cultural interests in common.

990a. 8. *Spoleto:* 60 miles north of Rome.

23. *Belisarius or Narses:* Byzantine generals of the sixth century, who defeated the Goths in Italy.

26. *the cataract:* Terni is 43 miles north of Rome.—The falls of the river Velino which Shelley admired are, as Baedecker says, "no longer of interest, as on week-days almost the entire volume of water is drawn off by the hydro-electric works and the factories of armor-plate, ordnance, and small arms."

27. *the glaciers of Montanvert:* those celebrated in Shelley's *Mont Blanc.* See the note on the poem, *Anth.,* p. 864.

991a. 9. *ilex:* an evergreen oak.

17. *arbutus:* an evergreen shrub of the heath family.

42. *Rome:* DISC.—Compare Shelley's descriptions and sentiments with Byron's in *Childe Harold, Anth.,* p. 575 ff.

991b. 31. *Christian reptile:* The emperor Constantine caused Christianity to be recognized by the state (c. 320 A.D.), but he was a Christian in only a rudimentary sense.

992a. 10. *English burying-place:* where the remains of both Keats and Shelley were to be interred within less than four years from the date of this letter. See the note on *Adonais, Anth.,* p. 963. **439.**

26. *these delightful regions:* the environs of the Bay of Naples, one of the most beautiful scenes in the world. See the map in any good guidebook of Italy.

37. *Inarime:* the island of Ischia, on the northern entrance of the bay, opposite Capri on the southern.

993a. 12. *C——:* Claire Clairmont.

16. *palanquin:* a litter borne on poles.

LEIGH HUNT (1784-1859)

I. EDITIONS

*Milford, H. S., ed. *Poetical Works,* 1923.
Blunden, Edmund, ed. *Autobiography* (World's Classics), 1928.
*Johnson, R. B., ed. *Essays and Poems,* 2 vols. (Temple Libr.), 1891.
Johnson, R. B., ed. *Prefaces,* 1927.
Brewer, Luther A., ed. *My Leigh Hunt Library: The Holograph Letters,* 1938.

II. BIOGRAPHY AND CRITICISM

Johnson, R. B. *Leigh Hunt,* 1896.
Saintsbury, George. *Essays in English Literature: First Series,* 1896.
Symons, Arthur. *The Romantic Movement in English Poetry,* 1909.
Miller, Barnette. *Leigh Hunt's Relations with Byron, Shelley, and Keats,* 1910.
Saintsbury, George. "The Landors, Leigh Hunt, De Quincey," in *Cambridge History of English Literature,* XII, 226-256; 1916.
Pierce, F. E. "The Eddy Around Leigh Hunt," in *Currents and Eddies in the English Romantic Generation,* 1918.
*Blunden, Edmund. *Leigh Hunt and His Circle,* 1930.
Wheeler, P. M. "The Great Quarterlies of the Early Nineteenth Century and Leigh Hunt," SAQ, XXIX, 282; 1930.
Brightfield, M. F. *Univ. of California Essays in Criticism, Second Series,* 1934.
*Landré, Louis. *Leigh Hunt: Contribution à l'Histoire du Romantisme Anglais,* 2 vols., 1935-1936.
Strout, A. L. "Leigh Hunt and Maga," ELH, IV, 151; 1937.
Aspinall, Arthur. "The Social Status of Journalists at the Beginning of the Nineteenth Century," RES, XXI, 216; 1945.

III. BIBLIOGRAPHY

Brewer, Luther A. *My Leigh Hunt Library,* 1932.

NOTES, COMMENTS, AND TOPICS FOR DISCUSSION

995.　　　　　　　　　　　　TO HAMPSTEAD

Hunt's cottage was near Hampstead Heath, the scene of Keats's *I Stood Tiptoe; Anth.*, p. 748.

996.　　　　　　　　　　　　THE POETS.

996. 3. *Pulci:* Italian poet (1432-1487), author of the half-serious, half-comic epic, *Morgante Maggiore,* which influenced Byron; see *Don Juan, Anth.*, p. 703, l. 43. Hunt was a great admirer of Italian literature.
　　6. *luxury:* (in a good sense) luxuriance, richness of style.
　　8. *society:* multitude of characters.

996.　　　　　　　　　　　THE STORY OF RIMINI

The scene is in Italy.—The style influenced Keats in his early work, in some respects disadvantageously.—**DISC.**—Distinguish between the graceful passages and the occasional commonplace or awkward ones.

997. 432. *Places of nestling green:* Chosen by Keats for the motto of *I Stood Tiptoe.*
　　462. *Alcina or Morgana:* In Ariosto and other poets, the names of fays who tempted knights to sensual indulgence.

998.　　　　　　　TO THE GRASSHOPPER AND THE CRICKET

Written in playful competition with Keats. See *Anth.*, p. 757.

998.　　　　　　　　　　　　THE NILE

998. 7. *Sesostris:* a legendary Egyptian king and world conquerer.
　　8. *laughing queen:* Shakspeare's Cleopatra.

DISC.—Contrast Shelley's *Ozymandias, Anth.*, p. 869.

998.　　　　　　　　ON A LOCK OF MILTON'S HAIR

The lock was a gift from Keats.

999.　　　　　　　　　　　　THE NYMPHS

Written in loving regard for the lesser deities of the trees, waters, and hills—the Hamadryads, Naiads, Oreads, etc. "What a delightful poem," wrote Shelley, "it is truly *poetical*, in the intense and emphatic sense of the word." But he adds, "it is not as faultless as it is beautiful." **DISC.**—Contrast the tone and style with that of Landor's *The Hamadryad* and Keats's *Endymion; Anth.*, pp. 514 and 758.

1000.　　　　　　　　　　THE PRAYER IN THE BOWER

1000. 4. *Priapus:* a god of fertility, protector of herdsmen.

1001.　　　　　　　　　　　ABOU BEN ADHEM

Hunt quotes the anecdote on which he based this poem, from D'Herbelot's *Bibliothèque Orientale* (1697). In the source Abou Ben Adhem is represented as asking the angel, "Pray set me down as one who loves those that love God." The humanitarian Hunt characteristically changed this to present Abou as one who loved *all* mankind. (See Leisy and Mabbott, EXP Nov., 1946; Mch., 1947.)

1002. RONDEAU

Jenny is commonly said to have been Mrs. Thomas (Jane) Carlyle, on an occasion when Hunt announced that a publisher had accepted one of Carlyle's works; but the anecdote may be fanciful (see Edmund Blunden, *Leigh Hunt*, p. 254).

1002. THE OLD LADY

1003a. 8. *The Spectator*, etc.: Observe that her books were becoming somewhat old fashioned even in her time, *The Turkish Spy* being of the seventeenth century. *Sir Charles Grandison* is a novel by Samuel Richardson presenting his conception of an ideal gentleman. *John Buncle* is an eccentric and sentimental novel by Thomas Amory; its lying in the pantry suggests that it had fallen into neglect.

37. *calash:* a hood that could be drawn over the head.

38. *pattens:* overshoes with wooden soles.

44. *Granby:* Probably she preferred him because he was handsomer (two portraits by Reynolds) and less gruff than the great Duke.

55. *minuet:* a more old fashioned dance than the waltz.

1003. ON BYRON'S "DON JUAN"

Since Leigh Hunt's critical essays are sometimes spoken of condescendingly, as superficial though pleasing, attention should be called to his sound common sense in this defense of Byron, and his close reasoning.—It first appeared in *The Examiner*, No. 618.

1005. GETTING UP ON COLD MORNINGS

1005a. 54. *decumbency:* posture of lying down (humorous Latinism).

1006a. 16. *his mother:* the brilliant Lady Mary Wortley Montagu.

1006b. 7. *Holborn:* then one of the longest streets in London.

1006. ON THE REALITIES OF IMAGINATION

Is there anywhere a better brief explanation of the function of literature in human life?

1007a. 36. *Humboldt:* Alexander von Humboldt (1769-1859), one of the greatest naturalists and explorers of the romantic period, celebrated for his brilliant accounts of his journeys to Mexico, South America. etc.

1007. ON AN ATTACK ON SHELLEY'S "PROMETHEUS UNBOUND"

First appeared in *The Examiner*, No. 752.

1007b. 44. *verbatim et literatim:* word for word and letter for letter.

1008a. 13. *great poem: The Divine Comedy.* The translator was Henry Francis Cary {1772-1844).

31. *The lines in question:* They are at the end of Act III, *Anth.*, p. 922.

1009a. 2. *Gifford:* William Gifford (1757-1826), editor of the *Quarterly Review*.

8. *Croker:* John Wilson Croker, a leading contributor.

17. *immoral and anti-christian:* said of course ironically, like "infidel" (l. 47) below.

45. *the Spaniards:* Hunt implies that, though they "were injured," they were Christian enough not to make, after Napoleon's defeat, a vengeful peace.

1009. WHAT IS POETRY?

One of the clearest and most comprehensive, though not the profoundest, treatment of the subject by any of the Romantics.—**DISC.**—Compare this, both the substance and the manner of presentation, with the greater treatises—Wordsworth's *Preface to the Lyrical Ballads* (*Anth.*, p. 300), Coleridge's *Biographia Literaria* (p. 331), and Shelley's *Defense of Poetry* (p. 975).

Which ideas of Wordsworth, Coleridge, and Shelley, does Hunt also set forth?   Which does he omit?   With which, if any, does he differ?   Contrast the styles, and the illustrations.

1011a. **3.** *walters:* rolls about, grovels.
15. *wonning:* dwelling.

1011b. **3.** *Priam:* the king of Troy in Homer.
26. *So the two brothers:* Keats's *Isabella,* l. 209; *Anth.,* p. 788.
41. *Italian poet:* Boiardo (c. 1434-1494).
50. *Imogen:* In Shakspeare's *Cymbeline,* II, ii.

1012a. **21.** *Friar of Orders Grey:* by Bishop Percy.
39. *Life, like a dome: Adonais,* l. 462; *Anth.,* p. 963.
59. *Peter Wilkins:* A fantastic romance (1757) by Robert Paltock.

1012.   **COLERIDGE**

1012b. **34.** *complexional:* constitutional, temperamental.
36. *subtler tone to criticism:* i.e., Coleridge helped the Germans, like Schlegel, to give profundity to *English* criticism.
48. *of pure poetry . . . the greatest master:* A noteworthy judgment, which should be discussed.

1013a. **25.** *a disinterested politician:* in the sense that he sought no office.
33. *the collection of Bishop Percy: Reliques of Ancient English Poetry* (1765).

1013.   **KEATS**

1013b. **54.** *morbidity:* The allusion is to Porphyro's faintness (l. 224; *Anth.,* p. 810).   Do you agree with this opinion?

1014b. **11.** *Gifford:* The editor of the *Quarterly Review,* long mistakenly believed the author of the hostile article on *Endymion* which appeared therein, April, 1818.   See the introductory note on Shelley's *Adonais, Anth.,* p. 954.

The last three selections first appeared in an anthology entitled *Imagination and Fancy* (1844); *What Is Poetry?* was the general introduction, and the essays on Coleridge and Keats prefaced the selections from their works.   The other authors represented were Spenser, Marlowe, Shakspeare, Jonson, Beaumont and Fletcher, Middleton, Decker, Webster, Milton, and Shelley. The purpose, in Hunt's words, was "to show what sort of poetry is to be considered *as poetry of the most poetical kind*" (Hunt's italics); and the title emphasized that imagination and fancy were considered "the first requisites of the poets' art."

THOMAS DE QUINCEY (1785-1859)

I. EDITIONS

*Masson, David, ed.   *Collected Writings,* 14 vols., 1889-1890.
Eaton, H. A., ed.   *A Diary of Thomas De Quincey: 1803,* 1927.
Darbishire, Helen, ed.   *Literary Criticism,* 1909.
*Jerrold, Walter, ed.   *The Confessions of an English Opium-Eater* (Temple Classics), 1899.
Bonner, W. H., ed.   *De Quincey At Work* [Letters], 1936.

Selections by:
M. H. Turk (Athenaeum Press Series), 1902.
W. R. Ridley (with essays by Leslie Stephen and Francis Thompson), 1927.
A. H. R. Ball, 1932.
*P. V. D. Stern, 1937.

II. BIOGRAPHY AND CRITICISM

Stephen, Leslie.   *Hours In A Library,* Vol. I, 1874.
Saintsbury, George.   *Essays in English Literature, First Series,* 1890.

Salt, Henry. *De Quincey*, 1904.
Fowler, J. H. *De Quincey As Literary Critic*, 1922.
Abrams, M. H. *The Milk of Paradise*, 1934.
*Eaton, H. A. *Thomas De Quincey: A Biography*, 1936.
Sackville-West, Edward. *A Flame in Sunlight: The Life and Work of Thomas De Quincey*, 1936.
Sehrt, Ernst T. *Geschichtliches und Religiöses Denken bei Thomas De Quincey*, 1936.
*Metcalf, J. C. *De Quincey: A Portrait*, 1940.
*Proctor, Sigmund K. *De Quincey's Theory of Literature*, 1943.
Wellek, René. "De Quincey's Status in the History of Ideas," PQ, XXIII, 248; 1944.
Schneider Elisabeth. "The Dream of Kubla Khan," PMLA, LX, 784; 1945.
Hendricks, Cecilia H. "De Quincey, Symptomatologist," PMLA, LX, 828; 1945.

NOTES, COMMENTS, AND TOPICS FOR DISCUSSION

1015. CONFESSIONS OF AN ENGLISH OPIUM-EATER

First appeared in the *London Magazine*, Sept. and Oct., 1821; reprinted in book form in 1822; revised and enlarged to nearly three times its original length in 1855.

As Elisabeth Schneider has shown (PMLA, LX, 784; 1945), De Quincey attached too much importance to opium. It was not the cause of his dreams nor a shaping influence upon their substance. The peculiar characteristics mistakenly attributed to opium are found in ordinary dreams. Years before he took to opium De Quincey was, so to speak, a connoisseur in dreams, reveries, and visions. His originality lay in attaching great significance to such experiences, long before the days of Freud and Jung, and in interpreting them powerfully. He was the first of the Romantics to give a conspicuous place in his work to the dream-story, a genre which was to be cultivated increasingly by nineteenth-century writers (e.g., Morris, Pater, Carroll, Stevenson, Thompson, Yeats, "A. E.," and Sharp).

The sub-title, *The Life of a Scholar*, often omitted, is significant not only with respect to the *Confessions* but also as an indication of the purpose of all his work. As M. R. Ridley says (Intr. to *Selections*), he "has always the scholar's belief in the pursuit of truth by the alliance of the intellect and the imagination,"—which is the Romantic's concept of perfect scholarship.

1015b. 13. *Trophonius:* Those who consulted this Grecian oracle returned from the cave dejected.

1016a. 18. *Behmenism, quietism,* etc.: various mystical cults which belittled common sense and rationalizing, and exalted religious contemplation and spiritual vision.

20. *Sir H. Vane:* Milton's contemporary, Sir Henry Vane (see his sonnet on him); who was Governor of Massachusetts in 1636, and who took a tolerant attitude toward the persecuted religious enthusiast, Anne Hutchinson.

59. *Wrongs unredressed:* Wordsworth, *The Excursion*, III, 305.

1016b. 9. *Hekatompylos:* Thebes, Egypt (hundred-gated).

1016. THE PAINS OF OPIUM

DISC.—Compare Coleridge's *The Pains of Sleep*, *Anth.*, p. 183.

1016b. 36. *Piranesi:* A brilliant and imaginative Italian engraver (1720-1778).

1017a. 57. *officina gentium:* workshop of nations.

1017b. 30. *Brama, Vishnu, Seeva:* In Hinduism, they respectively represent the creative, the preservative, and the destructive aspects of the godhead.

32. *Isis:* The Egyptian fertility goddess, sister and wife of Osiris, god of the underworld.

1018. ON THE KNOCKING AT THE GATE IN MACBETH

Before reading this, read the **murder scene** in *Macbeth*, II, II-III.

1018b. 44. *never to pay any attention:* Illustrates De Quincey's tendency to carry romantic doctrines to extremes.

1019a. 46. *Mr. Williams:* A murderer. De Quincey wrote *On Murder Considered As One Oj The Fine Arts* (1827 ff.), in which with mock gravity he compares the craftsmanship exhibited by various murderers—perhaps his most brilliant performance in a lighter vein.

1020a. 31. *funeral pomp:* such as the national funeral of Nelson in 1805, and of Pitt in 1806.

DISC.—Can you recall any dramas or novels in which, as in *Macbeth*, the villain is for the time being "insulated from ordinary human affairs"? Is Dostoevsky's *Crime and Punishment* one of them?

Compare De Quincey's opinions about Shakspeare, and his method of discussing his work, with the opinions and methods of other romantic critics, e.g., Coleridge's (*Anth.*, p. 368), Lamb's (p. 378), and Hazlitt's (p. 402).

In 1838 De Quincey was chosen to write the article on Shakspeare for the seventh edition of the *Encyclopaedia Britannica* (rptd. in his *Collected Writings*), still worth reading.

1020. DREAM-VISION OF THE INFINITE

A version of the *Dream Upon The Universe* by Jean Paul Richter, on whom see Carlyle's essay (*Anth.*, p. 1038). First appeared in the *London Magazine*, and in 1854 added to the *System of the Heavens*, De Quincey's most elaborate description of nature.

A strong effort of the imagination is necessary if you would comprehend what "infinite" meant to De Quincey here and to the Romantics in general. To them the "infinite" was not something that lasted so long and extended so far as to be immeasurable; it was not what the dictionary calls "boundless space and duration." It was that which, like God, has neither time nor space, has neither beginning nor end. Those phenomena—however ancient or endless or vast—which seem to us conceivably to have a beginning or an end are not infinite. They are, at best, imperfectly disclosed or imperfectly perceived manifestations of the timeless and space-less Infinite. Such is the Infinite which De Quincey shadows forth in this sublime parable.

1021a. 7. *Zaarahs:* Saharas.

DISC.—Read this selection aloud, mark the most conspicuous instances of the use of balanced clauses and strongly emphasized rhythm, and discuss their function and value. Other selections which should be read aloud, fully to appreciate De Quincey's prose, are *Levana* and *Joan of Arc.*

1021. AUTOBIOGRAPHIC SKETCHES

An important illustration of three characteristic interests of Romanticism—autobiography, reverie, and childhood. Especially noteworthy is the contribution to child psychology.

1021b. 32. *galleries:* De Quincey notes their symbolic value, saying: "Condemned by restorers of authentic church architecture, [they] have one advantage, that when the *height* of a church is that dimension which most of all expresses its sacred character, galleries expound and interpret that height."

1022a. 52. *truths and services of a national church:* Much of De Quincey's work was devoted to the elucidation of Christianity and of the Church of England.

54. *solitude:* The Christian (and romantic) doctrine of the worth of the individual soul is logically inseparable from its solitariness and from the pains and values of solitude This theme is also considered in the next selection.

1022. SUSPIRIA DE PROFUNDIS

These "sighs from the depths of the soul" were a sequel to the *Confessions.*

1023a. 11-13. *dream . . . reverie:* the latter is a *waking* dream, an exercise of the fancy or imagination. The main point of the selection is that modern life is hostile to wholesome imagination.

48. *too constantly in company:* In American literature, the golden passage on this theme is ch. 5 of Thoreau's *Walden.* Elsewhere Thoreau says, "We live too thick."

1023. THE PALIMPSEST OF THE HUMAN BRAIN

1023b. 9. *palimpsest:* A parchment is the skin (membrane) of a sheep or goat, prepared for writing on; a palimpsest is a parchment which has been written on twice or three times.

19. *Western Empire:* It fell A.D. 476, and was followed by several centuries of the "Dark Ages."

1024a. 2. *Paracelsus:* an alchemist and philosopher (1493-1541).

18. *exorcised:* called up *from* the shades, sometimes by "the torturing coercion of mystic adjurations" (De Quincey).

20. *Pharsalia:* Book VI is the correct reference.

25. *Phoenix:* the mythical Arabian bird, which every five hundred years flew to Egypt, and left there its burnt ashes, out of which its sole successor arose.

54. *diplomata:* historical documents.

1024b. 20. *a lady:* perhaps De Quincey's mother.

54. *Apostle:* St. Paul; see *Acts* 9, 1-18.

1025a. 24. *by opium:* nowadays by psychiatry.

DISC.—The importance of childhood impressions as described by De Quincey, and by Wordsworth in his *Ode: Intimations of Immortality from Recollections of Early Childhood,* Anth., p. 232.

1025. LEVANA AND OUR LADIES OF SORROW

"Perhaps, all in all, the finest thing that De Quincey ever wrote . . . Certainly the most perfect specimen he has left us of his peculiar art of English prose-poetry, and one of the most magnificent pieces of prose in English or in any other language" (David Masson).

The name of the Roman goddess Levana had been used as the title of Jean Paul Richter's *Erziehungslehre* (*Doctrine of Education,* 1807).

1026a. 14. *restless spokes:* De Quincey acknowledges that he borrowed "this fine image" from Wordsworth.

31. *on the foundation:* holding a scholarship.

1026b. 10. *individual sorrow:* Since the Romantics are accused of preoccupation with their own personal sorrows, this disclaimer is noteworthy.

1027a. 2. *Rama . . . Rachel:* See *Jeremiah,* 31, 15; and *Matthew,* 2, 16.

41. *the Czar:* the daughter of Czar Nicholas died in 1844.

1027b. 23. *Norfolk Island:* a penal settlement in the South Pacific.

DISC.—Which of the three Ladies of Sorrow do you think akin to so-called Byronic melancholy?

Can you imagine three outstanding varieties of human happiness that might be similarly personified? How would you describe them?

1028. JOAN OF ARC

The peasant girl (1412-1431) who, at the behest of what seemed to her supernatural voices, led an army to astounding victories, and liberated much of France from English dominion. Having been captured, she was accused of heresy, the Bishop of Beauvais presiding at her trial; and was burned at the stake, May 30, 1431. To Romantics her career had an irresistible appeal because it illustrated both the possibility of supernatural inspiration and the dignity of humble life. Southey and Schiller had preceded De Quincey in celebrating Joan of Arc; and during the past century and a half she has been a center of controversy between the Romantics and their opponents.—**DISC.**—The anti-romantic interpretations of Joan of Arc by Anatole France and Bernard Shaw.

1028a. 47. *shepherd boy:* David; see *I Samuel,* 18.

1028b. 37. *en contumace:* in default; failing to appear.

1030. THE LITERATURE OF KNOWLEDGE AND THE LITERATURE OF POWER

Observe that what De Quincey says is that the literature of power is not merely whatever moves you, but what moves you to "sympathy with truth" and to "sympathy with the infinite" (ll. 13b and 43b).

1030a. 46. *dry light:* "The light that a man receiveth by counsel from another is drier, and purer, than that which cometh from his own understanding and judgment, which is ever infused and drenched in his affections and customs" (Bacon, *Essay on Friendship*).

1031a. 16. *the heart, the great intuitive organ:* Compare Carlyle's "An open loving Heart is the beginning of all Knowledge" (*Biography, Anth.,* p. 1046b. 8-12).
    56. *quamdiu bene se gesserit:* as long as it may wear well.

1031b. 11. *La Place:* an eighteenth-century mathematician and astronomer whose *Celestial Mechanics* was supposed to have corrected Newton. Today it would be Einstein who was cited.

    DISC.—Make a list of what you have read in recent months, in courses or outside of them. Discuss which items belong to the literature of knowledge, and which to that of power.

1031.　　　　　　　　GOING DOWN WITH VICTORY

    This is the most realistic of the selections from De Quincey; but observe that he discerns an ideal significance in what to the ordinary eye would seem merely a strenuous practical activity.
    The victories began with Trafalgar, Oct. 21, 1805, and concluded with Waterloo, June 18, 1815. The intermediate ones were mostly those of the Spanish Peninsular War; see Southey, *Anth.,* p. 481.

1032a. 37. *Lombard Street:* in the center of London,—its "Wall Street."
    42. *attelage:* horses and coach.

1032b. 58. *Badajoz:* a Spanish frontier fort, which the French had taken in 1811, and which Wellington stormed in 1812. *Salamanca:* a Spanish city, near which Wellington totally defeated the French in 1812.

1033b. 17. *Be thou whole!* spoken by Christ to the ailing woman who secretly touched the border of his garment and was healed. *St. Luke,* 8, 43).

    DISC.—What points of resemblance and difference do you discern in Coleridge and De Quincey?
    Distinguish between De Quincey's style and the kind of style Hazlitt calls "familiar" (see *On Familiar Style, Anth.,* p. 405).
    Virginia Woolf says De Quincey could combine the record of external events with that profounder kind of writing in which "suddenly the smooth narrative parts fly asunder, arch opens beyond arch, the vision of something for ever flying, for ever escaping, is revealed, and *time stands still.*" Find and discuss such passages.
    Among moderns influenced by De Quincey's style are Virginia Woolf (see her tribute in the Preface to *Orlando*), Osbert Sitwell, and many others. Cite passages showing this influence, and consider why some of these authors like his style but turn away from his romantic philosophy.

THE YOUNG CARLYLE (1759-c. 1840)

I. EDITIONS

In the *Centenary Edition* (1898 ff.) the works prior to 1840, including:
    German Romance: Translations from the German
    Translation of Goethe's Wilhelm Meister
    Critical and Miscellaneous Essays

Karkaria, R. P., ed. (or Greene, J. R., ed.). *Lectures on the History of Literature,* 1892.
Creek, H. LeS., ed. *The Best of Carlyle,* 1929.
MacMechan, Archibald, ed. *Sartor Resartus* (Athenaeum Press Series), 1896.—Harrold, C. F., ed.; do., 1937.
Rose, J. Holland, ed. (or Fletcher, C. R. L., ed.). *The French Revolution,* 1902.
MacMechan, Archibald, ed. *Heroes and Hero-Worship* (Athenaeum Press Series) 1902.
Norton, C. E., ed. *The Letters of Carlyle: 1826-1836,* 1889.
Norton, C. E., ed. *Correspondence Between Goethe and Carlyle,* 1887.
Norton, C. E., ed. *Correspondence of Carlyle and Emerson. 1834-1872,* 1883.

II. BIOGRAPHY AND CRITICISM

*Carlyle, Thomas. *Reminiscenses*, ed. C. E. Norton, 2 vols., 1887.
Froude, J. A. *Thomas Carlyle: A History of the First Forty Years* and *A History of His Life in London*, 2 vols., 1882 ff.
*Garnett, Richard. *Life of Carlyle*, 1887.
Johnson, W. S. *Carlyle: A Study of his Literary Apprenticeship; 1814-31*, 1911.
Perry, Bliss. *Carlyle: How to Know Him*, 1915.
Cazamian, L. F. *Carlyle*, 1913; transl., 1932.
*Wilson, D. A. *Carlyle Till Marriage*, 1923; *Carlyle to "The French Revolution,"* 1924; *Carlyle on Cromwell and Others*, 1925.
Drew, Elizabeth A. *Jane Welsh and Jane Carlyle*, 1928.
*Neff, Emery. *Carlyle*, 1932.
Harrold, C. F. "The Mystical Element in Carlyle: 1827-1834," MP, xxix, 459; 1932.
*Harrold, C. F. *Carlyle and German Thought: 1819-1834*, 1934.
Thrall, Miriam M. H. *Rebellious Fraser's*, 1934.
Harrold, C. F. "The Nature of Carlyle's Calvinism," SP, xxxiii, 475; 1936.
Vance, W. S. "Carlyle in America Before Sartor Resartus," AL, 363; 1936.
Taylor, Alan C. *Carlyle et la Pensée Latine*, 1937.
*Shine, Hill. *Carlyle's Fusion of Poetry, History, and Religion by 1834*, 1938.
Scudder, Townsend. *Jane Welsh Carlyle*, 1939.
Moore, Carlisle. "Carlyle and Fiction: 1822-1834," *Nineteenth Century Studies* (Cornell), 1940.
*Shine, Hill. *Carlyle and the Saint-Simonians: The Concept of Historical Periodicity*, 1941.

III. MISCELLANEOUS

Ralli, Augustus. *Guide to Carlyle*, 1920.
Dyer, I. W. *A Bibliography of Carlyle's Writings and Ana*, 1928.

NOTES, COMMENTS, AND TOPICS FOR DISCUSSION

1036.   LONDON A MONSTROUS WEN

1036a. 3. *Alexander Carlyle:* his brother.
    5. *Pentonville:* a dreary part of London.
    16. *our father:* James Carlyle, country stonemason, one of nature's noblemen; see the grateful characterization of him in Carlyle's *Reminiscences*, ch. 1.
    42. *Cobbett:* William Cobbett (1766-1835), a sturdy democrat and realistic writer of political and social topics. His masterpiece is *Rural Rides* (1830).
1036b. 45. *Robinson:* Friend of many English and German Romantics; important is his *Diary, Reminiscences, and Correspondence* (1869).

1037a. 2. *Procter and Cunningham:* lesser Romantics—the former, Bryan Waller Procter, is better known as "Barry Cornwall"; the latter, an author of Scottish songs.
    9. *Campbell:* Thomas Campbell; see the Introduction to the Selections from his work; *Anth.*, p. 491.

1037.   PLAIN LIVING AND HIGH THINKING

    The most famous description of De Quincey was to be Carlyle's (*Reminiscences*), ending "*Eccovi*, this child has been in hell!" De Quincey was ten years older, and in 1824 had reviewed Carlyle's translation of *Wilhelm Meister* rather harshly, but no grudge was nursed.

1037b. 19. *a sort of colony:* The description curiously foreshadows some of the features of the admirable MacDowell Colony of artists and writers in Peterborough, New Hampshire.

1038a. 44. *Golconda and Potosi:* alluding to the diamonds of India and silver of Bolivia.
    49. *Brighton Teapot:* the Pavilion, a fashionable place of amusement at the seaside resort of Brighton.

1038b. 6. *eclipsed in clouds:* tactfully alluding to De Quincey's many troubles in Edinburgh.

DISC.—With Carlyle's attitude toward city life, compare Blake's *London, (Anth.,* p. 127); Wordsworth's *The Prelude,* Book VII (p. 257); and Lamb's *Letter to Wordsworth* (p. 377).

1038.   JEAN PAUL FRIEDRICH RICHTER

Richter (1763-1825) was the author of astounding romantic prose-fictions, *Hesperus, Titan,* etc.—fantasies by turns philosophical, humorous, and sentimental; sometimes like Rabelais, more often like Sterne. Two of them were translated by Carlyle, *Quintus Fixlein* and *Schmelzles Reise.* Carlyle's interpretation of Richter is confirmed by modern critics; see, for example, B. Boesch's Swiss *Deutsche Literaturgeschichte* (1946), pp. 272-274. The chief importance of this essay is that it shows what the Romantics admired in an author's personality, choice of themes, attitudes, and style; and what kind of original prose-fictions they would welcome.

1038b. 51. *Corinthian brass:* an ancient alloy of gold, silver, and copper.

1040a. 51. *fuliginous limbecs:* smoky alembic (still).

1040b. 10. *wind-harps:* again one of the favorite romantic symbols; see the Note on Coleridge, *The Aeolian Harp, Anth.,* p. 139.
  25. *Herder:* J. G. von Herder, an important early German Romantic, widely influential, to whom Richter was devoted.
  26. *mild Bramin:* the Bramins were the priests of Hinduism, and taught compassion toward all living creatures.

1040.   REVIEW OF LOCKHART'S LIFE OF BURNS

See M. H. Goldberg, "Jeffrey, Mutilator of Carlyle's 'Burns'?", *PMLA,* LVI, 466; 1941.—Lockhart was Scott's son-in-law.

1040b. 57. *Socrates,* etc.: Socrates was condemned to death for allegedly "corrupting" the youth of Athens; Roger Bacon's works and Galileo's discoveries were condemned by the Church.

1041a. 24. *implanting the strength needful:* a point of the romantic faith—circumstances do not completely dominate.

1041b. 1. *Restaurateur:* disher-up of popular literature.
  40. *Locke banished:* the famous philosopher (1632-1704) was not really banished, but found it prudent to flee from England and remain abroad for some years.
  52. *Araucana:* the best heroic poem in Spanish, by Ercilla y Zuniga (c. 1535-1595).

1042a. 24. *the wedge:* the metaphor of a stonemason's son.
  42. *New and Old Light:* The point is that the quarrel between these two sects—New Licht and Auld Licht—was more important than religion itself.

1042b. 29. *Jean Paul:* the Richter of the preceding Selection.

1043a. 14. *Byron:* **Disc.**—Compare Hazlitt's views on Byron; *Anth.,* p. 407.

1043b. 20. *He who would write:* The correct quotation is "He who would not be frustrate of his hope to write well hereafter in laudable things ought himself to be a true poem" (*Apology for Smectymnus*).

1044a. 6. *Plebiscita:* decision of the public.
  27. *gin-horse:* horse in a treadmill.
  51. *Valclusa Fountain:* near Avignon, France; associated with the poet Petrarch.

DISC.—Compare Carlyle's characterization of Burns, and his idea of a true poet, with Burns's *A Bard's Epitaph (Anth.,* p. 89), and Wordsworth's *At The Grave of Burns* (p. 298).

1044.   SIGNS OF THE TIMES

The earlier part of this essay restates the romantic doctrine that overvaluation of material and mechanical progress results in worldliness, slavery to practical circumstances and mass opinions, and paralysis of individual freedom and of the sense of personal responsibility.

1044b. 31. *Heraclides and Pelasgi:* prehistoric, semimythical peoples of the Eastern Mediterranean.
  49. *not from Nature:* Progress is not natural or inevitable (as, by a misapprehension of evolution, was after c. 1860 to be supposed) but is within man's own power. For his progress or retrogression he is responsible.

1045a. 38. *Carbonari:* literally "charcoal burners"—the underground revolutionary groups in Italy, and later in France, who (c. 1805-1830) resisted Napoleonic and Bourbon oppressors.

60. *higher freedom:* cultural progress is even more important than political.

DISC.—Mechanism ("faith in the all-importance of physical things") in our own times: what forms it takes, and how it may be counteracted.

1045. BIOGRAPHY

First appeared in *Fraser's Magazine,* which had been founded in 1830 as a progressive liberal organ; see Miriam Thrall, *Rebellious Fraser's,* 1934.

1046a. 30. *Calista:* Perhaps the intriguing woman of the court in Scott's *Talisman;* but more likely the "fair penitent" in Rowe's tragedy of that title.

41. *on its being really seen:* i.e., seen in its inwardness. Carlyle harps on this, e.g. "The whole thing I want to write seems lying in my mind, but I cannot get my eye on it" (Journal; Apr. 23, 1831); of Oliver Cromwell, "I begin to see him at times in some measure" (Froude, *Life in London,* I, 188); and "The seeing eye!" passage in *Heroes, Anth.,* p. 1056b, 20.

1046b. 8. *an open loving heart:* Compare De Quincey, *Literature of Knowledge, Anth.,* p. 1031a. 16.

1047a. 13. *pitiful Image of their own pitiful Self:* This helps to explain what Carlyle disliked in Byron (*Anth.,* p. 1043a, 14.)

44. *Parson White:* Gilbert White; see the selections from his *Natural History of Selborne, Anth.,* p. 95.

1047. THE DEATH OF GOETHE

Carlyle's estimate of Goethe has been vindicated by time, which has given him a most influential place in the literatures of Western civilization, as may be seen in authors as different as Matthew Arnold and Thomas Mann.—A useful introduction is Carré's *Goethe en Angleterre* (1920).

1048b. 17. *David Hume:* The keen skeptical philosopher (1711-1776), who with Gibson, Voltaire, and others of that school, created the anti-spiritual and anti-idealistic intellectual world through the darkness of which Goethe (in Carlyle's view of the matter) had to find his way—even as Carlyle himself had to do, in a later generation, and with the advantage of Goethe's guidance.

1049a. 1. *a Wise Man:* Goethe.

52. *Werter: Werther* was a sentimental and melancholy novel of Goethe's period of storm-and-stress.

56. *Meisters Lehrjahre: Wilhelm Meisters Lehrjahre,* a philosophical novel recounting the development of a frothy and vacillating youth toward self-recognition and self-limitation. Carlyle had translated it eight years previously.

57. *Hafiz:* Poems in an Oriental setting.

1049b. 4. *the laws,* etc.: The practices rather than the laws of Renaissance Italy are revealed in the amazing autobiography of the sculptor Cellini, which Goethe translated.

1050a. 44. *Mignon:* The beautiful and pathetic Italian maiden in *Wilhelm Meister.*

45. *Mephistopheles:* The devil who tries to seduce Faust.

1050b. 19. *Carl August:* The Duke of Sachsen-Weimar-Eisenach, whom Goethe served in public affairs for many years.

29. *higher Literature of Germany:* Observe that Carlyle, like his contemporary, Mme. de Staël, in her *L'Allmagne,* exalts German literature over French. The latter, except for Rousseau, he regarded as inferior in earnestness and profundity.

1051a. 5. *Im Ganzen, Guten, Wahren:* In this passage Goethe wrote "Schönen" (the beautiful) instead of "Wahren" (the true); and Carlyle has been reproached by Mr. Norwood Young and others for misrepresenting Goethe's meaning, and for substituting what was dearer to him for what was dearer to Goethe. In other passages, however, Goethe includes the true. In the *Doctrine of Colors,* which Carlyle had read, he speaks of the Platonic "everlasting Whole, Good, True, and Beautiful"; and elsewhere he speaks of

Schiller as penetrating the eternal world of "the true, the good, and the beautiful." It seems to me less likely that Carlyle should have deliberately changed the wording of Goethe's passage than that his memory had confused other passages with it (see TLS, Mch. 1, May 3 and 23, 1929). Many of the Romantics—Coleridge, Hazlitt, Shelley, Leigh Hunt, and De Quincey—are remarkably inaccurate quoters.

1051.   SARTOR RESARTUS

The title means "The Tailor Retailored" or "Patched." This prose-fiction, a fantasy with autobiographical elements like the Everlasting Yea passage, Emery Neff calls "the culmination of Carlyle's romantic tendencies" (*Carlyle*, p. 122). In this selection much is drawn from Goethe's *Wilhelm Meister*, including the doctrines of renunciation (1051b, 15) and of the nearest duty (1052a, 19.).—A German professor is supposed to be speaking.

1051a. 29. *Hochheimer:* A white wine of the professor's own country. In England it is called hock.

30. *Ophiuchus:* The serpent or dragon of the constellation Serpentarius.

1051b. 34. *Close thy Byron: open thy Goethe:* Here, again, Carlyle expresses the feeling that Byron fosters egotism and therefore despair. Goethe, whose influence on *Sartor Resartus* was great, encouraged, on the other hand, self-limitation and an impersonal interest in permanent realities.

1052a. 31. *America is here or nowhere:* Lothario, following the craving for the enchantingly distant, had gone to America; but comes to realize that his duty and opportunity lie at home. "In my house, amid my fields, among my people," he writes, "I will say, 'Here or nowhere is America.'"

38. *the Ideal is in thyself:* It is important to observe the close connection between this idea and the doctrine of work, *Anth.*, p. 1052b, 16. What Carlyle means by work is not any kind of labor, as seems sometimes to be supposed, but only the working out of one's *ideal* so far as possible amid those conditions in which one has been placed.

1052.   THE FRENCH REVOLUTION

G. M. Dutcher's authoritative *Guide to Historical Literature* says: "So eminent an authority as Professor Aulard regards Carlyle's work as good history. He believes that Carlyle was a true interpreter who discerned in the common people the real hero of the epic struggle . . . The opinion of the two most recent English editors is substantially the same. Rose remarks that Carlyle 'shows us the workings of the human heart as no other historian of institutions and no microscopic analyst like Taine, has ever done or ever will do'."—See C. F. Harrold, "Carlyle's General Method in 'The French Revolution'," PMLA, XLIII, 1150 (1928); Louise M. Young, *Carlyle and the Art of History* (1939); F. A. Lea, in *Adelphi*, XVIII, 20 and 36 (1941); the two books by Hill Shine (1938 and 1941) listed in the Bibliography; and René Wellek's "Carlyle and the Philosophy of History," PQ, XXIII, 55 (1944).

In accord with the romantic viewpoint, Carlyle interprets the past as mainly a conflict of personal forces rather than of political, social, economic, or physical circumstances. It is not history that makes men, but the inner spirit of men that makes history; that is why he calls history "the essence of innumerable biographies (*On History*). Hence the emphasis in this selection is on the character of the King and on that of his captor.

1053a. 24. *That Lady:* the queen, Marie Antoinette.

46. *Grosse-Tête:* Large-Head i.e., the king, Louis XVI.

1053b. 7. *fusils:* guns.

30. *Bouille:* a young royalist officer, who was waiting with fresh horses for the fugitives.

1054a. 26. *es-tu bon,* etc.: "Are you a loyal citizen of the Republic?" "I certainly am!"

1054b. 46. *the best Burgundy he ever drank:* To Carlyle, this interest in what under the circumstances should have been too trivial to mention, was a clear sign of a feeble personality. (Some other interpretation is of course possible.)

DISC.—Compare other pictures of the French Revolution,—e.g., Blake's, *Anth.*, p. 120, and Wordsworth's, *Prelude* IX and XI, *Anth.*, p. 267.

Is Carlyle's philosophy of history reconcilable with Arnold J. Toynbee's in *A Study of History* (1947)?

HEROES AND HERO-WORSHIP

The selection deals mainly with Shakspeare; but the book as a whole is concerned with the hero as god, prophet, poet or man of letters, and ruler; i.e., with the problem: What is a true leader; what are his functions, rights, and duties?   Since these questions are related to the philosophy of history, the references given for the previous selection, are also useful here.   Add thereto the following: B. H. Lehman, *Carlyle's Theory of the Hero* (1929); F. M. Smith, "Whitman's Poet-Prophet and Carlyle's Hero," PMLA, LV, 1146 (1940); Sidney Hook, *The Hero in History* (1943); E. R. Bentley, *A Century of Hero-Worship* (1944); Ernst Cassirer, *The Myth of the State* (1946); Max Weber, *The Theory of Social and Economic Organization* (1947), and A. J. Toynbee, *A Study of History* (1947).   There is involved the conflict between democratic and totalitarian ideas of leadership.

1055a. **29.** *melodious:* would "rhythmical" be a better term?

1055b. **34.** *Skeptical Dilettantism:* See the note on David Hume, above, p. 1048b. 17.—The combination of skepticism with frivolous amateurishness is precisely what the contemporary French Romantic, Mme. de Staël, attacked in her own country.   Carlyle admired her book, *L'Allemagne* (See R. C. Whitford, *Mme. de Staël's Literary Reputation in England*, (1918, p. 51).

1056b. **6.** *Novum Organum:* Bacon's ambitiously designed work, intended to institute a new scientific method of investigating nature.   The contrast is in some degree that between the literature of knowledge and the literature of power.

28. *genially:* generatively, creatively.

44. *discern the inner heart of things, and the harmony that dwells there:* An appropriate conclusion for Selections from the Romantic Movement.

DISC.—What, if anything, is new in Carlyle's interpretation of Shakspeare, compared with Coleridge's (*Anth.*, p. 368), Lamb's (p. 378), Hazlitt's (p. 402), and De Quincey's (p. 1018)?

In view of this essay, and the one on Burns, which one of the greater Romantics do you think Carlyle might have chosen for a hero?

DISC.—Carlyle's free use of capitalization—does it help or hinder?   It may be defended as a means of giving personification, or vitality, to what would otherwise seem merely general terms or abstractions).

As writers of prose, which of the Romantics seem to you closest to Carlyle's style, and which most remote?

When that classic of epicurean pessimism, Fitzgerald's translation of Omar Khayyam, appeared, Carlyle remarked: "I think my old friend Fitzgerald might have spent his time to much better purpose than in busying himself with the verses of that old Mohammedan blackguard." Why is that reaction characteristic of the romantic element in Carlyle's temperament?

Can you discern in the Selections any ideas or tendencies which might explain why Carlyle, in his post-romantic period, became an admirer of strong rulers like Frederick the Great?

INDEX TO AUTHORS, TITLES, AND FIRST LINES

First lines are in ordinary type; titles, in *italics;* and names of authors in **bold type.**

1229